MW01492464

THE NORTON ANTHOLOGY OF

AFRICAN AMERICAN LITERATURE

FOURTH EDITION

VOLUME 1

THE VERNACULAR TRADITION

McCARTHY

THE LITERATURE OF SLAVERY AND FREEDOM

ANDREWS • FOSTER

LITERATURE OF THE RECONSTRUCTION TO THE NEW NEGRO RENAISSANCE

FOSTER • ANDREWS

HARLEM RENAISSANCE

EDWARDS

REALISM, NATURALISM, MODERNISM

McDOWELL • SPILLERS

THE BLACK ARTS ERA

BENSTON

THE CONTEMPORARY PERIOD

GRIFFIN • McCARTHY

THE NORTON ANTHOLOGY OF AFRICAN AMERICAN LITERATURE

FOURTH EDITION

Henry Louis Gates Jr., *General Editor*
ALPHONSE FLETCHER UNIVERSITY PROFESSOR AND
DIRECTOR OF THE HUTCHINS CENTER
FOR AFRICAN AND AFRICAN AMERICAN RESEARCH
Harvard University

Valerie Smith, *General Editor*
PRESIDENT
Swarthmore College

VOLUME 1

W. W. NORTON & COMPANY
Independent Publishers Since 1923

W. W. Norton & Company has been independent since its founding in 1923, when William Warder Norton and Mary D. Herter Norton first published lectures delivered at the People's Institute, the adult education division of New York City's Cooper Union. The firm soon expanded its program beyond the Institute, publishing books by celebrated academics from America and abroad. By midcentury, the two major pillars of Norton's publishing program—trade books and college texts—were firmly established. In the 1950s, the Norton family transferred control of the company to its employees, and today—with a staff of five hundred and hundreds of trade, college, and professional titles published each year—W. W. Norton & Company stands as the largest and oldest publishing house owned wholly by its employees.

Printed in the United States of America.

Editor: Marian Johnson
Media Editor, Literature: Sarah Rose Aquilina
Assistant Editors: Serin Lee and Joseph Payne
Managing Editors, College: Carla Talmadge, Kim Yi
Project Editor, Digital Media: Diane Cipollone
Marketing Manager, Literature: Eleanor Lilly
Senior Associate Media Editor: Jessica Awad
Assistant Media Editor: Emma Daugherty
Production Manager: Benjamin Reynolds
Photo Editor: Ted Szczepanski
College Text Permissions, Manager: Elizabeth Trammell
Permissions Clearing: Nancy Rodwan
Composition: The Westchester Book Group
Manufacturing: Lakeside Book Company—Crawfordsville, IN

ISBN: 978-1-324-04704-9

W. W. Norton & Company, Inc., 500 Fifth Avenue, New York, NY 10110-0017
wwnorton.com

W. W. Norton & Company Ltd., 15 Carlisle Street, London W1D 3BS

10 9 8 7 6 5 4 3 2 1

In memory of Nellie Y. McKay,
Barbara T. Christian, and Cheryl A. Wall

Contents

VOLUME 1: BEGINNINGS THROUGH THE HARLEM RENAISSANCE

The Vernacular Tradition, Part 1

The Literature of Slavery and Freedom 1746–1865

Literature of the Reconstruction to the New Negro Renaissance, 1865–1919

Harlem Renaissance, 1919–1940

Preface to the Fourth Edition

In the fall of 1986, eleven scholars gathered on the campus of Cornell University to discuss the need for a *Norton Anthology of African American Literature* and to consider how best to execute the mammoth task of editing such a historic anthology, should we collectively decide to embark upon it. These scholars, chosen for their leadership in the field, represented a wide array of methodological approaches to the study of literature; each had a particular expertise in at least one historical period in the African American literary tradition. We were accompanied in our deliberations by M. H. Abrams, the "father" of Norton Anthologies, and John Benedict, vice president and editor at Norton, both of whom had championed our project during its two-year gestation period from proposal to approval.

Two things struck us all about our discussions. First was a certain sense of history-in-the-making, in which we were participating by editing this anthology. While anthologies of African American literature had been published at least since 1845, ours would be the first Norton Anthology, and Norton—along with just a few other publishers—had become synonymous to our generation with canon formation. Because of its scope and size, a Norton Anthology could serve as "a course in a book," as John Benedict was fond of saying. So, in spite of the existence of dozens of anthologies of Black literature—a tradition of which we were keenly aware since we had all studied the tables of contents and editorial introductions of each of these—none was ample enough to include the range of texts necessary to satisfy the requirements of an entire survey course. To meet this need was our goal.

This was crucial if we were going to make the canon of African American literature as readily accessible to teachers and students as were, say, the canons of American or English literature. Too often, we had heard colleagues complain that they would teach African American literature "if only the texts were available" in a form affordable to their students, meaning in a one- or two-volume anthology, rather than in a half dozen or more individual volumes. Were we successful in our endeavor, we believed, then not only could teachers teach African American literature, but they would do so eagerly, and new courses would be created in four- and two-year institutions and at the high school level. A well-edited, affordable anthology democratizes access. And broader access was essential for the permanent institutionalization of the Black literary tradition within departments of English, American Studies, and African American Studies.

The second surprise of our Ithaca meeting was how "un-theoretical" the process of editing would be. Many of us were deeply engaged in the passionate theoretical debates that would define "the canon wars," as they came to be called. It soon became apparent to us that editing an anthology is not primarily a process concerned with theorizing canon formation; rather, it is about forming a canon itself. If we were successful, we would be canon-makers, not canon-breakers. Our theories about the canon, no matter how intricately woven, were not as important as the actual practice of agreeing upon the periodization of African American literature published (principally in English) in England and the United States between 1746 and the present and then selecting the signal texts in the tradition that comprise its canon.

Ironically, we were embarking upon a process of canon formation precisely when many of our poststructuralist colleagues were questioning the value of a canon itself. Our argument was that the scholars of our literary tradition needed first to construct a canon before it could be deconstructed! For while the scores of anthologies of African American literature published since 1845 had each, in a way, made claims to canon formation, few, if any, had been widely embraced in the college curriculum. And that process of adoption for use in college courses is a necessary aspect of canon formation.

So, setting aside our individual passions for theorizing, we collectively got down to the nuts and bolts of editorial policymaking, addressing fundamental questions such as how many pages to devote to each period, where those periods should start and stop, and what principles of selection would guide us in gathering works that were essential both in the formation of our tradition and to its teaching and explication. Though readily available elsewhere, certain core texts, such as Frederick Douglass's 1845 slave narrative, we agreed, must be included, since our goal was to respond to our Norton editor's challenge to produce "a course in a book." Our task, then, was not primarily to bring lost or obscure texts back into print; rather, it was to make available in one representative anthology the major texts in the tradition and to construct a canon inductively, text by text, period by period, rather than deductively—that is, rather than through a priori ideological or thematic principles agreed upon in advance, which would function like a straitjacket for our selections. Further, through carefully written introductions and headnotes, we wanted to help students see how these texts "speak to," or signify upon, each other, just as they had "spoken" to each other across time, space, and genre, as authors read and revised each other's representations of the experiences, feelings, and beliefs of persons of African descent pondering the ironies of being at once Black, American, and human. We wanted the anthology to give full voice to the key tropes and topoi that repeat—are echoed and riffed and signified upon—so strikingly across the African American literary tradition, thereby allowing formal linkages to be foregrounded in the classroom. Most importantly, we agreed that each period editor would have the final say about the texts selected for her or his period. A full decade would follow our organizational meeting in Ithaca, but in 1997, the first edition of *The Norton Anthology of African American Literature* was born.

To our surprise, the anthology was widely reviewed in both trade and academic publications, commencing with a major feature in the *New York Times*. Perhaps even more surprising, the trade edition was purchased in great numbers by nonacademics, often members of the growing African American reading public, hungry for texts about themselves. Within the academy, thousands of colleges and universities worldwide have adopted the anthology since its publication in 1997. The first anthology to allow the oral tradition to "speak" for itself through the inclusion of music and spoken-word texts and performances, *The Norton Anthology of African American Literature* has made an important statement about the crucial role of the vernacular in shaping our written tradition.

In this Fourth Edition of *The Norton Anthology of African American Literature*, two new editors have joined the team: Farah Jasmine Griffin, William B. Ransford Professor of English and Comparative Literature and African American Studies, Columbia University, and Jesse McCarthy, John L. Loeb Associate Professor of the Humanities and of the Social Sciences, Harvard University. Professors Griffin and McCarthy succeed the late Cheryl Wall in editing the Contemporary Period, and Jesse McCarthy worked as well on the Vernacular Tradition section in each volume, which had previously been edited by Robert O'Meally. Each editor, new or continuing, is an expert in the relevant field or period and had ultimate responsibility for his or her section of the anthology, but we have worked collaboratively from first to last.

The Fourth Edition has benefited from a wealth of suggestions from instructors and students using the book in the classroom. It includes the work of close to two hundred writers, representing African American vernacular traditions, poetry, drama, short fiction, the novel, slave narratives, essays, memoirs, and autobiographies. In keeping with the practical goal of offering "a course in a book," we have included the following longer texts in their entirety: Venture Smith, *A Narrative of the Life and Adventures of Venture, A Native of Africa*; Frederick Douglass, *Narrative of the Life of Frederick Douglass, an American Slave*; James Weldon Johnson, *Autobiography of an Ex-Colored Man*; Jean Toomer, *Cane*; Nella Larsen, *Passing*; Gwendolyn Brooks, *Maud Martha*; Lorraine Hansberry, *A Raisin in the Sun*; Amiri Baraka, *Dutchman*; Toni Morrison, *Sula*; Adrienne Kennedy, *Funnyhouse of a Negro*; August Wilson, *The Piano Lesson*; and Suzan-Lori Parks, *Topdog/Underdog*. Likewise, we continue to make available, where possible, texts that we believe represent the origins of a genre: among these are Lucy Terry's "Bars Fight" (1746), the earliest known poem by an African American; "The Last & Dying Words of MARK" (1755), the earliest extant slave narrative published in North America (new to this edition); Victor Séjour's "The Mulatto," the earliest short story by an African American (published in Paris in 1837); selections from the first African American novel, William Wells Brown's *Clotel* (1853); and a selection from Hannah Crafts's *The Bondwoman's Narrative* (1858), a novel written by a Black woman who was a fugitive from slavery. We have also tried to select texts that fully reflect the technical and rhetorical development of the various genres over time. In addition, *The Norton Anthology of African American Literature* features more than seventy-five illustrations across the volumes.

The Fourth Edition includes many fresh selections. **Volume 1, Beginnings through the Harlem Renaissance**, opens with the first of two parts devoted to **The Vernacular Tradition**; the earliest forms—spirituals, secular rhymes and songs, ballads, work songs, the blues, and folktales are included in Part 1, and it is expanded, with sixteen new selections, including a cluster of ring shouts, the tradition of call and response performance kept alive to this day by the Geechee Gullah communities of coastal Georgia. **The Literature of Slavery and Freedom, 1746–1865,** introduces "The Last & Dying Words of MARK," the earliest known slave narrative published in North America, an extraordinary example of the subgenre of criminal confession narratives; a new chapter from Frederick Douglass's *My Bondage and My Freedom* that describes an enslaved woman's heroic battle with a brutal overseer; and a map showing the status of the U.S. states and territories with regard to slavery in 1860. To **The Literature of the Reconstruction to the New Negro Renaissance, 1865–1919,** have been added an entry from Charlotte Grimké's journal in which she describes meeting Harriet Tubman in 1863, Victoria Earle Matthews's prescient essay "The Value of Race Literature," and a wide-ranging cluster of texts on the emigration of Black Americans between 1852 and 1880. **The Harlem Renaissance**, dramatically revised in the Third Edition, continues its attention to modernist innovation and debate in the period. New to this edition are an amusing and culturally rich map of Harlem nightclubs, Alain Locke's seminal essay "The Legacy of the Ancestral Arts," Claude McKay's "The Lynching," Paul Robeson's "The Culture of the Negro," and Zora Neale Hurston's "The Eatonville Anthology" and "What White Publishers Won't Print."

In **Volume 2, Realism, Naturalism, Modernism to the Present, The Vernacular Tradition** features three new gospel songs, Tracy Chapman's "Thinkin' Bout a Revolution" in songs of social protest, three new songs in rhythm and blues, and new lyrics in the hip-hop section by Kendrick Lamar, Nas, Digable Planets, Chika, and Nicki Minaj. **Realism, Naturalism, Modernism, 1940–1960,** now offers Ann Petry's "Like a Winding Sheet" and a deepened representation of James Baldwin, with the addition of "Stranger in the Village" and chapter 1 from *Giovanni's Room*. New selections in **The Black Arts Era, 1960–1975,** include Audre Lorde's "The Master's Tools Will Never Dismantle the Master's House," Toni Cade Bambara's "The Lesson," James Alan McPherson's "A Solo Song: For Doc," and a moving and wonderfully teachable cluster of poems inspired by John Coltrane, among them Amiri Baraka's "Am/Trak," which is new to the anthology. Now edited by Farah Jasmine Griffin and Jesse McCarthy, **The Contemporary Period** features an array of new authors and new works: new prose writers Percival Everett, Ta-Nehisi Coates, Teju Cole, Rachel Kaadzi Ghansah, and Jesmyn Ward; new selections for August Wilson, Octavia Butler, Gloria Naylor, Edward P. Jones, Essex Hemphill, and Colson Whitehead; new poets M. NourbeSe Philip, Christopher Gilbert, Claudia Rankine, John Keene, Gregory Pardlo, and Terrance Hays; and new poems for Maya Angelou, Lucille Clifton, Yusef Komunyakaa, Nathaniel Mackey, Rita Dove, Elizabeth Alexander, Natasha Trethewey, and Tracy K. Smith. Truly the richness of the literature in this period, both returning and new, is extraordinary.

Another exciting thing about the Fourth Edition is the availability of the complete anthology in ebook format, with an ebook for each volume. Dynamic features exclusive to the Norton Ebook Reader platform—including audio of the anthology editors reading the period introductions and embedded videos that highlight various themes—give students new ways to engage with the anthology's valuable contextual material. In addition to encouraging close reading, annotation tools enable instructors to share notes, links, and videos with their whole class right on the page. Given the wide range of multimedia content used in various courses, this feature makes the anthology more customizable than ever. Instructors can link directly to specific readings in the ebook from their learning management system (LMS), making it easy to organize a course thematically or chronologically. Also exclusive to the Norton Ebook Reader platform is an introduction to reading and annotation that walks students through the general *whats*, *whys*, and *hows* of annotation before they delve into the works in the anthology. Many of the black-and-white images in the print version appear in color in the ebook, and matching page references ensure that everyone in the course stays on the same page, no matter their chosen format. Search functionality allows readers to search not only by keyword throughout the ebook but also by author or work within the table of contents. To access or learn more about the ebook, reach out to your Norton representative or contact us at literature@wwnorton.com.

Additional Resources from the Publisher

To give instructors even greater flexibility, the publisher is making available the full list of Norton Library editions, including such frequently assigned works as Harriet Jacobs's *Incidents in the Life of a Slave Girl*, Harriet Beecher Stowe's *Uncle Tom's Cabin*, Booker T. Washington's *Up from Slavery*, and Charles Chesnutt's *The Marrow of Tradition*. Any Norton Library edition can be packaged with the anthology for free. The volumes in the Norton Library give students authoritative, carefully annotated texts with rich introductions written by compelling and creative scholars. Instructors may also package Norton Critical Editions with the anthology at a reduced price.

Along with the interactive ebook features described above, the Fourth Edition is accompanied by a Student Site. Included with all new copies of the book or available as an affordable standalone purchase option for students with used copies, the Student Site contains the videos from the Norton Ebook Reader platform, a curated selection of links to Spotify recordings, bibliographies for the anthology's individual authors, writing resources, and more. Students can easily access the site from the book's digital landing page or via their instructor's LMS. Instructors who adopt the anthology for class use also have access to a robust set of teaching materials. *Teaching with* The Norton Anthology of African American Literature: *A Guide for Instructors* features tips and strategies for each section of the anthology as well as discussion questions and lists of teaching resources. A handy resource for new and seasoned instructors alike, the downloadable guide is easily searchable. Reading comprehension quizzes for often-taught works from the anthology can be accessed in Norton Testmaker. Export ready-to-use quizzes to Microsoft Word or as Common Cartridge files for your LMS. All the images from the anthology are available in PowerPoint with alt text and in JPEG format.

Editorial Procedures

In each literary period, the anthology presents the writers in the order of their birth dates and the works of each writer in the order of publication, with this ordering breaking down only slightly when we gather works in clusters. Thus, the overall organization facilitates a chronological approach to African American authors as well as generic or thematic approaches. Each editor has been responsible for defining the canonical writings of his or her period and for writing the introductory essays, headnotes, and footnotes. As in other Norton anthologies, period introductions and author headnotes are meant to be self-sufficient, thereby minimizing the student's need for supplementary biographical, political, or cultural material. After each work, we cite the date of first publication on the right and occasionally, when it differs significantly from publication, the date of composition on the left. When a work has been excerpted, *From* appears before the title; the omissions are indicated in the text by three asterisks; and, when necessary, summaries of deleted material are provided. The bibliographies for each period, now available at the Student Site, have been updated, as has the timeline.

Producing and revising this anthology has been a truly collaborative effort. The project has moved forward with the help of hundreds of colleagues in the field, who evaluated its general merits, made early recommendations for individual selections, and later proposed refinements and expansions based on their and their students' classroom experience. The editors are deeply indebted to these teachers. A list of Acknowledgments names advisors who prepared detailed critiques of the selections and responded to the extensive user survey that helped us shape the Fourth Edition.

The editors would like to thank the late M. H. Abrams and the late John Benedict for believing in this project and supporting it from its inception, as did Donald Lamm, then chairman of W. W. Norton & Company. The late Barry Wade eagerly accepted editorship upon the untimely death of John Benedict. Julia Reidhead, our longtime inhouse editor, continues to deserve our gratitude, as does Marian Johnson, who edited this edition. We also give special thanks to Sarah Rose Aquilina, Media Editor, who reimagined the digital media for this edition. We thank too Harry Haskell and Katharine Ings, manuscript editors; Ben Reynolds, production manager; Eleanor Lilly, literature marketer; Serin Lee and Joseph Payne, assistant editors; Megan Schindel, Elizabeth Trammell, and Nancy Rodwan, permissions experts (we also thank Nancy for her help with art research for the covers and packaging); Jessica Awad, who edited the instructor's resources, including the teaching manual; Ted Szcepanski, for his expert image research; and Debra Morton Hoyt and Mike Wood, for creating the inspiring covers.

We have attempted to present the African American literary heritage without pretending to completeness. Limitations of space and prohibitions on copyright have prevented us from including several authors whose texts are important to the canon and whose level of excellence warrants inclusion here. Despite these limitations, we believe that we have represented justly the African American literary tradition by re-printing many of its most historically important and aesthetically sophisticated works. The authors of these works (whose birth dates range from 1730 to 1981) have made the text of Western letters speak in voices and timbres resonant, resplendent, and variously "Black." Taken together, they form a literary tradition in which African American authors collectively affirm that the will to power is the will to write and to testify eloquently in aesthetic forms never far removed from the language of music and the rhythmic resonance of the spoken word.

HENRY LOUIS GATES JR.
Cambridge, Massachusetts

VALERIE SMITH
Swarthmore, Pennsylvania

September 2024

Acknowledgments

Among our many critics, advisors, and friends, the following were of especial help in the preparation of the Fourth Edition: Erica Edwards (Yale University) and Stephanie Li (Duke University), who provided incisive reviews of the Third Edition, which helped shape the Fourth; Vincent Carretta (University of Maryland), who allowed us to draw on his expertise with regard to Phillis Wheatley; Sarah Lewis (Harvard University), who assisted us in selecting new material by Alain Locke; Eliza Richards (University of North Carolina at Chapel Hill), who advised us on representing the complex career of George Moses Horton; and Adam Bradley (UCLA), who contributed much good information from his wide-ranging knowledge of hip-hop. Deep thanks go also to Chana Cohen-Mungan (Haverford College) and to Phoebe Braithwaite, Kevin Burke, Amy Gusdanian, Robert Heinrich, Namwali Serpell, and Marial Iglesias Utset—all of Harvard University.

We gratefully acknowledge the thoughtful comments and suggestions of our survey respondents for this edition: Lena Ampadu (Towson University), Paige Anderson (Pensacola State College), Joyce Bahhouth (Bladen Community College), Balthazar Beckett (American University in Cairo), Tanya Bennett (University of North Georgia), Dan Bergeron (St. Johns River State College), Alex Beringer (University of Montevallo), Kimberly Blockett (Penn State University), Mary Anne Boelcskevy (Boston University), Ellen Bonds (Villanova University), Michael Borshuk (Texas Tech University), Birdena Brookins (Rowan College at Gloucester County), Marne Campbell (Loyola Marymount University), Mary Paniccia Carden (Edinboro University of Pennsylvania), Bryan Carter (University of Arizona), Robert Cataliotti (Coppin State University), Corrie Claiborne (Morehouse College), Alanna Cotch (Prairie State College), Margaret Cox (Savannah State University), Shelby L. Crosby (University of Memphis), Susan Muaddi Darraj (Harford Community College), Karen Dillon (Blackburn College), Ray DiSanza (Suffolk County Community College), Ira Dworkin (Texas A&M University), Kalenda Eaton (Arcadia University), Crystal Edmonds (Robeson Community College), Africa Fine (Palm Beach State College), Theresa Ford (Grossmont College), Dan J. Giancola (Suffolk County Community College), Jurgen E. Grandt (University of North Georgia), Gurleen Grewal (University of South Florida, Tampa), Eric Hairston (Elon University), Lucy Harkness (SUNY Broome), Scott Hicks (University of North Caroline, Pembroke), Sara Hildreth (Regis Jesuit), Bev Hogue (Marietta College), Rashidah Jaami' Muhammad (Governors State University), Audrey Kerr (Southern Connecticut State University), Leigh Kellmann Kolb (East Central College), Heidi M. Kunz (Randolph College), Kristen Lillvis (Marshall University), April Logan

(Salisbury University), Christopher Love (The University of Alabama), Sharon Luk (University of Oregon), Matthew Luter (St. Andrew's Episcopal School), Jessica Magnani (St. Petersburg College), Joseph Malizia (Bloom Township High School District 206), Kathy Essick Martinez (Sandhill Community College), Barbara McCaskill (University of Georgia), Amber Metz (Geneva High School), Robert Milde (Eastern Kentucky University), Vernon Miles (Henderson State University), Geneva Cobb Moore (University of Wisconsin, Whitewater), Joshua Murray (Fayetteville State University), Taura Napier (Wingate University), Wayne Partridge (Albany State University), Robert Patterson (Georgetown University), Tony Prichard (Western Washington University), Aurelius Raines (Prairie State College), Ashraf Rushdy (Wesleyan University), Theresa Scott (Hillsborough Community College), Jorge Serrano (University of Delaware), Jolie Sheffer (Bowling Green State University), Sarah Sillin (Gettysburg College), Bianca Spriggs (Ohio University), Delia Steverson (University of Florida), Sonja Taylor (Morse High School), Steven Tracy (University of Massachusetts, Amherst), Gregg Ventello (Kansas City Kansas Community College), Peter Walker (Salem State University), K. Blaine Wall (Pensacola State College), Wendy Walters (Emerson College), Adrienne Akins Warfield (Mars Hill University), Charles Williams (Chaffey College), and Elizabeth Wurz (College of Coastal Georgia).

Introduction

Talking Books

> The lesson to be drawn from this cursory glance at what I may call the past, present and future of our Race Literature apart from its value as first beginnings, not only to us as a people but literature in general, is that unless earnest and systematic effort be made to procure and preserve for transmission to our successors, the records, books and various publications already produced by us, not only will the sturdy pioneers who paved the way and laid the foundation for our Race Literature be robbed of their just due, but an irretrievable wrong will be inflicted upon the generations that shall come after us.
>
> —VICTORIA EARLE MATTHEWS, 1895

> A people may become great through many means, but there is only one measure by which its greatness is recognized and acknowledged. The final measure of the greatness of all peoples is the amount and standard of the literature and art they have produced. The world does not know that a people is great until that people produces great literature and art. No people that has produced great literature and art has ever been looked upon by the world as distinctly inferior.
>
> —JAMES WELDON JOHNSON, 1922

In the history of world literature, few traditions have origins as curious as that created by enslaved and recently emancipated African women and men writing in the English language in the third quarter of the eighteenth century. In the stubbornly durable history of human slavery, it was only this small cadre of Black authors in England and the United States who created a genre of literature that, at once, *testified* against their captors and *bore witness* to the urge to be free and literate, to embrace the European Enlightenment's dream of reason and the American Enlightenment's dream of civil liberty, wedded together gloriously in a great republic of letters.

For what could be more peculiar to the institution of human slavery than liberal learning, than "the arts and sciences," as the French philosophes put it? Slavery, as Lucius C. Matlock argued in 1845 in a review of Frederick Douglass's now classic *Narrative of the Life*, "naturally and necessarily" is "the enemy of literature." Despite that antagonistic relation, Matlock continued, slavery had by the middle of the nineteenth century "become the prolific theme of much that is profound in argument, sublime in poetry, and thrilling in narrative." What's more, he concluded with as much astonishment as satisfaction, "the soil of slavery itself"—and the demands for its abolition—had turned out to be an ironically fertile ground for the creation of a new literature, a literature indicting oppression, a literature created by the oppressed: "From the soil of slavery itself have sprung forth some of the most brilliant productions, whose logical levers will ultimately upheave and overthrow the system." It will be from "the pen of self-emancipated slaves," Matlock predicted, that "startling incidents authenticated, far excelling fiction in their touching pathos," will "secure the execrations of all good men and become a monument more enduring than marble, in testimony strong as sacred wit. . . ."

A bold group of enslaved African Americans, remarkably, sought to write themselves out of slavery by mastering the Anglo-American bellettristic tradition. To say that they did so against the greatest odds does not begin to suggest the heroic proportions that the task of registering a Black voice in printed letters entailed. James Albert Ukawsaw Gronniosaw, author of the first full-length Black autobiography, *A narrative of the most remarkable particulars in the life of James Albert Ukawsaw Gronniosaw, an African Prince* (1772), and the source of the genre of the book-length slave narrative, accounted for this antagonism, as well as the slave's anxiety before it, in a story that he appropriated from Garcilaso de la Vega's account of the Inca emperor Atahualpa's fatal confrontation with the Spanish conquistador Francisco Pizarro, and which literary scholars now call "the trope of the talking book":

> [My Master] used to read prayers in public to the ship's crew every Sabbath day; and then I saw him read. I was never so surprised in my life, as when I saw the book talk to my master, for I thought it did as I observed him to look upon it, and move his lips. I wished it would do so with me. As soon as my master had done reading, I followed him to the place where he put the book, being mightily delighted with it, and when nobody saw me, I opened it, and put my ear down close upon it, in great hopes that it would say something to me; but I was sorry, and greatly disappointed, when I found that it would not speak. This thought immediately presented itself to me, that every body and every thing despised me because I was black.

The text of Western letters refused to speak to the person of African descent; paradoxically, we read about that refusal in a text narrated by that very person of African descent. In a very real sense, the Anglo-African literary tradition was created two and a half centuries ago in order to demonstrate that persons of African descent possessed the requisite degrees of reason and wit to create literature, that they were, indeed, full and equal members of the community of rational, sentient beings, that they could, indeed, publish books. With Gronniosaw's "*narrative of the most remarkable particulars*," a distinctively "African" voice registered its presence in the republic of letters; it was a text that both talked "Black" and, through its unrelenting indictment of the institution of slavery, talked back.

Making the text "speak" in the full range of timbres that the African enslaved in England and America brought to the process of writing became the dominant urge of the ex-slave authors. So compelling did Gronniosaw's trope of the talking book prove to be that, between 1770 and 1815, no fewer than five authors of the genre that we now call "the slave narratives" used the same metaphor as a crucial scene of instruction to dramatize the author's own road to literacy, initially, and to authorship, ultimately. John

Marrant in 1785, Ottobah Cugoano in 1787, Olaudah Equiano in 1789, and John Jea in 1816—all *riffed upon* Gronniosaw's figure of the talking book as the signal structural element of their autobiographical narratives, thereby providing the formal links of repetition and revision that, in part, define any literary tradition. So related, in theme and structure, were these texts that by 1790 Gronniosaw's Dublin publisher also included John Marrant's *Narrative* on his list and advertised its sale on Gronniosaw's endpapers. It is clear that these authors read and revised this trope from each other's texts, making "literary signification" one of the founding features of the Anglo-African literary tradition. And "signifying," as we shall see, "double-voiced" formal revision and "riffing," has remained a hallmark of the African American literary tradition well into the twenty-first century.

Still, the resistance even to the idea that an African could create literature proved to be stubbornly resilient. As early as 1680, Morgan Godwyn, the self-described "Negro and Indian's Advocate," had accounted for the resistance in this way:

> [a] disingenuous and unmanly *Position* had been formed; and privately (*as it were in the dark*) handed to and again, which is this, That the Negro's though in their Figure they carry some resemblances of manhood, yet are indeed not men . . . the consideration of the shape and figure of our Negro's Bodies, their Limbs and members; their Voice and Countenance, in all things according with other mens; together with their *Risibility* and *Discourse* (man's *peculiar* Faculties) should be sufficient Conviction. How should they otherwise be capable of Trades, and other no less manly imployments; as also of *Reading* and *Writing*, or show so much Discretion in management of Business; . . . but wherein (we know) that many of our People are *deficient*, were they not truly Men?

Godwyn's account of the claims that Africans were not human beings and his use of the possession of reason and its manifestations through "*Reading* and *Writing*" to refute these claims were widely debated during the Enlightenment, generally at the African's expense.

The putative relation between literacy and the quest for freedom provided the subtext for this larger debate over the African's "place in nature," his or her place in the great chain of being, an ancient construct that arranged all of creation on a vertical scale ascending from plants, insects, and animals through human beings to the angels and God. Following the Stono Rebellion of 1739 in South Carolina, the largest uprising of enslaved people in the colonies before the American Revolution, legislators there enacted a draconian body of public laws, making two forms of literacy punishable by law: the mastery of writing, and the mastery of the drum. The law against learning to write read as follows:

> And *whereas* the having of slaves taught to write, or suffering them to be employed in writing, may be attending with great inconveniences; *Be it enacted,* that all and every person and persons whatsoever, who shall hereafter teach, or cause any slave or slaves to be taught to write, or shall use or employ any slave as a scribe in any manner of writing whatsoever, hereafter taught to write; every such person or persons shall, for every offense, forfeit the sum of one hundred pounds current money.

The law against the use of the talking drum was just as strong:

> And for that as it is absolutely necessary to the safety of this Province, that all due care be taken to restrain the wanderings and meetings of negroes and other slaves, at all times, and more especially on Saturday nights, Sundays and other holidays, and their using and carrying wooden swords, and other mischievous and dangerous weapons, or using or keeping of drums, horns, or other loud instruments, which may call together or give sign or notice to one another of their wicked designs and purposes. . . . And whatsoever master, owner or overseer shall permit or suffer his or their negro or other slave or slaves, at any time hereafter, to beat drums, blow horns, or use any other loud instruments, or whosoever shall suffer and countenance any public meetings or seatings or strange negroes or slaves in their plantations, shall forfeit 10 current money, for every such offence.

In the Stono Rebellion, both forms of literacy—mastery of English letters and the use of African vernacular forms such as the talking drum—had been pivotal to the slave's capacity to rebel.

Writing, many philosophers argued in the Enlightenment, stood alone among the fine arts as the most salient repository of "genius," the visible sign of reason itself. In this subordinate role, however, writing, although secondary to reason, was nevertheless the *medium* of reason's expression. We *know* reason by its representations. Such representations could assume spoken or written form. Eighteenth-century European writers privileged *writing*—in their writings about Africans, at least—as the principal measure of the Africans' humanity, their capacity for progress, their very place in the great chain of being. As the Scottish philosopher David Hume put it in a footnote to the 1754 second edition of his widely read essay "Of National Characters":

> I am apt to suspect the negroes, and in general all the other species of men (for there are four or five different kinds) to be naturally inferior to the whites. There never was a civilized nation of any other complexion than white, nor even any individual eminent either in action or speculation. No ingenious manufacturers amongst them, no arts, no sciences. On the other hand, the most rude and barbarous of the whites, such as the ancient *Germans*, the present *Tartars*, have still something eminent about them, in their valour, form of government, or some other particular.
>
> Such a uniform and constant difference could not happen, in so many countries and ages, if nature had not made an original distinction betwixt these breeds of men. Not to mention our colonies, there are *negro* slaves dispersed all over *Europe*, of which none ever discovered any symptoms of ingenuity; tho' low people, without education, will start up amongst us, and distinguish themselves in every profession. In *Jamaica* indeed they talk of one negro as a man of parts and learning [the brilliant, wealthy, and widely known free Black man, Francis Williams, who pursued studies in England and wrote poetry in Latin]; but 'tis likely he is admired for every slender accomplishment, like a parrot, who speaks a few words plainly.

Immanuel Kant, the German philosopher, responding to Hume's essay a decade later, had this to say:

> The negroes of Africa have by nature no feeling that rises above the trifling. Mr. Hume challenges anyone to cite a single example in which a Negro has shown talents, and asserts that among the hundreds of thousands of blacks who are transported elsewhere from the countries, although many of them have been set free, still not a single one was ever found who presented anything great in art or science or any other praise-worthy quality, even though among the whites some continually rise aloft from the lowest rabble, and through superior gifts earn respect in the world. So fundamental is the difference between these two races of man, and it appears to be as great in regard to mental capacities as in color. The religion of fetishes so wide-spread among them is perhaps a sort of idolatry that sinks as deeply into the trifling as appears to be possible to human nature. A bird feather, a cow horn, a conch shell, or any other common object, as soon as it becomes consecrated by a few words, is an object of veneration and of invocation in swearing oaths. The blacks are very vain but in the Negro's way, and so talkative that they must be driven apart from each other with thrashings.

Thomas Jefferson, in his *Notes on the State of Virginia* (1785), echoed this discourse in his disparaging remarks about Phillis Wheatley's book of poems:

> Misery is often the parent of the most affecting touches in poetry. Among the blacks is misery enough, God knows, but no poetry. Love is the peculiar oestrum of the poet. Their love is ardent, but it kindles the senses only, not the imagination. Religion, indeed, has produced a Phillis Wheatley; but it could not produce a poet. The compositions published under her name are below the dignity of criticism.

To test assertions such as these, in the spirit of the Enlightenment's privileging of scientific experimentation, a handful of curious (dare we say "enlightened?") Europeans and Americans educated enslaved Black boys and girls along with their own children. "El negro Juan Latino," who published three books of poetry in Latin between 1573 and 1585, was one of the earliest examples of such an experiment, followed by the university-educated philosophers Wilhelm Amo and Jacobus Capitein, and the statesman, Angelo Soliman, in the first half of the eighteenth century. Phillis Wheatley, the first Black person to publish a book of poetry in English, although still enslaved, is perhaps the most famous subject of such an experiment.

The seven-year-old girl arrived in Boston, Massachusetts, on the slave ship *Phillis* in 1761. She was sold to the merchant John Wheatley, who purchased her as a gift for his wife, Susanna. They named the child Phillis, a grim reminder of her capture and voyage of suffering across the Atlantic Ocean. Unlike most enslavers, the Wheatleys did not believe that at least this one enslaved girl should remain illiterate, and thus they taught Phillis to read; by 1765 she was writing poetry. Phillis Wheatley's first published poem appeared in the *Newport Mercury* newspaper in December 1767. In 1770, she published a widely read poem on the Boston Massacre. That same year she rose to international prominence with "On the Death of Mr. George Whitefield," an elegy for a British Methodist evangelical preacher who helped launch the Great Awakening in Massachusetts.

By 1772 Wheatley was ready to publish a collection of her poems. The Wheatleys advertised in the local press to solicit subscribers to fund the book. Anticipating that white patrons would struggle to believe that an enslaved Black teenager could write such elegant poetry, the Wheatleys' advertisement in *The Censor* on February 29, 1772, emphasized that "[t]he Poems having been seen and read by the best Judges, who think them well worthy of the Publick View; and upon critical examination, they find that the declared Author was capable of writing them."

On October 28, 1772, the scholar Joanna Brooks has convincingly argued, eighteen prominent Bostonians, including John Hancock and Thomas Hutchinson (fourteen were graduates of Harvard; seven owned slaves themselves), signed an attestation to "assure the World, that the POEMS specified in the following Page, were (as we verily believe) written by PHILLIS, a young Negro Girl, who was but a few Years since, brought as an uncultivated Barbarian from *Africa*, and has ever since been, and now is, under the Disadvantage of serving as a Slave in a Family of this Town." No scholar actually knows how the poems' "critical examination," in fact, took place, although that matter has generated an enormous amount of speculation, including the representation of two literal "trial" scenes in plays written by African American feminists Mary Church Terrell in 1932 and Shirley Graham (soon to be the second wife of W. E. B. Du Bois) in 1949, but a group examination most probably did not take place. Nevertheless, evidence that a Black author "prove" that they possessed the requisite intelligence to have written their own book—that their work had been "written by himself" or "written by herself"—became a key feature of the authenticating apparatus of the narratives published by escaped slaves before the Civil War and has remained a troubling metaphor for Black authorship and the innate intelligence of African Americans since, features set in motion by Wheatley's curious letter of attestation.

Still, Wheatley's work apparently could not entice three hundred subscribers. Undeterred, John and Susanna Wheatley sent Phillis to England in the summer of 1773 to meet reformer and antislavery advocate Selina Hastings, Countess of Huntingdon, who had already subsidized the publication of Gronniosaw's narrative and would do so again for the captivity narrative of John Marrant and for Olaudah Equiano's slave narrative. Although Phillis and the Countess did not meet (the Countess was ill), Wheatley's *Poems on Various Subjects, Religious and Moral* was published in London in September 1773 by Archibald Bell, no doubt with the Countess's patronage and, not surprisingly, dedicated to her. Soon after returning from London (where, had she chosen to remain, she would have been free) to Boston, Wheatley gained her freedom. In a very real sense, Phillis Wheatley had written her way from slavery to freedom.

This curious anecdote is only a tiny part of a larger, and even more curious, episode in the Enlightenment. At least since the end of the seventeenth century, Europeans had wondered aloud whether the African "species of men," as they commonly put it, could ever create formal literature, could ever master "the arts and sciences." If they could, the argument ran, then the African variety of humanity and the European variety were fundamentally related. If not, then it seemed clear that the African was destined by nature to be enslaved, rightly relegated to a low place in the great chain of being. By 1750, the chain had become minutely calibrated; the human scale rose from "the lowliest Hottentot" (Black South African) to "glorious Milton and Newton." If Black people could write and publish imaginative literature, then they could, in effect, take a few "giant steps" up the chain of being, in a pernicious metaphysical game of "Mother, May I?" For example, some favorable reviewers of Wheatley's book argued that the publication of her poems meant that the African was indeed a human being and should not be enslaved. Indeed, Wheatley was manumitted soon after her poems were published. Wheatley's fate would be quite different from that of another poet, living in the slave-state of North Carolina.

George Moses Horton had, by the mid-1820s, gained a considerable reputation at Chapel Hill as the "slave-poet." With the urging of a "gentleman" who had come across some poems that Horton had written, *Freedom's Journal*, the first African American newspaper, launched a short-lived campaign between August 29 and October 3, 1828, with the stated endorsement of the Black Boston abolitionist David Walker, encouraging its readers to send donations for "assistance in paying the price his master may demand for him," because Horton was a slave with impressive "poetic talent." "There were a total of four campaigns in the 1820s to secure Horton's freedom," scholar Eliza Richards explains, "three in the South and one in the North. None of them was successful."

The Hope of Liberty, a twenty-two-page pamphlet, would be published in 1829 by Joseph Gales, the editor of the *Raleigh Register* newspaper, as "an undertaking of the Raleigh auxiliary of the American Colonization Society," which also wanted to purchase Horton and send him to the new colony of Liberia. Horton's text "was probably distributed free in churches and elsewhere," Richards says, "in the hopes that people would donate money for Horton's manumission via the Colonization Society." Unlike Wheatley, Horton, in the end, was unable to write his way to freedom, even though his literacy's commodity value was at the heart of the aborted campaign to free him. Although *Freedom Journal's* campaign "to effect the emancipation" of this writer was not successful, "Horton's enslaver did allow him to settle in Chapel Hill and hire his time by working as a professional writer, waiter, and handyman," as Horton's headnote in this anthology attests. Horton would become free only after the 9th Michigan Cavalry arrived in Chapel Hill in April of 1865, liberating all enslaved people living there, under the terms of the Emancipation Proclamation.

Two hundred and twenty years separate the publication of Phillis Wheatley's book of poems and Toni Morrison's receipt of the Nobel Prize for literature in 1993. This fitting acknowledgment of the brilliance of Morrison's novels was part of a much larger phenomenon. African American literature had been enjoying a renaissance in quality and quantity for the previous three decades, one even vaster than the New Negro, or Harlem, Renaissance of the 1920s, dating from the Black Arts movement of the 1960s, then taking a bold new direction in 1970, a year that saw the publication of two astonishingly accomplished novels, Toni Morrison's *The Bluest Eye* and Alice Walker's *The Third Life of Grange Copeland,* and the canon-forming anthology *The Black Woman,* edited by Toni Cade Bambara, all published a year after Maya Angelou's best-selling autobiography, *I Know Why the Caged Bird Sings.* Together, these texts seem to have given rise to an astonishing burst of creative production through the seventies, eighties, and into the nineties, one that can rightly be seen as a *belle epoque* of African American women's writing, a veritable "renaissance" of its own, one which continues to this day. In parallel, the writing of Black male authors since 1970 has been just as strong and just as sophisticated, and both "traditions," as it were, are indicative of a multigenerational, consistent level of production that is formally quite impressive, perhaps a literary "coming of age," to revert to language that W. E. B. Du Bois or Alain Locke might have used during the Harlem Renaissance.

The number of literary prizes won by Black authors in the past few decades, including Pulitzer Prizes and National and American Book Awards, to name just a few, is impressively long, a measure of critical praise and acceptance, of course, unprecedented before the seventies. And more than a few times since 1990, several Black authors have appeared simultaneously on the best-seller list of the *New York Times*. While the audience for this flowering of Black literature crosses all racial boundaries, Black readers—to some degree, a result of the growth of the Black middle class—have never been more numerous than they are today: as early as June 1996 the *Times* reported that African Americans were purchasing 160 million books a year; nearly three decades later, that figure has certainly increased significantly.

This prominence in the marketplace has had an astounding counterpart in the curriculum. Black literature courses, and professors of African American literature, have become a central part of English departments and departments of American studies, African American studies, ethnic studies, and women's studies, to a degree that we could scarcely have imagined when we published the first edition of *The Norton Anthology of African American Literature*. No anthology of "American literature" would be regarded as complete today without a significant representation of African American writing. Maya Angelou's delivery of "On the Pulse of Morning" at Bill Clinton's inauguration in 1993 (she was the first poet to read at a presidential inauguration since Robert Frost did so for John F. Kennedy in 1961), Elizabeth Alexander's delivery of "Praise Song for the Day" at Barack Obama's inauguration in 2009, and Amanda Gorman's delivery of "The Hill We Climb" at Joe Biden's inauguration in 2021, as well as Rita Dove's, Natasha Trethewey's, and Tracy K. Smith's two-term appointments as Poet Laureate of the United States, are all further signs of the strong presence of African American literature in American society. Without doubt, the globalization of hip-hop, the dominant form of American popular music for the past three decades, has contributed to the unprecedented popularity of Black poetry, starting with the "Spoken Word" movement (a truly international and postmodern version of coffeehouse readings by the Beat poets during the 1950s and the Black Arts movement of the late sixties) and continuing with the quotation of canonical Black poetry and the "sampling" of rhythm and blues and soul lyrics from the 1960s and 1970s in hip-hop.

Sampling, a fundamental structuring principle of hip-hop, both imitates and impacts the formal literary tradition in various creative ways, and is a version of forms of repetition and revision practiced by Black canonical writers, underscoring how contemporary Black literature and Black music are related. Like signifying in the African American literary tradition, sampling in hip-hop is an attempt to render the *simultaneity* of the texts in the tradition, to unveil, to make explicit, the principle at work, implicitly, in all artistic traditions, as T. S. Eliot noted over a century ago about the works in the Western literary tradition. Sampling is defined as absorbing short passages of other music into or quoting them in one's own composition or performance. Such "borrowing" is actually a part of all musical traditions (think of the triad of imitation, repetition, revision), just as it is also a key aspect of all literary traditions.

One type of sampling that relates to the patterns of allusion and revision in the African American literary tradition is the quotation of four- or eight-bar passages from earlier African American music—"My daddy's music" or "My mother's music," as hip-hop artists often say, such as Isaac Hayes's "Hot Buttered Soul" or anything by James Brown, generally thought to be the most sampled artist of all time—which has the effect of making discrete periods seem simultaneous, as it were, collapsing the timeline, almost like musical time travel. This is akin to Eliot's insight, in "Tradition and the Individual Talent," that the canonical works in a tradition comprise a "simultaneous existence" and a "simultaneous order," and that new works in that tradition affect how we read older works, just as those older works affect how we read a new work, somewhat like a reversible reaction in chemistry. We can also see Eliot's definition of the role of "simultaneity" at work in the way jazz is structured. In a jazz ensemble, each musician improvises within a shared structure, responding to and building upon the others in real time. The simultaneous order is found in the way each instrument plays off the others, creating a collective sound that is both spontaneous and deeply interconnected. The ensemble embodies the simultaneous existence of tradition through its balance of individual expression and communal harmony, allowing for both innovation and shared musical language. Or think of a row of dominoes falling over from the first one to the last one, but then falling backward in exactly the same, but reversed, way. Sampling does this as well. To draw on Eliot again, sampling underscores "the pastness of the past, but of its presence" in music and in literature, both in the way that forms morph into other forms, and in the way that actual quotation *names* this fascinating process. In fact, sampling leads to something like musical immortality for sampled passages. Looked at this way, sampling is a loving salute to canonical works and a testament to the fact that "tradition" is a living, continuous thing, its texts speaking to each other. Because of the astonishing popularity of hip-hop, we might call the last quarter-century "the age of sampling," as an extension of the larger rhetorical strategy of literary signifying. It certainly is safe to say that Black poetry is "listened to" today more than ever before, because of the popularity of hip-hop. And it is also true that its popularity over the last few decades has both contributed to the fact, and is a reflection of the fact, that Black writers have been published, reviewed, and read far more than in the past. We might say that Black literature has become institutionalized, that, as the saying goes, it is here to stay.

It often surprises students that this broad acceptance of the authority of African American writing was, of course, not always the case. Leonard Deutsch, a professor of English at Marshall University, recalls the harsh resistance that greeted his request to write a Ph.D. dissertation on Ralph Ellison at Kent State University in 1970. When his prospectus was approved, a member of his thesis committee—a well-known Melville scholar—resigned in protest, arguing that

> To write this dissertation is bad on two counts: for Len Deutsch himself, and subsequently for the university. A doctoral dissertation implies substance, weight (stuffiness often accompanying this), and spread, and not concentration upon the wings of a gnat. If it be concentration, the dissertation must by concentration bring together and sum-up worlds of thought and material—the dissertation as metonymy or synecdoche,

> which it generally is. One could, for instance, write about Hemingway, Faulkner, or Bellow (recently living or still kicking) because men like them have established a respectable and accepted corpus of work ranging sufficiently to call for comment.

Ellison's work, he concluded, was not of the stature to warrant being studied for a Ph.D. in English. Other stories of white professors and predominantly white institutions of higher education discouraging scholarly interests and careers in African American literature abound in academic folklore.

The resistance to the literary merits of Black literature, as we have seen, has its origins in the Enlightenment and in justifications of the peculiar institution of slavery. The social and political uses to which this literature has been put have placed a tremendous burden on these writers, casting an author and her or his works in the role of synecdoche, a part standing for the ethnic whole, signifying who "the Negro" was, what his or her "inherent" intellectual potential might be, and whether or not the larger group was entitled to the full range of rights and responsibilities of American citizenship. Because of the perilous stature of African Americans in American society, their literature has labored under tremendous extra-literary burdens.

Writing in the preface to *An Anthology of American Negro Literature* (1929), V. F. Calverton, a Marxist critic, argued that Black literature was primarily a reflection of the Negro's historical economic exploitation:

> In a subtle way, Negro art and literature in America have had an *economic origin*. All that is original in Negro folklore, or singular in Negro spirituals and Blues, can be traced to the economic institution of slavery and its influence upon the Negro soul.

Richard Wright would echo these sentiments in his "Blueprint for Negro Writing," published in 1937. Calverton went on to argue that the Negro's music and folk art were never "purely imitative," and that Black vernacular cultural forms were "definitely and unequivocally American," the only "original" American culture yet created. Wright, too, would repeat this claim. If Black writers turned to their own vernacular traditions, he concluded, Black literature could be as original and as compelling as Black music and folklore. The literary movement of the 1920s, he maintained, was more important for what it implied about what historian Carter G. Woodson called "the public Negro mind" than for what it had contributed to the canon of the world's great literatures:

> If this new literature of the Negro in America does not constitute a renaissance, it does signify rapid growth in racial art and culture. It is a growth that is as yet unfinished. Indeed we may say it illustrates a growth that in a dynamic sense has just begun. It indicates more than the rise of a literature. It marks the rise of an entire people.

Calverton's argument about the production of literary arts and "the rise of an entire people" echoed the eloquent argument that the poet James Weldon Johnson had made in his important anthology, *The Book of American Negro Poetry*, published in 1922, at the beginning of the Harlem Renaissance. Johnson's preface remains one of the major critical essays on the nature and function of Black literature. In it Johnson states explicitly what had been implicit in the critical reception of Black literary production since Phillis

Wheatley: Blacks must create literature because it is, inevitably, a fundamental aspect of their larger struggle for civil rights, and it can never escape this role because it serves as *prima facie* evidence of the Negro's intellectual potential.

Johnson here was drawing upon Ralph Waldo Emerson's claim (made in his 1844 speech "On the Emancipation of the West Indies") about the necessity for Blacks to contribute "an indispensable element" to the American nation's cultural mix before they would be granted full citizenship:

> If the black man carries in his bosom an indispensable element of a new and coming civilization, for the sake of that element, no money, nor strength, nor circumstance can hurt him; he will survive and play his part. . . . The intellect—that is miraculous! Who has it, has the talisman. His skin and bones, though they were the color of night, are transparent, and the everlasting stars shine through with attractive beams.

In large part because of these extra-literary expectations—and because of the pernicious withholding of literary and formal education from Blacks—African American literature did not come of age until well into the twentieth century. As Sylvestre C. Watkins put it in his *Anthology of American Negro Literature* (1944),

> Negro history and Negro literature have maintained a very close relationship through the years. In his struggle for a better way of life, the Negro has, through necessity, made his literature a purposeful thing born of his great desire to become a full-fledged citizen of the United States. His late start did not allow him the pleasure of creating a new phrase, or a more beautiful expression. The struggle against ignorance, indifference and racial bigotry had first claim upon his time and energy.

Indeed, the tension in the African American tradition between even the most private utterances of a poet such as Phillis Wheatley—whose mastery of the English language and grace under pressure as *the* synecdoche for the African in Western culture would merit her a place in the canon, even if her work were not as layered as it is—and the political uses to which those utterances are put obtains to this day. What is the "black voice" that Gronniosaw sought to place in his text? What, exactly, accounts for the "African" element in African American literature? What is the relation between vernacular literature, the blues, gospel, the sermon, and jazz and the formal African American literary tradition? And what relation does the canon of African American literature bear to that of the American tradition? To begin to address these questions, eleven scholars in the middle of the decade of the 1980s decided to edit a Norton anthology that would define the African American literary tradition, including its stunningly inventive vernacular tradition.

While *The Norton Anthology of African American Literature* is a celebration of over two and a half centuries of imaginative writing in English by persons of African descent in the United States and England, it is most certainly not the first anthology seeking to define the canon of African American literature. But it is the most comprehensive; its sheer scope and inclusiveness enable readers to trace the patterns of formal repetition and revision that have defined the tradition from its eighteenth-century "talking book" roots to the genre of "neo-slave narrative" in the twentieth and twenty-first in such texts as *Flight to Canada* by Ishmael Reed, *Kindred* by Octavia Butler, *The Autobiography of Miss Jane Pittman* by Ernest Gaines, *The Known World* by Edward P. Jones, *The Underground Railroad* by Colson Whitehead, *Beloved* by Toni Morrison, and Percival Everett's signifying riff on Mark Twain's *Huckleberry Finn,* entitled *James,* all the way to the legion of other self-referential allusions, echoes, and borrowings that characterize works by contemporary Black writers.

Why have Black writers done this with texts by other Black authors? Because "Blackness" is a socially constructed category, it must be learned through imitation, and its literary representations—how one structures the tale of a Black subject in print, how one creates what we might think of as a "literary Black self"—must be learned in the same way, through imitation, repetition, and revision. The African American literary tradition exists as a formal entity because of this practice, which the editors of the anthology *The Negro Caravan* (1944) called "a sort of literary inbreeding which causes Negro writers to be influenced by other Negroes more than should ordinarily be expected." Virginia Woolf was correct when she claimed that "books speak to other books," in the same way, as Kwame Anthony Appiah recently put it, that "the history of art is the history of people borrowing and adapting techniques and tropes from earlier work." And while it is true that works of literature created by African Americans often "speak to," or signify upon, canonical works in other literary traditions, it is also the case that they do so—and have done so since the eighteenth century—in fascinating ways with works in the Black tradition, both structurally and thematically. Tracing these formal connections can be enlightening and pleasurable in the classroom and is most certainly one of the guiding organizational principles of this anthology.

If African American literature is flourishing in the twenty-first century, so too is academic study of the field. Critical studies and monographs, critical editions, anthologies, encyclopedias, biographical dictionaries, dictionaries of "Black English," textual companions, concordances, literary histories, the recovery of long-lost texts by Black writers, reprint series, and reference works of all sorts are enabling us to reassemble the fragmented history of African American writing, much of which was buried in what one commentator in 1854 called "the ephemeral caskets" of periodical literature, pamphlets, occasional publications, and limited, even vanity, editions of works published for a targeted readership such as churches or professional associations. The scholarly work of bibliographical recovery will most likely, and blessedly, end the cycle of generations of scholars being forced to reinvent the proverbial wheel. Such duplication of effort has been the great curse confronting scholars of African American culture. These tools—the collective work of the last several decades—will enable even more sophisticated future scholarship and an even deeper appreciation of the genius of the African American literary tradition.

The Norton Anthology of African American Literature builds upon a distinguished tradition of anthology editing that began at least as early as the mid-nineteenth century, with the publication of *Les Cenelles: Choix de Poesies Indigenes* in New Orleans in 1845. These forays into canon formation—for every anthology defines a canon—were also acts of love, arduously grafted together under difficult circumstances. Often, a Black writer's work survives today only because of his or her presence in a scarce or rare anthology. Robert Thomas Kerlin's superbly edited *Negro Poets and Their Poems* (1923), for example, includes works by J. Monrad Allen, Joshua Henry Jones Jr., Eva A. Jessye, Irvin W. Underhill, and Andre Razafkeriefo, poets whose poems are seldom, if ever, taught or anthologized today. One generation's or one anthologist's canonical figures sometimes become another generation's footnote to literary history. The point is that now, because of the revolution (and that is the right word) in Black literary scholarship in the academy, even the most obscure Black writers will not be lost again, and that surely is cause for celebration.

In making selections for this anthology, the editors listened carefully to a caution made by the writer and social critic Victoria Earle Matthews in 1895 in her important speech "The Value of Race Literature":

> Race Literature does not mean things uttered in praise, thoughtless praise of ourselves, wherein each goose thinks her gosling a swan. We have had too much of this. . . . Race Literature does mean, though, the preserving of all records of a Race, and thus cherishing the material, saving from destruction and obliteration what is good, helpful and stimulating. But for our Race Literature, how will future generations know of the pioneers in Literature, our statesmen, soldiers, divines, musicians, artists, lawyers, critics, and scholars?

We have endeavored to choose for the Norton Anthology works of such quality that they merit preservation and sustain classroom interest. Like several historically important anthologies—Kerlin's *Negro Poets and Their Poetry*, Calverton's *Anthology of American Negro Literature*, Sterling Brown, Arthur P. Davis, and Ulysses Lee's *Negro Caravan*, among others—we have given a prominent place to the Black vernacular tradition, placing it at the beginning of our text because, historically, anonymous vernacular literature preceded the tradition of written letters among African Americans, and because *all* of the world's literatures have developed from an oral base. In our literary tradition, the oral, or the vernacular, is never far from the written. Oral expression—the dozens, signifying, sampling in the poetry of hip-hop—surrounds the written tradition rather as a Möbius strip intertwines above and below a plane, in the traditional antiphonal "call and response" structures peculiar to African and African American expressive cultural forms. Not only has the vernacular tradition served as the foundation of the written tradition, but it continues to nurture it, comment upon it, and criticize it in a dialectical, reciprocal relation that surely obtained historically in every major literary tradition. (A visit today to a Black beauty parlor, or barbershop, or other ritual sites in Black neighborhoods, verifies this claim.) The vernacular tradition, however, does not take its existence from the printed page, but in community and in performance and in recordings. The Norton Anthology was the first anthology to offer side by side the written and oral traditions, thus illuminating the connections between them, in the form of a CD, in our first edition, and now in the form of links to recordings and performances. This historically unique feature of our anthology, we are proud to note, was the editors' way of underscoring the signal importance of James Gronniosaw's foundational trope: by making our anthology a veritable "talking book," by pairing oral texts with written texts, and thus doing our best to literalize the Black tradition's first structuring metaphor and to emphasize the continuing importance of orality, of "voice," to the unfolding tradition. In this way, our anthology demonstrates, we have come full circle from Gronniosaw's astonishingly enduring mise-en-scène.

As we go to press for this Fourth Edition, we continue to witness an especially active and fecund period for African American literature, as evidenced by the dazzling work produced by Black authors across the full range of literary forms, far too many to list without risking serious omissions. But what is especially fascinating about the current phase of the tradition is the extent to which Black writers are exploring transnational and bi-/multi-racial themes and revising the works of other contemporary Black authors in what we might call a truly "pan-African tradition," and doing so with dazzling invention (often drawing creatively on emerging digital technologies). This mode of international literary influence is occurring simultaneously with the literary production of first-generation African, Caribbean, and Afro-Latin American immigrants (including feminist, gay, and lesbian writers), and all sorts of even more localized Black hyphenations, such as Haitian-African Americans, Nigerian-African Americans, Dominican-African Americans, Ethiopian-African Americans, and Somali-African Americans, as a result of recent immigration patterns from African, Caribbean, and Latin American countries to the United States. Through the work of these first- and second-generation Black Americans, what we mean by "African American identity" or "African American literature" is being called into question in fresh and exciting ways that challenge essentialist notions of ethnicity, gender, sexuality, national identity, and even "race" and "literary tradition." These writers embody and express "new" ways to be "Black" within the context of traditional American racial and artistic definitions. With this new generation and their cross-cultural formal influences, the Black diaspora, which has been a key part of African American literature since the eighteenth century, especially in the Harlem Renaissance and the Black Arts movement, has rooted even more deeply in rich new literary soil.

It is important to remember that the broad and deep influence upon contemporary African American writing of spoken Black English and popular vernacular forms, as we have discussed regarding poetry and hip-hop, has long been a fundamental aspect of Black literary cultural production, as readers can see in W. E. B. Du Bois's use of the spirituals in *The Souls of Black Folk* or Langston Hughes's and Sterling A. Brown's use of the blues and jazz as poetic dictions in their innovative poetry. But the relation between the oral and the written, between Black vernacular and Black written forms, has also been a consistent concern in Black aesthetic theoretical debates, including in Paul Laurence Dunbar's anxieties about the merits of his dialect poetry versus those of his standard English poetry, but perhaps most notably in James Weldon Johnson's worry that the imitation of Black speech in "dialect poetry," as he put it in the introduction to *The Book of American Negro Poetry,* could be fatal to genuine literary creativity, which the Negro must draw upon, as he indicates in the second epigraph to our introduction, to bring about a renaissance of literature and art to combat the Jim Crow racism so prevalent at the time. One can argue, then, that the canon, in the twenty-first century, has returned to its roots, and that the trope of the talking book, literalized in Toni Morrison's astonishingly subtle narrative technique in *Jazz,* but also at work in intertextual sampling and signifying, has never in the history of the African American literary tradition been more varied, vital, and compelling.

The fundamental premise of *The Norton Anthology of African American Literature* is that the works included here, the canonical works in the African American literary tradition, compose a tradition because they "speak" to each other, intertextually, in formal signifying riffs that trace a continuous line of literary descent between the eighteenth and the twenty-first centuries. These works represent—for the most part—Black people struggling to define themselves in a society where their ancestors had been enslaved, and then, when they were freed, where "Blackness" was devalued, mocked, derided, and negated. In the end, these works, as James Weldon Johnson argued almost exactly a century ago, help to define not only a people's place at the grand welcome table of world civilization, but also the depths of their humanity, their dignity, their belief that the will to power is the will to write, and their irrepressible urge to create beauty.

HENRY LOUIS GATES JR.

VALERIE SMITH

THE NORTON ANTHOLOGY OF

AFRICAN AMERICAN LITERATURE

FOURTH EDITION

VOLUME 1

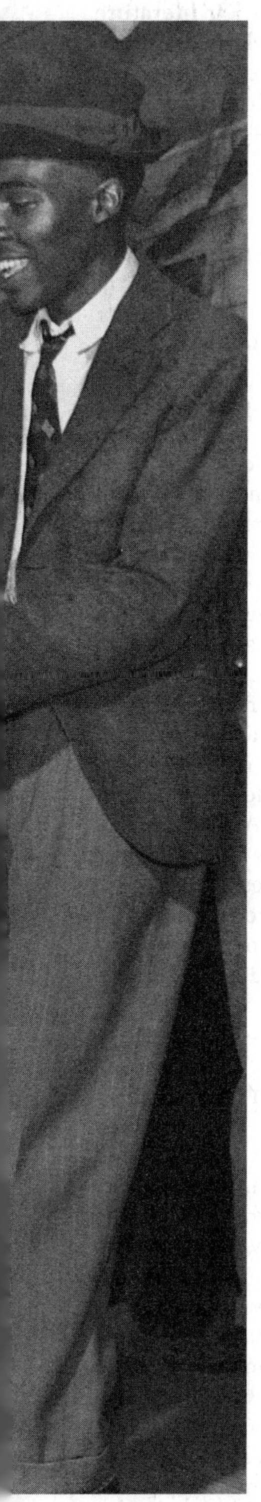

The Vernacular Tradition Part 1

In African American literature, *the vernacular* refers to the church songs, blues, ballads, sermons, stories, and, in our own era, hip-hop songs that are part of the oral, not primarily the literate (or written-down) tradition of Black expression. What distinguishes this body of work is its in-group and, at times, secretive, defensive, and aggressive character: it is not, generally speaking, produced for circulation beyond the Black group itself (though it sometimes is bought and sold by those outside its circle). This highly charged material has been extraordinarily influential for writers of poetry, fiction, drama, and other genres. What would the work of Langston Hughes, Sterling A. Brown, Zora Neale Hurston, and Toni Morrison be like without its Black vernacular ingredients? What, for that matter, would the writing of Mark Twain or William Faulkner be without these same elements? Still, this vernacular material has its own shapes, its own integrity, its own place in the Black literary canon: *the literature of the vernacular.*

Defining the vernacular and delineating it as a category of African American literary studies have been difficult and controversial projects. Some critics note the vernacular's typical demarcation as a category of things that are male, attached only to lower-class groups, and otherwise simplistically expressive of a vast and complexly layered and dispersed group of people. Others

Juke Joint, Clarksdale, Mississippi, 1939. "Musically speaking," wrote Zora Neale Hurston in 1934, "the Jook is the most important place in America. For in its smelly, shoddy confines has been born the secular music known as blues, and on blues has been founded jazz."

warn both against the sentimentalization of a stereotyped "folk" and their "lore" and against the impulse to define Black people and their literature solely in terms of the production of unconscious but somehow definitive work from the bottom of the social hierarchy. With these critiques often come warnings against forming too easy an idea about the shape and direction of African American literary history. Most emphatic is the argument against a "modernist" view that would posit an almost sacred set of foundational vernacular texts by "black and unknown bards" (to borrow James Weldon Johnson's ringing phrase) leading to ever more complex works by higher and higher artists marching into the future. Is contemporary music really more "progressive" or "complex" than the work of Bessie Smith, Robert Johnson, or Louis Armstrong?

And yet even after these questions and criticisms have been raised, somehow such distinctive forms as church songs, blues, tall tales, work songs, games, jokes, dozens, and rap songs—along with myriad other such forms, past and present—persist among African Americans, as they have for decades. They are, as a Langston Hughes poem announces, *still here*. Indeed, the vernacular is not a body of quaint, folksy items. It is not an exclusive male province. Nor is it associated with a particular level of society or with a particular historical era. It is neither long ago, far away, nor fading. Instead, the vernacular encompasses vigorous, dynamic processes of expression, past and present. It makes up a rich storehouse of materials wherein the values, styles, and character types of Black American life are reflected in language that is highly energized and often marvelously eloquent.

Ralph Ellison and Toni Morrison argued that vernacular art accounts, to a large degree, for the Black American's legacy of self-awareness and endurance. For Black performers and listeners (as well as readers) it has often served the classic function of teaching as it delights. Refusing to subscribe wholly to the white American's ethos and worldview, African Americans expressed in these vernacular forms their own ways of seeing the world, its history, and its meanings. The vernacular comprises, Ellison said, nothing less than another instance of humanity's "triumph over chaos." In it experiences of the past are remembered and evaluated; through it African Americans attempt to humanize an often harsh world, and to do so with honesty, with toughness, and often with humor.

THE VERNACULAR: A BRIEF HISTORY

Eighteenth- and nineteenth-century observers, Black and white, recorded their fascination with Black oral forms. Thomas Jefferson, for example, observed that musically the enslaved "are more generally gifted than the whites with accurate ears for tune and time." Nearly fifty years later, a Mississippi planter used conventionally racialized language to inform Frederick Law Olmsted that "niggers is allers good singers nat'rally. I reckon they got better lungs than white folks, they hev such powerful voices." Frederick Douglass took pains in his autobiographies to define the meaning of the songs of slaves. He points out, for instance, that those who hear the music as evidence that enslaved people are happy with their station in life miss the songs' deeper, troubled moanings and meanings. By the end of the nineteenth century, some Black writers were declaring these forms evidence of special "Negro genius," a keystone proof of Black contribution to world culture and of Black readiness for full U.S. citizenship.

Early landmark anthologies of Black literature, *The New Negro* (1925), *The Book of American Negro Poetry* (1931), and *The Negro Caravan* (1941), included careful discussions of Black songs and stories; *Caravan* presented vernacular texts as forms to be enjoyed and studied both as art and as part of the usually unseen historical record. These books opened the way to the realization that Black writers, most obviously poets, were sometimes strongly influenced by vernacular forms. Certain Negro writers of the 1920s and 1930s (and their literary offspring of later decades) consciously sought to draw artistic power from the vernacular into their writing. In some cases—one thinks of works by Langston Hughes, Sterling Brown, and Zora Neale Hurston as examples—writers celebrated such forms as blues and sermons and tried to capture them on the page with as little intrusion as possible.

By the late 1930s, however, Richard Wright, Ralph Ellison, and other African American writers who were close students of the Black vernacular warned against the sentimentalization of "the folk" and declared that the writer's responsibility was to do what they saw Eliot, Stein, and Joyce (along with Louis Armstrong, Jelly Roll Morton, and Duke Ellington) doing in their art: capturing the note and trick of the vernacular at the same time that they transformed it into something new by drawing on artistic sources and traditions beyond the vernacular. Wright and others warned too against the danger of winning audiences for Black writing with the "easy tears" of a simplified Black folklore at the expense of political engagement. What Ellison in particular advocated was a literature as conscious of the best new thinking in political science and modern writing as it was of the ways of Brer Rabbit and the down-home blues. Sounding a similar note in the late 1970s, Albert Murray pronounced what he termed (with a reference to literary critic Kenneth Burke) the "vernacular imperative" for writers: all writers, said Murray, must be thoroughly knowledgeable of the local materials surrounding them (what else could they write about with true authority?) as well as of the artistic traditions for transforming those materials—the vernacular—into the silver and gold of personalized modern artistic expression.

The Black Arts movement of the 1960s and 1970s reflected many of these controversies and convictions about the vernacular. It was a period of the rediscovery of Hurston, who was widely celebrated by the rising new group of feminist writers as well as by various factions of the male-centered Black aesthetic group. At the same time, it was a period of rediscovery of Wright and Hughes, whose radical politics and celebration of the potential within Black working-class communities were widely heralded and imitated. More than ever there was a general sense of Black vernacular expression as something of current value not just among working classes but throughout the African American "nation." Such students of Black speech and story as Roger Abrahams, John Szwed, and Geneva Smitherman helped define the peculiarities of Black vernacular expression and noted its relation to Black oral forms throughout the Americas and in Africa. By the 1980s and 1990s, many scholars and writers recognized the Black vernacular as an enormously rich and various source. Key books by Lawrence Levine, Sterling Stuckey, Albert Murray, Ralph Ellison, Houston A. Baker Jr.,

Henry Louis Gates Jr., Cheryl Wall, and others paved the way for the ongoing contemporary analysis of the forms as sources for historical and critical insight and also as wellsprings for the writer. In the first years of the twenty-first century, scholars across the disciplines, including Farah Jasmine Griffin, Brent Hayes Edwards, Fred Moten, Adam Bradley, Kobena Mercer, Greg Tate, Robin D. G. Kelley, Michael Veal, Lawrence P. Jackson, George E. Lewis, Daphne Brooks, Richard Iton, and Tiya Miles, have charted new directions in Black American vernacular studies.

In the first decades of the twenty-first century, *all* of these vernacular forms have continued to exist and, in some cases, to flourish. On a given weekend in New York City, for example, one might hear live performances of blues, jazz, and gospel as well as several contemporary forms related to R&B. As hip-hop culture has increased in commercial value and worldwide visibility, one wonders how much Black vernacular remains. But this is always a key question for students of these forms. How to evaluate a creolized form once it hits the marketplace, once the marketers have, in Langston Hughes's phrase, "taken our blues and gone"? How to separate and celebrate the fire and ice of hip-hop at its best from the bland imitations and marketeering hoaxes? With this is the mystery that for all the tawdry caprice and relentlessness of the marketplace, somehow the impulse to create vernacular forms that are fresh, independently produced, and recognizably Black has persisted.

DEFINING THE VERNACULAR

What is the vernacular? According to *Webster's* second edition, the term comes from the Latin—"*vernaculus:* Born in one's house, native, from *verna,* a slave born in his master's house, a native"—and counts among its meanings the following: (1) "belonging to, developed in, and spoken or used by the people of a particular place, region, or country; native; indigenous . . . (2) characteristic of a locality; local." In the context of American art, the vernacular may be defined as expression that springs from the creative interaction between the received or learned traditions and that which is locally invented, "made in America." This definition, derived from Ralph Ellison and American cultural historian John A. Kouwenhoven, sees Manhattan's skyscrapers as well as Appalachian quilts as vernacular because they use modern techniques and forms (machines, factory-made materials, etc.), along with what Ellison calls the play-it-by-ear methods and local products that give American forms their distinctive resonances and power. What, then, is the African American vernacular? It consists of forms sacred—songs, prayers, and sermons—and secular—work songs, secular rhymes and songs, blues, jazz, and stories of many kinds. It also consists of dances, wordless musical performances, stage shows, and visual art forms of many sorts.

As the American scholar Houston A. Baker Jr. noted, the word *vernacular* as a cultural term has been used most frequently to describe developments in the world of architecture. In contrast to the exalted, refined, or learned styles of designing buildings, the vernacular in architecture refers both to local styles by builders unaware of or unconcerned with developments beyond their particular province and to works by inspired, cosmopolitan architects such as Frank Lloyd Wright, a careful student of architecture as a worldwide enterprise and of the latest technologies but also one who wanted his buildings custom-made for their surroundings.

This example from architecture is relevant insofar as the makers of Black vernacular art used the American language and everything at their disposal to make art that paid a minimum of attention to the thou-shalt-nots of the academy or the arbiters of high style. Coming from the bottom of the American social ladder, Blacks have been relatively free from scrutiny by the official cultural monitors. As a group they tended to care little about such opinions; what the Black social dance called the Black Bottom looked like to the proctors at the local ballet class (be they white or Black) was of little interest to them. Thus it is no surprise that the Black inventors of this rich array of definitively American forms have had such a potent impact on America's cultural life and history. Consider, for example, the worldwide impact of the social dances called the cake-walk (with its strong impulses to parody) and the Lindy-Hop (the aerial dance taking its name from Charles Lindbergh's daring nonstop airplane voyage from New York to Paris, 1927).

The forms included here are varied and resist aesthetic generalizations. One is drawn nonetheless to parts of Zora Neale Hurston's wonderful catalog of the "Characteristics of Negro Expression": "angularity," "asymmetry," a tendency toward "mimicry," and the "will to adorn." In addition, the forms share traits that reflect their African background: call–response patterns of many kinds; group creation; and a polyrhythmically percussive, dance-beat orientation not only in musical forms but in the rhythm of a line, tale, or rhyme. It is not surprising that improvisation is a highly prized aspect of vernacular performance. Here too one finds European, European American, and Native American forms reshaped to African American purposes and sensibilities. For example, like Black folktales, tales from Europe often lack clear delineations of sacred and profane, good and evil, righteous punishers and righteously punished. Similarly, the blues offer few such consolations, solutions, or even scapegoats. At times what seems revealed is the starkness of a life that is real, that is tough, and that must be confronted without the convenience of formulaic dodges or wishful escapes. Even the spirituals admit that "I've been 'buked and I've been scorned, I've been talked about, / Sure as you're born." And the church songs involve—along with the yearning for heaven's peace—confrontation with real troubles of the world and the will to do something about them.

One of the most compelling efforts at generalization about African American aesthetics is drawn by Henry Louis Gates Jr. from the vernacular itself. Drawing on linguistic research by Geneva Smitherman and others, Gates has defined *signifying*—the often competitively figurative, subversively parodying speech of tales and of less formalized talk as well as of various forms of music—as an impulse that operates not only between contesting tale tellers but between writers (and painters, and dancers, et al.) as well. According to this view, Toni Morrison signifies on writers who precede her by revising their conceptions of character and scene, for example, or perhaps she even signifies on aspects of the novelistic tradition itself. In Gates's complex formulations about how African Americans create, the vernacular meets not only formal art but the world of scholarly criticism as well.

This leaves us with a battery of concerns from postmodern cultural criticism: Is the idea of the vernacular "essentialist," that is, dependent on definitions of racial essences that are not knowable outside the Black circle? What is *Black* about the Black vernacular? When is "American" culture not *Black* and *vernacular*? What stake do cultural observers have in this terminology, or, for that matter, in its rejection?

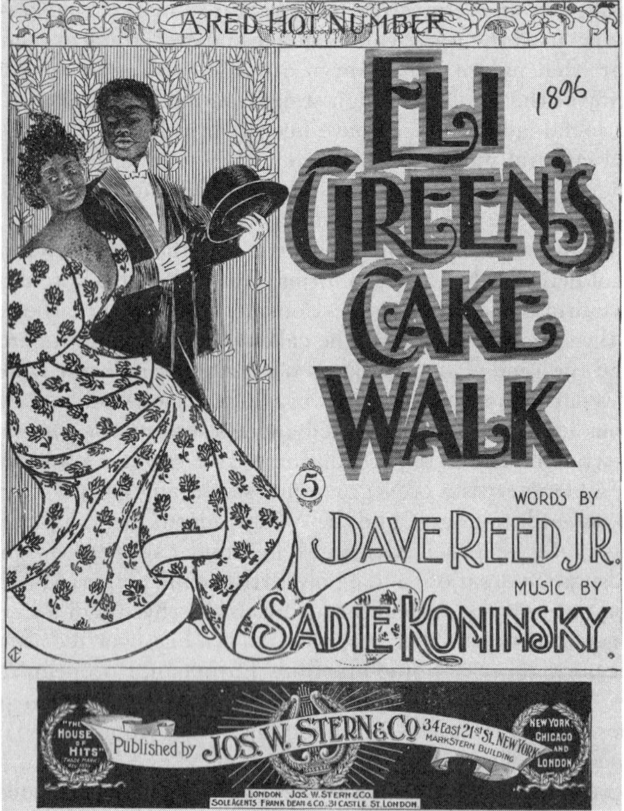

The Cakewalk. In the late nineteenth century, this Black dance, with its strong elements of parody, found its way to New York stage shows and became a citywide and then a national craze.

This leads us to ask, How were this section's entries selected? Whence came these particular texts? Poring over dozens of anthologies and collections, hymnals, songbooks, recordings, and literary works yielded texts that are not only historically representative but also distinctive and resonant with aesthetic power. One problem with capturing such works is that they were not originally constructed for the printed page but for performance within complicated social and often highly ritualized settings. Nonstandard pronunciations in texts transcribed from records are generally represented with a minimum of invented spellings—the "eye dialect" so often used by American writers to designate déclassé or politically disempowered groups. This effort was informed by those of writers who captured Black speech by getting the rhythms right, the pauses, the special emphases and colors. But contractions and new spellings were allowed when they seemed called for.

What determines the order of the vernacular selections, genre by genre? Whenever possible, works are presented in chronological order and are clustered according to authorship. But because authorship and chronology are often unknown or ambiguous (for example, who first told the tale of the rabbit and the tar baby?), we simply have done our best to ascertain credits and dates when they are available. In the folktales section, works are credited and dated in footnotes, but—recognizing that in this instance the "authors" are the recorders (brilliantly artistic ones though they may be) of works created incrementally by many, many voices over many, many years—they are listed not by date or writer but by subject: the animal tales precede the ones with human characters and follow a general chronological arc. Such broad thematic and timeline concerns govern all of the vernacular section's orderings—even when specific dates and authors are given. For even in the case of a Duke Ellington song or a Martin Luther King sermon/speech, for which date and author seem so specific, what we reproduce here is one particular text or version of a performance given over and over, according to changing settings and moments. And both Ellington and King draw on rich vernacular traditions (on Black and unknown bards) to fashion and project their works. (In Ellington's case, the best text may be the recorded "text," with its performance by the sixteen members of his band, each of whom adds much more to the creative process than is the case with European "classical" music.) More than any other form of Black literature, the vernacular resists being captured on a page or in a historical frame: by definition, it is about gradual group creation; it is about *change*.

Clearly, the selections here are not meant to be definitive but to invite further explorations and findings. Black vernacular forms are works in progress, experiments in a still new country. They have not survived because they are perfect, polished jewels but because they are vigorous fountains of expression. Not only are they influential for writers but they are wonderful creations on their own. In the Black tradition, no forms are more quick or overflowing with power and meaning.

Spirituals

Negro spirituals are the religious songs sung by African Americans since the earliest days of slavery and first gathered in a book in 1801 by the Black church leader Richard Allen. As scholars have observed, this term, whether abbreviated to *spirituals* or not, is somewhat misleading: for many enslaved people, and for their offspring, the divisions between secular and sacred were not as definite as the designation *spirituals* would suggest. Certainly these religious songs were not sung only in churches or in religious ritual settings. Travelers in the Old South and the enslaved themselves reported that music about God and the Bible was sung during work time, play time, and rest time as well as on Sundays at praise meetings. As historian Lawrence Levine observed, for those who were enslaved the concept of the sacred signified a strong will to incorporate "within this world all the elements of the divine."

That the songs were sung not just in ritual worship but throughout the day meant that they served as powerful shields against the values of the slaveholders and their killing definitions of Black humanity. For one thing, along with a sense of the enslaved

"A Negro Camp Meeting in the South." This 1872 engraving by Solomon Eytinge depicts a church meeting held outdoors. Families gathered to praise God in sermon and song and to consider their "rolling through an unfriendly world" (as one spiritual puts it) toward "a bright side, somewhere."

people's personal self-worth as children of a mighty God, the spirituals offered them much-needed psychic escape from the workaday world of slavery's restrictions and cruelties. Certainly, "this world is not my home" was a steady theme in the spirituals, one that offered its singer–hearers visions of a peaceful, loving realm beyond the one in which they labored. Some of the songs bespoke the dream of flying away, leaving the world of care behind:

> I've got two wings for to veil my face
> I've got two wings for to fly away . . .

Along with such visions of displacement and escape, many of the spirituals offered images of a steady and just King Jesus who had a comfortable space around his altar where those in Heaven could rest a while (significant for people forced to work all day), a place where they would be reunited with "friends and kindreds" who had gone before. One song makes clear the vision of familiarity and ease:

> A-settin' down with Jesus
> Eatin' hone and drinkin' wine
> Marchin' round de throne
> Wid Peter, James, and John.

And:

> I'm gonna tell God all my troubles,
> When I get home . . .
> I'm gonna tell him the road was rocky
> When I get home.

In such visions of justice and peace resided both a healthful impulse to escape the sorrowful world and an implied criticism of life's earthly overwork, injustice, and violence.

Most of the spirituals were not about easeful King Jesus at all, however, but about the Old Testament God and his heroes and prophets. Moses, Job, Daniel, Samson, and Ezekiel are celebrated in scores of spirituals along with the chosen people, protected by their furiously watchful god. According to poet and critic Sterling A. Brown, "Fairly easy allegories identified Egypt-land with the South, Pharaoh with the masters, the Israelites with themselves and Moses with their leader." It is not surprising that some of the songs offered not just psychic escapes and veiled criticisms but calls for this-worldly attentiveness and direct action:

Didn't my Lord deliver Daniel,
And why not every man?

Frederick Douglass and others spoke of references in the spirituals to escapes not to heaven but to freedomland, whether in the non-slaveholding states or all the way to Canada. "Swing low sweet chariot, Coming for to carry me home" was evidently one of those songs that referred to the urge, and perhaps the specific plan, to make a run out of the jaws of slavery into the land of freedom. Many songs, doubtless sung well out of the master's earshot, celebrated the coming of freedom:

O Freedom;
O Freedom!
And before I'll be a slave,
I'll be buried in my grave!
And go home to my Lord and be free.

Other secret songs were equally direct and stark:

No more driver's lash for me;
No more, no more . . .
No more peck of corn for me;
Many thousands go.

In terms of form, these songs employ the call–response patterns of West and Central Africa, patterns that were encouraged by the lining-out (that is, the calling out of the song lyrics in anticipation of the group's singing of the lyrics) of hymns that the New World Africans encountered in the Protestant services of America. The single voice of the chorus would be answered by a group of singers, usually the entire group gathered together. The songs varied in rhythm. Dirgelike "sorrow songs," rightly named by W. E. B. Du Bois in his extraordinary chapter on the music in *The Souls of Black Folk,* were quite appropriate for such plaintive lyrics as

Don't know what my mother wants to stay here fuh,
Dis ole world ain't been no friend to huh.

Only slightly less dark was the meditative poetry that clergyman, writer, and army officer Thomas Wentworth Higginson, one of the first to pay respectful attention to the spiritual, heard among Black Civil War soldiers:

I'll lie in de grave
And stretch out my arms,
When I lay dis body down.

Elsewhere, the spirituals presented a drivingly percussive vision of Judgment Day. "That Great Gittin' Up Morning!," a song of Gabriel, trumpet song, and jubilation, might have been used in a ring shout where the possessed worshippers were inspired to raise their voices and move their bodies in praise of the Lord.

Further study of spirituals will investigate efforts to capture their sounds on the printed page—by Du Bois, James Weldon Johnson, Zora Neale Hurston, John W. Work, Howard Thurman, and many others. New work will explore the spirituals' African, European, and Native American sources; the debates over the originality of their forms and verses; their presentation in minstrel shows and other commercial venues; their fund-raising importance for nineteenth- and twentieth-century Black schools; their uses by classically trained Black composers and arrangers as concert "art music"; their uses by Antonín Dvořák, William Grant Still, Duke Ellington, and other composers in search of an indigenous American music that used large forms; their importance for "race men and women" of the last two hundred years, who often pointed to the songs as evidence of "Negro genius"; and their relation to gospel and other African American musics. Suffice it to say that even when read spirituals are both moving and inspiring in their complex expression of sorrow and hope for far-off joy.

Been in the Storm So Long[1]

I've been in the storm so long,
You know I've been in the storm so long,
Oh Lord, give me more time to pray,
I've been in the storm so long.

I am a motherless child,
Singin' I am a motherless child,
Singin' Oh Lord, give me more time to pray,
I've been in the storm so long.

This is a needy time,
This is a needy time,
Singin' Oh Lord, give me more time to pray,
I've been in the storm so long.

Lord, I need you now,
Lord, I need you now,
Singin' Oh Lord, give me more time to pray,
I've been in the storm so long.

My neighbors need you now,
My neighbors need you now,
Singin' Oh Lord, give me more time to pray,
I've been in the storm so long.

My children need you now,
My children need you now,
Singin' Oh Lord, give me more time to pray,
I've been in the storm so long.

Just look what a shape I'm in,
Just look what a shape I'm in,
Cryin' Oh Lord, give me more time to pray,
I've been in the storm so long.

1. That this song can be found in many versions illustrates the dynamism of the oral form. Here and throughout this vernacular section, no single, final authoritative text exists.

Go Down, Moses[1]

Go down, Moses,
Way down in Egyptland
Tell old Pharaoh
To let my people go.

When Israel was in Egyptland
Let my people go
Oppressed so hard they could not stand
Let my people go.

Go down, Moses,
Way down in Egyptland
Tell old Pharaoh
"Let my people go."

"Thus saith the Lord," bold Moses said,
"Let my people go;
If not I'll smite your first-born dead
Let my people go.

"No more shall they in bondage toil,
Let my people go;
Let them come out with Egypt's spoil,
Let my people go."

The Lord told Moses what to do
Let my people go;
To lead the children of Israel through,
Let my people go.

Go down, Moses,
Way down in Egyptland,
Tell old Pharaoh,
"Let my people go!"

Ezekiel Saw de Wheel[1]

Ezekiel saw de wheel
'Way up in de middle of de air
Ezekiel saw de wheel
'Way in de middle of the air

The big wheel run by faith
And de little wheel run by de grace of God
A wheel in a wheel
'Way in de middle of de air

1. The scholar and poet Sterling A. Brown observed in 1953 that this song was so direct in its protest that it was banned on many slave plantations.

1. A Negro spiritual inspired by the biblical book of Ezekiel and arranged by William L. Dawson (1899–1990), a musicologist and professor at the Tuskegee Institute.

Better mind my brother how you walk on de cross
'Way in de middle of de air
Your foot might slip and your soul get lost
'Way in de middle of de air

Old Satan wears a club foot shoe
'Way in de middle of de air
If you don't mind he'll slip it on you
'Way in de middle of the air

Ezekiel saw de wheel
'Way up in de middle of de air
Ezekiel saw de wheel
'Way in de middle of the air

The big wheel run by faith
And de little wheel run by de grace of God
A wheel in a wheel
'Way in de middle of de air

Ezekiel saw de wheel
'Way up in de middle of de air
Ezekiel saw de wheel
'Way in de middle of de air

Deep River

Deep river, my home is over Jordan,[1]
Deep river, Lord, I want to cross over into campground, Lord.
I want to cross over into campground, Lord.
I want to cross over into campground.

Oh, don't you want to go to that Gospel feast?
That promised land where all is peace?

Roll, Jordan, Roll

Roll, Jordan, roll, roll, Jordan,
I want to go to heaven when I die,
To hear Jordan roll.

Oh, brothers, you ought t'have been there,
Yes, my Lord!
A sitting in the Kingdom,
To hear Jordan roll.

Roll, Jordan, roll, roll, Jordan,
I want to go to heaven when I die,
To hear Jordan roll.

1. A river in the Middle East. "Crossing over Jordan" is a metaphor for going to heaven.

Swing Low, Sweet Chariot[1]

Swing low, sweet chariot,
Coming for to carry me home,
Swing low, sweet chariot,
Coming for to carry me home.

I looked over Jordan[2] and what did I see
Coming for to carry me home,
A band of angels, coming after me,
Coming for to carry me home.

If you get there before I do,
Coming for to carry me home,
Tell all my friends I'm coming too,
Coming for to carry me home.

Swing low, sweet chariot,
Coming for to carry me home,
Swing low, sweet chariot,
Coming for to carry me home.

Steal Away to Jesus[1]

Steal away, steal away, steal away to Jesus,
Steal away, steal away home,
I ain't got long to stay here.

My Lord, He calls me,
He calls me by the thunder,
The trumpet sounds within-a my soul,
I ain't got long to stay here.

Steal away, steal away, steal away to Jesus,
Steal away, steal away home,
I ain't got long to stay here.

Green trees a-bending,
Po' sinner stands a-trembling,
The trumpet sounds within-a my soul,
I ain't got long to stay here.

Steal away, steal away, steal away to Jesus,
Steal away, steal away home,
I ain't got long to stay here.

1. This song is often cited as not just celebrating the hope of release into heaven but signaling the plan or the moment—or the general aspiration—to be carried "home" to freedom by the Underground Railroad.

2. Again, the river.

1. Often cited as a signal song for enslaved people who had run away. If so, its lyrics—especially using the dangerous word *steal*—must have been kept secret from white supporters of slavery.

Didn't My Lord Deliver Daniel?[1]

Didn't my Lord deliver Daniel,
Deliver Daniel, deliver Daniel?
Didn't my Lord deliver Daniel?
An' why not everyman?

He delivered Daniel from de lion's den,
Jonah[2] from de belly of de whale.
And de Hebrew children from de fiery furnace,
An' why not everyman?

Didn't my Lord deliver Daniel,
Deliver Daniel, deliver Daniel?
Didn't my Lord deliver Daniel?
An' why not everyman?

De moon run down in a purple stream,
De sun forbear to shine,
And every star disappear,
King Jesus shall be mine.

Didn't my Lord deliver Daniel,
Deliver Daniel, deliver Daniel?
Didn't my Lord deliver Daniel?
An' why not everyman?

De wind blows east and de wind blows west,
It blows like de judgment day,
And every poor soul dat never did pray'll
Be glad to pray dat day.

Didn't my Lord deliver Daniel,
Deliver Daniel, deliver Daniel?
Didn't my Lord deliver Daniel?
An' why not everyman?

I set my foot on de Gospel ship,
An' de ship begin to sail.
It landed me over on Canaan's[3] shore
And I'll never come back no more.

Didn't my Lord deliver Daniel,
Deliver Daniel, deliver Daniel?
Didn't my Lord deliver Daniel?
An' why not everyman?

1. When the Babylonians threw Daniel into a lions' den, God sent an angel to shut the lions' mouths, thus delivering him from harm (Daniel 6:22).
2. After being swallowed by a great fish, Jonah was saved when God heard his prayers (Jonah 2:7–10).
3. The Promised Land, encompassing present-day Israel and parts of Syria; here, a symbol of heaven.

My Lord, What a Morning

My Lord, what a morning,
My Lord, what a morning,
My Lord, what a morning,
When the stars begin to fall.

You'll hear the trumpet sound,
To wake the nations underground,
Looking to my God's right hand,
When the stars begin to fall.

You'll hear the sinner mourn,
To wake the nations underground,
Looking to my God's right hand,
When the stars begin to fall.

You'll hear the Christian shout,
To wake the nations underground,
Looking to my God's right hand
When the stars begin to fall.

Wade in the Water

Wade in the water,
Wade in the water, children,
Wade in the water,
God's a-going to trouble the water.

See that band all dressed in white,
God's a-going to trouble the water.
Leader looks like the Israelite,[1]
God's a-going to trouble the water.

See that band all dressed in red,
God's a-going to trouble the water.
Looks like the band that Moses led,
God's a-going to trouble the water.

Look over yonder what do I see?
God's a-going to trouble the water.
The Holy Ghost a-coming on me,
God's a-going to trouble the water.

You don't believe I've been redeemed?
God's a-going to trouble the water.
Just follow me down to Jordan's stream,
God's a going to trouble the water.

1. That is, Moses.

Since I Laid My Burden Down

I been shoutin',
I been shoutin'
Since I laid my burden down;
I been shoutin',
I been shoutin'
Since I laid my burden down.

[CHORUS]

Glory, glory, hallelujah,
Since I laid my burden down;
Glory, glory, hallelujah,
Since I laid my burden down.

I been prayerin',
I been prayerin'
Since I laid my burden down;
I been prayerin',
I been prayerin'
Since I laid my burden down.

[CHORUS]

Glory, glory, hallelujah,
Since I laid my burden down;
Glory, glory, hallelujah,
Since I laid my burden down.

Ride On, King Jesus[1]

Ride on, King Jesus,
No man can a hinder me;
Ride on, King Jesus,
No man can a hinder me.

I was but young when I begun,
No man can a hinder me;
But now my race is almost done,
No man can a hinder me.

King Jesus rides on a milk-white horse,
No man can a hinder me;
The river of Jordan he did cross,
No man can a hinder me.

If you want to find your way to God,
No man can a hinder me;
The gospel highway must be trod,
No man can a hinder me.

1. Sung by the Jubilee Singers in the late 19th century.

Secular Rhymes and Songs

Secular forms of expression were nearly as important as sacred forms for enslaved African Americans. Perhaps over time such forms have become *more* important than sacred ones; certainly, this seems to be the case for many Black people of the second half of the twentieth century and of the early twenty-first century as well.

Enslaved narrators reported mock-prayers, mock-sermons, and other parodies of the forms celebrated in church. Doubtless these provided a kind of outlet for the deeply faithful: Black laughter may have humanized an awesome God and his earthly saints (along with a powerful preacher, the subject of many a joke in this category) and thereby ironically *sustained* belief. Elsewhere, aside from religion and its purposes, such secular parodies of sacred texts contained their own stinging elements of truth:

> "Our Fadder, Which are in Heaben!"—
> White man owe me leben and pay me seben
> "D'y Kingdom come! D'y Will be done!"—
> An' if I hadn't tuck dat, I wouldn' git none.

In addition, they expressed with humor the bitter disappointments of enslaved existence:

> My ole Mistiss promise me,
> W'en she died, she'd set me free.
> She lived so long dat 'er head got bal',
> An' she give out 'n de notion a dyin' at all.

Superb narrative rhymes, sometimes framed as songs, also enliven this group. Here one finds praise songs to such fast-moving heroes as Travelin' Man; Long Gone Lost John; Railroad Bill; Po' Lazarus; and John Henry, the hard-muscled steel driver who died trying to outhammer the steam-driven hammer machine. Their more contemporary (that is, current and dating back to the beginning of the twentieth century) cousins are Shine and Stackolee, who, like certain earlier heroic ballad figures, are fast-talking figures of action and, if necessary, violence. Badman figures who "don't mind dying" became more numerous in twentieth-century lore. These hero and badman forms have had a strong impact on the blues, that other stronghold of secular expression, and, in current times, on rap music, in which modern wish-fulfillment avengers roam, bragging, daring trouble, ready for war.

In this broad category of the secular, one finds children's game songs, rhyming snatches of advice ("a still tongue makes a wise head"), and other miscellaneous pieces. All are materials of play, which is sometimes fun and frivolous, sometimes instructive, sometimes frighteningly reflective of the violence of American society.

Work songs of slavery and (relative) freedom also fall within this space of secular Black vernacular expression. These often ruggedly eloquent songs functioned to pass the time, to synchronize the work pace, and to reflect on the scene the workers witnessed. These story songs and rhymes were often expressed by virtuoso singers and wordsmiths whose underground talents, unseen by the broader society, are celebrated in the worlds in which they reign as "men of words," power figures. Doubtless their energy and unofficial artistry are part of the story of how Africans in America have managed to survive and even to prevail.

Ain't But Me One

My mother is gone,
Ain't but me one;
My mother is gone,
Ain't but me one;
My mother is gone,
Ain't but me one;
Oh Lord, ain't but me one.

Me and My Captain

Me an my captain don't agree,
But he don't know, 'cause he don't ask me;
He don't know, he don't know my mind,
When he see me laughing
Just laughing to keep from crying.

Oh what's the matter now,
Me and my captain can't get along nohow;
He don't know, he don't know my mind,
When he see me laughing
Just laughing to keep from crying.

He call me low down I just laugh,
Kick seat of my pants and that ain't half;
He don't know, he don't know my mind,
When he see me laughing
Just laughing to keep from crying.

Got one mind for white folks to see,
'Nother for what I know is me;
He don't know, he don't know my mind,
When he see me laughing
Just laughing to keep from crying.

Dere's a Man Goin' Roun' Takin' Names

Dere's a man goin' roun' takin' names,
Dere's a man goin' roun' takin' names,
He's a-taken mah mother's name,
An has left mah heart in pain,
Dere's a man goin' roun' takin' names.

Oh, Death is de man takin' names,
Oh, Death is de man takin' names,
He's a-taken mah father's name,
An' has left mah heart in pain,
Dere's a man goin' roun' takin' names.

Promises of Freedom

My ole Mistiss promise me,
W'en she died, she'd set me free.
She lived so long dat 'er head got bal',
An' she give out'n de notion a dyin' at all.

My ole Mistiss say to me:
"Sambo, I'se gwine ter set you free."
But w'en dat head git slick an' bal',
De Lawd couldn' a' killed 'er wid a big green maul.[1]

My ole Mistiss never die,
Wid 'er nose all hooked an' skin all dry.
But my ole Miss, she's somehow gone,
An' she lef' "Uncle Sambo" a-hillin' up co'n.

Ole Mosser lakwise promise me,
W'en he died, he'd set me free.
But ole Mosser go an' make his Will
Fer to leave me a-plowin' ole Beck still.

Yes, my ole Mosser promise me;
But "his papers" didn't leave me free.
A dose of pizen he'ped 'im along.
May de Devil preach 'is fūner'l song.

No More Auction Block[1]

No more auction block for me
No more, no more
No more auction block for me
Many thousand gone

No more peck of corn for me
No more, no more
No more peck of corn for me
Many thousand gone

No more driver's lash for me
No more, no more
No more driver's lash for me
Many thousand gone

No more pint of salt for me
No more, no more
No more pint of salt for me
Many thousand gone

1. A heavy club, mallet, or staff.
1. By Gustavus D. Pike (1873); performed by the Jubilee Singers.

No more hundred lash for me
No more, no more
No more hundred lash for me
Many thousand gone

No more mistress call for me
No more, no more
No more mistress call for me
Many thousand gone

Jack and Dinah Want Freedom

Ole Aunt Dinah, she's jes lak me.
She wuk so hard dat she want to be free.
But, you know, Aunt Dinah's gittin' sorter ole;
An' she's feared to go to Canada, caze it's so cōl'.

Dar wus ole Uncle Jack, he want to git free.
He find de way Norf by de moss on de tree.
He cross dat river a-floatin' in a tub.
Dem Patterollers[1] give 'im a mighty close rub.

Dar is ole Uncle Billy, he's a mighty good Nigger.
He tote all de news to Mosser a little bigger.
When you tells Uncle Billy, you wants free fer a fac';
De nex' day de hide drap off'n yō' back.

Run, Nigger, Run

Run, nigger run; de patter-roller catch you;
Run, nigger, run, it's almost day.
Run, nigger, run; de patter-roller catch you;
Run, nigger, run, and try to get away.

Dis nigger run, he run his best,
Stuck his head in a hornet's nest,
Jumped de fence and run fru de paster;
White man run, but nigger run faster.

Dat nigger run, dat nigger flew,
Dat nigger tore his shirt in two.

1. Formally and informally appointed police agents charged with intercepting fugitive slaves.

Another Man Done Gone

Another man done gone,
Another man done gone,
Uh—from the county farm,
Another man done gone.

I didn't know his name,
I didn't know his name,
I didn't know his name,
I didn't know his name.

He had a long chain on,
He had a long chain on,
He had a long chain on,
He had a long chain on.

He killed another man,
He killed another man,
He killed another man,
He killed another man.

I don' know where he's gone,
I don' know where he's gone,
I don' know where he's gone,
I don' know where he's gone.

I'm going to walk your log,
I'm going to walk your log,
I'm going to walk your log,
I'm going to walk your log.

You May Go But This Will Bring You Back[1]

You may leave and go to Hali-ma-fack,[2]
But my slow-drag will-a bring you back,
A-well-a you may go but this will bring you back.

Ahhh, I been in the country but I moved to town,
I'm a toe-low shaker[3] from a-head on down,
Well-a you may go but this will bring you back.

Ahh, some folks call me a toe-low shaker,
It's a doggone lie, I'm a backbone breaker,
Well-a you may go but this will bring you back.

1. Sung by Zora Neale Hurston in 1935 during an interview at the Library of Congress.
2. Facetious reference to the Halifax River in Florida and/or to Halifax in Nova Scotia; used here to mean a long distance. It also refers to a faraway mythic realm, such as the "Philamayork" of many tales.
3. Juke-house dancer; see also "backbone breaker," line 8, below.

Aw, you like my peaches but you don't like me,
Don't you like my peaches, don't you shake my tree,
Well-a you may go but this will bring you back.

A-hoodoo, a-hoodoo, a-hoodoo working,
My heels are popping and my toenails cracking,
Well-a you may go but this will bring you back.

Ring Shouts

Samuel A. Floyd Jr., a preeminent twentieth-century musicologist in the field of African American music and folk culture, describes the ring shout as "the foundation of Afro-American music." The ring shout draws on biblical parables, images, and themes to generate a collective performance, with members of the group arranged in a circle, sounding a dynamic call and response between a lead shouter who sets phrases or verses, often with variations, that are then echoed and reprised by basers, an ensemble who keep the original phrase circulating through the ring. With its combination of dance, chant, singing, clapping, and rhythmic shuffle, the ring shout is arguably the matrix for all African American music. The ring shout was—and still is—continued by some church groups, notably in the Geechee Gullah communities of coastal Georgia, where performers like the Georgia Sea Island Singers or the McIntosh County Shouters have helped to galvanize popular interest in the practice and keep its traditions alive.

Watch That Star

[CHORUS (LEADER AND BASERS)]

Oh, watch that star, see how it run
Watch that star, see how it run,
If the stars run down in the western hills,
You oughtta watch that star, see how it run,

[LEADER]

Everybody—

[CHORUS (LEADER AND BASERS)]

Oh, watch that star, see how it run
Watch that star, see how it run,
If the stars run down in the western hills,
You oughtta watch that star, see how it run,
Oh, members—

[CHORUS (LEADER AND BASERS)]

Oh, watch that star, see how it run
Watch that star, see how it run,
If the stars run down in the western hills,
You oughtta watch that star, see how it run,

[LEADER]

Well the days is past and gone
The evenin' shadow 'pear,
Oh may we all remember well
The night of death drawin' near
Everybody—

[CHORUS (LEADER AND BASERS)]

Oh, watch that star, see how it run
Watch that star, see how it run,
If the stars run down in the western hills,
You oughtta watch that star, see how it run,

[LEADER]

Oh, members—

[CHORUS (LEADER AND BASERS)]

Oh, watch that star, see how it run
Watch that star, see how it run,
If the stars run down in the western hills,
You oughtta watch that star, see how it run,

[LEADER]

Well we lay our garment by,
Upon our bed to res':
Oh death will soon rob us all
Of what we have possess'
Everybody—

[CHORUS (AS ABOVE, AND REPEAT PREVIOUS VERSE AND CHORUS)]

[LEADER]

Must Jesus bear the cross alone,
An' all this world go free?
No, he bears the cross for everyone
And bears the cross for me.

[CHORUS (LEADER AND BASERS)]

Oh, watch that star, see how it run
Watch that star, see how it run,
If the stars run down in the western hills,
You oughtta watch that star, see how it run.

The Georgia Sea Island Singers at the Newport Folk Festival in July 1963. Since the group came together in the early twentieth century, it has featured various performers, including the legendary Bessie Jones, here playing the tambourine.

Kneebone Bend

[LEADER]

Kneebone, kneebone

[BASERS]

Oh, Lord, kneebone

[LEADER]

Kneebone, kneebone

[BASERS]

Oh, Lord, kneebone bend

[SIMILARLY]

Kneebone hear God call you
    Oh, Lord, kneebone
Kneebone hear God call you
    Oh, Lord, kneebone bend.

Kneebone, kneebone
    Oh, Lord, kneebone

Kneebone, kneebone
  Oh, Lord, kneebone bend.

Kneebone, what's the matter?
  Oh, Lord, kneebone
Kneebone, what's the matter?
  Oh, Lord, kneebone bend.

Kneebone, kneebone
  Oh, Lord, kneebone
Kneebone, kneebone
  Oh, Lord, kneebone bend.

Kneebone in the wil'erness
  Oh, Lord, kneebone
Kneebone in the wil'erness
  Oh, Lord, kneebone bend.

Kneebone, hear God call you
  Oh, Lord, kneebone
Kneebone, hear God call you
  Oh, Lord, kneebone bend.

Kneebone, kneebone
  Oh, Lord, kneebone
Kneebone, kneebone
  Oh, Lord, kneebone bend.
Kneebone ben' to save m' soul

Farewell, Las' Goin'

[LEADER]

This is the las'

[BASERS]

Farewell, las' goin', farewell

[LEADER]

This is the las'

[BASERS]

Farewell, las' goin', farewell

[LEADER]

Goodbye, members / Goodbye, members /
I hate to leave you / I hope to see you /
Goodbye, members / Goodbye, members /
This is the las' / This is the las' /

We had a good time / I hate to leave you /
I hope to see you / Another time /
This is the las' / Goodbye, members /
Goodbye, members / I hate to leave you /
I hope to see you / Oh, this is the las' /
Oh, this is the las' / This is the las' /
Goodbye, members / Ah, members /
Bye-bye, members / I hate to leave you /
I hope to see you / We had a good time /
We had a good time / I hate to leave you /
I hope to see you / Oh, this is the las'
This is the las' / This is the las' /
Oh, this is the las' / This is the las' /
Goodbye, members!

Ballads

John Henry

When John Henry was a little fellow,
  You could hold him in the palm of your hand,
He said to his pa, "When I grow up
  I'm gonna be a steel-driving man.
    Gonna be a steel-driving man."

When John Henry was a little baby,
  Setting on his mammy's knee,
He said "The Big Bend Tunnel on the C. & O. Road[1]
  Is gonna be the death of me,
    Gonna be the death of me."

One day his captain told him,
  How he had bet a man
That John Henry would beat his steam-drill down,
  Cause John Henry was the best in the land,
    John Henry was the best in the land.

John Henry kissed his hammer,
  White man turned on steam,
Shaker held John Henry's trusty steel,
  Was the biggest race the world had ever seen,
    Lord, biggest race the world ever seen.

John Henry on the right side
  The steam drill on the left,
"Before I'll let your steam drill beat me down,
  I'll hammer my fool self to death,
    Hammer my fool self to death."

1. The Chesapeake and Ohio Railroad line.

John Henry walked in the tunnel,
His captain by his side,
The mountain so tall, John Henry so small,
He laid down his hammer and he cried,
Laid down his hammer and he cried.

Captain heard a mighty rumbling,
Said "The mountain must be caving in,"
John Henry said to the captain,
"It's my hammer swinging in de wind,
My hammer swinging in de wind."

John Henry said to his shaker,[2]
"Shaker, you'd better pray;
For if ever I miss this piece of steel,
Tomorrow'll be your burial day,
Tomorrow'll be your burial day."

John Henry said to his shaker,
"Lordy, shake it while I sing,
I'm pulling my hammer from my shoulders down,
Great Gawdamighty, how she ring,
Great Gawdamighty, how she ring!"

John Henry said to his captain,
"Before I ever leave town,
Gimme one mo' drink of dat tom-cat gin,
And I'll hammer dat steam driver down,
I'll hammer dat steam driver down."

John Henry said to his captain,
"Before I ever leave town,
Gimme a twelve-pound hammer wid a whale-bone handle,
And I'll hammer dat steam driver down,
I'll hammer dat steam drill on down."

John Henry said to his captain,
"A man ain't nothin' but a man,
But before I'll let dat steam drill beat me down,
I'll die wid my hammer in my hand,
Die wid my hammer in my hand."

The man that invented the steam drill
He thought he was mighty fine,
John Henry drove down fourteen feet,
While the steam drill only made nine,
Steam drill only made nine.

"Oh, lookaway over yonder, captain,
You can't see like me,"
He gave a long and loud and lonesome cry,

2. The railroad worker who holds the drill upright and rotates it between the blows of the hammer.

"Lawd, a hammer be the death of me,
A hammer be the death of me!"

John Henry had a little woman,
Her name was Polly Ann,
John Henry took sick, she took his hammer,
She hammered like a natural man,
Lawd, she hammered like a natural man.

John Henry hammering on the mountain
As the whistle blew for half-past two,
The last words his captain heard him say,
"I've done hammered my insides in two,
Lawd, I've hammered my insides in two."

The hammer that John Henry swung
It weighed over twelve pound,
He broke a rib in his left hand side
And his intrels fell on the ground,
And his intrels fell on the ground.

John Henry, O, John Henry,
His blood is running red,
Fell right down with his hammer to the ground,
Said, "I beat him to the bottom but I'm dead,
Lawd, beat him to the bottom but I'm dead."

When John Henry was laying there dying,
The people all by his side,
The very last words they heard him say,
"Give me a cool drink of water 'fore I die,
Cool drink of water 'fore I die."

John Henry had a little woman,
The dress she wore was red,
She went down the track, and she never looked back,
Going where her man fell dead,
Going where her man fell dead.

John Henry had a little woman,
The dress she wore was blue,
De very last words she said to him,
"John Henry, I'll be true to you,
John Henry, I'll be true to you."

"Who's gonna shoes yo' little feet,
Who's gonna glove yo' hand,
Who's gonna kiss yo' pretty, pretty cheek,
Now you done lost yo' man?
Now you done lost yo' man?"

"My mammy's gonna shoes my little feet,
Pappy gonna glove my hand,

My sister's gonna kiss my pretty, pretty cheek,
  Now I done lost my man,
    Now I done lost my man."

They carried him down by the river,
  And buried him in the sand,
And everybody that passed that way,
  Said, "There lies that steel-driving man,
    There lies a steel-driving man."

They took John Henry to the river,
  And buried him in the sand,
And every locomotive come a-roaring by,
  Says "There lies that steel-drivin' man,
    Lawd, there lies a *steel*-drivin' man."

Some say he came from Georgia,
  And some from Alabam,
But its wrote on the rock at the Big Bend Tunnel,
  That he was an East Virginia man,
    Lord, Lord, an East Virginia man.

Frankie and Johnny

Frankie and Johnny were lovers,
  Lordy, how they could love,
Swore to be true to each other,
  True as the stars up above,
    He was her man, but he done her wrong.

Frankie went down to the corner,
  To buy her a bucket of beer,
Frankie says "Mister Bartender,
  Has my lovin' Johnnie been here?
    He is my man, but he's doing me wrong."

"I don't want to cause you no trouble
  Don't want to tell you no lie,
I saw your Johnnie half-an-hour ago
  Making love to Nelly Bly.
    He is your man, but he's doing you wrong."

Frankie went down to the hotel
  Looked over the transom so high,
There she saw her lovin' Johnnie
  Making love to Nelly Bly
    He was her man; he was doing her wrong.

Frankie threw back her kimono,
  Pulled out her big forty-four;
Rooty-toot-toot: three times she shot

Right through that hotel door,
She shot her man, who was doing her wrong.

"Roll me over gently,
Roll me over slow,
Roll me over on my right side,
Cause these bullets hurt me so,
I was your man, but I done you wrong."

Bring all your rubber-tired hearses
Bring all your rubber-tired hacks,
They're carrying poor Johnny to the burying ground
And they ain't gonna bring him back,
He was her man, but he done her wrong.

Frankie says to the sheriff,
"What are they going to do?"
The sheriff he said to Frankie,
"It's the 'lectric chair for you.
He was your man, and he done you wrong."

"Put me in that dungeon,
Put me in that cell,
Put me where the northeast wind
Blows from the southeast corner of hell,
I shot my man, 'cause he done me wrong."

The Signifying Monkey[1]

The Monkey and the Lion
Got to talking one day.
Monkey looked down and said, Lion,
I hear you's king in every way.
But I know somebody
Who do not think that is true—
He told me he could whip
The living daylights out of you.
Lion said, Who?
Monkey said, Lion,
He talked about your mama
And talked about your grandma, too,
And I'm too polite to tell you
What he said about you.
Lion said, Who said what? Who?
Monkey in the tree,
Lion on the ground.

1. This somewhat sanitized version was presented by Langston Hughes and Arna Bontemps in *The Book of American Negro Folklore* (1958). "Signifying": a wide variety of African American verbal games involving ritual insult, competition, innuendo, parody, and other forms of loaded expression.

Monkey kept on signifying
But he didn't come down.
Monkey said, His name is Elephant—
He stone sure is not your friend.
Lion said, He don't need to be
Because today will be his end.
Lion took off through the jungle
Lickity-split,
Meaning to grab Elephant
And tear him bit to bit. Period!
He come across Elephant copping a righteous nod
Under a fine cool shady tree.
Lion said, You big old no-good so-and-so,
It's either you or me.
Lion let out a solid roar
And bopped Elephant with his paw.
Elephant just took his trunk
And busted old Lion's jaw.
Lion let out another roar,
Reared up six feet tall.
Elephant just kicked him in the belly
And laughed to see him drop and fall.
Lion rolled over,
Copped Elephant by the throat.
Elephant just shook him loose
And butted him like a goat,
Then he tromped him and he stomped him
Till the Lion yelled, Oh, no!
And it was near-nigh sunset
When Elephant let Lion go.
The signifying Monkey
Was still setting in his tree
When he looked down and saw the Lion.
Said, Why, Lion, who can that there be?
Lion said, It's me.
Monkey rapped, Why, Lion,
You look more dead than alive!
Lion said, Monkey, I don't want
To hear your jive-end jive.
Monkey just kept on signifying,
Lion, you for sure caught hell—
Mister Elephant's done whipped you
To a fare-thee-well!
Why, Lion, you look like to me
You been in the precinct station
And had the third-degree,
Else you look like
You been high on gage[2]
And done got caught
In a monkey cage!

2. Marijuana.

You ain't no king to me.
Facts, I don't think that you
Can even as much as roar—
And if you try I'm liable
To come down out of this tree and
Whip your tail some more.
The Monkey started laughing
And jumping up and down.
But he jumped so hard the limb broke
And he landed—*bam!*—on the ground.
When he went to run, his foot slipped
And he fell flat down.
Grrr-rrr-rr-r! The Lion was on him
With his front feet and his hind.
Monkey hollered, Ow!
I didn't mean it, Mister Lion!
Lion said, You little flea-bag you!
Why, I'll eat you up alive.
I wouldn't a-been in this fix a-tall
Wasn't for your signifying jive.
Please, said Monkey, Mister Lion,
If you'll just let me go,
I got something to tell you, *please,*
I think you ought to know.
Lion let the Monkey loose
To see what his tale could be—
And Monkey jumped right back on up
Into his tree.
What I was gonna tell you, said Monkey,
Is you square old so-and-so,
If you fool with me I'll get
Elephant to whip your head some more.
Monkey, said the Lion,
Beat to his unbooted knees,
You and all your signifying children
Better stay up in them trees.
Which is why today
Monkey does his signifying
A-*way-up* out of the way.

Stackolee

One dark and dusty day
I was strolling down the street.
I thought I heard some old dog bark,
But it warn't nothing but Stackolee gambling in the dark.
Stackolee threw seven.
Billy said, It ain't that way.
You better go home and come back another day.
Stackolee shot Billy four times in the head
And left that fool on the floor damn near dead.

Stackolee decided he'd go up to Sister Lou's.
Said, Sister Lou! Sister Lou, guess what I done done?
I just shot and killed Billy, your big-head son.
Sister Lou said, Stackolee, that can't be true!
You and Billy been friends for a year or two.
Stackolee said, Woman, if you don't believe what I said,
Go count the bullet holes in that son-of-a-gun's head.
Sister Lou got frantic and all in a rage,
Like a tea hound dame on some frantic gage.
She got on the phone, Sheriff, Sheriff, I want you to help poor me.
I want you to catch that bad son-of-a-gun they call Stackolee.
Sheriff said, My name might begin with an *s* and end with an *f*
But if you want that bad Stackolee you got to get him yourself.
So Stackolee left, he went walking down the New Haven track.
A train come along and flattened him on his back.
He went up in the air and when he fell
Stackolee landed right down in hell.
He said, Devil, devil, put your fork up on the shelf
'Cause I'm gonna run this devilish place myself.
There came a rumbling on the earth and a tumbling on the ground,
That bad son-of-a-gun, Stackolee, was turning hell around.
He ran across one of his ex-girl friends down there.
She was Chock-full-o'-nuts and had pony-tail hair.
She said, Stackolee, Stackolee, wait for me.
I'm trying to please you, can't you see?
She said, I'm going around the corner but I'll be right back.
I'm gonna see if I can't stack my sack.
Stackolee said, Susie Belle, go on and stack your sack.
But I just might not be here when you get back.
Meanwhile, Stackolee went with the devil's wife and with his girl friend, too.
Winked at the devil and said, I'll go with you.
The devil turned around to hit him a lick.
Stackolee knocked the devil down with a big black stick.
Now, to end this story, so I heard tell,
Stackolee, all by his self, is running hell.

Sinking of the *Titanic*[1]

It was 1912 when the awful news got around
That the great *Titanic* was sinking down.
Shine came running up on deck, told the Captain, "Please,
The water in the boiler room is up to my knees."

Captain said, "Take your black self on back down there!
I got a hundred-fifty pumps to keep the boiler room clear."
Shine went back in the hole, started shovelling coal,
Singing, "Lord, have mercy, Lord, on my soul!"

1. This sanitized version was presented by Langston Hughes and Arna Bontemps in *The Book of American Negro Folklore* (1958).

Just then half the ocean jumped across the boiler room deck.
Shine yelled to the Captain, "The water's 'round my neck!"
Captain said, "Go back! Neither fear nor doubt!
I got a hundred more pumps to keep the water out."

"Your words sound happy and your words sound true,
But this is one time, Cap, your words won't do.
I don't like chicken and I don't like ham—
And I don't believe your pumps is worth a damn!"

The old *Titanic* was beginning to sink.
Shine pulled off his clothes and jumped in the brink.
He said, "Little fish, big fish, and shark fishes, too,
Get out of my way because I'm coming through."

Captain on bridge hollered, "Shine, Shine, save poor me,
And I'm make you as rich as any man can be."
Shine said, "There's more gold on land than there is on sea."
And he swimmed on.

Big fat banker begging, "Shine, Shine, save poor me!
I'll give you a thousand shares of T and T."
Shine said, "More stocks on land than there is on sea."
And he swimmed on.

When all them white folks went to heaven,
Shine was in Sugar Ray's Bar drinking Seagrams Seven.

Shine and the *Titanic*[1]

One day when the great *Titanic* was sinking away,
Captain was in his quarters one lonely night,
This old man came up the port side.
He said, "Captain, Captain, the water's over the first fireroom door."
He said, "Shine, Shine, have no doubt.
We got forty-nine pumps to pump the water out."
Shine went down and he came up again.
He said, "Captain, look! That damn water's still coming in."
Captain said, "Shine, Shine, have no doubt,
Now we have ninety-nine pumps to pump the water out."
He said, "Captain, there was a time when your word might be true,
But this is one damn time your word won't do."
So Shine he jumped overboard. He took two kicks, one stroke,
He was off like a PT boat.[2]
Captain came up on the deck. He said, "Shine, Shine, save poor me.
I'll give you more money than any black man want to see."
Shine said, "You know my color and you guessed my race.
Come in here and give these sharks a chase."
Captain's daughter came up on deck,

1. This typically bawdy version was recorded as spoken in Philadelphia and published in Roger Abrahams' *Deep Down in the Jungle* (1964).

2. A fast, maneuverable U.S. fighting vessel that specialized in torpedoing enemy ships.

Drawers in her hand, brassiere around her neck.
She said, "Shine, Shine, save poor me.
Give you more pregnant pussy than a black man want to see."
Shine said, "I know you're pregnant, 'bout to have a kid,
But if that boat sink two more inches, you'll swim this coast just like Shine did."
The Captain's wife came up on deck. She said, "Shine, Shine, save poor me.
I'll let you eat pussy like a rat eats cheese."
Shine said, "I like pussy, I ain't no rat.
I like cock, but not like that."
Shine kept a-swimming.
Shine came past the whale's den.
The whale invited old Shine in.
Shine said, "I know you're king of the ocean, king of the sea,
But you gotta be a water-splashing motherfucker to outswim me."
So Shine kept on stroking.
Now Shine met up with the shark.
Shark said, "Shine, Shine, can't you see.
When you jump in these waters you belongs to me."
Shine said, "I know you outswim the barracuda, outsmart every fish in the sea,
But you gotta be a stroking motherfucker to outswim me."
Shine kept a-swimming.
When the word got to Washington that the great *Titanic* had sunk,
Shine was on Broadway, one-third drunk.

Work Songs

Pick a Bale of Cotton

Jump down, turn around to pick a bale of cotton.
Jump down, turn around, pick a bale a day.

Jump down, turn around to pick a bale of cotton.
Jump down, turn around, pick a bale a day.

Oh, Lordy, pick a bale of cotton!
Oh, Lordy, pick a bale a day!

Me and my gal can pick a bale of cotton,
Me and my gal can pick a bale a day. . . .
Me and my wife can pick a bale of cotton,
Me and my wife can pick a bale a day. . . .

Me and my friend can pick a bale of cotton,
Me and my friend can pick a bale a day. . . .

Me and my poppa can pick a bale of cotton,
Me and my poppa can pick a bale a day.
Oh, Lordy, pick a bale of cotton!
Oh, Lordy, pick a bale a day!

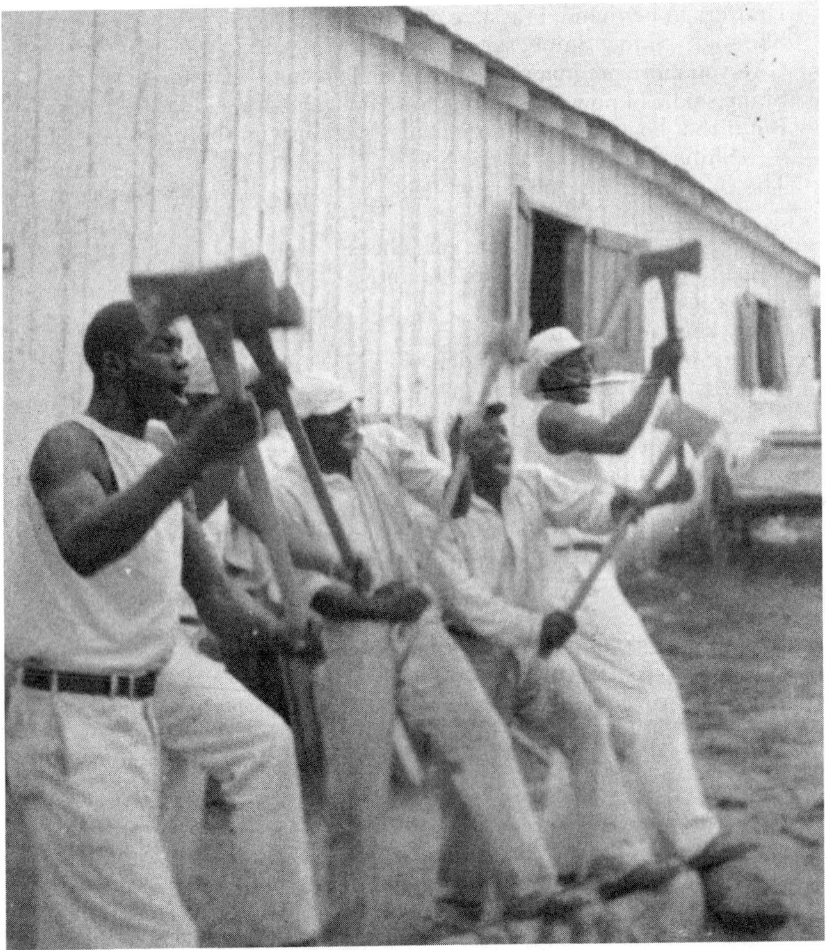

Inmate "Lightnin'" Washington and others singing at Darrington State Prison Farm, Sandy Point, Texas, 1934. Photograph by Alan Lomax.

Go Down, Old Hannah[1]

Go down, old Hannah,
  Won't you rise no more?
Go down, old Hannah,
  Won't you rise no more?

Lawd, if you rise,
  Bring judgment on.
Lawd, if you rise,
  Bring judgment on.

Oh, did you hear
  What the captain said?

1. The sun.

Oh, did you hear
What the captain said?

That if you work
He'll treat you well,
And if you don't
He'll give you hell.

Oh, go down, old Hannah,
Won't you rise no more?
Won't you go down, old Hannah,
Won't you rise no more?

Oh, long-time man,
Hold up your head.
Well, you may get a pardon
And you may drop dead.

Lawdy, nobody feels sorry
For the life-time man.
Nobody feels sorry
For the life-time man.

Can't You Line It?[1]

When I get in Illinois
I'm going to spread the news about the Florida boys.

[CHORUS]

(All men straining at rail in concert.)
Shove it over! Hey, hey, can't you line it?
(Shaking rail.) Ah, shack-a-lack-a-lack-a-lack-a-lack-a-lack-a-lack.
(Grunt as they move rail.) Can't you move it? Hey, hey, can't you try.

Tell what the hobo told the bum,
If you get any corn-bread save me some.

[CHORUS]

A nickle's worth of bacon, and a dime's worth of lard,
I would buy more but the time's too hard.

[CHORUS]

Wonder what's the matter with the walking boss,
It's done five-thirty and he won't knock off.

1. This song is common to the railroad camps. It is suited to the "lining" rhythm. That is, it fits the straining of the men at the lining bars as the rail is placed in position to be spiked down [*Zora Neale Hurston's note*].

[CHORUS]

I ast my Cap'n what's the time of day,
He got mad and throwed his watch away.

[CHORUS]

Cap'n got a pistol and he try to play bad,
But I'm going to take it if he make me mad.

[CHORUS]

Cap'n got a burner[2] I'd like to have,
A 32:20 with a shiny barrel.

[CHORUS]

De Cap'n can't read, de Cap'n can't write,
How do he know that the time is right?

[CHORUS]

Me and my buddy and two three more,
Going to ramshack Georgy everywhere we go.

[CHORUS]

Here come a woman walking 'cross the field,
Her mouth exhausting like an automobile.

Rosie

Be my woman gal, I'll
Be your man
Be my woman, gal, I'll
Be your man
Be my woman, gal, I'll
Be your man
Every day's a Sunday, dollar
In your hand

In your hand, Lordy
In your hand
Every day's a Sunday, dollar
In your hand

Stick to the promise, gal, that
You made me
Stick to the promise, gal, that
You made me
Stick to the promise, gal, that
You made me

2. Gun [*Hurston's note*].

Wasn't gonna marry till I
I go free

I go free, Lordy
I go free
Wasn't gonna marry till I
I go free

Well, Rosie
Oh Lord, gal
Well, Rosie
Oh Lord, gal

When she walks she reels and
Rocks behind
When she walks she reels and
Rocks behind

Ain't that enough to worry
Convict's mind
Ain't that enough to worry
Convict's mind

Well, Rosie
Oh Lord, gal
Well, Rosie
Oh Lord, gal

The Blues

At the beginning of the twentieth century, observers in New Orleans and elsewhere in the South began to notice a new kind of music. This music borrowed harmonic and structural devices and vocal techniques from work songs and spirituals. But unlike these other forms, this music was usually sung not by a chorus but by a single voice accompanied by one or more instruments. Like the earlier forms, blues, as this music came to be known, involved a compellingly rhythmical sound that relied on patterns of call–response between singer and audience, and at times between singer and instrument, too. In spite of all the affinities with church songs, blues music was decidedly secular; it promised no heavenly grace or home but offered instead a stylized complaint about earthly trials and troubles, a complaint countered, if at all, by the hope of better days back in some "sweet home" like Chicago or in another town or by the flickering promise of a "do-right" loving companion. Its dances were not the holy possession dances of church ritual but the courtship dances of Saturday night revelry and after-hours fun that held at bay, albeit temporarily, the melancholia typically described in blues lyrics.

Philosophically, the blues speak of a hard-won, wry optimism in the face of the immutable fact that life on earth involves a steady diet of trouble and pain. Songwriter and bandleader W. C. Handy (1873–1958) is called "the father of the blues" because he took careful note of this form of expression and transcribed its songs. But Handy was more than just a copyist. Having mastered the idiomatic forms, he combined and extended them to produce the first storehouse of blues compositions that were both true to their beginnings and inventive. Like the earlier blues of uncertain authorship—so widely circulated and so often reinvented that they may somewhat justly be termed group creations—Handy's blues were most often twelve-bar forms: three lines of four beats each, the first line repeated twice and followed by a third end-rhymed line:

> I hate to see the evening sun go down.
> I hate to see that evening sun go down.
> 'Cause my baby, he done left this town.

Other blues songs vary from the pattern we see here in Handy's "St. Louis Blues" but still are defined as blues because of their use of "blue notes" and other characteristic blues patterns and sounds. All blues songs involve improvisation, sometimes just in terms of timing and emphasis, sometimes more elaborate reinvention of melodies and even meanings. They also involve particular sounds: train bells and whistles, sexual groans, conversational whispers, rhapsodies, shouts, stories, talk to band members and audiences, and—especially in their first rural incarnations—barnyard squawks and squeals as well.

A full discussion of the blues would take into account the early southern farms where Black singing flourished; the background in African and European forms; the impact of minstrelsy, medicine shows, and carnivals on the music; the importance of dance to the music; early blues centers such as New Orleans, Memphis, and the Mississippi Delta; the movement of the blues to the Southwest, the Midwest, and up the eastern seaboard; and the persistence of the blues in jazz and other American musics, including, some would argue, hip-hop music. Worth noting here is how this powerful form inspired writers, choreographers, and visual artists throughout the twentieth century. In 1953, as a headnote to his first published fiction, Albert Murray wrote: "We all learn from Mann, Joyce, Hemingway, Eliot, and the rest, but I'm also trying to write in terms of the tradition I grew up in, the Negro tradition of blues, stomps, ragtimes, jumps, and swing. After all, very few writers have done as much with American experience as Jelly Roll Morton, Count Basie, and Duke Ellington." Ralph Ellison said that Richard Wright's *Black Boy* was like the blues in "its refusal to offer solutions"; he also composed the following compelling definition of the form:

> The blues is an impulse to keep the painful detail and episodes of a brutal existence alive in one's aching consciousness, to finger its jagged grain, and to transcend it, not by the consolation of philosophy but by squeezing from it a near-tragic, near-comic lyricism. As a form, the blues is an autobiographical chronicle of personal catastrophe expressed lyrically.

As Murray's and Ellison's words show, to term a poem, play, or work of fiction a "blues piece" or to note blues influence within it is to associate it with modern Black American vernacular expression at its finest.

In the heyday of the blues, the 1920s and early 1930s, the most popular artists were blueswomen like Gertrude "Ma" Rainey, Mamie Smith, Ethel Waters, Sippie Wallace, and Bessie Smith, often called "the Empress of the Blues." In *Blues Legacies and Black Feminism* (1998), Angela Davis shows how the music of this generation reveals "unacknowledged traditions of feminist consciousness in working-class black communities." As Davis notes, for popular music this music displays an astonishing "intellectual independence and representational freedom." Its lyrics present a frank, and sometimes even raunchy, female sexuality willingly traversed by contradictory desires. The songs and cabaret performances of these blueswomen flouted conventional norms and patriarchal attitudes and often included unabashed expressions of queer desire. The transformations these Black women wrought upon popular culture through their vernacular interventions, what Daphne Brooks calls the "insurgent musicking" of Black feminist sound, are, as Brooks argues, nothing short of revolutionary. In the provocations and paradoxes of contemporary divas like Rihanna,

Cardi B, Beyoncé, Lil' Kim, and Missy Elliott, when we listen closely, we can hear how the blues idiom and the blueswomen's vernacular live on.

Good Morning, Blues[1]

Good mornin', blues,
Blues, how do you do?
Good mornin', blues,
Blues, how do you do?
Good morning, how are you?

I laid down last night,
Turning from side to side;
Yes, I was turning from side to side,
I was not sick,
I was just dissatisfied.

When I got up this mornin',
Blues walking round my bed;
Yes, the blues walkin' round my bed,
I went to eat my breakfast,
The blues was all in my bread.

I sent for you yesterday baby,
Here you come a walking today;
Yes, here you come a walking today,
Got your mouth wide open,
You don't know what to say.

Good mornin', blues,
Blues, how do you do?
Yes, blues, how do you do?
I'm doing all right,
Good morning, how are you?

Hellhound on My Trail[1]

I've got to keep moving
I've got to keep moving
blues falling down like hail
blues falling down like hail
Ummmmmmmmmmmmmmmmmmmmm
blues falling down like hail
blues falling down

1. By Jimmy Rushing, who recorded it in 1937. As with many works in the vernacular tradition, this classic blues has been sung in many different versions.

1. By Robert Johnson, who recorded it in 1937. Eric Sackheim arranged this song on the page as a modern poet might have done; his arrangement emphasizes the idea that blues are part of contemporary poetic expression.

like hail
And the days keeps on 'minding me
it's a hellhound on my trail
hellhound on
my trail
hellhound on my trail
If today was Christmas Eve
If today was Christmas Eve
and tomorrow was Christmas Day
If today was Christmas Eve
and tomorrow was Christmas Day
(aw wouldn't we have a
time baby)
All I would need my little sweet rider just
to pass the time away
uh huh
to pass the
time away
You sprinkled hot foot powder[2]
umm around my door
all around my door
You sprinkled hot foot powder
all around your daddy's door
hmmm hmmm hmmm
It keeps me with a rambling mind, rider,
every old place I go
every old place I go
I can tell the wind is rising
the leaves trembling on the trees
trembling on the trees
I can tell the wind is rising
leaves trembling on the trees
umm hmm hmm hmm
All I need my little sweet woman
and to keep my company
hmmm hmmm hmmm
hmmm
my company

C. C. Rider[1]

C. C. Rider, see what you done done!
Lord, Lord, Lord!

2. Magic, goopher, or hoodoo powder, presumed to have special powers when prescribed by a conjure doctor.

1. By Ma Rainey; first recorded in 1924 as "See, See Rider." The origins of the often-used title "C. C. Rider" are unclear. Some authorities call it a slightly censored reworking of "Easy Rider"—considered a more unambiguously sexual reference to a callously promiscuous lover, a "rider." Others note a relation to Blind Lemon Jefferson's blues "Corinna Corinna" (shortened to "C. C."). Does the song refer to some sort of a playboy or playgirl circuit traveler (rider)? Or is it an offspring of a children's ring game song—with the words "C. C. Rider, *satisfied*"—perhaps preceding the blues with, as the folk-music scholar Harold Courlander describes it, its "generalized blues statement of discontent"? Although spelling may seem insignificant in an oral form, here it may suggest some of the song's history and its variety of echoing references.

You made me love you, now your gal done come.
You made me love you, now your gal done come.

I'm goin' away, baby, I won't be back till fall.
Lord, Lord, Lord!
Goin' away, baby, won't be back till fall.
If I find me a good man, I won't be back at all.

I'm gonna buy me a pistol just as long as I am tall.
Lord, Lord, Lord!
Kill my man and catch the Cannon Ball.[2]
If he won't have me, he won't have no gal at all.

C. C. Rider, where did you stay last night?
Lord, Lord, Lord!
Your shoes ain't buttoned, clothes don't fit you right.
You didn't come home till the sun was shinin' bright.

Backwater Blues[1]

When it rain five days an' de skies turned dark as night
When it rain five days an' de skies turned dark as night
Then trouble taken place in the lowland that night

I woke up this mornin', can't even get outa mah do'
I woke up this mornin', can't even get outa mah do'
That's enough trouble to make a po' girl wonder where she wanta go

Then they rowed a little boat about five miles 'cross the pond
They rowed a little boat about five miles 'cross the pond
I packed all mah clothes, th'owed 'em in, an' they rowed me along

When it thunder an' a-lightnin', an' the wind begin to blow
When it thunder an' a-lightnin', an' the wind begin to blow
An' thousan' people ain' got no place to go

Then I went an' stood up on some high ol' lonesome hill
I went an' stood up on some high ol' lonesome hill
An' looked down on the house where I used to live

Backwater blues done cause me to pack mah things an' go
Backwater blues done cause me to pack mah things an' go
Cause mah house fell down an' I cain' live there no mo'

O-o-o-oom, I cain' move no mo'
O-o-o-oom, I cain' move no mo'
There ain' no place fo' a po' ol' girl to go

2. A train; either the Wabash Cannonball or the express line from Cincinnati to New Orleans.

1. By Bessie Smith; first recorded in 1927. Used in Sterling A. Brown's poem "Ma Rainey" (1932).

Down-Hearted Blues[1]

Gee, but it's hard to love someone, when that someone don't love you,
I'm so disgusted, heartbroken too,
I've got those down-hearted blues.
Once I was crazy about a man, he mistreated me all the time,
The next man I see, he's got to promise to be mine, all mine.

Trouble, trouble, I've had it all my days,
Trouble, trouble, I've had it all my days,
It seems that trouble's going to follow me to my grave.

If I could only find the man, oh, how happy I would be,
To the Good Lord ev'rynight I pray, please send my man back to me
I've almost worried myself to death wond'ring why he went away,
But just wait and see, he's gonna want me back some sweet day.

World in a jug, the stopper's in my hand,
Got the world in a jug, the stopper's in my hand,[2]
Going to hold it baby till you come under my command.

Say, I ain't never loved but three men in my life,
No, I ain't never loved but three men in my life,
T'was my father, my brother, and the man who wrecked my life.

'Cause he mistreated me and he drove me from his door,
Yes, he mistreated me and he drove me from his door
But the Good Book says you'll reap just what you sow.

Oh, it may be a week and it may be a month or two,
Yes, it may be a week and it may be a month or two,
But the day you quit me honey, it's coming home to you.
Oh, I walked the floor and I wrung my hands and cried,
Yes, I walked the floor and I wrung my hands and cried,
Had the down-hearted blues and couldn't be satisfied.

Empty Bed Blues[1]

I woke up this morning with a awful aching head
I woke up this morning with a awful aching head
My new man had left me, just a room and a empty bed

Bought me a coffee grinder, that's the best one I could find
Bought me a coffee grinder, that's the best one I could find
Oh, he could grind my coffee, 'cause he had a brand-new grind

1. By Alberta Hunter and Louie Austin, written in 1922. This was a big hit for Bessie Smith in 1923.

2. A traditional couplet, alluded to by Ralph Ellison in "The World and the Jug" (1964).

1. By Bessie Smith (1928).

He's a deep sea diver with a stroke that can't go wrong
He's a deep sea diver with a stroke that can't go wrong
He can stay at the bottom and his wind holds out so long

He knows how to thrill me and he thrills me night and day
Oh, he knows how to thrill me, he thrills me night and day
He's got a new way of loving, almost takes my breath away

Lord, he's got that sweet somethin' and I told my girlfriend Lou
He's got that sweet somethin' and I told my girlfriend Lou
From the way she's raving, she must have gone and tried it too

Prove It on Me Blues[1]

Went out last night, and a great big fight
Everything seemed to go on wrong
I looked up, to my surprise
The gal I was with was gone

Where she went, I don't know
I mean to follow everywhere she goes
Folks say I'm crooked, I didn't know where she took it
I want the whole world to know

They said I do it, ain't nobody caught me
Sure got to prove it on me
Went out last night with a crowd of my friends
They must've been women, 'cause I don't like no men

It's true I wear collar and a tie
Make the wind blow all the while
'Cause they say I do it, ain't nobody caught me
They sure got to prove it on me

Wear my clothes just like a fan
Talk to the gals just like any old man
'Cause they say I do it, ain't nobody caught me
Sure got to prove it on me

1. Written and performed by Ma Rainey (1928). This song is notable for its forthright lesbian references.

Trouble in Mind[1]

Trouble in mind, I'm blue,
But I won't be blue always,
For the sun will shine in my backdoor someday.

Trouble in mind, that's true,
I have almost lost my mind;
Life ain't worth livin', feel like I could die,

I'm gonna lay my head on some lonesome railroad line:
Let the two nineteen train ease my troubled mind.

Trouble in mind, I'm blue,
My poor heart is beatin' slow;
Never had no trouble in my life before.

I'm all alone at midnight,
And my lamp is burning low,
Never had so much trouble in my life before.

I'm gonna lay my head
On that lonesome railroad track,
But when I hear the whistle,
Lord, I'm gonna pull it back.

I'm goin' down to the river
Take along my rocking chair,
And if the blues don't leave me,
I'll rock on away from there.

Well, trouble, oh, trouble,
Trouble on my worried mind,
When you see me laughin',
I'm laughin' just to keep from cryin'.[2]

How Long Blues[1]

How long, how long, has that evenin' train been gone?
How long, how long, baby, how long?
Heard the whistle blowin', couldn't see no train,
'Way down in my heart I had an achin' pain,
How long, how long, baby, how long?

I'm sad and lonely the whole day through,
Why don't you write me and give me the news?
You have left me singin' those how long blues.

1. By Richard M. Jones; published in 1926. Gayl Jones refers to this song in her novel *Corregidora* (1975).
2. A traditional line, used by Langston Hughes as the title of his 1952 novel.

1. By Leroy Carr; recorded in 1928. This song is sometimes compared with lines in the Bible about long suffering.

If I could holler like a Mountain Jack,
I'd go up on the mountain and call my baby back,
How long, how long, baby, how long?

I went up on the mountain looked as far as I could see,
The man had my woman and the blues had poor me,
How long, how long, how long?

I can see the green grass growing on the hill,
But I ain't seen the green grass on a dollar bill,
For so long, so long, baby, so long.

If you don't believe I'm sinkin' see what a hole I'm in,
If you don't believe I love you, baby, look what a fool I've been,
Well, I'm gone how long, baby, how long?

I'm goin' down to Georgia, been up in Tennessee,
So look me over, baby, the last you'll see of me,
For so long, so long, baby, so long.

The brook runs into the river, the river runs into the sea,
If I don't run into my baby, a train is goin' to run into me,
How long, how long, how long?

Death Letter Blues[1]

I got a letter this morning, how do you reckon it read?
Say, "Hurry, hurry! The gal you love is dead."
I got a letter this morning, I say how you reckon it read?
It say, "Hurry, hurry! mmm, 'cause the gal you love is dead"

You know I grabbed up my suitcase, took off down the road
When I got there, she was laying on the cooling board
I grabbed up my suitcase, I said I took off down the road
I said when I got there, mmm she's laying on the cooling board

Lord, I walked up close, I looked down in her face
She's a good old girl, got to lay her to Judgment Day
I say I walked up close, I looked down in her face
I say she's a good old girl, got to lay her to Judgment Day

Lord I fold up my arms, I slowly walked away
I said, "Farewell, Honey, I'll see ya Judgment Day!"
I fold up my arms, ah yes, I walked away
And I said, "Farewell, farewell, hmm, I'll see you Judgment Day!"

You know, I went in my room, and I bowed to pray
But the priest came along, and drive my spirit away
I went in my room, yeah, I bowed to pray
I said, well, the blues came along, and drive my spirit away

1. By Son House.

You know, I thought I'd never love but four women in my life
My mother, my sister, dead gal, and my wife
I thought I'd never love, and I said, but four women in my life
I said my mother and my sister, my dead gal, and my wife

(You know, looked like ten thousand people
Were standin' round the buryin' ground
I didn't know I loved her, until I let her down
Looked like ten thousand standin' around the buryin' ground
You know I didn't know that I loved her
Until I began to let her down)

You know I didn't feel so bad
Till the good Lord turned me down
I didn't have a soul to throw my arms around
I didn't feel so bad until the good Lord's sun went down
I say I didn't have a soul to throw my arms around

You know I's cryin' last night, the night before
I'm gonna change my way of living
So I won't be cryin' no more
You know I cried last night, I said, all the night before
I said I'm gone change my way of living so I won't cry no more

(You know it's so hard to love when someone don't love you
Don't look like satisfaction, don't care what you do
It's so hard to love someone that don't love you
You know you don't get no satisfaction
Don't care what you do

You know love had a fault
Make you do things you don't want to do
Love sometimes leave you feelin' sad and blue)

It's a Sin to Be Rich, It's a Low-Down Shame to Be Poor[1]

You know that it's a sin to be rich but it's a low-down shame
to be poor
It's a sin to be rich, you know that it's a low-down shame
to be poor
You know a rich man ain't got a chance to go to heaven and a
poor man got a hard way to go

You know I don't wanna be rich, I just wanna stay between
rich and poor
No, I don't wanna be rich, I just wanna live between rich and poor
Yes, when I die you know I wanna go to heaven,
That's when Po' Lightnin' will have a chance to go

Gabriel gonna be the next man to blow that trumpet,
I wants to be there when he blow (blow, Gabriel, blow)

1. By Lightnin' Hopkins.

Whoa, he gonna be the next man blow that trumpet,
I wants to be there when po' Gabriel blow
Whoa, that's when the world be off with the people
And I can lay there and rest for sure

Hard Time Killing Floor Blues[1]

Hard times is here
An ev'rywhere you go
Times are harder
Than th'ever been befo'

You know that people
They are driftin' from door to door
But they can't find no heaven
I don't care where they go

People, if I ever can get up
Off a-this old hard killin' flo'
Lord, I'll never get down
This low no mo'

Well, you hear me singin'
This old lonesome song
People, you know these hard times
Can't last us so long

You know, you'll say you had money
You better be sho'
But these hard times gon' kill you
Just drive a lonely soul

St. Louis Blues[1]

I hate to see de evenin' sun go down
I hate to see de evenin' sun go down
Cause mah baby, he done lef' dis town

Feelin' tomorrow lak I feel today
Feelin' tomorrow lak I feel today
I'll pack mah trunk, an' make mah getaway

St. Louis woman wid her diamon' rings
Pulls dat man aroun' by her apron strings
'Twant for powder an' for store-bought hair
De man I love would not gone nowhere

Got de St. Louis blues, jes as blue as I can be
Dat man got a heart lak a rock cast in de sea
Or else he wouldn't have gone so far from me

1. By Skip James (1931).

1. By W. C. Handy; published in 1914.

Been to de gypsy to get mah fortune tol'
To de gypsy, done got mah fortune tol'
Cause I'm most wild 'bout mah jelly roll

Gypsy done tol' me, "Don't you wear no black"
Yes, she done tol' me, "Don't you wear no black.
Go to St. Louis, you can win him back"

Help me to Cairo;[2] make St. Louis by mahself
Git to Cairo, find mah ol' frien', Jeff
Gwine to pin mahself close to his side
If I flag his train, I sho can ride

I loves dat man lak a schoolboy loves his pie
Lak a Kentucky Colonel loves his mint an' rye
I'll love mah baby till de day I die

You ought to see dat stovepipe brown o' mine
Lak he owns de Dimon' Joseph line
He'd make a cross-eyed 'oman go stone blind

Blacker than midnight, teeth lak flags of truce
Blackest man in de whole St. Louis
Blacker de berry, sweeter is de juice. . . .

A black headed gal make a freight train jump de track
Said, a black headed gal make a freight train jump de track
But a long tall gal makes a preacher "Ball de Jack"[3]

Lawd, a blond headed woman makes a good man leave the town
I said, blond headed woman makes a good man leave the town
But a red headed woman make a boy slap his papa down. . . .

Beale Street Blues[1]

I've seen the lights of gay Broadway,
Old Market Street, down by the Frisco Bay,
I've strolled the Prado,[2]
I've gambled on the Bourse,[3]
The seven wonders of the world I've seen,
And many are the places I have been.

Take my advice folks
And see Beale Street[4] first.

You'll see pretty browns in beautiful gowns,
You'll see tailor-mades and hand-me-downs,

2. Town in Illinois.
3. Social dance step of the 1920s.
1. By W. C. Handy; published in 1917.
2. Spanish national museum in Madrid.
3. Paris money market; equivalent of the New York Stock Exchange.
4. The main Black street of Memphis, Tennessee, lined with commercial buildings, churches, theaters, parks, and houses. The writer Stanley Crouch suggested a connection between this song's lyrics and aspects of F. Scott Fitzgerald's *The Great Gatsby* (1925).

You'll meet honest men and pick-pockets skilled,
You'll find that business never closes till somebody gets killed.

I'd rather be here than any place I know,
I'd rather be here than any place I know.
It's goin' to take the Sergeant
For to make me go.

Goin' to the river
Maybe, by and by,
Goin' to the river,
And there's a reason why:
Because the river's wet,
and Beale Street's gone dry.

You'll see Hog Nose rest'rants and Chitlin'[5] Cafes,
You'll see jugs that tell of by-gone days,
And places, once places, now just a sham,
You'll see Golden Balls enough to pave the New Jerusalem.[6]

Goin' to the river
Maybe, by and by,
Goin' to the river,
And there's a reason why:
Because the river's wet,
and Beale Street's gone dry.

I'd rather be here than any place I know,
I'd rather be here than any place I know.
It's goin' to take the Sergeant
For to make me go

Goin' to the river
Maybe, by and by,
Goin' to the river,
And there's a reason why:
Because the river's wet,
and Beale Street's gone dry.

If Beale Street could talk,[7] if Beale Street could talk
Married men would have to take their beds and walk,
Except one or two, who never drink booze,
And the blind man on the corner who sings the Beale Street Blues.

I'd rather be here than any place I know,
I'd rather be here than any place I know.
It's goin' to take the Sergeant
For to make me go

5. Dish made with the small intestines of hogs.
6. Heaven. "Golden Balls": signs of pawnshops.
7. James Baldwin's novel *If Beale Street Could Talk* (1974) takes its title from this line.

Hoochie Coochie[1]

The gypsy woman told my mother
Before I was born
I got a boy child's coming
Gonna be a son of a gun
He gonna make pretty womens
Jump and shout
Then the world wanna know
What this all about

'Cause you know I'm here
Everybody knows I'm here
Yeah, you know I'm a hoochie coochie man
Everybody knows I'm here

I got a black cat bone
I got a mojo[2] too
I got the John the Conqueroo[3]
I'm gonna mess with you
I'm gonna make you girls
Lead me by the hand
Then the world'll know
The hoochie coochie man

But you know I'm here
Everybody knows I'm here
Yeah, you know I'm a hoochie coochie man
Everybody knows I'm here

On a seven hours
On the seventh day
On the seventh month
The seven doctors said
He was born for good luck
And that you'll see
I got seven hundred dollars
Don't you mess with me

But you know I'm here
Everybody knows I'm here
Well you know I'm a hoochie coochie man
Everybody knows I'm here

1. This song is associated with Muddy Waters, who first recorded it in 1954.
2. Conjurer's potion.
3. A root prepared by a conjurer to grant extraordinary powers.

Chickasaw Train Blues[1]

I'm goin' tell everybody, what that Chickasaw has done done
for me
I'm goin' tell everybody, what that Chickasaw has done done
for me
She done stole my man away, and blow that doggone smoke
on me
She's a low-down dirty dog

I ain't no woman, like to ride that Chickasaw
Ain't no woman, like to ride that Chickasaw
Because everywhere she stop, she's stealing some woman's
good man, oh
She's a low-down dirty dog

I told the depot this mornin', I don't think he treats me right
Told the depot this mornin', I don't think he treats me right
He done sold my man a ticket, and I know that Chickasaw
leavin' town tonight
He's a low-down dirty dog

I walk down a railroad track, that Chickasaw wouldn't even
let me ride the blind
I walk down a railroad track, that Chickasaw wouldn't even
let me ride the blind
And she stop picking up men, all up and down the line
She's a low-down dirty dog

Mmm-mmm, Chickasaw don't pay no woman no mind
Mmm-mmm, that Chickasaw don't pay no woman no mind
And she stop and pickin' up men, all up and down the line

1. By Memphis Minnie.

Folktales

In his novel *Train-Whistle Guitar* (1974), Albert Murray introduces a character named Scooter who delights in the rare chances he gets to sit at the front room fireside within earshot of family and neighborhood elders when the mood and moonlight are right for the telling of tales. The novel's setting is Black semirural Alabama of the 1920s, but the ritual moment of telling and retelling lifts it into an almost timeless zone. The group's jewels of wisdom (along with some highfalutin play-talk and sheer nonsense) are handed around with an attitude that combines high solemnity and playfulness. Elders entertain elders with traditional tales (with topical twists and variations), but no one is unaware of the presence of the eleven-year-old boy who needs to hear these stories—their styles of telling and their substantive values along with their mysteries, silences, and incongruities. Since their arrival in the New World from Africa (and elsewhere), the tales have been a key part of the African American's equipment for survival and sustenance.

Many new Black arrivals, whether in the seventeenth, the eighteenth, or the nineteenth century, quickly developed local creoles and other means of facilitating communication. What is clearer than ever is that the Africans also brought with

Brer Rabbit and Brer Fox. Illustration from an 1893 printing of *Uncle Remus and His Friends* by Joel Chandler Harris.

them a vast storehouse of stories—along with other such expressive forms as songs, dances, styles of worship, games, patterns of adornment, and the like that helped them maintain on the new continent at least the broad outlines of their original worldview. (These forms were what Black people had instead of freedom. They had *rites* and not *rights,* as Ralph Ellison once put it; rhythmic freedom if not political freedom, said Cornel West.) Despite the ravages of the Middle Passage and the violence of slavery as an institution, one finds among African Americans story types, characters, motifs, and styles of telling that bear the distinctive traits of south Saharan Africa's ways of making stories. One finds, for example, many kinds of trickster tales (forerunners of the Brer Rabbit cycle) along with tales of metamorphoses and wonder that have distinctive counterparts in the New World.

Before long, African Americans had taken hold of Native American and Euro-American tales and passed them around the fireside. But whatever the sources—Old or New World; Black, white, red—African Americans hammered these myriad tales into unmistakably Black American shapes and themes. The voices of the stories (sometimes one story could involve several voices—of Bear, perhaps, or Sis Cat, or Brer Fox—operating in different octaves and vocal timbres) marked them as African American. So did the particular turns of the plot as well as the particular heroes, dupes, and villains, and their values.

This section contains several kinds of tales: animal trickster tales, tales of slave tricksters, tales explaining how things came to be as they are, tales with other lessons about life in the tough briar patch of the United States, and tales where there's simply one darned thing happening after another. All of them invite us along for the narrative ride.

One warning: do not accept any simplistic explanation for the stories' meanings. Watch for the easy interpretation of trickster tales as Weak-but-Cunning Black versus Strong-but-Duller White. This formula often will hold. But then again it will not. Frequently, the "weak" rabbits of these tales are (like tricksters the world over) greedy monsters of selfish pride, dangerously out of sync with their surroundings and fellow creatures. Or the rabbits can be just plain pretentious. In a sense, that is what gets Brer Rabbit into trouble in the famous Tar-Baby Tale: he arrogantly insists on being addressed with genteel etiquette, and to say the least, the effort fails (temporarily!). Often the rabbits' *foes* are infinitely more community-minded and responsible than the rabbits themselves. At times, as in tales of Rabbit and Fox, both antagonists are tricksters; in such cases, both may embody characteristics closer to those of the slaveholder, as usually imagined, than to those of the enslaved person. Both Rabbit and Fox often serve more as warnings than as exemplars of how to live.

Be aware too that like other oral forms these tales were originally invented not for the printed page but for spoken performance. Something vital is lost when we are not at the fireside with Scooter, hearing the sounds, watching the physical movements of the tellers: their whispery asides, silences, dramatic songs, clicks, calls, and other story sounds. Without being there we miss the sense of the tale as part of a process of verbal exchange that involves audience responses and sometimes a competitive round of tale set against tale. Some of these actual performances would surely have consisted not of complete and finished products but of fragments and loose bits of a familiar yarn handed around in brief before the next talk takes over. Some tales might have been introduced by one teller and finished off by one or more others. Some might have been hooted down before they got off the ground.

Keeping in mind this sense of the tales as part of a lived performance process, note in particular the entries reported by Zora Neale Hurston, who did her best to let her readers see and hear the work in its complex social and ritual contexts. But even while reading Hurston, remember that she was a literary intellectual who came to the party with pen (and/or tape recorder) in hand; even her best efforts to catch the dancing spirit of the thrice-told tale on paper betray her own sense of life and, alas, her identity as something of an outsider.

Because of the unavoidable difficulties of translation from oral to written forms, purity cannot be a central concern in choosing selections. Joel Chandler Harris, the late-nineteenth-century collector, is here with all his bags and baggages as a white southerner of his era. Harris invents his own frame to encase the tales—in his case as stories told by a somewhat stereotyped Uncle Remus to a curious white boy in his charge. Other literary renderings of the tales, including ones by Black writers like Hurston and Julius Lester, also are here along with more unvarnished (and in this sense scientific) reports by such scholars as Roger Abrahams. Sometimes the literary renderings of the tales involve phonetical spellings, which at first obscure meaning but—once the reader breaks the code—can help bring the work to life. Sometimes, on the other hand, faithful scientific renderings of the material can lie stillborn on the page. (In their naked authenticity, such transcribed tales will delight some readers and offend others.) All these efforts are now part of a tradition in which modern readers, like Albert Murray's Scooter, can pull up as close as we can to the spirit of the tales and their tellers.

All God's Chillen Had Wings[1]

Once all Africans could fly like birds; but owing to their many transgressions, their wings were taken away. There remained, here and there, in the sea islands and out-of-the-way places in the low country, some who had been overlooked, and had retained the power of flight, though they looked like other men.

There was a cruel master on one of the sea islands who worked his people till they died. When they died he bought others to take their places. These also he killed with overwork in the burning summer sun, through the middle hours of the day, although this was against the law.

One day, when all the worn-out Negroes were dead of overwork, he bought, of a broker in the town, a company of native Africans just brought into the country, and put them at once to work in the cottonfield.

1. As told by Caesar Grant, of John's Island, carter and laborer. Published in John Bennet's *Doctor to the Dead* (1943, 1946) and in Langston Hughes and Arna Bontemps's *Book of Negro Folklore* (1958). Tales of Black flight inspired Toni Morrison's *Song of Solomon*, among other works by African American writers.

He drove them hard. They went to work at sunrise and did not stop until dark. They were driven with unsparing harshness all day long, men, women and children. There was no pause for rest during the unendurable heat of the midsummer noon, though trees were plenty and near. But through the hardest hours, when fair plantations gave their Negroes rest, this man's driver pushed the work along without a moment's stop for breath, until all grew weak with heat and thirst.

There was among them one young woman who had lately borne a child. It was her first; she had not fully recovered from bearing, and should not have been sent to the field until her strength had come back. She had her child with her, as the other women had, astraddle on her hip, or piggyback.

The baby cried. She spoke to quiet it. The driver could not understand her words. She took her breast with her hand and threw it over her shoulder that the child might suck and be content. Then she went back to chopping knot-grass; but being very weak, and sick with the great heat, she stumbled, slipped and fell.

The driver struck her with his lash until she rose and staggered on.

She spoke to an old man near her, the oldest man of them all, tall and strong, with a forked beard. He replied; but the driver could not understand what they said; their talk was strange to him.

She returned to work; but in a little while she fell again. Again the driver lashed her until she got to her feet. Again she spoke to the old man. But he said: "Not yet, daughter; not yet." So she went on working, though she was very ill.

Soon she stumbled and fell again. But when the driver came running with his lash to drive her on with her work, she turned to the old man and asked: "Is it time yet, daddy?" He answered: "Yes, daughter; the time has come. Go; and peace be with you!" . . . and stretched out his arms toward her . . . so.

With that she leaped straight up into the air and was gone like a bird, flying over field and wood.

The driver and overseer ran after her as far as the edge of the field; but she was gone, high over their heads, over the fence, and over the top of the woods, gone, with her baby astraddle of her hip, sucking at her breast.

Then the driver hurried the rest to make up for her loss; and the sun was very hot indeed. So hot that soon a man fell down. The overseer himself lashed him to his feet. As he got up from where he had fallen the old man called to him in an unknown tongue. My grandfather told me the words that he said; but it was a long time ago, and I have forgotten them. But when he had spoken, the man turned and laughed at the overseer, and leaped up into the air, and was gone, like a gull, flying over field and wood.

Soon another man fell. The driver lashed him. He turned to the old man. The old man cried out to him, and stretched out his arms as he had done for the other two; and he, like them, leaped up, and was gone through the air, flying like a bird over field and wood.

Then the overseer cried to the driver, and the master cried to them both: "Beat the old devil! He is the doer!"

The overseer and the driver ran at the old man with lashes ready; and the master ran too, with a picket pulled from the fence, to beat the life out of the old man who had made those Negroes fly.

But the old man laughed in their faces, and said something loudly to all the Negroes in the field, the new Negroes and the old Negroes.

And as he spoke to them they all remembered what they had forgotten, and recalled the power which once had been theirs. Then all the Negroes, old and new, stood up together; the old man raised his hands; and they all leaped up into the air with a great shout; and in a moment were gone, flying, like a flock of crows, over the field, over the fence, and over the top of the wood; and behind them flew the old man.

The men went clapping their hands; and the women went singing; and those who had children gave them their breasts; and the children laughed and sucked as their mothers flew, and were not afraid.

The master, the overseer, and the driver looked after them as they flew, beyond the wood, beyond the river, miles on miles, until they passed beyond the last rim of the world and disappeared in the sky like a handful of leaves. They were never seen again.

Where they went I do not know; I never was told. Nor what it was that the old man said . . . that I have forgotten. But as he went over the last fence he made a sign in the master's face, and cried "Kuli-ba! Kuli-ba!" I don't know what that means.

But if I could only find the old wood sawyer, he could tell you more; for he was there at the time, and saw the Africans fly away with their women and children. He is an old, old man, over ninety years of age, and remembers a great many strange things.

Br'er Rabbit Learns What Trouble Is

Br'er Rabbit approached the King. "O, King," he began, "teach me what is trouble. I hear the people talk of trouble, but I have never seen it."

Then the King said thoughtfully, "Br'er Rabbit, if you would always be happy, give up this desire of yours to know trouble—for it brings tears and much weeping. Return to the brier patch and be a good rabbit child."

But Br'er Rabbit was not so to be put off—and seeing that he was determined, the King slowly brought forth a small tightly covered box.

"Do not open it until you have almost reached the further end of the open field near the brier patch. There is trouble in this box," cautioned the King.

"As Br'er Rabbit ran down the path he thought of his box—he ran faster; as his pace increased, so did his curiosity. He paused a second and held the box to his ear—what was it he heard? he thought. It must be a baby crying. "Hush, baby!" he said, but as the racket continued he thought he would take just the merest peep inside. He turned just to see if anyone were watching. The King was following him.

"Don't you open that box, Br'er Rabbit!" he cried.

"Oh, no! no! no!" Br'er Rabbit prevaricated. "I just only looked to see how close behind me you were!"

Br'er Rabbit ran on—again he paused to listen—and to peep—again the King shouted and Br'er Rabbit refrained. He had run now as long as he could—his curiosity burned him past endurance. He would raise the top and peep inside so quickly that even the King, as he followed, should not notice. His little paw scarcely moved the cover. Oh, wow! if you will excuse me for saying so. "Br-r-r! Bow-wow-wow-wow!!" and "B-r-r-r!" Two hungry hounds burst out and upon poor little Br'er Rabbit, giving him a pretty chase over the fields until he finally reached the welcome brier-patch worn and breathless. The dogs did not catch Br'er Rabbit—but to this day just the sight of a dog means *trouble* to Br'er Rabbit.

Big Talk[1]

During slavery time two ole niggers wuz talkin' an' one said tuh de other one, "Ole Massa made me so mad yistiddy till Ah give 'im uh good cussin' out. Man, Ah called 'im everything wid uh handle on it."

De other one says, "You didn't cuss *Ole Massa,* didja? Good God! Whut did he do tuh you?"

"He didn't do *nothin',* an' man, Ah laid one cussin' on 'im! Ah'm uh man lak dis, Ah won't stan' no hunchin'. Ah betcha he won't bother *me* no mo'."

"Well, if you cussed 'im an' he didn't do nothin' tuh you, de nex' time he make me mad Ah'm goin' tuh lay uh hearin' on him."

Nex' day de nigger did somethin'. Ole Massa got in behind 'im and he turnt 'round an' give Ole Massa one good cussin' an Ole Massa had 'im took down and whipped nearly tuh death. Nex' time he saw dat other nigger he says tuh 'im. "Thought you tole me, you cussed Ole Massa out and he never opened his mouf."

"Ah did."

"Well, how come he never did nothin' tuh yuh? Ah did it an' he come nigh uh killin' *me.*"

"Man, you didn't go cuss 'im tuh his face, didja?"

"Sho Ah did. Ain't dat whut you tole me you done?"

"Naw, Ah didn't say Ah cussed 'im tuh his face. You sho is crazy. Ah thought you had mo' sense than dat. When Ah cussed Ole Massa he wuz settin' on de front porch an' Ah wuz down at de big gate."

De other nigger wuz mad but he didn't let on. Way after while he 'proached de nigger dat got 'im de beatin' an' tole 'im, "Know whut Ah done tuhday?"

"Naw, whut you done? Give Ole Massa 'nother cussin'?"

"Naw, Ah ain't never goin' do dat no mo'. Ah peeped up under Ole Miss's drawers."

"Man, hush yo' mouf! You knows you ain't looked up under Ole Miss's clothes!"

"Yes, Ah did too. Ah looked right up her very drawers."

"You better hush dat talk! Somebody goin' hear you and Ole Massa'll have you kilt."

"Well, Ah sho done it an' she never done nothin' neither."

"Well, whut did she say?"

"Not uh mumblin' word, an' Ah stopped and looked jus' as long as Ah wanted tuh an' went on 'bout mah business."

"Well, de nex' time Ah see her settin' out on de porch Ah'm goin' tuh look too."

"Help yo'self."

1. From Zora Neale Hurston's *Mules and Men* (1935).

Dat very day Ole Miss wuz settin' out on de porch in de cool uh de evenin' all dressed up in her starchy white clothes. She had her legs all crossed up and de nigger walked up tuh de edge uh de porch and peeped up under Ole Miss's clothes. She took and hollored an' Ole Massa come out an' had dat nigger almost kilt alive.

When he wuz able tuh be 'bout again he said tuh de other nigger; "Thought you tole me you peeped up under Ole Miss's drawers?"

"Ah sho did."

"Well, how come she never done nothin' tuh *you*? She got me nearly kilt."

"Man, when Ah looked under Ole Miss's drawers they wuz hangin' out on de clothes line. You didn't go look up in 'em while she had 'em on, didja? You sho is uh fool! Ah thought you had mo' sense than dat, Ah claire Ah did. It's uh wonder he didn't kill yuh dead. Umph, umph, umph. You sho ain't got no sense atall."

" 'Member Youse a Nigger"[1]

Ole John was a slave, you know. Ole Massa and Ole Missy and de two li' children—a girl and a boy.

Well, John was workin' in de field and he seen de children out on de lake in a boat, just a hollerin'. They had done lost they oars and was 'bout to turn over. So then he went and tole Ole Massa and Ole Missy.

Well, Ole Missy, she hollered and said: "It's so sad to lose these 'cause Ah ain't never goin' to have no more children." Ole Massa made her hush and they went down to de water and follered de shore on 'round till they found 'em. John pulled off his shoes and hopped in and swum out and got in de boat wid de children and brought 'em to shore.

Well, Massa and John take 'em to de house. So they was all so glad 'cause de children got saved. So Massa told 'im to make a good crop dat year and fill up de barn, and den when he lay by de crops nex' year, he was going to set him free.

So John raised so much crop dat year he filled de barn and had to put some of it in de house.

So Friday come, and Massa said, "Well, de day done come that I said I'd set you free. I hate to do it, but I don't like to make myself out a lie. I hate to git rid of a good nigger lak you."

So he went in de house and give John one of his old suits of clothes to put on. So John put it on and come in to shake hands and tell 'em goodbye. De children they cry, and Ole Missy she cry. Didn't want to see John go. So John took his bundle and put it on his stick and hung it crost his shoulder.

Well, Ole John started on down de road. Well, Ole Massa said, "John, de children love yuh."

"Yassuh."

"John, I love yuh."

"Yassuh."

"And Missy *like* yuh!"

"Yassuh."

1. From Zora Neale Hurston's *Mules and Men* (1935).

"But 'member, John, youse a nigger."

"Yassuh."

Fur as John could hear 'im down de road he wuz hollerin', "John, Oh John! De children loves you. And I love you. De Missy *like* you."

John would holler back, "Yassuh."

"But 'member youse a nigger, tho!"

Ole Massa kept callin' 'im and his voice was pitiful. But John kept right on steppin' to Canada. He answered Old Massa every time he called 'im, but he consumed on wid his bag.

Why the Sister in Black Works Hardest[1]

Know how it happened? After God got thru makin' de world and de varmints and de folks, he made up a great big bundle and let it down in de middle of de road. It laid dere for thousands of years, then Ole Missus said to Ole Massa: "Go pick up dat box, Ah want to see whut's in it." Ole Massa look at de box and it look so heavy dat he says to de nigger, "Go fetch me dat big ole box out dere in de road." De nigger been stumblin' over de box a long time so he tell his wife:

"'Oman, go git dat box." So de nigger 'oman she runned to git de box. She says:

"Ah always lak to open up a big box 'cause there's nearly always something good in great big boxes." So she run and grabbed a-hold of de box and opened it up and it was full of hard work.

Dat's de reason de sister in black works harder than anybody else in de world. De white man tells de nigger to work and he takes and tells his wife.

You Talk Too Much, Anyhow[1]

Once, during the time of slavery, the pond was somewhat low. A negro happened to walk down there and found this turtle down there about the size of the bottom of a big tin tub, lying on the bank. So the negro said to the turtle, "Good morning, Mr. Turtle." The turtle at first didn't say anything, but finally said, "Good morning, Mr. Man." The negro said, "My, Mr. Turtle, I didn't know you could talk." Turtle said, "What I say about you niggers is you talk too much." So the negro goes back to his house and tells Old Massa about the turtle. He said, "Massa, don't you know, I was down at the creek this morning, and there was a great big turtle on the bank, and he could talk." Massa said, "Get away from here, you're just lying." The negro said he was telling the truth, but Master told him he lied like a dog. But the negro said, "No sir, he can really talk."

So the master said he would go down to see this turtle, but if he didn't talk he was going to beat the slave half to death. Both of them went back down to the creek and they found the turtle lying on the bank. The negro

1. From Zora Neale Hurston's *Mules and Men* (1935).

1. As published in Roger D. Abrahams, ed., *Afro-American Folktales* (1985).

walked right up to the turtle and said, "Good morning, Mr. Turtle." Turtle didn't say anything, so the negro repeated, "I say, good morning, Mr. Turtle." Turtle still didn't say anything. This time the negro got scared. He said, "Please sir, Mr. Turtle, please say good morning," but Turtle wouldn't talk.

The Master took the negro back to the house and beat him half to death. After he got his beating, he went on back to the creek. He saw the turtle again and said to him, "Why didn't you say good morning? You knew I was going to get a beating if you didn't talk." Turtle said, "Well, that's what I say about you negroes, you talk too much anyhow."

A Flying Fool[1]

This colored man died and went up there to meet his Maker. But when he got to the gates, St. Peter said that God wasn't home or having any visitors—by which he meant no negroes allowed. Well, this old boy, he had been a good man all his life and his preacher had told him that Heaven would be his place, so he didn't exactly know what to do. So he just kind of hung around the gates, until one time St. Peter just had to go and take a pee. So while Pete was gone, this old boy slipped through, stole himself a pair of wings, and he really took off. Sailed around the trees, in and out of those golden houses and all, swooped down and buzzed some of those heavenly singers and all, and had himself a good old time. Meanwhile, of course, St. Pete came back and found out what had happened and called out the heavenly police force to go get him. Well, this guy was just getting the feel of wearing wings, and he really took off, zoomed off. They had some little time bringing him down, him flying all over Heaven fast as he could go. Finally, they got him cornered and he racked up on one of those trees, and I tell you, he looked like a mess with broken wings and all. So they took him and threw him out the gates. Now here comes one of his friends, who asked him, "What happened, man?" He said, "Oh, man, when I got here they wouldn't let me in to the white man's Heaven, but I grabbed me some wings and I had me a fly." He said, "Oh yeah?" Man said, "Yeah, they may not let any colored folks in, but while I was there I was a flying fool."

Brer Rabbit Tricks Brer Fox Again[1]

When all the animals saw how well Brer Rabbit and Brer Fox were getting along, they decided to patch up their quarrels.

One hot day Brer Rabbit, Brer Fox, Brer Coon, Brer Bear, and a whole lot of the other animals were clearing new ground so they could plant corn and have some roasting ears when autumn came.

Brer Rabbit got tired about three minutes after he started, but he couldn't say anything if he didn't want the other animals calling him lazy. So he kept carrying off the weeds and brambles the others were pulling out of the

1. This tale, included in Roger D. Abrahams, ed., *Afro-American Folktales* (1985), is often referred to in novels, poems, and short stories. See Richard Wright's *Lawd Today,* Ralph Ellison's "Flying Home," and Sterling Brown's "Slim in Hell."

1. From *The Tales of Uncle Remus: The Adventures of Brer Rabbit,* as told by Julius Lester (1987).

ground. After a while he screamed real loud and said a briar was stuck in his hand. He wandered off, picking at his hand. As soon as he was out of sight, he started looking for a shady place where he could take a nap.

He saw a well with a bucket in it. That was the very thing he'd been looking for. He climbed, jumped in, and whoops! The bucket went down, down, down until—SPLASH!—it hit the water.

Now, I know you don't know nothing about no well. You probably think that when God made water, He made the faucet too. Well, God don't know nothing about no faucet, and I don't care too much for them myself. When I was coming up, everybody had their own well. Over the well was a pulley with a rope on it. Tied to each end of the rope was a bucket, and when you pulled one bucket up, the other one went down. Brer Rabbit found out about them kind of wells as he looked up at the other bucket.

He didn't know what he was going to do. He couldn't even move around very much or else he'd tip over and land in the water.

Brer Fox and Brer Rabbit might've made up and become friends, but that didn't mean Brer Fox trusted Brer Rabbit. Brer Fox had seen him sneaking off, so he followed. He watched Brer Rabbit get in the bucket and go to the bottom of the well. That was the most astonishing thing he had ever seen. Brer Rabbit had to be up to something.

"I bet you anything that's where Brer Rabbit hides all his money. Or he's probably discovered a gold mine down there!"

Brer Fox peeked down into the well. "Hey, Brer Rabbit! What you doing down there?"

"Who? Me? Fishing. I thought I'd surprise everybody and catch a mess of fish for dinner."

"Many of 'em down there?"

"Is there stars in the sky? I'm glad you come, 'cause there's more fish down here than I can haul up. Why don't you come on down and give me a hand?"

"How do I get down there?"

"Jump in the bucket."

Brer Fox did that and started going down. The bucket Brer Rabbit was in started up. As Brer Rabbit passed Brer Fox, he sang out:

Goodbye, Brer Fox, take care of your clothes,
For this is the way the world goes;
Some goes up and some goes down,
You'll get to the bottom all safe and sound.

Just as Brer Fox hit the water—SPLASH!—Brer Rabbit jumped out at the top. He ran and told the other animals that Brer Fox was muddying up the drinking water.

They ran to the well and hauled Brer Fox out, chastising him for muddying up some good water. Wasn't nothing he could say.

Everybody went back to work, and every now and then Brer Rabbit looked at Brer Fox and laughed. Brer Fox had to give a little dry grin himself.

The Wonderful Tar-Baby Story[1]

"Didn't the fox *never* catch the rabbit, Uncle Remus?" asked the little boy the next evening.

"He come mighty nigh it, honey, sho's you bawn—Brer Fox did. One day atter Brer Rabbit fool 'im wid dat calamus[2] root, Brer Fox went ter wuk en got 'im some tar, en mix it wid some turbentime, en fix up a contrapshun wat he call a Tar-Baby, en he tuck dish yer Tar-Baby en he sot 'er in de big road, en den he lay off in de bushes fer ter see wat de news wuz gwineter be. En he didn't hatter wait long, nudder, kaze bimeby here come Brer Rabbit pacin' down de road—lippity-clippity, clippity-lippity—dez ez sassy ez a jay-bird. Brer Fox, he lay low. Brer Rabbit come prancin' 'long twel he spy de Tar-Baby, en den he fotch up on his behime legs like he wuz 'stonished. De Tar-Baby, she sot dar, she did, en Brer Fox, he lay low.

" 'Mawnin'!' sez Brer Rabbit, sezee—'nice wedder dis mawnin',' sezee.

"Tar-Baby ain't sayin' nuthin', en Brer Fox, he lay low.

" 'How duz yo' sym'tums seem ter segashuate?' sez Brer Rabbit, sezee.

"Brer Fox, he wink his eye slow, en lay low, en de Tar-Baby, she ain't sayin' nuthin'.

" 'How you come on, den? Is you deaf?' sez Brer Rabbit, sezee. 'Kaze if you is, I kin holler louder,' sezee.

"Tar-Baby stay still, en Brer Fox, he lay low.

" 'Youer stuck up, dat's w'at you is,' says Brer Rabbit, sezee, 'en I'm gwineter kyore you, dat's w'at I'm a gwineter do,' sezee.

"Brer Fox, he sorter chuckle in his stummuck, he did, but Tar-Baby ain't sayin' nuthin'.

" 'I'm gwineter larn you howter talk ter 'specttubble fokes ef hit's de las' ack,' sez Brer Rabbit, sezee. 'Ef you don't take off dat hat en tell me howdy, I'm gwineter bus' you wide open,' sezee.

"Tar-Baby stay still, en Brer Fox, he lay low.

"Brer Rabbit keep on axin' 'im, en de Tar-Baby, she keep on sayin' nuthin', twel present'y Brer Rabbit draw back wid his fis', he did, en blip he tuck 'er side er de head. Right dar's whar he broke his merlasses jug. His fis' stuck, en he can't pull loose. De tar hilt 'im. But Tar-Baby, she stay still, en Brer Fox, he lay low.

" 'Ef you don't lemme loose, I'll knock you agin,' sez Brer Rabbit, sezee, en wid dat he fotch 'er a wipe wid de udder han', en dat stuck. Tar-Baby, she ain't sayin' nuthin', en Brer Fox, he lay low.

" 'Tu'n me loose, fo' I kick de natal stuffin' outen you,' sez Brer Rabbit, sezee, but de Tar-Baby, she ain't sayin' nuthin'. She des hilt on, en den Brer Rabbit lose de use er his feet in de same way. Brer Fox, he lay low. Den Brer Rabbit squall out dat ef de Tar-Baby don't tu'n 'im loose he butt 'er crank-sided. En den he butted, en his head got stuck. Den Brer Fox, he sa'ntered fort', lookin' des ez innercent ez wunner yo' mammy's mockin'-birds.

" 'Howdy, Brer Rabbit,' sez Brer Fox, sezee. 'You look sorter stuck up dis mawnin',' sezee, en den he rolled on de groun', en laft en laft twel he couldn't laff no mo'. 'I speck you'll take dinner wid me dis time, Brer Rabbit. I done laid in some calamus root, en I ain't gwineter take no skuse,' sez Brer Fox, sezee."

1. From Joel Chandler Harris, *Uncle Remus: His Songs and Sayings* (1880).

2. A tropical plant, also called sweet flag.

Here Uncle Remus paused, and drew a two-pound yam out of the ashes.

"Did the fox eat the rabbit?" asked the little boy to whom the story had been told.

"Dat's all de fur de tale goes," replied the old man. "He mout, en den agin he mountent. Some say Jedge B'ar come 'long en loosed 'im—some say he didn't. I hear Miss Sally callin'. You better run 'long."

How Mr. Rabbit Was Too Sharp for Mr. Fox[1]

"Uncle Remus," said the little boy one evening, when he had found the old man with little or nothing to do, "did the fox kill and eat the rabbit when he caught him with the Tar-Baby?"

"Law, honey, ain't I tell you 'bout dat?" replied the old darkey, chuckling slyly. "I 'clar ter grashus I ought er tole you dat, but ole man Nod wuz ridin' on my eyeleds 'twel a leetle mo'n I'd a dis'member'd my own name, en den on to dat here come yo' mammy hollerin' atter you.

"W'at I tell you w'en I fus' begin? I tole you Brer Rabbit wuz a monstus soon beas'; leas'ways dat's w'at I laid out fer ter tell you. Well, den, honey, don't you go en make no udder kalkalashuns, kaze in dem days Brer Rabbit en his fambly wuz at de head er de gang w'en enny racket wuz on han', en dar dey stayed. 'Fo' you begins fer ter wipe yo' eyes 'bout Brer Rabbit, you wait en see whar'bouts Brer Rabbit gwineter fetch up at. But dat's needer yer ner dar.

"W'en Brer Fox fine Brer Rabbit mixt up wid de Tar-Baby, he feel mighty good, en he roll on de groun' en laff. Bimeby he up'n say, sezee:

"'Well, I speck I got you dis time, Brer Rabbit,' sezee; 'maybe I ain't, but I speck I is. You been runnin' roun' here sassin' atter me a mighty long time, but I speck you done come ter de een' er de row. You bin cuttin' up yo' capers en bouncin' 'roun' in dis naberhood ontwel you come ter b'leeve yo'se'f de boss er de whole gang. En den youer allers some'rs whar you got no bizness,' sez Brer Fox, sezee. 'Who ax you fer ter come en strike up a 'quaintence wid dish yer Tar-Baby? En who stuck you up dar whar you iz? Nobody in de roun' worril. You des tuck en jam yo'se'f on dat Tar-Baby widout waitin' fer enny invite,' sez Brer Fox, sezee, 'en dar you is, en dar you'll stay twel I fixes up a bresh-pile and fires her up, kaze I'm gwineter bobbycue you dis day, sho,' sez Brer Fox, sezee.

"Den Brer Rabbit talk mighty 'umble.

"'I don't keer w'at you do wid me, Brer Fox,' sezee, 'so you don't fling me in dat brier-patch. Roas' me, Brer Fox,' sezee, 'but don't fling me in dat brier-patch,' sezee.

"'Hit's so much trouble fer ter kindle a fire,' sez Brer Fox, sezee, 'dat I speck I'll hatter hang you,' sezee.

"'Hang me des ez high ez you please, Brer Fox,' sez Brer Rabbit, sezee, 'but do fer de Lord's sake don't fling me in that brier-patch,' sezee.

"'I ain't got no string,' sez Brer Fox, sezee, 'en now I speck I'll hatter drown you,' sezee.

"'Drown me des ez deep ez you please, Brer Fox,' sez Brer Rabbit, sezee, 'but do don't fling me in dat brier-patch,' sezee.

1. From Joel Chandler Harris, *Uncle Remus: His Songs and Sayings* (1880).

"'Dey ain't no water nigh,' sez Brer Fox, sezee, 'en now I speck I'll hatter skin you,' sezee.

"'Skin me, Brer Fox,' sez Brer Rabbit, sezee, 'snatch out my eyeballs, t'ar out my years by de roots, en cut off my legs,' sezee, 'but do please, Brer Fox, don't fling me in dat brier-patch,' sezee.

"Co'se Brer Fox wanter hurt Brer Rabbit bad ez he kin, so he cotch 'im by de behime legs en slung 'im right in de middle er de brier-patch. Dar was a considerbul flutter whar Brer Rabbit struck de bushes, en Brer Fox sorter hang 'roun' fer ter see w'at wuz gwineter happen. Bimeby he hear somebody call 'im, en way up de hill he see Brer Rabbit settin' cross-legged on a chinkapin log koamin' de pitch outen his har wid a chip. Den Brer Fox know dat he bin swop off mighty bad. Brer Rabbit wuz bleedzed fer ter fling back some er his sass, en he holler out:

"'Bred en bawn in a brier-patch, Brer Fox—bred en bawn in a brier-patch!' en wid dat he skip out des ez lively ez a cricket in de embers."

The Awful Fate of Mr. Wolf[1]

Uncle Remus was half-soling[2] one of his shoes, and his Miss Sally's little boy had been handling his awls, his hammers, and his knives to such an extent that the old man was compelled to assume a threatening attitude; but peace reigned again, and the little boy perched himself on a chair, watching Uncle Remus driving in pegs.

"Folks w'at's allers pesterin' people, en bodderin' 'longer dat w'at ain't dern, don't never come ter no good eend. Dar wuz Brer Wolf; stidder mindin' un his own bizness, he hatter take en go in pardnerships wid Brer Fox, en dey want skacely a minnit in de day dat he want atter Brer Rabbit, en he kep' on en kep' on twel fus' news you knowed he got kotch up wid—en he got kotch up wid monstus bad."

"Goodness, Uncle Remus! I thought the Wolf let the Rabbit alone, after he tried to fool him about the Fox being dead."

"Better lemme tell dish yer my way. Bimeby hit'll be yo' bed time, en Miss Sally'll be a hollerin' atter you, en you'll be a whimplin' roun', en den Mars John'll fetch up de re'r wid dat ar strop w'at I made fer 'im."

The child laughed, and playfully shook his fist in the simple, serious face of the venerable old darkey, but said no more. Uncle Remus waited awhile to be sure there was to be no other demonstration, and then proceeded:

"Brer Rabbit ain't see no peace w'atsumever. He can't leave home 'cep' Brer Wolf 'ud make a raid en tote off some er de fambly. Brer Rabbit b'ilt 'im a straw house, en hit wuz tored down; den he made a house outen pine-tops, en dat went de same way; den he made 'im a bark house, en dat wuz raided on, en eve'y time he los' a house he los' wunner his chilluns. Las' Brer Rabbit got mad, he did, en cust, en den he went off, he did, en got some kyarpinters, en dey b'ilt 'im a plank house wid rock foundashuns. Atter dat he could have some peace en quietness. He could go out en pass de time er day wid his nabers, en come back en set by de fier, en smoke his pipe, en read de newspapers same like enny man w'at got a fambly. He made a hole, he

1. From Joel Chandler Harris, *Uncle Remus: His Songs and Sayings* (1880). Note the contrast between the outer tale's ostensible peace and the inner tale's extraordinary violence.
2. Performing a shoe repair.

did, in de cellar whar de little Rabbits could hide out w'en dar wuz much uv a racket in de naberhood, en de latch er de front do' kotch on de inside. Brer Wolf, he see how de lan' lay, he did, en he lay low. De little Rabbits wuz mighty skittish, but hit got so dat cole chills ain't run up Brer Rabbit's back no mo' w'en he heerd Brer Wolf go gallopin' by.

"Bimeby, one day w'en Brer Rabbit wuz fixin' fer ter call on Miss Coon, he heerd a monstus fuss en clatter up de big road, en 'mos' 'fo' he could fix his years fer ter lissen, Brer Wolf run in de do'. De little Rabbits dey went inter dere hole in de cellar, dey did, like blowin' out a cannle. Brer Wolf wuz far'ly kivver'd wid mud, en mighty nigh outer win'.

"'Oh, do pray save me, Brer Rabbit!' sez Brer Wolf, sezee. 'Do please, Brer Rabbit! de dogs is atter me, en dey'll t'ar me up. Don't you year um comin'? Oh, do please save me, Brer Rabbit! Hide me some'rs whar de dogs won't git me.'

"No quicker sed dan done.

"'Jump in dat big chist dar, Brer Wolf,' sez Brer Rabbit, sezee; 'jump in dar en make yo'se'f at home.'

"In jump Brer Wolf, down come de led, en inter de hasp went de hook, en dar Mr. Wolf wuz. Den Brer Rabbit went ter de lookin' glass, he did, en wink at hisse'f, en den he drawd de rockin'-cheer in front er de fier, he did, en tuck a big chaw terbarker."

"Tobacco, Uncle Remus?" asked the little boy, incredulously.

"Rabbit terbarker, honey. You know dis yer life ev'lastin' w'at Miss Sally puts 'mong de cloze in de trunk; well, dat's rabbit terbarker. Den Brer Rabbit sot dar long time, he did, turnin' his mine over en wukken his thinkin' masheen. Bimeby he got up, en sorter stir 'roun'. Den Brer Wolf open up.

"'Is de dogs all gone, Brer Rabbit?'

"'Seem like I hear one un um smellin' roun' de chimbly-cornder des now.'

"Den Brer Rabbit git de kittle en fill it full er water, en put it on de fier.

"'W'at you doin' now, Brer Rabbit?'

"'I'm fixin' fer ter make you a nice cup er tea, Brer Wolf.'

"Den Brer Rabbit went ter de cubberd en git de gimlet,[3] en commence fer ter bo' little holes in de chist-led.

"'W'at you doin' now, Brer Rabbit?'

"'I'm a bo'in' little holes so you kin get bref, Brer Wolf.'

"Den Brer Rabbit went out en git some mo' wood, en fling it on de fier.

"'W'at you doin' now, Brer Rabbit?'

"'I'm a chunkin' up de fier so you won't git cole, Brer Wolf.'

"Den Brer Rabbit went down inter de cellar en fotch out all his chilluns.

"'W'at you doin' now, Brer Rabbit?'

"'I'm a tellin' my chilluns w'at a nice man you is, Brer Wolf.'

"En de chilluns, dey had ter put der han's on der moufs fer ter keep fum laffin'. Den Brer Rabbit he got de kittle en commenced fer ter po' de hot water on de chist-lid.

"'W'at dat I hear, Brer Rabbit?'

"'You hear de win' a blowin', Brer Wolf.'

"Den de water begin fer ter sif' thoo.

"'W'at dat I feel, Brer Rabbit?'

"'You feels de fleas a bitin', Brer Wolf.'

"'Dey er bitin' mighty hard, Brer Rabbit.'

3. A small hand tool for boring holes.

"'Tu'n over on de udder side, Brer Wolf.'

"'W'at dat I feel now, Brer Rabbit?'

"'Still you feels de fleas, Brer Wolf.'

"'Dey er eatin' me up, Brer Rabbit,' en dem wuz de las' words er Brer Wolf, kase de scaldin' water done de bizness.

"Den Brer Rabbit call in his nabers, he did, en dey hilt a reg'lar juberlee; en ef you go ter Brer Rabbit's house right now, I dunno but w'at you'll fine Brer Wolf's hide hangin' in de back-po'ch, en all bekaze he wuz so bizzy wid udder fo'kses doin's."

What the Rabbit Learned[1]

So they had a convention. De rabbit took de floor and said they was tired of runnin', and dodgin' all de time, and they asted de dogs to please leave rabbits alone and run somethin' else. So de dogs put it to a vote and 'greed to leave off runnin' rabbits.

So after de big meetin' Brer Dog invites de rabbit over to his house to have dinner wid him.

He started on thru de woods wid Brer Dog but every now and then he'd stop and scratch his ear and listen. He stop right in his tracks. Dog say:

"Aw, come on Brer Rabbit, you too suscautious. Come on."

Kept dat up till they come to de branch just 'fore they got to Brer Dog's house. Just as Brer Rabbit started to step out on de foot-log, he heard some dogs barkin' way down de creek. He heard de old hound say, "How o-l-d is he?" and the young dogs answer him: "Twenty-one or two, twenty-one or two!" So Brer Rabbit say, "Excuse me, but Ah don't reckon Ah better go home wid you today, Brer Dog."

"Aw, come on, Brer Rabbit, you always gitten scared for nothin'. Come on."

"Ah hear dogs barkin', Brer Dog."

"Naw, you don't, Brer Rabbit."

"Yes, Ah do. Ah know, dat's dogs barkin'."

"S'posin' it is, it don't make no difference. Ain't we done held a convention and passed a law dogs run no mo' rabbits? Don't pay no 'tention to every li'l bit of barkin' you hear."

Rabbit scratch his ear and say,

"Yeah, but all de dogs ain't been to no convention, and anyhow some of dese fool dogs ain't got no better sense than to run all over dat law and break it up. De rabbits didn't go to school much and he didn't learn but three letter, and that's trust no mistake. Run every time de bush shake."

So he raced on home without breakin' another breath wid de dog.

1. From Zora Neale Hurston's *Mules and Men* (1935).

The Literature of Slavery and Freedom 1746–1865

THE RELIGIOUS AND POLITICAL MISSION OF AFRICAN AMERICAN LITERATURE

The engendering impulse of African American literature is resistance to human tyranny. The earliest known text of African American literature, *The Last & Dying Words of MARK* (1755), attests to a spirit that has distinguished this literature from its outset: opposition through word or deed to any form of enslavement, physical or psychological. Mark's story recounts the rebellion of a Black man and two Black women against their Massachusetts enslaver. Later works of eighteenth-century African American literature speak out against other forms of injustice and oppression experienced by people of African descent in the Americas. As resistance to tyranny and dedication to liberty became increasingly synonymous with the early American republic itself, early African American writers identified themselves as Americans with a special mission. They would articulate the spiritual and political ideals of America to inspire and justify the struggle of Blacks for their birthright as American citizens. They would demand fidelity to those same ideals from whites whose moral complacency and racial prejudices had blinded them to the obligations of their own heritage. They would also warn whites of the potentially cataclysmic consequences

Photograph of an African American soldier, thought to be Sergeant Samuel Smith of the 119th U.S. Colored Infantry, his wife, Mollie, and their daughters, Mary and Maggie.

of failing to live up to the ideals of liberty and egalitarianism that the United States professed to revere.

The ideals of equality and liberty celebrated by the founders of the United States drew their legitimacy from intertwined religious and political traditions. But the racial chauvinism of most white Americans in the early republic forced a separation of their religious and political responsibilities to Blacks. In the realm of the spirit, most whites were content with African American claims to an equal right to God's grace, as long as African American salvation did not entail a radical redemption of the white-dominated social order. In the political sphere, however, whites presumed themselves alone to be the arbiters of rights and privileges.

Recognizing this contradiction in white America's attitude toward Black advancement, early African American writers in the United States appealed to the traditional Christian gospel of the universal brotherhood of humanity as a way of initiating a discussion with whites that did not directly confront their prejudices and anxieties. Readers of Phillis Wheatley's *Poems on Various Subjects, Religious and Moral* (1773), which won international attention as an inaugural text of African American literature, found much more evidence of the enslaved Boston poet's piety than her politics. Even in one of her rare poems about her personal experience as an African American, "On Being Brought from Africa to America," Wheatley spoke of Black equality to whites in terms that appeared limited to matters of the spirit:

> Some view our sable race with scornful eye,
> "Their colour is a diabolic die."
> Remember, *Christians, Negros,* black as *Cain,*
> May be refin'd, and join th' angelic train.

Despite the self-deprecating treatment of color in this poem, by insisting that color is no barrier to Black ascension to spiritual heights, Wheatley may have been inviting her white readers to consider whether color should bar African Americans from rising in the social and political scale either.

Wheatley and her fellow pioneers in African American poetry, Massachusetts balladeer Lucy Terry and Jupiter Hammon, born enslaved in New York, as well as Briton Hammon, who produced a ground-breaking autobiography, *A Narrative of the Uncommon Sufferings and Surprising Deliverance of Briton Hammon, a Negro Man* (1760), all seem to have been motivated primarily by a desire to win a popular Christian readership. Nevertheless, their appearance on the American literary scene, however conventional their piety and its expression may seem today, had social significance. As currently or formerly enslaved persons, all placed their white readers on notice that even the least advantaged of Black Americans had compelling feelings to voice and absorbing stories to tell the public at large. Moreover, as *writers* who employed the arts of literacy with independent purpose—which the white-authored preface to Wheatley's *Poems* was at pains to attest—poets such as Wheatley and Jupiter Hammon contradicted a widespread European prejudice that Black people were incapable of sophisticated literary expression. Mastery of language, the essential sign of a civilized mind to the European, implicitly qualified a Black writer, and by analogy those whom he or she represented, for self-mastery and a place of respect within white civilization.

From the outset, African American literature challenged the dominant culture's attempt to segregate the religious from the political, the spirit from the flesh, insofar as racial affairs were concerned. Within two years of the publication of her landmark book of poems, Wheatley was articulating without equivocation the holistic view of spiritual and political issues that pervades later generations of African American writing. In 1774 she announced that she could discern "more and more clearly, the glorious Dispensation of civil and religious Liberty, which are so inseparably united, that there is little or no Enjoyment of one without the other." By the early nineteenth century, civil rights activists like Maria W. Stewart felt no compunction in affirming God's investment in both the eternal redemption and the earthly progress of Black people. Echoing, perhaps even alluding to, Wheatley's famous quatrain in "On Being Brought from Africa to America," Stewart announced to African Americans in 1831: "Many think, because your skins are tinged with a sable hue, that you are an inferior race of beings; but God does not consider you as such." By invoking divine sanction for African American social strivings, writers like Stewart brought to fruition the efforts of many earlier Black writers to dignify Black experience with spiritual significance and divinely ordained importance.

In the eyes of the standard-bearers of early African American literature, all of God's laws were indivisible because all of God's people were one. Jesus, the suffering servant, bore powerful witness to God's love of mercy; Moses, the deliverer of the Israelites from bondage in Egypt, testified just as compellingly to God's devotion to justice. Spurred by a conviction of their own special calling to witness against America's spiritual and political degeneration, early Black writers such as Olaudah Equiano, David Walker, Maria Stewart, and ultimately Frederick Douglass exhorted their white readers like preachers imploring a backsliding congregation to live up to the standards of their reputed religion and their professed political principles. "O, ye nominal Christians!" Equiano thundered to the white readers of his *Interesting Narrative of the Life of Olaudah Equiano, or Gustavus Vassa, the African, Written by Himself* (1789) after surveying the horrors of the notorious Middle Passage endured by millions of Africans before they were sold into slavery in the Americas: "might not an African ask you—Learned you this from your God, who says unto you, Do unto all men as you would men should do unto you?" In a similar vein, Benjamin Banneker, a Black mathematician and almanac maker, wrote Secretary of State Thomas Jefferson in 1791 to ask how the author of the Declaration of Independence could denounce Britain's tyranny over its American colonies in 1776 without also opposing "that state of tyrannical thraldom and inhuman captivity to which too many of my brethren are doomed" in the newly formed United States. Are you not also "guilty of that most criminal act which you professedly detested in others?" Banneker inquired with unassailable logic.

Representing themselves as faithful adherents to the humanitarian ideals of Christianity and the American Revolution, early African American writers explored through various forms of irony the chasm between white America's words and its deeds, between its propaganda about freedom and its widespread practice of slavery. *David Walker's Appeal in Four Articles; Together with a Preamble, to the Coloured Citizens of the World* (1829) is predicated on a structural irony anticipated in its very title. Like the U.S. Constitution, Walker's *Appeal* begins with a preamble followed by four articles. Unlike the Constitution, which legalized slavery in the United States, Walker's text demands slavery's abolition and warns of the deconstitution of the United States by God's avenging power if slavery is not outlawed. One of the most famous instances of irony in early African American literature appears in James M. Whitfield's "America" (1853), which opens with a bitter parody of the popular patriotic hymn "America" ("My Country, 'Tis of Thee"). The initial lines of Whitfield's poem declare:

> America, it is to thee,
> Thou boasted land of liberty,—
> It is to thee I raise my song,
> Thou land of blood, and crime, and wrong.

Whitfield's cry of betrayal at the hands of America summarized decades of increasingly vocal Black outrage over the fundamental hypocrisy of the United States' self-congratulatory image as the "land of the free."

The grotesque inconsistency between the United States' championing of "life, liberty, and the pursuit of happiness" in its own Declaration of Independence and its sanctioning of the crime of chattel slavery furnished early African American literature with its most enduring theme. Initially, writers like Benjamin Banneker used the egalitarian language of the Declaration of Independence to try to shame white America into abolishing slavery. But as early as the expatriate Victor Séjour's pioneering short story "The Mulatto" (1837), and with increasing vehemence in the speeches of mid-century Black America's most eloquent platform orators, such as Henry Highland Garnet and Frederick Douglass, the right of African Americans to armed resistance to slavery was proclaimed. The Founding Fathers' justification of revolution—particularly Patrick Henry's "Give me liberty or give me death" speech in 1775 in Virginia—gave ample precedent for violent action in the name of freedom. Regardless of the means of rhetorical attack, African American literature throughout the pre–Civil War era maintained as its central priorities the abolition of slavery and the promotion of the Black man and woman to a status in the civil and cultural order equal to that of whites.

SLAVERY IN THE AMERICAS

To prosecute their war of words against slavery, early Black advocates of freedom became students of the long and sordid history of human bondage, which dates back to ancient Egypt, Greece, and Rome. One such self-educated historian, David Walker, acknowledged that slavery had long been practiced in Africa, but he charged white Christian slaveholders with greater crimes against humanity and greater hypocrisy in justifying those crimes than any prior slave system had been guilty of. Twenty-first-century scholarship has lent much support to the contentions of Walker and others in the African American antislavery vanguard that slavery as perpetrated by the European colonizers of Africa and the Americas brought man's inhumanity to man to a level of technological efficiency unimagined by previous generations.

The transatlantic slave trade was not the first international system of human trafficking for forced labor, but its magnitude and effects were unprecedented. This era in the history of international slave trading is generally dated from 1501, when Spanish vessels began carrying African captives for sale in the West Indies, to 1867, when the last slave ship from Africa is believed to have discharged its human cargo in Cuba. During the 366 years of the transatlantic trade, an estimated 12.5 million captives were conveyed from Africa to Europe and the Americas. Scholars believe that about 15 percent of those who embarked on the horrific Middle Passage did not complete

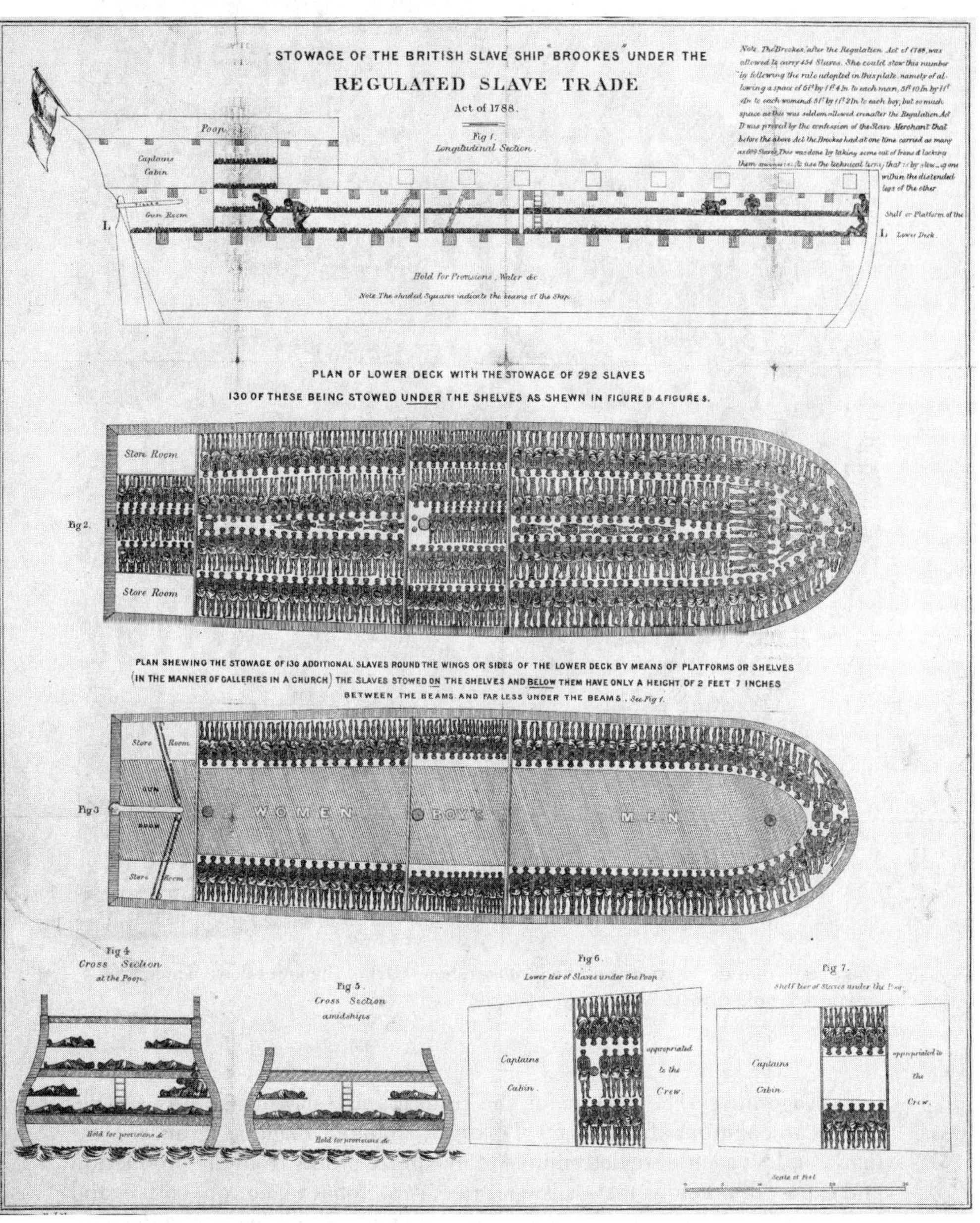

The Slave Ship *Brookes*. This engraving of the plan of a Liverpool-based slave ship, stowed with its human cargo, was published in 1789 by the Society for Effecting the Abolition of the Trade in Slaves. According to leading British abolitionist Thomas Clarkson, the image made "an instantaneous impression of horror upon all who saw it." The ship was designed to transport 454 enslaved people through the Middle Passage to the Western Hemisphere. See p. 76 for a detail.

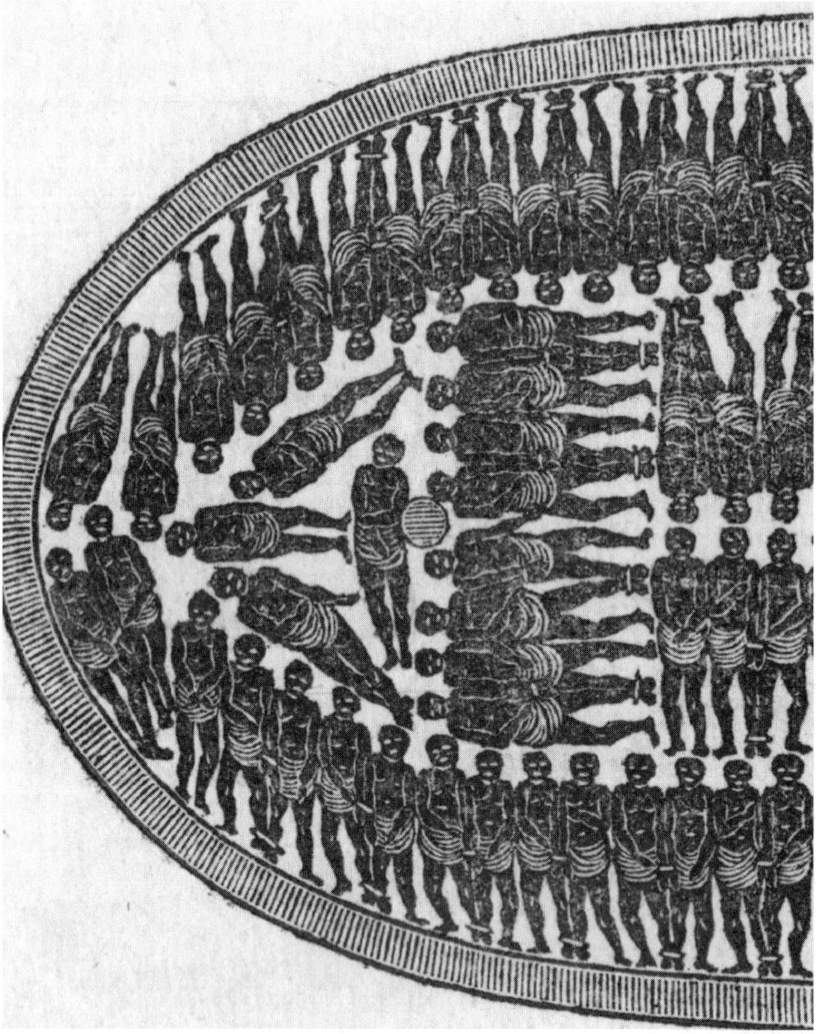

This detail from the engraving of the *Brookes* shows part of the lower deck, which was designed to hold close to 300 enslaved people.

the voyage alive. The reason for the transatlantic slave trade was simple. European colonizers from Spain, Portugal, Holland, England, France, Denmark, and Sweden were determined to maximize profits from the production and export of precious metals, sugar, rice, rum, tobacco, cotton, coffee, and indigo in the Americas. Through trial and error, which led to the decimation of the populations of enslaved native peoples especially in the Caribbean during the sixteenth century, Europeans concluded that Africans could provide the cheapest and hardiest labor for the high-mortality mining and agricultural enterprises that fueled the economic exploitation of the Western Hemisphere. Ironically, the ghastly effects of the Spanish enslavement of the indigenous peoples of the Caribbean triggered the first importation of African slaves into the Western Hemisphere. In 1517 Bartolomé de las Casas, a Spanish missionary to the Caribbean island of Hispaniola, recommended to his political superiors that Africans be imported to the Spanish colonies to relieve the appalling mistreatment of the native peoples of New Spain. By 1820 African slaves constituted roughly 80 percent of all immigrants to the Americas since 1500. Brazil and the Caribbean took 90 percent of the captive migrants. Only about 8 percent of the transatlantic slave trade disembarked in North America. Sugar plantations became the destinations of the large majority of the Africans trafficked against their wills to the so-called New World.

"AM I NOT A MAN ..." A popular antislavery image among abolitionists in Great Britain and North America, based on a 1787 medallion designed by Josiah Wedgwood.

The first people of African descent who came to North America were explorers. Among the most famous were the enslaved Moroccan Estevanico (or Esteban) (d. 1539), who opened up what is now New Mexico and Arizona for Spanish settlement, and Jean Baptiste Point du Sable (1745?–1818), a French-educated Haitian who founded a trading post on the southern shore of Lake Michigan from which the city of Chicago grew. The first Africans in British North America were brought to work as laborers. They arrived at Jamestown, Virginia, in 1619 aboard a Dutch slave ship. Only twenty in number, including at least three women, these people were neither free nor classified as slaves. They were purchased as indentured servants who, whether white or Black, could become free if they worked satisfactorily for their masters for a stipulated number of years. By 1700, however, the expanding plantation economy of Virginia demanded a workforce that was cheaper than free or indentured labor and more easily controlled and replenished. By establishing the institution of chattel slavery, in which a Black person became not just a temporary servant but the lifetime property of his or her enslaver, the tobacco, cotton, and rice planters of British North America ensured their rise to economic and political preeminence over the southern half of what would become the United States.

Under chattel slavery, the African imported to North America was divested as much as possible of his or her culture. The newly minted slave was relegated to a condition that the historian Orlando Patterson has termed "social death." Although much evidence demonstrates that some African religious beliefs, cultural practices, and linguistic forms survived the Middle Passage, chattel slavery was designed to prevent Africans and their descendants from building a new identity except in accordance with the dictates of their oppressors. Instead of an individual, slavery devised what Patterson calls "a social nonperson," a being that by legal definition could have no family, no personal honor, no past, and no future. The intention of slavery was to vitiate, if not dissolve, normal familial and communal ties among the enslaved, supplanting them with an absolute dependence on and identification with the enslaver's will. Self-reliance, a cardinal tenet of the popular American doctrine of rugged individualism, was forbidden the enslaved. Denying surnames and a knowledge of birthdays to the enslaved was a way to suppress the very notion of selfhood among those who could not even possess themselves. However, from the beginning of African American literature, *The Last & Dying Words of MARK* refuted the notion that chattel slavery could divest the enslaved of their will to assert themselves by making common cause against their oppressors.

SLAVERY AND AMERICAN RACISM

What gave American chattel slavery its uniquely oppressive character and power was its insistence that enslavement was the natural and proper condition for particular *races* of people. Reinforced by theories of racial difference promoted by such prestigious European philosophers as Friedrich Hegel, Immanuel Kant, and David Hume, most Europeans and Americans assumed that differences in externals—complexion, hair, and other physical features—between Blacks and whites signified differences in the inherent character—intelligence, morality, and spirituality—of the two groups. When Thomas Jefferson reviewed what he considered to be the major differences between whites and Blacks, he concluded that these differences were so deep and ineradicable that only complete separation of the races, with whites in control until such time as Blacks could be removed from the country, could avert race war in the United States.

Jefferson's *Notes on the State of Virginia* (1787) contained a powerful condemnation of slavery, but the book also became an influential statement of early American racism because of Jefferson's persistent association of Blackness with absence. After celebrating "the fine mixtures of red and white" that endowed the complexions of whites with their "superior beauty," Jefferson contemplated with an almost palpable shudder "that eternal monotony, which reigns in the countenances [of Black people], that immoveable veil of black which covers all the emotions of the other race." Thus darkness of skin symbolized for Jefferson an absence of light within the African American, a void that made Blackness the sign not merely of skin difference but also of an unknowable alien, a suspicious if not threatening other. Providing intellectual and moral cover for slavery's naked politics of exploitation, a sizable school of racist writers in the first half of the nineteenth century in the United States followed Jefferson in arguing that the physical, psychological, and cultural differences they perceived in African Americans amounted to an intellectual, spiritual, and moral otherness that only slavery could turn to some productive account.

RESISTANCE TO SLAVERY AND RACISM

After the United States won its war for independence from Britain in 1783, the cause of African American freedom earned a number of notable regional victories despite being stymied in the national political arena. To win the endorsement of the southern states, the framers of the U.S. Constitution wrote into law in 1787 several measures that protected slavery, in particular the infamous "three-fifths compromise," which stipulated that a slave could be counted as three-fifths of a person for the purpose of apportioning representation in congressional districts. Since the enslaved could not vote, the three-fifths compromise did nothing but augment the size and power of the southern bloc in the U.S. House of Representatives. Undaunted, antislavery advocates in Pennsylvania and New York, supported by the Society of Friends (Quakers), the most vocal religious group to oppose slavery in the North American colonies, issued a call for the gradual abolition of slavery in the new republic. The gradualism of those known as "moral suasionists" enjoyed genuine success when Vermont banned slavery in 1777 and abolitionists pushed through gradual emancipation or abolition laws in Pennsylvania (1780), New Hampshire and Massachusetts (1783), Rhode Island (1784), and Connecticut (1784), New Jersey (1804), and New York (1827). By the end of the first decade of the nineteenth century, slavery was effectively a dead letter in all the states of the North and in the burgeoning Northwest Territory. Bowing to antislavery pressure in 1807, the U.S. Congress went so far as to outlaw the African slave trade, though it did nothing to curb the internal slave trade.

In the early decades of the nineteenth century, African Americans in the North joined with fair-minded whites to bring about additional social and political advances. African American newspapers, inaugurated by *Freedom's Journal* in 1827, urged through essays, poetry, and fiction as well as more conventional journalism the achievements of Black people in the North and the need for an end to slavery in the South. Committed to improved educational opportunity, African Americans pushed for the admission of their children to the early public schools of the North and vigorously protested against laws that excluded them. Independent Black Methodist and Baptist churches, led by thoughtful and respected Black pastors, bore witness to the solidarity and progressive outlook of northern Black communities, as did the rise of various mutual-aid, fraternal, and debating societies in cities such as New York, Philadelphia, and Boston. Racial prejudice, discrimination, and segregation remained endemic in the states of the North, however, indifferent to the evidence of the self-improvement and good citizenship of many African Americans.

In the South, where racism provided the cornerstone of the social, economic, and political order, African Americans could do little to alter their circumstances. The living conditions of slaves remained almost totally dependent on the disposition of individual enslavers. The legal status of free persons of color deteriorated as their numbers shrank in the South after 1800. Antislavery proponents in the upper South were able to liberalize laws that made it easier to emancipate enslaved persons. But the expansion of the British textile industry, together with changes in the farming and processing of cotton in the United States during the 1790s, wedded the South more and more tightly to slavery. The invention of the cotton gin in 1794, a labor-saving device that provided a cheap means of separating cotton fiber from its seed, turned southern agriculture into "the cotton kingdom." Cotton plantations, on which a hundred or more enslaved men and women labored from dawn to dusk six days a week, sprang up over the lower South and in the opening territories of the trans-Mississippi Valley. Slaveholding seemed the key to unlocking vast new wealth from the land. As a consequence, the enslaved population in the South grew rapidly, from seven hundred thousand in 1790 to two million in 1830.

In late August 1831, in Southampton County, Virginia, a rebellion of the enslaved, fomented by a Black preacher named Nat Turner, crystallized the impending crisis into which slavery was taking the South. Convinced that he had been called by God to usher in the biblically prophesied Day of Judgment, Turner led his followers, who numbered between sixty and eighty, in a bloody march toward Jerusalem, the county seat, where he probably intended to seize its arsenal and munitions supply. Before the rebels were scattered and apprehended by state and federal troops, Turner and his adherents had put to death fifty-five whites, including Prophet Nat's enslaver as well as his family. In subsequent reprisals and trials during the summer and fall of 1831, local whites executed more than fifty enslaved persons. Turner remained at large until his capture in late October near where the rebellion had begun. After dictating a narrative hurried into publication under the title *The Confessions of Nat Turner,* the leader of the most notorious slave rebellion in U.S. history was hanged on November 11, 1831. It is estimated that fifty thousand copies of Turner's decidedly unrepentant "confessions" were printed, making this the most widely read African American personal narrative since Equiano's in 1789.

The slaveholding South was permanently traumatized by Turner's rebellion. The Virginia state legislature debated whether to abolish slavery or make it more repressive, deciding in the end to follow the latter course. Throughout the South tighter restrictions were placed on free Blacks; on Black opportunities to assemble, especially in church; on Black ministers; and on the access of enslaved people to books (even the Bible) as well as to literacy. Those who held the reins of power in the South became increasingly belligerent in their defense of slavery and their determination to see it extended into new territories beyond the Mississippi River that were lobbying for statehood. Regarding each other with heightening acrimony, representatives of the slave and the free states in the U.S. Congress fed sectional grievances that accelerated the polarization of the two regions of the country. Various compromises were enacted—the most controversial of which was the Compromise of 1850, which among other things instituted the Fugitive Slave Law—so that a balance of power might be maintained between the North and South. Nevertheless, compromise only intensified the feeling in each section that the opposition was gaining an unfair, if not a controlling, share of power.

RADICAL ABOLITIONISM AND THE FUGITIVE SLAVE NARRATIVE

In the aftermath of the Turner rebellion and the South's iron-fisted response to it, a new generation of reformers in the North proclaimed their absolute and uncompromising opposition to slavery. Led by the crusading white journalist William Lloyd Garrison, these abolitionists demanded the immediate end of slavery throughout the United States. Free Blacks in the North lent crucial support to Garrison's American Anti-Slavery Society, editing newspapers, holding conventions, circulating petitions, and investing their money and their energies in protest actions. Searching for a means of galvanizing public concern for the slave as "a man and a brother," this generation of Black and white radical abolitionists sponsored a new departure in African American literature, the fugitive slave narrative. From 1825 to the end of the slavery era, the fugitive slave narrative dominated the literary landscape of antebellum Black America, far outnumbering the autobiographies

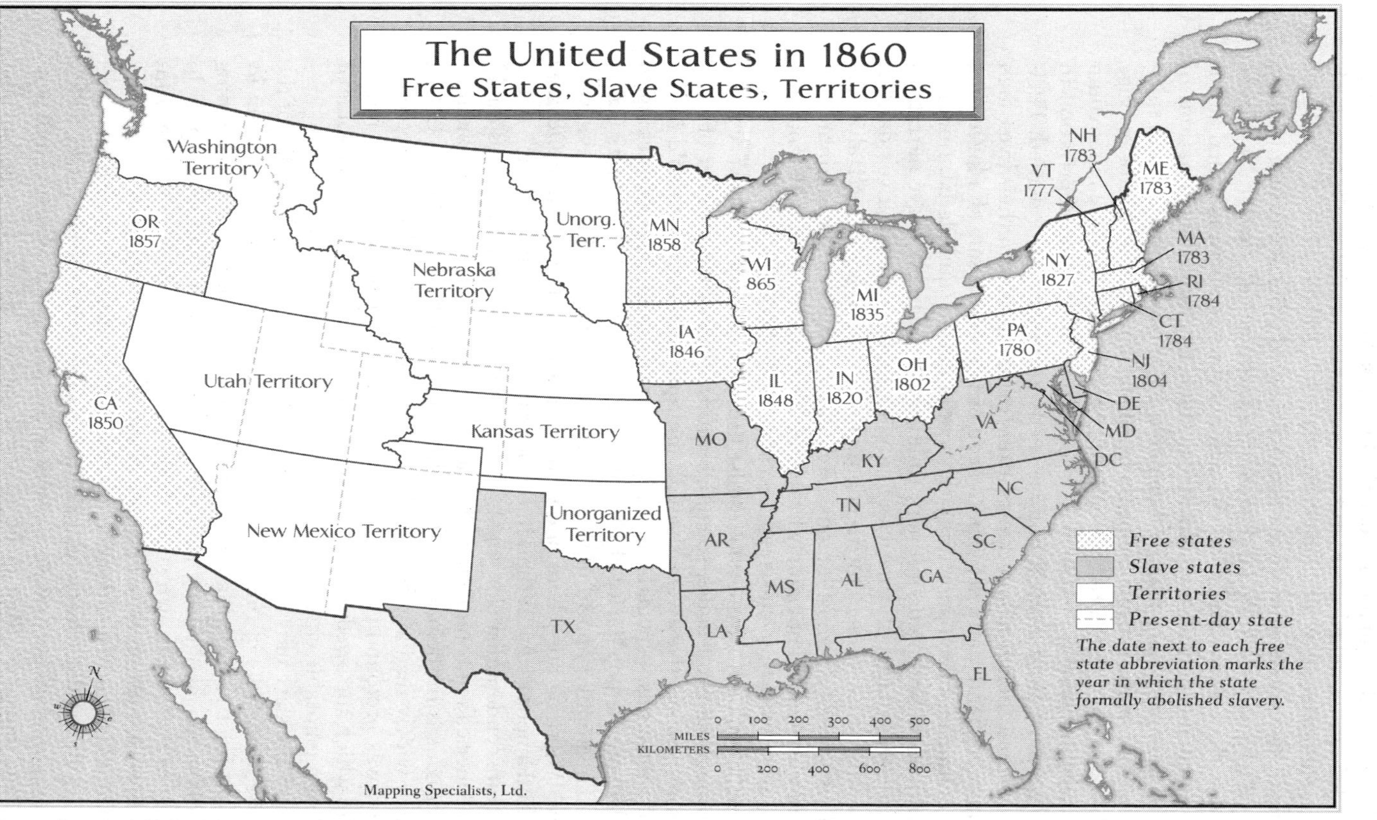

From the 1860 U.S. Census: Total white population of the fifteen slaveholding states: 8,039,000
Total free Black population of the fifteen slaveholding states: 251,000
Total enslaved population of the fifteen slaveholding states: 3,953,000
Total white population of the eighteen free states and seven territories: 18,920,000
Total free Black population of the eighteen free states and seven territories: 237,000

of free people of color, not to mention the handful of novels published by African Americans. Major authors of African American literature before 1865, including Olaudah Equiano, Frederick Douglass, William Wells Brown, and Harriet Jacobs, launched their writing careers via narratives of their experiences while enslaved.

Typically the antebellum slave narrative carried a Black message inside a white envelope. Prefatory (and sometimes appended) matter by whites attested to the veracity and good character of the narrator and called attention to what the narrative would reveal about the moral abominations of slavery. These narratives usually focus on the fugitive's emotional and spiritual preparation for escape, followed by his or her arduous rite of passage from bondage in the South to freedom in the North. Usually antebellum slave narrators portrayed slavery as a condition of extreme deprivation in which the most fundamental human needs and rights were denied. Fugitives launched their freedom quests after turning points in their lives such as an unprecedented atrocity experienced or witnessed, sale of a loved one, or a propitious escape opportunity that could not be squandered. Impelled by faith in God and a commitment to liberty comparable (slave narratives often stressed) to that of America's Founding Fathers, the fugitive's dangerous, usually solitary quest for freedom climaxed in a joyous arrival in the North. In some of the most famous antebellum narratives, the attainment of freedom was signaled not simply by reaching the free states but by renaming oneself and dedicating one's future to antislavery activism.

Advertised mostly in the abolitionist press and sold at antislavery meetings throughout the English-speaking world, a significant number of antebellum slave narratives went through multiple editions. Some sold in the tens of thousands, especially those published by trade presses seeking to capitalize on the popularity of Harriet Beecher Stowe's *Uncle Tom's Cabin* (1852). The popular appeal of slave narratives is reflected in this reviewer's praise: "We know not where one who wished to write a modern Odyssey could find a better subject than in the adventures of a fugitive slave." To the noted transcendentalist clergyman Theodore Parker, slave narratives qualified as America's only indigenous literary form, for "all the original romance of Americans is in them, not in the white man's novel." *Uncle Tom's Cabin*, the most widely read and hotly debated American novel of the nineteenth century, was profoundly influenced by its author's reading of slave narratives, to which she owed many graphic incidents and the models for some of her most memorable characters.

In 1845 the slave narrative reached its epitome with the publication of the *Narrative of the Life of Frederick Douglass, an American Slave, Written by Himself*. A fugitive from Maryland slavery, Douglass spent four years honing his skills as an abolitionist lecturer before writing his autobiography. In deciding to author his own story rather than enlist a white editor to transcribe his oral testimony and fashion that into a book, Douglass risked public censure for egotism and incompetence because he had never had a day's schooling in his life. Resolved, nevertheless, to write his own story in his own way, Douglass bore witness to the self-awareness, intellectual independence, and literary authority he claimed as a rightfully free man. After Douglass's immensely successful *Narrative*, the presence of the subtitle *Written by Himself* on a slave narrative bore increasing significance as an indicator of a narrator's political and literary self-reliance. In the late 1840s well-known fugitive slaves such as William Wells Brown, William and Ellen Craft, and James W. C. Pennington reinforced the rhetorical self-consciousness of the slave narrative by incorporating into their stories trickster motifs from African American folk culture, extensive literary and biblical allusion, and a realistic, picaresque perspective on the challenges fugitives had to overcome on their way to freedom.

As social and political conflict in the United States at mid-century centered increasingly on the fate of slavery and the human rights of African Americans, the slave narrative took on an unprecedented urgency and candor. Narrators probed as never before the moral and social complexities of the American caste and class system in the North as well as the South. *My Bondage and My Freedom* (1855), Douglass's second autobiography, conducted a fresh inquiry into the meaning of slavery and freedom, adopting the standpoint of one who had spent enough time in the so-called free states to understand how pervasive racism and racist paternalism were, even among the most liberal whites, the Garrisonians themselves. Harriet Jacobs, the earliest known enslaved African American woman to author her own narrative, also challenged conventional ideas about slavery and freedom in her strikingly original *Incidents in the Life of a Slave Girl* (1861). Jacobs was determined to show how sexual exploitation made slavery especially oppressive for Black women. But by demonstrating how she fought back and ultimately gained her own freedom and that of her two children, Jacobs proudly claimed agency, purpose, and triumph for herself and for African American women, exemplified in *Incidents* by her resilient and resourceful female kin, both enslaved and free. The writing of Jacobs; the oratory of the abolitionist-feminist Sojourner Truth; and the renowned example of Harriet Tubman, the fearless conductor of runaways on the Underground Railroad, enriched African American literature with new models of female self-expression and heroism.

THE FIRST AFRICAN AMERICAN LITERARY RENAISSANCE

These developments in the slave narrative, along with the publication of several pioneering experiments in fiction, justify calling the 1850s and early 1860s the first renaissance in African American letters. Martin R. Delany, a journalist, physician, and social activist, articulated the mood of the new literature when he stated in *The Condition, Elevation, Emigration and Destiny of the Colored People of the United States* (1852): "Our elevation must be the result of *self-efforts,* and work of our *own hands.*" Calls for a renewed national spirit among African Americans helped spur intellectual independence on a wide range of fronts, including the expansion of literary horizons in both form and theme. In 1853 Frederick Douglass published a historical novella, *The Heroic Slave,* in his own newspaper, *Frederick Douglass' Paper.* The protagonist of Douglass's story, Madison Washington, who led a successful mutiny on a slave ship in 1841, gave American readers a model of Black manhood that carefully balanced the violent desire for justice of Nat Turner and the Christian pacifism of Stowe's Uncle Tom. Soon after *The Heroic Slave,* the first full-length African American novel was published in England under the title *Clotel; or, The President's Daughter* (1853). Authored by William Wells Brown, who had already distinguished himself as the writer of an internationally celebrated slave narrative as well as the first travel book by an African American, *Clotel* blurred the line between fact and fiction. Clotel, a beautiful and idealized light-skinned enslaved woman, is identified in the novel as the daughter of Thomas Jefferson and his enslaved mistress. *Clotel* helped popularize the sentimental image of the "tragic mulatta" in American fiction by white as well as Black authors. But the ultimate outcome of her story, in which Clotel transforms herself into a combative trickster to rescue her daughter from slavery, shows Brown testing the limits of gender conventions in fiction. Five years later, Brown contributed again to the outpouring of literary creativity among Black Americans at mid-century by fashioning the first African American play, *The Escape; or, A Leap for Freedom,* based on scenes and themes familiar to readers of fugitive slave narratives.

In 1859 Delany infused a pan-African consciousness into his serialized novel *Blake; or, The Huts of America,* which celebrates a fugitive from slavery who plots war against whites in both the American South and the Caribbean. Delany's Blake represents the first Black nationalist culture hero in African American literature. In the same year two African American women published innovative works of fiction: "The Two Offers," a short story by Frances Ellen Watkins Harper, and *Our Nig; or, Sketches from the Life of a Free Black,* an autobiographical novel by Harriet E. Wilson. Among the poetic voices of Black America, Harper's was preeminent at mid-century. The African American reading community embraced her as a writer who spoke to the needs and aspirations of the enslaved and free people alike in verse that was direct, impassioned, and morally inspiring. "The Two Offers" appeared in a well-known African American magazine and bolstered Harper's considerable reputation for addressing women's concerns seriously and sympathetically. In contrast, *Our Nig* received little or no public notice, despite (or perhaps because of) its author's unprecedented, tough-minded exposure of the socioeconomic realities of life for a Black working-class woman in the North. Wilson's novel is now regarded as a foundational text of African American women's literature.

FOLK TRADITIONS

Behind the achievements of individual African American writers during the antislavery period lies the communal consciousness of millions of enslaved people, whose oral traditions in song and story have given form and substance to literature by Black Americans since they first began writing in English. In his *Narrative* Frederick Douglass recalled having received his first glimmering sense of the awful evil of slavery after hearing work songs of enslaved people on the Maryland plantation of his birth. Later in his life Douglass revealed that the familiar spiritual "Run to Jesus" had first suggested to him the thought of making his escape from slavery. The genius of the spirituals rests in their double meaning, their blending of religious inspiration and political aspiration. When slaves sang "I thank God I'm free at las'," only they knew whether they were referring to freedom from sin or from slavery. Even in those spirituals that express a poignant yearning for deliverance in heaven from earthly burdens, one can hear a powerful complaint against the institutions that forced many African Americans to believe that only in the next world would they find justice.

A second great fund of southern Black folklore, the animal tales, testified to the slaves' commonsense understanding of human psychology and everyday social relations in their world. Many of these tales explain in comic fashion how the world came to be as it is. But many more feature the exploits of trickster figures, most notably Brer (Brother) Rabbit, who use their wits to stymie or deceive stronger animal antagonists. Tales that celebrate the trickster, whether in animal or human form, are universal in human folklore. Still, the popularity of wily Brer Rabbit and his enslaved human counterpart, devious John, in the folklore of the enslaved attests to the enduring faith of Black Americans in the power of mind over matter. The spirit of Brer Rabbit or crafty John lived in every slave who soothed his master with a smile of loyalty while stealing from his storehouse or making plans for escape.

THE CIVIL WAR AND EMANCIPATION

In 1860 the avowedly antislavery Republican Party elected its candidate for president, Abraham Lincoln of Illinois, after one of the bitterest political campaigns ever waged in the United States. Southern extremists began to beat the drum for secession. Lincoln promised the South that he would not seek the abolition of slavery, but he warned the secessionists that he would not allow them to split the Union apart. When South Carolina bombarded federal troops at Fort Sumter in Charleston on April 12, 1861, Lincoln issued a call for seventy-five thousand volunteers to help put down what northerners called the southern rebellion. During the next four years, while the American Civil War raged on, African Americans played an increasingly important role in the Union cause. During the course of the war in the upper South, thousands of enslaved people fled their bondage in search of freedom under the protection of approaching Union armies. The longer the war dragged on, the more the southern economy contracted due to the steady departure of its Black workforce. Initially forbidden to serve in the Union army, African American men in the North waited until the summer of 1862, when Lincoln finally heeded the counsel of advisers like Frederick Douglass and permitted Blacks in liberated portions of Louisiana and South Carolina to form regiments. When two South Carolina regiments, combining both free Blacks and formerly enslaved men, captured and occupied Jacksonville, Florida, in March 1863, Lincoln authorized the full-scale recruitment of Black soldiers and sailors for the war effort. By the war's end, more than 186,000 Blacks had served in the artillery, cavalry, engineers, and infantry as well as in the U.S. Navy. African American troops left a notable record of valor in major battles throughout the South in the last two years of the war even though they were routinely paid less than the wages white soldiers received. More than 38,000 African Americans gave their lives for the Union cause.

Although Northern whites joined the Union Army for many reasons, African Americans fought for one overriding purpose—to bring an end to slavery. For more than two years after the outbreak of hostilities, African Americans waited for their president to link the Union cause with the extinction of slavery. When Lincoln issued the Emancipation Proclamation in the summer of 1862, which declared all enslaved persons in the

Sergeant Nimrod Burke (1836–1914), Company F, 23rd U.S. Colored Infantry, a Virginia-born scout during the Civil War.

rebellious states to be free as of January 1, 1863, African Americans in the North felt that, at long last, their country had committed itself to an ideal worth dying for. Few African Americans criticized Lincoln for failing to declare freedom for the slaves in the border states, such as Kentucky and Maryland, that had not joined the Southern Confederacy. Charlotte Forten, daughter of an influential Philadelphia civil rights activist and author of the most widely read African American diary of the nineteenth century, probably spoke for most in the Black American leadership class when she entered in her diary on January 1, 1863: "Ah, what a grand, glorious day this has been. The dawn of freedom which it heralds may not break upon us at once; but it will surely come, and sooner, I believe, than we have ever dared hope before." When the main army of the Southern slaveocracy surrendered at Appomattox, Virginia, on April 9, 1865, African Americans pressed for the enactment of laws ensuring a new era of freedom and opportunity for every Black American. On December 6, 1865, the Thirteenth Amendment to the U.S. Constitution, which abolished "slavery and involuntary servitude" throughout the country, was ratified by the newly united states of America, including eight from the former Confederacy. But the long-anticipated era of freedom, equality, and opportunity for all Americans would prove much more difficult to bring into reality.

THE LAST & DYING WORDS OF MARK

The Last & Dying Words of MARK is the earliest extant slave narrative published in North America. It appeared in September 1755 as a broadside—a popular form of street literature printed as a one-page poster—in the Boston area shortly after the spectacular execution of its purported narrator, Mark, an enslaved man convicted of murdering his enslaver by poison. Mark's *Dying Words* is the oldest surviving example of a sub-genre of the African American slave narrative known as the criminal confession narrative. The confessions of criminals, white as well as Black, usually awaiting executions, were widely disseminated in broadsides, tracts, and short pamphlets in eighteenth-century Great Britain and New England. The most famous representative of the criminal confession narrative in African American letters appeared in 1831 in Baltimore under the title *The Confessions of Nat Turner, the Leader of the Late Insurrection in Southampton, Va.* In many ways Turner and Mark were very different, but both were convicted of murdering whites. Laws in colonial North America and in the antebellum United States treated the killing of a white person by an enslaved person as a heinous crime for which death was the standard punishment. After trial, both Mark and Turner were hanged.

The Last & Dying Words of MARK displays many features characteristic of later criminal confession narratives purportedly dictated by African American men, the large majority enslaved, to white amanuenses in New England. Scholars have not determined the roles that the Black narrators of these New England narratives played in their composition. (The author of Turner's *Confessions* was a white Virginia lawyer who interviewed Turner shortly before his execution.) However, Mark's *Dying Words* echoes in several places the testimony he gave to the Massachusetts court officials who interrogated him prior to his trial. Thus, to a recognizable extent, *Dying Words* contains some of the thoughts and oral expression of Mark. The trial record also notes that Mark signed his deposition, an indication that he was literate and able to read the transcript of what he stated during the interrogation. *Dying Words* states that he was born in Barbados and had been enslaved by a succession of men, whose beneficence and "kindness" are noted, before John Codman, a sea captain and merchant, acquired Mark.

Dying Words presents Mark as relatively privileged, for an enslaved person at least. The text states that "my master let me live in Boston with my Wife, and go out to work" (probably as a blacksmith). Evidently, Codman permitted Mark to hire himself out for wages in Boston instead of living apart from his wife in Codman's residence in Charlestown. In his famous *Narrative* (1845), Frederick Douglass recalled gaining "the privilege of hiring my time" in Baltimore, although he had to pay most of the wages he earned to his enslaver. Typically, confessional narratives like Mark's portray their enslaved narrators as well treated and their enslavement as a normal condition for people of African descent. These narratives were not published to attack slavery but to justify it.

In 1883, a Massachusetts scholar who studied Mark's case argued that John Codman's "rigid discipline" became "unendurable" to Mark and two women whom Codman enslaved, Phillis and Phebe. *Dying Words*, however, says nothing about Codman's treatment of any of his enslaved men or women. Instead, as is characteristic of later criminal confessions, Mark deplores his own waywardness, lamenting his self-indulgence in base desires and anarchic behavior, "drinking and Carousing" on Sundays and other sinful failings, that culminated in the "fatal Delusion" that led him to "this horrid Crime." Court records of the trial of Mark and Phillis indicate that he pled not guilty to the charge of murder. But *Dying Words*, like later African American criminal confessions, declares Mark's belief in the justness of his death sentence. With great penitence, he beseeches "my Fellow-Servants (especially the Women)" to "shun those Vices which have proved my Ruin."

A particularly striking feature of *Dying Words* is the prominent roles that Phillis and Phebe play in the text. Harsh and biased though their portraits are, Phillis and Phebe emerge as ardent rebels against their enslavement. These determined women are the real protagonists of *Dying Words*. Mark is portrayed as "enticed" by his female co-workers into joining a murder conspiracy that they had already engineered two years before he had been purchased by Codman. *Dying Words* portrays Phebe, a trusted domestic slave in the Codman household, as duplicitous, cruel, and remorseless, the antithesis of the pacific, self-sacrificial Christian woman whom white patriarchal colonial culture publicly extolled. In Mark's presence, Phebe dances in gleeful anticipation of Codman's death, indifferent to his suffering "in great Misery" in a nearby room. Together, Phebe and Phillis seem single-mindedly focused on ending their enslavement by any means necessary. Their words and actions in *Dying Words* represent Black women working as a team to achieve a subversive goal, resolutely undeterred by white authorities or laws.

In her deposition to the Middlesex County, Massachusetts, court, Phillis claimed that Mark was the originator and leader of the conspiracy. Mark's deposition pictures him as the dupe of the two women. The jurors in the case concluded that Phillis, despite her plea of innocence, was guilty of Codman's murder and that Mark "did advise & incite procure & abet the said Phillis" in the poisoning of Codman. In exchange for evidence against other conspirators, Phebe was spared execution but was sold to the West Indies, where conditions were so oppressive that most enslaved workers died within five years.

Mark and Phillis were both executed in a fashion that suited a crime that in Massachusetts was considered not only homicide but an act of treason against the English state. For "feloniously and Traiterously" killing Codman, Phillis was sentenced to the most agonizing form of execution practiced in the colony. She was burnt at the stake. Mark was hanged and his corpse gibbeted (wrapped in chains and suspended from a post for public exhibition) in the Charlestown commons. In a letter recounting his famous 1775 "midnight ride," Paul Revere recalled stopping "opposite where Mark was hung in chains" before plunging into the darkness of the Charlestown road to warn Massachusetts patriots of an approaching British force.

The Last & Dying Words of MARK, Aged about 30 Years, A Negro Man who belonged to the late Captain *John Codman*, of *Charlestown*; Who was executed at *Cambridge*, the 18th of *September*, 1755, for Poysoning his abovesaid Master; is as follows, *viz.*

As I am condemn'd to die by the just Law of GOD and Man, for the heinous Sin of Murther, so I would give Glory to GOD in confessing many of my innumerable Crimes, whereby I have justly incur'd the highest Displeasure of the omnipotent Being, who in Anger has left me to the perpetrating such Crimes as to bring me to this shameful, awful Punishment, which may be a dreadful Warning to the Partners of my crimson Crimes, and by the Blessing of GOD may prove beneficial to all my Fellow Mortals.

I was Born in *Barbados*[1] some-time in the Year 1725, in a reputuble Family, and leaving my native Place very Young, came to *Boston*, where Mr. *Henry Caswell* bought me, with whom I tarried some Time, and then was sold to Mr. *Salter*, the Braizer,[2] who learn'd me to read, and educated me as tenderly as one of his own Children. Then I was sold to Mr. *Joseph Thomas* of *Plimtown*, who treated me with the same Kindness that Mr. *Salter* did. Then Mr. *John Codman* of Charlestown bought me, with whom I continued till my fatal Delusion by two Negro Women, *Phillis* and *Phebe*, my Fellow Servants, who wickedly enticed me to procure them Poyson to destroy my Master; for which Crime I am heartily sorry, and would fly to the Blood of *Jesus*

1. A British colony and slave-trading port located in the Windward Islands of the Lesser Antilles, northeast of Venezuela.
2. A person who works in brass.

THE

Last & Dying Words of

M A R K, Aged about 30 Years,

A Negro Man who belonged to the late Captain *John Codman*, of *Charlestown*;

Who was executed at *Cambridge*, the 18th of *September*, 1755, for Poysoning his abovesaid Master; is as follows, *viz.*

AS I am condemn'd to die by the just Law of GOD and Man, for the heinous Sin of Murther, so I would give Glory to GOD in confessing many of my innumerable Crimes, whereby I have justly incur'd the highest Displeasure of the omnipotent Being, who in Anger has left me to the perpetrating such Crimes as to bring me to this shameful, awful Punishment, which may be a dreadful Warning to the Partners of my crimson Crimes, and by the Blessing of GOD may prove beneficial to all my Fellow Mortals.

I WAS Born in *Barbados* some-time in the Year 1725, in a reputable Family, and leaving my native Place very Young, came to *Boston*, where Mr. *Henry Caswell* bought me, with whom I tarried some Time, and then was sold to Mr. *Salter*, the Braizer, who learn'd me to read, and educated me as tenderly as one of his own Children. Then I was sold to Mr. *Joseph Thomas* of *Plimtown*, who treated me with the same Kindness that Mr. *Salter* did. Then Mr. *John Codman* of *Charlestown* bought me, with whom I continued till my fatal Delusion by two Negro Women, *Phillis* and *Phebe*, my Fellow Servants, who wickedly enticed me to procure them Poyson to destroy my Master; for which Crime I am heartily sorry, and would fly to the Blood of *Jesus Christ*, which is able to wash me from the Iniquity and Pollution of my innumerable Crimes, and cleanse me from the Blood of my poor Master, which I unjustly and [illegible] not only for thus destroying my Master, but for breaking up his Family, and leaving so many innocent Children Orphans.

My Master let me live in *Boston* with my Wife, and go out to work. I have most grievously provoked the great GOD to Anger, by repeatedly breaking his holy Day, in going out of his House and resorting to private Places with my wicked Companions in drinking and Carousing on that holy Day, a Time that I should have improv'd in Meditation and Prayer. I have most sinfully abus'd and misimprov'd his manifold Favours to my fatal Disadvantage, and have wilfully neglected to work out my Salvation; all which Sins GOD has call'd in to Remembrance, and has justly left me to the perpetrating this horrid Crime.

I was entic'd by those two Negro Women to procure them Poyson, and being left of God at that Time, for my former Iniquities, I went to Dr. *Clarke's* Negro Fellow, *Robbin*, and entic'd him to get me some Poyson, to whom I told horrid Lies before I could get it of him, which must be no other than the Work of the Devil. I told him I wanted it to kill three Pigs, and he being wholly ignorant of my bloody Design, gave it me accordingly.

As to the being accessary to the Death of any other besides my poor Master, I absolutely deny, nor did I ever hear of it till I was confin'd in Prison.

As to the Crime for which I am to die, i.e. of destroying my Master in procuring Poyson for the Negro Women, is as follows:

The two Negro Women, my Fellow Servants (one of which suffers Death with me) enticed me to get the Poyson for them, for which horrible Fact we both deserve Death; it has been contriving this two Years by those two Negro Women *Phillis* and *Phebe*, *Phebe* confess'd to me she had been given it to my Master these two Years past at different Times.

After I was detected and put in Goal, *Phebe* (who was an Evidence in Behalf of the KING,) intended to poison me, that I might not bring both out, but I had taken it from her and hid it amongst the Coal, behind the Bellows in my Master's Blacksmith's Shop; and when I had been in Goal about four Days I confess'd where I had put said Poyson, and Mr. *Kettle* went and found it in the Place where I said it was. *Phebe* came to the Prison Grates to desire me not to confess any Thing for they could not hurt me. The Day I was committed, I call'd my Fellow-Servant *Pompey* to show him the Viol of Poyson which I had taken from *Phillis*, which *Phebe* let her have to hide, but the Officer took me before I had an Opportunity of letting *Pompey* see it. *Phebe* the Day before my Master died, danc'd about in the abovementioned Blacksmith's Shop, mocking my Master when in the bitter Pangs of Death, and came to me after that on the Wharff, while I was in the Necessary House; and I asked her how my Master did? she made answer, the *old Dog* was just gone, and she would stick as close to him as his Shirt to his Back, and not only so, but she would cut down the *Old Tree*, and then would hew off the Branches.—— *Phebe* had Poyson in the House long before I procur'd her any, and beg'd to give my Master Copperas which [illegible] Pain in his Belly, which I thought very Cruel, seeing Master treated her better than any of us Servants. The Night before my Master died, she watched with him, who was in great Misery until the Time of his Death.—Next Morning after watching with my Master, she went up to his Chamber to see him, and he ask'd her how she did after Watching, she told him she was very well, and wish'd he was as well as she was.——My two young Mistresses being then present, who put so much Confidence in her as to trust her with the Teas my Master drank; little thinking of her fatal Design against him.— Some Time before this, she told her Husband, (*Quaco*) when at *Charlestown* to see her, to desire me to get some more of that Trade, for it was a good Opportunity now her Master was already Sick, which I accordingly got twice for her from Dr. *Gibbins's* Negro, *Carr*; and to my certain Knowledge went once her self to this Negro to get more, but he had not an Opportunity then to get any; so she sent me to him another Time for it, and he (the said *Carr*) told me he would send her none, because *Phebe* had told him she had a Design to Poyson somebody in the House; and he told me, he'd ask her Husband (*Quaco*) first, whether he was willing, and then pretended to me that he was angry with her; (though I believe he was as knowing in this Affair as I was;) for he was contriving all he could to get her over to *Boston* to live with him, and said, he would not value *Forty Pounds* if he could do it.——

Now concerning the burning of my Master's Shop, I can declare I was sick in Bed, which *Phillis* can witness to; Notwithstanding People thinking hard of me, when the Fire was raging I got out of my Bed, though sick and weak, and saved my Master several Pair of Wheels, and let out two Horses which would have been burnt, and at the same Time had like to have lost my own Life in the Attempt. *Phebe* first prepar'd a Chaffin Dish of Coals in the Dwelling-House Cellar, and call'd *Phillis* to set the Shop on Fire.——I observ'd in *Phebe's* Countenance at the Time of the Fire, she looked Guilty, and upon asking her about it, she confess'd that she had prepar'd the Coals for *Phillis* to burn the Shop.

Phebe that Night, in the midst of the Hurry and Confusion, while the Shop was burning, wickedly stole some of the Cloaths thrown out of the Window to be sav'd; which *Phillis* told me of, and to my certain Knowledge, she was a great Thief: She stole Money from my Master, in which I brought her out; and since that, *Phillis* and she stole *One Hundred Pounds* in Money, Part of which I believe to be in *Phebe's* Sister's Hands; the Truth of which *Phillis* has declar'd to me in our Confinement.

Thus I have given you a true, but awful Account of mine and my Accomplices wicked Proceedings: I have justly provok'd GOD to leave me to myself— My heinous Sins of Sabbath-breaking, Lying, Drinking, Uncleanness, Eye-Service, Neglect of secret and publick Prayer, and the shedding of innocent Blood, loudly call for divine Vengeance. I now sadly experience what a dreadful Thing it is to fall into the Hands of the living GOD— Tho' I am a great Sinner, yet I despair not of the unmerited Mercy of G O D, through JESUS CHRIST; tho' my Sins exceed the Hairs of my Head in Number, and all of a crimson and a scarlet Dye; yet I hope to find Mercy with that GOD, whose Mercies and Loving-Kindnesses exceed my Sins in Number— Let me beseech you all, my Fellow-Servants, (especially the Women) to take Warning by me, and shun those Vices which have prov'd my Ruin; and which have most grievously provoked a mild God.— I once pursu'd a Course of Vice and Wickedness with some of you, and have been guilty of notorious Crimes: But God has singled me out from amongst you all, that I might not only be a Monument of awful Justice, but hope of his sharing Mercy too.

I freely forgive all my Enemies, and fly to JESUS CHRIST, who is willing to save undone Sinners. I heartily thank all the godly Ministers that have visited me while under Confinement, in order to direct me in the Way to eternal Life and Happiness; and can now, Thanks be to GOD, undauntedly look Death in the Face.

GOD be merciful to me a great Sinner. *Amen.*

Mark.

We the Subscribers were present, when Mark *acknowledged this to be his last and dying Words.*

Isaac Bradish,
James Boyd,
David Cutter,
Samuel Hide.

Sold next to the Prison in Queen-Street.

The Last & Dying Words of MARK. This broadside was sold "next to the Prison in Queen-Street" following Mark's execution in September 1755.

Christ, which is able to wash me from the Impurity and Pollution of my innumerable Crimes, and cleanse me from the Blood of my poor Master, which I unjustly and wilfully shed; and am heartily sorry not only for thus destroying my Master, but for breaking up his Family, and leaving so many innocent Children Orphans.

My Master let me live in *Boston* with my Wife, and go out to work. I have most grievously provoked the great GOD to Anger, by repeatedly breaking his holy Day, in going out of his House and resorting to private Places with my wicked Companions in drinking and Carousing on that holy Day, a Time that I should have improv'd in Meditation and Prayer. I have most sinfully abus'd and misimprov'd his manifold Favours to my fatal Disadvantage, and have wilfully neglected to work out my Salvation; all which Sins GOD has call'd in to Remembrance, and has justly left me to the perpetrating this horrid Crime.

I was entic'd by those two Negro Women to procure them Poyson, and being left of God at that Time, for my former Iniquities, I went to Dr. *Clarke*'s Negro Fellow, *Robbin*, and entic'd him to get me some Poyson, to whom I told horrid Lies before I could get it of him, which must be no other than the Work of the Devil. I told him I wanted it to kill three Pigs, and he being wholly ignorant of my bloody Design, gave it to me accordingly.

As to the being accessary to the Death of any other besides my poor Master, I absolutely deny, nor did I ever hear of it till I was confin'd in Prison.

As to the Crime for which I am to die, i.e. of destroying my Master in procuring Poyson for the Negro Women, is as follows:

The two Negro Women, my Fellow Servants (one of which suffers Death with me) enticed me to get the Poyson for them, for which horrible Fact we both deserve Death; it has been contriving this two Years by those two Negro Women *Phillis* and *Phebe*, *Phebe* confess'd to me she had been given it to my Master these two Years past at different Times. After I was detected and put in Gaol, *Phebe* (who was an Evidence in Behalf of the KING) intended to poison me, that I might not bring both out, but I had taken it from her and hid it amongst the Coal, behind the Bellows in my Master's Blacksmith's Shop; and when I had been put in Gaol about four Days I confess'd where I had put said Poyson, and Mr. *Kettle* went and found it in the Place where I said it was. *Phebe* came to the Prison Grates to desire me not to confess any Thing for they could not hurt me. The Day I was committed, I call'd my Fellow-Servant *Pompey* to show him the Viol of Poyson which I had taken away from *Phillis*, which *Phebe* let her have to hide, but the Officer took me before I had an Opportunity of letting *Pompey* see it. *Phebe* the Day before my Master died, danc'd about in the abovementioned Blacksmith's Shop, mocking my Master when in the bitter Pangs of Death, and came to me after that on the Wharff, while I was in the Necessary House; and I asked her how my Master did? she made answer, the *old Dog* was just gone, and she would stick as close to him as his Shirt to his Back, and not only so, but she would cut down the *Old Tree*, and then would hew off the Branches.—*Phebe* had Poyson in the House long before I procur'd her any, and us'd to give my Master Copperas[3] which caus'd a wracking Pain in his Belly, which I thought very Cruel, seeing Master treated her better than any of us Servants. The Night before my Master died, she watched with him, who was in great Mis-

3. Ferrous sulfate—a salt used in making ink and pigments; sometimes given to treat anemia.

ery until the Time of his Death.—Next Morning after watching with my Master, she went up to his Chamber to see him, and he ask'd her how she did after Watching, she told him she was very well, and wish'd he was as well as she was.—My two young Mistresses being then present, who put so much Confidence in her as to trust her with the Teas my Master drank; little thinking of her fatal Design against him.—Some Time before this, she told her Husband (*Quaco*) when at *Charlestown* to see her, to desire me to get some more of that Trade, for it was a good Opportunity now her Master was already Sick, which I accordingly got twice for her from Dr. *Gibbins*'s Negro, *Carr*; and to my certain Knowledge went once her self to this Negro to get more, but he had not an Opportunity then to get any; so she sent me to him another Time for it, and he (the said *Carr*) told me he would send her none, because *Phebe* had told him she had a Design to Poyson somebody in the House; and he told me, he'd ask her Husband (*Quaco*) first, whether he was willing, and then pretended to me that he was angry with her (though I believe he was as knowing in this Affair as I was;) for he was contriving all he could to get her over to *Boston* to live with him, and said, he would not value *Forty Pounds* if he could do it.—

Now concerning the burning of my Master's Shop, I can declare I was sick in Bed, which *Phillis* can witness to; Notwithstanding People thinking hard of me, when the Fire was raging I got out of my Bed, though sick and weak, and saved my Master several Pair of Wheels, and let out two Horses which would have been burnt, and at the same Time had like to have lost my own Life in the Attempt. *Phebe* first prepar'd a chafing dish[4] of Coals in the Dwelling-House Cellar, and call'd *Phillis* to set the Shop on Fire.—I observ'd in *Phebe*'s Countenance at the Time of the Fire, she looked Guilty, and upon asking her about it, she confess'd that she had prepar'd the Coals for *Phillis* to burn the shop.

Phebe that Night, in the midst of the Hurry and Confusion, while the Shop was burning, wickedly stole some of the Cloaths thrown out of the Window to be sav'd; which *Phillis* told me of, and to my certain Knowledge, she was a great Thief: She stole Money from my Master, in which I brought her out; and since that, *Phillis* and she stole *One Hundred Pounds* in Money, Part of which I believe to be in *Phebe*'s Sister's Hands; the Truth of which *Phillis* has declar'd to me in our Confinement.

Thus I have given you a true, but awful Account of mine and my Accomplices wicked Proceedings: I have justly provoked GOD to leave me to myself—My heinous Sins of Sabbath-breaking, Lying, Drinking, Uncleanness, Eye-Service,[5] Neglect of secret and publick Prayer, and the shedding of innocent Blood, loudly call for divine Vengeance. I now sadly experience what a dreadful Thing it is to fall into the Hands of the living GOD—Tho' I am a great Sinner, yet I despair not of the unmerited Mercy of GOD, through JESUS CHRIST; tho' my Sins exceed the Hairs of my Head in Number, and all of a crimson and a scarlet Dye; yet I hope to find Mercy with that God, whose Mercies and Loving-Kindnesses exceed my Sins in Number—Let me beseech you all, my Fellow-Servants, (especially the Women) to take Warning by me, and shun those Vices which have prov'd my Ruin; and which have most grievously provoked a mild God.—I once pursu'd a Course of Vice and Wickedness with some of you, and have been

4. Dish used for cooking or keeping food warm.

5. Attending to duty only when watched.

guilty of notorious Crimes: But God has singled me out from amongst you all, that I might not only be a Monument of awful Justice, but hope of his sharing Mercy too.

I freely forgive all my Enemies, and fly to JESUS CHRIST, who is willing to save undone Sinners. I heartily thank all the godly Ministers that have visited me while under Confinement, in order to direct me in the Way to eternal Life and Happiness; and can now, Thanks be to GOD, undauntedly look Death in the Face.

GOD be merciful to me a great Sinner. *Amen.*

Mark.

We the Subscribers were present, when Mark *acknowledged this to be his last and dying Words.*

Isaac Bradish,
James Boyd,
David Cutter,
Samuel Hide.

Sold next to the Prison in Queen-Street.

JUPITER HAMMON
1711–1790/1806

An entry in a wealthy enslaver's business ledger lists Jupiter Hammon's birth date as October 17, 1711. The same document suggests that Hammon was born at the Queen's Village Manor, home of Henry Lloyd, on Long Island, New York, Hammon's residence for almost all his life. Throughout his life Hammon was enslaved by members of the Lloyd family, whom he served as a clerk and bookkeeper. Although little is known about Hammon's life or exactly when he died, evidence indicates that in his youth he received private tutoring at his enslaver's expense. Some scholars suggest that Hammon also attended a local school run by the Society for the Propagation of the Gospel. Sometime in his early adulthood, Hammon was converted to Wesleyan Christianity. He probably served as an exhorter—an unofficial preacher—to a local Methodist congregation. Hammon's evangelical faith inspired much of his writings, which articulate a fervent dedication to Christian ideals and an impressive knowledge of the Bible.

The four prose pieces and five poems that are extant show that Jupiter Hammon's publishing career spanned at least twenty-six years. His earliest known publication, "An Evening Thought," appeared in 1760, the same year in which Briton Hammon published his *Narrative of the Uncommon Sufferings and Surprizing Deliverance.* The two men were probably not related. Critics have recognized Jupiter Hammon as one of the first published writers in African American literary history, but many have disparaged his poetry as "rhymed doggerel" or "derivative of hymnology" and faulted him for focusing too much on spiritual salvation and too little on political resistance to slavery and racism. Recent scholars have challenged these judgments, arguing that Hammon's poetry shows an emerging Black nationalism in its use of biblical texts to bolster claims to racial equality and to support early struggles to create strong African American communities. Critics now recognize Hammon's "psalmic" poetic style as a creative engagement with early Methodist hymns, whose rhyming alternate lines facilitate recitation. The antiphonal harmonies that characterize much of his poetry echo elements of early African American sermons and spirituals.

Hammon intended his work to influence other African Americans. He dedicated "An Address to the Negroes in the State of New York" (1786), his earliest extant prose work, to the African Society of New York. His colonial readers must have thought that Hammon's writings were helpful in the abolitionist cause, for "An Address . . ." was reprinted in 1787 under the auspices of a Pennsylvania abolitionist society. The "Address" suggests that Hammon favored gradual emancipation and hoped that "by our good conduct" enslavers would be induced "to set us free." Hammon's admiring "Address to Miss Phillis Wheatly" exhorts her to become "perfect in the word" through Christian piety. Published on behalf of "a number of his friends," Hammon's address to his fellow African American poet indicates not only that Wheatley was esteemed by colonial African Americans, some of whom assumed a responsibility for directing as well as praising and encouraging her, but also that Jupiter Hammon's poetic vocation was respected by his peers.

An Evening Thought

Salvation by Christ,
with
Penitential Cries:

COMPOSED BY JUPITER HAMMON, A NEGRO BELONGING TO MR LLOYD, OF QUEEN'S-VILLAGE, ON LONG ISLAND, THE 25TH OF DECEMBER, 1760.

Salvation comes by Jesus Christ alone,
  The only Son of God;
Redemption now to every one,
  That love his holy Word.
Dear Jesus we would fly to Thee,
  And leave off every Sin,
Thy tender Mercy well agree;
  Salvation from our King.
Salvation comes now from the Lord,
  Our victorious King;
His holy Name be well ador'd,
  Salvation surely bring.
Dear Jesus give thy Spirit now,
  Thy Grace to every Nation,
That han't° the Lord to whom we bow, *have not*
  The Author of Salvation.
Dear Jesus unto Thee we cry,
  Give us thy Preparation;
Turn not away thy tender Eye;
  We seek thy true Salvation.
Salvation comes from God we know,
  The true and only One;
It's well agreed and certain true,
  He gave his only Son.

Lord hear our penitential° Cry: *sorrowful; ashamed*
Salvation from above;
It is the Lord that doth supply,
With his Redeeming Love.
Dear Jesus by thy precious Blood,
The World Redemption have:
Salvation comes now from the Lord,
He being thy captive Slave.
Dear Jesus let the Nations cry,
And all the People say,
Salvation comes from Christ on high,
Haste on Tribunal° Day. *judgment*
We cry as Sinners to the Lord,
Salvation to obtain;
It is firmly fixt° his holy Word, *fixed*
Ye shall not cry in vain.
Dear Jesus unto Thee we cry,
And make our Lamentation:
O let our Prayers ascend on high;
We felt thy Salvation.
Lord turn our dark benighted[1] Souls;
Give us a true Motion,
And let the Hearts of all the World,
Make Christ their Salvation.
Ten Thousand Angels cry to Thee,
Yea louder than the Ocean.
Thou are the Lord, we plainly see;
Thou art the true Salvation.
Now is the Day, excepted Time;
The Day of Salvation;
Increase your Faith, do not repine:[2]
Awake ye every Nation.
Lord unto whom now shall we go,
Or seek a safe Abode;
Thou hast the Word Salvation too
The only Son of God.
Ho! every one that hunger hath,
Or pineth° after me, *yearn intensely*
Salvation be thy leading Staff,[3]
To set the Sinner free.
Dear Jesus unto Thee we fly;
Depart, depart from Sin,
Salvation doth at length supply,
The Glory of our King.
Come ye Blessed of the Lord,
Salvation gently given;
O turn your Hearts, accept the Word,
Your Souls are fit for Heaven.

1. Morally or intellectually backward, unenlightened.
2. Fret in discontent.
3. A pole used as a weapon or a symbol of authority.

Dear Jesus we now turn to Thee,
  Salvation to obtain;
Our Hearts and Souls do meet again,
  To magnify thy Name.
Come holy Spirit, Heavenly Dove,
  The Object of our Care;
Salvation doth increase our Love;
  Our Hearts hath felt thy fear.
Now Glory be to God on High,
  Salvation high and low;
And thus the Soul on Christ rely,
  To Heaven surely go.
Come Blessed Jesus, Heavenly Dove,
  Accept Repentance here;
Salvation give, with tender Love;
  Let us with Angels share.

FINIS

1760

An Address to Miss Phillis Wheatly

HARTFORD, AUGUST 4, 1778

AN ADDRESS TO MISS PHILLIS WHEATLY, ETHIOPIAN POETESS, IN BOSTON, WHO CAME FROM AFRICA AT EIGHT YEARS OF AGE, AND SOON BECAME ACQUAINTED WITH THE GOSPEL OF JESUS CHRIST.

Miss WHEATLY; pray give leave to express as follows:

1.

O Come you pious youth! adore
  The wisdom of thy God, *Eccles. xii.*
In bringing thee from distant shore,
  To learn his holy word.

2.

Thou mightst been left behind,
  Amidst a dark abode;[1] *Psal. cxxxv. 2, 3.*
God's tender mercy still combin'd,
  Thou hast the holy word.

3.

Fair wisdom's ways are paths of peace,
  And they that walk therein, *Psal. i. 1, 2.*
Shall reap the joys that never cease, *Prov. iii. 7.*
  And Christ shall be their king.

1. A living place or residence.

4.
God's tender mercy brought thee here,
Tost o'er the raging main;[2] *Psal. ciii. 1, 3, 4.*
In Christian faith thou hast a share,
Worth all the gold of Spain.

5.
While thousands tossed by the sea,
And others settled down, *Death.*
God's tender mercy set thee free
From danger still unknown.

6.
That thou a pattern still might be,
To youth of Boston town, *2 Cor. v. 10.*
The blessed Jesus set thee free,
From every sinful wound.

7.
The blessed Jesus, who came down,
Unvail'd[3] his sacred face, *Rom. v. 21.*
To cleanse the soul of every wound,
And give repenting grace.

8.
That we poor sinners may obtain
The pardon of our sin; *Psal. xxxiv. 6, 7, 8.*
Dear blessed Jesus now constrain,
And bring us flocking in.

9.
Come you, Phillis, now aspire,
And seek the living God, *Matth. vii. 7, 8.*
So step by step thou mayst go higher,
Till perfect in the word.

10.
While thousands mov'd to distant shore,
And others left behind, *Psal. lxxxix. 1.*
The blessed Jesus still adore,
Implant this in thy mind.

11.
Thou hast left the heathen shore,
Thro' mercy of the Lord, *Psal. xxxiv. 1, 2, 3.*
Among the heathen live no more,
Come magnify thy God.

12.
I pray the living God may be,

2. Ocean. "Tost": tossed.

3. Unveiled or uncovered.

The shepherd of thy soul; *Psal. lxxi. 1, 2, 3.*
His tender mercies still are free,
His mysteries to unfold.

13.

Thou, Phillis, when thou hunger hast,
Or pantest for thy God; *Psal. xlii. 1, 2, 3.*
Jesus Christ is thy relief,
Thou hast the holy word.

14.

The bounteous mercies of the Lord,
Are hid beyond the sky, *Psal. xvi. 10, 11.*
And holy souls that love his word,
Shall taste them when they die.

15.

These bounteous mercies are from God,
The merits of his Son; *Psal. xxxiv. 15.*
The humble soul that loves his word,
He chooses for his own.

16.

Come, dear Phillis, be advis'd,
To drink Samaria's[4] flood. *John iv. 13, 14.*
There nothing is that shall suffice,
But Christ's redeeming blood.

17.

While thousands muse with earthly toys,
And range about the street, *Matth. vi. 33.*
Dear Phillis, seek for heaven's joys,
Where we do hope to meet.

18.

When God shall send his summons down,
And number saints together, *Psal. cxvi. 15.*
Blest angels chant, (triumphant sound)
Come live with me for ever.

19.

The humble soul shall fly to God,
And leave the things of time, *Matth. v. 3, 8.*
Start forth as 'twere at the first word,
To taste things more divine.

20.

Behold! the soul shall waft[5] away,
Whene'er we come to die, *Cor. xv. 51, 52, 53.*
And leave its cottage made of clay,
In twinkling of an eye.

4. A part of Palestine during biblical times.

5. Float or drift.

21.

Now glory be to the Most High,
United praises given, *Psal. cl. 6.*
By all on earth, incessantly,
And all the host of heav'n.

Composed by JUPITER HAMMON, a Negro Man belonging to Mr. Joseph Lloyd, of Queen's-Village, on Long Island, now in Hartford.

The above lines are published by the Author, and a number of his friends, who desire to join with him in their best regards to Miss Wheatly.

1778

VENTURE SMITH

1729?–1805

Compared to the internationally famous autobiography of Olaudah Equiano, *A Narrative of the Life and Adventures of Venture, A Native of Africa* drew little notice when it appeared in New London, Connecticut, in 1798. Equiano, whom the scholar Vincent Carretta called "a master of self-promotion through the book trade" in Great Britain, was able to parlay his royalties from *The Interesting Narrative of the Life of Olaudah Equiano* (1789) into profits that made him probably the wealthiest man of African descent in England in the last decade of the eighteenth century. By contrast, Venture Smith seems to have realized little, if any, monetary gain from the publication of his narrative, which, unlike Equiano's, was never reprinted during Smith's lifetime. Surveying all his "griefs," "pains," and "losses" at the hands of "knaves," "false hearted friends," and even "my own countrymen whom I have assisted and redeemed from bondage," Smith ended his story grimly echoing the preacher in Ecclesiastes: "Vanity of vanities, all is vanity." Equiano's upbeat story of assimilation and success won him many English and American readers. But Smith's matter of fact, at times embittered, recollections of a lifetime of struggle for a hard-earned freedom and subsequent social respect and economic security were undoubtedly more representative of the experience of most eighteenth-century African Americans. In many ways an extraordinary man—"a Franklin, or a Washington, in a state of nature, or, rather, in a state of slavery," observed Smith's white amanuensis—Smith narrated his story almost like a deposition submitted to the court of American public opinion. His *Narrative of the Life and Adventures* attests to the harshness of slavery in New England during the early Republic while recounting one Black man's disillusioning test of the myth of America as a land of liberty, opportunity, and equality.

Like Equiano, Smith traced his origins to the savannah region of West Africa, where he was born the eldest son of a "Prince of the tribe of Dukandarra" around 1729. In keeping with the anxious, often gloomy mood of his *Narrative,* Smith's portrayal of his boyhood in Africa has little in common with the idyllic image of life among the Ibo that distinguishes the opening chapter of Equiano's autobiography. Family separation, marauding invaders, and his father's death by torture plunge young Broteer (Smith's African name) into tragedy even before he is captured by African slavers and later transported to the West Indies. A key to the stoic character of Smith is his laconic remark about the dreadful Middle Passage: "After an ordinary passage, except great mortality by the smallpox, which broke out on board, we arrived at the island of Barbadoes: but when we reached it, there were found out of the two hundred and sixty that sailed from Africa, not more than two hundred alive. These were all sold, except myself and three more, to the planters there."

Broteer, renamed Venture by his first North American enslaver when the boy was about ten years old, ended up on Fishers Island, off the Connecticut coast. There he grew up doing both domestic and agricultural labor. In his early twenties, Venture married Meg (surname unknown), with whom he had four children. Around this time he also made an abortive escape attempt. Venture's punishment was sale, which separated him for eighteen months from his wife and daughter. His new enslaver, Thomas Stanton of Stonington Point, Connecticut, eventually purchased Venture's wife and daughter. But Stanton and his wife proved intolerably demanding and violent, which led to Venture's defiant decision to refuse to work until he was purchased by another white man who Venture believed would give him a chance to buy his freedom. When this enslaver did not keep his word, Venture arranged to have himself sold again, to Colonel Oliver Smith of Stonington, who allowed Venture to hire his time as a wood cutter, farmer, and fisherman so he could raise the money for his purchase price. After five years of working night and day, at the age of thirty-six, Venture finally was allowed to buy himself, though, as he pointedly noted, he had been obliged to pay "an enormous sum for my freedom." As a free man, Venture adopted Oliver Smith's last name for his own.

Unlike most nineteenth-century slave narratives, which portray the achievement of freedom as glorious and inspiring, Smith's *Narrative* pictures his release from slavery almost anticlimactically. The final and perhaps most somber chapter of his autobiography discloses Smith's many frustrations in pursuit of the American dream. He amasses considerable material wealth and property in an effort to garner security, independence, and most of all respect and just treatment in Connecticut's white supremacist society. The ironic upshot of his striving, however, makes the *Narrative of the Life and Adventures* one of the earliest and most touching cautionary tales in the long, often-conflicted tradition of autobiography by middle-class African Americans.

A Narrative of the Life and Adventures of Venture, A Native of Africa: But Resident above Sixty Years in the United States of America

Related by Himself

Preface[1]

The following account of the life of VENTURE, is a relation of simple facts, in which nothing is added in substance to what he related himself. Many other interesting and curious passages of his life might have been inserted; but on account of the bulk to which they must necessarily have swelled this narrative, they were omitted. If any should suspect the truth of what is here related, they are referred to people now living who are acquainted with most of the facts mentioned in the narrative.

The reader is here presented with an account, not of a renowned politician or warrior, but of an untutored African slave, brought into this Christian

1. An 1897 reprint of Smith's *Narrative* identifies his original amanuensis as Elisha Niles, a soldier in the American Revolution and later a schoolteacher.

country at eight years of age, wholly destitute of all education but what he received in common with other domesticated animals, enjoying no advantages that could lead him to suppose himself superior to the beasts, his fellow servants. And if he shall derive no other advantage from perusing this narrative, he may experience those sensations of shame and indignation, that will prove him to be not wholly destitute of every noble and generous feeling.

The subject of the following pages, had he received only a common education, might have been a man of high respectability and usefulness; and had his education been suited to his genius, he might have been an ornament and an honor to human nature. It may perhaps, not be unpleasing to see the efforts of a great mind wholly uncultivated, enfeebled and depressed by slavery, and struggling under every disadvantage.—The reader may here see a Franklin and a Washington,[2] in a state of nature, or rather in a state of slavery. Destitute as he is of all education, and broken by hardships and infirmities of age, he still exhibits striking traces of native ingenuity and good sense.

This narrative exhibits a pattern of honesty, prudence and industry, to people of his own colour; and perhaps some white people would not find themselves degraded by imitating such an example.

The following account is published in compliance with the earnest desire of the subject of it, and likewise a number of respectable persons who are acquainted with him.

Chapter I

CONTAINING AN ACCOUNT OF HIS LIFE, FROM HIS BIRTH TO THE TIME OF HIS LEAVING HIS NATIVE COUNTRY

I was born at Dukandarra, in Guinea,[3] about the year 1729. My father's name was Saungm Furro, Prince of the Tribe of Dukandarra. My father had three wives. Polygamy was not uncommon in that country, especially among the rich, as every man was allowed to keep as many wives as he could maintain. By his first wife he had three children. The eldest of them was myself, named by my father, Broteer. The other two were named Cundazo and Soozaduka. My father had two children by his second wife, and one by his third. I descended from a very large, tall and stout race of beings, much larger than the generality of people in other parts of the globe, being commonly considerable above six feet in height, and every way well proportioned.

The first thing worthy of notice which I remember was, a contention between my father and mother, on account of my father's marrying his third wife without the consent of his first and eldest, which was contrary to the custom generally observed among my countrymen. In consequence of this rupture, my mother left her husband and country, and travelled away with her three children to the eastward. I was then five years old. She took not the least sustenance along with her, to support either herself or children. I was able to travel along by her side; the other two of her offspring she carried one on her back, and the other being a sucking child, in her arms. When we became hungry, my mother used to set us down on the ground, and gather some of the fruits which grew spontaneously in that climate. These served us for food on the way. At night we all lay down together in the most secure place we could

2. George Washington (1732–1799), first president of the United States (1789–98). Benjamin Franklin (1706–1790), American statesman, inventor, and author.

3. In Smith's time, a crescent of countries that ran roughly from today's Senegal to Nigeria.

find, and reposed ourselves until morning. Though there were many noxious animals there; yet so kind was our Almighty protector, that none of them were ever permitted to hurt or molest us. Thus we went on our journey until the second day after our departure from Dukandarra, when we came to the entrance of a great desert. During our travel in that [land] we were often affrighted with the doleful howlings and yellings of wolves, lions, and other animals. After five days travel we came to the end of this desert, and immediately entered into a beautiful and extensive interval country. Here my mother was pleased to stop and seek a refuge for me. She left me at the house of a very rich farmer. I was then, as I should judge, not less than one hundred and forty miles from my native place, separated from all my relations and acquaintance. At this place my mother took her farewel of me, and set out for her own country. My new guardian, as I shall call the man with whom I was left, put me into the business of tending sheep, immediately after I was left with him. The flock which I kept with the assistance of a boy, consisted of about forty. We drove them every morning between two and three miles to pasture, into the wide and delightful plains. When night drew on, we drove them home and secured them in the cote.[4] In this round I continued during my stay there. One incident which befel me when I was driving my flock from pasture, was so dreadful to me in that age, and is to this time so fresh in my memory, that I cannot help noticing it in this place. Two large dogs sallied out of a certain house and set upon me. One of them took me by the arm, and the other by the thigh, and before their master could come and relieve me, they lacerated my flesh to such a degree, that the scars are very visible to the present day. My master was immediately sent for. He came and carried me home, as I was unable to go myself on account of my wounds. Nothing remarkable happened afterwards until my father sent for me to return home.

Before I dismiss this country, I must just inform my reader what I remember concerning this place. A large river runs through this country in a westerly course. The land for a great way on each side is flat and level, hedged in by a considerable rise of the country at a great distance from it. It scarce ever rains there, yet the land is fertile; great dews fall in the night which refresh the soil. About the latter end of June or first of July, the river begins to rise, and gradually increases until it has inundated the country for a great distance, to the height of seven or eight feet. This brings on a slime which enriches the land surprisingly. When the river has subsided, the natives begin to sow and plant, and the vegetation is exceeding rapid. Near this rich river my guardian's land lay. He possessed, I cannot exactly tell how much, yet this I am certain of respecting it, that he owned an immense tract. He possessed likewise a great many cattle and goats. During my stay with him I was kindly used, and with as much tenderness, for what I saw, as his only son, although I was an entire stranger to him, remote from friends and relations. The principal occupations of the inhabitants there, were the cultivation of the soil and the care of their flocks. They were a people pretty similar in every respect to that of mine, except in their persons, which were not so tall and stout. They appeared to be very kind and friendly. I will now return to my departure from that place.

My father sent a man and horse after me. After settling with my guardian for keeping me, he took me away and went for home. It was then about one year since my mother brought me here. Nothing remarkable occured to us on our journey until we arrived safe home.

4. A shelter for sheep.

I found then that the difference between my parents had been made up previous to their sending for me. On my return, I was received both by my father and mother with great joy and affection, and was once more restored to my paternal dwelling in peace and happiness. I was then about six years old.

Not more than six weeks had passed after my return, before a message was brought by an inhabitant of the place where I lived the preceding year to my father, that that place had been invaded by a numerous army, from a nation not far distant, furnished with musical instruments, and all kinds of arms then in use; that they were instigated by some white nation who equipped and sent them to subdue and possess the country; that his nation had made no preparation for war, having been for a long time in profound peace that they could not defend themselves against such a formidable train of invaders, and must therefore necessarily evacuate their lands to the fierce enemy, and fly to the protection of some chief; and that if he would permit them they should come under his rule and protection when they had to retreat from their own possessions. He was a kind and merciful prince, and therefore consented to these proposals.

He had scarcely returned to his nation with the message, before the whole of his people were obliged to retreat from their country, and come to my father's dominions.

He gave them every privilege and all the protection his government could afford. But they had not been there longer than four days before news came to them that the invaders had laid waste their country, and were coming speedily to destroy them in my father's territories. This affrighted them, and therefore they immediately pushed off to the southward, into the unknown countries there, and were never more heard of.

Two days after their retreat, the report turned out to be but too true. A detachment from the enemy came to my father and informed him, that the whole army was encamped not far out of his dominions, and would invade the territory and deprive his people of their liberties and rights, if he did not comply with the following terms. These were to pay them a large sum of money, three hundred fat cattle, and a great number of goats, sheep, asses, &c.

My father told the messenger he would comply rather than that his subjects should be deprived of their rights and privileges, which he was not then in circumstances to defend from so sudden an invasion. Upon turning out those articles, the enemy pledged their faith and honor that they would not attack him. On these he relied and therefore thought it unnecessary to be on his guard against the enemy. But their pledges of faith and honor proved no better than those of other unprincipled hostile nations; for a few days after a certain relation of the king came and informed him, that the enemy who sent terms of accommodation to him and received tribute to their satisfaction, yet meditated an attack upon his subjects by surprise, and that probably they would commence their attack in less than one day, and concluded with advising him, as he was not prepared for war, to order a speedy retreat of his family and subjects. He complied with this advice.

The same night which was fixed upon to retreat, my father and his family set off about break of day. The king and his two younger wives went in one company, and my mother and her children in another. We left our dwellings in succession, and my father's company went on first. We directed our course for a large shrub plain, some distance off, where we intended to conceal ourselves from the approaching enemy, until we could refresh and rest ourselves a little. But we presently found that our retreat was not secure. For having struck up a little fire for the purpose of cooking victuals, the enemy who happened to be encamped a little distance off, had sent out a scouting party who discovered us by the smoke of the fire, just as we were extinguishing it, and about to eat. As soon as we had finished eating, my father discovered the party, and immediately began to discharge arrows at them. This was what I first saw, and it alarmed both me and the women, who being unable to make any resistance, immediately betook ourselves to the tall thick reeds not far off, and left the old king to fight alone. For some time I beheld him from the reeds defending himself with great courage and firmness, till at last he was obliged to surrender himself into their hands.

They then came to us in the reeds, and the very first salute I had from them was a violent blow on the head with the fore part of a gun, and at the same time a grasp round the neck. I then had a rope put about my neck, as had all the women in the thicket with me, and were immediately led to my father, who was likewise pinioned and haltered for leading. In this condition we were all led to the camp. The women and myself being pretty submissive, had tolerable treatment from the enemy, while my father was closely interrogated respecting his money which they knew he must have. But as he gave them no account of it, he was instantly cut and pounded on his body with great inhumanity, that he might be induced by the torture he suffered to make the discovery. All this availed not in the least to make him give up his money, but he despised all the tortures which they inflicted, until the continued exercise and increase of torment, obliged him to sink and expire.

He thus died without informing his enemies of the place where his money lay. I saw him while he was thus tortured to death. The shocking scene is to this day fresh in my mind, and I have often been overcome while thinking on it. He was a man of remarkable stature. I should judge as much as six feet and six or seven inches high, two feet across his shoulders, and every way well proportioned. He was a man of remarkable strength and resolution, affable, kind and gentle, ruling with equity and moderation.

The army of the enemy was large, I should suppose consisting of about six thousand men. Their leader was called Baukurre. After destroying the old prince, they decamped and immediately marched towards the sea, lying to the west, taking with them myself and the women prisoners. In the march a scouting party was detached from the main army. To the leader of this party I was made waiter, having to carry his gun, &c.—As we were a scouting we came across a herd of fat cattle, consisting of about thirty in number. These we set upon, and immediately wrested from their keepers, and afterwards converted them into food for the army. The enemy had remarkable success in destroying the country wherever they went. For as far as they had penetrated, they laid the habitations waste and captured the people. The distance they had now brought me was about four hundred miles. All the march I had very hard tasks imposed on me, which I must perform on pain of punishment. I was obliged to carry on my head a large flat stone used for grinding our corn, weighing as I should suppose, as much as 25 pounds; besides victuals, mat and cooking utensils. Though I was pretty large and stout of my age, yet these burthens were very grievous to me, being only about six years and an half old.

We were then come to a place called Malagasco.—When we entered the place we could not see the least appearance of either houses or inhabitants, but upon stricter search found, that instead of houses above ground they had dens in the sides of hillocks, contiguous to ponds and streams of water. In these we perceived they had all hid themselves, as I suppose they usually did upon such occasions. In order to compel them to surrender, the enemy contrived to smoke them out with faggots.[5] These they put to the entrance of the caves and set them on fire. While they were engaged in this business, to their great surprise some of them were desperately wounded with arrows which fell from above on them. This mystery they soon found out. They perceived that the enemy discharged these arrows through holes on the top of the dens directly into the air.—Their weight brought them back, point downwards on their enemies' heads, whilst they were smoking the inhabitants out. The points of their arrows were poisoned, but their enemy had an antidote for it, which they instantly applied to the wounded part. The smoke at last obliged the people to give themselves up. They came out of their caves, first spatting[6] the palms of their hands together, and immediately after extended their arms, crossed at their wrists, ready to be bound and pinioned. I should judge that the dens above mentioned were extended about eight feet horizontally into the earth, six feet in height and as many wide. They were arched over head and lined with earth, which was of the clay kind, and made the surface of their walls firm and smooth.

The invaders then pinioned the prisoners of all ages and sexes indiscriminately, took their flocks and all their effects, and moved on their way towards the sea. On the march the prisoners were treated with clemency, on account of their being submissive and humble. Having come to the next tribe, the enemy laid siege and immediately took men, women, children, flocks, and all their valuable effects. They then went on to the next district which was contiguous to the sea, called in Africa, Anamaboo.[7] The enemies' provisions were then almost spent, as well as their strength. The inhabitants knowing what conduct they had pursued, and what were their present intentions, improved the favorable opportunity, attacked them, and took enemy, prisoners, flocks and all their effects. I was then taken a second time. All of us were then put into the castle, and kept for market. On a certain time I and other prisoners were put on board a canoe, under our master, and rowed away to a vessel belonging to Rhode-Island, commanded by capt. Collingwood, and the mate Thomas Mumford. While we were going to the vessel, our master told us all to appear to the best possible advantage for sale. I was bought on board by one Robertson Mumford, steward of said vessel, for four gallons of rum, and a piece of calico, and called VENTURE, on account of his having purchased me with his own private venture. Thus I came by my name. All the slaves that were bought for that vessel's cargo, were two hundred and sixty.

Chapter II

CONTAINING AN ACCOUNT OF HIS LIFE, FROM THE TIME OF HIS LEAVING AFRICA, TO THAT OF HIS BECOMING FREE

After all the business was ended on the coast of Africa, the ship sailed from thence to Barbadoes.[8] After an ordinary passage, except great mortality by the small pox, which broke out on board, we arrived at the island of Barbadoes: but when we reached it, there were found out of the two hundred and sixty that sailed from Africa, not more than two hundred alive. These were all sold, except myself and three more, to the planters there.

5. A bundle of sticks bound together for use as fuel.
6. Clapping.
7. A slave port on the coast of Ghana.
8. A British colony and slave-trading port located in the Windward Islands of the Lesser Antilles, northeast of Venezuela.

The vessel then sailed for Rhode-Island, and arrived there after a comfortable passage. Here my master sent me to live with one of his sisters, until he could carry me to Fisher's Island, the place of his residence. I had then completed my eighth year. After staying with his sister some time I was taken to my master's place to live.

When we arrived at Narraganset,[9] my master went ashore in order to return a part of the way by land, and gave me the charge of the keys of his trunks on board the vessel, and charged me not to deliver them up to any body, not even to his father without his orders. To his directions I promised faithfully to conform. When I arrived with my master's articles at his house, my master's father asked me for his son's keys, as he wanted to see what his trunks contained. I told him that my master intrusted me with the care of them until he should return, and that I had given him my word to be faithful to the trust, and could not therefore give him or any other person the keys without my master's directions. He insisted that I should deliver to him the keys, threatening to punish me if I did not. But I let him know that he should not have them let him say what he would. He then laid aside trying to get them. But notwithstanding he appeared to give up trying to obtain them from me, yet I mistrusted that he would take some time when I was off my guard, either in the day time or at night to get them, therefore I slung them round my neck, and in the day time concealed them in my bosom, and at night I always lay with them under me, that no person might take them from me without being apprized of it. Thus I kept the keys from every body until my master came home. When he returned he asked where VENTURE was. As I was then within hearing, I came, and said, here sir, at your service. He asked me for his keys, and I immediately took them off my neck and reached them out to him. He took them, stroked my hair, and commended me, saying in presence of his father that his young VENTURE was so faithful that he never would have been able to have taken the keys from him but by violence; that he should not fear to trust him with his whole fortune, for that he had been in his native place so habituated to keeping his word, that he would sacrifice even his life to maintain it.

The first of the time of living at my master's own place, I was pretty much employed in the house at carding wool and other houshold business. In this situation I continued for some years, after which my master put me to work out of doors. After many proofs of my faithfulness and honesty, my master began to put great confidence in me. My behavior to him had as yet been submissive and obedient. I then began to have hard tasks imposed on me. Some of these were to pound four bushels of ears of corn every night in a barrel for the poultry, or be rigorously punished. At other seasons of the year I had to card wool until a very late hour. These tasks I had to perform when I was about nine years old. Some time after I had another difficulty and oppression which was greater than any I had ever experienced since I came into this country. This was to serve two masters. James Mumford, my master's son, when his father had gone from home in the morning, and given me a stint to perform that day, would order me to do *this* and *that* business different from what my master directed me. One day in particular, the authority which my master's son had set up, had like to have produced melancholy effects. For my master having set me off my business to perform that day and then left me to perform it, his son came up to me in the course of the

9. A town in southern Rhode Island.

day, big with authority, and commanded me very arrogantly to quit my present business and go directly about what he should order me. I replied to him that my master had given me so much to perform that day, and that I must therefore faithfully complete it in that time. He then broke out into a great rage, snatched a pitchfork and went to lay me over the head therewith; but I as soon got another and defended myself with it, or otherwise he might have murdered me in his outrage. He immediately called some people who were within hearing at work for him, and ordered them to take his hair rope and come and bind me with it. They all tried to bind me but in vain, tho' there were three assistants in number. My upstart master then desisted, put his pocket handkerchief before his eyes and went home with a design to tell his mother of the struggle with young VENTURE. He told her that their young VENTURE had become so stubborn that he could not control him, and asked her what he should do with him. In the mean time I recovered my temper, voluntarily caused myself to be bound by the same men who tried in vain before, and carried before my young master, that he might do what he pleased with me. He took me to a gallows made for the purpose of hanging cattle on, and suspended me on it. Afterwards he ordered one of his hands to go to the peach orchard and cut him three dozen of whips to punish me with. These were brought to him, and that was all that was done with them, as I was released and went to work after hanging on the gallows about an hour.

After I had lived with my master thirteen years, being then about twenty two years old, I married Meg, a slave of his who was about my age. My master owned a certain Irishman, named Heddy,[1] who about that time formed a plan of secretly leaving his master. After he had long had this plan in meditation he suggested it to me. At first I cast a deaf ear to it, and rebuked Heddy for harboring in his mind such a rash undertaking. But after he had persuaded and much enchanted me with the prospect of gaining my freedom by such a method, I at length agreed to accompany him. Heddy next inveigled two of his fellow servants to accompany us. The place to which we designed to go was the Mississippi. Our next business was to lay in a sufficient store of provisions for our voyage. We privately collected out of our master's store, six great old cheeses, two firkins[2] of butter, and one whole batch of new bread. When we had gathered all our own clothes and some more, we took them all about midnight, and went to the water side. We stole our master's boat, embarked, and then directed our course for the Mississippi river.

We mutually confederated not to betray or desert one another on pain of death. We first steered our course for Montauk point, the east end of Long-Island. After our arrival there we landed, and Heddy and I made an incursion into the island after fresh water, while our two comrades were left at a little distance from the boat, employed at cooking. When Heddy and I had sought some time for water, he returned to our companions, and I continued on looking for my object. When Heddy had performed his business with our companions who were engaged in cooking, he went directly to the boat, stole all the clothes in it, and then travelled away for East-Hampton, as I was informed. I returned to my fellows not long after. They informed me that our clothes were stolen, but could not determine who was the thief, yet they suspected Heddy as he was missing. After reproving my two comrades for not taking care of our things which were in the boat, I advertised Heddy

1. Likely an indentured servant who, in exchange for service to his master for a stipulated number of years, would be provided food, clothing, and lodging and, on completion of his indenture, some form of payment.

2. Small casks.

and sent two men in search of him. They pursued and overtook him at Southampton and returned him to the boat. I then thought it might afford some chance for my freedom, or at least a palliation for my running away, to return Heddy immediately to his master, and inform him that I was induced to go away by Heddy's address. Accordingly I set off with him and the rest of my companions for our master's, and arrived there without any difficulty. I informed my master that Heddy was the ringleader of our revolt, and that he had used us ill. He immediately put Heddy into custody, and myself and companions were well received and went to work as usual.

Not a long time passed after that, before Heddy was sent by my master to New-London gaol.[3] At the close of that year I was sold to a Thomas Stanton, and had to be separated from my wife and one daughter, who was about one month old. He resided at Stonington-point.[4] To this place I brought with me from my late master's, two johannes, three old Spanish dollars, and two thousand of coppers,[5] besides five pounds of my wife's money. This money I got by cleaning gentlemen's shoes and drawing boots, by catching musk-rats and minks, raising potatoes and carrots, &c. and by fishing in the night, and at odd spells.

All this money amounting to near twenty-one pounds York currency,[6] my master's brother, Robert Stanton, hired of me, for which he gave me his note. About one year and a half after that time, my master purchased my wife and her child, for seven hundred pounds old tenor.[7] One time my master sent me two miles after a barrel of molasses, and ordered me to carry it on my shoulders. I made out to carry it all the way to my master's house. When I lived with Captain George Mumford, only to try my strength, I took up on my knees a tierce[8] of salt containing seven bushels, and carried it two or three rods. Of this fact there are several eye witnesses now living.

Towards the close of the time that I resided with this master, I had a falling out with my mistress. This happened one time when my master was gone to Long-Island a gunning. At first the quarrel began between my wife and her mistress. I was then at work in the barn, and hearing a racket in the house, induced me to run there and see what had broken out. When I entered the house, I found my mistress in a violent passion with my wife, for what she informed me was a mere trifle; such a small affair that I forbear to put my mistress to the shame of having it known. I earnestly requested my wife to beg pardon of her mistress for the sake of peace, even if she had given no just occasion for offence. But whilst I was thus saying my mistress turned the blows which she was repeating on my wife to me. She took down her horse-whip, and while she was glutting her fury with it, I reached out my great black hand, raised it up and received the blows of the whip on it which were designed for my head. Then I immediately committed the whip to the devouring fire.

When my master returned from the island, his wife told him of the affair, but for the present he seemed to take no notice of it, and mentioned not a word about it to me. Some days after his return, in the morning as I was putting on a log in the fire-place, not suspecting harm from any one, I received a most violent stroke on the crown of my head with a club two feet long and as

3. Jail.
4. Near the town of Stonington in eastern Connecticut.
5. British pennies. "Johannes": Portuguese gold coins.
6. Money issued by the colonial government in New York.
7. Money issued by the Rhode Island and Massachusetts colonies before 1741.
8. A forty-two-gallon cask.

large round as a chair-post. This blow very badly wounded my head, and the scar of it remains to this day. The first blow made me have my wits about me you may suppose, for as soon as he went to renew it, I snatched the club out of his hands and dragged him out of the door. He then sent for his brother to come and assist him, but I presently left my master, took the club he wounded me with, carried it to a neighboring Justice of the Peace, and complained of my master. He finally advised me to return to my master, and live contented with him till he abused me again, and then complain. I consented to do accordingly. But before I set out for my master's, up he come and his brother Robert after me. The Justice improved this convenient opportunity to caution my master. He asked him for what he treated his slave thus hastily and unjustly, and told him what would be the consequence if he continued the same treatment towards me. After the Justice had ended his discourse with my master, he and his brother set out with me for home, one before and the other behind me. When they had come to a bye place, they both dismounted their respective horses, and fell to beating me with great violence. I became enraged at this and immediately turned them both under me, laid one of them across the other, and stamped both with my feet what I would.

This occasioned my master's brother to advise him to put me off. A short time after this I was taken by a constable and two men. They carried me to a blacksmith's shop and had me hand-cuffed. When I returned home my mistress enquired much of her waiters, whether VENTURE was hand-cuffed. When she was informed that I was, she appeared to be very contented and was much transported with the news. In the midst of this content and joy, I presented myself before my mistress, shewed her my hand-cuffs, and gave her thanks for my gold rings. For this my master commanded a negro of his to fetch him a large ox chain. This my master locked on my legs with two padlocks. I continued to wear the chain peaceably for two or three days, when my master asked me with contemptuous hard names whether I had not better be freed from my chains and go to work. I answered him, No. Well then, said he, I will send you to the West-Indies or banish you, for I am resolved not to keep you. I answered him I crossed the waters to come here, and I am willing to cross them to return.

For a day or two after this not any one said much to me, until one Hempsted Miner, of Stonington, asked me if I would live with him. I answered him that I would. He then requested me to make myself discontented and to appear as unreconciled to my master as I could before that he bargained with him for me; and that in return he would give me a good chance to gain my freedom when I came to live with him. I did as he requested me. Not long after Hempsted Miner purchased me of my master for fifty-six pounds lawful. He took the chain and padlocks from off me immediately after.

It may here be remembered, that I related a few pages back, that I hired out a sum of money to Mr. Robert Stanton, and took his note for it. In the fray between my master Stanton and myself, he broke open my chest containing his brother's note to me, and destroyed it. Immediately after my present master bought me, he determined to sell me at Hartford. As soon as I became apprized of it, I bethought myself that I would secure a certain sum of money which lay by me, safer than to hire it out to a Stanton. Accordingly I buried it in the earth, a little distance from Thomas Stanton's, in the road over which he passed daily. A short time after my master carried me to Hartford, and first proposed to sell me to one William Hooker of that place. Hooker asked whether I would go to the German Flats with him. I answered, No. He said

I should, if not by fair means I should by foul. If you will go by no other measures, I will tie you down in my sleigh. I replied to him, that if he carried me in that manner, no person would purchase me, for it would be thought that he had a murderer for sale. After this he tried no more, and said he would not have me as a gift.

My master next offered me to Daniel Edwards, Esq. of Hartford, for sale. But not purchasing me, my master pawned me to him for ten pounds, and returned to Stonington. After some trial of my honesty, Mr. Edwards placed considerable trust and confidence in me. He put me to serve as his cup-bearer and waiter. When there was company at his house, he would send me into his cellar and other parts of his house to fetch wine and other articles occasionally for them. When I had been with him some time, he asked me why my master wished to part with such an honest negro, and why he did not keep me himself. I replied that I could not give him the reason, unless it was to convert me into cash, and speculate with me as with other commodities. I hope that he can never justly say it was on account of my ill conduct that he did not keep me himself. Mr. Edwards told me that he should be very willing to keep me himself, and that he would never let me go from him to live, if it was not unreasonable and inconvenient for me to be parted from my wife and children; therefore he would furnish me with a horse to return to Stonington, if I had a mind for it. As Miner did not appear to redeem me I went, and called at my old master Stanton's first to see my wife, who was then owned by him. As my old master appeared much ruffled at my being there, I left my wife before I had spent any considerable time with her, and went to Colonel O. Smith's. Miner had not as yet wholly settled with Stanton for me, and had before my return from Hartford given Col. Smith a bill of sale of me. These men once met to determine which of them should hold me, and upon my expressing a desire to be owned by Col. Smith, and upon my master's settling the remainder of the money which was due to Stanton for me, it was agreed that I should live with Col. Smith. This was the third time of my being sold, and I was then thirty-one years old. As I never had an opportunity of redeeming myself whilst I was owned by Miner, though he promised to give me a chance, I was then very ambitious of obtaining it. I asked my master one time if he would consent to have me purchase my freedom. He replied that he would. I was then very happy, knowing that I was at that time able to pay part of the purchase money, by means of the money which I some time since buried. This I took out of the earth and tendered to my master, having previously engaged a free negro man to take his security for it, as I was the property of my master, and therefore could not safely take his obligation myself. What was wanting in redeeming myself, my master agreed to wait on me for, until I could procure it for him. I still continued to work for Col. Smith. There was continually some interest accruing on my master's note to my friend the free negro man above named, which I received, and with some besides which I got by fishing, I laid out in land adjoining my old master Stanton's. By cultivating this land with the greatest diligence and economy, at times when my master did not require my labor, in two years I laid up ten pounds. This my friend tendered my master for myself, and received his note for it.

Being encouraged by the success which I had met in redeeming myself, I again solicited my master for a further chance of completing it. The chance for which I solicited him was that of going out to work the ensuing winter. He agreed to this on condition that I would give him one quarter of my earnings. On these terms I worked the following winter, and earned four pounds sixteen shillings, one quarter of which went to my master for the privilege, and the rest was paid him on my own account. This added to the other payments made up forty four pounds, eight shillings, which I had paid on my own account. I was then about thirty five years old.

The next summer I again desired he would give me a chance of going out to work. But he refused and answered that he must have my labor this summer, as he did not have it the past winter. I replied that I considered it as hard that I could not have a chance to work out when the season became advantageous, and that I must only be permitted to hire myself out in the poorest season of the year. He asked me after this what I would give him for the privilege per month. I replied that I would leave it wholly with his own generosity to determine what I should return him a month. Well then, said he, if so two pounds a month. I answered him that if that was the least he would take I would be contented.

Accordingly I hired myself out at Fisher's Island, and earned twenty pounds; thirteen pounds six shillings of which my master drew for the privilege, and the remainder I paid him for my freedom. This made fifty-one pounds two shillings which I paid him. In October following I went and wrought six months at Long-Island. In that six month's time I cut and corded four hundred cords of wood, besides threshing out seventy-five bushels of grain, and received of my wages down only twenty pounds, which left remaining a larger sum. Whilst I was out that time, I took up on my wages only one pair of shoes. At night I lay on the hearth, with one coverlet over and another under me. I returned to my master and gave him what I received of my six months labor. This left only thirteen pounds eighteen shillings to make up the full sum for my redemption. My master liberated me, saying that I might pay what was behind if I could ever make it convenient, otherwise it would be well. The amount of the money which I had paid my master towards redeeming my time, was seventy-one pounds two shillings. The reason of my master for asking such an unreasonable price, was he said, to secure himself in case I should ever come to want. Being thirty-six years old, I left Col. Smith once for all. I had already been sold three different times, made considerable money with seemingly nothing to derive it from, been cheated out of a large sum of money, lost much by misfortunes, and paid an enormous sum for my freedom.

Chapter III

CONTAINING AN ACCOUNT OF HIS LIFE, FROM THE TIME OF HIS PURCHASING HIS FREEDOM TO THE PRESENT DAY

My wife and children were yet in bondage to Mr. Thomas Stanton. About this time I lost a chest, containing besides clothing, about thirty-eight pounds in paper money. It was burnt by accident. A short time after I sold all my possessions at Stonington, consisting of a pretty piece of land and one dwelling house thereon, and went to reside at Long-Island. For the first four years of my residence there, I spent my time in working for various people on that and at the neighboring islands. In the space of six months I cut and corded upwards of four hundred cords of wood. Many other singular and wonderful labors I performed in cutting wood there, which would not be inferior to those just recited, but for brevity sake I must omit them. In the aforementioned four years what wood I cut at Long-Island amounted to several thousand cords, and the money which I earned thereby amounted to two hundred and seven pounds ten shillings. This money I laid up carefully by me. Perhaps some may enquire what maintained me all the time I was laying up money. I would inform them that I bought nothing which I did not absolutely want. All fine clothes I despised in comparison with my interest, and never kept but just what clothes were comfortable for common days, and perhaps I would have a garment or two which I did not have on at all times, but as for superfluous finery I never thought it to be compared with a decent homespun dress, a good supply of money and prudence. Expensive gatherings of my mates I commonly shunned, and all kinds of luxuries I was perfectly a stranger to; and during the time I was employed in cutting the aforementioned quantity of wood, I never was at the expence of six-pence worth of spirits.[9] Being after this labour forty years of age, I worked at various places, and in particular on Ram-Island, where I purchased Solomon and Cuff, two sons of mine, for two hundred dollars each.

It will here be remembered how much money I earned by cutting wood in four years. Besides this I had considerable money, amounting in all to near three hundred pounds. When I had purchased my two sons, I had then left more than one hundred pounds. After this I purchased a negro man, for no other reason than to oblige him, and gave for him sixty pounds. But in a short time after he run away from me, and I thereby lost all that I gave for him, except twenty pounds which he paid me previous to his absconding. The rest of my money I laid out in land, in addition to a farm which I owned before, and a dwelling house thereon. Forty-four years had then completed their revolution since my entrance into this existence of servitude and misfortune. Solomon my eldest son, being then in his seventeenth year, and all my hope and dependence for help, I hired him out to one Charles Church, of Rhode-Island, for one year, on consideration of his giving him twelve pounds and an opportunity of acquiring some learning. In the course of the year, Church fitted out a vessel for a whaling voyage, and being in want of hands to man her, he induced my son to go, with the promise of giving him on his return, a pair of silver buckles, besides his wages. As soon as I heard of his going to sea, I immediately set out to go and prevent it if possible.—But on my arrival at Church's, to my great grief, I could only see the vessel my son was in almost out of sight going to sea. My son died of the scurvy[1] in this voyage, and Church has never yet paid me the least of his wages. In my son, besides the loss of his life, I lost equal to seventy-five pounds.

My other son being but a youth, still lived with me. About this time I chartered a sloop of about thirty tons burthen, and hired men to assist me in navigating her. I employed her mostly in the wood trade to Rhode-Island, and made clear of all expences above one hundred dollars with her in better than one year. I had then become something forehanded,[2] and being in my forty-fourth year, I purchased my wife Meg, and thereby prevented having another child to buy, as she was then pregnant. I gave forty pounds for her.

During my residence at Long-Island, I raised one year with another, ten cart loads of water-melons, and lost a great many every year besides by the thievishness of the sailors. What I made by the water-melons I sold there, amounted to nearly five hundred dollars. Various other methods I pursued in order to enable me to redeem my family. In the night time I fished with

9. Alcoholic beverages.
1. A disease caused by a diet lacking in vitamin C.
2. Well-to-do.

set-nets and pots for eels and lobsters, and shortly after went [on] a whaling voyage in the service of Col. Smith.—After being out seven months, the vessel returned, laden with four hundred barrels of oil. About this time, I become possessed of another dwelling-house, and my temporal affairs were in a pretty prosperous condition. This and my industry was what alone saved me from being expelled [from] that part of the island in which I resided, as an act was passed by the select-men of the place, that all negroes residing there should be expelled.

Next after my wife, I purchased a negro man for four hundred dollars. But he having an inclination to return to his old master, I therefore let him go. Shortly after I purchased another negro man for twenty-five pounds, whom I parted with shortly after.

Being about forty-six years old, I bought my oldest child Hannah, of Ray Mumford, for forty-four pounds, and she still resided with him. I had already redeemed from slavery, myself, my wife and three children, besides three negro men.

About the forty-seventh year of my life, I disposed of all my property at Long-Island, and came from thence into East-Haddam. I hired myself out at first to Timothy Chapman, for five weeks, the earnings of which time I put up carefully by me. After this I wrought[3] for Abel Bingham about six weeks. I then put my money together and purchased of said Bingham ten acres of land, lying at Haddam neck, where I now reside.—On this land I labored with great diligence for two years, and shortly after purchased six acres more of land contiguous to my other. One year from that time I purchased seventy acres more of the same man, and paid for it mostly with the produce of my other land. Soon after I bought this last lot of land, I set up a comfortable dwelling house on my farm, and built it from the produce thereof. Shortly after I had much trouble and expence with my daughter Hannah, whose name has before been mentioned in this account. She was married soon after I redeemed her, to one Isaac, a free negro, and shortly after her marriage fell sick of a mortal disease; her husband a dissolute and abandoned wretch, paid but little attention to her in her illness. I therefore thought it best to bring her to my house and nurse her there. I procured her all the aid mortals could afford, but notwithstanding this she fell a prey to her disease, after a lingering and painful endurance of it.

The physician's bills for attending her during her illness amounted to forty pounds. Having reached my fifty-fourth year, I hired two negro men, one named William Jacklin, and the other Mingo. Mingo lived with me one year, and having received his wages, run in debt to me eight dollars, for which he gave me his note. Presently after he tried to run away from me without troubling himself to pay up his note. I procured a warrant, took him, and requested him to go to Justice Throop's of his own accord, but he refusing, I took him on my shoulders, and carried him there, distant about two miles. The justice asking me if I had my prisoner's note with me, and replying that I had not, he told me that I must return with him and get it. Accordingly I carried Mingo back on my shoulders, but before we arrived at my dwelling, he complained of being hurt, and asked me if this was not a hard way of treating our fellow creatures. I answered him that it would be hard thus to treat our honest fellow creatures. He then told me that if I would let him off my shoulders, he had a pair of silver shoe-buckles, one shirt and a pocket handker-

3. Worked

chief, which he would turn out to me. I agreed, and let him return home with me on foot; but the very following night, he slipped from me, stole my horse and has never paid me even his note. The other negro man, Jacklin, being a comb-maker by trade, he requested me to set him up, and promised to reward me well with his labor. Accordingly I bought him a set of tools for making combs, and procured him stock. He worked at my house about one year, and then run away from me with all his combs, and owed me for all his board.

Since my residence at Haddam neck, I have owned of boats, canoes and sail vessels, not less than twenty. These I mostly employed in the fishing and trafficking business, and in these occupations I have been cheated out of considerable money by people whom I traded with taking advantage of my ignorance of numbers.

About twelve years ago, I hired a whale-boat and four black men, and proceeded to Long-Island after a load of round clams. Having arrived there, I first purchased of James Webb, son of Orange Webb, six hundred and sixty clams, and afterwards, with the help of my men, finished loading my boat. The same evening, however, this Webb stole my boat, and went in her to Connecticut river, and sold her cargo for his own benefit. I thereupon pursued him, and at length, after an additional expence of nine crowns, recovered the boat; but for the proceeds of her cargo I never could obtain any compensation.

Four years after, I met with another loss, far superior to this in value, and I think by no less wicked means. Being going to New-London with a grandchild, I took passage in an Indian's boat, and went there with him. On our return, the Indian took on board two hogsheads[4] of molasses, one of which belonged to Capt. Elisha Hart, of Saybrook, to be delivered on his wharf. When we arrived there, and while I was gone, at the request of the Indian, to inform Captain Hart of his arrival, and receive the freight for him, one hogshead of the molasses had been lost overboard by the people in attempting to land it on the wharf. Although I was absent at the time, and had no concern whatever in the business, as was known to a number of respectable witnesses, I was nevertheless prosecuted by this conscientious gentleman, (the Indian not being able to pay for it) and obliged to pay upwards of ten pounds lawful money, with all the costs of court. I applied to several gentlemen for counsel in this affair, and they advised me, as my adversary was rich, and threatened to carry the matter from court to court till it would cost me more than the first damages would be to pay the sum and submit to the injury; which I accordingly did, and he has often since insultingly taunted me with my unmerited misfortune. Such a proceeding as this, committed on a defenceless stranger, almost worn out in the hard service of the world, without any foundation in reason or justice, whatever it may be called in a christian land, would in my native country have been branded as a crime equal to highway robbery. But Captain Hart was a *white gentleman,* and I a *poor African,* therefore it was *all right, and good enough for the black dog.*

I am now sixty-nine years old. Though once strait and tall, measuring without shoes six feet one inch and an half, and every way well proportioned, I am now bowed down with age and hardship. My strength which was once equal if not superior to any man whom I have ever seen, is now enfeebled so that life is a burden, and it is with fatigue that I can walk a

4. Large casks.

couple of miles, stooping over my staff. Other griefs are still behind, on account of which some aged people, at least, will pity me. My eye-sight has gradually failed, till I am almost blind, and whenever I go abroad one of my grand-children must direct my way; besides for many years I have been much pained and troubled with an ulcer on one of my legs. But amidst all my griefs and pains, I have many consolations; Meg, the wife of my youth, whom I married for love, and bought with my money, is still alive. My freedom is a privilege which nothing else can equal. Notwithstanding all the losses I have suffered by fire, by the injustice of knaves, by the cruelty and oppression of false hearted friends, and the perfidy of my own countrymen whom I have assisted and redeemed from bondage, I am now possessed of more than one hundred acres of land, and three habitable dwelling houses. It gives me joy to think that I *have* and that I *deserve* so good a character, especially for *truth* and *integrity*. While I am now looking to the grave as my home, my joy for this world would be full—If my children, Cuff for whom I paid two hundred dollars when a boy, and Solomon who was born soon after I purchased his mother—If Cuff and Solomon—O! that they had walked in the way of their father. But a father's lips are closed in silence and in grief!—Vanity of vanities, all is vanity![5]

FINIS.

CERTIFICATE.

STONINGTON, *NOVEMBER* 3, 1793.

These certify, that VENTURE, a free negro man, aged about 69 years, and was, as we have ever understood, a native of Africa, and formerly a slave to Mr. James Mumford, of Fisher's-Island, in the state of New-York; who sold him to Mr. Thomas Stanton, 2d, of Stonington, in the state of Connecticut, and said Stanton sold said VENTURE to Col. Oliver Smith, of the aforesaid place. That said VENTURE hath sustained the character of a faithful servant, and that of a temperate, honest and industrious man, and being ever intent on obtaining his freedom, he was indulged by his masters after the ordinary labour on the days of his servitude, to improve the nights in fishing and other employments to his own emolument, in which time he procured so much money as to purchase his freedom from his late master Col. Smith; after which he took upon himself the name of VENTURE SMITH, and has since his freedom purchased a negro woman, called Meg, to whom he was previously married, and also his children who were slaves, and said VENTURE has since removed himself and family to the town of East-Haddam, in this state, where he hath purchased lands on which he hath built a house, and there taken up his abode.

NATHANIEL MINOR, Esq.
ELIJAH PALMER, Esq.
Capt. AMOS PALMER,
ACORS SHEFFIELD,
EDWARD SMITH.

5. Ecclesiastes 1:2.

LUCY TERRY
ca. 1724–1821

Lucy Terry's only poem, "Bars Fight," is the earliest known work of literature in English by an African American. Composed in rhymed tetrameter couplets and probably designed to be sung, Terry's ballad records an American Indian ambush of two settler families on August 25, 1746, in a section of Deerfield, Massachusetts, known as "the Bars," a colonial term for meadows. Although Terry had grown up enslaved in Deerfield, her poem appears sympathetic to the white men and women who died in the fight. The poem was preserved in local memory and recorded in one speech delivered by a Deerfield lawyer in 1819 before finally being published in Josiah G. Holland's *History of Western Massachusetts* in 1855.

Terry was born in Africa, captured and enslaved around the age of five, and after enduring the Middle Passage, arrived in the port of Boston in the late 1720s. She was first enslaved in North America by Samuel Terry of Enfield, Connecticut, in whose household she became known as Lucy Terry. Soon thereafter, Ebenezer and Abigail Wells of Deerfield purchased her. In this northern-frontier British settlement in the Connecticut River Valley, Terry lived for more than thirty years. In 1735 she was converted to Christianity; she joined her enslaver's church in 1744. Abijah Prince, an enterprising Black man, married Lucy Terry in 1756 and, more than likely, purchased her freedom subsequently. Around 1775, the Princes moved to Guilford, Vermont, where the couple raised a family of six children on a nearby homestead. The presence of this Black family aroused complaints and sometimes violent resistance from local townspeople. In 1785 Lucy Terry Prince responded to the discrimination and threats that her family had received by arguing a case for judicial redress before the Vermont Governor's Council. The council ordered Guilford authorities to protect the Prince family's civil rights and property.

After her husband's death in 1794, Terry Prince and four of her adult children moved to Sunderland, Vermont, where her claims for land her husband had owned met with local white resistance. Over seven years in proceedings all the way to the Vermont Supreme Court, the dauntless Terry Prince demanded justice, which was decided in her favor in June 1799. The rhetorical eloquence of Terry Prince's courtroom oratory gave rise to legends that scholars cannot document. She was reputed to have encouraged her oldest son, Caesar, a Revolutionary War veteran, to apply for admission to Williams College. When he was refused, according to oral tradition, she traveled to Williamstown, Massachusetts, and delivered a three-hour argument to the college's trustees against Williams's policy of racial discrimination. Another popular but unproven tribute to Terry Prince placed her before the U.S. Supreme Court arguing a land dispute. These stories augmented the regional reputation Terry Prince enjoyed in her lifetime as a skilled orator and indefatigable defender of African American civil rights. When she died on July 11, 1821, on her Sunderland land, her obituary in the *Vermont Gazette* reported that Rev. Lemuel Haynes, a leading African American minister and abolitionist in New England, delivered the eulogy. The *Gazette* praised her as a "prodigy" whose "fluency of speech captivated all around her."

Bars° Fight

meadows

August, 'twas the twenty-fifth,
Seventeen hundred forty-six,
The Indians did in ambush lay,
Some very valient men to slay,
The names of whom I'll not leave out:
Samuel Allen like a hero fout,° *fought*
And though he was so brave and bold,
His face no more shall we behold.

Eleazer Hawks was killed outright,
Before he had time to fight,—
Before he did the Indians see,
Was shot and killed immediately.
Oliver Amsden he was slain,
Which caused his friends much grief and pain.
Simeon Amsden they found dead
Not many rods distant from his head.

Adonijah Gillett, we do hear,
Did lose his life which was so dear.
John Sadler fled across the water,
And thus escaped the dreadful slaughter.

Eunice Allen see the Indians coming,
And hopes to save herself by running;
And had not her petticoats stopped her,
The awful creatures had not catched her,
Nor tommy hawked her on the head,
And left her on the ground for dead.
Young Samuel Allen, Oh, lack-a-day!
Was taken and carried to Canada.

1746 1855

OLAUDAH EQUIANO

ca. 1745–1797

The Interesting Narrative of the Life of Olaudah Equiano, or Gustavus Vassa, the African, Written by Himself (1789) is widely regarded as the prototype of the slave narrative, a form of autobiography that in the first half of the nineteenth century gained a wide international readership because of its compelling firsthand testimony against slavery. In its two bulky volumes, Olaudah Equiano's *Interesting Narrative* tells a richly detailed story of an idyllic African boyhood, kidnapping and enslavement in Africa, terror and adventure on the high seas, Christian conversion in England, and ultimate economic success in a variety of occupations, including authorship. Equiano was what one historian has termed "an Atlantic creole," a cosmopolitan figure whose sense of identity embraced Africa, the Americas, and England.

Equiano's ability to espouse the highest ideals of his era in the language of the everyday man and woman had much to do with the impressive popularity of the *Interesting Narrative*. It went through seventeen editions between 1789 and 1827 and was translated into Dutch and German. Equiano's was the most influential work of English prose by an African American in the eighteenth century. With Phillis Wheatley's *Poems on Various Subjects, Religious and Moral* (1773), Equiano's autobiography verified the claim, much disputed during the Enlightenment, that Black people could represent themselves effectively through writing. Equiano's seriousness of purpose, sophisticated self-analysis, and sustained attention to the craft of storytelling have identified his autobiography as an inaugural text of African American letters.

Portrait of Equiano on the frontispiece to the eighth edition of *The Interesting Narrative of the Life of Olaudah Equiano, or Gustavus Vassa, the African* (1794).

Equiano was not the first African-born formerly enslaved man to recount his experiences in bondage and freedom. But he was the first to write the story of his life without the aid or direction of white ghostwriters or editors, whom his predecessors in the slave narrative had relied on. Equiano signaled his independence of thought, purpose, and expression by making *Written by Himself* part of the title of his book. The man known from age twelve by his slave name, Gustavus Vassa, brought a complex personal and political agenda to the publication of the *Interesting Narrative*. An unmistakable feature of Equiano's moral and social purpose was his life story's outspoken emphasis on the atrocities of the international slave trade, which linked west Africa, the Caribbean, Europe, and North America in an unprecedented system of African despoliation for European and American profit and power. The *Interesting Narrative* pled more compellingly for the abolition of the slave trade than any previous slave narrative.

Most slave narrators of Equiano's era impressed their white sponsors with their piety and their willingness to forgive those who had once oppressed and exploited them. Although Equiano made much of his conversion to Christianity in his narrative, he made clear his dedication to social change by venting his moral outrage toward slavery and by structuring his story so that freedom, not the consolations of religion, emerges as his top priority and goal while he was enslaved. Equiano's twin desires at the end of the *Interesting Narrative*—to become a Christian missionary to Africa and to end the African slave trade—suggest that Christianity and abolitionism, the pursuit of individual and social perfection, go hand in hand. This mating of the spiritual and the secular in the *Interesting Narrative* was prophetic of the ideological orientation of most nineteenth-century African American protest literature.

One of Equiano's more remarkable rhetorical strategies is his use of African origins to establish his credibility as a critic of European imperialism in Africa. The *Interesting Narrative* pictures Equiano's having been born around 1745 in Essaka, a village located in the interior of modern-day eastern Nigeria. The book recounts its author's growing up among a peaceful, pastoral Ibo people before being kidnapped at the age of eleven and sold as a slave to other Africans. However, the most thoroughly researched of Equiano's biographies, authored by Vincent Carretta, has raised questions about whether Equiano was actually born in Africa. After locating the church record of Equiano's baptism on February 9, 1759, in Westminster, England, Carretta discovered Equiano listed as "Gustavus Vassa a Black born in Carolina 12 years old." Scholars have debated whether Equiano's account of Ibo life in his autobiography is based on the author's reading rather than on memory. Inconsistencies between historical records and the *Interesting Narrative*'s claims about Equiano's early life have produced no scholarly consensus on where he was born or whether his account of the Middle Passage was based on firsthand experience or knowledge gleaned from other sources, such as eyewitness accounts Equiano may have heard.

Most scholars of Equiano's autobiography recognize, nevertheless, how crucial his rendition of his early boyhood, kidnapping, and enslavement was to establishing his moral authority as an opponent of the slave trade. The *Interesting Narrative* strongly counters European myths about Africa as spiritually benighted and socially backward. Equiano represents the harmonious and just African society he grew up in as a moral judgment against the "polished and haughty European" whose callous ethnocentrism the opening chapters of the *Interesting Narrative* deplore. Even Equiano's months with his first enslaver, an African chieftain, are portrayed as benign when compared to his grisly initiation into the savagery of European slavery. Recreating the terror and awe he felt on seeing "those white men with horrible looks, red faces, and loose hair" engaged in packing the slave ships with their human cargo, Equiano thrusts his white reader into the mind and heart of a Black youth innocent of the horrors that were about to befall him on the Middle Passage and in the Americas. In this way Equiano attempted to liberate his white reader from a culturally enforced sense of superiority that prevented many whites from feeling a common bond of humanity with people of African descent.

Equiano survived his early years in slavery by tempering his fear of whites with a self-interested desire to master their technology and thus carve out a place for himself in their world. The major part of Equiano's autobiography describes his successful assimilation into practically every sphere of economic activity to which he applied himself. As the personal servant of a lieutenant in the English navy and later as a ship's steward during campaigns in the Mediterranean and off the coast of France, the enslaved youth made the most of his maritime opportunities. Expecting from his enslaver's assurances to be freed after six years of good service, Equiano was instead sold to a West Indian trader in 1762, who soon sold him to Robert King, a Philadelphia Quaker and merchant. Working for King taught Equiano, by that time a well-trained seaman, a good deal about seagoing commercial practices, so that by 1766, at the age of twenty-one, the ambitious Black man was able not only to buy his freedom but also to launch his own business career. In 1767 Equiano returned to England to work as a hairdresser for affluent Londoners, during which time he learned the French horn and expanded his study of mathematics. In 1773, after participating in an expedition in search of the North Pole, the world-traveling Equiano underwent a profound religious conversion and became a Methodist. Later voyages took Equiano to ports as far away as Central America and Turkey, before he settled in London in 1777. During the next few years he became increasingly interested in relief work in Africa and in the abolition of the transatlantic slave trade. In 1786 Equiano was rewarded with an appointment as a "comissary of provisions and stores" for a colonization venture in Sierra Leone on the west coast of Africa. Political infighting occasioned by his public criticism of the management of this venture prevented Equiano from making this journey to Africa.

After the publication of his autobiography in 1789, in which he claimed for the first time publicly to be a native of Africa, Equiano traveled extensively in England and Ireland promoting his book. Selling nine editions of the *Interesting Narrative* during his lifetime enabled the self-styled "son of Africa" to prosper as an English gentleman. Equiano married an Englishwoman, Susanna Cullen, in 1792, with whom he had two daughters. He died in London on March 31, 1797, leaving his surviving daughter a handsome estate. Equiano was the best-known and most successful author of African descent in the English-speaking world in the eighteenth century. Through his *Interesting Narrative* he bequeathed to modern African American literature a prescient and provocative example of what W. E. B. Du Bois would later call "double-consciousness"—the African American's fateful sense of "twoness" born of a bicultural identification with both an African heritage and a European way of life.

From The Interesting Narrative of the Life of Olaudah Equiano, or Gustavus Vassa, the African, Written by Himself

Volume I

> Behold, God is my salvation; I will trust and not be afraid, for the Lord Jehovah is my strength and my song; he also is become my salvation. And in that day shall ye say, Praise the Lord, call upon his name, declare his doings among the people.
>
> —Isaiah 12:2, 4

To the Lords Spiritual and Temporal, and the Commons of the Parliament of Great Britain.

My Lords and Gentlemen,

Permit me, with the greatest deference and respect, to lay at your feet the following genuine Narrative; the chief design of which is to excite in your august assemblies a sense of compassion for the miseries which the Slave-Trade has entailed on my unfortunate countrymen. By the horrors of that trade was I first torn away from all the tender connexions that were naturally dear to my heart; but these, through the mysterious ways of Providence, I ought to regard as infinitely more than compensated by the introduction I have thence obtained to the knowledge of the Christian religion, and of a nation which, by its liberal sentiments, its humanity, the glorious freedom of its government, and its proficiency in arts and sciences, has exalted the dignity of human nature.

I am sensible I ought to entreat your pardon for addressing to you a work so wholly devoid of literary merit; but, as the production of an unlettered African, who is actuated by the hope of becoming an instrument towards the relief of his suffering countrymen, I trust that *such a man,* pleading in *such a cause,* will be acquitted of boldness and presumption.

May the God of heaven inspire your hearts with peculiar benevolence on that important day when the question of Abolition is to be discussed, when thousands, in consequence of your Determination, are to look for Happiness or Misery!

I am,
My Lords and Gentlemen,
Your most obedient,
And devoted humble Servant,

Olaudah Equiano,
or
Gustavus Vassa.

Union-Street, Mary-le-bone,
March 24, 1789.

Chapter I

I believe it is difficult for those who publish their own memoirs to escape the imputation of vanity; nor is this the only disadvantage under which they labour: it is also their misfortune, that what is uncommon is rarely, if ever, believed, and what is obvious we are apt to turn from with disgust, and to charge the writer with impertinence. People generally think those memoirs only worthy to be read or remembered which abound in great or striking events, those, in short, which in a high degree excite either admiration or pity: all others they consign to contempt and oblivion. It is therefore, I confess, not a little hazardous in a private and obscure individual, and a stranger too, thus to solicit the indulgent attention of the public; especially when I own I offer here the history of neither a saint, a hero, nor a tyrant. I believe there are few events in my life, which have not happened to many: it is true the incidents of it are numerous; and, did I consider myself an European, I might say my sufferings were great: but when I compare my lot with that of most of my countrymen, I regard myself as a *particular favourite of Heaven,* and acknowledge the mercies of Providence in every occurrence of my life. If then the following narrative does not appear sufficiently interesting to engage general attention, let my motive be some excuse for its publication. I am not so foolishly vain as to expect from it either immortality or literary reputation. If it affords any satisfaction to my numerous friends, at whose request it has been written, or in the smallest degree promotes the interests of humanity, the ends for which it was undertaken will be fully attained, and every wish of my heart gratified. Let it therefore be remembered, that, in wishing to avoid censure, I do not aspire to praise.

That part of Africa, known by the name of Guinea, to which the trade for slaves is carried on, extends along the coast above 3400 miles, from the Senegal to Angola, and includes a variety of kingdoms. Of these the most considerable is the kingdom of Benen,[1] both as to extent and wealth, the richness and cultivation of the soil, the power of its king, and the number and warlike disposition of the inhabitants. It is situated nearly under the line,[2] and extends along the coast about 170 miles, but runs back into the interior part of Africa to a distance hitherto I believe unexplored by any traveller; and seems only terminated at length by the empire of Abyssinia,[3] near 1500 miles from its beginning. This kingdom is divided into many provinces or districts: in one of the most remote and fertile of which, called Eboe,[4] I was born, in the year 1745, in a charming fruitful vale, named Essaka. The distance of this province from the capital of Benin and the sea coast must be very considerable; for I had never heard of white men or Europeans, nor of the sea: and our subjection to the king of Benin was little more than nominal; for every transaction of the government, as far as my slender observation extended, was conducted by the chiefs or elders of the place. The manners and government of a people who have little commerce with other countries are generally very simple; and the history of what passes in one family or village may serve as a specimen of a nation. My father was one of those elders or chiefs I have spoken of, and was styled Embrenche; a term, as I remember, importing the highest distinction, and signifying in our language a *mark* of grandeur. This mark is conferred on the person entitled to it, by cutting the skin across at the top of the forehead,

1. Or Benin, a West African country, home of the kingdom of Dahomey.
2. South of the equator.
3. An African kingdom comprising modern-day Ethiopia and parts of the Sudan.
4. The Ibo people live in what is now southern Nigeria.

and drawing it down to the eye-brows; and while it is in this situation applying a warm hand, and rubbing it until it shrinks up into a thick *weal* across the lower part of the forehead. Most of the judges and senators were thus marked; my father had long born it: I had seen it conferred on one of my brothers, and I was also *destined* to receive it by my parents. Those Embrence, or chief men, decided disputes and punished crimes; for which purpose they always assembled together. The proceedings were generally short; and in most cases the law of retaliation prevailed. I remember a man was brought before my father, and the other judges, for kidnapping a boy; and, although he was the son of a chief or senator, he was condemned to make recompense by a man or woman slave. Adultery, however, was sometimes punished with slavery or death; a punishment which I believe is inflicted on it throughout most of the nations of Africa:[5] so sacred among them is the honour of the marriage bed, and so jealous are they of the fidelity of their wives. Of this I recollect an instance:—a woman was convicted before the judges of adultery, and delivered over, as the custom was, to her husband to be punished. Accordingly he determined to put her to death: but it being found, just before her execution, that she had an infant at her breast; and no woman being prevailed on to perform the part of a nurse, she was spared on account of the child. The men, however, do not preserve the same constancy to their wives, which they expect from them; for they indulge in a plurality, though seldom in more than two. Their mode of marriage is thus:—both parties are usually betrothed when young by their parents, (though I have known the males to betroth themselves). On this occasion a feast is prepared, and the bride and bridegroom stand up in the midst of all their friends, who are assembled for the purpose, while he declares she is thenceforth to be looked upon as his wife, and that no other person is to pay any addresses to her. This is also immediately proclaimed in the vicinity, on which the bride retires from the assembly. Some time after she is brought home to her husband, and then another feast is made, to which the relations of both parties are invited: her parents then deliver her to the bridegroom, accompanied with a number of blessings, and at the same time they tie round her waist a cotton string of the thickness of a goose-quill, which none but married women are permitted to wear: she is now considered as completely his wife; and at this time the dowry is given to the new married pair, which generally consists of portions of land, slaves, and cattle, household goods, and implements of husbandry. These are offered by the friends of both parties; besides which the parents of the bridegroom present gifts to those of the bride, whose property she is looked upon before marriage; but after it she is esteemed the sole property of her husband. The ceremony being now ended the festival begins, which is celebrated with bonefires, and loud acclamations of joy, accompanied with music and dancing.

We are almost a nation of dancers, musicians, and poets. Thus every great event, such as a triumphant return from battle, or other cause of public rejoicing is celebrated in public dances, which are accompanied with songs and music suited to the occasion. The assembly is separated into four divisions, which dance either apart or in succession, and each with a character peculiar to itself. The first division contains the married men, who in their dances frequently exhibit feats of arms, and the representation of a battle. To these succeed the married women, who dance in the second division. The young

5. See Benezet's "Account of Guinea" throughout [*Equiano's note*]. Anthony Benezet (1713–1784), American antislavery activist and author of *Some Historical Account of Guinea, with an Inquiry into the Rise and Progress of the Slave Trade* (1772).

men occupy the third; and the maidens the fourth. Each represents some interesting scene of real life, such as a great achievement, domestic employment, a pathetic story, or some rural sport; and as the subject is generally founded on some recent event, it is therefore ever new. This gives our dances a spirit and variety which I have scarcely seen elsewhere.[6] We have many musical instruments, particularly drums of different kinds, a piece of music which resembles a guitar, and another much like a stickado.[7] These last are chiefly used by betrothed virgins, who play on them on all grand festivals.

As our manners are simple, our luxuries are few. The dress of both sexes is nearly the same. It generally consists of a long piece of callico, or muslin, wrapped loosely round the body, somewhat in the form of a highland plaid. This is usually dyed blue, which is our favourite colour. It is extracted from a berry, and is brighter and richer than any I have seen in Europe. Besides this, our women of distinction wear golden ornaments; which they dispose with some profusion on their arms and legs. When our women are not employed with the men in tillage, their usual occupation is spinning and weaving cotton, which they afterwards dye, and make it into garments. They also manufacture earthen vessels, of which we have many kinds. Among the rest tobacco pipes, made after the same fashion, and used in the same manner, as those in Turkey.[8]

Our manner of living is entirely plain; for as yet the natives are unacquainted with those refinements in cookery which debauch the taste: bullocks, goats, and poultry, supply the greatest part of their food. These constitute likewise the principal wealth of the country, and the chief articles of its commerce. The flesh is usually stewed in a pan; to make it savoury we sometimes use also pepper, and other spices, and we have salt made of wood ashes. Our vegetables are mostly plantains, eadas, yams, beans, and Indian corn.[9] The head of the family usually eats alone; his wives and slaves have also their separate tables. Before we taste food we always wash our hands: indeed our cleanliness on all occasions is extreme; but on this it is an indispensable ceremony. After washing, libation is made, by pouring out a small portion of the food, in a certain place, for the spirits of departed relations, which the natives suppose to preside over their conduct, and guard them from evil. They are totally unacquainted with strong or spirituous liquors; and their principal beverage is palm wine. This is gotten from a tree of that name by tapping it at the top, and fastening a large gourd to it; and sometimes one tree will yield three or four gallons in a night. When just drawn it is of a most delicious sweetness; but in a few days it acquires a tartish and more spirituous flavour: though I never saw any one intoxicated by it. The same tree also produces nuts and oil. Our principal luxury is in perfumes; one sort of these is an odoriferous wood of delicious fragrance: the other a kind of earth; a small portion of which thrown into the fire diffuses a most powerful odour.[1] We beat this wood into powder, and mix it with palm oil; with which both men and women perfume themselves.

6. When I was in Smyrna I have frequently seen the Greeks dance after this manner [*Equiano's note*]. Smyrna is a city in western Turkey founded by the Greeks.

7. The sticcado pastorale, an Italian musical instrument resembling a xylophone.

8. The bowl is earthen, curiously figured, to which a long reed is fixed as a tube. This tube is sometimes so long as to be borne by one, and frequently out of grandeur by two boys [*Equiano's note*].

9. Also known as maize, a New World plant cultivated by Native American peoples and brought to Africa in the 16th century by the Portuguese, where it quickly became a staple. "Eadas": types of yams.

1. When I was in Smyrna I saw the same kind of earth, and brought some of it with me to England; it resembles musk in strength, but is more delicious in scent, and is not unlike the smell of a rose [*Equiano's note*].

In our buildings we study convenience rather than ornament. Each master of a family has a large square piece of ground, surrounded with a moat or fence, or enclosed with a wall made of red earth tempered; which, when dry, is as hard as brick. Within this are his houses to accommodate his family and slaves; which, if numerous, frequently present the appearance of a village. In the middle stands the principal building, appropriated to the sole use of the master, and consisting of two apartments; in one of which he sits in the day with his family, the other is left apart for the reception of his friends. He has besides these a distinct apartment in which he sleeps, together with his male children. On each side are the apartments of his wives, who have also their separate day and night houses. The habitations of the slaves and their families are distributed throughout the rest of the enclosure. These houses never exceed one story in height: they are always built of wood, or stakes driven into the ground, crossed with wattles,[2] and neatly plastered within, and without. The roof is thatched with reeds. Our day-houses are left open at the sides; but those in which we sleep are always covered, and plastered in the inside, with a composition mixed with cowdung, to keep off the different insects, which annoy us during the night. The walls and floors also of these are generally covered with mats. Our beds consist of a platform, raised three or four feet from the ground, on which are laid skins, and different parts of a spungy tree called plaintain. Our covering is calico or muslin, the same as our dress. The usual seats are a few logs of wood; but we have benches, which are generally perfumed, to accommodate strangers: these compose the greater part of our household furniture. Houses so constructed and furnished require but little skill to erect them. Every man is a sufficient architect for the purpose. The whole neighbourhood afford their unanimous assistance in building them and in return receive, and expect no other recompense than a feast.

As we live in a country where nature is prodigal of her favours, our wants are few and easily supplied; of course we have few manufactures. They consist for the most part of calicoes, earthern ware, ornaments, and instruments of war and husbandry. But these make no part of our commerce, the principal articles of which, as I have observed, are provisions. In such a state money is of little use; however we have some small pieces of coin, if I may call them such. They are made something like an anchor; but I do not remember either their value or denomination. We have also markets, at which I have been frequently with my mother. These are sometimes visited by stout mahogany-coloured men from the south west of us: we call them Oye-Eboe, which term signifies red men living at a distance. They generally bring us fire-arms, gunpowder, hats, beads, and dried fish. The last we esteemed a great rarity, as our waters were only brooks and springs. These articles they barter with us for odoriferous woods and earth, and our salt of wood ashes. They always carry slaves through our land; but the strictest account is exacted of their manner of procuring them before they are suffered to pass. Sometimes indeed we sold slaves to them, but they were only prisoners of war, or such among us as had been convicted of kidnapping, or adultery, and some other crimes, which we esteemed heinous. This practice of kidnapping induces me to think, that, notwithstanding all our strictness, their principal business among us was to trepan[3] our people. I remember too they carried great sacks along with them, which not long after I had an opportunity of fatally seeing applied to that infamous purpose.

2. Slender branches or reeds.

3. To trap by trickery.

Our land is uncommonly rich and fruitful, and produces all kinds of vegetables in great abundance. We have plenty of Indian corn, and vast quantities of cotton and tobacco. Our pine apples grow without culture; they are about the size of the largest sugar-loaf,[4] and finely flavoured. We have also spices of different kinds, particularly pepper; and a variety of delicious fruits which I have never seen in Europe; together with gums of various kinds, and honey in abundance. All our industry is exerted to improve those blessings of nature. Agriculture is our chief employment; and every one, even the children and women, are engaged in it. Thus we are all habituated to labour from our earliest years. Every one contributes something to the common stock; and as we are unacquainted with idleness, we have no beggars. The benefits of such a mode of living are obvious. The West India planters prefer the slaves of Benin or Eboe to those of any other part of Guinea, for their hardiness, intelligence, integrity, and zeal. Those benefits are felt by us in the general healthiness of the people, and in their vigour and activity; I might have added too in their comeliness. Deformity is indeed unknown amongst us, I mean that of shape. Numbers of the natives of Eboe now in London might be brought in support of this assertion: for, in regard to complexion, ideas of beauty are wholly relative. I remember while in Africa to have seen three negro children, who were tawny, and another quite white, who were universally regarded by myself, and the natives in general, as far as related to their complexions, as deformed. Our women too were in my eyes at least uncommonly graceful, alert, and modest to a degree of bashfulness; nor do I remember to have ever heard of an instance of incontinence amongst them before marriage. They are also remarkably cheerful. Indeed cheerfulness and affability are two of the leading characteristics of our nation.

Our tillage is exercised in a large plain or common, some hours walk from our dwellings, and all the neighbours resort thither in a body. They use no beasts of husbandry; and their only instruments are hoes, axes, shovels, and beaks, or pointed iron to dig with. Sometimes we are visited by locusts, which come in large clouds, so as to darken the air, and destroy our harvest. This however happens rarely, but when it does, a famine is produced by it. I remember an instance or two wherein this happened. This common is often the theatre of war; and therefore when our people go out to till their land, they not only go in a body, but generally take their arms with them for fear of a surprise; and when they apprehend an invasion they guard the avenues to their dwellings, by driving sticks into the ground, which are so sharp at one end as to pierce the foot, and are generally dipped in poison. From what I can recollect of these battles, they appear to have been irruptions of one little state or district on the other, to obtain prisoners or booty. Perhaps they were incited to this by those traders who brought the European goods I mentioned amongst us. Such a mode of obtaining slaves in Africa is common; and I believe more are procured this way and by kidnapping, than any other.[5] When a trader wants slaves, he applies to a chief for them, and tempts him with his wares. It is not extraordinary, if on this occasion he yields to the temptation with as little firmness, and accepts the price of his fellow creatures liberty with as little reluctance as the enlightened merchant. Accordingly he falls on his neighbours, and a desperate battle ensues. If he prevails and takes prisoners, he gratifies his avarice by selling them; but, if his party be vanquished, and he falls into the hands of the enemy, he is put to death:

4. Refined sugar molded into a cone.
5. See Benezet's "Account of Africa" throughout [*Equiano's note*].

for, as he has been known to foment their quarrels, it is thought dangerous to let him survive, and no ransom can save him, though all other prisoners may be redeemed. We have firearms, bows and arrows, broad two-edged swords and javelins: we have shields also which cover a man from head to foot. All are taught the use of these weapons; even our women are warriors, and march boldly out to fight along with the men. Our whole district is a kind of militia: on a certain signal given, such as the firing of a gun at night, they all rise in arms and rush upon their enemy. It is perhaps something remarkable, that when our people march to the field a red flag or banner is borne before them. I was once a witness to a battle in our common. We had been all at work in it one day as usual, when our people were suddenly attacked. I climbed a tree at some distance, from which I beheld the fight. There were many women as well as men on both sides; among others my mother was there, and armed with a broad sword. After fighting for a considerable time with great fury, and after many had been killed our people obtained the victory, and took their enemy's Chief prisoner. He was carried off in great triumph, and, though he offered a large ransom for his life, he was put to death. A virgin of note among our enemies had been slain in the battle, and her arm was exposed in our market-place, where our trophies were always exhibited. The spoils were divided according to the merit of the warriors. Those prisoners which were not sold or redeemed we kept as slaves: but how different was their condition from that of the slaves in the West Indies! With us they do no more work than other members of the community, even their masters; their food, clothing and lodging were nearly the same as theirs, (except that they were not permitted to eat with those who were free-born); and there was scarce any other difference between them, than a superior degree of importance which the head of a family possesses in our state, and that authority which, as such, he exercises over every part of his household. Some of these slaves have even slaves under them as their own property, and for their own use.

As to religion, the natives believe that there is one Creator of all things, and that he lives in the sun, and is girted round with a belt that he may never eat or drink; but, according to some, he smokes a pipe, which is our own favourite luxury. They believe he governs events, especially our deaths or captivity; but, as for the doctrine of eternity, I do not remember to have ever heard of it: some however believe in the transmigration of souls[6] in a certain degree. Those spirits, which are not transmigrated, such as our dear friends or relations, they believe always attend them, and guard them from the bad spirits or their foes. For this reason they always before eating, as I have observed, put some small portion of the meat, and pour some of their drink, on the ground for them; and they often make oblations of the blood of beasts or fowls at their graves. I was very fond of my mother, and almost constantly with her. When she went to make these oblations at her mother's tomb, which was a kind of small solitary thatched house, I sometimes attended her. There she made her libations, and spent most of the night in cries and lamentations. I have been often extremely terrified on these occasions. The loneliness of the place, the darkness of the night, and the ceremony of libation, naturally awful and gloomy, were heightened by my mother's lamentations; and these, concuring with the cries of doleful birds, by which these places were frequented, gave an inexpressible terror to the scene.

6. A concept of reincarnation in which the soul is reborn into successive existences that may be human, animal, or vegetable.

We compute the year from the day on which the sun crosses the line, and on its setting that evening there is a general shout throughout the land; at least I can speak from my own knowledge throughout our vicinity. The people at the same time make a great noise with rattles, not unlike the basket rattles used by children here, though much larger, and hold up their hands to heaven for a blessing. It is then the greatest offerings are made; and those children whom our wise men foretell will be fortunate are then presented to different people. I remember many used to come to see me, and I was carried about to others for that purpose. They have many offerings, particularly at full moons; generally two at harvest before the fruits are taken out of the ground: and when any young animals are killed, sometimes they offer up part of them as a sacrifice. These offerings, when made by one of the heads of a family, serve for the whole. I remember we often had them at my father's and my uncle's, and their families have been present. Some of our offerings are eaten with bitter herbs. We had a saying among us to any one of a cross temper, "That if they were to be eaten, they should be eaten with bitter herbs."

We practised circumcision like the Jews, and made offerings and feasts on that occasion in the same manner as they did. Like them also, our children were named from some event, some circumstance, or fancied foreboding at the time of their birth. I was named *Olaudah,* which, in our language, signifies vicissitude or fortune also, one favoured, and having a loud voice and well spoken. I remember we never polluted the name of the object of our adoration; on the contrary, it was always mentioned with the greatest reverence; and we were totally unacquainted with swearing, and all those terms of abuse and reproach which find their way so readily and copiously into the languages of more civilized people. The only expressions of that kind I remember were "May you rot, or may you swell, or may a beast take you."

I have before remarked that the natives of this part of Africa are extremely cleanly. This necessary habit of decency was with us a part of religion, and therefore we had many purifications and washings; indeed almost as many, and used on the same occasions, if my recollection does not fail me, as the Jews. Those that touched the dead at any time were obliged to wash and purify themselves before they could enter a dwelling-house. Every woman too, at certain times, was forbidden to come into a dwelling-house, or touch any person, or any thing we ate. I was so fond of my mother I could not keep from her, or avoid touching her at some of those periods, in consequence of which I was obliged to be kept out with her, in a little house made for that purpose, till offering was made, and then we were purified.

Though we had no places of public worship, we had priests and magicians, or wise men. I do not remember whether they had different offices, or whether they were united in the same persons, but they were held in great reverence by the people. They calculated our time, and foretold events, as their name imported, for we called them Ah-affoe-way-cah, which signifies calculators or yearly men, our year being called Ah-affoe. They wore their beards, and when they died they were succeeded by their sons. Most of their implements and things of value were interred along with them. Pipes and tobacco were also put into the grave with the corpse, which was always perfumed and ornamented, and animals were offered in sacrifice to them. None accompanied their funerals but those of the same profession or tribe. These buried them after sunset, and always returned from the grave by a different way from that which they went.

These magicians were also our doctors or physicians. They practised bleeding by cupping;[7] and were very successful in healing wounds and expelling poisons. They had likewise some extraordinary method of discovering jealousy, theft, and poisoning; the success of which no doubt they derived from their unbounded influence over the credulity and superstition of the people. I do not remember what those methods were, except that as to poisoning: I recollect an instance or two, which I hope it will not be deemed impertinent here to insert, as it may serve as a kind of specimen of the rest, and is still used by the negroes in the West Indies. A virgin had been poisoned, but it was not known by whom: the doctors ordered the corpse to be taken up by some persons, and carried to the grave. As soon as the bearers had raised it on their shoulders, they seemed seized with some[8] sudden impulse, and ran to and fro unable to stop themselves. At last, after having passed through a number of thorns and prickly bushes unhurt, the corpse fell from them close to a house, and defaced it in the fall; and, the owner being taken up, he immediately confessed the poisoning.[9]

The natives are extremely cautious about poison. When they buy any eatable the seller kisses it all round before the buyer, to shew him it is not poisoned; and the same is done when any meat or drink is presented, particularly to a stranger. We have serpents of different kinds, some of which are esteemed ominous when they appear in our houses, and these we never molest. I remember two of those ominous snakes, each of which was as thick as the calf of a man's leg, and in colour resembling a dolphin in the water, crept at different times into my mother's night-house, where I always lay with her, and coiled themselves into folds, and each time they crowed like a cock. I was desired by some of our wise men to touch these, that I might be interested in the good omens, which I did, for they were quite harmless, and would tamely suffer themselves to be handled; and then they were put into a large open earthen pan, and set on one side of the highway. Some of our snakes, however, were poisonous: one of them crossed the road one day when I was standing on it, and passed between my feet without offering to touch me, to the great surprise of many who saw it; and these incidents were accounted by the wise men, and therefore by my mother and the rest of the people, as remarkable omens in my favour.

Such is the imperfect sketch my memory has furnished me with of the manners and customs of a people among whom I first drew my breath. And here I cannot forbear suggesting what has long struck me very forcibly, namely, the strong analogy which even by this sketch, imperfect as it is, appears to prevail in the manners and customs of my countrymen and those of the Jews, before they reached the Land of Promise, and particularly the patriarchs[1]

7. Drawing blood with a heated glass vessel.

8. See also Leut. Matthew's Voyage, p. 123 [*Equiano's note*]. John Matthews's *A Voyage to the River Sierra Leone* (1788).

9. An instance of this kind happened at Montserrat in the West Indies in the year 1763. I then belonged to the Charming Sally, Capt. Doran.—The chief mate, Mr. Mansfield, and some of the crew being one day on shore, were present at the burying of a poisoned negro girl. Though they had often heard of the circumstance of the running in such cases, and had even seen it, they imagined it to be a trick of the corpse-bearers. The mate therefore desired two of the sailors to take up the coffin, and carry it to the grave. The sailors, who were all of the same opinion, readily obeyed; but they had scarcely raised it to their shoulders, before they began to run furiously about, quite unable to direct themselves, till, at last, without intention, they came to the hut of him who had poisoned the girl. The coffin then immediately fell from their shoulders against the hut, and damaged part of the wall. The owner of the hut was taken into custody on this, and confessed the poisoning.—I give this story as it was related by the mate and crew on their return to the ship. The credit which is due to it I leave with the reader [*Equiano's note*].

1. The forefathers of the Israelites, including Abraham, Isaac, Jacob, and Jacob's twelve sons. "Land of Promise": Canaan, which God promised to the ancient Israelites after their exodus from Egypt.

while they were yet in that pastoral state which is described in Genesis—an analogy, which alone would induce me to think that the one people had sprung from the other. Indeed this is the opinion of Dr. Gill,[2] who, in his commentary on Genesis, very ably deduces the pedigree of the Africans from Aster and Asra, the descendants of Abraham by Keturah his wife and concubine (for both these titles are applied to her). It is also comformable to the sentiments of Dr. John Clarke, formerly Dean of Sarum,[3] in his Truth of the Christian Religion: both these authors concur in ascribing to us this original. The reasonings of these gentlemen are still further confirmed by the scripture chronology; and if any further corroboration were required, this resemblance in so many respects is a strong evidence in support of the opinion. Like the Israelites in their primitive state, our government was conducted by our chiefs or judges, our wise men and elders; and the head of a family with us enjoyed a similar authority over his household with that which is ascribed to Abraham and the other patriarchs. The law of retaliation obtained almost universally with us as with them: and even their religion appeared to have shed upon us a ray of its glory, though broken and spent in its passage, or eclipsed by the cloud with which time, tradition, and ignorance might have enveloped it; for we had our circumcision (a rule I believe peculiar to that people:) we had also our sacrifices and burnt-offerings, our washings and purifications, on the same occasions as they had.

As to the difference of colour between the Eboan Africans and the modern Jews, I shall not presume to account for it. It is a subject which has engaged the pens of men of both genius and learning, and is far above my strength. The most able and Reverend Mr. T. Clarkson, however, in his much admired Essay on the Slavery and Commerce of the Human Species,[4] has ascertained the cause, in a manner that at once solves every objection on that account, and, on my mind at least, has produced the fullest conviction. I shall therefore refer to that performance for the theory,[5] contenting myself with extracting a fact as related by Dr. Mitchel.[6] "The Spaniards, who have inhabited America, under the torrid zone, for any time, are become as dark coloured as our native Indians of Virginia; of which *I myself have been a witness.*" There is also another instance of a Portuguese settlement at Mitomba, a river in Sierra Leona;[7] where the inhabitants are bred from a mixture of the first Portuguese discoverers with the natives, and are now become in their complexion, and in the woolly quality of their hair, *perfect negroes,* retaining however a smattering of the Portuguese language.

These instances, and a great many more which might be adduced, while they shew how the complexions of the same persons vary in different climates, it is hoped may tend also to remove the prejudice that some conceive against the natives of Africa on account of their colour. Surely the minds of the Spaniards did not change with their complexions! Are there not causes enough to which the apparent inferiority of an African may be ascribed, without limiting the goodness of God, and supposing he forbore to stamp understanding on certainly his own image, because "carved in ebony." Might

2. John Gill (1697–1771), English Baptist theologian.
3. The ecclesiastical name for Salisbury, England. John Clarke (1682–1757), mathematician and theologian, author of *The Truth of the Christian Religion* (1711).
4. Thomas Clarkson (1760–1846), antislavery agitator, wrote his essay in 1785.
5. Page 178 to 216 [*Equiano's note*].
6. Philos. Trans. No. 476, Set. 4, cited by Mr. Clarkson, p. 205 [*Equiano's note*].
7. A West African port for the Portuguese ivory and slave trade, later a colony established by British abolitionists for the resettlement of freed slaves. "Another instance": Same page [*Equiano's note*].

it not naturally be ascribed to their situation? When they come among Europeans, they are ignorant of their language, religion, manners, and customs. Are any pains taken to teach them these? Are they treated as men? Does not slavery itself depress the mind, and extinguish all its fire and every noble sentiment? But, above all, what advantages do not a refined people possess over those who are rude and uncultivated. Let the polished and haughty European recollect that his ancestors were once, like the Africans, uncivilized, and even barbarous. Did Nature make *them* inferior to their sons? and should *they too* have been made slaves? Every rational mind answers, No. Let such reflections as these melt the pride of their superiority into sympathy for the wants and miseries of their sable[8] brethren, and compel them to acknowledge, that understanding is not confined to feature or colour. If, when they look round the world, they feel exultation, let it be tempered with benevolence to others, and gratitude to God, "who hath made of one blood all nations of men for to dwell on all the face of the earth;[9] and whose wisdom is not our wisdom, neither are our ways his ways."[1]

Chapter II

I hope the reader will not think I have trespassed on his patience in introducing myself to him with some account of the manners and customs of my country. They had been implanted in me with great care, and made an impression on my mind, which time could not erase, and which all the adversity and variety of fortune I have since experienced served only to rivet and record; for, whether the love of one's country be real or imaginary, or a lesson of reason, or an instinct of nature, I still look back with pleasure on the first scenes of my life, though that pleasure has been for the most part mingled with sorrow.

I have already acquainted the reader with the time and place of my birth. My father, besides many slaves, had a numerous family, of which seven lived to grow up, including myself and a sister, who was the only daughter. As I was the youngest of the sons, I became, of course, the greatest favourite with my mother, and was always with her; and she used to take particular pains to form my mind. I was trained up from my earliest years in the art of war; my daily exercise was shooting and throwing javelins; and my mother adorned me with emblems, after the manner of our greatest warriors. In this way I grew up till I was turned the age of eleven, when an end was put to my happiness in the following manner:—Generally when the grown people in the neighbourhood were gone far in the fields to labour, the children assembled together in some of the neighbours' premises to play; and commonly some of us used to get up a tree to look out for any assailant, or kidnapper, that might come upon us; for they sometimes took those opportunities of our parents' absence to attack and carry off as many as they could seize. One day, as I was watching at the top of a tree in our yard, I saw one of those people come into the yard of our next neighbour but one, to kidnap, there being many stout young people in it. Immediately on this I gave the alarm of the rogue, and he was surrounded by the stoutest of them, who entangled him with cords, so that he could not escape till some of the grown people came and secured him. But alas! ere long it was my fate to be thus attacked, and to be carried off, when none of the grown people were nigh. One day, when all our people

8. Black.
9. Acts 17:26.
1. See Isaiah 55:8: "For my thoughts are not your thoughts, neither are your ways my ways, saith the Lord."

were gone out to their works as usual, and only I and my dear sister were left to mind the house, two men and a woman got over our walls, and in a moment seized us both, and, without giving us time to cry out, or make resistance, they stopped our mouths, and ran off with us into the nearest wood. Here they tied our hands, and continued to carry us as far as they could, till night came on, when we reached a small house, where the robbers halted for refreshment, and spent the night. We were then unbound, but were unable to take any food; and, being quite overpowered by fatigue and grief, our only relief was some sleep, which allayed our misfortune for a short time. The next morning we left the house, and continued travelling all the day. For a long time we had kept the woods, but at last we came into a road which I believed I knew. I had now some hopes of being delivered; for we had advanced but a little way before I discovered some people at a distance, on which I began to cry out for their assistance: but my cries had no other effect than to make them tie me faster and stop my mouth, and then they put me into a large sack. They also stopped my sister's mouth, and tied her hands; and in this manner we proceeded till we were out of the sight of these people. When we went to rest the following night they offered us some victuals;[2] but we refused it; and the only comfort we had was in being in one another's arms all that night, and bathing each other with our tears. But alas! we were soon deprived of even the small comfort of weeping together. The next day proved a day of greater sorrow than I had yet experienced; for my sister and I were then separated, while we lay clasped in each other's arms. It was in vain that we besought them not to part us; she was torn from me, and immediately carried away, while I was left in a state of distraction not to be described. I cried and grieved continually; and for several days I did not eat any thing but what they forced into my mouth. At length, after many days travelling, during which I had often changed masters, I got into the hands of a chieftain, in a very pleasant country. This man had two wives and some children, and they all used me extremely well, and did all they could to comfort me; particularly the first wife, who was something like my mother. Although I was a great many days journey from my father's house, yet these people spoke exactly the same language with us. This first master of mine, as I may call him, was a smith, and my principal employment was working his bellows, which were the same kind as I had seen in my vicinity. They were in some respects not unlike the stoves here in gentlemen's kitchens; and were covered over with leather, and in the middle of that leather a stick was fixed, and a person stood up, and worked it, in the same manner as is done to pump water out of a cask with a hand pump. I believe it was gold he worked, for it was of a lovely bright yellow colour, and was worn by the women on their wrists and ankles. I was there I suppose about a month, and they at last used to trust me some little distance from the house. This liberty I used in embracing every opportunity to inquire the way to my own home: and I also sometimes, for the same purpose, went with the maidens, in the cool of the evenings, to bring pitchers of water from the springs for the use of the house. I had also remarked where the sun rose in the morning, and set in the evening, as I had travelled along; and I had observed that my father's house was towards the rising of the sun. I therefore determined to seize the first opportunity of making my escape, and to shape my course for that quarter; for I was quite oppressed and weighed down by

2. Food.

grief after my mother and friends; and my love of liberty, ever great, was strengthened by the mortifying circumstance of not daring to eat with the free-born children, although I was mostly their companion. While I was projecting my escape, one day an unlucky event happened, which quite disconcerted my plan, and put an end to my hopes. I used to be sometimes employed in assisting an elderly woman slave to cook and take care of the poultry; and one morning, while I was feeding some chickens, I happened to toss a small pebble at one of them, which hit it on the middle and directly killed it. The old slave, having soon after missed the chicken, inquired after it; and on my relating the accident (for I told her the truth, because my mother would never suffer me to tell a lie) she flew into a violent passion, threatened that I should suffer for it; and, my master being out, she immediately went and told her mistress what I had done. This alarmed me very much, and I expected an instant flogging, which to me was uncommonly dreadful; for I had seldom been beaten at home. I therefore resolved to fly; and accordingly I ran into a thicket that was hard by, and hid myself in the bushes. Soon afterwards my mistress and the slave returned, and, not seeing me, they searched all the house, but not finding me, and I not making answer when they called to me, they thought I had run away, and the whole neighbourhood was raised in the pursuit of me. In that part of the country (as in ours) the houses and villages were skirted with woods, or shrubberies, and the bushes were so thick that a man could readily conceal himself in them, so as to elude the strictest search. The neighbours continued the whole day looking for me, and several times many of them came within a few yards of the place where I lay hid. I then gave myself up for lost entirely, and expected every moment, when I heard a rustling among the trees, to be found out, and punished by my master: but they never discovered me, though they were often so near that I even heard their conjectures as they were looking about for me; and I now learned from them, that any attempt to return home would be hopeless. Most of them supposed I had fled towards home; but the distance was so great, and the way so intricate, that they thought I could never reach it, and that I should be lost in the woods. When I heard this I was seized with a violent panic, and abandoned myself to despair. Night too began to approach, and aggravated all my fears. I had before entertained hopes of getting home, and I had determined when it should be dark to make the attempt; but I was now convinced it was fruitless, and I began to consider that, if possibly I could escape all other animals, I could not those of the human kind; and that, not knowing the way, I must perish in the woods. Thus was I like the hunted deer:

—Ev'ry leaf and ev'ry whisp'ring breath
Convey'd a foe, and ev'ry foe a death.[3]

I heard frequent rustlings among the leaves; and being pretty sure they were snakes I expected every instant to be stung by them. This increased my anguish, and the horror of my situation became now quite insupportable. I at length quitted the thicket, very faint and hungry, for I had not eaten or drank any thing all the day; and crept to my master's kitchen, from whence I set out at first, and which was an open shed, and laid myself down in the ashes with an anxious wish for death to relieve me from all my pains. I was scarcely awake in the morning when the old woman slave, who was the first up, came to light the fire, and saw me in the fire place. She was very much

3. From John Denham's *Cooper's Hill* (1642), lines 287–88.

surprised to see me, and could scarcely believe her own eyes. She now promised to intercede for me, and went for her master, who soon after came, and, having slightly reprimanded me, ordered me to be taken care of, and not to be ill-treated.

Soon after this my master's only daughter, and child by his first wife, sickened and died, which affected him so much that for some time he was almost frantic, and really would have killed himself, had he not been watched and prevented. However, in a small time afterwards he recovered, and I was again sold. I was now carried to the left of the sun's rising, through many different countries, and a number of large woods. The people I was sold to used to carry me very often, when I was tired, either on their shoulders or on their backs. I saw many convenient well-built sheds along the roads, at proper distances, to accommodate the merchants and travellers, who lay in those buildings along with their wives, who often accompany them; and they always go well armed.

From the time I left my own nation I always found somebody that understood me till I came to the sea coast. The languages of different nations did not totally differ, nor were they so copious as those of the Europeans, particularly the English. They were therefore easily learned; and, while I was journeying thus through Africa, I acquired two or three different tongues. In this manner I had been travelling for a considerable time, when one evening, to my great surprise, whom should I see brought to the house where I was but my dear sister! As soon as she saw me she gave a loud shriek, and ran into my arms—I was quite overpowered: neither of us could speak; but, for a considerable time, clung to each other in mutual embraces, unable to do any thing but weep. Our meeting affected all who saw us; and indeed I must acknowledge, in honour of those sable destroyers of human rights, that I never met with any ill treatment, or saw any offered to their slaves, except tying them, when necessary, to keep them from running away. When these people knew we were brother and sister they indulged us [to be] together; and the man, to whom I supposed we belonged, lay with us, he in the middle, while she and I held one another by the hands across his breast all night; and thus for a while we forgot our misfortunes in the joy of being together: but even this small comfort was soon to have an end; for scarcely had the fatal morning appeared, when she was again torn from me for ever! I was now more miserable, if possible, than before. The small relief which her presence gave me from pain was gone, and the wretchedness of my situation was redoubled by my anxiety after her fate, and my apprehensions lest her sufferings should be greater than mine, when I could not be with her to alleviate them. Yes, thou dear partner of all my childish sports! thou sharer of my joys and sorrows! happy should I have ever esteemed myself to encounter every misery for you, and to procure your freedom by the sacrifice of my own. Though you were early forced from my arms, your image has been always rivetted in my heart, from which neither *time nor fortune* have been able to remove it; so that, while the thoughts of your sufferings have damped my prosperity, they have mingled with adversity and increased its bitterness. To that Heaven which protects the weak from the strong, I commit the care of your innocence and virtues, if they have not already received their full reward, and if your youth and delicacy have not long since fallen victims to the violence of the African trader, the pestilential stench of a Guinea ship, the seasoning[4] in the European colonies, or the lash and lust of a brutal and unrelenting overseer.

4. Rigorous preparation for use. "Guinea": west coast of Africa (archaic).

I did not long remain after my sister. I was again sold, and carried through a number of places, till, after travelling a considerable time, I came to a town called Tinmah, in the most beautiful country I had yet seen in Africa. It was extremely rich, and there were many rivulets which flowed through it, and supplied a large pond in the centre of the town, where the people washed. Here I first saw and tasted cocoa-nuts, which I thought superior to any nuts I had ever tasted before; and the trees, which were loaded, were also interspersed amongst the houses, which had commodious shades adjoining, and were in the same manner as ours, the insides being neatly plastered and whitewashed. Here I also saw and tasted for the first time sugar-cane. Their money consisted of little white shells, the size of the finger nail. I was sold here for one hundred and seventy-two of them by a merchant who lived and brought me there. I had been about two or three days at his house, when a wealthy widow, a neighbour of his, came there one evening, and brought with her an only son, a young gentleman about my own age and size. Here they saw me; and, having taken a fancy to me, I was bought of the merchant, and went home with them. Her house and premises were situated close to one of those rivulets I have mentioned, and were the finest I ever saw in Africa: they were very extensive, and she had a number of slaves to attend her. The next day I was washed and perfumed, and when meal-time came I was led into the presence of my mistress, and ate and drank before her with her son. This filled me with astonishment; and I could scarce help expressing my surprise that the young gentleman should suffer me, who was bound, to eat with him who was free; and not only so, but that he would not at any time either eat or drink till I had taken first, because I was the eldest, which was agreeable to our custom. Indeed every thing here, and all their treatment of me, made me forget that I was a slave. The language of these people resembled ours so nearly, that we understood each other perfectly. They had also the very same customs as we. There were likewise slaves daily to attend us, while my young master and I with other boys sported with our darts and bows and arrows, as I had been used to do at home. In this resemblance to my former happy state I passed about two months; and I now began to think I was to be adopted into the family, and was beginning to be reconciled to my situation, and to forget by degrees my misfortunes, when all at once the delusion vanished; for, without the least previous knowledge, one morning early, while my dear master and companion was still asleep, I was wakened out of my reverie to fresh sorrow, and hurried away even amongst the uncircumcised.

Thus, at the very moment I dreamed of the greatest happiness, I found myself most miserable; and it seemed as if fortune wished to give me this taste of joy, only to render the reverie more poignant. The change I now experienced was as painful as it was sudden and unexpected. It was a change indeed from a state of bliss to a scene which is inexpressible by me, as it discovered to me an element I had never before beheld, and till then had no idea of, and wherein such instances of hardship and cruelty continually occurred as I can never reflect on but with horror.

All the nations and people I had hitherto passed through resembled our own in their manners, customs, and language: but I came at length to a country, the inhabitants of which differed from us in all those particulars. I was very much struck with this difference, especially when I came among a people who did not circumcise, and are without washing their hands. They cooked also in iron pots, and had European cutlasses and cross bows, which were unknown to us, and fought with their fists amongst themselves. Their women were not so modest as ours, for they ate, and drank, and slept, with their men. But, above all, I was amazed to see no sacrifices or offerings among them. In some of those places the people ornamented themselves with scars, and likewise filed their teeth very sharp. They wanted sometimes to ornament me in the same manner, but I would not suffer them; hoping that I might some time be among a people who did not thus disfigure themselves, as I thought they did. At last I came to the banks of a large river, which was covered with canoes, in which the people appeared to live with their household utensils and provisions of all kinds. I was beyond measure astonished at this, as I had never before seen any water larger than a pond or a rivulet: and my surprise was mingled with no small fear when I was put into one of these canoes, and we began to paddle and move along the river. We continued going on thus till night; and when we came to land, and made fires on the banks, each family by themselves, some dragged their canoes on shore, others stayed and cooked in theirs, and laid in them all night. Those on the land had mats, of which they made tents, some in the shape of little houses: in these we slept; and after the morning meal we embarked again and proceeded as before. I was often very much astonished to see some of the women, as well as the men, jump into the water, dive to the bottom, come up again, and swim about. Thus I continued to travel, sometimes by land, sometimes by water, through different countries and various nations, till, at the end of six or seven months after I had been kidnapped, I arrived at the sea coast. It would be tedious and uninteresting to relate all the incidents which befell me during this journey, and which I have not yet forgotten; of the various hands I passed through, and the manners and customs of all the different people among whom I lived: I shall therefore only observe, that in all the places where I was the soil was exceedingly rich; the pomkins, eadas, plantains, yams, etc., etc. were in great abundance, and of incredible size. There were also vast quantities of different gums, though not used for any purpose; and every where a great deal of tobacco. The cotton even grew quite wild; and there was plenty of red-wood.[5] I saw no mechanics whatever in all the way, except such as I have mentioned. The chief employment in all these countries was agriculture, and both the males and females, as with us, were brought up to it, and trained in the arts of war.

The first object which saluted my eyes when I arrived on the coast was the sea, and a slave ship, which was then riding at anchor, and waiting for its cargo. These filled me with astonishment, which was soon converted into terror when I was carried on board. I was immediately handled and tossed up to see if I were sound by some of the crew; and I was now persuaded that I had gotten into a world of bad spirits, and that they were going to kill me. Their complexions too differing so much from ours, their long hair, and the language they spoke, (which was very different from any I had ever heard) united to confirm me in this belief. Indeed such were the horrors of my views and fears at the moment, that, if ten thousand worlds had been my own, I would have freely parted with them all to have exchanged my condition with that of the meanest slave in my own country. When I looked round the ship too and saw a large furnace or copper boiling, and a multitude of black people of every description chained together, every one of their countenances expressing dejection and sorrow, I no longer doubted of my fate; and, quite overpowered with horror and anguish, I fell motionless on the deck and fainted. When I recovered a little I found some black people about

5. Probably mahogany.

me, who I believed were some of those who brought me on board, and had been receiving their pay; they talked to me in order to cheer me, but all in vain. I asked them if we were not to be eaten by those white men with horrible looks, red faces, and loose hair. They told me I was not; and one of the crew brought me a small portion of spirituous liquor in a wine glass; but, being afraid of him, I would not take it out of his hand. One of the blacks therefore took it from him and gave it to me, and I took a little down my palate, which, instead of reviving me, as they thought it would, threw me into the greatest consternation at the strange feeling it produced, having never tasted any such liquor before. Soon after this the blacks who brought me on board went off, and left me abandoned to despair. I now saw myself deprived of all chance of returning to my native country, or even the least glimpse of hope of gaining the shore, which I now considered as friendly; and I even wished for my former slavery in preference to my present situation, which was filled with horrors of every kind, still heightened by my ignorance of what I was to undergo. I was not long suffered to indulge my grief; I was soon put down under the decks, and there I received such a salutation in my nostrils as I had never experienced in my life: so that, with the loathsomeness of the stench, and crying together, I became so sick and low that I was not able to eat, nor had I the least desire to taste any thing. I now wished for the last friend, death, to relieve me; but soon, to my grief, two of the white men offered me eatables; and, on my refusing to eat, one of them held me fast by the hands, and laid me across I think the windlass, and tied my feet, while the other flogged me severely. I had never experienced any thing of this kind before; and although, not being used to the water, I naturally feared that element the first time I saw it, yet nevertheless, could I have got over the nettings, I would have jumped over the side, but I could not; and, besides, the crew used to watch us very closely who were not chained down to the decks, lest we should leap into the water: and I have seen some of these poor African prisoners most severely cut for attempting to do so, and hourly whipped for not eating. This indeed was often the case with myself. In a little time after, amongst the poor chained men, I found some of my own nation, which in a small degree gave ease to my mind. I inquired of these what was to be done with us; they gave me to understand we were to be carried to these white people's country to work for them. I then was a little revived, and thought, if it were no worse than working, my situation was not so desperate: but still I feared I should be put to death, the white people looked and acted, as I thought, in so savage a manner; for I had never seen among any people such instances of brutal cruelty; and this not only shewn towards us blacks, but also to some of the whites themselves. One white man in particular I saw, when we were permitted to be on deck, flogged so unmercifully with a large rope near the foremast, that he died in consequence of it; and they tossed him over the side as they would have done a brute. This made me fear these people the more; and I expected nothing less than to be treated in the same manner. I could not help expressing my fears and apprehensions to some of my countrymen: I asked them if these people had no country, but lived in this hollow place (the ship): they told me they did not, but came from a distant one. "Then," said I, "how comes it in all our country we never heard of them?" They told me because they lived so very far off. I then asked where were their women? had they any like themselves? I was told they had: "and why," said I, "do we not see them?" they answered, because they were left behind. I asked how the vessel could go? they told me they could not tell; but that there were cloths put upon the masts by the help of the ropes I saw, and then the vessel went on; and the white men had some spell or magic they put in the water when they liked in order to stop the vessel. I was exceedingly amazed at this account, and really thought they were spirits. I therefore wished much to be from amongst them, for I expected they would sacrifice me: but my wishes were vain; for we were so quartered that it was impossible for any of us to make our escape. While we stayed on the coast I was mostly on deck; and one day, to my great astonishment, I saw one of these vessels coming in with the sails up. As soon as the whites saw it, they gave a great shout, at which we were amazed; and the more so as the vessel appeared larger by approaching nearer. At last she came to an anchor in my sight, and when the anchor was let go I and my countrymen who saw it were lost in astonishment to observe the vessel stop; and were now convinced it was done by magic. Soon after this the other ship got her boats out, and they came on board of us, and the people of both ships seemed very glad to see each other. Several of the strangers also shook hands with us black people, and made motions with their hands, signifying I suppose we were to go to their country; but we did not understand them. At last, when the ship we were in had got in all her cargo, they made ready with many fearful noises, and we were all put under deck, so that we could not see how they managed the vessel. But this disappointment was the least of my sorrow. The stench of the hold while we were on the coast was so intolerably loathsome, that it was dangerous to remain there for any time, and some of us had been permitted to stay on the deck for the fresh air; but now that the whole ship's cargo were confined together, it became absolutely pestilential. The closeness of the place, and the heat of the climate, added to the number in the ship, which was so crowded that each had scarcely room to turn himself, almost suffocated us. This produced copious perspirations, so that the air soon became unfit for respiration, from a variety of loathsome smells, and brought on a sickness among the slaves, of which many died, thus falling victims to the improvident avarice, as I may call it, of their purchasers. This wretched situation was again aggravated by the galling of the chains, now become insupportable; and the filth of the necessary tubs,[6] into which the children often fell, and were almost suffocated. The shrieks of the women, and the groans of the dying, rendered the whole a scene of horror almost inconceivable. Happily perhaps for myself I was soon reduced so low here that it was thought necessary to keep me almost always on deck; and from my extreme youth I was not put in fetters. In this situation I expected every hour to share the fate of my companions, some of whom were almost daily brought upon deck at the point of death, which I began to hope would soon put an end to my miseries. Often did I think many of the inhabitants of the deep much more happy than myself. I envied them the freedom they enjoyed, and as often wished I could change my condition for theirs. Every circumstance I met with served only to render my state more painful, and heighten my apprehensions, and my opinion of the cruelty of the whites. One day they had taken a number of fishes; and when they had killed and satisfied themselves with as many as they thought fit, to our astonishment who were on the deck, rather than give any of them to us to eat as we expected, they tossed the remaining fish into the sea again, although we begged and prayed for some as well as we could, but in vain; and some of my countrymen, being pressed by hunger, took an opportunity, when they thought no one saw them, of trying to get a little privately; but they were discovered, and the

6. That is, human waste.

attempt procured them some very severe floggings. One day, when we had a smooth sea and moderate wind, two of my wearied countrymen who were chained together (I was near them at the time), preferring death to such a life of misery, somehow made through the nettings and jumped into the sea: immediately another quite dejected fellow, who, on account of his illness, was suffered to be out of irons, also followed their example; and I believe many more would very soon have done the same if they had not been prevented by the ship's crew, who were instantly alarmed. Those of us that were the most active were in a moment put down under the deck, and there was such a noise and confusion amongst the people of the ship as I never heard before, to stop her, and get the boat out to go after the slaves. However two of the wretches were drowned, but they got the other, and afterwards flogged him unmercifully for thus attempting to prefer death to slavery. In this manner we continued to undergo more hardships than I can now relate, hardships which are inseparable from this accursed trade. Many a time we were near suffocation from the want of fresh air, which we were often without for whole days together. This, and the stench of the necessary tubs, carried off many. During our passage I first saw flying fishes, which surprised me very much: they used frequently to fly across the ship, and many of them fell on the deck. I also now first saw the use of the quadrant;[7] I had often with astonishment seen the mariners make observations with it, and I could not think what it meant. They at last took notice of my surprise; and one of them, willing to increase it, as well as to gratify my curiosity, made me one day look through it. The clouds appeared to me to be land, which disappeared as they passed along. This heightened my wonder; and I was now more persuaded than ever that I was in another world, and that every thing about me was magic. At last we came in sight of the island of Barbadoes,[8] at which the whites on board gave a great shout, and made many signs of joy to us. We did not know what to think of this; but as the vessel drew nearer we plainly saw the harbour, and other ships of different kinds and sizes; and we soon anchored amongst them off Bridge Town.[9] Many merchants and planters now came on board, though it was in the evening. They put us in separate parcels, and examined us attentively. They also made us jump, and pointed to the land, signifying we were to go there. We thought by this we should be eaten by these ugly men, as they appeared to us; and, when soon after we were all put down under the deck again, there was much dread and trembling among us, and nothing but bitter cries to be heard all the night from these apprehensions, insomuch that at last the white people got some old slaves from the land to pacify us. They told us we were not to be eaten, but to work, and were soon to go on land, where we should see many of our country people. This report eased us much; and sure enough, soon after we were landed, there came to us Africans of all languages. We were conducted immediately to the merchant's yard, where we were all pent up together like so many sheep in a fold, without regard to sex or age. As every object was new to me every thing I saw filled me with surprise. What struck me first was that the houses were built with stories, and in every other respect different from those in Africa: but I was still more astonished on seeing people on horseback. I did not know what this could mean; and indeed I thought these people were full of nothing but

7. A navigation instrument used for measuring altitudes.
8. Or Barbados, the most easterly of the Caribbean islands.
9. The capital of Barbados.

magical arts. While I was in this astonishment one of my fellow prisoners spoke to a countryman of his about the horses, who said they were the same kind they had in their country. I understood them, though they were from a distant part of Africa, and I thought it odd I had not seen any horses there; but afterwards, when I came to converse with different Africans, I found they had many horses amongst them, and much larger than those I then saw. We were not many days in the merchant's custody before we were sold after their usual manner, which is this:—On a signal given, (as the beat of a drum) the buyers rush at once into the yard where the slaves are confined, and make choice of that parcel they like best. The noise and clamour with which this is attended, and the eagerness visible in the countenances of the buyers, serve not a little to increase the apprehensions of the terrified Africans, who may well be supposed to consider them as the ministers of that destruction to which they think themselves devoted. In this manner, without scruple, are relations and friends separated, most of them never to see each other again. I remember in the vessel in which I was brought over, in the men's apartment, there were several brothers, who, in the sale, were sold in different lots; and it was very moving on this occasion to see and hear their cries at parting. O, ye nominal Christians! might not an African ask you, learned you this from your God, who says unto you, Do unto all men as you would men should do unto you?[1] Is it not enough that we are torn from our country and friends to toil for your luxury and lust of gain? Must every tender feeling be likewise sacrificed to your avarice? Are the dearest friends and relations, now rendered more dear by their separation from their kindred, still to be parted from each other, and thus prevented from cheering the gloom of slavery with the small comfort of being together and mingling their sufferings and sorrows? Why are parents to lose their children, brothers their sisters, or husbands their wives? Surely this is a new refinement in cruelty, which, while it has no advantage to atone for it, thus aggravates distress, and adds fresh horrors even to the wretchedness of slavery.

From *Chapter III*

I now totally lost the small remains of comfort I had enjoyed in conversing with my countrymen; the women too, who used to wash and take care of me, were all gone different ways, and I never saw one of them afterwards.

I stayed in this island for a few days; I believe it could not be above a fortnight; when I, and some few more slaves, that were not saleable amongst the rest, from very much fretting, were shipped off in a sloop for North America. On the passage we were better treated than when we were coming from Africa, and we had plenty of rice and fat pork. We were landed up a river a good way from the sea, about Virginia county, where we saw few or none of our native Africans, and not one soul who could talk to me. I was a few weeks weeding grass, and gathering stones in a plantation; and at last all my companions were distributed different ways, and only myself was left. I was now exceedingly miserable, and thought myself worse off than any of the rest of my companions, for they could talk to each other, but I had no person to speak to that I could understand. In this state, I was constantly grieving and pining,

1. See Matthew 7.12: "Therefore all things whatsoever ye would that men should do to you, do ye even so to them."

and wishing for death rather than anything else. While I was in this plantation the gentleman, to whom I suppose the estate belonged, being unwell, I was one day sent for to his dwelling-house to fan him; when I came into the room where he was I was very much affrighted at some things I saw, and the more so as I had seen a black woman slave as I came through the house, who was cooking the dinner, and the poor creature was cruelly loaded with various kinds of iron machines; she had one particularly on her head, which locked her mouth so fast that she could scarcely speak; and could not eat nor drink. I was much astonished and shocked at this contrivance, which I afterwards learned was called the iron muzzle. Soon after I had a fan put in my hand, to fan the gentleman while he slept; and so I did indeed with great fear. While he was fast asleep I indulged myself a great deal in looking about the room, which to me appeared very fine and curious. The first object that engaged my attention was a watch which hung on the chimney, and was going. I was quite surprised at the noise it made, and was afraid it would tell the gentleman anything I might do amiss; and when I immediately after observed a picture hanging in the room, which appeared constantly to look at me, I was still more affrighted, having never seen such things as these before. At one time I thought it was something relative to magic; and not seeing it move I thought it might be some way the whites had to keep their great men when they died, and offer them libations as we used to do to our friendly spirits. In this state of anxiety I remained till my master awoke, when I was dismissed out of the room, to my no small satisfaction and relief; for I thought that these people were all made up of wonders. In this place I was called Jacob; but on board the *African Snow,* I was called Michael. I had been some time in this miserable, forlorn, and much dejected state, without having anyone to talk to, which made my life a burden, when the kind and unknown hand of the Creator (who in very deed leads the blind in a way they know not) now began to appear, to my comfort; for one day the captain of a merchant ship, called the *Industrious Bee,* came on some business to my master's house. This gentleman, whose name was Michael Henry Pascal, was a lieutenant in the royal navy, but now commanded this trading ship, which was somewhere in the confines of the county many miles off. While he was at my master's house it happened that he saw me, and liked me so well that he made a purchase of me. I think I have often heard him say he gave thirty or forty pounds sterling for me; but I do not now remember which. However, he meant me for a present to some of his friends in England: and as I was sent accordingly from the house of my then master (one Mr. Campbell) to the place where the ship lay; I was conducted on horseback by an elderly black man (a mode of travelling which appeared very odd to me). When I arrived I was carried on board a fine large ship, loaded with tobacco, etc., and just ready to sail for England. I now thought my condition much mended; I had sails to lie on, and plenty of good victuals to eat; and everybody on board used me very kindly, quite contrary to what I had seen of any white people before; I therefore began to think that they were not all of the same disposition. A few days after I was on board we sailed for England. I was still at a loss to conjecture my destiny. By this time, however, I could smatter a little imperfect English; and I wanted to know as well as I could where we were going. Some of the people of the ship used to tell me they were going to carry me back to my own country, and this made me very happy. I was quite rejoiced at the sound of going back; and thought if I should get home what wonders I should have to tell. But I was reserved for another fate, and was soon undeceived when we came within sight of the English coast. While I was on board this ship, my captain and master named me *Gustavus Vassa.*[2] I at that time began to understand him a little, and refused to be called so, and told him as well as I could that I would be called Jacob; but he said I should not, and still called me Gustavus: and when I refused to answer to my new name, which at first I did, it gained me many a cuff; so at length I submitted, and was obliged to bear the present name, by which I have been known ever since.

* * *

It was about the beginning of the spring 1757, when I arrived in England and I was near twelve years of age at that time. I was very much struck with the buildings and the pavement of the streets in Falmouth; and, indeed, every object I saw, filled me with new surprise. One morning, when I got upon deck, I saw it covered all over with the snow that fell over-night. As I had never seen anything of the kind before, I thought it was salt; so I immediately ran down to the mate and desired him, as well as I could, to come and see how somebody in the night had thrown salt all over the deck. He, knowing what it was, desired me to bring some of it down to him. Accordingly I took up a handful of it, which I found very cold indeed; and when I brought it to him he desired me to taste it. I did so, and I was surprised beyond measure. I then asked him what it was; he told me it was snow, but I could not in anywise understand him. He asked me if we had no such thing in my country; I told him, No. I then asked him the use of it, and who made it; he told me a great man in the heavens, called God. But here again I was to all intents and purposes at a loss to understand him; and the more so, when a little after I saw the air filled with it, in a heavy shower, which fell down on the same day. After this I went to church; and having never been at such a place before, I was again amazed at seeing and hearing the service. I asked all I could about it; and they gave me to understand it was worshipping God, who made us and all things. I was still at a great loss, and soon got into an endless field of inquiries, as well as I was able to speak and ask about things. However, my little friend Dick[3] used to be my best interpreter; for I could make free with him, and he always instructed me with pleasure. And from what I could understand by him of this God, and in seeing these white people did not sell one another as we did, I was much pleased; and in this I thought they were much happier than we Africans. I was astonished at the wisdom of the white people in all things I saw; but was amazed at their not sacrificing, or making any offerings, and eating with unwashed hands, and touching the dead. I likewise could not help remarking the particular slenderness of their women, which I did not at first like; and I thought they were not so modest and shamefaced as the African women.

I had often seen my master and Dick employed in reading; and I had a great curiosity to talk to the books, as I thought they did; and so to learn how all things had a beginning: for that purpose I have often taken up a book, and have talked to it, and then put my ears to it, when alone, in hopes it would answer me; and I have been very much concerned when I found it remained silent.

2. Gustavus Vassa became king of Sweden in 1523.

3. Richard Baxter, a white American youth whom Equiano met on his first voyage to England.

From *Chapter IV*

It was now between two and three years since I first came to England, a great part of which I had spent at sea; so that I became inured to that service, and began to consider myself as happily situated; for my master treated me always extremely well; and my attachment and gratitude to him were very great. From the various scenes I had beheld on ship-board, I soon grew a stranger to terror of every kind, and was, in that respect at least, almost an Englishman. I have often reflected with surprise that I never felt half the alarm at any of the numerous dangers I have been in, that I was filled with at the first sight of the Europeans, and at every act of theirs, even the most trifling, when I first came among them, and for some time afterwards. That fear, however, which was the effect of my ignorance, wore away as I began to know them. I could now speak English tolerably well, and I perfectly understood every thing that was said. I now not only felt myself quite easy with these new countrymen, but relished their society and manners. I no longer looked upon them as spirits, but as men superior to us; and therefore I had the stronger desire to resemble them; to imbibe their spirit, and imitate their manners; I therefore embraced every occasion of improvement; and every new thing that I observed I treasured up in my memory. I had long wished to be able to read and write; and for this purpose I took every opportunity to gain instruction, but had made as yet very little progress. However, when I went to London with my master, I had soon an opportunity of improving myself, which I gladly embraced. Shortly after my arrival, he sent me to wait upon the Miss Guerins, who had treated me with much kindness when I was there before; and they sent me to school.

While I was attending these ladies their servants told me I could not go to Heaven unless I was baptized. This made me very uneasy; for I had now some faint idea of a future state: accordingly I communicated my anxiety to the eldest Miss Guerin, with whom I was become a favourite, and pressed her to have me baptized; when to my great joy she told me I should. She had formerly asked my master to let me be baptized, but he had refused; however she now insisted on it; and he being under some obligation to her brother complied with her request; so I was baptized in St. Margaret's church, Westminster, in February 1759, by my present name.

* * *

1789

PHILLIS WHEATLEY
1753?–1784

Phillis Wheatley, the first African American to publish a book and the first to achieve an international reputation as a writer, has been one of the most controversial and enigmatic figures in the history of African American literature. She seems to have had little taste for controversy herself, but with a pen in her hand and a book

PROPOSALS

For Printing by SUBSCRIPTION,

A Collection of POEMS, wrote at several times, and upon various occasions, by PHILLIS, a Negro Girl, from the Strength of her own Genius, it being but a few Years since she came to this Town an uncultivated Barbarian from *Africa*. The Poems having been seen and read by the best Judges, who think them well worthy of the Publick View; and upon critical examination, they find that the declared Author was capable of writing them.

The Order in which they were penned, together with the Occasion, are as follows;

On the Death of the Rev. Dr. *Sewell*, when sick, 1765.—On virtue, 1766.—On two Friends, who were cast away, do. To the University of Cambrige, 1767.——An Address to the Atheist, do.——An Address to the Deist, do.——On America, 1768.——On the KING, do.——On Friendship, do.——Thoughts on being brought from Africa to America, do.——On the Nuptials of Mr. *Spence* to Miss *Hooper*, do. On the Hon. Commodore Hood, on his pardoning a Deserter, 1769.——On the Death of the Reverend Dr. *Sewell*, do.—— On the Death of Master *Seider*, who was killed by *Ebenezer Richardson*, 1770.——On the Death of the Rev. *George Whitefield*, do.——On the Death of a young Miss, aged 5 years, do. On the Arrival of the Ships of War, and landing of the Troops.——On the Affray in King-Street, on the Evening of the 5th of March.——On the death of a young Gentleman. To *Samuel Quincy*, Esq; a Panegyrick.——To a Lady on her coming to America for her Health.——To Mrs. *Leonard*, on the Death of her Husband.——To Mrs. Boylston and Children, on the Death of her Son and their Brother.——To a Gentleman and Lady on the Death of their Son, aged 9 Months.——To a Lady on her remarkable Deliverance in a Hurricane.——To *James Sullivan*, Esq; and Lady on the Death of her Brother and Sister, and a Child *Avis*, aged 12 Months.——*Goliah* of Gath.——On the Death of Dr. *Samuel Marshall*.

It is supposed they will make one small Octavo Volume, and will contain about 200 Pages.

They will be printed on Demy Paper, and beautiful Types.

The Price to Subscribers, handsomely bound and lettered, will be Four Shillings.——Stiched in blue, Three Shillings.

It is hoped Encouragement will be given to this Publication, as a reward to a very uncommon Genius, at present a Slave.

The Work will be put to the Press as soon as three Hundred Copies are subscribed for, and and shall be published with all Speed.

Subscriptions are taken in by E. RUSSELL, in Marlborough Street.

This proposal to print Wheatley's poems ran in early February 1772 in *The Censor*, a weekly newspaper published in Boston. The printing would be financed by subscription, meaning that those who paid three or four shillings would receive a copy upon publication. This is the first document to state that Wheatley's poems were submitted to "critical examination" by "the best judges," who found them "well worthy" of publication.

Etching of an ink portrait of Wheatley by African American painter Scipio Moorhead (fl. 1773) on the frontispiece to *Poems on Various Subjects, Religious and Moral* (1773).

in her name, Wheatley became, inevitably, a point of contention for others. Born south of Senegambia in West Africa and brought to North America in 1761 to be enslaved, Wheatley grew up in a fixed and prejudged position in the white social order. She was the alien, the dependent, the talking chattel. But before she was a teenager Wheatley decided, on her own, to add to the list of her predetermined social identities—the Negro, the woman, the slave—a new name, that of poet. Ever since that decision, the question of how to interpret and evaluate Wheatley the poet in light of her status as an enslaved Black woman in eighteenth-century New England has been the critical crux, the first order of business, for students of Wheatley and the beginnings of African American literature.

The mere fact of an African-born enslaved woman's writing poetry in English, her adopted language, must have been stunning news to whites who encountered *Poems on Various Subjects, Religious and Moral by Phillis Wheatley, Negro Servant to Mr. John Wheatley, of Boston, in New England* when it first appeared in London in September 1773. Since the revolution in European thought and expression known as the Enlightenment, the assumption among even the educated white elite was that dark-skinned Africans were incapable of the highest forms of civilization, such as poetic expression and mathematical calculation, and were, therefore, fit for enslavement by their supposed superiors in Europe. To the whites of Europe and the Americas, writing provided demonstrable evidence of reason. Creative writing, of which poetry was considered the highest expression, constituted indisputable proof of genius. Because Europeans knew little about the written literatures of Africa and considered the oral traditions of the continent sub-literary, slavery's defenders claimed that Blacks lacked the imagination, originality, and vision to qualify as fully human, the equals of whites. Wheatley's landmark volume of poetry challenged these prejudices on its title page alone. How could poems, especially serious verse on profound matters of the spirit, be written by a "Negro" and a "servant"? "It was not natural," twentieth-century African American poet June Jordan ironically observed in a tribute to the literary foremother she called "Phillis Miracle." Because Wheatley wrote her poems and saw to their publication, exploitative assumptions about the African's "nature" would never again be so easy to maintain in European and American letters.

The white sponsors of *Poems on Various Subjects,* chiefly the poet's enslaver, John Wheatley, a respected and well-to-do Boston merchant, realized that publishing Phillis's book represented an act of potentially disturbing intervention into an established literary and cultural tradition. White readers discovering the unprecedented example of an enslaved Black woman poet would not be satisfied merely to read and ponder her verse. They would have to be convinced that it was truly hers;

they would require an explanation as to how and why she had taken to writing in the first place. Thus *Poems on Various Subjects* offers its reader several introductory documents designed to authenticate Phillis Wheatley and her poetry and to legitimate her literary motives. These prefatory materials helped establish a convention, a kind of interracial literary etiquette, that white readers soon came to expect when encountering an African American author. The authenticating documents that preface Wheatley's poems attest to the extent of the challenge facing the emerging African American writer, when even her friends and sponsors could not see how a Black writer's work could speak for itself without first being spoken for by whites.

Among the documents that introduce *Poems on Various Subjects* is a short biographical sketch of the poet written by Nathaniel Wheatley and signed by his father, John Wheatley. John knew nothing of the personal history of the frail girl whom he purchased on July 11, 1761, from the human cargo transported from West Africa aboard the slave ship *Phillis*. Judging the child "between seven and eight years of age," John turned Phillis over to his wife, Susanna, to serve as her personal maid. Responding to early indications of intellectual precociousness in Phillis, the Wheatley family encouraged her to study the Bible and to read English and translated Latin literature as well as history and geography. After only four years' exposure to the English language, Phillis began to write poetry, which Susanna encouraged her to continue. Phillis's first published poem appeared in a Newport, Rhode Island newspaper in 1767. Impressed by the Black teenager's literary dedication and anxious about her delicate health, the Wheatleys reduced Phillis's work obligations to relatively light duties around the house.

In the fall of 1770 Phillis Wheatley earned her first extensive fame as a poet with an elegy on the death of the Reverend George Whitefield, an internationally popular Methodist evangelist. Phillis boldly sent a copy of the often-reprinted poem to Selina Hastings, the Countess of Huntingdon, with whom Susanna Wheatley had a regular correspondence. After publishing several more well-received elegies in broadsides and newspapers in North America and England, Phillis sailed to England in the spring of 1773 to see through to publication a volume of her poetry financed by the countess's patronage. In London the poet received a warm welcome from such dignitaries as Benjamin Franklin, Granville Sharp, a leading English abolitionist, and Sir Brook Watson, a future mayor of London. Susanna Wheatley's serious illness required Phillis's return to Boston a little more than a month before *Poems on Various Subjects* came out from a British publisher. Soon after her arrival in Boston in September 1773, and probably at the strong urging of Phillis backed by her friends in England, John Wheatley emancipated the twenty-year-old poet made famous by her unprecedented book.

Phillis Wheatley remained in her former enslavers' household for the next five years, attending to Susanna and John until their deaths in 1774 and 1778, respectively. The poet's letters from this time acknowledge her continuing regard for the Wheatley family and her keen interest in the business side of publishing poetry. An unusually forthright statement of her opposition to slavery, originally included in a 1774 personal letter, was reprinted in at least eleven New England newspapers. As popular agitation against British rule mounted into cries for revolution, Wheatley undertook patriotic poetry as a way to affirm her allegiance to the cause of liberty. In October 1775, while living in Providence, Rhode Island, where both Nathaniel Wheatley and his twin sister, Mary Wheatley Lathrop, had moved during the British occupation of Boston, Phillis wrote to George Washington, commander in chief of the American Revolutionary Army, enclosing a poem of praise and encouragement. General Washington acknowledged receipt of the poem and invited the poet to visit him at his headquarters in Cambridge. Whether she did so is not known.

Soon after John Wheatley died, Phillis Wheatley married a free Black man, John Peters, on November 26, 1778. Formerly enslaved, Peters had been successful in business, but in the wake of the American Revolution, his fortunes soured. The Peters family had at least one child but none survived early childhood. As the family gradually descended into poverty, Wheatley tried to publish a new volume of poetry. In 1779 she published a set of "Proposals" for the volume, but the project failed to attract subscribers. In the last year of her life, the poet published two elegies and "Liberty and Peace," a tribute to the triumphant American Revolution. However, her attempt in September 1784 to secure financial backing for a collection of her poems was unsuccessful. On December 5, 1784, Phillis Wheatley Peters died, probably of complications from asthma, on the outskirts of Boston. An American edition of *Poems on Various Subjects* was not published until two years after her death.

The literary reputation of Phillis Wheatley rests primarily on the thirty-eight poems in *Poems on Various Subjects.* Composed largely of neoclassical occasional and elegiac verse in the heroic couplet form popularized by Alexander Pope, *Poems* testifies to Wheatley's devout Christianity, her knowledge of the classic Greek, Latin, and English poets, and her desire to write a poetry that addressed current events and prominent people of the day as well as weighty life-and-death matters. In general, reviewers of *Poems* complimented Wheatley on an achievement that promised much from a poet barely out of her teens. As the abolitionist movement progressed in the first half of the nineteenth century, Wheatley became almost an icon, a model of native "African genius," proof positive of "the capacity of the African's intellect for improvement." But Wheatley the sociological symbol gradually eclipsed Wheatley the individual poet in the nineteenth century.

Since the twentieth-century revival of scholarly interest in her work, Wheatley's poems have sometimes been criticized for failing to live up to standards of self-expressiveness and political engagement that seem appropriate expectations of poetry today but were not nearly so aesthetically acceptable in her own time. To some readers Wheatley's poetry seems conventional and conformist; to others it has a detached correctness that lacks feeling. Her harshest critics have faulted Wheatley for failing to use her gifts in the service of antislavery or to identify herself plainly enough with African American people and their sociopolitical aspirations. Wheatley's defenders maintain that her poetry is a good deal more politically subversive and individually expressive than it appears at first glance. Some of Wheatley's most overtly political and antislavery writings, which she aimed to include in her second volume of poems, remained unpublished during her lifetime. In one of these poems, an unpublished elegy "On the Death of General Wooster," a Revolutionary War hero, Wheatley foresaw an America blessed with "freedom's charms" once it had rejected the "disgrace" of holding "in bondage Afric's blameless race."

Wherever critical debates over Wheatley lead, it remains important to remember the task that Wheatley had before her when she undertook a career as a Black woman poet in a white man's country. Wheatley had first to write her way *into* American literature before she or any other Black writer could claim a special mission and purpose for an *African* American literature. She had no models other than European American ones for her poetry. She could not assume that her white readers would want to know what an enslaved woman thought or felt unless she could demonstrate her capacity to express her ideas and feelings in a manner sanctioned by the dominant culture. In response to these conditions, Wheatley adopted a literary persona and style that affirmed her seriousness as an African American artist and created a precedent on which subsequent Black poets could build with confidence. No single writer has contributed more to the founding of African American literature.

From Poems on Various Subjects, Religious and Moral

Preface

The following Poems were written originally for the Amusement of the Author, as they were the products of her leisure Moments. She had no Intention ever to have published them; nor would they now have made their Appearance, but at the Importunity of many of her best, and most generous Friends; to whom she considers herself, as under the greatest Obligations.

As her Attempts in Poetry are now sent into the World, it is hoped the Critic will not severely censure their Defects; and we presume they have too much Merit to be cast aside with Contempt, as worthless and trifling Effusions.

As to the Disadvantages she has laboured under, with Regard to Learning, nothing needs to be offered, as her Master's Letter in the following Page will sufficiently shew the Difficulties in this Respect she had to encounter.

With all their Imperfections, the Poems are now humbly submitted to the Perusal of the Public.

[Letter Sent by the Author's Master to the Publisher]

Phillis was brought from *Africa* to *America* in the Year 1761, between Seven and Eight Years of Age. Without any Assistance from School Education, and by only what she was taught in the Family, she, in sixteen Months Time from her Arrival, attained the English Language, to which she was an utter Stranger before, to such a Degree, as to read any, the most difficult Parts of the Sacred Writings, to the great Astonishment of all who heard her.

As to her Writing, her own Curiosity led her to it; and this she learnt in so short a Time, that in the Year 1765, she wrote a Letter to the Rev. Mr. Occom,[1] the *Indian* Minister, while in *England*.

She has a great Inclination to learn the Latin Tongue, and has made some Progress in it. This Relation is given by her Master who bought her, and with whom she now lives.

John Wheatley

Boston, Nov. 14, 1772.

To the Publick

As it has been repeatedly suggested to the Publisher, by Persons, who have seen the Manuscript, that Numbers would be ready to suspect they were not really the Writings of PHILLIS, he has procured the following attestation, from the most respectable Characters in *Boston*, that none might have the least Ground for Disputing their *Original*.

1. Samson Occom (1723–1792), a member of the Mohegan nation who was ordained a Presbyterian minister.

We whose Names are under-written, do assure the World, that the POEMS specified in the following Page, were (as we verily believe) written by PHILLIS, a young Negro Girl, who was but a few Years since, brought an uncultivated Barbarian from *Africa*, and has ever since been, and now is, under the Disadvantage of serving as a Slave in a Family in this Town. She has been examined by some of the best Judges, and is thought qualified to write them.

His Excellency Thomas Hutchinson,[1] *Governor*

The Hon. Andrew Oliver, *Lieutenant-Governor.*
The Hon. Thomas Hubbard,
The Hon. John Erving,
The Hon. James Pitts,
The Hon. Harrison Gray,
The Hon. James Bowdoin,
John Hancock, *Esq;*
Joseph Green, *Esq;*
Richard Carey *Esq;*
The Rev. Charles Chauncy *D.D.*
The Rev. Mather Byles *D.D.*
The Rev. Ed. Pemberton *D.D.*
The Rev. Andrew Elliot *D.D.*
The Rev. Samuel Cooper *D.D.*
The Rev. Mr. Samuel Mather,
The Rev. Mr. Joon Moorhead,
Mr. John Wheatley, *her Master.*

N.B. The original Attestations, signed by the above Gentlemen, may be seen by applying to *Archibald Bell,* Bookseller, No. 8, *Aldgate-Street.*

1773

To Mæcenas[1]

Mæcenas, you, beneath the myrtle[2] shade,
Read o'er what poets sung, and shepherds play'd.
What felt those poets but you feel the same?
Does not your soul possess the sacred flame?
Their noble strains your equal genius shares
In softer language, and diviner airs.

While *Homer*[3] paints lo! circumfus'd in air,
Celestial Gods in mortal forms appear;
Swift as they move hear each recess rebound,
Heav'n quakes, earth trembles, and the shores resound.
Great Sire of verse, before my mortal eyes,
The lightnings blaze across the vaulted skies,
And, as the thunder shakes the heav'nly plains,
A deep-felt horror thrills through all my veins.
When gentler strains demand they graceful song,
The length'ning line moves languishing along.
When great *Patroclus* courts *Achilles'*[4] aid,

1. Hutchinson (1711–1780), governor of Massachusetts from 1771 to 1774. The following list includes the names of some of the most prominent political and religious leaders in Boston.
1. A Roman aristocrat (74–8 B.C.E.) who befriended and supported the poets Horace and Virgil.
2. An evergreen held sacred to the worship of Venus, the Roman goddess of love.
3. The epic poet of ancient Greece.
4. The hero of the Greeks in Homer's *Iliad*. Patroclus was his favorite companion.

The grateful tribute of my tears is paid;
Prone on the shore he feels the pangs of love,
And stern *Pelides*[5] tend'rest passions move.

Great *Maro's*[6] strain in heav'nly numbers flows,
The *Nine*[7] inspire, and all the bosom glows.
O could I rival thine and *Virgil's* page,
Or claim the *Muses* with the *Mantuan*[8] Sage;
Soon the same beauties should my mind adorn,
And the same ardors in my soul should burn:
Then should my song in bolder notes arise,
And all my numbers pleasingly surprize;
But here I sit, and mourn a grov'ling mind,
That fain would mount, and ride upon the wind.

Not you, my friend, these plaintive strains become,
Not you, whose bosom is the *Muses* home;
When they from tow'ring *Helicon*[9] retire,
They fan in you the bright immortal fire,
But I less happy, cannot raise the song,
The fault'ring music dies upon my tongue.

The happier *Terence*[1] all the choir inspir'd,
His soul replenish'd, and his bosom fir'd;
But say, ye *Muses,* why this partial grace,
To one alone of *Afric's* sable° race; *black*
From age to age transmitting thus his name
With the first glory in the rolls of fame?

Thy virtues, great *Mæcenas!* shall be sung
In praise of him, from whom those virtues sprung;
While blooming wreaths around thy temples spread,
I'll snatch a laurel[2] from thine honour'd head,
While you indulgent smile upon the deed.

As long as *Thames*[3] in streams majestic flows,
Or *Naiads*[4] in their oozy beds repose,
While Phœbus[5] reigns above the starry train,
While bright *Aurora*[6] purples o'er the main,
So long, great Sir, the muse thy praise shall sing,
So long thy praise shall make *Parnassus*[7] ring:
Then grant, *Mæcenas,* they paternal rays,
Hear me propitious; and defend my lays.° *songs*

1773

5. That is, Achilles, son of Peleus.
6. The family name of the Roman epic poet Virgil.
7. That is, the nine Muses, Greek goddesses of literature and the arts.
8. Mantua was thought to be the birthplace of Virgil.
9. Mount Helicon in Greece, the legendary home of the Muses.
1. He was an *African* by birth [*Wheatley's note*]. Terence was a celebrated Roman comic dramatist of the 2nd century B.C.E.
2. Emblem of honor and distinction.
3. A river that runs through London.
4. In Greek folklore, nymphs (fairylike women) of springs, rivers, and lakes.
5. That is, Apollo, Greek god of the sun.
6. The Roman goddess of the dawn.
7. A mountain in Greece associated with the worship of Apollo and the nine Muses, Greek deities of inspiration and artistic creation.

To the University of Cambridge,° in New-England *Harvard*

While an intrinsic ardor prompts to write,
The muses promise to assist my pen;
'Twas not long since I left my native shore
The land of errors, and *Egyptian* gloom:
Father of mercy, 'twas thy gracious hand
Brought me in safety from those dark abodes.

Students, to you 'tis giv'n to scan the heights
Above, to traverse the ethereal° space, *heavenly*
And mark the systems of revolving worlds.
Still more, ye sons of science ye receive
The blissful news by messengers from heav'n,
How *Jesus'* blood for your redemption flows.
See him with hands out-stretcht upon the cross;
Immense compassion in his bosom glows;
He hears revilers, nor resents their scorn:
What matchless mercy in the Son of God!
When the whole human race by sin had fall'n,
He deign'd to die that they might rise again,
And share with him in the sublimest skies,
Life without death, and glory without end.

Improve your privileges while they stay,
Ye pupils, and each hour redeem, that bears
Or good or bad report of you to heav'n.
Let sin, that baneful evil to the soul,
By you be shunn'd, nor once remit your guard;
Suppress the deadly serpent in its egg.
Ye blooming plants of human race devine,
An *Ethiop*° tells you 'tis your greatest foe; *black African*
Its transient sweetness turns to endless pain,
And in immense perdition° sinks the soul. *eternal damnation*

1773

On Being Brought from Africa to America

'Twas mercy brought me from my *Pagan* land;
Taught my benighted soul to understand
That there's a God, that there's a *Saviour* too:
Once I redemption neither sought nor knew.
Some view our sable° race with scornful eye; *black*
"Their colour is a diabolic die."
Remember, *Christians, Negros,* black as *Cain,*[1]
May be refin'd, and join th' angelic train.

1773

1. Because he murdered his brother Abel (Genesis 4:1–15), Cain is said to have been "marked" by God. Some readers of the Bible thought that Cain thereby became the first Black man.

On the Death of the Rev. Mr. George Whitefield[1] 1770

Hail, happy saint, on thine immortal throne,
Possest of glory, life, and bliss unknown;
We hear no more the music of thy tongue,
Thy wonted° auditories cease to throng. *accustomed*
Thy sermons in unequall'd accents flow'd,
And ev'ry bosom with devotion glow'd;
Thou didst in strains of eloquence refin'd
Inflame the heart, and captivate the mind.
Unhappy we the setting sun deplore,
So glorious once, but ah! it shines no more.

Behold the prophet in his tow'ring flight!
He leaves the earth for heav'n's unmeasur'd height,
And worlds unknown receive him from our sight.
There *Whitefield* wings with rapid course his way,
And sails to *Zion*[2] through vast seas of day.
Thy pray'rs, great saint, and thine incessant cries
Have pierc'd the bosom of thy native skies.
Thou moon hast seen, and all the stars of light,
How he has wrestled with his God by night.
He pray'd that grace in ev'ry heart might dwell,
He long'd to see *America* excel;
He charg'd° its youth that ev'ry grace divine *exhorted*
Should with full lustre in their conduct shine;
That Saviour,° which his soul did first receive, *Christ*
The greatest gift that ev'n a God can give,
He freely offer'd to the num'rous throng,
That on his lips with list'ning pleasure hung.

"Take him, ye wretched, for your only good,
"Take him ye starving sinners, for your food;
"Ye thirsty, come to this life-giving stream;
"Ye preachers, take him for your joyful theme;
"Take him my dear *Americans,* he said,
"Be your complaints on his kind bosom laid:
"Take him, ye *Africans,* he longs for you,
"*Impartial Saviour* is his title due:
"Wash'd in the fountain of redeeming blood,
"You shall be sons, and kings, and priests to God."[3]

Great *Countess,*[4] we *Americans* revere
Thy name, and mingle in thy grief sincere;
New England deeply feels, the *Orphans* mourn,
Their more than father will no more return.

1. An English Methodist evangelist (1714–1770), one of the most famous revivalists in America and Great Britain during the 18th century. This was Wheatley's first published poem, and it gave her considerable notoriety.
2. Here, the heavenly city of God.
3. In a version of this poem published in London in 1771, this line reads "He'll make you free, and King and Priests to God."
4. The Countess of *Huntingdon,* to whom Mr. *Whitefield* was Chaplain [*Wheatley's note*]. Selina Shirley Hastings (1707–1791), Countess of Huntingdon, was a strong supporter of Whitefield. Wheatley visited her in England in 1773. and dedicated her *Poems* to the countess.

But, though arrested by the hand of death,
Whitefield no more exerts his lab'ring breath,
Yet let us view him in th' eternal skies,
Let ev'ry heart to this bright vision rise;
While the tomb safe retains its sacred trust,
Till life divine re-animates his dust.

1773

To the Right Honourable William,[1] Earl of Dartmouth, His Majesty's Principal Secretary of State for North-America, Etc.

Hail, happy day, when, smiling like the morn,
Fair *Freedom* rose *New-England* to adorn:
The northern clime[2] beneath her genial ray, *region*
Dartmouth, congratulates thy blissful sway:
Elate with hope her race no longer mourns,
Each soul expands, each grateful bosom burns.
While in thine hand with pleasure we behold
The silken reins, and *Freedom's* charms unfold.
Long lost to realms beneath the northern skies
She shines supreme, while hated *faction* dies:
Soon as appear'd the *Goddess*° long desir'd, *freedom*
Sick at the view, she[2] languish'd and expir'd;
Thus from the splendors of the morning light
The owl in sadness seeks the caves of night.

No more, *America*, in mournful strain
Of wrongs, and grievance unredress'd complain,
No longer shalt thou dread the iron chain,
Which wanton *Tyranny* with lawless hand
Had made, and with it meant t' enslave the land.

Should you, my lord, while you peruse my song,
Wonder from whence my love of *Freedom* sprung,
Whence flow these wishes for the common good,
By feeling hearts alone best understood,
I, young in life, by seeming cruel fate
Was snatch'd from *Afric's* fancy'd happy seat:[3]
What pangs excruciating must molest,
What sorrows labour in my parent's breast?
Steel'd was that soul and by no misery mov'd
That from a father seiz'd his babe belov'd:
Such, such my case. And can I then but pray
Others may never feel tyrannic sway?

1. William Legge, Lord Dartmouth, was appointed secretary in charge of the American colonies in August 1772. Wheatley hoped that Dartmouth would prove more amenable to the grievances of the colonists.
2. That is, faction (internal conflict).
3. Abode or home. "Fancy'd": imagined.

For favours past, great Sir, our thanks are due,
And thee we ask thy favours to renew,
Since in thy pow'r, as in thy will before,
To sooth the griefs, which thou did'st once deplore.
May heav'nly grace the sacred sanction give
To all thy works, and thou for ever live
Not only on the wings of fleeting *Fame*,
Though praise immortal crowns the patriot's name,
But to conduct to heav'ns refulgent fane,° *shining temple*
May fiery coursers° sweep th' ethereal plain, *horses*
And bear thee upwards to that blest abode,
Where, like the prophet,[4] thou shalt find thy God.

1773

On Imagination

Thy various works, imperial queen, we see,
How bright their forms! how deck'd with pomp by thee!
Thy wond'rous acts in beauteous order stand,
And all attest how potent is thine hand.

From *Helicon's* refulgent heights attend,
Ye sacred choir,[1] and my attempts befriend:
To tell her glories with a faithful tongue,
Ye blooming graces, triumph in my song.

Now here, now there, the roving *Fancy* flies,
Till some lov'd object strikes her wand'ring eyes,
Whose silken fetters all the senses bind,
And soft captivity involves the mind.

Imagination! who can sing thy force?
Or who describe the swiftness of thy course?
Soaring through air to find the bright abode,
Th' empyreal° palace of the thund'ring God, *celestial*
We on thy pinions can surpass the wind,
And leave the rolling universe behind:
From star to star the mental optics rove,
Measure the skies, and range the realms above.
There in one view we grasp the mighty whole,
Or with new worlds amaze th' unbounded soul.

Though *Winter* frowns to *Fancy's* raptur'd eyes
The fields may flourish, and gay scenes arise;
The frozen deeps may break their iron bands,
And bid their waters murmur o'er the sands.
Fair *Flora*[2] may resume her fragrant reign,

4. Elijah, who was carried to heaven in a chariot of fire (2 Kings 2:11).
1. That is, the nine Muses, whose legendary home was Mount Helicon, in Greece.
2. Roman goddess of fertility and flowers.

And with her flow'ry riches deck the plain;
Sylvanus[3] may diffuse his honours round,
And all the forest may with leaves be crown'd:
Show'rs may descend, and dews their gems disclose,
And nectar sparkle on the blooming rose.

Such is thy pow'r, nor are thine orders vain,
O thou the leader of the mental train:
In full perfection all thy works are wrought,
And thine the sceptre o'er the realms of thought.
Before thy throne the subject-passions bow,
Of subject-passions sov'reign ruler Thou,
At thy command joy rushes on the heart,
And through the glowing veins the spirits dart.

Fancy might now her silken pinions try
To rise from earth, and sweep th' expanse on high;
From *Tithon's* bed now might *Aurora*[4] rise,
Her cheeks all glowing with celestial dies,° *colors*
While a pure stream of light o'erflows the skies.
The monarch of the day I might behold,
And all the mountains tipt with radiant gold,
But I reluctant leave the pleasing views,
Which *Fancy* dresses to delight the *Muse;*
Winter austere forbids me to aspire,
And northern tempests damp the rising fire;
They chill the tides of *Fancy's* flowing sea,
Cease then, my song, cease the unequal lay.° *ballad*

1773

To S. M.[1] a Young *African* Painter, on Seeing His Works

To show the lab'ring bosom's deep intent,
And thought in living characters to paint,
When first thy pencil did those beauties give,
And breathing figures learnt from thee to live,
How did those prospects give my soul delight,
A new creation rushing on my sight?
Still, wond'rous youth! each noble path pursue,
On deathless glories fix thine ardent view:
Still may the painter's and the poet's fire
To aid thy pencil, and thy verse conspire!
And may the charms of each seraphic° theme *angelic*
Conduct thy footsteps to immortal fame!
High to the blissful wonders of the skies

3. Roman goddess of the forest.
4. Roman goddess of dawn, who, according to Greek myth, loved Tithonus, a Trojan.

1. Scipio Moorhead, enslaved by Reverend John Moorhead of Boston.

Elate thy soul, and raise thy wishful eyes.
Thrice happy, when exalted to survey
That splendid city, crown'd with endless day,
Whose twice six gates on radiant hinges ring:
Celestial *Salem*[2] blooms in endless spring.

Calm and serene thy moments glide along,
And may the muse inspire each future song!
Still, with the sweets of contemplation bless'd,
May peace with balmy wings your soul invest!
But when these shades of time are chas'd away,
And darkness ends in everlasting day,
On what seraphic pinions shall we move,
And view the landscapes in the realms above?
There shall thy tongue in heav'nly murmurs flow,
And there my muse with heav'nly transport glow:
No more to tell of *Damon's*[3] tender sighs,
Or rising radiance of *Aurora's*[4] eyes,
For nobler themes demand a nobler strain,
And purer language on th' ethereal plain.
Cease, gentle muse! the solemn gloom of night
Now seals the fair creation from my sight.

1773

To Samson Occom[1]

Rev'd and honor'd Sir,

I have this Day received your obliging kind Epistle, and am greatly satisfied with your Reasons respecting the Negroes, and think highly reasonable what you offer in Vindication of their natural Rights: Those that invade them cannot be insensible that the divine Light is chasing away the thick Darkness which broods over the Land of Africa; and the Chaos which has reign'd so long, is converting into beautiful Order, and [r]eveals more and more clearly, the glorious Dispensation of civil and religious Liberty, which are so inseparably united, that there is little or no Enjoyment of one without the other: Otherwise, perhaps, the Israelites[2] had been less solicitous for their Freedom from Egyptian slavery; I do not say they would have been contented without it, by no means, for in every human Breast, God has implanted a Principle, which we call Love of Freedom; it is impatient of Oppression, and pants for Deliverance; and by the Leave of our modern Egyptians I will assert, that the same Principle lives in us. God grant Deliverance in his own Way and Time, and get him honour upon all those whose Avarice impels them to countenance and help forward the Calamities

2. Heavenly Jerusalem, which Revelation 21.12 describes as having twelve gates ("twice six gates").
3. In classical mythology, he pledged his life for his friend Pythias.
4. The Roman goddess of the dawn.
1. A member of the Mohegan nation (1723–1792); he was ordained a Presbyterian minister and had written an indictment of slaveholding Christian ministers with which Wheatley, who was his friend, strongly concurred.
2. The Hebrews held in bondage to the ancient Egyptians.

of their fellow Creatures. This I desire not for their Hurt, but to convince them of the strange Absurdity of their Conduct whose Words and Actions are so diametrically opposite. How well the Cry for Liberty, and the reverse Disposition for the exercise of oppressive Power over others agree,—I humbly think it does not require the Penetration of a Philosopher to determine.—

1774

To His Excellency General Washington[1]

Sir,

I have taken the freedom to address your Excellency in the enclosed poem, and entreat your acceptance, though I am not insensible of its inaccuracies. Your being appointed by the Grand Continental Congress to be Generalissimo of the armies of North America, together with the fame of your virtues, excite sensations not easy to suppress. Your generosity, therefore, I presume, will pardon the attempt. Wishing your Excellency all possible success in the great cause you are so generously engaged in. I am,

Your Excellency's most obedient humble servant,

Phillis Wheatley

1776

Celestial choir! [2]enthron'd in realms of light,
Columbia's[3] scenes of glorious toils I write.
While freedom's cause her anxious breast alarms,
She flashes dreadful in refulgent arms.
See mother earth her offspring's fate bemoan,
And nations gaze at scenes before unknown!
See the bright beams of heaven's revolving light
Involved in sorrows and veil of night!

The goddess comes, she moves divinely fair,
Olive and laurel[4] bind her golden hair:
Wherever shines this native of the skies,
Unnumber'd charms and recent graces rise.

Muse! bow propitious while my pen relates
How pour her armies through a thousand gates,
As when Eolus[5] heaven's fair face deforms,
Enwrapp'd in tempest and a night of storms;

1. As a demonstration of her patriotism, Wheatley sent this introductory letter and the following poem to Washington four months after he had been named commander in chief of the American Revolutionary Army. On February 28, 1776, Washington replied, thanking Wheatley for the poem and inviting her to visit him.
2. The nine Muses, goddesses of literature and art.
3. This reference to America as the land of Columbus is thought to be the first in print.
4. Emblems of victory.
5. In classical mythology, the keeper of the winds.

Astonish'd ocean feels the wild uproar,
The refluent surges beat the sounding shore;
Or thick as leaves in Autumn's golden reign,
Such, and so many, moves the warrior's train.
In bright array they seek the work of war,
Where high unfurl'd the ensign° waves in air. *flag or banner*
Shall I to Washington their praise recite?
Enough thou know'st them in the fields of fight.
Thee, first in peace and honours,—we demand
The grace and glory of thy martial band.
Fam'd for thy valour, for thy virtues more,
Hear every tongue thy guardian aid implore!

One century scarce perform'd its destined round,
When Gallic[6] powers Columbia's fury found;
And so may you, whoever dares disgrace
The land of freedom's heaven-defended race!
Fix'd are the eyes of nations on the scales,
For in their hopes Columbia's arm prevails.
Anon Britannia droops the pensive head,
While round increase the rising hills of dead.
Ah! cruel blindness to Columbia's state!
Lament thy thirst of boundless power too late.

Proceed, great chief, with virtue on thy side,
Thy ev'ry action let the goddess guide.
A crown, a mansion, and a throne that shine,
With gold unfading, WASHINGTON! be thine.

1776

6. French; a reference to the French and Indian War (1754–1763) in North America.

S

early nineteenth century

January 18, 1828, began the serialization of "Theresa, A Haytien Tale" in *Freedom's Journal,* the earliest extant newspaper for, by, and about African Americans. This four-part story is acknowledged as the earliest extant short story attributed to an African American author. Like Victor Séjour's *The Mulatto* (1841), which it predates by more than a decade, its setting is Haiti. But unlike Séjour's unfortunate Georges (or the multitude of mixed-race protagonists who emerge later in the century), Theresa is anything but tragic. Anticipating Frederick Douglass's *The Heroic Slave* (1853), "Theresa, A Haytien Tale" is historical fiction set during the armed revolt against slavery that erupted in 1791 in the French colony of Saint-

Domingue. Like William Wells Brown's *Clotel* (1853), the plot of "Theresa" revolves around a mother and two daughters who cast aside the restraints of gender to save themselves and their Black revolutionary compatriots. In several ways Theresa challenges and complicates stereotypical notions of identity and agency in African American literature during the slavery era. Most prominently, the title character, though raised to observe every standard of self-abnegating decorum for ladies, sacrifices her mother's protection and risks her own life to warn the leader of the revolution, Toussaint L'Ouverture (1743–1803) himself, about the threat of a French attack. Theresa's heroism and dedication to an independent Haiti mark her as perhaps the first female embodiment of Black nationalism in African American fiction.

S, the author of "Theresa," has not been identified. Not knowing who S was poses problems similar to those that faced mid-twentieth-century readers who pondered the identity of Linda Brent, narrator of *Incidents in the Life of a Slave Girl* (1861), and researchers attempting to determine the identity of Hannah Crafts, putative author of *The Bondwoman's Narrative* (2002). One could argue that anonymous or authorially indeterminate fiction in African American literary history should be assessed in much the same way as slavery-era spirituals and folk tales. Though we have no proof as to the racial heritage or identity of S, we have good reason to consider "Theresa" African American fiction simply because it appeared in an African American venue and features African American characters during an event of major impact on African American life. Many, if not most, contributors to *Freedom's Journal* signified their authorship with letters, such as E, V, and J. T. E., whereas others assumed a literary persona: Ophelia, Civis, Arion, Rosa, and Mr. Observer, to cite just a few. Pseudonyms ranging from single letters to phrases to fictitious names were in the nineteenth century what our online IDs are in the twenty-first. Readers of *Freedom's Journal*, like those of most early African American periodicals, generally assumed the writer was African American, unless otherwise stated or implied in the article itself. Such assumptions were based on general affirmations by editors as well as by the mission statements of African American periodicals.

In its first issue, the editors of *Freedom's Journal* stated: "We wish to plead our own cause. Too long have others spoken for us." One purpose of the paper, the editors noted, was to develop and demonstrate literary talent in African America. Not every item in the paper was originally for or by African Americans. However, when reprinting articles or reporting on events outside African America, *Freedom's Journal*, following standard journalistic procedure of the time, usually cited the original source. By captioning each episode of "Theresa" with "Original Communications" or "For the Freedom's Journal," the editors sent a widely recognized signal designed to authenticate the story's African American provenance.

Readers of the original text in 1828 probably needed no reassurance of authorial racial affiliation. Before "Theresa" appeared, S was already known as a frequent contributor of provocative essays on gender, racial equality, and African history. Six months earlier, S had argued in an essay titled "Female Tenderness" that a woman's love could assuage the trials and tribulations, prejudices, and white man's scorn that a Black man could experience in life. S's "African Genealogy," a serialized essay published in August 1827, offered a scholarly account of the ancestral nations, peoples, and families of Africa because, although "Africa's former greatness is buried with time in forgetfulness," "Ethiopia shall stretch forth her arms" again. S's December 1827 contribution to *Freedom's Journal*, "Christmas," asked readers to use the "holy-days" to give "serious thought" to religion, education, freedom, generosity and other means by which "the sons of Africa" might claim their "natural rights."

Scholars have speculated that S was Prince Saunders (ca. 1780–1839), a Connecticut-born teacher, writer, abolitionist, and adviser to Haitian emperor Henri Christophe. In 1816 Saunders published *Haytian Papers*, a volume celebrating Haitian independence, monarchy, laws, and commerce. S may have been James McCune Smith (1813–1865), physician, abolitionist, author, and mentor to Frederick Douglass. Smith earned his medical degree from the University of Glasgow and in 1841 published a famous lecture on Toussaint L'Ouverture and the Haitian Revolution. Until further archival research reveals the identity of S, "Theresa" remains a pioneering contribution to African American literature, particularly with regard to its focus on Haiti and its revolution as models of Black sociopolitical achievement. The story is also representative of the many stories, poems, essays, and articles contributed anonymously by African American writers to early African American print culture.

Theresa, A Haytien Tale

During the long and bloody contest, in St. Domingo,[1] between the white man, who flourished the child of sensuality, rioting on the miseries of his slaves; had the sons of Africa, who, provoked to madness, and armed themselves against French barbarity; Madame Paulina was left a widow, unhappy—unprotected, and exposed to all the horrors of the revolution. Not without much unhappiness, she saw that if she would save her life from the inhumanity of her country's enemy, she must depart from the endeared village of her innocent childhood; still dear to her, though now it was become a theatre of many tragic scenes. The once verdant plains, round its environs had been crimsoned with the blood of innocence, and the nature of the times afforded no security to the oppressed natives of Saint Nicholas.[2]

Famine which had usurped the place of plenty and happiness, with her associate security, were banished from the humble dwellings of the injured Haytiens.

After much unpleasant reflections on her pitiable situation, Madame Paulina resolved to address a letter, soliciting the advice of her brother, then at Cape Marie, and at the head of a party of his patriot brethren, who like him, disdained slavery, and were determined to live free men, or expire in the attempts for liberty and independence. But reason had scarce approved this suggestion of her mind, when suddenly she heard a simultaneous volley of musketry, and the appalling roaring of heavy artillery rumbling along the mountain's ridge, like terrifying thunders; to this distant warfare, the lapse of fifteen minutes brought cessation, which announced, that on either side, many that were, had ceased to be. Silence having ensued, there was a stillness in the air. All at Saint Nicholas, desirous to know the issue of the combat, remained in doubtful anxiety.

Each one's heart was the abode of fear and doubt, while the dense smoke, escaping the despot's fury, and evading the implacable resentment of those armed in the justice of their cause, was seen to overtop the dusky hills, winding its way upwards in the sulphureous columns, as if, to supplicate at the Eternal's Throne, and plead the cause of the injured.

The French in this combat with the Revolutionists, suffered much, both from the extreme sultriness of the day, and the courage of those with whom

1. The French colony on the Caribbean island of Hispaniola from 1659 to 1809.

2. Môle-Saint-Nicolas is a port in northwestern Haiti.

they contended; disappointed and harassed by the Islanders; they thought it a principle of policy, to resort to acts of cruelty; and to intimidate them, resolved, that none of them should be spared; but that the sword should annihilate, or compel them to submit to their wonted degradations; and St. Nicholas was the unfortunate village, first to be devoted to the resentful rage of the cruel enemy. All the natives were doomed to suffer; the mother and the infant that reposed on her bosom, fell by the same sword, while groans of the sick served only as the guides which discovered them to the inhumanity of the inexorable, at whose hands they met a miserable death.

The sun was fast receding to the west, as if ashamed of man's transactions, boasting itself in the dark mantle of twilight, when Gen. Le——, fired the few dwellings, then remaining in the village. Misery was now garbed in her most terrifying robes, and terror possessed itself the heart of all, except the French, in whose hands were placed the weapons of destruction. The intelligence of defeat of the army recently stationed at Cape Marie, reached the ears of the unhappy Paulina, and with horror she heard that her beloved brother in his attempt to regain St. Nicholas, breathed out his valuable life in the cause of freedom, and for his country. But it was now no time to indulge in grief—Safety was the object of the wretched villagers.

To effect an escape from the horrors of this ominous night, was difficult in the extreme; for the passes leading out into the country were all occupied by the enemy's troops, who were not only vigilant, but relentless and cruel. Madame Paulina apprehended her own danger, but her greatest solicitude was of the safety of her daughters, who in the morning of life, were expanding, like the foliages of the rose into elegance and beauty. She had kept them long concealed from the knowledge of the enemy, whose will she knew was their law, and whose law was injustice—the mother's wretchedness, and the daughter's shame and ruin. In happier days, when peace blessed her native island, she had seen a small hut, during a summer's excursion, in an unfrequented spot, in the delightful valley of Vega Real, and on the eastern bank of the beautiful Yuma; and now she resolved if possible, to retreat thither with both her daughters.

Necessity being the source of human inventions, was now ready to commune with her mind on subjects of moment, and to give birth to the events of its decision—and in the midst of the general uproar in which the village now was—The shrieks of the defenceless, the horrible clashing of arms, and the expiring groans of the aged, Paulina hurried herself in the execution of her plans for escaping.

With a feigned passport and letter, she ingeniously contrived to pass out of the village conducting her daughters, like the pious Aeneas,[3] through all the horrors, in which St. Nicholas was now involved.

But though protected by the mantle of night, Madame was hastening on her way to safety and quiet; she frequently would turn her eyes bathed with the dew of sorrow, and heave her farewell sigh towards her ill-fated village; and like Lot when departing out of Sodom,[4] Paulina prayed for mercy for the enemies of her country, and the destroyers of her peace. She and her

3. The hero of Virgil's epic poem, *The Aeneid* (29–19 B.C.E.), who led Trojan refugees to Italy after the fall of Troy.

4. See Genesis 19:17–26.

daughters, driven by cruel ambition, from their peaceful abodes were wretched. Their souls were occupied by fearful doubts and anxiety. Every whisper of the winds among the leaves of the plantain and orange trees, caused her daughters to apprehend the approach of danger, and she to heave the anxious sigh.

The green lizard crossed not the road in the way to its hole, at the noise of the fugitives feet, but they beheld through the shade of the night a body of the enemy; the distant glare of the firefly, was a light which pointed to the enemies camps; while the bat beating the [word indecipherable] in its nocturnal ranges, often was the false messenger of danger to the fair adventurers. Every tree kissed by the zephyrs,[5] that ruffled its leaves, was an army approaching, and in the trunk of every decored [*sic*] mahogany, was seen a Frenchman in ambush—not less alarming to the fugitives, were the ripe fruit that frequently fell to the earth. Then having turned into a by-path, Paulina felt herself more secure; and with a soul oppressed with mingled grief and joy, she with maternal affection embraced her daughters, and observed to them, that however just may be the cause which induces us to practice duplicity, or the laudable object which gives birth to hypocrisy. Truth alone can make us happy, and prevent the Internal Judge of the human mind, filling us with fearful apprehensions, and painting to our Imaginations the result which would attend detection.

Morning had just began to peep forth, and the golden rays of the returning sun were seen to burnish the tops of the majestic Cibao mountains,[6] when the bewildered adventurers were suddenly startled by the shrill blast of a bugle; their surprise was not less than their wretchedness, when at no great distance, they beheld approaching them a detachment of the enemy's cavalry. At this unexpected crisis Madame Paulina overcome with fearful apprehensions, trembled lest she should be wanting in the discharge of her difficult undertaking. But it was not too late; she must either act well her part or be reconducted by the foe to St. Nicholas, and there, after witnessing the destruction of those for whose happiness, she was more concerned, than for her own, receive a cruel and ignominious death.

The party of horsemen being now very near, she gave necessary instructions to her daughters, and conducted them onward with no little confidence in her success. The lieutenant, by whom the French were commanded, observing her attired in the uniform of a French officer, took her for what she was so well affected to be—(a captain of the French army) he made to her the order of the day, and enquired the time she left St. Nicholas, and whether conducting the two prisoners, (for Paulina had the presence of mind to disguise her daughters as such) she replied, and taking forth her letter, she handed it to the lieutenant. Succeeding thus far admirably, our adventuress was led to make some enquiries relative to the welfare of the French troops, stationed west of St. Nicholas, and having collected much valuable information, they parted, and Madame Paulina favoured by a ready address, and with much fortitude, escaped death—conducting the dear objects of her tender solicitude far, from the ill-fated village of their infancy.

Being informed by the lieutenant, that at the distance of a few miles, there were encamped a company of the French, she thought it judicious to avoid all

5. Mild winds.

6. In the northern Dominican Republic.

public roads, and having turned into a thick grove of the Pimento trees, she proposed to her daughters to rest in this spot until darkness again should unfold her mantle.

In this grove of quiet security, the troubled souls of the fugitives ceased partially to be oppressed with fear—the milky juice of the cocoanut allayed their thirst and moistened their parched lips, and the delicious orange, and luxurious mango, in spontaneous abundance, yielded a support to their nearly exhausted natures.

Madame Paulina and her daughters were now seated under the shade of a majestic spreading Guava. The day was fast declining, and though the heat of July was intensely oppressive; in this secluded spot, the air was rendered fragrant with the variety of arometic shrubs, that grew spontaneously in this grove of peace. The hummingbird skipping capriciously from blossom to blossom, displayed its magnificent plumage, and for a while diverted the minds of the unhappy fugitives from grief and from ominous forebodings; wearied and fatigued by a journey which was not less tiresome than hazardous, their much exhausted natures, were greatly refreshed by the cool breeze which gave to their whole bodies a calm sensation, in which their souls soon participated and Madame and her eldest daughter were now lost in the arms of sleep, the kind restorer of vigour to the minds and bodies of men. All around was now still, save the western woodpecker was heard at times to peck the hollow trunk of some decayed tree, or the distant roaring of heavy cannon, which announced that all creative beings were born to enjoy peace, but man, who stimulated by ambition, is more cruel than the beasts of the forest, which soil he ever renders fertile with the blood of his victims. But Mademoiselle Theresa, the youngest of the three adventurers, greeted not sleep. The vigour of her body was indeed much exhausted, but the emotions of her mind were more active than ever; she saw with the mind's eye the great services which might be rendered to her country; she brought to her imagination the once delightful fields of her native Hayti, now dy'd with the blood of her countrymen in their righteous struggle for liberty and for independence.

Not less did she contemplate the once flourishing plantations ruined and St. Domingo once the granary of the West Indies, reduced to famine, now the island of misery, and the abode of wretchedness.

It was but the last night, that she witnessed the most terrifying scenes of her life—when the shrieks of her dying friends made her apprehend justly what her own fate must be, should she fail to effect an escape from the village of her happiest days. Theresa thought of the brave St. Clair; she imagined she saw her beloved uncle weltering in his blood, and the barbarous French fixing his venerable head on a pole, and it exposed on a cross road, as the head of a rebel. She shuddered at this thought; her soul was subdued, and the fount of grief issued from her eyes in copious streams, bathing her febrile[7] cheeks with the dews of sorrow. "Why," said she, "O, my God! hast thou suffered thy creatures to be thus afflicted in all thy spacious earth? Are not we too thy children? And didst thou not cover us with this sable exterior, by which our race is distinguished, and for which they are contemned and ever been cruelly persecuted! O, my God!—my God!—be propitious to the cause

7. Feverish.

of justice—Be near to the Haytiens in their righteous struggle, to obtain those rights which thou hast graciously bestowed on all thy children. Raise up some few of those, who have been long degraded—give to them dominion, and enable them to govern a state of their own—so that the proud and cruel may know that thou art alike the Father of the native of the burning desert, and of the more temperate region."

It was in the presence of Theresa that the conversation between M. L'Motelle and her heroic mother took place. Madame Paulina, on her part leaving nothing undone, which might serve to accomplish the object for which she had been induced to practice duplicity; M. L'Motelle regarded her for what she really appeared to be; and unhesitatingly spoke of matters concerning the nature of the times; of the military and local situations of the French troops: their condition and strength were topics of interest; and Theresa learned that the distance to the camp of the brave Touissant L'Ouverture, was a single league[8] from the place where he communicated the intelligence. Seeming to be inattentive, she pensively bent her eyes towards the earth, listening the while as he unconsciously developed many military schemes, which were about being executed, and if successful, would, in all probability, terminate in the destruction of the Revolutionists, and, in the final success of the French power in this island. These were invaluable discoveries, and could they be made known in due time to those against whose rights, their injustice was intended, it would not fail to give success to Haytien independence, disappoint the arch-enemy, and aid the cause of humanity. But, alas! important as they were to the cause of freedom, by whom shall they be carried.

Who shall reveal them to the Revolutionists. No one interested was near, and they were in the possession of none friendly to the cause of justice, except the three defenceless ones. Theresa herself must be the bearer, or survive only to witness them executed agreeably to the desires of the enemy. In what manner must she act? The salvation of her oppressed country to her, was an object of no little concern; but she also owed a duty to that mother, whose tender solicitude for her happiness, could not be surpassed by any parent, and a sister too, whom she tenderly loved, and whose attachment to her was undivided. Her absence from the grove, she was confidently assured, would be to them their greatest source of affliction; it would probably terminate the already much exhausted life of her dear mother, and complete the measure of Amanda's wretchedness. Her own inexperience in the manner, she should conduct in an affair so important and hazardous, was an obstacle which in connexion with her sense of duty, and care for her mother's happiness, would deter her from embarking in it. She paused, then as if aroused by some internal agent, exclaimed, "Oh Hayti!—be independent, and let Theresa be the unworthy sacrifice offered to that God, who shall raise his mighty arm in defence of thy injured children. She drew from her bosom a pencil and wrote on a piece of bark of the Gourd tree, telling her mother and Amanda, whither she was gone—her errand; begged that, they would not be unhappy on account of her absence; that they would remain at their place of peace and quiet, until she should return to them with an escort, who should conduct them to a safer retreat, and commit them to the protection of friends. This

8. Approximately 3.5 miles. L'Ouverture (1743–1803) led the revolt that overthrew slavery in Haiti and in 1801 established himself as head of the first Black government in the Western Hemisphere.

scroll, Theresa pinned on her mother's coat, while she and Amanda were yet indulging in repose, and like an heroine of the age of chivalry, she forsook the grove of Pimento and hastened her way to the camp of L'Ouverture. She had scarce reached the third part of her journey, when her mother dreaming, that one of her daughters had been borne off by an officer of the enemy, awoke from sleep and missing Theresa, believed her dream prophetic. It was now that the keenest anguish filled her soul. Paulina wished not to live. Life to a mother thus sorely afflicted, is misery—she would go in search of the dear object of all her affliction, but where, she knew not. Keen is the grief of a mother, whose child has been forced from her. She is extremely wretched, and her affliction then, cannot be less severe, than it was when in the anguish and sorrow of her soul the dear object of her tenderest solicitude was introduced into the world, to take its station among the Probationers for eternity. Amanda was now awakened by the unhappy and pitiful grief of her bewildered mother. Hastily she enquired for her sister; Paulina in a burst of grief and wild despair, told her, she had been borne off while they slept; with half articulated accents, she related her ominous dream, and the fact was now realized in her absence from the grove. An icy chillness pervaded her whole nature—a dark mist covered her eyes—all the objects by which she was surrounded seemed to recede—her senses were bewildered, and Amanda, unobserved by her mother, swooned and fell to the earth. But soon recovering, she beheld the piece of Gourd bark pinned to the skirt of her mother's coat—she hastened to unpin—it was the hand writing of Theresa they read it with avidity—joyful in the happy discovery, the mother and the daughter embraced each other. From neither, words found utterance. Silence was perched upon their tongues, while the tears of mingled joy and sorrow poured from their eyes; The troubles of their souls were greatly subsided, but happiness could not be restored, until the success of Theresa be ascertained, and she again be encircled in their arms.

It was uncertain whether she could, in safety reach the camp of the Revolutionists; the roads were at all times traveled by reconnoitering parties of the French; and what would be the fate of the heroic Theresa, if taken by any of them! How cruel would be her usage, particularly, if her intentions and the circumstances, which gave them birth be known. Death inevitable would deprive the world of one so fair, virtuous, and so noble.

Such were the thoughts of the mother and sister of the noble adventuress. But while they were thus grieving, Theresa, favoured by fortune, had safely arrived at the military quarters of the great Toussaint: had communicated to the chieftain the object of her visit to his camp, and was receiving all the distinctions due her exalted virtue, and which her dauntless resolution so justly merited.

The sun was now fast receding behind the loft Cibao, whose rugged summits in the morning, appeared burnished by its resplendent rays, and darkness was out-stretching here spacious mantle. The orange and citron groves, and all the rich enameled luxuriance of torrid luxuries, now began to wear a sombre aspect, while the chattering Paroquet ceased to imitate man, and disturb the sweets of solitude, with prating garrulity, had retired to her roost on the sturdy logwood. Now it was, that Theresa, under a strong military escort, left the general's camp of hospitality, retracing her steps towards the grove of Pimento, where, at her departure, she left her dear mother and

Amanda, enjoying calm repose; seated in a close carriage, her thoughts reverted to the deplorable state of her country; with a prophetic eye she saw the destruction of the French, and their final expulsion from her native island. She entreated the Creator, that he would bless the means, which through her agency, he had been pleased to put in the possession of her too long oppressed countrymen, and that all might be made useful to the cause of freedom. But turning her thoughts toward her mother and sister, Theresa was conscious, that her absence from the grove could not fail to have given them extreme sorrow and unhappiness; her gentle nature recoiled at the recollection, and she gave way to a flood of tears. But recollecting again the important services, she had rendered her aggrieved country and to the Haytien people—the objects which prompted her to disobedience, which induced her to overstep the bounds of modesty, and expose to immediate dangers her life and sex. She felt that her conduct was exculpated, and self-reproach was lost in the consciousness of her laudable efforts to save St. Domingo. Her noble soul reanimated, recovered its wonted calm, as the ocean its quiet motion when the gentle breeze, and the returned sunshine, succeed a tempestuous sky and boisterous winds.

Fated to experience trials, she was now to be made more wretched than ever. St. Lewis was now near the forward progressing company of his brethren in arms. He had been despatched to the Pimento grove, to acquaint Madame Paulina and Amanda of the approach of their dear Theresa. But, alas! by whom, or how was the doleful news to be reported to the heroine? Her mother and sister were not to be found at the place where she had left them: and who shall keep the shocking intelligence from her! Already she saw him approaching; he was now near. She observed the gloomy melancholy, which settled on his brow, that plainly foretold all were not well. She inquired into the result of his journey to the grove, and as an earthquake rends the bosom of the earth, so the intelligence her gentle soul.

"Oh! Theresa!—Theresa!" said she in bitter grief, "thou art the murderer of a mother and a loving sister! Where! where shall I hide me from the displeasure of heaven and the curse of man!—Oh, matricide! matricide! whither shalt thou flee from thy accusing conscience! In life I shall be wretched, and after death, oh! who shall release this soul from the bonds of self-condemnation! Oh my affectionate mother! Hast Theresa rewarded thee thus, for thy tender solicitude for her; was it for this, that thou saved me from the devouring flames of my native St. Nicholas! Was it for this, that thou didst exert all thy ingenuity, and saved me from the uplifted sword of the enemy of St. Domingo!—Oh God! forgive this matricide! Forgive Theresa, who to save her country, sacrificed a mother and a sister—Wretched Amanda! and thrice wretched is thy sister, who devoted thee to misery and death!"

The body of escorts were now arrived at the Pimento grove—Theresa sprang from her carriage; hastened to the place where her mother and sister reposed at her departure. She cried in the anguish of her soul "My mother, my mother! where art thou!—Come forth—let Theresa embrace thee to her wretched bosom. Come Amanda! dear Amanda, come, and save thy loving sister from black despair! Where, cruel enemy, where have ye conducted them! If ye have murdered my dear mother and sister, let Theresa but embrace their clayey bodies, and while I bless the enemies of the Haytiens!" But her grief was unheard by those, the loss of whom she bitterly deplored; solemn silence occupied the grove, interrupted only by intervals with the moans and sobs of the men of arms, who marked her anguish of soul, and were absorbed into pity. Whither now shall Theresa bend her steps! No kind mother to guide her in life, or affectionate sister, to whom to impart the sorrow of her soul, or participate with in innocent pleasure; friendless and disconsolate, she was now left exposed to many evils, and at a time too when the assiduous care of a mother was most essential in the preservation of her well being. Theresa was on her way back to the camp of the kind Toussaint L'Ouverture to claim his fatherly protection, and seek a home in the bosom of those, to whom she had rendered herself dear by her wisdom and virtue. The trampling of many horses was heard rapidly approaching, and bending its way towards the same direction. It was a party of the French troops, and she was now to witness war in all its horrors. The enemy of Haytien freedom was now near. The war trumpet now sounded the terrible blast for the engagement, and the Revolutionists like lions, rushed on to the fight with a simultaneous cry of "Freedom or Death!" The French, great in number, fought in obedience to a cruel master. The Haytiens for liberty and independence, and to obtain their rights of which they long have been unjustly deprived.

The pass between the Mole and the village St. Nicholas, drank up the lives of hundreds in their blood. The French retreated with precipitance, leaving their baggage with their gasping friends, on the spot where victory perched on the standard of freedom: And now the conquerors had began to examine the property deserted by the vanquished. A faint but mournful groan issued from a baggage cart forsaken by the enemy; directed by the light of a flambeau,[9] captain Inginac bent thither his nimble steps. Curiosity is lost in surprise—joy succeeds sorrow—the lost ones are regained. It was Madame Paulina and Amanda, the mother and sister of the unhappy THERESA.

S.

1828

9. A flaming torch.

DAVID WALKER
ca. 1796–1830

The most militant voice among the early African American protest writers belonged to David Walker, whose call for violent resistance against slavery so alarmed authorities in the South that they were reputed to have put a $10,000 bounty on his head. *David Walker's Appeal,* published by its author in 1829, shocked and alarmed many white readers in the North as well as the South because of Walker's insistence on white racism as a national problem, of which slavery was the most egregious manifestation. Most Black readers found the *Appeal* an inspiring articulation of African American pride and a fearless call to radical action in the name of those principles of justice to which the American republic was purportedly dedicated.

In an ironically patriotic spirit, Walker, a self-avowed "restless disturber of the peace," took pains to pattern the title and structure of his *Appeal* on the U.S. Constitution. Hence the formal and stately character of the full title of the text:

David Walker's Appeal in Four Articles; Together with a Preamble, to the Coloured Citizens of the World, but in Particular and Very Expressly, to Those of the United States of America. In addition to drawing on American political precedent for his argument for Black nationalism, Walker also allied himself with the biblical tradition of the prophet crying in the wilderness, denouncing the hypocrisy of the prevailing religious practice and calling for divine punishment "in behalf of the oppressed." Walker's devastating historical analysis of slavery and racism in Europe and the Americas, set forth in the Preamble and Article I of the *Appeal,* is probably the most memorable part of his writing. But subsequent articles of the *Appeal* urge a program of African American educational, spiritual, and political renewal that proves Walker's dedication to constructive social change, not just retribution. By demonstrating that biblical as well as American history amply justified forcible resistance against tyranny, Walker tried to galvanize into unity of purpose both the religious and the worldly communities of Black America. No wonder, therefore, that white southerners demanded the *Appeal* be suppressed and took stringent measures to keep it out of the hands of the enslaved.

Born in Wilmington, North Carolina, possibly to an enslaved father and a free mother, David Walker, though never actually enslaved, became thoroughly acquainted with the South's "peculiar institution" during his youth and early manhood, which were spent in Wilmington and in Charleston, South Carolina. In these coastal cities he realized the contributions of the enslaved to the key industries of the southern seaboard and came to feel deeply the injustice of subjecting such industrious and resourceful people to bondage. Boston became Walker's home in 1825; a year later he married and was inducted into North America's first Black Masonic lodge. Walker also joined a Black Methodist congregation headed by a vehemently antislavery pastor. He supported his family well as a secondhand clothes dealer while devoting much of his available time to studying the history of slavery. In Boston's Black community Walker became a leader, gaining local recognition for his antislavery speeches, one of which was printed in 1828 in *Freedom's Journal,* the first African American newspaper published in the United States. Growing in militancy and outspokenness during the last two years of his life, Walker published three editions of the *Appeal* in 1829 and 1830, each one increasingly urgent and frank in its denunciation of racial injustice. Southern hysteria in response to the appearance of the *Appeal* made Walker a marked man. His death on August 6, 1830, generated rumors of assassination by poison, but his death certificate indicates that he died of tuberculosis, a widely fatal disease in the nineteenth century.

Walker did not live to read about Nat Turner's rebellion in Southampton County, Virginia, in August 1831, only fourteen months after the publication of the last edition of the *Appeal.* But slaveholders were convinced that Turner had put into action what Walker had proposed in words. Efforts in Virginia to bar Black ministers from preaching to their own people—on the supposition that some would use the *Appeal* as their text—were only some of the many repressive measures taken in that state to keep the ideas of Walker and the example of Turner from inciting the enslaved to revolt. Nevertheless, Walker's admirers in the North, such as the fiery antislavery minister Henry Highland Garnet, kept the *Appeal* and Walker's compelling story in print well into the middle of the nineteenth century. In the twentieth and twenty-first centuries, particularly during times of crisis and heightened Black consciousness, *David Walker's Appeal* reclaims our attention as a prophetic text. The *Appeal* launched a tradition extending from Garnet's own "Call to Rebellion" speech in 1843 through *The Autobiography of Malcolm X* (1965) and Eldridge Cleaver's *Soul on Ice* (1967) in the Black Power era. Contemporary hip-hop expressions of cultural nationalism by the Last Poets and Public Enemy also pay witness to a Black historical consciousness that Walker advocated. Whites, northern and southern, antislavery and proslavery, widely deplored or denounced the *Appeal* in the 1830s, but countless readers continue to respond to Walker as did the Black people of Boston, according to an 1830 editorial in the *Boston Evening Transcript.* "We have noticed a marked difference in the deportment of our colored population. It is evident they have read this pamphlet, and that they glory in its principles, as if it were a star in the east, guiding them to freedom and emancipation."

From David Walker's Appeal in Four Articles; Together with a Preamble, to the Coloured Citizens of the World

Preamble

My dearly beloved Brethren and Fellow Citizens.

Having travelled over a considerable portion of these United States, and having, in the course of my travels, taken the most accurate observations of things as they exist—the result of my observations has warranted the full and unshaken conviction, that we, (coloured people of these United States,) are the most degraded, wretched, and abject set of beings that ever lived since the world began; and I pray God that none like us ever may live again until time shall be no more. They tell us of the Israelites in Egypt, the Helots[1] in Sparta, and of the Roman Slaves, which last were made up from almost every nation under heaven, whose sufferings under those ancient and heathen nations, were, in comparison with ours, under this enlightened and Christian nation, no more than a cypher[2]—or, in other words, those heathen nations of antiquity, had but little more among them than the name and form of slavery; while wretchedness and endless miseries were reserved, apparently in a phial, to be poured out upon our fathers, ourselves and our children, by *Christian* Americans!

These positions I shall endeavour, by the help of the Lord, to demonstrate in the course of this *Appeal,* to the satisfaction of the most incredulous mind—and may God Almighty, who is the Father of our Lord Jesus Christ, open your hearts to understand and believe the truth.

The *causes,* my brethren, which produce our wretchedness and miseries, are so very numerous and aggravating, that I believe the pen only of a Josephus or a Plutarch,[3] can well enumerate and explain them. Upon subjects, then, of such incomprehensible magnitude, so impenetrable, and so notorious, I shall be obliged to omit a large class of, and content myself with giving you an exposition of a few of those, which do indeed rage to such an alarming pitch, that they cannot but be a perpetual source of terror and dismay to every reflecting mind.

I am fully aware, in making this appeal to my much afflicted and suffering brethren, that I shall not only be assailed by those whose greatest earthly desires are, to keep us in abject ignorance and wretchedness, and who are of the firm conviction that Heaven has designed us and our children to be slaves and *beasts of burden* to them and their children. I say, I do not only expect to be held up to the public as an ignorant, impudent and restless disturber of the public peace, by such avaricious creatures, as well as a mover of insubordination—and perhaps put in prison or to death, for giving a superficial exposition of our miseries, and exposing tyrants. But I am persuaded, that many of my brethren, particularly those who are ignorantly in league with slave-holders or tyrants, who acquire their daily bread by the

1. State-owned serfs in the ancient Greek city-state of Sparta.
2. Something of no consequence.
3. Greek biographer and moral philosopher (46 C.E.–120?). Josephus (37 C.E.–100?), Jewish statesman and historian.

blood and sweat of their more ignorant brethren—and not a few of those too, who are too ignorant to see an inch beyond their noses, will rise up and call me cursed—Yea, the jealous ones among us will perhaps use more abject subtlety, by affirming that this work is not worth perusing, that we are well situated, and there is no use in trying to better our condition, for we cannot. I will ask one question here.—Can our condition be any worse?—Can it be more mean and abject? If there are any changes, will they not be for the better, though they may appear for the worst at first? Can they get us any lower? Where can they get us? They are afraid to treat us worse, for they know well, the day they do it they are gone. But against all accusations which may or can be preferred against me, I appeal to Heaven for my motive in writing—who knows that my object is, if possible, to awaken in the breasts of my afflicted, degraded and slumbering brethren, a spirit of inquiry and investigation respecting our miseries and wretchedness in this *Republican Land of Liberty*!!!!!!

The sources from which our miseries are derived, and on which I shall comment, I shall not combine in one, but shall put them under distinct heads and expose them in their turn; in doing which, keeping truth on my side, and not departing from the strictest rules of morality, I shall endeavour to penetrate, search out, and lay them open for your inspection. If you cannot or will not profit by them, I shall have done *my* duty to you, my country and my God.

And as the inhuman system of *slavery,* is the *source* from which most of our miseries proceed, I shall begin with that *curse to nations,* which has spread terror and devastation through so many nations of antiquity, and which is raging to such a pitch at the present day in Spain and in Portugal. It had one tug in England, in France, and in the United States of America; yet the inhabitants thereof, do not learn wisdom, and erase it entirely from their dwellings and from all with whom they have to do. The fact is, the labour of slaves comes so cheap to the avaricious usurpers, and is (as they think) of such great utility to the country where it exists, that those who are actuated by sordid avarice only, overlook the evils, which will as sure as the Lord lives, follow after the good. In fact, they are so happy to keep in ignorance and degradation, and to receive the homage and the labour of the slaves, they forget that God rules in the armies of heaven and among the inhabitants of the earth, having his ears continually open to the cries, tears and groans of his oppressed people; and being a just and holy Being will at one day appear fully in behalf of the oppressed, and arrest the progress of the avaricious oppressors; for although the destruction of the oppressors God may not effect by the oppressed, yet the Lord our God will bring other destructions upon them—for not unfrequently will he cause them to rise up one against another, to be split and divided, and to oppress each other, and sometimes to open hostilities with sword in hand. Some may ask, what is the matter with this united and happy people?—Some say it is the cause of political usurpers, tyrants, oppressors, etc. But has not the Lord an oppressed and suffering people among them? Does the Lord condescend to hear their cries and see their tears in consequence of oppression? Will he let the oppressors rest comfortably and happy always? Will he not cause the very children of the oppressors to rise up against them, and oftimes put them to death? "God works in many ways his wonders to perform."[4]

4. Slightly adapted from William Cowper's hymn "Walking with God" (1779).

I will not here speak of the destructions which the Lord brought upon Egypt, in consequence of the oppression and consequent groans of the oppressed—of the hundreds and thousands of Egyptians whom God hurled into the Red Sea for afflicting his people in their land—of the Lord's suffering people in Sparta or Lacedaemon, the land of the truly famous Lycurgus[5]—nor have I time to comment upon the cause which produced the fierceness with which Sylla usurped the title, and absolutely acted as dictator of the Roman people—the conspiracy of Cataline—the conspiracy against, and murder of Cæsar in the Senate house—the spirit with which Marc Antony made himself master of the commonwealth—his associating Octavius and Lipidus with himself in power—their dividing the provinces of Rome among themselves—their attack and defeat, on the plains of Phillippi, of the last defenders of their liberty, (Brutus and Cassius)—the tyranny of Tiberius,[6] and from him to the final overthrow of Constantinople by the Turkish Sultan, Mahomed II,[7] A.D. 1453. I say, I shall not take up time to speak of the *causes* which produced so much wretchedness and massacre among those heathen nations, for I am aware that you know too well, that God is just, as well as merciful!—I shall call your attention a few moments to that *Christian* nation, the Spaniards—while I shall leave almost unnoticed, that avaricious and cruel people, the Portuguese, among whom all true hearted Christians and lovers of Jesus Christ, must evidently see the judgments of God displayed. To show the judgments of God upon the Spaniards, I shall occupy but a little time, leaving a plenty of room for the candid and unprejudiced to reflect.

All persons who are acquainted with history, and particularly the Bible, who are not blinded by the God of this world, and are not actuated solely by avarice—who are able to lay aside prejudice long enough to view candidly and impartially, things as they were, are, and probably will be—who are willing to admit that God made man to serve Him *alone,* and that man should have no other Lord or Lords but Himself—that God Almighty is the *sole proprietor* or *master* of the WHOLE human family, and will not on any consideration admit of a colleague, being unwilling to divide his glory with another—and who can dispense with prejudice long enough to admit that we are *men,* notwithstanding our *improminent noses* and *woolly heads,* and believe that we feel for our fathers, mothers, wives and children, as well as the whites do for theirs.—I say, all who are permitted to see and believe these things, can easily recognize the judgments of God among the Spaniards. Though others may lay the cause of the fierceness with which they cut each other's throats, to some other circumstance, yet they who believe that God is a God of justice, will believe that SLAVERY *is the principal cause.*

While the Spaniards are running about upon the field of battle cutting each other's throats, has not the Lord an afflicted and suffering people in the midst of them, whose cries and groans in consequence of oppression are continually pouring into the ears of the God of justice? Would they not cease to cut each other's throats, if they could? But how can they? The very support which they draw from government to aid them in perpetrating such enormities, does it not arise in a great degree from the wretched victims of oppression among them? And yet they are calling for *Peace!—Peace!!* Will any peace be given unto them? Their destruction may indeed be procrastinated

5. A legendary reformer and legislator of Sparta.
6. Walker is tracing the major events and leaders of the civil wars that, during the last century before Christ, transformed Rome from a republic into a dictatorship under the emperor Augustus and his successor, Tiberius.
7. Muhammad II (1429–1481) conquered the Byzantine Empire in 1453.

awhile, but can it continue long, while they are oppressing the Lord's people? Has He not the hearts of all men in His hand? Will he suffer one part of his creatures to go on oppressing another like brutes always, with impunity? And yet, those avaricious wretches are calling for *Peace!!!!* I declare, it does appear to me, as though some nations think God is asleep, or that he made the Africans for nothing else but to dig their mines and work their farms, or they cannot believe history, sacred or profane. I ask every man who has a heart, and is blessed with the privilege of believing—Is not God a God of justice to *all* his creatures? Do you say he is? Then if he gives peace and tranquillity to tyrants, and permits them to keep our fathers, our mothers, ourselves and our children in eternal ignorance and wretchedness, to support them and their families, would he be to us a God of *justice?* I ask, O ye *Christians!!!* who hold us and our children in the most abject ignorance and degradation, that ever a people were afflicted with since the world began—I say, if God gives you peace and tranquillity, and suffers you thus to go on afflicting us, and our children, who have never given you the least provocation—would he be to us *a God of justice?* If you will allow that we are MEN, who feel for each other, does not the blood of our fathers and of us their children, cry aloud to the Lord of Sabaoth against you, for the cruelties and murders with which you have, and do continue to afflict us. But it is time for me to close my remarks on the suburbs, just to enter more fully into the interior of this system of cruelty and oppression.

Article I

OUR WRETCHEDNESS IN CONSEQUENCE OF SLAVERY

My beloved brethren:—The Indians of North and of South America—the Greeks—the Irish, subjected under the king of Great Britain—the Jews, that ancient people of the Lord—the inhabitants of the islands of the sea—in fine, all the inhabitants of the earth, (except however, the sons of Africa) are called *men,* and of course are, and ought to be free. But we, (coloured people) and our children are *brutes!!* and of course are, and *ought to be* SLAVES to the American people and their children forever!! to dig their mines and work their farms; and thus go on enriching them, from one generation to another with our *blood* and our *tears!!!!*

I promised in a preceding page to demonstrate to the satisfaction of the most incredulous, that we, (coloured people of these United States of America) are the *most wretched, degraded* and *abject* set of beings that *ever lived* since the world began, and that the white Americans having reduced us to the wretched state of *slavery,* treat us in that condition *more cruel* (they being an enlightened and Christian people,) than any heathen nation did any people whom it had reduced to our condition. These affirmations are so well confirmed in the minds of all unprejudiced men, who have taken the trouble to read histories, that they need no elucidation from me. But to put them beyond all doubt, I refer you in the first place to the children of Jacob, or of Israel in Egypt, under Pharaoh and his people. Some of my brethren do not know who Pharaoh and the Egyptians were—I know it to be a fact, that some of them take the Egyptians to have been a gang of *devils,* not knowing any better, and that they (Egyptians) having got possession of the Lord's people, treated them *nearly* as cruel as *Christian Americans* do us, at the present day. For the information of such, I would only mention that the Egyptians, were

Africans or coloured people, such as we are—some of them yellow and others dark—a mixture of Ethiopians and the natives of Egypt—about the same as you see the coloured people of the United States at the present day.—I say, I call your attention then, to the children of Jacob, while I point out particularly to you his son Joseph, among the rest, in Egypt.

"And Pharaoh, said unto Joseph, . . . thou shalt be over my house, and according unto thy word shall all my people be ruled: only in the throne will I be greater than thou."[8]

"And Pharaoh said unto Joseph, see, I have set thee over all the land of Egypt."[9]

"And Pharaoh said unto Joseph, I am Pharaoh, and without thee shall no man lift up his hand or foot in all the land of Egypt."[1]

Now I appeal to heaven and to earth, and particularly to the American people themselves, who cease not to declare that our condition is not *hard,* and that we are comparatively satisfied to rest in wretchedness and misery, under them and their children. Not, indeed, to show me a coloured President, a Governor, a Legislator, a Senator, a Mayor, or an Attorney at the Bar.—But to show me a man of colour, who holds the low office of a Constable, or one who sits in a Juror Box, even on a case of one of his wretched brethren, throughout this great Republic! !—But let us pass Joseph the son of Israel a little farther in review, as he existed with that heathen nation.

"And Pharaoh called Joseph's name Zaphnathpaaneah; and he gave him to wife Asenath the daughter of Potipherah priest of On. And Joseph went out over all the land of Egypt."[2]

Compare the above, with the American institutions. Do they not institute laws to prohibit us from marrying among the whites? I would wish, candidly, however, before the Lord, to be understood, that I would not give a *pinch of snuff* to be married to any white person I ever saw in all the days of my life. And I do say it, that the black man, or man of colour, who will leave his own colour (provided he can get one, who is good for any thing) and marry a white woman, to be a double slave to her, just because she is *white,* ought to be treated by her as he surely will be, viz: as a NIGGER!!!! It is not, indeed, what I care about inter-marriages with the whites, which induced me to pass this subject in review; for the Lord knows, that there is a day coming when they will be glad enough to get into the company of the blacks, notwithstanding, we are, in this generation, levelled by them, almost on a level with the brute creation: and some of us they treat even worse than they do the brutes that perish. I only made this extract to show how much lower we are held, and how much more cruel we are treated by the Americans, than were the children of Jacob, by the Egyptians.—We will notice the sufferings of Israel some further, under *heathen Pharaoh,* compared with ours under the *enlightened Christians of America.*

"And Pharaoh spoke unto Joseph, saying, thy father and thy brethren are come unto thee:

"The land of Egypt is before thee: in the best of the land make thy father and brethren to dwell; in the land of Goshen let them dwell: and if thou knowest any men of activity among them, then make them rulers over my cattle."[3]

I ask those people who treat us so *well,* Oh! I ask them, where is the most barren spot of land which they have given unto us? Israel had the most fertile

8. See Genesis, chap. xli [*Walker's note*]. The verses are 39–40.

9. xli. 41 [*Walker's note*].

1. xli. 44 [*Walker's note*].

2. Genesis xli. 45 [*Walker's note*].

3. Genesis, chap. xlvii. 5, 6 [*Walker's note*].

land in all Egypt. Need I mention the very notorious fact, that I have known a poor man of colour, who laboured night and day, to acquire a little money, and having acquired it, he vested it in a small piece of land, and got him a house erected thereon, and having paid for the whole, he moved his family into it, where he was suffered to remain but nine months, when he was cheated out of his property by a white man, and driven out of door! And is not this the case generally? Can a man of colour buy a piece of land and keep it peaceably? Will not some white man try to get it from him, even if it is in a *mud hole?* I need not comment any farther on a subject, which all, both black and white, will readily admit. But I must, really, observe that in this very city, when a man of colour dies, if he owned any real estate it most generally falls into the hands of some white person. The wife and children of the deceased may weep and lament if they please, but the estate will be kept snug enough by its white possessor.

But to prove farther that the condition of the Israelites was better under the Egyptians than ours is under the whites. I call upon the professing Christians, I call upon the philanthropist, I call upon the very tyrant himself, to show me a page of history, either sacred or profane, on which a verse can be found, which maintains, that the Egyptians heaped the *insupportable insult* upon the children of Israel, by telling them that they were not of the *human family*. Can the whites deny this charge? Have they not, after having reduced us to the deplorable condition of slaves under their feet, held us up as descending originally from the tribes of *Monkeys* or *Orang-Outangs*? O! my God! I appeal to every man of feeling—is not this insupportable? Is it not heaping the most gross insult upon our miseries, because they have got us under their feet and we cannot help ourselves? Oh! pity us we pray thee, Lord Jesus, Master.—Has Mr. Jefferson declared to the world, that we are inferior to the whites, both in the endowments of our bodies and our minds?[4] It is indeed surprising, that a man of such great learning, combined with such excellent natural parts, should speak so of a set of men in chains. I do not know what to compare it to, unless, like putting one wild deer in an iron cage, where it will be secured, and hold another by the side of the same, then let it go, and expect the one in the cage to run as fast as the one at liberty. So far, my brethren, were the Egyptians from heaping these insults upon their slaves, that Pharaoh's daughter took Moses, a son of Israel for her own, as will appear by the following.

"And Pharaoh's daughter said unto her, [Moses' mother] take this child away, and nurse it for me, and I will pay thee thy wages. And the woman took the child [Moses] and nursed it.

"And the child grew, and she brought him unto Pharaoh's daughter and he became her son. And she called his name Moses: and she said because I drew him out of the water."[5]

In all probability, Moses would have become Prince Regent to the throne, and no doubt, in process of time but he would have been seated on the throne of Egypt. But he had rather suffer shame, with the people of God, than to enjoy pleasures with that wicked people for a season. O! that the coloured people were long since of Moses' excellent disposition, instead of courting favour with, and telling news and lies to our *natural enemies*, against each other—aiding them to keep their hellish chains of slavery upon us. Would we not long before this time, have been respectable men, instead of such

4. In his *Notes on the State of Virginia* (1787), Thomas Jefferson judged Black people both less beautiful than whites and intellectually inferior to them.

5. See Exodus, chap. ii. 9, 10 [*Walker's note*].

wretched victims of oppression as we are? Would they be able to drag our mothers, our fathers, our wives, our children and ourselves, around the world in chains and hand-cuffs as they do, to dig up gold and silver for them and theirs? This question, my brethren, I leave for you to digest; and may God Almighty force it home to your hearts. Remember that unless you are united, keeping your tongues within your teeth, you will be afraid to trust your secrets to each other, and thus perpetuate our miseries under the *Christians*!!!! ☞ ADDITION.—Remember, also to lay humble at the feet of our Lord and Master Jesus Christ, with prayers and fastings. Let our enemies go on with their butcheries, and at once fill up their cup. Never make an attempt to gain our freedom or *natural right,* from under our cruel oppressors and murderers, until you see your way clear[6]—when that hour arrives and you move, be not afraid or dismayed; for be you assured that Jesus Christ the King of heaven and of earth who is the God of justice and of armies, will surely go before you. And those enemies who have for hundreds of years stolen our *rights,* and kept us ignorant of Him and His divine worship, he will remove. Millions of whom, are this day, so ignorant and avaricious, that they cannot conceive how God can have an attribute of justice, and show mercy to us because it pleased Him to make us black—which colour, Mr. Jefferson calls unfortunate!!!!!! As though we are not as thankful to our God, for having made us as it pleased himself, as they, (the whites,) are for having made them white. They think because they hold us in their infernal chains of slavery, that we wish to be white, or of their color—but they are dreadfully deceived—we wish to be just as it pleased our Creator to have made us, and no avaricious and unmerciful wretches, have any business to make slaves of, or hold us in slavery. How would they like for us to make slaves of, and hold them in cruel slavery, and murder them as they do us?—But is Mr. Jefferson's assertions true? viz. "that it is unfortunate for us that our Creator has been pleased to make us *black*." We will not take his say so, for the fact. The world will have an opportunity to see whether it is unfortunate for us, that our Creator *has made us* darker than the *whites*.

Fear not the number and education of our *enemies,* against whom we shall have to contend for our lawful right; guaranteed to us by our Maker; for why should we be afraid, when God is, and will continue, (if we continue humble) to be on our side?

The man who would not fight under our Lord and Master Jesus Christ, in the glorious and heavenly cause of freedom and of God—to be delivered from the most wretched, abject and servile slavery, that ever a people was afflicted with since the foundation of the world, to the present day—ought to be kept with all of his children or family, in slavery, or in chains, to be butchered by his *cruel enemies.* ☜

I saw a paragraph, a few years since, in a South Carolina paper, which, speaking of the barbarity of the Turks, it said: "The Turks are the most barbarous people in the world—they treat the Greeks more like *brutes* than human beings." And in the same paper was an advertisement, which said: "Eight well

6. It is not to be understood here, that I mean for us to wait until God shall take us by the hair of our heads and drag us out of abject wretchedness and slavery, nor do I mean to convey the idea for us to wait until our enemies shall make preparations, and call us to seize those preparations, take it away from them, and put every thing before us to death, in order to gain our freedom which God has given us. For you must remember that we are men as well as they. God has been pleased to give us two eyes, two hands, two feet, and some sense in our heads as well as they. They have no more right to hold us in slavery than we have to hold them, we have just as much right, in the sight of God, to hold them and their children in slavery and wretchedness, as they have to hold us, and no more [*Walker's note*].

built Virginia and Maryland *Negro fellows* and four *wenches* will positively be *sold* this day, *to the highest bidder!*" And what astonished me still more was, to see in this same *humane* paper!! the cuts of three men, with clubs and budgets[7] on their backs, and an advertisement offering a considerable sum of money for their apprehension and delivery. I declare, it is really so amusing to hear the Southerners and Westerners of this country talk about *barbarity,* that it is positively, enough to make a man *smile.*

The sufferings of the Helots among the Spartans, were somewhat severe, it is true, but to say that theirs, were as severe as ours among the Americans, I do most strenuously deny—for instance, can any man show me an article on a page of ancient history which specifies, that, the Spartans chained, and handcuffed the Helots, and dragged them from their wives and children, children from their parents, mothers from their suckling babes, wives from their husbands, driving them from one end of the country to the other? Notice the Spartans were heathens, who lived long before our Divine Master made his appearance in the flesh. Can Christian Americans deny these barbarous cruelties? Have you not, Americans, having subjected us under you, added to these miseries, by insulting us in telling us to our face, because we are helpless, that we are not of the human family? I ask you, O! Americans, I ask you, in the name of the Lord, can you deny these charges? Some perhaps may deny, by saying, that they never thought or said that we were not men. But do not actions speak louder than words?—have they not made provisions for the Greeks, and Irish? Nations who have never done the least thing for them, while *we,* who have enriched their country with our blood and tears—have dug up gold and silver for them and their children, from generation to generation, and are in more miseries than any other people under heaven, are not seen, but by comparatively, a handful of the American people? There are indeed, more ways to kill a dog, besides choking it to death with butter. Further—The Spartans or Lacedaemonians, had some frivolous pretext, for enslaving the Helots, for they (Helots) while being free inhabitants of Sparta, stirred up an intestine commotion, and were, by the Spartans subdued, and made prisoners of war. Consequently they and their children were condemned to perpetual slavery.[8]

I have been for years troubling the pages of historians, to find out what our fathers have done to the *white Christians of America,* to merit such condign punishment as they have inflicted on them, and do continue to inflict on us their children. But I must aver, that my researches have hitherto been to no effect. I have therefore, come to the immoveable conclusion, that they (Americans) have, and do continue to punish us for nothing else, but for enriching them and their country. For I cannot conceive of anything else. Nor will I ever believe otherwise, until the Lord shall convince me.

The world knows, that slavery as it existed among the Romans, (which was the primary cause of their destruction) was, comparatively speaking, no more than a *cypher,* when compared with ours under the Americans. Indeed I should not have noticed the Roman slaves, had not the very learned and penetrating Mr. Jefferson said, "when a master was murdered, all his slaves in the same house, or within hearing, were condemned to death."[9]—Here let me ask Mr. Jefferson, (but he is gone to answer at the bar of God, for the

7. Leather bags. "Cuts": images from woodcuts.
8. See Dr. Goldsmith's History of Greece—page 9. See also, Plutarch's Lives. The Helots subdued by Agis, king of Sparta [*Walker's note*]. Walker's citation is to Oliver Goldsmith's *A History of Greece* (1774).
9. See his Notes on Virginia, page 210 [*Walker's note*].

deeds done in his body while living,) I therefore ask the whole American people, had I not rather die, or be put to death, than to be a slave to any tyrant, who takes not only my own, but my wife and children's lives by the inches? Yea, would I meet death with avidity far! far!! in preference to such *servile submission* to the murderous hands of tyrants. Mr. Jefferson's very severe remarks on us have been so extensively argued upon by men whose attainments in literature, I shall never be able to reach, that I would not have meddled with it, were it not to solicit each of my brethren, who has the spirit of a man, to buy a copy of Mr. Jefferson's "Notes on Virginia," and put it in the hand of his son. For let no one of us suppose that the refutations which have been written by our white friends are enough—they are *whites*—we are *blacks*. We, and the world wish to see the charges of Mr. Jefferson refuted by the blacks *themselves,* according to their chance; for we must remember that what the whites have written respecting this subject, is other men's labours, and did not emanate from the blacks. I know well, that there are some talents and learning among the coloured people of this country, which we have not a chance to develope, in consequence of oppression; but our oppression ought not to hinder us from acquiring all we can. For we will have a chance to develope them by and by. God will not suffer us, always to be oppressed. Our sufferings will come to an *end,* in spite of all the Americans this side of *eternity.* Then we will want all the learning and talents among ourselves, and perhaps more, to govern ourselves.—"Every dog must have its day," the American's is coming to an end.

But let us review Mr. Jefferson's remarks respecting us some further. Comparing our miserable fathers, with the learned philosophers of Greece, he says: "Yet notwithstanding these and other discouraging circumstances among the Romans, their slaves were often their rarest artists. They excelled too, in science, insomuch as to be usually employed as tutors to their master's children; Epictetus, Terence and Phædrus,[1] were slaves,—but they were of the race of whites. It is not their *condition* then, but *nature,* which has produced the distinction."[2] See this, my brethren!! Do you believe that this assertion is swallowed by millions of the whites? Do you know that Mr. Jefferson was one of as great characters as ever lived among the whites? See his writings for the world, and public labours for the United States of America. Do you believe that the assertions of such a man, will pass away into oblivion unobserved by this people and the world? If you do you are much mistaken—See how the American people treat us—have we souls in our bodies? Are we men who have any spirits at all? I know that there are many *swell-bellied* fellows among us, whose greatest object is to fill their stomachs. Such I do not mean—I am after those who know and feel, that we are MEN, as well as other people; to them, I say, that unless we try to refute Mr. Jefferson's arguments respecting us, we will only establish them.

But the slaves among the Romans. Every body who has read history, knows, that as soon as a slave among the Romans obtained his freedom, he could rise to the greatest eminence in the State, and there was no law instituted to hinder a slave from buying his freedom. Have not the Americans instituted laws to hinder us from obtaining our freedom? Do any deny this charge? Read the laws of Virginia, North Carolina, etc. Further: have not the Americans instituted laws to prohibit a man of colour from obtaining

1. A classical Roman philosopher, dramatist, and author of fables, respectively, each one born into slavery.

2. See his Notes on Virginia, page 211 [*Walker's note*].

and holding any office whatever, under the government of the United States of America? Now, Mr. Jefferson tells us, that our condition is not so hard, as the slaves were under the Romans!!!!!!

It is time for me to bring this article to a close. But before I close it, I must observe to my brethren that at the close of the first Revolution in this country, with Great Britain, there were but thirteen States in the Union, now there are twenty-four, most of which are slave-holding States, and the whites are dragging us around in chains and in handcuffs, to their new States and Territories to work their mines and farms, to enrich them and their children—and millions of them believing firmly that we being a little darker than they, were made by our Creator to be an inheritance to them and their children for ever—the same as a parcel of *brutes*.

Are we MEN!!—I ask you, O my brethren! are we MEN? Did our Creator make us to be slaves to dust and ashes like ourselves? Are they not dying worms as well as we? Have they not to make their appearance before the tribunal of Heaven, to answer for the deeds done in the body, as well as we? Have we any other Master but Jesus Christ alone? Is he not their Master as well as ours?—What right then, have we to obey and call any other Master, but Himself? How we could be so *submissive* to a gang of men, whom we cannot tell whether they are *as good* as ourselves or not, I never could conceive. However, this is shut up with the Lord, and we cannot precisely tell—but I declare, we judge men by their works.

The whites have always been an unjust, jealous, unmerciful, avaricious and blood-thirsty set of beings, always seeking after power and authority.—We view them all over the confederacy of Greece, where they were first known to be any thing, (in consequence of education) we see them there, cutting each other's throats—trying to subject each other to wretchedness and misery—to effect which, they used all kinds of deceitful, unfair, and unmerciful means. We view them next in Rome, where the spirit of tyranny and deceit raged still higher. We view them in Gaul,[3] Spain, and in Britain.—In fine, we view them all over Europe, together with what were scattered about in Asia and Africa, as heathens, and we see them acting more like devils than accountable men. But some may ask, did not the blacks of Africa, and the mulattoes of Asia, go on in the same way as did the whites of Europe. I answer, no—they never were half so avaricious, deceitful and unmerciful as the whites, according to their knowledge.

But we will leave the whites or Europeans as heathens, and take a view of them as Christians, in which capacity we see them as cruel, if not more so than ever. In fact, take them as a body, they are ten times more cruel, avaricious and unmerciful than ever they were; for while they were heathens, they were bad enough it is true, but it is positively a fact that they were not quite so audacious as to go and take vessel loads of men, women and children, and in cold blood, and through devilishness, throw them into the sea, and murder them in all kinds of ways. While they were heathens, they were too ignorant for such barbarity. But being Christians, enlightened and sensible, they are completely prepared for such hellish cruelties. Now suppose God were to give them more sense, what would they do? If it were possible, would they not *dethrone* Jehovah[4] and seat themselves upon his throne? I therefore, in the name and fear of the Lord God of Heaven and of earth, divested of prejudice either on the side of my colour or that of the whites,

3. France.

4. God.

advance my suspicion of them, whether they are *as good by nature* as we are or not. Their actions, since they were known as a people, have been the reverse, I do indeed suspect them, but this, as I before observed, is shut up with the Lord, we cannot exactly tell, it will be proved in succeeding generations.—The whites have had the essence of the gospel as it was preached by my master and his apostles—the Ethiopians have not, who are to have it in its meridian splendor—the Lord will give it to them to their satisfaction. I hope and pray my God, that they will make good use of it, that it may be well with them.[5]

1830

5. It is my solemn belief, that if ever the world becomes Christianized, (which must certainly take place before long) it will be through the means, under God of the *Blacks,* who are now held in wretchedness, and degradation, by the white *Christians* of the world, who before they learn to do justice to us before our Maker—and be reconciled to us, and reconcile us to them, and by that means have clear consciences before God and man.—Send out Missionaries to convert the Heathens, many of whom after they cease to worship gods, which neither see nor hear, become ten times more the children of Hell, than ever they were, why what is the reason? Why the reason is obvious, they must learn to do justice at home, before they go into distant lands, to display their charity, Christianity, and benevolence; when they learn to do justice, God will accept their offering, (no man may think that I am against Missionaries for I am not, my object is to see justice done at home, before we go to convert the Heathens) [*Walker's note*].

GEORGE MOSES HORTON
1797?–1883?

For most of his persistent, often frustrated life, George Moses Horton was both enslaved and a poet. Unlike Phillis Wheatley, his only significant predecessor in the history of African American poetry, Horton made the conflict between the condition of his birth and the aspiration of his life a salient and individualizing theme of his writing. In 1925 Countee Cullen became Harlem's most famous poet by composing the poignant and plainly self-referential couplet: "Yet do I marvel at this curious thing: / To make a poet black, and bid him sing." It was Horton, however, who introduced to American verse the agonizing contradiction epitomized in Cullen's lines. Not only Black but also enslaved, not just a versifier but a poet intent on a professional literary career in a society that denied him the right to write, Horton's experience and articulation of the contradictory status of the Black poet in the United States were paradigmatic, a crucial reference point in the history of African American literature.

Enslaved from birth in Northampton County, North Carolina, Horton endured bondage to three generations of the William Horton family until Union victory in the Civil War finally liberated him in 1865. George grew up working on his enslavers' farms in Chatham County but discovered by the age of ten a strong affinity toward music and verse. After teaching himself to read, the teenager began composing hymns in his head. By the time he was twenty years old he had begun to make a reputation at the state university at Chapel Hill, an eight-mile walk from his home, because of his ability to create made-to-order love poems for students willing to pay twenty-five to seventy-five cents per lyric, depending on the length and complexity desired. Some students compensated Horton for his work by giving him collections of poetry by Homer, Virgil, Shakespeare, Milton, Byron, and other classic English authors, all of whom provided models for Horton's own verse. Caroline Lee Hentz, a Chapel Hill professor's wife and novelist, helped Horton learn to write sometime around 1830.

She also helped him break into print in 1828 by sending two poems critical of slavery to the Lancaster, Massachusetts, *Gazette,* Hentz's hometown newspaper.

In 1828 an unlikely biracial coalition of southerners and northerners tried to raise money for Horton's freedom by sponsoring his first volume of poetry, *The Hope of Liberty,* which was published in Raleigh, North Carolina, in 1829. *The Hope of Liberty* was the first book of African American poetry in more than half a century as well as the first book authored by a Black southerner. Only three of the twenty-one poems in *The Hope of Liberty* shed light on Horton's feelings about his enslavement; the rest are concerned with romantic love, religion, and death. But the poem titled "On Hearing of the Intention of a Gentleman to Purchase the Poet's Freedom" proved that the facile creator of sentimental complaints like "The Lover's Farewell" had also been through depths of "deep despair" in his pursuit of a "dismal path" toward freedom.

Although *The Hope of Liberty* did not accomplish its purpose, Horton's enslaver did allow him to hire his time by working in Chapel Hill as a professional poet, waiter, and handyman. Apparently he was not punished after publishing his verse in various abolitionist periodicals, such as the *Liberator,* the *North Star,* and the *National Anti-Slavery Standard.* In 1845 Horton saw his second book into print, *The Poetical Works of George M. Horton, The Colored Bard of North Carolina.* Published in Hillsborough, North Carolina, *The Poetical Works* did not risk the goodwill Horton enjoyed among local southern whites by opposing slavery overtly. But the most remarkable poem in the volume, "Division of an Estate," has impressed a number of modern critics with its subtle rhetoric of protest and its pathetic rendition of the plight of enslaved families at the moment of auction and separation.

During the last months of the Civil War, Horton managed to interest Captain William H. S. Banks, a Michigan cavalry officer in the occupying Union Army, in his plans for the publication of a third book of poems. Shortly after the fall of the Confederacy, *Naked Genius,* a compendium of 133 poems, ninety of which were new, appeared from a Raleigh printer. The subjects addressed in Horton's final book of poetry are diverse, ranging from patriotic celebrations of President Lincoln, General Grant, and Union soldiers to the plight of a dying carriage horse "by the cruel driver pressed, / Push along, push along." In poems like "Death of a Carriage Horse," Horton decried the injustices, rather than simply complaining about the constraints, of slavery and racism. Perhaps the poet felt finally at liberty to speak his mind not only about slavery but also about the trammels that had bound him and his poetic talents. If so, "George Moses Horton, Myself," one of the relatively few noted poems in *Naked Genius,* stands as a fitting autobiographical summary of the life and work of the poet. Although freedom brought him the opportunity to move to Philadelphia, recent scholarship suggests that Horton soon became disillusioned by his experience of segregation and racial discrimination in the North. His last known poem, "Let Us Go, Song for the Emigrant," urges his Black reader: "Let us desert this friendless place, / To stay is nothing but disgrace." By the time "Let Us Go" appeared in print in January 1867, George Moses Horton had made his way to the West African republic of Liberia, determined to start a new life. What became of him either in Africa or in the land of his birth remains unknown.

The Lover's Farewell

And wilt thou, love, my soul display,
And all my secret thoughts betray?
I strove but could not hold thee fast,
My heart flies off with thee at last.

The favorite daughter of the dawn,
On love's mild breeze will soon be gone

I strove but could not cease to love,
Nor from my heart the weight remove.

And wilt thou, love, my soul beguile,
And gull° thy fav'rite with a smile? *trick, cheat*
Nay, soft affection answers, nay,
And beauty wings my heart away.

I steal on tiptoe from these bowers,
All spangled with a thousand flowers;
I sigh, yet leave them all behind,
To gain the object of my mind.

And wilt thou, love, command my soul,
And waft me with a light controul?—
Adieu to all the blooms of May,
Farewell—I fly with love away!

I leave my parents here behind,
And all my friends—to love resigned—
'Tis grief to go, but death to stay:
Farewell—I'm gone with love away!

1829

On Hearing of the Intention of a Gentleman to Purchase the Poet's Freedom

When on life's ocean first I spread my sail,
I then implored a mild auspicious gale;
And from the slippery strand I took my flight,
And sought the peaceful haven of delight.

Tyrannic storms arose upon my soul,
And dreadful did their mad'ning thunders roll;
The pensive muse[1] was shaken from her sphere,
And hope, it vanish'd in the clouds of fear.

At length a golden sun broke thro' the gloom,
And from his smiles arose a sweet perfume—
A calm ensued, and birds began to sing,
And lo! the sacred muse resumed her wing.

With frantic joy she chaunted° as she flew, *chanted*
And kiss'd the clement° hand that bore her thro' *kind, tender*
Her envious foes did from her sight retreat,
Or prostrate fall beneath her burning feet.

'Twas like a proselyte,[2] allied to Heaven—
Or rising spirits' boast of sins forgiven,
Whose shout dissolves the adamant away
Whose melting voice the stubborn rocks obey.

1. Greek goddess of literature.

2. A new convert to a religion.

'Twas like the salutation of the dove,
Borne on the zephyr° thro' some lonesome grove, *breeze, wind*
When Spring returns, and Winter's chill is past,
And vegetation smiles above the blast.

'Twas like the evening of a nuptial pair,
When love pervades the hour of sad despair—
'Twas like fair Helen's sweet return to Troy,[3]
When every Grecian bosom swell'd with joy.

The silent harp which on the osiers[4] hung,
Was then attuned, and manumission[5] sung:
Away by hope the clouds of fear were driven,
And music breathed my gratitude to heaven.

Hard was the race to reach the distant goal,
The needle oft was shaken from the pole;
In such distress, who could forbear to weep?
Toss'd by the headlong billows of the deep!

The tantalizing beams which shone so plain,
Which turn'd my former pleasures into pain—
Which falsely promised all the joys of fame,
Gave way, and to a more substantial flame.

Some philanthropic souls as from afar,
With pity strove to break the slavish bar;
To whom my floods of gratitude shall roll,
And yield with pleasure to their soft control.

And sure of Providence this work begun—.
He shod my feet this rugged race to run;
And in despite of all the swelling tide,
Along the dismal path will prove my guide.

Thus on the dusky verge of deep despair,
Eternal Providence was with me there;
When pleasure seemed to fade on life's gay dawn,
And the last beam of hope was almost gone.

1829

Division of an Estate

It well bespeaks a man beheaded, quite
Divested of the laurel[1] robe of life,
When every member struggles for its base,
The head; the power of order now recedes,
Unheeded efforts rise on every side,

3. In Homer's *Iliad*, the Greeks went to war with Troy to return the beautiful Helen.
4. Branches of a willow tree.
5. Emancipation, freedom.
1. An emblem of respect and honor.

With dull emotion rolling through the brain
Of apprehending slaves. The flocks and herds,
In sad confusion, now run to and fro,
And seem to ask, distressed, the reason why
That they are thus prostrated. Howl, ye dogs!
Ye cattle, low! ye sheep, astonish'd, bleat!
Ye bristling swine, trudge squealing through the glades,
Void of an owner to impart your food!
Sad horses, lift your heads and neigh aloud,
And caper frantic from the dismal scene:
Mow the last food upon your grass-clad lea.° *meadow*
And leave a solitary home behind,
In hopeless widowhood no longer gay!
The trav'ling sun of gain his journey ends
In unavailing pain; he sets with tears;
A king sequester'd sinking from his throne,
Succeeded by a train of busy friends.
Like stars which rise with smiles, to mark the flight
Of awful Phoebus[2] to another world;
Stars after stars in fleet succession rise
Into the wide empire of fortune clear,
Regardless of the donor of their lamps;
Like heirs forgetful of parental care,
Without a grateful smile or filial tear,
Redound in rev'rence to expiring age.
But soon parental benediction flies
Like vivid meteors; in a moment gone,
As though they ne'er had been. But O! the state,
The dark suspense in which poor vassals[3] stand
Each mind upon the spire of chance hangs fluctuant;
The day of separation is at hand;
Imagination lifts her gloomy curtains,
Like ev'ning's mantle at the flight of day,
Thro' which the trembling pinnacle we spy,
On which we soon must stand with hopeful smiles,
Or apprehending frowns; to tumble on
The right or left forever.

1845

George Moses Horton, Myself

I feel myself in need
  Of the inspiring strains of ancient lore,
My heart to lift, my empty mind to feed,
  And all the world explore.

I know that I am old
  And never can recover what is past,

2. The bright; a Greek epithet associated with Apollo, god of the sun.

3. Here, the enslaved.

But for the future may some light unfold
  And soar from ages blast.

I feel resolved to try,
  My wish to prove, my calling to pursue,
Or mount up from the earth into the sky,
  To show what Heaven can do.

My genius from a boy,
  Has fluttered like a bird within my heart;
But could not thus confined her powers employ,
  Impatient to depart.

She like a restless bird,
  Would spread her wing, her power to be unfurl'd,
And let her songs be loudly heard,
  And dart from world to world.

1865

SOJOURNER TRUTH
ca. 1799–1883

More than any other African American of her era, Sojourner Truth was the stuff of antislavery legend. She is said to have been accosted once by a white policeman in Rochester, New York, as she walked alone, cane in hand, from Corinthian Hall, having delivered an antislavery lecture that evening. The policeman demanded that she identify herself. Truth paused, planted her cane firmly, drew herself up to her full six-foot height, and in her deep, resonant voice, replied, *"I am that I am."* The unnerved officer vanished. Sojourner Truth went on to her destination undisturbed.

A leading exponent of liberty in both the abolitionist and the feminist movements in the mid-nineteenth century, Sojourner Truth was an extraordinarily self-possessed person. The singularity of her identity and the impossibility of labeling her are epitomized in her appropriation of "I am that I am," the words God speaks in the Bible in answer to Moses's attempt to give the Lord a name. Sojourner Truth was the name triumphantly adopted by Isabella Van Wagenen after forty years of struggle first to escape enslavement and then to settle on the mission she felt God intended for her.

Isabella Van Wagenen's experience in slavery was harsh. Born in Ulster County, New York, to a wealthy Dutch enslaver, she was separated from her parents as a child and sold to a succession of owners who exploited her unusual strength and did not hesitate to enforce their discipline with beatings. Married in her teens, she bore at least five children in slavery and took one of them with her when she walked away from her final enslaver in 1826, seizing her freedom a year before she would have been emancipated by New York law in 1827. Two years later Van Wagenen sued successfully for the return of her son Peter from enslavement in Alabama. Attracted to New York City, she moved there in 1828 to work as a domestic. She pursued both unorthodox and conventional religious paths toward the spiritual fulfillment she longed for. In

1843 Van Wagenen became convinced that God had called her to leave the city and go out into the countryside "testifying of the hope that was in her." Her hope was that others, regardless of color, sex, or condition, could experience the spiritual conversion and empowerment that had given her a new mission in life. She renamed herself Sojourner Truth to signify the new person she had become, a traveler dedicated to speaking a spiritually and socially redemptive truth as God revealed it to her.

Early in her career as an itinerant preacher, Sojourner Truth met William Lloyd Garrison, Frederick Douglass, and other prominent antislavery activists in Massachusetts. By 1851 she had joined their ranks, earning fame for her ability to deliver folksy as well as fiery speeches that denounced slavery as a moral abomination that tempted the wrath of God to be brought down on America. This commitment to human rights impelled Truth into the budding feminist movement of the 1850s as well. By the onset of the Civil War, Sojourner Truth had come to represent a brand of female, communitarian, vernacular African American leadership that rivaled the masculine, individualist, self-consciously literary model of Black spokesman exemplified by Douglass himself.

In 1863 Harriet Beecher Stowe gave Truth lasting celebrity in an *Atlantic Monthly* tribute titled "Sojourner Truth, the Libyan Sibyl," in which Stowe declared, "I do not recollect ever to have been conversant with any one who had more of that silent and subtle power which we call personal presence than this woman." However, Stowe's article also reduces Truth, in the words of one of her biographers, to "a quaint and innocent exotic," more preacher than social reformer and definitely not a feminist. Despite mischaracterizations like this as well as advancing age and infirmities brought on by the rigors of slavery, Truth worked tirelessly on several civil and women's rights fronts in the 1860s. She recruited Black troops in Michigan; helped with relief efforts for the freedmen and women escaping from the South; led a successful effort to desegregate the streetcars of Washington, D.C.; and campaigned for President Abraham Lincoln's re-election. In the early 1870s she lectured widely in favor of a federally funded homeland in Kansas for African American refugees from southern violence and oppression. Truth died at her home in Battle Creek, Michigan, in 1883, an icon of American progressivism and reform. In 2009 Sojourner Truth became the first African American woman to be honored with a bust in the U.S. Capitol.

Sojourner Truth never learned to read or write. "I cannot read a book, but I can read the people," she asserted. Two efforts were made during her lifetime to preserve her biography and the flavor of her remarkable manner of self-expression. In 1850 Truth worked with Olive Gilbert, a sympathetic white abolitionist, to write and publish the *Narrative of Sojourner Truth*, a contribution to both the slave narrative and the female spiritual autobiography traditions of African American literature. In 1875, with the editorial aid of a white friend, Frances Titus, Truth reprinted her *Narrative*, supplementing it with her *Book of Life*, which includes personal correspondence, newspaper accounts of her activities, and tributes from her admirers. This expanded edition of Truth's biography was reprinted in 1878, 1881, and 1884 under the title *Narrative of Sojourner Truth; A Bondswoman of Olden Time, with a History of Her Labors and Correspondence Drawn from Her "Book of Life."* Yet it is not her lengthy life story but rather a single speech that has preserved Sojourner Truth in cultural memory.

In the early summer of 1851 during a women's rights convention in Akron, Ohio, Truth took the podium to defend the dignity of women against theological attacks from a group of ministers. The president of the convention, Frances Gage, recalled some years later the pressure applied by white women to keep Truth from speaking lest she antagonize the ministers' racial as well as gender prejudices. But Truth spoke nonetheless. Her extemporaneous oration, scarcely more than three hundred words punctuated by homely metaphors and a deceptively simple argument for women's unique role in the liberation struggles of the day, was transcribed in the Salem, Ohio, *Anti-Slavery Bugle* on June 21, 1851. In 1863 a second and more elaborate version of the speech, as Gage recollected it, was published and later incorporated into the "Book of Life" section of the *Narrative of Sojourner Truth* (1875). The rhetorical question that Gage claimed Truth asked repeatedly in her speech—

"and ar'n't I a woman?"—became not only the de facto title of Truth's most famous oration but also the crux of her challenge as a Black woman to racial and sexual stereotypes. However, as scholarly study of Truth's ideas and public image has advanced, the reliability of Gage's 1863 account of the famed "Ar'n't I a Woman?" speech has been seriously challenged. The Sojourner Truth in the *Anti-Slavery Bugle*'s report does not speak in the southern dialectal English that Gage attributed to Truth a dozen years after her Ohio speech. Nor does the 1851 report contain the query "ar'n't I a woman?" that made Gage's version of the speech so famous. Today the two versions of the 1851 oration remain for readers of Truth to ponder. By comparing these renditions of a classic oral text of African American literature, we can usefully reconsider Truth's message from two perspectives and thereby appreciate its complex impact on those in her own time who tried, with varying agendas, to convey the ineffable power of her verbal artistry..

Ar'n't I a Woman?
Speech to the Women's Rights Convention in Akron, Ohio, 1851

From the *Anti-Slavery Bugle,* June 21, 1851

One of the most unique and interesting speeches of the Convention was made by Sojourner Truth, an emancipated slave. It is impossible to transfer it to paper, or convey any adequate idea of the effect it produced upon the audience. Those only can appreciate it who saw her powerful form, her whole-souled, earnest gesture, and listened to her strong and truthful tones. She came forward to the platform and addressing the President said with great simplicity: "May I say a few words?" Receiving an affirmative answer, she proceeded:

I want to say a few words about this matter. I am a woman's rights. I have as much muscle as any man, and can do as much work as any man. I have plowed and reaped and husked and chopped and mowed, and can any man do more than that? I have heard much about the sexes being equal. I can carry as much as any man, and can eat as much too, if I can get it. I am as strong as any man that is now. As for intellect, all I can say is, if woman have a pint, and man a quart—why can't she have her little pint full? You need not be afraid to give us our rights for fear we will take too much,—for we can't take more than our pint'll hold. The poor men seem to be all in confusion, and don't know what to do. Why children, if you have woman's rights, give it to her and you will feel better. You will have your own rights, and they won't be so much trouble. I can't read, but I can hear. I have heard the bible and have learned that Eve caused man to sin. Well, if woman upset the world, do give her a chance to set it right side up again. The Lady has spoken about Jesus, how he never spurned woman from him, and she was right. When Lazarus died, Mary and Martha came to him with faith and love and besought him to raise their brother.[1] And Jesus wept and Lazarus came forth. And how came Jesus into the world? Through God who created him and a woman who bore him. Man, where is your part? But the women are coming up blessed be God and a few of the men are coming up with them. But man is in a tight place, the poor slave is on him, woman is coming on him, he is surely between a hawk and a buzzard.

1. John 11:1–44 records the story of Jesus's raising of Lazarus, the brother of the disciples Mary and Martha, from the dead.

From *The Narrative of Sojourner Truth*, 1878

In the year 1851 she left her home in Northampton, Mass., for a lecturing tour in Western New York, accompanied by the Hon. George Thompson of England, and other distinguished abolitionists. To advocate the cause of the enslaved at this period was both unpopular and unsafe. Their meetings were frequently disturbed or broken up by the pro-slavery mob, and their lives imperiled. At such times, Sojourner fearlessly maintained her ground, and by her dignified manner and opportune remarks would disperse the rabble and restore order.

She spent several months in Western New York, making Rochester her head-quarters. Leaving this State, she traveled westward, and the next glimpse we get of her is in a Woman's Rights Convention at Akron, Ohio. Mrs. Frances D. Gage, who presided at that meeting, relates the following:—

"The cause was unpopular then. The leaders of the movement trembled on seeing a tall, gaunt black woman, in a gray dress and white turban, surmounted by an uncouth sun-bonnet, march deliberately into the church, walk with the air of a queen up the aisle, and take her seat upon the pulpit steps. A buzz of disapprobation was heard all over the house, and such words as these fell upon listening ears:—

"'An abolition affair!' 'Woman's rights and niggers!' 'We told you so!' 'Go it, old darkey!'

"I chanced upon that occasion to wear my first laurels in public life as president of the meeting. At my request, order was restored and the business of the hour went on. The morning session was held; the evening exercises came and went. Old Sojourner, quiet and reticent as the 'Libyan Statue,'[2] sat crouched against the wall on the corner of the pulpit stairs, her sun-bonnet shading her eyes, her elbows on her knees, and her chin resting upon her broad, hard palm. At intermission she was busy, selling 'The Life of Sojourner Truth,'[3] a narrative of her own strange and adventurous life. Again and again timorous and trembling ones came to me and said with earnestness, 'Don't let her speak, Mrs. Gage, it will ruin us. Every newspaper in the land will have our cause mixed with abolition and niggers, and we shall be utterly denounced.' My only answer was, 'We shall see when the time comes.'

"The second day the work waxed warm. Methodist, Baptist, Episcopal, Presbyterian, and Universalist ministers came in to hear and discuss the resolutions presented. One claimed superior rights and privileges for man on the ground of superior intellect; another, because of the manhood of Christ. 'If God had desired the equality of woman, he would have given some token of his will through the birth, life, and death of the Saviour.' Another gave us a theological view of the sin of our first mother. There were few women in those days that dared to 'speak in meeting,' and the august teachers of the people were seeming to get the better of us, while the boys in the galleries and the sneerers among the pews were hugely enjoying the discomfiture, as they supposed, of the 'strong minded.' Some of the tender-skinned friends were on the point of losing dignity, and the atmosphere of the convention betokened a storm.

"Slowly from her seat in the corner rose Sojourner Truth, who, till now, had scarcely lifted her head. 'Don't let her speak!' gasped half a dozen in my ear. She moved slowly and solemnly to the front, laid her old bonnet at her

2. A reference to the title of Harriet Beecher Stowe's "Sojourner Truth, the Libyan Sibyl," which was published in the *Atlantic Monthly* (April 1863).

3. *Narrative of Sojourner Truth* (1850).

feet, and turned her great, speaking eyes to me. There was a hissing sound of disapprobation above and below. I rose and announced 'Sojourner Truth,' and begged the audience to keep silence for a few moments. The tumult subsided at once, and every eye was fixed on this almost Amazon form, which stood nearly six feet high, head erect, and eye piercing the upper air, like one in a dream. At her first word, there was a profound hush. She spoke in deep tones, which, though not loud, reached every ear in the house, and away through the throng at the doors and windows:—

"'Well, chilern, whar dar is so much racket dar must be something out o' kilter. I tink dat 'twixt de niggers of de Souf and de women at de Norf all a talkin' 'bout rights, de white men will be in a fix pretty soon. But what's all dis here talkin' 'bout? Dat man ober dar say dat women needs to be helped into carriages, and lifted ober ditches, and to have de best place every whar. Nobody eber help me into carriages, or ober mud puddles, or gives me any best place [and raising herself to her full height and her voice to a pitch like rolling thunder, she asked], and ar'n't I a woman? Look at me! Look at my arm! [And she bared her right arm to the shoulder, showing her tremendous muscular power.] I have plowed, and planted, and gathered into barns, and no man could head me—and ar'n't I a woman? I could work as much and eat as much as a man (when I could get it), and bear de lash as well—and ar'n't I a woman? I have borne thirteen chilern and seen 'em mos' all sold off into slavery, and when I cried out with a mother's grief, none but Jesus heard—and ar'n't I a woman? Den dey talks 'bout dis ting in de head—what dis dey call it?' 'Intellect,' whispered some one near. 'Dat's it honey. What's dat got to do with women's rights or niggers' rights? If my cup won't hold but a pint and yourn holds a quart, would n't ye be mean not to let me have my little half-measure full?' And she pointed her significant finger and sent a keen glance at the minister who had made the argument. The cheering was long and loud.

"'Den dat little man in black dar, he say women can't have as much rights as man, cause Christ want a woman. Whar did your Christ come from?' Rolling thunder could not have stilled that crowd as did those deep, wonderful tones, as she stood there with outstretched arms and eye of fire. Raising her voice still louder, she repeated, 'Whar did your Christ come from? From God and a woman. Man had nothing to do with him.' Oh! what a rebuke she gave the little man.

"'Turning again to another objector, she took up the defense of mother Eve. I cannot follow her through it all. It was pointed, and witty, and solemn, eliciting at almost every sentence deafening applause; and she ended by asserting that 'if de fust woman God ever made was strong enough to turn the world upside down, all 'lone, dese togedder [and she glanced her eye over us], ought to be able to turn it back and get it right side up again, and now dey is asking to do it, de men better let em.' Long-continued cheering. 'Bleeged to ye for hearin' on me, and now ole Sojourner ha'n't got nothing more to say.'

"Amid roars of applause, she turned to her corner, leaving more than one of us with streaming eyes and hearts beating with gratitude. She had taken us up in her strong arms and carried us safely over the slough of difficulty, turning the whole tide in our favor. I have never in my life seen anything like the magical influence that subdued the mobbish spirit of the day and turned the jibes and sneers of an excited crowd into notes of respect and admiration. Hundreds rushed up to shake hands, and congratulate the glorious old mother and bid her God speed on her mission of 'testifying again concerning the wickedness of this 'ere people.'"

MARIA W. STEWART
1803–1879

Maria Stewart has been called America's first Black woman political writer. Her *Productions of Mrs. Maria W. Stewart* (1835), a collection of speeches and essays on such topics as slavery, women's rights, and African American uplift, opened the door through which subsequent Black women activists of the pen—Frances Ellen Watkins Harper and Mary Ann Shadd, to name just two—marched. Stewart is also thought to have been the first American woman of any color to step onto a lecture platform and speak her political mind to what was then called "a promiscuous audience," that is, an audience of men as well as women. The date of this bold foray into new territory for women, especially Black women, was September 21, 1832. The place was Franklin Hall in Boston, the site of the regular monthly meeting of the New England Anti-Slavery Society. Stewart knew that this audience, composed of some of the most liberal-minded people in the northern states, would be attentive rather than appalled by her direct defiance of accepted nineteenth-century ideas about "woman's place." Rather than congratulating them on their progressive views, however, Stewart challenged her audience, irrespective of color or gender, to greater efforts on behalf of educational and economic opportunity for young Black women as well as men in the city of Boston. When it was published in her *Productions*, Stewart called her remarks at Franklin Hall a lecture. But it might just as well have been received as a political sermon, for it is certainly a vintage decanter of piety, political exhortation, and social prophesy poured out in a distinctively nineteenth-century African American rhetorical vein.

Maria Miller was born in Hartford, Connecticut, and orphaned at the age of five. With no other means of support, she went to work as a domestic servant in a minister's family, where she received religious instruction but little else in the way of an education. In her teens she moved to Boston, where she worked as a domestic and, through her own efforts, made up somewhat for her lack of schooling. In 1826 she married James W. Stewart, a prosperous shipping agent in the Boston fishing industry, who left her a widow three years later. The publication of David Walker's *Appeal* in Boston in 1829 gave strong impetus to Maria Stewart's desire to address the issues facing African American men and women on the eve of the most militant phase of the antislavery struggle in America. A conversion experience in 1830 galvanized Stewart into action, confident that she possessed "that spirit of independence that, were I called upon, I would willingly sacrifice my life for the cause of God and my brethren." In the early 1830s, Stewart introduced herself as a writer of religious tracts designed to edify and inspire Black people. In 1832 and 1833 she moved into the world of secular controversy, undertaking a series of lectures and essays advertised and sometimes published in William Lloyd Garrison's new antislavery periodical, *The Liberator*, which were collected in 1835 as her *Productions*.

Stewart's social criticism in the *Productions* is usually couched in traditional appeals to Christian charity and individual moral reform. Her feminist agenda is at times predicated on pleas to women to rededicate themselves to their familial duties as mothers and wives. Nevertheless, Stewart's conviction that "religion and the pure principles of morality" were "the sure foundation" on which African Americans should build for the future did not keep her from recommending a blueprint for a new social order that was radically opposed to the hierarchies of social class and racial caste that dominated the world in which she lived. For Stewart, the egalitarianism of the Christian gospel demanded a fundamental rethinking of the roles that men and women as well as Blacks and whites assumed were natural, God-given, and inevitable. At the end of the *Productions*, Stewart proclaimed "a mighty work of reformation" in the minds of her people, particularly among women of color, even as she admitted that public opposition to her strident message of reform had grown to such proportions as to compel her to move from Boston to New York. If she was dispirited by the response to her speaking and writing in Boston, Stewart's career in New York does not show permanent evidence of it. She joined women's organizations and attended antislavery conventions while working as a schoolteacher in Brooklyn and Long Island and, after 1852, in Baltimore. At the outbreak of the Civil War, Stewart moved to Washington, D.C. seeking better teaching opportunities. During the early years of Reconstruction, she opened her own small academies in the District of Columbia, intent on educating the children of the African American working poor. She played a significant role in the founding of the first African American Episcopal church, St. Mary's Chapel for Colored People, in the District in 1865. Sometime in the late 1870s, Stewart became matron of the Freedmen's Hospital and Asylum. In 1879, just months before her death, Stewart brought out a reprinted edition of her essays, speeches, and meditations of the 1830s, adding to this material a short memoir, which she titled *Sufferings during the War.* The message of the new book, *Meditations from the Pen of Mrs. Maria W. Stewart,* is summarized in an observation that brought the memoir, and Stewart's career, to a fitting conclusion: "by grace I overcame."

From Religion and the Pure Principles of Morality, the Sure Foundation on Which We Must Build

Introduction

Feeling a deep solemnity of soul, in view of our wretched and degraded situation, and sensible of the gross ignorance that prevails among us, I have thought proper thus publicly to express my sentiments before you. I hope my friends will not scrutinize these pages with too severe an eye, as I have not calculated to display either elegance or taste in their composition, but have merely written the meditations of my heart as far as my imagination led; and have presented them before you in order to arouse you to exertion, and to enforce upon your minds the great necessity of turning your attention to knowledge and improvement.

I was born in Hartford, Connecticut, in 1803; was left an orphan at five years of age; was bound out in a clergyman's family; had the seeds of piety and virtue early sown in my mind, but was deprived of the advantages of education, though my soul thirsted for knowledge. Left them at fifteen years of age; attended Sabbath schools[1] until I was twenty; in 1826 was married to James W. Stewart; was left a widow in 1829; was, as I humbly hope and trust, brought to the knowledge of the truth, as it is in Jesus, in 1830; in 1831 made a public profession of my faith in Christ.

From the moment I experienced the change, I felt a strong desire, with the help and assistance of God, to devote the remainder of my days to piety and virtue, and now possess that spirit of independence that, were I called upon, I would willingly sacrifice my life for the cause of God and my brethren.

All the nations of the earth are crying out for liberty and equality. Away, away with tyranny and oppression! And shall Afric's sons be silent any longer? Far be it from me to recommend to you either to kill, burn, or destroy. But I

1. Sunday schools.

would strongly recommend to you to improve your talents; let not one lie buried in the earth. Show forth your powers of mind. Prove to the world that

> Though black your skins as shades of night,
> your hearts are pure, your souls are white.

This is the land of freedom. The press is at liberty. Every man has a right to express his opinion. Many think, because your skins are tinged with a sable hue, that you are an inferior race of beings; but God does not consider you as such. He hath formed and fashioned you in his own glorious image, and hath bestowed upon you reason and strong powers of intellect. He hath made you to have dominion over the beasts of the field, the fowls of the air, and the fish of the sea.[2] He hath crowned you with glory and honor; hath made you but a little lower than the angels.[3] and according to the Constitution of these United States, he hath made all men free and equal. Then why should one worm say to another, "Keep you down there, while I sit up yonder; for I am better than thou?"[4] It is not the color of the skin that makes the man, but it is the principles formed within the soul.

Many will suffer for pleading the cause of oppressed Africa, and I shall glory in being one of her martyrs; for I am firmly persuaded, that the God in whom I trust is able to protect me from the rage and malice of mine enemies, and from them that will rise up against me; and if there is no other way for me to escape, he is able to take me to himself, as he did the most noble, fearless, and undaunted David Walker.[5]

1831

Lecture Delivered at the Franklin Hall

Boston, September 21, 1832

Why sit ye here and die? If we say we will go to a foreign land, the famine and the pestilence are there, and there we shall die. If we sit here, we shall die. Come let us plead our cause before the whites: if they save us alive, we shall live—and if they kill us, we shall but die.[1]

Methinks I heard a spiritual interrogation—"Who shall go forward, and take off the reproach that is cast upon the people of color? Shall it be a woman?" And my heart made this reply—"If it is thy will, be it even so, Lord Jesus!"

I have heard much respecting the horrors of slavery; but may Heaven forbid that the generality of my color throughout these United States should experience any more of its horrors than to be a servant of servants, or hewers of wood and drawers of water![2] Tell us no more of southern slavery; for with few exceptions, although I may be very erroneous in my opinion, yet I consider our condition but little better than that. Yet, after all, methinks there are no chains so galling as those that bind the soul, and exclude it from the vast field of useful and scientific knowledge. O, had I received the advantages of an early education, my ideas would, ere now, have expanded

2. Genesis 1:26.
3. Psalms 8:5.
4. An ironic allusion to Isaiah 65:5: "Stand by thyself, come not near to me; for I am holier than thou."
5. African American polemicist (1785–1830), author of *David Walker's Appeal* (1829).

1. A paraphrase of 2 Kings 7:4.
2. Joshua 9:23: "Now therefore ye are cursed, and there shall none of you be freed from being bondmen, and hewers of wood and drawers of water for the house of my God."

far and wide; but, alas! I possess nothing but moral capability—no teachings but the teachings of the Holy Spirit.

I have asked several individuals of my sex, who transact business for themselves, if providing our girls were to give them the most satisfactory references, they would not be willing to grant them an equal opportunity with others? Their reply has been—for their own part, they had no objection; but as it was not the custom, were they to take them into their employ, they would be in danger of losing the public patronage.

And such is the powerful force of prejudice. Let our girls possess whatever amiable qualities of soul they may; let their characters be fair and spotless as innocence itself; let their natural taste and ingenuity be what they may; it is impossible for scarce an individual of them to rise above the condition of servants. Ah! why is this cruel and unfeeling distinction? Is it merely because God has made our complexion to vary? If it be, O shame to soft, relenting humanity! "Tell it not in Gath! publish it not in the streets of Askelon!"[3] Yet, after all, methinks were the American free people of color to turn their attention more assiduously to moral worth and intellectual improvement, this would be the result: prejudice would gradually diminish, and the whites would be compelled to say, unloose those fetters!

Though black their skins as shades of night
Their hearts are pure, their souls are white.

Few white persons of either sex, who are calculated for anything else, are willing to spend their lives and bury their talents in performing mean, servile labor. And such is the horrible idea that I entertain respecting a life of servitude, that if I conceived of their [*sic*] being no possibility of my rising above the condition of servant, I would gladly hail death as a welcome messenger. O, horrible idea, indeed! to possess noble souls aspiring after high and honorable acquirements, yet confined by the chains of ignorance and poverty to lives of continual drudgery and toil. Neither do I know of any who have enriched themselves by spending their lives as house-domestics, washing windows, shaking carpets, brushing boots, or tending upon gentlemen's tables. I can but die for expressing my sentiments: and I am as willing to die by the sword as the pestilence; for I am a true born American; your blood flows in my veins, and your spirit fires my breast.

I observed a piece in the Liberator a few months since, stating that the colonizationists[4] had published a work respecting us, asserting that we were lazy and idle. I confute them on that point. Take us generally as a people, we are neither lazy nor idle; and considering how little we have to excite or stimulate us, I am almost astonished that there are so many industrious and ambitious ones to be found; although I acknowledge, with extreme sorrow, that there are some who never were and never will be serviceable to society. And have you not a similar class among yourselves?

Again. It was asserted that we were "a ragged set, crying for liberty." I reply to it, the whites have so long and so loudly proclaimed the theme of equal rights and privileges, that our souls have caught the flame also, ragged as we are. As far as our merit deserves, we feel a common desire to rise above the condition of servants and drudges. I have learnt, by bitter experience, that

3. 2 Samuel 1:20.
4. People who believed that the enslaved should be freed on the condition that they return to Africa. "The Liberator": official journal of the American Anti-Slavery Society, edited by William Lloyd Garrison.

continual hard labor deadens the energies of the soul, and benumbs the faculties of the mind; the ideas become confined, the mind barren, and, like the scorching sands of Arabia, produces nothing; or like the uncultivated soil, brings forth thorns and thistles.

Again, continual and hard labor irritates our tempers and sours our dispositions; the whole system becomes worn out with toil and fatigue; nature herself becomes almost exhausted, and we care but little whether we live or die. It is true, that the free people of color throughout these United States are neither bought nor sold, nor under the lash of the cruel driver; many obtain a comfortable support; but few, if any, have an opportunity of becoming rich and independent; and the enjoyments we most pursue are as unprofitable to us as the spider's web or the floating bubbles that vanish into air. As servants, we are respected; but let us presume to aspire any higher, our employer regards us no longer. And were it not that the King eternal has declared that Ethiopia shall stretch forth her hands unto God,[5] I should indeed despair.

I do not consider it derogatory, my friends, for persons to live out to service. There are many whose inclination leads them to aspire no higher; and I would highly commend the performance of almost anything for an honest livelihood; but where constitutional strength is wanting, labor of this kind, in its mildest form, is painful. And doubtless many are the prayers that have ascended to Heaven from Afric's daughters for strength to perform their work. Oh, many are the tears that have been shed for the want of that strength! Most of our color have dragged out a miserable existence of servitude from the cradle to the grave. And what literary acquirement can be made, or useful knowledge derived, from either maps, books, or charts, by those who continually drudge from Monday morning until Sunday noon? O, ye fairer sisters, whose hands are never soiled, whose nerves and muscles are never strained, go learn by experience! Had we had the opportunity that you have had, to improve our moral and mental faculties, what would have hindered our intellects from being as bright, and our manners from being as dignified as yours? Had it been our lot to have been nursed in the lap of affluence and ease, and to have basked beneath the smiles and sunshine of fortune, should we not have naturally supposed that we were never made to toil? And why are not our forms as delicate, and our constitutions as slender, as yours? Is not the workmanship as curious and complete? Have pity upon us, have pity upon us, O ye who have hearts to feel for other's woes; for the hand of God has touched us. Owing to the disadvantages under which we labor, there are many flowers among us that are

> . . . born to bloom unseen
> And waste their fragrance on the desert air.[6]

My beloved brethren, as Christ has died in vain for those who will not accept his offered mercy, so will it be vain for the advocates of freedom to spend their breath in our behalf, unless with united hearts and souls you make some mighty efforts to raise your sons and daughters from the horrible state of servitude and degradation in which they are placed. It is upon you that woman depends; she can do but little besides using her influence; and it is for her sake and yours that I have come forward and made myself a

5. Psalms 68:31.
6. See Thomas Gray's "Elegy Written in a Country Churchyard" (1751), lines 55–56: "born to blush unseen, / And waste its sweetness on the desert air."

hissing and a reproach among the people;[7] for I am also one of the wretched and miserable daughters of the descendants of fallen Africa. Do you ask, why are you wretched and miserable? I reply, look at many of the most worthy and most interesting of us doomed to spend our lives in gentlemen's kitchens. Look at our young men, smart, active and energetic, with souls filled with ambitious fire; if they look forward, alas! What are their prospects? They can be nothing but the humblest laborers, on account of their dark complexions; hence many of them lose their ambition, and become worthless. Look at our middle-aged men, clad in their rusty plaids and coats; in winter, every cent they earn goes to buy their wood and pay their rents; the poor wives also toil beyond their strength, to help support their families. Look at our aged sires, whose heads are whitened with the frosts of seventy winters, with their old wood-saws on their backs. Alas, what keeps us so? Prejudice, ignorance and poverty. But ah! methinks our oppression is soon to come to an end; yea, before the Majesty of heaven, our groans and cries have reached the ears of the Lord of Sabaoth.[8] As the prayers and tears of Christians will avail the finally impenitent nothing; neither will the prayers and tears of the friends of humanity avail us anything, unless we possess a spirit of virtuous emulation within our breasts. Did the pilgrims, when they first landed on these shores, quietly compose themselves and say, "The Britons have all the money and all the power, and we must continue their servants forever?" Did they sluggishly sigh and say, "Our lot is hard, the Indians own the soil, and we cannot cultivate it?" No; they first made powerful efforts to raise themselves, and then God raised up those illustrious patriots, WASHINGTON and LAFAYETTE,[9] to assist and defend them. And, my brethren, have you made a powerful effort? Have you prayed the legislature for mercy's sake to grant you all the rights and privileges of free citizens, that your daughters may rise to that degree of respectability which true merit deserves, and your sons above the servile situations which most of them fill?

1832 1835

7. Jeremiah 29:18: "And I will . . . deliver them to be removed to all the kingdoms of the earth, to be a curse, and an astonishment, and an hissing, and a reproach, among all the nations whither I have driven them."

8. James 5:4.

9. Marquis de Lafayette (1757–1834), Frenchman who served as an aide to General George Washington, commander in chief of the American Revolutionary Army.

SOLOMON NORTHUP
1807–?

Twelve Years a Slave, the narrative of Solomon Northup's kidnapping and enslavement in Louisiana from 1841 through 1853, struck the United States like a literary thunderbolt in the spring of 1853. None other than Harriet Beecher Stowe, to whom *Twelve Years a Slave* was dedicated, declared that Northup's story of survival furnished a "striking parallel" to what her fictional creation, Uncle Tom, endures in *Uncle Tom's Cabin*, published barely a year before Northup's narrative. Like *Uncle Tom's Cabin*, *Twelve Years a Slave* became a best seller; an estimated 30,000 copies

Used as the frontispiece for *Twelve Years a Slave,* this is the only known image of Solomon Northup. African American slave narratives usually portray their authors dressed as prosperous free persons.

were purchased during the first two years of its existence. During this period of time, the combined sales of Thoreau's *Walden* (1854), Whitman's *Leaves of Grass* (1855), Longfellow's *The Song of Hiawatha* (1855), and Emerson's *English Traits* (1856) would not have equaled those of *Twelve Years a Slave*.

"It is a strange history," Frederick Douglass mused about *Twelve Years a Slave* in a review in *Frederick Douglass' Paper*. But "its truth is far greater than fiction. Think of it! For thirty years *a man*, with all a man's hopes, fears and aspirations—with a wife and children to call him by the endearing names of husband and father—with a home, humble it may be, but still a *home*, beneath the shelter of whose roof none had a right to molest or make him afraid—then for twelve years *a thing*, a chattel personal, classed with mules and horses, and treated with less consideration than they, torn from his home and family, and the free labor by which he earned their bread, and driven to unremitting, unrequited toil in a cotton field, under a burning

Southern sun, by the lash of an inhuman master. Oh! It is horrible. It chills the blood to think that such are."

Chilling and astounding though *Twelve Years a Slave* was, the book was supported by ample evidence, both internal and external. The writer of *Twelve Years a Slave*, a white professional author and sometime novelist named David Wilson, whom Northup had collaborated with to produce the book in less than six months, asserted in his preface: "Many of the statements contained in the following pages are corroborated by abundant evidence—others rest entirely upon Solomon's assertion. That he has adhered strictly to the truth the editor, at least, who has had an opportunity of detecting any contradiction or discrepancy in his statements, is well satisfied. He has invariably repeated the same story without deviating in the slightest particular, and has also carefully perused the manuscript, dictating an alteration wherever the most trivial inaccuracy has appeared." Over the last fifty years, scholars have authenticated virtually all the important details of *Twelve Years a Slave* as a reliable record of Northup's life before, during, and after his ordeal as an enslaved person in the Deep South.

Solomon Northup was born free on his parents' farm near Minerva, New York, in the Adirondack Mountains. By the time Solomon was a teenager, his father, Mintus, formerly enslaved, had become a property owner in Fort Edward, New York, able to send his son to school while also training him to become a farmer. In 1828, Solomon married Anne Hampton, a free-born upstate New Yorker like himself. The couple settled in Fort Edward, where Solomon developed skills in lumbering, carpentry, and masonry. As their family grew, Solomon's talents as a fiddler brought in needed extra income. Though "happy and prosperous" on their small farm, the Northups moved in 1834 to Saratoga, a popular tourist destination in the summers, where Solomon found work in a variety of part-time and seasonal occupations, always supplemented by income from his musicianship. Anne's employment as a cook in a well-known local hotel meant that the Northup family enjoyed a modest, but what Northup called a "comfortable," niche within the small African American population of Saratoga.

In late March 1841, Northup met two white men who identified themselves as Brown and Hamilton, supposedly circus performers seeking a high-quality fiddler for engagements in New York City. Once there, they persuaded him to journey on with them to Washington, D.C. Eager for extra income, Northup obtained his free papers from the Custom House in New York before traveling farther south. But after an afternoon and evening of drinking with Brown and Hamilton in Washington, Northup fell ill and returned to his room. When he woke up, he thought he was being taken to a doctor but the next day found himself in chains in a slave pen in the nation's capital, with his free papers missing.

Northup's protests and insistence on his free identity led to severe beatings followed by transfer to Richmond, Virginia, where the kidnap victim, now renamed Platt, and thirty-nine other enslaved people were placed on a transport ship that conveyed them down the eastern coast to New Orleans. There a cotton planter named William Prince Ford purchased Northup at auction for $900 in June 1841 and took him to Ford's plantation in central Louisiana. Northup's initiation into slavery began under unusually favorable circumstances. *Twelve Years a Slave* portrays Ford as a comparatively humane slaveholder who spurned the whip and allowed those he enslaved to have their own Bibles. Ford treated his newly acquired Negro Platt with uncommon respect due to Platt's multiple skills, good business sense, and initiative. Unfortunately for Northup, he spent scarcely more than six months under Ford before Ford, needing money, sold him to a local carpenter with whom Northup clashed. After a fight in which Northup bested and beat his own enslaver, Northup barely escaped lynching. But he maintained a good reputation as a "Jack at all trades" among local planters who recruited him to work on a variety of jobs, such as lumbering, rail splitting, and sugar cane cutting. So valuable had Platt become that his third enslaver, Edwin Epps, paid $1,500 for him in the spring of 1843.

The latter half of *Twelve Years a Slave* recounts Northup's ten years under the control of Epps, as sadistic and despicable a slaveholder as any depicted in an African

American novel or autobiography before 1865. Yet few enslavers are rendered in more individual detail in the nineteenth-century slave narrative tradition than the bullying, mercurial, near-psychotic Edwin Epps. His twisted, pathological attachment to his enslaved victim, Patsey, fascinated Northup. Celebrated for much more than physical beauty or traditional womanly virtue, the noble Patsey becomes in *Twelve Years a Slave* a genuinely tragic and pitiable figure, a multitalented person of accomplishment and leadership driven to despondency and hopelessness by Epps's desire, fear, and rage.

After two years of toil in the cotton fields, Northup became the foreman on Epps's plantation, the field boss over the nine workers enslaved by Epps. Just as he had distinguished himself in the eyes of William Ford, Northup impressed Epps with his work ethic, skills, and steady temperament—"'he's a reg'lar genius,'" Epps told another white man in Northup's presence. Northup's post placed him in a position of oversight and responsibility above Epps's other enslaved workers, but below Epps and his wife. *Twelve Years a Slave* is rare among pre-Civil War slave narratives in articulating the point of view of a "slave driver," whose complex status in the plantation pecking order often protected the driver from punishments inflicted on ordinary enslaved people but only if he acceded to the enslaver's demand that the driver administer those punishments himself. The excruciating moral crux of Northup's career in slavery arrived sometime around 1850 when he was ordered by Epps to whip Patsey insensible for leaving the plantation for the one thing his wife had jealously denied her: soap.

In the summer of 1852, Samuel Bass, a compassionate white Canadian who had been hired to do carpentry work for Epps, wrote three letters on Northup's behalf, indentifying his enslavement and location. The one that reached a pair of white shopkeepers in upstate New York found its way to Northup's wife, Anne Hampton, who then forwarded it to Henry Northup, a white lawyer who had known Solomon since childhood. It was this Northup who gathered the necessary documentation to authorize Solomon's rescue, which took place on January 3, 1853. Restored to his family a little less than three weeks later, Northup became front-page news in the *New York Daily Times*, which reported on both the free Negro's enslavement and his recent attempt to prosecute the Washington, D.C., trader who had ignored his protests and sold him to New Orleans. But the trial of James H. Birch yielded Northup no satisfaction, partly because he was prohibited from testifying against Birch, the testimony of a Black man against a white being inadmissible in District of Columbia court. Northup's later efforts to bring his kidnappers to justice were frustrated through the indifference of New York authorities as well as legal technicalities over jurisdictional disputes. A celebrity in abolitionist circles, Northup appeared before New York and New England antislavery audiences as a speaker and a performer in two plays that dramatized his ordeal. These activities along with royalties from *Twelve Years a Slave* earned Northup a satisfactory income for a few years, but after the fall of 1857, the fifty-year-old Northup disappeared from the public record. He may have participated in the Underground Railroad in the late 1850s, but the time, place, and cause of his death remain unknown.

From Twelve Years a Slave

[Lured to Washington, D.C. by two slave traders, Alexander Merrill and Joseph Russell, posing as circus performers under the names of Brown and Hamilton, Northup is wined, dined, and drugged into submission.]

When consciousness returned I found myself alone, in utter darkness, and in chains.

The pain in my head had subsided in a measure, but I was very faint and weak. I was sitting upon a low bench, made of rough boards, and without coat or hat. I was hand cuffed. Around my ankles also were a pair of heavy fetters. One end of a chain was fastened to a large ring in the floor, the other to the fetters on my ankles. I tried in vain to stand upon my feet. Waking from such a painful trance, it was some time before I could collect my thoughts. Where was I? What was the meaning of these chains? Where were Brown and Hamilton? What had I done to deserve imprisonment in such a dungeon? I could not comprehend. There was a blank of some indefinite period, preceding my awakening in that lonely place, the events of which the utmost stretch of memory was unable to recall. I listened intently for some sign or sound of life, but nothing broke the oppressive silence, save the clinking of my chains, whenever I chanced to move. I spoke aloud, but the sound of my voice startled me. I felt of my pockets, so far as the fetters would allow—far enough, indeed, to ascertain that I had not only been robbed of liberty, but that my money and free papers were also gone! Then did the idea begin to break upon my mind, at first dim and confused, that I had been kidnapped. But that I thought was incredible. There must have been some misapprehension—some unfortunate mistake. It could not be that a free citizen of New-York, who had wronged no man, nor violated any law, should be dealt with thus inhumanly. The more I contemplated my situation, however, the more I became confirmed in my suspicions. It was a desolate thought, indeed. I felt there was no trust or mercy in unfeeling man; and commending myself to the God of the oppressed, bowed my head upon my fettered hands, and wept most bitterly.

* * *

[Northup is shipped from Washington, D.C., to New Orleans, where he and two others, Harry and Eliza, are purchased by a Baptist minister and planter named William Ford. Ford takes them to his small plantation in Avoyelles parish "situated on the right bank of Red River, in the heart of Louisiana."]

Throughout the whole parish of Avoyelles, and especially along both shores of Bayou Boeuf, where [Ford] is more intimately known, he is accounted by his fellow-citizens as a worthy minister of God. In many northern minds, perhaps, the idea of a man holding his brother man in servitude, and the traffic in human flesh, may seem altogether incompatible with their conceptions of a moral or religious life. From descriptions of such men as Burch and Freeman,[1] and others hereinafter mentioned, they are led to despise and execrate the whole class of slaveholders, indiscriminately. But I was sometime his slave, and had an opportunity of learning well his character and disposition, and it is but simple justice to him when I say, in my opinion, there never was a more kind, noble, candid, Christian man than William Ford. The influences and associations that had always surrounded him, blinded him to the inherent wrong at the bottom of the system of Slavery. He never doubted the moral right of one man holding another in subjection. Looking through the same medium with his fathers before him, he saw things in the same light. Brought up under other circumstances and other influences, his notions would undoubtedly have been different. Nevertheless, he was a model master, walking uprightly, according to the light

1. James H. Birch was a Washington, D.C., trader who purchased Northup from Merrill and Russell. Theophilus Freeman was a New Orleans trader from whom William Ford bought Northup for $900 in late June 1841.

of his understanding, and fortunate was the slave who came to his possession. Were all men such as he, Slavery would be deprived of more than half its bitterness.

* * *

Much wearied with our walk [to Ford's plantation], as soon as it was dark, Harry and I wrapped our blankets round us, and laid down upon the cabin floor. My thoughts, as usual, wandered back to my wife and children. The consciousness of my real situation; the hopelessness of any effort to escape through the wide forests of Avoyelles, pressed heavily upon me, yet my heart was at home in Saratoga.

I was awakened early in the morning by the voice of Master Ford, calling Rose. She hastened into the house to dress the children, Sally to the field to milk the cows, while John was busy in the kitchen preparing breakfast. In the meantime Harry and I were strolling about the yard, looking at our new quarters. Just after breakfast a colored man, driving three yoke of oxen, attached to a wagon load of lumber, drove into the opening. He was a slave of Ford's, named Walton, the husband of Rose. By the way, Rose was a native of Washington, and had been brought from thence five years before. She had never seen Eliza, but she had heard of Berry,[2] and they knew the same streets, and the same people, either personally, or by reputation. They became fast friends immediately, and talked a great deal together of old times, and of friends they had left behind.

Ford was at that time a wealthy man. Besides his seat in the Pine Woods, he owned a large lumbering establishment on Indian Creek, four miles distant, and also, in his wife's right, an extensive plantation and many slaves on Bayou Boeuf.

Walton had come with his load of lumber from the mills on Indian Creek. Ford directed us to return with him, saying he would follow us as soon as possible. Before leaving, Mistress Ford called me into the storeroom, and handed me, as it is there termed, a tin bucket of molasses for Harry and myself.

Eliza was still [w]ringing her hands and deploring the loss of her children.[3] Ford tried as much as possible to console her—told her she need not work very hard; that she might remain with Rose, and assist the madam in the house affairs.

Riding with Walton in the wagon, Harry and I became quite well acquainted with him long before reaching Indian Creek. He was a "born thrall" of Ford's, and spoke kindly and affectionately of him, as a child would speak of his own father. In answer to his inquiries from whence I came, I told him from Washington. Of that city, he had heard much from his wife, Rose, and all the way plied me with many extravagant and absurd questions.

On reaching the mills at Indian Creek, we found two more of Ford's slaves, Sam and Antony. Sam, also, was a Washingtonian, having been brought out in the same gang with Rose. He had worked on a farm near Georgetown. Antony was a blacksmith, from Kentucky, who had been in his present master's service about ten years. Sam knew Burch, and when informed that he was the trader who had sent me on from Washington, it

2. Eliza's surname.
3. Eliza Berry's older child, Randall, was sold away from her by Theophilus Freeman. When William Ford bought Eliza, she implored him to purchase her daughter Emily as well. Ford tried to, but Freeman refused his offer, claiming that he could make far more money by selling her later as a concubine.

was remarkable how well we agreed upon the subject of his superlative rascality. He had forwarded Sam, also.

On Ford's arrival at the mill, we were employed in piling lumber, and chopping logs, which occupation we continued during the remainder of the summer.

We usually spent our Sabbaths at the opening, on which days our master would gather all his slaves about him, and read and expound the Scriptures. He sought to inculcate in our minds feelings of kindness towards each other, of dependence upon God—setting forth the rewards promised unto those who lead an upright and prayerful life. Seated in the doorway of his house, surrounded by his man-servants and his maid-servants, who looked earnestly into the good man's face, he spoke of the loving kindness of the Creator, and of the life that is to come. Often did the voice of prayer ascend from his lips to heaven, the only sound that broke the solitude of the place.

In the course of the summer Sam became deeply convicted, his mind dwelling intensely on the subject of religion. His mistress gave him a Bible, which he carried with him to his work. Whatever leisure time was allowed him, he spent in perusing it, though it was only with great difficulty that he could master any part of it. I often read to him, a favor which he well repaid me by many expressions of gratitude. Sam's piety was frequently observed by white men who came to the mill, and the remark it most generally provoked was, that a man like Ford, who allowed his slaves to have Bibles, was "not fit to own a nigger."

He, however, lost nothing by his kindness. It is a fact I have more than once observed, that those who treated their slaves most leniently, were rewarded by the greatest amount of labor. I know it from my own experience. It was a source of pleasure to surprise Master Ford with a greater day's work than was required, while, under subsequent masters, there was no prompter to extra effort but the overseer's lash.

It was the desire of Ford's approving voice that suggested to me an idea that resulted to his profit. The lumber we were manufacturing was contracted to be delivered at Lamourie. It had hitherto been transported by land, and was an important item of expense. Indian Creek, upon which the mills were situated, was a narrow but deep stream emptying into Bayou Boeuf. In some places it was not more than twelve feet wide, and much obstructed with trunks of trees. Bayou Boeuf was connected with Bayou Lamourie. I ascertained the distance from the mills to the point on the latter bayou, where our lumber was to be delivered, was but a few miles less by land than by water. Provided the creek could be made navigable for rafts, it occurred to me that the expense of transportation would be materially diminished.

Adam Taydem, a little white man who had been a soldier in Florida, and had strolled into that distant region, was foreman and superintendent of the mills. He scouted[4] the idea; but Ford, when I laid it before him, received it favorably, and permitted me to try the experiment.

Having removed the obstructions, I made up a narrow raft, consisting of twelve cribs. At this business I think I was quite skillful, not having forgotten my experience years before on the Champlain canal.[5] I labored hard, being extremely anxious to succeed, both from a desire to please my master,

4. Rejected the idea with scorn.
5. Opened in 1823, the Champlain canal connected the south end of Lake Champlain to the Hudson River in New York.

and to show Adam Taydem, that my scheme was not such a visionary one as he incessantly pronounced it. One hand could manage three cribs. I took charge of the forward three, and commenced poling down the creek. In due time we entered the first bayou, and finally reached our destination in a shorter period of time than I had anticipated.

The arrival of the raft at Lamourie created a sensation, while Mr. Ford loaded me with commendation. On all sides I heard Ford's Platt pronounced the "smartest nigger in the Pine Woods"—in fact I was the Fulton[6] of Indian Creek. I was not insensible to the praise bestowed upon me, and enjoyed, especially, my triumph over Taydem, whose half-malicious ridicule had stung my pride. From this time the entire control of bringing the lumber to Lamourie was placed in my hands until the contract was fulfilled.

* * *

Edwin Epps, of whom much will be said during the remainder of this history, is a large, portly, heavybodied man with light hair, high cheek bones, and a Roman nose of extraordinary dimensions. He has blue eyes, a fair complexion, and is, as I should say, full six feet high. He has the sharp, inquisitive expression of a jockey. His manners are repulsive and coarse, and his language gives speedy and unequivocal evidence that he has never enjoyed the advantages of an education. He has the faculty of saying most provoking things, in that respect even excelling old Peter Tanner.[7] At the time I came into his possession, Edwin Epps was fond of the bottle, his "sprees" sometimes extending over the space of two whole weeks. Latterly, however, he had reformed his habits, and when I left him, was as strict a specimen of temperance as could be found on Bayou Boeuf. When "in his cups,"[8] Master Epps was a roystering,[9] blustering, noisy fellow, whose chief delight was in dancing with his "niggers," or lashing them about the yard with his long whip, just for the pleasure of hearing them screech and scream, as the great welts were planted on their backs. When sober, he was silent, reserved and cunning, not beating us indiscriminately, as in his drunken moments, but sending the end of his rawhide to some tender spot of a lagging slave, with a sly dexterity peculiar to himself.

He had been a driver and overseer in his younger years, but at this time was in possession of a plantation on Bayou Huff Power, two and a half miles from Holmesville, eighteen from Marksville, and twelve from Cheneyville. It belonged to Joseph B. Roberts, his wife's uncle, and was leased by Epps. His principal business was raising cotton.

* * *

Patsey was slim and straight. She stood erect as the human form is capable of standing. There was an air of loftiness in her movement, that neither labor, nor weariness, nor punishment could destroy. Truly, Patsey was a splendid animal, and were it not that bondage had enshrouded her intellect in utter and everlasting darkness, would have been chief among ten thousand of her people. She could leap the highest fences, and a fleet hound it was indeed, that could outstrip her in a race. No horse could fling her from his back. She was a skillful teamster. She turned as true a furrow as the best, and at splitting rails there were none who could excel her. When the

6. American engineer Robert Fulton (1765–1815) developed the first commercial steamboat.
7. William Ford's brother-in-law and owner of a large plantation on Bayou Boeuf.
8. Drunk.
9. Swaggering, boisterous.

order to halt was heard at night, she would have her mules at the crib, unharnessed, fed and curried before uncle Abram had found his hat. Not, however, for all or any of these, was she chiefly famous. Such lightning-like motion was in her fingers as no other fingers ever possessed, and therefore it was, that in cotton picking time, Patsey was queen of the field.

She had a genial and pleasant temper, and was faithful and obedient. Naturally, she was a joyous creature, a laughing, light-hearted girl, rejoicing in the mere sense of existence. Yet Patsey wept oftener, and suffered more, than any of her companions. She had been literally excoriated. Her back bore the scars of a thousand stripes; not because she was backward in her work, nor because she was of an unmindful and rebellious spirit, but because it had fallen to her lot to be the slave of a licentious master [Epps] and a jealous mistress [Mrs. Mary Epps]. She shrank before the lustful eye of the one, and was in danger even of her life at the hands of the other, and between the two, she was indeed accursed. In the great house, for days together, there were high and angry words, poutings and estrangement, whereof she was the innocent cause. Nothing delighted the mistress so much as to see her suffer, and more than once, when Epps had refused to sell her, has she tempted me with bribes to put her secretly to death, and bury her body in some lonely place in the margin of the swamp. Gladly would Patsey have appeased this unforgiving spirit, if it had been in her power, but not like Joseph, dared she escape from Master Epps, leaving her garment in his hand.[1] Patsey walked under a cloud. If she uttered a word in opposition to her master's will, the lash was resorted to at once, to bring her to subjection; if she was not watchful when about her cabin, or when walking in the yard, a billet of wood,[2] or a broken bottle perhaps, hurled from her mistress' hand, would smite her unexpectedly in the face. The enslaved victim of lust and hate, Patsey had no comfort of her life.

* * *

Besides the overseer, there are drivers under him [the overseer], the number being in proportion to the number of hands in the field. The drivers are black, who, in addition to the performance of their equal share of work, are compelled to do the whipping of their several gangs. Whips hang around their necks, and if they fail to use them thoroughly, are whipped themselves. They have a few privileges, however; for example, in cane-cutting the hands are not allowed to sit down long enough to eat their dinners. Carts filled with corn cake, cooked at the kitchen, are driven into the field at noon. The cake is distributed by the drivers, and must be eaten with the least possible delay.

When the slave ceases to perspire, as he often does when taxed beyond his strength, he falls to the ground and becomes entirely helpless. It is then the duty of the driver to drag him into the shade of the standing cotton or cane, or of a neighboring tree, where he dashes buckets of water upon him, and uses other means of bringing out perspiration again, when he is ordered to his place, and compelled to continue his labor.

At Huff Power, when I first came to Epps', Tom, one of Roberts' negroes, was driver. He was a burly fellow, and severe in the extreme. After Epps' removal to Bayou Boeuf, that distinguished honor was conferred upon myself. Up to the time of my departure I had to wear a whip about my neck

1. In Genesis 39:1–12, Joseph, son of Israel (Jacob) and Rachel, escapes the advances of the wife of Potiphar, captain of the Egyptian Pharaoh's army, by slipping out of his coat as she tries to lay hands on him.
2. A chunky piece of wood.

in the field. If Epps was present, I dared not show any lenity, not having the Christian fortitude of a certain well-known Uncle Tom[3] sufficiently to brave his wrath, by refusing to perform the office. In that way, only, I escaped the immediate martyrdom he suffered, and, withal, saved my companions much suffering, as it proved in the end. Epps, I soon found, whether actually in the field or not, had his eyes pretty generally upon us. From the piazza,[4] from behind some adjacent tree, or other concealed point of observation, he was perpetually on the watch. If one of us had been backward or idle through the day, we were apt to be told all about it on returning to the quarters, and as it was a matter of principle with him to reprove every offence of that kind that came within his knowledge, the offender not only was certain of receiving a castigation for his tardiness, but I likewise was punished for permitting it.

If, on the other hand, he had seen me use the lash freely, the man was satisfied. "Practice makes perfect," truly; and during my eight years' experience as a driver, I learned to handle the whip with marvelous dexterity and precision, throwing the lash within a hair's breadth of the back, the ear, the nose, without, however, touching either of them. If Epps was observed at a distance, or we had reason to apprehend he was as sneaking somewhere in the vicinity, I would commence plying the lash vigorously, when, according to arrangement, they would squirm and screech as if in agony, although not one of them had in fact been even grazed. Patsey would take occasion, if he made his appearance presently, to mumble in his hearing some complaints that Platt was lashing them the whole time, and Uncle Abram, with an appearance of honesty peculiar to himself, would declare roundly I had just whipped them worse than General Jackson whipped the enemy at New-Orleans.[5] If Epps was not drunk, and in one of his beastly humors, this was, in general, satisfactory. If he was, some one or more of us must suffer, as a matter of course. Sometimes his violence assumed a dangerous form, placing the lives of his human stock in jeopardy. On one occasion the drunken madman thought to amuse himself by cutting my throat.

He had been absent at Holmesville, in attendance at a shooting-match, and none of us were aware of his return. While hoeing by the side of Patsey, she exclaimed in a low voice, suddenly, "Platt, d'ye see old Hog-Jaw beckoning me to come to him?"

Glancing sideways, I discovered him in the edge of the field, motioning and grimacing, as was his habit when half-intoxicated. Aware of his lewd intentions, Patsey began to cry. I whispered her not to look up, and to continue at her work, as if she had not observed him. Suspecting the truth of the matter, however, he soon staggered up to me in a great rage.

"What did you say to Pats?" he demanded, with an oath. I made him some evasive answer, which only had the effect of increasing his violence.

"How long have you owned this plantation, *say*, you d—d nigger?" he inquired, with a malicious sneer, at the same time taking hold of my shirt collar with one hand, and thrusting the other into his pocket. "Now I'll cut your black throat; that's what I'll do," drawing his knife from his pocket as he said it. But with one hand he was unable to open it, until finally seizing the blade in his teeth, I saw he was about to succeed, and felt the necessity

3. The long-suffering and self-sacrificial hero of Harriet Beecher Stowe's *Uncle Tom's Cabin* (1852).

4. The veranda of a house.

5. On January 8, 1815, Major General Andrew Jackson (1767–1845) led a U.S. victory over a British force at New Orleans in the final battle of the War of 1812.

of escaping from him, for in his present reckless state, it was evident he was not joking, by any means. My shirt was open in front, and as I turned round quickly and sprang from him, while he still retained his gripe, it was stripped entirely from my back. There was no difficulty now in eluding him. He would chase me until out of breath, then stop until it was recovered, swear, and renew the chase again. Now he would command me to come to him, now endeavor to coax me, but I was careful to keep at a respectful distance. In this manner we made the circuit of the field several times, he making desperate plunges, and I always dodging them, more amused than frightened, well knowing that when his sober senses returned, he would laugh at his own drunken folly. At length I observed the mistress standing by the yard fence, watching our half-serious, half-comical maneuvres. Shooting past him, I ran directly to her. Epps, on discovering her, did not follow. He remained about the field an hour or more, during which time I stood by the mistress, having related the particulars of what had taken place. Now, *she* was aroused again, denouncing her husband and Patsey about equally. Finally, Epps came towards the house, by this time nearly sober, walking demurely, with his hands behind his back, and attempting to look as innocent as a child.

* * *

On a Sabbath day in hoeing time, not long ago, we were on the bayou bank, washing our clothes, as was our usual custom. Presently Patsey was missing. Epps called aloud, but there was no answer. No one had observed her leaving the yard, and it was a wonder with us whither she had gone. In the course of a couple of hours she was seen approaching from the direction of Shaw's.[6] This man, as has been intimated, was a notorious profligate, and withal not on the most friendly terms with Epps. Harriet, his wife, knowing Patsey's troubles, was kind to her, in consequence of which the latter was in the habit of going over to see her every opportunity. Her visits were prompted by friendship merely, but the suspicion gradually entered the brain of Epps, that another and a baser passion led her thither—that it was not Harriet she desired to meet, but rather the unblushing libertine, his neighbor. Patsey found her master in a fearful rage on her return. His violence so alarmed her that at first she attempted to evade direct answers to his questions, which only served to increase his suspicions. She finally, however, drew herself up proudly, and in a spirit of indignation boldly denied his charges.

"Missus don't give me soap to wash with, as she does the rest," said Patsey, "and you know why. I went over to Harriet's to get a piece," and saying this, she drew it forth from a pocket in her dress and exhibited it to him. "That's what I went to Shaw's for, Massa Epps," continued she; "the Lord knows that was all."

"You lie, you black wench!" shouted Epps.

"I *don't* lie, massa. If you kill me, I'll stick to that."

"Oh! I'll fetch you down. I'll learn you to go to Shaw's. I'll take the starch out of ye," he muttered fiercely through his shut teeth.

Then turning to me, he ordered four stakes to be driven into the ground, pointing with the toe of his boot to the places where he wanted them. When the stakes were driven down, he ordered her to be stripped of every article

6. A neighboring plantation owner.

of dress. Ropes were then brought, and the naked girl was laid upon her face, her wrists and feet each tied firmly to a stake. Stepping to the piazza, he took down a heavy whip, and placing it in my hands, commanded me to lash her. Unpleasant as it was, I was compelled to obey him. Nowhere that day, on the face of the whole earth, I venture to say, was there such a demoniac exhibition witnessed as then ensued.

Mistress Epps stood on the piazza among her children, gazing on the scene with an air of heartless satisfaction. The slaves were huddled together at a little distance, their countenances indicating the sorrow of their hearts. Poor Patsey prayed piteously for mercy, but her prayers were vain. Epps ground his teeth, and stamped upon the ground, screaming at me, like a mad fiend, to strike *harder*.

"Strike harder, or *your* turn will come next, you scoundrel," he yelled.

"Oh, mercy, massa!—oh! have mercy, *do*. Oh, God! pity me," Patsey exclaimed continually, struggling fruitlessly, and the flesh quivering at every stroke.

When I had struck her as many as thirty times, I stopped, and turned round toward Epps, hoping he was satisfied; but with bitter oaths and threats, he ordered me to continue. I inflicted ten or fifteen blows more. By this time her back was covered with long welts, intersecting each other like net work. Epps was yet furious and savage as ever, demanding if she would like to go to Shaw's again, and swearing he would flog her until she wished she was in h—l. Throwing down the whip, I declared I could punish her no more. He ordered me to go on, threatening me with a severer flogging than she had received, in case of refusal. My heart revolted at the inhuman scene, and risking the consequences, I absolutely refused to raise the whip. He then seized it himself, and applied it with ten-fold greater force than I had. The painful cries and shrieks of the tortured Patsey, mingling with the loud and angry curses of Epps, loaded the air. She was terribly lacerated—I may say, without exaggeration, literally flayed. The lash was wet with blood, which flowed down her sides and dropped upon the ground. At length she ceased struggling. Her head sank listlessly on the ground. Her screams and supplications gradually decreased and died away into a low moan. She no longer writhed and shrank beneath the lash when it bit out small pieces of her flesh. I thought that she was dying!

It was the Sabbath of the Lord. The fields smiled in the warm sunlight—the birds chirped merrily amidst the foliage of the trees—peace and happiness seemed to reign everywhere, save in the bosoms of Epps and his panting victim and the silent witnesses around him. The tempestuous emotions that were raging there were little in harmony with the calm and quiet beauty of the day. I could look on Epps only with unutterable loathing and abhorrence, and thought within myself—"Thou devil, sooner or later, somewhere in the course of eternal justice, thou shalt answer for this sin!"

Finally, he ceased whipping from mere exhaustion, and ordered Phebe to bring a bucket of salt and water. After washing her thoroughly with this, I was told to take her to her cabin. Untying the ropes, I raised her in my arms. She was unable to stand, and as her head rested on my shoulder, she repeated many times, in a faint voice scarcely perceptible, "Oh, Platt—oh, Platt!" but nothing further. Her dress was replaced, but it clung to her back, and was soon stiff with blood. We laid her on some boards in the hut, where she remained a long time, with eyes closed and groaning in agony. At night

Phebe applied melted tallow to her wounds, and so far as we were able, all endeavored to assist and console her. Day after day she lay in her cabin upon her face, the sores preventing her resting in any other position.

A blessed thing it would have been for her—days and weeks and months of misery it would have saved her—had she never lifted up her head in life again. Indeed, from that time forward she was not what she had been. The burden of a deep melancholy weighed heavily on her spirits. She no longer moved with that buoyant and elastic step—there was not that mirthful sparkle in her eyes that formerly distinguished her. The bounding vigor—the sprightly, laughter-loving spirit of her youth, were gone. She fell into a mournful and desponding mood, and often times would start up in her sleep, and with raised hands, plead for mercy. She became more silent than she was, toiling all day in our midst, not uttering a word. A care-worn, pitiful expression settled on her face, and it was her humor now to weep, rather than rejoice. If ever there was a broken heart— one crushed and blighted by the rude grasp of suffering misfortune—it was Patsey's.

1853

MARTIN R. DELANY
1812–1885

Martin Robison Delany had the most varied, extensive, and impressive résumé of any African American leader of the nineteenth century. At one time or another in his life, and in some cases simultaneously, he was an editor, a physician, a lecturer, a fundraiser, a novelist, an explorer, an army officer, a government bureaucrat, a politician, a real estate agent, a jurist, an ethnographer, and withal a social activist and reformer. Three great themes unified his life's work. First and foremost, an abiding conviction of the dignity and equality, if not the superiority, of those he called "the colored people of the United States" when compared to "the European race." Second, a commitment to the empowerment of the African American "nation within a nation." And third, a sense of Delany's own mission as a bold, tough-minded leader intent on molding the thinking and mobilizing the aspirations of the people he loved. Alternately visionary and pragmatic, Delany had a devotion to the social, political, and economic advancement of African Americans that found expression in voluminous speeches and writing in multiple genres, the totality of which has never been fully collected. No single text from a writing career that spanned more than thirty-five years can adequately represent the complex, and not always fully consistent, pattern of Delany's thinking on the issues that stirred him the most. *The Condition, Elevation, Emigration and Destiny of the Colored People of the United States* (1852) comes closest to a summary statement of his ideas about racial identity and advancement and African American nationhood before the Civil War. *The Condition* also exemplifies Delany's intellectual leadership through a writing style aimed at "expressing our mind freely, and with candor, as we are determined that as far as we can at present do so, the minds of our readers shall be enlightened."

Born free in Charles Town in what was later West Virginia, ten-year-old Martin Delany received an early lesson in the political value of mental enlightenment for

Black people when his mother, Pati Delany, removed her five children to Chambersburg, Pennsylvania, in 1822 to avoid threats of possible imprisonment for teaching Martin and his siblings to read. At the age of nineteen, Martin moved to Pittsburgh in search of better educational opportunity and a strong African American community. Pittsburgh's Black leaders fostered racial pride in Delany, while antislavery whites helped him begin the study of medicine. Active in a variety of reform movements in Pittsburgh and well established in his medical practice in the early 1840s, Delany married Catherine Richards, a seamstress who supported his interest in public affairs, in 1843 and launched in the same year the *Mystery,* the first African American newspaper west of the Alleghenies. In 1847, Delany set aside his independent journalistic career in favor of coediting the *North Star* with Frederick Douglass. Writing for this newspaper helped Delany attain a national readership for the first time. Delany's contributions to the *North Star* were sent from the various locales he visited while working as the paper's prime subscription agent in the North and Midwest. On his travels Delany took special pleasure in reporting on the successful African American farmers, tradesmen, businessmen, and teachers whom he met in such towns as Columbus, Ohio, and Harrisburg, Pennsylvania. The *North Star* also gave Delany a forum from which to attack the colonization of African Americans to the republic of Liberia in West Africa, a program that Delany, along with most African American leaders in the later 1840s, regarded as degrading to Black Americans.

Delany's resignation from the staff of the *North Star* in June 1849 signaled growing disaffection between Douglass and himself. Delany's willingness to advocate violent resistance to slavery, which Douglass refused to support until the early 1850s, and Delany's criticism of Douglass's receptiveness to financial support for the *North Star* from white abolitionists exposed serious differences between the two men. These became more apparent when they argued publicly over the merits of Harriet Beecher Stowe's *Uncle Tom's Cabin* in 1853. Douglass welcomed the novel for having drawn unprecedented popular attention to the antislavery cause. Delany deplored Stowe's paternalistic portrayal of Black people and her sympathy to African colonization as a solution to America's slavery problem. By the time of this debate, however, Delany had himself taken a stand in favor of African American emigration as a proper and justifiable alternative for Blacks who refused to wait any longer for the United States to treat its citizens of color with equal justice. "That country is the best," Delany declaimed in *The Condition*, "in which our manhood can be best developed; and that is Central and South America, and the West Indies." "We love our country," Delany insisted, "dearly love her, but she don't love us—she despises us, and bids us begone, driving us from her embraces." The only alternative for self-respecting, progressive Black Americans was expatriation.

What pushed Delany to become the most eloquent spokesman for African American emigration in the mid-nineteenth century was a combination of personal and political factors. His resentment of American racism had surged in 1851 after he was asked to withdraw from Harvard's medical school, which a few months earlier had admitted Delany and a handful of other Black students to attend lectures. Passage of the Fugitive Slave Law in 1850, which made a criminal offense out of helping fugitive enslaved people escape, spurred Delany's declaration that he would shoot anyone who tried to enter his home to capture a fugitive. News of the success of formerly enslaved and enterprising free African Americans in founding Black towns and settlements in Canada helped convince Delany of the viability of emigration, at least to Canada. Nevertheless, the largest proportion of *The Condition* is not devoted to promoting plans for leaving the United States but to asserting the achievements of Black Americans in their native land and propounding the bases on which further successes, individually and communally, could be built.

Among the more remarkable features of Delany's first book are his class-based, rather than race-based, analyses of the socioeconomic situation of Black people in antebellum America. He linked African American elevation to "self-efforts" in the marketplace rather than to sociopolitical agitation in partnership with whites. He issued frank criticisms of misplaced African American priorities, often the result of undue imitation of whites and "a want of a sense of propriety or *self-respect*." Delany also stressed the importance of education for Black American women. *The Condition* emphasized themes of Black pride, self-help, and nationhood that also surfaced in the writing of David Walker, Maria W. Stewart, Henry Highland Garnet, Alexander Crummell, and Booker T. Washington. For these reasons, twentieth-century scholars often identified Delany as the father of Black nationalism, an intellectual progenitor of Marcus Garvey and Malcolm X.

Treated with skepticism by Douglass and other Black integrationists who saw emigration as a separatist solution bought at the price of voluntary exile from their birthright as Americans, Delany maintained his commitment to Black nationalism throughout the 1850s. Practicing what he preached, he moved his family to Chatham, Ontario in 1856 in solidarity with the more than fifty thousand African Americans who left the United States for Canada before the Civil War. In Chatham he worked as a physician and a journalist, was politically active, and met with John Brown, leader of the 1859 raid on the federal arsenal at Harpers Ferry, Virginia, to discuss the latter's plans for guerilla action against the slaveholders of the South. Reversing himself on his previous preference for Central and South America as sites for emigrating Black Americans, Delany sailed to Liberia in 1859. There he praised the work of that nation's African American leadership and went on to Lagos and Abeokuta (in what is now the Republic of Nigeria) to negotiate a treaty that granted arable land for African American settlement. Delany recorded his positive firsthand account of his travels in West Africa in his *Official Report of the Niger Valley Exploring Party* (1861), which was published in New York soon after he returned to his home in Canada.

While Delany was abroad, his novel *Blake; or, The Huts of America* appeared serially, first in the *Anglo-African Magazine* in 1859 and later in the *Weekly Anglo-African* from November 1861 to June 1862. The final six chapters of the original eighty that Delany planned for *Blake* have not been found, but what exists attests to its author's creation of the first Black nationalist hero in American fiction. Dedicated to fomenting insurrection among the enslaved, Henrico Blacus, a.k.a. Henry Blake, journeys through the American slaveocracy, creating the kind of revolutionary *imperium in imperio* that would become the focus, as well as the title, of an important African American novel by Sutton E. Griggs in 1899. By the end of the story Blake is in Cuba engaged in a conspiracy to overthrow international white supremacy in the Americas.

The outbreak of the Civil War and problems with the king of Abeokuta over the treaty forced Delany to reconsider his efforts to resettle Black Canadians in West Africa. In 1862, having become convinced that the war could bring an end to slavery, Delany went to work for the U.S. government as a full-time recruiter of Black soldiers. Before the end of the war he had been commissioned a major, the first African American field officer in U.S. military history. From 1865 to the early 1870s he tried through his appointments at the Freedmen's Bureau to make Reconstruction a success in South Carolina. His political pragmatism, which led him to make common cause with Northern capitalists and former slaveholders as well as with the formerly enslaved Black people of the state, sparked criticism from powerful Republicans who ruled South Carolina after the war. In the gubernatorial campaign of 1876 Delany further alienated South Carolina's Black rank and file by supporting the Democratic candidate, Wade Hampton, a former slaveholder and Confederate army officer, who, Delany was convinced, would bring good government and racial harmony to the state. For supporting Hampton's successful campaign publicly, Delany received a political patronage appointment as a trial justice until 1879. By this time, he could see that his professional and political prospects in the post-Reconstruction South were dim. He left the South, returning to Washington, D.C., in the hope of securing a civil service job. In 1879 a respected white-owned publisher, Harper & Brothers, brought out Delany's ethnographic treatise, *Principia of Ethnology: The Origin of Races and Color.* The book affirmed its author's bedrock beliefs in inherent racial differences and the greatness of the African and African-descended peoples. The *Principia* also warned against the intermixing of races that, in Delany's view, had been created by God for special destinies. During his last years, profoundly pessimistic about the future for Black people in post-Reconstruction America, Delany sought fruitlessly to finance his and his family's emigration to Liberia. He died at home in Xenia, Ohio.

From The Condition, Elevation, Emigration and Destiny of the Colored People of the United States

Chapter I.

CONDITION OF MANY CLASSES IN EUROPE CONSIDERED.

That there have been in all ages and in all countries, in every quarter of the habitable globe, especially among those nations laying the greatest claim to civilization and enlightenment, classes of people who have been deprived of equal privileges, political, religious and social, cannot be denied, and that this deprivation on the part of the ruling classes is cruel and unjust, is also equally true. Such classes have ever been looked upon as inferior to their oppressors, and have ever been mainly the domestics and menials of society, doing the low offices and drudgery of those among whom they lived, moving about and existing by mere sufferance, having no rights nor privileges but those conceded by the common consent of their political superiors. These are historical facts that cannot be controverted, and therefore proclaim in tones more eloquently than thunder, the listful attention of every oppressed man, woman, and child under the government of the people of the United States of America.

In the past ages there were many such classes, as the Israelites in Egypt, the Gladiators in Rome, and similar classes in Greece; and in the present age, the Gipsies in Italy and Greece, the Cossacs in Russia and Turkey, the Sclaves and Croats[1] in the Germanic States, and the Welsh and Irish among the British, to say nothing of various other classes among other nations.

That there have in all ages, in almost every nation, existed a nation within a nation—a people who although forming a part and parcel of the population, yet were from force of circumstances, known by the peculiar position they occupied, forming in fact, by the deprivation of political equality with others, no part, and if any, but a restricted part of the body politic of such nations, is also true.

Such then are the Poles in Russia, the Hungarians in Austria, the Scotch, Irish, and Welsh in the United Kingdom, and such also are the Jews, scattered throughout not only the length and breadth of Europe, but almost the habitable globe, maintaining their national characteristics, and looking forward in high hopes of seeing the day when they may return to their former national position of self-government and independence, let that be in what-

1. Southeastern European peoples constituting part of the Slavic ethnic group. "Gipsies": or Gypsies, now called "Roma," nomadic peoples who migrated originally from India and settled in various parts of Europe. "Cossacs": groups of Slavs who lived in the southern part of czarist Russia.

ever part of the habitable world it may. This is the lot of these various classes of people in Europe, and it is not our intention here, to discuss the justice or injustice of the causes that have contributed to their degradation, but simply to set forth the undeniable facts, which are as glaring as the rays of a noonday's sun, thereby to impress them indelibly on the mind of every reader of this pamphlet.

It is not enough, that these people are deprived of equal privileges by their rulers, but, the more effectually to succeed, the equality of these classes must be denied, and their inferiority by nature as distinct races, actually asserted. This policy is necessary to appease the opposition that might be interposed in their behalf. Wherever there is arbitrary rule, there must of necessity, on the part of the dominant classes, superiority be assumed. To assume superiority, is to deny the equality of others, and to deny their equality, is to premise their incapacity for self-government. Let this once be conceded, and there will be little or no sympathy for the oppressed, the oppressor being left to prescribe whatever terms at discretion for their government, suits his own purpose.

Such then is the condition of various classes in Europe; yes, nations, for centuries within nations, even without the hope of redemption among those who oppress them. And however unfavorable their condition, there is none more so than that of the colored people of the United States.

Chapter II.

COMPARATIVE CONDITION OF THE COLORED PEOPLE OF THE UNITED STATES.

The United States, untrue to her trust and unfaithful to her professed principles of republican equality, has also pursued a policy of political degradation to a large portion of her native born countrymen, and that class is the Colored People. Denied an equality not only of political, but of natural rights, in common with the rest of our fellow citizens, there is no species of degradation to which we are not subject.

Reduced to abject slavery is not enough, the very thought of which should awaken every sensibility of our common nature; but those of their descendants who are freemen even in the non-slaveholding States, occupy the very same position politically, religiously, civilly and socially, (with but few exceptions,) as the bondman occupies in the slave States.

In those States, the bondman is disfranchised, and for the most part so are we. He is denied all civil, religious, and social privileges, except such as he gets by mere sufferance, and so are we. They have no part nor lot in the government of the country, neither have we. They are ruled and governed without representation, existing as mere nonentities among the citizens, and excrescences[2] on the body politic—a mere dreg in community, and so are we. Where then is our political superiority to the enslaved? none, neither are we superior in any other relation to society, except that we are defacto[3] masters of ourselves and joint rulers of our own domestic household, while the bondman's self is claimed by another, and his relation to his family denied him. What the unfortunate classes are in Europe, such are we in the United States, which is folly to deny, insanity not to understand, blindness not to

2. Abnormal outgrowths.

3. In reality (Latin).

see, and surely now full time that our eyes were opened to these startling truths, which for ages have stared us full in the face.

It is time that we had become politicians, we mean, to understand the political economy and domestic policy of nations; that we had become as well as moral theorists, also the practical demonstrators of equal rights and self-government. Except we do, it is idle to talk about rights, it is mere chattering for the sake of being seen and heard—like the slave, saying something because his so called "master" said it, and saying just what he told him to say. Have we not now sufficient intelligence among us to understand our true position, to realise our actual condition, and determine for ourselves what is best to be done? If we have not now, we never shall have, and should at once cease prating[4] about our equality, capacity, and all that.

Twenty years ago, when the writer was a youth, his young and yet uncultivated mind was aroused, and his tender heart made to leap with anxiety in anticipation of the promises then held out by the prime movers in the cause of our elevation.

In 1830 the most intelligent and leading spirits among the colored men in the United States, such as James Forten, Robert Douglass, I. Bowers, A. D. Shadd, John Peck, Joseph Cassey, and John B. Vashon of Pennsylvania; John T. Hilton, Nathaniel and Thomas Paul, and James G. Barbadoes of Massachusetts; Henry Sipkins, Thomas Hamilton, Thomas L. Jennings, Thomas Downing, Samuel E. Cornish,[5] and others of New York; R. Cooley and others of Maryland, and representatives from other States which cannot now be recollected, the data not being at hand, assembled in the city of Philadelphia, in the capacity of a National Convention, to "devise ways and means for the bettering of our condition." These Conventions determined to assemble annually, much talent, ability, and energy of character being displayed; when in 1831 at a sitting of the Convention in September, from their previous pamphlet reports, much interest having been created throughout the country, they were favored by the presence of a number of whites, some of whom were able and distinguished men, such as Rev. R. R. Gurley, Arthur Tappan, Elliot Cresson, John Rankin, Simeon Jocelyn and others, among them William Lloyd Garrison, then quite a young man, all of whom were staunch and ardent Colonizationists,[6] young Garrison at that time, doing his mightiest in his favorite work.

Among other great projects of interest brought before the convention at a previous sitting, was that of the expediency of a general emigration, as far

4. Babbling.

5. Editor and founding member of the American Anti-Slavery Society (1795–1858). Forten (1766–1842), businessman and abolitionist. Douglass (1776–1849), founder of Philadelphia's first African Presbyterian Church. Thomas J. Bowers (1836–1885?), opera singer and civil rights activist. Abraham Doras Shadd (1801–1883), businessman and founding member of the American Anti-Slavery Society. Peck (b. 1801), restauranteur and abolitionist. Cassey was a businessman and abolitionist. Vashon (ca. 1790–1853), barber and abolitionist. Hilton (1801–1864), Black Masonic leader in Boston. Nathaniel Paul (1793?–1839), clergyman and abolitionist. Thomas Paul (1773–1831), clergyman and missionary. Barbadoes (ca. 1796–1841), barber and founding member of the American Anti-Slavery Society. Sipkins was president of the 1832 National Black Convention. Hamilton (1823–1865), editor of the *Anglo-African Magazine*. Jennings (1791–1859), inventor and abolitionist. George Thomas Downing (1819–1903), caterer and civil rights activist.

6. Supporters of the idea, espoused by the American Colonization Society, that African Americans, especially those who had been enslaved, should be colonized in Africa rather than be allowed to reside in the United States. Ralph Randolph Gurley (1797–1872), minister and head of the American Colonization Society. Tappan (1786–1865), philanthropist and reformer. Cresson (1796–1854), merchant and philanthropist. Rankin (1793–1886), minister and abolitionist author. Jocelyn (1799–1879), minister and abolitionist. Garrison (1805–1879), editor and abolitionist leader.

as it was practicable, of the colored people to the British Provinces of North America. Another was that of raising sufficient means for the establishment and erection of a College for the proper education of the colored youth. These gentlemen long accustomed to observation and reflection on the condition of their people, saw at once, that there must necessarily be means used adequate to the end to be attained—that end being an unqualified equality with the ruling class of their fellow citizens. He saw that as a class, the colored people of the country were ignorant, degraded and oppressed, by far the greater portion of them being abject slaves in the South, the very condition of whom was almost enough, under the circumstances, to blast the remotest hope of success, and those who were freemen, whether in the South or North, occupied a subservient, servile, and menial position, considering it a favor to get into the service of the whites, and do their degrading offices. That the difference between the whites and themselves, consisted in the superior advantages of the one over the other, in point of attainments. That if a knowledge of the arts and sciences, the mechanical occupations, the industrial occupations, as farming, commerce, and all the various business enterprises, and learned professions were necessary for the superior position occupied by their rulers, it was also necessary for them. And very reasonably too, the first suggestion which occurred to them was, the advantages of a location, then the necessity of a qualification. They reasoned with themselves, that all distinctive differences made among men on account of their origin, is wicked, unrighteous, and cruel, and never shall receive countenance in any shape from us, therefore, the first acts of the measures entered into by them, was to protest, solemnly protest, against every unjust measure and policy in the country, having for its object the proscription of the colored people, whether state, national, municipal, social, civil, or religious.

But being far-sighted, reflecting, discerning men, they took a political view of the subject, and determined for the good of their people to be governed in their policy according to the facts as they presented themselves. In taking a glance at Europe, they discovered there, however unjustly, as we have shown in another part of this pamphlet, that there are and have been numerous classes proscribed and oppressed, and it was not for them to cut short their wise deliberations, and arrest their proceedings in contention, as to the cause, whether on account of language, the color of eyes, hair, skin, or their origin of country—because all this is contrary to reason, a contradiction to common sense, at war with nature herself, and at variance with facts as they stare us every day in the face, among all nations, in every country—this being made the pretext as a matter of *policy* alone—a fact worthy of observation, that wherever the objects of oppression are the most easily distinguished by any peculiar or general characteristics, these people are the more easily oppressed, because the war of oppression is the more easily waged against them. This is the case with the modern Jews and many other people who have strongly-marked, peculiar, or distinguishing characteristics. This arises in this wise. The policy of all those who proscribe any people, induces them to select as the objects of proscription, those who differed as much as possible, in some particulars, from themselves. This is to ensure the greater success, because it engenders the greater prejudice, or in other words, elicits less interest on the part of the oppressing class, in their favor. This fact is well understood in national conflicts, as the soldier or civilian, who is distinguished by his dress, mustache, or any other peculiar appendage, would certainly prove himself a madman, if he did not take the precaution to change his dress, remove his mustache, and conceal as much as possible his peculiar characteristics, to give him access among the repelling party. This is mere policy, nature having nothing to do with it. Still, it is a fact, a great truth well worthy of remark, and as such we adduce it for the benefit of those of our readers, unaccustomed to an enquiry into the policy of nations.

In view of these truths, our fathers and leaders in our elevation, discovered that as a policy, we the colored people were selected as the subordinate class in this country, not on account of any actual or supposed inferiority on their part, but simply because, in view of all the circumstances of the case, they were the very best class that could be selected. They would have as readily had any other class as subordinates in the country, as the colored people, but the condition of society *at the time*, would not admit of it. In the struggle for American Independence, there were among those who performed the most distinguished parts, the most common-place peasantry of the Provinces. English, Danish, Irish, Scotch, and others, were among those whose names blazoned forth as heroes in the American Revolution. But a single reflection will convince us, that no course of policy could have induced the proscription of the parentage and relatives of such men as Benjamin Franklin the printer, Roger Sherman[7] the cobbler, the tinkers, and others of the signers of the Declaration of Independence. But as they were determined to have a subservient class, it will readily be conceived, that according to the state of society at the time, the better policy on their part was, to select some class, who from their political position—however much they may have contributed their aid as we certainly did, in the general struggle for liberty by force of arms—who had the least claims upon them, or who had the *least chance*, or was the *least potent* in urging their claims. This class of course was the colored people and Indians.

The Indians who in the early settlement of the continent, before an African captive had ever been introduced thereon, were reduced to the most abject slavery, toiling day and night in the mines, under the relentless hands of heartless Spanish taskmasters, but being a race of people raised to the sports of fishing, the chase, and of war, were wholly unaccustomed to labor, and therefore sunk under the insupportable weight, two millions and a half having fallen victims to the cruelty of oppression and toil suddenly placed upon their shoulders. And it was only this that prevented their farther enslavement as a class, after the provinces were absolved from the British Crown. It is true that their general enslavement took place on the islands and in the mining districts of South America, where indeed, the Europeans continued to enslave them, until a comparatively recent period; still, the design, the feeling, and inclination from policy, was the same to do so here, in this section of the continent.

Nor was it until their influence became too great, by the political position occupied by their brethren in the new republic, that the German and Irish peasantry ceased to be sold as slaves for a term of years fixed by law, for the repayment of their passage-money, the descendants of these classes of people for a long time being held as inferiors, in the estimation of the ruling class, and it was not until they assumed the rights and privileges guaran-

7. American statesman (1721–1793). Franklin (1706–1790), American statesman, inventor, and author.

teed to them by the established policy of the country, among the leading spirits of whom were their relatives, that the policy towards them was discovered to be a bad one, and accordingly changed. Nor was it, as is frequently very erroneously asserted, by colored as well as white persons, that it was on account of hatred to the African, or in other words, on account of hatred to his color, that the African was selected as the subject of oppression in this country. This is sheer nonsense; being based on policy and nothing else, as shown in another place. The Indians, who being the most foreign to the sympathies of the Europeans on this continent, were selected in the first place, who, being unable to withstand the hardships, gave way before them.

But the African race had long been known to Europeans, in all ages of the world's history, as a long-lived, hardy race, subject to toil and labor of various kinds, subsisting mainly by traffic, trade, and industry, and consequently being as foreign to the sympathies of the invaders of the continent as the Indians, they were selected, captured, brought here as a laboring class, and as a matter of policy held as such. Nor was the absurd idea of natural inferiority of the African ever dreamed of, until recently adduced by the slaveholders and their abettors, in justification of their policy. This, with contemptuous indignation, we fling back into their face, as a scorpion to a vulture. And so did our patriots and leaders in the cause of regeneration know better, and never for a moment yielded to the base doctrine. But they had discovered the great fact, that a cruel policy was pursued towards our people, and that they possessed distinctive characteristics which made them the objects of proscription. These characteristics being strongly marked in the colored people, as in the Indians, by color, character of hair and so on, made them the more easily distinguished from other Americans, and the policies more effectually urged against us. For this reason they introduced the subject of emigration to Canada, and a proper institution for the education of the youth.

At this important juncture of their proceedings, the afore named white gentlemen were introduced to the notice of the Convention, and after gaining permission to speak, expressed their gratification and surprise at the qualification and talent manifested by different members of the Convention, all expressing their determination to give the cause of the colored people more serious reflection. Mr. Garrison, the youngest of them all, and none the less honest on account of his youthfulness, being but 26 years of age at the time, (1831) expressed his determination to change his course of policy at once, and espouse the cause of the elevation of the colored people here in their own country. We are not at present well advised upon this point, it now having escaped our memory, but we are under the impression that Mr. Jocelyn also, at once changed his policy.

During the winter of 1832, Mr. Garrison issued his "Thoughts on African Colonization," and near about the same time or shortly after, issued the first number of the "Liberator,"[8] in both of which, his full convictions of the enormity of American slavery, and the wickedness of their policy towards the colored people, were fully expressed. At the sitting of the Convention in this year, a number, perhaps all of these gentlemen were present, and those who had denounced the Colonization scheme, and espoused the cause of the elevation of the colored people in this country, or the Anti-Slavery cause, as it was now termed, expressed themselves openly and without reserve.

8. Published in Boston from 1831 to 1865, a leading organ of the most uncompromising abolitionists.

Sensible of the high-handed injustice done to the colored people in the United States, and the mischief likely to emanate from the unchristian proceedings of the deceptious Colonization scheme, like all honest hearted penitents, with the ardor only known to new converts, they entreated the Convention, whatever they did, not to entertain for a moment, the idea of recommending emigration to their people, nor the establishment of separate institutions of learning. They earnestly contended, and doubtless honestly meaning what they said, that they (the whites) had been our oppressors and injurers, they had obstructed our progress to the high positions of civilization, and now, it was their bounden duty to make full amends for the injuries thus inflicted on an unoffending people. They exhorted the Convention to cease; as they had laid on the burden, they would also take it off; as they had obstructed our pathway, they would remove the hindrance. In a word, as they had oppressed and trampled down the colored people, they would now elevate them. These suggestions and promises, good enough to be sure, after they were made, were accepted by the Convention—though some gentlemen were still in favor of the first project as the best policy, Mr. A. D. Shadd of West Chester, Pa., as we learn from himself, being one among that number—ran through the country like wild-fire, no one thinking, and if he thought, daring to speak above his breath of going any where out of certain prescribed limits, or of sending a child to school, if it should but have the name of "colored" attached to it, without the risk of being termed a "traitor" to the cause of his people, or an enemy to the Anti-Slavery cause.

At this important point in the history of our efforts, the colored men stopped suddenly, and with their hands thrust deep in their breeches-pockets, and their mouths gaping open, stood gazing with astonishment, wonder, and surprise, at the stupendous moral colossal statues of our Anti-Slavery friends and brethren, who in the heat and zeal of honest hearts, from a desire to make atonement for the many wrongs inflicted, promised a great deal more than they have ever been able half to fulfill, in thrice the period in which they expected it. And in this, we have no fault to find with our Anti-Slavery friends, and here wish it to be understood, that we are not laying any thing to their charge as blame, neither do we desire for a moment to reflect on them, because we heartily believe that all that they did at the time, they did with the purest and best of motives, and further believe that they now are, as they then were, the truest friends we have among the whites in this country. And hope, and desire, and request, that our people should always look upon *true* anti-slavery people, Abolitionists we mean, as their friends, until they have just cause for acting otherwise. It is true, that the Anti-Slavery, like all good causes, has produced some recreants, but the cause itself is no more to be blamed for that, than Christianity is for the malconduct of any professing hypocrite, nor the society of Friends, for the conduct of a broad-brimmed hat and shad-belly coated[9] horse-thief, because he spoke *thee* and *thou* before stealing the horse. But what is our condition even amidst our Anti-Slavery friends? And here, as our sole intention is to contribute to the elevation of our people, we must be permitted to express our opinion freely, without being thought uncharitable.

In the first place, we should look at the objects for which the Anti-Slavery cause was commenced, and the promises or inducements it held out at the

9. Wearing a coat made of brown broadcloth. "Friends": Quakers.

commencement. It should be borne in mind, that Anti-Slavery took its rise among *colored men*, just at the time they were introducing their greatest projects for their own elevation, and that our Anti-Slavery brethren were converts of the colored men, in behalf of their elevation. Of course, it would be expected that being baptized into the new doctrines, their faith would induce them to embrace the principles therein contained, with the strictest possible adherence.

The cause of dissatisfaction with our former condition, was, that we were proscribed, debarred, and shut out from every respectable position, occupying the places of inferiors and menials.

It was expected that Anti-Slavery, according to its professions, would extend to colored persons, as far as in the power of its adherents, those advantages nowhere else to be obtained among white men. That colored boys would get situations in their shops and stores, and every other advantage tending to elevate them as far as possible, would be extended to them. At least, it was expected, that in Anti-Slavery establishments, colored men would have the preference. Because, there was no other ostensible object in view, in the commencement of the Anti-Slavery enterprise, than the *elevation* of the *colored man*, by facilitating his efforts in attaining to equality with the white man. It was urged, and it was true, that the colored people were susceptible of all that the whites were, and all that was required was to give them a fair opportunity, and they would prove their capacity. That it was unjust, wicked, and cruel, the result of an unnatural prejudice, that debarred them from places of respectability, and that public opinion could and should be corrected upon this subject. That it was only necessary to make a sacrifice of feeling, and an innovation on the customs of society, to establish a different order of things,—that as Anti-Slavery men, they were willing to make these sacrifices, and determined to take the colored man by the hand, making common cause with him in affliction, and bear a part of the odium heaped upon him. That his cause was the cause of God—that "In as much as ye did it not unto the least of these my little ones, ye did it not unto me,"[1] and that as Anti-Slavery men, they would "do right if the heavens fell."[2] Thus, was the cause espoused, and thus did we expect much. But in all this, we were doomed to disappointment, sad, sad disappointment. Instead of realising what we had hoped for, we find ourselves occupying the very same position in relation to our Anti-Slavery friends, as we do in relation to the pro-slavery part of the community—a mere secondary, underling position, in all our relations to them, and any thing more than this, is not a matter of course affair—it comes not by established anti-slavery custom or right, but like that which emanates from the proslavery portion of the community, by mere sufferance.

It is true, that the "Liberator" office, in Boston, has got Elijah Smith, a colored youth, at the cases—the "Standard," in New York, a young colored man, and the "Freeman," in Philadelphia, William Still,[3] another, in the publication office, as "packing clerk;" yet these are but three out of the hosts that fill these offices in their various departments, all occupying places that

1. Matthew 25:45.
2. English translation of a popular Latin maxim: *Fiat justitia, ruat coelum*.
3. Still (1821–1902), abolitionist, businessman, and author of *The Underground Railroad* (1872). "Standard": the *National Anti-Slavery Standard* (1840–70), published in New York City. "Freeman": the *Pennsylvania Freeman*, antislavery newspaper founded in Philadelphia in 1836 and edited after 1838 by the antislavery poet John Greenleaf Whittier.

could have been, and as we once thought, would have been, easily enough, occupied by colored men. Indeed, we can have no other idea about anti-slavery in this country, than that the legitimate persons to fill any and every position about an anti-slavery establishment are colored persons. Nor will it do to argue in extenuation, that white men are as justly entitled to them as colored men; because white men do not from *necessity* become anti-slavery men in order to get situations; they being white men, may occupy any position they are capable of filling—in a word, their chances are endless, every avenue in the country being opened to them. They do not therefore become abolitionists, for the sake of employment—at least, it is not the song that anti-slavery sung, in the first love of the new faith, proclaimed by its disciples.

And if it be urged that colored men are incapable as yet to fill these positions, all that we have to say is, that the cause has fallen far short; almost equivalent to a failure, of a tithe,[4] of what it promised to do in half the period of its existence, to this time, if it have not as yet, now a period of twenty years, raised up colored men enough, to fill the offices within its patronage. We think it is not unkind to say, if it had been half as faithful to itself, as it should have been—its professed principles we mean; it could have reared and tutored from childhood, colored men enough by this time, for its own especial purpose. These we know could have been easily obtained, because colored people in general, are favorable to the anti-slavery cause, and wherever there is an adverse manifestation, it arises from sheer ignorance; and we have now but comparatively few such among us. There is one thing certain, that no colored person, except such as would reject education altogether, would be adverse to putting their child with an anti-slavery person, for educational advantages. This then, could have been done. But it has not been done, and let the cause of it be whatever it may, and let whoever may be to blame, we are willing to let all that pass, and extend to our anti-slavery brethren the right-hand of fellowship, bidding them God-speed in the propagation of good and wholesome sentiments—for whether they are practically carried out or not, the professions are in themselves all right and good. Like Christianity, the principles are holy and of divine origin. And we believe, if ever a man started right, with pure and holy motives, Mr. Garrison did; and that, had he the power of making the cause what it should be, it would all be right, and there never would have been any cause for the remarks we have made, though in kindness, and with the purest of motives. We are nevertheless, still occupying a miserable position in the community, wherever we live; and what we most desire is, to draw the attention of our people to this fact, and point out what, in our opinion, we conceive to be a proper remedy.

* * *

Chapter V.

MEANS OF ELEVATION.

Moral theories have long been resorted to by us, as a means of effecting the redemption of our brethren in bonds, and the elevation of the free colored people in this country. Experience has taught us, that speculations are not

4. A levy of produce or income as an obligation for support of a church.

enough; that the *practical* application of principles adduced, the thing carried out, is the only true and proper course to pursue.

We have speculated and moralised much about equality—claiming to be as good as our neighbors, and every body else—all of which, may do very well in ethics—but not in politics. We live in society among men, conducted by men, governed by rules and regulations. However arbitrary, there are certain policies that regulate all well organized institutions and corporate bodies. We do not intend here to speak of the legal political relations of society, for those are treated on elsewhere. The business and social, or voluntary and mutual policies, are those that now claim our attention. Society regulates itself—being governed by mind, which like water, finds its own level. "Like seeks like," is a principle in the laws of matter, as well as of mind. There is such a thing as inferiority of things, and positions; at least society has made them so, and while we continue to live among men, we must agree to all *just* measures—all those we mean, that do not necessarily infringe on the rights of others. By the regulations of society, there is no equality of persons, where there is not an equality of attainments. By this, we do not wish to be understood as advocating the actual equal attainments of every individual; but we mean to say, that if these attainments be necessary for the elevation of the white man, they are necessary for the elevation of the colored man. That some colored men and women, in a like proportion to the whites, should be qualified in all the attainments possessed by them. It is one of the regulations of society the world over, and we shall have to conform to it, or be discarded as unworthy of the associations of our fellows.

Cast our eyes about us and reflect for a moment, and what do we behold! every thing that presents to view gives evidence of the skill of the white man. Should we purchase a pound of groceries, a yard of linen, a vessel of crockeryware, a piece of furniture, the very provisions that we eat,—all, all are the products of the white man, purchased by us from the white man, consequently, our earnings and means, are all given to the white man.

Pass along the avenues of any city or town, in which you live—behold the trading shops—the manufactories—see the operations of the various machinery—see the stage-coaches coming in, bringing the mails of intelligence—look at the railroads interlining every section, bearing upon them their mighty trains, flying with the velocity of the swallow, ushering in the hundreds of industrious, enterprising travellers. Cast again your eyes widespread over the ocean—see the vessels in every direction with their white sheets spread to the winds of heaven, freighted with the commerce, merchandise and wealth of many nations. Look as you pass along through the cities, at the great and massive buildings—the beautiful and extensive structures of architecture—behold the ten thousand cupolas, with their spires all reared up towards heaven, intersecting the territory of the clouds—all standing as mighty living monuments, of the industry, enterprise, and intelligence of the white man. And yet, with all these living truths, rebuking us with scorn, we strut about, place our hands akimbo,[5] straighten up ourselves to our greatest height, and talk loudly about being "as good as any body." How do we compare with them? Our fathers are their coachmen, our brothers their cookmen, and ourselves their waiting-men. Our mothers their nurse-women, our sisters their scrub-women, our daughters their maid-women, and our wives their washer-women. Until colored men, attain to a

5. With hands on hips and elbows bent outward.

position above permitting their mothers, sisters, wives, and daughters, to do the drudgery and menial offices of other men's wives and daughters; it is useless, it is nonsense, it is pitiable mockery, to talk about equality and elevation in society. The world is looking upon us, with feelings of commisseration, sorrow, and contempt. We scarcely deserve sympathy, if we peremptorily refuse advice, bearing upon our elevation.

We will suppose a case for argument: In this city reside, two colored families, of three sons and three daughters each. At the head of each family, there is an old father and mother. The opportunities of these families, may or may not be the same for educational advantages—be that as it may, the children of the one go to school, and become qualified for the duties of life. One daughter becomes [a] school-teacher, another a mantua[6]-maker, and a third a fancy shop-keeper; while one son becomes a farmer, another a merchant, and a third a mechanic. All enter into business with fine prospects, marry respectably, and settle down in domestic comfort—while the six sons and daughters of the other family, grow up without educational and business qualifications, and the highest aim they have, is to apply to the sons and daughters of the first named family, to hire for domestics! Would there be an equality here between the children of these two families? Certainly not. This, then, is precisely the position of the colored people generally in the United States, compared with the whites. What is necessary to be done, in order to attain an equality, is to change the condition, and the person is at once changed. If, as before stated, a knowledge of all the various business enterprises, trades, professions, and sciences, is necessary for the elevation of the white, a knowledge of them also is necessary for the elevation of the colored man; and he cannot be elevated without them.

White men are producers—we are consumers. They build houses, and we rent them. They raise produce, and we consume it. They manufacture clothes and wares, and we garnish ourselves with them. They build coaches, vessels, cars, hotels, saloons, and other vehicles and places of accommodation, and we deliberately wait until they have got them in readiness, then walk in, and contend with as much assurance for a "right," as though the whole thing was bought by, paid for, and belonged to us. By their literary attainments, they are the contributors to, authors and teachers of, literature, science, religion, law, medicine, and all other useful attainments that the world now makes use of. We have no reference to ancient times—we speak of modern things.

These are the means by which God intended man to succeed: and this discloses the secret of the white man's success with all of his wickedness, over the head of the colored man, with all of his religion. We have been pointed and plain, on this part of the subject, because we desire our readers to see persons and things in their true position. Until we are determined to change the condition of things, and raise ourselves above the position in which we are now prostrated, we must hang our heads in sorrow, and hide our faces in shame. It is enough to know that these things are so; the causes we care little about. Those we have been examining, complaining about, and moralizing over, all our life time. This we are weary of. What we desire to learn now is, how to effect a *remedy;* this we have endeavored to point out. Our elevation must be the result of *self-efforts*, and work of our *own hands*. No other human power can accomplish it. If we but determine it shall be so,

6. A loose, sleeveless cloak.

it will be so. Let each one make the case his own, and endeavor to rival his neighbor, in honorable competition.

These are the proper and only means of elevating ourselves and attaining equality in this country or any other, and it is useless, utterly futile, to think about going any where, except we are determined to use these as the necessary means of developing our manhood. The means are at hand, within our reach. Are we willing to try them? Are we willing to raise ourselves superior to the condition of slaves, or continue the meanest underlings, subject to the beck and call of every creature bearing a pale complexion? If we are, we had as well remained in the South, as to have come to the North in search of more freedom. What was the object of our parents in leaving the South, if it were not for the purpose of attaining equality in common with others of their fellow citizens, by giving their children access to all the advantages enjoyed by others? Surely this was their object. They heard of liberty and equality here, and they hastened on to enjoy it, and no people are more astonished and disappointed than they, who for the first time, on beholding the position we occupy here in the free North—what is called, and what they expect to find, the free States. They at once tell us, that they have as much liberty in the South as we have in the North—that there as free people, they are protected in their rights—that we have nothing more—that in other respects they have the same opportunity, indeed the preferred opportunity, of being their maids, servants, cooks, waiters, and menials in general, there, as we have here—that had they known for a moment, before leaving, that such was to be the only position they occupied here, they would have remained where they were, and never left. Indeed, such is the disappointment in many cases, that they immediately return back again, completely insulted at the idea, of having us here at the north, assume ourselves to be their superiors. Indeed, if our superior advantages of the free States, do not induce and stimulate us to the higher attainments in life, what in the name of degraded humanity will do it? Nothing, surely nothing. If, in fine, the advantages of free schools in Massachusetts, New York, Pennsylvania, Ohio, Michigan, and wherever else we may have them, do not give us advantages and pursuits superior to our slave brethren, then are the unjust assertions of Messrs. Henry Clay, John C. Calhoun, Theodore Frelinghuysen, late Governor Poindexter of Mississippi, George McDuffy, Governor Hammond of South Carolina, Extra Billy (present Governor) Smith,[7] of Virginia, and the host of our oppressors, slave-holders and others, true, that we are insusceptible and incapable of elevation to the more respectable, honorable, and higher attainments among white men. But this we do not believe—neither do you, although our whole life and course of policy in this country are such, that it would seem to prove otherwise. The degradation of the slave parent has been entailed upon the child, induced by the subtle policy of the oppressor, in regular succession handed down from father to son—a system of regular submission and servitude, menialism and dependence, until it has become almost a physiological function of our system, an actual condition of our nature. Let this no longer be so, but let us determine to equal the whites among whom we live, not by declarations and unexpressed self-opinion, for

7. William Smith (1797–1887), governor of Virginia (1846–49, 1864–65). Clay (1777–1852), U.S. senator from Kentucky, who served several terms from 1806 to 1852. Calhoun (1782–1850), U.S. senator from South Carolina (1832–43, 1845–50). Frelinghuysen (1787–1862), U.S. senator from New Jersey (1829–35). George Poindexter (1779–1853), governor of Mississippi (1820–22). McDuffie (1790–1851), U.S. senator from South Carolina (1842–46). James Hammond (1807–1864), governor of South Carolina (1842–44).

we have always had enough of that, but by actual proof in acting, doing, and carrying out practically, the measures of equality. Here is our nativity, and here have we the natural right to abide and be elevated through the measures of our own efforts.

* * *

Chapter XXIII.

THINGS AS THEY ARE.

"And if thou boast TRUTH to utter,
SPEAK, and leave the rest to God."[8]

In presenting this work, we have but a single object in view, and that is, to inform the minds of the colored people at large, upon many things pertaining to their elevation, that but few among us are acquainted with. Unfortunately for us, as a body, we have been taught to believe, that we must have some person to think for us, instead of thinking for ourselves. So accustomed are we to submission and this kind of training, that it is with difficulty, even among the most intelligent of the colored people, an audience may be elicited for any purpose whatever, if the expounder is to be a colored person; and the introduction of any subject is treated with indifference, if not contempt, when the originator is a colored person. Indeed, the most ordinary white person, is almost revered, while the most qualified colored person is totally neglected. Nothing from them is appreciated.

We have been standing comparatively still for years, following in the footsteps of our friends, believing that what they promise us can be accomplished, just because they say so, although our own knowledge should long since, have satisfied us to the contrary. Because even were it possible, with the present hate and jealousy that the whites have towards us in this country, for us to gain equality of rights with them; we never could have an equality of the exercise and enjoyment of those rights—because, the great odds of numbers are against us. We might indeed, as some at present, have the right of the elective franchise—nay, it is not the elective franchise, because the *elective franchise* makes the enfranchised, *eligible* to any position attainable; but we may exercise the right of *voting* only, which to us, is but poor satisfaction; and we by no means care to cherish the privilege of voting somebody into office, to help to make laws to degrade us.

In religion—because they are both *translators* and *commentators*, we must believe nothing, however absurd, but what our oppressors tell us. In Politics, nothing but such as they promulge; in Anti-Slavery, nothing but what our white brethren and friends say we must; in the mode and manner of our elevation, we must do nothing, but that which may be laid down to be done by our white brethren from some quarter or other; and now, even on the subject of emigration, there are some colored people to be found, so lost to their own interest and self-respect, as to be gulled by slave owners and colonizationists, who are led to believe there is no other place in which they can become elevated, but Liberia,[9] a government of American slave-holders, as we have shown—simply, because white men have told them so.

8. From *Truth and Freedom,* by William D. Gallagher (1808–1894).

9. A republic on the West African coast, founded in 1822 by formerly enslaved American sponsored by the American Colonization Society.

Upon the possibility, means, mode and manner, of our Elevation in the United States—Our Original Rights and Claims as Citizens—Our Determination not to be Driven from our Native Country—the Difficulties in the Way of our Elevation—Our Position in Relation to our Anti-Slavery Brethren—the Wicked Design and Injurious Tendency of the American Colonization Society—Objections to Liberia—Objections to Canada—Preferences to South America, &c., &c., all of which we have treated without reserve; expressing our mind freely, and with candor, as we are determined that as far as we can at present do so, the minds of our readers shall be enlightened. The custom of concealing information upon vital and important subjects, in which the interest of the people is involved, we do not agree with, nor favor in the least; we have therefore, laid this cursory treatise before our readers, with the hope that it may prove instrumental in directing the attention of our people in the right way, that leads to their Elevation. Go or stay—of course each is free to do as he pleases—one thing is certain; our Elevation is the work of our own hands. And Mexico, Central America, the West Indies, and South America, all present now, opportunities for the individual enterprise of our young men, who prefer to remain in the United States, in preference to going where they can enjoy real freedom, and equality of rights. Freedom of Religion, as well as of politics, being tolerated in all of these places.

Let our young men and women, prepare themselves for usefulness and business; that the men may enter into merchandise, trading, and other things of importance; the young women may become teachers of various kinds, and otherwise fill places of usefulness. Parents must turn their attention more to the education of their children. We mean, to educate them for useful practical business purposes. Educate them for the Store and the Counting House—to do every-day practical business. Consult the children's propensities, and direct their education according to their inclinations. It may be, that there is too great a desire on the part of parents, to give their children a professional education, before the body of the people, are ready for it. A people must be a business people, and have more to depend upon than mere help in people's houses and Hotels, before they are either able to support, or capable of properly appreciating the services of professional men among them. This has been one of our great mistakes—we have gone in advance of ourselves. We have commenced at the superstructure of the building, instead of the foundation—at the top instead of the bottom. We should first be mechanics and common tradesmen, and professions as a matter of course would grow out of the wealth made thereby. Young men and women, must now prepare for usefulness—the day of our Elevation is at hand—all the world now gazes at us—and Central and South America, and the West Indies, bid us come and be men and women, protected, secure, beloved and Free.

The branches of Education most desirable for the preparation of youth, for practical useful every-day life, are Arithmetic and good Penmanship, in order to be Accountants; and a good rudimental knowledge of Geography—which has ever been neglected, and under estimated—and of Political Economy; which without the knowledge of the first, no people can ever become adventurous—nor of the second, never will be an enterprising people. Geography, teaches a knowledge of the world, and Political Economy, a knowledge of the wealth of nations; or how to make money. These are not abstruse sciences, or learning not easily acquired or understood; but simply, common School Primer learning, that every body may get. And, although it is the very Key to prosperity and success in common life, but few know any thing about it. Unfortunately for our people, so soon as their children learn to read a Chapter in the New Testament, and scribble a miserable hand, they are pronounced to have "Learning enough;" and taken away from School, no use to themselves, nor community. This is apparent in our Public Meetings, and Official Church Meetings; of the great number of men present, there are but few capable of filling a Secretaryship. Some of the large cities may be an exception to this. Of the multitudes of Merchants, and Business men throughout this country, Europe, and the world, few are qualified, beyond the branches here laid down by us as necessary for business. What did John Jacob Astor, Stephen Girard,[1] or do the millionaires and the greater part of the merchant princes, and mariners, know about Latin and Greek, and the Classics? Precious few of them know any thing. In proof of this, in 1841, during the Administration of President Tyler,[2] when the mutiny was detected on board of the American Man of War Brig Somers, the names of the Mutineers, were recorded by young S—a Midshipman in Greek. Captain Alexander Slidell McKenzie, Commanding, was unable to read them; and in his despatches to the Government, in justification of his policy in executing the criminals, said that he "discovered some curious characters which he was unable to read," &c.; showing thereby, that that high functionary, did not understand even the Greek Alphabet, which was only necessary, to have been able to read proper names written in Greek.

What we most need then, is a good business practical Education; because, the Classical and Professional education of so many of our young men, before their parents are able to support them, and community ready to patronize them, only serves to lull their energy, and cripple the otherwise, praiseworthy efforts they would make in life. A Classical education, is only suited to the wealthy, or those who have a prospect of gaining a livelihood by it. The writer does not wish to be understood, as underrating a Classical and Professional education; this is not his intention; he fully appreciates them, having had some such advantages himself; but he desires to give a proper guide, and put a check to the extravagant idea that is fast obtaining, among our people especially, that a Classical, or as it is termed, a "finished education," is necessary to prepare one for usefulness in life. Let us have an education, that shall practically develope our thinking faculties and manhood; and then, and not until then, shall we be able to vie with our oppressors, go where we may. We as heretofore, have been on the extreme; either no qualification at all, or a Collegiate education. We jumped too far; taking a leap from the deepest abyss to the highest summit; rising from the ridiculous to the sublime; without medium or intermission.

Let our young women have an education; let their minds be well informed; well stored with useful information and practical proficiency, rather than the light superficial acquirements, popularly and fashionably called accomplishments. We desire accomplishments, but they must be *useful*.

Our females must be qualified, because they are to be the mothers of our children. As mothers are the first nurses and instructors of children; from them children consequently, get their first impressions, which being always the most lasting, should be the most correct. Raise the mothers above the level of degradation, and the offspring is elevated with them. In a word, instead of our young men, transcribing in their blank books, recipes for *Cooking;* we desire

1. American businessman and philanthropist (1750–1831). Astor (1763–1848), German American merchant and financier.

2. John Tyler (1790–1862), president of the United States from 1841 to 1845.

to see them making the transfer of *Invoices of Merchandise*. Come to our aid then; the *morning* of our *Redemption* from degradation, adorns the horizon.

In our selection of individuals,[3] it will be observed, that we have confined ourself entirely to those who occupy or have occupied positions among the whites, consequently having a more general bearing as useful contributors to society at large. While we do not pretend to give all such worthy cases, we gave such as we possessed information of, and desire it to be understood, that a large number of our most intelligent and worthy men and women, have not been named, because from their more private position in community, it was foreign to the object and design of this work. If we have said aught to offend, "take the will for the deed,"[4] and be assured, that it was given with the purest of motives, and best intention, from a true hearted man and brother; deeply lamenting the sad fate of his race in this country, and sincerely desiring the elevation of man, and submitted to the serious consideration of all, who favor the promotion of the cause of God and humanity.

Chapter XXIV.

A GLANCE AT OURSELVES—CONCLUSION.

With broken hopes—sad devastation;
A race *resigned* to DEGRADATION!

We have said much of our young men and women, about their vocation and calling; we have dwelt much upon the menial position of our people in this country. Upon this point we cannot say too much, because there is a seeming satisfaction and seeking after such positions manifested on their part, unknown to any other people. There appears to be, a want of a sense of propriety or *self-respect*, altogether inexplicable; because young men and women among us, many of whom have good trades and homes, adequate to their support, voluntarily leave them, and seek positions, such as servants, waiting maids, coachmen, nurses, cooks in gentlemens' kitchen, or such like occupations, when they can gain a livelihood at something more respectable, or elevating in character. And the worse part of the whole matter is, that they have become so accustomed to it, it has become so "fashionable," that it seems to have become second nature, and they really become offended, when it is spoken against.

Among the German, Irish, and other European peasantry who come to this country, it matters not what they were employed at before and after they come; just so soon as they can better their condition by keeping shops, cultivating the soil, the young men and women going to night-schools, qualifying themselves for usefulness, and learning trades—they do so. Their first and last care, object and aim is, to better their condition by raising themselves above the condition that necessity places them in. We do not say too much, when we say, as an evidence of the deep degradation of our race, in the United States, that there are those among us, the wives and daughters, some of the *first ladies*, (and who dare say they are not the "first," because they belong to the "first class" and associate where any body among us can?) whose husbands are industrious, able and willing to support them, who

3. Earlier chapters of the book feature short biographies of successful African American women and men in a variety of occupations and professions.
4. Appearing in 19th-century novels by Lydia Maria Child, James Fenimore Cooper, and Charles Dickens, this popular phrase originates from *A Treatise on Polite Conversation*, Dialogue 2 (1738), by Jonathan Swift.

voluntarily leave home, and become chamber-maids, and stewardesses, upon vessels and steamboats, in all probability, to enable them to obtain some more fine or costly article of dress or furniture.

We have nothing to say against those whom *necessity* compels to do these things, those who can do no better; we have only to do with those who can, and will not, or do not do better. The whites are always in the advance, and we either standing still or retrograding; as that which does not go forward, must either stand in one place or go back. The father in all probability is a farmer, mechanic, or man of some independent business; and the wife, sons and daughters, are chamber-maids, on vessels, nurses and waiting-maids, or coachmen and cooks in families. This is retrogradation. The wife, sons, and daughters should be elevated above this condition as a necessary consequence.

If we did not love our race superior to others, we would not concern ourself about their degradation; for the greatest desire of our heart is, to see them stand on a level with the most elevated of mankind. No people are ever elevated above the condition of their *females;* hence, the condition of the *mother* determines the condition of the child. To know the position of a people, it is only necessary to know the *condition* of their *females;* and despite themselves, they cannot rise above their level. Then what is our condition? Our *best ladies* being washerwomen, chamber-maids, children's traveling nurses, and common house servants, and menials, we are all a degraded, miserable people, inferior to any other people as a whole, on the face of the globe.

These great truths, however unpleasant, must be brought before the minds of our people in its true and proper light, as we have been too delicate about them, and too long concealed them for fear of giving offence. It would have been infinitely better for our race, if these facts had been presented before us half a century ago—we would have been now proportionably benefitted by it.

As an evidence of the degradation to which we have been reduced, we dare premise, that this chapter will give offence to many, very many, and why? Because they may say, "He dared to say that the occupation of a *servant* is a degradation." It is not necessarily degrading; it would not be, to one or a few people of a kind; but a *whole race of servants* are a degradation to that people.

Efforts made by men of qualifications for the toiling and degraded millions among the whites, neither gives offence to that class, nor is it taken unkindly by them; but received with manifestations of gratitude; to know that they are thought to be, equally worthy of, and entitled to stand on a level with the elevated classes; and they have only got to be informed of the way to raise themselves, to make the effort and do so as far as they can. But how different with us. Speak of our position in society, and it at once gives insult. Though we are servants; among ourselves we claim to be *ladies* and *gentlemen*, equal in standing, and as the popular expression goes, "Just as good as any body"—and so believing, we make no efforts to raise above the common level of menials; because the *best* being in that capacity, all are content with the position. We cannot at the same time, be domestic and lady; servant and gentleman. We must be the one or the other. Sad, sad indeed, is the thought, that hangs drooping in our mind, when contemplating the picture drawn before us. Young men and women, "we write these things unto you, because ye are strong,"[5] because the writer, a few years ago, gave unpardonable offence to many of the young people of Philadelphia and other places, because he dared

5. 1 John 2:14.

tell them, that he thought too much of them, to be content with seeing them the servants of other people. Surely, she that could be the mistress, would not be the maid; neither would he that could be the master, be content with being the servant; then why be offended, when we point out to you, the way that leads from the menial to the mistress or the master. All this we seem to reject with fixed determination, repelling with anger, every effort on the part of our intelligent men and women to elevate us, with true Israelitish degradation, in reply to any suggestion or proposition that may be offered, "Who made thee a ruler and judge?"[6]

The writer is no "Public Man," in the sense in which this is understood among our people, but simply an humble individual, endeavoring to seek a livelihood by a profession obtained entirely by his own efforts, without relatives and friends able to assist him; except such friends as he gained by the merit of his course and conduct, which he here gratefully acknowledges; and whatever he has accomplished, other young men may, by making corresponding efforts, also accomplish.

We have advised an emigration to Central and South America, and even to Mexico and the West Indies, to those who prefer either of the last named places, all of which are free countries, Brazil being the only real slave-holding State in South America—there being nominal slavery in Dutch Guiana,[7] Peru, Buenos Ayres, Paraguay, and Uraguay, in all of which places colored people have equality in social, civil, political, and religious privileges; Brazil making it punishable with death to import slaves into the empire.

Our oppressors, when urging us to go to Africa, tell us that we are better adapted to the climate than they—that the physical condition of the constitution of colored people better endures the heat of warm climates than that of the whites; this we are willing to *admit*, without argument, without adducing the physiological reason why, that colored people can and do stand warm climates better than whites; and find an answer fully to the point in the fact, that they also stand *all other* climates, cold, temperate, and modified, that white people can stand; therefore, according to our oppressors' own showing, we are a *superior race*, being endowed with properties fitting us for *all parts* of the earth, while they are only adapted to *certain* parts. Of course, this proves our right and duty to live wherever we may *choose;* while the white race may only live where they *can*. We are content with the fact, and have ever claimed it. Upon this rock, they and we shall ever agree.

Of the West India Islands, Santa Cruz, belonging to Denmark; Porto Rico, and Cuba with its little adjuncts, belonging to Spain, are the only slave-holding Islands among them—three-fifths of the whole population of Cuba being colored people, who cannot and will not much longer endure the burden and the yoke. They only want intelligent leaders of their own color, when they are ready at any moment to charge to the conflict—to liberty or death. The remembrance of the noble mulatto, PLACIDO, the gentleman, scholar, poet, and intended Chief Engineer of the Army of Liberty and Freedom in Cuba; and the equally noble black, CHARLES BLAIR, who was to have been Commander-in-Chief, who were shamefully put to death in 1844, by that living monster, Captain General O'Donnell,[8] is still fresh and indelible to the mind of every bondman of Cuba.

6. Acts 7:27.
7. Today, the nation of Suriname.
8. Leopoldo O'Donnell (1809–1867), governor of Cuba from 1843 to 1848. "Placido": pen name of Gabriel de la Concepción Valdés (1809–1844), a mixed-race poet and revolutionary executed in Cuba on June 28, 1844. Belair (1778–1802), general under Toussaint L'Ouverture during the Haitian Revolution.

In our own country, the United States, there are *three million five hundred thousand slaves;* and we, the nominally free colored people, are *six hundred thousand* in number; estimating one-sixth to be men, we have *one hundred thousand* able bodied freemen, which will make a powerful auxiliary in any country to which we may become adopted—an ally not to be despised by any power on earth. We love our country, dearly love her, but she don't love us—she despises us, and bids us begone, driving us from her embraces; but we shall not go where she desires us; but when we do go, whatever love we have for her, we shall love the country none the less that receives us as her adopted children.

For the want of business habits and training, our energies have become paralyzed; our young men never think of business, any more than if they were so many bondmen, without the right to pursue any calling they may think most advisable. With our people in this country, dress and good appearances have been made the only test of gentleman and ladyship, and that vocation which offers the best opportunity to dress and appear well, has generally been preferred, however menial and degrading, by our young people, without even, in the majority of cases, an effort to do better; indeed, in many instances, refusing situations equally lucrative, and superior in position; but which would not allow as much display of dress and personal appearance. This, if we ever expect to rise, must be discarded from among us, and a high and respectable position assumed.

One of our great temporal curses is our consummate poverty. We are the poorest people, as a class, in the world of civilized mankind—abjectly, miserably poor, no one scarcely being able to assist the other. To this, of course, there are noble exceptions; but that which is common to, and the very process by which white men exist, and succeed in life, is unknown to colored men in general. In any and every considerable community may be found, some one of our white fellow-citizens, who is worth more than all the colored people in that community put together. We consequently have little or no efficiency. We must have means to be practically efficient in all the undertakings of life; and to obtain them, it is necessary that we should be engaged in lucrative pursuits, trades, and general business transactions. In order to be thus engaged, it is necessary that we should occupy positions that afford the facilities for such pursuits. To compete now with the mighty odds of wealth, social and religious preferences, and political influences of this country, at this advanced stage of its national existence, we never may expect. A new country, and new beginning, is the only true, rational, politic remedy for our disadvantageous position; and that country we have already pointed out, with triple golden advantages, all things considered, to that of any country to which it has been the province of man to embark.

Every other than we, have at various periods of necessity, been a migratory people; and all when oppressed, shown a greater abhorrence of oppression, if not a greater love of liberty, than we. We cling to our oppressors as the objects of our love. It is true that our enslaved brethren are here, and we have been led to believe that it is necessary for us to remain, on that account. Is it true, that all should remain in degradation, because a part are degraded? We believe no such thing. We believe it to be the duty of the Free, to elevate themselves in the most speedy and effective manner possible; as the redemption of the bondman depends entirely upon the elevation of the freeman; therefore, to elevate the free colored people of America, anywhere upon this continent; forebodes the speedy redemption of the slaves. We shall hope to hear no more of so fallacious a doctrine—the necessity of the free remaining in degradation, for the sake of the oppressed. Let us apply, first, the lever to ourselves; and the force that elevates us to the position of manhood's considerations and honors, will cleft the manacle of every slave in the land.

When such great worth and talents—for want of a better sphere—of men like Rev. Jonathan Robinson, Robert Douglass, Frederick A. Hinton,[9] and a hundred others that might be named, were permitted to expire in a barber-shop; and such living men as may be found in Boston, New York, Philadelphia, Baltimore, Richmond, Washington City, Charleston, (S. C.) New Orleans, Cincinnati, Louisville, St. Louis, Pittsburg, Buffalo, Rochester, Albany, Utica, Cleveland, Detroit, Milwaukie, Chicago, Columbus, Zanesville, Wheeling, and a hundred other places, confining themselves to Barbar-shops and waiterships in Hotels; certainly the necessity of such a course as we have pointed out, must be cordially acknowledged; appreciated by every brother and sister of oppression; and not rejected as heretofore, as though they preferred inferiority to equality. These minds must become "unfettered," and have "space to rise." This cannot be in their present positions. A continuance in any position, becomes what is termed "Second Nature;" it begets an *adaptation*, and *reconciliation* of *mind* to such condition. It changes the whole physiological condition of the system, and adapts man and woman to a higher or lower sphere in the pursuits of life. The offsprings of slaves and peasantry, have the general characteristics of their parents; and nothing but a different course of training and education, will change the character.

The slave may become a lover of his master, and learn to forgive him for continual deeds of maltreatment and abuse; just as the Spaniel would c[r]ouch and fondle at the feet that kick him; because he has been taught to reverence them, and consequently, becomes adapted in body and mind to his condition. Even the shrubbery-loving Canary, and lofty-soaring Eagle, may be tamed to the cage, and learn to love it from habit of confinement. It has been so with us in our position among our oppressors; we have been so prone to such positions, that we have learned to love them. When reflecting upon this all important, and to us, all absorbing subject; we feel in the agony and anxiety of the moment, as though we could cry out in the language of a Prophet of old: "Oh that my head were waters, and mine eyes a fountain of tears, that I might weep day and night for the" degradation "of my people! Oh that I had in the wilderness a lodging place of way-faring men; that I might leave my people, and go from them!"[1]

The Irishman and German in the United States, are very different persons to what they were when in Ireland and Germany, the countries of their nativity. There their spirits were depressed and downcast; but the instant they set their foot upon unrestricted soil; free to act and untrammeled to move; their physical condition undergoes a change, which in time becomes physiological, which is transmitted to the offspring, who when born under such circumstances, is a decidedly different being to what it would have been, had it been born under different circumstances.

A child born under oppression, has all the elements of servility in its constitution; who when born under favorable circumstances, has to the contrary, all the elements of freedom and independence of feeling. Our children then, may not be expected, to maintain that position and manly bearing; born under the

9. Head of the American Moral Reform Society, an antislavery organization founded in 1837.

1. Jeremiah 9:1–2.

unfavorable circumstances with which we are surrounded in this country; that we so much desire. To use the language of the talented Mr. Whipper,[2] "they cannot be raised in this country, without being stoop shouldered." Heaven's pathway stands unobstructed, which will lead us into a Paradise of bliss. Let us go on and possess the land,[3] and the God of Israel will be our God.

The lessons of every school book, the pages of every history, and columns of every newspaper, are so replete with stimuli to nerve us on to manly aspirations, that those of our young people, who will now refuse to enter upon this great theatre of Polynesian adventure, and take their position on the stage of Central and South America, where a brilliant engagement, of certain and most triumphant success, in the drama of human equality awaits them; then, with the blood of *slaves,* write upon the lintel of every door in sterling Capitals, to be gazed and hissed at by every passer by—

Doomed by the Creator
To servility and degradation;
The SERVANT of the *white man,*
And despised of every nation!

1852

2. William Whipper (1804?–1876), African American businessman, editor, and abolitionist.

3. See Deuteronomy 8:1: "Go in and possess the land which the Lord sware unto your fathers."

HARRIET JACOBS
ca. 1813–1897

Harriet Jacobs was the first African American woman to author and publish a slave narrative in the United States. Before the publication of *Incidents in the Life of a Slave Girl* (1861), several free-born African American women, such as Jarena Lee and Zilpha Elaw, had proudly portrayed their spiritual journeys and social struggles in autobiographies that featured the trials and triumphs of Christian women determined to follow a calling to preach despite opposition. Jacobs's successful struggle for freedom, not only for herself but for her two children, represented no less profoundly a Black woman's dauntless spirit. Yet nowhere in her autobiography, not even on its title page, did Jacobs disclose her own identity as the subject and author of her story. Instead, she called herself "Linda Brent" and masked the important places and persons in her story in the manner of a novelist. "I had no motive for secrecy on my own account," Jacobs insisted in the preface to her autobiography. But given the harrowing and sensational story she had decided to tell, the one-time fugitive from slavery felt she had little alternative but to shield herself from a readership whose empathy she could not take for granted.

Jacobs's task in writing her narrative was considerably more complicated than that of Lee or Elaw. Jacobs felt obliged to disclose through her firsthand example the special injustices that women suffered under what sentimental defenders of slavery often referred to as the "patriarchal institution." Famous male fugitive slave narrators like Frederick Douglass and William Wells Brown had called attention to the sexual victimization of enslaved women by white men. But male-authored slave narratives tend not to elaborate the means by which enslaved women resisted sexual exploitation. Jacobs knew that she risked losing her white reader's respect by speaking frankly about sex and slavery. Nevertheless, she refused to suppress the truth about the sexual threats enslaved women, including herself, experienced from white men. Even riskier was her acknowledgment of how she had used her own sexuality as a weapon against white male domination. Writing an unprecedented mixture of confession, societal exposé, and defense of Black womanhood, Jacobs turned her autobiography into a unique analysis of the myths and the realities that defined the situation of the African American woman and her outsider's relationship to the nineteenth century's "cult of true [white] womanhood." As a result, *Incidents in the Life of a Slave Girl* occupies a crucial turning point in the history of both African American and white American women's literature.

Harriet Ann Jacobs was born enslaved in the coastal town of Edenton, North Carolina, around 1813. Orphaned as a child, she grew up under the care of her loving and protective grandmother and a white female enslaver who taught her to read and sew. The death of this relatively kind enslaver when Jacobs was eleven conveyed her into the hands of the licentious and abusive Dr. James Norcom, who is called, appropriately, Dr. Flint in *Incidents.* During her early teenage years, Jacobs was subjected to relentless sexual harassment from Norcom. In desperation she formed a clandestine liaison with Samuel Tredwell Sawyer, a white attorney (the shifty Mr. Sands in *Incidents*), with whom Jacobs had two children by the time she was twenty years old. Hoping that by seeming to run away she could induce Norcom to sell her children to their father, Jacobs hid herself in a crawl space above a storeroom in her grandmother's house in the summer of 1835. In that "little dismal hole" she remained for almost seven years, sewing, reading the Bible, keeping watch over her children as best she could, and writing occasional letters to Norcom designed to confuse him as to her actual whereabouts. In 1842 Jacobs escaped by sea to the North, where she obtained employment as a nursemaid, and set about reclaiming her daughter, Louisa, from Sawyer, who had purchased the child and sent her to Brooklyn, New York, without emancipating her. In New York, Jacobs was reunited with Louisa, and secured a place for her son, Joseph, to live in Boston.

For ten years after her escape from North Carolina, Harriet Jacobs lived the tense and uncertain life of a still-enslaved fugitive. In 1844 she moved to Boston to avoid recapture. She supported herself and her children as a seamstress or a nursemaid to the baby daughter of Mary Stace Willis, wife of the popular editor, poet, and magazine writer Nathaniel Parker Willis. Norcom's attempts to apprehend Jacobs in New York forced her to keep on the move. Enlisting the aid of antislavery activists in Rochester, New York, in 1849 she went to work with her brother, John S. Jacobs, also a fugitive from slavery, in an antislavery office and bookstore above the office of Frederick Douglass's newspaper, *The North Star.* In Rochester Jacobs met and began to confide in Amy Post, an abolitionist and feminist who gently urged her to consider making public her story of struggle and triumph. After the tremendous response to *Uncle Tom's Cabin* (1852), Jacobs thought of asking the novel's author, Harriet Beecher Stowe, for help in creating her life story. But Stowe had little interest in the project. After receiving, early in 1852, the gift of her freedom from Cornelia Grinnell Willis, the second wife of her employer, Jacobs decided to write her autobiography herself.

Incidents in the Life of a Slave Girl is the only nineteenth-century slave narrative whose genesis and production can be ascertained through surviving documents, namely, a series of letters from Jacobs to various friends and advisors, including Post and the eventual editor of *Incidents,* Lydia Maria Child, a noted American novelist. Discovered and published by Jean Fagan Yellin in her pioneering scholarly edition of *Incidents in the Life of a Slave Girl* (1987), Jacobs's correspondence with Child helps lay to rest the long-time charge made by several scholars and critics that *Incidents* was at worst an outright fiction and at best the product of Child's pen, not Jacobs's. Extant letters between Child and Jacobs make clear that the white woman's role as editor was no more than she acknowledged in her introduction to *Incidents*: ensuring the orderly arrangement of events in the narrative without adding anything to the text or altering in any significant way Jacobs's manner of recounting her story.

Incidents in the Life of a Slave Girl appeared inauspiciously in early 1861, its publication underwritten by its author. The narrative was favorably reviewed in the abolitionist press, but after the onset of the Civil War in April of that year, Jacobs's book claimed little attention beyond antislavery circles. From 1862 to 1866 the author turned to social work on behalf of African Americans from the South. She devoted herself to relief efforts in and around Washington, D.C., among formerly enslaved men and women who had become refugees from the war. In the war's immediate aftermath Jacobs moved to Savannah, Georgia, to engage in further relief work among the freedmen and freedwomen. Returning to Boston with Louisa in 1868, Jacobs opened a boarding house in Cambridge, Massachusetts. By the mid-1880s mother and daughter had returned to Washington, D.C., where except for a short-lived boarding-house venture Harriet worked as a housekeeper and a caterer until she was almost eighty years old. When she died on March 7, 1897, her pastor, Rev. Francis Grimké, eulogized her as "a woman of marked individuality" and "strong character," who "did her own thinking; had opinions of her own, and held to them with great tenacity." Another eulogist, the white feminist-reformer and writer Edna Dow Cheney, who had been a friend and supporter of Jacobs for thirty years, said of *Incidents*: "It should be carefully preserved in our libraries, for it is a wonderful record of the suffering and heroism of those never to be forgotten days."

Two excerpts from a letter, ca. 1852, from Harriet Jacobs to her friend and confidant Amy Kirby Post (1802–1899), in which Jacobs reflects on Post's "proposal" that Jacobs write her autobiography. A larger selection of the letter is transcribed here:

your proposal to me has been thought over and over again but not with out some most painful rememberances dear Amy if it was the life of a Heroine with no degradation associated with it far better to have been one of the starving poor of Ireland whose bones had to bleach on the highways than to have been a slave with the curse of slavery stamped upon yourself and Children your purity of heart and kindly sympathies won me at one time to speak of my children it is the only words that has passed my lips since I left my Mothers door I had determined to let others think as they pleased but my lips should be sealed and no one had a right to question me for this reason when I first came North I avoided the Antislavery people as much as possible because I felt that I could not be honest and tell the whole truth often have I gone to my poor Brother with my gurived [grieved] and mortified spirits he would mingle his tears with mine while he would advise me to do what was right my conscience approved it but my stubborn pride would not yeild [sic] I have tried for the past two years to conquer it and I felt that God has helped me or I never would consent to give my past life to any one for I would not do it with out giving the whole truth if it could help save another from my fate it would be selfish and unchristian in me to keep it back. . . .

From Incidents in the Life of a Slave Girl

Preface

BY THE AUTHOR

Reader, be assured this narrative is no fiction. I am aware that some of my adventures may seem incredible; but they are, nevertheless, strictly true. I have not exaggerated the wrongs inflicted by Slavery; on the contrary, my descriptions fall far short of the facts. I have concealed the names of places, and given persons fictitious names. I had no motive for secrecy on my own account, but I deemed it kind and considerate towards others to pursue this course.

I wish I were more competent to the task I have undertaken. But I trust my readers will excuse deficiencies in consideration of circumstances. I was born and reared in Slavery; and I remained in a Slave State twenty-seven years. Since I have been at the North, it has been necessary for me to work diligently for my own support, and the education of my children. This has not left me much leisure to make up for the loss of early opportunities to improve myself; and it has compelled me to write these pages at irregular intervals, whenever I could snatch an hour from household duties.

When I first arrived in Philadelphia, Bishop Paine[1] advised me to publish a sketch of my life, but I told him I was altogether incompetent to such an undertaking. Though I have improved my mind somewhat since that time, I still remain of the same opinion; but I trust my motives will excuse what might otherwise seem presumptuous. I have not written my experiences in order to attract attention to myself; on the contrary, it would have been more pleasant to me to have been silent about my own history. Neither do I care to excite sympathy for my own sufferings. But I do earnestly desire to arouse the women of the North to a realizing sense of the condition of two millions of women at the South, still in bondage, suffering what I suffered, and most of them far worse. I want to add my testimony to that of abler pens to convince the people of the Free States what Slavery really is. Only by experience can any one realize how deep, and dark, and foul is that pit of abominations. May the blessing of God rest on this imperfect effort in behalf of my persecuted people!

LINDA BRENT.

I. Childhood

I was born a slave; but I never knew it till six years of happy childhood had passed away. My father was a carpenter, and considered so intelligent and

1. Daniel A. Payne (1811–1893), bishop of the African Methodist Episcopal Church. Jacobs met him in Philadelphia in 1842.

skillful in his trade, that, when buildings out of the common line were to be erected, he was sent for from long distances, to be head workman. On condition of paying his mistress two hundred dollars a year, and supporting himself, he was allowed to work at his trade, and manage his own affairs. His strongest wish was to purchase his children; but, though he several times offered his hard earnings for that purpose, he never succeeded. In complexion my parents were a light shade of brownish yellow, and were termed mulattoes. They lived together in a comfortable home; and, though we were all slaves, I was so fondly shielded that I never dreamed I was a piece of merchandise, trusted to them for safe keeping, and liable to be demanded of them at any moment. I had one brother, William, who was two years younger than myself—a bright, affectionate child. I had also a great treasure in my maternal grandmother, who was a remarkable woman in many respects. She was the daughter of a planter in South Carolina, who, at his death, left her mother and his three children free, with money to go to St. Augustine, where they had relatives. It was during the Revolutionary War; and they were captured on their passage, carried back, and sold to different purchasers. Such was the story my grandmother used to tell me; but I do not remember all the particulars. She was a little girl when she was captured and sold to the keeper of a large hotel. I have often heard her tell how hard she fared during childhood. But as she grew older she evinced so much intelligence, and was so faithful, that her master and mistress could not help seeing it was for their interest to take care of such a valuable piece of property. She became an indispensable personage in the household, officiating in all capacities, from cook and wet nurse to seamstress. She was much praised for her cooking; and her nice crackers became so famous in the neighborhood that many people were desirous of obtaining them. In consequence of numerous requests of this kind, she asked permission of her mistress to bake crackers at night, after all the household work was done; and she obtained leave to do it, provided she would clothe herself and her children from the profits. Upon these terms, after working hard all day for her mistress, she began her midnight bakings, assisted by her two oldest children. The business proved profitable; and each year she laid by a little, which was saved for a fund to purchase her children. Her master died, and the property was divided among his heirs. The widow had her dower in the hotel, which she continued to keep open. My grandmother remained in her service as a slave; but her children were divided among her master's children. As she had five, Benjamin, the youngest one, was sold, in order that each heir might have an equal portion of dollars and cents. There was so little difference in our ages that he seemed more like my brother than my uncle. He was a bright, handsome lad, nearly white; for he inherited the complexion my grandmother had derived from Anglo-Saxon ancestors. Though only ten years old, seven hundred and twenty dollars were paid for him. His sale was a terrible blow to my grandmother; but she was naturally hopeful, and she went to work with renewed energy, trusting in time to be able to purchase some of her children. She had laid up three hundred dollars, which her mistress one day begged as a loan, promising to pay her soon. The reader probably knows that no promise or writing given to a slave is legally binding; for, according to Southern laws, a slave, *being* property, can *hold* no property. When my grandmother lent her hard earnings to her mistress, she trusted solely to her honor. The honor of a slaveholder to a slave!

To this good grandmother I was indebted for many comforts. My brother Willie and I often received portions of the crackers, cakes, and preserves, she made to sell; and after we ceased to be children we were indebted to her for many more important services.

Such were the unusually fortunate circumstances of my early childhood. When I was six years old, my mother died; and then, for the first time, I learned, by the talk around me, that I was a slave. My mother's mistress was the daughter of my grandmother's mistress. She was the foster sister of my mother; they were both nourished at my grandmother's breast. In fact, my mother had been weaned at three months old, that the babe of the mistress might obtain sufficient food. They played together as children; and, when they became women, my mother was a most faithful servant to her whiter foster sister. On her death-bed her mistress promised that her children should never suffer for any thing; and during her lifetime she kept her word. They all spoke kindly of my dead mother, who had been a slave merely in name, but in nature was noble and womanly. I grieved for her, and my young mind was troubled with the thought who would now take care of me and my little brother. I was told that my home was now to be with her mistress; and I found it a happy one. No toilsome or disagreeable duties were imposed upon me. My mistress was so kind to me that I was always glad to do her bidding, and proud to labor for her as much as my young years would permit. I would sit by her side for hours, sewing diligently, with a heart as free from care as that of any free-born white child. When she thought I was tired, she would send me out to run and jump; and away I bounded, to gather berries or flowers to decorate her room. Those were happy days—too happy to last. The slave child had no thought for the morrow; but there came that blight, which too surely waits on every human being born to be a chattel.

When I was nearly twelve years old, my kind mistress sickened and died. As I saw the cheek grow paler, and the eye more glassy, how earnestly I prayed in my heart that she might live! I loved her; for she had been almost like a mother to me. My prayers were not answered. She died, and they buried her in the little churchyard, where, day after day, my tears fell upon her grave.

I was sent to spend a week with my grandmother. I was now old enough to begin to think of the future; and again and again I asked myself what they would do with me. I felt sure I should never find another mistress so kind as the one who was gone. She had promised my dying mother that her children should never suffer for any thing; and when I remembered that, and recalled her many proofs of attachment to me, I could not help having some hopes that she had left me free. My friends were almost certain it would be so. They thought she would be sure to do it, on account of my mother's love and faithful service. But, alas! we all know that the memory of a faithful slave does not avail much to save her children from the auction block.

After a brief period of suspense, the will of my mistress was read, and we learned that she had bequeathed me to her sister's daughter, a child of five years old. So vanished our hopes. My mistress had taught me the precepts of God's Word: "Thou shalt love thy neighbor as thyself."[2] "Whatsoever ye would that men should do unto you, do ye even so unto them."[3] But I was her slave, and I suppose she did not recognize me as her neighbor. I would give much to blot out from my memory that one great wrong. As a child, I loved my mistress; and, looking back on the happy days I spent with her, I try to

2. Mark 12:31.

3. Matthew 7:12.

think with less bitterness of this act of injustice. While I was with her, she taught me to read and spell; and for this privilege, which so rarely falls to the lot of a slave, I bless her memory.

She possessed but few slaves; and at her death those were all distributed among her relatives. Five of them were my grandmother's children, and had shared the same milk that nourished her mother's children. Notwithstanding my grandmother's long and faithful service to her owners, not one of her children escaped the auction block. These God-breathing machines are no more, in the sight of their masters, than the cotton they plant, or the horses they tend.

II. The New Master and Mistress

Dr. Flint, a physician in the neighborhood, had married the sister of my mistress, and I was now the property of their little daughter. It was not without murmuring that I prepared for my new home; and what added to my unhappiness, was the fact that my brother William was purchased by the same family. My father, by his nature, as well as by the habit of transacting business as a skillful mechanic, had more of the feelings of a freeman than is common among slaves. My brother was a spirited boy; and being brought up under such influences, he early detested the name of master and mistress. One day, when his father and his mistress had happened to call him at the same time, he hesitated between the two; being perplexed to know which had the strongest claim upon his obedience. He finally concluded to go to his mistress. When my father reproved him for it, he said, "You both called me, and I didn't know which I ought to go to first."

"You are *my* child," replied our father, "and when I call you, you should come immediately, if you have to pass through fire and water."

Poor Willie! He was now to learn his first lesson of obedience to a master. Grandmother tried to cheer us with hopeful words, and they found an echo in the credulous hearts of youth.

When we entered our new home we encountered cold looks, cold words, and cold treatment. We were glad when the night came. On my narrow bed I moaned and wept, I felt so desolate and alone.

I had been there nearly a year, when a dear little friend of mine was buried. I heard her mother sob, as the clods fell on the coffin of her only child, and I turned away from the grave, feeling thankful that I still had something left to love. I met my grandmother, who said, "Come with me, Linda;" and from her tone I knew that something sad had happened. She led me apart from the people, and then said, "My child, your father is dead." Dead! How could I believe it? He had died so suddenly I had not even heard that he was sick. I went home with my grandmother. My heart rebelled against God, who had taken from me mother, father, mistress, and friend. The good grandmother tried to comfort me. "Who knows the ways of God?" said she. "Perhaps they have been kindly taken from the evil days to come." Years afterwards I often thought of this. She promised to be a mother to her grandchildren, so far as she might be permitted to do so; and strengthened by her love, I returned to my master's. I thought I should be allowed to go to my father's house the next morning; but I was ordered to go for flowers, that my mistress's house might be decorated for an evening party. I spent the day gathering flowers and weaving them into festoons, while the dead body of my father was lying within a mile of me. What cared my owners for that?

he was merely a piece of property. Moreover, they thought he had spoiled his children, by teaching them to feel that they were human beings. This was blasphemous doctrine for a slave to teach; presumptuous in him, and dangerous to the masters.

The next day I followed his remains to a humble grave beside that of my dear mother. There were those who knew my father's worth, and respected his memory.

My home now seemed more dreary than ever. The laugh of the little slave-children sounded harsh and cruel. It was selfish to feel so about the joy of others. My brother moved about with a very grave face. I tried to comfort him, by saying, "Take courage, Willie; brighter days will come by and by."

"You don't know any thing about it, Linda," he replied. "We shall have to stay here all our days; we shall never be free."

I argued that we were growing older and stronger, and that perhaps we might, before long, be allowed to hire our own time, and then we could earn money to buy our freedom. William declared this was much easier to say than to do; moreover, he did not intend to *buy* his freedom. We held daily controversies upon this subject.

Little attention was paid to the slaves' meals in Dr. Flint's house. If they could catch a bit of food while it was going, well and good. I gave myself no trouble on that score, for on my various errands I passed my grandmother's house, where there was always something to spare for me. I was frequently threatened with punishment if I stopped there; and my grandmother, to avoid detaining me, often stood at the gate with something for my breakfast or dinner. I was indebted to *her* for all my comforts, spiritual or temporal. It was *her* labor that supplied my scanty wardrobe. I have a vivid recollection of the linsey-woolsey[4] dress given me every winter by Mrs. Flint. How I hated it! It was one of the badges of slavery.

While my grandmother was thus helping to support me from her hard earnings, the three hundred dollars she had lent her mistress were never repaid. When her mistress died, her son-in-law, Dr. Flint, was appointed executor. When grandmother applied to him for payment, he said the estate was insolvent, and the law prohibited payment. It did not, however, prohibit him from retaining the silver candelabra, which had been purchased with that money. I presume they will be handed down in the family, from generation to generation.

My grandmother's mistress had always promised her that, at her death, she should be free; and it was said that in her will she made good the promise. But when the estate was settled, Dr. Flint told the faithful old servant that, under existing circumstances, it was necessary she should be sold.

On the appointed day, the customary advertisement was posted up, proclaiming that there would be a "public sale of negroes, horses, etc." Dr. Flint called to tell my grandmother that he was unwilling to wound her feelings by putting her up at auction, and that he would prefer to dispose of her at private sale. My grandmother saw through his hypocrisy; she understood very well that he was ashamed of the job. She was a very spirited woman, and if he was base enough to sell her, when her mistress intended she should be free, she was determined the public should know it. She had for a long time supplied many families with crackers and preserves; consequently,

4. A cheap fabric made of linen and wool.

"Aunt Marthy," as she was called, was generally known, and every body who knew her respected her intelligence and good character. Her long and faithful service in the family was also well known, and the intention of her mistress to leave her free. When the day of sale came, she took her place among the chattels, and at the first call she sprang upon the auction-block. Many voices called out, "Shame! Shame! Who is going to sell *you*, aunt Marthy? Don't stand there! That is no place for *you*." Without saying a word, she quietly awaited her fate. No one bid for her. At last, a feeble voice said, "Fifty dollars." It came from a maiden lady, seventy years old, the sister of my grandmother's deceased mistress. She had lived forty years under the same roof with my grandmother; she knew how faithfully she had served her owners, and how cruelly she had been defrauded of her rights; and she resolved to protect her. The auctioneer waited for a higher bid; but her wishes were respected; no one bid above her. She could neither read nor write; and when the bill of sale was made out, she signed it with a cross. But what consequence was that, when she had a big heart overflowing with human kindness? She gave the old servant her freedom.

At that time, my grandmother was just fifty years old. Laborious years had passed since then; and now my brother and I were slaves to the man who had defrauded her of her money, and tried to defraud her of her freedom. One of my mother's sisters, called Aunt Nancy, was also a slave in his family. She was a kind, good aunt to me; and supplied the place of both housekeeper and waiting maid to her mistress. She was, in fact, at the beginning and end of every thing.

Mrs. Flint, like many southern women, was totally deficient in energy. She had not strength to superintend her household affairs; but her nerves were so strong, that she could sit in her easy chair and see a woman whipped, till the blood trickled from every stroke of the lash. She was a member of the church; but partaking of the Lord's supper did not seem to put her in a Christian frame of mind. If dinner was not served at the exact time on that particular Sunday, she would station herself in the kitchen, and wait till it was dished, and then spit in all the kettles and pans that had been used for cooking. She did this to prevent the cook and her children from eking out their meagre fare with the remains of the gravy and other scrapings. The slaves could get nothing to eat except what she chose to give them. Provisions were weighed out by the pound and ounce, three times a day. I can assure you she gave them no chance to eat wheat bread from her flour barrel. She knew how many biscuits a quart of flour would make, and exactly what size they ought to be.

Dr. Flint was an epicure.[5] The cook never sent a dinner to his table without fear and trembling; for if there happened to be a dish not to his liking, he would either order her to be whipped, or compel her to eat every mouthful of it in his presence. The poor, hungry creature might not have objected to eating it; but she did object to having her master cram it down her throat till she choked.

They had a pet dog, that was a nuisance in the house. The cook was ordered to make some Indian mush[6] for him. He refused to eat, and when his head was held over it, the froth flowed from his mouth into the basin. He died a few minutes after. When Dr. Flint came in, he said the mush had

5. A person with discriminating taste in food and drink.

6. A mush made of corn, or maize.

not been well cooked, and that was the reason the animal would not eat it. He sent for the cook, and compelled her to eat it. He thought that the woman's stomach was stronger than the dog's; but her sufferings afterwards proved that he was mistaken. This poor woman endured many cruelties from her master and mistress; sometimes she was locked up, away from her nursing baby, for a whole day and night.

When I had been in the family a few weeks, one of the plantation slaves was brought to town, by order of his master. It was near night when he arrived, and Dr. Flint ordered him to be taken to the work house, and tied up to the joist, so that his feet would just escape the ground. In that situation he was to wait till the doctor had taken his tea. I shall never forget that night. Never before, in my life, had I heard hundreds of blows fall, in succession, on a human being. His piteous groans, and his "O, pray don't, massa," rang in my ear for months afterwards. There were many conjectures as to the cause of this terrible punishment. Some said master accused him of stealing corn; others said the slave had quarrelled with his wife, in presence of the overseer, and had accused his master of being the father of her child. They were both black, and the child was very fair.

I went into the work house next morning, and saw the cowhide still wet with blood, and the boards all covered with gore. The poor man lived, and continued to quarrel with his wife. A few months afterwards Dr. Flint handed them both over to a slavetrader. The guilty man put their value into his pocket, and had the satisfaction of knowing that they were out of sight and hearing. When the mother was delivered into the trader's hands, she said, "You *promised* to treat me well." To which he replied, "You have let your tongue run too far; damn you!" She had forgotten that it was a crime for a slave to tell who was the father of her child.

From others than the master persecution also comes in such cases. I once saw a young slave girl dying soon after the birth of a child nearly white. In her agony she cried out, "O Lord, come and take me!" Her mistress stood by, and mocked at her like an incarnate fiend. "You suffer, do you?" she exclaimed. "I am glad of it. You deserve it all, and more too."

The girl's mother said, "The baby is dead, thank God; and I hope my poor child will soon be in heaven, too."

"Heaven!" retorted the mistress. "There is no such place for the like of her and her bastard."

The poor mother turned away, sobbing. Her dying daughter called her, feebly, and as she bent over her, I heard her say, "Don't grieve so, mother; God knows all about it; and HE will have mercy upon me."

Her sufferings, afterwards, became so intense, that her mistress felt unable to stay; but when she left the room, the scornful smile was still on her lips. Seven children called her mother. The poor black woman had but the one child, whose eyes she saw closing in death, while she thanked God for taking her away from the greater bitterness of life.

* * *

V. The Trials of Girlhood

During the first years of my service in Dr. Flint's family, I was accustomed to share some indulgences with the children of my mistress. Though this seemed to me no more than right, I was grateful for it, and tried to merit the kindness by the faithful discharge of my duties. But I now entered on my fifteenth year—a sad epoch in the life of a slave girl. My master began to whisper foul words in my ear. Young as I was, I could not remain ignorant of their import. I tried to treat them with indifference or contempt. The master's age, my extreme youth, and the fear that his conduct would be reported to my grandmother, made him bear this treatment for many months. He was a crafty man, and resorted to many means to accomplish his purposes. Sometimes he had stormy, terrific ways, that made his victims tremble; sometimes he assumed a gentleness that he thought must surely subdue. Of the two, I preferred his stormy moods, although they left me trembling. He tried his utmost to corrupt the pure principles my grandmother had instilled. He peopled my young mind with unclean images, such as only a vile monster could think of. I turned from him with disgust and hatred. But he was my master. I was compelled to live under the same roof with him—where I saw a man forty years my senior daily violating the most sacred commandments of nature. He told me I was his property; that I must be subject to his will in all things. My soul revolted against the mean tyranny. But where could I turn for protection? No matter whether the slave girl be as black as ebony or as fair as her mistress. In either case, there is no shadow of law to protect her from insult, from violence, or even from death; all these are inflicted by fiends who bear the shape of men. The mistress, who ought to protect the helpless victim, has no other feelings towards her but those of jealousy and rage. The degradation, the wrongs, the vices, that grow out of slavery, are more than I can describe. They are greater than you would willingly believe. Surely, if you credited one half the truths that are told you concerning the helpless millions suffering in this cruel bondage, you at the north would not help to tighten the yoke. You surely would refuse to do for the master, on your own soil, the mean and cruel work which trained bloodhounds and the lowest class of whites do for him at the south.

Every where the years bring to all enough of sin and sorrow; but in slavery the very dawn of life is darkened by these shadows. Even the little child, who is accustomed to wait on her mistress and her children, will learn, before she is twelve years old, why it is that her mistress hates such and such a one among the slaves. Perhaps the child's own mother is among those hated ones. She listens to violent outbreaks of jealous passion, and cannot help understanding what is the cause. She will become prematurely knowing in evil things. Soon she will learn to tremble when she hears her master's footfall. She will be compelled to realize that she is no longer a child. If God has bestowed beauty upon her, it will prove her greatest curse. That which commands admiration in the white woman only hastens the degradation of the female slave. I know that some are too much brutalized by slavery to feel the humiliation of their position; but many slaves feel it most acutely, and shrink from the memory of it. I cannot tell how much I suffered in the presence of these wrongs, nor how I am still pained by the retrospect. My master met me at every turn, reminding me that I belonged to him, and swearing by heaven and earth that he would compel me to submit to him. If I went out for a breath of fresh air, after a day of unwearied toil, his footsteps dogged me. If I knelt by my mother's grave, his dark shadow fell on me even there. The light heart which nature had given me became heavy with sad forebodings. The other slaves in my master's house noticed the change. Many of them pitied me; but none dared to ask the cause. They had no need to inquire. They knew too well the guilty practices under that roof; and they were aware that to speak of them was an offence that never went unpunished.

I longed for some one to confide in. I would have given the world to have laid my head on my grandmother's faithful bosom, and told her all my troubles. But Dr. Flint swore he would kill me, if I was not as silent as the grave. Then, although my grandmother was all in all to me, I feared her as well as loved her. I had been accustomed to look up to her with a respect bordering upon awe. I was very young, and felt shamefaced about telling her such impure things, especially as I knew her to be very strict on such subjects. Moreover, she was a woman of a high spirit. She was usually very quiet in her demeanor; but if her indignation was once roused, it was not very easily quelled. I had been told that she once chased a white gentleman with a loaded pistol, because he insulted one of her daughters. I dreaded the consequences of a violent outbreak; and both pride and fear kept me silent. But though I did not confide in my grandmother, and even evaded her vigilant watchfulness and inquiry, her presence in the neighborhood was some protection to me. Though she had been a slave, Dr. Flint was afraid of her. He dreaded her scorching rebukes. Moreover, she was known and patronized by many people; and he did not wish to have his villainy made public. It was lucky for me that I did not live on a distant plantation, but in a town not so large that the inhabitants were ignorant of each other's affairs. Bad as are the laws and customs in a slaveholding community, the doctor, as a professional man, deemed it prudent to keep up some outward show of decency.

O, what days and nights of fear and sorrow that man caused me! Reader, it is not to awaken sympathy for myself that I am telling you truthfully what I suffered in slavery. I do it to kindle a flame of compassion in your hearts for my sisters who are still in bondage, suffering as I once suffered.

I once saw two beautiful children playing together. One was a fair white child; the other was her slave, and also her sister. When I saw them embracing each other, and heard their joyous laughter, I turned sadly away from the lovely sight. I foresaw the inevitable blight that would fall on the little slave's heart. I knew how soon her laughter would be changed to sighs. The fair child grew up to be a still fairer woman. From childhood to womanhood her pathway was blooming with flowers, and overarched by a sunny sky. Scarcely one day of her life had been clouded when the sun rose on her happy bridal morning.

How had those years dealt with her slave sister, the little playmate of her childhood? She, also, was very beautiful; but the flowers and sunshine of love were not for her. She drank the cup of sin, and shame, and misery, whereof her persecuted race are compelled to drink.

In view of these things, why are ye silent, ye free men and women of the north? Why do your tongues falter in maintenance of the right? Would that I had more ability! But my heart is so full, and my pen is so weak! There are noble men and women who plead for us, striving to help those who cannot help themselves. God bless them! God give them strength and courage to go on! God bless those, every where, who are laboring to advance the cause of humanity!

[After appealing futilely to Dr. Flint's jealous wife for protection, Brent receives a marriage proposal from a free Black carpenter, but Dr. Flint refuses to let her purchase her freedom.]

X. A Perilous Passage in the Slave Girl's Life

After my lover went away, Dr. Flint contrived a new plan. He seemed to have an idea that my fear of my mistress was his greatest obstacle. In the blandest tones, he told me that he was going to build a small house for me, in a secluded place, four miles away from the town. I shuddered; but I was constrained to listen, while he talked of his intention to give me a home of my own, and to make a lady of me. Hitherto, I had escaped my dreaded fate, by being in the midst of people. My grandmother had already had high words with my master about me. She had told him pretty plainly what she thought of his character, and there was considerable gossip in the neighborhood about our affairs, to which the open-mouthed jealousy of Mrs. Flint contributed not a little. When my master said he was going to build a house for me, and that he could do it with little trouble and expense, I was in hopes something would happen to frustrate his scheme; but I soon heard that the house was actually begun. I vowed before my Maker that I would never enter it. I had rather toil on the plantation from dawn till dark; I had rather live and die in jail, than drag on, from day to day, through such a living death. I was determined that the master, whom I so hated and loathed, who had blighted the prospects of my youth, and made my life a desert, should not, after my long struggle with him, succeed at last in trampling his victim under his feet. I would do any thing, every thing, for the sake of defeating him. What *could* I do? I thought and thought, till I became desperate, and made a plunge into the abyss.

And now, reader, I come to a period in my unhappy life, which I would gladly forget if I could. The remembrance fills me with sorrow and shame. It pains me to tell you of it; but I have promised to tell you the truth, and I will do it honestly, let it cost me what it may. I will not try to screen myself behind the plea of compulsion from a master; for it was not so. Neither can I plead ignorance or thoughtlessness. For years, my master had done his utmost to pollute my mind with foul images, and to destroy the pure principles inculcated by my grandmother, and the good mistress of my childhood. The influences of slavery had had the same effect on me that they had on other young girls; they had made me prematurely knowing, concerning the evil ways of the world. I knew what I did, and I did it with deliberate calculation.

But, O, ye happy women, whose purity has been sheltered from childhood, who have been free to choose the objects of your affection, whose homes are protected by law, do not judge the poor desolate slave girl too severely! If slavery had been abolished, I, also, could have married the man of my choice; I could have had a home shielded by the laws; and I should have been spared the painful task of confessing what I am now about to relate; but all my prospects had been blighted by slavery. I wanted to keep myself pure; and, under the most adverse circumstances, I tried hard to preserve my self-respect; but I was struggling alone in the powerful grasp of the demon Slavery; and the monster proved too strong for me. I felt as if I was forsaken by God and man; as if all my efforts must be frustrated; and I became reckless in my despair.

I have told you that Dr. Flint's persecutions and his wife's jealousy had given rise to some gossip in the neighborhood. Among others, it chanced that a white unmarried gentleman had obtained some knowledge of the circumstances in which I was placed. He knew my grandmother, and often spoke to me in the street. He became interested for me, and asked questions about my master, which I answered in part. He expressed a great deal of sympathy, and a wish to aid me. He constantly sought opportunities to see me, and wrote to me frequently. I was a poor slave girl, only fifteen years old.

So much attention from a superior person was, of course, flattering; for human nature is the same in all. I also felt grateful for his sympathy, and encouraged by his kind words. It seemed to me a great thing to have such a friend. By degrees, a more tender feeling crept into my heart. He was an educated and eloquent gentleman; too eloquent, alas, for the poor slave girl who trusted in him. Of course I saw whither all this was tending. I knew the impassable gulf between us; but to be an object of interest to a man who is not married, and who is not her master, is agreeable to the pride and feelings of a slave, if her miserable situation has left her any pride or sentiment. It seems less degrading to give one's self, than to submit to compulsion. There is something akin to freedom in having a lover who has no control over you, except that which he gains by kindness and attachment. A master may treat you as rudely as he pleases, and you dare not speak; moreover, the wrong does not seem so great with an unmarried man, as with one who has a wife to be made unhappy. There may be sophistry[7] in all this; but the condition of a slave confuses all principles of morality, and, in fact, renders the practice of them impossible.

When I found that my master had actually begun to build the lonely cottage, other feelings mixed with those I have described. Revenge, and calculations of interest, were added to flattered vanity and sincere gratitude for kindness. I knew nothing would enrage Dr. Flint so much as to know that I favored another; and it was something to triumph over my tyrant even in that small way. I thought he would revenge himself by selling me, and I was sure my friend, Mr. Sands, would buy me. He was a man of more generosity and feeling than my master, and I thought my freedom could be easily obtained from him. The crisis of my fate now came so near that I was desperate. I shuddered to think of being the mother of children that should be owned by my old tyrant. I knew that as soon as a new fancy took him, his victims were sold far off to get rid of them; especially if they had children. I had seen several women sold, with his babies at the breast. He never allowed his offspring by slaves to remain long in sight of himself and his wife. Of a man who was not my master I could ask to have my children well supported; and in this case, I felt confident I should obtain the boon.[8] I also felt quite sure that they would be made free. With all these thoughts revolving in my mind, and seeing no other way of escaping the doom I so much dreaded, I made a headlong plunge. Pity me, and pardon me, O virtuous reader! You never knew what it is to be a slave; to be entirely unprotected by law or custom; to have the laws reduce you to the condition of a chattel, entirely subject to the will of another. You never exhausted your ingenuity in avoiding the snares, and eluding the power of a hated tyrant; you never shuddered at the sound of his footsteps, and trembled within hearing of his voice. I know I did wrong. No one can feel it more sensibly than I do. The painful and humiliating memory will haunt me to my dying day. Still, in looking back, calmly, on the events of my life, I feel that the slave woman ought not to be judged by the same standard as others.

The months passed on. I had many unhappy hours. I secretly mourned over the sorrow I was bringing on my grandmother, who had so tried to

7. Subtly deceptive reasoning.

8. Favor.

shield me from harm. I knew that I was the greatest comfort of her old age, and that it was a source of pride to her that I had not degraded myself, like most of the slaves. I wanted to confess to her that I was no longer worthy of her love; but I could not utter the dreaded words.

As for Dr. Flint, I had a feeling of satisfaction and triumph in the thought of telling *him*. From time to time he told me of his intended arrangements, and I was silent. At last, he came and told me the cottage was completed, and ordered me to go to it. I told him I would never enter it. He said, "I have heard enough of such talk as that. You shall go, if you are carried by force; and you shall remain there."

I replied, "I will never go there. In a few months I shall be a mother."

He stood and looked at me in dumb amazement, and left the house without a word. I thought I should be happy in my triumph over him. But now that the truth was out, and my relatives would hear of it, I felt wretched. Humble as were their circumstances, they had pride in my good character. Now, how could I look them in the face? My self-respect was gone! I had resolved that I would be virtuous, though I was a slave. I had said, "Let the storm beat! I will brave it till I die." And now, how humiliated I felt!

I went to my grandmother. My lips moved to make confession, but the words stuck in my throat. I sat down in the shade of a tree at her door and began to sew. I think she saw something unusual was the matter with me. The mother of slaves is very watchful. She knows there is no security for her children. After they have entered their teens she lives in daily expectation of trouble. This leads to many questions. If the girl is of a sensitive nature, timidity keeps her from answering truthfully, and this well-meant course has a tendency to drive her from maternal counsels. Presently, in came my mistress, like a mad woman, and accused me concerning her husband. My grandmother, whose suspicions had been previously awakened, believed what she said. She exclaimed, "O Linda! has it come to this? I had rather see you dead than to see you as you now are. You are a disgrace to your dead mother." She tore from my fingers my mother's wedding ring and her silver thimble. "Go away!" she exclaimed, "and never come to my house, again." Her reproaches fell so hot and heavy, that they left me no chance to answer. Bitter tears, such as the eyes never shed but once, were my only answer. I rose from my seat, but fell back again, sobbing. She did not speak to me; but the tears were running down her furrowed cheeks, and they scorched me like fire. She had always been so kind to me! *So* kind! How I longed to throw myself at her feet, and tell her all the truth! But she had ordered me to go, and never to come there again. After a few minutes, I mustered strength, and started to obey her. With what feelings did I now close that little gate, which I used to open with such an eager hand in my childhood! It closed upon me with a sound I never heard before.

Where could I go? I was afraid to return to my master's. I walked on recklessly, not caring where I went, or what would become of me. When I had gone four or five miles, fatigue compelled me to stop. I sat down on the stump of an old tree. The stars were shining through the boughs above me. How they mocked me, with their bright, calm light! The hours passed by, and as I sat there alone a chilliness and deadly sickness came over me. I sank on the ground. My mind was full of horrid thoughts. I prayed to die; but the prayer was not answered. At last, with great effort I roused myself, and walked some distance further, to the house of a woman who had been a friend of my mother. When I told her why I was there, she spoke soothingly to me; but I could not be comforted. I thought I could bear my shame if I could only be reconciled to my grandmother. I longed to open my heart to her. I thought if she could know the real state of the case, and all I had been bearing for years, she would perhaps judge me less harshly. My friend advised me to send for her. I did so; but days of agonizing suspense passed before she came. Had she utterly forsaken me? No. She came at last. I knelt before her, and told her the things that had poisoned my life; how long I had been persecuted; that I saw no way of escape; and in an hour of extremity I had become desperate. She listened in silence. I told her I would bear any thing and do any thing, if in time I had hopes of obtaining her forgiveness. I begged of her to pity me, for my dead mother's sake. And she did pity me. She did not say, "I forgive you;" but she looked at me lovingly, with her eyes full of tears. She laid her old hand gently on my head, and murmured, "Poor child! Poor child!"

[Outraged when he learns that Brent is pregnant, Dr. Flint threatens her but fails to coerce Brent into revealing the identity of her lover. Brent gives birth to a son, Benjamin, and goes to live with Aunt Martha.]

XII. Fear of Insurrection

Not far from this time Nat Turner's insurrection broke out;[9] and the news threw our town into great commotion. Strange that they should be alarmed, when their slaves were so "contented and happy"! But so it was.

It was always the custom to have a muster every year. On that occasion every white man shouldered his musket. The citizens and the so-called country gentlemen wore military uniforms. The poor whites took their places in the ranks in every-day dress, some without shoes, some without hats. This grand occasion had already passed; and when the slaves were told there was to be another muster, they were surprised and rejoiced. Poor creatures! They thought it was going to be a holiday. I was informed of the true state of affairs, and imparted it to the few I could trust. Most gladly would I have proclaimed it to every slave; but I dared not. All could not be relied on. Mighty is the power of the torturing lash.

By sunrise, people were pouring in from every quarter within twenty miles of the town. I knew the houses were to be searched; and I expected it would be done by country bullies and the poor whites. I knew nothing annoyed them so much as to see colored people living in comfort and respectability; so I made arrangements for them with especial care. I arranged every thing in my grandmother's house as neatly as possible. I put white quilts on the beds, and decorated some of the rooms with flowers. When all was arranged, I sat down at the window to watch. Far as my eye could reach, it rested on a motley crowd of soldiers. Drums and fifes were discoursing martial music. The men were divided into companies of sixteen, each headed by a captain. Orders were given, and the wild scouts rushed in every direction, wherever a colored face was to be found.

It was a grand opportunity for the low whites, who had no negroes of their own to scourge. They exulted in such a chance to exercise a little brief authority, and show their subserviency to the slaveholders; not reflecting

9. A bloody rebellion of enslaved people led by Turner in Southampton County, Virginia (August 21–22, 1831). White fear and paranoia generated reprisals, such as those Jacobs recounts, in many southern communities in the aftermath of the rebellion.

that the power which trampled on the colored people also kept themselves in poverty, ignorance, and moral degradation. Those who never witnessed such scenes can hardly believe what I know was inflicted at this time on innocent men, women, and children, against whom there was not the slightest ground for suspicion. Colored people and slaves who lived in remote parts of the town suffered in an especial manner. In some cases the searchers scattered powder and shot among their clothes, and then sent other parties to find them, and bring them forward as proof that they were plotting insurrection. Every where men, women, and children were whipped till the blood stood in puddles at their feet. Some received five hundred lashes; others were tied hands and feet, and tortured with a bucking paddle, which blisters the skin terribly. The dwellings of the colored people, unless they happened to be protected by some influential white person, who was nigh at hand, were robbed of clothing and every thing else the marauders thought worth carrying away. All day long these unfeeling wretches went round, like a troop of demons, terrifying and tormenting the helpless. At night, they formed themselves into patrol bands, and went wherever they chose among the colored people, acting out their brutal will. Many women hid themselves in woods and swamps, to keep out of their way. If any of the husbands or fathers told of these outrages, they were tied up to the public whipping post, and cruelly scourged for telling lies about white men. The consternation was universal. No two people that had the slightest tinge of color in their faces dared to be seen talking together.

I entertained no positive fears about our household, because we were in the midst of white families who would protect us. We were ready to receive the soldiers whenever they came. It was not long before we heard the tramp of feet and the sound of voices. The door was rudely pushed open; and in they tumbled, like a pack of hungry wolves. They snatched at every thing within their reach. Every box, trunk, closet, and corner underwent a thorough examination. A box in one of the drawers containing some silver change was eagerly pounced upon. When I stepped forward to take it from them, one of the soldiers turned and said angrily, "What d'ye foller us fur? D'ye s'pose white folks is come to steal?"

I replied, "You have come to search; but you have searched that box, and I will take it, if you please."

At that moment I saw a white gentleman who was friendly to us; and I called to him, and asked him to have the goodness to come in and stay till the search was over. He readily complied. His entrance into the house brought in the captain of the company, whose business it was to guard the outside of the house, and see that none of the inmates left it. This officer was Mr. Litch,[1] the wealthy slaveholder whom I mentioned, in the account of neighboring planters, as being notorious for his cruelty. He felt above soiling his hands with the search. He merely gave orders; and, if a bit of writing was discovered, it was carried to him by his ignorant followers, who were unable to read.

My grandmother had a large trunk of bedding and table cloths. When that was opened, there was a great shout of surprise; and one exclaimed, "Where'd the damned niggers git all dis sheet an' table clarf?"

My grandmother, emboldened by the presence of our white protector, said, "You may be sure we didn't pilfer 'em from *your* houses."

1. Mentioned in Chapter IX.

"Look here, mammy," said a grim-looking fellow without any coat, "you seem to feel mighty gran' 'cause you got all them 'ere fixens. White folks oughter have 'em all."

His remarks were interrupted by a chorus of voices shouting, "We's got 'em! We's got 'em! Dis 'ere yaller gal's got letters!"

There was a general rush for the supposed letter, which, upon examination, proved to be some verses written to me by a friend. In packing away my things, I had overlooked them. When their captain informed them of their contents, they seemed much disappointed. He inquired of me who wrote them. I told him it was one of my friends. "Can you read them?" he asked. When I told him I could, he swore, and raved, and tore the paper into bits. "Bring me all your letters!" said he, in a commanding tone. I told him I had none. "Don't be afraid," he continued, in an insinuating way. "Bring them all to me. Nobody shall do you any harm." Seeing I did not move to obey him, his pleasant tone changed to oaths and threats. "Who writes to you? half free niggers?" inquired he. I replied, "O, no; most of my letters are from white people. Some request me to burn them after they are read, and some I destroy without reading."

An exclamation of surprise from some of the company put a stop to our conversation. Some silver spoons which ornamented an old-fashioned buffet had just been discovered. My grandmother was in the habit of preserving fruit for many ladies in the town, and of preparing suppers for parties; consequently she had many jars of preserves. The closet that contained these was next invaded, and the contents tasted. One of them, who was helping himself freely, tapped his neighbor on the shoulder, and said, "Wal done! Don't wonder de niggers want to kill all de white folks, when dey live on 'sarves" [meaning preserves]. I stretched out my hand to take the jar, saying, "You were not sent here to search for sweetmeats."

"And what *were* we sent for?" said the captain, bristling up to me. I evaded the question.

The search of the house was completed, and nothing found to condemn us. They next proceeded to the garden, and knocked about every bush and vine, with no better success. The captain called his men together, and, after a short consultation, the order to march was given. As they passed out of the gate, the captain turned back, and pronounced a malediction on the house. He said it ought to be burned to the ground, and each of its inmates receive thirty-nine lashes. We came out of this affair very fortunately; not losing any thing except some wearing apparel.

Towards evening the turbulence increased. The soldiers, stimulated by drink, committed still greater cruelties. Shrieks and shouts continually rent the air. Not daring to go to the door, I peeped under the window curtain. I saw a mob dragging along a number of colored people, each white man, with his musket upraised, threatening instant death if they did not stop their shrieks. Among the prisoners was a respectable old colored minister. They had found a few parcels of shot in his house, which his wife had for years used to balance her scales. For this they were going to shoot him on Court House Green. What a spectacle was that for a civilized country! A rabble, staggering under intoxication, assuming to be the administrators of justice!

The better class of the community exerted their influence to save the innocent, persecuted people; and in several instances they succeeded, by keeping them shut up in jail till the excitement abated. At last the white citizens found that their own property was not safe from the lawless rabble they had summoned to protect them. They rallied the drunken swarm, drove them back into the country, and set a guard over the town.

The next day, the town patrols were commissioned to search colored people that lived out of the city; and the most shocking outrages were committed with perfect impunity. Every day for a fortnight, if I looked out, I saw horsemen with some poor panting negro tied to their saddles, and compelled by the lash to keep up with their speed, till they arrived at the jail yard. Those who had been whipped too unmercifully to walk were washed with brine, tossed into a cart, and carried to jail. One black man, who had not fortitude to endure scourging, promised to give information about the conspiracy. But it turned out that he knew nothing at all. He had not even heard the name of Nat Turner. The poor fellow had, however, made up a story, which augmented his own sufferings and those of the colored people.

The day patrol continued for some weeks, and at sundown a night guard was substituted. Nothing at all was proved against the colored people, bond or free. The wrath of the slaveholders was somewhat appeased by the capture of Nat Turner. The imprisoned were released. The slaves were sent to their masters, and the free were permitted to return to their ravaged homes. Visiting was strictly forbidden on the plantations. The slaves begged the privilege of again meeting at their little church in the woods, with their burying ground around it. It was built by the colored people, and they had no higher happiness than to meet there and sing hymns together, and pour out their hearts in spontaneous prayer. Their request was denied, and the church was demolished. They were permitted to attend the white churches, a certain portion of the galleries being appropriated to their use. There, when every body else had partaken of the communion, and the benediction had been pronounced, the minister said, "Come down, now, my colored friends." They obeyed the summons, and partook of the bread and wine, in commemoration of the meek and lowly Jesus, who said, "God is your Father, and all ye are brethren."[2]

* * *

XIV. Another Link to Life

I had not returned to my master's house since the birth of my child. The old man raved to have me thus removed from his immediate power; but his wife vowed, by all that was good and great, she would kill me if I came back; and he did not doubt her word. Sometimes he would stay away for a season. Then he would come and renew the old threadbare discourse about his forbearance and my ingratitude. He labored, most unnecessarily, to convince me that I had lowered myself. The venomous old reprobate[3] had no need of descanting on that theme. I felt humiliated enough. My unconscious babe was the ever-present witness of my shame. I listened with silent contempt when he talked about my having forfeited *his* good opinion; but I shed bitter tears that I was no longer worthy of being respected by the good and pure. Alas! slavery still held me in its poisonous grasp. There was no chance for me to be respectable. There was no prospect of being able to lead a better life.

Sometimes, when my master found that I still refused to accept what he called his kind offers, he would threaten to sell my child. "Perhaps that will humble you," said he.

2. See Matthew 23:8: "For one is your Master, even Christ; and all ye are brethren."

3. A depraved, vicious person.

Humble *me!* Was I not already in the dust? But his threat lacerated my heart. I knew the law gave him power to fulfill it; for slaveholders have been cunning enough to enact that "the child shall follow the condition of the *mother,*" not of the *father;* thus taking care that licentiousness shall not interfere with avarice. This reflection made me clasp my innocent babe all the more firmly to my heart. Horrid visions passed through my mind when I thought of his liability to fall into the slave trader's hands. I wept over him, and said, "O my child! perhaps they will leave you in some cold cabin to die, and then throw you into a hole, as if you were a dog."

When Dr. Flint learned that I was again to be a mother, he was exasperated beyond measure. He rushed from the house, and returned with a pair of shears. I had a fine head of hair; and he often railed about my pride of arranging it nicely. He cut every hair close to my head, storming and swearing all the time. I replied to some of his abuse, and he struck me. Some months before, he had pitched me down stairs in a fit of passion; and the injury I received was so serious that I was unable to turn myself in bed for many days. He then said, "Linda, I swear by God I will never raise my hand against you again;" but I knew that he would forget his promise.

After he discovered my situation, he was like a restless spirit from the pit. He came every day; and I was subjected to such insults as no pen can describe. I would not describe them if I could; they were too low, too revolting. I tried to keep them from my grandmother's knowledge as much as I could. I knew she had enough to sadden her life, without having my troubles to bear. When she saw the doctor treat me with violence, and heard him utter oaths terrible enough to palsy a man's tongue, she could not always hold her peace. It was natural and motherlike that she should try to defend me; but it only made matters worse.

When they told me my new-born babe was a girl, my heart was heavier than it had ever been before. Slavery is terrible for men; but it is far more terrible for women. Superadded to the burden common to all, *they* have wrongs, and sufferings, and mortifications peculiarly their own.

Dr. Flint had sworn that he would make me suffer, to my last day, for this new crime against *him,* as he called it; and as long as he had me in his power he kept his word. On the fourth day after the birth of my babe, he entered my room suddenly, and commanded me to rise and bring my baby to him. The nurse who took care of me had gone out of the room to prepare some nourishment, and I was alone. There was no alternative. I rose, took up my babe, and crossed the room to where he sat. "Now stand there," said he, "till I tell you to go back!" My child bore a strong resemblance to her father, and to the deceased Mrs. Sands, her grandmother. He noticed this; and while I stood before him, trembling with weakness, he heaped upon me and my little one every vile epithet he could think of. Even the grandmother in her grave did not escape his curses. In the midst of his vituperations[4] I fainted at his feet. This recalled him to his senses. He took the baby from my arms, laid it on the bed, dashed cold water in my face, took me up, and shook me violently, to restore my consciousness before any one entered the room. Just then my grandmother came in, and he hurried out of the house. I suffered in consequence of this treatment; but I begged my friends to let me die, rather than send for the doctor. There was nothing I dreaded so much as his presence. My life was spared; and I was glad for the sake of my little ones. Had

4. Bitter, abusive language.

it not been for these ties to life, I should have been glad to be released by death, though I had lived only nineteen years.

Always it gave me a pang that my children had no lawful claim to a name. Their father offered his; but, if I had wished to accept the offer, I dared not while my master lived. Moreover, I knew it would not be accepted at their baptism. A Christian name they were at least entitled to; and we resolved to call my boy for our dear good Benjamin, who had gone far away from us.

My grandmother belonged to the church; and she was very desirous of having the children christened. I knew Dr. Flint would forbid it, and I did not venture to attempt it. But chance favored me. He was called to visit a patient out of town, and was obliged to be absent during Sunday. "Now is the time," said my grandmother; "we will take the children to church, and have them christened."

When I entered the church, recollections of my mother came over me, and I felt subdued in spirit. There she had presented me for baptism, without any reason to feel ashamed. She had been married, and had such legal rights as slavery allows to a slave. The vows had at least been sacred to *her,* and she had never violated them. I was glad she was not alive, to know under what different circumstances her grandchildren were presented for baptism. Why had my lot been so different from my mother's? *Her* master had died when she was a child; and she remained with her mistress till she married. She was never in the power of any master; and thus she escaped one class of the evils that generally fall upon slaves.

When my baby was about to be christened, the former mistress of my father stepped up to me, and proposed to give it her Christian name. To this I added the surname of my father, who had himself no legal right to it; for my grandfather on the paternal side was a white gentleman. What tangled skeins are the genealogies of slavery! I loved my father; but it mortified me to be obliged to bestow his name on my children.

When we left the church, my father's old mistress invited me to go home with her. She clasped a gold chain around my baby's neck. I thanked her for this kindness; but I did not like the emblem. I wanted no chain to be fastened on my daughter, not even if its links were of gold. How earnestly I prayed that she might never feel the weight of slavery's chain, whose iron entereth into the soul![5]

[To remind her of his power over her, Dr. Flint compels Brent to work at his son's plantation. She forms a plan to get her freedom by hiding in the house of a local friend until Flint gives up hope of finding her. Brent hopes that Flint will eventually sell her along with her children to their father, Mr. Sands.]

XVII. *The Flight*

Mr. Flint[6] was hard pushed for house servants, and rather than lose me he had restrained his malice. I did my work faithfully, though not, of course, with a willing mind. They were evidently afraid I should leave them. Mr. Flint wished that I should sleep in the great house instead of the servants' quarters. His wife agreed to the proposition, but said I mustn't bring my bed into the house, because it would scatter feathers on her carpet. I knew when I went there that they would never think of such a thing as furnishing a bed of any

5. Psalm 105:18 in the Anglican Book of Common Prayer.
6. Dr. Flint's son.

kind for me and my little one. I therefore carried my own bed, and now I was forbidden to use it. I did as I was ordered. But now that I was certain my children were to be put in their power, in order to give them a stronger hold on me, I resolved to leave them that night. I remembered the grief this step would bring upon my dear old grandmother; and nothing less than the freedom of my children would have induced me to disregard her advice. I went about my evening work with trembling steps. Mr. Flint twice called from his chamber door to inquire why the house was not locked up. I replied that I had not done my work. "You have had time enough to do it," said he. "Take care how you answer me!"

I shut all the windows, locked all the doors, and went up to the third story, to wait till midnight. How long those hours seemed, and how fervently I prayed that God would not forsake me in this hour of utmost need! I was about to risk every thing on the throw of a die; and if I failed, O what would become of me and my poor children? They would be made to suffer for my fault.

At half past twelve I stole softly down stairs. I stopped on the second floor, thinking I heard a noise. I felt my way down into the parlor, and looked out of the window. The night was so intensely dark that I could see nothing. I raised the window very softly and jumped out. Large drops of rain were falling, and the darkness bewildered me. I dropped on my knees, and breathed a short prayer to God for guidance and protection. I groped my way to the road, and rushed towards the town with almost lightning speed. I arrived at my grandmother's house, but dared not see her. She would say, "Linda, you are killing me;" and I knew that would unnerve me. I tapped softly at the window of a room, occupied by a woman, who had lived in the house several years. I knew she was a faithful friend, and could be trusted with my secret. I tapped several times before she heard me. At last she raised the window, and I whispered, "Sally, I have run away. Let me in, quick." She opened the door softly, and said in low tones, "For God's sake, don't. Your grandmother is trying to buy you and de chillern. Mr. Sands was here last week. He tole her he was going away on business, but he wanted her to go ahead about buying you and de chillern, and he would help her all he could. Don't run away, Linda. Your grandmother is all bowed down wid trouble now."

I replied, "Sally, they are going to carry my children to the plantation to-morrow; and they will never sell them to any body so long as they have me in their power. Now, would you advise me to go back?"

"No, chile, no," answered she. "When dey finds you is gone, dey won't want de plague ob de chillern; but where is you going to hide? Dey knows ebery inch ob dis house."

I told her I had a hiding-place, and that was all it was best for her to know. I asked her to go into my room as soon as it was light, and take all my clothes out of my trunk, and pack them in hers; for I knew Mr. Flint and the constable would be there early to search my room. I feared the sight of my children would be too much for my full heart; but I could not go out into the uncertain future without one last look. I bent over the bed where lay my little Benny and baby Ellen. Poor little ones! fatherless and motherless! Memories of their father came over me. He wanted to be kind to them; but they were not all to him, as they were to my womanly heart. I knelt and prayed for the innocent little sleepers. I kissed them lightly, and turned away.

As I was about to open the street door, Sally laid her hand on my shoulder, and said, "Linda, is you gwine all alone? Let me call your uncle."

"No, Sally," I replied, "I want no one to be brought into trouble on my account."

I went forth into the darkness and rain. I ran on till I came to the house of the friend who was to conceal me.

Early the next morning Mr. Flint was at my grandmother's inquiring for me. She told him she had not seen me, and supposed I was at the plantation. He watched her face narrowly, and said, "Don't you know any thing about her running off?" She assured him that she did not. He went on to say, "Last night she ran off without the least provocation. We had treated her very kindly. My wife liked her. She will soon be found and brought back. Are her children with you?" When told that they were, he said, "I am very glad to hear that. If they are here, she cannot be far off. If I find out that any of my niggers have had any thing to do with this damned business, I'll give 'em five hundred lashes." As he started to go to his father's, he turned round and added, persuasively, "Let her be brought back, and she shall have her children to live with her."

The tidings made the old doctor rave and storm at a furious rate. It was a busy day for them. My grandmother's house was searched from top to bottom. As my trunk was empty, they concluded I had taken my clothes with me. Before ten o'clock every vessel northward bound was thoroughly examined, and the law against harboring fugitives was read to all on board. At night a watch was set over the town. Knowing how distressed my grandmother would be, I wanted to send her a message; but it could not be done. Every one who went in or out of her house was closely watched. The doctor said he would take my children, unless she became responsible for them; which of course she willingly did. The next day was spent in searching. Before night, the following advertisement was posted at every corner, and in every public place for miles round:—

> "$300 Reward! Ran away from the subscriber, an intelligent, bright, mulatto girl, named Linda, 21 years of age. Five feet four inches high. Dark eyes, and black hair inclined to curl; but it can be made straight. Has a decayed spot on a front tooth. She can read and write, and in all probability will try to get to the Free States. All persons are forbidden, under penalty of the law, to harbor or employ said slave. $150 will be given to whoever takes her in the state, and $300 if taken out of the state and delivered to me, or lodged in jail.
>
> Dr. Flint."

[A handful of sympathetic Black and white women keep Brent in safe hiding. Dr. Flint retaliates by selling Brent's children and her brother, William, to a trader, unaware that the trader represents Mr. Sands. A permanent hiding place is secured in Brent's grandmother's house.]

XXI. The Loophole of Retreat

A small shed had been added to my grandmother's house years ago. Some boards were laid across the joists at the top, and between these boards and the roof was a very small garret, never occupied by any thing but rats and mice. It was a pent roof, covered with nothing but shingles, according to the southern custom for such buildings. The garret was only nine feet long and seven wide. The highest part was three feet high, and sloped down abruptly to the loose board floor. There was no admission for either light or air. My uncle Phillip, who was a carpenter, had very skillfully made a concealed trap-door, which communicated with the storeroom. He had been doing this while I was waiting in the swamp. The storeroom opened upon a piazza.[7] To this hole I was conveyed as soon as I entered the house. The air was stifling; the darkness total. A bed had been spread on the floor. I could sleep quite comfortably on one side; but the slope was so sudden that I could not turn on the other without hitting the roof. The rats and mice ran over my bed; but I was weary, and I slept such sleep as the wretched may, when a tempest has passed over them. Morning came. I knew it only by the noises I heard; for in my small den day and night were all the same. I suffered for air even more than for light. But I was not comfortless. I heard the voices of my children. There was joy and there was sadness in the sound. It made my tears flow. How I longed to speak to them! I was eager to look on their faces; but there was no hole, no crack, through which I could peep. This continued darkness was oppressive. It seemed horrible to sit or lie in a cramped position day after day, without one gleam of light. Yet I would have chosen this, rather than my lot as a slave, though white people considered it an easy one; and it was so compared with the fate of others. I was never cruelly over-worked; I was never lacerated with the whip from head to foot; I was never so beaten and bruised that I could not turn from one side to the other; I never had my heel-strings cut to prevent my running away; I was never chained to a log and forced to drag it about, while I toiled in the fields from morning till night; I was never branded with hot iron, or torn by bloodhounds. On the contrary, I had always been kindly treated, and tenderly cared for, until I came into the hands of Dr. Flint. I had never wished for freedom till then. But though my life in slavery was comparatively devoid of hardships, God pity the woman who is compelled to lead such a life!

My food was passed up to me through the trap-door my uncle had contrived; and my grandmother, my uncle Phillip, and aunt Nancy would seize such opportunities as they could, to mount up there and chat with me at the opening. But of course this was not safe in the daytime. It must all be done in darkness. It was impossible for me to move in an erect position, but I crawled about my den for exercise. One day I hit my head against something, and found it was a gimlet. My uncle had left it sticking there when he made the trap-door. I was as rejoiced as Robinson Crusoe[8] could have been at finding such a treasure. It put a lucky thought into my head. I said to myself, "Now I will have some light. Now I will see my children." I did not dare to begin my work during the daytime, for fear of attracting attention. But I groped round; and having found the side next the street, where I could frequently see my children, I stuck the gimlet in and waited for evening. I bored three rows of holes, one above another; then I bored out the interstices between. I thus succeeded in making one hole about an inch long and an inch broad. I sat by it till late into the night, to enjoy the little whiff of air that floated in. In the morning I watched for my children. The first person I saw in the street was Dr. Flint. I had a shuddering, superstitious feeling that it was a bad omen. Several familiar faces passed by. At last I heard the merry laugh of children, and presently two sweet little faces

7. A large covered porch.
8. The shipwrecked hero of Daniel Defoe's novel *Robinson Crusoe* (1719).

were looking up at me, as though they knew I was there, and were conscious of the joy they imparted. How I longed to *tell* them I was there!

My condition was now a little improved. But for weeks I was tormented by hundreds of little red insects, fine as a needle's point, that pierced through my skin, and produced an intolerable burning. The good grandmother gave me herb teas and cooling medicines, and finally I got rid of them. The heat of my den was intense, for nothing but thin shingles protected me from the scorching summer's sun. But I had my consolations. Through my peeping-hole I could watch the children, and when they were near enough, I could hear their talk. Aunt Nancy brought me all the news she could hear at Dr. Flint's. From her I learned that the doctor had written to New York to a colored woman, who had been born and raised in our neighborhood, and had breathed his contaminating atmosphere. He offered her a reward if she could find out any thing about me. I know not what was the nature of her reply; but he soon after started for New York in haste, saying to his family that he had business of importance to transact. I peeped at him as he passed on his way to the steamboat. It was a satisfaction to have miles of land and water between us, even for a little while; and it was a still greater satisfaction to know that he believed me to be in the Free States. My little den seemed less dreary than it had done. He returned, as he did from his former journey to New York, without obtaining any satisfactory information. When he passed our house next morning, Benny was standing at the gate. He had heard them say that he had gone to find me, and he called out, "Dr. Flint, did you bring my mother home? I want to see her." The doctor stamped his foot at him in a rage, and exclaimed, "Get out of the way, you little damned rascal! If you don't, I'll cut off your head."

Benny ran terrified into the house, saying, "You can't put me in jail again. I don't belong to you now." It was well that the wind carried the words away from the doctor's ear. I told my grandmother of it, when we had our next conference at the trap-door; and begged of her not to allow the children to be impertinent to the irascible old man.

Autumn came, with a pleasant abatement of heat. My eyes had become accustomed to the dim light, and by holding my book or work in a certain position near the aperture I contrived to read and sew. That was a great relief to the tedious monotony of my life. But when winter came, the cold penetrated through the thin shingle roof, and I was dreadfully chilled. The winters there are not so long, or so severe, as in northern latitudes; but the houses are not built to shelter from cold, and my little den was peculiarly comfortless. The kind grandmother brought me bed-clothes and warm drinks. Often I was obliged to lie in bed all day to keep comfortable; but with all my precautions, my shoulders and feet were frostbitten. O, those long, gloomy days, with no object for my eye to rest upon, and no thoughts to occupy my mind, except the dreary past and the uncertain future! I was thankful when there came a day sufficiently mild for me to wrap myself up and sit at the loophole to watch the passers by. Southerners have the habit of stopping and talking in the streets, and I heard many conversations not intended to meet my ears. I heard slave-hunters planning how to catch some poor fugitive. Several times I heard allusions to Dr. Flint, myself, and the history of my children, who, perhaps, were playing near the gate. One would say, "I wouldn't move my little finger to catch her, as old Flint's property." Another would say, "I'll catch *any* nigger for the reward. A man ought to have what belongs to him, if he *is* a damned brute." The opinion was often expressed that I was in the Free States. Very rarely did any one suggest that I might be in the vicinity. Had the least suspicion rested on my grandmother's house, it would have been burned to the ground. But it was the last place they thought of. Yet there was no place, where slavery existed, that could have afforded me so good a place of concealment.

Dr. Flint and his family repeatedly tried to coax and bribe my children to tell something they had heard said about me. One day the doctor took them into a shop, and offered them some bright little silver pieces and gay handkerchiefs if they would tell where their mother was. Ellen shrank away from him, and would not speak; but Benny spoke up, and said, "Dr. Flint, I don't know where my mother is. I guess she's in New York; and when you go there again, I wish you'd ask her to come home, for I want to see her; but if you put her in jail, or tell her you'll cut her head off, I'll tell her to go right back."

[Brent passes the years hidden in her garret, suffering from exposure, lack of exercise, poor ventilation, and illness. Mr. Sands is elected to Congress. Risking discovery, Brent pleads with him to free their children. He does not live up to his promises to do so but instead conveys their daughter, Ellen, to some of his relatives in Brooklyn, New York. Meanwhile Dr. Flint continues to search for Brent both locally and in New York.]

XXIX. *Preparations for Escape*

I hardly expect that the reader will credit me, when I affirm that I lived in that little dismal hole, almost deprived of light and air, and with no space to move my limbs, for nearly seven years. But it is a fact; and to me a sad one, even now; for my body still suffers from the effects of that long imprisonment, to say nothing of my soul. Members of my family, now living in New York and Boston, can testify to the truth of what I say.

Countless were the nights that I sat late at the little loophole scarcely large enough to give me a glimpse of one twinkling star. There, I heard the patrols and slave-hunters conferring together about the capture of runaways, well knowing how rejoiced they would be to catch me.

Season after season, year after year, I peeped at my children's faces, and heard their sweet voices, with a heart yearning all the while to say, "Your mother is here." Sometimes it appeared to me as if ages had rolled away since I entered upon that gloomy, monotonous existence. At times, I was stupefied and listless; at other times I became very impatient to know when these dark years would end, and I should again be allowed to feel the sunshine, and breathe the pure air.

After Ellen left us, this feeling increased. Mr. Sands had agreed that Benny might go to the north whenever his uncle Phillip could go with him; and I was anxious to be there also, to watch over my children, and protect them so far as I was able. Moreover, I was likely to be drowned out of my den, if I remained much longer; for the slight roof was getting badly out of repair, and uncle Phillip was afraid to remove the shingles, lest some one should get a glimpse of me. When storms occurred in the night, they spread mats and bits of carpet, which in the morning appeared to have been laid out to dry; but to cover the roof in the daytime might have attracted attention. Consequently, my clothes and bedding were often drenched; a process by which the pains and aches in my cramped and stiffened limbs were greatly increased. I revolved various plans of escape in my mind, which I sometimes imparted to my grandmother, when she came to whisper with me at the trap-door. The kind-hearted old woman had an intense sympathy for runaways. She had known too much of the cruelties inflicted on those who were captured. Her memory always flew back at once to the sufferings of her bright and handsome son, Benjamin, the youngest and dearest of her flock. So, whenever I alluded to the subject, she would groan out, "Oh, don't think of it, child. You'll break my heart." I had no good old aunt Nancy now to encourage me; but my brother William and my children were continually beckoning me to the north.

And now I must go back a few months in my story. I have stated that the first of January was the time for selling slaves, or leasing them out to new masters. If time were counted by heart-throbs, the poor slaves might reckon years of suffering during that festival so joyous to the free. On the New Year's day preceding my aunt's death, one of my friends, named Fanny, was to be sold at auction, to pay her master's debts. My thoughts were with her during all the day, and at night I anxiously inquired what had been her fate. I was told that she had been sold to one master, and her four little girls to another master, far distant; that she had escaped from her purchaser, and was not to be found. Her mother was the old Aggie I have spoken of. She lived in a small tenement belonging to my grandmother, and built on the same lot with her own house. Her dwelling was searched and watched, and that brought the patrols so near me that I was obliged to keep very close in my den. The hunters were somehow eluded; and not long afterwards Benny accidentally caught sight of Fanny in her mother's hut. He told his grandmother, who charged him never to speak of it, explaining to him the frightful consequences; and he never betrayed the trust. Aggie little dreamed that my grandmother knew where her daughter was concealed, and that the stooping form of her old neighbor was bending under a similar burden of anxiety and fear; but these dangerous secrets deepened the sympathy between the two old persecuted mothers.

My friend Fanny and I remained many weeks hidden within call of each other; but she was unconscious of the fact. I longed to have her share my den, which seemed a more secure retreat than her own; but I had brought so much trouble on my grandmother, that it seemed wrong to ask her to incur greater risks. My restlessness increased. I had lived too long in bodily pain and anguish of spirit. Always I was in dread that by some accident, or some contrivance, slavery would succeed in snatching my children from me. This thought drove me nearly frantic, and I determined to steer for the North Star at all hazards. At this crisis, Providence opened an unexpected way for me to escape. My friend Peter came one evening, and asked to speak with me. "Your day has come, Linda," said he. "I have found a chance for you to go to the Free States. You have a fortnight to decide." The news seemed too good to be true; but Peter explained his arrangements, and told me all that was necessary was for me to say I would go. I was going to answer him with a joyful yes, when the thought of Benny came to my mind. I told him the temptation was exceedingly strong, but I was terribly afraid of Dr. Flint's alleged power over my child, and that I could not go and leave him behind. Peter remonstrated earnestly. He said such a good chance might never occur again; that Benny was free, and could be sent to me; and that for the sake of my children's welfare I ought not to hesitate a moment. I told him I would consult with uncle Phillip. My uncle rejoiced in the plan, and bade me go by all means. He promised, if his life was spared, that he would either bring or send my son to me as soon as I reached a place of safety. I resolved to go, but thought nothing had better be said to my grandmother till very near the time of departure. But my uncle thought she would feel it more keenly if I left her so suddenly. "I will reason with her," said he, "and convince her how necessary it is, not only for your sake, but for hers also. You cannot be blind to the fact that she is sinking under her burdens." I was not blind to it. I knew that my concealment was an ever-present source of anxiety, and that the older she grew the more nervously fearful she was of discovery. My uncle talked with her, and finally succeeded in persuading her that it was absolutely necessary for me to seize the chance so unexpectedly offered.

The anticipation of being a free woman proved almost too much for my weak frame. The excitement stimulated me, and at the same time bewildered me. I made busy preparations for my journey, and for my son to follow me. I resolved to have an interview with him before I went, that I might give him cautions and advice, and tell him how anxiously I should be waiting for him at the north. Grandmother stole up to me as often as possible to whisper words of counsel. She insisted upon my writing to Dr. Flint, as soon as I arrived in the Free States, and asking him to sell me to her. She said she would sacrifice her house, and all she had in the world, for the sake of having me safe with my children in any part of the world. If she could only live to know *that* she could die in peace. I promised the dear old faithful friend that I would write to her as soon as I arrived, and put the letter in a safe way to reach her; but in my own mind I resolved that not another cent of her hard earnings should be spent to pay rapacious slaveholders for what they called their property. And even if I had not been unwilling to buy what I had already a right to possess, common humanity would have prevented me from accepting the generous offer, at the expense of turning my aged relative out of house and home, when she was trembling on the brink of the grave.

I was to escape in a vessel; but I forbear to mention any further particulars. I was in readiness, but the vessel was unexpectedly detained several days. Meantime, news came to town of a most horrible murder committed on a fugitive slave, named James. Charity, the mother of this unfortunate young man, had been an old acquaintance of ours. I have told the shocking particulars of his death,[9] in my description of some of the neighboring slaveholders. My grandmother, always nervously sensitive about runaways, was terribly frightened. She felt sure that a similar fate awaited me, if I did not desist from my enterprise. She sobbed, and groaned, and entreated me not to go. Her excessive fear was somewhat contagious, and my heart was not proof against her extreme agony. I was grievously disappointed, but I promised to relinquish my project.

When my friend Peter was apprised of this, he was both disappointed and vexed. He said, that judging from our past experience, it would be a long time before I had such another chance to throw away. I told him it need not be thrown away; that I had a friend concealed near by, who would be glad enough to take the place that had been provided for me. I told him about poor Fanny, and the kind-hearted, noble fellow, who never turned his back upon any body in distress, white or black, expressed his readiness to help her. Aggie was much surprised when she found that we knew her secret. She was rejoiced to hear of such a chance for Fanny, and arrangements were made for her to go on board the vessel the next night. They both supposed

9. To illustrate the cruelty of enslavers, Jacobs recalled, earlier in her narrative, the tortures suffered by a local enslaved man named James.

that I had long been at the north, therefore my name was not mentioned in the transaction. Fanny was carried on board at the appointed time, and stowed away in a very small cabin. This accommodation had been purchased at a price that would pay for a voyage to England. But when one proposes to go to fine old England, they stop to calculate whether they can afford the cost of the pleasure; while in making a bargain to escape from slavery, the trembling victim is ready to say, "Take all I have, only don't betray me!"

The next morning I peeped through my loophole, and saw that it was dark and cloudy. At night I received news that the wind as ahead, and the vessel had not sailed. I was exceedingly anxious about Fanny, and Peter too, who was running a tremendous risk at my instigation. Next day the wind and weather remained the same. Poor Fanny had been half dead with fright when they carried her on board, and I could readily imagine how she must be suffering now. Grandmother came often to my den, to say how thankful she was I did not go. On the third morning she rapped for me to come down to the storeroom. The poor old sufferer was breaking down under her weight of trouble. She was easily flurried now. I found her in a nervous, excited state, but I was not aware that she had forgotten to lock the door behind her, as usual. She was exceedingly worried about the detention of the vessel. She was afraid all would be discovered, and then Fanny, and Peter, and I, would all be tortured to death, and Phillip would be utterly ruined, and her house would be torn down. Poor Peter! If he should die such a horrible death as the poor slave James had lately done, and all for his kindness in trying to help me, how dreadful it would be for us all! Alas, the thought was familiar to me, and had sent many a sharp pang through my heart. I tried to suppress my own anxiety, and speak soothingly to her. She brought in some allusion to aunt Nancy, the dear daughter she had recently buried, and then she lost all control of herself. As she stood there, trembling and sobbing, a voice from the piazza called out, "Whar is you, aunt Marthy?" Grandmother was startled, and in her agitation opened the door, without thinking of me. In stepped Jenny, the mischievous housemaid, who had tried to enter my room, when I was concealed in the house of my white benefactress. "I's bin huntin ebery whar for you, aunt Marthy," said she. "My missis wants you to send her some crackers." I had slunk down behind a barrel, which entirely screened me, but I imagined that Jenny was looking directly at the spot, and my heart beat violently. My grandmother immediately thought what she had done, and went out quickly with Jenny to count the crackers locking the door after her. She returned to me, in a few minutes, the perfect picture of despair. "Poor child!" she exclaimed, "my carelessness has ruined you. The boat ain't gone yet. Get ready immediately, and go with Fanny. I ain't got another word to say against it now; for there's no telling what may happen this day."

Uncle Phillip was sent for, and he agreed with his mother in thinking that Jenny would inform Dr. Flint in less than twenty-four hours. He advised getting me on board the boat, if possible; if not, I had better keep very still in my den, where they could not find me without tearing the house down. He said it would not do for him to move in the matter, because suspicion would be immediately excited; but he promised to communicate with Peter. I felt reluctant to apply to him again, having implicated him too much already; but there seemed to be no alternative. Vexed as Peter had been by my indecision, he was true to his generous nature, and said at once that he would do his best to help me, trusting I should show myself a stronger woman this time.

He immediately proceeded to the wharf, and found that the wind had shifted, and the vessel was slowly beating down stream. On some pretext of urgent necessity, he offered two boatmen a dollar apiece to catch up with her. He was of lighter complexion than the boatmen he hired, and when the captain saw them coming so rapidly, he thought officers were pursuing his vessel in search of the runaway slave he had on board. They hoisted sails, but the boat gained upon them, and the indefatigable Peter sprang on board.

The captain at once recognized him. Peter asked him to go below, to speak about a bad bill he had given him. When he told his errand, the captain replied, "Why, the woman's here already; and I've put her where you or the devil would have a tough job to find her."

"But it is another woman I want to bring," said Peter. "*She* is in great distress, too, and you shall be paid any thing within reason, if you'll stop and take her."

"What's her name?" inquired the captain.

"Linda," he replied.

"That's the name of the woman already here," rejoined the captain. "By George! I believe you mean to betray me."

"O!" exclaimed Peter, "God knows I wouldn't harm a hair of your head. I am too grateful to you. But there really *is* another woman in great danger. Do have the humanity to stop and take her!"

After a while they came to an understanding. Fanny, not dreaming I was any where about in that region, had assumed my name, though she had called herself Johnson. "Linda is a common name," said Peter, "and the woman I want to bring is Linda Brent."

The captain agreed to wait at a certain place till evening, being handsomely paid for his detention.

Of course, the day was an anxious one for us all. But we concluded that if Jenny had seen me, she would be too wise to let her mistress know of it; and that she probably would not get a chance to see Dr. Flint's family till evening, for I knew very well what were the rules in that household. I afterwards believed that she did not see me; for nothing ever came of it, and she was one of those base characters that would have jumped to betray a suffering fellow being for the sake of thirty pieces of silver.

I made all my arrangements to go on board as soon as it was dusk. The intervening time I resolved to spend with my son. I had not spoken to him for seven years, though I had been under the same roof, and seen him every day, when I was well enough to sit at the loophole. I did not dare to venture beyond the storeroom; so they brought him there, and locked us up together, in a place concealed from the piazza door. It was an agitating interview for both of us. After we had talked and wept together for a little while, he said, "Mother, I'm glad you're going away. I wish I could go with you. I knew you was here; and I have been *so* afraid they would come and catch you!"

I was greatly surprised, and asked him how he had found it out.

He replied, "I was standing under the eaves, one day, before Ellen went away, and I heard somebody cough up over the wood shed. I don't know what made me think it was you, but I did think so. I missed Ellen, the night before she went away; and grandmother brought her back into the room in the night; and I thought maybe she'd been to see *you*, before she went, for I heard grandmother whisper to her, 'Now go to sleep; and remember never to tell.'"

I asked him if he ever mentioned his suspicions to his sister. He said he never did; but after he heard the cough, if he saw her playing with other children on that side of the house, he always tried to coax her round to the other side, for fear they would hear me cough, too. He said he had kept a close lookout for Dr. Flint, and if he saw him speak to a constable, or a patrol, he always told grandmother. I now recollected that I had seen him manifest uneasiness, when people were on that side of the house, and I had at the time been puzzled to conjecture a motive for his actions. Such prudence may seem extraordinary in a boy of twelve years, but slaves, being surrounded by mysteries, deceptions, and dangers, early learn to be suspicious and watchful, and prematurely cautious and cunning. He had never asked a question of grandmother, or uncle Phillip, and I had often heard him chime in with other children, when they spoke of my being at the north.

I told him I was now really going to the Free States, and if he was a good, honest boy, and a loving child to his dear old grandmother, the Lord would bless him, and bring him to me, and we and Ellen would live together. He began to tell me that grandmother had not eaten any thing all day. While he was speaking, the door was unlocked, and she came in with a small bag of money, which she wanted me to take. I begged her to keep a part of it, at least, to pay for Benny's being sent to the north; but she insisted, while her tears were falling fast, that I should take the whole. "You may be sick among strangers," she said, "and they would send you to the poorhouse to die." Ah, that good grandmother!

For the last time I went up to my nook. Its desolate appearance no longer chilled me, for the light of hope had risen in my soul. Yet, even with the blessed prospect of freedom before me, I felt very sad at leaving forever that old homestead, where I had been sheltered so long by the dear old grandmother; where I had dreamed my first young dream of love; and where, after that had faded away, my children came to twine themselves so closely round my desolate heart. As the hour approached for me to leave, I again descended to the storeroom. My grandmother and Benny were there. She took me by the hand, and said, "Linda, let us pray." We knelt down together, with my child pressed to my heart, and my other arm round the faithful, loving old friend I was about to leave forever. On no other occasion has it ever been my lot to listen to so fervent a supplication for mercy and protection. It thrilled through my heart, and inspired me with trust in God.

Peter was waiting for me in the street. I was soon by his side, faint in body, but strong of purpose. I did not look back upon the old place, though I felt that I should never see it again.

[Brent escapes to Philadelphia by boat. She goes to New York and visits her daughter, who is being trained to become a lady's personal servant instead of receiving schooling and her freedom. Brent finds employment in New York providing child care for Mary, the infant daughter of Mrs. Bruce, "a true and sympathizing friend." Mrs. Bruce's death heightens Brent's insecurity and she is forced to flee to Boston, where she supports her children by working as a seamstress.]

XXXIX. The Confession

For two years my daughter and I supported ourselves comfortably in Boston. At the end of that time, my brother William offered to send Ellen to a boarding school. It required a great effort for me to consent to part with her, for I had few near ties, and it was her presence that made my two little rooms seem home-like. But my judgment prevailed over my selfish feelings. I made preparations for her departure. During the two years we had lived together I had often resolved to tell her something about her father; but I had never been able to muster sufficient courage. I had a shrinking dread of diminishing my child's love. I knew she must have curiosity on the subject, but she had never asked a question. She was always very careful not to say any thing to remind me of my troubles. Now that she was going from me, I thought if I should die before she returned, she might hear my story from some one who did not understand the palliating circumstances; and that if she were entirely ignorant on the subject, her sensitive nature might receive a rude shock.

When we retired for the night, she said, "Mother, it is very hard to leave you alone. I am almost sorry I am going, though I do want to improve myself. But you will write to me often; won't you, mother?"

I did not throw my arms round her. I did not answer her. But in a calm, solemn way, for it cost me great effort, I said, "Listen to me, Ellen; I have something to tell you!" I recounted my early sufferings in slavery, and told her how nearly they had crushed me. I began to tell her how they had driven me into a great sin, when she clasped me in her arms, and exclaimed, "Oh, don't, mother! Please don't tell me any more."

I said, "But, my child, I want you to know about your father."

"I know all about it, mother," she replied; "I am nothing to my father, and he is nothing to me. All my love is for you. I was with him five months in Washington, and he never cared for me. He never spoke to me as he did to his little Fanny. I knew all the time he was my father, for Fanny's nurse told me so; but she said I must never tell any body, and I never did. I used to wish he would take me in his arms and kiss me, as he did Fanny; or that he would sometimes smile at me, as he did at her. I thought if he was my own father, he ought to love me. I was a little girl then, and didn't know any better. But now I never think any thing about my father. All my love is for you." She hugged me closer as she spoke, and I thanked God that the knowledge I had so much dreaded to impart had not diminished the affection of my child. I had not the slightest idea she knew that portion of my history. If I had, I should have spoken to her long before; for my pent-up feelings had often longed to pour themselves out to some one I could trust. But I loved the dear girl better for the delicacy she had manifested towards her unfortunate mother.

The next morning, she and her uncle started on their journey to the village in New York, where she was to be placed at school. It seemed as if all the sunshine had gone away. My little room was dreadfully lonely. I was thankful when a message came from a lady, accustomed to employ me, requesting me to come and sew in her family for several weeks. On my return, I found a letter from brother William. He thought of opening an anti-slavery reading room in Rochester, and combining with it the sale of some books and stationery; and he wanted me to unite with him. We tried it, but it was not successful. We found warm anti-slavery friends there, but the feeling was not general enough to support such an establishment. I passed nearly a year in the family of Isaac and Amy Post,[1] practical believers in the Christian doctrine of human brotherhood. They measured a man's worth by his character, not by his complexion. The memory of those beloved and honored friends will remain with me to my latest hour.

1. Quaker abolitionists living in Rochester, New York. Amy Post was a participant in the first Woman's Rights Convention held at Seneca Falls, New York, in 1848.

XL. The Fugitive Slave Law[2]

My brother, being disappointed in his project, concluded to go to California; and it was agreed that Benjamin should go with him. Ellen liked her school, and was a great favorite there. They did not know her history, and she did not tell it, because she had no desire to make capital out of their sympathy. But when it was accidentally discovered that her mother was a fugitive slave, every method was used to increase her advantages and diminish her expenses.

I was alone again. It was necessary for me to be earning money, and I preferred that it should be among those who knew me. On my return from Rochester, I called at the house of Mr. Bruce, to see Mary, the darling little babe that had thawed my heart, when it was freezing into a cheerless distrust of all my fellow-beings. She was growing a tall girl now, but I loved her always. Mr. Bruce had married again, and it was proposed that I should become nurse to a new infant. I had but one hesitation, and that was my feeling of insecurity in New York, now greatly increased by the passage of the Fugitive Slave Law. However, I resolved to try the experiment. I was again fortunate in my employer. The new Mrs. Bruce was an American, brought up under aristocratic influences, and still living in the midst of them; but if she had any prejudice against color, I was never made aware of it; and as for the system of slavery, she had a most hearty dislike of it. No sophistry of Southerners could blind her to its enormity. She was a person of excellent principles and a noble heart. To me, from that hour to the present, she has been a true and sympathizing friend. Blessings be with her and hers!

About the time that I reentered the Bruce family, an event occurred of disastrous import to the colored people. The slave Hamlin, the first fugitive that came under the new law, was given up by the bloodhounds of the north to the bloodhounds of the south. It was the beginning of a reign of terror to the colored population. The great city rushed on in its whirl of excitement, taking no note of the "short and simple annals of the poor."[3] But while fashionables were listening to the thrilling voice of Jenny Lind[4] in Metropolitan Hall, the thrilling voices of poor hunted colored people went up, in an agony of supplication, to the Lord, from Zion's church. Many families, who had lived in the city for twenty years, fled from it now. Many a poor washerwoman, who, by hard labor, had made herself a comfortable home, was obliged to sacrifice her furniture, bid a hurried farewell to friends, and seek her fortune among strangers in Canada. Many a wife discovered a secret she had never known before—that her husband was a fugitive, and must leave her to insure his own safety. Worse still, many a husband discovered that his wife had fled from slavery years ago, and as "the child follows the condition of its mother," the children of his love were liable to be seized and carried into slavery. Every where, in those humble homes, there was consternation and anguish. But what cared the legislators of the "dominant race" for the blood they were crushing out of trampled hearts?

When my brother William spent his last evening with me, before he went to California, we talked nearly all the time of the distress brought on our oppressed people by the passage of this iniquitous law; and never had I seen him manifest such bitterness of spirit, such stern hostility to our oppressors.

2. The most controversial feature of the Compromise of 1850, the Fugitive Slave Law made any action that aided a runaway enslaved person a federal crime.

3. From Thomas Gray's "Elegy Written in a Country Churchyard" (1751), line 32.

4. Internationally popular Swedish singer.

He was himself free from the operation of the law; for he did not run from any Slaveholding State, being brought into the Free States by his master.[5] But I was subject to it; and so were hundreds of intelligent and industrious people all around us. I seldom ventured into the streets; and when it was necessary to do an errand for Mrs. Bruce, or any of the family, I went as much as possible through back streets and by-ways. What a disgrace to a city calling itself free, that inhabitants, guiltless of offence, and seeking to perform their duties conscientiously, should be condemned to live in such incessant fear, and have nowhere to turn for protection! This state of things, of course, gave rise to many impromptu vigilance committees. Every colored person, and every friend of their persecuted race, kept their eyes wide open. Every evening I examined the newspapers carefully, to see what Southerners had put up at the hotels. I did this for my own sake, thinking my young mistress and her husband might be among the list; I wished also to give information to others, if necessary; for if many were "running to and fro," I resolved that "knowledge should be increased."[6]

This brings up one of my Southern reminiscences, which I will here briefly relate. I was somewhat acquainted with a slave named Luke, who belonged to a wealthy man in our vicinity. His master died, leaving a son and daughter heirs to his large fortune. In the division of the slaves, Luke was included in the son's portion. This young man became a prey to the vices growing out of the "patriarchal institution," and when he went to the north, to complete his education, he carried his vices with him. He was brought home, deprived of the use of his limbs, by excessive dissipation. Luke was appointed to wait upon his bed-ridden master, whose despotic habits were greatly increased by exasperation at his own helplessness. He kept a cowhide beside him, and, for the most trivial occurrence, he would order his attendant to bare his back, and kneel beside the couch, while he whipped him till his strength was exhausted. Some days he was not allowed to wear any thing but his shirt, in order to be in readiness to be flogged. A day seldom passed without his receiving more or less blows. If the slightest resistance was offered, the town constable was sent for to execute the punishment, and Luke learned from experience how much more the constable's strong arm was to be dreaded than the comparatively feeble one of his master. The arm of his tyrant grew weaker, and was finally palsied; and then the constable's services were in constant requisition. The fact that he was entirely dependent on Luke's care, and was obliged to be tended like an infant, instead of inspiring any gratitude or compassion towards his poor slave, seemed only to increase his irritability and cruelty. As he lay there on his bed, a mere degraded wreck of manhood, he took into his head the strangest freaks of despotism; and if Luke hesitated to submit to his orders, the constable was immediately sent for. Some of these freaks were of a nature too filthy to be repeated. When I fled from the house of bondage, I left poor Luke still chained to the bedside of this cruel and disgusting wretch.

One day, when I had been requested to do an errand for Mrs. Bruce, I was hurrying through back streets, as usual, when I saw a young man approaching, whose face was familiar to me. As he came nearer, I recognized Luke. I always rejoiced to see or hear of any one who had escaped from the black pit; but, remembering this poor fellow's extreme hardships, I was peculiarly glad

5. William escaped from his master, Mr. Sands, when Sands moved to Washington, D.C.

6. Daniel 12:4.

to see him on Northern soil, though I no longer called it *free* soil. I well remembered what a desolate feeling it was to be alone among strangers, and I went up to him and greeted him cordially. At first, he did not know me; but when I mentioned my name, he remembered all about me. I told him of the Fugitive Slave Law, and asked him if he did not know that New York was a city of kidnappers.

He replied, "De risk ain't so bad for me, as 'tis fur you. 'Cause I runned away from de speculator, and you runned away from de massa. Dem speculators vont spen dar money to come here fur a runaway, if dey ain't sartin sure to put dar hans right on him. An I tell you I's tuk good car 'bout dat. I had too hard times down dar, to let 'em ketch dis nigger."

He then told me of the advice he had received, and the plans he had laid. I asked if he had money enough to take him to Canada. "'Pend upon it, I hab," he replied. "I tuk car fur dat. I'd bin workin all my days fur dem cussed whites, an got no pay but kicks and cuffs. So I tought dis nigger had a right to money nuff to bring him to de Free States. Massa Henry he lib till ebery body vish him dead; an ven he did die, I knowed de debbil would hab him, an vouldn't vant him to bring his money 'long too. So I tuk some of his bills, and put 'em in de pocket of his old trousers. An ven he was buried, dis nigger ask fur dem ole trousers, an dey gub 'em to me." With a low, chuckling laugh, he added, "You see I didn't *steal* it; dey *gub* it to me. I tell you, I had mighty hard time to keep de speculator from findin it; but he didn't git it."

This is a fair specimen of how the moral sense is educated by slavery. When a man has his wages stolen from him, year after year, and the laws sanction and enforce the theft, how can he be expected to have more regard to honesty than has the man who robs him? I have become somewhat enlightened, but I confess that I agree with poor, ignorant, much-abused Luke, in thinking he had a *right* to that money, as a portion of his unpaid wages. He went to Canada forthwith, and I have not since heard from him.

All that winter I lived in a state of anxiety. When I took the children out to breathe the air, I closely observed the countenances of all I met. I dreaded the approach of summer, when snakes and slaveholders make their appearance. I was, in fact, a slave in New York, as subject to slave laws as I had been in a Slave State. Strange incongruity in a State called free!

Spring returned, and I received warning from the south that Dr. Flint knew of my return to my old place, and was making preparations to have me caught. I learned afterwards that my dress, and that of Mrs. Bruce's children, had been described to him by some of the Northern tools, which slaveholders employ for their base purposes, and then indulge in sneers at their cupidity and mean servility.

I immediately informed Mrs. Bruce of my danger, and she took prompt measures for my safety. My place as nurse could not be supplied immediately, and this generous, sympathizing lady proposed that I should carry her baby away. It was a comfort to me to have the child with me; for the heart is reluctant to be torn away from every object it loves. But how few mothers would have consented to have one of their own babes become a fugitive, for the sake of a poor, hunted nurse, on whom the legislators of the country had let loose the bloodhounds! When I spoke of the sacrifice she was making, in depriving herself of her dear baby, she replied, "It is better for you to have baby with you, Linda; for if they get on your track, they will be obliged to bring the child to me; and then, if there is a possibility of saving you, you shall be saved."

This lady had a very wealthy relative, a benevolent gentleman in many respects, but aristocratic and pro-slavery. He remonstrated with her for harboring a fugitive slave; told her she was violating the laws of her country; and asked her if she was aware of the penalty. She replied, "I am very well aware of it. It is imprisonment and one thousand dollars fine. Shame on my country that it *is* so! I am ready to incur the penalty. I will go to the state's prison, rather than have any poor victim torn from *my* house, to be carried back to slavery."

The noble heart! The brave heart! The tears are in my eyes while I write of her. May the God of the helpless reward her for her sympathy with my persecuted people!

I was sent into New England, where I was sheltered by the wife of a senator, whom I shall always hold in grateful remembrance. This honorable gentleman would not have voted for the Fugitive Slave Law, as did the senator in "Uncle Tom's Cabin";[7] on the contrary, he was strongly opposed to it; but he was enough under its influence to be afraid of having me remain in his house many hours. So I was sent into the country, where I remained a month with the baby. When it was supposed that Dr. Flint's emissaries had lost track of me, and given up the pursuit for the present, I returned to New York.

XLI. Free at Last

Mrs. Bruce, and every member of her family, were exceedingly kind to me. I was thankful for the blessings of my lot, yet I could not always wear a cheerful countenance. I was doing harm to no one; on the contrary, I was doing all the good I could in my small way; yet I could never go out to breathe God's free air without trepidation at my heart. This seemed hard; and I could not think it was a right state of things in any civilized country.

From time to time I received news from my good old grandmother. She could not write; but she employed others to write for her. The following is an extract from one of her last letters:—

> "Dear Daughter: I cannot hope to see you again on earth; but I pray to God to unite us above, where pain will no more rack this feeble body of mine; where sorrow and parting from my children will be no more. God has promised these things if we are faithful unto the end. My age and feeble health deprive me of going to church now; but God is with me here at home. Thank your brother for his kindness. Give much love to him, and tell him to remember the Creator in the days of his youth,[8] and strive to meet me in the Father's kingdom. Love to Ellen and Benjamin. Don't neglect him. Tell him for me, to be a good boy. Strive, my child, to train them for God's children. May he protect and provide for you, is the prayer of your loving old mother."

These letters both cheered and saddened me. I was always glad to have tidings from the kind, faithful old friend of my unhappy youth; but her messages of love made my heart yearn to see her before she died, and I mourned over the fact that it was impossible. Some months after I returned from my flight to New England, I received a letter from her, in which she wrote, "Dr. Flint is dead. He has left a distressed family. Poor old man! I hope he made his peace with God."

7. An allusion to Senator Bird of Ohio in Harriet Beecher Stowe's *Uncle Tom's Cabin* (1852).
8. Ecclesiastes 12:1.

I remembered how he had defrauded my grandmother of the hard earnings she had loaned; how he had tried to cheat her out of the freedom her mistress had promised her, and how he had persecuted her children; and I thought to myself that she was a better Christian than I was, if she could entirely forgive him. I cannot say, with truth, that the news of my old master's death softened my feelings towards him. There are wrongs which even the grave does not bury. The man was odious to me while he lived, and his memory is odious now.

His departure from this world did not diminish my danger. He had threatened my grandmother that his heirs should hold me in slavery after he was gone; that I never should be free so long as a child of his survived. As for Mrs. Flint, I had seen her in deeper afflictions than I supposed the loss of her husband would be, for she had buried several children; yet I never saw any signs of softening in her heart. The doctor had died in embarrassed circumstances, and had little to will to his heirs, except such property as he was unable to grasp. I was well aware what I had to expect from the family of Flints; and my fears were confirmed by a letter from the south, warning me to be on my guard, because Mrs. Flint openly declared that her daughter could not afford to lose so valuable a slave as I was.

I kept close watch of the newspapers for arrivals; but one Saturday night, being much occupied, I forgot to examine the Evening Express as usual. I went down into the parlor for it, early in the morning, and found the boy about to kindle a fire with it. I took it from him and examined the list of arrivals. Reader, if you have never been a slave, you cannot imagine the acute sensation of suffering at my heart, when I read the names of Mr. and Mrs. Dodge, at a hotel in Courtland Street. It was a third-rate hotel, and that circumstance convinced me of the truth of what I had heard, that they were short of funds and had need of my value, as *they* valued me; and that was by dollars and cents. I hastened with the paper to Mrs. Bruce. Her heart and hand were always open to every one in distress, and she always warmly sympathized with mine. It was impossible to tell how near the enemy was. He might have passed and repassed the house while we were sleeping. He might at that moment be waiting to pounce upon me if I ventured out of doors. I had never seen the husband of my young mistress, and therefore I could not distinguish him from any other stranger. A carriage was hastily ordered; and, closely veiled, I followed Mrs. Bruce, taking the baby again with me into exile. After various turnings and crossings, and returnings, the carriage stopped at the house of one of Mrs. Bruce's friends, where I was kindly received. Mrs. Bruce returned immediately, to instruct the domestics what to say if any one came to inquire for me.

It was lucky for me that the evening paper was not burned up before I had a chance to examine the list of arrivals. It was not long after Mrs. Bruce's return to her house, before several people came to inquire for me. One inquired for me, another asked for my daughter Ellen, and another said he had a letter from my grandmother, which he was requested to deliver in person.

They were told, "She *has* lived here, but she has left."

"How long ago?"

"I don't know, sir."

"Do you know where she went?"

"I do not, sir." And the door was closed.

This Mr. Dodge, who claimed me as his property, was originally a Yankee pedler in the south; then he became a merchant, and finally a slaveholder.

He managed to get introduced into what was called the first society, and married Miss Emily Flint. A quarrel arose between him and her brother, and the brother cowhided him. This led to a family feud, and he proposed to remove to Virginia. Dr. Flint left him no property, and his own means had become circumscribed, while a wife and children depended upon him for support. Under these circumstances, it was very natural that he should make an effort to put me into his pocket.

I had a colored friend, a man from my native place, in whom I had the most implicit confidence. I sent for him, and told him that Mr. and Mrs. Dodge had arrived in New York. I proposed that he should call upon them to make inquiries about his friends at the south, with whom Dr. Flint's family were well acquainted. He thought there was no impropriety in his doing so, and he consented. He went to the hotel, and knocked at the door of Mr. Dodge's room, which was opened by the gentleman himself, who gruffly inquired, "What brought you here? How came you to know I was in the city?"

"Your arrival was published in the evening papers, sir; and I called to ask Mrs. Dodge about my friends at home. I didn't suppose it would give any offence."

"Where's that negro girl, that belongs to my wife?"

"What girl, sir?"

"You know well enough. I mean Linda, that ran away from Dr. Flint's plantation, some years ago. I dare say you've seen her, and know where she is."

"Yes, sir, I've seen her, and know where she is. She is out of your reach, sir."

"Tell me where she is, or bring her to me, and I will give her a chance to buy her freedom."

"I don't think it would be of any use, sir. I have heard her say she would go to the ends of the earth, rather than pay any man or woman for her freedom, because she thinks she has a right to it. Besides, she couldn't do it, if she would, for she has spent her earnings to educate her children."

This made Mr. Dodge very angry, and some high words passed between them. My friend was afraid to come where I was; but in the course of the day I received a note from him. I supposed they had not come from the south, in the winter, for a pleasure excursion; and now the nature of their business was very plain.

Mrs. Bruce came to me and entreated me to leave the city the next morning. She said her house was watched, and it was possible that some clew to me might be obtained. I refused to take her advice. She pleaded with an earnest tenderness, that ought to have moved me; but I was in a bitter, disheartened mood. I was weary of flying from pillar to post. I had been chased during half my life, and it seemed as if the chase was never to end. There I sat, in that great city, guiltless of crime, yet not daring to worship God in any of the churches. I heard the bells ringing for afternoon service, and, with contemptuous sarcasm, I said, "Will the preachers take for their text, 'Proclaim liberty to the captive, and the opening of prison doors to them that are bound'?[9] or will they preach from the text, 'Do unto others as ye would they should do unto you'?"[1] Oppressed Poles and Hungarians could find a safe refuge in that city; John Mitchell[2] was free to proclaim in the City Hall his desire for "a plantation well stocked with slaves"; but there I sat, an oppressed American, not daring to show my face. God forgive the

9. Isaiah 61:1.

1. See Matthew 7:12: "Therefore all things whatsoever ye would that men should do to you, do ye even so to them."

2. Irish nationalist and advocate of slavery.

black and bitter thoughts I indulged on that Sabbath day! The Scripture says, "Oppression makes even a wise man mad";[3] and I was not wise.

I had been told that Mr. Dodge said his wife had never signed away her right to my children, and if he could not get me, he would take them. This it was, more than any thing else, that roused such a tempest in my soul. Benjamin was with his uncle William in California, but my innocent young daughter had come to spend a vacation with me. I thought of what I had suffered in slavery at her age, and my heart was like a tiger's when a hunter tries to seize her young.

Dear Mrs. Bruce! I seem to see the expression of her face, as she turned away discouraged by my obstinate mood. Finding her expostulations[4] unavailing, she sent Ellen to entreat me. When ten o'clock in the evening arrived and Ellen had not returned, this watchful and unwearied friend became anxious. She came to us in a carriage, bringing a well-filled trunk for my journey—trusting that by this time I would listen to reason. I yielded to her, as I ought to have done before.

The next day, baby and I set out in a heavy snow storm, bound for New England again. I received letters from the City of Iniquity, addressed to me under an assumed name. In a few days one came from Mrs. Bruce, informing me that my new master was still searching for me, and that she intended to put an end to this persecution by buying my freedom. I felt grateful for the kindness that prompted this offer, but the idea was not so pleasant to me as might have been expected. The more my mind had become enlightened, the more difficult it was for me to consider myself an article of property; and to pay money to those who had so grievously oppressed me seemed like taking from my sufferings the glory of triumph. I wrote to Mrs. Bruce, thanking her, but saying that being sold from one owner to another seemed too much like slavery; that such a great obligation could not be easily cancelled; and that I preferred to go to my brother in California.

Without my knowledge, Mrs. Bruce employed a gentleman in New York to enter into negotiations with Mr. Dodge. He proposed to pay three hundred dollars down, if Mr. Dodge would sell me, and enter into obligations to relinquish all claim to me or my children forever after. He who called himself my master said he scorned so small an offer for such a valuable servant. The gentleman replied, "You can do as you choose, sir. If you reject this offer you will never get any thing; for the woman has friends who will convey her and her children out of the country."

Mr. Dodge concluded that "half a loaf was better than no bread," and he agreed to the proffered terms. By the next mail I received this brief letter from Mrs. Bruce: "I am rejoiced to tell you that the money for your freedom has been paid to Mr. Dodge. Come home to-morrow. I long to see you and my sweet babe."

My brain reeled as I read these lines. A gentleman near me said, "It's true; I have seen the bill of sale." "The bill of sale!" Those words struck me like a blow. So I was *sold* at last! A human being *sold* in the free city of New York! The bill of sale is on record, and future generations will learn from it that women were articles of traffic in New York, late in the nineteenth century of the Christian religion. It may hereafter prove a useful document to antiquaries,[5] who are seeking to measure the progress of civilization in the

3. Ecclesiastes 7:7.
4. Earnest reasoning designed to change someone's conduct.
5. Those who study rare, old things.

United States. I well know the value of that bit of paper; but much as I love freedom, I do not like to look upon it. I am deeply grateful to the generous friend who procured it, but I despise the miscreant who demanded payment for what never rightfully belonged to him or his.

I had objected to having my freedom bought, yet I must confess that when it was done I felt as if a heavy load had been lifted from my weary shoulders. When I rode home in the cars I was no longer afraid to unveil my face and look at people as they passed. I should have been glad to have met Daniel Dodge himself; to have had him seen me and known me, that he might have mourned over the untoward circumstances which compelled him to sell me for three hundred dollars.

When I reached home, the arms of my benefactress were thrown round me, and our tears mingled. As soon as she could speak, she said, "O Linda, I'm *so* glad it's all over! You wrote to me as if you thought you were going to be transferred from one owner to another. But I did not buy you for your services. I should have done just the same, if you had been going to sail for California tomorrow. I should, at least, have the satisfaction of knowing that you left me a free woman."

My heart was exceedingly full. I remembered how my poor father had tried to buy me, when I was a small child, and how he had been disappointed. I hoped his spirit was rejoicing over me now. I remembered how my good old grandmother had laid up her earnings to purchase me in later years, and how often her plans had been frustrated. How that faithful, loving old heart would leap for joy, if she could look on me and my children now that we were free! My relatives had been foiled in all their efforts, but God had raised me up a friend among strangers, who had bestowed on me the precious, long-desired boon. Friend! It is a common word, often lightly used. Like other good and beautiful things, it may be tarnished by careless handling; but when I speak of Mrs. Bruce as my friend, the word is sacred.

My grandmother lived to rejoice in my freedom; but not long after, a letter came with a black seal. She had gone "where the wicked cease from troubling, and the weary are at rest."[6]

Time passed on, and a paper came to me from the south, containing an obituary notice of my uncle Phillip. It was the only case I ever knew of such an honor conferred upon a colored person. It was written by one of his friends, and contained these words: "Now that death has laid him low, they call him a good man and a useful citizen; but what are eulogies to the black man, when the world has faded from his vision? It does not require man's praise to obtain rest in God's kingdom." So they called a colored man a *citizen!* Strange words to be uttered in that region!

Reader, my story ends with freedom; not in the usual way, with marriage. I and my children are now free! We are as free from the power of slaveholders as are the white people of the north; and though that, according to my ideas, is not saying a great deal, it is a vast improvement in *my* condition. The dream of my life is not yet realized. I do not sit with my children in a home of my own. I still long for a hearthstone of my own, however humble. I wish it for my children's sake far more than for my own. But God so orders circumstances as to keep me with my friend Mrs. Bruce. Love, duty, gratitude, also bind me to her side. It is a privilege to serve her who pities my oppressed people, and who has bestowed the inestimable boon of freedom on me and my children.

6. Job 3.17.

It has been painful to me, in many ways, to recall the dreary years I passed in bondage. I would gladly forget them if I could. Yet the retrospection is not altogether without solace; for with those gloomy recollections come tender memories of my good old grandmother, like light, fleecy clouds floating over a dark and troubled sea.

1861

WILLIAM WELLS BROWN
1814?–1884

William Wells Brown is generally regarded as the first African American to achieve distinction in what the nineteenth century called *belles lettres,* or "fine letters." A number of Black Americans contemporary with Brown, most notably Frederick Douglass, enjoyed popular success as journalists and orators. In addition to these forms of expression, however, Brown tried his hand at genres considered more "literary," authoring the first novel, *Clotel; or, The President's Daughter* (1853) and the first drama, *The Escape; or, A Leap for Freedom* (1858), in African American literature. Less well known but still remarkable works from Brown include *Three Years in Europe* (1852), the first travel book by a Black American, and two volumes of history, *The Black Man: His Antecedents, His Genius, and His Achievements* (1863) and *The Negro in the American Rebellion* (1867), the latter of which is the first African American history of the Civil War. Brown was an antislavery lecturer and an activist long before he became a literary man. He saw *belles lettres* as a fresh and potent way to dramatize his case against slavery while promoting a sympathetic image of African Americans in both the United States and England. Brown's critics have sometimes seen his fiction and poetry as burdened by abolitionist propaganda and sentimentality, but few deny that he originated some of the most persistent and provocative character types and motifs in the African American narrative tradition.

William Wells Brown was born on a plantation in Montgomery County, Kentucky, the son of a white man who never acknowledged his fatherhood and an enslaved woman whose only name was Elizabeth. Light complexioned and quick witted, William spent his boyhood in Marthasville on the Missouri frontier and his teenage years mainly in St. Louis, Missouri, and its vicinity. He worked as a house servant, a field hand, a tavernkeeper's assistant, a printer's helper, an assistant in a medical office, and finally a handyman for James Walker—a Missouri slave trader with whom William made three trips up and down the Mississippi River between St. Louis and the New Orleans slave market. After a year's service to Walker, William returned to his enslaver in January 1832, only to learn that he was to be sold. This news precipitated William's first escape attempt, which failed in part because he was determined to take his mother with him. The captured fugitive suffered the usual punishment for trying to run away—beatings, hard labor as a field hand, and sale. In the fall of 1833 he fell into the hands of slaveholders who were so unwary as to take him on a family excursion to Cincinnati in the last weeks of the year. On New Year's Day, 1834, William made his escape, traveling by night alone in the cold from Cincinnati across Ohio to Cleveland. On his way, the fugitive was befriended by Mr. and Mrs. Wells Brown, a Quaker couple whose kindness William acknowledged by adding their names to his own.

After seizing his freedom, William Wells Brown worked for nine years as a steamboatman on Lake Erie and conductor for the Underground Railroad in Cleveland, Ohio, and Buffalo, New York. In 1843 Brown became a lecturing agent for the Western New York Anti-Slavery Society. Moving to Boston in 1847, Brown found an enthusiastic publisher, the American Anti-Slavery Society, happy to print and promote his autobiography, *Narrative of William W. Brown, a Fugitive Slave.* Going through multiple American and British editions and printings before 1850, Brown's *Narrative* was exceeded in popularity and sales only by the *Narrative of the Life of Frederick Douglass, an American Slave,* which had appeared in 1845. Brown's *Narrative* and his skills on the anti slavery platform earned him international acclaim.

The contrasts between Brown's self-portrait and Douglass's are mirrored in the differences between the styles of the two men's narratives. Douglass's storytelling incorporates the rhetorical conventions of nineteenth-century platform oratory and the structure of Protestant conversion narratives to emphasize how Douglass had fashioned himself into an exemplary figure. Brown's modest, understated plain style, displaying few flourishes and little self-reflection, refuses to make great claims for the man himself. Instead, it is often the ordinary, the representative, and the nonheroic—even the antiheroic—that come to the fore in Brown's narrative of his life. We discover a striking brand of realism in Brown's willingness to portray himself as an enslaved trickster and to explore the conflicts between the survival ethic he adopted while enslaved and the dominant morality of his time.

In the summer of 1849 Brown went abroad to attend the International Peace Congress in Paris and to encourage British support for the antislavery movement in the United States. He remained in England until 1854, delivering more than one thousand antislavery lectures and publishing *Three Years in Europe* and *Clotel* in London. *Clotel,* Brown's panoramic story of the fate of a mixed-race daughter of Thomas Jefferson, draws substantially on its author's personal experience in bondage as well as on the slave narrative and antislavery novel traditions. But in the development of the character of Clotel, Brown's book moves beyond the stereotypes and conventions of its time. While Clotel, like many a "tragic mulatta" in nineteenth-century American fiction, is distinguished by her beauty, her idealism, her barely traceable African ancestry, and her disappointments in love, she also proves herself an active and combative figure by the end of her story. Like many of his Black literary contemporaries during the 1850s, Brown felt obliged to create characters that epitomized the ideals of aspiring African American men and women in order to educate an American readership that saw much defamation of African American character in newspapers, magazines, and books. The real and the ideal maintain at best an uncertain balance in Brown's writing. But the tension between them and the problematic ways Brown tried to resolve it tell us much about the conflicting aesthetic and ideological agendas underlying early African American *belles lettres.*

After Brown's friends purchased his freedom in 1854, he returned to the United States and continued agitating for abolitionism until the end of the Civil War. After the war, he practiced medicine in Boston and promoted temperance among African Americans, believing that abstinence from alcohol was key to the social and economic advancement of the freedpeople of the South. During the Reconstruction era, Brown produced several significant books, among them *Clotelle; or, The Colored Heroine* (1867), a revision of *Clotel* that left Brown's heroine in charge of a school for freedmen and freedwomen at the end of the Civil War. In 1874 Brown wrote and self-published his most comprehensive work of African American history, *The Rising Son; or, The Antecedents and Advancement of the Colored Race,* which contains biographical sketches of 110 prominent Black Americans. In 1880 the last of Brown's books appeared under the curiously nostalgic title (for one who had escaped slavery), *My Southern Home.* The most perplexing of all Brown's first-person narratives, *My Southern Home* starts with rosy reminiscences of life on a pre-Civil War Missouri plantation followed by a hard-hitting report on the reversal of Reconstruction reforms and the pernicious rise of Jim Crow in the postwar South. Brown died at his home in Chelsea, a suburb of Boston, on November 6, 1884.

Obituaries in Boston's major newspapers praised him as "one of the foremost men of the colored race" in America, one of "the most intelligent, earnest, and active" veterans of the antislavery struggle, and in his later years a tireless proponent of "every phase of reform—temperance, woman suffrage, and the rights of labor."

From Narrative of William W. Brown, a Fugitive Slave

Chapter V

My master[1] had family worship, night and morning. At night, the slaves were called in to attend; but in the mornings, they had to be at their work, and master did all the praying. My master and mistress were great lovers of mint julep, and every morning, a pitcherfull was made, of which they all partook freely, not excepting little master William. After drinking freely all round, they would have family worship, and then breakfast. I cannot say but I loved the julep as well as any of them, and during prayer was always careful to seat myself close to the table where it stood, so as to help myself when they were all busily engaged in their devotions. By the time prayer was over, I was about as happy as any of them. A sad accident happened one morning. In helping myself, and at the same time keeping an eye on my old mistress, I accidentally let the pitcher fall upon the floor, breaking it in pieces, and spilling the contents. This was a bad affair for me; for as soon as prayer was over, I was taken and severely chastised.

My master's family consisted of himself, his wife, and their nephew, William Moore. He was taken into the family, when only a few weeks of age. His name being that of my own, mine was changed,[2] for the purpose of giving precedence to his, though I was his senior by ten or twelve years. The plantation being four miles from the city, I had to drive the family to church. I always dreaded the approach of the Sabbath; for, during service, I was obliged to stand by the horses in the hot broiling sun, or in the rain, just as it happened.

One Sabbath, as we were driving past the house of D.D. Page, a gentleman who owned a large baking establishment, as I was sitting upon the box of the carriage, which was very much elevated, I saw Mr. Page pursuing a slave around the yard, with a long whip, cutting him at every jump. The man soon escaped from the yard, and was followed by Mr. Page. They came running past us, and the slave perceiving that he would be overtaken, stopped suddenly, and Page stumbled over him, and falling on the stone pavement, fractured one of his legs, which crippled him for life. The same gentleman, but a short time previous, tied up a woman of his, by the name of Delphia, and whipped her nearly to death; yet he was a deacon in the Baptist church, in good and regular standing. Poor Delphia! I was well acquainted with her, and called to see her while upon her sick bed; and I shall never forget her appearance. She was a member of the same church with her master.

Soon after this, I was hired out to Mr. Walker; the same man whom I have mentioned as having carried a gang of slaves down the river, on the steamboat Enterprize. Seeing me in the capacity of steward on the boat, and thinking that I would make a good hand to take care of slaves, he determined to

1. Dr. John Young, a St. Louis physician and plantation owner, was Brown's enslaver from his birth until 1834.

2. To Sanford.

have me for that purpose; and finding that my master would not sell me, he hired me for the term of one year.

When I learned the fact of my having been hired to a negro speculator, or a "soul-driver" as they are generally called among slaves, no one can tell my emotions. Mr. Walker had offered a high price for me, as I afterwards learned, but I suppose my master was restrained from selling me by the fact that I was a near relative of his. On entering the service of Mr. Walker, I found that my opportunity of getting to a land of liberty was gone, at least for the time being. He had a gang of slaves in readiness to start for New Orleans, and in a few days we were on our journey. I am at a loss for language to express my feelings on that occasion. Although my master had told me that he had not sold me, and Mr. Walker had told me that he had not purchased me, I did not believe them; and not until I had been to New Orleans, and was on my return, did I believe that I was not sold.

There was on the boat a large room on the lower deck, in which the slaves were kept, men and women, promiscuously—all chained two and two, and a strict watch kept that they did not get loose; for cases have occurred in which slaves have got off their chains, and made their escape at landing-places, while the boats were taking in wood;—and with all our care, we lost one woman who had been taken from her husband and children, and having no desire to live without them, in the agony of her soul jumped overboard, and drowned herself. She was not chained.

It was almost impossible to keep that part of the boat clean.

On landing at Natchez,[3] the slaves were all carried to the slavepen, and there kept one week, during which time, several of them were sold. Mr. Walker fed his slaves well. We took on board, at St. Louis, several hundred pounds of bacon (smoked meat) and cornmeal, and his slaves were better fed than slaves generally were in Natchez, so far as my observation extended.

At the end of a week, we left for New Orleans, the place of our final destination, which we reached in two days. Here the slaves were placed in a negro-pen, where those who wished to purchase could call and examine them. The negro-pen is a small yard, surrounded by buildings, from fifteen to twenty feet wide, with the exception of a large gate with iron bars. The slaves are kept in the buildings during the night, and turned out into the yard during the day. After the best of the stock was sold at private sale at the pen, the balance were taken to the Exchange Coffee House Auction Rooms, kept by Isaac L. McCoy, and sold at public auction. After the sale of this lot of slaves, we left New Orleans for St. Louis.

From *Chapter VI*

On our arrival at St. Louis, I went to Dr. Young, and told him that I did not wish to live with Mr. Walker any longer. I was heart-sick at seeing my fellow-creatures bought and sold. But the Dr. had hired me for the year, and stay I must. Mr. Walker again commenced purchasing another gang of slaves. He bought a man of Colonel John O'Fallon, who resided in the suburbs of the city. This man had a wife and three children. As soon as the purchase was made, he was put in jail for safe keeping, until we should be ready to start for New Orleans. His wife visited him while there, several times, and several times when she went for that purpose was refused admittance.

3. In Mississippi.

In the course of eight or nine weeks Mr. Walker had his cargo of human flesh made up. There was in this lot a number of old men and women, some of them with gray locks. We left St. Louis in the steamboat Carlton, Captain Swan, bound for New Orleans. On our way down, and before we reached Rodney,[4] the place where we made our first stop, I had to prepare the old slaves for market. I was ordered to have the old men's whiskers shaved off, and the gray hairs plucked out where they were not too numerous, in which case he had a preparation of blacking to color it, and with a blacking-brush we would put it on. This was new business to me, and was performed in a room where the passengers could not see us. These slaves were also taught how old they were by Mr. Walker, and after going through the blacking process, they looked ten or fifteen years younger; and I am sure that some of those who purchased slaves of Mr. Walker, were dreadfully cheated, especially in the ages of the slaves which they bought.

We landed at Rodney, and the slaves were driven to the pen in the back part of the village. Several were sold at this place, during our stay of four or five days, when we proceeded to Natchez. There we landed at night, and the gang were put in the warehouse until morning, when they were driven to the pen. As soon as the slaves are put in these pens, swarms of planters may be seen in and about them. They knew when Walker was expected, as he always had the time advertised beforehand when he would be in Rodney, Natchez, and New Orleans. These were the principal places where he offered his slaves for sale.

When at Natchez the second time, I saw a slave very cruelly whipped. He belonged to a Mr. Broadwell, a merchant who kept a store on the wharf. The slave's name was Lewis. I had known him several years, as he was formerly from St. Louis. We were expecting a steamboat down the river, in which we were to take passage for New Orleans. Mr. Walker sent me to the landing to watch for the boat, ordering me to inform him on its arrival. While there, I went into the store to see Lewis. I saw a slave in the store, and asked him where Lewis was. Said he, "They have got Lewis hanging between the heavens and the earth." I asked him what he meant by that. He told me to go into the warehouse and see. I went in, and found Lewis there. He was tied up to a beam, with his toes just touching the floor. As there was no one in the warehouse but himself, I inquired the reason of his being in that situation. He said Mr. Broadwell had sold his wife to a planter six miles from the city, and that he had been to visit her,—that he went in the night, expecting to return before daylight, and went without his master's permission. The patrol had taken him up before he reached his wife. He was put in jail, and his master had to pay for his catching and keeping, and that was what he was tied up for.

Just as he finished his story, Mr. Broadwell came in, and inquired what I was doing there. I knew not what to say, and while I was thinking what reply to make, he struck me over the head with the cowhide, the end of which struck me over my right eye, sinking deep into the flesh, leaving a scar which I carry to this day. Before I visited Lewis, he had received fifty lashes. Mr. Broadwell gave him fifty more after I came out, as I was afterwards informed by Lewis himself.

The next day we proceeded to New Orleans, and put the gang in the same negro-pen which we occupied before. In a short time, the planters came flocking to the pen to purchase slaves. Before the slaves were exhibited for sale, they were dressed and driven out into the yard. Some were set to dancing, some to jumping, some to singing, and some to playing cards. This was

4. Also in Mississippi.

done to make them appear cheerful and happy. My business was to see that they were placed in those situations before the arrival of the purchasers, and I have often set them to dancing when their cheeks were wet with tears. As slaves were in good demand at that time, they were all soon disposed of, and we again set out for St. Louis.

On our arrival, Mr. Walker purchased a farm five or six miles from the city. He had no family, but made a housekeeper of one of his female slaves. Poor Cynthia! I knew her well. She was a quadroon,[5] and one of the most beautiful women I ever saw. She was a native of St. Louis, and bore an irreproachable character for virtue and propriety of conduct. Mr. Walker bought her for the New Orleans market, and took her down with him on one of the trips that I made with him. Never shall I forget the circumstances of that voyage! On the first night that we were on board the steamboat, he directed me to put her into a state-room he had provided for her, apart from the other slaves. I had seen too much of the workings of slavery, not to know what this meant. I accordingly watched him into the state-room, and listened to hear what passed between them. I heard him make his base offers, and her reject them. He told her that if she would accept his vile proposals, he would take her back with him to St. Louis, and establish her as his housekeeper at his farm. But if she persisted in rejecting them, he would sell her as a field hand on the worst plantation on the river. Neither threats nor bribes prevailed, however, and he retired, disappointed of his prey.

The next morning, poor Cynthia told me what had past, and bewailed her sad fate with floods of tears. I comforted and encouraged her all I could; but I foresaw but too well what the result must be. Without entering into any farther particulars, suffice it to say that Walker performed his part of the contract, at that time. He took her back to St. Louis, established her as his mistress and housekeeper at his farm, and before I left, he had two children by her. But, mark the end! Since I have been at the North, I have been credibly informed that Walker has been married, and, as a previous measure, sold poor Cynthia and her four children (she having had two more since I came away) into hopeless bondage!

He soon commenced purchasing to make up the third gang. We took steamboat, and went to Jefferson City, a town on the Missouri river. Here we landed, and took stage for the interior of the State. He bought a number of slaves as he passed the different farms and villages. After getting twenty-two or twenty-three men and women, we arrived at St. Charles, a village on the banks of the Missouri. Here he purchased a woman who had a child in her arms, appearing to be four or five weeks old.

We had been travelling by land for some days, and were in hopes to have found a boat at this place for St. Louis, but were disappointed. As no boat was expected for some days, we started for St. Louis by land. Mr. Walker had purchased two horses. He rode one, and I the other. The slaves were chained together, and we took up our line of march, Mr. Walker taking the lead, and I bringing up the rear. Though the distance was not more than twenty miles, we did not reach it the first day. The road was worse than any that I have ever travelled.

Soon after we left St. Charles, the young child grew very cross, and kept up a noise during the greater part of the day. Mr. Walker complained of its crying several times, and told the mother to stop the child's d—d noise, or

5. A person who has one-quarter African American ancestry.

he would. The woman tried to keep the child from crying, but could not. We put up at night with an acquaintance of Mr. Walker, and in the morning, just as we were about to start, the child again commenced crying. Walker stepped up to her, and told her to give the child to him. The mother tremblingly obeyed. He took the child by one arm, as you would a cat by the leg, walked into the house, and said to the lady,

"Madam, I will make you a present of this little nigger; it keeps such a noise that I can't bear it."

"Thank you, sir," said the lady.

The mother, as soon as she saw that her child was to be left, ran up to Mr. Walker, and falling upon her knees begged him to let her have her child; she clung around his legs, and cried, "Oh, my child! my child! master, do let me have my child! oh, do, do, do. I will stop its crying, if you will only let me have it again." When I saw this woman crying for her child so piteously, a shudder,—a feeling akin to horror, shot through my frame. I have often since in imagination heard her crying for her child:—

O, master, let me stay to catch
My baby's sobbing breath,
His little glassy eye to watch,
And smooth his limbs in death,

And cover him with grass and leaf,
Beneath the large oak tree:
It is not sullenness, but grief,—
O, master, pity me!

The morn was chill—I spoke no word,
But feared my babe might die,
And heard all day, or thought I heard,
My little baby cry.

At noon, oh, how I ran and took
My baby to my breast!
I lingered—and the long lash broke
My sleeping infant's rest.

I worked till night—till darkest night,
In torture and disgrace;
Went home and watched till morning light,
To see my baby's face.

Then give me but one little hour—
O! do not lash me so!
One little hour—one little hour—
And gratefully I'll go.[6]

Mr. Walker commanded her to return into the ranks with the other slaves. Women who had children were not chained, but those that had none were. As soon as her child was disposed of, she was chained in the gang.

The following song I have often heard the slaves sing, when about to be carried to the far south. It is said to have been composed by a slave.

6. An abridged version of Charlotte Elizabeth, "The Slave and Her Babe" in *The Liberty Minstrel* (1845), ed. George W. Clark.

See these poor souls from Africa
Transported to America;
We are stolen, and sold to Georgia,
Will you go along with me?
We are stolen, and sold to Georgia,
Come sound the jubilee!

See wives and husbands sold apart,
Their children's screams will break my heart;—
There's a better day a coming,
Will you go along with me?
There's a better day a coming,
Go sound the jubilee!

O, gracious Lord! when shall it be,
That we poor souls shall all be free;
Lord, break them slavery powers—
Will you go along with me?
Lord break them slavery powers,
Go sound the jubilee!

Dear Lord, dear Lord, when slavery'll cease,
Then we poor souls will have our peace;—
There's a better day a coming,
Will you go along with me?
There's a better day a coming,
Go sound the jubilee!"

We finally arrived at Mr. Walker's farm. He had a house built during our absence to put slaves in. It was a kind of domestic jail. The slaves were put in the jail at night, and worked on the farm during the day. They were kept here until the gang was completed, when we again started for New Orleans, on board the steamboat North America, Capt. Alexander Scott. We had a large number of slaves in this gang. One, by the name of Joe, Mr. Walker was training up to take my place, as my time was nearly out, and glad was I. We made our first stop at Vicksburg,[7] where we remained one week and sold several slaves.

Mr. Walker, though not a good master, had not flogged a slave since I had been with him, though he had threatened me. The slaves were kept in the pen, and he always put up at the best hotel, and kept his wines in his room, for the accommodation of those who called to negotiate with him for the purchase of slaves. One day while we were at Vicksburg, several gentlemen came to see him for this purpose, and as usual the wine was called for. I took the tray and started around with it, and having accidentally filled some of the glasses too full, the gentlemen spilled the wine on their clothes as they went to drink. Mr. Walker apologized to them for my carelessness, but looked at me as though he would see me again on this subject.

After the gentlemen had left the room, he asked me what I meant by my carelessness, and said that he would attend to me. The next morning, he gave me a note to carry to the jailer, and a dollar in money to give to him. I suspected that all was not right, so I went down near the landing where I met with a sailor, and walking up to him, asked him if he would be so kind as to

7. In Mississippi.

read the note for me. He read it over, and then looked at me. I asked him to tell me what was in it. Said he,

"They are going to give you hell."

"Why?" said I.

He said, "This is a note to have you whipped, and says that you have a dollar to pay for it."

He handed me back the note, and off I started. I knew not what to do, but was determined not to be whipped. I went up to the jail—took a look at it, and walked off again. As Mr. Walker was acquainted with the jailer, I feared that I should be found out if I did not go, and be treated in consequence of it still worse.

While I was meditating on the subject, I saw a colored man about my size walk up, and the thought struck me in a moment to send him with my note. I walked up to him, and asked him who he belonged to. He said he was a free man, and had been in the city but a short time. I told him I had a note to go into the jail, and get a trunk to carry to one of the steamboats; but was so busily engaged that I could not do it, although I had a dollar to pay for it. He asked me if I would not give him the job. I handed him the note and the dollar, and off he started for the jail.

I watched to see that he went in, and as soon as I saw the door close behind him, I walked around the corner, and took my station, intending to see how my friend looked when he came out. I had been there but a short time, when a colored man came around the corner, and said to another colored man with whom he was acquainted—

"They are giving a nigger scissors[8] in the jail."

"What for?" said the other. The man continued,

"A nigger came into the jail, and asked for the jailer. The jailer came out, and he handed him a note, and said he wanted to get a trunk. The jailer told him to go with him, and he would give him the trunk. So he took him into the room, and told the nigger to give up the dollar. He said a man had given him the dollar to pay for getting the trunk. But that lie would not answer. So they made him strip himself, and then they tied him down, and are now whipping him."

I stood by all the while listening to their talk, and soon found out that the person alluded to was my customer. I went into the street opposite the jail, and concealed myself in such a manner that I could not be seen by any one coming out. I had been there but a short time, when the young man made his appearance, and looked around for me. I, unobserved, came forth from my hiding-place, behind a pile of brick, and he pretty soon saw me and came up to me complaining bitterly, saying that I had played a trick upon him. I denied any knowledge of what the note contained, and asked him what they had done to him. He told me in substance what I heard the man tell who had come out of the jail.

"Yes," said he, "they whipped me and took my dollar, and gave me this note."

He showed me the note which the jailer had given him, telling him to give it to his master. I told him I would give him fifty cents for it,—that being all the money I had. He gave it to me, and took his money. He had received twenty lashes on his bare back, with the negro-whip.

I took the note and started for the hotel where I had left Mr. Walker. Upon reaching the hotel, I handed it to a stranger whom I had not seen

8. That is, giving him a lashing.

before, and requested him to read it to me. As near as I can recollect, it was as follows:—

> Dear Sir:—By your direction, I have given your boy twenty lashes. He is a very saucy boy, and tried to make me believe that he did not belong to you, and I put it on to him well for lying to me.
>
> I remain,
>
> Your obedient servant.

It is true that in most of the slave-holding cities, when a gentleman wishes his servants whipped, he can send him to the jail and have it done. Before I went in where Mr. Walker was, I wet my cheeks a little, as though I had been crying. He looked at me, and inquired what was the matter. I told him that I had never had such a whipping in my life, and handed him the note. He looked at it and laughed;—"and so you told him that you did not belong to me." "Yes, sir," said I. "I did not know that there was any harm in that." He told me I must behave myself, if I did not want to be whipped again.

This incident shows how it is that slavery makes its victims lying and mean; for which vices it afterwards reproaches them, and uses them as arguments to prove that they deserve no better fate. I have often, since my escape, deeply regretted the deception I practised upon this poor fellow; and I heartily desire that it may be, at some time or other, in my power to make him amends for his vicarious sufferings in my behalf.

* * *

1847

From Clotel; or, The President's Daughter

Chapter I. The Negro Sale

Why stands she near the auction stand,
That girl so young and fair?
What brings her to this dismal place,
Why stands she weeping there?[1]

With the growing population of slaves in the Southern States of America, there is a fearful increase of half whites, most of whose fathers are slaveowners, and their mothers slaves. Society does not frown upon the man who sits with his mulatto child upon his knee, whilst its mother stands a slave behind his chair. The late Henry Clay, some years since, predicted that the abolition of negro slavery would be brought about by the amalgamation of the races. John Randolph,[2] a distinguished slaveholder of Virginia, and a prominent statesman, said in a speech in the legislature of his native state, that "the blood of the first American statesmen coursed through the veins of the slave of the South." In all the cities and towns of the slave states, the real negro, or clear black, does not amount to more than one in every four of the slave popula-

1. A quatrain from "The Slave Auction – A Fact" in William Wells Brown's *The Anti-Slavery Harp* (1848). The poem may have been composed by Brown himself. Most of the verses that serve as epigraphs and conclusions to chapters in *Clotel* were taken from popular American antislavery poetry published in the periodical press and in collections such as *The Anti-Slavery Harp*.

2. U.S. congressperson and defender of states' rights (1773–1833). Clay was a U.S. senator from Kentucky and leader of the Whig Party (1777–1852).

tion. This fact is, of itself, the best evidence of the degraded and immoral condition of the relation of master and slave in the United States of America.

In all the slave states, the law says:—"Slaves shall be deemed, sold, taken, reputed, and adjudged in law to be chattels personal in the hands of their owners and possessors, and their executors, administrators and assigns, to all intents, constructions, and purposes whatsoever." A slave is one who is in the power of a master to whom he belongs. The master may sell him, dispose of his person, his industry, and his labour. He can do nothing, possess nothing, nor acquire anything, but what must belong to his master. The slave is entirely subject to the will of his master, who may correct and chastise him, though not with unusual rigour, or so as to maim and mutilate him, or expose him to the danger of loss of life, or to cause his death. The slave, to remain a slave, must be sensible that there is no appeal from his master. Where the slave is placed by law entirely under the control of the man who claims him, body and soul, as property, what else could be expected than the most depraved social condition? The marriage relation, the oldest and most sacred institution given to man by his Creator, is unknown and unrecognised in the slave laws of the United States. Would that we could say, that the moral and religious teaching in the slave states were better than the laws; but, alas! we cannot. A few years since, some slaveholders became a little uneasy in their minds about the rightfulness of permitting slaves to take to themselves husbands and wives, while they still had others living, and applied to their religious teachers for advice; and the following will show how this grave and important subject was treated:—

> Is a servant, whose husband or wife has been sold by his or her master into a distant country, to be permitted to marry again?

The query was referred to a committee, who made the following report; which, after discussion, was adopted:—

> That, in view of the circumstances in which servants in this country are placed, the committee are unanimous in the opinion, that it is better to permit servants thus circumstanced to take another husband or wife.

Such was the answer from a committee of the "Shiloh Baptist Association;" and instead of receiving light, those who asked the question were plunged into deeper darkness!

A similar question was put to the "Savannah River Association," and the answer, as the following will show, did not materially differ from the one we have already given:—

> Whether, in a case of involuntary separation, of such a character as to preclude all prospect of future intercourse, the parties ought to be allowed to marry again.

Answer—

> That such separation among persons situated as our slaves are, is civilly a separation by death; and they believe that, in the sight of God, it would be so viewed. To forbid second marriages in such cases would be to expose the parties, not only to stronger hardships and strong temptation, but to church-censure for acting in obedience to their masters, who cannot be expected to acquiesce in a regulation at variance with justice to the slaves, and to the spirit of that command which regulates marriage among Christians. The slaves are not free agents;

> and a dissolution by death is not more entirely without their consent, and beyond their control, than by such separation.

Although marriage, as the above indicates, is a matter which the slaveholders do not think is of any importance, or of any binding force with their slaves; yet it would be doing that degraded class an injustice, not to acknowledge that many of them do regard it as a sacred obligation, and show a willingness to obey the commands of God on this subject. Marriage is, indeed, the first and most important institution of human existence—the foundation of all civilisation and culture—the root of church and state. It is the most intimate covenant of heart formed among mankind; and for many persons the only relation in which they feel the true sentiments of humanity. It gives scope for every human virtue, since each of these is developed from the love and confidence which here predominate. It unites all which ennobles and beautifies life,—sympathy, kindness of will and deed, gratitude, devotion, and every delicate, intimate feeling. As the only asylum for true education, it is the first and last sanctuary of human culture. As husband and wife through each other become conscious of complete humanity, and every human feeling, and every human virtue; so children, at their first awakening in the fond covenant of love between parents, both of whom are tenderly concerned for the same object, find an image of complete humanity leagued in free love. The spirit of love which prevails between them acts with creative power upon the young mind, and awakens every germ of goodness within it. This invisible and incalculable influence of parental life acts more upon the child than all the efforts of education, whether by means of instruction, precept, or exhortation. If this be a true picture of the vast influence for good of the institution of marriage, what must be the moral degradation of that people to whom marriage is denied? Not content with depriving them of all the higher and holier enjoyments of this relation, by degrading and darkening their souls, the slaveholder denies to his victim even that slight alleviation of his misery, which would result from the marriage relation being protected by law and public opinion. Such is the influence of slavery in the United States, that the ministers of religion, even in the so-called free states, are the mere echoes, instead of the correctors, of public sentiment.

We have thought it advisable to show that the present system of chattel slavery in America undermines the entire social condition of man, so as to prepare the reader for the following narrative of slave life, in that otherwise happy and prosperous country.

In all the large towns in the Southern States, there is a class of slaves who are permitted to hire their time of their owners, and for which they pay a high price. These are mulatto women, or quadroons,[3] as they are familiarly known, and are distinguished for their fascinating beauty. The handsomest usually pays the highest price for her time. Many of these women are the favourites of persons who furnish them with the means of paying their owners, and not a few are dressed in the most extravagant manner. Reader, when you take into consideration the fact, that amongst the slave population no safeguard is thrown around virtue, and no inducement held out to slave women to be chaste, you will not be surprised when we tell you that immorality and vice pervade the cities of the Southern States in a manner unknown in the cities and towns of the Northern States. Indeed most of the slave women have no

3. Those who have one-quarter African American ancestry.

higher aspiration than that of becoming the finely-dressed mistress of some white man. And at negro balls and parties, this class of women usually cut the greatest figure.

At the close of the year—the following advertisement appeared in a newspaper published in Richmond, the capital of the state of Virginia:—"Notice: Thirty-eight negroes will be offered for sale on Monday, November 10th, at twelve o'clock, being the entire stock of the late John Graves Esq. The negroes are in good condition, some of them very prime; among them are several mechanics, able-bodied field hands, plough-boys, and women with children at the breast, and some of them very prolific in their generating qualities, affording a rare opportunity to any one who wishes to raise a strong and healthy lot of servants for their own use. Also several mulatto girls of rare personal qualities: two of them very superior. Any gentleman or lady wishing to purchase, can take any of the above slaves on trial for a week, for which no charge will be made." Amongst the above slaves to be sold were Currer and her two daughters, Clotel and Althesa; the latter were the girls spoken of in the advertisement as "very superior." Currer was a bright mulatto, and of prepossessing appearance, though then nearly forty years of age. She had hired her time for more than twenty years, during which time she had lived in Richmond. In her younger days Currer had been the housekeeper of a young slaveholder; but of later years had been a laundress or washerwoman, and was considered to be a woman of great taste in getting up linen. The gentleman for whom she had kept house was Thomas Jefferson,[4] by whom she had two daughters. Jefferson being called to Washington to fill a government appointment, Currer was left behind, and thus she took herself to the business of washing, by which means she paid her master, Mr. Graves, and supported herself and two children. At the time of the decease of her master, Currer's daughters, Clotel and Althesa, were aged respectively sixteen and fourteen years, and both, like most of their own sex in America, were well grown. Currer early resolved to bring her daughters up as ladies, as she termed it, and therefore imposed little or no work upon them. As her daughters grew older, Currer had to pay a stipulated price for them; yet her notoriety as a laundress of the first class enabled her to put an extra price upon her charges, and thus she and her daughters lived in comparative luxury. To bring up Clotel and Althesa to attract attention, and especially at balls and parties, was the great aim of Currer. Although the term "negro ball" is applied to most of these gatherings, yet a majority of the attendants are often whites. Nearly all the negro parties in the cities and towns of the Southern States are made up of quadroon and mulatto girls, and white men. These are democratic gatherings, where gentlemen, shopkeepers, and their clerks, all appear upon terms of perfect equality. And there is a degree of gentility and decorum in these companies that is not surpassed by similar gatherings of white people in the Slave States. It was at one of these parties that Horatio Green, the son of a wealthy gentleman of Richmond, was first introduced to Clotel. The young man had just returned from college, and was in his twenty-second year. Clotel was sixteen, and was admitted by all to be the most beautiful girl, coloured or white, in the city. So attentive was the young man to the quadroon during the evening that it was noticed by all, and became a matter of general conversation; while Currer appeared delighted beyond measure at

4. During the presidential campaign of 1804, Jefferson (1743–1826), third president of the United States, was accused by the Federalist press of having fathered several children by Sally Hemings (1773–1835), a light-skinned enslaved woman.

her daughter's conquest. From that evening, young Green became the favourite visitor at Currer's house. He soon promised to purchase Clotel, as speedily as it could be effected, and make her mistress of her own dwelling; and Currer looked forward with pride to the time when she should see her daughter emancipated and free. It was a beautiful moonlight night in August, when all who reside in tropical climes are eagerly gasping for a breath of fresh air, that Horatio Green was seated in the small garden behind Currer's cottage, with the object of his affections by his side. And it was here that Horatio drew from his pocket the newspaper, wet from the press, and read the advertisement for the sale of the slaves to which we have alluded; Currer and her two daughters being of the number. At the close of the evening's visit, and as the young man was leaving, he said to the girl, "You shall soon be free and your own mistress."

As might have been expected, the day of sale brought an unusual large number together to compete for the property to be sold. Farmers who make a business of raising slaves for the market were there; slave-traders and speculators were also numerously represented; and in the midst of this throng was one who felt a deeper interest in the result of the sale than any other of the bystanders; this was young Green. True to his promise, he was there with a blank bank check in his pocket, awaiting with impatience to enter the list as a bidder for the beautiful slave. The less valuable slaves were first placed upon the auction block, one after another, and sold to the highest bidder. Husbands and wives were separated with a degree of indifference that is unknown in any other relation of life, except that of slavery. Brothers and sisters were torn from each other; and mothers saw their children leave them for the last time on this earth.

It was late in the day, when the greatest number of persons were thought to be present, that Currer and her daughters were brought forward to the place of sale. Currer was first ordered to ascend the auction stand, which she did with a trembling step. The slave mother was sold to a trader. Althesa, the youngest, and who was scarcely less beautiful than her sister, was sold to the same trader for one thousand dollars. Clotel was the last, and, as was expected, commanded a higher price than any that had been offered for sale that day. The appearance of Clotel on the auction block created a deep sensation amongst the crowd. There she stood, with a complexion as white as most of those who were waiting with a wish to become her purchasers; her features as finely defined as any of her sex of pure Anglo-Saxon; her long black wavy hair done up in the neatest manner; her form tall and graceful, and her whole appearance indicating one superior to her position. The auctioneer commenced by saying, that "Miss Clotel had been reserved for the last, because she was the most valuable. How much, gentlemen? Real Albino, fit for a fancy girl for any one. She enjoys good health, and has a sweet temper. How much do you say?" "Five hundred dollars." "Only five hundred for such a girl as this? Gentlemen, she is worth a deal more than that sum; you certainly don't know the value of the article you are bidding upon. Here, gentlemen, I hold in my hand a paper certifying that she has a good moral character." "Seven hundred." "Ah, gentlemen, that is something like. This paper also states that she is very intelligent." "Eight hundred." "She is a devoted Christian, and perfectly trustworthy." "Nine hundred." "Nine fifty." "Ten." "Eleven." "Twelve hundred." Here the sale came to a dead stand. The auctioneer stopped, looked around, and began in a rough manner to relate some anecdotes relative to the sale of slaves, which, he said, had come under his own observation. At this juncture the scene was indeed strange. Laughing, joking, swearing, smoking, spitting, and talking kept up a continual hum and noise amongst the crowd; while the slave-girl stood with tears in her eyes, at one time looking towards her mother and sister, and at another towards the young man whom she hoped would become her purchaser. "The chastity of this girl is pure; she has never been from under her mother's care; she is a virtuous creature." "Thirteen." "Fourteen." "Fifteen." "Fifteen hundred dollars," cried the auctioneer, and the maiden was struck for that sum. This was a Southern auction, at which the bones, muscles, sinews, blood, and nerves of a young lady of sixteen were sold for five hundred dollars; her moral character for two hundred; her improved intellect for one hundred; her Christianity for three hundred; and her chastity and virtue for four hundred dollars more. And this, too, in a city thronged with churches, whose tall spires look like so many signals pointing to heaven, and whose ministers preach that slavery is a God-ordained institution!

What words can tell the inhumanity, the atrocity, and the immorality of that doctrine which, from exalted office, commends such a crime to the favour of enlightened and Christian people? What indignation from all the world is not due to the government and people who put forth all their strength and power to keep in existence such an institution? Nature abhors it; the age repels it; and Christianity needs all her meekness to forgive it.

Clotel was sold for fifteen hundred dollars, but her purchaser was Horatio Green. Thus closed a negro sale, at which two daughters of Thomas Jefferson, the writer of the Declaration of American Independence, and one of the presidents of the great republic, were disposed of to the highest bidder!

O God! my every heart-string cries,
Dost thou these scenes behold
In this our boasted Christian land,
And must the truth be told?

Blush, Christian, blush! for e'en the dark,
Untutored heathen see
Thy inconsistency; and, lo!
They scorn thy God, and thee![5]

Chapter II. Going to the South

My country, shall thy honoured name,
Be as a bye-word through the world?
Rouse! for, as if to blast thy fame,
This keen reproach is at thee hurled;
The banner that above thee waves,
Is floating o'er three million slaves.[6]

Dick Walker, the slave speculator, who had purchased Currer and Althesa, put them in prison until his gang was made up, and then, with his forty slaves, started for the New Orleans market. As many of the slaves had been brought up in Richmond, and had relations residing there, the slave trader determined to leave the city early in the morning, so as not to witness any of those scenes so common where slaves are separated from their relatives and friends, when about departing for the Southern market. This plan was

5. Final quatrains of "The Slave Auction – A Fact."
6. Robert C. Waterston, "Freedom's Banner" in *Anti-Slavery Melodies* (1843), ed. Jairus Lincoln.

successful, for not even Clotel, who had been every day at the prison to see her mother and sister, knew of their departure. A march of eight days through the interior of the state, and they arrived on the banks of the Ohio river, where they were all put on board a steamer, and then speedily sailed for the place of their destination.

Walker had already advertised in the New Orleans papers, that he would be there at a stated time with "a prime lot of able-bodied slaves ready for field service; together with a few extra ones, between the ages of fifteen and twenty-five." But, like most who make a business of buying and selling slaves for gain, he often bought some who were far advanced in years, and would always try to sell them for five or ten years younger than they actually were. Few persons can arrive at anything like the age of a negro, by mere observation, unless they are well acquainted with the race. Therefore the slave-trader very frequently carried out this deception with perfect impunity. After the steamer had left the wharf, and was fairly on the bosom of the Father of Waters,[7] Walker called his servant Pompey to him, and instructed him as to "getting the negroes ready for market." Amongst the forty negroes were several whose appearance indicated that they had seen some years, and had gone through some services. Their grey hair and whiskers at once pronounced them to be above the ages set down in the trader's advertisement. Pompey had long been with the trader, and knew his business; and if he did not take delight in discharging his duty, he did it with a degree of alacrity, so that he might receive the approbation of his master. "Pomp," as Walker usually called him, was of real negro blood, and would often say, when alluding to himself, "Dis nigger is no countefit; he is de genewine artekil." Pompey was of low stature, round face, and, like most of his race, had a set of teeth, which for whiteness and beauty could not be surpassed; his eyes large, lips thick, and hair short and woolly. Pompey had been with Walker so long, and had seen so much of the buying and selling of slaves, that he appeared perfectly indifferent to the heartrending scenes which daily occurred in his presence. It was on the second day of the steamer's voyage that Pompey selected five of the old slaves, took them into a room by themselves, and commenced preparing them for the market. "Well," said Pompey, addressing himself to the company, "I is de gentman dat is to get you ready, so dat you will bring marser a good price in de Orleans market. How old is you?" addressing himself to a man who, from appearance, was not less than forty. "If I live to see next corn-planting time I will either be forty-five or fifty-five, I don't know which." "Dat may be," replied Pompey; "But now you is only thirty years old; dat is what marser says you is to be." "I know I is more den dat," responded the man. "I knows nothing about dat," said Pompey; "but when you get in de market, an anybody axe you how old you is, an you tell 'em forty-five, marser will tie you up an gib you de whip like smoke. But if you tell 'em dat you is only thirty, den he wont." "Well den, I guess I will only be thirty when dey axe me," replied the chattel.

"What your name?" inquired Pompey. "Geemes," answered the man. "Oh, Uncle Jim, is it?" "Yes." "Den you must have off dem dare whiskers of yours, and when you get to Orleans you must grease dat face an make it look shiney." This was all said by Pompey in a manner which clearly showed that he knew what he was about. "How old is you?" asked Pompey of a tall, strong-looking man. "I was twenty-nine last potato-digging time," said the man.

7. The Mississippi River.

"What's your name?" "My name is Tobias, but dey call me 'Toby.'" "Well, Toby, or Mr. Tobias, if dat will suit you better, you is now twenty-three years old, an no more. Dus you hear dat?" "Yes," responded Toby. Pompey gave each to understand how old he was to be when asked by persons who wished to purchase, and then reported to his master that the "old boys" were all right. At eight o'clock on the evening of the third day, the lights of another steamer were seen in the distance, and apparently coming up very fast. This was a signal for a general commotion on the Patriot, and everything indicated that a steamboat race was at hand. Nothing can exceed the excitement attendant upon a steamboat on the Mississippi river. By the time the boats had reached Memphis, they were side by side, and each exerting itself to keep the ascendancy in point of speed. The night was clear, the moon shining brightly, and the boats so near to each other that the passengers were calling out from one boat to the other. On board the Patriot, the firemen were using oil, lard, butter, and even bacon, with the wood, for the purpose of raising the steam to its highest pitch. The blaze, mingled with the black smoke, showed plainly that the other boat was burning more than wood. The two boats soon locked, so that the hands of the boats were passing from vessel to vessel, and the wildest excitement prevailed throughout amongst both passengers and crew. At this moment the engineer of the Patriot was seen to fasten down the safety-valve, so that no steam should escape. This was, indeed, a dangerous resort. A few of the boat hands who saw what had taken place, left that end of the boat for more secure quarters.

The Patriot stopped to take in passengers, and still no steam was permitted to escape. At the starting of the boat cold water was forced into the boilers by the machinery, and, as might have been expected, one of the boilers immediately exploded. One dense fog of steam filled every part of the vessel, while shrieks, groans, and cries were heard on every hand. The saloons and cabins soon had the appearance of a hospital. By this time the boat had landed, and the Columbia, the other boat, had come alongside to render assistance to the disabled steamer. The killed and scalded (nineteen in number) were put on shore, and the Patriot, taken in tow by the Columbia, was soon again on its way.

It was now twelve o'clock at night, and instead of the passengers being asleep the majority were gambling in the saloons. Thousands of dollars change hands during a passage from Louisville or St. Louis to New Orleans on a Mississippi steamer, and many men, and even ladies, are completely ruined. "Go call my boy, steward," said Mr. Smith, as he took his cards one by one from the table. In a few moments a fine looking, bright-eyed mulatto boy, apparently about fifteen years of age, was standing by his master's side at the table. "I will see you, and five hundred dollars better," said Smith, as his servant Jerry approached the table. "What price do you set on that boy?" asked Johnson, as he took a roll of bills from his pocket. "He will bring a thousand dollars, any day, in the New Orleans market," replied Smith. "Then you bet the whole of the boy, do you?" "Yes." "I call you, then," said Johnson, at the same time spreading his cards out upon the table. "You have beat me," said Smith, as soon as he saw the cards. Jerry, who was standing on top of the table, with the bank notes and silver dollars round his feet, was now ordered to descend from the table. "You will not forget that you belong to me," said Johnson, as the young slave was stepping from the table to a chair. "No, sir," replied the chattel. "Now go back to your bed, and be up in time to-morrow morning to brush my clothes and clean my boots, do you hear?" "Yes, sir," responded Jerry, as he wiped the tears from his eyes.

Smith took from his pocket the bill of sale and handed it to Johnson; at the same time saying, "I claim the right of redeeming that boy, Mr. Johnson. My father gave him to me when I came of age, and I promised not to part with him." "Most certainly, sir, the boy shall be yours, whenever you hand me over a cool thousand," replied Johnson. The next morning, as the passengers were assembling in the breakfast saloons and upon the guards of the vessel, and the servants were seen running about waiting upon or looking for their masters, poor Jerry was entering his new master's state-room with his boots. "Who do you belong to?" said a gentleman to an old black man, who came along leading a fine dog that he had been feeding. "When I went to sleep last night, I belonged to Governor Lucas; but I understand dat he is bin gambling all night, so I don't know who owns me dis morning." Such is the uncertainty of a slave's position. He goes to bed at night the property of the man with whom he has lived for years, and gets up in the morning the slave of some one whom he has never seen before! To behold five or six tables in a steamboat's cabin, with half-a-dozen men playing at cards, and money, pistols, bowie-knives, etc. all in confusion on the tables, is what may be seen at almost any time on the Mississippi river.

On the fourth day, while at Natchez, taking in freight and passengers, Walker, who had been on shore to see some of his old customers, returned, accompanied by a tall, thin-faced man, dressed in black, with a white neckcloth, which immediately proclaimed him to be a clergyman. "I vant a good, trusty woman for house service," said the stranger, as they entered the cabin where Walker's slaves were kept. "Here she is, and no mistake," replied the trader. "Stand up, Currer, my gal; here's a gentleman who wishes to see if you will suit him." Althesa clung to her mother's side, as the latter rose from her seat. "She is a rare cook, a good washer, and will suit you to a T, I am sure." "If you buy me, I hope you will buy my daughter too," said the woman, in rather an excited manner. "I only want one for my own use and would not need another," said the man in black, as he and the trader left the room. Walker and the parson went into the saloon, talked over the matter, the bill of sale was made out, the money paid over, and the clergyman left, with the understanding that the woman should be delivered to him at his house. It seemed as if poor Althesa would have wept herself to death, for the first two days after her mother had been torn from her side by the hand of the ruthless trafficker in human flesh. On the arrival of the boat at Baton Rouge, an additional number of passengers were taken on board; and, amongst them, several persons who had been attending the races. Gambling and drinking were now the order of the day. Just as the ladies and gentlemen were assembling at the suppertable, the report of a pistol was heard in the direction of the Social Hall, which caused great uneasiness to the ladies, and took the gentlemen to that part of the cabin. However, nothing serious had occurred. A man at one of the tables where they were gambling had been seen attempting to conceal a card in his sleeve, and one of the party seized his pistol and fired; but fortunately the barrel of the pistol was knocked up, just as it was about to be discharged, and the ball passed through the upper deck, instead of the man's head, as intended. Order was soon restored; all went on well the remainder of the night, and the next day, at ten o'clock, the boat arrived at New Orleans, and the passengers went to the hotels and the slaves to the market!

Our eyes are yet on Afric's shores,
Her thousand wrongs we still deplore;

We see the grim slave trader there;
We hear his fettered victim's prayer;
And hasten to the sufferer's aid,
Forgetful of *our own "slave trade."*

The Ocean "Pirate's" fiend-like form
Shall sink beneath the vengeance-storm;
His heart of steel shall quake before
The battle-din and havoc roar:
The knave shall die, the Law hath said,
While it protects *our own "slave trade."*

What earthly eye presumes to scan
The wily Proteus[8]-heart of man?—
What potent hand will e'er unroll
The mantled treachery of his soul!—
O where is he who hath surveyed
The horrors of *our own "slave trade?"*

There is an eye that wakes in light,
There is a hand of peerless might;
Which, soon or late, shall yet assail
And rend dissimulation's veil:
Which *will* unfold the masquerade
Which justifies *our own "slave trade."*

* * *

Chapter IV. The Quadroon's Home

How sweetly on the hill-side sleeps
  The sunlight with its quickening rays!
The verdant trees that crown the steeps,
  Grow greener in its quivering blaze.[9]

About three miles from Richmond is a pleasant plain, with here and there a beautiful cottage surrounded by trees so as scarcely to be seen. Among them was one far retired from the public roads, and almost hidden among the trees. It was a perfect model of rural beauty. The piazzas[1] that surrounded it were covered with clematis and passion flower. The pride of China mixed its oriental looking foliage with the majestic magnolia, and the air was redolent with the fragrance of flowers, peeping out of every nook and nodding upon you with a most unexpected welcome. The tasteful hand of art had not learned to imitate the lavish beauty and harmonious disorder of nature, but they lived together in loving amity, and spoke in accordant tones. The gateway rose in a gothic arch, with graceful tracery in iron work, surmounted by a cross, round which fluttered and played the mountain fringe, that lightest and most fragile of vines. This cottage was hired by Horatio Green for Clotel, and the quadroon girl soon found herself in her new home.

The tenderness of Clotel's conscience, together with the care her mother had with her and the high value she placed upon virtue, required an outward

8. A Greek god of the sea who has the power to assume different shapes.
9. William H. Burleigh, "A Summer Morning in the Country," in *Voices of the True-Hearted* (1846).
1. Large covered porches.

marriage; though she well knew that a union with her proscribed race was unrecognised by law, and therefore the ceremony would give her no legal hold on Horatio's constancy. But her high poetic nature regarded reality rather than the semblance of things; and when he playfully asked how she could keep him if he wished to run away, she replied, "If the mutual love we have for each other, and the dictates of your own conscience do not cause you to remain my husband, and your affections fall from me, I would not, if I could, hold you by a single fetter." It was indeed a marriage sanctioned by heaven, although unrecognised on earth. There the young couple lived secluded from the world, and passed their time as happily as circumstances would permit. It was Clotel's wish that Horatio should purchase her mother and sister, but the young man pleaded that he was unable, owing to the fact that he had not come into possession of his share of property, yet he promised that when he did, he would seek them out and purchase them. Their first-born was named Mary, and her complexion was still lighter than her mother. Indeed she was not darker than other white children. As the child grew older, it more and more resembled its mother. The iris of her large dark eye had the melting mezzotinto,[2] which remains the last vestige of African ancestry, and gives that plaintive expression, so often observed, and so appropriate to that docile and injured race. Clotel was still happier after the birth of her dear child; for Horatio, as might have been expected, was often absent day and night with his friends in the city, and the edicts of society had built up a wall of separation between the quadroon and them. Happy as Clotel was in Horatio's love, and surrounded by an outward environment of beauty, so well adapted to her poetic spirit, she felt these incidents with inexpressible pain. For herself she cared but little; for she had found a sheltered home in Horatio's heart, which the world might ridicule, but had no power to profane. But when she looked at her beloved Mary, and reflected upon the unavoidable and dangerous position which the tyranny of society had awarded her, her soul was filled with anguish. The rare loveliness of the child increased daily, and was evidently ripening into most marvellous beauty. The father seemed to rejoice in it with unmingled pride; but in the deep tenderness of the mother's eye, there was an indwelling sadness that spoke of anxious thoughts and fearful foreboding. Clotel now urged Horatio to remove to France or England, where both her and her child would be free, and where colour was not a crime. This request excited but little opposition, and was so attractive to his imagination, that he might have overcome all intervening obstacles, had not "a change come over the spirit of his dreams."[3] He still loved Clotel; but he was now becoming engaged in political and other affairs which kept him oftener and longer from the young mother; and ambition to become a statesman was slowly gaining the ascendancy over him.

Among those on whom Horatio's political success most depended was a very popular and wealthy man, who had an only daughter. His visits to the house were at first purely of a political nature; but the young lady was pleasing, and he fancied he discovered in her a sort of timid preference for himself. This excited his vanity, and awakened thoughts of the great worldly advantages connected with a union. Reminiscences of his first love kept these vague ideas in check for several months; for with it was associated the

2. A delicate half-tint.
3. See Byron's "The Dream" (stanza 3, line 75): "A change came o'er the spirit of my dream."

idea of restraint. Moreover, Gertrude, though inferior in beauty, was yet a pretty contrast to her rival. Her light hair fell in silken ringlets down her shoulders, her blue eyes were gentle though inexpressive, and her healthy cheeks were like opening rosebuds. He had already become accustomed to the dangerous experiment of resisting his own inward convictions; and this new impulse to ambition, combined with the strong temptation of variety in love, met the ardent young man weakened in moral principle, and unfettered by laws of the land. The change wrought upon him was soon noticed by Clotel.

[Currer becomes a cook in the home of John Peck, a transplanted Connecticut clergyman turned slaveholder. The courtship of Peck's antislavery daughter, Georgiana, by Mr. Carlton, a freethinker, arouses much debate about abolition among the principal white characters. Meanwhile Horatio discards Clotel and Mary for marriage to a white woman. Although initially purchased by a New Orleans bank teller, Althesa wins the love of a white man, Henry Morton, who buys, frees, and marries her.]

Chapter XV. To-Day a Mistress, To-Morrow a Slave

I promised thee a sister tale
Of man's perfidious cruelty;
Come, then, and hear what cruel wrong
Befel the dark ladie.

—Coleridge[4]

Let us return for a moment to the home of Clotel. While she was passing lonely and dreary hours with none but her darling child, Horatio Green was trying to find relief in that insidious enemy of man, the intoxicating cup. Defeated in politics, forsaken in love by his wife, he seemed to have lost all principle of honour, and was ready to nerve himself up to any deed, no matter how unprincipled. Clotel's existence was now well known to Horatio's wife, and both her and her father demanded that the beautiful quadroon and her child should be sold and sent out of the state. To this proposition he at first turned a deaf ear; but when he saw that his wife was about to return to her father's roof, he consented to leave the matter in the hands of his father-in-law. The result was, that Clotel was immediately sold to the slave-trader, Walker, who, a few years previous, had taken her mother and sister to the far South. But, as if to make her husband drink of the cup of humiliation to its very dregs, Mrs. Green resolved to take his child under her own roof for a servant. Mary was, therefore, put to the meanest work that could be found, and although only ten years of age, she was often compelled to perform labour, which, under ordinary circumstances, would have been thought too hard for one much older. One condition of the sale of Clotel to Walker was, that she should be taken out of the state, which was accordingly done. Most quadroon women who are taken to the lower countries to be sold are either purchased by gentlemen for their own use, or sold for waiting-maids; and Clotel, like her sister, was fortunate enough to be bought for the latter purpose. The town of Vicksburgh stands on the left bank of the Mississippi, and is noted for the severity with which slaves are treated. It was here that Clotel was sold to Mr. James French, a merchant.

4. Samuel Taylor Coleridge's "Introduction to the Tale of the Dark Ladie" (1799).

Mrs. French was severe in the extreme to her servants. Well dressed, but scantily fed, and overworked were all who found a home with her. The quadroon had been in her new home but a short time ere she found that her situation was far different from what it was in Virginia. What social virtues are possible in a society of which injustice is the primary characteristic? in a society which is divided into two classes, masters and slaves? Every married woman in the far South looks upon her husband as unfaithful, and regards every quadroon servant as a rival. Clotel had been with her new mistress but a few days, when she was ordered to cut off her long hair. The negro, constitutionally, is fond of dress and outward appearance. He that has short, woolly hair, combs it and oils it to death. He that has long hair, would sooner have his teeth drawn than lose it. However painful it was to the quadroon, she was soon seen with her hair cut as short as any of the full-blooded negroes in the dwelling.

Even with her short hair, Clotel was handsome. Her life had been a secluded one, and though now nearly thirty years of age, she was still beautiful. At her short hair, the other servants laughed, "Miss Clo needn't strut round so big, she got short nappy har well as I," said Nell, with a broad grin that showed her teeth. "She tinks she white, when she come here wid dat long har of hers," replied Mill. "Yes," continued Nell; "missus make her take down her wool so she no put it up to-day."

The fairness of Clotel's complexion was regarded with envy as well by the other servants as by the mistress herself. This is one of the hard features of slavery. To-day the woman is mistress of her own cottage; to-morrow she is sold to one who aims to make her life as intolerable as possible. And be it remembered, that the house servant has the best situation which a slave can occupy. Some American writers have tried to make the world believe that the condition of the labouring classes of England is as bad as the slaves of the United States.

The English labourer may be oppressed, he may be cheated, defrauded, swindled, and even starved; but it is not slavery under which he groans. He cannot be sold; in point of law he is equal to the prime minister. "It is easy to captivate the unthinking and the prejudiced, by eloquent declamation about the oppression of English operatives being worse than that of American slaves, and by exaggerating the wrongs on one side and hiding them on the other. But all informed and reflecting minds, knowing that bad as are the social evils of England, those of Slavery are immeasurably worse." But the degradation and harsh treatment that Clotel experienced in her new home was nothing compared with the grief she underwent at being separated from her dear child. Taken from her without scarcely a moment's warning, she knew not what had become of her. The deep and heartfelt grief of Clotel was soon perceived by her owners, and fearing that her refusal to take food would cause her death, they resolved to sell her. Mr. French found no difficulty in getting a purchaser for the quadroon woman, for such are usually the most marketable kind of property. Clotel was sold at private sale to a young man for a housekeeper; but even he had missed his aim.

[On the death of Rev. Peck, Georgiana marries Carlton and establishes on their plantation "a system of gradual emancipation" that includes cash bonuses for superior work. Currer dies from yellow fever.]

Chapter XIX. Escape of Clotel

The fetters galled my weary soul—
A soul that seemed but thrown away:
I spurned the tyrant's base control,
Resolved at least the man to play.[5]

No country has produced so much heroism in so short a time, connected with escapes from peril and oppression, as has occurred in the United States among fugitive slaves, many of whom show great shrewdness in their endeavours to escape from this land of bondage. A slave was one day seen passing on the high road from a border town in the interior of the state of Virginia to the Ohio river. The man had neither hat upon his head or coat upon his back. He was driving before him a very nice fat pig, and appeared to all who saw him to be a labourer employed on an adjoining farm. "No negro is permitted to go at large in the Slave States without a written pass from his or her master, except on business in the neighbourhood." "Where do you live, my boy?" asked a white man of the slave, as he passed a white house with green blinds. "Jist up de road, sir," was the answer. "That's a fine pig." "Yes, sir, marser like dis choat[6] berry much." And the negro drove on as if he was in great haste. In this way he and the pig travelled more than fifty miles before they reached the Ohio river. Once at the river they crossed over; the pig was sold; and nine days after the runaway slave passed over the Niagara river,[7] and, for the first time in his life, breathed the air of freedom. A few weeks later, and, on the same road, two slaves were seen passing; one was on horseback, the other was walking before him with his arms tightly bound, and a long rope leading from the man on foot to the one on horseback. "Oh, ho, that's a runaway rascal, I suppose," said a farmer, who met them on the road. "Yes, sir, he bin runaway, and I got him fast. Marser will tan his jacket for him nicely when he gets him." "You are a trustworthy fellow, I imagine," continued the farmer. "Oh yes, sir; marser puts a heap of confidence in dis nigger." And the slaves travelled on. When the one on foot was fatigued they would change positions, the other being tied and driven on foot. This they called "ride and tie." After a journey of more than two hundred miles they reached the Ohio river, turned the horse loose, told him to go home, and proceeded on their way to Canada. However they were not to have it all their own way. There are men in the Free States, and especially in the states adjacent to the Slave States, who make their living by catching the runaway slave, and returning him for the reward that may be offered. As the two slaves above mentioned were travelling on towards the land of freedom, led by the North Star, they were set upon by four of these slave-catchers, and one of them unfortunately captured. The other escaped. The captured fugitive was put under the torture, and compelled to reveal the name of his owner and his place of residence. Filled with delight, the kidnappers started back with their victim. Overjoyed with the prospect of receiving a large reward, they gave themselves up on the third night to pleasure. They put up at an inn. The negro was chained to the bed-post, in the same room with his captors. At dead of night, when all was still, the slave arose from the floor upon which he had been lying, looked around, and saw that the white men were fast asleep. The brandy punch had done its work. With palpitating heart and trembling

5. Elizur Wright, Jr., "The Fugitive Slave to the Christian" in *The Liberty Minstrel*.
6. Or shoat, a young hog.
7. A river that flows along the New York-Canada border.

limbs he viewed his position. The door was fast, but the warm weather had compelled them to leave the window open. If he could but get his chains off, he might escape through the window to the piazza, and reach the ground by one of the posts that supported the piazza. The sleeper's clothes hung upon chairs by the bedside; the slave thought of the padlock key, examined the pockets and found it. The chains were soon off, and the negro stealthily making his way to the window: he stopped and said to himself, "These men are villains, they are enemies to all who like me are trying to be free. Then why not I teach them a lesson?" He then undressed himself, took the clothes of one of the men, dressed himself in them, and escaped through the window, and, a moment more, he was on the high road to Canada. Fifteen days later, and the writer of this gave him a passage across Lake Erie, and saw him safe in her Britannic Majesty's dominions.

We have seen Clotel sold to Mr. French in Vicksburgh, her hair cut short, and everything done to make her realise her position as a servant. Then we have seen her re-sold, because her owners feared she would die through grief. As yet her new purchaser treated her with respectful gentleness, and sought to win her favour by flattery and presents, knowing that whatever he gave her he could take back again. But she dreaded every moment lest the scene should change, and trembled at the sound of every footfall. At every interview with her new master Clotel stoutly maintained that she had left a husband in Virginia, and would never think of taking another. The gold watch and chain, and other glittering presents which he purchased for her, were all laid aside by the quadroon, as if they were of no value to her. In the same house with her was another servant, a man, who had from time to time hired himself from his master. William was his name. He could feel for Clotel, for he, like her, had been separated from near and dear relatives, and often tried to console the poor woman. One day the quadroon observed to him that her hair was growing out again. "Yes," replied William, "you look a good deal like a man with your short hair." "Oh," rejoined she, "I have often been told that I would make a better looking man than a woman. If I had the money," continued she, "I would bid farewell to this place." In a moment more she feared that she had said too much, and smilingly remarked, "I am always talking nonsense." William was a tall, full-bodied negro, whose very countenance beamed with intelligence. Being a mechanic, he had, by his own industry, made more than what he paid his owner; this he laid aside, with the hope that some day he might get enough to purchase his freedom. He had in his chest one hundred and fifty dollars. His was a heart that felt for others, and he had again and again wiped the tears from his eyes as he heard the story of Clotel as related by herself. "If she can get free with a little money, why not give her what I have?" thought he, and then he resolved to do it. An hour after, he came into the quadroon's room, and laid the money in her lap, and said, "There, Miss Clotel, you said if you had the means you would leave this place; there is money enough to take you to England, where you will be free. You are much fairer than many of the white women of the South, and can easily pass for a free white lady." At first Clotel feared that it was a plan by which the negro wished to try her fidelity to her owner; but she was soon convinced by his earnest manner, and the deep feeling with which he spoke, that he was honest. "I will take the money only on one condition," said she; "and that is, that I effect your escape as well as my own." "How can that be done?" he inquired. "I will assume the disguise of a gentleman and you that of a servant, and we will take passage on a steamboat and go to Cincinnati, and thence to Canada."[8] Here William put in several objections to the plan. He feared detection, and he well knew that, when a slave is once caught when attempting to escape, if returned is sure to be worse treated than before. However, Clotel satisfied him that the plan could be carried out if he would only play his part.

The resolution was taken, the clothes for her disguise procured, and before night everything was in readiness for their departure. That night Mr. Cooper, their master, was to attend a party, and this was their opportunity. William went to the wharf to look out for a boat, and had scarcely reached the landing ere he heard the puffing of a steamer. He returned and reported the fact. Clotel had already packed her trunk, and had only to dress and all was ready. In less than an hour they were on board the boat. Under the assumed name of "Mr. Johnson," Clotel went to the clerk's office and took a private state room for herself, and paid her own and servant's fare. Besides being attired in a neat suit of black, she had a white silk handkerchief tied round her chin, as if she was an invalid. A pair of green glasses covered her eyes; and fearing that she would be talked to too much and thus render her liable to be detected, she assumed to be very ill. On the other hand, William was playing his part well in the servants' hall; he was talking loudly of his master's wealth. Nothing appeared as good on the boat as in his master's fine mansion. "I don't like dees steamboats no how," said William; "I hope when marser goes on a journey agin he will take de carriage and de hosses." Mr. Johnson (for such was the name by which Clotel now went) remained in his room, to avoid, as far as possible, conversation with others. After a passage of seven days they arrived at Louisville, and put up at Gough's Hotel. Here they had to await the departure of another boat for the North. They were now in their most critical position. They were still in a slave state, and John C. Calhoun,[9] a distinguished slave-owner, was a guest at this hotel. They feared, also, that trouble would attend their attempt to leave this place for the North, as all persons taking negroes with them have to give bail that such negroes are not runaway slaves. The law upon this point is very stringent: all steamboats and other public conveyances are liable to a fine for every slave that escapes by them, besides paying the full value for the slave. After a delay of four hours, Mr. Johnson and servant took passage on the steamer Rodolph, for Pittsburgh. It is usual, before the departure of the boats, for an officer to examine every part of the vessel to see that no slave secretes himself on board. "Where are you going?" asked the officer of William, as he was doing his duty on this occasion. "I am going with marser," was the quick reply. "Who is your master?" "Mr. Johnson, sir, a gentleman in the cabin." "You must take him to the office and satisfy that captain that all is right, or you can't go on this boat." William informed his master what the officer had said. The boat was on the eve of going, and no time could be lost, yet they knew not what to do. At last they went to the office, and Mr. Johnson, addressing the captain, said, "I am informed that my boy can't go with me unless I give security that he belongs to me." "Yes," replied the captain, "that is the law." "A very strange law indeed," rejoined Mr. Johnson, "that one can't take his property with him." After a conversation of some minutes, and a plea on the part of Johnson that he did not wish to be delayed owing to his illness, they were permitted to take their passage without farther trouble,

8. The escape of Clotel and William is based on the actual escape of Ellen and William Craft from Georgia in 1848.

9. U.S. senator from South Carolina and a leading proponent of states' rights (1782–1850).

and the boat was soon on its way up the river. The fugitives had now passed the Rubicon,[1] and the next place at which they would land would be in a Free State. Clotel called William to her room, and said to him, "We are now free, you can go on your way to Canada, and I shall go to Virginia in search of my daughter." The announcement that she was going to risk her liberty in a Slave State was unwelcome news to William. With all the eloquence he could command, he tried to persuade Clotel that she could not escape detection, and was only throwing her freedom away. But she had counted the cost, and made up her mind for the worst. In return for the money he had furnished, she had secured for him his liberty, and their engagement was at an end.

After a quick passage the fugitives arrived at Cincinnati, and there separated. William proceeded on his way to Canada, and Clotel again resumed her own apparel, and prepared to start in search of her child. As might have been expected, the escape of those two valuable slaves created no little sensation in Vicksburgh. Advertisements and messages were sent in every direction in which the fugitives were thought to have gone. It was soon, however, known that they had left the town as master and servant; and many were the communications which appeared in the newspapers, in which the writers thought, or pretended, that they had seen the slaves in their disguise. One was to the effect that they had gone off in a chaise; one as master, and the other as servant. But the most probable was an account given by a correspondent of one of the Southern newspapers, who happened to be a passenger in the same steamer in which the slaves escaped, and which we here give:—

> One bright starlight night, in the month of December last, I found myself in the cabin of the steamer Rodolph, then lying in the port of Vicksburgh, and bound to Louisville. I had gone early on board, in order to select a good berth, and having got tired of reading the papers, amused myself with watching the appearance of the passengers as they dropped in, one after another, and I being a believer in physiognomy,[2] formed my own opinion of their characters.
>
> The second bell rang, and as I yawningly returned my watch to my pocket, my attention was attracted by the appearance of a young man who entered the cabin supported by his servant, a strapping negro.
>
> The man was bundled up in a capacious overcoat; his face was bandaged with a white handkerchief, and its expression entirely hid by a pair of enormous spectacles.
>
> There was something so mysterious and unusual about the young man as he sat restless in the corner, that curiosity led me to observe him more closely.
>
> He appeared anxious to avoid notice, and before the steamer had fairly left the wharf, requested, in a low, womanly voice, to be shown his berth, as he was an invalid, and must retire early: his name he gave as Mr. Johnson. His servant was called, and he was put quietly to bed. I paced the deck until Tybee light[3] grew dim in the distance, and then went to my berth.
>
> I awoke in the morning with the sun shining in my face; we were then just passing St. Helena.[4] It was a mild beautiful morning, and most of the passengers were on deck, enjoying the freshness of the air, and stimulating

1. Figuratively, the point of no turning back.
2. The practice of judging personality and mental ability by observing facial characteristics.
3. Light from the Tybee Lighthouse on the Georgia coast.
4. One of the sea islands off the South Carolina coast.

their appetites for breakfast. Mr. Johnson soon made his appearance, arrayed as on the night before, and took his seat quietly upon the guard of the boat.

From the better opportunity afforded by daylight, I found that he was a slight built, apparently handsome young man, with black hair and eyes, and of a darkness of complexion that betokened Spanish extraction. Any notice from others seemed painful to him; so to satisfy my curiosity, I questioned his servant, who was standing near, and gained the following information.

His master was an invalid—he had suffered for a long time under a complication of diseases, that had baffled the skill of the best physicians in Mississippi, he was now suffering principally with the "rheumatism," and he was scarcely able to walk or help himself in any way. He came from Vicksburgh, and was now on his way to Philadelphia, at which place resided his uncle, a celebrated physician, and through whose means he hoped to be restored to perfect health.

This information, communicated in a bold, off-hand manner, enlisted my sympathies for the sufferer, although it occurred to me that he walked rather too gingerly for a person afflicted with so many ailments.

After thanking Clotel for the great service she had done him in bringing him out of slavery, William bade her farewell. The prejudice that exists in the Free States against coloured persons, on account of their colour, is attributable solely to the influence of slavery, and is but another form of slavery itself. And even the slave who escapes from the Southern plantations, is surprised when he reaches the North, at the amount and withering influence of this prejudice. William applied at the railway station for a ticket for the train going to Sandusky,[5] and was told that if he went by that train he would have to ride in the luggage-van. "Why?" asked the astonished negro. "We don't send a Jim Crow carriage but once a day, and that went this morning." The "Jim Crow" carriage is the one in which the blacks have to ride. Slavery is a school in which its victims learn much shrewdness, and William had been an apt scholar. Without asking any more questions, the negro took his seat in one of the first-class carriages. He was soon seen and ordered out. Afraid to remain in the town longer, he resolved to go by that train; and consequently seated himself on a goods' box in the luggage-van. The train started at its proper time, and all went on well. Just before arriving at the end of the journey, the conductor called on William for his ticket. "I have none," was the reply. "Well, then, you can pay your fare to me," said the officer. "How much is it?" asked the black man. "Two dollars." "What do you charge those in the passenger-carriage?" "Two dollars." "And do you charge me the same as you do those who ride in the best carriages?" asked the negro. "Yes," was the answer. "I shan't pay it," returned the man. "You black scamp, do you think you can ride on this road without paying your fare?" "No, I don't want to ride for nothing; I only want to pay what's right." "Well, launch out two dollars, and that's right." "No, I shan't; I will pay what I ought, and won't pay any more." "Come, come, nigger, your fare and be done with it," said the conductor, in a manner that is never used except by Americans to blacks. "I won't pay you two dollars, and that enough," said William. "Well, as you have come all the way in the luggage-van, pay me a dollar and a half and you may

5. A town in Ohio on Lake Erie, often the destination of fugitives from slavery bound for Canada.

go." "I shan't do any such thing." "Don't you mean to pay for riding?" "Yes, but I won't pay a dollar and a half for riding up here in the freight-van. If you had let me come in the carriage where others ride, I would have paid you two dollars." "Where were you raised? You seem to think yourself as good as white folks." "I want nothing more than my rights." "Well, give me a dollar, and I will let you off." "No, sir, I shan't do it." "What do you mean to do then—don't you wish to pay anything?" "Yes, sir, I want to pay you the full price." "What do you mean by full price?" "What do you charge per hundred-weight for goods?" inquired the negro with a degree of gravity that would have astonished Diogenes[6] himself. "A quarter of a dollar per hundred," answered the conductor. "I weigh just one hundred and fifty pounds," returned William, "and will pay you three eighths of a dollar." "Do you expect that you will pay only thirty-seven cents for your ride?" "This, sir, is your own price. I came in a luggage-van, and I'll pay for luggage." After a vain effort to get the negro to pay more, the conductor took the thirty-seven cents, and noted in his cash-book, "Received for one hundred and fifty pounds of luggage, thirty-seven cents." This, reader, is no fiction; it actually occurred in the railway above described.

Thomas Corwin,[7] a member of the American Congress, is one of the blackest white men in the United States. He was once on his way to Congress, and took passage in one of the Ohio river steamers. As he came just at the dinner hour, he immediately went into the dining saloon, and took his seat at the table. A gentleman with his whole party of five ladies at once left the table. "Where is the captain," cried the man in an angry tone. The captain soon appeared, and it was sometime before he could satisfy the old gent. that Governor Corwin was not a nigger. The newspapers often have notices of mistakes made by innkeepers and others who undertake to accommodate the public, one of which we give below.

On the 6th inst., the Hon. Daniel Webster and family entered Edgartown,[8] on a visit for health and recreation. Arriving at the hotel, without alighting from the coach, the landlord was sent for to see if suitable accommodation could be had. That dignitary appearing, and surveying Mr. Webster, while the hon. senator addressed him, seemed woefully to mistake the dark features of the traveller as he sat back in the corner of the carriage, and to suppose him a *coloured man*, particularly as there were two coloured servants of Mr. W. outside. So he promptly declared that there was no room for him and his family, and he could not be accommodated there—at the same time suggesting that he might perhaps find accommodation at some of the huts "up back," to which he pointed. So deeply did the prejudice of looks possess him, that he appeared not to notice that the stranger introduced himself to him as Daniel Webster, or to be so ignorant as not to have heard of such a personage; and turning away, he expressed to the driver his astonishment that he should bring *black* people there for *him* to take in. It was not till he had been repeatedly assured and made to understand that the said Daniel Webster was a real live senator of the United States, that he perceived his awkward mistake and the distinguished honour which he and his house were so near missing.

In most of the Free States, the coloured people are disfranchised on account of their colour. The following scene, which we take from a newspaper in the state of Ohio, will give some idea of the extent to which this prejudice is carried.

6. Greek philosopher (d. ca. 320 B.C.E.).
7. U.S. congressman and senator from Ohio (1794–1865).
8. On the island of Martha's Vineyard, Massachusetts. Webster (1782–1852), U.S. senator from Massachusetts and leader of the Whig Party.

> The whole of Thursday last was occupied by the Court of Common Pleas for this county in trying to find out whether one Thomas West was of the VOTING COLOUR, as some had very *constitutional doubts* as to whether his colour was orthodox, and whether his hair was of the official crisp! Was it not a dignified business? Four profound judges, four acute lawyers, twelve grave jurors, and I don't know how many venerable witnesses, making in all about thirty men, perhaps, all engaged in the profound, laborious, and illustrious business, of finding out whether a man who pays tax, works on the road, and is an industrious farmer, has been born according to the republican, Christian constitution of Ohio—so that he can vote! And they wisely, gravely, and "JUDGMATICALLY" decided that he should not vote! What wisdom—what research it must have required to evolve this truth! It was left for the Court of Common Pleas for Columbian county, Ohio, in the United States of North America, to find out what Solomon[9] never dreamed of—the courts of all civilised, heathen, or Jewish countries, never contemplated. Lest the wisdom of our courts should be circumvented by some such men as might be named, who are so near being born constitutionally that they might be taken for white by sight, I would suggest that our court be invested with SMELLING powers, and that if a man don't exhale the constitutional smell, he shall not vote! This would be an additional security to our liberties.

William found, after all, that liberty in the so-called Free States was more a name than a reality; that prejudice followed the coloured man into every place that he might enter. The temples erected for the worship of the living God are no exception. The finest Baptist church in the city of Boston has the following paragraph in the deed that conveys its seats to pewholders:[1]

> And it is a further condition of these presents, that if the owner or owners of said pew shall determine hereafter to sell the same, it shall first be offered, in writing, to the standing committee of said society for the time being, at such price as might otherwise be obtained for it; and the said committee shall have the right, for ten days after such offer, to purchase said pew for said society, at that price, first deducting therefrom all taxes and assessments on said pew then remaining unpaid. And if the said committee shall not so complete such purchase within said ten days, then the pew may be sold by the owner or owners thereof (after payment of all such arrears) to any one respectable *white person*, but upon the same conditions as are contained in this instrument; and immediate notice of such sale shall be given in writing, by the vendor, to the treasurer of said society.

Such are the conditions upon which the Rowe Street Baptist Church, Boston, disposes of its seats. The writer of this is able to put that whole congregation, minister and all, to flight, by merely putting his coloured face in that church. We once visited a church in New York that had a place set apart for the sons of Ham.[2] It was a dark, dismal looking place in one corner of the gallery, grated in front like a hen-coop, with a black border around it. It had two doors; over one was B.M.—black men; over the other B.W.—black women.

9. King of Israel, celebrated in the Bible for his wisdom (d. 922 B.C.E.).

1. Persons who rent or own a pew in a church.

2. Son of the biblical patriarch Noah, who was thought to be the progenitor of African peoples.

* * *

[Dying of consumption, Georgiana Carlton frees the enslaved people whom she had inherited. Disguised as a "Spanish or Italian gentleman," Clotel goes to Richmond to find her daughter. Althesa and her husband die in a yellow fever epidemic in New Orleans. Their two daughters are sold into slavery and soon die tragically. Clotel is apprehended in Richmond and conveyed to Washington, D.C., to be sold back into slavery. When her dramatic escape attempt is thwarted, she chooses to drown herself in the Potomac River, within sight of the White House. Clotel's daughter, Mary, ultimately marries the light-skinned George Green, a fugitive from slavery with whom she is providentially reunited in France after a ten-year separation.]

1853

HENRY HIGHLAND GARNET
1815–1882

Growing up enslaved in Maryland, Henry Highland Garnet was inspired by a family tradition that identified his grandfather as a tribal ruler in the legendary Mandingo Empire of West Africa. The example of that grandfather, as well as that of Garnet's father, George, who successfully engineered the escape of his entire family from slavery in 1825, gave young Henry a model of Black manhood based in African as well as African American styles of leadership. To this model he remained dedicated throughout his life. In New York City, where his family lived after leaving Maryland, Garnet received an unusually thorough preparation for the role he would play in the antislavery struggle. He was befriended by such influential African American activists as the Reverend Theodore S. Wright and the teachers of the New York African Free School. Garnet's classmates at the school included Alexander Crummell, who would become one of the leading Black intellectuals of the mid-nineteenth century, and Ira Aldridge, later to achieve international acclaim as a Shakespearean actor. Garnet studied at the Noyes Academy in Canaan, New Hampshire, before being driven out by bigoted whites, and at the Oneida Institute in Whitesboro, New York, where he decided on a career as a Presbyterian minister. Licensed to preach in 1842, the Reverend Mr. Garnet assumed the pastorate of the predominately white Liberty Street Presbyterian church of Troy, New York. Soon he became famous as one of Black America's most eloquent and controversial platform orators and radical political leaders.

In 1843 at the National Negro Convention in Buffalo, New York, Garnet delivered the speech that defined him as an unabashed revolutionary in support of the African American struggle for liberation in the United States. Garnet's "Address to the Slaves of the United States of America" began by taking stock of what the antislavery moment had accomplished by the 1840s. Neither appeals to Christian humanitarianism nor efforts to shame the U.S. government into fulfilling the liberty and equality rhetoric of its Declaration of Independence had weakened slavery's hold on the new nation. The only way to defeat slavery, Garnet concluded, was direct action on the part of the enslaved themselves. He urged mass noncompliance through a general strike. If violent retaliation by their enslavers ensued, Garnet urged the enslaved to adopt the battle cry of the American revolutionaries, "LIBERTY OR DEATH." Garnet's justification of violent resistance in his "Call to Rebellion" speech, as the address has come to be known, sparked a strong denunciation from Frederick Douglass, at that time an adherent of the nonviolent "moral suasion" school of abolitionism. The speech fell only a single vote short of being approved as an official resolution of the 1843 convention. But in 1847, the National Negro Convention endorsed Garnet's militance, as would Douglass by the mid-1850s. With the financial aid of abolitionist John Brown, Garnet in 1848 combined his hitherto unpublished "Call to Rebellion" speech with *David Walker's Appeal* to form a pamphlet uniquely prophetic of the armed conflict over slavery to which the United States was fatefully committed.

During the Civil War, Garnet was among the first to urge President Lincoln to authorize the enlistment of African American troops. After accepting a call in 1864 to lead the storied Fifteenth Street Presbyterian Church of Washington, D.C., the Black minister became the first man of color to deliver a sermon to the U.S. House of Representatives. He called on the legislators to "emancipate, enfranchise, and educate" not only African Americans but "every American citizen." Despite his advocacy of Black emigration to Africa and the Caribbean from the late 1850s until his death, Garnet never ceased to agitate for reform at home on both the social and the political fronts. His witness for justice in the economic arena led him to oppose post–Civil War land monopolies held by southern whites, which Garnet felt would perpetuate free African Americans in second-class citizenship. In 1881 Garnet's long devotion to pan-Africanism reached its culmination in his appointment as U.S. minister to Liberia. Hoping to help build a Black nation, Garnet sailed to Monrovia but died after only three months in office. He was buried in a Liberian cemetery overlooking the Atlantic Ocean.

An Address to the Slaves of the United States of America

Brethren and Fellow Citizens: Your brethren of the North, East, and West have been accustomed to meet together in National Conventions,[1] to sympathize with each other, and to weep over your unhappy condition. In these meetings we have addressed all classes of the free, but we have never, until this time, sent a word of consolation and advice to you. We have been contented in sitting still and mourning over your sorrows, earnestly hoping that before this day your sacred liberties would have been restored. But, we have hoped in vain. Years have rolled on, and tens of thousands have been borne on streams of blood and tears to the shores of eternity. While you have been oppressed, we have also been partakers with you; nor can we be free while you are enslaved. We, therefore, write to you as being bound with you.

Many of you are bound to us, not only by the ties of a common humanity, but we are connected by the more tender relations of parents, wives, husbands, and sisters, and friends. As such we most affectionately address you.

Slavery has fixed a deep gulf between you and us, and while it shuts out from you the relief and consolation which your friends would willingly render, it afflicts and persecutes you with a fierceness which we might not expect to see in the fiends of hell. But still the Almighty Father of mercies has left to us a glimmering ray of hope, which shines out like a lone star in a cloudy sky. Mankind are becoming wiser, and better—the oppressor's power is fading, and you, every day, are becoming better informed, and more numerous. Your grievances, brethren, are many. We shall not attempt, in this short address, to present to

1. In 1830 African Americans began to hold national conventions to consider social, economic, and political issues and to promote measures for the advancement of African-descended people in the United States.

the world all the dark catalogue of the nation's sins, which have been committed upon an innocent people. Nor is it indeed necessary, for you feel them from day to day, and all the civilized world looks upon them with amazement.

Two hundred and twenty-seven years ago the first of our injured race were brought to the shores of America. They came not with glad spirits to select their homes in the New World. They came not with their own consent, to find an unmolested enjoyment of the blessings of this fruitful soil. The first dealings they had with men calling themselves Christians exhibited to them the worst features of corrupt and sordid hearts: and convinced them that no cruelty is too great, no villainy and no robbery too abhorrent for even enlightened men to perform, when influenced by avarice and lust. Neither did they come flying upon the wings of liberty to a land of freedom. But they came with broken hearts, from their beloved native land, and were doomed to unrequited toil and deep degradation. Nor did the evil of their bondage end at their emancipation by death. Succeeding generations inherited their chains, and millions have come from eternity into time, and have returned again to the world of spirits, cursed and ruined by American slavery.

The propagators of the system, or their immediate successors, very soon discovered its growing evil, and its tremendous wickedness, and secret promises were made to destroy it. The gross inconsistency of a people holding slaves, who had themselves "ferried o'er the wave" for freedom's sake, was too apparent to be entirely overlooked. The voice of Freedom cried, "Emancipate your slaves." Humanity supplicated with tears for the deliverance of the children of Africa. Wisdom urged her solemn plea. The bleeding captive plead his innocence, and pointed to Christianity who stood weeping at the cross. Jehovah frowned upon the nefarious institution, and thunderbolts, red with vengeance, struggled to leap forth to blast the guilty wretches who maintained it. But all was vain. Slavery had stretched its dark wings of death over the land, the Church stood silently by—the priests prophesied falsely, and the people loved to have it so. Its throne is established, and now it reigns triumphant.

Nearly three millions of your fellow-citizens are prohibited by law and public opinion (which in this country is stronger than law) from reading the Book of Life.[2] Your intellect has been destroyed as much as possible, and every ray of light they have attempted to shut out from your minds. The oppressors themselves have become involved in the ruin. They have become weak, sensual, and rapacious—they have cursed you—they have cursed themselves—they have cursed the earth which they have trod.

The colonies threw the blame upon England. They said that the mother country entailed the evil upon them, and they would rid themselves of it if they could. The world thought they were sincere, and the philanthropic pitied them. But time soon tested their sincerity. In a few years the colonists grew strong, and severed themselves from the British Government. Their independence was declared, and they took their station among the sovereign powers of the earth. The declaration was a glorious document. Sages admired it, and the patriotic of every nation reverenced the God-like sentiments which it contained. When the power of Government returned to their hands, did they emancipate the slaves? No; they rather added new links to our chains. Were they ignorant of the principles of Liberty? Certainly they were not. The sentiments of their revolutionary orators fell in burning eloquence upon their hearts, and with one voice they cried, LIBERTY OR DEATH. Oh, what a sentence

2. The Bible.

was that! It ran from soul to soul like electric fire, and nerved the arms of thousands to fight in the holy cause of Freedom. Among the diversity of opinions that are entertained in regard to physical resistance, there are but a few found to gainsay the stern declaration. We are among those who do not.

SLAVERY! How much misery is comprehended in that single word. What mind is there that does not shrink from its direful effects? Unless the image of God be obliterated from the soul, all men cherish the love of liberty. The nice discerning political economist does not regard the sacred right more than the untutored African who roams in the wilds of Congo. Nor has the one more right to the full enjoyment of his freedom than the other. In every man's mind the good seeds of liberty are planted, and he who brings his fellow down so low, as to make him contented with a condition of slavery, commits the highest crime against God and man. Brethren, your oppressors aim to do this. They endeavor to make you as much like brutes as possible. When they have blinded the eyes of your mind—when they have embittered the sweet waters of life—when they have shut out the light which shines from the word of God—then, and not till then, has American slavery done its perfect work.

TO SUCH DEGRADATION IT IS SINFUL IN THE EXTREME FOR YOU TO MAKE VOLUNTARY SUBMISSION. The divine commandments you are in duty bound to reverence and obey. If you do not obey them, you will surely meet with the displeasure of the Almighty. He requires you to love Him supremely, and your neighbor as yourself—to keep the Sabbath day holy—to search the Scriptures—and bring up your children with respect for His laws, and to worship no other God but Him. But slavery sets all these at nought, and hurls defiance in the face of Jehovah. The forlorn condition in which you are placed does not destroy your obligation to God. You are not certain of heaven, because you allow yourselves to remain in a state of slavery, where you cannot obey the commandments of the Sovereign of the universe. If the ignorance of slavery is a passport to heaven, then it is a blessing, and no curse, and you should rather desire its perpetuity than its abolition. God will not receive slavery, nor ignorance, nor any other state of mind, for love and obedience to Him. Your condition does not absolve you from your moral obligation. The diabolical injustice by which your liberties are cloven[3] down, NEITHER GOD NOR ANGELS, OR JUST MEN, COMMAND YOU TO SUFFER FOR A SINGLE MOMENT. THEREFORE IT IS YOUR SOLEMN AND IMPERATIVE DUTY TO USE EVERY MEANS, BOTH MORAL, INTELLECTUAL, AND PHYSICAL, THAT PROMISES SUCCESS. If a band of heathen men should attempt to enslave a race of Christians, and to place their children under the influence of some false religion, surely Heaven would frown upon the men who would not resist such aggression, even to death. If, on the other hand, a band of Christians should attempt to enslave a race of heathen men, and to entail slavery upon them, and to keep them in heathenism in the midst of Christianity, the God of heaven would smile upon every effort which the injured might make to disenthral themselves.

Brethren, it is as wrong for your lordly oppressors to keep you in slavery as it was for the man thief to steal our ancestors from the coast of Africa. You should therefore now use the same manner of resistance as would have been just in our ancestors when the bloody foot-prints of the first remorseless soul-thief was placed upon the shores of our fatherland. The humblest peasant is as free in the sight of God as the proudest monarch that ever swayed a sceptre. Liberty is a spirit sent out from God, and like its great Author, is no respecter of persons.

3. Split or cut by a sharp blow.

Brethren, the time has come when you must act for yourselves. It is an old and true saying that, "if hereditary bondmen would be free, they must themselves strike the blow."[4] You can plead your own cause, and do the work of emancipation better than any others. The nations of the Old World are moving in the great cause of universal freedom, and some of them at least will, ere long, do you justice. The combined powers of Europe have placed their broad seal of disapprobation upon the African slave-trade. But in the slaveholding parts of the United States the trade is as brisk as ever. They buy and sell you as though you were brute beasts. The North has done much—her opinion of slavery in the abstract is known. But in regard to the South, we adopt the opinion of the *New York Evangelist*—"We have advanced so far, that the cause apparently waits for a more effectual door to be thrown open than has been yet." We are about to point you to that more effectual door. Look around you, and behold the bosoms of your loving wives heaving with untold agonies! Hear the cries of your poor children! Remember the stripes your fathers bore. Think of the torture and disgrace of your noble mothers. Think of your wretched sisters, loving virtue and purity, as they are driven into concubinage and are exposed to the unbridled lusts of incarnate devils. Think of the undying glory that hangs around the ancient name of Africa—and forget not that you are native-born American citizens, and as such you are justly entitled to all the rights that are granted to the freest. Think how many tears you have poured out upon the soil which you have cultivated with unrequited toil and enriched with your blood; and then go to your lordly enslavers and tell them plainly, that you *are determined to be free.* Appeal to their sense of justice, and tell them that they have no more right to oppress you than you have to enslave them. Entreat them to remove the grievous burdens which they have imposed upon you, and to remunerate you for your labor. Promise them renewed diligence in the cultivation of the soil, if they will render to you an equivalent for your services. Point them to the increase of happiness and prosperity in the British West Indies since the Act of Emancipation.[5] Tell them in language which they cannot misunderstand of the exceeding sinfulness of slavery, and of a future judgment, and of the righteous retributions of an indignant God. Inform them that all you desire is FREEDOM, and that nothing else will suffice. Do this, and forever after cease to toil for the heartless tyrants, who give you no other reward but stripes and abuse. If they then commence work of death, they, and not you, will be responsible for the consequences. You had far better all die—*die immediately,* than live slaves, and entail your wretchedness upon your posterity. If you would be free in this generation, here is your only hope. However much you and all of us may desire it, there is not much hope of redemption without the shedding of blood. If you must bleed, let it all come at once—rather *die freemen than live to be the slaves.* It is impossible, like the children of Israel, to make a grand exodus from the land of bondage. The Pharaohs are on both sides of the blood-red waters! You cannot move *en masse* to the dominions of the British Queen—nor can you pass through Florida and overrun Texas, and at last find peace in Mexico. The propagators of American slavery are spending their blood and treasure that they may plant the black flag in the heart of Mexico and riot in the halls of the Montezumas.[6] In language of the Reverend Robert Hall,[7] when addressing the volunteers of Bristol, who

4. See Byron's *Childe Harold's Pilgrimage* 2.76: "Hereditary bondsmen! Know ye not/ Who would be free themselves must strike the blow?"

5. Slavery was abolished in the British Empire in 1833.

6. Montezuma (1408?–1520) was Aztec emperor at the time of the Spanish conquest. A reference to proslavery imperialists anxious to seize Mexican territory for slavery.

7. English Baptist clergyman (1764–1831).

were rushing forth to repel the invasion of Napoleon, who threatened to lay waste the fair homes of England, "Religion is too much interested in your behalf not to shed over you her most gracious influences."

You will not be compelled to spend much time in order to become inured to hardships. From the first movement that you breathed the air of heaven, you have been accustomed to nothing else but hardships. The heroes of the American Revolution were never put upon harder fare than a peck of corn and few herrings per week. You have not become enervated by the luxuries of life. Your sternest energies have been beaten out upon the anvil of severe trial. Slavery has done this to make you subservient to its own purposes; but it has done more than this, it has prepared you for any emergency. If you receive good treatment, it is what you can hardly expect; if you meet with pain, sorrow, and even death, these are the common lot of the slaves.

Fellowmen! patient sufferers! behold your dearest rights crushed to the earth! See your sons murdered, and your wives, mothers and sisters doomed to prostitution. In the name of the merciful God, and by all that life is worth, let it no longer be a debatable question, whether it is better to choose *liberty* or *death*.

In 1822, Denmark Veazie,[8] of South Carolina, formed a plan for the liberation of his fellowmen. In the whole history of human efforts to overthrow slavery, a more complicated and tremendous plan was never formed. He was betrayed by the treachery of his own people, and died a martyr to freedom. Many a brave hero fell, but history, faithful to her high trust, will transcribe his name on the same monument with Moses, Hampden, Tell, Bruce and Wallace, Toussaint L'Ouverture, Lafayette, and Washington.[9] That tremendous movement shook the whole empire of slavery. The guilty soul-thieves were overwhelmed with fear. It is a matter of fact that at this time, and in consequence of the threatened revolution, the slave States talked strongly of emancipation. But they blew but one blast of the trumpet of freedom, and then laid it aside. As these men became quiet, the slaveholders ceased to talk about emancipation: and now behold your condition to-day! Angels sigh over it, and humanity has long since exhausted her tears in weeping on your account!

The patriotic Nathaniel Turner[1] followed Denmark Veazie. He was goaded to desperation by wrong and injustice. By despotism, his name has been recorded on the list of infamy, and future generations will remember him among the noble and brave.

Next arose the immortal Joseph Cinque,[2] the hero of the Amistad. He was a native African, and by the help of God he emancipated a whole shipload of his fellowmen on the high seas. And he now sings of liberty on the sunny hills of Africa and beneath his native palm-trees, where he hears the lion roar and feels himself as free as the king of the forest.

Next arose Madison Washington,[3] that bright star of freedom, and took his station in the constellation of true heroism. He was a slave on board the

8. Denmark Vesey (ca. 1767– 1822), a self-purchased formerly enslaved carpenter accused of and executed for plotting a Black coup d'état in Charleston.

9. George Washington (1732–1799), commander in chief of the army that won the North American colonies' revolution against Great Britain in 1781. Moses led the Hebrews out of Egyptian bondage in the 13th century B.C.E. John Hampden (1594–1643) fought against Charles I in the English Civil War. William Tell, legendary Swiss patriot in Switzerland's struggle against Austrian domination. Robert the Bruce, king of Scotland (1274–1329), and Sir William Wallace (1270–1305) led their country in wars of independence against England. Toussaint L'Ouverture (1743–1803) led the revolution that freed the Black population of Haiti from French rule in 1803. Marquis de Lafayette (1757–1834) volunteered his services to the American revolutionaries and became a major general in the Revolutionary Army.

1. Leader of a rebellion of enslaved people in Southampton, Virginia, in 1831.

2. Leader of a successful mutiny of African captives aboard the Spanish schooner *Amistad* in 1839.

3. Leader of a successful mutiny of enslaved people aboard the U.S. brig *Creole* in 1841.

brig *Creole,* of Richmond, bound to New Orleans, that great slave mart, with a hundred and four others. Nineteen struck for liberty or death. But one life was taken, and the whole were emancipated, and the vessel was carried into Nassau, New Providence.

Noble men! Those who have fallen in freedom's conflict, their memories will be cherished by the true-hearted and the God-fearing in all future generations; those who are living, their names are surrounded by a halo of glory.

Brethren, arise, arise! Strike for your lives and liberties. Now is the day and the hour. Let every slave throughout the land do this, and the days of slavery are numbered. You cannot be more oppressed than you have been—you cannot suffer greater cruelties than you have already. *Rather die freemen than live to be slaves.* Remember that you are FOUR MILLIONS!

It is in your power so to torment the God-cursed slaveholders that they will be glad to let you go free. If the scale was turned, and black men were the masters and white men the slaves, every destructive agent and element would be employed to lay the oppressor low. Danger and death would hang over their heads day and night. Yes, the tyrants would meet with plagues more terrible than those of Pharaoh. But you are a patient people. You act as though you were made for the special use of these devils. You act as though your daughters were born to pamper the lusts of your masters and overseers. And worse than all, you tamely submit while your lords tear your wives from your embraces and defile them before your eyes. In the name of God, we ask, are you men? Where is the blood of your fathers? Has it all run out of your veins? Awake, awake; millions of voices are calling you! Your dead fathers speak to you from their graves. Heaven, as with a voice of thunder, calls on you to arise from the dust.

Let your motto be resistance! *resistance!* RESISTANCE! No oppressed people have ever secured their liberty without resistance. What kind of resistance you had better make you must decide by the circumstances that surround you, and according to the suggestion of expediency. Brethren, adieu! Trust in the living God. Labor for the peace of the human race, and remember that you are FOUR MILLIONS!

1843 1848

VICTOR SÉJOUR
1817–1874

Victor Séjour's chilling short story "Le Mulâtre" (The mulatto) is the earliest known work of fiction authored by an identifiable African American. "Theresa, A Haytien Tale" (1828), which also appears in this anthology, antedates Séjour's story, but while the author of "Theresa" was likely to have been an American of African descent, scholars have not yet identified this person specifically. By contrast, we know a good deal about the author of "Le Mulâtre" as well as why he wrote the story in French and published it in 1837 in a Parisian journal, *La Revue des Colonies,* sponsored by an antislavery society of men of color. This anthology prints the first English translation of Séjour's pioneering story of racial exploitation and violent revenge.

Juan Victor Séjour Marcou et Ferrand was born in New Orleans, Louisiana, the son of a free man of color of Haitian origins and a free mixed-race woman of New Orleans. Séjour's parents were sufficiently prosperous to send their son to a private school, where he came under the influence of a respected Black journalist who wrote for French newspapers in New Orleans. Following a custom of New Orleans's free Black class, Séjour went to Paris when he was nineteen to further his education. He stayed on to launch a literary career unhampered by the racial proscriptions of the antebellum American South.

Soon after his arrival in Paris, Séjour made the acquaintance of influential literary men of color, such as Alexandre Dumas *père*, the popular French novelist, and abolitionist Cyrille Bisette, who edited *La Revue des Colonies*. Turning away from fiction after "Le Mulâtre," Séjour wrote an intensely nationalistic ode, "Le Retour de Napoléon," which expressed his admiration for Napoléon and his identification with France. After its initial publication in Paris in 1841, "Le Retour de Napoléon" was reprinted in *Les Cenelles* (1845), the first anthology of African American poetry, edited by the Black New Orleans writer Armand Lanusse. Like all the contributors to *Les Cenelles,* Séjour wrote in French, the language he grew up speaking in New Orleans.

In 1844 Séjour's first play, a verse drama set in fifteenth-century Spain, was accepted for production by the French national theater. During the next twenty-five years, Séjour's plays were regularly staged in Paris and, until 1865, enjoyed considerable popular success. After initial success as a historical dramatist, he specialized in the 1850s in lavishly staged melodramas, heroic adventure plays, and romantic comedies, at least three of which were performed in New Orleans. However, in his 1859 play, *La Tireuse de cartes* (the Fortune Teller), Séjour issued a dramatic protest against an act that had led to an international uproar: the kidnapping of an Italian Jewish boy by guards acting on the orders of the papacy. Shakespeare, whose works were often featured in the New Orleans theater of Séjour's youth, was a major influence on Séjour's most acclaimed drama, *Richard III* (1852). During the late 1860s Séjour's brand of costume drama fell out of fashion in France. Ill health and a changing social and cultural climate contributed to a major decline in Séjour's fortunes in the last years of his life.

Séjour was the first in a series of distinguished African American literary expatriates who settled and wrote in Paris. Unlike Chester Himes, Richard Wright, and James Baldwin in the twentieth century, Séjour seems to have gone to France not only to find a social refuge but also to create himself anew as a Continental man of letters unburdened by the responsibility his Black literary contemporaries in America felt to speak directly to racial issues. After "Le Mulâtre" Séjour published little directly concerned with color or caste and evidently nothing concerned with slavery in the United States. Nevertheless, "Le Mulâtre" provided a remarkable precedent for the tradition of African American antislavery protest fiction that, a decade and a half later, made an auspicious start in English with Frederick Douglass's *The Heroic Slave* (1853) and William Wells Brown's *Clotel* (1853).

Publishing "Le Mulâtre" in French probably cost its author an American readership outside the city of his birth. Even the most cosmopolitan of African American writers, such as Douglass and Brown, seem to have known nothing about Séjour's early foray into antislavery fiction. Yet who is to say that Séjour's decision to publish in a Black-owned journal in France was not the right—indeed, the only—way to ensure that his explicit and grisly tale of racial exploitation, rape, murder, and suicide would ever see print? Even William Faulkner and Richard Wright, whose fictional accounts of perverse desire and sadistic retribution look back to Séjour's melodramatic tragedy of Black–white relationships under slavery, were attacked in the twentieth century for writing in veins first probed by "Le Mulâtre." Edgar Allan Poe had some success in the mid-nineteenth century United States writing about violent death, sexual obsession, and the human psyche under extreme mental or emotional strain. But in "Le Mulâtre" Séjour took a literary risk his white American contemporary never attempted. Séjour grounded his study of similarly extreme manifestations of individual pathology in a *social* reality, the system of slavery, which the African American writer treated as the source of the depravity and misery that infect the minds and hearts of all, Black and white alike, in his story.

The Mulatto[1]

I

The first rays of dawn were just beginning to light the black mountaintops when I left the Cape for Saint-Marc, a small town in St. Domingue, now known as Haiti.[2] I had seen so many exquisite landscapes and thick, tall forests that, truth to tell, I had begun to believe myself indifferent to these virile beauties of creation. But at the sight of this town, with its picturesque vegetation, its bizarre and novel nature, I was stunned; I stood dumbstruck before the sublime diversity of God's works. The moment I arrived, I was accosted by an old negro, at least seventy years of age; his step was firm, his head held high, his form imposing and vigorous; save the remarkable whiteness of his curly hair, nothing betrayed his age. As is common in that country, he wore a large straw hat and was dressed in trousers of coarse gray linen, with a kind of jacket made from plain batiste.[3]

"Good day, Master," he said, tipping his hat when he saw me.

"Ah! There you are . . . ," and I offered him my hand, which he shook in return.

"Master," he said, "that's quite noble-hearted of you. . . . But you know, do you not, that a negro's as vile as a dog; society rejects him; men detest him; the laws curse him. . . . Yes, he's a most unhappy being, who hasn't even the consolation of always being virtuous. . . . He may be born good, noble, and generous; God may grant him a great and loyal soul; but despite all that, he often goes to his grave with bloodstained hands, and a heart hungering after yet more vengeance. For how many times has he seen the dreams of his youth destroyed? How many times has experience taught him that his good deeds count for nothing, and that he should love neither his wife nor his son; for one day the former will be seduced by the master, and his own flesh and blood will be sold and transported away despite his despair. What, then, can you expect him to become? Shall he smash his skull against the paving stones? Shall he kill his torturer? Or do you believe the human heart can find a way to bear such misfortune?"

The old negro fell silent a moment, as if awaiting my response.

"You'd have to be mad to believe that," he continued, heatedly. "If he continues to live, it can only be for vengeance; for soon he shall rise . . . and, from the day he shakes off his servility, the master would do better to have a starving tiger raging beside him than to meet that man face to face." While the old man spoke, his face lit up, his eyes sparkled, and his heart pounded forcefully. I would not have believed one could discover that much life and power beneath such an aged exterior. Taking advantage of this moment of excitement, I said to him: "Antoine, you promised you'd tell me the story of your friend Georges."

"Do you want to hear it now?"

1. First published in French in *La Revue des Colonies* in 1837. This translation is by Philip Barnard.

2. A republic occupying the western third of the island of Hispaniola in the Caribbean Sea.

3. A fine plain-woven fabric.

"Certainly . . ." We sat down, he on my trunk, myself on my valise. Here is what he told me:

"Do you see this edifice that rises so graciously toward the sky and whose reflection seems to rise from the sea; this edifice that in its peculiarity resembles a temple and in its pretense a palace? This is the house of Saint-M***. Each day, in one of this building's rooms, one finds an assemblage of hangers-on, men of independent means, and the great plantation owners. The first two groups play billiards or smoke the delicious cigars of Havana, while the third purchases negroes; that is, free men who have been torn from their country by ruse or by force, and who have become, by violence, the goods, the property of their fellow men. . . . Over here we have the husband without the wife; there, the sister without the brother; farther on, the mother without the children. This makes you shudder? Yet this loathsome commerce goes on continuously. Soon, in any case, the offering is a young Senegalese[4] woman, so beautiful that from every mouth leaps the exclamation: 'How pretty!' Everyone there wants her for his mistress, but not one of them dares dispute the prize with the young Alfred, now twenty-one years old and one of the richest planters in the country.

"'How much do you want for this woman?'

"'Fifteen hundred piasters,' replied the auctioneer.

"'Fifteen hundred piasters,' Alfred rejoined dryly.

"'Yes indeed, Sir.'

"'That's your price?'

"'That's my price.'

"'That's awfully expensive.'

"'Expensive?' replied the auctioneer, with an air of surprise. 'But surely you see how pretty she is; how clear her skin is, how firm her flesh is. She's eighteen years old at the most. . . .' Even as he spoke, he ran his shameless hands all over the ample and half-naked form of the beautiful African.

"'Is she guaranteed?' asked Alfred, after a moment of reflection.

"'As pure as the morning dew,' the auctioneer responded. But, for that matter, you yourself can. . . .'

"'No no, there's no need,' said Alfred, interrupting him. 'I trust you.'

"'I've never sold a single piece of bad merchandise,' replied the vendor, twirling his whiskers with a triumphant air. When the bill of sale had been signed and all formalities resolved, the auctioneer approached the young slave.

"'This man is now your master,' he said, pointing toward Alfred.

"'I know it,' the negress answered coldly.

"'Are you content?'

"'What does it matter to me . . . him or some other. . . .'

"'But surely. . . .' stammered the auctioneer, searching for some answer.

"'But surely what?' said the African, with some humor. 'And if he doesn't suit me?'

"'My word, that would be unfortunate, for everything is finished. . . .'

"'Well then, I'll keep my thoughts to myself.'

"Ten minutes later, Alfred's new slave stepped into a carriage that set off along the *chemin des quepes,* a well-made road that leads out into those delicious fields that surround Saint-Marc like young virgins at the foot of the altar. A somber melancholy enveloped her soul, and she began to weep. The driver understood only too well what was going on inside her, and thus made

4. From Senegal, a country in West Africa.

no attempt to distract her. But when he saw Alfred's white house appear in the distance, he involuntarily leaned down toward the unfortunate girl and, with a voice full of tears, said to her: 'Sister, what's your name?'

"'Laïsa,' she answered, without raising her head.

"At the sound of this name, the driver shivered. Then, gaining control of his emotions, he asked: 'Your mother?'

"'She's dead. . . .'

"'Your father?'

"'He's dead. . . .'

"'Poor child,' he murmured. 'What country are you from, Laïsa?'

"'From Senegal. . . .'

"Tears rose in his eyes; she was a fellow countrywoman.

"'Sister,' he said, wiping his eyes, 'perhaps you know old Chambo and his daughter. . . .'

"'Why?' answered the girl, raising her head quickly.

"'Why?' continued the driver, in obvious discomfort, 'well, old Chambo is my father, and . . .'

"'My God,' cried out the orphan, cutting off the driver before he could finish. 'You are?'

"'Jacques Chambo.'

"'You're my brother!'

"'Laïsa!'

"They threw themselves into each other's arms. They were still embracing when the carriage passed through the main entrance to Alfred's property. The overseer was waiting. . . . 'What's this I see,' he shouted, uncoiling an immense whip that he always carried on his belt; 'Jacques kissing the new arrival before my very eyes. . . . What impertinence!' With this, lashes began to fall on the unhappy man, and spurts of blood leaped from his face."

II

"Alfred may have been a decent man, humane and loyal with his equals; but you can be certain he was a hard, cruel man toward his slaves. I won't tell you everything he did in order to possess Laïsa; for in the end she was virtually raped. For almost a year, she shared her master's bed. But Alfred was already beginning to tire of her; he found her ugly, cold, and insolent. About this time the poor woman gave birth to a boy and gave him the name Georges. Alfred refused to recognize him, drove the mother from his presence, and relegated her to the most miserable hut on his lands, despite the fact that he knew very well, as well as one can, that he was the child's father.

"Georges grew up without ever hearing the name of his father; and when, at times, he attempted to penetrate the mystery surrounding his birth, his mother remained inflexible, never yielding to his entreaties. On one occasion only, she said to him: 'My son, you shall learn your name only when you reach twenty-five, for then you will be a man; you will be better able to guard its secret. You don't realize that he has forbidden me to speak to you about him and threatens you if I do. . . . And Georges, don't you see, this man's hatred would be your death.'

"'What does that matter,' Georges shouted impetuously. 'At least I could reproach him for his unspeakable conduct.'

"'Hush. . . . Hush, Georges. The walls have ears and someone will talk,' moaned the poor mother as she trembled.

"A few years later this unhappy woman died, leaving to Georges, her only son, as his entire inheritance, a small leather pouch containing a portrait of the boy's father. But she exacted a promise that the pouch not be opened until his twenty-fifth year; then she kissed him, and her head fell back onto the pillow. . . . She was dead. The painful cries that escaped the orphan drew the other slaves around him. . . . They all set to crying, they beat their chests, they tore their hair in agony. Following these gestures of suffering, they bathed the dead woman's body and laid it out on a kind of long table, raised on wooden supports. The dead woman is placed on her back, her face turned to the East, dressed in her finest clothing, with her hands folded on her chest. At her feet is a bowl filled with holy water, in which a sprig of jasmine is floating; and, finally, at the four corners of this funereal bed, the flames of torches rise up. . . . Each of them, having blessed the remains of the deceased, kneels and prays; for most of the negro races, despite their fetishism,[5] have profound faith in the existence of God. When this first ceremony is finished, another one, no less singular, commences. . . . There are shouts, tears, songs, and then funeral dances!"

III

"Georges had all the talents necessary for becoming a well-regarded gentleman; yet he was possessed of a haughty, tenacious, willful nature; he had one of those oriental sorts of dispositions, the kind that, once pushed far enough from the path of virtue, will stride boldly down the path of crime. He would have given ten years of his life to know the name of his father, but he dared not violate the solemn oath he had made to his dying mother. It was as if nature pushed him toward Alfred; he liked him, as much as one can like a man; and Alfred esteemed him, but with that esteem that the horseman bears for the most handsome and vigorous of his chargers. In those days, a band of thieves was spreading desolation through the region; already several of the settlers had fallen victim to them. One night, by what chance I know not, Georges learned of their plans. They had sworn to murder Alfred. The slave ran immediately to his master's side.

"'Master, master,' he shouted. . . . 'In heaven's name, follow me.'

"Alfred raised his eyebrows.

"'Please! come, come, master,' the mulatto insisted passionately.

"'Good God,' Alfred replied, 'I believe you're commanding me.'

"'Forgive me, master . . . forgive me . . . I'm beside myself . . . I don't know what I'm saying . . . but in heaven's name, come, follow me, because. . . .'

"'Explain yourself,' said Alfred, in an angry tone. . . .

"The mulatto hesitated.

"'At once; I order you,' continued Alfred, as he rose menacingly.

"'Master, you're to be murdered tonight.'

"'By the Virgin, you're lying. . . .'

"'Master, they mean to take your life.'

"'Who?'

"'The bandits.'

"'Who told you this?'

"'Master, that's my secret. . . .' said the mulatto in a submissive voice.

"'Do you have weapons?' rejoined Alfred, after a moment of silence.

5. Worship or belief in objects thought to have magical powers.

"'The mulatto pulled back a few of the rags that covered him, revealing an axe and a pair of pistols.

"'Good,' said Alfred, hastily arming himself.

"'Master, are you ready?'

"'Let's go. . . .'

"'Let's go,' repeated the mulatto as he stepped toward the door.

"Alfred held him back by the arm.

"'But where to?'

"'To your closest friend, Monsieur Arthur.'

"As they were about to leave the room, there was a ferocious pounding at the door.

"'The devil,' exclaimed the mulatto, 'it's too late. . . .'

"'What say you?'

"'They're here,' replied Georges, pointing at the door. . . .

"'Ah!'

"'Master, what's wrong?'

"'Nothing . . . a sudden pain. . . .'

"'Don't worry, master, they'll have to walk over my body before they get to you,' said the slave with a calm and resigned air.

"This calm, this noble devotion, were calculated to reassure the most cowardly of men. Yet at these last words, Alfred trembled even more, overwhelmed by a horrible thought. He reckoned that Georges, despite his generosity, was an accomplice of the murderers. Such is the tyrant: he believes all other men incapable of elevated sentiments or selfless dedication, for they must be small-minded, perfidious souls. . . . Their souls are but uncultivated ground, where nothing grows but thorns and weeds. The door shook violently. At this point, Alfred could no longer control his fears; he had just seen the mulatto smiling, whether from joy or anger he knew not.

"'Scoundrel!' he shouted, dashing into the next room; 'you're trying to have me murdered, but your plot will fail'—upon which he disappeared. Georges bit his lips in rage, but had no time to think, for the door flew open and four men stood in the threshold. Like a flash of lightning, the mulatto drew his pistols and pressed his back to the wall, crying out in a deep voice:

"'Wretches! What do you want?'

"'We want to have a talk with you,' rejoined one of them, firing a bullet at Georges from point-blank range.

"'A fine shot,' muttered Georges, shaking.

"The bullet had broken his left arm. Georges let off a shot. The brigand whirled three times about and fell stone dead. A second followed instantly. At this point, like a furious lion tormented by hunters, Georges, with his axe in his fist and his dagger in his teeth, threw himself upon his adversaries. . . . A hideous struggle ensues. . . . The combatants grapple . . . collide again . . . they seem bound together. . . . The axe blade glistens. . . . The dagger, faithful to the hand that guides it, works its way into the enemy's breast. . . . But never a shout, not a word . . . not a whisper escapes the mouths of these three men, wallowing among the cadavers as if at the heart of some intoxicating orgy. . . . To see them thus, pale and blood-spattered, silent and full of desperation, one must imagine three phantoms throwing themselves against each other, tearing themselves to pieces, in the depths of a grave. . . . Meanwhile, Georges is covered with wounds; he can barely hold himself up. . . . Oh! the intrepid mulatto has reached his end; the severing axe is lifted above his head. . . . Suddenly two explosions are heard, and the two brigands slump to the floor, blaspheming God as they drop. At the same moment, Alfred returns, followed by a young negro. He has the wounded man carried to his hut, and instructs his doctor to attend to him. Now, how is it that Georges was saved by the same man who had just accused him of treachery? As he ran off, Alfred heard the sound of a gun, and the clash of steel; blushing at his own cowardice, he awoke his valet de chambre and flew to the aid of his liberator. Ah, I've forgotten to tell you that Georges had a wife, by the name Zelia, whom he loved with every fiber of his being; she was a mulatto about eighteen or twenty years old, standing very straight and tall, with black hair and a gaze full of tenderness and love. Georges lay for twelve days somewhere between life and death. Alfred visited him often; and, driven on by some fateful chance, he became enamored of Zelia. But, unfortunately for him, she was not one of these women who sell their favors or use them to pay tribute to their master. She repelled Alfred's propositions with humble dignity; for she never forgot that this was a master speaking to a slave. Instead of being moved by this display of a virtue that is so rare among women, above all among those who, like Zelia, are slaves, and who, every day, see their shameless companions prostitute themselves to the colonists, thereby only feeding more licentiousness; instead of being moved, as I said, Alfred flew into a rage. . . . What!—him, the despot, the Bey, the Sultan of the Antilles,[6] being spurned by a slave . . . how ironic! Thus he swore he would possess her. . . . A few days before Georges was recovered, Alfred summoned Zelia to his chamber. Then, attending to nothing but his criminal desires, he threw his arms around her and planted a burning kiss on her face. The young slave begged, pleaded, resisted; but all in vain. . . . Already he draws her toward the adulterous bed; already. . . . Then, the young slave, filled with a noble indignation, repulses him with one final effort, but one so sudden, so powerful, that Alfred lost his balance and struck his head as he fell. . . . At this sight, Zelia began to tear her hair in despair, crying tears of rage; for she understood perfectly, the unhappy girl, that death was her fate for having drawn the blood of a being so vile. After crying for some time, she left to be at her husband's side. He must have been dreaming about her, for there was a smile on his lips.

"'Georges . . . Georges. . . .' she cried out in agony.

"The mulatto opened his eyes; and his first impulse was to smile at the sight of his beloved. Zelia recounted for him everything that had happened. He didn't want to believe it, but soon he was convinced of his misfortune; for some men entered his hut and tied up his wife while she stood sobbing. . . . Georges made an effort to rise up; but, still weakened, he fell back onto his bed, his eyes haggard, his hands clenched, his mouth gasping for air."

IV

"Ten days later, two white creole[7] children were playing in the street.

"'Charles,' one said to the other: 'is it true that the mulatto woman who wanted to kill her master is to be hung tomorrow?'

"'At eight o'clock,' answered the other.

"'Will you go?'

"'Oh yes, certainly.'

6. The main island group of the West Indies. "Bey": Turkish title for a lord or a prince. "Sultan": ruler of a Muslim country.

7. Someone of European descent born in the West Indies.

"'Won't that be fine, to see her pirouetting between the earth and the sky,' rejoined the first, laughing as they walked off.

"Does it surprise you to hear two children, at ten years of age, conversing so gayly on the death of another? This is, perhaps, an inevitable consequence of their education. From their earliest days, they have heard it ceaselessly repeated, that we were born to serve them, that we were created to attend to their whims, and that they need have no more or less consideration for us than for a dog. . . . Indeed, what is our agony and suffering to them? Have they not, just as often, seen their best horses die? They don't weep for them, for they're rich, and tomorrow they'll buy others. . . . While these two children were speaking, Georges was at the feet of his master.

"'Master, have mercy . . . mercy. . . .' he cried out, weeping. . . . 'Have pity on her . . . Master, pardon her. . . . Oh! yes, pardon her, it is in your power . . . oh! speak . . . you have only to say the word . . . just one word . . . and she will live.'

"Alfred made no answer.

"'Oh! for pity's sake . . . master . . . for pity's sake, tell me you pardon her . . . oh! speak . . . answer me, master . . . won't you pardon her. . . .' The unhappy man was bent double with pain. . . .

"Alfred remained impassive, turning his head aside. . . .

"'Oh!' continued Georges, begging, 'please answer . . . just one word . . . please say something; you see how your silence is tearing my heart in two . . . it's killing me. . . .'

"'There's nothing I can do,' Alfred finally answered, in an icy tone.

"The mulatto dried his tears, and raised himself to his full height.

"'Master,' he continued in a hollow voice, 'do you remember what you said to me, as I lay twisting in agony on my bed?'

"'No . . .'

"'Well! I can remember . . . the master said to the slave: you saved my life; what can I grant you in return? Do you want your freedom? 'Master,' answered the slave, 'I can never be free, while my son and my wife are slaves.' To which the master replied: 'If ever you ask me, I swear that your wishes shall be granted'; and the slave did not ask, for he was content that he had saved his master's life . . . but today, today when he knows that, in eighteen hours, his wife will no longer be among the living, he flies to throw himself at your feet, and to call out to you: master, in God's name, save my wife.' And the mulatto, his hands clasped, with a supplicating gaze, fell to his knees and began to cry, his tears falling like rain. . . .

"Alfred turned his head away. . . .

"'Master . . . master . . . for pity, give me an answer. . . . Oh! say that you want her to live . . . in God's name . . . in your mother's name . . . mercy . . . have mercy upon us. . . .' and the mulatto kissed the dust at his feet.

"Alfred stood silent.

"'But speak, at least, to this poor man who begs you,' he said, sobbing.

"Alfred said nothing.

"'My God . . . my God! how miserable I am . . .' and he rolled on the floor, pulling at his hair in torment.

"Finally, Alfred decided to speak: 'I have already told you that it is no longer up to me to pardon her.'

"'Master,' murmured Georges, still crying, 'she will probably be condemned; for only you and I know that she is innocent.'

"At these words from the mulatto, the blood rose to Alfred's face, and fury to his heart. . . .

"Georges understood that it was no longer time to beg, for he had raised the veil that covered his master's crime; thus he stood up resolutely.

" 'Leave . . . get out,' Alfred shouted at him.

"Instead of leaving, the mulatto crossed his arms on his chest and, with a fierce look, eyed his master scornfully from head to foot.

" 'Get out! get out, I say,' continued Alfred, more and more angrily.

" 'I'm not leaving,' answered Georges.

" 'This is defiance, you wretch.' He made a motion to strike him, but his hand remained at his side, so full of pride and hatred was George's gaze.

" 'What! you can leave her to be killed, to have her throat cut, to be murdered,' said the mulatto, 'when you know her to be innocent . . . when, like a coward, you wanted to seduce her?'

" 'Insolent! What are you saying?'

" 'I'm saying that it would be an infamous deed to let her die . . .'

" 'Georges . . . Georges. . . .'

" 'I am saying that you're a scoundrel,' screamed Georges, giving full rein to his anger, and seizing Alfred by the arm . . . 'ah! she'll die . . . she will die because she didn't prostitute herself to you . . . because you're white . . . because you're her master . . . you lying coward.'

" 'Careful, Georges,' replied Alfred, trying to take a tone of assurance. 'Be careful that instead of one victim tomorrow, the executioner does not find two.'

" 'You talk of victim and executioner, wretch,' shouted Georges. . . . 'So that means she dies . . . her . . . my Zella . . . but you should know that her life is linked to your own.'

" 'Georges!'

" 'You should know that your head will remain on your shoulders only so long as she lives.'

" 'Georges . . . Georges!'

" 'You should know that I will kill you, that I'll drink your blood, if even a hair on her head is harmed.'

"During all this time, the mulatto was shaking Alfred with all his strength.

" 'Let me go,' cried Alfred.

" 'Ah! she's dying . . . she's dying' . . . the mulatto screamed deliriously.

" 'Georges, let me go!'

" 'Shut your mouth . . . shut it, you scoundrel . . . ah! she's dying . . . well then, should the executioner put an end to my wife . . .' he continued with a hideous smile.

"Alfred was so agitated he didn't even know that Georges had left. He went directly to his hut, where his child of two years was sleeping in a light cradle made from lianas;[8] taking up the child, he slipped away. In order to understand what follows, you must know that there was only a small river to cross from Alfred's home before one arrives in the midst of those thick forests that seem to hold the new world in their arms.

"For six long hours, Georges walked without a rest; at last he stopped, a few steps from a hut built in the deepest heart of the forest; you'll understand the joy that shone in his eyes when you realize that this tiny hut, isolated as it is, is the camp of the Maroons; that is, of slaves who have fled the tyranny of their masters. At this moment the hut was filled with murmurs; for a rustling

8. A woody vine common in the tropics.

had been heard in the forest, and the leader, swearing that the noise was not that of any animal, had taken his rifle and gone out. . . . Suddenly the underbrush parted before him and he found himself face to face with a stranger.

"'By my freedom,' he cried, looking over the newcomer, 'you found our recess all too easily.'

"'Africa and freedom,' Georges replied calmly, as he pushed aside the barrel of the rifle. . . . 'I'm one of you.'

"'Your name.'

"'Georges, slave of Alfred.'

"They shook hands and embraced.

"The next day the crowd clamored round a scaffold, from which hung the body of a young mulatto woman. . . . When she had expired, the executioner let her corpse down into a pine coffin and, ten minutes later, body and coffin were thrown into a ditch that was opened at the edge of the forest.

"Thus this woman, for having been too virtuous, died the kind of death meted out to the vilest criminal. Would this alone not suffice to render the gentlest of men dangerous and bloodthirsty?"

V

"Three years had passed since the death of the virtuous Zelia. For a time, Alfred was in extreme torment; by day, he seemed to see a vengeful hand descending toward his head; he trembled at night because the darkness brought him hideous, frightful dreams. Soon, however, he banished from his thoughts both the painful memory of the martyr and the terrible threat Georges had made; he married and became a father. . . . Oh! how gratified he felt, when he was told that his prayers were answered, he who had humbly kissed the church floor each evening, beseeching the Virgin of Sorrows to grant him a son.

"For Georges also, there was happiness in this child's arrival. For if he had hoped for three years without attempting to strike back at his wife's executioner; if he had lain sleepless so many nights, with fury in his heart and a hand on his dagger, it was because he was waiting for Alfred to find himself, like Georges, with a wife and a son. It was because he wished to kill him only when dear and precious bonds linked him to this world. . . . Georges had always maintained close ties with one of Alfred's slaves; indeed, he visited him each week; and that slave had never given Georges any news more important than that of the newborn's arrival. . . . He immediately set out for the house of his enemy. On his way he met a negress who was bringing a cup of broth to Madame Alfred; he stopped her, exchanged a few insignificant words, and went on. . . . After many difficulties, he managed to slip his way, like a snake, into Alfred's rooms; once there, hidden in the space between the bed and the wall, he awaited his master. . . . A moment later, Alfred entered the room, humming a tune; he opened his secretary and took out a superb jewel box, set with diamonds, that he had promised his wife, should she give him a son; but, filled with joy and happiness, he sat down and put his head between his hands, like a man who can't believe his unexpected good fortune. Then, on raising his head, he saw before him a kind of motionless shadow, with arms crossed on its breast and two burning eyes that possessed all the ferocity of a tiger preparing to tear its prey to pieces. Alfred made a motion to stand, but a powerful arm held him down in his chair.

"'What do you want with me,' Alfred whispered, in a trembling voice.

"'To compliment you on the birth of your child,' answered a voice that seemed to emerge from the tomb.

"Alfred shook from head to toe, his hair stood on end, and a cold sweat poured over his limbs.

"'I don't know you,' Alfred muttered weakly. . . .

"'Georges is the name.'

"'You. . . .'

"'You thought I was dead, I suppose,' said the mulatto with a convulsive laugh.

"'Help . . . help,' cried Alfred.

"'Who will help you,' rejoined the mulatto . . . haven't you dismissed your servants, haven't you closed your doors, to be alone with your wife . . . so you see, your cries are useless . . . you should commend your soul to God.'

"Alfred had begun to rise from his chair, but at these last words he fell back, pale and trembling.

"'Oh! have pity, Georges . . . don't kill me, not today.'

"Georges shrugged his shoulders. 'Master, isn't it horrible to die when you're happy; to lie down in the grave at the moment you see your fondest dreams coming true . . . oh! it's horrible, isn't it,' said the mulatto with an infernal laugh. . . .

"'Mercy, Georges. . . .'

"'And yet,' he continued, 'such is your destiny . . . you shall die today, this hour, this minute, without giving your wife your last farewell. . . .'

"'Have pity . . . pity. . . .'

"'Without kissing your newborn son a second time. . . .'

"'Oh! mercy . . . mercy.'

"'I think my vengeance is worthy of your own . . . I would have sold my soul to the Devil, had he promised me this moment.'

"'Oh! mercy . . . please take pity on me,' said Alfred, throwing himself at the feet of the mulatto.

"Georges shrugged his shoulders and raised his axe.

"'Oh! one more hour of life!'

"'To embrace your wife, is that it?'

"'One minute. . . .'

"'To see your son again, right?'

"'Oh! have pity. . . .'

"'You might as well plead with the starving tiger to let go his prey.'

"'In God's name, Georges.'

"'I don't believe in that any longer.'

"'In the name of your father. . . .'

"At this, Georges's fury subsided.

"'My father . . . my father,' repeated the mulatto, tears in his eyes. 'Do you know him . . . oh! tell me his name. . . . What's his name . . . oh! tell me, tell me his name . . . I'll pardon you . . . I'll bless you.'

"And the mulatto nearly fell on his knees before his master. But suddenly, sharp cries were heard. . . .

"'Good heavens . . . that's my wife's voice,' cried Alfred, dashing toward the sounds. . . .

"As if he were coming back to his senses, the mulatto remembered that he had come to the house of his master, not to learn the name of his father, but to settle accounts with him for his wife's blood. Holding Alfred back, he told him with a hideous grin: 'Hold on, master; it's nothing.'

"'Jesus and Mary . . . don't you hear her calling for help.'

"'It's nothing, I tell you.'

"'Let me go . . . let me go . . . it's my wife's voice.'

"'No, it's the gasps of a dying woman.'

"'Wretch, you're lying. . . .'

"'I poisoned her. . . .'

"'Oh!'

"'Do you hear those cries . . . they're hers.'

"'The Devil. . . .'

"'Do you hear those screams . . . they're hers.'

"'A curse. . . .'

"During all this time, Alfred had been trying to shake free of the mulatto's grip; but he held him fast, tighter and tighter. As he did, his head rose higher, his heart beat fiercely, he steadied himself for his awful task.

"'Alfred . . . help . . . water . . . I'm suffocating,' shouted a woman, as she threw herself into the middle of the room. She was pale and disheveled, her eyes were starting out of her head, her hair was in wild disarray.

"'Alfred, Alfred . . . for heaven's sake, help me . . . some water . . . I need water . . . my blood is boiling . . . my heart is twitching . . . oh! water, water. . . .'

"Alfred struggled mightily to help her, but Georges held him fast with an iron hand. Laughing like one of the damned, he cried out: 'No, master . . . I'm afraid not . . . I want your wife to die . . . right there . . . before your eyes . . . right in front of you . . . do you understand, master; right in front of you, asking you for water, for air, while you can do nothing to help her.'

"'Damnation . . . may you be damned,' howled Alfred, as he struggled like a madman.

"'You can curse and blaspheme all you want,' answered the mulatto . . . 'this is the way it's going to be. . . .'

"'Alfred,' the dying woman moaned again, 'good-bye . . . good-bye . . . I'm dying. . . .'

"'Look well,' responded the mulatto, still laughing. . . . 'Look . . . she's gasping . . . goodness! a single drop of this water would restore her to life.' He showed him a small vial.

"'My entire fortune for that drop of water. . . .' cried Alfred.

"'Have you gone mad, master. . . .'

"'Ah! that water . . . that water . . . don't you see she's dying . . . give it to me . . . please give it to me. . . .'

"'Here . . .' and the mulatto flung the vial against the wall.

"'Accursed,' screamed Alfred, seizing Georges by the neck. 'Oh! my entire life, my soul, for a dagger. . . .'

"Georges released Alfred's hands.

"'Now that she's dead, it's your turn, master,' he said as he lifted his axe.

"'Strike, executioner . . . strike . . . after poisoning her, you might as well kill your own fa—.' The ax fell, and Alfred's head rolled across the floor, but, as it rolled, the head distinctly pronounced the final syllable, '—ther . . .' Georges at first believed he had misheard, but the word *father,* like a funeral knell, rang in his ears. To be certain, he opened the fateful pouch. . . . 'Ah!' he cried out, 'I'm cursed. . . .' An explosion was heard; and the next day, near the corpse of Alfred, was discovered the corpse of the unhappy Georges. . . ."

1837

ELIZABETH HOBBS KECKLY
ca. 1818–1907

Elizabeth Keckly's assertion early in her autobiography, "My life, so full of romance, may sound like a dream," belies the nightmarish quality of much of her early life. Enslaved from her birth in Dinwiddie County, Virginia, during her childhood and teenage years she was separated from her parents, beaten, raped by a wealthy slaveholder, and violated in countless ways. While working for her enslaver full time as a seamstress in St. Louis, she toiled late into the night to earn the funds to purchase freedom for herself and her son. An unfulfilling marriage led to further heartache, compounded in 1861 by the death of her son George (who had enlisted in the Union army as a white man) in an early Civil War battle. Nevertheless, by the start of the war, Keckly had launched her own unlikely American dream by leaving her husband and establishing a successful independent career as a dressmaker who, with a staff of twenty, catered to the wives of Washington's political elite. Among her clients were Varina Davis, wife of soon-to-be Confederate president Jefferson Davis, and Mary Todd Lincoln, wife of U.S. president Abraham Lincoln.

The relationship between Keckly and the First Lady gradually evolved from professional to personal, with the former becoming friend, confidante, and, in the wake of Lincoln's assassination, comforter of Mary Todd Lincoln. In 1867 Keckly set aside her own business to come to the aid of Mrs. Lincoln, whose protracted debts had led her to concoct a scheme whereby she hoped, with her friend's help, to sell anonymously clothes and jewelry she had purchased and worn when she was in the White House. Exposed and humiliated in the New York press, Lincoln ended up losing money in the "Old Clothes Scandal," which placed such a financial hardship on Keckly that in 1868 she turned to a New York commercial publisher to bring out her sensational memoir, *Behind the Scenes; or, Thirty Years a Slave and Four Years in the White House*.

Behind the Scenes does not soft-pedal the cruelty and exploitation its author experienced while enslaved. But Keckly focused her memoir on how her thirty-seven years in bondage had taught her "to rely upon myself, and to prepare myself to render assistance to others." Her story presents her as an exemplar of the aspiring leadership cohort of post-emancipation Black America intent on taking their rightful place as self-respecting, forward-looking contributors to a new American socioeconomic order. Both a social and an economic entrepreneur, Keckly recalled in *Behind the Scenes* how she organized the Contraband Relief Association in 1862 to aid the self-liberated freed people (termed "contrabands of war" by Union army generals) who had flocked to the District of Columbia. Keckly's circle of activist colleagues and friends included Frederick Douglass, Rev. Francis Grimké, Henry Highland Garnet, and Anna Julia Cooper, as well as many white political and military figures. Keckly's decision to characterize slavery as a crucible in which she had proved her mettle and confirmed her credentials as a constructive leader anticipated a similar strategy among many Reconstruction-era autobiographers who had once been enslaved. Rather than engage in bitter recriminations about her enslaved past, Keckly articulated the optimism of the early years of Reconstruction when the abolition of slavery and the promise of equal rights encouraged many early post-Civil War African American writers to stress their dedication to racial reconciliation and mutual progress with whites.

The first nationally recognized African American autobiography to be published after slavery's abolition, *Behind the Scenes* was a notable literary experiment, an African American woman's success story for a new era. Keckly's publisher energetically advertised the book and ensured that it was widely noticed and reviewed. But Keckly came to regret the attention, much of it negative, that *Behind the Scenes* received. Feeling betrayed by her publisher, whom she sued for royalties she had not received, Keckly was disheartened by the knowledge that Mary Todd Lincoln had disavowed her and her book. Dismissed by many as mere White House gossip, the most remarkable African American autobiography of the Reconstruction era faded from public view. Keckly never again wrote for publication. She stayed out of the public eye except when journalists asked for interviews about her connections to the Lincolns. Ten years before her death in 1907, ill health and poverty obliged Keckly to become a resident of the National Home for Destitute Colored Women and Children in Washington, D.C., an institution founded with funds contributed by her Contraband Relief Association. At her funeral she was eulogized as "a commanding figure," a woman of "unusual intelligence" and "remarkable energy and push," who had always "thoroughly respected herself."

From Behind the Scenes; or, Thirty Years a Slave and Four Years in the White House

Chapter I

WHERE I WAS BORN

My life has been an eventful one. I was born a slave—was the child of slave parents—therefore I came upon the earth free in God-like thought, but fettered in action. My birthplace was Dinwiddie Court-House, in Virginia. My recollections of childhood are distinct, perhaps for the reason that many stirring incidents are associated with that period. I am now on the shady side of forty, and as I sit alone in my room the brain is busy, and a rapidly moving panorama brings scene after scene before me, some pleasant and others sad; and when I thus greet old familiar faces, I often find myself wondering if I am not living the past over again. The visions are so terribly distinct that I almost imagine them to be real. Hour after hour I sit while the scenes are being shifted; and as I gaze upon the panorama of the past, I realize how crowded with incidents my life has been. Every day seems like a romance within itself, and the years grow into ponderous volumes. As I cannot condense, I must omit many strange passages in my history. From such a wilderness of events it is difficult to make a selection, but as I am not writing altogether the history of myself, I will confine my story to the most important incidents which I believe influenced the moulding[1] of my character. As I glance over the crowded sea of the past, these incidents stand forth prominently, the guide-posts of memory. I presume that I must have been four years old when I first began to remember; at least, I cannot now recall anything occurring previous to this period. My master, Col. A. Burwell, was somewhat unsettled in his business

1. Forming.

affairs, and while I was yet an infant he made several removals. While living at Hampton Sidney College, Prince Edward County, Va., Mrs. Burwell gave birth to a daughter, a sweet, black-eyed baby, my earliest and fondest pet. To take care of this baby was my first duty. True, I was but a child myself—only four years old—but then I had been raised in a hardy school—had been taught to rely upon myself, and to prepare myself to render assistance to others. The lesson was not a bitter one, for I was too young to indulge in philosophy, and the precepts that I then treasured and practised I believe developed those principles of character which have enabled me to triumph over so many difficulties. Notwithstanding all the wrongs that slavery heaped upon me, I can bless it for one thing—youth's important lesson of self-reliance. The baby was named Elizabeth, and it was pleasant to me to be assigned a duty in connection with it, for the discharge of that duty transferred me from the rude cabin to the household of my master. My simple attire was a short dress and a little white apron. My old mistress encouraged me in rocking the cradle, by telling me that if I would watch over the baby well, keep the flies out of its face, and not let it cry, I should be its little maid. This was a golden promise, and I required no better inducement for the faithful performance of my task. I began to rock the cradle most industriously, when lo! out pitched little pet on the floor. I instantly cried out, "Oh! the baby is on the floor;" and, not knowing what to do, I seized the fire-shovel in my perplexity, and was trying to shovel up my tender charge, when my mistress called to me to let the child alone, and then ordered that I be taken out and lashed for my carelessness. The blows were not administered with a light hand, I assure you, and doubtless the severity of the lashing has made me remember the incident so well. This was the first time I was punished in this cruel way, but not the last. The black-eyed baby that I called my pet grew into a self-willed girl, and in after years was the cause of much trouble to me. I grew strong and healthy, and, notwithstanding I knit socks and attended to various kinds of work, I was repeatedly told, when even fourteen years old, that I would never be worth my salt. When I was eight, Mr. Burwell's family consisted of six sons and four daughters, with a large family of servants. My mother was kind and forbearing; Mrs. Burwell a hard task-master; and as mother had so much work to do in making clothes, etc., for the family, besides the slaves, I determined to render her all the assistance in my power, and in rendering her such assistance my young energies were taxed to the utmost. I was my mother's only child, which made her love for me all the stronger. I did not know much of my father, for he was the slave of another man, and when Mr. Burwell moved from Dinwiddie he was separated from us, and only allowed to visit my mother twice a year—during the Easter holidays and Christmas. At last Mr. Burwell determined to reward my mother, by making an arrangement with the owner of my father, by which the separation of my parents could be brought to an end. It was a bright day, indeed, for my mother when it was announced that my father was coming to live with us. The old weary look faded from her face, and she worked as if her heart was in every task. But the golden days did not last long. The radiant dream faded all too soon.

In the morning my father called me to him and kissed me, then held me out at arms' length as if he were regarding his child with pride. "She is growing into a large fine girl," he remarked to my mother. "I dun no which I like best, you or Lizzie, as both are so dear to me." My mother's name was Agnes, and my father delighted to call me his "Little Lizzie." While yet my father and mother were speaking hopefully, joyfully of the future, Mr. Burwell came to the cabin, with a letter in his hand. He was a kind master in some things, and as gently as possible informed my parents that they must part; for in two hours my father must join his master at Dinwiddie, and go with him to the West, where he had determined to make his future home. The announcement fell upon the little circle in that rude-log cabin like a thunderbolt. I can remember the scene as if it were but yesterday;—how my father cried out against the cruel separation; his last kiss; his wild straining of my mother to his bosom; the solemn prayer to Heaven; the tears and sobs—the fearful anguish of broken hearts. The last kiss, the last good-by; and he, my father, was gone, gone forever. The shadow eclipsed the sunshine, and love brought despair. The parting was eternal. The cloud had no silver lining, but I trust that it will be all silver in heaven. We who are crushed to earth with heavy chains, who travel a weary, rugged, thorny road, groping through midnight darkness on earth, earn our right to enjoy the sunshine in the great hereafter. At the grave, at least, we should be permitted to lay our burdens down, that a new world, a world of brightness, may open to us. The light that is denied us here should grow into a flood of effulgence[2] beyond the dark, mysterious shadows of death. Deep as was the distress of my mother in parting with my father, her sorrow did not screen her from insult. My old mistress said to her: "Stop your nonsense; there is no necessity for you putting on airs. Your husband is not the only slave that has been sold from his family, and you are not the only one that has had to part. There are plenty more men about here, and if you want a husband so badly, stop your crying and go and find another." To these unfeeling words my mother made no reply. She turned away in stoical silence, with a curl of that loathing scorn upon her lips which swelled in her heart.

My father and mother never met again in this world. They kept up a regular correspondence for years, and the most precious mementoes of my existence are the faded old letters that he wrote, full of love, and always hoping that the future would bring brighter days. In nearly every letter is a message for me. "Tell my darling little Lizzie," he writes, "to be a good girl, and to learn her book. Kiss her for me, and tell her that I will come to see her some day." Thus he wrote time and again, but he never came. He lived in hope, but died without ever seeing his wife and child.

I note a few extracts from one of my father's letters to my mother, following copy literally:

"Shelbyvile, Sept. 6, 1833.

"Mrs. Agnes Hobbs.

"Dear Wife: My dear biloved wife I am more than glad to meet with opportunty writee thes few lines to you by my Mistress who ar now about starterng to virginia, and sevl others of my old friends are with her; in compeney Mrs. Ann Rus the wife of master Thos Rus and Dan Woodiard and his family and I am very sorry that I havn the chance to go with them as I feele Determid to see you If life last again. I am now here and out at this pleace so I am not abble to get of at this time. I am write well and hearty and all the rest of masters family. I heard this eveng by Mistress that ar just from theree all sends love to you and all my old frends. I am a living in a town called Shelbyville and I have wrote a greate many letters since Ive beene here and almost been ready to my selfe that its out of the question to write any more at tall: my dear wife I dont feeld no

2. Radiance.

> whys like giving out writing to you as yet and I hope when you get this letter that you be Inncougege to write me a letter. I am well satisfied at my living at this place I am a making money for my own benifit and I hope that its to yours also If I live to see Nexct year I shall heve my own time from master by giving him 100 and twenty Dollars a year and I thinke I shall be doing good bisness at that and heve something more thean all that. I hope with gods helpe that I may be abble to rejoys with you on the earth and In heaven lets meet when will I am detemnid to nuver stope praying, not in this earth and I hope to praise god In glory there weel meet to part no more forever. So my dear wife I hope to meet you In paradase to prase god forever * * * * * I want Elizabeth to be a good girl and not to thinke that becasue I am bound so fare that gods not abble to open the way * * * *
>
> "GEORGE PLEASANT,"
>
> *"Hobbs a servant of Grum."*

The last letter that my mother received from my father was dated Shelbyville, Tennessee, March 20, 1839. He writes in a cheerful strain, and hopes to see her soon. Alas! he looked forward to a meeting in vain. Year after year the one great hope swelled in his heart, but the hope was only realized beyond the dark portals of the grave.

When I was about seven years old I witnessed, for the first time, the sale of a human being. We were living at Prince Edward, in Virginia, and master had just purchased his hogs for the winter, for which he was unable to pay in full. To escape from his embarrassment it was necessary to sell one of the slaves. Little Joe, the son of the cook, was selected as the victim. His mother was ordered to dress him up in his Sunday clothes, and send him to the house. He came in with a bright face, was placed in the scales, and was sold, like the hogs, at so much per pound. His mother was kept in ignorance of the transaction, but her suspicions were aroused. When her son started for Petersburgh in the wagon, the truth began to dawn upon her mind, and she pleaded piteously that her boy should not be taken from her; but master quieted her by telling her that he was simply going to town with the wagon, and would be back in the morning. Morning came, but little Joe did not return to his mother. Morning after morning passed, and the mother went down to the grave without ever seeing her child again. One day she was whipped for grieving for her lost boy. Colonel Burwell never liked to see one of his slaves wear a sorrowful face, and those who offended in this particular way were always punished. Alas! the sunny face of the slave is not always an indication of sunshine in the heart. Colonel Burwell at one time owned about seventy slaves, all of which were sold, and in a majority of instances wives were separated from husbands and children from their parents. Slavery in the Border States forty years ago was different from what it was twenty years ago. Time seemed to soften the hearts of master and mistress, and to insure kinder and more humane treatment to bondsmen and bondswomen. When I was quite a child, an incident occurred which my mother afterward impressed more strongly on my mind. One of my uncles, a slave of Colonel Burwell, lost a pair of ploughlines,[3] and when the loss was made known the master gave him a new pair, and told him that if he did not take care of them he would punish him severely. In a few weeks the second pair

3. Straps used on a plow.

of lines was stolen, and my uncle hung himself rather than meet the displeasure of his master. My mother went to the spring in the morning for a pail of water, and on looking up into the willow tree which shaded the bubbling crystal stream, she discovered the lifeless form of her brother suspended beneath one of the strong branches. Rather than be punished the way Colonel Burwell punished his servants, he took his own life. Slavery had its dark side as well as its bright side.

Chapter II

GIRLHOOD AND ITS SORROWS

I must pass rapidly over the stirring events of my early life. When I was about fourteen years old I went to live with my master's eldest son, a Presbyterian minister. His salary was small, and he was burdened with a helpless wife, a girl that he had married in the humble walks of life. She was morbidly sensitive, and imagined that I regarded her with contemptuous feelings because she was of poor parentage. I was their only servant, and a gracious loan at that. They were not able to buy me, so my old master sought to render them assistance by allowing them the benefit of my services. From the very first I did the work of three servants, and yet I was scolded and regarded with distrust. The years passed slowly, and I continued to serve them, and at the same time grew into strong, healthy womanhood. I was nearly eighteen when we removed from Virginia to Hillsboro', North Carolina, where young Mr. Burwell took charge of a church. The salary was small, and we still had to practise the closest economy. Mr. Bingham, a hard, cruel man, the village schoolmaster, was a member of my young master's church, and he was a frequent visitor to the parsonage. She whom I called mistress seemed to be desirous to wreak vengeance on me for something, and Bingham became her ready tool. During this time my master was unusually kind to me; he was naturally a good-hearted man, but was influenced by his wife. It was Saturday evening, and while I was bending over the bed, watching the baby that I had just hushed into slumber, Mr. Bingham came to the door and asked me to go with him to his study. Wondering what he meant by his strange request, I followed him, and when we had entered the study he closed the door, and in his blunt way remarked: "Lizzie, I am going to flog you." I was thunderstruck, and tried to think if I had been remiss in anything. I could not recollect of doing anything to deserve punishment, and with surprise exclaimed: "Whip me, Mr. Bingham! what for?"

"No matter," he replied, "I am going to whip you, so take down your dress this instant."

Recollect, I was eighteen years of age, was a woman fully developed, and yet this man coolly bade me take down my dress. I drew myself up proudly, firmly, and said: "No, Mr. Bingham, I shall not take down my dress before you. Moreover, you shall not whip me unless you prove the stronger. Nobody has a right to whip me but my own master, and nobody shall do so if I can prevent it."

My words seemed to exasperate him. He seized a rope, caught me roughly, and tried to tie me. I resisted with all my strength, but he was the stronger of the two, and after a hard struggle succeeded in binding my hands and tearing my dress from my back. Then he picked up a rawhide,[4] and began to

4. A rope or whip made of untanned cattle skin.

ply it freely over my shoulders. With steady hand and practised eye he would raise the instrument of torture, nerve himself for a blow, and with fearful force the rawhide descended upon the quivering flesh. It cut the skin, raised great welts, and the warm blood trickled down my back. Oh God! I can feel the torture now—the terrible, excruciating agony of those moments. I did not scream; I was too proud to let my tormentor know what I was suffering. I closed my lips firmly, that not even a groan might escape from them, and I stood like a statue while the keen lash cut deep into my flesh. As soon as I was released, stunned with pain, bruised and bleeding, I went home and rushed into the presence of the pastor and his wife, wildly exclaiming: "Master Robert, why did you let Mr. Bingham flog me? What have I done that I should be so punished?"

"Go away," he gruffly answered, "do not bother me."

I would not be put off thus. "What *have* I done? I *will* know why I have been flogged."

I saw his cheeks flush with anger, but I did not move. He rose to his feet, and on my refusing to go without an explanation, seized a chair, struck me, and felled me to the floor. I rose, bewildered, almost dead with pain, crept to my room, dressed my bruised arms and back as best I could, and then lay down, but not to sleep. No, I could not sleep, for I was suffering mental as well as bodily torture. My spirit rebelled against the unjustness that had been inflicted upon me, and though I tried to smother my anger and to forgive those who had been so cruel to me, it was impossible. The next morning I was more calm, and I believe that I could then have forgiven everything for the sake of one kind word. But the kind word was not proffered, and it may be possible that I grew somewhat wayward and sullen. Though I had faults, I know now, as I felt then, harshness was the poorest inducement for the correction of them. It seems that Mr. Bingham had pledged himself to Mrs. Burwell to subdue what he called my "stubborn pride." On Friday following the Saturday on which I was so savagely beaten, Mr. Bingham again directed me to come to his study. I went, but with the determination to offer resistance should he attempt to flog me again. On entering the room I found him prepared with a new rope and a new cowhide. I told him that I was ready to die, but that he could not conquer me. In struggling with him I bit his finger severely, when he seized a heavy stick and beat me with it in a shameful manner. Again I went home sore and bleeding, but with pride as strong and defiant as ever. The following Thursday Mr. Bingham again tried to conquer me, but in vain. We struggled, and he struck me many savage blows. As I stood bleeding before him, nearly exhausted with his efforts, he burst into tears, and declared that it would be a sin to beat me any more. My suffering at last subdued his hard heart; he asked my forgiveness, and afterwards was an altered man. He was never known to strike one of his servants from that day forward. Mr. Burwell, he who preached the love of Heaven, who glorified the precepts and examples of Christ, who expounded the Holy Scriptures Sabbath after Sabbath from the pulpit, when Mr. Bingham refused to whip me any more, was urged by his wife to punish me himself. One morning he went to the wood-pile, took an oak broom, cut the handle off, and with this heavy handle attempted to conquer me. I fought him, but he proved the strongest. At the sight of my bleeding form, his wife fell upon her knees and begged him to desist. My distress even touched her cold, jealous heart. I was so badly bruised that I was unable to leave my bed for five days. I will not dwell upon the bitter anguish of these hours, for even the thought of them now makes me shudder. The Rev. Mr. Burwell was not yet satisfied. He resolved to make another attempt to subdue my proud, rebellious spirit—made the attempt and again failed, when he told me, with an air of penitence, that he should never strike me another blow; and faithfully he kept his word. These revolting scenes created a great sensation at the time, were the talk of the town and neighborhood, and I flatter myself that the actions of those who had conspired against me were not viewed in a light to reflect much credit upon them.

The savage efforts to subdue my pride were not the only things that brought me suffering and deep mortification during my residence at Hillsboro'. I was regarded as fair-looking for one of my race, and for four years a white man[5]—I spare the world his name—had base designs upon me. I do not care to dwell upon this subject, for it is one that is fraught with pain. Suffice it to say, that he persecuted me for four years, and I—I—became a mother. The child of which he was the father was the only child that I ever brought into the world. If my poor boy[6] ever suffered any humiliating pangs on account of birth, he could not blame his mother, for God knows that she did not wish to give him life; he must blame the edicts of that society which deemed it no crime to undermine the virtue of girls in my then position.

Among the old letters preserved by my mother I find the following, written by myself while at Hillsboro'. In this connection I desire to state that Rev. Robert Burwell is now living[7] at Charlotte, North Carolina:—

"Hillsboro', April 10, 1838.

"My Dear Mother:—I have been intending to write to you for a long time, but numerous things have prevented, and for that reason you must excuse me.

"I thought very hard of you for not writing to me, but hope that you will answer this letter as soon as you receive it, and tell me how you like Marsfield, and if you have seen any of my old acquaintances, or if you yet know any of the brick-house people who I think so much of. I want to hear of the family at home very much, indeed. I really believe you and all the family have forgotten me, if not I certainly should have heard from some of you since you left Boyton, if it was only a line; nevertheless I love you all very dearly, and shall, although I may never see you again, nor do I ever expect to. Miss Anna is going to Petersburgh next winter, but she says that she does not intend to take me; what reason she has for leaving me I cannot tell. I have often wished that I lived where I knew I never could see you, for then I would not have my hopes raised, and to be disappointed in this manner; however, it is said that a bad beginning makes a good ending, but I hardly expect to see that happy day at this place. Give my love to all the family, both white and black. I was very much obliged to you for the presents you sent me last summer, though it is quite late in the day to be thanking for them. Tell Aunt Bella that I was very much obliged to her for her present; I have been so particular with it that I have only worn it once.

"There have been six weddings since October; the most respectable[8] one was about a fortnight ago; I was asked to be the first attendant, but, as usual with all my expectations, I was disappointed, for on the wedding-day I felt more like being locked up in a three-cornered box

5. Alexander McKenzie Kirkland (1807–1843), the violent, dissolute son of a prominent family in Hillsborough.

6. George Hobbs (1841–1861).

7. March, 1868 [*Keckly's note*].

8. Noteworthy, special.

than attending a wedding. About a week before Christmas I was bridesmaid for Ann Nash; when the night came I was in quite a trouble; I did not know whether my frock was clean or dirty; I only had a week's notice, and the body and sleeves to make, and only one hour every night to work on it, so you can see with these troubles to overcome my chance was rather slim. I must now close, although I could fill ten pages with my griefs and misfortunes; no tongue could express them as I feel; don't forget me though; and answer my letters soon. I will write you again, and would write more now, but Miss Anna says it is time I had finished. Tell Miss Elizabeth that I wish she would make haste and get married, for mistress says that I belong to her when she gets married.

"I wish you would send me a pretty frock this summer; if you will send it to Mrs. Robertson's Miss Bet will send it to me.

"Farewell, darling mother.
"Your affectionate daughter,

"Elizabeth Hobbs."

Chapter III

HOW I GAINED MY FREEDOM

The years passed and brought many changes to me, but on these I will not dwell, as I wish to hasten to the most interesting part of my story. My troubles in North Carolina were brought to an end by my unexpected return to Virginia, where I lived with Mr. Garland, who had married Miss Ann Burwell, one of my old master's daughters. His life was not a prosperous one, and after struggling with the world for several years he left his native State, a disappointed man. He moved to St. Louis, hoping to improve his fortune in the West; but ill luck followed him there, and he seemed to be unable to escape from the influence of the evil star of his destiny. When his family, myself included, joined him in his new home on the banks of the Mississippi, we found him so poor that he was unable to pay the dues on a letter advertised as in the post-office for him. The necessities of the family were so great, that it was proposed to place my mother out at service.[9] The idea was shocking to me. Every gray hair in her old head was dear to me, and I could not bear the thought of her going to work for strangers. She had been raised in the family, had watched the growth of each child from infancy to maturity; they had been the objects of her kindest care, and she was wound round about them as the vine winds itself about the rugged oak. They had been the central figures in her dream of life—a dream beautiful to her, since she had basked in the sunshine of no other. And now they proposed to destroy each tendril of affection, to cloud the sunshine of her existence when the day was drawing to a close, when the shadows of solemn night were rapidly approaching. My mother, my poor aged mother, go among strangers to toil for a living! No, a thousand times no! I would rather work my fingers to the bone, bend over my sewing till the film of blindness gathered in my eyes; nay, even beg from street to street. I told Mr. Garland so, and he gave me permission to see what I could do. I was fortunate in obtaining work, and in a short time I had acquired something of a reputation as a seamstress and dress-maker. The best ladies in St. Louis were my patrons,

9. To rent or lease someone's labor.

and when my reputation was once established I never lacked for orders. With my needle I kept bread in the mouths of seventeen persons for two years and five months. While I was working so hard that others might live in comparative comfort, and move in those circles of society to which their birth gave them entrance, the thought often occurred to me whether I was really worth my salt or not; and then perhaps the lips curled with a bitter sneer. It may seem strange that I should place so much emphasis upon words thoughtlessly, idly spoken; but then we do many strange things in life, and cannot always explain the motives that actuate[1] us. The heavy task was too much for me, and my health began to give way. About this time Mr. Keckley,[2] whom I had met in Virginia, and learned to regard with more than friendship, came to St. Louis. He sought my hand in marriage, and for a long time I refused to consider his proposal; for I could not bear the thought of bringing children into slavery—of adding one single recruit to the millions bound to hopeless servitude, fettered and shackled with chains stronger and heavier than manacles of iron. I made a proposition to buy myself and son; the proposition was bluntly declined, and I was commanded never to broach the subject again. I would not be put off thus, for hope pointed to a freer, brighter life in the future. Why should my son be held in slavery? I often asked myself. He came into the world through no will of mine, and yet, God only knows how I loved him. The Anglo-Saxon blood as well as the African flowed in his veins; the two currents commingled—one singing of freedom, the other silent and sullen with generations of despair. Why should not the Anglo-Saxon triumph—why should it be weighed down with the rich blood typical of the tropics? Must the life-current of one race bind the other race in chains as strong and enduring as if there had been no Anglo-Saxon taint? By the laws of God and nature, as interpreted by man, one-half of my boy was free, and why should not this fair birthright of freedom remove the curse from the other half—raise it into the bright, joyous sunshine of liberty? I could not answer these questions of my heart that almost maddened me, and I learned to regard human philosophy with distrust. Much as I respected the authority of my master, I could not remain silent on a subject that so nearly concerned me. One day, when I insisted on knowing whether he would permit me to purchase myself, and what price I must pay for myself, he turned to me in a petulant[3] manner, thrust his hand into his pocket, drew forth a bright silver quarter of a dollar, and proffering it to me, said:

"Lizzie, I have told you often not to trouble me with such a question. If you really wish to leave me, take this: it will pay the passage of yourself and boy on the ferry-boat, and when you are on the other side of the river you will be free. It is the cheapest way that I know of to accomplish what you desire."

I looked at him in astonishment, and earnestly replied: "No, master, I do not wish to be free in such a manner. If such had been my wish, I should never have troubled you about obtaining your consent to my purchasing myself. I can cross the river any day, as you well know, and have frequently done so, but will never leave you in such a manner. By the laws of the land I am your slave—you are my master, and I will only be free by such means as the laws of the country provide." He expected this answer, and I knew

1. Activate.
2. James "Judge" Keckley (d. 1868), popular St. Louis caterer. Although James spelled his name Keckley, considerable documentary evidence indicates that Elizabeth Hobbs spelled her married name Keckly. The publisher of *Behind the Scenes* erroneously printed her name as Keckley throughout the book.
3. Impatiently, irritated.

that he was pleased. Some time afterwards he told me that he had reconsidered the question; that I had served his family faithfully; that I deserved my freedom, and that he would take $1200 for myself and boy.

This was joyful intelligence[4] for me, and the reflection of hope gave a silver lining to the dark cloud of my life—faint, it is true, but still a silver lining.

Taking a prospective glance at liberty, I consented to marry. The wedding was a great event in the family. The ceremony took place in the parlor, in the presence of the family and a number of guests. Mr. Garland gave me away, and the pastor, Bishop Hawks, performed the ceremony, who had solemnized the bridals of Mr. G.'s own children. The day was a happy one, but it faded all too soon. Mr. Keckley—let me speak kindly of his faults—proved dissipated,[5] and a burden instead of a helpmate. More than all, I learned that he was a slave instead of a free man, as he represented himself to be. With the simple explanation that I lived with him eight years, let charity draw around him the mantle of silence.

I went to work in earnest to purchase my freedom, but the years passed, and I was still a slave. Mr. Garland's family claimed so much of my attention—in fact, I supported them—that I was not able to accumulate anything. In the mean time Mr. Garland died, and Mr. Burwell, a Mississippi planter, came to St. Louis to settle up the estate. He was a kind-hearted man, and said I should be free, and would afford me every facility to raise the necessary amount to pay the price of my liberty. Several schemes were urged upon me by my friends. At last I formed a resolution to go to New York, state my case, and appeal to the benevolence of the people. The plan seemed feasible, and I made preparations to carry it out. When I was almost ready to turn my face northward, Mrs. Garland told me that she would require the names of six gentlemen who would vouch for my return, and become responsible for the amount at which I was valued. I had many friends in St. Louis, and as I believed that they had confidence in me, I felt that I could readily obtain the names desired. I started out, stated my case, and obtained five signatures to the paper, and my heart throbbed with pleasure, for I did not believe that the sixth would refuse me. I called, he listened patiently, then remarked:

"Yes, yes, Lizzie; the scheme is a fair one, and you shall have my name. But I shall bid you good-by when you start."

"Good-by for a short time," I ventured to add.

"No, good-by for all time," and he looked at me as if he would read my very soul with his eyes.

I was startled. "What do you mean, Mr. Farrow? Surely you do not think that I do not mean to come back?"

"No."

"No, what then?"

"Simply this: you *mean* to come back, that is, you *mean* so *now*, but you never will. When you reach New York the abolitionists will tell you what savages we are, and they will prevail on you to stay there; and we shall never see you again."

"But I assure you, Mr. Farrow, you are mistaken. I not only *mean* to come back, but *will* come back, and pay every cent of the twelve hundred dollars for myself and child."

I was beginning to feel sick at heart, for I could not accept the signature of this man when he had no faith in my pledges. No; slavery, eternal slavery rather than be regarded with distrust by those whose respect I esteemed.

4. News.
5. To have indulged in intemperate or dissolute pleasures, especially by drinking or gambling.

"But—I am not mistaken," he persisted. "Time will show. When you start for the North I shall bid you good-by."

The heart grew heavy. Every ray of sunshine was eclipsed. With humbled pride, weary step, tearful face, and a dull, aching pain, I left the house. I walked along the street mechanically. The cloud had no silver lining now. The rosebuds of hope had withered and died without lifting up their heads to receive the dew kiss of morning. There was no morning for me—all was night, dark night.

I reached my own home, and weeping threw myself upon the bed. My trunk was packed, my luncheon was prepared by mother, the cars were ready to bear me where I would not hear the clank of chains, where I would breathe the free, invigorating breezes of the glorious North. I had dreamed such a happy dream, in imagination had drunk of the water, the pure, sweet crystal water of life, but now—now—the flowers had withered before my eyes; darkness had settled down upon me like a pall, and I was left alone with cruel mocking shadows.

The first paroxysm[6] of grief was scarcely over, when a carriage stopped in front of the house; Mrs. Le Bourgois, one of my kind patrons, got out of it and entered the door. She seemed to bring sunshine with her handsome cheery face. She came to where I was, and in her sweet way said:—

"Lizzie, I hear that you are going to New York to beg for money to buy your freedom. I have been thinking over the matter, and told Ma it would be a shame to allow you to go North to *beg* for what we should *give* you. You have many friends in St. Louis, and I am going to raise the twelve hundred dollars required among them. I have two hundred dollars put away for a present; am indebted to you one hundred dollars; mother owes you fifty dollars, and will add another fifty to it; and as I do not want the present, I will make the money a present to you. Don't start for New York now until I see what I can do among your friends."

Like a ray of sunshine she came, and like a ray of sunshine she went away. The flowers no longer were withered, drooping. Again they seemed to bud and grow in fragrance and beauty. Mrs. Le Bourgois, God bless her dear good heart, was more than successful. The twelve hundred dollars were raised, and at last my son and myself were free. Free, free! what a glorious ring to the word. Free! the bitter heart-struggle was over. Free! the soul could go out to heaven and to God with no chains to clog its flight or pull it down. Free! the earth wore a brighter look, and the very stars seemed to sing with joy. Yes, free! free by the laws of man and the smile of God—and Heaven bless them who made me so!

The following, copied from the original papers, contain, in brief, the history of my emancipation:—

> "I promise to give Lizzie and her son George their freedom, on the payment of $1200.
>
> "ANNE P. GARLAND.
>
> "June 27, 1855."
>
> "LIZZY:—I send you this note to sign for the sum of $75, and when I give you the whole amount you will then sign the other note for $100.
>
> "ELLEN M. DOAN.

6. Sudden outburst.

"In the paper you will find $25; see it is all right before the girl leaves."

"I have received of Lizzy Keckley $950, which I have deposited with Darby & Barksdale for her—$600 on the 21st July, $300 on the 27th and 28th of July, and $50 on 13th August, 1855.

"I have and shall make use of said money for Lizzy's benefit, and hereby guarantee to her one per cent. per month—as much more as can be made she shall have. The one per cent., as it may be checked out, I will be responsible for myself, as well as for the whole amount, when it shall be needed by her.

"WILLIS L. WILLIAMS.

"St. Louis, 13th August, 1855."

"Know all men by these presents, that for and in consideration of the love and affection we bear towards our sister, Anne P. Garland, of St. Louis, Missouri, and for the further consideration of $5 in hand paid, we hereby sell and convey unto her, the said Anne P. Garland, a negro woman named Lizzie, and a negro boy, her son, named George; said Lizzie now resides at St. Louis, and is a seamstress, known there as Lizzie Garland, the wife of a yellow man named James, and called James Keckley; said George is a bright mulatto boy, and is known in St. Louis as Garland's George. We warrant these two slaves to be slaves for life, but make no representations as to age or health.

"Witness our hands and seals, this 10th day of August, 1855.

"JAS. R. PUTNAM, [L.S.]
"E. M. PUTNAM, [L.S.]
"A. BURWELL, [L.S.]"

"The State of Mississippi, Warren County, City of Vicksburg. } *ss.*

"Be it remembered, that on the tenth day of August, in the year of our Lord one thousand eight hundred and fifty-five, before me, Francis N. Steele, a Commissioner, resident in the city of Vicksburg, duly commissioned and qualified by the executive authority, and under the laws of the State of Missouri, to take the acknowledgment of deeds, etc., to be used or recorded therein, personally appeared James R. Putnam and E. M. Putnam, his wife, and Armistead Burwell, to me known to be the individuals named in, and who executed the foregoing conveyance, and acknowledged that they executed the same for the purposes therein mentioned; and the E. M. Putnam being by me examined apart from her husband, and being fully acquainted with the contents of the foregoing conveyance, acknowledged that she executed the same freely, and relinquished her dower,[7] and any other claim she might have in and to the property therein mentioned, freely, and without fear, compulsion, or undue influence of her said husband.

"In witness whereof I have hereunto set my hand and affixed my official seal, this 10th day of August, A.D. 1855.

[L.S.] "F. N. STEELE,
"Commissioner for Missouri."

7. Dowry.

"Know all men that I, Anne P. Garland, of the County and City of St. Louis, State of Missouri, for and in consideration of the sum of $1200, to me in hand paid this day in cash, hereby emancipate my negro woman Lizzie, and her son George; the said Lizzie is known in St. Louis as the wife of James, who is called James Keckley; is of light complexion, about 37 years of age, by trade a dress-maker, and called by those who know her Garland's Lizzie. The said boy, George, is the only child of Lizzie, is about 16 years of age, and is almost white, and called by those who know him Garland's George.

"Witness my hand and seal, this 13th day of November, 1855.

"ANNE P. GARLAND, [L.S.]

"Witness:—JOHN WICKHAM,

"WILLIS L. WILLIAMS."

In St. Louis Circuit Court, October Term, 1855.
November 15, 1855.

"State of Missouri,
County of St. Louis. } *ss.*

"Be it remembered, that on this fifteenth day of November, eighteen hundred and fifty-five, in open court came John Wickham and Willis L. Williams, these two subscribing witnesses, examined under oath to that effect, proved the execution and acknowledgment of said deed by Anne P. Garland to Lizzie and her son George, which said proof of acknowledgment is entered on the record of the court of that day.

"In testimony whereof I hereto set my hand and affix the seal of said court, at office in the City of St. Louis, the day and year last aforesaid.

[L.S.] "WM J. HAMMOND, *Clerk.*"

"State of Missouri,
County of St. Louis. } *ss.*

"I, Wm. J. Hammond, Clerk of the Circuit Court within and for the county aforesaid, certify the foregoing to be a true copy of a deed of emancipation from Anne P. Garland to Lizzie and her son George, as fully as the same remain in my office.

"In testimony whereof I hereto set my hand and affix the seal of said court, at office in the City of St. Louis, this fifteenth day of November, 1855.

"WM J. HAMMOND, *Clerk.*

"By WM. A. PENNINGTON, D.C."

"State of Missouri,
County of St. Louis. } *ss.*

"I, the undersigned Recorder of said county, certify that the foregoing instrument of writing was filed for record in my office on the 14th day of November, 1855; it is truly recorded in Book No. 169, page 288.

"Witness my hand and official seal, date last aforesaid.

[L.S.] "C. KEEMLE, *Recorder.*"

Chapter IV

IN THE FAMILY OF SENATOR JEFFERSON DAVIS

The twelve hundred dollars with which I purchased the freedom of myself and son I consented to accept only as a loan. I went to work in earnest, and in a short time paid every cent that was so kindly advanced by my lady patrons of St Louis. All this time my husband was a source of trouble to me, and a burden. Too close occupation with my needle had its effects upon my health, and feeling exhausted with work, I determined to make a change. I had a conversation with Mr. Keckley; informed him that since he persisted in dissipation we must separate; that I was going North, and that I should never live with him again, at least until I had good evidence of his reform. He was rapidly debasing himself, and although I was willing to work for him, I was not willing to share his degradation. Poor man; he had his faults, but over these faults death has drawn a veil. My husband is now sleeping in his grave, and in the silent grave I would bury all unpleasant memories of him.

I left St. Louis in the spring of 1860, taking the cars direct for Baltimore, where I stopped six weeks, attempting to realize a sum of money by forming classes of young colored women, and teaching them my system of cutting and fitting dresses. The scheme was not successful, for after six weeks of labor and vexation, I left Baltimore with scarcely money enough to pay my fare to Washington. Arriving in the capital, I sought and obtained work at two dollars and a half per day. However, as I was notified that I could only remain in the city ten days without obtaining a license to do so, such being the law, and as I did not know whom to apply to for assistance, I was sorely troubled. I also had to have some one vouch to the authorities that I was a free woman. My means were too scanty, and my profession too precarious to warrant my purchasing license. In my perplexity I called on a lady for whom I was sewing, Miss Ringold, a member of Gen. Mason's family, from Virginia. I stated my case, and she kindly volunteered to render me all the assistance in her power. She called on Mayor Burritt with me, and Miss Ringold succeeded in making an arrangement for me to remain in Washington without paying the sum required for a license; moreover, I was not to be molested. I rented apartments in a good locality, and soon had a good run of custom.[8] The summer passed, winter came, and I was still in Washington. Mrs. Davis, wife of Senator Jefferson Davis, came from the South in November of 1860, with her husband. Learning that Mrs. Davis wanted a modiste,[9] I presented myself, and was employed by her on the recommendation of one of my patrons and her intimate friend, Mrs. Captain Hetsill. I went to the house to work, but finding that they were such late risers, and as I had to fit many dresses on Mrs. Davis, I told her that I should prefer giving half the day to her, working the other in my own room for some of my other lady patrons. Mrs. D. consented to the proposition, and it was arranged that I should come to her own house every day after 12 M. It was the winter before the breaking out of that fierce and bloody war between the two sections of the country; and as Mr. Davis occupied a leading position, his house was the resort of politicians and statesmen from the South. Almost every night, as I learned from the servants and other members of the family, secret meetings were held at the house; and

8. Clientele.
9. A woman who makes or sells fashionable clothes.

some of these meetings were protracted[1] to a very late hour. The prospects of war were freely discussed in my presence by Mr. and Mrs. Davis and their friends. The holidays were approaching, and Mrs. Davis kept me busy in manufacturing articles of dress for herself and children. She desired to present Mr. Davis on Christmas with a handsome dressing-gown. The material was purchased, and for weeks the work had been under way. Christmas eve came, and the gown had been laid aside so often that it was still unfinished. I saw that Mrs. D. was anxious to have it completed, so I volunteered to remain and work on it. Wearily the hours dragged on, but there was no rest for my busy fingers. I persevered in my task, notwithstanding my head was aching. Mrs. Davis was busy in the adjoining room, arranging the Christmas tree for the children. I looked at the clock, and the hands pointed to a quarter of twelve. I was arranging the cords on the gown when the Senator came in; he looked somewhat careworn, and his step seemed to be a little nervous. He leaned against the door, and expressed his admiration of the Christmas tree, but there was no smile on his face. Turning round, he saw me sitting in the adjoining room, and quickly exclaimed:

"That you, Lizzie! why are you here so late? Still at work; I hope that Mrs. Davis is not too exacting!"[2]

"No, sir," I answered. "Mrs. Davis was very anxious to have this gown finished to-night, and I volunteered to remain and complete it."

"Well, well, the case must be urgent," and he came slowly towards me, took the gown in his hand, and asked the color of the silk, as he said the gaslight was so deceptive to his old eyes.

"It is a drab changeable silk, Mr. Davis," I answered; and might have added that it was rich and handsome, but did not, well knowing that he would make the discovery in the morning.

He smiled curiously, but turned and walked from the room without another question. He inferred that the gown was for him, that it was to be the Christmas present from his wife, and he did not wish to destroy the pleasure that she would experience in believing that the gift would prove a surprise. In this respect, as in many others, he always appeared to me as a thoughtful, considerate man in the domestic circle. As the clock struck twelve I finished the gown, little dreaming of the future that was before it. It was worn, I have not the shadow of a doubt, by Mr. Davis during the stormy years that he was the President of the Confederate States.

The holidays passed, and before the close of January the war was discussed in Mr. Davis's family as an event certain to happen in the future. Mrs. Davis was warmly attached to Washington, and I often heard her say that she disliked the idea of breaking up old associations, and going South to suffer from trouble and deprivation. One day, while discussing the question in my presence with one of her intimate friends, she exclaimed: "I would rather remain in Washington and be kicked about, than go South and be Mrs. President." Her friend expressed surprise at the remark, and Mrs. Davis insisted that the opinion was an honest one.

While dressing her one day, she said to me: "Lizzie, you are so very handy that I should like to take you South with me."

"When do you go South, Mrs. Davis?" I inquired.

"Oh, I cannot tell just now, but it will be soon. You know there is going to be war, Lizzie?"

1. Extended.

2. Demanding.

"No!"

"But I tell you yes."

"Who will go to war?" I asked.

"The North and South," was her ready reply. "The Southern people will not submit to the humiliating demands of the Abolition party; they will fight first."

"And which do you think will whip?"

"The South, of course. The South is impulsive, is in earnest, and the Southern soldiers will fight to conquer. The North will yield, when it sees the South is in earnest, rather than engage in a long and bloody war."

"But, Mrs. Davis, are you certain that there will be war?"

"Certain!—I know it. You had better go South with me; I will take good care of you. Besides, when the war breaks out, the colored people will suffer in the North. The Northern people will look upon them as the cause of the war, and I fear, in their exasperation, will be inclined to treat you harshly. Then, I may come back to Washington in a few months, and live in the White House. The Southern people talk of choosing Mr. Davis for their President. In fact, it may be considered settled that he will be their President. As soon as we go South and secede from the other States, we will raise an army and march on Washington, and then I shall live in the White House."

I was bewildered with what I heard. I had served Mrs. Davis faithfully, and she had learned to place the greatest confidence in me. At first I was almost tempted to go South with her, for her reasoning seemed plausible. At the time the conversation was closed, with my promise to consider the question.

I thought over the question much, and the more I thought the less inclined I felt to accept the proposition so kindly made by Mrs. Davis. I knew the North to be strong, and believed that the people would fight for the flag that they pretended to venerate[3] so highly. The Republican party had just emerged from a heated campaign, flushed with victory, and I could not think that the hosts composing the party would quietly yield all they had gained in the Presidential canvass. A show of war from the South, I felt, would lead to actual war in the North; and with the two sections bitterly arrayed against each other, I preferred to cast my lot among the people of the North.

I parted with Mrs. Davis kindly, half promising to join her in the South if further deliberation should induce me to change my views. A few weeks before she left Washington I made two chintz[4] wrappers for her. She said that she must give up expensive dressing for a while; and that she, with the Southern people, now that war was imminent, must learn to practise lessons of economy. She left some fine needle-work in my hands, which I finished, and forwarded to her at Montgomery, Alabama, in the month of June, through the assistance of Mrs. Emory, one of her oldest and best friends.

Since bidding them good-by at Washington, early in the year 1860, I have never met any of the Davis family. Years of excitement, years of bloodshed, and hundreds of thousands of graves intervene between the months I spent in the family and now. The years have brought many changes; and in view of these terrible changes even I, who was once a slave, who have been punished with the cruel lash, who have experienced the heart and soul tortures of a slave's life, can say to Mr. Jefferson Davis, "Peace! you have suffered! Go in peace."

3. Respect, revere.

4. An inexpensive cotton print fabric.

In the winter of 1865 I was in Chicago, and one day visited the great charity fair held for the benefit of the families of those soldiers who were killed or wounded during the war. In one part of the building was a wax figure of Jefferson Davis, wearing over his other garments the dress in which it was reported that he was captured. There was always a great crowd around this figure, and I was naturally attracted towards it. I worked my way to the figure, and in examining the dress made the pleasing discovery that it was one of the chintz wrappers that I had made for Mrs. Davis, a short time before she departed from Washington for the South. When it was announced that I recognized the dress as one that I had made for the wife of the late Confederate President there was great cheering and excitement, and I at once became an object of the deepest curiosity. Great crowds followed me, and in order to escape from the embarrassing situation I left the building.

I believe it now is pretty well established that Mr. Davis had on a waterproof cloak instead of a dress, as first reported, when he was captured. This does not invalidate any portion of my story. The dress on the wax figure at the fair in Chicago unquestionably was one of the chintz wrappers that I made for Mrs. Davis in January, 1860, in Washington; and I infer, since it was not found on the body of the fugitive President of the South, it was taken from the trunks of Mrs. Davis, captured at the same time. Be this as it may, the coincidence is none the less striking and curious.

1868

FREDERICK DOUGLASS
1818–1895

In his introduction to Frederick Douglass's second autobiography, *My Bondage and My Freedom* (1855), James McCune Smith, an African American physician and abolitionist, hailed Douglass as "a Representative American man—a type of his countrymen." To Smith, Douglass's record of "self-elevation" from the lowest to the highest condition in society marked him as a "noble example" for all Americans to emulate. Rising through the ranks of the antislavery movement in the 1840s and 1850s to become Black America's most electrifying speaker and commanding writer, Douglass by the outbreak of the Civil War was generally recognized as the premier African American leader and spokesman for his people. Through the latter half of the nineteenth century Douglass dedicated his leadership to building a racially integrated America in which skin color would cease to determine an individual's social respectability and economic opportunities. As the most highly regarded African American man of letters in the nineteenth century, Douglass devoted his literary efforts primarily to the creation of a heroic image of himself that would inspire in Blacks the belief that color need not be a permanent bar to their achievement of the American Dream, while reminding whites of their obligation as Americans to support free and equal access to that dream for all Americans.

The man who became internationally famous as Frederick Douglass was born in the backcountry of Maryland's Eastern Shore, the son of Harriet Bailey, an enslaved agricultural worker, and an unknown white man. Throughout his adult life, Douglass tried futilely to obtain reliable information about the date of his birth, which as far as he knew was never recorded. Biographical scholarship, however, has uncovered the property book of Douglass's first enslaver, Aaron Anthony, in which Frederick Augustus Washington Bailey's birth is listed as February 1818. In his first autobiography, *Narrative of the Life of Frederick Douglass* (1845), Douglass cited the resentment he felt over not knowing his birthday as early evidence of "a restless spirit" that would goad him into increasing defiance of the institution into which he had been born. But in many respects Douglass's childhood in slavery was not as miserable as it might have been, despite the fact that his mother died when he was about seven years old. In his *Narrative* Douglass recalled having suffered much more from hunger and cold as a child than from beatings or other forms of overt abuse.

Before he was old enough to do fieldwork, Frederick was selected to go to Baltimore in 1826 to become a domestic worker in the home of Sophia and Hugh Auld. Like her sister-in-law, Lucretia Anthony Auld, who had befriended Frederick on the Eastern Shore plantation where he spent his early childhood, Sophia Auld treated her obviously talented new servant with unusual kindness. She went so far as to begin reading lessons for Frederick, until her husband angrily closed the books on further efforts to brighten the mental outlook of the enslaved boy. Refusing to accept Hugh Auld's dictates, Frederick took his first covertly rebellious steps by teaching himself to read and write.

In 1833 a quarrel between Hugh Auld and his brother Thomas, Frederick's legal owner, resulted in Frederick's return to his original home in St. Michaels, Maryland. Tensions between the recalcitrant Black youth and his owner convinced Auld to hire Frederick out as a farm worker in January 1834 under the supervision of Edward Covey, a local slave breaker. After six months of unstinting labor, relentless whippings, and persistent humiliations, the desperate sixteen-year-old fought back, resisting one of Covey's attempted beatings and intimidating his tormentor sufficiently to forestall future attacks. Douglass's dramatic account of his battle with Covey would become the heroic turning point of his future autobiographies and one of the most celebrated scenes in all of antebellum African American literature.

In the spring of 1836 Thomas Auld sent Frederick back to Baltimore to learn the calking trade in the city's shipyards. What Hugh Auld did not take from his earnings Frederick invested in a scheme to seize his freedom. Aided by his future spouse, Anna Murray, a free woman, and masquerading as a free merchant sailor, Frederick Bailey took a northbound train out of Baltimore on September 3, 1838. He arrived safely in New York City the next day. Before a month had passed he and Anna were reunited, married, and living in New Bedford, Massachusetts, as Mr. and Mrs. Frederick Douglass, the new last name recommended by a friend in New Bedford's thriving Black community. Less than three years later Douglass joined the abolitionist movement as a full-time lecturer. His natural brilliance, imposing physique, and rhetorical skill soon brought him national notoriety.

Although he was best known in his own time as a speaker, Douglass worked hard to deserve the recognition he enjoys today as a writer. Rumors that a man of such accomplished address could never have been enslaved drove Douglass to the decision to put his life's story into print in 1845. He was far from the first fugitive from slavery to produce an account of his experiences in bondage. But the *Narrative of the Life of Frederick Douglass, an American Slave, Written by Himself* was unquestionably the epitome of the antebellum fugitive slave narrative. Selling more than thirty thousand copies in the first five years of its existence, Douglass's *Narrative* became an international bestseller, its contemporary readership far outstripping that of such classic white autobiographies as Henry David Thoreau's *Walden* (1854). The abolitionist leader William Lloyd Garrison introduced Douglass's *Narrative* by stressing how representative Douglass's experience of slavery had been. But Garrison could not help but note the extraordinary individuality of the Black author's manner of rendering that experience. What makes the *Narrative* so memorable is Douglass's style of self-presentation, through which he dramatized the evolution of his sense of self via conflict with the mental as well as physical bonds of slavery. After the *Narrative,* the presence of the subtitle, *Writ-*

Daguerreotype of Frederick Douglass taken in Akron, Ohio, by Samuel J. Miller sometime between 1847 and 1852.

ten by Himself, on a slave narrative bore increasing political and literary significance as an indicator of a narrator's self-determination and intellectual self-reliance. Fearing that the added attention that his *Narrative* would attract would make him an easy target for slave catchers, Douglass went on a lecture tour in England and Ireland immediately after the publication of his *Narrative*. When he came back to the United States in the spring of 1847, he had resolved, against the advice of many of his associates in Garrison's American Anti-Slavery Society, to launch his own newspaper, *The North Star*. In part Douglass wanted to prove that a Black-run newspaper could succeed; in part he needed a forum from which to express himself freely, without having to consult his former mentors and sponsors in Garrison's antislavery circle. Douglass kept his newspaper going from 1847 to 1863, authoring most of the articles and editorials himself. One of the literary highlights of his newspaper was a novella he wrote and published in March 1853, under the title *The Heroic Slave*. Based on an actual mutiny of enslaved captives off the coast of the United States, *The Heroic Slave* brought Douglass, and with him Black America, into the war of words that Harriet Beecher Stowe's *Uncle Tom's Cabin* (1852) precipitated in American literary fiction.

During the early 1850s the once close relationship between Douglass and Garrison ruptured in a split that forced the Black reformer to reassess his philosophy and goals. Out of this time of soul searching came Douglass's second autobiography, *My Bondage and My Freedom* (1855). In this remarkable reevaluation of his life from the standpoint of almost fifteen years of freedom, Douglass addressed the injustices of slavery in the South and racism in the North with unprecedented candor. Much more than the 1845 *Narrative*, *My Bondage and My Freedom* unmasks caste and class structures nationwide to expose the nexus of prejudice and privilege underlying American social, economic, and political life. Having become an outspoken advocate for women's rights, Douglass wrote into *My Bondage and My Freedom* the story of an enslaved female rebel whose heroic fight with an overseer does not appear in the 1845 *Narrative*. *My Bondage and My Freedom* also recounts Douglass's early years in the abolitionist movement more critically than does the *Narrative*. In the last pages of his second autobiography, Douglass acknowledged that his search for freedom had not reached its fulfillment. "Progress is yet possible," he asserted. But the ending of *My Bondage and My Freedom* also indicates Douglass's realization that anchoring himself in the northern Black community was essential to his attaining a fully liberated and fulfilled sense of self.

After the outbreak of the Civil War, Douglass lobbied President Lincoln to admit Black troops into the Union army and navy. When mass recruitment of African Americans finally began in the spring of 1863, Douglass's speeches rallied northern Black men to war against the southern slaveocracy. After victory in 1865, Douglass pleaded in vain with Lincoln's presidential successor, Andrew Johnson, for a national voting rights act that would allow African American men to vote in all states. Douglass's loyalty to the Republican Party, whose candidates he supported throughout his later years, won him appointment to the highest political offices that any Black man from the North had ever won: federal marshal and recorder of deeds for the District of Columbia, president of the Freedmen's Bureau Bank, consul to Haiti, and chargé d'affaires for the Dominican Republic. The income he earned from these civil and diplomatic service positions, coupled with the fees he received for his popular lectures, most notably one titled "Self-Made Men," allowed Douglass and his family to live in comfort in Washington, D.C., during the last two decades of his life. His final memoir, *Life and Times of Frederick Douglass*, first published in 1881 and expanded in 1892, did not excite the admiration of reviewers or sell widely, as his first two autobiographies had. But it was enough for Douglass to express through *Life and Times* his confidence that his had been a "life of victory, if not complete, at least assured." Douglass died of a heart attack on February 20, 1895, a few hours after he had delivered a rousing speech to a women's rights rally.

Although the early twentieth century heard an occasional plea for the recognition of Frederick Douglass as a major contributor to the tradition of American autobiographical literature, not until the Civil Rights movement of the 1950s and the agitation for Black Studies in the 1960s did the *Narrative of the Life of Frederick Douglass* begin its ascent into the highest echelons of nineteenth-century American prose. After years of obscurity, *My Bondage and My Freedom* is now regarded as one of the crucial "I-narratives" of the American 1850s, comparable in significance to the first-person writings of such renowned figures as Thoreau and Walt Whitman. In the history of African American literature, Douglass's importance and influence are virtually immeasurable. His *Narrative* gave the English-speaking world the most compelling and sophisticated rendition of African American selfhood ever fashioned by a Black writer up to that time. Douglass's literary artistry invested this model of selfhood with a moral and political authority that subsequent aspirants to the role of African American culture hero—from the conservative Booker T. Washington to the radical W. E. B. Du Bois—would seek to appropriate for their own autobiographical self-portraits. "Frederick Douglass's mighty, leonine gaze," as President Barack Obama put it in 2016, informs and inspires twentieth- and twenty-first-century African American literature—from Paul

Laurence Dunbar's brooding poetic tribute "Douglass" (1903) to the idealistic Ned Douglass in Ernest J. Gaines's novel *The Autobiography of Miss Jane Pittman* (1971) and the fugitive seekers in Colson Whitehead's *The Underground Railroad* (2016), Ta-Nehisi Coates's *The Water Dancer* (2019), and Rivers Solomon's *The Deep* (2019).

Narrative of the Life of Frederick Douglass, an American Slave, Written by Himself[1]

Preface[2]

In the month of August, 1841, I attended an anti-slavery convention in Nantucket, at which it was my happiness to become acquainted with FREDERICK DOUGLASS, the writer of the following Narrative. He was a stranger to nearly every member of that body; but, having recently made his escape from the southern prison-house of bondage, and feeling his curiosity excited to ascertain the principles and measures of the abolitionists,—of whom he had heard a somewhat vague description while he was a slave,—he was induced to give his attendance, on the occasion alluded to, though at that time a resident in New Bedford.[3]

Fortunate, most fortunate occurrence!—fortunate for the millions of his manacled brethren, yet panting for deliverance from their awful thraldom!—fortunate for the cause of negro emancipation, and of universal liberty!—fortunate for the land of his birth, which he has already done so much to save and bless!—fortunate for a large circle of friends and acquaintances, whose sympathy and affection he has strongly secured by the many sufferings he has endured, by his virtuous traits of character, by his ever-abiding remembrance of those who are in bonds, as being bound with them!—fortunate for the multitudes, in various parts of our republic, whose minds he has enlightened on the subject of slavery, and who have been melted to tears by his pathos, or roused to virtuous indignation by his stirring eloquence against the enslavers of men!—fortunate for himself, as it at once brought him into the field of public usefulness, "gave the world assurance of a MAN,"[4] quickened the slumbering energies of his soul, and consecrated him to the great work of breaking the rod of the oppressor, and letting the oppressed go free!

I shall never forget his first speech at the convention—the extraordinary emotion it excited in my own mind—the powerful impression it created upon a crowded auditory, completely taken by surprise—the applause which followed from the beginning to the end of his felicitous remarks. I think I never hated slavery so intensely as at that moment; certainly, my perception of the enormous outrage which is inflicted by it, on the godlike nature of its victims, was rendered far more clear than ever. There stood one, in physical proportion and stature commanding and exact—in intellect richly endowed—in natural eloquence a prodigy—in soul manifestly "created but a little lower than the angels"[5]—yet a slave, ay, a fugitive slave,—trembling for his safety,

1. First printed in May 1845 by the Anti-Slavery Office in Boston, the source of the present text.
2. The preface is by William Lloyd Garrison (1805–1879), American journalist and social reformer, and one of the most uncompromising spokesmen for radical abolition in the United States.
3. Douglass escaped from Baltimore on September 3, 1838, and settled in New Bedford, Massachusetts, where he eventually became active in the antislavery movement.
4. Shakespeare's *Hamlet* 3.4.62.
5. God created humans "a little lower than the angels" to have authority over all other living creatures (Psalms 8:5). Paul calls the Hebrews to look at Christ, who was made "a little lower than the angels" (Hebrews 2:7, 9).

hardly daring to believe that on the American soil, a single white person could be found who would befriend him at all hazards, for the love of God and humanity! Capable of high attainments as an intellectual and moral being—needing nothing but a comparatively small amount of cultivation to make him an ornament to society and a blessing to his race—by the law of the land, by the voice of the people, by the terms of the slave code, he was only a piece of property, a beast of burden, a chattel personal, nevertheless!

A beloved friend[6] from New Bedford prevailed on Mr. Douglass to address the convention: He came forward to the platform with a hesitancy and embarrassment, necessarily the attendants of a sensitive mind in such a novel position. After apologizing for his ignorance, and reminding the audience that slavery was a poor school for the human intellect and heart, he proceeded to narrate some of the facts in his own history as a slave, and in the course of his speech gave utterance to many noble thoughts and thrilling reflections. As soon as he had taken his seat, filled with hope and admiration, I rose, and declared that Patrick Henry[7] of revolutionary fame, never made a speech more eloquent in the cause of liberty, than the one we had just listened to from the lips of that hunted fugitive. So I believed at that time—such is my belief now. I reminded the audience of the peril which surrounded this self-emancipated young man at the North,—even in Massachusetts, on the soil of the Pilgrim Fathers, among the descendants of revolutionary sires; and I appealed to them, whether they would ever allow him to be carried back into slavery,—law or no law, constitution or no constitution. The response was unanimous and in thunder tones "NO!" "Will you succor and protect him as a brother-man—a resident of the old Bay State."[8] "YES!" shouted the whole mass, with an energy so startling, that the ruthless tyrants south of Mason and Dixon's line might almost have heard the mighty burst of feeling, and recognized it as the pledge of an invincible determination, on the part of those who gave it, never to betray him that wanders, but to hide the outcast, and firmly to abide the consequences.

It was at once deeply impressed upon my mind, that, if Mr. Douglass could be persuaded to consecrate his time and talents to the promotion of the anti-slavery enterprise, a powerful impetus would be given to it, and a stunning blow at the same time inflicted on northern prejudice against a colored complexion. I therefore endeavored to instill hope and courage into his mind, in order that he might dare to engage in a vocation so anomalous and responsible for a person in his situation; and I was seconded in this effort by warm-hearted friends, especially by the late General Agent of the Massachusetts Anti-Slavery Society, Mr. John A. Collins, whose judgment in this instance entirely coincided with my own. At first, he could give no encouragement; with unfeigned diffidence, he expressed his conviction that he was not adequate to the performance of so great a task; the path marked out was wholly an untrodden one; he was sincerely apprehensive that he should do more harm than good. After much deliberation, however, he consented to make a trial; and ever since that period, he has acted as a lecturing agent, under the auspices either of the American or the Massachusetts Anti-Slavery Society. In labors he has been most abundant; and his success in combating

6. William C. Coffin, New Bedford's leading abolitionist at the time.
7. American patriot (1736–1799), famous for the words: "I know not what course others may take, but as for me, give me liberty or give me death."
8. That is, Massachusetts.

prejudice, in gaining proselytes, in agitating the public mind, has far surpassed the most sanguine expectations that were raised at the commencement of his brilliant career. He has borne himself with gentleness and meekness, yet with true manliness of character. As a public speaker, he excels in pathos, wit, comparison, imitation, strength of reasoning, and fluency of language. There is in him that union of head and heart, which is indispensable to an enlightenment of the heads and a winning of the hearts of others. May his strength continue to be equal to his day! May he continue to "grow in grace, and in the knowledge of God,"[9] that he may be increasingly serviceable in the cause of bleeding humanity, whether at home or abroad!

It is certainly a very remarkable fact, that one of the most efficient advocates of the slave population, now before the public, is a fugitive slave, in the person of FREDERICK DOUGLASS; and that the free colored population of the United States are as ably represented by one of their own number, in the person of CHARLES LENOX REMOND,[1] whose eloquent appeals have extorted the highest applause of multitudes on both sides of the Atlantic. Let the calumniators[2] of the colored race despise themselves for their baseness and illiberality of spirit, and henceforth cease to talk of the natural inferiority of those who require nothing but time and opportunity to attain to the highest point of human excellence.

It may, perhaps, be fairly questioned, whether any other portion of the population of the earth could have endured the privations, sufferings and horrors of slavery, without having become more degraded in the scale of humanity than the slaves of African descent. Nothing has been left undone to cripple their intellects, darken their minds, debase their moral nature, obliterate all traces of their relationship to mankind; and yet how wonderfully they have sustained the mighty load of a most frightful bondage, under which they have been groaning for centuries! To illustrate the effect of slavery on the white man,—to show that he has no powers of endurance, in such a condition, superior to those of his black brother,—DANIEL O'CONNELL,[3] the distinguished advocate of universal emancipation, and the mightiest champion of prostrate but not conquered Ireland, relates the following anecdote in a speech delivered by him in the Conciliation Hall, Dublin, before the Loyal National Repeal Association, March 31, 1845. "No matter," said Mr. O'CONNELL, "under what specious term it may disguise itself, slavery is still hideous. *It has a natural, an inevitable tendency to brutalize every noble faculty of man.* An American sailor, who was cast away on the shore of Africa, where he was kept in slavery for three years, was at the expiration of that period, found to be imbruted and stultified—he had lost all reasoning power; and having forgotten his native language, could only utter some savage gibberish between Arabic and English, which nobody could understand, and which even he himself found difficulty in pronouncing. So much for the humanizing influence of THE DOMESTIC INSTITUTION!" Admitting this to have been an extraordinary case of mental deterioration, it proves at least that the white slave can sink as low in the scale of humanity as the black one.

9. 2 Peter 3:18.
1. A free-born Black man (1810–1873), the first African American employed by the Massachusetts Anti-Slavery Society as a lecturer. He toured with Douglass in 1842.
2. Those who make malicious false charges.
3. Irish statesman (1775–1847), fighter for Catholic emancipation and Irish independence, called "the Liberator."

Mr. DOUGLASS has very properly chosen to write his own Narrative, in his own style, and according to the best of his ability, rather than to employ some one else. It is, therefore, entirely his own production; and, considering how long and dark was the career he had to run as a slave,—how few have been his opportunities to improve his mind since he broke his iron fetters,—it is, in my judgment, highly creditable to his head and heart. He who can peruse it without a tearful eye, a heaving breast, an afflicted spirit,—without being filled with an unutterable abhorrence of slavery and all its abettors, and animated with a determination to seek the immediate overthrow of that execrable system,—without trembling for the fate of this country in the hands of a righteous God, who is ever on the side of the oppressed, and whose arm is not shortened that it cannot save,—must have a flinty heart, and be qualified to act the part of a trafficker "in slaves and the souls of men."[4] I am confident that it is essentially true in all its statements; that nothing has been set down in malice, nothing exaggerated, nothing drawn from the imagination; that it comes short of the reality, rather than overstates a single fact in regard to SLAVERY AS IT IS. The experience of FREDERICK DOUGLASS, as a slave, was not a peculiar one; his lot was not especially a hard one; his case may be regarded as a very fair specimen of the treatment of slaves in Maryland, in which State it is conceded that they are better fed and less cruelly treated than in Georgia, Alabama, or Louisiana. Many have suffered incomparably more, while very few on the plantations have suffered less, than himself. Yet how deplorable was his situation! what terrible chastisements were inflicted upon his person! what still more shocking outrages were perpetrated upon his mind! with all his noble powers and sublime aspirations, how like a brute was he treated, even by those professing to have the same mind in them that was in Christ Jesus! to what dreadful liabilities was he continually subjected! how destitute of friendly counsel and aid, even in his greatest extremities! how heavy was the midnight of woe which shrouded in blackness the last ray of hope, and filled the future with terror and gloom! what longings after freedom took possession of his breast, and how his misery augmented, in proportion as he grew reflective and intelligent,—thus demonstrating that a happy slave is an extinct man! how he thought, reasoned, felt, under the lash of the driver, with the chains upon his limbs! what perils he encountered in his endeavors to escape from his horrible doom! and how signal have been his deliverance and preservation in the midst of a nation of pitiless enemies!

This Narrative contains many affecting incidents, many passages of great eloquence and power; but I think the most thrilling one of them all is the description DOUGLASS gives of his feelings, as he stood soliloquizing respecting his fate, and the chances of his one day being a freeman, on the banks of the Chesapeake Bay—view in the receding vessels as they flew with their white wings before the breeze, and apostrophizing[5] them as animated by the living spirit of freedom. Who can read that passage, and be insensible to its pathos and sublimity? Compressed into it is a whole Alexandrian library[6] of thought, feeling, and sentiment—all that can, all that need be urged, in the form of expostulation, entreaty, rebuke, against that crime of crimes,—making man the property of his fellow-man! O, how accursed is that system, which entombs the godlike mind of man, defaces the divine image, reduces those who by creation were crowned with glory and honor to a level

4. See Revelation 18:13.
5. Addressing a personified thing (in this case, the Chesapeake Bay) in eloquent speech.
6. Alexandria, in Egypt, housed the great library center of the Greco-Roman world.

with four-footed beasts, and exalts the dealer in human flesh above all that is called God! Why should its existence be prolonged one hour? Is it not evil, only evil, and that continually? What does its presence imply but the absence of all fear of God, all regard for man, on the part of the people of the United States? Heaven speed its eternal overthrow!

So profoundly ignorant of the nature of slavery are many persons, that they are stubbornly incredulous whenever they read or listen to any recital of the cruelties which are daily inflicted on its victims. They do not deny that the slaves are held as property; but that terrible fact seems to convey to their minds no idea of injustice, exposure to outrage, or savage barbarity. Tell them of cruel scourgings, of mutilations and brandings, of scenes of pollution and blood, of the banishment of all light and knowledge, and they affect to be greatly indignant at such enormous exaggerations, such wholesale misstatements, such abominable libels on the character of the southern planters! As if all these direful outrages were not the natural results of slavery! As if it were less cruel to reduce a human being to the condition of a thing, than to give him a severe flagellation, or to deprive him of necessary food and clothing! As if whips, chains, thumb-screws, paddles, bloodhounds, overseers, drivers, patrols, were not all indispensable to keep the slaves down, and to give protection to their ruthless oppressors! As if, when the marriage institution is abolished, concubinage, adultery, and incest, must not necessarily abound; when all the rights of humanity are annihilated, any barrier remains to protect the victim from the fury of the spoiler; when absolute power is assumed over life and liberty, it will not be wielded with destructive sway! Skeptics of this character abound in society. In some few instances, their incredulity arises from a want of reflection; but, generally, it indicates a hatred of the light, a desire to shield slavery from the assaults of its foes, a contempt of the colored race, whether bond or free. Such will try to discredit the shocking tales of slaveholding cruelty which are recorded in this truthful Narrative; but they will labor in vain. Mr. Douglass has frankly disclosed the place of his birth, the names of those who claimed ownership in his body and soul, and the names also of those who committed the crimes which he has alleged against them. His statements, therefore, may easily be disproved, if they are untrue.

In the course of his Narrative, he relates two instances of murderous cruelty,—in one of which a planter deliberately shot a slave belonging to a neighboring plantation, who had unintentionally gotten within his lordly domain in quest of fish; and in the other, an overseer blew out the brains of a slave who had fled to a stream of water to escape a bloody scourging. Mr. Douglass states that in neither of these instances was any thing done by way of legal arrest or judicial investigation. The Baltimore American, of March 17, 1845, relates a similar case of atrocity, perpetrated with similar impunity—as follows:—"*Shooting a Slave.*—We learn, upon the authority of a letter from Charles county, Maryland, received by a gentleman of this city, that a young man, named Matthews, a nephew of General Matthews, and whose father, it is believed, holds an office at Washington, killed one of the slaves upon his father's farm by shooting him. The letter states that young Matthews had been left in charge of the farm; that he gave an order to the servant, which was disobeyed, when he proceeded to the house, *obtained a gun, and, returning, shot the servant.* He immediately, the letter continues, fled to his father's residence, where he still remains unmolested."—Let it never be forgotten, that no slaveholder or overseer can be convicted of any outrage perpetrated on the person of a slave, however diabolical it may be, on the testimony of colored witnesses, whether bond or free. By the slave code, they are adjudged to be as incompetent to testify against a white man, as though they were indeed a part of the brute creation. Hence, there is no legal protection in fact, whatever there may be in form, for the slave population; and any amount of cruelty may be inflicted on them with impunity. Is it possible for the human mind to conceive of a more horrible state of society?

The effect of a religious profession on the conduct of southern masters is vividly described in the following Narrative, and shown to be any thing but salutary. In the nature of the case, it must be in the highest degree pernicious. The testimony of Mr. Douglass, on this point, is sustained by a cloud of witnesses, whose veracity is unimpeachable. "A slaveholder's profession of Christianity is a palpable imposture. He is a felon of the highest grade. He is a manstealer. It is of no importance what you put in the other scale."

Reader! are you with the man-stealers in sympathy and purpose, or on the side of their down-trodden victims? If with the former, then are you the foe of God and man. If with the latter, what are you prepared to do and dare in their behalf? Be faithful, be vigilant, be untiring in your efforts to break every yoke, and let the oppressed go free.[7] Come what may—cost what it may—inscribe on the banner which you unfurl to the breeze, as your religious and political motto—"No Compromise with Slavery! No Union with Slaveholders!"

WM. LLOYD GARRISON

Boston, *May* 1, 1845.

Letter from Wendell Phillips, Esq.[8]

BOSTON, April 22, 1845.

My Dear Friend:

You remember the old fable of "The Man and the Lion" where the lion complained that he should not be so misrepresented "when the lions wrote history."

I am glad the time has come when the "lions write history." We have been left long enough to gather the character of slavery from the involuntary evidence of the masters. One might, indeed, rest sufficiently satisfied with what, it is evident, must be, in general, the results of such a relation, without seeking farther to find whether they have followed in every instance. Indeed, those who stare at the half-peck of corn a week, and love to count the lashes on the slave's back, are seldom the "stuff" out of which reformers and abolitionists are to be made. I remember that, in 1838, many were waiting for the results of the West India experiment,[9] before they could come into our ranks. Those "results" have come long ago; but, alas! few of that number have come with them, as converts. A man must be disposed to judge of emancipation by other tests than whether it has increased the produce of sugar,—and to hate

7. Isaiah 58:6.
8. A leading abolitionist (1811–1884).
9. Slavery was officially abolished in the West Indies and throughout the British Empire in 1833. The process of emancipation was completed in 1838.

slavery for other reasons than because it starves men and whips women,—before he is ready to lay the first stone of his anti-slavery life.

I was glad to learn, in your story, how early the most neglected of God's children waken to a sense of their rights, and of the injustice done them. Experience is a keen teacher; and long before you had mastered your A B C, or knew where the "white sails" of the Chesapeake were bound, you began, I see, to gauge the wretchedness of the slave, not by his hunger and want, not by his lashes and toil, but by the cruel and blighting death which gathers over his soul.

In connection with this, there is one circumstance which makes your recollections peculiarly valuable, and renders your early insight the more remarkable. You come from that part of the country where we are told slavery appears with its fairest features. Let us hear, then, what it is at its best estate—gaze on its bright side, if it has one; and then imagination may task her powers to add dark lines to the picture, as she travels southward to that (for the colored man) Valley of the Shadow of Death,[1] where the Mississippi sweeps along.

Again, we have known you long, and can put the most entire confidence in your truth, candor, and sincerity. Every one who has heard you speak has felt, and, I am confident, every one who reads your book will feel, persuaded that you give them a fair specimen of the whole truth. No one-sided portrait,—no wholesale complaints,—but strict justice done, whenever individual kindliness has neutralized, for a moment, the deadly system with which it was strangely allied. You have been with us, too, some years, and can fairly compare the twilight of rights, which your race enjoy at the North, with that "noon of night" under which they labor south of Mason and Dixon's line. Tell us whether, after all, the half-free colored man of Massachusetts is worse off than the pampered slave of the rice swamps!

In reading your life, no one can say that we have unfairly picked out some rare specimens of cruelty. We know that the bitter drops, which even you have drained from the cup, are no incidental aggravations, no individual ills, but such as must mingle always and necessarily in the lot of every slave. They are the essential ingredients, not the occasional results, of the system.

After all, I shall read your book with trembling for you. Some years ago, when you were beginning to tell me your real name and birthplace, you may remember I stopped you, and preferred to remain ignorant of all. With the exception of a vague description, so I continued, till the other day, when you read me your memoirs. I hardly knew, at the time, whether to thank you or not for the sight of them, when I reflected that it was still dangerous, in Massachusetts, for honest men to tell their names! They say the fathers, in 1776, signed the Declaration of Independence with the halter about their necks. You, too, publish your declaration of freedom with danger compassing you around. In all the broad lands which the Constitution of the United States overshadows, there is no single spot,—however narrow or desolate,—where a fugitive slave can plant himself and say, "I am safe." The whole armory of Northern Law has no shield for you. I am free to say that, in your place, I should throw the MS. into the fire.

You, perhaps, may tell your story in safety, endeared as you are to so many warm hearts by rare gifts, and a still rarer devotion of them to the service of others. But it will be owing only to your labors, and the fearless efforts of

1. Psalms 23:4.

those who, trampling the laws and Constitution of the country under their feet, are determined that they will "hide the outcast,"[2] and that their hearths shall be, spite of the law, an asylum for the oppressed, if, some time or other, the humblest may stand in our streets, and bear witness in safety against the cruelties which he has been the victim.

Yet it is sad to think, that these very throbbing hearts which welcome your story, and form your best safeguard in telling it, are all beating contrary to the "statute in such case made and provided." Go on, my dear friend, till you, and those who, like you, have been saved, so as by fire, from the dark prison-house, shall stereotype these free, illegal pulses into statutes; and New England, cutting loose from a blood-stained Union, shall glory in being the house of refuge for the oppressed;—till we no longer merely "*hide* the outcast," or make a merit of standing idly by while he is hunted in our midst; but, consecrating anew the soil of the Pilgrims as an asylum for the oppressed, proclaim our *welcome* to the slave so loudly, that the tones shall reach every hut in the Carolinas, and make the broken-hearted bondman leap up at the thought of old Massachusetts.

God speed the day!
Till then, and ever,
Yours truly,

WENDELL PHILLIPS

Chapter I

I was born in Tuckahoe, near Hillsborough, and about twelve miles from Easton, in Talbot county, Maryland. I have no accurate knowledge of my age, never having seen any authentic record containing it. By far the larger part of the slaves know as little of their ages as horses know of theirs, and it is the wish of most masters within my knowledge to keep their slaves thus ignorant. I do not remember to have ever met a slave who could tell of his birthday. They seldom come nearer to it than planting-time, harvest-time, cherry-time, spring-time, or fall-time. A want of information concerning my own was a source of unhappiness to me even during childhood. The white children could tell their ages. I could not tell why I ought to be deprived of the same privilege. I was not allowed to make any inquiries of my master concerning it. He deemed all such inquiries on the part of a slave improper and impertinent, and evidence of a restless spirit. The nearest estimate I can give makes me now between twenty-seven and twenty-eight years of age. I come to this, from hearing my master say, some time during 1835, I was about seventeen years old.

My mother was named Harriet Bailey. She was the daughter of Isaac and Betsey Bailey, both colored, and quite dark. My mother was of a darker complexion than either my grandmother or grandfather.

My father was a white man. He was admitted to be such by all I ever heard speak of my parentage. The opinion was also whispered that my master was my father; but of the correctness of this opinion, I know nothing; the means of knowing was withheld from me. My mother and I were separated when I was but an infant—before I knew her as my mother. It is a common custom, in the part of Maryland from which I ran away, to part children from their

2. Isaiah 16:3.

mothers at a very early age. Frequently, before the child has reached its twelfth month, its mother is taken from it, and hired out on some farm a considerable distance off, and the child is placed under the care of an old woman, too old for field labor. For what this separation is done, I do not know, unless it be to hinder the development of the child's affection toward its mother, and to blunt and destroy the natural affection of the mother for the child. This is the inevitable result.

I never saw my mother, to know her as such, more than four or five times in my life; and each of these times was very short in duration, and at night. She was hired by a Mr. Stewart, who lived about twelve miles from my home. She made her journeys to see me in the night, travelling the whole distance on foot, after the performance of her day's work. She was a field hand, and a whipping is the penalty of not being in the field at sunrise, unless a slave has special permission from his or her master to the contrary—a permission which they seldom get, and one that gives to him that gives it the proud name of being a kind master. I do not recollect of ever seeing my mother by the light of day. She was with me in the night. She would lie down with me, and get me to sleep, but long before I waked she was gone. Very little communication ever took place between us. Death soon ended what little we could have while she lived, and with it her hardships and suffering. She died when I was about seven years old, on one of my master's farms, near Lee's Mill. I was not allowed to be present during her illness, at her death, or burial. She was gone long before I knew anything about it. Never having enjoyed, to any considerable extent, her soothing presence, her tender and watchful care, I received the tidings of her death with much the same emotions I should have probably felt at the death of a stranger.

Called thus suddenly away, she left me without the slightest intimation of who my father was. The whisper that my master was my father, may or may not be true; and, true or false, it is of but little consequence to my purpose whilst the fact remains, in all its glaring odiousness, that slaveholders have ordained, and by law established, that the children of slave women shall in all cases follow the condition of their mothers; and this is done too obviously to administer to their own lusts, and make a gratification of their wicked desires profitable as well as pleasureable; for by this cunning arrangement, the slaveholder, in cases not a few, sustains to his slaves the double relation of master and father.

I know of such cases; and it is worthy of remark that such slaves invariably suffer greater hardships, and have more to contend with, than others. They are, in the first place, a constant offence to their mistress. She is ever disposed to find fault with them; they can seldom do any thing to please her; she is never better pleased than when she sees them under the lash, especially when she suspects her husband of showing to his mulatto children favors which he withholds from his black slaves. The master is frequently compelled to sell this class of his slaves, out of deference to the feelings of his white wife; and, cruel as the deed may strike any one to be, for a man to sell his own children to human flesh-mongers, it is often the dictate of humanity for him to do so; for, unless he does this, he must not only whip them himself, but must stand by and see one white son tie up his brother, of but few shades darker complexion than himself, and ply the gory lash to his naked back; and if he lisp one word of disapproval, it is set down to his parental partiality, and only makes a bad matter worse, both for himself and the slave whom he would protect and defend.

Every year brings with it multitudes of this class of slaves. It was doubtless in consequence of a knowledge of this fact, that one great statesman of the south predicted the downfall of slavery by the inevitable laws of population. Whether this prophecy is ever fulfilled or not, it is nevertheless plain that a very different-looking class of people are springing up at the south, and are now held in slavery, from those originally brought to this country from Africa; and if their increase will do no other good, it will do away the force of the argument, that God cursed Ham,[3] and therefore American slavery is right. If the lineal descendants of Ham are alone to be scripturally enslaved, it is certain that slavery at the south must soon become unscriptural; for thousands are ushered into the world, annually, who, like myself, owe their existence to white fathers, and those fathers most frequently their own masters.

I have had two masters. My first master's name was Anthony. I do not remember his first name. He was generally called Captain Anthony—a title which, I presume, he acquired by sailing a craft on the Chesapeake Bay. He was not considered a rich slaveholder. He owned two or three farms, and about thirty slaves. His farms and slaves were under the care of an overseer. The overseer's name was Plummer. Mr. Plummer was a miserable drunkard, a profane swearer, and a savage monster. He always went armed with a cowskin and a heavy cudgel.[4] I have known him to cut and slash the women's heads so horribly, that even master would be enraged at his cruelty, and would threaten to whip him if he did not mind himself. Master, however, was not a humane slaveholder. It required extraordinary barbarity on the part of an overseer to affect him. He was a cruel man, hardened by a long life of slaveholding. He would at times seem to take great pleasure in whipping a slave. I have often been awakened at the dawn of day by the most heartrending shrieks of an own aunt of mine, whom he used to tie up to a joist, and whip upon her naked back till she was literally covered with blood. No words, no tears, no prayers, from his gory victim, seemed to move his iron heart from its bloody purpose. The louder she screamed, the harder he whipped; and where the blood ran fastest, there he whipped longest. He would whip her to make her scream, and whip her to make her hush; and not until overcome by fatigue, would he cease to swing the blood-clotted cowskin. I remember the first time I ever witnessed this horrible exhibition. I was quite a child, but I well remember it. I never shall forget it whilst I remember any thing. It was the first of a long series of such outrages, of which I was doomed to be a witness and a participant. It struck me with awful force. It was the blood-stained gate, the entrance to the hell of slavery, through which I was about to pass. It was a most terrible spectacle. I wish I could commit to paper the feelings with which I beheld it.

This occurrence took place very soon after I went to live with my old master, and under the following circumstances. Aunt Hester went out one night,—where or for what I do not know,—and happened to be absent when my master desired her presence. He had ordered her not to go out evenings, and warned her that she must never let him catch her in company with a young man, who was paying attention to her, belonging to Colonel Lloyd.[5] The young man's name was Ned Roberts, generally called Lloyd's Ned. Why master was so careful of her, may be safely left to conjecture. She was a woman

3. The specious argument referred to is based on an interpretation of Genesis 9:20–27, in which Noah curses his son Ham and condemns him to bondage to his brothers.

4. A short, thick stick of wood. "Cowskin": a whip made of raw cowhide.

5. Colonel Edward Lloyd V (1779–1834), who served as governor of the state and a U.S. senator from Maryland.

of noble form, and of graceful proportions, having very few equals, and fewer superiors, in personal appearance, among the colored or white women of our neighborhood.

Aunt Hester had not only disobeyed his orders in going out, but had been found in company with Lloyd's Ned; which circumstance, I found, from what he said while whipping her, was the chief offence. Had he been a man of pure morals himself, he might have been thought interested in protecting the innocence of my aunt; but those who knew him will not suspect him of any such virtue. Before he commenced whipping Aunt Hester, he took her into the kitchen, and stripped her from neck to waist, leaving her neck, shoulders, and back, entirely naked. He then told her to cross her hands, calling her at the same time a d——d b——h. After crossing her hands, he tied them with a strong rope, and led her to a stool under a large hook in the joist, put in for the purpose. He made her get upon the stool, and tied her hands to the hook. She now stood fair for his infernal purpose. Her arms were stretched up at their full length, so that she stood upon the ends of her toes. He then said to her, "Now, you d——d b——h, I'll learn you how to disobey my orders!" and after rolling up his sleeves, he commenced to lay on the heavy cowskin, and soon the warm, red blood (amid heart-rending shrieks from her, and horrid oaths from him) came dripping to the floor. I was so terrified and horror-stricken at the sight, that I hid myself in a closet, and dared not venture out till long after the bloody transaction was over. I expected it would be my turn next. It was all new to me. I had never seen any thing like it before. I had always lived with my grandmother on the outskirts of the plantation, where she was put to raise the children of the younger women. I had therefore been, until now, out of the way of the bloody scenes that often occurred on the plantation.

Chapter II

My master's family consisted of two sons, Andrew and Richard; one daughter, Lucretia, and her husband, Captain Thomas Auld. They lived in one house, upon the home plantation of Colonel Edward Lloyd. My master was Colonel Lloyd's clerk and superintendent. He was what might be called the overseer of the overseers. I spent two years of childhood on this plantation in my old master's family. It was here that I witnessed the bloody transaction recorded in the first chapter; and as I received my first impressions of slavery on this plantation, I will give some description of it, and of slavery as it there existed. The plantation is about twelve miles north of Easton, in Talbot county, and is situated on the border of Miles River. The principal products raised upon it were tobacco, corn, and wheat. These were raised in great abundance; so that, with the products of this and the other farms belonging to him, he was able to keep in almost constant employment a large sloop, in carrying them to market at Baltimore. This sloop was named Sally Lloyd, in honor of one of the colonel's daughters. My master's son-in-law, Captain Auld, was master of the vessel; she was otherwise manned by the colonel's own slaves. Their names were Peter, Isaac, Rich, and Jake. These were esteemed very highly by the other slaves, and looked upon as the privileged ones of the plantation; for it was no small affair, in the eyes of the slaves, to be allowed to see Baltimore.

Colonel Lloyd kept from three to four hundred slaves on his home plantation, and owned a large number more on the neighboring farms belonging to him. The names of the farms nearest to the home plantation were

Wye Town and New Design. "Wye Town" was under the overseership of a man named Noah Willis. New Design was under the overseership of a Mr. Townsend. The overseers of these, and all the rest of the farms, numbering over twenty, received advice and direction from the managers of the home plantation. This was the great business place. It was the seat of government for the whole twenty farms. All disputes among the overseers were settled here. If a slave was convicted of any high misdemeanor, became unmanageable, or evinced a determination to run away, he was brought immediately here, severely whipped, put on board the sloop, carried to Baltimore, and sold to Austin Woolfolk, or some other slave-trader, as a warning to the slaves remaining.

Here, too, the slaves of all the other farms received their monthly allowance of food, and their yearly clothing. The men and women slaves received, as their monthly allowance of food, eight pounds of pork, or its equivalent in fish, and one bushel of corn meal. Their yearly clothing consisted of two coarse linen shirts, one pair of linen trousers, like the shirts, one jacket, one pair of trousers for winter, made of coarse negro cloth, one pair of stockings, and one pair of shoes; the whole of which could not have cost more than seven dollars. The allowance of the slave children was given to their mothers, or the old women having the care of them. The children unable to work in the field had neither shoes, stockings, jackets, nor trousers, given to them; their clothing consisted of two coarse linen shirts per year. When these failed them, they went naked until the next allowance-day. Children from seven to ten years old, of both sexes, almost naked, might be seen at all seasons of the year.

There were no beds given the slaves, unless one coarse blanket be considered such, and none but the men and women had these. This, however, is not considered a very great privation. They find less difficulty from the want of beds, than from the want of time to sleep; for when their day's work in the field is done, the most of them having their washing, mending, and cooking to do, and having few or none of the ordinary facilities for doing either of these, very many of their sleeping hours are consumed in preparing for the field the coming day; and when this is done, old and young, male and female, married and single, drop down side by side; on one common bed,—the cold, damp floor,—each covering himself or herself with their miserable blankets; and here they sleep till they are summoned to the field by the driver's horn. At the sound of this, all must rise, and be off to the field. There must be no halting; every one must be at his or her post; and woe betides them who hear not this morning summons to the field; for if they are not awakened by the sense of hearing, they are by the sense of feeling: no age nor sex finds any favor. Mr. Severe, the overseer, used to stand by the door of the quarter, armed with a large hickory stick and heavy cowskin, ready to whip any one who was so unfortunate as not to hear, or, from any other cause, was prevented from being ready to start for the field at the sound of the horn.

Mr. Severe was rightly named: he was a cruel man. I have seen him whip a woman, causing the blood to run half an hour at the time; and this, too, in the midst of her crying children, pleading for their mother's release. He seemed to take pleasure in manifesting his fiendish barbarity. Added to his cruelty, he was a profane swearer. It was enough to chill the blood and stiffen the hair of an ordinary man to hear him talk. Scarce a sentence escaped him but that was commenced or concluded by some horrid oath. The field was the place to witness his cruelty and profanity. His presence made it both the field of blood and of blasphemy. From the rising till the going down of the sun, he was cursing, raving, cutting, and slashing among the slaves of the field, in the most frightful manner. His career was short. He died very soon after I went to Colonel Lloyd's; and he died as he lived, uttering, with his dying groans, bitter curses and horrid oaths. His death was regarded by the slaves as the result of a merciful providence.

Mr. Severe's place was filled by a Mr. Hopkins. He was a very different man. He was less cruel, less profane, and made less noise, than Mr. Severe. His course was characterized by no extraordinary demonstrations of cruelty. He whipped, but seemed to take no pleasure in it. He was called by the slaves a good overseer.

The home plantation of Colonel Lloyd wore the appearance of a country village. All the mechanical operations for all the farms were performed here. The shoemaking and mending, the blacksmithing, cartwrighting, coopering, weaving, and grain-grinding, were all performed by the slaves on the home plantation. The whole place wore a business-like aspect very unlike the neighboring farms. The number of houses, too, conspired to give it advantage over the neighboring farms. It was called by the slaves the *Great House Farm.* Few privileges were esteemed higher, by the slaves of the out-farms, than that of being selected to do errands at the Great House Farm. It was associated in their minds with greatness. A representative could not be prouder of his election to a seat in the American Congress, than a slave on one of the out-farms would be of his election to do errands at the Great House Farm. They regarded it as evidence of great confidence reposed in them by their overseers; and it was on this account, as well as a constant desire to be out of the field from under the driver's lash, that they esteemed it a high privilege, one worth careful living for. He was called the smartest and most trusty fellow, who had this honor conferred upon him the most frequently. The competitors for this office sought as diligently to please their overseers, as the office-seekers in the political parties seek to please and deceive the people. The same traits of character might be seen in Colonel Lloyd's slaves, as are seen in the slaves of the political parties.

The slaves selected to go to the Great House Farm, for the monthly allowance for themselves and their fellow-slaves, were peculiarly enthusiastic. While on their way, they would make the dense old woods, for miles around, reverberate with their wild songs, revealing at once the highest joy and the deepest sadness. They would compose and sing as they went along, consulting neither time nor tune. The thought that came up, came out—if not in the word, in the sound;—and as frequently in the one as in the other. They would sometimes sing the most pathetic sentiment in the most rapturous tone, and the most rapturous sentiment in the most pathetic tone. Into all of their songs they would manage to weave something of the Great House Farm. Especially would they do this, when leaving home. They would then sing most exultingly the following words:—

> "I am going away to the Great House Farm!
> O, yea! O, yea! O!"

This they would sing, as a chorus, to words which to many would seem unmeaning jargon, but which, nevertheless, were full of meaning to themselves. I have sometimes thought that the mere hearing of those songs would do more to impress some minds with the horrible character of slavery, than the reading of whole volumes of philosophy on the subject could do.

I did not, when a slave, understand the deep meaning of those rude and apparently incoherent songs. I was myself within the circle; so that I neither saw nor heard as those without might see and hear. They told a tale of woe which was then altogether beyond my feeble comprehension; they were tones loud, long, and deep; they breathed the prayer and complaint of souls boiling over with the bitterest anguish. Every tone was a testimony against slavery, and a prayer to God for deliverance from chains. The hearing of those wild notes always depressed my spirit, and filled me with ineffable sadness. I have frequently found myself in tears while hearing them. The mere recurrence to those songs, even now, afflicts me; and while I am writing these lines, an expression of feeling has already found its way down my cheek. To those songs I trace my first glimmering conception of the dehumanizing character of slavery. I can never get rid of that conception. Those songs still follow me, to deepen my hatred of slavery, and quicken my sympathies for my brethren in bonds. If any one wishes to be impressed with the soul-killing effects of slavery, let him go to Colonel Lloyd's plantation, and, on allowance-day, place himself in the deep pine woods, and there let him, in silence, analyze the sounds that shall pass through the chambers of his soul,—and if he is not thus impressed, it will only be because "there is no flesh in his obdurate heart."[6]

I have often been utterly astonished, since I came to the north, to find persons who could speak of the singing, among slaves, as evidence of their contentment and happiness. It is impossible to conceive of a greater mistake. Slaves sing most when they are most unhappy. The songs of the slave represent the sorrows of his heart; and he is relieved by them, only as an aching heart is relieved by its tears. At least, such is my experience. I have often sung to drown my sorrow, but seldom to express my happiness. Crying for joy, and singing for joy, were alike uncommon to me while in the jaws of slavery. The singing of a man cast away upon a desolate island might be as appropriately considered as evidence of contentment and happiness, as the singing of a slave; the songs of the one and of the other are prompted by the same emotion.

Chapter III

Colonel Lloyd kept a large and finely cultivated garden, which afforded almost constant employment for four men, besides the chief gardener, (Mr. M'Durmond.) This garden was probably the greatest attraction of the place. During the summer months, people came from far and near—from Baltimore, Easton, and Annapolis—to see it. It abounded in fruits of almost every description, from the hardy apple of the north to the delicate orange of the south. This garden was not the least source of trouble on the plantation. Its excellent fruit was quite a temptation to the hungry swarms of boys, as well as the older slaves, belonging to the colonel, few of whom had the virtue or the vice to resist it. Scarcely a day passed, during the summer, but that some slave had to take the lash for stealing fruit. The colonel had to resort to all kinds of stratagems to keep his slaves out of the garden. The last and most successful one was that of tarring his fence all around, after which, if

6. From William Cowper's popular poem *The Task* (1785): "*The Time-Piece,*" line 2.8.

a slave was caught with any tar upon his person, it was deemed sufficient proof that he had either been into the garden, or had tried to get in. In either case, he was severely whipped by the chief gardener. This plan worked well; the slaves became as fearful of tar as of the lash. They seemed to realize the impossibility of touching *tar* without being defiled.

The colonel also kept a splendid riding equipage. His stable and carriage-house presented the appearance of some of our large city livery establishments. His horses were of the finest form and noblest blood. His carriage-house contained three splendid coaches, three or four gigs, besides dearborns and barouches[7] of the most fashionable style.

This establishment was under the care of two slaves—old Barney and young Barney—father and son. To attend to this establishment was their sole work. But it was by no means an easy employment; for in nothing was Colonel Lloyd more particular than in the management of his horses. The slightest inattention to these was unpardonable, and was visited upon those, under whose care they were placed, with the severest punishment; no excuse could shield them, if the colonel only suspected any want of attention to his horses—a supposition which he frequently indulged, and one which, of course, made the office of old and young Barney a very trying one. They never knew when they were safe from punishment. They were frequently whipped when least deserving, and escaped whipping when most deserving it. Every thing depended upon the looks of the horses, and the state of Colonel Lloyd's own mind when his horses were brought to him for use. If a horse did not move fast enough, or hold his head high enough, it was owing to some fault of his keepers. It was painful to stand near the stable door, and hear the various complaints against the keepers when a horse was taken out for use. "This horse has not had proper attention. He has not been sufficiently rubbed and curried, or he has not been properly fed; his food was too wet or too dry; he got it too soon or too late; he was too hot or too cold; he had too much hay, and not enough of grain; or he had too much grain, and not enough of hay; instead of old Barney's attending to the horse, he had very improperly left it to his son." To all these complaints, no matter how unjust, the slave must answer never a word. Colonel Lloyd could not brook any contradiction from a slave. When he spoke, a slave must stand, listen, and tremble; and such was literally the case. I have seen Colonel Lloyd make old Barney, a man between fifty and sixty years of age, uncover his bald head, kneel down upon the cold, damp ground, and receive upon his naked and toil-worn shoulders more than thirty lashes at the time. Colonel Lloyd had three sons—Edward, Murray, and Daniel,—and three sons-in-law, Mr. Winder, Mr. Nicholson, and Mr. Lowndes. All of these lived at the Great House Farm, and enjoyed the luxury of whipping the servants when they pleased, from old Barney down to William Wilkes, the coach-driver. I have seen Winder make one of the house-servants stand off from him a suitable distance to be touched with the end of his whip, and at every stroke raise great ridges upon his back.

To describe the wealth of Colonel Lloyd would be almost equal to describing the riches of Job. He kept from ten to fifteen house-servants. He was said to own a thousand slaves, and I think this estimate quite within the truth. Colonel Lloyd owned so many that he did not know them when he saw them; nor did all the slaves of the out-farms know him. It is reported of him,

7. Different kinds of carriages.

that, while riding along the road one day, he met a colored man, and addressed him in the usual manner of speaking to colored people on the public highways of the south: "Well, boy, whom do you belong to?" "To Colonel Lloyd," replied the slave. "Well, does the colonel treat you well?" "No, sir," was the ready reply. "What, does he work you too hard?" "Yes, sir." "Well, don't he give you enough to eat?" "Yes, sir, he gives me enough, such as it is."

The colonel, after ascertaining where the slave belonged, rode on; the man also went on about his business, not dreaming that he had been conversing with his master. He thought, said, and heard nothing more of the matter, until two or three weeks afterwards. The poor man was then informed by his overseer that, for having found fault with his master, he was now to be sold to a Georgia trader. He was immediately chained and handcuffed; and thus, without a moment's warning, he was snatched away, and forever sundered, from his family and friends, by a hand more unrelenting than death. This is the penalty of telling the truth, of telling the simple truth, in answer to a series of plain questions.

It is partly in consequence of such facts, that slaves, when inquired of as to their condition and the character of their masters, almost universally say they are contented, and that their masters are kind. The slaveholders have been known to send in spies among their slaves, to ascertain their views and feelings in regard to their condition. The frequency of this has had the effect to establish among the slaves the maxim, that a still tongue makes a wise head. They suppress the truth rather than take the consequences of telling it, and in so doing prove themselves a part of the human family. If they have any thing to say of their masters, it is generally in their master's favor, especially when speaking to an untried man. I have been frequently asked, when a slave, if I had a kind master, and do not remember ever to have given a negative answer; nor did I, in pursuing this course, consider myself as uttering what was absolutely false; for I always measured the kindness of my master by the standard of kindness set up among slaveholders around us. Moreover, slaves are like other people, and imbibe prejudices quite common to others. They think their own better than that of others. Many, under the influence of this prejudice, think their own masters are better than the masters of other slaves; and this, too, in some cases, when the very reverse is true. Indeed, it is not uncommon for slaves even to fall out and quarrel among themselves about the relative goodness of their masters, each contending for the superior goodness of his own over that of the others. At the very same time, they mutually execrate their masters when viewed separately. It was so on our plantation. When Colonel Lloyd's slaves met the slaves of Jacob Jepson, they seldom parted without a quarrel about their masters; Colonel Lloyd's slaves contending that he was the richest, and Mr. Jepson's slaves that he was the smartest, and most of a man. Colonel Lloyd's slaves would boast his ability to buy and sell Jacob Jepson. Mr. Jepson's slaves would boast his ability to whip Colonel Lloyd. These quarrels would almost always end in a fight between the parties, and those that whipped were supposed to have gained the point at issue. They seemed to think that the greatness of their masters was transferable to themselves. It was considered as being bad enough to be a slave; but to be a poor man's slave was deemed a disgrace indeed!

Chapter IV

Mr. Hopkins remained but a short time in the office of overseer. Why his career was so short, I do not know, but suppose he lacked the necessary severity to suit Colonel Lloyd. Mr. Hopkins was succeeded by Mr. Austin Gore, a man possessing, in an eminent degree, all those traits of character indispensable to what is called a first-rate overseer. Mr. Gore had served Colonel Lloyd, in the capacity of overseer, upon one of the out-farms, and had shown himself worthy of the high station of overseer upon the home or Great House Farm.

Mr. Gore was proud, ambitious, and persevering. He was artful, cruel, and obdurate. He was just the man for such a place, and it was just the place for such a man. It afforded scope for the full exercise of all his powers, and he seemed to be perfectly at home in it. He was one of those who could torture the slightest look, word, or gesture, on the part of the slave, into impudence, and would treat it accordingly. There must be no answering back to him; no explanation was allowed a slave, showing himself to have been wrongfully accused. Mr. Gore acted fully up to the maxim laid down by slaveholders,—"It is better that a dozen slaves suffer under the lash, than that the overseer should be convicted, in the presence of the slaves, of having been at fault." No matter how innocent a slave might be—it availed him nothing, when accused by Mr. Gore of any misdemeanor. To be accused was to be convicted, and to be convicted was to be punished; the one always following the other with immutable certainty. To escape punishment was to escape accusation; and few slaves had the fortune to do either, under the overseership of Mr. Gore. He was just proud enough to demand the most debasing homage of the slave, and quite servile enough to crouch, himself, at the feet of the master. He was ambitious enough to be contented with nothing short of the highest rank of overseers, and persevering enough to reach the height of his ambition. He was cruel enough to inflict the severest punishment, artful enough to descend to the lowest trickery, and obdurate enough to be insensible to the voice of a reproving conscience. He was, of all the overseers, the most dreaded by the slaves. His presence was painful; his eye flashed confusion; and seldom was his sharp, shrill voice heard, without producing horror and trembling in their ranks.

Mr. Gore was a grave man, and, though a young man, he indulged in no jokes, said no funny words, seldom smiled. His words were in perfect keeping with his looks, and his looks were in perfect keeping with his words. Overseers will sometimes indulge in a witty word, even with the slaves; not so with Mr. Gore. He spoke but to command, and commanded but to be obeyed; he dealt sparingly with his words, and bountifully with his whip, never using the former where the latter would answer as well. When he whipped, he seemed to do so from a sense of duty, and feared no consequences. He did nothing reluctantly, no matter how disagreeable; always at his post, never inconsistent. He never promised but to fulfil. He was, in a word, a man of the most inflexible firmness and stone-like coolness.

His savage barbarity was equalled only by the consummate coolness with which he committed the grossest and most savage deeds upon the slaves under his charge. Mr. Gore once undertook to whip one of Colonel Lloyd's slaves, by the name of Demby. He had given Demby but a few stripes, when, to get rid of the scourging, he ran and plunged himself into a creek, and stood there at the depth of his shoulders, refusing to come out. Mr. Gore told him that he would give him three calls, and that, if he did not come out at the third call, he would shoot him. The first call was given. Demby made no response, but stood his ground. The second and third calls were given with the same result. Mr. Gore then, without consultation or deliberation with any one, not even giving Demby an additional call, raised his musket to his face, taking deadly aim at his standing victim, and in an instant poor Demby was no more. His mangled body sank out of sight, and blood and brains marked the water where he had stood.

A thrill of horror flashed through every soul upon the plantation, excepting Mr. Gore. He alone seemed cool and collected. He was asked by Colonel Lloyd and my old master, why he resorted to this extraordinary expedient. His reply was, (as well as I can remember,) that Demby had become unmanageable. He was setting a dangerous example to the other slaves,—one which, if suffered to pass without some such demonstration on his part, would finally lead to the total subversion of all rule and order upon the plantation. He argued that if one slave refused to be corrected, and escaped with his life, the other slaves would soon copy the example; the result of which would be, the freedom of the slaves, and the enslavement of the whites. Mr. Gore's defence was satisfactory. He was continued in his station as overseer upon the home plantation. His fame as an overseer went abroad. His horrid crime was not even submitted to judicial investigation. It was committed in the presence of slaves, and they of course could neither institute a suit, nor testify against him; and thus the guilty perpetrator of one of the bloodiest and most foul murders goes unwhipped of justice, and uncensured by the community in which he lives. Mr. Gore lived in St. Michael's, Talbot county, Maryland, when I left there; and if he is still alive, he very probably lives there now; and if so, he is now as he was then, as highly esteemed and as much respected as though his guilty soul had not been stained with his brother's blood.

I speak advisedly when I say this,—that killing a slave, or any colored person, in Talbot county, Maryland, is not treated as a crime, either by the courts or the community. Mr. Thomas Lanman, of St. Michael's, killed two slaves, one of whom he killed with a hatchet, by knocking his brains out. He used to boast of the commission of the awful and bloody deed. I have heard him do so laughingly, saying, among other things, that he was the only benefactor of his country in the company, and that when others would do as much as he had done, we should be relieved of "the d—d niggers."

The wife of Mr. Giles Hicks, living but a short distance from where I used to live, murdered my wife's cousin, a young girl between fifteen and sixteen years of age, mangling her person in the most horrible manner, breaking her nose and breastbone with a stick, so that the poor girl expired in a few hours afterward. She was immediately buried, but had not been in her untimely grave but a few hours before she was taken up and examined by the coroner, who decided that she had come to her death by severe beating. The offence for which this girl was thus murdered was this:—She had been set that night to mind Mrs. Hicks's baby, and during the night she fell asleep, and the baby cried. She, having lost her rest for several nights previous, did not hear the crying. They were both in the room with Mrs. Hicks. Mrs. Hicks, finding the girl slow to move, jumped from her bed, seized an oak stick of wood by the fireplace, and with it broke the girl's nose and breastbone, and thus ended her life. I will not say that this most horrid murder produced no sensation in the community. It did produce sensation, but not enough to bring the murderess to punishment. There was a warrant issued for her arrest, but it was never served. Thus she escaped not only punishment, but even the pain of being arraigned before a court for her horrid crime.

Whilst I am detailing bloody deeds which took place during my stay on Colonel Lloyd's plantation, I will briefly narrate another, which occurred about the same time as the murder of Demby by Mr. Gore.

Colonel Lloyd's slaves were in the habit of spending a part of their nights and Sundays in fishing for oysters, and in this way made up the deficiency of their scanty allowance. An old man belonging to Colonel Lloyd, while thus engaged, happened to get beyond the limits of Colonel Lloyd's, and on the premises of Mr. Beal Bondly. At this trespass, Mr. Bondly took offence, and with his musket came down to the shore, and blew its deadly contents into the poor old man.

Mr. Bondly came over to see Colonel Lloyd the next day, whether to pay him for his property, or to justify himself in what he had done, I know not. At any rate, this whole fiendish transaction was soon hushed up. There was very little said about it at all, and nothing done. It was a common saying, even among little white boys, that it was worth a half-cent to kill a "nigger," and a half-cent to bury one.

Chapter V

As to my own treatment while I lived on Colonel Lloyd's plantation, it was very similar to that of the other slave children. I was not old enough to work in the field, and there being little else than field work to do, I had a great deal of leisure time. The most I had to do was to drive up the cows at evening, keep the fowls out of the garden, keep the front yard clean, and run of errands for my old master's daughter, Mrs. Lucretia Auld. The most of my leisure time I spent in helping Master Daniel Lloyd in finding his birds, after he had shot them. My connection with Master Daniel was of some advantage to me. He became quite attached to me, and was a sort of protector of me. He would not allow the older boys to impose upon me, and would divide his cakes with me.

I was seldom whipped by my old master, and suffered little from any thing else than hunger and cold. I suffered much from hunger, but much more from cold. In hottest summer and coldest winter, I was kept almost naked—no shoes, no stockings, no jacket, no trousers, nothing on but a coarse tow linen shirt, reaching only to my knees. I had no bed. I must have perished with cold, but that, the coldest nights, I used to steal a bag which was used for carrying corn to the mill. I would crawl into this bag, and there sleep on the cold, damp, clay floor, with my head in and feet out. My feet have been so cracked with the frost, that the pen with which I am writing might be laid in the gashes.

We were not regularly allowanced. Our food was coarse corn meal boiled. This was called *mush*. It was put into a large wooden tray or trough, and set down upon the ground. The children were then called, like so many pigs, and like so many pigs they would come and devour the mush; some with oystershells, others with pieces of shingle, some with naked hands, and none with spoons. He that ate fastest got most; he that was strongest secured the best place; and few left the trough satisfied.

I was probably between seven and eight years old when I left Colonel Lloyd's plantation. I left it with joy. I shall never forget the ecstasy with which I received the intelligence that my old master (Anthony) had determined to let me go to Baltimore, to live with Mr. Hugh Auld, brother to my old master's son-in-law, Captain Thomas Auld. I received this information about three days before my departure. They were three of the happiest days I ever enjoyed. I spent the most part of all these three days in the creek, washing off the plantation scurf,[8] and preparing myself for my departure.

The pride of appearance which this would indicate was not my own. I spent the time in washing, not so much because I wished to, but because Mrs. Lucretia had told me I must get all the dead skin off my feet and knees before I could go to Baltimore; for the people of Baltimore were very cleanly, and would laugh at me if I looked dirty. Besides, she was going to give me a pair of trousers, which I should not put on unless I got all the dirt off me. The thought of owning a pair of trousers was great indeed! It was almost a sufficient motive, not only to make me take off what would be called by pigdrovers the mange, but the skin itself. I went at it in good earnest, working for the first time with the hope of reward.

The ties that ordinarily bind children to their homes were all suspended in my case. I found no severe trial in my departure. My home was charmless; it was not home to me; on parting from it, I could not feel that I was leaving any thing which I could have enjoyed by staying. My mother was dead, my grandmother lived far off, so that I seldom saw her. I had two sisters and one brother, that lived in the same house with me; but the early separation of us from our mother had well nigh blotted the fact of our relationship from our memories. I looked for home elsewhere, and was confident of finding none which I should relish less than the one which I was leaving. If, however, I found in my new home hardship, hunger, whipping, and nakedness, I had the consolation that I should not have escaped any one of them by staying. Having already had more than a taste of them in the house of my old master, and having endured them there, I very naturally inferred my ability to endure them elsewhere, and especially at Baltimore; for I had something of the feeling about Baltimore that is expressed in the proverb, that "being hanged in England is preferable to dying a natural death in Ireland." I had the strongest desire to see Baltimore. Cousin Tom, though not fluent in speech, had inspired me with that desire by his eloquent description of the place. I could never point out any thing at the Great House, no matter how beautiful or powerful, but that he had seen something at Baltimore far exceeding, both in beauty and strength, the object which I pointed out to him. Even the Great House itself, with all its pictures, was far inferior to many buildings in Baltimore. So strong was my desire, that I thought a gratification of it would fully compensate for whatever loss of comforts I should sustain by the exchange. I left without a regret, and with the highest hopes of future happiness.

We sailed out of Miles River for Baltimore on a Saturday morning. I remember only the day of the week, for at that time I had no knowledge of the days of the month, nor the months of the year. On setting sail, I walked aft, and gave to Colonel Lloyd's plantation what I hoped would be the last look. I then placed myself in the bows of the sloop, and there spent the remainder of the day in looking ahead, interesting myself in what was in the distance rather than in things near or behind.

8. A scaly deposit attached to the epidermis.

In the afternoon of that day, we reached Annapolis, the capital of the State. We stopped but a few moments, so that I had no time to go on shore. It was the first large town that I had ever seen, and though it would look small compared with some of our New England factory villages, I thought it a wonderful place for its size—more imposing even than the Great House Farm!

We arrived at Baltimore early on Sunday morning, landing at Smith's Wharf, not far from Bowley's Wharf. We had on board the sloop a large flock of sheep; and after aiding in driving them to the slaughterhouse of Mr. Curtis on Louden Slater's Hill, I was conducted by Rich, one of the hands belonging on board of the sloop to my new home in Alliciana Street near Mr. Gardner's ship-yard, on Fells Point.

Mr. and Mrs. Auld were both at home, and met me at the door with their little son Thomas, to take care of whom I had been given. And here I saw what I had never seen before; it was a white face beaming with the most kindly emotions; it was the face of my new mistress, Sophia Auld. I wish I could describe the rapture that flashed through my soul as I beheld it. It was a new and strange sight to me, brightening up my pathway with the light of happiness. Little Thomas was told, there was his Freddy,—and I was told to take care of little Thomas; and thus I entered upon the duties of my new home with the most cheering prospect ahead.

I look upon my departure from Colonel Lloyd's plantation as one of the most interesting events of my life. It is possible, and even quite probable, that but for the mere circumstance of being removed from that plantation to Baltimore, I should have to-day, instead of being here seated by my own table, in the enjoyment of freedom and the happiness of home, writing this Narrative, been confined in the galling chains of slavery. Going to live at Baltimore laid the foundation, and opened the gateway, to all my subsequent prosperity. I have ever regarded it as the first plain manifestation of that kind providence which has ever since attended me, and marked my life with so many favors. I regarded the selection of myself as being somewhat remarkable. There were a number of slave children that might have been sent from the plantation to Baltimore. There were those younger, those older, and those of the same age. I was chosen from among them all, and was the first, last, and only choice.

I may be deemed superstitious, and even egotistical, in regarding this event as a special interposition of divine Providence in my favor. But I should be false to the earliest sentiments of my soul, if I suppressed the opinion. I prefer to be true to myself, even at the hazard of incurring the ridicule of others, rather than to be false, and incur my own abhorrence. From my earliest recollection, I date the entertainment of a deep conviction that slavery would not always be able to hold me within its foul embrace; and in the darkest hours of my career in slavery, this living word of faith and spirit of hope departed not from me, but remained like ministering angels to cheer me through the gloom. This good spirit was from God, and to him I offer thanksgiving and praise.

Chapter VI

My new mistress proved to be all she appeared when I first met her at the door,—a woman of the kindest heart and finest feelings. She had never had a slave under her control previously to myself, and prior to her marriage she had been dependent upon her own industry for a living. She was by trade a weaver; and by constant application to her business, she had been in a good degree preserved from the blighting and dehumanizing effects of slavery. I was utterly astonished at her goodness. I scarcely knew how to behave towards her. She was entirely unlike any other white woman I had ever seen. I could not approach her as I was accustomed to approach other white ladies. My early instruction was all out of place. The crouching servility, usually so acceptable a quality in a slave, did not answer when manifested toward her. Her favor was not gained by it; she seemed to be disturbed by it. She did not deem it impudent or unmannerly for a slave to look her in the face. The meanest slave was put fully at ease in her presence, and none left without feeling better for having seen her. Her face was made of heavenly smiles, and her voice of tranquil music.

But, alas! this kind heart had but a short time to remain such. The fatal poison of irresponsible power was already in her hands; and soon commenced its infernal work. That cheerful eye, under the influence of slavery, soon became red with rage; that voice, made all of sweet accord, changed to one of harsh and horrid discord; and that angelic face gave place to that of a demon.

Very soon after I went to live with Mr. and Mrs. Auld, she very kindly commenced to teach me the A, B, C. After I had learned this, she assisted me in learning to spell words of three or four letters. Just at this point of my progress, Mr. Auld found out what was going on, and at once forbade Mrs. Auld to instruct me further, telling her, among other things, that it was unlawful, as well as unsafe, to teach a slave to read. To use his own words, further, he said, "If you give a nigger an inch, he will take an ell.[9] A nigger should know nothing but to obey his master—to do as he is told to do. Learning would *spoil* the best nigger in the world. Now," said he, "if you teach that nigger (speaking of myself) how to read, there would be no keeping him. It would forever unfit him to be a slave. He would at once become unmanageable, and of no value to his master. As to himself, it could do him no good, but a great deal of harm. It would make him discontented and unhappy." These words sank deep into my heart, stirred up sentiments within that lay slumbering, and called into existence an entirely new train of thought. It was a new and special revelation, explaining dark and mysterious things, with which my youthful understanding had struggled, but struggled in vain. I now understood what had been to me a most perplexing difficulty—to wit, the white man's power to enslave the black man. It was a grand achievement, and I prized it highly. From that moment, I understood the pathway from slavery to freedom. It was just what I wanted, and I got it at a time when I the least expected it. Whilst I was saddened by the thought of losing the aid of my kind mistress, I was gladdened by the invaluable instruction which, by the merest accident, I had gained from my master. Though conscious of the difficulty of learning without a teacher, I set out with high hope, and a fixed purpose, at whatever cost of trouble, to learn how to read. The very decided manner with which he spoke, and strove to impress his wife with the evil consequences of giving me instruction, served to convince me that he was deeply sensible of the truths he was uttering. It gave me the best assurance that I might rely with the utmost confidence on the results which, he said, would flow from teaching me to read. What he most dreaded, that I most desired. What he most loved, that I most hated. That

9. An old measure of length, about 45 inches.

which to him was a great evil, to be carefully shunned, was to me a great good, to be diligently sought; and the argument which he so warmly urged, against my learning to read, only served to inspire me with a desire and determination to learn. In learning to read, I owe almost as much to the bitter opposition of my master, as to the kindly aid of my mistress. I acknowledge the benefit of both.

I had resided but a short time in Baltimore before I observed a marked difference, in the treatment of slaves, from that which I had witnessed in the country. A city slave is almost a freeman, compared with a slave on the plantation. He is much better fed and clothed, and enjoys privileges altogether unknown to the slave on the plantation. There is a vestige of decency, a sense of shame, that does much to curb and check those outbreaks of atrocious cruelty so commonly enacted upon the plantation. He is a desperate slaveholder, who will shock the humanity of his non-slaveholding neighbors with the cries of his lacerated slave. Few are willing to incur the odium attaching to the reputation of being a cruel master; and above all things, they would not be known as not giving a slave enough to eat. Every city slaveholder is anxious to have it known of him, that he feeds his slaves well; and it is due to them to say, that most of them do give their slaves enough to eat. There are, however, some painful exceptions to this rule. Directly opposite to us, on Philpot Street, lived Mr. Thomas Hamilton. He owned two slaves. Their names were Henrietta and Mary. Henrietta was about twenty-two years of age, Mary was about fourteen; and of all the mangled and emaciated creatures I ever looked upon, these two were the most so. His heart must be harder than stone, that could look upon these unmoved. The head, neck, and shoulders of Mary were literally cut to pieces. I have frequently felt her head, and found it nearly covered with festering sores, caused by the lash of her cruel mistress. I do not know that her master ever whipped her, but I have been an eye-witness to the cruelty of Mrs. Hamilton. I used to be in Mr. Hamilton's house nearly every day. Mrs. Hamilton used to sit in a large chair in the middle of the room, with a heavy cowskin always by her side, and scarce an hour passed during the day but was marked by the blood of one of these slaves. The girls seldom passed her without her saying, "Move faster, you *black gip!*" at the same time giving them a blow with the cowskin over the head or shoulders, often drawing the blood. She would then say, "Take that, you *black gip!*"—continuing, "If you don't move faster, I'll move you!" Added to the cruel lashings to which these slaves were subjected, they were kept nearly half-starved. They seldom knew what it was to eat a full meal. I have seen Mary contending with the pigs for the offal thrown into the street. So much was Mary kicked and cut to pieces, that she was oftener called *"pecked"* than by her name.

Chapter VII

I lived in Master Hugh's family about seven years. During this time, I succeeded in learning to read and write. In accomplishing this, I was compelled to resort to various stratagems. I had no regular teacher. My mistress, who had kindly commenced to instruct me, had, in compliance with the advice and direction of her husband, not only ceased to instruct, but had set her face against my being instructed by any one else. It is due, however, to my mistress to say of her, that she did not adopt this course of treatment immediately. She at first lacked the depravity indispensable to shutting me up in mental darkness. It was at least necessary for her to have some training in the exercise of irresponsible power, to make her equal to the task of treating me as though I were a brute.

My mistress was, as I have said, a kind and tender-hearted woman; and in the simplicity of her soul she commenced, when I first went to live with her, to treat me as she supposed one human being ought to treat another. In entering upon the duties of a slaveholder, she did not seem to perceive that I sustained to her the relation of a mere chattel, and that for her to treat me as a human being was not only wrong, but dangerously so. Slavery proved as injurious to her as it did to me. When I went there, she was a pious, warm, and tender-hearted woman. There was no sorrow or suffering for which she had not a tear. She had bread for the hungry, clothes for the naked, and comfort for every mourner that came within her reach. Slavery soon proved its ability to divest her of these heavenly qualities. Under its influence, the tender heart became stone, and the lamblike disposition gave way to one of tigerlike fierceness. The first step in her downward course was in her ceasing to instruct me. She now commenced to practise her husband's precepts. She finally became even more violent in her opposition than her husband himself. She was not satisfied with simply doing as well as he had commanded; she seemed anxious to do better. Nothing seemed to make her more angry than to see me with a newspaper. She seemed to think that here lay the danger. I have had her rush at me with a face made all up of fury, and snatch from me a newspaper, in a manner that fully revealed her apprehension. She was an apt woman; and a little experience soon demonstrated, to her satisfaction, that education and slavery were incompatible with each other.

From this time I was most narrowly watched. If I was in a separate room any considerable length of time, I was sure to be suspected of having a book and was at once called to give an account of myself. All this, however, was too late. The first step had been taken. Mistress, in teaching me the alphabet, had given me the *inch,* and no precaution could prevent me from taking the *ell.*

The plan which I adopted, and the one by which I was most successful, was that of making friends of all the little white boys whom I met in the street. As many of these as I could, I converted into teachers. With their kindly aid obtained at different times and in different places, I finally succeeded in learning to read. When I was sent of errands, I always took my book with me, and by going one part of my errand quickly, I found time to get a lesson before my return. I used also to carry bread with me, enough of which was always in the house, and to which I was always welcome; for I was much better off in this regard than many of the poor white children in our neighborhood. This bread I used to bestow upon the hungry little urchins, who, in return, would give me that more valuable bread of knowledge. I am strongly tempted to give the names of two or three of those little boys, as a testimonial of the gratitude and affection I bear them; but prudence forbids;—not that it would injure me, but it might embarrass them; for it is almost an unpardonable offence to teach slaves to read in this Christian country. It is enough to say of the dear little fellows, that they lived on Philpot Street, very near Durgin and Bailey's ship-yard. I used to talk this matter of slavery over with them. I would sometimes say to them, I wished I could be as free as they would be when they got to be men. "You will be free as soon as you are twenty-one, *but I am a slave for life!* Have not I as good a right to be free as you have?" These words used to trouble them; they would express for me the liveliest sympathy, and console me with the hope that something would occur by which I might be free.

I was now about twelve years old, and the thought of being *a slave for life* began to bear heavily upon my heart. Just about this time, I got hold of a book entitled "The Columbian Orator."[1] Every opportunity I got, I used to read this book. Among much of other interesting matter, I found in it a dialogue between a master and his slave. The slave was represented as having run away from his master three times. The dialogue represented the conversation which took place between them, when the slave was retaken the third time. In this dialogue, the whole argument in behalf of slavery was brought forward by the master, all of which was disposed of by the slave. The slave was made to say some very smart as well as impressive things in reply to his master—things which had the desired though unexpected effect; for the conversation resulted in the voluntary emancipation of the slave on the part of the master.

In the same book, I met with one of Sheridan's mighty speeches on and in behalf of Catholic emancipation.[2] These were choice documents to me. I read them over and over again with unabated interest. They gave tongue to interesting thoughts of my own soul, which had frequently flashed through my mind, and died away for want of utterance. The moral which I gained from the dialogue was the power of truth over the conscience of even a slaveholder. What I got from Sheridan was a bold denunciation of slavery, and a powerful vindication of human rights. The reading of these documents enabled me to utter my thoughts, and to meet the arguments brought forward to sustain slavery; but while they relieved me of one difficulty, they brought on another even more painful than the one of which I was relieved. The more I read, the more I was led to abhor and detest my enslavers. I could regard them in no other light than a band of successful robbers, who had left their homes, and gone to Africa, and stolen us from our homes, and in a strange land reduced us to slavery. I loathed them as being the meanest as well as the most wicked of men. As I read and contemplated the subject, behold! that very discontentment which Master Hugh had predicted would follow my learning to read had already come, to torment and sting my soul to unutterable anguish. As I writhed under it, I would at times feel that learning to read had been a curse rather than a blessing. It had given me a view of my wretched condition, without the remedy. It opened my eyes to the horrible pit, but to no ladder upon which to get out. In moments of agony, I envied my fellow-slaves for their stupidity. I have often wished myself a beast. I preferred the condition of the meanest reptile to my own. Any thing, no matter what, to get rid of thinking! It was this everlasting thinking of my condition that tormented me. There was no getting rid of it. It was pressed upon me by every object within sight or hearing, animate or inanimate. The silver trump of freedom had roused my soul to eternal wakefulness. Freedom now appeared, to disappear no more forever. It was heard in every sound, and seen in every thing. It was ever present to torment

1. A popular collection of classic poems, dialogues, plays, and speeches that Douglass used as a model for his own speeches. "Columbian": American.

2. The speech in the *Columbian Orator* to which Douglass refers was actually made by the Irish patriot Arthur O'Connor. Richard Brinsley Sheridan (1751–1816), Irish dramatist and political leader.

me with a sense of my wretched condition. I saw nothing without seeing it, I heard nothing without hearing it, and felt nothing without feeling. It looked from every star, it smiled in every calm, breathed in every wind, and moved in every storm.

I often found myself regretting my own existence, and wishing myself dead; and but for the hope of being free, I have no doubt but that I should have killed myself, or done something for which I should have been killed. While in this state of mind, I was eager to hear any one speak of slavery. I was a ready listener. Every little while, I could hear something about the abolitionists. It was some time before I found what the word meant. It was always used in such connections as to make it an interesting word to me. If a slave ran away and succeeded in getting clear, or if a slave killed his master, set fire to a barn, or did any thing very wrong in the mind of a slaveholder, it was spoken of as the fruit of *abolition*. Hearing the word in this connection very often, I set about learning what it meant. The dictionary afforded me little or no help. I found it was "the act of abolishing;" but then I did not know what was to be abolished. Here I was perplexed. I did not dare to ask any one about its meaning, for I was satisfied that it was something they wanted me to know very little about. After a patient waiting, I got one of our city papers, containing an account of the number of petitions from the north, praying for the abolition of slavery in the District of Columbia, and of the slave trade between the States. From this time I understood the words *abolition* and *abolitionist,* and always drew near when that word was spoken, expecting to hear something of importance to myself and fellow-slaves. The light broke in upon me by degrees. I went one day down on the wharf of Mr. Waters; and seeing two Irishmen unloading a scow of stone, I went, unasked and helped them. When we had finished, one of them came to me and asked me if I were a slave. I told him I was. He asked, "Are ye a slave for life?" I told him that I was. The good Irishman seemed to be deeply affected by the statement. He said to the other that it was a pity so fine a little fellow as myself should be a slave for life. He said it was a shame to hold me. They both advised me to run away to the north; that I should find friends there, and that I should be free. I pretended not to be interested in what they said, and treated them as if I did not understand them; for I feared they might be treacherous. White men have been known to encourage slaves to escape, and then, to get the reward, catch them and return them to their masters. I was afraid that these seemingly good men might use me so; but I nevertheless remembered their advice, and from that time I resolved to run away. I looked forward to a time at which it would be safe for me to escape. I was too young to think of doing so immediately; besides, I wished to learn how to write, as I might have occasion to write my own pass. I consoled myself with the hope that I should one day find a good chance. Meanwhile, I would learn to write.

The idea as to how I might learn to write was suggested to me by being in Durgin and Bailey's ship-yard, and frequently seeing the ship carpenters, after hewing, and getting a piece of timber ready for use, write on the timber the name of that part of the ship for which it was intended. When a piece of timber was intended for the larboard side, it would be marked thus—"L." When a piece was for the starboard side, it would be marked thus—"S." A piece for the larboard side forward, would be marked thus—"L.F." When a piece was for starboard side forward, it would be marked thus—"S.F." For larboard aft, it would be marked thus—"L.A." For starboard aft, it would be marked thus—"S.A." I soon learned the names of these letters, and for what they were intended when placed upon a piece of timber in the ship-yard. I immediately commenced copying them, and in a short time was able to make the four letters named. After that, when I met with any boy who I knew could write, I would tell him I could write as well as he. The next word would be, "I don't believe you. Let me see you try it." I would then make the letters which I had been so fortunate as to learn, and ask him to beat that. In this way I got a good many lessons in writing, which it is quite possible I should never have gotten in any other way. During this time, my copy-book was the board fence, brick wall, and pavement; my pen and ink was a lump of chalk. With these, I learned mainly how to write. I then commenced and continued copying the Italics in Webster's Spelling Book,[3] until I could make them all without looking on the book. By this time, my little Master Thomas had gone to school, and learned how to write, and had written over a number of copy-books. These had been brought home, and shown to some of our near neighbors, and then laid aside. My mistress used to go to class meeting at the Wilk Street meeting-house every Monday afternoon, and leave me to take care of the house. When left thus, I used to spend the time in writing in the spaces left in Master Thomas's copy-book, copying what he had written. I continued to do this until I could write a hand very similar to that of Master Thomas. Thus, after a long, tedious effort for years, I finally succeeded in learning how to write.

Chapter VIII

In a very short time after I went to live at Baltimore, my old master's youngest son Richard died; and in about three years and six months after his death, my old master, Captain Anthony died, leaving only his son, Andrew, and daughter, Lucretia, to share his estate. He died while on a visit to see his daughter at Hillsborough. Cut off thus unexpectedly, he left no will as to the disposal of his property. It was therefore necessary to have a valuation of the property, that it might be equally divided between Mrs. Lucretia and Master Andrew. I was immediately sent for, to be valued with the other property. Here again my feelings rose up in detestation of slavery. I had now a new conception of my degraded condition. Prior to this, I had become, if not insensible to my lot, at least partly so. I left Baltimore with a young heart overborne with sadness, and a soul full of apprehension. I took passage with Captain Rowe, in the schooner Wild Cat, and, after a sail of about twenty-four hours, I found myself near the place of my birth. I had now been absent from it almost, if not quite, five years. I, however, remembered the place very well. I was only about five years old when I left it, to go and live with my old master on Colonel Lloyd's plantation; so that I was now between ten and eleven years old.

We were all ranked together at the valuation. Men and women, old and young, married and single, were ranked with horses, sheep, and swine. There were horses and men, cattle and women, pigs and children, all holding the same rank in the scale of being, and were all subjected to the same narrow examination. Silvery-headed age and sprightly youth, maids and matrons, had to undergo the same indelicate inspection. At this moment, I saw more

3. The *American Spelling Book* (1783), by Noah Webster (1758–1843), the leading American lexicographer of the time.

clearly than ever the brutalizing effects of slavery upon both slave and slaveholder.

After the valuation, then came the division. I have no language to express the high excitement and deep anxiety which were felt among us poor slaves during this time. Our fate for life was now to be decided. We had no more voice in that decision than the brutes among whom we were ranked. A single word from the white men was enough—against all our wishes, prayers, and entreaties—to sunder forever the dearest friends, dearest kindred, and strongest ties known to human beings. In addition to the pain of separation, there was the horrid dread of falling into the hands of Master Andrew. He was known to us all as being a most cruel wretch,—a common drunkard, who had, by his reckless mismanagement and profligate dissipation, already wasted a large portion of his father's property. We all felt that we might as well be sold at once to the Georgia traders, as to pass into his hands; for we knew that that would be our inevitable condition,—a condition held by us all in the utmost horror and dread.

I suffered more anxiety than most of my fellow-slaves. I had known what it was to be kindly treated; they had known nothing of the kind. They had seen little or nothing of the world. They were in very deed men and women of sorrow, and acquainted with grief.[4] Their backs had been made familiar with the bloody lash, so that they had become callous; mine was yet tender; for while at Baltimore I got few whippings, and few slaves could boast of a kinder master and mistress than myself; and the thought of passing out of their hands into those of Master Andrew—a man who, but a few day before, to give me a sample of his bloody disposition, took my little brother by the throat, threw him on the ground, and with the heel of his boot stamped upon his head till the blood gushed from his nose and ears—was well calculated to make me anxious as to my fate. After he had committed this savage outrage upon my brother, he turned to me, and said that was the way he meant to serve me one of these days,—meaning, I suppose, when I came into his possession.

Thanks to a kind Providence, I fell to the portion of Mrs. Lucretia, and was sent immediately back to Baltimore, to live again in the family of Master Hugh.[5] Their joy at my return equalled their sorrow at my departure. It was a glad day to me. I had escaped a [fate] worse than lion's jaws. I was absent from Baltimore, for the purpose of valuation and division, just about one month, and it seemed to have been six.

Very soon after my return to Baltimore, my mistress, Lucretia, died, leaving her husband and one child, Amanda; and in a very short time after her death, Master Andrew died. Now all the property of my old master, slaves included, was in the hands of strangers,—strangers who had had nothing to do with accumulating it. Not a slave was left free. All remained slaves, from the youngest to the oldest. If any one thing in my experience, more than another, served to deepen my conviction of the infernal character of slavery, and to fill me with unutterable loathing of slaveholders, it was their base ingratitude to my poor old grandmother. She had served my old master faithfully from youth to old age. She had been the source of all his wealth; she had peopled his plantation with slaves; she had become a great grandmother in his service. She had rocked him in infancy, attended him in childhood, served him through life, and at his death wiped from his icy brow the cold

4. See Isaiah 53:3.
5. Douglass returned to Baltimore in November 1827.

death-sweat, and closed his eyes forever. She was nevertheless left a slave—a slave for life—a slave in the hands of strangers; and in their hands she saw her children, her grandchildren, and her great-grandchildren, divided, like so many sheep, without being gratified with the small privilege of a single word, as to their or her own destiny. And, to cap the climax of their base ingratitude and fiendish barbarity, my grandmother, who was now very old, having outlived my old master and all his children, having seen the beginning and end of all of them, and her present owners finding she was of but little value, her frame already racked with the pains of old age, and complete helplessness fast stealing over her once active limbs, they took her to the woods, built her a little hut, put up a little mud-chimney, and then made her welcome to the privilege of supporting herself there in perfect loneliness; thus virtually turning her out to die! If my poor old grandmother now lives, she lives to suffer in utter loneliness; she lives to remember and mourn over the loss of children, the loss of grandchildren, and the loss of great-grandchildren. They are, in the language of the slave's poet, Whittier,[6]—

"Gone, gone, sold and gone
To the rice swamp dank and lone,
Where the slave-whip ceaseless swings,
Where the noisome insect stings,
Where the fever-demon strews
Poison with the falling dews,
Where the sickly sunbeams glare
Through the hot and misty air:—
  Gone, gone, sold and gone
  To the rice swamp dank and lone,
  From Virginia hills and waters—
  Woe is me, my stolen daughters!"

The hearth is desolate. The children, the unconscious children, who once sang and danced in her presence, are gone. She gropes her way, in the darkness of age, for a drink of water. Instead of the voices of her children, she hears by day the moans of the dove, and by night the screams of the hideous owl. All is gloom. The grave is at the door. And now, when weighed down by the pains and aches of old age, when the head inclines to the feet, when the beginning and ending of human existence meet, and helpless infancy and painful old age combine together—at this time, this most needful time, the time for the exercise of that tenderness and affection which children only can exercise toward a declining parent—my poor old grandmother, the devoted mother of twelve children, is left all alone, in yonder little hut, before a few dim embers. She stands—she sits—she staggers—she falls—she groans—she dies—and there are none of her children or grandchildren present, to wipe from her wrinkled brow the cold sweat of death, or to place beneath the sod her fallen remains. Will not a righteous God visit for these things?

In about two years after the death of Mrs. Lucretia, Master Thomas married his second wife. Her name was Rowena Hamilton. She was the eldest daughter of Mr. William Hamilton. Master now lived in St. Michael's. Not long after his marriage, a misunderstanding took place between himself and Master Hugh; and as a means of punishing his brother, he took me

6. John Greenleaf Whittier (1807–1892), American poet and abolitionist. The lines Douglass quotes are from Whittier's poem "The Farewell of a Virginia Slave Mother to Her Daughters, Sold into Southern Bondage" (1838).

from him to live with himself at St. Michael's. Here I underwent another most painful separation. It, however, was not so severe as the one I dreaded at the division of property; for, during this interval, a great change had taken place in Master Hugh and his once kind and affectionate wife. The influence of brandy upon him, and of slavery upon her, had effected a disastrous change in the characters of both; so that, as far as they were concerned, I thought I had little to lose by the change. But it was not to them that I was attached. It was to those little Baltimore boys that I felt the strongest attachment. I had received many good lessons from them, and was still receiving them, and the thought of leaving them was painful indeed. I was leaving, too, without the hope of ever being allowed to return. Master Thomas had said he would never let me return again. The barrier betwixt himself and brother he considered impassable.

I then had to regret that I did not at least make the attempt to carry out my resolution to run away; for the chances of success are tenfold greater from the city than from the country.

I sailed from Baltimore for St. Michael's in the sloop Amanda, Captain Edward Dodson. On my passage, I paid particular attention to the direction which the steamboats took to go to Philadelphia. I found, instead of going down, on reaching North Point they went up the bay, in a north-easterly direction. I deemed this knowledge of the utmost importance. My determination to run away was again revived. I resolved to wait only so long as the offering of a favorable opportunity. When that came, I was determined to be off.

Chapter IX

I have now reached a period of my life when I can give dates. I left Baltimore, and went to live with Master Thomas Auld, at St. Michael's in March, 1832.[7] It was now more than seven years since I lived with him in the family of my old master, on Colonel Lloyd's plantation. We of course were now almost entire strangers to each other. He was to me a new master, and I to him a new slave. I was ignorant of his temper and disposition; he was equally so of mine. A very short time, however brought us into full acquaintance with each other. I was made acquainted with his wife not less than with himself. They were well matched, being equally mean and cruel. I was now, for the first time during a space of more than seven years, made to feel the painful gnawings of hunger—a something which I had not experienced before since I left Colonel Lloyd's plantation. It went hard enough with me then, when I could look back to no period at which I had enjoyed a sufficiency. It was tenfold harder after living in Master Hugh's family, where I had always had enough to eat, and of that which was good. I have said Master Thomas was a mean man. He was so. Not to give a slave enough to eat, is regarded as the most aggravated development of meanness even among slaveholders. The rule is, no matter how coarse the food, only let there be enough of it. This is the theory; and in the part of Maryland from which I came, it is the general practice,—though there are many exceptions. Master Thomas gave us enough of neither coarse nor fine food. There were four slaves of us in the kitchen—my sister Eliza, my aunt Priscilla, Henny, and myself; and we were allowed less than half of a bushel of cornmeal per week, and very little else, either in the shape of meat or vegetables. It was not

7. Douglass actually returned to Thomas Auld's control in March 1833.

enough for us to subsist upon. We were therefore reduced to the wretched necessity of living at the expense of our neighbors. This we did by begging and stealing, whichever came handy in the time of need, the one being considered as legitimate as the other. A great many times have we poor creatures been nearly perishing with hunger, when food in abundance lay mouldering in the safe and smoke-house,[8] and our pious mistress was aware of the fact; and yet that mistress and her husband would kneel every morning, and pray that God would bless them in basket and store!

Bad as all slaveholders are, we seldom meet one destitute of every element of character commanding respect. My master was one of this rare sort. I do not know of one single noble act ever performed by him. The leading trait in his character was meanness; and if there were any other element in his nature, it was made subject to this. He was mean; and, like most other mean men, he lacked the ability to conceal his meanness. Captain Auld was not born a slaveholder. He had been a poor man, master only of a Bay craft. He came into possession of all his slaves by marriage; and of all men, adopted slaveholders are the worst. He was cruel, but cowardly. He commanded without firmness. In the enforcement of his rules he was at times rigid, and at times lax. At times, he spoke to his slaves with the firmness of Napoleon and the fury of a demon; at other times, he might well be mistaken for an inquirer who had lost his way. He did nothing of himself. He might have passed for a lion, but for his ears. In all things noble which he attempted, his own meanness shone most conspicuous. His airs, words, and actions, were the airs, words, and actions of born slaveholders, and, being assumed, were awkward enough. He was not even a good imitator. He possessed all the disposition to deceive, but wanted the power. Having no resources within himself, he was compelled to be the copyist of many, and being such, he was forever the victim of inconsistency; and of consequence he was an object of contempt, and was held as such even by his slaves. The luxury of having slaves of his own to wait upon him was something new and unprepared for. He was a slaveholder without the ability to hold slaves. He found himself incapable of managing his slaves either by force, fear, or fraud. We seldom called him "master;" we generally called him "Captain Auld," and were hardly disposed to title him at all. I doubt not that our conduct had much to do with making him appear awkward, and of consequence fretful. Our want of reverence for him must have perplexed him greatly. He wished to have us call him master, but lacked the firmness necessary to command us to do so. His wife used to insist upon our calling him so, but to no purpose. In August, 1832, my master attended a Methodist camp-meeting[9] held in the Bay-side, Talbot county, and there experienced religion. I indulged a faint hope that his conversion would lead him to emancipate his slaves, and that, if he did not do this, it would at any rate, make him more kind and humane. I was disappointed in both these respects. It neither made him to be humane to his slaves, nor to emancipate them. If it had any effect on his character, it made him more cruel and hateful in all his ways; for I believe him to have been a much worse man after his conversion than before. Prior to his conversion, he relied upon his own depravity to shield and sustain him in his savage barbarity; but after his conversion, he found religious sanction and support for his slaveholding cruelty. He made the greatest pre-

8. Used both to cure and to store meat and fish. "Safe": that is, a meat safe, a structure for preserving food.

9. A popular form of 19th-century evangelical religious gathering held in rural areas.

tensions to piety. His house was the house of prayer. He prayed morning, noon, and night. He very soon distinguished himself among his brethren, and was soon made a class-leader and exhorter. His activity in revivals was great, and he proved himself an instrument in the hands of the church in converting many souls. His house was the preachers' home. They used to take great pleasure in coming there to put up; for while he starved us, he stuffed them. We have had three or four preachers there at a time. The names of those who used to come most frequently while I lived there, were Mr. Storks, Mr. Ewery, Mr. Humphry, and Mr. Hickey. I have also seen Mr. George Cookman at our house. We slaves loved Mr. Cookman. We believed him to be a good man. We thought him instrumental in getting Mr. Samuel Harrison, a very rich slaveholder, to emancipate his slaves; and by some means got the impression that he was laboring to effect the emancipation of all the slaves. When he was at our house, we were sure to be called in to prayers. When the others were there, we were sometimes called in and sometimes not. Mr. Cookman took more notice of us than either of the other ministers. He could not come among us without betraying his sympathy for us, and, stupid as we were, we had the sagacity to see it.

While I lived with my master in St. Michael's, there was a white young man, a Mr. Wilson, who proposed to keep a Sabbath school for the instruction of such slaves as might be disposed to learn to read the New Testament. We met but three times, when Mr. West and Mr. Fairbanks, both class-leaders, with many others, came upon with us with sticks and other missiles, drove us off, and forbade us to meet again. Thus ended our little Sabbath school in the pious town of St. Michael's.

I have said my master found religious sanction for his cruelty. As an example, I will state one of many facts going to prove the charge. I have seen him tie up a lame young woman, and whip her with a heavy cowskin upon her naked shoulders, causing the warm red blood to drip; and, in justification of the bloody deed, he would quote this passage of Scripture—"He that knoweth his master's will, and doeth it not, shall be beaten with many stripes."[1]

Master would keep this lacerated young woman tied up in this horrid situation four or five hours at a time. I have known him to tie her up early in the morning, and whip her before breakfast; leave her, go to his store, return at dinner, and whip her again, cutting her in the places already made raw with his cruel lash. The secret of master's cruelty toward "Henny" is found in the fact of her being almost helpless. When quite a child, she fell into the fire, and burned herself horribly. Her hands were so burnt that she never got the use of them. She could do very little but bear heavy burdens. She was to master a bill of expense; and as he was a mean man, she was a constant offence to him. He seemed desirous of getting the poor girl out of existence. He gave her away once to his sister; but, being a poor gift, she was not disposed to keep her. Finally, my benevolent master, to use his own words, "set her adrift to take care of herself." Here was a recently-converted man, holding on upon the mother, and at the same time turning out her helpless child, to starve and die! Master Thomas was one of the many pious slaveholders who hold slaves for the very charitable purpose of taking care of them.

My master and myself had quite a number of differences. He found me unsuitable to his purpose. My city life, he said, had had a very pernicious

1. Luke 12:47.

effect upon me. It had almost ruined me for every good purpose, and fitted me for every thing which was bad. One of my greatest faults was that of letting his horse run away, and go down to his father-in-law's farm, which was about five miles from St. Michael's. I would then have to go after it. My reason for this kind of carelessness, or carefulness, was, that I could always get something to eat when I went there. Master William Hamilton, my master's father-in-law, always gave his slaves enough to eat. I never left there hungry, no matter how great the need of my speedy return. Master Thomas at length said he would stand it no longer. I had lived with him nine months, during which time he had given me a number of severe whippings, all to no good purpose. He resolved to put me out, as he said, to be broken; and, for this purpose, he let me for one year to a man named Edward Covey. Mr. Covey was a poor man, a farm-renter. He rented the place upon which he lived, as also the hands with which he tilled it. Mr. Covey had acquired a very high reputation for breaking young slaves, and this reputation was of immense value to him. It enabled him to get his farm tilled with much less expense to himself than he could have had it done without such a reputation. Some slaveholders thought it not much loss to allow Mr. Covey to have their slaves one year, for the sake of training to which they were subjected, without any other compensation. He could hire young help with great ease, in consequence of this reputation. Added to the natural good qualities of Mr. Covey, he was a professor of religion—a pious soul—a member and a class-leader in the Methodist church. All of this added weight to his reputation as a "nigger-breaker." I was aware of all the facts, having been made acquainted with them by a young man who had lived there. I nevertheless made the change gladly; for I was sure of getting enough to eat, which is not the smallest consideration to a hungry man.

Chapter X

I left Master Thomas's house, and went to live with Mr. Covey, on the 1st of January, 1833. I was now, for the first time in my life, a field hand. In my new employment, I found myself even more awkward than a country boy appeared to be in a large city. I had been at my new home but one week before Mr. Covey gave me a very severe whipping, cutting my back, causing the blood to run, and raising ridges on my flesh as large as my little finger. The details of this affair are as follows: Mr. Covey sent me, very early in the morning of one of our coldest days in the month of January, to the woods, to get a load of wood. He gave me a team of unbroken oxen. He told me which was the in-hand ox, and which the off-hand one.[2] He then tied the end of a large rope around the horns of the in-hand-ox, and gave me the other end of it, and told me, if the oxen started to run, that I must hold on upon the rope. I had never driven oxen before, and of course I was very awkward. I, however, succeeded in getting to the edge of the woods with little difficulty; but I had got a very few rods into the woods, when the oxen took fright, and started full tilt, carrying the cart against trees, and over stumps, in the most frightful manner. I expected every moment that my brains would be dashed out against the trees. After running thus for a considerable distance, they finally upset the cart, dashing it with great force against a tree, and threw themselves into a dense thicket. How I escaped death, I do not know. There

2. That is, the ox to the right of a pair hitched to a wagon. "The in-hand ox": the one to the left.

I was, entirely alone, in a thick wood, in a place new to me. My cart was upset and shattered, my oxen were entangled among the young trees, and there was none to help me. After a long spell of effort, I succeeded in getting my cart righted, my oxen disentangled, and again yoked to the cart. I now proceeded with my team to the place where I had, the day before, been chopping wood, and loaded my cart pretty heavily, thinking in this way to tame my oxen. I then proceeded on my way home. I had now consumed one half of the day. I got out of the woods safely, and now felt out of danger. I stopped my oxen to open the woods gate; and just as I did so, before I could get hold of my ox-rope, the oxen again started, rushed through the gate, catching it between the wheel and the body of the cart, tearing it to pieces, and coming within a few inches of crushing me against the gate-post. Thus twice, in one short day, I escaped death by the merest chance. On my return, I told Mr. Covey what had happened, and how it happened. He ordered me to return to the woods again immediately. I did so, and he followed on after me. Just as I got into the woods, he came up and told me to stop my cart, and that he would teach me how to trifle away my time, and break gates. He then went to a large gum-tree, and with his axe cut three large switches, and, after trimming them up neatly with his pocketknife, he ordered me to take off my clothes. I made him no answer, but stood with my clothes on. He repeated his order. I still made him no answer, nor did I move to strip myself. Upon this he rushed at me with the fierceness of a tiger, tore off my clothes, and lashed me till he had worn out his switches, cutting me so savagely as to leave the marks visible for a long time after. This whipping was the first of a number just like it, and for similar offences.

I lived with Mr. Covey one year. During the first six months, of that year, scarce a week passed without his whipping me. I was seldom free from a sore back. My awkwardness was almost always his excuse for whipping me. We were worked fully up to the point of endurance. Long before day we were up, our horses fed, and by the first approach of day we were off to the field with our hoes and ploughing teams. Mr. Covey gave us enough to eat, but scarce time to eat it. We were often less than five minutes taking our meals. We were often in the field from the first approach of day till its last lingering ray had left us; and at saving-fodder time, midnight often caught us in the field binding blades.[3]

Covey would be out with us. The way he used to stand it, was this. He would spend the most of his afternoons in bed. He would then come out fresh in the evening, ready to urge us on with his words, example, and frequently with the whip. Mr. Covey was one of the few slaveholders who could and did work with his hands. He was a hard-working man. He knew by himself just what a man or a boy could do. There was no deceiving him. His work went on in his absence almost as well as in his presence; and he had the faculty of making us feel that he was ever present with us. This he did by surprising us. He seldom approached the spot where we were at work openly, if he could do it secretly. He always aimed at taking us by surprise. Such was his cunning, that we used to call him, among ourselves, "the snake." When we were at work in the cornfield, he would sometimes crawl on his hands and knees to avoid detection, and all at once he would rise nearly in our midst, and scream out, "Ha, ha! Come, come! Dash on, dash on!" This being his mode of attack, it was never safe to stop a single minute. His com-

3. That is, of wheat or other crops. "Saving-fodder time": a reference to the harvest of the crops.

ings were like a thief in the night. He appeared to us as being ever at hand. He was under every tree, behind every stump, in every bush, and at every window, on the plantation. He would sometimes mount his horse, as if bound to St. Michael's, a distance of seven miles, and in half an hour afterwards you would see him coiled up in the corner of the wood-fence, watching every motion of the slaves. He would, for this purpose, leave his horse tied up in the woods. Again, he would sometimes walk up to us, and give us orders as though he was upon the point of starting on a long journey, turn his back upon us, and make as though he was going to the house to get ready; and, before he would get half way thither, he would turn short and crawl into a fence-corner, or behind some tree, and there watch us till the going down of the sun.

Mr. Covey's *forte* consisted in his power to deceive. His life was devoted to planning and perpetrating the grossest deceptions. Every thing he possessed in the shape of learning or religion, he made conform to his disposition to deceive. He seemed to think himself equal to deceiving the Almighty. He would make a short prayer in the morning, and a long prayer at night; and, strange as it may seem, few men would at times appear more devotional than he. The exercises of his family devotions were always commenced with singing; and, as he was a very poor singer himself, the duty of raising the hymn generally came upon me. He would read his hymn, and nod at me to commence. I would at times do so; at others, I would not. My non-compliance would almost always produce much confusion. To show himself independent of me, he would start and stagger through with his hymn in the most discordant manner. In this state of mind, he prayed with more than ordinary spirit. Poor man! such was his disposition, and success at deceiving, I do verily believe that he sometimes deceived himself into the solemn belief, that he was a sincere worshiper of the most high God; and this, too, at a time when he may be said to have been guilty of compelling his woman slave to commit the sin of adultery. The facts in the case are these: Mr. Covey was a poor man; he was just commencing in life; he was only able to buy one slave; and, shocking as is the fact, he bought her, as he said, for a *breeder*. This woman was named Caroline. Mr. Covey bought her from Mr. Thomas Lowe, about six miles from St. Michael's. She was a large, able-bodied woman, about twenty years old. She had already given birth to one child, which proved her to be just what he wanted. After buying her, he hired a married man of Mr. Samuel Harrison, to live with him one year; and him he used to fasten up with her every night! The result was, that, at the end of the year, the miserable woman gave birth to twins. At this result Mr. Covey seemed to be highly pleased, both with the man and the wretched woman. Such was his joy, and that of his wife, that nothing they could do for Caroline during her confinement was too good, or too hard to be done. The children were regarded as being quite an addition to his wealth.

If at any one time of my life more than another, I was made to drink the bitterest dregs of slavery, that time was during the first six months of my stay with Mr. Covey. We were worked in all weathers. It was never too hot or too cold; it could never rain, blow, hail, or snow, too hard for us to work in the field. Work, work, work, was scarcely more the order of the day than of the night. The longest days were too short for him, and the shortest nights too long for him. I was somewhat unmanageable when I first went there, but a few months of this discipline tamed me. Mr. Covey succeed in breaking me. I was broken in body, soul, and spirit. My natural elasticity was crushed, my intellect languished, the disposition to read departed, the cheerful spark that lingered about my eye died; the dark night of slavery closed in upon me, and behold a man transformed into a brute!

Sunday was my only leisure time. I spent this in a sort of beastlike stupor, between sleep and wake, under some large tree. At times I would rise up, a flash of energetic freedom would dart through my soul, accompanied with a faint beam of hope, that flickered for a moment, and then vanished. I sank down again, mourning over my wretched condition. I was sometimes prompted to take my life, and that of Covey, but was prevented by a combination of hope and fear. My sufferings on this plantation seem now like a dream rather than a stern reality.

Our house stood within a few rods of the Chesapeake Bay, whose broad bosom was ever white with sails from every quarter of the habitable globe. These beautiful vessels, robed in purest white, so delightful to the eye of freemen, were to me so many shrouded ghosts, to terrify and torment me with thoughts of my wretched condition. I have often, in the deep stillness of a summer's Sabbath, stood all alone upon the lofty banks of that noble bay, and traced, with saddened heart and tearful eye, the countless number of sails moving off to the mighty ocean. The sight of these always affected me powerfully. My thoughts would compel utterance; and there, with no audience but the Almighty, I would pour out my soul's complaint, in my rude way, with an apostrophe to the moving multitude of ships:—

"You are loosed from your moorings, and are free; I am fast in my chains, and am a slave! You move merrily before the gentle gale, and I sadly before the bloody whip! You are freedom's swift-winged angels, that fly round the world; I am confined in bands of iron! O that I were free! Oh, that I were on one of your gallant decks, and under your protecting wing! Alas! betwixt me and you, the turbid waters roll. Go on, go on. O that I could also go! Could I but swim! If I could fly! Oh, why was I born a man, of whom to make a brute! The glad ship is gone; she hides in the dim distance. I am left in the hottest hell of unending slavery. O God, save me! God, deliver me! Let me be free! Is there any God? Why am I a slave? I will run away. I will not stand it. Get caught, or get clear, I'll try it. I had as well die with ague as the fever. I have only one life to lose. I had as well be killed running as die standing. Only think of it; one hundred miles straight north, and I am free! Try it? Yes! God helping me, I will. It cannot be that I shall live and die a slave. I will take to the water. This very bay shall yet bear me into freedom. The steamboats steered in a north-east course from North Point. I will do the same; and when I get to the head of the bay, I will turn my canoe adrift, and walk straight through Delaware into Pennsylvania. When I get there, I shall not be required to have a pass; I can travel without being disturbed. Let but the first opportunity offer, and, come what will, I am off. Meanwhile, I will try to bear up under the yoke. I am not the only slave in the world. Why should I fret? I can bear as much as any one of them. Besides, I am but a boy, and all boys are bound to some one. It may be that my misery in slavery will only increase my happiness when I get free. There is a better day coming."

Thus I used to think, and thus I used to speak to myself; goaded almost to madness at one moment, and at the next reconciling myself to my wretched lot.

I have already intimated that my condition was much worse, during the first six months of my stay at Mr. Covey's, than in the last six. The circumstances leading to the change in Mr. Covey's course toward me form an epoch in my humble history. You have seen how a man was made a slave; you shall see how a slave was made a man. On one of the hottest days of the month of August, 1833, Bill Smith, William Hughes, a slave named Eli, and myself, were engaged in fanning wheat.[4] Hughes was clearing the fanned wheat from before the fan. Eli was turning, Smith was feeding, and I was carrying wheat to the fan. The work was simple, requiring strength rather than intellect; yet, to one entirely unused to such work, it came very hard. About three o'clock of that day, I broke down; my strength failed me; I was seized with a violent aching of the head, attended with extreme dizziness; I trembled in every limb. Finding what was coming, I nerved myself up, feeling it would never do to stop work. I stood as long as I could stagger to the hopper with grain. When I could stand no longer, I fell, and felt as if held down by an immense weight. The fan of course stopped; every one had his own work to do; and no one could do the work of the other, and have his own go on at the same time.

Mr. Covey was at the house, about one hundred yards from the treading-yard where we were fanning. On hearing the fan stop, he left immediately, and came to the spot where we were. He hastily inquired what the matter was. Bill answered that I was sick, and there was no one to bring wheat to the fan. I had by this time crawled away under the side of the post and rail-fence by which the yard was enclosed, hoping to find relief by getting out of the sun. He then asked where I was. He was told by one of the hands. He came to the spot, and, after looking at me awhile, asked me what was the matter. I told him as well as I could, for I scarce had strength to speak. He then gave me a savage kick in the side, and told me to get up. I tried to do so, but fell back in the attempt. He gave me another kick, and again told me to rise. I again tried, and succeeded in gaining my feet; but, stooping to get the tub with which I was feeding the fan, I again staggered and fell. While down in this situation, Mr. Covey took up the hickory slat with which Hughes had been striking off the half-bushel measure, and with it gave me a heavy blow upon the head, making a large wound, and the blood ran freely; and with this again told me to get up. I made no effort to comply, having now made up my mind to let him do his worst. In a short time after receiving this blow, my head grew better. Mr. Covey had now left me to my fate. At this moment I resolved, for the first time, to go to my master, enter a complaint, and ask his protection. In order to do this, I must that afternoon walk seven miles; and this, under the circumstances, was truly a severe undertaking. I was exceedingly feeble; made so as much by the kicks and blows which I received, as by the severe fit of sickness to which I had been subjected. I, however, watched my chance, while Covey was looking in an opposite direction, and started for St. Michael's. I succeeded in getting a considerable distance on my way to the woods, when Covey discovered me, and called after me to come back, threatening what he would do if I did not come. I disregarded both his calls and his threats, and made my way to the woods as fast as my feeble state would allow; and thinking I might be overhauled by him if I kept the road, I walked through the woods, keeping far enough from the road to avoid detection, and near enough to prevent losing my way. I had not gone far before my little strength again failed me. I could go no farther. I fell down, and lay for a considerable time. The blood was yet oozing from the wound

4. That is, separating the wheat from the chaff.

on my head. For a time I thought I should bleed to death; and think now that I should have done so, but that the blood so matted my hair as to stop the wound. After lying there about three quarters of an hour, I nerved myself up again, and started on my way, through bogs and briers, barefooted and bareheaded, tearing my feet sometimes at nearly every step; and after a journey of about seven miles, occupying some five hours to perform it, I arrived at master's store. I then presented an appearance enough to affect any but a heart of iron. From the crown of my head to my feet, I was covered with blood. My hair was all clotted with dust and blood; my shirt was stiff with blood. My legs and feet were torn in sundry places with briers and thorns, and were also covered with blood. I suppose I looked like a man who had escaped a den of wild beasts, and barely escaped them. In this state I appeared before my master, humbly entreating him to interpose his authority for my protection. I told him all the circumstances as well as I could, and it seemed, as I spoke, at times to affect him. He would then walk the floor, and seek to justify Covey by saying he expected I deserved it. He asked me what I wanted. I told him, to let me get a new home; that as sure as I lived with Mr. Covey again, I should live with but to die with him; that Covey would surely kill me; he was in a fair way for it. Master Thomas ridiculed the idea that there was any danger of Mr. Covey's killing me, and said that he knew Mr. Covey; that he was a good man, and that he could not think of taking me from him; that, should he do so, he would lose the whole year's wages; that I belonged to Mr. Covey for one year, and that I must go back to him, come what might; and that I must not trouble him with any more stories, or that he would himself *get hold of me.* After threatening me thus, he gave me a very large dose of salts, telling me that I might remain in St. Michael's that night, (it being quite late,) but that I must be off back to Mr. Covey's early in the morning; and that if I did not, he would *get hold of me,* which meant that he would whip me. I remained all night, and, according to his orders I started off to Covey's in the morning, (Saturday morning), wearied in body and broken in spirit. I got no supper that night, or breakfast that morning. I reached Covey's about nine o'clock; and just as I was getting over the fence that divided Mrs. Kemp's fields from ours, out ran Covey with his cowskin, to give me another whipping. Before he could reach me, I succeeded in getting to the cornfield; and as the corn was very high, it afforded me the means of hiding. He seemed very angry, and searched for me a long time. My behavior was altogether unaccountable. He finally gave up the chase, thinking, I suppose, that I must come home for something to eat; he would give himself no further trouble in looking for me. I spent that day mostly in the woods, having the alternative before me,—to go home and be whipped to death, or stay in the woods and be starved to death. That night, I fell in with Sandy Jenkins, a slave with whom I was somewhat acquainted. Sandy had a free wife[5] who lived about four miles from Mr. Covey's; and it being Saturday, he was on his way to see her. I told him my circumstances, and he very kindly invited me to go home with him. I went home with him, and talked this whole matter over, and got his advice as to what course it was best for me to pursue. I found Sandy an old adviser. He told me, with great solemnity, I must go back to Covey; but that before I went, I must go with him into another part of the woods, where there was a certain *root,* which, if I would take some of it with me, carrying it *always on my right side,* would render it impossible for

5. That is, she was not enslaved by anyone.

Mr. Covey, or any other white man, to whip me. He said he had carried it for years; and since he had done so, he had never received a blow, and never expected to while he carried it. I at first rejected the idea, that the simple carrying of a root in my pocket would have any such effect as he had said, and was not disposed to take it; but Sandy impressed the necessity with much earnestness, telling me it could do no harm, if it did no good. To please him, I at length took the root, and, according to his direction, carried it upon my right side. This was Sunday morning. I immediately started for home; and upon entering the yard gate, out came Mr. Covey on his way to meeting. He spoke to me very kindly, bade me drive the pigs from a lot near by, and passed on towards the church. Now, this singular conduct of Mr. Covey really made me begin to think that there was something in the *root* which Sandy had given me; and had it been on any other day than Sunday, I could have attributed the conduct to no other cause than the influence of that root; and as it was, I was half inclined to think the *root* to be something more than I at first had taken it to be. All went well till Monday morning. On this morning, the virtue of the *root* was fully tested. Long before daylight, I was called to go and rub, curry, and feed, the horses. I obeyed, and was glad to obey. But whilst thus engaged, whilst in the act of throwing down some blades from the loft, Mr. Covey entered the stable with a long rope; and just as I was half out of the loft, he caught hold of my legs, and was about tying me. As soon as I found what he was up to, I gave a sudden spring, and as I did so, he holding to my legs, I was brought sprawling on the stable floor. Mr. Covey seemed now to think he had me, and could do what he pleased; but at this moment—from whence came the spirit I don't know—I resolved to fight; and, suiting my action to the resolution, I seized Covey hard by the throat; and as I did so, I rose. He held on to me, and I to him. My resistance was so entirely unexpected, that Covey seemed taken all aback. He trembled like a leaf. This gave me assurance, and I held him uneasy, causing the blood to run where I touched him with the ends of my fingers. Mr. Covey soon called out to Hughes for help. Hughes came, and while Covey held me, attempted to tie my right hand. While he was in the act of doing so, I watched my chance, and gave him a heavy kick close under the ribs. This kick fairly sickened Hughes, so that he left me in the hands of Mr. Covey. This kick had the effect of not only weakening Hughes, but Covey also. When he saw Hughes bending over with pain, his courage quailed. He asked me if I meant to persist in my resistance. I told him I did, come what might; that he had used me like a brute for six months, and that I was determined to be used so no longer. With that, he strove to drag me to a stick that was lying just out of the stable door. He meant to knock me down. But just as he was leaning over to get the stick, I seized him with both hands by his collar, and brought him by a sudden snatch to the ground. By this time, Bill came. Covey called upon him for assistance. Bill wanted to know what he could do. Covey said, "Take hold of him, take hold of him!" Bill said his master hired him out to work, and not to help to whip me; so he left Covey and myself to fight our own battle out. We were at it for nearly two hours. Covey at length let me go, puffing and blowing at a great rate, saying that if I had not resisted, he would not have whipped me half so much. The truth was, that he had not whipped me at all. I considered him as getting entirely the worst end of the bargain; for he had drawn no blood from me, but I had from him. The whole six months afterwards, that I spent with Mr. Covey, he never laid the weight of his finger upon me in anger. He would occasionally say, he didn't want to get hold of me again. "No," thought I, "you need not; for you will come off worse than you did before."

This battle with Mr. Covey was the turning-point in my career as a slave. It rekindled the few expiring embers of freedom, and revived within me a sense of my own manhood. It recalled the departed self-confidence, and inspired me again with a determination to be free. The gratification afforded by the triumph was a full compensation for whatever else might follow, even death itself. He only can understand the deep satisfaction which I experienced, who has himself repelled by force the bloody arm of slavery. I felt as I never felt before. It was a glorious resurrection, from the tomb of slavery, to the heaven of freedom. My long-crushed spirit rose, cowardice departed, bold defiance took its place; and I now, resolved that, however long I might remain a slave in form, the day had passed forever when I could be a slave in fact. I did not hesitate to let it be known of me, that the white man who expected to succeed in whipping, must also succeed in killing me.

From this time I was never again what might be called fairly whipped, though I remained a slave four years afterwards. I had several fights, but was never whipped.

It was for a long time a matter of surprise to me why Mr. Covey did not immediately have me taken by the constable to the whipping-post, and there regularly whipped for the crime of raising my hand against a white man in defence of myself. And the only explanation I can now think of does not entirely satisfy me; but such as it is, I will give it. Mr. Covey enjoyed the most unbounded reputation for being a first-rate overseer and negro-breaker. It was of considerable importance to him. That reputation was at stake; and had he sent me—a boy about sixteen years old—to the public whipping post, his reputation would have been lost; so, to save his reputation, he suffered me to go unpunished.

My term of actual service to Mr. Edward Covey ended on Christmas day, 1833. The days between Christmas and New Year's day are allowed as holidays; and, accordingly, we were not required to perform any labor, more than to feed and take care of the stock. This time we regarded as our own, by the grace of our masters; and we therefore used or abused it nearly as we pleased. Those of us who had families at a distance, were generally allowed to spend the whole six days in their society. This time, however, was spent in various ways. The staid, sober, thinking and industrious ones of our number would employ themselves in making corn-brooms, mats, horse-collars, and baskets; and another class of us would spend the time hunting opossums, hares, and coons. But by far the larger part engaged in such sports and merriments as playing ball, wrestling, running foot-races, fiddling, dancing, and drinking whisky; and this latter mode of spending the time was by far the most agreeable to the feelings of our master. A slave who would work during the holidays was considered by our masters as scarcely deserving them. He was regarded as one who rejected the favor of his master. It was deemed a disgrace not to get drunk at Christmas; and he was regarded as lazy indeed, who had not provided himself with the necessary means, during the year, to get whisky enough to last him through Christmas.

From what I know of the effect of these holidays upon the slave, I believe them to be among the most effective means in the hands of the slaveholder in keeping down the spirit of insurrection. Were the slaveholders at once to abandon this practice, I have not the slightest doubt it would lead to an immediate insurrection among the slaves. These holidays serve as conductors, or safety-valves, to carry off the rebellious spirit of enslaved humanity. But for these, the slave would be forced up to the wildest desperation; and woe betide the slaveholder, the day he ventures to remove or hinder the operation of those conductors! I warn him that, in such an event, a spirit will go forth in their midst, more to be dreaded than the most appalling earthquake.

The holidays are part and parcel of the gross fraud, wrong, and inhumanity of slavery. They are professedly a custom established by the benevolence of the slaveholders; but I undertake to say, it is the result of selfishness, and one of the grossest fraud committed upon the down-trodden slave. They do not give the slaves this time because they would not like to have their work during its continuance, but because they know it would be unsafe to deprive them of it. This will be seen by the fact, that the slaveholders like to have their slaves spend those days just in such a manner as to make them as glad of their ending as of their beginning. Their object seems to be, to disgust their slaves with freedom, by plunging them into the lowest depths of dissipation. For instance, the slaveholders not only like to see the slave drink of his own accord, but will adopt various plans to make him drunk. One plan is, to make bets on their slaves, as to who can drink the most whisky without getting drunk; and in this way they succeed in getting whole multitudes to drink to excess. Thus, when the slave asks for virtuous freedom, the cunning slaveholder, knowing his ignorance, cheats him with a dose of vicious dissipation, artfully labelled with the name of liberty. The most of us used to drink it down, and the result was just what might be supposed: many of us were led to think that there was little to choose between liberty and slavery. We felt, and very properly too, that we had almost as well be slaves to man as to rum. So, when the holidays ended, we staggered up from the filth of our wallowing, took a long breath, and marched to the field,—feeling, upon the whole, rather glad to go, from what our master had deceived us into a belief was freedom, back to the arms of slavery.

I have said that this mode of treatment is a part of the whole system of fraud and inhumanity of slavery. It is so. The mode here adopted to disgust the slave with freedom, by allowing him to see only the abuse of it, is carried out in other things. For instance, a slave loves molasses; he steals some. His master, in many cases, goes off to town, and buys a large quantity; he returns, takes his whip, and commands the slave to eat the molasses, until the poor fellow is made sick at the very mention of it. The same mode is sometimes adopted to make the slaves refrain from asking for more food than their regular allowance. A slave runs through his allowance, and applies for more. His master is enraged at him; but, not willing to send him off without food, gives more than is necessary, and compels him to eat it within a given time. Then, if he complains that he cannot eat it, he is said to be satisfied neither full nor fasting, and is whipped for being hard to please! I have an abundance of such illustrations of the same principle, drawn from my own observation, but think the cases I have cited sufficient. The practice is a very common one.

On the first of January, 1834, I left Mr. Covey, and went to live with Mr. William Freeland, who lived about three miles from St. Michael's. I soon found Mr. Freeland a very different man from Mr. Covey. Though not rich, he was what would be called an educated southern gentleman. Mr. Covey, as I have shown, was a well-trained negro-breaker and slave-driver. The former (slaveholder though he was) seemed to possess some regard for honor, some reverence for justice, and some respect for humanity. The latter seemed totally insensible to all such sentiments. Mr. Freeland had many of the faults peculiar to slaveholders, such as being very passionate and fretful; but I must do him the justice to say, that he was exceedingly free from those degrading vices to which Mr. Covey was constantly addicted. The one was open and frank, and we always knew where to find him. The other was a most artful deceiver, and could be understood only by such as were skilful enough to detect his cunningly-devised frauds. Another advantage I gained in my new master was, he made no pretensions to, or profession of, religion; and this, in my opinion, was truly a great advantage. I assert most unhesitatingly, that the religion of the south is a mere covering for the most horrid crimes,—a justifier of the most appalling barbarity,—a sanctifier of the most hateful frauds,—and a dark shelter under, which the darkest, foulest, grossest, and most infernal deeds of slaveholders find the strongest protection. Were I to be again reduced to the chains of slavery, next to that enslavement, I should regard being the slave of a religious master the greatest calamity that could befall me. For of all slaveholders with whom I have ever met, religious slaveholders are the worst. I have ever found them the meanest and basest, the most cruel and cowardly, of all others. It was my unhappy lot not only to belong to a religious slaveholder, but to live in a community of such religionists. Very near Mr. Freeland lived the Rev. Daniel Weeden, and in the same neighborhood lived the Rev. Rigby Hopkins. These were members and ministers in the Reformed Methodist Church. Mr. Weeden owned, among others, a woman slave, whose name I have forgotten. This woman's back, for weeks, was kept literally raw, made so by the lash of this merciless, *religious* wretch. He used to hire hands. His maxim was, Behave well or behave ill, it is the duty of a master occasionally to whip a slave, to remind him of his master's authority. Such was his theory, and such his practice.

Mr. Hopkins was even worse than Mr. Weeden. His chief boast was his ability to manage slaves. The peculiar feature of his government was that of whipping slaves in advance of deserving it. He always managed to have one or more of his slaves to whip every Monday morning. He did this to alarm their fears, and strike terror into those who escaped. His plan was to whip for the smallest offences, to prevent the commission of large ones. Mr. Hopkins could always find some excuse for whipping a slave. It would astonish one, unaccustomed to a slave-holding life, to see with what wonderful ease a slave-holder can find things, of which to make occasion to whip a slave. A mere look, word, or motion,—a mistake, accident, or want of power,—are all matters for which a slave may be whipped at any time. Does a slave look dissatisfied? It is said, he has the devil in him, and it must be whipped out. Does he speak loudly when spoken to by his master? Then he is wanting in reverence, and should be whipped for it. Does he ever venture to vindicate his conduct, when censured for it? Then he is guilty of impudence,—one of the greatest crimes of which a slave can be guilty. Does he ever venture to suggest a different mode of doing things from that pointed out by his master? He is indeed presumptuous, and getting above himself; and nothing less than a flogging will do for him. Does he, while ploughing, break a plough,—or, while hoeing, break a hoe? It is owing to his carelessness, and for it a slave must always be whipped. Mr. Hopkins could always find something of this sort to justify the use of the lash, and he seldom failed to embrace such opportunities. There was not a man in the whole county, with whom the slaves who had the getting their own home, would not prefer to live, rather than with this Rev. Mr. Hopkins. And yet there was not a man any where round, who made higher professions of religion, or was more active in revivals—more attentive to the class, love-feast, prayer and preaching meetings, or more devotional in his family,—that prayed earlier, later, louder, and longer,—than this same reverend slave-driver, Rigby Hopkins.

But to return to Mr. Freeland, and to my experience while in his employment. He, like Mr. Covey, gave us enough to eat; but unlike Mr. Covey, he also gave us sufficient time to take our meals. He worked us hard, but always between sunrise and sunset. He required a good deal of work to be done, but gave us good tools with which to work. His farm was large, but he employed hands enough to work it, and with ease, compared with many of his neighbors. My treatment, while in his employment, was heavenly, compared with what I experienced at the hands of Mr. Edward Covey.

Mr. Freeland was himself the owner of but two slaves. Their names were Henry Harris and John Harris. The rest of his hands he hired. These consisted of myself, Sandy Jenkins[6] and Handy Caldwell. Henry and John were quite intelligent, and in a very little while after I went there, I succeeded in creating in them a strong desire to learn how to read. This desire soon sprang up in the others also. They very soon mustered up some old spelling-books, and nothing would do but that I must keep a Sabbath school. I agreed to do so, and accordingly devoted my Sundays to teaching these my loved fellow-slaves how to read. Neither of them knew his letters when I went there. Some of the slaves of the neighboring farms found what was going on, and also availed themselves of this little opportunity to learn to read. It was understood, among all who came, that there must be as little display about it as possible. It was necessary to keep our religious masters at St. Michael's unacquainted with the fact, that, instead of spending the Sabbath in wrestling, boxing, and drinking whisky, we were trying to learn how to read the will of God; for they had much rather see us engaged in those degrading sports, than to see us behaving like intellectual, moral, and accountable beings. My blood boils as I think of the bloody manner in which Messrs. Wright Fairbanks and Garrison West, both class-leaders, in connection with many others, rushed in upon us with sticks and stones, and broke up our virtuous little Sabbath school, at St. Michael's—all calling themselves Christians! humble followers of the Lord Jesus Christ! But I am again digressing.

I held my Sabbath school at the house of a free colored man, whose name I deem it imprudent to mention; for should it be known, it might embarrass him greatly, though the crime of holding the school was committed ten years ago. I had at one time over forty scholars, and those of the right sort, ardently desiring to learn. They were of all ages, though mostly men and women. I look back to those Sundays with an amount of pleasure not to be expressed. They were great days to my soul. The work of instructing my dear fellow-slaves was the sweetest engagement with which I was ever

6. This is the same man who gave me the roots to prevent my being whipped by Mr. Covey. He was "a clever soul." We used frequently to talk about the fight with Covey, and as often as we did so, he would claim my success as the result of the roots he gave me. This superstition is very common among the more ignorant slaves. A slave seldom dies but that his death is attributed to trickery [*Douglass's note*].

blessed. We loved each other, and to leave them at the close of the Sabbath was a severe cross indeed. When I think that those precious souls are to-day shut up in the prison-house of slavery, my feelings overcome me, and I am almost ready to ask, "Does a righteous God govern the universe? and for what does he hold the thunders in his right hand, if not to smite the oppressor, and deliver the spoiled out of the hand of the spoiler?" These dear souls came not to Sabbath school because it was popular to do so, nor did I teach them because it was reputable to be thus engaged. Every moment they spent in that school, they were liable to be taken up, and given thirty-nine lashes. They came because they wished to learn. Their minds had been starved by their cruel masters. They had been shut up in mental darkness. I taught them, because it was the delight of my soul to be doing something that looked like bettering the condition of my race. I kept up my school nearly the whole year I lived with Mr. Freeland; and, beside my Sabbath school, I devoted three evenings in the week, during the winter, to teaching the slaves at home. And I have the happiness to know, that several of those who came to Sabbath school learned how to read; and that one, at least, is now free through my agency.

The year passed off smoothly. It seemed only about half as long as the year which preceded it. I went through it without receiving a single blow. I will give Mr. Freeland the credit of being the best master I ever had, *till I became my own master*. For the ease with which I passed the year, I was, however, somewhat indebted to the society of my fellow-slaves. They were noble souls; they not only possessed loving hearts, but brave ones. We were linked and interlinked with each other. I loved them with a love stronger than any thing I have experienced since. It is sometimes said that we slaves do not love and confide in each other. In answer to this assertion, I can say, I never loved any or confided in any people more than my fellow-slaves, and especially those with whom I lived at Mr. Freeland's. I believe we would have died for each other. We never undertook to do any thing, of any importance, without a mutual consultation. We never moved separately. We were one; and as much so by our tempers and dispositions, as by the mutual hardships to which we were necessarily subjected by our condition as slaves.

At the close of the year 1834, Mr. Freeland again hired me of my master, for the year 1835. But, by this time, I began to want to live *upon free land* as well as *with Freeland;* and I was no longer content, therefore, to live with him or any slaveholder. I began, with the commencement of the year, to prepare myself for a final struggle, which should decide my fate one way or the other. My tendency was upward. I was fast approaching manhood, and year after year had passed, and I was still a slave. These thoughts roused me—I must do something. I therefore resolved that 1835 should not pass without witnessing an attempt, on my part, to secure my liberty. But I was not willing to cherish this determination alone. My fellow-slaves were dear to me. I was anxious to have them participate with me in this, my life-giving determination. I therefore, though with great prudence, commenced early to ascertain their views and feelings in regard to their condition, and to imbue their minds with thoughts of freedom. I bent myself to devising ways and means for our escape, and meanwhile strove, on all fitting occasions, to impress them with the gross fraud and inhumanity of slavery. I went first to Henry, next to John, then to the others. I found, in them all, warm hearts and noble spirits. They were ready to hear, and ready to act when a feasible plan should be proposed. This was what I wanted. I talked to them of our want of manhood, if we submitted to our enslavement without at least one noble effort to be free. We met often, and consulted frequently, and told our hopes and fears, recounted the difficulties, real and imagined, which we should be called on to meet. At times we were almost disposed to give up and try to content ourselves with our wretched lot; at others, we were firm and unbending in our determination to go. Whenever we suggested any plan, there was shrinking—the odds were fearful. Our path was beset with the greatest obstacles; and if we succeeded in gaining the end of it, our right to be free was yet questionable—we were yet liable to be returned to bondage. We could see no spot, this side of the ocean, where we could be free. We knew nothing about Canada. Our knowledge of the north did not extend farther than New York; and to go there, and be forever harassed with the frightful liability of being returned to slavery—with the certainty of being treated tenfold worse than before—the thought was truly a horrible one, and one which it was not easy to overcome. The case sometimes stood thus: At every gate through which we were to pass, we saw a watchman—at every ferry a guard—on every bridge a sentinel—and in every wood a patrol. We were hemmed in upon every side. Here were the difficulties, real or imagined—the good to be sought, and the evil to be shunned. On the one hand, there stood slavery, a stern reality, glaring frightfully upon us,—its robes already crimsoned with the blood of millions, and even now feasting itself greedily upon our own flesh. On the other hand, away back in the dim distance, under the flickering light of the north star, behind some craggy hill or snow-covered mountain, stood a doubtful freedom—half frozen—beckoning us to come and share its hospitality. This in itself was sometimes enough to stagger us; but when we permitted ourselves to survey the road, we were frequently appalled. Upon either side we saw grim death, assuming the most horrid shapes. Now it was starvation, causing us to eat our own flesh;—now we were contending with the waves, and were drowned;—now we were overtaken, and torn to pieces by the fangs of the terrible bloodhound. We were stung by scorpions, chased by wild beasts, bitten by snakes, and finally, after having nearly reached the desired spot,—after swimming rivers, encountering wild beasts, sleeping in the woods, suffering hunger and nakedness,—we were overtaken by our pursuers, and in our resistance, we were shot dead upon the spot! I say, this picture sometimes appalled us, and made us

"rather bear those ills we had,
Than fly to others, that we knew not of."[7]

In coming to a fixed determination to run away, we did more than Patrick Henry, when he resolved upon liberty or death. With us it was a doubtful liberty at most, and almost certain death if we failed. For my part, I should prefer death to hopeless bondage.

Sandy, one of our number, gave up the notion, but still encouraged us. Our company then consisted of Henry Harris, John Harris, Henry Bailey, Charles Roberts, and myself. Henry Bailey was my uncle, and belonged to my master. Charles married my aunt: he belonged to my master's father-in-law, Mr. William Hamilton.

The plan we finally concluded upon was, to get a large canoe belonging to Mr. Hamilton, and upon the Saturday night previous to Easter holidays,

7. Shakespeare's *Hamlet* 3.1.81–82.

paddle directly up the Chesapeake Bay. On our arrival at the head of the bay, a distance of seventy or eighty miles from where we lived, it was our purpose to turn our canoe adrift, and follow the guidance of the north star till we got beyond the limits of Maryland. Our reason for taking the water route was, that we were less liable to be suspected as runaways; we hoped to be regarded as fishermen; whereas, if we should take the land route, we should be subjected to interruptions of almost every kind. Any one having a white face, and being so disposed, could stop us, and subject us to examination.

The week before our intended start, I wrote several protections, one for each of us. As well as I can remember they were in the following words, to wit:—

> "This is to certify that I, the undersigned, have given the bearer, my servant, full liberty to go to Baltimore, and spend the Easter holidays. Written with mine own hand, etc., 1835
>
> "WILLIAM HAMILTON,
> Near St. Michael's, in Talbot county, Maryland."

We were not going to Baltimore; but, in going up the bay, we went toward Baltimore, and these protections were only intended to protect us while on the bay.

As the time drew near for our departure, our anxiety became more and more intense. It was truly a matter of life and death with us. The strength of our determination was about to be fully tested. At this time, I was very active in explaining every difficulty, removing every doubt, dispelling every fear, and inspiring all with the firmness indispensable to success in our undertaking; assuring them that half was gained the instant we made the move; we had talked long enough; we were now ready to move; if not now, we never should be; and if we did not intend to move now, we had as well fold our arms, sit down, and acknowledge ourselves fit only to be slaves. This, none of us were prepared to acknowledge. Every man stood firm; and at our last meeting, we pledged ourselves afresh, in the most solemn manner, that at the time appointed, we would certainly start in pursuit of freedom. This was in the middle of the week, at the end of which we were to be off. We went, as usual, to our several fields of labor, but with bosoms highly agitated with thoughts of our truly hazardous undertaking. We tried to conceal our feelings as much as possible; and I think we succeeded very well.

After a painful waiting, the Saturday morning, whose night was to witness our departure, came. I hailed it with joy, bring what of sadness it might. Friday night was a sleepless one for me. I probably felt more anxious than the rest, because I was, by common consent, at the head of the whole affair. The responsibility of success or failure lay heavily upon me. The glory of the one, and the confusion of the other, were alike mine. The first two hours of that morning were such as I never experienced before, and hope never to again. Early in the morning, we went, as usual, to the field. We were spreading manure; and all at once, while thus engaged, I was overwhelmed with an indescribable feeling, in the fulness of which I turned to Sandy, who was near by, and said, "We are betrayed!" "Well," said he, "that thought has this moment struck me." We said no more. I was never more certain of any thing.

The horn was blown as usual, and we went up from the field to the house for breakfast. I went for the form, more than for want of any thing to eat that morning. Just as I got to the house, in looking out at the lane gate, I saw four white men, with two colored men. The white men were on horseback, and the colored ones were walking behind, as if tied. I watched them a few moments till they got up to our lane gate. Here they halted, and tied the colored men to the gate-post. I was not yet certain as to what the matter was. In a few moments, in rode Mr. Hamilton, with a speed betokening great excitement. He came to the door, and inquired if Master William was in. He was told he was at the barn. Mr. Hamilton, without dismounting, rode up to the barn with extraordinary speed. In a few moments, he and Mr. Freeland returned to the house. By this time, the three constables rode up, and in great haste dismounted, tied their horses, and met Master William and Mr. Hamilton returning from the barn; and after talking awhile, they all walked up to the kitchen door. There was no one in the kitchen but myself and John. Henry and Sandy were up at the barn. Mr. Freeland put his head in at the door, and called me by name, saying, there were some gentlemen at the door who wished to see me. I stepped to the door, and inquired what they wanted. They at once seized me, and, without giving me any satisfaction, tied me—lashing my hands closely together. I insisted upon knowing what the matter was. They at length said, that they had learned I had been in a "scrape," and that I was to be examined before my master; and if their information proved false, I should not be hurt.

In a few moments, they succeeded in tying John. They then turned to Henry, who had by this time returned, and commanded him to cross his hands. "I won't!" said Henry, in a firm tone, indicating his readiness to meet the consequences of his refusal. "Won't you?" said Tom Graham, the constable. "No, I won't!" said Henry, in a still stronger tone. With this, two of the constables pulled out their shining pistols, and swore, by their Creator, that they would make him cross his hands or kill him. Each cocked his pistol, and, with fingers on the trigger, walked up to Henry, saying, at the same time, if he did not cross his hands, they would blow his damned heart out. "Shoot me, shoot me!" said Henry; "you can't kill me but once. Shoot, shoot,—and be damned! *I won't be tied!"* This he said in a tone of loud defiance; and at the same time, with a motion as quick as lightning, he with one single stroke dashed the pistols from the hand of each constable. As he did this, all hands fell upon him, and, after beating him some time, they finally overpowered him, and got him tied.

During the scuffle, I managed, I know not how, to get my pass out, and, without being discovered, put it into the fire. We were all now tied; and just as we were to leave for Easton jail, Betsy Freeland, mother of William Freeland, came to the door with her hands full of biscuits, and divided them between Henry and John. She then delivered herself of a speech, to the following effect:—addressing herself to me, she said, *"You devil! You yellow devil!* it was you that put it into the heads of Henry and John to run away. But for you, you long-legged mulatto devil! Henry nor John would never have thought of such a thing." I made no reply, and was immediately hurried off towards St. Michael's. Just a moment previous to the scuffle with Henry, Mr. Hamilton suggested the propriety of making a search for the protections which he had understood Frederick had written for himself and the rest. But, just at the moment he was about carrying his proposal into effect, his aid was needed in helping to tie Henry; and the excitement attending the scuffle caused them either to forget, or to deem it unsafe, under the circumstances, to search. So we were not yet convicted of the intention to run away.

When we got about half way to St. Michael's, while the constables having us in charge were looking ahead, Henry inquired of me what he should do with his pass. I told him to eat it with his biscuit, and own nothing; and we passed the word around, "*Own nothing;*" and "*Own nothing!*" said we all. Our confidence in each other was unshaken. We were resolved to succeed or fail together, after the calamity had befallen us as much as before. We were now prepared for any thing. We were to be dragged that morning fifteen miles behind horses, and then to be placed in the Easton jail. When we reached St. Michael's, we underwent a sort of examination. We all denied that we ever intended to run away. We did this more to bring out the evidence against us, than from any hope of getting clear of being sold; for, as I have said, we were ready for that. The fact was, we cared but little where we went, so we went together. Our greatest concern was about separation. We dreaded that more than any thing this side of death. We found the evidence against us to be the testimony of one person; our master would not tell who it was; but we came to a unanimous decision among ourselves as to who their informant was. We were sent off to the jail at Easton. When we got there, we were delivered up to the sheriff, Mr. Joseph Graham, and by him placed in jail. Henry, John, and myself, were placed in one room together—Charles, and Henry Bailey, in another. Their object in separating us was to hinder concert.[8]

We had been in jail scarcely twenty minutes, when a swarm of slave traders, and agents for slave traders, flocked into jail to look at us, and to ascertain if we were for sale. Such a set of beings I never saw before! I felt myself surrounded by so many fiends from perdition. A band of pirates never looked more like their father, the devil. They laughed and grinned over us, saying, "Ah, my boys! we have got you, haven't we?" And after taunting us in various ways, they one by one went into an examination of us, with intent to ascertain our value. They would impudently ask us if we would not like to have them for our masters. We would make them no answer, and leave them to find out as best they could. Then they would curse and swear at us, telling us that they could take the devil out of us in a very little while, if we were only in their hands.

While in jail, we found ourselves in much more comfortable quarters than we expected when we went there. We did not get much to eat, nor that which was very good; but we had a good clean room, from the windows of which we could see what was going on in the street, which was very much better than though we had been placed in one of the dark, damp cells. Upon the whole, we got along very well, so far as the jail and its keeper were concerned. Immediately after the holidays were over, contrary to all our expectations, Mr. Hamilton and Mr. Freeland came up to Easton, and took Charles, the two Henrys, and John, out of jail, and carried them home, leaving me alone. I regarded this separation as a final one. It caused me more pain than any thing else in the whole transaction. I was ready for any thing rather than separation. I supposed that they had consulted together, and had decided that, as I was the whole cause of the intention of the others to run away, it was hard to make the innocent suffer with the guilty; and that they had, therefore, concluded to take the others home, and sell me, as a warning to the others that remained. It is due to the noble Henry to say, he seemed almost as reluctant at leaving the prison as at leaving home to come to the prison. But we knew we should, in all probability, be separated, if we were sold; and since he was in their hands, he concluded to go peaceably home.

8. Agreement in design or plan.

I was now left to my fate. I was all alone, and within the walls of a stone prison. But a few days before, and I was full of hope. I expected to have been safe in a land of freedom; but now I was covered with gloom, sunk down to the utmost despair. I thought the possibility of freedom was gone. I was kept in this way about one week, at the end of which, Captain Auld, my master, to my surprise and utter astonishment, came up, and took me out, with the intention of sending me, with a gentleman of his acquaintance, into Alabama. But, from some cause or other, he did not send me to Alabama, but concluded to send me back to Baltimore, to live again with his brother Hugh, and to learn a trade.

Thus, after an absence of three years and one month, I was once more permitted to return to my old home at Baltimore. My master sent me away, because there existed against me a very great prejudice in the community, and he feared I might be killed.

In a few weeks after I went to Baltimore, Master Hugh hired me to Mr. William Gardner, an extensive ship-builder, on Fell's Point. I was put there to learn how to calk. It, however, proved a very unfavorable place for the accomplishment of this object. Mr. Gardner was engaged that spring in building two large man-of-war brigs, professedly for the Mexican government. The vessels were to be launched in the July of that year,[9] and in failure thereof, Mr. Gardner was to lose a considerable sum; so that when I entered, all was hurry. There was no time to learn any thing. Every man had to do that which he knew how to do. In entering the shipyard, my orders from Mr. Gardner were, to do whatever the carpenters commanded me to do. This was placing me at the beck and call of about seventy-five men. I was to regard all these as masters. Their word was to be my law. My situation was a most trying one. At times I needed a dozen pair of hands. I was called a dozen ways in the space of a single minute. Three or four voices would strike my ear at the same moment. It was—"Fred., come help me to cant this timber here."—"Fred., come carry this timber yonder."—"Fred., bring that roller here."—"Fred., go get a fresh can of water."—"Fred., come help saw off the end of this timber."—"Fred., go quick, and get the crowbar."—"Fred., hold on the end of this fall."[1]—"Fred., go to the blacksmith's shop, and get a new punch."—"Hurra, Fred.! run and bring me a cold chisel."—"I say, Fred., bear a hand, and get up a fire as quick as lightning under that steam-box."—"Halloo, nigger! come, turn this grindstone."—"Come, come! move, move! and *bowse*[2] this timber forward."—"I say, darky, blast your eyes, why don't you heat up some pitch?"—"Halloo! halloo! halloo!" (Three voices at the same time.) "Come here!—Go there!—Hold on where you are! Damn you, if you move, I'll knock your brains out!"

This was my school for eight months; and I might have remained there longer, but for a most horrid fight I had with four of the white apprentices, in which my left eye was nearly knocked out, and I was horribly mangled in other respects. The facts in the case were these: Until a very little while after I went there, white and black ship-carpenters worked side by side, and no one seemed to see any impropriety in it. All hands seemed to be very well satisfied. Many of the black carpenters were freemen. Things seemed to be going on very well. All at once, the white carpenters knocked off, and said they would not work with free colored workmen. Their reason for this, as

9. 1836.
1. Nautical term for the free end of a rope of a tackle or hoisting device.
2. To haul the timber by pulling on the rope.

alleged, was, that if free colored carpenters were encouraged, they would soon take the trade into their own hands, and poor white men would be thrown out of employment. They therefore felt called upon at once to put a stop to it. And, taking advantage of Mr. Gardner's necessities, they broke off, swearing they would work no longer, unless he would discharge his black carpenters. Now, though this did not extend to me in form, it did reach me in fact. My fellow-apprentices very soon began to feel it degrading to them to work with me. They began to put on airs, and talk about the "niggers" taking the country, saying we all ought to be killed; and, being encouraged by the journeymen, they commenced making my condition as hard as they could, by hectoring me around, and sometimes striking me. I, of course, kept the vow I made after the fight with Mr. Covey, and struck back again, regardless of consequences; and while I kept them from combining, I succeeded very well; for I could whip the whole of them, taking them separately. They, however, at length combined, and came upon me, armed with sticks, stones, and heavy handspikes. One came in front with a half brick. There was one at each side of me, and one behind me. While I was attending to those in front, and on either side, the one behind ran up with the handspike, and struck me a heavy blow upon the head. It stunned me. I fell, and with this they all ran upon me, and fell to beating me with their fists. I let them lay on for a while, gathering strength. In an instant, I gave a sudden surge, and rose to my hands and knees. Just as I did that, one of their number gave me, with his heavy boot, a powerful kick in the left eye. My eyeball seemed to have burst. When they saw my eye closed, and badly swollen, they left me. With this I seized the handspike, and for a time pursued them. But here the carpenters interfered, and I thought I might as well give it up. It was impossible to stand my hand against so many. All this took place in sight of not less than fifty white ship-carpenters, and not one interposed a friendly word; but some cried, "Kill the damned nigger! Kill him! kill him! He struck a white person." I found my only chance for life was in flight. I succeeded in getting away without an additional blow, and barely so, for to strike a white man is death by Lynch law,[3]—and that was the law in Mr. Gardner's ship-yard; nor is there much of any other out of Mr. Gardner's ship-yard.

I went directly home, and told the story of my wrongs to Master Hugh; and I am happy to say of him, irreligious as he was, his conduct was heavenly, compared with that of his brother Thomas under similar circumstances. He listened attentively to my narration of the circumstances leading to the savage outrage, and gave many proofs of his strong indignation at it. The heart of my once overkind mistress was again melted into pity. My puffed-out eye and blood-covered face moved her to tears. She took a chair by me, washed the blood from my face, and, with a mother's tenderness, bound up my head, covering the wounded eye with a lean piece of fresh beef. It was almost compensation for my suffering to witness, once more, a manifestation of kindness from this, my once affectionate old mistress. Master Hugh was very much enraged. He gave expression to his feelings by pouring out curses upon the heads of those who did the deed. As soon as I got a little the better of my bruises, he took me with him to Esquire Watson's, on Bond Street, to see what could be done about the matter. Mr. Watson inquired who saw the assault committed. Master Hugh told him it was done in Mr. Gardner's ship-yard, at midday, where there were a large

3. That is, to be subject to lynching, without benefit of legal procedures.

company of men at work. "As to that," he said, "the deed was done, and there was no question as to who did it." His answer was, he could do nothing in the case, unless some white man would come forward and testify. He could issue no warrant on my word. If I had been killed in the presence of a thousand colored people, their testimony combined would have been insufficient to have arrested one of the murderers. Master Hugh, for once, was compelled to say this state of things was too bad. Of course, it was impossible to get any white man to volunteer his testimony in my behalf, and against the white young men. Even those who may have sympathized with me were not prepared to do this. It required a degree of courage unknown to them to do so; for just at that time, the slightest manifestation of humanity toward a colored person was denounced as abolitionism, and that name subjected its bearer to frightful liabilities. The watchwords of the bloody-minded in that region, and in those days, were, "Damn the abolitionists!" and "Damn the niggers!" There was nothing done, and probably nothing would have been done if I had been killed. Such was, and such remains, the state of things in the Christian city of Baltimore.

Master Hugh, finding he could get no redress, refused to let me go back again to Mr. Gardner. He kept me himself, and his wife dressed my wound till I was again restored to health. He then took me into the ship-yard of which he was foreman, in the employment of Mr. Walter Price. There I was immediately set to calking, and very soon learned the art of using my mallet and irons. In the course of one year from the time I left Mr. Gardner's, I was able to command the highest wages given to the most experienced calkers. I was now of some importance to my master. I was bringing him from six to seven dollars per week. I sometimes brought him nine dollars per week: my wages were a dollar and a half a day. After learning how to calk, I sought my own employment, made my own contracts, and collected the money which I earned. My pathway became much more smooth than before; my condition was now much more comfortable. When I could get no calking to do, I did nothing. During these leisure times, those old notions about freedom would steal over me again. When in Mr. Gardner's employment, I was kept in such a perpetual whirl of excitement, I could think of nothing, scarcely, but my life; and in thinking of my life, I almost forgot my liberty. I have observed this in my experience of slavery,—that whenever my condition was improved, instead of its increasing my contentment, it only increased my desire to be free, and set me to thinking of plans to gain my freedom. I have found that, to make a contented slave, it is necessary to make a thoughtless one. It is necessary to darken his moral and mental vision, and, as far as possible, to annihilate the power of reason. He must be able to detect no inconsistencies in slavery; he must be made to feel that slavery is right; and he can be brought to that only when he ceases to be a man.

I was now getting, as I have said, one dollar and fifty cents per day. I contracted for it; I earned it; it was paid to me; it was rightfully my own; yet, upon each returning Saturday night, I was compelled to deliver every cent of that money to Master Hugh. And why? Not because he earned it,—not because he had any hand in earning it,—not because I owed it to him,—nor because he possessed the slightest shadow of a right to it; but solely because he had the power to compel me to give it up. The right of the grim-visaged pirate upon the high seas is exactly the same.

Chapter XI

I now come to that part of my life during which I planned, and finally succeeded in making, my escape from slavery. But before narrating any of the peculiar circumstances, I deem it proper to make known my intention not to state all the facts connected with the transaction. My reasons for pursuing this course may be understood from the following: First, were I to give a minute statement of all the facts, it is not only possible but quite probable, that others would thereby be involved in the most embarrassing difficulties. Secondly, such a statement would most undoubtedly induce greater vigilance on the part of slaveholders than has existed heretofore among them; which would, of course, be the means of guarding a door whereby some dear brother bondman might escape his galling chains. I deeply regret the necessity that impels me to suppress any thing of importance connected with my experience in slavery. It would afford me great pleasure indeed, as well as materially add to the interest of my narrative, were I at liberty to gratify a curiosity, which I know exists in the minds of many, by an accurate statement of all the facts pertaining to my most fortunate escape. But I must deprive myself of this pleasure, and the curious of the gratification which such a statement would afford. I would allow myself to suffer under the greatest imputations which evil-minded men might suggest, rather than exculpate myself, and thereby run the hazard of closing the slightest avenue by which a brother slave might clear himself of the chains and fetters of slavery.

I have never approved of the very public manner in which some of our western friends have conducted what they call the *underground railroad,* but which I think, by their own declarations, had been made most emphatically the *upperground railroad.* I honor those good men and women for their noble daring; and applaud them for willingly subjecting themselves to bloody persecution, by openly avowing their participation in the escape of slaves. I, however, can see very little good resulting from such a course, either to themselves or the slaves escaping; while, upon the other hand, I see and feel assured that those open declarations are a positive evil to the slaves remaining, who are seeking to escape. They do nothing towards enlightening the slave, whilst they do much towards enlightening the master. They stimulate him to greater watchfulness, and enhance his power to capture his slave. We owe something to the slave south of the line as well as to those north of it; and in aiding the latter on their way to freedom, we should be careful to do nothing which would be likely to hinder the former from escaping from slavery. I would keep the merciless slaveholder profoundly ignorant of the means of flight adopted by the slave. I would leave him to imagine himself surrounded by myriads of invisible tormentors, ever ready to snatch from his infernal grasp his trembling prey. Let him be left to feel his way in the dark; let darkness commensurate with his crime hover over him; and let him feel that at every step he takes, in pursuit of the flying bondman, he is running the frightful risk of having his hot brains dashed out by an invisible agency. Let us render the tyrant no aid; let us not hold the light by which he can trace the footprints of our flying brother. But enough of this. I will now proceed to the statement of those facts, connected with my escape, for which I am alone responsible, and for which no one can be made to suffer but myself.

In the early part of the year 1838, I became quite restless. I could see no reason why I should, at the end of each week, pour the reward of my toil into the purse of my master. When I carried to him my weekly wages, he would, after counting the money, look me in the face with a robber-like fierceness, and say, "Is this all?" He was satisfied with nothing less than the last cent. He would, however, when I made him six dollars, sometimes give me six cents, to encourage me. It had the opposite effect. I regarded it as a sort of admission of my right to the whole. The fact that he gave me any part of my wages was proof, to my mind, that he believed me entitled to the whole of them. I always felt worse for having received any thing; for I feared that the giving me a few cents would ease his conscience, and make him feel himself to be a pretty honorable sort of robber. My discontent grew upon me. I was ever on the lookout for means of escape; and, finding no direct means, I determined to try to hire my time, with a view of getting money with which to make my escape. In the spring of 1838, when Master Thomas came to Baltimore to purchase his spring goods, I got an opportunity, and applied to him to allow me to hire my time. He unhesitatingly refused my request, and told me this was another stratagem by which to escape. He told me I could go nowhere but that he could get me; and that, in the event of my running away, he should spare no pains in his efforts to catch me. He exhorted me to content myself, and be obedient. He told me, if I would be happy, I must lay out no plans for the future. He said, if I behaved myself properly, he would take care of me. Indeed, he advised me to complete thoughtlessness of the future, and taught me to depend solely upon him for happiness. He seemed to see fully the pressing necessity of setting aside my intellectual nature, in order to [insure] contentment in slavery. But in spite of him, and even in spite of myself, I continued to think, and to think about the injustice of my enslavement, and the means of escape.

About two months after this, I applied to Master Hugh for the privilege of hiring my time. He was not acquainted with the fact that I had applied to Master Thomas, and had been refused. He too, at first, seemed disposed to refuse; but, after some reflection, he granted me the privilege, and proposed the following terms: I was to be allowed all my time, make all contracts with those for whom I worked, and find my own employment; and, in return for this liberty, I was to pay him three dollars at the end of each week; find myself in calking tools, and in board and clothing. My board was two dollars and a half per week. This, with the wear and tear of clothing and calking tools, made my regular expenses about six dollars per week. This amount I was compelled to make up, or relinquish the privilege of hiring my time. Rain or shine, work or no work, at the end of each week the money must be forthcoming, or I must give up my privilege. This arrangement, it will be perceived, was decidedly in my master's favor. It relieved him of all needs of looking after me. His money was sure. He received all the benefits of slaveholding without its evils; while I endured all the evils of a slave, and suffered all the care and anxiety of a freeman. I found it a hard bargain. But, hard as it was I thought it better than the old mode of getting along. It was a step towards freedom to be allowed to bear the responsibilities of a freeman, and I was determined to hold on upon it. I bent myself to the work of making money. I was ready to work at night as well as day, and by the most untiring perseverance and industry, I made enough to meet my expenses, and lay up a little money each week. I went on thus from May till August. Master Hugh then refused to allow me to hire my time longer. The ground for his refusal was a failure on my part, one Saturday night, to pay him for my week's time. This failure was occasioned by my attending a camp meeting about ten miles from Baltimore. During the week, I had entered into an engagement with a number of young friends to start from Baltimore to the camp ground early Saturday evening; and being detained by my employer, I was unable to get down to Master Hugh's without disappointing the company. I knew that Master Hugh was in no special need of the money that night. I therefore decided to go to camp meeting, and upon my return pay him the three dollars. I staid at the camp meeting one day longer than I intended when I left. But as soon as I returned, I called upon him to pay him what he considered his due. I found him very angry; he could scarce restrain his wrath. He said he had a great mind to give me a severe whipping. He wished to know how I dared go out of the city without asking his permission. I told him I hired my time, and while I paid him the price which he asked for it, I did not know that I was bound to ask him when and where I should go. This reply troubled him; and, after reflecting a few moments, he turned to me, and said I should hire my time no longer; that the next thing he should know of, I would be running away. Upon the same plea, he told me to bring my tools and clothing home forthwith. I did so; but instead of seeking work, as I had been accustomed to do previously to hiring my time, I spent the whole week without the performance of a single stroke of work. I did this in retaliation. Saturday night, he called upon me as usual for my week's wages. I told him I had no wages; I had done no work that week. Here we were upon the point of coming to blows. He raved, and swore his determination to get hold of me. I did not allow myself a single word; but was resolved, if he laid the weight of his hand upon me, it should be blow for blow. He did not strike me, but told me that he would find me in constant employment in future. I thought the matter over during the next day, Sunday, and finally resolved upon the third day of September, as the day upon which I would make a second attempt to secure my freedom. I now had three weeks during which to prepare for my journey. Early on Monday morning, before Master Hugh had time to make any engagement for me, I went out and got employment of Mr. Butler, at his ship-yard near the draw-bridge, upon what is called the City Block, thus making it unnecessary for him to seek employment for me. At the end of the week, I brought him between eight and nine dollars. He seemed very well pleased, and asked why I did not do the same the week before. He little knew what my plans were. My object in working steadily was to remove any suspicion he might entertain of my intent to run away; and in this I succeeded admirably. I suppose he thought I was never better satisfied with my condition than at the very time during which I was planning my escape. The second week passed, and again I carried him my full wages; and so well pleased was he, that he gave me twenty-five cents, (quite a large sum for a slaveholder to give a slave), and bade me to make a good use of it. I told him I would.

Things went on without very smoothly indeed, but within there was trouble. It is impossible for me to describe my feelings as the time of my contemplated start drew near. I had a number of warm-hearted friends in Baltimore,—friends that I loved almost as I did my life,—and the thought of being separated from them forever was painful beyond expression. It is my opinion that thousands would escape from slavery, who now remain, but for the strong cords of affection that bind them to their friends. The thought of leaving my friends was decidedly the most painful thought with which I had to contend. The love of them was my tender point, and shook my decision more than all things else. Besides the pain of separation, the dread and apprehension of a failure exceeded what I had experienced at my first attempt. The appalling defeat I then sustained returned to torment me. I felt assured that, if I failed in this attempt, my case would be a hopeless one—it would seal my fate as a slave forever. I could not hope to get off with any thing less than the severest punishment, and being placed beyond the means of escape. It required no very vivid imagination to depict the most frightful scenes through which I should have to pass, in case I failed. The wretchedness of slavery, and the blessedness of freedom, were perpetually before me. It was life and death with me. But I remained firm, and, according to my resolution, on the third day of September, 1838, I left my chains, and succeeded in reaching New York without the slightest interruption of any kind. How I did so,—what means I adopted,—what direction I travelled, and by what mode of conveyance,—I must leave unexplained, for the reasons before mentioned.

I have been frequently asked how I felt when I found myself in a free State. I have never been able to answer the question with any satisfaction to myself. It was a moment of the highest excitement I ever experienced. I suppose I felt as one may imagine the unarmed mariner to feel when he is rescued by a friendly man-of-war from the pursuit of a pirate. In writing to a dear friend, immediately after my arrival at New York, I said I felt like one who had escaped a den of hungry lions. This state of mind, however, very soon subsided; and I was again seized with a feeling of great insecurity and loneliness. I was yet liable to be taken back, and subjected to all the tortures of slavery. This in itself was enough to damp the ardor of my enthusiasm. But the loneliness overcame me. There I was in the midst of thousands, and yet a perfect stranger; without home and without friends, in the midst of thousands of my own brethren—children of a common Father, and yet I dared not to unfold to any one of them my sad condition. I was afraid to speak to any one for fear of speaking to the wrong one, and thereby falling into the hands of money-loving kidnappers, whose business it was to lie in wait for the panting fugitive, as the ferocious beasts of the forest lie in wait for their prey. The motto which I adopted when I started from slavery was this—"Trust no man!" I saw in every white man an enemy, and in almost every colored man cause for distrust. It was a most painful situation; and, to understand it, one must needs experience it, or imagine himself in similar circumstances. Let him be a fugitive slave in a strange land—a land given up to be the hunting-ground for slaveholders—whose inhabitants are legalized kidnappers—where he is every moment subjected to the terrible liability of being seized upon by his fellowmen, as the hideous crocodile seizes upon his prey!—I say, let him place himself in my situation—without home or friends—without money or credit—wanting shelter, and no one to give it—wanting bread, and no money to buy it,—and at the same time let him feel that he is pursued by merciless men-hunters, and in total darkness as to what to do, where to go, or where to stay,—perfectly helpless both as to the means of defence and means of escape,—in the midst of plenty, yet suffering the terrible gnawings of hunger,—in the midst of houses, yet having no home,—among fellow-men, yet feeling as if in the midst of wild beasts, whose greediness to swallow up the trembling and half-famished fugitive is only equalled by that with which the monsters of the deep swallow up the helpless fish upon which they subsist,—I say, let him be placed in this most trying situation,—the situation in which I was placed,—then, and not till then, will he fully appreciate the hardships of, and know how to sympathize with, the toil-worn and whip-scarred fugitive slave.

Thank Heaven, I remained but a short time in this distressed situation. I was relieved from it by the humane hand of MR. DAVID RUGGLES,[4] whose vigilance, kindness, and perseverance, I shall never forget. I am glad of an opportunity to express, as far as words can, the love and gratitude I bear him. Mr. Ruggles is now afflicted with blindness, and is himself in need of the same kind offices which he was once so forward in the performance of toward others. I had been in New York but a few days, when Mr. Ruggles sought me out, and very kindly took me to his boarding-house at the corner of Church and Lespenard Streets. Mr. Ruggles was then very deeply engaged in the memorable *Darg* case,[5] as well as attending to a number of other fugitive slaves; devising ways and means for their successful escape; and, though watched and hemmed in on almost every side, he seemed to be more than a match for his enemies.

Very soon after I went to Mr. Ruggles, he wished to know of me where I wanted to go; as he deemed it unsafe for me to remain in New York. I told him I was a calker, and should like to go where I could get work. I thought of going to Canada; but he decided against it, and in favor of my going to New Bedford,[6] thinking I should be able to get work there at my trade. At this time, Anna,[7] my intended wife, came on; for I wrote to her immediately after my arrival at New York, (notwithstanding my homeless, houseless, and helpless condition,) informing her of my successful flight, and wishing her to come on forthwith. In a few days after her arrival, Mr. Ruggles called in the Rev. J. W. C. Pennington, who, in the presence of Mr. Ruggles, Mrs. Michaels, and two or three others, performed the marriage ceremony, and gave us a certificate, of which the following is an exact copy:—

> "This may certify, that I joined together in holy matrimony Frederick Johnson[8] and Anna Murray, as man and wife, in the presence of Mr. David Ruggles and Mrs. Michaels.
>
> "JAMES W. C. PENNINGTON[9]
> *New York, Sept.* 15, 1838."

Upon receiving this certificate, and a five-dollar bill from Mr. Ruggles, I shouldered one part of our baggage, and Anna took up the other, and we set out forthwith to take passage on board of the steamboat John W. Richmond for Newport, on our way to New Bedford. Mr. Ruggles gave me a letter to a Mr. Shaw in Newport, and told me, in case my money did not serve me to New Bedford, to stop in Newport and obtain further assistance; but upon our arrival at Newport, we were so anxious to get to a place of safety, that, notwithstanding we lacked the necessary money to pay our fare, we decided to take seats in the stage, and promise to pay when we got to New Bedford. We were encouraged to do this by two excellent gentlemen, residents of New Bedford, whose names I afterward ascertained to be Joseph Ricketson

4. A journalist and abolitionist (1810–1849) who helped Douglass escape from Maryland and in whose house Douglass stayed on his way to New Bedford in 1838.
5. Ruggles had been arrested in 1839 and charged with harboring a fugitive slave who had escaped from John P. Darg of Arkansas.
6. A seaport on the southern coast of Massachusetts.
7. She was free [*Douglass's note*]. Anna Murray (d. 1882) had been a self-supporting domestic worker before moving to New York to marry.
8. I had changed my name from Frederick *Bailey* to that of *Johnson* [*Douglass's note*].
9. A fugitive from Maryland slavery, abolitionist orator, writer, and Congregationalist pastor (1807–1870).

and William C. Taber. They seemed at once to understand our circumstances, and gave us such assurance of their friendliness as put us fully at ease in their presence. It was good indeed to meet with such friends, at such a time. Upon reaching New Bedford, we were directed to the house of Mr. Nathan Johnson, by whom we were kindly received, and hospitably provided for. Both Mr. and Mrs. Johnson took a deep and lively interest in our welfare. They proved themselves quite worthy of the name of abolitionists. When the stage-driver found us unable to pay our fare, he held on upon our baggage as security for the debt. I had but to mention the fact to Mr. Johnson, and he forthwith advanced the money.

We now began to feel a degree of safety, and to prepare ourselves for the duties and responsibilities of a life of freedom. On the morning after our arrival at New Bedford, while at the breakfast-table, the question arose as to what name I should be called by. The name given me by my mother was, "Frederick Augustus Washington Bailey." I, however, had dispensed with the two middle names long before I left Maryland so that I was generally known by the name of "Frederick Bailey." I started from Baltimore bearing the name of "Stanley." When I got to New York, I again changed my name to "Frederick Johnson," and thought that would be the last change. But when I got to New Bedford, I found it necessary again to change my name. The reason of this necessity was, that there were so many Johnsons in New Bedford, it was already quite difficult to distinguish between them. I gave Mr. Johnson the privilege of choosing me a name, but told him he must not take from me the name of "Frederick." I must hold on to that, to preserve a sense of my identity. Mr. Johnson had just been reading the "Lady of the Lake," and at once suggested that my name be "Douglass."[1] From that time until now I have been called "Frederick Douglass;" and as I am more widely known by that name than by either of the others, I shall continue to use it as my own.

I was quite disappointed at the general appearance of things in New Bedford. The impression which I had received respecting the character and condition of the people of the north, I found to be singularly erroneous. I had very strangely supposed, while in slavery, that few of the comforts, and scarcely any of the luxuries, of life were enjoyed at the north; compared with what were enjoyed by the slaveholders of the south. I probably came to this conclusion from the fact that northern people owned no slaves. I supposed that they were about upon a level with the non-slaveholding population of the south. I knew *they* were exceedingly poor, and I had been accustomed to regard their poverty as the necessary consequence of their being non-slaveholders. I had somehow imbibed the opinion that, in the absence of slaves, there could be no wealth, and very little refinement. And upon coming to the north, I expected to meet with a rough, hard-handed, and uncultivated population, living in the most Spartanlike simplicity, knowing nothing of the ease, luxury, pomp, and grandeur of southern slaveholders. Such being my conjectures, any one acquainted with the appearance of New Bedford may very readily infer how palpably I must have seen my mistake.

In the afternoon of the day when I reached New Bedford, I visited the wharves, to take a view of the shipping. Here I found myself surrounded with the strongest proofs of wealth. Lying at the wharves, and riding in the

1. Sir Walter Scott's poem *Lady of the Lake* (1810) is a historical romance set in the Scottish highlands in the 16th century. Douglass is named after the wrongfully exiled Lord James of Douglas, a Scottish chieftain revered for his bravery and virtue.

stream, I saw many ships of the finest model, in the best order, and of the largest size. Upon the right and left, I was walled in by granite warehouses of the widest dimensions, stowed to their utmost capacity with the necessaries and comforts of life. Added to this, almost every body seemed to be at work, but noiselessly so, compared with what I had been accustomed to in Baltimore. There were no loud songs heard from those engaged in loading and unloading ships. I heard no deep oaths or horrid curses on the laborer. I saw no whipping of men; but all seemed to go smoothly on. Every man appeared to understand his work, and went at it with a sober, yet cheerful earnestness, which betokened the deep interest which he felt in what he was doing, as well as a sense of his own dignity as a man. To me this looked exceedingly strange. From the wharves I strolled around and over the town, gazing with wonder and admiration at the splendid churches, beautiful dwellings, and finely-cultivated gardens; evincing an amount of wealth, comfort, taste, and refinement, such as I had never seen in any part of slaveholding Maryland.

Every thing looked clean, new, and beautiful. I saw few or no dilapidated houses, with poverty-stricken inmates; no half-naked children and barefooted women, such as I had been accustomed to see in Hillsborough, Easton, St. Michael's, and Baltimore. The people looked more able, stronger, healthier, and happier, than those of Maryland. I was for once made glad by a view of extreme wealth, without being saddened by seeing extreme poverty. But the most astonishing as well as the most interesting thing to me was the condition of the colored people, a great many of whom, like myself, had escaped thither as a refuge from the hunters of men. I found many, who had not been seven years out of their chains, living in finer houses, and evidently enjoying more of the comforts of life, than the average of slaveholders in Maryland. I will venture to assert, that my friend Mr. Nathan Johnson (of whom I can say with a grateful heart, "I was hungry, and he gave me meat; I was thirsty, and he gave me drink; I was a stranger, and he took me in"[2]) lived in a neater house, dined at a better table; took, paid for, and read, more newspapers; better understood the moral, religious, and political character of the nation,—than nine tenths of the slaveholders in Talbot county Maryland. Yet Mr. Johnson was a working man. His hands were hardened by toil, and not his alone, but those also of Mrs. Johnson. I found the colored people much more spirited than I had supposed they would be. I found among them a determination to protect each other from the blood-thirsty kidnapper, at all hazards. Soon after my arrival, I was told a circumstance which illustrated their spirit. A colored man and a fugitive slave were on unfriendly terms. The former was heard to threaten the latter with informing his master of his whereabouts. Straightway a meeting was called among the colored people, under the stereotyped notice, "Business of importance!" The betrayer was invited to attend. The people came at the appointed hour, and organized the meeting by appointing a very religious old gentleman as president, who, I believe, made a prayer, after which he addressed the meeting as follows: *"Friends, we have got him here, and I would recommend that you young men just take him outside the door, and kill him!"* With this, a number of them bolted at him; but they were intercepted by some more timid than themselves, and the betrayer escaped their vengeance, and has not been seen in New Bedford since. I believe there have been no more such

2. Matthew 25:35.

threats, and should there be hereafter, I doubt not that death would be the consequence.

I found employment, the third day after my arrival, in stowing a sloop with a load of oil. It was new, dirty, and hard work for me; but I went at it with a glad heart and a willing hand. I was now my own master. It was a happy moment, the rapture of which can be understood only by those who have been slaves. It was the first work, the reward of which was to be entirely my own. There was no Master Hugh standing ready, the moment I earned the money, to rob me of it. I worked that day with a pleasure I had never before experienced. I was at work for myself and newly-married wife. It was to me the starting-point of a new existence. When I got through with that job, I went in pursuit of a job of calking; but such was the strength of prejudice against color, among the white calkers, that they refused to work with me, and of course I could get no employment.[3] Finding my trade of no immediate benefit, I threw off my calking habiliments, and prepared myself to do any kind of work I could get to do. Mr. Johnson kindly let me have his wood-horse and saw, and I very soon found myself, a plenty of work. There was no work too hard—none too dirty. I was ready to saw wood, shovel coal, carry the hod,[4] sweep the chimney, or roll oil casks,—all of which I did for nearly three years in New Bedford, before I became known to the anti-slavery world.

In about four months after I went to New Bedford, there came a young man to me, and inquired if I did not wish to take the "Liberator."[5] I told him I did; but, just having made my escape from slavery, I remarked that I was unable to pay for it then. I, however, finally became a subscriber to it. The paper came, and I read it from week to week with such feelings as it would be quite idle for me to attempt to describe. The paper became my meat and my drink. My soul was set all on fire. Its sympathy for my brethren in bonds—its scathing denunciations of slaveholders—its faithful exposures of slavery—and its powerful attacks upon the upholders of the institution—sent a thrill of joy through my soul, such as I had never felt before!

I had not long been a reader of the "Liberator," before I got a pretty correct idea of the principles, measures and spirit of the anti-slavery reform. I took right hold of the cause. I could do but little; but what I could, I did with a joyful heart, and never felt happier than when in an anti-slavery meeting. I seldom had much to say at the meetings, because what I wanted to say was said so much better by others. But, while attending an anti-slavery convention at Nantucket, on the 11th of August, 1841, I felt strongly moved to speak, and was at the same time much urged to do so by Mr. William C. Coffin, a gentleman who had heard me speak in the colored people's meeting at New Bedford.[6] It was a severe cross, and I took it up reluctantly. The truth was, I felt myself a slave, and the idea of speaking to white people weighed me down. I spoke but a few moments, when I felt a degree of freedom, and said what I desired with considerable ease. From that time until now, I have been engaged in pleading the cause of my brethren—with what success, and with what devotion, I leave those acquainted with my labors to decide.

3. I am told that colored persons can now get employment at calking in New Bedford—a result of anti-slavery effort [*Douglass's note*].
4. Carrying supplies to bricklayers or stonemasons.
5. Edited by William Lloyd Garrison, the *Liberator* was a widely read abolitionist newspaper.
6. Douglass was licensed as a preacher in the African Methodist Episcopal Zion Church in 1839.

Appendix

I find, since reading over the foregoing Narrative, that I have, in several instances, spoken in such a tone and manner, respecting religion, as may possibly lead those unacquainted with my religious views to suppose me an opponent of all religion. To remove the liability of such misapprehension, I deem it proper to append the following brief explanation. What I have said respecting and against religion, I mean strictly to apply to the *slaveholding religion* of this land, and with no possible reference to Christianity proper; for, between the Christianity of this land, and the Christianity of Christ, I recognize the widest possible difference—so wide, that to receive the one as good, pure, and holy, is of necessity to reject the other as bad, corrupt, and wicked. To be the friend of the one, is of necessity to be the enemy of the other. I love the pure, peaceable, and impartial Christianity of Christ: I therefore hate the corrupt, slaveholding, women-whipping, cradle-plundering, partial and hypocritical Christianity of this land. Indeed, I can see no reason, but the most deceitful one, for calling the religion of this land Christianity. I look upon it as the climax of all misnomers, the boldest of all frauds, and the grossest of all libels. Never was there a clearer case of "stealing the livery of the court of heaven to serve the devil in."[7] I am filled with unutterable loathing when I contemplate the religious pomp and show, together with the horrible inconsistencies, which every where surround me. We have men-stealers for ministers, women-whippers for missionaries, and cradle-plunderers for church members. The man who wields the blood-clotted cowskin during the week fills the pulpit on Sunday, and claims to be a minister of the meek and lowly Jesus. The man who robs me of my earnings at the end of each week meets me as a class-leader on Sunday morning, to show me the way of life, and the path of salvation. He who sells my sister, for purposes of prostitution, stands forth as the pious advocate of purity. He who proclaims it a religious duty to read the Bible denies me the right of learning to read the name of the God who made me. He who is the religious advocate of marriage robs whole millions of its sacred influence, and leaves them to the ravages of wholesale pollution. The warm defender of the sacredness of the family relation is the same that scatters whole families,—sundering husbands and wives, parents and children, sisters and brothers,—leaving the hut vacant, and the hearth desolate. We see the thief preaching against theft, and the adulterer against adultery. We have men sold to build churches, women sold to support the gospel, and babies sold to purchase Bibles for the *poor heathen! all for the glory of God and the good of souls!* The slave auctioneer's bell and the church-going bell chime in with each other, and the bitter cries of the heartbroken slave are drowned in the religious shouts of his pious master. Revivals of religion and revivals in the slave-trade go hand in hand together. The slave prison and the church stand near each other. The clanking of fetters and the rattling of chains in the prison, and the pious psalm and solemn prayer in the church, may be heard at the same time. The dealers in the bodies and souls of men erect their stand in the presence of the pulpit, and they mutually help each other. The dealer gives his blood-stained gold to support the pulpit, and the pulpit, in return, covers his infernal business with the garb of Christianity. Here we have

7. See Robert Pollok's *The Course of Time* (1827) 8.616–18: "He was a man / Who stole the livery of the court of Heaven / To serve the Devil in."

religion and robbery the allies of each other—devils dressed in angels' robes, and hell presenting the semblance of paradise.

"Just God! and these are they,
  Who minister at thine altar, God of right!
Men who their hands, with prayer and blessing, lay
  On Israel's ark of light.[8]

"What! preach, and kidnap men?
  Give thanks, and rob thy own afflicted poor?
Talk of thy glorious liberty, and then
  Bolt hard the captive's door?

"What! servants of thy own
  Merciful Son, who came to seek and save
The homeless and the outcast, fettering down
  The tasked and plundered slave!

"Pilate and Herod[9] friends!
  Chief priests and rulers, as of old, combine!
Just God and holy! is that church which lends
  Strength to the spoiler thine?"[1]

The Christianity of America is a Christianity, of whose votaries it may be as truly said, as it was of the ancient scribes and Pharisees, "They bind heavy burdens, and grievous to be borne, and lay them on men's shoulders, but they themselves will not move them with one of their fingers. All their works they do for to be seen of men.——They love the uppermost rooms at feasts, and the chief seats in the synagogues, ... and to be called of men, Rabbi, Rabbi.——But woe unto you, scribes and Pharisees, hypocrites! for ye shut up the kingdom of heaven against men; for ye neither go in yourselves, neither suffer ye them that are entering to go in. Ye devour widows' houses, and for a pretence make long prayers; therefore ye shall receive the greater damnation. Ye compass sea and land to make one proselyte, and when he is made, ye make him twofold more the child of hell than yourselves.——Woe unto you, scribes and Pharisees, hypocrites! for ye pay tithe of mint, and anise, and cumin, and have omitted the weightier matters of the law, judgment, mercy, and faith; these ought ye to have done, and not to leave the other undone. Ye blind guides! which strain at a gnat, and swallow a camel. Woe unto you, scribes and Pharisees, hypocrites! for ye make clean the outside of the cup and of the platter; but within, they are full of extortion and excess.——Woe unto you, scribes[2] and Pharisees, hypocrites! for ye are like unto whited sepulchres, which indeed appear beautiful outward, but are within full of dead men's bones, and of all uncleanness. Even so ye also outwardly appear righteous unto men, but within ye are full of hypocrisy and iniquity."[3]

Dark and terrible as is this picture, I hold it to be strictly true of the overwhelming mass of professed Christians in America. They strain at a gnat,

8. That is, the Holy Ark containing the Torah; by extension, the entire body of law as contained in the Old Testament of the Bible and in the Talmud.
9. Herod Antipas, ruler of Galilee, ordered the execution of John the Baptist and participated in the trial of Christ. Pontius Pilate was the Roman authority who condemned Christ to death.
1. From Whittier's antislavery poem "*Clerical Oppressors*" (1836).
2. Members of a powerful Jewish sect that insisted on strict observance of written and oral religious laws. "Scribes": Jewish Scholars who taught Jewish law and edited and interpreted the Bible.
3. Jesus's denunciation of the Scribes and Pharisees in Matthew 23:4–28.

and swallow a camel. Could any thing be more true of our churches? They would be shocked at the proposition of fellowshipping a *sheep*-stealer; and at the same time they hug to their communion a *man*-stealer, and brand me with being an infidel, if I find fault with them for it. They attend with Pharisaical strictness to the outward forms of religion, and at the same time neglect the weightier matters of the law, judgment, mercy, and faith. They are always ready to sacrifice, but seldom to show mercy. They are they who are represented as professing to love God whom they have not seen, whilst they hate their brother whom they have seen. They love the heathen on the other side of the globe. They can pray for him, pay money to have the Bible put into his hand, and missionaries to instruct him; while they despise and totally neglect the heathen at their own doors.

Such is, very briefly, my view of the religion of this land; and to avoid any misunderstanding, growing out of the use of general terms, I mean, by the religion of this land, that which is revealed in the words, deeds, and actions, of those bodies, north and south, calling themselves Christian churches, and yet in union with slaveholders. It is against religion, as presented by these bodies, that I have felt it my duty to testify.

I conclude these remarks by copying the following portrait of the religion of the south, (which is, by communion and fellowship, the religion of the north,) which I soberly affirm is "true to the life," and without caricature or the slightest exaggeration. It is said to have been drawn, several years before the present anti-slavery agitation began, by a northern Methodist preacher, who, while residing at the south, had an opportunity to see slaveholding morals, manners, and piety, with his own eyes. "Shall I not visit for these things? saith the Lord. Shall not my soul be avenged on such a nation as this?"[4]

A PARODY[5]

"Come, saints and sinners, hear me tell
How pious priests whip Jack and Nell,
And women buy and children sell,
And preach all sinners down to hell,
  And sing of heavenly union.

"They'll bleat and baa, dona like goats,
Gorge down black sheep, and strain at motes,
Array their backs in fine black coats,
Then seize their negroes by their throats,
  And choke, for heavenly union.

"They'll church you if you sip a dram,[6]
And damn you if you steal a lamb;
Yet rob old Tony, Doll, and Sam,
Of human rights, and bread and ham;
  Kidnapper's heavenly union.

"They'll loudly talk of Christ's reward,
And bind his image with a cord,

4. Jeremiah speaks God's charges against the sins of the House of Israel (Jeremiah 5:9).

5. A parody of "The Heavenly Union," a Protestant hymn popular in the South.

6. One-eighth of a liquid ounce.

And scold, and swing the lash abhorred,
And sell their brother in the Lord
To handcuffed heavenly union.

"They'll read and sing a sacred song,
And make a prayer both loud and long,
And teach the right and do the wrong,
Hailing the brother, sister throng,
With words of heavenly union.

"We wonder how such saints can sing,
Or praise the Lord upon the wing,
Who roar, and scold, and whip, and sting,
And to their slaves and mammon cling,
In guilty conscience union.

"They'll raise tobacco, corn, and rye,
And drive, and thieve, and cheat, and lie,
And lay up treasures in the sky,
By making switch and cowskin fly,
In hope of heavenly union.

"They'll crack old Tony on the skull,
And preach and roar like Bashan[7] bull
Or braying ass, of mischief full,
Then seize old Jacob by the wool,
And pull for heavenly union.

"A roaring, ranting, sleek man-thief,
Who lived on mutton, veal, and beef,
Yet never would afford relief
To needy, sable sons of grief,
Was big with heavenly union.

"'Love not the world,' the preacher said,
And winked his eye, and shook his head;
He seized on Tom, and Dick, and Ned,
Cut short their meat, and clothes, and bread,
Yet still loved heavenly union.

"Another preacher whining spoke
Of One whose heart for sinners broke:
He tied old Nanny to an oak,
And drew the blood at every stroke,
And prayed for heavenly union.

"Two others oped their iron jaws,
And waved their children-stealing paws;
There sat their children in gewgaws;
By stinting negroes' backs and maws,[8]
They kept up heavenly union.

7. Strong bulls mentioned in the Bible.

8. Mouths.

"All good from Jack another takes,
And entertains their flirts and rakes,
Who dress as sleek as glossy snakes,
And cram their mouths with sweetened cakes;
And this goes down for union."

Sincerely and earnestly hoping that this little book may do something toward throwing light on the American slave system, and hastening the glad day of deliverance to the millions of my brethren in bonds—faithfully relying upon the power of truth, love, and justice, for success in my humble efforts—and solemnly pledging my self anew to the sacred cause,—I subscribe myself,

FREDERICK DOUGLASS

LYNN, *Mass., April 28, 1845.*

1845

From My Bondage and My Freedom

From *Chapter VI. Treatment of Slaves on Lloyd's Plantation*

* * *

Up to the time of the brutal flogging of my Aunt Esther[1]—for she was my own aunt—and the horrid plight in which I had seen my cousin from Tuckahoe, who had been so badly beaten by the cruel Mr. Plummer, my attention had not been called, especially, to the gross features of slavery. I had, of course, heard of whippings, and of savage *rencontres*[2] between overseers and slaves, but I had always been out of the way at the times and places of their occurrences. My plays and sports, most of the time, took me from the corn and tobacco fields, where the great body of the hands were at work, and where scenes of cruelty were enacted and witnessed. But, after the whipping of Aunt Esther, I saw many cases of the same shocking nature, not only in my master's house, but on Col. Lloyd's plantation.[3] One of the first which I saw, and which greatly agitated me, was the whipping of a woman belonging to Col. Lloyd named Nelly.[4] The offense alleged against Nelly was one of the commonest and most indefinite in the whole catalogue of offenses usually laid to the charge of slaves, viz: "impudence." This may mean almost anything, or nothing at all, just according to the caprice of the master or overseer at the moment. But, whatever it is, or is not, if it gets the name of "impudence," the party charged with it is sure of a flogging. This offense may be committed in various ways; in the tone of an answer; in answering at all; in not answering; in the expression of countenance; in the motion of the head; in the gait, manner and bearing of the slave. In the case under consideration, I can easily believe that, according to all slaveholding standards, here was a genuine instance of impudence. In Nelly there were all the necessary conditions for committing the offense. She was a bright mulatto,[5] the recognized wife of a favorite "hand" on board Col. Lloyd's sloop,

1. Aunt Hester in Douglass's *Narrative.*
2. Encounters (French).
3. The Wye House plantation on the Eastern Shore of Maryland owned by Colonel Edward Lloyd V (1779–1834), who served as governor of the state and a U.S. senator from Maryland.
4. Nelly's surname was Kellem.
5. A light-skinned, mixed-race person.

and the mother of five sprightly children. She was a vigorous and spirited woman, and one of the most likely, on the plantation, to be guilty of impudence. My attention was called to the scene by the noise, curses and screams that proceeded from it; and on going a little in that direction, I came upon the parties engaged in the skirmish. Mr. Sevier,[6] the overseer, had hold of Nelly when I caught sight of them; he was endeavoring to drag her toward a tree, which endeavor Nelly was sternly resisting; but to no purpose, except to retard the progress of the overseer's plans. Nelly—as I have said—was the mother of five children; three of them were present, and though quite small (from seven to ten years old, I should think), they gallantly came to their mother's defense, and gave the overseer an excellent pelting with stones. One of the little fellows ran up, seized the overseer by the leg and bit him; but the monster was too busily engaged with Nelly to pay any attention to the assaults of the children. There were numerous bloody marks on Mr. Sevier's face when I first saw him, and they increased as the struggle went on. The imprints of Nelly's fingers were visible, and I was glad to see them. Amidst the wild screams of the children—*"Let my mammy go"*—*"let my mammy go"*—there escaped, from between the teeth of the bullet-headed overseer, a few bitter curses, mingled with threats, that "he would teach the d—d b—h how to give a white man impudence." There is no doubt that Nelly felt herself superior, in some respects, to the slaves around her. She was a wife and a mother; her husband was a valued and favorite slave. Besides, he was one of the first hands on board the sloop, and the sloop hands—since they had to represent the plantation abroad—were generally treated tenderly. The overseer never was allowed to whip Harry; why then should he be allowed to whip Harry's wife? Thoughts of this kind, no doubt, influenced her; but, for whatever reason, she nobly resisted, and, unlike most of the slaves, seemed determined to make her whipping cost Mr. Sevier as much as possible. The blood on his (and her) face attested her skill, as well as her courage and dexterity in using her nails. Maddened by her resistance, I expected to see Mr. Sevier level her to the ground by a stunning blow; but no; like a savage bull-dog—which he resembled both in temper and appearance—he maintained his grip, and steadily dragged his victim toward the tree, disregarding alike her blows, and the cries of the children for their mother's release. He would, doubtless, have knocked her down with his hickory stick, but that such act might have cost him his place. It is often deemed advisable to knock a *man* slave down, in order to tie him, but it is considered cowardly and inexcusable, in an overseer, thus to deal with a *woman*. He is expected to tie her up, and to give her what is called in southern parlance, a "genteel flogging," without any very great outlay of strength or skill. I watched, with palpitating interest, the course of the preliminary struggle, and was saddened by every new advantage gained over her by the ruffian.[7] There were times when she seemed likely to get the better of the brute, but he finally overpowered her, and succeeded in getting his rope around her arms, and in firmly tying her to the tree, at which he had been aiming. This done, and Nelly was at the mercy of his merciless lash; and now what followed, I have no heart to describe. The cowardly creature made good his every threat; and wielded the lash with all the hot zest of furious revenge. The cries of the woman, while undergoing the terrible infliction, were mingled with those of the children, sounds which I hope the reader may never

6. William Sevier's name is spelled Severe in Douglass's *Narrative*.
7. A thug.

be called upon to hear. When Nelly was untied, her back was covered with blood. The red stripes were all over her shoulders. She was whipped—severely whipped; but she was not subdued, for she continued to denounce the overseer, and to call him every vile name. He had bruised her flesh, but had left her invincible spirit undaunted. Such floggings are seldom repeated by the same overseer. They prefer to whip those who are most easily whipped. The old doctrine that submission is the best cure for outrage and wrong does not hold good on the slave plantation. He is whipped oftenest, who is whipped easiest; and that slave who has the courage to stand up for himself against the overseer, although he may have many hard stripes at the first, becomes, in the end, a freeman, even though he sustain the formal relation of a slave. "You can shoot me but you can't whip me," said a slave to Rigby Hopkins; and the result was that he was neither whipped nor shot. If the latter had been his fate, it would have been less deplorable than the living and lingering death to which cowardly and slavish souls are subjected. I do not know that Mr. Sevier ever undertook to whip Nelly again. He probably never did, for it was not long after his attempt to subdue her that he was taken sick, and died. The wretched man died as he had lived, unrepentant; and it was said—with how much truth I know not—that in the very last hours of his life, his ruling passion showed itself, and that when wrestling with death, he was uttering horrid oaths, and flourishing the cowskin, as though he was tearing the flesh off some helpless slave.

* * *

Chapter XXIII. Introduced to the Abolitionists

In the summer of 1841, a grand anti-slavery convention was held in Nantucket,[8] under the auspices of Mr. Garrison[9] and his friends. Until now, I had taken no holiday since my escape from slavery.[1] Having worked very hard that spring and summer, in Richmond's brass foundery—sometimes working all night as well as all day—and needing a day or two of rest, I attended this convention, never supposing that I should take part in the proceedings. Indeed, I was not aware that any one connected with the convention even so much as knew my name. I was, however, quite mistaken. Mr. William C. Coffin, a prominent abolitionist in those days of trial, had heard me speaking to my colored friends, in the little schoolhouse on Second street, New Bedford, where we worshiped. He sought me out in the crowd, and invited me to say a few words to the convention. Thus sought out, and thus invited, I was induced to speak out the feelings inspired by the occasion, and the fresh recollection of the scenes through which I had passed as a slave. My speech on this occasion is about the only one I ever made, of which I do not remember a single connected sentence. It was with the utmost difficulty that I could stand erect, or that I could command and articulate two words without hesitation and stammering. I trembled in every limb. I am not sure that my embarrassment was not the most effective part of my speech, if speech it could be called. At any rate, this is about the only part of my performance that I now distinctly remember. But excited and convulsed as I was, the audience, though remarkably quiet before, became

8. An island town in southeastern Massachusetts.
9. William Lloyd Garrison (1805–1879), American journalist, reformer, and one of the most uncompromising spokesmen for radical abolition in the United States.
1. Douglass escaped from Baltimore on September 3, 1838, and settled in New Bedford, Massachusetts.

as much excited as myself. Mr. Garrison followed me, taking me as his text; and now, whether I had made an eloquent speech in behalf of freedom or not, his was one never to be forgotten by those who heard it. Those who had heard Mr. Garrison oftenest, and had known him longest, were astonished. It was an effort of unequaled power, sweeping down, like a very tornado, every opposing barrier, whether of sentiment or opinion. For a moment, he possessed that almost fabulous inspiration, often referred to but seldom attained, in which a public meeting is transformed, as it were, into a single individuality—the orator wielding a thousand heads and hearts at once, and by the simple majesty of his all controlling thought, converting his hearers into the express image of his own soul. That night there were at least one thousand Garrisonians in Nantucket! At the close of this great meeting, I was duly waited on by Mr. John A. Collins—then the general agent of the Massachusetts anti-slavery society—and urgently solicited by him to become an agent of that society, and to publicly advocate its anti-slavery principles. I was reluctant to take the proffered position. I had not been quite three years from slavery—was honestly distrustful of my ability—wished to be excused; publicity exposed me to discovery and arrest by my master; and other objections came up, but Mr. Collins was not to be put off, and I finally consented to go out for three months, for I supposed that I should have got to the end of my story and my usefulness, in that length of time.

Here, opened upon me a new life—a life for which I had had no preparation. I was a "graduate from the peculiar institution," Mr. Collins used to say, when introducing me, *"with my diploma written on my back!"* The three years of my freedom had been spent in the hard school of adversity. My hands had been furnished by nature with something like a solid leather coating, and I had bravely marked out for myself a life of rough labor, suited to the hardness of my hands, as a means of supporting myself and rearing my children.

Now what shall I say of this fourteen years' experience as a public advocate of the cause of my enslaved brothers and sisters? The time is but as a speck, yet large enough to justify a pause for retrospection—and a pause it must only be.

Young, ardent, and hopeful, I entered upon this new life in the full gush of unsuspecting enthusiasm. The cause was good; the men engaged in it were good; the means to attain its triumph, good; Heaven's blessing must attend all, and freedom must soon be given to the pining millions under a ruthless bondage. My whole heart went with the holy cause, and my most fervent prayer to the Almighty Disposer of the hearts of men, were continually offered for its early triumph. "Who or what," thought I, "can withstand a cause so good, so holy, so indescribably glorious. The God of Israel is with us. The might of the Eternal is on our side. Now let but the truth be spoken, and a nation will start forth at the sound!" In this enthusiastic spirit, I dropped into the ranks of freedom's friends, and went forth to the battle. For a time I was made to forget that my skin was dark and my hair crisped. For a time I regretted that I could not have shared the hardships and dangers endured by the earlier workers for the slave's release. I soon, however, found that my enthusiasm had been extravagant; that hardships and dangers were not yet passed; and that the life now before me, had shadows as well as sunbeams.

Among the first duties assigned me, on entering the ranks, was to travel, in company with Mr. George Foster, to secure subscribers to the "Anti-slavery Standard" and the "Liberator."[2] With him I traveled and lectured

2. Newspapers that espoused immediate abolition.

through the eastern counties of Massachusetts. Much interest was awakened—large meetings assembled. Many came, no doubt, from curiosity to hear what a negro could say in his own cause. I was generally introduced as a *"chattel"*—a *"thing"*—a piece of southern *"property"*—the chairman assuring the audience that *it* could speak. Fugitive slaves, at that time, were not so plentiful as now; and as a fugitive slave lecturer, I had the advantage of being a *"brand new fact"*—the first one out. Up to that time, a colored man was deemed a fool who confessed himself a runaway slave, not only because of the danger to which he exposed himself of being retaken, but because it was a confession of a very *low* origin! Some of my colored friends in New Bedford thought very badly of my wisdom for thus exposing and degrading myself. The only precaution I took, at the beginning, to prevent Master Thomas[3] from knowing where I was, and what I was about, was the withholding my former name, my master's name, and the name of the state and county from which I came. During the first three or four months, my speeches were almost exclusively made up of narrations of my own personal experience as a slave. "Let us have the facts," said the people. So also said Friend George Foster, who always wished to pin me down to my simple narrative. "Give us the facts," said Collins, "we will take care of the philosophy." Just here arose some embarrassment. It was impossible for me to repeat the same old story month after month, and to keep up my interest in it. It was new to the people, it is true, but it was an old story to me; and to go through with it night after night, was a task altogether too mechanical for my nature. "Tell your story, Frederick," would whisper my then revered friend, William Lloyd Garrison, as I stepped upon the platform. I could not always obey, for I was now reading and thinking. New views of the subject were presented to my mind. It did not entirely satisfy me to *narrate* wrongs; I felt like *denouncing* them. I could not always curb my moral indignation for the perpetrators of slaveholding villainy, long enough for a circumstantial statement of the facts which I felt almost everybody must know. Besides, I was growing, and needed room. "People won't believe you ever was a slave, Frederick, if you keep on this way," said Friend Foster. "Be yourself," said Collins, "and tell your story." It was said to me, "Better have a *little* of the plantation manner of speech than not; 'tis not best that you seem too learned." These excellent friends were actuated by the best of motives, and were not altogether wrong in their advice; and still I must speak just the word that seemed to *me* the word to be spoken *by* me.

At last the apprehended trouble came. People doubted if I had ever been a slave. They said I did not talk like a slave, look like a slave, nor act like a slave, and that they believed I had never been south of Mason and Dixon's line. "He don't tell us where he came from—what his master's name was—how he got away—nor the story of his experience. Besides, he is educated, and is, in this, a contradiction of all the facts we have concerning the ignorance of the slaves." Thus, I was in a pretty fair way to be denounced as an impostor. The committee of the Massachusetts anti-slavery society knew all the facts in my case, and agreed with me in the prudence of keeping them private. They, therefore, never doubted my being a genuine fugitive; but going down the aisles of the churches in which I spoke, and hearing the free spoken Yankees saying, repeatedly, *"He's never been a slave, I'll warrant ye,"* I resolved to dispel all doubt, at no distant day, by such a revelation of facts as could not be made by any other than a genuine fugitive.

3. Douglass's former enslaver, Thomas Auld.

In a little less than four years, therefore, after becoming a public lecturer, I was induced to write out the leading facts connected with my experience in slavery, giving names of persons, places, and dates[4]—thus putting it in the power of any who doubted, to ascertain the truth or falsehood of my story of being a fugitive slave. This statement soon became known in Maryland, and I had reason to believe that an effort would be made to recapture me.

It is not probable that any open attempt to secure me as a slave could have succeeded, further than the obtainment, by my master, of the money value of my bones and sinews. Fortunately for me, in the four years of my labors in the abolition cause, I had gained many friends, who would have suffered themselves to be taxed to almost any extent to save me from slavery. It was felt that I had committed the double offense of running away, and exposing the secrets and crimes of slavery and slaveholders. There was a double motive for seeking my reenslavement—avarice and vengeance; and while, as I have said, there was little probability of successful recapture, if attempted openly, I was constantly in danger of being spirited away, at a moment when my friends could render me no assistance. In traveling about from place to place—often alone—I was much exposed to this sort of attack. Any one cherishing the design to betray me, could easily do so, by simply tracing my whereabouts through the anti-slavery journals, for my meetings and movements were promptly made known in advance. My true friends, Mr. Garrison and Mr. Phillips,[5] had no faith in the power of Massachusetts to protect me in my right to liberty. Public sentiment and the law, in their opinion, would hand me over to the tormentors. Mr. Phillips, especially, considered me in danger, and said, when I showed him the manuscript of my story, if in my place, he would throw it into the fire. Thus, the reader will observe, the settling of one difficulty only opened the way for another; and that though I had reached a free state, and had attained a position for public usefulness, I was still tormented with the liability of losing my liberty. How this liability was dispelled, will be related, with other incidents, in the next chapter.

Chapter XXIV. Twenty-One Months in Great Britain

The allotments of Providence, when coupled with trouble and anxiety, often conceal from finite vision the wisdom and goodness in which they are sent; and, frequently, what seemed a harsh and invidious dispensation, is converted by after experience into a happy and beneficial arrangement. Thus, the painful liability to be returned again to slavery, which haunted me by day, and troubled my dreams by night, proved to be a necessary step in the path of knowledge and usefulness. The writing of my pamphlet, in the spring of 1845, endangered my liberty, and led me to seek a refuge from republican slavery in monarchical England. A rude, uncultivated fugitive slave was driven, by stern necessity, to that country to which young American gentlemen go to increase their stock of knowledge, to seek pleasure, to have their rough, democratic manners softened by contact with English aristocratic refinement. On applying for a passage to England, on board the Cambria, of the Cunard line, my friend, James N. Buffum,[6] of Lynn, Massachusetts, was informed that I could not be received on board as a cabin passenger. American prejudice against color triumphed over British liberality and civilization,

4. That is, the *Narrative of the Life of Frederick Douglass* (1845).
5. Massachusetts reformer, antislavery agitator, and orator (1811–1884).
6. Businessman, Massachusetts politician, and civil rights activist (1807–1887).

and erected a color test and condition for crossing the sea in the cabin of a British vessel. The insult was keenly felt by my white friends, but to me, it was common, expected, and therefore, a thing of no great consequence, whether I went in the cabin or in the steerage. Moreover, I felt that if I could not go into the first cabin, first-cabin passengers could come into the second cabin, and the result justified my anticipations to the fullest extent. Indeed, I soon found myself an object of more general interest than I wished to be; and so far from being degraded by being placed in the second cabin, that part of the ship became the scene of as much pleasure and refinement, during the voyage, as the cabin itself. The Hutchinson Family, celebrated vocalists—fellow-passengers—often came to my rude forecastle deck, and sung their sweetest songs, enlivening the place with eloquent music, as well as spirited conversation, during the voyage. In two days after leaving Boston, one part of the ship was about as free to me as another. My fellow-passengers not only visited me, but invited me to visit them, on the saloon deck. My visits there, however, were but seldom. I preferred to live within my privileges, and keep upon my own premises. I found this quite as much in accordance with good policy, as with my own feelings. The effect was, that with the majority of the passengers, all color distinctions were flung to the winds, and I found myself treated with every mark of respect, from the beginning to the end of the voyage, except in a single instance; and in that, I came near being mobbed, for complying with an invitation given me by the passengers, and the captain of the "Cambria," to deliver a lecture on slavery. Our New Orleans and Georgia passengers were pleased to regard my lecture as an insult offered to them, and swore I should not speak. They went so far as to threaten to throw me overboard, and but for the firmness of Captain Judkins, probably would have (under the inspiration of *slavery* and *brandy*) attempted to put their threats into execution. I have no space to describe this scene, although its tragic and comic peculiarities are well worth describing. An end was put to the *melee,* by the captain's calling the ship's company to put the salt water mobocrats in irons. At this determined order, the gentlemen of the lash scampered, and for the rest of the voyage conducted themselves very decorously.

This incident of the voyage, in two days after landing at Liverpool, brought me at once before the British public, and that by no act of my own. The gentlemen so promptly snubbed in their meditated violence, flew to the press to justify their conduct, and to denounce me as a worthless and insolent negro. This course was even less wise than the conduct it was intended to sustain; for, besides awakening something like a national interest in me, and securing me an audience, it brought out counter statements, and threw the blame upon themselves, which they had sought to fasten upon me and the gallant captain of the ship.

Some notion may be formed of the difference in my feelings and circumstances, while abroad, from the following extract from one of a series of letters addressed by me to Mr. Garrison, and published in the Liberator. It was written on the first day of January, 1846:

> "My Dear Friend Garrison: Up to this time, I have given no direct expression of the views, feelings, and opinions which I have formed, respecting the character and condition of the people of this land. I have refrained thus, purposely. I wish to speak advisedly, and in order to do this, I have waited till, I trust, experience has brought my opinions to

an intelligent maturity. I have been thus careful, not because I think what I say will have much effect in shaping the opinions of the world, but because whatever of influence I may possess, whether little or much, I wish it to go in the right direction, and according to truth. I hardly need say that, in speaking of Ireland, I shall be influenced by no prejudices in favor of America. I think my circumstances all forbid that. I have no end to serve, no creed to uphold, no government to defend; and as to nation, I belong to none. I have no protection at home, or resting-place abroad. The land of my birth welcomes me to her shores only as a slave, and spurns with contempt the idea of treating me differently; so that I am an outcast from the society of my childhood, and an outlaw in the land of my birth. 'I am a stranger with thee, and a sojourner, as all my fathers were.'[7] That men should be patriotic, is to me perfectly natural; and as a philosophical fact, I am able to give it an *intellectual* recognition. But no further can I go. If ever I had any patriotism, or any capacity for the feeling, it was whipped out of me long since, by the lash of the American soul-drivers.

"In thinking of America, I sometimes find myself admiring her bright blue sky, her grand old woods, her fertile fields, her beautiful rivers, her mighty lakes, and star-crowned mountains. But my rapture is soon checked, my joy is soon turned to mourning. When I remember that all is cursed with the infernal spirit of slaveholding, robbery, and wrong; when I remember that with the waters of her noblest rivers, the tears of my brethren are borne to the ocean, disregarded and forgotten, and that her most fertile fields drink daily of the warm blood of my outraged sisters; I am filled with unutterable loathing, and led to reproach myself that anything could fall from my lips in praise of such a land. America will not allow her children to love her. She seems bent on compelling those who would be her warmest friends, to be her worst enemies. May God give her repentance, before it is too late, is the ardent prayer of my heart. I will continue to pray, labor, and wait, believing that she cannot always be insensible to the dictates of justice, or deaf to the voice of humanity.

"My opportunities for learning the character and condition of the people of this land have been very great. I have traveled almost from the Hill of Howth[8] to the Giant's Causeway, and from the Giant's Causeway to Cape Clear. During these travels, I have met with much in the character and condition of the people to approve, and much to condemn; much that has thrilled me with pleasure, and very much that has filled me with pain. I will not, in this letter, attempt to give any description of those scenes which have given me pain. This I will do hereafter. I have enough, and more than your subscribers will be disposed to read at one time, of the bright side of the picture. I can truly say, I have spent some of the happiest moments of my life since landing in this country. I seem to have undergone a transformation. I live a new life. The warm and generous cooperation extended to me by the friends of my despised race; the prompt and liberal manner with which the press has rendered me its aid; the glorious enthusiasm with which thousands have flocked to hear the cruel wrongs of my down-trodden and long-enslaved fellow-countrymen portrayed; the deep sympathy for

7. Psalms 39:12.
8. A peak on a peninsula northeast of Dublin, Ireland; "Cape Clear": an island off the southwest coast of County Cork, Ireland.

the slave, and the strong abhorrence of the slaveholder, everywhere evinced; the cordiality with which members and ministers of various religious bodies, and of various shades of religious opinion, have embraced me, and lent me their aid; the kind hospitality constantly proffered to me by persons of the highest rank in society; the spirit of freedom that seems to animate all with whom I come in contact, and the entire absence of everything that looked like prejudice against me, on account of the color of my skin—contrasted so strongly with my long and bitter experience in the United States, that I look with wonder and amazement on the transition. In the southern part of the United States, I was a slave, thought of and spoken of as property; in the language of the Law, *'held, taken, reputed, ajudged to be a chattel in the hands of my owners and possessors, and their executors, administrators, and assigns, to all intents, constructions, and purposes whatsoever.'* (Brev. Digest, 224.) In the northern states, a fugitive slave, liable to be hunted at any moment, like a felon, and to be hurled into the terrible jaws of slavery—doomed by an inveterate prejudice against color to insult and outrage on every hand, (Massachusetts out of the question)—denied the privileges and courtesies common to others in the use of the most humble means of conveyance—shut out from the cabins on steamboats—refused admission to respectable hotels—caricatured, scorned, scoffed, mocked, and maltreated with impunity by any one, (no matter how black his heart,) so he has a white skin. But now behold the change! Eleven days and a half gone, and I have crossed three thousand miles of the perilous deep. Instead of a democratic government, I am under a monarchical government. Instead of the bright, blue sky of America, I am covered with the soft, grey fog of the Emerald Isle.[9] I breathe, and lo! the chattel becomes a man. I gaze around in vain for one who will question my equal humanity, claim me as his slave, or offer me an insult. I employ a cab—I am seated beside white people—I reach the hotel—I enter the same door—I am shown into the same parlor—I dine at the same table—and no one is offended. No delicate nose grows deformed in my presence. I find no difficulty here in obtaining admission into any place of worship, instruction, or amusement, on equal terms with people as white as any I ever saw in the United States. I meet nothing to remind me of my complexion. I find myself regarded and treated at every turn with the kindness and deference paid to white people. When I go to church, I am met by no upturned nose and scornful lip to tell me, *'We don't allow niggers in here!'*

"I remember, about two years ago, there was in Boston, near the southwest corner of Boston Common, a menagerie. I had long desired to see such a collection as I understood was being exhibited there. Never having had an opportunity while a slave, I resolved to seize this, my first, since my escape. I went, and as I approached the entrance to gain admission, I was met and told by the door-keeper, in a harsh and contemptuous tone, *'We don't allow niggers in here.'* I also remember attending a revival meeting in the Rev. Henry Jackson's meeting-house, at New Bedford, and going up the broad aisle to find a seat, I was met by a good deacon, who told me, in a pious tone, *'We don't allow niggers in here!'* Soon after my arrival in New Bedford, from the south, I had a

9. That is, Ireland.

strong desire to attend the Lyceum,[1] but was told, *'They don't allow niggers in here!'* While passing from New York to Boston, on the steamer Massachusetts, on the night of the 9th of December, 1843, when chilled almost through with the cold, I went to the cabin to get a little warm. I was soon touched upon the shoulder, and told, *'We don't allow niggers in here!'* On arriving in Boston, from an anti-slavery tour, hungry and tired, I went into an eating-house, near my friend, Mr. Campbell's, to get some refreshments. I was met by a lad in a white apron, *'We don't allow niggers in here!'* A week or two before leaving the United States, I had a meeting appointed at Weymouth, the home of that glorious hand of true abolitionists, the Weston family, and others. On attempting to take a seat in the omnibus to that place, I was told by the driver, (and I never shall forget his fiendish hate,) *'I don't allow niggers in here!'* Thank heaven for the respite I now enjoy! I had been in Dublin but a few days, when a gentleman of great respectability kindly offered to conduct me through all the public buildings of that beautiful city; and a little afterward, I found myself dining with the lord mayor of Dublin. What a pity there was not some American democratic christian at the door of his splendid mansion, to bark out at my approach, *'They don't allow niggers in here!'* The truth is, the people here know nothing of the republican negro hate prevalent in our glorious land. They measure and esteem men according to their moral and intellectual worth, and not according to the color of their skin. Whatever may be said of the aristocracies here, there is none based on the color of a man's skin. This species of aristocracy belongs preeminently to 'the land of the free, and the home of the brave.' I have never found it abroad, in any but Americans. It sticks to them wherever they go. They find it almost as hard to get rid of, as to get rid of their skins.

"The second day after my arrival at Liverpool, in company with my friend, Buffum, and several other friends, I went to Eaton Hall, the residence of the Marquis of Westminster, one of the most splendid buildings in England. On approaching the door, I found several of our American passengers, who came out with us in the Cambria, waiting for admission, as but one party was allowed in the house at a time. We all had to wait till the company within came out. And of all the faces, expressive of chagrin, those of the Americans were preeminent. They looked as sour as vinegar, and as bitter as gall when they found I was to be admitted on equal terms with themselves. When the door was opened, I walked in, on an equal footing with my white fellow-citizens, and from all I could see, I had as much attention paid me by the servants that showed us through the house, as any with a paler skin. As I walked through the building, the statuary did not fall down, the pictures did not leap from their places, the doors did not refuse to open, and the servants did not say, *'We don't allow niggers in here!'*

"A happy new-year to you, and all the friends of freedom."

My time and labors, while abroad, were divided between England, Ireland, Scotland, and Wales. Upon this experience alone, I might write a book twice the size of this, *"My Bondage and my Freedom."* I visited and lectured in nearly all the large towns and cities in the United Kingdom,

1. The lyceum movement brought popular education to the United States, particularly Northeast and Midwest, through lectures, debates, concerts, and scientific demonstrations.

and enjoyed many favorable opportunities for observation and information. But books on England are abundant, and the public may, therefore, dismiss any fear that I am meditating another infliction in that line; though, in truth, I should like much to write a book on those countries, if for nothing else, to make grateful mention of the many dear friends, whose benevolent actions toward me are ineffaceably stamped upon my memory, and warmly treasured in my heart. To these friends I owe my freedom in the United States. On their own motion, without any solicitation from me (Mrs. Henry Richardson, a clever lady, remarkable for her devotion to every good work, taking the lead,) they raised a fund sufficient to purchase my freedom, and actually paid it over, and placed the papers[2] of my manumission in my hands, before they would tolerate the idea of my returning to this, my native country. To this commercial transaction I owe my exemption from the democratic operation of the fugitive slave bill of 1850.[3] But for this, I might at any time become a victim of this most cruel and scandalous enactment, and be doomed to end my life, as I began it, a slave. The sum paid for my freedom was one hundred and fifty pounds sterling.[4]

Some of my uncompromising anti-slavery friends in this country failed to see the wisdom of this arrangement, and were not pleased that I consented to it, even by my silence. They thought it a violation of anti-slavery principles—conceding a right of property in man—and a wasteful expenditure of money. On the other hand, viewing it simply in the light of a ransom, or as money extorted by a robber, and my liberty of more value than one hundred and fifty pounds sterling, I could not see either a violation of the laws of morality, or those of economy, in the transaction.

It is true, I was not in the possession of my claimants, and could have easily remained in England, for the same friends who had so generously purchased my freedom, would have assisted me in establishing myself in

2. The following is a copy of these curious papers, both of my transfer from Thomas to Hugh Auld, and from Hugh to myself:

"Know all men by these Presents, That I, Thomas Auld, of Talbot county, and state of Maryland, for and in consideration of the sum of one hundred dollars, current money, to me paid by Hugh Auld, of the city of Baltimore, in the said state, at and before the sealing and delivery of these presents, the receipt whereof, I, the said Thomas Auld, do hereby acknowledge, have granted, bargained, and sold, and by these presents do grant, bargain, and sell unto the said Hugh Auld, his executors, administrators, and assigns, ONE NEGRO MAN, by the name of FREDERICK BAILY, or DOUGLASS, as he calls himself—he is now about twenty-eight years of age—to have and to hold the said negro man for life. And I, the said Thomas Auld, for myself, my heirs, executors, and administrators, all and singular, the said FREDERICK BAILY, *alias* DOUGLASS, unto the said Hugh Auld, his executors, administrators, and assigns, against me, the said Thomas Auld, my executors, and administrators, and against all and every other person or persons whatsoever, shall and will warrant and forever defend by these presents. In witness whereof, I set my hand and seal, this thirteenth day of November, eighteen hundred and forty-six. THOMAS AULD.

"Signed, sealed, and delivered in presence of Wrightson Jones.

"JOHN C. LEAS."

The authenticity of this bill of sale is attested by N. Harrington, a justice of the peace of the state of Maryland, and for the county of Talbot, dated same day as above.

"To all whom it may concern: Be it known, that I, Hugh Auld, of the city of Baltimore, in Baltimore county, in the state of Maryland, for divers good causes and considerations, me thereunto moving, have released from slavery, liberated, manumitted, and set free, and by these presents do hereby release from slavery, liberate, manumit, and set free, MY NEGRO MAN, named FREDERICK BAILY, otherwise called DOUGLASS, being of the age of twenty-eight years, or thereabouts, and able to work and gain a sufficient livelihood and maintenance; and him the said negro man, named FREDERICK BAILY, otherwise called FREDERICK DOUGLASS, I do declare to be henceforth free, manumitted, and discharged from all manner of servitude to me, my executors, and administrators forever.

"In witness whereof, I, the said Hugh Auld, have hereunto set my hand and seal, the fifth of December, in the year one thousand eight hundred and forty-six. HUGH AULD

"Sealed and delivered in the presence of T. Hanson Belt.

"JAMES N. S. T. WRIGHT" [*Douglass's note*].

3. A provision of the Compromise of 1850, the Fugitive Slave Act criminalized any interference with an attempt to recapture an escaped enslaved person anywhere in the United States.

4. The equivalent of $711.66 in U.S. currency at that time.

that country. To this, however, I could not consent. I felt that I had a duty to perform—and that was, to labor and suffer with the oppressed in my native land. Considering, therefore, all the circumstances—the fugitive slave bill included—I think the very best thing was done in letting Master Hugh have the hundred and fifty pounds sterling and leaving me free to return to my appropriate field of labor. Had I been a private person, having no other relations or duties than those of a personal and family nature, I should never have consented to the payment of so large a sum for the privilege of living securely under our glorious republican form of government. I could have remained in England, or have gone to some other country; and perhaps I could even have lived unobserved in this. But to this I could not consent. I had already become somewhat notorious; and withal quite as unpopular as notorious; and I was, therefore, much exposed to arrest and recapture.

1855

From What to the Slave Is the Fourth of July?: An Address Delivered in Rochester, New York, on 5 July 1852

Mr. President, Friends and Fellow Citizens: He who could address this audience without a quailing sensation, has stronger nerves than I have. I do not remember ever to have appeared as a speaker before any assembly more shrinkingly, nor with greater distrust of my ability, than I do this day. A feeling has crept over me, quite unfavorable to the exercise of my limited powers of speech. The task before me is one which requires much previous thought and study for its proper performance. I know that apologies of this sort are generally considered flat and unmeaning. I trust, however, that mine will not be so considered. Should I seem at ease, my appearance would much misrepresent me. The little experience I have had in addressing public meetings, in country school houses, avails me nothing on the present occasion.

The papers and placards say, that I am to deliver a 4th [of] July oration. This certainly sounds large, and out of the common way, for me. It is true that I have often had the privilege to speak in this beautiful Hall, and to address many who now honor me with their presence. But neither their familiar faces, nor the perfect gage I think I have of Corinthian Hall, seems to free me from embarrassment.

The fact is, ladies and gentlemen, the distance between this platform and the slave plantation, from which I escaped, is considerable—and the difficulties to be overcome in getting from the latter to the former, are by no means slight. That I am here to-day is, to me, a matter of astonishment as well as of gratitude. You will not, therefore, be surprised, if in what I have to say, I evince no elaborate preparation, nor grace my speech with any high sounding exordium.[1] With little experience and with less learning, I have been able to throw my thoughts hastily and imperfectly together; and trusting to your patient and generous indulgence, I will proceed to lay them before you.

This, for the purpose of this celebration, is the 4th of July. It is the birthday of your National Independence, and of your political freedom. This, to

1. The beginning of or introduction to a discourse.

you, is what the Passover[2] was to the emancipated people of God. It carries your minds back to the day, and to the act of your great deliverance; and to the signs, and to the wonders, associated with that act, and that day. This celebration also marks the beginning of another year of your national life; and reminds you that the Republic of America is now 76 years old. I am glad, fellow-citizens, that your nation is so young. Seventy-six years, though a good old age for a man, is but a mere speck in the life of a nation. Three score years and ten is the allotted time for individual men; but nations number their years by thousands. According to this fact, you are, even now, only in the beginning of your national career, still lingering in the period of childhood. I repeat, I am glad this is so. There is hope in the thought, and hope is much needed, under the dark clouds which lower above the horizon. The eye of the reformer is met with angry flashes, portending disastrous times; but his heart may well beat lighter at the thought that America is young, and that she is still in the impressible stage of her existence. May he not hope that high lessons of wisdom, of justice and of truth, will yet give direction to her destiny? Were the nation older, the patriot's heart might be sadder, and the reformer's brow heavier. Its future might be shrouded in gloom, and the hope of its prophets go out in sorrow. There is consolation in the thought that America is young. Great streams are not easily turned from channels, worn deep in the course of ages. They may sometimes rise in quiet and stately majesty, and inundate the land, refreshing and fertilizing the earth with their mysterious properties. They may also rise in wrath and fury, and bear away, on their angry waves, the accumulated wealth of years of toil and hardship. They, however, gradually flow back to the same old channel, and flow on as serenely as ever. But, while the river may not be turned aside, it may dry up, and leave nothing behind but the withered branch, and the unsightly rock, to howl in the abyss-sweeping wind, the sad tale of departed glory. As with rivers so with nations.

Fellow-citizens, I shall not presume to dwell at length on the associations that cluster about this day. The simple story of it is that, 76 years ago, the people of this country were British subjects. The style and title of your "sovereign people" (in which you now glory) was not then born. You were under the British Crown. Your fathers esteemed the English Government as the home government; and England as the fatherland. This home government, you know, although a considerable distance from your home, did, in the exercise of its parental prerogatives, impose upon its colonial children, such restraints, burdens and limitations, as, in its mature judgement, it deemed wise, right and proper.

But, your fathers, who had not adopted the fashionable idea of this day, of the infallibility of government, and the absolute character of its acts, presumed to differ from the home government in respect to the wisdom and the justice of some of those burdens and restraints. They went so far in their excitement as to pronounce the measures of government unjust, unreasonable, and oppressive, and altogether such as ought not to be quietly submitted to. I scarcely need say, fellow-citizens, that my opinion of those measures fully accords with that of your fathers. Such a declaration of agreement on my part would not be worth much to anybody. It would, certainly, prove nothing, as to what part I might have taken, had I lived during the great controversy of 1776. To say *now* that America was right, and England wrong,

2. A Jewish festival celebrating the Jews' deliverance from bondage in Egypt.

is exceedingly easy. Everybody can say it; the dastard, not less than the noble brave, can flippantly discant on the tyranny of England towards the American Colonies. It is fashionable to do so; but there was a time when to pronounce against England, and in favor of the cause of the colonies, tried men's souls.[3] They who did so were accounted in their day, plotters of mischief, agitators and rebels, dangerous men. To side with the right, against the wrong, with the weak against the strong, and with the oppressed against the oppressor! *here* lies the merit, and the one which, of all others, seems unfashionable in our day. The cause of liberty may be stabbed by the men who glory in the deeds of your fathers. But, to proceed.

Feeling themselves harshly and unjustly treated by the home government, your fathers, like men of honesty, and men of spirit, earnestly sought redress. They petitioned and remonstrated; they did so in a decorous, respectful, and loyal manner. Their conduct was wholly unexceptionable. This, however, did not answer the purpose. They saw themselves treated with sovereign indifference, coldness and scorn. Yet they persevered. They were not the men to look back.

As the sheet anchor takes a firmer hold, when the ship is tossed by the storm, so did the cause of your fathers grow stronger, as it breasted the chilling blasts of kingly displeasure. The greatest and best of British statesmen admitted its justice, and the loftiest eloquence of the British Senate came to its support. But, with that blindness which seems to be the unvarying characteristic of tyrants, since Pharoah and his hosts were drowned in the Red Sea, the British Government persisted in the exactions complained of.

The madness of this course, we believe, is admitted now, even by England; but we fear the lesson is wholly lost on our present rulers.

Oppression makes a wise man mad. Your fathers were wise men, and if they did not go mad, they became restive under this treatment. They felt themselves the victims of grievous wrongs, wholly incurable in their colonial capacity. With brave men there is always a remedy for oppression. Just here, the idea of a total separation of the colonies from the crown was born! It was a startling idea, much more so, than we, at this distance of time, regard it. The timid and the prudent (as has been intimated) of that day, were, of course, shocked and alarmed by it.

Such people lived then, had lived before, and will, probably, ever have a place on this planet; and their course, in respect to any great change, (no matter how great the good to be attained, or the wrong to be redressed by it), may be calculated with as much precision as can be the course of the stars. They hate all changes, but silver, gold and copper change! Of this sort of change they are always strongly in favor.

These people were called tories in the days of your fathers; and the appellation, probably, conveyed the same idea that is meant by a more modern, though a somewhat less euphonious term,[4] which we often find in our papers, applied to some of our old politicians.

Their opposition to the then dangerous thought was earnest and powerful; but, amid all their terror and affrighted vociferations against it, the alarming and revolutionary idea moved on, and the country with it.

3. An allusion to the famous opening of Thomas Paine's revolutionary pamphlet *The American Crisis* (1776): "These are the times that try men's souls."

4. Douglass is probably referring to the term *Hunker*, which was applied to conservative Democrats. "Euphonious": having a pleasant sound.

On the 2d of July, 1776, the old Continental Congress, to the dismay of the lovers of ease, and the worshippers of property, clothed that dreadful idea with all the authority of national sanction. They did so in the form of a resolution; and as we seldom hit upon resolutions, drawn up in our day, whose transparency is at all equal to this, it may refresh your minds and help my story if I read it.

> "Resolved, That these united colonies *are,* and of right, ought to be free and Independent States; that they are absolved from all allegiance to the British Crown; and that all political connection between them and the State of Great Britain *is,* and ought to be, dissolved."

Citizens, your fathers made good that resolution. They succeeded; and to-day you reap the fruits of their success. The freedom gained is yours; and you, therefore, may properly celebrate this anniversary. The 4th of July is the first great fact in your nation's history—the very ring-bolt in the chain of your yet undeveloped destiny.

Pride and patriotism, not less than gratitude, prompt you to celebrate and to hold it in perpetual remembrance. I have said that the Declaration of Independence is the RING-BOLT to the chain of your nation's destiny; so, indeed, I regard it. The principles contained in that instrument are saving principles. Stand by those principles, be true to them on all occasions, in all places, against all foes, and at whatever cost.

From the round top of your ship of state, dark and threatening clouds may be seen. Heavy billows, like mountains in the distance, disclose to the leeward huge forms of flinty rocks! That *bolt* drawn, that *chain* broken, and all is lost. *Cling to this day—cling to it,* and to its principles, with the grasp of a storm-tossed mariner to a spar at midnight.

The coming into being of a nation, in any circumstances, is an interesting event. But, besides general considerations, there were peculiar circumstances which make the advent of this republic an event of special attractiveness.

The whole scene, as I look back to it, was simple, dignified and sublime.

The population of the country, at the time, stood at the insignificant number of three millions. The country was poor in the munitions of war. The population was weak and scattered, and the country a wilderness unsubdued. There were then no means of concert and combination, such as exist now. Neither steam nor lightning had then been reduced to order and discipline. From the Potomac to the Delaware was a journey of many days. Under these, and innumerable other disadvantages, your fathers declared for liberty and independence and triumphed.

Fellow Citizens, I am not wanting in respect for the fathers of this republic. The signers of the Declaration of Independence were brave men. They were great men too—great enough to give fame to a great age. It does not often happen to a nation to raise, at one time, such a number of truly great men. The point from which I am compelled to view them is not, certainly, the most favorable; and yet I cannot contemplate their great deeds with less than admiration. They were statesmen, patriots and heroes, and for the good they did, and the principles they contended for, I will unite with you to honor their memory.

They loved their country better than their own private interests; and, though this is not the highest form of human excellence, all will concede that it is a rare virtue, and that when it is exhibited, it ought to command respect. He who will, intelligently, lay down his life for his country, is a man whom it is not in human nature to despise. Your fathers staked their lives, their fortunes, and their sacred honor, on the cause of their country. In their admiration of liberty, they lost sight of all other interests.

They were peace men; but they preferred revolution to peaceful submission to bondage. They were quiet men; but they did not shrink from agitating against oppression. They showed forbearance; but that they knew its limits. They believed in order; but not in the order of tyranny. With them, nothing was *"settled"* that was not right. With them, justice, liberty and humanity were *"final"*; not slavery and oppression. You may well cherish the memory of such men. They were great in their day and generation. Their solid manhood stands out the more as we contrast it with these degenerate times.

How circumspect, exact and proportionate were all their movements! How unlike the politicians of an hour! Their statesmanship looked beyond the passing moment, and stretched away in strength into the distant future. They seized upon eternal principles, and set a glorious example in their defence. Mark them!

Fully appreciating the hardship to be encountered, firmly believing in the right of their cause, honorably inviting the scrutiny of an on-looking world, reverently appealing to heaven to attest their sincerity, soundly comprehending the solemn responsibility they were about to assume, wisely measuring the terrible odds against them, your fathers, the fathers of this republic, did, most deliberately, under the inspiration of a glorious patriotism, and with a sublime faith in the great principles of justice and freedom, lay deep the corner-stone of the national superstructure, which has risen and still rises in grandeur around you.

Of this fundamental work, this day is the anniversary. Our eyes are met with demonstrations of joyous enthusiasm. Banners and pennants wave exultingly on the breeze. The din of business, too, is hushed. Even Mammon[5] seems to have quitted his grasp on this day. The ear-piercing fife and the stirring drum unite their accents with the ascending peal of a thousand church bells. Prayers are made, hymns are sung, and sermons are preached in honor of this day; while the quick martial tramp of a great and multitudinous nation, echoed back by all the hills, valleys and mountains of a vast continent, bespeak the occasion one of thrilling and universal interest—a nation's jubilee.

Friends and citizens, I need not enter further into the causes which led to this anniversary. Many of you understand them better than I do. You could instruct me in regard to them. That is a branch of knowledge in which you feel, perhaps, a much deeper interest than your speaker. The causes which led to the separation of the colonies from the British crown have never lacked for a tongue. They have all been taught in your common schools, narrated at your firesides, unfolded from your pulpits, and thundered from your legislative halls, and are as familiar to you as household words. They form the staple of your national poetry and eloquence.

I remember, also, that, as a people, Americans are remarkably familiar with all facts which make in their own favor. This is esteemed by some as a national trait—perhaps a national weakness. It is a fact, that whatever makes for the wealth or for the reputation of Americans, and can be had *cheap!* will be found by Americans. I shall not be charged with slandering Americans, if I say I think the American side of any question may be safely left in American hands.

5. The false god of riches and greed.

I leave, therefore, the great deeds of your fathers to other gentlemen whose claim to have been regularly descended will be less likely to be disputed than mine!

The Present

My business, if I have any here to-day, is with the present. The accepted time with God and his cause is the ever-living now.

> "Trust no future, however pleasant,
> Let the dead past bury its dead;
> Act, act in the living present,
> Heart within, and God overhead."[6]

We have to do with the past only as we can make it useful to the present and to the future. To all inspiring motives, to noble deeds which can be gained from the past, we are welcome. But now is the time, the important time. Your fathers have lived, died, and have done their work, and have done much of it well. You live and must die, and you must do your work. You have no right to enjoy a child's share in the labor of your fathers, unless your children are to be blest by your labors. You have no right to wear out and waste the hard-earned fame of your fathers to cover your indolence. Sydney Smith[7] tells us that men seldom eulogize the wisdom and virtues of their fathers, but to excuse some folly or wickedness of their own. This truth is not a doubtful one. There are illustrations of it near and remote, ancient and modern. It was fashionable, hundreds of years ago, for the children of Jacob to boast, we have "Abraham to our father,"[8] when they had long lost Abraham's faith and spirit. That people contented themselves under the shadow of Abraham's great name, while they repudiated the deeds which made his name great. Need I remind you that a similar thing is being done all over this country to-day? Need I tell you that the Jews are not the only people who built the tombs of the prophets, and garnished the sepulchres of the righteous? Washington could not die till he had broken the chains of his slaves.[9] Yet his monument is built up by the price of human blood, and the traders in the bodies and souls of men, shout—"We have Washington to *our father*." Alas! that it should be so; yet so it is.

> "The evil that men do, lives after them,
> The good is oft' interred with their bones."[1]

Fellow-citizens, pardon me, allow me to ask, why am I called upon to speak here to-day? What have I, or those I represent, to do with your national independence? Are the great principles of political freedom and of natural justice, embodied in that Declaration of Independence, extended to us? and am I, therefore, called upon to bring our humble offering to the national altar, and to confess the benefits and express devout gratitude for the blessings resulting from your independence to us?

Would to God, both for your sakes and ours, that an affirmative answer could be truthfully returned to these questions! Then would my task be

6. From Henry Wadsworth Longfellow's poem "A Psalm of Life" (1838).
7. English minister and satirical essayist (1771–1845).
8. Luke 3:8. Abraham was the first patriarch of the Hebrews. Jacob, whose sons were the ancestors of the twelve tribes of Israel, was Abraham's grandson.
9. In his 1799 will George Washington authorized the eventual emancipation of 123 people whom he had enslaved, but only upon the death of his wife, Martha Custis Washington.
1. Shakespeare's *Julius Caesar* 3.2.76.

light, and my burden easy and delightful. For *who* is there so cold, that a nation's sympathy could not warm him? Who so obdurate and dead to the claims of gratitude, that would not thankfully acknowledge such priceless benefits? Who so stolid and selfish, that would not give his voice to swell the hallelujahs of a nation's jubilee, when the chains of servitude had been torn from his limbs? I am not that man. In a case like that, the dumb might eloquently speak, and the "lame man leap as an hart."[2]

But, such is not the state of the case. I say it with a sad sense of the disparity between us. I am not included within the pale of this glorious anniversary! Your high independence only reveals the immeasurable distance between us. The blessings in which you, this day, rejoice, are not enjoyed in common. The rich inheritance of justice, liberty, prosperity and independence, bequeathed by your fathers, is shared by you, not by me. The sunlight that brought life and healing to you, has brought stripes and death to me. This Fourth [of] July is *yours*, not *mine*. *You* may rejoice, *I* must mourn. To drag a man in fetters into the grand illuminated temple of liberty, and call upon him to join you in joyous anthems, were inhuman mockery and sacrilegious irony. Do you mean, citizens, to mock me, by asking me to speak to-day? If so, there is a parallel to your conduct. And let me warn you that it is dangerous to copy the example of a nation whose crimes, towering up to heaven, were thrown down by the breath of the Almighty, burying that nation in irrecoverable ruin! I can to-day take up the plaintive lament of a peeled and woe-smitten people!

"By the rivers of Babylon, there we sat down. Yea! we wept when we remembered Zion. We hanged our harps upon the willows in the midst thereof. For there, they that carried us away captive, required of us a song; and they who wasted us required of us mirth, saying, Sing us one of the songs of Zion. How can we sing the Lord's song in a strange land? If I forget thee, O Jerusalem, let my right hand forget her cunning. If I do not remember thee, let my tongue cleave to the roof of my mouth."[3]

Fellow-citizens; above your national, tumultuous joy, I hear the mournful wail of millions! whose chains, heavy and grievous yesterday, are, to-day, rendered more intolerable by the jubilee shouts that reach them. If I do forget, if I do not faithfully remember those bleeding children of sorrow this day, "may my right hand forget her cunning, and may my tongue cleave to the roof of my mouth!" To forget them, to pass lightly over their wrongs, and to chime in with the popular theme, would be treason most scandalous and shocking, and would make me a reproach before God and the world. My subject, then fellow-citizens, is AMERICAN SLAVERY. I shall see, this day, and its popular characteristics, from the slave's point of view. Standing, there, identified with the American bondman, making his wrongs mine, I do not hesitate to declare, with all my soul, that the character and conduct of this nation never looked blacker to me than on this 4th of July! Whether we turn to the declarations of the past, or to the professions of the present, the conduct of the nation seems equally hideous and revolting. America is false to the past, false to the present, and solemnly binds herself to be false to the future. Standing with God and the crushed and bleeding slave on this occasion, I will, in the name of humanity which is outraged, in the name of liberty which is fettered, in the name of the constitution and the Bible, which are disregarded and trampled upon, dare to call in question

2. Isaiah 35:6.

3. Psalms 137:1–6.

and to denounce, with all the emphasis I can command, everything that serves to perpetuate slavery—the great sin and shame of America! "I will not equivocate; I will not excuse";[4] I will use the severest language I can command; and yet not one word shall escape me that any man, whose judgement is not blinded by prejudice, or who is not at heart a slaveholder, shall not confess to be right and just.

But I fancy I hear some one of my audience say, it is just in this circumstance that you and your brother abolitionists fail to make a favorable impression on the public mind. Would you argue more, and denounce less, would you persuade more, and rebuke less, your cause would be much more likely to succeed. But, I submit, where all is plain there is nothing to be argued. What point in the anti-slavery creed would you have me argue? On what branch of the subject do the people of this country need light? Must I undertake to prove that the slave is a man? That point is conceded already. Nobody doubts it. The slaveholders themselves acknowledge it in the enactment of laws for their government. They acknowledge it when they punish disobedience on the part of the slave. There are seventy-two crimes in the State of Virginia, which, if committed by a black man, (no matter how ignorant he be), subject him to the punishment of death; while only two of the same crimes will subject a white man to the like punishment. What is this but the acknowledgement that the slave is a moral, intellectual and responsible being? The manhood of the slave is conceded. It is admitted in the fact that Southern statute books are covered with enactments forbidding, under severe fines and penalties, the teaching of the slave to read or to write. When you can point to any such laws, in reference to the beasts of the field, then I may consent to argue the manhood of the slave. When the dogs in your streets, when the fowls of the air, when the cattle on your hills, when the fish of the sea, and the reptiles that crawl, shall be unable to distinguish the slave from a brute, *then* will I argue with you that the slave is a man!

For the present, it is enough to affirm the equal manhood of the negro race. Is it not astonishing that, while we are ploughing, planting and reaping, using all kinds of mechanical tools, erecting houses, constructing bridges, building ships, working in metals of brass, iron, copper, silver and gold; that, while we are reading, writing and cyphering, acting as clerks, merchants and secretaries, having among us lawyers, doctors, ministers, poets, authors, editors, orators and teachers; that, while we are engaged in all manner of enterprises common to other men, digging gold in California, capturing the whale in the Pacific, feeding sheep and cattle on the hill-side, living, moving, acting, thinking, planning, living in families as husbands, wives and children, and, above all, confessing and worshipping the Christian's God, and looking hopefully for life and immortality beyond the grave, we are called upon to prove that we are men!

Would you have me argue that man is entitled to liberty? that he is the rightful owner of his own body? You have already declared it. Must I argue the wrongfulness of slavery? Is that a question for Republicans? Is it to be settled by the rules of logic and argumentation, as a matter beset with great difficulty, involving a doubtful application of the principle of justice, hard to be understood? How should I look to-day, in the presence of Americans, dividing, and subdividing a discourse, to show that men have a natural right to freedom? speaking of it relatively, and positively, negatively, and

4. From the first issue of William Lloyd Garrison's pioneering antislavery newspaper, *The Liberator*.

affirmatively. To do so, would be to make myself ridiculous, and to offer an insult to your understanding. There is not a man beneath the canopy of heaven, that does not know that slavery is wrong *for him*.

What, am I to argue that it is wrong to make men brutes, to rob them of their liberty, to work them without wages, to keep them ignorant of their relations to their fellow men, to beat them with sticks, to flay their flesh with the lash, to load their limbs with irons, to hunt them with dogs, to sell them at auction, to sunder their families, to knock out their teeth, to burn their flesh, to starve them into obedience and submission to their masters? Must I argue that a system thus marked with blood, and stained with pollution, is *wrong*? No! I will not. I have better employments for my time and strength, than such arguments would imply.

What, then, remains to be argued? Is it that slavery is not divine; that God did not establish it; that our doctors of divinity are mistaken? There is blasphemy in the thought. That which is inhuman, cannot be divine! *Who* can reason on such a proposition? They that can, may; I cannot. The time for such argument is past.

At a time like this, scorching irony, not convincing argument, is needed. O! had I the ability, and could I reach the nation's ear, I would, to-day, pour out a fiery stream of biting ridicule, blasting reproach, withering sarcasm, and stern rebuke. For it is not light that is needed, but fire; it is not the gentle shower, but thunder. We need the storm, the whirlwind, and the earthquake. The feeling of the nation must be quickened; the conscience of the nation must be roused; the propriety of the nation must be startled; the hypocrisy of the nation must be exposed; and its crimes against God and man must be proclaimed and denounced.

What, to the American slave, is your 4th of July? I answer: a day that reveals to him, more than all other days in the year, the gross injustice and cruelty to which he is the constant victim. To him, your celebration is a sham; your boasted liberty, an unholy license; your national greatness, swelling vanity; your sounds of rejoicing are empty and heartless; your denunciations of tyrants, brass fronted impudence; your shouts of liberty and equality, hollow mockery; your prayers and hymns, your sermons and thanksgivings, with all your religious parade, and solemnity, are, to him, mere bombast, fraud, deception, impiety, and hypocrisy—a thin veil to cover up crimes which would disgrace a nation of savages. There is not a nation on the earth guilty of practices, more shocking and bloody, than are the people of these United States, at this very hour.

Go where you may, search where you will, roam through all the monarchies and despotisms of the old world, travel through South America, search out every abuse, and when you have found the last, lay your facts by the side of the everyday practices of this nation, and you will say with me, that, for revolting barbarity and shameless hypocrisy, America reigns without a rival.

The Internal Slave Trade

* * *

Americans! your republican politics, not less than your republican religion, are flagrantly inconsistent. You boast of your love of liberty, your superior civilization, and your pure Christianity, while the whole political power of the nation (as embodied in the two great political parties), is solemnly pledged to support and perpetuate the enslavement of three millions of your countrymen. You hurl your anathemas[5] at the crowned headed tyrants of Russia and Austria, and pride yourselves on your Democratic institutions, while you yourselves consent to be the mere *tools* and *body-guards* of the tyrants of Virginia and Carolina. You invite to your shores fugitives of oppression from abroad, honor them with banquets, greet them with ovations, cheer them, toast them, salute them, protect them, and pour out your money to them like water; but the fugitives from your own land you advertise, hunt, arrest, shoot and kill. You glory in your refinement and your universal education; yet you maintain a system as barbarous and dreadful as ever stained the character of a nation—a system begun in avarice, supported in pride, and perpetuated in cruelty. You shed tears over fallen Hungary,[6] and make the sad story of her wrongs the theme of your poets, statesmen and orators, till your gallant sons are ready to fly to arms to vindicate her cause against her oppressors; but, in regard to the ten thousand wrongs of the American slave, you would enforce the strictest silence, and would hail him as an enemy of the nation who dares to make those wrongs the subject of public discourse! You are all on fire at the mention of liberty for France or for Ireland; but are as cold as an iceberg at the thought of liberty for the enslaved of America. You discourse eloquently on the dignity of labor; yet, you sustain a system which, in its very essence, casts a stigma upon labor. You can bare your bosom to the storm of British artillery to throw off a threepenny tax on tea; and yet wring the last hard-earned farthing from the grasp of the black laborers of your country. You profess to believe "that, of one blood, God made all nations of men to dwell on the face of all the earth,"[7] and hath commanded all men, everywhere to love one another; yet you notoriously hate, (and glory in your hatred), all men whose skins are not colored like your own. You declare, before the world, and are understood by the world to declare, that you *"hold these truths to be self evident, that all men are created equal; and are endowed by their Creator with certain inalienable rights; and that, among these are, life, liberty, and the pursuit of happiness"*;[8] and yet, you hold securely, in a bondage which, according to your own Thomas Jefferson, *"is worse than ages of that which your fathers rose in rebellion to oppose,"*[9] *a seventh part* of the inhabitants of your country.

Fellow-citizens! I will not enlarge further on your national inconsistencies. The existence of slavery in this country brands your republicanism as a sham, your humanity as a base pretence, and your Christianity as a lie. It destroys your moral power abroad; it corrupts your politicians at home. It saps the foundation of religion; it makes your name a hissing, and a by-word to a mocking earth. It is the antagonistic force in your government, the only thing that seriously disturbs and endangers your *Union*. It fetters your progress; it is the enemy of improvement, the deadly foe of education; it fosters pride; it breeds insolence; it promotes vice; it shelters crime; it is a curse to the earth that supports it; and yet, you cling to it, as if it were the sheet anchor of all your hopes. Oh! be warned! be warned! a horrible reptile is coiled up in your nation's bosom; the venomous creature is nursing at the tender breast of your youthful republic; *for the love of God, tear away,* and

5. Denunciations or curses.
6. In August 1849 the republic of Hungary was overthrown by invading Russian and Austrian troops.
7. Acts 17:26.
8. From the U.S. Declaration of Independence.
9. See Jefferson's June 26, 1786, letter to Nicholas Demeunier: "Who can endure toil, famine, stripes, imprisonment or death itself in vindication of his own liberty . . . and inflict upon his fellow men a bondage, one hour of which is fraught with more misery than ages of that which he rose in rebellion to oppose."

fling from you the hideous monster, and *let the weight of twenty millions crush and destroy it forever!*

The Constitution

* * *

Allow me to say, in conclusion, notwithstanding the dark picture I have this day presented of the state of the nation, I do not despair of this country. There are forces in operation, which must inevitably work the downfall of slavery. *"The arm of the Lord is not shortened,"*[1] and the doom of slavery is certain. I, therefore, leave off where I began, with *hope.* While drawing encouragement from the Declaration of Independence, the great principles it contains, and the genius of American Institutions, my spirit is also cheered by the obvious tendencies of the age. Nations do not now stand in the same relation to each other that they did ages ago. No nation can now shut itself up from the surrounding world, and trot round in the same old path of its fathers without interference. The time *was* when such could be done. Long established customs of hurtful character could formerly fence themselves in, and do their evil work with social impunity. Knowledge was then confined and enjoyed by the privileged few, and the multitude walked on in mental darkness. But a change has now come over the affairs of mankind. Walled cities and empires have become unfashionable. The arm of commerce has borne away the gates of the strong city. Intelligence is penetrating the darkest corners of the globe. It makes its pathway over and under the sea, as well as on the earth. Wind, steam, and lightning are its chartered agents. Oceans no longer divide, but link nations together. From Boston to London is now a holiday excursion. Space is comparatively annihilated. Thoughts expressed on one side of the Atlantic are distinctly heard on the other.

The far off and almost fabulous Pacific rolls in grandeur at our feet. The Celestial Empire, the mystery of ages, is being solved. The fiat of the Almighty, *"Let there be Light,"*[2] has not yet spent its force. No abuse, no outrage whether in taste, sport or avarice, can now hide itself from the all-pervading light. The iron shoe, and crippled foot of China must be seen, in contrast with nature. *Africa must rise and put on her yet unwoven garment. "Ethiopia shall stretch out her hand unto God."*[3] In the fervent aspirations of William Lloyd Garrison, I say, and let every heart join in saying it:

God speed the year of jubilee
  The wide world o'er!
When from their galling chains set free,
Th' oppress'd shall vilely bend the knee,
And wear the yoke of tyranny
  Like brutes no more.
That year will come, and freedom's reign,
To man his plundered rights again
  Restore.

God speed the day when human blood
  Shall cease to flow!

1. See Isaiah 59:1: "Behold the Lord's hand is not shortened, that it cannot save; neither his ear heavy, that it cannot hear."
2. Genesis 1:3.
3. See Psalms 68:31: "Princes shall come out of Egypt; Ethiopia shall soon stretch out her hands unto God."

In every clime be understood,
The claims of human brotherhood,
And each return for evil, good,
  Not blow for blow;
That day will come all feuds to end,
And change into a faithful friend
  Each foe.

God speed the hour, the glorious hour,
  When none on earth
Shall exercise a lordly power,
Nor in a tyrant's presence cower;
But all to manhood's stature tower,
  By equal birth!
THAT HOUR WILL COME, to each, to all,
And from his prison-house, the thrall
  Go forth.

Until that year, day, hour, arrive,
With head, and heart, and hand I'll strive,
To break the rod, and rend the gyve,
The spoiler of his prey deprive—
  So witness Heaven!
And never from my chosen post,
Whate'er the peril or the cost,
  Be driven.[4]

1852

From Life and Times of Frederick Douglass

From *Second Part*

FROM CHAPTER XV. WEIGHED IN THE BALANCE

The most of my story is now before the reader. Whatever of good or ill the future may have in store for me, the past at least is secure. As I review the last decade up to the present writing, I am impressed with a sense of completeness; a sort of rounding up of the arch to the point where the keystone may be inserted, the scaffolding removed, and the work, with all its perfections or faults, left to speak for itself. This decade, from 1871 to 1881, has been crowded, if time is capable of being thus described, with incidents and events which may well enough be accounted remarkable. To me they certainly appear strange, if not wonderful. My early life not only gave no visible promise, but no hint of such experience. On the contrary, that life seemed to render it, in part at least, impossible. In addition to what is narrated in the foregoing chapter, I have, as belonging to this decade, to speak of my mission to Santo Domingo; of my appointment as a member of the council for the government of the District of Columbia; of my election as elector at large for the State of New York; of my invitation to speak at the monument

4. William Lloyd Garrison's "The Triumph of Freedom" (1845).

of the unknown loyal dead, at Arlington, on Decoration day;[1] of my address on the unveiling of Lincoln monument, at Lincoln Park, Washington; of my appointment to bring the electoral vote from New York to the national capital; of my invitation to speak near the statue of Abraham Lincoln, Madison Square, New York; of my accompanying the body of Vice-President Wilson from Washington to Boston; of my conversations with Senator Sumner and President Grant; of my welcome to the receptions of Secretary Hamilton Fish; of my appointment by President R. B. Hayes to the office of Marshal of the District of Columbia; of my visit to Thomas Auld, the man who claimed me as his slave, and from whom I was purchased by my English friends; of my visit, after an absence of fifty-six years, to Lloyd's plantation, the home of my childhood; and of my appointment by President James A. Garfield[2] to the office of Recorder of Deeds of the District of Columbia.

Those who knew of my more than friendly relations with Hon. Charles Sumner, and of his determined opposition to the annexation of Santo Domingo to the United States, were surprised to find me earnestly taking sides with General Grant upon that question. Some of my white friends, and a few of those of my own color—who, unfortunately, allow themselves to look at public questions more through the medium of feeling than of reason, and who follow the line of what is grateful to their friends rather than what is consistent with their own convictions—thought my course was an ungrateful return for the eminent services of the Massachusetts senator. I am free to say that, had I been guided only by the promptings of my heart, I should in this controversy have followed the lead of Charles Sumner. He was not only the most clearsighted, brave, and uncompromising friend of my race who had ever stood upon the floor of the Senate, but was to me a loved, honored, and precious personal friend; a man possessing the exalted and matured intellect of a statesman, with the pure and artless heart of a child. Upon any issue, as between him and others, when the right seemed in anywise doubtful, I should have followed his counsel and advice. But the annexation of Santo Domingo, to my understanding, did not seem to be any such question. The reasons in its favor were many and obvious; and those against it, as I thought, were easily answered. To Mr. Sumner, annexation was a measure to extinguish a colored nation, and to do so by dishonorable means and for selfish motives. To me it meant the alliance of a weak and defenseless people, having few or none of the attributes of a nation, torn and rent by internal feuds and unable to maintain order at home or command respect abroad, to a government which would give it peace, stability, prosperity, and civilization, and make it helpful to both countries. To favor annexation at the time when Santo Domingo asked for a place in our union, was a very different thing from what it was when Cuba and Central America were sought by fillibustering expeditions.[3] When the slave power bore rule, and a spirit of injustice and oppression animated and controlled every part of our government, I was for limiting our dominion to the smallest possible margin; but since liberty and equality have become the law of our land, I am for

1. Now called Memorial Day. Douglass spoke on May 30, 1871. Santo Domingo is the capital of the Dominican Republic on the island of Hispaniola in the Caribbean Sea.

2. Served in 1881 as twentieth president of the United States. Charles Sumner, Republican Party leader and U.S. senator. Ulysses S. Grant, eighteenth president of the United States (1869–77). Fish, U.S. secretary of state (1869–77). Rutherford B. Hayes, nineteenth president of the United States (1877–81).

3. Private American citizens intent on seizing governmental control of Latin American countries such as Cuba, Nicaragua, and Costa Rica between 1830 and 1860.

extending our dominion whenever and wherever such extension can peaceably and honorably, and with the approval and desire of all the parties concerned, be accomplished. Santo Domingo wanted to come under our government upon the terms thus described; and for more reasons than I can stop here to give, I then believed, and do now believe, it would have been wise to have received her into our sisterhood of States.

The idea that annexation meant degradation to a colored nation was altogether fanciful; there was no more dishonor to Santo Domingo in making her a State of the American Union, than in making Kansas, Nebraska, or any other territory such a State. It was giving to a part the strength of the whole, and lifting what must be despised for its isolation into an organization and relationship which would compel consideration and respect.

* * *

An appointment to any important and lucrative office under the United States government usually brings its recipient a large measure of praise and congratulation on the one hand, and much abuse and disparagement on the other; and he may think himself singularly fortunate if the censure does not exceed the praise. I need not dwell upon the causes of this extravagance, but I may say that there is no office of any value in the country which is not desired and sought by many persons equally meritorious and equally deserving. But as only one person can be appointed to any one office, only one can be pleased, while many are offended. Unhappily, resentment follows disappointment, and this resentment often finds expression in disparagement and abuse of the successful man. As in most else that I have said, I borrow this reflection from my own experience.

My appointment as United States Marshal of the District of Columbia,[4] was in keeping with the rest of my life, as a free-man. It was an innovation upon long established usage, and opposed to the general current of sentiment in the community. It came upon the people of the District as a gross surprise, and almost a punishment; and provoked something like a scream—I will not say a *yell*—of popular displeasure. As soon as I was named by President Hayes for the place, efforts were made by members of the bar to defeat my confirmation before the Senate. All sorts of reasons against my appointment, but the true one, were given, and that was withheld more from a sense of shame, than from a sense of justice. The apprehension doubtless was, that if appointed marshal, I would surround myself with colored deputies, colored bailiffs and colored messengers and pack the jury-box with colored jurors; in a word, Africanize the courts. But the most dreadful thing threatened, was a colored man at the *Executive Mansion* in white kid gloves, sparrow-tailed coat, patent-leather boots, and alabaster cravat, performing the ceremony—a very empty one—of introducing the aristocratic citizens of the republic to the President of the United States. This was something entirely too much to be borne; and men asked themselves in view of it, To what is the world coming? and where will these things stop? Dreadful! Dreadful!

It is creditable to the manliness of the American Senate, that it was moved by none of these things, and that it lost no time in the matter of my confirmation. I learn, and believe my information correct, that foremost among those who supported my confirmation against the objections made to it, was Hon. Roscoe Conkling of New York. His speech in executive session is said by the senators who heard it, to have been one of the most masterly and eloquent

4. From 1877 to 1881.

ever delivered on the floor of the Senate; and this too I readily believe, for Mr. Conkling possesses the ardor and fire of Henry Clay, the subtlety of Calhoun, and the massive grandeur of Daniel Webster.[5]

* * *

In all my forty years of thought and labor to promote the freedom and welfare of my race, I never found myself more widely and painfully at variance with leading colored men of the country than when I opposed the effort to set in motion a wholesale exodus of colored people of the South to the Northern States;[6] and yet I never took a position in which I felt myself better fortified by reason and necessity. It was said of me, that I had deserted to the old master class, and that I was a traitor to my race; that I had run away from slavery myself, and yet I was opposing others in doing the same. When my opponents condescended to argue, they took the ground that the colored people of the South needed to be brought into contact with the freedom and civilization of the North; that no emancipated and persecuted people ever had or ever could rise in the presence of the people by whom they had been enslaved, and that the true remedy for the ills which the freedmen were suffering, was to initiate the Israelitish departure from our modern Egypt to a land abounding, if not in "milk and honey,"[7] certainly in pork and hominy.

Influenced, no doubt, by the dazzling prospects held out to them by the advocates of the exodus movement, thousands of poor, hungry, naked and destitute colored people were induced to quit the South amid the frosts and snows of a dreadful winter in search of a better country. I regret to say that there was something sinister in this so-called exodus, for it transpired that some of the agents most active in promoting it had an understanding with certain railroad companies, by which they were to receive one dollar per head upon all such passengers. Thousands of these poor people, traveling only so far as they had money to bear their expenses, were dropped in the extremest destitution on the levees of St. Louis, and their tales of woe were such as to move a heart much less sensitive to human suffering than mine. But while I felt for these poor deluded people, and did what I could to put a stop to their ill-advised and ill-arranged stampede, I also did what I could to assist such of them as were within my reach, who were on their way to this land of promise. Hundreds of these people came to Washington, and at one time there were from two to three hundred lodgers here unable to get further for the want of money. I lost no time in appealing to my friends for the means of assisting them.

* * *

From *Third Part*

CHAPTER I. LATER LIFE

Ten years ago when the preceding chapters of this book were written,[8] having then reached in the journey of life the middle of the decade beginning

5. Henry Clay, John C. Calhoun, and Daniel Webster were pre–Civil War national political leaders renowned for their oratory.
6. The migration of African Americans from the South to the Midwest, especially Kansas, in search of economic opportunity and legal protection, gained national attention in 1879. Lengthier excerpts from Douglass's paper, "The Negro Exodus from the Gulf States," which was read to the American Social Sciences Association at Saratoga, New York, on September 12, 1879, are reprinted later in this volume.
7. Numbers 13:27.
8. The first edition of *Life and Times of Frederick Douglass* was published in 1881. In 1892 Douglass revised and updated the *Life and Times*.

at sixty and ending at seventy, and naturally reminded that I was no longer young, I laid aside my pen with some such sense of relief as might be felt by a weary and over-burdened traveler when arrived at the desired end of a long journey, or as an honest debtor wishing to be square with all the world might feel when the last dollar of an old debt was paid off. Not that I wished to be discharged from labor and service in the cause to which I have devoted my life, but from this peculiar kind of labor and service. I hardly need say to those who know me, that writing for the public eye never came quite as easily to me as speaking to the public ear. It is a marvel to me that under the circumstances I learned to write at all. It has been a still greater marvel that in the brief working period in which they lived and wrought, such men as Dickens, Dumas, Carlyle and Sir Walter Scott[9] could have produced the works ascribed to them. But many have been the impediments with which I have had to struggle. I have, too, been embarrassed by the thought of writing so much about myself when there was so much else of which to write. It is far easier to write about others than about one's self. I write freely of myself, not from choice, but because I have, by my cause, been morally forced into thus writing. Time and events have summoned me to stand forth both as a witness and an advocate for a people long dumb, not allowed to speak for themselves, yet much misunderstood and deeply wronged. In the earlier days of my freedom, I was called upon to expose the direful nature of the slave system, by telling my own experience while a slave, and to do what I could thereby to make slavery odious and thus to hasten the day of emancipation. It was no time to mince matters or to stand upon a delicate sense of propriety, in the presence of a crime so gigantic as our slavery was, and the duty to oppose it so imperative. I was called upon to expose even my stripes, and with many misgivings obeyed the summons and tried thus to do my whole duty in this my first public work and what I may say proved to be the best work of my life.

Fifty years have passed since I entered upon that work, and now that it is ended, I find myself summoned again by the popular voice and by what is called the negro problem, to come a second time upon the witness stand and give evidence upon disputed points concerning myself and my emancipated brothers and sisters who, though free, are yet oppressed and are in as much need of an advocate as before they were set free. Though this is not altogether as agreeable to me as was my first mission, it is one that comes with such commanding authority as to compel me to accept it as a present duty. In it I am pelted with all sorts of knotty questions, some of which might be difficult even for Humboldt, Cuvier or Darwin,[1] were they alive, to answer. They are questions which range over the whole field of science, learning and philosophy, and some descend to the depths of impertinent, unmannerly and vulgar curiosity. To be able to answer the higher range of these questions I should be profoundly versed in psychology, anthropology, ethnology, sociology, theology, biology, and all the other ologies, philosophies and sciences. There is no disguising the fact that the American people are much interested and mystified about the mere matter of color as connected with manhood. It seems to them that color has some moral or immoral qualities and especially the latter. They do not feel quite reconciled to the idea that a

9. Charles Dickens, Alexandre Dumas, Thomas Carlyle, and Sir Walter Scott were all 19th-century European literary figures.

1. Nineteenth-century scientists. Alexander von Humboldt, German naturalist. George Cuvier, French zoologist. Charles Darwin, English naturalist and evolutionist.

man of different color from themselves should have all the human rights claimed by themselves. When an unknown man is spoken of in their presence, the first question that arises in the average American mind concerning him and which must be answered is, Of what color is he? and he rises or falls in estimation by the answer given. It is not whether he is a good man or a bad man. That does not seem of primary importance. Hence I have often been bluntly and sometimes very rudely asked, of what color my mother was, and of what color was my father? In what proportion does the blood of the various races mingle in my veins, especially how much white blood and how much black blood entered into my composition? Whether I was not part Indian as well as African and Caucasian? Whether I considered myself more African than Caucasian, or the reverse? Whether I derived my intelligence from my father, or from my mother, from my white, or from my black blood? Whether persons of mixed blood are as strong and healthy as persons of either of the races whose blood they inherit? Whether persons of mixed blood do permanently remain of the mixed complexion or finally take on the complexion of one or the other of the two or more races of which they may be composed? Whether they live as long and raise as large families as other people? Whether they inherit only evil from both parents and good from neither? Whether evil dispositions are more transmissible than good? Why did I marry a person of my father's complexion instead of marrying one of my mother's complexion? How is the race problem to be solved in this country? Will the negro go back to Africa or remain here? Under this shower of purely American questions, more or less personal, I have endeavored to possess my soul in patience and get as much good out of life as was possible with so much to occupy my time; and, though often perplexed, seldom losing my temper, or abating heart or hope for the future of my people. Though I cannot say I have satisfied the curiosity of my countrymen on all the questions raised by them, I have, like all honest men on the witness stand, answered to the best of my knowledge and belief, and I hope I have never answered in such wise as to increase the hardships of any human being of whatever race or color.

When the first part of this book was written, I was, as before intimated, already looking toward the sunset of human life and thinking that my children would probably finish the recital of my life, or that possibly some other persons outside of family ties to whom I am known might think it worth while to tell what he or she might know of the remainder of my story. I considered, as I have said, that my work was done. But friends and publishers concur in the opinion that the unity and completeness of the work require that it shall be finished by the hand by which it was begun.

Many things touched me and employed my thoughts and activities between the years 1881 and 1891. I am willing to speak of them. Like most men who give the world their autobiographies I wish my story to be told as favorably towards myself as it can be with a due regard to truth. I do not wish it to be imagined by any that I am insensible to the singularity of my career, or to the peculiar relation I sustain to the history of my time and country. I know and feel that it is something to have lived at all in this Republic during the latter part of this eventful century, but I know it is more to have had some small share in the great events which have distinguished it from the experience of all other centuries. No man liveth unto himself,[2] or ought to live unto

2. Romans 14:7.

himself. My life has conformed to this Bible saying, for, more than most men, I have been the thin edge of the wedge to open for my people a way in many directions and places never before occupied by them. It has been mine, in some degree, to stand as their defense in moral battle against the shafts of detraction, calumny and persecution, and to labor in removing and overcoming those obstacles which, in the shape of erroneous ideas and customs, have blocked the way to their progress. I have found this to be no hardship, but the natural and congenial vocation of my life. I had hardly become a thinking being when I first learned to hate slavery, and hence I was no sooner free than I joined the noble band of Abolitionists in Massachusetts, headed by William Lloyd Garrison and Wendell Phillips. Afterward, by voice and pen, in season and out of season, it was mine to stand for the freedom of people of all colors, until in our land the last yoke was broken and the last bondsman was set free. In the war for the Union I persuaded the colored man to become a soldier. In the peace that followed, I asked the Government to make him a citizen. In the construction of the rebellious States I urged his enfranchisement.

Much has been written and published during the last ten years purporting to be a history of the anti-slavery movement and of the part taken by the men and women engaged in it, myself among the number. In some of these narrations I have received more consideration and higher estimation than I perhaps deserved. In others I have not escaped undeserved disparagement, which I may leave to the reader and to the judgment of those who shall come after me to reply to and to set right.

The anti-slavery movement, that truly great moral conflict which rocked the land during thirty years, and the part taken by the men and women engaged in it, are not quite far enough removed from us in point of time to admit at present of an impartial history. Some of the sects and parties that took part in it still linger with us and are zealous for distinction, for priority and superiority. There is also the disposition to unduly magnify the importance of some men and to diminish the importance of others. While over all this I spread the mantle of charity, it may in a measure explain whatever may seem like prejudice, bigotry and partiality in some attempts already made at the history of the anti-slavery movement. As in a great war, amid the roar of cannon, the smoke of powder, the rising dust and the blinding blaze of fire and counterfire of battle, no one participant may be blamed for not being able to see and correctly to measure and report the efficiency of the different forces engaged, and to render honor where honor is due; so we may say of the late historians who have essayed to write the history of the anti-slavery movement. It is not strange that those who write in New England from the stand occupied by William Lloyd Garrison and his friends, should fail to appreciate the services of the political abolitionists and of the Free Soil and Republican parties. Perhaps a political abolitionist would equally misjudge and underrate the value of the non-voting and moral-suasion party, of which Mr. Garrison was the admitted leader; while in fact the two were the halves necessary to make the whole. Without Adams, Giddings, Hale, Chase, Wade, Seward, Wilson and Sumner[3] to plead our cause in the councils of the nation, the taskmasters would have remained the contented and undisturbed rulers of the Union, and no condition of things would have been brought about autho-

3. John Quincy Adams, Joshua R. Giddings, John Parker Hale, Salmon P. Chase, Benjamin F. Wade, William H. Seward, Henry Wilson, and Charles Sumner were leading figures in the American antislavery movement.

rizing the Federal Government to abolish slavery in the country's defense. As one of those whose bonds have been broken, I cannot see without pain any attempt to disparage and undervalue any man's work in this cause.

Hereafter, when we get a little farther away from the conflict, some brave and truth-loving man, with all the facts before him, uninfluenced by filial love and veneration for men, or party associations, or pride of name, will gather from here and there the scattered fragments, my small contribution perhaps among the number, and give to those who shall come after us an impartial history of this the grandest moral conflict of the century. Truth is patient and time is just. With these and like reflections, which have often brought consolation to better men than myself, when upon them has fallen the keen edge of censure, and with the scrupulous justice done me in the biography of myself lately written by Mr. Frederick May Holland[4] of Concord, Massachusetts, I can easily rest contented.

1892

4. *Frederick Douglass, the Colored Orator* (1891).

JAMES M. WHITFIELD
1822–1871

Admired and endorsed by both Frederick Douglass and William Wells Brown, James Monroe Whitfield's artistry and commitment to his people's advancement earned him lasting recognition as the standard bearer of Black America's antislavery poets. Yet even in his own time Whitfield's achievement was sometimes measured more by what he and others felt he could have attained than by what he actually did accomplish as a poet. Douglass was perhaps the first to declare Whitfield a disheartening example of genius shackled to an uninspiring job—that of barbering—that sapped the poet's energies and consumed his time while returning to him and his family only minimal financial reward. Some of Whitfield's contemporaries, including Martin R. Delany, thought the barber-poet had the potential to become another Edgar Allan Poe, the epitome of blighted genius among antebellum white American poets, or John Greenleaf Whittier, the leading white antislavery poet of the time. Though never enslaved, Whitfield may have felt affinities with George Moses Horton, who pictured himself in some of his poems as unfairly handicapped and frustrated by the white supremacist United States. But it is also possible that Whitfield's sense of himself was more in line with Langston Hughes's self-characterization in his poem "Me and the Mule," which concludes by the poet's affirming, unapologetically, that like his mule he's "Black—and don't give a damn! / You got to take me / Like I am."

James M. Whitfield was born free in Exeter, New Hampshire, in 1822. His father had escaped Virginia slavery; his mother was the sister of influential Black ministers in Massachusetts whose antislavery activism shaped James's early social and political consciousness. After moving to Buffalo, New York, in his teens, Whitfield became active in the city's Union Moral and Mental Improvement Society, which had been founded by African Americans. In his late teens he became a barber, working in a basement shop in Buffalo. His business prospered, allowing him to purchase a house for himself and his family. Active in progressive causes, Whitfield met both Douglass and Delany at the 1848 national convention of the Free-Soil party held in Buffalo. From 1849 to 1852, readers of Douglass's newspapers, the *North Star* and *Frederick Douglass' Paper,* found Whitfield's impassioned antislavery poetry published on a regular basis. In 1852, Delany's landmark volume, *The Condition . . . of the Colored People of the United States*, hailed Whitfield as "one of the purest poets in America."

In 1853 Whitfield assembled the book for which he is remembered, *America and Other Poems,* seeing it through to publication at his own expense in Buffalo. The anonymous writer of the introduction to the volume, probably Whitfield himself, appealed to the buying public for support so that the poet, "a poor colored man," might "fully develop the talent which God hath given him." Although *America and Other Poems* was well received in the antislavery press, it did not compensate Whitfield sufficiently to enable him to devote himself full time to writing. The collection did demonstrate that an important self- and socially conscious African American poet had arrived. Reviewers in Whitfield's own time as well as more recent critics have recognized the poet's craftsmanship, especially in his use of classical imagery, his high seriousness, and his engagement with both political and lyric traditions of British and American poetry. Whitfield's distinctive powers of satire and invective have been praised frequently. The title poem of the collection, the 160-line "America," begins as a sardonic parody of "America," a nationalistic hymn familiar to all Whitfield's countrymen. Whitfield's "America" develops a systematic and trenchant analysis of the hypocrisies and lies that undergirded "slavery's accursed plan" for the nation. Despite the moral outrage and bitterness of the poet's attack on slavery, however, "America" closes in the spirit of a prayer of supplication to a just God and "the sacred name of peace, / Of justice, virtue, love and truth" to "burst the bonds of every slave." Some readers have called Whitfield a cynical and pessimistic poet imitative of Byron in both the form and mood of his verse. But in "Self-Reliance," Whitfield rejected despair and self-seeking, exalting instead those dedicated to "the eternal good of all alike, the high or low." Of the twenty-four poems in *America and Other Poems*, half address nonracial themes, celebrating music, romantic love, the founding of churches, and holidays such as Christmas. Urgent political and social issues of his day made Whitfield a "Black nationalist bard," as one critic has termed him, but the range of his verse shows that he aimed to be recognized and respected as a multi-faceted artist.

In 1854 Whitfield affiliated himself with Martin R. Delany, one of the foremost champions of Black emigration, and helped to organize that year's National Emigration Convention of Colored People in Cleveland, Ohio. Later in the decade Whitfield may have traveled to Central America or Haiti, commissioned to search for likely settlement locales for African Americans disenchanted with the United States. The outbreak of the Civil War found Whitfield and his family in San Francisco, where he operated his own barbershop and joined a local Black Masonic lodge. He traveled extensively in the Northwest in the 1860s, but spent most of his time in San Francisco. For the *San Francisco Elevator,* an African American newspaper, he wrote occasional poems until the spring 1870. His last poems register Whitfield's optimism about the prospects for liberty and democracy in Reconstruction America. Whitfield remains nineteenth-century Black America's most eloquent example of the poet as tribune of his people, "wielding, with unfaltering arm, / The utmost power which God has given."

America

America, it is to thee,
Thou boasted land of liberty,—
It is to thee I raise my song,
Thou land of blood, and crime, and wrong.
It is to thee, my native land,
From whence has issued many a band

To tear the black man from his soil,
And force him here to delve and toil;
Chained on your blood-bemoistened sod,
Cringing beneath a tyrant's rod,
Stripped of those rights which Nature's God
  Bequeathed to all the human race,
Bound to a petty tyrant's nod,
  Because he wears a paler face.
Was it for this, that freedom's fires
Were kindled by your patriot sires?
Was it for this, they shed their blood,
On hill and plain, on field and flood?
Was it for this, that wealth and life
Were staked upon that desperate strife,
Which drenched this land for seven long years
With blood of men, and women's tears?
When black and white fought side by side,
  Upon the well-contested field,—
Turned back the fierce opposing tide,
  And made the proud invader yield—
When, wounded, side by side they lay,
  And heard with joy the proud hurrah
From their victorious comrades say
  That they had waged successful war,
The thought ne'er entered in their brains
That they endured those toils and pains,
To forge fresh fetters, heavier chains
For their own children, in whose veins
Should flow that patriotic blood,
So freely shed on field and flood.
Oh no; they fought, as they believed,
  For the inherent rights of man;
But mark, how they have been deceived
  By slavery's accursed plan.
They never thought, when thus they shed
  Their heart's best blood, in freedom's cause.
That their own sons would live in dread,
  Under unjust, oppressive laws:
That those who quietly enjoyed
  The rights for which they fought and fell,
Could be the framers of a code,
  That would disgrace the fiends of hell!
Could they have looked, with prophet's ken,° *knowledge*
  Down to the present evil time,
  Seen free-born men, uncharged with crime,
Consigned unto a slaver's pen,—
Or thrust into a prison cell,
With thieves and murderers to dwell—
While that same flag whose stripes and stars
Had been their guide through freedom's wars
As proudly waved above the pen
Of dealers in the souls of men!
Or could the shades° of all the dead, *spirits*
  Who fell beneath that starry flag,

Visit the scenes where they once bled,
  On hill and plain, on vale and crag,
By peaceful brook, or ocean's strand,
  By inland lake, or dark green wood,
Where'er the soil of this wide land
  Was moistened by their patriot blood,—
And then survey the country o'er,
  From north to south, from east to west,
And hear the agonizing cry
Ascending up to God on high,
From western wilds to ocean's shore,
  The fervent prayer of the oppressed;
The cry of helpless infancy
  Torn from the parent's fond caress
By some base tool of tyranny,
  And doomed to woe and wretchedness;
The indignant wail of fiery youth,
  Its noble aspirations crushed,
Its generous zeal, its love of truth,
  Trampled by tyrants in the dust;
The aerial piles which fancy reared,
  And hopes too bright to be enjoyed,
Have passed and left his young heart scared,
  And all its dreams of bliss destroyed.
The shriek of virgin purity,
  Doomed to some libertine's embrace,
Should rouse the strongest sympathy
  Of each one of the human race;
And weak old age, oppressed with care,
  As he reviews the scene of strife,
Puts up to God a fervent prayer,
  To close his dark and troubled life.
The cry of fathers, mothers, wives,
  Severed from all their hearts hold dear,
And doomed to spend their wretched lives
  In gloom, and doubt, and hate, and fear;
And manhood, too, with soul of fire,
And arm of strength, and smothered ire,
Stands pondering with brow of gloom,
Upon his dark unhappy doom,
Whether to plunge in battle's strife,
And buy his freedom with his life,
And with stout heart and weapon strong,
Pay back the tyrant wrong for wrong,
Or wait the promised time of God,
  When his Almighty ire shall wake,
And smite the oppressor in his wrath,
And hurl red ruin in his path,
And with the terrors of his rod,
  Cause adamantine° hearts to quake. *unyielding*
Here Christian writhes in bondage still,
  Beneath his brother Christian's rod,
And pastors trample down at will,
  The image of the living God.

While prayers go up in lofty strains,
And pealing hymns ascend to heaven,
The captive, toiling in his chains,
With tortured limbs and bosom riven,
Raises his fettered hand on high,
And in the accents of despair,
To him who rules both earth and sky,
Puts up a sad, a fervent prayer,
To free him from the awful blast
Of slavery's bitter galling shame—
Although his portion should be cast
With demons in eternal flame!
Almighty God! 'tis this they call
The land of liberty and law;
Part of its sons in baser thrall
Than Babylon[1] or Egypt saw—
Worse scenes of rapine, lust and shame,
Than Babylonian ever knew,
Are perpetrated in the name
Of God, the holy, just, and true;
And darker doom than Egypt felt,[2]
May yet repay this nation's guilt.
Almighty God! thy aid impart,
And fire anew each faltering heart,
And strengthen every patriot's hand,
Who aims to save our native land.
We do not come before thy throne,
With carnal weapons drenched in gore,
Although our blood has freely flown,
In adding to the tyrant's store.
Father! before thy throne we come,
Not in the panoply of war,
With pealing trump, and rolling drum,
And cannon booming loud and far;
Striving in blood to wash out blood,
Through wrong to seek redress for wrong;
For while thou'rt holy, just and good,
The battle is not to the strong;
But in the sacred name of peace,
Of justice, virtue, love and truth,
We pray, and never mean to cease,
Till weak old age and fiery youth
In freedom's cause their voices raise,
And burst the bonds of every slave;
Till, north and south, and east and west,
The wrongs we bear shall be redressed.

1853

1. Ancient city of Mesopotamia and center of an empire that flourished in the 6th century B.C.E.

2. A reference to the plagues described in Exodus 7–12 suffered by Egypt because of its resistance to the liberation of the Hebrews.

Self-Reliance

I love the man whose lofty mind
  On God and its own strength relies;
Who seeks the welfare of his kind,
  And dare be honest though he dies;
Who cares not for the world's applause,
  But, to his own fixed purpose true,
The path which God and nature's laws
  Point out, doth earnestly pursue.
When adverse clouds around him lower,
  And stern oppression bars his way,
When friends desert in trial's hour,
  And hope sheds but a feeble ray;
When all the powers of earth and hell
  Combine to break his spirit down,
And strive, with their terrific yell,
  To crush his soul beneath their frown—
When numerous friends, whose cheerful tone
  In happier hours once cheered him on,
With visions that full brightly shone,
  But now, alas! are dimmed and gone!
When love, which in his bosom burned
  With all the fire of ardent youth,
And which he fondly thought returned
  With equal purity and truth,
Mocking his hopes, falls to the ground,
  Like some false vision of the night,
Its vows a hollow, empty sound,
  Scathing his heart with deadly blight,
Choking that welling spring of love,
Which lifts the soul to God above,
In bonds mysterious to unite
The finite with the infinite;
And draw a blessing from above,
Of infinite on finite love.
When hopes of better, fear of worse,
  Alike are fled, and naught remains
To stimulate him on his course:
  No hope of bliss, no fear of pains
Fiercer than what already rend,
  With tortures keen, his inmost heart,
Without a hope, without a friend,
  With nothing to allay the smart
From blighted love, affections broken,
  From blasted hopes and cankering care,
When every thought, each word that's spoken
  Urges him onward to despair.
When through the opening vista round,
  Shines on him no pellucid° ray, *transparent*
Like beam of early morning found,
  The harbinger of perfect day;

But like the midnight's darkening frown,
  When stormy tempests rear on high,
When pealing thunder shakes the ground,
  And lurid lightning rends the sky!
When clothed in more than midnight gloom,
Like some foul specter from the tomb,
Despair, with stern and fell control,
Sits brooding o'er his inmost soul—
'Tis then the faithful mind is proved,
  That, true alike to man and God,
By all the ills of life unmoved,
  Pursues its straight and narrow road.
For such a man the siren song
  Of pleasure hath no lasting charm;
Nor can the mighty and the strong
  His spirit tame with powerful arm.
His pleasure is to wipe the tear
  Of sorrow from the mourner's cheek,
The languid, fainting heart to cheer,
  To succor and protect the weak.
When the bright face of fortune smiles
  Upon his path with cheering ray,
And pleasure, with alluring wiles,
  Flatters, to lead his heart astray,
His soul in conscious virtue strong,
  And armed with innate rectitude,
Loving the right, detesting wrong,
  And seeking the eternal good
Of all alike, the high or low,
His dearest friend, or direst foe,
Seeks out the brave and faithful few,
Who, to themselves and Maker true,
Dare, in the name and fear of God,
To spread the living truth abroad!
Armed with the same sustaining power,
Against adversity's dark hour,
And from the deep deceitful guile
Which lurks in pleasure's hollow smile,
Or from the false and fitful beam
  That marks ambition's meteor fire,
Or from the dark and lurid gleam
  Revealing passion's deadly ire.
His steadfast soul fearing no harm,
  But trusting in the aid of Heaven,
And wielding, with unfaltering arm,
  The utmost power which God has given—
Conscious that the Almighty power
  Will nerve the faithful soul with might,
Whatever storms may round him lower,
  Strikes boldly for the true and right.

1853

WILLIAM CRAFT
1824–1900

ELLEN CRAFT
1826–1891

Perhaps the most sensational story of the escape of enslaved people from the South came to light on January 4, 1849, when William Wells Brown announced in a letter to the *Liberator* the first account of what would become *Running a Thousand Miles for Freedom; or, the Escape of William and Ellen Craft from Slavery*. Brown's sketch of the Crafts and their flight anticipated the images and themes that the antislavery movement would publicize extensively about the couple over the next decade throughout North America and Great Britain:

> One of the most interesting cases of the escape of fugitives from American slavery that have ever come before the American people, has just occurred, under the following circumstances: – William and Ellen Crapt [sic], man and wife, lived with different masters in the State of Georgia. Ellen is so near white, that she can pass without suspicion for a white woman. Her husband is much darker. He is a mechanic, and by working nights and Sundays, he laid up money enough to bring himself and his wife out of slavery. Their plan was without precedent; and though novel, was the means of getting them their freedom. Ellen dressed in man's clothing, and passed as the master, while her husband passed as the servant. In this way they travelled from Georgia to Philadelphia. They are now out of the reach of the blood-hounds of the South. On their journey, they put up at the best hotels where they stopped. Neither of them can read or write. And Ellen, knowing that she would be called upon to write her name at the hotels, &c., tied her right hand up as though it was lame, which proved of some service to her, as she was called upon several times at hotels to 'register' her name. In Charleston, S.C., they put up at the hotel which Gov. M'Duffie and John C. Calhoun generally make their home, yet these distinguished advocates of the 'peculiar institution' say that the slaves cannot take care of themselves. They arrived in Philadelphia, in four days from the time they started. Their history, especially that of their escape, is replete with interest. They will be at the meeting of the Massachusetts Anti-Slavery Society, in Boston, in the latter part of this month, where I know the history of their escape will be listened to with great interest. They are very intelligent. They are young, Ellen 22, and Wm. 24 years of age. Ellen is truly a heroine.

Brown's prediction that "the history of their escape will be listened to with great interest" proved a considerable understatement. As news of their story spread, antislavery activists quickly enlisted the Crafts in the cause and put them on the lecture circuit in Massachusetts, where they were commonly exhibited to curious crowds, fascinated as much by the contrast between Ellen's and William's complexions as by the story of their intrepid escape. They married and settled in Boston. Denied by racism to engage in the carpentry trade he had learned while enslaved, William opened a used-furniture business. Within a year, however, after the passage of the Fugitive Slave Act in 1850, the Crafts had to take flight to find refuge ultimately in England. There they pursued their educations and bought a home in a West London suburb while lecturing for the British antislavery movement. In 1860 they brought out *Running a Thousand Miles for Freedom* from a British publisher. The book was popular enough to go through at least two editions in England alone.

Returning to the United States in 1869, the Crafts opened a school near Savannah, Georgia, which was destroyed by Ku Klux Klan arsonists in 1871. Two years later,

Portrait of Ellen Craft in the men's clothes that she wore for her and her husband's 1848 escape; this was the frontispiece to *Running a Thousand Miles for Freedom* (1860).

William raised enough money from Bostonians to purchase a farm near Savannah, Georgia, where he and Ellen established a co-operative school for the formerly enslaved. In 1876 some of the school's financial backers accused William of misappropriating funds. William's suit for libel was turned down by a Boston court in 1878. Gradually the school sank into bankruptcy and closed by 1880. In 1890 the Crafts moved to Charleston, where Ellen died a year later in their daughter's home. William continued to struggle financially, losing his remaining land to bank foreclosure in 1899. He died a year later in Charleston.

Because Ellen and William Craft had been comparatively fortunate to have been enslaved in a town and had not been subjected to the harsh regime of plantation life, *Running a Thousand Miles for Freedom* says little about slavery as an institution but a great deal about white supremacy as an all-pervading code not only in the slaveholding South but also in the supposedly more enlightened North. The Crafts' bid for sympathy and justice based on their experience does not derive from the physical suffering and deprivation that Frederick Douglass, William Wells Brown, and Harriet Jacobs detailed in their narratives. *Running a Thousand Miles for Freedom* emphasizes the threat that slavery represented to the love and mutual devotion of African American spouses. Heart-rending scenes of families separated on the auction plot punctuate many slave narratives and the antislavery fiction, such as Harriet Beecher Stowe's *Uncle Tom's Cabin* (1852), that emerged from such narratives. But the Crafts riveted their readers' attention to their plight by dramatizing the threats to their union that confronted them every step of their four-day, thousand-mile journey. Their story also demonstrates the bravery and grace under pressure, as well as the loving commitment, that sustained the Crafts through every trial. By attributing their shrewd plotting, elaborate disguises, and calculated deceit to their dedication to their marriage, the Crafts lured readers into a sympathetic response to the most socially transgressive aspects of the couple's flight—Ellen's flouting of gender as well as racial norms through her deliberate, and quite expert, passing for a white male southern enslaver. Brown's praise of Ellen as "truly a heroine" undoubtedly stems as much from his appreciation of her consummate trickster performance on the road as from her equally convincing assumption of a traditionally lady-like demeanor once she reached freedom. Brown's novel, *Clotel* (1853), pays tribute to Ellen's famous example by recounting a similar journey by his cross-dressing, near-white title character, accompanied by a dark-skinned stalwart named William, from Mississippi to Cincinnati.

A salient difference between *Running a Thousand Miles for Freedom* and *Clotel* emerges in Part II of the Crafts' narrative. While most pre-1865 slave narratives focus on the rigors of the flight to freedom and climax in the fugitive's fulfilling transition into a new life in the North, the Crafts' quest for freedom in the North reaches an at best ironic conclusion. No sooner do they arrive in Philadelphia than they feel in danger of recapture and soon move on to Boston, the epicenter of anti-slavery activism in the United States. After settling in Boston, where William works as a cabinetmaker and Ellen a seamstress, their former enslavers' efforts to reclaim them oblige the couple to "fly from under the Stars and Stripes to save our liberties and our lives." Arriving in New Brunswick, Canada, on their way to Nova Scotia, the Crafts encounter repeated discrimination and harassment because their differences in skin color lead hotel keepers and ticket agents to assume that Ellen could not be the wife of any man as dark as William. That the fugitives waited till they had settled in England to start their family represents the culmination of their odyssey and their marriage, both finally and fully liberated from what their narrative terms "Yankee" colorphobia in Canada as well as the United States.

From Running a Thousand Miles for Freedom

From *Part I*

"God gave us only over beast, fish, fowl,
Dominion absolute; that right we hold
By his donation. But man over man
He made not lord; such title to himself
Reserving, human left from human free."
MILTON[1]

My wife and myself were born in different towns in the State of Georgia, which is one of the principal slave States. It is true, our condition as slaves was not by any means the worst; but the mere idea that we were held as chattels, and deprived of all legal rights—the thought that we had to give up our hard earnings to a tyrant, to enable him to live in idleness and luxury—the thought that we could not call the bones and sinews that God gave us our own: but above all, the fact that another man had the power to tear from our cradle the new-born babe and sell it in the shambles like a brute, and then scourge us if we dared to lift a finger to save it from such a fate, haunted us for years.

But in December, 1848, a plan suggested itself that proved quite successful, and in eight days after it was first thought of we were free from the horrible trammels of slavery, rejoicing and praising God in the glorious sunshine of liberty.

My wife's first master was her father, and her mother his slave, and the latter is still the slave of his widow.

Notwithstanding my wife being of African extraction on her mother's side, she is almost white—in fact, she is so nearly so that the tyrannical old lady to whom she first belonged became so annoyed, at finding her frequently mistaken for a child of the family, that she gave her when eleven years of age to a daughter, as a wedding present. This separated my wife from her mother, and also from several other dear friends. But the incessant cruelty of her old mistress made the change of owners or treatment so desirable, that she did not grumble much at this cruel separation.

* * *

[William Craft, apprenticed to a cabinetmaker in Macon, Georgia, married Ellen Smith in 1846.]

After puzzling our brains for years, we were reluctantly driven to the sad conclusion, that it was almost impossible to escape from slavery in Georgia,

1. John Milton (1608–1674), *Paradise Lost*, book 12, lines 67–71.

and travel 1,000 miles across the slave States. We therefore resolved to get the consent of our owners, be married, settle down in slavery, and endeavour to make ourselves as comfortable as possible under that system; but at the same time ever to keep our dim eyes steadily fixed upon the glimmering hope of liberty, and earnestly pray God mercifully to assist us to escape from our unjust thraldom.

We were married, and prayed and toiled on till December, 1848, at which time (as I have stated) a plan suggested itself that proved quite sucessful, and in eight days after it was first thought of we were free from the horrible trammels of slavery, and glorifying God who had brought us safely out of a land of bondage.

Knowing that slaveholders have the privilege of taking their slaves to any part of the country they think proper, it occurred to me that, as my wife was nearly white, I might get her to disguise herself as an invalid gentleman, and assume to be my master, while I could attend as his slave, and that in this manner we might effect our escape. After I thought of the plan, I suggested it to my wife, but at first she shrank from the idea. She thought it was almost impossible for her to assume that disguise, and travel a distance of 1,000 miles across the slave States. However, on the other hand, she also thought of her condition. She saw that the laws under which we lived did not recognize her to be a woman, but a mere chattel, to be bought and sold, or otherwise dealt with as her owner might see fit. Therefore the more she contemplated her helpless condition, the more anxious she was to escape from it. So she said, "I think it is almost too much for us to undertake; however, I feel that God is on our side, and with his assistance, notwithstanding all the difficulties, we shall be able to succeed. Therefore, if you will purchase the disguise, I will try to carry out the plan."

But after I concluded to purchase the disguise, I was afraid to go to any one to ask him to sell me the articles. It is unlawful in Georgia for a white man to trade with slaves without the master's consent. But, notwithstanding this, many persons will sell a slave any article that he can get the money to buy. Not that they sympathize with the slave, but merely because his testimony is not admitted in court against a free white person.

Therefore, with little difficulty I went to different parts of the town, at odd times, and purchased things piece by piece, (except the trowsers which she found necessary to make,) and took them home to the house where my wife resided. She being a ladies' maid, and a favourite slave in the family, was allowed a little room to herself; and amongst other pieces of furniture which I had made in my overtime, was a chest of drawers; so when I took the articles home, she locked them up carefully in these drawers. No one about the premises knew that she had anything of the kind. So when we fancied we had everything ready the time was fixed for the flight. But we knew it would not do to start off without first getting our master's consent to be away for a few days. Had we left without this, they would soon have had us back into slavery, and probably we should never have got another fair opportunity of even attempting to escape.

Some of the best slaveholders will sometimes give their favourite slaves a few days' holiday at Christmas time; so, after no little amount of perseverance on my wife's part, she obtained a pass from her mistress, allowing her to be away for a few days. The cabinet-maker with whom I worked gave me a similar paper, but said that he needed my services very much, and wished me to return as soon as the time granted was up. I thanked him kindly; but somehow I have not been able to make it convenient to return yet; and, as the free air of good old England agrees so well with my wife and our dear little ones, as well as with myself, it is not at all likely we shall return at present to the "peculiar institution" of chains and stripes.

* * *

At first, we were highly delighted at the idea of having gained permission to be absent for a few days; but when the thought flashed across my wife's mind, that it was customary for travellers to register their names in the visitors' book at hotels, as well as in the clearance or Custom-house book at Charleston, South Carolina—it made our spirits droop within us.

So, while sitting in our little room upon the verge of despair, all at once my wife raised her head, and with a smile upon her face, which was a moment before bathed in tears, said, "I think I have it!" I asked what it was. She said, "I think I can make a poultice[2] and bind up my right hand in a sling, and with propriety ask the officers to register my name for me." I thought that would do.

It then occurred to her that the smoothness of her face might betray her; so she decided to make another poultice, and put it in a white handkerchief to be worn under the chin, up the cheeks, and to tie over the head. This nearly hid the expression of the countenance, as well as the beardless chin.

The poultice is left off in the engraving, because the likeness could not have been taken well with it on.

My wife, knowing that she would be thrown a good deal into the company of gentlemen, fancied that she could get on better if she had something to go over the eyes; so I went to a shop and bought a pair of green spectacles. This was in the evening.

We sat up all night discussing the plan, and making preparations. Just before the time arrived, in the morning, for us to leave, I cut off my wife's hair square at the back of the head, and got her to dress in the disguise and stand out on the floor. I found that she made a most respectable looking gentleman.

My wife had no ambition whatever to assume this disguise, and would not have done so had it been possible to have obtained our liberty by more simple means; but we knew it was not customary in the South for ladies to travel with male servants; and therefore, notwithstanding my wife's fair complexion, it would have been a very difficult task for her to have come off as a free white lady, with me as her slave; in fact, her not being able to write would have made this quite impossible. We knew that no public conveyance would take us, or any other slave, as a passenger, without our master's consent. This consent could never be obtained to pass into a free State. My wife's being muffled in the poultices, &c., furnished a plausible excuse for avoiding general conversation, of which most Yankee travellers are passionately fond.

* * *

When the time had arrived for us to start, we blew out the lights, knelt down, and prayed to our Heavenly Father mercifully to assist us, as he did his people of old, to escape from cruel bondage; and we shall ever feel that God heard and answered our prayer. Had we not been sustained by a kind, and I sometimes think special, providence, we could never have overcome the mountainous difficulties which I am now about to describe.

2. A soft medicated mass placed on a bandage and applied to a sore.

After this we rose and stood for a few moments in breathless silence,—we were afraid that some one might have been about the cottage listening and watching our movements. So I took my wife by the hand, stepped softly to the door, raised the latch, drew it open, and peeped out. Though there were trees all around the house, yet the foliage scarcely moved; in fact, everything appeared to be as still as death. I then whispered to my wife, "Come my dear, let us make a desperate leap for liberty!" But poor thing, she shrank back, in a state of trepidation. I turned and asked what was the matter; she made no reply, but burst into violent sobs, and threw her head upon my breast. This appeared to touch my very heart, it caused me to enter into her feelings more fully than ever. We both saw the many mountainous difficulties that rose one after the other before our view, and knew far too well what our sad fate would have been, were we caught and forced back into our slavish den. Therefore on my wife's fully realizing the solemn fact that we had to take our lives, as it were, in our hands, and contest every inch of the thousand miles of slave territory over which we had to pass, it made her heart almost sink within her, and, had I known them at that time, I would have repeated the following encouraging lines, which may not be out of place here—

"The hill, though high, I covet to ascend,
The *difficulty will not me offend;*
For I perceive the way to life lies here:
Come, pluck up heart, let's neither faint nor fear;
Better, though difficult, the right way to go,—
Than wrong, though easy, where the end is woe."[3]

However, the sobbing was soon over, and after a few moments of silent prayer she recovered her self-possession, and said, "Come, William, it is getting late, so now let us venture upon our perilous journey."

* * *

[Traveling separately, William and Ellen, whom he dubs "my master" while she is in disguise, converge on the railway station in Macon. Ellen purchases tickets for the first leg of the journey, a two hundred-mile trip to Savannah, Georgia. Stepping into her car, she discovers an old friend of her master's family on board. Her fears gradually calm as she realizes that the white man does not recognize her. On arrival in Savannah, Ellen retrieves her husband from the Negro car and books passage on a steamer bound for Charleston, South Carolina. After receiving a slave trader's advice against taking a slave to the North, Ellen retires to the eating cabin.]

On my master entering the cabin he found at the breakfast-table a young southern military officer, with whom he had travelled some distance the previous day.

After passing the usual compliments the conversation turned upon the old subject,—niggers.

The officer, who was also travelling with a man-servant, said to my master, "You will excuse me, Sir, for saying I think you are very likely to spoil your boy by saying 'thank you' to him. I assure you, sir, nothing spoils a slave so soon as saying, 'thank you' and 'if you please' to him. The only way to make a nigger toe the mark, and to keep him in his place, is to storm at him like thunder, and keep him trembling like a leaf. Don't you see, when I speak to my Ned, he darts like lightning; and if he didn't I'd skin him."

3. From *The Pilgrim's Progress* (1678) by John Bunyan (1628–1688).

Just then the poor dejected slave came in, and the officer swore at him fearfully, merely to teach my master what he called the proper way to treat me.

After he had gone out to get his master's luggage ready, the officer said, "That is the way to speak to them. If every nigger was drilled in this manner, they would be as humble as dogs, and never dare to run away.

The gentleman urged my master not to go to the North for the restoration of his health, but to visit the Warm Springs in Arkansas.

My master said, he thought the air of Philadelphia would suit his complaint best; and, not only so, he thought he could get better advice there.

The boat had now reached the wharf. The officer wished my master a safe and pleasant journey, and left the saloon.

* * *

When we left Macon, it was our intention to take a steamer at Charleston through to Philadelphia; but on arriving there we found that the vessels did not run during the winter, and I have no doubt it was well for us they did not; for on the very last voyage the steamer made that we intended to go by, a fugitive was discovered secreted on board, and sent back to slavery. However, as we had also heard of the Overland Mail Route, we were all right. So I ordered a fly[4] to the door, had the luggage placed on; we got in, and drove down to the Custom-house Office, which was near the wharf where we had to obtain tickets, to take a steamer for Wilmington, North Carolina. When we reached the building, I helped my master into the office, which was crowded with passengers. He asked for a ticket for himself and one for his slave to Philadelphia. This caused the principal officer—a very mean-looking, cheese-coloured fellow, who was sitting there—to look up at us very suspiciously, and in a fierce tone of voice he said to me, "Boy, do you belong to that gentleman?" I quickly replied, "Yes, sir" (which was quite correct). The tickets were handed out, and as my master was paying for them the chief man said to him, "I wish you to register your name here, sir, and also the name of your nigger, and pay a dollar duty on him."

My master paid the dollar, and pointing to the hand that was in the poultice, requested the officer to register his name for him. This seemed to offend the "high-bred" South Carolinian. He jumped up, shaking his head; and, cramming his hands almost through the bottom of his trousers pockets, with a slave-bullying air, said, "I shan't do it."

This attracted the attention of all the passengers. Just then the young military officer with whom my master travelled and conversed on the steamer from Savannah stepped in, somewhat the worse for brandy; he shook hands with my master, and pretended to know all about him. He said, "I know his kin (friends) like a book;" and as the officer was known in Charleston, and was going to stop there with friends, the recognition was very much in my master's favour.

The captain of the steamer, a good-looking jovial fellow, seeing that the gentleman appeared to know my master, and perhaps not wishing to lose us as passengers, said in an off-hand sailor-like manner, "I will register the gentleman's name, and take the responsibility upon myself." He asked my master's name. He said, "William Johnson." The names were put down, I think, "Mr. Johnson and slave." The captain said, "It's all right now, Mr. Johnson." He thanked him kindly, and the young officer begged my master to go with

4. A carriage.

him, and have something to drink and a cigar; but as he had not acquired these accomplishments, he excused himself, and we went on board and came off to Wilmington, North Carolina. When the gentleman finds out his mistake, he will, I have no doubt, be careful in future not to pretend to have an intimate acquaintance with an entire stranger. During the voyage the captain said, "It was rather sharp shooting this morning, Mr. Johnson. It was not out of any disrespect to you, sir; but they make it a rule to be very strict at Charleston. I have known families to be detained there with their slaves till reliable information could be received respecting them. If they were not very careful, any d—d abolitionist might take off a lot of valuable niggers."

My master said, "I suppose so," and thanked him again for helping him over the difficulty.

We reached Wilmington the next morning, and took the train for Richmond, Virginia.

* * *

At Richmond, a stout elderly lady, whose whole demeanour indicated that she belonged (as Mrs. Stowe's Aunt Chloe[5] expresses it) to one of the "firstest families," stepped into the carriage, and took a seat near my master. Seeing me passing quickly along the platform, she sprang up as if taken by a fit, and exclaimed, "Bless my soul! there goes my nigger, Ned!"

My master said, "No; that is my boy."

The lady paid no attention to this; she poked her head out of the window, and bawled to me, "You Ned, come to me, sir, you runaway rascal!"

On my looking round she drew her head in, and said to my master, "I beg your pardon, sir, I was sure it was my nigger; I never in my life saw two black pigs more alike than your boy and my Ned."

After the disappointed lady had resumed her seat, and the train had moved off, she closed her eyes, slightly raising her hands, and in a sanctified tone said to my master, "Oh! I hope, sir, your boy will not turn out to be so worthless as my Ned has. Oh! I was as kind to him as if he had been my own son. Oh! sir, it grieves me very much to think that after all I did for him he should go off without having any cause whatever."

"When did he leave you?" asked Mr. Johnson.

"About eighteen months ago, and I have never seen hair or hide of him since."

"Did he have a wife?" enquired a very respectable-looking young gentleman, who was sitting near my master and opposite to the lady.

"No, sir; not when he left, though he did have one a little before that. She was very unlike him; she was as good and as faithful a nigger as any one need wish to have. But, poor thing! she became so ill, that she was unable to do much work; so I thought it would be best to sell her, to go to New Orleans, where the climate is nice and warm."

"I suppose she was very glad to go South for the restoration of her health?" said the gentleman.

"No; she was not," replied the lady, "for niggers never know what is best for them. She took on a great deal about leaving Ned and the little nigger; but, as she was so weakly, I let her go."

"Was she good-looking?" asked the young passenger, who was evidently not of the same opinion as the talkative lady, and therefore wished her to tell all she knew.

5. The wife of Uncle Tom in Harriet Beecher Stowe's *Uncle Tom's Cabin* (1852).

"Yes; she was very handsome, and much whiter than I am; and therefore will have no trouble in getting another husband. I am sure I wish her well. I asked the speculator who bought her to sell her to a good master. Poor thing! she has my prayers, and I know she prays for me. She was a good Christian, and always used to pray for my soul. It was through her earliest prayers," continued the lady, "that I was first led to seek forgiveness of my sins, before I was converted at the great camp-meeting."[6]

This caused the lady to snuffle and to draw from her pocket a richly embroidered handkerchief, and apply it to the corner of her eyes. But my master could not see that it was at all soiled.

The silence which prevailed for a few moments was broken by the gentleman's saying, "As your 'July' was such a very good girl, and had served you so faithfully before she lost her health, don't you think it would have been better to have emancipated her?"

"No, indeed I do not!" scornfully exclaimed the lady, as she impatiently crammed the fine handkerchief into a little work-bag. "I have no patience with people who set niggers at liberty. It is the very worst thing you can do for them. My dear husband just before he died willed all his niggers free. But I and all our friends knew very well that he was too good a man to have ever thought of doing such an unkind and foolish thing, had he been in his right mind, and, therefore we had the will altered as it should have been in the first place."

"Did you mean, madam," asked my master, "that willing the slaves free was unjust to yourself, or unkind to them?"

"I mean that it was decidedly unkind to the servants themselves. It always seems to me such a cruel thing to turn niggers loose to shift for themselves, when there are so many good masters to take care of them. As for myself," continued the considerate lady, "I thank the Lord my dear husband left me and my son well provided for. Therefore I care nothing for the niggers, on my own account, for they are a great deal more trouble than they are worth, I sometimes wish that there was not one of them in the world; for the ungrateful wretches are always running away. I have lost no less than ten since my poor husband died. It's ruinous, sir!"

"But as you are well provided for, I suppose you do not feel the loss very much," said the passenger.

"I don't feel it at all," haughtily continued the good soul; "but that is no reason why property should be squandered. If my son and myself had the money for those valuable niggers, just see what a great deal of good we could do for the poor, and in sending missionaries abroad to the poor heathen, who have never heard the name of our blessed Redeemer. My dear son who is a good Christian minister has advised me not to worry and send my soul to hell for the sake of niggers; but to sell every blessed one of them for what they will fetch, and go and live in peace with him in New York. This I have concluded to do. I have just been to Richmond and made arrangements with my agent to make clean work of the forty that are left."

"Your son being a good Christian minister," said the gentleman, "It's strange he did not advise you to let the poor negroes have their liberty and go North."

"It's not at all strange, sir; it's not at all strange. My son knows what's best for the niggers; he has always told me that they were much better off than

6. An evangelical, often multiracial, religious assembly, usually held in frontier or rural areas, where believers camped for an extended period of worship, testimony, and prayer.

the free niggers in the North. In fact, I don't believe there are any white labouring people in the world who are as well off as the slaves."

"You are quite mistaken, madam," said the young man. "For instance, my own widowed mother, before she died, emancipated all her slaves, and sent them to Ohio, where they are getting along well. I saw several of them last summer myself."

"Well," replied the lady, "freedom may do for your ma's niggers, but it will never do for mine; and, plague them, they shall never have it; that is the word, with the bark on it."

"If freedom will not do for your slaves," replied the passenger, "I have no doubt your Ned and the other nine negroes will find out their mistake, and return to their old home.

"Blast them!" exclaimed the old lady, with great emphasis, "if I ever get them, I will cook their infernal hash, and tan their accursed black hides well for them! God forgive me," added the old soul, "the niggers will make me lose all my religion!"

By this time the lady had reached her destination. The gentleman got out at the next station beyond. As soon as she was gone, the young Southerner said to my master, "What a d——d shame it is for that old whining hypocritical humbug to cheat the poor negroes out of their liberty! If she has religion, may the devil prevent me from ever being converted!"

* * *

[From Richmond, Virginia, the Crafts continue by train to Washington, D.C., and then board another to Baltimore, Maryland.]

We left our cottage on Wednesday morning, the 21st of December, 1848, and arrived at Baltimore, Saturday evening, the 24th (Christmas Eve). Baltimore was the last slave port of any note at which we stopped.

On arriving there we felt more anxious than ever, because we knew not what that last dark night would bring forth. It is true we were near the goal, but our poor hearts were still as if tossed at sea; and, as there was another great and dangerous bar to pass, we were afraid our liberties would be wrecked, and, like the ill-fated *Royal Charter*,[7] go down for ever just off the place we longed to reach.

They are particularly watchful at Baltimore to prevent slaves from escaping into Pennsylvania, which is a free State. After I had seen my master into one of the best carriages, and was just about to step into mine, an officer, a full-blooded Yankee of the lower order, saw me. He came quickly up, and, tapping me on the shoulder, said in his unmistakable native twang, together with no little display of his authority, "Where are you going, boy?" "To Philadelphia, sir," I humbly replied. "Well, what are you going there for?" "I am travelling with my master, who is in the next carriage, sir." "Well, I calculate you had better get him out; and be mighty quick about it, because the train will soon be starting. It is against my rules to let any man take a slave past here, unless he can satisfy them in the office that he has a right to take him along."

The officer then passed on and left me standing upon the platform, with my anxious heart apparently palpitating in the throat. At first I scarcely knew which way to turn. But it soon occurred to me that the good God, who

7. A steam clipper bound for Liverpool, England, that was wrecked in a storm off the coast of Wales on October 26, 1859.

had been with us thus far, would not forsake us at the eleventh hour. So with renewed hope I stepped into my master's carriage, to inform him of the difficulty. I found him sitting at the farther end, quite alone. As soon as he looked up and saw me, he smiled. I also tried to wear a cheerful countenance, in order to break the shock of the sad news. I knew what made him smile. He was aware that if we were fortunate we should reach our destination at five o'clock the next morning, and this made it the more painful to communicate what the officer had said; but, as there was no time to lose, I went up to him and asked him how he felt. He said "Much better," and that he thanked God we were getting on so nicely. I then said we were not getting on quite so well as we had anticipated. He anxiously and quickly asked what was the matter. I told him. He started as if struck by lightning, and exclaimed, "Good Heavens! William, is it possible that we are, after all, doomed to hopeless bondage?" I could say nothing, my heart was too full to speak, for at first I did not know what to do. However we knew it would never do to turn back to the "City of Destruction," like Bunyan's *Mistrust* and *Timorous*, because they saw lions in the narrow way after ascending the hill Difficulty; but press on, like noble *Christian* and *Hopeful*, to the great city in which dwelt a few "shining ones."[8] So, after a few moments, I did all I could to encourage my companion, and we stepped out and made for the office: but how or where my master obtained sufficient courage to face the tyrants who had power to blast all we held dear, heaven only knows! Queen Elizabeth could not have been more terror-stricken, on being forced to land at the traitors' gate leading to the Tower,[9] than we were on entering that office. We felt that our very existence was at stake, and that we must either sink or swim. But, as God was our present and mighty helper in this as well as in all former trials, we were able to keep our heads up and press forwards.

On entering the room we found the principal man, to whom my master said, "Do you wish to see me, sir?" "Yes," said this eagle-eyed officer; and he added, "It is against our rules, sir, to allow any person to take a slave out of Baltimore into Philadelphia, unless he can satisfy us that he has a right to take him along." "Why is that?" asked my master," with more firmness than could be expected. "Because, sir," continued he, in a voice and manner that almost chilled our blood, "if we should suffer any gentleman to take a slave past here into Philadelphia; and should the gentleman with whom the slave might be travelling turn out not to be his rightful owner; and should the proper master come and prove that his slave escaped on our road, we shall have him to pay for; and, therefore, we cannot let any slave pass here without receiving security to show, and to satisfy us, that it is all right."

This conversation attracted the attention of the large number of bustling passengers. After the officer had finished, a few of them said, "Chit, chit, chit;" not because they thought we were slaves endeavouring to escape, but merely because they thought my master was a slaveholder and invalid gentleman, and therefore it was wrong to detain him. The officer, observing that the passengers sympathised with my master, asked him if he was not acquainted with some gentleman in Baltimore that he could get to endorse for him, to

8. In *Pilgrim's Progress*, the protagonist, Christian, along with a character named Hopeful, makes an arduous journey from the City of Destruction to the Celestial City. Along the way persons such as Mistrust and his companion Timorous attempt to divert Christian from his goal, but he is supported by, among others, the "shining ones," that is, angels.

9. The Tower of London, a castle on the Thames River in central London, where Elizabeth I was imprisoned before she became queen in 1558.

show that I was his property, and that he had a right to take me off. He said, "No;" and added, "I bought tickets in Charleston to pass us through to Philadelphia, and therefore you have no right to detain us here." "Well, sir," said the man, indignantly, "right or no right, we shan't let you go." These sharp words fell upon our anxious hearts like the crack of doom,[1] and made us feel that hope only smiles to deceive.

For a few moments perfect silence prevailed. My master looked at me, and I at him, but neither of us dared to speak a word, for fear of making some blunder that would tend to our detection. We knew that the officers had power to throw us into prison, and if they had done so we must have been detected and driven back, like the vilest felons, to a life of slavery, which we dreaded far more than sudden death.

We felt as though we had come into deep waters and were about being overwhelmed, and that the slightest mistake would clip asunder the last brittle thread of hope by which we were suspended, and let us down for ever into the dark and horrible pit of misery and degradation from which we were straining every nerve to escape. While our hearts were crying lustily unto Him who is ever ready and able to save, the conductor of the train that we had just left stepped in. The officer asked if we came by the train with him from Washington; he said we did, and left the room. Just then the bell rang for the train to leave; and had it been the sudden shock of an earthquake it could not have given us a greater thrill. The sound of the bell caused every eye to flash with apparent interest, and to be more steadily fixed upon us than before. But, as God would have it, the officer all at once thrust his fingers through his hair, and in a state of great agitation said, "I really don't know what to do; I calculate it is all right." He then told the clerk to run and tell the conductor to "let this gentleman and slave pass;" adding, "As he is not well, it is a pity to stop him here. We will let him go." My master thanked him, and stepped out and hobbled across the platform as quickly as possible. I tumbled him unceremoniously into one of the best carriages, and leaped into mine just as the train was gliding off towards our happy destination.

We thought of this plan about four days before we left Macon; and as we had our daily employment to attend to, we only saw each other at night. So we sat up the four long nights talking over the plan and making preparations.

We had also been four days on the journey; and as we travelled night and day, we got but very limited opportunities for sleeping. I believe nothing in the world could have kept us awake so long but the intense excitement, produced by the fear of being retaken on the one hand, and the bright anticipation of liberty on the other.

We left Baltimore about eight o'clock in the evening; and not being aware of a stopping-place of any consequence between there and Philadelphia, and also knowing that if we were fortunate we should be in the latter place early the next morning, I thought I might indulge in a few minutes' sleep in the car; but I, like Bunyan's Christian in the arbour, went to sleep at the wrong time, and took too long a nap. So, when the train reached Havre de Grace,[2] all the first-class passengers had to get out of the carriages and into a ferry-boat, to be ferried across the Susquehanna river, and take the train on the opposite side.

1. A term associated with the Christian Day of Judgment.

2. At the mouth of the Susquehanna River in Maryland.

The road was constructed so as to be raised or lowered to suit the tide. So they rolled the luggage-vans on to the boat, and off on the other side; and as I was in one of the apartments adjoining a baggage-car, they considered it unnecessary to awaken me, and tumbled me over with the luggage. But when my master was asked to leave his seat, he found it very dark, and cold, and raining. He missed me for the first time on the journey. On all previous occasions, as soon as the train stopped, I was at hand to assist him. This caused many slaveholders to praise me very much: they said they had never before seen a slave so attentive to his master: and therefore my absence filled him with terror and confusion; the children of Israel could not have felt more troubled on arriving at the Red Sea.[3] So he asked the conductor if he had seen anything of his slave. The man being somewhat of an abolitionist, and believing that my master was really a slaveholder, thought he would tease him a little respecting me. So he said, "No, sir; I haven't seen anything of him for some time: I have no doubt he has run away, and is in Philadelphia, free, long before now." My master knew that there was nothing in this; so he asked the conductor if he would please to see if he could find me. The man indignantly replied, "I am no slave-hunter; and as far as I am concerned everybody must look after their own niggers." He went off and left the confused invalid to fancy whatever he felt inclined. My master at first thought I must have been kidnapped into slavery by some one, or left, or perhaps killed on the train. He also thought of stopping to see if he could hear anything of me, but he soon remembered that he had no money. That night all the money we had was consigned to my own pocket, because we thought, in case there were any pickpockets about, a slave's pocket would be the last one they would look for. However, hoping to meet me some day in a land of liberty, and as he had the tickets, he thought it best upon the whole to enter the boat and come off to Philadelphia, and endeavour to make his way alone in this cold and hollow world as best he could. The time was now up, so he went on board and came across with feelings that can be better imagined than described.

After the train had got fairly on the way to Philadelphia, the guard came into my car and gave me a violent shake, and bawled out at the same time, "Boy, wake up!" I started, almost frightened out of my wits. He said, "Your master is scared half to death about you." That frightened me still more—I thought they had found him out; so I anxiously inquired what was the matter. The guard said, "He thinks you have run away from him." This made me feel quite at ease. I said, "No, sir; I am satisfied my good master doesn't think that." So off I started to see him. He had been fearfully nervous, but on seeing me he at once felt much better. He merely wished to know what had become of me.

On returning to my seat, I found the conductor and two or three other persons amusing themselves very much respecting my running away. So the guard said, "Boy, what did your master want?[4] I replied, "He merely wished to know what had become of me." "No," said the man, "that was not it; he thought you had taken French leave,[5] for parts unknown. I never saw a fellow so badly scared about losing his slave in my life. Now," continued the guard,

3. See Exodus 14.

4. I may state here that every man slave is called boy till he is very old, then the more respectable slaveholders call him uncle. The women are all girls till they are aged, then they are called aunts. This is the reason why Mrs. Stowe calls her characters Uncle Tom, Aunt Chloe, Uncle Tiff, &c. [*Craft's note*].

5. An unannounced departure without saying goodbye.

"let me give you a little friendly advice. When you get to Philadelphia, run away and leave that cripple, and have your liberty." "No, sir," I indifferently replied, "I can't promise to do that." "Why not?" said the conductor, evidently much surprised; "don't you want your liberty?" "Yes, sir," I replied; "but I shall never run away from such a good master as I have at present."

One of the men said to the guard, "Let him alone; I guess he will open his eyes when he gets to Philadelphia, and see things in another light." After giving me a good deal of information, which I afterwards found to be very useful, they left me alone.

I also met with a coloured gentleman on this train, who recommended me to a boarding-house that was kept by an abolitionist, where he thought I would be quite safe, if I wished to run away from my master. I thanked him kindly, but of course did not let him know who we were. Late at night, or rather early in the morning, I heard a fearful whistling of the steam-engine; so I opened the window and looked out, and saw a large number of flickering lights in the distance, and heard a passenger in the next carriage—who also had his head out of the window—say to his companion, "Wake up, old horse, we are at Philadelphia!"

The sight of those lights and that announcement made me feel almost as happy as Bunyan's Christian must have felt when he first caught sight of the cross. I, like him, felt that the straps that bound the heavy burden to my back began to pop, and the load to roll off. I also looked, and looked again, for it appeared very wonderful to me how the mere sight of our first city of refuge should have all at once made my hitherto sad and heavy heart become so light and happy. As the train speeded on, I rejoiced and thanked God with all my heart and soul for his great kindness and tender mercy, in watching over us, and bringing us safely through.

As soon as the train had reached the platform, before it had fairly stopped, I hurried out of my carriage to my master, whom I got at once into a cab, placed the luggage on, jumped in myself, and we drove off to the boarding-house which was so kindly recommended to me. On leaving the station, my master—or rather my wife, as I may now say—who had from the commencement of the journey borne up in a manner that much surprised us both, grasped me by the hand, and said, "Thank God, William, we are safe!" then burst into tears, leant upon me, and wept like a child. The reaction was fearful. So when we reached the house, she was in reality so weak and faint that she could scarcely stand alone. However, I got her into the apartments that were pointed out, and there we knelt down, on this Sabbath, and Christmas-day,—a day that will ever be memorable to us,—and poured out our heartfelt gratitude to God, for his goodness in enabling us to overcome so many perilous difficulties, in escaping out of the jaws of the wicked.[6]

From *Part II*

After my wife had a little recovered herself, she threw off the disguise and assumed her own apparel. We then stepped into the sitting-room, and asked to see the landlord. The man came in, but he seemed thunderstruck on finding a fugitive slave and his wife, instead of a "young cotton planter and his nigger." As his eyes travelled round the room, he said to me. "Where is your master?" I pointed him out. The man gravely replied, "I am not joking,

6. Job 29:17.

I really wish to see your master." I pointed him out again, but at first he could not believe his eyes; he said "he knew that was not the gentleman that came with me."

But, after some conversation, we satisfied him that we were fugitive slaves, and had just escaped in the manner I have described. We asked him if he thought it would be safe for us to stop in Philadelphia. He said he thought not, but he would call in some persons who knew more about the laws than himself. He then went out, and kindly brought in several of the leading abolitionists of the city, who gave us a most hearty and friendly welcome amongst them. As it was in December, and also as we had just left a very warm climate, they advised us not to go to Canada as we had intended, but to settle at Boston in the United States. It is true that the constitution of the Republic has always guaranteed the slaveholders the right to come into any of the so-called free States, and take their fugitives back to southern Egypt. But through the untiring, uncompromising, and manly efforts of Mr. Garrison, Wendell Phillips, Theodore Parker,[7] and a host of other noble abolitionists of Boston and the neighbourhood, public opinion in Massachusetts had become so much opposed to slavery and to kidnapping, that it was almost impossible for any one to take a fugitive slave out of that State.

So we took the advice of our good Philadelphia friends, and settled at Boston. I shall have something to say about our sojourn there presently.

Among other friends we met with at Philadelphia, was Robert Purves, Esq.,[8] a well educated and wealthy coloured gentleman, who introduced us to Mr. Barkley Ivens, a member of the Society of Friends, and a noble and generous-hearted farmer, who lived at some distance in the country.

This good Samaritan at once invited us to go and stop quietly with his family, till my wife could somewhat recover from the fearful reaction of the past journey. We most gratefully accepted the invitation, and at the time appointed we took a steamer to a place up the Delaware river, where our new and dear friend met us with his snug little cart, and took us to his happy home. This was the first act of great and disinterested kindness we had ever received from a white person.

The gentleman was not of the fairest complexion, and therefore, as my wife was not in the room when I received the information respecting him and his anti-slavery character, she thought of course he was a quadroon like herself. But on arriving at the house, and finding out her mistake, she became more nervous and timid than ever.

As the cart came into the yard, the dear good old lady, and her three charming and affectionate daughters, all came to the door to meet us. We got out, and the gentleman said, "Go in, and make yourselves at home; I will see after the baggage." But my wife was afraid to approach them. She stopped in the yard, and said to me, "William, I thought we were coming among coloured people?" I replied, "It is all right; these are the same." "No," she said, "it is not all right, and I am not going to stop here; I have no confidence whatever in white people, they are only trying to get us back to slavery." She turned round and said, "I am going right off." The old lady then came out, with her sweet, soft, and winning smile, shook her heartily by the hand, and kindly said, "How art thou, my dear? We are all very glad to see thee and thy husband. Come in, to the fire; I dare say thou art cold and hungry after thy journey."

7. William Lloyd Garrison (1805–1879), Phillips (1811–1884), and Parker (1810–1860) were all white antislavery leaders in Boston.

8. Robert Purvis, a prominent, Northern-born African American antislavery lecturer, editor, and author (1810–1898).

We went in, and the young ladies asked if she would like to go upstairs and "fix" herself before tea. My wife said, "No, I thank you; I shall only stop a little while." "But where art thou going this cold night?" said Mr. Ivens, who had just stepped in. "I don't know," was the reply. "Well, then," he continued, "I think thou hadst better take off thy things and sit near the fire; tea will soon be ready. "Yes, come Ellen," said Mrs. Ivens, "let me assist thee;" (as she commenced undoing my wife's bonnet-strings); "don't be frightened, Ellen, I shall not hurt a single hair of thy head. We have heard with much pleasure of the marvellous escape of thee and thy husband, and deeply sympathise with thee in all that thou hast undergone. I don't wonder at thee, poor thing, being timid; but thou needs not fear us; we would as soon send one of our own daughters into slavery as thee; so thou mayest make thyself quite at ease!" These soft and soothing words fell like balm upon my wife's unstrung nerves, and melted her to tears; her fears and prejudices vanished, and from that day she has firmly believed that there are good and bad persons of every shade of complexion.

After seeing Sally Ann and Jacob, two coloured domestics, my wife felt quite at home. After partaking of what Mrs. Stowe's Mose and Pete called a "busting supper," the ladies wished to know whether we could read. On learning we could not, they said if we liked they would teach us. To this kind offer, of course, there was no objection. But we looked rather knowingly at each other, as much as to say that they would have rather a hard task to cram anything into our thick and matured sculls.

However, all hands set to and quickly cleared away the tea-things, and the ladies and their good brother brought out the spelling and copy books and slates, &c., and commenced with their new and green pupils. We had, by stratagem, learned the alphabet while in slavery, but not the writing characters; and, as we had been such a time learning so little, we at first felt that it was a waste of time for any one at our ages to undertake to learn to read and write. But, as the ladies were so anxious that we should learn, and so willing to teach us, we concluded to give our whole minds to the work, and see what could be done. By so doing, at the end of the three weeks we remained with the good family we could spell and write our names quite legibly. They all begged us to stop longer; but, as we were not safe in the State of Pennsylvania, and also as we wished to commence doing something for a livelihood, we did not remain.

When the time arrived for us to leave for Boston, it was like parting with our relatives. We have since met with many very kind and hospitable friends, both in America and England; but we have never been under a roof where we were made to feel more at home, or where the inmates took a deeper interest in our well-being, than Mr. Barkley Ivens and his dear family. May God ever bless them, and preserve each one from every reverse of fortune!

We finally, as I have stated, settled at Boston, where we remained nearly two years, I employed as cabinet-maker and furniture broker, and my wife at her needle; and, as our little earnings in slavery were not all spent on the journey, we were getting on very well, and would have made money, if we had not been compelled by the General Government, at the bidding of the slaveholders, to break up business, and fly from under the Stars and Stripes to save our liberties and our lives.

* * *

1860

FRANCES E. W. HARPER
1825–1911

Author of at least four novels, several volumes of poetry, and numerous separately published stories, poems, essays, and letters, Frances Ellen Watkins Harper was one of the most prolific and popular American writers prior to the twentieth century. As with her contemporaries William Wells Brown, Frederick Douglass, John Greenleaf Whittier, Harriet Beecher Stowe, and Harriet Jacobs, Harper's life and literature were entwined. Local and national newspapers regularly noted her activities and advertised her lecture tours. Histories such as Brown's *The Rising Son; or, The Antecedents and Advances of the Colored Race* (1873) and Phebe A. Hanaford's *Daughters of America; or, Women of the Century* (1883) referred to her accomplishments. Many African American women's service clubs named themselves in her honor, and across the nation, in cities such as St. Louis, St. Paul, and Pittsburgh, F. E. W. Harper Leagues and Frances E. Harper Women's Christian Temperance Unions thrived well into the twentieth century.

Harper was born Frances Ellen Watkins on September 24, 1825, in Baltimore, Maryland. The Watkins family were free, but Maryland was a slave state. By the age of three, Harper was orphaned and living with relatives, most likely her uncle and aunt, William and Henrietta Watkins. A deeply religious and politically active man, William Watkins was a writer, educator, and minister. Harper received an uncommonly thorough education at her uncle's school, where she showed promise in writing and elocution, a strong interest in radical politics and religion, and a special sense of social and civic responsibility.

As with all but the most privileged African American children, while still an adolescent, Harper had to leave school and find work. Her employers allowed her access to their library and she read voraciously and began writing poetry. She published her first collection of poems, titled *Forest Leaves*, not long before she was hired to teach domestic arts at Union Seminary, a school newly established by the African Methodist Episcopal Church near Columbus, Ohio. The next year she took another teaching position, this time in York, Pennsylvania, but her frequent encounters with fugitive slaves and her own refugee status (the result of a Maryland law that made it a crime, punishable by enslavement, for a free Black person to enter the state) led her to quit teaching, move to Philadelphia, and devote herself to the antislavery movement.

Harper fervently believed in the power of literature to change lives, a belief that led her to write and publish on a variety of topics. Among her admiring editors were Frederick Douglass, who often published Harper's poems prefaced with flattering remarks about her lectures and recommendations of her books, and William Lloyd Garrison, who regularly allocated space in the *Liberator* for her writings and notices of her activities.

When Harper was hired by the Maine Anti-Slavery Society, her schedule was grueling. In the first six weeks of fall 1854, she traveled to twenty cities and gave at least thirty-one lectures. Yet she continued to make time to write. In 1854 her book *Poems on Miscellaneous Subjects,* a collection of poems and essays prefaced by William Lloyd Garrison, was published both in Boston and in Philadelphia. The book was an immediate success, selling more than ten thousand copies and meriting reprinting in an enlarged version within three years. During Harper's lifetime the collection was revised and reprinted at least twenty times.

Poems on Miscellaneous Subjects includes several of the works for which she is most famous, poems that are generally agreed to have ushered in the tradition of African American protest poetry. A classic example is "The Slave Mother," which focuses on the separation of families and the devastating pain that mothers, in particular, suffered in bondage. The works in *Poems on Miscellaneous Subjects* address the need to end slavery and the importance of Christian living, equal rights, and racial pride, ideals that Harper advocated throughout her career.

Although Harper was often characterized as "a noble Christian woman" and "one of the most scholarly and well-read women of her day," she did not shy away from difficult daily work. Her position with the Maine Anti-Slavery Society took her to parts of Canada and most of New England. The ordinary difficulties of travel were compounded by the danger posed to abolitionists by slavery advocates and by people opposed to both women and African Americans speaking publicly. Despite these dangers Harper next signed on as an agent and lecturer for the Pennsylvania Society for Promoting the Abolition of Slavery and proceeded on a series of tours across the old Northwest.

As the repressive measures against African Americans increased, Harper's activism and writings became increasingly militant. When a group of armed men led by famed abolitionist John Brown stormed the arsenal at Harpers Ferry, West Virginia, in October 1859, Harper solicited support for the captured men and their families. She wrote letters, one of which is anthologized here, and joined efforts to raise money for the families of the jailed men. "It is not enough to express our sympathy by words," she wrote; "we should be ready to crystallize it into actions." She violated the Fugitive Slave Law herself by actively working with the Underground Railroad.

In 1859 Harper published in the newly created *Anglo-African Magazine* several prose pieces, including "The Two Offers" and "Our Greatest Want." "The Two Offers" argues against social complacency and asserts that marriage is but one option for a woman of intelligence and social conscience. "Our Greatest Want" argues that acquisition of material wealth was necessary for African Americans but that their development as "true men and true women" was a higher priority. As in several early poems, Harper emphasizes the importance of personal faith and self-discipline.

In November 1860, Frances Watkins married Fenton Harper, a widower with three children, and moved to a farm near Columbus, Ohio. The Harpers had one child, Mary. Despite the demands of family life, Frances Harper still found time to write and deliver occasional lectures. When Fenton Harper died in 1864, creditors claimed their property and most of their belongings. To support her family, the widowed mother returned to the lecture circuit, where she attracted large and receptive audiences. Shortly thereafter, Harper joined Frederick Douglass, Robert and Harriet Purvis, Sojourner Truth, Susan B. Anthony, Lucretia Mott, and Elizabeth Cady Stanton in the newly founded American Equal Rights Association. But Harper's equal rights advocacy was complicated by the racism of her feminist colleagues and the sexism of some of her African American brothers. During the debate over the Fifteenth Amendment to the Constitution, this group divided over support for African American men's suffrage if women's suffrage were not included. Harper, then as later, tried to mediate between sometimes naive, often competitive, and frequently hostile sectors. "We are all bound up together in one great bundle of humanity," she repeatedly admonished.

After the Civil War, educated northern women from many racial backgrounds traveled to the South to teach and to provide other social services for the newly freed slaves. From 1866 to 1871, Harper crossed and recrossed the South, teaching and lecturing to southern audiences and recording her impressions for northern readers. In her lectures Harper argued that the future of the nation depended on the ability of its citizens to unite behind a common goal. "Between the white people and the colored there is a community of interests," she asserted, "and the sooner they find it out, the better it will be for both parties." Her other theme, and the one that increasingly dominated her published writings, was that Emancipation had opened a new era, a time for African Americans, particularly African American women, to "consecrate their lives to the work of upbuilding the race." Her first serialized novel, *Minnie's Sacrifice* (1869), advocated this type of personal commitment and devotion to higher ideals.

Harper published three collections of poetry during the decade following Emancipation. *Moses: A Story of the Nile* (1869), approximately seven hundred lines of free verse, is a remarkable departure from Harper's typical four-line, rhymed stanzas. Here Harper uses an especially common African American trope, the enslavement of the Hebrews in Egypt, to create an example of personal sacrifice. Two years later Harper published *Poems* (1871), which explores themes similar to those of *Poems on Miscellaneous Subjects* but updated for a new era. From the horrific and unnatural experiences of slavery, like the work of many post-emancipation era activist/authors, her writings turned to the redemptive suffering of divinely ordained trials and promoted the Reconstruction ideal of heroic effort, sacrifice, and courage rewarded, striking a more hopeful tone than during the slave era.

The following year Harper published *Sketches of Southern Life,* a significant marker in African American literature as well as in Harper's career. Unlike the slave narratives and much of Harper's antebellum writings, *Sketches* treats slavery as a literary construct. The heart of this volume is a series of six poems, narrated by Aunt Chloe, that form at once the autobiography of a formerly enslaved person and an oral history of slavery and Reconstruction. Aunt Chloe may prove to be Harper's most important contribution to American letters. Although she is sixty years old, Aunt Chloe learns to read, takes an active interest in politics (though she cannot vote), and does what she can to ensure that the men "voted clean." She helps build schools and churches for the community, and she works to buy herself a cabin, which she enlarges to accommodate her children after they are reunited.

Sometime around 1871 Harper settled in Philadelphia, where she continued to interweave her literary production with her political commitment. In 1873 she began a newspaper column (first named *Fancy Etchings,* then *Fancy Sketches*) that discussed contemporary issues, moral dilemmas, and aesthetics through the conversations and activities of Jenny, a recent college graduate who wants to be a poet; Jenny's Aunt Jane, who encourages her to use her talent to improve society; and a variety of other fictitious characters. Later, other African American writers, including Olivia Ward Bush-Banks and Langston Hughes, created similar series. Two of her next three novels, *Sowing and Reaping: A Temperance Story* (1876) and *Trial and Triumph* (1888–89), as well as numerous essays and poems, deal with temperance, which had become one of her top priorities. *Trial* is also one of Harper's most obvious attempts to combat the mythology of the chivalrous South, the happy slave, and the treacherous free Black then being created by plantation school literature. *Iola Leroy* (1892), Harper's best-known novel, builds on both her own corrective work in *Trial* and the methods, characters, and plots of earlier African American novels. Although Iola is superficially similar to the figure of the tragic mulatta, she is not a suffering victim. In addition, Harper pairs her mulatto characters with "pure African" counterparts who are generally superior to their noble and accomplished lighter-skinned friends. Further extending the conventions of earlier African American fiction, Harper includes several folk characters whose intelligence, dedication, and resourcefulness are models for the emerging Black middle class.

After *Iola Leroy* Harper published at least five collections of poetry. Even in her seventies, she continued to be active, working with the National Council of Women, the Universal Peace Union, the Women's Christian Temperance Union, and other organizations, and writing essays and poems for their journals. In 1892 she addressed the Women's Congress at the Columbian Exposition. In 1896, she helped create the National Association of Colored Women, for which she served as vice president and as consultant for several years.

Harper died on February 20, 1911. During her career, she worked in virtually every literary genre available to her. Although she appreciated beauty and enjoyed the honors she received, she believed that literature that could not be used to represent, to reprimand, and to revise was useless. Born during slavery, Harper was buried during the period that historians now refer to as the nadir of American race relations. Through it all she combined pragmatic idealism, courageous action, and lyrical words to dispel the shadows and usher in what she knew would be brighter coming days.

Ethiopia[1]

Yes! Ethiopia yet shall stretch
  Her bleeding hands abroad;
Her cry of agony shall reach
  The burning throne of God.[2]

The tyrant's yoke from off her neck,
  His fetters from her soul,
The mighty hand of God shall break,
  And spurn the base control.

Redeemed from dust and freed from chains,
  Her sons shall lift their eyes;
From cloud-capt hills and verdant plains
  Shall shouts of triumph rise.

Upon her dark, despairing brow,
  Shall play a smile of peace;
For God shall bend unto her woe,
  And bid her sorrows cease.

'Neath sheltering vines and stately palms
  Shall laughing children play,
And aged sires with joyous psalms
  Shall gladden every day.

Secure by night, and blest by day,
  Shall pass her happy hours;
Nor human tigers hunt for prey
  Within her peaceful bowers.

Then, Ethiopia! stretch, oh! stretch
  Thy bleeding hands abroad;
Thy cry of agony shall reach
  And find redress from God.

1853?

1. If Kletzing and Crogman (*Progress of a Race; or, The Remarkable Advancement of the Afro-American*, 1897) are correct, this poem was published before 1853 and is Harper's earliest extant poem. It also appears in *Frederick Douglass' Paper*, March 31, 1854, and in *Poems on Miscellaneous Subjects* (1854). In the 19th century, the term *Ethiopia* was often considered synonymous with "Black Africa."

2. An allusion to Psalms 68:31–35. Psalms 68 was often quoted and revised in 19th-century African American literature.

Eliza Harris[1]

Like a fawn from the arrow, startled and wild,
A woman swept by us, bearing a child;
In her eye was the night of a settled despair,
And her brow was o'ershaded with anguish and care.

She was nearing the river—in reaching the brink,
She heeded no danger, she paused not to think!
For she is a mother—her child is a slave—
And she'll give him his freedom, or find him a grave!

It was a vision to haunt us, that innocent face—
So pale in its aspect, so fair in its grace;
As the tramp of the horse and the bay of the hound,
With the fetters that gall, were trailing the ground!

She was nerv'd by despair, and strengthened by woe,
As she leap'd o'er the chasms that yawn'd from below;
Death howl'd in the tempest, and rav'd in the blast,
But she heard not the sound till the danger was past.

Oh! how shall I speak of my proud country's shame?
Of the stains on her glory, how give them their name?
How say that her banner in mockery waves—
Her "star spangled banner"—o'er millions of slaves?

How say that the lawless may torture and chase
A woman whose crime is the hue of her face?
How the depths of the forest may echo around
With the shrieks of despair, and the bay of the hound?

With her step on the ice, and her arm on her child,
The danger was fearful, the pathway was wild;
But, aided by Heaven, she gained a free shore,
Where the friends of humanity open'd their door.

So fragile and lovely, so fearfully pale,
Like a lily that bends to the breath of the gale,
Save the heave of her breast, and the sway of her hair,
You'd have thought her a statue of fear and despair.

In agony close to her bosom she press'd
The life of her heart, the child of her breast:—
Oh! love from its tenderness gathering might,
Had strengthen'd her soul for the dangers of flight.

1. Versions of this poem appeared in the *Liberator* on December 16, 1853, and in *Frederick Douglass' Paper* on December 23, 1853. Some references cite an even earlier publication in the *Aliened American*. Stanzas 11 and 12, reprinted here from the *Liberator,* were included in the early versions but not in *Poems on Miscellaneous Subjects*. Both the *Liberator* and *Frederick Douglass' Paper* reprinted "Eliza Harris" in 1860. Like Harriet Beecher Stowe in *Uncle Tom's Cabin* and other writers of the time, Harper based her poem on an incident that occurred in Cincinnati, Ohio.

But she's free—yes, free from the land where the slave
From the hand of oppression must rest in the grave;
Where bondage and torture, where scourges and chains,
Have plac'd on our banner indelible stains.

Did a fever e'er burning through bosom and brain,
Send a lava-like flood through every vein,
Till it suddenly cooled 'neath a healing spell,
And you knew, oh! the joy! you knew you were well?

So felt this young mother, as a sense of the rest
Stole gently and sweetly o'er *her* weary breast,
As her boy looked up, and, wondering, smiled
On the mother whose love had freed her child.

The bloodhounds have miss'd the scent of her way;
The hunter is rifled and foil'd of his prey;
Fierce jargon and cursing, with clanking of chains,
Make sounds of strange discord on Liberty's plains.

With the rapture of love and fulness of bliss,
She plac'd on his brow a mother's fond kiss:—
Oh! poverty, danger and death she can brave,
For the child of her love is no longer a slave!

1853

The Slave Mother

Heard you that shriek? It rose
  So wildly on the air,
It seemed as if a burden'd heart
  Was breaking in despair.

Saw you those hands so sadly clasped—
  The bowed and feeble head—
The shuddering of that fragile form—
  That look of grief and dread?

Saw you the sad, imploring eye?
  Its every glance was pain,
As if a storm of agony
  Were sweeping through the brain.

She is a mother, pale with fear,
  Her boy clings to her side,
And in her kirtle[1] vainly tries
  His trembling form to hide.

He is not hers, although she bore
  For him a mother's pains;

[1] *loose gown*

He is not hers, although her blood
  Is coursing through his veins!

He is not hers, for cruel hands
  May rudely tear apart
The only wreath of household love
  That binds her breaking heart.

His love has been a joyous light
  That o'er her pathway smiled,
A fountain gushing ever new,
  Amid life's desert wild.

His lightest word has been a tone
  Of music round her heart,
Their lives a streamlet blent in one—
  Oh, Father! must they part?

They tear him from her circling arms,
  Her last and fond embrace.
Oh! never more may her sad eyes
  Gaze on his mournful face.

No marvel, then, these bitter shrieks
  Disturb the listening air:
She is a mother, and her heart
  Is breaking in despair.

1854

Vashti[1]

She leaned her head upon her hand
  And heard the king's decree—
"My lords are feasting in my halls,
  Bid Vashti come to me.

"I've shown the treasures of my house,
  My costly jewels rare,
But with the glory of her eyes
  No rubies can compare.

"Adorn'd and crown'd I'd have her come,
  With all her queenly grace,
And, 'mid my lords and mighty men,
  Unveil her lovely face.

1. Published in *Poems* (1857) and in *New National Era* on September 22, 1870. The poem is based on an incident in Esther 1:13–22.

"Each gem that sparkles in my crown,
   Or glitters on my throne,
Grows poor and pale when she appears,
   My beautiful, my own!"

All waiting stood the chamberlains
   To hear the Queen's reply,
They saw her cheek grow deathly pale,
   But light flash'd to her eye:

"Go, tell the King," she proudly said,
   "That I am Persia's° Queen, *now Iran*
And by his crowds of merry men
   I never will be seen.

"I'll take the crown from off my head
   And tread it 'neath my feet
Before their rude and careless gaze
   My shrinking eyes shall meet.

"A queen unveil'd before the crowd!—
   Upon each lip my name!—
Why, Persia's women all would blush
   And weep for Vashti's shame!

"Go back!" she cried, and waived her hand,
   And grief was in her eye:
"Go, tell the King," she sadly said,
   "That I would rather die."

They brought her message to the King,
   Dark flash'd his angry eye;
'Twas as the lightning ere the storm
   Hath swept in fury by.

Then bitterly outspoke the King,
   Through purple lips of wrath—
"What shall be done to her who dares
   To cross your monarch's path?"

Then spake his wily counsellors—
   "O King of this fair land!
From distant Ind° to Ethiop, *that is, India*
   All bow to thy command.

"But if, before thy servants' eyes,
   This thing they plainly see,
That Vashti doth not heed thy will
   Nor yield herself to thee,

"The women, restive 'neath our rule,
   Would learn to scorn our name,
And from her deed to us would come
   Reproach and burning shame.

"Then, gracious King, sign with thy hand
This stern but just decree,
That Vashti lay aside her crown,
Thy Queen no more to be."

She heard again the King's command,
And left her high estate,
Strong in her earnest womanhood,
She calmly met her fate,

And left the palace of the King,
Proud of her spotless name—
A woman who could bend to grief,
But would not bow to shame.

1857

Bury Me in a Free Land[1]

Make me a grave where'er you will,
In a lowly plain or a lofty hill;
Make it among earth's humblest graves,
But not in a land where men are slaves.

I could not rest, if around my grave
I heard the steps of a trembling slave;
His shadow above my silent tomb
Would make it a place of fearful gloom.

I could not sleep, if I heard the tread
Of a coffle-gang to the shambles[2] led,
And the mother's shriek of wild despair
Rise, like a curse, on the trembling air.

I could not rest, if I saw the lash
Drinking her blood at each fearful gash;
And I saw her babes torn from her breast,
Like trembling doves from their parent nest.

I'd shudder and start, if I heard the bay
Of a bloodhound seizing his human prey;
And I heard the captive plead in vain,
As they bound, afresh, his galling° chain. *chafing, irritating*

If I saw young girls from their mother's arms
Bartered and sold for their youthful charms,
My eye would flash with a mournful flame,
My death-pale cheek grow red with shame.

1. Published in the *Liberator* on January 14, 1864. Harper included a copy of this poem in a letter she wrote to one of John Brown's men who was awaiting execution for his part in the raid on Harpers Ferry.

2. Slaughterhouse. "Coffle-gang": a group of enslaved people who are chained together.

I would sleep, dear friends, where bloated Might
Can rob no man of his dearest right;
My rest shall be calm in any grave
Where none can call his brother a slave.

I ask no monument, proud and high,
To arrest the gaze of the passers by;
All that my yearning spirit craves
Is—*Bury me not in a land of slaves!*

1864

Aunt Chloe's Politics

Of course, I don't know very much
  About these politics,
But I think that some who run 'em
  Do mighty ugly tricks.

I've seen 'em honey-fugle[1] round,
  And talk so awful sweet,
That you'd think them full of kindness,
  As an egg is full of meat.

Now I don't believe in looking
  Honest people in the face,
And saying when you're doing wrong,
  That "I haven't sold my race."[2]

When we want to school our children,
  If the money isn't there,
Whether black or white have took it,
  The loss we all must share.

And this buying up each other[3]
  Is something worse than mean,
Though I thinks a heap of voting,
  I go for voting clean.

1872

Learning to Read

Very soon the Yankee teachers
  Came down and set up school;
But, oh! how the Rebs[1] did hate it,—
  It was agin' their rule.

1. Or honey fogle; act in an ingratiating manner so as to deceive or cheat.
2. Betrayed one's own group or culture.
3. Paying someone to vote a certain way.
1. Rebel, or Confederate, forces during the Civil War.

Our masters always tried to hide
  Book learning from our eyes;
Knowledge did'nt agree with slavery—
  'Twould make us all too wise.

But some of us would try to steal
  A little from the book,
And put the words together,
  And learn by hook or crook.

I remember Uncle Caldwell,
  Who took pot-liquor[2] fat
And greased the pages of his book,
  And hid it in his hat.

And had his master ever seen
  The leaves upon his head,
He'd have thought them greasy papers,
  But nothing to be read.

And there was Mr. Turner's Ben,
  Who heard the children spell,
And picked the words right up by heart,
  And learned to read 'em well.

Well, the Northern folks kept sending
  The Yankee teachers down;
And they stood right up and helped us,
  Though Rebs did sneer and frown.

And, I longed to read my Bible,
  For precious words it said;
But when I begun to learn it,
  Folks just shook their heads,

And said there is no use trying,
  Oh! Chloe, you're too late;
But as I was rising sixty,
  I had no time to wait.

So I got a pair of glasses,
  And straight to work I went,
And never stopped till I could read
  The hymns and Testament.° *the Bible*

Then I got a little cabin—
  A place to call my own—
And I felt as independent
  As the queen upon her throne.

1872

2. Fatty broth from cooking meat and vegetables.

A Double Standard

Do you blame me that I loved him?
If when standing all alone
I cried for bread a careless world
Pressed to my lips a stone.

Do you blame me that I loved him,
That my heart beat glad and free,
When he told me in the sweetest tones
He loved but only me?

Can you blame me that I did not see
Beneath his burning kiss
The serpent's wiles, nor even hear
The deadly adder hiss?

Can you blame me that my heart grew cold
That the tempted, tempter turned;
When he was feted and caressed
And I was coldly spurned?

Would you blame him, when you draw from me
Your dainty robes aside,
If he with gilded baits should claim
Your fairest as his bride?

Would you blame the world if it should press
On him a civic crown;
And see me struggling in the depth
Then harshly press me down?

Crime has no sex and yet to-day
I wear the brand of shame;
Whilst he amid the gay and proud
Still bears an honored name.

Can you blame me if I've learned to think
Your hate of vice a sham,
When you so coldly crushed me down
And then excused the man?

Would you blame me if to-morrow
The coroner should say,
A wretched girl, outcast, forlorn,
Has thrown her life away?

Yes, blame me for my downward course,
But oh! remember well,
Within your homes you press the hand
That led me down to hell.

I'm glad God's ways are not our ways,
He does not see as man;

Within His love I know there's room
   For those whom others ban.

I think before His great white throne,
   His throne of spotless light,
That whited sepulchres[1] shall wear
   The hue of endless night.

That I who fell, and he who sinned,
   Shall reap as we have sown;
That each the burden of his loss
   Must bear and bear alone.

No golden weights can turn the scale
   Of justice in His sight;
And what is wrong in woman's life
   In man's cannot be right.

1895

Songs for the People

Let me make the songs for the people,
   Songs for the old and young;
Songs to stir like a battle-cry
   Wherever they are sung.

Not for the clashing of sabres,
   For carnage nor for strife;
But songs to thrill the hearts of men
   With more abundant life.

Let me make the songs for the weary,
   Amid life's fever and fret,
Till hearts shall relax their tension,
   And careworn brows forget.

Let me sing for little children,
   Before their footsteps stray,
Sweet anthems of love and duty,
   To float o'er life's highway.

I would sing for the poor and aged,
   When shadows dim their sight;
Of the bright and restful mansions,
   Where there shall be no night.

Our world, so worn and weary,
   Needs music, pure and strong,

1. Crypts or tombs. See Matthew 23:27.

To hush the jangle and discords
Of sorrow, pain, and wrong.

Music to soothe all its sorrow,
Till war and crime shall cease;
And the hearts of men grown tender
Girdle the world with peace.

1895

An Appeal to My Country Women

You can sigh o'er the sad-eyed Armenian
Who weeps in her desolate home.
You can mourn o'er the exile of Russia
From kindred and friends doomed to roam.

You can pity the men who have woven
From passion and appetite chains
To coil with a terrible tension
Around their heartstrings and brains.

You can sorrow o'er little children
Disinherited from their birth,
The wee waifs and toddlers neglected,
Robbed of sunshine, music and mirth.

For beasts you have gentle compassion;
Your mercy and pity they share.
For the wretched, outcast and fallen
You have tenderness, love and care.

But hark! from our Southland are floating
Sobs of anguish, murmurs of pain,
And women heart-stricken are weeping
Over their tortured and their slain.

On their brows the sun has left traces;
Shrink not from their sorrow in scorn.
When they entered the threshold of being
The children of a King were born.

Each comes as a guest to the table
The hand of our God has outspread,
To fountains that ever leap upward,
To share in the soil we all tread.

When we plead for the wrecked and fallen,
The exile from far-distant shores,
Remember that men are still wasting
Life's crimson around our own doors.

Have ye not, oh, my favored sisters,
  Just a plea, a prayer or a tear,
For mothers who dwell 'neath the shadows
  Of agony, hatred and fear?

Men may tread down the poor and lowly,
  May crush them in anger and hate,
But surely the mills of God's justice
  Will grind out the grist of their fate.

Oh, people sin-laden and guilty,
  So lusty and proud in your prime,
The sharp sickles of God's retribution
  Will gather your harvest of crime.

Weep not, oh my well-sheltered sisters,
  Weep not for the Negro alone,
But weep for your sons who must gather
  The crops which their fathers have sown.

Go read on the tombstones of nations
  Of chieftains who masterful trod,
The sentence which time has engraven,
  That they had forgotten their God.

'Tis the judgment of God that men reap
  The tares[1] which in madness they sow,
Sorrow follows the footsteps of crime,
  And Sin is the consort of Woe.

1900

The Two Offers

"What is the matter with you, Laura, this morning? I have been watching you this hour, and in that time you have commenced a half dozen letters and torn them all up. What matter of such grave moment is puzzling your dear little head, that you do not know how to decide?"

"Well, it is an important matter: I have two offers for marriage, and I do not know which to choose."

"I should accept neither, or to say the least, not at present."

"Why not?"

"Because I think a woman who is undecided between two offers, has not love enough for either to make a choice; and in that very hesitation, indecision, she has a reason to pause and seriously reflect, lest her marriage, instead of being an affinity of souls or a union of hearts, should only be a mere matter of bargain and sale, or an affair of convenience and selfish interest."

"But I consider them both very good offers, just such as many a girl would gladly receive. But to tell you the truth, I do not think that I regard either as

1. Plants, especially poisonous weeds.

a woman should the man she chooses for her husband. But then if I refuse, there is the risk of being an old maid, and that is not to be thought of."

"Well, suppose there is, is that the most dreadful fate that can befall a woman? Is there not more intense wretchedness in an ill-assorted marriage—more utter loneliness in a loveless home, than in the lot of the old maid who accepts her earthly mission as a gift from God, and strives to walk the path of life with earnest and unfaltering steps?"

"Oh! what a little preacher you are. I really believe that you were cut out for an old maid; that when nature formed you, she put in a double portion of intellect to make up for a deficiency of love; and yet you are kind and affectionate. But I do not think that you know anything of the grand, overmastering passion, or the deep necessity of woman's heart for loving."

"Do you think so?" resumed the first speaker; and bending over her work she quietly applied herself to the knitting that had lain neglected by her side, during this brief conversation; but as she did so, a shadow flitted over her pale and intellectual brow, a mist gathered in her eyes, and a slight quivering of the lips, revealed a depth of feeling to which her companion was a stranger.

But before I proceed with my story, let me give you a slight history of the speakers. They were cousins, who had met life under different auspices. Laura Lagrange, was the only daughter of rich and indulgent parents, who had spared no pains to make her an accomplished lady. Her cousin, Janette Alston, was the child of parents, rich only in goodness and affection. Her father had been unfortunate in business, and dying before he could retrieve his fortunes, left his business in an embarrassed state. His widow was unacquainted with his business affairs, and when the estate was settled, hungry creditors had brought their claims and the lawyers had received their fees, she found herself homeless and almost penniless, and she who had been sheltered in the warm clasp of loving arms, found them too powerless to shield her from the pitiless pelting storms of adversity. Year after year she struggled with poverty and wrestled with want, till her toil-worn hands became too feeble to hold the shattered chords of existence, and her tear-dimmed eyes grew heavy with the slumber of death. Her daughter had watched over her with untiring devotion, had closed her eyes in death, and gone out into the busy, restless world, missing a precious tone from the voices of earth, a beloved step from the paths of life. Too self reliant to depend on the charity of relations, she endeavored to support herself by her own exertions, and she had succeeded. Her path for a while was marked with struggle and trial, but instead of uselessly repining, she met them bravely, and her life became not a thing of ease and indulgence, but of conquest, victory, and accomplishments. At the time when this conversation took place, the deep trials of her life had passed away. The achievements of her genius had won her a position in the literary world, where she shone as one of its bright particular stars. And with her fame came a competence of worldly means, which gave her leisure for improvement, and the riper development of her rare talents. And she, that pale intellectual woman, whose genius gave life and vivacity to the social circle, and whose presence threw a halo of beauty and grace around the charmed atmosphere in which she moved, had at one period of her life, known the mystic and solemn strength of an all-absorbing love. Years faded into the misty past, had seen the kindling of her eye, the quick flushing of her cheek, and the wild throbbing of her heart, at tones of a voice long since hushed to the stillness of death. Deeply, wildly, passionately, she had loved. Her whole life seemed like the pouring out of rich, warm and gushing affections. This love quickened her talents, inspired her genius, and threw over her life a tender and spiritual earnestness. And then came a fearful shock, a mournful waking from that "dream of beauty and delight." A shadow fell around her path; it came between her and the object of her heart's worship; first a few cold words, estrangement, and then a painful separation; the old story of woman's pride—digging the sepulchre of her happiness, and then a new-made grave, and her path over it to the spirit world; and thus faded out from that young heart her bright, brief and saddened dream of life. Faint and spirit-broken, she turned from the scenes associated with the memory of the loved and lost. She tried to break the chain of sad associations that bound her to the mournful past; and so, pressing back the bitter sobs from her almost breaking heart, like the dying dolphin, whose beauty is born of its death anguish, her genius gathered strength from suffering and wonderous power and brilliancy from the agony she hid within the desolate chambers of her soul. Men hailed her as one of earth's strangely gifted children, and wreathed the garlands of fame for her brow, when it was throbbing with a wild and fearful unrest. They breathed her name with applause, when through the lonely halls of her stricken spirit, was an earnest cry for peace, a deep yearning for sympathy and heart-support.

But life, with its stern realities, met her; its solemn responsibilities confronted her, and turning, with an earnest and shattered spirit, to life's duties and trials, she found a calmness and strength that she had only imagined in her dreams of poetry and song. We will now pass over a period of ten years, and the cousins have met again. In that calm and lovely woman, in whose eyes is a depth of tenderness, tempering the flashes of her genius, whose looks and tones are full of sympathy and love, we recognize the once smitten and stricken Janette Alston. The bloom of her girlhood had given way to a higher type of spiritual beauty, as if some unseen hand had been polishing and refining the temple in which her lovely spirit found its habitation; and this had been the fact. Her inner life had grown beautiful, and it was this that was constantly developing the outer. Never, in the early flush of womanhood, when an absorbing love had lit up her eyes and glowed in her life, had she appeared so interesting as when, with a countenance which seemed overshadowed with a spiritual light, she bent over the death-bed of a young woman, just lingering at the shadowy gates of the unseen land.

"Has he come?" faintly but eagerly exclaimed the dying woman. "Oh! how I have longed for his coming, and even in death he forgets me."

"Oh, do not say so, dear Laura, some accident may have detained him," said Janette to her cousin; for on that bed, from whence she will never rise, lies the once-beautiful and light-hearted Laura Lagrange, the brightness of whose eyes has long since been dimmed with tears, and whose voice had become like a harp whose every chord is tuned to sadness—whose faintest thrill and loudest vibrations are but the variations of agony. A heavy hand was laid upon her once warm and bounding heart, and a voice came whispering through her soul, that she must die. But, to her, the tidings was a message of deliverance—a voice, hushing her wild sorrows to the calmness of resignation and hope. Life had grown so weary upon her head—the future looked so hopeless—she had no wish to tread again the track where thorns had pierced her feet, and clouds overcast her sky; and she hailed the coming of death's angel as the footsteps of a welcome friend. And yet, earth had one object so very dear to her weary heart. It was her absent and recreant husband; for, since that conversation, she had accepted one of her offers, and become a wife. But, before she married, she learned that great lesson of human experience and woman's life, to love the man who bowed at her shrine, a willing worshipper. He had a pleasing address, raven hair, flashing eyes, a voice of thrilling sweetness, and lips of persuasive eloquence; and being well versed in the ways of the world, he won his way to her heart, and she became his bride, and he was proud of his prize. Vain and superficial in his character, he looked upon marriage not as a divine sacrament for the soul's development and human progression, but as the title-deed that gave him possession of the woman he thought he loved. But alas for her, the laxity of his principles had rendered him unworthy of the deep and undying devotion of a pure-hearted woman; but, for awhile, he hid from her his true character, and she blindly loved him, and for a short period was happy in the consciousness of being beloved; though sometimes a vague unrest would fill her soul, when, overflowing with a sense of the good, the beautiful, and the true, she would turn to him, but find no response to the deep yearnings of her soul—no appreciation of life's highest realities—its solemn grandeur and significant importance. Their souls never met, and soon she found a void in her bosom, that his earth-born love could not fill. He did not satisfy the wants of her mental and moral nature—between him and her there was no affinity of minds, no intercommunion of souls.

Talk as you will of woman's deep capacity for loving, of the strength of her affectional nature. I do not deny it; but will the mere possession of any human love, fully satisfy all the demands of her whole being? You may paint her in poetry or fiction, as a frail vine, clinging to her brother man for support, and dying when deprived of it; and all this may sound well enough to please the imaginations of school-girls, or love-lorn maidens. But woman—the true woman—if you would render her happy, it needs more than the mere development of her affectional nature. Her conscience should be enlightened, her faith in the true and right established, and scope given to her Heaven-endowed and God-given faculties. The true aim of female education should be, not a development of one or two, but all the faculties of the human soul, because no perfect womanhood is developed by imperfect culture. Intense love is often akin to intense suffering, and to trust the whole wealth of a woman's nature on the frail bark of human love, may often be like trusting a cargo of gold and precious gems, to a bark that has never battled with the storm, or buffetted the waves. Is it any wonder, then, that so many life-barks go down, paving the ocean of time with precious hearts and wasted hopes? that so many float around us, shattered and dismasted wrecks? that so many are stranded on the shoals of existence, mournful beacons and solemn warnings for the thoughtless, to whom marriage is a careless and hasty rushing together of the affections? Alas that an institution so fraught with good for humanity should be so perverted, and that state of life, which should be filled with happiness, become so replete with misery. And this was the fate of Laura Lagrange. For a brief period after her marriage her life seemed like a bright and beautiful dream, full of hope and radiant with joy. And then there came a change—he found other attractions that lay beyond the pale of home influences. The gambling saloon had power to win him from her side, he had lived in an element of unhealthy and unhallowed excitements, and the society of a loving wife, the pleasures of a well-regulated home, were enjoyments too tame for one who had vitiated his tastes by the pleasures of sin. There were charmed houses of vice, built upon dead men's loves, where, amid a flow of song, laughter, wine, and careless mirth, he would spend hour after hour, forgetting the cheek that was paling through his neglect, heedless of the tear-dimmed eyes, peering anxiously into the darkness, waiting, or watching his return.

The influence of old associations was upon him. In early life, home had been to him a place of ceilings and walls, not a true home, built upon goodness, love and truth. It was a place where velvet carpets hushed his tread, where images of loveliness and beauty invoked into being by painter's art and sculptor's skill, pleased the eye and gratified the taste, where magnificence surrounded his way and costly clothing adorned his person; but it was not the place for the true culture and right development of his soul. His father had been too much engrossed in making money, and his mother in spending it, in striving to maintain a fashionable position in society, and shining in the eyes of the world, to give the proper direction to the character of their wayward and impulsive son. His mother put beautiful robes upon his body, but left ugly scars upon his soul; she pampered his appetite, but starved his spirit. Every mother should be a true artist, who knows how to weave into her child's life images of grace and beauty, the true poet capable of writing on the soul of childhood the harmony of love and truth, and teaching it how to produce the grandest of all poems—the poetry of a true and noble life. But in his home, a love for the good, the true and right, had been sacrificed at the shrine of frivolity and fashion. That parental authority which should have been preserved as a string of precious pearls, unbroken and unscattered, was simply the administration of chance. At one time obedience was enforced by authority, at another time by flattery and promises, and just as often it was not enforced at all. His early associations were formed as chance directed, and from his want of home-training, his character received a bias, his life a shade, which ran through every avenue of his existence, and darkened all his future hours. Oh, if we would trace the history of all the crimes that have o'ershadowed this sin-shrouded and sorrow-darkened world of ours, how many might be seen arising from the wrong home influences, or the weakening of the home ties. Home should always be the best school for the affections, the birthplace of high resolves, and the altar upon which lofty aspirations are kindled, from whence the soul may go forth strengthened, to act its part aright in the great drama of life, with conscience enlightened, affections cultivated, and reason and judgment dominant. But alas for the young wife. Her husband had not been blessed with such a home. When he entered the arena of life, the voices from home did not linger around his path as angels of guidance about his steps; they were not like so many messages to invite him to deeds of high and holy worth. The memory of no sainted mother arose between him and deeds of darkness; the earnest prayers of no father arrested him in his downward course; and before a year of his married life had waned, his young wife had learned to wait and mourn his frequent and uncalled-for absence. More than once had she seen him come home from his midnight haunts, the bright intelligence of his eye displaced by the drunkard's stare, and his manly gait changed to the inebriate's stagger; and she was beginning to know the bitter agony that is compressed in the mournful words, a drunkard's wife. And then there came a bright but brief episode in her experience; the angel of life gave to her existence a deeper meaning and loftier significance: she sheltered in the warm clasp of her loving arms, a dear babe, a precious child, whose love filled every chamber of her heart, and felt the fount of maternal love gushing so new within her soul. That child was hers. How overshadowing was the love with which she bent over its helplessness, how much it helped to fill the void and chasms in her soul. How many lonely hours were beguiled by its winsome ways, its answering smiles and fond caresses. How exquisite and solemn was the feeling that thrilled her heart when she clasped the tiny hands together and taught her dear child to call God "Our Father."

What a blessing was that child. The father paused in his headlong career, awed by the strange beauty and precocious intellect of his child; and the mother's life had a better expression through her ministrations of love. And then there came hours of bitter anguish, shading the sunlight of her home and hushing the music of her heart. The angel of death bent over the couch of her child and beaconed it away. Closer and closer the mother strained her child to her wildly heaving breast, and struggled with the heavy hand that lay upon its heart. Love and agony contended with death, and the language of the mother's heart was,

"Oh, Death, away! that innocent is mine;
  I cannot spare him from my arms
To lay him, Death, in thine.
  I am a mother, Death; I gave that darling birth
I could not bear his lifeless limbs
  Should moulder in the earth."

But death was stronger than love and mightier than agony and won the child for the land of crystal founts and deathless flowers, and the poor, stricken mother sat down beneath the shadow of her mighty grief, feeling as if a great light had gone out from her soul, and that the sunshine had suddenly faded around her path. She turned in her deep anguish to the father of her child, the loved and cherished dead. For awhile his words were kind and tender, his heart seemed subdued, and his tenderness fell upon her worn and weary heart like rain on perishing flowers, or cooling waters to lips all parched with thirst and scorched with fever; but the change was evanescent, the influence of unhallowed associations and evil habits had vitiated and poisoned the springs of his existence. They had bound him in their meshes, and he lacked the moral strength to break his fetters, and stand erect in all the strength and dignity of a true manhood, making life's highest excellence his ideal, and striving to gain it.

And yet moments of deep contrition would sweep over him, when he would resolve to abandon the wine-cup forever, when he was ready to forswear the handling of another card, and he would try to break away from the associations that he felt were working his ruin; but when the hour of temptation came his strength was weakness, his earnest purposes were cobwebs, his well-meant resolutions ropes of sand, and thus passed year after year of the married life of Laura Lagrange. She tried to hide her agony from the public gaze, to smile when her heart was almost breaking. But year after year her voice grew fainter and sadder, her once light and bounding step grew slower and faltering. Year after year she wrestled with agony, and strove with despair, till the quick eyes of her brother read, in the paling of her cheek and the dimming eye, the secret anguish of her worn and weary spirit. On that wan, sad face, he saw the death-tokens, and he knew the dark wing of the mystic angel swept coldly around her path. "Laura," said her brother to her one day, "you are not well, and I think you need our mother's tender care and nursing. You are daily losing strength, and if you will go I will accompany you." At first, she hesitated, she shrank almost instinctively from presenting that pale sad face to the loved ones at home. That face was such a tell-tale; it told of heart-sickness, of hope deferred, and the mournful story of unrequited love. But then a deep yearning for home sympathy woke within her a passionate longing for love's kind words, for tenderness and heart-support, and she resolved to seek the home of her childhood, and lay her weary head upon her mother's bosom, to be folded again in her loving arms, to lay that poor, bruised and aching heart where it might beat and throb closely to the loved ones at home. A kind welcome awaited her. All that love and tenderness could devise was done to bring the bloom to her cheek and the light to her eye; but it was all in vain; her's was a disease that no medicine could cure, no earthly balm would heal. It was a slow wasting of the vital forces, the sickness of the soul. The unkindness and neglect of her husband, lay like a leaden weight upon her heart, and slowly oozed away its life-drops. And where was he that had won her love, and then cast it aside as a useless thing, who rifled her heart of its wealth and spread bitter ashes upon its broken altars? He was lingering away from her when the death-damps were gathering on her brow, when his name was trembling on her lips! lingering away! when she was watching his coming, though the death films were gathering before her eyes, and earthly things were fading from her vision. "I think I hear him now," said the dying woman, "surely that is his step;" but the sound died away in the distance. Again she started from an uneasy slumber, "That is his voice! I am so glad he has come." Tears gathered in the eyes of the sad watchers by that dying bed, for they knew that she was deceived. He had not returned. For her sake they wished his coming. Slowly the hours waned away, and then came the sad, soul-sickening thought that she was forgotten, forgotten in the last hour of human need, forgotten when the spirit, about to be dissolved, paused for the last time on the threshold of existence, a weary watcher at the gates of death. "He has forgotten me," again she faintly murmured, and the last tears she would ever shed on earth sprung to her mournful eyes, and clasping her hands together in silent anguish, a few broken sentences issued from her pale and quivering lips. They were prayers for strength and earnest pleading for him who had desolated her young life, by turning its sunshine to shadows, its smiles to tears. "He has forgotten me," she murmured again, "but I can bear it, the bitterness of death is passed, and soon I hope to exchange the shadows of death for the brightness of eternity, the rugged paths of life for the golden streets of glory, and the care and turmoils of earth for the peace and rest of heaven." Her voice grew fainter and fainter, they saw the shadows that never deceive flit over her pale and faded face, and knew that the death angel waited to soothe their weary one to rest, to calm the throbbing of her bosom and cool the fever of her brain. And amid the silent hush of their grief the freed spirit, refined through suffering, and brought into divine harmony through the spirit of the living Christ, passed over the dark waters of death as on a bridge of light, over whose radiant arches hovering angels bent. They parted the dark locks from her marble brow, closed the waxen lids over the once bright and laughing eye, and left her to the dreamless slumber of the grave. Her cousin turned from that deathbed a sadder and wiser woman. She resolved more earnestly than ever to make the world better by her example, gladder by her presence, and to kindle the fires of her genius on the altars of universal love and truth. She had a higher and better object in all her writings than the mere acquisition of gold, or acquirement of fame. She felt that she had a high and holy mission on the battle-field of existence, that life was not given her to be frittered away in nonsense, or wasted away in trifling pursuits. She would willingly espouse an unpopular cause but not an unrighteous one. In her the down-trodden slave found an earnest advocate; the flying fugitive remembered her kindness as he stepped cautiously through our Republic, to gain his freedom in a monarchial land, having broken the chains on which the rust of centuries had gathered. Little children learned to name her with affection, the poor called her blessed, as she broke her bread to the pale lips of hunger. Her life was like a beautiful story, only it was clothed with the dignity of reality and invested with the sublimity of truth. True, she was an old maid, no husband brightened her life with his love, or shaded it with his neglect. No children nestling lovingly in her arms called her mother. No one appended Mrs. to her name; she was indeed an old maid, not vainly striving to keep up an appearance of girlishness, when departed was written on her youth. Not vainly pining at her loneliness and isolation: the world was full of warm, loving hearts, and her own beat in unison with them. Neither was she always sentimentally sighing for something to love, objects of affection were all around her, and the world was not so wealthy in love that it had no use for her's; in blessing others she made a life and benediction, and as old age descended peacefully and gently upon her, she had learned one of life's most precious lessons, that true happiness consists not so much in the fruition of our wishes as in the regulation of desires and the full development and right culture of our whole natures.

1859

Our Greatest Want

Leading ideas impress themselves upon communities and countries. A thought is evolved and thrown out among the masses, they receive it and it becomes interwoven with their mental and moral life—if the thought be good the receivers are benefited, and helped onward to the truer life; if it is not, the reception of the idea is a detriment. A few earnest thinkers, and workers infuse into the mind of Great Britain, a sentiment of human brotherhood. The hue and cry of opposition is raised against it. Avarice and cupidity oppose it, but the great heart of the people throbs for it. A healthy public opinion dashes and surges against the British throne, the idea gains ground and progresses till hundreds of thousands of men, women and children arise, redeemed from bondage, and freed from chains, and the nation gains moral power by the act.[1] Visions of dominion, proud dreams of conquest fill the soul of Napoleon Bonaparte, and he infuses them into the mind of

1. Great Britain had abolished slavery in the British Empire in 1833.

France, and the peace of Europe is invaded. His bloodstained armies dazzled and misled, follow him through carnage and blood, to shake earth's proudest kingdoms to their base, and the march of a true progression is stayed by a river of blood. In America, where public opinion exerts such a sway, a leading is success. The politician who chooses for his candidate not the best man but the most available one.—The money getter, who virtually says let me make money, though I coin it from blood and extract it from tears—The minister, who stoops from his high position to the slave power, and in a word all who barter principle for expediency, the true and right for the available and convenient, are worshipers at the shrine of success. And we, or at least some of us, upon whose faculties the rust of centuries has lain, are beginning to awake and worship at the same altar, and bow to the idols. The idea if I understand it aright, that is interweaving itself with our thoughts, is that the greatest need of our people at present is money, and that as money is a symbol of power, the possession of it will gain for us the rights which power and prejudice now deny us.—And it may be true that the richer we are the nearer we are to social and political equality; but somehow, (and I may not fully comprehend the idea,) it does not seem to me that money, as little as we possess of it, is our greatest want. Neither do I think that the possession of intelligence and talent is our greatest want. If I understand our greatest wants aright they strike deeper than any want that gold or knowledge can supply. We want more soul, a higher cultivation of all our spiritual faculties. We need more unselfishness, earnestness and integrity. Our greatest need is not gold or silver, talent or genius, but true men and true women. We have millions of our race in the prison house of slavery, but have we yet a single Moses in freedom. And if we had who among us would be led by him?

I like the character of Moses. He is the first disunionist[2] we read of in the Jewish Scriptures. The magnificence of Pharaoh's throne loomed up before his vision, its oriental splendors glittered before his eyes; but he turned from them all and chose rather to suffer with the enslaved, than rejoice with the free. He would have no union with the slave power of Egypt. When we have a race of men whom this blood stained government cannot tempt or flatter, who would sternly refuse every office in the nation's gift, from a president down to a tide-waiter,[3] until she shook her hands from complicity in the guilt of cradle plundering and man stealing, then for us the foundations of an historic character will have been laid. We need men and women whose hearts are the homes of a high and lofty enthusiasm, and a noble devotion to the cause of emancipation, who are ready and willing to lay time, talent and money on the altar of universal freedom. We have money among us, but how much of it is spent to bring deliverance to our captive brethren? Are our wealthiest men the most liberal sustainers of the Anti-slavery enterprise? Or does the bare fact of their having money, really help mould public opinion and reverse its sentiments? We need what money cannot buy and what affluence is too beggarly to purchase. Earnest, self sacrificing souls that will stamp themselves not only on the present but the future. Let us not then defer all our noble opportunities till we get rich. And here I am not aiming to enlist a fanatical crusade against the desire for riches, but I do protest against chaining down the soul, with

2. In the antebellum period, anyone who advocated secession from or dissolution of the United States.
3. A dock laborer who tows boats.

its Heaven endowed faculties and God given attributes to the one idea of getting money as stepping into power or even gaining our rights in common with others. The respect that is only bought by gold is not worth much. It is no honor to shake hands politically with men who whip women and steal babies. If this government has no call for our services, no aim for your children, we have the greater need of them to build up a true manhood and womanhood for ourselves. The important lesson we should learn and be able to teach, is how to make every gift, whether gold or talent, fortune or genius, subserve the cause of crushed humanity and carry out the greatest idea of the present age, the glorious idea of human brotherhood.

1859

From Fancy Etchings

2/20/73

[ENTHUSIASM AND LOFTY ASPIRATIONS]

"Aunt Jane? Aunt Jane?"

I lifted up my eyes as a fresh young voice sang out my name in tones of pleasurable excitement, and before me stood my niece; her face aglow with one of those beautiful enthusiasms which ever lend a charm to the plainest face.

"What is it, darling?"

"Why Aunty, I want you to immortalize yourself. I want you to write a book, a good book, full of hard, earnest thoughts. A book that will make people better and happier because they read it. I wish I had your power of utterance, and I would write such a book. I am just from College and I mean to do something for my race."

I said, "What do you mean to do?" for her words had awakened my interest.

"I hardly know what I shall succeed in doing, but I want to be a living loving force, not a mere intellectual force, eager about and excited only for my own welfare; but a moral and spiritual force. A woman who can and will do something for women, especially for our own women because they will need me most."

"I am glad, very glad, Jenny, that you have concluded to make something out of your young life. I am always delighted when I see young people full of enthusiasm and lofty aspirations. Our women have been treated as the 'fag' end[1] women of the country; but now that advantages are thrown open to you, which were denied to us older women, I hope that you will prove that your minds are widening with the cycles of the sun. Jenny, darling, permit me to say to you, set your mark high; aim at perfection, and if you would succeed yourself, always be ready to acknowledge the success of others, and do not place the culture of your intellect before the development of your soul. The culture of the intellect may bring you money and applause, but the right training of your soul will give you character and influence; but really Jenny you did not ask me for a sermon and I will stop moralizing."

1. The last part or the very end of something.

"Oh! no dear Aunty, I love to hear you talk. You often regret your limited knowledge of books; but you are a book yourself, and I am passionately fond of reading you."

"Thank you, darling, you are quite complimentary to me this morning, but I suppose you like to say pleasant things to Aunty."

"But Aunty if they are pleasant, they are true. If some of us younger women have more learning, you have more knowledge; and if we know more of books, you know more of life; and one knowledge should supplement the other. I felt rather provoked, when Thomas Pemroy, who was discussing with you on some disputed point, asked you in such a tone of conceited superiority, 'Don't you know any better than that?' and, I thought that you felt a little sensitive when Mary Talbot took the liberty to correct a mispronounced word of yours in the presence of several persons."

"Of course I did not feel as if she were treating me very politely; but I attributed it to her lack of social training. Of course I don't suppose that any of us like to be treated as if our words were mice, and that a critic sat beside us like a watchful cat, ever ready to pounce upon a mishap or slipshod word. I think an undue cultivation of the spirit of criticism becomes a kill joy to genial conversation, and a repressive force in society."

"I think Aunty, that conversation ought to be made one of the finest and most excellent of all arts. Have you not met with some people with whom you feel it easy to converse? They seem to unlock your heart and loosen your lips. Then there are others who do not talk to you; they make speeches at you; they step through their sentences as if their words were eggs and they were afraid of hatching them, and they convey to your mind an idea of a self-consciousness that annoys you."

"Yes, I have met with just such people; but how I do enjoy those genial souls, whose fine social tact, and generous appreciation, unloosen your lips and make you feel at home with them. I often desire these people with tact, more than I do the people of mere talent; but when both are combined, I think it creates a delightful companionship. But Jenny we have wandered from our original subject, what do you intend doing in the future."

"Well Aunty I will tell you when I come again. It is a pleasant little secret, but it will keep; and I must go now for I have an engagement at eleven o'clock, and it is now half past ten, so good-bye Aunty."

"Good-bye, Jenny, come again soon, and unfold to Aunty's willing ear, all the wise schemes and loving plans you have for the good of our people, and in the meantime rest assured of my hearty sympathy for the cause in which you are interested."

1873

Woman's Political Future[1]

If before sin had cast its deepest shadows or sorrow had distilled its bitterest tears, it was true that it was not good for man to be alone,[2] it is no less true, since the shadows have deepened and life's sorrows have increased, that the

1. Speech given at the World's Congress of Representative Women at the Columbian Exposition, the 1893 World's Fair commemorating the "discovery" of the Americas. Harper was one of four African American women to address this audience.

2. Genesis 2:18.

world has need of all the spiritual aid that woman can give for the social advancement and moral development of the human race. The tendency of the present age, with its restlessness, religious upheavals, failures, blunders, and crimes, is toward broader freedom, an increase of knowledge, the emancipation of thought, and a recognition of the brotherhood of man; in this movement woman, as the companion of man, must be a sharer. So close is the bond between man and woman that you can not raise one without lifting the other. The world can not move without woman's sharing in the movement, and to help give a right impetus to that movement is woman's highest privilege.

If the fifteenth century discovered America to the Old World, the nineteenth is discovering woman to herself. Little did Columbus imagine, when the New World broke upon his vision like a lovely gem in the coronet of the universe, the glorious possibilities of a land where the sun should be our engraver, the winged lightning our messenger, and steam our beast of burden. But as mind is more than matter, and the highest ideal always the true real, so to woman comes the opportunity to strive for richer and grander discoveries than ever gladdened the eye of the Genoese mariner.

Not the opportunity of discovering new worlds, but that of filling this old world with fairer and higher aims than the greed of gold and the lust of power, is hers. Through weary, wasting years men have destroyed, dashed in pieces, and overthrown, but to-day we stand on the threshold of woman's era, and woman's work is grandly constructive. In her hand are possibilities whose use or abuse must tell upon the political life of the nation, and send their influence for good or evil across the track of unborn ages.

As the saffron tints and crimson flushes of morn herald the coming day, so the social and political advancement which woman has already gained bears the promise of the rising of the full-orbed sun of emancipation. The result will be not to make home less happy, but society more holy; yet I do not think the mere extension of the ballot a panacea for all the ills of our national life. What we need to-day is not simply more voters, but better voters. To-day there are red-handed men[3] in our republic, who walk unwhipped of justice, who richly deserve to exchange the ballot of the freeman for the wristlets of the felon; brutal and cowardly men, who torture, burn, and lynch their fellow-men, men whose defenselessness should be their best defense and their weakness an ensign of protection. More than the changing of institutions we need the development of a national conscience, and the upbuilding of national character. Men may boast of the aristocracy of blood, may glory in the aristocracy of talent, and be proud of the aristocracy of wealth, but there is one aristocracy which must ever outrank them all, and that is the aristocracy of character; and it is the women of a country who help to mold its character, and to influence if not determine its destiny; and in the political future of our nation woman will not have done what she could if she does not endeavor to have our republic stand foremost among the nations of the earth, wearing sobriety as a crown and righteousness as a garment and a girdle. In coming into her political estate woman will find a mass of illiteracy to be dispelled. If knowledge is power, ignorance is also power. The power that educates wickedness may manipulate and dash against the pillars of any state when they are undermined and honeycombed by injustice.

3. That is, those in the act of committing a crime or wrongdoing.

I envy neither the heart nor the head of any legislator who has been born to an inheritance of privileges, who has behind him ages of education, dominion, civilization, and Christianity, if he stands opposed to the passage of a national education bill, whose purpose is to secure education to the children of those who were born under the shadow of institutions which made it a crime to read.

To-day women hold in their hands influence and opportunity, and with these they have already opened doors which have been closed to others. By opening doors of labor woman has become a rival claimant for at least some of the wealth monopolized by her stronger brother. In the home she is the priestess, in society the queen, in literature she is a power, in legislative halls law-makers have responded to her appeals, and for her sake have humanized and liberalized their laws. The press has felt the impress of her hand. In the pews of the church she constitutes the majority; the pulpit has welcomed her, and in the school she has the blessed privilege of teaching children and youth. To her is apparently coming the added responsibility of political power; and what she now possesses should only be the means of preparing her to use the coming power for the glory of God and the good of mankind; for power without righteousness is one of the most dangerous forces in the world.

Political life in our country has plowed in muddy channels, and needs the infusion of clearer and cleaner waters. I am not sure that women are naturally so much better than men that they will clear the stream by the virtue of their womanhood; it is not through sex but through character that the best influence of women upon the life of the nation must be exerted.

I do not believe in unrestricted and universal suffrage for either men or women. I believe in moral and educational tests. I do not believe that the most ignorant and brutal man is better prepared to add value to the strength and durability of the government than the most cultured, upright, and intelligent woman. I do not think that willful ignorance should swamp earnest intelligence at the ballot-box, nor that educated wickedness, violence, and fraud should cancel the votes of honest men. The unsteady hands of a drunkard can not cast the ballot of a freeman. The hands of lynchers are too red with blood to determine the political character of the government for even four short years. The ballot in the hands of woman means power added to influence. How well she will use that power I can not foretell. Great evils stare us in the face that need to be throttled by the combined power of an upright manhood and an enlightened womanhood; and I know that no nation can gain its full measure of enlightenment and happiness if one-half of it is free and the other half is fettered. China compressed the feet of her women and thereby retarded the steps of her men. The elements of a nation's weakness must ever be found at the hearthstone.

More than the increase of wealth, the power of armies, and the strength of fleets is the need of good homes, of good fathers, and good mothers.

The life of a Roman citizen was in danger in ancient Palestine, and men had bound themselves with a vow that they would eat nothing until they had killed the Apostle Paul. Pagan Rome threw around that imperiled life a bulwark of living clay consisting of four hundred and seventy human hearts, and Paul was saved.[4] Surely the life of the humblest American citizen should be as well protected in America as that of a Roman citizen was in heathen

4. Because he was a Roman citizen, the Roman government went to great lengths to protect Paul from physical assault by those who disagreed with his teachings. See Acts 23–26.

Rome. A wrong done to the weak should be an insult to the strong. Woman coming into her kingdom will find enthroned three great evils, for whose overthrow she should be as strong in a love of justice and humanity as the warrior is in his might. She will find intemperance sending its flood of shame, and death, and sorrow to the homes of men, a fretting leprosy in our politics, and a blighting curse in our social life; the social evil sending to our streets women whose laughter is sadder than their tears, who slide from the paths of sin and shame to the friendly shelter of the grave; and lawlessness enacting in our republic deeds over which angels might weep, if heaven knows sympathy.

How can any woman send petitions to Russia against the horrors of Siberian prisons if, ages after the Inquisition has ceased to devise its tortures, she has not done all she could by influence, tongue, and pen to keep men from making bonfires of the bodies of real or supposed criminals?

O women of America! into your hands God has pressed one of the sublimest opportunities that ever came into the hands of the women of any race or people. It is yours to create a healthy public sentiment; to demand justice, simple justice, as the right of every race; to brand with everlasting infamy the lawless and brutal cowardice that lynches, burns, and tortures your own countrymen.

To grapple with the evils which threaten to undermine the strength of the nation and to lay magazines of powder under the cribs of future generations is no child's play.

Let the hearts of the women of the world respond to the song of the herald angels of peace on earth and good will to men. Let them throb as one heart unified by the grand and holy purpose of uplifting the human race, and humanity will breathe freer, and the world grow brighter. With such a purpose Eden would spring up in our path, and Paradise be around our way.

1893

HARRIET E. WILSON
1825–1900

The first novel by an African American woman, Harriet E. Wilson's *Our Nig; or, Sketches from the Life of a Free Black, in a Two-Story White House, North* (1859), is also pioneering because of its realistic examination of life among free Blacks in the North. The central figure in *Our Nig* is based on Wilson herself, a working-class woman who set out to reveal from her actual experience in the North that "slavery's shadows fall even there." The mockery of freedom that northern Black people had to endure during the antebellum era first received serious attention in fiction in Frank J. Webb's *The Garies and Their Friends* (1857), the third novel, after Douglass's *The Heroic Slave* (1853) and Brown's *Clotel* (1853), authored by an African American. But Wilson's fictionalized autobiography makes a more convincing case than Webb's novel for the connection between racism and the economic subordination of Blacks to whites in the antebellum North. Moreover, Wilson's sensitivity to gender in her representation of a Black servant girl as a sympathetic and admirable figure makes *Our Nig* a key intervention in the history of American fiction's treatment of women of color.

Little was known about the identity or the biography of Harriet E. Wilson until Henry Louis Gates, Jr., undertook research on her and her novel in the early 1980s. Gates's ground-breaking 1983 edition of *Our Nig* restored the novel to African American literary history and catalyzed widespread biographical research and critical re-assessments of the origins of African American women's fiction. Thanks to subsequent work by several scholars, particularly P. Gabrielle Foreman and Reginald Pitts, the outlines of Harriet Adams Wilson's life have become clearer. Harriet Adams was born in Milford, New Hampshire, in 1825 and grew up in a white household, working as an indentured servant from the time that she was a child. She married Thomas Wilson, an itinerant lecturer, in her hometown in 1851 and gave birth to a son, George Mason Wilson, in the spring of 1852. Deserted by her husband, Wilson struggled to support herself; early in 1860 she suffered the death of her son. By the time her novel was published in Boston at her own expense in the fall of 1859, she had launched a business in that city selling hair products. During the Civil War, Wilson reinvented herself as Dr. Hattie E. Wilson, "the colored medium," becoming a rising star in the Spiritualist movement in Massachusetts in the late 1860s. In 1870 Wilson married John Gallatin Robinson in Boston. For the next three decades she enjoyed recognition for her work as a healer, trance medium, and lecturer while also negotiating racial prejudice within Spiritualist communities. Wilson died in Quincy, Massachusetts, on June 28, 1900.

The correspondences between *Our Nig,* the letters of recommendation that append it, and the facts that have been uncovered about its author's youth, suggest that Wilson's years as an indentured servant in Milford were harsh and dispiriting, as were the childhood and teens of Alfrado, the much-mistreated protagonist of *Our Nig.* That Wilson married a reputed fugitive from slavery, as Alfrado does in the novel, and was abandoned in pregnancy by her husband, as Alfrado notes in her story, is also attested to by one of the writers of a recommendation letter for *Our Nig.* Wilson's and Alfrado's struggles for dignity and self-sufficiency finally dovetail in the literary and economic venture that was *Our Nig.* After years of emotional and physical abuse at the hands of her white female employer, which left her so weakened that she had to depend on public assistance for herself and her son, Wilson turned to novel writing as a means of earning a living and supporting her family. Thus African American women's fiction originated in necessity, if not virtual desperation, but took form and meaning in Wilson's eloquent testimony to the economics of class as well as race and gender in her life.

Our Nig is a woman's growing-up story. More than one critic has noted its similarities to white American women's fiction of the mid-nineteenth century, particularly its focus on the struggles of a young single woman to achieve economic independence and self-respect. Alfrado's fundamental motivation through most of her story is to defend herself against the assaults on her psyche as well as her body perpetrated by her mistress, Mrs. Bellmont. A later goal for Alfrado is to find some means by which she might "succeed in providing for her own wants." A lack of money and social connections handicaps Alfrado profoundly. But unlike white working-class girls, she must also negotiate fierce racial prejudice, manifested in Mrs. Bellmont's determined resistance to any aspiration Alfrado has for a life no longer subjected to whites. Although Mrs. Bellmont and her daughter Mary dedicate themselves to breaking Alfrado's spirit, they never succeed in doing so.

Our Nig joins forces with antebellum Black women's spiritual autobiographies by Jarena Lee and Zilpha Elaw and Harriet Jacobs's pioneering slave narrative to pay special tribute to the strength of character and moral resolution of African American women. Alfrado's out-of-wedlock birth to a white woman and a Black man, which Wilson records with rare candor and understanding, would have disqualified her from serious attention at the hands of almost any conventional novelist of the era. By focusing on Alfrado's struggle to attain dignity and self-assurance founded in religious faith, Wilson asserted her decision to depart from literary norms and invest in her Black female protagonist qualities of genuine heroism. Consistent with a view of Christianity put forward in much nineteenth-century African American writing, Alfrado's faith transforms her self-estimate, endows her with an undaunted sense of power and hope, and spurs her toward direct confrontation with her oppressor. Like Douglass's famous battle with Covey the slave breaker, Alfrado's climactic defiance of Mrs. Bellmont is represented as an act of self-reclamation and spiritual regeneration. Wilson signals her female hero's victory in classic slave narrative fashion: escaping the "two-story white house, North," Alfrado sets out in quest of economic, intellectual, and spiritual "self-improvement." Marriage, ironically, does not bring her the security that it often symbolizes for women in sentimental fiction of the time. But Alfrado does not give in to hopelessness. Instead she concludes her story with a promise to her reader that "nothing turns her from her steadfast purpose of elevating herself." In the voice of the narrator of *Our Nig*, Wilson articulated a self-confidence and an unswerving commitment to a brighter future that remain a hallmark of Black women's fiction in the United States.

From Our Nig; or, Sketches from the Life of a Free Black, in a Two-Story White House, North

Preface

In offering to the public the following pages, the writer confesses her inability to minister to the refined and cultivated, the pleasure supplied by abler pens. It is not for such these crude narrations appear. Deserted by kindred, disabled by failing health, I am forced to some experiment which shall aid me in maintaining myself and child without extinguishing this feeble life. I would not from these motives even palliate slavery at the South, by disclosures of its appurtenances North. My mistress was wholly imbued with *southern* principles. I do not pretend to divulge every transaction in my own life, which the unprejudiced would declare unfavorable in comparison with treatment of legal bondmen; I have purposely omitted what would most provoke shame in our good anti-slavery friends at home.

My humble position and frank confession of errors will, I hope, shield me from severe criticism. Indeed, defects are so apparent it requires no skilful hand to expose them.

I sincerely appeal to my colored brethren universally for patronage, hoping they will not condemn this attempt of their sister to be erudite, but rally around me a faithful band of supporters and defenders.

H. E. W.

Chapter I. Mag Smith, My Mother

Oh, Grief beyond all other griefs, when fate
First leaves the young heart lone and desolate
In the wide world, without that only tie
For which it loved to live or feared to die;
Lorn as the hung-up lute, that ne'er hath spoken
Since the sad day its master-chord was broken!
Moore.[1]

1. From Thomas Moore's popular "Oriental Romance" in verse, *Lalla Rookh* (1817).

Lonely Mag Smith! See her as she walks with downcast eyes and heavy heart. It was not always thus. She *had* a loving, trusting heart. Early deprived of parental guardianship, far removed from relatives, she was left to guide her tiny boat over life's surges alone and inexperienced. As she merged into womanhood, unprotected, uncherished, uncared for, there fell on her ear the music of love, awakening an intensity of emotion long dormant. It whispered of an elevation before unaspired to; of ease and plenty her simple heart had never dreamed of as hers. She knew the voice of her charmer, so ravishing, sounded far above her. It seemed like an angel's, alluring her upward and onward. She thought she could ascend to him and become an equal. She surrendered to him a priceless gem, which he proudly garnered as a trophy, with those of other victims, and left her to her fate. The world seemed full of hateful deceivers and crushing arrogance. Conscious that the great bond of union to her former companions was severed, that the disdain of others would be insupportable, she determined to leave the few friends she possessed, and seek an asylum among strangers. Her offspring came unwelcomed, and before its nativity numbered weeks, it passed from earth, ascending to a purer and better life.

"God be thanked," ejaculated Mag, as she saw its breathing cease; "no one can taunt *her* with my ruin."

Blessed release! may we all respond. How many pure, innocent children not only inherit a wicked heart of their own, claiming life-long scrutiny and restraint, but are heirs also of parental disgrace and calumny, from which only long years of patient endurance in paths of rectitude can disencumber them.

Mag's new home was soon contaminated by the publicity of her fall; she had a feeling of degradation oppressing her; but she resolved to be circumspect, and try to regain in a measure what she had lost. Then some foul tongue would jest of her shame, and averted looks and cold greetings disheartened her. She saw she could not bury in forgetfulness her misdeed, so she resolved to leave her home and seek another in the place she at first fled from.

Alas, how fearful are we to be first in extending a helping hand to those who stagger in the mires of infamy; to speak the first words of hope and warning to those emerging into the sunlight of morality! Who can tell what numbers, advancing just far enough to hear a cold welcome and join in the reserved converse of professed reformers, disappointed, disheartened, have chosen to dwell in unclean places, rather than encounter these "holier-than-thou" of the great brotherhood of man!

Such was Mag's experience; and disdaining to ask favor or friendship from a sneering world, she resolved to shut herself up in a hovel she had often passed in better days, and which she knew to be untenanted. She vowed to ask no favors of familiar faces; to die neglected and forgotten before she would be dependent on any. Removed from the village, she was seldom seen except as upon your introduction, gentle reader, with downcast visage, returning her work to her employer, and thus providing herself with the means of subsistence. In two years many hands craved the same avocation; foreigners who cheapened toil and clamored for a livelihood, competed with her, and she could not thus sustain herself. She was now above no drudgery. Occasionally old acquaintances called to be favored with help of some kind, which she was glad to bestow for the sake of the money it would bring her; but the association with them was such a painful reminder of by-gones, she returned to her hut morose and revengeful, refusing all offers of a better home than she possessed. Thus she lived for years, hugging her wrongs, but making no effort to escape. She had never known plenty, scarcely competency; but the present was beyond comparison with those innocent years when the coronet of virtue was hers.

Every year her melancholy increased, her means diminished. At last no one seemed to notice her, save a kind-hearted African, who often called to inquire after her health and to see if she needed any fuel, he having the responsibility of furnishing that article, and she in return mending or making garments.

"How much you earn dis week, Mag?" asked he one Saturday evening.

"Little enough, Jim. Two or three days without any dinner. I washed for the Reeds, and did a small job for Mrs. Bellmont; that's all. I shall starve soon, unless I can get more to do. Folks seem as afraid to come here as if they expected to get some awful disease. I don't believe there is a person in the world but would be glad to have me dead and out of the way."

"No, no, Mag! don't talk so. You shan't starve so long as I have barrels to hoop. Peter Greene boards me cheap. I'll help you, if nobody else will."

A tear stood in Mag's faded eye. "I'm glad," she said, with a softer tone than before, "if there is *one* who isn't glad to see me suffer. I b'lieve all Singleton wants to see me punished, and feel as if they could tell when I've been punished long enough. It's a long day ahead they'll set it, I reckon."

After the usual supply of fuel was prepared, Jim returned home. Full of pity for Mag, he set about devising measures for her relief. "By golly!" said he to himself one day—for he had become so absorbed in Mag's interest that he had fallen into a habit of musing aloud—"By golly! I wish she'd *marry* me."

"Who?" shouted Pete Greene, suddenly starting from an unobserved corner of the rude shop.

"Where you come from, you sly nigger!" exclaimed Jim.

"Come, tell me, who is 't?" said Pete; "Mag Smith, you want to marry?"

"Git out, Pete! and when you come in dis shop again, let a nigger know it. Don't steal in like a thief."

Pity and love know little severance. One attends the other. Jim acknowledged the presence of the former, and his efforts in Mag's behalf told also of a finer principle.

This sudden expedient which he had unintentionally disclosed, roused his thinking and inventive powers to study upon the best method of introducing the subject to Mag.

He belted his barrels, with many a scheme revolving in his mind, none of which quite satisfied him, or seemed, on the whole, expedient. He thought of the pleasing contrast between her fair face and his own dark skin; the smooth, straight hair, which he had once, in expression of pity, kindly stroked on her now wrinkled but once fair brow. There was a tempest gathering in his heart, and at last, to ease his pent-up passion, he exclaimed aloud, "By golly!" Recollecting his former exposure, he glanced around to see if Pete was in hearing again. Satisfied on this point, he continued: "She'd be as much of a prize to me as she'd fall short of coming up to the mark with white folks. I don't care for past things. I've done things 'fore now I's 'shamed of. She's good enough for me, any how."

One more glance about the premises to be sure Pete was away.

The next Saturday night brought Jim to the hovel again. The cold was fast coming to tarry its apportioned time. Mag was nearly despairing of meeting its rigor.

"How's the wood, Mag?" asked Jim.

"All gone; and no more to cut, any how," was the reply.

"Too bad!" Jim said. His truthful reply would have been, I'm glad.

"Anything to eat in the house?" continued he.

"No," replied Mag.

"Too bad!" again, orally, with the same *inward* gratulation as before.

"Well, Mag," said Jim, after a short pause, "you's down low enough. I don't see but I've got to take care of ye. 'Sposin' we marry!"

Mag raised her eyes, full of amazement, and uttered a sonorous "What?"

Jim felt abashed for a moment. He knew well what were her objections.

"You's had trial of white folks, any how. They run off and left ye, and now none of 'em come near ye to see if you's dead or alive. I's black outside, I know, but I's got a white heart inside. Which you rather have, a black heart in a white skin, or a white heart in a black one?"

"Oh, dear!" sighed Mag; "Nobody on earth cares for *me*—"

"I do," interrupted Jim.

"I can do but two things," said she, "beg my living, or get it from you."

"Take me, Mag. I can give you a better home than this, and not let you suffer so."

He prevailed; they married. You can philosophize, gentle reader, upon the impropriety of such unions, and preach dozens of sermons on the evils of amalgamation. Want is a more powerful philosopher and preacher. Poor Mag. She has sundered another bond which held her to her fellows. She has descended another step down the ladder of infamy.

Chapter II. My Father's Death

Misery! we have known each other,
Like a sister and a brother,
Living in the same lone home
Many years—we must live some
Hours or ages yet to come.

Shelley.[2]

Jim, proud of his treasure,—a white wife,—tried hard to fulfil his promises; and furnished her with a more comfortable dwelling, diet, and apparel. It was comparatively a comfortable winter she passed after her marriage. When Jim could work, all went on well. Industrious, and fond of Mag, he was determined she should not regret her union to him. Time levied an additional charge upon him, in the form of two pretty mulattos, whose infantile pranks amply repaid the additional toil. A few years, and a severe cough and pain in his side compelled him to be an idler for weeks together, and Mag had thus a reminder of by-gones. She cared for him only as a means to subserve her own comfort; yet she nursed him faithfully and true to marriage vows till death released her. He became the victim of consumption.[3] He loved Mag to the last. So long as life continued, he stifled his sensibility to pain, and toiled for her sustenance long after he was able to do so.

2. From "Invocation to Misery" (1832) by English Romantic poet Percy Bysshe Shelley (1792–1822).

3. Tuberculosis.

A few expressive wishes for her welfare; a hope of better days for her; an anxiety lest they should not all go to the "good place"; brief advice about their children; a hope expressed that Mag would not be neglected as she used to be; the manifestation of Christian patience; these were *all* the legacy of miserable Mag. A feeling of cold desolation came over her, as she turned from the grave of one who had been truly faithful to her.

She was now expelled from companionship with white people; this last step—her union with a black—was the climax of repulsion.

Seth Shipley, a partner in Jim's business, wished her to remain in her present home; but she declined, and returned to her hovel again, with obstacles threefold more insurmountable than before. Seth accompanied her, giving her a weekly allowance which furnished most of the food necessary for the four inmates. After a time, work failed; their means were reduced.

How Mag toiled and suffered, yielding to fits of desperation, bursts of anger, and uttering curses too fearful to repeat. When both were supplied with work, they prospered; if idle, they were hungry together. In this way their interests became united; they planned for the future together. Mag had lived an outcast for years. She had ceased to feel the gushings of penitence; she had crushed the sharp agonies of an awakened conscience. She had no longings for a purer heart, a better life. Far easier to descend lower. She entered the darkness of perpetual infamy. She asked not the rite of civilization or Christianity. Her will made her the wife of Seth. Soon followed scenes familiar and trying.

"It's no use," said Seth one day; "we must give the children away, and try to get work in some other place."

"Who'll take the black devils?" snarled Mag.

"They're none of mine," said Seth; "what you growling about?"

"Nobody will want any thing of mine, or yours either," she replied.

"We'll make 'em, p'r'aps," he said. "There's Frado's six years old, and pretty, if she is yours, and white folks'll say so. She'd be a prize somewhere," he continued, tipping his chair back against the wall, and placing his feet upon the rounds, as if he had much more to say when in the right position.

Frado, as they called one of Mag's children, was a beautiful mulatto, with long, curly black hair, and handsome, roguish eyes, sparkling with an exuberance of spirit almost beyond restraint.

Hearing her name mentioned, she looked up from her play, to see what Seth had to say of her.

"Wouldn't the Bellmonts take her?" asked Seth.

"Bellmonts?" shouted Mag. "His wife is a right she-devil! and if—"

"Hadn't they better be all together?" interrupted Seth, reminding her of a like epithet used in reference to her little ones.

Without seeming to notice him, she continued, "She can't keep a girl in the house over a week; and Mr. Bellmont wants to hire a boy to work for him, but he can't find one that will live in the house with her; she's so ugly, they can't."

"Well, we've got to make a move soon," answered Seth; "if you go with me, we shall go right off. Had you rather spare the other one?" asked Seth, after a short pause.

"One's as bad as t' other," replied Mag. "Frado is such a wild, frolicky thing, and means to do jest as she's a mind to; she won't go if she don't want to. I don't want to tell her she is to be given away."

"I will," said Seth. "Come here, Frado?"

The child seemed to have some dim foreshadowing of evil, and declined.

"Come here," he continued; "I want to tell you something."

She came reluctantly. He took her hand and said: "We're going to move, by-'m-bye; will you go?"

"No!" screamed she; and giving a sudden jerk which destroyed Seth's equilibrium, left him sprawling on the floor, while she escaped through the open door.

"She's a hard one," said Seth, brushing his patched coat sleeve. "I'd risk her at Bellmont's."

They discussed the expediency of a speedy departure. Seth would first seek employment, and then return for Mag. They would take with them what they could carry, and leave the rest with Pete Greene, and come for them when they were wanted. They were long in arranging affairs satisfactorily, and were not a little startled at the close of their conference to find Frado missing. They thought approaching night would bring her. Twilight passed into darkness, and she did not come. They thought she had understood their plans, and had, perhaps, permanently withdrawn. They could not rest without making some effort to ascertain her retreat. Seth went in pursuit, and returned without her. They rallied others when they discovered that another little colored girl was missing, a favorite playmate of Frado's. All effort proved unavailing. Mag felt sure her fears were realized, and that she might never see her again. Before her anxieties became realities, both were safely returned, and from them and their attendant they learned that they went to walk, and not minding the direction soon found themselves lost. They had climbed fences and walls, passed through thickets and marshes, and when night approached selected a thick cluster of shrubbery as a covert for the night. They were discovered by the person who now restored them, chatting of their prospects, Frado attempting to banish the childish fears of her companion. As they were some miles from home, they were kindly cared for until morning. Mag was relieved to know her child was not driven to desperation by their intentions to relieve themselves of her, and she was inclined to think severe restraint would be healthful.

The removal was all arranged; the few days necessary for such migrations passed quickly, and one bright summer morning they bade farewell to their Singleton hovel, and with budgets and bundles commenced their weary march. As they neared the village, they heard the merry shouts of children gathered around the schoolroom, awaiting the coming of their teacher.

"Halloo!" screamed one, "Black, white and yeller!" "Black, white and yeller," echoed a dozen voices.

It did not grate so harshly on poor Mag as once it would. She did not even turn her head to look at them. She had passed into an insensibility no childish taunt could penetrate, else she would have reproached herself as she passed familiar scenes, for extending the separation once so easily annihilated by steadfast integrity. Two miles beyond lived the Bellmonts, in a large, old fashioned, two-story white house, environed by fruitful acres, and embellished by shrubbery and shade trees. Years ago a youthful couple consecrated it as home; and after many little feet had worn paths to favorite fruit trees, and over its green hills, and mingled at last with brother man in the race which belongs neither to the swift or strong, the sire became grey-haired and decrepid, and went to his last repose. His aged consort soon followed him. The old homestead thus passed into the hands of a son, to whose wife Mag had applied the epithet "she-devil," as may be remembered. John, the son, had not in his family arrangements departed from the example of the father. The pastimes of his boyhood were ever freshly revived by witnessing the games of his own sons as they rallied about the same goal his youthful feet had often won; as well as by the amusements of his daughters in their imitations of maternal duties.

At the time we introduce them, however, John is wearing the badge of age. Most of his children were from home; some seeking employment; some were already settled in homes of their own. A maiden sister shared with him the estate on which he resided, and occupied a portion of the house.

Within sight of the house, Seth seated himself with his bundles and the child he had been leading, while Mag walked onward to the house leading Frado. A knock at the door brought Mrs. Bellmont, and Mag asked if she would be willing to let that child stop there while she went to the Reed's house to wash, and when she came back she would call and get her. It seemed a novel request, but she consented. Why the impetuous child entered the house, we cannot tell; the door closed, and Mag hastily departed. Frado waited for the close of day, which was to bring back her mother. Alas! it never came. It was the last time she ever saw or heard of her mother.

Chapter III. A New Home for Me

Oh! did we but know of the shadows so nigh,
The world would indeed be a prison of gloom;
All light would be quenched in youth's eloquent eye,
And the prayer-lisping infant would ask for the tomb.

For if Hope be a star that may lead us astray,
And "deceiveth the heart," as the aged ones preach;
Yet 'twas Mercy that gave it, to beacon our way,
Though its halo illumes where it never can reach.
Eliza Cook.[4]

As the day closed and Mag did not appear, surmises were expressed by the family that she never intended to return. Mr. Bellmont was a kind, humane man, who would not grudge hospitality to the poorest wanderer, nor fail to sympathize with any sufferer, however humble. The child's desertion by her mother appealed to his sympathy, and he felt inclined to succor her. To do this in opposition to Mrs. Bellmont's wishes, would be like encountering a whirlwind charged with fire, daggers and spikes. She was not as susceptible of fine emotions as her spouse. Mag's opinion of her was not without foundation. She was self-willed, haughty, undisciplined, arbitrary and severe. In common parlance, she was a *scold,* a thorough one. Mr. B. remained silent during the consultation which follows, engaged in by mother, Mary and John, or Jack, as he was familiarly called.

"Send her to the County House,"[5] said Mary, in reply to the query what should be done with her, in a tone which indicated self-importance in the speaker. She was indeed the idol of her mother, and more nearly resembled her in disposition and manners than the others.

Jane, an invalid daughter, the eldest of those at home, was reclining on a sofa apparently uninterested.

4. Stanzas from "The Future" (1845) by English poet Eliza Cook (1818–1889).

5. A county poorhouse.

"Keep her," said Jack. "She's real handsome and bright, and not very black, either."

"Yes," rejoined Mary; "that's just like you, Jack. She'll be of no use at all these three years, right under foot all the time."

"Poh! Miss Mary; if she should stay, it wouldn't be two days before you would be telling the girls about *our* nig, *our* nig!" retorted Jack.

"I don't want a nigger 'round *me,* do you, mother?" asked Mary.

"I don't mind the nigger in the child. I should like a dozen better than one," replied her mother. "If I could make her do my work in a few years, I would keep her. I have so much trouble with girls I hire, I am almost persuaded if I have one to train up in my way from a child, I shall be able to keep them awhile. I am tired of changing every few months."

"Where could she sleep?" asked Mary. "I don't want her near me."

"In the L chamber," answered the mother.

"How'll she get there?" asked Jack. "She'll be afraid to go through that dark passage, and she can't climb the ladder safely."

"She'll have to go there; it's good enough for a nigger," was the reply.

Jack was sent on horseback to ascertain if Mag was at her home. He returned with the testimony of Pete Greene that they were fairly departed, and that the child was intentionally thrust upon their family.

The imposition was not at all relished by Mrs. B., or the pert, haughty Mary, who had just glided into her teens.

"Show the child to bed, Jack," said his mother. "You seem most pleased with the little nigger, so you may introduce her to her room."

He went to the kitchen, and, taking Frado gently by the hand, told her he would put her in bed now; perhaps her mother would come the next night after her.

It was not yet quite dark, so they ascended the stairs without any light, passing through nicely furnished rooms, which were a source of great amazement to the child. He opened the door which connected with her room by a dark, unfinished passage-way. "Don't bump your head," said Jack, and stepped before to open the door leading into her apartment,—an unfinished chamber over the kitchen, the roof slanting nearly to the floor, so that the bed could stand only in the middle of the room. A small half window furnished light and air. Jack returned to the sitting room with the remark that the child would soon outgrow those quarters.

"When she *does,* she'll outgrow the house," remarked the mother.

"What can she do to help you?" asked Mary. "She came just in the right time, didn't she? Just the very day after Bridget left," continued she.

"I'll see what she can do in the morning," was the answer.

While this conversation was passing below, Frado lay, revolving in her little mind whether she would remain or not until her mother's return. She was of wilful, determined nature, a stranger to fear, and would not hesitate to wander away should she decide to. She remembered the conversation of her mother with Seth, the words "given away" which she heard used in reference to herself; and though she did not know their full import, she thought she should, by remaining, be in some relation to white people she was never favored with before. So she resolved to tarry, with the hope that mother would come and get her some time. The hot sun had penetrated her room, and it was long before a cooling breeze reduced the temperature so that she could sleep.

Frado was called early in the morning by her new mistress. Her first work was to feed the hens. She was shown how it was *always* to be done, and in no other way; any departure from this rule to be punished by a whipping. She was then accompanied by Jack to drive the cows to pasture, so she might learn the way. Upon her return she was allowed to eat her breakfast, consisting of a bowl of skimmed milk, with brown bread crusts, which she was told to eat, standing, by the kitchen table, and must not be over ten minutes about it. Meanwhile the family were taking their morning meal in the dining-room. This over, she was placed on a cricket[6] to wash the common dishes; she was to be in waiting always to bring wood and chips, to run hither and thither from room to room.

A large amount of dish-washing for small hands followed dinner. Then the same after tea and going after the cows finished her first day's work. It was a new discipline to the child. She found some attractions about the place, and she retired to rest at night more willing to remain. The same routine followed day after day, with slight variation; adding a little more work, and spicing the toil with "words that burn," and frequent blows on her head. These were great annoyances to Frado, and had she known where her mother was, she would have gone at once to her. She was often greatly wearied, and silently wept over her sad fate. At first she wept aloud, which Mrs. Bellmont noticed by applying a rawhide, always at hand in the kitchen. It was a symptom of discontent and complaining which must be "nipped in the bud," she said.

Thus passed a year. No intelligence of Mag. It was now certain Frado was to become a permanent member of the family. Her labors were multiplied; she was quite indispensable, although but seven years old. She had never learned to read, never heard of a school until her residence in the family.

Mrs. Bellmont was in doubt about the utility of attempting to educate people of color, who were incapable of elevation. This subject occasioned a lengthy discussion in the family. Mr. Bellmont, Jane and Jack arguing for Frado's education; Mary and her mother objecting. At last Mr. Bellmont declared decisively that she *should* go to school. He was a man who seldom decided controversies at home. The word once spoken admitted of no appeal; so, notwithstanding Mary's objection that she would have to attend the same school she did, the word became law.

It was to be a new scene to Frado, and Jack had many queries and conjectures to answer. He was himself too far advanced to attend the summer school, which Frado regretted, having had too many opportunities of witnessing Miss Mary's temper to feel safe in her company alone.

The opening day of school came. Frado sauntered on far in the rear of Mary, who was ashamed to be seen "walking with a nigger." As soon as she appeared, with scanty clothing and bared feet, the children assembled, noisily published her approach: "See that nigger," shouted one. "Look! look!" cried another. "I won't play with her," said one little girl. "Nor I neither," replied another.

Mary evidently relished these sharp attacks, and saw a fair prospect of lowering Nig where, according to her views, she belonged. Poor Frado, chagrined and grieved, felt that her anticipations of pleasure at such a place were far from being realized. She was just deciding to return home, and never come there again, when the teacher appeared, and observing the downcast looks of the child, took her by the hand, and led her into the school-room. All followed, and, after the bustle of securing seats was over, Miss Marsh inquired if the children knew "any cause for the sorrow of that

6. A footstool.

little girl?" pointing to Frado. It was soon all told. She then reminded them of their duties to the poor and friendless; their cowardice in attacking a young innocent child; referred them to one who looks not on outward appearances, but on the heart. "She looks like a good girl; I think I shall love her, so lay aside all prejudice, and vie with each other in shewing kindness and good-will to one who seems different from you," were the closing remarks of the kind lady. Those kind words! The most agreeable sound which ever meets the ear of sorrowing, grieving childhood.

Example rendered her words efficacious. Day by day there was a manifest change of deportment towards "Nig." Her speeches often drew merriment from the children; no one could do more to enliven their favorite pastimes than Frado. Mary could not endure to see her thus noticed, yet knew not how to prevent it. She could not influence her schoolmates as she wished. She had not gained their affections by winning ways and yielding points of controversy. On the contrary, she was self-willed, domineering; every day reported "mad" by some of her companions. She availed herself of the only alternative, abuse and taunts, as they returned from school. This was not satisfactory; she wanted to use physical force "to subdue her," to "keep her down."

There was, on their way home, a field intersected by a stream over which a single plank was placed for a crossing. It occurred to Mary that it would be a punishment to Nig to compel her to cross over; so she dragged her to the edge, and told her authoritatively to go over. Nig hesitated, resisted. Mary placed herself behind the child, and, in the struggle to force her over, lost her footing and plunged into the stream. Some of the larger scholars being in sight, ran, and thus prevented Mary from drowning and Frado from falling. Nig scampered home fast as possible, and Mary went to the nearest house, dripping, to procure a change of garments. She came loitering home, half crying, exclaiming, "Nig pushed me into the stream!" She then related the particulars. Nig was called from the kitchen. Mary stood with anger flashing in her eyes. Mr. Bellmont sat quietly reading his paper. He had witnessed too many of Miss Mary's outbreaks to be startled. Mrs. Bellmont interrogated Nig.

"I didn't do it! I didn't do it!" answered Nig, passionately, and then related the occurrence truthfully.

The discrepancy greatly enraged Mrs. Bellmont. With loud accusations and angry gestures she approached the child. Turning to her husband, she asked,

"Will you sit still, there, and hear that black nigger call Mary a liar?"

"How do we know but she has told the truth? I shall not punish her," he replied, and left the house, as he usually did when a tempest threatened to envelop him. No sooner was he out of sight than Mrs. B. and Mary commenced beating her inhumanly; then propping her mouth open with a piece of wood, shut her up in a dark room, without any supper. For employment, while the tempest raged within, Mr. Bellmont went for the cows, a task belonging to Frado, and thus unintentionally prolonged her pain. At dark Jack came in, and seeing Mary, accosted her with, "So you thought you'd vent your spite on Nig, did you? Why can't you let her alone? It was good enough for you to get a ducking, only you did not stay in half long enough."

"Stop!" said his mother. "You shall never talk so before me. You would have that little nigger trample on Mary, would you? She came home with a lie; it made Mary's story false."

"What was Mary's story?" asked Jack.

It was related.

"Now," said Jack, sallying into a chair, "the school-children happened to see it all, and they tell the same story Nig does. Which is most likely to be true, what a dozen agree they saw, or the contrary?"

"It is very strange you will believe what others say against your sister," retorted his mother, with flashing eye. "I think it is time your father subdued you."

"Father is a sensible man," argued Jack. "He would not wrong a dog. Where *is* Frado?" he continued.

"Mother gave her a good whipping and shut her up," replied Mary.

Just then Mr. Bellmont entered, and asked if Frado was "shut up yet."

The knowledge of her innocence, the perfidy of his sister, worked fearfully on Jack. He bounded from his chair, searched every room till he found the child; her mouth wedged apart, her face swollen, and full of pain.

How Jack pitied her! He relieved her jaws, brought her some supper, took her to her room, comforted her as well as he knew how, sat by her till she fell asleep, and then left for the sitting room. As he passed his mother, he remarked, "If that was the way Frado was to be treated, he hoped she would never wake again!" He then imparted her situation to his father, who seemed untouched, till a glance at Jack exposed a tearful eye. Jack went early to her next morning. She awoke sad, but refreshed. After breakfast Jack took her with him to the field, and kept her through the day. But it could not be so generally. She must return to school, to her household duties. He resolved to do what he could to protect her from Mary and his mother. He bought her a dog, which became a great favorite with both. The invalid, Jane, would gladly befriend her; but she had not the strength to brave the iron will of her mother. Kind words and affectionate glances were the only expressions of sympathy she could safely indulge in. The men employed on the farm were always glad to hear her prattle; she was a great favorite with them. Mrs. Bellmont allowed them the privilege of talking with her in the kitchen. She did not fear but she should have ample opportunity of subduing her when they were away. Three months of schooling, summer and winter, she enjoyed for three years. Her winter over-dress was a cast-off overcoat, once worn by Jack, and a sun-bonnet. It was a source of great merriment to the scholars, but Nig's retorts were so mirthful, and their satisfaction so evident in attributing the selection to "Old Granny Bellmont," that it was not painful to Nig or pleasurable to Mary. Her jollity was not to be quenched by whipping or scolding. In Mrs. Bellmont's presence she was under restraint; but in the kitchen, and among her schoolmates, the pent up fires burst forth. She was ever at some sly prank when unseen by her teacher, in school hours; not unfrequently some outburst of merriment, of which she was the original, was charged upon some innocent mate, and punishment inflicted which she merited. They enjoyed her antics so fully that any of them would suffer wrongfully to keep open the avenues of mirth. She would venture far beyond propriety, thus shielded and countenanced.

The teacher's desk was supplied with drawers, in which were stored his books and other *et ceteras*[7] of the profession. The children observed Nig very busy there one morning before school, as they flitted in occasionally from their play outside. The master came; called the children to order; opened a drawer to take the book the occasion required; when out poured a

7. Additional things.

volume of smoke. "Fire! fire!" screamed he, at the top of his voice. By this time he had become sufficiently acquainted with the peculiar odor, to know he was imposed upon. The scholars shouted with laughter to see the terror of the dupe, who, feeling abashed at the needless fright, made no very strict investigation, and Nig once more escaped punishment. She had provided herself with cigars, and puffing, puffing away at the crack of the drawer, had filled it with smoke, and then closed it tightly to deceive the teacher, and amuse the scholars. The interim of terms was filled up with a variety of duties new and peculiar. At home, no matter how powerful the heat when sent to rake hay or guard the grazing herd, she was never permitted to shield her skin from the sun. She was not many shades darker than Mary now; what a calamity it would be ever to hear the contrast spoken of. Mrs. Bellmont was determined the sun should have full power to darken the shade which nature had first bestowed upon her as best befitting.

[Mrs. Bellmont halts Frado's schooling when she reaches the age of nine. Mr. Bellmont's unmarried sister, Abby, and James Bellmont, a grown son home for a recuperative visit, befriend Frado in the face of Mrs. Bellmont's violent persecution of the Black girl. In defiance of her mother, Jane Bellmont marries modest George Means instead of Henry Reed, a wealthy suitor, and moves away. Not long after, Jack Bellmont heads west to seek his fortune.]

From *Chapter VIII. Visitor and Departure*

* * *

Frado, under the instructions of Aunt Abby and the minister, became a believer in a future existence—one of happiness or misery. Her doubt was, *is* there a heaven for the black? She knew there was one for James, and Aunt Abby, and all good white people; but was there any for blacks? She had listened attentively to all the minister said, and all Aunt Abby had told her; but then it was all for white people.

As James approached that blessed world, she felt a strong desire to follow, and be with one who was such a dear, kind friend to her.

While she was exercised with these desires and aspirations, she attended an evening meeting with Aunt Abby, and the good man urged all, young or old, to accept the offers of mercy, to receive a compassionate Jesus as their Saviour. "Come to Christ," he urged, "all, young or old, white or black, bond or free, come all to Christ for pardon; repent, believe."

This was the message she longed to hear; it seemed to be spoken for her. But he had told them to repent; "what was that?" she asked. She knew she was unfit for any heaven, made for whites or blacks. She would gladly repent, or do anything which would admit her to share the abode of James.

Her anxiety increased; her countenance bore marks of solicitude unseen before; and though she said nothing of her inward contest, they all observed a change.

James and Aunt Abby hoped it was the springing of good seed sown by the Spirit of God. Her tearful attention at the last meeting encouraged his aunt to hope that her mind was awakened, her conscience aroused. Aunt Abby noticed that she was particularly engaged in reading the Bible; and this strengthened her conviction that a heavenly Messenger was striving with her. The neighbors dropped in to inquire after the sick, and also if Frado was *"serious?"* They noticed she seemed very thoughtful and tearful at the meetings. Mrs. Reed was very inquisitive; but Mrs. Belmont saw no appearance of change for the better. She did not feel responsible for her spiritual culture, and hardly believed she had a soul.

Nig was in truth suffering much; her feelings were very intense on any subject, when once aroused. She read her Bible carefully, and as often as an opportunity presented, which was when entirely secluded in her own apartment, or by Aunt Abby's side, who kindly directed her to Christ, and instructed her in the way of salvation.

Mrs. Bellmont found her one day quietly reading her Bible. Amazed and half crediting the reports of officious neighbors, she felt it was time to interfere. Here she was, reading and shedding tears over the Bible. She ordered her to put up the book, and go to work, and not be snivelling about the house, or stop to read again.

But there was one little spot seldom penetrated by her mistress' watchful eye: this was her room, uninviting and comfortless; but to herself a safe retreat. Here she would listen to the pleadings of a Saviour, and try to penetrate the veil of doubt and sin which clouded her soul, and long to cast off the fetters of sin, and rise to the communion of saints.

Mrs. Bellmont, as we before said, did not trouble herself about the future destiny of her servant. If she did what she desired for *her* benefit, it was all the responsibility she acknowledged. But she seemed to have great aversion to the notice Nig would attract should she become pious. How could she meet this case? She resolved to make her complaint to John. Strange, when she was always foiled in this direction, she should resort to him. It was time something was done; she had begun to read the Bible openly.

The night of this discovery, as they were retiring, Mrs. Bellmont introduced the conversation, by saying:

"I want your attention to what I am going to say. I have let Nig go out to evening meetings a few times, and, if you will believe it, I found her reading the Bible to-day, just as though she expected to turn pious nigger, and preach to white folks. So now you see what good comes of sending her to school. If she should get converted she would have to go to meeting: at least, as long as James lives. I wish he had not such queer notions about her. It seems to trouble him to know he must die and leave her. He says if he should get well he would take her home with him, or educate her here. Oh, how awful! What can the child mean? So careful, too, of her! He says we shall ruin her health making her work so hard, and sleep in such a place. O, John! do you think he is in his right mind?"

"Yes, yes; she is slender."

"Yes, *yes!*" she repeated sarcastically, "you know these niggers are just like black snakes; you *can't* kill them. If she wasn't tough she would have been killed long ago. There was never one of my girls could do half the work."

"Did they ever try?" interposed her husband. "I think she can do more than all of them together."

"What a man!" said she, peevishly. "But I want to know what is going to be done with her about getting pious?"

"Let her do just as she has a mind to. If it is a comfort to her, let her enjoy the privilege of being good. I see no objection."

"I should think *you* were crazy, sure. Don't you know that every night she will want to go toting off to meeting? and Sundays, too? and you know we have a great deal of company Sundays, and she can't be spared."

"I thought you Christians held to going to church," remarked Mr. B.

"Yes, but who ever thought of having a nigger go, except to drive others there? Why, according to you and James, we should very soon have her in the parlor, as smart as our own girls. It's of no use talking to you or James. If you should go on as you would like, it would not be six months before she would be leaving me; and that won't do. Just think how much profit she was to us last summer. We had no work hired out; she did the work of two girls—"

"And got the whippings for two with it!" remarked Mr. Bellmont.

"I'll beat the money out of her, if I can't get her worth any other way," retorted Mrs. B. sharply. While this scene was passing, Frado was trying to utter the prayer of the publican, "God be merciful to me a sinner."[8]

[Frado is disconsolate on the death of James Bellmont, but clings to the religious hope he encourages in her.]

Chapter X. Perplexities.—Another Death

Neath the billows of the ocean,
Hidden treasures wait the hand,
That again to light shall raise them
With the diver's magic wand.[9]
G. W. Cook.

The family, gathered by James' decease, returned to their homes. Susan and Charles[1] returned to Baltimore. Letters were received from the absent, expressing their sympathy and grief. The father bowed like a "bruised reed,"[2] under the loss of his beloved son. He felt desirous to die the death of the righteous; also, conscious that he was unprepared, he resolved to start on the narrow way, and some time solicit entrance through the gate which leads to the celestial city. He acknowledged his too ready acquiescence with Mrs. B., in permitting Frado to be deprived of her only religious privileges for weeks together. He accordingly asked his sister to take her to meeting once more, which she was ready at once to do.

The first opportunity they once more attended meeting together. The minister conversed faithfully with every person present. He was surprised to find the little colored girl so solicitous, and kindly directed her to the flowing fountain[3] where she might wash and be clean. He inquired of the origin of her anxiety, of her progress up to this time, and endeavored to make Christ, instead of James, the attraction of Heaven. He invited her to come to his house, to speak freely her mind to him, to pray much, to read her Bible often.

The neighbors, who were at meeting,—among them Mrs. Reed,—discussed the opinions Mrs. Bellmont would express on the subject. Mrs. Reed called and informed Mrs. B. that her colored girl "related her experience the other night at the meeting."

"What experience?" asked she, quickly, as if she expected to hear the number of times she had whipped Frado, and the number of lashes set forth in plain Arabic numbers.

"Why, you know she is serious, don't you? She told the minister about it."

8. Luke 18:13.
9. From "A Mother's Love," published in *Godey's Lady's Book* (1859) by George W. Cook.
1. Wife and son of James Bellmont.
2. Matthew 12:20.
3. That is, Christ.

Mrs. B. made no reply, but changed the subject adroitly. Next morning she told Frado she "should not go out of the house for one while, except on errands; and if she did not stop trying to be religious, she would whip her to death."

Frado pondered; her mistress was a professor of religion; was *she* going to heaven? then she did not wish to go. If she should be near James, even, she could not be happy with those fiery eyes watching her ascending path. She resolved to give over all thought of the future world, and strove daily to put her anxiety far from her.

Mr. Bellmont found himself unable to do what James or Jack could accomplish for her. He talked with her seriously, told her he had seen her many times punished undeservedly; he did not wish to have her saucy or disrespectful, but when she was *sure* she did not deserve a whipping, to avoid it if she could. "You are looking sick," he added, "you cannot endure beating as you once could."

It was not long before an opportunity offered of profiting by his advice. She was sent for wood, and not returning as soon as Mrs. B. calculated, she followed her, and, snatching from the pile a stick, raised it over her.

"Stop!" shouted Frado, "strike me, and I'll never work a mite more for you;" and throwing down what she had gathered, stood like one who feels the stirring of free and independent thoughts.

By this unexpected demonstration, her mistress, in amazement, dropped her weapon, desisting from her purpose of chastisement. Frado walked towards the house, her mistress following with the wood she herself was sent after. She did not know, before, that she had a power to ward off assaults. Her triumph in seeing her enter the door with *her* burden, repaid her for much of her former suffering.

It was characteristic of Mrs. B. never to rise in her majesty, unless she was sure she should be victorious.

This affair never met with an "after clap," like many others.

Thus passed a year. The usual amount of scolding, but fewer whippings. Mrs. B. longed once more for Mary's return, who had been absent over a year; and she wrote imperatively for her to come quickly to her. A letter came in reply, announcing that she would comply as soon as she was sufficiently recovered from an illness which detained her.

No serious apprehensions were cherished by either parent, who constantly looked for notice of her arrival, by mail. Another letter brought tidings that Mary was seriously ill; her mother's presence was solicited.

She started without delay. Before she reached her destination, a letter came to the parents announcing her death.

No sooner was the astounding news received, than Frado rushed into Aunt Abby's, exclaiming:—

"She's dead, Aunt Abby!"

"Who?" she asked, terrified by the unprefaced announcement.

"Mary; they've just had a letter."

As Mrs. B. was away, the brother and sister could freely sympathize, and she sought him in this fresh sorrow, to communicate such solace as she could, and to learn particulars of Mary's untimely death, and assist him in his journey thither.

It seemed a thanksgiving to Frado. Every hour or two she would pop in into Aunt Abby's room with some strange query:

"She got into the *river* again, Aunt Abby, didn't she; the Jordan[4] is a big one to tumble into, any how. S'posen she goes to hell, she'll be as black as I am. Wouldn't mistress be mad to see her a nigger!" and others of a similar stamp, not at all acceptable to the pious, sympathetic dame; but she could not evade them.

The family returned from their sorrowful journey, leaving the dead behind. Nig looked for a change in her tyrant; what could subdue her, if the loss of her idol could not?

Never was Mrs. B. known to shed tears so profusely, as when she reiterated to one and another the sad particulars of her darling's sickness and death. There was, indeed, a season of quiet grief; it was the lull of the fiery elements. A few weeks revived the former tempests, and so at variance did they seem with chastisement sanctified, that Frado felt them to be unbearable. She determined to flee. But where? Who would take her? Mrs. B. had always represented her ugly. Perhaps every one thought her so. Then no one would take her. She was black, no one would love her. She might have to return, and then she would be more in her mistress' power than ever.

She remembered her victory at the wood-pile. She decided to remain to do as well as she could; to assert her rights when they were trampled on; to return once more to her meeting in the evening, which had been prohibited. She had learned how to conquer; she would not abuse the power while Mr. Bellmont was at home.

But had she not better run away? Where? She had never been from the place far enough to decide what course to take. She resolved to speak to Aunt Abby. *She* mapped the dangers of her course, her liability to fail in finding so good friends as John and herself. Frado's mind was busy for days and nights. She contemplated administering poison to her mistress, to rid herself and the house of so detestable a plague.

But she was restrained by an overruling Providence; and finally decided to stay contentedly through her period of service,[5] which would expire when she was eighteen years of age.

In a few months Jane returned home with her family, to relieve her parents, upon whom years and affliction had left the marks of age. The years intervening since she had left her home, had, in some degree, softened the opposition to her unsanctioned marriage with George. The more Mrs. B. had about her, the more energetic seemed her directing capabilities, and her fault-finding propensities. Her own, she had full power over; and Jane after vain endeavors, became disgusted, weary, and perplexed, and decided that, though her mother might suffer, she could not endure her home. They followed Jack to the West. Thus vanished all hopes of sympathy or relief from this source to Frado. There seemed no one capable of enduring the oppressions of the house but her. She turned to the darkness of the future with the determination previously formed, to remain until she should be eighteen. Jane begged her to follow her so soon as she should be released; but so wearied out was she by her mistress, she felt disposed to flee from any and every one having her similitude of name or feature.

[Frado completes her long term of service to the Bellmonts and departs with one dress and a Bible. She finds work as a seamstress but illness compounded by years

4. The Jordan River of the Mideast, used here figuratively to represent the transition from death to the afterlife.

5. Frado is an indentured servant, obliged to remain with the Bellmonts until she reaches adulthood.

of mistreatment compels her to return to the Bellmont house, where Abby nurses her back to a fragile health. Frado takes a job as a domestic, but soon suffers a physical breakdown. Aided by charity, she is able to continue her efforts at self-support by sewing and bonnet making.]

Chapter XII. The Winding Up of the Matter

Nothing new under the sun.
Solomon.[6]

A few years ago, within the compass of my narrative, there appeared often in some of our New England villages, professed fugitives from slavery, who recounted their personal experience in homely phrase, and awakened the indignation of non-slaveholders against brother Pro.[7] Such a one appeared in the new home of Frado; and as people of color were rare there, was it strange she should attract her dark brother; that he should inquire her out; succeed in seeing her; feel a strange sensation in his heart towards her; that he should toy with her shining curls, feel proud to provoke her to smile and expose the ivory concealed by thin, ruby lips; that her sparkling eyes should fascinate; that he should propose; that they should marry? A short acquaintance was indeed an objection, but she saw him often, and thought she knew him. He never spoke of his enslavement to her when alone, but she felt that, like her own oppression, it was painful to disturb oftener than was needful.

He was a fine, straight negro, whose back showed no marks of the lash, erect as if it never crouched beneath a burden. There was a silent sympathy which Frado felt attracted her, and she opened her heart to the presence of love—that arbitrary and inexorable tyrant.

She removed to Singleton, her former residence, and there was married. Here were Frado's first feelings of trust and repose on human arm. She realized, for the first time, the relief of looking to another for comfortable support. Occasionally he would leave her to "lecture."

Those tours were prolonged often to weeks. Of course he had little spare money. Frado was again feeling her self-dependence, and was at last compelled to resort alone to that. Samuel was kind to her when at home, but made no provision for his absence, which was at last unprecedented.

He left her to her fate—embarked at sea, with the disclosure that he had never seen the South, and that his illiterate harangues were humbugs for hungry abolitionists. Once more alone! Yet not alone. A still newer companionship would soon force itself upon her. No one wanted her with such prospects. Herself was burden enough; who would have an additional one?

The horrors of her condition nearly prostrated her, and she was again thrown upon the public for sustenance. Then followed the birth of her child. The long absent Samuel unexpectedly returned, and rescued her from charity. Recovering from her expected illness, she once more commenced toil for herself and child, in a room obtained of a poor woman, but with better fortune. One so well known would not be wholly neglected. Kind friends watched her when Samuel was from home, prevented her from suffering,

6. King of Israel during the 10th century B.C.E. and traditionally credited with authorship of the Book of Ecclesiastes. The epigraph is after Ecclesiastes 1:9: "There is no new thing under the sun."

7. Proslavery.

and when the cold weather pinched the warmly clad, a kind friend took them in, and thus preserved them. At last Samuel's business became very engrossing, and after long desertion, news reached his family that he had become a victim of yellow fever, in New Orleans.

So much toil as was necessary to sustain Frado, was more than she could endure. As soon as her babe could be nourished without his mother, she left him in charge of a Mrs. Capon, and procured an agency,[8] hoping to recruit her health, and gain an easier livelihood for herself and child. This afforded her better maintenance than she had yet found. She passed into the various towns of the State she lived in, then into Massachusetts. Strange were some of her adventures. Watched by kidnappers, maltreated by professed abolitionists, who didn't want slaves at the South, nor niggers in their own houses, North. Faugh! to lodge one; to eat with one; to admit one through the front door; to sit next one; awful!

Traps slyly laid by the vicious to ensnare her, she resolutely avoided. In one of her tours, Providence favored her with a friend who, pitying her cheerless lot, kindly provided her with a valuable recipe, from which she might herself manufacture a useful article for her maintenance. This proved a more agreeable, and an easier way of sustenance.

And thus, to the present time, may you see her busily employed in preparing her merchandise; then sallying forth to encounter many frowns, but some kind friends and purchasers. Nothing turns her from her steadfast purpose of elevating herself. Reposing on God, she has thus far journeyed securely. Still an invalid, she asks your sympathy, gentle reader. Refuse not, because some part of her history is unknown, save by the Omniscient God. Enough has been unrolled to demand your sympathy and aid.

Do you ask the destiny of those connected with her *early* history? A few years only have elapsed since Mr. and Mrs. B. passed into another world. As age increased, Mrs. B. became more irritable, so that no one, even her own children, could remain with her; and she was accompanied by her husband to the home of Lewis,[9] where, after an agony in death unspeakable, she passed away. Only a few months since, Aunt Abby entered heaven. Jack and his wife rest in heaven, disturbed by no intruders; and Susan and her child are yet with the living. Jane has silver locks in place of auburn tresses, but she has the early love of Henry still, and has never regretted her exchange of lovers. Frado has passed from their memories, as Joseph from the butler's,[1] but she will never cease to track them till beyond mortal vision.

1859

8. Got a job as a traveling agent.
9. One of the Bellmonts' sons.
1. In Genesis 40:23, the chief butler of Pharoah in Egypt forgets the help rendered him by the imprisoned slave Joseph, the youngest son of the Hebrew patriarch Jacob.

HANNAH CRAFTS
(Hannah Bond)
1826–ca. 1905

In 1948, Dorothy Porter Wesley, a pioneering African American librarian, bibliographer, and curator, spent eighty-five dollars to buy an intriguing 301-page cloth-bound manuscript from a New York City bookseller. *The Bondwoman's Narrative by Hannah Crafts a Fugitive Slave Recently Escaped from North Carolina* had arrested her attention because, as she wrote in a letter, "from internal evidence, it appears to be the work of a Negro and the time of composition was before the Civil War." Porter Wesley was never able to undertake research about the text or its author, except to suggest that the surname of the central male character in the novel was the same as a minor North Carolina government official named John Hill Wheeler, whose name she had found listed in a directory.

The text next resurfaced in 2001, when the literary scholar Henry Louis Gates Jr. bought the manuscript at auction, intrigued by the text's title and the author's claim that she was a fugitive slave. A friend of Gates, Porter Wesley had mentioned the novel to him after Gates authenticated and published *Our Nig* by Harriet E. Wilson, the first novel published by a Black woman in the United States. After researching this unprecedented text from multiple standpoints, Gates became convinced that Hannah Crafts was an African American female fugitive who had once been enslaved by a prominent North Carolina family headed by John Hill Wheeler (1806–1882), who plays a prominent role in *The Bondwoman's Narrative*, as does his wife, Ellen. Careful forensic study of the manuscript commissioned by Gates indicated it was written in the mid-to-late 1850s, before the Civil War, as Porter had surmised. What remained to be determined was which of the enslaved people held by Wheeler actually had written the novel.

Time, circumstance, and indifference had buried Hannah Crafts' fugitive narrative for almost a century and a half, waiting to be resurrected so that scholars and critics, following Gates's path-breaking lead, could finally appreciate this remarkable literary experiment. The 2002 publishing debut of *The Bondwoman's Narrative*, edited by Gates, was widely hailed by critics and scholars as a double-barreled first in African American literature: the earliest known novel by an African American woman and the first novel to have been authored by an enslaved woman in the United States.

Researchers such as Hollis Robbins were quick to publish valuable discoveries disclosing Hannah Crafts' reading and literary influences. Purposely drawing from Charles Dickens's *Bleak House*, Charlotte Brontë's *Jane Eyre*, and other works by nineteenth-century British writers such as Sir Walter Scott and Lord Byron, Crafts seemed intent on contributing to a major transatlantic debate at midcentury: whether enslaved African Americans were better off than the British underclass. Moreover, it was clear that *The Bondwoman's Narrative* had been a designed intervention into the African American fugitive slave narrative, which, by the mid-1850s, was in its heyday as the most widely read and celebrated genre of Black American writing in U.S. history. That Hannah Crafts was aware of this African American tradition was undeniable, if for no other reasons than the author's strong critique of slavery and the plotting of the story around two attempted escapes from bondage. The success of the second escape depended greatly on the narrator's adopting a male disguise, thereby emulating the notorious example of Ellen Craft, who had dressed as a man when accompanying her husband, William, on their sensational 1848 journey from Georgia to Boston.

Since 2002 no other facet of this fascinating text has generated more speculation than its tantalizing central mystery—the historical identity of the person who wore the mask of Hannah Crafts. In 2023, after years of historical sleuthing, literary scholar Gregg Hecimovich put the speculation to rest by publishing his exhaustively researched biography, *The Life and Times of Hannah Crafts*. Hecimovich confirmed Gates's earlier deduction that one of those enslaved by John Hill Wheeler was the author of *The Bondwoman's Narrative*. Focusing on Hannah Bond, one of the Wheelers' domestic workers who escaped from their eastern North Carolina plantation, Hecimovich's book provides ample evidence identifying Hannah Bond as the "Bondwoman." Bond's blending of autobiography and fiction in her novel is just one reason why it should be recognized as a foundational text in African American literature.

Hannah Bond was born in 1826 and first enslaved on the plantation of Lewis and Catherine Pugh Bond in Bertie County, North Carolina. Light-skinned and highly prized, Bond, like the near-white Hannah Crafts, found that her domestic duties gave her access to books in her enslavers' homes. In the novel, Crafts' stealthy means of learning to read testifies to Bond's seizing both literacy and the tools of writing, likely purloined from an enslaver. During her twenties, Hannah Bond had to adjust to the demands of two new enslavers, daughters of Lewis and Catherine Bond. At age thirty, Hannah was sold to pay a debt and conveyed into the hands of John Hill Wheeler, who made her the personal servant of his spouse, Ellen Sully Wheeler, the vain and shallow "Mrs. Wheeler" targeted for satirical attack in *The Bondwoman's Narrative*.

Like Crafts, Hannah Bond lived with the Wheelers in Washington, D.C., in 1856 and early 1857 while her enslaver, a former U.S. minister to Nicaragua, hunted for a government appointment. The hilarious scene in *The Bondwoman's Narrative* in which Mrs. Wheeler gets her sallow face embarrassingly blackened by a "beautifying powder" may have its origins in a story in an 1851 issue of *Scientific American*, to which John Hill Wheeler subscribed. Crafts' clandestine reading in her enslaver's library is likely based on Bond's access to and familiarity with Wheeler's library, the contents of which Gates initially established. This library contained copies of the novels and Shakespeare plays from which the author of *The Bondwoman's Narrative* borrowed.

In the spring of 1857 Hannah Bond fled the Wheeler family's plantation outside Murfreesboro, North Carolina. Disguised as a man and more than likely hiding a manuscript of her novel, Bond, like Crafts, made her way north. In McGrawville, New York, Horace Craft, a local farmer, hid the fugitive from her pursuing enslaver. In honor of and gratitude to the two Crafts who had done so much to inspire and facilitate her escape, Hannah Bond chose Crafts as her pen name. Settling in the all-Black community of Timbuctoo, New Jersey, where she finished her novel in 1858, Hannah Crafts, like the protagonist of her novel, married a minister and became a school teacher. Hecimovich's biography suggests that Hannah Crafts Vincent died sometime between 1905 and 1910. What she did with her manuscript after its completion, or whether she ever tried to find a publisher for it, is still unknown. Nor is there evidence that anyone ever read *The Bondwoman's Narrative* or even knew of its existence during its author's lifetime. How it survived, who treasured and transmitted it over the generations, and for what reasons—all this too remains in the darker corners of history. That this unprecedented autobiographical novel was preserved, passed on, and finally authenticated speaks to the tenacity and vision of its author and to the vitality and commitment of African American literary scholarship in the twentieth and twenty-first centuries.

The following selections from *The Bondwoman's Narrative* reproduce the text of the holograph manuscript, including words struck through apparently after the author changed her mind in the process of composition. Spelling, punctuation, and grammar in these selections correspond exactly to what appears in the holograph except that periods at the ends of sentences have been inserted when needed to enhance readability. Brackets [ ] are inserted around letters, words, and punctuation that appear to have been inadvertently omitted by the author during composition of the manuscript. In a few instances, a word has been inserted in brackets to clarify a word in the text that is not spelled according to twenty-first-century usage.

The Bondwoman's Narrative

From *Chapter 1*

IN CHILDHOOD

It may be that I assume to[o] much responsibility in attempting to write these pages. The world will probably say so, and I am aware of my deficiencies. I am neither clever, nor learned, nor talented. When a child they used to scold and find fault with me because they said I was dull and stupid. Perhaps under other circumstances and with more encouragement I might have appeared better; for I was shy and reserved and scarce dared open my lips to any one I had none of that quickness and animation which are so much admired in children, but rather a silent unobtrusive way of observing things and events, and wishing to understand them better than I could.

I was not brought up by any body in particular that I know of. I had no training, no cultivation. The birds of the air, or beasts of the feild are not freer from moral culture than I was. No one seemed to care for me till I was able to work, and then it was Hannah do this and Hannah do that, but I never complained as I found a sort of pleasure and something to divert my thoughts in employment. Of my relatives I knew nothing. No one ever spoke of my father or mother, but I soon learned what a curse was attached to my race, soon learned that the African blood in my veins would forever exclude me from the higher walks of life. That toil unremitted unpaid toil must be my lot and portion, without even the hope or expectation of any thing better. This seemed the harder to be borne, because my complexion was almost white, and the obnoxious descent could not be readily traced, though it gave a rotundity to my person, a wave and curl to my hair, and perhaps led me to fancy pictorial illustrations and flaming colors.

The busiest life has its leisure moments; it was so with mine. I had from the first an instinctive desire for knowledge and the means of mental improvement. Though neglected and a slave, I felt the immortal longings in me. In the absence of books and teachers and schools I determined to learn if not in a regular, approved, and scientific way. I was aware that this plan would meet with opposition, perhaps with punishment. My master never permitted his slaves to be taught. Education in his view tended to enlarge and expand their ideas; made them less subservient to their superiors, and besides that its blessings were destined to be conferred exclusively on the higher and nobler race. Indeed though he was generally easy and good-tempered, there was nothing liberal or democratic in his nature. Slaves were slaves to him, and nothing more. Practically he regarded them not as men and women, but in the same light as horses or other domestic animals. He ~~furnished~~ supplied their necessities of food and clothing from ~~the same~~ motives of policy, but [di]scounted the ideas of equality and fraternity as preposterous and absurd. Of course I had nothing to expect from him, yet "where there's a will there's a way."

I was employed about the house, consequently my labors were much easier than those of the field servants, and I enjoyed intervals of repose and rest unknown to them. Then, too, I was a mere child and some hours of each day were allotted to play. On such occasions, and while the other children of the house were amusing themselves I would quietly steal away from their company to ponder over the pages of some old book or newspaper that chance had thrown in [my] way. Though I knew not the meaning of a single letter, and had not the means of finding out I loved to look at them and think that some day I should probably understand them all.

My dream was destined to be realized. One day while ~~I was~~ sitting on a little bank, beneath the shade of some large trees, at a short distance from my playmates, ~~when~~ an aged woman approached me. She was white, and looked venerable with her grey hair smoothly put back beneath a plain sun bonnet, and I recollected having seen her once or twice at my master's house whither she came to sell salves and ointments, and hearing it remarked that she was the wife of a sand-digger[1] and very poor.

She smiled benevolently and inquired why I concealed my book, and with child-like artlessness I told her all. How earnestly I desired knowledge, how our Master interdicted it, and how I was trying to teach myself. She stood for a few moments apparently buried in deep thought, but I interpreted her looks and actions favorably, and an idea struck me that perhaps she could read, and would become my teacher. She seemed to understand my wish before I expressed it.

"Child" she said "I was thinking of our Saviour's words to Peter where he commands the latter to 'feed his lambs.[2] I will dispense to you such knowledge as I possess. Come to me each day. I will teach you to read in the hope and trust that you will thereby be made better in this world and that to come.["] Her demeanor like her words was very grave and solemn.

"Where do you live?["] I inquired.

"In the little cottage just around the foot of the hill" she replied.

"I will come! Oh how eagerly, how joyfully" I answered "but if master finds it out his anger will be terrible; and then I have no means of paying you."

She smiled quietly, bade me fear nothing, and went her way. I returned home that evening with a light heart. Pleased, delighted, overwhelmed with my good fortune in prospective I felt like a being to whom a new world with all its mysteries and marvels was opening, and could scarcely repress my tears of joy and thankfulness.

[Hannah, a an enslaved domestic worker in "the ancient mansion of Lindendale," accompanies her mistress (unnamed in the novel) when the latter, on the verge of marriage to the aristocratic bachelor who owns Lindendale, decides to run away, fearing exposure of her racial heritage by a menacing lawyer, Mr. Trappe. Trappe catches the two women and threatens to sell them to a slave trader. The mistress dies of shock; Hannah is sold. After a wagon accident kills the trader and frees Hannah, she is befriended by Mrs. Henry, an antislavery lady who has inherited enslaved people from her father. Mrs. Henry sells Hannah to a "distant relative in North Carolina," who, Mrs. Henry assures the disconcerted young Black woman, is "very kind and humane" to those she enslaves.]

From *Chapter 12*

A NEW MISTRESS

Mrs Wheeler complained of feeble health, and required the most incessant attendance. Her two waiting maids had ran [sic] off to the North, and she had been thus far unable to suit herself with another. Now that Charlotte was absent[3] Mrs Henry could not supply her wants, unless I consented to perform the ~~service~~ service. This I readily engaged to do, wishing not only to

1. Possibly a person who digs wild roots for food.
2. John 21:15.
3. Charlotte, one of the highly favored enslaved people who worked in Mrs. Henry's house, has escaped with her fiancé.

oblige the lady, but to show my gratitude to Mrs Henry. The next morning Mrs Wheeler sent for me to her room. She was languidly reclining in a large chamber chair deeply cushioned, loosely enveloped in a light morning wrapper. She made an effort to smile as I advanced, and inquired in a particularly bland, soft, insinuating voice if I could perform the duties of Lady's maid.

"I can try, madam" I answered.

"But trying will not suit me, unless you succeed" she answered quickly. "Can you dress hair?"

"I have done something at it."

"Did you do it well and as it should be done?"

"There was no fault found."

"Well, that I may be enabled to judge of your skill in that fashionable art I wish you to dress my hair this morning."

"But Madam."

"What?"

"There are many styles of dressing hair."

"Certainly, put mine in the most graceful style of morning costume you know."

"Yes, Madam." And I went to work with combs, brushes and pomatum [pomade].

"Be careful" she exclaimed. "My hair, I expect, is excessively tangled, as it hasn't been combed for more than a week."

"Indeed, Madam."

~~It's more than a week I think, yes I know it is~~

"I was too feeble to think of attempting it myself, and since Jane ran off, there has been no one to whom I could think of entrusting my head, till Mrs Henry so warmly recommended you."

"I am much obliged to Mrs Henry I am sure.["]

"Jane was very handy at almost everything" she continued. "You will seldom find a slave so handy, but she grew discontented and dissatisfied with her condition, thought she could do better in a land of freedom, and such like I watched her closely you may depend; there, there, how you pull." The comb had caught in a snarl of hair.

"Forgive me, madam, but I could not help it; the hair is actually matted."

"Oh dear, this is what I have to endure from losing Jane, but she'll have to suffer more, probably. I didn't much like the idea of bringing her to Washington. It was all Mr Wheeler's fault. He wanted me to come, and I couldn't think of doing without her in my feeble health. Are you getting the tangles most out?"

"I believe so."

"My husband, you are aware, occupies a high official position in the Federal City, which gives us access to the best society the Capital affords. While there my time was chiefly occupied in giving and receiving visits, attending parties, and going to places of amusement. As I knew that Washington was swarming with the enemies of our domestic institution[4] I told Catharine, my second maid, to keep a sharp eye on Jane, and if strangers called on her during my absence, or she received messages from them to inform me. Hannah Hannah, why I can't stand such rough usage.["]

"I do my best, madam, but your hair is in a dreadful state."

"I know that, but do be careful" and she continued the rehearsal of Jane's conduct.

4. Slavery.

Those who suppose that southern ladies keep their attendants at a distance, scarcely speaking to them, or only to give commands have a very erroneous impression. Between the mistress and her slave a freedom exists probably not to be found elsewhere. A northern woman would have recoiled at the idea of communicating a private history to one of my race, and in my condition, whereas such a thought never occurred to Mrs Wheeler. I was near her. She was not fond of silence when there was a listener, and I was pleased with her apparent sociality.

"Catharine, however" she went on "was false to her trust, but I had a little page, or errand boy, who discovered that something was not right, and so came to me one day, with the information that both Jane and Catharine had received a letter from somebody. [']And who were they from?['] I inquired.

"[']Can't tell for certain, but I think['] he answered, scratching his head.

"[']And what do you think?[']

"[']Why Missus, to tell you all about it. The 'Hio man's servant has been here good many times, and Jane said he was her brother, but I knowed better and told her so; then she wanted me not to tell you, but I told her that I should. And to[-]day he was skulking round here and then they both had letters, and that's just what I know.[']"

"Who did he mean by the 'Hio man?"

"The Senator from Ohio, whose name I forget, but who professed a great regard for slaves and negroes, I don't know why, unless because he was so black himself, his mulatto servant being much the whitest, and best looking man of the two. This fellow was thought to have his master's concurrence in persuading servants to abandon their masters; it was even suspected that the grave senator assisted in spiriting them away."

"Did many go?"

"I should think so. Nearly every family lost two or more, and these generally speaking the most valuable ones they possessed. I told my husband that there was something in the wind, but he only laughed at me, said there was no danger of our servants going, that they were too well off, and knew it, and so one night when I was attending a party at the Russian Minister's they took themselves ~~away~~ off.["]

"Did you try to recover them?["]

"Oh, no: Mr Wheeler said that it would be of no use, and then he disliked making a hue and cry about a slave at the Federal Capital, so we said little as possible about it."

"Well Madam, your hair is completed; will you tell me how you like it?" said I, bringing forward a mirror. "To me it looks well."

"So it does, why Hannah I must retain you in my service."

I bowed, but said nothing. Notwithstanding her sociality and freedom of conversation there was something in her manner that I did not like. Her voice ~~had that low~~ was soft and low, but the tone was rather artificial than natural. Her manner was exceedingly pleasant and kind, though I could not help fearing that it was affected. Then there was a sparkle in her eye, and a tremor in her frame when she became agitated that indicated an effort to keep down strong passion.

While assisting at her toilet[5] I was greatly amused with the gossip and titbits of Washington scandal she related, yet my heart did not yearn

5. Here, the process of dressing and grooming someone.

towards her as it [did] to Mrs Henry, and I felt a certain presentiment that ~~by acquaintance with her~~ she must be less good.

Her toilet preperations being finished she retired to her breakfast room, a dainty little boudoir, with a great bow window, completely trellised by climbing rose vines. Here she was joined by Mrs Henry, and they partook together the~~ir~~ morning meal.

"You find Hannah right handy, don't you?" inquired Mrs Henry.

"Oh, very, I have serious thoughts of dictating a letter to that gentleman this day, if you will give me his name and address. I must endeavor to secure her. She could fill the place of Jane so exactly."

"She would do more" said Mrs Henry. "Hannah is a good girl; she has good principles, and is I believe a consistent Christian. I don't think your Jane was either."

"Oh, as to that" said Mrs Wheeler ["]it makes little difference. I never trouble myself about the principles of my girls; so they are obedient is all I require."

After breakfast Mrs Henry went out to give the servants their orders for the day, while Mrs ~~Wheeler se~~ Wheeler requested me to read for her. I had not gone over two pages, when she called for pillows, which were to be disposed about her person to facilitate slumber; then she inquired if I was musical, adding that Jane used to soothe her to sleep with the guitar. I had played a little on the harp, and so I told her. She bade me get it, and play softly, very softly on account of her nerves. Then settling her person among the pillows, but in such a manner as not to derange her hair she prepared to take a nap. My music, however, did not suit her. It was sharp, or flat, or dull, or insipid anything but what she wished.

I was sorry at my inability to please her, and apologised of course in the best language I was able to command.

It was singular, indeed, but there was something imperative in her manner. Her requests, though made in the softest voice, implied command. You were not forced, but awed to obedience.

From *Chapter 13*

THE BEAUTIFYING POWDER

Mrs Wheeler conceived her beauty to be on the wane. She had been a belle in youth, and the thought of her fading charms was unendurable. That very day an antiquated lady, with a large mouth filled with false teeth, a head covered with false hair, and a thin scrawny neck, beneath which swelled out a false bust, had called on my mistress with what she designated very highly important information. I supposed at first that the President's wife was dead, or the secretary's daughter about to be married, but it was something more interesting to fashionable ladies than even that. Some great Italian chemist, a Signor with an unpronounceable name had discovered or rather invented an impalpable powder, fine, highly scented, and luxurious, that applied to the hands and face was said to produce the most marvellous effect. The skin, however sallow and unbeautiful, would immediately acquire the softness and delicacy of childhood. Tan, or freckless [freckles], or wrinkles, or other unseemly blotches would simultaneously disappear, and to render the article still more attractive it was said that only two or three boxes of it yet remained. Of course Mrs Wheeler was all impatience to obtain one of them, and her visitor was scarcely out of hearing when I was summoned, and directed to go at once to the Chemist's, and get a box of the Italian Medicated Powder. No hesitancy on account of mud or bad weather was allowable. I went, purchased the last box, and when returning passed two gentlemen, standing in a somewhat sheltered place apparently conversing on some subject of deep interest. There was something in the coat of seedy black, and the general bearing and manner of one of them, which instantly arrested my attention, but the driving mist and sleet was full in my face, with the gloom momentarily thickening, so that I failed to obtain a perfect view of his features. It was certainly very ill-mannered, but stimulated by curiosity I even turned back to look at them, and not minding my footing through pre-occupation of mind I slipped very suddenly and came down with all my weight on the rough paving stones. The two gentlemen immediately came forward, and one of them assisting me to rise, kindly inquired if I was hurt. I looked into the face of the other I knew. ~~I knew him on the instant~~ Oh then I knew him on the instant, I could have remembered his eyes and countenance among a thousand. It was Mr Trapp[e].

Whether or not the recognition was mutual I had no means of ascertaining, but his presence to me seemed ominous of evil, and hastily murmuring my thanks I hastened home.

Mr Wheeler was in the apartment of his wife when I entered it. He was a little dapper man, very quick in his motions, and with little round piercing black eyes set far back in his head. He had the exact air and manner of a Frenchman, but was reputed to be very obstinate in his way, and to have little respect for constituted authorities in his moments of passion. Report said that he had actually quarreled with the President, and challenged a senator to fight a duel, besides laying a cowhide on a certain occasion over the broad shoulders of a member of Congress. At any rate he had been turned out of office, and now was busily engaged in hunting another. Consequently he was seldom at home, being usually to be found haunting the bureau of some department or other, and striving to engage attention by talking in sharp shrill voice, accompanied with violent gesticulation of what should be done in one place, or had been left undone in another. He knows exactly where a screw is loose, and he understands perfectly to tighten it again. On many matters he is better informed than the President. He could give instructions to the secretaries of the army and navy, but they are old, obstinate, and headstrong, and won't listen to his advice.

* * *

On the present occasion Mr Wheeler came to ask a favor of his wife. Another vacancy had occurred, but the gift was in the power of a gentleman, with whom at some time or another of his life Mr Wheeler had some disturbance, and much as he desired the office he dreaded still more the humiliation of asking for it. Could not his wife be induced to make the request? He thought with a little well-timed flattery she might. Ladies of great consideration not unfrequently petitioned for their husbands. The President had been importuned by them till he almost feared the sight of a woman. The Secretaries had fared little better; indeed all who had offices to bestow had been coaxed, and flattered, and addled by female tongues untill they scarcely knew what they were about. They said, too, that female petitioners were likeliest to succeed. Perhaps that was the reason of his frequent failure. Had he brought his wife sooner into the field, in all probability he would have secured a prize with far less trouble. The experiment is worth trying at any rate, though he is not positive that the lady will concur.

* * *

"I regret to say, my dear" continued Mr Wheeler "that I am the object of continued opposition. Men of attainment in a high position of society always have their enemies of course. I have mine. Not so with you. You, I am proud to say it, are universally admired. Then no gentleman would think for a moment of opposing a lady. Certainly not. Now a vacancy has just occurred, and Mrs Piper is intriguing to have it filled by her husband. It is a very important office, worth about two thousand a year."

"Then she expects to get it, does she?—and a failure would mortify her exceedingly. She is so haughty, vain, and conceited. Wouldn't it be pleasant to disappoint her?"

"It would, indeed."

"Who makes the appointment?"

Mr Wheeler gave the desired information.

The lady sate [sat] a few moments in profound silence, then she spoke though rather as talking to herself than any one else. "Mrs Piper, indeed, going to obtain a situation for her husband when mine has none. But I'll disappoint her, that I will. Mr Wheeler you shall have this office. I'll see to it that you do."

Mr Wheeler bowed complacently. Nothing could suit his purpose better.

"I'll go now, this very evening" continued the lady. "The weather is so bad that probably the gentleman will be at home. And then he will be more likely to be disengaged. Hannah you can prepare my toilet."

"Certainly."

"My rich antique moire,[6] and purple velvent [velvet] mantilla. Mr Wheeler be so good as to order the carriage."

Two bows, and two expressions of "certainly Madam" were the response to this.

Mrs Wheeler did not forget her beautifying powder.

"How lucky" she exclaimed ["]that I sent for it just when I did. Don't be sparing of it Hannah, dear, as I wish to look particularly well."

The powder was very fine, soft, and white, and certainly did add much to the beauty of her appearance. I had never seen her look better. Mr Wheeler complimented her, hoped that she would be careful of herself and not take cold, and actually kissed her hand as he assisted her into the carriage, observing to me as he stepped back on the pavement "She is a dear, good, noble woman."

The next moment I heard my voice called, and turning round beheld Mrs Wheeler leaning from the carriage window and beckoning.

"Hannah, dear" she cried on my approach. "I forgot my smelling-bottle,[7] go and bring it, that new one I obtained purchased yesterday."

"Yes Madam" and back I went to the house, procured the smelling-bottle, Mr Wheeler advanced to meet me, took the little delicate supporter of weak nerves, and handing it to his wife, the carriage drove off.

In two hours a carriage stopped at the door; the bell was rung with a hasty jerk, and the servant admitted a lady, who came directly to Mrs Wheeler's

6. A silk fabric with a rippled appearance.
7. A bottle containing smelling salts, used as a stimulant or restorative.

apartment. I was greatly surprised; for though the vail, the bonnet, and the dress were those of that lady, or exactly similar, the face was black.

I stood gazing in mute amazement, when a voice not in the least languid called out "What are you gazing at me in that manner for? Am I to be insulted by my own slaves?"

Mr Wheeler just that moment stepped in. She turned towards him, and the mixture of surprise and curiosity with which he regarded her was most ludicrous.

"Are you all gone mad?" inquired the not now languid voice. "Or what is the matter?"

"You may well ask that question" exclaimed Mr Wheeler, sobbing with suppressed laughter. "Why, Madam, I didn't know you. Your face is black as Tophet."[8]

"Black?" said the lady, the expression of astonishment on his countenance transferred to hers.

"Hannah bring the mirror."

I complied.

She gazed a moment, and then her mingled emotions of grief, rage, and shame were truly awful. To all Mr Wheeler's inquiries of "how did it happen, my dear?["] and ["]how came your face to turn black, my dear?" she only answered that she did not know, had no idea, and then she wept and moaned, and finally went into a fit of strong hysterics. Mr Wheeler and myself quickly flew to her assistance. To tell the truth he was now more concerned about his wife than the office ~~now~~,

"Heaven help me" he said bending over her. "I fear that her beauty has gone forever. What a dreadful thing it is. I never heard of the like."

"It must have been the powder."

"The powder was white I thought."

"The powder certainly is white, and yet it may posses such chemical properties as occasion blackness. Indeed I recently saw in the newspapers some accounts of a chemist who having been jilted by a lady very liberal in the application of powder to her face had invented as a method of revenge a certain kind of smelling bottles, of which the fumes would suddenly blacken the whitest skin provided the said cosmetic had been previously applied."

"You wretch" exclaimed the lady suddenly opening her eyes. "Why didn't you tell me of this before?"

"I—I—didn't think of it, didn't know it was necessary" I stammered in extenuation.

"Oh no: you didn't think of it, you never think of anything that you ought to, and I must be insulted on account of your thoughtlessness, right before Mrs Piper, too. Get out of my sight this instant. I never want to see you again."

"My dear Madam" I said, kneeling at her feet, and attempting to kiss her hand "how should I know that those mentioned in the papers were identical with those you purchased."

Here Mr Wheeler interposed and told her that he did not see how I could be to blame.

"Of course, you don't" she replied mockingly eager to vent her spleen on somebody "of course, you don't. No: no: ~~what husband ever could agree with his wife~~ Slaves generally are far preferable to wives in husbands' eyes."

8. A place of punishment for the wicked; hell.

Mr Wheeler's face flushed with anger. The allusion was most uncalled for, and ungenerous. However recovering his serenity in a moment he inquired who had insulted her.

"Why everybody" she replied, making another demonstration of hysterics.

"Don't have another fit, pray" said the husband, applying the camphor to her nose. "Hannah bring some water and wash off this hedious stuff."

I procured the water, brought a basin, soap, napkin, and cloth, and went to work. Gradually and by little and little the skin resumed its natural color.

* * *

Finding themselves the subjects of such unwelcome notoriety they concluded to forsake the capital and remove to their estate. The splendid mansion they occupied having been taken only temporarily could be abandoned at any time. Suddenly and without any previous intimation a certain circle was astounded with the intelligence that the Wheeler's [sic] had gone.

[The "victim of a conspiracy" among envious enslaved domestic workers at the Wheelers' North Carolina plantation, Hannah is banished to the agricultural workers' quarters to live and work as a field hand. Insulted by Mrs. Wheeler, disgusted by the prospect of living among the field workers, and fearful of rape, Hannah escapes "in a suit of male apparel." Sustained by her faith in God, the fugitive makes her way to freedom in New Jersey.]

From *Chapter 21*

IN FREEDOM

There is a hush on my spirit in these days, a deep repose a blest and holy quietude. I found a life of freedom all my fancy had pictured it to be. I found the friends of the slave in the free state just as good as kind and hospitable as I had always heard they were. I dwell now in a neat little Cottage, and keep a school for colored children. It is well attended, and I enjoy myself almost as well in imparting knowledge to others, as I did in obtaining it when a child myself. Can you guess who lives with me? You never could—my own dear mother, aged and venerable, yet so smart and lively and active, and Oh; so fond of me. There was a hand of Providence in our meeting as we did. I am sure of it. Her history is most affecting and eventful. During my infancy she was transferred from Lindendale to the owner of a plantation in Mississippi, yet she never forgot me nor certain marks on my body, by which I might be identified in after years. She found a hard master, but he soon died, and she became the property of his daughter who dwelt in Maryland, and thither she was removed. Here she became acquainted with a free mulatto from New Jersey, who persuaded her to escape to his native state with him, where they might be married and live in freedom and happiness. She consented. Their plan of escape proved successful, and they lived together very happyly many years when the husband died.

* * *

I have yet another companion quite as dear—a fond and affectionate husband. He sits by my side even as I write and sometimes, shakes his head, and sometimes laughs, saying, "There, there, my dear. I fear you grow prosy, you cannot expect the public to take the same interest in me that you do" when I answer "of course not, I should be jealous if it did." He is and has always been a free man, is a regularly ordained preacher of the Methodist persuasion, and I believe and hope that many through his means, under Providence, have been led into wisdom's ways, which are those of pleasantness.[9]

* * *

Need I describe the little church where we all go to meeting, and the happiness we experience in listening to the words of Gospel truth; and as I could not, if I tried, sufficiently set forth the goodness of those about me, the tenderness and love with which my children of the school regard me, and the undeviating happiness I find in the society of my mother, my husband, and my friends, I will let the reader picture it all to his imagination and say farewell

1858

9. See Proverbs 3:13–17: "Happy is the man that findeth wisdom . . . for her ways are ways of pleasantness and all her paths are peace."

Literature of the Reconstruction to the New Negro Renaissance 1865–1919

"THE BONDS OF PEACE"

Sitting in church in Richmond, Virginia, the capital of the Confederate States of America, on Sunday, April 2, 1865, Jefferson Davis, the president of the Confederacy, received the news he had been dreading. The Union army was advancing, and he must leave immediately. As the Confederate military fled, they set fire to the city. On Tuesday, April 4, a party of Union political dignitaries, military officers, and close associates accompanied President Abraham Lincoln to review the still smoldering ruins. Elizabeth Keckly was among the group. In her autobiography, *Behind the Scenes; or, Thirty Years a Slave and Four Years in the White House* (1868), Keckly writes that as the *River Queen* approached the city, she "wondered, now that Richmond had fallen, and Virginia had been restored to the clustering stars of the Union, if the people would come together in the bonds of peace."

Keckly's meditation was a bit premature. Richmond had indeed fallen, but Virgina was not readmitted into the United States of America until January 26, 1870. A week after Richmond fell, on April 9, 1865, Union general Ulysses S. Grant's army defeated Confederate general Robert E. Lee in the Battle of Appomattox Court

Chapel at Tuskegee Institute filled with female students, 1902.

Collage of images of African American troops during the Civil War by C. F .F. Hillen, published in *Frank Leslie's Illustrated Newspaper.*

House. The two generals negotiated terms of surrender and the Union Army had basically won the Civil War. But the fighting continued as the country plunged deeper into chaos. Lincoln was assassinated, Andrew Johnson became president, and the United States Constitution added the Thirteenth Amendment (1865) abolishing slavery and involuntary servitude, except as punishment for a crime. The Civil War officially ended on August 20, 1866, when President Andrew Johnson signed Proclamation 157 declaring that "Peace, Order, Tranquility, and Civil Authority Now Exists in and Throughout the Whole of the United States of America." That statement was also premature.

The Civil War had not been fought over abolition per se, but it had in fact broken slavery's bonds. Abraham Lincoln had called the Civil War (1861–65) a test of whether the United States or any nation "conceived in liberty and dedicated to the proposition that all men are created equal . . . could long endure." It was also a war to determine the power relationship between the federal and the state governments, and the nature and control of the economy. It was a war catalyzed by the challenges of ascendency of scientific inquiry and technological advances combined with increased immigration and migration and the resultant tensions of diverse religious, legal, and cultural theories and practices. African Americans, both former slaves and longtime free citizens; Euro-Americans, whether newly immigrated or descendants of the founding families; Asians and other immigrants, as well as the indigenous peoples of the territories now claimed as Mexico, Canada, and the United States were all affected. Keckly's concern about the bonds of peace was apt.

Despite the hundreds of thousands of lives lost and millions of acres devastated in the Civil War, most agreed that the United States had in fact passed its test. The postwar challenge was to make real President Johnson's proclamation that "Peace, Order, Tranquility, and Civil Authority" actually existed and that they would continue to exist in the re-United States of America. Civil War survivors wanted to reconstruct a United States of America that was faithful to the language and intent of the Constitution but open to new opportunities and knowledge. The dominant desire was to salvage from the past the best and truest ideals, and—using the spirit, experience, and technology of the present—to fashion a better, more *United* States of America. Many wanted to remove the debris of war and shore up weight-bearing beams, following the same design as before. Others insisted upon replacing or redesigning certain structural elements evident before the war and those created by the war itself. For example, slavery had been abolished, in word if not in deed, but the societal role of the freedpeople was yet to be determined. Redefinition of roles was not a question only for those who had once been legally enslaved. Freeborn Americans of African descent, nominally free indigenous Americans, recent immigrants, and women of all cultures worked to ensure that their civil and human rights were incorporated into the fundamental architecture of the reconstructed country.

The desire to remake, not merely repair, the country was especially apparent in discussions of gender roles and rights. The Civil War had forced women to become more independent, and the fervor of Reconstruction motivated them to secure their independence. For example, by organizing themselves and developing financial and political savvy, women had supported families, run businesses and farms, established hospitals, schools, recreation centers, and other institutions to care for newly freed people as well as themselves and others. Many had become accomplished speakers and writers who recognized and articulated comparisons between their own status and that of enslaved African Americans and others who were indentured or conscripted and denied civil rights. Most were entirely unwilling to return silently to the patriarchal hierarchies that reserved liberty and equality solely for the Fraternal Order of Men. In addition, the increased diversity and urbanization had made some women more cosmopolitan, and they wanted to continue to work with people regardless of differences in gender, religion, national origin, and class. Such women applauded Frances E. W. Harper at the Eleventh National Woman's Rights Convention in May 1866, when she proclaimed:

> We are all bound up together in one great bundle of humanity, and society cannot trample on the weakest and feeblest of its members without receiving the curse in its own soul. . . . This grand and glorious revolution which has commenced, will fail to reach its climax of success, until throughout the length and brea[d]th of the American Republic, the nation shall be so color-blind, as to know no man by the color of his skin or the curl of his hair. It will then have no privileged class, trampling upon and outraging the underprivileged classes, but will be then one great privileged nation, whose privilege will be to produce the loftiest manhood and womanhood that humanity can attain.

While some poets and activists agreed with Harper, hers was not a majority position. Knowing that the nation was at a historical watershed, that the war had settled the question of whether the agricultural South, supported by slave labor, would dominate the economy or whether the mercantile North, a magnet for European immigrants, would determine the national future, some people envisioned a reconstructed economy that would integrate southern agriculture with northern manufacturing and exploit the opportunities of the western frontier. They recognized the possibilities of applying scientific knowledge to burgeoning technology and thereby establishing the United States as a world power. The argument for a shared community of interests and a classless society represented by Harper's "we are all bound up together" speech directly conflicted with the rugged and sometimes rapacious individualism that imperialistic expansion required.

The conflict in vision for the future of the United States was not simply regional nor was it entirely along racial lines. The Civil War had wrecked many individual fortunes but had not dismantled the plantation system; postwar industrial expansion enabled it to be refigured as sharecropping and tenant farming. The changes wrought by war and mobility had opened many areas to virtually anyone with the desire and design to exploit them. A compelling factor was completion of the first transcontinental railroad in 1869. Built by exploited African Americans, Asians, and other poor people, the railroad opened up the frontier and made the distribution of minerals and raw materials, as well as meat, produce, and finished goods, quicker and easier than ever before. Soon the nation boasted four transcontinental railroads as well as an impressive array of canals. Both forms of transportation encouraged transformation from a land of small towns and rural communities to one of urban metropolises. Gradually, as the western territories beckoned, coastal New England's position as the cultural and commercial center diminished. At the same time, immigration was doubling, tripling, and quadrupling the size of some cities. Between 1860 and 1900 an estimated fourteen million immigrants, primarily from Europe, settled in the Northeast and Midwest. In 1850 New York counted 500,000 residents. By 1900 it was home to three and a half million. During the same period Chicago went from a small outpost of 20,000 to the center of the meatpacking and other industries, with two million inhabitants.

Never before had people from so many different cultures lived so close to one another. Though westward expansion allowed greater than usual class and cultural interaction and assimilation, that same expansion, class and cultural interaction, and assimilation practically destroyed other cultures, particularly those of Native Americans, as well as the environments that had sustained them. Moreover, the physical space of the United States, while vast, was nevertheless limited; as the pioneers and refugees reached the Pacific, they had to settle down and live with one another. Increased cultural diversity in a finite physical territory multiplied the normal pressures to conform. Many saw the answer in a "melting pot" concept, but their tastes favored a stew characterized by meat and potatoes, mildly flavored with a little salt and almost no pepper. Rice, yams, and maize were excluded from the recipe, and the rice, yam, or maize eaters were allowed at the table only to serve.

A DECADE OF RECONSTRUCTION

Reconstruction is generally identified as the years between 1865 and 1877. Actually, it began even before the end of the Civil War, when numerous volunteers, including the sons of Frederick Douglass and Elizabeth Keckly, joined the Union Army and Charlotte Forten, Anna Julia Cooper, and Harriet Jacobs, among others, helped create refugee centers, hospitals, schools, and other social services. In March 1867 the Republican-dominated Congress passed the Reconstruction Act, which struck down many restrictive codes that had targeted African Americans. In addition, it established the Freedmen's Bureau to protect the rights and the lives of African American people in the

School for the Formerly Enslaved. Harriet Jacobs and her daughter, Louisa, taught at this school in Alexandria, Virginia, 1864.

South. Through the Freedmen's Bureau, thousands of northerners—men and women, African American and white—traveled to the South to set up schools, establish cooperatives, and train the newly freed people in the rituals and responsibilities of citizenship. During its brief history, from 1865 to about 1870, the bureau established nearly four thousand schools. Some of these schools, along with those founded by churches and by visionary philanthropists, became independent colleges. Between 1866 and 1868, for example, Fisk, Morehouse, Howard, Atlanta, Talladega, and Hampton were established.

The most significant pieces of Reconstruction legislation were three Constitutional amendments. The Thirteenth Amendment (1865) outlawed slavery, the Fourteenth (1868) provided equal protection to African Americans under the law, and the Fifteenth (1870) granted suffrage to African American men. These three amendments provided limited but dramatic results. The passage of the Fifteenth Amendment gave African American men some political clout. In Louisiana, for instance, they had enough voting strength to elect an African American governor. Newly enfranchised African Americans sent sixteen of their number to Congress and significantly influenced several state legislatures. However, in many places African Americans never actually obtained the vote. And the Constitutional amendments, like other reform legislation, were neither uniformly enforced nor even recognized in all parts of the country. Consequently, the daily lives of far too many African Americans were not substantially different in freedom from what they had been under slavery. For example, under new institutions such as sharecropping and the convict-lease system, most African Americans, especially those living in the states of the former Confederacy, continued to work on farms, often in service to the same people who had once owned them. Their bosses still exercised considerable authority over their actions and their activities. The limited social and economic gains that African Americans experienced immediately after the war were quickly reversed when, in 1877, the withdrawal of federal troops, the reversal by state and federal courts of protective legislation for African Americans, and the return to power of the Democrats in the South signaled the end of Reconstruction. Vigilante and white supremacist terrorist organizations embarked on a campaign of brutal suppression that the federal government did little to suppress.

SEPARATE AS THE FINGERS

It took very little time to deconstruct the institutions and to repeal or replace the legislation of the Reconstruction decade. Random violence and systematic oppression were supported by Jim Crow laws, which legalized racial segregation in virtually every area of life. The last part of the nineteenth century and the first decades of the twentieth, known in African American history as "the Nadir "of African American experience, were particularly violent as lynching and race riots became increasingly common. According to historians such as John Hope Franklin, during the last sixteen years of the nineteenth century there were more than twenty-five hundred lynchings, mostly of African Americans in the South. When one recalls that lynchings often entailed not just death by hanging but also torture and burning alive, and that such horrible events were sometimes advertised in advance and attracted large crowds of white men, women, and children, the pre–World War I years almost make the antebellum South seem like a dress rehearsal.

The reasons were many. For example, the majority of northern whites, whose support had been crucial for the abolition of slavery, wanted to put sectional divisions behind them and turned their attention to issues such as suffrage, temperance, and pacifism. Moreover, issues of equal rights were complicated. For example, when it appeared that Congress would grant the vote to African American men but not to any women, white suffragist Elizabeth Cady Stanton declared, "I will cut off this right arm of mine before I will ever work for or demand the ballot for the Negro and not the woman." Whereupon Stanton, Susan B. Anthony, and others left the American Equal Rights Association and created the National Woman Suffrage Association. As the century progressed, abolitionist leaders such as Charles Sumner, Frederick Douglass, Lydia Maria Child, and William Lloyd Garrison died. Other activists, such as Harriet Tubman and Frances Harper, became old and infirm. More important, their prestige and influence, founded as it had been on conditions that no longer existed, had seriously eroded. The new generation of leaders came of age after emancipation. Although they fought against repressive legislation, they tended to focus upon preserving present progress and achieving, at least, a segregated version of the American Dream.

In 1881, when Booker T. Washington arrived in Tuskegee, he was joining one of the rare and rapidly disappearing attempts at interracial cooperation. He was to preside over one of the first schools for African Americans financially sponsored by both African Americans and whites but headed by an African American and with an African American faculty. Tuskegee was built on a philosophy of thrift, hard work, self-reliance, and patience. Its emphasis on vocational training and manual labor did not challenge segregation. Although Washington included "commerce" and "the professions" among the fountains from which southern African Americans might nourish their ambitions, agriculture, mechanics, and domestic service dominated Tuskegee's curriculum and the minds of philanthropists who supported the institution. While Washington acknowledged that it was "important and right" that African Americans

The Library Reading Room at Booker T. Washington's Tuskegee Institute.

share the "privileges of the law," his caveat that it "is vastly more important" that African Americans "be *prepared* for the exercise of those privileges" (emphasis added) implied that they were not yet ready for equal protection under the law, for suffrage, or for other manifestations of citizenship.

In 1883, two years after the opening of Tuskegee, the Supreme Court outlawed the Civil Rights Act of 1875. In rapid succession, state and federal courts supported laws and changes in state constitutions segregating public transportation and buildings, disenfranchising African American men, and making illegal integrated schools and many gatherings. By 1896, with the Supreme Court in *Plessy v. Ferguson* affirming the legality of the "separate but equal" ideology, a hold had been placed on real progress for African Americans, a hold that was to withstand serious legal challenge until the middle of the twentieth century.

LIFTING AS WE CLIMB

The decades just before and after the start of the twentieth century are characterized in many U.S. history books as the Progressive Period. For African Americans they are more accurately called the Decades of Disappointment, years marked by a "great migration" from south to north and from farmlands to cities in search of succor and sufferance, if not success. Still, the turn of the century did see the establishment of nationwide reform movements and the enactment of laws that ameliorated working conditions and hours, provided worker's compensation, and improved the health, education, and welfare of the poor and the working classes. Some African Americans participated effectively in groups such as the Populist Party, the Knights of Labor, the women's suffrage movement, and the Women's Christian Temperance Union, though often as part of the "colored" section. Inventors such as Jan E. Matzeliger, Elijah McCoy, and Granville T. Woods received patents for important mechanical and electrical devices. During the Spanish-American War, two African American military units, the 9th and 10th Cavalries, were said to have saved Teddy Roosevelt's Rough Riders from "complete annihilation" in Cuba. Though their experiences were often traumatic, individuals such as Anna Julia Cooper, W. E. B. Du Bois, Pauline Elizabeth Hopkins, James Weldon Johnson, and Ida B. Wells-Barnett participated in integrated efforts as well as projects by and for African Americans. A fortunate few attended colleges, founded theater groups, traveled abroad, edited and published periodicals, and established educational, civic, and political organizations they believed would, in fact, ensure upward mobility.

As the nation moved into the twentieth century, wealth and power were still far from evenly distributed. Tenements teemed with migrants and immigrants struggling to gain a foothold on the success ladder, struggling too often simply to survive. To investigate and address this inequity, philanthropists funded an increasing number of reform movements. Writers stirred the public to protest the most blatant abuses. That most of these efforts were segregated did not concern most white Americans. And African Americans, having endured decades of disappointment, were generally less interested in integration than in their physical safety and economic security. They were convinced that they too had rights to life, liberty, and the pursuit of happiness. They believed they could enjoy those rights for themselves—if their fellow citizens would stop the violence and live up to their constitutional promises.

In 1895 Frederick Douglass died, Booker T. Washington catapulted to fame with his Atlanta Exposition speech, and W. E. B. Du Bois graduated from Harvard with a Ph.D. in sociology. Washington and Du Bois offered two seemingly different options for civil rights. In the ensuing years, the dominant debate was the merits of Washington's privileging industrial education and economic advancement over Du Bois's advocacy of political agitation and the leadership of the "talented tenth." This was, of course, oversimplification. Washington stated time and again that he would "set no limits to the attainments of the Negro in arts, in letters or statesmanship," but he argued that "knowledge must be harnessed to the things of real life," and he "pleaded for industrial education and development "as the foundation on which the race could prosper. Du Bois stated that "the Negro race, like all races, is going to be saved by its exceptional men" educated on a curriculum that made "manhood the object of the work of the schools—intelligence, broad sympathy, knowledge of that world that was and is, and the relation of men to it." This, Du Bois asserted, was the foundation on which to "build bread winning, the skill of hand and the quickness of brain, with never a fear lest the child and man mistake the means of living for the object of life." There were, of course, other leaders with other options. For example, many African American women proclaimed the time was now the "Woman's Era." Anna Julia Cooper's declaration that "Only the Black woman can say when and where I enter, in the quiet, undisputed dignity of my womanhood, without violence and without suing or special patronage, then and there the whole Negro race enters with me" is a fair summary of their attitudes.

The rise of capitalism and industrialization, a growing division between the wealth of a few and scarcity for others, and natural disasters such as a plague of boll weevils destroying the entire cotton crop of 1914 contributed to a floundering economy in the South. African American tenant farmers were plunged further into debt, and laborers saw their daily wages decrease to seventy-five cents a day and below. Despite Washington's admonition to "cast down your buckets where you are," large numbers left the South seeking work in Chicago, Detroit, New York, Pittsburgh, St. Louis, Oakland, and other cities. African Americans left to purchase farms in the Midwest or to explore opportunities on the Pacific Coast. With the advent of World War I, the steady stream of migrants became a flood as the military accepted more African Americans, and factories, railroads, and major employers found themselves desperate for workers to fill the positions left vacant by enlisted men. In 1916, for example, the Pennsylvania Railroad hired twelve thousand African Americans, the majority of whom they had recruited in the South and transported north by the trainload.

Despite the violence and blatant inequalities in the "separate but equal" United States, African Americans generally declared they were "Lifting as We Climb," as stated in the National Council of Negro Women's motto. Literacy increased, businesses were started. An African American middle class began to emerge, and the small but wealthy social elite grew in number and influence. Throughout the country, African American communities and institutions made significant changes. Many churches, for example, were centers for political action. They created kindergartens and homes for the elderly, credit unions, employment bureaus, housing projects, and orphanages. Organizations such as the Afro-American League, the Negro Business League, and the National Council of Negro Women worked through the churches and independently to create educational, economic, social, and recreational opportunities. Still, though African Americans paid market rates and were taxed as if they had equal access to the wealth and privileges of the nation, they did not. Discrimination in education and in job opportunities increased as the twentieth century neared. And to make matters worse, not only were African Americans unwelcome outside their neighborhoods, but often they were not safe even in their own communities. Migration brought them closer to freedom, but they had not arrived in the Promised Land. Nonetheless, they knew themselves to be starting new lives. Some called themselves "New Negroes."

THE NEW NEGRO

In his foreword to *The New Negro: An Interpretation* (1925), Alain Locke wrote, "There is ample evidence of a New Negro in the latest phases of social change and progress, but still more in the internal world of the Negro mind and spirit." "New Negroes" were more about attitude and action in the present than apology for the past. However, extolling ancestral heroism, courage, and fortitude was important to creating and maintaining these new attitudes. Books with titles such as A *New Negro for a New Century: An Accurate and Up-to-Date Record of the Upward Struggles of the Negro Race* (1900) by Booker T. Washington, Fannie Barrier Williams, and Norman Barton Wood; essays such as Pauline Hopkins's "Famous Women of the Negro Race: Literary Workers" (1902); and proclamations like Victoria Earle Matthews's "The Value of Race Literature" (1895) exemplify efforts to correct misapprehensions about the past and inspire visions for the future. The New Negroes presented themselves as self-assured, self-reliant, and self-identified, as race proud and resilient. Considering Booker T. Washington along with Anna Julia Cooper, James Weldon

Johnson in conversation with Paul Laurence Dunbar and Charles Chesnutt, W. E. B. Du Bois organizing the NAACP and Marcus Garvey founding the Universal Negro Improvement Association and African Communities, and Ida B. Wells-Barnett, Charlotte Forten, and Alice Dunbar-Nelson reading one another's work shows how capacious was the term "New Negro."

WRITING THINGS RIGHT

From its colonial beginnings, American literature has been inextricably connected with its perceived political and religious usefulness. From the Puritan sermons and hymnals that were the first products of the American printing presses to the captivity and conversion narratives that proved Divine Providence's intervention in individual lives to the novels, poems, and sketches that demonstrated the efficacy of moral and mannerly living, the most popular literature in the United States was that which taught and affirmed social mores. Yet increasingly the artist's obligation to instruct was accompanied by the desire that it be done both pleasingly and also in a manner that showed off the writer's familiarity with the literary canon. Thus nineteenth-century American literature tried not merely to delight and instruct but also to highlight intellectual achievement and aesthetic sophistication.

African Americans generally understood these expectations. For them, as for their Anglo-American contemporaries, writing was a primary means of instructing themselves and others and of correcting the historical record. However, for African American writers, the challenge of producing literature both *utile* and *dulce* ("useful" and "sweet" [Latin]) was exacerbated by external disparagement of their intellectual and creative capacities and by the exoticization and marginalization of African American culture. Such had been the circumstances when William Wells Brown wrote, in his introduction to *The Black Man, His Genius and His Achievements* (1863), "If this work shall aid in vindicating the Negro's character, and show that he is endowed with those intellectual and amiable qualities which adorn and dignify human nature, it will meet the most sanguine hopes of the writer." Such were also catalysts for Victoria Earle Matthews's declaration in "The Value of Race Literature" (1895) that there was

> indubitable evidence of the need of thoughtful, well-defined and intelligently placed efforts on our part, to serve as counterirritants against all such writing that shall stand, having as an aim the supplying of influential and accurate information, on all subjects relating to the Negro and his environments, to inform the American mind at least, for literary purposes. We cannot afford any more than any other people to be indifferent to the fact, that the surest road to real fame is through literature.

Thus, African American literature in the mid-nineteenth and early twentieth centuries was used to confirm and to manifest creativity and genius while also documenting and shaping social, political, and spiritual aspirations and conditions.

ACTIVIST AUTOBIOGRAPHIES

Before the Civil War, personal narratives played a vital role in influencing public attitudes. The autobiographical writings of formerly enslaved people had been critical to the abolitionist effort. Small wonder then that in the

Reconstruction period, African American literature relied heavily on personal testimony. In the fifty years after the Civil War, the number of extant published autobiographies by formerly enslaved people doubled that of the one hundred years before it. Postbellum narratives of freedpeople tended to recast the sin and suffering of slavery as trials and tribulations from which they emerged wiser and stronger and to represent the slave era as a warning. Slavery was, in Elizabeth Keckly's words, "a cruel custom" and a "plant of evil" that had been allowed to grow until it had choked and nearly destroyed the nation. Activist autobiographies championed the rugged individualism and successful transcendence that characterized the American Dream, as exemplified by Benjamin Franklin, Abraham Lincoln, and the Horatio Alger myth put forth in popular literature. But the postbellum narrators usually combined these capitalist possibilities with the strong spirit of community and mutual effort that the social, political, and religious sentiments promulgated, if not practiced, in postbellum America. Especially during Reconstruction, narrators concentrated on the lessons learned from slavery and the progress made after emancipation that would entitle African Americans to full participation in the building and maintaining of a new and improved "City upon a Hill." This is shown clearly in the titles of works such as *Life and Adventures of James Williams, a Fugitive Slave, with a Full Description of the Underground Railroad* (1874); *From Slave Cabin to Pulpit, the Autobiography of Peter Randolph* (1893); *From the Virginia Plantation to the National Capitol; or, The First and Only Negro Representative in Congress from the Old Dominion* by John Mercer Langston (1894); Henry Clay Bruce's *The New Man: Twenty-Nine Years a Slave, Twenty-Nine Years a Free Man* (1895); *Thirty Years a Slave: From Bondage to Freedom* by Louis Hughes (1896); and Booker T. Washington's *Up From Slavery* (1901).

Of course, not all African Americans had been enslaved, nor was slavery the only way in which freedpeople defined their lives or shaped their narratives. During this period, biographies, memoirs, and other life stories ranged in focus from those of religious leaders such as Julia Foote (1879) and Daniel Payne (1888) and prominent community activist leaders including Martin Delany (1883), Mary Ellen Pleasant (1902), and Fanny Jackson Coppin (1913), to domestic servants and professional attendants such as Paul Jennings (1865) and Eliza Potter (1859), and explorers and travelers such as David Augustus Straker (1896) and Nat Love (Deadwood Dick) (1907). As social and economic conditions changed and as legal segregation and racial persecution increased, so too did the number of African Americans who presented their experiences in overcoming past adversity as models for the present and as blueprints for a better future. "Progress report autobiographies"—that is, personal accounts by individuals who could not claim unmitigated success but whose achievements thus far were deemed sufficient to instruct and to inspire others—became their own genre. These include works such as *Early Recollections and Life of Dr. James Still* (1877), *The Colored Cadet at West Point* by Henry Ossian Flipper (1878), *Meditations from the Pen of Mrs. Maria W. Stewart* (1879), Susie King Taylor's *Reminiscences of My Life with the 33rd United States Colored Troops* (1902), William Pickens's *The Heir of Slaves* (1910), and James David Corrothers's *In Spite of the Handicap* (1916). Individual stories of those who had endured trials but experienced triumph assuaged the fears of whites and others who worried about revenge or dependency. These autobiographical texts served also to instruct other African Americans that they could and should buy into the American Dream.

LITERACY AS LIBERATION

Because African American literature depended upon African American literacy, many African American writers aimed to educate and inspire students as well as other readers. As public education developed across the country and with the advent of the schools for freedpeople particularly, the need for relevant and accurate texts grew. A few schools had curricula that stressed Greek, rhetoric, elocution, and higher mathematics. African American scholars such as William Sanders Scarborough and Anna Julia Cooper published textbooks of Greek grammar and translations of literature originally in French, German, and other languages. The majority of the schools that African Americans attended, however, offered reading, writing, arithmetic, and vocational skills. Yet, even for these institutions, writers saw a need for books that adequately expressed the history, position, and aspirations of African Americans and published individual biographies and compendia of African American contributions. Among the biographies by African Americans about African Americans are *Life and Public Services of Martin R. Delany* (1868) by Frances Anne Rollin, *Frederick Douglass* (1899) by Charles Chesnutt, and *Norris Wright Cuney: A Tribune of the Black People* (1913) by Maud Cuney Hare. Generally, these texts were designed for at least two purposes: to show white readers that African Americans had contributed to the rebuilding of the nation, and also to inform, inspire, and instruct other African Americans of the way to a more satisfying future. This dual purpose is clearly stated in Martin Robison Delany's preface to his *Condition, Elevation, Emigration and Destiny of the Colored People of the United States* (1852). Delany's "sole purpose," he wrote, was "to place before the public in general, and the colored people of the United States in particular, great truths concerning this class of citizens, which appears [*sic*] to have been heretofore avoided, as well by friends as enemies to their elevation."

During Reconstruction, Delany's efforts were joined by those such as William Wells Brown's *The Negro in the American Rebellion* (1867) and *The Rising Son; or, The Antecedents and Advancement of the Colored Race* (1874), and William Still's *The Underground Rail Road: A Record of Facts, Authentic Narratives, Letters, &c* (1872). As the century advanced, the projects became more grand and more diverse. Alexander Crummell compiled *The Greatness of Christ, and Other Sermons* (1882), and Albery A. Whitman versified on *Twasinta's Seminoles; or, The Rape of Florida* (1884). Daniel Payne accepted the challenge of writing *The History of the African American Episcopal Church* (1891) and George Washington Williams needed two volumes for his *History of the Negro Race in America from 1619 to 1880* (1893). W. E. B. Du Bois offered a sociological study, *The Philadelphia Negro* (1899); and Charles Fred White offered *Who's Who in Philadelphia* (1912). Pauline Hopkins's *Primer of Facts Pertaining to the Early Greatness of the African Race* (1905), Alice Dunbar Nelson's *Masterpieces of Negro Eloquence* (1914), and Delilah L. Beasley's *Negro Trail Blazers of California* (1919) were all attempts to enlighten and inspire.

PUBLISHING FOR THE PEOPLE

The intended readership for African American literature was not limited by race, class, or cultural aspiration. African American writers in general wrote what Roy Harvey Pearce calls "popular literature," that is, a literature accessible to all, composed and produced for maximum readership while not unduly compromising its aesthetics or its mission. African American writers participated in the major literary trends that appeared between the two wars. They tried virtually every genre and every style. They wrote in realistic, naturalistic, sentimental styles. They published romances, science fiction, mysteries, and fantasy fiction. They created epics and lyrics in dialect and in elaborate or formalized diction. Often, they subtly revised the themes and techniques of white writers. For example, although the folktales told by Charles Chesnutt and by Joel Chandler Harris have obvious similarities, Chesnutt's Uncle Julius more clearly recognizes the power of his words and uses them to his own ends. African American writers revised character types and situations to reflect African Americans more positively or, at least, more accurately. One such case is that of the mixed-race protagonist, the depictions of whom moved from the tragic mulatto victimization of William Wells Brown's *Clotel* (1853) to the proud claiming of heritage in Frances Ellen Watkins Harper's *Iola Leroy* (1892) and presented possibilities of racial and personal identity that ranged from Paul Laurence Dunbar's "The Colored Soldiers (1895) to the pathetic self-betrayal of the protagonist in James Weldon Johnson's *Autobiography of an Ex-Coloured Man* (1912).

Finding a publisher can be a major problem for any writer. For African American writers this obstacle was often insurmountable. Sometimes special-interest presses, such as those dedicated to temperance, peace, and other social reform movements, published writers whose work accorded with their goals and did not overtly challenge their assumptions about African Americans. For example, her affiliations with the Women's Christian Temperance Union, the Unitarian Church, and the YWCA often allowed Frances E. W. Harper to publish in such journals as the *Englishwoman's Review,* the *Woman's Journal*, and the *Peacemaker and Board of Arbitration.* Others, such as Frederick Douglass and Booker T. Washington, enjoyed extensive political ties and such elevated national stature that their essays were sometimes commissioned or reprinted by newspapers and magazines that catered almost exclusively to white readers. During the period when realism and local color were in vogue, stories and poems in dialect or about folk figures enjoyed enthusiastic acceptance. Writers such as Paul Laurence Dunbar and Charles Chesnutt were welcomed in the pages of the *Atlantic Monthly*, favorably reviewed in the *North American Quarterly*, and published by established presses such as Houghton Mifflin and Dodd, Mead. Occasionally, a book was printed and marketed not as the production of an African American writer but in a series also containing texts by white Americans. This was the case with William Wells Brown, whose third revision of *Clotel* was included in James Redpath's Campfire Series, and with Amelia Johnson, whose *Clarence and Corrine; or, God's Way* (1890) and *The Hazeley Family* (1894) were part of the Sunday School material produced by the American Baptist Publication Society. William Stanley Braithwaite's success within the white publishing industry was such that he subordinated his own writing to his editing of the *Anthology of Magazine*

Verse (1913–29), *The Book of Elizabethan Verse, The Book of Restoration Verse*, and other such collections. The majority of African American writers, however, were published first and most frequently in an outlet largely ignored by most literary scholars, the African American press.

THE AFRICAN AMERICAN PRESS

The African American press was not a single company but a diverse group of African American individuals and institutions unified by two basic attributes. First, their goal was to promulgate the writings of African Americans among a readership that was primarily African American. Second, their publications were, as Frankie Hutton characterizes them, "uplifting, positive, and forward thinking both in the messages conveyed and in spirit." African American press publications encouraged African Americans to write stories, poems, essays, and letters by sponsoring contests, by advertising, and often by distributing the resulting volumes. From *Freedom's Journal* (1827) to *The Mystery* (1843), the *North Star* (1847), which was re-created as *Frederick Douglass's Paper* (1851), and the *Anglo African Magazine* (1859), African American writers created their own audiences for their artistic and philosophical utterances as well as their theological and political declarations. After slavery was abolished, African American publications flourished. By 1896 more than 150 newspapers and magazines had been founded. Most originated from Massachusetts, New York, and Pennsylvania, but Ohio, Minnesota, and California also entered the publishing stream, and its tributaries flowed through Alabama, Louisiana, Kansas, Iowa, and the Oklahoma Territory with much passion and purpose. Like the ventures of white Americans and others, most were undercapitalized, short-lived, and local; but many merged with other papers and had a significant impact on national and international perspectives.

It was through the African American press that journalists such as Ida B. Wells-Barnett, T. Thomas Fortune, Phillip A. Bell, and Victoria Earle Matthews gained their audiences. Some, such as Thomas Detter, author of *Nellie Brown; or, The Jealous Wife* (1871), and Pauline Hopkins, were not only journalists but also fiction writers. And it was as serializations in the pages of the African American press that Julia Collins's *The Curse of Caste* (1865) first appeared, Frances E. W. Harper published three of her four novels, and Clarissa Minnie Thompson presented *Treading the Winepress* (1885).

In *The Afro American Press and Its Editors* (1891), I. Garland Penn makes it clear that art was also politics and that quantity was not to be confused with quality:

> That the measure of a people's literary qualifications is its press facilities has been accepted, we think, as a fact; yet a people's literary worth is not to be estimated solely by the number of its newspapers, magazines and periodicals. . . . Press facilities may be a measure of a people's literary worth only insomuch as the press is able, practical, and efficient; and so far as it expresses itself clearly and produces sentiment in accordance with the principles of right, truth and justice.

The African American press included publications by special-interest groups such as churches, labor unions, sororities, and fraternities. An unusual number of these groups did not limit their aspirations to providing mere in-house organs. Among the influential members of the African American press in the second half of the nineteenth century were McGirt's Publishing Company, which printed *McGirt's Magazine* as well as individual books, and the Colored Co-Operative Publishing Company, which serialized novels in its periodical, the *Colored American*, and published individual titles as well. In the spirit of its motto—"Lifting as We Climb"—the National Association of Colored Women began publishing *Women's Era* in 1894. The NAACP founded *The Crisis* in 1910 and published a magazine for children called with *The Brownie's Book*. The Urban League created *Opportunity*, which, along with *The Crisis*, provided publishing outlets that were foundational to the artistic innovations and the renaissances that were to follow. Sutton Griggs, using the expertise gained by privately publishing his own five novels, founded the Public Welfare League in 1914 as a means of encouraging African American talent and influencing public opinion. W. E. B. Du Bois, though living in Georgia, invested in a printing company in Tennessee. Of particular interest is the period between 1890 and 1910, a time known to many as "the women's era." In 1892, for example, there appeared *Iola Leroy; or, Shadows Uplifted* by Frances E. W. Harper, *A Voice from the South by an African American Woman of the South* by Anna Julia Cooper, *From Darkness Cometh the Light; or, Struggles for Freedom* by Lucy A. Delaney, and *Southern Horrors: Lynch Law in All Its Phases* by Ida B. Wells. In fiction, in essays, in autobiographies, and in investigative reporting, African American women were voicing their perspectives and recording their activities. Nor were their voices alone, for there appeared during this time volumes testifying to the women now claiming the era for themselves and their race. Their tenor is evident in titles such as Monroe Majors's *Noted Negro Women: Their Triumphs and Activities* (1893) and Gertrude Mossell's *The Work of the Afro-American Woman* (1894).

The lines between secular and special-interest presses were not so clearly drawn as they are today, and it is true that the African American press was, to a great extent, created by and strongly dependent on African American church leaders. The AME Book Concern, for example, was established in 1817 not only to provide the disciplines, hymnals, and records of the newly organized African Methodist Episcopal Church but also to publish educational materials for church literacy programs. From that enterprise developed bookstores, national distribution systems, and a variety of texts of literary and social importance. The Book Concern supported the *Repository of Religion and Literature and of Science and Art* (1858); the *Christian Recorder*, whose masthead proclaimed that it was published "for the dissemination of Religion, Morality, Literature and Science"; and the *A.M.E. Church Review*, which was founded as a literary magazine in 1884. While no copies are known to have survived, the AME Book Concern is also said to have published *The Ladies' Magazine* and *The Children's Recorder*. Similar influence was offered by other denominations. Beginning in 1896 the National Baptist Publishing Company became a major conduit for songs, poems, autobiographies, histories, and fiction composed by African American writers. It was from the offices of the *South Western Christian Advocate* that Victoria Rogers Albert's *House of Bondage* (1900) was presented. Generally, the newspapers and magazines of the Afro-Protestant press championed abolition, temperance, suffrage, education, and economic development and encouraged the editorials, essays, and letters as well as the poems, plays, short stories, and serialized novels of African Americans. They held literary contests, published book reviews, argued points of aesthetics, and advertised books by and for African Americans. Recently, scholars have argued convincingly for enlarging the history of African American literature by recognizing the autobiographical contributions of published cookbooks and other self-help works. As early as 1827, Robert Roberts published *The House Servant's Directory,* but as Elizabeth McHenry points out in *To Make Negro Literature: Writing, Literary Practice and African American Authorship* (2021), between 1890 and 1920 a plethora of innovative publications undertook deliberate interventions in literacy and literary appreciation. One such genre was "racial schoolbooks," generally sold by subscription, especially in the rural South. Such books, McHenry argues, were creative self-help volumes teaching literature, history, and aesthetic appreciation by allowing illiterate and semiliterate readers to move sequentially from "reading" illustrations to reading "curated bits of text" to thinking and analyzing critically.

World War I began, and African Americans were reading and writing, publishing, and pontificating in virtually every genre and in every literary style. African American writers had become skilled at correcting misinformation and challenging literary movements such as the Plantation School and other revisionist, even repulsive literary trends. Some, such as Alice Moore Dunbar Nelson, Daniel Webster Davis, and Charles Chesnutt, had contributed to the local color movement. Others had written biographies, histories, autobiographies, sermons, meditations, and patriotic poems. Many had achieved both national and international prominence. Others were known and celebrated primarily within their communities or through the national African American press. All had set the stage and established the stories from (and against) which the next generations could create their own renaissance.

CHARLOTTE FORTEN GRIMKÉ

1837–1914

Charlotte Forten was born into a prominent Philadelphia family that had been free, educated, and highly esteemed social activists for four generations. Rather than participate in the racially segregated educational system, the Fortens homeschooled their children. When Charlotte was sixteen years old, she was sent to Salem, Massachusetts, home to a tight-knit community of African American activists that included Sarah Parker Remond, Charles Lenox Remond, and Caroline Remond Putnam, with whom Charlotte lived and socialized. In the integrated schools of Salem, Charlotte Forten was an honor student whose poem "A Parting Hymn" was selected over thirty-nine other entries to become the class song. After graduating, Forten became the first African American to teach in the Salem school system; she left that post during the Civil War as one of the first northern African Americans to go south to teach newly freed people. In 1864 the *Atlantic Monthly* published "Life in the Sea Islands," her account of her wartime experiences teaching in coastal South Carolina, which was held by Union troops. Later, she taught in Philadelphia and Washington, D.C., until ill health forced her to accept a less demanding but prestigious position as clerk in the Treasury Department. In 1876 she married the Reverend Francis James Grimké, a former fugitive enslaved person and a graduate of the Princeton Theological Seminary. For the next thirty-six years, the Grimké home was a center for friends such as Anna Julia Cooper and others who loved literature, art, and music and hated racism and oppression.

Charlotte Forten Grimké enjoyed a modest reputation as a poet, essayist, and translator of Emile Erckmann and Alexandre Chatrain's novel *Madame Therese; or, The Volunteers of '92*. These days, however, she is best known for works she never intended for publication, the journals that she kept between 1854 and 1889. Beginning with her arrival in Salem and her abolitionist activities, and chronicling her experiences during the Civil War and Reconstruction, Grimké's journals provide rare insight into the coming of age of a free Black woman in the nineteenth century; the culture and traditions of middle-class African Americans; freedman's schools during the Civil War; and lesser-known activities of individuals such as Frederick Douglass, Harriet Tubman, John Greenleaf Whittier, Wendell Phillips, Mary Shepard, and Laura Towne.

A Parting Hymn

When Winter's royal robes of white
 From hill and vale are gone,
And the glad voices of the spring
 Upon the air are borne,
Friends, who have met with us before,
Within these walls shall meet no more.

Forth to a noble work they go:
 O, may their hearts keep pure,
And hopeful zeal and strength be theirs
 To labor and endure,
That they an earnest faith may prove
By words of truth and deeds of love.

May those, whose holy task it is
 To guide impulsive youth,
Fail not to cherish in their souls
 A reverence for truth;
For teachings which the lips impart
Must have their source within the heart.

May all who suffer share their love—
 The poor and the oppressed;
So shall the blessing of our God
 Upon their labors rest.
And may we meet again where all
Are blest and freed from every thrall.

1856

Journals

A wish to record the passing events of my life, which, even if quite unimportant to others, naturally possess great interest to myself, and of which it will be pleasant to have some remembrance, has induced me to commence this journal. I feel that keeping a diary will be a pleasant and profitable employment of my leisure hours, and will afford me much pleasure in other years, by recalling to my mind the memories of other days, thoughts of much-loved friends from whom I may then be separated, with whom I now pass many happy hours, in taking delightful walks, and holding "sweet converse"; the interesting books that I read; and the different people, places and things that I am permitted to see.

Besides this, it will doubtless enable me to judge correctly of the growth and improvement of my mind from year to year.

—C. L. F., *Salem, May 1854.*

From *Journal One*

Wednesday, May 24, 1854

Rose at five. The sun was shining brightly through my window, and I felt vexed with myself that he should have risen before me; I shall not let him have that advantage again very soon. How bright and beautiful are these May mornings! The air is so pure and balmy, the trees are in full blossom, and the little birds sing sweetly. I stand by the window listening to their music, but suddenly remember that I have an Arithmetic lesson which employes me until breakfast; then to school, recited my lessons, and commenced my journal. After dinner practised a music lesson, did some sewing, and then took a pleasant walk by the water. I stood for some time admiring the waves as they rose and fell, sparkling in the sun, and could not help envying a party of boys who were enjoying themselves in a sailing boat. On my way home, I stopped at Mrs. [Caroline] Putnam's and commenced reading "Hard Times," a new story by Dickens. The scene opens in a very matter-of-fact school, where teacher and committee deal in stern facts, and allow no flights of fancy in the youthful minds committed to their charge. One interesting little girl is severely reprimanded for wishing a carpet of flowers (not natural ones); while a repulsive looking boy receives much praise for a very long definition of the word "horse," which seems quite unintelligible to every one else. I anticipate to much pleasure in reading this story.—Saw some agreeable friends, [Jonathan] McBuffum and his family from Lynn, prepared tea, and spent the evening in writing.

Thursday, May 25

Did not intend to write this evening, but have just heard of something that is worth recording;—something which must ever rouse in the mind of every true friend of liberty and humanity, feelings of the deepest indignation and sorrow. Another fugitive [Anthony Burns] from bondage has been arrested; a poor man, who for two short months has trod the soil and breathed the air of the "Old Bay State," was arrested like a criminal in the streets of her capital, and is now kept strictly guarded,—a double police force is required, the military are in readiness; and all this is done to prevent a man, whom God has created in his own image, from regaining that freedom with which, he, in common with every other human being, is endowed. I can only hope and pray most earnestly that Boston will not again disgrace herself by sending him back to a bondage worse than death; or rather that she will redeem herself from the disgrace which his arrest alone has brought upon her.[1] The weather is gloomy and my feelings correspond with it, how applicable now are the words of the immortal Cowper,[2]

> "My ear is pained,
> My soul is sick with every day's report
> Of wrong and outrage, with which earth is filled;
> There is no flesh in man's obdurate heart,
> It does not feel for man; the nat'ral bond
> Of brotherhood, is severed as the flax.
> He finds his fellow guilty of a skin
> Not coloured like his own; and having power
> T'enforce the wrong, for such a worthy cause
> Dooms and devotes him as his lawful prey."

Friday, May 26

Had a conversation with Miss Mary Shepard about slavery; she is, as I thought, thoroughly opposed to it, but does not agree with me in thinking that the churches and ministers are generally supporters of the infamous system; I believe it firmly. Mr. [Albert] Barnes, one of the most prominent of the Philadelphia clergy, who does not profess to be an abolitionist, has declared his belief that 'the American church is the bulwark of slavery.' Words cannot express all that I feel; all that is felt by the friends of Freedom, when thinking of this great obstacle to the removal of slavery from our land. Alas! that it should be so. I was much disappointed in not seeing the eclipse, which, it [*sic*] was expected to be the most entire that has taken place for years, but the weather was rainy and the sky obscured by clouds, so after spending half the afternoon on the roof of the house in eager expectation, I saw nothing; heard since that the sun made his appearance for a minute or two, but I was not fortunate enough to catch even the momentary glimpse of him. Father left yesterday for Providence and N.[ew] Bedford; thinks he will return tomorrow evening. I write to the sound of music sweet; Sarah [Cassey Smith] is playing the "Bords Du Rhin," and I imagine myself standing on the banks of that beautiful river which flows so placidly past the happy homes of Germany. All around is lovely and calm; the sun is shedding his last rays upon the distant hills, and the gentle warbling of the shepherd's flute is heard as he returns home with his flock. I wish that this delightful day-dream could last, but it cannot, and I must rouse myself from it and return to sober reality. It is already time that I should be indulging in nightly dreams.—

> "Ah—visions less beguiling far,
> Than waking dreams by daylight are."

Saturday, May 27

Have been very busy all morning, sweeping, dusting, sewing, and doing sundry other little things which are always to be done on Saturday.—Spent a delightful hour in the afternoon at Miss [Mary] Shepard's, looking with her and Miss [Elizabeth] Church, over some beautiful engravings, representing

1. The federal court, citing the Fugitive Slave Act of 1850, decided that Anthony Burns was the property of Charles F. Suttle and should be immediately returned to him. So intense was the opposition to the decision that the Marines had to provide security for the transfer.

2. William Cowper (1731–1800), English poet. The quotation is from *The Task: A Poem in Six Books*, book 2, "The Time-Piece," lines 5–15. The quotation at the end of the May 26 entry (below) is from "Night" by English poet James Montgomery (1771–1854).

those parts of France, Italy and Switzerland in which the persecuted Waldenses[3] lived. . . . Miss Shepard showed us some of her beautiful books, and read one or two exquisite pieces of poetry. I enjoyed myself very much.—Returned home, read the Anti-Slavery papers, and then went down to the depot to meet father; he had arrived in Boston early in the morning, regretted very much that he had not reached there in the evening before to attend the great meeting at Faneuil Hall. He says that the excitement in Boston is very great; the trial of the poor man takes place on Monday. We scarcely dare to think of what may be the result; there seems to be nothing too bad for those Northern tools of slavery to do.

Tuesday, May 30

Rose very early and was busy until nine o'clock; then, at Mrs. Putnam's urgent request, went to keep store for her while she went to Boston to attend the Anti-Slavery Convention. I was very anxious to go, and will certainly do so to-morrow; the arrest of the alleged fugitive will give additional interest to the meetings, I should think. His trial is still going on and I can scarcely think of anything else; read again to-day as most suitable to my feelings and to the times, "The Runaway Slave at Pilgrim's Point," by Elizabeth B. Browning;[4] how powerfully it is written! how earnestly and touchingly does the writer portray the bitter anguish of the poor fugitive as she thinks over all the wrongs and sufferings that she has endured, and of the sin to which tyrants have driven her but which they alone must answer for! It seems as if no one could read this poem without having his sympathies roused to the utmost on behalf of the oppressed. After a long conversation with my friends on their return, on this all-absorbing subject, we separated for the night, and I went to bed, weary and sad.

Wednesday, May 31

The last day of spring. She has not been very pleasant this year, until within a few weeks, during which her smiles have been so bountiful and bright, her character so very lovable, that we part from her with regret. Sarah [Cassey Smith] and I went to Boston in the morning. Everything was much quieter—outwardly than we expected, but still much real indignation and excitement prevail. We walked past the Court-House, which is now lawlessly converted into a prison, and filled with soldiers, some of whom were looking from the windows, with an air of insolent authority, which made my blood boil, while I felt the strongest contempt for their cowardice and servility. We went to the meeting, but the best speakers were absent, engaged in the most arduous and untiring efforts in behalf of the poor fugitive; but though we missed the glowing eloquence of [Wendell] Phillips, [William Lloyd] Garrison, and [Theodore] Parker,[5] still there were excellent speeches made, and our hearts responded to the exalted sentiments of Truth and Liberty which were uttered. The exciting intelligence which occasionally came in relation to the trial, added fresh zeal to the speakers, of whom Stephen Foster and his wife [Abigail Kelley][6] were the principal. The latter

3. Protestant religious sect of medieval origin.
4. British poet (1806–1861).
5. All prominent abolitionists.
6. Equal rights activist (1810–1887) whose election to the executive board of the American Anti-Slavery Society led to a split in the organization and the formation of the American and Foreign Anti-Slavery Society. Stephen Seymonds Foster (1809–1881), New England equal rights activist.

addressed, in the most eloquent language, the women present, entreating them to urge their husbands and brothers to action, and also to give their aid on all occasions in our just and holy cause.—I did not see father the whole day; he, of course, was deeply interested in the trial.—Dined at Mr. Garrison's; his wife is one of the loveliest persons I have ever seen, worthy of such a husband. At the table, I watched earnestly the expression of that noble face, as he spoke beautifully in support of the non-resistant principles to which he has kept firm; his is indeed the very highest Christian spirit, to which I cannot hope to reach, however, for I believe in resistance to tyrants, and would fight for liberty until death. We came home in the evening, and felt sick at heart as we passed through the streets of Boston on our way to the depot, seeing the military as they rode along, ready at any time to prove themselves the minions of the South.

Thursday, June 1

I am keeping store for Mrs. Putnam again. Miss [Sarah Parker] Remond is still in Boston, and Mrs. [Nancy] R.[emond] has gone also; father and Aunt Harriet [Purvis] are there. The trial is over at last; the commissioner's decision will be given to-morrow. We are all in the greatest suspense; what will that decision be? Alas! that any one should have the power to decide the right of a fellow being to himself! It is thought by many that he will be acquitted of the *great crime* of leaving a life of bondage, as the legal evidence is not thought sufficient to convict him. But it is only too probable that they will sacrifice him to propitiate the South, since so many at the North dared oppose the passage of the infamous Nebraska Bill.[7] Miss [Helen] Putnam was married this evening. Mr. [Octavius B.] Frothingham performed the ceremony, and in his prayer alluded touchingly to the events of this week; he afterwards in conversation with the bridegroom, (Mr. [Jacob] Gilliard), spoke in the most feeling manner about this case,—his sympathies are on the right side. The wedding was a pleasant one; the bride looked very lovely; and we enjoyed ourselves as much as is possible in these exciting times. It is impossible to be happy now.

Friday, June 2

Our worst fears are realized; the decision was against poor [Anthony] Burns, and he has been sent back to a bondage worse, a thousand times worse than death. Even an attempt at rescue was utterly impossible; the prisoner was completely surrounded by soldiers with bayonets fixed, a canon loaded, ready to be fired at the slightest sign. To-day Massachusetts has again been disgraced; again has she showed her submissions to the Slave Power; and Oh! with what deep sorrow do we think of what will doubtless be the fate of that poor man, when he is again consigned to the horrors of slavery. With what scorn must that government be regarded which cowardly assembles thousands of soldiers to satisfy the demands of slaveholders; to deprive of his freedom a man, created in God's own image, whose sole offense is the color of his skin! And if resistance is offered to this outrage, these soldiers are to shoot down American citizens without mercy; and this by express

7. That is, the Kansas-Nebraska Act of 1854, which provided for the organization of Kansas and Nebraska into territories but led to great controversy over the status of slavery within them.

orders of a government which proudly boasts of being the freest in the world; this on the very soil where the Revolution of 1776 began; in sight of the battlefield, where thousands of brave men fought and died in opposing British tyranny, which was nothing compared with the American oppression of today. In looking over my diary, I perceive that I did not mention that there was on the Friday night after the man's arrest, an attempt made to rescue him, but although it failed, on account of there not being men enough engaged in it, all honor should be given to those who bravely made the attempt. I can write no more. A cloud seems hanging over me, over all our persecuted race, which nothing can dispel.

Sunday, June 4

A beautiful day. The sky is cloudless, the sun shines warm and bright, and a delicious breeze fans my cheeks as I sit by the window writing. How strange it is that in a world so beautiful, there can be so much wickedness, on this delightful day, while many are enjoying themselves in their happy homes, not poor Burns only, but millions beside are suffering in chains; and how many Christian ministers to-day will mention him, or those who suffer with him? How many will speak from the pulpit against the cruel outrage on humanity which has just been committed, or against the many, even worse ones, which are committed in this country every day? Too well do we know that there are but very few, and these few alone deserve to be called the ministers of Christ, whose doctrine was 'Break every yoke, and let the oppressed go free.'[8]—During the past week, we have had a vacation, which I had expected to enjoy very much, but it was, of course, impossible for me to do so. To-morrow school commences, and although the pleasure I shall feel in again seeing my beloved teacher, and in resuming my studies will be much saddened by recent events, yet they shall be a fresh incentive to more earnest study, to aid me in fitting myself for laboring in a holy cause, for enabling me to do much towards changing the condition of my oppressed and suffering people. Would that those with whom I shall recite to-morrow could sympathize with me in this; would that they could look upon all God's creatures without respect to color, feeling that it is character alone which makes the true man or woman! I earnestly hope that the time will come when they will feel thus.

* * *

From *Journal Three*

Tuesday Night [October 28, 1862]

'Twas a strange sight as our boat approached the landing at Hilton Head.[1] On the wharf was a motley assemblage,—soldiers, officers, and "contrabands"[2] of every hue and size. They were mostly black, however, and certainly the most dismal specimens I ever saw. H.[ilton] H.[ead] looks like a very desolate place; just a long low, sandy point running out into the sea with no visible dwellings upon it but the soldiers' white roofed tents.

8. Isaiah 58:6.
1. South Carolina port.
2. When enslaved persons were abandoned or escaped during the war, the U.S. government declared them "contraband of war" and placed them under its supervision.

Thence, after an hour's delay, during which we signed a paper, which was virtually taking the oath of allegiance, we left the "United States," most rocking of rockety propellers,—and took a steamboat for Beaufort.[3] On board the boat was General [Rufus] Saxton to whom we were introduced. I like his face exceedingly. And his manners were very courteous and affable. He looks like a thoroughly *good* man.—From H.[ilton] H.[ead] to B.[eaufort] the same low line of sandy shore bordered by trees[,] almost the only object of interest to me were the remains of an old Huguenot Fort,[4] built many, many years ago.

Arrived at B.[eaufort;] we found that we had yet not reached our home. Went to Mr. [Mansfield] French's, and saw there Reuben T.[omlinson] whom I was very glad to meet, and Mrs. [Francis] Gage, who seemed to be in rather a dismal state of mind. B.[eaufort] looks like a pleasant place. The houses are large and quite handsome, built in the usual Southern style with verandahs around them, and beautiful trees. One magnolia tree in Mr. F.[rench]'s yard is splendid,—quite as large as some of our large shade trees, and with the most beautiful foliage, a dark rich glossy green.

Went into the Commissary's Office to wait for the boat which was to take us to St. Helena's Island which is about six miles from B[eaufort]. Tis here that Miss [Laura] Towne has her school, in which I am to teach and that Mr. Hunn will have his store. While waiting in the office we saw several military gentleman [*sic*], *not* very creditable specimens, I sh'ld say. The little Commissary himself, Capt. T. is a perfect little popinjay, and he and a Colonel somebody who didn't look any too sensible, talked in a very smart manner, evidently for our especial benefit. The word "nigger" was plentifully used, whereupon I set them down at once as *not* gentleman [*sic*]. Then they talked a great deal about rebel attacks and yellow fever, and other alarming things, with significant nods and looks at each other. We saw through them at once, and were not at all alarmed by any of their representations. But if they are a fair example of army officers, I sh'ld pray to see as little of them as possible.

To my great joy found that we were to be rowed by a crew of negro boatmen. Young Mr. F.[rench—]whom I like—accompanied us, while Mr. H.[unn] went with a flat to get our baggage. The row was delightful. It was just at sunset—a grand Southern sunset; and the gorgeous clouds of crimson and gold were reflected in the waters below, which were smooth and calm as a mirror. Then, as we glided along, the rich sonorous tones of the boatmen broke upon the evening stillness. Their singing impressed me much. It was so sweet and strange and solemn. "Roll, Jordan, Roll" was grand, and another

> "Jesus make de blind to see
> Jesus make de deaf to hear
> Jesus make de cripple walk
> Walk in, dear Jesus,"

and the refrain

> "No man can hender me."

It was very, very impressive. I want to hear these men sing [John Greenleaf] Whittier's[5] "Song of the Negro Boatmen." I am going to see if it can't be brought about in some way.

3. In South Carolina.
4. A fort built by early French Protestant settlers.
5. American poet and abolitionist (1807–1892).

It was nearly dark when we reached St. Helena's, where we found Miss T.[owne]'s carriage awaiting us, and then we three and our driver, had a long drive along the lonely roads in the dark night. How easy it sh'ld have been for a band of guerillas—had any chanced that way—to seize and hang us. But we found nothing of the kind. We were in a jubilant state of mind and sang "John Brown"[6] with a will as we drove through the pines and palmettos. Arrived at the Superintendent's house[;] we were kindly greeted by him and the ladies and shown into a lofty *ceilinged* parlor where a cheerful wood fire glowed in the grate, and we soon began to feel quite at home in the very heart of Rebeldom; only that I do not at all realize yet that we are in S.[outh] C[arolina]. It is all a strange wild dream, from which I am constantly expecting to awake. But I can write no more now. I am tired, and still feel the motion of the ship in my poor head. Good night, dear A.!

Wednesday, October 29

A lovely day, but rather cool, I sh'ld think, for the "sunny South." The ship still reals [*sic*] in my head, and everything is most unreal, yet I went to drive . . . We drove to Oaklands, our future home. It is very pleasantly situated, but the house is in rather a dilapidated condition, as are most of the houses here, and the and the [*sic*] yard and garden have a neglected look, when it is cleaned up, and the house made habitable I think it will be quite a pleasant place. There are some lovely roses growing there and quantities of ivy creeping along the ground, even under the house, in wild luxuriance—The negroes on the place are very kind and polite. I think I shall get on amicably with them[.]

After walking about and talking with them, and plucking some roses and ivy to send home, we left Oaklands and drove to the school. It is kept by Miss [Ellen] Murray and Miss Towne in the little Baptist Church, which is beautifully situated in a grove of live oaks. Never saw anything more beautiful than these trees. It is strange that we do not hear of them at the North. They are the first objects that attract one's attention here. They are large, noble trees with small glossy green leaves. Their beauty consists in the long bearded moss with which every branch is heavily draped. This moss is singularly beautiful, and gives a solemn almost funeral aspect to the trees.

We went into the school, and heard the children read and spell. The teachers tell us that they have made great improvement in a very short time, and I noticed with pleasure how bright, how eager to learn many of them seem. The singing delighted me most. They sang beautifully in their rich, sweet clear tones, and with that peculiar swaying motion which I had noticed before in the older people, and which seems to make their singing all the more effective. Besides several other tunes they sang "Marching Along" with much spirit, and then one of their own hymns "Down in the Lonesome Valley," which is sweetly solemn and most beautiful. Dear children! born in slavery, but free at last? May God preserve to you all the blessings of freedom, and may you be in every possible way fitted to enjoy them. My heart goes out to you. I shall be glad to do all that I can to help you.—

As we drove homeward I noticed that the trees are just beginning to turn; some beautiful scarlet berries were growing along the roadside, and everywhere the beautiful live oak with its moss drapery. The palmettos disappoint

6. "John Brown's Body," a marching song for Union soldiers in the Civil War.

me much. Most of them have a very jagged appearance, and are yet stiff and ungraceful. The country is very level—as flat as that in eastern Penn[sylvania]. There are plenty of woods, but I think they have not the grandeur of our Northern woods. The cotton fields disappoint me too. They have a very straggling look, and the pods are small, not at all the great snowballs that I had imagined. Altogether the country w'ld be rather desolate looking were it not for my beautiful and evergreen live oaks.

Friday, October 31

Miss T.[owne] went to B.[eaufort] to-day, and I taught for her. I enjoyed it much. The children are well-behaved and eager to learn. It will be a happiness to teach here. I like Miss [Ellen] Murray so much. She is of English parentage, born in the Provinces. She is one of the most whole-souled warm-hearted women I ever met. I felt drawn to her from the first (before I knew she was English) and of course I like her none the less for that. Miss Towne also is a delightful person. "A charming lady" Gen. Saxton calls her and my heart echoes the words. She is housekeeper, physician, everything, here. The most indispensable person on the place, and the people are devoted to her. And indeed she is quite a remarkable young lady. She is one of the earliest comers, and has done much good in teaching and superintending the negroes. She is quite young; not more than twenty-two or three I sh'ld think, and is superintendent of two plantations. I like her energy and decision of character. Her appearance too is very interesting. Mr. [Richard] S.[oule] the superintendent, is a very kind, agreeable person. I like him.

Sunday, November 2

Drove to church to-day—to the same little Baptist Church that the school is held in. The people came in slowly. They have no way of telling the time. About eleven they had all assembled; the church was full. Old and young were there assembled in their Sunday dresses. Clean gowns on, clean head handkerchiefs, bright colored, of course, I noticed that some had even reached the dignity of straw hats, with bright feathers. The services were very interesting. The minister, Mr. P.[hillips?] is an earnest N.[ew] E.[ngland] man. The singing was very beautiful, sat there in a kind of trance and listened to it, and while I listened looked through the open windows into the beautiful grove of oaks with their moss drapery. "Ah w'ld that my tongue c'ld utter the thoughts that arise in me."[7] But it cannot. The sermon was quite good. But I enjoyed nothing so much as the singing—the wonderful, beautiful singing. There can be no doubt that these people have a great deal of musical talent. It was a beautiful sight,—their enthusiasm. After the service two couples were married. Then the meeting was out. The various groups under the trees forming a very pretty picture. We drove to the Episcopal Church afterward where the aristocracy of Rebeldom was to worship. The building is much smaller than the others, but there is a fine organ there on which Miss W.[ay?] played while some of the young superintendents sang very finely, and then we came home. It is all like a dream still, and will be for a long time, I suppose; a strange wild dream. When we get settled in our own house and I have fairly entered into teaching, perhaps I shall begin to

7. Quoting Tennyson's "Break, Break, Break" (1842).

realize it all. What we are to do for furniture I know not. Our sole possessions now consist of two bureaus and a bedstead. Mr. H.[unn] had not time to get the mattresses in N.[ew] York. So I suppose we must use blanket substitutes till we can do better. I am determined not to be discouraged at anything. I have never felt more hopeful, more cheerful than I do now.

Oaklands. Tuesday, November 4

Came to our new home to-day. Felt sorry to leave the friends who have been so kind to us, but as they are only three miles distant[,] hope to see them occasionally. But nobody here has much time for visiting. Our home looks rather desolate; the only furniture consisting of two bureaus, three small pine tables and two chairs, one of which has a broken back. L.[izzie] and I have manufactured a tolerable drugget[8] out of some woollen stuff, red and black plaid which will give our "parlor" a somewhat more comfortable look. I have already hung up my lovely Evangeline, and two or three other prints and gathered some beautiful roses. This has been a busy day. A few more such and we hope that our home will begin to look homelike. I am tired, dear A. Good night, and God be with you.

Wednesday, November 5

Had my first regular teaching experience, and to you and you only friend beloved, will acknowledge that it was *not* a very pleasant one. Part of my scholars are very tiny,—babies, I call them—and it is hard to keep them quiet and interested while I am hearing the larger ones. They are too young even for the alphabet, it seems to me. I think I must write home and ask somebody to send me picture-books and toys to amuse them with. I fancied Miss T.[owne] looked annoyed when, at one time the little ones were usually restless. Perhaps it was only my fancy. Dear Miss M.[urray] was kind and considerate as usual. She is very lovable. Well I *must* not be discouraged. Perhaps things will go on better to-morrow. I am sure I enjoyed the walk to school. Through those lovely woods, just brightening to scarlet now. Met the ladies about halfway, and they gave me a drive to the church. Lizzie H.[unn] tells me that the store has been crowded all day. Her father hasn't had time to arrange his goods. I foresee that his store, to which people from all the neighboring plantations come,—will be a source of considerable interest and amusement. We've established our household on—as we hope—a firm basis. We have *Rose* for our little maid-of-all-work, *Amoretta* for cook, washer, and ironer, and *Cupid*, yes, Cupid himself, for clerk, oysterman and future coachman. I must also inform you dear A., that we have made ourselves a bed, whereon we hope to rest to-night, for rest *I* certainly did not last night, despite innumerable blankets designed to conceal and render inactive the bones of the bed. But said bones did so protrude that sleep was almost an impossibility to our poor little body. Everything is still very, very strange. I am not at all homesick, but it does seem *so* long since I saw some who are very dear, and I believe *I* am quite sick for want of a letter. But patience! patience! *That* is a luxury which cannot possibly be enjoyed before the last of next week.

8. A floor covering.

Thursday, November 6

Rained all day so that I c'ldn't go to school. Attended store part of the day. 'Twas crowded nearly all the time. It was quite amusing to see how eager the people are to buy. The bright handkerchiefs—imitation Madras[9]—are an especial attraction. I think they were very quiet and orderly considering how crowded the place was. This afternoon made another bed; and this eve. finished a very long letter to father, the first part of which was begun last month. I wish I c'ld see them all. It w'ld be such a happiness. My dear, dear Quincy [Forten]—I wonder if he w'ld know me now, God bless him! God be with him! Cut out a dress to-day for an old woman—Venus,—who thanked and blessed me enough poor old soul. It was a pleasure to hear her say what a happy year this has been for her[:] "Nobody to whip me nor dribe me, and plenty to eat. Nebber had such a happy year in my life before." Promised to make a little dress for her great-grandchild—only a few weeks old. It shall be a bright pink calico, such as will delight the little free baby's eyes, when it shall be old enough to appreciate it.

Friday, November 7

Had a lovely walk to school. The trees,—a few of them are thinning beautifully now, but they have not the general brilliant hues of the northern woods. The mocking birds were singing sweetly this morn. I think my "babies" were rather more manageable to-day, but they were certainly troublesome enough. This afternoon L.[izzie] and I went round to the "quarters." Some of the people are really quite interesting, and all were pleasant and seemed glad to see us. One poor woman has a very sick child. The poor little thing is only a few months old, and is suffering dreadfully with whooping cough. It is pitiful to hear it moan. If our good doctor Miss T.[owne] were only here. But she does not come to-day.

Monday, November 10

We taught—or rather commenced teaching the children "John Brown"[1] which they entered into eagerly. I felt to the full the significance of *that* song being sung here in S.[outh] C.[arolina] by little negro children, by those whom he—the glorious old man—died to save. Miss [Laura] T.[owne] told them about him. A poor mulatto man is in one of our people's houses, a man from the North, who assisted Mr. [Samuel D.] Phillips (a nephew of Wendell P.[hillips]) when he was here, in teaching school; he seems to be quite an intelligent man. He is suffering from fever. I shall be glad to take as good care of him as I can. It is so sad to be ill, helpless and poor, and so far away from home. This eve. though I felt wretchedly, had a long exercise in irregular French verbs. The work of reviewing did me good. Forgot bodily ills—even so great an ill as a bad cold in the head for a while.

Thursday, November 13

Was there ever a lovelier road than that through part of my way to school lies? Oh, I wish you were here to go with me, *cher ami.*[2] It is lined with woods on

9. Cotton fabric, often with a design or pattern.
1. Brown (1800–1859) was a prominent abolitionist who led a revolt of enslaved persons at Harpers Ferry, Virginia, and was tried and hanged for it.
2. Dear friend (French).

both sides. On the one tall stately pines, on the other the noble live oaks with their graceful moss drapery. And the road is captured with those brown odorous pine leaves that I love so well. It is perfectly lovely. I forgot that I was almost ill to-day, while sauntering along, listening to the birds and breathing the soft delicious air. Of the last part of the walk, through sun and sand, the less said the better. Talked to the children a little while to-day about the noble Toussaint.[3] They listened very attentively. It is well that they sh'ld know what one of their own color c'ld do for his race. I long to inspire them with courage and ambition (of a noble sort), and high purposes. It is noticeable how very few mulattoes[4] there are here. Indeed in our school, with one or two exceptions, the children are all black. A little mulatto child strayed into the school house yesterday—a pretty little thing with large beautiful black eyes and lovely long lashes. But so dirty! I longed to seize and thoroughly cleanse her. The mother is a good-looking woman, but quite black. "Thereby," I doubt not, "hangs a tale."[5] This eve. Harry, one of the men on the place, came in for a lesson. He is most eager to learn, and is really a scholar to be proud of. He learns rapidly. I gave him his first lesson in writing to-night, and his progress was wonderful. He held his pen almost perfectly right the first time. He will very soon learn to write, I think. I must inquire who w'ld like to take lessons at night. Whenever I am well enough it will be a real pleasure to teach them. Finished translating into French Adelaide Proctor's[6] poem "A Woman's Question," which I like so much. It was an experiment, and I assure you, *mon ami*, tis a queer translation. But it was good practice in French. Shall finish this eve. by copying some of my Journal for my dear Mary [Shepard].

Monday, November 17

Had a dreadfully wearying day in school, of which the less said the better. Afterward drove the ladies to "The Corner," a collection of negro houses, whither Miss T.[owne] went on a doctoring expedition. The people there are very pleasant. Saw a little baby, just borne [*sic*] today—and another—old Venus' great grandchild for whom I made the little pink frock. These people are very grateful. The least kindness that you do them they insist on repaying in some way. We have had a quantity of eggs and potatoes brought us despite our remonstrances. Today one of the women gave me some Tanias. Tania is a queer looking root. After it is boiled it looks a little like potato, but is much larger. I don't like the taste.

Tuesday, November 18

After school went to the Corner again. Stopped at old Susy's house to see some sick children. Old Susy is a character. Miss T.[owne] asked her if she wanted her old master to come back again. Most emphatically she answered. "No *indeed*, missus, no indeed dey treat we too bad. Dey tuk ebery one of my chilen away from me. When we sick and c'ldnt work dey tuk away all our food from us; gib us nutten to eat. Dey's orful hard Missis." When Miss T.[owne] told her that some of the people wanted their old masters to come back, a look of supreme contempt came to old Susy's withered face. "That's

3. Toussaint L'Ouverture (1750?–1803), slave leader who not only freed his people but helped establish Haiti as an independent nation.
4. People of mixed white and Black ancestry.
5. Shakespeare, *As You Like It* 2.7.28.
6. British writer and activist (1825–1864). "A Woman's Question" was in her *Legends and Lyrics* (1858).

cause dey's got no sense den, missus," she said indignantly. Susy has any quantity of children and grandchildren, and she thanks God that she can now have some of them with her in her old age. To-night gave Cupid a lesson in the alphabet. He is not a brilliant scholar, but he tries hard to learn, and so I am sure will succeed in time. A man from another plantation came in for a lesson. L.[izzie Hunn] attended to him while I had Cupid. He knows his letters, and seems very bright.

Thursday, November 20

Had letters from Aunt M.[argaretta], Annie [Woods Webb], and Sarah P.[itman?] Was delighted to hear from them, but so disappointed at not hearing from my dear brother Henry [Cassey]. Aunt M.[argaretta] writes me that he did not receive any letter from me. Strange! When I wrote to him the same time that I wrote to her. Am very sorry. Wrote to-night to Aunt M.[argaretta], Lizzie C.[hurch?], Charlotte, E.[llen Shearman?], Sarah P.[itman?] and to Whittier asking him to write a little Christmas hymn for our children to sing. I hope he will do it. Asked Aunt M.[argaretta] to see Mrs. Rachel Moore about sending some thick clothing for the people, and some blocks, etc. for our "babies." I hope they can get here by Christmas. It w'ld be so nice to distribute them for Christmas presents.

January 31, 1863

In B.[eaufort] we spent nearly all our time at Harriet Tubman's otherwise [*sic*] "Moses."[7] She is a wonderful woman—a real heroine. Has helped off a large number of slaves, after taking her own freedom. She told us that she used to hide them in the woods during the day and go around to get provisions for them. Once she had with her a man named Joe, for whom a reward of $1,500 was offered. Frequently, in different places she found handbills exactly describing him, but at last they reached in safety the Suspension Bridge over the Falls[8] and found themselves in Canada. Until then, she said, Joe had been very silent. In vain had she called his attention to the glory of the Falls. He sat perfectly still—moody, it seemed, and w[ou]ld not even glance at them. But when she said, "Now we are in Can.[ada]" he sprang to his feet—with a great shout and sang and clapped his hands in a perfect delirium of joy. So when they got out, and he first touched *free* soil, he shouted and hurrahed "as if he were crazy"—she said. How exciting it was to hear her tell the story. And to hear her sing the very scraps of jubilant hymns that he sang. She said the ladies crowded around them, and some laughed and some cried. My own eyes were full as I listened to her—the heroic woman! A reward of $10,000 was offered for her by Southerners, and her friends deemed it best that she sh[ou]ld, for a time find refuge in Can[ada]. And she did so, but only for a short time. She came back and was soon at the good brave work again. She is living in B.[eaufort] now; keeping an eating house. But she wants to go North, and will probably do so ere long. I am glad I saw her—*very* glad.

1988

7. Tubman (1822–1913) was a formerly enslaved Underground Railroad conductor, Union army spy, feminist, and humanitarian. She was known as "Moses" for her many journeys to her native Maryland to lead more than one hundred enslaved persons northward to freedom.
8. That is, the suspension bridge across the Niagara River between New York and Ontario, Canada.

BOOKER T. WASHINGTON
1856–1915

After witnessing the systematic legalization of racial segregation throughout the South in the 1890s, many African Americans concluded that self-reliance and racial solidarity were their last best hopes for a decent life in the United States. These people embraced Booker T. Washington as their champion and adopted his autobiography, *Up From Slavery* (1901), as their guide to a better future. In 1895, the year that Frederick Douglass died, Washington gave a speech at the Cotton States Exposition in Atlanta, Georgia, that helped catapult him to fame, especially among European Americans, as an African American spokesperson and role model. In that speech the once-enslaved school principal from Tuskegee, Alabama, declared the best way to ensure progress and peace in the South was for European Americans to respect African Americans' desire for improved economic opportunities and for African Americans to accept European Americans' desire for social separation of the races. Washington advised his fellow African Americans that accepting, at least temporarily, the political status quo while proving themselves valuable, productive members of society who deserved fair treatment before the law would eventually gain them civil rights. Washington's supporters welcomed *Up From Slavery* as a demonstration of the good that an African American could do for self and society, if given a chance to obtain an education and engage in useful, productive work.

Washington was born in Franklin County, Virginia, in what he described in *Up From Slavery* as "the most miserable, desolate, and discouraging surroundings." He never knew his white father and was raised by his enslaved mother, Jane. After the Civil War, Washington moved with his mother and three siblings to Malden, West Virginia, where he went to work at a salt furnace and later in the coal mines. Determined to get an education, he attended night school and fit classes into his daily work schedule until the fall of 1872, when he embarked on an arduous, five-hundred-mile journey to seek admission to the Hampton Institute, an industrial school for Blacks and American Indians in Virginia. After graduating with honors in 1875, Washington served on the faculty of Hampton until 1881, when the Alabama legislature authorized him to found a school for Black teachers in the heart of Alabama's "Black belt."

From July 4, 1881, the official opening date of the Tuskegee Normal and Industrial Institute, until his death in 1915, Washington concentrated on making Tuskegee a major African American institution and on promoting and defending his philosophy of African American progress through industrial education; accommodation of southern white supremacy; and a focus on racial pride, solidarity, and self-help. This idea was not new, but the Tuskegeean was a master publicist who knew how to use his connections among the white business, philanthropic, and political elite to advance his enterprises on a national front. A commanding speaker and tireless traveler, Washington made a name for himself as an author, hiring ghostwriters to help him churn out a large quantity of magazine articles and essays, a two-volume history of African America, a biography of Frederick Douglass, and his greatest literary assets, two versions of his own life story.

Washington's first "autobiography" was *The Story of My Life and Work* (1900), a ghostwritten account published by an African American firm and marketed primarily to a Black audience. Seeking a wider readership, Washington authorized a serialized version of his life that appeared as *Up From Slavery* in *Outlook*, a popular national family magazine. Washington exercised careful editorial control over the writing of this narrative and its subsequent publication as a book because, as he confided to the publisher of his first autobiography, this version was designed to appeal to "a class of people who have money and to whom I must look for money for endowment and other purposes."

What virtually guaranteed *Up From Slavery*'s popularity among whites was Washington's deftness in masking his personal and social agenda behind an apparently simple, almost folksy, brand of unassuming storytelling. His style in the most popular portions of *Up From Slavery* is almost drained of personal emotion or self-reference. The overall impression that the book left on its white readers—that of an almost saintly self-forgetfulness balanced by a businesslike worldliness in the art of getting things done—went a long way toward creating the myth of the Tuskegeean as the Moses of his people.

Up From Slavery won praise from prestigious literary magazines for its inspirational tone, its lucidity of style, and its solution to racial problems in the South. More than one reviewer likened *Up From Slavery* to the archetypal American success story, Benjamin Franklin's *Autobiography*. Translations of *Up From Slavery* into French, Spanish, German, Russian, and a half-dozen other European languages testified to the interest that Washington's story aroused worldwide. Many African American readers responded favorably to *Up From Slavery; but others*, whom Washington scornfully labeled "the intellectuals," doubted the effectiveness of the author's conciliatory approach to race relations in the South.

Up From Slavery quickly eclipsed the narratives by formerly enslaved individuals such as Frederick Douglass and Harriet Jacobs. Like Elizabeth Keckly and other postbellum narrators, Washington termed slavery a "school" from which he and others had graduated with honors, so to speak, with the will and the skill to keep progressing in the American way. Such postbellum revisionism epitomizes the double-edged interpretive rhetorical possibilities of postbellum narratives by formerly enslaved people. On the one hand, in portraying enslavement and all the injustices attendant on it as ultimately helpful in tempering rugged individualism, Washington and others came close to implying that slavery and racism had not really been so bad for African Americans after all. On the other hand, the same revisionist treatment of slavery and race could be read as a rejoinder to long-standing assumptions among whites that under slavery Black people suffered a disabling demoralization that left them, in freedom, unfit for any role except as wards of the state.

The problem of how to interpret such perspectives on African American history and post–Civil War struggles for dignity and opportunity continues to be debated. To some, Washington's memoirs seem to mitigate centuries of accumulated white responsibility for the evils of slavery. Instead of demanding reform of white American institutions, they call for African Americans to pull themselves up by their bootstraps even if they must first make their own boots. To some, *Up From Slavery* is a strategy for creating better lives when other Americans refuse to acknowledge responsibility for slavery and systemic racism or to tolerate any form of Black leadership that does not seem to subscribe to the ideology of the dominant order. No small part of the genius of *Up From Slavery* lies in the fact that neither those who reject postbellum authors like Washington as cynical sellouts nor those who praise them as shrewd power brokers have ever fully persuaded readers as to the true identities of writers such as Washington, who was known contradictorily as both "the Sage of Tuskegee" and "the Wizard of the Tuskegee Machine."

From Up From Slavery

Chapter I. A Slave among Slaves

I was born a slave on a plantation in Franklin County, Virginia. I am not quite sure of the exact place or exact date of my birth, but at any rate I suspect I must have been born somewhere and at some time. As nearly as I have been able to learn, I was born near a cross-roads post-office called Hale's Ford, and the year was 1858 or 1859.[1] I do not know the month or the day. The earliest impressions I can now recall are of the plantation and the slave quarters—the latter being the part of the plantation where the slaves had their cabins.

My life had its beginning in the midst of the most miserable, desolate, and discouraging surroundings. This was so, however, not because my owners were especially cruel, for they were not, as compared with many others. I was born in a typical log cabin, about fourteen by sixteen feet square. In this cabin I lived with my mother and a brother and sister till after the Civil War, when we were all declared free.

Of my ancestry I know almost nothing. In the slave quarters, and even later, I heard whispered conversations among the coloured people of the tortures which the slaves, including, no doubt, my ancestors on my mother's side, suffered in the middle passage of the slave ship while being conveyed from Africa to America. I have been unsuccessful in securing any information that would throw any accurate light upon the history of my family beyond my mother. She, I remember, had a half-brother and a half-sister. In the days of slavery not very much attention was given to family history and family records—that is, black family records. My mother, I suppose, attracted the attention of a purchaser who was afterward my owner and hers. Her addition to the slave family attracted about as much attention as the purchase of a new horse or cow. Of my father I know even less than of my mother. I do not even know his name. I have heard reports to the effect that he was a white man who lived on one of the near-by plantations. Whoever he was, I never heard of his taking the least interest in me or providing in any way for my rearing. But I do not find especial fault with him. He was simply another unfortunate victim of the institution which the Nation unhappily had engrafted upon it at that time.

The cabin was not only our living-place, but was also used as the kitchen for the plantation. My mother was the plantation cook. The cabin was without glass windows; it had only openings in the side which let in the light, and also the cold, chilly air of winter. There was a door to the cabin—that is, something that was called a door—but the uncertain hinges by which it was hung, and the large cracks in it, to say nothing of the fact that it was too small, made the room a very uncomfortable one. In addition to these openings there was, in the lower right-hand corner of the room, the "cat-hole,"—a contrivance which almost every mansion or cabin in Virginia possessed during the ante-bellum period.[2] The "cat-hole" was a square opening, about seven by eight inches, provided for the purpose of letting the cat pass in and out of the house at will during the night. In the case of our particular cabin I could never understand the necessity for this convenience, since there were at least a half-dozen other places in the cabin that would have

1. According to biographer Louis H. Harlan, Washington was born in 1856.

2. The era before the Civil War began in 1861.

accommodated the cats. There was no wooden floor in our cabin, the naked earth being used as a floor. In the centre of the earthen floor there was a large, deep opening covered with boards, which was used as a place in which to store sweet potatoes during the winter. An impression of this potato-hole is very distinctly engraved upon my memory, because I recall that during the process of putting the potatoes in or taking them out I would often come into possession of one or two, which I roasted and thoroughly enjoyed. There was no cooking-stove on our plantation, and all the cooking for the whites and slaves my mother had to do over an open fireplace, mostly in pots and "skillets." While the poorly built cabin caused us to suffer with cold in the winter, the heat from the open fireplace in summer was equally trying.

The early years of my life, which were spent in the little cabin, were not very different from those of thousands of other slaves. My mother, of course, had little time in which to give attention to the training of her children during the day. She snatched a few moments for our care in the early morning before her work began, and at night after the day's work was done. One of my earliest recollections is that of my mother cooking a chicken late at night, and awakening her children for the purpose of feeding them. How or where she got it I do not know. I presume, however, it was procured from our owner's farm. Some people may call this theft. If such a thing were to happen now, I should condemn it as theft myself. But taking place at the time it did, and for the reason that it did, no one could ever make me believe that my mother was guilty of thieving. She was simply a victim of the system of slavery. I cannot remember having slept in a bed until after our family was declared free by the Emancipation Proclamation.[3] Three children—John, my older brother, Amanda, my sister, and myself—had a pallet on the dirt floor, or, to be more correct, we slept in and on a bundle of filthy rags laid upon the dirt floor.

I was asked not long ago to tell something about the sports and pastimes that I engaged in during my youth. Until that question was asked it had never occurred to me that there was no period of my life that was devoted to play. From the time that I can remember anything, almost every day of my life has been occupied in some kind of labour; though I think I would now be a more useful man if I had had time for sports. During the period that I spent in slavery I was not large enough to be of much service, still I was occupied most of the time in cleaning the yards, carrying water to the men in the fields, or going to the mill, to which I used to take the corn, once a week, to be ground. The mill was about three miles from the plantation. This work I always dreaded. The heavy bag of corn would be thrown across the back of the horse, and the corn divided about evenly on each side; but in some way, almost without exception, on these trips, the corn would so shift as to become unbalanced and would fall off the horse, and often I would fall with it. As I was not strong enough to reload the corn upon the horse, I would have to wait, sometimes for many hours, till a chance passer-by came along who would help me out of my trouble. The hours while waiting for some one were usually spent in crying. The time consumed in this way made me late in reaching the mill, and by the time I got my corn ground and reached home it would be far into the night. The road was a lonely one,

3. President Lincoln's Emancipation Proclamation (1863) freed enslaved people in the Confederate States of America; however, the Confederacy considered itself a separate nation—thus, Lincoln's proclamation was null within its borders.

and often led through dense forests. I was always frightened. The woods were said to be full of soldiers who had deserted from the army, and I had been told that the first thing a deserter did to a Negro boy when he found him alone was to cut off his ears. Besides, when I was late in getting home I knew I would always get a severe scolding or a flogging.

I had no schooling whatever while I was a slave, though I remember on several occasions I went as far as the schoolhouse door with one of my young mistresses to carry her books. The picture of several dozen boys and girls in a schoolroom engaged in study made a deep impression upon me, and I had the feeling that to get into a schoolhouse and study in this way would be about the same as getting into paradise.

So far as I can now recall, the first knowledge that I got of the fact that we were slaves, and that freedom of the slaves was being discussed, was early one morning before day, when I was awakened by my mother kneeling over her children and fervently praying that Lincoln and his armies might be successful, and that one day she and her children might be free. In this connection I have never been able to understand how the slaves throughout the South, completely ignorant as were the masses so far as books or newspapers were concerned, were able to keep themselves so accurately and completely informed about the great National questions that were agitating the country. From the time that Garrison, Lovejoy,[4] and others began to agitate for freedom, the slaves throughout the South kept in close touch with the progress of the movement. Though I was a mere child during the preparation for the Civil War and during the war itself, I now recall the many late-at-night whispered discussions that I heard my mother and the other slaves on the plantation indulge in. These discussions showed that they understood the situation, and that they kept themselves informed of events by what was termed the "grape-vine" telegraph.

During the campaign when Lincoln was first a candidate for the Presidency, the slaves on our far-off plantation, miles from any railroad or large city or daily newspaper, knew what the issues involved were. When war was begun between the North and the South, every slave on our plantation felt and knew that, though other issues were discussed, the primal one was that of slavery. Even the most ignorant members of my race on the remote plantations felt in their hearts, with a certainty that admitted of no doubt, that the freedom of the slaves would be the one great result of the war, if the Northern armies conquered. Every success of the Federal armies and every defeat of the Confederate forces was watched with the keenest and most intense interest. Often the slaves got knowledge of the results of great battles before the white people received it. This news was usually gotten from the coloured man who was sent to the post-office for the mail. In our case the post-office was about three miles from the plantation, and the mail came once or twice a week. The man who was sent to the office would linger about the place long enough to get the drift of the conversation from the group of white people who naturally congregated there, after receiving their mail, to discuss the latest news. The mail-carrier on his way back to our master's house would as naturally retail [*sic*] the news that he had secured

4. Elijah P. Lovejoy (1802–1837), antislavery editor who was murdered while defending his press from a mob in Alton, Illinois. William Lloyd Garrison (1805–1879), uncompromising editor of the *Liberator* and leader of the American Anti-Slavery Society.

among the slaves, and in this way they often heard of important events before the white people at the "big house," as the master's house was called.

I cannot remember a single instance during my childhood or early boyhood when our entire family sat down to the table together, and God's blessing was asked, and the family ate a meal in a civilized manner. On the plantation in Virginia, and even later, meals were gotten by the children very much as dumb animals get theirs. It was a piece of bread here and a scrap of meat there. It was a cup of milk at one time and some potatoes at another. Sometimes a portion of our family would eat out of the skillet or pot, while some one else would eat from a tin plate held on the knees, and often using nothing but the hands with which to hold the food. When I had grown to sufficient size, I was required to go to the "big house" at mealtimes to fan the flies from the table by means of a large set of paper fans operated by a pulley. Naturally much of the conversation of the white people turned upon the subject of freedom and the war, and I absorbed a good deal of it. I remember that at one time I saw two of my young mistresses and some lady visitors eating ginger-cakes, in the yard. At that time those cakes seemed to me to be absolutely the most tempting and desirable things that I had ever seen; and I then and there resolved that, if I ever got free, the height of my ambition would be reached if I could get to the point where I could secure and eat ginger-cakes in the way that I saw those ladies doing.

Of course as the war was prolonged the white people, in many cases, often found it difficult to secure food for themselves. I think the slaves felt the deprivation less than the whites, because the usual diet for the slaves was corn bread and pork, and these could be raised on the plantation; but coffee, tea, sugar, and other articles which the whites had been accustomed to use could not be raised on the plantation, and the conditions brought about by the war frequently made it impossible to secure these things. The whites were often in great straits. Parched corn was used for coffee, and a kind of black molasses was used instead of sugar. Many times nothing was used to sweeten the so-called tea and coffee.

The first pair of shoes that I recall wearing were wooden ones. They had rough leather on the top, but the bottoms, which were about an inch thick, were of wood. When I walked they made a fearful noise, and besides this they were very inconvenient, since there was no yielding to the natural pressure of the foot. In wearing them one presented an exceedingly awkward appearance. The most trying ordeal that I was forced to endure as a slave boy, however, was the wearing of a flax[5] shirt. In the portion of Virginia where I lived it was common to use flax as part of the clothing for the slaves. That part of the flax from which our clothing was made was largely the refuse, which of course was the cheapest and roughest part. I can scarcely imagine any torture, except, perhaps, the pulling of a tooth, that is equal to that caused by putting on a new flax shirt for the first time. It is almost equal to the feeling that one would experience if he had a dozen or more chestnut burrs, or a hundred small pin-points, in contact with his flesh. Even to this day I can recall accurately the tortures that I underwent when putting on one of these garments. The fact that my flesh was soft and

5. A coarse fiber used for rope and clothes until replaced by softer textiles made of cotton.

tender added to the pain. But I had no choice. I had to wear the flax shirt or none; and had it been left to me to choose, I should have chosen to wear no covering. In connection with the flax shirt, my brother John, who is several years older than I am, performed one of the most generous acts that I ever heard of one slave relative doing for another. On several occasions when I was being forced to wear a new flax shirt, he generously agreed to put it on in my stead and wear it for several days, till it was "broken in." Until I had grown to be quite a youth this single garment was all that I wore.

One may get the idea, from what I have said, that there was bitter feeling toward the white people on the part of my race, because of the fact that most of the white population was away fighting in a war which would result in keeping the Negro in slavery if the South was successful. In the case of the slaves on our place this was not true, and it was not true of any large portion of the slave population in the South where the Negro was treated with anything like decency. During the Civil War one of my young masters was killed, and two were severely wounded. I recall the feeling of sorrow which existed among the slaves when they heard of the death of "Mars' Billy." It was no sham sorrow, but real. Some of the slaves had nursed "Mars' Billy"; others had played with him when he was a child. "Mars' Billy" had begged for mercy in the case of others when the overseer or master was thrashing them. The sorrow in the slave quarter was only second to that in the "big house." When the two young masters were brought home wounded, the sympathy of the slaves was shown in many ways. They were just as anxious to assist in the nursing as the family relatives of the wounded. Some of the slaves would even beg for the privilege of sitting up at night to nurse their wounded masters. This tenderness and sympathy on the part of those held in bondage was a result of their kindly and generous nature. In order to defend and protect the women and children who were left on the plantations when the white males went to war, the slaves would have laid down their lives. The slave who was selected to sleep in the "big house" during the absence of the males was considered to have the place of honour. Any one attempting to harm "young Mistress" or "old Mistress" during the night would have had to cross the dead body of the slave to do so. I do not know how many have noticed it, but I think that it will be found to be true that there are few instances, either in slavery or freedom, in which a member of my race has been known to betray a specific trust.

As a rule, not only did the members of my race entertain no feelings of bitterness against the whites before and during the war, but there are many instances of Negroes tenderly caring for their former masters and mistresses who for some reason have become poor and dependent since the war. I know of instances where the former masters of slaves have for years been supplied with money by their former slaves to keep them from suffering. I have known of still other cases in which the former slaves have assisted in the education of the descendants of their former owners. I know of a case on a large plantation in the South in which a young white man, the son of the former owner of the estate, has become so reduced in purse and self-control by reason of drink that he is a pitiable creature; and yet, notwithstanding the poverty of the coloured people themselves on this plantation, they have for years supplied this young white man with the necessities of life. One sends him a little coffee or sugar, another a little meat, and so on. Nothing that the coloured people possess is too good for the son of "old Mars' Tom," who will perhaps never be permitted to suffer while any remain on the place who knew directly or indirectly of "old Mars' Tom."

I have said that there are few instances of a member of my race betraying a specific trust. One of the best illustrations of this which I know of is in the case of an ex-slave from Virginia whom I met not long ago in a little town in the state of Ohio. I found that this man had made a contract with his master, two or three years previous to the Emancipation Proclamation, to the effect that the slave was to be permitted to buy himself, by paying so much per year for his body; and while he was paying for himself, he was to be permitted to labour where and for whom he pleased. Finding that he could secure better wages in Ohio, he went there. When freedom came, he was still in debt to his master some three hundred dollars. Notwithstanding that the Emancipation Proclamation freed him from any obligation to his master, this black man walked the greater portion of the distance back to where his old master lived in Virginia, and placed the last dollar, with interest, in his hands. In talking to me about this, the man told me that he knew that he did not have to pay the debt, but that he had given his word to his master, and his word he had never broken. He felt that he could not enjoy his freedom till he had fulfilled his promise.

From some things that I have said one may get the idea that some of the slaves did not want freedom. This is not true. I have never seen one who did not want to be free, or one who would return to slavery.

I pity from the bottom of my heart any nation or body of people that is so unfortunate as to get entangled in the net of slavery. I have long since ceased to cherish any spirit of bitterness against the Southern white people on account of the enslavement of my race. No one section of our country was wholly responsible for its introduction, and, besides, it was recognized and protected for years by the General Government. Having once got its tentacles fastened on to the economic and social life of the Republic, it was no easy matter for the country to relieve itself of the institution. Then, when we rid ourselves of prejudice, or racial feeling, and look facts in the face, we must acknowledge that, notwithstanding the cruelty and moral wrong of slavery, the ten million Negroes inhabiting this country, who themselves or whose ancestors went through the school of American slavery, are in a stronger and more hopeful condition, materially, intellectually, morally, and religiously, than is true of an equal number of black people in any other portion of the globe. This is so to such an extent that Negroes in this country, who themselves or whose forefathers went through the school of slavery, are constantly returning to Africa as missionaries to enlighten those who remained in the fatherland. This I say, not to justify slavery—on the other hand, I condemn it as an institution, as we all know that in America it was established for selfish and financial reasons, and not from a missionary motive—but to call attention to a fact, and to show how Providence so often uses men and institutions to accomplish a purpose. When persons ask me in these days how, in the midst of what sometimes seem hopelessly discouraging conditions, I can have such faith in the future of my race in this country, I remind them of the wilderness through which and out of which, a good Providence has already led us.

Ever since I have been old enough to think for myself, I have entertained the idea that, notwithstanding the cruel wrongs inflicted upon us, the black man got nearly as much out of slavery as the white man did. The hurtful influences of the institution were not by any means confined to the Negro. This was fully illustrated by the life upon our own plantation. The whole machinery of slavery was so constructed as to cause labour, as a rule, to be looked upon as a badge of degradation, of inferiority. Hence labour was something that both races on the slave plantation sought to escape. The slave system on our place, in a large measure, took the spirit of self-reliance and self-help out of the white people. My old master had many boys and girls, but not one, so far as I know, ever mastered a single trade or special line of productive industry. The girls were not taught to cook, sew, or to take care of the house. All of this was left to the slaves. The slaves, of course, had little personal interest in the life of the plantation, and their ignorance prevented them from learning how to do things in the most improved and thorough manner. As a result of the system, fences were out of repair, gates were hanging half off the hinges, doors creaked, window-panes were out, plastering had fallen but was not replaced, weeds grew in the yard. As a rule, there was food for whites and blacks, but inside the house, and on the dining-room table, there was wanting that delicacy and refinement of touch and finish which can make a home the most convenient, comfortable, and attractive place in the world. Withal there was a waste of food and other materials which was sad. When freedom came, the slaves were almost as well fitted to begin life anew as the master, except in the matter of book-learning and ownership of property. The slave owner and his sons had mastered no special industry. They unconsciously had imbibed the feeling that manual labour was not the proper thing for them. On the other hand, the slaves, in many cases, had mastered some handicraft, and none were ashamed, and few unwilling, to labour.

Finally the war closed, and the day of freedom came. It was a momentous and eventful day to all upon our plantation. We had been expecting it. Freedom was in the air, and had been for months. Deserting soldiers returning to their homes were to be seen every day. Others who had been discharged, or whose regiments had been paroled, were constantly passing near our place. The "grape-vine telegraph" was kept busy night and day. The news and mutterings of great events were swiftly carried from one plantation to another. In the fear of "Yankee" invasions, the silverware and other valuables were taken from the "big house," buried in the woods, and guarded by trusted slaves. Woe be to any one who would have attempted to disturb the buried treasure. The slaves would give the Yankee soldiers food, drink, clothing—anything but that which had been specifically intrusted to their care and honour. As the great day drew nearer, there was more singing in the slave quarters than usual. It was bolder, had more ring, and lasted later into the night. Most of the verses of the plantation songs had some reference to freedom. True, they had sung those same verses before, but they had been careful to explain that the "freedom" in these songs referred to the next world, and had no connection with life in this world. Now they gradually threw off the mask, and were not afraid to let it be known that the "freedom" in their songs meant freedom of the body in this world. The night before the eventful day, word was sent to the slave quarters to the effect that something unusual was going to take place at the "big house" the next morning. There was little, if any, sleep that night. All was excitement and expectancy. Early the next morning word was sent to all the slaves, old and young, to gather at the house. In company with my mother, brother, and sister, and a large number of other slaves, I went to the master's house. All of our master's family were either standing or seated on the veranda of the house, where they could see what was to take place and hear what was said. There was a feeling of deep interest, or perhaps sadness, on their faces, but not bitterness. As I now recall the impression they made upon me, they did not at the moment seem to be sad because of the loss of property, but rather because of parting with those whom they had reared and who were in many ways very close to them. The most distinct thing that I now recall in connection with the scene was that some man who seemed to be a stranger (a United States officer, I presume) made a little speech and then read a rather long paper—the Emancipation Proclamation, I think. After the reading we were told that we were all free, and could go when and where we pleased. My mother, who was standing by my side, leaned over and kissed her children, while tears of joy ran down her cheeks. She explained to us what it all meant, that this was the day for which she had been so long praying, but fearing that she would never live to see.

For some minutes there was great rejoicing, and thanksgiving, and wild scenes of ecstasy. But there was no feeling of bitterness. In fact, there was pity among the slaves for our former owners. The wild rejoicing on the part of the emancipated coloured people lasted but for a brief period, for I noticed that by the time they returned to their cabins there was a change in their feelings. The great responsibility of being free, of having charge of themselves, of having to think and plan for themselves and their children, seemed to take possession of them. It was very much like suddenly turning a youth of ten or twelve years out into the world to provide for himself. In a few hours the great questions with which the Anglo-Saxon race had been grappling for centuries had been thrown upon these people to be solved. These were the questions of a home, a living, the rearing of children, education, citizenship, and the establishment and support of churches. Was it any wonder that within a few hours the wild rejoicing ceased and a feeling of deep gloom seemed to pervade the slave quarters? To some it seemed that, now that they were in actual possession of it, freedom was a more serious thing than they had expected to find it. Some of the slaves were seventy or eighty years old; their best days were gone. They had no strength with which to earn a living in a strange place and among strange people, even if they had been sure where to find a new place of abode. To this class the problem seemed especially hard. Besides, deep down in their hearts there was a strange and peculiar attachment to "old Marster" and "old Missus," and to their children, which they found it hard to think of breaking off. With these they had spent in some cases nearly a half-century, and it was no light thing to think of parting. Gradually, one by one, stealthily at first, the older slaves began to wander from the slave quarters back to the "big house" to have a whispered conversation with their former owners as to the future.

Chapter II. Boyhood Days

After the coming of freedom there were two points upon which practically all the people on our place were agreed, and I find that this was generally true throughout the South: that they must change their names, and that they must leave the old plantation for at least a few days or weeks in order that they might really feel sure that they were free.

In some way a feeling got among the coloured people that it was far from proper for them to bear the surname of their former owners, and a great many of them took other surnames. This was one of the first signs of freedom. When they were slaves, a coloured person was simply called "John" or "Susan." There was seldom occasion for more than the use of the one name. If "John" or "Susan" belonged to a white man by the name of "Hatcher," sometimes he was called "John Hatcher," or as often "Hatcher's John." But there was a feeling that "John Hatcher" or "Hatcher's John" was not the proper title by which to denote a freeman; and so in many cases "John Hatcher" was changed to "John S. Lincoln" or "John S. Sherman," the initial "S" standing for no name, it being simply a part of what the coloured man proudly called his "entitles."

As I have stated, most of the coloured people left the old plantation for a short while at least, so as to be sure, it seemed, that they could leave and try their freedom on to see how it felt. After they had remained away for a time, many of the older slaves, especially, returned to their old homes and made some kind of contract with their former owners by which they remained on the estate.

My mother's husband, who was the stepfather of my brother John and myself, did not belong to the same owners as did my mother. In fact, he seldom came to our plantation. I remember seeing him there perhaps once a year, that being about Christmas time. In some way, during the war, by running away and following the Federal soldiers, it seems, he found his way into the new state of West Virginia. As soon as freedom was declared, he sent for my mother to come to the Kanawha Valley, in West Virginia. At that time a journey from Virginia over the mountains to West Virginia was rather a tedious and in some cases a painful undertaking. What little clothing and few household goods we had were placed in a cart, but the children walked the greater portion of the distance, which was several hundred miles.

I do not think any of us ever had been very far from the plantation, and the taking of a long journey into another state was quite an event. The parting from our former owners and the members of our own race on the plantation was a serious occasion. From the time of our parting till their death we kept up a correspondence with the older members of the family, and in later years we have kept in touch with those who were the younger members. We were several weeks making the trip, and most of the time we slept in the open air and did our cooking over a log fire out-of-doors. One night I recall that we camped near an abandoned log cabin, and my mother decided to build a fire in that for cooking, and afterward to make a "pallet" on the floor for our sleeping. Just as the fire had gotten well started a large black snake fully a yard and a half long dropped down the chimney and ran out on the floor. Of course we at once abandoned that cabin. Finally we reached our destination—a little town called Maiden, which is about five miles from Charleston, the present capital of the state.

At that time salt-mining was the great industry in that part of West Virginia, and the little town of Maiden was right in the midst of the salt-furnaces. My stepfather had already secured a job at a salt-furnace, and he had also secured a little cabin for us to live in. Our new house was no better than the one we had left on the old plantation in Virginia. In fact, in one respect it was worse. Notwithstanding the poor condition of our plantation cabin, we were at all times sure of pure air. Our new home was in the midst of a cluster of cabins crowded closely together, and as there were no sanitary regulations, the filth about the cabins was often intolerable. Some of our neighbours were coloured people, and some were the poorest and most ignorant and degraded white people. It was a motley mixture. Drinking, gambling, quarrels, fights, and shockingly immoral practices were frequent. All who lived in the little town were in one way or another connected with the salt business. Though I was a mere child, my stepfather put me and my brother at work in one of the furnaces. Often I began work as early as four o'clock in the morning.

The first thing I ever learned in the way of book knowledge was while working in this salt-furnace. Each salt-packer had his barrels marked with a certain number. The number allotted to my stepfather was "18." At the close of the day's work the boss of the packers would come around and put "18" on each of our barrels, and I soon learned to recognize that figure wherever I saw it, and after a while got to the point where I could make that figure, though I knew nothing about any other figures or letters.

From the time that I can remember having any thoughts about anything, I recall that I had an intense longing to learn to read. I determined, when quite a small child, that, if I accomplished nothing else in life, I would in some way get enough education to enable me to read common books and newspapers. Soon after we got settled in some manner in our new cabin in West Virginia, I induced my mother to get hold of a book for me. How or where she got it I do not know, but in some way she procured an old copy of Webster's[6] "blue-black" spelling-book, which contained the alphabet, followed by such meaningless words as "ab," "ba," "ca," "da." I began at once to devour this book, and I think that it was the first one I ever had in my hands. I had learned from somebody that the way to begin to read was to learn the alphabet, so I tried in all the ways I could think of to learn it,—all of course without a teacher, for I could find no one to teach me. At that time there was not a single member of my race anywhere near us who could read, and I was too timid to approach any of the white people. In some way, within a few weeks, I mastered the greater portion of the alphabet. In all my efforts to learn to read my mother shared fully my ambition, and sympathized with me and aided me in every way that she could. Though she was totally ignorant, so far as mere book knowledge was concerned, she had high ambitions for her children, and a large fund of good, hard, common sense which seemed to enable her to meet and master every situation. If I have done anything in life worth attention, I feel sure that I inherited the disposition from my mother.

In the midst of my struggles and longing for an education, a young coloured boy who had learned to read in the state of Ohio came to Maiden. As soon as the coloured people found out that he could read, a newspaper was secured, and at the close of nearly every day's work this young man would be surrounded by a group of men and women who were anxious to hear him read the news contained in the papers. How I used to envy this man! He seemed to me to be the one young man in all the world who ought to be satisfied with his attainments.

6. Noah Webster (1758–1843), author of the most widely used spelling books in the 19th-century United States.

About this time the question of having some kind of a school opened for the coloured children in the village began to be discussed by members of the race. As it would be the first school for Negro children that had ever been opened in that part of Virginia, it was, of course, to be a great event, and the discussion excited the widest interest. The most perplexing question was where to find a teacher. The young man from Ohio who had learned to read the papers was considered, but his age was against him. In the midst of the discussion about a teacher, another young coloured man from Ohio, who had been a soldier, in some way found his way into town. It was soon learned that he possessed considerable education, and he was engaged by the coloured people to teach their first school. As yet no free schools had been started for coloured people in that section, hence each family agreed to pay a certain amount per month, with the understanding that the teacher was to "board 'round"—that is, spend a day with each family. This was not bad for the teacher, for each family tried to provide the very best on the day the teacher was to be its guest. I recall that I looked forward with an anxious appetite to the "teacher's day" at our little cabin.

This experience of a whole race beginning to go to school for the first time, presents one of the most interesting studies that has ever occurred in connection with the development of any race. Few people who were not right in the midst of the scenes can form any exact idea of the intense desire which the people of my race showed for an education. As I have stated, it was a whole race trying to go to school. Few were too young, and none too old, to make the attempt to learn. As fast as any kind of teachers could be secured, not only were day-schools filled, but night-schools as well. The great ambition of the older people was to try to learn to read the Bible before they died. With this end in view, men and women who were fifty or seventy-five years old would often be found in the night-school. Sunday-schools were formed soon after freedom, but the principal book studied in the Sunday-school was the spelling-book. Day-school, night-school, Sunday-school, were always crowded, and often many had to be turned away for want of room.

The opening of the school in the Kanawha Valley, however, brought to me one of the keenest disappointments that I ever experienced. I had been working in a salt-furnace for several months, and my stepfather had discovered that I had a financial value, and so, when the school opened, he decided that he could not spare me from my work. This decision seemed to cloud my every ambition. The disappointment was made all the more severe by reason of the fact that my place of work was where I could see the happy children passing to and from school, mornings and afternoons. Despite this disappointment, however, I determined that I would learn something, anyway. I applied myself with greater earnestness than ever to the mastering of what was in the "blue-back" speller.

My mother sympathized with me in my disappointment, and sought to comfort me in all the ways she could, and to help me find a way to learn. After a while I succeeded in making arrangements with the teacher to give me some lessons at night, after the day's work was done. These night lessons were so welcome that I think I learned more at night than the other children did during the day. My own experiences in the night-school gave me faith in the night-school idea, with which, in after years, I had to do both at Hampton and Tuskegee. But my boyish heart was still set upon going to the day-school, and I let no opportunity slip to push my case. Finally I won, and was permitted to go to the school in the day for a few months, with the understanding that I was to rise early in the morning and work in the furnace till nine o'clock, and return immediately after school closed in the afternoon for at least two more hours of work.

The schoolhouse was some distance from the furnace, and as I had to work till nine o'clock, and the school opened at nine, I found myself in a difficulty. School would always be begun before I reached it, and sometimes my class had recited. To get around this difficulty I yielded to a temptation for which most people, I suppose, will condemn me; but since it is a fact, I might as well state it. I have great faith in the power and influence of facts. It is seldom that anything is permanently gained by holding back a fact. There was a large clock in a little office in the furnace. This clock, of course, all the hundred or more workmen depended upon to regulate their hours of beginning and ending the day's work. I got the idea that the way for me to reach school on time was to move the clock hands from half-past eight up to the nine o'clock mark. This I found myself doing morning after morning, till the furnace "boss" discovered that something was wrong, and locked the clock in a case. I did not mean to inconvenience anybody. I simply meant to reach that schoolhouse in time.

When, however, I found myself at the school for the first time, I also found myself confronted with two other difficulties. In the first place, I found that all of the other children wore hats or caps on their heads, and I had neither hat nor cap. In fact, I do not remember that up to the time of going to school I had ever worn any kind of covering upon my head, nor do I recall that either I or anybody else had even thought anything about the need of covering for my head. But, of course, when I saw how all the other boys were dressed, I began to feel quite uncomfortable. As usual, I put the case before my mother, and she explained to me that she had no money with which to buy a "store hat," which was a rather new institution at that time among the members of my race and was considered quite the thing for young and old to own, but that she would find a way to help me out of the difficulty. She accordingly got two pieces of "homespun" (jeans) and sewed them together, and I was soon the proud possessor of my first cap.

The lesson that my mother taught me in this has always remained with me, and I have tried as best I could to teach it to others. I have always felt proud, whenever I think of the incident, that my mother had strength of character enough not to be led into the temptation of seeming to be that which she was not—of trying to impress my schoolmates and others with the fact that she was able to buy me a "store hat" when she was not. I have always felt proud that she refused to go into debt for that which she did not have the money to pay for. Since that time I have owned many kinds of caps and hats, but never one of which I have felt so proud as of the cap made of the two pieces of cloth sewed together by my mother. I have noted the fact, but without satisfaction, I need not add, that several of the boys who began their careers with "store hats" and who were my schoolmates and used to join in the sport that was made of me because I had only a "homespun" cap, have ended their careers in the penitentiary, while others are not able now to buy any kind of hat.

My second difficulty was with regard to my name, or rather *a* name. From the time when I could remember anything, I had been called simply

"Booker." Before going to school it had never occurred to me that it was needful or appropriate to have an additional name. When I heard the school-roll called, I noticed that all of the children had at least two names, and some of them indulged in what seemed to me the extravagance of having three. I was in deep perplexity, because I knew that the teacher would demand of me at least two names, and I had only one. By the time the occasion came for the enrolling of my name, an idea occurred to me which I thought would make me equal to the situation; and so, when the teacher asked me what my full name was, I calmly told him "Booker Washington," as if I had been called by that name all my life; and by that name I have since been known. Later in my life I found that my mother had given me the name of "Booker Taliaferro" soon after I was born, but in some way that part of my name seemed to disappear and for a long while was forgotten, but as soon as I found out about it I revived it, and made my full name "Booker Taliaferro Washington." I think there are not many men in our country who have had the privilege of naming themselves in the way that I have.

More than once I have tried to picture myself in the position of a boy or man with an honoured and distinguished ancestry which I could trace back through a period of hundreds of years, and who had not only inherited a name, but fortune and a proud family homestead; and yet I have sometimes had the feeling that if I had inherited these, and had been a member of a more popular race, I should have been inclined to yield to the temptation of depending upon my ancestry and my colour to do that for me which I should do for myself. Years ago I resolved that because I had no ancestry myself I would leave a record of which my children would be proud, and which might encourage them to still higher effort.

The world should not pass judgment upon the Negro, and especially the Negro youth, too quickly or too harshly. The Negro boy has obstacles, discouragements, and temptations to battle with that are little known to those not situated as he is. When a white boy undertakes a task, it is taken for granted that he will succeed. On the other hand, people are usually surprised if the Negro boy does not fail. In a word, the Negro youth starts out with the presumption against him.

The influence of ancestry, however, is important in helping forward any individual or race, if too much reliance is not placed upon it. Those who constantly direct attention to the Negro youth's moral weaknesses, and compare his advancement with that of white youths, do not consider the influence of the memories which cling about the old family homesteads. I have no idea, as I have stated elsewhere, who my grandmother was. I have, or have had, uncles and aunts and cousins, but I have no knowledge as to where most of them are. My case will illustrate that of hundreds of thousands of black people in every part of our country. The very fact that the white boy is conscious that, if he fails in life, he will disgrace the whole family record, extending back through many generations, is of tremendous value in helping him to resist temptations. The fact that the individual has behind and surrounding him proud family history and connection serves as a stimulus to help him to overcome obstacles when striving for success.

The time that I was permitted to attend school during the day was short, and my attendance was irregular. It was not long before I had to stop attending day-school altogether, and devote all of my time again to work. I resorted to the night-school again. In fact, the greater part of the education

I secured in my boyhood was gathered through the night-school after my day's work was done. I had difficulty often in securing a satisfactory teacher. Sometimes, after I had secured some one to teach me at night, I would find, much to my disappointment, that the teacher knew but little more than I did. Often I would have to walk several miles at night in order to recite my night-school lessons. There was never a time in my youth, no matter how dark and discouraging the days might be, when one resolve did not continually remain with me, and that was a determination to secure an education at any cost.

Soon after we moved to West Virginia, my mother adopted into our family, notwithstanding our poverty, an orphan boy, to whom afterward we gave the name of James B. Washington. He has ever since remained a member of the family.

After I had worked in the salt-furnace for some time, work was secured for me in a coal-mine which was operated mainly for the purpose of securing fuel for the salt-furnace. Work in the coal-mine I always dreaded. One reason for this was that any one who worked in a coal-mine was always unclean, at least while at work, and it was a very hard job to get one's skin clean after the day's work was over. Then it was fully a mile from the opening of the coal-mine to the face of the coal, and all, of course, was in the blackest darkness. I do not believe that one ever experiences anywhere else such darkness as he does in a coal-mine. The mine was divided into a large number of different "rooms" or departments, and, as I never was able to learn the location of all these "rooms," I many times found myself lost in the mine. To add to the horror of being lost, sometimes my light would go out, and then, if I did not happen to have a match, I would wander about in the darkness until by chance I found some one to give me a light. The work was not only hard, but it was dangerous. There was always the danger of being blown to pieces by a premature explosion of powder, or of being crushed by falling slate. Accidents from one or the other of these causes were frequently occurring, and this kept me in constant fear. Many children of the tenderest years were compelled then, as is now true I fear, in most coal-mining districts, to spend a large part of their lives in these coal-mines, with little opportunity to get an education; and, what is worse, I have often noted that, as a rule, young boys who begin life in a coal-mine are often physically and mentally dwarfed. They soon lose ambition to do anything else than to continue as a coal-miner.

In those days, and later as a young man, I used to try to picture in my imagination the feelings and ambitions of a white boy with absolutely no limit placed upon his aspirations and activities. I used to envy the white boy who had no obstacles placed in the way of his becoming a Congressman, Governor, Bishop, or President by reason of the accident of his birth or race. I used to picture the way that I would act under such circumstances; how I would begin at the bottom and keep rising until I reached the highest round of success.

In later years, I confess that I do not envy the white boy as I once did. I have learned that success is to be measured not so much by the position that one has reached in life as by the obstacles which he has overcome while trying to succeed. Looked at from this standpoint, I almost reach the conclusion that often the Negro boy's birth and connection with an unpopular race is an advantage, so far as real life is concerned. With few exceptions, the Negro youth must work harder and must perform his tasks even better than a white youth in order to secure recognition. But out of the hard and unusual struggle through which he is compelled to pass, he gets a strength, a confidence, that one misses whose pathway is comparatively smooth by reason of birth and race.

From any point of view, I had rather be what I am, a member of the Negro race, than be able to claim membership with the most favoured of any other race. I have always been made sad when I have heard members of any race claiming rights and privileges, or certain badges of distinction, on the ground simply that they were members of this or that race, regardless of their own individual worth or attainments. I have been made to feel sad for such persons because I am conscious of the fact that mere connection with what is known as a superior race will not permanently carry an individual forward unless he has individual worth, and mere connection with what is regarded as an inferior race will not finally hold an individual back if he possesses intrinsic, individual merit. Every persecuted individual and race should get much consolation out of the great human law, which is universal and eternal, that merit, no matter under what skin found, is, in the long run, recognized and rewarded. This I have said here, not to call attention to myself as an individual, but to the race to which I am proud to belong.

Chapter III. The Struggle for an Education

One day, while at work in the coal-mine, I happened to overhear two miners talking about a great school for coloured people somewhere in Virginia. This was the first time that I had ever heard anything about any kind of school or college that was more pretentious than the little coloured school in our town.

In the darkness of the mine I noiselessly crept as close as I could to the two men who were talking. I heard one tell the other that not only was the school established for the members of my race, but that opportunities were provided by which poor but worthy students could work out all or a part of the cost of board, and at the same time be taught some trade or industry.

As they went on describing the school, it seemed to me that it must be the greatest place on earth, and not even Heaven presented more attractions for me at that time than did the Hampton Normal and Agricultural Institute[7] in Virginia, about which these men were talking. I resolved at once to go to that school, although I had no idea where it was, or how many miles away, or how I was going to reach it; I remembered only that I was on fire constantly with one ambition, and that was to go to Hampton. This thought was with me day and night.

After hearing of the Hampton Institute, I continued to work for a few months longer in the coal-mine. While at work there, I heard of a vacant position in the household of General Lewis Ruffner, the owner of the salt-furnace and coal-mine. Mrs. Viola Ruffner, the wife of General Ruffner, was a "Yankee" woman from Vermont. Mrs. Ruffner had a reputation all through the vicinity for being very strict with her servants, and especially with the boys who tried to serve her. Few of them had remained with her

7. Founded in 1868, a school that offered industrial, agricultural, and teacher training for African Americans and American Indians.

more than two or three weeks. They all left with the same excuse: she was too strict. I decided, however, that I would rather try Mrs. Ruffner's house than remain in the coal-mine, and so my mother applied to her for the vacant position. I was hired at a salary of $5 per month.

I had heard so much about Mrs. Ruffner's severity that I was almost afraid to see her, and trembled when I went into her presence. I had not lived with her many weeks, however, before I began to understand her. I soon began to learn that, first of all, she wanted everything kept clean about her, that she wanted things done promptly and systematically, and that at the bottom of everything she wanted absolute honesty and frankness. Nothing must be sloven or slipshod; every door, every fence, must be kept in repair.

I cannot now recall how long I lived with Mrs. Ruffner before going to Hampton, but I think it must have been a year and a half. At any rate, I here repeat what I have said more than once before, that the lessons that I learned in the home of Mrs. Ruffner were as valuable to me as any education I have ever gotten anywhere since. Even to this day I never see bits of paper scattered around a house or in the street that I do not want to pick them up at once. I never see a filthy yard that I do not want to clean it, a paling off of a fence that I do not want to put it on, an unpainted or unwhitewashed house that I do not want to paint or whitewash it, or a button off one's clothes, or a grease-spot on them or on a floor, that I do not want to call attention to it.

From fearing Mrs. Ruffner I soon learned to look upon her as one of my best friends. When she found that she could trust me she did so implicitly. During the one or two winters that I was with her she gave me an opportunity to go to school for an hour in the day during a portion of the winter months, but most of my studying was done at night, sometimes alone, sometimes under some one whom I could hire to teach me. Mrs. Ruffner always encouraged and sympathized with me in all my efforts to get an education. It was while living with her that I began to get together my first library. I secured a dry-goods box, knocked out one side of it, put some shelves in it, and began putting into it every kind of book that I could get my hands upon, and called it my "library."

Notwithstanding my success at Mrs. Ruffner's I did not give up the idea of going to the Hampton Institute. In the fall of 1872 I determined to make an effort to get there, although, as I have stated, I had no definite idea of the direction in which Hampton was, or of what it would cost to go there. I do not think that any one thoroughly sympathized with me in my ambition to go to Hampton unless it was my mother, and she was troubled with a grave fear that I was starting out on a "wild-goose chase." At any rate, I got only a half-hearted consent from her that I might start. The small amount of money that I had earned had been consumed by my stepfather and the remainder of the family, with the exception of a very few dollars, and so I had very little with which to buy clothes and pay my travelling expenses. My brother John helped me all that he could, but of course that was not a great deal, for his work was in the coal-mine, where he did not earn much, and most of what he did earn went in the direction of paying the household expenses.

Perhaps the thing that touched and pleased me most in connection with my starting for Hampton was the interest that many of the older coloured people took in the matter. They had spent the best days of their lives in slavery, and hardly expected to live to see the time when they would see a member of their race leave home to attend a boarding-school. Some of these older people would give me a nickel, others a quarter, or a handkerchief.

Finally the great day came, and I started for Hampton. I had only a small, cheap satchel that contained what few articles of clothing I could get. My mother at the time was rather weak and broken in health. I hardly expected to see her again, and thus our parting was all the more sad. She, however, was very brave through it all. At that time there were no through trains connecting that part of West Virginia with eastern Virginia. Trains ran only a portion of the way, and the remainder of the distance was travelled by stage-coaches.

The distance from Malden to Hampton is about five hundred miles. I had not been away from home many hours before it began to grow painfully evident that I did not have enough money to pay my fare to Hampton. One experience I shall long remember. I had been travelling over the mountains most of the afternoon in an old-fashioned stagecoach, when, late in the evening, the coach stopped for the night at a common, unpainted house called a hotel. All the other passengers except myself were whites. In my ignorance I supposed that the little hotel existed for the purpose of accommodating the passengers who travelled on the stage-coach. The difference that the colour of one's skin would make I had not thought anything about. After all the other passengers had been shown rooms and were getting ready for supper, I shyly presented myself before the man at the desk. It is true I had practically no money in my pocket with which to pay for bed or food, but I had hoped in some way to beg my way into the good graces of the landlord, for at that season in the mountains of Virginia the weather was cold, and I wanted to get indoors for the night. Without asking as to whether I had any money, the man at the desk firmly refused to even consider the matter of providing me with food or lodging. This was my first experience in finding out what the colour of my skin meant. In some way I managed to keep warm by walking about, and so got through the night. My whole soul was so bent upon reaching Hampton that I did not have time to cherish any bitterness toward the hotel-keeper.

By walking, begging rides both in wagons and in the cars, in some way, after a number of days, I reached the city of Richmond, Virginia, about eighty-two miles from Hampton. When I reached there, tired, hungry, and dirty, it was late in the night. I had never been in a large city, and this rather added to my misery. When I reached Richmond, I was completely out of money. I had not a single acquaintance in the place, and, being unused to city ways, I did not know where to go. I applied at several places for lodging, but they all wanted money, and that was what I did not have. Knowing nothing else better to do, I walked the streets. In doing this I passed by many foodstands where fried chicken and half-moon apple pies were piled high and made to present a most tempting appearance. At that time it seemed to me that I would have promised all that I expected to possess in the future to have gotten hold of one of those chicken legs or one of those pies. But I could not get either of these, nor anything else to eat.

I must have walked the streets till after midnight. At last I became so exhausted that I could walk no longer. I was tired, I was hungry, I was everything but discouraged. Just about the time when I reached extreme physical exhaustion, I came upon a portion of a street where the board sidewalk was considerably elevated. I waited for a few minutes, till I was sure that no passers-by could see me, and then crept under the sidewalk and lay for the night upon the ground, with my satchel of clothing for a pillow. Nearly all night I could hear the tramp of feet over my head. The next morning I found myself somewhat refreshed, but I was extremely hungry, because it had been a long time since I had had sufficient food. As soon as it became light enough for me to see my surroundings I noticed that I was near a large ship, and that this ship seemed to be unloading a cargo of pig iron.[8] I went at once to the vessel and asked the captain to permit me to help unload the vessel in order to get money for food. The captain, a white man, who seemed to be kind-hearted, consented. I worked long enough to earn money for my breakfast, and it seems to me, as I remember it now, to have been about the best breakfast that I have ever eaten.

My work pleased the captain so well that he told me if I desired I could continue working for a small amount per day. This I was very glad to do. I continued working on this vessel for a number of days. After buying food with the small wages I received there was not much left to add to the amount I must get to pay my way to Hampton. In order to economize in every way possible, so as to be sure to reach Hampton in a reasonable time, I continued to sleep under the same sidewalk that gave me shelter the first night I was in Richmond. Many years after that the coloured citizens of Richmond very kindly tendered me a reception at which there must have been two thousand people present. This reception was held not far from the spot where I slept the first night I spent in that city, and I must confess that my mind was more upon the sidewalk that first gave me shelter than upon the reception, agreeable and cordial as it was.

When I had saved what I considered enough money with which to reach Hampton, I thanked the captain of the vessel for his kindness, and started again. Without any unusual occurrence I reached Hampton, with a surplus of exactly fifty cents with which to begin my education. To me it had been a long, eventful journey; but the first sight of the large, three-story, brick school building seemed to have rewarded me for all that I had undergone in order to reach the place. If the people who gave the money to provide that building could appreciate the influence the sight of it had upon me, as well as upon thousands of other youths, they would feel all the more encouraged to make such gifts. It seemed to me to be the largest and most beautiful building I had ever seen. The sight of it seemed to give me new life. I felt that a new kind of existence had now begun—that life would now have a new meaning. I felt that I had reached the promised land, and I resolved to let no obstacle prevent me from putting forth the highest effort to fit myself to accomplish the most good in the world.

As soon as possible after reaching the grounds of the Hampton Institute, I presented myself before the head teacher for assignment to a class. Having been so long without proper food, a bath, and change of clothing, I did not, of course, make a very favourable impression upon her, and I could see at once that there were doubts in her mind about the wisdom of admitting me as a student. I felt that I could hardly blame her if she got the idea that I was a worthless loafer or tramp. For some time she did not refuse to admit me, neither did she decide in my favour, and I continued to linger about her, and to impress her in all the ways I could with my worthiness. In the meantime I saw her admitting other students, and that added greatly to my dis-

8. Crude iron used in the production of steel.

comfort, for I felt, deep down in my heart, that I could do as well as they, if I could only get a chance to show what was in me.

After some hours had passed, the head teacher said to me: "The adjoining recitation-room needs sweeping. Take the broom and sweep it."

It occurred to me at once that here was my chance. Never did I receive an order with more delight. I knew that I could sweep, for Mrs. Ruffner had thoroughly taught me how to do that when I lived with her.

I swept the recitation-room three times. Then I got a dusting-cloth and I dusted it four times. All the woodwork around the walls, every bench, table, and desk, I went over four times with my dusting-cloth. Besides, every piece of furniture had been moved and every closet and corner in the room had been thoroughly cleaned. I had the feeling that in a large measure my future depended upon the impression I made upon the teacher in the cleaning of that room. When I was through, I reported to the head teacher. She was a "Yankee" woman who knew just where to look for dirt. She went into the room and inspected the floor and closets; then she took her handkerchief and rubbed it on the woodwork about the walls, and over the table and benches. When she was unable to find one bit of dirt on the floor, or a particle of dust on any of the furniture, she quietly remarked, "I guess you will do to enter this institution."

I was one of the happiest souls on earth. The sweeping of that room was my college examination, and never did any youth pass an examination for entrance into Harvard or Yale that gave him more genuine satisfaction. I have passed several examinations since then, but I have always felt that this was the best one I ever passed.

I have spoken of my own experience in entering the Hampton Institute. Perhaps few, if any, had anything like the same experience that I had, but about that same period there were hundreds who found their way to Hampton and other institutions after experiencing something of the same difficulties that I went through. The young men and women were determined to secure an education at any cost.

The sweeping of the recitation-room in the manner that I did it seems to have paved the way for me to get through Hampton. Miss Mary F. Mackie, the head teacher, offered me a position as janitor. This, of course, I gladly accepted, because it was a place where I could work out nearly all the cost of my board. The work was hard and taxing, but I stuck to it. I had a large number of rooms to care for, and had to work late into the night, while at the same time I had to rise by four o'clock in the morning, in order to build the fires and have a little time in which to prepare my lessons. In all my career at Hampton, and ever since I have been out in the world, Miss Mary F. Mackie, the head teacher to whom I have referred, proved one of my strongest and most helpful friends. Her advice and encouragement were always helpful and strengthening to me in the darkest hour.

I have spoken of the impression that was made upon me by the buildings and general appearance of the Hampton Institute, but I have not spoken of that which made the greatest and most lasting impression upon me, and that was a great man—the noblest, rarest human being that it has ever been my privilege to meet. I refer to the late General Samuel C. Armstrong.[9]

9. Former officer in the Union Army, educational reformer, and founder of Hampton Institute (1839–1893).

It has been my fortune to meet personally many of what are called great characters, both in Europe and America, but I do not hesitate to say that I never met any man who, in my estimation, was the equal of General Armstrong. Fresh from the degrading influences of the slave plantation and the coal-mines, it was a rare privilege for me to be permitted to come into direct contact with such a character as General Armstrong. I shall always remember that the first time I went into his presence he made the impression upon me of being a perfect man; I was made to feel that there was something about him that was superhuman. It was my privilege to know the General personally from the time I entered Hampton till he died, and the more I saw of him the greater he grew in my estimation. One might have removed from Hampton all the buildings, class-rooms, teachers, and industries, and given the men and women there the opportunity of coming into daily contact with General Armstrong, and that alone would have been a liberal education. The older I grow, the more I am convinced that there is no education which one can get from books and costly apparatus that is equal to that which can be gotten from contact with great men and women. Instead of studying books so constantly, how I wish that our schools and colleges might learn to study men and things!

General Armstrong spent two of the last six months of his life in my home at Tuskegee. At that time he was paralyzed to the extent that he had lost control of his body and voice in a very large degree. Notwithstanding his affliction, he worked almost constantly night and day for the cause to which he had given his life. I never saw a man who so completely lost sight of himself. I do not believe he ever had a selfish thought. He was just as happy in trying to assist some other institution in the South as he was when working for Hampton. Although he fought the Southern white man in the Civil War, I never heard him utter a bitter word against him afterward. On the other hand, he was constantly seeking to find ways by which he could be of service to the Southern whites.

It would be difficult to describe the hold that he had upon the students at Hampton, or the faith they had in him. In fact, he was worshipped by his students. It never occurred to me that General Armstrong could fail in anything that he undertook. There is almost no request that he could have made that would not have been complied with. When he was a guest at my home in Alabama, and was so badly paralyzed that he had to be wheeled about in an invalid's chair, I recall that one of the General's former students had occasion to push his chair up a long, steep hill that taxed his strength to the utmost. When the top of the hill was reached, the former pupil, with a glow of happiness on his face, exclaimed, "I am so glad that I have been permitted to do something that was real hard for the General before he dies!" While I was a student at Hampton, the dormitories became so crowded that it was impossible to find room for all who wanted to be admitted. In order to help remedy the difficulty, the General conceived the plan of putting up tents to be used as rooms. As soon as it became known that General Armstrong would be pleased if some of the older students would live in the tents during the winter, nearly every student in school volunteered to go.

I was one of the volunteers. The winter that we spent in those tents was an intensely cold one, and we suffered severely—how much I am sure General Armstrong never knew, because we made no complaints. It was enough for us to know that we were pleasing General Armstrong, and that we were making it possible for an additional number of students to secure an education. More than once, during a cold night, when a stiff gale would be blowing, our tent was lifted bodily, and we would find ourselves in the open air. The General would usually pay a visit to the tents early in the morning, and his earnest, cheerful, encouraging voice would dispel any feeling of despondency.

I have spoken of my admiration for General Armstrong, and yet he was but a type of that Christlike body of men and women who went into the Negro schools at the close of the war by the hundreds to assist in lifting up my race. The history of the world fails to show a higher, purer, and more unselfish class of men and women than those who found their way into those Negro schools.

Life at Hampton was a constant revelation to me; was constantly taking me into a new world. The matter of having meals at regular hours, of eating on a tablecloth, using a napkin, the use of the bathtub and of the toothbrush, as well as the use of sheets upon the bed, were all new to me.

I sometimes feel that almost the most valuable lesson I got at the Hampton Institute was in the use and value of the bath. I learned there for the first time some of its value, not only in keeping the body healthy, but in inspiring self-respect and promoting virtue. In all my travels in the South and elsewhere since leaving Hampton I have always in some way sought my daily bath. To get it sometimes when I have been the guest of my own people in a single-roomed cabin has not always been easy to do, except by slipping away to some stream in the woods. I have always tried to teach my people that some provision for bathing should be a part of every house.

For some time, while a student at Hampton, I possessed but a single pair of socks, but when I had worn these till they became soiled, I would wash them at night and hang them by the fire to dry, so that I might wear them again the next morning.

The charge for my board at Hampton was ten dollars per month. I was expected to pay a part of this in cash and to work out the remainder. To meet this cash payment, as I have stated, I had just fifty cents when I reached the institution. Aside from a very few dollars that my brother John was able to send me once in a while, I had no money with which to pay my board. I was determined from the first to make my work as janitor so valuable that my services would be indispensable. This I succeeded in doing to such an extent that I was soon informed that I would be allowed the full cost of my board in return for my work. The cost of tuition was seventy dollars a year. This, of course, was wholly beyond my ability to provide. If I had been compelled to pay the seventy dollars for tuition, in addition to providing for my board, I would have been compelled to leave the Hampton school. General Armstrong, however, very kindly got Mr. S. Griffitts Morgan,[1] of New Bedford, Mass., to defray the cost of my tuition during the whole time that I was at Hampton. After I finished the course at Hampton and had entered upon my lifework at Tuskegee, I had the pleasure of visiting Mr. Morgan several times.

After having been for a while at Hampton, I found myself in difficulty because I did not have books and clothing. Usually, however, I got around

1. A merchant.

the trouble about books by borrowing from those who were more fortunate than myself. As to clothes, when I reached Hampton I had practically nothing. Everything that I possessed was in a small hand satchel. My anxiety about clothing was increased because of the fact that General Armstrong made a personal inspection of the young men in ranks, to see that their clothes were clean. Shoes had to be polished, there must be no buttons off the clothing, and no grease-spots. To wear one suit of clothes continually, while at work and in the schoolroom, and at the same time keep it clean, was rather a hard problem for me to solve. In some way I managed to get on till the teachers learned that I was in earnest and meant to succeed, and then some of them were kind enough to see that I was partly supplied with second-hand clothing that had been sent in barrels from the North. These barrels proved a blessing to hundreds of poor but deserving students. Without them I question whether I should ever have gotten through Hampton.

When I first went to Hampton I do not recall that I had ever slept in a bed that had two sheets on it. In those days there were not many buildings there, and room was very precious. There were seven other boys in the same room with me; most of them, however, students who had been there for some time. The sheets were quite a puzzle to me. The first night I slept under both of them, and the second night I slept on top of both of them; but by watching the other boys I learned my lesson in this, and have been trying to follow it ever since and to teach it to others.

I was among the youngest of the students who were in Hampton at that time. Most of the students were men and women—some as old as forty years of age. As I now recall the scene of my first year, I do not believe that one often has the opportunity of coming into contact with three or four hundred men and women who were so tremendously in earnest as these men and women were. Every hour was occupied in study or work. Nearly all had had enough actual contact with the world to teach them the need of education. Many of the older ones were, of course, too old to master the text-books very thoroughly, and it was often sad to watch their struggles; but they made up in earnestness much of what they lacked in books. Many of them were as poor as I was, and, besides having to wrestle with their books, they had to struggle with a poverty which prevented their having the necessities of life. Many of them had aged parents who were dependent upon them, and some of them were men who had wives whose support in some way they had to provide for.

The great and prevailing idea that seemed to take possession of every one was to prepare himself to lift up the people at his home. No one seemed to think of himself. And the officers and teachers, what a rare set of human beings they were! They worked for the students night and day, in season and out of season. They seemed happy only when they were helping the students in some manner. Whenever it is written—and I hope it will be—the part that the Yankee teachers played in the education of the Negroes immediately after the war will make one of the most thrilling parts of the history of this country. The time is not far distant when the whole South will appreciate this service in a way that it has not yet been able to do.

* * *

Chapter XIV. The Atlanta Exposition[2] Address

The Atlanta Exposition, at which I had been asked to make an address as a representative of the Negro race, as stated in the last chapter, was opened with a short address from Governor Bullock.[3] After other interesting exercises, including an invocation from Bishop Nelson, of Georgia, a dedicatory ode by Albert Howell, Jr., and addresses by the President of the Exposition and Mrs. Joseph Thompson,[4] the President of the Woman's Board, Governor Bullock introduced me with the words, "We have with us to-day a representative of Negro enterprise and Negro civilization."

When I arose to speak, there was considerable cheering, especially from the coloured people. As I remember it now, the thing that was uppermost in my mind was the desire to say something that would cement the friendship of the races and bring about hearty cooperation between them. So far as my outward surroundings were concerned, the only thing that I recall distinctly now is that when I got up, I saw thousands of eyes looking intently into my face. The following is the address which I delivered:—

MR. PRESIDENT AND GENTLEMEN OF THE BOARD OF DIRECTORS AND CITIZENS.

One-third of the population of the South is of the Negro race. No enterprise seeking the material, civil, or moral welfare of this section can disregard this element of our population and reach the highest success. I but convey to you, Mr. President and Directors, the sentiment of the masses of my race when I say that in no way have the value and manhood of the American Negro been more fittingly and generously recognized than by the managers of this magnificent Exposition at every stage of its progress. It is a recognition that will do more to cement the friendship of the two races than any occurrence since the dawn of our freedom.

Not only this, but the opportunity here afforded will awaken among us a new era of industrial progress. Ignorant and inexperienced, it is not strange that in the first years of our new life we began at the top instead of at the bottom; that a seat in Congress or the state legislature was more sought than real estate or industrial skill; that the political convention or stump speaking had more attractions than starting a dairy farm or truck garden.

A ship lost at sea for many days suddenly sighted a friendly vessel. From the mast of the unfortunate vessel was seen a signal, "Water, water; we die of thirst!" The answer from the friendly vessel at once came back, "Cast down your bucket where you are." A second time the signal, "Water, water; send us water!" ran up from the distressed vessel, and was answered, "Cast down your bucket where you are." And a third and fourth signal for water was answered, "Cast down your bucket where you are." The captain of the distressed vessel, at last heeding the injunction, cast down his bucket, and it came up full of fresh, sparkling water from the mouth of the Amazon

2. The Cotton States and International Exposition, which officially opened on September 18, 1895, was a trade fair for the promotion of the New South.

3. Rufus B. Bullock (1834–1907), governor of Georgia from 1868 to 1871 and president of the exposition.

4. An active clubwoman and president of the Woman's Board of the Atlanta Exposition.

River. To those of my race who depend on bettering their condition in a foreign land or who underestimate the importance of cultivating friendly relations with the Southern white man, who is their next-door neighbour, I would say: "Cast down your bucket where you are"—cast it down in making friends in every manly way of the people of all races by whom we are surrounded.

Cast it down in agriculture, mechanics, in commerce, in domestic service, and in the professions. And in this connection it is well to bear in mind that whatever other sins the South may be called to bear, when it comes to business, pure and simple, it is in the South that the Negro is given a man's chance in the commercial world, and in nothing is this Exposition more eloquent than in emphasizing this chance. Our greatest danger is that in the great leap from slavery to freedom we may overlook the fact that the masses of us are to live by the productions of our hands, and fail to keep in mind that we shall prosper in proportion as we learn to dignify and glorify common labour and put brains and skill into the common occupations of life; shall prosper in proportion as we learn to draw the line between the superficial and the substantial, the ornamental gewgaws of life and the useful. No race can prosper till it learns that there is as much dignity in tilling a field as in writing a poem. It is at the bottom of life we must begin, and not at the top. Nor should we permit our grievances to overshadow our opportunities.

To those of the white race who look to the incoming of those of foreign birth and strange tongue and habits for the prosperity of the South, were I permitted I would repeat what I say to my own race, "Cast down your bucket where you are." Cast it down among the eight millions of Negroes whose habits you know, whose fidelity and love you have tested in days when to have proved treacherous meant the ruin of your firesides. Cast down your bucket among these people who have, without strikes and labour wars, tilled your fields, cleared your forests, builded your railroads and cities, and brought forth treasures from the bowels of the earth, and helped make possible this magnificent representation of the progress of the South. Casting down your bucket among my people, helping and encouraging them as you are doing on these grounds, and to education of head, hand, and heart, you will find that they will buy your surplus land, make blossom the waste places in your fields, and run your factories. While doing this, you can be sure in the future, as in the past, that you and your families will be surrounded by the most patient, faithful, law-abiding, and unresentful people that the world has seen. As we have proved our loyalty to you in the past, in nursing your children, watching by the sick-bed of your mothers and fathers, and often following them with tear-dimmed eyes to their graves, so in the future, in our humble way, we shall stand by you with a devotion that no foreigner can approach, ready to lay down our lives, if need be, in defence of yours, interlacing our industrial, commercial, civil, and religious life with yours in a way that shall make the interests of both races one. In all things that are purely social we can be as separate as the fingers, yet one as the hand in all things essential to mutual progress.

There is no defence or security for any of us except in the highest intelligence and development of all. If anywhere there are efforts tending to curtail the fullest growth of the Negro, let these efforts be turned into stimulating, encouraging, and making him the most useful and intelligent citizen. Effort or means so invested will pay a thousand per cent interest. These efforts will be twice blessed—"blessing him that gives and him that takes."[5]

There is no escape through law of man or God from the inevitable:—

The laws of changeless justice bind
Oppressor with oppressed;
And close as sin and suffering joined
We march to fate abreast.[6]

Nearly sixteen millions of hands will aid you in pulling the load upward, or they will pull against you the load downward. We shall constitute one-third and more of the ignorance and crime of the South, or one-third its intelligence and progress; we shall contribute one-third to the business and industrial prosperity of the South, or we shall prove a veritable body of death,[7] stagnating, depressing, retarding every effort to advance the body politic.

Gentlemen of the Exposition, as we present to you our humble effort at an exhibition of our progress, you must not expect overmuch. Starting thirty years ago with ownership here and there in a few quilts and pumpkins and chickens (gathered from miscellaneous sources), remember the path that has led from these to the inventions and production of agricultural implements, buggies, steam-engines, newspapers, books, statuary, carving, paintings, the management of drug-stores and banks, has not been trodden without contact with thorns and thistles. While we take pride in what we exhibit as a result of our independent efforts, we do not for a moment forget that our part in this exhibition would fall far short of your expectations but for the constant help that has come to our educational life, not only from the Southern states, but especially from Northern philanthropists, who have made their gifts a constant stream of blessing and encouragement.

The wisest among my race understand that the agitation of questions of social equality is the extremest folly, and that progress in the enjoyment of all the privileges that will come to us must be the result of severe and constant struggle rather than of artificial forcing. No race that has anything to contribute to the markets of the world is long in any degree ostracized. It is important and right that all privileges of the law be ours, but it is vastly more important that we be prepared for the exercises of these privileges. The opportunity to earn a dollar in a factory just now is worth infinitely more than the opportunity to spend a dollar in an opera-house.

In conclusion, may I repeat that nothing in thirty years has given us more hope and encouragement, and drawn us so near to you of the white race, as this opportunity offered by the Exposition; and here bending, as it were, over the altar that represents the results of the struggles of your race and mine, both starting practically empty-handed three decades ago, I pledge that in your effort to work out the great and intricate problem which God has laid at the doors of the South, you shall have at all times the patient, sympathetic help of my race; only let this be constantly in mind, that, while from representations in these buildings of the product of field, of forest, of mine, of factory, letters, and art, much good will come, yet far above and beyond material benefits will be that higher good, that, let us pray God, will

5. Shakespeare's *The Merchant of Venice* 4.1.182.

6. From "The Song of the Negro Boatmen" in *At Port Royal* (1862) by the American antislavery poet John Greenleaf Whittier.

7. "Who shall deliver me from the body of this death?" (Romans 7:24).

come, in a blotting out of sectional differences and racial animosities and suspicions, in a determination to administer absolute justice, in a willing obedience among all classes to the mandates of law. This, this, coupled with our material prosperity, will bring into our beloved South a new heaven and a new earth.

The first thing that I remember, after I had finished speaking, was that Governor Bullock rushed across the platform and took me by the hand, and that others did the same. I received so many and such hearty congratulations that I found it difficult to get out of the building. I did not appreciate to any degree, however, the impression which my address seemed to have made, until the next morning, when I went into the business part of the city. As soon as I was recognized, I was surprised to find myself pointed out and surrounded by a crowd of men who wished to shake hands with me. This was kept up on every street on to which I went, to an extent which embarrassed me so much that I went back to my boarding-place. The next morning I returned to Tuskegee. At the station in Atlanta, and at almost all of the stations at which the train stopped between that city and Tuskegee, I found a crowd of people anxious to shake hands with me.

The papers in all parts of the United States published the address in full, and for months afterward there were complimentary editorial references to it. Mr. Clark Howell, the editor of the Atlanta *Constitution*, telegraphed to a New York paper, among other words, the following, "I do not exaggerate when I say that Professor Booker T. Washington's address yesterday was one of the most notable speeches, both as to character and as to the warmth of its reception, ever delivered to a Southern audience. The address was a revelation. The whole speech is a platform upon which blacks and whites can stand with full justice to each other."

The Boston *Transcript* said editorially: "The speech of Booker T. Washington at the Atlanta Exposition, this week, seems to have dwarfed all the other proceedings and the Exposition itself. The sensation that it has caused in the press has never been equalled."

I very soon began receiving all kinds of propositions from lecture bureaus, and editors of magazines and papers, to take the lecture platform, and to write articles. One lecture bureau offered me fifty thousand dollars, or two hundred dollars a night and expenses, if I would place my services at its disposal for a given period. To all these communications I replied that my life-work was at Tuskegee; and that whenever I spoke it must be in the interests of the Tuskegee school and my race, and that I would enter into no arrangements that seemed to place a mere commercial value upon my services.

Some days after its delivery I sent a copy of my address to the President of the United States, the Hon. Grover Cleveland. I received from him the following autograph reply:—

Gray Gables, Buzzard's Bay, Mass.,
October 6, 1895.

Booker T. Washington, Esq.:

My Dear Sir: I thank you for sending me a copy of your address delivered at the Atlanta Exposition.

I thank you with much enthusiasm for making the address. I have read it with intense interest, and I think the Exposition would be fully justified if it did not do more than furnish the opportunity for its delivery. Your words cannot fail to delight and encourage all who wish well for your race; and if our coloured fellow-citizens do not from your utterances gather new hope and form new determinations to gain every valuable advantage offered them by their citizenship, it will be strange indeed.

Yours very truly,
GROVER CLEVELAND.

Later I met Mr. Cleveland, for the first time, when, as President, he visited the Atlanta Exposition. At the request of myself and others he consented to spend an hour in the Negro Building, for the purpose of inspecting the Negro exhibit and of giving the coloured people in attendance an opportunity to shake hands with him. As soon as I met Mr. Cleveland I became impressed with his simplicity, greatness, and rugged honesty. I have met him many times since then, both at public functions and at his private residence in Princeton, and the more I see of him the more I admire him. When he visited the Negro Building in Atlanta he seemed to give himself up wholly, for that hour, to the coloured people. He seemed to be as careful to shake hands with some old coloured "auntie" clad partially in rags, and to take as much pleasure in doing so, as if he were greeting some millionnaire. Many of the coloured people took advantage of the occasion to get him to write his name in a book or on a slip of paper. He was as careful and patient in doing this as if he were putting his signature to some great state document.

Mr. Cleveland has not only shown his friendship for me in many personal ways, but has always consented to do anything I have asked of him for our school. This he has done, whether it was to make a personal donation or to use his influence in securing the donations of others. Judging from my personal acquaintance with Mr. Cleveland, I do not believe that he is conscious of possessing any colour prejudice. He is too great for that. In my contact with people I find that, as a rule, it is only the little, narrow people who live for themselves, who never read good books, who do not travel, who never open up their souls in a way to permit them to come into contact with other souls—with the great outside world. No man whose vision is bounded by colour can come into contact with what is highest and best in the world. In meeting men, in many places, I have found that the happiest people are those who do the most for others; the most miserable are those who do the least. I have also found that few things, if any, are capable of making one so blind and narrow as race prejudice. I often say to our students, in the course of my talks to them on Sunday evenings in the chapel, that the longer I live and the more experience I have of the world, the more I am convinced that, after all, the one thing that is most worth living for—and dying for, if need be—is the opportunity of making some one else more happy and more useful.

The coloured people and the coloured newspapers at first seemed to be greatly pleased with the character of my Atlanta address, as well as with its reception. But after the first burst of enthusiasm began to die away, and the coloured people began reading the speech in cold type, some of them seemed to feel that they had been hypnotized. They seemed to feel that I had been too liberal in my remarks toward the Southern whites, and that I had not spoken out strongly enough for what they termed the "rights" of the race. For a while there was a reaction, so far as a certain element of my own race was concerned, but later these reactionary ones seemed to have been won over to my way of believing and acting.

While speaking of changes in public sentiment, I recall that about ten years after the school at Tuskegee was established, I had an experience that I shall never forget. Dr. Lyman Abbott,[8] then the pastor of Plymouth Church, and also editor of the *Outlook* (then the *Christian Union*), asked me to write a letter for his paper giving my opinion of the exact condition, mental and moral, of the coloured ministers in the South, as based upon my observations. I wrote the letter, giving the exact facts as I conceived them to be. The picture painted was a rather black one—or, since I am black, shall I say "white"? It could not be otherwise with a race but a few years out of slavery, a race which had not had time or opportunity to produce a competent ministry.

What I said soon reached every Negro minister in the country, I think, and the letters of condemnation which I received from them were not few. I think that for a year after the publication of this article every association and every conference or religious body of any kind, of my race, that met, did not fail before adjourning to pass a resolution condemning me, or calling upon me to retract or modify what I had said. Many of these organizations went so far in their resolutions as to advise parents to cease sending their children to Tuskegee. One association even appointed a "missionary" whose duty it was to warn the people against sending their children to Tuskegee. This missionary had a son in the school, and I noticed that, whatever the "missionary" might have said or done with regard to others, he was careful not to take his son away from the institution. Many of the coloured papers, especially those that were the organs of religious bodies, joined in the general chorus of condemnation or demands for retraction.

During the whole time of the excitement, and through all the criticism, I did not utter a word of explanation or retraction. I knew that I was right, and that time and the sober second thought of the people would vindicate me. It was not long before the bishops and other church leaders began to make a careful investigation of the conditions of the ministry, and they found out that I was right. In fact, the oldest and most influential bishop in one branch of the Methodist Church said that my words were far too mild. Very soon public sentiment began making itself felt, in demanding a purifying of the ministry. While this is not yet complete by any means, I think I may say, without egotism, and I have been told by many of our most influential ministers, that my words had much to do with starting a demand for the placing of a higher type of men in the pulpit. I have had the satisfaction of having many who once condemned me thank me heartily for my frank words.

The change of the attitude of the Negro ministry, so far as regards myself, is so complete that at the present time I have no warmer friends among any class than I have among the clergymen. The improvement in the character and life of the Negro ministers is one of the most gratifying evidences of the progress of the race. My experience with them, as well as other events in my

8. American editor and writer (1835–1922) who was the minister of the Plymouth Congregational Church in Brooklyn, New York.

life, convince me that the thing to do, when one feels sure that he has said or done the right thing, and is condemned, is to stand still and keep quiet. If he is right, time will show it.

In the midst of the discussion which was going on concerning my Atlanta speech, I received the letter which I give below, from Dr. Gilman, the President of Johns Hopkins University, who had been made chairman of the judges of award in connection with the Atlanta Exposition:—

Johns Hopkins University, Baltimore,
President's Office, September 30, 1895.

DEAR MR. WASHINGTON:

Would it be agreeable to you to be one of the Judges of Award in the Department of Education at Atlanta? If so, I shall be glad to place your name upon the list. A line by telegraph will be welcomed.

Yours very truly,
D. C. GILMAN.

I think I was even more surprised to receive this invitation than I had been to receive the invitation to speak at the opening of the Exposition. It was to be a part of my duty, as one of the jurors, to pass not only upon the exhibits of the coloured schools, but also upon those of the white schools. I accepted the position, and spent a month in Atlanta in performance of the duties which it entailed. The board of jurors was a large one, consisting in all of sixty members. It was about equally divided between Southern white people and Northern white people. Among them were college presidents, leading scientists and men of letters, and specialists in many subjects. When the group of jurors to which I was assigned met for organization, Mr. Thomas Nelson Page,[9] who was one of the number, moved that I be made secretary of that division, and the motion was unanimously adopted. Nearly half of our division were Southern people. In performing my duties in the inspection of the exhibits of white schools I was in every case treated with respect, and at the close of our labours I parted from my associates with regret.

I am often asked to express myself more freely than I do upon the political condition and the political future of my race. These recollections of my experience in Atlanta give me the opportunity to do so briefly. My own belief is, although I have never before said so in so many words, that the time will come when the Negro in the South will be accorded all the political rights which his ability, character, and material possessions entitle him to. I think, though, that the opportunity to freely exercise such political rights will not come in any large degree through outside or artificial forcing, but will be accorded to the Negro by the Southern white people themselves, and that they will protect him in the exercise of those rights. Just as soon as the South gets over the old feeling that it is being forced by "foreigners," or "aliens," to do something which it does not want to do, I believe that the change in the direction that I have indicated is going to begin. In fact, there are indications that it is already beginning in a slight degree.

9. Popular Virginia author (1853–1922) who wrote *In Ole Virginia* (1887) and other southern romances.

Let me illustrate my meaning. Suppose that some months before the opening of the Atlanta Exposition there had been a general demand from the press and public platform outside the South that a Negro be given a place on the opening programme, and that a Negro be placed upon the board of jurors of award. Would any such recognition of the race have taken place? I do not think so. The Atlanta officials went as far as they did because they felt it to be a pleasure, as well as a duty, to reward what they considered merit in the Negro race. Say what we will, there is something in human nature which we cannot blot out, which makes one man, in the end, recognize and reward merit in another, regardless of colour or race.

I believe it is the duty of the Negro—as the greater part of the race is already doing—to deport himself modestly in regard to political claims, depending upon the slow but sure influences that proceed from the possession of property, intelligence, and high character for the full recognition of his political rights. I think that the according of the full exercise of political rights is going to be a matter of natural, slow growth, not an over-night, gourd-vine affair. I do not believe that the Negro should cease voting, for a man cannot learn the exercise of self-government by ceasing to vote, any more than a boy can learn to swim by keeping out of the water, but I do believe that in his voting he should more and more be influenced by those of intelligence and character who are his next-door neighbours.

I know coloured men who, through the encouragement, help, and advice of Southern white people, have accumulated thousands of dollars' worth of property, but who, at the same time, would never think of going to those same persons for advice concerning the casting of their ballots. This, it seems to me, is unwise and unreasonable, and should cease. In saying this I do not mean that the Negro should truckle, or not vote from principle, for the instant he ceases to vote from principle he loses the confidence and respect of the Southern white man even.

I do not believe that any state should make a law that permits an ignorant and poverty-stricken white man to vote, and prevents a black man in the same condition from voting. Such a law is not only unjust, but it will react, as all unjust laws do, in time; for the effect of such a law is to encourage the Negro to secure education and property, and at the same time it encourages the white man to remain in ignorance and poverty. I believe that in time, through the operation of intelligence and friendly race relations, all cheating at the ballot-box in the South will cease. It will become apparent that the white man who begins by cheating a Negro out of his ballot soon learns to cheat a white man out of his, and that the man who does this ends his career of dishonesty by the theft of property or by some equally serious crime. In my opinion, the time will come when the South will encourage all of its citizens to vote. It will see that it pays better, from every standpoint, to have healthy, vigorous life than to have that political stagnation which always results when one-half of the population has no share and no interest in the Government.

As a rule, I believe in universal, free suffrage, but I believe that in the South we are confronted with peculiar conditions that justify the protection of the ballot in many of the states, for a while at least, either by an educational test, a property test, or by both combined; but whatever tests are required, they should be made to apply with equal and exact justice to both races.

1901

CHARLES W. CHESNUTT
1858–1932

Charles W. Chesnutt was the first African American writer of fiction to enlist the white-controlled publishing industry in the service of his social message. From 1899 to 1905, during which time he published two collections of short stories and three novels, Chesnutt was the most influential and widely respected African American fiction writer in the United States, reaching a significant portion of the national reading audience with his probing analyses and compelling indictments of racism.

Born in Cleveland, Ohio, in 1858, the son of free Black émigrés from the South, Charles Waddell Chesnutt grew up in Fayetteville, North Carolina, during the turbulent Reconstruction era. An inquisitive, bookish boy, he attended school regularly at an institution founded by the Freedmen's Bureau. In his late teens he was appointed assistant principal of a school in Fayetteville for the training of Black teachers, which had been established by the North Carolina State Legislature. But his marriage in 1878 and his impatience with the restrictions of life in the South fueled his ambitions to find better opportunities elsewhere. Before his twenty-first birthday he had confided to his journal a plan to move to the North, where he would "strike for an entering wedge in the literary world." Confident that he could succeed, Chesnutt moved to New York City in 1883 and to Cleveland in 1884, where he settled his family, passed the Ohio State bar, and launched a successful business career as a legal stenographer.

In August 1887, the *Atlantic Monthly* printed Chesnutt's "The Goophered Grapevine," his first important work of fiction. Set in North Carolina and featuring a formerly enslaved raconteur adept at spinning wonderful tales about antebellum southern life, "The Goophered Grapevine" appeared to be part of the "plantation tradition" of contemporary southern literature, typified in the work of white writers such as Joel Chandler Harris and Thomas Nelson Page, who had made their fame writing nostalgic tales of the Old South in Negro dialect. But Chesnutt's story was singular in two respects. It presented the lore of "conjuration," African American hoodoo beliefs and practices, to a white reading public largely ignorant of Black folk culture. It also introduced a new kind of Black storytelling protagonist, Uncle Julius McAdoo, who shrewdly designs his recollections of the past to secure his economic advantage in the present, sometimes at the expense of his white employer.

In October 1889, a more penetrating and disturbing story by Chesnutt appeared in the *Atlantic*. Framed in the manner of "The Goophered Grapevine" but without the conjure motif, "Dave's Neckliss" revealed the new author probing the mind of McAdoo himself and the psyche of his friend in slavery, a preacher named Dave, whose downward spiral into delusion, madness, and suicide makes him one of the most pathetic of Chesnutt's tragic protagonists. Through Dave's fate, Chesnutt invited his white readers to consider the corrosive effects of stigmatizing on the otherwise healthy mind and body of a sympathetic Black man. "Dave's Neckliss" represents one of Chesnutt's earliest attempts in fiction to trace the effects of the ultimate stigma in America—dark skin—imposed on African Americans by a racist white culture. Dave's undeserved suffering and death demonstrate how damaging a prejudicially stigmatized identity could be to an individual or an entire people.

Chesnutt's first book, *The Conjure Woman*, a collection of "conjure stories" based on the model established in "The Goophered Grapevine," made its debut in March 1899, delighting reviewers with its peculiar blend of realism and fantasy. The most memorable stories in the collection, such as "The Goophered Grapevine" and

Charles W. Chesnutt (left) went from pupil to principal of the **Howard School** (right), now Fayetteville State University in Fayetteville, North Carolina.

"Po' Sandy," portray enslaved Black people under almost unbearable psychological pressures, which demanded of them tenacity of purpose, firmness of character, and imaginative ingenuity to preserve themselves, their families, and their communities. Appearing during a time when most whites questioned the African American's capacity for full and equal civil rights, the stories of *The Conjure Woman* implicitly argued that, having confirmed their human dignity and heroic fortitude in the face of the worst that slavery could do, African Americans were amply qualified for the rights and responsibilities of American citizenship.

Pleased with the critical reception of *The Conjure Woman*, its publisher, Houghton Mifflin, brought out a second collection of Chesnutt's short fiction in the fall of 1899. The majority of the stories in *The Wife of His Youth and Other Stories of the Color Line* explore the moral conflicts and psychological strains experienced by those who lived closest to the color line in Chesnutt's day, namely mixed-race persons like himself. The title story of the volume typifies its creator's sensitive depiction of the manners and mores of the African American urban elite in the post–Civil War North. "The Passing of Grandison," a clever burlesque of sentimental white southern images of master–slave relationships, evokes the antebellum South with a comic exuberance rare in Chesnutt's fiction. After reading *The Wife of His Youth*, some critics, like the noted white novelist William Dean Howells, praised Chesnutt as a literary realist of the first order. But other reviewers were put off by his inquiries into topics such as racial segregation and interracial marriage, which many whites, especially in the South, considered too delicate or volatile for fiction.

In the fall of 1899, Chesnutt closed his prosperous court-reporting business in Cleveland to pursue his lifelong dream—a career as a full-time author. In the next six years he published three novels of purpose, *The House behind the Cedars* (1900), *The Marrow of Tradition* (1901), and *The Colonel's Dream* (1905). Each surveyed racial problems in the postwar South and tested various social, economic, and political solutions. *The House behind the Cedars*, whose central character is an African American woman who attempts unsuccessfully to pass for white, was generally well received. *The Marrow of Tradition* was more socially and politically confrontational. In this roman à clef, Chesnutt engaged in a searching analysis of the causes and effects of the 1898 Wilmington, North Carolina, white supremacist coup d'état and racial massacre. Hoping to write the *Uncle Tom's Cabin* of his generation, Chesnutt made a forceful plea for social justice in the face of surging Jim

Crow laws that by 1900 had denied basic civil rights to Blacks across the South. *The Marrow of Tradition* was reviewed extensively throughout the country as a troubling but timely study of the contemporary South in the throes of racist reactionism. But Chesnutt was disillusioned by its sluggish sales. By the time he began writing *The Colonel's Dream,* he doubted whether his brand of realism could sell well enough to sustain his experimental literary career. Rather than subject himself and his family to a permanently diminished standard of living, Chesnutt reopened his court-reporting business. He continued writing and speaking on various social and political issues affecting African Americans in the early twentieth century. During the last twenty-five years of his life, he tried to interest publishers in several novels, but none saw print until more than a half century after Chesnutt's death.

Among African American readers admiration for his achievement never waned. In 1928 the National Association for the Advancement of Colored People awarded Chesnutt its Spingarn Medal for his "pioneer work as a literary artist depicting the life and struggles of Americans of Negro descent, and for his long and useful career as scholar, worker, and freeman of one of America's greatest cities." In his 1931 essay in literary autobiography, "Post-Bellum—Pre-Harlem," Chesnutt accepted the fact that writing fashions had passed him by. But he took pride in pointing out how far African American literature and the attitude of the white literary world toward it had come since the days when he first broke into print. Although he was too modest to do so, Chesnutt might have claimed an important role in preparing the American public for the advent of the New Negro author of the 1920s. These new modernist writers followed Chesnutt's precedent in unmasking the false poses and images of their era to refocus attention on more substantive racial issues facing their America.

Historians of African American writing today recognize Charles Chesnutt for almost singlehandedly inaugurating a truly African American literary tradition in the short story. He was the first writer to make the broad range of African American experience his artistic province and to consider practically every issue and problem endemic to the American color line worthy of literary attention. He developed a mode of realism that enabled him to satirize as well as sympathize with upwardly mobile African Americans like himself. Chesnutt left to his successors a rich formal legacy that underlies major trends in Black fiction, from the ironies of James Weldon Johnson's classic fiction of manners to the magical realism of neo-slave narratives of the late twentieth and early twenty-first centuries.

The Goophered Grapevine

Some years ago my wife was in poor health, and our family doctor, in whose skill and honesty I had implicit confidence, advised a change of climate. I shared, from an unprofessional standpoint, his opinion that the raw winds, the chill rains, and the violent changes of temperature that characterized the winters in the region of the Great Lakes tended to aggravate my wife's difficulty, and would undoubtedly shorten her life if she remained exposed to them. The doctor's advice was that we seek, not a temporary place of sojourn, but a permanent residence, in a warmer and more equable climate. I was engaged at the time in grape-culture in northern Ohio, and, as I liked the business and had given it much study, I decided to look for some other locality suitable for carrying it on. I thought of sunny France, of sleepy Spain, of Southern California, but there were objections to them all. It occurred to me that I might find what I wanted in some one of our own Southern States. It was a sufficient time after the war for conditions in the South to have become somewhat settled; and I was enough of a pioneer to start a new industry, if I could not find a place where grape-culture had been tried. I wrote to a cousin who had gone into the turpentine business in central North Carolina. He assured me, in response to my inquiries, that no better place could be found in the South than the State and neighborhood where he lived; the climate was perfect for health, and, in conjunction with the soil, ideal for grape-culture; labor was cheap, and land could be bought for a mere song. He gave us a cordial invitation to come and visit him while we looked into the matter. We accepted the invitation, and after several days of leisurely travel, the last hundred miles of which were up a river on a side-wheel steamer, we reached our destination, a quaint old town, which I shall call Patesville, because, for one reason, that is not its name. There was a red brick market-house in the public square, with a tall tower, which held a four-faced clock that struck the hours, and from which there pealed out a curfew at nine o'clock. There were two or three hotels, a court-house, a jail, stores, offices, and all the appurtenances of a county seat and a commercial emporium; for while Patesville numbered only four or five thousand inhabitants, of all shades of complexion, it was one of the principal towns in North Carolina, and had a considerable trade in cotton and naval stores. This business activity was not immediately apparent to my unaccustomed eyes. Indeed, when I first saw the town, there brooded over it a calm that seemed almost sabbatic in its restfulness, though I learned later on that underneath its somnolent exterior the deeper currents of life—love and hatred, joy and despair, ambition and avarice, faith and friendship—flowed not less steadily than in livelier latitudes.

We found the weather delightful at that season, the end of summer, and were hospitably entertained. Our host was a man of means and evidently regarded our visit as a pleasure, and we were therefore correspondingly at our ease, and in a position to act with the coolness of judgment desirable in making so radical a change in our lives. My cousin placed a horse and buggy at our disposal, and himself acted as our guide until I became somewhat familiar with the country.

I found that grape-culture, while it had never been carried on to any great extent, was not entirely unknown in the neighborhood. Several planters thereabouts had attempted it on a commercial scale, in former years, with greater or less success; but like most Southern industries, it had felt the blight of war and had fallen into desuetude.[1]

I went several times to look at a place that I thought might suit me. It was a plantation of considerable extent, that had formerly belonged to a wealthy man by the name of McAdoo. The estate had been for years involved in litigation between disputing heirs, during which period shiftless cultivation had well-nigh exhausted the soil. There had been a vineyard of some extent on the place, but it had not been attended to since the war, and had lapsed into utter neglect. The vines—here partly supported by decayed and broken-down trellises, there twining themselves among the branches of the slender saplings which had sprung up among them—grew in wild and unpruned luxuriance, and the few scattered grapes they bore were the undisputed prey of the first comer. The site was admirably adapted to grape-raising; the soil, with a little attention, could not have been better; and with the native grape, the luscious scuppernong, as my main reliance in the beginning, I felt sure that I could introduce and cultivate successfully a number of other varieties.

1. Disuse.

One day I went over with my wife to show her the place. We drove out of the town over a long wooden bridge that spanned a spreading mill-pond, passed the long whitewashed fence surrounding the county fair-ground, and struck into a road so sandy that the horse's feet sank to the fetlocks.[2] Our route lay partly up hill and partly down, for we were in the sand-hill county; we drove past cultivated farms, and then by abandoned fields grown up in scrub-oak and short-leaved pine, and once or twice through the solemn aisles of the virgin forest, where the tall pines, well-nigh meeting over the narrow road, shut out the sun, and wrapped us in cloistral solitude. Once, at a cross-roads, I was in doubt as to the turn to take, and we sat there waiting ten minutes—we had already caught some of the native infection of restfulness—for some human being to come along, who could direct us on our way. At length a little negro girl appeared, walking straight as an arrow, with a piggin[3] full of water on her head. After a little patient investigation, necessary to overcome the child's shyness, we learned what we wished to know, and at the end of about five miles from the town reached our destination.

We drove between a pair of decayed gateposts—the gate itself had long since disappeared—and up a straight sandy lane, between two lines of rotting rail fence, partly concealed by jimsonweeds and briers, to the open space where a dwelling-house had once stood, evidently a spacious mansion, if we might judge from the ruined chimneys that were still standing, and the brick pillars on which the sills rested. The house itself, we had been informed, had fallen a victim to the fortunes of war.

We alighted from the buggy, walked about the yard for a while, and then wandered off into the adjoining vineyard. Upon Annie's complaining of weariness I led the way back to the yard, where a pine log, lying under a spreading elm, afforded a shady though somewhat hard seat. One end of the log was already occupied by a venerable-looking colored man. He held on his knees a hat full of grapes, over which he was smacking his lips with great gusto, and a pile of grapeskins near him indicated that the performance was no new thing. We approached him at an angle from the rear, and were close to him before he perceived us. He respectfully rose as we drew near, and was moving away, when I begged him to keep his seat.

"Don't let us disturb you," I said. "There is plenty of room for us all."

He resumed his seat with somewhat of embarrassment. While he had been standing, I had observed that he was a tall man, and, though slightly bowed by the weight of years, apparently quite vigorous. He was not entirely black, and this fact, together with the quality of his hair, which was about six inches long and very bushy, except on the top of his head, where he was quite bald, suggested a slight strain of other than negro blood. There was a shrewdness in his eyes, too, which was not altogether African, and which, as we afterwards learned from experience, was indicative of a corresponding shrewdness in his character. He went on eating the grapes, but did not seem to enjoy himself quite so well as he had apparently done before he became aware of our presence.

"Do you live around here?" I asked, anxious to put him at his ease.

"Yas, suh. I lives des ober yander, behine de nex' san'-hill, on de Lumberton plank-road."

2. Hair on the back of a horse's leg above the hoof.

3. A small wooden pail or tub.

"Do you know anything about the time when this vineyard was cultivated?"

"Lawd bless you, suh, I knows all about it. Dey ain' na'er a man in dis settlement w'at won' tell you ole Julius McAdoo 'uz bawn en raise' on dis yer same plantation. Is you de Norv'n gemman w'at's gwine ter buy de ole vimya'd?"

"I am looking at it," I replied; "but I don't know that I shall care to buy unless I can be reasonably sure of making something out of it."

"Well, suh, you is a stranger ter me, en I is a stranger ter you, en we is bofe strangers ter one anudder, but 'f I 'uz in yo' place, I would n' buy dis vimya'd."

"Why not?" I asked.

"Well, I dunno whe'r you b'lieves in cunj'in' er not,—some er de w'ite folks don't, er says dey don't,—but de truf er de matter is dat dis yer ole vimya'd is goophered."

"Is what?" I asked, not grasping the meaning of this unfamiliar word.

"Is goophered,—cunju'd, bewitch'."

He imparted this information with such solemn earnestness, and with such an air of confidential mystery, that I felt somewhat interested, while Annie was evidently much impressed, and drew closer to me.

"How do you know it is bewitched?" I asked.

"I would n' spec' fer you ter b'lieve me 'less you know all 'bout de fac's. But ef you en young miss dere doan' min' lis'nin' ter a ole nigger run on a minute er two w'ile you er restin', I kin 'splain to you how it all happen'."

We assured him that we would be glad to hear how it all happened, and he began to tell us. At first the current of his memory—or imagination—seemed somewhat sluggish; but as his embarrassment wore off, his language flowed more freely, and the story acquired perspective and coherence. As he became more and more absorbed in the narrative, his eyes assumed a dreamy expression, and he seemed to lose sight of his auditors, and to be living over again in monologue his life on the old plantation.

"Ole Mars Dugal' McAdoo," he began, "bought dis place long many years befo' de wah, en I 'member well w'en he sot out all dis yer part er de plantation in scuppernon's. De vimes growed monst'us fas', en Mars Dugal' made a thousan' gallon er scuppernon' wine eve'y year.

"Now, ef dey's an'thing a nigger lub, nex' ter 'possum, en chick'n, en water-millyums, it's scuppernon's. Dey ain' nuffin dat kin stan' up side'n de scuppernon' fer sweetness; sugar ain't a suckumstance ter scuppernon'. W'en de season is nigh 'bout ober, en de grapes begin ter swivel up des a little wid de wrinkles er ole age,—w'en de skin git sof' en brown,—den de scuppernon' make you smack yo' lip en roll yo' eye en wush fer mo'; so I reckon it ain' very 'stonishin' dat niggers lub scuppernon'.

"Dey wuz a sight er niggers in de naberhood er de vimya'd. Dere wuz ole Mars Henry Brayboy's niggers, en ole Mars Jeems McLean's niggers, en Mars Dugal's own niggers; den dey wuz a settlement er free niggers en po' buckrahs[4] down by de Wim'l'ton Road, en Mars Dugal' had de only vimya'd in de naberhood. I reckon it ain' so much so nowadays, but befo' de wah, in slab'ry times, a nigger did n' mine goin' fi' er ten mile in a night, w'en dey wuz sump'n good ter eat at de yuther een'.

"So atter a w'ile Mars Dugal' begin ter miss his scuppernon's. Co'se he 'cuse' de niggers er it, but dey all 'nied it ter de las'. Mars Dugal' sot spring

4. White men (regionalism).

guns en steel traps, en he en de oberseah sot up nights once't er twice't, tel one night Mars Dugal'—he 'uz a monst'us keerless man—got his leg shot full er cow-peas. But somehow er nudder dey could n' nebber ketch none er de niggers. I dunner how it happen, but it happen des like I tell you, en de grapes kep' on a-goin' des de same.

"But bimeby ole Mars Dugal' fix' up a plan ter stop it. Dey wuz a cunjuh 'oman livin' down 'mongs' de free niggers on de Wim'l'ton Road, en all de darkies fum Rockfish ter Beaver Crick wuz feared er her. She could wuk de mos' powerfulles' kin' er goopher,—could make people hab fits, er rheumatiz, er make 'em des dwinel away en die; en dey say she went out ridin' de niggers at night, fer she wuz a witch 'sides bein' a cunjuh 'oman. Mars Dugal' hearn 'bout Aun' Peggy's doin's, en begun ter 'flect whe'r er no he could n' git her ter he'p him keep de niggers off'n de grapevimes. One day in de spring er de year, ole miss pack' up a basket er chick'n en poun'-cake, en a bottle er scuppernon' wine, en Mars Dugal' tuk it in his buggy en driv ober ter Aun' Peggy's cabin. He tuk de basket in, en had a long talk wid Aun' Peggy.

"De nex' day Aun' Peggy come up ter de vimya'd. De niggers seed her slippin' 'roun', en dey soon foun' out what she 'uz doin' dere. Mars Dugal' had hi'ed her ter goopher de grapevimes. She sa'ntered 'roun' 'mongs' de vimes, en tuk a leaf fum dis one, en a grape-hull fum dat one, en a grape-seed fum anudder one; en den a little twig fum here, en a little pinch er dirt fum dere,—en put it all in a big black bottle, wid a snake's toof en a speckle' hen's gall en some ha'rs fum a black cat's tail, en den fill' de bottle wid scuppernon' wine. W'en she got de goopher all ready en fix', she tuk 'n went out in de woods en buried it under de root uv a red oak tree, en den come back en tole one er de niggers she done goopher de grapevines, en a'er a nigger w'at eat dem grapes 'ud be sho ter die inside'n twel' mont's.

"Atter dat de niggers let de scuppernon's 'lone, en Mars Dugal' did n' hab no 'casion ter fine no mo' fault; en de season wuz mos' gone, w'en a strange gemman stop at de plantation one night ter see Mars Dugal' on some business; en his coachman, seein' de scuppernon's growin' so nice en sweet, slip 'roun' behine de smoke-house, en et all de scuppernon's he could hole. Nobody did n' notice it at de time, but dat night, on de way home, de gemman's hoss runned away en kill' de coachman. Wen we hearn de noos, Aun' Lucy, de cook, she up 'n say she seed de strange nigger eat'n' er de scuppernon's behine de smokehouse; en den we knowed de goopher had b'en er wukkin'. Den one er de nigger chilluns runned away fum de quarters one day, en got in de scuppernon's, en died de nex' week. W'ite folks say he die' er de fevuh, but de niggers knowed it wuz de goopher. So you k'n be sho de darkies did n' hab much ter do wid dem scuppernon' vimes.

"W'en de scuppernon' season 'uz ober fer dat year, Mars Dugal' foun' he had made fifteen hund'ed gallon er wine; en one er de niggers hearn him laffin' wid de oberseah fit ter kill, en sayin' dem fifteen hund'ed gallon er wine wuz monst'us good intrus' on de ten dollars he laid out on de vimya'd. So I 'low ez he paid Aun' Peggy ten dollars fer to goopher de grapevimes.

"De goopher did n' wuk no mo' tel de nex' summer, w'en 'long to'ds de middle er de season one er de fiel' han's died; en ez dat lef' Mars Dugal' sho't er han's, he went off ter town fer ter buy anudder. He fotch de noo nigger home wid 'im. He wuz er ole nigger, er de color er a gingy-cake, en ball ez a hoss-apple on de top er his head. He wuz a peart ole nigger, do', en could do a big day's wuk.

"Now it happen dat one er de niggers on de nex' plantation, one er ole Mars Henry Brayboy's niggers, had runned away de day befo', en tuk ter de swamp, en ole Mars Dugal' en some er de yuther nabor w'ite folks had gone out wid dere guns en dere dogs fer ter he'p 'em hunt fer de nigger; en de han's on our own plantation wuz all so flusterated dat we fuhgot ter tell de noo han' 'bout de goopher on de scuppernon' vimes. Co'se he smell de grapes en see de vimes, an atter dahk de fus' thing he done wuz ter slip off ter de grapevimes 'dout sayin' nuffin ter nobody. Nex' mawnin' he tole some er de niggers 'bout de fine bait er scuppernon' he et de night befo'.

"W'en dey tole 'im 'bout de goopher on de grapevimes, he 'uz dat tarrified dat he turn pale, en look des like he gwine ter die right in his tracks. De oberseah come up en axed w'at 'uz de matter; en w'en dey tole 'im Henry be'n eatin' er de scuppernon's, en got de goopher on 'im, he gin Henry a big drink er w'iskey, en 'low dat de nex' rainy day he take 'im ober ter Aun' Peggy's, en see ef she would n' take de goopher off'n him, seein' ez he did n' know nuffin erbout it tel he done et de grapes.

"Sho nuff, it rain de nex' day, en de oberseah went ober ter Aun' Peggy's wid Henry. En Aun' Peggy say dat bein' ez Henry did n' know 'bout de goopher, en et de grapes in ign'ance er de conseq'ences, she reckon she mought be able fer ter take de goopher off'n him. So she fotch out er bottle wid some cunjuh medicine in it, en po'd some out in a go'd fer Henry ter drink. He manage ter git it down; he say it tas'e like whiskey wid sump'n bitter in it. She 'lowed dat 'ud keep de goopher off'n him tel de spring; but w'en de sap begin ter rise in de grapevimes he ha' ter come en see her ag'in, en she tell him w'at e's ter do.

"Nex' spring, w'en de sap commence' ter rise in de scuppernon' vime, Henry tuk a ham one night. Whar'd he git de ham? *I* doan know; dey wa'n't no hams on de plantation 'cep'n' w'at 'uz in de smoke-house, but *I* never see Henry 'bout de smoke-house. But ez I wuz a-sayin', he tuk de ham ober ter Aun' Peggy's; en Aun' Peggy tole 'im dat w'en Mars Dugal' begin ter prune de grapevimes, he mus' go en take 'n scrape off de sap whar it ooze out'n de cut een's er de vimes, en 'n'int his ball head wid it; en ef he do dat once't a year de goopher would n' wuk agin 'im long ez he done it. En bein' ez he fotch her de ham, she fix' it so he kin eat all de scuppernon' he want.

"So Henry 'n'int his head wid de sap out'n de big grapevime des ha'f way 'twix' de quarters en de big house, en de goopher nebber wuk agin him dat summer. But de beatenes' thing you eber see happen ter Henry. Up ter dat time he wuz ez ball ez a sweeten' 'tater, but des ez soon ez de young leaves begun ter come out on de grapevimes, de ha'r begun ter grow out on Henry's head, en by de middle er de summer he had de bigges' head er ha'r on de plantation. Befo' dat, Henry had tol'able good ha'r 'roun' de aidges, but soon ez de young grapes begun ter come, Henry's ha'r begun to quirl all up in little balls, des like dis yer reg'lar grapy ha'r, en by de time de grapes got ripe his head look des like a bunch er grapes. Combin' it did n' do no good; he wuk at it ha'f de night wid er Jim Crow,[5] en think he git it straighten' out, but in de mawnin' de grapes 'ud be dere des de same. So he gin it up, en tried ter keep de grapes down by havin' his ha'r cut sho't.

5. A small card, resembling a currycomb in construction, and used by negroes in the rural districts instead of a comb [*Chesnutt's note*].

"But dat wa'n't de quares' thing 'bout de goopher. When Henry come ter de plantation, he wuz gittin' a little ole an stiff in de j'ints. But dat summer he got des ez spry en libely ez any young nigger on de plantation; fac', he got so biggity dat Mars Jackson, de oberseah, ha' ter th'eaten ter whip 'im, ef he did n' stop cuttin' up his didos en behave hisse'f. But de mos' cur'ouses' thing happen' in de fall, when de sap begin ter go down in de grapevimes. Fus', when de grapes 'uz gethered, de knots begun ter straighten out'n Henry's ha'r; en w'en de leaves begin ter fall, Henry's ha'r 'mence' ter drap out; en when de vimes 'uz bar', Henry's head wuz baller'n it wuz in de spring, en he begin ter git ole en stiff in de j'ints ag'in, en paid no mo' 'tention ter de gals dyoin' er de whole winter. En nex' spring, w'en he rub de sap on ag'in, he got young ag'in, en so soopl en libely dat none er de young niggers on de plantation could n' jump, ner dance, ner hoe ez much cotton ez Henry. But in de fall er de year his grapes 'mence' ter straighten out, en his j'ints ter git stiff, en his ha'r drap off, en de rheumatiz begin ter wrastle wid 'im.

"Now, ef you'd 'a' knowed ole Mars Dugal' McAdoo, you'd 'a' knowed dat it ha' ter be a mighty rainy day when he could n' fine sump'n fer his niggers ter do, en it ha' ter be a mighty little hole he could n' crawl thoo, en ha' ter be a monst'us cloudy night when a dollar git by him in de dahkness; en w'en he see how Henry git young in de spring en ole in de fall, he 'lowed ter hisse'f ez how he could make mo' money out'n Henry dan by wukkin' him in de cotton-fiel'. 'Long de nex' spring, atter de sap 'mence' ter rise, en Henry 'n'int 'is head en sta'ted fer ter git young en soopl, Mars Dugal' up 'n tuk Henry ter town, en sole 'im fer fifteen hunder' dollars. Co'se de man w'at bought Henry did n' know nuffin 'bout de goopher, en Mars Dugal' did n' see no 'casion fer ter tell 'im. Long to'ds de fall, w'en de sap went down, Henry begin ter git ole ag'in same ez yuzhal, en his noo marster begin ter git skeered les'n he gwine ter lose his fifteen-hunder'-dollar nigger. He sent fer a mighty fine doctor, but de med'cine did n' 'pear ter do no good; de goopher had a good holt. Henry tole de doctor 'bout de goopher, but de doctor des laff at 'im.

"One day in de winter Mars Dugal' went ter town, en wuz santerin' 'long de Main Street, when who should he meet but Henry's noo marster. Dey said 'Hoddy,' en Mars Dugal' ax 'im ter hab a seegyar; en atter dey run on awhile 'bout de craps en de weather, Mars Dugal' ax 'im, sorter keerless, like ez ef he des thought of it,—

"'How you like de nigger I sole you las' spring?'

"Henry's marster shuck his head en knock de ashes off'n his seegyar.

"'Spec' I made a bad bahgin when I bought dat nigger. Henry done good wuk all de summer, but sence de fall set in he 'pears ter be sorter pinin' away. Dey ain' nuffin pertickler de matter wid 'im—leastways de doctor say so—'cep'n' a tech er de rheumatiz; but his ha'r is all fell out, en ef he don't pick up his strenk mighty soon, I spec' I'm gwine ter lose 'im.'

"Dey smoked on awhile, en bimeby ole mars say, 'Well, a bahgin's a bahgin, but you en me is good fren's, en I doan wan' ter see you lose all de money you paid fer dat nigger; en ef w'at you say is so, en I ain't 'sputin' it, he ain't wuf much now. I 'spec's you wukked him too ha'd dis summer, er e'se de swamps down here don't agree wid de san'-hill nigger. So you des lemme know, en ef he gits any wusser I'll be willin' ter gib yer five hund'ed dollars fer 'im, en take my chances on his livin'.'

"Sho 'nuff, when Henry begun ter draw up wid de rheumatiz en it look like he gwine ter die fer sho, his noo marster sen' fer Mars Dugal', en Mars Dugal' gin him what he promus, en brung Henry home ag'in. He tuk good keer uv 'im dyoin' er de winter,—give 'im w'iskey ter rub his rheumatiz, en terbacker ter smoke, en all he want ter eat,—'caze a nigger w'at he could make a thousan' dollars a year off'n did n' grow on eve'y huckleberry bush.

"Nex' spring, w'en de sap ris en Henry's ha'r commence' ter sprout, Mars Dugal' sole 'im ag'in, down in Robeson County dis time; en he kep' dat sellin' business up fer five year er mo'. Henry nebber say nuffin 'bout de goopher ter his noo marsters, 'caze he know he gwine ter be tuk good keer uv de nex' winter, w'en Mars Dugal' buy him back. En Mars Dugal' made 'nuff money off'n Henry ter buy anudder plantation ober on Beaver Crick.

"But 'long 'bout de een' er dat five year dey come a stranger ter stop at de plantation. De fus' day he 'uz dere he went out wid Mars Dugal' en spent all de mawnin' lookin' ober de vimya'd, en atter dinner dey spent all de evenin' playin' kya'ds. De niggers soon 'skiver' dat he wuz a Yankee, en dat he come down ter Norf C'lina fer ter l'arn de w'ite folks how to raise grapes en make wine. He promus Mars Dugal' he c'd make de grapevimes b'ar twice't ez many grapes, en dat de noo winepress he wuz a-sellin' would make mo' d'n twice't ez many gallons er wine. En ole Mars Dugal' des drunk it all in, des 'peared ter be bewitch' wid dat Yankee. W'en de darkies see dat Yankee runnin' 'roun' de vimya'd en diggin' under de grapevimes, dey shuk dere heads, en 'lowed dat dey feared Mars Dugal' losin' his min'. Mars Dugal' had all de dirt dug away fum under de roots er all de scuppernon' vimes, an' let 'em stan' dat away fer a week er mo'. Den dat Yankee made de niggers fix up a mixtry er lime en ashes en manyo,[6] en po' it 'roun' de roots er de grapevimes. Den he 'vise Mars Dugal' fer ter trim de vimes close't, en Mars Dugal' tuck 'n done eve'ything de Yankee tole him ter do. Dyoin' all er dis time, mind yer, dis yer Yankee wuz libbin' off'n de fat er de lan', at de big house, en playin' kya'ds wid Mars Dugal' eve'y night; en dey say Mars Dugal' los' mo'n a thousan' dollars dyoin' er de week dat Yankee wuz a-ruinin' de grapevimes.

"W'en de sap ris nex' spring, ole Henry 'n'inted his head ez yuzhal, en his ha'r 'mence' ter grow des de same ez it done eve'y year. De scuppernon' vimes growed monst's fas', en de leaves wuz greener en thicker dan dey eber be'n dyoin' my rememb'ance; en Henry's ha'r growed out thicker dan eber, en he 'peared ter git younger 'n younger, en soopler 'n soopler; en seein' ez he wuz sho't er han's dat spring, havin' tuk in consid'able noo groun', Mars Dugal' 'cluded he would n' sell Henry 'tel he git de crap in en de cotton chop'. So he kep' Henry on de plantation.

"But 'long 'bout time fer de grapes ter come on de scuppernon' vimes, dey 'peared ter come a change ober 'em; de leaves withered en swivel' up, en de young grapes turn' yaller, en bimeby eve'ybody on de plantation could see dat de whole vimya'd wuz dyin'. Mars Dugal' tuk'n water de vimes en done all he could, but't wa'n' no use: dat Yankee had done bus' de watermillyum. One time de vimes picked up a bit, en Mars Dugal' 'lowed

6. Manure.

dey wuz gwine ter come out ag'in; but dat Yankee done dug too close under de roots, en prune de branches too close ter de vime, en all dat lime en ashes done burn' de life out'n de vimes, en dey des kep' a-with'in' en a-swivelin'.

"All dis time de goopher wuz a-wukkin'. When de vimes sta'ted ter wither, Henry 'mence' ter complain er his rheumatiz; en when de leaves begin ter dry up, his ha'r 'mence' ter drap out. When de vimes fresh' up a bit, Henry 'd git peart ag'in, en when de vimes wither' ag'in, Henry 'd git ole ag'in, en des kep' gittin' mo' en mo' fitten fer nuffin; he des pined away, en pined away, en fine'ly tuk ter his cabin; en when de big vime whar he got de sap ter 'n'int his head withered en turned yaller en died, Henry died too,—des went out sorter like a cannel. Dey did n't 'pear ter be nuffin de matter wid 'im, 'cep'n' de rheumatiz, but his strenk des dwinel' away 'tel he did n' hab ernuff lef' ter draw his bref. De goopher had got de under holt, en th'owed Henry dat time fer good en all.

"Mars Dugal' tuk on might'ly 'bout losin' his vimes en his nigger in de same year; en he swo' dat ef he could git holt er dat Yankee he'd wear 'im ter a frazzle, en den chaw up de frazzle; en he'd done it, too, for Mars Dugal' 'uz a monst'us brash man w'en he once git started. He sot de vimya'd out ober ag'in, but it wuz th'ee er fo' year befo' de vimes got ter b'arin' any scuppernon's.

"W'en de wah broke out, Mars Dugal' raise' a comp'ny, en went off ter fight de Yankees. He say he wuz mighty glad dat wah come, en he des want ter kill a Yankee fer eve'y dollar he los' 'long er dat grape-raisin' Yankee. En I 'spec' he would 'a' done it, too, ef de Yankees had n' s'picioned sump'n, en killed him fus'. Atter de s'render ole miss move' ter town, de niggers all scattered 'way fum de plantation, en de vimya'd ain' be'n cultervated sence."

"Is that story true?" asked Annie doubtfully, but seriously, as the old man concluded his narrative.

"It's des ez true ez I 'm a-settin' here, miss. Dey's a easy way ter prove it: I kin lead de way right ter Henry's grave ober yander in de plantation buryin'-groun'. En I tell yer w'at, marster, I would n' 'vise you to buy dis yer ole vimya'd, 'caze de goopher's on it yit, en dey ain' no tellin' w'en it's gwine ter crap out."

"But I thought you said all the old vines died."

"Dey did 'pear ter die, but a few un 'em come out ag'in, en is mixed in 'mongs' de yuthers. I ain' skeered ter eat de grapes, 'caze I knows de old vimes fum de noo ones; but wid strangers dey ain' no tellin' w'at mought happen. I would n' 'vise yer ter buy dis vimya'd."

I bought the vineyard, nevertheless, and it has been for a long time in a thriving condition, and is often referred to by the local press as a striking illustration of the opportunities open to Northern capital in the development of Southern industries. The luscious scuppernong holds first rank among our grapes, though we cultivate a great many other varieties, and our income from grapes packed and shipped to the Northern markets is quite considerable. I have not noticed any developments of the goopher in the vineyard, although I have a mild suspicion that our colored assistants do not suffer from want of grapes during the season.

I found, when I bought the vineyard, that Uncle Julius had occupied a cabin on the place for many years, and derived a respectable revenue from the product of the neglected grapevines. This, doubtless, accounted for his advice to me not to buy the vineyard, though whether it inspired the goopher story I am unable to state. I believe, however, that the wages I paid him for his services as coachman, for I gave him employment in that capacity, were more than an equivalent for anything he lost by the sale of the vineyard.

1899

The Passing of Grandison

I

When it is said that it was done to please a woman, there ought perhaps to be enough said to explain anything; for what a man will not do to please a woman is yet to be discovered. Nevertheless, it might be well to state a few preliminary facts to make it clear why young Dick Owens tried to run one of his father's negro men off to Canada.

In the early fifties, when the growth of anti-slavery sentiment and the constant drain of fugitive slaves into the North had so alarmed the slaveholders of the border States as to lead to the passage of the Fugitive Slave Law,[1] a young white man from Ohio, moved by compassion for the sufferings of a certain bondman who happened to have a "hard master," essayed to help the slave to freedom. The attempt was discovered and frustrated; the abductor was tried and convicted for slave-stealing, and sentenced to a term of imprisonment in the penitentiary. His death, after the expiration of only a small part of the sentence, from cholera contracted while nursing stricken fellow prisoners, lent to the case a melancholy interest that made it famous in anti-slavery annals.

Dick Owens had attended the trial. He was a youth of about twenty-two, intelligent, handsome, and amiable, but extremely indolent, in a graceful and gentlemanly way; or, as old Judge Fenderson put it more than once, he was lazy as the Devil,—a mere figure of speech, of course, and not one that did justice to the Enemy of Mankind. When asked why he never did anything serious, Dick would good-naturedly reply, with a well-modulated drawl, that he didn't have to. His father was rich; there was but one other child, an unmarried daughter, who because of poor health would probably never marry, and Dick was therefore heir presumptive to a large estate. Wealth or social position he did not need to seek, for he was born to both. Charity Lomax had shamed him into studying law, but notwithstanding an hour or so a day spent at old Judge Fenderson's office, he did not make remarkable headway in his legal studies.

"What Dick needs," said the judge, who was fond of tropes,[2] as became a scholar, and of horses, as was befitting a Kentuckian, "is the whip of necessity, or the spur of ambition. If he had either, he would soon need the snaffle[3] to hold him back."

But all Dick required, in fact, to prompt him to the most remarkable thing he accomplished before he was twenty-five, was a mere suggestion from

1. This law made a federal crime any action that aided a runaway enslaved person and was the most controversial feature of the Compromise of 1850.

2. Figures of speech.

3. The bit of a bridle.

Charity Lomax. The story was never really known to but two persons until after the war, when it came out because it was a good story and there was no particular reason for its concealment.

Young Owens had attended the trial of this slave-stealer, or martyr,—either or both,—and, when it was over, had gone to call on Charity Lomax, and, while they sat on the veranda after sundown, had told her all about the trial. He was a good talker, as his career in later years disclosed, and described the proceedings very graphically.

"I confess," he admitted, "that while my principles were against the prisoner, my sympathies were on his side. It appeared that he was of good family, and that he had an old father and mother, respectable people, dependent upon him for support and comfort in their declining years. He had been led into the matter by pity for a negro whose master ought to have been run out of the county long ago for abusing his slaves. If it had been merely a question of old Sam Briggs's negro, nobody would have cared anything about it. But father and the rest of them stood on the principle of the thing, and told the judge so, and the fellow was sentenced to three years in the penitentiary."

Miss Lomax had listened with lively interest.

"I've always hated old Sam Briggs," she said emphatically, "ever since the time he broke a negro's leg with a piece of cordwood. When I hear of a cruel deed it makes the Quaker blood that came from my grandmother assert itself. Personally I wish that all Sam Briggs's negroes would run away. As for the young man, I regard him as a hero. He dared something for humanity. I could love a man who would take such chances for the sake of others."

"Could you love me, Charity, if I did something heroic?"

"You never will, Dick. You're too lazy for any use. You'll never do anything harder than playing cards or fox-hunting."

"Oh, come now, sweetheart! I've been courting you for a year, and it's the hardest work imaginable. Are you never going to love me?" he pleaded.

His hand sought hers, but she drew it back beyond his reach.

"I'll never love you, Dick Owens, until you have done something. When that time comes, I'll think about it."

"But it takes so long to do anything worth mentioning, and I don't want to wait. One must read two years to become a lawyer, and work five more to make a reputation. We shall both be gray by then."

"Oh, I don't know," she rejoined. "It doesn't require a lifetime for a man to prove that he is a man. This one did something, or at least tried to."

"Well, I'm willing to attempt as much as any other man. What do you want me to do, sweetheart? Give me a test."

"Oh, dear me!" said Charity, "I don't care what you *do*, so you do *something*. Really, come to think of it, why should I care whether you do anything or not?"

"I'm sure I don't know why you should, Charity," rejoined Dick humbly, "for I'm aware that I'm not worthy of it."

"Except that I do hate," she added, relenting slightly, "to see a really clever man so utterly lazy and good for nothing."

"Thank you, my dear; a word of praise from you has sharpened my wits already. I have an idea! Will you love me if *I* run a negro off to Canada?"

"What nonsense!" said Charity scornfully. "You must be losing your wits. Steal another man's slave, indeed, while your father owns a hundred!"

"Oh, there'll be no trouble about that," responded Dick lightly; "I'll run off one of the old man's; we've got too many anyway. It may not be quite as difficult as the other man found it, but it will be just as unlawful, and will demonstrate what I am capable of."

"Seeing's believing," replied Charity. "Of course, what you are talking about now is merely absurd. I'm going away for three weeks, to visit my aunt in Tennessee. If you're able to tell me, when I return, that you've done something to prove your quality, I'll—well, you may come and tell me about it."

II

Young Owens got up about nine o'clock next morning, and while making his toilet put some questions to his personal attendant, a rather bright looking young mulatto of about his own age.

"Tom," said Dick.

"Yas, Mars Dick," responded the servant.

"I'm going on a trip North. Would you like to go with me?"

Now, if there was anything that Tom would have liked to make, it was a trip North. It was something he had long contemplated in the abstract, but had never been able to muster up sufficient courage to attempt in the concrete. He was prudent enough, however, to dissemble his feelings.

"I wouldn't min' it, Mars Dick, ez long ez you'd take keer er me an' fetch me home all right."

Tom's eyes belied his words, however, and his young master felt well assured that Tom needed only a good opportunity to make him run away. Having a comfortable home, and a dismal prospect in case of failure, Tom was not likely to take any desperate chances; but young Owens was satisfied that in a free State but little persuasion would be required to lead Tom astray. With a very logical and characteristic desire to gain his end with the least necessary expenditure of effort, he decided to take Tom with him, if his father did not object.

Colonel Owens had left the house when Dick went to breakfast, so Dick did not see his father till luncheon.

"Father," he remarked casually to the colonel, over the fried chicken, "I'm feeling a trifle run down. I imagine my health would be improved somewhat by a little travel and change of scene."

"Why don't you take a trip North?" suggested his father. The colonel added to paternal affection a considerable respect for his son as the heir of a large estate. He himself had been "raised" in comparative poverty, and had laid the foundations of his fortune by hard work; and while he despised the ladder by which he had climbed, he could not entirely forget it, and unconsciously manifested, in his intercourse with his son, some of the poor man's deference toward the wealthy and well-born.

"I think I'll adopt your suggestion, sir," replied the son, "and run up to New York; and after I've been there awhile I may go on to Boston for a week or so. I've never been there, you know."

"There are some matters you can talk over with my factor[4] in New York," rejoined the colonel, "and while you are up there among the Yankees, I hope

4. A business agent or broker.

you'll keep your eyes and ears open to find out what the rascally abolitionists are saying and doing. They're becoming altogether too active for our comfort, and entirely too many ungrateful niggers are running away. I hope the conviction of that fellow yesterday may discourage the rest of the breed. I'd just like to catch any one trying to run off one of my darkeys. He'd get short shrift; I don't think any Court would have a chance to try him."

"They are a pestiferous lot," assented Dick, "and dangerous to our institutions. But say, father, if I go North I shall want to take Tom with me."

Now, the colonel, while a very indulgent father, had pronounced views on the subject of negroes, having studied them, as he often said, for a great many years, and, as he asserted oftener still, understanding them perfectly. It is scarcely worth while to say, either, that he valued more highly than if he had inherited them the slaves he had toiled and schemed for.

"I don't think it safe to take Tom up North," he declared, with promptness and decision. "He's a good enough boy, but too smart to trust among those low-down abolitionists. I strongly suspect him of having learned to read, though I can't imagine how. I saw him with a newspaper the other day, and while he pretended to be looking at a woodcut, I'm almost sure he was reading the paper. I think it by no means safe to take him."

Dick did not insist, because he knew it was useless. The colonel would have obliged his son in any other matter, but his negroes were the outward and visible sign of his wealth and station, and therefore sacred to him.

"Whom do you think it safe to take?" asked Dick. "I suppose I'll have to have a body-servant."

"What's the matter with Grandison?" suggested the colonel. "He's handy enough, and I reckon we can trust him. He's too fond of good eating, to risk losing his regular meals; besides, he's sweet on your mother's maid, Betty, and I've promised to let 'em get married before long. I'll have Grandison up, and we'll talk to him. Here, you boy Jack," called the colonel to a yellow youth in the next room who was catching flies and pulling their wings off to pass the time, "go down to the barn and tell Grandison to come here."

"Grandison," said the colonel, when the negro stood before him, hat in hand.

"Yas, marster."

"Haven't I always treated you right?"

"Yas, marster."

"Haven't you always got all you wanted to eat?"

"Yas, marster."

"And as much whiskey and tobacco as was good for you, Grandison?"

"Y-a-s, marster."

"I should just like to know, Grandison, whether you don't think yourself a great deal better off than those poor free negroes down by the plank road, with no kind master to look after them and no mistress to give them medicine when they're sick and—and"—

"Well, I sh'd jes' reckon I is better off, suh, dan dem low-down free niggers, suh! Ef anybody ax 'em who dey b'long ter, dey has ter say nobody, er e'se lie erbout it. Anybody ax me who I b'longs ter, I ain' got no 'casion ter be shame' ter tell 'em, no, suh, 'deed I ain', suh!"

The colonel was beaming. This was true gratitude, and his feudal heart thrilled at such appreciative homage. What cold-blooded, heartless monsters they were who would break up this blissful relationship of kindly protection on the one hand, of wise subordination and loyal dependence on the other! The colonel always became indignant at the mere thought of such wickedness.

"Grandison," the colonel continued, "your young master Dick is going North for a few weeks, and I am thinking of letting him take you along. I shall send you on this trip, Grandison, in order that you may take care of your young master. He will need some one to wait on him, and no one can ever do it so well as one of the boys brought up with him on the old plantation. I am going to trust him in your hands, and I'm sure you'll do your duty faithfully, and bring him back home safe and sound—to old Kentucky."

Grandison grinned. "Oh yas, marster, I'll take keer er young Mars Dick."

"I want to warn you, though, Grandison," continued the colonel impressively, "against these cussed abolitionists, who try to entice servants from their comfortable homes and their indulgent masters, from the blue skies, the green fields, and the warm sunlight of their southern home, and send them away off yonder to Canada, a dreary country, where the woods are full of wildcats and wolves and bears, where the snow lies up to the eaves of the houses for six months of the year, and the cold is so severe that it freezes your breath and curdles your blood; and where, when runaway niggers get sick and can't work, they are turned out to starve and die, unloved and uncared for. I reckon, Grandison, that you have too much sense to permit yourself to be led astray by any such foolish and wicked people."

"'Deed, suh, I would n' low none er dem cussed, low-down abolitioners ter come nigh me, suh. I'd—I'd—would I be 'lowed ter hit 'em, suh?"

"Certainly, Grandison," replied the colonel, chuckling, "hit 'em as hard as you can. I reckon they'd rather like it. Begad, I believe they would! It would serve 'em right to be hit by a nigger!"

"Er ef I didn't hit 'em, suh," continued Grandison reflectively, "I'd tell Mars Dick, en *he'd* fix 'em. He'd smash de face off'n 'em, suh, I jes' knows he would."

"Oh yes, Grandison, your young master will protect you. You need fear no harm while he is near."

"Dey won't try ter steal me, will dey, marster?" asked the negro, with sudden alarm.

"I don't know, Grandison," replied the colonel, lighting a fresh cigar. "They're a desperate set of lunatics, and there's no telling what they may resort to. But if you stick close to your young master, and remember always that he is your best friend, and understands your real needs, and has your true interests at heart, and if you will be careful to avoid strangers who try to talk to you, you'll stand a fair chance of getting back to your home and your friends. And if you please your master Dick, he'll buy you a present, and a string of beads for Betty to wear when you and she get married in the fall."

"Thanky, marster, thanky, suh," replied Grandison, oozing gratitude at every pore; "you is a good marster, to be sho', suh; yas, 'deed you is. You kin jes' bet me and Mars Dick gwine git 'long jes' lack I wuz own boy ter Mars Dick. En it won't be my fault ef he don' want me fer his boy all de time, w'en we come back home ag'in."

"All right, Grandison, you may go now. You needn't work any more to-day, and here's a piece of tobacco for you off my own plug."

"Thanky, marster, thanky, marster! You is de bes' marster any nigger ever had in dis worl'." And Grandison bowed and scraped and disappeared round the corner, his jaws closing around a large section of the colonel's best tobacco.

"You may take Grandison," said the colonel to his son. "I allow he's abolitionist-proof."

III

Richard Owens, Esq., and servant, from Kentucky, registered at the fashionable New York hostelry for Southerners in those days, a hotel where an atmosphere congenial to Southern institutions was sedulously maintained. But there were negro waiters in the dining-room, and mulatto bell-boys, and Dick had no doubt that Grandison, with the native gregariousness and garrulousness of his race, would foregather and palaver with them sooner or later, and Dick hoped that they would speedily inoculate him with the virus of freedom. For it was not Dick's intention to say anything to his servant about his plan to free him, for obvious reasons. To mention one of them, if Grandison should go away, and by legal process be recaptured, his young master's part in the matter would doubtless become known, which would be embarrassing to Dick, to say the least. If, on the other hand, he should merely give Grandison sufficient latitude, he had no doubt he would eventually lose him. For while not exactly skeptical about Grandison's perfervid loyalty, Dick had been a somewhat keen observer of human nature, in his own indolent way, and based his expectations upon the force of the example and argument that his servant could scarcely fail to encounter. Grandison should have a fair chance to become free by his own initiative; if it should become necessary to adopt other measures to get rid of him, it would be time enough to act when the necessity arose; and Dick Owens was not the youth to take needless trouble.

The young master renewed some acquaintances and made others, and spent a week or two very pleasantly in the best society of the metropolis, easily accessible to a wealthy, well-bred young Southerner, with proper introductions. Young women smiled on him, and young men of convivial habits pressed their hospitalities; but the memory of Charity's sweet, strong face and clear blue eyes made him proof against the blandishments of the one sex and the persuasions of the other. Meanwhile he kept Grandison supplied with pocket-money, and left him mainly to his own devices. Every night when Dick came in he hoped he might have to wait upon himself, and every morning he looked forward with pleasure to the prospect of making his toilet unaided. His hopes, however, were doomed to disappointment, for every night when he came in Grandison was on hand with a bootjack, and a nightcap mixed for his young master as the colonel had taught him to mix it, and every morning Grandison appeared with his master's boots blacked and his clothes brushed, and laid his linen out for the day.

"Grandison," said Dick one morning, after finishing his toilet, "this is the chance of your life to go around among your own people and see how they live. Have you met any of them?"

"Yas, suh, I's seen some of 'em. But I don' keer nuffin fer 'em, suh. Dey 're diffe'nt f'm de niggers down ou' way. Dey 'lows dey 're free, but dey ain' got sense 'nuff ter know dey ain' half as well off as dey would be down Souf, whar dey'd be 'preciated."

When two weeks had passed without any apparent effect of evil example upon Grandison, Dick resolved to go on to Boston, where he thought the atmosphere might prove more favorable to his ends. After he had been at the Revere House for a day or two without losing Grandison, he decided upon slightly different tactics.

Having ascertained from a city directory the addresses of several well-known abolitionists, he wrote them each a letter something like this:—

Dear Friend and Brother:—

A wicked slaveholder from Kentucky, stopping at the Revere House, has dared to insult the liberty-loving people of Boston by bringing his slave into their midst. Shall this be tolerated? Or shall steps be taken in the name of liberty to rescue a fellow-man from bondage? For obvious reasons I can only sign myself,

A Friend of Humanity.

That his letter might have an opportunity to prove effective, Dick made it a point to send Grandison away from the hotel on various errands. On one of these occasions Dick watched him for quite a distance down the street. Grandison had scarcely left the hotel when a long-haired, sharp-featured man came out behind him, followed him, soon overtook him, and kept along beside him until they turned the next corner. Dick's hopes were roused by this spectacle, but sank correspondingly when Grandison returned to the hotel. As Grandison said nothing about the encounter, Dick hoped there might be some self-consciousness behind this unexpected reticence, the results of which might develop later on.

But Grandison was on hand again when his master came back to the hotel at night, and was in attendance again in the morning, with hot water, to assist at his master's toilet.[5] Dick sent him on further errands from day to day, and upon one occasion came squarely up to him—inadvertently of course—while Grandison was engaged in conversation with a young white man in clerical garb. When Grandison saw Dick approaching, he edged away from the preacher and hastened toward his master, with a very evident expression of relief upon his countenance.

"Mars Dick," he said, "dese yer abolitioners is jes' pesterin' de life out er me tryin' ter git me ter run away. I don' pay no 'tention ter 'em, but dey riles me so sometimes dat I'm feared I'll hit some of 'em some er dese days, an' dat mought git me inter trouble. I ain' said nuffin' ter you 'bout it, Mars Dick, fer I did n' wanter 'sturb yo' min'; but I don' like it, suh; no, suh, I don'! Is we gwine back home 'fo' long, Mars Dick?"

"We'll be going back soon enough," replied Dick somewhat shortly, while he inwardly cursed the stupidity of a slave who could be free and would not, and registered a secret vow that if he were unable to get rid of Grandison without assassinating him, and were therefore compelled to take him back to Kentucky, he would see that Grandison got a taste of an article of slavery that would make him regret his wasted opportunities. Meanwhile he determined to tempt his servant yet more strongly.

"Grandison," he said next morning, "I'm going away for a day or two, but I shall leave you here. I shall lock up a hundred dollars in this drawer and give you the key. If you need any of it, use it and enjoy yourself,—spend it

5. Dressing and grooming.

all if you like,—for this is probably the last chance you'll have for some time to be in a free State, and you'd better enjoy your liberty while you may."

When he came back a couple of days later and found the faithful Grandison at his post, and the hundred dollars intact, Dick felt seriously annoyed. His vexation was increased by the fact that he could not express his feelings adequately. He did not even scold Grandison; how could he, indeed, find fault with one who so sensibly recognized his true place in the economy of civilization, and kept it with such touching fidelity?

"I can't say a thing to him," groaned Dick. "He deserves a leather medal, made out of his own hide tanned. I reckon I'll write to father and let him know what a model servant he has given me."

He wrote his father a letter which made the colonel swell with pride and pleasure. "I really think," the colonel observed to one of his friends, "that Dick ought to have the nigger interviewed by the Boston papers, so that they may see how contented and happy our darkeys really are."

Dick also wrote a long letter to Charity Lomax, in which he said, among many other things, that if she knew how hard he was working, and under what difficulties, to accomplish something serious for her sake, she would no longer keep him in suspense, but overwhelm him with love and admiration.

Having thus exhausted without result the more obvious methods of getting rid of Grandison, and diplomacy having also proved a failure, Dick was forced to consider more radical measures. Of course he might run away himself, and abandon Grandison, but this would be merely to leave him in the United States, where he was still a slave, and where, with his notions of loyalty, he would speedily be reclaimed. It was necessary, in order to accomplish the purpose of his trip to the North, to leave Grandison permanently in Canada, where he would be legally free.

"I might extend my trip to Canada," he reflected, "but that would be too palpable. I have it! I'll visit Niagara Falls on the way home, and lose him on the Canada side. When he once realizes that he is actually free, I'll warrant that he'll stay."

So the next day saw them westward bound, and in due course of time, by the somewhat slow conveyances of the period, they found themselves at Niagara. Dick walked and drove about the Falls for several days, taking Grandison along with him on most occasions. One morning they stood on the Canadian side, watching the wild whirl of the waters below them.

"Grandison," said Dick, raising his voice above the roar of the cataract, "do you know where you are now?"

"I's wid you, Mars Dick; dat's all I keers."

"You are now in Canada, Grandison, where your people go when they run away from their masters. If you wished, Grandison, you might walk away from me this very minute, and I could not lay my hand upon you to take you back."

Grandison looked around uneasily.

"Let's go back ober de ribber, Mars Dick. I's feared I'll lose you ovuh heah, an' den I won' hab no marster, an' won't nebber be able to git back home no mo'."

Discouraged, but not yet hopeless, Dick said, a few minutes later,—

"Grandison, I'm going up the road a bit, to the inn over yonder. You stay here until I return. I'll not be gone a great while."

Grandison's eyes opened wide and he looked somewhat fearful.

"Is dey any er dem dadblasted abolitioners roun' heah, Mars Dick?"

"I don't imagine that there are," replied his master, hoping there might be. "But I'm not afraid of *your* running away, Grandison. I only wish I were," he added to himself.

Dick walked leisurely down the road to where the whitewashed inn, built of stone, with true British solidity, loomed up through the trees by the roadside. Arrived there he ordered a glass of ale and a sandwich, and took a seat at a table by a window, from which he could see Grandison in the distance. For a while he hoped that the seed he had sown might have fallen on fertile ground, and that Grandison, relieved from the restraining power of a master's eye, and finding himself in a free country, might get up and walk away; but the hope was vain, for Grandison remained faithfully at his post, awaiting his master's return. He had seated himself on a broad flat stone, and, turning his eyes away from the grand and awe-inspiring spectacle that lay close at hand, was looking anxiously toward the inn where his master sat cursing his ill-timed fidelity.

By and by a girl came into the room to serve his order, and Dick very naturally glanced at her; and as she was young and pretty and remained in attendance, it was some minutes before he looked for Grandison. When he did so his faithful servant had disappeared.

To pay his reckoning and go away without the change was a matter quickly accomplished. Retracing his footsteps toward the Falls, he saw, to his great disgust, as he approached the spot where he had left Grandison, the familiar form of his servant stretched out on the ground, his face to the sun, his mouth open, sleeping the time away, oblivious alike to the grandeur of the scenery, the thunderous roar of the cataract, or the insidious voice of sentiment.

"Grandison," soliloquized his master, as he stood gazing down at his ebony encumbrance, "I do not deserve to be an American citizen; I ought not to have the advantages I possess over you; and I certainly am not worthy of Charity Lomax, if I am not smart enough to get rid of you. I have an idea! You shall yet be free, and I will be the instrument of your deliverance. Sleep on, faithful and affectionate servitor, and dream of the blue grass and the bright skies of old Kentucky, for it is only in your dreams that you will ever see them again!"

Dick retraced his footsteps towards the inn. The young woman chanced to look out of the window and saw the handsome young gentleman she had waited on a few minutes before, standing in the road a short distance away, apparently engaged in earnest conversation with a colored man employed as hostler[6] for the inn. She thought she saw something pass from the white man to the other, but at that moment her duties called her away from the window, and when she looked out again the young gentleman had disappeared, and the hostler, with two other young men of the neighborhood, one white and one colored, were walking rapidly towards the Falls.

IV

Dick made the journey homeward alone, and as rapidly as the conveyances of the day would permit. As he drew near home his conduct in going back

6. A person who takes care of horses.

without Grandison took on a more serious aspect than it had borne at any previous time, and although he had prepared the colonel by a letter sent several days ahead, there was still the prospect of a bad quarter of an hour with him; not, indeed, that his father would upbraid him, but he was likely to make searching inquiries. And notwithstanding the vein of quiet recklessness that had carried Dick through his preposterous scheme, he was a very poor liar, having rarely had occasion or inclination to tell anything but the truth. Any reluctance to meet his father was more than offset, however, by a stronger force drawing him homeward, for Charity Lomax must long since have returned from her visit to her aunt in Tennessee.

Dick got off easier than he had expected. He told a straight story, and a truthful one, so far as it went.

The colonel raged at first, but rage soon subsided into anger, and anger moderated into annoyance, and annoyance into a sort of garrulous sense of injury. The colonel thought he had been hardly used; he had trusted this negro, and he had broken faith. Yet, after all, he did not blame Grandison so much as he did the abolitionists, who were undoubtedly at the bottom of it.

As for Charity Lomax, Dick told her, privately of course, that he had run his father's man, Grandison, off to Canada, and left him there.

"Oh, Dick," she had said with shuddering alarm, "what have you done? If they knew it they'd send you to the penitentiary, like they did that Yankee."

"But they don't know it," he had replied seriously; adding, with an injured tone, "you don't seem to appreciate my heroism like you did that of the Yankee; perhaps it's because I wasn't caught and sent to the penitentiary. I thought you wanted me to do it."

"Why, Dick Owens!" she exclaimed. "You know I never dreamed of any such outrageous proceeding.

"But I presume I'll have to marry you," she concluded, after some insistence on Dick's part, "if only to take care of you. You are too reckless for anything; and a man who goes chasing all over the North, being entertained by New York and Boston society and having negroes to throw away, needs some one to look after him."

"It's a most remarkable thing," replied Dick fervently, "that your views correspond exactly with my profoundest convictions. It proves beyond question that we were made for one another."

They were married three weeks later. As each of them had just returned from a journey, they spent their honeymoon at home.

A week after the wedding they were seated, one afternoon, on the piazza of the colonel's house, where Dick had taken his bride, when a negro from the yard ran down the lane and threw open the big gate for the colonel's buggy to enter. The colonel was not alone. Beside him, ragged and travel-stained, bowed with weariness, and upon his face a haggard look that told of hardship and privation, sat the lost Grandison.

The colonel alighted at the steps.

"Take the lines, Tom," he said to the man who had opened the gate, "and drive round to the barn. Help Grandison down,—poor devil, he's so stiff he can hardly move!—and get a tub of water and wash him and rub him down, and feed him, and give him a big drink of whiskey, and then let him come round and see his young master and his new mistress."

The colonel's face wore an expression compounded of joy and indignation,—joy at the restoration of a valuable piece of property; indignation for reasons he proceeded to state.

"It's astounding, the depths of depravity the human heart is capable of! I was coming along the road three miles away, when I heard some one call me from the roadside. I pulled up the mare, and who should come out of the woods but Grandison. The poor nigger could hardly crawl along, with the help of a broken limb. I was never more astonished in my life. You could have knocked me down with a feather. He seemed pretty far gone,—he could hardly talk above a whisper,—and I had to give him a mouthful of whiskey to brace him up so he could tell his story. It's just as I thought from the beginning, Dick; Grandison had no notion of running away; he knew when he was well off, and where his friends were. All the persuasions of abolition liars and runaway niggers did not move him. But the desperation of those fanatics knew no bounds; their guilty consciences gave them no rest. They got the notion somehow that Grandison belonged to a nigger-catcher, and had been brought North as a spy to help capture ungrateful runaway servants. They actually kidnaped him—just think of it!—and gagged him and bound him and threw him rudely into a wagon, and carried him into the gloomy depths of a Canadian forest, and locked him in a lonely hut, and fed him on bread and water for three weeks. One of the scoundrels wanted to kill him, and persuaded the others that it ought to be done; but they got to quarreling about how they should do it, and before they had their minds made up Grandison escaped, and, keeping his back steadily to the North Star, made his way, after suffering incredible hardships, back to the old plantation, back to his master, his friends, and his home. Why, it's as good as one of Scott's novels! Mr. Simms[7] or some other one of our Southern authors ought to write it up."

"Don't you think, sir," suggested Dick, who had calmly smoked his cigar throughout the colonel's animated recital, "that that kidnaping yarn sounds a little improbable? Isn't there some more likely explanation?"

"Nonsense, Dick; it's the gospel truth! Those infernal abolitionists are capable of anything—everything! Just think of their locking the poor, faithful nigger up, beating him, kicking him, depriving him of his liberty, keeping him on bread and water for three long, lonesome weeks, and he all the time pining for the old plantation!"

There were almost tears in the colonel's eyes at the picture of Grandison's sufferings that he conjured up. Dick still professed to be slightly skeptical, and met Charity's severely questioning eye with bland unconsciousness.

The colonel killed the fatted calf for Grandison, and for two or three weeks the returned wanderer's life was a slave's dream of pleasure. His fame spread throughout the county, and the colonel gave him a permanent place among the house servants, where he could always have him conveniently at hand to relate his adventures to admiring visitors.

About three weeks after Grandison's return the colonel's faith in sable humanity was rudely shaken, and its foundations almost broken up. He came near losing his belief in the fidelity of the negro to his master,—the servile virtue most highly prized and most sedulously cultivated by the

7. William Gilmore Simms (1806–1870), the most widely read novelist of the antebellum South. Sir Walter Scott (1771–1832), popular British historical novelist.

colonel and his kind. One Monday morning Grandison was missing. And not only Grandison, but his wife, Betty the maid; his mother, aunt Eunice; his father, uncle Ike; his brothers, Tom and John, and his little sister Elsie, were likewise absent from the plantation; and a hurried search and inquiry in the neighborhood resulted in no information as to their whereabouts. So much valuable property could not be lost without an effort to recover it, and the wholesale nature of the transaction carried consternation to the hearts of those whose ledgers were chiefly bound in black. Extremely energetic measures were taken by the colonel and his friends. The fugitives were traced, and followed from point to point, on their northward run through Ohio. Several times the hunters were close upon their heels, but the magnitude of the escaping party begot unusual vigilance on the part of those who sympathized with the fugitives, and strangely enough, the underground railroad seemed to have had its tracks cleared and signals set for this particular train. Once, twice, the colonel thought he had them, but they slipped through his fingers.

One last glimpse he caught of his vanishing property, as he stood, accompanied by a United States marshal, on a wharf at a port on the south shore of Lake Erie. On the stern of a small steamboat which was receding rapidly from the wharf, with her nose pointing toward Canada, there stood a group of familiar dark faces, and the look they cast backward was not one of longing for the fleshpots of Egypt.[8] The colonel saw Grandison point him out to one of the crew of the vessel, who waved his hand derisively toward the colonel. The latter shook his fist impotently—and the incident was closed.

1899

The Wife of His Youth

I

Mr. Ryder was going to give a ball. There were several reasons why this was an opportune time for such an event.

Mr. Ryder might aptly be called the dean of the Blue Veins. The original Blue Veins were a little society of colored persons organized in a certain Northern city shortly after the war. Its purpose was to establish and maintain correct social standards among a people whose social condition presented almost unlimited room for improvement. By accident, combined perhaps with some natural affinity, the society consisted of individuals who were, generally speaking, more white than black. Some envious outsider made the suggestion that no one was eligible for membership who was not white enough to show blue veins. The suggestion was readily adopted by those who were not of the favored few, and since that time the society, though possessing a longer and more pretentious name, had been known far and wide as the "Blue Vein Society," and its members as the "Blue Veins."

The Blue Veins did not allow that any such requirement existed for admission to their circle, but, on the contrary, declared that character and culture were the only things considered; and that if most of their members were light-colored, it was because such persons, as a rule, had had better

8. An allusion to Exodus 16:2–3.

opportunities to qualify themselves for membership. Opinions differed, too, as to the usefulness of the society. There were those who had been known to assail it violently as a glaring example of the very prejudice from which the colored race had suffered most; and later, when such critics had succeeded in getting on the inside, they had been heard to maintain with zeal and earnestness that the society was a lifeboat, an anchor, a bulwark and a shield,—a pillar of cloud by day and of fire by night,[1] to guide their people through the social wilderness. Another alleged prerequisite for Blue Vein membership was that of free birth; and while there was really no such requirement, it is doubtless true that very few of the members would have been unable to meet it if there had been. If there were one or two of the older members who had come up from the South and from slavery, their history presented enough romantic circumstances to rob their servile origin of its grosser aspects.

While there were no such tests of eligibility, it is true that the Blue Veins had their notions on these subjects, and that not all of them were equally liberal in regard to the things they collectively disclaimed. Mr. Ryder was one of the most conservative. Though he had not been among the founders of the society, but had come in some years later, his genius for social leadership was such that he had speedily become its recognized adviser and head, the custodian of its standards, and the preserver of its traditions. He shaped its social policy, was active in providing for its entertainment, and when the interest fell off, as it sometimes did, he fanned the embers until they burst again into a cheerful flame.

There were still other reasons for his popularity. While he was not as white as some of the Blue Veins, his appearance was such as to confer distinction upon them. His features were of a refined type, his hair was almost straight; he was always neatly dressed; his manners were irreproachable, and his morals above suspicion. He had come to Groveland a young man, and obtaining employment in the office of a railroad company as messenger had in time worked himself up to the position of stationery clerk, having charge of the distribution of the office supplies for the whole company. Although the lack of early training had hindered the orderly development of a naturally fine mind, it had not prevented him from doing a great deal of reading or from forming decidedly literary tastes. Poetry was his passion. He could repeat whole pages of the great English poets; and if his pronunciation was sometimes faulty, his eye, his voice, his gestures, would respond to the changing sentiment with a precision that revealed a poetic soul and disarmed criticism. He was economical, and had saved money; he owned and occupied a very comfortable house on a respectable street. His residence was handsomely furnished, containing among other things a good library, especially rich in poetry, a piano, and some choice engravings. He generally shared his house with some young couple, who looked after his wants and were company for him; for Mr. Ryder was a single man. In the early days of his connection with the Blue Veins he had been regarded as quite a catch, and young ladies and their mothers had manoeuvred with much ingenuity to capture him. Not, however, until Mrs. Molly Dixon visited Groveland had any woman ever made him wish to change his condition to that of a married man.

Mrs. Dixon had come to Groveland from Washington in the spring, and before the summer was over she had won Mr. Ryder's heart. She possessed

1. An allusion to Exodus 13:21.

many attractive qualities. She was much younger than he; in fact, he was old enough to have been her father, though no one knew exactly how old he was. She was whiter than he, and better educated. She had moved in the best colored society of the country, at Washington, and had taught in the schools of that city. Such a superior person had been eagerly welcomed to the Blue Vein Society, and had taken a leading part in its activities. Mr. Ryder had at first been attracted by her charms of person, for she was very good looking and not over twenty-five; then by her refined manners and the vivacity of her wit. Her husband had been a government clerk, and at his death had left a considerable life insurance. She was visiting friends in Groveland, and, finding the town and the people to her liking, had prolonged her stay indefinitely. She had not seemed displeased at Mr. Ryder's attentions, but on the contrary had given him every proper encouragement; indeed, a younger and less cautious man would long since have spoken. But he had made up his mind, and had only to determine the time when he would ask her to be his wife. He decided to give a ball in her honor, and at some time during the evening of the ball to offer her his heart and hand. He had no special fears about the outcome, but, with a little touch of romance, he wanted the surroundings to be in harmony with his own feelings when he should have received the answer he expected.

Mr. Ryder resolved that this ball should mark an epoch in the social history of Groveland. He knew, of course,—no one could know better,—the entertainments that had taken place in past years, and what must be done to surpass them. His ball must be worthy of the lady in whose honor it was to be given, and must, by the quality of its guests, set an example for the future. He had observed of late a growing liberality, almost a laxity, in social matters, even among members of his own set, and had several times been forced to meet in a social way persons whose complexions and callings in life were hardly up to the standard which he considered proper for the society to maintain. He had a theory of his own.

"I have no race prejudice," he would say, "but we people of mixed blood are ground between the upper and the nether millstone. Our fate lies between absorption by the white race and extinction in the black. The one doesn't want us yet, but may take us in time. The other would welcome us, but it would be for us a backward step. 'With malice towards none, with charity for all,'[2] we must do the best we can for ourselves and those who are to follow us. Self-preservation is the first law of nature."

His ball would serve by its exclusiveness to counteract leveling tendencies, and his marriage with Mrs. Dixon would help to further the upward process of absorption he had been wishing and waiting for.

II

The ball was to take place on Friday night. The house had been put in order, the carpets covered with canvas, the halls and stairs decorated with palms and potted plants; and in the afternoon Mr. Ryder sat on his front porch, which the shade of a vine running up over a wire netting made a cool and pleasant lounging place. He expected to respond to the toast "The Ladies" at the supper, and from a volume of Tennyson[3]—his favorite poet—

2. From Abraham Lincoln's second inaugural address (1865).
3. Alfred, Lord Tennyson (1809–1892), poet laureate of England. He published "A Dream of Fair Women" in 1832.

was fortifying himself with apt quotations. The volume was open at "A Dream of Fair Women." His eyes fell on these lines, and he read them aloud to judge better of their effect:—

"At length I saw a lady within call,
  Stiller than chisell'd marble, standing there;
A daughter of the gods, divinely tall,
  And most divinely fair."

He marked the verse, and turning the page read the stanza beginning,—

"O sweet pale Margaret,
  O rare pale Margaret."[4]

He weighed the passage a moment, and decided that it would not do. Mrs. Dixon was the palest lady he expected at the ball, and she was of a rather ruddy complexion, and of lively disposition and buxom build. So he ran over the leaves until his eye rested on the description of Queen Guinevere:[5]—

"She seem'd a part of joyous Spring:
A gown of grass-green silk she wore,
Buckled with golden clasps before;
A light-green tuft of plumes she bore
Closed in a golden ring.

"She look'd so lovely, as she sway'd
The rein with dainty finger-tips,
A man had given all other bliss,
And all his worldly worth for this,
To waste his whole heart in one kiss
Upon her perfect lips."[6]

As Mr. Ryder murmured these words audibly, with an appreciative thrill, he heard the latch of his gate click, and a light footfall sounding on the steps. He turned his head, and saw a woman standing before his door.

She was a little woman, not five feet tall, and proportioned to her height. Although she stood erect, and looked around her with very bright and restless eyes, she seemed quite old; for her face was crossed and recrossed with a hundred wrinkles, and around the edges of her bonnet could be seen protruding here and there a tuft of short gray wool. She wore a blue calico gown of ancient cut, a little red shawl fastened around her shoulders with an old-fashioned brass brooch, and a large bonnet profusely ornamented with faded red and yellow artificial flowers. And she was very black,—so black that her toothless gums, revealed when she opened her mouth to speak, were not red, but blue. She looked like a bit of the old plantation life, summoned up from the past by the wave of a magician's wand, as the poet's fancy had called into being the gracious shapes of which Mr. Ryder had just been reading.

He rose from his chair and came over to where she stood.

"Good-afternoon, madam," he said.

"Good-evenin', suh," she answered, ducking suddenly with a quaint curtsy. Her voice was shrill and piping, but softened somewhat by age. "Is dis yere whar Mistuh Ryduh lib, suh?" she asked, looking around her doubtfully, and

4. Tennyson's "Margaret" (1832).
5. Wife of the legendary King Arthur.
6. Tennyson's "Sir Launcelot and Queen Guinevere" (1842).

glancing into the open windows, through which some of the preparations for the evening were visible.

"Yes," he replied, with an air of kindly patronage, unconsciously flattered by her manner, "I am Mr. Ryder. Did you want to see me?"

"Yas, suh, ef I ain't 'sturbin' of you too much."

"Not at all. Have a seat over here behind the vine, where it is cool. What can I do for you?"

"'Scuse me, suh," she continued, when she had sat down on the edge of a chair, "'scuse me, suh, I's lookin' for my husban'. I heerd you wuz a big man an' had libbed heah a long time, an' I 'lowed you would n't min' ef I'd come roun' an' ax you ef you 'd ever heerd of a merlatter[7] man by de name er Sam Taylor 'quirin' roun' in de chu'ches ermongs' de people fer his wife 'Liza Jane?"

Mr. Ryder seemed to think for a moment.

"There used to be many such cases right after the war," he said, "but it has been so long that I have forgotten them. There are very few now. But tell me your story, and it may refresh my memory."

She sat back farther in her chair so as to be more comfortable, and folded her withered hands in her lap.

"My name 's 'Liza," she began, "'Liza Jane. Wen I wuz young I us'ter b'long ter Marse Bob Smif, down in ole Missoura. I wuz bawn down dere. W'en I wuz a gal I wuz married ter a man named Jim. But Jim died, an' after dat I married a merlatter man named Sam Taylor. Sam wuz freebawn, but his mammy and daddy died, an' de w'ite folks 'prenticed him ter my marster fer ter work fer 'im 'tel he wuz growed up. Sam worked in de fiel', an' I wuz de cook. One day Ma'y Ann, ole miss's maid, came rushin' out ter de kitchen, an' says she, ''Liza Jane, ole marse gwine sell yo' Sam down de ribber.'

"'Go way f'm yere,' says I; 'my husban' 's free!'

"'Don' make no diff'ence. I heerd ole marse tell ole miss he wuz gwine take yo' Sam 'way wid 'im ter-morrow, fer he needed money, an' he knowed whar he could git a t'ousan' dollars fer Sam an' no questions axed.'

"W'en Sam come home f'm de fiel' dat night, I tole him 'bout ole marse gwine steal 'im, an' Sam run erway. His time wuz mos' up, an' he swo' dat w'en he wuz twenty-one he would come back an' he'p me run erway, er else save up de money ter buy my freedom. An' I know he'd 'a' done it, fer he thought a heap er me, Sam did. But w'en he come back he did n' fin' me, fer I wuz n' dere. Ole marse had heerd dat I warned Sam, so he had me whip' an' sol' down de ribber.

"Den de wah broke out, an' w'en it wuz ober de cullud folks wuz scattered. I went back ter de ole home; but Sam wuz n' dere, an' I could n' l'arn nuffin' 'bout 'im. But I knowed he 'd be'n dere to look fer me an' had n' foun' me, an' had gone erway ter hunt fer me.

"I's be'n lookin' fer 'im eber sence," she added simply, as though twenty-five years were but a couple of weeks, "an' I knows he 's be'n lookin' fer me. Fer he sot a heap er sto' by me, Sam did, an' I know he 's be'n huntin' fer me all dese years,—'less'n he 's be'n sick er sump'n, so he could n' work, er out'n his head, so he could n' 'member his promise. I went back down de ribber, fer I 'lowed he'd gone down dere lookin' fer me. I's be'n ter Noo Orleens, an'

7. Mulatto.

Atlanty, an' Charleston, an' Richmon'; an' w'en I'd be'n all ober de Souf I come ter de Norf. Fer I knows I'll fin' 'im some er dese days," she added softly, "er he 'll fin' me, an' den we 'll bofe be as happy in freedom as we wuz in de ole days befo' de wah." A smile stole over her withered countenance as she paused a moment, and her bright eyes softened into a faraway look.

This was the substance of the old woman's story. She had wandered a little here and there. Mr. Ryder was looking at her curiously when she finished.

"How have you lived all these years?" he asked.

"Cookin', suh. I's a good cook. Does you know anybody w'at needs a good cook, suh? I's stoppin' wid a cullud fam'ly roun' de corner yonder 'tel I kin git a place."

"Do you really expect to find your husband? He may be dead long ago."

She shook her head emphatically. "Oh no, he ain' dead. De signs an' de tokens tells me. I dremp three nights runnin' on'y dis las' week dat I foun' him."

"He may have married another woman. Your slave marriage would not have prevented him, for you never lived with him after the war, and without that your marriage doesn't count."[8]

"Would n' make no diff'ence wid Sam. He would n' marry no yuther 'ooman 'tel he foun' out 'bout me. I knows it," she added. "Sump'n 's be'n tellin' me all dese years dat I's gwine fin' Sam 'fo' I dies."

"Perhaps he's outgrown you, and climbed up in the world where he would n't care to have you find him."

"No, indeed, suh," she replied, "Sam ain' dat kin' er man. He wuz good ter me, Sam wuz, but he wuz n' much good ter nobody e'se, fer he wuz one er de triflin'es' han's on de plantation. I 'spec's ter haf ter suppo't 'im w'en I fin' 'im, fer he nebber would work 'less'n he had ter. But den he wuz free, an' he did n' git no pay fer his work, an' I don' blame 'im much. Mebbe he 's done better sence he run erway, but I ain' 'spectin' much."

"You may have passed him on the street a hundred times during the twenty-five years, and not have known him; time works great changes."

She smiled incredulously. "I'd know 'im 'mongs' a hund'ed men. Fer dey wuz n' no yuther merlatter man like my man Sam, an' I could n' be mistook. I's toted his picture roun' wid me twenty-five years."

"May I see it?" asked Mr. Ryder. "It might help me to remember whether I have seen the original."

As she drew a small parcel from her bosom he saw that it was fastened to a string that went around her neck. Removing several wrappers, she brought to light an old-fashioned daguerreotype in a black case. He looked long and intently at the portrait. It was faded with time, but the features were still distinct, and it was easy to see what manner of man it had represented.

He closed the case, and with a slow movement handed it back to her.

"I don't know of any man in town who goes by that name," he said, "nor have I heard of any one making such inquiries. But if you will leave me your address, I will give the matter some attention, and if I find out anything I will let you know."

8. Although marriages between enslaved men and women had no legal standing before 1865, after the fall of the Confederacy many formerly enslaved couples—previously separated by sale or war—made serious efforts to reunite and register themselves formally as husband and wife.

She gave him the number of a house in the neighborhood, and went away, after thanking him warmly.

He wrote the address on the fly-leaf of the volume of Tennyson, and, when she had gone, rose to his feet and stood looking after her curiously. As she walked down the street with mincing step, he saw several persons whom she passed turn and look back at her with a smile of kindly amusement. When she had turned the corner, he went upstairs to his bedroom, and stood for a long time before the mirror of his dressing-case, gazing thoughtfully at the reflection of his own face.

III

At eight o'clock the ballroom was a blaze of light and the guests had begun to assemble; for there was a literary programme and some routine business of the society to be gone through with before the dancing. A black servant in evening dress waited at the door and directed the guests to the dressing-rooms.

The occasion was long memorable among the colored people of the city; not alone for the dress and display, but for the high average of intelligence and culture that distinguished the gathering as a whole. There were a number of school-teachers, several young doctors, three or four lawyers, some professional singers, an editor, a lieutenant in the United States army spending his furlough in the city, and others in various polite callings; these were colored, though most of them would not have attracted even a casual glance because of any marked difference from white people. Most of the ladies were in evening costume, and dress coats and dancing pumps were the rule among the men. A band of string music, stationed in an alcove behind a row of palms, played popular airs while the guests were gathering.

The dancing began at half past nine. At eleven o'clock supper was served. Mr. Ryder had left the ballroom some little time before the intermission, but reappeared at the supper-table. The spread was worthy of the occasion, and the guests did full justice to it. When the coffee had been served, the toast-master, Mr. Solomon Sadler, rapped for order. He made a brief introductory speech, complimenting host and guests, and then presented in their order the toasts of the evening. They were responded to with a very fair display of after-dinner wit.

"The last toast," said the toast-master, when he reached the end of the list, "is one which must appeal to us all. There is no one of us of the sterner sex who is not at some time dependent upon woman,—in infancy for protection, in manhood for companionship, in old age for care and comforting. Our good host has been trying to live alone, but the fair faces I see around me to-night prove that he too is largely dependent upon the gentler sex for most that makes life worth living,—the society and love of friends,—and rumor is at fault if he does not soon yield entire subjection to one of them. Mr. Ryder will now respond to the toast,—The Ladies."

There was a pensive look in Mr. Ryder's eyes as he took the floor and adjusted his eyeglasses. He began by speaking of woman as the gift of Heaven to man, and after some general observations on the relations of the sexes he said: "But perhaps the quality which most distinguishes woman is her fidelity and devotion to those she loves. History is full of examples, but has recorded none more striking than one which only to-day came under my notice."

He then related, simply but effectively, the story told by his visitor of the afternoon. He gave it in the same soft dialect, which came readily to his lips, while the company listened attentively and sympathetically. For the story had awakened a responsive thrill in many hearts. There were some present who had seen, and others who had heard their fathers and grandfathers tell, the wrongs and sufferings of this past generation, and all of them still felt, in their darker moments, the shadow hanging over them. Mr. Ryder went on:—

"Such devotion and confidence are rare even among women. There are many who would have searched a year, some who would have waited five years, a few who might have hoped ten years; but for twenty-five years this woman has retained her affection for and her faith in a man she has not seen or heard of in all that time.

"She came to me to-day in the hope that I might be able to help her find this long-lost husband. And when she was gone I gave my fancy rein, and imagined a case I will put to you.

"Suppose that this husband, soon after his escape, had learned that his wife had been sold away, and that such inquiries as he could make brought no information of her whereabouts. Suppose that he was young, and she much older than he; that he was light, and she was black; that their marriage was a slave marriage, and legally binding only if they chose to make it so after the war. Suppose, too, that he made his way to the North, as some of us have done, and there, where he had larger opportunities, had improved them, and had in the course of all these years grown to be as different from the ignorant boy who ran away from fear of slavery as the day is from the night. Suppose, even, that he had qualified himself, by industry, by thrift, and by study, to win the friendship and be considered worthy the society of such people as these I see around me to-night, gracing my board and filling my heart with gladness; for I am old enough to remember the day when such a gathering would not have been possible in this land. Suppose, too, that, as the years went by, this man's memory of the past grew more and more indistinct, until at last it was rarely, except in his dreams, that any image of this bygone period rose before his mind. And then suppose that accident should bring to his knowledge the fact that the wife of his youth, the wife he had left behind him,—not one who had walked by his side and kept pace with him in his upward struggle, but one upon whom advancing years and a laborious life had set their mark,—was alive and seeking him, but that he was absolutely safe from recognition or discovery, unless he chose to reveal himself. My friends, what would the man do? I will presume that he was one who loved honor, and tried to deal justly with all men. I will even carry the case further, and suppose that perhaps he had set his heart upon another, whom he had hoped to call his own. What would he do, or rather what ought he to do, in such a crisis of a lifetime?

"It seemed to me that he might hesitate, and I imagined that I was an old friend, a near friend, and that he had come to me for advice; and I argued the case with him. I tried to discuss it impartially. After we had looked upon the matter from every point of view, I said to him, in words that we all know:—

'This above all: to thine own self be true,
And it must follow, as the night the day,
Thou canst not then be false to any man.'[9]

Then, finally, I put the question to him, 'Shall you acknowledge her?'

"And now, ladies and gentlemen, friends and companions, I ask you, what should he have done?"

There was something in Mr. Ryder's voice that stirred the hearts of those who sat around him. It suggested more than mere sympathy with an imaginary situation; it seemed rather in the nature of a personal appeal. It was observed, too, that his look rested more especially upon Mrs. Dixon, with a mingled expression of renunciation and inquiry.

She had listened, with parted lips and streaming eyes. She was the first to speak: "He should have acknowledged her."

"Yes," they all echoed, "he should have acknowledged her."

"My friends and companions," responded Mr. Ryder, "I thank you, one and all. It is the answer I expected, for I knew your hearts."

He turned and walked toward the closed door of an adjoining room, while every eye followed him in wondering curiosity. He came back in a moment, leading by the hand his visitor of the afternoon, who stood startled and trembling at the sudden plunge into this scene of brilliant gayety. She was neatly dressed in gray, and wore the white cap of an elderly woman.

"Ladies and gentlemen," he said, "this is the woman, and I am the man, whose story I have told you. Permit me to introduce to you the wife of my youth."

1899

Dave's Neckliss

"Have some dinner, Uncle Julius?" said my wife.

It was a Sunday afternoon in early autumn. Our two women-servants had gone to a camp-meeting[1] some miles away, and would not return until evening. My wife had served the dinner, and we were just rising from the table, when Julius came up the lane, and, taking off his hat, seated himself on the piazza.[2]

The old man glanced through the open door at the dinner-table, and his eyes rested lovingly upon a large sugar-cured ham, from which several slices had been cut, exposing a rich pink expanse that would have appealed strongly to the appetite of any hungry Christian.

"Thanky, Miss Annie," he said, after a momentary hesitation, "I dunno ez I keers ef I does tas'e a piece er dat ham, ef yer'll cut me off a slice un it."

"No," said Annie, "I won't. Just sit down to the table and help yourself; eat all you want, and don't be bashful."

Julius drew a chair up to the table, while my wife and I went out on the piazza. Julius was in my employment; he took his meals with his own family, but when he happened to be about our house at meal-times, my wife never let him go away hungry.

9. Shakespeare, *Hamlet* 1.3.

1. An evangelical, often multiracial, religious assembly, usually held in rural areas, where believers camped for an extended period of worship, testimony, and prayer.

2. A verandah or front porch.

I threw myself into a hammock, from which I could see Julius through an open window. He ate with evident relish, devoting his attention chiefly to the ham, slice after slice of which disappeared in the spacious cavity of his mouth. At first the old man ate rapidly, but after the edge of his appetite had been taken off he proceeded in a more leisurely manner. When he had cut the sixth slice of ham (I kept count of them from a lazy curiosity to see how much he *could* eat) I saw him lay it on his plate; as he adjusted the knife and fork to cut it into smaller pieces, he paused, as if struck by a sudden thought, and a tear rolled down his rugged cheek and fell upon the slice of ham before him. But the emotion, whatever the thought that caused it, was transitory, and in a moment he continued his dinner. When he was through eating, he came out on the porch, and resumed his seat with the satisfied expression of countenance that usually follows a good dinner.

"Julius," I said, "you seemed to be affected by something, a moment ago. Was the mustard so strong that it moved you to tears?"

"No, suh, it wa'n't de mustard; I wuz studyin' 'bout Dave."

"Who was Dave, and what about him?" I asked.

The conditions were all favorable to story-telling. There was an autumnal languor in the air, and a dreamy haze softened the dark green of the distant pines and the deep blue of the Southern sky. The generous meal he had made had put the old man in a very good humor. He was not always so, for his curiously undeveloped nature was subject to moods which were almost childish in their variableness. It was only now and then that we were able to study, through the medium of his recollection, the simple but intensely human inner life of slavery. His way of looking at the past seemed very strange to us; his view of certain sides of life was essentially different from ours. He never indulged in any regrets for the Arcadian[3] joyousness and irresponsibility which was a somewhat popular conception of slavery; his had not been the lot of the petted house-servant, but that of the toiling field-hand. While he mentioned with a warm appreciation the acts of kindness which those in authority had shown to him and his people, he would speak of a cruel deed, not with the indignation of one accustomed to quick feeling and spontaneous expression, but with a furtive disapproval which suggested to us a doubt in his own mind as to whether he had a right to think or to feel, and presented to us the curious psychological spectacle of a mind enslaved long after the shackles had been struck off from the limbs of its possessor. Whether the sacred name of liberty ever set his soul aglow with a generous fire; whether he had more than the most elementary ideas of love, friendship, patriotism, religion,—things which are half, and the better half, of life to us; whether he even realized, except in a vague, uncertain way, his own degradation, I do not know. I fear not; and if not, then centuries of repression had borne their legitimate fruit. But in the simple human feeling, and still more in the undertone of sadness, which pervaded his stories, I thought I could see a spark which, fanned by favoring breezes and fed by the memories of the past, might become in his children's children a glowing flame of sensibility, alive to every thrill of human happiness or human woe.

"Dave use' ter b'long ter my ole marster," said Julius; "he wuz raise' on dis yer plantation, en I kin 'member all erbout 'im, fer I wuz ole 'nuff ter chop

3. Bucolic, peaceful.

cotton w'en it all happen'. Dave wuz a tall man, en monst'us strong: he could do mo' wuk in a day dan any yuther two niggers on de plantation. He wuz one er dese yer solemn kine er men, en nebber run on wid much foolishness, like de yuther darkies. He use' ter go out in de woods en pray; en w'en he hear de han's on de plantation cussin' en gwine on wid dere dancin' en foolishness, he use' ter tell 'em 'bout religion en jedgmen'-day, w'en dey would haf ter gin account fer eve'y idle word en all dey yuther sinful kyarin's-on.

"Dave had l'arn' how ter read de Bible. Dey wuz a free nigger boy in de settlement w'at wuz monst'us smart, en could write en cipher, en wuz alluz readin' books er papers. En Dave had hi'ed dis free boy fer ter l'arn 'im how ter read. Hit wuz 'g'in' de law, but co'se none er de niggers did n' say nuffin ter de w'ite folks 'bout it. Howsomedever, one day Mars Walker—he wuz de oberseah—foun' out Dave could read. Mars Walker wa'n't nuffin but a po' bockrah,[4] en folks said he couldn' read ner write hisse'f, en co'se he didn' lack ter see a nigger w'at knowed mo' d'n he did; so he went en tole Mars Dugal'. Mars Dugal' sont fer Dave, en ax' 'im 'bout it.

"Dave didn't hardly knowed w'at ter do; but he couldn' tell no lie, so he 'fessed he could read de Bible a little by spellin' out de words. Mars Dugal' look' mighty solemn.

"'Dis yer is a se'ious matter,' sezee; 'it's 'g'in' de law ter l'arn niggers how ter read, er 'low 'em ter hab books. But w'at yer l'arn out'n dat Bible, Dave?'

"Dave wa'n't no fool, ef he wuz a nigger, en sezee:—

"'Marster, I l'arns dat it's a sin fer ter steal, er ter lie, er fer ter want w'at doan b'long ter yer; en I l'arns fer ter love de Lawd en ter 'bey my marster.'

"Mars Dugal' sorter smile' en laf' ter hisse'f, like he 'uz might'ly tickle' 'bout sump'n, en sezee:—

"'Doan 'pear ter me lack readin' de Bible done yer much harm, Dave. Dat's w'at I wants all my niggers fer ter know. Yer keep right on readin', en tell de yuther han's w'at yer be'n tellin' me. How would yer lack fer ter preach ter de niggers on Sunday?'

"Dave say he'd be glad fer ter do w'at he could. So Mars Dugal' tole de oberseah fer ter let Dave preach ter de niggers, en tell 'em w'at wuz in de Bible, en it would he'p ter keep 'em fum stealin' er runnin' erway.

"So Dave 'mence' ter preach, en done de han's on de plantation a heap er good, en most un 'em lef' off dey wicked ways, en 'mence' ter love ter hear 'bout God, en religion, en de Bible; en dey done dey wuk better, en didn' gib de oberseah but mighty little trouble fer ter manage 'em.

"Dave wuz one er dese yer men w'at didn' keer much fer de gals,—leastways he didn' 'tel Dilsey come ter de plantation. Dilsey wuz a monst'us peart, good-lookin', gingybread-colored gal,—one er dese yer high-steppin' gals w'at hol's dey heads up, en won' stan' no foolishness fum no man. She had b'long' ter a gemman over on Rockfish, w'at died, en whose 'state ha' ter be sol' fer ter pay his debts. En Mars Dugal' had be'n ter de oction, en w'en he seed dis gal a-cryin' en gwine on 'bout bein' sol' erway fum her ole mammy, Aun' Mahaly, Mars Dugal' bid 'em bofe in, en fotch 'em ober ter our plantation.

"De young nigger men on de plantation wuz des wil' atter Dilsey, but it didn' do no good, en none un 'em couldn' git Dilsey fer dey junesey,[5] 'tel Dave 'mence' fer ter go roun' Aun' Mahaly's cabin. Dey wuz a fine-lookin' couple, Dave en Dilsey wuz, bofe tall, en well-shape', en soopl'. En dey sot a heap by

4. Variant of "buckra," African American vernacular for a low-class white man.

5. Sweetheart [*Chesnutt's note*].

one ernudder. Mars Dugal' seed 'em tergedder one Sunday, en de nex' time he seed Dave atter dat, sezee:—

"Dave, w'en yer en Dilsey gits ready fer ter git married, I ain' got no rejections. Dey's a poun' er so er chawin'-terbacker up at de house, en I reckon yo' mist'iss kin fine a frock en a ribbin er two fer Dilsey. Youer bofe good niggers, en yer neenter be feared er bein' sol' 'way fum one ernudder long ez I owns dis plantation; en I 'spec's ter own it fer a long time yit.'

"But dere wuz one man on de plantation w'at didn' lack ter see Dave en Dilsey tergedder ez much ez ole marster did. W'en Mars Dugal' went ter de sale whar he got Dilsey en Mahaly, he bought ernudder han', by de name er Wiley. Wiley wuz one er dese yer shiny-eyed, double-headed[6] little niggers, sha'p ez a steel trap, en sly ez de fox w'at keep out'n it. Dis yer Wiley had be'n pesterin' Dilsey 'fo' she come ter our plantation, en had nigh 'bout worried de life out'n her. She didn' keer nuffin fer 'im, but he pestered her so she ha' ter th'eaten ter tell her marster fer ter make Wiley let her 'lone. W'en he come ober to our place it wuz des ez bad, 'tel bimeby Wiley seed dat Dilsey had got ter thinkin' a heap 'bout Dave, en den he sorter hilt off aw'ile, en purten' lack he gin Dilsey up. But he wuz one er dese yer 'ceitful niggers, en w'ile he wuz laffin' en jokin' wid de yuther han's 'bout Dave en Dilsey, he wuz settin' a trap fer ter ketch Dave en git Dilsey back fer hisse'f.

"Dave en Dilsey made up dere min's fer ter git married long 'bout Christmas time, w'en dey'd hab mo' time fer a weddin'. But 'long 'bout two weeks befo' dat time ole mars 'mence' ter lose a heap er bacon. Eve'y night er so somebody 'ud steal a side er bacon, er a ham, er a shoulder, er sump'n, fum one er de smoke-'ouses. De smoke-'ouses wuz lock', but somebody had a key, en manage' ter git in some way er 'nudder. Dey's mo' ways 'n one ter skin a cat, en dey's mo' d'n one way ter git in a smoke-'ouse,—leastways dat's w'at I hearn say. Folks w'at had bacon fer ter sell didn' hab no trouble 'bout gittin' rid un it. Hit wuz 'g'in' de law fer ter buy things fum slabest; but Lawd! dat law didn' 'mount ter a hill er peas. Eve'y week er so one er dese yer big covered waggins would come 'long de road, peddlin' terbacker en w'iskey. Dey wuz a sight er room in one er dem big waggins, en it wuz monst'us easy fer ter swop off bacon fer sump'n ter chaw er ter wa'm yer up in de winter-time. I s'pose de peddlers didn' knowed dey wuz breakin' de law, caze de niggers alluz went at night, en stayed on de dark side er de waggin; en it wuz mighty hard fer ter tell *w'at* kine er folks dey wuz.

"Atter two er th'ee hund'ed er meat had be'n stole', Mars Walker call all de niggers up one ebenin', en tol' 'em dat de fus' nigger he cot stealin' bacon on dat plantation would git sump'n fer ter 'member it by long ez he lib'. En he say he'd gin fi' dollars ter de nigger w'at 'skiver' de rogue. Mars Walker say he s'picion' one er two er de niggers, but he couldn' tell fer sho, en co'se dey all 'nied it w'en he 'cuse em un it.

"Dey wa'n't no bacon stole' fer a week er so, 'tel one dark night w'en somebody tuk a ham fum one er de smoke-'ouses. Mars Walker des cusst awful w'en he foun' out de ham wuz gone, en say he gwine ter sarch all de niggers' cabins; w'en dis yer Wiley I wuz tellin' yer 'bout up'n say he s'picion' who tuk de ham, fer he seed Dave comin' 'cross de plantation fum to'ds de smoke-'ouse de night befo'. W'en Mars Walker hearn dis fum Wiley, he went en sarch' Dave's cabin, en foun' de ham hid under de flo'.

6. Deceitful, two-faced.

"Eve'ybody wuz 'stonish'; but dere wuz de ham. Co'se Dave 'nied it ter de las', but dere wuz de ham. Mars Walker say it wuz des ez he 'spected: he did n' b'lieve in dese yer readin' en prayin' niggers; it wuz all 'pocrisy, en sarve' Mars Dugal' right fer 'lowin' Dave ter be readin' books w'en it wuz 'g'in' de law.

"W'en Mars Dugal' hearn 'bout de ham, he say he wuz might'ly 'ceived en disapp'inted in Dave. He say he wouldn' nebber hab no mo' conferdence in no nigger, en Mars Walker could do des ez he wuz a mineter wid Dave er any er de res' er de niggers. So Mars Walker tuk'n tied Dave up en gin 'im forty;[7] en den he got some er dis yer wire clof w'at dey uses fer ter make sifters out'n, en tuk'n wrap' it roun' de ham en fasten it tergedder at de little een'. Den he tuk Dave down ter de blacksmif-shop, en had Unker Silas, de plantation blacksmif, fasten a chain ter de ham, en den fasten de yuther een' er de chain roun' Dave's neck. En den he says ter Dave, sezee:—

"'Now, suh, yer'll wear dat neckliss fer de nex' six mont's; en I 'spec's yer ner none er de yuther niggers on dis plantation won' steal no mo' bacon dyoin' er dat time.'

"Well, it des 'peared ez if fum dat time Dave didn' hab nuffin but trouble. De niggers all turnt ag'in' 'im, caze he be'n de 'casion er Mars Dugal' turnin' 'em all ober ter Mars Walker. Mars Dugal' wa'n't a bad marster hisse'f, but Mars Walker wuz hard ez a rock. Dave kep' on sayin' he didn' take de ham, but none un 'em did n' b'lieve 'im.

"Dilsey wa'n't on de plantation w'en Dave wuz 'cused er stealin' de bacon. Ole mist'iss had sont her ter town fer a week er so fer ter wait on one er her darters w'at had a young baby, en she didn' fine out nuffin 'bout Dave's trouble 'tel she got back ter de plantation. Dave had patien'ly endyoed de finger er scawn, en all de hard words w'at de niggers pile' on 'im, caze he wuz sho' Dilsey would stan' by 'im, en wouldn' b'lieve he wuz a rogue, ner none er de yuther tales de darkies wuz tellin' 'bout 'im.

"W'en Dilsey come back fum town, en got down fum behine de buggy whar she b'en ridin' wid ole mars, de fus' nigger 'ooman she met says ter her,—

"'Is yer seed Dave, Dilsey?'

"'No, I ain' seed Dave,' says Dilsey.

"'Yer des oughter look at dat nigger; reckon yer wouldn' want 'im fer yo' junesey no mo'. Mars Walker cotch 'im stealin' bacon, en gone en fasten' a ham roun' his neck, so he can't git it off'n hisse'f. He sut'nly do look quare.' En den de 'ooman bus' out laffin' fit ter kill herse'f. W'en she got thoo laffin' she up'n tole Dilsey all 'bout de ham, en all de yuther lies w'at de niggers be'n tellin' on Dave.

"W'en Dilsey started down ter de quarters, who should she meet but Dave, comin' in fum de cotton-fiel'. She turnt her head ter one side, en purten' lack she did n' seed Dave.

"'Dilsey!' sezee.

"Dilsey walk' right on, en didn' notice 'im.

"'*Oh*, Dilsey!'

"Dilsey didn' paid no 'tention ter 'im, en den Dave knowed some er de niggers be'n tellin' her 'bout de ham. He felt monst'us bad, but he 'lowed ef he could des git Dilsey fer ter listen ter 'im, fer a minute er so, he could make her b'lieve he didn' stole de bacon. It wuz a week er two befo' he could git a

7. Forty lashes from a whip.

chance ter speak ter her ag'in; but fine'ly he cotch her down by de spring one day, en sezee:—

"'Dilsey, w'at fer yer won' speak ter me, en purten' lack yer doan see me? Dilsey, yer knows me too well fer ter b'lieve I'd steal, er do dis yuther wick'ness de niggers is all layin' ter me,—yer *knows* I would n' do dat, Dilsey. Yer ain' gwine back on yo' Dave, is yer?'

"But w'at Dave say didn' hab no 'fec' on Dilsey. Dem lies folks b'en tellin' her had p'isen' her min' 'g'in' Dave.

"'I doan wanter talk ter no nigger,' says she, 'w'at be'n whip' fer stealin', en w'at gwine roun' wid sich a lookin' thing ez dat hung roun' his neck. I's a 'spectable gal, *I* is. W'at yer call dat, Dave? Is dat a cha'm fer ter keep off witches, er is it a noo kine er neckliss yer got?'

"Po' Dave didn' knowed w'at ter do. De las' one he had 'pended on fer ter stan' by 'im, had gone back on 'im, en dey didn' 'pear ter be nuffin mo' wuf libbin' fer. He couldn' hol' no mo' pra'r-meetin's, fer Mars Walker wouldn' 'low 'im ter preach, en de darkies wouldn' 'a' listen' ter 'im ef he had preach'. He didn' eben hab his Bible fer ter comfort hisse'f wid, fer Mars Walker had tuk it erway fum 'im en burnt it up, en say ef he ketch any mo' niggers wid Bibles on de plantation he'd do 'em wuss'n he done Dave.

"En ter make it still harder fer Dave, Dilsey tuk up wid Wiley. Dave could see him gwine up ter Aun' Mahaly's cabin, en settin' out on de bench in de moonlight wid Dilsey, en singin' sinful songs en playin' de banjer. Dave use' ter scrouch down behine de bushes, en wonder w'at de Lawd sen' 'im all dem tribbelations fer.

"But all er Dave's yuther troubles wa'n't nuffin side er dat ham. He had wrap' de chain roun' wid a rag, so it did n' hurt his neck; but w'eneber he went ter wuk, dat ham would be in his way; he had ter do his task, howsomedever, des de same ez ef he didn' hab de ham. W'eneber he went ter lay down, dat ham would be in de way. Ef he turn ober in his sleep, dat ham would be tuggin' at his neck. It wuz de las' thing he seed at night, en de fus' thing he seed in de mawnin'. W'eneber he met a stranger, de ham would be de fus' thing de stranger would see. Most un 'em would 'mence' ter laf, en whareber Dave went he could see folks p'intin' at him, en year 'em sayin':—

"'W'at kine er collar dat nigger got roun' his neck?' er, ef dey knowed 'im, 'Is yer stole any mo' hams lately?' er 'W'at yer take fer yo' neckliss, Dave?' er some joke er 'nuther 'bout dat ham.

"Fus' Dave didn' mine it so much, caze he knowed he hadn' done nuffin. But bimeby he got so he couldn' stan' it no longer, en he'd hide hisse'f in de bushes w'eneber he seed anybody comin', en alluz kep' hisse'f shet up in his cabin atter he come in fum wuk.

"It wuz monst'us hard on Dave, en bimeby, w'at wid dat ham eberlastin' en etarnally draggin' roun' his neck, he 'mence' fer ter do en say quare things, en make de niggers wonder ef he wa'n't gittin' out'n his mine. He got ter gwine roun' talkin' ter hisse'f, en singin' corn-shuckin' songs, en laffin' fit ter kill 'bout nuffin. En one day he tole one er de niggers he had 'skivered a noo way fer ter raise hams,—gwine ter pick 'em off'n trees, en save de expense er smoke-'ouses by kyoin' 'em in de sun. En one day he up'n tole Mars Walker he got sump'n pertickler fer ter say ter 'im; en he tuk Mars Walker off ter one side, en tole 'im he wuz gwine ter show 'im a place in de swamp whar dey wuz a whole trac' er lan' covered wid ham-trees.

"Wen Mars Walker hearn Dave talkin' dis kine er fool-talk, en w'en he seed how Dave wuz 'mencin' ter git behine in his wuk, en wen he ax' de niggers en dey tole 'im, how Dave be'n gwine on, he 'lowed he reckon' he'd punish' Dave ernuff, en it mou't do mo' harm dan good fer ter keep de ham on his neck any longer. So he sont Dave down ter de blacksmif-shop en had de ham tuk off. Dey wa'n't much er de ham lef' by dat time, fer de sun had melt all de fat, en de lean had all swivel' up, so dey wa'n't but th'ee er fo' poun's lef'.

"W'en de ham had be'n tuk off'n Dave, folks kinder stopped talkin' 'bout 'im so much. But de ham had be'n on his neck so long dat Dave had sorter got use' ter it. He look des lack he'd los' sump'n fer a day er so atter de ham wuz tuk off, en didn' 'pear ter know w'at ter do wid hisse'f; en fine'ly he up'n tuk'n tied a lighterd-knot[8] ter a string, en hid it under de flo' er his cabin, en w'en nobody wuzn' lookin' he'd take it out en hang it roun' his neck, en go off in de woods en holler en sing; en he allus tied it roun' his neck w'en he went ter sleep. Fac', it 'peared lack Dave done gone clean out'n his mine. En atter a w'ile he got one er de quarest notions you eber hearn tell un. It wuz 'bout dat time dat I come back ter de plantation fer ter wuk,—I had be'n out ter Mars Dugal's yuther place on Beaver Crick for a mont' er so. I had hearn 'bout Dave en de bacon, en 'bout w'at wuz gwine on on de plantation; but I didn' b'lieve w'at dey all say 'bout Dave, fer I knowed Dave wa'n't dat kine er man. One day atter I come back, me'n Dave wuz choppin' cotton tergedder, w'en Dave lean' on his hoe, en motion' fer me ter come ober close ter 'im; en den he retch' ober en w'ispered ter me.

"'Julius,' sezee, 'did yer knowed yer wuz wukkin' long yer wid a ham?'

"I couldn' 'magine w'at he meant. 'G'way fum yer, Dave,' says I. 'Yer ain' wearin' no ham no mo'; try en fergit 'bout dat; 't ain' gwine ter do yer no good fer ter 'member it.'

"'Look a-yer, Julius,' sezee, 'kin yer keep a secret?'

"'Co'se I kin, Dave,' says I. 'I doan go roun' tellin' people w'at yuther folks says ter me.'

"'Kin I trus' yer, Julius? Will yer cross yo' heart?'

"I cross' my heart. 'Wush I may die ef I tells a soul,' says I.

"Dave look' at me des lack he wuz lookin' thoo me en 'way on de yuther side er me, en sezee:—

"'Did yer knowed I wuz turnin' ter a ham, Julius?'

"I tried ter 'suade Dave dat dat wuz all foolishness, en dat he oughtn't ter be talkin' dat-a-way,—hit wa'n't right. En I tole 'im ef he'd des be patien', de time would sho'ly come w'en eve'ything would be straighten' out, en folks would fine out who de rale rogue wuz w'at stole de bacon. Dave 'peared ter listen ter w'at I say, en promise' ter do better, en stop gwine on dat-a-way; en it seem lack he pick' up a bit w'en he seed dey wuz one pusson didn' b'lieve dem tales 'bout 'im.

"Hit wa'n't long atter dat befo' Mars Archie McIntyre, ober on de Wimbleton road, 'mence' ter complain 'bout somebody stealin' chickens fum his hen-'ouse. De chickens kep' on gwine, en at las' Mars Archie tole de han's on his plantation dat he gwine ter shoot de fus' man he ketch in his hen-'ouse. In less'n a week atter he gin dis warnin', he cotch a nigger in de hen-'ouse, en fill' 'im full er squir'l-shot. W'en he got a light, he 'skivered it wuz a strange nigger; en w'en he call' one er his own sarven's, de nigger tole 'im it wuz our

8. A piece of kindling made from a resinous pine stump or root.

Wiley. W'en Mars Archie foun' dat out, he sont ober ter our plantation fer ter tell Mars Dugal' he had shot one er his niggers, en dat he could sen' ober dere en git w'at wuz lef un 'im.

"Mars Dugal' wuz mad at fus'; but w'en he got ober dere en hearn how it all happen', he didn' hab much ter say. Wiley wuz shot so bad he wuz sho' he wuz gwine ter die, so he up'n says ter ole marster:—

"'Mars Dugal',' sezee, 'I knows I's be'n a monst'us bad nigger, but befo' I go I wanter git sump'n off'n my mine. Dave didn' steal dat bacon w'at wuz tuk out'n de smoke-'ouse. *I* stole it all, en I hid de ham under Dave's cabin fer ter th'ow de blame on him—en may de good Lawd fergib me fer it.'

"Mars Dugal' had Wiley tuk back ter de plantation, en sont fer a doctor fer ter pick de shot out'n 'im. En de ve'y nex' mawnin' Mars Dugal' sont fer Dave ter come up ter de big house; he felt kinder sorry fer de way Dave had be'n treated. Co'se it wa'n't no fault er Mars Dugal's, but he wuz gwine ter do w'at he could fer ter make up fer it. So he sont word down ter de quarters fer Dave en all de yuther han's ter 'semble up in de yard befo' de big house at sun-up nex' mawnin'.

"Yearly in de mawnin' de niggers all swarm' up in de yard. Mars Dugal' wuz feelin' so kine dat he had brung up a bairl er cider, en tole de niggers all fer ter he'p deyselves.

"All de han's on de plantation come but Dave; en bimeby, w'en it seem lack he wa'n't comin', Mars Dugal' sont a nigger down ter de quarters ter look fer 'im. De sun wuz gittin' up, en dey wuz a heap er wuk ter be done, en Mars Dugal' sorter got ti'ed waitin'; so he up'n says:—

"'Well, boys en gals, I sont fer yer all up yer fer ter tell yer dat all dat 'bout Dave's stealin' er de bacon wuz a mistake, ez I s'pose yer all done hearn befo' now, en I's mighty sorry it happen'. I wants ter treat all my niggers right, en I wants yer all ter know dat I sets a heap by all er my han's w'at is hones' en smart. En I want yer all ter treat Dave des lack yer did befo' dis thing happen', en mine w'at he preach ter yer; fer Dave is a good nigger, en has had a hard row ter hoe. En de fus' one I ketch sayin' anythin' 'g'in Dave, I'll tell Mister Walker ter gin 'im forty. Now take ernudder drink er cider all roun', en den git at dat cotton, fer I wanter git dat Persimmon Hill trac' all pick' ober ter-day.'

"W'en de niggers wuz gwine 'way, Mars Dugal' tole me fer ter go en hunt up Dave, en bring 'im up ter de house. I went down ter Dave's cabin, but couldn' fine 'im dere. Den I look' roun' de plantation, en in de aidge er de woods, en 'long de road; but I couldn' fine no sign er Dave. I wuz 'bout ter gin up de sarch, w'en I happen' fer ter run 'cross a foot-track w'at look' lack Dave's. I had wukked 'long wid Dave so much dat I knowed his tracks: he had a monst'us long foot, wid a holler instep, w'ich wuz sump'n skase 'mongs' black folks. So I follered dat track 'cross de fiel' fum de quarters 'tel I got ter de smoke-'ouse. De fus' thing I notice' wuz smoke comin' out'n de cracks; it wuz cu'ous, caze dey hadn' be'n no hogs kill' on de plantation fer six mont' er so, en all de bacon in de smoke-'ouse wuz done kyoed. I couldn' 'magine fer ter sabe my life w'at Dave wuz doin' in dat smoke-'ouse. I went up ter de do' en hollered:—

"'Dave!'

"Dey didn' nobody answer. I didn' wanter open de do', fer w'ite folks is monst'us pertickler 'bout dey smoke-'ouses; en ef de oberseah had a-come up en cotch me in dere, he mou't not wanter b'lieve I wuz des lookin' fer Dave. So I sorter knock at de do' en call' out ag'in:—

"'O Dave, hit's me—Julius! Doan be skeered. Mars Dugal' wants yer ter come up ter de big house,—he done 'skivered who stole de ham.'

"But Dave didn' answer. En w'en I look' roun' ag'in en didn' seed none er his tracks gwine way fum de smoke-'ouse, I knowed he wuz in dere yit, en I wuz 'termine' fer ter fetch 'im out; so I push de do' open en look in.

"Dey wuz a pile er bark burnin' in de middle er de flo', en right ober de fier, hangin' fum one er de rafters, wuz Dave; dey wuz a rope roun' his neck, en I didn' haf ter look at his face mo' d'n once fer ter see he wuz dead.

"Den I knowed how it all happen'. Dave had kep' on gittin' wusser en wusser in his mine, 'tel he des got ter b'lievin' he wuz all done turnt ter a ham; en den he had gone en built a fier, en tied a rope roun' his neck, des lack de hams wuz tied, en had hung hisse'f up in de smoke-'ouse fer ter kyo.

"Dave wuz buried down by de swamp, in de plantation buryin'-groun'. Wiley didn' died fum de woun' he got in Mars McIntyre's hen-'ouse; he got well atter a w'ile, but Dilsey wouldn' hab nuffin mo' ter do wid 'im, en 't wa'n't long 'fo' Mars Dugal' sol' 'im ter a spekilater on his way souf,—he say he didn' want no sich a nigger on de plantation, ner in de county, ef he could he'p it. En w'en de een er de year come, Mars Dugal' turnt Mars Walker off, en run de plantation hisse'f atter dat.

"Eber sence den," said Julius in conclusion, "w'eneber I eats ham, it min's me er Dave. I lacks ham, but I nebber kin eat mo' d'n two er th'ee poun's befo' I gits ter studyin' 'bout Dave, en den I has ter stop en leab de res' fer ernudder time."

There was a short silence after the old man had finished his story, and then my wife began to talk to him about the weather, on which subject he was an authority. I went into the house. When I came out, half an hour later, I saw Julius disappearing down the lane, with a basket on his arm.

At breakfast, next morning, it occurred to me that I should like a slice of ham. I said as much to my wife.

"Oh, no, John," she responded, "you shouldn't eat anything so heavy for breakfast."

I insisted.

"The fact is," she said, pensively, "I couldn't have eaten any more of that ham, and so I gave it to Julius."

1889

ANNA JULIA COOPER
1858?–1964

Anna Julia Cooper was born into slavery in North Carolina, the daughter of Hannah Haywood and a white man said to be her mother's owner. She lived more than a century, during which time she became one of the most well-respected activist authors on the African American cultural scene. Cooper published essays, lectures, sociological pamphlets, and a biography of the Grimké family; however, she is best known for *A Voice from the South by a Black Woman of the South* (1892) and especially the declaration that "Only the Black Woman can say 'when and where I enter, in the quiet undisputed dignity of my womanhood, then and there the whole Negro race enters with me.'"

Cooper's remarkable career began when she was about nine years old and received a scholarship to St. Augustine's Normal School, a North Carolina institution developed to train teachers for service among formerly enslaved people. She stayed there fourteen years, eventually joining the faculty. In 1881 Cooper entered Oberlin College, graduating three years later. After teaching briefly at Wilberforce College and again at St. Augustine's, Cooper earned a master's degree in mathematics from Oberlin. In 1887 she began a long and sometimes difficult tenure at Washington Colored High School, also known as M Street School, an institution in Washington, D.C., renowned for graduating many well-known African American professionals, artists, and politicians. Cooper began there as a teacher of math and science, but in 1902 she became the school's principal. She later attended Columbia University, and in 1925, at nearly sixty-seven years old, she earned her Ph.D. in French from the University of Paris. Among her other accomplishments were serving as president of Frelinghuysen University, a school dedicated to serving working Black residents of Washington, D.C., and raising five adopted children.

Cooper's associates included Charlotte Forten Grimké, Frances E. W. Harper, and W. E. B. Du Bois, with whose educational philosophies she was often identified despite her own advocacy of ideas more akin to those of Booker T. Washington. In fact, like Harper, Fannie Jackson Coppin, and others, Anna Julia Cooper's educational and social attitudes interwove strongly feminist ideas with particularly compelling aspects of Washington's and Du Bois's platforms. Published the same year as Harper's *Iola* and Ida B. Wells-Barnett's famous editorial on lynching, Cooper's *A Voice from the South* is a complicated example of activist writing during the "Women's Era," as the 1890s were called. "Womanhood a Vital Element in the Regeneration and Progress of a Race," which we excerpt from *A Voice from the South*, argues that the education and elevation of Black women are crucial to racial uplift because societies can best be evaluated by the status of their female members. In Cooper's words, "The fundamental agency under God in the regeneration, the retraining of the race, as well as the groundwork and starting point of its progress upward, must be the *black woman*." Black women, Cooper believed, were especially well situated to analyze and offer solutions to society's injustices because of their position as women in a sexist society and as Black people in a racist society. Cooper thus considered the development of Black women's faculties through higher education crucial not only to the "regeneration of a race" but to the progress of the nation and the world.

Womanhood a Vital Element in the Regeneration and Progress of a Race[1]

The two sources from which, perhaps, modern civilization has derived its noble and ennobling ideal of woman are Christianity and the Feudal System.

In Oriental[2] countries woman has been uniformly devoted to a life of ignorance, infamy, and complete stagnation. The Chinese shoe of to-day does not more entirely dwarf, cramp, and destroy her physical powers, than have the customs, laws, and social instincts, which from remotest ages have governed our Sister of the East, enervated and blighted her mental and moral life.

1. Read before the convocation of colored clergy of the Protestant Episcopal Church at Washington, D.C., 1886 [*Cooper's note*].

2. Includes the Mideast and North Africa as well as East Asia.

Mahomet[3] makes no account of woman whatever in his polity. The Koran, which, unlike our Bible, was a product and not a growth, tried to address itself to the needs of Arabian civilization as Mahomet with his circumscribed powers saw them. The Arab was a nomad. Home to him meant his present camping place. That deity who, according to our western ideals, makes and sanctifies the home, was to him a transient bauble to be toyed with so long as it gave pleasure and then to be thrown aside for a new one. As a personality, an individual soul, capable of eternal growth and unlimited development, and destined to mould and shape the civilization of the future to an incalculable extent, Mahomet did not know woman. There was no hereafter, no paradise for her. The heaven of the Mussulman[4] is peopled and made gladsome not by the departed wife, or sister, or mother, but by *houri*[5]—a figment of Mahomet's brain, partaking of the ethereal qualities of angels, yet imbued with all the vices and inanity of Oriental women. The harem here, and—"dust to dust" hereafter, this was the hope, the inspiration, the *summum bonum*[6] of the Eastern woman's life! With what result on the life of the nation, the "Unspeakable Turk,"[7] the "sick man" of modern Europe can to-day exemplify.

Says a certain writer: "The private life of the Turk is vilest of the vile, unprogressive, unambitious, and inconceivably low." And yet Turkey is not without her great men. She has produced most brilliant minds; men skilled in all the intricacies of diplomacy and statesmanship; men whose intellects could grapple with the deep problems of empire and manipulate the subtle agencies which check-mate kings. But these minds were not the normal outgrowth of a healthy trunk. They seemed rather ephemeral excrescencies[8] which shoot far out with all the vigor and promise, apparently, of strong branches; but soon alas fall into decay and ugliness because there is no soundness in the root, no life-giving sap, permeating, strengthening and perpetuating the whole. There is a worm at the core! The homelife is impure! and when we look for fruit, like apples of Sodom,[9] it crumbles within our grasp into dust and ashes.

It is pleasing to turn from this effete and immobile civilization to a society still fresh and vigorous, whose seed is in itself, and whose very name is synonymous with all that is progressive, elevating and inspiring, viz., the European bud and the American flower of modern civilization.

And here let me say parenthetically that our satisfaction in American institutions rests not on the fruition we now enjoy, but springs rather from the possibilities and promise that are inherent in the system, though as yet, perhaps, far in the future.

"Happiness," says Madame de Stael,[1] "consists not in perfections attained, but in a sense of progress, the result of our own endeavor under conspiring circumstances *toward* a goal which continually advances and broadens and deepens till it is swallowed up in the Infinite." Such conditions in embryo are all that we claim for the land of the West. We have not yet reached our ideal in American civilization. The pessimists even declare that we are not marching in that direction. But there can be no doubt that here in America

3. Muhammad.
4. Muslim.
5. One of the beautiful virgins promised to faithful Muslim men in Paradise.
6. Highest good (Latin).
7. Quoting Thomas Carlyle (1795–1835).
8. Short-lived abnormalities.
9. Biblical city known for the unnatural wickedness of its citizens.
1. Germaine de Staël (1766–1817), French-Swiss woman of letters.

is the arena in which the next triumph of civilization is to be won; and here too we find promise abundant and possibilities infinite.

Now let us see on what basis this hope for our country primarily and fundamentally rests. Can any one doubt that it is chiefly on the homelife and on the influence of good women in those homes? Says Macaulay:[2] "You may judge a nation's rank in the scale of civilization from the way they treat their women." And Emerson,[3] "I have thought that a sufficient measure of civilization is the influence of good women." Now this high regard for woman, this germ of a prolific idea which in our own day is bearing such rich and varied fruit, was ingrafted into European civilization, we have said, from two sources, the Christian Church and the Feudal System. For although the Feudal System can in no sense be said to have originated the idea, yet there can be no doubt that the habits of life and modes of thought to which Feudalism gave rise, materially fostered and developed it; for they gave us chivalry, than which no institution has more sensibly magnified and elevated woman's position in society.

Tacitus[4] dwells on the tender regard for woman entertained by these rugged barbarians before they left their northern homes to overrun Europe. Old Norse legends too, and primitive poems, all breathe the same spirit of love of home and veneration for the pure and noble influence there presiding—the wife, the sister, the mother.

And when later on we see the settled life of the Middle Ages "oozing out," as M. Guizot[5] expresses it, from the plundering and pillaging life of barbarism and crystallizing into the Feudal System, the tiger of the field is brought once more within the charmed circle of the goddesses of his castle, and his imagination weaves around them a halo whose reflection possibly has not yet altogether vanished.

It is true the spirit of Christianity had not yet put the seal of catholicity on this sentiment. Chivalry, according to Bascom,[6] was but the toning down and softening of a rough and lawless period. It gave a roseate glow to a bitter winter's day. Those who looked out from castle windows revelled in its "amethyst tints." But God's poor, the weak, the unlovely, the commonplace were still freezing and starving none the less in unpitied, unrelieved loneliness.

Respect for woman, the much lauded chivalry of the Middle Ages, meant what I fear it still means to some men in our own day—respect for the elect few among whom they expect to consort.

The idea of the radical amelioration of womankind, reverence for woman as woman regardless of rank, wealth, or culture, was to come from that rich and bounteous fountain from which flow all our liberal and universal ideas—the Gospel of Jesus Christ.

And yet the Christian Church at the time of which we have been speaking would seem to have been doing even less to protect and elevate woman than the little done by secular society. The Church as an organization committed a double offense against woman in the Middle Ages. Making of marriage a sacrament and at the same time insisting on the celibacy of

2. Thomas Babington Macaulay (1800–1859), British writer and statesman.
3. Ralph Waldo Emerson (1803–1882), American essayist and poet.
4. Publius Cornelius Tacitus (ca. 55–ca. 120), Roman historian.
5. Francois Pierre Guillaume Guizot (1787–1874), French historian and statesman.
6. John Bascom (1827–1911), author of *Philosophy of English Literature: A Course of Lectures Delivered in the Lowel Institute* (1874).

the clergy and other religious orders, she gave an inferior if not an impure character to the marriage relation, especially fitted to reflect discredit on woman. Would this were all or the worst! but the Church by the licentiousness of its chosen servants invaded the household and established too often as vicious connections those relations which it forbade to assume openly and in good faith. "Thus," to use the words of our authority, "the religious corps became as numerous, as searching, and as unclean as the frogs of Egypt, which penetrated into all quarters, into the ovens and kneading troughs, leaving their filthy trail wherever they went." Says Chaucer[7] with characteristic satire, speaking of the Friars:

"Women may now go safely up and doun,
In every bush, and under every tree,
Ther is non other incubus but he,
And he ne will don hem no dishonour."

Henry, Bishop of Liege, could unblushingly boast the birth of twenty-two children in fourteen years.[8]

It may help us under some of the perplexities which beset our way in "the one Catholic and Apostolic Church" to-day, to recall some of the corruptions and incongruities against which the Bride of Christ has had to struggle in her past history and in spite of which she has kept, through many vicissitudes, the faith once delivered to the saints. Individuals, organizations, whole sections of the Church militant may outrage the Christ whom they profess, may ruthlessly trample under foot both the spirit and the letter of his precepts, yet not till we hear the voices audibly saying "Come let us depart hence," shall we cease to believe and cling to the promise, "*I am with you to the end of the world.*"

"Yet saints their watch are keeping,
The cry goes up 'How long!'
And soon the night of weeping
Shall be the morn of song."[9]

However much then the facts of any particular period of history may seem to deny it, I for one do not doubt that the source of the vitalizing principle of woman's development and amelioration is the Christian Church, so far as that church is coincident with Christianity.

Christ gave ideals not formulae. The Gospel is a germ requiring millennia for its growth and ripening. It needs and at the same time helps to form around itself a soil enriched in civilization, and perfected in culture and insight without which the embryo can neither be unfolded or comprehended. With all the strides our civilization has made from the first to the nineteenth century, we can boast not an idea, not a principle of action, not a progressive social force but was already mutely foreshadowed, or directly enjoined in that simple tale of a meek and lowly life. The quiet face of the Nazarene[1] is ever seen a little way ahead, never too far to come down to and touch the life of the lowest in days the darkest, yet ever leading onward, still onward, the tottering childish feet of our strangely boastful civilization.

7. Geoffrey Chaucer (ca. 1340–1400), English poet. The quotation is from his *Canterbury Tales*.
8. Bascom [*Cooper's note*].
9. From "The Church's One Foundation," a hymn written in 1866 by S. J. Stone. The Bible quotations above are from John 14:31 and Matthew 28:20.
1. Jesus Christ.

By laying down for woman the same code of morality, the same standard of purity, as for man; by refusing to countenance the shameless and equally guilty monsters who were gloating over her fall,—graciously stooping in all the majesty of his own spotlessness to wipe away the filth and grime of her guilty past and bid her go in peace and sin no more; and again in the moments of his own careworn and footsore dejection, turning trustfully and lovingly, away from the heartless snubbing and sneers, away from the cruel malignity of mobs and prelates in the dusty marts of Jerusalem to the ready sympathy, loving appreciation and unfaltering friendship of that quiet home at Bethany;[2] and even at the last, by his dying bequest to the disciple whom he loved, signifying the protection and tender regard to be extended to that sorrowing mother and ever afterward to the sex she represented;—throughout his life and in his death he has given to men a rule and guide for the estimation of woman as an equal, as a helper, as a friend, and as a sacred charge to be sheltered and cared for with a brother's love and sympathy, lessons which nineteen centuries' gigantic strides in knowledge, arts, and sciences, in social and ethical principles have not been able to probe to their depth or to exhaust in practice.

It seems not too much to say then of the vitalizing, regenerating, and progressive influence of womanhood on the civilization of today, that, while it was foreshadowed among Germanic nations in the far away dawn of their history as a narrow, sickly and stunted growth, it yet owes its catholicity and power, the deepening of its roots and broadening of its branches to Christianity.

The union of these two forces, the Barbaric and the Christian, was not long delayed after the Fall of the Empire. The Church, which fell with Rome, finding herself in danger of being swallowed up by barbarism, with characteristic vigor and fertility of resources, addressed herself immediately to the task of conquering her conquerors. The means chosen does credit to her power of penetration and adaptability, as well as to her profound, unerring, all-compassing diplomacy; and makes us even now wonder if aught human can successfully and ultimately withstand her far-seeing designs and brilliant policy, or gainsay her well-earned claim to the word *Catholic*.

She saw the barbarian, little more developed than a wild beast. She forbore to antagonize and mystify his warlike nature by a full blaze of the heart-searching and humanizing tenets of her great Head. She said little of the rule "If thy brother smite thee on one cheek, turn to him the other also;"[3] but thought it sufficient for the needs of those times, to establish the so-called "Truce of God" under which men were bound to abstain from butchering one another for three days of each week and on Church festivals. In other words, she respected their individuality: non-resistance pure and simple being for them an utter impossibility, she contented herself with less radical measures calculated to lead up finally to the full measure of the benevolence of Christ.

Next she took advantage of the barbarian's sensuous love of gaudy display and put all her magnificent garments on. She could not capture him by physical force, she would dazzle him by gorgeous spectacles. It is said that Romanism gained more in pomp and ritual during this trying period of the Dark Ages than throughout all her former history.

2. Village associated with the final scenes of Jesus's life.

3. Matthew 5:39.

The result was she carried her point. Once more Rome laid her ambitious hand on the temporal power, and allied with Charlemagne,[4] aspired to rule the world through a civilization dominated by Christianity and permeated by the traditions and instincts of those sturdy barbarians.

Here was the confluence of the two streams we have been tracing, which, united now, stretch before us as a broad majestic river. In regard to woman it was the meeting of two noble and ennobling forces, two kindred ideas the resultant of which, we doubt not, is destined to be a potent force in the betterment of the world.

Now after our appeal to history comparing nations destitute of this force and so destitute also of the principle of progress, with other nations among whom the influence of woman is prominent coupled with a brisk, progressive, satisfying civilization,—if in addition we find this strong presumptive evidence corroborated by reason and experience, we may conclude that these two equally varying concomitants are linked as cause and effect; in other words, that the position of woman in society determines the vital elements of its regeneration and progress.

Now that this is so on *a priori* grounds[5] all must admit. And this not because woman is better or stronger or wiser than man, but from the nature of the case, because it is she who must first form the man by directing the earliest impulses of his character.

Byron and Wordsworth[6] were both geniuses and would have stamped themselves on the thought of their age under any circumstances; and yet we find the one a savor of life unto life, the other of death unto death. "Byron, like a rocket, shot his way upward with scorn and repulsion, flamed out in wild, explosive, brilliant excesses and disappeared in darkness made all the more palpable."[7]

Wordsworth lent of his gifts to reinforce that "power in the Universe which makes for righteousness" by taking the harp handed him from Heaven and using it to swell the strains of angelic choirs. Two locomotives equally mighty stand facing opposite tracks; the one to rush headlong to destruction with all its precious freight, the other to toil grandly and gloriously up the steep embattlements to Heaven and to God. Who—who can say what a world of consequences hung on the first placing and starting of these enormous forces!

Woman, Mother,—your responsibility is one that might make angels tremble and fear to take hold! To trifle with it, to ignore or misuse it, is to treat lightly the most sacred and solemn trust ever confided by God to human kind. The training of children is a task on which an infinity of weal[8] or woe depends. Who does not covet it? Yet who does not stand awe-struck before its momentous issues! It is a matter of small moment, it seems to me, whether that lovely girl in whose accomplishments you take such pride and delight, can enter the gay and crowded salon with the ease and elegance of this or that French or English gentlewoman, compared with the decision as to whether her individuality is going to reinforce the good or the evil elements of the world. The lace and the diamonds, the dance and the theater, gain a new significance when scanned in their bearings on such issues.

4. King of the Franks (742–814) and emperor of the Holy Roman Empire.
5. That is, based on theoretical reasoning, rather than on experience or observation.
6. George Gordon, Lord Byron (1788–1824) and William Wordsworth (1770–1850), English poets.
7. Bascom's Eng. Lit. p. 253 [*Cooper's note*].
8. Happiness.

Their influence on the individual personality, and through her on the society and civilization which she vitalizes and inspires—all this and more must be weighed in the balance before the jury can return a just and intelligent verdict as to the innocence or banefulness of these apparently simple amusements.

Now the fact of woman's influence on society being granted, what are its practical bearings on the work which brought together this conference of colored clergy and laymen in Washington? "We come not here to talk." Life is too busy, too pregnant with meaning and far reaching consequences to allow you to come this far for mere intellectual entertainment.

The vital agency of womanhood in the regeneration and progress of a race, as a general question, is conceded almost before it is fairly stated. I confess one of the difficulties for me in the subject assigned lay in its obviousness. The plea is taken away by the opposite attorney's granting the whole question.

"Woman's influence on social progress"—who in Christendom doubts or questions it? One may as well be called on to prove that the sun is the source of light and heat and energy to this many-sided little world.

Nor, on the other hand, could it have been intended that I should apply the position when taken and proven, to the needs and responsibilities of the women of our race in the South. For is it not written, "Cursed is he that cometh after the king?" and has not the King already preceded me in "The Black Woman of the South"?[9]

They have had both Moses and the Prophets in Dr. Crummell and if they hear not him, neither would they be persuaded though one came up from the South.

I would beg, however, with the Doctor's permission, to add my plea for the *Colored Girls* of the South:—that large, bright, promising fatally beautiful class that stand shivering like a delicate plantlet before the fury of tempestuous elements, so full of promise and possibilities, yet so sure of destruction; often without a father to whom they dare apply the loving term, often without a stronger brother to espouse their cause and defend their honor with his life's blood; in the midst of pitfalls and snares, waylaid by the lower classes of white men, with no shelter, no protection nearer than the great blue vault above, which half conceals and half reveals the one Care-Taker they know so little of. Oh, save them, help them, shield, train, develop, teach, inspire them! Snatch them, in God's name, as brands[1] from the burning! There is material in them well worth your while, the hope in germ of a staunch, helpful, regenerating womanhood on which, primarily, rests the foundation stones of our future as a race.

It is absurd to quote statistics showing the Negro's bank account and rent rolls, to point to the hundreds of newspapers edited by colored men and lists of lawyers, doctors, professors, D.D.'s, LL.D.'s, etc., etc., etc., while the source from which the life-blood of the race is to flow is subject to taint and corruption in the enemy's camp.

True progress is never made by spasms. Real progress is growth. It must begin in the seed. Then, "first the blade, then the ear, after that the full corn in the ear."[2] There is something to encourage and inspire us in the

9. "Pamphlet published by Dr. Alex. Crummell" [*Cooper's note*]. Alexander Crummell (1819–1898), American essayist, theologian, and political spokesperson who was "proud of his unmixed African blood."

1. Partly burned pieces of wood.

2. Mark 4:28.

advancement of individuals since their emancipation from slavery. It at least proves that there is nothing irretrievably wrong in the shape of the black man's skull, and that under given circumstances his development, downward or upward, will be similar to that of other average human beings.

But there is no time to be wasted in mere felicitation. That the Negro has his niche in the infinite purposes of the Eternal, no one who has studied the history of the last fifty years in America will deny. That much depends on his own right comprehension of his responsibility and rising to the demands of the hour, it will be good for him to see; and how best to use his present so that the structure of the future shall be stronger and higher and brighter and nobler and holier than that of the past, is a question to be decided each day by every one of us.

The race is just twenty-one years removed from the conception and experience of a chattel, just at the age of ruddy manhood. It is well enough to pause a moment for retrospection, introspection, and prospection. We look back, not to become inflated with conceit because of the depths from which we have arisen, but that we may learn wisdom from experience. We look within that we may gather together once more our forces, and, by improved and more practical methods, address ourselves to the tasks before us. We look forward with hope and trust that the same God whose guiding hand led our fathers through and out of the gall and bitterness of oppression, will still lead and direct their children, to the honor of His name, and for their ultimate salvation.

But this survey of the failures or achievements of the past, the difficulties and embarrassments of the present, and the mingled hopes and fears for the future, must not degenerate into mere dreaming nor consume the time which belongs to the practical and effective handling of the crucial questions of the hour; and there can be no issue more vital and momentous than this of the womanhood of the race.

Here is the vulnerable point, not in the heel, but at the heart of the young Achilles;[3] and here must the defenses be strengthened and the watch redoubled.

We are the heirs of a past which was not our fathers' moulding. "Every man the arbiter of his own destiny" was not true for the American Negro of the past: and it is no fault of his that he finds himself to-day the inheritor of a manhood and womanhood impoverished and debased by two centuries and more of compression and degradation.

But weaknesses and malformations, which to-day are attributable to a vicious schoolmaster and a pernicious system, will a century hence be rightly regarded as proofs of innate corruptness and radical incurability.

Now the fundamental agency under God in the regeneration, the retraining of the race, as well as the ground work and starting point of its progress upward, must be the *black woman*.

With all the wrongs and neglects of her past, with all the weakness, the debasement, the moral thralldom of her present, the black woman of to-day stands mute and wondering at the Herculean task devolving upon her. But the cycles wait for her. No other hand can move the lever. She must be loosed from her bands and set to work.

3. In Greek mythology, the foremost hero of the Trojan War. His vulnerable spot was the heel by which his mother held him when she dipped him in the river Styx to make him immortal.

Our meager and superficial results from past efforts prove their futility; and every attempt to elevate the Negro, whether undertaken by himself or through the philanthropy of others, cannot but prove abortive unless so directed as to utilize the indispensable agency of an elevated and trained womanhood.

A race cannot be purified from without. Preachers and teachers are helps, and stimulants and conditions as necessary as the gracious rain and sunshine are to plant growth. But what are rain and dew and sunshine and cloud if there be no life in the plant germ? We must go to the root and see that that is sound and healthy and vigorous; and not deceive ourselves with waxen flowers and painted leaves of mock chlorophyll.

We too often mistake individuals' honor for race development and so are ready to substitute pretty accomplishments for sound sense and earnest purpose.

A stream cannot rise higher than its source. The atmosphere of homes is no rarer and purer and sweeter than are the mothers in those homes. A race is but a total of families. The nation is the aggregate of its homes. As the whole is sum of all its parts, so the character of the parts will determine the characteristics of the whole. These are all axioms and so evident that it seems gratuitous to remark it; and yet, unless I am greatly mistaken, most of the unsatisfaction from our past results arises from just such a radical and palpable error, as much almost on our own part as on that of our benevolent white friends.

The Negro is constitutionally hopeful and proverbially irrepressible; and naturally stands in danger of being dazzled by the shimmer and tinsel of superficials. We often mistake foliage for fruit and overestimate or wrongly estimate brilliant results.

The late Martin R. Delany,[4] who was an unadulterated black man, used to say when honors of state fell upon him, that when he entered the council of kings the black race entered with him; meaning, I suppose, that there was no discounting his race identity and attributing his achievements to some admixture of Saxon blood. But our present record of eminent men, when placed beside the actual status of the race in America to-day, proves that no man can represent the race. Whatever the attainments of the individual may be, unless his home has moved on *pari passu*,[5] he can never be regarded as identical with or representative of the whole.

Not by pointing to sun-bathed mountain tops do we prove that Phœbus[6] warms the valleys. We must point to homes, average homes, homes of the rank and file of horny handed toiling men and women of the South (where the masses are) lighted and cheered by the good, the beautiful, and the true,—then and not till then will the whole plateau be lifted into the sunlight.

Only the Black Woman can say "when and where I enter, in the quiet, undisputed dignity of my womanhood, without violence and without suing or special patronage, then and there the whole *Negro race enters with me.*" Is it not evident then that as individual workers for this race we must address ourselves with no half-hearted zeal to this feature of our mission. The need is felt and must be recognized by all. There is a call for workers, for missionaries, for men and women with the double consecration of a fundamental love of humanity and a desire for its melioration through the Gospel;

4. African American medical doctor, abolitionist, and writer (1812–1885).

5. At the same pace (Latin).

6. Apollo, god of the sun.

but superadded to this we demand an intelligent and sympathetic comprehension of the interests and special needs of the Negro.

I see not why there should not be an organized effort for the protection and elevation of our girls such as the White Cross League[7] in England. English women are strengthened and protected by more than twelve centuries of Christian influences, freedom and civilization; English girls are dispirited and crushed down by no such all-levelling prejudice as that supercilious caste spirit in America which cynically assumes "A Negro woman cannot be a lady." English womanhood is beset by no such snares and traps as betray the unprotected, untrained colored girl of the South, whose only crime and dire destruction often is her unconscious and marvelous beauty. Surely then if English indignation is aroused and English manhood thrilled under the leadership of a Bishop of the English church to build up bulwarks around their wronged sisters, Negro sentiment cannot remain callous and Negro effort nerveless in view of the imminent peril of the mothers of the next generation. "*I am my Sister's keeper!*" should be the hearty response of every man and woman of the race, and this conviction should purify and exalt the narrow, selfish and petty personal aims of life into a noble and sacred purpose.

We need men who can let their interest and gallantry extend outside the circle of their aesthetic appreciation; men who can be a father, a brother, a friend to every weak, struggling unshielded girl. We need women who are so sure of their own social footing that they need not fear leaning to lend a hand to a fallen or falling sister. We need men and women who do not exhaust their genius splitting hairs on aristocratic distinctions and thanking God they are not as others; but earnest, unselfish souls, who can go into the highways and byways, lifting up and leading, advising and encouraging with the truly catholic benevolence of the Gospel of Christ.

As Church workers we must confess our path of duty is less obvious; or rather our ability to adapt our machinery to our conception of the peculiar exigencies of this work as taught by experience and our own consciousness of the needs of the Negro, is as yet not demonstrable. Flexibility and aggressiveness are not such strong characteristics of the Church to-day as in the Dark Ages.

As a Mission field for the Church the Southern Negro is in some aspects most promising; in others, perplexing. Aliens neither in language and customs, nor in associations and sympathies, naturally of deeply rooted religious instincts and taking most readily and kindly to the worship and teachings of the Church, surely the task of proselytizing the American Negro is infinitely less formidable than that which confronted the Church in the Barbarians of Europe. Besides, this people already look to the Church as the hope of their race. Thinking colored men almost uniformly admit that the Protestant Episcopal Church with its quiet, chaste dignity and decorous solemnity, its instructive and elevating ritual, its bright chanting and joyous hymning, is eminently fitted to correct the peculiar faults of worship—the rank exuberance and often ludicrous demonstrativeness of their people. Yet, strange to say, the Church, claiming to be missionary and Catholic, urging that schism is sin and denominationalism inexcusable, has made in all these years almost no inroads upon this semi-civilized religionism.

7. Founded in the early 1800s in England, it was also known as the White Cross Army or Bishop of Durham's Movement—an organization of men who vowed to uphold chastity and purity.

Harvests from this over ripe field of home missions have been gathered in by Methodists, Baptists, and not least by Congregationalists, who were unknown to the Freedmen before their emancipation.

Our clergy numbers less than two dozen[8] priests of Negro blood and we have hardly more than one self-supporting colored congregation in the entire Southland. While the organization known as the A. M. E. Church[9] has 14,063 ministers, itinerant and local, 4,069 self-supporting churches, 4,275 Sunday-schools, with property valued at $7,772,284, raising yearly for church purposes $1,427,000.

Stranger and more significant than all, the leading men of this race (I do not mean demagogues and politicians, but men of intellect, heart, and race devotion, men to whom the elevation of their people means more than personal ambition and sordid gain—and the men of that stamp have not all died yet) the Christian workers for the race, of younger and more cultured growth, are noticeably drifting into sectarian churches, many of them declaring all the time that they acknowledge the historic claims of the Church, believe her apostolicity, and would experience greater personal comfort, spiritual and intellectual, in her revered communion. It is a fact which any one may verify for himself, that representative colored men, professing that in their heart of hearts they are Episcopalians, are actually working in Methodist and Baptist pulpits, while the ranks of the Episcopal clergy are left to be filled largely by men who certainly suggest the propriety of a "*perpetual* Diaconate"[1] if they cannot be said to have created the necessity for it.

Now where is the trouble? Something must be wrong. What is it?

A certain Southern Bishop of our Church reviewing the situation, whether in Godly anxiety or in "Gothic antipathy" I know not, deprecates the fact that the colored people do not seem *drawn* to the Episcopal Church, and comes to the sage conclusion that the Church is not adapted to the rude untutored minds of the Freedmen, and that they may be left to go to the Methodists and Baptists whither their racial proclivities undeniably tend. How the good Bishop can agree that all-foreseeing Wisdom, and Catholic Love[2] would have framed his Church as typified in his seamless garment and unbroken body, and yet not leave it broad enough and deep enough and loving enough to seek and save and hold seven millions of God's poor, I cannot see.

But the doctors while discussing their scientifically conclusive diagnosis of the disease, will perhaps not think it presumptuous in the patient if he dares to suggest where at least the pain is. If this be allowed, a *Black woman of the South* would beg to point out two possible oversights in this southern work which may indicate in part both a cause and a remedy for some failure. The first is *not calculating for the Black man's personality*; not having respect, if I may so express it, to his manhood or deferring at all to his conceptions of the needs of his people. When colored persons have been employed it was too often as machines or as manikins. There has been no disposition, generally, to get the black man's ideal or to let his individuality

8. The published report of '91 shows 26 priests for the entire country, including one not engaged in work and one a professor in a non-sectarian school, since made Dean of an episcopal Annex to Howard University known as King Hall [*Cooper's note*].

9. African Methodist Episcopal Church, the oldest independent Black church in the United States.

1. The subordinate officers of a church, usually in charge of its day-to-day operations.

2. That is, love that is universal and inclusive.

work by its own gravity, as it were. A conference of earnest Christian men have met at regular intervals for some years past to discuss the best methods of promoting the welfare and development of colored people in this country. Yet, strange as it may seem, they have never invited a colored man or even intimated that one would be welcome to take part in their deliberations. Their remedial contrivances are purely theoretical or empirical, therefore, and the whole machinery devoid of soul.

The second important oversight in my judgment is closely allied to this and probably grows out of it, and that is not developing Negro womanhood as an essential fundamental for the elevation of the race, and utilizing this agency in extending the work of the Church.

Of the first I have possibly already presumed to say too much since it does not strictly come within the province of my subject. However, Macaulay somewhere criticises the Church of England as not knowing how to use fanatics, and declares that had Ignatius Loyola[3] been in the Anglican instead of the Roman communion, the Jesuits would have been schismatics instead of Catholics; and if the religious awakenings of the Wesleys[4] had been in Rome, she would have shaven their heads, tied ropes around their waists, and sent them out under her own banner and blessing. Whether this be true or not, there is certainly a vast amount of force potential for Negro evangelization rendered latent, or worse, antagonistic by the halting, uncertain, I had almost said, *trimming* policy of the Church in the South. This may sound both presumptuous and ungrateful. It is mortifying, I know, to benevolent wisdom, after having spent itself in the execution of well conned theories for the ideal development of a particular work, to hear perhaps the weakest and humblest element of that work asking "what doest thou?"[5]

Yet so it will be in life. The "thus far and no farther" pattern cannot be fitted to any growth in God's kingdom. The universal law of development is "onward and upward." It is God-given and inviolable. From the unfolding of the germ in the acorn to reach the sturdy oak, to the growth of a human soul into the full knowledge and likeness of its Creator, the breadth and scope of the movement in each and all are too grand, too mysterious, too like God himself, to be encompassed and locked down in human molds.

After all the Southern slave owners were right: either the very alphabet of intellectual growth must be forbidden and the Negro dealt with absolutely as a chattel having neither rights nor sensibilities; or else the clamps and irons of mental and moral, as well as civil compression must be riven asunder and the truly enfranchised soul led to the entrance of that boundless vista through which it is to toil upwards to its beckoning God as the buried seed germ to meet the sun.

A perpetual colored diaconate, carefully and kindly superintended by the white clergy; congregations of shiny faced peasants with their clean white aprons and sunbonnets catechised at regular intervals and taught to recite the creed, the Lord's prayer and the ten commandments—duty towards God and duty towards neighbor, surely such well tended sheep ought to be grateful to their shepherds and content in that station of life to which it pleased God to call them. True, like the old professor lecturing to his solitary student, we make no provision here for irregularities. "Questions must

3. Spanish priest (1491–1556), founder of the Jesuit order.
4. English preacher (1703–1791), founder of Methodism.
5. Job 38:11.

be kept till after class," or dispensed with altogether. That some do ask questions and insist on answers, in class too, must be both impertinent and annoying. Let not our spiritual pastors and masters however be grieved at such self-assertion as merely signifies we have a destiny to fulfill and as men and women we must *be about our Father's business.*[6]

It is a mistake to suppose that the Negro is prejudiced against a white ministry. Naturally there is not a more kindly and implicit follower of a white man's guidance than the average colored peasant. What would to others be an ordinary act of friendly or pastoral interest he would be more inclined to regard gratefully as a condescension. And he never forgets such kindness. Could the Negro be brought near to his white priest or bishop, he is not suspicious. He is not only willing but often longs to unburden his soul to this intelligent guide. There are no reservations when he is convinced that you are his friend. It is a saddening satire on American history and manners that it takes something to convince him.

That our people are not "drawn" to a church whose chief dignitaries they see only in the chancel, and whom they reverence as they would a painting or an angel, whose life never comes down to and touches theirs with the inspiration of an objective reality, may be "perplexing" truly (American caste and American Christianity both being facts) but it need not be surprising. There must be something of human nature in it, the same as that which brought about that "the Word was made flesh and dwelt among us"[7] that He might "draw" us towards God.

Men are not "drawn" by abstractions. Only sympathy and love can draw, and until our Church in America realizes this and provides a clergy that can come in touch with our life and have a fellow feeling for our woes, without being imbedded and frozen up in their "Gothic antipathies," the good bishops are likely to continue "perplexed" by the sparsity of colored Episcopalians.

A colored priest of my acquaintance recently related to me, with tears in his eyes, how his reverend Father in God, the Bishop who had ordained him, had met him on the cars on his way to the diocesan convention and warned him, not unkindly, not to take a seat in the body of the convention with the white clergy. To avoid disturbance of their godly placidity he would of course please sit back and somewhat apart. I do not imagine that that clergyman had very much heart for the Christly (!) deliberations of that convention.

To return, however, it is not on this broader view of Church work, which I mentioned as a primary cause of its halting progress with the colored people, that I am to speak. My proper theme is the second oversight of which in my judgment our Christian propagandists have been guilty: or, the necessity of church training, protecting and uplifting our colored womanhood as indispensable to the evangelization of the race.

Apelles[8] did not disdain even that criticism of his lofty art which came from an uncouth cobbler; and may I not hope that the writer's oneness with her subject both in feeling and in being may palliate undue obtrusiveness of opinions here. That the race cannot be effectually lifted up till its women are truly elevated we take as proven. It is not for us to dwell on the needs, the neglects, and the ways of succor, pertaining to the black woman of the

6. Luke 2:49.
7. John 1:14.
8. Greek painter (360?–315? B.C.E.).

South. The ground has been ably discussed and an admirable and practical plan proposed by the oldest Negro priest in America, advising and urging that special organizations such as Church Sisterhoods and industrial schools be devised to meet her pressing needs in the Southland. That some such movements are vital to the life of this people and the extension of the Church among them, is not hard to see. Yet the pamphlet fell still-born from the press. So far as I am informed the Church has made no motion towards carrying out Dr. Crummell's suggestion.

The denomination which comes next our own in opposing the proverbial emotionalism of Negro worship in the South, and which in consequence like ours receives the cold shoulder from the old heads, resting as we do under the charge of not "having religion" and not believing in conversion—the Congregationalists—have quietly gone to work on the young, have established industrial and training schools, and now almost every community in the South is yearly enriched by a fresh infusion of vigorous young hearts, cultivated heads, and helpful hands that have been trained at Fisk, at Hampton, in Atlanta University, and in Tuskegee, Alabama.

These young people are missionaries actual or virtual both here and in Africa. They have learned to love the methods and doctrines of the Church which trained and educated them; and so Congregationalism surely and steadily progresses.

Need I compare these well known facts with results shown by the Church in the same field and during the same or even a longer time.

The institution of the Church in the South to which she mainly looks for the training of her colored clergy and for the help of the "Black Woman" and "Colored Girl" of the South, has graduated since the year 1868, when the school was founded, *five young women*,[9] and while yearly numerous young men have been kept and trained for the ministry by the charities of the Church, the number of indigent females who have here been supported, sheltered and trained, is phenomenally small. Indeed, to my mind, the attitude of the Church toward this feature of her work is as if the solution of the problem of Negro missions depended solely on sending a quota of deacons and priests into the field, girls being a sort of *tertium quid*[1] whose development may be promoted if they can pay their way and fall in with the plans mapped out for the training of the other sex. Now I would ask in all earnestness, does not this force potential deserve by education and stimulus to be made dynamic? Is it not a solemn duty incumbent on all colored churchmen to make it so? Will not the aid of the Church be given to prepare our girls in head, heart, and hand for the duties and responsibilities that await the intelligent wife, the Christian mother, the earnest, virtuous, helpful woman, at once both the lever and the fulcrum for uplifting the race.

As Negroes and churchmen we cannot be indifferent to these questions. They touch us most vitally on both sides. We believe in the Holy Catholic[2] Church. We believe that however gigantic and apparently remote the consummation, the Church will go on conquering and to conquer till the kingdoms of this world, not excepting the black man and the black woman of the South, shall have become the kingdoms of the Lord and of his Christ.

9. Five have been graduated since '86, two in '91, two in '92 [*Cooper's note*].

1. Related to two things but distinctly different from both (Latin).

2. Here meaning "universal."

That past work in this direction has been unsatisfactory we must admit. That without a change of policy results in the future will be as meagre, we greatly fear. Our life as a race is at stake. The dearest interests of our hearts are in the scales. We must either break away from dear old landmarks and plunge out in any line and every line that enables us to meet the pressing need of our people, or we must ask the Church to allow and help us, untrammelled by the prejudices and theories of individuals, to work aggressively under her direction as we alone can, with God's help, for the salvation of our people.

The time is ripe for action. Self-seeking and ambition must be laid on the altar. The battle is one of sacrifice and hardship, but our duty is plain. We have been recipients of missionary bounty in some sort for twenty-one years. Not even the senseless vegetable is content to be a mere reservoir. Receiving without giving is an anomaly in nature. Nature's cells are all little workshops for manufacturing sunbeams, the product to be *given out* to earth's inhabitants in warmth, energy, thought, action. Inanimate creation always pays back an equivalent.

Now, *How much owest thou my Lord*?[3] Will his account be overdrawn if he call for singleness of purpose and self-sacrificing labor for your brethren? Having passed through your drill school, will you refuse a general's commission even if it entail responsibility, risk and anxiety, with possibly some adverse criticism? Is it too much to ask you to step forward and direct the work for your race along those lines which you know to be of first and vital importance?

Will you allow these words of Ralph Waldo Emerson? "In ordinary," says he, "we have a snappish criticism which watches and contradicts the opposite party. We want the will which advances and dictates [acts]. Nature has made up her mind that what cannot defend itself, shall not be defended. Complaining never so loud and with never so much reason, is of no use. What cannot stand must fall; *and the measure of our sincerity and therefore of the respect of men is the amount of health and wealth we will hazard in the defense of our right.*"[4]

1892

3. Luke 16:5.
4. Cooper is quoting from Ralph Waldo Emerson's "Courage," published in *Society and Solitude* in 1881.

PAULINE E. HOPKINS
1859–1930

Born in Portland, Maine, in 1859, the daughter of Benjamin and Sarah Allen Northup, Pauline Elizabeth Hopkins was a fifth-generation African American New Englander. Her mother's family included Thomas Paul, a minister and one of the founders of *Freedom's Journal*, Susan Paul, a teacher and the author of one of the earliest African American biographies, *Memoirs of James Jackson* (1831), and poet James Monroe Whitfield. Her parents moved to Boston and soon divorced; as a young girl, Pauline took the name of her stepfather, William Hopkins, with whom she shared a love of art, activism, and education. Hopkins graduated from Boston's Girls' High School. When fifteen-year-old Pauline Hopkins's essay "The Evils of Intemperance and Their Remedy" won the Congregational Publishing Society Prize, the pioneering African American author William Wells Brown presented her award, a $10 gold piece. In 1877 Hopkins's stage debut in *The Belle of Saratoga* sparked her interest in playwriting, and the eighteen-year-old applied for copyright of two plays, *Aristocracy* and *Winona*. Two years later, Hopkins wrote her best-known play, *The Slaves' Escape; or, the Underground-Rail-road*, and with the family theatrical group, known as the Hopkins Colored Troubadours, she appeared at Boston's Oakland Garden on July 5, 1880, in the premiere of what became an extremely long run for the play, which featured revised stereotypes of slavery's legacy by emphasizing freedom, family, and community.

Between 1892 and 1900 Hopkins worked as a stenographer, and during her free time, she read her fiction for literary societies and lectured on African American history and social issues for various Black community organizations. Her career as a journalist and author began in earnest when she joined the staff of Boston's *Colored American Magazine*, a crucial forum for creative writing, reportage, scholarship, and progressive political commentary. Hopkins purchased ownership shares in the magazine, served on the board of directors, and became a prolific contributing writer. In June 1900 she became editor of the Women's Department, and in May 1903 she became the magazine's literary editor. As one of the few women who edited important periodicals, her influence extended beyond the articles she actually authored.

From 1900 through 1904, Hopkins published an astounding body of diverse prose, including short fiction, historical articles, and biographical sketches. Today, her position in the African American literary canon rests primarily on the four novels that she produced during this period, three of which were serialized in the *Colored American* (one under the pseudonym Sarah A. Allen, derived from her mother's maiden name). The best known of these works is *Contending Forces: A Romance of Negro Life North and South* (1900). Hopkins favored the sentimental romance forms with surprise endings and heavy overtones of the Gothic. Her work generally features female protagonists who are strikingly beautiful, extremely talented, well educated, strongly courageous, and indelibly virtuous. As critic Claudia Tate wrote, Hopkins generally "entangled her heroines and heroes in interracial plots whose conflicts were initiated by villains." Miscegenation and the absurdity of racial prejudice are constant themes. The short stories "Talma Gordon" (1900) and "Bro'r Abr'm Jimson's Wedding" (1901), both published in the *Colored American*, are examples of the breadth of stylistic and thematic concerns that Hopkins developed in her fiction.

In 1904 Hopkins left the *Colored American*, supposedly for medical reasons. However, her departure coincided with the magazine's falling under the control of Booker T. Washington, whose politics and priorities differed significantly from hers. Hopkins continued to publish; she contributed articles to periodicals including *New Era*, which she later edited, and *Voice of the Negro*. In 1905 she published *A Primer of Facts Pertaining to the Early Greatness of the African Race and the Possibility of Restoration by Its Descendants—with Epilogue*.

Pauline Elizabeth Hopkins was one of the most versatile and prolific writers of her generation; however, in later life, she again had to work as a stenographer to support herself. She died August 13, 1930, from injuries suffered in a house fire. Like many African American women writers, Hopkins's life and work were rescued from mid-twentieth-century obscurity by dedicated scholars, and recent publications have revealed fascinating details about Hopkins's life, literature, and the author/activist community in which she lived and of which she wrote.

Talma Gordon

The Canterbury Club of Boston was holding its regular monthly meeting at the palatial Beacon-street residence of Dr. William Thornton, expert medical practitioner and specialist. All the members were present, because some rare opinions were to be aired by men of profound thought on a question of vital importance to the life of the Republic, and because the club celebrated its anniversary in a home usually closed to society. The Doctor's winters, since his marriage, were passed at his summer home near his celebrated sanatorium. This winter found him in town with his wife and two boys. We had heard much of the beauty of the former, who was entirely unknown to social life, and about whose life and marriage we felt sure a romantic interest attached. The Doctor himself was too bright a luminary of the professional world to remain long hidden without creating comment. We had accepted the invitation to dine with alacrity, knowing that we should be welcomed to a banquet that would feast both eye and palate; but we had not been favored by even a glimpse of the hostess. The subject for discussion was: "Expansion: Its Effect upon the Future Development of the Anglo-Saxon throughout the World."

Dinner was over, but we still sat about the social board discussing the question of the hour. The Hon. Herbert Clapp, eminent jurist and politician, had painted in glowing colors the advantages to be gained by the increase of wealth and the exalted position which expansion would give the United States in the councils of the great governments of the world. In smoothly flowing sentences marshalled in rhetorical order, with compact ideas, and incisive argument, he drew an effective picture with all the persuasive eloquence of the trained orator.

Joseph Whitman, the theologian of world-wide fame, accepted the arguments of Mr. Clapp, but subordinated all to the great opportunity which expansion would give to the religious enthusiast. None could doubt the sincerity of this man, who looked once into the idealized face on which heaven had set the seal of consecration.

Various opinions were advanced by the twenty-five men present, but the host said nothing; he glanced from one to another with a look of amusement in his shrewd gray-blue eyes. "Wonderful eyes," said his patients who came under their magic spell. "A wonderful man and a wonderful mind," agreed his contemporaries, as they heard in amazement of some great cure of chronic or malignant disease which approached the supernatural.

"What do you think of this question, Doctor?" finally asked the president, turning to the silent host.

"Your arguments are good; they would convince almost anyone."

"But not Doctor Thornton," laughed the theologian.

"I acquiesce which ever way the result turns. Still, I like to view both sides of a question. We have considered but one tonight. Did you ever think that in spite of our prejudices against amalgamation, some of our descendants, indeed many of them, will inevitably intermarry among those far-off tribes of dark-skinned peoples, if they become a part of this great Union?"

"Among the lower classes that may occur, but not to any great extent," remarked a college president.

"My experience teaches me that it will occur among all classes, and to an appalling extent," replied the Doctor.

"You don't believe in intermarriage with other races?"

"Yes, most emphatically, when they possess decent moral development and physical perfection, for then we develop a superior being in the progeny born of the intermarriage. But we are not ready to receive and assimilate the new material which will be brought to mingle with our pure Anglo-Saxon stream, we should call a halt in our expansion policy."

"I must confess, Doctor, that in the idea of amalgamation you present a new thought to my mind. Will you not favor us with a few of your main points?" asked the president of the club, breaking the silence which followed the Doctor's remarks.

"Yes, Doctor, give us your theories on the subject. We may not agree with you, but we are all open to conviction."

The Doctor removed the half-consumed cigar from his lips, drank what remained in his glass of the choice Burgundy, and leaning back in his chair contemplated the earnest faces before him.

We may make laws, but laws are but straws in the hands of Omnipotence.

"There's a divinity that shapes our ends,
Rough-hew them how we will."[1]

And no man may combat fate. Given a man, propinquity, opportunity fascinating femininity, and there you are. Black, white, green, yellow—nothing will prevent intermarriage. Position, wealth, family, friends—all sink into insignificance before the God-implanted instinct that made Adam, awakening from a deep sleep and finding the woman beside him, accept Eve as bone of his bone; he cared not nor questioned whence she came. So it is with the sons of Adam ever since, through the law of heredity which makes us all one common family. And so it will be with us in our re-formation of this old Republic. Perhaps I can make my meaning clearer by illustration, and with your permission I will tell you a story which came under my observation as a practitioner.

Doubtless all of you heard of the terrible tragedy which occurred at Gordonville, Mass., some years ago, when Capt. Jonathan Gordon, his wife and little son were murdered. I suppose that I am the only man on this side the Atlantic, outside of the police, who can tell you the true story of that crime.

I knew Captain Gordon well; it was through his persuasions that I bought a place in Gordonville and settled down to spending my summers in that charming rural neighborhood. I had rendered the Captain what he was pleased to call valuable medical help, and I became his family physician. Captain Gordon was a retired sea captain, formerly engaged in the East India trade. All his ancestors had been such; but when the bottom fell out of that business he established the Gordonville Mills with his first wife's money, and settled down as a money-making manufacturer of cotton cloth. The Gordons were old New England Puritans who had come over in the "Mayflower"; they had owned Gordon Hall for more than a hundred years. It was a baronial-like pile of granite with towers, standing on a hill which commanded a superb view of Massachusetts Bay and the surrounding coun-

1. Shakespeare, *Hamlet* 5.2.

try. I imagine the Gordon star was under a cloud about the time Captain Jonathan married his first wife, Miss Isabel Franklin of Boston, who brought to him the money which mended the broken fortunes of the Gordon house, and restored this old Puritan stock to its rightful position. In the person of Captain Gordon the austerity of manner and indomitable will-power that he had inherited were combined with a temper that brooked no contradiction.

The first wife died at the birth of her third child, leaving him two daughters, Jeannette and Talma. Very soon after her death the Captain married again. I have heard it rumored that the Gordon girls did not get on very well with their stepmother. She was a woman with no fortune of her own, and envied the large portion left by the first Mrs. Gordon to her daughters.

Jeannette was tall, dark, and stern like her father; Talma was like her dead mother, and possessed of great talent, so great that her father sent her to the American Academy at Rome, to develop the gift. It was the hottest of July days when her friends were bidden to an afternoon party on the lawn and a dance in the evening, to welcome Talma Gordon among them again. I watched her as she moved about among her guests, a fairylike blonde in floating white draperies, her face a study in delicate changing tints, like the heart of a flower, sparkling in smiles about the mouth to end in merry laughter in the clear blue eyes. There were all the subtle allurements of birth, wealth and culture about the exquisite creature:

> "Smiling, frowning evermore,
> Thou art perfect in love-lore,
> Ever varying Madeline,"[2]

quoted a celebrated writer as he stood apart with me, gazing upon the scene before us. He sighed as he looked at the girl.

"Doctor, there is genius and passion in her face. Sometime our little friend will do wonderful things. But is it desirable to be singled out for special blessings by the gods? Genius always carries with it intense capacity for suffering: 'Whom the gods love die young.'"

"Ah," I replied, "do not name death and Talma Gordon together. Cease your dismal croakings; such talk is rank heresy."

The dazzling daylight dropped slowly into summer twilight. The merriment continued; more guests arrived; the great dancing pagoda built for the occasion was lighted by myriads of Japanese lanterns. The strains from the band grew sweeter and sweeter, and "all went merry as a marriage bell."[3] It was a rare treat to have this party at Gordon Hall, for Captain Jonathan was not given to hospitality. We broke up shortly before midnight, with expressions of delight from all the guests.

I was a bachelor then, without ties. Captain Gordon insisted upon my having a bed at the Hall. I did not fall asleep readily; there seemed to be something in the air that forbade it. I was still awake when a distant clock struck the second hour of the morning. Suddenly the heavens were lighted by a sheet of ghastly light; a terrific midsummer thunderstorm was breaking over the sleeping town. A lurid flash lit up all the landscape, painting the trees in grotesque shapes against the murky sky, and defining clearly the sullen blackness of the waters of the bay breaking in grandeur against

2. Quoting "Madeline" by Alfred, Lord Tennyson (1809–1892).

3. Quoting "Eve of Waterloo" by Byron (1788–1824).

the rocky coast. I had arisen and put back the draperies from the windows, to have an unobstructed view of the grand scene. A low muttering coming nearer and nearer, a terrific roar, and then a tremendous downpour. The storm had burst.

Now the uncanny howling of a dog mingled with the rattling volleys of thunder. I heard the opening and closing of doors; the servants were about looking after things. It was impossible to sleep. The lightning was more vivid. There was a blinding flash of a greenish-white tinge mingled with the crash of falling timbers. Then before my startled gaze arose columns of red flames reflected against the sky. "Heaven help us!" I cried; "it is the left tower; it has been struck and is on fire!"

I hurried on my clothes and stepped into the corridor; the girls were there before me. Jeannette came up to me instantly with anxious face. "Oh, Doctor Thornton, what shall we do? papa and mamma and little Johnny are in the old left tower. It is on fire. I have knocked and knocked, but get no answer."

"Don't be alarmed," said I soothingly. "Jenkins, ring the alarm bell," I continued, turning to the butler who was standing near; "the rest follow me. We will force the entrance to the Captain's room."

Instantly, it seemed to me, the bell boomed out upon the now silent air, for the storm had died down as quickly as it arose: and as our little procession paused before the entrance to the old left tower, we could distinguish the sound of the fire engines already on their way from the village.

The door resisted all our efforts; there seemed to be a barrier against it which nothing could move. The flames were gaining headway. Still the same deathly silence within the rooms.

"Oh, will they never get here?" cried Talma, ringing her hands in terror. Jeannette said nothing, but her face was ashen. The servants were huddled together in a panic-stricken group. I can never tell you what a relief it was when we heard the first sound of the firemen's voices, saw their quick movements, and heard the ringing of the axes with which they cut away every obstacle to our entrance to the rooms. The neighbors who had just enjoyed the hospitality of the house were now gathered around offering all the assistance in their power. In less than fifteen minutes the fire was out, and the men began to bear the unconscious inmates from the ruins. They carried them to the pagoda so lately the scene of mirth and pleasure, and I took up my station there, ready to assume my professional duties. The Captain was nearest me; and as I stooped to make the necessary examination I reeled away from the ghastly sight which confronted me—*gentlemen, across the Captain's throat was a deep gash that severed the jugular vein!*

The Doctor paused, and the hand with which he refilled his glass trembled violently.

"What is it, Doctor?" cried the men gathering about me.

"Take the women away; this is murder!"

"Murder!" cried Jeannette, as she fell against the side of the pagoda.

"Murder!" screamed Talma, staring at me as if unable to grasp my meaning.

I continued my examination of the bodies, and found that the same thing had happened to Mrs. Gordon and to little Johnny.

The police were notified; and when the sun rose over the dripping town he found them in charge of Gordon Hall, the servants standing in excited knots talking over the crime, the friends of the family confounded, and the two girls trying to comfort each other and realize the terrible misfortune that had overtaken them.

Nothing in the rooms of the left tower seemed to have been disturbed. The door of communication between the rooms of the husband and wife was open, as they had arranged it for the night. Little Johnny's crib was placed beside his mother's bed. In it he was found as though never awakened by the storm. It was quite evident that the assassin was no common ruffian. The chief gave strict orders for a watch to be kept on all strangers or suspicious characters who were seen in the neighborhood. He made inquiries among the servants, seeing each one separately, but there was nothing gained from them. No one had heard anything suspicious; all had been awakened by the storm. The chief was puzzled. Here was a triple crime for which no motive could be assigned.

"What do you think of it?" I asked him, as we stood together on the lawn.

"It is my opinion that the deed was committed by one of the higher classes, which makes the mystery more difficult to solve. I tell you, Doctor, there are mysteries that never come to light, and this, I think, is one of them."

While we were talking Jenkins, the butler, an old and trusted servant, came up to the chief and saluted respectfully. "Want to speak with me, Jenkins?" he asked. The man nodded, and they walked away together.

The story of the inquest was short, but appalling. It was shown that Talma had been allowed to go abroad to study because she and Mrs. Gordon did not get on well together. From the testimony of Jenkins it seemed that Talma and her father had quarrelled bitterly about her lover, a young artist whom she had met at Rome, who was unknown to fame, and very poor. There had been terrible things said by each, and threats even had passed, all of which now rose up in judgment against the unhappy girl. The examination of the family solicitor revealed the fact that Captain Gordon intended to leave his daughters only a small annuity, the bulk of the fortune going to his son Jonathan, junior. This was a monstrous injustice, as everyone felt. In vain Talma protested her innocence. Someone must have done if. No one would be benefited so much by these deaths as she and her sister. Moreover, the will, together with other papers, was nowhere to be found. Not the slightest clue bearing upon the disturbing elements in this family, if any there were, was to be found. As the only surviving relatives, Jeannette and Talma became joint heirs to an immense fortune, which only for the bloody tragedy just enacted would, in all probability, have passed them by. Here was the motive. The case was very black against Talma. The foreman stood up. The silence was intense: We "find that Capt. Jonathan Gordon, Mary E. Gordon and Jonathan Gordon, junior, all deceased, came to their deaths by means of a knife or other sharp instrument in the hands of Talma Gordon." The girl was like one stricken with death. The flower-like mouth was drawn and pinched; the great sapphire-blue eyes were black with passionate anguish, terror and despair. She was placed in jail to await her trial at the fall session of the criminal court. The excitement in the hitherto quiet town rose to fever heat. Many points in the evidence seemed incomplete to thinking men. The weapon could not be found, nor could it be divined what had become of it. No reason could be given for the murder except the quarrel between Talma and her father and the ill will which existed between the girl and her stepmother.

When the trial was called Jeannette sat beside Talma in the prisoner's dock; both were arrayed in deepest mourning. Talma was pale and careworn, but seemed uplifted, spiritualized, as it were. Upon Jeannette the full realization of her sister's peril seemed to weigh heavily. She had changed much too: hollow cheeks, tottering steps, eyes blazing with fever, all suggestive of rapid and premature decay. From far-off Italy Edward Turner, growing famous in the art world, came to stand beside his girl-love in this hour of anguish.

The trial was a memorable one. No additional evidence had been collected to strengthen the prosecution; when the attorney-general rose to open the case against Talma he knew, as everyone else did, that he could not convict solely on the evidence adduced. What was given did not always bear upon the case, and brought out strange stories of Captain Jonathan's methods. Tales were told of sailors who had sworn to take his life, in revenge for injuries inflicted upon them by his hand. One or two clues were followed, but without avail. The judge summed up the evidence impartially, giving the prisoner the benefit of the doubt. The points in hand furnished valuable collateral evidence, but were not direct proof. Although the moral presumption was against the prisoner, legal evidence was lacking to actually convict. The jury found the prisoner "Not Guilty," owing to the fact that the evidence was entirely circumstantial. The verdict was received in painful silence; then a murmur of discontent ran through the great crowd.

"She must have done it," said one; "who else has been benefited by the horrible deed?"

"A poor woman would not have fared so well at the hands of the jury, nor a homely one either, for that matter," said another.

The great Gordon trial was ended; innocent or guilty, Talma Gordon could not be tried again. She was free; but her liberty, with blasted prospects and fair fame gone forever, was valueless to her. She seemed to have but one object in her mind: to find the murderer or murderers of her parents and half-brother. By her direction the shrewdest of detectives were employed and money flowed like water, but to no purpose; the Gordon tragedy remained a mystery. I had consented to act as one of the trustees of the immense Gordon estates and business interests, and by my advice the Misses Gordon went abroad. A year later I received a letter from Edward Turner, saying that Jeannette Gordon had died suddenly at Rome, and that Talma, after refusing all his entreaties for an early marriage, had disappeared, leaving no clue as to her whereabouts. I could give the poor fellow no comfort, although I had been duly notified of the death of Jeannette by Talma, in a letter telling me where to forward her remittances, and at the same time requesting me to keep her present residence secret, especially from Edward.

I had established a sanitarium for the cure of chronic diseases at Gordonville, and absorbed in the cares of my profession I gave little thought to the Gordons. I seemed fated to be involved in mysteries.

A man claiming to be an Englishman, and fresh from the California gold fields, engaged board and professional service at my retreat. I found him suffering in the grasp of the tubercle[4] fiend—the last stages. He called himself Simon Cameron. Seldom have I seen so fascinating and wicked a face.

4. Tuberculosis.

The lines of the mouth were cruel, the eyes cold and sharp, the smile mocking and evil. He had money in plenty but seemed to have no friends, for he had received no letters and had had no visitors in the time he had been with us. He was an enigma to me; and his nationality puzzled me, for of course I did not believe his story of being English. The peaceful influence of the house seemed to sooth him in a measure, and make his last steps to the mysterious valley[5] as easy as possible. For a time he improved, and would sit or walk about the grounds and sing sweet songs for the pleasure of the other inmates. Strange to say, his malady only affected his voice at times. He sang quaint songs in a silvery tenor of great purity and sweetness that was delicious to the listening ear:

"A wet sheet and a flowing sea,
A wind that follows fast,
And fills the white and rustling sail
And bends the gallant mast;
And bends the gallant mast, my Boys;
While like the eagle free,
Away the good ship flies, and leaves
Old England on the lea."[6]

There are few singers on the lyric stage who could surpass Simon Cameron.

One night, a few weeks after Cameron's arrival, I sat in my office making up my accounts when the door opened and closed; I glanced up, expecting to see a servant. A lady advanced toward me. She threw back her veil, and then I saw that Talma Gordon, or her ghost, stood before me. After the first excitement of our meeting was over, she told me she had come direct from Paris, to place herself in my care. I had studied her attentively during the first moments of our meeting, and I felt that she was right; unless something unforeseen happened to arouse her from the stupor into which she seemed to have fallen, the last Gordon was doomed to an early death. The next day I told her I had cabled Edward Turner to come to her.

"It will do no good; I cannot marry him," was her only comment.

"Have you no feeling of pity for that faithful fellow?" I asked her sternly, provoked by her seeming indifference. I shall never forget the varied emotions depicted on her speaking face. Fully revealed to my gaze was the sight of a human soul tortured beyond the point of endurance; suffering all things, enduring all things, in the silent agony of despair.

In a few days Edward arrived and Talma consented to see him and explain her refusal to keep her promise to him. You must be present, Doctor; it is due your long, tried friendship to know that I have not been fickle, but have acted from the best and strongest motives.

I shall never forget that day. It was directly after lunch that we met in the library. I was greatly excited, expecting I knew not what. Edward was agitated, too. Talma was the only calm one. She handed me what seemed to be a letter, with the request that I would read it. Even now I think I can repeat every word of the document, so indelibly are the words engraved upon my mind:

My darling Sister Talma: When you read these lines I shall be no more, for I shall not live to see your life blasted by the same knowledge that has blighted mine.

5. Death.
6. An adaptation of "A Wet and Flowing Sheet and a Flowing Sea" (1837), by Scottish poet Allan Cunningham (1784–1842).

One evening, about a year before your expected return from Rome, I climbed into a hammock in one corner of the veranda outside the breakfast-room windows, intending to spend the twilight hours in lazy comfort, for it was very hot, enervating August weather. I fell asleep. I was awakened by voices. Because of the heat the rooms had been left in semi-darkness. As I lay there, lazily enjoying the beauty of the perfect summer night, my wandering thoughts were arrested by words spoken by our father to Mrs. Gordon, for they were the occupants of the breakfast-room.

"Never fear, Mary; Johnny shall have it all—money, houses, land and business."

"But if you do go first, Jonathan, what will happen if the girls contest the will? People will think that they ought to have the money as it appears to be theirs by law. I never could survive the terrible disgrace of the story."

"Don't borrow trouble; all you would need to do would be to show them papers I have drawn up, and they would be glad to take their annuity and say nothing. After all, I do not think it is so bad. Jeannette can teach; Talma can paint; six hundred dollars a year is quite enough for them."

I had been somewhat mystified by the conversation until now. This last remark solved the riddle. What could he mean? teach, paint, six hundred a year! With my usual impetuosity I sprang from my resting-place, and in a moment stood in the room confronting my father, and asking what he meant. I could see plainly that both were disconcerted by my unexpected appearance.

"Ah, wretched girl! you have been listening. But what could I expect of your mother's daughter?"

At these words I felt the indignant blood rush to my head in a torrent. So it had been all my life. Before you could remember, Talma, I had felt my little heart swell with anger at the disparaging hints and slurs concerning our mother. Now was my time. I determined that tonight I would know why she was looked upon as an outcast, and her children subjected to every humiliation. So I replied to my father in bitter anger:

"I was not listening; I fell asleep in the hammock. What do you mean by a paltry six hundred a year each to Talma and to me? 'My mother's daughter' demands an explanation from you, sir, of the meaning of the monstrous injustice that you have always practised toward my sister and me."

"Speak more respectfully to your father, Jeannette," broke in Mrs. Gordon.

"How is it, madam, that you look for respect from one whom you have delighted to torment ever since you came into this most unhappy family?"

"Hush, both of you," said Captain Gordon, who seemed to have recovered from the dismay into which my sudden appearance and passionate words had plunged him. "I think I may as well tell you as to wait. Since you know so much you may as well know the whole miserable story." He motioned me to a seat. I could see that he was deeply agitated. I seated myself in a chair he pointed out, in wonder and expectation,—expectation of I knew not what. I trembled. This was a supreme moment in my life; I felt it. The air was heavy with the intense stillness that had settled over us as the common sounds of day gave place to the early quiet of the rural evening. I could see Mrs. Gordon's face as she sat within the radius of the lighted hallway. There was a smile of triumph upon it. I clinched my hands and bit my lips until the blood came, in the effort to keep from screaming. What was I about to hear? At last he spoke:

"I was disappointed at your birth, and also at the birth of Talma. I wanted a male heir. When I knew that I should again be a father I was torn by hope and fear, but I comforted myself with the thought that luck would be with me in the birth of the third child. When the doctor brought me word that a son was born to the house of Gordon, I was wild with delight, and did not notice his disturbed countenance. In the midst of my joy he said to me:

'Captain Gordon, there is something strange about this birth. I want you to see this child.'

Quelling my exultation I followed him to the nursery, and there, lying in the cradle, I saw a child dark as a mulatto, with the characteristic features of the Negro! I was stunned. Gradually it dawned upon me that there was something radically wrong. I turned to the doctor for an explanation.

'There is but one explanation, Captain Gordon; there is Negro blood in the child.'

'There is no Negro blood in my veins,' I said proudly. Then I paused—*the mother!*—I glanced at the doctor. He was watching me intently. The same thought was in his mind. I must have lived a thousand years in that cursed five seconds that I stood there confronting the physician and trying to think. 'Come,' said I to him, 'let us end this suspense.' Without thinking of consequences, I hurried away to your mother and accused her of infidelity to her marriage vows. I raved like a madman. Your mother fell into convulsions; her life was despaired of. I sent for Mr. and Mrs. Franklin, and then I learned the truth. They were childless. One year while on a Southern tour, they befriended an octoroon[7] girl who had been abandoned by her white lover. Her child was a beautiful girl baby. They, being Northern born, thought little of caste distinction because the child showed no trace of Negro blood. They determined to adopt it. They went abroad, secretly sending back word to their friends at a proper time, of the birth of a little daughter. No one doubted the truth of the statement. They made Isabel their heiress, and all went well until the birth of your brother. Your mother and the unfortunate babe died. This is the story which, if known, would bring dire disgrace upon the Gordon family.

To appease my righteous wrath, Mr. Franklin left a codicil to his will by which all the property is left at my disposal save a small annuity to you and your sister."

I sat there after he had finished his story, stunned by what I had heard. I understood, now, Mrs. Gordon's half contemptuous toleration and lack of consideration for us both. As I rose from my seat to leave the room, I said to Captain Gordon:

"Still, in spite of all, sir, I am a Gordon, legally born. I will not tamely give up my birthright."

I left that room a broken-hearted girl, filled with a desire for revenge upon this man, my father, who, by his manner disowned us without regret. Not once in that remarkable interview did he speak of our mother as his wife. He quietly repudiated her and us with all the cold cruelty of relentless caste prejudice. I heard the treatment of your lover's proposal; I knew why Captain Gordon's consent to your marriage was withheld.

7. Person with one-eighth African or African American ancestry.

The night of the reception and dance was the chance for which I had waited, planned and watched. I crept from my window into the ivy-vines, and down, down, until I stood upon the window-sill of Captain Gordon's room in the old left tower. How did I do it, you ask? I do not know. The house was silent after the revel; the darkness of the gathering storm favored me, too. The lawyer was there that day. The will was signed and put safely away among my father's papers. I was determined to have the will and the other documents bearing upon the case, and I would have revenge, too, for the cruelties we had suffered. With the old East Indian dagger firmly grasped I entered the room and found—that my revenge had been forestalled! The horror of the discovery I made that night restored me to reason and a realization of the crime I meditated. Scarce knowing what I did, I sought and found the papers, and crept back to my room as I had come. Do you wonder that my disease is past medical aid?"

I looked at Edward as I finished. He sat, his face covered with his hands. Finally he looked up with a glance of haggard despair: "God! Doctor, but this is too much. I could stand the stigma of murder, but add to that the pollution of Negro blood! No man is brave enough to face such a situation."

"It is as I thought it would be," said Talma sadly, while the tears poured over her white face. "I do not blame you, Edward."

He rose from his chair, rung my hand in a convulsive clasp, turned to Talma and bowed profoundly, with his eyes fixed upon the floor, hesitated, turned, paused, bowed again and abruptly left the room. So those two who had been lovers, parted. I turned to Talma, expecting her to give way. She smiled a pitiful smile, and said: "You see, Doctor, I knew best."

From that moment on she failed rapidly. I was restless. If only I could rouse her to an interest in life, she might live to old age. So rich, so young, so beautiful, so talented, so pure; I grew savage thinking of the injustice of the world. I had not reckoned on the power that never sleeps. Something was about to happen.

On visiting Cameron next morning I found him approaching the end. He had been sinking for a week very rapidly. As I sat by the bedside holding his emaciated hand, he fixed his bright, wicked eyes on me, and asked: "How long have I got to live?"

"Candidly, but a few hours."

"Thank you; well, I want death; I am not afraid to die. Doctor, Cameron is not my name."

"I never supposed it was."

"No? You are sharper than I thought. I heard all your talk yesterday with Talma Gordon. Curse the whole race!"

He clasped his bony fingers around my arm and gasped: *"I murdered the Gordons!"*

Had I the pen of a Dumas[8] I could not paint Cameron as he told his story. It is a question with me whether this wheeling planet, home of the suffering, doubting, dying, may not hold worse agonies on its smiling surface than those of the conventional hell. I sent for Talma and a lawyer. We gave him stimulants, and then with broken intervals of coughing and prostration we got the story of the Gordon murder. I give it to you in a few words:

"I am an East Indian, but my name does not matter, Cameron is as good as any. There is many a soul crying in heaven and hell for vengeance on

8. Alexandre Dumas is the name of two popular French novelists and playwrights: *Dumas père*, the father (1802–1870), and *Dumas fils*, the son (1824–1895).

Jonathan Gordon. Gold was his idol; and many a good man walked the plank, and many a gallant ship was stripped of her treasure, to satisfy his lust for gold. His blackest crime was the murder of my father, who was his friend, and had sailed with him for many a year as mate. One night these two went ashore together to bury their treasure. My father never returned from that expedition. His body was afterward found with a bullet through the heart on the shore where the vessel stopped that night. It was the custom then among pirates for the captain to kill the men who helped bury their treasure. Captain Gordon was no better than a pirate. An East Indian never forgets, and I swore by my mother's deathbed to hunt Captain Gordon down until I had avenged my father's murder. I had the plans of the Gordon estate, and fixed on the night of the reception in honor of Talma as the time for my vengeance. There is a secret entrance from the shore to the chambers where Captain Gordon slept; no one knew of it save the Captain and trusted members of his crew. My mother gave me the plans, and entrance and escape were easy."

"So the great mystery was solved. In a few hours Cameron was no more. We placed the confession in the hands of the police, and there the matter ended."

"But what became of Talma Gordon?" questioned the president. "Did she die?"

"Gentlemen," said the Doctor, rising to his feet and sweeping the faces of the company with his eagle gaze, "gentlemen, if you will follow me to the drawing-room, I shall have much pleasure in introducing you to my wife—*nee*[9] Talma Gordon."

1900

Bro'r Abr'm Jimson's Wedding

A Christmas Story

It was a Sunday in early spring the first time that Caramel Johnson dawned on the congregation of —— Church in a populous New England city.

The Afro-Americans of that city are well-to-do, being of a frugal nature, and considering it a lasting disgrace for any man among them, desirous of social standing in the community, not to make himself comfortable in this world's goods against the coming time, when old age creeps on apace and renders him unfit for active business.

Therefore the members of the said church had not waited to be exhorted by reformers to own their unpretentious homes and small farms outside the city limits, but they vied with each other in efforts to accumulate a small competency urged thereto by a realization of what pressing needs the future might bring, or it might have been because of the constant example of white neighbors, and a due respect for the dignity which *their* foresight had brought to the superior race.

Of course, these small Vanderbilts and Astors of a darker hue must have a place of worship in accord with their worldly prosperity, and so it fell out that —— church was the richest plum in the ecclesiastical pudding, and

9. Formerly known as.

greatly sought by scholarly divines as a resting place for four years,—the extent of the time-limit allowed by conference to the men who must be provided with suitable charges according to the demands of their energy and scholarship.

The attendance was unusually large for morning service, and a restless movement was noticeable all through the sermon. How strange a thing is nature; the change of the seasons announces itself in all humanity as well as in the trees and flowers, the grass, and in the atmosphere. Something within us responds instantly to the touch of kinship that dwells in all life.

The air soft and balmy, laden with rich promise for the future, came through the massive, half-open windows, stealing in refreshing waves upon the congregation. The sunlight fell through the colored glass of the windows in prismatic hues, and dancing all over the lofty star-gemmed ceiling, painted the hue of the broad vault of heaven, creeping down in crinkling shadows to touch the deep garnet cushions of the sacred desk, and the rich wood of the altar with a hint of gold.

The offertory[1] was ended. The silvery cadences of a rich soprano voice still lingered on the air, "O, Worship the Lord in the beauty of holiness."[2] There was a suppressed feeling of expectation, but not the faintest rustle as the minister rose in the pulpit, and after a solemn pause, gave the usual invitation:

"If there is anyone in this congregation desiring to unite with this church, either by letter or on probation, please come forward to the altar."

The words had not died upon his lips when a woman started from her seat near the door and passed up the main aisle. There was a sudden commotion on all sides. Many heads were turned—it takes so little to interest a church audience. The girls in the choir-box leaned over the rail, nudged each other and giggled, while the men said to one another, "She's a stunner,[3] and no mistake."

The candidate for membership, meanwhile, had reached the altar railing and stood before the man of God, to whom she had handed her letter from a former Sabbath home, with head decorously bowed as became the time and the holy place. There was no denying the fact that she was a pretty girl; brown of skin, small of feature, with an ever-lurking gleam of laughter in eyes coal black. Her figure was slender and beautifully moulded, with a seductive grace in the undulating walk and erect carriage. But the chief charm of the sparkling dark face lay in its intelligence, and the responsive play of facial expression which was enhanced by two mischievous dimples pressed into the rounded cheeks by the caressing fingers of the god of Love.

The minister whispered to the candidate, coughed, blew his nose on his snowy clerical handkerchief, and, finally, turned to the expectant congregation:

"Sister Chocolate Caramel Johnson—"

He was interrupted by a snicker and a suppressed laugh, again from the choir-box, and an audible whisper which sounded distinctly throughout the quiet church,—

"I'd get the Legislature to change that if it was mine, 'deed I would!" then silence profound caused by the reverend's stern glance of reproval bent on the offenders in the choir-box.

1. Communion or Holy Eucharist, also known as "The Lord's Supper."

2. From a hymn by Robert Lowry (1826–1899).

3. That is, a stunningly beautiful person.

"Such levity will not be allowed among the members of the choir. If it occurs again, I shall ask the choir master for the names of the offenders and have their places taken by those more worthy to be gospel singers."

Thereupon Mrs. Tilly Anderson whispered to Mrs. Nancy Tobias that, "them choir gals is the mos' deceivines' hussies in the church, an' for my part, I'm glad the pastor called 'em down. That sister's too good lookin' fer 'em, an' they'll be after her like er pack o' houn's, min' me, Sis' Tobias."

Sister Tobias ducked her head in her lap and shook her fat sides in laughing appreciation of the sister's foresight.

Order being restored the minister proceeded:

"Sister Chocolate Caramel Johnson brings a letter to us from our sister church in Nashville, Tennessee. She has been a member in good standing for ten years, having been received into fellowship at ten years of age. She leaves them now, much to their regret, to pursue the study of music at one of the large conservatories in this city, and they recommend her to our love and care. You know the contents of the letter. All in favor of giving Sister Johnson the right hand of fellowship, please manifest the same by a rising vote." The whole congregation rose.

"Contrary minded? None. The ayes have it. Be seated, friends. Sister Johnson, it gives me great pleasure to receive you into this church. I welcome you to its joys and sorrows. May God bless you, Brother Jimson?" (Brother Jimson stepped from his seat to the pastor's side.) "I assign this sister to your class.[4] Sister Johnson, this is Brother Jimson, your future spiritual teacher."

Brother Jimson shook the hand of his new member, warmly, and she returned to her seat. The minister pronounced the benediction over the waiting congregation; the organ burst into richest melody. Slowly the crowd of worshippers dispersed.

Abraham Jimson had made his money as a janitor for the wealthy people of the city. He was a bachelor, and when reproved by some good Christian brother for still dwelling in single blessedness always offered as an excuse that he had been too busy to think of a wife, but that now he was "well fixed," pecuniarily,[5] he would begin to "look over" his lady friends for a suitable companion.

He owned a house in the suburbs and a fine brick dwelling-house in the city proper. He was a trustee of prominence in the church; in fact, its "solid man," and his opinion was sought and his advice acted upon by his associates on the Board. It was felt that any lady in the congregation would be proud to know herself his choice.

When Caramel Johnson received the right hand of fellowship, her aunt, the widow Maria Nash, was ahead in the race for the wealthy class-leader. It had been neck-and-neck for a while between her and Sister Viney Peters, but, finally it had settled down to Sister Maria with a hundred to one, among the sporting members of the Board, that she carried off the prize, for Sister Maria owned a house adjoining Brother Jimson's in the suburbs, and property counts these days.

Sister Nash had "no idea" when she sent for her niece to come to B. that the latter would prove a rival; her son Andy was as good as engaged to Caramel. But it is always the unexpected that happens. Caramel came, and Brother

4. Subset of a congregation under the leadership of a class leader, or teacher and spiritual guide.
5. Financially.

Jimson had no eyes for the charms of other women after he had gazed into her coal black orbs, and watched her dimples come and go.

Caramel decided to accept a position as housemaid in order to help defray the expenses of her tuition at the conservatory, and Brother Jimson interested himself so warmly in her behalf that she soon had a situation in the home of his richest patron where it was handy for him to chat with her about the business of the church, and the welfare of her soul, in general. Things progressed very smoothly until the fall, when one day Sister Maria had occasion to call, unexpectedly, on her niece and found Brother Jimson basking in her smiles while he enjoyed a sumptuous dinner of roast chicken and fixings.

To say that Sister Maria was "set way back" would not accurately describe her feelings: but from that time Abraham Jimson knew that he had a secret foe in the Widow Nash.

Before many weeks had passed it was publicly known that Brother Jimson would lead Caramel Johnson to the altar "come Christmas." There was much sly speculation as to the "widder's gittin' left," and how she took it from those who had cast hopeless glances toward the chief man of the church. Great preparations were set on foot for the wedding festivities. The bride's trousseau was a present from the groom and included a white satin wedding gown and a costly gold watch. The town house was refurnished, and a trip to New York was in contemplation.

"Hump!" grunted Sister Nash when told the rumors, "there's no fool like an ol' fool. Car'mel's a han'ful he'll fin', ef he gits her."

"I reckon he'll git her all right, Sis' Nash," laughed the neighbor, who had run in to talk over the news.

"I've said my word an' I ain't goin' change it, Sis'r. Min' me, I says, *ef he gits her*, an, I mean it."

Andy Nash was also a member of Brother Jimson's class; he possessed, too, a strong sweet baritone voice which made him of great value to the choir. He was an immense success in the social life of the city, and had created sad havoc with the hearts of the colored girls; he could have his pick of the best of them because of his graceful figure and fine easy manners. Until Caramel had been dazzled by the wealth of her elderly lover, she had considered herself fortunate as the lady of his choice.

It was Sunday, three weeks before the wedding, that Andy resolved to have it out with Caramel.

"She's been hot an' she's been col', an' now she's luke warm, an' today ends it before this gent-man sleeps." he told himself as he stood before the glass and tied his pale blue silk tie in a stunning knot, and settled his glossy tile[6] at a becoming angle.

Brother Jimson's class was a popular one and had a large membership; the hour spent there was much enjoyed, even by visitors. Andy went into the vestry early, resolved to meet Caramel if possible. She was there, at the back of the room sitting alone on a settee. Andy immediately seated himself in the vacant place by her side. There were whispers and much head-shaking among the few early worshippers, all of whom knew the story of the young fellow's romance and his disappointment.

6. Hat or cap.

As he dropped into the seat beside her, Caramel turned her large eyes on him intently, speculatively, with a doubtful sort of curiosity suggested in her expression, as to how he took her flagrant desertion.

"Howdy, Car'mel?" was his greeting without a shade of resentment.

"I'm well; no need to ask how you are," was the quick response. There was a mixture of cordiality and coquetry in her manner. Her eyes narrowed and glittered under lowered lids, as she gave him a long side-glance. How could she help showing her admiration for the supple young giant beside her? "Surely," she told herself, "I'll have long time enough to git sick of old rheumatics,"[7] her pet name for her elderly lover.

"I ain't sick much," was Andy's surly reply.

He leaned his elbow on the back of the settee and gave his recreant sweetheart a flaming glance of mingled love and hate, oblivious to the presence of the assembled class-members.

"You ain't over friendly these days, Car'mel, but I gits news of your capers 'roun' 'bout some of the members."

"My—Yes?" she answered as she flashed her great eyes at him in pretended surprise. He laughed a laugh not good to hear.

"Yes," he drawled. Then he added with sudden energy, "Are you goin' to tie up to old Rheumatism sure 'nuff, come Chris'mas?"

"Come Chris'mas, Andy, I be. I hate to tell you but I have to do it."

He recoiled as from a blow. As for the girl, she found a keen relish in the situation: it flattered her vanity.

"How comes it you've changed your mind, Car'mel, 'bout you an' me? You've tol' me often that I was your first choice."

"We—ll," she drawled, glancing uneasily about her and avoiding her aunt's gaze, which she knew was bent upon her every movement. "I did reckon once I would. But a man with money suits me best, an' you ain't got a cent."

"No more have you. You ain't no better than other women to work an' help a man along, is you?"

The color flamed an instant in her face turning the dusky skin to a deep, dull red.

"Andy Nash, you always was a fool, an' as ignerunt as a wil' Injun. I mean to have a sure nuff brick house an' plenty of money. That makes people respec' you. Why don' you quit bein' so shifless and save your money. You ain't worth your salt."[8]

"Your head's turned with pianorer-playin' an' livin' up North. Ef you'll turn *him* off an' come back home, I'll turn over a new leaf, Car'mel," his voice was soft and persuasive enough now.

She had risen to her feet; her eyes flashed, her face was full of pride.

"I won't. I've quit likin' you, Andy Nash."

"Are you in earnest?" he asked, also rising from his seat.

"Dead earnes'."

"Then there's no more to be said."

He spoke calmly, not raising his voice above a whisper. She stared at him in surprise. Then he added as he swung on his heel preparatory to leaving her:

7. Persons suffering from rheumatism (arthritis).
8. That is, worthless; see Bible verses such as Matthew 5:13.

"You ain't got him yet, my gal. But remember, I'm waitin' for you when you need me."

While this whispered conference was taking place in the back part of the vestry, Brother Jimson had entered, and many an anxious glance he cast in the direction of the couple. Andy made his way slowly to his mother's side as Brother Jimson rose in his place to open the meeting. There was a commotion on all sides as the members rustled down on their knees for prayer. Widow Nash whispered to her son as they knelt side by side:

"How did you make out, Andy?"

"Didn't make out at all, mammy;[9] she's as obstinate as a mule."

"Well, then, there's only one thing mo' to do."

Andy was unpleasant company for the remainder of the day. He sought, but found nothing to palliate Caramel's treachery. He had only surly, bitter words for his companions who ventured to address him, as the outward expression of inward tumult. The more he brooded over his wrongs the worse he felt. When he went to work on Monday morning he was feeling vicious. He had made up his mind to do something desperate. The wedding should not come off. He would be avenged.

Andy went about his work at the hotel in gloomy silence unlike his usual gay hilarity. It happened that all the female help at the great hostelry was white, and on that particular Monday morning it was the duty of Bridget McCarthy's watch to clean the floors. Bridget was also not in the best of humors, for Pat McClosky, her special company,[1] had gone to the priest's with her rival, Kate Connerton, on Sunday afternoon, and Bridget had not yet got over the effects of a strong rum punch taken to quiet her nerves after hearing the news.

Bridget had scrubbed a wide swath of the marble floor when Andy came through with a rush order carried in scientific style high above his head, balanced on one hand. Intent upon satisfying the guest who was princely in his "tips," Andy's unwary feet became entangled in the maelstrom[2] of brooms, scrubbing-brushes and pails. In an instant the "order" was sliding over the floor in a general mix-up.

To say Bridget was mad wouldn't do her state justice.[3] She forgot herself and her surroundings and relieved her feelings in elegant Irish, ending a tirade of abuse by calling Andy a "wall-eyed, bandy-legged[4] nagur."

Andy couldn't stand that from "common, po' white trash," so calling all his science into play he struck out straight from the shoulder with his right, and brought her a swinging blow on the mouth, which seated her neatly in the five-gallon bowl of freshly made lobster salad which happened to be standing on the floor behind her.

There was a wail from the kitchen force that reached to every department. It being the busiest hour of the day when they served dinner, the dish-washers and scrubbers went on a strike against the "nagur who struck Bridget McCarthy, the baste," mingled with cries of "lynch him!" Instantly the great basement floor was a battle ground. Every colored man seized whatever was handiest and ranged himself by Andy's side, and stood ready to receive the onslaught of the Irish brigade. For the sake of peace, and sorely against his inclinations, the proprietor surrendered Andy to the police on a charge of assault and battery.

9. Generally considered derogatory now, at the time of the story "Mammy" was a term of endearment comparable to "Mama."
1. Boyfriend or suitor.
2. Confusion, disorder.
3. That is, would be an understatement.
4. That is, eyes turned outward from the nose, and legs bowed outward from the knees.

On Wednesday morning of that eventful week, Brother Jimson wended his way to his house in the suburbs to collect the rent. Unseen by the eye of man, he was wrestling with a problem that had shadowed his life for many years. No one on earth suspected him unless it might be the widow. Brother Jimson boasted of his consistent Christian life—rolled his piety like a sweet morsel beneath his tongue, and had deluded himself into thinking that *he* could do no sin. There were scoffers in the church who doubted the genuineness of his pretentions, and he believed that there was a movement on foot against his power led by Widow Nash.

Brother Jimson groaned in bitterness of spirit.[5] His only fear was that he might be parted from Caramel. If he lost her he felt that all happiness in life was over for him, and anxiety gave him a sickening feeling of unrest. He was tormented, too, by jealousy; and when he was called upon by Andy's anxious mother to rescue her son from the clutches of the law, he had promised her fair enough, but in reality resolved to do nothing but—tell the judge that Andy was a dangerous character whom it was best to quell by severity. The pastor and all the other influential members of the church were at court on Tuesday, but Brother Jimson was conspicuous by his absence.

Today Brother Jimson resolved to call on Sister Nash, and, as he had heard nothing of the outcome of the trial, make cautious inquiries concerning that, and also sound her on the subject nearest his heart.

He opened the gate and walked down the side path to the back door. From within came the rythmic sound of a rubbing board. The brother knocked, and then cleared his throat with a preliminary cough.

"Come," called a voice within. As the door swung open it revealed the spare form of the widow, who with sleeves rolled above her elbows stood at the tub cutting her way through piles of foaming suds.

"Mornin', Sis' Nash! How's all?"

"That you, Bro'r Jimson? How's yourself? Take a cheer an' make yourself to home."

"Cert'nly, Sis' Nash; don' care ef I do," and the good brother scanned the sister with an eagle eye. "Yas'm, I'm purty tol'rable these days, thank God. Bleeg'd to you, Sister, I jes' will stop an' res' myself befo' I repair myself back to the city." He seated himself in the most comfortable chair in the room, tilted it on the two back legs against the wall, lit his pipe and with a grunt of satisfaction settled back to watch the white rings of smoke curl about his head.

"These are mighty ticklish times, Sister. How's you continue on the journey? Is you strong in the faith?"

"I've got the faith, my brother, but I ain't on no mountain top this week. I'm way down in the valley: I'm jes' coaxin' the Lord to keep me sweet," and Sister Nash wiped the ends from her hands and prodded the clothes in the boiler with the clothes-stick, added fresh pieces and went on with her work.

"This is a worl' strewed with wrecks an' floatin' with tears. It's the valley of tribulation. May your faith continue. I hear Jim Jinkins has bought a farm up Taunton way."

"Wan' ter know!"

"Doctor tells me Bro'r Waters is comin' after Chris-mus. They do say as how he's stirrin' up things turrible; he's easin' his min' on this lynchin' business, an' it's high time—high time."

5. Resentment, anger.

"Sho! Don' say so! What you reck'n he's goin' tell us now, Brother Jimson?"

"Suthin' 'stonishin', Sister; it'll stir the country from end to end. Yes'm, the Council is powerful strong as an organ'zation."

"Sho! sho!" and the "thrub, thrub" of the board could be heard a mile away.

The conversation flagged. Evidently Widow Nash was not in a talkative mood that morning. The brother was disappointed.

"Well, it's mighty comfort'ble here, but I mus' be goin'."

"What's your hurry, Brother Jimson?"

"Business, Sister, business," and the brother brought his chair forward preparatory to rising. "Where's Andy? How'd he come out of that little difficulty?"

"Locked up."

"You don' mean to say he's in jail?"

"Yes; he's in jail 'tell I git's his bail."

"What might the sentence be, Sister?"

"Twenty dollars fine or six months at the Islan'."[6] There was silence for a moment, broken only by the "thrub, thrub" of the washboard, while the smoke curled upward from Brother Jimson's pipe as he enjoyed a few last puffs.

"These are mighty ticklish times, Sister. Po' Andy, the way of the transgressor is hard."

Sister Nash took her hands out of the tub and stood with arms akimbo, a statue of Justice carved in ebony. Her voice was like the trump of doom.

"Yes; an' men like you is the cause of it. You leadin' men with money an' chances don' do your duty. I arst you, I arst you fair, to go down to the jedge an' bail that po' chile out. Did you go? No; you hard-faced old devil, you lef him be there, an' I had to git the money from my white folks. Yes, an' I'm breakin' my back now, over that pile of clo's to pay that twenty dollars. Um! all the trouble comes to us women."

"That's so, Sister; that's the livin' truth," murmured Brother Jimson furtively watching the rising storm and wondering where the lightning of her speech would strike next.

"I tell you what it is our receiptfulness to each other is the reason we don' prosper an' God's a-punishin' us with fire an' with sward 'cause we's so jealous an' snaky[7] to each other."

"That's so, Sister; that's the livin' truth."

"Yes, sir; a nigger's boun' to be a nigger 'tell the trump of doom. You kin skin him, but he's a nigger still. Broad-cloth, biled shirts an' money won' make him more or less, no, sir."

"That's so, Sister; that's jes' so."

"A nigger can't holp himself. White folks can run agin the law all the time an' they never gits caught, but a nigger! Every time he opens his mouth he puts his foot in it—got to hit that po' white trash gal in the mouth an' git jailed, an' leave his po'r ol' mother to work her fingers to the secon' jint to git him out. Um!"

"These are mighty ticklish times, Sister. Man's boun' to sin; it's his nat'ral state. I hope this will teach Andy humility of the sperit."

6. Deer Island Prison in Boston Harbor.

7. Deceitful.

"A little humility'd be good for yourself, Abra'm Jimson." Sister Nash ceased her sobs and set her teeth hard.

"Lord, Sister Nash, what compar'son is there 'twixt me an' a worthless nigger like Andy? My business is with the salt of the earth, an' so I have dwelt ever since I was consecrated."

"Salt, of the earth! But ef the salt have los' its saver how you goin' salt it ergin'?[8] No, sir, you cain't do it; it mus' be cas' out an' trodded under foot of men. That's who's goin' happen you Abe Jimson, hyar me? An' I'd like to trod on you with my foot, an' every ol' good fer nuthin' bag o' salt like you," shouted Sister Nash. "You're a snake in the grass; you done stole the boy's gal an' then try to git him sent to the Islan'. You cain't deny it, fer the jedge done tol' me all you said, you ol' rhinoceros-hided hypercrite. Salt of the earth! You!"

Brother Jimson regretted that Widow Nash had found him out. Slowly he turned, settling his hat on the back of his head.

"Good mornin', Sister Nash. I ain't no hard feelin's agains' you. I'm too near to the kindom to let trifles jar me. My bowels of compassion yearns over you, Sister, a pilgrim an' a stranger in this unfriendly worl'."[9]

No answer from Sister Nash. Brother Jimson lingered.

"Good mornin', Sister," still no answer.

"I hope to see you at the weddin', Sister."

"Keep on hopin'; I'll be there. That gal's my own sister's chile. What in time she wants of a rheumatic ol' sap-head like you for, beats me. I wouldn't marry you for no money, myself; no, sir; it's my belief that you've done goophered[1] her."

"Yes, Sister; I've hearn tell of people refusin' befo' they was ask'd," he retorted, giving her a sly look.

For answer the widow grabbed the clothes-stick and flung it at him in speechless rage.

"My, what a temper it's got," remarked Brother Jimson soothingly as he dodged the shovel, the broom, the coal-hod and the stove-covers. But he sighed with relief as he turned into the street and caught the faint sound of the washboard now resumed.

To a New Englander the season of snow and ice with its clear biting atmosphere, is the ideal time for the great festival. Christmas morning dawned in royal splendor; the sun kissed the snowy streets and turned the icicles into brilliant stalactites. The bells rang a joyous call from every steeple, and soon the churches were crowded with eager worshippers—eager to hear again the oft-repeated, the wonderful story on which the heart of the whole Christian world feeds its faith and hope. Words of tender faith, marvellous in their simplicity fell from the lips of a world-renowned preacher, and touched the hearts of the listening multitude:

"The winter sunshine is not more bright and clear than the atmosphere of living joy, which stretching back between our eyes and that picture of Bethlehem, shows us its beauty in unstained freshness. And as we open once again those chapters of the gospel in which the ever fresh and living

8. See Matthew 5:13–14—"Ye are the salt of the earth: but if the salt have lost its savour, wherewith shall it be salted? It is thenceforth good for nothing, but to be cast out, and to be trodden under foot of men."

9. The bowels were considered the source of passions such as anger, love, and mercy. This conversation is a collage of references to biblical passages including Luke 8:17 and Matthew 10:26.

1. Bewitched.

picture stands, there seems from year to year always to come some newer, brighter meaning into the words that tell the tale.

"St. Matthew says that when Jesus was born in Bethlehem the wise men came from the East to Jerusalem. The East means man's search after God; Jerusalem means God's search after man. The East means the religion of the devout soul; Jerusalem means the religion of the merciful God. The East means Job's cry, 'Oh, that I knew where I might find him!' Jerusalem means 'Immanuel—God with us.'"

Then the deep-toned organ joined the grand chorus of human voices in a fervent hymn of praise and thanksgiving:

"Lo! the Morning Star appeareth,
  O'er the world His beams are cast;
He the Alpha and Omega,
  He, the Great, the First the Last!
Hallelujah! hallelujah!
  Let the heavenly portal ring!
Christ is born, the Prince of glory!
  Christ the Lord, Messiah, King!"[2]

Everyone of prominence in church circles had been bidden to the Jimson wedding. The presents were many and costly. Early after service on Christmas morning the vestry rooms[3] were taken in hand by leading sisters to prepare the tables for the supper, for on account of the host of friends bidden to the feast, the reception was to be held in the vestry.

The tables groaned beneath their loads of turkey, salads, pies, puddings, cakes and fancy ices.

Yards and yards of evergreen wreaths encircled the granite pillars; the altar was banked with potted plants and cut flowers. It was a beautiful sight. The main aisle was roped off for the invited guests, with white satin ribbons.

Brother Jimson's patrons were to be present in a body, and they had sent the bride a solid silver service, so magnificent that the sisters could only sigh with envy.

The ceremony was to take place at seven sharp. Long before that hour the ushers in full evening dress were ready to receive the guests. Sister Maria Nash was among the first to arrive, and even the Queen of Sheba was not arrayed like unto her. At fifteen minutes before the hour, the organist began an elaborate instrumental performance. There was an expectant hush and much head-turning when the music changed to the familiar strains of the "Wedding March." The minister took his place inside the railing ready to receive the party. The groom waited at the altar.

First came the ushers, then the maids of honor, then the flower girl—daughter of a prominent member—carrying a basket of flowers which she scattered before the bride, who was on the arm of the best man. In the bustle and confusion incident to the entrance of the wedding party no one noticed a group of strangers accompanied by Andy Nash, enter and occupy seats near the door.

The service began. All was quiet. The pastor's words fell clearly upon the listening ears. He had reached the words:

2. Lyrics to hymn (1897) by Fanny Crosby.
3. Rooms in a church for storing robes or holding meetings and classes.

"If any man can show just cause," etc., when like a thunder-clap came a voice from the back part of the house—an angry excited voice, and a woman of ponderous avoirdupois[4] advanced up the aisle.

"Hol' on thar, pastor, hol'on! A man cain't have but one wife 'cause it's agin' the law. I'm Abe Jimson's lawful wife, an' hyars his six children—all boys—to pint out their daddy." In an instant the assembly was in confusion.

"My soul," exclaimed Viney Peters, "the ol' sarpen'! An' to think how near I come to takin' up with him. I'm glad I ain't Car'mel."

Sis'r Maria said nothing, but a smile of triumph lit up her countenance.

"Brother Jimson, is this true?" demanded the minister, sternly. But Abraham Jimson was past answering. His face was ashen, his teeth chattering, his hair standing on end. His shaking limbs refused to uphold his weight; he sank upon his knees on the steps of the altar.

But now a hand was laid upon his shoulder and Mrs. Jimson hauled him upon his feet with a jerk.

"Abe Jimson, you know me. You run'd 'way from me up North fifteen year ago, an' you hid yourself like a groun' hog in a hole, but I've got you. There'll be no new wife in the Jimson family this week. I'm yer fus' wife an' I'll be yer las' one. Git up hyar now, you mis'able sinner an' tell the pastor who I be." Brother Jimson meekly obeyed the clarion voice. His sanctified air had vanished; his pride humbled into the dust.

"Pastor," came in trembling tones from his quivering lips. "These are mighty ticklish times." He paused. A deep silence followed his words. "I'm a weak-kneed, mis'able sinner. I have fallen under temptation. This is Ma' Jane, my wife, an' these hyar boys is my sons, God forgive me."

The bride, who had been forgotten now, broke in:

"Abraham Jimson, you ought to be hung. I'm goin' to sue you for breach of promise." It was a fatal remark. Mrs. Jimson turned upon her.

"You will, will you? Sue him, will you? I'll make a choc'late Car'mel of you befo' I'm done with you, you 'ceitful hussy, hoodooin'[5] hones' men from thar wives."

She sprang upon the girl, tearing, biting, rendering. The satin gown and gossamar veil were reduced to rags. Caramel emitted a series of ear-splitting shrieks, but the biting and tearing went on. How it might have ended no one can tell if Andy had not sprang over the backs of the pews and grappled with the infuriated woman.

The excitement was intense. Men and women struggled to get out of the church. Some jumped from the windows and others crawled under the pews, where they were secure from violence. In the midst of the melee, Brother Jimson disappeared and was never seen again, and Mrs. Jimson came into possession of his property by due process of law.

In the church Abraham Jimson's wedding and his fall from grace is still spoken of in eloquent whispers.

In the home of Mrs. Andy Nash a motto adorns the parlor walls worked in scarlet wool and handsomely framed in gilt. The text reads: "Ye are the salt of the earth; there is nothing hidden that shall not be revealed."[6]

1901

4. Heaviness.
5. Bewitching.
6. From Matthew 5:13 and Luke 8:17.

From Famous Men of the Negro Race

Booker T. Washington

The subject of this sketch is probably the most talked of Afro-American in the civilized world today, and the influence of his words and acts on the future history of the Negro race will be carefully scrutinized by future generations.

Dr. Washington's life-story has been rehearsed so frequently by writers of both races, that it has become familiar in the households of the land.

We all know that he was born a slave on a plantation in Franklin County, Virginia, in 1858 or 1859. He describes Hale's Ford, near his birthplace, as a town with one house and a post-office. His master's name was John Burroughs, for whose family his mother cooked.[1]

Dr. Washington's[2] early life and struggles are stories common to thousands of Negroes,—freedom, poverty, a desire for education, the hardships encountered to compass the coveted end, his admission to Hampton and his final graduation from that college, a year at Wayland Seminary, Washington, D.C., and his "slumbering ambition"[3] to become a lawyer. We read with pleasure the account of his life as a teacher at Malden, West Virginia, where he had received his first training in the three r's "reading, 'riting and 'rithmetic." His own description of his work there is highly entertaining:

"I not only taught school in the day, but for a great portion of the time taught night school. In addition to this I had two Sunday schools: the average attendance in my day school was, I think, between 80 and 90. As I had no assistant it was a very difficult task to keep all the pupils interested and to see that they made progress in their work.

"One thing that gave me great satisfaction and pleasure in teaching this school was the conducting of a debating society, which met weekly and was largely attended by the young and older people."

After an interval of successful work in this field, Dr. Washington tells of his work as a teacher at Hampton. He says: "I was surprised by being asked by Gen. Armstrong[4] to return to Hampton Institute and take a position, partly as a teacher and partly as a post-graduate student. This, I gladly consented to do. Gen. Armstrong had decided to start a night class at Hampton for students who wanted to work all day and study for two hours at night. He asked me to organize and teach this class. At first there were only about a half dozen students, but the number soon grew to about thirty. The night class at Hampton has since grown to the point where it numbers six or seven hundred.

"At the end of my second year at Hampton as a teacher, in 1881, there came a call from the little town of Tuskegee, Alabama, to Gen. Armstrong for some one to organize and become the Principal of a Normal School, which the people wanted to start in that town. Gen. Armstrong asked me to give up my work at Hampton and go to Tuskegee in answer to this call. I decided to undertake the work, and after spending a few days at my old home in Malden, West Virginia, I proceeded to the town of Tuskegee."

1. Jane (Washington's mother) was a cook for Burroughs, who claimed to own her. Most biographies say that Washington's father was an "unknown" white man who lived nearby.
2. Washington received honorary degrees from Harvard (1896) and Dartmouth (1901).
3. The autobiographical passages in Hopkins's essay are quoted from Washington's first autobiography, *The Story of My Life and Work*, not from his more famous *Up from Slavery*, published in 1901.
4. General Samuel Chapman Armstrong (1839–1893), founder in 1868 of the Hampton Institute, a school for African Americans and Native Americans.

No one will question the assertion that Dr. Washington and Tuskegee are one.

Tuskegee Institute is the soul of the man outlined in wood, in brick and stone, pulsating with the life of the human hive within on whom he has stamped his individuality.

As the absorbing topic of two continents, wherever the Negro is discussed, is the "Washington Industrial Propaganda," which has gained proselytes in every section of our country among influential and wealthy citizens, we shall trace the growth of the Institute from its inception, quoting from the founder's story as given in his book, "The Story of My Life and Work."

"When I reached Tuskegee, the only thing that had been done toward starting the school was the securing of $2,000. There was no land, building, or apparatus. I opened the school on July 4, 1881, in an old church and a shanty that was almost ready to fall down from decay. On the first day there was an attendance of thirty students, mainly those engaged in teaching in the public schools of the vicinity. I remember that, during the first months I taught in this little shanty, it was in such a dilapidated condition that, when it rained, one of the larger pupils would cease his lessons and hold the umbrella over me while I heard the recitation. After the school had been in session for several months, I began to see the necessity of having a permanent location for the institution, where we could have the students not only in their class rooms, but get hold of them in their home life, and teach them how to take care of their bodies in the matter of general cleanliness. It was rather noticeable that, notwithstanding the poverty of most of the students who came to us in the earlier months of the institution, most of them had the idea of getting an education in order that they might find some method of living without manual labor; that is, they had the feeling that to work with the hands was not conducive to being of the highest type of lady or gentleman."

We can well believe this prejudice against labor was true of the Negro, and we ought to expect nothing different from a class so long accustomed to see nought but excellence in the behavior of the white race. "Massa Charles" lolled in his hammock while the slave worked. All the training of the Negro was in the direction that despised labor and made it a crime for a gentleman to labor.

Irony of fate! that sees the Southern gentleman adopting today, for the salvation of his section, the despised tactics of the "greasy Northern mechanic."[5]

Feeling that it was necessary to make a great effort to improve the school, Dr. Washington secured a loan of $500 from Gen. J. F. B. Marshall, treasurer of Hampton Institute, and with this money bought an abandoned farm of 100 acres. Purchases of adjacent land and gifts of the same have increased the site to 2,460 acres.

Speaking of the great amount of assistance given him by the white inhabitants of the town, Dr. Washington says:

"I have been in a good many Southern towns, but I think I have never seen one where the general average of culture and intelligence is so high as that of the people of Tuskegee. We have in this town and its surroundings a good example of the friendly relations that exist between the two races when both races are enlightened and educated."

5. Reference to William G. Cambridge's *The Mechanic's Bride* (1857).

Through the efforts of Miss Davidson, Dr. Washington's first assistant teacher at Tuskegee in the North, money enough was secured to repay Gen. Marshall's loan and build Porter Hall, the first building on the grounds, which was dedicated on Thanksgiving Day, 1882. From this time on the school's reputation grew, and it soon became a problem what to do with the increasing number of applicants, anxious to secure an education.

In May, 1882, Dr. Washington had married Miss Fannie N. Smith of Maiden, W. Virginia; she died in 1884, leaving one child, Miss Portia Washington, recently graduated from the Normal School at Framingham, Mass. In 1885, Miss Olivia Davidson became Mrs. Washington; this estimable woman died in 1889. Two sons survive her—Baker Taliaferro and Ernest Davidson.

In 1893, Dr. Washington married Miss Maggie James Murray, a graduate of Fisk University,[6] who is well known to the public in all sections of the country.

In February, 1883, the State Legislature of Alabama was so impressed with the excellent character of the school that they voted to increase the annual appropriation from two to three thousand dollars. That summer a four-room cottage was put up to hold sixteen young men, and three board shanties were rented which would accommodate thirty-six additional students.

In September, 1885, $1,100 was secured through Rev. R. C. Bedford from the Trustees of the States of the Slater Fund. "I might add right here that the interest of the Trustees of the Slater Fund, now under the control of Dr. J. L. M. Curry, special agent, has continued from that time until this, so that now the institution receives $11,000 from the Fund," says Dr. Washington; also: "With this impetus a carpenter shop was built, a windmill set up to pump water into the school building, a sewing machine bought for girls' industrial room, mules and wagons for the farm, and work on the new buildings, Alabama Hall, was vigorously pushed."

In March, 1884, through influence of Gen. Armstrong, meetings were held in Baltimore, Philadelphia, New York and Boston, having for their object the completion of Alabama Hall, and by much hard work funds were secured, $10,000 in all.

In the spring of same year Dr. Washington was invited by Hon. Thomas W. Bicknall, of Boston, President of the National Educational Association, to address that body at its session during the summer at Madison, Wisconsin. At that assembly there were at least five thousand teachers present, representing every State in the Union. This was the first great meeting, national in character, at which the doctor had had an opportunity of presenting his work.

Between 1884 and 1894, the hardest work was done in securing money for Tuskegee. This was the period of growth. In 1884, the enrollment was 169. In 1894 the enrollment had increased to 712, and 54 officers and teachers employed, and 30 buildings practically all built by the labor of the students.

In 1883, they received their first donation of $500 from the Peabody Fund through Dr. J. L. M. Curry, general agent. This amount has been increased to twelve or fifteen hundred dollars each year.

In 1895, Dr. Washington lectured on "Industrial Education," under the auspices of the Students' Lecture Bureau of Fisk University. We give two

6. Founded in 1866 in Nashville, Tennessee, for African Americans.

extracts from the speech: "Despite all our disadvantages and hardships ever since our forefathers set foot upon the American soil as slaves, our pathway has been marked by progress. Think of it: We went into slavery pagans; we came out Christians. We went into slavery pieces of property; we came out American citizens. We went into slavery without a language; we came out speaking the proud Anglo-Saxon tongue. We went into slavery with slave chains clanking about our wrists; we came out with the American ballot in our hands." Continuing his speech, he said: "As a race there are two things we must learn to do—one is to put brains into the common occupations of life, and the other is to dignify common labor. Twenty years ago every large and paying barber shop was in the hands of black men; today in all the large cities you cannot find a single large or first-class barber shop operated by colored men. The black man had had a monopoly of that industry, but had gone on from day to day in the same old monotonous way without improving anything about the industry. As a result, the white man has taken it up, put brains into it, watched all the fine points, improved and progressed, until his shop today is not known as a barber shop, but as a tonsorial parlor, and he is no longer called a barber, but a tonsorial artist."

In the spring of 1895 he accompanied a committee of Atlanta, Ga., people to Washington to appear before the Committee on Appropriation for the purpose of inducing Congress to help forward the Exposition which the citizens of Atlanta were planning to have. The bill passed with little opposition.

Dr. Washington was proposed for chief commissioner, but declined to serve, accepting instead the position of commissioner for the State of Alabama, and was also made one of the judges of award in the Department of Education. Tuskegee Normal and Industrial Institute prepared a large and creditable exhibit, having with one exception (Hampton Institute) the largest exhibit in the Negro building. Three gold medals were awarded to institutions of learning, and Tuskegee got one of them.

On September 18, Dr. Washington made his great speech,[7] tendering the Negro exhibit of which the New York World said that it was one of the most notable speeches, both as to character and the warmth of its reception, ever delivered to a Southern audience. For this address Dr. Washington received many flattering encomiums from leading men all over the country.

In 1896, Harvard College conferred the honorary degree of Master of Arts upon him. Mr. Washington is the first of his race to receive an honorary degree from a New England University.

In 1897 occurred the dedication of the Robert Gould Shaw[8] monument in Boston. The dedicatory exercises were held in Music Hall, Boston, which was packed from top to bottom with a distinguished audience. Many old anti-slavery men were there. Hon. Roger Wolcott, Governor of Massachusetts, presided. Again Mr. Washington's address was the feature of the occasion, and he scored another great hit.

By dint of hard work and much persuasive eloquence, Dr. Washington secured the honor of a visit from President McKinley[9] to Tuskegee, at the time of the Atlanta Peace Jubilee, December 14 and 15, 1898. On the morning of December 16, at eight o'clock, the President, Mrs. McKinley, with his

7. That is, Washington's 1895 Atlanta Exposition address.
8. White commander of the Black 54th Massachusetts Volunteer Infantry unit in the Civil War.
9. William McKinley (1843–1901), the twenty-fifth president of the United States.

cabinet, their families and distinguished generals, including Generals Shafter, Joseph Wheeler, Lawton, etc., were met by Governor Joseph F. Johnston of Alabama, and his staff and the Alabama Legislature, at Tuskegee. The morning was spent in a parade and inspection of the grounds, all of which were witnessed by more than six thousand visitors. After this they retired to the large chapel, where the President and others made addresses.

Dr. Washington's public career as a speaker is full of interest: we can, of course, in an article like this, give but a bare outline of many brilliant occasions in which he has participated as the central figure. His speeches on the Negro problem, and in behalf of the Institute, are able and teem with humor, and they possess also the essential property of attracting the attention of the monied element, for Dr. Washington is without a peer in this particular line, and as a result Tuskegee is the richest Negro educational plant in the world.

Immediately after the public meeting held at the Hollis Street Theatre in 1899, friends quietly started a movement to raise a certain sum of money, to be used in sending Dr. and Mrs. Washington to Europe. They remained abroad from May 10 until August 5, gaining much needed rest. While abroad lynching was especially frequent in the South, and Mr. Washington addressed a letter to the Southern people through the medium of the press. We give an excerpt:

"With all the earnestness of my heart I want to appeal, not to the President of the United States, Mr. McKinley, not to the people of New York nor of the New England States, but to the citizens of our Southern States, to assist in creating a public sentiment such as will make human life here just as safe and sacred as it is anywhere else in the world.

"For a number of years the South has appealed to the North and to Federal authorities, through the public press, from the public platform and most eloquently through the late Henry W. Grady,[1] to leave the whole matter of the rights and protection of the Negro to the South, declaring that it would see to it that the Negro would be made secure in his citizenship. During the last half dozen years the whole country, from the President down, has been inclined more than ever to pursue this policy, leaving the whole matter of the destiny of the Negro to the Negro himself and to the Southern white people among whom the great bulk of the Negroes live.

"By the present policy of non-interference on the part of the North and the Federal Government, the South is given a sacred trust. How will she execute this trust?" It is all very well to talk of the Negro's immorality and illiteracy, and that raising him out of the Slough of Despond will benefit the South and remove unpleasantness between the races, but until the same course is pursued with the immoral and illiterate *white* Southerner that is pursued with the Negro, there will be no peace in that section. Ignorance is as harmful in one race as in another. The South keeps on in her mad carnage of blood: she refuses to be conciliated. The influence and wealth which have flowed into Hampton and Tuskegee have awakened jealous spite. She doesn't care a rap for the "sacred trust" of Grady or any other man. We hear a lot of talk against the methods of the anti-slavery leaders, but no abolitionist ever used stronger language than the Rev. Quincy Ewing of Mississippi, in his recent great speech against

1. Journalist and actor; he promoted the idea of the "New South," adding industry to agriculture, but also argued in favor of white supremacy.

lynching. We wonder how they like it down that way? Will they hang him or burn him?

The effect of that speech has been as electrical as was the first gun from Sumter. We could shout for joy over the words: "I have always been and am now a States-right Democrat; but I say with no sort of hesitation that if Mississippi cannot put a stop to the lynching of Negroes within her borders—Negroes, let us remember, who are citizens of the United States as well as of Mississippi—then the Federal Government ought to take a hand in this business!" The reverend gentleman does not believe in treating a cancer with rose water.

Through the generosity of wealthy friends, Tuskegee has now an endowment fund of $150,000, from which the school is receiving interest.

The site of the Institute is now 835 acres. The other large tract is about four miles southeast of the Institute and is composed of 800 acres and known as "Marshall farm." Upon the home farm is located forty-two buildings. Of these, Alabama, Davidson, Huntington, Cassidy and Science Halls, the Agricultural Trades and Laundry Buildings, and the chapel are built of brick. There are also two large frame halls—Porter and Phelps Halls, small frame buildings and cottages used for commissary storerooms, recitation rooms, dormitories and teachers' residences. There are also the shop and saw-mill, with engine rooms and dynamo in conjunction. The brickyard, where the bricks needed in the construction of all brick buildings are made by pupils, turned out 1,500,000 bricks in 1899.

The Agricultural Department, Prof. G. W. Carver,[2] of the Iowa State University, in charge, attracts much attention on account of changes wrought in old methods by scientific agriculture. The building is well-equipped at a cost of $10,000, and contains a fine chemical laboratory. Agriculture is an important feature in the life of the school. 135 acres of the home farm are devoted to raising vegetables, strawberries, grapes and other fruits. The Marshall farm is worked by student labor, keeping from thirty to forty-five boys on it constantly. It produces a large amount of the farm products used by the school and 800 head of live stock.

The Mechanical Department is in the Slater-Armstrong Memorial Trades' Building, dedicated in 1900. It is built entirely of brick, and contains twenty-seven rooms. The bricks were made by student labor. The building contains directors' office, reading room, exhibit room, wheelwright shop, blacksmith shop, tin shop, printing office, carpenter shop, repair shop, wood-working machine room, iron-working machine room, foundry, brick-making and plastering rooms, general stock and supply room, and a boiler and engine room. The second floor contains the mechanical drawing room, harness shop, paint shop, tailor shop, shoe shop, and electrical laboratory, and a room for carriage trimming and upholstering.

The Department of Domestic Science is directed by Mrs. Booker T. Washington, and embraces laundering, cooking, dressmaking, plain sewing, millinery and mattress making. A training school for nurses has for instructors the resident physician and a competent trained nurse.

There is also a division of music, a Bible training department and an academic department, all of which are carried on extensively with elaborate equipments.

2. George Washington Carver (1864–1943), African American scientist who joined the Tuskegee faculty in 1896.

From this brief review of the life of the founder of Tuskegee Institute and the prodigious growth of the work there we can but conclude that this is a phenomenal age in which we are living, and one of the most remarkable features of this age is Booker T. Washington,—his humble birth and rise to eminence and wealth.

View his career in whatever light we may, be we for or against his theories, his personality is striking, his life uncommon, and the magnetic influence which radiates from him in all direction, bending and swaying great minds and pointing the ultimate conclusion of colossal schemes as the wind the leaves of the trees, is stupendous. When the happenings of the Twentieth Century have become matters of history, Dr. Washington's motives will be open to as many constructions and discussions as are those of Napoleon today, or of other men of extraordinary ability, whether for good or evil, who have had like phenomenal careers.

1901

From Famous Women of the Negro Race

V. Literary Workers (Concluded)

In presenting to our readers a short sketch of the labors of Frances Ellen Watkins Harper[1] we feel more than glad of an opportunity to add our mead of praise to the just encomiums[2] of many other writers for the noble deeds of an eminent Christian woman. We need give but the simple facts of the many acts that composed her life work, but these speak in trumpet tones, louder than extravagant praise or fulsome compliment.

Mrs. Harper was born in Baltimore, Maryland, in 1825; freeborn she yet partook of the cup of woe under the oppressive influence which was the heritage of bond and free alike under slave laws. She was an only child and was left an orphan at the tender age of three years. Happily an aunt took charge of her, and until she was thirteen she was sent to a private school for free colored children in Baltimore kept by an uncle, the Rev. William Watkins. At the conclusion of this period the little girl was deemed fit for labor and was put out to work in order that she might earn her own living. She endured many trials, but in the midst of the most trying ordeals preserved her desire for knowledge. She possessed a remarkable talent for composition, and when but fourteen wrote an article which attracted the attention of the lady for whom she was working. To the honor of this woman be it said that she appreciated the girl's extraordinary talent, and while she was zealously taught sewing, housework and the care of children, books were furnished her and many leisure hours were permitted her in which she was able to indulge her longing for intellectual food.

At eighteen the young girl published her first volume, called "Forest Leaves."[3] Some of her productions were also published in the newspapers, attracting much attention.

In 1851 she left Baltimore and resided a short time in Ohio, where she was engaged in teaching. Becoming dissatisfied with her surroundings, she

1. African American author and reformer (1825–1911).
2. Written tributes, praise. "Mead": portion or offering.
3. A copy of *Forest Leaves* was discovered, dated 1849; however, an 1846 text is rumored to have been published.

removed to Little York, Penn., and engaged in teaching again. While there she saw much of the underground railroad and her mind became imbued with the desire to help her people in some way. About this time Maryland enacted a law forbidding free people of color from the North from coming into the State on pain of being imprisoned and sold into slavery. A free man violated this law and was sold to Georgia; he escaped, was discovered and remanded to slavery. He died soon after from the effects of exposure and suffering. In a letter to a friend, referring to this outrage, Mrs. Harper wrote: "Upon that grave I pledged myself to the Anti-Slavery cause." In another letter she wrote: "It may be that God himself has written upon both my heart and brain a commission to use time, talent and energy in the cause of freedom." In this faith she began the study of Anti-Slavery methods and documents, finally visiting Boston, where she was received with great kindness by the Anti-Slavery people. From there she proceeded to New Bedford, where she addressed a public meeting on the "Education and Elevation of the Colored Race." The following month she was engaged by the State Anti-Slavery Society of Maine, with what success is shown from one of her letters:

"Bucksport Centre,
"Sept. 28, 1854.

"The agent of the State Anti-Slavery Society travels with me, and she is a pleasant, sweet lady. I do like her so. We eat together, sleep together. (She is a white woman.) In fact, I have not been in one colored person's house since I left Massachusetts; but I have a pleasant time. My life reminds me of a beautiful dream. What a difference between this and York! I have lectured three times this week. I have met with some of the kindest treatment I have ever received."

Her ability and labors were everywhere appreciated, and her meetings largely attended. She breakfasted with the Governor of Maine.

For a year and a half she continued speaking in the Eastern States with marked success; the papers commending her efforts highly. The following extract is from the Portland Daily Press respecting a lecture delivered after the war:

"She spoke for nearly an hour and a half, her subject being 'The Mission of the War, and the Demands of the Colored Race in the Work of Reconstruction.' Mrs. Harper has a splendid articulation, uses chaste, pure language, has a pleasant voice, and allows no one to tire of hearing her. We shall attempt no abstract of her address; none that we could make would do her justice. It was one of which any lecturer might feel proud, and her reception by a Portland audience was all that could be desired. We have seen no praises of her that were overdrawn. We have heard Miss Dickinson,[4] and do not hesitate to award the palm to her darker colored sister."

In 1856, desiring to see the fugitives in Canada, she visited the Upper Province.[5] While in Toronto she lectured, where she was well received and listened to with great interest. We give an extract from a letter unfolding her mind and showing her impressions of the land where her race found a refuge:

"Well, I have gazed for the first time upon Free Land, and, would you believe it, tears sprang to my eyes, and I wept. Oh, it was a glorious sight to

4. Probably Anna E. Dickinson (1842–1932), advocate for women's suffrage and civil rights for Blacks.

5. British colonies in what is now Ontario.

gaze for the first time on a land where a poor slave flying from our glorious land of liberty would in a moment find his fetters broken, his shackles loosed, and whatever he was in the land of Washington, beneath the shadow of Bunker Hill Monument or even Plymouth Rock, 'here he becomes a man and a brother.' I have gazed on Harper's Ferry, or rather the rock at the Ferry; I have seen it towering up in simple grandeur, with the gentle Potomac gliding peacefully at its feet, and felt that it was God's masonry, and my soul had expanded in gazing on its sublimity. I have seen the ocean singing its wild chorus of sounding waves, and ecstacy has thrilled upon the living chords of my heart. I have since then seen the rainbow crowned Niagara chanting the choral hymn of Omnipotence, girdled with grandeur and robed with glory; but none of these things have melted me as the first sight of Free Land. Towering mountains lifting their hoary summits to catch the first faint flush of day when the sunbeams kiss the shadows from morning's drowsy face may expand and exalt your soul. The first view of the ocean may fill you with strange delight. Niagara—the great, the glorious Niagara—may hush your spirit with its ceaseless thunder; it may charm you with its robe of crested spray and rainbow crown; but the Land of Freedom was a lesson of deeper significance than foaming waves or towering mounts."

Mrs. Harper was not contented to make speeches and receive plaudits, but was ready to do the rough work, and gave freely of all the moneys that her literary labors brought her. Indeed, it was often found necessary to restrain her open hand and to counsel her to be more careful of her hard-earned income.

When the John Brown[6] episode was agitating the nation, no one was more deeply affected than Mrs. Harper. To John Brown's wife she sent a letter saying: "May God, our God, sustain you in the hour of trial. If there is one thing on earth I can do for you or yours, let me be apprized. I am at your service."

Not forgetting Brown's comrades, then in prison under sentence of death, true to the impulses of her generous heart, she wrote to their relations offering financial aid—sending clothing and money. "Spare no expense," she says, "to make their last hours as bright as possible. Now, my friend, fulfil this to the letter. Oh, is it not a privilege, if you are sisterless and lonely, to be a sister to the human race and to place your heart where it may throb close to down-trodden humanity?" In the fall of 1860, in Cincinnati, O., Mrs. Harper married Fenton Harper, a widower. She then retired to a small farm bought from the accumulated sales of her books, etc., and for a time was absorbed by the cares of married life. Mr. Harper died May 23, 1864.

After this event Mrs. Harper again appeared as an advocate for her race. She had battled for freedom under slavery and through the war. She now began laboring as earnestly for equality before the law—education, and a higher manhood, especially in the South.

She traveled for several years, extensively through Southern cities, visiting the plantations and lowly cabin homes, addressing schools, churches, meetings in Court Houses and Legislative Halls, under most trying conditions.

6. White militant abolitionist (1800–1859) who was hanged as a result of the attack he led in 1859 on a federal arsenal at Harpers Ferry, Virginia.

Her private lectures to freedwomen are particularly worthy of notice. Desiring to speak to women, along the objects of wrong and abuse under slavery, and whom emancipation found in deepest ignorance, Mrs. Harper made it her business to talk to them of their morals and general improvement, giving them the wisest counsel in her possession. For all this work she made no charge, working and preaching as did the Master—for the love of humanity.

After her labors in the South ceased, Mrs. Harper returned to Philadelphia and began active work in the Sabbath schools. Her work in the temperance field must also be noticed.

Mrs. Harper has always read the best magazines and ablest weeklies published; she is familiar with the best authors, including De Tocqueville, Mill, Ruskin, Buckle, Guizot, etc.[7]

Before the learned and unlearned Mrs. Harper has spoken in behalf of her race; during seventeen years of public speaking she has never once been other than successful in delivering thousands of speeches. By personal effort alone she has removed mountains of prejudice. At least we may be allowed to hope that the rising generation will be encouraged by her example to renewed courage in surmounting prejudice and racial difficulties. Fifty thousand copies of her four books have been sold. They have been used to entertain and delight hundreds of audiences.

Grace Greenwood,[8] in noticing a course of lectures in which Mrs. Harper spoke, pays her this tribute:

"Next on the course was Mrs. Harper, a colored woman; about as colored as some of the Cuban belles I have met at Saratoga. She has a noble head, this bronze muse; a strong face, with a shadowed glow upon it, indicative of thoughtful fervor, and of a nature most femininely sensitive, but not in the least morbid. Her form is delicate, her hands daintily small. She stands quietly beside her desk, and speaks without notes, with gestures few and fitting. Her manner is marked by dignity and composure. She is never assuming, never theatrical. Every glance of her sad eyes was a mournful remonstrance against injustice and wrong. Feeling in her soul, as she must have felt it, the chilling weight of caste, she seemed to say:

'I lift my heart up solemnly,
As once Electra her sepulchral urn.'[9]

As I listened to her there swept over me a chill wave of horror, the realization that this noble woman, had she not been rescued from her mother's condition, might have been sold on the auction block to the highest bidder—her intellect, fancy, eloquence, the flashing wit that might make the delight of a Parisian salon, and her pure, Christian character all thrown in—the recollection that women like her could be dragged out of public conveyances in our own city, so frowned out of fashionable churches by Anglo-Saxon saints."

Mrs. Harper is still living in Philadelphia; she is eighty odd years old, and is lovingly spoken of and known to her friends and acquaintances as "Mother Harper."

7. Alexis de Tocqueville (1805–1859), French author. John Stuart Mill (1806–1873), British philosopher. John Ruskin (1819–1900), British philosopher and reformer. Henry Thomas Buckle (1821–1862), British historian. François Pierre Guillaume Guizot (1787–1874), French politician and historian.
8. Pen name of American author and social activist Sara Jane Lippincott (1823–1904).
9. Quoting Elizabeth Barrett Browning's Sonnet 5.

We append her poem published in 1871, "Words for the Hour," because it fits the times and our present needs:

Men of the North! it is no time
  To quit the battle-field;
When danger fronts your rear and van
  It is no time to yield.

No time to bend the battle's crest
  Before the wily foe,
And, ostrich-like, to hide your heads
  From the impending blow.

The minions of a baffled wrong
  Are marshalling their clan;
Rise up! rise up enchanted North!
  And strike for God and man.

This is no time for careless ease;
  No time for idle sleep;
Go light the fires in every camp,
  And solemn sentries keep.

The foe you foiled upon the field
  Has only changed his base;
New dangers crowd around you
  And stare you in the face.

O Northern men! within your hands
  Is held no common trust;
Secure the victories won by blood
  When treason bit the dust.

'Tis yours to banish from the land
  Oppression's iron rule;
And o'er the ruined auction block
  Erect the common school.

To wipe from labor's branded brow
  The curse that shamed the land,
And teach the Freedman how to wield
  The ballot in his hand.

This is the nation's golden hour,
  Nerve every heart and hand,
To build on Justice as a rock,
  The future of the land.

True to your trust, oh, never yield
  One citadel of right!
With Truth and Justice clasping hands
  Ye yet shall win the fight!

1902

Letter from Cordelia A. Condict[1] and Pauline Hopkins's Reply (March 1903)

We are constantly in receipt of letters from our readers in all sections of the country, in fact of the world, and it gives us a great deal of pleasure to note how warm a reception is given our publication among all classes and races. Some friends offer kindly suggestions as to how we can improve and make more helpful "The Colored American Magazine," while others tell of the grand work already accomplished by our periodical. The following letter, recently received from one of our *white* readers, is of more than passing interest to us all:

Dear Sirs:—

With Miss Floto I have been taking and reading with interest the COLORED AMERICAN MAGAZINE.

If I found it more helpful to Christian work among your people I would continue to take it.

May I make a comment on the stories, especially those that have been serial. Without exception they have been of love between the colored and whites. Does that mean that your novelists can imagine no love beautiful and sublime within the range of the colored race, for each other? I have seen beautiful home life and love in families altogether of Negro blood.

The stories of these tragic mixed loves will not commend themselves to your white readers and will not elevate the colored readers. I believe your novelists could do with a consecrated[2] imagination and pen, more for the elevation of home life and love, than perhaps any other one class of writers.

What Dickens[3] did for the neglected working class of England, some writer could do for the neglected colored people of America.

For several years I worked (superintended a Sunday school) among a greatly mixed people, Indian, Negro, Spanish and Anglo-Saxon.

My sympathies are with the earnest and spiritual work that is being done for your people, by yourselves or others.

We have kindred who are cultured Christian ladies, who for years have borne the ostracism of the white women of the South for the sake of the colored girls and women of the great South land.

Very respectfully,
CORNELIA A. CONDICT.

Following is Miss Hopkins' reply, which we feel will be of general interest:—

With regard to your enclosure (letter from Mrs. Condict) will say, it is the same old story. One religion for the whites and another for the blacks. The story of Jesus for us, that carries with it submission to the abuses of our people and blindness to the degrading of our youth. I think Mrs. Condict has a great work to do—greater than she can accomplish, I fear—to carry religion to the Southern whites.

1. Condict (1835–1926) was a Presbyterian missionary and Sunday School teacher.

2. Sacred.

3. Charles Dickens (1812–1870), British novelist.

My stories are definitely planned to show the obstacles persistently placed in our paths by a dominant race to subjugate us spiritually. Marriage is made illegal between the races and yet the mulattoes increase. Thus the shadow of corruption falls on the blacks and on the whites, without whose aid the mulattoes would not exist. And then the hue and cry goes abroad of the immorality of the Negro and the disgrace that the mulattoes are to this nation. Amalgamation[4] is an institution designed by God for some wise purpose, and mixed bloods have always exercised a great influence on the progress of human affairs. I sing of the *wrongs* of a race that ignorance of their pitiful condition may be changed to intelligence and must awaken compassion in the hearts of the just.

The home life of Negroes is beautiful in many instances; warm affection is there between husband and wife, and filial and paternal tenderness in them is not surpassed by any other race of the human family. But Dickens wrote not of the joys and beauties of English society; I believe he was the author of "Bleak House" and "David Copperfield."[5] If he had been an American, and with his trenchant pen had exposed the abuses practiced by the Southern whites upon the blacks—had told the true story of how wealth, intelligence and femininity has stooped to choose for a partner in sin, the degraded (?) Negro whom they affect to despise, Dickens would have been advised to shut up or get out. I believe Jesus Christ when on earth rebuked the Pharisees in this wise:[6] "Ye hypocrites, ye expect to be heard for your much speaking"; "O wicked and adulterous (?) nation, how can ye escape the damnation of hell?" He didn't go about patting those old sinners on the back and saying, "All right, boys, fix me up and the Jews will get there all right. Money talks. Divy on the money you take in the exchange business of the synagogue, and it'll be all right with God." Jesus told the thing as it was and the Jews crucified him! I am glad to receive this criticism for it shows more clearly than ever that white people don't understand *what pleases Negroes.* You are between Scylla and Charybdis:[7] If you please the author of this letter and your white clientele, you will lose your Negro patronage. If you cater to the *demands* of the Negro trade, away goes Mrs.——. I have sold to many whites and have received great praise for the work I am doing in exposing the social life of the Southerners and the wickedness of their caste prejudice.

Let the good work go on. Opposition is the life of an enterprise; criticism tells you that you are doing something.

Respect.,
PAULINE E. HOPKINS.

4. Joining or blending of two entities, here referring to interracial marriage.
5. Dickens's novels, published in 1852–53 and 1849–50, respectively.
6. What follows is a blending of New Testament verses, including Matthew 23:33 and Matthew 16:4 and 5:13.
7. Monsters in Greek mythology. Scylla is usually depicted as a ravenous six-headed sea creature and Charybdis as a whirlpool. They are associated with the perilous Strait of Messina between Italy and Sicily.

VICTORIA EARLE MATTHEWS
1861–1907

Victoria Earle Matthews was born Victoria Smith in Georgia during the era of slavery. At birth, she was defined as property. As an adult, she changed her name to "Victoria Earle" and became an exemplar of the New Negro Woman. Like Frances E. W. Harper, Ida B. Wells, Anna Julia Cooper, and other determined and talented women, Matthews was celebrated as a public intellectual who spoke, wrote, and organized in support of many groups of people. She wrote stories that challenged popular images of African American women and emphasized the value of the less fortunate. She gave lectures at conferences large and small, segregated and integrated. She edited a collection of essays by Booker T. Washington. And she was renowned as a journalist who published in many periodicals, including the *New York Times*, *Washington Bee*, *Boston Advocate*, *Cleveland Gazette*, *A.M.E. Church Review*, *Woman's Era*, and *Catholic Tribune*.

Matthews's achievements were all the more impressive given that she completed only four years of school before having to find work to help support her family, who had migrated to New York City. Like Frances E. W. Harper, she was hired as a domestic servant by an employer who allowed her access to the family library. Self-taught and highly ambitious, Victoria married coachman William Matthews at age eighteen and went on to have a son, but from the start she eschewed the life of hearth and home that was typical for women at the time. In 1892 Matthews helped organize a testimonial dinner for journalist Ida B. Wells, whose powerful anti-lynching campaign had aroused ire in the South, thereby forcing her to seek exile in New York. That dinner led to her founding of the Women's Loyal Union of New York and Brooklyn. In 1895, Matthews and others created the National Federation of Afro-American Women, which merged with the National Colored Women's League to become the National Association of Colored Women. In 1897 she opened a community center where girls were taught "right living and self-help" with a curriculum that included sewing, math, reading, writing, and African history and literature. Incensed by the "employment centers" and pimps who lured migrant women into prostitution and sexual slavery, Matthews organized volunteers to meet incoming trains and guide migrants to safe quarters. And she drew on the support of notable African Americans, among them W. E. B. Du Bois, James Weldon Johnson, and Rev. Adam Clayton Powell, to buy a house at 217 East 86th Street in New York, which came to be called the White Rose Home for Working Class Negro Girls.

As a lecturer, Matthews traveled extensively, giving speeches to audiences ranging from students at Hampton Institute in Virginia to visitors at the Columbian Exposition in Chicago to the (white) Christian Endeavor Society, which invited her to "represent the Negro Women of America" at its convention in San Francisco. Her most famous lecture, "The Value of Race Literature," was delivered at the First Congress of Colored Women of the United States, in Boston, on July 30, 1895. Professor Fred Miller Robinson notes that this "eloquent" essay, "one of the first commentaries by any critic on the treatment of Blacks by white writers in American literature, has both "bite" and "hopefulness." Matthews, like many of her time, believed that the literature produced by any given group was its most important achievement. Though critical of the literature written by African Americans up to the late nineteenth century, she argued that the circumstances under which these authors lived had been and continued to be hostile to the development of artistry, and she asserted that what they wrote deserved respect, especially for what it revealed about African

American life in the United States, and should become a foundation upon which others could build. Matthews's vitriolic comments about Washington Irving, William Dean Howells, and Mark Twain support her declaration that such "impious" writers are ignorant of African American lives and that their work is one reason why African Americans must create truthful counternarratives. Proudly, she lists the African Americans writers who are creating "history, poetry, novel writing, speeches, orations . . . sermons, and so on." In this influential work, Matthews speaks of race literature as a socially constructed category but one that recounts the past, impacts the present, and has liberating promise for the future.

The Value of Race Literature

> "If the black man carries in his bosom an indispensable element of a new and coming civilization, for the sake of that element, no money, nor strength, nor circumstance can hurt him; he will survive and play his part. . . . If you have *man*, black or white is an insignificance. The intellect—that is miraculous! who has it, has the talisman. His skin and bones, though they were the color of night, are transparent, and the everlasting stars shine through with attractive beams."
>
> —Ralph Waldo Emerson[1]

By Race Literature, we mean ordinarily all the writings emanating from a distinct class—not necessarily race matter; but a general collection of what has been written by the men and women of that Race: History, Biographies, Scientific Treatises, Sermons, Addresses, Novels, Poems, Books of Travel, miscellaneous essays and the contributions to magazines and newspapers.

Literature, according to Webster, is learning: acquaintance with books or letters: the collective body of literary productions, embracing the entire results of knowledge and fancy, preserved in writing, *also the whole body of literature*, productions or writings upon any given subject, or in reference to a particular science, a branch of knowledge, as the Literature of Biblical Customs, the Literature of Chemistry, Etc.

In the light of this definition, many persons may object to the term, Race Literature, questioning seriously the need, doubting if there be any, or indeed whether there can be a Race Literature in a country like ours apart from the general American Literature. Others may question the correctness of the term American Literature, since our civilization in its essential features is a reproduction of all that is most desirable in the civilizations of the Old World. English being the language of America, they argue in favor of the general term, English Literature.

While I have great respect for the projectors of this theory, yet it is a limited definition; it does not express the idea in terms sufficiently clear.

The conditions which govern the people of African descent in the United States have been and still are such as create a very marked difference in the limitations, characteristics, aspirations and ambitions of this class of people, in decidedly strong contrast with the more or less powerful races which dominate it.

Laws were enacted denying and restricting their mental development in such pursuits, which engendered servility and begot ox-like endurance; and

1. Quoted from Emerson's "Address on the Anniversary of Emancipation in the British West Indies" (1844).

though statutes were carefully, painstakingly prepared by the most advanced and learned American jurists to perpetuate ignorance, yet they were powerless to keep all the race out from the Temple of Learning. Many though in chains mastered the common rudiments and others possessing talent of higher order—like the gifted Phyllis Wheatley, who dared to express her meditations in poetic elegance which won recognition in England and America, from persons distinguished in letters and statesmanship—dared to seek the sources of knowledge and wield a pen.

While oppressive legislation, aided by grossly inhuman customs, successfully retarded all general efforts toward improvement, the race suffered physically and mentally under a great wrong, an appalling evil, in contrast with which the religious caste prejudice of India appears as a glimmering torch to a vast consuming flame.

The prejudice of color! Not condition, not character, not capacity for artistic development, not the possibility of emerging from savagery into Christianity, not these, but the "Prejudice of Color." Washington Irving's Life of Columbus contains a translation from the contemporaries of Las Casas, in which this prejudice is plainly evident. Since our reception on this continent, men have cried out against this inhuman prejudice; granting that, a man may improve his condition, accumulate wealth, become wise and upright, merciful and just as an infidel or Christian, but they despair because he can not change his color, as if it were possible for the victim to change his organic structure, and impossible for the oppressor to change his wicked heart.

But all this impious wrong has made a Race Literature a possibility, even a necessity to dissipate the odium conjured up by the term "colored" persons, not originally perhaps designed to humiliate, but unfortunately still used to express not only an inferior order, but to accentuate and call unfavorable attention to the most ineradicable difference between the races.

So well was this understood and deplored by liberal minded men, regardless of affiliation, that the editor of "Freedom's Journal," published in New York City in 1827, the first paper published in this country by Americans of African descent, calls special attention to this prejudice by quoting from the great Clarkson, where he speaks of a master not only looking with disdain upon a slave's features, but hating his very color.

The effect of this unchristian disposition was like the merciless scalpel about the very heart of the people, a sword of Damocles,[2] at all times hanging above and threatening all that makes life worth living. Why they should not develop and transmit stealthy, vicious and barbaric natures under such conditions is a question that able metaphysicians, ethnologists and scientists will, most probably in the future, investigate with a view of solving what to-day is considered in all quarters a profound mystery, the Negro's many-sided, happy, hopeful enduring character.

Future investigations may lead to the discovery of what to-day seems lacking, what has deformed the manhood and womanhood in the Negro. What is bright, hopeful and encouraging is in reality the source of an original school of race literature, of racial psychology, of potent possibilities, an amalgam needed for this great American race of the future.

Dr. Dvorak[3] claims this for the original Negro melodies of the South as every student of music is well aware. On this subject he says, "I am now

2. From a parable by Cicero (7 B.C.E.–43 C.E.), the sword of Damocles has come to mean impending danger or death.

3. Antonin Leopold Dvorak (1841–1904), Czech composer.

satisfied that the future music of this continent must be founded upon what are called the Negro melodies. This can be the foundation of a serious and original school of composition to be developed in the United States.

"When I first came here, I was impressed with this idea, and it has developed into a settled conviction. The beautiful and varied themes are the product of the soil. *They are American, they are the folk songs of America, and our composers must turn to them.* All of the great musicians have borrowed from the songs of the common people.

"Beethoven's most charming *scherzo* is based upon what might now be considered a skilfully handled Negro melody. I have myself gone to the simple half-forgotten tunes of the Bohemian peasants for hints in my most serious work. Only in this way can a musician express the true sentiment of a people. He gets into touch with common humanity of the country.

"*In the Negro melodies of America I discover all that is needed for a great and noble school of music. They are pathetic, tender, passionate and melancholy, solemn, religious, bold, merry, gay, gracious, or what you will. It is music that suits itself to any work or any purpose. There is nothing in the whole range of composition that cannot find a themetic source here.*"

When the literature of our race is developed, it will of necessity be different in all essential points of greatness, true heroism and real Christianity from what we may at the present time, for convenience, call American Literature. When some master hand writes the stories as Dr. Dvorak has caught the melodies when, amid the hearts of the people, there shall live a George Eliot,[4] moving this human world by the simple portrayal of the scenes of our ordinary existence; or when the pure, ennobling touch of a black Hannah More[5] shall rightly interpret our unappreciated contribution to Christianity and make it into universal literature, such writers will attain and hold imperishable fame.

The novelists most read at the present time in this country find a remunerative source for their doubtful literary productions based upon the wrongly interpreted and too often grossly exaggerated frailties. This is patent to all intelligent people. The Negro need not envy such reputation, nor feel lost at not revelling in its ill-gotten wealth or repute. We are the only people most distinctive from those who have civilized and governed this country, who have become typical Americans, and we rank next to the Indians in originality of soil, and yet remain a distinct people.

In this connection, Joseph Wilson, in the Black Phalanx[6] says:

"The Negro race is the only race that has ever come in contact with the European race that has proved itself able to withstand its atrocities and oppression. All others like the Indians whom they could not make subservient to their use they have destroyed."

Prof. Sampson in his "Mixed Races" says, "The American Negro is a new race, and is not the direct descent of any people that has ever flourished."

On this supposition, and relying upon finely developed, native imaginative powers, and humane tendencies, I base my expectation that our Race Literature when developed will not only compare favorably with many, but will stand out preeminent, not only in the limited history of colored people, but in the broader field of universal literature.

4. Pen name of Mary Ann Evans (1819–1880), British novelist.
5. British poet, playwright, abolitionist, and philanthropist (1845–1883).
6. A military history of African American soldiers in the Civil War published in 1888 by Joseph T. Wilson (1837–1891), African American journalist and politician.

Though Race Literature be founded upon the traditionary history of a people yet its fullest and largest development ought not to be circumscribed by the narrow limits of race or creed for the simple reason that literature in its loftiest development reaches out to the utmost limits of soul enlargement and outstrips all earthly limitations. Our history and individuality as a people, not only provides material for masterly treatment; but would seem to make a Race Literature a necessity as an outlet for the unnaturally suppressed inner lives which our people have been compelled to lead.

The literature of any people of varied nationality who have won a place in the literature of the world, presents certain cardinal points. French literature for instance, is said to be "not the wisest, not the weightiest, not certainly the purest and loftiest, but by odds the most brilliant and the most interesting literature in the world."

Ours, when brought out, and we must admit in reverence to truth that, as yet, we have done nothing distinctive, but may when we have built upon our own individuality, win a place by the simplicity of the story, thrown into strong relief by the multiplicity of its dramatic situations; the spirit of romance, and even tragedy, shadowy and as yet ill-defined, but from which our race on this continent can never be disassociated.

When the foundations of such a literature shall have been properly laid, the benefit to be derived will be at once apparent. There will be a revelation to our people, and it will enlarge our scope, make us better known wherever real lasting culture exists, will undermine and utterly drive out the traditional Negro in dialect,—the subordinate, the servant as the type representing a race whose numbers are now far into the millions. It would suggest to the world the wrong and contempt with which the lion viewed the picture that the hunter and famous painter besides, had drawn of the King of the Forest.

As a matter of history the only high-type Negro that has been put before the American people by a famous writer, is the character Dred founded upon the deeds of Nat Turner, in Mrs. Stowe's novel.[7]

Except the characters sketched by the writers of folk-lore, I know of none more representative of the spirit of the writers of to-day, wherein is infiltrated in the public mind that false sense of the Negro's meaning of inalienable rights, so far as actual practice is concerned, than is found in a story in "Harper's Magazine" some years ago. Here a pathetic picture is drawn of a character generally known as the typical "Darkey."

The man, old and decrepit, had labored through long years to pay for an humble cabin and garden patch; in fact, he had paid double and treble the original price, but dashing "Marse Wilyum" quieted his own conscience by believing, so the writer claimed, that the old Darkey should be left free to pay him all he felt the cabin was worth to him. The old man looked up to him, trusted him implicitly, and when he found at last he had been deceived, the moment he acknowledged to himself that "Marse Wilyum" had cheated him, a dejected listlessness settled upon him, an expression weak and vacant came in his dull eyes and hung around his capacious but characterless mouth, an exasperatingly meek smile trembled upon his features, and casting a helpless look around the cabin that he thought his own, nay, knew it was, with dragging steps he left the place! "Why did you not stand out for your rights?" a sympathizing friend questioned some years afterwards. To this the writer makes the old man say:

"Wid white folks dat's de way, but wid niggers its dif'unt."

7. *Dred: A Tale of the Great Dismal Swamp* (1856), a novel by Harriet Beecher Stowe (1811–1896), author of *Uncle Tom's Cabin* (1852).

Here the reader is left to infer whatever his or her predilection will incline to accept, as to the meaning of the old man's words. The most general view is that the old man had no manhood, not the sense, nothing to even suggest to his inner conscience aught that could awaken a comprehension of the word man, much less its rightful price; no moral responsibility, no spirit or, as the Negro-hating Mark Twain would say, no capacity of kicking at real or imaginary wrongs, which in his estimation makes the superior clan. In a word, there was nothing within the old man's range of understanding to make him feel his inalienable rights.

We know the true analysis of the old man's words was that faith, once destroyed, can never be regained, and the blow to his faith in the individual and the wound to his honest esteem so overwhelming, rendered it out of the question to engage further with a fallen idol.

With one sweep of mind he had seen the utter futility of even hoping for justice from a people who would take advantage of an aged honest man. That is the point, and this reveals neglected subject for analytical writers to dissect in the interest of truth the real meaning of the so-called cowardice, self-negation and lack of responsibility so freely referred to by those in positions calculated to make lasting impressions on the public, that by custom scoffs at the meaning introduced in Mrs. Stowe's burning words, when she repeated a question before answering;—"What can any individual do?" "There is one thing every individual can do. They can see to it that they feel right—an atmosphere of sympathetic influence encircles every human being; and the man or woman who feels strongly, healthily and justly on the great interests of humanity, is a constant benefactor to the human race."

Think of the moral status of the Negro, that Mr. Ridpath[8] in his history degrades before the world. Consider the political outline of the Negro, sketched with extreme care in "Bryce's Commonwealth,"[9] and the diatribes of Mr. Froude.[1] From these, turn to the play, where impressions are made upon a heterogeneous assemblage—Mark Twain's "Pudd'n Head Wilson,"[2] which Beaumount Fletcher claims as "among the very best of those productions which gives us hope for a distinctive American drama."

In this story we have education and fair environment attended by the most deplorable results, an educated octoroon is made out to be a most despicable, cowardly villain. "The one compensation for all this," my friend Professor Greener wittily remarks, "is that the white nigger in the story, though actually a pure white man, is indescribably worse in all his characteristics than the real nigger, using the vernacular of the play, was ever known to be, and just here Mark Twain unconsciously avenges the Negro while trying his best to disparage him."

In "Imperative Duty," Mr. Howells,[3] laboriously establishes for certain minds, the belief that the Negro possesses an Othello like charm in his ignorance which education and refinement destroys, or at best makes repulsive.

In explaining why Dr. Olney loves Rhoda, whose training was imparted by good taste, refined by wealth, and polished by foreign travel, he says: "It was the elder world, the beauty of antiquity which appealed to him in the luster and sparkle of this girl, and *the remote taint* of her servile and savage

8. John Clark Ridpath (1840–1900), American educator and historian.
9. James Bryce (1838–1922), British politician; author of *The American Commonwealth* (1888).
1. James Anthony Froude (1818–1894), British historian and essayist.
2. *Pudd'nhead Wilson* (1894), a novel by Mark Twain, was adapted for the theater in 1895.
3. William Dean Howells (1837–1920), American novelist and editor, author of *An Imperative Duty* (1892).

origin, *gave her a fascination* which refuses to let itself be put in words, it was the grace of a limp, the occult, indefinable, lovableness of deformity, but transcending these by its allurements, in indefinite degree, and going for the reason of its effect deep into the mysterious places of being, where the spirit and animal meet and part in us. . . .

"The mood was of his emotional nature alone, it sought and could have won no justification from the moral sense which indeed it simply submerged, and blotted out for all time."

All this tergiversation[4] and labored explanation of how a white man came to love a girl with a remote tingle of Negro blood! But he must have recourse to this tortuous jugglery of words because one of his characters in the story had taken pains to assert, "That so far as society in the society sense is concerned we have frankly simplified the matter, and no more consort with the Negroes than we do with lower animals, so that one would be quite as likely to meet a cow or a horse in an American drawing-room, as a person of color." This is the height of enlightenment! and from Dean Howells too, litterateur, diplomat, journalist, altruist!

Art, goodness, and beauty are assaulted in order to stimulate or apologize for prejudice against the educated Negro!

In Dr. Huguet, we have as a type a man pitifully trying to be self-conscious, struggling to feel within himself, what prejudice and custom demand that he feel.

In "A Question of Color" the type is a man of splendid English training, that of an English gentleman, surrounded from his birth by wealth, and accepted in the most polished society, married to a white girl, who sells herself for money, and after the ceremony like an angelic Sunday-school child, shudders and admits the truth, that she can never forget that he is a Negro, and he is cad enough to say, so says the writer, that he will say his prayers at her feet night and morning notwithstanding!

We all know, no man, negro or other, ever enacted such a part; it is wholly inconsistent with anything short of a natural-born idiot! And yet a reputable house offers this trash to the public, but thanks to a sensible public, it has been received with jeers, And so stuff like this comes apace, influencing the reading-world, not indeed thinkers and scholars; but the indiscriminate reading-world, upon whom rests, unfortunately, the bulk of senseless prejudice.

Conan Doyle,[5] like Howells, also pays his thoughtful attention to the educated negro—making him in this case more bloodthirsty and treacherous and savage than the Seminole. One more, and these are mentioned only to show the kind of types of Negro characters eminent writers have taken exceeding care to place before the world as representing us.

In the "Condition of Women in the United States," Mme. Blanc,[6] in a volume of 285 pages, devotes less than 100 words to negro women; after telling ironically of a "Black Damsel" in New Orleans engaged in teaching Latin, she describes her attire, the arrangement of her hair, and concludes, "I also saw a class of little Negro girls with faces like monkeys studying Greek, and the disgust expressed by their former masters seemed quite justified."

Her knowledge of history is as imperfect so far as veracity goes as her avowal in the same book of her freedom from prejudice against the Negro.

4. Evasive or equivocal statements.
5. Arthur Conan Doyle (1859–1930), British writer and physician; creator of the detective Sherlock Holmes.
6. Marie-Therese Blanc (1840–1907), French journalist, essayist, and author of *The Condition of Woman in the United States* (1895).

The "little girls" must have been over thirty years old to have had any former masters even at their birth! And all this is the outcome in the nineteeth century of the highest expressions of Anglo-Saxon acumen, criticism and understanding of the powers of Negroes of America!

The point of all this is the indubitable evidence of the need of thoughtful, well-defined and intelligently placed efforts on our part, to serve as counter-irritants against all such writing that shall stand, having as an aim the supplying of influential and accurate information, on all subjects relating to the Negro and his environments, to inform the American mind at least, for literary purposes.

We cannot afford any more than any other people to be indifferent to the fact, that the surest road to real fame is through literature. Who is so well known and appreciated by the cultured minds as Dumas of France,[7] and Pushkin of Russia?[8] I need not say to this thoughtful and intelligent gathering that, any people without a literature is valued lightly the world round. Who knows or can judge of our intrinsic worth without actual evidence of our breadth of mind, our boundless humanity? Appearing well and weighted with many degrees of titles will not raise us in our own estimation while color is the white elephant in America. Yet, America is but a patch on the universe: if she ever produces a race out of her cosmopolitan population, that can look beyond mere money-getting to more permanent qualities of true greatness as a nation, it will call this age her unbalanced stage.

No one thinks of mere color when looking upon the Chinese, but the dignified character of the literature of his race, and he for monotony of expression, color and undesirable individual habits is far inferior in these points to the ever-varying American Negro. So our people must awaken to the fact, that our task is a conquest for a place for ourselves, and is a legitimate ground for action for us, if we shall resolve to conquer it.

While we of to-day view with increasing dissatisfaction the trend of the literary productions of this country, concerning us, yet are we standing squarely on the foundation laid for us by our immediate predecessors?

This is the question I would bring to your minds. Are we adding to the structure planned for us by our pioneers? Do we know our dwelling and those who under many hardships, at least, gathered the material for its upbuilding? Knowing them do we honor—do we love them—what have they done that we should love? Your own Emerson says—"To judge the production of a people you must transplant the spirit of the times in which they lived."

In the ten volumes of American Literature edited by H. L. Stoddard only Phyllis Wheatley and George W. Williams[9] find a place. This does not show that we have done nothing in literature; far from it, but it does show that we have done nothing so brilliant, so effective, so startling as to attract the attention of these editors. Now it is a fact that thoughtful, scholarly white people do not look for literature in its highest sense, from us any more than they look for high scholarship, profound and critical learning on any one point, nor for any eminent judicial acumen or profound insight into causes and effects.

These are properly regarded as the results only of matured intellectual growth or abundant leisure and opportunity, when united with exceptional

7. Either Alexandre Dumas *pere* (1802–1870), French novelist and playwright of African descent, or Alexandre Dumas *fils* (1824–1895), also a French novelist and playwright.

8. Alexander Pushkin (1799–1837), Russian novelist, poet, and playwright of African descent.

9. George Washington Williams (1849–1891), African American minister, politician, and author of *The History of the Negro Race in America, 1619–1880* (1882).

talents, and this is the world's view and it is in the main a correct one. Even the instances of precocious geniuses and the rare examples of extraordinary talent appearing from humble and unpromising parentage and unfortuitous surroundings are always recognized as brilliant, sporadic cases, exceptions.

Consequently our success in Race Literature will be looked upon with curiosity and only a series of projected enterprises in various directions—history, poetry, novel writing, speeches, orations, forensic effort, sermons, and so on, will have the result of gaining for us recognition.

You recall Poteghine's remark in Turgenef's novel of "Smoke."[1] How well it applies to us.

"For heaven's sake do not spread the idea in Russia that we can achieve success without preparation. No, if your brow be seven spans in width *study*, begin with the alphabet or *else remain quiet* and say nothing. Oh! it excites me to think of these things."

Dr. Blyden's essay, Dr. Crummell's sermons and addresses, and Professor Greener's[2] orations all are high specimens of sustained English, good enough for anyone to read, and able to bear critical examination, and reflect the highest credit on the race.

Your good city of Boston deserves well for having given us our first real historian, William C. Nell—his history of "The colored Patriots of the Revolution"—not sufficiently read nowadays or appreciated by the present generation; a scholarly, able, accurate book, second to none written by any other colored man.

William Wells Brown's "Black Man" was worthy of tribute in its day, the precursor of more elaborate books, and should be carefully studied now; his "Sights and Scenes Abroad" was probably the first book of travel written by an American Negro. The same is doubtless true of his novel, "Clotilde." The "Anglo-African" magazine published in New York City in 1859, is adjudged by competent authority to be the highest, best, most scholarly written of all the literature published by us in fifty years.

We have but to read the graphic descriptions and eloquent passages in the first edition of the "Life and Times" of Frederick Douglass to see the high literary qualities of which the race is capable. "Light and Truth," a valuable volume published many years ago; Dr. Perry's "Cushite!"; "Bond and Free, or Under the Yoke," by John S. Ladue; "The Life of William Lloyd Garrison," by Archibald Grimke; Joseph Wilson's "Black Phalanx"; and "Men of Mark," by Rev. W. J. Simmons; "Noted Women," by Dr. Scruggs; "The Negro Press and Its Editors," by I. Garland Penn; "Paul Dunbar's Dialect Poems," which have lately received high praise from the Hoosier Poet, James Whitcomb Reilly; "Johnson's School History"; "From a Virginia Cabin to the Capitol," by Hon. J. M. Langston; "Iola Leroy," by Mrs. F. E. W. Harper; "Music and Some Highly Musical People," by James M. Trotter, are specimen books within easy reach of the public, that will increase in interest with time.

Professor R. T. Greener as a metaphysician, logician, orator, and prize essayist, holds an undisputed position in the annals of our literature second to none. His defense of the Negro in the "National Quarterly Review," 1880, in reply to Mr. Parton's strictures, has been an arsenal from which many have since supplied their armor. It was quoted extensively in this country and England.

1. Published in 1867, *Smoke* was a novel by Russian fiction writer and poet Ivan Turgenev (1818–1883).

2. Richard T. Greener (1844–1922), African American scholar and diplomat; Edward Wilmot Blyden (1832–1912), Liberian educator, minister, and author; Alexander Crummell (1819–1898), African American minister, abolitionist, and Pan-Africanist.

And it is not generally known that one of the most valuable contributions to Race Literature has appeared in the form of a scientific treatise on "Incandescent Lighting" published by Van Nostrand of New York, and thus another tribute is laid to Boston's credit by Lewis H. Latimer.

In the ecclesiastical line we have besides those already mentioned, the writings of the learned Dr. Pennington, Bishops Payne and Tanner of the A.M.E. Church.

The poems, songs and addresses by our veteran literary women F. E. W. Harper, Charlotte Forten Grimke, H. Cordelia Ray, Gertrude Mossell, "Clarence and Corinne," "The Hazeltone Family" by Mrs. G. E. Johnson, and "Appointed" by W. H. Stowers, and W. H. Anderson are a few of the publications on similar subjects; all should be read and placed in our libraries, as first beginnings it is true, but they compare favorably with similar work of the most advanced people.

Our journalism has accomplished more than can now be estimated; in fact not until careful biographers make special studies drawn from the lives of the pioneer journalists shall we or those contemporary with them ever know the actual meed[3] of good work accomplished by them under almost insurmountable difficulties.

Beginning with the editors of the first newspapers published in this country by colored men, we New Yorkers take pride in the fact that Messrs. Cornish and Russwurm of "Freedom's Journal," New York City, 1827, edited the first paper in this country devoted to the upbuilding of the Negro. Philip A. Bell of the "Weekly Advocate," 1837, was named by contemporaries "the Nestor of African American journalists." The gifted Dr. James McCune Smith was associated with him. The "Weekly Advocate" later became the "Colored American." And in 1839, on Mr. Bell's retirement Dr. Charles Ray assumed the editorial chair and continued until 1842, making an enviable record for zeal on all matters of race interest. These men were in very truth the Pioneers of Race Journalism.

Their lives and record should be zealously guarded for the future use of our children, for they familiarized the public with the idea of the Negro owning and doing the brain work of a newspaper. The people of other sections became active in establishing journals, which did good work all along the line. Even the superficial mind must accept the modest claim that "These journals proved a powerful lever in diverting public opinion, public sympathy, and public support towards the liberation of the slave."

Papers were edited by such men as Dr. H. H. Garnet, David Ruggles, W. A. Hodges, and T. Van Rensselaer, of the "Ram's Horn." In 1847 our beloved and lofty minded Frederick Douglass edited his own paper "The North Star," in the City of Rochester, where his mortal remains now peacefully rest. His paper was noted for its high class matter—and it had the effect of raising the plane of journalism thereafter. About this time, Samuel Ringold Ward of the "Impartial Citizen," published in Syracuse, N.Y., "forged to the front," winning in years after from Mr. Douglass a most flattering tribute. "Samuel Ringold Ward," the sage of Anacostia once said to the writer, "was one of the smartest men I ever knew if not the smartest."

The prevailing sentiment at that time was sympathy for the ambitious Negro. At a most opportune time, "The Anglo African," the finest effort in the way of a magazine by the race up to that time, was established in January of

3. Share.

1859 in New York City, with Thomas Hamilton as editor and proprietor. The columns were opened to the most experienced writers of the day. Martin R. Delaney contributed many important papers on astronomy, among which was one on "Comets," another on "The Attraction of the Planets." George B. Vashon wrote "The Successive Advances of Astronomy," James McCune Smith wrote his comments "On the Fourteenth Query of Thomas Jefferson's Notes on Virginia" and his "German Invasion"—every number contained gems that to-day are beyond price. In these pages also appeared "Afric-American Picture Gallery," by "Ethiope"—Wm. J. Wilson; Robert Gordon's "Personality of the First Cause;" Dr. Pennington on "The Self-Redeeming Power of the Colored Races of the World;" Dr. Blyden on "The Slave Traffic;" and on the current questions of the day, such brave minds as Frederick Douglass, William C. Nell, John Mercer Langston, Theodore Holly, J. Sella Martin, Frances Ellen Watkins, Jane Rustic, Sarah M. Douglass, and Grace A. Mapps! What a galaxy! The result was a genuine race newspaper, one that had the courage to eliminate everything of personal interest and battle for the rights of the whole people, and while its history, like many other laudable enterprises, may be little known beyond the journalistic fraternity, to such men as Wendell Phillips and William Lloyd Garrison, the paper and staff were well known and appreciated. In those days, the Negro in literature was looked upon as a prodigy; he was encouraged in many ways by white people particularly, as he was useful in serving the cause of philanthropic agitators for the liberation of the slave. The earnest, upright character and thoughtful minds of the early pioneers acted as a standing argument in favor of the cause for which the abolitionists were then bending every nerve when the slave was liberated and the Civil War brought to a close. The spirit of Mr. Lincoln's interview with a committee of colored citizens of the District of Columbia, in August, 1862, as told by William Wells Brown, in which Mr. Lincoln said, "But for your people among us, there would be no war," reacted upon the public, and from that time until the present a vicious oppression, under the name of natural prejudice, has succeeded immeasurably in retarding our progress.

As a matter of history we have nothing to compare with weekly publications of 25 or 30 years ago. The unequal contest waged between Negro journals and their white contemporaries is lost sight of by the people, as only those connected with various publications are aware of the condition and difficulties surrounding the managements of such journals.

Our struggling journalists not only find themselves on the losing side, but as if to add to their thankless labor, they oftentimes receive the contemptuous regard of the people who should enthusiastically rally to their support. The journalist is spurred with the common sense idea that every enterprise undertaken and carried on by members of the race is making a point in history for that entire race, and the historians of the future will not stop to consider our discontented and sentimental whys and wherefores when they critically examine our race enterprises; but they will simply record their estimate of what the men and women journalists of to-day not only represented, but actually accomplished.

It is so often claimed that colored newspapers do not amount to anything. People even who boast of superior attainments, voice such sentiments with the most ill-placed indifference; the most discreditable phase of race disloyalty imaginable—one that future historians will have no alternative but to censure.

If our newspapers and magazines do not amount to anything, it is because our people do not demand anything of better quality from their own. It is because they strain their purses supporting those white papers that are and always will be independent of any income derived from us. Our contributions to such journals are spasmodic and uncertain, like fluctuating stocks, and are but an excess of surplus. It is hard for the bulk of our people to see this; it is even hard to prove to them that in supporting such journals, published by the dominant class, we often pay for what are not only vehicles of insult to our manhood and womanhood, but we assist in propagating or supporting false impressions of ourselves or our less fortunate brothers.

Our journalistic leader is unquestionably T. Thomas Fortune, editor of "The New York Age," and a regular contributor of signed articles to the "New York Sun," one of the oldest and ablest daily newspapers in the United States, noted on two continents for its rare excellence.

For many years Mr. Fortune has given his best efforts to the cause of race advancement, and the splendid opportunities now opening to him on the great journals of the day, attest the esteem in which he is held by men who create public opinion in this country.

If John E. Bruce, "Bruce-Grit," "John Mitchell, Jr." W. H. A. Moore, Augustus M. Hodge "B Square," were members of any other race, they would be famous the country over. Joe Howard or "Bill Nye" have in reality done no more for their respective clientage than these bright minds and corresponding wits have done for theirs.

T. T. Fortune of "The Age," Ida Wells-Barnet of the "Free Speech," and John Mitchell of the "Richmond Planet" have made a nobler fight than the brilliant Parnel in his championship of Ireland's cause, for the reason that the people for whom he battled better knew and utilized more the strength obtained only by systematic organization, not so is the case with the constituents of the distinguished journalists I have mentioned.

Depressing as this fact is, it should not deter those who know that Race Literature should be cultivated for the sake of the formation of habits. First efforts are always crude, each succeeding one becomes better or should be so. Each generation by the law of heredity receives the impulse or impression for good or ill from its predecessors, and since this is the law, we must begin to form habits of observation and commence to build a plan for posterity by synthesis, analysis, ourselves aiming and striving after the highest, whether we attain it or not. Such are the attempts of our journalists of to-day, and they shall reap if they faint not.

Race Literature does not mean things uttered in praise, thoughtless praise of ourselves, wherein each goose thinks her gosling a swan. We have had too much of this, too much that is crude, rude, pompous, and literary nothings, which ought to have been strangled before they were written much less printed; and this does not only apply to us; for it is safe to say that, only an infinitesimal percentage of the so-called literature filling the book shelves to-day, will survive a half century.

In the words of a distinguished critic, "It is simply amazing how little of all that is written and printed in these days that makes for literature; how small a part is permanent, how much purely ephemeral, famous to-day on account of judicious advertising, forgotten to-morrow. We should clear away the under-brush of self-deception which makes the novice think because sentences are strung together and ordinary ideas evolved, dilated upon and printed, that such trash is literature." If this is claimed for the more favored class, it should have a tendency with us to encourage our work, even though the results do not appear at once.

It should serve the student by guarding him against the fulsome praise of "great men," "great writers," "great lawyers," "great ministers," who in reality have never done one really great or meritorious thing.

Rather should the student contemplate the success of such as Prof. Dubois who won the traveling fellowship at Harvard on metaphysical studies, and has just received his Ph.D., at the last commencement, on account of his work. For such facts demonstrate that it is the character of the work we do, rather than the quantity of it, which counts for real Race Literature.

Race Literature does mean though the preserving of all the records of a Race, and thus cherishing the materials saving from destruction and obliteration what is good, helpful and stimulating. But for our Race Literature, how will future generations know of the pioneers in Literature, our statesmen, soldiers, divines, musicians, artists, lawyers, critics, and scholars? True culture in Race Literature will enable us to discriminate and not to write hasty thoughts and unjust and ungenerous criticism often of our superiors in knowledge and judgment.

And now comes the question, What part shall we women play in the Race Literature of the future? I shall best answer that question by calling your attention to the glorious part which they have already performed in the columns of the "Woman's Era," edited by Josephine St. P. Ruffin.

Here within the compass of one small journal we have struck out a new line of departure—a journal, a record of Race interests gathered from all parts of the United States, carefully selected, moistened, winnowed and garnered by the ablest intellects of educated colored women, shrinking at no lofty theme, shirking no serious duty, aiming at every possible excellence, and determined to do their part in the future uplifting of the race.

If twenty women, by their concentrated efforts in one literary movement, can meet with such success as has engendered, planned out, and so successfully consummated this convention, what much more glorious results, what wider spread success, what grander diffusion of mental light will not come forth at the bidding of the enlarged hosts of women writers, already called into being by the stimulus of your efforts?

And here let me speak one word for my journalistic sisters who have already entered the broad arena of journalism. Before the "Woman's Era" had come into existence, no one except themselves can appreciate the bitter experience and sore disappointments under which they have at all times been compelled to pursue their chosen vocations.

If their brothers of the press have had their difficulties to contend with, I am here as a sister journalist to state, from the fullness of knowledge, that their task has been an easy one compared with that of the colored woman in journalism.

Woman's part in Race Literature, as in Race building, is the most important part and has been so in all ages. It is for her to receive impressions and transmit them. All through the most remote epochs she has done her share in literature. When not an active singer like Sappho,[4] she has been the means of producing poets, statesmen, and historians, understandingly as Napoleon's mother worked on Homeric tapestry while bearing the future conqueror of the world.

When living up to her highest development, woman has done much to make lasting history, by her stimulating influence and there can be no greater responsibility than that, and this is the highest privilege granted to her by the Creator of the Universe.

4. Greek poet (ca. 630–570 B.C.E.).

Such are some brief outlines of the vast problem of Race Literature. Never was the outlook for Race Literature brighter. Questions of vast importance to succeeding generations on all lines are now looming up to be dissected and elucidated.

Among the students of the occult, certain powers are said to be fully developed innately in certain types of the Negro, powers that when understood and properly directed will rival if not transcend those of Du Maurier's Svengali.[5]

The medical world recognizes this especially when investigating the science of neurology,—by the merest chance it was discovered that certain types of our nurses—male and female—possessed invaluable qualities for quieting and controlling patients afflicted with the self-destructive mania. This should lead our physicians to explore and investigate so promising a field.

American artists find it easy to caricature the Negro, but find themselves baffled when striving to depict the highest characteristics of a Sojourner Truth. If he lacks the required temperament, there is thus offered a field for the race-loving Negro artist to compete with his elder brother in art, and succeed where the other has failed.

American and even European historians have often proved themselves much enchained by narrow local prejudice, hence there is a field for the unbiased historian of this closing century.

The advance made during the last fifteen or twenty years in mechanical science is the most encouraging nature possible for our own ever-increasing class of scientific students.

The scholars of the race, linguists and masters of the dead languages have a wide field before them, which when fully explored, will be of incalculable interest to the whole people—I mean particularly the translators of the writings of the ancient world, on all that pertains to the exact estimate in which our African ancestors were held by contemporaries. This will be of interest to all classes, and especially to our own.

Until our scholars shall apply themselves to these greatly neglected fields, we must accept the perverted and indifferent translations of those prejudiced against us.

Dr. Le Plongeon, an eminent explorer and archaeologist, in his Central American studies, has made startling discoveries, which, if he succeeds in proving, will mean that the cradle of man's primitive condition is situated in Yucatan, and the primitive race was the ancestor of the Negro.

The "Review of Reviews" of July has this to say: "That such a tradition should have been handed down to the modern Negro is not so improbable in view of the fact that the inhabitants of Africa appear certainly to have had communication with the people of the Western world up to the destruction of the Island of Atlanta, concerning which even Dr. Le Plongeon has much to tell us."

Think of it! What a scope for our scholars not only in archaeology, but in everything that goes to make up literature!

Another avenue of research that commands dignified attention is the possibility that Negroes were among those who embarked with Columbus. Prominent educators are giving serious attention to this. Prof. Wright, of Georgia, lately sailed to England with the express purpose of investigating the subject, during his vacation, in some of the famous old libraries of Europe.

5. Svengali is a character in the novel *Trilby* (1894) by George Du Maurier (1834–1896); the name has come to mean an evil manipulator or excessively dominating person.

The lesson to be drawn from this cursory glance at what I may call the past, present and future of our Race Literature apart from its value as first beginnings, not only to us as a people but literature in general, is that unless earnest and systematic effort be made to procure and preserve for transmission to our successors, the records, books and various publications already produced by us, not only will the sturdy pioneers who paved the way and laid the foundation for our Race Literature be robbed of their just due, but an irretrievable wrong will be inflicted upon the generations that shall come after us.

1895

IDA B. WELLS-BARNETT
1862–1931

Ida B. Wells-Barnett is best known as a courageous, tenacious, consciousness-raising investigative journalist who published factual reports and scholarly analyses on lynching. However, it is more accurate to consider her a literary activist who wrote stirring essays on a variety of political subjects, including education and equal rights. Born to enslaved parents, Jim and Elizabeth Warrenton Wells, six months before Emancipation, Ida Baker Wells was the oldest of eight children. When the Freedman's Aid association opened a school in Holly Springs, Mississippi, Jim Wells became a member of the trustee board and Ida B. Wells became one of its first students. When her parents died in the yellow fever epidemic of 1878, sixteen-year-old Ida dropped out of school and found work as a teacher in order to support her siblings. Later she moved to Memphis where the salaries were higher, and during the summer breaks she attended Fisk University. An outspoken critic of substandard education for African Americans, Wells-Barnett began her journalism career as a contributor to the *Evening Star*, a paper affiliated with her Friday evening "lyceum," one of several informal educational endeavors in African America that provided experience in elocution and reading through discussion of current events and literature. In 1884 she became editor of the *Living Way*, a weekly Black Baptist newspaper. Wells-Barnett later wrote, "I had an instinctive feeling that the people who had little or no school training should have something coming into their homes weekly which dealt with their problems in a simple, helpful way. So in weekly letters to the *Living Way*, I wrote in a plain, common-sense way on the things which concerned our people." One subject was her own lawsuit against the Chesapeake, Ohio, and Southwestern Railroad. Wells-Barnett had sued the railroad company for attempting to expel her from the women's car. Though she won her case in a lower court, the Tennessee Supreme Court later overturned the ruling. Her columns written under the pen name "Iola" were reprinted in newspapers throughout the country. When she was twenty-seven, Wells-Barnett became editor and part owner of the *Memphis Free Speech*. Two years later, when she wrote an article denouncing inadequate schools for Black children, she was fired from her teaching position. Not long afterward another article almost cost her life. In March 1892 three Black businessmen opened a grocery store that competed with a white merchant. They were lynched. Outraged, Wells-Barnett wrote a scathing report that challenged the purported cause of the lynching with this statement: "Nobody in this section believes the old thread-bare lie that Negro men assault white women. If southern white men are not careful they will over-reach themselves and a conclusion will be reached which will be very damaging to the moral reputation of their women." Fortunately, Wells-Barnett was out of town visiting Frances E. W. Harper when the white mob destroyed the office of the *Free Speech*. Her partner, J. C. Fleming, was run out of town and Wells-Barnett was advised not to return.

Making the best of her exile, Wells-Barnett made a new home for herself and soon became writer, editor, and part owner of the *New York Age*. She continued to develop her critiques of lynch law and to publicize events in the South, believing that northerners would be moved to action if they were made aware of what was happening. *A Red Record* was one of several publications written to inspire her readers to take positive action. Among her other well-publicized crusades was one she undertook with Frederick Douglass, Ferdinand Lee Barnett, and I. Garland Penn, for which Wells-Barnett wrote and distributed a pamphlet titled *The Reason Why the Colored American Is Not in the World's Columbian Exposition*.

She later married Ferdinand Lee Barnett and had four children, but Wells-Barnett persisted with her activism. She continued to edit newspapers and to write provocative essays. She became nationally prominent in the women's club movement and was part of the founding group of the National Association for the Advancement of Colored People. In 1913 she organized one of the first suffrage groups made up of Black women, and in 1930 she ran as an independent candidate for Illinois state senator.

Ida B. Wells-Barnett is remembered as an outspoken and articulate advocate of equal rights and a fearlessly feminist pioneer in journalism. However, as her diary demonstrates, her literary aspirations included becoming a serious novelist. Realizing that her contributions were being ignored, belittled, or usurped by men such as Carter G. Woodson and W. E. B. Du Bois, Wells-Barnett wrote her own autobiography, *A Crusade for Justice*, which was published after her death, by her daughter, Alfreda B. Duster.

From A Red Record

Chapter I

THE CASE STATED

The student of American sociology will find the year 1894 marked by a pronounced awakening of the public conscience to a system of anarchy and outlawry which had grown during a series of ten years to be so common, that scenes of unusual brutality failed to have any visible effect upon the humane sentiments of the people of our land.

Beginning with the emancipation of the Negro, the inevitable result of unbridled power exercised for two and a half centuries, by the white man over the Negro, began to show itself in acts of conscienceless outlawry. During the slave regime, the Southern white man owned the Negro body and soul. It was to his interest to dwarf the soul and preserve the body. Vested with unlimited power over his slave, to subject him to any and all kinds of physical punishment, the white man was still restrained from such punishment as tended to injure the slave by abating his physical powers and thereby reducing his financial worth. While slaves were scourged mercilessly, and in countless cases inhumanly treated in other respects, still the white owner rarely permitted his anger to go so far as to take a life, which would entail upon him a loss of several hundred dollars. The slave was rarely killed, he was too valuable; it was easier and quite as effective, for discipline or revenge, to sell him "Down South."

But Emancipation came and the vested interests of the white man in the Negro's body were lost. The white man had no right to scourge the emancipated Negro, still less has he a right to kill him. But the Southern white people had been educated so long in that school of practice, in which might makes right, that they disdained to draw strict lines of action in dealing with the Negro. In slave times the Negro was kept subservient and submissive by the frequency and severity of the scourging, but, with freedom, a new system of intimidation came into vogue; the Negro was not only whipped and scourged; he was killed.

Not all nor nearly all of the murders done by white men, during the past thirty years in the South, have come to light, but the statistics as gathered and preserved by white men, and which have not been questioned, show that during these years more than ten thousand Negroes have been killed in cold blood, without the formality of judicial trial and legal execution. And yet, as evidence of the absolute impunity with which the white man dares to kill a Negro, the same record shows that during all these years, and for all these murders only three white men have been tried, convicted, and executed. As no white man has been lynched for the murder of colored people, these three executions are the only instances of the death penalty being visited upon white men for murdering Negroes.

Naturally enough the commission of these crimes began to tell upon the public conscience, and the Southern white man, as a tribute to the nineteenth century civilization, was in a manner compelled to give excuses for his barbarism. His excuses have adapted themselves to the emergency, and are aptly outlined by that greatest of all Negroes, Frederick Douglass, in an article of recent date, in which he shows that there have been three distinct eras of Southern barbarism, to account for which three distinct excuses have been made.

The first excuse given to the civilized world for the murder of unoffending Negroes was the necessity of the white man to repress and stamp out alleged "race riots." For years immediately succeeding the war there was an appalling slaughter of colored people, and the wires usually conveyed to northern people and the world the intelligence, first, that an insurrection was being planned by Negroes, which, a few hours later, would prove to have been vigorously resisted by white men, and controlled with a resulting loss of several killed and wounded. It was always a remarkable feature in these insurrections and riots that only Negroes were killed during the rioting, and that all the white men escaped unharmed.

From 1865 to 1872, hundreds of colored men and women were mercilessly murdered and the almost invariable reason assigned was that they met their death by being alleged participants in an insurrection or riot. But this story at last wore itself out. No insurrection ever materialized; no Negro rioter was ever apprehended and proven guilty, and no dynamite ever recorded the black man's protest against oppression and wrong. It was too much to ask thoughtful people to believe this transparent story, and the southern white people at last made up their minds that some other excuse must be had.

Then came the second excuse, which had its birth during the turbulent times of reconstruction. By an amendment to the Constitution the Negro was given the right of franchise, and, theoretically at least, his ballot became his invaluable emblem of citizenship. In a government "of the people, for the people, and by the people," the Negro's vote became an important factor in all matters of state and national politics. But this did not last long. The southern white man would not consider that the Negro had any right[1] which a white man was bound to respect, and the idea of a republican form of government[2] in the southern states grew into general contempt. It was maintained that "This is a white man's government," and regardless of numbers the white man should rule. "No Negro domination" became the new legend on the sanguinary[3] banner of the sunny South, and under it rode the Ku Klux Klan, the Regulators, and the lawless mobs, which for any cause chose to murder one man or a dozen as suited their purpose best. It was a long, gory campaign; the blood chills and the heart almost loses faith in Christianity when one thinks of Yazoo, Hamburg, Edgefield, Copiah, and the countless massacres of defenseless Negroes, whose only crime was the attempt to exercise their right to vote.

But it was a bootless strife for colored people. The government which had made the Negro a citizen found itself unable to protect him. It gave him the right to vote, but denied him the protection which should have maintained that right. Scourged from his home; hunted through the swamps; hung by midnight raiders, and openly murdered in the light of day, the Negro clung to his right of franchise with a heroism which would have wrung admiration from the hearts of savages. He believed that in that small white ballot there was a subtle something which stood for manhood as well as citizenship, and thousands of brave black men went to their graves, exemplifying the one by dying for the other.

The white man's victory soon became complete by fraud, violence, intimidation and murder. The franchise vouchsafed to the Negro grew to be a "barren ideality,"[4] and regardless of numbers, the colored people found themselves voiceless in the councils of those whose duty it was to rule. With no longer the fear of "Negro Domination" before their eyes, the white man's second excuse became valueless. With the Southern governments all subverted and the Negro actually eliminated from all participation in state and national elections, there could be no longer an excuse for killing Negroes to prevent "Negro Domination."

Brutality still continued; Negroes were whipped, scourged, exiled, shot and hung whenever and wherever it pleased the white man so to treat them, and as the civilized world with increasing persistency held the white people of the South to account for its outlawry, the murderers invented the third excuse—that Negroes had to be killed to avenge their assaults upon women. There could be framed no possible excuse more harmful to the Negro and more unanswerable if true in its sufficiency for the white man.

Humanity abhors the assailant of womanhood, and this charge upon the Negro at once placed him beyond the pale of human sympathy. With such unanimity, earnestness and apparent candor was this charge made and reiterated that the world has accepted the story that the Negro is a monster which the Southern white man has painted him. And to-day, the Christian world feels, that while lynching is a crime, and lawlessness and anarchy the certain precursors of a nation's fall, it can not by word or deed, extend sympathy or help to a race of outlaws, who might mistake their plea for justice and deem it an excuse for their continued wrongs.

1. A reference to the Supreme Court decision in *Dred Scott v. Sandford* (1857), which declared that African Americans were not citizens.
2. Government deriving its power from its citizens.
3. Bloodthirsty.
4. Quoted from "The Southern Problem and Its Solution" by Lewis Harvie Blair (1834–1916), an antislavery white southern reformer.

The Negro has suffered much and is willing to suffer more. He recognizes that the wrongs of two centuries can not be righted in a day, and he tries to bear his burden with patience for to-day and be hopeful for to-morrow. But there comes a time when the veriest worm will turn, and the Negro feels today that after all the work he has done, all the sacrifices he has made, and all the suffering he has endured, if he did not, now, defend his name and manhood from this vile accusation, he would be unworthy even of the contempt of mankind. It is to this charge he now feels he must make answer.

If the Southern people in defense of their lawlessness, would tell the truth and admit that colored men and women are lynched for almost any offense, from murder to a misdemeanor, there would not now be the necessity for this defense. But when they intentionally, maliciously and constantly belie the record and bolster up these falsehoods by the words of legislators, preachers, governors and bishops, then the Negro must give to the world his side of the awful story.

A word as to the charge itself. In considering the third reason assigned by the Southern white people for the butchery of blacks, the question must be asked, what the white man means when he charges the black man with rape. Does he mean the crime which the statutes of the civilized states describe as such? Not by any means. With the Southern white man, any mesalliance[5] existing between a white woman and a colored man is a sufficient foundation for the charge of rape. The Southern white man says that it is impossible for a voluntary alliance to exist between a white woman and a colored man, and therefore, the fact of an alliance is a proof of force. In numerous instances where colored men have been lynched on the charge of rape, it was positively known at the time of lynching, and indisputably proven after the victim's death, that the relationship sustained between the man and woman was voluntary and clandestine, and that in no court of law could even the charge of assault have been successfully maintained.

It was for the assertion of this fact, in the defense of her own race, that the writer hereof became an exile; her property destroyed and her return to her home forbidden under penalty of death, for writing the following editorial which was printed in her paper, the Free Speech, in Memphis, Tenn., May 21, 1892:

"Eight Negroes lynched since last issue of the 'Free Speech' one at Little Rock, Ark., last Saturday morning where the citizens broke (?) into the penitentiary and got their man; three near Anniston, Ala., one near New Orleans; and three at Clarksville, Ga., the last three for killing a white man, and five on the same old racket—the new alarm about raping white women. The same programme of hanging, then shooting bullets into the lifeless bodies was carried out to the letter. Nobody in this section of the country believes the old threadbare lie that Negro men rape white women. If Southern white men are not careful, they will over-reach themselves and public sentiment will have a reaction; a conclusion will then be reached which will be very damaging to the moral reputation of their women."

But threats cannot suppress the truth, and while the Negro suffers the soul deformity, resultant from two and a half centuries of slavery, he is no more guilty of this vilest of all vile charges than the white man who would blacken his name.

5. Marriage to a person of lower social status.

During all the years of slavery, no such charge was ever made, not even during the dark days of the rebellion, when the white man, following the fortunes of war went to do battle for the maintenance of slavery. While the master was away fighting to forge the fetters upon the slave, he left his wife and children with no protectors save the Negroes themselves. And yet during those years of trust and peril, no Negro proved recreant to his trust and no white man returned to a home that had been dispoiled.

Likewise during the period of alleged "insurrection," and alarming "race riots," it never occurred to the white man, that his wife and children were in danger of assault. Nor in the Reconstruction era, when the hue and cry was against "Negro Domination," was there ever a thought that the domination would ever contaminate a fireside or strike to death the virtue of womanhood. It must appear strange indeed, to every thoughtful and candid man, that more than a quarter of a century elapsed before the Negro began to show signs of such infamous degeneration.

In his remarkable apology for lynching, Bishop Haygood, of Georgia,[6] says: "No race, not the most savage, tolerates the rape of woman, but it may be said without reflection upon any other people that the Southern people are now and always have been most sensitive concerning the honor of their women—their mothers, wives, sisters and daughters." It is not the purpose of this defense to say one word against the white women of the South. Such need not be said, but it is their misfortune that the chivalrous white men of that section, in order to escape the deserved execration of the civilized world, should shield themselves by their cowardly and infamously false excuse, and call into question that very honor about which their distinguished priestly apologist claims they are most sensitive. To justify their own barbarism they assume a chivalry which they do not possess. True chivalry respects all womanhood, and no one who reads the record, as it is written in the faces of the million mulattoes in the South, will for a minute conceive that the southern white man had a very chivalrous regard for the honor due the women of his own race or respect for the womanhood which circumstances placed in his power. That chivalry which is "most sensitive concerning the honor of women" can hope for but little respect from the civilized world, when it confines itself entirely to the women who happen to be white. Virtue knows no color line, and the chivalry which depends upon complexion of skin and texture of hair can command no honest respect.

When emancipation came to the Negroes, there arose in the northern part of the United States an almost divine sentiment among the noblest, purest and best white women of the North, who felt called to a mission to educate and Christianize the millions of southern ex-slaves. From every nook and corner of the North, brave young white women answered that call and left their cultured homes, their happy associations and their lives of ease, and with heroic determination went to the South to carry light and truth to the benighted blacks. It was a heroism no less than that which calls for volunteers for India, Africa and the Isles of the sea. To educate their unfortunate charges; to teach them the Christian virtues and to inspire in them the moral sentiments manifest in their own lives, these young women braved dangers whose record reads more like fiction than fact. They became

6. Atticus G. Haygood (1839–1896), bishop of the Methodist church and president of Emory College in Atlanta.

social outlaws in the South. The peculiar sensitiveness of the southern white men for women, never shed its protecting influence about them. No friendly word from their own race cheered them in their work; no hospitable doors gave them the companionship like that from which they had come. No chivalrous white man doffed his hat in honor or respect. They were "Nigger teachers"—unpardonable offenders in the social ethics of the South, and were insulted, persecuted and ostracised, not by Negroes, but by the white manhood which boasts of its chivalry toward women.

And yet these northern women worked on, year after year, unselfishly, with a heroism which amounted almost to martyrdom. Threading their way through dense forests, working in schoolhouse, in the cabin and in the church, thrown at all times and in all places among the unfortunate and lowly Negroes, whom they had come to find and to serve, these northern women, thousands and thousands of them, have spent more than a quarter of a century in giving to the colored people their splendid lessons for home and heart and soul. Without protection, save that which innocence gives to every good woman, they went about their work, fearing no assault and suffering none. Their chivalrous protectors were hundreds of miles away in their northern homes, and yet they never feared any "great dark faced mobs," they dared night or day to "go beyond their own roof trees." They never complained of assaults, and no mob was ever called into existence to avenge crimes against them. Before the world adjudges the Negro a moral monster, a vicious assailant of womanhood and a menace to the sacred precincts of home, the colored people ask the consideration of the silent record of gratitude, respect, protection and devotion of the millions of the race in the South, to the thousands of northern white women who have served as teachers and missionaries since the war.

The Negro may not have known what chivalry was, but he knew enough to preserve inviolate[7] the womanhood of the South which was entrusted to his hands during the war. The finer sensibilities of his soul may have been crushed out by years of slavery, but his heart was full of gratitude to the white women of the North, who blessed his home and inspired his soul in all these years of freedom. Faithful to his trust in both of these instances, he should now have the impartial ear of the civilized world, when he dares to speak for himself as against the infamy wherewith he stands charged.

It is his regret, that, in his own defense, he must disclose to the world that degree of dehumanizing brutality which fixes upon America the blot of a national crime. Whatever faults and failings other nations may have in their dealings with their own subjects or with other people, no other civilized nation stands condemned before the world with a series of crimes so peculiarly national. It becomes a painful duty of the Negro to reproduce a record which shows that a large portion of the American people avow anarchy, condone murder and defy the contempt of civilization.

These pages are written in no spirit of vindictiveness, for all who give the subject consideration must concede that far too serious is the condition of that civilized government in which the spirit of unrestrained outlawry constantly increases in violence, and casts its blight over a continually growing area of territory. We plead not for the colored people alone, but for all victims of the terrible injustice which puts men and women to death without form of law. During the year 1894, there were 132 persons executed in the

7. Safe from harm.

United States by due form of law, while in the same year, 197 persons were put to death by mobs who gave the victims no opportunity to make a lawful defense. No comment need be made upon a condition of public sentiment responsible for such alarming results.

The purpose of the pages which follow shall be to give the record which has been made, not by colored men, but that which is the result of compilations made by white men, of reports sent over the civilized world by white men in the South. Out of their own mouths shall the murderers be condemned. For a number of years the Chicago Tribune, admittedly one of the leading journals of America, has made a specialty of the compilation of statistics touching upon lynching. The data compiled by that journal and published to the world January 1st, 1894, up to the present time has not been disputed. In order to be safe from the charge of exaggeration, the incidents hereinafter reported have been confined to those vouched for by the Tribune.

* * *

Chapter X

THE REMEDY

It is a well established principle of law that every wrong has a remedy. Herein rests our respect for law. The Negro does not claim that all of the one thousand black men, women and children, who have been hanged, shot and burned alive during the past ten years, were innocent of the charges made against them. We have associated too long with the white man not to have copied his vices as well as his virtues. But we do insist that the punishment is not the same for both classes of criminals. In lynching, opportunity is not given the Negro to defend himself against the unsupported accusations of white men and women. The word of the accuser is held to be true and the excited bloodthirsty mob demands that the rule of law be reversed and instead of proving the accused to be guilty, the victim of their hate and revenge must prove himself innocent. No evidence he can offer will satisfy the mob; he is bound hand and foot and swung into eternity. Then to excuse its infamy, the mob almost invariably reports the monstrous falsehood that its victim made a full confession before he was hanged.

With all military, legal and political power in their hands, only two of the lynching States have attempted a check by exercising the power which is theirs. Mayor Trout, of Roanoke, Virginia, called out the militia in 1893, to protect a Negro prisoner, and in so doing nine men were killed and a number wounded. Then the mayor and militia withdrew, left the Negro to his fate and he was promptly lynched. The business men realized the blow to the town's financial interests, called the mayor home, the grand jury indicted and prosecuted the ringleaders of the mob. They were given light sentences, the highest being one of twelve months in State prison. The day he arrived at the penitentiary, he was pardoned by the governor of the State.

The only other real attempt made by the authorities to protect a prisoner of the law, and which was more successful, was that of Gov. McKinley, of Ohio, who sent the militia to Washington Courthouse, O., in October, 1894, and five men were killed and twenty wounded in maintaining the principle that the law must be upheld.

In South Carolina, in April, 1893, Gov. Tillman aided the mob by yielding up to be killed, a prisoner of the law, who had voluntarily placed himself under the Governor's protection. Public sentiment by its representatives has encouraged Lynch Law, and upon the revolution of this sentiment we must depend for its abolition.

Therefore, we demand a fair trial by law for those accused of crime, and punishment by law after honest conviction. No maudlin sympathy for criminals is solicited, but we do ask that the law shall punish all alike. We earnestly desire those that control the forces which make public sentiment to join with us in the demand. Surely the humanitarian spirit of this country which reaches out to denounce the treatment of the Russian Jews, the Armenian Christians, the laboring poor of Europe, the Siberian exiles and the native women of India—will not longer refuse to lift its voice on this subject. If it were known that the cannibals or the savage Indians had burned three human beings alive in the past two years, the whole of Christendom would be roused, to devise ways and means to put a stop to it. Can you remain silent and inactive when such things are done in our own community and country? Is your duty to humanity in the United States less binding?

What can you do, reader, to prevent lynching, to thwart anarchy and promote law and order throughout our land?

1st. You can help disseminate the facts contained in this book by bringing them to the knowledge of every one with whom you come in contact, to the end that public sentiment may be revolutionized. Let the facts speak for themselves, with you as a medium.

2d. You can be instrumental in having churches, missionary societies, Y.M.C.A.'s, W.C.T.U.'s[8] and all Christian and moral forces in connection with your religious and social life, pass resolutions of condemnation and protest every time a lynching takes place; and see that they are sent to the place where these outrages occur.

3d. Bring to the intelligent consideration of Southern people the refusal of capital to invest where lawlessness and mob violence hold sway. Many labor organizations have declared by resolution that they would avoid lynch infested localities as they would the pestilence when seeking new homes. If the South wishes to build up its waste places quickly, there is no better way than to uphold the majesty of the law by enforcing obedience to the same, and meting out the same punishment to all classes of criminals, white as well as black. "Equality before the law," must become a fact as well as a theory before America is truly the "land of the free and the home of the brave."

4th. Think and act on independent lines in this behalf, remembering that after all, it is the white man's civilization and the white man's government which are on trial. This crusade will determine whether that civilization can maintain itself by itself, or whether anarchy shall prevail; whether this Nation shall write itself down a success at self government, or in deepest humiliation admit its failure complete; whether the precepts and theories of Christianity are professed and practiced by American white people as Golden Rules of thought and action, or adopted as a system of morals to be preached to heathen until they attain to the intelligence which needs the system of Lynch Law.

8. Women's Christian Temperance Union, a movement to abolish alcoholic beverages.

5th. Congressman Blair offered a resolution in the House of Representatives, August, 1894. The organized life of the country can speedily make this a law by sending resolutions to Congress indorsing Mr. Blair's bill and asking Congress to create the commission. In no better way can the question be settled, and the Negro does not fear the issue. The following is the resolution:

"Resolved, By the House of Representatives and Senate in congress assembled, That the committee on labor be instructed to investigate and report the number, location and date of all alleged assaults by males upon females throughout the country during the ten years last preceding the passing of this joint resolution, for or on account of which organized but unlawful violence has been inflicted or attempted to be inflicted. Also to ascertain and report all facts of organized but unlawful violence to the person, with the attendant facts and circumstances, which have been inflicted upon accused persons alleged to have been guilty of crimes punishable by due process of law which have taken place in any part of the country within the ten years last preceding the passage of this resolution. Such investigation shall be made by the usual methods and agencies of the Department of Labor, and report made to Congress as soon as the work can be satisfactorily done, and the sum of $25,000, or so much thereof as may be necessary, is hereby appropriated to pay the expenses out of any money in the treasury not otherwise appropriated."

The belief has been constantly expressed in England that in the United States, which has produced Wm. Lloyd Garrison, Henry Ward Beecher, James Russell Lowell, John G. Whittier and Abraham Lincoln[9] there must be those of their descendants who would take hold of the work of inaugurating an era of law and order. The colored people of this country who have been loyal to the flag believe the same, and strong in that belief have begun this crusade. To those who still feel they have no obligation in the matter, we commend the following lines of Lowell on "Freedom."

Men! whose boast it is that ye
Come of fathers brave and free,
If there breathe on earth a slave
Are ye truly free and brave?
If ye do not feel the chain,
When it works a brother's pain,
Are ye not base slaves indeed,
Slaves unworthy to be freed?

Women! who shall one day bear
Sons to breathe New England air,
If ye hear without a blush,
Deeds to make the roused blood rush
Like red lava through your veins,
For your sisters now in chains,—
Answer! are ye fit to be
Mothers of the brave and free?

9. Lincoln (1809–1865), president of the United States (1861–65). Garrison (1805–1879), antislavery leader. Beecher (1813–1887), antislavery preacher. Lowell (1819–1891), poet, editor, and antislavery activist. Whittier (1807–1892), poet and reformer.

Is true freedom but to break
Fetters for our own dear sake,
And, with leathern hearts, forget
That we owe mankind a debt?
No! true freedom is to share
All the chains our brothers wear,
And, with heart and hand, to be
Earnest to make others free!

There are slaves who fear to speak
For the fallen and the weak;
They are slaves who will not choose
Hatred, scoffing, and abuse,
Rather than in silence shrink
From the truth they needs must think;
They are slaves who dare not be
In the right with two or three.

A FIELD FOR PRACTICAL WORK

The very frequent inquiry made after my lectures by interested friends is, "What can I do to help the cause?" The answer always is, "Tell the world the facts." When the Christian world knows the alarming growth and extent of outlawry in our land, some means will be found to stop it.

The object of this publication is to tell the facts, and friends of the cause can lend a helping hand by aiding in the distribution of these books. When I present our cause to a minister, editor, lecturer, or representative of any moral agency, the first demand is for facts and figures. Plainly, I can not then hand out a book with a twenty-five cent tariff on the information contained. This would be only a new method in the book agents' art. In all such cases it is a pleasure to submit this book for investigation, with the certain assurance of gaining a friend to the cause.

There are many agencies which may be enlisted in our cause by the general circulation of the facts herein contained. The preachers, teachers, editors and humanitarians of the white race, at home and abroad, must have facts laid before them, and it is our duty to supply these facts. The Central Anti-Lynching League, Room 9, 128 Clark St., Chicago, has established a Free Distribution Fund, the work of which can be promoted by all who are interested in this work.

Anti-lynching leagues, societies and individuals can order books from this fund at agents' rates. The books will be sent to their order, or, if desired, will be distributed by the League among those whose co-operative aid we so greatly need. The writer hereof assures prompt distribution of books according to order, and public acknowledgment of all orders through the public press.

1895

African American Migration Debates, 1852–1880

The land is free, and it is nobody's business,
if there is land enough, where the people go.
—Benjamin Singleton, 1879

African American migration has always been a leap of faith, requiring more than resilience, determination, stamina, and imagination. Despite the iconic literary characterizations of the North Star, the Drinking Gourd, and the Underground Railroad that ran from South to North, African Americans migrated in any direction that offered the possibility of taking them to a better life. In 1536, people of African ancestry in the Spanish colony of San Miguel de Gualdape in the Carolina area went to live with Native American tribes. Others, especially those in the slave-holding South and commonly referred to as "maroons," created hidden communities on nearby islands or in the wilderness and swamps. For decades, Spanish Floridians encouraged African American migration by offering citizenship, employment, and housing in return for help in defending their colonies against British invasion. Still others, known as "Exodusters," migrated to Kansas in 1879, the first large-scale exodus following the Civil War. Black migrants could also look beyond the United States: in 1811 Paul Cuffee, African American merchant and shipbuilder, transported a group of Black settlers from the United States to Sierra Leone. The literature of African Americans has long chronicled their multiple and unceasing migrations, codified often as searches for the Promised Land. The writings in this cluster tell and retell the complex stories of and attitudes toward African American migration both before and after the Civil War.

It is an understatement to say that very few Africans had any choice about coming to North America. And few had any choice about migrating anywhere before or even after slavery was abolished. But some did, and the debate about whether and where to go was complex. In addition to challenges surrounding finances, transportation, food, shelter, and employment, African American migrants faced other obstacles. During the era of legal enslavement, they were required to show "free papers," "slave badges," or "passes" upon demand. Self-emancipated individuals had none of these forms of identification. And it was not unusual for the papers of legally free people to be confiscated or destroyed and for those people to be enslaved, especially after the abolition of the slave trade in 1808 and the passage of the Fugitive Slave Act of 1850. After the Civil War, African American migrants faced "Black Codes." For example, before Black Americans could live in certain cities, they had to produce paperwork such as documents signed by local white people testifying to their "good character," payment of annual fees and bonds to ensure they would not violate laws and customs or seek government assistance, or cash to purchase or lease land and housing since most banks did not loan to African Americans. Despite incredible obstacles, before the Civil War, African American migrants created Black communities in the free states of the northern United States, in the border states of the western frontier, and in California and the territories north of it. Migrants settled together, in part because they often traveled in groups of friends and family, but also for mutual aid and protection against hostile European Americans or Native Americans. Though some white Americans welcomed and helped them, discriminatory laws and practices restricted where and when and how they could work or live, go to school, or even gather in groups of more than four.

African American migrant literature displays the resilience and determination of the people who sought a new life. Its creative and historical themes have long focused on the means and modes of survival and transcendence. It describes or imagines places of care, safety, and satisfaction and extols the feats of those who succeed against the odds. Among the earliest such pieces are the "Flying African" stories that blur boundaries of fact and fiction, such as "All God's Chillen Had Wings." Drawing on African American religion, spirituals such as "Steal Away," "Swing Low, Sweet Chariot," and "I Got Shoes" offered complex messages both of religious devotion and of the deep desire for liberation from enslavement. But what is probably the best-known African American migrant literature is rarely acknowledged as such. Popularly known as "slave narratives" or "freedom narratives," the autobiographical accounts of formerly enslaved individuals describe life in bondage and desperate journeys to places where freedom is possible. Those published before the Civil War often include a pivot point when the narrator decides that the promise of life outside of slavery justifies the risks of escape. One needs only a slight shift of focus to recast "the slave" as running or escaping *from* something to acknowledge the fact that they are deliberately moving *to* somewhere. Focusing on a narrator's decision to go to a better place, rather than on the idea of a fugitive escaping the prison house of slavery, allows "the slave" to become "a migrant," one who is self-directed and courageous.

Still, dreams of a better life do not always come true. Harriet Jacobs's *Incidents in the Life of a Slave Girl* (1861) shows patient planning, assistance of friends and family, and continuing sacrifices, yet when Jacobs published her narrative, she concludes with a sigh: "The dream of my life is not yet realized. I do not sit with my children in a home of my own." Some went in search of friends and relatives that slavery had separated, though as Charles Chesnutt's "The Wife of His Youth" (1898) shows, such reunions could be complicated. Moving out of the war years and into the era of Reconstruction, many formerly enslaved people were anxious to leave behind the horrors of bondage, and moving geographically was one way of trying to do so. Also significant, and often motivating physical relocation, was professional and economic improvement. In *Behind the Scenes: Thirty Years a Slave and Four Years in the White House* (1868), Elizabeth Keckly gives her long years of enslavement a cursory summary and her relatively few years as a self-emancipated woman much detailed attention. Likewise, Peter Randolph, Henry Clay Bruce, Booker T. Washington, and others expand upon their lives after enslavement in *From Slave Cabin to the Pulpit* (1893), *The New Man* (1895), and *Up From Slavery* (1900).

African American media also intended to educate, inspire, manage, and celebrate people of African ancestry while countering the often demeaning literature of non–African Americans. The titles of newspapers, many printed in church basements, affirm ideas of brighter days: *Freedom's Journal* (1827–29), *The North Star* (1847–51), *The Afro-American* (1892). Such periodicals published speeches and essays by and news of African Americans, encouraging concepts of nationhood or new communities. Indeed, African American media was a primary source of information for African American migration. David Walker's *Appeal . . . to the Coloured Citizens of the World* (1829) and Martin R. Delany's *The Condition, Elevation, Emigration and Destiny of the Colored People of the United States* (1852) championed or excoriated, debated and interpreted arguments for migration and considered which locations held out the best chance for a better life.

The selections in this cluster offer glimpses of what was at stake for African American migrants both in the difficult decision to move and in the challenging process of resettling. Mary Ann Shadd, who emigrated to Canada, published *A Plea for Emigration*, a compilation of arguments and information passed along in antislavery publications as well as in speeches and conversations. Thomas P. Detter's two postbellum essays represent migration literature promoting the western states. Henry McNeal Turner's solutions harken back to Martin Delany while presaging Marcus Garvey's "back to Africa" movement. Sojourner Truth, a traveling preacher, called for a "colony" to be established in the West. Benjamin Singleton practiced entrepreneurialism, economic advancement, and land ownership, establishing Black settlements in Kansas. Frederick Douglass and Richard T. Greener, two "Representative Men" because of their oratorical skills and social status, publicly disagreed on migration: Douglass thought it should be "a last resort" while Greener responded that it "leads peoples and individuals toward peace, protection and happiness."

MARY ANN SHADD

Mary Ann Shadd (1823–1893) published *A Plea for Emigration; or, Notes of Canada West* after the U.S. Congress passed the Fugitive Slave Act of 1850, which legalized capturing the "property" of enslavers in states where slavery was illegal. Since capture required little more than claiming that a person fit the description of a fugitive, the bill endangered not only the self-emancipated but also the legally free. It prompted migration of African Americans within and from the United States. For those in the northern states, Canada was an obvious choice, but the western frontier, Africa, Mexico, and South America were also suggested as sanctuaries. Mary Ann Shadd and her brother, Isaac, moved to Canada West (Ontario) in 1851 to join Henry and Mary Bibb, Josiah Henson, and other African American author/activists in helping migrants obtain food, shelter, and employment.

A Plea for Emigration speaks eloquently of Canada as a land of promise and progress. It was not, however, Shadd's first widely read publication. Some years earlier, when Frederick Douglass queried readers of the *North Star* about how to free enslaved people and gain equal rights for African Americans, she had replied with a long letter advising the famed orator that "We should do more and talk less." Conferences and resolutions, lectures and publications were well and good, she advised, but there was no substitute for action.

Like Douglass, Shadd was a regular participant in national and international conferences, but she also initiated or participated in political protests and taught in and founded schools and organizations for abolition, suffrage, civil rights, and gender equality.

Shadd's rebuke of Douglass was not her first public disagreement with Black leaders. She debated Bibb, Henson, and others over issues of integration versus separation, management of the Refugee Home Society, and the reliance upon "begging" for donations. In opposition to their strategies, she founded the *Provincial Freeman,* a rival to Bibb's *Voice of the Fugitive.* Anticipating displeasure with a female editor, she enlisted African American author/activist Samuel Ringgold Ward and white Congregational minister Alexander McArthur as contributors and "co-editors." The *Provincial Freeman*'s motto, "Self-reliance is the true road to independence," is evident in *A Plea for Emigration.* When the Civil War began, Shadd returned to the United States and in another gender-challenging action accepted appointment by Martin Delany as a recruiter of Black soldiers for the Union Army. With the end of the Civil War, Mary Ann Shadd, now a widowed mother of two (her husband, Thomas Cary, had died in 1856, just four years after they married), entered Howard University Law School and became a lawyer—many believe she was the first Black woman to do so. She founded the Colored Women's Progressive Franchise Association, was a member of the National Woman Suffrage Association, and worked until her death in Washington, D.C., in 1893.

During her lifetime, Shadd was respected and reviled, awarded and rejected because as a woman she dared to do more and speak more—in the public sphere. In "The Damnation of Women," W. E. B. Du Bois thought it important to say, "Mary Shadd" was "a ravishing dream-born beauty," but also acknowledged that she was "Well educated, vivacious, with determination shining from her sharp eye, she threw herself singlehanded into the great Canadian pilgrimage," and as teacher, editor, and lecturer tramped through winter snows, pushed "without blot or blemish through crowd and turmoil to conventions and meetings," and was an apt example of "human sympathy and sacrifice as characteristic of Negro womanhood." Several statues and plaques honor her in Canada, and in September 2023, her papers were included in the Canada section of UNESCO's Memory of the World Register.

From A Plea for Emigration; or, Notes of Canada West[1]

Introductory Remarks

The increasing desire on the part of the colored people to become thoroughly informed respecting the Canadas, and particularly that part of the province called Canada West—to learn of the climate, soil and productions, and of the inducements offered generally to emigrants, and to them particularly, since that the passage of the odious Fugitive Slave Law[2] has made a residence in the United States to many of them dangerous in the extreme—this consideration, and the absence of condensed information accessible to all, is my excuse for offering this tract to the notice of the public. The people are in a strait—on the one hand, a pro-slavery administration,

1. In the mid-19th century, "Canada West" generally meant what is now Ontario. "Canada East" was generally French-speaking Quebec.
2. Part of the congressional Compromise of 1850, which included the right (and obligation) to capture and return those who had escaped enslavement to whomever claimed ownership regardless of whether they were in "free states" or not.

with its entire controllable force, is bearing upon them with fatal effect; on the other, the Colonization Society, in the garb of *Christianity* and *Philanthropy*, is seconding the efforts of the first named power, by bringing into the lists a vast social and immoral influence, thus making more effective the agencies employed. Information is needed.—Tropical Africa, the land of promise of the colonizationists, teeming as she is with the breath of pestilence, a burning sun and fearful maladies, bids them welcome;—she feelingly invites [them] to moral and physical death, under a voluntary escort of their most bitter enemies at home. Again, many look with dreadful forebodings to the probability of worse than inquisitorial inhumanity in the Southern States, from the operation of the Fugitive Law. Certain that neither a home in Africa, nor in the Southern States, is desirable under present circumstances, inquiry is made respecting Canada. I have endeavored to furnish information to a certain extent, to that end, and believing that more reliance would be placed upon a statement of facts obtained in the country, from reliable sources and from observation, than upon a repetition of current statements made elsewhere, however honestly made, I determined to visit Canada, and to there collect such information as most persons desire. These pages contain the result of much inquiry—matter obtained both from individuals and from documents and papers of unquestionable character in the Province.

M. A. S.

* * *

Settlements—Dawn—Elgin—the "Institution"

Much has been said of the Canada colored settlements, and fears have been expressed by many, that by encouraging exclusive settlements, the attempt to identify colored men with degraded men of like color in the States would result, and as a consequence, estrangement, suspicion, and distrust would be induced. Such would inevitably be the result, and will be, shall they determine to have entirely proscriptive settlements. Those in existence, so far as I have been able to get at facts, do not exclude whites from their vicinity; but that settlements may not be established of that character is not so certain. Dawn, on the Suydenham river, Elgin, or King's Settlement, as it is called, situated about ten miles from Chatham, are settlements in which there are regulations in regard to morals, the purchase of lands, etc., bearing only on the colored people; but whites are not excluded because of dislike. When purchase was made of the lands, many white families were residents,—at least, locations were not selected in which none resided. At first, a few sold out, fearing that such neighbors might not be agreeable; others, and they the majority, concluded to remain, and the result attests their superior judgment. Instead of an increase of vice, prejudice, improvidence, laziness, or a lack of energy, that many feared would characterize them, the infrequency of violations of law among so many is unprecedented; due attention to moral and intellectual culture has been given; the former prejudices on the part of the whites has given place to a perfect reciprocity of religious and social intercommunication. Schools are patronized equally; the gospel is common, and hospitality is shared alike by all. The school for the settlers, at Elgin, is so far superior to the one established for white children, that the latter was discontinued, and, as before said, all send together, and visit in common the Presbyterian church, there established. So of Dawn; that settlement is exceedingly flourishing, and the moral influence it exerts is good, though, owing to some recent arrangements, regulations designed to further promote its importance are being made. Land has increased in value in those settlements. Property that was worth but little, from the superior culture given by colored persons over the method before practiced, and the increasing desires for country homes, is held much higher. Another fact that is worth a passing notice is that a spirit of competition is active in their vicinity. Efforts are now put forth to produce more to the acre, and to have the land and tenements present a tidy appearance. That others than those designed to be benefited by the organization should be is not reasonable, else might persons not members of a society justly claim equal benefits with members. If Irishmen should subscribe to certain regulations on purchasing land, no neighboring landholders could rightfully share with them in the result of that organization. But prejudice would not be the cause of exclusion. So it is of those two settlements; it cannot be said of them that they are caste institutions so long as they do not express hostility to the whites; but the question of their necessity in the premises may be raised, and often is, by the settlers in Canada as well as in the States. The "Institution"[3] is a settlement under the direction of the A. M. E. Church; it contains, at present, two hundred acres, and is sold out in ten acre farms, at one dollar and fifty cents per acre, or one shilling less than cost. They have recently opened a school, and there is a log meeting house in an unfinished state, also a burying ground. There are about fifteen families settled on the land, most of whom have cleared away a few trees, but it is not in a very prosperous condition, owing, it is said, to bad management of agents—a result to be looked for when a want of knowledge characterizes them. This "Institution" bids fair to be one nucleus around which caste settlements will cluster in Canada.

* * *

The Thirty Thousand Colored Freemen of Canada

The colored subjects of her Majesty in the Canadas are, in the general, in good circumstances, that is, there are few cases of positive destitution to be found among those permanently settled. They are settled promiscuously in cities, towns, villages, and the farming districts; and no equal number of colored men in the States, north or south, can produce more freeholders.[4] They are settled on and own portions of the best farming lands in the province, and own much valuable property in the several cities, etc. There is, of course, a difference in the relative prosperity and deportment in different sections, but a respect for, and observance of the laws, is conceded to them by all; indeed, much indifference on the part of whites has given place to genuine sympathy, and the active abolitionists and liberal men of the country

3. Probably referring to a settlement in what would become Oro, Ontario, Canada, near Lake Huron. The settlement was established in 1815 by African Americans who fought with the British during the War of 1812. As the British troops retreated, many of those who fought with them relocated to the Oro area.

4. Owners of real estate.

look upon that element in their character as affording ground for hope of a bright future for them, and as evidence that their sympathy for the *free* man is not misplaced, as more than compensation for their own exertions for those yet in bonds. I have said, there is but little actual poverty among them. They are engaged in the different trades and other manual occupations. They have a paper conducted by the Rev. Henry Bibb,[5] and other able men, white and colored, are laboring among them, and in view of the protection afforded, there is no good reason why they should not prosper. After the passage of the Fugitive Law, the sudden emigration of several thousand in a few months, destitute as they necessarily were, from having, in many instances, to leave behind them all they possessed, made not a little suffering for a brief period (only among them), and the report of *their* condition had an injurious bearing upon all the colored settlers. Clothing, provisions, and other articles were sent them, but often so disposed of, or appropriated, as not to benefit those for whom intended. Distrust of agents, indiscriminately, and altogether but little real good has followed from the charity. The sensible men among them, seeing the bad results from a general character for poverty and degradation, have not been slow to express their disapprobation in the social circle, in meetings, and through the public papers. The following extracts express fully the sentiments of nine-tenths of the colored men of Canada; they think they are fully able to live without begging. There are others (very ignorant people) who think differently, as there will be in all communities, though they are in the minority. There are those, also, and they are a respectable minority (in point of numbers), who are in favor of distinctive churches and schools, and of being entirely to themselves; they will come in for especial notice, but first, let us hear the people of Buxton and other places:

> "If facts would bear out the statements made, the fugitives would have little to choose between slavery on one side of the line, and starvation on the other; but we rejoice that he is not reduced to the alternative. The man who is willing to work need not suffer, and unless a man supports himself he will neither be independent nor respectable in any country. . . . The cry that has been often raised, that we could not support ourselves, is a foul slander, got up by our enemies, and circulated both on this and the other side of the line, to our prejudice. Having lived many years in Canada, we hesitate not to say that all who are able and willing to work, can make a good living. . . . It is time the truth should be known concerning the relief that has been sent to the 'suffering fugitives in Canada,' and to what extent it has been applied. The boxes of clothing and barrels of provisions which have been sent in, from time to time, by the praiseworthy but misguided zeal of friends in the United States, have been employed to support the idle, who are too lazy to work, and who form but a small portion of the colored population in Canada. There are upwards of thirty thousand colored persons in Canada West, and not more than three thousand of them have ever received aid, and not more than half of them required it had they been willing to work. We do not think it right that twenty-seven thousand

5. Bibb (1815–1854) was an African American author. Born into slavery, he escaped to Detroit and then Canada, where he founded the abolitionist newspaper *The Voice of the Fugitive*. Bibb was a passionate supporter of Canadian emigration.

colored persons, who are supporting themselves by their own industry, should lie under the disgrace of being called public beggars, when they receive nothing, and don't want anything. . . . We wish the people of the United States to know that there is one portion of Canada West where the colored people are self-supporting, and they wish them to send neither petticoat nor pantaloons to the county of Kent. . . . The few cases of real want which arise from sickness or old age can, with a trifling effort, be relieved here, without making it a pretext for a system of wholesale begging in the United States."

Edward R. Grants,
Samuel Wickham,
Robert Harris. } Committee.

"As to the state of things in Toronto and Hamilton, I can say, from actual observation, that extreme suffering is scarcely known among the black people, while some who are far from being as industrious and deserving as they ought to be receive aid to which they would hardly seem entitled."—*S. R. Ward's Letter to the Voice of the Fugitive.*[6]

Notwithstanding the prosperity and liberal sentiment of the majority, there is yet a great deal of ignorance, bigotry, prejudice, and idleness. There are those who are only interested in education so far as the establishment of separate schools, churches, &c., tend to make broad the line of separation they wish to make between them and the whites; and they are active to increase their numbers, and to perpetuate, in the minds of the newly arrived emigrant or refugee, prejudices, originating in slavery, and as strong and objectionable in their manifestations as those entertained by whites towards them. Every casual remark by whites is tortured into a decided and effective negro hate. The expressions of an individual are made to infer the existence of prejudice on the part of the whites, and partiality by the administrators of public affairs. The recently arrived fugitives, unacquainted with the true state of things, are "*completely convinced*" by the noisy philippic[7] against all the "white folks," and all colored ones who think differently from them, and he is thus prepared to aid demagogues in preventing the adoption of proper measures for the spread of education and general intelligence, to maintain an ascendency over the inferior minds around them, and to make the way of the missionary a path of thorns. Among that portion, generally, may those be found, who by their indolent habits, tend to give point to what of prejudice is lingering in the minds of the whites; and it is to be feared that they may take some misguided step now, the consequences of which will entail evil on the many who will hereafter settle in Canada. The only ground of hope is in the native good sense of those who are now making use of the same instrumentalities for improvement as are the whites around them.

6. Samuel Ringgold Ward (1817–1866) was the author of *Autobiography of a Fugitive Negro* (1855), a minister, an abolitionist, and the co-editor of *Provincial Freeman* (Shadd's newspaper).

7. Tirade, rant, bitter criticism.

The French and Foreign Population

The population of Canada consists of English, Scotch, French, Irish and Americans; and, including colored persons, numbers about 1,582,000. Of the whites, the French are in the majority, but the increasing emigration of Irish, Scotch, English and other Europeans is fast bringing about an equality in point of numbers that will be felt in political circles. In Canada West the French are in the minority.

The disposition of the people generally towards colored emigrants, that is, so far as the opinions of old settlers may be taken, and my own observation may be allowed, is as friendly as could be looked for under the circumstances. The Yankees,[8] in the country and in the States adjoining, leave no opportunity unimproved to embitter their minds against them. The result is, in some sections, a contemptible sort of prejudice, which, among English, is powerless beyond the individual entertaining it—not even affecting *his circle*. This grows out of the constitution of English society, in which people are not obliged to think as others do. There is more independent thought and free expression than among Americans. The affinity between the Yankees and French is strong; said to grow out of similar intentions with respect to political affairs: and they express most hostility, but it is not of a complexional character only, as that serves as a mark to identify men of a different policy. Leaving out Yankees—having but little practical experience of colored people—they (the French) are predisposed, from the influence alluded to, to deal roughly with them; but in the main benevolence and a sense of justice are elements in their character. They are not averse to truth. There is a prevailing hostility to chattel slavery, and an honest representation of the colored people: their aims and progressive character, backed by uniform good conduct on their part, would in a very short time destroy every vestige of prejudice in the Province.[9]

> "The public mind literally thirsts for the truth, and honest listeners, and anxious inquirers will travel many miles, crowd our country chapels, and remain for hours eagerly and patiently seeking the light. . . . Let the ignorance now prevalent on the subject of slavery be met by fair and full discussion, and open and thorough investigation, and the apathy and prejudice now existing will soon disappear."
> —*S. R. Ward.*

Colored persons have been refused entertainment in taverns (invariably of an inferior class), and on some boats distinction is made; but in all cases, it is that kind of distinction that is made between poor foreigners and other passengers on the cars and steamboats of the Northern States. There are the emigrant train and the forward deck in the United States. In Canada, colored persons, holding the same relation to the Canadians, are in some cases treated similarly. It is an easy matter to make out a case of prejudice in any country. We naturally look for it, and the conduct of many is calculated to cause unpleasant treatment and to make it difficult for well-mannered persons to get comfortable accommodations. There is a medium between servility and presumption that recommends itself to all persons of common sense, of whatever rank or complexion; and if colored people would avoid

8. Residents of the United States, especially New England.
9. Administrative division of a country.

the two extremes, there would be but few cases of prejudice to complain of in Canada. In cases in which tavern keepers and other public characters persist in refusing to entertain them, they can, in common with the traveling public generally, get redress[1] at law.

Persons emigrating to Canada, need not hope to find the general state of society as it is in the States. There is as in the old country a strong class feeling—lines are as completely drawn between the different classes, and aristocracy in the Canadas is the same in its manifestations as aristocracy in England, Scotland and elsewhere. There is no approach to Southern chivalry, nor the sensitive democracy prevalent at the North; but there is an aristocracy of birth, not of skin, as with Americans. In the ordinary arrangements of society, from wealthy and titled immigrants and visitors from the mother country, down through the intermediate circles to Yankees and Indians, it appears to have been settled by common consent that one class should not "see any trouble over another" but the common ground on which all honest and respectable men meet is that of innate hatred of American slavery.

* * *

Vancouver's Island[2]—Concluding Remarks

This island is situated between 49° and 51° north latitude, or on the southern boundary of British America; and between 122° and 127° west longitude. It is about three hundred miles long, and between ninety and one hundred miles broad, and contains about twenty-eight thousand square miles. Though remotely situated, and comparatively uninhabited (there not being more than twenty thousand persons on it), it will, it is said, be the first island in importance on the globe. It has a fine climate, being in the same latitude as the south of England, Germany, and the north of France: the soil is also of the best description. But it is not as an agricultural island that it will surpass all others. The Western Continent, and particularly the northern part, say "wise men of the east," must eventually leave the eastern far in the distance (a fact that should not be lost sight of by colored men), and that over the Pacific will the trade with eastern nations be prosecuted. It is important now as a stopping place for whale ships visiting the Northern Seas, and is directly in the route to the East Indies, Japan Isles, and China, from Oregon and British America. The overland route to the Pacific terminating near that point, the great Atlantic trade of Western Europe and America will find there the most practicable outlet and the shortest distance to Eastern Asia; consequently the people there settled, of whatever complexion, will be the "merchant princes of the world," and under the protection of Great Britain. Now, there are two weighty reasons why the people settled there should be colored principally; the first, because by that means they would become more fully involved in the destiny of this Continent; any eastern move of magnitude, as for instance to Africa, if *possible*, would appear a retrograde step now that the current of affairs is so clearly setting west: and, secondly, in no more effectual way could a check be given to the encroachments of slavery on free soil. The purely American sympathy

1. Compensation.
2. George Vancouver (1757–1798) was a British naval explorer of the Pacific Northwest.

for "kith and kin"[3] only would experience unmistakable obstacles to its free exercise, in the event of a contemplated annexation of that delightful Western country.

It will be seen that the possibility of a pretty extensive emigration to those countries has been the prominent feature throughout this tract, and for that reason direct reference has been made to other points, under British jurisdiction, than Canada. The preference given to these (Canada, West Indies, and Vancouver's Island), over British Colonies elsewhere, has been because of their strong position and availability in every way. There would not be as in Africa, Mexico, or South America, hostile tribes to annoy the settler or destroy at will towns and villages with their inhabitants: the strong arm of British power would summarily punish depredations made, of whatever character, and the emigrants would naturally assume the responsibility of British freemen.

The question whether or not an extensive emigration by the free colored people of the United States would affect the institution of slavery would then be answered. I have here taken the affirmative of that question, because that view of the case seems to me most clear. The free colored people have steadily discountenanced[4] any rational scheme of emigration, in the hope that by remaining in the States, a powerful miracle for the overthrow of slavery would be wrought. What are the facts? More territory[5] has been given up to slavery, the Fugitive Law has passed, and a concert of measures, seriously affecting their personal liberty, has been entered into by several of the free states; so subtle, unseen and effective have been their movements that, were it not that we remember there is a Great Britain, we would be overwhelmed, powerless, from the force of such successive shocks; and the end may not be yet, if we persist in remaining for targets, while they are strengthening themselves in the Northwest, and in the Gulf. There would be more of the right spirit, and infinitely more of real manliness, in a peaceful but decided demand for freedom to the slave from the Gulf of Mexico, than in a miserable scampering from state to state, in a vain endeavor to gather the crumbs of freedom that a pro-slavery besom[6] may sweep away at any moment. May a selection for the best be made, now that there are countries between which and the United States a comparison may be instituted. A little folding of the hands, and there may be no retreat from the clutches of the slave power.

1852

3. Friends and relatives.
4. Disfavored, refused approval.
5. Area controlled by a country but not a state or province.
6. A broom made of twigs.

THOMAS DETTER

Thomas P. Detter (1829–1891) was an activist writer, an innovator in African American fiction, and a pioneer of the African American press. He was born and raised in the Washington, D.C., area and migrated to San Francisco in 1852. He was a regular correspondent for two African American newspapers, the *San Francisco Elevator* and the *Pacific Appeal*. His published commentaries on social and political issues as well as eulogies for local community leaders and writers and national figures were often reprinted in other periodicals. In 1862, he joined 219 other African American Californians in urging the government to condemn racial discrimination and, should that fail, strongly suggesting migration to countries where color was not considered "a badge of degradation." This seems to have been the only time Detter supported migration *outside* the United States. From then on, he fought for civil rights *in* the United States by writing, speaking, and participating in lawsuits to end discrimination locally and nationally. Detter was the Sacramento County delegate to the Colored Citizens of the State of California Convention; served on the executive committee of that and other civil rights organizations; and campaigned in California, Nevada, Washington, and the Idaho Territory for public education, voting rights, and the admission of testimony by African Americans in court cases.

Detter's only extant book, *Nellie Brown; or, The Jealous Wife, with Other Sketches* (1871), includes fiction and sketches set in antebellum Virginia and Maryland, Louisiana and Cuba, Idaho and California. "Boise City" and "Idaho City" are two of the sketches. Like Mary Ann Shadd's *A Plea for Emigration*, these pieces were written to advise prospective migrants of likely homesteads by answering questions about flora, fauna, accommodations, politics, and economic prospects. Detter's book was written for those seeking alternatives to the increasingly hostile Black Codes and Jim Crow laws with which Reconstruction was being replaced. As "Boise" demonstrates, his writings were candid, often personal, generally opinionated, but ultimately optimistic. In his newspaper columns, his speeches, and *Nellie Brown*, whether he was evaluating the impact of the "Central Pacific Railroad," discussing the prospects of "Idaho City," or relating the painful folly of racial discrimination in "Boise," Detter wrote to inspire and to inform his readers.

Boise City

We shall not attempt to give a graphic description of the place. It is a neat little burg, situated in a beautiful and fertile valley, and is the capital of Idaho Territory.[1] It contains many permanent buildings, including neat and handsome cottages. It being a central point, it has many advantages over its sister towns. It contains a population ranging from nine to twelve hundred inhabitants. Many of its citizens are afflicted with the terrible disease of Negrophobia.[2] The very air seems to be pregnated with this disease. A respectable colored man can scarcely get accommodations at any of the hotels or restaurants. I was compelled, on my way from Idaho City to Silver City, to lay over from five P.M. until two A.M. the following morning. A few moments before the stage started for Silver City, I was invited by a swarthy, but generous-looking

1. Idaho was not yet a state.
2. Hatred or fear of African Americans.

Spaniard, to take a cigar. We started down the street. The most of the saloons at this unseasonable hour being closed, my companion saw a light in a saloon kept by Mr. J. Old. We entered and called for what we wanted. The polite and accommodating Mr. Old bent over the counter and said, in a low tone of voice: "Detter, I cannot accommodate you." I regarded it as a polite insult, and walked out. He was the last man I expected that would treat me thus. Had I approached him with my hat in my hand, trembling like a quarry slave, I have no doubt this proud Saxon would have accommodated me. I have seen many like Mr. Old come to naught, and who would gladly accept a favor, though extended by a Negro. I have lived in mountain towns where the lowest and basest females, white and colored, could be served with meals. If a respectable colored man desired a meal, the landlord would politely invite him to be seated in the kitchen. I ever have and ever will take issue against any such treatment. In my travels wherever I have met gentlemen, they have always treated me as a man, and not as a thing. The rough usages and insults that colored men receive, invariably come from that class of whites who have little to recommend them outside of a white skin. Were I to say that there are no good feeling men in Boise City, I would be doing an injustice, to many. I appreciate my friends. I never can condescend to lick the hand that smites me, nor respect the man that insults me.

Idaho City–Its Customs and Future Prospects

Idaho City is a noted mountain town, situated in a basin. Its citizens are liberal and generous. The mines are inexhaustible. The future prospects of the city are flattering. We expect it to become the terminus of every railroad in the Territory as well as the emporium[1] of the North. Why the Territorial Fathers don't introduce gas-lights in the city is really astonishing. Property is advancing in value daily. The lumbermen are the chief benefactors of the city. Conflagrations[2] lay it waste about once a year. We can stand it! Every property-holder is able to rebuild and meet his demands promptly. They seldom allow a bill to be presented the second time. The pioneers of the country have amassed large fortunes and retired from business. Merchants keep up the old customs of former days. They never fail to present their bill on Monday morning with a pleasant smile. If not paid, their countenances change. Miners are exceptions. They are all honorable, and will have plenty of cash when the birds sing and the waters run. Clerks, by strict economy, may soon be able to buy out their employers. Saloon keepers do an extensive business, especially in the Winter. They have lots of stove customers, who seldom make room for others, or spend a dime. It don't cost anything to run a saloon in the Winter! Butchers and bakers know not the want of money. Your patronage is solicited by all business men If you have cash and ask no credit!

We have an institution called the "Cold-water Tank."[3] All of 'em are joining it, 'cept de Niggers; they can fill their kegs until it runs out of their eyes. They are of no use to the community, and the sooner whiskey kills 'em, the better.

Barbers are a fine set of fellows; they never condescend to speak disparagingly of each other. They are all finished workmen, and have received the

1. Department store.
2. Large fires.
3. A temperance group.

Tonsorial Diploma. Some of them are a little selfish, and claim to do better work than any one else, and of course they know it all, because they have had a better opportunity of receiving a finished education than some others; consequently they are better than others and are ready to condemn their efforts, but do but little themselves.

1871

HENRY McNEAL TURNER

Born free but poor, as a young man Henry McNeal Turner (1834–1915) picked cotton alongside enslaved people. His efforts to learn to read and write were thwarted by law and discrimination until he became a janitor at a law firm and a few lawyers surreptitiously helped him gain a liberal arts education. By 1872, when he gave the lecture excerpted here, Turner was not yet forty years old, but he had fought in the Civil War, helped establish the Georgia Republican Party, and been elected twice to the Georgia State Legislature. Both politician and preacher, he sought to persuade his audience that it was God's divine plan for African Americans to rise and contribute to the world at large, especially to Africa. As early as 1870, Turner had begun declaring that some African Americans had been divinely chosen to migrate to Africa (their "fatherland") and, by proclaiming a "free, religious, civil, and political gospel," help bring that continent into its rightful place as a leader in the civilized world. As an ordained minister of the African Methodist Episcopal Church assigned to Washington, D.C., he presided over a large congregation and gained substantial political power with leaders of various ethnic and religious groups. When the Compromise of 1877 effectively ended Reconstruction by granting the former Confederate states both amnesty and the power to govern themselves, Turner became increasingly passionate about migration. The first southern-born bishop in the A.M.E. Church, he used his position to expand the church's outreach to Africa by leading study tours for ministers and lay leaders and establishing a student exchange program between Wilberforce College and African students. He founded and edited *Voice of Missions*, a monthly periodical to protest racism in the United States and to recruit African American missionaries to Africa, who would not only spread the gospel of Christianity but also teach subjects such as scientific agriculture, engineering, medicine, business, art, music, and literature as well as nurture self-respect, dignity, responsibility, and appreciation of self-governance and intercultural democracy. He founded an international migration society, traveled to Africa at least four times, debated leaders like Booker T. Washington, and presaged the Pan-Africanism of thinkers like W. E. B. Du Bois and Marcus Garvey.

From A Speech on the Present Duties and Future Destiny of the Negro Race[1]

* * *

I would like to state another thing just here, that is, I have grave doubts about this being the ultimate home of the colored race any way. I do not

1. Delivered to and published by the "Lyceum for the benefit of the young colored men who are laboring to make themselves intelligent and useful."

believe we are ever to be expatriated[2] from this country; but I am of the opinion that our people will one day turn their attention to Africa and go to it. I fear we cannot, for a great while, hold our own against the whites, with their numerical strength on the one hand and their fearful competition on the other. Besides the land and the money are theirs, and we are not going to be satisfied always in the capacity of water-carriers and wood-hewers. We must have railroads, stock in telegraph companies, insurance companies, factories, &c. This is essential to our growth, up-building, and material advancement. How are we to acquire it? Either by going to Africa or out West and settling on new territory. It is utterly impossible for menial laborers to ever acquire wealth; one here and one there may overcome the obstacles and rise up a little, but the masses will go from bad to worse. I think the Dutch and Irish are setting us good examples if we would but see and heed it. They land in New York today, poor and degraded, but tomorrow they are on the cars going out West, there they squat[3] on a piece of land, which does not cost one cent per acre; they work all day and fish and hunt at night for their meat. In a few years they are off to New York again to lay in $15,000 or $30,000 worth of goods. You ask what's up now? Well, I will tell you: he is a wealthy merchant; he lives in great style; one son is going to Congress, one is a lawyer, the other a doctor, and the old man himself is being talked of for the next Governor. Had this Irishman remained in New York and driven a cart, carried a hod or blacked boots, he would have always been at the point of starvation, his sons drunkards or gamblers, and his daughters night strollers,[4] with his wife in the grave.

Africa holds out the greatest inducements to the colored man of any other spot on God's green earth; her resources are boundless; her climate unsurpassed; her minerals incomprehensible; her productive resources amply sufficient to feed the world ten thousand years; and her territory ample enough to give every human being a homestead on the face of the globe, whose value would defy dollars and cents.

Can any sane man presume for a moment that Providence will allow these garnered treasures to lie in the bowels of the earth forever? The idea is preposterous in the extreme. No sir; the time will come when the negro race will thirst for those climes as the hart does for the water brook, and omniscient skill will provide the means for his importation. Mr. McQueen, when speaking of the superstition which infested that country, made the following remark: "It is in Africa this evil must be rooted out—by African hands and African exertions chiefly that it can be destroyed." Wm. Pitt, the great English statesman, in a gust of patriotic eloquence, uses the following language: "We may live to behold the nations of Africa engaged in the calm occupations of industry, and in the pursuits of a just and legitimate commerce; we may behold the beams of science and philosophy breaking in upon their land, which at some happier period, in still later times, may blaze with full luster, and, joining their influence to that of *pure religion*, may illuminate and invigorate the most distant extremities of that immense continent."

Mr. Pitt speaks as if touched by the same finger of prophetic inspiration which was hovering over David, when he, by a higher claim to infallibility, stood gazing in the future and exclaimed, "Ethiopia shall soon stretch out

2. Exiled from the country of one's birth.
3. Live on without title or permission.
4. Involved with prostitution.

her hands to God; Sing, ye kingdoms of the earth, sing praises to the Lord; for they shall drink at noon the palm's rich nectar, and lie down at eve in the green pastures of remembered days, and walk to wonder and weep no more on Congo's mountain coast, or Guinea's golden shore."[5]

Africa will rise, as sure as e'er a nation rose, through transverses and inexplicabilities the path may lie. But as Wordsworth says, while soaring on the wings of the muses: "In the unreasoning progress of the world—

A wiser spirit is at work,
A better eye than ours sees."[6]

I once read an ode, said to have been written by some Rev. Dr. Croswell.[7] I have often repeated it, and if I can I will do so now, and let that suffice for what I have to say about Africa. * * * The time is not far distant when millions of redeemed and refined Africans will devour every item of our history in this country, and still thirst for more.

Joy to thy savage realm, O, Africa.
A sign is on thee that the Great I AM[8]
Shall work new wonders in the land of Ham;
And while He tarries for the glorious day
To bring again His people, there shall be
A remnant left from Chusan[9] to the sea.
And though the Ethiope[1] cannot change his skin,
Or bleach the outward stain, He yet shall roll
The darkness off that overshades the soul,
And wash the deeper dyes of sin.
Princes submissive to the Gospel sway
Shall come from Egypt and the Morian land,[2]
In holy transport stretch to God its hand.
Joy to thy savage realm, O, Africa!

* * *

1872

5. A paraphrase of Psalm 68:31–32.
6. From *The Prelude* (1850), Book V, lines 359–61.
7. Rev. William Croswell, poet and rector of the Old North Church, Boston.
8. God.
9. British colony in China.
1. Ethiopian or Black person.
2. That is, the land of the Moors; northwest Africa.

SOJOURNER TRUTH

Sojourner Truth (1799–1883) was the youngest of ten or twelve children born to enslaved parents in upstate New York. She was named Isabella, spoke Dutch, and by the time she was fourteen years old had been sold several times. She learned English by wit and whip. When she didn't understand an order, she would be whipped, a method that accelerated her language acquisition to the point that today she is known for her oratorical skills. Renowned for her lectures, she was spoken of by Harriet Beecher Stowe and others as the "Libyan Sybil." Though her speech was often published in a parody of southern dialect, according to historian Nell Irvin

Painter, "Truth took pride in speaking correct English and objected to accounts of her speeches in heavy southern dialect."

Isabella was married and the mother of five children when New York State began the gradual emancipation of enslaved people. She made a bargain with her owner to be freed a year early, but he changed his mind. Not long afterward, Isabella says God told her to self-emancipate. Taking her baby daughter with her, she left, staying with various religious communities as she worked her way to New York City. On June 1, 1843, having been "called in spirit" to go and preach, she changed her name to Sojourner (roughly translated as "migrant missionary") Truth and set out to do God's work. Truth became an indefatigable activist, but her words come to us from journalists and others with whom she worked to produce both *Narrative of Sojourner Truth* and the *Narrative* supplemented with her *Book of Life*.

Truth is known primarily for her antislavery and women's rights advocacy; she was also deeply involved in matters of migration. Working in Washington, D.C., with newly emancipated refugees, she was keenly aware of their needs for food, shelter, safety, and employment. She deplored the sins that had been committed against them, but she also feared that the freedpeople's despair would drive them to sin themselves. She proposed that the U.S. government should allocate land in the West for African Americans. In her usual fashion, she took it upon herself to make this happen with the help of prominent northern friends. Though her attempt to collect enough signatures on a petition to Congress failed, the grassroots surge of "Kansas Fever Exodus" in 1871 encouraged her to keep trying. Eventually, despite her age and declining health, Sojourner Truth accompanied a migrating group to Kansas. Though Truth's mission required continual traveling and speaking, she did establish a home in Battle Creek, Michigan, and reunited with as many of her family as she could locate. She is buried in Battle Creek's Oak Hill Cemetery.

From Sojourner Truth's Narrative and Book of Life

* * *

As she looked about upon the imposing public edifices that grace the District of Columbia, all built at the nation's expense, she said, "*We helped* to pay this cost. We have been a source of wealth to this republic. Our labor supplied the country with cotton, until villages and cities dotted the enterprising North for its manufacture, and furnished employment and support for a multitude, thereby becoming a revenue to the government. Beneath a burning southern sun have we toiled, in the canebrake and the rice swamp, urged on by the merciless driver's lash, earning millions of money; and so highly were we valued there, that should one poor wretch venture to escape from this hell of slavery, no exertion of man or trained blood-hound was spared to seize and return him to his field of unrequited labor.

"The overseer's horn awoke us at the dawning of day from our half-finished slumbers to pick the disgusting worm from the tobacco plant, which was an added source of wealth. Our nerves and sinews, our tears and blood, have been sacrificed on the altar of this nation's avarice. Our unpaid labor has been a stepping-stone to its financial success. Some of its dividends must surely be ours."

Who can deny the logic of her reasoning? The prophet[1] of the nineteenth century said, many years ago, that "our nation will yet be obliged to pay sigh

1. Parker Pillsbury [*Sojourner Truth's note*].

for sigh, groan for groan, and dollar for dollar, to this wronged and outraged race." Ah, me! what an awful debt when we consider that every mill of interest will surely be added! Did mothers and wives whose husbands and sons languished and died in Libby and Andersonville[2] ever think of that prophecy? Does this nation realize that the debt is still unpaid? the note not taken up yet?

She knew that the United States owned countless acres of unoccupied land, which by cultivation would become a source of wealth to it. She also saw that it was given to build railroads, and that large reservations were apportioned to the Indians. Why not give a tract of land to those colored people who would rather become independent through their own exertions than longer clog the wheels of government?

It seemed to Sojourner that the money expended upon officials, in just this District alone, to convict and punish these vagabond children, would be ample to provide for them homes with the accessories of church and school-house and all the necessary requirements of civilization. With God's blessing, they might yet become an honor to the country which had so cruelly wronged them. This scheme presented itself to her mind as a divine revelation, and she made haste to lay her plan before the leading men of the government. They heard her patiently, expressed themselves willing to do the people's bidding; but manifested no enthusiasm. She regretted now, as ever, that women had no political rights under government; for she knew that could the voice of maternity be heard in the advocacy of this measure, the welfare, not only of the present generation, but of future ones, would be assured.

As it requires both the male and female element to propagate and successfully rear a family, so the State, being only the larger family, demands both for its life and proper development. As those who had the power to legislate for the carrying out of this measure, regarded it indifferently, and those who would gladly work for its accomplishment lacked political opportunity, some other measure must be adopted. She thought that whatever else had been denied to woman, she had ever been allowed to stand on praying ground, and that through petition she might be able to reach the head and heart of the government, or rather half the head and half the heart, as only in this proportion have they ever been represented in our country's legislation. She therefore dictated the following petition:—

"To the Senate and House of Representatives, in Congress assembled:—

"*Whereas*, From the faithful and earnest representations of Sojourner Truth (who has personally investigated the matter), we believe that the freed colored people in and about Washington, dependent upon government for support, would be greatly benefited and might become useful citizens by being placed in a position to support themselves: We, the undersigned, therefore earnestly request your honorable body to set apart for them a portion of the public land in the West, and erect buildings thereon for the aged and infirm, and otherwise legislate so as to secure the desired results."

2. Libby (Richmond, Virginia) and Andersonville (Andersonville, Georgia) were Confederate prisons with extremely high death tolls for Union soldiers.

The vitalizing forces of her nature were now fully aroused and deeply earnest. She felt that her life culminated at this point, and that all her previous experiences had been needful to prepare her for this crowning work. Being convinced of the feasibility and justice of this plan, she hastened to present her petition to the public, and solicit signatures. Her first lecture for this object was delivered in Providence, R.I., in Feb., 1870, to a large and appreciative audience.

* * *

From The N.Y. Tribune

"SOJOURNER TRUTH AT WORK

"To the Editor of the Tribune:—

"Sir: Seeing an item in your paper about me, I thought I would give you the particulars of what I am trying to do, in hopes that you would print a letter about it and so help on the good cause. I am urging the people to sign petitions to Congress to have a grant of land set apart for the freed people to earn their living on, and not be dependent on the government for their bread. I have had fifty petitions printed at my own expense, and have been urging the people of the Eastern States for the past seven months. I have been crying out in the East, and now an answer comes to me from the West, as you will see from the following letter. The gentleman who writes it I have never seen or heard of before, but the Lord has raised him up to help me.[3] Bless the Lord! I made up my mind last winter, when I saw able men and women taking dry bread from the government to keep from starving, that I would devote myself to the cause of getting land for these people, where they can work and earn their own living in the West, where the land is so plenty. Instead of going home from Washington to take rest, I am traveling around getting it before the people.

"Instead of sending these people to Liberia,[4] why can't they have a colony in the West? This is why I am contending so in my old age. It is to teach the people that this colony can just as well be in this country as in Liberia. Everybody says this is a good work, but nobody helps. How glad I will be if you will take hold and give it a good lift. Please help me with these petitions. Yours truly,

"Sojourner Truth.

"Florence, Mass., Feb. 18, 1871.

"P.S. I should have said that the Rev. Gilbert Haven of Boston is kindly aiding me in getting petitions signed, and will receive all petitions signed in Massachusetts and send them to Congress. S. T."

1875

3. Byron M. Smith was a realtor from Topeka, Kansas, who posed as an admirer of Truth's and offered to pay her travel expenses to Topeka, hoping to sell land. She went but there was no deal.

4. Founded by the American Colonization Society and settled by free and formerly enslaved African Americans, Liberia became an independent republic in 1847.

BENJAMIN SINGLETON

Tennessee native Benjamin Singleton (1809–1900) self-emancipated and moved to Ontario, Canada, in 1846. Soon afterward, he migrated across the river from Windsor, Ontario, to Detroit, Michigan, where he ran a boarding house that served also as a station on the Underground Railroad. When the Union Army gained control of Tennessee in 1862, Singleton returned there determined to teach freedpeople how to stay free by acquiring land and avoiding debt. In 1869, he partnered with Columbus M. Johnson to found Edgefield Real Estate, which focused on helping African Americans buy farms. When white southern realtors and bankers refused to sell or provide financial backing to African Americans, he added "homestead association" to the firm's name and shifted the company's focus to recruiting homesteaders to Kansas. In 1874 the first Singleton group of several hundred settled in Dunlap, Kansas.

Historians consistently connect Singleton with the "Kansas Fever Exodus of 1879–80" (or "the Negro Exodus"), calling him the "Moses of Kansas." Singleton accepted this title but with a caveat because as the "Exodusters," as they were called, became a mass movement, they included "hordes" of indigent, unskilled, and desperate people whose arrival placed great burdens on local and federal government resources, fueling racial hostility. Singleton insisted that his organization accepted only "hard workers with the means to pay for the trip." He became increasingly nationalistic when a U.S. Senate committee investigating the migration of African Americans from southern states, concluded, after interviewing more than 150 people, white and Black, including him, that migration was not prompted by persecution and violations of personal and political rights. He endorsed schemes such as migrating to Cyprus or Canada and creating all-Black communities. Singleton's last major project was establishing the United Trans-Atlantic Society to bring African Americans to Africa.

Testimony before the U.S. Senate[1]

Washington, D.C., April 17, 1880, Before the Senate Select Committee Investigating the "Negro Exodus from the Southern States"

Benjamin Singleton (colored) sworn and examined. By Mr. Windom:

QUESTION. Where were you born, Mr. Singleton? ANSWER. I was born in the State of Tennessee, sir.

Q. Where do you now live? A. In Kansas.

Q. What part of Kansas? A. I have a colony sixty miles from Topeka, sir.

Q. Which way from Topeka—west? A. Yes, sir; sixty miles from Topeka, west.

Q. What is your colony called? A. Singleton colony is the name of it, sir.

Q. How long has it been since you have formed that colony? A. I have two colonies in Kansas—one in Cherokee County, and one in Lyon, Morris County.

Q. When did you commence the formation of that colony—the first one? A. It was in 1875, perhaps.

1. Singleton's testimony appears in part 3 of the Senate report on "Causes of the Removal of the Negroes from the Southern States to the Northern States."

Q. That is, you first began this colonizing business in 1875? A. No; when I first commenced working at this it was in 1869.

Q. You commenced your colony, then, in 1869? A. No, I commenced getting the emigration up in 1875; I think it was in 1875.

Q. When did you leave Tennessee, Mr. Singleton? A. This last time; do you mean?

Q. No; when you moved from there to Kansas? A. It has been a year this month, just about now.

Q. You misunderstand me; you say you were born in Tennessee? A. Yes, sir.

Q. And you now live in Kansas? A. Yes, sir.

Q. When did you change your home from Tennessee to Kansas? A. I have been going there for the last six or seven years, sir.

Q. Going between Tennessee and Kansas, at different times? A. Yes, sir; several times.

Q. Well, tell us about it. A. I have been fetching out people; I believe I fetched out 7,432 people.

Q. You have brought out 7,432 people from the South to Kansas? A. Yes, sir; brought and sent.

Q. That is, they came out to Kansas under your influence? A. Yes, sir; I was the cause of it.

Q. How long have you been doing that—ever since 1869? A. Yes, sir; ever since 1869.

Q. Did you go out there yourself in 1869, before you commenced sending them out? A. No, sir.

Q. How did you happen to send them out? A. The first cause, do you mean, of them going?

Q. Yes; what was the cause of your going out, and in the first place how did you happen to go there, or to send these people there? A. Well, my people, for the want of land—we needed land for our children—and their disadvantages—that caused my heart to grieve and sorrow; pity for my race, sir, that was coming down, instead of going up—that caused me to go to work for them. I sent out there perhaps in '66—perhaps so; or in '65, any way—my memory don't recollect which; and they brought back tolerable favorable reports; then I jacked up three or four hundred, and went into Southern Kansas, and found it was a good country, and I thought Southern Kansas was congenial to our nature, sir; and I formed a colony there, and bought about a thousand acres of ground—the colony did—my people.

Q. And they went upon it and settled there? A. Yes, sir; they went and settled there.

Q. Were they men with some means or without means? A. I never carried none there without means.

Q. They had some means to start with? A. Yes; I prohibited my people leaving their country and going there without they had money—some money to start with and go on with a while.

Q. You were in favor of their going there if they had some means? A. Yes, and not staying at home.

Q. Tell us how these people are getting on in Kansas. A. I am glad to tell you, sir.

Ho for Kansas!

Brethren, Friends, & Fellow Citizens:
I feel thankful to inform you that the
REAL ESTATE
AND
Homestead Association,
Will Leave Here the
15th of April, 1878,
In pursuit of Homes in the Southwestern Lands of America, at Transportation Rates, cheaper than ever was known before.
For full information inquire of
Benj. Singleton, better known as old Pap,
NO. 5 NORTH FRONT STREET.
Beware of Speculators and Adventurers, as it is a dangerous thing to fall in their hands.
Nashville, Tenn., March 18, 1878.

"Exodusters." Advertisement distributed in 1878 in Tennessee to encourage emigration to Kansas.

Q. Have they any property now? A. Yes; I have carried some people in there that when they got there they didn't have fifty cents left, and now they have got in my colony—Singleton colony—a house, nice cabins, their milch cows, and pigs, and sheep, perhaps a span of horses, and trees before their yards, and some three or four or ten acres broken up, and all of them has got little houses that I carried there. They didn't go under no relief assistance; they went on their own resources; and when they went in there first the country was not overrun with them; you see they could get good wages; the country was not overstocked with people; they went to work, and I never helped them as soon as I put them on the land.

Q. Well, they have been coming continually, and adding from time to time to your colony these few years past, have they? A. Yes, sir; I have spent, perhaps, nearly six hundred dollars flooding the country with circulars.

Q. You have sent the circulars yourself, have you? A. Yes, sir; all over these United States.

Q. Did you send them into other Southern States besides Tennessee? A. O, yes, sir.

Q. Did you do that at the instance of Governor St. John and others in Kansas? A. O, no, sir; no white men. This was gotten up by colored men in purity and confidence; not a political negro was in it; they would want to pilfer and rob at the cents before they got the dollars. O, no, it was the muscle of the arm, the men that worked that we wanted.

Q. Well, tell us all about it. A. These men would tell all their grievances to me in Tennessee—the sorrows of their heart. You know I was an undertaker there in Nashville, and worked in the shop. Well, actually, I would have to go and bury their fathers and mothers. You see we have the same heart and feelings as any other race and nation. (The land is free, and it is nobody's business, if there is land enough, where the people go. I put that in my people's heads.) Well, that man would die, and I would bury him; and the next morning maybe a woman would go to that man (meaning the landlord), and she would have six or seven children, and he would say to her, "Well, your husband owed me before he died" and they would say that to every last one of them, "You owe me." Suppose he would? Then he would say, "You must go to some other place; I cannot take care of you." Now, you see, that is something I would take notice of, that woman had to go out, and these little children was left running through the streets, and the next place you would find them in a disorderly house, and their children in the State's prison.

Well, now, sir, you will find that I have a charter here. You will find that I called on the white people in Tennessee about that time. I called conventions about it, and they sat with me in my conventions, and "Old man," they said, "you are right." The white people said, "You are right; take your people away." And let me tell you, it was the white people—the ex-governor of the State, felt like I did, and they said to me, "You have tooken a great deal on to yourself, but if these negroes, instead of deceiving one another and running for office, would take the same idea that you have in your head, you will be a people."

I then went out to Kansas, and advised them all to go to Kansas; and, sir they are going to leave the Southern country. The Southern country is out of joint. The blood of a white man runs through my veins. That is congenial, you know, to my nature, that is my choice. Right emphatically, I tell you today, I woke up the millions right through me! The great God of glory has worked in me. I have had open air interviews with the living spirit of God for my people; and we are going to leave the South. We are going to leave it if there ain't an alteration and signs of change. I am going to advise the people who left that country (Kansas) to go back.

Q. What do you mean by a change? A. Well, I am not going to stand bulldozing[2] and half pay and all those things. Gentlemen, allow me to tell you the truth; it seems to me that they have picked out the negroes from the Southern country to come here and testify who are in good circumstances and own their homes and not the poor ones who don't study their own interests. Let them go and pick up the men that has to walk when they goes, and not those who have money.

2. Coercing or restraining by threats of brute force.

There is good white men in the Southern country, but it ain't the minority (majority); they can't do nothing; the bulldozers has got possession of the country, and they have got to go in there and stop them; if they don't the last colored man will leave them. I see colored men testifying to a positive lie, for they told me out there all their interests were in Louisiana and Mississippi. Said I, "You are right to protect your own country," and they would tell me, "I am obliged to do what I am doing." Of course I have done the same, but I am clear footed.

Q. Now you say that during these years you have been getting up this colony you have spent, yourself, some six hundred dollars in circulars, and in sending them out; where did you send them, Mr. Singleton? A. Into Mississippi, Alabama, South Carolina, Georgia, Kentucky, Virginia, North Carolina, Texas, Tennessee, and all those countries.

Q. To whom did you send them; how were they circulated? A. Every man that would come into my country, and I could get a chance, I would put one in his hand, and the boys that started from my country on the boats, and the porters in the cars. That is the way I circulated them.

Q. Did you send any out by mail? A. I think I sent some perhaps to North Carolina by mail—I think I did. I sent them out by people, you see.

Q. Yes; by colored people, generally? A. Some white people, too. There was Mrs. Governor Brown, the first Governor Brown of Tennessee—Mrs. Sanders, she was a widow, and she married the governor.[3] He had thirty on his place. I went to him, and he has given me advice. And Ex-Governor Brown, he is there too.

Q. You say your circulars were sent all over these States? A. Yes, sir; to all of 'em.

Q. Did you ever hear from them; did anybody ever write to you about them? A. O, yes.

Q. And you attribute this movement to the information you gave in your circulars? A. Yes, sir; I am the whole cause of the Kansas immigration!

Q. You take all that responsibility on yourself? A. I do, and I can prove it; and I think I have done a good deal of good, and I feel relieved!

Q. You are proud of your work? A. Yes, sir; I am! (*Uttered emphatically.*)

1880

3. Cynthia Pillow Saunders (1810–1892), wife of Aaron V. Brown, Tennessee governor (1845–47).

FREDERICK DOUGLASS

In 1879, Frederick Douglass (1818–1885) was about seventy years old, in the later stages of his remarkable journey from three-fifths human to internationally famous author, lecturer, and politician. He was considered a Representative Man, a symbol of what was possible for all Americans regardless of race, class, or ethnicity. However, because of his stance on African American mass migration, Douglass was revered and honored more as a Grand Old Man than as a Man of the People.

Having left the slave South for the free North, Douglass had no problem with individual migrants seeking better lives in new locations. Indeed, he wrote and spoke often on "the right of locomotion, the right of migration" as a "universal and indestructible" human right. He was in accord with most African American leaders in denouncing colonization schemes to deport African Americans rather than accept their rights to equal protection and participation in society. In 1861, when it seemed as if the U.S. government was not going to abolish slavery or grant equal protection and privileges to free people of African descent, he had publicly encouraged group migration to Haiti. In 1867, Douglass campaigned relentlessly for Chinese immigration and citizenship in the United States.

It was Douglass's stance on what he called the "Negro Exodus" that contributed to his diminishing authority, especially among African American leaders who had emerged after the Civil War. Despite the major failure of Reconstruction, the creation of Black Codes and Jim Crow laws by the increasingly powerful former Confederate states, Douglass believed it was a "solemn obligation and duty" to force the nation "to protect its citizens where they are, not to transport them where they will not need protection."

For the first time, Douglass realized he was "painfully at variance with leading colored men of the country." At a meeting in New York, he rose to speak against what he termed "a wholesale exodus of colored people" only to hear the audience hiss at him. Hurt and humiliated, Douglass lashed out at his critics and former allies in public letters and essays, explaining that "Exodus is medicine, not food; it is for disease, not health; it is not to be taken from choice, but necessity." But Douglass was fighting an uphill battle. Though the majority of freedpeople had remained in the South, the post-emancipation migration movements had had significant negative effects upon the economy and racial attitudes. Feelings were strong, apprehensions numerous, and divisiveness increasing. This was the context for the American Social Science Association's invitation to Douglass to present his views at its general meeting. He accepted but at the last minute did not go. Instead, he sent a speech (below), which was read by Yale Law School dean Francis Wayland III.

From The Negro Exodus from the Gulf States

* * *

Nothing has occurred since the abolition of slavery, which has excited a deeper interest among thoughtful men in all sections of the country, than has this Exodus. In the simple fact that a few thousand freedmen have deliberately laid down the shovel and the hoe, quitted the sugar and cotton fields of Mississippi and Louisiana, and sought homes in Kansas, and that thousands more are seriously meditating upon following their example, the sober-thinking minds of the South have discovered a new and startling peril to the welfare and civilization of that section of our country.

* * *

Important as manual labor is everywhere, it is nowhere near more important, and absolutely indispensable to the existence of civilization, than in the more southern of the United States. Machinery may continue to do, as it has done, much of the work of the North, but the work of the South requires bone, sinew, and muscle of the strongest and most enduring kind for its performance. * * *

It is now seen that nothing less powerful than the naked iron arm of the negro can save her. For him, as a southern laborer, there is no competitor or substitute. The thought of filling his place by any other variety of the human family will be found utterly impracticable. Neither Chinaman, German, Norwegian nor Swede can drive him from the sugar and cotton fields of Louisiana and Mississippi. * * *

Hence, it is seen that the dependence of the planters, landowners, and old master-class of the South upon the negro, however galling and humiliating to Southern pride and power, is nearly complete and perfect. There is only one mode of escape for them, and that mode they will certainly not adopt. It is to take off their own coats, cease to whittle sticks and talk politics at the cross-roads, and go themselves to work in their broad and sunny fields of cotton and sugar. An invitation to do this is about as harsh and distasteful to all their inclinations, as would be an invitation to step down into their graves. With the negro, all this is different. Neither natural, artificial, nor traditional causes stand in the way of the freedman to such labor in the South. Neither heat, nor the fever demon that lurks in her tangled and oozy swamps affrights him, and he stands today the admitted author of whatever prosperity, beauty, and civilization are now possessed by the South. He is the arbiter[1] of her destiny.

This, then, is the high vantage ground of the negro; he has labor, the South wants it, and must have it or perish. Since he is free he can now give it, or withhold it; use it where he is, or take it elsewhere, as he pleases. His labor made him a slave, and his labor can, if he will, make him free, comfortable, and independent. It is more to him than either fire, sword, ballot-boxes, or bayonets. It touches the heart of the South through its pocket.

* * *

Political tricksters, land speculators, defeated office seekers, Northern malignants,[2] speeches and resolutions in the Senate, unaided by other causes, could not, of themselves, have set such a multitudinous Exodus in motion. The colored race is a remarkably home-loving race. It has done little in the way of voluntary colonization. It shrinks from the untried and unknown. It thinks its own locality the best in the world. Of all the galling conditions to which the negro was subjected in the days of his bondage, the worst was the liability of separation from home and friends. His love of home and his dread of change made him even partially content in slavery. He could endure the smart of the lash, work to the utmost of his power, and be content till the thought of being sent away from the scenes of his childhood and youth was thrust upon his heart.

But argument is less needed upon this point than testimony. We have the story of the emigrants themselves, and if any can reveal the true cause of this Exodus *they* can. They have spoken, and their story is before the country. It is a sad story, disgraceful and scandalous to our age and country. Much of their testimony has been given under the solemnity of an oath. They tell us with great unanimity that they are very badly treated at the South. The land owners, planters, and the old master-class generally, deal unfairly with them, having had their labor for nothing when they were slaves. These men, now they are free, endeavor by various devices to get it for next to nothing; work as hard, faithfully and constantly as they may, live as plainly and as sparingly as they may, they are no better off at the end of

1. Controller, determiner.

2. Malicious individuals.

the year than at the beginning. They say that they are the dupes[3] and victims of cunning and fraud in signing contracts which they cannot read and cannot fully understand; that they are compelled to trade at stores owned in whole or in part by their employers, and that they are paid with orders and not with money. They say that they have to pay double the value of nearly everything they buy; that they are compelled to pay a rental of ten dollars a year for an acre of ground that will not bring thirty dollars under the hammer; that land owners are in league to prevent land-owning by negroes; that when they work the land on shares they barely make a living; that outside the towns and cities no provision is made for education, and, ground down[4] as they are, they cannot themselves employ teachers to instruct their children; that they are not only the victims of fraud and cunning, but of violence and intimidation; that from their very poverty the temples of justice are not open to them; that the jury box is virtually closed; that the murder of a black man by a white man is followed by no conviction or punishment. They say further, that a crime for which a white man goes free a black man is severely punished; that impunity and encouragement are given by the wealthy and respectable classes to men of the baser sort who delight in midnight raids upon the defenceless; that their ignorance of letters has put them at the mercy of men bent upon making their freedom a greater evil to them than was their slavery; that the law is the refuge of crime rather than of innocence; that even the old slave driver's whip has reappeared, and the inhuman and disgusting spectacle of the chain-gang is beginning to be seen; that the government of every Southern State is now in the hands of the old slave oligarchy,[5] and that both departments of the National Government soon will be in the same hands. They believe that when the Government, State and National, shall be in the control of the old masters of the South, they will find means for reducing the freedmen to a condition analogous to slavery. They despair of any change for the better, declaring that everything is waxing worse for the negro, and that his only means of safety is to leave the South.

It must be admitted, if this brief statement of complaints be only half true, the explanation of the Exodus and the justification of the persons composing it, are full and ample. The complaints they make against Southern society are such as every man of common honesty and humanity must wish ill founded; unhappily, however, there is nothing in the nature of these complaints to make them doubtful or surprising. The unjust conduct charged against the late slaveholders is eminently probable. It is an inheritance from the long exercise of irresponsible power by man over man. It is not a question of the natural inferiority of the negro, or the color of his skin. Tyranny is the same proud and selfish thing everywhere, and with all races and colors. What the negro is now suffering at the hands of his former master, the white emancipated serfs of Russia are now suffering from the lords and nobles by whom they were formerly held as slaves. In form and appearance the emancipation of the latter was upon better terms than in the case of the negro. The Empire, unlike the Republic, gave the free serfs[6] three acres of land,—a start in the world. But the selection and bestowment of this land was unhappily confided to the care

3. Innocents, tricked.
4. Overwhelmed, worn out.
5. Rule by a small group of people.
6. Slaves.

of the lords and nobles, their former masters. Thus the lamb was committed to the care of the wolf; hence the organized assassination now going on in that country, and it will be well for our Southern States if they escape a like fate.

* * *

The Exodus as a Policy

Very evidently there are to be asked and answered many important questions, before the friends of humanity can be properly called upon to give their support to this emigration movement. A natural and primary enquiry is: What does it mean? How much ground is it meant to cover? Is the total removal of the whole five millions of colored people from the South contemplated? Or is it proposed to remove only a part? And if only a part, why a part and not the whole? A vindication of the rights of the many can not be less important than the same to the few. If the few are to be removed because of the intolerable oppression which prevails in the South, why not the many, also? If exodus is good for any, must it not be equally good for all? Then, if the whole five millions are to leave the South, as a doomed country,—left as Lot left Sodom,[7] or driven out as the Moors[8] were driven out of Spain.—there is next a question of ways and means to be considered. Has any definite estimate of the cost of this removal been made? How shall the one or two hundred millions of dollars which such removal would require be obtained? Shall it be appropriated by Congress, or voluntarily be contributed by the public? Manifestly, with such a debt upon the nation as the war for the Union has created, Congress is not likely to be in a hurry to make any such appropriation. It would much more willingly and readily enact the necessary legislation to protect the freedmen where they are, than appropriate $200,000,000 to help them away to Kansas, or elsewhere in the North.

* * *

Voluntary, spontaneous, self-sustained emigration on the part of the freedmen, may or may not be commendable. It is a matter with which they alone have to do. The public is not called upon to say or do anything for or against it; but when the public is called upon to take sides, declare its views, organize emigration societies, appoint and send out agents to make speeches and collect money,—to help the freedmen from the South,—it may very properly object. The public may not wish to be responsible for the measure, or for the disheartening doctrines by which the measure is supported. Objection may properly be made upon many grounds. It may well enough be said that the negro question is not so desperate as the advocates of this Exodus would have the public believe; that there is still hope that the negro will ultimately have his rights as a man, and be fully protected in the South; that in several of the old slave States his citizenship and his right to vote are already respected and protected; that the same, in time, will be secured for the negro in the other States; that the world was not the work of a day; that

7. In the Old Testament, Sodom is a wicked city that was destroyed by fire, except for the family of Lot (Genesis 19).

8. North Africans.

even in free New England, all the evils generated by slavery did not disappear in a century after the abolition of the system, if, indeed, they have yet entirely disappeared.

Within the last forty years, a dark and shocking picture might be given of the persecution of the negro and his friends, even in the now preeminently free State of Massachusetts. It is not more than twenty years ago that Boston supplied a pistol club, if not a rifle club, to break up an abolition meeting; and that one of her most eminent citizens had to be guarded to and from his house (Wendell Phillips) to escape the hand of mobocratic assassins, armed in the interest of slavery. The negro on the Sound boats[9] between New York and Boston, though a respectable educated gentleman, was driven forward of the wheels, and must sleep, if he slept at all, upon the naked deck in the open air. Upon no condition except that of a servant or slave could he be permitted to go into a cabin. All the handicrafts[1] of New England were closed to him. The appearance of a black man in any workshop or ship yard, as a mechanic, would have scattered the whole gang of white hands at once. The poor negro was not admitted into the factories to work, or as an apprentice to any trade. He was barber, waiter, whitewasher and wood-sawer. All of what were called respectable employments, by a power superior to legal enactments, were denied him. But none of these things have moved the negro from New England, and it is well for him that he has remained there. Bad as is the condition of the negro today at the South, there was a time when it was flagrantly and incomparably worse. A few years ago he had nothing; he did not have himself, his labor and his rights to dispose of as should best suit his own happiness. But he has now even more. He has a standing in the supreme law of the land, in the Constitution of the United States, not to be changed or affected by any conjunction of circumstances likely to occur in the immediate or remote future. The Fourteenth Amendment makes him a citizen, and the Fifteenth makes him a voter. With power behind him at work for him, and which cannot be taken from him, the negro of the South may wisely bide his time.

The situation at this moment is exceptional and transient. The permanent powers of the Government are all on his side. What though for the moment the hand of violence strikes down the negro's rights in the South? Those rights will revive, survive and flourish again. They are not the only people who have been in a moment of popular passion maltreated and driven from the polls. The Irish and Dutch have frequently been so treated; Boston, Baltimore and New York have been the scenes of this lawless violence; but those scenes have now disappeared. A Hebrew may even now be rudely repulsed from the door of a hotel; but he will not on that account get up another exodus, as he did three thousand years ago, but will quietly "put money in his purse" and bide his time, knowing that the rising tide of civilization will eventually float him, as it floats all other varieties of the human family, to whom floating in any condition is possible. Of one thing we may be certain (and it is a thing which is destined to be made very prominent not long hence), the negro will either be counted at the polls, or not counted in the basis of representation. The South must let the negro vote, or surrender its representation in Congress. The

9. Ferryboats.
1. Manual labor or skills.

chosen horn of this dilemma will finally be to let the negro vote, and vote unmolested.

* * *

There is a growing recognition of the duty and obligation of the American people to guard, protect and defend the personal and political rights of all the people of the States; to uphold the principles upon which rebellion was suppressed, slavery abolished, and the country saved from dismemberment and ruin. * * *

It is manifest that the public and noisy advocacy of a general stampede of the colored people from the South to the North, is necessarily an abandonment of the great and paramount principle of protection to person and property in every State of the Union. It is an evasion of a solemn obligation and duty. The business of this nation is to protect its citizens where they are, not to transport them where they will not need protection. The best that can be said of this Exodus in this respect, is that it is an attempt to climb up some other than the right way; it is an expedient, a half-way measure, and tends to weaken in the public mind a sense of the absolute right, power and duty of the Government, inasmuch as it concedes, by implication at least, that on the soil of the South, the law of the land cannot command obedience; the ballot box cannot be kept pure; peaceable elections cannot be held; the Constitution cannot be enforced; and the lives and liberties of loyal and peaceable citizens cannot be protected. It is a surrender, a premature, disheartening surrender, since it would make freedom and free institutions depend upon migration rather than protection; by flight, rather than by right; by going into a strange land, rather than by staying in one's own. It leaves the whole question of equal rights on the soil of the South open and still to be settled, with the moral influence of exodus against us; since it is a confession of the utter impracticability of equal rights and equal protection in any State, where those rights may be struck down by violence.

* * *

Better to Stay Than to Go

While necessity often compels men to migrate; to leave their old homes and seek new ones; to sever old ties and create new ones; to do this the necessity should be obvious and imperative. It should be a last resort and only adopted after carefully considering what is against the measure as well as what is in favor of it. There are prodigal sons[2] everywhere, who are ready to demand the portion of goods that would fall to them and betake themselves to a strange country. Something is ever lost in the process of migration, and much is sacrificed at home for what is gained abroad. A world of wisdom is in the saying of Mr. Emerson,[3] "that those who made Rome worth going to stayed there." Three moves from house to house are said to be worse than a fire. That a rolling stone gathers no moss has passed into the world's wisdom. The colored people of the South, just beginning to accumulate a

2. In the New Testament, Luke 15:11–32 includes the parable of the "prodigal son"—that is, the dissolute son who returns repentant.

3. Ralph Waldo Emerson (1803–1882), American transcendentalist, essayist, and poet.

little property, and to lay the foundation of families, should not be in haste to sell that little and be off to the banks of the Mississippi. The habit of roaming from place to place in pursuit of better conditions of existence is by no means a good one. A man should never leave his home for a new one till he has earnestly endeavored to make his immediate surroundings accord with his wishes. The time and energy expended in wandering about from place to place, if employed in making him comfortable where he is, will, in nine cases out of ten, prove the best investment. No people ever did much for themselves or for the world, without the sense and inspiration of native land; of a fixed home; of a familiar neighborhood, and common associations. * * *

The South the Best Market for the Black Man's Labor

Not only is the South the best locality for the negro on the ground of his political powers and possibilities, but it is best for him as a field of labor. He is there, as he is nowhere else, an absolute necessity. He has a monopoly of the labor market. His labor is the only labor which can successfully offer itself for sale in that market. This, with a little wisdom and firmness, will enable him to sell his labor there on terms more favorable to himself than he can elsewhere. As there are no competitors or substitutes, he can demand living prices with the certainty that the demand will be complied with. Exodus would deprive him of this advantage. It would take him from a country where the land owners and planters must have his labor, or allow their fields to go untilled and their purses unsupplied with cash; to a country where the land owners are able and proud to do their own work, and do not need to hire hands except for limited periods at certain seasons of the year. The effect of this will be to send the negro to the towns and cities to compete with white labor. With what result, let the past tell. They will be crowded into lanes and alleys, cellars and garrets, poorly provided with the necessaries of life, and will gradually die out. The negro, as already intimated, is preëminently a Southern man. He is so both in constitution and habits, in body as well as mind. He will not only take with him to the North, Southern modes of labor, but Southern modes of life. The careless and improvident habits of the South cannot be set aside in a generation. If they are adhered to in the North, in the fierce winds and snows of Kansas and Nebraska, the emigration must be large to keep up their numbers. It would appear, therefore, that neither the laws of polities, labor nor climate favor this Exodus. * * *

The North Gate of the South Must Be Kept Open

As an assertion of power by a people hitherto held in bitter contempt; as an emphatic and stinging protest against high-handed, greedy and shameless injustice to the weak and defenceless; as a means of opening the blind eyes of oppressors to their folly and peril, the Exodus has done valuable service. Whether it has accomplished all of which it is capable in this particular direction for the present, is a question which may well be considered. With a moderate degree of intelligent leadership among the laboring class at the South, properly handling the justice of their cause, and wisely using the Exodus example, they can easily exact better terms for their labor than ever before. Exodus is medicine, not food; it is for disease, not health; it is not to be taken from choice, but necessity. In anything like a normal condition of things the South is the best place for the negro. Nowhere else is there for him a promise of a happier future. Let him stay there if he can, and save both the South and himself to civilization. While, however, it may be the highest wisdom under the circumstances for the freedmen to stay where they are, no encouragement should be given to any measures of coercion to keep them there. The American people are bound, if they are or can be bound to anything, to keep the North gate of the South open to black and white, and to all the people. The time to assert a right, Webster[4] says, is when it is called in question. If it is attempted by force or fraud to compel the colored people to stay, then they should by all means go; go quickly, and die, if need be, in the attempt. Thus far and to this extent any man may be an emigrationist, and thus far and to this extent I certainly am an emigrationist. * * *

1880

4. Daniel Webster (1782–1852), American lawyer, politician, and statesman.

RICHARD THEODORE GREENER

Born in Philadelphia, Richard T. Greener (1844–1922) grew up in Cambridge, Massachusetts. When his father joined the California Gold Rush and did not return, Greener dropped out of school to help support his family. Nonetheless, he became the first African American male to graduate from Harvard; he went on to become both dean of the Howard University Law School and a U.S. diplomat.

Once a coeditor of a newspaper founded by Frederick Douglass, Greener came to disagree publicly with Douglass's politics. Douglass opposed migration from the South, wanting African Americans to stay and fight for their rights as outlined in the Constitution and promised by Republicans. Greener, however, argued against relying on the promises of the Constitution, the Republican Party, and white benefactors to do the right things for African Americans. He blamed not just the former slave states but also the not-so-free North for the poverty and vulnerability of freedpeople at the end of the Civil War. Greener strenuously advocated migration to other parts of the United States because the freedpeople needed food, shelter, security, and employment immediately, not later, and because he wanted to remove African Americans from what he considered an immoral environment.

Both Greener and Douglass were eloquent orators and persuasive writers whose public debates were popular not merely for their well-conceived arguments but also as entertainment, as their contests increasingly tended toward personal sparring. Perhaps that is why the all-white American Social Science Association (ASSA) invited Douglass and Greener to present their views at its annual meeting in 1879. Douglass accepted but did not attend. Instead, he sent a paper to be read aloud, saying in his accompanying letter, "I hope to meet you in the spirit of Social Science and not in a spirit of controversy." The texts of both Douglass and Greener included here are excerpted from the versions published in the ASSA's *Journal of Social Science* in May 1880.

From The Emigration of Colored Citizens from the Southern States

* * *

It has been fourteen years since the Confederacy collapsed, and eleven years since reconstruction. The South has now had for three years home rule, "Autonomy"; and yet, instead of the renewed prosperity, harmony of races, and absence of political violence and lawlessness, which we were promised, we find demoralized credit, shameless repudiation, and organized lawlessness—rendering the condition of the negro tenant class worse than at any period since slavery. So deplorable and abject indeed is it that expatriation[1] and escape to Liberia, or the West, seems the only hope, as it is the continued dream of the negroes, old and young, in the six Southern States. We are accustomed to blame the Southern whites for the ultimate and approximate causes of this sad state of affairs. They are deeply responsible. I do not hesitate to place upon their shoulders all they deserve; but the North is not wholly innocent. We legislate for the interests of four million blacks just freed from bondage, demoralized by four years of war, and for two million rebellious whites, landless, hopeless, thankful at that time, even if their lives were spared, and we ignore all the precedents of history—the West Indies, Ireland, Russia and Germany. We threw the negro without anything, the carpet-bagger[2] with his musket, the ex-Confederate disarmed, pell-mell together, and told them to work out the problem. * * *

Immediate Causes of the Exodus

To quote from the *St. Louis Memorial:* "The story is about the same, in each instance; great privation and want from excessive rent exacted for land; connected with the murder of colored neighbors and friends, and threats of personal violence to themselves; the tenor of which statement is that of suffering and terror. Election days and Christmas, by the concurrent testimony, seem to have been preferred for killing the 'smart man,'[3] while robbery and personal violence, in one form and another, seem to have run the year around. Here they are in multitudes, not often alone, but women and children, old and middle-aged and young, and with common consent, leaving their old home for an unnatural climate, and facing storms and unknown dangers to go to northern Kansas. Why? Among them little is said of hope in the future; it is all of fear in the past. They are not drawn by the attractions of Kansas, they are driven by the terrors of Mississippi and Louisiana." * * *

Again, the political difference of opinion which exists in the South, is another important cause. There, political convictions rank with religious opinions in intensity. The over-production of cotton is another cause, by the low price of that staple. Then the fact that the negro owns neither land, nor presses, cotton-gin, and implements, but buys mules, rents land, and purchases his provisions at an advance, often of thirty and forty per cent., is sufficient cause for the Exodus.

1. Removal from one's native land to another country.
2. Derogatory term for migrants to the South who participated in Reconstruction, some to effect reforms, others for financial or political gain.
3. Smart aleck, impertinent.

* * *

Advantages of the Exodus to the Negro

This emigration will benefit the negro, who is now too much inclined to stay where he is put. At the South he never knows his own possibilities. Then again, the South is a wretched place for any people to develop in, and this is especially true of the negro; because, like all subject races, he imitates the life about him. * * * I need not enumerate the demoralizing features of Southern life, the reckless disregard for human life, the lack of thrift, drinking customs, gaming, horse-racing, etc. The negro needs contact with all that is healthful and developing in modern civilization, and by emigration the negro will learn to love thrift, and unlearn many bad habits and improvident notions acquired from preceding generations.

The exclusive devotion of the negro to the culture of cotton and rice is demoralizing to him. They drag women and children into the field, with no commissioner of labor to look out for outraged childhood and impaired maternity. I do not expect this argument to find favor with those who think the negro has no other future before him than to cultivate sugar, cotton and rice. On the politico-economic side a partial Exodus will benefit those who remain, by raising the wage fund, increasing the demand, and insuring better treatment to those who are left; the fact of the Exodus being a preventive check, if I may borrow a phrase from Mr. Malthus.[4] It will remove the negro from the incessant whirl of politics, in which, like all dark races, he is governed more by feeling than selfish interest. * * *

Objections to the Exodus

There are few opponents of the Exodus. Most of them are only negative objectors. The only class positively objecting is the planting class. At Vicksburg, and in Washington County (Miss.), they objected vehemently and loudly. Foreign labor, they say, would cost money. Not one planter in ten is able to make further outlay. During the change of laborers, even, they would go to rack and ruin.[5] The negro is the only one who can do their work. To go now will ruin the cotton crop, and, hence, affect the North as well as the South.

No one disputes the right of the negro to go West, now that he is free. We accord to all men the right to improve their condition, by change of residence or employment. Nearly all of the objectors, white and black, have grave doubts as to our ability to stand this severe Northern climate. They fear we may not find work adapted to our limited and peculiar powers; may not meet with kind friends and genial sympathy. We must endure privations and meet with ostracism[6] at the North. Mechanics will not work with negroes. The negro remembers Slavery, Black Codes, Ku-Klux, Sister Sallie's plan, tissue ballots, the murder of Dr. Dostie and Randolph in South Carolina, Caldwell and Dixon in Mississippi, and says:

"My relatives and friends who have gone North since the war tell a different story. They have held no offices, but they are free. They sleep in peace at night; what they earn is paid them, if not, they can appeal to the courts. They vote without fear of the shot-gun, and their children go to school. It is

4. Thomas Malthus (1766–1834), English economist and demographer.

5. Complete destruction.

6. Exclusion.

true the Northern people do not love us so well as you did, and hence the intermixture of races is not so promiscuous there as here. This we shall try to endure, if we go North, with patience and Christian resignation. We have never heard of the people at the North paying in ten, twenty-five and fifty cent scrip, payable four years hence, nor charging $2.00 a plug for tobacco, and $2.50 for witnessing a contract. While we may not have so much social equality as with you, we shall have more political equality and man to man justice. You charge $15.00 and $25.00 per acre for worn-out land; we can buy better in Kansas and Nebraska at $2.50 an acre. We had rather die free at the North than live as paupers and pariahs here, only nominally free. You thought Kansas not too cold for us in 1854–5; we are not afraid to try it now."

The most important opponent of the Exodus is Marshal Frederick Douglass,[7] my distinguished antagonist in this discussion, who, I sincerely regret, is not here, to lend to his able and ingenious argument the magic of his presence and the influence of his eloquent voice. The greatest negro whom America has produced, having suffered all that our race could endure, and having been elevated higher than any other negro, he cannot lack sympathy with any movement which concerns his race, and hence, any objection coming from him challenges attention, and demands to be answered. Age, long service, and a naturally keen and analytic mind, would presume a soundness of view on almost any topic of national importance or race interest. It is, therefore, with the highest regard for the honesty of Mr. Douglass's views that I venture to reply to some of his objections. * * *

Mr. Douglass's arguments, as I have been able to find them in speeches, resolutions, and the paper just read, are briefly these:—

1. Emigration is not the proper nor permanent remedy.

2. The Government ought to protect colored citizens at the South; to encourage emigration gives the Government a chance to shirk its duty; while the advocates of the measure leave Equal Rights, Protection and Allegiance open questions.

3. The colored race should be warned against a nomadic life and habits of wandering.

4. African emigration and migration to the West are analogous;[8] the failure of the one is prophetic of the other.

5. The negro now is potentially able to elect some members of his race at the South to Congress; this is impossible at the North.

6. At the South he has a monopoly of the supply of labor; at the West he would not have it. At the South, land owners must have laborers or starve; Western land owners are independent.

7. The Exodus does not conform to "the laws of civilizing emigration," as the carrying of a language, literature, etc. of a superior race to an inferior; nor does it conform to "the laws of geography." These, according to Mr. Douglass, "require for healthy emigration that it proceed from East to West, not from South to North, and not far away from latitudes and climates in which the emigrants were born."

To these objections first, it may be said, no favorer of migration claims it as the sole, proper or only permanent remedy for the aggravated relation of landlord and tenant at the South. It is approved of as one remedy, thus far the most salutary, in stopping lawlessness and exactions. * * *

7. Douglass was appointed a U.S. Marshal in 1877 by President Rutherford B. Hayes.
8. Comparable, similar

The failure of the analogy drawn between African colonization and migration to the West may be stated in this way: the one was worked up by slave-owners in the interest of slavery; this one springs spontaneously, according to Mr. Douglass's view, from the class considering itself aggrieved; one led out of the country to a comparative wilderness; the other directs to better land and larger opportunities here at home. The one took the negro to contend with barbarism. This places him under more civilizing influences than he has ever enjoyed, involving no change of allegiance nor serious differences of climate. If the colored people are "potentially" able to elect one of their own race to Congress, they cannot now make that potentiality possible. Emigration surely cannot lessen the potentiality, since the emigrants will remain citizens. I am inclined to think it will not diminish the probability. * * *

Mr. Douglass is rather misleading and fails again in his analogy, when he infers that the negro must go West as a civilizer or not go at all. He goes out from the house of bondage up from the land of Egypt, directed, I am inclined to think, by the same mighty hand which pointed out the way to Israel. * * *

If by the laws of geography, to which, unfortunately, this new Exodus does not conform, Mr. Douglass means that colonization, migration or civilization proceed best within the isothermal lines,[9] we may concede the law, but all history shows exceptions remarkable and instructive.

The Phoenicians sailed West and North; the Greek colonies were at all known points; the Dutch and English have not been hindered by isothermal lines, penetrating far away from the latitudes in which they were born. Magna Graecia,[1] in distinction from Hellas, and Mr. Dilke's "Greater Britain," are pertinent illustrations of the unsoundness of this seeming historical statement. If it were even philosophically correct, there is no analogy in the examples; the Southern negro, if he emigrate to Washington Territory or Arizona, would not be as far from home as the Aryan race now is by its excessive waves of migration from the Black and Caspian Seas. When Mr. Douglass grants in his paper that if the half is true of what the negro suffers, the Exodus is justified,—he grants all that any advocate of it asks. It is from causes, which he condemns, denounces, deplores and considers disgraceful, that we say, "emigrate, and if you can, better your condition."

The Exodus is complained of as a "policy." We might answer, it is a result, not a policy in the ordinary sense, although, as a safe check to certain ulterior causes, we might well commend it to oppressed people anywhere as a measure of policy.

We are told, aphoristically,[2] that the negro's labor made him free, and therefore, it can make him "free, comfortable, and independent." The assumed fact is not exactly clear, and the conclusion is scarcely warranted by the negro's statements of his condition, according to Mr. Douglass.

We are called upon to say whether we would remove a part, or all of the colored people from the South. "A part," we answer, "if that will insure protection and just treatment for the rest; the whole, if they can be protected in no other way." * * *

We are assured that there will be misery and want resulting from this "ill-timed" movement. Doubtless there will be; every movement having in it the elements of good, has brought some hardship. * * * The crucial test,

9. That is, lines connecting places on a map that have the same temperatures on an average over a given period of time.

1. Greek colonies in ancient Italy.

2. Concisely, briefly.

however, is whether there will be more misery and want by migrating than by remaining; we think not. * * *

* * *

How Will They Be Treated in the West?

Governor St. John, of Kansas,[3] is authority on this point. "Up to the present writing, about 3,000 destitute refugees have arrived, the most of whom have been cared for by our committee. We have been very successful in securing for them employment, and thus placed them in a position that they soon became self-sustaining, and no longer required aid. These people seem to be honest, and of good habits; are certainly industrious and anxious to work, and, so far as they have been tried, have proved to be faithful and excellent laborers." * * *

What is true of Kansas is true of the Indian Territory.[4] A recent traveller there, writes: "The cozy homes and promising fields were the property of freedmen; every ploughboy you see has been a slave. *All* the farms along our route today belong to freedmen, to whom the Creeks accord every right and privilege they enjoy themselves,—annuity lands, offices and honors. . . .

Every home gives proof of thrift. New fences, addition to the cabins, new barns and out-houses, catch the eye on every hand, except the schoolhouse and church; these appear to be going to decay, but it is only in the rude buildings that this is true. Both church and school are prosperous."

* * *

Emigration is no new thing, beginning with Senator Windom's speech.[5] It began in 1840 and has kept up ever since. You may remember some of the old pictures of the emigrant with bundle on his shoulder. He went alone formerly, and was often taken back at the Government's expense; now he takes his family, and cannot be taken back against his will. In Kansas there are now five or six colonies, some of them established since 1870; Baxter Springs, Nicodemus, Morton City and Singleton. The reports from all are favorable. * * *

The Political Side of the Exodus

* * *

It is estimated that 15,000 have gone West within eight months; 150 leave New Orleans each week. All are not going to Kansas. Many are wisely pushing farther North. As a class, they differ from the West India negroes after their emancipation. The Southern negro did not relapse into barbarism; he manifests a disposition and an adaptability to work. That he is industrious is shown by the immense cotton crop, just reported as contributing to the exportable products of the nation, $189,000,000 per annum.

No view of the movement would be complete which did not notice the relation of the colored people of the country to this flight from oppression. The first stage is passed, the appeal to white philanthropists. My notion is the second is here, the appeal to ourselves. We must organize societies,

3. John Pearce St. John (1833–1916).
4. Lands granted to resettled Native peoples in what became the state of Oklahoma in 1907.
5. Minnesota senator William Windom (1827–1891) gave a speech supporting Black emigration from the South in 1879.

contribute our dimes, and form a network of communication between the South and every principal point North and West. We should raise $200,000 to form a company; we should have a National Executive Committee, and have agents to buy land, procure cheap transportation, disseminate accurate information, and see to it that they are neither deluded nor defrauded. Such an organization, working through our churches and benevolent societies, would do more to develop our race than all the philanthropic measures designed to aid us since the war.

The Exodus Will Go On

The little rill[6] has started on its course toward the great sea of humanity. It moves slowly on by virtue of the eternal law of gravitation, which leads peoples and individuals toward peace, protection and happiness. Today it is a slender thread and makes way with difficulty amid the rocks and tangled growth; but it has already burst through serious impediments, showing itself possessed of a mighty current. It started in Mississippi, but it is even now being rapidly fed by other rills and streams from the territory through which it flows. Believing that it comes from God, and feeling convinced that it bears only blessings in its course for that race so long tossed, so ill-treated, so sadly misunderstood, I greet its tiny line, and almost see in the near future its magnificent broad bosom, bearing proudly onward, until at last, like the travel-worn and battle-scarred Greeks of old, there bursts upon its sight the sea, the broad sea of universal freedom and protection.

1880

6. Small stream.

W. E. B. DU BOIS
1868–1963

The first decades of the twentieth century saw the emergence of many acclaimed, educated, activist leaders, commonly called "the New Negro." Among those women and men, William Edward Burghardt Du Bois was renowned as *the* Renaissance man of African American letters. Today he is still considered one of the most multifaceted, prolific, and influential scholar/activists that black America has produced, a man with as wide-ranging an intellect as that of any American of his era. Because of his extensive publications in the sociology and history of African Americans and in tribute to his pioneering editing of numerous journals of opinion devoted to racial issues, Du Bois has been called, with justification, the founder of Black studies in American academic life. His work and his example inspired a twentieth-century African American intelligentsia proud of its heritage and committed to a social as well as an intellectual mission.

Du Bois believed that ideas and principles, not slogans and personalities, were essential to the eradication of the many forms of bigotry and inequality that had perverted what he called "the ideal of human brotherhood" in America. While

Men of the African American Niagara Movement. Changing the African American Niagara Movement into an integrated National Association for the Advancement of Colored People was both a racial and a gendered action.

engaged in full-time university teaching, scholarly research, and lecturing, he played a pivotal role in the organization of the Niagara Movement, which in 1910 became the National Association for the Advancement of Colored People (NAACP). A radical democrat, Du Bois was not afraid to espouse unpopular notions of socialism and communism in the name of full socioeconomic equality. Yet his unflagging critique of the material injustices of America arose from his commitment to spiritual ideals, to "the striving in the souls of black folk" to become "co-worker[s] in the kingdom of culture," creators of an America in which the "best powers" and "latent genius" that Du Bois believed were inherent in all races could find expression and fulfillment. Thus, although Du Bois was educated as a scholar and his manner of

Women of the African American Niagara Movement.

writing was often professorial, he repeatedly turned to traditional literary forms, such as poetry, fiction, and an introspective, impressionistic prose when impelled by the need to express his most deeply felt emotions.

On his twenty-fifth birthday, while studying for his Ph.D. at the University of Berlin, Du Bois confided in his journal the following goals: "to make a name in science, to make a name in art and thus to raise my race." From his childhood in Great Barrington, Massachusetts, he had cherished a fondness for books and a desire for intellectual distinction. His mother, Mary Burghardt Du Bois, and her extended family (which could trace its ancestry back to the earliest settlers of the valley where Du Bois grew up), protected and encouraged William after his father, Alfred Du Bois, deserted his family when his son was still an infant. Attending predominantly white schools and churches, Du Bois graduated with honors from the local high school in 1884 with "no thought of discrimination on the part of my [white] fellows," as he recalled in his autobiography, *Dusk of Dawn*, in 1940.

In 1885 the "quite thoroughly New England" youth went to Fisk University in Nashville, Tennessee, his first foray into the South, his first direct encounter with southern racism, and, more important, his first deep immersion in the lives of African Americans. Earning his bachelor's degree in 1888, Du Bois applied to Harvard University for a scholarship, which he won; he graduated from Harvard with another bachelor's degree in 1890 and a master's degree the next year. Between 1892 and 1894, he pursued his education at the University of Berlin. In 1895 Du Bois earned his doctorate in history from Harvard; his dissertation, "The Suppression of the African Slave-Trade to the United States," was published in 1896, the first volume in the Harvard Historical Studies series.

By the time his first book saw print, Du Bois was busy at his first teaching post, at Wilberforce University, a black institution established by the African Methodist Episcopal church in central Ohio. In 1896 he married Nina Gomer, a Wilberforce student, and soon thereafter accepted an offer from the University of Pennsylvania to do research on the Black people of Philadelphia. Despite a low salary, no assistance, and not even an office, Du Bois did his work in exemplary fashion, producing *The Philadelphia Negro* (1899), reputedly the first sociological text on an African American community published in the United States. In 1897 Du Bois joined the faculty of Atlanta University, where for the next thirteen years through his teaching and research he laid the foundation for twentieth-century African American sociology with a series of academic conferences and empirically based annual reports on such topics as Black landowners, the Black church, the Black family, Black urbanization, and Black mortality.

Increasingly alarmed by the incidence of white violence against Blacks in the South and chafing against the restraints of segregation, Du Bois sought forums beyond academe from which he could address fundamental problems of race and justice in the United States. In articles for such magazines as the *Atlantic Monthly*, *The Dial*, and *World's Work*, Du Bois wrote not as a detached social scientist but as a cultural interpreter, historian, advocate, and oracle of his people. By the turn of the century, he had become convinced that the distinctive artistic traditions, expressive culture, and communal values of African Americans—what he called the "soul" of the Black folk in the United States—had to be recognized, respected, and conserved by white and Black Americans alike. In 1903 Du Bois voiced this conviction and this plea in the eloquent and experimental book for which he is now best known, *The Souls of Black Folk*.

Ostensibly a collection of essays on African American history, sociology, religion, politics, and music, *The Souls of Black Folk* reads in important respects like a personal exposition of a collective experience, "life within the Veil," as Du Bois termed it. The metaphor of the veil denotes throughout *The Souls of Black Folk* the shadowy yet substantial line that separated whites from persons of African descent in the turn-of-the-century United States. "The problem of the Twentieth Century is the problem of the color-line," Du Bois announced prophetically in the "forethought" to *The Souls of Black Folk*. But it was Du Bois's genius to realize that to protest the color line most effectively and originally in a new century, he had to find ways to personalize it, to make its reality not merely a social and legal fact but a profound psychological factor in the African American's sense of self and relationship to society. Thus, from the beginning of his book, Du Bois introduces his white reader to peculiar dualities and conflicts in African American self-perception—known ever since by Du Bois's term *double-consciousness*—which for Du Bois defined both the crux of Black Americans' struggle to identify themselves and the crucible in which their African and American identities could be merged into a unity of which they and the nation could be proud. "Of Mr. Booker T. Washington and Others"—the most influential essay in *The Souls of Black Folk*—attacked the political program of another acknowledged African American leader in a way that gave Du Bois a national following as an uncompromising civil rights champion. *The Souls of Black Folk* begins and ends in a prose more evocative than provocative, as Du Bois celebrates spiritual aspirations of African America through its folklore, its music, and its "simple faith and reverence" in "the ultimate justice of things," when "America shall rend the Veil and the prisoned shall go free."

Between 1903 and 1910 Du Bois wrote some of his memorable work in poetry and narrative prose. He published his prose poem "A Litany of Atlanta" in the wake of a brutal outbreak of violence against African Americans in Atlanta in September 1906. A year later "The Song of the Smoke" testified to Du Bois's desire for an alternative to the traditional deity he prayed to in the "Litany," while also pioneering an aesthetic of unabashed Blackness. In 1909, the same year in which Du Bois and others founded the National Association for the Advancement of Colored People (NAACP), Du Bois published a biography of John Brown in an attempt to plumb the mysteries of the mind of the radical abolitionist martyr. A year later Du Bois launched the *Crisis*, the official organ of the NAACP, which, as its editor, he fashioned into the most widely read African American magazine of its time. Du Bois also tried his hand at long fiction. His novel *The Quest of the Silver Fleece* (1911), partly an exposé of the southern cotton industry, partly a romantic love story, and partly a brief for socialism, did not receive much notice, but its unhackneyed depiction of Black women and its barely disguised political radicalism were remarkable in African American fiction. Du Bois's feminism, though imperfect by today's standards, came to the fore again in his essay "The Damnation of Women," one of the most notable essays in *Darkwater: Voices within the Veil* (1920).

Although the *Crisis* served Du Bois well as a forum for his ideas on American racial issues, he devoted considerable energy during the 1910s and 1920s to international questions. In 1915 he published *The Negro*, a study that embraced peoples of African descent worldwide. Attempting to combat colonialism, Du Bois helped organize several Pan-African congresses in Europe and New York. His second novel, *Dark Princess* (1928), imagined an international "Great Council of Darker Peoples" poised to overthrow European imperialism and American racism. The blend of socialist propaganda and romantic fantasy at the heart of *Dark Princess* was designed to illustrate Du Bois's contention in "Criteria of Negro Art" (1926) that art and propaganda were one. Du Bois felt obliged to insist on this because many writers of the New Negro Renaissance in the 1920s were unsympathetic to the explicitly political agenda of his fiction and to what they saw as his outmoded Victorian values in writing about love and sex. Despite the friction between Du Bois and some of the firebrands of the New Negro Renaissance, the editor of the *Crisis* published several of the best of the new writers, especially Langston Hughes and Countee Cullen. Hughes and other notable writers such as Jessie Fauset also made important contributions to the *Brownie's Book*, a magazine for African American children that Du Bois initiated in 1920.

The Depression of the 1930s confirmed in Du Bois's mind the need for fundamental socioeconomic change in America according to Marxist principles. He resigned from the NAACP in 1934 and returned to Atlanta University. His massive history, *Black Reconstruction* (1935), revised conventional accounts of Reconstruction in the South as a debacle and emphasized the efforts of the freed people to transform the South into a society free of social and economic exploitation. In 1940 Du Bois published his first full-length autobiography, *Dusk of Dawn: An Autobiography of a Concept of Race*, in which he focused on the evolution of his ideas about race, "human difference," and social justice, concluding with an argument for Black "voluntary segregation" as the most effective means of organizing and advancing African Americans socially and economically. Although *Dusk of Dawn* firmly stated that its author was not a communist, Du Bois's writing later in the 1940s affirmed his growing affinities to Marxism, his admiration of the Soviet Union, his vigorous anticolonialism, and his heightened militancy in the struggle for African American civil rights in the United States.

Du Bois's left-wing politics had more than a little to do with his forced retirement from Atlanta University in 1944 and his firing in 1948 by the NAACP from his position as director of special research. In 1951 the U.S. government indicted, as subversive agents of a foreign power, Du Bois and his colleagues in the New York–based Peace Information Center, an organization that promoted the banning of atomic weapons. Acquitted in November 1951, Du Bois found himself ostracized by many African American leaders and civil rights organizations. But he went on writing (although most of his outlets were now limited to the left-wing press): *In Battle for Peace* (1952), an autobiography; *The Black Flame*, a trilogy of novels: *The Ordeal of Mansart* (1957), *Mansart Builds a School* (1959), and *Worlds of Color* (1961); and *The Autobiography of W. E. B. Du Bois* (1968), posthumously published. In 1963 Du Bois renounced his American citizenship and became a citizen of Ghana, where he had moved in 1961. When he died he was planning the multivolume *Encyclopaedia Africana*.

A Litany of Atlanta[1]

Done of Atlanta, in the Day of Death, 1906.

O Silent God, Thou whose voice afar in mist and mystery hath left our ears an-hungered in these fearful days—
Hear us, good Lord!

Listen to us, Thy children: our faces dark with doubt, are made a mockery in Thy sanctuary. With uplifted hands we front Thy heaven, O God, crying:
We beseech Thee to hear us, good Lord!

We are not better than our fellows, Lord, we are but weak and human men. When our devils do deviltry, curse Thou the doer and the deed: curse them as we curse them, do to them all and more than ever they have done to innocence and weakness, to womanhood and home.
Have mercy upon us, miserable sinners!

And yet whose is the deeper guilt? Who made these devils? Who nursed them in crime and fed them on injustice? Who ravished and debauched their mothers and their grandmothers? Who bought and sold their crime, and waxed fat and rich on public iniquity?
Thou knowest, good God!

Is this Thy justice, O Father, that guile be easier than innocence, and the innocent crucified for the guilt of the untouched guilty?
Justice, O Judge of men!

Wherefore do we pray? Is not the God of the fathers dead? Have not seers seen in Heaven's halls Thine hearsed and lifeless form stark amidst the black and rolling smoke of sin, where all along bow bitter forms of endless dead?
Awake, Thou that sleepest!

Thou art not dead, but flown afar, up hills of endless light, thru blazing corridors of suns, where worlds do swing of good and gentle men, of women strong and free—far from the cozenage,[2] black hypocrisy and chaste prostitution of this shameful speck of dust!
Turn again, O Lord, leave us not to perish in our sin!

From lust of body and lust of blood
Great God deliver us!

From lust of power and lust of gold,
Great God deliver us!

From the leagued lying of despot and of brute,
Great God deliver us!

A city lay in travail, God our Lord, and from her loins sprang twin Murder and Black Hate. Red was the midnight; clang, crack and cry of death and

1. From September 24 to 26, 1906, the Atlanta Race Massacre, perpetuated by white mobs, raged through Georgia's capital. Du Bois wrote this poem on a train as he returned to the city, unsure of the fate of his family there. "Litany": a prayer of entreaty in which a minister and a congregation alternately speak.
2. Fraud, trickery.

fury filled the air and trembled underneath the stars when church spires pointed silently to Thee. And all this was to sate the greed of greedy men who hide behind the veil of vengeance!

Bend us Thine ear, O Lord!

In the pale, still morning we looked upon the deed. We stopped our ears and held our leaping hands, but they—did they not wag their heads and leer and cry with bloody jaws: *Cease from Crime!* The word was mockery, for thus they train a hundred crimes while we do cure one.

Turn again our captivity, O Lord!

Behold this maimed and broken thing; dear God it was an humble black man who toiled and sweat to save a bit from the pittance paid him. They told him: *Work and Rise.* He worked. Did this man sin? Nay, but some one told how some one said another did—one whom he had never seen nor known. Yet for that man's crime this man lieth maimed and murdered, his wife naked to shame, his children, to poverty and evil.

Hear us, O heavenly Father!

Doth not this justice of hell stink in Thy nostrils, O God? How long shall the mounting flood of innocent blood roar in Thine ears and pound in our hearts for vengeance? Pile the pale frenzy of blood-crazed brutes who do such deeds high on Thine altar, Jehovah Jireh,[3] and burn it in hell forever and forever!

Forgive us, good Lord; we know not what we say!

Bewildered we are, and passion-tost, mad with the madness of a mobbed and mocked and murdered people; straining at the armposts of Thy Throne, we raise our shackled hands and charge Thee, God, by the bones of our stolen fathers, by the tears of our dead mothers, by the very blood of Thy crucified Christ: *What meaneth this?* Tell us the Plan; give us the Sign!

Keep not thou silence, O God!

Sit no longer blind, Lord God, deaf to our prayer and dumb to our dumb suffering. Surely Thou too art not white, O Lord, a pale, bloodless, heartless thing?

Ah! Christ of all the Pities!

Forgive the thought! Forgive these wild, blasphemous words. Thou art still the God of our black fathers, and in Thy soul's soul sit some soft darkenings of the evening, some shadowings of the velvet night.

But whisper—speak—call, great God, for Thy silence is white terror to our hearts! The way, O God, show us the way and point us the path.

Whither? North is greed and South is blood; within, the coward, and without, the liar. Whither? To death?

Amen! Welcome dark sleep!

3. God.

Whither? To life? But not this life, dear God, not this. Let the cup pass from us, tempt us not beyond our strength, for there is that clamoring and clawing within, to whose voice we would not listen, yet shudder lest we must, and it is red, Ah! God! It is a red and awful shape.
Selah.[4]

In yonder East trembles a star.
Vengeance is mine; I will repay, saith the Lord!

Thy will, O Lord, be done!
Kyrie Eleison![5]

Lord, we have done these pleading, wavering words.
We beseech Thee to hear us, good Lord!

We bow our heads and hearken soft to the sobbing of women and little children.
We beseech Thee to hear us, good Lord!

Our voices sink in silence and in night.
Hear us, good Lord!

In night, O God of a godless land!
Amen!

In silence, O Silent God.
Selah!

1906

The Song of the Smoke

I am the Smoke King
I am black!
I am swinging in the sky,
I am wringing worlds awry;
I am the thought of the throbbing mills,
I am the soul of the soul-toil kills,
Wraith of the ripple of trading rills;
Up I'm curling from the sod,
I am whirling home to God;
I am the Smoke King
I am black.

I am the Smoke King,
I am black!
I am wreathing broken hearts,
I am sheathing love's light darts;

4. Du Bois uses this Hebrew word, perhaps meaning "God has spoken," to invoke the reverential mood of the Old Testament Psalms, in which the word often appears.
5. Lord, have mercy on us (Greek).

Inspiration of iron times
Wedding the toil of toiling climes,
Shedding the blood of bloodless crimes—
Lurid lowering 'mid the blue,
Torrid towering toward the true,
I am the Smoke King,
I am black.

I am the Smoke King,
I am black!
I am darkening with song,
I am hearkening to wrong!
I will be black as blackness can—
The blacker the mantle, the mightier the man!
For blackness was ancient ere whiteness began.
I am daubing God in night,
I am swabbing Hell in white:
I am the Smoke King
I am black.

I am the Smoke King,
I am black!
I am cursing ruddy morn,
I am hearsing hearts unborn:
Souls unto me are as stars in a night,
I whiten my black men—I blacken my white!
What's the hue of a hide to a man in his might?
Hail! great, gritty, grimy hands—
Sweet Christ, pity toiling lands!
I am the Smoke King
I am black.

1907

From The Souls of Black Folk

The Forethought

Herein lie buried many things which if read with patience may show the strange meaning of being black here in the dawning of the Twentieth Century. This meaning is not without interest to you, Gentle Reader; for the problem of the Twentieth Century is the problem of the color-line.

I pray you, then, receive my little book in all charity, studying my words with me, forgiving mistake and foible for sake of the faith and passion that is in me, and seeking the grain of truth hidden there.

I have sought here to sketch, in vague, uncertain outline, the spiritual world in which ten thousand thousand Americans live and strive. First, in two chapters I have tried to show what Emancipation meant to them, and what was its aftermath. In a third chapter I have pointed out the slow rise of personal leadership, and criticised candidly the leader who bears the chief burden of his race to-day. Then, in two other chapters I have sketched in swift outline the two worlds within and without the Veil, and thus have come to the central problem of training men for life. Venturing now into deeper detail, I have in two chapters studied the struggles of the massed millions of the black peasantry, and in another have sought to make clear the present relations of the sons of master and man.

Leaving, then, the world of the white man, I have stepped within the Veil, raising it that you may view faintly its deeper recesses,—the meaning of its religion, the passion of its human sorrow, and the struggle of its greater souls. All this I have ended with a tale twice told but seldom written.

Some of these thoughts of mine have seen the light before in other guise. For kindly consenting to their republication here, in altered and extended form, I must thank the publishers of *The Atlantic Monthly, The World's Work, The Dial, The New World*, and the *Annals of the American Academy of Political and Social Science*.

Before each chapter, as now printed, stands a bar of the Sorrow Songs,[1]—some echo of haunting melody from the only American music which welled up from black souls in the dark past. And, finally, need I add that I who speak here am bone of the bone and flesh of the flesh of them that live within the Veil?

W. E. B. Du B.

Atlanta, Ga., Feb. 1, 1903.

I. Of Our Spiritual Strivings

O water, voice of my heart, crying in the sand,
  All night long crying with a mournful cry,
As I lie and listen, and cannot understand
    The voice of my heart in my side or the voice of the sea,
  O water, crying for rest, is it I, is it I?
    All night long the water is crying to me.

Unresting water, there shall never be rest
  Till the last moon droop and the last tide fail,
And the fire of the end begin to burn in the west;
    And the heart shall be weary and wonder and cry like the sea,
  All life long crying without avail,
    As the water all night long is crying to me.

Arthur Symons[2]

Between me and the other world there is ever an unasked question: unasked by some through feelings of delicacy; by others through the difficulty of rightly framing it. All, nevertheless, flutter round it. They approach me in a half-hesitant sort of way, eye me curiously or compassionately, and then, instead of saying directly, How does it feel to be a problem? they say, I know an excellent colored man in my town; or, I fought at Mechanicsville;[3] or, Do not these Southern outrages make your blood boil? At these I smile, or am interested, or reduce the boiling to a simmer, as the occasion may require.

1. Du Bois's term for African American spirituals communally composed by southern slaves.
2. English poet (1865–1945). The quotation is from "The Crying of Water" (1903).
3. A Civil War battlesite in Virginia.

To the real question, How does it feel to be a problem? I answer seldom a word.

And yet, being a problem is a strange experience,—peculiar even for one who has never been anything else, save perhaps in babyhood and in Europe. It is in the early days of rollicking boyhood that the revelation first bursts upon one, all in a day, as it were. I remember well when the shadow swept across me. I was a little thing, away up in the hills of New England, where the dark Housatonic[4] winds between Hoosac and Taghkanic to the sea. In a wee wooden schoolhouse, something put it into the boys' and girls' heads to buy gorgeous visiting-cards—ten cents a package—and exchange. The exchange was merry, till one girl, a tall newcomer, refused my card,—refused it peremptorily, with a glance. Then it dawned upon me with a certain suddenness that I was different from the others; or like, mayhap, in heart and life and longing, but shut out from their world by a vast veil. I had thereafter no desire to tear down that veil, to creep through; I held all beyond it in common contempt, and lived above it in a region of blue sky and great wandering shadows. That sky was bluest when I could beat my mates at examination-time, or beat them at a foot-race, or even beat their stringy heads. Alas, with the years all this fine contempt began to fade; for the worlds I longed for, and all their dazzling opportunities, were theirs, not mine. But they should not keep these prizes, I said; some, all, I would wrest from them. Just how I would do it I could never decide: by reading law, by healing the sick, by telling the wonderful tales that swam in my head,—some way. With other black boys the strife was not so fiercely sunny: their youth shrunk into tasteless sycophancy, or into silent hatred of the pale world about them and mocking distrust of everything white; or wasted itself in a bitter cry, Why did God make me an outcast and a stranger in mine own house? The shades of the prison-house closed round about us all: walls strait and stubborn to the whitest, but relentlessly narrow, tall, and unscalable to sons of night who must plod darkly on in resignation, or beat unavailing palms against the stone, or steadily, half hopelessly, watch the streak of blue above.

After the Egyptian and Indian, the Greek and Roman, the Teuton and Mongolian, the Negro is a sort of seventh son, born with a veil, and gifted with second-sight[5] in this American world,—a world which yields him no true self-consciousness, but only lets him see himself through the revelation of the other world. It is a peculiar sensation, this double-consciousness, this sense of always looking at one's self through the eyes of others, of measuring one's soul by the tape of a world that looks on in amused contempt and pity. One ever feels his two-ness,—an American, a Negro; two souls, two thoughts, two unreconciled strivings; two warring ideals in one dark body, whose dogged strength alone keeps it from being torn asunder.

The history of the American Negro is the history of this strife,—this longing to attain self-conscious manhood, to merge his double self into a better and truer self. In this merging he wishes neither of the older selves to be lost. He would not Africanize America, for America has too much to teach the world and Africa. He would not bleach his Negro soul in a flood of white Americanism, for he knows that Negro blood has a message for the world. He simply wishes to make it possible for a man to be both a Negro

4. A river in western Massachusetts.
5. Characteristics of people believed to be gifted with special powers of perception and clairvoyance.

and an American, without being cursed and spit upon by his fellows, without having the doors of Opportunity closed roughly in his face.

This, then, is the end of his striving: to be a co-worker in the kingdom of culture, to escape both death and isolation, to husband and use his best powers and his latent genius. These powers of body and mind have in the past been strangely wasted, dispersed, or forgotten. The shadow of a mighty Negro past flits through the tale of Ethiopia the Shadowy and of Egypt the Sphinx. Throughout history, the powers of single black men flash here and there like falling stars, and die sometimes before the world has rightly gauged their brightness. Here in America, in the few days since Emancipation, the black man's turning hither and thither in hesitant and doubtful striving has often made his very strength to lose effectiveness, to seem like absence of power, like weakness. And yet it is not weakness,—it is the contradiction of double aims. The double-aimed struggle of the black artisan—on the one hand to escape white contempt for a nation of mere hewers of wood and drawers of water, and on the other hand to plough and nail and dig for a poverty-stricken horde—could only result in making him a poor craftsman, for he had but half a heart in either cause. By the poverty and ignorance of his people, the Negro minister or doctor was tempted toward quackery and demagogy; and by the criticism of the other world, toward ideals that made him ashamed of his lowly tasks. The would-be black *savant* was confronted by the paradox that the knowledge his people needed was a twice-told tale to his white neighbors, while the knowledge which would teach the white world was Greek to his own flesh and blood. The innate love of harmony and beauty that set the ruder souls of his people a-dancing and a-singing raised but confusion and doubt in the soul of the black artist; for the beauty revealed to him was the soul-beauty of a race which his larger audience despised, and he could not articulate the message of another people. This waste of double aims, this seeking to satisfy two unreconciled ideals, has wrought sad havoc with the courage and faith and deeds of ten thousand thousand people,—has sent them often wooing false gods and invoking false means of salvation, and at times has even seemed about to make them ashamed of themselves.

Away back in the days of bondage they thought to see in one divine event the end of all doubt and disappointment; few men ever worshipped Freedom with half such unquestioning faith as did the American Negro for two centuries. To him, so far as he thought and dreamed, slavery was indeed the sum of all villainies, the cause of all sorrow, the root of all prejudice; Emancipation was the key to a promised land of sweeter beauty than ever stretched before the eyes of wearied Israelites. In song and exhortation swelled one refrain—Liberty; in his tears and curses the God he implored had Freedom in his right hand. At last it came,—suddenly, fearfully, like a dream. With one wild carnival of blood and passion came the message in his own plaintive cadences:—

"Shout, O children!
Shout, you're free!
For God has bought your liberty!"[6]

Years have passed away since then,—ten, twenty, forty; forty years of national life, forty years of renewal and development, and yet the swarthy

6. African American spiritual.

spectre sits in its accustomed seat at the Nation's feast. In vain do we cry to this our vastest social problem:—

> "Take any shape but that, and my firm nerves
> Shall never tremble!"[7]

The Nation has not yet found peace from its sins; the freedman has not yet found in freedom his promised land. Whatever of good may have come in these years of change, the shadow of a deep disappointment rests upon the Negro people,—a disappointment all the more bitter because the unattained ideal was unbounded save by the simple ignorance of a lowly people.

The first decade was merely a prolongation of the vain search for freedom, the boon that seemed ever barely to elude their grasp,—like a tantalizing will-o'-the-wisp,[8] maddening and misleading the headless host. The holocaust of war, the terrors of the Ku-Klux Klan, the lies of carpet-baggers,[9] the disorganization of industry, and the contradictory advice of friends and foes, left the bewildered serf with no new watchword beyond the old cry for freedom. As the time flew, however, he began to grasp a new idea. The ideal of liberty demanded for its attainment powerful means, and these the Fifteenth Amendment[1] gave him. The ballot, which before he had looked upon as a visible sign of freedom, he now regarded as the chief means of gaining and perfecting the liberty with which war had partially endowed him. And why not? Had not votes made war and emancipated millions? Had not votes enfranchised the freedmen? Was anything impossible to a power that had done all this? A million black men started with renewed zeal to vote themselves into the kingdom. So the decade flew away, the revolution of 1876[2] came, and left the half-free serf weary, wondering, but still inspired. Slowly but steadily, in the following years, a new vision began gradually to replace the dream of political power,—a powerful movement, the rise of another ideal to guide the unguided, another pillar of fire by night after a clouded day. It was the ideal of "book-learning"; the curiosity, born of compulsory ignorance, to know and test the power of the cabalistic letters of the white man, the longing to know. Here at last seemed to have been discovered the mountain path to Canaan;[3] longer than the highway of Emancipation and law, steep and rugged, but straight, leading to heights high enough to over-look life.

Up the new path the advance guard toiled, slowly, heavily, doggedly; only those who have watched and guided the faltering feet, the misty minds, the dull understandings, of the dark pupils of these schools know how faithfully, how piteously, this people strove to learn. It was weary work. The cold statistician wrote down the inches of progress here and there, noted also where here and there a foot had slipped or some one had fallen. To the tired climbers, the horizon was ever dark, the mists were often cold, the Canaan was always dim and far away. If, however, the vistas disclosed as yet no goal, no resting-place, little but flattery and criticism, the journey at least gave leisure for reflection and self-examination; it changed the child of

7. Shakespeare, *Macbeth* 3.4.124–25.
8. A delusive hope or goal. "Boon": a favor.
9. Northerners, often viewed as opportunists, who moved to the South to participate in Reconstruction. "Ku-Klux Klan": a secret society founded in the post–Civil War South to reestablish white supremacy.
1. Ratified in 1870, this amendment to the U.S. Constitution guaranteed voting rights to African American men.
2. Opposition to continuing the Reconstruction policy after the 1876 national elections.
3. In the Bible, the Promised Land of the Israelites. "Cabalistic": mystical, esoteric.

Emancipation to the youth with dawning self-consciousness, self-realization, self-respect. In those sombre forests of his striving his own soul rose before him, and he saw himself,—darkly as through a veil; and yet he saw in himself some faint revelation of his power, of his mission. He began to have a dim feeling that, to attain his place in the world, he must be himself, and not another. For the first time he sought to analyze the burden he bore upon his back, that dead-weight of social degradation partially masked behind a half-named Negro problem. He felt his poverty; without a cent, without a home, without land, tools, or savings, he had entered into competition with rich, landed, skilled neighbors. To be a poor man is hard, but to be a poor race in a land of dollars is the very bottom of hardships. He felt the weight of his ignorance,—not simply of letters, but of life, of business, of the humanities; the accumulated sloth and shirking and awkwardness of decades and centuries shackled his hands and feet. Nor was his burden all poverty and ignorance. The red stain of bastardy, which two centuries of systematic legal defilement of Negro women had stamped upon his race, meant not only the loss of ancient African chastity, but also the hereditary weight of a mass of corruption from white adulterers, threatening almost the obliteration of the Negro home.

A people thus handicapped ought not to be asked to race with the world, but rather allowed to give all its time and thought to its own social problems. But alas! while sociologists gleefully count his bastards and his prostitutes, the very soul of the toiling, sweating black man is darkened by the shadow of a vast despair. Men call the shadow prejudice, and learnedly explain it as the natural defence of culture against barbarism, learning against ignorance, purity against crime, the "higher" against the "lower" races. To which the Negro cries Amen! and swears that to so much of this strange prejudice as is founded on just homage to civilization, culture, righteousness, and progress, he humbly bows and meekly does obeisance.[4] But before that nameless prejudice that leaps beyond all this he stands helpless, dismayed, and well-nigh speechless; before that personal disrespect and mockery, the ridicule and systematic humiliation, the distortion of fact and wanton license of fancy, the cynical ignoring of the better and the boisterous welcoming of the worse, the all-pervading desire to inculcate disdain for everything black, from Toussaint[5] to the devil,—before this there rises a sickening despair that would disarm and discourage any nation save that black host to whom "discouragement" is an unwritten word.

But the facing of so vast a prejudice could not but bring the inevitable self-questioning, self-disparagement, and lowering of ideals which ever accompany repression and breed in an atmosphere of contempt and hate. Whisperings and portents came borne upon the four winds: Lo! we are diseased and dying, cried the dark hosts; we cannot write, our voting is vain; what need of education, since we must always cook and serve? And the Nation echoed and enforced this self-criticism, saying: Be content to be servants, and nothing more; what need of higher culture for half-men? Away with the black man's ballot, by force or fraud,—and behold the suicide of a race! Nevertheless, out of the evil came something of good,—the more careful adjustment of education to real life, the clearer perception of

4. A gesture of obedience and respect.
5. Toussaint L'Ouverture (1743–1803), leader of a successful revolution of the enslaved in Haiti.

the Negroes' social responsibilities, and the sobering realization of the meaning of progress.

So dawned the time of *Sturm und Drang*:[6] storm and stress to-day rocks our little boat on the mad waters of the world-sea; there is within and without the sound of conflict, the burning of body and rending of soul; inspiration strives with doubt, and faith with vain questionings. The bright ideals of the past,—physical freedom, political power, the training of brains and the training of hands,—all these in turn have waxed and waned, until even the last grows dim and overcast. Are they all wrong,—all false? No, not that, but each alone was over-simple and incomplete,—the dreams of a credulous race-childhood, or the fond imaginings of the other world which does not know and does not want to know our power. To be really true, all these ideals must be melted and welded into one. The training of the schools we need to-day more than ever,—the training of deft hands, quick eyes and ears, and above all the broader, deeper, higher culture of gifted minds and pure hearts. The power of the ballot we need in sheer self-defence,—else what shall save us from a second slavery? Freedom, too, the long-sought, we still seek,—the freedom of life and limb, the freedom to work and think, the freedom to love and aspire. Work, culture, liberty,—all these we need, not singly but together, not successively but together, each growing and aiding each, and all striving toward that vaster ideal that swims before the Negro people, the ideal of human brotherhood, gained through the unifying ideal of Race; the ideal of fostering and developing the traits and talents of the Negro, not in opposition to or contempt for other races, but rather in large conformity to the greater ideals of the American Republic, in order that some day on American soil two world-races may give each to each those characteristics both so sadly lack. We the darker ones come even now not altogether empty-handed: there are to-day no truer exponents of the pure human spirit of the Declaration of Independence than the American Negroes; there is no true American music but the wild sweet melodies of the Negro slave; the American fairy tales and folk-lore are Indian and African; and, all in all, we black men seem the sole oasis of simple faith and reverence in a dusty desert of dollars and smartness. Will America be poorer if she replace her brutal dyspeptic blundering with light-hearted but determined Negro humility? or her coarse and cruel wit with loving jovial good-humor? or her vulgar music with the soul of the Sorrow Songs?

Merely a concrete test of the underlying principles of the great republic is the Negro Problem, and the spiritual striving of the freedmen's sons is the travail of souls whose burden is almost beyond the measure of their strength, but who bear it in the name of an historic race, in the name of this the land of their fathers' fathers, and in the name of human opportunity.

And now what I have briefly sketched in large outline let me on coming pages tell again in many ways, with loving emphasis and deeper detail, that men may listen to the striving in the souls of black folk.

* * *

6. Storm and stress (German).

III. Of Mr. Booker T. Washington and Others

From birth till death enslaved; in word, in deed, unmanned!

Hereditary bondsmen! Know ye not
Who would be free themselves must strike the blow?

BYRON[7]

Easily the most striking thing in the history of the American Negro since 1876 is the ascendancy of Mr. Booker T. Washington. It began at the time when war memories and ideals were rapidly passing; a day of astonishing commercial development was dawning; a sense of doubt and hesitation overtook the freedmen's sons,—then it was that his leading began. Mr. Washington came, with a simple definite programme, at the psychological moment when the nation was a little ashamed of having bestowed so much sentiment on Negroes, and was concentrating its energies on Dollars. His programme of industrial education, conciliation of the South, and submission and silence as to civil and political rights, was not wholly original; the Free Negroes from 1830 up to wartime had striven to build industrial schools, and the American Missionary Association had from the first taught various trades; and Price[8] and others had sought a way of honorable alliance with the best of the Southerners. But Mr. Washington first indissolubly linked these things; he put enthusiasm, unlimited energy, and perfect faith into this programme, and changed it from a by-path into a veritable Way of Life. And the tale of the methods by which he did this is a fascinating study of human life.

It startled the nation to hear a Negro advocating such a programme after many decades of bitter complaint; it startled and won the applause of the South, it interested and won the admiration of the North; and after a confused murmur of protest, it silenced if it did not convert the Negroes themselves.

To gain the sympathy and cooperation of the various elements comprising the white South was Mr. Washington's first task; and this, at the time Tuskegee[9] was founded, seemed, for a black man, well-nigh impossible. And yet ten years later it was done in the word spoken at Atlanta: "In all things purely social we can be as separate as the five fingers, and yet one as the hand in all things essential to mutual progress." This "Atlanta Compromise" is by all odds the most notable thing in Mr. Washington's career. The South interpreted it in different ways: the radicals received it as a complete surrender of the demand for civil and political equality; the conservatives, as a generously conceived working basis for mutual understand-

7. George Gordon, Lord Byron (1788–1824), British poet. The quotation is from *Childe Harold's Pilgrimage* (1812).

8. Joseph Charles Price (1854–1893), southern orator, educator, and moderate civil rights spokesman.

9. Tuskegee Normal and Industrial Institute, a school for African Americans founded by Booker T. Washington in Tuskegee, Alabama, in 1881.

ing. So both approved it, and to-day its author is certainly the most distinguished Southerner since Jefferson Davis, and the one with the largest personal following.

Next to this achievement comes Mr. Washington's work in gaining place and consideration in the North. Others less shrewd and tactful had formerly essayed to sit on these two stools and had fallen between them; but as Mr. Washington knew the heart of the South from birth and training, so by singular insight he intuitively grasped the spirit of the age which was dominating the North. And so thoroughly did he learn the speech and thought of triumphant commercialism, and the ideals of material prosperity, that the picture of a lone black boy poring over a French grammar amid the weeds and dirt of a neglected home soon seemed to him the acme of absurdities. One wonders what Socrates and St. Francis of Assisi[1] would say to this.

And yet this very singleness of vision and thorough oneness with his age is a mark of the successful man. It is as though Nature must needs make men narrow in order to give them force. So Mr. Washington's cult has gained unquestioning followers, his work has wonderfully prospered, his friends are legion, and his enemies are confounded. To-day he stands as the one recognized spokesman of his ten million fellows, and one of the most notable figures in a nation of seventy millions. One hesitates, therefore, to criticise a life which, beginning with so little, has done so much. And yet the time is come when one may speak in all sincerity and utter courtesy of the mistakes and shortcomings of Mr. Washington's career, as well as of his triumphs, without being thought captious or envious, and without forgetting that it is easier to do ill than well in the world.

The criticism that has hitherto met Mr. Washington has not always been of this broad character. In the South especially has he had to walk warily to avoid the harshest judgments,—and naturally so, for he is dealing with the one subject of deepest sensitiveness to that section. Twice—once when at the Chicago celebration of the Spanish-American War he alluded to the color-prejudice that is "eating away the vitals of the South," and once when he dined with President Roosevelt[2]—has the resulting Southern criticism been violent enough to threaten seriously his popularity. In the North the feeling has several times forced itself into words, that Mr. Washington's counsels of submission overlooked certain elements of true manhood, and that his educational programme was unnecessarily narrow. Usually, however, such criticism has not found open expression, although, too, the spiritual sons of the Abolitionists have not been prepared to acknowledge that the schools founded before Tuskegee, by men of broad ideals and self-sacrificing spirit, were wholly failures or worthy of ridicule. While, then, criticism has not failed to follow Mr. Washington, yet the prevailing public opinion of the land has been but too willing to deliver the solution of a wearisome problem into his hands, and say, "If that is all you and your race ask, take it."

Among his own people, however, Mr. Washington has encountered the strongest and most lasting opposition, amounting at times to bitterness, and even to-day continuing strong and insistent even though largely silenced

1. Italian cleric (1181?–1226), founder of the Franciscan religious order. Socrates (470?–399 B.C.E.), Athenian philosopher and teacher.

2. Theodore Roosevelt (1858–1919), U.S. president from 1901 to 1909.

in outward expression by the public opinion of the nation. Some of this opposition is, of course, mere envy; the disappointment of displaced demagogues and the spite of narrow minds. But aside from this, there is among educated and thoughtful colored men in all parts of the land a feeling of deep regret, sorrow, and apprehension at the wide currency and ascendancy which some of Mr. Washington's theories have gained. These same men admire his sincerity of purpose, and are willing to forgive much to honest endeavor which is doing something worth the doing. They coöperate with Mr. Washington as far as they conscientiously can; and, indeed, it is no ordinary tribute to this man's tact and power that, steering as he must between so many diverge interests and opinions, he so largely retains the respect of all.

But the hushing of the criticism of honest opponents is a dangerous thing. It leads some of the best of the critics to unfortunate silence and paralysis of effort, and others to burst into speech so passionately and intemperately as to lose listeners. Honest and earnest criticism from those whose interests are most nearly touched,—criticism of writers by readers, of government by those governed, of leaders by those led,—this is the soul of democracy and the safeguard of modern society. If the best of the American Negroes receive by outer pressure a leader whom they had not recognized before, manifestly there is here a certain palpable gain. Yet there is also irreparable loss,—a loss of that peculiarly valuable education which a group receives when by search and criticism it finds and commissions its own leaders. The way in which this is done is at once the most elementary and the nicest problem of social growth. History is but the record of such group-leadership; and yet how infinitely changeful is its type and character! And of all types and kinds, what can be more instructive than the leadership of a group within a group?—that curious double movement where real progress may be negative and actual advance be relative retrogression. All this is the social student's inspiration and despair.

Now in the past the American Negro has had instructive experience in the choosing of group leaders, founding thus a peculiar dynasty which in the light of present conditions is worth while studying. When sticks and stones and beasts form the sole environment of a people, their attitude is largely one of determined opposition to and conquest of natural forces. But when to earth and brute is added an environment of men and ideas, then the attitude of the imprisoned group may take three main forms,—a feeling of revolt and revenge; an attempt to adjust all thought and action to the will of the greater group; or, finally, a determined effort at self-realization and self-development despite environing opinion. The influence of all of these attitudes at various times can be traced in the history of the American Negro, and in the evolution of his successive leaders.

Before 1750, while the fire of African freedom still burned in the veins of the slaves, there was in all leadership or attempted leadership but the one motive of revolt and revenge,—typified in the terrible Maroons, the Danish blacks, and Cato of Stono,[3] and veiling all the Americas in fear of insurrection. The liberalizing tendencies of the latter half of the eighteenth century brought, along with kindlier relations between black and white, thoughts of

3. Leader of an insurrection of enslaved people in Stono, South Carolina, in 1739. "Maroons": fugitive slave communities in the South that often raided nearby farms and plantations. "Danish blacks": enslaved people who mounted an insurrection and took control of the island of St. John in the Danish West Indies (now the Virgin Islands) in 1723.

ultimate adjustment and assimilation. Such aspiration was especially voiced in the earnest songs of Phyllis, in the martyrdom of Attucks, the fighting of Salem and Poor, the intellectual accomplishments of Banneker and Derham, and the political demands of the Cuffes.[4]

Stern financial and social stress after the war cooled much of the previous humanitarian ardor. The disappointment and impatience of the Negroes at the persistence of slavery and serfdom voiced itself in two movements. The slaves in the South, aroused undoubtedly by vague rumors of the Haytian revolt, made three fierce attempts at insurrection,—in 1800 under Gabriel in Virginia, in 1822 under Vesey in Carolina, and in 1831 again in Virginia under the terrible Nat Turner.[5] In the Free States, on the other hand, a new and curious attempt at self-development was made. In Philadelphia and New York color-prescription led to a withdrawal of Negro communicants from white churches and the formation of a peculiar socio-religious institution among the Negroes known as the African Church,—an organization still living and controlling in its various branches over a million of men.

Walker's wild appeal[6] against the trend of the times showed how the world was changing after the coming of the cotton-gin. By 1830 slavery seemed hopelessly fastened on the South, and the slaves thoroughly cowed into submission. The free Negroes of the North, inspired by the mulatto immigrants from the West Indies, began to change the basis of their demands; they recognized the slavery of slaves, but insisted that they themselves were freemen, and sought assimilation and amalgamation with the nation on the same terms with other men. Thus, Forten and Purvis of Philadelphia, Shad of Wilmington, Du Bois of New Haven, Barbadoes[7] of Boston, and others, strove singly and together as men, they said, not as slaves; as "people of color," not as "Negroes." The trend of the times, however, refused them recognition save in individual and exceptional cases, considered them as one with all the despised blacks, and they soon found themselves striving to keep even the rights they formerly had of voting and working and moving as freemen. Schemes of migration and colonization arose among them; but these they refused to entertain, and they eventually turned to the Abolition movement as a final refuge.

Here, led by Remond, Nell, Wells-Brown,[8] and Douglass, a new period of self-assertion and self-development dawned. To be sure, ultimate freedom and assimilation was the ideal before the leaders, but the assertion of the

4. Paul Cuffe (1759–1817), merchant-mariner and author who in 1780 with his brother John protested Massachusetts laws that withheld the vote from African Americans and American Indians. Phillis Wheatley (1753–1784), internationally acclaimed African-born poet who grew up enslaved in Boston. Crispus Attucks (1723?–1770), a fugitive from slavery, was the first person to die in the Boston Massacre, a prelude to the American Revolution. Peter Salem (1750–1816), born enslaved, became a distinguished American Revolutionary War soldier. Salem Poor (1747–1802), distinguished free-born American Revolutionary War soldier. Benjamin Banneker (1731–1806), surveyor, astronomer, and almanac maker. James Durham or Derham (1762–1802?), born enslaved, was the earliest known African American physician.

5. Gabriel Prosser (1775–1800), Denmark Vesey (ca. 1767–1822), and Nat Turner (1800–1831) were leaders of insurrections inspired to some extent by the successful revolt that established the independent nation of Haiti in 1804.

6. David Walker (1785–1830), author of *David Walker's Appeal* (1829), a revolutionary antislavery tract.

7. James G. Barbadoes (1796–1841), abolitionist and leader among the free African Americans of Boston. James Forten Sr. (1766–1842), wealthy Philadelphia businessman and civil rights activist. Robert Purvis Sr. (1810–1898), wealthy Philadelphia reformer and abolitionist. Mary Ann Shadd (1823–1893), newspaper editor and antislavery lecturer. Alexander Du Bois, W. E. B. Du Bois's grandfather.

8. William Wells Brown (ca. 1814–1884), internationally famous fugitive enslaved person, lecturer, and author. Charles Lenox Remond (1810–1874), journalist and antislavery lecturer. William C. Nell (1816–1874), abolitionist journalist and active participant in the Underground Railroad.

manhood rights of the Negro by himself was the main reliance, and John Brown's raid was the extreme of its logic. After the war and emancipation, the great form of Frederick Douglass, the greatest of American Negro leaders, still led the host. Self-assertion, especially in political lines, was the main programme, and behind Douglass came Elliot, Bruce, and Langston, and the Reconstruction politicians, and, less conspicuous but of greater social significance Alexander Crummell and Bishop Daniel Payne.[9]

Then came the Revolution of 1876, the suppression of the Negro votes, the changing and shifting of ideals, and the seeking of new lights in the great night. Douglass, in his old age, still bravely stood for the ideals of his early manhood,—ultimate assimilation *through* self-assertion, and on no other terms. For a time Price arose as a new leader, destined, it seemed, not to give up, but to re-state the old ideals in a form less repugnant to the white South. But he passed away in his prime. Then came the new leader. Nearly all the former ones had become leaders by the silent suffrage of their fellows, had sought to lead their own people alone, and were usually, save Douglass, little known outside their race. But Booker T. Washington arose as essentially the leader not of one race but of two,—a compromiser between the South, the North, and the Negro. Naturally the Negroes resented, at first bitterly, signs of compromise which surrendered their civil and political rights, even though this was to be exchanged for larger chances of economic development. The rich and dominating North, however, was not only weary of the race problem, but was investing largely in Southern enterprises, and welcomed any method of peaceful cooperation. Thus, by national opinion, the Negroes began to recognize Mr. Washington's leadership; and the voice of criticism was hushed.

Mr. Washington represents in Negro thought the old attitude of adjustment and submission; but adjustment at such a peculiar time as to make his programme unique. This is an age of unusual economic development, and Mr. Washington's programme naturally takes an economic cast, becoming a gospel of Work and Money to such an extent as apparently almost completely to overshadow the higher aims of life. Moreover, this is an age when the more advanced races are coming in closer contact with the less developed races, and the race-feeling is therefore intensified; and Mr. Washington's programme practically accepts the alleged inferiority of the Negro races. Again, in our own land, the reaction from the sentiment of war time has given impetus to race-prejudice against Negroes, and Mr. Washington withdraws many of the high demands of Negroes as men and American citizens. In other periods of intensified prejudice all the Negro's tendency to self-assertion has been called forth; at this period a policy of submission is advocated. In the history of nearly all other races and peoples the doctrine preached at such crises has been that manly self-respect is worth more than lands and houses, and that a people who voluntarily surrender such respect, or cease striving for it, are not worth civilizing.

In answer to this, it has been claimed that the Negro can survive only through submission. Mr. Washington distinctly asks that black people give up, at least for the present, three things,—

9. Daniel A. Payne (1811–1893), African Methodist Episcopal church leader and educator. Robert Brown Elliott (1842–1884), congressperson from South Carolina (1870–74). Blanche Kelso Bruce (1841–1898), U.S. senator from Mississippi (1875–81). John Mercer Langston (1829–1897), congressperson from Virginia (1890–91).

First, political power,

Second, insistence on civil rights,

Third, higher education of Negro youth,—and concentrate all their energies on industrial education, the accumulation of wealth, and the conciliation of the South.[1] This policy has been courageously and insistently advocated for over fifteen years, and has been triumphant for perhaps ten years. As a result of this tender of the palm-branch,[2] what has been the return? In these years there have occurred:

1. The disfranchisement of the Negro.
2. The legal creation of a distinct status of civil inferiority for the Negro.
3. The steady withdrawal of aid from institutions for the higher training of the Negro.

These movements are not, to be sure, direct results of Mr. Washington's teachings; but his propaganda has, without a shadow of doubt, helped their speedier accomplishment. The question then comes: Is it possible, and probable, that nine millions of men can make effective progress in economic lines if they are deprived of political rights, made a servile caste, and allowed only the most meagre chance for developing their exceptional men? If history and reason give any distinct answer to these questions, it is an emphatic *No*. And Mr. Washington thus faces the triple paradox of his career:

1. He is striving nobly to make Negro artisans business men and property-owners; but it is utterly impossible, under modern competitive methods, for workingmen and property-owners to defend their rights and exist without the right of suffrage.
2. He insists on thrift and self-respect, but at the same time counsels a silent submission to civic inferiority such as is bound to sap the manhood of any race in the long run.
3. He advocates common-school[3] and industrial training, and depreciates institutions of higher learning; but neither the Negro common-schools, nor Tuskegee itself, could remain open a day were it not for teachers trained in Negro colleges, or trained by their graduates.

This triple paradox in Mr. Washington's position is the object of criticism by two classes of colored Americans. One class is spiritually descended from Toussaint the Savior, through Gabriel, Vesey, and Turner, and they represent the attitude of revolt and revenge; they hate the white South blindly and distrust the white race generally, and so far as they agree on definite action, think that the Negro's only hope lies in emigration beyond the borders of the United States. And yet, by the irony of fate, nothing has more effectually made this programme seem hopeless than the recent course of the United States toward weaker and darker peoples in the West Indies, Hawaii, and the Philippines,—for where in the world may we go and be safe from lying and brute force?

The other class of Negroes who cannot agree with Mr. Washington has hitherto said little aloud. They deprecate the sight of scattered counsels, of internal disagreement; and especially they dislike making their just criticism of a useful and earnest man an excuse for a general discharge of venom from small-minded opponents. Nevertheless, the questions involved are so

1. Alluding to a famous speech made at Atlanta Cotton States and International Exposition, Sept. 19, 1895.

2. A gesture acknowledging victory.

3. Public elementary school.

fundamental and serious that it is difficult to see how men like the Grimkes, Kelly Miller, J. W. E. Bowen,[4] and other representatives of this group, can much longer be silent. Such men feel in conscience bound to ask of this nation three things:

1. The right to vote.
2. Civic equality.
3. The education of youth according to ability.

They acknowledge Mr. Washington's invaluable service in counselling patience and courtesy in such demands; they do not ask that ignorant black men vote when ignorant whites are debarred, or that any reasonable restrictions in the suffrage should not be applied; they know that the low social level of the mass of the race is responsible for much discrimination against it, but they also know, and the nation knows, that relentless color-prejudice is more often a cause than a result of the Negro's degradation; they seek the abatement of this relic of barbarism, and not its systematic encouragement and pampering by all agencies of social power from the Associated Press to the Church of Christ. They advocate, with Mr. Washington, a broad system of Negro common schools supplemented by thorough industrial training; but they are surprised that a man of Mr. Washington's insight cannot see that no such educational system ever has rested or can rest on any other basis than that of the well-equipped college and university, and they insist that there is a demand for a few such institutions throughout the South to train the best of the Negro youth as teachers, professional men, and leaders.

This group of men honor Mr. Washington for his attitude of conciliation toward the white South; they accept the "Atlanta Compromise" in its broadest interpretation; they recognize, with him, many signs of promise, many men of high purpose and fair judgment, in this section; they know that no easy task has been laid upon a region already tottering under heavy burdens. But, nevertheless, they insist that the way to truth and right lies in straightforward honesty, not in indiscriminate flattery; in praising those of the South who do well and criticising uncompromisingly those who do ill; in taking advantage of the opportunities at hand and urging their fellows to do the same, but at the same time in remembering that only a firm adherence to their higher ideals and aspirations will ever keep those ideals within the realm of possibility. They do not expect that the free right to vote, to enjoy civic rights, and to be educated, will come in a moment; they do not expect to see the bias and prejudices of years disappear at the blast of a trumpet; but they are absolutely certain that the way for a people to gain their reasonable rights is not by voluntarily throwing them away and insisting that they do not want them; that the way for a people to gain respect is not by continually belittling and ridiculing themselves; that, on the contrary, Negroes must insist continually, in season and out of season, that voting is necessary to modern manhood, that color discrimination is barbarism, and that black boys need education as well as white boys.

In failing thus to state plainly and unequivocally the legitimate demands of their people, even at the cost of opposing an honored leader, the thinking

4. John Wesley Edward Bowen (1855–1933), Methodist church leader and popular lecturer. Archibald H. Grimké (1849–1930), attorney and journalist, and Francis J. Grimké (1850–1937), clergyman and educator, both civil rights activists in the North. Kelly Miller (1863–1939), professor at Howard University and a mediator between conservatives and militants among African Americans.

classes of American Negroes would shirk a heavy responsibility,—a responsibility to themselves, a responsibility to the struggling masses, a responsibility to the darker races of men whose future depends so largely on this American experiment, but especially a responsibility to this nation,—this common Fatherland. It is wrong to encourage a man or a people in evil-doing; it is wrong to aid and abet a national crime simply because it is unpopular not to do so. The growing spirit of kindliness and reconciliation between the North and South after the frightful differences of a generation ago ought to be a source of deep congratulation to all, and especially to those whose mistreatment caused the war; but if that reconciliation is to be marked by the industrial slavery and civic death of those same black men, with permanent legislation into a position of inferiority, then those black men, if they are really men, are called upon by every consideration of patriotism and loyalty to oppose such a course by all civilized methods, even though such opposition involves disagreement with Mr. Booker T. Washington. We have no right to sit silently by while the inevitable seeds are sown for a harvest of disaster to our children, black and white.

First, it is the duty of black men to judge the South discriminatingly. The present generation of Southerners are not responsible for the past, and they should not be blindly hated or blamed for it. Furthermore, to no class is the indiscriminate endorsement of the recent course of the South toward Negroes more nauseating than to the best thought of the South. The South is not "solid"; it is a land in the ferment of social change, wherein forces of all kinds are fighting for supremacy; and to praise the ill the South is to-day perpetrating is just as wrong as to condemn the good. Discriminating and broad-minded criticism is what the South needs,—needs it for the sake of her own white sons and daughters, and for the insurance of robust, healthy mental and moral development.

To-day even the attitude of the Southern whites toward the blacks is not, as so many assume, in all cases the same; the ignorant Southerner hates the Negro, the workingmen fear his competition, the money-makers wish to use him as a laborer, some of the educated see a menace in his upward development, while others—usually the sons of the masters—wish to help him to rise. National opinion has enabled this last class to maintain the Negro common schools, and to protect the Negro partially in property, life, and limb. Through the pressure of the money-makers, the Negro is in danger of being reduced to semi-slavery, especially in the country districts; the workingmen, and those of the educated who fear the Negro, have united to disfranchise him, and some have urged his deportation; while the passions of the ignorant are easily aroused to lynch and abuse any black man. To praise this intricate whirl of thought and prejudice is nonsense; to inveigh indiscriminately against "the South" is unjust; but to use the same breath in praising Governor Aycock, exposing Senator Morgan, arguing with Mr. Thomas Nelson Page, and denouncing Senator Ben Tillman,[5] is not only sane, but the imperative duty of thinking black men.

It would be unjust to Mr. Washington not to acknowledge that in several instances he has opposed movements in the South which were unjust to the

5. Benjamin Ryan Tillman (1847–1918), white supremacist governor of South Carolina (1890–94) and U.S. senator (1895–1918). Charles Brantley Aycock (1859–1912), reformist governor of North Carolina (1901–05). John Tyler Morgan (1824–1907), white supremacist senator from Alabama (1876–1907). Thomas Nelson Page (1853–1922), author of sentimental fiction about slavery in the pre–Civil War South.

Negro; he sent memorials to the Louisiana and Alabama constitutional conventions, he has spoken against lynching, and in other ways has openly or silently set his influence against sinister schemes and unfortunate happenings. Notwithstanding this, it is equally true to assert that on the whole the distinct impression left by Mr. Washington's propaganda is, first, that the South is justified in its present attitude toward the Negro because of the Negro's degradation; secondly, that the prime cause of the Negro's failure to rise more quickly is his wrong education in the past; and, thirdly, that his future rise depends primarily on his own efforts. Each of these propositions is a dangerous half-truth. The supplementary truths must never be lost sight of: first, slavery and race-prejudice are potent if not sufficient causes of the Negro's position; second, industrial and common-school training were necessarily slow in planting because they had to await the black teachers trained by higher institutions,—it being extremely doubtful if any essentially different development was possible, and certainly a Tuskegee was unthinkable before 1880; and, third, while it is a great truth to say that the Negro must strive and strive mightily to help himself, it is equally true that unless his striving be not simply seconded, but rather aroused and encouraged, by the initiative of the richer and wiser environing group, he cannot hope for great success.

In his failure to realize and impress this last point, Mr. Washington is especially to be criticised. His doctrine has tended to make the whites, North and South, shift the burden of the Negro problem to the Negro's shoulders and stand aside as critical and rather pessimistic spectators; when in fact the burden belongs to the nation, and the hands of none of us are clean if we bend not our energies to righting these great wrongs.

The South ought to be led, by candid and honest criticism, to assert her better self and do her full duty to the race she has cruelly wronged and is still wronging. The North—her co-partner in guilt—cannot salve her conscience by plastering it with gold. We cannot settle this problem by diplomacy and suaveness, by "policy" alone. If worse come to worst, can the moral fibre of this country survive the slow throttling and murder of nine millions of men?

The black men of America have a duty to perform, a duty stern and delicate,—a forward movement to oppose a part of the work of their greatest leader. So far as Mr. Washington preaches Thrift, Patience, and Industrial Training for the masses, we must hold up his hands and strive with him, rejoicing in his honors and glorying in the strength of this Joshua[6] called of God and of man to lead the headless host. But so far as Mr. Washington apologizes for injustice, North or South, does not rightly value the privilege and duty of voting, belittles the emasculating effects of caste distinctions, and opposes the higher training and ambition of our brighter minds,—so far as he, the South, or the Nation, does this,—we must unceasingly and firmly oppose them. By every civilized and peaceful method we must strive for the rights which the world accords to men, clinging unwaveringly to those great words which the sons of the Fathers would fain forget: "We hold these truths to be self-evident: That all men are created equal; that they are endowed by their Creator with certain unalienable rights; that among these are life, liberty, and the pursuit of happiness."

6. Biblical leader who brought the Israelites into the Promised Land.

IV. *Of the Meaning of Progress*

Willst Du Deine Macht verkünden,
Wähle sie die frei von Sünden,
Steh'n in Deinem ew'gen Haus!
Deine Geister sende aus!
Die Unsterblichen, die Reinen,
Die nicht fühlen, die nicht weinen!
Nicht die zarte Jungfrau wähle,
Nicht der Hirtin weiche Seele!

SCHILLER[7]

Once upon a time I taught school in the hills of Tennessee, where the broad dark vale of the Mississippi begins to roll and crumple to greet the Alleghanies. I was a Fisk student then, and all Fisk men thought that Tennessee—beyond the Veil—was theirs alone, and in vacation time they sallied forth in lusty bands to meet the county school-commissioners. Young and happy, I too went, and I shall not soon forget that summer, seventeen years ago.

First, there was a Teachers' Institute at the county-seat; and there distinguished guests of the superintendent taught the teachers fractions and spelling and other mysteries,—white teachers in the morning, Negroes at night. A picnic now and then, and a supper, and the rough world was softened by laughter and song. I remember how—But I wander.

There came a day when all the teachers left the Institute and began the hunt for schools. I learn from hearsay (for my mother was mortally afraid of fire-arms) that the hunting of ducks and bears and men is wonderfully interesting, but I am sure that the man who has never hunted a country school has something to learn of the pleasures of the chase. I see now the white, hot roads lazily rise and fall and wind before me under the burning July sun; I feel the deep weariness of heart and limb as ten, eight, six miles stretch relentlessly ahead; I feel my heart sink heavily as I hear again and again, "Got a teacher? Yes." So I walked on and on—horses were too expensive—until I had wandered beyond railways, beyond stage lines, to a land of "varmints" and rattlesnakes, where the coming of a stranger was an event, and men lived and died in the shadow of one blue hill.

Sprinkled over hill and dale lay cabins and farmhouses, shut out from the world by the forests and the rolling hills toward the east. There I found at last a little school. Josie told me of it; she was a thin, homely girl of twenty, with a dark-brown face and thick, hard hair. I had crossed the stream at Watertown,[8] and rested under the great willows; then I had gone to the little cabin in the lot where Josie was resting on her way to town. The gaunt farmer made me welcome, and Josie, hearing my errand, told me anxiously

7. Friedrich von Schiller (1759–1805), German poet and dramatist. The quotation is from "The Maid of Orleans" (1801): "Would thou proclaim thy high command, Make choice of those who, free from sin, In thy eternal mansions stand; send forth thy flaming cherubim! Immortal ones, thy law they keep, They do not feel, they do not weep! Choose not a tender woman's aid, Not the frail soul of shepherd maid!" (4.1)

8. A village in eastern Tennessee.

that they wanted a school over the hill; that but once since the war had a teacher been there; that she herself longed to learn,—and thus she ran on, talking fast and loud, with much earnestness and energy.

Next morning I crossed the tall round hill, lingered to look at the blue and yellow mountains stretching toward the Carolinas, then plunged into the wood, and came out at Josie's home. It was a dull frame cottage with four rooms, perched just below the brow of the hill, amid peach-trees. The father was a quiet, simple soul, calmly ignorant, with no touch of vulgarity. The mother was different,—strong, bustling, and energetic, with a quick, restless tongue, and an ambition to live "like folks." There was a crowd of children. Two boys had gone away. There remained two growing girls; a shy midget of eight; John, tall, awkward, and eighteen; Jim, younger, quicker, and better looking; and two babies of indefinite age. Then there was Josie herself. She seemed to be the centre of the family: always busy at service, or at home, or berry-picking; a little nervous and inclined to scold, like her mother, yet faithful, too, like her father. She had about her a certain fineness, the shadow of an unconscious moral heroism that would willingly give all of life to make life broader, deeper, and fuller for her and hers. I saw much of this family afterwards, and grew to love them for their honest efforts to be decent and comfortable, and for their knowledge of their own ignorance. There was with them no affectation. The mother would scold the father for being so "easy"; Josie would roundly berate the boys for carelessness; and all knew that it was a hard thing to dig a living out of a rocky sidehill.

I secured the school. I remember the day I rode horseback out to the commissioner's house with a pleasant young white fellow who wanted the white school. The road ran down the bed of a stream; the sun laughed and the water jingled, and we rode on. "Come in," said the commissioner,—"come in. Have a seat. Yes, that certificate will do. Stay to dinner. What do you want a month?" "Oh," thought I, "this is lucky"; but even then fell the awful shadow of the Veil, for they ate first, then I—alone.

The schoolhouse was a log hut, where Colonel Wheeler used to shelter his corn. It sat in a lot behind a rail fence and thorn bushes, near the sweetest of springs. There was an entrance where a door once was, and within, a massive rickety fireplace; great chinks between the logs served as windows. Furniture was scarce. A pale blackboard crouched in the corner. My desk was made of three boards, reinforced at critical points, and my chair, borrowed from the landlady, had to be returned every night. Seats for the children—these puzzled me much. I was haunted by a New England vision of neat little desks and chairs, but, alas! the reality was rough plank benches without backs, and at times without legs. They had the one virtue of making naps dangerous,—possibly fatal, for the floor was not to be trusted.

It was a hot morning late in July when the school opened. I trembled when I heard the patter of little feet down the dusty road, and saw the growing row of dark solemn faces and bright eager eyes facing me. First came Josie and her brothers and sisters. The longing to know, to be a student in the great school at Nashville, hovered like a star above this child-woman amid her work and worry, and she studied doggedly. There were the Dowells from their farm over toward Alexandria,—Fanny, with her smooth black face and wondering eyes; Martha, brown and dull; the pretty girl-wife of a brother, and the younger brood.

There were the Burkes,—two brown and yellow lads, and a tiny haughty-eyed girl. Fat Reuben's little chubby girl came, with golden face and old-gold hair, faithful and solemn. 'Thenie was on hand early,—a jolly, ugly, good-hearted girl, who slyly dipped snuff[9] and looked after her little bowlegged brother. When her mother could spare her, 'Tildy came,—a midnight beauty, with starry eyes and tapering limbs; and her brother, correspondingly homely. And then the big boys,—the hulking Lawrences; the lazy Neills, unfathered sons of mother and daughter; Hickman, with a stoop in his shoulders; and the rest.

There they sat, nearly thirty of them, on the rough benches, their faces shading from a pale cream to a deep brown, the little feet bare and swinging, the eyes full of expectation, with here and there a twinkle of mischief, and the hands grasping Webster's blue-back spelling-book.[1] I loved my school, and the fine faith the children had in the wisdom of their teacher was truly marvellous. We read and spelled together, wrote a little, picked flowers, sang, and listened to stories of the world beyond the hill. At times the school would dwindle away, and I would start out. I would visit Mun Eddings, who lived in two very dirty rooms, and ask why little Lugene, whose flaming face seemed ever ablaze with the dark-red hair uncombed, was absent all last week, or why I missed so often the inimitable rags of Mack and Ed. Then the father, who worked Colonel Wheeler's farm on shares, would tell me how the crops needed the boys; and the thin, slovenly mother, whose face was pretty when washed, assured me that Lugene must mind the baby. "But we'll start them again next week." When the Lawrences stopped, I knew that the doubts of the old folks about book-learning had conquered again, and so, toiling up the hill, and getting as far into the cabin as possible, I put Cicero "pro Archia Poeta"[2] into the simplest English with local applications, and usually convinced them—for a week or so.

On Friday nights I often went home with some of the children,—sometimes to Doc Burke's farm. He was a great, loud, thin Black, ever working, and trying to buy the seventy-five acres of hill and dale where he lived; but people said that he would surely fail, and the "white folks would get it all." His wife was a magnificent Amazon,[3] with saffron face and shining hair, uncorseted and barefooted, and the children were strong and beautiful. They lived in a one-and-a-half-room cabin in the hollow of the farm, near the spring. The front room was full of great fat white beds, scrupulously neat; and there were bad chromos[4] on the walls, and a tired centretable. In the tiny back kitchen I was often invited to "take out and help" myself to fried chicken and wheat biscuit, "meat" and corn pone,[5] string-beans and berries. At first I used to be a little alarmed at the approach of bedtime in the one lone bedroom, but embarrassment was very deftly avoided. First, all the children nodded and slept, and were stowed away in one great pile of goose feathers; next, the mother and the father discreetly slipped away to the kitchen while I went to bed; then, blowing out the dim light, they retired in the dark. In the morning all were up and away before I thought of awaking.

9. Placed pinches of powdered tobacco between the cheek and gums.
1. The most popular spelling book of the 19th century, authored by Noah Webster (1758–1843).
2. Defense of the poet Archias by Marcus Tullius Cicero (106–43 B.C.E.), Roman statesman and orator.
3. A large, strong woman.
4. Colored pictures printed by a lithographic process.
5. A simple type of corn bread.

Across the road, where fat Reuben lived, they all went outdoors while the teacher retired, because they did not boast the luxury of a kitchen.

I liked to stay with the Dowells, for they had four rooms and plenty of good country fare. Uncle Bird had a small, rough farm, all woods and hills, miles from the big road; but he was full of tales,—he preached now and then,—and with his children, berries, horses, and wheat he was happy and prosperous. Often, to keep the peace, I must go where life was less lovely; for instance, 'Tildy's mother was incorrigibly dirty, Reuben's larder was limited seriously, and herds of untamed insects wandered over the Eddingses' beds. Best of all I loved to go to Josie's, and sit on the porch, eating peaches, while the mother bustled and talked: how Josie had bought the sewing-machine; how Josie worked at service in winter, but that four dollars a month was "mighty little" wages; how Josie longed to go away to school, but that it "looked like" they never could get far enough ahead to let her; how the crops failed and the well was yet unfinished; and, finally, how "mean" some of the white folks were.

For two summers I lived in this little world; it was dull and humdrum. The girls looked at the hill in wistful longing, and the boys fretted and haunted Alexandria. Alexandria was "town,"—a straggling, lazy village of houses, churches, and shops, and an aristocracy of Toms, Dicks, and Captains. Cuddled on the hill to the north was the village of the colored folks, who lived in three- or four-room unpainted cottages, some neat and homelike, and some dirty. The dwellings were scattered rather aimlessly, but they centred about the twin temples of the hamlet, the Methodist, and the Hard-Shell[6] Baptist churches. These, in turn, leaned gingerly on a sad-colored school-house. Hither my little world wended its crooked way on Sunday to meet other worlds, and gossip, and wonder, and make the weekly sacrifice with frenzied priest at the altar of the "old-time religion." Then the soft melody and mighty cadences of Negro song fluttered and thundered.

I have called my tiny community a world, and so its isolation made it; and yet there was among us but a half-awakened common consciousness, sprung from common joy and grief, at burial, birth, or wedding; from a common hardship in poverty, poor land, and low wages; and, above all, from the sight of the Veil that hung between us and Opportunity. All this caused us to think some thoughts together; but these, when ripe for speech, were spoken in various languages. Those whose eyes twenty-five and more years before had seen "the glory of the coming of the Lord,"[7] saw in every present hindrance or help a dark fatalism bound to bring all things right in His own good time. The mass of those to whom slavery was a dim recollection of childhood found the world a puzzling thing: it asked little of them, and they answered with little, and yet it ridiculed their offering. Such a paradox they could not understand, and therefore sank into listless indifference, or shiftlessness, or reckless bravado. There were, however, some—such as Josie, Jim, and Ben—to whom War, Hell, and Slavery were but childhood tales, whose young appetites had been whetted to an edge by school and story and half-awakened thought. Ill could they be content, born without and beyond the World. And their weak wings beat against their barriers,—barriers of caste, of youth, of life; at last, in dangerous moments, against everything that opposed even a whim.

6. Uncompromising.
7. From the opening line of Julia Ward Howe's "Battle Hymn of the Republic" (1861).

The ten years that follow youth, the years when first the realization comes that life is leading somewhere,—these were the years that passed after I left my little school. When they were past, I came by chance once more to the walls of Fisk University, to the halls of the chapel of melody. As I lingered there in the joy and pain of meeting old school-friends, there swept over me a sudden longing to pass again beyond the blue hill, and to see the homes and the school of other days, and to learn how life had gone with my schoolchildren; and I went.

Josie was dead, and the gray-haired mother said simply, "We've had a heap of trouble since you've been away." I had feared for Jim. With a cultured parentage and a social caste to uphold him, he might have made a venturesome merchant or a West Point cadet. But here he was, angry with life and reckless; and when Farmer Durham charged him with stealing wheat, the old man had to ride fast to escape the stones which the furious fool hurled after him. They told Jim to run away; but he would not run, and the constable came that afternoon. It grieved Josie, and great awkward John walked nine miles every day to see his little brother through the bars of Lebanon jail. At last the two came back together in the dark night. The mother cooked supper, and Josie emptied her purse, and the boys stole away. Josie grew thin and silent, yet worked the more. The hill became steep for the quiet old father, and with the boys away there was little to do in the valley. Josie helped them to sell the old farm, and they moved nearer town. Brother Dennis, the carpenter, built a new house with six rooms; Josie toiled a year in Nashville, and brought back ninety dollars to furnish the house and change it to a home.

When the spring came, and the birds twittered, and the stream ran proud and full, little sister Lizzie, bold and thoughtless, flushed with the passion of youth, bestowed herself on the tempter, and brought home a nameless child. Josie shivered and worked on, with the vision of schooldays all fled, with a face wan and tired,—worked until, on a summer's day, some one married another; then Josie crept to her mother like a hurt child, and slept—and sleeps.

I paused to scent the breeze as I entered the valley. The Lawrences have gone,—father and son forever,—and the other son lazily digs in the earth to live. A new young widow rents out their cabin to fat Reuben. Reuben is a Baptist preacher now, but I fear as lazy as ever, though his cabin has three rooms; and little Ella has grown into a bouncing woman, and is ploughing corn on the hot hillside. There are babies a-plenty, and one half-witted girl. Across the valley is a house I did not know before, and there I found, rocking one baby and expecting another, one of my schoolgirls, a daughter of Uncle Bird Dowell. She looked somewhat worried with her new duties, but soon bristled into pride over her neat cabin and the tale of her thrifty husband, the horse and cow, and the farm they were planning to buy.

My log schoolhouse was gone. In its place stood Progress; and Progress, I understand, is necessarily ugly. The crazy foundation stones still marked the former site of my poor little cabin, and not far away, on six weary boulders, perched a jaunty board house, perhaps twenty by thirty feet, with three windows and a door that locked. Some of the window-glass was broken, and part of an old iron stove lay mournfully under the house. I peeped through the window half reverently, and found things that were more familiar. The blackboard had grown by about two feet, and the seats were still without backs. The county owns the lot now, I hear, and every year there is a session of school. As I sat by the spring and looked on the Old and the New I felt glad, very glad, and yet—

After two long drinks I started on. There was the great double log-house on the corner. I remembered the broken, blighted family that used to live there. The strong, hard face of the mother, with its wilderness of hair, rose before me. She had driven her husband away, and while I taught school a strange man lived there, big and jovial, and people talked. I felt sure that Ben and 'Tildy would come to naught from such a home. But this is an odd world; for Ben is a busy farmer in Smith County, "doing well, too," they say, and he had cared for little 'Tildy until last spring, when a lover married her. A hard life the lad had led, toiling for meat, and laughed at because he was homely and crooked. There was Sam Carlon, an impudent old skinflint, who had definite notions about "niggers," and hired Ben a summer and would not pay him. Then the hungry boy gathered his sacks together, and in broad daylight went into Carlon's corn; and when the hard-fisted farmer set upon him, the angry boy flew at him like a beast. Doc Burke saved a murder and a lynching that day.

The story reminded me again of the Burkes, and an impatience seized me to know who won in the battle, Doc or the seventy-five acres. For it is a hard thing to make a farm out of nothing, even in fifteen years. So I hurried on, thinking of the Burkes. They used to have a certain magnificent barbarism about them that I liked. They were never vulgar, never immoral, but rather rough and primitive, with an unconventionality that spent itself in loud guffaws, slaps on the back, and naps in the corner. I hurried by the cottage of the misborn Neill boys. It was empty, and they were grown into fat, lazy farm-hands. I saw the home of the Hickmans, but Albert, with his stooping shoulders, had passed from the world! Then I came to the Burkes' gate and peered through; the inclosure looked rough and untrimmed, and yet there were the same fences around the old farm save to the left, where lay twenty-five other acres. And lo! the cabin in the hollow had climbed the hill and swollen to a half-finished six-room cottage.

The Burkes held a hundred acres, but they were still in debt. Indeed, the gaunt father who toiled night and day would scarcely be happy out of debt, being so used to it. Some day he must stop, for his massive frame is showing decline. The mother wore shoes, but the lion-like physique of other days was broken. The children had grown up. Rob, the image of his father, was loud and rough with laughter. Birdie, my school baby of six, had grown to a picture of maiden beauty, tall and tawny. "Edgar is gone," said the mother, with head half bowed,—"gone to work in Nashville; he and his father couldn't agree."

Little Doc, the boy born since the time of my school, took me horseback down the creek next morning toward Farmer Dowell's. The road and the stream were battling for mastery, and the stream had the better of it. We splashed and waded, and the merry boy, perched behind me, chattered and laughed. He showed me where Simon Thompson had bought a bit of ground and a home; but his daughter Lana, a plump, brown, slow girl, was not there. She had married a man and a farm twenty miles away. We wound on down the stream till we came to a gate that I did not recognize, but the boy insisted that it was "Uncle Bird's." The farm was fat with the growing crop. In that little valley was a strange stillness as I rode up; for death and marriage had stolen youth and left age and childhood there. We sat and talked that night after the chores were done. Uncle Bird was grayer, and his eyes did not see so well, but he was still jovial. We talked of the acres bought,—one hundred and twenty-five,—of the new guest-chamber added, of Martha's marrying. Then we talked of death: Fanny and Fred were gone; a shadow hung over the other daughter, and when it lifted she was to go to Nashville to school. At last we spoke of the neighbors, and as night fell, Uncle Bird told me how, on a night like that, 'Thenie came wandering back to her home over yonder, to escape the blows of her husband. And next morning she died in the home that her little bow-legged brother, working and saving, had bought for their widowed mother.

My journey was done, and behind me lay hill and dale, and Life and Death. How shall man measure Progress there where the dark-faced Josie lies? How many heartfuls of sorrow shall balance a bushel of wheat? How hard a thing is life to the lowly, and yet how human and real! And all this life and love and strife and failure,—is it the twilight of nightfall or the flush of some faint-dawning day?

Thus sadly musing, I rode to Nashville in the Jim Crow car.[8]

V. *Of the Wings of Atalanta*

O black boy of Atlanta!
  But half was spoken;
The slave's chains and the master's
  Alike are broken;
The one curse of the races
  Held both in tether;
They are rising—all are rising—
  The black and white together.

WHITTIER[9]

South of the North, yet north of the South, lies the City of a Hundred Hills, peering out from the shadows of the past into the promise of the future. I have seen her in the morning, when the first flush of day had half-roused her; she lay gray and still on the crimson soil of Georgia; then the blue smoke began to curl from her chimneys, the tinkle of bell and scream of whistle broke the silence, the rattle and roar of busy life slowly gathered and swelled, until the seething whirl of the city seemed a strange thing in a sleepy land.

Once, they say, even Atlanta slept dull and drowsy at the foot-hills of the Alleghanies, until the iron baptism of war awakened her with its sullen waters, aroused and maddened her, and left her listening to the sea. And the sea cried to the hills and the hills answered the sea, till the city rose like a widow and cast away her weeds, and toiled for her daily bread; toiled steadily, toiled cunningly,—perhaps with some bitterness, with a touch of *réclame*,[1]—and yet with real earnestness, and real sweat.

8. A railroad car on which African Americans were compelled to ride because of segregation laws.

9. John Greenleaf Whittier (1807–1892), anti-slavery poet. The quotation is from "Howard at Atlanta" (1869).

1. Publicity.

It is a hard thing to live haunted by the ghost of an untrue dream; to see the wide vision of empire fade into real ashes and dirt; to feel the pang of the conquered, and yet know that with all the Bad that fell on one black day, something was vanquished that deserved to live, something killed that in justice had not dared to die; to know that with the Right that triumphed, triumphed something of Wrong, something sordid and mean, something less than the broadest and best. All this is bitter hard; and many a man and city and people have found in it excuse for sulking, and brooding, and listless waiting.

Such are not men of the sturdier make; they of Atlanta turned resolutely toward the future; and that future held aloft vistas of purple and gold:—Atlanta, Queen of the cotton kingdom; Atlanta, Gateway to the Land of the Sun; Atlanta, the new Lachesis,[2] spinner of web and woof for the world. So the city crowned her hundred hills with factories, and stored her shops with cunning handiwork, and stretched long iron ways to greet the busy Mercury[3] in his coming. And the Nation talked of her striving.

Perhaps Atlanta was not christened for the winged maiden of dull Bœotia; you know the tale,—how swarthy Atalanta, tall and wild, would marry only him who out-raced her; and how the wily Hippomenes laid three apples of gold in the way. She fled like a shadow, paused, startled over the first apple, but even as he stretched his hand, fled again; hovered over the second, then, slipping from his hot grasp, flew over river, vale, and hill; but as she lingered over the third, his arms fell round her, and looking on each other, the blazing passion of their love profaned the sanctuary of Love, and they were cursed. If Atlanta be not named for Atalanta, she ought to have been.

Atlanta is not the first or the last maiden whom greed of gold has led to defile the temple of Love; and not maids alone, but men in the race of life, sink from the high and generous ideals of youth to the gambler's code of the Bourse,[4] and in all our Nation's striving is not the Gospel of Work befouled by the Gospel of Pay? So common is this that one-half think it normal; so unquestioned, that we almost fear to question if the end of racing is not gold, if the aim of man is not rightly to be rich. And if this is the fault of America, how dire a danger lies before a new land and a new city, lest Atlanta, stooping for mere gold, shall find that gold accursed!

It was no maiden's idle whim that started this hard racing; a fearful wilderness lay about the feet of that city after the War,—feudalism, poverty, the rise of the Third Estate,[5] serfdom, the re-birth of Law and Order, and above and between all, the Veil of Race. How heavy a journey for weary feet! what wings must Atalanta have to flit over all this hollow and hill, through sour wood and sullen water, and by the red waste of sun-baked clay! How fleet must Atalanta be if she will not be tempted by gold to profane the Sanctuary!

The Sanctuary of our fathers has, to be sure, few Gods,—some sneer, "all too few." There is the thrifty Mercury of New England, Pluto of the North, and Ceres of the West; and there, too, is the half-forgotten Apollo of the South, under whose ægis the maiden ran,—and as she ran she forgot him,

2. In Greek mythology, one of the three Fates who preside over the birth, life, and death of humankind.

3. Roman god of trade.

4. The stock exchange.

5. The middle class.

even as there in Bœotia Venus[6] was forgot. She forgot the old ideal of the Southern gentleman,—that new-world heir of the grace and courtliness of patrician,[7] knight, and noble; forgot his honor with his foibles, his kindliness with his carelessness, and stooped to apples of gold,—to men busier and sharper, thriftier and more unscrupulous. Golden apples are beautiful—I remember the lawless days of boyhood, when orchards in crimson and gold tempted me over fence and field—and, too, the merchant who has dethroned the planter is no despicable *parvenu*.[8] Work and wealth are the mighty levers to lift this old new land; thrift and toil and saving are the highways to new hopes and new possibilities; and yet the warning is needed lest the wily Hippomenes tempt Atalanta to thinking that golden apples are the goal of racing, and not mere incidents by the way.

Atlanta must not lead the South to dream of material prosperity as the touchstone of all success; already the fatal might of this idea is beginning to spread; it is replacing the finer type of Southerner with vulgar money-getters; it is burying the sweeter beauties of Southern life beneath pretence and ostentation. For every social ill the panacea of Wealth has been urged,—wealth to overthrow the remains of the slave feudalism; wealth to raise the "cracker"[9] Third Estate; wealth to employ the black serfs, and the prospect of wealth to keep them working; wealth as the end and aim of politics, and as the legal tender for law and order; and, finally, instead of Truth, Beauty, and Goodness, wealth as the ideal of the Public School.

Not only is this true in the world which Atlanta typifies, but it is threatening to be true of a world beneath and beyond that world,—the Black World beyond the Veil. To-day it makes little difference to Atlanta, to the South, what the Negro thinks or dreams or wills. In the soul-life of the land he is to-day, and naturally will long remain, unthought of, half forgotten; and yet when he does come to think and will and do for himself,—and let no man dream that day will never come,—then the part he plays will not be one of sudden learning, but words and thoughts he has been taught to lisp in his race-childhood. To-day the ferment of his striving toward self-realization is to the strife of the white world like a wheel within a wheel: beyond the Veil are smaller but like problems of ideals, of leaders and the led, of serfdom, of poverty, of order and subordination, and, through all, the Veil of Race. Few know of these problems, few who know notice them; and yet there they are, awaiting student, artist, and seer,—a field for somebody sometime to discover. Hither has the temptation of Hippomenes penetrated; already in this smaller world, which now indirectly and anon directly must influence the larger for good or ill, the habit is forming of interpreting the world in dollars. The old leaders of Negro opinion, in the little groups where there is a Negro social consciousness, are being replaced by new; neither the black preacher nor the black teacher leads as he did two decades ago. Into their places are pushing the farmers and gardeners, the well-paid porters and artisans, the businessmen,—all those with property and money. And with all this change, so curiously parallel to that of the Other-world, goes too the same inevitable change in ideals. The South laments to-day the slow, steady disappearance of a certain

6. Roman goddess of love. Pluto is the Roman god of the underworld. Ceres is the Roman goddess of agriculture. Apollo is the Greek god of music and poetry.

7. An aristocrat.

8. A wealthy upstart.

9. A poor white person.

type of Negro,—the faithful, courteous slave of other days, with his incorruptible honesty and dignified humility. He is passing away just as surely as the old type of Southern gentleman is passing, and from not dissimilar causes,—the sudden transformation of a fair far-off ideal of Freedom into the hard reality of bread-winning and the consequent deification of Bread.

In the Black World, the Preacher and Teacher embodied once the ideals of this people,—the strife for another and a juster world, the vague dream of righteousness, the mystery of knowing; but to-day the danger is that these ideals, with their simple beauty and weird inspiration, will suddenly sink to a question of cash and a lust for gold. Here stands this black young Atalanta, girding herself for the race that must be run; and if her eyes be still toward the hills and sky as in the days of old, then we may look for noble running; but what if some ruthless or wily or even thoughtless Hippomenes lay golden apples before her? What if the Negro people be wooed from a strife for righteousness, from a love of knowing, to regard dollars as the be-all and end-all of life? What if to the Mammonism[1] of America be added the rising Mammonism of the re-born South, and the Mammonism of this South be reinforced by the budding Mammonism of its half-awakened black millions? Whither, then, is the new-world quest of Goodness and Beauty and Truth gone glimmering? Must this, and that fair flower of Freedom which, despite the jeers of latter-day striplings, sprung from our fathers' blood, must that too degenerate into a dusty quest of gold,—into lawless lust with Hippomenes?

The hundred hills of Atlanta are not all crowned with factories. On one, toward the west, the setting sun throws three buildings in bold relief against the sky. The beauty of the group lies in its simple unity:—a broad lawn of green rising from the red street with mingled roses and peaches; north and south, two plain and stately halls; and in the midst, half hidden in ivy, a larger building, boldly graceful, sparingly decorated, and with one low spire. It is a restful group,—one never looks for more; it is all here, all intelligible. There I live, and there I hear from day to day the low hum of restful life. In winter's twilight, when the red sun glows, I can see the dark figures pass between the halls to the music of the nightbell. In the morning, when the sun is golden, the clang of the day-bell brings the hurry and laughter of three hundred young hearts from hall and street, and from the busy city below,—children all dark and heavy-haired,—to join their clear young voices in the music of the morning sacrifice. In a half-dozen class-rooms they gather then,—here to follow the love-song of Dido, here to listen to the tale of Troy divine,[2] there to wander among the stars, there to wander among men and nations,—and elsewhere other well-worn ways of knowing this queer world. Nothing new, no time-saving devices,—simply old time-glorified methods of delving for Truth, and searching out the hidden beauties of life, and learning the good of living. The riddle of existence is the college curriculum that was laid before the Pharaohs, that was taught in the groves by Plato, that formed the *trivium* and *quadrivium*,[3] and is to-day laid before the freedmen's sons by Atlanta University. And this course of

1. The worship of riches.
2. That is, Homer's epic *The Iliad*. In Virgil's epic *The Aeneid*, Dido was the queen of Carthage who loved Aeneas and committed suicide when he left her.
3. Together, the seven liberal arts of the Middle Ages (Latin). Plato (ca. 427–348 B.C.E.), Greek philosopher and founder of the Academy in Athens.

study will not change; its methods will grow more deft and effectual, its content richer by toil of scholar and sight of seer; but the true college will ever have one goal,—not to earn meat, but to know the end and aim of that life which meat nourishes.

The vision of life that rises before these dark eyes has in it nothing mean or selfish. Not at Oxford or at Leipsic, not at Yale or Columbia,[4] is there an air of higher resolve or more unfettered striving; the determination to realize for men, both black and white, the broadest possibilities of life, to seek the better and the best, to spread with their own hands the Gospel of Sacrifice,—all this is the burden of their talk and dream. Here, amid a wide desert of caste and proscription, amid the heart-hurting slights and jars and vagaries of a deep race-dislike, lies this green oasis, where hot anger cools, and the bitterness of disappointment is sweetened by the springs and breezes of Parnassus,[5] and here men may lie and listen, and learn of a future fuller than the past, and hear the voice of Time:

"Entbehren sollst du, sollst entbehren."[6]

They made their mistakes, those who planted Fisk and Howard and Atlanta before the smoke of battle had lifted; they made their mistakes, but those mistakes were not the things at which we lately laughed somewhat uproariously. They were right when they sought to found a new educational system upon the University: where, forsooth, shall we ground knowledge save on the broadest and deepest knowledge? The roots of the tree, rather than the leaves, are the sources of its life; and from the dawn of history, from Academus to Cambridge,[7] the culture of the University has been the broad foundation-stone on which is built the kindergarten's A B C.

But these builders did make a mistake in minimizing the gravity of the problem before them; in thinking it a matter of years and decades; in therefore building quickly and laying their foundation carelessly, and lowering the standard of knowing, until they had scattered haphazard through the South some dozen poorly equipped high schools and miscalled them universities. They forgot, too, just as their successors are forgetting, the rule of inequality:—that of the million black youth, some were fitted to know and some to dig; that some had the talent and capacity of university men, and some the talent and capacity of blacksmiths; and that true training meant neither that all should be college men nor all artisans, but that the one should be made a missionary of culture to an untaught people, and the other a free workman among serfs. And to seek to make the blacksmith a scholar is almost as silly as the more modern scheme of making the scholar a blacksmith; almost, but not quite.

The function of the university is not simply to teach bread-winning, or to furnish teachers for the public schools, or to be a centre of polite society; it is, above all, to be the organ of that fine adjustment between real life, and the growing knowledge of life, an adjustment which forms the secret of

4. All world-renowned universities, in England, Germany, Connecticut, and New York, respectively.
5. A mountain in Greece considered the wellspring of poetry and music.
6. Deny yourself, you must deny yourself (German); from Johann Wolfgang von Goethe's *Faust* (1808) I.
7. The site of Cambridge University in England and Harvard University in the United States. Academus is the site of Plato's ancient academy.

civilization. Such an institution the South of to-day sorely needs. She has religion, earnest, bigoted:—religion that on both sides the Veil often omits the sixth, seventh, and eighth commandments,[8] but substitutes a dozen supplementary ones. She has, as Atlanta shows, growing thrift and love of toil; but she lacks that broad knowledge of what the world knows and knew of human living and doing, which she may apply to the thousand problems of real life to-day confronting her. The need of the South is knowledge and culture,—not in dainty limited quantity, as before the war, but in broad busy abundance in the world of work; and until she has this, not all the Apples of Hesperides, be they golden and bejewelled, can save her from the curse of the Bœotian lovers.

The Wings of Atalanta are the coming universities of the South. They alone can bear the maiden past the temptation of golden fruit. They will not guide her flying feet away from the cotton and gold; for—ah, thoughtful Hippomenes!—do not the apples lie in the very Way of Life? But they will guide her over and beyond them, and leave her kneeling in the Sanctuary of Truth and Freedom and broad Humanity, virgin and undefiled. Sadly did the Old South err in human education, despising the education of the masses, and niggardly in the support of colleges. Her ancient university foundations dwindled and withered under the foul breath of slavery; and even since the war they have fought a failing fight for life in the tainted air of social unrest and commercial selfishness, stunted by the death of criticism, and starving for lack of broadly cultured men. And if this is the white South's need and danger, how much heavier the danger and need of the freedmen's sons! how pressing here the need of broad ideals and true culture, the conservation of soul from sordid aims and petty passions! Let us build the Southern university—William and Mary, Trinity, Georgia, Texas, Tulane, Vanderbilt, and the others—fit to live; let us build, too, the Negro universities:—Fisk, whose foundation was ever broad; Howard, at the heart of the Nation; Atlanta at Atlanta, whose ideal of scholarship has been held above the temptation of numbers. Why not here, and perhaps elsewhere, plant deeply and for all time centres of learning and living, colleges that yearly would send into the life of the South a few white men and a few black men of broad culture, catholic tolerance, and trained ability, joining their hands to other hands, and giving to this squabble of the Races a decent and dignified peace?

Patience, Humility, Manners, and Taste, common schools and kindergartens, industrial and technical schools, literature and tolerance,—all these spring from knowledge and culture, the children of the university. So must men and nations build, not otherwise, not upside down.

Teach workers to work,—a wise saying; wise when applied to German boys and American girls; wiser when said of Negro boys, for they have less knowledge of working and none to teach them. Teach thinkers to think,—a needed knowledge in a day of loose and careless logic; and they whose lot is gravest must have the carefulest training to think aright. If these things are so, how foolish to ask what is the best education for one or seven or sixty million souls! shall we teach them trades, or train them in liberal arts? Neither and both: teach the workers to work and the thinkers to think; make carpenters of carpenters, and philosophers of philosophers, and fops of fools. Nor can we pause here. We are training not isolated men but a living

8. The prohibitions against killing, adultery, and theft, respectively, from the Ten Commandments.

group of men,—nay, a group within a group. And the final product of our training must be neither a psychologist nor a brickmason, but a man. And to make men, we must have ideals, broad, pure, and inspiring ends of living,—not sordid money-getting, not apples of gold. The worker must work for the glory of his handiwork, not simply for pay; the thinker must think for truth, not for fame. And all this is gained only by human strife and longing; by ceaseless training and education; by founding Right on righteousness and Truth on the unhampered search for Truth; by founding the common school on the university, and the industrial school on the common school; and weaving thus a system, not a distortion, and bringing a birth, not an abortion.

When night falls on the City of a Hundred Hills, a wind gathers itself from the seas and comes murmuring westward. And at its bidding, the smoke of the drowsy factories sweeps down upon the mighty city and covers it like a pall, while yonder at the University the stars twinkle above Stone Hall. And they say that yon gray mist is the tunic of Atalanta pausing over her golden apples. Fly, my maiden, fly, for yonder comes Hippomenes!

VI. *Of the Training of Black Men*

Why, if the Soul can fling the Dust aside,
And naked on the Air of Heaven ride,
Were 't not a Shame—were 't not a Shame for him
In this clay carcase crippled to abide?

OMAR KHAYYÁM (FITZGERALD)[9]

From the shimmering swirl of waters where many, many thoughts ago the slave-ship first saw the square tower of Jamestown,[1] have flowed down to our day three streams of thinking: one swollen from the larger world here and overseas, saying, the multiplying of human wants in culture-lands calls for the world-wide cooperation of men in satisfying them. Hence arises a new human unity, pulling the ends of earth nearer, and all men, black, yellow, and white. The larger humanity strives to feel in this contact of living Nations and sleeping hordes a thrill of new life in the world, crying, "If the contact of Life and Sleep be Death, shame on such Life." To be sure, behind this thought lurks the afterthought of force and dominion,—the making of brown men to delve when the temptation of beads and red calico cloys.

The second thought streaming from the death-ship and the curving river is the thought of the older South,—the sincere and passionate belief that somewhere between men and cattle, God created a *tertium quid*,[2] and

9. Khayyám (fl. 1000 C.E.), Persian poet. The quotation is from Edward FitzGerald's translation of "The Rubaiyat of Omar Khayyam" (1859).

1. Site of early English settlement in Virginia.
2. A third something (Latin).

called it a Negro,—a clownish, simple creature, at times even lovable within its limitations, but straitly foreordained to walk within the Veil. To be sure, behind the thought lurks the afterthought,—some of them with favoring chance might become men, but in sheer self-defence we dare not let them, and we build about them walls so high, and hang between them and the light a veil so thick, that they shall not even think of breaking through.

And last of all there trickles down that third and darker thought,—the thought of the things themselves, the confused, half-conscious mutter of men who are black and whitened, crying "Liberty, Freedom, Opportunity—vouchsafe[3] to us, O boastful World, the chance of living men!" To be sure, behind the thought lurks the afterthought,—suppose, after all, the World is right and we are less than men? Suppose this mad impulse within is all wrong, some mock mirage from the untrue?

So here we stand among thoughts of human unity, even through conquest and slavery; the inferiority of black men, even if forced by fraud; a shriek in the night for the freedom of men who themselves are not yet sure of their right to demand it. This is the tangle of thought and afterthought wherein we are called to solve the problem of training men for life.

Behind all its curiousness, so attractive alike to sage and *dilettante*,[4] lie its dim dangers, throwing across us shadows at once grotesque and awful. Plain it is to us that what the world seeks through desert and wild we have within our threshold,—a stalwart laboring force, suited to the semi-tropics; if, deaf to the voice of the Zeitgeist,[5] we refuse to use and develop these men, we risk poverty and loss. If, on the other hand, seized by the brutal afterthought, we debauch the race thus caught in our talons, selfishly sucking their blood and brains in the future as in the past, what shall save us from national decadence? Only that saner selfishness, which Education teaches men, can find the rights of all in the whirl of work.

Again, we may decry the color-prejudice of the South, yet it remains a heavy fact. Such curious kinks of the human mind exist and must be reckoned with soberly. They cannot be laughed away, nor always successfully stormed at, nor easily abolished by act of legislature. And yet they must not be encouraged by being let alone. They must be recognized as facts, but unpleasant facts; things that stand in the way of civilization and religion and common decency. They can be met in but one way,—by the breadth and broadening of human reason, by catholicity of taste and culture. And so, too, the native ambition and aspiration of men, even though they be black, backward, and ungraceful, must not lightly be dealt with. To stimulate wildly weak and untrained minds is to play with mighty fires; to flout their striving idly is to welcome a harvest of brutish crime and shameless lethargy in our very laps. The guiding of thought and the deft coördination of deed is at once the path of honor and humanity.

And so, in this great question of reconciling three vast and partially contradictory streams of thought, the one panacea of Education leaps to the lips of all:—such human training as will best use the labor of all men without enslaving or brutalizing; such training as will give us poise to encourage the prejudices that bulwark society, and to stamp out those that in sheer barbarity deafen us to the wail of prisoned souls within the Veil, and the mounting fury of shackled men.

3. Grant.
4. A dabbler in arts or science (French).
5. The spirit of the age (German).

But when we have vaguely said that Education will set this tangle straight, what have we uttered but a truism? Training for life teaches living; but what training for the profitable living together of black men and white? A hundred and fifty years ago our task would have seemed easier. Then Dr. Johnson[6] blandly assured us that education was needful solely for the embellishments of life, and was useless for ordinary vermin. To-day we have climbed to heights where we would open at least the outer courts of knowledge to all, display its treasures to many, and select the few to whom its mystery of Truth is revealed, not wholly by birth or the accidents of the stock market, but at least in part according to deftness and aim, talent and character. This programme, however, we are sorely puzzled in carrying out through that part of the land where the blight of slavery fell hardest, and where we are dealing with two backward peoples. To make here in human education that ever necessary combination of the permanent and the contingent—of the ideal and the practical in workable equilibrium—has been there, as it ever must be in every age and place, a matter of infinite experiment and frequent mistakes.

In rough approximation we may point out four varying decades of work in Southern education since the Civil War. From the close of the war until 1876, was the period of uncertain groping and temporary relief. There were army schools, mission schools, and schools of the Freedman's Bureau in chaotic disarrangement seeking system and cooperation. Then followed ten years of constructive definite effort toward the building of complete school systems in the South. Normal schools and colleges[7] were founded for the freedmen, and teachers trained there to man the public schools. There was the inevitable tendency of war to underestimate the prejudices of the master and the ignorance of the slave, and all seemed clear sailing out of the wreckage of the storm. Meantime, starting in this decade yet especially developing from 1885 to 1895, began the industrial revolution of the South. The land saw glimpses of a new destiny and the stirring of new ideals. The educational system striving to complete itself saw new obstacles and a field of work ever broader and deeper. The Negro colleges, hurriedly founded, were inadequately equipped, illogically distributed, and of varying efficiency and grade; the normal and high schools were doing little more than common-school work, and the common schools were training but a third of the children who ought to be in them, and training these too often poorly. At the same time the white South, by reason of its sudden conversion from the slavery ideal, by so much the more became set and strengthened in its racial prejudice, and crystallized it into harsh law and harsher custom; while the marvellous pushing forward of the poor white daily threatened to take even bread and butter from the mouths of the heavily handicapped sons of the freedmen. In the midst, then, of the larger problem of Negro education sprang up the more practical question of work, the inevitable economic quandary that faces a people in the transition from slavery to freedom, and especially those who make that change amid hate and prejudice, lawlessness and ruthless competition.

The industrial school springing to notice in this decade, but coming to full recognition in the decade beginning with 1895, was the proffered answer to this combined educational and economic crisis, and an answer of

6. Samuel Johnson (1709–1784), English writer and critic.

7. Schools for the training of teachers.

singular wisdom and timeliness. From the very first in nearly all the schools some attention had been given to training in handiwork, but now was this training first raised to a dignity that brought it in direct touch with the South's magnificent industrial development, and given an emphasis which reminded black folk that before the Temple of Knowledge swing the Gates of Toil.

Yet after all they are but gates, and when turning our eyes from the temporary and the contingent in the Negro problem to the broader question of the permanent uplifting and civilization of black men in America, we have a right to inquire, as this enthusiasm for material advancement mounts to its height, if after all the industrial school is the final and sufficient answer in the training of the Negro race; and to ask gently, but in all sincerity, the ever-recurring query of the ages, Is not life more than meat, and the body more than raiment?[8] And men ask this to-day all the more eagerly because of sinister signs in recent educational movements. The tendency is here, born of slavery and quickened to renewed life by the crazy imperialism of the day, to regard human beings as among the material resources of a land to be trained with an eye single to future dividends. Race-prejudices, which keep brown and black men in their "places," we are coming to regard as useful allies with such a theory, no matter how much they may dull the ambition and sicken the hearts of struggling human beings. And above all, we daily hear that an education that encourages aspiration, that sets the loftiest of ideals and seeks as an end culture and character rather than breadwinning, is the privilege of white men and the danger and delusion of black.

Especially has criticism been directed against the former educational efforts to aid the Negro. In the four periods I have mentioned, we find first, boundless, planless enthusiasm and sacrifice; then the preparation of teachers for a vast public-school system; then the launching and expansion of that school system amid increasing difficulties; and finally the training of workmen for the new and growing industries. This development has been sharply ridiculed as a logical anomaly and flat reversal of nature. Soothly[9] we have been told that first industrial and manual training should have taught the Negro to work, then simple schools should have taught him to read and write, and finally, after years, high and normal schools could have completed the system, as intelligence and wealth demanded.

That a system logically so complete was historically impossible, it needs but a little thought to prove. Progress in human affairs is more often a pull than a push, surging forward of the exceptional man, and the lifting of his duller brethren slowly and painfully to his vantage-ground. Thus it was no accident that gave birth to universities centuries before the common schools, that made fair Harvard the first flower of our wilderness. So in the South: the mass of the freedmen at the end of the war lacked the intelligence so necessary to modern workingmen. They must first have the common school to teach them to read, write, and cipher; and they must have higher schools to teach teachers for the common schools. The white teachers who flocked South went to establish such a common-school system. Few held the idea of founding colleges; most of them at first would have laughed at the idea. But they faced, as all men since them have faced, that central paradox of the South,—the social separation of the races. At that time it was the sudden volcanic rupture of nearly all relations between black and white, in work and

8. Matthew 6:25.

9. In truth.

government and family life. Since then a new adjustment of relations in economic and political affairs has grown up,—an adjustment subtle and difficult to grasp, yet singularly ingenious, which leaves still that frightful chasm at the color-line across which men pass at their peril. Thus, then and now, there stand in the South two separate worlds; and separate not simply in the higher realms of social intercourse, but also in church and school, on railway and street-car, in hotels and theatres, in streets and city sections, in books and newspapers, in asylums and jails, in hospitals and graveyards. There is still enough of contact for large economic and group coöperation, but the separation is so thorough and deep that it absolutely precludes for the present between the races anything like that sympathetic and effective group-training and leadership of the one by the other, such as the American Negro and all backward peoples must have for effectual progress.

This the missionaries of '68 soon saw; and if effective industrial and trade schools were impracticable before the establishment of a common-school system, just as certainly no adequate common schools could be founded until there were teachers to teach them. Southern whites would not teach them; Northern whites in sufficient numbers could not be had. If the Negro was to learn, he must teach himself, and the most effective help that could be given him was the establishment of schools to train Negro teachers. This conclusion was slowly but surely reached by every student of the situation until simultaneously, in widely separated regions, without consultation or systematic plan, there arose a series of institutions designed to furnish teachers for the untaught. Above the sneers of critics at the obvious defects of this procedure must ever stand its one crushing rejoinder: in a single generation they put thirty thousand black teachers in the South; they wiped out the illiteracy of the majority of the black people of the land, and they made Tuskegee possible.

Such higher training-schools tended naturally to deepen broader development: at first they were common and grammar schools, then some became high schools. And finally, by 1900, some thirty-four had one year or more of studies of college grade. This development was reached with different degrees of speed in different institutions: Hampton is still a high school, while Fisk University started her college in 1871, and Spelman Seminary[1] about 1896. In all cases the aim was identical,—to maintain the standards of the lower training by giving teachers and leaders the best practicable training; and above all, to furnish the black world with adequate standards of human culture and lofty ideals of life. It was not enough that the teachers of teachers should be trained in technical normal methods; they must also, so far as possible, be broad-minded, cultured men and women, to scatter civilization among a people whose ignorance was not simply of letters, but of life itself.

It can thus be seen that the work of education in the South began with higher institutions of training, which threw off as their foliage common schools, and later industrial schools, and at the same time strove to shoot their roots ever deeper toward college and university training. That this was an inevitable and necessary development, sooner or later, goes without saying; but there has been, and still is, a question in many minds if the natural growth was not forced, and if the higher training was not either overdone or done with cheap and unsound methods. Among white Southerners this

1. A school for Black women founded in 1881 in Atlanta.

feeling is widespread and positive. A prominent Southern journal voiced this in a recent editorial.

"The experiment that has been made to give the colored students classical training has not been satisfactory. Even though many were able to pursue the course, most of them did so in a parrot-like way, learning what was taught, but not seeming to appropriate the truth and import of their instruction, and graduating without sensible aim or valuable occupation for their future. The whole scheme has proved a waste of time, efforts, and the money of the state."

While most fair-minded men would recognize this as extreme and overdrawn, still without doubt many are asking, Are there a sufficient number of Negroes ready for college training to warrant the undertaking? Are not too many students prematurely forced into this work? Does it not have the effect of dissatisfying the young Negro with his environment? And do these graduates succeed in real life? Such natural questions cannot be evaded, nor on the other hand must a Nation naturally skeptical as to Negro ability assume an unfavorable answer without careful inquiry and patient openness to conviction. We must not forget that most Americans answer all queries regarding the Negro *a priori*, and that the least that human courtesy can do is to listen to evidence.

The advocates of the higher education of the Negro would be the last to deny the incompleteness and glaring defects of the present system: too many institutions have attempted to do college work, the work in some cases has not been thoroughly done, and quantity rather than quality has sometimes been sought. But all this can be said of higher education throughout the land; it is the almost inevitable incident of educational growth, and leaves the deeper question of the legitimate demand for the higher training of Negroes untouched. And this latter question can be settled in but one way,—by a first-hand study of the facts. If we leave out of view all institutions which have not actually graduated students from a course higher than that of a New England high school, even though they be called colleges; if then we take the thirty-four remaining institutions, we may clear up many misapprehensions by asking searchingly, What kind of institutions are they? what do they teach? and what sort of men do they graduate?

And first we may say that this type of college, including Atlanta, Fisk, and Howard, Wilberforce and Lincoln, Biddle, Shaw,[2] and the rest, is peculiar, almost unique. Through the shining trees that whisper before me as I write, I catch glimpses of a boulder of New England granite, covering a grave, which graduates of Atlanta University have placed there, with this inscription:

"IN GRATEFUL MEMORY OF THEIR
FORMER TEACHER AND FRIEND
AND OF THE UNSELFISH LIFE HE
LIVED, AND THE NOBLE WORK HE
WROUGHT; THAT THEY, THEIR
CHILDREN, AND THEIR CHIL-
DREN'S CHILDREN MIGHT BE
BLESSED."[3]

2. Colleges for African Americans in, respectively, Georgia (Atlanta) and Tennessee (Fisk); Washington, D.C. (Howard) and Ohio (Wilberforce); Pennsylvania (Lincoln) and North Carolina (Biddle and Shaw).

3. A memorial to Edmund Asa Ware, founder of Atlanta University.

This was the gift of New England to the freed Negro: not alms, but a friend; not cash, but character. It was not and is not money these seething millions want, but love and sympathy, the pulse of hearts beating with red blood;—a gift which to-day only their own kindred and race can bring to the masses, but which once saintly souls brought to their favored children in the crusade of the sixties, that finest thing in American history, and one of the few things untainted by sordid greed and cheap vainglory. The teachers in these institutions came not to keep the Negroes in their place, but to raise them out of the defilement of the places where slavery had wallowed them. The colleges they founded were social settlements; homes where the best of the sons of the freedmen came in close and sympathetic touch with the best traditions of New England. They lived and ate together, studied and worked, hoped and harkened in the dawning light. In actual formal content their curriculum was doubtless old-fashioned, but in educational power it was supreme, for it was the contact of living souls.

From such schools about two thousand Negroes have gone forth with the bachelor's degree. The number in itself is enough to put at rest the argument that too large a proportion of Negroes are receiving higher training. If the ratio to population of all Negro students throughout the land, in both college and secondary training, be counted, Commissioner Harris assures us "it must be increased to five times its present average" to equal the average of the land.

Fifty years ago the ability of Negro students in any appreciable numbers to master a modern college course would have been difficult to prove. Today it is proved by the fact that four hundred Negroes, many of whom have been reported as brilliant students, have received the bachelor's degree from Harvard, Yale, Oberlin, and seventy other leading colleges. Here we have, then, nearly twenty-five hundred Negro graduates, of whom the crucial query must be made, How far did their training fit them for life? It is of course extremely difficult to collect satisfactory data on such a point,—difficult to reach the men, to get trustworthy testimony, and to gauge that testimony by any generally acceptable criterion of success. In 1900, the Conference at Atlanta University undertook to study these graduates, and published the results. First they sought to know what these graduates were doing, and succeeded in getting answers from nearly two-thirds of the living. The direct testimony was in almost all cases corroborated by the reports of the colleges where they graduated, so that in the main the reports were worthy of credence. Fifty-three per cent of these graduates were teachers,—presidents of institutions, heads of normal schools, principals of city school-systems, and the like. Seventeen per cent were clergymen; another seventeen per cent were in the professions, chiefly as physicians. Over six per cent were merchants, farmers, and artisans, and four per cent were in the government civil-service. Granting even that a considerable proportion of the third unheard from are unsuccessful, this is a record of usefulness. Personally I know many hundreds of these graduates, and have corresponded with more than a thousand; through others I have followed carefully the life-work of scores; I have taught some of them and some of the pupils whom they have taught, lived in homes which they have builded, and looked at life through their eyes. Comparing them as a class with my fellow students in New England and in Europe, I cannot hesitate in saying that nowhere have I met men and women with a broader spirit of helpfulness, with deeper devotion to their life-work, or with more consecrated determination to succeed in the face of bitter difficulties than among Negro college-bred men. They have, to be sure, their proportion of ne'er-do-wells, their pedants and lettered fools, but they have a surprisingly small proportion of them; they have not that culture of manner which we instinctively associate with university men, forgetting that in reality it is the heritage from cultured homes, and that no people a generation removed from slavery can escape a certain unpleasant rawness and *gaucherie*,[4] despite the best of training.

With all their larger vision and deeper sensibility, these men have usually been conservative, careful leaders. They have seldom been agitators, have withstood the temptation to head the mob, and have worked steadily and faithfully in a thousand communities in the South. As teachers, they have given the South a commendable system of city schools and large numbers of private normal-schools and academies. Colored college-bred men have worked side by side with white college graduates at Hampton; almost from the beginning the backbone of Tuskegee's teaching force has been formed of graduates from Fisk and Atlanta. And to-day the institute is filled with college graduates, from the energetic wife of the principal down to the teacher of agriculture, including nearly half of the executive council and a majority of the heads of departments. In the professions, college men are slowly but surely leavening the Negro church, are healing and preventing the devastations of disease, and beginning to furnish legal protection for the liberty and property of the toiling masses. All this is needful work. Who would do it if Negroes did not? How could Negroes do it if they were not trained carefully for it? If white people need colleges to furnish teachers, ministers, lawyers, and doctors, do black people need nothing of the sort?

If it is true that there are an appreciable number of Negro youth in the land capable by character and talent to receive that higher training, the end of which is culture, and if the two and a half thousand who have had something of this training in the past have in the main proved themselves useful to their race and generation, the question then comes, What place in the future development of the South ought the Negro college and college-bred man to occupy? That the present social separation and acute race-sensitiveness must eventually yield to the influences of culture, as the South grows civilized, is clear. But such transformation calls for singular wisdom and patience. If, while the healing of this vast sore is progressing, the races are to live for many years side by side, united in economic effort, obeying a common government, sensitive to mutual thought and feeling, yet subtly and silently separate in many matters of deeper human intimacy,—if this unusual and dangerous development is to progress amid peace and order, mutual respect and growing intelligence, it will call for social surgery at once the delicatest and nicest in modern history. It will demand broad-minded, upright men, both white and black, and in its final accomplishment American civilization will triumph. So far as white men are concerned, this fact is to-day being recognized in the South, and a happy renaissance of university education seems imminent. But the very voices that cry hail to this good work are, strange to relate, largely silent or antagonistic to the higher education of the Negro.

Strange to relate! for this is certain, no secure civilization can be built in the South with the Negro as an ignorant, turbulent proletariat. Suppose we

4. Uncouthness (French).

seek to remedy this by making them laborers and nothing more: they are not fools, they have tasted of the Tree of Life, and they will not cease to think, will not cease attempting to read the riddle of the world. By taking away their best equipped teachers and leaders, by slamming the door of opportunity in the faces of their bolder and brighter minds, will you make them satisfied with their lot? or will you not rather transfer their leading from the hands of men taught to think to the hands of untrained demagogues? We ought not to forget that despite the pressure of poverty, and despite the active discouragement and even ridicule of friends, the demand for higher training steadily increases among Negro youth: there were, in the years from 1875 to 1880, 22 Negro graduates from Northern colleges; from 1885 to 1890 there were 43, and from 1895 to 1900, nearly 100 graduates. From Southern Negro colleges there were, in the same three periods, 143, 413, and over 500 graduates. Here, then, is the plain thirst for training; by refusing to give this Talented Tenth the key to knowledge, can any sane man imagine that they will lightly lay aside their yearning and contentedly become hewers of wood and drawers of water?

No. The dangerously clear logic of the Negro's position will more and more loudly assert itself in that day when increasing wealth and more intricate social organization preclude the South from being, as it so largely is, simply an armed camp for intimidating black folk. Such waste of energy cannot be spared if the South is to catch up with civilization. And as the black third of the land grows in thrift and skill, unless skilfully guided in its larger philosophy, it must more and more brood over the red past and the creeping, crooked present, until it grasps a gospel of revolt and revenge and throws its new-found energies athwart the current of advance. Even to-day the masses of the Negroes see all too clearly the anomalies of their position and the moral crookedness of yours. You may marshal strong indictments against them, but their counter-cries, lacking though they be in formal logic, have burning truths within them which you may not wholly ignore, O Southern Gentlemen! If you deplore their presence here, they ask, Who brought us? When you cry, Deliver us from the vision of intermarriage, they answer that legal marriage is infinitely better than systematic concubinage[5] and prostitution. And if in just fury you accuse their vagabonds of violating women, they also in fury quite as just may reply: The wrong which your gentlemen have done against helpless black women in defiance of your own laws is written on the foreheads of two millions of mulattoes, and written in ineffaceable blood. And finally, when you fasten crime upon this race as its peculiar trait, they answer that slavery was the arch-crime, and lynching and lawlessness its twin abortion; that color and race are not crimes, and yet they it is which in this land receives most unceasing condemnation, North, East, South, and West.

I will not say such arguments are wholly justified,—I will not insist that there is no other side to the shield; but I do say that of the nine millions of Negroes in this nation, there is scarcely one out of the cradle to whom these arguments do not daily present themselves in the guise of terrible truth. I insist that the question of the future is how best to keep these millions from brooding over the wrongs of the past and the difficulties of the present, so that all their energies may be bent toward a cheerful striving and

5. Cohabitation without legal marriage.

cooperation with their white neighbors toward a larger, juster, and fuller future. That one wise method of doing this lies in the closer knitting of the Negro to the great industrial possibilities of the South is a great truth. And this the common schools and the manual training and trade schools are working to accomplish. But these alone are not enough. The foundations of knowledge in this race, as in others, must be sunk deep in the college and university if we would build a solid, permanent structure. Internal problems of social advance must inevitably come,—problems of work and wages, of families and homes, of morals and the true valuing of the things of life; and all these and other inevitable problems of civilization the Negro must meet and solve largely for himself, by reason of his isolation; and can there be any possible solution other than by study and thought and an appeal to the rich experience of the past? Is there not, with such a group and in such a crisis, infinitely more danger to be apprehended from half-trained minds and shallow thinking than from over-education and over-refinement? Surely we have wit enough to found a Negro college so manned and equipped as to steer successfully between the *dilettante* and the fool. We shall hardly induce black men to believe that if their stomachs be full, it matters little about their brains. They already dimly perceive that the paths of peace winding between honest toil and dignified manhood call for the guidance of skilled thinkers, the loving, reverent comradeship between the black lowly and the black men emancipated by training and culture.

The function of the Negro college, then, is clear: it must maintain the standards of popular education, it must seek the social regeneration of the Negro, and it must help in the solution of problems of race contact and cooperation. And finally, beyond all this, it must develop men. Above our modern socialism, and out of the worship of the mass, must persist and evolve that higher individualism which the centres of culture protect; there must come a loftier respect for the sovereign human soul that seeks to know itself and the world about it; that seeks a freedom for expansion and self-development; that will love and hate and labor in its own way, untrammeled alike by old and new. Such souls aforetime have inspired and guided worlds, and if we be not wholly bewitched by our Rhine-gold,[6] they shall again. Herein the longing of black men must have respect: the rich and bitter depth of their experience, the unknown treasures of their inner life, the strange rendings of nature they have seen, may give the world new points of view and make their loving, living, and doing precious to all human hearts. And to themselves in these the days that try their souls, the chance to soar in the dim blue air above the smoke is to their finer spirits boon and guerdon[7] for what they lose on earth by being black.

I sit with Shakespeare and he winces not. Across the color line I move arm in arm with Balzac and Dumas, where smiling men and welcoming women glide in gilded halls. From out the caves of evening that swing between the strong-limbed earth and the tracery of the stars, I summon Aristotle and Aurelius[8] and what soul I will, and they come all graciously with no scorn nor condescension. So, wed with Truth, I dwell above the Veil. Is this the life you grudge us, O knightly America? Is this the life you long to change into the dull red hideousness of Georgia? Are you so afraid

6. A reference to Richard Wagner's opera *The Reingold* (1853–54); a mass of pure gold hidden in the Rhine River.

7. A reward.

8. Marcus Aurelius Antoninus (121–180 C.E.), Roman emperor and philosopher. Aristotle (384–322 B.C.E.), Greek philosopher.

lest peering from this high Pisgah, between Philistine and Amalekite,[9] we sight the Promised Land?

* * *

X. *Of the Faith of the Fathers*

Dim face of Beauty haunting all the world,
Fair face of Beauty all too fair to see,
Where the lost stars adown the heavens are hurled,—
There, there alone for thee
May white peace be.

Beauty, sad face of Beauty, Mystery, Wonder,
What are these dreams to foolish babbling men
Who cry with little noises 'neath the thunder
Of Ages ground to sand,
To a little sand.

FIONA MACLEOD[1]

It was out in the country, far from home, far from my foster home, on a dark Sunday night. The road wandered from our rambling log-house up the stony bed of a creek, past wheat and corn, until we could hear dimly across the fields a rhythmic cadence of song,—soft, thrilling, powerful, that swelled and died sorrowfully in our ears. I was a country school-teacher then, fresh from the East, and had never seen a Southern Negro revival. To be sure, we in Berkshire were not perhaps as stiff and formal as they in Suffolk of olden time; yet we were very quiet and subdued, and I know not what would have happened those clear Sabbath mornings had some one punctuated the sermon with a wild scream, or interrupted the long prayer with a loud Amen! And so most striking to me, as I approached the village and the little plain church perched aloft, was the air of intense excitement that possessed that mass of black folk. A sort of suppressed terror hung in the air and seemed to seize us,—a pythian madness,[2] a demoniac possession, that lent terrible reality to song and word. The black and massive form of the preacher swayed and quivered as the words crowded to his lips and flew at us in singular eloquence. The people moaned and fluttered, and then the gaunt-cheeked brown woman beside me suddenly leaped straight into the air and shrieked like a lost soul, while round about came wail and groan and outcry, and a scene of human passion such as I had never conceived before.

Those who have not thus witnessed the frenzy of a Negro revival in the untouched backwoods of the South can but dimly realize the religious feeling of the slave; as described, such scenes appear grotesque and funny, but as seen they are awful. Three things characterized this religion of the slave,—the Preacher, the Music, and the Frenzy. The Preacher is the most

9. Peoples who repeatedly warred with the Israelites for control of Canaan, the Promised Land. Pisgah is a mountain from which Moses could see the Promised Land.

1. Pseudonym of William Sharp (1855–1905), English poet and novelist.

2. A trance in which the priestess Pythia uttered the oracles at Delphi in Greece.

unique personality developed by the Negro on American soil. A leader, a politician, an orator, a "boss," an intriguer, an idealist,—all these he is, and ever, too, the centre of a group of men, now twenty, now a thousand in number. The combination of a certain adroitness with deep-seated earnestness, of tact with consummate ability, gave him his preëminence, and helps him maintain it. The type, of course, varies according to time and place, from the West Indies in the sixteenth century to New England in the nineteenth, and from the Mississippi bottoms to cities like New Orleans or New York.

The Music of Negro religion is that plaintive rhythmic melody, with its touching minor cadences, which, despite caricature and defilement, still remains the most original and beautiful expression of human life and longing yet born on American soil. Sprung from the African forests, where its counterpart can still be heard, it was adapted, changed, and intensified by the tragic soul-life of the slave, until, under the stress of law and whip, it became the one true expression of a people's sorrow, despair, and hope.

Finally the Frenzy or "Shouting," when the Spirit of the Lord passed by, and, seizing the devotee, made him mad with supernatural joy, was the last essential of Negro religion and the one more devoutly believed in than all the rest. It varied in expression from the silent rapt countenance or the low murmur and moan to the mad abandon of physical fervor,—the stamping, shrieking, and shouting, the rushing to and fro and wild waving of arms, the weeping and laughing, the vision and the trance. All this is nothing new in the world, but old as religion, as Delphi and Endor.[3] And so firm a hold did it have on the Negro, that many generations firmly believed that without this visible manifestation of the God there could be no true communion with the Invisible.

These were the characteristics of Negro religious life as developed up to the time of Emancipation. Since under the peculiar circumstances of the black man's environment they were the one expression of his higher life, they are of deep interest to the student of his development, both socially and psychologically. Numerous are the attractive lines of inquiry that here group themselves. What did slavery mean to the African savage? What was his attitude toward the World and Life? What seemed to him good and evil,—God and Devil? Whither went his longings and strivings, and wherefore were his heart-burnings and disappointments? Answers to such questions can come only from a study of Negro religion as a development, through its gradual changes from the heathenism of the Gold Coast to the institutional Negro church of Chicago.

Moreover, the religious growth of millions of men, even though they be slaves, cannot be without potent influence upon their contemporaries. The Methodists and Baptists of America owe much of their condition to the silent but potent influence of their millions of Negro converts. Especially is this noticeable in the South, where theology and religious philosophy are on this account a long way behind the North, and where the religion of the poor whites is a plain copy of Negro thought and methods. The mass of "gospel" hymns which has swept through American churches and well-nigh ruined our sense of song consists largely of debased imitations of Negro melodies made by ears that caught the jingle but not the music, the body

3. In Palestine where King Saul spoke to the dead prophet Samuel via a sorceress's power (1 Samuel 28). Delphi was the site of a shrine to Apollo and the most important oracle in ancient Greece.

but not the soul, of the Jubilee songs.[4] It is thus clear that the study of Negro religion is not only a vital part of the history of the Negro in America, but no uninteresting part of American history.

The Negro church of to-day is the social centre of Negro life in the United States, and the most characteristic expression of African character. Take a typical church in a small Virginian town: it is the "First Baptist"—a roomy brick edifice seating five hundred or more persons, tastefully finished in Georgia pine, with a carpet, a small organ, and stained-glass windows. Underneath is a large assembly room with benches. This building is the central club-house of a community of a thousand or more Negroes. Various organizations meet here,—the church proper, the Sunday-school, two or three insurance societies, women's societies, secret societies, and mass meetings of various kinds. Entertainments, suppers, and lectures are held beside the five or six regular weekly religious services. Considerable sums of money are collected and expended here, employment is found for the idle, strangers are introduced, news is disseminated and charity distributed. At the same time this social, intellectual, and economic centre is a religious centre of great power. Depravity, Sin, Redemption, Heaven, Hell, and Damnation are preached twice a Sunday with much fervor, and revivals take place every year after the crops are laid by; and few indeed of the community have the hardihood to withstand conversion. Back of this more formal religion, the Church often stands as a real conserver of morals, a strengthener of family life, and the final authority on what is Good and Right.

Thus one can see in the Negro church to-day, reproduced in microcosm, all that great world from which the Negro is cut off by color-prejudice and social condition. In the great city churches the same tendency is noticeable and in many respects emphasized. A great church like the Bethel of Philadelphia[5] has over eleven hundred members, an edifice seating fifteen hundred persons and valued at one hundred thousand dollars, an annual budget of five thousand dollars, and a government consisting of a pastor with several assisting local preachers, an executive and legislative board, financial boards and tax collectors; general church meetings for making laws; sub-divided groups led by class leaders, a company of militia, and twenty-four auxiliary societies. The activity of a church like this is immense and far-reaching, and the bishops who preside over these organizations throughout the land are among the most powerful Negro rulers in the world.

Such churches are really governments of men, and consequently a little investigation reveals the curious fact that, in the South, at least, practically every American Negro is a church member. Some, to be sure, are not regularly enrolled, and a few do not habitually attend services; but, practically, a proscribed people must have a social centre, and that centre for this people is the Negro church. The census of 1890 showed nearly twenty-four thousand Negro churches in the country, with a total enrolled membership of over two and a half millions, or ten actual church members to every twenty-eight persons, and in some Southern States one in every two persons. Besides these there is the large number who, while not enrolled as members, attend and take part in many of the activities of the church. There is

4. Southern African American religious folk songs expressing joyful hope.

5. "Mother" Bethel was the founding church of the African Methodist Episcopal denomination in the United States.

an organized Negro church for every sixty black families in the nation, and in some States for every forty families, owning, on an average, a thousand dollars' worth of property each, or nearly twenty-six million dollars in all.

Such, then, is the large development of the Negro church since Emancipation. The question now is, What have been the successive steps of this social history and what are the present tendencies? First, we must realize that no such institution as the Negro church could rear itself without definite historical foundations. These foundations we can find if we remember that the social history of the Negro did not start in America. He was brought from a definite social environment,—the polygamous clan life[6] under the headship of the chief and the potent influence of the priest. His religion was nature-worship, with profound belief in invisible surrounding influences, good and bad, and his worship was through incantation and sacrifice. The first rude change in this life was the slave ship and the West Indian sugar-fields. The plantation organization replaced the clan and tribe, and the white master replaced the chief with far greater and more despotic powers. Forced and long-continued toil became the rule of life, the old ties of blood relationship and kinship disappeared, and instead of the family appeared a new polygamy and polyandry,[7] which, in some cases, almost reached promiscuity. It was a terrific social revolution, and yet some traces were retained of the former group life, and the chief remaining institution was the Priest or Medicineman. He early appeared on the plantation and found his function as the healer of the sick, the interpreter of the Unknown, the comforter of the sorrowing, the supernatural avenger of wrong, and the one who rudely but picturesquely expressed the longing, disappointment, and resentment of a stolen and oppressed people. Thus, as bard, physician, judge, and priest, within the narrow limits allowed by the slave system, rose the Negro preacher, and under him the first Afro-American institution, the Negro church. This church was not at first by any means Christian nor definitely organized; rather it was an adaptation and mingling of heathen rites among the members of each plantation, and roughly designated as Voodooism.[8] Association with the masters, missionary effort and motives of expediency gave these rites an early veneer of Christianity, and after the lapse of many generations the Negro church became Christian.

Two characteristic things must be noticed in regard to this church. First, it became almost entirely Baptist and Methodist in faith; secondly, as a social institution it antedated by many decades the monogamic[9] Negro home. From the very circumstances of its beginning, the church was confined to the plantation, and consisted primarily of a series of disconnected units; although, later on, some freedom of movement was allowed, still this geographical limitation was always important and was one cause of the spread of the decentralized and democratic Baptist faith among the slaves. At the same time, the visible rite of baptism appealed strongly to their mystic temperament. To-day the Baptist Church is still largest in membership among Negroes, and has a million and a half communicants. Next in popu-

6. A society made up of extended family groups that allows men to have more than one wife at the same time.

7. Having more than one husband at the same time.

8. An underground religion combining African spiritualism with Christian symbols, and featuring the casting of spells and charms.

9. Having only one spouse at a time.

larity came the churches organized in connection with the white neighboring churches, chiefly Baptist and Methodist, with a few Episcopalian and others. The Methodists still form the second greatest denomination, with nearly a million members. The faith of these two leading denominations was more suited to the slave church from the prominence they gave to religious feeling and fervor. The Negro membership in other denominations has always been small and relatively unimportant, although the Episcopalians and Presbyterians are gaining among the more intelligent classes to-day, and the Catholic Church is making headway in certain sections. After Emancipation, and still earlier in the North, the Negro churches largely severed such affiliations as they had had with the white churches, either by choice or by compulsion. The Baptist churches became independent, but the Methodists were compelled early to unite for purposes of episcopal government. This gave rise to the great African Methodist Church, the greatest Negro organization in the world, to the Zion Church and the Colored Methodist, and to the black conferences and churches in this and other denominations.

The second fact noted, namely, that the Negro church antedates the Negro home, leads to an explanation of much that is paradoxical in this communistic institution and in the morals of its members. But especially it leads us to regard this institution as peculiarly the expression of the inner ethical life of a people in a sense seldom true elsewhere. Let us turn, then, from the outer physical development of the church to the more important inner ethical life of the people who compose it. The Negro has already been pointed out many times as a religious animal,—a being of that deep emotional nature which turns instinctively toward the supernatural. Endowed with a rich tropical imagination and a keen, delicate appreciation of Nature, the transplanted African lived in a world animate with gods and devils, elves and witches; full of strange influences,—of Good to be implored, of Evil to be propitiated. Slavery, then, was to him the dark triumph of Evil over him. All the hateful powers of the Under-world were striving against him, and a spirit of revolt and revenge filled his heart. He called up all the resources of heathenism to aid,—exorcism and witchcraft, the mysterious Obi worship with its barbarous rites, spells, and blood-sacrifice even, now and then, of human victims. Weird midnight orgies and mystic conjurations were invoked, the witch-woman and the voodoo-priest became the centre of Negro group life, and that vein of vague superstition which characterizes the unlettered Negro even to-day was deepened and strengthened.

In spite, however, of such success as that of the fierce Maroons, the Danish blacks, and others, the spirit of revolt gradually died away under the untiring energy and superior strength of the slave masters. By the middle of the eighteenth century the black slave had sunk, with hushed murmurs, to his place at the bottom of a new economic system, and was unconsciously ripe for a new philosophy of life. Nothing suited his condition then better than the doctrines of passive submission embodied in the newly learned Christianity. Slave masters early realized this, and cheerfully aided religious propaganda within certain bounds. The long system of repression and degradation of the Negro tended to emphasize the elements in his character which made him a valuable chattel: courtesy became humility, moral strength degenerated into submission, and the exquisite native appreciation of the beautiful became an infinite capacity for dumb suffering. The Negro, losing the joy of this world, eagerly seized upon the offered conceptions of the next; the avenging Spirit of the Lord enjoining patience in this world, under sorrow and tribulation until the Great Day when He should lead His dark children home,—this became his comforting dream. His preacher repeated the prophecy, and his bards sang,—

"Children, we all shall be free
When the Lord shall appear!"[1]

This deep religious fatalism, painted so beautifully in "Uncle Tom,"[2] came soon to breed, as all fatalistic faiths will, the sensualist side by side with the martyr. Under the lax moral life of the plantation, where marriage was a farce, laziness a virtue, and property a theft, a religion of resignation and submission degenerated easily, in less strenuous minds, into a philosophy of indulgence and crime. Many of the worst characteristics of the Negro masses of to-day had their seed in this period of the slave's ethical growth. Here it was that the Home was ruined under the very shadow of the Church, white and black; here habits of shiftlessness took root, and sullen hopelessness replaced hopeful strife.

With the beginning of the abolition movement and the gradual growth of a class of free Negroes came a change. We often neglect the influence of the freedman before the war, because of the paucity of his numbers and the small weight he had in the history of the nation. But we must not forget that his chief influence was internal,—was exerted on the black world; and that there he was the ethical and social leader. Huddled as he was in a few centres like Philadelphia, New York, and New Orleans, the masses of the freedmen sank into poverty and listlessness; but not all of them. The free Negro leader early arose and his chief characteristic was intense earnestness and deep feeling on the slavery question. Freedom became to him a real thing and not a dream. His religion became darker and more intense, and into his ethics crept a note of revenge, into his songs a day of reckoning close at hand. The "Coming of the Lord" swept this side of Death, and came to be a thing to be hoped for in this day. Through fugitive slaves and irrepressible discussion this desire for freedom seized the black millions still in bondage, and became their one ideal of life. The black bards caught new notes, and sometimes even dared to sing,—

"O Freedom, O Freedom, O Freedom over me!
Before I'll be a slave
I'll be buried in my grave,
And go home to my Lord
And be free."[3]

For fifty years Negro religion thus transformed itself and identified itself with the dream of Abolition, until that which was a radical fad in the white North and an anarchistic plot in the white South had become a religion to the black world. Thus, when Emancipation finally came, it seemed to the freedman a literal Coming of the Lord. His fervid imagination was stirred as never before, by the tramp of armies, the blood and dust of battle, and

1. From "Children, We Shall All Be Free," an African American spiritual.
2. The pious, long-suffering enslaved hero of *Uncle Tom's Cabin* by Harriet Beecher Stowe (1852).
3. From "O Freedom!," an African American spiritual.

the wail and whirl of social upheaval. He stood dumb and motionless before the whirlwind: what had he to do with it? Was it not the Lord's doing, and marvellous in his eyes? Joyed and bewildered with what came, he stood awaiting new wonders till the inevitable Age of Reaction swept over the nation and brought the crisis of to-day.

It is difficult to explain clearly the present critical stage of Negro religion. First, we must remember that living as the blacks do in close contact with a great modern nation, and sharing, although imperfectly, the soul-life of that nation, they must necessarily be affected more or less directly by all the religious and ethical forces that are to-day moving the United States. These questions and movements are, however, overshadowed and dwarfed by the (to them) all-important question of their civil, political, and economic status. They must perpetually discuss the "Negro Problem,"—must live, move, and have their being in it, and interpret all else in its light or darkness. With this come, too, peculiar problems of their inner life,—of the status of women, the maintenance of Home, the training of children, the accumulation of wealth, and the prevention of crime. All this must mean a time of intense ethical ferment, of religious heart-searching and intellectual unrest. From the double life every American Negro must live, as a Negro and as an American, as swept on by the current of the nineteenth while yet struggling in the eddies of the fifteenth century,—from this must arise a painful self-consciousness, an almost morbid sense of personality and a moral hesitancy which is fatal to self-confidence. The worlds within and without the Veil of Color are changing, and changing rapidly, but not at the same rate, not in the same way; and this must produce a peculiar wrenching of the soul, a peculiar sense of doubt and bewilderment. Such a double life, with double thoughts, double duties, and double social classes, must give rise to double words and double ideals, and tempt the mind to pretence or to revolt, to hypocrisy or to radicalism.

In some such doubtful words and phrases can one perhaps most clearly picture the peculiar ethical paradox that faces the Negro of to-day and is tingeing and changing his religious life. Feeling that his rights and his dearest ideals are being trampled upon, that the public conscience is ever more deaf to his righteous appeal, and that all the reactionary forces of prejudice, greed, and revenge are daily gaining new strength and fresh allies, the Negro faces no enviable dilemma. Conscious of his impotence, and pessimistic, he often becomes bitter and vindictive; and his religion, instead of a worship, is a complaint and a curse, a wail rather than a hope, a sneer rather than a faith. On the other hand, another type of mind, shrewder and keener and more tortuous too, sees in the very strength of the anti-Negro movement its patent weaknesses, and with Jesuitic casuistry[4] is deterred by no ethical considerations in the endeavor to turn this weakness to the black man's strength. Thus we have two great and hardly reconcilable streams of thought and ethical strivings; the danger of the one lies in anarchy, that of the other in hypocrisy. The one type of Negro stands almost ready to curse God and die, and the other is too often found a traitor to right and a coward before force; the one is wedded to ideals remote, whimsical, perhaps impossible of realization; the other forgets that life is more than meat and the body more than raiment. But, after all, is not this

4. Subtle but misleading or false reasoning.

simply the writhing of the age translated into black,—the triumph of the Lie which to-day, with its false culture, faces the hideousness of the anarchist assassin?

To-day the two groups of Negroes, the one in the North, the other in the South, represent these divergent ethical tendencies, the first tending toward radicalism, the other toward hypocritical compromise. It is no idle regret with which the white South mourns the loss of the old-time Negro,—the frank, honest, simple old servant who stood for the earlier religious age of submission and humility. With all his laziness and lack of many elements of true manhood, he was at least open-hearted, faithful, and sincere. To-day he is gone, but who is to blame for his going? Is it not those very persons who mourn for him? Is it not the tendency, born of Reconstruction and Reaction, to found a society on lawlessness and deception, to tamper with the moral fibre of a naturally honest and straightforward people until the whites threaten to become ungovernable tyrants and the blacks criminals and hypocrites? Deception is the natural defence of the weak against the strong, and the South used it for many years against its conquerors; to-day it must be prepared to see its black proletariat turn that same two-edged weapon against itself. And how natural this is! The death of Denmark Vesey and Nat Turner proved long since to the Negro the present hopelessness of physical defence. Political defence is becoming less and less available, and economic defence is still only partially effective. But there is a patent defence at hand,—the defence of deception and flattery, of cajoling and lying. It is the same defence which the Jews of the Middle Age used and which left its stamp on their character for centuries. To-day the young Negro of the South who would succeed cannot be frank and outspoken, honest and self-assertive, but rather he is daily tempted to be silent and wary, politic and sly; he must flatter and be pleasant, endure petty insults with a smile, shut his eyes to wrong; in too many cases he sees positive personal advantage in deception and lying. His real thoughts, his real aspirations, must be guarded in whispers; he must not criticise, he must not complain. Patience, humility, and adroitness must, in these growing black youth, replace impulse, manliness, and courage. With this sacrifice there is an economic opening, and perhaps peace and some prosperity. Without this there is riot, migration, or crime. Nor is this situation peculiar to the Southern United States,—is it not rather the only method by which undeveloped races have gained the right to share modern culture? The price of culture is a Lie.

On the other hand, in the North the tendency is to emphasize the radicalism of the Negro. Driven from his birthright in the South by a situation at which every fibre of his more outspoken and assertive nature revolts, he finds himself in a land where he can scarcely earn a decent living amid the harsh competition and the color discrimination. At the same time, through schools and periodicals, discussions and lectures, he is intellectually quickened and awakened. The soul, long pent up and dwarfed, suddenly expands in new-found freedom. What wonder that every tendency is to excess,—radical complaint, radical remedies, bitter denunciation or angry silence. Some sink, some rise. The criminal and the sensualist leave the church for the gambling-hell and the brothel, and fill the slums of Chicago and Baltimore; the better classes segregate themselves from the group-life of both white and black, and form an aristocracy, cultured but pessimistic, whose bitter criticism stings while it points out no way of escape. They despise the submission and subserviency of the Southern Negroes, but offer no other means by which a poor and oppressed minority can exist side by side with its masters. Feeling deeply and keenly the tendencies and opportunities of the age in which they live, their souls are bitter at the fate which drops the Veil between; and the very fact that this bitterness is natural and justifiable only serves to intensify it and make it more maddening.

Between the two extreme types of ethical attitude which I have thus sought to make clear wavers the mass of the millions of Negroes, North and South; and their religious life and activity partake of this social conflict within their ranks. Their churches are differentiating,—now into groups of cold, fashionable devotees, in no way distinguishable from similar white groups save in color of skin; now into large social and business institutions catering to the desire for information and amusement of their members, warily avoiding unpleasant questions both within and without the black world, and preaching in effect if not in word: *Dum vivimus, vivamus.*[5]

But back of this still broods silently the deep religious feeling of the real Negro heart, the stirring, unguided might of powerful human souls who have lost the guiding star of the past and are seeking in the great night a new religious ideal. Some day the Awakening will come, when the pent-up vigor of ten million souls shall sweep irresistibly toward the Goal, out of the Valley of the Shadow of Death, where all that makes life worth living—Liberty, Justice, and Right—is marked "For White People Only."

XI. Of the Passing of the First-Born

O sister, sister, thy first-begotten,
The hands that cling and the feet that follow,
The voice of the child's blood crying yet,
Who hath remembered me? who hath forgotten?
Thou hast forgotten, O summer swallow,
But the world shall end when I forget.

SWINBURNE[6]

"Unto you a child is born," sang the bit of yellow paper that fluttered into my room one brown October morning. Then the fear of fatherhood mingled wildly with the joy of creation; I wondered how it looked and how it felt,—what were its eyes, and how its hair curled and crumpled itself. And I thought in awe of her,—she who had slept with Death to tear a man-child from underneath her heart, while I was unconsciously wandering. I fled to my wife and child, repeating the while to myself half wonderingly, "Wife and child? Wife and child?"—fled fast and faster than boat and steamcar, and yet must ever impatiently await them; away from the hard-voiced city,

5. While we live, let us live (Latin).
6. Charles Algernon Swinburne (1837–1909), British poet. The quotation is from "Itylus" (1866).

away from the flickering sea into my own Berkshire Hills that sit all sadly guarding the gates of Massachusetts.

Up the stairs I ran to the wan mother and whimpering babe, to the sanctuary on whose altar a life at my bidding had offered itself to win a life, and won. What is this tiny formless thing, this new-born wail from an unknown world,—all head and voice? I handle it curiously, and watch perplexed its winking, breathing, and sneezing. I did not love it then; it seemed a ludicrous thing to love; but her I loved, my girl-mother, she whom now I saw unfolding like the glory of the morning—the transfigured woman.

Through her I came to love the wee thing, as it grew and waxed strong; as its little soul unfolded itself in twitter and cry and half-formed word, and as its eyes caught the gleam and flash of life. How beautiful he was, with his olive-tinted flesh and dark gold ringlets, his eyes of mingled blue and brown, his perfect little limbs, and the soft voluptuous roll which the blood of Africa had moulded into his features! I held him in my arms, after we had sped far away to our Southern home,—held him, and glanced at the hot red soil of Georgia and the breathless city of a hundred hills, and felt a vague unrest. Why was his hair tinted with gold? An evil omen was golden hair in my life. Why had not the brown of his eyes crushed out and killed the blue?—for brown were his father's eyes, and his father's father's. And thus in the Land of the Color-line I saw, as it fell across my baby, the shadow of the Veil.

Within the Veil was he born, said I; and there within shall he live,—a Negro and a Negro's son. Holding in that little head—ah, bitterly!—the unbowed pride of a hunted race, clinging with that tiny dimpled hand—ah, wearily!—to a hope not hopeless but unhopeful, and seeing with those bright wondering eyes that peer into my soul a land whose freedom is to us a mockery and whose liberty a lie. I saw the shadow of the Veil as it passed over my baby, I saw the cold city towering above the blood-red land. I held my face beside his little cheek, showed him the star-children and the twinkling lights as they began to flash, and stilled with an even-song the unvoiced terror of my life.

So sturdy and masterful he grew, so filled with bubbling life so tremulous with the unspoken wisdom of a life but eighteen months distant from the All-life,—we were not far from worshipping this revelation of the divine, my wife and I. Her own life builded and moulded itself upon the child; he tinged her every dream and idealized her every effort. No hands but hers must touch and garnish those little limbs; no dress or frill must touch them that had not wearied her fingers; no voice but hers could coax him off to Dreamland, and she and he together spoke some soft and unknown tongue and in it held communion. I too mused above his little white bed; saw the strength of my own arm stretched onward through the ages through the newer strength of his; saw the dream of my black fathers stagger a step onward in the wild phantasm of the world; heard in his baby voice the voice of the Prophet that was to rise within the Veil.

And so we dreamed and loved and planned by fall and winter, and the full flush of the long Southern spring, till the hot winds rolled from the fetid Gulf, till the roses shivered and the still stern sun quivered its awful light over the hills of Atlanta. And then one night the little feet pattered wearily to the wee white bed, and the tiny hands trembled; and a warm flushed face tossed on the pillow, and we knew baby was sick. Ten days he lay there,—a swift week and three endless days, wasting, wasting away. Cheerily the mother nursed him the first days, and laughed into the little eyes that smiled again. Tenderly then she hovered round him, till the smile fled away and Fear crouched beside the little bed.

Then the day ended not, and night was a dreamless terror, and joy and sleep slipped away. I hear now that Voice at midnight calling me from dull and dreamless trance,—crying, "The Shadow of Death! The Shadow of Death!" Out into the starlight I crept, to rouse the gray physician,—the Shadow of Death, the Shadow of Death. The hours trembled on; the night listened; the ghastly dawn glided like a tired thing across the lamplight. Then we two alone looked upon the child as he turned toward us with great eyes, and stretched his string-like hands,—the Shadow of Death! And we spoke no word, and turned away.

He died at eventide, when the sun lay like a brooding sorrow above the western hills, veiling its face; when the winds spoke not, and the trees, the great green trees he loved, stood motionless. I saw his breath beat quicker and quicker, pause, and then his little soul leapt like a star that travels in the night and left a world of darkness in its train. The day changed not; the same tall trees peeped in at the windows, the same green grass glinted in the setting sun. Only in the chamber of death writhed the world's most piteous thing—a childless mother.

I shirk not. I long for work. I pant for a life full of striving. I am no coward, to shrink before the rugged rush of the storm, nor even quail before the awful shadow of the Veil. But hearken, O Death! Is not this my life hard enough,—is not that dull land that stretches its sneering web about me cold enough,—is not all the world beyond these four little walls pitiless enough, but that thou must needs enter here,—thou, O Death? About my head the thundering storm beat like a heartless voice, and the crazy forest pulsed with the curses of the weak; but what cared I, within my home beside my wife and baby boy? Wast thou so jealous of one little coign of happiness that thou must needs enter there,—thou, O Death?

A perfect life was his, all joy and love, with tears to make it brighter,—sweet as a summer's day beside the Housatonic. The world loved him; the women kissed his curls, the men looked gravely into his wonderful eyes, and the children hovered and fluttered about him. I can see him now, changing like the sky from sparkling laughter to darkening frowns, and then to wondering thoughtfulness as he watched the world. He knew no color-line, poor dear,—and the Veil, though it shadowed him, had not yet darkened half his sun. He loved the white matron, he loved his black nurse; and in his little world walked souls alone, uncolored and unclothed. I—yea, all men—are larger and purer by the infinite breadth of that one little life. She who in simple clearness of vision sees beyond the stars said when he had flown, "He will be happy There; he ever loved beautiful things." And I, far more ignorant, and blind by the web of mine own weaving, sit alone winding words and muttering, "If still he be, and he be There, and there be a There, let him be happy, O Fate!"

Blithe was the morning of his burial, with bird and song and sweet-smelling flowers. The trees whispered to the grass, but the children sat with hushed faces. And yet it seemed a ghostly unreal day,—the wraith of Life. We seemed to rumble down an unknown street behind a little white bundle of posies, with the shadow of a song in our ears. The busy city dinned about us; they did not say much, those pale-faced hurrying men and women; they did not say much,—they only glanced and said, "Niggers!"

We could not lay him in the ground there in Georgia, for the earth there is strangely red; so we bore him away to the northward, with his flowers and his little folded hands. In vain, in vain!—for where, O God! beneath thy broad blue sky shall my dark baby rest in peace,—where Reverence dwells, and Goodness, and a Freedom that is free?

All that day and all that night there sat an awful gladness in my heart,—nay, blame me not if I see the world thus darkly through the Veil,—and my soul whispers ever to me, saying, "Not dead, not dead, but escaped; not bond, but free." No bitter meanness now shall sicken his baby heart till it die a living death, no taunt shall madden his happy boyhood. Fool that I was to think or wish that this little soul should grow choked and deformed within the Veil! I might have known that yonder deep unworldly look that ever and anon floated past his eyes was peering far beyond this narrow Now. In the poise of his little curl-crowned head did there not sit all that wild pride of being which his father had hardly crushed in his own heart? For what, forsooth, shall a Negro want with pride amid the studied humiliations of fifty million fellows? Well sped, my boy, before the world had dubbed your ambition insolence, had held your ideals unattainable, and taught you to cringe and bow. Better far this nameless void that stops my life than a sea of sorrow for you.

Idle words; he might have borne his burden more bravely than we,—aye, and found it lighter too, some day; for surely, surely this is not the end. Surely there shall yet dawn some mighty morning to lift the Veil and set the prisoned free. Not for me,—I shall die in my bonds,—but for fresh young souls who have not known the night and waken to the morning; a morning when men ask of the workman, not "Is he white?" but "Can he work?" When men ask artists, not "Are they black?" but "Do they know?" Some morning this may be, long, long years to come. But now there wails, on that dark shore within the Veil, the same deep voice, *Thou shalt forego!* And all have I foregone at that command, and with small complaint,—all save that fair young form that lies so coldly wed with death in the nest I had builded.

If one must have gone, why not I? Why may I not rest me from this restlessness and sleep from this wide waking? Was not the world's alembic,[7] Time, in his young hands, and is not my time waning? Are there so many workers in the vineyard that the fair promise of this little body could lightly be tossed away? The wretched of my race that line the alleys of the nation sit fatherless and unmothered; but Love sat beside his cradle, and in his ear Wisdom waited to speak. Perhaps now he knows the All-love, and needs not to be wise. Sleep, then, child,—sleep till I sleep and waken to a baby voice and the ceaseless patter of little feet—above the Veil.

7. Something that purifies as if by distillation.

XII. *Of Alexander Crummell*[8]

Then from the Dawn it seemed there came, but faint
As from beyond the limit of the world,
Like the last echo born of a great cry,
Sounds, as if some fair city were one voice
Around a king returning from his wars.[9]

TENNYSON

This is the history of a human heart,—the tale of a black boy who many long years ago began to struggle with life that he might know the world and know himself. Three temptations he met on those dark dunes that lay gray and dismal before the wonder-eyes of the child: the temptation of Hate, that stood out against the red dawn; the temptation of Despair, that darkened noonday; and the temptation of Doubt, that ever steals along with twilight. Above all, you must hear of the vales he crossed,—the Valley of Humiliation and the Valley of the Shadow of Death.

I saw Alexander Crummell first at a Wilberforce commencement season, amid its bustle and crush. Tall, frail, and black he stood, with simple dignity and an unmistakable air of good breeding. I talked with him apart, where the storming of the lusty young orators could not harm us. I spoke to him politely, then curiously, then eagerly, as I began to feel the fineness of his character,—his calm courtesy, the sweetness of his strength, and his fair blending of the hope and truth of life. Instinctively I bowed before this man, as one bows before the prophets of the world. Some seer he seemed, that came not from the crimson Past or the gray To-come, but from the pulsing Now,—that mocking world which seemed to me at once so light and dark, so splendid and sordid. Four-score years had he wandered in this same world of mine, within the Veil.

He was born with the Missouri Compromise and lay adying amid the echoes of Manila and El Caney:[1] stirring times for living, times dark to look back upon, darker to look forward to. The black-faced lad that paused over his mud and marbles seventy years ago saw puzzling vistas as he looked down the world. The slave-ship still groaned across the Atlantic, faint cries burdened the Southern breeze, and the great black father whispered mad tales of cruelty into those young ears. From the low doorway the mother silently watched her boy at play, and at nightfall sought him eagerly lest the shadows bear him away to the land of slaves.

So his young mind worked and winced and shaped curiously a vision of Life; and in the midst of that vision ever stood one dark figure alone,—

8. Clergyman, antislavery activist, and African missionary (1819–1898).

9. From Tennyson's "The Passing of Arthur" in *Idylls of the King* (1869).

1. Sites of U.S. victories in the Philippines and Cuba, respectively, during the Spanish-American War in 1898. "Missouri Compromise": passed by the U.S. Congress in 1820 to keep a balance of free and slave states by allowing Missouri to enter the Union as a slave state.

ever with the hard, thick countenance of that bitter father, and a form that fell in vast and shapeless folds. Thus the temptation of Hate grew and shadowed the growing child,—gliding stealthily into his laughter, fading into his play, and seizing his dreams by day and night with rough, rude turbulence. So the black boy asked of sky and sun and flower the never-answered Why? and loved, as he grew, neither the world nor the world's rough ways.

Strange temptation for a child, you may think; and yet in this wide land to-day a thousand thousand dark children brood before this same temptation, and feel its cold and shuddering arms. For them, perhaps, some one will some day lift the Veil,—will come tenderly and cheerily into those sad little lives and brush the brooding hate away, just as Beriah Green strode in upon the life of Alexander Crummell. And before the bluff, kind-hearted man the shadow seemed less dark. Beriah Green had a school in Oneida County, New York, with a score of mischievous boys. "I'm going to bring a black boy here to educate," said Beriah Green, as only a crank and an abolitionist would have dared to say. "Oho!" laughed the boys. "Ye-es," said his wife; and Alexander came. Once before, the black boy had sought a school, had travelled, cold and hungry, four hundred miles up into free New Hampshire, to Canaan. But the godly farmers hitched ninety yoke of oxen to the abolition schoolhouse and dragged it into the middle of the swamp. The black boy trudged away.

The nineteenth was the first century of human sympathy,—the age when half wonderingly we began to descry in others that transfigured spark of divinity which we call Myself; when clodhoppers and peasants, and tramps and thieves, and millionaires and—sometimes—Negroes, became throbbing souls whose warm pulsing life touched us so nearly that we half gasped with surprise, crying, "Thou too! Hast Thou seen Sorrow and the dull waters of Hopelessness? Hast Thou known Life?" And then all helplessly we peered into those Other-worlds, and wailed, "O World of Worlds, how shall man make you one?"

So in that little Oneida school there came to those schoolboys a revelation of thought and longing beneath one black skin, of which they had not dreamed before. And to the lonely boy came a new dawn of sympathy and inspiration. The shadowy, formless thing—the temptation of Hate, that hovered between him and the world—grew fainter and less sinister. It did not wholly fade away, but diffused itself and lingered thick at the edges. Through it the child now first saw the blue and gold of life,—the sun-swept road that ran 'twixt heaven and earth until in one far-off wan wavering line they met and kissed. A vision of life came to the growing boy,—mystic, wonderful. He raised his head, stretched himself, breathed deep of the fresh new air. Yonder, behind the forests, he heard strange sounds; then glinting through the trees he saw, far, far away, the bronzed hosts of a nation calling,—calling faintly, calling loudly. He heard the hateful clank of their chains, he felt them cringe and grovel, and there rose within him a protest and a prophecy. And he girded himself to walk down the world.

A voice and vision called him to be a priest,—a seer to lead the uncalled out of the house of bondage. He saw the headless host turn toward him like the whirling of mad waters,—he stretched forth his hands eagerly, and then, even as he stretched them, suddenly there swept across the vision the temptation of Despair.

They were not wicked men,—the problem of life is not the problem of the wicked,—they were calm, good men, Bishops of the Apostolic Church of God, and strove toward righteousness. They said slowly, "It is all very natural—it is even commendable; but the General Theological Seminary of the Episcopal Church cannot admit a Negro." And when that thin, half-grotesque figure still haunted their doors, they put their hands kindly, half sorrowfully, on his shoulders, and said, "Now,—of course, we—we know how *you* feel about it; but you see it is impossible,—that is—well—it is premature. Sometime, we trust—sincerely trust—all such distinctions will fade away; but now the world is as it is."

This was the temptation of Despair; and the young man fought it doggedly. Like some grave shadow he flitted by those halls, pleading, arguing, half angrily demanding admittance, until there came the final *No*; until men hustled the disturber away, marked him as foolish, unreasonable, and injudicious, a vain rebel against God's law. And then from that Vision Splendid all the glory faded slowly away, and left an earth gray and stern rolling on beneath a dark despair. Even the kind hands that stretched themselves toward him from out the depths of that dull morning seemed but parts of the purple shadows. He saw them coldly, and asked, "Why should I strive by special grace when the way of the world is closed to me?" All gently yet, the hands urged him on,—the hands of young John Jay,[2] that daring father's daring son; the hands of the good folk of Boston, that free city. And yet, with a way to the priesthood of the Church open at last before him, the cloud lingered there; and even when in old St. Paul's the venerable Bishop raised his white arms above the Negro deacon—even then the burden had not lifted from that heart, for there had passed a glory from the earth.

And yet the fire through which Alexander Crummell went did not burn in vain. Slowly and more soberly he took up again his plan of life. More critically he studied the situation. Deep down below the slavery and servitude of the Negro people he saw their fatal weaknesses, which long years of mistreatment had emphasized. The dearth of strong moral character, of unbending righteousness, he felt, was their great shortcoming, and here he would begin. He would gather the best of his people into some little Episcopal chapel and there lead, teach, and inspire them, till the leaven spread, till the children grew, till the world hearkened, till—till—and then across his dream gleamed some faint after-glow of that first fair vision of youth—only an after-glow, for there had passed a glory from the earth.

One day—it was in 1842, and the springtide was struggling merrily with the May winds of New England—he stood at last in his own chapel in Providence, a priest of the Church. The days sped by, and the dark young clergyman labored; he wrote his sermons carefully; he intoned his prayers with a soft, earnest voice; he haunted the streets and accosted the wayfarers; he visited the sick, and knelt beside the dying. He worked and toiled, week by week, day by day, month by month. And yet month by month the congregation dwindled, week by week the hollow walls echoed more sharply, day by day the calls came fewer and fewer, and day by day the third temptation sat clearer and still more clearly within the Veil; a temptation, as it were, bland and smiling, with just a shade of mockery in its smooth tones. First it came casually, in the cadence of a voice: "Oh, colored folks? Yes." Or perhaps more

2. Antislavery activist and politician (1817–1894), grandson of John Jay, the first Chief Justice of the United States, and son of William Jay, a prominent antislavery and peace activist.

definitely: "What do you *expect*?" In voice and gesture lay the doubt—the temptation of Doubt. How he hated it, and stormed at it furiously! "Of course they are capable," he cried; "of course they can learn and strive and achieve—" and "Of course," added the temptation softly, "they do nothing of the sort." Of all the three temptations, this one struck the deepest. Hate? He had outgrown so childish a thing. Despair? He had steeled his right arm against it, and fought it with the vigor of determination. But to doubt the worth of his lifework,—to doubt the destiny and capability of the race his soul loved because it was his; to find listless squalor instead of eager endeavor; to hear his own lips whispering, "They do not care; they cannot know; they are dumb driven cattle,—why cast your pearls before swine?"—this, this seemed more than man could bear; and he closed the door, and sank upon the steps of the chancel, and cast his robe upon the floor and writhed.

The evening sunbeams had set the dust to dancing in the gloomy chapel when he arose. He folded his vestments, put away the hymn-books, and closed the great Bible. He stepped out into the twilight, looked back upon the narrow little pulpit with a weary smile, and locked the door. Then he walked briskly to the Bishop, and told the Bishop what the Bishop already knew. "I have failed," he said simply. And gaining courage by the confession, he added: "What I need is a larger constituency. There are comparatively few Negroes here, and perhaps they are not of the best. I must go where the field is wider, and try again." So the Bishop sent him to Philadelphia, with a letter to Bishop Onderdonk.

Bishop Onderdonk lived at the head of six white steps,—corpulent, red-faced, and the author of several thrilling tracts on Apostolic Succession.[3] It was after dinner, and the Bishop had settled himself for a pleasant season of contemplation, when the bell must needs ring, and there must burst in upon the Bishop a letter and a thin, ungainly Negro. Bishop Onderdonk read the letter hastily and frowned. Fortunately, his mind was already clear on this point; and he cleared his brow and looked at Crummell. Then he said, slowly and impressively: "I will receive you into this diocese on one condition: no Negro priest can sit in my church convention, and no Negro church must ask for representation there."

I sometimes fancy I can see that tableau: the frail black figure, nervously twitching his hat before the massive abdomen of Bishop Onderdonk; his threadbare coat thrown against the dark woodwork of the book-cases, where Fox's "Lives of the Martyrs" nestled happily beside "The Whole Duty of Man."[4] I seem to see the wide eyes of the Negro wander past the Bishop's broadcloth to where the swinging glass doors of the cabinet glow in the sunlight. A little blue fly is trying to cross the yawning keyhole. He marches briskly up to it, peers into the chasm in a surprised sort of way, and rubs his feelers reflectively; then he essays its depths, and, finding it bottomless, draws back again. The dark-faced priest finds himself wondering if the fly too has faced its Valley of Humiliation, and if it will plunge into it,—when lo! it spreads its tiny wings and buzzes merrily across, leaving the watcher wingless and alone.

3. The Christian doctrine that the religious authority conferred by Jesus on St. Peter extends through an unbroken succession of Apostles, bishops, and popes. "Bishop Onderdonk" (below): Henry Ustick Onderdonk (1789–1858).

4. A Christian devotional book (1658) by an anonymous English author. John Foxe (1516–1578), English clergyman who wrote *Acts and Monuments of These Latter and Perilous Days* (popularly known as *The Book of Martyrs*).

Then the full weight of his burden fell upon him. The rich walls wheeled away, and before him lay the cold rough moor winding on through life, cut in twain by one thick granite ridge,—here, the Valley of Humiliation; yonder, the Valley of the Shadow of Death. And I know not which be darker,—no, not I. But this I know: in yonder Vale of the Humble stand to-day a million swarthy men, who willingly would

> ". . . bear the whips and scorns of time,
> The oppressor's wrong, the proud man's contumely,
> The pangs of despised love, the law's delay,
> The insolence of office, and the spurns
> That patient merit of the unworthy takes,"[5]

all this and more would they bear did they but know that this were sacrifice and not a meaner thing. So surged the thought within that lone black breast. The Bishop cleared his throat suggestively; then, recollecting that there was really nothing to say, considerately said nothing, only sat tapping his foot impatiently. But Alexander Crummell said, slowly and heavily: "I will never enter your diocese on such terms." And saying this, he turned and passed into the Valley of the Shadow of Death. You might have noted only the physical dying, the shattered frame and hacking cough; but in that soul lay deeper death than that. He found a chapel in New York,—the church of his father; he labored for it in poverty and starvation, scorned by his fellow priests. Half in despair, he wandered across the sea, a beggar with outstretched hands. Englishmen clasped them,—Wilberforce and Stanley, Thirwell and Ingles, and even Froude and Macaulay; Sir Benjamin Brodie[6] bade him rest awhile at Queen's College in Cambridge, and there he lingered, struggling for health of body and mind, until he took his degree in '53. Restless still and unsatisfied, he turned toward Africa, and for long years, amid the spawn of the slave-smugglers, sought a new heaven and a new earth.

So the man groped for light; all this was not Life,—it was the world-wandering of a soul in search of itself, the striving of one who vainly sought his place in the world, ever haunted by the shadow of a death that is more than death,—the passing of a soul that has missed its duty. Twenty years he wandered,—twenty years and more; and yet the hard rasping question kept gnawing within him, "What, in God's name, am I on earth for?" In the narrow New York parish his soul seemed cramped and smothered. In the fine old air of the English University he heard the millions wailing over the sea. In the wild fever-cursed swamps of West Africa he stood helpless and alone.

You will not wonder at his weird pilgrimage,—you who in the swift whirl of living, amid its cold paradox and marvellous vision, have fronted life and asked its riddle face to face. And if you find that riddle hard to read, remember that yonder black boy finds it just a little harder; if it is difficult for you to find and face your duty, it is a shade more difficult for him; if your heart sickens in the blood and dust of battle, remember that to him the dust is thicker and the battle fiercer. No wonder the wanderers fall! No wonder we point to thief and murderer, and haunting prostitute, and the never-ending

5. Shakespeare, *Hamlet* 3.1.78–82.

6. Sir Benjamin Collins Brodie (1783–1862), English surgeon. William Wilberforce (1759–1833), English politician and antislavery leader. Arthur Penrhyn Stanley (1815–1881), English Episcopal leader. Connop Thirwall (1797–1875), English Episcopal bishop. James Anthony Froude (1818–1894), English historian. Thomas Babington Macaulay (1800–1859), English historian.

throng of unhearsed dead! The Valley of the Shadow of Death gives few of its pilgrims back to the world.

But Alexander Crummell it gave back. Out of the temptation of Hate, and burned by the fire of Despair, triumphant over Doubt, and steeled by Sacrifice against Humiliation, he turned at last home across the waters, humble and strong, gentle and determined. He bent to all the gibes and prejudices, to all hatred and discrimination, with that rare courtesy which is the armor of pure souls. He fought among his own, the low, the grasping, and the wicked, with that unbending righteousness which is the sword of the just. He never faltered, he seldom complained; he simply worked, inspiring the young, rebuking the old, helping the weak, guiding the strong.

So he grew, and brought within his wide influence all that was best of those who walk within the Veil. They who live without knew not nor dreamed of that full power within, that mighty inspiration which the dull gauze of caste decreed that most men should not know. And now that he is gone, I sweep the Veil away and cry, Lo! the soul to whose dear memory I bring this little tribute. I can see his face still, dark and heavy-lined beneath his snowy hair; lighting and shading, now with inspiration for the future, now in innocent pain at some human wickedness, now with sorrow at some hard memory from the past. The more I met Alexander Crummell, the more I felt how much that world was losing which knew so little of him. In another age he might have sat among the elders of the land in purple-bordered toga;[7] in another country mothers might have sung him to the cradles.

He did his work,—he did it nobly and well; and yet I sorrow that here he worked alone, with so little human sympathy. His name to-day, in this broad land, means little, and comes to fifty million ears laden with no incense of memory or emulation. And herein lies the tragedy of the age: not that men are poor,—all men know something of poverty; not that men are wicked,—who is good? not that men are ignorant,—what is Truth? Nay, but that men know so little of men.

He sat one morning gazing toward the sea. He smiled and said, "The gate is rusty on the hinges." That night at star-rise a wind came moaning out of the west to blow the gate ajar, and then the soul I loved fled like a flame across the Seas, and in its seat sat Death.

I wonder where he is to-day? I wonder if in that dim world beyond, as he came gliding in, there rose on some wan throne a King,—a dark and pierced Jew, who knows the writhings of the earthly damned, saying, as he laid those heart-wrung talents down, "Well done!" while round about the morning stars sat singing.

XIII. Of the Coming of John

What bring they 'neath the midnight,
  Beside the River-sea?
They bring the human heart wherein
  No nightly calm can be;
That droppeth never with the wind,
  Nor drieth with the dew;

7. A robe denoting high office in ancient Rome.

O calm it, God; thy calm is broad
 To cover spirits too.
 The river floweth on.[8]
 MRS. BROWNING

Carlisle street runs westward from the centre of Johnstown, across a great black bridge, down a hill and up again, by little shops and meat-markets, past single-storied homes, until suddenly it stops against a wide green lawn. It is a broad, restful place, with two large buildings outlined against the west. When at evening the winds come swelling from the east, and the great pall of the city's smoke hangs wearily above the valley, then the red west glows like a dreamland down Carlisle Street, and, at the tolling of the supper-bell, throws the passing forms of students in dark silhouette against the sky. Tall and black, they move slowly by, and seem in the sinister light to flit before the city like dim warning ghosts. Perhaps they are; for this is Wells Institute, and these black students have few dealings with the white city below.

And if you will notice, night after night, there is one dark form that ever hurries last and late toward the twinkling lights of Swain Hall,—for Jones is never on time. A long, straggling fellow he is, brown and hard-haired, who seems to be growing straight out of his clothes, and walks with a half-apologetic roll. He used perpetually to set the quiet dining-room into waves of merriment, as he stole to his place after the bell had tapped for prayers; he seemed so perfectly awkward. And yet one glance at his face made one forgive him much,—that broad, good-natured smile in which lay no bit of art or artifice, but seemed just bubbling good-nature and genuine satisfaction with the world.

He came to us from Altamaha, away down there beneath the gnarled oaks of Southeastern Georgia, where the sea croons to the sands and the sands listen till they sink half drowned beneath the waters, rising only here and there in long, low islands. The white folk of Altamaha voted John a good boy,—fine plough-hand, good in the rice-fields, handy everywhere, and always good-natured and respectful. But they shook their heads when his mother wanted to send him off to school. "It'll spoil him,—ruin him," they said; and they talked as though they knew. But full half the black folk followed him proudly to the station, and carried his queer little trunk and many bundles. And there they shook and shook hands, and the girls kissed him shyly and the boys clapped him on the back. So the train came, and he pinched his little sister lovingly, and put his great arms about his mother's neck, and then was away with a puff and a roar into the great yellow world

8. From "A Romance of the Ganges" (1838) by British poet Elizabeth Barrett Browning (1806–1861).

that flamed and flared about the doubtful pilgrim. Up the coast they hurried, past the squares and palmettos of Savannah, through the cotton-fields and through the weary night, to Millville, and came with the morning to the noise and bustle of Johnstown.

And they that stood behind, that morning in Altamaha, and watched the train as it noisily bore playmate and brother and son away to the world, had thereafter one ever-recurring word,—"When John comes." Then what parties were to be, and what speakings in the churches; what new furniture in the front room,—perhaps even a new front room; and there would be a new schoolhouse, with John as teacher; and then perhaps a big wedding; all this and more—when John comes. But the white people shook their heads.

At first he was coming at Christmas-time,—but the vacation proved too short; and then, the next summer,—but times were hard and schooling costly, and so, instead, he worked in Johnstown. And so it drifted to the next summer, and the next,—till playmates scattered, and mother grew gray, and sister went up to the Judge's kitchen to work. And still the legend lingered,—"When John comes."

Up at the Judge's they rather liked this refrain; for they too had a John—a fair-haired, smooth-faced boy, who had played many a long summer's day to its close with his darker name-sake. "Yes, sir! John is at Princeton, sir," said the broad-shouldered gray-haired Judge every morning as he marched down to the post-office. "Showing the Yankees what a Southern gentleman can do," he added; and strode home again with his letters and papers. Up at the great pillared house they lingered long over the Princeton letter,—the Judge and his frail wife, his sister and growing daughters. "It'll make a man of him," said the Judge, "college is the place." And then he asked the shy little waitress, "Well, Jennie, how's your John?" and added reflectively, "Too bad, too bad your mother sent him off,—it will spoil him." And the waitress wondered.

Thus in the far-away Southern village the world lay waiting, half consciously, the coming of two young men, and dreamed in an inarticulate way of new things that would be done and new thoughts that all would think. And yet it was singular that few thought of two Johns,—for the black folk thought of one John, and he was black; and the white folk thought of another John, and he was white. And neither world thought the other world's thought, save with a vague unrest.

Up in Johnstown, at the Institute, we were long puzzled at the case of John Jones. For a long time the clay seemed unfit for any sort of moulding. He was loud and boisterous, always laughing and singing, and never able to work consecutively at anything. He did not know how to study; he had no idea of thoroughness; and with his tardiness, carelessness, and appalling good-humor, we were sore perplexed. One night we sat in faculty-meeting, worried and serious; for Jones was in trouble again. This last escapade was too much, and so we solemnly voted "that Jones, on account of repeated disorder and inattention to work, be suspended for the rest of the term."

It seemed to us that the first time life ever struck Jones as a really serious thing was when the Dean told him he must leave school. He stared at the gray-haired man blankly, with great eyes. "Why,—why," he faltered, "but—I haven't graduated!" Then the Dean slowly and clearly explained, reminding him of the tardiness and the carelessness, of the poor lessons and neglected work, of the noise and disorder, until the fellow hung his head in confusion.

Then he said quickly, "But you won't tell mammy and sister,—you won't write mammy, now will you? For if you won't I'll go out into the city and work, and come back next term and show you something." So the Dean promised faithfully, and John shouldered his little trunk, giving neither word nor look to the giggling boys, and walked down Carlisle Street to the great city, with sober eyes and a set and serious face.

Perhaps we imagined it, but someway it seemed to us that the serious look that crept over his boyish face that afternoon never left it again. When he came back to us he went to work with all his rugged strength. It was a hard struggle, for things did not come easily to him,—few crowding memories of early life and teaching came to help him on his new way; but all the world toward which he strove was of his own building, and he builded slow and hard. As the light dawned lingeringly on his new creations, he sat rapt and silent before the vision, or wandered alone over the green campus peering through and beyond the world of men into a world of thought. And the thoughts at times puzzled him sorely; he could not see just why the circle was not square, and carried it out fifty-six decimal places one midnight,—would have gone further, indeed, had not the matron rapped for lights out. He caught terrible colds lying on his back in the meadows of nights, trying to think out the solar system; he had grave doubts as to the ethics of the Fall of Rome, and strongly suspected the Germans of being thieves and rascals, despite his text-books; he pondered long over every new Greek word, and wondered why this meant that and why it couldn't mean something else, and how it must have felt to think all things in Greek. So he thought and puzzled along for himself,—pausing perplexed where others skipped merrily, and walking steadily through the difficulties where the rest stopped and surrendered.

Thus he grew in body and soul, and with him his clothes seemed to grow and arrange themselves; coat sleeves got longer, cuffs appeared, and collars got less soiled. Now and then his boots shone, and a new dignity crept into his walk. And we who saw daily a new thoughtfulness growing in his eyes began to expect something of this plodding boy. Thus he passed out of the preparatory school into college, and we who watched him felt four more years of change, which almost transformed the tall, grave man who bowed to us commencement morning. He had left his queer thought-world and come back to a world of motion and of men. He looked now for the first time sharply about him, and wondered he had seen so little before. He grew slowly to feel almost for the first time the Veil that lay between him and the white world; he first noticed now the oppression that had not seemed oppression before, differences that erstwhile seemed natural, restraints and slights that in his boyhood days had gone unnoticed or been greeted with a laugh. He felt angry now when men did not call him "Mister," he clenched his hands at the "Jim Crow" cars, and chafed at the color-line that hemmed in him and his. A tinge of sarcasm crept into his speech, and a vague bitterness into his life; and he sat long hours wondering and planning a way around these crooked things. Daily he found himself shrinking from the choked and narrow life of his native town. And yet he always planned to go back to Altamaha,—always planned to work there. Still, more and more as the day approached he hesitated with a nameless dread; and even the day after graduation he seized with eagerness the offer of the Dean to send him North with the quartette during the summer vacation, to sing for the Institute. A breath of air before the plunge, he said to himself in half apology.

It was a bright September afternoon, and the streets of New York were brilliant with moving men. They reminded John of the sea, as he sat in the square and watched them, so changelessly changing, so bright and dark, so grave and gay. He scanned their rich and faultless clothes, the way they carried their hands, the shape of their hats; he peered into the hurrying carriages. Then, leaning back with a sigh, he said, "This is the World." The notion suddenly seized him to see where the world was going; since many of the richer and brighter seemed hurrying all one way. So when a tall, light-haired young man and a little talkative lady came by, he rose half hesitatingly and followed them. Up the street they went, past stores and gay shops, across a broad square, until with a hundred others they entered the high portal of a great building.

He was pushed toward the ticket-office with the others, and felt in his pocket for the new five-dollar bill he had hoarded. There seemed really no time for hesitation, so he drew it bravely out, passed it to the busy clerk, and received simply a ticket but no change. When at last he realized that he had paid five dollars to enter he knew not what, he stood stock-still amazed. "Be careful," said a low voice behind him; "you must not lynch the colored gentleman simply because he's in your way," and a girl looked up roguishly into the eyes of her fair-haired escort. A shade of annoyance passed over the escort's face. "You *will* not understand us at the South," he said half impatiently, as if continuing an argument. "With all your professions, one never sees in the North so cordial and intimate relations between white and black as are everyday occurrences with us. Why, I remember my closest playfellow in boyhood was a little Negro named after me, and surely no two,—*well*!" The man stopped short and flushed to the roots of his hair, for there directly beside his reserved orchestra chairs sat the Negro he had stumbled over in the hallway. He hesitated and grew pale with anger, called the usher and gave him his card, with a few peremptory words, and slowly sat down. The lady deftly changed the subject.

All this John did not see, for he sat in a half-maze minding the scene about him; the delicate beauty of the hall, the faint perfume, the moving myriad of men, the rich clothing and low hum of talking seemed all a part of a world so different from his, so strangely more beautiful than anything he had known, that he sat in dreamland, and started when, after a hush, rose high and clear the music of Lohengrin's swan.[9] The infinite beauty of the wail lingered and swept through every muscle of his frame, and put it all a-tune. He closed his eyes and grasped the elbows of the chair, touching unwittingly the lady's arm. And the lady drew away. A deep longing swelled in all his heart to rise with that clear music out of the dirt and dust of that low life that held him prisoned and befouled. If he could only live up in the free air where birds sang and setting suns had no touch of blood! Who had called him to be the slave and butt of all? And if he had called, what right had he to call when a world like this lay open before men?

Then the movement changed, and fuller, mightier harmony swelled away. He looked thoughtfully across the hall, and wondered why the beautiful gray-haired woman looked so listless, and what the little man could be whispering about. He would not like to be listless and idle, he thought, for he felt with the music the movement of power within him. If he but had

9. The guide for the hero of Richard Wagner's opera *Lohengrin* (1850).

some master-work, some life-service, hard,—aye, bitter hard, but without the cringing and sickening servility, without the cruel hurt that hardened his heart and soul. When at last a soft sorrow crept across the violins, there came to him the vision of a far-off home,—the great eyes of his sister, and the dark drawn face of his mother. And his heart sank below the waters, even as the sea-sand sinks by the shores of Altamaha, only to be lifted aloft again with that last ethereal wail of the swan that quivered and faded away into the sky.

It left John sitting so silent and rapt that he did not for some time notice the usher tapping him lightly on the shoulder and saying politely, "Will you step this way, please, sir?" A little surprised, he arose quickly at the last tap, and, turning to leave his seat, looked full into the face of the fair-haired young man. For the first time the young man recognized his dark boyhood playmate, and John knew that it was the Judge's son. The white John started, lifted his hand, and then froze into his chair; the black John smiled lightly, then grimly, and followed the usher down the aisle. The manager was sorry, very, very sorry,—but he explained that some mistake had been made in selling the gentleman a seat already disposed of; he would refund the money, of course,—and indeed felt the matter keenly, and so forth, and—before he had finished John was gone, walking hurriedly across the square and down the broad streets, and as he passed the park he buttoned his coat and said, "John Jones, you're a natural-born fool." Then he went to his lodgings and wrote a letter, and tore it up; he wrote another, and threw it in the fire. Then he seized a scrap of paper and wrote: "Dear Mother and Sister—I am coming—John."

"Perhaps," said John, as he settled himself on the train, "perhaps I am to blame myself in struggling against my manifest destiny simply because it looks hard and unpleasant. Here is my duty to Altamaha plain before me; perhaps they'll let me help settle the Negro problems there,—perhaps they won't. 'I will go in to the King, which is not according to the law; and if I perish, I perish.'"[1] And then he mused and dreamed, and planned a life-work; and the train flew south.

Down in Altamaha, after seven long years, all the world knew John was coming. The homes were scrubbed and scoured,—above all, one; the gardens and yards had an unwonted trimness, and Jennie bought a new gingham. With some finesse and negotiation, all the dark Methodists and Presbyterians were induced to join in a monster welcome at the Baptist Church; and as the day drew near, warm discussions arose on every corner as to the exact extent and nature of John's accomplishments. It was noontide on a gray and cloudy day when he came. The black town flocked to the depot, with a little of the white at the edges,—a happy throng, with "Good-mawnings" and "Howdys" and laughing and joking and jostling. Mother sat yonder in the window watching; but sister Jennie stood on the platform, nervously fingering her dress,—tall and lithe, with soft brown skin and loving eyes peering from out a tangled wilderness of hair. John rose gloomily as the train stopped, for he was thinking of the "Jim Crow" car; he stepped to the platform, and paused: a little dingy station, a black crowd gaudy and dirty, a half-mile of dilapidated shanties along a straggling ditch of mud. An overwhelming sense of the sordidness and narrowness of it all seized him; he looked in vain for his mother, kissed coldly the tall, strange girl who

1. Esther 4:16.

called him brother, spoke a short, dry word here and there; then, lingering neither for hand-shaking nor gossip, started silently up the street, raising his hat merely to the last eager old aunty, to her open-mouthed astonishment. The people were distinctly bewildered. This silent, cold man,—was this John? Where was his smile and hearty handgrasp? "'Peared kind o' down in the mouf," said the Methodist preacher thoughtfully. "Seemed monstus stuck up," complained a Baptist sister. But the white postmaster from the edge of the crowd expressed the opinion of his folks plainly. "That damn Nigger," said he, as he shouldered the mail and arranged his tobacco, "has gone North and got plum full o' fool notions; but they won't work in Altamaha." And the crowd melted away.

The meeting of welcome at the Baptist Church was a failure. Rain spoiled the barbecue, and thunder turned the milk in the ice-cream. When the speaking came at night, the house was crowded to overflowing. The three preachers had especially prepared themselves, but somehow John's manner seemed to throw a blanket over everything,—he seemed so cold and preoccupied, and had so strange an air of restraint that the Methodist brother could not warm up to his theme and elicited not a single "Amen"; the Presbyterian prayer was but feebly responded to, and even the Baptist preacher, though he wakened faint enthusiasm, got so mixed up in his favorite sentence that he had to close it by stopping fully fifteen minutes sooner than he meant. The people moved uneasily in their seats as John rose to reply. He spoke slowly and methodically. The age, he said, demanded new ideas; we were far different from those men of the seventeenth and eighteenth centuries,—with broader ideas of human brotherhood and destiny. Then he spoke of the rise of charity and popular education, and particularly of the spread of wealth and work. The question was, then, he added reflectively, looking at the low discolored ceiling, what part the Negroes of this land would take in the striving of the new century. He sketched in vague outline the new Industrial School that might rise among these pines, he spoke in detail of the charitable and philanthropic work that might be organized, of money that might be saved for banks and business. Finally he urged unity, and deprecated especially religious and denominational bickering. "To-day," he said, with a smile, "the world cares little whether a man be Baptist or Methodist, or indeed a churchman at all, so long as he is good and true. What difference does it make whether a man be baptized in river or wash-bowl, or not at all? Let's leave all that littleness, and look higher." Then, thinking of nothing else, he slowly sat down. A painful hush seized that crowded mass. Little had they understood of what he said, for he spoke an unknown tongue, save the last word about baptism; that they knew, and they sat very still while the clock ticked. Then at last a low suppressed snarl came from the Amen corner, and an old bent man arose, walked over the seats, and climbed straight up into the pulpit. He was wrinkled and black, with scant gray and tufted hair; his voice and hands shook as with palsy; but on his face lay the intense rapt look of the religious fanatic. He seized the Bible with his rough, huge hands; twice he raised it inarticulate, and then fairly burst into the words, with rude and awful eloquence. He quivered, swayed, and bent; then rose aloft in perfect majesty, till the people moaned and wept, wailed and shouted, and a wild shrieking arose from the corners where all the pent-up feeling of the hour gathered itself and rushed into the air. John never knew clearly what the old man said; he only felt himself held up to scorn and scathing denunciation for trampling on the true Religion, and he realized with amazement that all unknowingly he had put rough, rude hands on something this little world held sacred. He arose silently, and passed out into the night. Down toward the sea he went, in the fitful starlight, half conscious of the girl who followed timidly after him. When at last he stood upon the bluff, he turned to his little sister and looked upon her sorrowfully, remembering with sudden pain how little thought he had given her. He put his arm about her and let her passion of tears spend itself on his shoulder.

Long they stood together, peering over the gray unresting water.

"John," she said, "does it make every one—unhappy when they study and learn lots of things?"

He paused and smiled. "I am afraid it does," he said.

"And, John, are you glad you studied?"

"Yes," came the answer, slowly but positively.

She watched the flickering lights upon the sea, and said thoughtfully, "I wish I was unhappy,—and—and," putting both arms about his neck, "I think I am, a little, John."

It was several days later that John walked up to the Judge's house to ask for the privilege of teaching the Negro school. The Judge himself met him at the front door, stared a little hard at him, and said brusquely, "Go 'round to the kitchen door, John, and wait." Sitting on the kitchen steps, John stared at the corn, thoroughly perplexed. What on earth had come over him? Every step he made offended some one. He had come to save his people, and before he left the depot he had hurt them. He sought to teach them at the church, and had outraged their deepest feelings. He had schooled himself to be respectful to the Judge, and then blundered into his front door. And all the time he had meant right,—and yet, and yet, somehow he found it so hard and strange to fit his old surroundings again, to find his place in the world about him. He could not remember that he used to have any difficulty in the past, when life was glad and gay. The world seemed smooth and easy then. Perhaps,—but his sister came to the kitchen door just then and said the Judge awaited him.

The Judge sat in the dining-room amid his morning's mail, and he did not ask John to sit down. He plunged squarely into the business. "You've come for the school, I suppose. Well, John, I want to speak to you plainly. You know I'm a friend to your people. I've helped you and your family, and would have done more if you hadn't got the notion of going off. Now I like the colored people, and sympathize with all their reasonable aspirations; but you and I both know, John, that in this country the Negro must remain subordinate, and can never expect to be the equal of white men. In their place, your people can be honest and respectful; and God knows, I'll do what I can to help them. But when they want to reverse nature, and rule white men, and marry white women, and sit in my parlor, then, by God! we'll hold them under if we have to lynch every Nigger in the land. Now, John, the question is, are you, with your education and Northern notions, going to accept the situation and teach the darkies to be faithful servants and laborers as your fathers were,—I knew your father, John, he belonged to my brother, and he was a good Nigger. Well—well, are you going to be like him, or are you going to try to put fool ideas of rising and equality into these folks' heads, and make them discontented and unhappy?"

"I am going to accept the situation, Judge Henderson," answered John, with a brevity that did not escape the keen old man. He hesitated a moment, and then said shortly, "Very well,—we'll try you awhile. Good-morning."

It was a full month after the opening of the Negro school that the other John came home, tall, gay, and headstrong. The mother wept, the sisters sang. The whole white town was glad. A proud man was the Judge, and it was a goodly sight to see the two swinging down Main Street together. And yet all did not go smoothly between them, for the younger man could not and did not veil his contempt for the little town, and plainly had his heart set on New York. Now the one cherished ambition of the Judge was to see his son mayor of Altamaha, representative to the legislature, and—who could say?—governor of Georgia. So the argument often waxed hot between them. "Good heavens, father," the younger man would say after dinner, as he lighted a cigar and stood by the fireplace, "you surely don't expect a young fellow like me to settle down permanently in this—this God-forgotten town with nothing but mud and Negroes?" "*I* did," the Judge would answer laconically; and on this particular day it seemed from the gathering scowl that he was about to add something more emphatic, but neighbors had already begun to drop in to admire his son, and the conversation drifted.

"Heah that John is livenin' things up at the darky school," volunteered the postmaster, after a pause.

"What now?" asked the Judge, sharply.

"Oh, nothin' in particulah,—just his almighty air and uppish ways. B'lieve I did heah somethin' about his givin' talks on the French Revolution, equality, and such like. He's what I call a dangerous Nigger."

"Have you heard him say anything out of the way?"

"Why, no,—but Sally, our girl, told my wife a lot of rot. Then, too, I don't need to heah: a Nigger what won't say 'sir' to a white man, or—"

"Who is this John?" interrupted the son.

"Why, it's little black John, Peggy's son,—your old playfellow."

The young man's face flushed angrily, and then he laughed.

"Oh," said he, "it's the darky that tried to force himself into a seat beside the lady I was escorting—"

But Judge Henderson waited to hear no more. He had been nettled all day, and now at this he rose with a half-smothered oath, took his hat and cane, and walked straight to the schoolhouse.

For John, it had been a long, hard pull to get things started in the rickety old shanty that sheltered his school. The Negroes were rent into factions for and against him, the parents were careless, the children irregular and dirty, and books, pencils, and slates largely missing. Nevertheless, he struggled hopefully on, and seemed to see at last some glimmering of dawn. The attendance was larger and the children were a shade cleaner this week. Even the booby class in reading showed a little comforting progress. So John settled himself with renewed patience this afternoon.

"Now, Mandy," he said cheerfully, "that's better; but you mustn't chop your words up so: 'If—the—man—goes.' Why, your little brother even wouldn't tell a story that way, now would he?"

"Naw, suh, he cain't talk."

"All right; now let's try again: 'If the man—'"

"John!"

The whole school started in surprise, and the teacher half arose, as the red, angry face of the Judge appeared in the open doorway.

"John, this school is closed. You children can go home and get to work. The white people of Altamaha are not spending their money on black folks to have their heads crammed with impudence and lies. Clear out! I'll lock the door myself."

Up at the great pillared house the tall young son wandered aimlessly about after his father's abrupt departure. In the house there was little to interest him; the books were old and stale, the local newspaper flat, and the women had retired with headaches and sewing. He tried a nap, but it was too warm. So he sauntered out into the fields, complaining disconsolately, "Good Lord! how long will this imprisonment last!" He was not a bad fellow,—just a little spoiled and self-indulgent, and as headstrong as his proud father. He seemed a young man pleasant to look upon, as he sat on the great black stump at the edge of the pines idly swinging his legs and smoking. "Why, there isn't even a girl worth getting up a respectable flirtation with," he growled. Just then his eye caught a tall, willowy figure hurrying toward him on the narrow path. He looked with interest at first, and then burst into a laugh as he said, "Well, I declare, if it isn't Jennie, the little brown kitchen-maid! Why, I never noticed before what a trim little body she is. Hello, Jennie! Why, you haven't kissed me since I came home," he said gaily. The young girl stared at him in surprise and confusion,—faltered something inarticulate, and attempted to pass. But a wilful mood had seized the young idler, and he caught at her arm. Frightened, she slipped by; and half mischievously he turned and ran after her through the tall pines.

Yonder, toward the sea, at the end of the path, came John slowly, with his head down. He had turned wearily homeward from the schoolhouse; then, thinking to shield his mother from the blow, started to meet his sister as she came from work and break the news of his dismissal to her. "I'll go away," he said slowly; "I'll go away and find work, and send for them. I cannot live here longer." And then the fierce, buried anger surged up into his throat. He waved his arms and hurried wildly up the path.

The great brown sea lay silent. The air scarce breathed. The dying day bathed the twisted oaks and mighty pines in black and gold. There came from the wind no warning, not a whisper from the cloudless sky. There was only a black man hurrying on with an ache in his heart, seeing neither sun nor sea, but starting as from a dream at the frightened cry that woke the pines, to see his dark sister struggling in the arms of a tall and fair-haired man.

He said not a word, but, seizing a fallen limb, struck him with all the pent-up hatred of his great black arm; and the body lay white and still beneath the pines, all bathed in sunshine and in blood. John looked at it dreamily, then walked back to the house briskly, and said in a soft voice, "Mammy, I'm going away,—I'm going to be free."

She gazed at him dimly and faltered, "No'th, honey, is yo' gwine No'th agin?"

He looked out where the North Star glistened pale above the waters, and said, "Yes, mammy, I'm going—North."

Then, without another word, he went out into the narrow lane, up by the straight pines, to the same winding path, and seated himself on the great black stump, looking at the blood where the body had lain. Yonder in the gray past he had played with that dead boy, romping together under the solemn trees. The night deepened; he thought of the boys at Johnstown. He wondered how Brown had turned out, and Carey? And Jones,—Jones? Why, *he* was Jones, and he wondered what they would all say when they knew, when they knew, in that great long dining-room with its hundreds of merry eyes. Then as the sheen of the starlight stole over him, he thought of the gilded ceiling of that vast concert hall, and heard stealing toward him the faint sweet music of the swan. Hark! was it music, or the hurry and shouting of men? Yes, surely! Clear and high the faint sweet melody rose and fluttered like a living thing, so that the very earth trembled as with the tramp of horses and murmur of angry men.

He leaned back and smiled toward the sea, whence rose the strange melody, away from the dark shadows where lay the noise of horses galloping, galloping on. With an effort he roused himself, bent forward, and looked steadily down the pathway, softly humming the "Song of the Bride,"—

"Freudig geführt, ziehet dahin."[2]

Amid the trees in the dim morning twilight he watched their shadows dancing and heard their horses thundering toward him, until at last they came sweeping like a storm, and he saw in front that haggard white-haired man, whose eyes flashed red with fury. Oh, how he pitied him,—pitied him,—and wondered if he had the coiling twisted rope. Then, as the storm burst round him, he rose slowly to his feet and turned his closed eyes toward the Sea.

And the world whistled in his ears.

XIV. The Sorrow Songs

I walk through the churchyard
    To lay this body down;
I know moon-rise, I know star-rise;
I walk in the moonlight, I walk in the starlight;
I'll lie in the grave and stretch out my arms,
I'll go to judgment in the evening of the day,
And my soul and thy soul shall meet that day,
    When I lay this body down.[3]

NEGRO SONG

They that walked in darkness sang songs in the olden days—Sorrow Songs—for they were weary at heart. And so before each thought that I have written in this book I have set a phrase, a haunting echo of these weird old songs in which the soul of the black slave spoke to men. Ever since I was a child these songs have stirred me strangely. They came out of the South unknown to me, one by one, and yet at once I knew them as of me and of mine. Then in after years when I came to Nashville I saw the great temple builded of these songs towering over the pale city. To me Jubilee Hall[4] seemed ever made of the songs themselves, and its bricks were red

2. Joyfully led, enter within (German); an adaptation of the opening line of the "Wedding March" in Wagner's *Lohengrin*.
3. From "Lay This Body Down," an African American spiritual.
4. The central building on the Fisk University campus.

with the blood and dust of toil. Out of them rose for me morning, noon, and night, bursts of wonderful melody, full of the voices of my brothers and sisters, full of the voices of the past.

Little of beauty has America given the world save the rude grandeur God himself stamped on her bosom; the human spirit in this new world has expressed itself in vigor and ingenuity rather than in beauty. And so by fateful chance the Negro folk-song—the rhythmic cry of the slave—stands today not simply as the sole American music, but as the most beautiful expression of human experience born this side the seas. It has been neglected, it has been, and is, half despised, and above all it has been persistently mistaken and misunderstood; but notwithstanding, it still remains as the singular spiritual heritage of the nation and the greatest gift of the Negro people.

Away back in the thirties the melody of these slave songs stirred the nation, but the songs were soon half forgotten. Some, like "Near the lake where drooped the willow," passed into current airs and their source was forgotten; others were caricatured on the "minstrel" stage and their memory died away. Then in war-time came the singular Port Royal experiment after the capture of Hilton Head, and perhaps for the first time the North met the Southern slave face to face and heart to heart with no third witness. The Sea Islands of the Carolinas, where they met, were filled with a black folk of primitive type, touched and moulded less by the world about them than any others outside the Black Belt. Their appearance was uncouth, their language funny, but their hearts were human and their singing stirred men with a mighty power. Thomas Wentworth Higginson hastened to tell of these songs, and Miss McKim[5] and others urged upon the world their rare beauty. But the world listened only half credulously until the Fisk Jubilee Singers[6] sang the slave songs so deeply into the world's heart that it can never wholly forget them again.

There was once a blacksmith's son born at Cadiz, New York, who in the changes of time taught school in Ohio and helped defend Cincinnati from Kirby Smith.[7] Then he fought at Chancellorsville and Gettysburg and finally served in the Freedman's Bureau at Nashville. Here he formed a Sunday-school class of black children in 1866, and sang with them and taught them to sing. And then they taught him to sing, and when once the glory of the Jubilee songs passed into the soul of George L. White,[8] he knew his life-work was to let those Negroes sing to the world as they had sung to him. So in 1871 the pilgrimage of the Fisk Jubilee Singers began. North to Cincinnati they rode,—four half-clothed black boys and five girl-women,—led by a man with a cause and a purpose. They stopped at Wilberforce, the oldest of Negro schools, where a black bishop blessed them. Then they went, fighting cold and starvation, shut out of hotels, and cheerfully sneered at, ever northward; and ever the magic of their song kept thrilling hearts, until a burst of applause in the Congregational Council at Oberlin revealed them to the world. They came to New York and Henry Ward Beecher[9] dared to welcome them, even though the metropolitan dailies sneered at his "Nigger Minstrels." So their songs conquered till they sang across the land

5. Lucy McKim Garrison, co-editor of *Slave Songs of the United States* (1867). Higginson (1823–1911), commander of the first Black regiment in the Civil War and early commentator on spirituals.

6. A traveling singing troupe founded in 1871 to raise funds for Fisk University.

7. Confederate general who laid siege to Cincinnati in 1862.

8. Creator and leader of the Fisk Jubilee Singers (1838–1895).

9. Clergyman and antislavery crusader (1813–1887), brother of Harriet Beecher Stowe (author of *Uncle Tom's Cabin*).

and across the sea, before Queen and Kaiser, in Scotland and Ireland, Holland and Switzerland. Seven years they sang, and brought back a hundred and fifty thousand dollars to found Fisk University.

Since their day they have been imitated—sometimes well, by the singers of Hampton and Atlanta, sometimes ill, by straggling quartettes. Caricature has sought again to spoil the quaint beauty of the music, and has filled the air with many debased melodies which vulgar ears scarce know from the real. But the true Negro folk-song still lives in the hearts of those who have heard them truly sung and in the hearts of the Negro people.

What are these songs, and what do they mean? I know little of music and can say nothing in technical phrase, but I know something of men, and knowing them, I know that these songs are the articulate message of the slave to the world. They tell us in these eager days that life was joyous to the black slave, careless and happy. I can easily believe this of some, of many. But not all the past South, though it rose from the dead, can gainsay the heart-touching witness of these songs. They are the music of an unhappy people, of the children of disappointment; they tell of death and suffering and unvoiced longing toward a truer world, of misty wanderings and hidden ways.

The songs are indeed the siftings of centuries; the music is far more ancient than the words, and in it we can trace here and there signs of development. My grandfather's grandmother was seized by an evil Dutch trader two centuries ago; and coming to the valleys of the Hudson and Housatonic,[1] black, little, and lithe, she shivered and shrank in the harsh north winds, looked longingly at the hills, and often crooned a heathen melody to the child between her knees, thus:

The child sang it to his children and they to their children's children, and so two hundred years it has travelled down to us and we sing it to our children, knowing as little as our fathers what its words may mean, but knowing well the meaning of its music.

This was primitive African music; it may be seen in larger form in the strange chant which heralds "The Coming of John":

"You may bury me in the East,
You may bury me in the West,
But I'll hear the trumpet sound in that morning,"

—the voice of exile.

Ten master songs, more or less, one may pluck from this forest of melody—songs of undoubted Negro origin and wide popular currency, and

1. Rivers in New England.

songs peculiarly characteristic of the slave. One of these I have just mentioned. Another whose strains begin this book is "Nobody knows the trouble I've seen." When, struck with a sudden poverty, the United States refused to fulfil its promises of land to the freedmen, a brigadier-general went down to the Sea Islands to carry the news. An old woman on the outskirts of the throng began singing this song; all the mass joined with her, swaying. And the soldier wept.

The third song is the cradle-song of death which all men know,—"Swing low, sweet chariot,"—whose bars begin the life story of "Alexander Crummell." Then there is the song of many waters, "Roll, Jordan, roll," a mighty chorus with minor cadences. There were many songs of the fugitive like that which opens "The Wings of Atalanta," and the more familiar "Been a-listening." The seventh is the song of the End and the Beginning—"My Lord, what a mourning! when the stars begin to fall"; a strain of this is placed before "The Dawn of Freedom." The song of groping—"My way's cloudy"—begins "The Meaning of Progress"; the ninth is the song of this chapter—"Wrestlin' Jacob, the day is a-breaking,"—a pæan of hopeful strife. The last master song is the song of songs—"Steal away,"—sprung from "The Faith of the Fathers."

There are many others of the Negro folk-songs as striking and characteristic as these, as, for instance, the three strains in the third, eighth, and ninth chapters; and others I am sure could easily make a selection on more scientific principles. There are, too, songs that seem to me a step removed from the more primitive types: there is the maze-like medley, "Bright sparkles," one phrase of which heads "The Black Belt"; the Easter carol, "Dust, dust and ashes"; the dirge, "My mother's took her flight and gone home"; and that burst of melody hovering over "The Passing of the First-Born"—"I hope my mother will be there in that beautiful world on high."

These represent a third step in the development of the slave song, of which "You may bury me in the East" is the first, and songs like "March on" (chapter six) and "Steal away" are the second. The first is African music, the second Afro-American, while the third is a blending of Negro music with the music heard in the foster land. The result is still distinctively Negro and the method of blending original, but the elements are both Negro and Caucasian. One might go further and find a fourth step in this development, where the songs of white America have been distinctively influenced by the slave songs or have incorporated whole phrases of Negro melody, as "Swanee River" and "Old Black Joe."[2] Side by side, too, with the growth has gone the debasements and imitations—the Negro "minstrel" songs, many of the "gospel" hymns, and some of the contemporary "coon" songs,—a mass of music in which the novice may easily lose himself and never find the real Negro melodies.

In these songs, I have said, the slave spoke to the world. Such a message is naturally veiled and half articulate. Words and music have lost each other and new and cant phrases of a dimly understood theology have displaced the older sentiment. Once in a while we catch a strange word of an unknown tongue, as the "Mighty Myo," which figures as a river of death; more often slight words or mere doggerel are joined to music of singular sweetness. Purely secular songs are few in number, partly because many of them were

2. "Old Folks at Home" (1851), also known as "Swanee River," and "Old Black Joe" (1860) were popular songs by Stephen Foster (1826–1864).

turned into hymns by a change of words, partly because the frolics were seldom heard by the stranger, and the music less often caught. Of nearly all the songs, however, the music is distinctly sorrowful. The ten master songs I have mentioned tell in word and music of trouble and exile, of strife and hiding; they grope toward some unseen power and sigh for rest in the End.

The words that are left to us are not without interest, and, cleared of evident dross, they conceal much of real poetry and meaning beneath conventional theology and unmeaning rhapsody. Like all primitive folk, the slave stood near to Nature's heart. Life was a "rough and rolling sea" like the brown Atlantic of the Sea Islands; the "Wilderness" was the home of God, and the "lonesome valley" led to the way of life. "Winter'll soon be over," was the picture of life and death to a tropical imagination. The sudden wild thunderstorms of the South awed and impressed the Negroes,—at times the rumbling seemed to them "mournful," at times imperious:

"My Lord calls me,
He calls me by the thunder,
The trumpet sounds it in my soul."

The monotonous toil and exposure is painted in many words. One sees the ploughmen in the hot, moist furrow, singing:

"Deres no rain to wet you,
Dere's no sun to burn you,
Oh, push along, believer,
I want to go home."

The bowed and bent old man cries, with thrice-repeated wail:

"O Lord, keep me from sinking down,"

and he rebukes the devil of doubt who can whisper:

"Jesus is dead and God's gone away."

Yet the soul-hunger is there, the restlessness of the savage, the wail of the wanderer, and the plaint is put in one little phrase:

My soul wants some thing that's new, that's new

Over the inner thoughts of the slaves and their relations one with another the shadow of fear ever hung, so that we get but glimpses here and there, and also with them, eloquent omissions and silences. Mother and child are sung, but seldom father; fugitive and weary wanderer call for pity and affection, but there is little of wooing and wedding; the rocks and the mountains are well known, but home is unknown. Strange blending of love and helplessness sings through the refrain:

"Yonder's my ole mudder,
Been waggin' at de hill so long;
'Bout time she cross over,
Git home bime-by."

Elsewhere comes the cry of the "motherless" and the "Farewell, farewell, my only child."

Love-songs are scarce and fall into two categories—the frivolous and light, and the sad. Of deep successful love there is ominous silence, and in one of the oldest of these songs there is a depth of history and meaning:

Poor Ro - sy, poor gal; Poor Ro - sy,
poor gal; Ro - sy break my poor heart.
Heav'n shall - a - be my home.

A black woman said of the song, "It can't be sung without a full heart and a troubled sperrit." The same voice sings here that sings in the German folksong:

"Jetz Geh i' an's brunele, trink' aber net."[3]

Of death the Negro showed little fear, but talked of it familiarly and even fondly as simply a crossing of the waters, perhaps—who knows?—back to his ancient forests again. Later days transfigured his fatalism, and amid the dust and dirt the toiler sang:

"Dust, dust and ashes, fly over my grave,
But the Lord shall bear my spirit home."

The things evidently borrowed from the surrounding world undergo characteristic change when they enter the mouth of the slave. Especially is this true of Bible phrases. "Weep, O captive daughter of Zion," is quaintly turned into "Zion, weep-a-low," and the wheels of Ezekiel are turned every way in the mystic dreaming of the slave, till he says:

"There's a little wheel a-turnin' in-a-my heart."

As in olden time, the words of these hymns were improvised by some leading minstrel of the religious band. The circumstances of the gathering, however, the rhythm of the songs, and the limitations of allowable thought, confined the poetry for the most part to single or double lines, and they seldom were expanded to quatrains or longer tales, although there are some few examples of sustained efforts, chiefly paraphrases of the Bible. Three short series of verses have always attracted me,—the one that heads this chapter, of one line of which Thomas Wentworth Higginson[4] has fittingly said, "Never, it seems to me, since man first lived and suffered was his infinite longing for peace uttered more plaintively." The second and third are descriptions of the Last Judgment,—the one a late improvisation, with some traces of outside influence:

"Oh, the stars in the elements are falling,
And the moon drips away into blood,

3. Now I'm going to the well, but I'm not going to drink (German).
4. Unitarian minister and abolitionist (1823–1911).

And the ransomed of the Lord are returning unto God,
Blessed be the name of the Lord."

And the other earlier and homelier picture from the low coast lands:

"Michael, haul the boat ashore,
Then you'll hear the horn they blow,
Then you'll hear the trumpet sound,
Trumpet sound the world around,
Trumpet sound for rich and poor,
Trumpet sound the Jubilee,
Trumpet sound for you and me."

Through all the sorrow of the Sorrow Songs there breathes a hope—a faith in the ultimate justice of things. The minor cadences of despair change often to triumph and calm confidence. Sometimes it is faith in life, sometimes a faith in death, sometimes assurance of boundless justice in some fair world beyond. But whichever it is, the meaning is always clear: that sometime, somewhere, men will judge men by their souls and not by their skins. Is such a hope justified? Do the Sorrow Songs sing true?

The silently growing assumption of this age is that the probation of races is past, and that the backward races of to-day are of proven inefficiency and not worth the saving. Such an assumption is the arrogance of peoples irreverent toward Time and ignorant of the deeds of men. A thousand years ago such an assumption, easily possible, would have made it difficult for the Teuton to prove his right to life. Two thousand years ago such dogmatism, readily welcome, would have scouted the idea of blond races ever leading civilization. So wofully unorganized is sociological knowledge that the meaning of progress, the meaning of "swift" and "slow" in human doing, and the limits of human perfectability, are veiled, unanswered sphinxes on the shores of science. Why should Æschylus[5] have sung two thousand years before Shakespeare was born? Why has civilization flourished in Europe, and flickered, flamed, and died in Africa? So long as the world stands meekly dumb before such questions, shall this nation proclaim its ignorance and unhallowed prejudices by denying freedom of opportunity to those who brought the Sorrow Songs to the Seats of the Mighty?

Your country? How came it yours? Before the Pilgrims landed we were here. Here we have brought our three gifts and mingled them with yours: a gift of story and song—soft, stirring melody in an ill-harmonized and unmelodious land; the gift of sweat and brawn to beat back the wilderness, conquer the soil, and lay the foundations of this vast economic empire two hundred years earlier than your weak hands could have done it; the third, a gift of the Spirit. Around us the history of the land has centred for thrice a hundred years; out of the nation's heart we have called all that was best to throttle and subdue all that was worst; fire and blood, prayer and sacrifice, have billowed over this people, and they have found peace only in the altars of the God of Right. Nor has our gift of the Spirit been merely passive. Actively we have woven ourselves with the very warp and woof of this nation,—we fought their battles, shared their sorrow, mingled our blood with theirs, and generation after generation have pleaded with a headstrong, careless people to despise not Justice, Mercy, and Truth, lest the nation be

5. Greek tragic dramatist (525–456 B.C.E.).

smitten with a curse. Our song, our toil, our cheer, and warning have been given to this nation in blood-brotherhood. Are not these gifts worth the giving? Is not this work and striving? Would America have been America without her Negro people?

Even so is the hope that sang in the songs of my fathers well sung. If somewhere where in this whirl and chaos of things there dwells Eternal Good, pitiful yet masterful, then anon in His good time America shall rend the Veil and the prisoned shall go free. Free, free as the sunshine trickling down the morning into these high windows of mine, free as yonder fresh young voices welling up to me from the caverns of brick and mortar below—swelling with song, instinct with life, tremulous treble and darkening bass. My children, my little children, are singing to the sunshine, and thus they sing:

And the traveller girds himself, and sets his face toward the Morning, and goes his way.

The After-Thought[6]

Hear my cry, O God the Reader; vouchsafe that this my book fall not still-born into the world-wilderness. Let there spring, Gentle One, from out its leaves vigor of thought and thoughtful deed to reap the harvest wonderful. (Let the ears of a guilty people tingle with truth, and seventy millions sigh for the righteousness which exalteth nations, in this drear day when human brotherhood is mockery and a snare.) Thus in Thy good time may infinite reason turn the tangle straight, and these crooked marks on a fragile leaf be not indeed

THE END

1903

The Damnation of Women

I remember four women of my boyhood: my mother, cousin Inez, Emma, and Ide Fuller. They represented the problem of the widow, the wife, the maiden, and the outcast. They were, in color, brown and light-brown, yellow with brown freckles, and white. They existed not for themselves, but for men; they were named after the men to whom they were related and not after the fashion of their own souls.

They were not beings, they were relations and these relations were enfilmed with mystery and secrecy. We did not know the truth or believe it when we heard it. Motherhood! What was it? We did not know or greatly care. My mother and I were good chums. I liked her. After she was dead I loved her with a fierce sense of personal loss.

Inez was a pretty, brown cousin who married. What was marriage? We did not know, neither did she, poor thing! It came to mean for her a litter of children, poverty, a drunken, cruel companion, sickness, and death. Why?

There was no sweeter sight than Emma,—slim, straight, and dainty, darkly flushed with the passion of youth; but her life was a wild, awful struggle to crush her natural, fierce joy of love. She crushed it and became a cold, calculating mockery.

Last there was that awful outcast of the town, the white woman, Ide Fuller. What she was, we did not know. She stood to us as embodied filth and wrong,—but whose filth, whose wrong?

Grown up I see the problem of these women transfused; I hear all about me the unanswered call of youthful love, none the less glorious because of its clean, honest, physical passion. Why unanswered? Because the youth are too poor to marry or if they marry, too poor to have children. They turn aside, then, in three directions: to marry for support, to what men call shame, or to that which is more evil than nothing. It is an unendurable paradox; it must be changed or the bases of culture will totter and fall.

The world wants healthy babies and intelligent workers. Today we refuse to allow the combination and force thousands of intelligent workers to go childless at a horrible expenditure of moral force, or we damn them if they break our idiotic conventions. Only at the sacrifice of intelligence and the

6. Paraphrases of various Psalms and Proverbs, including Psalms 61:1–4 and Proverbs 14:34.

chance to do their best work can the majority of modern women bear children. This is the damnation of women.

All womanhood is hampered today because the world on which it is emerging is a world that tries to worship both virgins and mothers and in the end despises motherhood and despoils virgins.

The future woman must have a life work and economic independence. She must have knowledge. She must have the right of motherhood at her own discretion. The present mincing horror at free womanhood must pass if we are ever to be rid of the bestiality of free manhood; not by guarding the weak in weakness do we gain strength, but by making weakness free and strong.

The world must choose the free woman or the white wraith of the prostitute. Today it wavers between the prostitute and the nun. Civilization must show two things: the glory and beauty of creating life and the need and duty of power and intelligence. This and this only will make the perfect marriage of love and work.

God is Love,
Love is God;
There is no God but Love
And Work is His Prophet!

All this of woman,—but what of black women?

The world that wills to worship womankind studiously forgets its darker sisters. They seem in a sense to typify that veiled Melancholy:

"Whose saintly visage is too bright
To hit the sense of human sight,
And, therefore, to our weaker view
O'er-laid with black."[1]

Yet the world must heed these daughters of sorrow, from the primal black All-Mother of men down through the ghostly throng of mighty womanhood, who walked in the mysterious dawn of Asia and Africa; from Neith,[2] the primal mother of all, whose feet rest on hell, and whose almighty hands uphold the heavens; all religion, from beauty to beast, lies on her eager breasts; her body bears the stars, while her shoulders are necklaced by the dragon; from black Neith down to

"That starr'd Ethiop queen who strove
To set her beauty's praise above
The sea-nymphs,"[3]

through dusky Cleopatras, dark Candaces, and darker, fiercer Zinghas, to our own day and our own land,—in gentle Phillis; Harriet, the crude Moses; the sybil, Sojourner Truth; and the martyr, Louise De Mortie.[4]

The father and his worship is Asia; Europe is the precocious, self-centered, forward-striving child; but the land of the mother is and was

1. English poet John Milton's "Il Penseroso" (ca. 1631).
2. Or Net, ancient Egyptian creator goddess.
3. Milton's "Il Penseroso."
4. Teacher, lecturer, and social worker among the freed people in New Orleans (1833–1867). Cleopatra (69–30 B.C.E.), queen of Egypt. Candace was the title for queens in ancient Ethiopia. Ana Nzinga (ca. 1583–1663), queen of Ndongo and Matamba (present-day northern Angola). Phillis Wheatley (1735–1784), internationally acclaimed African-born poet who grew up enslaved in Boston. Harriet Tubman (1822–1913), formerly enslaved Underground Railroad conductor, Union army spy, and feminist. Sojourner Truth (ca. 1799–1883), antislavery and women's rights activist; born enslaved.

Africa. In subtle and mysterious way, despite her curious history, her slavery, polygamy, and toil, the spell of the African mother pervades her land. Isis,[5] the mother, is still titular goddess, in thought if not in name, of the dark continent. Nor does this all seem to be solely a survival of the historic matriarchate[6] through which all nations pass,—it appears to be more than this,—as if the great black race in passing up the steps of human culture gave the world, not only the Iron Age,[7] the cultivation of the soil, and the domestication of animals, but also, in peculiar emphasis, the mother-idea.

"No mother can love more tenderly and none is more tenderly loved than the Negro mother," writes Schneider. Robin tells of the slave who bought his mother's freedom instead of his own. Mungo Park[8] writes: "Everywhere in Africa, I have noticed that no greater affront can be offered a Negro than insulting his mother. 'Strike me,' cries a Mandingo to his enemy, 'but revile not my mother!'" And the Krus and Fantis say the same. The peoples on the Zambezi and the great lakes cry in sudden fear or joy: "O, my mother!" And the Herero swear (endless oath) "By my mother's tears!" "As the mist in the swamps," cries the Angola[9] Negro, "so lives the love of father and mother."

A student of the present Gold Coast[1] life describes the work of the village headman, and adds: "It is a difficult task that he is set to, but in this matter he has all-powerful helpers in the female members of the family, who will be either the aunts or the sisters or the cousins or the nieces of the headman, and as their interests are identical with his in every particular, the good women spontaneously train up their children to implicit obedience to the headman, whose rule in the family thus becomes a simple and an easy matter. 'The hand that rocks the cradle rules the world.' What a power for good in the native state system would the mothers of the Gold Coast and Ashanti[2] become by judicious training upon native lines!"

Schweinfurth declares of one tribe: "A bond between mother and child which lasts for life is the measure of affection shown among the Dyoor" and Ratzel[3] adds:

"Agreeable to the natural relation the mother stands first among the chief influences affecting the children. From the Zulus to the Waganda, we find the mother the most influential counsellor at the court of ferocious sovereigns, like Chaka or Mtesa;[4] sometimes sisters take her place. Thus even with chiefs who possess wives by hundreds the bonds of blood are the strongest and that the woman, though often heavily burdened, is in herself held in no small esteem among the Negroes is clear from the numerous Negro queens, from the medicine women, from the participation in public meetings permitted to women by many Negro peoples."

As I remember through memories of others, backward among my own family, it is the mother I ever recall,—the little, far-off mother of my grand-

5. Principal goddess of ancient Egypt.
6. A family or tribe headed by a woman.
7. The period beginning in about 4000 B.C.E. in Egypt when human beings began making things of iron.
8. British explorer of Africa (1771–1806).
9. A country on the southwest coast of Africa. The Mandingo people inhabit the Niger River region in western Sudan. The Zambezi is the largest African river flowing into the Indian Ocean. The Herero people live in Botswana and Namibia.
1. The name of the British colony in West Africa that became the nation of Ghana.
2. A people who live in Ghana.
3. Friedrich Ratzel (1844–1904), originator of anthropogeography. Georg August Schweinfurth (1836–1925), African explorer and botanist, collaborator with Ratzel. The Dyoor people lived along the Dyoor River in central Africa.
4. Late-19th-century king of Uganda. The Zulu people live in South Africa. The Waganda are Bantu people from Nigeria. Chaka Zulu (1787?–1828), leader of southeast African Zulus.

mothers, who sobbed her life away in song, longing for her lost palm-trees and scented waters; the tall and bronzen grandmother, with beaked nose and shrewish eyes, who loved and scolded her black and laughing husband as he smoked lazily in his high oak chair; above all, my own mother, with all her soft brownness,—the brown velvet of her skin, the sorrowful black-brown of her eyes, and the tiny brown-capped waves of her midnight hair as it lay new parted on her forehead. All the way back in these dim distances it is mothers and mothers of mothers who seem to count, while fathers are shadowy memories.

Upon this African mother-idea, the westward slave trade and American slavery struck like doom. In the cruel exigencies of the traffic in men and in the sudden, unprepared emancipation the great pendulum of social equilibrium swung from a time, in 1800,—when America had but eight or less black women to every ten black men,—all too swiftly to a day, in 1870,—when there were nearly eleven women to ten men in our Negro population. This was but the outward numerical fact of social dislocation; within lay polygamy, polyandry, concubinage,[5] and moral degradation. They fought against all this desperately, did these black slaves in the West Indies, especially among the half-free artisans; they set up their ancient household gods, and when Toussaint and Cristophe[6] founded their kingdom in Haiti, it was based on old African tribal ties and beneath it was the mother-idea.

The crushing weight of slavery fell on black women. Under it there was no legal marriage, no legal family, no legal control over children. To be sure, custom and religion replaced here and there what the law denied, yet one has but to read advertisements like the following to see the hell beneath the system:

> "One hundred dollars reward will be given for my two fellows, Abram and Frank. Abram has a wife at Colonel Stewart's, in Liberty County, and a mother at Thunderbolt, and a sister in Savannah.
>
> "William Roberts."
>
> "Fifty dollars reward—Ran away from the subscriber a Negro girl named Maria. She is of a copper color, between thirteen and fourteen years of age—bare headed and barefooted. She is small for her age—very sprightly and very likely. She stated she was going to see her mother at Maysville.
>
> "Sanford Thomson."
>
> Fifty dollars reward—Ran away from the subscriber his Negro man Pauladore, commonly called Paul. I understand General R. Y. Hayne has purchased his wife and children from H. L. Pinckney, Esq., and has them now on his plantation at Goose Creek, where, no doubt, the fellow is frequently lurking.
>
> "T. Davis."

The Presbyterian synod of Kentucky said to the churches under its care in 1835: "Brothers and sisters, parents and children, husbands and wives, are torn asunder and permitted to see each other no more. These acts are daily

5. Cohabitation without legal marriage. "Polygamy": having more than one wife at the same time. "Polyandry": having more than one husband at the same time.

6. Henri Christophe (1767–1820), dictator of Haiti (1811–20). Toussaint L'Ouverture (1743?–1803), leader of a successful by the enslaved people of revolution Haiti.

occurring in the midst of us. The shrieks and agony often witnessed on such occasions proclaim, with a trumpet tongue, the iniquity of our system. There is not a neighborhood where these heartrending scenes are not displayed. There is not a village or road that does not behold the sad procession of manacled outcasts whose mournful countenances tell that they are exiled by force from all that their hearts hold dear."

A sister of a president of the United States declared: "We Southern ladies are complimented with the names of wives, but we are only the mistresses of seraglios."[7]

Out of this, what sort of black women could be born into the world of today? There are those who hasten to answer this query in scathing terms and who say lightly and repeatedly that out of black slavery came nothing decent in womanhood; that adultery and uncleanness were their heritage and are their continued portion.

Fortunately so exaggerated a charge is humanly impossible of truth. The half-million women of Negro descent who lived at the beginning of the 19th century had become the mothers of two and one-fourth million daughters at the time of the Civil War and five million granddaughters in 1910. Can all these women be vile and the hunted race continue to grow in wealth and character? Impossible. Yet to save from the past the shreds and vestiges of self-respect has been a terrible task. I most sincerely doubt if any other race of women could have brought its fineness up through so devilish a fire.

Alexander Crummell[8] once said of his sister in the blood: "In her girlhood all the delicate tenderness of her sex has been rudely outraged. In the field, in the rude cabin, in the press-room, in the factory she was thrown into the companionship of coarse and ignorant men. No chance was given her for delicate reserve or tender modesty. From her childhood she was the doomed victim of the grossest passion. All the virtues of her sex were utterly ignored. If the instinct of chastity asserted itself, then she had to fight like a tiger for the ownership and possession of her own person and ofttimes had to suffer pain and lacerations for her virtuous self-assertion. When she reached maturity, all the tender instincts of her womanhood were ruthlessly violated. At the age of marriage,—always prematurely anticipated under slavery—she was mated as the stock of the plantation were mated, not to be the companion of a loved and chosen husband, but to be the breeder of human cattle for the field or the auction block.

Down in such mire has the black motherhood of this race struggled,—starving its own wailing offspring to nurse to the world their swaggering masters; welding for its children chains which affronted even the moral sense of an unmoral world. Many a man and woman in the South have lived in wedlock as holy as Adam and Eve and brought forth their brown and golden children, but because the darker woman was helpless, her chivalrous and whiter mate could cast her off at his pleasure and publicly sneer at the body he had privately blasphemed.

I shall forgive the white South much in its final judgment day: I shall forgive its slavery, for slavery is a world-old habit; I shall forgive its fighting for a well-lost cause, and for remembering that struggle with tender tears; I shall forgive its so-called "pride of race," the passion of its hot blood, and

7. Harems.
8. Clergyman, antislavery activist, and African missionary (1819–1898).

even its dear, old, laughable strutting and posing; but one thing I shall never forgive, neither in this world nor the world to come: its wanton and continued and persistent insulting of the black womanhood which it sought and seeks to prostitute to its lust. I cannot forget that it is such Southern gentlemen into whose hands smug Northern hypocrites of today are seeking to place our women's eternal destiny,—men who insist upon withholding from my mother and wife and daughter those signs and appellations of courtesy and respect which elsewhere he withholds only from bawds and courtesans.

The result of this history of insult and degradation has been both fearful and glorious. It has birthed the haunting prostitute, the brawler, and the beast of burden; but it has also given the world an efficient womanhood, whose strength lies in its freedom and whose chastity was won in the teeth of temptation and not in prison and swaddling clothes.

To no modern race does its women mean so much as to the Negro nor come so near to the fulfilment of its meaning. As one of our women writes: "Only the black woman can say 'when and where I enter, in the quiet, undisputed dignity of my womanhood, without violence and without suing or special patronage, then and there the whole Negro race enters with me.'"[9]

They came first, in earlier days, like foam flashing on dark, silent waters,—bits of stern, dark womanhood here and there tossed almost carelessly aloft to the world's notice. First and naturally they assumed the panoply[1] of the ancient African mother of men, strong and black, whose very nature beat back the wilderness of oppression and contempt. Such a one was that cousin of my grandmother, whom western Massachusetts remembers as "Mum Bett."[2] Scarred for life by a blow received in defense of a sister, she ran away to Great Barrington and was the first slave, or one of the first, to be declared free under the Bill of Rights of 1780. The son of the judge who freed her, writes:

> "Even in her humble station, she had, when occasion required it, an air of command which conferred a degree of dignity and gave her an ascendancy over those of her rank, which is very unusual in persons of any rank or color. Her determined and resolute character, which enabled her to limit the ravages of Shay's mob,[3] was manifested in her conduct and deportment during her whole life. She claimed no distinction, but it was yielded to her from her superior experience, energy, skill, and sagacity. Having known this woman as familiarly as I knew either of my parents, I cannot believe in the moral or physical inferiority of the race to which she belonged. The degradation of the African must have been otherwise caused than by natural inferiority."

It was such strong women that laid the foundations of the great Negro church of today, with its five million members and ninety millions of dollars in property. One of the early mothers of the church, Mary Still, writes thus quaintly, in the forties:

> "When we were as castouts and spurned from the large churches, driven from our knees, pointed at by the proud, neglected by the careless, with-

9. Anna Julia Cooper's *A Voice from the South* (1892).
1. A complete set of armor.
2. Elizabeth Freeman (ca. 1744–1829) sued for her freedom and won.
3. Daniel Shays (1747–1825) led an armed insurrection of debt-ridden farmers in western Massachusetts in 1786–87 to protest foreclosure of mortgages and imprisonment for debt.

> out a place of worship, Allen,[4] faithful to the heavenly calling, came forward and laid the foundation of this connection. The women, like the women at the sepulcher, were early to aid in laying the foundation of the temple and in helping to carry up the noble structure and in the name of their God set up their banner; most of our aged mothers are gone from this to a better state of things. Yet some linger still on their staves, watching with intense interest the ark as it moves over the tempestuous waves of opposition and ignorance. . . .
>
> "But the labors of these women stopped not here, for they knew well that they were subject to affliction and death. For the purpose of mutual aid, they banded themselves together in society capacity, that they might be better able to administer to each others' sufferings and to soften their own pillows. So we find the females in the early history of the church abounding in good works and in acts of true benevolence."[5]

From such spiritual ancestry came two striking figures of war-time,—Harriet Tubman and Sojourner Truth.

For eight or ten years previous to the breaking out of the Civil War, Harriet Tubman was a constant attendant at anti-slavery conventions, lectures, and other meetings; she was a black woman of medium size, smiling countenance, with her upper front teeth gone, attired in coarse but neat clothes, and carrying always an old-fashioned reticule[6] at her side. Usually as soon as she sat down she would drop off in sound sleep.

She was born a slave in Maryland, in 1820, bore the marks of the lash on her flesh; and had been made partially deaf, and perhaps to some degree mentally unbalanced by a blow on the head in childhood. Yet she was one of the most important agents of the Underground Railroad and a leader of fugitive slaves. She ran away in 1849 and went to Boston in 1854, where she was welcomed into the homes of the leading abolitionists and where every one listened with tense interest to her strange stories. She was absolutely illiterate, with no knowledge of geography, and yet year after year she penetrated the slave states and personally led North over three hundred fugitives without losing a single one. A standing reward of $10,000 was offered for her, but as she said: "The whites cannot catch us, for I was born with the charm, and the Lord has given me the power." She was one of John Brown's closest advisers and only severe sickness prevented her presence at Harper's Ferry.[7]

When the war cloud broke, she hastened to the front, flitting down along her own mysterious paths, haunting the armies in the field, and serving as guide and nurse and spy. She followed Sherman in his great march to the sea and was with Grant at Petersburg, and always in the camps the Union officers silently saluted her!

The other woman belonged to a different type,—a tall, gaunt, black, unsmiling sybil, weighted with the woe of the world. She ran away from slavery and giving up her own name took the name of Sojourner Truth. She says: "I can remember when I was a little, young girl, how my old mammy would sit out of doors in the evenings and look up at the stars and groan, and I would say, 'Mammy, what makes you groan so?' And she would say, 'I

4. Bishop Richard Allen (1760–1831), founder of the African Methodist Episcopal church.
5. Mary Still's *An Appeal to the Females of the African Methodist Episcopal Church* (1857).
6. A small woman's handbag.
7. Site in Virginia of abolitionist John Brown's failed attempt in 1859 to seize the U.S. arsenal and instigate a rebellion of the enslaved people.

am groaning to think of my poor children; they do not know where I be and I don't know where they be. I look up at the stars and they look up at the stars!' "[8]

Her determination was founded on unwavering faith in ultimate good. Wendell Phillips says that he was once in Faneuil Hall, when Frederick Douglass[9] was one of the chief speakers. Douglass had been describing the wrongs of the Negro race and as he proceeded he grew more and more excited and finally ended by saying that they had no hope of justice from the whites, no possible hope except in their own right arms. It must come to blood! They must fight for themselves. Sojourner Truth was sitting, tall and dark, on the very front seat facing the platform, and in the hush of feeling when Douglass sat down she spoke out in her deep, peculiar voice, heard all over the hall:

"Frederick, is God dead?"

Such strong, primitive types of Negro womanhood in America seem to some to exhaust its capabilities. They know less of a not more worthy, but a finer type of black woman wherein trembles all of that delicate sense of beauty and striving for self-realization, which is as characteristic of the Negro soul as is its quaint strength and sweet laughter. George Washington wrote in grave and gentle courtesy to a Negro woman, in 1776, that he would "be happy to see" at his headquarters at any time, a person "to whom nature has been so liberal and beneficial in her dispensations." This child, Phillis Wheatley, sang her trite and halting strain to a world that wondered and could not produce her like. Measured today her muse was slight and yet, feeling her striving spirit, we call to her still in her own words:

> "Through thickest glooms look back, immortal shade."[1]

Perhaps even higher than strength and art loom human sympathy and sacrifice as characteristic of Negro womanhood. Long years ago, before the Declaration of Independence, Kate Ferguson[2] was born in New York. Freed, widowed, and bereaved of her children before she was twenty, she took the children of the streets of New York, white and black, to her empty arms, taught them, found them homes, and with Dr. Mason of Murray Street Church established the first modern Sunday School in Manhattan.

Sixty years later came Mary Shadd[3] up out of Delaware. She was tall and slim, of that ravishing dream-born beauty,—that twilight of the races which we call mulatto. Well-educated, vivacious, with determination shining from her sharp eyes, she threw herself singlehanded into the great Canadian pilgrimage when thousands of hunted black men hurried northward and crept beneath the protection of the lion's paw. She became teacher, editor, and lecturer; tramping afoot through winter snows, pushing without blot or blemish through crowd and turmoil to conventions and meetings, and finally becoming recruiting agent for the United States government in gathering Negro soldiers in the West.

After the war the sacrifice of Negro women for freedom and uplift is one of the finest chapters in their history. Let one life typify all: Louise De

8. From *Narrative of Sojourner Truth* (1850).
9. A fugitive from enslavement and an abolitionist speaker (1818–1895). Wendell Phillips (1811–1884), American abolitionist speaker.
1. Wheatley's "On the Death of Dr. Samuel Marshall" (1773).
2. Catherine Ferguson (ca. 1774–1854), whose integrated Sunday school was launched in 1793.
3. Mary Ann Shadd (1823–1893), antislavery activist in Canada.

Mortie, a free-born Virginia girl, had lived most of her life in Boston. Her high forehead, swelling lips, and dark eyes marked her for a woman of feeling and intellect. She began a successful career as a public reader. Then came the War and the Call. She went to the orphaned colored children of New Orleans,—out of freedom into insult and oppression and into the teeth of the yellow fever. She toiled and dreamed. In 1887 she had raised money and built an orphan home and that same year, in the thirty-fourth of her young life, she died, saying simply: "I belong to God."

As I look about me today in this veiled world of mine, despite the noisier and more spectacular advance of my brothers, I instinctively feel and know that it is the five million women of my race who really count. Black women (and women whose grandmothers were black) are today furnishing our teachers; they are the main pillars of those social settlements which we call churches; and they have with small doubt raised three-fourths of our church property. If we have today, as seems likely, over a billion dollars of accumulated goods, who shall say how much of it has been wrung from the hearts of servant girls and washerwomen and women toilers in the fields? As makers of two million homes these women are today seeking in marvelous ways to show forth our strength and beauty and our conception of the truth.

In the United States in 1910 there were 4,931,882 women of Negro descent; over twelve hundred thousand of these were children, another million were girls and young women under twenty, and two and a half-million were adults. As a mass these women were unlettered,—a fourth of those from fifteen to twenty-five years of age were unable to write. These women are passing through, not only a moral, but an economic revolution. Their grandmothers married at twelve and fifteen, but twenty-seven per cent of these women today who have passed fifteen are still single.

Yet these black women toil and toil hard. There were in 1910 two and a half million Negro homes in the United States. Out of these homes walked daily to work two million women and girls over ten years of age,—over half of the colored female population as against a fifth in the case of white women. These, then, are a group of workers, fighting for their daily bread like men; independent and approaching economic freedom! They furnished a million farm laborers, 80,000 farmers, 22,000 teachers, 600,000 servants and washerwomen, and 50,000 in trades and merchandizing.

The family group, however, which is the ideal of the culture with which these folk have been born, is not based on the idea of an economically independent working mother. Rather its ideal harks back to the sheltered harem with the mother emerging at first as nurse and homemaker, while the man remains the sole breadwinner. What is the inevitable result of the clash of such ideals and such facts in the colored group? Broken families.

Among native white women one in ten is separated from her husband by death, divorce, or desertion. Among Negroes the ratio is one in seven. Is the cause racial? No, it is economic, because there is the same high ratio among the white foreign-born. The breaking up of the present family is the result of modern working and sex conditions and it hits the laborers with terrible force. The Negroes are put in a peculiarly difficult position, because the wage of the male breadwinner is below the standard, while the openings for colored women in certain lines of domestic work, and now in industries, are many. Thus while toil holds the father and brother in country and town at low wages, the sisters and mothers are called to the city. As a result the Negro women outnumber the men nine or ten to eight in many cities, making what Charlotte Gilman[4] bluntly calls "cheap women."

What shall we say to this new economic equality in a great laboring class? Some people within and without the race deplore it. "Back to the homes with the women," they cry, "and higher wage for the men." But how impossible this is has been shown by war conditions. Cessation of foreign migration has raised Negro men's wages, to be sure—but it has not only raised Negro women's wages, it has opened to them a score of new avenues of earning a living. Indeed, here, in microcosm and with differences emphasizing sex equality, is the industrial history of labor in the 19th and 20th centuries. We cannot abolish the new economic freedom of women. We cannot imprison women again in a home or require them all on pain of death to be nurses and housekeepers.

What is today the message of these black women to America and to the world? The uplift of women is, next to the problem of the color line and the peace movement, our greatest modern cause. When, now, two of these movements—woman and color—combine in one, the combination has deep meaning.

In other years women's way was clear: to be beautiful, to be petted, to bear children. Such has been their theoretic destiny and if perchance they have been ugly, hurt, and barren, that has been forgotten with studied silence. In partial compensation for this narrowed destiny the white world has lavished its politeness on its womankind,—its chivalry and bows, its uncoverings and courtesies—all the accumulated homage disused for courts and kings and craving exercise. The revolt of white women against this preordained destiny has in these latter days reached splendid proportions, but it is the revolt of an aristocracy of brains and ability,—the middle class and rank and file still plod on in the appointed path, paid by the homage, the almost mocking homage, of men.

From black women of America, however, (and from some others, too, but chiefly from black women and their daughters' daughters) this gauze has been withheld and without semblance of such apology they have been frankly trodden under the feet of men. They are and have been objected to, apparently for reasons peculiarly exasperating to reasoning human beings. When in this world a man comes forward with a thought, a deed, a vision, we ask not, how does he look,—but what is his message? It is of but passing interest whether or not the messenger is beautiful or ugly,—the *message* is the thing. This, which is axiomatic among men, has been in past ages but partially true if the messenger was a woman. The world still wants to ask that a woman primarily be pretty and if she is not, the mob pouts and asks querulously, "What else are women for?" Beauty "is its own excuse for being,"[5] but there are other excuses, as most men know, and when the white world objects to black women because it does not consider them beautiful, the black world of right asks two questions: "What is beauty?" and, "Suppose you think them ugly, what then? If ugliness and unconventionality and

4. Charlotte Perkins Gilman (1860–1935), feminist author and lecturer.
5. See Ralph Waldo Emerson's "The Rhodora" (1839): "Tell them, dear, that if eyes were made for seeing / Then Beauty is its own excuse for being."

eccentricity of face and deed do not hinder men from doing the world's work and reaping the world's reward, why should it hinder women?"

Other things being equal, all of us, black and white, would prefer to be beautiful in face and form and suitably clothed; but most of us are not so, and one of the mightiest revolts of the century is against the devilish decree that no woman is a woman who is not by present standards a beautiful woman. This decree the black women of America have in large measure escaped from the first. Not being expected to be merely ornamental, they have girded themselves for work, instead of adorning their bodies only for play. Their sturdier minds have concluded that if a woman be clean, healthy, and educated, she is as pleasing as God wills and far more useful than most of her sisters. If in addition to this she is pink and white and straight-haired, and some of her fellow-men prefer this, well and good; but if she is black or brown and crowned in curled mists (and this to us is the most beautiful thing on earth), this is surely the flimsiest excuse for spiritual incarceration or banishment.

The very attempt to do this in the case of Negro Americans has strangely over-reached itself. By so much as the defective eyesight of the white world rejects black women as beauties, by so much the more it needs them as human beings,—an enviable alternative, as many a white woman knows. Consequently, for black women alone, as a group, "handsome is that handsome does" and they are asked to be no more beautiful than God made them, but they are asked to be efficient, to be strong, fertile, muscled, and able to work. If they marry, they must as independent workers be able to help support their children, for their men are paid on a scale which makes sole support of the family often impossible.

On the whole, colored working women are paid as well as white working women for similar work, save in some higher grades, while colored men get from one-fourth to three-fourths less than white men. The result is curious and three-fold: the economic independence of black women is increased, the breaking up of Negro families must be more frequent, and the number of illegitimate children is decreased more slowly among them than other evidences of culture are increased, just as was once true in Scotland and Bavaria.

What does this mean? It forecasts a mighty dilemma which the whole world of civilization, despite its will, must one time frankly face: the unhusbanded mother or the childless wife. God send us a world with woman's freedom and married motherhood inextricably wed, but until He sends it, I see more of future promise in the betrayed girl-mothers of the black belt than in the childless wives of the white North, and I have more respect for the colored servant who yields to her frank longing for motherhood than for her white sister who offers up children for clothes. Out of a sex freedom that today makes us shudder will come in time a day when we will no longer pay men for work they do not do, for the sake of their harem; we will pay women what they earn and insist on their working and earning it; we will allow those persons to vote who know enough to vote, whether they be black or female, white or male; and we will ward race suicide, not by further burdening the over-burdened, but by honoring motherhood, even when the sneaking father shirks his duty.

"Wait till the lady passes," said a Nashville white boy.

"She's no lady; she's a nigger," answered another.

So some few women are born free, and some amid insult and scarlet letters[6] achieve freedom; but our women in black had freedom thrust contemptuously upon them. With that freedom they are buying an untrammeled independence and dear as is the price they pay for it, it will in the end be worth every taunt and groan. Today the dreams of the mothers are coming true. We have still our poverty and degradation, our lewdness and our cruel toil; but we have, too, a vast group of women of Negro blood who for strength of character, cleanness of soul, and unselfish devotion of purpose, is today easily the peer of any group of women in the civilized world. And more than that, in the great rank and file of our five million women we have the upworking of new revolutionary ideals, which must in time have vast influence on the thought and action of this land.

For this, their promise, and for their hard past, I honor the women of my race. Their beauty,—their dark and mysterious beauty of midnight eyes, crumpled hair, and soft, full-featured faces—is perhaps more to me than to you, because I was born to its warm and subtle spell; but their worth is yours as well as mine. No other women on earth could have emerged from the hell of force and temptation which once engulfed and still surrounds black women in America with half the modesty and womanliness that they retain. I have always felt like bowing myself before them in all abasement, searching to bring some tribute to these long-suffering victims, these burdened sisters of mine, whom the world, the wise, white world, loves to affront and ridicule and wantonly to insult. I have known the women of many lands and nations,—I have known and seen and lived beside them, but none have I known more sweetly feminine, more unswervingly loyal, more desperately earnest, and more instinctively pure in body and in soul than the daughters of my black mothers. This, then,—a little thing—to their memory and inspiration.

1920

Criteria of Negro Art

I do not doubt but there are some in this audience who are a little disturbed at the subject of this meeting, and particularly at the subject I have chosen. Such people are thinking something like this: "How is it that an organization like this, a group of radicals trying to bring new things into the world, a fighting organization which has come up out of the blood and dust of battle, struggling for the right of black men to be ordinary human beings—how is it that an organization of this kind can turn aside to talk about Art? After all, what have we who are slaves and black to do with Art?"

Or perhaps there are others who feel a certain relief and are saying, "After all it is rather satisfactory after all this talk about rights and fighting to sit and dream of something which leaves a nice taste in the mouth."

Let me tell you that neither of these groups is right. The thing we are talking about tonight is part of the great fight we are carrying on and it represents a forward and an upward look—a pushing onward. You and I

6. In Nathaniel Hawthorne's *The Scarlet Letter* (1851), the protagonist is convicted of adultery and compelled by Puritan authorities to wear a scarlet *A*.

have been breasting[1] hills; we have been climbing upward; there has been progress and we can see it day by day looking back along blood-filled paths. But as you go through the valleys and over the foothills, so long as you are climbing, the direction,—north, south, east or west,—is of less importance. But when gradually the vista widens and you begin to see the world at your feet and the far horizon, then it is time to know more precisely whither you are going and what you really want.

What do we want? What is the thing we are after? As it was phrased last night it had a certain truth: We want to be Americans, full-fledged Americans, with all the rights of other American citizens. But is that all? Do we want simply to be Americans? Once in a while through all of us there flashes some clairvoyance, some clear idea, of what America really is. We who are dark can see America in a way that white Americans can not. And seeing our country thus, are we satisfied with its present goals and ideals?

In the high school where I studied we learned most of Scott's "Lady of the Lake"[2] by heart. In after life once it was my privilege to see the lake. It was Sunday. It was quiet. You could glimpse the deer wandering in unbroken forests; you could hear the soft ripple of romance on the waters. Around me fell the cadence of that poetry of my youth. I fell asleep full of the enchantment of the Scottish border. A new day broke and with it came a sudden rush of excursionists. They were mostly Americans and they were loud and strident. They poured upon the little pleasure boat,—men with their hats a little on one side and drooping cigars in the wet corners of their mouths; women who shared their conversation with the world. They all tried to get everywhere first. They pushed other people out of the way. They made all sorts of incoherent noises and gestures so that the quiet home folk and the visitors from other lands silently and half-wonderingly gave way before them. They struck a note not evil but wrong. They carried, perhaps, a sense of strength and accomplishment, but their hearts had no conception of the beauty which pervaded this holy place.

If you tonight suddenly should become full-fledged Americans; if your color faded, or the color line here in Chicago was miraculously forgotten; suppose, too, you became at the same time rich and powerful;—what is it that you would want? What would you immediately seek? Would you buy the most powerful of motor cars and outrace Cook County?[3] Would you buy the most elaborate estate on the North Shore? Would you be a Rotarian or a Lion[4] or a What-not of the very last degree? Would you wear the most striking clothes, give the richest dinners and buy the longest press notices?

Even as you visualize such ideals you know in your hearts that these are not the things you really want. You realize this sooner than the average white American because, pushed aside as we have been in America, there has come to us not only a certain distaste for the tawdry and flamboyant but a vision of what the world could be if it were really a beautiful world; if we had the true spirit; if we had the Seeing Eye, the Cunning Hand, the Feeling Heart; if we had, to be sure, not perfect happiness, but plenty of good hard work, the inevitable suffering that always comes with life; sacrifice and waiting, all that—but, nevertheless, lived in a world where men

1. Ascending, moving forward or across.
2. Sir Walter Scott (1771–1832) wrote the poem "Lady of the Lake" in 1810.
3. Chicago is the seat of Cook County, Illinois. "North Shore": an affluent area outside of the city along Lake Michigan.
4. That is, a member of a civic organization comprised mainly of professional people (these clubs were predominantly male at the time).

know, where men create, where they realize themselves and where they enjoy life. It is that sort of a world we want to create for ourselves and for all America.

After all, who shall describe Beauty? What is it? I remember tonight four beautiful things: The Cathedral at Cologne,[5] a forest in stone, set in light and changing shadow, echoing with sunlight and solemn song; a village of the Veys[6] in West Africa, a little thing of mauve and purple, quiet, lying content and shining in the sun; a black and velvet room where on a throne rests, in old and yellowing marble, the broken curves of the Venus of Milo;[7] a single phrase of music in the Southern South—utter melody, haunting and appealing, suddenly arising out of night and eternity, beneath the moon.

Such is Beauty. Its variety is infinite, its possibility is endless. In normal life all may have it and have it yet again. The world is full of it; and yet today the mass of human beings are choked away from it, and their lives distorted and made ugly. This is not only wrong, it is silly. Who shall right this well-nigh universal failing? Who shall let this world be beautiful? Who shall restore to men the glory of sunsets and the peace of quiet sleep?

We black folk may help for we have within us as a race new stirrings; stirrings of the beginning of a new appreciation of joy, of a new desire to create, of a new will to be; as though in this morning of group life we had awakened from some sleep that at once dimly mourns the past and dreams a splendid future; and there has come the conviction that the Youth that is here today, the Negro Youth, is a different kind of Youth, because in some new way it bears this mighty prophecy on its breast, with a new realization of itself, with new determination for all mankind.

What has this Beauty to do with the world? What has Beauty to do with Truth and Goodness—with the facts of the world and the right actions of men? "Nothing," the artists rush to answer. They may be right. I am but an humble disciple of art and cannot presume to say. I am one who tells the truth and exposes evil and seeks with Beauty and for Beauty to set the world right. That somehow, somewhere eternal and perfect Beauty sits above Truth and Right I can conceive, but here and now and in the world in which I work they are for me unseparated and inseparable.

This is brought to us peculiarly when as artists we face our own past as a people. There has come to us—and it has come especially through the man we are going to honor tonight[8]—a realization of that past, of which for long years we have been ashamed, for which we have apologized. We thought nothing could come out of that past which we wanted to remember; which we wanted to hand down to our children. Suddenly, this same past is taking on form, color and reality, and in a half shamefaced way we are beginning to be proud of it. We are remembering that the romance of the world did not die and lie forgotten in the Middle Age; that if you want romance to deal with you must have it here and now and in your own hands.

I once knew a man and woman. They had two children, a daughter who was white and a daughter who was brown; the daughter who was white married a white man; and when her wedding was preparing the daughter who was brown prepared to go and celebrate. But the mother said, "No!"

5. A Gothic cathedral in Germany.
6. One of the Mandingo peoples of Senegal.
7. A Greek statue of the goddess Venus (ca. 100 B.C.E.).
8. "Carter Godwin Woodson, 12th Spingarn Medallist" [*Du Bois's note*]. Woodson (1875–1950), African American historian and author; he received the NAACP medal in 1926.

and the brown daughter went into her room and turned on the gas and died. Do you want Greek tragedy swifter than that?

Or again, here is a little Southern town and you are in the public square. On one side of the square is the office of a colored lawyer and on all the other sides are men who do not like colored lawyers. A white woman goes into the black man's office and points to the white-filled square and says, "I want five hundred dollars now and if I do not get it I am going to scream."

Have you heard the story of the conquest of German East Africa? Listen to the untold tale: There were 40,000 black men and 4,000 white men who talked German. There were 20,000 black men and 12,000 white men who talked English. There were 10,000 black men and 400 white men who talked French. In Africa then where the Mountains of the Moon[9] raised their white and snow-capped heads into the mouth of the tropic sun, where Nile and Congo[1] rise and the Great Lakes swim, these men fought; they struggled on mountain, hill and valley, in river, lake and swamp, until in masses they sickened, crawled and died; until the 4,000 white Germans had become mostly bleached bones; until nearly all the 12,000 white Englishmen had returned to South Africa, and the 400 Frenchmen to Belgium and Heaven; all except a mere handful of the white men died; but thousands of black men from East, West and South Africa, from Nigeria and the Valley of the Nile, and from the West Indies still struggled, fought and died. For four years they fought and won and lost German East Africa; and all you hear about it is that England and Belgium conquered German Africa for the allies!

Such is the true and stirring stuff of which Romance is born and from this stuff come the stirrings of men who are beginning to remember that this kind of material is theirs; and this vital life of their own kind is beckoning them on.

The question comes next as to the interpretation of these new stirrings, of this new spirit: Of what is the colored artist capable? We have had on the part of both colored and white people singular unanimity of judgment in the past. Colored people have said: "This work must be inferior because it comes from colored people." White people have said: "It is inferior because it is done by colored people." But today there is coming to both the realization that the work of the black man is not always inferior. Interesting stories come to us. A professor in the University of Chicago read to a class that had studied literature a passage of poetry and asked them to guess the author. They guessed a goodly company from Shelley and Robert Browning down to Tennyson and Masefield. The author was Countée Cullen.[2] Or again the English critic John Drinkwater went down to a Southern seminary, one of the sort which "finishes" young white women of the South. The students sat with their wooden faces while he tried to get some response out of them. Finally he said, "Name me some of your Southern poets". They hesitated. He said finally, "I'll start out with your best: Paul Laurence Dunbar!"[3]

With the growing recognition of Negro artists in spite of the severe handicaps, one comforting thing is occurring to both white and black. They are whispering, "Here is a way out. Here is the real solution of the color prob-

9. Legendary source of the Nile River; possibly the Rwenzori Mountains in Uganda.
1. The Nile and Congo are major African rivers.
2. African American poet (1903–1946). Percy Bysshe Shelley (1792–1822); Robert Browning (1812–1889); Alfred, Lord Tennyson (1809–1892); and John Masefield (1878–1967) were all English poets.
3. African American poet (1872–1906).

lem. The recognition accorded Cullen, Hughes, Fauset, White[4] and others shows there is no real color line. Keep quiet! Don't complain! Work! All will be well!"

I will not say that already this chorus amounts to a conspiracy. Perhaps I am naturally too suspicious. But I will say that there are today a surprising number of white people who are getting great satisfaction out of these younger Negro writers because they think it is going to stop agitation of the Negro question. They say, "What is the use of your fighting and complaining; do the great thing and the reward is there". And many colored people are all too eager to follow this advice; especially those who are weary of the eternal struggle along the color line, who are afraid to fight and to whom the money of philanthropists and the alluring publicity are subtle and deadly bribes. They say, "What is the use of fighting? Why not show simply what we deserve and let the reward come to us?"

And it is right here that the National Association for the Advancement of Colored People comes upon the field, comes with its great call to a new battle, a new fight and new things to fight before the old things are wholly won; and to say that the Beauty of Truth and Freedom which shall some day be our heritage and the heritage of all civilized men is not in our hands yet and that we ourselves must not fail to realize.

There is in New York tonight a black woman molding clay by herself in a little bare room, because there is not a single school of sculpture in New York where she is welcome. Surely there are doors she might burst through, but when God makes a sculptor He does not always make the pushing sort of person who beats his way through doors thrust in his face. This girl is working her hands off to get out of this country so that she can get some sort of training.

There was Richard Brown. If he had been white he would have been alive today instead of dead of neglect. Many helped him when he asked but he was not the kind of boy that always asks. He was simply one who made colors sing.

There is a colored woman in Chicago who is a great musician. She thought she would like to study at Fontainebleau this summer where Walter Damrosch[5] and a score of leaders of Art have an American school of music. But the application blank of this school says: "I am a white American and I apply for admission to the school."

We can go on the stage; we can be just as funny as white Americans wish us to be; we can play all the sordid parts that America likes to assign to Negroes; but for any thing else there is still small place for us.

And so I might go on. But let me sum up with this: Suppose the only Negro who survived some centuries hence was the Negro painted by white Americans in the novels and essays they have written. What would people in a hundred years say of black Americans? Now turn it around. Suppose you were to write a story and put in it the kind of people you know and like and imagine. You might get it published and you might not. And the "might not" is still far bigger than the "might". The white publishers catering to white folk would say, "It is not interesting"—to white folk, naturally not. They

4. Walter White (1893–1955), author and civil rights leader. Langston Hughes (1902–1967), poet, dramatist, and fiction writer. Jessie Redmon Fauset (1882–1961), editor and novelist.

5. German-American conductor and composer (1862–1950). The Fontainebleau is a French resort.

want Uncle Toms, Topsies,[6] good "darkies" and clowns. I have in my office a story with all the earmarks of truth. A young man says that he started out to write and had his stories accepted. Then he began to write about the things he knew best about, that is, about his own people. He submitted a story to a magazine which said, "We are sorry, but we cannot take it." "I sat down and revised my story, changing the color of the characters and the locale and sent it under an assumed name with a change of address and it was accepted by the same magazine that had refused it, the editor promising to take anything else I might send in providing it was good enough."

We have, to be sure, a few recognized and successful Negro artists; but they are not all those fit to survive or even a good minority. They are but the remnants of that ability and genius among us whom the accidents of education and opportunity have raised on the tidal waves of chance. We black folk are not altogether peculiar in this. After all, in the world at large, it is only the accident, the remnant, that gets the chance to make the most of itself; but if this is true of the white world it is infinitely more true of the colored world. It is not simply the great clear tenor of Roland Hayes[7] that opened the ears of America. We have had many voices of all kinds as fine as his and America was and is as deaf as she was for years to him. Then a foreign land heard Hayes and put its imprint on him and immediately America with all its imitative snobbery woke up. We approved Hayes because London, Paris and Berlin approved him and not simply because he was a great singer.

Thus it is the bounden duty of black America to begin this great work of the creation of Beauty, of the preservation of Beauty, of the realization of Beauty, and we must use in this work all the methods that men have used before. And what have been the tools of the artist in times gone by? First of all, he has used the Truth—not for the sake of truth, not as a scientist seeking truth, but as one upon whom Truth eternally thrusts itself as the highest handmaid of imagination, as the one great vehicle of universal understanding. Again artists have used Goodness—goodness in all its aspects of justice, honor and right—not for sake of an ethical sanction but as the one true method of gaining sympathy and human interest.

The apostle of Beauty thus becomes the apostle of Truth and Right not by choice but by inner and outer compulsion. Free he is but his freedom is ever bounded by Truth and Justice; and slavery only dogs[8] him when he is denied the right to tell the Truth or recognize an ideal of Justice.

Thus all Art is propaganda and ever must be, despite the wailing of the purists. I stand in utter shamelessness and say that whatever art I have for writing has been used always for propaganda for gaining the right of black folk to love and enjoy. I do not care a damn for any art that is not used for propaganda. But I do care when propaganda is confined to one side while the other is stripped and silent.

In New York we have two plays: "White Cargo" and "Congo."[9] In "White Cargo" there is a fallen woman. She is black. In "Congo" the fallen woman is white. In "White Cargo" the black woman goes down further and further and in "Congo" the white woman begins with degradation but in the end is one of the angels of the Lord.

6. Uncle Tom and Topsy are characters from Harriet Beecher Stowe's *Uncle Tom's Cabin* (1852).

7. Internationally acclaimed African American singer (1887–1976).

8. Pursues or troubles relentlessly.

9. Or *Kongo* (1926) by Kilbourn Gordon and Chester DeVonde. "White Cargo": *A Play of the Primitive* (1925) by Leon Gordon.

You know the current magazine story: A young white man goes down to Central America and the most beautiful colored woman there falls in love with him. She crawls across the whole isthmus to get to him. The white man says nobly, "No." He goes back to his white sweetheart in New York.

In such cases, it is not the positive propaganda of people who believe white blood divine, infallible and holy to which I object. It is the denial of a similar right of propaganda to those who believe black blood human, lovable and inspired with new ideals for the world. White artists themselves suffer from this narrowing of their field. They cry for freedom in dealing with Negroes because they have so little freedom in dealing with whites. DuBose Heywood writes "Porgy"[1] and writes beautifully of the black Charleston underworld. But why does he do this? Because he cannot do a similar thing for the white people of Charleston, or they would drum him out of town. The only chance he had to tell the truth of pitiful human degradation was to tell it of colored people. I should not be surprised if Octavius Roy Cohen[2] had approached the *Saturday Evening Post* and asked permission to write about a different kind of colored folk than the monstrosities he has created; but if he has, the *Post* has replied, "No. You are getting paid to write about the kind of colored people you are writing about."

In other words, the white public today demands from its artists, literary and pictorial, racial pre-judgment which deliberately distorts Truth and Justice, as far as colored races are concerned, and it will pay for no other.

On the other hand, the young and slowly growing black public still wants its prophets almost equally unfree. We are bound by all sorts of customs that have come down as second-hand soul clothes of white patrons. We are ashamed of sex and we lower our eyes when people will talk of it. Our religion holds us in superstition. Our worst side has been so shamelessly emphasized that we are denying we have or ever had a worst side. In all sorts of ways we are hemmed in and our new young artists have got to fight their way to freedom.

The ultimate judge has got to be you and you have got to build yourselves up into that wide judgment, that catholicity[3] of temper which is going to enable the artist to have his widest chance for freedom. We can afford the Truth. White folk today cannot. As it is now we are handing everything over to a white jury. If a colored man wants to publish a book, he has got to get a white publisher and a white newspaper to say it is great; and then you and I say so. We must come to the place where the work of art when it appears is reviewed and acclaimed by our own free and unfettered judgment. And we are going to have a real and valuable and eternal judgment only as we make ourselves free of mind, proud of body and just of soul to all men.

And then do you know what will be said? It is already saying. Just as soon as true Art emerges; just as soon as the black artist appears, someone touches the race on the shoulder and says, "He did that because he was an American, not because he was a Negro; he was born here; he was trained here; he is not a Negro—what is a Negro anyhow? He is just human; it is the kind of thing you ought to expect."[4]

I do not doubt that the ultimate art coming from black folk is going to be just as beautiful, and beautiful largely in the same ways, as the art that comes from white folk, or yellow, or red; but the point today is that until the

1. A 1925 novel about southern African American life by Dubose Heyward (1885–1940).
2. Carolina humorist (1891–1959).
3. Broad sympathy, universality.
4. Quotation from *The Fire-Bringer* (1904), a play by William Vaughn Moody (1869–1910).

art of the black folk compells recognition they will not be rated as human. And when through art they compell recognition then let the world discover if it will that their art is as new as it is old and as old as new.

I had a classmate once who did three beautiful things and died. One of them was a story of a folk who found fire and then went wandering in the gloom of night seeking again the stars they had once known and lost; suddenly out of blackness they looked up and there loomed the heavens; and what was it that they said? They raised a mighty cry: "It is the stars, it is the ancient stars, it is the young and everlasting stars!"[5]

1926

5. By William Vaughan Moody.

JAMES WELDON JOHNSON

1871–1938

Born in Jacksonville, Florida, to freeborn middle-class parents from the North, James Weldon Johnson was groomed for success. As headwaiter at the luxurious St. James Hotel, his father, James Johnson, had the wherewithal to help his son become part of the "Talented Tenth." His schoolteacher mother, Helen Louise (Dillet) Johnson, also shared her considerable love and knowledge of English literature and the classical European tradition in music. Study at Atlanta University reinforced his familial values by emphasizing classical education as a trust given to the more fortunate so they could help the less fortunate, and after college Johnson responded to this sense of obligation by becoming principal of Stanton School in his hometown. There, in February 1900, he wrote "Lift Every Voice and Sing" for a school commemoration of Lincoln's birthday. Set to music by his brother, Rosamond, the song resonated throughout African America, becoming known within Johnson's lifetime as the "Negro National Anthem."

Stanton Institute. As principal, James Weldon Johnson wrote "Lift Every Voice and Sing" for students to commemorate Lincoln's birthday celebration.

In his autobiography, *Along This Way* (1933), written soon after he became a professor at Fisk University, James Weldon Johnson recalled his first foray into teaching, forty years earlier. In the summer of 1891, after his freshman year, Johnson had gone to a rural district in Georgia to instruct the children of formerly enslaved people. "In all of my experience there has been no period so brief that has meant so much in my education for life as the three months I spent in the backwoods of Georgia," Johnson wrote. "I was thrown for the first time on my own resources and abilities. I had my first lesson in dealing with men and conditions in the outside world. . . . It was this period that marked the beginning of my psychological change from boyhood to manhood. It was this period which marked also the beginning of my knowledge of my own people as a 'race.'" That experience "laid the first stones in the foundation of faith in [African Americans] on which I have stood ever since. . . . I discerned that the forces behind the slow but persistent movement forward of the race lie, ultimately, in them; that when the vanguard of that movement must fall back, it must fall back on them." Had he not recognized early on the importance of this identification with and reliance on the folk of African America, James Weldon Johnson probably could not have exemplified, as he eventually did with such confidence, the African American vanguard in letters and in social activism during the first third of the twentieth century.

In 1901 Johnson left Jacksonville for New York to collaborate with his brother, J. Rosamond, and their friend Bob Cole on the writing of popular songs and librettos. Enjoying unusual success as a songwriter for Broadway shows, Johnson moved easily in the upper echelons of African American society in Brooklyn, New York, where he met his future wife, Grace Nail. In 1906 Johnson abandoned songwriting for the diplomatic corps, serving first as U.S. consul at Puerto Cabello, Venezuela, and later (in 1909) as head of the U.S. consulate at Corinto, Nicaragua. During those years Johnson published poems in such national periodicals as the *Century Magazine* and the *Independent*, and he finished a novel, *The Autobiography of an Ex-Colored Man*, which was published in 1912, anonymously at his request. What little attention *The Autobiography of an Ex-Colored Man* received was generally positive, but sales of the novel were discouraging.

In the fall of 1913 Johnson resigned from the Foreign Service. A year later he took over the editorial page of the *New York Age*, an influential African American weekly that had supported Booker T. Washington in his struggle with W. E. B. Du Bois for leadership of African America in the early twentieth century. Johnson's gift for political writing soon made him nationally prominent. No ideologue himself, he excelled as a mediator of differences among those whose ideological agendas seemed to preclude unified, cooperative action, and in 1916 he became national organizer for the National Association for the Advancement of Colored People (NAACP). Opposing race riots in northern cities and the lynchings that pervaded the South during and following World War I, Johnson engaged the NAACP in highly visible tactics such as a silent protest parade of ten thousand African Americans down New York's Fifth Avenue on July 28, 1917. In 1920 Johnson was elected to head the NAACP, the first African American to hold this position.

In December 1930, Johnson resigned from the leadership of the NAACP to accept the Spence Chair of Creative Literature at Fisk University, which he held until his death in a car accident in 1938. The position had been especially created for him, largely out of recognition of his achievements as a poet, editor, and critic during the heyday of the Harlem Renaissance in the 1920s. As editor of *The Book of American Negro Poetry* (1922, rev. 1931), itself a landmark in the history of African American literature, Johnson stated unequivocally that African Americans had created "the only things artistic that have yet sprung from American soil and been universally acknowledged as distinctive American products." In characterizing the artistic achievements of African Americans, Johnson paid tribute first to the genius of the folk, to whom he attributed the beast fables associated with Uncle Remus, as well as the spirituals and other slave songs, ragtime music, and the cakewalk. Johnson believed that if African American poets (and by implication almost any other kind of African American artist) aligned themselves with the folk, their work would "express the racial spirit by symbols from within rather than by symbols from without." In his own poetic career, Johnson proved adept at many styles and forms of poetry, from the unaffected dialect of "Sence You Went Away" (1900) to the urbane sonnet "My City" (1923). But his best-known poems—the graphic, pulsating free-verse sermons collected in *God's Trombones* (1927)—drew on the spiritual aspirations and folk imagination of African Americans such as those Johnson met in the rural South.

In 1927 Johnson republished his novel, with the spelling of its title slightly altered to read *The Autobiography of an Ex-Coloured Man* and with its authorship now plainly acknowledged. These changes dramatized his theory of the roots of African American creativity in the story of an artist who rejects his gifts and his people in exchange for a masked identity in the white world. Johnson's novel of passing, though its subject was in some ways antagonistic to the more outspoken celebrants of blackness among the New Negroes of the 1920s, spoke tellingly, nevertheless, to the cultural concerns of the Harlem Renaissance. The protagonist of the *Autobiography* registers profoundly, if also pathetically and even tragically, the problematic exploration of racial identity and the conflicted relationship of "the Negro" to "the American" in the twentieth-century African American's struggle for self-definition in the United States. In *Along This Way* Johnson states that he was pleased when most of the reviewers of the 1912 edition of the *Autobiography* "accepted it as a human document," as a genuine autobiography, not a consciously crafted piece of fiction. "This was a tribute to the writing," Johnson concluded, "for I had done the book with the intention of its being so taken"—as a real account of a real man's interior odyssey toward an uneasy solution to his identity problems. The fact that so much has been argued and so little resolved about what motivates the Ex-Colored Man, and what Johnson intended him to signify, only confirms the *Autobiography*'s inexhaustible appeal as a narrative that evokes the crises of modernity for the early-twentieth-century African American man.

Sence You Went Away

Seems lak to me de stars don't shine so bright,
Seems lak to me de sun done loss his light,
Seems lak to me der's nothin' goin' right,
  Sence you went away.

Seems lak to me de sky ain't half so blue,
Seems lak to me dat eve'ything wants you,
Seems lak to me I don't know what to do,
  Sence you went away.

Seems lak to me dat eve'ything is wrong,
Seems lak to me de day's jes twice ez long,
Seems lak to me de bird's forgot his song,
  Sence you went away.

Seems lak to me I jes can't he'p but sigh,
Seems lak to me ma th'oat keeps gittin' dry,
Seems lak to me a tear stays in ma eye,
  Sence you went away.

1900

Lift Every Voice and Sing

Lift ev'ry voice and sing,
Till earth and heaven ring,
Ring with the harmonies of Liberty;
Let our rejoicing rise
High as the list'ning skies,
Let it resound loud as the rolling sea.
Sing a song full of the faith that the dark past has taught us,
Sing a song full of the hope that the present has brought us;
Facing the rising sun of our new day begun,
Let us march on till victory is won.

Stony the road we trod,
Bitter the chast'ning rod,
Felt in the days when hope unborn had died;
Yet with a steady beat,
Have not our weary feet
Come to the place for which our fathers sighed?
We have come over a way that with tears has been watered,
We have come, treading our path through the blood of the
slaughtered,
Out from the gloomy past,
Till now we stand at last
Where the white gleam of our bright star is cast.

God of our weary years,
God of our silent tears,
Thou who hast brought us thus far on the way;
Thou who hast by Thy might,
Led us into the light,
Keep us forever in the path, we pray.
Lest our feet stray from the places, our God, where we met Thee,
Lest our hearts, drunk with the wine of the world, we forget Thee;
Shadowed beneath Thy hand,
May we forever stand,
True to our God,
True to our native land.

1900 1921

O Black and Unknown Bards

O Black and unknown bards of long ago,
How came your lips to touch the sacred fire?
How, in your darkness, did you come to know
The power and beauty of the minstrel's lyre?
Who first from midst his bonds lifted his eyes?
Who first from out the still watch, lone and long,
Feeling the ancient faith of prophets rise
Within his dark-kept soul, burst into song?

Heart of what slave poured out such melody
As "Steal away to Jesus"?[1] On its strains
His spirit must have nightly floated free,
Though still about his hands he felt his chains.
Who heard great "Jordan roll"?[2] Whose starward eye
Saw chariot "swing low"?[3] And who was he
That breathed that comforting, melodic sigh,
"Nobody knows de trouble I see"?[4]

What merely living clod, what captive thing,
Could up toward God through all its darkness grope,
And find within its deadened heart to sing
These songs of sorrow, love, and faith, and hope?
How did it catch that subtle undertone,
That note in music heard not with the ears?
How sound the elusive reed, so seldom blown,
Which stirs the soul or melts the heart to tears?

Not that great German master[5] in his dream
Of harmonies that thundered 'mongst the stars
At the creation, ever heard a theme
Nobler than "Go down, Moses."[6] Mark its bars,
How like a mighty trumpet-call they stir
The blood. Such are the notes that men have sung,
Going to valorous deeds; such tones there were
That helped make history when Time was young.

There is a wide, wide wonder in it all,
That from degraded rest and service toil
The fiery spirit of the seer should call
These simple children of the sun and soil.
O black slave singers, gone, forgot, unfamed,
You—you alone, of all the long, long line
Of those who've sung untaught, unknown, unnamed,
Have stretched out upward, seeking the divine.

You sang not deeds of heroes or of kings;
No chant of bloody war, no exulting pæan[7]
Of arms-won triumphs; but your humble strings
You touched in chord with music empyrean.[8]
You sang far better than you knew; the songs
That for your listeners' hungry hearts sufficed
Still live,—but more than this to you belongs:
You sang a race from wood and stone to Christ.

1908

1. An African American spiritual.
2. "Roll, Jordan, Roll," an African American spiritual. The Jordan River is in Palestine.
3. "Swing Low, Sweet Chariot," an African American spiritual.
4. An African American spiritual.
5. Gottfried Wilhelm Leibniz (1646–1716), philosopher.
6. An African American spiritual.
7. A song of triumph.
8. From the highest heaven.

Fifty Years

Today Is the Fiftieth Anniversary of Lincoln's Emancipation Proclamation

O brothers mine, to-day we stand
  Where half a century sweeps our ken,° *knowledge*
Since God, through Lincoln's ready hand,
  Struck off our bonds and made us men.

Just fifty years—a Winter's day—
  As runs the history of a race;
Yet, as we look back o'er the way,
  How distant seems our starting-place!

Look farther back! Three centuries!
  To where a naked, shivering score,
Snatched from their haunts across the seas,
  Stood, wild-eyed, on Virginia's shore.

Far, far the way that we have trod,
  From heathen kraals[1] and jungle dens,
To freedmen, freemen, sons of God,
  Americans and Citizens.

A part of His unknown design,
  We've lived within a mighty age;
And we have helped to write a line
  On history's most wondrous page.

A few black bondmen strewn along
  The borders of our eastern coast,
Now grown a race, ten million strong,
  An upward, onward, marching host.

Then let us here erect a stone,
  To mark the place, to mark the time;
A witness to God's mercies shown,
  A pledge to hold this day sublime.

And let that stone an altar be
  Whereon thanksgivings we may lay—
Where we, in deep humility,
  For faith and strength renewed may pray,

With open hearts ask from above
  New zeal, new courage and new pow'rs,
That we may grow more worthy of
  This country and this land of ours.

1. African villages, especially in South Africa.

For never let the thought arise
  That we are here on sufferance° bare; *permission*
Outcasts, asylumed 'neath these skies,
  And aliens without part or share

This land is ours by right of birth,
  This land is ours by right of toil;
We helped to turn its virgin earth,
  Our sweat is in its fruitful soil.

Where once the tangled forest stood,
  Where flourished once rank weed and thorn,
Behold the path-traced, peaceful wood,
  The cotton white, the yellow corn.

To gain these fruits that have been earned,
  To hold these fields that have been won,
Our arms have strained, our backs have burned,
  Bent bare beneath a ruthless sun.

That Banner, which is now the type
  Of victory on field and flood—
Remember, its first crimson stripe
  Was dyed by Attucks'[2] willing blood.

And never yet has come the cry—
  When that fair flag has been assailed—
For men to do, for men to die,
  That have we faltered or have failed.

We've helped to bear it, rent and torn,
  Through many a hot-breath'd battle breeze;
Held in our hands, it has been borne
  And planted far across the seas.

And, never yet, O haughty Land—
  Let us, at least, for this be praised—
Has one black, treason-guided hand
  Ever against that flag been raised.

Then should we speak but servile words,
  Or shall we hang our heads in shame?
Stand back of new-come foreign hordes,
  And fear our heritage to claim?

No! Stand erect and without fear,
  And for our foes let this suffice—
We've bought a rightful sonship here,
  And we have more than paid the price.

2. Crispus Attucks (1723?–1770), a fugitive from slavery, was the first person to die in the Boston Massacre, a prelude to the American Revolution.

And yet, my brothers, well I know
  The tethered feet, the pinioned[3] wings,
The spirit bowed beneath the blow,
  The heart grown faint from wounds and stings;

The staggering force of brutish might,
  That strikes and leaves us stunned and dazed;
The long, vain waiting through the night
  To hear some voice for justice raised.

Full well I know the hour when hope
  Sinks dead, and 'round us everywhere
Hangs stifling darkness, and we grope
  With hands uplifted in despair.

Courage! Look out, beyond, and see
  The far horizon's beckoning span!
Faith in your God-known destiny!
  We are a part of some great plan.

Because the tongues of Garrison
  And Phillips[4] now are cold in death,
Think you their work can be undone?
  Or quenched the fires lit by their breath?

Think you that John Brown's spirit stops?
  That Lovejoy[5] was but idly slain?
Or do you think those precious drops
  From Lincoln's heart were shed in vain?

That for which millions prayed and sighed,
  That for which tens of thousands fought,
For which so many freely died,
  God cannot let it come to naught.

1913

3. Bound to prevent flying.
4. Wendell Phillips (1811–1884), antislavery orator. William Lloyd Garrison (1805–1879), crusading antislavery editor and orator.
5. Elijah P. Lovejoy (1802–1837), antislavery editor, killed by a proslavery mob in Alton, Illinois. John Brown (1800–1859) led an antislavery insurrection against the U.S. arsenal at Harpers Ferry, Virginia, resulting in his execution.

Brothers

See! There he stands; not brave, but with an air
Of sullen stupor. Mark him well! Is he
Not more like brute than man? Look in his eye!
No light is there, none, save the light that shines
In the now glaring, and now shifting orbs° *eyes*
Of some wild animal in the hunter's trap.

How came this beast in human shape and form?
Speak man!—We call you man because you wear
His shape—How are you thus? Are you not from
That docile, child-like, tender-hearted race
Which we have known three centuries? Not from
That more than faithful race which through three wars
Fed our dear wives and nursed our helpless babes
Without a single breach of trust? Speak out?

I am, and am not.

Then who, why are you?

I am a thing not new, I am as old
As human nature. I am that which lurks,
Ready to spring whenever a bar is loosed;
The ancient trait which fights incessantly
Against restraint, balks at the upward climb;
The weight forever seeking to obey
The law of downward pull,—and I am more:
The bitter fruit am I of planted seed,
The resultant, the inevitable end
Of evil forces and the powers of wrong.

Lessons in degradation, taught and learned,
The memories of cruel sights and deeds,
The pent up bitterness, the unspent hate
Filtered through fifteen generations have
Sprung up and found in me sporadic life.
In me the muttered curse of dying men,
On me the stain of conquered women, and
Consuming me the fearful fires of lust,
Lit long ago by other hands than mine.
In me the down-crushed spirit, the hurled-back prayers
Of wretches now long dead,—their dire bequests,—
In me the echo of the stifled cry
Of children for their bartered mothers' breasts.
I claim no race, no race claims me; I am
No more than human dregs; degenerate;
The monstrous offspring of the monster, Sin;
I am—just what I am—The race that fed
Your wives and nursed your babes would do the same
To-day, but I—

Enough, the brute must die!
Quick! Chain him to that oak! It will resist
The fire much longer than this slender pine.
Now bring the fuel! Pile it 'round him! Wait!
Pile not so fast or high! or we shall lose
The agony and terror in his face.
And now the torch! Good fuel that! the flames
Already leap head-high. Ha! hear that shriek!
And there's another wilder than the first.
Fetch water! Water! Pour a little on
The fire, lest it should burn too fast. Hold so!
Now let it slowly blaze again. See there!
He squirms, he groans, his eyes bulge wildly out,
Searching around in vain appeal for help.
Another shriek, the last! Watch how the flesh
Grows crisp and hangs till, turned to ash, it sifts
Down through the coils of chain that hold erect
The ghastly frame against the bark-scorched tree.

Stop! to each man no more than one man's share
You take that bone, and you this tooth; the chain
Let us divide its links; this skull, of course,
In fair division, to the leader comes.

And now his fiendish crime has been avenged;
Let us back to our wives and children.—Say,
What did he mean by those last muttered words,
"Brothers in spirit, brothers in deed are we"?

1916

The Creation

And God stepped out on space,
And he looked around and said:
I'm lonely—
I'll make me a world.

And far as the eye of God could see
Darkness covered everything,
Blacker than a hundred midnights
Down in a cypress swamp.

Then God smiled,
And the light broke,
And the darkness rolled up on one side,
And the light stood shining on the other,
And God said: That's good!

Then God reached out and took the light in his hands,
And God rolled the light around in his hands

Until he made the sun;
And he set that sun a-blazing in the heavens.
And the light that was left from making the sun
God gathered it up in a shining ball
And flung it against the darkness,
Spangling the night with the moon and stars.
Then down between
The darkness and the light
He hurled the world;
And God said: That's good!

Then God himself stepped down—
And the sun was on his right hand,
And the moon was on his left;
The stars were clustered about his head,
And the earth was under his feet.
And God walked, and where he trod
His footsteps hollowed the valleys out
And bulged the mountains up.

Then he stopped and looked and saw
That the earth was hot and barren.
So God stepped over to the edge of the world
And he spat out the seven seas—
He batted his eyes, and the lightnings flashed—
He clapped his hands, and the thunders rolled—
And the waters above the earth came down,
The cooling waters came down,

Then the green grass sprouted,
And the little red flowers blossomed,
The pine tree pointed his finger to the sky,
And the oak spread out his arms,
The lakes cuddled down in the hollows of the ground,
And the rivers ran down to the sea;
And God smiled again,
And the rainbow appeared,
And curled itself around his shoulder.

Then God raised his arm and he waved his hand
Over the sea and over the land,
And he said: Bring forth! Bring forth!
And quicker than God could drop his hand,
Fishes and fowls
And beasts and birds
Swam the rivers and the seas,
Roamed the forests and the woods,
And split the air with their wings.
And God said: That's good!

Then God walked around,
And God looked around
On all that he had made.
He looked at his sun,

And he looked at his moon,
And he looked at his little stars;
He looked on his world
With all its living things,
And God said: I'm lonely still.

Then God sat down—
On the side of a hill where he could think;
By a deep, wide river he sat down;
With his head in his hands,
God thought and thought,
Till he thought: I'll make me a man!

Up from the bed of the river
God scooped the clay;
And by the bank of the river
He kneeled him down;
And there the great God Almighty
Who lit the sun and fixed it in the sky,
Who flung the stars to the most far corner of the night,
Who rounded the earth in the middle of his hand;
This Great God,
Like a mammy bending over her baby,
Kneeled down in the dust
Toiling over a lump of clay
Till he shaped it in his own image;

Then into it he blew the breath of life,
And man became a living soul.
Amen. Amen.

1920

My City

When I come down to sleep death's endless night,
    The threshold of the unknown dark to cross,
    What to me then will be the keenest loss,
When this bright world blurs on my fading sight?
Will it be that no more I shall see the trees
    Or smell the flowers or hear the singing birds
    Or watch the flashing streams or patient herds?
No, I am sure it will be none of these.
But, ah! Manhattan's sights and sounds, her smells,
    Her crowds, her throbbing force, the thrill that comes
From being of her a part, her subtile spells,
    Her shining towers, her avenues, her slums—
    O God! the stark, unutterable pity,
To be dead, and never again behold my city!

1923

The Autobiography of an Ex-Colored Man

Preface to the Original Edition of 1912

This vivid and startlingly new picture of conditions brought about by the race question in the United States makes no special plea for the Negro, but shows in a dispassionate, though sympathetic, manner conditions as they actually exist between the whites and blacks to-day. Special pleas have already been made for and against the Negro in hundreds of books, but in these books either his virtues or his vices have been exaggerated. This is because writers, in nearly every instance, have treated the colored American as a *whole*; each has taken some one group of the race to prove his case. Not before has a composite and proportionate presentation of the entire race, embracing all of its various groups and elements, showing their relations with each other and to the whites, been made.

It is very likely that the Negroes of the United States have a fairly correct idea of what the white people of the country think of them, for that opinion has for a long time been and is still being constantly stated; but they are themselves more or less a sphinx to the whites. It is curiously interesting and even vitally important to know what are the thoughts of ten millions of them concerning the people among whom they live. In these pages it is as though a veil had been drawn aside: the reader is given a view of the inner life of the Negro in America, is initiated into the "freemasonry," as it were, of the race.

These pages also reveal the unsuspected fact that prejudice against the Negro is exerting a pressure which, in New York and other large cities where the opportunity is open, is actually and constantly forcing an unascertainable number of fair-complexioned colored people over into the white race.

In this book the reader is given a glimpse behind the scenes of this race-drama which is being here enacted,—he is taken upon an elevation where he can catch a bird's-eye view of the conflict which is being waged.

THE PUBLISHERS
[Sherman, French & Company]

I

I know that in writing the following pages I am divulging the great secret of my life, the secret which for some years I have guarded far more carefully than any of my earthly possessions; and it is a curious study to me to analyze the motives which prompt me to do it. I feel that I am led by the same impulse which forces the un-found-out criminal to take somebody into his confidence, although he knows that the act is likely, even almost certain, to lead to his undoing. I know that I am playing with fire, and I feel the thrill which accompanies that most fascinating pastime; and, back of it all, I think I find a sort of savage and diabolical desire to gather up all the little tragedies of my life, and turn them into a practical joke on society.

And, too, I suffer a vague feeling of unsatisfaction, of regret, of almost remorse, from which I am seeking relief, and of which I shall speak in the last paragraph of this account.

I was born in a little town of Georgia a few years after the close of the Civil War. I shall not mention the name of the town, because there are people still living there who could be connected with this narrative. I have only a faint recollection of the place of my birth. At times I can close my eyes and call up in a dreamlike way things that seem to have happened ages ago in some other world. I can see in this half vision a little house—I am quite sure it was not a large one—I can remember that flowers grew in the front yard, and that around each bed of flowers was a hedge of vari-colored glass bottles stuck in the ground neck down. I remember that once, while playing around in the sand, I became curious to know whether or not the bottles grew as the flowers did, and I proceeded to dig them up to find out; the investigation brought me a terrific spanking, which indelibly fixed the incident in my mind. I can remember, too, that behind the house was a shed under which stood two or three wooden wash-tubs. These tubs were the earliest aversion of my life, for regularly on certain evenings I was plunged into one of them and scrubbed until my skin ached. I can remember to this day the pain caused by the strong, rank soap's getting into my eyes.

Back from the house a vegetable garden ran, perhaps seventy-five or one hundred feet; but to my childish fancy it was an endless territory. I can still recall the thrill of joy, excitement, and wonder it gave me to go on an exploring expedition through it, to find the blackberries, both ripe and green, that grew along the edge of the fence.

I remember with what pleasure I used to arrive at, and stand before, a little enclosure in which stood a patient cow chewing her cud, how I would occasionally offer her through the bars a piece of my bread and molasses, and how I would jerk back my hand in half fright if she made any motion to accept my offer.

I have a dim recollection of several people who moved in and about this little house, but I have a distinct mental image of only two: one, my mother; and the other, a tall man with a small, dark mustache. I remember that his shoes or boots were always shiny, and that he wore a gold chain and a great gold watch with which he was always willing to let me play. My admiration was almost equally divided between the watch and chain and the shoes. He used to come to the house evenings, perhaps two or three times a week; and it became my appointed duty whenever he came to bring him a pair of slippers and to put the shiny shoes in a particular corner; he often gave me in return for this service a bright coin, which my mother taught me to promptly drop in a little tin bank. I remember distinctly the last time this tall man came to the little house in Georgia; that evening before I went to bed he took me up in his arms and squeezed me very tightly; my mother stood behind his chair wiping tears from her eyes. I remember how I sat upon his knee and watched him laboriously drill a hole through a ten-dollar gold piece, and then tie the coin around my neck with a string. I have worn that gold piece around my neck the greater part of my life, and still possess it, but more than once I have wished that some other way had been found of attaching it to me besides putting a hole through it.

On the day after the coin was put around my neck my mother and I started on what seemed to me an endless journey. I knelt on the seat and watched through the train window the corn and cotton fields pass swiftly by until I fell asleep. When I fully awoke, we were being driven through the streets of a large city—Savannah. I sat up and blinked at the bright lights. At Savannah we boarded a steamer which finally landed us in New York. From New York we went to a town in Connecticut, which became the home of my boyhood.

My mother and I lived together in a little cottage which seemed to me to be fitted up almost luxuriously; there were horse-hair-covered chairs in the parlor, and a little square piano; there was a stairway with red carpet on it leading to a half second story; there were pictures on the walls, and a few books in a glass-doored case. My mother dressed me very neatly, and I developed that pride which well-dressed boys generally have. She was careful about my associates, and I myself was quite particular. As I look back now I can see that I was a perfect little aristocrat. My mother rarely went to anyone's house, but she did sewing, and there were a great many ladies coming to our cottage. If I was around they would generally call me, and ask me my name and age and tell my mother what a pretty boy I was. Some of them would pat me on the head and kiss me.

My mother was kept very busy with her sewing; sometimes she would have another woman helping her. I think she must have derived a fair income from her work. I know, too, that at least once each month she received a letter; I used to watch for the postman, get the letter, and run to her with it; whether she was busy or not, she would take it and instantly thrust it into her bosom. I never saw her read one of these letters. I knew later that they contained money and what was to her more than money. As busy as she generally was, she found time, however, to teach me my letters and figures and how to spell a number of easy words. Always on Sunday evenings she opened the little square piano and picked out hymns. I can recall now that whenever she played hymns from the book her *tempo* was always decidedly *largo*.[1] Sometimes on other evenings, when she was not sewing, she would play simple accompaniments to some old Southern songs which she sang. In these songs she was freer, because she played them by ear. Those evenings on which she opened the little piano were the happiest hours of my childhood. Whenever she started toward the instrument, I used to follow her with all the interest and irrepressible joy that a pampered pet dog shows when a package is opened in which he knows there is a sweet bit for him. I used to stand by her side and often interrupt and annoy her by chiming in with strange harmonies which I found on either the high keys of the treble or the low keys of the bass. I remember that I had a particular fondness for the black keys. Always on such evenings, when the music was over, my mother would sit with me in her arms, often for a very long time. She would hold me close, softly crooning some old melody without words, all the while gently stroking her face against my head; many and many a night I thus fell asleep. I can see her now, her great dark eyes looking into the fire, to where? No one knew but her. The memory of that picture has more than once kept me from straying too far from the place of purity and safety in which her arms held me.

At a very early age I began to thump on the piano alone, and it was not long before I was able to pick out a few tunes. When I was seven years old, I could play by ear all of the hymns and songs that my mother knew. I had also learned the names of the notes in both clefs, but I preferred not to be hampered by notes. About this time several ladies for whom my mother

1. Slow and dignified (Italian).

sewed heard me play and they persuaded her that I should at once be put under a teacher; so arrangements were made for me to study the piano with a lady who was a fairly good musician; at the same time arrangements were made for me to study my books with this lady's daughter. My music teacher had no small difficulty at first in pinning me down to the notes. If she played my lesson over for me, I invariably attempted to reproduce the required sounds without the slightest recourse to the written characters. Her daughter, my other teacher, also had her worries. She found that, in reading, whenever I came to words that were difficult or unfamiliar, I was prone to bring my imagination to the rescue and read from the picture. She has laughingly told me, since then, that I would sometimes substitute whole sentences and even paragraphs from what meaning I thought the illustrations conveyed. She said she not only was sometimes amused at the fresh treatment I would give an author's subject, but, when I gave some new and sudden turn to the plot of the story, often grew interested and even excited in listening to hear what kind of a denouement I would bring about. But I am sure this was not due to dullness, for I made rapid progress in both my music and my books.

And so for a couple of years my life was divided between my music and my school books. Music took up the greater part of my time. I had no playmates, but amused myself with games—some of them my own invention—which could be played alone. I knew a few boys whom I had met at the church which I attended with my mother, but I had formed no close friendships with any of them. Then, when I was nine years old, my mother decided to enter me in the public school, so all at once I found myself thrown among a crowd of boys of all sizes and kinds; some of them seemed to me like savages. I shall never forget the bewilderment, the pain, the heart-sickness, of that first day at school. I seemed to be the only stranger in the place; every other boy seemed to know every other boy. I was fortunate enough, however, to be assigned to a teacher who knew me; my mother made her dresses. She was one of the ladies who used to pat me on the head and kiss me. She had the tact to address a few words directly to me; this gave me a certain sort of standing in the class and put me somewhat at ease.

Within a few days I had made one staunch friend and was on fairly good terms with most of the boys. I was shy of the girls, and remained so; even now a word or look from a pretty woman sets me all a-tremble. This friend I bound to me with hooks of steel in a very simple way. He was a big awkward boy with a face full of freckles and a head full of very red hair. He was perhaps fourteen years of age; that is, four or five years older than any other boy in the class. This seniority was due to the fact that he had spent twice the required amount of time in several of the preceding classes. I had not been at school many hours before I felt that "Red Head"—as I involuntarily called him—and I were to be friends. I do not doubt that this feeling was strengthened by the fact that I had been quick enough to see that a big, strong boy was a friend to be desired at a public school; and, perhaps, in spite of his dullness, "Red Head" had been able to discern that I could be of service to him. At any rate there was a simultaneous mutual attraction.

The teacher had strung the class promiscuously around the walls of the room for a sort of trial heat for places of rank; when the line was straightened out, I found that by skillful maneuvering I had placed myself third and had piloted "Red Head" to the place next to me. The teacher began by giving us to spell the words corresponding to our order in the line. "Spell *first*." "Spell *second*." "Spell *third*." I rattled off: "T-h-i-r-d, third," in a way which said: "Why don't you give us something hard?" As the words went down the line, I could see how lucky I had been to get a good place together with an easy word. As young as I was, I felt impressed with the unfairness of the whole proceeding when I saw the tailenders going down before *twelfth* and *twentieth*, and I felt sorry for those who had to spell such words in order to hold a low position. "Spell *fourth*." "Red Head," with his hands clutched tightly behind his back, began bravely: "F-o-r-t-h." Like a flash a score of hands went up, and the teacher began saying: "No snapping of fingers, no snapping of fingers." This was the first word missed, and it seemed to me that some of the scholars were about to lose their senses; some were dancing up and down on one foot with a hand above their heads, the fingers working furiously, and joy beaming all over their faces; others stood still, their hands raised not so high, their fingers working less rapidly, and their faces expressing not quite so much happiness; there were still others who did not move or raise their hands, but stood with great wrinkles on their foreheads, looking very thoughtful.

The whole thing was new to me, and I did not raise my hand, but slyly whispered the letter "u" to "Red Head" several times. "Second chance," said the teacher. The hands went down and the class became quiet. "Red Head," his face now red, after looking beseechingly at the ceiling, then pitiably at the floor, began very haltingly: "F-u—" Immediately an impulse to raise hands went through the class, but the teacher checked it, and poor "Red Head," though he knew that each letter he added only took him farther out of the way, went doggedly on and finished: "—r-t-h." The hand-raising was now repeated with more hubbub and excitement than at first. Those who before had not moved a finger were now waving their hands above their heads. "Red Head" felt that he was lost. He looked very big and foolish, and some of the scholars began to snicker. His helpless condition went straight to my heart, and gripped my sympathies. I felt that if he failed, it would in some way be my failure. I raised my hand, and, under cover of the excitement and the teacher's attempts to regain order, I hurriedly shot up into his ear twice, quite distinctly: "F-o-u-r-t-h, f-o-u-r-t-h." The teacher tapped on her desk and said: "Third and last chance." The hands came down, the silence became oppressive. "Red Head" began: "F—" Since that day I have waited anxiously for many a turn of the wheel of fortune, but never under greater tension than when I watched for the order in which those letters would fall from "Red's" lips—"o-u-r-t-h." A sigh of relief and disappointment went up from the class. Afterwards, through all our school days, "Red Head" shared my wit and quickness and I benefited by his strength and dogged faithfulness.

There were some black and brown boys and girls in the school, and several of them were in my class. One of the boys strongly attracted my attention from the first day I saw him. His face was as black as night, but shone as though it were polished; he had sparkling eyes, and when he opened his mouth, he displayed glistening white teeth. It struck me at once as appropriate to call him "Shiny Face," or "Shiny Eyes," or "Shiny Teeth," and I spoke of him often by one of these names to the other boys. These terms were finally merged into "Shiny," and to that name he answered good-naturedly during the balance of his public school days.

"Shiny" was considered without question to be the best speller, the best reader, the best penman—in a word, the best scholar, in the class. He was very quick to catch anything, but, nevertheless, studied hard; thus he possessed two powers very rarely combined in one boy. I saw him year after year, on up into the high school, win the majority of the prizes for punctuality, deportment, essay writing, and declamation. Yet it did not take me long to discover that, in spite of his standing as a scholar, he was in some way looked down upon.

The other black boys and girls were still more looked down upon. Some of the boys often spoke of them as "niggers." Sometimes on the way home from school a crowd would walk behind them repeating:

"Nigger, nigger, never die,
Black face and shiny eye."[2]

On one such afternoon one of the black boys turned suddenly on his tormentors and hurled a slate; it struck one of the white boys in the mouth, cutting a slight gash in his lip. At sight of the blood the boy who had thrown the slate ran, and his companions quickly followed. We ran after them pelting them with stones until they separated in several directions. I was very much wrought up over the affair, and went home and told my mother how one of the "niggers" had struck a boy with a slate. I shall never forget how she turned on me. "Don't you ever use that word again," she said, "and don't you ever bother the colored children at school. You ought to be ashamed of yourself." I did hang my head in shame, not because she had convinced me that I had done wrong, but because I was hurt by the first sharp word she had ever given me.

My school days ran along very pleasantly. I stood well in my studies, not always so well with regard to my behavior. I was never guilty of any serious misconduct, but my love of fun sometimes got me into trouble. I remember, however, that my sense of humor was so sly that most of the trouble usually fell on the head of the other fellow. My ability to play on the piano at school exercises was looked upon as little short of marvelous in a boy of my age. I was not chummy with many of my mates, but, on the whole, was about as popular as it is good for a boy to be.

One day near the end of my second term at school the principal came into our room and, after talking to the teacher, for some reason said: "I wish all of the white scholars to stand for a moment." I rose with the others. The teacher looked at me and, calling my name, said: "You sit down for the present, and rise with the others." I did not quite understand her, and questioned: "Ma'm?" She repeated, with a softer tone in her voice: "You sit down now, and rise with the others." I sat down dazed. I saw and heard nothing. When the others were asked to rise, I did not know it. When school was dismissed, I went out in a kind of stupor. A few of the white boys jeered me, saying: "Oh, you're a nigger too." I heard some black children say: "We knew he was colored." "Shiny" said to them: "Come along, don't tease him," and thereby won my undying gratitude.

I hurried on as fast as I could, and had gone some distance before I perceived that "Red Head" was walking by my side. After a while he said to me: "Le' me carry your books." I gave him my strap without being able to answer. When we got to my gate, he said as he handed me my books: "Say, you know

2. One of many derogatory folk rhymes; also lyrics to a song popularized in 1897 by Nellie Sylvester and William Osborne.

my big red agate? I can't shoot with it any more. I'm going to bring it to school for you tomorrow." I took my books and ran into the house. As I passed through the hallway, I saw that my mother was busy with one of her customers; I rushed up into my own little room, shut the door, and went quickly to where my looking-glass hung on the wall. For an instant I was afraid to look, but when I did, I looked long and earnestly. I had often heard people say to my mother: "What a pretty boy you have!" I was accustomed to hear remarks about my beauty; but now, for the first time, I became conscious of it and recognized it. I noticed the ivory whiteness of my skin, the beauty of my mouth, the size and liquid darkness of my eyes, and how the long, black lashes that fringed and shaded them produced an effect that was strangely fascinating even to me. I noticed the softness and glossiness of my dark hair that fell in waves over my temples, making my forehead appear whiter than it really was. How long I stood there gazing at my image I do not know. When I came out and reached the head of the stairs, I heard the lady who had been with my mother going out. I ran downstairs and rushed to where my mother was sitting, with a piece of work in her hands. I buried my head in her lap and blurted out: "Mother, mother, tell me, am I a nigger?" I could not see her face, but I knew the piece of work dropped to the floor and I felt her hands on my head. I looked up into her face and repeated: "Tell me, mother, am I a nigger?" There were tears in her eyes and I could see that she was suffering for me. And then it was that I looked at her critically for the first time. I had thought of her in a childish way only as the most beautiful woman in the world; now I looked at her searching for defects. I could see that her skin was almost brown, that her hair was not so soft as mine, and that she did differ in some way from the other ladies who came to the house; yet, even so, I could see that she was very beautiful, more beautiful than any of them. She must have felt that I was examining her, for she hid her face in my hair and said with difficulty: "No, my darling, you are not a nigger." She went on: "You are as good as anybody; if anyone calls you a nigger, don't notice them." But the more she talked, the less was I reassured, and I stopped her by asking: "Well, mother, am I white? Are you white?" She answered tremblingly: "No, I am not white, but you—your father is one of the greatest men in the country—the best blood of the South is in you—" This suddenly opened up in my heart a fresh chasm of misgiving and fear, and I almost fiercely demanded: "Who is my father? Where is he?" She stroked my hair and said: "I'll tell you about him some day." I sobbed: "I want to know now." She answered: "No, not now."

Perhaps it had to be done, but I have never forgiven the woman who did it so cruelly. It may be that she never knew that she gave me a sword-thrust that day in school which was years in healing.

II

Since I have grown older I have often gone back and tried to analyze the change that came into my life after that fateful day in school. There did come a radical change, and, young as I was, I felt fully conscious of it, though I did not fully comprehend it. Like my first spanking, it is one of the few incidents in my life that I can remember clearly. In the life of everyone there is a limited number of unhappy experiences which are not written upon the memory, but stamped there with a die; and in long years after, they can be called up in detail, and every emotion that was stirred by them can be lived through anew; these are the tragedies of life. We may grow to include some of them among the trivial incidents of childhood—a broken toy, a promise made to us which was not kept, a harsh, heart-piercing word—but these, too, as well as the bitter experiences and disappointments of mature years, are the tragedies of life.

And so I have often lived through that hour, that day, that week, in which was wrought the miracle of my transition from one world into another; for I did indeed pass into another world. From that time I looked out through other eyes, my thoughts were colored, my words dictated, my actions limited by one dominating, all-pervading idea which constantly increased in force and weight until I finally realized in it a great, tangible fact.

And this is the dwarfing, warping, distorting influence which operates upon each and every colored man in the United States. He is forced to take his outlook on all things, not from the viewpoint of a citizen, or a man, or even a human being, but from the viewpoint of a *colored* man. It is wonderful to me that the race has progressed so broadly as it has, since most of its thought and all of its activity must run through the narrow neck of this one funnel.

And it is this, too, which makes the colored people of this country, in reality, a mystery to the whites. It is a difficult thing for a white man to learn what a colored man really thinks; because, generally, with the latter an additional and different light must be brought to bear on what he thinks; and his thoughts are often influenced by considerations so delicate and subtle that it would be impossible for him to confess or explain them to one of the opposite race. This gives to every colored man, in proportion to his intellectuality, a sort of dual personality; there is one phase of him which is disclosed only in the freemasonry of his own race. I have often watched with interest and sometimes with amazement even ignorant colored men under cover of broad grins and minstrel antics maintain this dualism in the presence of white men.

I believe it to be a fact that the colored people of this country know and understand the white people better than the white people know and understand them.

I now think that this change which came into my life was at first more subjective than objective. I do not think my friends at school changed so much toward me as I did toward them. I grew reserved, I might say suspicious. I grew constantly more and more afraid of laying myself open to some injury to my feelings or my pride. I frequently saw or fancied some slight where, I am sure, none was intended. On the other hand, my friends and teachers were, if anything different, more considerate of me; but I can remember that it was against this very attitude in particular that my sensitiveness revolted. "Red" was the only one who did not so wound me; up to this day I recall with a swelling heart his clumsy efforts to make me understand that nothing could change his love for me.

I am sure that at this time the majority of my white schoolmates did not understand or appreciate any differences between me and themselves; but there were a few who had evidently received instructions at home on the matter, and more than once they displayed their knowledge in word and action. As the years passed, I noticed that the most innocent and ignorant among the others grew in wisdom.

I myself would not have so clearly understood this difference had it not been for the presence of the other colored children at school; I had learned what their status was, and now I learned that theirs was mine. I had had no particular like or dislike for these black and brown boys and girls; in fact, with the exception of "Shiny," they had occupied very little of my thought; but I do know that when the blow fell, I had a very strong aversion to being classed with them. So I became something of a solitary. "Red" and I remained inseparable, and there was between "Shiny" and me a sort of sympathetic bond, but my intercourse with the others was never entirely free from a feeling of constraint. I must add, however, that this feeling was confined almost entirely to my intercourse with boys and girls of about my own age; I did not experience it with my seniors. And when I grew to manhood, I found myself freer with elderly white people than with those near my own age.

I was now about eleven years old, but these emotions and impressions which I have just described could not have been stronger or more distinct at an older age. There were two immediate results of my forced loneliness: I began to find company in books, and greater pleasure in music. I made the former discovery through a big, gilt-bound, illustrated copy of the Bible, which used to lie in splendid neglect on the center table in our little parlor. On top of the Bible lay a photograph album. I had often looked at the pictures in the album, and one day, after taking the larger book down and opening it on the floor, I was overjoyed to find that it contained what seemed to be an inexhaustible supply of pictures. I looked at these pictures many times; in fact, so often that I knew the story of each one without having to read the subject, and then, somehow, I picked up the thread of history on which are strung the trials and tribulations of the Hebrew children; this I followed with feverish interest and excitement. For a long time King David, with Samson a close second, stood at the head of my list of heroes; he was not displaced until I came to know Robert the Bruce.[3] I read a good portion of the Old Testament, all that part treating of wars and rumors of wars, and then started in on the New. I became interested in the life of Christ, but became impatient and disappointed when I found that, notwithstanding the great power he possessed, he did not make use of it when, in my judgment, he most needed to do so. And so my first general impression of the Bible was what my later impression has been of a number of modern books, that the authors put their best work in the first part, and grew either exhausted or careless toward the end.

After reading the Bible, or those parts which held my attention, I began to explore the glass-doored bookcase which I have already mentioned. I found there *Pilgrim's Progress*, Peter Parley's *History of the United States*, Grimm's *Household Stories*, *Tales of a Grandfather*, a bound volume of an old English publication (I think it was called *The Mirror*), a little volume called *Familiar Science*,[4] and somebody's *Natural Theology*, which last, of course, I could not read, but which, nevertheless, I tackled, with the result of gaining a permanent dislike for all kinds of theology. There were several

3. Robert I (1274–1329), king of Scotland. David (ca. 1012–972 B.C.E.), biblical king of Israel. Samson was a tragic biblical hero of great strength (Judges 13–16).

4. R. E. Peterson's *Familiar Science, or the Scientific Explanation of Common Things* (1851). *Pilgrim's Progress* (1678) is a prose religious allegory by English author John Bunyan (1628–1688). "Parley's *History of the United States*": probably *A Pictorial History of the United States* (1844) by juvenile writer Samuel G. Goodrich (1793–1860). *Household Stories* (1812–15) is a collection of fairy tales by Wilhelm and Jacob Grimm. *Tales of a Grandfather* (1827–29) contains stories about the history of Scotland by novelist Sir Walter Scott (1771–1832). The Mirror Library series was published in the 1840s by Nathaniel Parker Willis.

other books of no particular name or merit, such as agents sell to people who know nothing of buying books. How my mother came by this little library which, considering all things, was so well suited to me I never sought to know. But she was far from being an ignorant woman and had herself, very likely, read the majority of these books, though I do not remember ever seeing her with a book in her hand, with the exception of the Episcopal Prayer book. At any rate she encouraged in me the habit of reading, and when I had about exhausted those books in the little library which interested me, she began to buy books for me. She also regularly gave me money to buy a weekly paper which was then very popular for boys.

At this time I went in for music with an earnestness worthy of maturer years; a change of teachers was largely responsible for this. I began now to take lessons of the organist of the church which I attended with my mother; he was a good teacher and quite a thorough musician. He was so skillful in his instruction and filled me with such enthusiasm that my progress—these are his words—was marvelous. I remember that when I was barely twelve years old I appeared on a program with a number of adults at an entertainment given for some charitable purpose, and carried off the honors. I did more, I brought upon myself through the local newspapers the handicapping title of "infant prodigy."

I can believe that I did astonish my audience, for I never played the piano like a child; that is, in the "one-two-three" style with accelerated motion. Neither did I depend upon mere brilliancy of technique, a trick by which children often surprise their listeners; but I always tried to interpret a piece of music; I always played with feeling. Very early I acquired that knack of using the pedals, which makes the piano a sympathetic, singing instrument, quite a different thing from the source of hard or blurred sounds it so generally is. I think this was due not entirely to natural artistic temperament, but largely to the fact that I did not begin to learn the piano by counting out exercises, but by trying to reproduce the quaint songs which my mother used to sing, with all their pathetic turns and cadences.

Even at a tender age, in playing I helped to express what I felt by some of the mannerisms which I afterwards observed in great performers; I had not copied them. I have often heard people speak of the mannerisms of musicians as affectations adopted for mere effect; in some cases they may be so; but a true artist can no more play upon the piano or violin without putting his whole body in accord with the emotions he is striving to express than a swallow can fly without being graceful. Often when playing I could not keep the tears which formed in my eyes from rolling down my cheeks. Sometimes at the end or even in the midst of a composition, as big a boy as I was, I would jump from the piano, and throw myself sobbing into my mother's arms. She, by her caresses and often her tears, only encouraged these fits of sentimental hysteria. Of course, to counteract this tendency to temperamental excesses I should have been out playing ball or in swimming with other boys of my age; but my mother didn't know that. There was only once when she was really firm with me, making me do what she considered was best; I did not want to return to school after the unpleasant episode which I have related, and she was inflexible.

I began my third term, and the days ran along as I have already indicated. I had been promoted twice, and had managed each time to pull "Red" along with me. I think the teachers came to consider me the only hope of his ever getting through school, and I believe they secretly conspired with me to bring about the desired end. At any rate, I know it became easier in each succeeding examination for me not only to assist "Red," but absolutely to do his work. It is strange how in some things honest people can be dishonest without the slightest compunction. I knew boys at school who were too honorable to tell a fib even when one would have been just the right thing, but could not resist the temptation to assist or receive assistance in an examination. I have long considered it the highest proof of honesty in a man to hand his street-car fare to the conductor who had overlooked it.

One afternoon after school, during my third term, I rushed home in a great hurry to get my dinner and go to my music teacher's. I was never reluctant about going there, but on this particular afternoon I was impetuous. The reason of this was I had been asked to play the accompaniment for a young lady who was to play a violin solo at a concert given by the young people of the church, and on this afternoon we were to have our first rehearsal. At that time playing accompaniments was the only thing in music I did not enjoy; later this feeling grew into positive dislike. I have never been a really good accompanist because my ideas of interpretation were always too strongly individual. I constantly forced my *accelerandos* and *rubatos*[5] upon the soloist, often throwing the duet entirely out of gear.

Perhaps the reader has already guessed why I was so willing and anxious to play the accompaniment to this violin solo; if not—the violinist was a girl of seventeen or eighteen whom I had first heard play a short time before on a Sunday afternoon at a special service of some kind, and who had moved me to a degree which now I can hardly think of as possible. At present I do not think it was due to her wonderful playing, though I judge she must have been a very fair performer, but there was just the proper setting to produce the effect upon a boy such as I was; the half-dim church, the air of devotion on the part of the listeners, the heaving tremor of the organ under the clear wail of the violin, and she, her eyes almost closing, the escaping strands of her dark hair wildly framing her pale face, and her slender body swaying to the tones she called forth, all combined to fire my imagination and my heart with a passion, though boyish, yet strong and, somehow, lasting. I have tried to describe the scene; if I have succeeded, it is only half success, for words can only partially express what I wish to convey. Always in recalling that Sunday afternoon I am subconscious of a faint but distinct fragrance which, like some old memory-awakening perfume, rises and suffuses my whole imagination, inducing a state of reverie so airy as just to evade the powers of expression.

She was my first love, and I loved her as only a boy loves. I dreamed of her, I built air castles for her, she was the incarnation of each beautiful heroine I knew; when I played the piano, it was to her, not even music furnished an adequate outlet for my passion; I bought a new note-book and, to sing her praises, made my first and last attempts at poetry. I remember one day at school, after we had given in our notebooks to have some exercises corrected, the teacher called me to her desk and said: "I couldn't correct your exercises because I found nothing in your book but a rhapsody on somebody's brown eyes." I had passed in the wrong note-book. I don't think

5. Departures from strict tempo during performance (literally, "robbed" in Italian). "*Accelerandos*": sections played with a gradual increase of speed (Italian).

I have felt greater embarrassment in my whole life than I did at that moment. I was ashamed not only that my teacher should see this nakedness of my heart, but that she should find out that I had any knowledge of such affairs. It did not then occur to me to be ashamed of the kind of poetry I had written.

Of course, the reader must know that all of this adoration was in secret; next to my great love for this young lady was the dread that in some way she would find it out. I did not know what some men never find out, that the woman who cannot discern when she is loved has never lived. It makes me laugh to think how successful I was in concealing it all; within a short time after our duet all of the friends of my dear one were referring to me as her "little sweetheart," or her "little beau," and she laughingly encouraged it. This did not entirely satisfy me; I wanted to be taken seriously. I had definitely made up my mind that I should never love another woman, and that if she deceived me I should do something desperate—the great difficulty was to think of something sufficiently desperate—and the heartless jade,[6] how she led me on!

So I hurried home that afternoon, humming snatches of the violin part of the duet, my heart beating with pleasurable excitement over the fact that I was going to be near her, to have her attention placed directly upon me; that I was going to be of service to her, and in a way in which I could show myself to advantage—this last consideration has much to do with cheerful service—. The anticipation produced in me a sensation somewhat between bliss and fear. I rushed through the gate, took the three steps to the house at one bound, threw open the door, and was about to hang my cap on its accustomed peg of the hall rack when I noticed that that particular peg was occupied by a black derby hat. I stopped suddenly and gazed at this hat as though I had never seen an object of its description. I was still looking at it in open-eyed wonder when my mother, coming out of the parlor into the hallway, called me and said there was someone inside who wanted to see me. Feeling that I was being made a party to some kind of mystery, I went in with her, and there I saw a man standing leaning with one elbow on the mantel, his back partly turned toward the door. As I entered, he turned and I saw a tall, handsome, well-dressed gentleman of perhaps thirty-five; he advanced a step toward me with a smile on his face. I stopped and looked at him with the same feelings with which I had looked at the derby hat, except that they were greatly magnified. I looked at him from head to foot, but he was an absolute blank to me until my eyes rested on his slender, elegant polished shoes; then it seemed that indistinct and partly obliterated films of memory began, at first slowly, then rapidly, to unroll, forming a vague panorama of my childhood days in Georgia.

My mother broke the spell by calling me by name and saying: "This is your father."

"Father, father," that was the word which had been to me a source of doubt and perplexity ever since the interview with my mother on the subject. How often I had wondered about my father, who he was, what he was like, whether alive or dead, and, above all, why she would not tell me about him. More than once I had been on the point of recalling to her the promise she had made me, but I instinctively felt that she was happier for not telling

6. A disreputable woman; flirtatious.

me and that I was happier for not being told; yet I had not the slightest idea what the real truth was. And here he stood before me, just the kind of looking father I had wishfully pictured him to be; but I made no advance toward him; I stood there feeling embarrassed and foolish, not knowing what to say or do. I am not sure but that he felt pretty much the same. My mother stood at my side with one hand on my shoulder, almost pushing me forward, but I did not move. I can well remember the look of disappointment, even pain, on her face; and I can now understand that she could expect nothing else but that at the name "father" I should throw myself into his arms. But I could not rise to this dramatic, or, better, melodramatic, climax. Somehow I could not arouse any considerable feeling of need for a father. He broke the awkward tableau by saying: "Well, boy, aren't you glad to see me?" He evidently meant the words kindly enough, but I don't know what he could have said that would have had a worse effect; however, my good breeding came to my rescue, and I answered: "Yes, sir," and went to him and offered him my hand. He took my hand into one of his, and, with the other, stroked my head, saying that I had grown into a fine youngster. He asked me how old I was; which, of course, he must have done merely to say something more, or perhaps he did so as a test of my intelligence. I replied: "Twelve, sir." He then made the trite observation about the flight of time, and we lapsed into another awkward pause.

My mother was all in smiles; I believe that was one of the happiest moments of her life. Either to put me more at ease or to show me off, she asked me to play something for my father. There is only one thing in the world that can make music, at all times and under all circumstances, up to its general standard; that is a hand-organ, or one of its variations. I went to the piano and played something in a listless, half-hearted way. I simply was not in the mood. I was wondering, while playing, when my mother would dismiss me and let me go; but my father was so enthusiastic in his praise that he touched my vanity—which was great—and more than that; he displayed that sincere appreciation which always arouses an artist to his best effort, and, too, in an unexplainable manner, makes him feel like shedding tears. I showed my gratitude by playing for him a Chopin waltz with all the feeling that was in me. When I had finished, my mother's eyes were glistening with tears; my father stepped across the room, seized me in his arms, and squeezed me to his breast. I am certain that for that moment he was proud to be my father. He sat and held me standing between his knees while he talked to my mother. I, in the mean time, examined him with more curiosity, perhaps, than politeness. I interrupted the conversation by asking: "Mother, is he going to stay with us now?" I found it impossible to frame the word "father"; it was too new to me; so I asked the question through my mother. Without waiting for her to speak, my father answered: "I've got to go back to New York this afternoon, but I'm coming to see you again." I turned abruptly and went over to my mother, and almost in a whisper reminded her that I had an appointment which I should not miss; to my pleasant surprise she said that she would give me something to eat at once so that I might go. She went out of the room and I began to gather from off the piano the music I needed. When I had finished, my father, who had been watching me, asked: "Are you going?" I replied: "Yes, sir, I've got to go to practice for a concert." He spoke some words of advice to me about being a good boy and taking care of my mother when I grew up, and added that he was going to send me something nice from New York. My mother called, and I said goodbye to him and went out. I saw him only once after that.

I quickly swallowed down what my mother had put on the table for me, seized my cap and music, and hurried off to my teacher's house. On the way I could think of nothing but this new father, where he came from, where he had been, why he was here, and why he would not stay. In my mind I ran over the whole list of fathers I had become acquainted with in my reading, but I could not classify him. The thought did not cross my mind that he was different from me, and even if it had, the mystery would not thereby have been explained; for, notwithstanding my changed relations with most of my schoolmates, I had only a faint knowledge of prejudice and no idea at all how it ramified and affected our entire social organism. I felt, however, that there was something about the whole affair which had to be hid.

When I arrived, I found that she of the brown eyes had been rehearsing with my teacher and was on the point of leaving. My teacher, with some expressions of surprise, asked why I was late, and I stammered out the first deliberate lie of which I have any recollection. I told him that when I reached home from school, I found my mother quite sick, and that I had stayed with her awhile before coming. Then unnecessarily and gratuitously—to give my words force of conviction, I suppose—I added: "I don't think she'll be with us very long." In speaking these words I must have been comical; for I noticed that my teacher, instead of showing signs of anxiety or sorrow, half hid a smile. But how little did I know that in that lie I was speaking a prophecy!

She of the brown eyes unpacked her violin, and we went through the duet several times. I was soon lost to all other thoughts in the delights of music and love. I saw delights of love without reservation; for at no time of life is love so pure, so delicious, so poetic, so romantic, as it is in boyhood. A great deal has been said about the heart of a girl when she stands "where the brook and river meet,"[7] but what she feels is negative; more interesting is the heart of a boy when just at the budding dawn of manhood he stands looking wide-eyed into the long vistas opening before him; when he first becomes conscious of the awakening and quickening of strange desires and unknown powers; when what he sees and feels is still shadowy and mystical enough to be intangible, and, so, more beautiful; when his imagination is unsullied, and his faith new and whole—then it is that love wears a halo. The man who has not loved before he was fourteen has missed a foretaste of Elysium.[8]

When I reached home, it was quite dark and I found my mother without a light, sitting rocking in a chair, as she so often used to do in my childhood days, looking into the fire and singing softly to herself. I nestled close to her, and, with her arms around me, she haltingly told me who my father was—a great man, a fine gentleman—he loved me and loved her very much; he was going to make a great man of me. All she said was so limited by reserve and so colored by her feelings that it was but half truth; and so I did not yet fully understand.

7. Chapter title in *Anne of Green Gables* (1908) by Lucy Maude Montgomery.

8. In Greek mythology, the home of the blessed after death.

III

Perhaps I ought not pass on in this narrative without mentioning that the duet was a great success, so great that we were obliged to respond with two encores. It seemed to me that life could hold no greater joy than it contained when I took her hand and we stepped down to the front of the stage bowing to our enthusiastic audience. When we reached the little dressing-room, where the other performers were applauding as wildly as the audience, she impulsively threw both her arms round me and kissed me, while I struggled to get away.

One day a couple of weeks after my father had been to see us, a wagon drove up to our cottage loaded with a big box. I was about to tell the men on the wagon that they had made a mistake, when my mother, acting darkly wise, told them to bring their load in; she had them unpack the box, and quickly there was evolved from the boards, paper, and other packing material a beautiful, brand-new, upright piano. Then she informed me that it was a present to me from my father. I at once sat down and ran my fingers over the keys; the full, mellow tone of the instrument was ravishing. I thought, almost remorsefully, of how I had left my father; but, even so, there momentarily crossed my mind a feeling of disappointment that the piano was not a grand. The new instrument greatly increased the pleasure of my hours of study and practice at home.

Shortly after this I was made a member of the boys' choir, it being found that I possessed a clear, strong soprano voice. I enjoyed the singing very much. About a year later I began the study of the pipe organ and the theory of music; and before I finished the grammar school, I had written out several simple preludes for organ which won the admiration of my teacher, and which he did me the honor to play at services.

The older I grew, the more thought I gave to the question of my mother's and my position, and what was our exact relation to the world in general. My idea of the whole matter was rather hazy. My study of United States history had been confined to those periods which were designated in my book as "Discovery," "Colonial," "Revolutionary," and "Constitutional." I now began to study about the Civil War, but the story was told in such a condensed and skipping style that I gained from it very little real information. It is a marvel how children ever learn any history out of books of that sort. And, too, I began now to read the newspapers; I often saw articles which aroused my curiosity, but did not enlighten me. But one day I drew from the circulating library a book that cleared the whole mystery, a book that I read with the same feverish intensity with which I had read the old Bible stories, a book that gave me my first perspective of the life I was entering; that book was *Uncle Tom's Cabin*.[9]

This work of Harriet Beecher Stowe has been the object of much unfavorable criticism. It has been assailed, not only as fiction of the most imaginative sort, but as being a direct misrepresentation. Several successful attempts have lately been made to displace the book from Northern school libraries. Its critics would brush it aside with the remark that there never was a Negro as good as Uncle Tom, nor a slave-holder as bad as Legree. For

9. Best-selling 1852 novel by Harriet Beecher Stowe (1811–1896).

my part, I was never an admirer of Uncle Tom, nor of his type of goodness; but I believe that there were lots of old Negroes as foolishly good as he; the proof of which is that they knowingly stayed and worked the plantations that furnished sinews for the army which was fighting to keep them enslaved. But in these later years several cases have come to my personal knowledge in which old Negroes have died and left what was a considerable fortune to the descendants of their former masters. I do not think it takes any great stretch of the imagination to believe there was a fairly large class of slave-holders typified in Legree. And we must also remember that the author depicted a number of worthless if not vicious Negroes, and a slave-holder who was as much of a Christian and a gentleman as it was possible for one in his position to be; that she pictured the happy, singing, shuffling "darky" as well as the mother wailing for her child sold "down river."

I do not think it is claiming too much to say that *Uncle Tom's Cabin* was a fair and truthful panorama of slavery; however that may be, it opened my eyes as to who and what I was and what my country considered me; in fact, it gave me my bearing. But there was no shock; I took the whole revelation in a kind of stoical way. One of the greatest benefits I derived from reading the book was that I could afterwards talk frankly with my mother on all the questions which had been vaguely troubling my mind. As a result, she was entirely freed from reserve, and often herself brought up the subject, talking of things directly touching her life and mine and of things which had come down to her through the "old folks." What she told me interested and even fascinated me, and, what may seem strange, kindled in me a strong desire to see the South. She spoke to me quite frankly about herself, my father, and myself: she, the sewing girl of my father's mother; he, an impetuous young man home from college; I, the child of this unsanctioned love. She told me even the principal reason for our coming north. My father was about to be married to a young lady of another great Southern family. She did not neglect to add that another reason for our being in Connecticut was that he intended to give me an education and make a man of me. In none of her talks did she ever utter one word of complaint against my father. She always endeavored to impress upon me how good he had been and still was, and that he was all to us that custom and the law would allow. She loved him; more, she worshiped him, and she died firmly believing that he loved her more than any other woman in the world. Perhaps she was right. Who knows?

All of these newly awakened ideas and thoughts took the form of a definite aspiration on the day I graduated from the grammar school. And what a day that was! The girls in white dresses, with fresh ribbons in their hair; the boys in new suits and creaky shoes; the great crowd of parents and friends; the flowers, the prizes and congratulations, made the day seem to me one of the greatest importance. I was on the program, and played a piano solo which was received by the audience with that amount of applause which I had come to look upon as being only the just due of my talent.

But the real enthusiasm was aroused by "Shiny." He was the principal speaker of the day, and well did he measure up to the honor. He made a striking picture, that thin little black boy standing on the platform, dressed in clothes that did not fit him any too well, his eyes burning with excitement, his shrill, musical voice vibrating in tones of appealing defiance, and his black face alight with such great intelligence and earnestness as to be positively handsome. What were his thoughts when he stepped forward and looked into that crowd of faces, all white with the exception of a score or so that were lost to view? I do not know, but I fancy he felt his loneliness. I think there must have rushed over him a feeling akin to that of a gladiator tossed into the arena and bade to fight for his life. I think that solitary little black figure standing there felt that for the particular time and place he bore the weight and responsibility of his race; that for him to fail meant general defeat; but he won, and nobly. His oration was Wendell Phillips's "Toussaint L'Ouverture,"[1] a speech which may now be classed as rhetorical—even, perhaps, bombastic; but as the words fell from "Shiny's" lips their effect was magical. How so young an orator could stir so great enthusiasm was to be wondered at. When, in the famous peroration,[2] his voice, trembling with suppressed emotion, rose higher and higher and then rested on the name "Toussaint L'Ouverture," it was like touching an electric button which loosed the pent-up feelings of his listeners. They actually rose to him.

I have since known of colored men who have been chosen as class orators in our leading universities, of others who have played on the varsity football and baseball teams, of colored speakers who have addressed great white audiences. In each of these instances I believe the men were stirred by the same emotions which actuated "Shiny" on the day of his graduation; and, too, in each case where the efforts have reached any high standard of excellence they have been followed by the same phenomenon of enthusiasm. I think the explanation of the latter lies in what is a basic, though often dormant, principle of the Anglo-Saxon heart, love of fair play. "Shiny," it is true, was what is so common in his race, a natural orator; but I doubt that any white boy of equal talent could have wrought the same effect. The sight of that boy gallantly waging with puny, black arms so unequal a battle touched the deep springs in the hearts of his audience, and they were swept by a wave of sympathy and admiration.

But the effect upon me of "Shiny's" speech was double; I not only shared the enthusiasm of his audience, but he imparted to me some of his own enthusiasm. I felt leap within me pride that I was colored; and I began to form wild dreams of bringing glory and honor to the Negro race. For days I could talk of nothing else with my mother except my ambitions to be a great man, a great colored man, to reflect credit on the race and gain fame for myself. It was not until years after that I formulated a definite and feasible plan for realizing my dreams.

I entered the high school with my class, and still continued my study of the piano, the pipe organ, and the theory of music. I had to drop out of the boys' choir on account of a changing voice; this I regretted very much. As I grew older, my love for reading grew stronger. I read with studious interest everything I could find relating to colored men who had gained prominence. My heroes had been King David, then Robert the Bruce; now Frederick Douglass was enshrined in the place of honor. When I learned that Alexandre Dumas[3] was a colored man, I re-read *Monte Cristo* and *The*

1. Born enslaved and freed in the 1770s, Toussaint (ca. 1743–1803) was the leader of the Haitian Revolution in the 1790s. Phillips (1811–1884), renowned U.S. antislavery orator, celebrated L'Ouverture in his speech.
2. Conclusion of an oration.
3. French novelist and dramatist (1802–1870), author of *The Count of Monte Cristo* and *The Three Musketeers* (1844–45). Douglass (1818–1895), African American orator, editor, and civil rights leader.

Three Guardsmen with magnified pleasure. I lived between my music and books, on the whole a rather unwholesome life for a boy to lead. I dwelt in a world of imagination, of dreams and air castles—the kind of atmosphere that sometimes nourishes a genius, more often men unfitted for the practical struggles of life. I never played a game of ball, never went fishing or learned to swim; in fact, the only outdoor exercise in which I took any interest was skating. Nevertheless, though slender, I grew well formed and in perfect health. After I entered the high school, I began to notice the change in my mother's health, which I suppose had been going on for some years. She began to complain a little and to cough a great deal; she tried several remedies, and finally went to see a doctor; but though she was failing in health, she kept her spirits up. She still did a great deal of sewing, and in the busy seasons hired two women to help her. The purpose she had formed of having me go through college without financial worries kept her at work when she was not fit for it. I was so fortunate as to be able to organize a class of eight or ten beginners on the piano, and so start a separate little fund of my own. As the time for my graduation from the high school grew nearer, the plans for my college career became the chief subject of our talks. I sent for catalogues of all the prominent schools in the East and eagerly gathered all the information I could concerning them from different sources. My mother told me that my father wanted me to go to Harvard or Yale; she herself had a half desire for me to go to Atlanta University,[4] and even had me write for a catalogue of that school. There were two reasons, however, that inclined her to my father's choice; the first, that at Harvard or Yale I should be near her; the second, that my father had promised to pay for a part of my college education.

Both "Shiny" and "Red" came to my house quite often of evenings, and we used to talk over our plans and prospects for the future. Sometimes I would play for them, and they seemed to enjoy the music very much. My mother often prepared sundry Southern dishes for them, which I am not sure but that they enjoyed more. "Shiny" had an uncle in Amherst, Mass., and he expected to live with him and work his way through Amherst College. "Red" declared that he had enough of school and that after he got his high school diploma, he would get a position in a bank. It was his ambition to become a banker and he felt sure of getting the opportunity through certain members of his family.

My mother barely had strength to attend the closing exercises of the high school when I graduated, and after that day she was seldom out of bed. She could no longer direct her work, and under the expense of medicines, doctors, and someone to look after her our college fund began to diminish rapidly. Many of her customers and some of the neighbors were very kind, and frequently brought her nourishment of one kind or another. My mother realized what I did not, that she was mortally ill, and she had me write a long letter to my father. For some time past she had heard from him only at irregular intervals; we never received an answer. In those last days I often sat at her bedside and read to her until she fell asleep. Sometimes I would leave the parlor door open and play on the piano, just loud enough for the music to reach her. This she always enjoyed.

4. Founded in 1865 by the American Missionary Association for liberal arts education of African Americans.

One night, near the end of July, after I had been watching beside her for some hours, I went into the parlor and, throwing myself into the big arm chair, dozed off into a fitful sleep. I was suddenly aroused by one of the neighbors, who had come in to sit with her that night. She said: "Come to your mother at once." I hurried upstairs, and at the bedroom door met the woman who was acting as nurse. I noted with a dissolving heart the strange look of awe on her face. From my first glance at my mother I discerned the light of death upon her countenance. I fell upon my knees beside the bed and, burying my face in the sheets, sobbed convulsively. She died with the fingers of her left hand entwined in my hair.

I will not rake over this, one of the two sacred sorrows of my life; nor could I describe the feeling of unutterable loneliness that fell upon me. After the funeral I went to the house of my music teacher; he had kindly offered me the hospitality of his home for so long as I might need it. A few days later I moved my trunk, piano, my music, and most of my books to his home; the rest of my books I divided between "Shiny" and "Red." Some of the household effects I gave to "Shiny's" mother and to two or three of the neighbors who had been kind to us during my mother's illness; the others I sold. After settling up my little estate I found that, besides a good supply of clothes, a piano, some books and trinkets, I had about two hundred dollars in cash.

The question of what I was to do now confronted me. My teacher suggested a concert tour; but both of us realized that I was too old to be exploited as an infant prodigy and too young and inexperienced to go before the public as a finished artist. He, however, insisted that the people of the town would generously patronize a benefit concert; so he took up the matter and made arrangements for such an entertainment. A more than sufficient number of people with musical and elocutionary talent volunteered their services to make a program. Among these was my brown-eyed violinist. But our relations were not the same as they were when we had played our first duet together. A year or so after that time she had dealt me a crushing blow by getting married. I was partially avenged, however, by the fact that, though she was growing more beautiful, she was losing her ability to play the violin.

I was down on the program for one number. My selection might have appeared at that particular time as a bit of affectation, but I considered it deeply appropriate; I played Beethoven's "Sonata Pathétique." When I sat down at the piano and glanced into the faces of the several hundreds of people who were there solely on account of love or sympathy for me, emotions swelled in my heart which enabled me to play the "Pathétique" as I could never again play it. When the last tone died away, the few who began to applaud were hushed by the silence of the others; and for once I played without receiving an encore.

The benefit yielded me a little more than two hundred dollars, thus raising my cash capital to about four hundred dollars. I still held to my determination of going to college; so it was now a question of trying to squeeze through a year at Harvard or going to Atlanta, where the money I had would pay my actual expenses for at least two years. The peculiar fascination which the South held over my imagination and my limited capital decided me in favor of Atlanta University; so about the last of September I bade farewell to the friends and scenes of my boyhood and boarded a train for the South.

IV

The farther I got below Washington, the more disappointed I became in the appearance of the country. I peered through the car windows, looking in vain for the luxuriant semi-tropical scenery which I had pictured in my mind. I did not find the grass so green, nor the woods so beautiful, nor the flowers so plentiful, as they were in Connecticut. Instead, the red earth partly covered by tough, scrawny grass, the muddy, straggling roads, the cottages of unpainted pine boards, and the clay-daubed huts imparted a "burnt up" impression. Occasionally we ran through a little white and green village that was like an oasis in a desert.

When I reached Atlanta, my steadily increasing disappointment was not lessened. I found it a big, dull, red town. This dull red color of that part of the South I was then seeing had much, I think, to do with the extreme depression of my spirits—no public squares, no fountains, dingy street-cars, and, with the exception of three or four principal thoroughfares, unpaved streets. It was raining when I arrived and some of these unpaved streets were absolutely impassable. Wheels sank to the hubs in red mire, and I actually stood for an hour and watched four or five men work to save a mule, which had stepped into a deep sink, from drowning, or, rather, suffocating in the mud. The Atlanta of today is a new city.

On the train I had talked with one of the Pullman car porters,[5] a bright young fellow who was himself a student, and told him that I was going to Atlanta to attend school. I had also asked him to tell me where I might stop for a day or two until the University opened. He said I might go with him to the place where he stopped during his "lay-overs" in Atlanta. I gladly accepted his offer and went with him along one of those muddy streets until we came to a rather rickety looking frame house, which we entered. The proprietor of the house was a big, fat, greasy-looking brown-skin man. When I asked him if he could give me accommodations, he wanted to know how long I would stay. I told him perhaps two days, not more than three. In reply he said: "Oh, dat's all right den," at the same time leading the way up a pair of creaky stairs. I followed him and the porter to a room, the door of which the proprietor opened while continuing, it seemed, his remark, "Oh, dat's all right den," by adding: "You kin sleep in dat cot in de corner der. Fifty cents, please." The porter interrupted by saying: "You needn't collect from him now, he's got a trunk." This seemed to satisfy the man, and he went down, leaving me and my porter friend in the room. I glanced around the apartment and saw that it contained a double bed and two cots, two wash-stands, three chairs, and a time-worn bureau, with a looking-glass that would have made Adonis[6] appear hideous. I looked at the cot in which I was to sleep and suspected, not without good reasons, that I should not be the first to use the sheets and pillow-case since they had last come from the wash. When I thought of the clean, tidy, comfortable surroundings in which I had been reared, a wave of homesickness swept over me that made me feel faint. Had it not been for the presence of my companion, and that I knew this much of his history—that he was not yet quite twenty, just three years older than myself, and that he had been fighting his own way in the world,

5. Pullman cars were sleeping compartments on railroads. Pullman porters, who served these passengers, were generally middle-class, educated African Americans.

6. In Greek mythology, a handsome youth loved by the goddess Aphrodite.

earning his own living and providing for his own education since he was fourteen—I should not have been able to stop the tears that were welling up in my eyes.

I asked him why it was that the proprietor of the house seemed unwilling to accommodate me for more than a couple of days. He informed me that the man ran a lodging house especially for Pullman porters, and, as their stays in town were not longer than one or two nights, it would interfere with his arrangements to have anyone stay longer. He went on to say: "You see this room is fixed up to accommodate four men at a time. Well, by keeping a sort of table of trips, in and out, of the men, and working them like checkers, he can accommodate fifteen or sixteen in each week and generally avoid having an empty bed. You happen to catch a bed that would have been empty for a couple of nights." I asked him where he was going to sleep. He answered: "I sleep in that other cot tonight; tomorrow night I go out." He went on to tell me that the man who kept the house did not serve meals, and that if I was hungry, we would go out and get something to eat.

We went into the street, and in passing the railroad station I hired a wagon to take my trunk to my lodging place. We passed along until, finally, we turned into a street that stretched away, up and down hill, for a mile or two; and here I caught my first sight of colored people in large numbers. I had seen little squads around the railroad stations on my way south, but here I saw a street crowded with them. They filled the shops and thronged the sidewalks and lined the curb. I asked my companion if all the colored people in Atlanta lived in this street. He said they did not and assured me that the ones I saw were of the lower class. I felt relieved, in spite of the size of the lower class. The unkempt appearance, the shambling, slouching gait and loud talk and laughter of these people aroused in me a feeling of almost repulsion. Only one thing about them awoke a feeling of interest; that was their dialect. I had read some Negro dialect and had heard snatches of it on my journey down from Washington; but here I heard it in all of its fullness and freedom. I was particularly struck by the way in which it was punctuated by such exclamatory phrases as "Lawd a mussy!" "G'wan, man!" "Bless ma soul!" "Look heah, chile!" These people talked and laughed without restraint. In fact, they talked straight from their lungs and laughed from the pits of their stomachs. And this hearty laughter was often justified by the droll humor of some remark. I paused long enough to hear one man say to another: "Wat's de mattah wid you an' yo' fr'en' Sam?" and the other came back like a flash: "Ma fr'en'? He ma fr'en'? Man! I'd go to his funeral jes' de same as I'd go to a minstrel show." I have since learned that this ability to laugh heartily is, in part, the salvation of the American Negro; it does much to keep him from going the way of the Indian.

The business places of the street along which we were passing consisted chiefly of low bars, cheap dry-goods and notion stores, barber shops, and fish and bread restaurants. We, at length, turned down a pair of stairs that led to a basement and I found myself in an eating-house somewhat better than those I had seen in passing; but that did not mean much for its excellence. The place was smoky, the tables were covered with oilcloth, the floor with sawdust, and from the kitchen came a rancid odor of fish fried over several times, which almost nauseated me. I asked my companion if this was the place where we were to eat. He informed me that it was the best place in town where a colored man could get a meal. I then wanted to know why somebody didn't open a place where respectable colored people who had money could be accommodated. He answered: "It wouldn't pay; all the respectable colored people eat at home, and the few who travel generally have friends in the towns to which they go, who entertain them." He added: "Of course, you could go in any place in the city; they wouldn't know you from white."

I sat down with the porter at one of the tables, but was not hungry enough to eat with any relish what was put before me. The food was not badly cooked; but the iron knives and forks needed to be scrubbed, the plates and dishes and glasses needed to be washed and well dried. I minced over what I took on my plate while my companion ate. When we finished, we paid the waiter twenty cents each and went out. We walked around until the lights of the city were lit. Then the porter said that he must get to bed and have some rest, as he had not had six hours' sleep since he left Jersey City. I went back to our lodging house with him.

When I awoke in the morning, there were, besides my newfound friend, two other men in the room, asleep in the double bed. I got up and dressed myself very quietly, so as not to awake anyone. I then drew from under the pillow my precious roll of greenbacks, took out a ten-dollar bill, and, very softly unlocking my trunk, put the remainder, about three hundred dollars, in the inside pocket of a coat near the bottom, glad of the opportunity to put it unobserved in a place of safety. When I had carefully locked my trunk, I tiptoed toward the door with the intention of going out to look for a decent restaurant where I might get something fit to eat. As I was easing the door open, my porter friend said with a yawn: "Hello! You're going out?" I answered him: "Yes." "Oh!" he yawned again, "I guess I've had enough sleep; wait a minute, I'll go with you." For the instant his friendship bored and embarrassed me. I had visions of another meal in the greasy restaurant of the day before. He must have divined my thoughts, for he went on to say: "I know a woman across town who takes a few boarders; I think we can go over there and get a good breakfast." With a feeling of mingled fears and doubts regarding what the breakfast might be, I waited until he had dressed himself.

When I saw the neat appearance of the cottage we entered, my fears vanished, and when I saw the woman who kept it, my doubts followed the same course. Scrupulously clean, in a spotless white apron and colored head-handkerchief, her round face beaming with motherly kindness, she was picturesquely beautiful. She impressed me as one broad expanse of happiness and good nature. In a few minutes she was addressing me as "chile" and "honey." She made me feel as though I should like to lay my head on her capacious bosom and go to sleep.

And the breakfast, simple as it was, I could not have had at any restaurant in Atlanta at any price. There was fried chicken, as it is fried only in the South, hominy boiled to the consistency where it could be eaten with a fork, and biscuits so light and flaky that a fellow with any appetite at all would have no difficulty in disposing of eight or ten. When I had finished, I felt that I had experienced the realization of, at least, one of my dreams of Southern life.

During the meal we found out from our hostess, who had two boys in school, that Atlanta University opened on that very day. I had somehow mixed my dates. My friend the porter suggested that I go out to the University at once and offered to walk over and show me the way. We had to walk because, although the University was not more than twenty minutes' distance from the center of the city, there were no streetcars running in that direction. My first sight of the school grounds made me feel that I was not far from home; here the red hills had been terraced and covered with green grass; clean gravel walks, well shaded, led up to the buildings; indeed, it was a bit of New England transplanted. At the gate my companion said he would bid me good-by, because it was likely that he would not see me again before his car went out. He told me that he would make two more trips to Atlanta and that he would come out and see me; that after his second trip he would leave the Pullman service for the winter and return to school in Nashville. We shook hands, I thanked him for all his kindness, and we said good-by.

I walked up to a group of students and made some inquiries. They directed me to the president's office in the main building. The president gave me a cordial welcome; it was more than cordial; he talked to me, not as the official head of a college, but as though he were adopting me into what was his large family, personally to look after my general welfare as well as my education. He seemed especially pleased with the fact that I had come to them all the way from the North. He told me that I could have come to the school as soon as I had reached the city and that I had better move my trunk out at once. I gladly promised him that I would do so. He then called a boy and directed him to take me to the matron, and to show me around afterwards. I found the matron even more motherly than the president was fatherly. She had me register, which was in effect to sign a pledge to abstain from the use of intoxicating beverages, tobacco, and profane language while I was a student in the school. This act caused me no sacrifice, as, up to that time, I was free from all three habits. The boy who was with me then showed me about the grounds. I was especially interested in the industrial building.

The sounding of a bell, he told me, was the signal for the students to gather in the general assembly hall, and he asked me if I would go. Of course I would. There were between three and four hundred students and perhaps all of the teachers gathered in the room. I noticed that several of the latter were colored. The president gave a talk addressed principally to newcomers; but I scarcely heard what he said, I was so much occupied in looking at those around me. They were of all types and colors, the more intelligent types predominating. The colors ranged from jet black to pure white, with light hair and eyes. Among the girls especially there were many so fair that it was difficult to believe that they had Negro blood in them. And, too, I could not help noticing that many of the girls, particularly those of the delicate brown shades, with black eyes and wavy dark hair, were decidedly pretty. Among the boys many of the blackest were fine specimens of young manhood, tall, straight, and muscular, with magnificent heads; these were the kind of boys who developed into the patriarchal "uncles" of the old slave regime.

When I left the University, it was with the determination to get my trunk and move out to the school before night. I walked back across the city with a light step and a light heart. I felt perfectly satisfied with life for the first time since my mother's death. In passing the railroad station I hired a wagon and rode with the driver as far as my stopping-place. I settled with my landlord and went upstairs to put away several articles I had left out. As soon as I opened my trunk, a dart of suspicion shot through my heart; the arrangement of things did not look familiar. I began to dig down excitedly to the bottom till I reached the coat in which I had concealed my treasure.

My money was gone! Every single bill of it. I knew it was useless to do so, but I searched through every other coat, every pair of trousers, every vest, and even each pair of socks. When I had finished my fruitless search, I sat down dazed and heartsick. I called the landlord up and informed him of my loss; he comforted me by saying that I ought to have better sense than to keep money in a trunk and that he was not responsible for his lodgers' personal effects. His cooling words brought me enough to my senses to cause me to look and see if anything else was missing. Several small articles were gone, among them a black and gray necktie of odd design upon which my heart was set; almost as much as the loss of my money I felt the loss of my tie.

After thinking for a while as best I could, I wisely decided to go at once back to the University and lay my troubles before the president. I rushed breathlessly back to the school. As I neared the grounds, the thought came across me, would not my story sound fishy? Would it not place me in the position of an impostor or beggar? What right had I to worry these busy people with the results of my carelessness? If the money could not be recovered, and I doubted that it could, what good would it do to tell them about it? The shame and embarrassment which the whole situation gave me caused me to stop at the gate. I paused, undecided, for a moment; then turned and slowly retraced my steps, and so changed the whole course of my life.

If the reader has never been in a strange city without money or friends, it is useless to try to describe what my feelings were; he could not understand. If he has been, it is equally useless, for he understands more than words could convey. When I reached my lodgings, I found in the room one of the porters who had slept there the night before. When he heard what misfortune had befallen me, he offered many words of sympathy and advice. He asked me how much money I had left. I told him that I had ten or twelve dollars in my pocket. He said: "That won't last you very long here, and you will hardly be able to find anything to do in Atlanta. I'll tell you what you do, go down to Jacksonville and you won't have any trouble to get a job in one of the big hotels there, or in St. Augustine." I thanked him, but intimated my doubts of being able to get to Jacksonville on the money I had. He reassured me by saying: "Oh, that's all right. You express your trunk on through, and I'll take you down in my closet." I thanked him again, not knowing then what it was to travel in a Pullman porter's closet. He put me under a deeper debt of gratitude by lending me fifteen dollars, which he said I could pay back after I had secured work. His generosity brought tears to my eyes, and I concluded that, after all, there were some kind hearts in the world.

I now forgot my troubles in the hurry and excitement of getting my trunk off in time to catch the train, which went out at seven o'clock. I even forgot that I hadn't eaten anything since morning. We got a wagon—the porter went with me—and took my trunk to the express office. My new friend then told me to come to the station at about a quarter of seven and walk straight to the car where I should see him standing, and not to lose my nerve. I found my role not so difficult to play as I thought it would be, because the train did not leave from the central station, but from a smaller one, where there were no gates and guards to pass. I followed directions, and the porter took me on his car and locked me in his closet. In a few minutes the train pulled out for Jacksonville.

I may live to be a hundred years old, but I shall never forget the agonies I suffered that night. I spent twelve hours doubled up in the porter's basket for soiled linen, not being able to straighten up on account of the shelves for clean linen just over my head. The air was hot and suffocating and the smell of damp towels and used linen was sickening. At each lurch of the car over the none-too-smooth track I was bumped and bruised against the narrow walls of my narrow compartment. I became acutely conscious of the fact that I had not eaten for hours. Then nausea took possession of me, and at one time I had grave doubts about reaching my destination alive. If I had the trip to make again, I should prefer to walk.

V

The next morning I got out of the car at Jacksonville with a stiff and aching body. I determined to ask no more porters, not even my benefactor, about stopping-places; so I found myself on the street not knowing where to go. I walked along listlessly until I met a colored man who had the appearance of a preacher. I asked him if he could direct me to a respectable boarding-house for colored people. He said that if I walked along with him in the direction he was going, he would show me such a place: I turned and walked at his side. He proved to be a minister, and asked me a great many direct questions about myself. I answered as many as I saw fit to answer; the others I evaded or ignored. At length we stopped in front of a frame house, and my guide informed me that it was the place. A woman was standing in the doorway, and he called to her saying that he had brought her a new boarder. I thanked him for his trouble, and after he had urged upon me to attend his church while I was in the city, he went on his way.

I went in and found the house neat and not uncomfortable. The parlor was furnished with cane-bottomed chairs, each of which was adorned with a white crocheted tidy. The mantel over the fireplace had a white crocheted cover; a marble-topped center table held a lamp, a photograph album and several trinkets, each of which was set upon a white crocheted mat. There was a cottage organ in a corner of the room, and I noted that the lamp-racks upon it were covered with white crocheted mats. There was a matting on the floor, but a white crocheted carpet would not have been out of keeping. I made arrangements with the landlady for my board and lodging; the amount was, I think, three dollars and a half a week. She was a rather fine-looking, stout, brown-skin woman of about forty years of age. Her husband was a light-colored Cuban, a man about one half her size, and one whose age could not be guessed from his appearance. He was small in size, but a handsome black mustache and typical Spanish eyes redeemed him from insignificance.

I was in time for breakfast, and at the table I had the opportunity to see my fellow boarders. There were eight or ten of them. Two, as I afterwards learned, were colored Americans. All of them were cigar makers and worked in one of the large factories—cigar making is one trade in which the color line is not drawn. The conversation was carried on entirely in Spanish, and my ignorance of the language subjected me more to alarm than embarrassment. I had never heard such uproarious conversation; everybody talked at once, loud exclamations, rolling "*carambas*,"[7] menacing gesticulations with knives, forks, and spoons. I looked every moment for the clash of blows.

7. Exclamation expressing surprise or annoyance (Spanish).

One man was emphasizing his remarks by flourishing a cup in his hand, seemingly forgetful of the fact that it was nearly full of hot coffee. He ended by emptying it over what was, relatively, the only quiet man at the table excepting myself, bringing from him a volley of language which made the others appear dumb by comparison. I soon learned that in all of this clatter of voices and table utensils they were discussing purely ordinary affairs and arguing about mere trifles, and that not the least ill feeling was aroused. It was not long before I enjoyed the spirited chatter and *badinage*[8] the table as much as I did my meals—and the meals were not bad.

I spent the afternoon in looking around the town. The streets were sandy, but were well-shaded by fine oak trees and far preferable to the clay roads of Atlanta. One or two public squares with green grass and trees gave the city a touch of freshness. That night after supper I spoke to my landlady and her husband about my intentions. They told me that the big winter hotels would not open within two months. It can easily be imagined what effect this news had on me. I spoke to them frankly about my financial condition and related the main fact of my misfortune in Atlanta. I modestly mentioned my ability to teach music and asked if there was any likelihood of my being able to get some scholars. My landlady suggested that I speak to the preacher who had shown me her house; she felt sure that through his influence I should be able to get up a class in piano. She added, however, that the colored people were poor, and that the general price for music lessons was only twenty-five cents. I noticed that the thought of my teaching white pupils did not even remotely enter her mind. None of this information made my prospects look much brighter.

The husband, who up to this time had allowed the woman to do most of the talking, gave me the first bit of tangible hope; he said that he could get me a job as a "stripper" in the factory where he worked, and that if I succeeded in getting some music pupils, I could teach a couple of them every night, and so make a living until something better turned up. He went on to say that it would not be a bad thing for me to stay at the factory and learn my trade as a cigar maker, and impressed on me that, for a young man knocking about the country, a trade was a handy thing to have. I determined to accept his offer and thanked him heartily. In fact, I became enthusiastic, not only because I saw a way out of my financial troubles, but also because I was eager and curious over the new experience I was about to enter. I wanted to know all about the cigar making business. This narrowed the conversation down to the husband and myself, so the wife went in and left us talking.

He was what is called a *regalía*[9] workman, and earned from thirty-five to forty dollars a week. He generally worked a sixty-dollar job; that is, he made cigars for which he was paid at the rate of sixty dollars per thousand. It was impossible for him to make a thousand in a week because he had to work very carefully and slowly. Each cigar was made entirely by hand. Each piece of filler and each wrapper had to be selected with care. He was able to make a bundle of one hundred cigars in a day, not one of which could be told from the others by any difference in size or shape, or even by any appreciable difference in weight. This was the acme of artistic skill in cigar making. Workmen of this class were rare, never more than three or four in one factory, and

8. Humorous banter or ridicule (French).

9. A large high-quality cigar.

it was never necessary for them to remain out of work. There were men who made two, three, and four hundred cigars of the cheaper grades in a day; they had to be very fast in order to make a decent week's wages. Cigar making was a rather independent trade; the men went to work when they pleased and knocked off when they felt like doing so. As a class the workmen were careless and improvident; some very rapid makers would not work more than three or four days out of the week, and there were others who never showed up at the factory on Mondays. "Strippers" were the boys who pulled the long stems from the tobacco leaves. After they had served at that work for a certain time they were given tables as apprentices.

All of this was interesting to me; and we drifted along in conversation until my companion struck the subject nearest his heart, the independence of Cuba. He was an exile from the island, and a prominent member of the Jacksonville Junta.[1] Every week sums of money were collected from juntas all over the country. This money went to buy arms and ammunition for the insurgents. As the man sat there nervously smoking his long, "green" cigar, and telling me of the Gómezes, both the white one and the black one, of Macéo and Bandera,[2] he grew positively eloquent. He also showed that he was a man of considerable education and reading. He spoke English excellently, and frequently surprised me by using words one would hardly expect from a foreigner. The first one of this class of words he employed almost shocked me, and I never forgot it; 'twas "ramify." We sat on the piazza until after ten o'clock. When we arose to go in to bed, it was with the understanding that I should start in the factory on the next day.

I began work the next morning seated at a barrel with another boy, who showed me how to strip the stems from the leaves, to smooth out each half leaf, and to put the "rights" together in one pile, and the "lefts" together in another pile on the edge of the barrel. My fingers, strong and sensitive from their long training, were well adapted to this kind of work, and within two weeks I was accounted the fastest "stripper" in the factory. At first the heavy odor of the tobacco almost sickened me, but when I became accustomed to it, I liked the smell. I was now earning four dollars a week, and was soon able to pick up a couple more by teaching a few scholars at night, whom I had secured through the good offices of the preacher I had met on my first morning in Jacksonville.

At the end of about three months, through my skill as a "stripper" and the influence of my landlord, I was advanced to a table and began to learn my trade; in fact, more than my trade; for I learned not only to make cigars, but also to smoke, to swear, and to speak Spanish. I discovered that I had a talent for languages as well as for music. The rapidity and ease with which I acquired Spanish astonished my associates. In a short time I was able not only to understand most of what was said at the table during meals, but to join in the conversation. I bought a method for learning the Spanish language, and with the aid of my landlord as a teacher, by constant practice with my fellow workmen, and by regularly reading the Cuban newspapers and finally some books of standard Spanish literature which were at the house, I was able in less than a year to speak like a native. In fact, it was my

1. Cuban exiles plotting the overthrow of the Spanish colonial government of the island.

2. Antonio Maceo (1845–1896) and his assistant Quintín Bandera (ca. 1843–1906) were officers in Cuban revolutionary armies of 1868–78 and 1895–98. José Miguel Gómez (1858–1921) and Máximo Gómez y Baez (1836–1905) were leaders in Cuba's War of Independence (1895–98).

pride that I spoke better Spanish than many of the Cuban workmen at the factory.

After I had been in the factory a little over a year, I was repaid for all the effort I had put forth to learn Spanish by being selected as "reader." The "reader" is quite an institution in all cigar factories which employ Spanish-speaking workmen. He sits in the center of the large room in which the cigar makers work and reads to them for a certain number of hours each day all the important news from the papers and whatever else he may consider would be interesting. He often selects an exciting novel and reads it in daily installments. He must, of course, have a good voice, but he must also have a reputation among the men for intelligence, for being well-posted and having in his head a stock of varied information. He is generally the final authority on all arguments which arise, and in a cigar factory these arguments are many and frequent, ranging from the respective and relative merits of rival baseball clubs to the duration of the sun's light and energy— Cigar making is a trade in which talk does not interfere with work. My position as "reader" not only released me from the rather monotonous work of rolling cigars, and gave me something more in accord with my tastes, but also added considerably to my income. I was now earning about twenty-five dollars a week, and was able to give up my peripatetic method of giving music lessons. I hired a piano and taught only those who could arrange to take their lessons where I lived. I finally gave up teaching entirely, as what I made scarcely paid for my time and trouble. I kept the piano, however, in order to keep up my own studies, and occasionally I played at some church concert or other charitable entertainment.

Through my music teaching and my not absolutely irregular attendance at church I became acquainted with the best class of colored people in Jacksonville. This was really my entrance into the race. It was my initiation into what I have termed the freemasonry of the race. I had formulated a theory of what it was to be colored; now I was getting the practice. The novelty of my position caused me to observe and consider things which, I think, entirely escaped the young men I associated with; or, at least, were so commonplace to them as not to attract their attention. And of many of the impressions which came to me then I have realized the full import only within the past few years, since I have had a broader knowledge of men and history, and a fuller comprehension of the tremendous struggle which is going on between the races in the South.

It is a struggle; for though the black man fights passively, he nevertheless fights; and his passive resistance is more effective at present than active resistance could possibly be. He bears the fury of the storm as does the willow tree.

It is a struggle; for though the white man of the South may be too proud to admit it, he is, nevertheless, using in the contest his best energies; he is devoting to it the greater part of his thought and much of his endeavor. The South today stands panting and almost breathless from its exertions.

And how the scene of the struggle has shifted! The battle was first waged over the right of the Negro to be classed as a human being with a soul; later, as to whether he had sufficient intellect to master even the rudiments of learning; and today it is being fought out over his social recognition.

I said somewhere in the early part of this narrative that because the colored man looked at everything through the prism of his relationship to society as a *colored* man, and because most of his mental efforts ran through the narrow channel bounded by his rights and his wrongs, it was to be wondered at that he has progressed so broadly as he has. The same thing may be said of the white man of the South; most of his mental efforts run through one narrow channel; his life as a man and a citizen, many of his financial activities, and all of his political activities are impassably limited by the ever present "Negro question." I am sure it would be safe to wager that no group of Southern white men could get together and talk for sixty minutes without bringing up the "race question." If a Northern white man happened to be in the group, the time could be safely cut to thirty minutes. In this respect I consider the conditions of the whites more to be deplored than that of the blacks. Here, a truly great people, a people that produced a majority of the great historic Americans from Washington to Lincoln, now forced to use up its energies in a conflict as lamentable as it is violent.

I shall give the observations I made in Jacksonville as seen through the light of after years; and they apply generally to every Southern community. The colored people may be said to be roughly divided into three classes, not so much in respect to themselves as in respect to their relations with the whites. There are those constituting what might be called the desperate class—the men who work in the lumber and turpentine camps, the ex-convicts, the bar-room loafers are all in this class. These men conform to the requirements of civilization much as a trained lion with low muttered growls goes through his stunts under the crack of the trainer's whip. They cherish a sullen hatred for all white men, and they value life as cheap. I have heard more than one of them say: "I'll go to hell for the first white man that bothers me." Many who have expressed that sentiment have kept their word, and it is that fact which gives such prominence to this class; for in numbers it is only a small proportion of the colored people, but it often dominates public opinion concerning the whole race. Happily, this class represents the black people of the South far below their normal physical and moral condition, but in its increase lies the possibility of grave dangers. I am sure there is no more urgent work before the white South, not only for its present happiness, but for its future safety, than the decreasing of this class of blacks. And it is not at all a hopeless class; for these men are but the creatures of conditions, as much so as the slum and criminal elements of all the great cities of the world are creatures of conditions. Decreasing their number by shooting and burning them off will not be successful; for these men are truly desperate, and thoughts of death, however terrible, have little effect in deterring them from acts the result of hatred or degeneracy. This class of blacks hate everything covered by a white skin, and in return they are loathed by the whites. The whites regard them just about as a man would a vicious mule, a thing to be worked, driven, and beaten, and killed for kicking.

The second class, as regards the relation between blacks and whites, comprises the servants, the washerwomen, the waiters, the cooks, the coachmen, and all who are connected with the whites by domestic service. These may be generally characterized as simple, kind-hearted, and faithful; not over-fine in their moral deductions, but intensely religious, and relatively—such matters can be judged only relatively—about as honest and wholesome in their lives as any other grade of society. Any white person is "good" who treats them kindly, and they love him for that kindness. In return, the white people with whom they have to do regard them with indulgent affection. They come into close daily contact with the whites, and may be called the connecting link between whites and blacks; in fact, it is through them that the whites know the rest of their colored neighbors. Between this class of the blacks and the whites there is little or no friction.

The third class is composed of the independent workmen and tradesmen, and of the well-to-do and educated colored people; and, strange to say, for a directly opposite reason they are as far removed from the whites as the members of the first class I mentioned. These people live in a little world of their own; in fact, I concluded that if a colored man wanted to separate himself from his white neighbors, he had but to acquire some money, education, and culture, and to live in accordance. For example, the proudest and fairest lady in the South could with propriety—and it is what she would most likely do—go to the cabin of Aunt Mary, her cook, if Aunt Mary was sick, and minister to her comfort with her own hands; but if Mary's daughter, Eliza, a girl who used to run round my lady's kitchen, but who has received an education and married a prosperous young colored man, were at death's door, my lady would no more think of crossing the threshold of Eliza's cottage than she would of going into a bar-room for a drink.

I was walking down the street one day with a young man who was born in Jacksonville, but had been away to prepare himself for a professional life. We passed a young white man, and my companion said to me: "You see that young man? We grew up together; we have played, hunted, and fished together; we have even eaten and slept together; and now since I have come back home, he barely speaks to me." The fact that the whites of the South despise and ill-treat the desperate class of blacks is not only explainable according to the ancient laws of human nature, but it is not nearly so serious or important as the fact that as the progressive colored people advance, they constantly widen the gulf between themselves and their white neighbors. I think that the white people somehow feel that colored people who have education and money, who wear good clothes and live in comfortable houses, are "putting on airs," that they do these things for the sole purpose of "spiting the white folks," or are, at best, going through a sort of monkey-like imitation. Of course, such feelings can only cause irritation or breed disgust. It seems that the whites have not yet been able to realize and understand that these people in striving to better their physical and social surroundings in accordance with their financial and intellectual progress are simply obeying an impulse which is common to human nature the world over. I am in grave doubt as to whether the greater part of the friction in the South is caused by the whites' having a natural antipathy to Negroes as a race, or an acquired antipathy to Negroes in certain relations to themselves. However that may be, there is to my mind no more pathetic side of this many-sided question than the isolated position into which are forced the very colored people who most need and who could best appreciate sympathetic coöperation; and their position grows tragic when the effort is made to couple them, whether or no, with the Negroes of the first class I mentioned.

This latter class of colored people are well-disposed towards the whites, and always willing to meet them more than half-way. They, however, feel keenly any injustice or gross discrimination, and generally show their resentment. The effort is sometimes made to convey the impression that the better class of colored people fight against riding in "Jim Crow" cars because they want to ride with white people or object to being with humbler members of their own race. The truth is they object to the humiliation of being forced to ride in a *particular* car, aside from the fact that that car is distinctly inferior, and that they are required to pay full first-class fare. To say that the whites are forced to ride in the superior car is less than a joke. And, too, odd as it may sound, refined colored people get no more pleasure out of riding with offensive Negroes than anybody else would get.

I can realize more fully than I could years ago that the position of the advanced element of the colored race is often very trying. They are the ones among the blacks who carry the entire weight of the race question; it worries the others very little, and I believe the only thing which at times sustains them is that they know that they are in the right. On the other hand, this class of colored people get a good deal of pleasure out of life; their existence is far from being one long groan about their condition. Out of a chaos of ignorance and poverty they have evolved a social life of which they need not be ashamed. In cities where the professional and well-to-do class is large they have formed society—society as discriminating as the actual conditions will allow it to be; I should say, perhaps, society possessing discriminating tendencies which become rules as fast as actual conditions allow. This statement will, I know, sound preposterous, even ridiculous, to some persons; but as this class of colored people is the least known of the race it is not surprising. These social circles are connected throughout the country, and a person in good standing in one city is readily accepted in another. One who is on the outside will often find it a difficult matter to get in. I know personally of one case in which money to the extent of thirty or forty thousand dollars and a fine house, not backed up by a good reputation, after several years of repeated effort, failed to gain entry for the possessor. These people have their dances and dinners and card parties, their musicals, and their literary societies. The women attend social affairs dressed in good taste, and the men in dress suits which they own; and the reader will make a mistake to confound these entertainments with the "Bellman's Balls" and "Whitewashers' Picnics" and "Lime-kiln Clubs" with which the humorous press of the country illustrates "Cullud Sassiety."

Jacksonville, when I was there, was a small town, and the number of educated and well-to-do colored people was small: so this society phase of life did not equal what I have since seen in Boston, Washington, Richmond, and Nashville; and it is upon what I have more recently seen in these cities that I have made the observations just above. However, there were many comfortable and pleasant homes in Jacksonville to which I was often invited. I belonged to the literary society—at which we generally discussed the race question—and attended all of the church festivals and other charitable entertainments. In this way I passed three years which were not at all the least enjoyable of my life. In fact, my joy took such an exuberant turn that I fell in love with a young school teacher and began to have dreams of matrimonial bliss; but another turn in the course of my life brought these dreams to an end.

I do not wish to mislead my readers into thinking that I led a life in Jacksonville which would make copy for the hero of a Sunday-school library book. I was a hail fellow well met with all of the workmen at the factory, most of whom knew little and cared less about social distinctions. From their example I learned to be careless about money, and for that reason I constantly postponed and finally abandoned returning to Atlanta University. It seemed impossible for me to save as much as two hundred dollars.

Several of the men at the factory were my intimate friends, and I frequently joined them in their pleasures. During the summer months we went almost every Monday on an excursion to a seaside resort called Pablo Beach. These excursions were always crowded. There was a dancing pavilion, a great deal of drinking, and generally a fight or two to add to the excitement. I also contracted the cigar maker's habit of riding around in a hack[3] on Sunday afternoons. I sometimes went with my cigar maker friends to public balls that were given at a large hall on one of the main streets. I learned to take a drink occasionally and paid for quite a number that my friends took; but strong liquors never appealed to my appetite. I drank them only when the company I was in required it, and suffered for it afterwards. On the whole, though I was a bit wild, I can't remember that I ever did anything disgraceful, or, as the usual standard for young men goes, anything to forfeit my claim to respectability.

At one of the first public balls I attended I saw the Pullman car porter who had so kindly assisted me in getting to Jacksonville. I went immediately to one of my factory friends and borrowed fifteen dollars with which to repay the loan my benefactor had made me. After I had given him the money, and was thanking him, I noticed that he wore what was, at least, an exact duplicate of my lamented black and gray tie. It was somewhat worn, but distinct enough for me to trace the same odd design which had first attracted my eye. This was enough to arouse my strongest suspicions, but whether it was sufficient for the law to take cognizance of I did not consider. My astonishment and the ironical humor of the situation drove everything else out of my mind.

These balls were attended by a great variety of people. They were generally given by the waiters of some one of the big hotels, and were often patronized by a number of hotel guests who came to "see the sights." The crowd was always noisy, but good-natured; there was much quadrille-dancing,[4] and a strong-lunged man called figures in a voice which did not confine itself to the limits of the hall. It is not worth the while for me to describe in detail how these people acted; they conducted themselves in about the same manner as I have seen other people at similar balls conduct themselves. When one has seen something of the world and human nature, one must conclude, after all, that between people in like stations of life there is very little difference the world over.

However, it was at one of these balls that I first saw the cake-walk.[5] There was a contest for a gold watch, to be awarded to the hotel head-waiter receiving the greatest number of votes. There was some dancing while the votes were being counted. Then the floor was cleared for the cake-walk. A half-dozen guests from some of the hotels took seats on the stage to act as judges, and twelve or fourteen couples began to walk for a sure enough, highly decorated cake, which was in plain evidence. The spectators crowded about the space reserved for the contestants and watched them with interest and excitement. The couples did not walk round in a circle, but in a square, with the men on the inside. The fine points to be considered were the bearing of the men, the precision with which they turned the corners, the grace of the women, and the ease with which they swung around the pivots. The men walked with stately and soldierly step, and the women with

3. A vehicle for hire.
4. A square dance performed by four couples.
5. A dance developed from a contest in stylish walking; a cake was offered as a prize.

considerable grace. The judges arrived at their decision by a process of elimination. The music and the walk continued for some minutes; then both were stopped while the judges conferred; when the walk began again, several couples were left out. In this way the contest was finally narrowed down to three or four couples. Then the excitement became intense; there was much partisan cheering as one couple or another would execute a turn in extra elegant style. When the cake was finally awarded, the spectators were about evenly divided between those who cheered the winners and those who muttered about the unfairness of the judges. This was the cake-walk in its original form, and it is what the colored performers on the theatrical stage developed into the prancing movements now known all over the world, and which some Parisian critics pronounced the acme of poetic motion.

There are a great many colored people who are ashamed of the cake-walk, but I think they ought to be proud of it. It is my opinion that the colored people of this country have done four things which refute the oft-advanced theory that they are an absolutely inferior race, which demonstrate that they have originality and artistic conception, and, what is more, the power of creating that which can influence and appeal universally. The first two of these are the Uncle Remus stories, collected by Joel Chandler Harris, and the Jubilee songs, to which the Fisk singers[6] made the public and the skilled musicians of both America and Europe listen. The other two are ragtime music[7] and the cake-walk. No one who has traveled can question the world-conquering influence of ragtime, and I do not think it would be an exaggeration to say that in Europe the United States is popularly known better by ragtime than by anything else it has produced in a generation. In Paris they call it American music. The newspapers have already told how the practice of intricate cake-walk steps has taken up the time of European royalty and nobility. These are lower forms of art, but they give evidence of a power that will some day be applied to the higher forms. In this measure, at least, and aside from the number of prominent individuals the colored people of the United States have produced, the race has been a world influence; and all of the Indians between Alaska and Patagonia[8] haven't done as much.

Just when I was beginning to look upon Jacksonville as my permanent home and was beginning to plan about marrying the young school teacher, raising a family, and working in a cigar factory the rest of my life, for some reason, which I do not now remember, the factory at which I worked was indefinitely shut down. Some of the men got work in other factories in town; some decided to go to Key West and Tampa, others made up their minds to go to New York for work. All at once a desire like a fever seized me to see the North again and I cast my lot with those bound for New York.

VI

We steamed up into New York Harbor late one afternoon in spring. The last efforts of the sun were being put forth in turning the waters of the bay to

6. A nine-person traveling singing troupe founded in 1871 to raise funds for Fisk University. Harris (1848–1908), African American folklore collector, published his *Uncle Remus: His Songs and His Sayings* in 1881. "Jubilee songs": southern African American religious folk songs of joy and hope.

7. African American instrumental musical style of the 1890s characterized by a syncopated melodic line and regularly accented accompaniment.

8. A region of southern Argentina.

glistening gold; the green islands on either side, in spite of their warlike mountings, looked calm and peaceful; the buildings of the town shone out in a reflected light which gave the city an air of enchantment; and, truly, it is an enchanted spot. New York City is the most fatally fascinating thing in America. She sits like a great witch at the gate of the country, showing her alluring white face and hiding her crooked hands and feet under the folds of her wide garments—constantly enticing thousands from far within, and tempting those who come from across the seas to go no farther. And all these become the victims of her caprice. Some she at once crushes beneath her cruel feet; others she condemns to a fate like that of galley slaves; a few she favors and fondles, riding them high on the bubbles of fortune; then with a sudden breath she blows the bubbles out and laughs mockingly as she watches them fall.

Twice I had passed through it, but this was really my first visit to New York; and as I walked about that evening, I began to feel the dread power of the city; the crowds, the lights, the excitement, the gaiety, and all its subtler stimulating influences began to take effect upon me. My blood ran quicker and I felt that I was just beginning to live. To some natures this stimulant of life in a great city becomes a thing as binding and necessary as opium is to one addicted to the habit. It becomes their breath of life; they cannot exist outside of it; rather than be deprived of it they are content to suffer hunger, want, pain, and misery; they would not exchange even a ragged and wretched condition among the great crowd for any degree of comfort away from it.

As soon as we landed, four of us went directly to a lodging house in Twenty-seventh Street, just west of Sixth Avenue. The house was run by a short, stout mulatto man, who was exceedingly talkative and inquisitive. In fifteen minutes he not only knew the history of the past life of each one of us, but had a clearer idea of what we intended to do in the future than we ourselves. He sought this information so much with an air of being very particular as to whom he admitted into his house that we tremblingly answered every question that he asked. When we had become located, we went out and got supper, then walked around until about ten o'clock. At that hour we met a couple of young fellows who lived in New York and were known to one of the members of our party. It was suggested we go to a certain place which was known by the proprietor's name. We turned into one of the cross streets and mounted the stoop of a house in about the middle of a block between Sixth and Seventh Avenues. One of the young men whom we had met rang a bell, and a man on the inside cracked the door a couple of inches; then opened it and let us in. We found ourselves in the hallway of what had once been a residence. The front parlor had been converted into a bar, and a half-dozen or so well-dressed men were in the room. We went in and after a general introduction had several rounds of beer. In the back parlor a crowd was sitting and standing around the walls of the room watching an exciting and noisy game of pool. I walked back and joined this crowd to watch the game, and principally to get away from the drinking party. The game was really interesting, the players being quite expert, and the excitement was heightened by the bets which were being made on the result. At times the antics and remarks of both players and spectators were amusing. When, at a critical point, a player missed a shot, he was deluged, by those financially interested in his making it, with a flood of epithets synonymous with "chump"; while from the others he would be jeered by such remarks as "Nigger, dat cue ain't no hoe-handle."

I noticed that among this class of colored men the word "nigger" was freely used in about the same sense as the word "fellow," and sometimes as a term of almost endearment; but I soon learned that its use was positively and absolutely prohibited to white men.

I stood watching this pool game until I was called by my friends, who were still in the bar-room, to go upstairs. On the second floor there were two large rooms. From the hall I looked into the one on the front. There was a large, round table in the center, at which five or six men were seated playing poker. The air and conduct here were greatly in contrast to what I had just seen in the pool-room; these men were evidently the aristocrats of the place; they were well, perhaps a bit flashily, dressed and spoke in low modulated voices, frequently using the word "gentlemen"; in fact, they seemed to be practicing a sort of Chesterfieldian politeness[9] towards each other. I was watching these men with a great deal of interest and some degree of admiration when I was again called by the members of our party, and I followed them on to the back room. There was a door-keeper at this room, and we were admitted only after inspection. When we got inside, I saw a crowd of men of all ages and kinds grouped about an old billiard table, regarding some of whom, in supposing them to be white, I made no mistake. At first I did not know what these men were doing; they were using terms that were strange to me. I could hear only a confusion of voices exclaiming: "Shoot the two!" "Shoot the four!" "Fate me! Fate me!" "I've got you fated!" "Twenty-five cents he don't turn!" This was the ancient and terribly fascinating game of dice, popularly known as "craps." I myself had played pool in Jacksonville—it is a favorite game among cigar makers—and I had seen others play cards; but here was something new. I edged my way in to the table and stood between one of my new-found New York friends and a tall, slender, black fellow, who was making side bets while the dice were at the other end of the table. My companion explained to me the principles of the game; and they are so simple that they hardly need to be explained twice. The dice came around the table until they reached the man on the other side of the tall, black fellow. He lost, and the latter said: "Gimme the bones."[1] He threw a dollar on the table and said: "Shoot the dollar." His style of play was so strenuous that he had to be allowed plenty of room. He shook the dice high above his head, and each time he threw them on the table, he emitted a grunt such as men give when they are putting forth physical exertion with a rhythmic regularity. He frequently whirled completely around on his heels, throwing the dice the entire length of the table, and talking to them as though they were trained animals. He appealed to them in short singsong phrases. "Come, dice," he would say. "Little Phoebe," "Little Joe," "'Way down yonder in the cornfield." Whether these mystic incantations were efficacious or not I could not say, but, at any rate, his luck was great, and he had what gamblers term "nerve." "Shoot the dollar!" "Shoot the two!" "Shoot the four!" "Shoot the eight!" came from his lips as quickly as the dice turned to his advantage. My companion asked me if I had ever played. I told him no. He said that I ought to try my luck: that everybody won at first. The tall man at my side was waving his arms in the air, exclaiming: "Shoot the sixteen!" "Shoot the sixteen!" "Fate me!"

9. A standard of urbane good manners represented by Philip Dormer Stanhope, fourth Earl of Chesterfield (1694–1773).

1. Dice.

Whether it was my companion's suggestion or some latent dare-devil strain in my blood which suddenly sprang into activity I do not know; but with a thrill of excitement which went through my whole body I threw a twenty-dollar bill on the table and said in a trembling voice: "I fate you."

I could feel that I had gained the attention and respect of everybody in the room, every eye was fixed on me, and the widespread question, "Who is he?" went around. This was gratifying to a certain sense of vanity of which I have never been able to rid myself, and I felt that it was worth the money even if I lost. The tall man, with a whirl on his heels and a double grunt, threw the dice; four was the number which turned up. This is considered as a hard "point" to make. He redoubled his contortions and his grunts and his pleadings to the dice; but on his third or fourth throw the fateful seven turned up, and I had won. My companion and all my friends shouted to me to follow up my luck. The fever was on me. I seized the dice. My hands were so hot that the bits of bone felt like pieces of ice. I shouted as loudly as I could: "Shoot it all!" but the blood was tingling so about my ears that I could not hear my own voice. I was soon "fated." I threw the dice—seven—I had won. "Shoot it all!" I cried again. There was a pause; the stake was more than one man cared to or could cover. I was finally "fated" by several men taking each a part of it. I then threw the dice again. Seven. I had won. "Shoot it all!" I shouted excitedly. After a short delay I was "fated." Again I rolled the dice. Eleven. Again I won. My friends now surrounded me and, much against my inclination, forced me to take down all of the money except five dollars. I tried my luck once more, and threw some small "point" which I failed to make, and the dice passed on to the next man.

In less than three minutes I had won more than two hundred dollars, a sum which afterwards cost me dearly. I was the hero of the moment and was soon surrounded by a group of men who expressed admiration for my "nerve" and predicted for me a brilliant future as a gambler. Although at the time I had no thought of becoming a gambler, I felt proud of my success. I felt a bit ashamed, too, that I had allowed my friends to persuade me to take down my money so soon. Another set of men also got around me and begged me for twenty-five or fifty cents to put them back into the game. I gave each of them something. I saw that several of them had on linen dusters,[2] and as I looked about, I noticed that there were perhaps a dozen men in the room similarly clad. I asked the fellow who had been my prompter at the dice table why they dressed in such a manner. He told me that men who had lost all the money and jewelry they possessed, frequently, in an effort to recoup their losses, would gamble away all their outer clothing and even their shoes; and that the proprietor kept on hand a supply of linen dusters for all who were so unfortunate. My informant went on to say that sometimes a fellow would become almost completely dressed and then, by a turn of the dice, would be thrown back into a state of semi-nakedness. Some of them were virtually prisoners and unable to get into the streets for days at a time. They ate at the lunch counter, where their credit was good so long as they were fair gamblers and did not attempt to jump their debts, and they slept around in chairs. They importuned friends and winners to put them back in the game, and kept at it until fortune again smiled on them. I

2. Long, loose-fitting linen coats.

laughed heartily at this, not thinking the day was coming which would find me in the same ludicrous predicament.

On passing downstairs I was told that the third and top floor of the house was occupied by the proprietor. When we passed through the bar, I treated everybody in the room—and that was no small number, for eight or ten had followed us down. Then our party went out. It was now about half past twelve, but my nerves were at such a tension that I could not endure the mere thought of going to bed. I asked if there was no other place to which we could go; our guides said yes, and suggested that we go to the "Club." We went to Sixth Avenue, walked two blocks, and turned to the west into another street. We stopped in front of a house with three stories and a basement. In the basement was a Chinese chop-suey restaurant. There was a red lantern at the iron gate to the areaway, inside of which the Chinaman's name was printed. We went up the steps of the stoop, rang the bell, and were admitted without any delay. From the outside the house bore a rather gloomy aspect, the windows being absolutely dark, but within, it was a veritable house of mirth. When we had passed through a small vestibule and reached the hallway, we heard mingled sounds of music and laughter, the clink of glasses, and the pop of bottles. We went into the main room and I was little prepared for what I saw. The brilliancy of the place, the display of diamond rings, scarf-pins, ear-rings, and breast-pins, the big rolls of money that were brought into evidence when drinks were paid for, and the air of gaiety that pervaded the place, all completely dazzled and dazed me. I felt positively giddy, and it was several minutes before I was able to make any clear and definite observations.

We at length secured places at a table in a corner of the room and, as soon as we could attract the attention of one of the busy waiters, ordered a round of drinks. When I had somewhat collected my senses, I realized that in a large back room into which the main room opened, there was a young fellow singing a song, accompanied on the piano by a short, thickset, dark man. After each verse he did some dance steps, which brought forth great applause and a shower of small coins at his feet. After the singer had responded to a rousing encore, the stout man at the piano began to run his fingers up and down the keyboard. This he did in a manner which indicated that he was master of a good deal of technique. Then he began to play; and such playing! I stopped talking to listen. It was music of a kind I had never heard before. It was music that demanded physical response, patting of the feet, drumming of the fingers, or nodding of the head in time with the beat. The barbaric harmonies, the audacious resolutions, often consisting of an abrupt jump from one key to another, the intricate rhythms in which the accents fell in the most unexpected places, but in which the beat was never lost, produced a most curious effect. And, too, the player—the dexterity of his left hand in making rapid octave runs and jumps was little short of marvelous; and with his right hand he frequently swept half the keyboard with clean-cut chromatics[3] which he fitted in so nicely as never to fail to arouse in his listeners a sort of pleasant surprise at the accomplishment of the feat.

This was ragtime music, then a novelty in New York, and just growing to be a rage, which has not yet subsided. It was originated in the questionable resorts about Memphis and St. Louis by Negro piano players who knew no

3. Series of twelve tones within an octave.

more of the theory of music than they did of the theory of the universe, but were guided by natural musical instinct and talent. It made its way to Chicago, where it was popular some time before it reached New York. These players often improvised crude and, at times, vulgar words to fit the melodies. This was the beginning of the ragtime song. Several of these improvisations were taken down by white men, the words slightly altered, and published under the names of the arrangers. They sprang into immediate popularity and earned small fortunes, of which the Negro originators got only a few dollars. But I have learned that since that time a number of colored men, of not only musical talent, but training, are writing out their own melodies and words and reaping the reward of their work. I have learned also that they have a large number of white imitators and adulterators.

American musicians, instead of investigating ragtime, attempt to ignore it, or dismiss it with a contemptuous word. But that has always been the course of scholasticism[4] in every branch of art. Whatever new thing the *people* like is pooh-poohed; whatever is *popular* is spoken of as not worth the while. The fact is, nothing great or enduring, especially in music, has ever sprung full-fledged and unprecedented from the brain of any master; the best that he gives to the world he gathers from the hearts of the people, and runs it through the alembic[5] of his genius. In spite of the bans which musicians and music teachers have placed upon it, the people still demand and enjoy ragtime. One thing cannot be denied; it is music which possesses at least one strong element of greatness: it appeals universally; not only the American, but the English, the French, and even the German people find delight in it. In fact, there is not a corner of the civilized world in which it is not known, and this proves its originality; for if it were an imitation, the people of Europe, anyhow, would not have found it a novelty. Anyone who doubts that there is a peculiar heel-tickling, smile-provoking, joy-awakening charm in ragtime needs only to hear a skillful performer play the genuine article to be convinced. I believe that it has its place as well as the music which draws from us sighs and tears.

I became so interested in both the music and the player that I left the table where I was sitting, and made my way through the hall into the back room, where I could see as well as hear. I talked to the piano player between the musical numbers and found out that he was just a natural musician, never having taken a lesson in his life. Not only could he play almost anything he heard, but he could accompany singers in songs he had never heard. He had, by ear alone, composed some pieces, several of which he played over for me; each of them was properly proportioned and balanced. I began to wonder what this man with such a lavish natural endowment would have done had he been trained. Perhaps he wouldn't have done anything at all; he might have become, at best, a mediocre imitator of the great masters in what they have already done to a finish, or one of the modern innovators who strive after originality by seeing how cleverly they can dodge about through the rules of harmony and at the same time avoid melody. It is certain that he would not have been so delightful as he was in ragtime.

I sat by, watching and listening to this man until I was dragged away by my friends. The place was now almost deserted; only a few stragglers hung

4. An insistence on traditional doctrines and methods. "Pooh-poohed" (below): judged as silly or not worth consideration.

5. Something that purifies as if by distillation.

on, and they were all the worse for drink. My friends were well up in this class. We passed into the street; the lamps were pale against the sky; day was just breaking. We went home and got into bed. I fell into a fitful sort of sleep, with ragtime music ringing continually in my ears.

VII

I shall take advantage of this pause in my narrative to describe more closely the "Club" spoken of in the latter part of the preceding chapter—to describe it as I afterwards came to know it, as an habitué.[6] I shall do this not only because of the direct influence it had on my life, but also because it was at that time the most famous place of its kind in New York, and was well known to both white and colored people of certain classes.

I have already stated that in the basement of the house there was a Chinese restaurant. The Chinaman who kept it did an exceptionally good business; for chop-suey was a favorite dish among the frequenters of the place. It is a food that, somehow, has the power of absorbing alcoholic liquors that have been taken into the stomach. I have heard men claim that they could sober up on chop-suey. Perhaps that accounted, in some degree, for its popularity. On the main floor there were two large rooms: a parlor about thirty feet in length, and a large, square back room into which the parlor opened. The floor of the parlor was carpeted; small tables and chairs were arranged about the room; the windows were draped with lace curtains, and the walls were literally covered with photographs or lithographs of every colored man in America who had ever "done anything." There were pictures of Frederick Douglass and of Peter Jackson,[7] of all the lesser lights of the prize-fighting ring, of all the famous jockeys and the stage celebrities, down to the newest song and dance team. The most of these photographs were autographed and, in a sense, made a really valuable collection. In the back room there was a piano, and tables were placed around the wall. The floor was bare and the center was left vacant for singers, dancers, and others who entertained the patrons. In a closet in this room which jutted out into the hall the proprietor kept his buffet. There was no open bar, because the place had no liquor license. In this back room the tables were sometimes pushed aside, and the floor given over to general dancing. The front room on the next floor was a sort of private party room; a back room on the same floor contained no furniture and was devoted to the use of new and ambitious performers. In this room song and dance teams practiced their steps, acrobatic teams practiced their tumbles, and many other kinds of "acts" rehearsed their "turns." The other rooms of the house were used as sleeping-apartments.

No gambling was allowed, and the conduct of the place was surprisingly orderly. It was, in short, a center of colored Bohemians and sports.[8] Here the great prize fighters were wont to come, the famous jockeys, the noted minstrels, whose names and faces were familiar on every bill-board in the country; and these drew a multitude of those who love to dwell in the shadow of greatness. There were then no organizations giving perfor-

6. A person who frequents a certain place (French).
7. Australian heavyweight boxing champion (1861–1901).
8. Flashy, good-time people. "Bohemians": unconventional, nonconforming people, especially artists and writers.

mances of such order as are now given by several colored companies; that was because no manager could imagine that audiences would pay to see Negro performers in any other role than that of Mississippi River roustabouts; but there was lots of talent and ambition. I often heard the younger and brighter men discussing the time when they would compel the public to recognize that they could do something more than grin and cut pigeon-wings.[9]

Sometimes one or two of the visiting stage professionals, after being sufficiently urged, would go into the back room and take the places of the regular amateur entertainers, but they were very sparing with these favors, and the patrons regarded them as special treats. There was one man, a minstrel, who, whenever he responded to a request to "do something," never essayed anything below a reading from Shakespeare. How well he read I do not know, but he greatly impressed me; and I can say that at least he had a voice which strangely stirred those who heard it. Here was a man who made people laugh at the size of his mouth, while he carried in his heart a burning ambition to be a tragedian; and so after all he did play a part in a tragedy.

These notables of the ring, the turf, and the stage, drew to the place crowds of admirers, both white and colored. Whenever one of them came in, there were awe-inspired whispers from those who knew him by sight, in which they enlightened those around them as to his identity, and hinted darkly at their great intimacy with the noted one. Those who were on terms of approach immediately showed their privilege over others less fortunate by gathering around their divinity. I was, at first, among those who dwelt in darkness. Most of these celebrities I had never heard of. This made me an object of pity among many of my new associates. I soon learned, however, to fake a knowledge for the benefit of those who were greener than I; and, finally, I became personally acquainted with the majority of the famous personages who came to the "Club."

A great deal of money was spent here, so many of the patrons were men who earned large sums. I remember one night a dapper little brown-skin fellow was pointed out to me and I was told that he was the most popular jockey of the day, and that he earned $12,000 a year. This latter statement I couldn't doubt, for with my own eyes I saw him spending at about thirty times that rate. For his friends and those who were introduced to him he bought nothing but wine—in sporting circles, "wine" means champagne—and paid for it at five dollars a quart. He sent a quart to every table in the place with his compliments; and on the table at which he and his party were seated there were more than a dozen bottles. It was the custom at the "Club" for the waiter not to remove the bottles when champagne was being drunk until the party had finished. There were reasons for this; it advertised the brand of wine, it advertised that the party was drinking wine, and advertised how much they had bought. This jockey had won a great race that day, and he was rewarding his admirers for the homage they paid him, all of which he accepted with a fine air of condescension.

Besides the people I have just been describing, there was at the place almost every night one or two parties of white people, men and women, who were out sight-seeing, or slumming. They generally came in cabs; some

9. A dance step performed by jumping up and striking the legs together.

of them would stay only for a few minutes, while others sometimes stayed until morning. There was also another set of white people who came frequently; it was made up of variety performers[1] and others who delineated "darky characters"; they came to get their imitations first hand from the Negro entertainers they saw there.

There was still another set of white patrons, composed of women; these were not occasional visitors, but five or six of them were regular habituées. When I first saw them, I was not sure that they were white. In the first place, among the many colored women who came to the "Club" there were several just as fair; and, secondly, I always saw these women in company with colored men. They were all good-looking and well-dressed, and seemed to be women of some education. One of these in particular attracted my attention; she was an exceedingly beautiful woman of perhaps thirty-five; she had glistening copper-colored hair, very white skin, and eyes very much like Du Maurier's[2] conception of Trilby's "twin gray stars." When I came to know her, I found that she was a woman of considerable culture; she had traveled in Europe, spoke French, and played the piano well. She was always dressed elegantly, but in absolute good taste. She always came to the "Club" in a cab, and was soon joined by a well-set-up, very black young fellow. He was always faultlessly dressed; one of the most exclusive tailors in New York made his clothes, and he wore a number of diamonds in about as good taste as they could be worn in by a man. I learned that she paid for his clothes and his diamonds. I learned, too, that he was not the only one of his kind. More that I learned would be better suited to a book on social phenomena than to a narrative of my life.

This woman was known at the "Club" as the rich widow. She went by a very aristocratic-sounding name, which corresponded to her appearance. I shall never forget how hard it was for me to get over my feelings of surprise, perhaps more than surprise, at seeing her with her black companion; somehow I never exactly enjoyed the sight. I have devoted so much time to this pair, the "widow" and her companion, because it was through them that another decided turn was brought about in my life.

VIII

On the day following our night at the "Club" we slept until late in the afternoon; so late that beginning search for work was entirely out of the question. This did not cause me much worry, for I had more than three hundred dollars, and New York had impressed me as a place where there was lots of money and not much difficulty in getting it. It is needless to inform my readers that I did not long hold this opinion. We got out of the house about dark, went to a restaurant on Sixth Avenue and ate something, then walked around for a couple of hours. I finally suggested that we visit the same places we had been in the night before. Following my suggestion, we started first to the gambling house. The man on the door let us in without any question; I accredited this to my success of the night before. We went straight to the "crap" room, and I at once made my way to a table, where I was rather flattered by the murmur of recognition which went around. I played in up and down luck for three or four hours; then, worn with nervous excitement,

1. Generally minstrel or vaudeville performers. "Habituees" (below): frequent visitors.
2. George Louis Du Maurier (1834–1896), English author of *Trilby* (1894), a popular novel about a famous singer.

quit, having lost about fifty dollars. But I was so strongly possessed with the thought that I would make up my losses the next time I played that I left the place with a light heart.

When we got into the street our party was divided against itself; two were for going home at once and getting to bed. They gave as a reason that we were to get up early and look for jobs. I think the real reason was that they had each lost several dollars in the game. I lived to learn that in the world of sport all men win alike, but lose differently; and so gamblers are rated, not by the way in which they win, but by the way in which they lose. Some men lose with a careless smile, recognizing that losing is a part of the game; others curse their luck and rail at fortune; and others, still, lose sadly; after each such experience they are swept by a wave of reform; they resolve to stop gambling and be good. When in this frame of mind it would take very little persuasion to lead them into a prayer-meeting. Those in the first class are looked upon with admiration; those in the second class are merely commonplace; while those in the third are regarded with contempt. I believe these distinctions hold good in all the ventures of life. After some minutes one of my friends and I succeeded in convincing the other two that a while at the "Club" would put us all in better spirits; and they consented to go, on our promise not to stay longer than an hour. We found the place crowded, and the same sort of thing going on which we had seen the night before. I took a seat at once by the side of the piano player, and was soon lost to everything except the novel charm of the music. I watched the performer with the idea of catching the trick, and during one of his intermissions I took his place at the piano and made an attempt to imitate him, but even my quick ear and ready fingers were unequal to the task on first trial.

We did not stay at the "Club" very long, but went home to bed in order to be up early the next day. We had no difficulty in finding work, and my third morning in New York found me at a table rolling cigars. I worked steadily for some weeks, at the same time spending my earnings between the "crap" game and the "Club." Making cigars became more and more irksome to me; perhaps my more congenial work as a "reader" had unfitted me for work at the table. And, too, the late hours I was keeping made such a sedentary occupation almost beyond the powers of will and endurance. I often found it hard to keep my eyes open and sometimes had to get up and move around to keep from falling asleep. I began to miss whole days from the factory, days on which I was compelled to stay at home and sleep.

My luck at the gambling table was varied; sometimes I was fifty to a hundred dollars ahead, and at other times I had to borrow money from my fellow workmen to settle my room rent and pay for my meals. Each night after leaving the dice game I went to the "Club" to hear the music and watch the gaiety. If I had won, this was in accord with my mood; if I had lost, it made me forget. I at last realized that making cigars for a living and gambling for a living could not both be carried on at the same time, and I resolved to give up the cigar making. This resolution led me into a life which held me bound more than a year. During that period my regular time for going to bed was somewhere between four and six o'clock in the mornings. I got up late in the afternoons, walked about a little, then went to the gambling house or the "Club." My New York was limited to ten blocks; the boundaries were Sixth Avenue from Twenty-third to Thirty-third Streets, with the cross streets one block to the west. Central Park was a distant forest, and the lower part of the city a foreign land. I look back upon the life I then led with a shudder when I think what would have been had I not escaped it. But had I not escaped it, I should have been no more unfortunate than are many young colored men who come to New York. During that dark period I became acquainted with a score of bright, intelligent young fellows who had come up to the great city with high hopes and ambitions and who had fallen under the spell of this under life, a spell they could not throw off. There was one popularly known as "the doctor"; he had had two years in the Harvard Medical School, but here he was, living this gas-light life, his will and moral sense so enervated and deadened that it was impossible for him to break away. I do not doubt that the same thing is going on now, but I have sympathy rather than censure for these victims, for I know how easy it is to slip into a slough from which it takes a herculean effort to leap.

I regret that I cannot contrast my views of life among colored people of New York; but the truth is, during my entire stay in this city I did not become acquainted with a single respectable family. I knew that there were several colored men worth a hundred or so thousand dollars each, and some families who proudly dated their free ancestry back a half-dozen generations. I also learned that in Brooklyn there lived quite a large colony in comfortable homes which they owned; but at no point did my life come in contact with theirs.

In my gambling experiences I passed through all the states and conditions that a gambler is heir to. Some days found me able to peel ten- and twenty-dollar bills from a roll, and others found me clad in a linen duster and carpet slippers. I finally caught up another method of earning money, and so did not have to depend entirely upon the caprices of fortune at the gaming table. Through continually listening to the music at the "Club," and through my own previous training, my natural talent and perseverance, I developed into a remarkable player of ragtime; indeed, I had the name at that time of being the best ragtime-player in New York. I brought all my knowledge of classic music to bear and, in so doing, achieved some novelties which pleased and even astonished my listeners. It was I who first made ragtime transcriptions of familiar classic selections. I used to play Mendelssohn's "Wedding March" in a manner that never failed to arouse enthusiasm among the patrons of the "Club." Very few nights passed during which I was not asked to play it. It was no secret that the great increase in slumming visitors was due to my playing. By mastering ragtime I gained several things: first of all, I gained the title of professor. I was known as "the professor" as long as I remained in that world. Then, too, I gained the means of earning a rather fair livelihood. This work took up much of my time and kept me almost entirely away from the gambling table. Through it I also gained a friend who was the means by which I escaped from this lower world. And, finally, I secured a wedge which has opened to me more doors and made me a welcome guest than my playing of Beethoven and Chopin could ever have done.

The greater part of the money I now began to earn came through the friend to whom I alluded in the foregoing paragraph. Among the other white "slummers" there came into the "Club" one night a clean-cut, slender, but athletic-looking man, who would have been taken for a youth had it not been for the tinge of gray about his temples. He was clean-shaven and had regular features, and all of his movements bore the indefinable but unmistakable stamp of culture. He spoke to no one, but sat languidly puffing cigarettes and sipping a glass of beer. He was the center of a great deal of attention; all of the old-timers were wondering who he was. When I had finished playing, he called a waiter and by him sent me a five-dollar bill. For about a month after that he was at the "Club" one or two nights each week, and each time after I had played, he gave me five dollars. One night he sent for me to come to his table; he asked me several questions about myself; then told me that he had an engagement which he wanted me to fill. He gave me a card containing his address and asked me to be there on a certain night.

I was on hand promptly and found that he was giving a dinner in his own apartments to a party of ladies and gentlemen and that I was expected to furnish the musical entertainment. When the grave, dignified man at the door let me in, the place struck me as being almost dark, my eyes had been so accustomed to the garish light of the "Club." He took my coat and hat, bade me take a seat, and went to tell his master that I had come. When my eyes were adjusted to the soft light, I saw that I was in the midst of elegance and luxury in a degree such as I had never seen; but not the elegance which makes one ill at ease. As I sank into a great chair, the subdued tone, the delicately sensuous harmony of my surroundings, drew from me a deep sigh of relief and comfort. How long the man was gone I do not know, but I was startled by a voice saying: "Come this way, if you please, sir," and I saw him standing by my chair. I had been asleep; and I awoke very much confused and a little ashamed, because I did not know how many times he may have called me. I followed him through into the diningroom, where the butler was putting the finishing touches to a table which already looked like a big jewel. The doorman turned me over to the butler, and I passed with the butler on back to where several waiters were busy polishing and assorting table utensils. Without being asked whether I was hungry or not, I was placed at a table and given something to eat. Before I had finished eating, I heard the laughter and talk of the guests who were arriving. Soon afterwards I was called in to begin my work.

I passed in to where the company was gathered and went directly to the piano. According to a suggestion from the host, I began with classic music. During the first number there was absolute quiet and appreciative attention, and when I had finished, I was given a round of generous applause. After that the talk and the laughter began to grow until the music was only an accompaniment to the chatter. This, however, did not disconcert me as it once would have done, for I had become accustomed to playing in the midst of uproarious noise. As the guests began to pay less attention to me, I was enabled to pay more to them. There were about a dozen of them. The men ranged in appearance from a girlish-looking youth to a big grizzled man whom everybody addressed as "Judge." None of the women appeared to be under thirty, but each of them struck me as being handsome. I was not long in finding out that they were all decidedly blasé. Several of the women smoked cigarettes, and with a careless grace which showed they were used to the habit. Occasionally a "Damn it!" escaped from the lips of some one of them, but in such a charming way as to rob it of all vulgarity. The most notable thing which I observed was that the reserve of the host increased in direct proportion with the hilarity of his guests. I thought that there was something going wrong which displeased him. I afterwards learned that it was his habitual manner on such occasions. He seemed to take cynical delight in watching and studying others indulging in excess. His guests were evidently accustomed to his rather non-participating attitude, for it did not seem in any degree to dampen their spirits.

When dinner was served, the piano was moved and the door left open, so that the company might hear the music while eating. At a word from the host I struck up one of my liveliest ragtime pieces. The effect was surprising, perhaps even to the host; the ragtime music came very near spoiling the party so far as eating the dinner was concerned. As soon as I began, the conversation suddenly stopped. It was a pleasure to me to watch the expression of astonishment and delight that grew on the faces of everybody. These were people—and they represented a large class—who were ever expecting to find happiness in novelty, each day restlessly exploring and exhausting every resource of this great city that might possibly furnish a new sensation or awaken a fresh emotion, and who were always grateful to anyone who aided them in their quest. Several of the women left the table and gathered about the piano. They watched my fingers and asked what kind of music it was that I was playing, where I had learned it, and a host of other questions. It was only by being repeatedly called back to the table that they were induced to finish their dinner. When the guests arose, I struck up my ragtime transcription of Mendelssohn's "Wedding March," playing it with terrific chromatic octave[3] runs in the bass. This raised everybody's spirits to the highest point of gaiety, and the whole company involuntarily and unconsciously did an impromptu cake-walk. From that time on until the time of leaving they kept me so busy that my arms ached. I obtained a little respite when the girlish-looking youth and one or two of the ladies sang several songs, but after each of these it was "back to ragtime."

In leaving, the guests were enthusiastic in telling the host that he had furnished them the most unusual entertainment they had ever enjoyed. When they had gone, my millionaire friend—for he was reported to be a millionaire—said to me with a smile: "Well, I have given them something they've never had before." After I had put on my coat and was ready to leave, he made me take a glass of wine; he then gave me a cigar and twenty dollars in bills. He told me that he would give me lots of work, his only stipulation being that I should not play any engagements such as I had just filled for him, except by his instructions. I readily accepted the proposition, for I was sure that I could not be the loser by such a contract.

I afterwards played for him at many dinners and parties of one kind or another. Occasionally he "loaned" me to some of his friends. And, too, I often played for him alone at his apartments. At such times he was quite a puzzle to me until I became accustomed to his manners. He would sometimes sit for three or four hours hearing me play, his eyes almost closed, making scarcely a motion except to light a fresh cigarette, and never commenting one way or another on the music. At first I sometimes thought he had fallen asleep and would pause in playing. The stopping of the music always aroused him enough to tell me to play this or that; and I soon learned that my task was not to be considered finished until he got up from his chair and said: "That will do." The man's powers of endurance in listening often exceeded mine in performing—yet I am not sure that he was always listening. At times I became so oppressed with fatigue and sleepiness that it took almost superhuman effort to keep my fingers going; in fact, I believe I sometimes did so while dozing. During such moments this man sitting there so mysteriously silent, almost hid in a cloud of heavy-scented smoke,

3. Musical scale usually with twelve pitches inserted as embellishment to the harmony.

filled me with a sort of unearthly terror. He seemed to be some grim, mute, but relentless tyrant, possessing over me a supernatural power which he used to drive me on mercilessly to exhaustion. But these feelings came very rarely; besides, he paid me so liberally I could forget much. There at length grew between us a familiar and warm relationship, and I am sure he had a decided personal liking for me. On my part, I looked upon him at that time as about all a man could wish to be.

The "Club" still remained my headquarters, and when I was not playing for my good patron, I was generally to be found there. However, I no longer depended on playing at the "Club" to earn my living; I rather took rank with the visiting celebrities and, occasionally, after being sufficiently urged, would favor my old and new admirers with a number or two. I say, without any egotistic pride, that among my admirers were several of the best-looking women who frequented the place, and who made no secret of the fact that they admired me as much as they did my playing. Among these was the "widow"; indeed, her attentions became so marked that one of my friends warned me to beware of her black companion, who was generally known as a "bad man." He said there was much more reason to be careful because the pair had lately quarreled and had not been together at the "Club" for some nights. This warning greatly impressed me and I resolved to stop the affair before it should go any further; but the woman was so beautiful that my native gallantry and delicacy would not allow me to repulse her; my finer feelings entirely overcame my judgment. The warning also opened my eyes sufficiently to see that though my artistic temperament and skill made me interesting and attractive to the woman, she was, after all, using me only to excite the jealousy of her companion and revenge herself upon him. It was this surly, black despot who held sway over her deepest emotions.

One night, shortly afterwards, I went into the "Club" and saw the "widow" sitting at a table in company with another woman. She at once beckoned for me to come to her. I went, knowing that I was committing worse than folly. She ordered a quart of champagne and insisted that I sit down and drink with her. I took a chair on the opposite side of the table and began to sip a glass of the wine. Suddenly I noticed by an expression on the "widow's" face that something had occurred. I instinctively glanced around and saw that her companion had just entered. His ugly look completely frightened me. My back was turned to him, but by watching the "widow's" eyes I judged that he was pacing back and forth across the room. My feelings were far from being comfortable; I expected every moment to feel a blow on my head. She, too, was very nervous; she was trying hard to appear unconcerned, but could not succeed in hiding her real feelings. I decided that it was best to get out of such a predicament even at the expense of appearing cowardly, and I made a motion to rise. Just as I partly turned in my chair, I saw the black fellow approaching; he walked directly to our table and leaned over. The "widow" evidently feared he was going to strike her, and she threw back her head. Instead of striking her he whipped out a revolver and fired; the first shot went straight into her throat. There were other shots fired, but how many I do not know; for the first knowledge I had of my surroundings and actions was that I was rushing through the chop-suey restaurant into the street. Just which streets I followed when I got outside I do not know, but I think I must have gone towards Eighth Avenue, then down towards Twenty-third

Street and across towards Fifth Avenue. I traveled, not by sight, but instinctively. I felt like one fleeing in a horrible nightmare.

How long and far I walked I cannot tell; but on Fifth Avenue, under a light, I passed a cab containing a solitary occupant, who called to me, and I recognized the voice and face of my millionaire friend. He stopped the cab and asked: "What on earth are you doing strolling in this part of the town?" For answer I got into the cab and related to him all that had happened. He reassured me by saying that no charge of any kind could be brought against me; then added: "But of course you don't want to be mixed up in such an affair." He directed the driver to turn around and go into the park, and then went on to say: "I decided last night that I'd go to Europe tomorrow. I think I'll take you along instead of Walter." Walter was his valet. It was settled that I should go to his apartments for the rest of the night and sail with him in the morning.

We drove around through the park, exchanging only an occasional word. The cool air somewhat calmed my nerves and I lay back and closed my eyes; but still I could see that beautiful white throat with the ugly wound. The jet of blood pulsing from it had placed an indelible red stain on my memory.

IX

I did not feel at ease until the ship was well out of New York harbor; and, notwithstanding the repeated reassurances of my millionaire friend and my own knowledge of the facts in the case, I somehow could not rid myself of the sentiment that I was, in a great degree, responsible for the "widow's" tragic end. We had brought most of the morning papers aboard with us, but my great fear of seeing my name in connection with the killing would not permit me to read the accounts, although, in one of the papers, I did look at the picture of the victim, which did not in the least resemble her. This morbid state of mind, together with sea-sickness, kept me miserable for three or four days. At the end of that time my spirits began to revive, and I took an interest in the ship, my fellow passengers, and the voyage in general. On the second or third day out we passed several spouting whales, but I could not arouse myself to make the effort to go to the other side of the ship to see them. A little later we ran in close proximity to a large iceberg. I was curious enough to get up and look at it, and I was fully repaid for my pains. The sun was shining full upon it, and it glistened like a mammoth diamond, cut with a million facets. As we passed, it constantly changed its shape; at each different angle of vision it assumed new and astonishing forms of beauty. I watched it through a pair of glasses, seeking to verify my early conception of an iceberg—in the geographies of my grammar school days the pictures of icebergs always included a stranded polar bear, standing desolately upon one of the snowy crags. I looked for the bear, but if he was there, he refused to put himself on exhibition.

It was not, however, until the morning that we entered the harbor of Havre[4] that I was able to shake off my gloom. Then the strange sights, the chatter in an unfamiliar tongue, and the excitement of landing and passing the customs officials caused me to forget completely the events of a few days before. Indeed, I grew so lighthearted that when I caught my first sight

4. A seaport in northwestern France.

of the train which was to take us to Paris, I enjoyed a hearty laugh. The toy-looking engine, the stuffy little compartment cars, with tiny, old-fashioned wheels, struck me as being extremely funny. But before we reached Paris my respect for our train rose considerably. I found that the "tiny" engine made remarkably fast time, and that the old-fashioned wheels ran very smoothly. I even began to appreciate the "stuffy" cars for their privacy. As I watched the passing scenery from the car window, it seemed too beautiful to be real. The bright-colored houses against the green background impressed me as the work of some idealistic painter. Before we arrived in Paris, there was awakened in my heart a love for France which continued to grow stronger, a love which to-day makes that country for me the one above all others to be desired.

We rolled into the station Saint Lazare about four o'clock in the afternoon and drove immediately to the Hôtel Continental. My benefactor, humoring my curiosity and enthusiasm, which seemed to please him very much, suggested that we take a short walk before dinner. We stepped out of the hotel and turned to the right into the rue de Rivoli. When the vista of the Place de la Concorde and the Champs Élysées suddenly burst on me, I could hardly credit my own eyes. I shall attempt no such supererogatory task as a description of Paris. I wish only to give briefly the impressions which that wonderful city made upon me. It impressed me as the perfect and perfectly beautiful city; and even after I had been there for some time, and seen not only its avenues and palaces, but its most squalid alleys and hovels, this impression was not weakened. Paris became for me a charmed spot, and whenever I have returned there, I have fallen under the spell, a spell which compels admiration for all of its manners and customs and justification of even its follies and sins.

We walked a short distance up the Champs Élysées and sat for a while in chairs along the sidewalk, watching the passing crowds on foot and in carriages. It was with reluctance that I went back to the hotel for dinner. After dinner we went to one of the summer theatres, and after the performance my friend took me to a large café on one of the Grands Boulevards. Here it was that I had my first glimpse of the French life of popular literature, so different from real French life. There were several hundred people, men and women, in the place drinking, smoking, talking, and listening to the music. My millionaire friend and I took seats at a table, where we sat smoking and watching the crowd. It was not long before we were joined by two or three good-looking, well-dressed young women. My friend talked to them in French and bought drinks for the whole party. I tried to recall my high-school French, but the effort availed me little. I could stammer out a few phrases, but, very naturally, could not understand a word that was said to me. We stayed at the café a couple of hours, then went back to the hotel. The next day we spent several hours in the shops and at the tailor's. I had no clothes except what I had been able to gather together at my benefactor's apartments the night before we sailed. He bought me the same kind of clothes which he himself wore, and that was the best; and he treated me in every way as he dressed me, as an equal, not as a servant. In fact, I don't think anyone could have guessed that such a relation existed. My duties were light and few, and he was a man full of life and vigor, who rather enjoyed doing things for himself. He kept me supplied with money far beyond what ordinary wages would have amounted to. For the first two weeks we were together almost constantly, seeing the sights, sights old to him, but from which he seemed to get new pleasure in showing them to me. During the day we took in the places of interest, and at night the theatres and cafés. This sort of life appealed to me as ideal, and I asked him one day how long he intended to stay in Paris. He answered: "Oh, until I get tired of it." I could not understand how that could ever happen. As it was, including several short trips to the Mediterranean, to Spain, to Brussels, and to Ostend,[5] we did remain there fourteen or fifteen months. We stayed at the Hôtel Continental about two months of this time. Then my millionaire took apartments, hired a piano, and lived almost the same life he lived in New York. He entertained a great deal, some of the parties being a good deal more blasé than the New York ones. I played for the guests at all of them with an effect which to relate would be but a tiresome repetition to the reader. I played not only for the guests, but continued, as I used to do in New York, to play often for the host when he was alone. This man of the world, who grew weary of everything and was always searching for something new, appeared never to grow tired of my music; he seemed to take it as a drug. He fell into a habit which caused me no little annoyance; sometimes he would come in during the early hours of the morning and, finding me in bed asleep, would wake me up and ask me to play something. This, so far as I can remember, was my only hardship during my whole stay with him in Europe.

After the first few weeks spent in sight-seeing I had a great deal of time left to myself; my friend was often I did not know where. When not with him, I spent the day nosing about all the curious nooks and corners of Paris; of this I never grew tired. At night I usually went to some theatre, but always ended up at the big café on the Grands Boulevards. I wish the reader to know that it was not alone the gaiety which drew me there; aside from that I had a laudable purpose. I had purchased an English-French conversational dictionary, and I went there every night to take a language lesson. I used to get three or four of the young women who frequented the place at a table and buy beer and cigarettes for them. In return I received my lesson. I got more than my money's worth, for they actually compelled me to speak the language. This, together with reading the papers every day, enabled me within a few months to express myself fairly well, and, before I left Paris, to have more than an ordinary command of French. Of course, every person who goes to Paris could not dare to learn French in this manner, but I can think of no easier or quicker way of doing it. The acquiring of another foreign language awoke me to the fact that with a little effort I could secure an added accomplishment as fine and as valuable as music; so I determined to make myself as much of a linguist as possible. I bought a Spanish newspaper every day in order to freshen my memory of that language, and, for French, devised what was, so far as I knew, an original system of study. I compiled a list which I termed "Three hundred necessary words." These I thoroughly committed to memory, also the conjugation of the verbs which were included in the list. I studied these words over and over, much as children of a couple of generations ago studied the alphabet. I also practiced a set of phrases like the following: "How?" "What did you say?" "What does the word —— mean?" "I understand all you say except ——." "Please repeat." "What do you call ——?" "How do you say ——?" These I called my working sentences. In an astonishingly short time I reached the point where

5. Brussels and Ostend are cities in Belgium.

the language taught itself—where I learned to speak merely by speaking. This point is the place which students taught foreign languages in our schools and colleges find great difficulty in reaching. I think the main trouble is that they learn too much of a language at a time. A French child with a vocabulary of two hundred words can express more spoken ideas than a student of French can with a knowledge of two thousand. A small vocabulary, the smaller the better, which embraces the common, everyday-used ideas, thoroughly mastered, is the key to a language. When that much is acquired the vocabulary can be increased simply by talking. And it is easy. Who cannot commit three hundred words to memory? Later I tried my method, if I may so term it, with German, and found that it worked in the same way.

I spent a good many evenings at the Opéra. The music there made me strangely reminiscent of my life in Connecticut; it was an atmosphere in which I caught a fresh breath of my boyhood days and early youth. Generally, in the morning after I had attended a performance, I would sit at the piano and for a couple of hours play the music which I used to play in my mother's little parlor.

One night I went to hear *Faust.*[6] I got into my seat just as the lights went down for the first act. At the end of the act I noticed that my neighbor on the left was a young girl. I cannot describe her either as to feature, or color of her hair, or of her eyes; she was so young, so fair, so ethereal, that I felt to stare at her would be a violation; yet I was distinctly conscious of her beauty. During the intermission she spoke English in a low voice to a gentleman and a lady who sat in the seats to her left, addressing them as father and mother. I held my program as though studying it, but listened to catch every sound of her voice. Her observations on the performance and the audience were so fresh and naïve as to be almost amusing. I gathered that she was just out of school, and that this was her first trip to Paris. I occasionally stole a glance at her, and each time I did so my heart leaped into my throat. Once I glanced beyond to the gentleman who sat next to her. My glance immediately turned into a stare. Yes, there he was, unmistakably, my father! looking hardly a day older than when I had seen him some ten years before. What a strange coincidence! What should I say to him? What would he say to me? Before I had recovered from my first surprise, there came another shock in the realization that the beautiful, tender girl at my side was my sister. Then all the springs of affection in my heart, stopped since my mother's death, burst out in fresh and terrible torrents, and I could have fallen at her feet and worshiped her. They were singing the second act, but I did not hear the music. Slowly the desolate loneliness of my position became clear to me. I knew that I could not speak, but I would have given a part of my life to touch her hand with mine and call her "sister." I sat through the opera until I could stand it no longer. I felt that I was suffocating. Valentine's[7] love seemed like mockery, and I felt an almost uncontrollable impulse to rise up and scream to the audience: "Here, here in your very midst, is a tragedy, a real tragedy!" This impulse grew so strong that I became afraid of myself, and in the darkness of one of the scenes I stumbled out of the theatre. I walked aimlessly about for an hour or so, my feelings divided between a desire to weep and a desire to curse. I finally took a

6. *Faust* (1859), an opera by French composer Charles Gounod (1818–1893).

7. The brother of Marguerite, the heroine of Gounod's *Faust.*

cab and went from café to café, and for one of the very few times in my life drank myself into a stupor.

It was unwelcome news for me when my benefactor—I could not think of him as employer—informed me that he was at last tired of Paris. This news gave me, I think, a passing doubt as to his sanity. I had enjoyed life in Paris, and, taking all things into consideration, enjoyed it wholesomely. One thing which greatly contributed to my enjoyment was the fact that I was an American. Americans are immensely popular in Paris; and this is not due solely to the fact that they spend lots of money there, for they spend just as much or more in London, and in the latter city they are merely tolerated because they do spend. The Londoner seems to think that Americans are people whose only claim to be classed as civilized is that they have money, and the regrettable thing about that is that the money is not English. But the French are more logical and freer from prejudices than the British; so the difference of attitude is easily explained. Only once in Paris did I have cause to blush for my American citizenship. I had become quite friendly with a young man from Luxemburg whom I had met at the big café. He was a stolid, slow-witted fellow, but, as we say, with a heart of gold. He and I grew attached to each other and were together frequently. He was a great admirer of the United States and never grew tired of talking to me about the country and asking for information. It was his intention to try his fortune there some day. One night he asked me in a tone of voice which indicated that he expected an authoritative denial of an ugly rumor: "Did they really burn a man alive in the United States?" I never knew what I stammered out to him as an answer. I should have felt relieved if I could even have said to him: "Well, only one."

When we arrived in London, my sadness at leaving Paris was turned into despair. After my long stay in the French capital, huge, ponderous, massive London seemed to me as ugly a thing as man could contrive to make. I thought of Paris as a beauty spot on the face of the earth, and of London as a big freckle. But soon London's massiveness, I might say its very ugliness, began to impress me. I began to experience that sense of grandeur which one feels when he looks at a great mountain or a mighty river. Beside London Paris becomes a toy, a pretty plaything. And I must own that before I left the world's metropolis I discovered much there that was beautiful. The beauty in and about London is entirely different from that in and about Paris; and I could not but admit that the beauty of the French city seemed handmade, artificial, as though set up for the photographer's camera, everything nicely adjusted so as not to spoil the picture; while that of the English city was rugged, natural, and fresh.

How these two cities typify the two peoples who built them! Even the sound of their names expresses a certain racial difference. Paris is the concrete expression of the gaiety, regard for symmetry, love of art, and, I might well add, of the morality of the French people. London stands for the conservatism, the solidarity, the utilitarianism, and, I might well add, the hypocrisy of the Anglo-Saxon. It may sound odd to speak of the morality of the French, if not of the hypocrisy of the English; but this seeming paradox impresses me as a deep truth. I saw many things in Paris which were immoral according to English standards, but the absence of hypocrisy, the absence of the spirit to do the thing if it might only be done in secret, robbed these very immoralities of the damning influence of the same evils in London. I have walked along the terrace cafés of Paris and seen hundreds of men and women sipping their wine and beer, without observing a sign of drunkenness. As they drank, they chatted and laughed and watched the passing crowds; the drinking seemed to be a secondary thing. This I have witnessed, not only in the cafés along the Grands Boulevards, but in the out-of-the-way places patronized by the working classes. In London I have seen in the "pubs" men and women crowded in stuffy little compartments, drinking seemingly only for the pleasure of swallowing as much as they could hold. I have seen there women from eighteen to eighty, some in tatters, and some clutching babes in their arms, drinking the heavy English ales and whiskies served to them by women. In the whole scene, not one ray of brightness, not one flash of gaiety, only maudlin joviality or grim despair. And I have thought, if some men and women will drink—and it is certain that some will—is it not better that they do so under the open sky, in the fresh air, than huddled together in some close, smoky room? There is a sort of frankness about the evils of Paris which robs them of much of the seductiveness of things forbidden, and with that frankness goes a certain cleanliness of thought belonging to things not hidden. London will do whatever Paris does, provided exterior morals are not shocked. As a result, Paris has the appearance only of being the more immoral city. The difference may be summed up in this: Paris practices its sins as lightly as it does its religion, while London practices both very seriously.

I should not neglect to mention what impressed me most forcibly during my stay in London. It was not St. Paul's nor the British Museum nor Westminster Abbey. It was nothing more or less than the simple phrase "Thank you," or sometimes more elaborated, "Thank you very kindly, sir." I was continually surprised by the varied uses to which it was put; and, strange to say, its use as an expression of politeness seemed more limited than any other. One night I was in a cheap music hall and accidentally bumped into a waiter who was carrying a tray-load of beer, almost bringing him to several shillings' worth of grief. To my amazement he righted himself and said: "Thank ye, sir," and left me wondering whether he meant that he thanked me for not completely spilling his beer, or that he would thank me for keeping out of his way.

I also found cause to wonder upon what ground the English accuse Americans of corrupting the language by introducing slang words. I think I heard more and more different kinds of slang during my few weeks' stay in London than in my whole "tenderloin"[8] life in New York. But I suppose the English feel that the language is theirs, and that they may do with it as they please without at the same time allowing that privilege to others.

My millionaire was not so long in growing tired of London as of Paris. After a stay of six or eight weeks we went across into Holland. Amsterdam was a great surprise to me. I had always thought of Venice as the city of canals; it had never entered my mind that I should find similar conditions in a Dutch town. I don't suppose the comparison goes far beyond the fact that there are canals in both cities—I have never seen Venice—but Amsterdam struck me as being extremely picturesque. From Holland we went to Germany, where we spent five or six months, most of the time in Berlin. I found Berlin more to my taste than London, and occasionally I had to admit that in some things it was superior to Paris.

8. A district of New York City below Forty-Second Street and west of Broadway, then noted for crime and corruption.

In Berlin I especially enjoyed the orchestral concerts, and I attended a large number of them. I formed the acquaintance of a good many musicians, several of whom spoke of my playing in high terms. It was in Berlin that my inspiration was renewed. One night my millionaire entertained a party of men composed of artists, musicians, writers, and, for aught I know, a count or two. They drank and smoked a great deal, talked art and music, and discussed, it seemed to me, everything that ever entered man's mind. I could only follow the general drift of what they were saying. When they discussed music, it was more interesting to me; for then some fellow would run excitedly to the piano and give a demonstration of his opinions, and another would follow quickly, doing the same. In this way, I learned that, regardless of what his specialty might be, every man in the party was a musician. I was at the same time impressed with the falsity of the general idea that Frenchmen are excitable and emotional, and that Germans are calm and phlegmatic. Frenchmen are merely gay and never overwhelmed by their emotions. When they talk loud and fast, it is merely talk, while Germans get worked up and red in the face when sustaining an opinion, and in heated discussions are likely to allow their emotions to sweep them off their feet.

My millionaire planned, in the midst of the discussion on music, to have me play the "new American music" and astonish everybody present. The result was that I was more astonished than anyone else. I went to the piano and played the most intricate ragtime piece I knew. Before there was time for anybody to express an opinion on what I had done, a big bespectacled, bushy-headed man rushed over, and, shoving me out of the chair, exclaimed: "Get up! Get up!" He seated himself at the piano, and, taking the theme of my ragtime, played it through first in straight chords; then varied and developed it through every known musical form. I sat amazed. I had been turning classic music into ragtime, a comparatively easy task; and this man had taken ragtime and made it classic. The thought came across me like a flash—It can be done, why can't I do it? From that moment my mind was made up. I clearly saw the way of carrying out the ambition I had formed when a boy.

I now lost interest in our trip. I thought: "Here I am a man, no longer a boy, and what am I doing but wasting my time and abusing my talent? What use am I making of my gifts? What future have I before me following my present course?" These thoughts made me feel remorseful and put me in a fever to get to work, to begin to do something. Of course I know now that I was not wasting time; that there was nothing I could have done at that age which would have benefited me more than going to Europe as I did. The desire to begin work grew stronger each day. I could think of nothing else. I made up my mind to go back into the very heart of the South, to live among the people, and drink in my inspiration firsthand. I gloated over the immense amount of material I had to work with, not only modern ragtime, but also the old slave songs—material which no one had yet touched.

The more decided and anxious I became to return to the United States, the more I dreaded the ordeal of breaking with my millionaire. Between this peculiar man and me there had grown a very strong bond of affection, backed up by a debt which each owed to the other. He had taken me from a terrible life in New York and, by giving me the opportunity of traveling and of coming in contact with the people with whom he associated, had made me a polished man of the world. On the other hand, I was his chief means of disposing of the thing which seemed to sum up all in life that he dreaded—time. As I remember him now, I can see that time was what he was always endeavoring to escape, to bridge over, to blot out; and it is not strange that some years later he did escape it forever, by leaping into eternity.

For some weeks I waited for just the right moment in which to tell my patron of my decision. Those weeks were a trying time to me. I felt that I was playing the part of a traitor to my best friend. At length, one day he said to me: "Well, get ready for a long trip; we are going to Egypt, and then to Japan." The temptation was for an instant almost overwhelming, but I summoned determination enough to say: "I don't think I want to go." "What!" he exclaimed, "you want to go back to your dear Paris? You still think that the only spot on earth? Wait until you see Cairo and Tokio, you may change your mind." "No," I stammered, "it is not because I want to go back to Paris. I want to go back to the United States." He wished to know my reason, and I told him, as best I could, my dreams, my ambition, and my decision. While I was talking, he watched me with a curious, almost cynical, smile growing on his lips. When I had finished he put his hand on my shoulder—this was the first physical expression of tender regard he had ever shown me—and looking at me in a big-brotherly way, said: "My boy, you are by blood, by appearance, by education, and by tastes a white man. Now, why do you want to throw your life away amidst the poverty and ignorance, in the hopeless struggle, of the black people of the United States? Then look at the terrible handicap you are placing on yourself by going home and working as a Negro composer; you can never be able to get the hearing for your work which it might deserve. I doubt that even a white musician of recognized ability could succeed there by working on the theory that American music should be based on Negro themes. Music is a universal art; anybody's music belongs to everybody; you can't limit it to race or country. Now, if you want to become a composer, why not stay right here in Europe? I will put you under the best teachers on the Continent. Then if you want to write music on Negro themes, why, go ahead and do it."

We talked for some time on music and the race question. On the latter subject I had never before heard him express any opinion. Between him and me no suggestion of racial differences had ever come up. I found that he was a man entirely free from prejudice, but he recognized that prejudice was a big stubborn entity which had to be taken into account. He went on to say: "This idea you have of making a Negro out of yourself is nothing more than a sentiment; and you do not realize the fearful import of what you intend to do. What kind of a Negro would you make now, especially in the South? If you had remained there, or perhaps even in your club in New York, you might have succeeded very well; but now you would be miserable. I can imagine no more dissatisfied human being than an educated, cultured, and refined colored man in the United States. I have given more study to the race question in the United States than you may suppose, and I sympathize with the Negroes there; but what's the use? I can't right their wrongs, and neither can you; they must do that themselves. They are unfortunate in having wrongs to right, and you would be foolish to take their wrongs unnecessarily on your shoulders. Perhaps some day, through study and observation, you will come to see that evil is a force, and, like the physical and chemical forces, we cannot annihilate it; we may only change its form. We light upon one evil and hit it with all the might of our civilization, but only succeed in scattering it into a dozen other forms. We hit slavery through a great civil war. Did we destroy it? No, we only changed it into hatred between sections of the country: in the South, into political corruption and chicanery, the degradation of the blacks through peonage,[9] unjust laws, unfair and cruel treatment; and the degradation of the whites by their resorting to these practices, the paralyzation of the public conscience, and the ever overhanging dread of what the future may bring. Modern civilization hit ignorance of the masses through the means of popular education. What has it done but turn ignorance into anarchy, socialism, strikes, hatred between poor and rich, and universal discontent? In like manner, modern philanthropy hit at suffering and disease through asylums and hospitals; it prolongs the sufferers' lives, it is true, but is, at the same time, sending down strains of insanity and weakness into future generations. My philosophy of life is this: make yourself as happy as possible, and try to make those happy whose lives come in touch with yours; but to attempt to right the wrongs and ease the sufferings of the world in general is a waste of effort. You had just as well try to bail the Atlantic by pouring the water into the Pacific."

This tremendous flow of serious talk from a man I was accustomed to see either gay or taciturn so surprised and overwhelmed me that I could not frame a reply. He left me thinking over what he had said. Whatever was the soundness of his logic or the moral tone of his philosophy, his argument greatly impressed me. I could see, in spite of the absolute selfishness upon which it was based, that there was reason and common sense in it. I began to analyze my own motives, and found that they, too, were very largely mixed with selfishness. Was it more a desire to help those I considered my people, or more a desire to distinguish myself, which was leading me back to the United States? That is a question I have never definitely answered.

For several weeks longer I was in a troubled state of mind. Added to the fact that I was loath to leave my good friend was the weight of the question he had aroused in my mind, whether I was not making a fatal mistake. I suffered more than one sleepless night during that time. Finally, I settled the question on purely selfish grounds, in accordance with my millionaire's philosophy. I argued that music offered me a better future than anything else I had any knowledge of, and, in opposition to my friend's opinion, that I should have greater chances of attracting attention as a colored composer than as a white one. But I must own that I also felt stirred by an unselfish desire to voice all the joys and sorrows, the hopes and ambitions, of the American Negro, in classic musical form.

When my mind was fully made up, I told my friend. He asked me when I intended to start. I replied that I would do so at once. He then asked me how much money I had. I told him that I had saved several hundred dollars out of sums he had given me. He gave me a check for five hundred dollars, told me to write to him in care of his Paris bankers if I ever needed his help, wished me good luck, and bade me good-by. All this he did almost coldly; and I often wondered whether he was in a hurry to get rid of what he considered a fool, or whether he was striving to hide deeper feelings.

And so I separated from the man who was, all in all, the best friend I ever had, except my mother, the man who exerted the greatest influence ever brought into my life, except that exerted by my mother. My affection for him was so strong, my recollections of him are so distinct, he was such a

9. A system of reducing to near-slavery Blacks convicted of crimes who were unable to pay their fines.

peculiar and striking character, that I could easily fill several chapters with reminiscences of him; but for fear of tiring the reader I shall go on with my narration.

I decided to go to Liverpool and take ship for Boston. I still had an uneasy feeling about returning to New York; and in a few days I found myself aboard ship headed for home.

X

Among the first of my fellow-passengers of whom I took any particular notice was a tall, broad-shouldered, almost gigantic, colored man. His dark-brown face was clean-shaven; he was well-dressed and bore a decidedly distinguished air. In fact, if he was not handsome, he at least compelled admiration for his fine physical proportions. He attracted general attention as he strode the deck in a sort of majestic loneliness. I became curious to know who he was and determined to strike up an acquaintance with him at the first opportune moment. The chance came a day or two later. He was sitting in the smoking-room, with a cigar, which had gone out, in his mouth, reading a novel. I sat down beside him and, offering him a fresh cigar, said: "You don't mind my telling you something unpleasant, do you?" He looked at me with a smile, accepted the proffered cigar, and replied in a voice which comported perfectly with his size and appearance: "I think my curiosity overcomes any objections I might have." "Well," I said, "have you noticed that the man who sat at your right in the saloon during the first meal has not sat there since?" He frowned slightly without answering my question. "Well," I continued, "he asked the steward to remove him; and not only that, he attempted to persuade a number of the passengers to protest against your presence in the dining-saloon." The big man at my side took a long draw from his cigar, threw his head back, and slowly blew a great cloud of smoke toward the ceiling. Then turning to me he said: "Do you know, I don't object to anyone's having prejudices so long as those prejudices don't interfere with my personal liberty. Now, the man you are speaking of had a perfect right to change his seat if I in any way interfered with his appetite or his digestion. I should have no reason to complain if he removed to the farthest corner of the saloon, or even if he got off the ship; but when his prejudice attempts to move *me* one foot, one inch, out of the place where I am comfortably located, then I object." On the word "object" he brought his great fist down on the table in front of us with such a crash that everyone in the room turned to look. We both covered up the slight embarrassment with a laugh and strolled out on the deck.

We walked the deck for an hour or more, discussing different phases of the Negro question. In referring to the race I used the personal pronoun "we"; my companion made no comment about it, nor evinced any surprise, except to raise his eyebrows slightly the first time he caught the significance of the word. He was the broadest-minded colored man I have ever talked with on the Negro question. He even went so far as to sympathize with and offer excuses for some white Southern points of view. I asked him what were his main reasons for being so hopeful. He replied: "In spite of all that is written, said, and done, this great, big, incontrovertible fact stands out—the Negro is progressing, and that disproves all the arguments in the world that he is incapable of progress. I was born in slavery, and at emancipation was set adrift a ragged, penniless bit of humanity. I have seen the

Negro in every grade, and I know what I am talking about. Our detractors point to the increase of crime as evidence against us; certainly we have progressed in crime as in other things; what less could be expected? And yet, in this respect, we are far from the point which has been reached by the more highly civilized white race. As we continue to progress, crime among us will gradually lose much of its brutal, vulgar, I might say healthy, aspect, and become more delicate, refined, and subtle. Then it will be less shocking and noticeable, although more dangerous to society." Then dropping his tone of irony, he continued with some show of eloquence: "But, above all, when I am discouraged and disheartened, I have this to fall back on: if there is a principle of right in the world, which finally prevails, and I believe that there is; if there is a merciful but justice-loving God in heaven, and I believe that there is, we shall win; for we have right on our side, while those who oppose us can defend themselves by nothing in the moral law, nor even by anything in the enlightened thought of the present age."

For several days, together with other topics, we discussed the race problem, not only of the United States, but as it affected native Africans and Jews. Finally, before we reached Boston, our conversation had grown familiar and personal. I had told him something of my past and much about my intentions for the future. I learned that he was a physician, a graduate of Howard University, Washington, and had done post-graduate work in Philadelphia; and this was his second trip abroad to attend professional courses. He had practiced for some years in the city of Washington, and though he did not say so, I gathered that his practice was a lucrative one. Before we left the ship, he had made me promise that I would stop two or three days in Washington before going on south.

We put up at a hotel in Boston for a couple of days and visited several of my new friend's acquaintances; they were all people of education and culture and, apparently, of means. I could not help being struck by the great difference between them and the same class of colored people in the South. In speech and thought they were genuine Yankees. The difference was especially noticeable in their speech. There was none of that heavy-tongued enunciation which characterizes even the best-educated colored people of the South. It is remarkable, after all, what an adaptable creature the Negro is. I have seen the black West Indian gentleman in London, and he is in speech and manners a perfect Englishman. I have seen natives of Haiti and Martinique[1] in Paris, and they are more Frenchy than a Frenchman. I have no doubt that the Negro would make a good Chinaman, with exception of the pigtail.

My stay in Washington, instead of being two or three days, was two or three weeks. This was my first visit to the national capital, and I was, of course, interested in seeing the public buildings and something of the working of the government; but most of my time I spent with the doctor among his friends and acquaintances. The social phase of life among colored people is more developed in Washington than in any other city in the country. This is on account of the large number of individuals earning good salaries and having a reasonable amount of leisure time to draw from. There are dozens of physicians and lawyers, scores of school teachers, and

1. A Caribbean island; formerly a French colony, Haiti is an independent republic that retains French as its official language, along with Haitian Creole, a French-based patois.

hundreds of clerks in the departments. As to the colored department clerks, I think it fair to say that in educational equipment they average above the white clerks of the same grade; for, whereas a colored college graduate will seek such a job, the white university man goes into one of the many higher vocations which are open to him.

In a previous chapter I spoke of social life among colored people; so there is no need to take it up again here. But there is one thing I did not mention: among Negroes themselves there is the peculiar inconsistency of a color question. Its existence is rarely admitted and hardly ever mentioned; it may not be too strong a statement to say that the greater portion of the race is unconscious of its influence; yet this influence, though silent, is constant. It is evidenced most plainly in marriage selection; thus the black men generally marry women fairer than themselves; while, on the other hand, the dark women of stronger mental endowment are very often married to light-complexioned men; the effect is a tendency toward lighter complexions, especially among the more active elements in the race. Some might claim that this is a tacit admission of colored people among themselves of their own inferiority judged by the color line. I do not think so. What I have termed an inconsistency is, after all, most natural; it is, in fact, a tendency in accordance with what might be called an economic necessity. So far as racial differences go, the United States puts a greater premium on color, or, better, lack of color, than upon anything else in the world. To paraphrase, "Have a white skin, and all things else may be added unto you."[2] I have seen advertisements in newspapers for waiters, bell-boys, or elevator men, which read: "Light-colored man wanted." It is this tremendous pressure which the sentiment of the country exerts that is operating on the race. There is involved not only the question of higher opportunity, but often the question of earning a livelihood; and so I say it is not strange, but a natural tendency. Nor is it any more a sacrifice of self-respect that a black man should give to his children every advantage he can which complexion of the skin carries than that the new or vulgar rich should purchase for their children the advantages which ancestry, aristocracy, and social position carry. I once heard a colored man sum it up in these words: "It's no disgrace to be black, but it's often very inconvenient."

Washington shows the Negro not only at his best, but also at his worst. As I drove around with the doctor, he commented rather harshly on those of the latter class which we saw. He remarked: "You see those lazy, loafing, good-for-nothing darkies; they're not worth digging graves for; yet they are the ones who create impressions of the race for the casual observer. It's because they are always in evidence on the street corners, while the rest of us are hard at work, and you know a dozen loafing darkies make a bigger crowd and a worse impression in this country than fifty white men of the same class. But they ought not to represent the race. We are the race, and the race ought to be judged by us, not by them. Every race and every nation should be judged by the best it has been able to produce, not by the worst."

The recollection of my stay in Washington is a pleasure to me now. In company with the doctor I visited Howard University,[3] the public schools, the excellent colored hospital, with which he was in some way connected, if

2. Luke 12:31: "But rather seek ye the kingdom of God; and all these things shall be added unto you."
3. African American university chartered by U.S. Congress in 1867.

I remember correctly, and many comfortable and even elegant homes. It was with some reluctance that I continued my journey south. The doctor was very kind in giving me letters to people in Richmond and Nashville when I told him that I intended to stop in both of these cities. In Richmond a man who was then editing a very creditable colored newspaper gave me a great deal of his time and made my stay there of three or four days very pleasant. In Nashville I spent a whole day at Fisk University, the home of the "Jubilee Singers," and was more than repaid for my time. Among my letters of introduction was one to a very prosperous physician. He drove me about the city and introduced me to a number of people. From Nashville I went to Atlanta, where I stayed long enough to gratify an old desire to see Atlanta University again. I then continued my journey to Macon.

During the trip from Nashville to Atlanta I went into the smoking-compartment of the car to smoke a cigar. I was traveling in a Pullman, not because of an abundance of funds, but because through my experience with my millionaire a certain amount of comfort and luxury had become a necessity to me whenever it was obtainable. When I entered the car, I found only a couple of men there; but in a half-hour there were half a dozen or more. From the general conversation I learned that a fat Jewish-looking man was a cigar manufacturer, and was experimenting in growing Havana tobacco in Florida; that a slender bespectacled young man was from Ohio and a professor in some State institution in Alabama; that a white-mustached, well-dressed man was an old Union soldier who had fought through the Civil War; and that a tall, raw-boned, red-faced man, who seemed bent on leaving nobody in ignorance of the fact that he was from Texas, was a cotton planter.

In the North men may ride together for hours in a "smoker"[4] and unless they are acquainted with each other never exchange a word; in the South men thrown together in such manner are friends in fifteen minutes. There is always present a warm-hearted cordiality which will melt down the most frigid reserve. It may be because Southerners are very much like Frenchmen in that they must talk; and not only must they talk, but they must express their opinions.

The talk in the car was for a while miscellaneous—on the weather, crops, business prospects; the old Union soldier had invested capital in Atlanta, and he predicted that that city would soon be one of the greatest in the country. Finally the conversation drifted to politics; then, as a natural sequence, turned upon the Negro question.

In the discussion of the race question the diplomacy of the Jew was something to be admired; he had the faculty of agreeing with everybody without losing his allegiance to any side. He knew that to sanction Negro oppression would be to sanction Jewish oppression and would expose him to a shot along that line from the old soldier, who stood firmly on the ground of equal rights and opportunity to all men; long traditions and business instincts told him when in Rome to act as a Roman. Altogether his position was a delicate one, and I gave him credit for the skill he displayed in maintaining it. The young professor was apologetic. He had had the same views as the G.A.R.[5] man; but a year in the South had opened his

4. Train compartment where smoking is allowed.
5. Grand Army of the Republic, the victorious federal army in the Civil War.

eyes, and he had to confess that the problem could hardly be handled any better than it was being handled by the Southern whites. To which the G.A.R. man responded somewhat rudely that he had spent ten times as many years in the South as his young friend and that he could easily understand how holding a position in a State institution in Alabama would bring about a change of views. The professor turned very red and had very little more to say. The Texan was fierce, eloquent, and profane in his argument, and, in a lower sense, there was a direct logic in what he said, which was convincing; it was only by taking higher ground, by dealing in what Southerners call "theories," that he could be combated. Occasionally some one of the several other men in the "smoker" would throw in a remark to reinforce what he said, but he really didn't need any help; he was sufficient in himself.

In the course of a short time the controversy narrowed itself down to an argument between the old soldier and the Texan. The latter maintained hotly that the Civil War was a criminal mistake on the part of the North and that the humiliation which the South suffered during Reconstruction could never be forgotten. The Union man retorted just as hotly that the South was responsible for the war and that the spirit of unforgetfulness on its part was the greatest cause of present friction; that it seemed to be the one great aim of the South to convince the North that the latter made a mistake in fighting to preserve the Union and liberate the slaves. "Can you imagine," he went on to say, "what would have been the condition of things eventually if there had been no war, and the South had been allowed to follow its course? Instead of one great, prosperous country with nothing before it but the conquests of peace, a score of petty republics, as in Central and South America, wasting their energies in war with each other or in revolutions."

"Well," replied the Texan, "anything—no country at all—is better than having niggers over you. But anyhow, the war was fought and the niggers were freed; for it's no use beating around the bush, the niggers, and not the Union, was the cause of it; and now do you believe that all the niggers on earth are worth the good white blood that was spilt? You freed the nigger and you gave him the ballot, but you couldn't make a citizen out of him. He don't know what he's voting for, and we buy 'em like so many hogs. You're giving 'em education, but that only makes slick rascals out of 'em."

"Don't fancy for a moment," said the Northern man, "that you have any monopoly in buying ignorant votes. The same thing is done on a larger scale in New York and Boston, and in Chicago and San Francisco; and they are not black votes either. As to education's making the Negro worse, you might just as well tell me that religion does the same thing. And, by the way, how many educated colored men do you know personally?"

The Texan admitted that he knew only one, and added that he was in the penitentiary. "But," he said, "do you mean to claim, ballot or no ballot, education or no education, that niggers are the equals of white men?"

"That's not the question," answered the other, "but if the Negro is so distinctly inferior, it is a strange thing to me that it takes such tremendous effort on the part of the white man to make him realize it, and to keep him in the same place into which inferior men naturally fall. However, let us grant for sake of argument that the Negro is inferior in every respect to the white man; that fact only increases our moral responsibility in regard to our actions toward him. Inequalities of numbers, wealth, and power, even of intelligence and morals, should make no difference in the essential rights of men."

"If he's inferior and weaker, and is shoved to the wall, that's his own lookout," said the Texan. "That's the law of nature; and he's bound to go to the wall; for no race in the world has ever been able to stand competition with the Anglo-Saxon. The Anglo-Saxon race has always been and always will be the masters of the world, and the niggers in the South ain't going to change all the records of history."

"My friend," said the old soldier slowly, "if you have studied history, will you tell me, as confidentially between white men, what the Anglo-Saxon has ever done?"

The Texan was too much astonished by the question to venture any reply.

His opponent continued: "Can you name a single one of the great fundamental and original intellectual achievements which have raised man in the scale of civilization that may be credited to the Anglo-Saxon? The art of letters, of poetry, of music, of sculpture, of painting, of the drama, of architecture; the science of mathematics, of astronomy, of philosophy, of logic, of physics, of chemistry, the use of the metals, and the principles of mechanics, were all invented or discovered by darker and what we now call inferior races and nations. We have carried many of these to their highest point of perfection, but the foundation was laid by others. Do you know the only original contribution to civilization we can claim is what we have done in steam and electricity and in making implements of war more deadly? And there we worked largely on principles which we did not discover. Why, we didn't even originate the religion we use. We are a great race, the greatest in the world today, but we ought to remember that we are standing on a pile of past races, and enjoy our position with a little less show of arrogance. We are simply having our turn at the game, and we were a long time getting to it. After all, racial supremacy is merely a matter of dates in history. The man here who belongs to what is, all in all, the greatest race the world ever produced, is almost ashamed to own it. If the Anglo-Saxon is the source of everything good and great in the human race from the beginning, why wasn't the German forest the birthplace of civilization, rather than the valley of the Nile?"

The Texan was somewhat disconcerted, for the argument had passed a little beyond his limits, but he swung it back to where he was sure of his ground by saying: "All that may be true, but it hasn't got much to do with us and the niggers here in the South. We've got 'em here, and we've got 'em to live with, and it's a question of white man or nigger, no middle ground. You want us to treat niggers as equals. Do you want to see 'em sitting around in our parlors? Do you want to see a mulatto South? To bring it right home to you, would you let your daughter marry a nigger?"

"No, I wouldn't consent to my daughter's marrying a nigger, but that doesn't prevent my treating a black man fairly. And I don't see what fair treatment has to do with niggers sitting around in your parlors; they can't come there unless they're invited. Out of all the white men I know, only a hundred or so have the privilege of sitting around in my parlor. As to the mulatto South, if you Southerners have one boast that is stronger than another, it is your women; you put them on a pinnacle of purity and virtue and bow down in a chivalric worship before them; yet you talk and act as though, should you treat the Negro fairly and take the anti-inter-marriage laws off your statute books, these same women would rush into the arms of black lovers and husbands. It's a wonder to me that they don't rise up and resent the insult."

"Colonel," said the Texan, as he reached into his handbag and brought out a large flask of whisky, "you might argue from now until hell freezes over, and you might convince me that you're right, but you'll never convince me that I'm wrong. All you say sounds very good, but it's got nothing to do with facts. You can say what men ought to be, but they ain't that; so there you are. Down here in the South we're up against facts, and we're meeting 'em like facts. We don't believe the nigger is or ever will be the equal of the white man, and we ain't going to treat him as an equal; I'll be damned if we will. Have a drink." Everybody except the professor partook of the generous Texan's flask, and the argument closed in a general laugh and good feeling.

I went back into the main part of the car with the conversation on my mind. Here I had before me the bald, raw, naked aspects of the race question in the South; and, in consideration of the step I was just taking, it was far from encouraging. The sentiments of the Texan—and he expressed the sentiments of the South—fell upon me like a chill. I was sick at heart. Yet I must confess that underneath it all I felt a certain sort of admiration for the man who could not be swayed from what he held as his principles. Contrasted with him, the young Ohio professor was indeed a pitiable character. And all along, in spite of myself, I have been compelled to accord the same kind of admiration to the Southern white man for the manner in which he defends not only his virtues, but his vices. He knows that, judged by a high standard, he is narrow and prejudiced, that he is guilty of unfairness, oppression, and cruelty, but this he defends as stoutly as he would his better qualities. This same spirit obtains in a great degree among the blacks; they, too, defend their faults and failings. This they generally do whenever white people are concerned. And yet among themselves they are their own most merciless critics. I have never heard the race so terribly arraigned as I have by colored speakers to strictly colored audiences. It is the spirit of the South to defend everything belonging to it. The North is too cosmopolitan and tolerant for such a spirit. If you should say to an Easterner that Paris is a gayer city than New York, he would be likely to agree with you, or at least to let you have your own way; but to suggest to a South Carolinian that Boston is a nicer city to live in than Charleston would be to stir his greatest depths of argument and eloquence.

But to-day, as I think over that smoking-car argument, I can see it in a different light. The Texan's position does not render things so hopeless, for it indicates that the main difficulty of the race question does not lie so much in the actual condition of the blacks as it does in the mental attitude of the whites; and a mental attitude, especially one not based on truth, can be changed more easily than actual conditions. That is to say, the burden of the question is not that the whites are struggling to save ten million despondent and moribund people from sinking into a hopeless slough of ignorance, poverty, and barbarity in their very midst, but that they are unwilling to open certain doors of opportunity and to accord certain treatment to ten million aspiring, education-and-property-acquiring people. In a word, the difficulty of the problem is not so much due to the facts presented as to the hypothesis assumed for its solution. In this it is similar to the problem of the solar system. By a complex, confusing, and almost contradictory mathematical process, by the use of zigzags instead of straight lines, the earth can be proved to be the center of things celestial; but by an operation so simple that it can be comprehended by a schoolboy, its position can be verified among the other worlds which revolve about the sun, and its movements harmonized with the laws of the universe. So, when the white race assumes as a hypothesis that it is the main object of creation and that all things else are merely subsidiary to its well-being, sophism,[6] subterfuge, perversion of conscience, arrogance, injustice, oppression, cruelty, sacrifice of human blood, all are required to maintain the position, and its dealings with other races become indeed a problem, a problem which, if based on a hypothesis of common humanity, could be solved by the simple rules of justice.

When I reached Macon, I decided to leave my trunk and all my surplus belongings, to pack my bag, and strike out into the interior. This I did; and by train, by mule and ox-cart. I traveled through many counties. This was my first real experience among rural colored people, and all that I saw was interesting to me; but there was a great deal which does not require description at my hands; for log cabins and plantations and dialect-speaking "darkies" are perhaps better known in American literature than any other single picture of our national life. Indeed, they form an ideal and exclusive literary concept of the American Negro to such an extent that it is almost impossible to get the reading public to recognize him in any other setting; so I shall endeavor to avoid giving the reader any already overworked and hackneyed descriptions. This generally accepted literary ideal of the American Negro constitutes what is really an obstacle in the way of the thoughtful and progressive element of the race. His character has been established as a happy-go-lucky, laughing, shuffling, banjo-picking being, and the reading public has not yet been prevailed upon to take him seriously. His efforts to elevate himself socially are looked upon as a sort of absurd caricature of "white civilization." A novel dealing with colored people who lived in respectable homes and amidst a fair degree of culture and who naturally acted "just like white folks" would be taken in a comic-opera sense. In this respect the Negro is much in the position of a great comedian who gives up the lighter roles to play tragedy. No matter how well he may portray the deeper passions, the public is loath to give him up in his old character; they even conspire to make him a failure in serious work, in order to force him back into comedy. In the same respect, the public is not too much to be blamed, for great comedians are far more scarce than mediocre tragedians; every amateur actor is a tragedian. However, this very fact constitutes the opportunity of the future Negro novelist and poet to give the country something new and unknown, in depicting the life, the ambitions, the struggles, and the passions of those of their race who are striving to break the narrow limits of traditions. A beginning has already been made in that remarkable book by Dr. Du Bois, *The Souls of Black Folk*.[7]

Much, too, that I saw while on this trip, in spite of my enthusiasm, was disheartening. Often I thought of what my millionaire had said to me, and wished myself back in Europe. The houses in which I had to stay were generally uncomfortable, sometimes worse. I often had to sleep in a division or compartment with several other people. Once or twice I was not so fortunate as to find divisions; everybody slept on pallets on the floor. Frequently I was able to lie down and contemplate the stars which were in their zenith. The food was at times so distasteful and poorly cooked that I could not eat

6. A plausible but deceiving argument.

7. A collection of essays chiefly about African Americans in the South, published by W. E. B. Du Bois (1868–1963) in 1903.

it. I remember that once I lived for a week or more on buttermilk,[8] on account of not being able to stomach the fat bacon, the rank turniptops, and the heavy damp mixture of meal, salt, and water which was called corn bread. It was only my ambition to do the work which I had planned that kept me steadfast to my purpose. Occasionally I would meet with some signs of progress and uplift in even one of these back-wood settlements—houses built of boards, with windows, and divided into rooms; decent food, and a fair standard of living. This condition was due to the fact that there was in the community some exceptionally capable Negro farmer whose thrift served as an example. As I went about among these dull, simple people—the great majority of them hard working, in their relations with the whites submissive, faithful, and often affectionate, negatively content with their lot—and contrasted them with those of the race who had been quickened by the forces of thought, I could not but appreciate the logic of the position held by those Southern leaders who have been bold enough to proclaim against the education of the Negro. They are consistent in their public speech with Southern sentiment and desires. Those public men of the South who have not been daring or heedless enough to defy the ideals of twentieth-century civilization and of modern humanitarianism and philanthropy, find themselves in the embarrassing situation of preaching one thing and praying for another. They are in the position of the fashionable woman who is compelled by the laws of polite society to say to her dearest enemy: "How happy I am to see you!"

And yet in this respect how perplexing is Southern character; for, in opposition to the above, it may be said that the claim of the Southern whites that they love the Negro better than the Northern whites do is in a manner true. Northern white people love the Negro in a sort of abstract way, as a race; through a sense of justice, charity, and philanthropy, they will liberally assist in his elevation. A number of them have heroically spent their lives in this effort (and just here I wish to say that when the colored people reach the monument-building stage, they should not forget the men and women who went South after the war and founded schools for them). Yet, generally speaking, they have no particular liking for individuals of the race. Southern white people despise the Negro as a race, and will do nothing to aid in his elevation as such; but for certain individuals they have a strong affection, and are helpful to them in many ways. With these individual members of the race they live on terms of the greatest intimacy; they entrust to them their children, their family treasures, and their family secrets; in trouble they often go to them for comfort and counsel; in sickness they often rely upon their care. This affectionate relation between the Southern whites and those blacks who come into close touch with them has not been overdrawn even in fiction.

This perplexity of Southern character extends even to the intermixture of the races. That is spoken of as though it were dreaded worse than smallpox, leprosy, or the plague. Yet, when I was in Jacksonville, I knew several prominent families there with large colored branches, which went by the same name and were known and acknowledged as blood relatives. And what is more, there seemed to exist between these black brothers and sisters and uncles and aunts a decidedly friendly feeling.

8. Fermented dairy drink.

I said above that Southern whites would do nothing for the Negro as a race. I know the South claims that it has spent millions for the education of the blacks, and that it has of its own free will shouldered this awful burden. It seems to be forgetful of the fact that these millions have been taken from the public tax funds for education, and that the law of political economy which recognizes the land owner as the one who really pays the taxes is not tenable. It would be just as reasonable for the relatively few land owners of Manhattan to complain that they had to stand the financial burden of the education of the thousands and thousands of children whose parents pay rent for tenements and flats. Let the millions of producing and consuming Negroes be taken out of the South, and it would be quickly seen how much less of public funds there would be to appropriate for education or any other purpose.

In thus traveling about through the country I was sometimes amused on arriving at some little railroad-station town to be taken for and treated as a white man, and six hours later, when it was learned that I was stopping at the house of the colored preacher or school teacher, to note the attitude of the whole town change. At times this led even to embarrassment. Yet it cannot be so embarrassing for a colored man to be taken for white as for a white man to be taken for colored; and I have heard of several cases of the latter kind.

All this while I was gathering material for work, jotting down in my note-book themes and melodies, and trying to catch the spirit of the Negro in his relatively primitive state. I began to feel the necessity of hurrying so that I might get back to some city like Nashville to begin my compositions and at the same time earn at least a living by teaching and performing before my funds gave out. At the last settlement in which I stopped I found a mine of material. This was due to the fact that "big meeting" was in progress. "Big meeting" is an institution something like camp-meeting, the difference being that it is held in a permanent church, and not in a temporary structure. All the churches of some one denomination—of course, either Methodist or Baptist—in a county, or, perhaps, in several adjoining counties, are closed, and the congregations unite at some centrally located church for a series of meetings lasting a week. It is really a social as well as a religious function. The people come in great numbers, making the trip, according to their financial status, in buggies drawn by sleek, fleet-footed mules, in ox-carts, or on foot. It was amusing to see some of the latter class trudging down the hot and dusty road, with their shoes, which were brand-new, strung across their shoulders. When they got near the church, they sat on the side of the road and, with many grimaces, tenderly packed their feet into those instruments of torture. This furnished, indeed, a trying test of their religion. The famous preachers come from near and far and take turns in warning sinners of the day of wrath. Food, in the form of those two Southern luxuries, fried chicken and roast pork, is plentiful, and no one need go hungry. On the opening Sunday the women are immaculate in starched stiff white dresses adorned with ribbons, either red or blue. Even a great many of the men wear streamers of vari-colored ribbons in the buttonholes of their coats. A few of them carefully cultivate a forelock of hair by wrapping it in twine, and on such festive occasions decorate it with a narrow ribbon streamer. Big meetings afford a fine opportunity to the younger people to meet each other dressed in their Sunday clothes, and much rustic courting, which is as enjoyable as any other kind, is indulged in.

This big meeting which I was lucky enough to catch was particularly well attended; the extra large attendance was due principally to two attractions, a man by the name of John Brown, who was renowned as the most powerful preacher for miles around; and a wonderful leader of singing, who was known as "Singing Johnson." These two men were a study and a revelation to me. They caused me to reflect upon how great an influence their types have been in the development of the Negro in America. Both these types are now looked upon generally with condescension or contempt by the progressive element among the colored people; but it should never be forgotten that it was they who led the race from paganism and kept it steadfast to Christianity through all the long, dark years of slavery.

John Brown was a jet-black man of medium size, with a strikingly intelligent head and face, and a voice like an organ peal. He preached each night after several lesser lights had successively held the pulpit during an hour or so. As far as subject-matter is concerned, all of the sermons were alike: each began with the fall of man, ran through various trials and tribulations of the Hebrew children, on to the redemption by Christ, and ended with a fervid picture of the judgment day and the fate of the damned. But John Brown possessed magnetism and an imagination so free and daring that he was able to carry through what the other preachers would not attempt. He knew all the arts and tricks of oratory, the modulation of the voice to almost a whisper, the pause for effect, the rise through light, rapid-fire sentences to the terrific, thundering outburst of an electrifying climax. In addition, he had the intuition of a born theatrical manager. Night after night this man held me fascinated. He convinced me that, after all, eloquence consists more in the manner of saying than in what is said. It is largely a matter of tone pictures.

The most striking example of John Brown's magnetism and imagination was his "heavenly march"; I shall never forget how it impressed me when I heard it. He opened his sermon in the usual way; then, proclaiming to his listeners that he was going to take them on the heavenly march, he seized the Bible under his arm and began to pace up and down the pulpit platform. The congregation immediately began with their feet a tramp, tramp, tramp, in time with the preacher's march in the pulpit, all the while singing in an undertone a hymn about marching to Zion. Suddenly he cried: "Halt!" Every foot stopped with the precision of a company of well-drilled soldiers, and the singing ceased. The morning star had been reached. Here the preacher described the beauties of that celestial body. Then the march, the tramp, tramp, tramp, and the singing were again taken up. Another "Halt!" They had reached the evening star. And so on, past the sun and moon—the intensity of religious emotion all the time increasing—along the milky way, on up to the gates of heaven. Here the halt was longer, and the preacher described at length the gates and walls of the New Jerusalem. Then he took his hearers through the pearly gates, along the golden streets, pointing out the glories of the city, pausing occasionally to greet some patriarchal members of the church, well-known to most of his listeners in life, who had had "the tears wiped from their eyes, were clad in robes of spotless white, with crowns of gold upon their heads and harps within their hands," and ended his march before the great white throne. To the reader this may sound ridiculous, but listened to under the circumstances, it was highly and effectively dramatic. I was a more or less sophisticated and non-religious man of the world, but the torrent of the preacher's words, moving with the rhythm and glowing with the eloquence of primitive poetry, swept me along, and I, too, felt like joining in the shouts of "Amen! Hallelujah!"

John Brown's powers in describing the delights of heaven were no greater than those in depicting the horrors of hell. I saw great, strapping fellows trembling and weeping like children at the "mourners' bench." His warnings to sinners were truly terrible. I shall never forget one expression that he used, which for originality and aptness could not be excelled. In my opinion, it is more graphic and, for us, far more expressive than St. Paul's "It is hard to kick against the pricks."[9] He struck the attitude of a pugilist and thundered out: "Young man, your arm's too short to box with God!"

Interesting as was John Brown to me, the other man, "Singing Johnson," was more so. He was a small, dark-brown, one-eyed man, with a clear, strong, high-pitched voice, a leader of singing, a maker of songs, a man who could improvise at the moment lines to fit the occasion. Not so striking a figure as John Brown, but, at "big meetings," equally important. It is indispensable to the success of the singing, when the congregation is a large one made up of people from different communities, to have someone with a strong voice who knows just what hymn to sing and when to sing it, who can pitch it in the right key, and who has all the leading lines committed to memory. Sometimes it devolves upon the leader to "sing down" a long-winded or uninteresting speaker. Committing to memory the leading lines of all the Negro spiritual songs is no easy task, for they run up into the hundreds. But the accomplished leader must know them all, because the congregation sings only the refrains and repeats; every ear in the church is fixed upon him, and if he becomes mixed in his lines or forgets them, the responsibility falls directly on his shoulders.

For example, most of these hymns are constructed to be sung in the following manner:

Leader. *Swing low, sweet chariot.*
Congregation. *Coming for to carry me home.*
Leader. *Swing low, sweet chariot.*
Congregation. *Coming for to carry me home.*
Leader. *I look over yonder, what do I see?*
Congregation. *Coming for to carry me home.*
Leader. *Two little angels coming after me.*
Congregation. *Coming for to carry me home. . . .*

The solitary and plaintive voice of the leader is answered by a sound like the roll of the sea, producing a most curious effect.

In only a few of these songs do the leader and the congregation start off together. Such a song is the well-known "Steal away to Jesus."

The leader and the congregation begin with part-singing:

Steal away, steal away,
Steal away to Jesus;
Steal away, steal away home,
I ain't got long to stay here.

Then the leader alone or the congregation in unison:

My Lord he calls me,
He calls me by the thunder,
The trumpet sounds within-a my soul.

9. See Acts 9:5: "It is hard for thee to kick against the pricks."

Then all together:

I ain't got long to stay here.

The leader and the congregation again take up the opening refrain; then the leader sings three more leading lines alone, and so on almost *ad infinitum.* It will be seen that even here most of the work falls upon the leader, for the congregation sings the same lines over and over, while his memory and ingenuity are taxed to keep the songs going.

Generally the parts taken up by the congregation are sung in a three-part harmony, the women singing the soprano and a transposed tenor, the men with high voices singing the melody, and those with low voices a thundering bass. In a few of these songs, however, the leading part is sung in unison by the whole congregation, down to the last line, which is harmonized. The effect of this is intensely thrilling. Such a hymn is "Go down, Moses." It stirs the heart like a trumpet call.

"Singing Johnson" was an ideal leader, and his services were in great demand. He spent his time going about the country from one church to another. He received his support in much the same way as the preachers—part of a collection, food and lodging. All of his leisure time he devoted to originating new words and melodies and new lines for old songs. He always sang with his eyes—or, to be more exact, his eye—closed, indicating the *tempo* by swinging his head to and fro. He was a great judge of the proper hymn to sing at a particular moment; and I noticed several times, when the preacher reached a certain climax, or expressed a certain sentiment, that Johnson broke in with a line or two of some appropriate hymn. The speaker understood and would pause until the singing ceased.

As I listened to the singing of these songs, the wonder of their production grew upon me more and more. How did the men who originated them manage to do it? The sentiments are easily accounted for; they are mostly taken from the Bible; but the melodies, where did they come from? Some of them so weirdly sweet, and others so wonderfully strong. Take, for instance, "Go down, Moses." I doubt that there is a stronger theme in the whole musical literature of the world. And so many of these songs contain more than mere melody; there is sounded in them that elusive undertone, the note in music which is not heard with the ears. I sat often with the tears rolling down my cheeks and my heart melted within me. Any musical person who has never heard a Negro congregation under the spell of religious fervor sing these old songs has missed one of the most thrilling emotions which the human heart may experience. Anyone who without shedding tears can listen to Negroes sing "Nobody knows de trouble I see, Nobody knows but Jesus" must indeed have a heart of stone.

As yet, the Negroes themselves do not fully appreciate these old slave songs. The educated classes are rather ashamed of them and prefer to sing hymns from books. This feeling is natural; they are still too close to the conditions under which the songs were produced; but the day will come when this slave music will be the most treasured heritage of the American Negro.

At the close of the "big meeting" I left the settlement where it was being held, full of enthusiasm. I was in that frame of mind which, in the artistic temperament, amounts to inspiration. I was now ready and anxious to get to some place where I might settle down to work, and give expression to the ideas which were teeming in my head; but I strayed into another deviation from my path of life as I had it marked out, which led me upon an entirely different road. Instead of going to the nearest and most convenient railroad station, I accepted the invitation of a young man who had been present the closing Sunday at the meeting to drive with him some miles farther to the town in which he taught school, and there take the train. My conversation with this young man as we drove along through the country was extremely interesting. He had been a student in one of the Negro colleges—strange coincidence, in the very college, as I learned through him, in which "Shiny" was now a professor. I was, of course, curious to hear about my boyhood friend; and had it not been vacation time, and that I was not sure that I should find him, I should have gone out of my way to pay him a visit; but I determined to write to him as soon as the school opened. My companion talked to me about his work among the people, of his hopes and his discouragements. He was tremendously in earnest; I might say, too much so. In fact, it may be said that the majority of intelligent colored people are, in some degree, too much in earnest over the race question. They assume and carry so much that their progress is at times impeded and they are unable to see things in their proper proportions. In many instances a slight exercise of the sense of humor would save much anxiety of soul. Anyone who marks the general tone of editorials in colored newspapers is apt to be impressed with this idea. If the mass of Negroes took their present and future as seriously as do the most of their leaders, the race would be in no mental condition to sustain the terrible pressure which it undergoes; it would sink of its own weight. Yet it must be acknowledged that in the making of a race overseriousness is a far lesser failing than its reverse, and even the faults resulting from it lean toward the right.

We drove into the town just before dark. As we passed a large, unpainted church, my companion pointed it out as the place where he held his school. I promised that I would go there with him the next morning and visit awhile. The town was of that kind which hardly requires or deserves description; a straggling line of brick and wooden stores on one side of the railroad track and some cottages of various sizes on the other side constituted about the whole of it. The young school teacher boarded at the best house in the place owned by a colored man. It was painted, had glass windows, contained "store bought" furniture, an organ, and lamps with chimneys. The owner held a job of some kind on the railroad. After supper it was not long before everybody was sleepy. I occupied the room with the school teacher. In a few minutes after we got into the room he was in bed and asleep; but I took advantage of the unusual luxury of a lamp which gave light, and sat looking over my notes and jotting down some ideas which were still fresh in my mind. Suddenly I became conscious of that sense of alarm which is always aroused by the sound of hurrying footsteps on the silence of the night. I stopped work and looked at my watch. It was after eleven. I listened, straining every nerve to hear above the tumult of my quickening pulse. I caught the murmur of voices, then the gallop of a horse, then of another and another. Now thoroughly alarmed, I woke my companion, and together we both listened. After a moment he put out the light and softly opened the window-blind, and we cautiously peeped out. We saw men moving in one direction, and from the mutterings we vaguely caught the rumor that some terrible crime had been committed. I put on my coat and hat. My friend did all in his power to dissuade me from venturing out, but it was impossible for me to remain in the house under such tense excitement. My nerves would not have stood it. Perhaps what bravery I exercised in going out was due to the fact that I felt sure my identity as a colored man had not yet become known in the town.

I went out and, following the drift,[1] reached the railroad station. There was gathered there a crowd of men, all white, and others were steadily arriving, seemingly from all the surrounding country. How did the news spread so quickly? I watched these men moving under the yellow glare of the kerosene lamps about the station, stern, comparatively silent, all of them armed, some of them in boots and spurs; fierce, determined men. I had come to know the type well, blond, tall, and lean, with ragged mustache and beard, and glittering gray eyes. At the first suggestion of daylight they began to disperse in groups, going in several directions. There was no extra noise or excitement, no loud talking, only swift, sharp words of command given by those who seemed to be accepted as leaders by mutual understanding. In fact, the impression made upon me was that everything was being done in quite an orderly manner. In spite of so many leaving, the crowd around the station continued to grow; at sunrise there were a great many women and children. By this time I also noticed some colored people; a few seemed to be going about customary tasks; several were standing on the outskirts of the crowd; but the gathering of Negroes usually seen in such towns was missing.

Before noon they brought him in. Two horsemen rode abreast; between them, half dragged, the poor wretch made his way through the dust. His hands were tied behind him, and ropes around his body were fastened to the saddle horns of his double guard. The men who at midnight had been stern and silent were now emitting that terror-instilling sound known as the "rebel yell." A space was quickly cleared in the crowd, and a rope placed about his neck, when from somewhere came the suggestion, "Burn him!" It ran like an electric current. Have you ever witnessed the transformation of human beings into savage beasts? Nothing can be more terrible. A railroad tie was sunk into the ground, the rope was removed, and a chain brought and securely coiled around the victim and the stake. There he stood, a man only in form and stature, every sign of degeneracy stamped upon his countenance. His eyes were dull and vacant, indicating not a single ray of thought. Evidently the realization of his fearful fate had robbed him of whatever reasoning power he had ever possessed. He was too stunned and stupefied even to tremble. Fuel was brought from everywhere, oil, the torch; the flames crouched for an instant as though to gather strength, then leaped up as high as their victim's head. He squirmed, he writhed, strained at his chains, then gave out cries and groans that I shall always hear. The cries and groans were choked off by the fire and smoke; but his eyes, bulging from their sockets, rolled from side to side, appealing in vain for help. Some of the crowd yelled and cheered, others seemed appalled at what they had done, and there were those who turned away sickened at the sight. I was fixed to the spot where I stood, powerless to take my eyes from what I did not want to see.

It was over before I realized that time had elapsed. Before I could make myself believe that what I saw was really happening, I was looking at a scorched post, a smoldering fire, blackened bones, charred fragments sifting down through coils of chain; and the smell of burnt flesh—human flesh—was in my nostrils.

1. Leaving, moving sideways in a controlled manner.

I walked a short distance away and sat down in order to clear my dazed mind. A great wave of humiliation and shame swept over me. Shame that I belonged to a race that could be so dealt with; and shame for my country, that it, the great example of democracy to the world, should be the only civilized, if not the only state on earth, where a human being would be burned alive. My heart turned bitter within me. I could understand why Negroes are led to sympathize with even their worst criminals and to protect them when possible. By all the impulses of normal human nature they can and should do nothing less.

Whenever I hear protests from the South that it should be left alone to deal with the Negro question, my thoughts go back to that scene of brutality and savagery. I do not see how a people that can find in its conscience any excuse whatever for slowly burning to death a human being, or for tolerating such an act, can be entrusted with the salvation of a race. Of course, there are in the South men of liberal thought who do not approve lynching, but I wonder how long they will endure the limits which are placed upon free speech. They still cower and tremble before "Southern opinion." Even so late as the recent Atlanta riot[2] those men who were brave enough to speak a word in behalf of justice and humanity felt called upon, by way of apology, to preface what they said with a glowing rhetorical tribute to the Anglo-Saxon's superiority and to refer to the "great and impassable gulf" between the races "fixed by the Creator at the foundation of the world." The question of the relative qualities of the two races is still an open one. The reference to the "great gulf" loses force in face of the fact that there are in this country perhaps three or four million people with the blood of both races in their veins; but I fail to see the pertinency of either statement subsequent to the beating and murdering of scores of innocent people in the streets of a civilized and Christian city.

The Southern whites are in many respects a great people. Looked at from a certain point of view, they are picturesque. If one will put oneself in a romantic frame of mind, one can admire their notions of chivalry and bravery and justice. In this same frame of mind an intelligent man can go to the theatre and applaud the impossible hero, who with his single sword slays everybody in the play except the equally impossible heroine. So can an ordinary peace-loving citizen sit by a comfortable fire and read with enjoyment of the bloody deeds of pirates and the fierce brutality of Vikings. This is the way in which we gratify the old, underlying animal instincts and passions; but we should shudder with horror at the mere idea of such practices being realities in this day of enlightened and humanitarianized thought. The Southern whites are not yet living quite in the present age; many of their general ideas hark back to a former century, some of them to the Dark Ages. In the light of other days they are sometimes magnificent. Today they are often cruel and ludicrous.

How long I sat with bitter thoughts running through my mind I do not know; perhaps an hour or more. When I decided to get up and go back to the house, I found that I could hardly stand on my feet. I was as weak as a man who had lost blood. However, I dragged myself along, with the central idea of a general plan well fixed in my mind. I did not find my school teacher

2. The Atlanta Race Massacre, which occurred September 24–26, 1906.

friend at home, so I did not see him again. I swallowed a few mouthfuls of food, packed my bag, and caught the afternoon train.

When I reached Macon, I stopped only long enough to get the main part of my luggage and to buy a ticket for New York. All along the journey I was occupied in debating with myself the step which I had decided to take. I argued that to forsake one's race to better one's condition was no less worthy an action than to forsake one's country for the same purpose. I finally made up my mind that I would neither disclaim the black race nor claim the white race; but that I would change my name, raise a mustache, and let the world take me for what it would; that it was not necessary for me to go about with a label of inferiority pasted across my forehead. All the while I understood that it was not discouragement or fear or search for a larger field of action and opportunity that was driving me out of the Negro race. I knew that it was shame, unbearable shame. Shame at being identified with a people that could with impunity be treated worse than animals. For certainly the law would restrain and punish the malicious burning alive of animals.

So once again I found myself gazing at the towers of New York and wondering what future that city held in store for me.

XI

I have now reached that part of my narrative where I must be brief and touch only on important facts; therefore the reader must make up his mind to pardon skips and jumps and meager details.

When I reached New York, I was completely lost. I could not have felt more a stranger had I been suddenly dropped into Constantinople.[3] I knew not where to turn or how to strike out. I was so oppressed by a feeling of loneliness that the temptation to visit my old home in Connecticut was well-nigh irresistible. I reasoned, however, that unless I found my old music teacher, I should be, after so many years of absence, as much of a stranger there as in New York; and, furthermore, that in view of the step which I had decided to take, such a visit would be injudicious. I remembered, too, that I had some property there in the shape of a piano and a few books, but decided that it would not be worth what it might cost me to take possession.

By reason of the fact that my living expenses in the South had been very small, I still had nearly four hundred dollars of my capital left. In contemplation of this, my natural and acquired Bohemian tastes asserted themselves, and I decided to have a couple of weeks' good time before worrying seriously about the future. I went to Coney Island[4] and the other resorts, took in the pre-season shows along Broadway, and ate at firstclass restaurants; but I shunned the old Sixth Avenue district as though it were pest-infected. My few days of pleasure made appalling inroads upon what cash I had, and caused me to see that it required a good deal of money to live in New York as I wished to live and that I should have to find, very soon, some more or less profitable employment. I was sure that unknown, without friends or prestige, it would be useless to try to establish myself as a teacher

3. Or Istanbul, largest city in Turkey.
4. A beach and amusement park in Brooklyn, New York, which was at that time racially segregated.

of music; so I gave that means of earning a livelihood scarcely any consideration. And even had I considered it possible to secure pupils, as I then felt, I should have hesitated about taking up a work in which the chances for any considerable financial success are necessarily so small. I had made up my mind that since I was not going to be a Negro, I would avail myself of every possible opportunity to make a white man's success; and that, if it can be summed up in any one word, means "money."

I watched the "want" columns in the newspapers and answered a number of advertisements, but in each case found the positions were such as I could not fill or did not want. I also spent several dollars for "ads" which brought me no replies. In this way I came to know the hopes and disappointments of a large and pitiable class of humanity in this great city, the people who look for work through the newspapers. After some days of this sort of experience I concluded that the main difficulty with me was that I was not prepared for what I wanted to do. I then decided upon a course which, for an artist, showed an uncommon amount of practical sense and judgment. I made up my mind to enter a business college. I took a small room, ate at lunch counters, in order to economize, and pursued my studies with the zeal that I have always been able to put into any work upon which I set my heart. Yet, in spite of all my economy, when I had been at the school for several months, my funds gave out completely. I reached the point where I could not afford sufficient food for each day. In this plight I was glad to get, through one of the teachers, a job as an ordinary clerk in a downtown wholesale house. I did my work faithfully, and received a raise of salary before I expected it. I even managed to save a little money out of my modest earnings. In fact, I began then to contract the money fever, which later took strong possession of me. I kept my eyes open, watching for a chance to better my condition. It finally came in the form of a position with a house which was at the time establishing a South American department. My knowledge of Spanish was, of course, the principal cause of my good luck; and it did more for me: it placed me where the other clerks were practically put out of competition with me. I was not slow in taking advantage of the opportunity to make myself indispensable to the firm.

What an interesting and absorbing game is money-making! After each deposit at my savings-bank I used to sit and figure out, all over again, my principal and interest, and make calculations on what the increase would be in such and such time. Out of this I derived a great deal of pleasure. I denied myself as much as possible in order to swell my savings. As much as I enjoyed smoking, I limited myself to an occasional cigar, and that was generally of a variety which in my old days at the "Club" was known as a "Henry Mud." Drinking I cut out altogether, but that was no great sacrifice.

The day on which I was able to figure up a thousand dollars marked an epoch in my life. And this was not because I had never before had money. In my gambling days and while I was with my millionaire I handled sums running high up into the hundreds; but they had come to me like fairy godmother's gifts, and at a time when my conception of money was that it was made only to spend. Here, on the other hand, was a thousand dollars which I had earned by days of honest and patient work, a thousand dollars which I had carefully watched grow from the first dollar; and I experienced, in owning them, a pride and satisfaction which to me was an entirely new sensation. As my capital went over the thousand-dollar mark, I was puzzled to know what to do with it, how to put it to the most advantageous use.

I turned down first one scheme and then another, as though they had been devised for the sole purpose of gobbling up my money. I finally listened to a friend who advised me to put all I had in New York real estate; and under his guidance I took equity in a piece of property on which stood a rickety old tenement-house. I did not regret following this friend's advice, for in something like six months I disposed of my equity for more than double my investment. From that time on I devoted myself to the study of New York real estate and watched for opportunities to make similar investments. In spite of two or three speculations which did not turn out well, I have been remarkably successful. Today I am the owner and part-owner of several flat-houses. I have changed my place of employment four times since returning to New York, and each change has been a decided advancement. Concerning the position which I now hold I shall say nothing except that it pays extremely well.

As my outlook on the world grew brighter, I began to mingle in the social circles of the men with whom I came in contact; and gradually, by a process of elimination, I reached a grade of society of no small degree of culture. My appearance was always good and my ability to play on the piano, especially ragtime, which was then at the height of its vogue, made me a welcome guest. The anomaly of my social position often appealed strongly to my sense of humor. I frequently smiled inwardly at some remark not altogether complimentary to people of color; and more than once I felt like declaiming: "I am a colored man. Do I not disprove the theory that one drop of Negro blood renders a man unfit?" Many a night when I returned to my room after an enjoyable evening, I laughed heartily over what struck me as the capital joke I was playing.

Then I met her, and what I had regarded as a joke was gradually changed into the most serious question of my life. I first saw her at a musical which was given one evening at a house to which I was frequently invited. I did not notice her among the other guests before she came forward and sang two sad little songs. When she began, I was out in the hallway, where many of the men were gathered; but with the first few notes I crowded with others into the doorway to see who the singer was. When I saw the girl, the surprise which I had felt at the first sound of her voice was heightened; she was almost tall and quite slender, with lustrous yellow hair and eyes so blue as to appear almost black. She was as white as a lily, and she was dressed in white. Indeed, she seemed to me the most dazzlingly white thing I had ever seen. But it was not her delicate beauty which attracted me most; it was her voice, a voice which made one wonder how tones of such passionate color could come from so fragile a body.

I determined that when the program was over, I would seek an introduction to her; but at the moment, instead of being the easy man of the world, I became again the bashful boy of fourteen, and my courage failed me. I contented myself with hovering as near her as politeness would permit; near enough to hear her voice, which in conversation was low, yet thrilling, like the deeper middle tones of a flute. I watched the men gather round her talking and laughing in an easy manner, and wondered how it was possible for them to do it. But destiny, my special destiny, was at work. I was standing near, talking with affected gaiety to several young ladies, who, however, must have remarked my preoccupation; for my second sense of hearing was alert to what was being said by the group of which the girl in white was the center, when I heard her say: "I think his playing of Chopin is exquisite."

And one of my friends in the group replied: "You haven't met him? Allow me—" Then turning to me, "Old man, when you have a moment I wish you to meet Miss ——." I don't know what she said to me or what I said to her. I can remember that I tried to be clever, and experienced a growing conviction that I was making myself appear more and more idiotic. I am certain, too, that, in spite of my Italian-like complexion, I was as red as a beet.

Instead of taking the car, I walked home. I needed the air and exercise as a sort of sedative. I am not sure whether my troubled condition of mind was due to the fact that I had been struck by love or to the feeling that I had made a bad impression upon her.

As the weeks went by, and when I had met her several more times, I came to know that I was seriously in love; and then began for me days of worry, for I had more than the usual doubts and fears of a young man in love to contend with.

Up to this time I had assumed and played my rôle as a white man with a certain degree of nonchalance, a carelessness as to the outcome, which made the whole thing more amusing to me than serious; but now I ceased to regard "being a white man" as a sort of practical joke. My acting had called for mere external effects. Now I began to doubt my ability to play the part. I watched her to see if she was scrutinizing me, to see if she was looking for anything in me which made me differ from the other men she knew. In place of an old inward feeling of superiority over many of my friends I began to doubt myself. I began even to wonder if I really was like the men I associated with; if there was not, after all, an indefinable something which marked a difference.

But, in spite of my doubts and timidity, my affair progressed, and I finally felt sufficiently encouraged to decide to ask her to marry me. Then began the hardest struggle of my life, whether to ask her to marry me under false colors or to tell her the whole truth. My sense of what was exigent[5] made me feel there was no necessity of saying anything; but my inborn sense of honor rebelled at even indirect deception in this case. But however much I moralized on the question, I found it more and more difficult to reach the point of confession. The dread that I might lose her took possession of me each time I sought to speak, and rendered it impossible for me to do so. That moral courage requires more than physical courage is no mere poetic fancy. I am sure I should have found it easier to take the place of a gladiator, no matter how fierce the Numidian[6] lion, than to tell that slender girl that I had Negro blood in my veins. The fact which I had at times wished to cry out, I now wished to hide forever.

During this time we were drawn together a great deal by the mutual bond of music. She loved to hear me play Chopin and was herself far from being a poor performer of his compositions. I think I carried her every new song that was published which I thought suitable to her voice, and played the accompaniment for her. Over these songs we were like two innocent children with new toys. She had never been anything but innocent; but my innocence was a transformation wrought by my love for her, love which melted away my cynicism and whitened my sullied soul and gave me back the wholesome dreams of my boyhood.

5. Urgent.
6. From Numidia, an ancient country in North Africa.

My artistic temperament also underwent an awakening. I spent many hours at my piano, playing over old and new composers. I also wrote several little pieces in a more or less Chopinesque style,[7] which I dedicated to her. And so the weeks and months went by. Often words of love trembled on my lips, but I dared not utter them, because I knew they would have to be followed by other words which I had not the courage to frame. There might have been some other woman in my set whom I could have fallen in love with and asked to marry me without a word of explanation; but the more I knew this girl, the less could I find it in my heart to deceive her. And yet, in spite of this specter that was constantly looming up before me, I could never have believed that life held such happiness as was contained in those dream days of love.

One Saturday afternoon, in early June, I was coming up Fifth Avenue, and at the corner of Twenty-third Street I met her. She had been shopping. We stopped to chat for a moment, and I suggested that we spend half an hour at the Eden Musée.[8] We were standing leaning on the rail in front of a group of figures, more interested in what we had to say to each other than in the group, when my attention became fixed upon a man who stood at my side studying his catalogue. It took me only an instant to recognize in him my old friend "Shiny." My first impulse was to change my position at once. As quick as a flash I considered all the risks I might run in speaking to him, and most especially the delicate question of introducing him to her. I confess that in my embarrassment and confusion I felt small and mean. But before I could decide what to do, he looked around at me and, after an instant, quietly asked: "Pardon me; but isn't this—?" The nobler part in me responded to the sound of his voice and I took his hand in a hearty clasp. Whatever fears I had felt were quickly banished, for he seemed, at a glance, to divine my situation, and let drop no word that would have aroused suspicion as to the truth. With a slight misgiving I presented him to her and was again relieved of fear. She received the introduction in her usual gracious manner, and without the least hesitancy or embarrassment joined in the conversation. An amusing part about the introduction was that I was upon the point of introducing him as "Shiny," and stammered a second or two before I could recall his name. We chatted for some fifteen minutes. He was spending his vacation north, with the intention of doing four or six weeks' work in one of the summer schools; he was also going to take a bride back with him in the fall. He asked me about myself, but in so diplomatic a way that I found no difficulty in answering him. The polish of his language and the unpedantic manner in which he revealed his culture greatly impressed her; and after we had left the Musée she showed it by questioning me about him. I was surprised at the amount of interest a refined black man could arouse. Even after changes in the conversation she reverted several times to the subject of "Shiny." Whether it was more than mere curiosity I could not tell, but I was convinced that she herself knew very little about prejudice.

Just why it should have done so I do not know, but somehow the "Shiny" incident gave me encouragement and confidence to cast the die of my fate.[9] I reasoned, however, that since I wanted to marry her only, and since it concerned her alone, I would divulge my secret to no one else, not even her parents.

7. That is, in the style of Polish composer and pianist Frederic Chopin (1810–1841).
8. A popular wax museum in downtown Manhattan.
9. Take a chance.

One evening, a few days afterwards, at her home we were going over some new songs and compositions when she asked me, as she often did, to play the Thirteenth Nocturne.[1] When I began, she drew a chair near to my right and sat leaning with her elbow on the end of the piano, her chin resting on her hand, and her eyes reflecting the emotions which the music awoke in her. An impulse which I could not control rushed over me, a wave of exultation, the music under my fingers sank almost to a whisper, and calling her for the first time by her Christian name, but without daring to look at her, I said: "I love you, I love you, I love you." My fingers were trembling so that I ceased playing. I felt her hand creep to mine, and when I looked at her, her eyes were glistening with tears. I understood, and could scarcely resist the longing to take her in my arms; but I remembered, remembered that which has been the sacrificial altar of so much happiness—Duty; and bending over her hand in mine, I said: "Yes, I love you; but there is something more, too, that I must tell you." Then I told her, in what words I do not know, the truth. I felt her hand grow cold, and when I looked up, she was gazing at me with a wild, fixed stare as though I was some object she had never seen. Under the strange light in her eyes I felt that I was growing black and thick-featured and crimp-haired. She appeared not to have comprehended what I had said. Her lips trembled and she attempted to say something to me, but the words stuck in her throat. Then, dropping her head on the piano, she began to weep with great sobs that shook her frail body. I tried to console her, and blurted out incoherent words of love, but this seemed only to increase her distress, and when I left her, she was still weeping.

When I got into the street, I felt very much as I did the night after meeting my father and sister at the opera in Paris, even a similar desperate inclination to get drunk; but my self-control was stronger. This was the only time in my life that I ever felt absolute regret at being colored, that I cursed the drops of African blood in my veins and wished that I were really white. When I reached my rooms, I sat and smoked several cigars while I tried to think out the significance of what had occurred. I reviewed the whole history of our acquaintance, recalled each smile she had given me, each word she had said to me that nourished my hope. I went over the scene we had just gone through, trying to draw from it what was in my favor and what was against me. I was rewarded by feeling confident that she loved me, but I could not estimate what was the effect upon her of my confession. At last, nervous and unhappy, I wrote her a letter, which I dropped into the mailbox before going to bed, in which I said:

> I understand, understand even better than you, and so I suffer even more than you. But why should either of us suffer for what neither of us is to blame for? If there is any blame, it belongs to me and I can only make the old, yet strongest plea that can be offered, I love you; and I know that my love, my great love, infinitely overbalances that blame and blots it out. What is it that stands in the way of our happiness? It is not what you feel or what I feel; it is not what you are or what I am. It is what others feel and are. But, oh! is that a fair price? In all the endeavors and struggles of life, in all our strivings and longings, there is only one thing worth seeking, only one thing worth winning, and that is love. It

1. A piano composition by Chopin.

is not always found; but when it is, there is nothing in all the world for which it can be profitably exchanged.

The second morning after, I received a note from her which stated briefly that she was going up into New Hampshire to spend the summer with relatives there. She made no reference to what had passed between us; nor did she say exactly when she would leave the city. The note contained no single word that gave me any clue to her feelings. I could gather hope only from the fact that she had written at all. On the same evening, with a degree of trepidation which rendered me almost frightened, I went to her house.

I met her mother, who told me that she had left for the country that very afternoon. Her mother treated me in her usual pleasant manner, which fact greatly reassured me; and I left the house with a vague sense of hope stirring in my breast, which sprang from the conviction that she had not yet divulged my secret. But that hope did not remain with me long. I waited one, two, three weeks, nervously examining my mail every day, looking for some word from her. All of the letters received by me seemed so insignificant, so worthless, because there was none from her. The slight buoyancy of spirit which I had felt gradually dissolved into gloomy heart-sickness. I became preoccupied; I lost appetite, lost sleep, and lost ambition. Several of my friends intimated to me that perhaps I was working too hard.

She stayed away the whole summer. I did not go to the house, but saw her father at various times, and he was as friendly as ever. Even after I knew that she was back in town, I did not go to see her. I determined to wait for some word or sign. I had finally taken refuge and comfort in my pride, pride which, I suppose, I came by naturally enough.

The first time I saw her after her return was one night at the theatre. She and her mother sat in company with a young man whom I knew slightly, not many seats away from me. Never did she appear more beautiful; and yet, it may have been my fancy, she seemed a trifle paler, and there was a suggestion of haggardness in her countenance. But that only heightened her beauty; the very delicacy of her charm melted down the strength of my pride. My situation made me feel weak and powerless, like a man trying with his bare hands to break the iron bars of his prison cell. When the performance was over, I hurried out and placed myself where, unobserved, I could see her as she passed out. The haughtiness of spirit in which I had sought relief was all gone, and I was willing and ready to undergo any humiliation.

Shortly afterward we met at a progressive card party, and during the evening we were thrown together at one of the tables as partners. This was really our first meeting since the eventful night at her house. Strangely enough, in spite of our mutual nervousness, we won every trick of the game, and one of our opponents jokingly quoted the old saw: "Lucky at cards, unlucky in love." Our eyes met and I am sure that in the momentary glance my whole soul went out to her in one great plea. She lowered her eyes and uttered a nervous little laugh. During the rest of the game I fully merited the unexpressed and expressed abuse of my various partners; for my eyes followed her wherever she was and I played whatever card my fingers happened to touch.

Later in the evening she went to the piano and began to play very softly, as to herself, the opening bars of the Thirteenth Nocturne. I felt that the psychic moment of my life had come, a moment which, if lost, could never be called back; and, in as careless a manner as I could assume, I sauntered over to the piano and stood almost bending over her. She continued playing, but, in a voice that was almost a whisper, she called me by my Christian name and said: "I love you, I love you. I love you." I took her place at the piano and played the Nocturne in a manner that silenced the chatter of the company both in and out of the room, involuntarily closing it with the major triad.

We were married the following spring, and went to Europe for several months. It was a double joy for me to be in France again under such conditions.

First there came to us a little girl, with hair and eyes dark like mine, but who is growing to have ways like her mother. Two years later there came a boy, who has my temperament, but is fair like his mother, a little golden-headed god, with a face and head that would have delighted the heart of an old Italian master. And this boy, with his mother's eyes and features, occupies an inner sanctuary of my heart; for it was for him that she gave all; and that is the second sacred sorrow of my life.

The few years of our married life were supremely happy, and perhaps she was even happier than I; for after our marriage, in spite of all the wealth of her love which she lavished upon me, there came a new dread to haunt me, a dread which I cannot explain and which was unfounded, but one that never left me. I was in constant fear that she would discover in me some shortcoming which she would unconsciously attribute to my blood rather than to a failing of human nature. But no cloud ever came to mar our life together; her loss to me is irreparable. My children need a mother's care, but I shall never marry again. It is to my children that I have devoted my life. I no longer have the same fear for myself of my secret's being found out, for since my wife's death I have gradually dropped out of social life; but there is nothing I would not suffer to keep the brand from being placed upon them.

It is difficult for me to analyze my feelings concerning my present position in the world. Sometimes it seems to me that I have never really been a Negro, that I have been only a privileged spectator of their inner life; at other times I feel that I have been a coward, a deserter, and I am possessed by a strange longing for my mother's people.

Several years ago I attended a great meeting in the interest of Hampton Institute[2] at Carnegie Hall. The Hampton students sang the old songs and awoke memories that left me sad. Among the speakers were R. C. Ogden, ex-Ambassador Choate, and Mark Twain; but the greatest interest of the audience was centered in Booker T. Washington,[3] and not because he so much surpassed the others in eloquence, but because of what he represented with so much earnestness and faith. And it is this that all of that small but gallant band of colored men who are publicly fighting the cause of their race have behind them. Even those who oppose them know that these men have the eternal principles of right on their side, and they will be victors even though they should go down in defeat. Beside them I feel small and selfish.

2. A school founded in Hampton, Virginia, for the training of African Americans and American Indians.

3. African American educator, political leader, and author (1856–1915). Robert Curtis Ogden (1836–1913), educational reformer. Joseph Hodges Choate (1832–1917), political reformer and ambassador to England. Mark Twain was the pen name of Samuel Clemens (1835–1910), popular American humorist and author.

I am an ordinarily successful white man who has made a little money. They are men who are making history and a race. I, too, might have taken part in a work so glorious.

My love for my children makes me glad that I am what I am and keeps me from desiring to be otherwise; and yet, when I sometimes open a little box in which I still keep my fast yellowing manuscripts, the only tangible remnants of a vanished dream, a dead ambition, a sacrificed talent, I cannot repress the thought that, after all, I have chosen the lesser part, that I have sold my birthright for a mess of pottage.[4]

1912

From The Book of American Negro Poetry

Preface

There is, perhaps, a better excuse for giving an Anthology of American Negro Poetry to the public than can be offered for many of the anthologies that have recently been issued. The public, generally speaking, does not know that there are American Negro poets—to supply this lack of information is, alone, a work worthy of somebody's effort.

Moreover, the matter of Negro poets and the production of literature by the colored people in this country involves more than supplying information that is lacking. It is a matter which has a direct bearing on the most vital of American problems.

A people may become great through many means, but there is only one measure by which its greatness is recognized and acknowledged. The final measure of the greatness of all peoples is the amount and standard of the literature and art they have produced. The world does not know that a people is great until that people produces great literature and art. No people that has produced great literature and art has ever been looked upon by the world as distinctly inferior.

The status of the Negro in the United States is more a question of national mental attitude toward the race than of actual conditions. And nothing will do more to change that mental attitude and raise his status than a demonstration of intellectual parity by the Negro through the production of literature and art.

Is there likelihood that the American Negro will be able to do this? There is, for the good reason that he possesses the innate powers. He has the emotional endowment, the originality and artistic conception, and, what is more important, the power of creating that which has universal appeal and influence.

I make here what may appear to be a more startling statement by saying that the Negro has already proved the possession of these powers by being the creator of the only things artistic that have yet sprung from American soil and been universally acknowledged as distinctive American products.[1]

4. A thick vegetable soup. In the Bible, Esau, son of Isaac, sold his birthright to his twin brother Jacob for bread and pottage. See Genesis 25:21–34.

1. This statement should probably be modified by the inclusion of American skyscraper architecture [*Johnson's note, 1931 edition*].

These creations by the American Negro may be summed up under four heads. The first two are the Uncle Remus stories, which were collected by Joel Chandler Harris, and the "spirituals" or slave songs, to which the Fisk Jubilee Singers[2] made the public and the musicians of both the United States and Europe listen. The Uncle Remus stories constitute the greatest body of folk lore that America has produced, and the "spirituals" the greatest body of folk song. I shall speak of the "spirituals" later because they are more than folk songs, for in them the Negro sounded the depths, if he did not scale the heights, of music.

The other two creations are the cakewalk and ragtime.[3] We do not need to go very far back to remember when cakewalking was the rage in the United States, Europe and South America. Society in this country and royalty abroad spent time in practicing the intricate steps. Paris pronounced it the "poetry of motion." The popularity of the cakewalk passed away but its influence remained. The influence can be seen today on any American stage where there is dancing.

The influence which the Negro has exercised on the art of dancing in this country has been almost absolute. For generations the "buck and wing" and the "stop-time" dances, which are strictly Negro, have been familiar to American theater audiences. A few years ago the public discovered the "turkey trot," the "eagle rock," "ballin' the jack,"[4] and several other varieties that started the modern dance craze. These dances were quickly followed by the "tango," a dance originated by the Negroes of Cuba and later transplanted to South America. (This fact is attested by no less authority than Vicente Blasco Ibañez[5] in his *Four Horsemen of the Apocalypse.*) Half the floor space in the country was then turned over to dancing, and highly paid exponents sprang up everywhere. The most noted, Mr. Vernon Castle,[6] and, by the way, an Englishman, never danced except to the music of a colored band, and he never failed to state to his audiences that most of his dances had long been done by "your colored people," as he put it.

Any one who witnesses a musical production in which there is dancing cannot fail to notice the Negro stamp on all the movements; a stamp which even the great vogue of Russian dances that swept the country about the time of the popular dance craze could not affect. That peculiar swaying of the shoulders which you see done everywhere by the blond girls of the chorus is nothing more than a movement from the Negro dance referred to above, the "eagle rock." Occasionally the movement takes on a suggestion of the now outlawed "shimmy."[7]

As for Ragtime, I go straight to the statement that it is the one artistic production by which America is known the world over. It has been all-conquering. Everywhere it is hailed as "American music."

For a dozen years or so there has been a steady tendency to divorce Ragtime from the Negro; in fact, to take from him the credit of having origi-

2. A nine-person traveling singing troupe founded in 1871 to raise funds for Fisk University. Harris (1848–1908) popularized African American folk tales in *Uncle Remus: His Songs and His Sayings* (1881).
3. African American instrumental musical style of the 1890s, characterized by a syncopated melodic line and regularly accented accompaniment. "Cakewalk": a dance developed from an African American contest in stylish walking; a cake was offered as a prize.
4. African American dance steps that became popular with the white public in the late 19th and early 20th centuries.
5. Spanish novelist (1867–1928).
6. Castle (1887–1918) and his wife, Irene (1894–1969), revolutionized ballroom dancing in the 1910s by introducing the one-step, turkey trot, and Castle walk.
7. Popular 1920s dance, characterized by shaking of the upper body, considered sexually suggestive.

nated it. Probably the younger people of the present generation do not know that Ragtime is of Negro origin. The change wrought in Ragtime and the way in which it is accepted by the country have been brought about chiefly through the change which has gradually been made in the words and stories accompanying the music. Once the text of all Ragtime songs was written in Negro dialect, and was about Negroes in the cabin or in the cotton field or on the levee or at a jubilee[8] or on Sixth Avenue or at a ball, and about their love affairs. Today, only a small proportion of Ragtime songs relate at all to the Negro. The truth is, Ragtime is now national rather than racial. But that does not abolish in any way the claim of the American Negro as its originator.

Ragtime music was originated by colored piano players in the questionable resorts of St. Louis, Memphis, and other Mississippi River towns. These men did not know any more about the theory of music than they did about the theory of the universe. They were guided by their natural musical instinct and talent, but above all by the Negro's extraordinary sense of rhythm. Any one who is familiar with Ragtime may note that its chief charm is not in melody, but in rhythms. These players often improvised crude and, at times, vulgar words to fit the music. This was the beginning of the Ragtime song.

Ragtime music got its first popular hearing at Chicago during the World's Fair[9] in that city. From Chicago it made its way to New York, and then started on its universal triumph.

The earliest Ragtime songs, like Topsy,[1] "jes' grew." Some of these earliest songs were taken down by white men, the words slightly altered or changed, and published under the names of the arrangers. They sprang into immediate popularity and earned small fortunes. The first to become widely known was "The Bully," a levee song which had been long used by roustabouts along the Mississippi. It was introduced in New York by Miss May Irwin,[2] and gained instant popularity. Another one of these "jes' grew" songs was one which for a while disputed for place with Yankee Doodle; perhaps, disputes it even today. That song was "A Hot Time in the Old Town Tonight"; introduced and made popular by the colored regimental bands during the Spanish-American War.[3]

Later there came along a number of colored men who were able to transcribe the old songs and write original ones. I was, about that time, writing words to music for the music show stage in New York. I was collaborating with my brother, J. Rosamond Johnson, and the late Bob Cole. I remember that we appropriated about the last one of the old "jes' grew" songs. It was a song which had been sung for years all through the South. The words were unprintable, but the tune was irresistible, and belonged to nobody. We took it, re-wrote the verses, telling an entirely different story from the original, left the chorus as it was, and published the song, at first under the name of "Will Handy." It became very popular with college boys, especially at football games, and perhaps still is. The song was "Oh, Didn't He Ramble!"

In the beginning, and for quite a while, almost all of the Ragtime songs that were deliberately composed were the work of colored writers. Now, the

8. A service of religious rejoicing.
9. World's Columbian Exhibition, held in 1893 to honor the first four hundred years of European settlement of America.
1. An orphaned enslaved girl in Harriet Beecher Stowe's *Uncle Tom's Cabin* (1852) who says of her past only that she "jes' grew."
2. Popular singer and Broadway performer in the 1890s.
3. An 1898 war that brought Cuba independence from Spain and transferred the Philippines, Puerto Rico, and Guam to U.S. possession.

colored composers, even in this particular field, are greatly outnumbered by the white.

The reader might be curious to know if the "jes' grew" songs have ceased to grow. No, they have not; they are growing all the time. The country has lately been flooded with several varieties of "The Blues." These "Blues," too, had their origin in Memphis, and the towns along the Mississippi. They are a sort of lament of a lover who is feeling "blue" over the loss of his sweetheart. The "Blues" of Memphis have been adulterated so much on Broadway that they have lost their pristine hue.

* * *

Of course, there are those who will deny that Ragtime is an artistic production. American musicians, especially, instead of investigating Ragtime, dismiss it with a contemptuous word. But this has been the course of scholasticism[4] in every branch of art. Whatever new thing the people like is pooh-poohed; whatever is popular is regarded as not worth while. The fact is, nothing great or enduring in music has ever sprung full-fledged from the brain of any master; the best he gives the world he gathers from the hearts of the people, and runs it through the alembic[5] of his genius.

* * *

Now, these dances which I have referred to and Ragtime music may be lower forms of art, but they are evidence of a power that will some day be applied to the higher forms. And even now we need not stop at the Negro's accomplishment through these lower forms. In the "spirituals," or slave songs, the Negro has given America not only its only folk songs, but a mass of noble music. I never think of this music but that I am struck by the wonder, the miracle of its production. How did the men who originated these songs manage to do it? The sentiments are easily accounted for; they are, for the most part, taken from the Bible. But the melodies, where did they come from? Some of them so weirdly sweet, and others so wonderfully strong. Take, for instance, "Go Down, Moses"; I doubt that there is a stronger theme in the whole musical literature of the world.

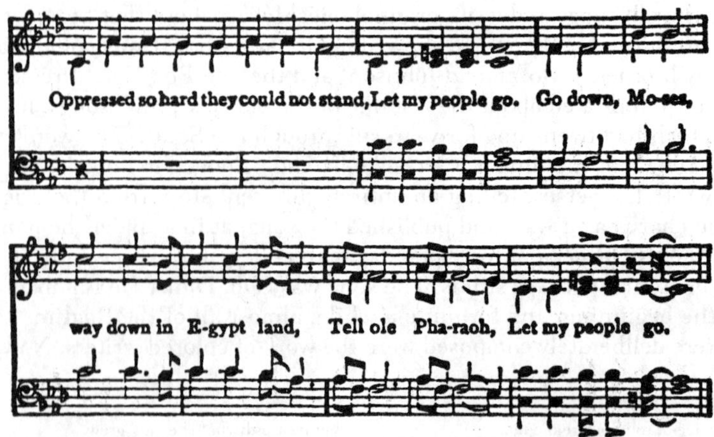
Oppressed so hard they could not stand, Let my people go. Go down, Mo-ses,
way down in E-gypt land, Tell ole Pha-raoh, Let my people go.

4. An insistence on traditional doctrines and methods.

5. Something that purifies as if by distillation.

It is to be noted that whereas the chief characteristic of Ragtime is rhythm, the chief characteristic of the "spirituals" is melody. The melodies of "Steal Away to Jesus," "Swing Low Sweet Chariot," "Nobody Knows de Trouble I See," "I Couldn't Hear Nobody Pray," "Deep River," "O, Freedom Over Me," and many others of these songs possess a beauty that is—what shall I say? poignant. In the riotous rhythms of Ragtime the Negro expressed his irrepressible buoyancy, his keen response to the sheer joy of living; in the "spirituals" he voiced his sense of beauty and his deep religious feeling.

Naturally, not as much can be said for the words of these songs as for the music. Most of the songs are religious. Some of them are songs expressing faith and endurance and a longing for freedom. In the religious songs, the sentiments and often the entire lines are taken bodily from the Bible. However, there is no doubt that some of these religious songs have a meaning apart from the Biblical text. It is evident that the opening lines of "Go Down, Moses,"

Go down, Moses,
'Way down in Egypt land;
Tell old Pharaoh,
Let my people go.

have a significance beyond the bondage of Israel in Egypt.

* * *

This power of the Negro to suck up the national spirit from the soil and create something artistic and original, which, at the same time, possesses the note of universal appeal, is due to a remarkable racial gift of adaptability; it is more than adaptability, it is a transfusive[6] quality. And the Negro has exercised this transfusive quality not only here in America, where the race lives in large numbers, but in European countries, where the number has been almost infinitesimal.

Is it not curious to know that the greatest poet of Russia is Alexander Pushkin, a man of African descent; that the greatest romancer of France is Alexandre Dumas,[7] a man of African descent; and that one of the greatest musicians of England is Coleridge-Taylor,[8] a man of African descent?

The fact is fairly well known that the father of Dumas was a Negro of the French West Indies, and that the father of Coleridge-Taylor was a native-born African; but the facts concerning Pushkin's African ancestry are not so familiar.

* * *

[T]he Negro has accomplished something in pure literature. The list of those who have done so would be surprising both by its length and the excellence of the achievements. One of the great books written in this country since the Civil War is the work of a colored man, *The Souls of Black Folk*, by W. E. B. Du Bois.[9]

6. The ability to permeate.
7. French novelist and dramatist (1802–1870). Pushkin (1799–1837), Russian man of letters.
8. Samuel Coleridge-Taylor (1875–1912), English composer.
9. Author, editor, and social activist (1868–1963); *Souls* was published in 1903.

Such a list begins with Phillis Wheatley.[1] In 1761 a slave ship landed a cargo of slaves in Boston. Among them was a little girl seven or eight years of age. She attracted the attention of John Wheatley, a wealthy gentleman of Boston, who purchased her as a servant for his wife. Mrs. Wheatley was a benevolent woman. She noticed the girl's quick mind and determined to give her opportunity for its development. Twelve years later Phillis published a volume of poems. The book was brought out in London, where Phillis was for several months an object of great curiosity and attention.

Phillis Wheatley has never been given her rightful place in American literature. By some sort of conspiracy she is kept out of most of the books, especially the text-books on literature used in the schools. Of course, she is not a *great* American poet—and in her day there were no great American poets—but she is an important American poet. Her importance, if for no other reason, rests on the fact that, save one, she is the first in order of time of all the women poets of America. And she is among the first of all American poets to issue a volume.

* * *

Thomas Jefferson said of Phillis: "Religion has produced a Phillis Wheatley, but it could not produce a poet; her poems are beneath contempt." It is quite likely that Jefferson's criticism was directed more against religion than against Phillis' poetry. On the other hand, General George Washington wrote her with his own hand a letter in which he thanked her for a poem which she had dedicated to him. He later received her with marked courtesy at his camp at Cambridge.

It appears certain that Phillis was the first person to apply to George Washington the phrase, "First in peace." The phrase occurs in her poem addressed to "His Excellency, General George Washington," written in 1775. The encomium, "First in war, first in peace, first in the hearts of his countrymen," was originally used in the resolutions presented to Congress on the death of Washington, December, 1799.

Phillis Wheatley's poetry is the poetry of the Eighteenth Century. She wrote when Pope and Gray[2] were supreme; it is easy to see that Pope was her model. Had she come under the influence of Wordsworth, Byron or Keats or Shelley,[3] she would have done greater work. As it is, her work must not be judged by the work and standards of a later day, but by the work and standards of her own day and her own contemporaries. By this method of criticism she stands out as one of the important characters in the making of American literature, without any allowances for her sex or her antecedents.

According to *A Bibliographical Checklist of American Negro Poetry*, compiled by Mr. Arthur A. Schomburg,[4] more than one hundred Negroes in the United States have published volumes of poetry ranging in size from pamphlets to books of from one hundred to three hundred pages. About thirty of these writers fill in the gap between Phillis Wheatley and Paul Laurence Dunbar.[5] Just here it is of interest to note that a Negro wrote and published a poem before Phillis Wheatley arrived in this country from Africa. He was

1. Author (1753–1784) of the first book written by an African American (1773).
2. Alexander Pope (1688–1744) and Thomas Gray (1716–1771), English poets.
3. William Wordsworth (1770–1850); George Gordon, Lord Byron (1788–1824); John Keats (1795–1821); and Percy Bysshe Shelley (1792–1822), English Romantic poets.
4. African American bibliophile, book collector, and writer (1874–1938).
5. The most popular African American poet of his era (1872–1906).

Jupiter Hammon,[6] a slave belonging to a Mr. Lloyd of Queens Village, Long Island. In 1760 Hammon published a poem, eighty-eight lines in length, entitled "An Evening Thought, Salvation by Christ, with Penitential Cries." In 1788 he published "An Address to Miss Phillis Wheatley, Ethiopian Poetess in Boston, who came from Africa at eight years of age, and soon became acquainted with the Gospel of Jesus Christ." These two poems do not include all that Hammon wrote.

The poets between Phillis Wheatley and Dunbar must be considered more in the light of what they attempted than of what they accomplished. Many of them showed marked talent, but barely a half dozen of them demonstrated even mediocre mastery of technique in the use of poetic material and forms. And yet there are several names that deserve mention. George M. Horton, Frances E. Harper, James M. Bell and Alberry A. Whitman,[7] all merit consideration when due allowances are made for their limitations in education, training and general culture. The limitations of Horton were greater than those of either of the others; he was born a slave in North Carolina in 1797, and as a young man began to compose poetry without being able to write it down. Later he received some instruction from professors of the University of North Carolina, at which institution he was employed as a janitor. He published a volume of poems, *The Hope of Liberty*, in 1829.

Mrs. Harper, Bell, and Whitman would stand out if only for the reason that each of them attempted sustained work. Mrs. Harper published her first volume of poems in 1854, but later she published "Moses, a Story of the Nile," a poem which ran to 52 closely printed pages. Bell in 1864 published a poem of 28 pages in celebration of President Lincoln's Emancipation Proclamation. In 1870 he published a poem of 32 pages in celebration of the ratification of the Fifteenth Amendment[8] to the Constitution. Whitman published his first volume of poems, a book of 253 pages, in 1877; but in 1884 he published "The Rape of Florida," an epic poem written in four cantos and done in the Spenserian stanza,[9] and which ran to 97 closely printed pages. The poetry of both Mrs. Harper and of Whitman had a large degree of popularity; one of Mrs. Harper's books went through more than twenty editions.

* * *

It is curious and interesting to trace the growth of individuality and race consciousness in this group of poets. Jupiter Hammon's verses were almost entirely religious exhortations. Only very seldom does Phillis Wheatley sound a native note. Four times in single lines she refers to herself as "Afric's muse." In a poem of admonition addressed to the students at the "University of Cambridge in New England" she refers to herself as follows:

> Ye blooming plants of human race divine,
> An Ethiop tells you 'tis your greatest foe.

6. New York poet (1711–1806?).
7. African Methodist Episcopal minister and author of long narrative verse (1851–1901). Horton (1797–1883?), poet born enslaved in North Carolina. Harper (1825–1911), reformist lecturer and novelist. Bell (1826–1902), antislavery poet from the Midwest.
8. Ratified in 1870, it guaranteed voting rights to African American men.
9. A stanzaic pattern of poetry developed by Edmund Spenser in his epic *The Faerie Queene* (1590).

But one looks in vain for some outburst or even complaint against the bondage of her people, for some agonizing cry about her native land. In two poems she refers definitely to Africa as her home, but in each instance there seems to be under the sentiment of the lines a feeling of almost smug contentment at her own escape therefrom. In the poem, "On Being Brought from Africa to America," she says:

'Twas mercy brought me from my pagan land,
Taught my benighted soul to understand
That there's a God and there's a Saviour too;
Once I redemption neither sought nor knew.
Some view our sable race with scornful eye—
"Their color is a diabolic dye."
Remember, Christians, Negroes black as Cain,
May be refined, and join th' angelic train.

In the poem addressed to the Earl of Dartmouth, she speaks of freedom and makes a reference to the parents from whom she was taken as a child, a reference which cannot but strike the reader as rather unimpassioned:

Should you, my lord, while you peruse my song,
Wonder from whence my love of Freedom sprung,
Whence flow these wishes for the common good,
By feeling hearts alone best understood;
I, young in life, by seeming cruel fate
Was snatch'd from Afric's fancy'd happy seat;
What pangs excruciating must molest,
What sorrows labor in my parents' breast?
Steel'd was that soul and by no misery mov'd
That from a father seiz'd his babe belov'd;
Such, such my case. And can I then but pray
Others may never feel tyrannic sway?

The bulk of Phillis Wheatley's work consists of poems addressed to people of prominence. Her book was dedicated to the Countess of Huntington, at whose house she spent the greater part of her time while in England. On his repeal of the Stamp Act,[1] she wrote a poem to King George III, whom she saw later; another poem she wrote to the Earl of Dartmouth, whom she knew. A number of her verses were addressed to other persons of distinction. Indeed, it is apparent that Phillis was far from being a democrat. She was far from being a democrat not only in her social ideas but also in her political ideas; unless a religious meaning is given to the closing lines of her ode to General Washington, she was a decided royalist:

A crown, a mansion, and a throne that shine
With gold unfading, Washington! be thine.

Nevertheless, she was an ardent patriot. Her ode to General Washington (1775), her spirited poem, "On Major General Lee" (1776), and her poem, "Liberty and Peace," written in celebration of the close of the war, reveal not only strong patriotic feeling but an understanding of the issues at stake.

* * *

1. A means of raising revenue imposed on the American colonies by the English government in 1765.

Horton, who was born three years after Phillis Wheatley's death, expressed in all of his poetry strong complaint at his condition of slavery and a deep longing for freedom. The following verses are typical of his style and his ability:

Alas! and am I born for this,
  To wear this slavish chain?
Deprived of all created bliss,
  Through hardship, toil, and pain?

Come, Liberty! thou cheerful sound,
  Roll through my ravished ears;
Come, let my grief in joys be drowned,
  And drive away my fears.

In Mrs. Harper we find something more than the complaint and the longing of Horton. We find an expression of a sense of wrong and injustice. The following stanzas are from a poem addressed to the white women of America:

You can sigh o'er the sad-eyed Armenian
  Who weeps in her desolate home.
You can mourn o'er the exile of Russia
  From kindred and friends doomed to roam.

But hark! from our Southland are floating
  Sobs of anguish, murmurs of pain;
And women heart-stricken are weeping
  O'er their tortured and slain.

Have ye not, oh, my favored sisters,
  Just a plea, a prayer or a tear
For mothers who dwell 'neath the shadows
  Of agony, hatred and fear?

Weep not, oh, my well sheltered sisters,
  Weep not for the Negro alone,
But weep for your sons who must gather
  The crops which their fathers have sown.

* * *

Paul Laurence Dunbar stands out as the first poet from the Negro race in the United States to show a combined mastery over poetic material and poetic technique, to reveal innate literary distinction in what he wrote, and to maintain a high level of performance. He was the first to rise to a height from which he could take a perspective view of his own race. He was the first to see objectively its humor, its superstitions, its shortcomings; the first to feel sympathetically its heart-wounds, its yearnings, its aspirations, and to voice them all in a purely literary form.

Dunbar's fame rests chiefly on his poems in Negro dialect. This appraisal of him is, no doubt, fair; for in these dialect poems he not only carried his art to the highest point of perfection, but he made a contribution to American literature unlike what any one else had made, a contribution which, perhaps, no one else could have made. Of course, Negro dialect poetry was written before Dunbar wrote, most of it by white writers; but the fact stands out that Dunbar was the first to use it as a medium for the true interpretation of Negro character and psychology. And yet, dialect poetry does not constitute the whole or even the bulk of Dunbar's work. In addition to a large number of poems of a very high order done in literary English, he was the author of four novels and several volumes of short stories.

Indeed, Dunbar did not begin his career as a writer of dialect. I may be pardoned for introducing here a bit of reminiscence. My personal friendship with Paul Dunbar began before he had achieved recognition, and continued to be close until his death. When I first met him he had published a thin volume, *Oak and Ivy*,[2] which was being sold chiefly through his own efforts. *Oak and Ivy* showed no distinctive Negro influence, but rather the influence of James Whitcomb Riley.[3] At this time Paul and I were together every day for several months. He talked to me a great deal about his hopes and ambitions. In these talks he revealed that he had reached a realization of the possibilities of poetry in the dialect, together with a recognition of the fact that it offered the surest way by which he could get a hearing. Often he said to me: "I've got to write dialect poetry; it's the only way I can get them to listen to me." I was with Dunbar at the beginning of what proved to be his last illness. He said to me then: "I have not grown. I am writing the same things I wrote ten years ago, and am writing them no better." His self-accusation was not fully true; he had grown, and he had gained a surer control of his art, but he had not accomplished the greater things of which he was constantly dreaming; the public had held him to the things for which it had accorded him recognition. If Dunbar had lived he would have achieved some of those dreams, but even while he talked so dejectedly to me he seemed to feel that he was not to live. He died when he was only thirty-three.

It has a bearing on this entire subject to note that Dunbar was of unmixed Negro blood; so, as the greatest figure in literature which the colored race in the United States has produced, he stands as an example at once refuting and confounding those who wish to believe that whatever extraordinary ability an Aframerican shows is due to an admixture of white blood.

As a man, Dunbar was kind and tender. In conversation he was brilliant and polished. His voice was his chief charm, and was a great element in his success as a reader of his own works. In his actions he was impulsive as a child, sometimes even erratic; indeed, his intimate friends almost looked upon him as a spoiled boy. He was always delicate in health. Temperamentally, he belonged to that class of poets who Taine[4] says are vessels too weak to contain the spirit of poetry, the poets whom poetry kills, the Byrons, the Burnses, the De Mussets,[5] the Poes.

To whom may he be compared, this boy who scribbled his early verses while he ran an elevator, whose youth was a battle against poverty, and who, in spite of almost insurmountable obstacles, rose to success? A comparison between him and Burns is not unfitting. The similarity between many phases of their lives is remarkable, and their works are not incom-

2. Dunbar's first poetry collection (1893).
3. Indiana regionalist and dialect poet (1849–1916).
4. Hippolyte Adolphe Taine (1828–1893), French literary critic and historian.
5. Louis Charles Alfred de Musset (1810–1857), French poet. Robert Burns (1759–1796), Scottish poet.

mensurable. Burns took the strong dialect of his people and made it classic; Dunbar took the humble speech of his people and in it wrought music.

Mention of Dunbar brings up for consideration the fact that, although he is the most outstanding figure in literature among the Aframericans of the United States, he does not stand alone among the Aframericans of the whole Western world. There are Plácido and Manzano in Cuba; Vieux and Durand in Haiti; Machado de Assis[6] in Brazil, and others still that might be mentioned, who stand on a plane with or even above Dunbar. Plácido and Machado de Assis rank as great in the literatures of their respective countries without any qualifications whatever. They are world figures in the literature of the Latin languages. Machado de Assis is somewhat handicapped in this respect by having as his tongue and medium the lesser known Portuguese, but Plácido, writing in the language of Spain, Mexico, Cuba and of almost the whole of South America, is universally known. His works have been republished in the original in Spain, Mexico and in most of the Latin-American countries; several editions have been published in the United States; translations of his works have been made into French and German.

* * *

In considering the Aframerican poets of the Latin languages I am impelled to think that, as up to this time the colored poets of greater universality have come out of the Latin-American countries rather than out of the United States, they will continue to do so for a good many years. The reason for this I hinted at in the first part of this preface. The colored poet in the United States labors within limitations which he cannot easily pass over. He is always on the defensive or the offensive. The pressure upon him to be propagandic is well nigh irresistible. These conditions are suffocating to breadth and to real art in poetry. In addition he labors under the handicap of finding culture not entirely colorless in the United States. On the other hand, the colored poet of Latin America can voice the national spirit without any reservations. And he will be rewarded without any reservations, whether it be to place him among the great or declare him the greatest.

* * *

The Negro in the United States has achieved or been placed in a certain artistic niche. When he is thought of artistically, it is as a happy-go-lucky, singing, shuffling, banjo-picking being or as a more or less pathetic figure. The picture of him is in a log cabin amid fields of cotton or along the levees. Negro dialect is naturally and by long association the exact instrument for voicing this phase of Negro life; and by that very exactness it is an instrument with but two full stops, humor and pathos. So even when he confines himself to purely racial themes, the Aframerican poet realizes that there are phases of Negro life in the United States which cannot be treated in the dialect either adequately or artistically. Take, for example, the phases rising out of life in Harlem, that most wonderful Negro city in the world. I do not deny that a Negro in a log cabin is more picturesque than a Negro in a Harlem flat, but the Negro in the Harlem flat is here, and he is but part of a

6. Brazilian writer (1839–1908). Plácido is the pen name of Gabriel de la Concepción Valdés (1809–1844), Cuban poet and revolutionary. Juan Francisco Manzano (1797–1854), Cuban poet and autobiographer. Antonio Vieux, early-20th-century Haitian experimental poet.

group growing everywhere in the country, a group whose ideals are becoming increasingly more vital than those of the traditionally artistic group, even if its members are less picturesque.

What the colored poet in the United States needs to do is something like what Synge[7] did for the Irish; he needs to find a form that will express the racial spirit by symbols from within rather than by symbols from without, such as the mere mutilation of English spelling and pronunciation. He needs a form that is freer and larger than dialect, but which will still hold the racial flavor; a form expressing the imagery, the idioms, the peculiar turns of thought, and the distinctive humor and pathos, too, of the Negro, but which will also be capable of voicing the deepest and highest emotions and aspirations, and allow of the widest range of subjects and the widest scope of treatment.

* * *

In stating the need for Aframerican poets in the United States to work out a new and distinctive form of expression I do not wish to be understood to hold any theory that they should limit themselves to Negro poetry, to racial themes; the sooner they are able to write *American* poetry spontaneously, the better. Nevertheless, I believe that the richest contribution the Negro poet can make to the American literature of the future will be the fusion into it of his own individual artistic gifts.

* * *

I offer this collection without making apology or asking allowance. I feel confident that the reader will find not only an earnest for the future, but actual achievement. The reader cannot but be impressed by the distance already covered. It is a long way from the plaints of George Horton to the invectives of Claude McKay, from the obviousness of Frances Harper to the complexness of Anne Spencer. Much ground has been covered, but more will yet be covered. It is this side of prophecy to declare that the undeniable creative genius of the Negro is destined to make a distinctive and valuable contribution to American poetry. * * *

1921

7. John Millington Synge (1871–1909), Irish dramatist whose works celebrate Irish traditions.

PAUL LAURENCE DUNBAR
1872–1906

Dubbed by Booker T. Washington as the "Poet Laureate of the Negro race" and praised by readers on both sides of the color line, Paul Laurence Dunbar was best known for his lively and often genial verse in a literary version of African American speech. Although he was not the first African American to write in this idiom, Dunbar demonstrated both the talent to "feel the Negro life aesthetically" and the craftsmanship to "express it lyrically," as the influential white critic William Dean Howells wrote in his introduction to Dunbar's *Lyrics of Lowly Life* (1896), the poet's best-selling book. Yet for all the unprecedented critical and commercial celebrity that Dunbar enjoyed during his heyday, his place at the welcome table of twentieth-century literary criticism was often challenged and sometimes denied. Although African American schools, cultural societies, and literary prizes are named in Dunbar's honor, during the twentieth century Dunbar was frequently represented as a cautionary example: an African American co-opted by white media hype, a poet who by singing "serenely sweet" to whites only postponed the bitter realization resonant in his most poignant line: "I know why the caged bird sings."

Dunbar's achievements, however, are impressive. He was a most unlikely candidate for literary fame in turn-of-the-century white-supremacist America, but he made his way to the top by appropriating the still popular regional, or local-color, school, with a folksy, nostalgic celebration of rural life and homey values that had charmed readers of American regional poetry and fiction since the end of the Civil War era. He adapted stereotypes made popular during the 1870s and 1880s in the work of white writers such as Irwin Russell and Joel Chandler Harris toward more socially redemptive roles. For example, as the poem "An Ante-bellum Sermon" shows, he altered the "old-time Negro"—an entertaining Black-face variant of a popular local-color persona—into a character of depth, dignity, and deliberation. Although he created a peculiar literary dialect that was not linguistically accurate, Dunbar's dialect lent an air of apparent authenticity to the stories he told of enslaved individuals who were quaint and amusing, but also loving and courageous. Dunbar's poetry capitalized on the appeal of southern African American folklife to the sizable national reading audience won over by Harris and other cultivators of the "plantation school" of literature that promoted a myth of benign southern race relations. A reading of Dunbar's most enduring poem, "We Wear the Mask," suggests that he was aware of the liability of allowing his own poetry to evoke an image of African American folk that played on thoughtless prejudices and degrading stereotypes, and that to tar all of Dunbar's dialect poetry with the brush of social accommodationism is to forget that wearing the mask let Dunbar "mouth with myriad subtleties" truths that whites refused to confront face to face.

Dunbar learned about African American rural folk from his parents, Joshua and Matilda, who had been enslaved on a Kentucky plantation and whose stories of their pre-Emancipation experiences gave the future writer much valuable material. A city dweller practically all his life, Dunbar was born in Dayton, Ohio, in 1872 and became a popular and high--achieving student at Dayton's Central High School; though the only African American in the school, he was elected president of his class and delivered the class's graduation poem in June 1891. Despite his popularity and abilities, after graduation, the only job made available to Dunbar was as an elevator operator. Like his friend James D. Corrothers, Dunbar persisted against such obstacles. In free moments he wrote poems and articles for various midwestern

Paul Laurence Dunbar's class photo in Dayton, Ohio, 1890.

newspapers while studying his favorite poets: Tennyson, Shakespeare, Keats, Poe, Longfellow, and the Midwest's most famous regionalist, James Whitcomb Riley.

In 1893 Dunbar took out a loan to subsidize the printing of his first book, *Oak and Ivy*, a collection of fifty-six poems. The risk was increased by the fact that Dunbar's collection combined poems that could be read as sentimental, even reactionary about the pre-Emancipation South, such as the dialect poem "Goin' Back," with others such as "Ode to Ethiopia" that proclaimed pride in his race's progress toward an expanding freedom. Fortunately, the range of matter and mood and the maturity of technique in *Oak and Ivy* impressed enough readers to make a successful beginning to Dunbar's career as a writer. In later writings, Dunbar seems to acknowledge a deliberate double-voiced strategy to such collections combining romanticized views of slavery written in his trademark version of dialect and more serious and brooding poems written in Standard English. In "Sympathy," Dunbar evokes the song of the caged bird that has an intense desire for free self-expression but is deliberately misheard by whites as merely "a carol of joy or glee."

Dunbar's detractors have argued that he regaled his public with too many easygoing, uncritical portrayals of African American life and character in his dialect poetry. Dunbar's defenders answer that although the largest proportion of his verse was not in dialect, whites showed little interest in this side of the poet's talent. Inevitably constrained by the tastes of the times, Dunbar, like many of his literary contemporaries, white as well as Black, tried to find ways to enlighten his readers without alienating them.

As the demand for his work grew, Dunbar cultivated literary friendships with prominent whites who in turn helped him publish and publicize his most famous volumes of poetry, *Majors and Minors* (1895) and *Lyrics of Lowly Life* (1896). Reading tours enhanced Dunbar's popularity and allowed his introduction to Alice Ruth Moore, whose own poetic fame had spread far beyond her native New Orleans. The couple married in 1898, by which time Paul Laurence Dunbar had achieved an international acclaim that earned him an appointment to a clerkship in the U.S. Library of Congress. In 1898 Dunbar began to make a name for himself as a fiction writer as well. During the next six years he published four books of short stories and four novels. As in his poetry, many of Dunbar's stories spoke frankly about racial injustice in the South while others employed fairly stereotyped images of African Americans and drew little upon authentic African American culture. But his final book, *The Sport of the Gods* (1903), is important for addressing a major question for Black America at the turn of the century—the advantages and disadvantages of migration from the rural South to the urban North. The concerns behind this grim foray into urban realism also impelled Dunbar to publish "The Fourth of July and Race Outrages" in the *New York Times* in 1903, a sardonic attack on the myopic indifference of American patriotism to the race riots, lynchings, peonage, and disfranchisement of African Americans in the South. By this time, however, Dunbar's steadily worsening health, together with his poor finances, allowed him little time or energy to undertake serious new departures in his writing.

At the end of Dunbar's life, his self-described disciple James Weldon Johnson congratulated him on having taken dialect poetry as far as it could go, giving it what Johnson called in his autobiography *Along This Way* (1933) "the fullest measure of charm, tenderness, and beauty." Johnson recalled that Dunbar's rueful reply to this compliment was simply, "I have never gotten to the things I really wanted to do."

Ode to Ethiopia

O Mother Race! to thee I bring
This pledge of faith unwavering,
  This tribute to thy glory.
I know the pangs which thou didst feel,
When Slavery crushed thee with its heel,
  With thy dear blood all gory.

Sad days were those—ah, sad indeed!
But through the land the fruitful seed
  Of better times was growing.
The plant of freedom upward sprung,
And spread its leaves so fresh and young—
  Its blossoms now are blowing.

On every hand in this fair land,
Proud Ethiope's swarthy children stand
  Beside their fairer neighbour;
The forests flee before their stroke,
Their hammers ring, their forges smoke,—
  They stir in honest labour.

They tread the fields where honour calls;
Their voices sound through senate halls
  In majesty and power.
To right they cling; the hymns they sing
Up to the skies in beauty ring,
  And bolder grow each hour.

Be proud, my Race, in mind and soul;
Thy name is writ on Glory's scroll
  In characters of fire.
High 'mid the clouds of Fame's bright sky

Thy banner's blazoned folds now fly,
And truth shall lift them higher.

Thou hast the right to noble pride,
Whose spotless robes were purified
By blood's severe baptism.
Upon thy brow the cross was laid,
And labour's painful sweat-beads made
A consecrating chrism.° *sacramental oil*

No other race, or white or black,
When bound as thou wert, to the rack,
So seldom stooped to grieving;
No other race, when free again,
Forgot the past and proved them men
So noble in forgiving.

Go on and up! Our souls and eyes
Shall follow thy continuous rise;
Our ears shall list thy story
From bards who from thy root shall spring,
And proudly tune their lyres to sing
Of Ethiopia's glory.

1893

Worn Out

You bid me hold my peace
And dry my fruitless tears,
Forgetting that I bear
A pain beyond my years.

You say that I should smile
And drive the gloom away;
I would, but sun and smiles
Have left my life's dark day.

All time seems cold and void,
And naught but tears remain;
Life's music beats for me
A melancholy strain.

I used at first to hope,
But hope is past and gone;
And now without a ray
My cheerless life drags on.

Like to an ash-stained hearth
When all its fires are spent;
Like to an autumn wood
By storm winds rudely shent,°— *damaged*

So sadly goes my heart,
  Unclothed of hope and peace;
It asks not joy again,
  But only seeks release.

1893

A Negro Love Song

Seen my lady home las' night,
  Jump back, honey, jump back.
Hel' huh han' an' sque'z it tight,
  Jump back, honey, jump back.
Hyeahd huh sigh a little sigh,
Seen a light gleam f'om huh eye,
An' a smile go flittin' by—
  Jump back, honey, jump back.

Hyeahd de win' blow thoo de pine,
  Jump back, honey, jump back.
Mockin'-bird was singin' fine,
  Jump back, honey, jump back.
An' my hea't was beatin' so,
When I reached my lady's do',
Dat I couldn't ba' to go—
  Jump back, honey, jump back.

Put my ahm aroun' huh wais',
  Jump back, honey, jump back.
Raised huh lips an' took a tase,
  Jump back, honey, jump back.
Love me, honey, love me true?
Love me well ez I love you?
An' she answe'd, "'Cose I do"—
  Jump back, honey, jump back.

1895

The Colored Soldiers

If the muse were mine to tempt it
  And my feeble voice were strong,
If my tongue were trained to measures,
  I would sing a stirring song.
I would sing a song heroic
  Of those noble sons of Ham,[1]

1. In the Old Testament, the second of Noah's three sons, traditionally labeled as the father of the black race.

Of the gallant colored soldiers
  Who fought for Uncle Sam!

In the early days you scorned them,
  And with many a flip and flout
Said "These battles are the white man's,
  And the whites will fight them out."
Up the hills you fought and faltered,
  In the vales you strove and bled,
While your ears still heard the thunder
  Of the foes' advancing tread.

Then distress fell on the nation,
  And the flag was drooping low;
Should the dust pollute your banner?
  No! the nation shouted, No!
So when War, in savage triumph,
  Spread abroad his funeral pall—
Then you called the colored soldiers,
  And they answered to your call.

And like hounds unleashed and eager
  For the life blood of the prey,
Sprung they forth and bore them bravely
  In the thickest of the fray.
And where'er the fight was hottest,
  Where the bullets fastest fell,
There they pressed unblanched and fearless
  At the very mouth of hell.

Ah, they rallied to the standard
  To uphold it by their might;
None were stronger in the labors,
  None were braver in the fight.
From the blazing breach of Wagner
  To the plains of Olustee,[2]
They were foremost in the fight
  Of the battles of the free.

And at Pillow![3] God have mercy
  On the deeds committed there,
And the souls of those poor victims
  Sent to Thee without a prayer.
Let the fulness of Thy pity
  O'er the hot wrought spirits sway
Of the gallant colored soldiers
  Who fell fighting on that day!

2. Site of a Union defeat in Florida on February 20, 1863, where three Black regiments nevertheless distinguished themselves. At Fort Wagner, in South Carolina, a Black Union regiment's bravery in defeat on July 18, 1863, earned widespread praise in the North.

3. Fort Pillow, in Tennessee, was the site of a massacre of Black Union soldiers by Confederate forces on April 12, 1864.

Yes, the Blacks enjoy their freedom,
  And they won it dearly, too;
For the life blood of their thousands
  Did the southern fields bedew.
In the darkness of their bondage,
  In the depths of slavery's night,
Their muskets flashed the dawning,
  And they fought their way to light.

They were comrades then and brothers,
  Are they more or less to-day?
They were good to stop a bullet
  And to front the fearful fray.
They were citizens and soldiers,
  When rebellion raised its head;
And the traits that made them worthy,—
  Ah! those virtues are not dead.

They have shared your nightly vigils,
  They have shared your daily toil;
And their blood with yours commingling
  Has enriched the Southern soil.
They have slept and marched and suffered
  'Neath the same dark skies as you,
They have met as fierce a foeman,
  And have been as brave and true.

And their deeds shall find a record
  In the registry of Fame;
For their blood has cleansed completely
  Every blot of Slavery's shame.
So all honor and all glory
  To those noble sons of Ham—
The gallant colored soldiers
  Who fought for Uncle Sam!

1895

An Ante-Bellum[1] Sermon

We is gathahed hyeah, my brothahs,
  In dis howlin' wildaness,
Fu' to speak some words of comfo't
  To each othah in distress.
An' we chooses fu' ouah subjic'
  Dis—we'll 'splain it by an' by;
"An' de Lawd said, 'Moses, Moses,'
  An' de man said, 'Hyeah am I.'"

Now ole Pher'oh, down in Egypt,
  Was de wuss man evah bo'n,

1. Before the U.S. Civil War (1861–65).

An' he had de Hebrew chillun
  Down dah wukin' in his co'n;
'Twell de Lawd got tiahed o' his foolin',
  An' sez he: "I'll let him know—
Look hyeah, Moses, go tell Pher'oh
  Fu' to let dem chillun go."

"An' ef he refuse to do it,
  I will make him rue de houah,° *hour*
Fu' I'll empty down on Egypt
  All de vials of my powah."
Yes, he did—an' Pher'oh's ahmy
  Wasn't wuth a ha'f a dime;
Fu' de Lawd will he'p his chillun,
  You kin trust him evah time.

An' yo' enemies may 'sail you
  In de back an' in de front;
But de Lawd is all aroun' you,
  Fu' to ba' de battle's brunt.
Dey kin fo'ge yo' chains an' shackles
  F'om de mountains to de sea;
But de Lawd will sen' some Moses
  Fu' to set his chillun free.

An' de lan' shall hyeah his thundah,
  Lak a blas' f'om Gab'el's[2] ho'n,
Fu' de Lawd of hosts is mighty
  When he girds his ahmor on.
But fu' feah some one mistakes me,
  I will pause right hyeah to say,
Dat I'm still a-preachin' ancient,
  I ain't talkin' 'bout to-day.

But I tell you, fellah christuns,
  Things'll happen mighty strange;
Now, de Lawd done dis fu' Isrul,
  An' his ways don't nevah change,
An' de love he showed to Isrul
  Wasn't all on Isrul spent;
Now don't run an' tell yo' mastahs
  Dat I's preachin' discontent.

'Cause I is n't; I 'se a-judgin'
  Bible people by deir ac's;
I 'se a-givin' you de Scriptuah,
  I 'se a-handin' you de fac's.
Cose ole Pher'oh b'lieved in slav'ry,
  But de Lawd he let him see,
Dat de people he put bref in,—
  Evah mothah's son was free.

2. In the Bible, Gabriel is the archangel who bears good news.

An' dahs othahs thinks lak Pher'oh,
  But dey calls de Scriptuah liar,
Fu' de Bible says "a servant
  Is a-worthy of his hire."
An' you cain't git roun' nor thoo dat,
  An' you cain't git ovah it,
Fu' whatevah place you git in,
  Dis hyeah Bible too 'll fit.

So you see de Lawd's intention,
  Evah sence de worl' began,
Was dat His almighty freedom
  Should belong to evah man,
But I think it would be bettah,
  Ef I'd pause agin to say,
Dat I'm talkin' 'bout ouah freedom
  In a Bibleistic way.

But de Moses is a-comin',
  An' he's comin', suah and fas'
We kin hyeah his feet a-trompin',
  We kin hyeah his trumpit blas'.
But I want to wa'n you people,
  Don't you git too brigity,° *biggety, self-important*
An' don't you git to braggin'
  'Bout dese things, you wait an' see.

But when Moses wif his powah
  Comes an' sets us chillun free,
We will praise de gracious Mastah° *Jesus Christ*
  Dat has gin us liberty;
An' we'll shout ouah halleluyahs,
  On dat mighty reck'nin' day,
When we'se reco'nised ez citiz'°— *citizens*
  Huh uh! Chillun, let us pray!

1895

Ere Sleep Comes Down to Soothe the Weary Eyes

Ere sleep comes down to soothe the weary eyes,
  Which all the day with ceaseless care have sought
The magic gold which from the seeker flies;
  Ere dreams put on the gown and cap of thought,
And make the waking world a world of lies,—
  Of lies most palpable, uncouth, forlorn,
That say life's full of aches and tears and sighs,—
  Oh, how with more than dreams the soul is torn,
Ere sleep comes down to soothe the weary eyes.

Ere sleep comes down to soothe the weary eyes,
  How all the griefs and heartaches we have known

Come up like pois'nous vapors that arise
From some base witch's caldron, when the crone,
To work some potent spell, her magic plies.
The past which held its share of bitter pain,
Whose ghost we prayed that Time might exorcise,
Comes up, is lived and suffered o'er again,
Ere sleep comes down to soothe the weary eyes.

Ere sleep comes down to soothe the weary eyes,
What phantoms fill the dimly lighted room;
What ghostly shades in awe-creating guise
Are bodied forth within the teeming gloom.
What echoes faint of sad and soul-sick cries,
And pangs of vague inexplicable pain
That pay the spirit's ceaseless enterprise,
Come thronging through the chambers of the brain,
Ere sleep comes down to soothe the weary eyes.

Ere sleep comes down to soothe the weary eyes,
Where ranges forth the spirit far and free?
Through what strange realms and unfamiliar skies
Tends her far course to lands of mystery?
To lands unspeakable—beyond surmise,
Where shapes unknowable to being spring,
Till, faint of wing, the Fancy fails and dies
Much wearied with the spirit's journeying,
Ere sleep comes down to soothe the weary eyes.

Ere sleep comes down to soothe the weary eyes,
How questioneth the soul that other soul,—
The inner sense which neither cheats nor lies,
But self exposes unto self, a scroll
Full writ with all life's acts unwise or wise,
In characters indelible and known;
So, trembling with the shock of sad surprise,
The soul doth view its awful self alone,
Ere sleep comes down to soothe the weary eyes.

When sleep comes down to seal the weary eyes,
The last dear sleep whose soft embrace is balm,
And whom sad sorrow teaches us to prize
For kissing all our passions into calm,
Ah, then, no more we heed the sad world's cries,
Or seek to probe th' eternal mystery,
Or fret our souls at long-withheld replies,
At glooms through which our visions cannot see,
When sleep comes down to seal the weary eyes.

1895

Not They Who Soar

Not they who soar, but they who plod
Their rugged way, unhelped, to God
Are heroes; they who higher fare,
And, flying, fan the upper air,
Miss all the toil that hugs the sod.
'Tis they whose backs have felt the rod,
Whose feet have pressed the path unshod,
May smile upon defeated care,
Not they who soar.

High up there are no thorns to prod,
Nor boulders lurking 'neath the clod
To turn the keenness of the share,
For flight is ever free and rare;
But heroes they the soil who've trod,
Not they who soar!

1895

When Malindy Sings

G'way an' quit dat noise, Miss Lucy—
Put dat music book away;
What's de use to keep on tryin'?
Ef you practise twell you're gray,
You cain't sta't no notes a-flyin'
Lak de ones dat rants and rings
F'om de kitchen to de big woods
When Malindy sings.

You ain't got de nachel° o'gans *natural*
Fu' to make de soun' come right,
You ain't got de tu'ns an' twistin's
Fu' to make it sweet an' light.
Tell you one thing now, Miss Lucy,
An' I'm tellin' you fu' true,
When hit comes to raal° right singin', *real*
'T ain't no easy thing to do.

Easy 'nough fu' folks to hollah,
Lookin' at de lines an' dots,
When dey ain't no one kin sence it,
An' de chune comes in, in spots;
But fu' real melojous music,
Dat jes' strikes you' hea't and clings,
Jes' you stan' an' listen wif me
When Malindy sings.

Ain't you nevah hyeahd Malindy?
  Blessed soul, tek up de cross!
Look hyeah, ain't you jokin', honey?
  Well, you don't know whut you los'.
Y' ought to hyeah dat gal a-wa'blin',
  Robins, la'ks, an' all dem things,
Heish dey moufs an' hides dey faces
  When Malindy sings.

Fiddlin' man jes' stop his fiddlin',
  Lay his fiddle on de she'f;
Mockin'-bird quit tryin' to whistle,
  'Cause he jes' so shamed hisse'f.
Folks a-playin' on de banjo
  Draps dey fingahs on de strings—
Bless yo' soul—fu'gits to move 'em,
  When Malindy sings.

She jes' spreads huh mouf and hollahs,
  "Come to Jesus,"° twell you hyeah — *popular hymn*
Sinnahs' tremblin' steps and voices,
  Timid-lak a-drawin' neah;
Den she tu'ns to "Rock of Ages,"° — *popular hymn*
  Simply to de cross she clings,
An' you fin' yo' teahs a-drappin'
  When Malindy sings.

Who dat says dat humble praises
  Wif de Master° nevah counts? — *Jesus Christ*
Heish yo' mouf, I hyeah dat music,
  Ez hit rises up an' mounts—
Floatin' by de hills an' valleys,
  Way above dis buryin' sod,
Ez hit makes its way in glory
  To de very gates of God!

Oh, hit's sweetah dan de music
  Of an edicated band;
An' hit's dearah dan de battle's
  Song o' triumph in de lan'.
It seems holier dan evenin'
  When de solemn chu'ch bell rings,
Ez I sit an' ca'mly listen
  While Malindy sings.

Towsah, stop dat ba'kin', hyeah me!
  Mandy, mek dat chile keep still;
Don't you hyeah de echoes callin'
  F'om de valley to de hill?
Let me listen, I can hyeah it,
  Th'oo de bresh of angels' wings,
Sof' an' sweet, "Swing Low, Sweet Chariot,"° — *spiritual*
  Ez Malindy sings.

1895

We Wear the Mask

We wear the mask that grins and lies,
It hides our cheeks and shades our eyes,—
This debt we pay to human guile;
With torn and bleeding hearts we smile,
And mouth with myriad subtleties.

Why should the world be overwise,
In counting all our tears and sighs?
Nay, let them only see us, while
    We wear the mask.

We smile, but, O great Christ, our cries
To thee from tortured souls arise.
We sing, but oh the clay is vile
Beneath our feet, and long the mile;
But let the world dream otherwise,
    We wear the mask!

1895

Little Brown Baby

Little brown baby wif spa'klin' eyes,
  Come to yo' pappy an' set on his knee.
What you been doin', suh—makin' san' pies?
  Look at dat bib—you's ez du'ty ez me.
Look at dat mouf—dat's merlasses, I bet;
  Come hyeah, Maria, an' wipe off his han's.
Bees gwine to ketch you an' eat you up yit,
  Bein' so sticky an' sweet—goodness lan's!

Little brown baby wif spa'klin' eyes,
  Who's pappy's darlin' an' who's pappy's chile?
Who is it all de day nevah once tries
  Fu' to be cross, er once loses dat smile?
Whah did you git dem teef? My, you's a scamp!
  Whah did dat dimple come f'om in yo' chin?
Pappy do' know you—I b'lieves you's a tramp;
  Mammy, dis hyeah's some ol' straggler got in!

Let's th'ow him outen de do' in de san',
  We do' want stragglers a-layin' 'roun' hyeah;
Let's gin him 'way to de big buggah-man;
  I know he's hidin' erroun' hyeah right neah.
Buggah-man, buggah-man, come in de do',
  Hyeah's a bad boy you kin have fu' to eat.
Mammy an' pappy do' want him no mo',
  Swaller him down f'om his haid to his feet!

Dah, now, I t'ought dat you'd hug me up close.
  Go back, ol' buggah, you sha'n't have dis boy.
He ain't no tramp, ner no straggler, of co'se;
  He's pappy's pa'dner an' playmate an' joy.
Come to you' pallet now—go to yo' res';
  Wisht you could allus know ease an' cleah skies;
Wisht you could stay jes' a chile on my breas'—
  Little brown baby wif spa'klin' eyes!

1897

Her Thought and His

The gray of the sea, and the gray of the sky,
A glimpse of the moon like a half-closed eye.
The gleam on the waves and the light on the land,
A thrill in my heart,—and—my sweetheart's hand.

She turned from the sea with a woman's grace,
And the light fell soft on her upturned face,
And I thought of the flood-tide of infinite bliss
That would flow to my heart from a single kiss.

But my sweetheart was shy, so I dared not ask
For the boon, so bravely I wore the mask.
But into her face there came a flame:—
I wonder could she have been thinking the same?

1899

A Cabin Tale

The Young Master Asks for a Story

Whut you say, dah? huh, uh! chile,
You's enough to dribe me wile.
Want a sto'y; jes' hyeah dat!
Whah' 'll I git a sto'y at?
Di'n' I tell you th'ee las' night?
Go 'way, honey, you ain't right.
I got somep'n' else to do,
'Cides jes' tellin' tales to you.
Tell you jes' one? Lem me see
Whut dat one's a-gwine to be.
When you's ole, yo membry fails;
Seems lak I do' know no tales.
Well, set down dah in dat cheer,
Keep still ef you wants to hyeah.
Tek dat chin up off yo' han's,
Set up nice now. Goodness lan's!
Hol' yo'se'f up lak yo' pa.

Bet nobidy evah saw
Him scrunched down lak you was den—
High-tone boys meks high-tone men.

Once dey was a ole black bah,
Used to live 'roun' hyeah somewhah
In a cave. He was so big
He could ca'y off a pig
Lak you picks a chicken up,
Er yo' leetles' bit o' pup.
An' he had two gread big eyes,
Jes' erbout a saucer's size.
Why, dey looked lak balls o' fiah
Jumpin' 'roun' erpon a wiah
W'en dat bah was mad; an' laws!
But you ought to seen his paws!
Did I see 'em? How you 'spec
I's a-gwine to ricollec'
Dis hyeah ya'n I's try'n' to spin
Ef you keeps on puttin' in?
You keep still an' don't you cheep
Less I'll sen' you off to sleep.
Dis hyeah bah'd go trompin' 'roun'
Eatin' evahthing he foun';
No one couldn't have a fa'm
But dat bah 'u'd do 'em ha'm;
And dey couldn't ketch de scamp.
Anywhah he wan'ed to tramp.
Dah de scoun'el 'd mek his track,
Do his du't an' come on back.
He was sich a sly ole limb,
Traps was jes' lak fun to him.

Now, down neah whah Mistah Bah
Lived, dey was a weasel dah;
But dey wasn't fren's a-tall
Case de weasel was so small.
An' de bah 'u'd, jes' fu' sass,
Tu'n his nose up w'en he'd pass.
Weasels's small o' cose, but my!
Dem air animiles is sly.
So dis hyeah one says, says he,
"I'll jes' fix dat bah, you see."
So he fixes up his plan
An' hunts up de fa'merman.
When de fa'mer see him come,
He 'mence lookin' mighty glum,
An' he ketches up a stick;
But de weasel speak up quick:
"Hol' on, Mistah Fa'mer man,
I wan' 'splain a little plan.
Ef you waits, I'll tell you whah
An' jes' how to ketch ol' Bah.
But I tell you now you mus'

Gin me one fat chicken fus'."
Den de man he scratch his haid,
Las' he say, "I'll mek de trade."
So de weasel et his hen,
Smacked his mouf and says, "Well, den,
Set yo' trap an' bait ternight,
An' I'll ketch de bah all right."
Den he ups an' goes to see
Mistah Bah, an' says, says he:
"Well, fren' Bah, we *ain't* been fren's,
But ternight ha'd feelin' en's.
Ef you ain't too proud to steal,
We kin git a splendid meal.
Cose I wouldn't come to you,
But it mus' be done by two;
Hit's a trap, but we kin beat
All dey tricks an' git de meat."
"Cose I's wif you," says de bah,
"Come on, weasel, show me whah."
Well, dey trots erlong ontwell
Dat air meat beginned to smell
In de trap. Den weasel say:
"Now you put yo' paw dis way
While I hoi' de spring back so,
Den you grab de meat an' go."
Well, de bah he had to grin
Ez he put his big paw in,
Den he juked up, but—kerbing!
Weasel done let go de spring.
"Dah now," says de weasel, "dah,
I done cotched you, Mistah Bah!"
O, dat bah did sno't and spout,
Try'n' his bestes' to git out,
But de weasel say, "Goo'-bye!
Weasel small, but weasel sly."
Den he tu'ned his back an' run
Tol' de fa'mer whut he done.
So de fa'mer come down dah,
Wif a axe and killed de bah.

Dah now, ain't dat sto'y fine?
Run erlong now, nevah min'.
Want some mo', you rascal, you?
No, suh! no, suh! dat'll do.

1899

Sympathy

I know what the caged bird feels, alas!
When the sun is bright on the upland slopes;
When the wind stirs soft through the springing grass,

And the river flows like a stream of glass;
When the first bird sings and the first bud opes,
And the faint perfume from its chalice° steals— *cup-shaped flower*
I know what the caged bird feels!

I know why the caged bird beats his wing
Till its blood is red on the cruel bars;
For he must fly back to his perch and cling
When he fain would be on the bough a-swing;
And a pain still throbs in the old, old scars
And they pulse again with a keener sting—
I know why he beats his wing!

I know why the caged bird sings, ah me,
When his wing is bruised and his bosom sore,—
When he beats his bars and he would be free;
It is not a carol of joy or glee,
But a prayer that he sends from his heart's deep core,
But a plea, that upward to Heaven he flings—
I know why the caged bird sings!

1899

Dinah Kneading Dough

I have seen full many a sight
Born of day or drawn by night:
Sunlight on a silver stream,
Golden lilies all a-dream,
Lofty mountains, bold and proud,
Veiled beneath the lacelike cloud;
But no lovely sight I know
Equals Dinah kneading dough.

Brown arms buried elbow-deep
Their domestic rhythm keep,
As with steady sweep they go
Through the gently yielding dough.
Maids may vaunt their finer charms—
Naught to me like Dinah's arms;
Girls may draw, or paint, or sew—
I love Dinah kneading dough.

Eyes of jet and teeth of pearl,
Hair, some say, too tight a-curl;
But the dainty maid I deem
Very near perfection's dream.
Swift she works, and only flings
Me a glance—the least of things.
And I wonder, does she know
That my heart is in the dough?

1899

The Haunted Oak

Pray why are you so bare, so bare,
  Oh, bough of the old oak-tree;
And why, when I go through the shade you throw,
  Runs a shudder over me?

My leaves were green as the best, I trow,° *believe*
  And sap ran free in my veins,
But I saw in the moonlight dim and weird
  A guiltless victim's pains.

I bent me down to hear his sigh;
  I shook with his gurgling moan,
And I trembled sore when they rode away,
  And left him here alone.

They'd charged him with the old, old crime,
  And set him fast in jail:
Oh, why does the dog howl all night long,
  And why does the night wind wail?

He prayed his prayer and he swore his oath,
  And he raised his hand to the sky;
But the beat of hoofs smote on his ear,
  And the steady tread drew nigh.

Who is it rides by night, by night,
  Over the moonlit road?
And what is the spur that keeps the pace,
  What is the galling goad?

And now they beat at the prison door,
  "Ho, keeper, do not stay!
We are friends of him whom you hold within,
  And we fain would take him away

"From those who ride fast on our heels
  With mind to do him wrong;
They have no care for his innocence,
  And the rope they bear is long."

They have fooled the jailer with lying words,
  They have fooled the man with lies;
The bolts unbar, the locks are drawn,
  And the great door open flies.

Now they have taken him from the jail,
  And hard and fast they ride,
And the leader laughs low down in his throat,
  As they halt my trunk beside.

Oh, the judge, he wore a mask of black,
And the doctor one of white,
And the minister, with his oldest son,
Was curiously bedight.° *dressed*

Oh, foolish man, why weep you now?
'T is but a little space,
And the time will come when these shall dread
The mem'ry of your face.

I feel the rope against my bark,
And the weight of him in my grain,
I feel in the throe of his final woe
The touch of my own last pain.

And never more shall leaves come forth
On a bough that bears the ban;
I am burned with dread, I am dried and dead,
From the curse of a guiltless man.

And ever the judge rides by, rides by,
And goes to hunt the deer,
And ever another rides his soul
In the guise of a mortal fear.

And ever the man he rides me hard,
And never a night stays he;
For I feel his curse as a haunted bough,
On the trunk of a haunted tree.

1903

Douglass

Ah, Douglass, we have fall'n on evil days,
Such days as thou, not even thou didst know,
When thee, the eyes of that harsh long ago
Saw, salient, at the cross of devious ways,
And all the country heard thee with amaze.
Not ended then, the passionate ebb and flow,
The awful tide that battled to and fro;
We ride amid a tempest of dispraise.

Now, when the waves of swift dissension swarm,
And Honor, the strong pilot, lieth stark,
Oh, for thy voice high-sounding o'er the storm,
For thy strong arm to guide the shivering bark,
The blast-defying power of thy form,
To give us comfort through the lonely dark.

1903

Philosophy

I been t'inkin' 'bout de preachah; whut he said de othah night,
'Bout hit bein' people's dooty, fu' to keep dey faces bright;
How one ought to live so pleasant dat ouah tempah never riles,
Meetin' evahbody roun' us wid ouah very nicest smiles.

Dat's all right, I ain't a-sputin' not a t'ing dat soun's lak fac',
But you don't ketch folks a-grinnin' wid a misery in de back;
An' you don't fin' dem a-smilin' w'en dey's hongry ez kin be,
Leastways, dat's how human natur' allus seems to 'pear to me.

We is mos' all putty likely fu' to have our little cares,
An' I think we's doin' fus' rate w'en we jes' go long and bears,
Widout breakin' up ouah faces in a sickly so't o' grin,
W'en we knows dat in ouah innards we is p'intly mad ez sin.

Oh dey's times fu' bein' pleasant an' fu' goin' smilin' roun',
'Cause I don't believe in people allus totin' roun' a frown,
But it's easy 'nough to titter w'en de stew is smokin' hot,
But hit's mighty ha'd to giggle w'en dey's nuffin' in de pot.

1903

Black Samson of Brandywine[1]

"In the fight at Brandywine, Black Samson, a giant negro armed with a scythe, sweeps his way through the red ranks. . . ."
—C. M. Skinner's *"Myths and Legends of Our Own Land"*

Gray are the pages of record,
Dim are the volumes of eld;
Else had old Delaware told us
More that her history held.
Told us with pride in the story,
Honest and noble and fine,
More of the tale of my hero,
Black Samson of Brandywine.

Sing of your chiefs and your nobles,
Saxon and Celt and Gaul,[2]
Breath of mine ever shall join you,
Highly I honor them all.
Give to them all of their glory,
But for this noble of mine,
Lend him a tithe° of your tribute, *one tenth*
Black Samson of Brandywine.

1. A creek in southeastern Pennsylvania; the site of a British victory in 1777 over the American Revolutionary Army.
2. One of the Celtic-speaking peoples of ancient France. The Saxons were a West Germanic people who invaded Britain in the 5th century C.E. The Celts were an ancient warlike Irish and Scottish people.

There in the heat of the battle,
  There in the stir of the fight,
Loomed he, an ebony giant,
  Black as the pinions° of night. *wings*
Swinging his scythe like a mower
  Over a field of grain,
Needless the care of the gleaners,[3]
  Where he had passed amain.° *furiously*

Straight through the human harvest,
  Cutting a bloody swath,
Woe to you, soldier of Briton!
  Death is abroad in his path.
Flee from the scythe of the reaper,
  Flee while the moment is thine,
None may with safety withstand him,
  Black Samson of Brandywine.

Was he a freeman or bondman?
  Was he a man or a thing?
What does it matter? His brav'ry
  Renders him royal—a king.
If he was only a chattel,° *enslaved*
  Honor the ransom may pay
Of the royal, the loyal black giant
  Who fought for his country that day.

Noble and bright is the story,
  Worthy the touch of the lyre,[4]
Sculptor or poet should find it
  Full of the stuff to inspire.
Beat it in brass and in copper,
  Tell it in storied line,
So that the world may remember
  Black Samson of Brandywine.

1903

The Poet

He sang of life, serenely sweet,
  With, now and then, a deeper note.
  From some high peak, nigh yet remote,
He voiced the world's absorbing beat.

He sang of love when earth was young,
  And Love, itself, was in his lays.
  But ah, the world, it turned to praise
A jingle in a broken tongue.

1903

3. People who gather grain missed by harvesters.
4. A small harp used, in ancient times, to accompany poetry.

The Fourth of July and Race Outrages

Belleville, Wilmington, Evansville, the Fourth of July, and Kishineff,[1] a curious combination and yet one replete with a ghastly humor. Sitting with closed lips over our own bloody deeds we accomplish the fine irony of a protest to Russia. Contemplating with placid eyes the destruction of all the Declaration of Independence and the Constitution stood for, we celebrate the thing which our own action proclaims we do not believe in.

But it is over and done. The Fourth is come and gone. The din has ceased and the smoke has cleared away. Nothing remains but the litter of all and a few reflections. The sky-rocket has ascended, the firecrackers have burst, the roman candles have sputtered, the "nigger chasers"—a pertinent American name—have run their courses, and we have celebrated the nation's birthday. Yes, and we black folks have celebrated.

Dearborn Street and Armour Avenue[2] have been all life and light. Not even the Jews and the Chinaman have been able to outdo us in the display of loyalty. And we have done it all because we have not stopped to think just how little it means to us.

The papers are full of the reports of peonage[3] in Alabama. A new and more dastardly slavery there has arisen to replace the old. For the sake of reenslaving the Negro, the Constitution has been trampled under feet, the rights of man have been laughed out of court, and the justice of God has been made a jest and we celebrate.

Every wire, no longer in the South alone, brings us news of a new hanging or a new burning, some recent outrage against a helpless people, some fresh degradation of an already degraded race. One man sins and a whole nation suffers, and we celebrate.

Like a dark cloud, pregnant with terror and destruction, disenfranchisement has spread its wings over our brethren of the South. Like the same dark cloud, industrial prejudice glooms above us in the North. We may not work save when the new-come foreigner refuses to, and then they, high prized above our sacrificial lives, may shoot us down with impunity. And yet we celebrate.

With citizenship discredited and scored, with violated homes and long unheeded prayers, with bleeding hands uplifted, still sore and smarting from long beating at the door of opportunity, we raise our voices and sing, "My Country, 'Tis of Thee"; we shout and sing while from the four points of the compass comes our brothers' unavailing cry, and so we celebrate.

With a preacher, one who a few centuries ago would have sold indulgences to the murderers on St. Bartholomew's Day,[4] with such a preacher in a Chicago pulpit, jingling his thirty pieces of silver, distorting the number and nature of our crimes, excusing anarchy, apologizing for murder, and tearing to tatters the teachings of Jesus Christ while he cries, "Release unto us Barabbas,"[5] we celebrate.

1. Sites of recent racial violence in Illinois, North Carolina, and Indiana, respectively, and of a pogrom against Jews in Moldavia, then a province of Russia in eastern Europe.
2. Streets in Chicago.
3. In parts of the late-19th-century South, a system of forcing into near enslavement black people convicted of crimes who were unable to pay their fines.
4. The August 1572 massacre of Protestants by Catholics in Paris.
5. The murderer released by Pilate in exchange for a judgment of death against Jesus (Luke 23.18–25).

But there are some who sit silent within their closed rooms and hear as from afar the din of joy come muffled to their ears as on some later day their children and their children's sons shall hear a nation's cry for succor in her need. Aye, there be some who on this festal day kneel in their private closets and with hands upraised and bleeding hearts cry out to God, if there still lives a God, "How long, O God, How long?"[6]

1903

6. From Psalm 13.

ALICE MOORE DUNBAR NELSON
1875–1935

Born in New Orleans, Alice Ruth Moore attended the local public schools, graduated from Straight College (now Dillard University) in 1892, and began teaching in her hometown. An accomplished violinist, cellist, and mandolin player; an amateur actor; and a writer of local acclaim, the spirited daughter of Joseph and Patricia Moore was a leader among the African American intelligentsia even before her first book, *Violets and Other Tales* (1895), was published. One of her poems caught the fancy of another rising literary star, Paul Laurence Dunbar, who began a correspondence that led to their marriage. Ironically, Paul became famous for his dialect poetry and minstrel song writing while Alice was sometimes criticized because her work was so "nonracial." Perhaps her attitude is best summarized in a letter she wrote to Paul in May 1895:

> You ask my opinion about the Negro dialect in literature? Well, frankly, I believe in everyone following his own bent. If it be so that one has a special aptitude for dialect work why it is only right that dialect work should be a specialty. But if one should be like me—absolutely devoid of the ability to manage dialect, I don't see the necessity of cramming and forcing oneself into that plane because one is a Negro or a Southerner.

Apparently, others shared the couple's respect for diversity, for Dodd, Mead & Company marketed Paul's *Poems of Cabin and Field* and Alice's second book, *The Goodness of St. Rocque* (1899), as companion pieces.

Dunbar Nelson's first two books are collections of poems, reviews, sketches, and short stories. She also gained distinction as an editor, a journalist, a literary critic, and a scholar. Two themes of great importance to her were race and gender, but she tried to make a firm distinction between imaginative literature and journalism, reserving her explicit political discussions for the latter. This was not always workable, and as her poem "I Sit and Sew" shows, she occasionally violated her dictum. She joined the Local Color movement, but in focusing as she did on Creole culture, New Orleans, and other aspects of her personal experience and in experimenting with different prose forms, Dunbar Nelson consciously attempted to expand notions of African American life and literature.

As a scholar she often wrote on issues of curriculum and literature. Her master's thesis at Cornell on the influence of Milton upon Wordsworth has been cited by a number of scholars. Both *Masterpieces of Negro Eloquence* (1914) and *The Dunbar Speaker and Entertainer* (1920) demonstrate her concern with promulgating African American literature. As a teacher and a writer, she was increasingly active in politics and civic affairs, and after eighteen years on the Howard High School faculty in Wilmington, Delaware, Dunbar Nelson was fired because, despite a rule forbidding her school district's employees to engage in political activities, she participated in a social justice conference convened by then-senator Warren G. Harding. Dunbar Nelson published a series of regular columns in papers such as the *Pittsburgh Courier, Washington Eagle, New York Sun*, and the *Chicago Daily News*. She was a co-editor of the *A.M.E. Church Review*, and with her husband, Robert Nelson, she owned and operated the *Wilmington Advocate*. When she died in 1935, she left a 2,000-page diary, screenplays, manuscripts for several novels, and other writings. While most critical attention has focused on her youthful poetry and short stories, Dunbar Nelson's contributions over her lifetime were many and diverse.

Violets[1]

I had not thought of violets of late,
The wild, shy kind that springs beneath your feet
In wistful April days, when lovers mate
And wander through the fields in raptures sweet.
And thought of violets meant florists' shops,
And bows and pins, and perfumed paper fine;
And garish lights, and mincing little fops[2]
And cabarets and songs, and deadening wine.
So far from sweet real things my thoughts had strayed,
I had forgot wide fields, and clear brown streams;
The perfect loveliness that God has made—
Wild violets shy and heaven-mounting dreams.
And now—unwittingly, you've made me dream
Of violets, and my soul's forgotten gleam.

1917

I Sit and Sew

I sit and sew—a useless task it seems,
My hands grown tired, my head weighed down with dreams—
The panoply of war, the martial tred of men,
Grim-faced, stern-eyed, gazing beyond the ken
Of lesser souls, whose eyes have not seen Death,
Nor learned to hold their lives but as a breath—
But—I must sit and sew.

I sit and sew—my heart aches with desire—
That pageant terrible, that fiercely pouring fire
On wasted fields, and writhing grotesque things
Once men. My soul in pity flings
Appealing cries, yearning only to go
There in that holocaust of hell, those fields of woe—
But—I must sit and sew.

1. Reportedly, when Alice Moore met Paul Laurence Dunbar after a two-year correspondence, she presented him with violets.

2. Men excessively concerned with their appearance, clothing, and manners.

The little useless seam, the idle patch;
Why dream I here beneath my homely thatch,
When there they lie in sodden mud and rain,
Pitifully calling me, the quick ones and the slain?
You need me, Christ! It is no roseate dream
That beckons me—this pretty futile seam,
It stifles me—God, must I sit and sew?

1920

April Is on the Way

April is on the way!
I saw the scarlet flash of a blackbird's wing
As he sang in the cold, brown February trees;
And children said that they caught a glimpse of the sky on a bird's wing from the far South.
(Dear God, was that a stark figure outstretched in the bare branches
Etched brown against the amethyst sky?)

April is on the way!
The ice crashed in the brown mud-pool under my tread,
The warning earth clutched my bloody feet with great fecund[1] fingers.
I saw a boy rolling a hoop up the road,
His little bare hands were red with cold,
But his brown hair blew backward in the southwest wind.
(Dear God! He screamed when he saw my awful woe-spent eyes.)

April is on the way!
I met a woman in the lane;
Her burden was heavy as it is always, but today her step was light,
And a smile drenched the tired look away from her eyes.
(Dear God, she had dreams of vengeance for her slain mate,
Perhaps the west wind has blown the mist of hate from her heart,
The dead man was cruel to her, you know that, God.)

April is on the way!
My feet spurn the ground now; instead of dragging on the bitter road.
I laugh in my throat as I see the grass greening beside the patches of snow
(Dear God, those were wild fears. Can there be hate when the southwest wind is blowing?)

April is on the way!
The crisp brown hedges stir with the bustle of bird wings.
There is business of building, and songs from brown thrust throats
As the bird-carpenters make homes against Valentine Day.
(Dear God, could they build me a shelter in the hedge from the icy winds that will come with the dark?)

1. Fertile.

April is on the way!
I sped through the town this morning. The florist shops have put
yellow flowers in the windows,
Daffodils and tulips and primroses, pale yellow flowers
Like the tips of her fingers when she waved me that frightened
farewell.
And the women in the market have stuck pussy willows in the long
necked bottles on their stands.
(Willow trees are kind, Dear God. They will not bear a body on their
limbs.)

April is on the way!
The soul within me cried that all the husk of indifference to sorrow
was but the crust of ice with which winter disguises life;
It will melt, and reality will burgeon forth like the crocuses in the glen.
(Dear God! Those thoughts were from long ago. When we read poetry
after the day's toil, and got religion together at the revival
meeting.)

April is on the way!
The infinite miracle of unfolding life in the brown February fields.
(Dear God, the hounds are baying!)
Murder and wasted love, lust and weariness, deceit and vainglory—
what are they but the spent breath of the runner?
(God, you know he laid hairy red hands on the golden loveliness of her
little daffodil body.)
Hate may destroy me, but from my brown limbs will bloom the golden
buds with which we once spelled love.
(Dear God! How their light eyes glow into black pin points of hate!)

April is on the way!
Wars are made in April, and they sing at Easter time of the
Resurrection.
Therefore I laugh in their faces.
(Dear God, give her the strength to join me before her golden petals
are fouled in the slime!)
April is on the way!

1927

Violets

I

"And she tied a bunch of violets with a tress of her pretty brown hair."

She sat in the yellow glow of the lamplight softly humming these words. It was Easter evening, and the newly risen spring world was slowly sinking to a gentle, rosy, opalescent slumber, sweetly tired of the joy which had pervaded it all day. For in the dawn of the perfect morn, it had arisen, stretched out its arms in glorious happiness to greet the Saviour and said its hallelujahs, merrily trilling out carols of bird, and organ and flower-song. But the evening had come, and rest.

There was a letter lying on the table, it read:

"Dear, I send you this little bunch of flowers as my Easter token. Perhaps you may not be able to read their meaning, so I'll tell you. Violets, you know, are my favorite flowers. Dear, little, human-faced things! They seem always as if about to whisper a love-word; and then they signify that thought which passes always between you and me. The orange blossoms—you know their meaning;[1] the little pinks are the flowers you love; the evergreen leaf is the symbol of the endurance of our affection; the tube-roses I put in, because once when you kissed and pressed me close in your arms, I had a bunch of tube-roses on my bosom, and the heavy fragrance of their crushed loveliness has always lived in my memory. The violets and pinks are from a bunch I wore to-day, and when kneeling at the altar, during communion, did I sin, dear, when I thought of you? The tube-roses and orange-blossoms I wore Friday night; you always wished for a lock of my hair, so I'll tie these flowers with them—but there, it is not stable enough; let me wrap them with a bit of ribbon, pale blue, from that little dress I wore last winter to the dance, when we had such a long, sweet talk in that forgotten nook. You always loved that dress, it fell in such soft ruffles away from the throat and bosom,—you called me your little forget-me-not, that night. I laid the flowers away for awhile in our favorite book,—Byron[2]—just at the poem we loved best, and now I send them to you. Keep them always in remembrance of me, and if aught should occur to separate us, press these flowers to your lips, and I will be with you in spirit, permeating your heart with unutterable love and happiness."

II

It is Easter again. As of old, the joyous bells clang out the glad news of the resurrection. The giddy, dancing sunbeams laugh riotously in field and street; birds carol their sweet twitterings everywhere, and the heavy perfume of flowers scents the golden atmosphere with inspiring fragrance. One long, golden sunbeam steals silently into the white-curtained window of a quiet room, and lay athwart a sleeping face. Cold, pale, still, its fair, young face pressed against the satin-lined casket. Slender, white fingers, idle now, they that had never known rest; locked softly over a bunch of violets; violets and tube-roses in her soft, brown hair, violets in the bosom of her long, white gown; violets and tube-roses and orange-blossoms banked everywhere, until the air was filled with the ascending souls of the human flowers. Some whispered that a broken heart had ceased to flutter in that still, young form, and that it was a mercy for the soul to ascend on the slender sunbeam. To-day she kneels at the throne of heaven, where one year ago she had communed at an earthly altar.

III

Far away in a distant city, a man, carelessly looking among some papers, turned over a faded bunch of flowers tied with a blue ribbon and a lock of hair. He paused meditatively awhile, then turning to the regal-looking woman lounging before the fire, he asked:

1. Chastity and nuptials.
2. Perhaps the lover's name. It could also refer to the author of the "favorite book"; perhaps a volume by Lord Byron (George Gordon Byron) (1788–1824), English Romantic poet.

"Wife, did you ever send me these?"

She raised her great, black eyes to his with a gesture of ineffable disdain, and replied languidly:

"You know very well I can't bear flowers. How could I ever send such sentimental trash to any one? Throw them into the fire."

And the Easter bells chimed a solemn requiem as the flames slowly licked up the faded violets. Was it merely fancy on the wife's part, or did the husband really sigh,—a long, quivering breath of remembrance?

1895

FENTON JOHNSON
1888–1958

Born in Chicago on May 7, 1888, to Elijah H. and Jessie Taylor Johnson, Fenton Johnson was raised in a relatively well-to-do environment and attended Northwestern University, the University of Chicago, and Columbia University. His first poem was published in a Chicago newspaper when Johnson was twelve years old, and his first plays were produced at a Chicago theater when he was only nineteen. James Weldon Johnson and others singled out "The Vision of Lazarus," a long poem in blank verse, for praise; otherwise, his first collection of poetry, *A Little Dreaming* (1913), merely marked him as promising. Fenton Johnson published (largely at his own expense) two more collections of verse, *Visions of the Dusk* (1915) and *Songs of the Soil* (1916), but focused his attention on editing two short-lived periodicals, *Champion Magazine* and *Favorite Magazine*. In 1920 Johnson published *For the Highest Good* and *Tales of Darkest America*, collections of essays and short stories, respectively. Though he lived until 1958 and continued to write poetry at least through the Depression, these two books represent Johnson's last major publications.

Fenton Johnson's poetry has been widely anthologized; however, he remains one of African American literature's lesser-known writers, probably because his work falls between the popular writing from the turn of the century and the writing identified with the New Negro Renaissance of the 1920s and 1930s. Ironically, Johnson's work is valuable in large measure precisely because it bridges, in style and theme, some of the chief defining characteristics of African American writing in these two periods. Although many pieces in his three volumes of verse merit serious attention, Johnson's reputation rests primarily on a small number of post–World War I poems, including "Tired" and "The Scarlet Woman." Fenton Johnson's role as a transitional figure in the African American literary tradition is significant, in part because his use of folk forms such as the spiritual and the blues anticipates and perhaps even enables the subsequent work of such better-known authors as Jean Toomer, James Weldon Johnson, Langston Hughes, and Sterling Brown.

Tired

I am tired of work; I am tired of building up somebody else's civilization.
Let us take a rest, M'Lissy Jane.
I will go down to the Last Chance Saloon, drink a gallon or two of gin, shoot a game or two of dice and sleep the rest of the night on one of Mike's barrels.
You will let the old shanty go to rot, the white people's clothes turn to dust, and the Calvary Baptist Church sink to the bottomless pit.
You will spend your days forgetting you married me and your nights hunting the warm gin Mike serves the ladies in the rear of the Last Chance Saloon.
Throw the children into the river; civilization has given us too many. It is better to die than to grow up and find that you are colored.
Pluck the stars out of the heavens. The stars mark our destiny. The stars marked my destiny.
I am tired of civilization.

1919

The Scarlet Woman

Once I was good like the Virgin Mary and the Minister's wife.
My father worked for Mr. Pullman[1] and white people's tips; but he died two days after his insurance expired.
I had nothing, so I had to go to work.
All the stock I had was a white girl's education and a face that enchanted the men of both races.
Starvation danced with me.
So when Big Lizzie, who kept a house for white men, came to me with tales of fortune that I could reap from the sale of my virtue I bowed my head to Vice.
Now I can drink more gin than any man for miles around.
Gin is better than all the water in Lethe.[2]

1922

1. George Pullman (1831–1897), inventor of the modern railroad sleeping and dining cars and founder of the Pullman Palace Car Company in 1865. Many Black men found employment as Pullman porters.

2. In Greek mythology, the river of forgetfulness in Hades, marking the boundary between life and death.

125
ST
APOLLO

Harlem Renaissance 1919–1940

A CULTURAL FLOWERING

Although the very existence of the Harlem Renaissance has been disputed, with some choosing to emphasize the national and international scope of the cultural phenomenon and thus downplaying its identification with one district in New York City, the term *Harlem Renaissance* has remained popular. It has remained so because most scholars and students agree that the 1920s was a decade of extraordinary creativity in the arts for Black Americans and that much of that creativity found its focus in the activities of African Americans living in New York City, particularly in Harlem.

Unquestionably, at least where the arts (including music and dance) are concerned, these years marked an especially brilliant moment in the history of Blacks in America. In particular, the second half of the decade witnessed an outpouring of publications by African Americans that was unprecedented in its variety and scope, so that it clearly qualifies as a moment of renaissance, as such moments of unusually fertile cultural activity are often called. In poetry, fiction, drama, and the essay, as in music, dance, painting, and sculpture, African Americans worked not only with a new sense of confidence and purpose but also with a sense of achievement never before experienced by so many Black artists in the long, troubled history of the peoples of African descent in North America.

Although the term *Harlem Renaissance* is convenient and defensible, it is important to remember that

125th Street in Harlem, 1935.

what took place in New York City was in many respects a heightened version of the unusual cultural productivity taking place elsewhere in the United States, especially in the major cities of the North. In addition, it is important not to draw artificial lines between "serious" and "popular" art, although many of the renaissance creators certainly did so. Expressed in various ways, the creativity of Black Americans undoubtedly came from a common source—the irresistible impulse of Blacks to create boldly expressive art of a high quality as a primary response to their social conditions, as an affirmation of their dignity and humanity in the face of poverty and racism.

What happened in the United States should also be linked to trends abroad. In the wake of World War I (1914–18), the Black population of the United States began to acquire an unprecedented worldliness, a sense (even if inchoate or idealistic) of the links between events within the nation and broader forces and currents around the globe. This was partly a matter of new experience—above all, through the eyes of the more than 350,000 African Americans who served in the armed forces during the war—but it was also a matter of exposure to new technologies (including mass transportation and media) and new ideas. Some of these ideas emerged out of the war effort itself: when President Woodrow Wilson justified the war as an effort to "make the world safe for democracy," African Americans living under segregation, rampant discrimination, and the terror of lynching wondered (as the socialist magazine the *Messenger* would phrase it in 1920) what the Negro needed to do to "make America safe for himself."

The all-Black 369th Infantry Regiment, known as **the "Harlem Hellfighters,"** returns in triumph to New York in 1919, marching past enormous crowds at Lenox Avenue and 135th Street.

Others were more abstract, including the notion that there were human rights and privileges that were universal, applicable to all regardless of race or creed. At the same time there was a growing sense that the world was in the process of being transformed, most visibly in the Russian Revolution of 1917. As much as this transformation was cataclysmic and terrifying in its unpredictability, it also demonstrated that major change was possible, even in the face of a powerful autocracy and entrenched injustice.

For Black writers and intellectuals, the attraction to international ideas cut across political divisions. On the one hand, there emerged a new generation of Black thinkers (many from the Caribbean) who were attracted by the promise of socialism. Even some of them, however, came to be convinced (as they observed struggles against British rule in places like Egypt and India) that class consciousness would not suffice without race consciousness. Thus in 1920 when the great Harlem radical editor and street speaker Hubert Henry Harrison counseled that "before the Negroes of the Western world can play any effective part they must first acquaint themselves with what is taking place in that larger world whose millions are in motion," he also insisted that "the international Fact to which Negroes in America are now reacting is not the exploitation of laborers by capitalists; but the social, political, and economic subjection of colored peoples by white." On the other hand, even the Black intellectuals who eschewed direct political involvement (in part out of a conviction that Black artistic accomplishment would itself provide a road to social advancement) were drawn to international concerns. Thus the philosopher Alain Locke noted in the period-defining anthology *The New Negro* that "as with the Jew, persecution is making the Negro international"; but even earlier (in his surprising if often overlooked 1924 article "Apropos of Africa") Locke had espoused the idea of "large-scale

Protest parade, 1924. James VanDerZee (1886–1983), who opened his first portrait studio in Harlem in 1917, was the preeminent Black photographer of the period.

cooperation between the variously separated branches of the Negro peoples," while cautioning that "it is rather against than with the wish of the interested governments, that the American Negro must reach out toward his rightful share in the solution of African problems and the development of Africa's resources."

From its inception, the cultural flowering of the renaissance was characterized by attempts to "reach out," whether in the form of Marcus Garvey's efforts to establish branches of the Universal Negro Improvement Association (UNIA) in the Caribbean and in Africa, or in the form of the extended series of articles that publisher Robert Abbott wrote for the *Chicago Defender* in 1923 recounting his trip through South America, or in the form of the Pan-African Congresses organized by W. E. B. Du Bois in 1919, 1921, 1923, and 1927, or in the form of Zora Neale Hurston's anthropological fieldwork in Jamaica and Haiti (1936–38). Appalled by the U.S. occupation of Haiti (1915–34), James Weldon Johnson not only published a four-part article defending Haiti's right to self-determination in the *Nation* (1920), but also built ties between the National Association for the Advancement of Colored People (NAACP) and Haitian leaders such as Dantès Bellegarde and Georges Sylvain. Numerous writers associated with the renaissance traveled extensively and made contact with Black writers elsewhere: as early as 1924, for example, Langston Hughes, Countee Cullen, Claude McKay, Jessie Fauset, and Alain Locke had met Black French writers such as the Martinican novelist René Maran and the Dahomean philosopher Kojo Tovalou Houénou in Paris, and these contacts led to exchanges among the key journals and newspapers in Harlem and their French-language counterparts in Paris. In the early 1930s, Hughes also established contact with writers in the Caribbean such as the Haitian Jacques Roumain and the Cuban Nicolás Guillén, both of whom he translated into English. This intermittent cross-fertilization continued through the inception of the *Négritude* movement among the generation of French Caribbean and African students (including Paulette Nardal, Aimé Césaire, Léon-Gontran Damas, and Léopold Sédar Senghor) who arrived in Paris in the late 1920s and early 1930s. At the same time, it must be remembered that even in Harlem itself, the renaissance was an international phenomenon due to the prominence of Caribbean writers such as McKay and Eric Walrond, in whose work Black life outside the United States remained a central focus.

Nevertheless, Harlem and New York were crucial to the movement in the United States. The history of the publication of books of poetry and novels, as well as the production of plays, attests to the fact that something new and significant was taking place. For example, when Harper & Brothers brought out Countee Cullen's first book of verse, *Color,* in 1925 in New York City, it was apparently the first book of poetry written by an African American to be published by a major American house since Dodd, Mead offered Paul Laurence Dunbar's books at the turn of the century (although in 1922, Harcourt, Brace had published the Jamaican Claude McKay's *Harlem Shadows*). In the same way, Jean Toomer's 1923 *Cane* was apparently the first book of fiction (sometimes called a novel, the work also contains poems and drama) by an American of African descent to arrive from a New York publisher since Doubleday, Page announced the appearance of Charles Chesnutt's *The Colonel's Dream* in 1905. Certainly a new day had arrived for the Black American writer in the 1920s in New York City.

MIGRATION NORTH

The cause or causes of a cultural renaissance are almost always difficult to trace precisely. However, New York City had become a magnet, perhaps the most powerful, for the thousands of Blacks fleeing the South in the aftermath of the entrenchment of segregation following the end of the Reconstruction era, which itself followed the Civil War, and the segregationist rulings of the U.S. Supreme Court, notably the landmark case *Plessy v. Ferguson* in 1896, which endorsed separation in transportation. As legal segregation made living conditions for Blacks in the South more and more intolerable, the widespread lynching of Blacks bitterly underscored the extent to which they were powerless before the law and less than human in the eyes of many whites. Migration to the North increasingly seemed an absolute necessity for Blacks seeking a better life for themselves and their children. In addition, swift industrial expansion in the North created a demand for labor that made many employers eager to recruit and hire Black workers. This demand intensified when the United States entered World War I in 1917 and jobs previously held by white males, themselves now serving in the armed forces, became available to newcomers from the South.

While Blacks settled in several northern cities, including Chicago, Philadelphia, and Cleveland, New York City was the destination of choice. Perhaps some migrants were enthralled by living in the largest, most cosmopolitan, and most renowned of American cities. More substantially, the district of Harlem had an additional attraction. Built originally to house middle-class and upper-middle-class whites, Harlem became available to Blacks when it seemed clear that the area was seriously overbuilt; facing economic hardship, real estate interests among both races in effect conspired to break the exclusionary practices that had hitherto kept Blacks out. Newcomers found grand avenues, broad sidewalks, and finely constructed houses that afforded Blacks the chance to live in housing stock far superior in quality to anything available to them elsewhere in the United States. Harlem became home to all classes of Blacks, including leading writers and artists. As the national interest in African American culture grew, encouraged by a variety of factors, such as the growing popularity of jazz and the blues, Harlem seemed well on its way to becoming, as the prominent writer and civil rights leader James Weldon Johnson put it, "the Negro capital of the world."

Harlem and New York quickly became the headquarters of many of the most important African American cultural and political national organizations, including the NAACP, the National Urban League, and Marcus Garvey's UNIA. Newspapers and magazines played a pivotal role in setting the renaissance in motion. Although a few important Black newspapers had been in existence since the turn of the century (for example the *New York Age*, the *Boston Guardian*, and the *Baltimore Afro-American*), many of the most powerful Black periodicals were founded in the early twentieth century and attained their high points of circulation and influence in the 1920s:

The Young Blood Hungers by Aaron Douglas. Cover illustration for *The Crisis*. Raised in Kansas City, Douglas moved to New York in 1925 and quickly established himself as the visual artist most closely connected to the literary renaissance.

especially notable were the *Chicago Defender*, the *Pittsburgh Courier*, the *New York Amsterdam News*, and the *Norfolk Journal and Guide*. Distributed beyond their cities of publication, the northern papers actively promoted the gospel of migration—or, in the famous catchphrase of the *Defender*, "Come to Chicago and Prosper!" Harlem itself hosted an eruption of newspapers, journals, and little magazines. Of these, the most important were almost certainly the house organs of the major Black political organizations based in the city: *The Crisis* (founded in 1910), edited by the brilliant scholar and propagandist W. E. B. Du Bois for the NAACP; *Negro World* (founded in 1919), edited by Marcus Garvey, Hubert Harrison, Eric Walrond, William Ferris, and others for the UNIA; and *Opportunity* (founded in 1923), edited by the urbane sociologist and cultural entrepreneur Charles S. Johnson for the National Urban League. Starting in 1917 with the *Voice* ("A Newspaper for the New Negro"), the paper of Hubert Harrison's Liberty League, there was also a group of smaller but vibrant periodicals associated with Black radical movements in the city, including the *Crusader*, edited by Cyril Briggs; the *Emancipator*, edited by W. A. Domingo; and most prominently the *Messenger*, edited by the socialists A. Philip Randolph and Chandler Owen.

Although there were heated political differences among these periodicals, there was not a pronounced divergence among the literary works featured in the *Crisis*, the *Negro World*, *Opportunity*, and the *Messenger*. Each was dedicated to political progress and social uplift for Black Americans and to the development of literary and artistic traditions of which the typical readers might be proud. Du Bois and the *Crisis* took the lead in calling for a cultural renaissance among Blacks that would prove the genius of Black America to the greater world, and especially to white Americans, who presumably would be moved to treat Blacks with greater justice and compassion. Indeed, between 1919 and 1926 the *Crisis* employed a literary editor, Jessie Fauset, a Phi Beta Kappa graduate of Cornell University who not only published four novels, starting with *There Is Confusion* (1924), but also discovered and nurtured several younger writers. The *Crisis, Opportunity*, and the *Negro World* all sponsored yearly literary prizes in the 1920s, drawing attention to a number of the writers who

An advertisement from the *Chicago Defender* (May 3, 1924) for the first concert appearance of Bessie Smith in Chicago.

went on to become key voices of the renaissance. It is worth noting as well that this promotional activity had a fundamental impact on Black writing in the period, not only in terms of subject matter but also in terms of form: it is a major reason for the preponderance of one-act plays and short stories.

THE NEW WRITERS

The first glimmerings of the new day in literature probably came not with the work of a Black writer but with that of a white—*Three Plays for a Negro Theatre,* by Ridgely Torrence. James Weldon Johnson called the premiere of these plays in 1917 "the most important single event in the entire history of the Negro in the American Theatre." Overturning the tradition of depicting Blacks in stereotypical minstrel forms, Torrence's plays featured Black actors representing complex human emotions and yearnings; in this sense they anticipated not only plays of the 1920s about Blacks such as *The Emperor Jones* (1920) and *All God's Chillun Got Wings* (1925) by the celebrated dramatist Eugene O'Neill but also the work of African American playwrights, poets, and fiction writers breaking with traditions that diminished and often insulted Black humanity. Another landmark came in 1919, a year marked nationally by several anti-Black riots, with the publication of the Jamaican-born poet Claude McKay's militant sonnet "If We Must Die." Although the poem never alludes to race, to Black readers it sounded a note of defiance against racism and racist violence unheard in Black literature in many years. Then, in 1921, the musical revue *Shuffle Along,* written and performed by Blacks, brought to the stage novel styles of song, dance, and comedy that captivated Blacks and whites alike and underscored the emergence of a new generation of Black artistry. Simultaneously, the rapid emergence of the recording industry, in no small part due to the enormous popularity of the blues and jazz (starting with Mamie Smith's hit recording of "Crazy Blues" in 1920), brought unprecedented fame to a generation of Black performers such as Louis Armstrong, Bessie Smith, and Duke Ellington, and proof of an eager African American market for what came

Duke Ellington and his orchestra accompany dancers from the Cotton Club in Harlem, in a still from the 1929 film *Black and Tan.*

to be called "race records." While some in the Black middle class found the blues and jazz debased and distasteful, a number of younger writers were entranced by Black popular music, both as an art that seemed to be defining the cutting edge of what was modern (and what the world saw as "American") and as a sign of their own revolt against the Victorian mores of their elders. In the literature of the renaissance, Black music and dance became flash points in larger debates about "primitivism" and propaganda.

In 1922, James Weldon Johnson's anthology of verse, the *Book of American Negro Poetry,* emphasized the youthful promise of the new writers and established some of the terms of the emerging movement. In his preface, Johnson attacked dialect verse, which had dominated Black American poetry until recently, and wrote of the need for the new Black artists to find "a form expressing the imagery, the idioms, the peculiar turns of thought, and the distinctive humor and pathos" of African Americans in a manner that could give voice to "the deepest and highest emotions and aspirations" and the "widest range of subjects and the widest scope of treatment."

"What the colored poet in the United States needs to do," Johnson wrote, "is something like what Synge did for the Irish." Thus Johnson sought to link what was happening among Blacks in the United States to the Irish Renaissance that had produced such internationally renowned figures as the poet William Butler Yeats and the playwright John Millington Synge. In alluding to "the racial spirit," he was identifying a counterpart to the so-called Celtic or Irish muse that was seen as quite distinct from the English literary imagination. In calling for a form "freer and larger than dialect," he challenged Black writers to disentangle themselves from the stereotypes that had reached their highest form of art in the poetry of the African American writer Paul Laurence Dunbar, who had died in 1906. Above all, Johnson set the manipulation of language and other patterns of signification, not the overt assertion of political ideals, as the heart of the African American poetic enterprise. And he did so while reminding the young Black writers, through his anthology, that they were also heirs to their own tradition—the tradition of African American literature from Phillis Wheatley in the eighteenth century down to his own work—on which they could draw with a measure of confidence as they moved into the future.

Even as he argued (on the first page of his preface) that "the final measure of the greatness of all peoples is the amount and standard of the literature and art they have produced," Johnson also demonstrated the profound challenge posed by Black popular music and dance for the literary renaissance. He argued that the American Negro was "the creator of the only things artistic that have yet sprung from American soil and been universally acknowledged as distinctive American products," and devoted the majority of his preface to a discussion of those products, which strikingly included not literature but popular culture: the spirituals, folk tales (the "Uncle Remus stories" collected by Joel Chandler Harris), the cakewalk (the alternately stately and exaggerated two-step that at the end of the nineteenth century gave rise to what was perhaps the first international "dance craze"), and ragtime (the densely syncopated style that Johnson called "the popular medium for our national expression musically").

In Johnson's anthology and in Robert Kerlin's *Negro Poets and Their Poems* (1923) appeared the work of some of the writers who would dominate the movement, although the younger generation is only sparsely represented (neither includes a selection by Countee Cullen, and only Kerlin's collection contains a single poem by Langston Hughes). As they began to publish over the next few years, Hughes and Cullen (like all the younger writers of the movement) tended not to see themselves as part of the radical modernist strain of literature set in motion in America mainly through the efforts of poets such as Ezra Pound, T. S. Eliot, H.D., and Wallace Stevens or by the Irish writer James Joyce, whose novel *Ulysses* appeared in 1923. Such crucial tenets of radical modernism as a learned allusiveness and a necessary complexity of expression that demands an exclusive literary audience attracted few African American writers. Like most white poets of the age, most Black poets were enthralled by traditional forms of verse as established by the major British and American Romantic poets and their admirers. Modernist verse that resembles the work of Pound, for example, would not appear until much later, and then on a highly restricted scale. Among major American poets after Whitman, only E. A. Robinson and Carl Sandburg would exert any degree of influence on the Harlem Renaissance. In part, this distance was owing, no doubt, to some inattentiveness on the part of the younger writers; in part, however, these writers were after a different business altogether. Most could not be completely taken, for example, by T. S. Eliot's epochal figuring of the entire modern world as a "Waste Land." For many of them, the 1920s was a decade of unrivaled optimism, and all through the generations of slavery and neo-slavery, Black American culture had of necessity emphasized the power of endurance and survival, of love and laughter, as the only effective response to the painful circumstances surrounding their lives.

Even more important than Johnson's anthology as a text helping to define the emerging ambition of the movement was another anthology, albeit one of a more varied sort: *The New Negro* (1925), edited by the Howard University professor Alain Locke. Locke's timely and definitive anthology combined essays, stories, poems, and artwork by older as well as younger writers, white as well as Black, into a book that defined with clarity and flair the spirit of the Harlem Renaissance. Merging racial awareness with a desire for literary and artistic excellence, the text exuded a confidence in the Black world emerging from generations of repression in the United States, and taking up Johnson's challenge, it conceived of Black America as linked not only to other African-based cultural movements around the world but also to other movements, such as the Irish or Czech, that fused ethnic pride or nationalism with a desire for a fresh achievement and independence in art, culture, and politics.

Between the appearance of Johnson's anthology and Locke's, the publication of Jean Toomer's *Cane* independently illustrated several of the peculiar challenges and opportunities of the developing movement. Opening with brief but hauntingly evocative portraits of the Black South, then moving to a powerful rendition of Blacks in northern cities, before returning to the South with a shrouded drama about a Black northerner of troubled, fatalistic consciousness terrorized by the threat of violence at the hands of whites, *Cane* is a text that few of the young writers could resist. Technically, the work embraced certain principles of modernism and even the avant-garde and yet was saturated with African American racial feeling offered now nostalgically, now militantly, but always in highly affecting language. Quite apart from the fiction in the book, the poems included almost casually were of a quality to challenge the best of the young Harlem writers, who read *Cane* and saw Toomer as an authentic star.

Certainly the first important young writers birthed by the movement accepted Toomer and his implicit challenge to them as an artist. These writers were Cullen, who had grown up in the city, and Hughes, who had spent most of his youth in Kansas but had come to Columbia University in 1921, ostensibly to be a student but really, he later insisted, to be in Harlem. Cullen's *Color* (1925) revealed an often dazzling lyrical facility that admitted racial feeling while preserving its author's commitment to conservative poetic forms born of his passion for English Romantic writers such as Keats and Shelley. Hughes, starting with his collection *The Weary Blues* (1926), sometimes matched Cullen's lyrical intensity but opened up a new front by advertising his worship of the blues and jazz, musical forms seldom seen as compatible with formal poetry but that Hughes accepted as perhaps the most authentic and moving expression in art of African American cultural feeling. Other writers, too, attempted to discover literary models in Black music and speech. In 1918 James Weldon Johnson wrote a poem called "The Creation" in which he attempted to capture in free verse the "imagery, color, abandon, sonorous diction, syncopated rhythms, and native idioms" of a Black preacher improvising a sermon (Johnson believed that the "primitive stuff" of the preacher's style "could be used in a way similar to that in which a composer uses a folk theme in writing a major composition"). But it was above all Hughes (and slightly later, Sterling Brown) who set the pace in attempts to find a poetic form that would, as Hughes put it, "grasp and hold some of the meanings and rhythms of jazz."

By the end of 1925, many of the major young artists identified their careers with the movement. The editor, novelist, and critic Wallace Thurman arrived from Los Angeles, as did the poet and novelist Arna Bontemps; from Washington, D.C., came the artist and fiction writer Richard Bruce Nugent, Rudolph Fisher (by training a physician, but also a talented writer of fiction), and the Florida-born Zora Neale Hurston, whose novel *Their Eyes Were Watching God* (1937), although published after the end of the movement, should nevertheless be seen as among its greatest achievements. Also drawn by the sense of excitement in Harlem were the artist and poet Gwendolyn Bennett, who came from Texas, and a little later, from New England, the poet Helene Johnson and her cousin Dorothy West, a writer of fiction and an editor. These were only some of the young artists drawn to Harlem. At the same time, some writers associated with the renaissance pulled away from the distractions of the city: in 1928 Hurston went back to the South to collect folklore, and Eric Walrond used a Guggenheim Award to go to Panama before living in France and England. Georgia Douglas Johnson, Marita Bonner, and Sterling Brown never lived in Harlem at all. Claude McKay wrote *Home to Harlem* (1928) in France, and would not return to New York until 1934; "I had done my best Harlem stuff when I was abroad," McKay wrote later, "seeing it from a long perspective."

PATRONS AND FRIENDS

The deliberate courting and inclusion of leading whites in the Harlem Renaissance have led to questions, at times acrimonious, about the role of patronage—that is, white patronage—in the movement and even about the authenticity of the movement as an expression of African American culture if the renaissance depended so heavily on the goodwill of whites. The truth probably is that such involvement was important and even necessary to the movement, so deep was the historic chasm in the United States between the races because of segregation and racist beliefs; if books by Blacks were to be published, something more than simple merit would have to be involved. In particular, Charles S. Johnson of *Opportunity* and the National Urban League, seeing nothing but benefits in an association between Blacks and whites, worked ingeniously to stimulate such contacts.

Perhaps the two leading white figures associated with the Harlem Renaissance were Carl Van Vechten and Charlotte Osgood Mason. Van Vechten's interracial parties broke new ground on the New York social scene, but he also used his influence as a novelist and critic to help launch certain careers, notably that of Langston Hughes. (Countee Cullen and a few other writers, however, were decidedly wary of Van Vechten's help.) Van Vechten's novel of Harlem life, *Nigger Heaven* (1926), became a best-seller, although many Blacks were utterly alienated by the title. Through the dispensing of money, Mason, an older woman of volatile temperament and sometimes arresting ideas, supported a number of Black artists in this period, including Hurston, Hughes, and Locke;

she did not hesitate to subject her beneficiaries to her powerful notions concerning parapsychology, the matchless force of folk culture, and the dangers of "civilization." In addition to Van Vechten and Mason, grant-awarding philanthropies such as the Julius Rosenwald Fund and the William E. Harmon Foundation as well as publishers and editors at houses such as Knopf, Macmillan, Macaulay, Harper, and Harcourt, Brace played a quieter but no less effective role in lowering the barriers between Black writers and the major means of publication in the United States. The Black writers eagerly seized these opportunities.

EMERGING CONFLICTS

Among the Black writers themselves certain tensions became more serious as the movement grew. One such tension was occupational, in the sense that the writers and artists lived with the uneasy knowledge that their world was in crucial ways distinct from that of the masses of Blacks, almost all of whom, as Langston Hughes once wryly observed, did not know that the Harlem Renaissance was going on. Another tension was generational—the growing antagonism between many of the older writers and editors and the younger set. James Weldon Johnson, among others of the old guard, had little difficulty with the new writers and actively supported their development. However, the most powerful voice among the old guard, that of W. E. B. Du Bois, was less conciliatory. Increasingly disturbed by the apparent "immorality" of some of the new works, as well as by their lack of political seriousness, Du Bois organized in the *Crisis* a symposium, *The Negro in Art,* which appeared over several issues in 1926. Evidently dissatisfied with many of the responses, he openly criticized several of the new works. He was especially hard on Claude McKay's 1928 novel *Home to Harlem,* which Du Bois linked caustically with Van Vechten's *Nigger Heaven,* previously dismissed in the *Crisis* as "an affront to the hospitality of Black folk and to the intelligence of white."

To most of the younger artists, including Thurman, Hughes, Hurston, Nugent, and even the relatively conservative Cullen, the essence of the renaissance was freedom—freedom for them to create as they saw fit, without regard to politics. What freedom meant practically was another matter. Hughes expressed his freedom by insisting on racial commitment on the part of the Black artist; Cullen expressed his by rejecting jazz and blues verse in favor of conservative forms. In his landmark 1926 essay, "The Negro Artist and the Racial Mountain," Hughes insisted that the Black artist must recognize that his or her link to Africa was a precious resource; Cullen preferred to suggest instead, as in his long poem "Heritage" (1925), that Africa was a source of confusion and ambivalence. Both, however, sought freedom from the political constraints that an older generation considered an essential part of the duty of the Black artist. In 1926, many of the younger artists banded together to produce a new magazine, *Fire!!,* which promised "to burn up a lot of old, dead conventional Negro-white ideas of the past." It included one of Hurston's best short stories, "Sweat," as well as selections the younger group expressly chose in an effort to shock, such as Thurman's "Cordelia the Crude" (about prostitution) and Nugent's singular "Smoke, Lilies and Jade" (about homosexual desire). It was no secret that one of the freedoms available in Harlem in the 1920s was sexual; like their peers in Greenwich Village, Black artists uptown took advantage of the license afforded by the Jazz Age to explore desires that transgressed the traditional boundaries of society (whether in terms of race, class, or sexual norms). A number of the writers of the renaissance had homosexual encounters and relationships; some (like the protagonist in Nugent's story) drifted between male and female lovers. Yet the period's atmosphere of exploration remained at best a muted element in their writings—as was the case in American literature as a whole. Nugent was the only important writer of the renaissance who openly identified as homosexual. And *Fire!!*, which was weakly supported by the public and, indeed, by the artists themselves, lasted only one number.

DRAMA, POETRY, FICTION

Many of the younger writers were interested in the theater, but few made it a priority during the most important years of the Harlem Renaissance. The success of *Shuffle Along* in 1921 led to a vogue of such revues and to many imitations of this compendium of song, dance, and humor. However, Black involvement in more traditional drama as part of the renaissance was far more restricted, and less successful. Throughout the 1920s, the best-known dramas of Black life were undoubtedly written by white artists such as Eugene O'Neill and Paul Green of North Carolina. The outstanding Black talent was probably Willis Richardson, whose best-known play is *The Chip Woman's Fortune* (1923), the first serious play by an African American to be staged on Broadway. Richardson was, however, a resident of Washington, D.C., where he had been moved to write plays after seeing, in 1916, Angelina Weld Grimké's highly controversial *Rachel,* about racial persecution and its psychological effects. This controversy, about propaganda versus art, stimulated the theater in Washington but produced few new plays of quality.

In 1926, responding to the dearth of serious drama in New York involving Blacks, Du Bois established the Krigwa Little Theatre movement. He asserted four basic principles: "The plays of a real Negro theatre must be: 1. *About us.* That is, they must have plots which reveal Negro life as it is. 2. *By us.* That is, they must be written by Negro authors who understand from birth and continual association just what it means to be a Negro today." The other principles called for the theater to be *"For us"*—catering mainly to Black audiences, and *"Near us"*—that is, in a Black neighborhood "near the masses of ordinary Negro people." But the first two Krigwa productions, *Compromise* and *The Broken Banjo,* were by Willis Richardson, and Krigwa failed to inspire any important young New York playwrights. In the 1930s, Langston Hughes would emphasize drama with some success, and his play about the South and miscegenation, *Mulatto* (1935), would have the longest run of any play by an African American on Broadway until Lorraine Hansberry's *A Raisin in the Sun* in the 1960s. Nevertheless, drama was almost certainly one of the weakest areas of achievement in the Harlem Renaissance. At the same time, the period saw the emergence of a brilliant generation of Black stage performers who flourished in plays (often by white authors such as Eugene O'Neill and DuBose Heyward), musicals, or revues (evening-length theatrical productions featuring suites of musical numbers, dance performances, comedy, and dramatic sketches), including Charles Gilpin, Opal Cooper, Rose McClendon, Ethel Waters, Nina Mae McKinney, Canada Lee, and above all Paul Robeson. A number of these figures were prominent Harlem presences, and as such very much part of the scene of the renaissance.

Around 1928, the emphasis seemed to shift decisively away from poetry toward fiction. Poets such as Cullen, Hughes, Bontemps, Waring Cuney, Anne Spencer, and Helene Johnson continued to publish in magazines, but far fewer books of verse appeared; perhaps the only notable event of this sort was the appearance of Sterling Brown's folk-inflected *Southern Road* in 1932. In 1928 came Du Bois's novel *Dark Princess,* which was in large part his attempt to exemplify the idealistic, politically engaged fiction he preferred. More authentic that year to the mood of the age, however, were Rudolph Fisher's *The Walls of Jericho;* Nella Larsen's *Quicksand,* about one woman's chronic unhappiness and her descent into a self-imposed, tawdry marriage; and Claude McKay's epochal *Home to Harlem,* which celebrated the pleasures as well as the complexities of Black urban life.

Still later in the renaissance came other novels by McKay, Jessie Fauset, and Thurman, including the latter's *The Blacker the Berry* (1929), about skin-color fixation within the Black community, a subject also of interest to Nella Larsen, as in her *Passing* (1929). In 1930 came Langston Hughes's *Not without Laughter,* about a young boy growing up in the Midwest. Arna Bontemps turned from poetry to write his first novel, *God Sends Sunday* (1931), based on the life of a beloved, fun-loving uncle whose approach to living contrasted with the strictness of Bontemps's Seventh Day Adventist religion. Also in 1931, the satirist George Schuyler, whose 1926 essay in the *Nation,* "The Negro-Art Hokum," ridiculing African American race consciousness, had provoked Hughes's "Negro Artist and the Racial Mountain," published the satirical novel *Black No More.* Satire was prominent again in Wallace Thurman's novel *Infants of the Spring* (1932), in which major figures are easily recognizable under thin disguises, as Thurman lampooned many of the excesses and posturings of the Harlem Renaissance.

THE GREAT DEPRESSION AND THE DECLINE OF THE HARLEM RENAISSANCE

Although it is convenient and even accurate to include Hurston's lyrical 1937 novel about one woman's growth into mature self-confidence and self-fulfillment, *Their Eyes Were Watching God,* within the boundaries of the movement, it is also clear that by that year the movement was finished, although the talent of many of its writers was hardly exhausted. The Harlem Renaissance had depended in large part on a special prosperity in the publishing industry, the theater, and the art world. The crash of Wall Street in 1929 was the beginning of the end for the movement, which swiftly declined as the country lurched toward the Great Depression in the early 1930s. Conditions for Blacks in New York City, and especially for Blacks in Harlem, made a mockery of the heady enthusiasms that had led to the characterization of the 1920s as the Jazz Age, an era of reckless fun. Unemployment and the rise of crime (although the latter was mild compared with conditions a half century later) damaged the image and the reality of Harlem as an artistic and cultural paradise. A civic explosion, often called the Harlem Riot of 1935, underscored the radically altered nature of the district and the lives of the people there.

The renaissance was over, to be revived in significantly different forms at later points in African American history. What did it achieve? Some critics, skeptical of the role of patronage and insistent on more militant and radical political approaches, have suggested that the movement achieved little. Such a view may be short-sighted, however. The art of the Harlem Renaissance—in poetry, fiction, drama, music, painting, and sculpture—represents a prodigious achievement for a people hardly more than a half-century removed from slavery and enmeshed in the chains of a dehumanizing segregation. In this movement, Black American artists took stock of the lives and destinies of their people against the backdrop not only of the United States but also of the world. A sense of the modern overhangs the period, although the African American approach to the modern was in many ways distinct from the pessimism and even despair of European attitudes to the same large topic. To look at it from another angle, the Harlem Renaissance can be understood as a conversation (and at times, a debate) among African American artists and intellectuals about the meaning of modernity from a Black perspective. This is readily apparent, for instance, in invocations of the period's touchstone figure of the "New Negro," which was defined in a dizzying variety of ways in the early twentieth century, from Booker T. Washington's sober advocate of respectability and self-help (on display in the 1900 volume *A New Negro for a New Century*) to W. E. B. Du Bois's progressive "Talented Tenth" vanguard, from the militant socialist "New Negro" espoused in the *Messenger* to Marcus Garvey's paragon of race consciousness and vindication.

In this period, Black American artists laid the foundations for the representation of their people in the modern world, with a complexity and a self-knowledge that proved durable even as the African American condition changed considerably with the unfolding of the twentieth century. Although there were occasional references to the "Harlem Renaissance" during the 1920s—for example, in a review of Du Bose Heyward's *Mamba's Daughters* published in the March 3, 1929 *Macon Telegraph*, the critic A. B. Bernd wrote that the novel "sketched the progress of the Harlem Renaissance"—the phrase became the predominant designation for the period only years later, in hindsight, through the influence of scholarship such as John Hope Franklin's masterful 1947 overview of African American history, *From Slavery to Freedom*. But the term *renaissance* is nevertheless entirely appropriate as a description of the remarkable flourishing of Black culture in the 1920s, for in that decade or so a loose but united gathering of Black artists, located most significantly in Harlem, rediscovered the ancient confidence and sense of destiny of their African ancestors and created a body of art on which future writers and musicians and artists might build and in which the masses of Blacks could see their own faces and features accurately and lovingly reflected.

A NIGHT-CLUB MAP OF HARLEM

E. Simms Campbell (1906–1971) drew this pictorial map showing entertainment venues, restaurants, and speakeasy facilities in Harlem. Created at the start of Campbell's career, the map appeared in the inaugural issue (1/18/1933) of *Manhattan*, a weekly periodical for "wakeful New Yorkers." Campbell, who had studied at the Chicago Art Institute, became one of the first successful African American commercial artists. He produced numerous watercolors and cartoons for *Esquire*, *Cosmopolitan*, and *The New Yorker*, among other publications, and illustrated advertisements for everything from waffle mix to shaving cream from the 1930s to the late 1960s. Full of life and humor, Campbell's map displays an insider's knowledge of and affection for Harlem. Every square inch tells a story that makes the viewer want to jump into its world.

The title panel includes the following text: "The stars indicate the places that are open all night. . . . The only important omission is the location of the various speakeasies but since there are about 500 of them you won't have much trouble. . . ."

Below the map appear two captions, in very small type. LEFT: "Points of interest underneath the Harlem Moon: A dozen Marahuana cigarettes guaranteed to give a three-day jag. If the Crab Man says 'Top or Bottom?' (meaning his basket) say 'Bottom' and you'll get a 'shorty of gin.' The white haired apostle who wanders about passing out benedictions and philosophy. Hot Peanuts, the Harlem National Food. When there's no room on the dance floor, they just stand still and shake—that's the 'bump.'" RIGHT: "The café au lait girls which are the color of coffee and cream. The waiters who tap dance to and fro with trays bearing glasses of water (and other liquids) and never spill a drop. The police dogs which the sheiks hire for the Sunday Parade. The eternal Harlem question: 'What's th' number?' meaning 3 Pari-mutuel digits of the seventh race, which all Harlem bets on. Most of the gamblers pick their numbers from dream books."

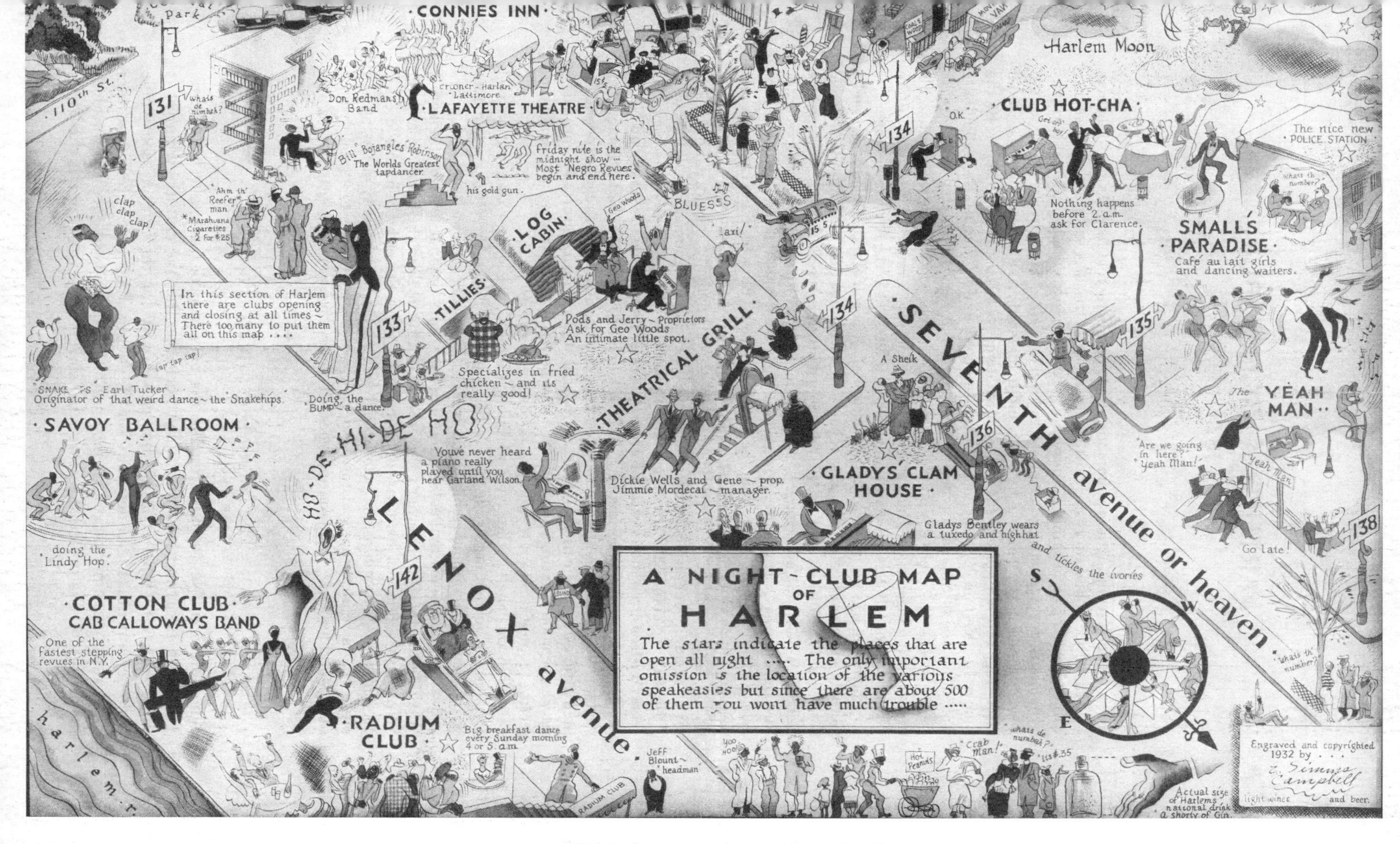
A NIGHT-CLUB MAP OF HARLEM
The stars indicate the places that are open all night ..... The only important omission is the location of the various speakeasies but since there are about 500 of them you wont have much trouble .....
Harlem Moon
110th St.
Park
CONNIES INN
Don Redmans Band
Crooner - Harlan Lattimore
LAFAYETTE THEATRE
Friday nite is the midnight show ... Most Negro Revues begin and end here.
his gold gun.
Bill "Bojangles" Robinson The Worlds Greatest tapdancer.
131
whats de numbah?
Ahm th' Reefer man
*Marahuana Cigarettes 2 for $.25
clap clap clap!
In this section of Harlem there are clubs opening and closing at all times ~ There too many to put them all on this map ....
"SNAKE-HIPS" Earl Tucker Originator of that weird dance ~ the Snakehips.
Doing the "BUMP" ~ a dance.
133
TILLIES
Specializes in fried chicken ~ and its really good!
LOG CABIN
Pods and Jerry ~ Proprietors Ask for Geo Woods An intimate little spot.
Geo Woods
BLUESSS
taxi!
134
O.K.
CLUB HOT-CHA
Nothing happens before 2 a.m. ask for Clarence.
The nice new POLICE STATION
whats th' number?
SMALLS PARADISE
Café au lait girls and dancing waiters.
135
SEVENTH avenue or heaven
The YEAH MAN
"Are we going in here?" "Yeah Man!"
Yeah Man
Go late!
138
whats th' number?
A Sheik
136
THEATRICAL GRILL
Dickie Wells and Gene ~ prop. Jimmie Mordecai ~ manager.
GLADYS' CLAM HOUSE
Gladys Bentley wears a tuxedo and highhat and tickles the ivories
SAVOY BALLROOM
doing the "Lindy Hop."
HO-DE-HI-DE HO
You've never heard a piano really played until you hear Garland Wilson.
LENOX avenue
142
COTTON CLUB CAB CALLOWAYS BAND
One of the fastest stepping revues in N.Y.
RADIUM CLUB
Big breakfast dance every Sunday morning 4 or 5 a.m.
RADIUM CLUB
Jeff Blount ~ "headman"
harlem r.
Yoo Hoo!
Hot Peanuts
"Crab Man!"
whats de numbah?
its $.35
Actual size of Harlems national drink a shorty of Gin
light wines and beer.
Engraved and copyrighted 1932 by E. Simms Campbell
S
W
E

ARTHUR A. SCHOMBURG
1874–1938

As an adolescent, Arthur Schomburg was apparently told by one of his teachers that Blacks had no history. In some respects, the urge to prove this teacher wrong drove the olive-skinned Puerto Rican youth to embrace his African heritage. Schomburg devoted most of his life both to recovering as much of the history of the Black peoples of the world as he could and to disseminating information that would discourage or even prevent such gross misstatements as that of his teacher. By the time of his death in 1938, he had amassed enough material to make the Schomburg Collection one of the major repositories of African American material in the world. In the process, he exerted a powerful influence on his contemporaries, particularly the young intelligentsia of Harlem. He left an enduring example and legacy to future generations of scholars, students, and readers interested in the African heritage.

Schomburg was born in San Juan, Puerto Rico, the son of a Black laundress and a German merchant. After attending school in Puerto Rico and the Virgin Islands, he arrived in New York in 1891. He first developed his research skills while working as a clerk for a New York law firm; politically concerned, he also served as the secretary of Los Dos Antillas, an organization advocating Cuban and Puerto Rican independence. In 1906, he began work in the mail room of the Bankers Trust Company and was soon made chief of the foreign mailing department. He stayed with the company in that capacity until 1929. From his modest salary he not only supported himself and his large family but also built his remarkable collection of documents and drawings.

In 1911, he cofounded the Negro Society for Historical Research, serving as its secretary-treasurer and librarian for several years. By the time the American Negro Academy elected him president in 1922, Schomburg's collection had become fairly well known. In addition to lending out his materials, Schomburg regularly contributed articles to publications interested in African American culture. So enthusiastic was he about sharing his knowledge that he rarely turned down an invitation to lecture, even if it meant traveling at his own expense.

In 1926, on behalf of the New York Public Library, the Carnegie Corporation paid $10,000 for Schomburg's collection of five thousand books, three thousand manuscripts, and two thousand etchings and drawings. The collection included such prizes as manuscript poems by Paul Laurence Dunbar and original texts by Booker T. Washington. In 1932, another grant from Carnegie enabled the library to appoint Schomburg curator of his own collection at its 135th Street branch. In the essay printed here, Schomburg characteristically argues for the necessity of having and preserving a sense of one's history, especially when one belongs to a group whose history and humanity were routinely denied under slavery and segregation.

The Negro Digs Up His Past

The American Negro must remake his past in order to make his future. Though it is orthodox to think of America as the one country where it is unnecessary to have a past, what is a luxury for the nation as a whole becomes a prime social necessity for the Negro. For him, a group tradition must supply compensation for persecution, and pride of race the antidote for prejudice. History must restore what slavery took away, for it is the social damage of slavery that the present generations must repair and offset. So among the rising democratic millions we find the Negro thinking more collectively, more retrospectively than the rest, and apt out of the very pressure of the present to become the most enthusiastic antiquarian of them all.

Vindicating evidences of individual achievement have as a matter of fact been gathered and treasured for over a century: Abbé Gregoire's[1] liberal-minded book on Negro notables in 1808 was the pioneer effort; it has been followed at intervals by less known and often less discriminating compendiums of exceptional men and women of African stock. But this sort of thing was on the whole pathetically over-corrective, ridiculously over-laudatory; it was apologetics turned into biography. A true historical sense develops slowly and with difficulty under such circumstances. But today, even if for the ultimate purpose of group justification, history has become less a matter of argument and more a matter of record. There is the definite desire and determination to have a history, well documented, widely known at least within race circles, and administered as a stimulating and inspiring tradition for the coming generations.

Gradually as the study of the Negro's past has come out of the vagaries of rhetoric and propaganda and become systematic and scientific, three outstanding conclusions have been established:

First, that the Negro has been throughout the centuries of controversy an active collaborator, and often a pioneer, in the struggle for his own freedom and advancement. This is true to a degree which makes it the more surprising that it has not been recognized earlier.

Second, that by virtue of their being regarded as something "exceptional," even by friends and well-wishers, Negroes of attainment and genius have been unfairly disassociated from the group, and group credit lost accordingly.

Third, that the remote racial origins of the Negro, far from being what the race and the world have been given to understand, offer a record of credible group achievement when scientifically viewed, and more important still, that they are of vital general interest because of their bearing upon the beginnings and early development of human culture.

With such crucial truths to document and establish, an ounce of fact is worth a pound of controversy. So the Negro historian today digs under the spot where his predecessor stood and argued. Not long ago, the Public Library of Harlem housed a special exhibition of books, pamphlets, prints and old engravings, that simply said, to skeptic and believer alike, to scholar and schoolchild, to proud black and astonished white, "Here is the evidence." Assembled from the rapidly growing collections of the leading Negro book-collectors and research societies, there were in these cases, materials not only for the first true writing of Negro history, but for the rewriting of many important paragraphs of our common American history. Slow though it be, historical truth is no exception to the proverb.

Here among the rarities of early Negro Americana was Jupiter Hammon's[2] Address to the Negroes of the State of New York, edition of 1787, with the first American Negro poet's famous "If we should ever get to Heaven, we shall find nobody to reproach us for being black, or for being slaves." Here was Phyllis Wheatley's Mss. poem of 1767 addressed to the students of Harvard, her spirited encomiums upon George Washington and

1. Henri Grégoire (1750–1831), French author of *De la littérature des nègres, ou Recherches sur leurs facultés intellectuelles, leurs qualités morales, et leur littérature* (1808).

2. Poet (ca. 1711–ca. 1806).

the Revolutionary Cause,[3] and John Marrant's[4] St. John's Day eulogy to the "Brothers of African Lodge No. 459" delivered at Boston in 1789. Here too were Lemuel Haynes'[5] Vermont commentaries on the American Revolution and his learned sermons to his white congregation in Rutland, Vermont, and the sermons of the year 1808 by the Rev. Absalom Jones of St. Thomas Church, Philadelphia, and Peter Williams of St. Philip's, New York, pioneer Episcopal rectors who spoke out in daring and influential ways on the Abolition of the Slave Trade. Such things and many others are more than mere items of curiosity: they educate any receptive mind.

Reinforcing these were still rarer items of Africana and foreign Negro interest, the volumes of Juan Latino,[6] the best Latinist of Spain in the reign of Philip V, incumbent of the chair of Poetry at the University of Granada, and author of Poems printed there in 1573 and a book on the Escurial[7] published 1576; the Latin and Dutch treatises of Jacobus Eliza Capitein, a native of West Coast Africa and graduate of the University of Leyden, Gustavus Vassa's celebrated autobiography that supplied so much of the evidence in 1796 for Granville Sharpe's attack on slavery in the British colonies, Julien Raymond's Paris exposé of the disabilities of the free people of color in the then (1791) French colony of Hayti, and Baron de Vastey's *Cry of the Fatherland,* the famous polemic by the secretary of Christophe[8] that precipitated the Haytian struggle for independence. The cumulative effect of such evidences of scholarship and moral prowess is too weighty to be dismissed as exceptional.

But weightier surely than any evidence of individual talent and scholarship could ever be, is the evidence of important collaboration and significant pioneer initiative in social service and reform, in the efforts toward race emancipation, colonization and race betterment. From neglected and rust-spotted pages comes testimony to the black men and women who stood shoulder to shoulder in courage and zeal, and often on a parity of intelligence and talent, with their notable white benefactors. There was the already cited work of Vassa that aided so materially the efforts of Granville Sharpe, the record of Paul Cuffee,[9] the Negro colonization pioneer, associated so importantly with the establishment of Sierra Leone as a British colony for the occupancy of free people of color in West Africa; the dramatic and history-making exposé of John Baptist Phillips,[1] African graduate of Edinburgh, who compelled through Lord Bathhurst in 1824 the enforcement of the articles of capitulation guaranteeing freedom to the blacks of Trinidad. There is the record of the pioneer colonization project of Rev. Daniel Coker in conducting a voyage of ninety expatriates to West Africa in 1820, of the missionary efforts of Samuel Crowther in Sierra Leone, first Anglican bishop of his diocese, and that of the work of John Russwurm, a leader in the work and foundation of the American Colonization Society.

When we consider the facts, certain chapters of American history will have to be reopened. Just as black men were influential factors in the

3. Wheatley's poem to Harvard is titled "To the University of Cambridge, in New England" and her poem to Washington, "To His Excellency General Washington."
4. Born 1755.
5. Haynes (1753–1833), a New England minister popular with white and Black congregations, published his sermon "Universal Salvation" in 1806.
6. Latino (ca. 1518–1594).
7. A palace and monastery outside Madrid.
8. Henri Christophe (1767–1820), king of Haiti from 1811 to 1820. Capitein (1717–1747), author of *De Vocatione Ethnicorum* (1737) and a thesis defending slavery (1742). Vassa (ca. 1745–1797), formerly named Olaudah Equiano, wrote his autobiographical *Interesting Narrative* in 1789. Granville Sharp (1735–1813), a leading British abolitionist. Vastey (d. 1820), author of *Le Cri de la Patrie* (1815).
9. Cuffee (ca. 1758–1817).
1. Phillips (1799–1851).

campaign against the slave trade, so they were among the earliest instigators of the abolition movement. Indeed there was a dangerous calm between the agitation for the suppression of the slave trade and the beginning of the campaign for emancipation. During that interval colored men were very influential in arousing the attention of public men who in turn aroused the conscience of the country. Continuously between 1808 and 1845, men like Prince Saunders, Peter Williams, Absalom Jones, Nathaniel Paul, and Bishops Varick and Richard Allen,[2] the founders of the two wings of African Methodism, spoke out with force and initiative, and men like Denmark Vesey (1822), David Walker (1828) and Nat Turner[3] (1831) advocated and organized schemes for direct action. This culminated in the generally ignored but important conventions of Free People of Color in New York, Philadelphia and other centers, whose platforms and efforts are to the Negro of as great significance as the nationally cherished memories of Faneuil and Independence Halls.[4] Then with Abolition comes the better documented and more recognized collaboration of Samuel R. Ward, William Wells Brown, Henry Highland Garnett, Martin Delany, Harriet Tubman, Sojourner Truth, and Frederick Douglass[5] with their great colleagues, Tappan, Phillips, Sumner, Mott, Stowe and Garrison.[6]

But even this latter group[7] who came within the limelight of national and international notice, and thus into open comparison with the best minds of their generation, the public too often regards as a group of inspired illiterates, eloquent echoes of their Abolitionist sponsors. For a true estimate of their ability and scholarship, however, one must go with the antiquarian to the files of the *Anglo-African Magazine,* where page by page comparisons may be made. Their writings show Douglass, McCune Smith, Wells Brown, Delany, Wilmot Blyden and Alexander Crummell[8] to have been as scholarly and versatile as any of the noted publicists with whom they were associated. All of them labored internationally in the cause of their fellows; to Scotland, England, France, Germany and Africa, they carried their brilliant offensive of debate and propaganda, and with this came instance upon instance of signal foreign recognition, from academic, scientific, public and official sources. Delany's *Principia of Ethnology* won public reception from learned societies, Pennington's[9] discourses an honorary doctorate from Heidelberg, Wells Brown's three year mission the entrée of the salons of London and Paris, and the tours of Frederick Douglass, receptions second only to Henry Ward Beecher's.[1]

After this great era of public interest and discussion, it was Alexander Crummell, who, with the reaction already setting in, first organized Negro brains defensively through the founding of the American Negro Academy in 1897 at Washington. A New York boy whose zeal for education had suffered

2. Allen (ca. 1750–1831). Saunders (1775–1839). Paul (1775–1834). James Varick (ca. 1750–1827).
3. Turner (1800–1831) and Vesey (1767?–1822) both led conspiracies among enslaved people to revolt in the South. Walker (1785–1830) published his *Appeal to the Colored Citizens of the World* in 1829.
4. Independence Hall (in Philadelphia) hosted both the Second Constitutional Congress and the federal convention of 1787. Faneuil Hall was the meeting place for the participants in the Boston Tea Party incident of 1773.
5. Brown (1815–1884), Garnet (1815–1882), Tubman (ca. 1820–1913), Sojourner Truth (ca. 1775–1883), and Douglass (1818–1895) escaped enslavement and joined Delany (1812–1885), a free man of the North, in fighting slavery.
6. Arthur Tappan (1786–1865), Wendell Phillips (1811–1884), Lucretia Mott (1793–1880), and William Lloyd Garrison (1805–1879) were prominent abolitionists. Charles Sumner (1811–1874), an important Radical Republican during the Reconstruction era. Harriet Beecher Stowe (1811–1896), author of *Uncle Tom's Cabin.*
7. That is, Ward, Brown, etc.
8. Crummell (1819–1898). James McCune Smith (1813–1865). Blyden (1832–1912).
9. James Pennington (1809–1870).
1. A prominent abolitionist (1813–1887).

a rude shock when refused admission to the Episcopal Seminary by Bishop Onderdonk, he had been befriended by John Jay[2] and sent to Cambridge University, England, for his education and ordination. On his return, he was beset with the idea of promoting race scholarship, and the Academy was the final result. It has continued ever since to be one of the bulwarks of our intellectual life, though unfortunately its members have had to spend too much of their energy and effort answering detractors and disproving popular fallacies. Only gradually have the men of this group been able to work toward pure scholarship. Taking a slightly different start, The Negro Society for Historical Research[3] was later organized in New York, and has succeeded in stimulating the collection from all parts of the world of books and documents dealing with the Negro. It has also brought together for the first time cooperatively in a single society African, West Indian and Afro-American scholars. Direct offshoots of this same effort are the extensive private collections[4] of Henry P. Slaughter of Washington, the Rev. Charles D. Martin of Harlem, of Arthur Schomburg of Brooklyn, and of the late John E. Bruce, who was the enthusiastic and far-seeing pioneer of this movement. Finally and more recently, the Association for the Study of Negro Life and History has extended these efforts into a scientific research project of great achievement and promise. Under the direction of Dr. Carter G. Woodson,[5] it has continuously maintained for nine years the publication of the learned quarterly, *The Journal of Negro History,* and with the assistance and recognition of two large educational foundations has maintained research and published valuable monographs in Negro history. Almost keeping pace with the work of scholarship has been the effort to popularize the results, and to place before Negro youth in the schools the true story of race vicissitude, struggle and accomplishment. So that quite largely now the ambition of Negro youth can be nourished on its own milk.

Such work is a far cry from the puerile controversy and petty braggadocio with which the effort for race history first started. But a general as well as a racial lesson has been learned. We seem lately to have come at last to realize what the truly scientific attitude requires, and to see that the race issue has been a plague on both our historical houses, and that history cannot be properly written with either bias or counterbias. The blatant Caucasian racialist with his theories and assumptions of race superiority and dominance has in turn bred his Ethiopian counterpart—the rash and rabid amateur who has glibly tried to prove half of the world's geniuses to have been Negroes and to trace the pedigree of nineteenth century Americans from the Queen of Sheba. But fortunately to-day there is on both sides of a really common cause less of the sand of controversy and more of the dust of digging.

Of course, a racial motive remains—legitimately compatible with scientific method and aim. The work our race students now regard as important, they undertake very naturally to overcome in part certain handicaps of disparagement and omission too well-known to particularize. But they do so not merely that we may not wrongfully be deprived of the spiritual nourishment of our cultural past, but also that the full story of human collaboration and interdependence may be told and realized. Especially is this likely to be

2. First U.S. Supreme Court chief justice (1745–1829). Benjamin T. Onderdonk (1791–1861).
3. Founded by Schomburg and John E. Bruce (1856–1924).
4. Schomburg's collection had been purchased by the New York Public Library in 1926, but he continued collecting materials and donating them to the library.
5. Woodson (1875–1950) began editing the *Journal of Negro History* in 1915. He founded Negro History Week, later Black History Month, in 1926.

the effect of the latest and most fascinating of all of the attempts to open up the closed Negro past, namely the important study of African cultural origins and sources. The bigotry of civilization which is the taproot of intellectual prejudice begins far back and must be corrected at its source. Fundamentally it has come about from that depreciation of Africa which has sprung up from ignorance of her true rôle and position in human history and the early development of culture. The Negro has been a man without a history because he has been considered a man without a worthy culture. But a new notion of the cultural attainment and potentialities of the African stocks has recently come about, partly through the corrective influence of the more scientific study of African institutions and early cultural history, partly through growing appreciation of the skill and beauty and in many cases the historical priority of the African native crafts, and finally through the signal recognition which first in France and Germany, but now very generally, the astonishing art of the African sculptures has received. Into these fascinating new vistas, with limited horizons lifting in all directions, the mind of the Negro has leapt forward faster than the slow clearings of scholarship will yet safely permit. But there is no doubt that here is a field full of the most intriguing and inspiring possibilities. Already the Negro sees himself against a reclaimed background, in a perspective that will give pride and self-respect ample scope, and make history yield for him the same values that the treasured past of any people affords.

1925

ANGELINA WELD GRIMKÉ
1880–1958

Few writers of the Harlem Renaissance had a family history as poignant as that of Angelina Grimké. Her paternal great-aunts were southern white abolitionist women—Sarah Moore Grimké and her sister Angelina, who married Theodore Dwight Weld. In a rare example of such honesty, these two independent-minded daughters of a wealthy South Carolina enslaver publicly acknowledged their ties to their brother's sons, Archibald Henry Grimké and Francis James Grimké, who had been born to Henry Grimké and Nancy Weston, a woman enslaved on the Grimkés' Caneacre plantation. Under the sponsorship of his aunts, Archibald took his law degree from Harvard in 1874. In 1879, he married a white woman, Sarah E. Stanley (although her father, a prominent Boston clergyman, opposed the marriage). Angelina Weld Grimké was born to the couple the following year.

The strain of the marriage soon proved too much for Sarah, who abandoned Archibald and Angelina and never saw her daughter again. Angelina, pampered by her father and educated at such liberal institutions as Cushing Academy in Ashburnham, Massachusetts, and Carleton Academy in Northfield, Minnesota, seems to have grown up fairly sheltered from racial discrimination. However, her description of her play *Rachel* (first produced in 1916) indicates that at some point she awoke to the reality of racism: "This is the first attempt to use the stage for race propaganda in order to enlighten the American people relating to the lamentable condition of ten millions of Colored citizens in this free republic."

Graduating from the Boston Normal School of Gymnastics in 1902, Grimké moved to Washington, D.C., where she taught English at the Armstrong Manual Training School until 1916. She then joined the faculty at the distinguished Dunbar High School, remaining there until shortly after her father's death in 1930. By that time, *Rachel* had been hailed, in the words of Alain Locke and Montgomery Gregory, as "apparently the first successful drama written by a Negro and interpreted by Negro actors." Frankly sentimental, it stressed the effects of racism on middle-class Blacks as well as the evil of lynching. Grimké also placed several of her delicate, traditional poems in magazines such as the *Crisis* and *Opportunity,* and in Countee Cullen's timely anthology *Caroling Dusk.* Her most important prose piece, "The Closing Door," reiterates one of the themes of *Rachel* in its insistence on the immorality of bringing Black children—particularly Black males—into a world that does not want them and is likely to warp or destroy them. The story ends with a hysterical Black woman killing the Black boy to whom she has just given birth in order to prevent the possibility of his dying at the hands of a lynch mob at some future date.

In her important study of Grimké, Gloria Hull suggests that Grimké's adult life was unhappy because of an overdependence on her father and possible repression of an attraction to women. After her father's death, Grimké's sense of direction seemed to leave her. She moved to New York, claiming that she intended to write, but nothing came of it. Apart from the friendship she kept up with the Washington poet Georgia Douglas Johnson, her remaining years seem to have been relatively desolate. Nevertheless, although her reputation rests mainly on a few lyric pieces repeatedly anthologized in collections of African American literature of the 1920s, that reputation seems likely to endure because of the refinement of her lyric sensibility and her consciousness as a woman and an artist in a literary culture then dominated by male writers.

A Winter Twilight

A silence slipping around like death,
Yet chased by a whisper, a sigh, a breath;
One group of trees, lean, naked and cold,
Inking their crest 'gainst a sky green-gold;
One path that knows where the corn flowers were;
Lonely, apart, unyielding, one fir;
And over it softly leaning down,
One star that I loved ere the fields went brown.

1923

The Black Finger

I have just seen a beautiful thing
    Slim and still,
Against a gold, gold sky,
    A straight cypress,
    Sensitive
    Exquisite,
A black finger
Pointing upwards.
Why, beautiful, still finger are you black?
And why are you pointing upwards?

1925

When the Green Lies over the Earth

When the green lies over the earth, my dear,
A mantle of witching° grace, *bewitching*
When the smile and the tear of the young child year
Dimple across its face,
And then flee, when the wind all day is sweet
With the breath of growing things,
When the wooing bird lights on restless feet
And chirrups and trills and sings
    To his lady-love
    In the green above,
Then oh! my dear, when the youth's in the year,
Yours is the face that I long to have near,
    Yours is the face, my dear.

But the green is hiding your curls, my dear,
Your curls so shining and sweet;
And the gold-hearted daisies this many a year
Have bloomed and bloomed at your feet,
And the little birds just above your head
With their voices hushed, my dear,
For you have sung and have prayed and have pled
    This many, many a year.
    And the blossoms fall,
    On the garden wall,
And drift like snow on the green below.
    But the sharp thorn grows
    On the budding rose,
And my heart no more leaps at the sunset glow,
For oh! my dear, when the youth's in the year,
Yours is the face that I long to have near,
Yours is the face, my dear.

1927

Tenebris°

in darkness (Latin)

There is a tree, by day,
That, at night,
Has a shadow,
A hand huge and black,
With fingers long and black.
    All through the dark,
Against the white man's house,
    In the little wind,
The black hand plucks and plucks
    At the bricks.
The bricks are the color of blood and very small.
    Is it a black hand,
    Or is it a shadow?

1927

ANNE SPENCER
1882–1975

Of the poetry of the Harlem Renaissance, Anne Spencer's work is perhaps the most modernist, not least of all in its enigmatic, allusive quality and its emphasis on privacy of vision. She wrote sparingly but to distinct effect, much as she cultivated the garden that became the focus of her life. Spencer and her husband, Edward, planted the garden in the backyard of their home in Lynchburg, Virginia, where they settled in 1901, two years after their graduation from the Virginia Seminary. During those two years Anne Spencer (born Annie Bethel Bannister) had taught public school in the Bramwell, West Virginia, area, which she knew well. Her mother, Sarah Scales, had taken her there after separating from Anne's father in 1887.

Though she began writing poetry at the Virginia Seminary, Spencer did not publish until 1920, after James Weldon Johnson accidentally learned of her writing while staying at her home during a trip on NAACP business (local Blacks had decided to form a chapter of the organization). He cajoled Spencer into allowing "Before the Feast of Shushan" to be published in the *Crisis*. He also introduced her to the celebrated editor of *American Mercury* magazine, H. L. Mencken; but she rejected Mencken's help because she denied his right (as a nonpoet) to criticize her work. Although most of her verse is about nature, Spencer's best poetry, marked by the irony and some of the complexity typical of literary modernism, tends to be more concerned with gender than with race. The 1920s saw her publish in such magazines as *Survey Graphic, Palms, Opportunity,* and *Lyric* as well as in a number of important anthologies, including Johnson's *Book of American Negro Poetry* and Countee Cullen's *Caroling Dusk*. However, fewer than thirty of her poems were published during her lifetime, and only one of those, a tribute to Johnson called "For Jim, Easter Eve," appeared after Johnson's untimely death in 1938.

After Johnson's death, fewer callers came to the Spencer home, which Claude McKay, W. E. B. Du Bois, Langston Hughes, Georgia Douglas Johnson, Paul Robeson, and many others had visited. Her husband's death in 1964 made Spencer a virtual recluse, and she stopped tending her beloved garden. She spent the last years of her life revising her poems in her own way, which often meant jotting down whatever alterations occurred to her on the scrap of paper nearest to hand. During her last illness in 1975, her friends, unable to make anything of these scraps, apparently discarded them. She died later that year in Lynchburg. Her home, its garden restored, has since been accorded the status of historic landmark. This is an appropriate honor. Spencer's voice as a poet was distinctive, assured, and complex; it deserves further study and appreciation.

Before the Feast of Shushan[1]

Garden of Shushan!
After Eden, all terrace, pool, and flower recollect thee:
Ye weavers in saffron and haze and Tyrian purple,[2]
Tell yet what range in color wakes the eye;
Sorcerer, release the dreams born here when
Drowsy, shifting palm-shade enspells the brain;
And sound! ye with harp and flute ne'er essay
Before these star-noted birds escaped from paradise awhile to
Stir all dark, and dear, and passionate desire, till mine
Arms go out to be mocked by the softly kissing body of the wind—
Slave, send Vashti to her King!

The fiery wattles of the sun startle into flame
The marbled towers of Shushan:
So at each day's wane, two peers—the one in
Heaven, the other on earth—welcome with their
Splendor the peerless beauty of the Queen.

Cushioned at the Queen's feet and upon her knee
Finding glory for mine head,—still, nearly shamed
Am I, the King, to bend and kiss with sharp
Breath the olive-pink of sandaled toes between;
Or lift me high to the magnet of a gaze, dusky,
Like the pool when but the moon-ray strikes to its depth;
Or closer press to crush a grape 'gainst lips redder
Than the grape, a rose in the night of her hair;
Then—Sharon's Rose[3] in my arms.

And I am hard to force the petals wide;
And you are fast to suffer and be sad.
Is any prophet come to teach a new thing
Now in a more apt time?
Have him 'maze how you say love is sacrament;
How says Vashti, love is both bread and wine;
How to the altar may not come to break and drink,
Hulky flesh nor fleshly spirit!

I, thy lord, like not manna for meat as a Judahn;[4]
I, thy master, drink, and red wine, plenty, and when
I thirst. Eat meat, and full, when I hunger.
I, thy King, teach you and leave you, when I list.
No woman in all Persia sets out strange action

1. This reflective monologue is based on an incident in the Book of Esther (1:2–12): "When the king Ahasuerus sat on the throne of his kingdom, which was in Shushan the palace, . . . he made a feast unto all his princes and his servants. . . . Also Vashti the queen made a feast for the women in the royal house which belonged to king Ahasuerus. On the seventh day, when the heart of the king was merry with wine, he commanded . . . the seven chamberlains that served [him] to bring Vashti the queen before the king with the crown royal, to shew the people and the princes her beauty: for she was fair to look on. But the queen Vashti refused to come at the king's commandment by his chamberlains: therefore was the king very wroth, and his anger burned in him."

2. Tyre was famous in antiquity for its purple dyes.

3. See Song of Solomon 2:1: "I am the rose of Sharon, and the lily of the valleys."

4. See Exodus 16:13–36.

To confuse Persia's lord—
Love is but desire and thy purpose fulfillment;
I, thy King, so say!

1920

The Wife-Woman[1]

Maker-of-Sevens[2] in the scheme of things
From earth to star;
Thy cycle holds whatever is fate, and
Over the border the bar.
Though rank and fierce the mariner
Sailing the seven seas,
He prays, as he holds his glass to his eyes,
Coaxing the Pleiades.[3]

I cannot love them; and I feel your glad
Chiding from the grave,
That my all was only worth at all, what
Joy to you it gave,
These seven links the *Law*[4] compelled
For the human chain—
I cannot love *them*; and *you*, oh,
Seven-fold months in Flanders[5] slain!

A jungle there, a cave here, bred six
And a million years,
Sure and strong, mate for mate, such
Love as culture fears;
I gave you clear the oil and wine;
You saved me your hob[6] and hearth—
See how *even* life may be ere the
Sickle comes and leaves a swath.

But I can wait the seven of moons,
Or years I spare,
Hoarding the heart's plenty, nor spend
A drop, nor share—
So long but outlives a smile and
A silken gown;
Then gayly I reach up from my shroud,
And you, glory-clad, reach down.

1931

1. The poem is written from the point of view of a woman with seven children who has lost her husband in World War I.
2. The god of luck.
3. A cluster of stars named after the seven daughters of Atlas, although only six stars are visible.
4. From the Old Testament, particularly "Be fruitful, and multiply" (Genesis 1:28). "Seven links": the speaker's children.
5. A region comprising western Belgium, northern France, and southwestern Netherlands; the site of prolonged fighting in World War I.
6. A shelf on the side of a fireplace used for keeping food warm.

HUBERT HARRISON
1883–1927

In a 1923 article in the *Amsterdam News*, William Pickens wrote that "it is not possible that Socrates could have outdone Hubert Harrison in making the most commonplace subject interesting. Here is a plain Black man who can speak more easily, effectively and interestingly, on a greater variety of subjects than any other man we have ever met, even in any of the great universities." The greatest soapbox orator in 1920s Harlem, Harrison was also a pioneering socialist organizer, a dazzling autodidact, an indefatigable editor and writer, and the "father of Negro radicalism," the major inspiration for the entire generation of Black intellectuals who emerged after World War I, from Marcus Garvey to Claude McKay to A. Philip Randolph. As Randolph observed simply: "Hubert Harrison was far more advanced than we were."

Both of Harrison's working-class parents died when he was young; after migrating to New York from his birthplace, St. Croix in the Danish West Indies, Harrison was forced to take a series of menial jobs (messenger, elevator operator, stock clerk, bellhop) to support himself while he attended high school at night. Nonetheless his intellectual gifts and fierce determination were immediately apparent. Omnivorous and free-thinking, with an extraordinary memory, he read constantly even outside of school, immersing himself in classic works in history, religion, philosophy, politics, and literature. Nor was he afraid to speak his mind in public. In late 1904, he sent a letter to the editor of the *New York Times* in which he criticized the paper for inflaming racial tensions with an editorial that referred to African Americans as "chicken-stealers." He was only a twenty-one-year-old fresh out of night school, but already his writing displayed a humor and devastating logic that would become characteristic: "I, as a Negro, can have no objection to a bit of news that reports a Jersey Negro, or many Jersey Negroes, as being dexterous stealers of chicken; but I strongly object to the sweeping opinion of any newspaper that we are a race of thieves—either of fowls or anything else." By the end of the decade he was publishing articles and reviews in the *Times* and elsewhere.

Unable to afford college, Harrison passed the exam for the postal service and settled in Harlem, but when in 1910 he published an article in the *New York Sun* criticizing Booker T. Washington, a politician beholden to Washington's infamous "Tuskegee Machine" connived to have Harrison fired. Harrison was subsequently hired to organize Blacks by the Socialist Party of New York and founded a colored Socialist Club in Harlem. He also wrote a five-part series of articles on "The Negro and Socialism" for the *New York Call* in which he contended that "the crucial test of Socialism's sincerity" would be its commitment to the cause of African American advancement. By 1913, Harrison was a featured speaker at Socialist events such as the famous Paterson, New Jersey, silk strike (where he appeared with "Big Bill" Haywood and Elizabeth Gurley Flynn), but already he was beginning to rail in public against entrenched racism in the party. By May 1914 he was suspended for his public complaints; Harrison left the Socialist Party soon thereafter, and began teaching at the Ferrer Modern School and giving street lectures on various topics.

He began to promote the idea of "Race First," and in the summer of 1917 immediately after the brutal race riots in East St. Louis, Illinois (in which African Americans defended themselves against unprovoked attacks by white mobs), Harrison founded the Liberty League at a meeting at Harlem's Bethel African Methodist Episcopal Church, where one of the speakers was a relatively unknown Jamaican named Marcus Garvey. Reflecting on the events in East St. Louis, Harrison argued

Unidentified streetcorner orator, 1938. Harrison was the most famous of the dozens of street speakers who, lecturing from a stepladder or soapbox, drew large crowds in Harlem throughout the period, especially along Lenox and Seventh avenues.

in powerful language that they demonstrated a new "temper" among the Black population: "If white men are to kill unoffending Negroes, Negroes must kill white men in defense of their lives and property."

Harrison published two books, *The Negro and the Nation* (1917) and *When Africa Awakes* (1920). Both were largely compilations of his brilliant newspaper writing. He was a master of the short form (the editorial, the review), and as Garvey's UNIA began to receive popular support, Harrison came to play a crucial role as the editor of the *Negro World*. He completely redesigned the paper and almost single-handedly launched a section of book and theater reviews. Very quickly, however, he became disillusioned with Garvey, incensed at his flamboyant megalomania, his compulsive self-aggrandizement and hunger for publicity, and his organizational sloppiness.

In 1923 Harrison took a position as a roving lecturer with the New York City Board of Education while continuing to publish on a remarkable breadth of topics. Two years later he founded another short-lived organization, the International Colored Unity League, and briefly edited a new journal called the *Voice of the Negro* before he died suddenly in 1927, reportedly from complications of appendicitis.

Harrison had a deep knowledge of literature and wrote many book reviews. But he was not seduced by the Harlem Renaissance, which he considered a mirage, at best a "fool's paradise" of promotional hot air. In his most devastating dismissal, a 1927 article in the *Pittsburgh Courier*, he dubbed the renaissance the "Cabaret School," a product of whites convinced that the Negro "existed to furnish entertainment to others." These white "discoverers of 'The New Negro,'" Harrison wrote, sought whatever was "quaint, queer, odd, bizarre and different," and built a pseudo-movement on that premise: "The grotesques antics of bibulous balloons furnished the esthetic principles upon which a 'new' art for the New Negro was predicated." When younger Black artists such as Zora Neale Hurston, Langston Hughes, and Helene Johnson pander to these stereotypes, Harrison wrote, they "often mistake the language of the gutter for the language of the common people and, since, 'spice' rhymes with 'nice,' they sometimes think that they are nifty when they are only being nasty." And despite all the noise and attention, for Harrison the real crime was that "nine-tenths of Negro life is still unrepresented by the artists of the Cabaret School, still waiting for those who have gumption and courage enough to eschew the namby-pamby colored Brahmins and the seductions of the midnight maniacs from downtown."

The East St. Louis Horror

This nation is now at war to make the world "safe for democracy,"[1] but the Negro's contention in the court of public opinion is that until this nation itself is made safe for twelve million of its subjects the Negro, at least, will refuse to believe in the democratic assertions of the country. The East St. Louis pogrom[2] gives point to this contention. Here, on the eve of the celebration of the Nation's birthday of freedom and equality, the white people, who are denouncing the Germans as Huns and barbarians, break loose in an orgy of unprovoked and villainous barbarism which neither Germans nor any other civilized people have ever equalled.

How can America hold up its hands in hypocritical horror at foreign barbarism while the red blood of the Negro is clinging to those hands? So long as the President and Congress of the United States remain dumb in the presence of barbarities in their own land which would tip their tongues with righteous indignation if they had been done in Belgium, Ireland, or Galicia?

And what are the Negroes to do? Are they expected to re-echo with enthusiasm the patriotic protestations of the boot-licking leaders whose pockets and positions testify to the power of the white man's gold? Let there be no mistake. Whatever the Negroes may be compelled by law to do and say, the resentment in their hearts will not down. Unbeknown to the white people of this land a temper is being developed among Negroes with which the American people will have to reckon.

At the present moment it takes this form: If white men are to kill unoffending Negroes, Negroes must kill white men in defense of their lives and property. This is the lesson of the East St. Louis massacre.

The press reports declare that "the troops who were on duty during the most serious disturbances were ordered not to shoot." The civil and military authorities are evidently winking at the work of the mobs—horrible as that was—and the Negroes of the city need not look to them for protection. They must protect themselves. And even the United States Supreme Court concedes them this right.

There is, in addition, a method of retaliation which we urge upon them. It is one which will hit those white men who have the power to prevent lawlessness just where they will feel it most, in the place where they keep their

1. On April 2, 1917, President Woodrow Wilson gave an address to a joint session of Congress requesting a Declaration of War against Germany in order that the world "be made safe for democracy."

2. Race riots erupted in East St. Louis on July 2, 1917, when whites, anxious over jobs and angry at the perceived competition from thousands of Blacks who had recently migrated there from the South, attacked Black neighborhoods, killing between 40 and 200 people and inflicting major property damage. Armed Blacks defended themselves with violence, and at least 9 whites were killed. The events in East St. Louis were the first and bloodiest in a series of racial clashes across the country in cities including Houston, Texas (1917), Knoxville, Tennessee (1919), Washington, D.C. (1919), Chicago, Illinois (1919), Omaha, Nebraska (1919), and Longview, Texas (1919).

consciences—the pocket-book. Let every Negro in East St. Louis and the other cities where race rioting occurs draw his money from the savings-bank and either bank it in the other cities or in the postal savings bank. The only part of the news reports with which we are well pleased is that which states that the property loss is already estimated at a million and a half dollars.

Another reassuring feature is the one suppressed in most of the news despatches. We refer to the evidences that the East St. Louis Negroes organized themselves during the riots and fought back under some kind of leadership. We Negroes will never know, perhaps, how many whites were killed by our enraged brothers in East St. Louis. It isn't the news-policy of the white newspapers (whether friendly or unfriendly) to spread such news broadcast. It might teach Negroes too much. But we will hope for the best.

The occurrence should serve to enlarge rapidly the membership of the Liberty League of Negro-Americans which was organized to take practical steps to help our people all over the land in the protection of their lives and liberties.

1917

Two Negro Radicalisms

Twenty years ago all Negroes known to the white publicists of America could be classed as conservatives on all the great questions on which thinkers differ. In matters of industry, commerce, politics, religion, they could be trusted to take the backward view. Only on the question of the Negro's "rights" could a small handful be found bold enough to be tagged as "radicals"—and they were howled down by both the white and colored adherents of the conservative point of view. Today Negroes differ on all those great questions on which white thinkers differ, and there are Negro radicals of every imaginable stripe—agnostics, atheists, I.W.W.'s, Socialists, Single Taxers,[1] and even Bolshevists.

In the good old days white people derived their knowledge of what Negroes were doing from those Negroes who were nearest to them, generally their own selected exponents of Negro activity or of their white point of view. A classic illustration of this kind of knowledge was afforded by the Republican Party; but the Episcopal Church, the Urban League, or the U.S. Government would serve as well. To-day the white world is vaguely, but disquietingly, aware that Negroes are awake, different and perplexingly uncertain. Yet the white world by which they are surrounded retains its traditional method of interpreting the mass by the Negro nearest to themselves in affiliation or contact. The Socialist party thinks that the "unrest" now apparent in the Negro masses is due to the propaganda which its adherents support, and believes that it will function largely along the lines of socialist political thought. The great dailies, concerned mainly with their

1. Proponents of the movement associated with the writings of the economist Henry George (1839–1897), who advocated the idea of a single tax on the value of land. "I.W.W's": the Industrial Workers of the World, known as the "Wobblies," an international union founded in 1905.

chosen task of being the mental bellwethers of the mob, scream "Bolshevist propaganda" and flatter themselves that they have found the true cause; while the government's unreliable agents envisage it as "disloyalty." The truth, as usual, is to be found in the depths: but they are all prevented from going by mental laziness and that traditional off-handed, easy contempt with which white men in America, from scholars like Lester Ward to scavengers like Stevenson,[2] deign to consider the colored population of 12 millions.

In the first place the cause of the "radicalism" among American Negroes is international. But it is necessary to cause clear distinctions at the outset. The function of the Christian church is international. So is art, war, the family, rum and exploitation of labor. But none of these is entitled to extend the mantle of its own peculiar "internationalism" to cover the present case of the Negro discontent—although this has been attempted. The international Fact to which Negroes in America are now reacting is not the exploitation of laborers by capitalists; but the social, political and economic subjection of colored peoples by white. It is not the Class Line, but the Color line, which is the incorrect but accepted expression for the Dead Line of racial inferiority. This fact is a fact of Negro consciousness as well as a fact of externals. The international Color Line is the practice and theory of that doctrine which holds that the best stocks of Africa, China, Egypt and the West Indies are inferior to the worst stocks of Belgium, England, and Italy, and must hold their lives, lands and liberties upon such terms and conditions as the white races may choose to grant them.

On the part of the whites, the motive was originally economic; but it is no longer purely so. All the available facts go to prove that, whether in the United States or in Africa or China, the economic subjection is without exception keener and more brutal when the exploited are black, brown and yellow, than when they are white. And the fact that black, brown, and yellow also exploit each other brutally whenever Capitalism has created the economic classes of plutocrat and proletarian should suffice to put purely economic subjection out of court as the prime cause of racial unrest. For the similarity of suffering has produced in all lands where whites rule colored races a certain similarity of sentiment, viz: a racial revulsion of racial feeling. The peoples of those lands begin to feel and realize that they are so subjected because they are members of races condemned as "inferior" by their Caucasian overlords. The fact presented to their minds is one of race, and in terms of race do they react to it. Put the case to any Negro by way of test and the answer will make this clear.

The great World War, by virtue of its great advertising campaign for democracy and the promises which were held out to subject peoples, fertilized the Race Consciousness of the Negro people into the stage of conflict with the dominant white idea of the Color Line. They took democracy at its face value—which is—Equality. So did the Hindus, Egyptians, and West Indians. This is what the hypocritical advertisers of democracy had not bargained for. The American Negroes, like the other darker peoples, are presenting their checques and trying to "cash in," and delays in that process,

2. Archibald E. Stevenson (1884–1961), lawyer who wrote the New York State Senate Lusk Committee report (1920) on "seditious activities," leading to police raids of Communist and Socialist organizations. Lester F. Ward (1841–1913), American sociologist.

however unavoidable to the paying tellers, are bound to beget a plentiful lack of belief in either their intention or in their ability to pay. Hence the run on Democracy's bank—"the Negro unrest" of the newspaper paragraphers.

This Race Consciousness takes many forms, some negative, others positive. On the one hand we balk at Jim Crow, object to educational starvation, refuse to accept good-will for good deeds, and scornfully reject our conservative leaders. On the other hand, we are seeking racial independence in business and reaching out into new fields of endeavor. One of the most taking enterprises at present is the Black Star Line, a steamship enterprise being floated by Mr. Marcus Garvey of New York. Garvey's project (whatever may be its ultimate fate) has attracted tens of thousands of Negroes. Where Negro "radicals" of the type known to white radicals can scarce get a handful of people, Garvey fills the largest halls and the Negro people rain money on him. This is not to be explained by the argument of "superior brains," for this man's education and intelligence are markedly inferior to those of the brilliant "radicals" whose "internationalism" is drawn from other than racial sources. But this man holds up to the Negro masses those things which bloom in their hearts—racialism, race-consciousness, racial solidarity—things taught first in 1917 by *THE VOICE* and The Liberty League. That is the secret of his success so far.

All over this land and in the West Indies Negroes are responding to the call of battle against the white man's Color Line. And, so long as this remains, the international dogma of the white race, so long will the new Negro war against it. This is the very Ethiopianism which England has been combatting from Cairo to the Cape.

Undoubtedly some of these newly-awakened Negroes will take to Socialism and Bolshevism. But here again the reason is racial. Since they suffer racially from the world as at present organized by the white race, some of their ablest hold that it is "good play" to encourage and give aid to every subversive movement within that white world which makes for its destruction "as it is." For by its subversion they have much to gain and nothing to lose. But they build on their own foundations. Parallel with the dogma of Class-Consciousness they run the dogma of Race-Consciousness. And they dig deeper. For the roots of Class-consciousness inhere in a temporary economic order; whereas the roots of Race-consciousness must of necessity survive any and all changes in the economic order. Accepting biology as a fact, their view is the more fundamental. At any rate, it is that view with which the white world will have to deal.

1919

JESSIE REDMON FAUSET
ca. 1884–1961

When Langston Hughes credited Jessie Redmon Fauset with being (along with Alain Locke and Charles S. Johnson) one of "the three people who mid-wifed the so-called New Negro literature into being," he captured something of her central importance to the Harlem Renaissance. Unfortunately, many critics have chosen to dwell on Fauset's discovery or encouragement of writers such as Hughes, Claude McKay, and Nella Larsen and ignored her own work. As brilliant an editor as she was, Fauset was also, with four novels between 1924 and 1933, the most prolific novelist of the Harlem Renaissance and a writer of genuine accomplishment as well as ambition.

Born in a New Jersey suburb of Philadelphia to the Reverend Redmon Fauset and his wife, Annie, Jessie Fauset grew up in a relatively poor but genteel family. Educated in Philadelphia public schools, she graduated from the High School for Girls in 1900. Although she hoped to attend the prestigious Bryn Mawr College, that institution sidestepped the thorny issue of admitting a Black by obtaining for her a scholarship to Cornell University. Fauset was an excellent student. In 1905, she became the first woman to graduate from Cornell with a Phi Beta Kappa key and the first Black woman in America to become a member of that society. Barred from teaching in Philadelphia because of her race, she found a one-year position with Douglass High School of Baltimore before moving on to Dunbar High School in Washington, D.C., where she taught French and Latin until 1918. She then devoted a year to completing her master's degree at the University of Pennsylvania. About this time, Fauset also began to work for the *Crisis* (the magazine of the NAACP) under W. E. B. Du Bois. In October 1919, she became its literary editor, serving in that capacity until 1926. Fauset was also important in the development of Du Bois's *The Brownies' Book,* a children's monthly.

As a vehicle for literature, the *Crisis* was certainly at its best during Fauset's seven-year tenure. As editor, she demonstrated a flair for detecting literary talent and a capacity for hard work; at the same time, she produced her own important essays and fiction. While a minor portion of her output, her essays in the *Crisis* are particularly intriguing albeit restrained in tone, taking up a range of concerns (the 1921 Pan-African Congress in London, Paris, and Brussels; the flea market on the outskirts of Paris; life in lodging houses in the French capital; the nostalgic longing of immigrants in the United States) that are not encountered anywhere else in the literature of the period. Unlike her fiction, Fauset's essays seek what she called "breathing-spells, in-between spaces where colored men and women work and love and go their ways with no thought of the 'problem.'"

Fauset's first novel, *There Is Confusion,* was published in 1924 as a response to *Birthright* (1922), a book about Blacks by T. S. Stribling, a white writer whose inadequate representation of the African American middle class, to which Fauset proudly belonged, made her determined to set the record straight. *Plum Bun: A Novel without a Moral* (1929) chronicles the complex story of Angela Murray, a light-skinned Black whose attempt to pass for white makes up most of the story. Two other books followed: *The Chinaberry Tree: A Novel of American Life* (1931), regarded by many critics as perhaps Fauset's weakest literary achievement, and *Comedy, American Style* (1933), in which she experimented with the relationship between drama and narrative. In 1948, Hugh Gloster called this last novel "the most penetrating study of color mania in American fiction"; however, it has not appealed consistently to readers.

In 1926, for reasons that are not clear (including possibly the decline in the circulation of the magazine and a strain in her relationship with Du Bois), Fauset resigned her position, leaving *Crisis* altogether a year later. She returned to teaching (at DeWitt Clinton High School in New York) in 1927. Fauset's 1929 marriage to Herbert E. Harris lasted until his death in 1958. They lived mainly in Montclair, New Jersey, but after Harris's death, Fauset returned to Philadelphia to live with her stepbrother, Arthur Huff Fauset, until her death in 1961. Jessie Fauset's reputation is shrouded unfairly by a sense of her as having been snobbish both as an artist and as an individual, despite the testimony of sympathetic observers such as Langston Hughes. More attention should be paid to her intellectual and artistic energy, the high standards she set for herself as a writer, and the achievement of her fiction when read with sympathy for and understanding of the legitimate issues and complex narratives that characterize them.

As the critic Deborah McDowell has argued, *Plum Bun* may seem to be "just another novel of racial passing," but it rewards the attentive reader because of its rich texture and complicated meanings. In the end, its heroine comes to accept her ties to the African American world. This return to her origins caps a narrative that probes the relationship among money, power, and sexuality from an African American woman's perspective. As in almost all of Fauset's writing, the social milieu is the middle class, which she explores with wisdom and artistic deftness.

From Plum Bun: A Novel without a Moral[1]

From *Home*

CHAPTER I [BLACK PHILADELPHIA]

Opal Street, as streets go, is no jewel of the first water.[2] It is merely an imitation, and none too good at that. Narrow, unsparkling, uninviting, it stretches meekly off from dull Jefferson Street to the dingy, drab market which forms the north side of Oxford Street. It has no mystery, no allure, either of exclusiveness or of downright depravity; its usages are plainly significant,—an unpretentious little street lined with unpretentious little houses, inhabited for the most part by unpretentious little people.

The dwellings are three stories high, and contain six boxes called by courtesy, rooms—a "parlor," a midget of a dining-room, a larger kitchen and, above, a front bedroom seemingly large only because it extends for the full width of the house, a mere shadow of a bathroom, and another back bedroom with windows whose possibilities are spoiled by their outlook on sad and diminutive back-yards. And above these two, still two others built in similar wise.

In one of these houses dwelt a father, a mother and two daughters. Here, as often happens in a home sheltering two generations, opposite, unevenly matched emotions faced each other. In the houses of the rich the satisfied ambition of the older generation is faced by the overwhelming ambition of the younger. Or the elders may find themselves brought in opposition to the blank indifference and ennui of youth engendered by the realization that there remain no more worlds to conquer; their fathers having already taken all. In houses on Opal Street these niceties of distinction are hardly to be

1. The title is taken from the nursery rhyme that serves as an epigraph to the novel: "To market, to market / To buy a Plum Bun; / Home again, Home again, / Market is done." *Plum Bun* is broken into five sections, each named after a word or phrase from the nursery rhyme. Included here are the two opening chapters of the first section.

2. No fine jewel. Opal Street is in Philadelphia.

found; there is a more direct and concrete contrast. The satisfied ambition of maturity is a foil for the restless despair of youth.

Affairs in the Murray household were advancing towards this stage; yet not a soul in that family of four could have foretold its coming. To Junius and Mattie Murray, who had known poverty and homelessness, the little house on Opal Street represented the *ne plus ultra*[3] of ambition; to their daughter Angela it seemed the dingiest, drabbest chrysalis that had ever fettered the wings of a brilliant butterfly. The stories which Junius and Mattie told of difficulties overcome, of the arduous learning of trades, of the pitiful scraping together of infinitesimal savings, would have made a latter-day Iliad,[4] but to Angela they were merely a description of a life which she at any cost would avoid living. Somewhere in the world were paths which lead to broad thoroughfares, large, bright houses, delicate niceties of existence. Those paths Angela meant to find and frequent. At a very early age she had observed that the good things of life are unevenly distributed; merit is not always rewarded; hard labor does not necessarily entail adequate recompense. Certain fortuitous endowments, great physical beauty, unusual strength, a certain unswerving singleness of mind,—gifts bestowed quite blindly and disproportionately by the forces which control life,—these were the qualities which contributed toward a glowing and pleasant existence.

Angela had no high purpose in life; unlike her sister Virginia, who meant some day to invent a marvelous method for teaching the pianoforte, Angela felt no impulse to discover, or to perfect. True she thought she might become eventually a distinguished painter, but that was because she felt within herself an ability to depict which as far as it went was correct and promising. Her eye for line and for expression was already good and she had a nice feeling for color. Moreover she possessed the instinct for self-appraisal which taught her that she had much to learn. And she was sure that the knowledge once gained would flower in her case to perfection. But her gift was not for her the end of existence; rather it was an adjunct to a life which was to know light, pleasure, gaiety and freedom.

Freedom! That was the note which Angela heard oftenest in the melody of living which was to be hers. With a wildness that fell just short of unreasonableness she hated restraint. Her father's earlier days as coachman in a private family, his later successful, independent years as boss carpenter, her mother's youth spent as maid to a famous actress, all this was to Angela a manifestation of the sort of thing which happens to those enchained it might be by duty, by poverty, by weakness or by color.

Color or rather the lack of it seemed to the child the one absolute prerequisite to the life of which she was always dreaming. One might break loose from a too hampering sense of duty; poverty could be overcome; physicians conquered weakness; but color, the mere possession of a black or a white skin, that was clearly one of those fortuitous endowments of the gods. Gratitude was no strong ingredient in this girl's nature, yet very often early she began thanking Fate for the chance which in that household of four had bestowed on her the heritage of her mother's fair skin. She might so easily have been, like her father, black, or have received the melange[5] which had resulted in Virginia's rosy bronzeness and her deeply waving black hair. But Angela had received not only her mother's creamy complexion and her soft

3. The highest point (Latin).
4. Ancient Greek epic poem (ca. 700 B.C.E.) of the Trojan War, attributed to Homer.
5. Or mélange; a mixture or medley (French).

cloudy, chestnut hair, but she had taken from Junius the aquiline nose, the gift of some remote Indian ancestor which gave to his face and his eldest daughter's that touch of chiselled immobility.

It was from her mother that Angela learned the possibilities for joy and freedom which seemed to her inherent in mere whiteness. No one would have been more amazed than that same mother if she could have guessed how her daughter interpreted her actions. Certainly Mrs. Murray did not attribute what she considered her happy, busy, sheltered life on tiny Opal Street to the accident of her color; she attributed it to her black husband whom she had been glad and proud to marry. It is equally certain that that white skin of hers had not saved her from occasional contumely and insult. The famous actress for whom she had worked was aware of Mattie's mixed blood and, boasting temperament rather than refinement, had often dubbed her "white nigger."

Angela's mother employed her color very much as she practiced certain winning usages of smile and voice to obtain indulgences which meant much to her and which took nothing from anyone else. Then, too, she was possessed of a keener sense of humor than her daughter; it amused her when by herself to take lunch at an exclusive restaurant whose patrons would have been panic-stricken if they had divined the presence of a "colored" woman no matter how little her appearance differed from theirs. It was with no idea of disclaiming her own that she sat in orchestra seats which Philadelphia denied to colored patrons. But when Junius or indeed any other dark friend accompanied her she was the first to announce that she liked to sit in the balcony or gallery, as indeed she did; her infrequent occupation of orchestra seats was due merely to a mischievous determination to flout a silly and unjust law.

Her years with the actress had left their mark, a perfectly harmless and rather charming one. At least so it seemed to Junius, whose weakness was for the qualities known as "essentially feminine." Mrs. Murray loved pretty clothes, she liked shops devoted to the service of women; she enjoyed being even on the fringe of a fashionable gathering. A satisfaction that was almost ecstatic seized her when she drank tea in the midst of modishly gowned women in a stylish tea-room. It pleased her to stand in the foyer of a great hotel or of the Academy of Music and to be part of the whirling, humming, palpitating gaiety. She had no desire to be of these people, but she liked to look on; it amused and thrilled and kept alive some unquenchable instinct for life which thrived within her. To walk through Wanamaker's[6] on Saturday, to stroll from Fifteenth to Ninth Street on Chestnut, to have her tea in the Bellevue Stratford, to stand in the lobby of the St. James' fitting on immaculate gloves; all innocent, childish pleasures pursued without malice or envy contrived to cast a glamour over Monday's washing and Tuesday's ironing, the scrubbing of kitchen and bathroom and the fashioning of children's clothes. She was endowed with a humorous and pungent method of presentation; Junius, who had had the wit not to interfere with these little excursions and the sympathy to take them at their face value, preferred one of his wife's sparkling accounts of a Saturday's adventure in "passing" to all the tall stories told by cronies at his lodge.

6. A famous department store, now closed.

Much of this pleasure, harmless and charming though it was, would have been impossible with a dark skin.

In these first years of marriage, Mattie, busied with the house and the two babies had given up those excursions. Later, when the children had grown and Junius had reached the stage where he could afford to give himself a half-holiday on Saturdays, the two parents inaugurated a plan of action which eventually became a fixed program. Each took a child, and Junius went off to a beloved but long since suspended pastime of exploring old Philadelphia, whereas Mattie embarked once more on her social adventures. It is true that Mattie accompanied by brown Virginia could not move quite as freely as when with Angela. But her maternal instincts were sound; her children, their feelings and their faith in her meant much more than the pleasure which she would have been first to call unnecessary and silly. As it happened the children themselves quite unconsciously solved the dilemma; Virginia found shopping tiring and stupid, Angela returned from her father's adventuring worn and bored. Gradually the rule was formed that Angela accompanied her mother and Virginia her father.

On such fortuities does life depend. Little Angela Murray, hurrying through Saturday morning's scrubbing of steps in order that she might have her bath at one and be with her mother on Chestnut Street at two, never realized that her mother took her pleasure among all these pale people because it was there that she happened to find it. It never occurred to her that the delight which her mother obviously showed in meeting friends on Sunday morning when the whole united Murray family came out of church was the same as she showed on Chestnut Street the previous Saturday, because she was finding the qualities which her heart craved, bustle, excitement and fashion. The daughter could not guess that if the economic status or the racial genius of colored people had permitted them to run modish hotels or vast and popular department stores her mother would have been there. She drew for herself certain clearly formed conclusions which her subconscious mind thus codified:

First, that the great rewards of life—riches, glamour, pleasure,—are for white-skinned people only. Secondly, that Junius and Virginia were denied these privileges because they were dark; here her reasoning bore at least an element of verisimilitude but she missed the essential fact that her father and sister did not care for this type of pleasure. The effect of her fallaciousness was to cause her to feel a faint pity for her unfortunate relatives and also to feel that colored people were to be considered fortunate only in the proportion in which they measured up to the physical standards of white people.

One Saturday excursion left a far-reaching impression. Mrs. Murray and Angela had spent a successful and interesting afternoon. They had browsed among the contents of the small exclusive shops in Walnut Street; they had had soda at Adams' on Broad Street and they were standing finally in the portico of the Walton Hotel deciding with fashionable and idle elegance what they should do next. A thin stream of people constantly passing threw an occasional glance at the quietly modish pair, the well-dressed, assured woman and the refined and no less assured daughter. The door-man knew them; it was one of Mrs. Murray's pleasures to proffer him a small tip, much appreciated since it was uncalled for. This was the atmosphere which she loved. Angela had put on her gloves and was waiting for her mother, who was drawing on her own with great care, when she glimpsed in the laughing, hurrying Saturday throng the figures of her father and of Virginia. They were close enough for her mother, who saw them too, to touch them by merely descending a few steps and stretching out her arm. In a second the pair had vanished. Angela saw her mother's face change—with trepidation she thought. She remarked: "It's a good thing Papa didn't see us, you'd have had to speak to him, wouldn't you?" But her mother, giving her a distracted glance, made no reply.

That night, after the girls were in bed, Mattie, perched on the arm of her husband's chair, told him about it. "I was at my old game of play-acting again today, June, passing you know, and darling, you and Virginia went by within arm's reach and we never spoke to you. I'm so ashamed."

But Junius consoled her. Long before their marriage he had known of his Mattie's weakness and its essential harmlessness. "My dear girl, I told you long ago that where no principle was involved, your passing means nothing to me. It's just a little joke; I don't think you'd be ashamed to acknowledge your old husband anywhere if it were necessary."

"I'd do that if people were mistaking me for a queen," she assured him fondly. But she was silent, not quite satisfied. "After all," she said with her charming frankness, "it isn't you, dear, who make me feel guilty. I really am ashamed to think that I let Virginia pass by without a word. I think I should feel very badly if she were to know it. I don't believe I'll ever let myself be quite as silly as that again."

But of this determination Angela, dreaming excitedly of Saturdays spent in turning her small olive face firmly away from peering black countenances was, unhappily, unaware.

1924

ALAIN LOCKE
1886–1954

The importance to the Harlem Renaissance of the March 1925 special issue of the *Survey Graphic*, a national magazine devoted to sociology and social work, is hard to overestimate. Paul Kellogg, editor of the magazine, had decided to devote that entire number to the question of race and Black New York. As special editor for this project he chose Alain Locke, who subtitled the issue "Harlem: Mecca of the New Negro" and imaginatively included a wide variety of articles, poems, stories, and other pieces by writers such as W. E. B. Du Bois, James Weldon Johnson, Countee Cullen, Langston Hughes, Claude McKay, Angelina Grimké, and Anne Spencer. The special issue was an extraordinary success. Eight months later, Locke brought out *The New Negro,* an anthology including most of what had appeared in the *Survey Graphic* (much of it revised) along with a good deal of new material, including stunning artwork depicting Blacks by the Bavarian artist Winold Reiss. Serving as a coherent and articulate announcement of a new spirit among Black Americans, *The New Negro* was virtually the central text of the Harlem Renaissance.

In his manifestolike introduction, Locke defined the "New Negro" as self-consciously modern, independent, and "dynamic," an effect of the migration of tens of thousands of African Americans from the rural U.S. South to the urban North in the first decades of the twentieth century. Above all, Locke linked the "New Negro" to Harlem, which he described as an international "race capital" drawing Blacks from around the world into "the laboratory of a great race-welding." If the new phenomenon was thoroughly American, Locke also insisted that the "inner life" of the "New Negro" was opening out into other channels, including a "new internationalism" that "has linked up with the growing group consciousness of the dark-peoples and is gradually learning their common interests." Even before *The New Negro*, Locke was as intrigued by the implications of political internationalism as any of his contemporaries. In February 1924, he published an essay entitled "Apropos of Africa" in *Opportunity*, which though instilled with his characteristic paternalism—as he put it in *The New Negro*, the American Negro was "the advance-guard of the African peoples in their contact with Twentieth Century civilization"—also argued that "we must realize that in some respects we need what Africa has to give us as much as, or even more than, Africa needs what we in turn have to give her."

The only son of a couple who belonged solidly to the Black elite of Philadelphia, Alain Locke excelled at Central High School and later (1902–04) at the Philadelphia School of Pedagogy, where his father taught. He then entered Harvard, from which he graduated magna cum laude three years later, in 1907. In that year, he became the first Black American to be awarded a Rhodes scholarship (he remained the only one for some sixty years). He earned a degree at Oxford in 1910, then spent a year studying philosophy at the University of Berlin. In 1912, he returned to the United States to begin teaching English, philosophy, and education at Howard University. From 1916 to 1917, he worked to complete his doctoral thesis at Harvard, after which he became the chair of the philosophy department at Howard. Except for a few months spent elsewhere, he remained at Howard for the rest of his life.

Aside from *The New Negro*, Locke also edited *Plays of Negro Life* (1927, with Montgomery Gregory), *Four Negro Poets* (1927), *The Negro in Art: A Pictorial Record of the Negro Artist and of the Negro Theme in Art* (1940), and *When Peoples Meet, a Study in Race and Culture Contacts* (1942, with Bernhard J. Stern). But perhaps more important than his own literary accomplishments was his influence on the younger Harlem intellectuals. With remarkable skill and devotion, he directed their energies, helped them to be published, and put several of them (such as Hughes, Hurston, and McKay) into contact with patrons—notably Mrs. Charlotte Osgood Mason, a wealthy, elderly white woman who provided financial and moral support for several struggling artists.

Locke died before completing what he considered to be his life's work—a comprehensive study of Black American culture. (However, with the guidelines and the materials he left at his death, Margaret Just Butcher was able to publish *The Negro in American Culture* in 1956.) An indefatigable proponent of the role of art as a bridge between individuals and cultures, Locke was one of the most influential of the contemporary champions of the Harlem Renaissance. Although he clashed eventually with various people—including Toomer, McKay, and Hughes (over matters that range from changes in their texts made without permission to, in Hughes's case, personal betrayal)—perhaps no other senior intellectual matched his zeal in personally meeting and encouraging younger artists or his learning and cosmopolitanism in illuminating the question of race, notably where African American culture is concerned.

From Apropos of Africa

Except from the point of view of religious missionarism, it has been until recently almost impossible to cultivate generally in the mind of the American Negro an abiding and serious interest in Africa. Politically, economically, scientifically, culturally, the great concerns of this great continent have engaged the Caucasian and primarily the European mind. The sooner we recognize as a fact this painful paradox, that those who have naturally the greatest interests in Africa have of all other peoples been least interested, the sooner will it be corrected. With notable exceptions, our interest in Africa has heretofore been sporadic, sentimental and unpractical. And,—as for every fact, there is of course a reason: the dark shadow of slavery has thrown Africa, in spite of our conscious wishes, into a sort of chilly and terrifying eclipse, against which only religious ardor could kindle an attractive and congenial glow of interest. The time has come, however, with the generation that knows slavery only as history, to cast off this spell, and see Africa at least with the interest of the rest of the world, if not indeed with a keener, more favored, regard. There are parallels, we must remember, for this: Except for the prosperous Tories, England was a bogey to the American colonists; from the thirties to the nineties, the average Irishman was half-ashamed of Erin[1] in spite of lapses into occasional fervent sentimentalism; and even with the sturdy Jewish sense of patrimony, Zionism[2] has had its difficulties in rekindling the concrete regard for the abandoned fatherland. Only prosperity looks backward. Adversity is afraid to look over its own shoulder. But eventually all peoples exhibit the homing instinct and turn back physically or mentally, hopefully and helpfully, to the land of their origin. And we American Negroes, in this respect cannot, will not, be an exception.

The very same facts that have frustrated the healthy, vigorous interest in Africa and things African, have focused whatever interest there was upon the West Coast,—erroneously regarded because of the accidents of the slave-trade as our especial patrimony, if we ever had any. But the colored millions of America represent every one of the many racial stocks of Africa, are descended from the peoples of almost every quarter of the continent, and are culturally the heirs of the entire continent. The history of the wide dispersion of the slave-trade and trading-posts will establish this in the mind of any open-minded person, and anthropological investigation of American Negro types would conclusively prove this. If the Negro is interested in Africa, he should be interested in the whole of Africa; if he is to link himself up again with his past and his kin, he must link himself up with all of the African peoples. As the physical composite of eighty-five per cent at least of the African stocks, the American Negro is in a real sense the true Pan-African, and certainly even apart from this, on the grounds of opportunity and strategic position, should be the leader in constructive Pan-African thought and endeavor. Enlightened imperialism,—but who can visualize enlightened imperialism,—would have seen in the American Negro just those resources of leadership and devoted interest which it would have needed, and could have utilized if its real aims had been the development, and not merely the exploitations of this great continent and its varied peoples. But it is rather against than with the wish of the interested governments, that the American Negro must reach out toward his rightful share in the solution of African problems and the development of Africa's resources.

1. English derivative of *Éirinn*, the Irish name for Ireland.

2. An international movement aimed at securing a homeland for the Jewish people.

II

With a more practical and enlightened vision, the question of the redemption of Africa has become with us the question of the regeneration of Africa. We now see that the missionary condescension of the past generations in their attitude toward Africa was a pious but sad mistake. In taking it, we have fallen into the snare of enemies and have given grievous offence to our brothers. We must realize that in some respects we need what Africa has to give us as much as, or even more than, Africa needs what we in turn have to give her; and that unless we approach Africa in the spirit of the finest reciprocity, our efforts will be ineffectual or harmful. We need to be the first of all Westerners to rid ourselves of the insulting prejudice, the insufferable bias of the attitude of "civilizing Africa"—for she is not only our mother but in the light of most recent science is beginning to appear as the mother of civilization in general. On the other hand, the average African of the enlightened classes has his characteristic bias,—his pride of blood and bias of clan,—so that the meeting of mind between the African and the Afro-American is dependent upon a broadening of vision and a dropping of prejudices from both sides. The African must dismiss his provincialism, his political-mindedness, his pride of clan; the Afro-American, his missionary condescension, his religious parochialism, and his pride of place. The meeting of the two will mean the inauguration of a new era for both. Above all, it must be recognized that for the present the best channels of cooperative effort lie along economic and educational lines, and that religion and politics, with their inevitable contentiousness and suspicions, are far less promising ways of approach and common effort. America offers the African his greatest educational opportunity; Africa offers the Afro-American his greatest economic opportunity. So we may truly say that the salvation of the one is in the other's hands. I am aware that this is not to many a self-evident proposition, but sober thought will prove to the far-sighted what the logic of the course of events must ultimately justify for the multitude.

But here on this point we have, strangely enough, the feeling of the masses, more ready and ripe for action than the minds of the leaders and the educated few. The Garvey movement has demonstrated that conclusively. Perhaps in the perspective of time, that will appear to have been its chief service and mission,—to have stirred the race mind to the depths with the idea of large-scale cooperation between the variously separated branches of the Negro peoples. This is without doubt the great constructive idea in the race life during the last decade, and must become the center of constructive endeavor for this and the next generation. Unfortunately obscured by the controversy between its radical exponents in the Garvey movement and its liberal exponents, Dr. Du Bois and the sponsors of the Pan-African Congress, and still more unfortunately but temporarily discredited by the financial mal-administration of Mr. Garvey's overambitious ventures, the idea has seemed to suffer a fatal set-back. But each branch of the movement has done yeoman service, in spite of great obstacles and unfortunate mistakes,—for publicity for the idea is for the present the main thing; its successful working out is a matter of painstaking experiment and endeavor. Each has temporarily failed in what it considered to be its main objective, and what, if realized, would have been a great service both to the cause of the race and humanity at large. The establishment of a great tropical

African State, under international mandate, was one of the most constructive and promising proposals in all the grand agenda of the Peace Conference.[3] If Mr. Wilson had sponsored it, fewer of his fourteen points[4] would have been shattered by selfish European diplomacy, and not only America, but the American Negro would have had an official share and a responsible opportunity in the guardianship and development of this great continent. Many forces combined to crush the idea; but when the secret history of the Conference becomes public, General Smuts[5] will probably appear as the most blameworthy opponent of the scheme. Time will, however, eventually justify this idea and acclaim this brilliant sponsor, and out of the desperate exigencies of the near future we may yet see it brought forward in altered form in the councils of the League of Nations, although the greatest practical opportunity, the disposal of the German colonies in Africa, has been irrevocably missed. Similarly, but for internal rather than external causes, the main objective of the Garvey movement has foundered. Wholly self-initiated and self-supported trade intercourse with Africa would have been in itself a wonderful demonstration of practical economic ability on the part of American Negroes as well as of a modern and constructive interest in their African brethren. It is more of a pity, more of a reproach, that this was not realized. But in both cases the idea has survived its initial defeat. Journalistically the Garvey movement has made a permanent contribution to the Afro-American press, and has built bridges of communication for the future. The first great span in the archway, communication, exchange of thought and information between American Negroes and their brothers in the West Indies, can be optimistically regarded as already established. With greater difficulty, three Pan-African Congresses have been trying to construct the broader spans of communication and publicity between us and Africa. The greatest difficulty is in bringing African interests together; that task once achieved, it will be comparatively easy to link up with the American groups. This is especially the problem of the Third Pan-African Congress,[6] which has just concluded its sessions. In the present situation when national feeling, especially that of the French and Belgian contingents, threatens to disrupt the feeble unity of action already achieved, it is very necessary that the American Negro, the most disinterested party, should assume very direct leadership and responsibility for the movement, insisting upon keeping dominant the Pan-African character of the scheme. This is Dr. Du Bois' purpose in holding the conference at what is considered by many formerly enthusiastic members as a singularly inappropriate time. Quixotic as it may seem to run counter to the wishes of many African delegates, such a course is undoubtedly right; but, pending its justification, the Pan-African idea is just now at the most critical point of its career. The European press and public opinion have always shown keenest interest,

3. The Paris Peace Conference (1919), at which the Allied victors met after World War I to set the peace terms for the defeated Central Powers (the German Empire, the Austro-Hungarian Empire, the Ottoman Empire, and Bulgaria).

4. January 1918 speech by President Woodrow Wilson to a joint session of Congress outlining principles and postwar aims, including free trade, democracy, and self-determination.

5. Jan Christiaan Smuts (1870–1950), South African and British Commonwealth military leader and statesman, participant in Peace Conference negotiations that led to the League of Nations and to South Africa being granted a mandate over the former German colony in South West Africa (now Namibia).

6. Meeting of Black political leaders organized by W. E. B. Du Bois in London and in Lisbon (1923).

appreciating the important potentialities of this movement; it is the apathy and disinterestedness of the American, and especially the Afro-American press, which is the strange and disappointing feature of the situation. If the movement should lag, it will be an indictment of the intelligence, perspicacity, and race-mindedness of the American Negro.

* * *

V

While our active interests in Africa must of necessity and of reason remain educational and eventually economic, there is every reason why we should be keenly interested in the political fortunes of all African peoples. The apathy of our general public opinion in the matter of the proposed American loan and economic protection to Liberia[7] was a shameful dereliction, which should not be allowed to repeat itself on any matter of African politics. Assessing at the lowest value, the motives of this project, and supposing even that it could have militated somewhat against Liberian sovereignty—a too pessimistic and undeserved assumption, especially in view of the moral force of the League of Nations, we may warrantably ask, what better guarantee of fair and considerate treatment could the Liberians have had than the force of the American Negro electorate, if properly awake and intelligently directed? Minorities have as their best protection today the court of world opinion; if they do not live on an international scale and in the eyes of the world, they are doomed even in the twentieth century to medieval conditions and hardships. Witness the effectiveness of that fine voice in the League of Nations, the former Haytian representative, Monsieur Bellegarde,[8] who ought to have the esteem and gratitude of the entire world of colored people. European statesmen and publicists felt and acknowledged the force of this man; his recall was a calamity to our larger international interest. The success and strength of the Jew, still very precariously situated in some parts of the world, has been his international scale of organization, promoted first of all by his religion, and latterly through many other channels of cooperative race effort, of which Zionism is only one phase. Mr. Ford's phrase is true,—the international Jew;[9] but it is an unwarrantable calumny because his inferences are wrong. In the first place, the Jew has been made international by persecution and forced dispersion,—and so, potentially, have we. In the second place, as a minority threatened here and there, its only intelligent safeguard has been international appeal and international organization. To relieve pressure in one place very often pressure has to be strategically applied in another, and the Jewish people have perforce become masters in this intelligent and modern strategy of group action. And if the international mind is to be for all people

7. Proposed $5 million loan from the U.S. government to Liberia to support infrastructure and development, rejected by the U.S. Senate in 1922; in 1926 the Liberia government negotiated to receive the loan from the Firestone Corporation in exchange for a million-acre concession of Liberian territory.

8. Dantès Bellegarde (1877–1966), Haitian historian and diplomat.

9. *The International Jew: The World's Foremost Problem* (1920), a collection of anti-Semitic writings by the automobile manufacturer Henry Ford (1863–1947) originally published as articles in the *Dearborn Independent*.

the eventual achievement, the Jew has simply the temporary advantage of having acquired it a little in advance of the rest of the world.

There is much value to us in this great example. We have for the present, in spite of Mr. Garvey's hectic efforts, no Zionistic hope or intention. But for protection and mutual development, we must develop the race mind and race interest on an international scale. For that reason, we should be most vitally interested in the idea of the League of Nations and all kindred movements. For that reason, it should be a matter of the profoundest satisfaction that an African State, with almost unassailable sovereignty, has recently achieved recognition and admittance; and on the basis of an enlightened initiative of its own. It was my privilege to meet and congratulate the able envoy,—His Excellency Belata Herony, in Egypt, on his way from Geneva to Adis Abeba; a man of modern view and twentieth century skill and what is more important, international vision. At a time when warrantably he might have been naturally and pardonably nationalistic and characteristic in sentiment, one found his dominant mood that of internationalism and the progressive interests of the darker races the world over. Politically he represents Abyssinia;[1] morally, however, I am sure, our interests and those of Negroes everywhere on progressive world legislation and in event of an appeal on any necessary question to the court of world opinion. We already know from the cordial and interested behavior of this man on his American visit, what a vivid sense of racial interest he has. Counselled in another direction, the entire mission regarded the colored people of America as brothers, and the feeling of kinship was warmly reciprocated. To congratulations offered in the name of our group, his reply, with greetings and assurances of warm interest, was a forecast of progressive reform and development for Abyssinia which proclaimed it, in my judgment, the most promising and stategic center of African development in the near future, a forecast that in itself was tantamount to a cordial invitation for closer relations and cooperative help. I repeat, of the many, here is a special reason for more active and enlightened interest in Africa.

1924

The New Negro

In the last decade something beyond the watch and guard of statistics has happened in the life of the American Negro and the three norns[1] who have traditionally presided over the Negro problem have a changeling in their laps. The Sociologist, the Philanthropist, the Race-leader are not unaware of the New Negro, but they are at a loss to account for him. He simply cannot be swathed in their formulæ. For the younger generation is vibrant with a new psychology; the new spirit is awake in the masses, and under the very eyes of the professional observers is transforming what has been a perennial problem into the progressive phases of contemporary Negro life.

1. Historical name in English for Ethiopia.

1. The three fates in Norse mythology.

Could such a metamorphosis have taken place as suddenly as it has appeared to? The answer is no; not because the New Negro is not here, but because the Old Negro had long become more of a myth than a man. The Old Negro, we must remember, was a creature of moral debate and historical controversy. His has been a stock figure perpetuated as an historical fiction partly in innocent sentimentalism, partly in deliberate reactionism. The Negro himself has contributed his share to this through a sort of protective social mimicry forced upon him by the adverse circumstances of dependence. So for generations in the mind of America, the Negro has been more of a formula than a human being—a something to be argued about, condemned or defended, to be "kept down," or "in his place," or "helped up," to be worried with or worried over, harassed or patronized, a social bogey or a social burden. The thinking Negro even has been induced to share this same general attitude, to focus his attention on controversial issues, to see himself in the distorted perspective of a social problem. His shadow, so to speak, has been more real to him than his personality. Through having had to appeal from the unjust stereotypes of his oppressors and traducers to those of his liberators, friends and benefactors he has had to subscribe to the traditional positions from which his case has been viewed. Little true social or self-understanding has or could come from such a situation.

But while the minds of most of us, black and white, have thus burrowed in the trenches of the Civil War and Reconstruction, the actual march of development has simply flanked these positions, necessitating a sudden reorientation of view. We have not been watching in the right direction; set North and South on a sectional axis, we have not noticed the East till the sun has us blinking.

Recall how suddenly the Negro spirituals revealed themselves; suppressed for generations under the stereotypes of Wesleyan hymn[2] harmony, secretive, half-ashamed, until the courage of being natural brought them out—and behold, there was folk-music. Similarly the mind of the Negro seems suddenly to have slipped from under the tyranny of social intimidation and to be shaking off the psychology of imitation and implied inferiority. By shedding the old chrysalis of the Negro problem we are achieving something like a spiritual emancipation. Until recently, lacking self-understanding, we have been almost as much of a problem to ourselves as we still are to others. But the decade[3] that found us with a problem has left us with only a task. The multitude perhaps feels as yet only a strange relief and a new vague urge, but the thinking few know that in the reaction the vital inner grip of prejudice has been broken.

With this renewed self-respect and self-dependence, the life of the Negro community is bound to enter a new dynamic phase, the buoyancy from within compensating for whatever pressure there may be of conditions from without. The migrant masses, shifting from countryside to city, hurdle several generations of experience at a leap, but more important, the same thing happens spiritually in the life-attitudes and self-expression of the Young Negro, in his poetry, his art, his education and his new outlook, with the

2. After Charles Wesley (1707–1788), English hymnist and brother of John Wesley, founder of Methodism.
3. The 1920s.

additional advantage, of course, of the poise and greater certainty of knowing what it is all about. From this comes the promise and warrant of a new leadership. As one of them[4] has discerningly put it:

We have tomorrow
Bright before us
Like a flame.

Yesterday, a night-gone thing
A sun-down name.

And dawn today
Broad arch above the road we came.
We march!

This is what, even more than any "most creditable record of fifty years of freedom," requires that the Negro of today be seen through other than the dusty spectacles of past controversy. The day of "aunties," "uncles" and "mammies" is equally gone. Uncle Tom and Sambo have passed on, and even the "Colonel" and "George"[5] play barnstorm roles from which they escape with relief when the public spotlight is off. The popular melodrama has about played itself out, and it is time to scrap the fictions, garret the bogeys and settle down to a realistic facing of facts.

First we must observe some of the changes which since the traditional lines of opinion were drawn have rendered these quite obsolete. A main change has been, of course, that shifting of the Negro population which has made the Negro problem no longer exclusively or even predominantly Southern. Why should our minds remain sectionalized, when the problem itself no longer is? Then the trend of migration has not only been toward the North and the Central Midwest, but city-ward and to the great centers of industry—the problems of adjustment are new, practical, local and not peculiarly racial. Rather they are an integral part of the large industrial and social problems of our present-day democracy. And finally, with the Negro rapidly in process of class differentiation, if it ever was warrantable to regard and treat the Negro *en masse* it is becoming with every day less possible, more unjust and more ridiculous.

In the very process of being transplanted, the Negro is becoming transformed.

The tide of Negro migration, northward and city-ward, is not to be fully explained as a blind flood started by the demands of war industry coupled with the shutting off of foreign migration, or by the pressure of poor crops coupled with increased social terrorism in certain sections of the South and Southwest. Neither labor demand, the bollweevil[6] nor the Ku Klux Klan is a basic factor, however contributory any or all of them may have been. The wash and rush of this human tide on the beach line of the northern city centers is to be explained primarily in terms of a new vision of opportunity, of social and economic freedom, of a spirit to seize, even in the face of an extortionate and heavy toll, a chance for the improvement of conditions. With each successive wave of it, the movement of the Negro becomes more and more a mass movement toward the larger and the more demo-

4. Langston Hughes (1902–1967). The following lines are from "Youth."
5. Typical forms of interracial address during slavery and segregation.
6. A snout beetle notorious for destroying cotton crops.

cratic chance—in the Negro's case a deliberate flight not only from countryside to city, but from medieval America to modern.

Take Harlem as an instance of this. Here in Manhattan is not merely the largest Negro community in the world, but the first concentration in history of so many diverse elements of Negro life. It has attracted the African, the West Indian, the Negro American; has brought together the Negro of the North and the Negro of the South; the man from the city and the man from the town and village; the peasant, the student, the business man, the professional man, artist, poet, musician, adventurer and worker, preacher and criminal, exploiter and social outcast. Each group has come with its own separate motives and for its own special ends, but their greatest experience has been the finding of one another. Proscription and prejudice have thrown these dissimilar elements into a common area of contact and interaction. Within this area, race sympathy and unity have determined a further fusing of sentiment and experience. So what began in terms of segregation becomes more and more, as its elements mix and react, the laboratory of a great race-welding. Hitherto, it must be admitted that American Negroes have been a race more in name than in fact, or to be exact, more in sentiment than in experience. The chief bond between them has been that of a common condition rather than a common consciousness; a problem in common rather than a life in common. In Harlem, Negro life is seizing upon its first chances for group expression and self-determination. It is—or promises at least to be—a race capital. That is why our comparison is taken with those nascent centers of folk-expression and self-determination which are playing a creative part in the world today. Without pretense to their political significance, Harlem has the same role to play for the New Negro as Dublin has had for the New Ireland or Prague for the New Czechoslovakia.

Harlem, I grant you, isn't typical—but it is significant, it is prophetic. No sane observer, however sympathetic to the new trend, would contend that the great masses are articulate as yet, but they stir, they move, they are more than physically restless. The challenge of the new intellectuals among them is clear enough—the "race radicals" and realists who have broken with the old epoch of philanthropic guidance, sentimental appeal and protest. But are we after all only reading into the stirrings of a sleeping giant the dreams of an agitator? The answer is in the migrating peasant. It is the "man farthest down" who is most active in getting up. One of the most characteristic symptoms of this is the professional man, himself migrating to recapture his constituency after a vain effort to maintain in some Southern corner what for years back seemed an established living and clientele. The clergyman following his errant flock, the physician or lawyer trailing his clients, supply the true clues. In a real sense it is the rank and file who are leading, and the leaders who are following. A transformed and transforming psychology permeates the masses.

When the racial leaders of twenty years ago spoke of developing race-pride and stimulating race-consciousness, and of the desirability of race solidarity, they could not in any accurate degree have anticipated the abrupt feeling that has surged up and now pervades the awakened centers. Some of the recognized Negro leaders and a powerful section of white opinion identified with "race work" of the older order have indeed attempted to discount this feeling as a "passing phase," an attack of "race nerves" so to speak, an "aftermath of the war," and the like. It has not abated, however, if we are to gauge by the present tone and temper of the Negro press, or by the shift in popular support from the officially recognized and orthodox spokesmen to those of the independent, popular, and often radical type who are unmistakable symptoms of a new order. It is a social disservice to blunt the fact that the Negro of the Northern centers has reached a stage where tutelage, even of the most interested and well-intentioned sort, must give place to new relationships, where positive self-direction must be reckoned with in ever increasing measure. The American mind must reckon with a fundamentally changed Negro.

The Negro too, for his part, has idols of the tribe to smash. If on the one hand the white man has erred in making the Negro appear to be that which would excuse or extenuate his treatment of him, the Negro, in turn, has too often unnecessarily excused himself because of the way he has been treated. The intelligent Negro of today is resolved not to make discrimination an extenuation for his shortcomings in performance, individual or collective; he is trying to hold himself at par, neither inflated by sentimental allowances nor depreciated by current social discounts. For this he must know himself and be known for precisely what he is, and for that reason he welcomes the new scientific rather than the old sentimental interest. Sentimental interest in the Negro has ebbed. We used to lament this as the falling off of our friends; now we rejoice and pray to be delivered both from self-pity and condescension. The mind of each racial group has had a bitter weaning, apathy or hatred on one side matching disillusionment or resentment on the other; but they face each other today with the possibility at least of entirely new mutual attitudes.

It does not follow that if the Negro were better known, he would be better liked or better treated. But mutual understanding is basic for any subsequent cooperation and adjustment. The effort toward this will at least have the effect of remedying in large part what has been the most unsatisfactory feature of our present stage of race relationships in America, namely the fact that the more intelligent and representative elements of the two race groups have at so many points got quite out of vital touch with one another.

The fiction is that the life of the races is separate, and increasingly so. The fact is that they have touched too closely at the unfavorable and too lightly at the favorable levels.

While inter-racial councils have sprung up in the South, drawing on forward elements of both races, in the Northern cities manual laborers may brush elbows in their everyday work, but the community and business leaders have experienced no such interplay or far too little of it. These segments must achieve contact or the race situation in America becomes desperate. Fortunately this is happening. There is a growing realization that in social effort the cooperative basis must supplant long-distance philanthropy, and that the only safeguard for mass relations in the future must be provided in the carefully maintained contacts of the enlightened minorities of both race groups. In the intellectual realm a renewed and keen curiosity is replacing the recent apathy; the Negro is being carefully studied, not just talked about and discussed. In art and letters, instead of being wholly caricatured, he is being seriously portrayed and painted.

To all of this the New Negro is keenly responsive as an augury of a new democracy in American culture. He is contributing his share to the new social understanding. But the desire to be understood would never in itself have been sufficient to have opened so completely the protectively closed portals of the thinking Negro's mind. There is still too much possibility of being snubbed or patronized for that. It was rather the necessity for fuller, truer self-expression, the realization of the unwisdom of allowing social discrimination to segregate him mentally, and a counter-attitude to cramp and fetter his own living—and so the "spite-wall" that the intellectuals built over the "color-line" has happily been taken down. Much of this reopening of intellectual contacts has centered in New York and has been richly fruitful not merely in the enlarging of personal experience, but in the definite enrichment of American art and letters and in the clarifying of our common vision of the social tasks ahead.

The particular significance in the re-establishment of contact between the more advanced and representative classes is that it promises to offset some of the unfavorable reactions of the past, or at least to re-surface race contacts somewhat for the future. Subtly the conditions that are molding a New Negro are molding a new American attitude.

However, this new phase of things is delicate; it will call for less charity but more justice; less help, but infinitely closer understanding. This is indeed a critical stage of race relationships because of the likelihood, if the new temper is not understood, of engendering sharp group antagonism and a second crop of more calculated prejudice. In some quarters, it has already done so. Having weaned the Negro, public opinion cannot continue to paternalize. The Negro today is inevitably moving forward under the control largely of his own objectives. What are these objectives? Those of his outer life are happily already well and finally formulated, for they are none other than the ideals of American institutions and democracy. Those of his inner life are yet in process of formation, for the new psychology at present is more of a consensus of feeling than of opinion, of attitude rather than of program. Still some points seem to have crystallized.

Up to the present one may adequately describe the Negro's "inner objectives" as an attempt to repair a damaged group psychology and reshape a warped social perspective. Their realization has required a new mentality for the American Negro. And as it matures we begin to see its effects; at first, negative, iconoclastic, and then positive and constructive. In this new group psychology we note the lapse of sentimental appeal, then the development of a more positive self-respect and self-reliance; the repudiation of social dependence, and then the gradual recovery from hyper-sensitiveness and "touchy" nerves, the repudiation of the double standard of judgment with its special philanthropic allowances and then the sturdier desire for objective and scientific appraisal; and finally the rise from social disillusionment to race pride, from the sense of social debt to the responsibilities of social contribution, and offsetting the necessary working and commonsense acceptance of restricted conditions, the belief in ultimate esteem and recognition. Therefore the Negro today wishes to be known for what he is, even in his faults and shortcomings, and scorns a craven and precarious survival at the price of seeming to be what he is not. He resents being spoken of as a social ward or minor, even by his own, and to being regarded a chronic patient for the sociological clinic, the sick man of American Democracy. For the same reasons, he himself is through with those social nostrums and panaceas, the so-called "solutions" of his "problem," with which he and the country have been so liberally dosed in the past. Religion, freedom, education, money—in turn, he has ardently hoped for and peculiarly trusted these things; he still believes in them, but not in blind trust that they alone will solve his life-problem.

Each generation, however, will have its creed, and that of the present is the belief in the efficacy of collective effort, in race cooperation. This deep feeling of race is at present the mainspring of Negro life. It seems to be the outcome of the reaction to proscription and prejudice; an attempt, fairly successful on the whole, to convert a defensive into an offensive position, a handicap into an incentive. It is radical in tone, but not in purpose and only the most stupid forms of opposition, misunderstanding or persecution could make it otherwise. Of course, the thinking Negro has shifted a little toward the left with the world-trend, and there is an increasing group who affiliate with radical and liberal movements. But fundamentally for the present the Negro is radical on race matters, conservative on others, in other words, a "forced radical," a social protestant rather than a genuine radical. Yet under further pressure and injustice iconoclastic thought and motives will inevitably increase. Harlem's quixotic radicalisms call for their ounce of democracy today lest tomorrow they be beyond cure.

The Negro mind reaches out as yet to nothing but American wants, American ideas. But this forced attempt to build his Americanism on race values is a unique social experiment, and its ultimate success is impossible except through the fullest sharing of American culture and institutions. There should be no delusion about this. American nerves in sections unstrung with race hysteria are often fed the opiate that the trend of Negro advance is wholly separatist, and that the effect of its operation will be to encyst the Negro as a benign foreign body in the body politic. This cannot be—even if it were desirable. The racialism of the Negro is no limitation or reservation with respect to American life; it is only a constructive effort to build the obstructions in the stream of his progress into an efficient dam of social energy and power. Democracy itself is obstructed and stagnated to the extent that any of its channels are closed. Indeed they cannot be selectively closed. So the choice is not between one way for the Negro and another way for the rest, but between American institutions frustrated on the one hand and American ideals progressively fulfilled and realized on the other.

There is, of course, a warrantably comfortable feeling in being on the right side of the country's professed ideals. We realize that we cannot be undone without America's undoing. It is within the gamut of this attitude that the thinking Negro faces America, but with variations of mood that are if anything more significant than the attitude itself. Sometimes we have it taken with the defiant ironic challenge of McKay:[7]

Mine is the future grinding down to-day
Like a great landslip moving to the sea,
Bearing its freight of débris far away
Where the green hungry waters restlessly
Heave mammoth pyramids, and break and roar
Their eerie challenge to the crumbling shore.

7. Claude McKay (1889–1948), Harlem Renaissance poet.

Sometimes, perhaps more frequently as yet, it is taken in the fervent and almost filial appeal and counsel of Weldon Johnson's:

O Southland, dear Southland!
Then why do you still cling
To an idle age and a musty page,
To a dead and useless thing?[8]

But between defiance and appeal, midway almost between cynicism and hope, the prevailing mind stands in the mood of the same author's *To America*,[9] an attitude of sober query and stoical challenge:

How would you have us, as we are?
  Or sinking 'neath the load we bear,
Our eyes fixed forward on a star,
  Or gazing empty at despair?

Rising or falling? Men or things?
  With dragging pace or footsteps fleet?
Strong, willing sinews in your wings,
  Or tightening chains about your feet?

More and more, however, an intelligent realization of the great discrepancy between the American social creed and the American social practice forces upon the Negro the taking of the moral advantage that is his. Only the steadying and sobering effect of a truly characteristic gentleness of spirit prevents the rapid rise of a definite cynicism and counter-hate and a defiant superiority feeling. Human as this reaction would be, the majority still deprecate its advent, and would gladly see it forestalled by the speedy amelioration of its causes. We wish our race pride to be a healthier, more positive achievement than a feeling based upon a realization of the shortcomings of others. But all paths toward the attainment of a sound social attitude have been difficult; only a relatively few enlightened minds have been able as the phrase puts it "to rise above" prejudice. The ordinary man has had until recently only a hard choice between the alternatives of supine and humiliating submission and stimulating but hurtful counter-prejudice. Fortunately from some inner, desperate resourcefulness has recently sprung up the simple expedient of fighting prejudice by mental passive resistance, in other words by trying to ignore it. For the few, this manna may perhaps be effective, but the masses cannot thrive upon it.

Fortunately there are constructive channels opening out into which the balked social feelings of the American Negro can flow freely.

Without them there would be much more pressure and danger than there is. These compensating interests are racial but in a new and enlarged way. One is the consciousness of acting as the advance-guard of the African peoples in their contact with Twentieth Century civilization; the other, the sense of a mission of rehabilitating the race in world esteem from that loss of prestige for which the fate and conditions of slavery have so largely been responsible. Harlem, as we shall see, is the center of both these movements; she is the home of the Negro's "Zionism."[1] The pulse of the Negro world has begun to beat in Harlem. A Negro newspaper carrying news material in English,

8. From "O Southland!" (1907).
9. Published in 1917.

1. An international movement aimed at securing a homeland for the Jewish people.

French and Spanish, gathered from all quarters of America, the West Indies and Africa has maintained itself in Harlem for over five years. Two important magazines,[2] both edited from New York, maintain their news and circulation consistently on a cosmopolitan scale. Under American auspices and backing, three pan-African congresses have been held abroad for the discussion of common interests, colonial questions and the future cooperative development of Africa. In terms of the race question as a world problem, the Negro mind has leapt, so to speak, upon the parapets of prejudice and extended its cramped horizons. In so doing it has linked up with the growing group consciousness of the dark-peoples and is gradually learning their common interests. As one of our writers has recently put it: "It is imperative that we understand the white world in its relations to the non-white world." As with the Jew, persecution is making the Negro international.

As a world phenomenon this wider race consciousness is a different thing from the much asserted rising tide of color. Its inevitable causes are not of our making. The consequences are not necessarily damaging to the best interests of civilization. Whether it actually brings into being new Armadas of conflict or argosies[3] of cultural exchange and enlightenment can only be decided by the attitude of the dominant races in an era of critical change. With the American Negro, his new internationalism is primarily an effort to recapture contact with the scattered peoples of African derivation. Garveyism[4] may be a transient, if spectacular, phenomenon, but the possible role of the American Negro in the future development of Africa is one of the most constructive and universally helpful missions that any modern people can lay claim to.

Constructive participation in such causes cannot help giving the Negro valuable group incentives, as well as increased prestige at home and abroad. Our greatest rehabilitation may possibly come through such channels, but for the present, more immediate hope rests in the revaluation by white and black alike of the Negro in terms of his artistic endowments and cultural contributions, past and prospective. It must be increasingly recognized that the Negro has already made very substantial contributions, not only in his folk-art, music especially, which has always found appreciation, but in larger, though humbler and less acknowledged ways. For generations the Negro has been the peasant matrix of that section of America which has most undervalued him, and here he has contributed not only materially in labor and in social patience, but spiritually as well. The South has unconsciously absorbed the gift of his folk-temperament. In less than half a generation it will be easier to recognize this, but the fact remains that a leaven of humor, sentiment, imagination and tropic nonchalance has gone into the making of the South from a humble, unacknowledged source. A second crop of the Negro's gifts promises still more largely. He now becomes a conscious contributor and lays aside the status of a beneficiary and ward for that of a collaborator and participant in American civilization. The great social gain in this is the releasing of our talented group from the arid fields of controversy and debate to the productive fields of creative expression. The especially cultural recognition they win should in turn prove the key to that revaluation of the Negro which must precede or accompany any considerable further betterment of

2. Probably *Opportunity* and the *Crisis*.
3. Merchant ships. "Armadas": fleets of warships.
4. The Back to Africa movement of Marcus Garvey (1887–1940).

race relationships. But whatever the general effect, the present generation will have added the motives of self-expression and spiritual development to the old and still unfinished task of making material headway and progress. No one who understandingly faces the situation with its substantial accomplishment or views the new scene with its still more abundant promise can be entirely without hope. And certainly, if in our lifetime the Negro should not be able to celebrate his full initiation into American democracy, he can at least, on the warrant of these things, celebrate the attainment of a significant and satisfying new phase of group development, and with it a spiritual Coming of Age.

1925

The Legacy of the Ancestral Arts*

Music and poetry, and to an extent the dance, have been the predominant arts of the American Negro. This is an emphasis quite different from that of the African cultures, where the plastic[1] and craft arts predominate; Africa being one of the great fountain sources of the arts of decoration and design. Except then in his remarkable carry-over of the rhythmic gift, there is little evidence of any direct connection of the American Negro with his ancestral arts. But even with the rude transplanting of slavery, that uprooted the technical elements of his former culture, the American Negro brought over as an emotional inheritance a deep-seated æsthetic endowment. And with a versatility of a very high order, this offshoot of the African spirit blended itself in with entirely different culture elements and blossomed in strange new forms.

There was in this more than a change of art-forms and an exchange of cultural patterns; there was a curious reversal of emotional temper and attitude. The characteristic African art expressions are rigid, controlled, disciplined, abstract, heavily conventionalized; those of the Aframerican—free, exuberant, emotional, sentimental and human. Only by the misinterpretation of the African spirit can one claim any emotional kinship between them—for the spirit of African expression, by and large, is disciplined, sophisticated, laconic and fatalistic. The emotional temper of the American Negro is exactly opposite. What we have thought primitive in the American Negro—his naïveté, his sentimentalism, his exuberance and his improvizing spontaneity—are then neither characteristically African nor to be explained as an ancestral heritage. They are the result of his peculiar experience in America and the emotional upheaval of its trials and ordeals. True, these are now very characteristic traits, and they have their artistic, and perhaps even their moral compensations; but they represent essentially the working of environmental forces rather than the outcropping of a race psychology; they are really the acquired and not the original artistic temperament.

A further proof of this is the fact that the American Negro, even when he confronts the various forms of African art expression with a sense of its

*The original publication of this essay in *The New Negro* included illustrations of African "plastic and craft arts" from the Barnes Foundation in Pennsylvania and from ethnographic museums in Germany and Belgium. The two photographs shown here, of an N'tomo mask and a brass head of a Beninese king, while similar to images in the 1925 text, have been added by the Norton editor, as have the captions.

1. That is, sculptural.

ethnic claims upon him, meets them in as alienated and misunderstanding an attitude as the average European Westerner. Christianity and all the other European conventions operate to make this inevitable. So there would be little hope of an influence of African art upon the western African descendants if there were not at present a growing influence of African art upon European art in general. But led by these tendencies, there is the possibility that the sensitive artistic mind of the American Negro, stimulated by a cultural pride and interest, will receive from African art a profound and galvanizing influence. The legacy is there at least, with prospects of a rich yield. In the first place, there is in the mere knowledge of the skill and unique mastery of the arts of the ancestors the valuable and stimulating realization that the Negro is not a cultural foundling without his own inheritance. Our timid and apologetic imitativeness and overburdening sense of cultural indebtedness have, let us hope, their natural end in such knowledge and realization.

Then possibly from a closer knowledge and proper appreciation of the African arts must come increased effort to develop our artistic talents in the discontinued and lagging channels of sculpture, painting and the decorative arts. If the forefathers could so adroitly master these mediums, why not we? And there may also come to some creative minds among us hints of a new technique to be taken as the basis of a characteristic expression in the plastic and pictorial arts; incentives to new artistic idioms as well as to a renewed mastery of these older arts. African sculpture has been for contemporary European painting and sculpture just such a mine of fresh *motifs,* just such a lesson in simplicity and originality of expression, and surely, once known and appreciated, this art can scarcely have less influence upon the blood descendants, bound to it by a sense of direct cultural kinship, than upon those who inherit by tradition only, and through the channels of an exotic curiosity and interest.

But what the Negro artist of today has most to gain from the arts of the forefathers is perhaps not cultural inspiration or technical innovations, but the lesson of a classic background, the lesson of discipline, of style, of technical control pushed to the limits of technical mastery. A more highly stylized art does not exist than the African. If after absorbing the new content of American life and experience, and after assimilating new patterns of art, the original artistic endowment can be sufficiently augmented to express itself with equal power in more complex patterns and substance, then the Negro may well become what some have predicted, the artist of American life.

As it is, African art has influenced modern art most considerably. It has been the most influential exotic art of our era, Chinese and Japanese art not excepted. The African art object, a half generation ago the most neglected of ethnological curios, is now universally recognized as a "notable instance of plastic representation," a genuine work of art, masterful over its material in a powerful simplicity of conception, design and effect. This artistic discovery of African art came at a time when there was a marked decadence and sterility in certain forms of European plastic art expression, due to generations of the inbreeding of style and idiom. Out of the exhaustion of imitating Greek classicism and the desperate exploitation in graphic art of all the technical possibilities of color by the Impressionists and Post Impressionists, the problem of form and decorative design became emphasized in one of those reactions which in art occur so repeatedly. And suddenly with this new problem and interest, the African representation of form, previously regarded as ridiculously crude and inadequate, appeared cunningly sophisticated and masterful. Once the strong stylistic conventions that had stood between it and a true æsthetic appreciation were thus broken through, Negro art instantly came into marked recognition. Roger Fry[2] in an essay on Negro sculpture has the following to say: "I have to admit that some of these things are great sculpture—greater, I think, than anything we produced in the Middle Ages. Certainly they have the special qualities of sculpture in a higher degree. They have indeed complete plastic freedom; that is to say, these African artists really can see form in three dimensions. Now this is rare in sculpture. . . . So—far from the clinging to two dimensions, as we tend to do, the African artist actually underlines, as it were, the three-dimensionalness of his forms. It is in some such way that he manages to give to his forms their disconcerting vitality, the suggestion that they make of being not mere echoes of actual figures, but of possessing an inner life of their own. . . . Besides the logical comprehension of plastic form which the Negro shows, he has also an exquisite taste in the handling of his material." The most authoritative contemporary Continental criticism quite thoroughly agrees with this verdict and estimate.

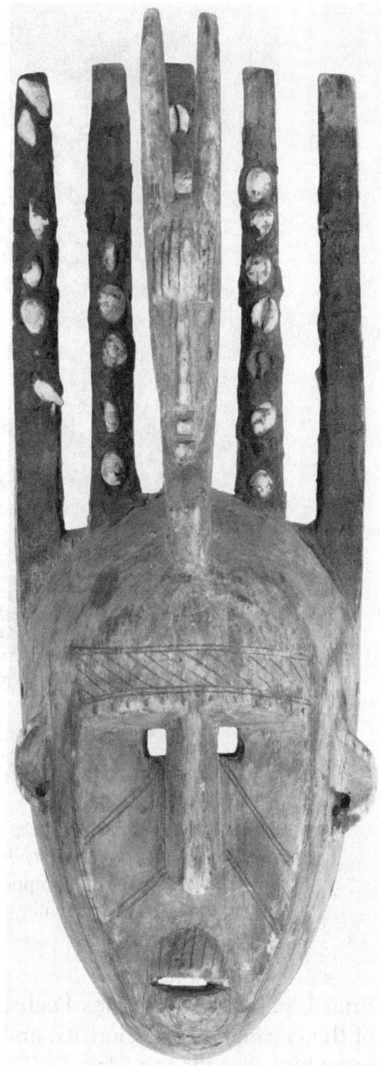

N'tomo masks are made by the Bambana people of West Africa, by an association, or school, called N'tomo. The masks represent a kind of demon-ghost, part human/part animal, and are worn during dances and rituals intended to protect young Bambana tribespeople, in particular boys who have not yet been circumcised. This mask was likely made in the early twentieth century and is decorated with shells.

Indeed there are many attested influences of African art in French and German modernist art. They are to be found in work of Matisse, Picasso, Derain, Modigliani and Utrillo among the

2. Fry (1866–1934) was an English art historian, critic, and painter, as well as a prominent advocate of modern art. The essay to which Locke refers, "Negro Sculpture," is collected in Fry's *Vision and Design* (1920).

Head of an Oba, or king. Ca. 1550. This cast-brass sculpture likely stood on an altar in a palace in Benin (present-day Nigeria). As part of a shrine, it played an important role in communications between the living king and the ruler who had preceded him.

French painters, upon Max Pechstein, Elaine Stern, Franz Marc and others of the German Expressionists, and upon Modigliani, Archipenko, Epstein, Lipschitz, Lembruch, and Zadkine and Faggi among sculptors. In Paris, centering around Paul Guillaume, one of its pioneer exponents, there has grown up an art coterie profoundly influenced by an æsthetic developed largely from the idioms of African art. And what has been true of the African sculptures has been in a lesser degree true of the influence of other African art forms—decorative design, musical rhythms, dance forms, verbal imagery and symbolism. Attracted by the appeal of African plastic art to the study of other modes of African expression, poets like Guillaume Apollinaire and Blaise Cendrars have attempted artistic re-expression of African idioms in poetic symbols and verse forms. So that what is a recognized school of modern French poetry professes the inspiration of African sources—Apollinaire, Reverdy, Salmon, Fargue and others. The bible of this coterie has been Cendrars' *Anthologie Nègre,* now in its sixth edition.

The starting point of an æsthetic interest in African musical idiom seems to have been H. A. Junod's work *Les Chants et les Contes des Barongas* (1897). From the double source of African folk song and the study of American

Negro musical rhythms, many of the leading French modernists have derived inspiration. Berard, Satie, Poulenc, Auric, and even Honneger, are all in diverse ways and degrees affected, but the most explicit influence has been upon the work of Darius Milhaud, who is an avowed propagandist of the possibilities of Negro musical idiom. The importance of these absorptions of African and Negro material by all of the major forms of contemporary art, some of them independently of any transfer that might be dismissed as a mere contagion of fad or vogue, is striking, and ought to be considered as a quite unanimous verdict of the modern creative mind upon the values, actual and potential, of this yet unexhausted reservoir of art material.

There is a vital connection between this new artistic respect for African idiom and the natural ambition of Negro artists for a racial idiom in their art expression. To a certain extent contemporary art has pronounced in advance upon this objective of the younger Negro artists, musicians and writers. Only the most reactionary conventions of art, then, stand between the Negro artist and the frank experimental development of these fresh idioms. This movement would, we think, be well under way in more avenues of advance at present but for the timid conventionalism which racial disparagement has forced upon the Negro mind in America. Let us take as a comparative instance, the painting of the Negro subject and notice the retarding effect of social prejudice. The Negro is a far more familiar figure in American life than in European, but American art, barring caricature and *genre*, reflects him scarcely at all. An occasional type sketch of Henri, or local color sketch of Winslow Homer represents all of a generation of painters. Whereas in Europe, with the Negro subject rarely accessible, we have as far back as the French romanticists a strong interest in the theme, an interest that in contemporary French, Belgian, German and even English painting has brought forth work of singular novelty and beauty. This work is almost all above the plane of *genre,* and in many cases represents sustained and lifelong study of the painting of the particularly difficult values of the Negro subject. To mention but a few, there is the work of Julius Hüther, Max Slevogt, Max Pechstein, Elaine Stern, von Ruckteschell among German painters; of Dinet, Lucie Cousturier, Bonnard, Georges Rouault, among the French; Klees van Dongen, the Dutch painter; most notably among the Belgians, Auguste Mambour; and among English painters, Neville Lewis, F. C. Gadell, John A. Wells, and Frank Potter. All these artists have looked upon the African scene and the African countenance, and discovered there a beauty that calls for a distinctive idiom both of color and modelling. The Negro physiognomy[3] must be freshly and objectively conceived on its own patterns if it is ever to be seriously and importantly interpreted. Art must discover and reveal the beauty which prejudice and caricature have overlaid. And all vital art discovers beauty and opens our eyes to that which previously we could not see. While American art, including the work of our own Negro artists, has produced nothing above the level of the *genre* study or more penetrating

3. The general form or appearance of something, often with specific reference to facial features; the practice of physiognomy held that the face could reveal a person's character—such pseudoscience was often applied to whole ethnic groups.

than a Nordicized[4] transcription, European art has gone on experimenting until the technique of the Negro subject has reached the dignity and skill of virtuoso treatment and a distinctive style. No great art will impose alien canons upon its subject matter. The work of Mambour[5] especially suggests this forceful new stylization; he has brought to the Negro subject a modelling of masses that is truly sculptural and particularly suited to the broad massive features and subtle value shadings of the Negro countenance. After seeing his masterful handling of mass and light and shade in bold solid planes, one has quite the conviction that mere line and contour treatment can never be the classical technique for the portrayal of Negro types.

The work of these European artists should even now be the inspiration and guide-posts of a younger school of American Negro artists. They have too long been the victims of the academy tradition and shared the conventional blindness of the Caucasian eye with respect to the racial material at their immediate disposal. Thus there have been notably successful Negro artists, but no development of a school of Negro art. Our Negro American painter of outstanding success is Henry O. Tanner.[6] His career is a case in point. Though a professed painter of types, he has devoted his art talent mainly to the portrayal of Jewish Biblical types and subjects, and has never maturely touched the portrayal of the Negro subject. Warrantable enough—for to the individual talent in art one must never dictate—who can be certain what field the next Negro artist of note will choose to command, or whether he will not be a landscapist or a master of still life or of purely decorative painting? But from the point of view of our artistic talent in bulk—it is a different matter. We ought and must have a school of Negro art, a local and a racially representative tradition. And that we have not, explains why the generation of Negro artists succeeding Mr. Tanner had only the inspiration of his great success to fire their ambitions, but not the guidance of a distinctive tradition to focus and direct their talents. Consequently they fumbled and fell short of his international stride and reach. The work of Henri Scott, Edwin A. Harleson, Laura Wheeler, in painting, and of Meta Warrick Fuller and May Howard Jackson in sculpture, competent as it has been, has nevertheless felt this handicap and has wavered between abstract expression which was imitative and not highly original, and racial expression which was only experimental. Lacking group leadership and concentration, they were wandering amateurs in the very field that might have given them concerted mastery.

A younger group of Negro artists is beginning to move in the direction of a racial school of art. The strengthened tendency toward representative group expression is shared even by the later work of the artists previously mentioned, as in Meta Warrick Fuller's "Ethiopia Awakening," to mention an outstanding example. But the work of young artists like Archibald Motley, Otto Farrill, Cecil Gaylord, John Urquhart, Samuel Blount, and especially that of Charles Keene and Aaron Douglas shows the promising beginning of an art movement instead of just the cropping out of isolated talent. The work of Winold Reiss, fellow-countryman of Slevogt and von Ruckteschell, which has supplied the main illustrative

4. That is, something that is remade or communicated in the style of the people of northern Europe.
5. Auguste Mambour (1896–1968), a Belgian painter who traveled to the Congo in 1923.
6. Though known for his depictions of Black life, especially *The Banjo Lesson* (1893), Tanner (1859–1937) is most famous for the many biblical scenes he painted.

material for this volume has been deliberately conceived and executed as a path-breaking guide and encouragement to this new foray of the younger Negro artists. In idiom, technical treatment and objective social angle, it is a bold iconoclastic break with the current traditions that have grown up about the Negro subject in American art. It is not meant to dictate a style to the young Negro artist, but to point the lesson that contemporary European art has already learned—that any vital artistic expression of the Negro theme and subject in art must break through the stereotypes to a new style, a distinctive fresh technique, and some sort of characteristic idiom.

While we are speaking of the resources of racial art, it is well to take into account that the richest vein of it is not that of portraitistic idiom after all, but its almost limitless wealth of decorative and purely symbolic material. It is for the development of this latter aspect of a racial art that the study and example of African art material is so important. The African spirit, as we said at the outset, is at its best in abstract decorative forms. Design, and to a lesser degree, color, are its original *fortes.* It is this aspect of the folk tradition, this slumbering gift of the folk temperament that most needs reachievement and reexpression. And if African art is capable of producing the ferment in modern art that it has, surely this is not too much to expect of its influence upon the culturally awakened Negro artist of the present generation. So that if even the present vogue of African art should pass, and the bronzes of Benin and the fine sculptures of Gabon and Baoulé, and the superb designs of the Bushongo should again become mere items of exotic curiosity, for the Negro artist they ought still to have the import and influence of classics in whatever art expression is consciously and representatively racial.

1925

GEORGIA DOUGLAS JOHNSON
1886–1966

Although she never lived in Harlem, Georgia Douglas Johnson was almost universally regarded as the foremost poet among the women of the Harlem Renaissance as well as among the most beloved because of her unstinting encouragement of younger writers, male and female. Johnson, a shy child, grew up in Rome, Georgia, and Atlanta, where she was a favorite among her teachers. At the Atlanta University Normal School, she overcame her loneliness by educating herself in the field of music. She regarded the university as a haven and regretted having to leave it after graduation.

Douglas then taught in Marietta, Georgia, served as an assistant school principal in Atlanta, and studied music at the Oberlin Conservatory and the Cleveland College of Music. She also wrote verse, but it was not until her marriage to Henry Lincoln Johnson in 1903 that she began submitting poetry and short fiction to newspapers and magazines. In 1910, the Johnsons moved to Washington, D.C., where Henry (a prominent Republican) was appointed recorder of deeds by President Taft in 1912. The Johnsons made their home (known as Halfway House) a gathering place for Black intellectuals and artists. They hosted a Saturday night salon that drew not only writers based in the area (including Jean Toomer, Angelina Weld Grimké, Willis Richardson, Alain Locke, Zora Neale Hurston, and Bruce Nugent) but also luminaries such as W. E. B. Du Bois and Langston Hughes when they visited Washington.

In 1918, Georgia Johnson published her first book, a slim collection of poems titled *The Heart of a Woman.* Despite praise from the best-known African American critic of poetry, William Stanley Braithwaite, a number of readers criticized Johnson for her apparent lack of concern for the theme of race. In 1922, she responded with *Bronze: A Book of Verse.* Dedicated entirely to racial themes, this volume enjoyed a friendlier reception. However, her main interest as a poet was clearly in romantic, sentimental, and brief commentaries on the human condition.

After her husband's death in 1925, and partly in appreciation of his service to the Republican Party, Calvin Coolidge appointed Johnson commissioner of conciliation in the Department of Labor. In 1928, she published her third volume of verse, *An Autumn Love Cycle,* in which she returned to her favorite subject, the role of love in women's lives. In the years that followed, the energetic Johnson wrote numerous short stories (many were never published), several well-received plays, and four newspaper columns: *Homely Philosophy, Wise Sayings, Beauty Hints,* and a column of interracial news for the *New York Amsterdam News.* For a while, she even sponsored a lonely hearts club, to help people meet one another in the hope of finding love. Her last book, *Share My World,* a small collection of poems, was privately published in 1962. In 1965, Atlanta University conferred on her an honorary doctoral degree.

Although Johnson sometimes regretted that she never had either the time or the money to finish the many projects that were so important to her, she was nevertheless one of the most prolific writers of the Harlem Renaissance and one of its more memorable personalities.

The Heart of a Woman

The heart of a woman goes forth with the dawn,
As a lone bird, soft winging, so restlessly on,
Afar o'er life's turrets and vales does it roam
In the wake of those echoes the heart calls home.

The heart of a woman falls back with the night,
And enters some alien cage in its plight,
And tries to forget it has dreamed of the stars,
While it breaks, breaks, breaks on the sheltering bars.

1918

I Want to Die While You Love Me[1]

I want to die while you love me,
While yet you hold me fair,
While laughter lies upon my lips
And lights are in my hair.

I want to die while you love me,
And bear to that still bed,
Your kisses turbulent, unspent,
To warm me when I'm dead.

I want to die while you love me,
Oh, who would care to live
Till love has nothing more to ask
And nothing more to give!

I want to die while you love me
And never, never see
The glory of this perfect day
Grow dim or cease to be.

1927

1. Set to music (sung by Harry Burleigh for Victor Records), this poem became a popular song.

MARCUS GARVEY
1887–1940

Marcus Garvey, whose name continues to evoke the glorious "Back to Africa" slogan with which it is linked, was easily the most controversial figure associated with Harlem in the 1920s. A hero to millions of Blacks, he was scorned by many of their other leaders and intellectuals. W. E. B. Du Bois clashed openly with Garvey over basic questions of leadership; and even Wallace Thurman, who professed to admire him, once described Garvey as "composed of charlatan, mountebank, saviour and fool." Many people who admired Garvey for his seemingly inexhaustible energy and vision were bewildered by his flamboyance and his apparent lack of business sense. No one can deny, however, that Garvey was a profound human force during the Harlem Renaissance, a mighty shaper of attitudes and molder of opinions concerning the rights and destiny of Black Americans.

Born in St. Ann's Bay, Jamaica, Marcus Garvey had to quit school at the age of fourteen to help support his family. He found work as a printer's apprentice in Kingston, the capital. Moved by the economic and social inequities he saw all around him, he helped lead a printer's union strike in 1907. Three years later, he founded *Garvey's Watchman,* a periodical that quickly failed. He moved on to Costa Rica, where, as a timekeeper on a banana plantation, he witnessed the exploitation of Black laborers by their lighter-skinned taskmasters. Further travels in Central America convinced him that wherever whites and Blacks were found together, the whites were sure to be exploiting the Blacks—a situation he was determined to change. In 1912, he traveled to London. While there, he read Booker T. Washington's *Up From Slavery* (1901), which changed his life. According to Garvey, after reading Washington's text he asked himself: "'Where is the Black man's government?' 'Where is his King and his kingdom?' 'Where is his president, his country, and his ambassador, his army, his navy, his men of big affairs?' I could not find them, and then I declared, 'I will help to make them.'"

With something approaching religious fervor, he returned to Jamaica in 1914. Later that year, he founded one of the most important organizations of the twentieth century, the Universal Negro Improvement Association (UNIA). Its principal objective, "the general uplift of the Negro peoples of the world," was identified at first with Garvey's struggle to provide Jamaicans with schools modeled on Washington's Tuskegee Institute in Alabama. Frustrated by his failure during the next two years to make progress toward his goals, Garvey traveled to the United States to raise money. Arriving in Harlem in 1916, he quickly decided to remain there. Within four years, he commanded a larger following than any other Black leader in America. Much of the extraordinary growth of the UNIA is attributable to the success of *Negro World,* the weekly newspaper that Garvey founded in 1918 and in which many of his speeches and essays (usually brief) appeared. At one point, *Negro World* probably enjoyed a circulation of nearly a quarter million readers—although most statistics relating to the UNIA are impossible to verify.

The UNIA reached the zenith of its prestige and influence in 1920, with a remarkable international convention in Harlem. After the convention, which attracted some twenty-five thousand delegates, even Garvey's most hostile critics could no longer dismiss him as a marginal demagogue.

The tide began to turn, however, with the failure of one of Garvey's pet projects, the Black Star Line. The shipping line, for which the UNIA raised well over $500,000, had the threefold objective of making a profit, employing Blacks in the important

Reverend J. C. Austin and Marcus Garvey, in ceremonial field marshal dress as the self-appointed "commander-in-chief of the African Legion," during a UNIA parade in Harlem, August 1922.

positions denied them in the traditionally white shipping industry, and serving as an economic means of transportation for Blacks interested in escaping white oppression by moving to Africa, particularly to Liberia. But the line was a fiasco almost from its inception in 1919. By 1922, despite Garvey's attempts to raise money for it through a mail campaign, the Black Star Line was past saving. Garvey was arrested on a federal charge of mail fraud that same year and convicted in 1925. Sentenced to a five-year prison term, he served nearly three years before he was deported to Jamaica in 1927.

Garvey spent the remainder of his life vainly attempting to recover the prestige that he and the UNIA had lost. Ironically, opposed by the major colonial powers, he died in 1940 (of a stroke) without ever having set foot in Africa. Even after his death, the UNIA continued to plan for racial "uplift."

Marcus Garvey's achievement is difficult to evaluate. Despite his lack of organization, his occasional meetings with the Ku Klux Klan, who shared his racially exclusive views of society, and his failure to achieve many of his long-term goals, his gospel of race pride and race solidarity (key themes of the Harlem Renaissance) endures as a sustaining force in Black cultures throughout the world.

Africa for the Africans

For five years the Universal Negro Improvement Association[1] has been advocating the cause of Africa for the Africans—that is, that the Negro peoples of the world should concentrate upon the object of building up for themselves a great nation in Africa.

When we started our propaganda toward this end several of the so-called intellectual Negroes who have been bamboozling the race for over half a century said that we were crazy, that the Negro peoples of the western world were not interested in Africa and could not live in Africa. One editor and leader went so far as to say at his so-called Pan-African Congress[2] that American Negroes could not live in Africa, because the climate was too hot. All kinds of arguments have been adduced by these Negro intellectuals against the colonization of Africa by the black race. Some said that the black man would ultimately work out his existence alongside of the white man in countries founded and established by the latter. Therefore, it was not necessary for Negroes to seek an independent nationality of their own. The old time stories of "African fever," "African bad climate," "African mosquitos," "African savages," have been repeated by these "brainless intellectuals" of ours as a scare against our people in America and the West Indies taking a kindly interest in the new program of building a racial empire of our own in our Motherland. Now that years have rolled by and the Universal Negro Improvement Association has made the circuit of the world with its propaganda, we find eminent statesmen and leaders of the white race coming out boldly advocating the cause of colonizing Africa with the Negroes of the western world. A year ago Senator MacCullum[3] of the Mississippi Legislature introduced a resolution in the House for the purpose of petitioning the Congress of the United States of America and the President to use their good influence in securing from the Allies sufficient territory in Africa in liquidation of the war debt, which territory should be used for the establishing of an independent nation for American Negroes. About the same time Senator France[4] of Maryland gave expression to a similar desire in the Senate of the United States. During a speech on the "Soldiers' Bonus," he said: "We owe a big debt to Africa and one which we have too long ignored. I need not enlarge upon our peculiar interest in the obligation to the people of Africa. Thousands of Americans have for years been contributing to the missionary work which has been carried out by the noble men and women who have been sent out in that field by the churches of America."

1. Founded by Garvey in 1916 with "the general uplift of the Negro peoples of the world" as its main objective.
2. W. E. B. Du Bois (1868–1963) organized the congress in 1919.
3. T. G. MacCallum, state senator for Mississippi (1932–36).
4. Joseph Irwin France (1873–1939), U.S. senator from 1917 to 1923.

Germany to the Front

This reveals a real change on the part of prominent statesmen in their attitude on the African question. Then comes another suggestion from Germany, for which Dr. Heinrich Schnee, a former Governor[5] of German East Africa, is author. This German statesman suggests in an interview given out in Berlin, and published in New York, that America takes over the mandatories of Great Britain and France in Africa for the colonization of American Negros. Speaking on the matter, he says, "As regards the attempt to colonize Africa with the surplus American colored population, this would in a long way settle the vexed problem, and under the plan such as Senator France has outlined, might enable France and Great Britain to discharge their duties to the United States, and simultaneously ease the burden of German reparations which is paralyzing economic life."

With expressions as above quoted from prominent world statesmen, and from the demands made by such men as Senators France and MacCullum, it is clear that the question of African nationality is not a far-fetched one, but is as reasonable and feasible as was the idea of an American nationality.

A "Program" at Last

I trust that the Negro peoples of the world are now convinced that the work of the Universal Negro Improvement Association is not a visionary one, but very practical, and that it is not so far fetched, but can be realized in a short while if the entire race will only co-operate and work toward the desired end. Now that the work of our organization has started to bear fruit we find that some of these "doubting Thomases" of three and four years ago are endeavoring to mix themselves up with the popular idea of rehabilitating Africa in the interest of the Negro. They are now advancing spurious "programs" and in a short while will endeavor to force themselves upon the public as advocates and leaders of the African idea.

It is felt that those who have followed the career of the Universal Negro Improvement Association will not allow themselves to be deceived by these Negro opportunists who have always sought to live off the ideas of other people.

The Dream of a Negro Empire

It is only a question of a few more years when Africa will be completely colonized by Negroes, as Europe is by the white race. What we want is an independent African nationality, and if America is to help the Negro peoples of the world establish such a nationality, then we welcome the assistance.

It is hoped that when the time comes for American and West Indian Negroes to settle in Africa, they will realize their responsibility and their duty. It will not be to go to Africa for the purpose of exercising an overlordship over the natives, but it shall be the purpose of the Universal Negro Improvement Association to have established in Africa that brotherly co-operation which will make the interests of the African native and the American and West Indian Negro one and the same, that is to say, we shall enter into a common partnership to build up Africa in the interests of our race.

5. From 1912 to 1918.

Oneness of Interests

Everybody knows that there is absolutely no difference between the native African and the American and West Indian Negroes, in that we are descendants from one common family stock. It is only a matter of accident that we have been divided and kept apart for over three hundred years, but it is felt that when the time has come for us to get back together, we shall do so in the spirit of brotherly love, and any Negro who expects that he will be assisted here, there or anywhere by the Universal Negro Improvement Association to exercise a haughty superiority over the fellows of his own race, makes a tremendous mistake. Such men had better remain where they are and not attempt to become in any way interested in the higher development of Africa.

The Negro has had enough of the vaunted practice of race superiority as inflicted upon him by others, therefore he is not prepared to tolerate a similar assumption on the part of his own people. In America and the West Indies, we have Negroes who believe themselves so much above their fellows as to cause them to think that any readjustment in the affairs of the race should be placed in their hands for them to exercise a kind of an autocratic and despotic control as others have done to us for centuries. Again I say, it would be advisable for such Negroes to take their hands and minds off the now popular idea of colonizing Africa in the interest of the Negro race, because their being identified with this new program will not in any way help us because of the existing feeling among Negroes everywhere not to tolerate the infliction of race or class superiority upon them, as is the desire of the self-appointed and self-created race leadership that we have been having for the last fifty years.

The Basis of an African Aristocracy

The masses of Negroes in America, the West Indies, South and Central America are in sympathetic accord with the aspirations of the native Africans. We desire to help them build up Africa as a Negro Empire, where every black man, whether he was born in Africa or in the Western world, will have the opportunity to develop on his own lines under the protection of the most favorable democratic institutions.

It will be useless, as before stated, for bombastic Negroes to leave America and the West Indies to go to Africa, thinking that they will have privileged positions to inflict upon the race that bastard aristocracy that they have tried to maintain in this Western world at the expense of the masses. Africa shall develop an aristocracy of its own, but it shall be based upon service and loyalty to race. Let all Negroes work toward that end. I feel that it is only a question of a few more years before our program will be accepted not only by the few statesmen of America who are now interested in it, but by the strong statesmen of the world, as the only solution to the great race problem. There is no other way to avoid the threatening war of the races that is bound to engulf all mankind, which has been prophesied by the world's greatest thinkers; there is no better method than by apportioning every race to its own habitat.

The time has really come for the Asiatics to govern themselves in Asia, as the Europeans are in Europe and the Western world, so also is it wise for the Africans to govern themselves at home, and thereby bring peace and satisfaction to the entire human family.

1923

The Future as I See It

It comes to the individual, the race, the nation, once in a life-time to decide upon the course to be pursued as a career. The hour has now struck for the individual Negro as well as the entire race to decide the course that will be pursued in the interest of our own liberty.

We who make up the Universal Negro Improvement Association have decided that we shall go forward, upward and onward toward the great goal of human liberty. We have determined among ourselves that all barriers placed in the way of our progress must be removed, must be cleared away for we desire to see the light of a brighter day.

The Negro Is Ready

The Universal Negro Improvement Association for five years has been proclaiming to the world the readiness of the Negro to carve out a pathway for himself in the course of life. Men of other races and nations have become alarmed at this attitude of the Negro in his desire to do things for himself and by himself. This alarm has become so universal that organizations have been brought into being here, there and everywhere for the purpose of deterring and obstructing this forward move of our race. Propaganda has been waged here, there and everywhere for the purpose of misinterpreting the intention of this organization; some have said that this organization seeks to create discord and discontent among the races; some say we are organized for the purpose of hating other people. Every sensible, sane and honest-minded person knows that the Universal Negro Improvement Association has no such intention. We are organized for the absolute purpose of bettering our condition, industrially, commercially, socially, religiously and politically. We are organized not to hate other men, but to lift ourselves, and to demand respect of all humanity. We have a program that we believe to be righteous; we believe it to be just, and we have made up our minds to lay down ourselves on the altar of sacrifice for the realization of this great hope of ours, based upon the foundation of righteousness. We declare to the world that Africa must be free, that the entire Negro race must be emancipated from industrial bondage, peonage and serfdom; we make no compromise, we make no apology in this our declaration. We do not desire to create offense on the part of other races, but we are determined that we shall be heard, that we shall be given the rights to which we are entitled.

The Propaganda of Our Enemies

For the purpose of creating doubts about the work of the Universal Negro Improvement Association, many attempts have been made to cast shadow and gloom over our work. They[1] have even written the most uncharitable things about our organization; they have spoken so unkindly of our effort, but what do we care? They spoke unkindly and uncharitably about all the reform movements that have helped in the betterment of humanity. They maligned the great movement of the Christian religion; they maligned the great liberation movements of America, of France, of England, of Russia; can we expect, then, to escape being maligned in this, our desire for the liberation of Africa and the freedom of four hundred million Negroes of the world?

We have unscrupulous men and organizations working in opposition to us. Some trying to capitalize the new spirit that has come to the Negro to make profit out of it to their own selfish benefit; some are trying to set back the Negro from seeing the hope of his own liberty, and thereby poisoning our people's mind against the motives of our organization; but every sensible far-seeing Negro in this enlightened age knows what propaganda means. It is the medium of discrediting that which you are opposed to, so that the propaganda of our enemies will be of little avail as soon as we are rendered able to carry to our peoples scattered throughout the world the true message of our great organization.

"Crocodiles" as Friends

Men of the Negro race, let me say to you that a greater future is in store for us; we have no cause to lose hope, to become faint-hearted. We must realize that upon ourselves depend our destiny, our future; we must carve out that future, that destiny, and we who make up the Universal Negro Improvement Association have pledged ourselves that nothing in the world shall stand in our way, nothing in the world shall discourage us, but opposition shall make us work harder, shall bring us closer together so that as one man the millions of us will march on toward that goal that we have set for ourselves. The new Negro shall not be deceived. The new Negro refuses to take advice from anyone who has not felt with him, and suffered with him. We have suffered for three hundred years, therefore we feel that the time has come when only those who have suffered with us can interpret our feelings and our spirit. It takes the slave to interpret the feelings of the slave; it takes the unfortunate man to interpret the spirit of his unfortunate brother; and so it takes the suffering Negro to interpret the spirit of his comrade. It is strange that so many people are interested in the Negro now, willing to advise him how to act, and what organizations he should join, yet nobody was interested in the Negro to the extent of not making him a slave for two hundred and fifty years, reducing him to industrial peonage and serfdom after he was freed; it is strange that the same people can be so interested in the Negro now, as to tell him what organization he should follow and what leader he should support.

Whilst we are bordering on a future of brighter things, we are also at our danger period, when we must either accept the right philosophy, or go down by following deceptive propaganda which has hemmed us in for many centuries.

1. That is, Garvey's opponents such as W. E. B. Du Bois.

Deceiving the People

There is many a leader of our race who tells us that everything is well, and that all things will work out themselves and that a better day is coming. Yes, all of us know that a better day is coming; we all know that one day we will go home to Paradise, but whilst we are hoping by our Christian virtues to have an entry into Paradise we also realize that we are living on earth, and that the things that are practiced in Paradise are not practiced here. You have to treat this world as the world treats you; we are living in a temporal, material age, an age of activity, an age of racial, national selfishness. What else can you expect but to give back to the world what the world gives to you, and we are calling upon the four hundred million Negroes of the world to take a decided stand, a determined stand, that we shall occupy a firm position; that position shall be an emancipated race and a free nation of our own. We are determined that we shall have a free country; we are determined that we shall have a flag; we are determined that we shall have a government second to none in the world.

An Eye for an Eye

Men may spurn the idea, they may scoff at it; the metropolitan press of this country may deride us; yes, white men may laugh at the idea of Negroes talking about government; but let me tell you there is going to be a government, and let me say to you also that whatsoever you give, in like measure it shall be returned to you.[2] The world is sinful, and therefore man believes in the doctrine of an eye for an eye, a tooth for a tooth.[3] Everybody believes that revenge is God's,[4] but at the same time we are men, and revenge sometimes springs up, even in the most Christian heart.

Why should man write down a history that will react against him? Why should man perpetrate deeds of wickedness upon his brother which will return to him in like measure? Yes, the Germans maltreated the French in the Franco-Prussian war of 1870, but the French got even with the Germans in 1918. It is history, and history will repeat itself. Beat the Negro, brutalize the Negro, kill the Negro, burn the Negro, imprison the Negro, scoff at the Negro, deride the Negro, it may come back to you one of these fine days, because the supreme destiny of man is in the hands of God. God is no respecter of persons, whether that person be white, yellow or black. Today the one race is up, tomorrow it has fallen; today the Negro seems to be the footstool of the other races and nations of the world; tomorrow the Negro may occupy the highest rung of the great human ladder.

But, when we come to consider the history of man, was not the Negro a power, was he not great once? Yes, honest students of history can recall the day when Egypt, Ethiopia and Timbuctoo towered in their civilizations, towered above Europe, towered above Asia. When Europe was inhabited by a race of cannibals, a race of savages, naked men, heathens and pagans, Africa was peopled with a race of cultured black men, who were masters in art, science and literature; men who were cultured and refined; men who, it

2. "For with the same measure that ye mete withal it shall be measured to you again" (Luke 6:38).

3. "Ye have heard that it hath been said, An eye for an eye, and a tooth for a tooth" (Matthew 5:38).

4. "To me belongeth vengeance, and recompence" (Deuteronomy 32:35).

was said, were like the gods. Even the great poets of old sang in beautiful sonnets of the delight it afforded the gods to be in companionship with the Ethiopians. Why, then, should we lose hope? Black men, you were once great; you shall be great again. Lose not courage, lose not faith, go forward. The thing to do is to get organized; keep separated and you will be exploited, you will be robbed, you will be killed. Get organized, and you will compel the world to respect you. If the world fails to give you consideration, because you are black men, because you are Negroes, four hundred millions of you shall, through organization, shake the pillars of the universe and bring down creation, even as Samson brought down the temple upon his head and upon the heads of the Philistines.[5]

An Inspiring Vision

So Negroes, I say, through the Universal Negro Improvement Association, that there is much to live for. I have a vision of the future, and I see before me a picture of a redeemed Africa, with her dotted cities, with her beautiful civilization, with her millions of happy children, going to and fro. Why should I lose hope, why should I give up and take a back place in this age of progress? Remember that you are men, that God created you Lords of this creation. Lift up yourselves, men, take yourselves out of the mire and hitch your hopes to the stars; yes, rise as high as the very stars themselves. Let no man pull you down, let no man destroy your ambition, because man is but your companion, your equal; man is your brother; he is not your lord; he is not your sovereign master.

We of the Universal Negro Improvement Association feel happy; we are cheerful. Let them connive to destroy us; let them organize to destroy us; we shall fight the more. Ask me personally the cause of my success, and I say opposition; oppose me, and I fight the more, and if you want to find out the sterling worth of the Negro, oppose him, and under the leadership of the Universal Negro Improvement Association he shall fight his way to victory, and in the days to come, and I believe not far distant, Africa shall reflect a splendid demonstration of the worth of the Negro, of the determination of the Negro, to set himself free and to establish a government of his own.

1923

5. Judges 16:29–30.

RENÉ MARAN
1887–1960

Along with James Weldon Johnson's *Book of American Negro Poetry* (1922) and Jean Toomer's *Cane* (1923), the English translation of René Maran's novel *Batouala* in the summer of 1922 was one of the major publishing events that gave early momentum to the Harlem Renaissance. The shocking news that a novel about

Africa written by an obscure Black Caribbean author had been awarded the 1921 Prix Goncourt, France's most prestigious book prize (given to Marcel Proust just two years earlier), stirred up excitement in every corner of Harlem. In the *Crisis* (which featured a portrait of Maran on its May 1922 cover), Jessie Fauset called it a "great novel" and lauded its "almost cinema-like sharpness of picturization." The very first issue of *Opportunity* in January 1923 promised "more about René Maran." In 1924 W. E. B. Du Bois wrote that Maran's "attack on France" in *Batouala* "marks an era. Never before have Negroes criticized the work of the French in Africa." Not to be outdone, Marcus Garvey's *Negro World* devoted multiple articles to *Batouala* in 1922 and 1923 (by Hubert Harrison, William Ferris, Mary White Ovington, J. A. Rogers, Alain Locke, and Eric Walrond), and by November one bookstore in Harlem was even offering free copies of the novel with the purchase of a subscription to the UNIA paper. Garvey himself, in an August 1922 speech, commented that Maran's book proved "the universality of the dissatisfaction that now exists among far-seeing, self-respecting Negroes, over the mis-Government and exploitation that is carried on in Africa by the so-called Colonizing and civilizing Governments of the world."

Painting of Maran by Albert Smith that appeared on the cover of *The Crisis*. A regular contributor of etchings and drawings to Harlem Renaissance periodicals, Smith spent most of the period living in Paris, where he worked both as a musician and singer and as a commercial printmaker and illustrator.

Maran himself had not anticipated either the prize or the controversy *Batouala* would arouse in French literary circles. Born in Fort-de-France, Martinique, where his Guyanese father was stationed in the French colonial administration, Maran was sent alone at the age of seven to Bordeaux to complete his studies in France. He excelled in school, and there was early evidence of his literary talent (he published a book of poetry just as he finished high school), but the death of his father in 1910 put further education out of reach financially. Maran followed his father's example and joined the colonial service, taking a position in French Equatorial Africa (now part of the Central African Republic).

He started work on *Batouala* in 1912 and devoted more than six years to revision, striving for unflinching realism in the model of Flaubert. In a letter to a friend, Maran insisted that as a writer he was only "a recording device," capturing "what the natives really think, and what they say *when they think that no one hears them.*" But upon the announcement of the Prix Goncourt, Maran was widely condemned in the French press, less for the novel's relatively straightforward tale of the chief Batouala's betrayal at the hands of his favorite wife Yassiguindiji and his best friend Bissibingui than for Maran's incendiary preface, which attacked the abuses and hypocrisies of French colonialism in unsparing terms: "Civilization, civilization, pride of the Europeans, and their slaughterhouse of innocents. . . . You build your kingdom on top of corpses."

Stung by the criticism and accusations of disloyalty, Maran left the colonial service in 1923 and settled in Paris. He continued to write, publishing articles and reviews at a prodigious rate, and in May 1924 helped to found (with the Dahomean Kojo Tovalou Houénou) one of the first Black newspapers in the metropole, the bi-monthly *Les Continents*. He continued to respond to attacks on *Batouala*, explaining that his criticism of colonial abuses was motivated only by his commitment to the ideals of the French empire. He considered it his duty to unmask the hypocrisy of the colonial administration, he wrote in *Les Continents* in July, "in order to render it innocuous, so that the people of the overseas territories might come to love the real France without reservations." But Maran was widely criticized as a traitor to the empire. When in October *Les Continents* published an unsigned article accusing the Senegalese deputy Blaise Diagne (the first African elected to the French legislature) of having accepted payments for each African conscripted into service during World War I, Diagne brought suit and the newspaper was forced to cease publication.

Nevertheless, during its brief lifetime *Les Continents* was a crucial link to the Harlem Renaissance. In June 1924 *Les Continents* printed Maran's "Open Letter" criticizing Alain Locke's naïve essay in *Opportunity* about the French African soldiers who had been stationed along the Rhine after the war to guard the German border. *Opportunity* published a translation of Maran's letter, and the men began a life-long correspondence. That summer, Maran met Langston Hughes in Paris, and *Les Continents* published poems by Hughes, Leslie Hill, and Countee Cullen, along with a short article by Locke extolling the younger generation of Negro poets. (This selection appeared nearly six months before the celebrated "New Negro" special issue of the *Survey Graphic*.) Cullen's contribution was called "The Dance of Love (After Reading René Maran's *Batouala*)."

In December 1925 Maran published a piece on "The Negro Literary Movement in the United States" in *Vient de Paraître* that was the first in Europe to cover the renaissance; it led to a French translation of Walter White's novel *The Fire in the Flint* in the fall of 1927. Maran tried without success to convince a French publisher to translate *The New Negro*, as well, and Locke in turn tried to interest American publishers in Maran's later novels such as *Le roman d'un nègre* (1927) and *Le livre de la brousse* (1933). Translations of articles by Maran continued to appear regularly in *Opportunity*, and Maran served as one of the judges for the *Crisis* short story prizes in 1925. Over the next decade and a half, Maran and his wife hosted a literary salon in Paris that drew almost every visiting Harlem Renaissance figure; in the 1930s it was Maran who introduced the writers of the renaissance to the Francophone graduate students, Paulette Nardal, Aimé Césaire, and Léopold Sédar Senghor, who would spearhead the *Négritude* movement.

While he continued to publish fiction and poetry, Maran had difficulty making a living as a writer, and by the late 1930s he had begun to write commissioned biographies of colonial luminaries under titles such as *The Pioneers of Empire*. He was given a smattering of prizes for career accomplishment, but he was overlooked or dismissed by younger Black French writers after World War II; most famously, Frantz Fanon devoted a chapter of *Black Skin, White Masks* (1952) to an analysis of one of Maran's autobiographical novels as "neurotic." Only Senghor—whose first publication was a 1935 essay on Maran—was compelled to argue after Maran's death in 1960 that the author of *Batouala* had been a "precursor of *Négritude*."

Alain Locke credited *Batouala* for forcibly pushing the colonial novel away from exoticism through a "revolutionary change from sentimentality to realism, from caricature to portraiture." For him, Maran's work was crucial for the younger generation of Harlem Renaissance fiction writers because they, too, were determined "to take their material objectively with detached artistic vision." For the younger writers, Locke concluded in *The New Negro*, "though *Batouala* is not of the American Negro either in substance or authorship, the influence of its daring realism and Latin frankness was educative and emancipating."

From Batouala[1]

Preface

Henri de Régnier, Jacques Boulenger,[2] sponsors of this book, I should consider myself unfeeling were I not to use the very first lines of my preface to acknowledge all I owe to your kindness and advice.

You know how earnestly I wish for the success of this novel. To be sure, it is merely a series of etchings. But I have taken six years to complete it. I have taken six years to translate what I have heard and to describe what I have seen.

During those six years I did not yield once to the temptation to express my views. I have carried my scruples regarding objectivity so far as to suppress any reflections that others might attribute to me.

As a matter of fact the Negroes of equatorial Africa are an unreflecting race. They have no critical faculties; and they never have had, nor ever will have, any intelligence. At least, so it is said. Wrongly, no doubt. For if the Negro were characterized by a lack of intelligence, there would be few Europeans in Africa.

So this novel is altogether objective. It makes no attempt to explain: it states. It voices no indignation: it records. No other method would have been possible. Moonlight nights, as I sat reclining in my chaise-longue on the verandah, I listened to the conversations of those poor people. Their joking proved their resignation. They suffered, and laughed at suffering.

Ah, Mr. Bruel, in your clever, ill-digested compilation[3] you stated, correctly enough, that the province of Ubangi-Shari[4] counted as many as 1,350,000 inhabitants. But you did not say—why didn't you?—that in a certain little village of Ouahm there were, in 1918, only 1080 souls of the 10,000 that had figured in the census seven years before. You spoke of the wealth of that immense region. How is it that you failed to remark that famine is queen there?

I know. Yes. What difference does it make to Sirius that in this time of unspeakable distress ten, twenty, or even a hundred natives were forced to make their meals by looking in the dung of the horses that belong to the pillagers who pretend to be their benefactors, hunting for undigested grains of maize or millet to eat!

Montesquieu[5] was right when he wrote on a page vibrating with restrained indignation veiled under a surface of cool irony: "They are black from head to foot; their noses are mashed down so flat that it is almost impossible to pity them."

1. *Batouala, véritable roman nègre* was published in Paris by Albin Michel in 1921. Maran dedicated the book to his friend Manoel Gahisto (b. 1878), a writer and translator. An English translation by Adele Seltzer was published in New York by Thomas Seltzer in 1922. This is a revised version of the Seltzer translation.

2. Boulenger, French literary critic and journalist (1870–1944); de Régnier, French symbolist poet (1864–1936).

3. *Afrique Equatoriale Française* (1918), by Georges Bruel (1871–1945), French colonial administrator.

4. Colony in French Equatorial Africa, now part of the independent Central African Republic.

5. French philosopher and political thinker (1689–1755).

After all, if they fall by the thousand like flies and rot in starvation, it is because their country is being "developed." The only ones that die are those who do not adapt themselves to civilization.

Civilization, civilization, pride of the Europeans and their slaughterhouse of innocents, Rabindranath Tagore, the Hindu poet, once, at Tokyo,[6] told what you were!

You build your kingdom on top of corpses. Whatever you want, whatever you do, you move in lies. At the sight of you, there are gushing tears and shrieks of agony. You are might prevailing over right. You are not a torch, you are a conflagration. You devour whatever you touch. . . .

O my brothers in France, writers of all persuasions, honor of the country that has given me everything, you who often squabble over nothing and wantonly rip each other up, then suddenly reconcile with each other every time a just and noble cause is to be championed, I call upon you for help: I have faith in your generosity.

My book is not a polemic. It comes, by chance, when its hour strikes. The Negro question is "of the moment." Who made it so? Why, the Americans. Why, the press campaigns on the other side of the Rhine.[7] Why, *Romulus Coucou* by Paul Reboux, *Le Visage de la Brousse* by Pierre Bonardi, and *l'Isolement* by that poor fellow Combette.[8] And wasn't it you, *Eve*, curious little one[9] who, at the beginning of the year when you were still a daily, carried on an investigation to find out whether a white woman might properly marry a Negro?

Since then, Jean Finot[1] published articles in the *Revue* on the employment of black troops. Since then, Dr. Huot devoted to the Negroes a study in the *Mercure de France*.[2] Since then *Les Lettres* have told of their martyrization in the United States. And in the course of an interpellation in the Chamber of Deputies, Mr. André Lefèvre, Minister of War, was not afraid to say that certain French officials felt they could behave in reconquered Alsace-Lorraine as if they were in the French Congo.

Such sentiments uttered in such a place are significant. They prove two things: that people are aware of what is going on in those distant lands, and that until now no attempt has been made to remedy the endless abuses, frauds, and atrocities. Moreover, "the best settlers have been not the professional colonials, but the European troops from the trenches." It is Mr. Diagne[3] who makes this statement.

My brothers in spirit, writers of France, it is only too true. And that is why it behooves you to come forward and declare that from now on, under no pretext will you have your compatriots who are stationed in Africa cast discredit upon the nation of which you are the upholders.

6. Bengali writer Rabindranath Tagore (1861–1941), who was awarded the Nobel Prize for literature in 1913. Possibly a reference to "The Spirit of Japan," a 1916 lecture in Tokyo in which Tagore stated that "the spirit of the Western civilization" emphasized "control by conquest," and taught people "to foster hatreds and ambitions by all kinds of means,—by the manufacture of half-truths and untruths in history, by persistent misrepresentation of other races and the culture of unfavourable sentiments towards them."

7. An allusion to racist efforts in the German press to portray the French African soldiers stationed along the Rhine River after World War I as potential rapists and criminals.

8. Novels by French writers Paul Reboux (1877–1963), Pierre Bonardi (1887–1964), and Bernard Combette (1878–1914) set in colonial Africa.

9. A French periodical.

1. Polish-born French author (1858–1922).

2. Louis Huot, whose *L'âme noire* (1921) was first published in the journal *Mercure de France*.

3. Blaise Diagne (1872–1934), Senegalese politician and the first African elected to the French Chamber of Deputies.

Let your voices be heard! It is right and necessary that you come to the aid of those who tell things as they are and not as we should like them to be. And, later, when the colonial Suburas[4] shall have been cleansed, I will describe some of these types. I have sketched a few, but am keeping them a while in my notebooks. I will tell you how, in certain parts, unfortunate Negroes have been obliged to sell their wives for as much as seventy-five francs and as little as twenty francs.[5] I will tell you. . . . But I shall speak then in my own name, not in the name of another. It will be my ideas that I shall set forth, not someone else's ideas. And I know even now that the Europeans at whom I shall take aim are so cowardly that not one of them will dare—I know it positively—not one of them will dare to give me the lie in so much as the faintest whisper.

If we knew of what vileness the great colonial life is composed, of what daily vileness, we should talk of it less, we should not talk of it at all. It degrades little by little. Even among the officials, the man who cultivates his mind is a rarity. The colonials haven't got the strength to resist the atmosphere. They take to drink. Before the war there were any number of Europeans capable of finishing off fifteen quarts of Pernod in a month. Since the war, alas, I have met one man who beat all records—he was able to drink eighty bottles of whiskey in a month.

These and other ignoble excesses reduce those who indulge in them to the most abject slackness. This abjection must be a matter of prime concern to those who are charged with representing France, the men who assume responsibility for the evils under which certain parts of Africa are at present suffering. But, if they are to be promoted to higher positions, they must have no tales to tell, and so, a prey to ambition, they have renounced pride, they have hesitated, temporized, concealed the truth, woven a tissue of lies. They have not wanted to see, they have not wanted to hear. They are too cowardly to speak out. And so, intellectual anemia joining hands with moral debility, they have deceived their country and felt no remorse.

What I urge upon you to set right is everything embraced in the administration's euphemism of "mistakes." It will be a hard struggle. You will attack the slave-drivers. Fighting them will be harder than tilting at windmills. Your task is a splendid one. To work, then, without waiting any longer. It is the will of France.

This novel takes place in Ubangi-Shari, one of the four colonies under the jurisdiction of the Gouvernement Général of French Equatorial Africa. It is bounded on the south by the Ubangi River, on the east by the watershed of the Congo and the Nile, on the north and west by the watershed of the Congo and the Shari. Like the other colonies in the group it is divided into circumscriptions and subdivisions. A circumscription is an administrative unit. It corresponds to a department.[6] And the districts of a department are its subdivisions.

The circumscription of Kemo is one of the most important in Ubangi-Shari. If the famous railway were ever started—the railway they are forever

4. "Subura": a poor and populous neighborhood in ancient Rome.
5. In the revised and "definitive" 1938 edition of *Batouala*, Maran added the explanatory phrase "in order to pay their poll taxes."
6. A *département* is an administrative unit in French government, the approximate equivalent of a province or state.

talking about but never getting at—Fort-Sibut, the chief town in the circumscription, might become the capital.

The circumscription of Kemo comprises four subdivisions: Fort-de-Possel, Fort-Sibut, Dakoa, and Grimari. The natives—and even the Europeans—know them only as Kémo, Krébédgé, Combélé, and Bamba. Fort-Sibut, otherwise known as Krébédgé, is situated about 190 kilometers north of Bangui, capital of Ubangi-Shari, the European population of which has never exceeded 150 persons.

The district of Grimari (or of Bamba or Kandjia, from the two names of the river near which the administrative post was built) is about 120 kilometers east of Krébédgé. This region used to be very rich in rubber and had a large population. It was covered with plantations of every kind and teemed with goats and poultry.

Seven years have been enough to work complete ruin. Villages have grown fewer and farther between, the plantations have disappeared, the goats and poultry have been exterminated. As for the natives, they have been broken by incessant, excessive, and unpaid toil, and robbed even of the time to plant their crops. They saw disease come and take up its abode with them, saw famine stalk their land, saw their numbers diminish.

And yet they are descended from a hardy, warrior tribe, inured to illness and fatigue. Neither raids by the Snoussi nor perpetual internal dissension could destroy them. Their family name was a guarantee of their vitality. Were they not Bandas? And doesn't "banda" mean "net"? For it is with nets that the tribe hunts in the season when the whole horizon is ablaze with the bush on fire.

Civilization passed that way. And all the Banda tribes, the Dacpas, M'bis, Maroubas, Langbassis, Sabangas and N'gapus, were decimated.

The subdivision of Grimari is fertile, picturesque and full of game. Wild bulls and boar abound, as well as guinea fowl, partridges, and turtle-doves.

Every part of the district is irrigated by streams. The trees are sparse and stunted, which is not surprising because the rainforest stops at Bangui. Beautiful trees are found only along the wooded corridors bordering the waterways.

The rivers snake between heights that the Bandas call "kagas." The three kagas nearest to Grimari are Kossegamba, Gobo, and Biga. The first is two or three kilometers to the southeast of the outpost and borders the valley of the Bamba. The other two are in the N'gapu country, twenty kilometers to the northeast.

Such, in brief description, is the region in which this novel of impersonal observation will unfold.

And now, as Verlaine said at the end of the prefatory verses of his *Poèmes saturniens*:

"Go, my book, wither chance may lead you."[7]

R.M.

Bordeaux, November 5, 1920.

7. From the "Prologue" to *Poèmes saturniens* (1866), the first book of French poet Paul Verlaine (1844–1896).

From *Chapter 1*

In the course of the night, the fire, which it is the custom to kindle every evening, had slowly burned down into a large heap of cinders that still retained some heat.

The circular wall of the hut sweats. A vague light filters through the opening that serves as a door. Under the thatch there sounds the steady, delicate rummaging of the termites, which, in the shelter of their corridors of brown earth, are making their way into the branch-work of the low roof, which gives them a refuge from the humidity and the sun.

Outside, the cocks crow. Their "kekerekes" mingle with the bleating of goats for the ewes, the cackling of the toucans, and—from farther away, from the depths of the high thickets bordering the Pombo and Bamba rivers—with the hoarse call of the "bacouyas," monkeys with elongated muzzles like dogs.

Day is coming.

Although heavy with sleep still, Batouala the chief—Batouala the mokoundji of so many villages—was quite conscious of these sounds.

He yawned, shivered, and stretched himself, not knowing whether to go back to sleep or to get up.

Get up, by N'Gakoura! Why get up? He did not even want to know, as he was scornful of overly simple decisions or overly complex solutions.

Now, merely to get up—didn't that require an enormous effort? The decision in itself seemed to be perfectly simple. As a matter of fact, it was hard; for getting up and working were one and the same thing, at least to the whites.

Not that work dismayed Batouala. He was vigorous, strong-limbed, a splendid walker, more than a match for any man in running, wrestling, and hurling the assegai and the throwing knife.

From one end of the vast Banda country to the other, his prowess had become a legend. Tradition had already invested his exploits in love and war, his agility and valor in hunting, with the glamour of the miraculous. And when "Ipeu," the moon, rose in the sky, then the M'bis, Dacpas, Dakouas and Langbassis in their distant villages chanted the valiant deeds of the great mokoundji Batouala to the tom-tom of the li'nghas, and the discords of the balafons and koundes.

So work had no terrors for him.

Only, in the language of the whites, work took on a very strange meaning. It meant getting tired without achieving immediate or tangible results, it meant trouble, annoyance, suffering, the squandering of health, the pursuit of imaginary ends.

Ah, the whites! They would do better to go back home, all of them. They would do better to confine their desire to their own households and to the cultivation of their own land, instead of setting their wishes upon the acquisition of stupid money.

Life is short. Work is for those who will never understand life. Idleness does not degrade a man. In the eyes of one who sees things truly, it differs from laziness. As for him, Batouala, until it was proven to the contrary, he would believe that to do nothing was simply to profit in everything that surrounds us. To live from day to day, without thought of yesterday or care for the morrow, without looking ahead—that is perfect.

Really, why get up? Sitting was better than standing, lying down was better than sitting.

The mat on which he slept smelled sweetly of dried grass, and was more softly yielding than the hide of a fresh-killed wild bull.

So, instead of lying there with closed eyes dreaming, why not try to go to sleep again? That would give him the chance to enjoy in full the soft perfection of his "bogbo."

First he would have to revive the fire.

A few dry twigs and a little straw would do. He blew, cheeks puffed, on the smoldering sparks. The smoke sent up its spirals, pungent, suffocating. There was a crackling, the flames burst forth, and warmth invaded the place.

Now, with his back to the fire, he could just fall asleep again stretched out like a boar. He could just bask in the glow like a lizard in the sunshine. All he had to do was imitate the "yassi" with whom he had been living so long.

She set an excellent example. She lay there peacefully, her head resting on a log, naked, her hands on her belly. "Gologolo," she said—snoring, in other words—with her side to a fire that had also burned down to ashes.

What a sound sleep! Sometimes she fumbled at her breasts—wrinkled, flabby breasts like dried tobacco leaves—and scratched herself with long-drawn sighs. Her lips moved. She made gentle little gestures. Then she calmed down again and resumed her even snoring . . .

In a nook behind the fagots, raised above the chickens, ducks and goats, slept Djouma, the sad little yellow dog. He slept curled up, head to tail, on a pile of rubber baskets.

All that was visible of his emaciated body were the ears, standing straight up, pointed, mobile. Every now and then, tickled by a flea or stung by a tick, he would shake them. Occasionally, he would growl without moving any more than Yassiguindja, the favorite yassi of her master, Batouala, the mokoundji. And sometimes, dreaming cynical dreams, he would inveigh against the silence with stifled barks, and open his jaws to snap at the void.

Batouala raised himself and leaned on his elbow. There was no use trying to sleep any more. Everything was in league against him. The mist drizzled in through the entrance to the hut. It was cold. He was hungry. And the day was coming on.

1921

CLAUDE McKAY
1889–1948

Often regarded as the first major poet of the Harlem Renaissance, Claude McKay probably did more than anyone else to shape the trends that would later define that literary movement. More than any other writer of his time, he was able to satisfy and even inspire two major groups of Black readers. Many African Americans were attracted to his poetry by its frequently explosive condemnations of bigotry and oppression, written invariably and ironically in such traditional poetic forms as the sonnet, McKay's favorite. Other readers, more easily moved by poetry in the genteel tradition, were also satisfied, even as they were often introduced at the same time to the power of race-conscious verse. These two groups sometimes seemed irreconcilable. Had it not been for McKay, they might have remained so in the renaissance. He helped uncover some of the unifying principles underlying the major conflicting themes of the writers of the Harlem Renaissance.

Born September 15, 1889, Festus Claudius McKay was the youngest of the eleven children of Thomas and Ann McKay, members of the peasant class in Jamaica. McKay was raised in Sunny Ville, in Clarendon Parish, by a compassionate mother and a stern father who did his best to pass on to his children elements of the customs and traditions of the Ashanti, the West African people from whom he was descended, at least as he understood those customs and traditions. Repeatedly sharing with his children the story of his own father's enslavement by whites, Thomas McKay sought to instill in his offspring a suspicion of whites that would become particularly evident in his son Claude's writing. Other impressions from McKay's childhood that left an indelible mark on his literary productions include his profound respect for the sense of community he encountered among rural Jamaican farmers and a somewhat skeptical attitude toward religion encouraged by his older brother Uriah Theophilus, an elementary-school teacher.

At seventeen, McKay received government sponsorship to become an apprentice to a wheelwright and cabinetmaker in Brown's Town. At nineteen, he moved to Kingston (Jamaica's capital) and served as a police constable for less than a year before his sympathy for the criminals, whom he often considered the victims of an unjust colonial order, led him to return to Clarendon Parish. During the two years that followed, he was encouraged to write poetry in the Jamaican dialect by his most important mentor, Walter Jekyll, an English collector of island folklore with whom McKay had forged a close relationship. In 1912, Jekyll helped him publish two books of dialect poetry: *Songs of Jamaica* (with an introduction by Jekyll and melodies for six selections in an appendix) and *Constab Ballads*. *Songs of Jamaica* is primarily a celebration of the Jamaican peasants, with their relative freedom from bigotry; *Constab Ballads* centers more on Kingston and the contempt and exploitation encountered there by dark-skinned Blacks at the hands of whites and people of mixed race. With their unique melding of traditional verse forms with vivid vernacular speech, the books are now considered foundational texts in the emergence of twentieth-century Caribbean literature. In recognition of their accomplishment, McKay became the first Black to receive the medal of the Jamaican Institute of Arts and Sciences, which came with a substantial cash award.

McKay, determined to use the prize money to finance an education at Booker T. Washington's Tuskegee Institute in Alabama, arrived in the United States in 1912, but he departed from Tuskegee in frustration at local conditions two months after his arrival. He went on to study agricultural science for two years at Kansas State College before he decided to resume his career as a writer. He left for Harlem.

Supporting himself at first as a waiter and a porter, McKay familiarized himself with the New York literary scene. He was soon befriended by such important white figures as the poet Edwin Arlington Robinson and Waldo Frank, a Jewish radical novelist and cultural critic. His first break came in 1917, when Frank published two of his sonnets, "The Harlem Dancer" and "Invocation," in the December issue of *The Seven Arts,* a highly respected avant-garde magazine. Short story writer Frank Harris, who published several of McKay's poems in *Pearson's,* another magazine, seems also to have made a major impression on the young poet. Unlike later Black writers, McKay did not rely primarily on such periodicals as the *Crisis* and *Opportunity* as outlets for his verse. Though he wrote for Black magazines on occasion, his most enduring literary ties were with white publications, particularly with the leftist magazines based in Greenwich Village. Indeed, Max Eastman, the dean of the American literary left in the early twentieth century, published McKay's "The Dominant White" in the April 1919 issue of *The Liberator* and nine more of his poems in the July issue. McKay later served on Eastman's editorial staff, contributing essays and reviews as well as poetry.

In 1919, McKay traveled to England, where he met George Bernard Shaw and worked for a time under Sylvia Pankhurst at *Workers Dreadnought*. C. K. Ogden included nearly two dozen of McKay's poems in the summer 1920 issue of *Cambridge Magazine*; and I. A. Richards, one of the foremost English literary critics of the century, wrote the preface for McKay's third book of verse, *Spring in New Hampshire*. According to Richards, McKay's was among "the best work that the present generation is producing" in Great Britain.

After his return to the United States in 1921, McKay continued to work for and contribute to a number of publications (including his fellow Jamaican Marcus Garvey's *Negro World*, until a political disagreement in 1922 severed their ties). In 1922, he published his most important collection of poetry, *Harlem Shadows*, which, in the opinion of some critics, virtually inaugurated the Harlem Renaissance. According to McKay, the book grew out of his urge to place the militant "If We Must Die," his most famous poem, "inside of a book." The racial violence that racked America in the summer of 1919 had inspired the sonnet, which later served as one of the unofficial rallying cries of the Allied Forces in World War II, particularly after it was recited by Winston Churchill in a speech against the Nazis. Although the poem offers no internal evidence to suggest that it is about race, McKay had refrained from including it in *Spring in New Hampshire* (which was deeply admired by Countee Cullen and Langston Hughes) because of his desire to avoid racial themes in that book. *Harlem Shadows*, however, marked a point of no return for several members of the literary set in Harlem, who saw in McKay's masterful treatment of racial issues evidence that a Black writer's insights into matters of race could serve on more than an occasional basis as suitable subjects for poetry.

In 1923, in Moscow, McKay addressed the Fourth Congress of the Communist International and, as a Black poet sympathetic to the Soviet cause (though not an official delegate), achieved instant popularity among most citizens of the U.S.S.R. as well as with Communist Party officials. He was introduced to Trotsky and other leaders, and his poem "Petrograd: May Day, 1923" was published in translation in *Pravda*. McKay also wrote a short book called *Negry v Amerike* (*The Negroes in America*; 1923) that was translated and published by the state publishing firm of the Soviet Union (the original manuscript has been lost, but an English translation of the Russian version was published in 1979). From the Soviet Union, McKay traveled briefly through Germany and then lived several years in France. There he produced his first novel, *Home to Harlem* (1928), and began work on his second, *Banjo* (1929), which he completed during travels in Spain and Morocco. He eventually settled in Tangier, where he lived from 1930 to 1934.

Home to Harlem was the first novel by a Black writer to become a best-seller. Reprinted five times in two months, it seems to have satisfied a consuming curiosity on the part of Americans for information about the nightlife—and the lowlife—of Harlem. The novel examines two characters, both of whom are seen by most critics as existing mainly for the purpose of taking the reader on a tour of Harlem. Jake is a hedonist who deserts the army to return to his beloved Harlem; he falls in love with a prostitute after she affectionately and surreptitiously returns the money he has paid her. Through Jake, the reader is introduced to Ray, a Haitian intellectual who envies Jake because his own desire to become a writer interferes with his enjoyment of life. Predictably, the stern W. E. B. Du Bois had little patience with McKay's presentation of Harlem. Du Bois declared that the book "for the most part nauseates me, and after the dirtier parts of its filth I feel distinctly like taking a bath." McKay's response was simply to accuse Du Bois of failing to make the proper distinction "between the task of propaganda and the work of art."

Banjo continues the story of Ray by matching him with a jovial, restless vagabond and would-be musician named Lincoln Agrippa Daily who is nicknamed "Banjo" after the instrument he plays. The novel did not sell well in the United States, perhaps not only due to the unfortunate timing of its appearance (on the cusp of the Great Depression) but also as a result of its picaresque form (the book is subtitled "A Story without a Plot") and unfamiliar setting among Black dockers and drifters in the Southern French port of Marseille. Nevertheless *Banjo* is one of the most extraordinary novels of the era, both for its cynical analysis of the impact of the grand forces of modernity (above all commerce and colonialism) on individual Black lives, and for its almost documentary depiction of interactions among a wide range of characters of African descent from the United States, the Caribbean, and Africa. *Banjo* may also have had the greatest international reach of any novel associated with the renaissance. Translated into French in 1931, it was the single book with the most significant impact on the generation of Caribbean and African students (including Aimé Césaire, Léopold Sédar Senghor, and Léon-Gontran Damas) that would later come to be known as the *Négritude* generation.

McKay's third novel, *Banana Bottom* (1933), is often regarded as his finest achievement in fiction. *Banana Bottom* tells the story of a Jamaican peasant girl, Bita Plant, who is rescued by the white missionaries Malcolm and Priscilla Craig after being raped. In taking refuge with the Craigs, however, Bita also becomes their prisoner and has their values (including an education in Britain) foisted on her. They even attempt to arrange her marriage. But Bita escapes and, overcoming the memory of rape, returns to her native town of Jubilee. Critical reception of *Banana Bottom* was warm, but sometimes misguided; some reviewers seemed primarily captivated by its descriptions of lush tropical scenery. Like the rest of McKay's prose, except for *Home to Harlem*, *Banana Bottom* did not make much of an impression on the reading public of McKay's time. A collection of short stories, *Gingertown* (1932), did not fare any better.

In 1934, McKay returned to Harlem after twelve years of wandering through Europe and North Africa. He struggled to find employment and even spent a short period in a camp for destitute men before joining the New York branch of the Federal Writers' Project, like many of the most talented Black writers of the time (including Dorothy West, Richard Nugent, Roi Ottley, and Ralph Ellison). While on staff there, McKay was able to complete his autobiography, *A Long Way from Home,* which appeared in 1937. He became a regular contributor of articles on race and politics to periodicals such as the *Amsterdam News* and *The New Leader,* and was a central figure in the effort to establish a Negro Writers' Guild (an effort that brought together a number of figures associated with the renaissance, such as Countee Cullen, James Weldon Johnson, and Arthur Schomburg). The last book he published was a study of Black life in New York, *Harlem: Negro Metropolis* (1940), which remains an important historical document, with well-wrought portraits of aspects of Harlem life in the 1930s (including the "numbers" racket and the religious leader Father Divine). Through Ellen Tarry, a friend who wrote children's books, McKay became involved in the activities of Friendship House, a Catholic-sponsored community center in Harlem. Tarry's influence on McKay culminated in his conversion to Roman Catholicism in 1944, after he had moved to Chicago, where he spent the remainder of his life teaching classes at the Catholic Youth Organization. Despite serious health problems after 1941, he continued to write poetry and completed at least one unpublished book-length fiction manuscript, *Amiable with Big Teeth,* which concerned efforts among Black political leaders in Harlem to organize support for Ethiopia after it had been invaded by Mussolini's Italy in the fall of 1935.

When McKay died in 1948, the world lost someone who, according to William Stanley Braithwaite, had once promised to be "the keystone of the new movement in racial poetic achievement." Unlike Countee Cullen, the other great figure of the

Harlem Renaissance who treated racial themes in conventional poetic forms, Claude McKay was not concerned with living up to the intellectual, political, or social expectations of Du Bois or Alain Locke. In fact, he once referred to Locke's anthology, *The New Negro,* as a "remarkable chocolate soufflé of art and politics." Concerned with political consequences, McKay was a worker for social change; and subtle though his poetry is on some levels, he believed strongly that too many Black poets had hidden behind lofty standards of poetic refinement to keep from offending white readers. He refused to mask his impatience with racism in this way. He managed to use traditional poetic forms as satisfying vehicles for the expression of that impatience; but at the same time, McKay refused to allow social relevance to become an excuse for the production of inferior art. McKay was a courageous thinker and writer who prized his intimate knowledge of all classes of people. His work rings with an authority and authenticity matched by few of his contemporaries.

The Harlem Dancer

Applauding youths laughed with young prostitutes
And watched her perfect, half-clothed body sway;
Her voice was like the sound of blended flutes
Blown by black players upon a picnic day.
She sang and danced on gracefully and calm,
The light gauze hanging loose about her form;
To me she seemed a proudly-swaying palm
Grown lovelier for passing through a storm.
Upon her swarthy neck black shiny curls
Luxuriant fell; and tossing coins in praise,
The wine-flushed, bold-eyed boys, and even the girls,
Devoured her shape with eager, passionate gaze;
But looking at her falsely-smiling face,
I knew her self was not in that strange place.

1917

Harlem Shadows

I hear the halting footsteps of a lass
  In Negro Harlem when the night lets fall
Its veil. I see the shapes of girls who pass
  To bend and barter at desire's call.
Ah, little dark girls who in slippered feet
Go prowling through the night from street to street!

Through the long night until the silver break
  Of day the little gray feet know no rest;
Through the lone night until the last snow-flake
  Has dropped from heaven upon the earth's white breast,
The dusky, half-clad girls of tired feet
Are trudging, thinly shod, from street to street.

Ah, stern harsh world, that in the wretched way
Of poverty, dishonor and disgrace,
Has pushed the timid little feet of clay,
The sacred brown feet of my fallen race!
Ah, heart of me, the weary, weary feet
In Harlem wandering from street to street.

1918

If We Must Die[1]

If we must die, let it not be like hogs
Hunted and penned in an inglorious spot,
While round us bark the mad and hungry dogs,
Making their mock at our accursed lot.
If we must die, O let us nobly die,
So that our precious blood may not be shed
In vain; then even the monsters we defy
Shall be constrained to honor us though dead!
O kinsmen! we must meet the common foe!
Though far outnumbered let us show us brave,
And for their thousand blows deal one deathblow!
What though before us lies the open grave?
Like men we'll face the murderous, cowardly pack,
Pressed to the wall, dying, but fighting back!

1919

To the White Fiends

Think you I am not fiend and savage too?
Think you I could not arm me with a gun
And shoot down ten of you for every one
Of my black brothers murdered, burnt by you?
Be not deceived, for every deed you do
I could match—out-match: am I not Afric's son,
Black of that black land where black deeds are done?
But the Almighty from the darkness drew
My soul and said: Even thou shalt be a light
Awhile to burn on the benighted earth,
Thy dusky face I set among the white
For thee to prove thyself of higher worth;
Before the world is swallowed up in night,
To show thy little lamp: go forth, go forth!

1919

1. Written following the "Red Summer" of 1919, when race riots broke out in several cities, notably Chicago. McKay later denied that the poem referred to Blacks and whites specifically.

Africa

The sun sought thy dim bed and brought forth light,
The sciences were sucklings at thy breast;
When all the world was young in pregnant night
Thy slaves toiled at thy monumental best.
Thou ancient treasure-land, thou modern prize,
New peoples marvel at thy pyramids!
The years roll on, thy sphinx of riddle eyes
Watches the mad world with immobile lids.
The Hebrews humbled them[2] at Pharaoh's name.
Cradle of Power! Yet all things were in vain!
Honor and Glory, Arrogance and Fame!
They went. The darkness swallowed thee again.
Thou art the harlot, now thy time is done,
Of all the mighty nations of the sun.

1921

America

Although she feeds me bread of bitterness,
And sinks into my throat her tiger's tooth,
Stealing my breath of life, I will confess
I love this cultured hell that tests my youth!
Her vigor flows like tides into my blood,
Giving me strength erect against her hate.
Her bigness sweeps my being like a flood.
Yet as a rebel fronts a king in state,
I stand within her walls with not a shred
Of terror, malice, not a word of jeer.
Darkly I gaze into the days ahead,
And see her might and granite wonders there,
Beneath the touch of Time's unerring hand,
Like priceless treasures sinking in the sand.

1921

The White House[3]

Your door is shut against my tightened face,
And I am sharp as steel with discontent;
But I possess the courage and the grace
To bear my anger proudly and unbent.
The pavement slabs burn loose beneath my feet,
A chafing savage, down the decent street;

2. That is, themselves. According to the Bible, Hebrew bondage in Egypt ended with the exodus led by Moses.

3. In *A Long Way from Home* (1937), McKay insisted that the title of this poem did not refer to the official residence of the U.S. president.

And passion rends my vitals as I pass,
Where boldly shines your shuttered door of glass.
Oh, I must search for wisdom every hour,
Deep in my wrathful bosom sore and raw,
And find in it the superhuman power
To hold me to the letter of your law!
Oh, I must keep my heart inviolate
Against the potent poison of your hate.

1922

The Lynching

His Spirit in smoke ascended to high heaven.
His father, by the cruelest way of pain,
Had bidden him to his bosom once again;
The awful sin remained still unforgiven.
All night a bright and solitary star
(Perchance the one that ever guided him,
Yet gave him up at last to Fate's wild whim)
Hung pitifully o'er the swinging char.
Day dawned, and soon the mixed crowds came to view
The ghastly body swaying in the sun
The women thronged to look, but never a one
Showed sorrow in her eyes of steely blue;
And little lads, lynchers that were to be,
Danced round the dreadful thing in fiendish glee.

1922

Outcast

For the dim regions whence my fathers came
My spirit, bondaged by the body, longs.
Words felt, but never heard, my lips would frame;
My soul would sing forgotten jungle songs.
I would go back to darkness and to peace,
But the great western world holds me in fee,[4]
And I may never hope for full release
While to its alien gods I bend my knee.
Something in me is lost, forever lost,
Some vital thing has gone out of my heart,
And I must walk the way of life a ghost
Among the sons of earth, a thing apart;
For I was born, far from my native clime,
Under the white man's menace, out of time.

1922

4. On condition of performing certain services.

From Home to Harlem

Chapter XVII. He Also Loved

It was in the winter of 1916 when I first came to New York to hunt for a job. I was broke. I was afraid I would have to pawn my clothes, and it was dreadfully cold. I didn't even know the right way to go about looking for a job. I was always timid about that. For five weeks I had not paid my rent. I was worried, and Ma Lawton, my landlady, was also worried. She had her bills to meet. She was a good-hearted old woman from South Carolina. Her face was all wrinkled and sensitive like finely-carved mahogany.

Every bed-space in the flat was rented. I was living in the small hall bedroom. Ma Lawton asked me to give it up. There were four men sleeping in the front room; two in an old, chipped-enameled brass bed, one on a davenport, and the other in a folding chair. The old lady put a little canvas cot in that same room, gave me a pillow and a heavy quilt, and said I should try and make myself comfortable there until I got work.

The cot was all right for me. Although I hate to share a room with another person and the fellows snoring disturbed my rest. Ma Lawton moved into the little room that I had had, and rented out hers—it was next to the front room—to a man and a woman.

The woman was above ordinary height, chocolate-colored. Her skin was smooth, too smooth, as if it had been pressed and fashioned out for ready sale like chocolate candy. Her hair was straightened out into an Indian Straight after the present style among Negro ladies. She had a mongoose sort of a mouth, with two top front teeth showing. She wore a long mink coat.

The man was darker than the woman. His face was longish, with the right cheek somewhat caved in. It was an interesting face, an attractive, salacious mouth, with the lower lip protruding. He wore a bottle-green peg-top suit, baggy at the hips. His coat hung loose from his shoulders and it was much longer than the prevailing style. He wore also a Mexican hat, and in his breast pocket he carried an Ingersoll watch attached to a heavy gold chain. His name was Jericho Jones, and they called him Jerco for short. And she was Miss Whicher—Rosalind Whicher.

Ma Lawton introduced me to them and said I was broke, and they were both awfully nice to me. They took me to a big feed of corned beef and cabbage at Burrell's on Fifth Avenue. They gave me a good appetizing drink of gin to commence with. And we had beer with the eats; not ordinary beer, either, but real Budweiser, right off the ice.

And as good luck sometimes comes pouring down like a shower, the next day Ma Lawton got me a job in the little free-lunch saloon right under her flat. It wasn't a paying job as far as money goes in New York, but I was glad to have it. I had charge of the free-lunch counter. You know the little dry crackers that go so well with beer, and the cheese and fish and the potato salad. And I served, besides, spare-ribs and whole boiled potatoes and corned beef and cabbage for those customers who could afford to pay for a lunch. I got no wages at all, but I got my eats twice a day. And I made a few tips, also. For there were about six big black men with plenty of money who used to eat lunch with us, specially for our spare-ribs and sweet potatoes. Each one of them gave me a quarter. I made enough to pay Ma Lawton for my canvas cot.

Strange enough, too, Jerco and Rosalind took a liking to me. And sometimes they came and ate lunch perched up there at the counter, with Rosalind the only woman there, all made up and rubbing her mink coat against the men. And when they got through eating, Jerco would toss a dollar bill at me.

We got very friendly, we three. Rosalind would bring up squabs and canned stuff from the German delicatessen in One Hundred and Twenty-fifth Street, and sometimes they asked me to dinner in their room and gave me good liquor.

I thought I was pretty well fixed for such a hard winter. All I had to do as extra work was keeping the saloon clean. . . .

One afternoon Jerco came into the saloon with a man who looked pretty near white. Of course, you never can tell for sure about a person's race in Harlem, nowadays, when there are so many high-yallers floating round—colored folks that would make Italian and Spanish people look like Negroes beside them. But I figured out from his way of talking and acting that the man with Jerco belonged to the white race. They went in through the family entrance into the back room, which was unusual, for the family room of a saloon, as you know, is only for women in the business and the men they bring in there with them. Real men don't sit in a saloon here as they do at home. I suppose it would be sissified. There's a bar for them to lean on and drink and joke as long as they feel like.

The boss of the saloon was a little fidgety about Jerco and his friend sitting there in the back. The boss was a short pumpkin-bellied brown man, a little bald off the forehead. Twice he found something to attend to in the back room, although there was nothing at all there that wanted attending to. . . . I felt better, and the boss, too, I guess, when Rosalind came along and gave the family room its respectable American character. I served Rosalind a Martini cocktail extra dry, and afterward all three of them, Rosalind, Jerco, and their friend, went up to Ma Lawton's.

The two fellows that slept together were elevator operators in a department store, so they had their Sundays free. On the afternoon of the Sunday of the same week that the white-looking man had been in the saloon with Jerco, I went upstairs to change my old shoes—they'd got soaking wet behind the counter—and I found Ma Lawton talking to the two elevator fellows.

The boys had given Ma Lawton notice to quit. They said they couldn't sleep there comfortably together on account of the goings-on in Rosalind's room. The fellows were members of the Colored Y. M. C. A. and were queerly quiet and pious. One of them was studying to be a preacher. They were the sort of fellows that thought going to cabarets a sin, and that parlor socials were leading Harlem straight down to hell. They only went to church affairs themselves. They had been rooming with Ma Lawton for over a year. She called them her gentlemen lodgers.

Ma Lawton said to me: "Have you heard anything phony outa the next room, dear?"

"Why, no, Ma," I said, "nothing more unusual than you can hear all over Harlem. Besides, I work so late, I am dead tired when I turn in to bed, so I sleep heavy."

"Well, it's the truth I do like that there Jerco an' Rosaline," said Ma Lawton. "They did seem quiet as lambs, although they was always havin' company. But Ise got to speak to them, 'cause I doana wanta lose ma young mens. . . . But theys a real nice-acting couple. Jerco him treats me like him was mah son. It's true that they doan work like all poah niggers, but they pays that rent down good and prompt ehvery week."

Jerco was always bringing in ice-cream and cake or something for Ma Lawton. He had a way about him, and everybody liked him. He was a sympathetic type. He helped Ma Lawton move beds and commodes and he fixed her clothes lines. I had heard somebody talking about Jerco in the saloon, however, saying that he could swing a mean fist when he got his dander up, and that he had been mixed up in more than one razor cut-up. He did have a nasty long razor scar on the back of his right hand.

The elevator fellows had never liked Rosalind and Jerco. The one who was studying to preach Jesus said he felt pretty sure that they were an ungodly-living couple. He said that late one night he had pointed out their room to a woman that looked white. He said the woman looked suspicious. She was perfumed and all powdered up and it appeared as if she didn't belong among colored people.

"There's no sure telling white from high-yaller these days," I said. "There are so many swell-looking quadroons and octoroons[1] of the race."

But the other elevator fellow said that one day in the tenderloin section he had run up against Rosalind and Jerco together with a petty officer of marines. And that just put the lid on anything favorable that could be said about them.

But Ma Lawton said: "Well, Ise got to run mah flat right an' try mah utmost to please youall, but I ain't wanta dip mah nose too deep in a lodger's affairs."

Late that night, toward one o'clock, Jerco dropped in at the saloon and told me that Rosalind was feeling badly. She hadn't eaten a bite all day and he had come to get a pail of beer, because she had asked specially for draught beer. Jerco was worried, too.

"I hopes she don't get bad," he said. "For we ain't got a cent o' money. Wese just in on a streak o' bad luck."

"I guess she'll soon be all right," I said.

The next day after lunch I stole a little time and went up to see Rosalind. Ma Lawton was just going to attend to her when I let myself in, and she said to me: "Now the poor woman is sick, poor chile, ahm so glad mah conscience is free and that I hadn't a said nothing evil t' her."

Rosalind was pretty sick. Ma Lawton said it was the grippe.[2] She gave Rosalind hot whisky drinks and hot milk, and she kept her feet warm with a hot-water bottle. Rosalind's legs were lead-heavy. She had a pain that pinched her side like a pair of pincers. And she cried out for thirst and begged for draught beer.

Ma Lawton said Rosalind ought to have a doctor. "You'd better go an' scares up a white one," she said to Jerco. "Ise nevah had no faith in these heah nigger doctors."

"I don't know how we'll make out without money," Jerco whined. He was sitting in the old Morris chair[3] with his head heavy on his left hand.

"You kain pawn my coat," said Rosalind. "Old man Greenbaum will give you two hundred down without looking at it."

"I won't put a handk'chief o' yourn in the hock shop," said Jerco. "You'll need you' stuff soon as you get better. Specially you' coat. You kain't go anywheres without it."

"S'posin' I don't get up again," Rosalind smiled. But her countenance changed suddenly as she held her side and moaned. Ma Lawton bent over and adjusted the pillows.

Jerco pawned his watch chain and his own overcoat, and called in a Jewish doctor from the upper Eighth Avenue fringe of the Belt.[4] But Rosalind

1. People of one-fourth and one-eighth African ancestry, respectively.
2. Influenza.
3. Popular furniture style designed by English craftsman and poet William Morris (1834–1896).
4. That is, the Black Belt, which then extended south to 125th Street.

did not improve under medical treatment. She lay there with a sad, tired look, as if she didn't really care what happened to her. Her lower limbs were apparently paralyzed. Jerco told the doctor that she had been sick unto death like that before. The doctor shot a lot of stuff into her system. But Rosalind lay there heavy and fading like a felled tree.

The elevator operators looked in on her. The student one gave her a Bible with a little red ribbon marking the chapter in St. John's Gospel about the woman taken in adultery.[5] He also wanted to pray for her recovery. Jerco wanted the prayer, but Rosalind said no. Her refusal shocked Ma Lawton, who believed in God's word.

The doctor stopped Rosalind from drinking beer. But Jerco slipped it in to her when Ma Lawton was not around. He said he couldn't refuse it to her when beer was the only thing she cared for. He had an expensive sweater. He pawned it. He also pawned their large suitcase. It was real leather and worth a bit of money.

One afternoon Jerco sat alone in the back room of the saloon and began to cry.

"I'd do anything. There ain't anything too low I wouldn't do to raise a little money," he said.

"Why don't you hock Rosalind's fur coat?" I suggested. "That'll give you enough money for a while."

"Gawd, no! I wouldn't touch none o' Rosalind's clothes. I jest kain't," he said. "She'll need them as soon as she's better."

"Well, you might try and find some sort of a job, then," I said.

"Me find a job? What kain I do? I ain't no good foh no job. I kain't work. I don't know how to ask for no job. I wouldn't know how. I wish I was a woman."

"Good God! Jerco," I said, "I don't see any way out for you but some sort of a job."

"What kain I do? What kain I do?" he whined. "I kain't do nothing. That's why I don't wanta hock Rosalind's fur coat. She'll need it soon as she's better. Rosalind's so wise about picking up good money. Just like that!" He snapped his fingers.

I left Jerco sitting there and went into the saloon to serve a customer a plate of corned beef and cabbage.

After lunch I thought I'd go up to see how Rosalind was making out. The door was slightly open, so I slipped in without knocking. I saw Jerco kneeling down by the open wardrobe and kissing the toe of one of her brown shoes. He started as he saw me, and looked queer kneeling there. It was a high old-fashioned wardrobe that Ma Lawton must have picked up at some sale. Rosalind's coat was hanging there, and it gave me a spooky feeling, for it looked so much more like the real Rosalind than the woman that was dozing there on the bed.

Her other clothes were hanging there, too. There were three gowns—a black silk, a glossy green satin, and a flimsy chiffon-like yellow thing. In a corner of the lowest shelf was a bundle of soiled champagne-colored silk stockings and in the other four pairs of shoes—one black velvet, one white kid, and another gold-finished. Jerco regarded the lot with dog-like affection.

5. "And the scribes and Pharisees brought unto [Jesus] a woman taken in adultery, and when they had set her in the midst, They say unto him, Master. . . . Moses in the law commanded us, that such should be stoned: but what sayest thou? . . . But Jesus . . . said unto them. He that is without sin among you, let him first cast a stone at her" (John 8:3–7).

"I wouldn't touch not one of her things until she's better," he said. "I'd sooner hock the shirt off mah back."

Which he was preparing to do. He had three expensive striped silk shirts, presents from Rosalind. He had just taken two out of the wardrobe and the other off his back, and made a parcel of them for old Greenbaum. . . . Rosalind woke up and murmured that she wanted some beer. . . .

A little later Jerco came to the saloon with the pail. He was shivering. His coat collar was turned up and fastened with a safety pin, for he only had an undershirt on.

"I don't know what I'd do if anything happens to Rosalind," he said. "I kain't live without her."

"Oh yes, you can," I said in a not very sympathetic tone. Jerco gave me such a reproachful pathetic look that I was sorry I said it.

The tall big fellow had turned into a scared, trembling baby. "You ought to buck up and hold yourself together," I told him. "Why, you ought to be game if you like Rosalind, and don't let her know you're down in the dumps."

"I'll try," he said. "She don't know how miserable I am. When I hooks up with a woman I treat her right, but I never let her know everything about me. Rosalind is an awful good woman. The straightest woman I ever had, honest."

I gave him a big glass of strong whisky.

Ma Lawton came in the saloon about nine o'clock that evening and said that Rosalind was dead. "I told Jerco we'd have to sell that theah coat to give the poah woman a decent fun'ral, an' he jest brokes down crying like a baby."

That night Ma Lawton slept in the kitchen and put Jerco in her little hall bedroom. He was all broken up. I took him up a pint of whisky.

"I'll nevah find another one like Rosalind," he said, "nevah!" He sat on an old black-framed chair in which a new yellow-varnished bottom had just been put. I put my hand on his shoulder and tried to cheer him up: "Buck up, old man. Never mind, you'll find somebody else." He shook his head. "Perhaps you didn't like the way me and Rosalind was living. But she was one naturally good woman, all good inside her."

I felt foolish and uncomfortable. "I always liked Rosalind, Jerco," I said, "and you, too. You were both awfully good scouts to me. I have nothing against her. I am nothing myself."

Jerco held my hand and whimpered: "Thank you, old top. Youse all right. Youse always been a regular fellar."

It was late, after two a.m. I went to bed. And, as usual, I slept soundly.

Ma Lawton was an early riser. She made excellent coffee and she gave the two elevator runners and another lodger, a porter who worked on Ellis Island, coffee and hot homemade biscuits every morning. The next morning she shook me abruptly out of my sleep.

"Ahm scared to death. Thar's moah tur'ble trouble. I kain't git in the barlroom and the hallway's all messy."

I jumped up, hauled on my pants, and went to the bathroom. A sickening purplish liquid coming from under the door had trickled down the hall toward the kitchen. I took Ma Lawton's rolling-pin and broke through the door.

Jerco had cut his throat and was lying against the bowl of the water-closet. Some empty coke papers[6] were on the floor. And he sprawled there like a great black boar in a mess of blood.

1928

6. Drug paraphernalia. "Water-closet": toilet.

ZORA NEALE HURSTON
1891–1960

Although all of her books appeared in the 1930s, Zora Neale Hurston was undoubtedly a product of the Harlem Renaissance as well as one of its most extraordinary writers. Some readers first encounter Hurston as a rather disconcerting figure in Langston Hughes's autobiography *The Big Sea* (1940), where Hughes depicts her as a somewhat eccentric, even occasionally bizarre character with the nerve to approach strangers in Harlem and measure their heads as part of an anthropological inquiry. In Wallace Thurman's roman à clef *Infants of the Spring* (1932), she appears as Sweetie Mae Carr, a woman who fundamentally cares nothing about art. For Alice Walker, however, as well as for thousands of Hurston's admirers, she is one of the greatest writers of the century. Walker has declared that if she were relegated to a desert island for the balance of her life with only ten books to sustain her, she "would choose, unhesitatingly, two of Zora's." Walker's choices, *Mules and Men* (1935) and *Their Eyes Were Watching God* (1937), are beyond question two of the finest achievements in African American literature.

Nevertheless, Hurston remains one of the more mysterious figures in that literature. In her autobiography, *Dust Tracks on a Road* (1942), she addressed the matter of her birth itself with characteristic aplomb: "This is all hearsay. Maybe some of the details of my birth as told me might be a little inaccurate, but it is pretty well established that I really did get born." For years, misled by Hurston herself, scholars set the year of her birth as 1901, when in fact she was born a decade earlier, on January 7, 1891. No scholar thus far has been able to account for this lost decade of Hurston's life. She was raised in Eatonville, Florida, the first Black township to be incorporated in the United States. An extraordinary place by any reckoning, Hurston's hometown takes on an almost mythic quality in her fiction and autobiographical writing. In her view, the absence of whites not only kept Eatonville free of racism but also freed Blacks to express themselves without reservation. She was also proud of her father's crucial role as mayor of and lawgiver to the town.

Zora Neale Hurston in Chicago, 1934. Photograph by Carl Van Vechten.

Despite the lively, comic stories of Eatonville, however, Hurston's childhood was far from perfect. Her parents' marriage was marred by tension, not least of all because of her father's many infidelities; and her mother died when Zora was only thirteen. When her father married again, she clashed repeatedly with her stepmother. Apparently, Hurston left school and was shuffled back and forth between relatives. Of the odd jobs she took to support herself in the years that followed, the most important took her away from Eatonville, when she became the personal maid of a kindly white actress in a traveling theatrical troupe. In Baltimore, Hurston left her employer and returned to school. She earned her high school diploma from Morgan Academy in 1918, then studied sporadically at Howard University between 1918 and 1924. In Washington, D.C., she came to know such literary figures as Alain Locke and Georgia Douglas Johnson. Locke paved the way for her migration to New York when he urged her to submit "Drenched in Light" to the editor of *Opportunity,* Charles S. Johnson, who published her story there in December 1924.

Arriving in New York City in 1925, Hurston soon established herself as one of the brightest of the young artists in Harlem. Her short play *Color Struck* (which would later appear in *Fire!!,* the magazine she co-founded with Hughes and a number of others) and her story "Spunk" (which appeared in the June 1925 issue of *Opportunity*) brought her to the attention of the novelist Fannie Hurst and the philanthropist Annie Nathan Meyer. Hurst hired Hurston as her personal secretary, and Meyer made it possible for Hurston to attend Barnard College.

While a student at Barnard, from which she graduated in 1928, she wrote a paper that her instructor passed on to Franz Boas, the foremost figure in anthropology in the United States at the time. Boas, then at Columbia University, was so impressed by her work that he convinced her to start graduate study in anthropology at Columbia. In turn, Hurston was thrilled by Boas's interest in the folktales (known to herself and the people who told them simply as "lies") that had kept her spellbound as a child in Eatonville. With a $1,400 grant and Boas's intellectual and moral support, Hurston returned to her native South. Also important to Hurston's development as a folklorist was Charlotte Mason, the wealthy, elderly white woman who also befriended and aided Hughes and Alain Locke as well as other writers and artists.

With Mason's support, Hurston was able to gather the material that would later comprise *Mules and Men* (1935), generally regarded as the first collection of African American folklore to be compiled and published by an African American. *Mules and Men* received mixed reviews, with some Black critics complaining that it was too easy on whites. According to Sterling A. Brown, for instance, Hurston's collection was "too pastoral" and would have been "nearer the truth" if it had been "more bitter." Nevertheless, the book was a popular success. Less successful was her second book of folklore, *Tell My Horse* (1938), which she began after joining the Depression-inspired Works Progress Administration in 1935. Many readers were disappointed to find that the purported collection of folklore actually emphasizes a comparison between the intraracial barriers in Black America and those in the Caribbean and makes relatively short shrift of the delightful tales that had made her first collection so endearing.

Hurston's trip to the Caribbean in connection with research on this book was also important because during her stay there she completed her second and finest novel: *Their Eyes Were Watching God* (1937). Her first novel, *Jonah's Gourd Vine* (1934), had been well received by both the critics and the public. The story of John Pearson, a Baptist minister who is unable to remain faithful to his wife between sabbaths, *Jonah's Gourd Vine* is loosely modeled on the infidelities of Hurston's father, who was also a preacher. But as impressive as it is for a first novel, it prepared few readers for the book that was to follow. In its chronicle of Janie Crawford, a Black woman who marries three times before she finds a man who is as concerned about her happiness as about his own, *Their Eyes Were Watching God* celebrates one individual's triumph over the limitations imposed on her mainly by sexism and poverty. Janie Crawford's ultimate attainment of contentment is based squarely on a mature understanding of life and of the acknowledgment of forces superior even to romantic love, which can blind women to the necessity of seeking emotional and intellectual independence as individuals in a complex world.

Throughout the 1930s, Hurston worked intermittently on musical productions that were generally based on the stories she collected in her travels. She also collaborated with Langston Hughes on the play *Mule Bone.* But a quarrel with Hughes kept the two from working together, and the play was never professionally staged during Hurston's lifetime. Her experience with the stage qualified her for a position as a drama instructor at the North Carolina College for Negroes at Durham, where she began working in 1939. Her third novel, *Moses, Man of the Mountain,* was published in November of that year. Most critics are perplexed by the book; typical of their ambivalent responses is the scholar Robert Hemenway's description of it as a "noble failure." Fascinating though this retelling of the Exodus story undoubtedly is, the transmuting of Israelites into African Americans and of Moses into a practitioner of hoodoo leaves many readers wondering whether Hurston was more interested in modernizing the biblical tale or parodying it. Nevertheless, *Moses, Man of the Mountain,* like the two novels before it, has proved attractive enough to have remained in print.

In fact, the only one of Hurston's novels not readily available is her last, *Seraph on the Suwanee* (1948), in which Hurston turns to the study of a fictional white woman, Arvay Henson. If readers were surprised by this dramatic change in subject matter, Hurston had her reasons. In a letter to Carl Van Vechten she wrote, "I have hopes of breaking that old silly rule about Negroes not writing about white people." Her readers, though surprised, were probably not as troubled by her sudden breaking of that "silly" rule as her critics; and the book sold well despite many critics' fears that Hurston was perhaps turning her back on her race—a charge that was almost bound to be brought against her because of apparent inconsistencies in her views on race as she expressed them during the 1940s.

For Hurston, a new stage of her career and reputation began with the publication of her popular autobiography *Dust Tracks on a Road* in 1942, which led unquestionably to controversies and misconceptions concerning her. Even though Hurston's publisher had specifically requested an autobiography from her, he refused to publish the book she gave him because of several potentially objectionable passages in which Hurston indicts white America for its hypocrisy and racism. Without those passages, the book was published. *Dust Tracks on a Road* won Hurston the Anisfield-Wolf award for its contribution to the amelioration of race relations; it also won her the contempt of many Black critics who considered it an unconscionably cheery portrayal of the life experience of a Black woman in America. In other words, *Dust Tracks on a Road* failed (for these critics at least) precisely where *Their Eyes Were Watching God* had succeeded. Nevertheless, Hurston found herself solicited for articles by numerous magazines. Soon she was appearing in such publications as the *Saturday Evening Post, Reader's Digest, American Mercury, World Telegram,* and *Negro Digest.* Her views were sometimes contradictory. In an article from 1943 she wrote that "the Jim Crow system works," but Hurston claimed just less than three years later that she was "all for the repeal of every Jim Crow law in the nation here and now." Ambivalence toward her deepened as the 1940s wore on, and she was probably relieved and a little surprised when *Seraph on the Suwanee* sold well.

But what might have been the beginning of a second phase in her career (it had been nearly a decade since the publication of her previous novel) was cut short by a personal calamity. In September 1948 Hurston was arrested on charges of having committed an immoral act with a ten-year-old boy. The fact that she had been out of the country when the crime was supposed to have taken place was not enough to keep the story out of the newspapers, and Hurston was humiliated. "My race," she wrote to Van Vechten, "has seen fit to destroy me without reason, and with the vilest tools conceived of by man so far." She never recovered from the incident, and wrote little in the remaining twelve years of her life. Discovered working as a cleaning woman in Florida in 1950, Hurston claimed unconvincingly that she was engaged in research for a piece she was planning to write about domestics.

Her brief stints of employment as librarian, reporter, and substitute teacher in the years that followed left her poor at her death in 1960, and her grave (in a segregated cemetery in Fort Pierce, Florida) was unmarked until 1973, when Alice Walker had a tombstone erected on the approximate location of the gravesite. The 1970s, in fact, saw a resurgence of interest in Hurston that continues to swell. Hurston has found a new audience, one composed of people far more ready than her contemporaries to accept the complex wisdom of this woman who refused to be "tragically colored." For Hurston, that refusal entailed not a denial of her race, but a joyful affirmation of infinite possibility in the scope of her own life.

The Eatonville[1] Anthology

I. The Pleading Woman

Mrs. Tony Roberts is the pleading woman. She just loves to ask for things. Her husband gives her all he can rake and scrape, which is considerably more than most wives get for their housekeeping, but she goes from door to door begging for things.

She starts at the store. "Mist' Clarke," she sing-songs in a high keening voice, "gimme lil' piece uh meat tuh boil a pot uh greens wid. Lawd knows me an' mah chillen is SO hongry! Hits uh SHAME! Tony don't fee-ee-eee-ed me!"

Mr. Clarke knows that she has money and that her larder[2] is well stocked, for Tony Roberts is the best provider on his list. But her keening annoys him and he arises heavily. The pleader at this shows all the joy of a starving man being seated at a feast.

"Thass right Mist' Clarke. De Lawd loveth de cheerful giver. Gimme jes' a lil' piece 'bout dis big (indicating the width of her hand) an' de Lawd'll bless yuh."

She follows this angel-on-earth to his meat tub and superintends the cutting, crying out in pain when he refuses to move the knife just a teeny bit mo'.

Finally, meat in hand, she departs remarking on the meanness of some people who give a piece of salt meat only two-fingers wide when they were plainly asked for a hand-wide piece. Clarke puts it down to Tony's account and resumes his reading.

With the slab of salt pork as a foundation, she visits various homes until she has collected all she wants for the day. At the Piersons, for instance: "Sister Pierson, plee-ee-ease gimme uh han'ful uh collard greens fuh me an' mah po' chillen! 'Deed, me an' mah chillen is SO hongry. Tony doan' fee-ee-eed me!"

Mrs. Pierson picks a bunch of greens for her, but she springs away from them as if they were poison. "Lawd a mussy, Mis' Pierson, you ain't gonna gimme dat lil' eye-full uh greens fuh me an' mah chillen, is you? Don't be so graspin'; Gawd won't bless yuh. Gimme uh hah'full mo'. Lawd, some folks is got everything, an' theys jes' as gripin' an stingy!"

Mrs. Pierson raises the ante, and the pleading woman moves on to the next place, and on and on. The next day, it commences all over.

II. Turpentine Love

Jim Merchant is always in good humor—even with his wife. He says he fell in love with her at first sight. That was some years ago. She has had all her teeth pulled out, but they still get along splendidly.

He says that first time he called on her he found out that she was subject to fits. This didn't cool his love, however. She had several in his presence.

One Sunday, while he was there, she had one, and her mother tried to give her a dose of turpentine to stop it. Accidently, she spilled it in her eye

1. Hurston grew up in Eatonville, Florida.
2. Pantry.

and it cured her. She never had another fit, so they got married and have kept each other in good humor ever since.

III

Becky Moore has eleven children of assorted colors and sizes. She has never been married, but that is not her fault. She has never stopped any of the fathers of her children from proposing, so if she has no father for her children it's not her fault. The men round about are entirely to blame.

The other mothers of the town are afraid that it is catching. They won't let their children play with hers.

IV. Tippy

Sykes Jones' family all shoot craps.[3] The most interesting member of the family—also fond of bones, but of another kind—is Tippy, the Jones' dog.

He is so thin, that it amazes one that he lives at all. He sneaks into village kitchens if the housewives are careless about the doors and steals meats, even off the stoves. He also sucks eggs.

For these offenses he has been sentenced to death dozens of times, and the sentences executed upon him, only they didn't work. He has been fed bluestone, strychnine, nux vomica, even an entire Peruna bottle beaten up. It didn't fatten him, but it didn't kill him. So Eatonville has resigned itself to the plague of Tippy, reflecting that it has erred in certain matters and is being chastened.

In spite of all the attempts upon his life, Tippy is still willing to be friendly with anyone who will let him.

V. The Way of a Man with a Train

Old Man Anderson lived seven or eight miles out in the country from Eatonville. Over by Lake Apopka. He raised feed-corn and cassava[4] and went to market with it two or three times a year. He bought all of his victuals wholesale so he wouldn't have to come to town for several months more.

He was different from us citybred folks. He had never seen a train. Everybody laughed at him for even the smallest child in Eatonville had either been to Maitland or Orlando and watched a train go by. On Sunday afternoons all of the young people of the village would go over to Maitland, a mile away, to see Number 35 whizz southward on its way to Tampa and wave at the passengers. So we looked down on him a little. Even we children felt superior in the presence of a person so lacking in worldly knowledge.

The grown-ups kept telling him he ought to go see a train. He always said he didn't have time to wait so long. Only two trains a day passed through Maitland. But patronage and ridicule finally had its effect and Old Man Anderson drove in one morning early. Number 78 went north to Jacksonville at 10:20. He drove his light wagon over in the woods beside the railroad below Maitland, and sat down to wait. He began to fear that his horse would get frightened and run away with the wagon. So he took him out and led him deeper into the grove and tied him securely. Then he returned to his wagon

3. Gamble with dice.
4. Plant whose tuberous roots can be used to make an edible starch.

and waited some more. Then he remembered that some of the train-wise villagers had said the engine belched fire and smoke. He had better move his wagon out of danger. It might catch afire. He climbed down from the seat and placed himself between the shafts to draw it away. Just then 78 came thundering over the trestle[5] spouting smoke, and suddenly began blowing for Maitland. Old Man Anderson became so frightened he ran away with the wagon through the woods and tore it up worse than the horse ever could have done. He doesn't know yet what a train looks like, and says he doesn't care.

VI. Coon Taylor

Coon Taylor never did any real stealing. Of course, if he saw a chicken or a watermelon or muskmelon or anything like that that he wanted he'd take it. The people used to get mad but they never could catch him. He took so many melons from Joe Clarke that he set up in the melon patch one night with his shotgun loaded with rock salt. He was going to fix Coon. But he was tired. It is hard work being a mayor, postmaster, storekeeper and everything. He dropped asleep sitting on a stump in the middle of the patch. So he didn't see Coon when he came. Coon didn't see him either, that is, not at first. He knew the stump was there, however. He had opened many of Clarke's juicy Florida Favorite on it. He selected his fruit, walked over to the stump and burst the melon on it. That is, he thought it was the stump until it fell over with a yell. Then he knew it was no stump and departed hastily from those parts. He had cleared the fence when Clarke came to, as it were. So the charge of rock-salt was wasted on the desert air.

During the sugar-cane season, he found he couldn't resist Clarke's soft green cane, but Clarke did not go to sleep this time. So after he had cut six or eight stalks by the moonlight, Clarke rose up out of the cane strippings with his shotgun and made Coon sit right down and chew up the last one of them on the spot. And the next day he made Coon leave his town for three months.

VII. Village Fiction

Joe Lindsay is said by Lum Boger to be the largest manufacturer of prevarications in Eatonville; Brazzle (late owner of the world's leanest and meanest mule) contends that his business is the largest in the state and his wife holds that he is the biggest liar in the world.

Exhibit A—He claims that while he was in Orlando one day he saw a doctor cut open a woman, remove everything—liver, lights[6] and heart included—clean each of them separately; the doctor then washed out the empty woman, dried her out neatly with a towel and replaced the organs so expertly that she was up and about her work in a couple of weeks.

VIII

Sewell is a man who lives all to himself. He moves a great deal. So often, that 'Lige Moseley says his chickens are so used to moving that every time he comes out into his backyard the chickens lie down and cross their legs, ready to be tied up again.

5. A framework of timber or steel built so that trains can travel over water or low-lying areas.
6. Lungs.

He is baldheaded; but he says he doesn't mind that, because he wants as little as possible between him and God.

IX

Mrs. Clarke is Joe Clarke's wife. She is a soft-looking, middle-aged woman, whose bust and stomach are always holding a get-together.

She waits on the store sometimes and cries every time he yells at her which he does every time she makes a mistake, which is quite often. She calls her husband "Jody." They say he used to beat her in the store when he was a young man, but he is not so impatient now. He can wait until he goes home.

She shouts in Church every Sunday and shakes the hand of fellowship with everybody in the Church with her eyes closed, but somehow always misses her husband.

X

Mrs. McDuffy goes to Church every Sunday and always shouts and tells her "determination." Her husband always sits in the back row and beats her as soon as they get home. He says there's no sense in her shouting, as big a devil as she is. She just does it to slur him. Elijah Moseley asked her why she didn't stop shouting, seeing she always got a beating out about it. She says she can't "squinch the sperrit." Then Elijah asked Mr. McDuffy to stop beating her, seeing that she was going to shout anyway. He answered that she just did it for spite and that his fist was just as hard as her head. He could last just as long as she. So the village let the matter rest.

XI. Double-Shuffle

Back in the good old days before the World War, things were very simple in Eatonville. People didn't fox-trot. When the town wanted to put on its Sunday clothes and wash behind the ears, it put on a "breakdown." The daring younger set would two-step and waltz, but the good church members and the elders stuck to the grand march. By rural canons dancing is wicked, but one is not held to have danced until the feet have been crossed. Feet don't get crossed when one grand marches.

At elaborate affairs the organ from the Methodist church was moved up to the hall and Lizzimore, the blind man, presided. When informal gatherings were held, he merely played his guitar assisted by any volunteer with mouth organs or accordions.

Among white people the march is as mild as if it had been passed on by Volstead.[7] But it still has a kick in Eatonville. Everybody happy, shining eyes, gleaming teeth. Feet dragged shhlap, shhlap! to beat out the time. No orchestra needed. Round and round! Back again, parse-me-la! shlap! shlap! Strut! Strut! Seaboard! Shlap! Shlap! Tiddy bumm! Mr. Clarke in the lead with Mrs. Mosely.

It's too much for some of the young folks. Double shuffling commences. Buck and wing. Lizzimore about to break his guitar. Accordion doing contortions. People fall back against the walls, and let the soloist have it, shouting as they clap the old, old double shuffle songs.

7. That is, the act of Congress that established the prohibition of alcoholic drinks (1919).

"Me an' mah honey got two mo' days
Two mo' days tuh do de buck"

Sweating bodies, laughing mouths, grotesque faces, feet drumming fiercely. Deacons clapping as hard as the rest.

"Great big nigger, black as tar
Trying tuh git tuh hebben on uh 'lectric car."

"Some love cabbage, some love kale
But I love a gal wid a short skirt tail."

"Long tall angel—steppin' down.
Long white robe an' starry crown."

"'Ah would not marry uh black gal (bumm bumm!)
Tell yuh de reason why
Every time she comb her hair
She make de goo-goo eye.

Would you not marry a yaller gal (bumm bumm!)
Tell yuh de reason why
Her neck so long an' stringy
Ahm 'fraid she'd never die.

Would you not marry uh preacher
Tell yuh de reason why
Every time he comes tuh town
He makes de chicken fly."

When the buck dance was over, the boys would give the floor to the girls and they would parse-me-la[8] with a sly eye out of the corner to see if anybody was looking who might "have them up in church" on conference night. Then there would be more dancing. Then Mr. Clarke would call for everybody's best attention and announce that *'freshments was served! Every gent'man would please take his lady by the arm and scorch her right up to de table fur a treat!*

Then the men would stick their arms out with a flourish and ask their ladies: "You lak chicken? Well, then, take a wing." And the ladies would take the proffered "wings" and parade up to the long table and be served. Of course most of them had brought baskets in which were heaps of jointed and fried chicken, two or three kinds of pies, cakes, potato pone and chicken purlo.[9] The hall would separate into happy groups about the baskets until time for more dancing.

But the boys and girls got scattered about during the war, and now they dance the fox-trot by a brand new piano. They do waltz and two-step still, but no one now considers it good form to lock his chin over his partner's shoulder and stick out behind. One night just for fun and to humor the old folks, they danced, that is, they grand marched, but everyone picked up their feet. *Bah!!*

XII. The Head of the Nail

Daisy Taylor was the town vamp. Not that she was pretty. But sirens were all but non-existent in the town. Perhaps she was forced to it by circumstances.

8. A type of dance.
9. Type of casserole with chicken and rice. "Pone": type of baked or fried bread.

She was quite dark, with little brushy patches of hair squatting over her head. These were held down by shingle-nails often. No one knows whether she did this for artistic effect or for lack of hair-pins, but there they were shining in the little patches of hair when she got all dressed for the afternoon and came up to Clarke's store to see if there was any mail for her.

It was seldom that anyone wrote to Daisy, but she knew that the men of the town would be assembled there by five o'clock, and some one could usually be induced to buy her some soda-water or peanuts.

Daisy flirted with married men. There were only two single men in town. Lum Boger, who was engaged to the assistant school-teacher, and Hiram Lester, who had been off to school at Tuskegee[1] and wouldn't look at a person like Daisy. In addition to other drawbacks, she was pigeon-toed and her petticoat was always showing so perhaps he was justified. There was nothing else to do except flirt with married men.

This went on for a long time. First one wife then another complained of her, or drove her from the preserves by threat.

But the affair with Crooms was the most prolonged and serious. He was even known to have bought her a pair of shoes.

Mrs. Laura Crooms was a meek little woman who took all of her troubles crying, and talked a great deal of leaving things in the hands of God.

The affair came to a head one night in orange picking time. Crooms was over at Oneido picking oranges. Many fruit pickers move from one town to the other during the season.

The *town* was collected at the store-post office as is customary on Saturday nights. The *town* has had its bath and with its week's pay in pocket fares forth to be merry. The men tell stories and treat the ladies to soda-water, peanuts and peppermint candy.

Daisy was trying to get treats, but the porch was cold to her that night.

"Ah don't keer if you don't treat me. What's a dirty lil nickel?" She flung this at Walter Thomas. "The ever-loving Mister Crooms will gimme anything atall Ah wants."

"You better shet up yo' mouf talking 'bout Albert Crooms. Heah his wife comes right now."

Daisy went akimbo.[2] "Who? Me! Ah don't keer whut Laura Crooms think. If she ain't a heavy hip-ted Mama enough to keep him, she don't need to come crying to me."

She stood making goo-goo eyes as Mrs. Crooms walked upon the porch. Daisy laughed loud, made several references to Albert Crooms, and when she saw the mail-bag come in from Maitland she said, "Ah better go in an' see if Ah ain't got a letter from Oneido."

The more Daisy played the game of getting Mrs. Crooms' goat,[3] the better she liked it. She ran in and out of the store laughing until she could scarcely stand. Some of the people present began to talk to Mrs. Crooms—to egg her on to halt Daisy's boasting, but she was for leaving it all in the hands of God. Walter Thomas kept on after Mrs. Crooms until she stiffened and resolved to fight. Daisy was inside when she came to this resolve and never dreamed anything of the kind could happen. She had gotten hold of an envelope and came laughing and shouting, "Oh, Ah can't stand to see Oneido lose!"

1. Town in Alabama where the Tuskegee Normal School (then Institute, then University) is located.
2. That is, she put her hands on her hips and turned her elbows outward.
3. That is, irritating her or making her mad.

There was a box of ax-handles on display on the porch, propped up against the door jamb. As Daisy stepped upon the porch, Mrs. Crooms leaned the heavy end of one of those handles heavily upon her head. She staggered from the porch to the ground and the timid Laura, fearful of a counterattack, struck her again and Daisy toppled into the town ditch. There was not enough water in there to do more than muss her up. Every time she tried to rise, down would come that ax-handle again. Laura was fighting a sacred fight. With Daisy thoroughly licked, she retired to the store porch and left her fallen enemy in the ditch. None of the men helped Daisy—even to get out of the ditch. But Elijah Moseley, who was some distance down the street when the trouble began, arrived as the victor was withdrawing. He rushed up and picked Daisy out of the mud and began feeling her head.

"Is she hurt much?" Joe Clarke asked from the doorway.

"I don't know," Elijah answered. "I was just looking to see if Laura had been lucky enough to hit one of those nails on the head and drive it in."

Before a week was up, Daisy moved to Orlando. There in a wider sphere, perhaps, her talents as a vamp were appreciated.

XIII. Pants and Cal'line

Sister Cal'line Potts was a silent woman. Did all of her laughing down inside, but did the thing that kept the town in an uproar of laughter. It was the general opinion of the village that Cal'line would do anything she had a mind to. And she had a mind to do several things.

Mitchell Potts, her husband, had a weakness for women. No one ever believed that she was jealous. She did things to the women, surely. But most any townsman would have said that she did them because she liked the novel situation and the queer things she could bring out of it.

Once he took up with Delphine—called Mis' Pheeny by the town. She lived on the outskirts on the edge of the piney woods. The town winked and talked. People don't make secrets of such things in the village. Cal'line went about her business with her thin black lips pursed tight as ever, and her shiny black eyes unchanged.

"Dat devil of a Cal'line's got somethin' up her sleeve!" The town smiled in anticipation.

"Delphine is too big a cigar for her to smoke. She ain't crazy," said some as the weeks went on and nothing happened. Even Pheeny herself would give an extra flirt to her over-starched petticoats as she rustled into church past her of Sundays.

Mitch Potts said furthermore, that he was tired of Cal'line's foolishness. She had to stay where he put her. His African soup-bone (arm) was too strong to let a woman run over him. 'Nough was 'nough. And he did some fancy cussing, and he was the fanciest cusser in the county.

So the town waited and the longer it waited, the odds changed slowly from the wife to the husband.

One Saturday, Mitch knocked off work at two o'clock and went over to Maitland. He came back with a rectangular box under his arm and kept straight on out to the barn and put it away. He ducked around the corner of the house quickly, but even so, his wife glimpsed the package. Very much like a shoe-box. So!

He put on the kettle and took a bath. She stood in her bare feet at the ironing board and kept on ironing. He dressed. It was about five o'clock but still very light. He fiddled around outside. She kept on with her ironing. As soon as the sun got red, he sauntered out to the barn, got the parcel and walked away down the road, past the store and into the piney woods. As soon as he left the house, Cal'line slipped on her shoes without taking time to don stockings, put on one of her husband's old Stetsons,[4] worn and floppy, slung the axe over her shoulder and followed in his wake. He was hailed cheerily as he passed the sitters on the store porch and answered smiling sheepishly and passed on. Two minutes later passed his wife, silently, unsmilingly, and set the porch to giggling and betting.

An hour passed perhaps. It was dark. Clarke had long ago lighted the swinging kerosene lamp inside.

[*XIV*]

Once 'way back yonder before the stars fell all the animals used to talk just like people. In them days dogs and rabbits was the best of friends—even tho both of them was stuck on the same gal—which was Miss Nancy Coon. She had the sweetest smile and the prettiest striped and bushy tail to be found anywhere.

They both run their legs nigh off trying to win her for themselves—fetching nice ripe persimmons and such. But she never give one or the other no satisfaction.

Finally one night Mr. Dog popped the question right out. "Miss Coon," he says, "Ma'am, also Ma'am, which would you ruther be—a lark flyin' or a dove a settin'?"

Course Miss Nancy blushed and laughed a little and hid her face behind her bushy tail for a spell. Then she said sorter shy like, "I does love yo' sweet voice, brother dawg—but—but I ain't jes' exactly set in my mind yit."

Her and Mr. Dog set on a spell, when up comes hopping Mr. Rabbit wid his tail fresh washed and his whiskers shining. He got right down to business and asked Miss Coon to marry him, too.

"Oh, Miss Nancy," he says, "Ma'am, also Ma'am, if you'd see me settin' straddle of a mud-cut leadin' a minnow, what would you think? Ma'am also Ma'am?" which is a out and out proposal as everybody knows.

"Youse awful nice, Brother Rabbit and a beautiful dancer, but you cannot sing like Brother Dog. Both you uns come back next week to gimme time for to decide."

They both left arm-in-arm. Finally Mr. Rabbit says to Mr. Dog, "Taint no use in me going back—she ain't gwinter have me. So I mought as well give up. She loves singing, and I ain't got nothing but a squeak."

"Oh, don't talk that a' way," says Mr. Dog, tho' he is glad Mr. Rabbit can't sing none.

"Thass all right, Brer Dog. But if I had a sweet voice like you got, I'd have it worked on and make it sweeter."

"How! How! How!" Mr. Dog cried, jumping up and down.

"Lemme fix it for you, like I do for Sister Lark and Sister Mocking-bird."

"When? Where?" asked Mr. Dog, all excited. He was figuring that if he could sing just a little better Miss Coon would be bound to have him.

"Just you meet me t'morrer in de huckleberry patch," says the rabbit and off they both goes to bed.

4. Hats.

The dog is there on time next day and after a while the rabbit comes loping up.

"Mawnin', Brer Dawg," he says kinder chippy like. "Ready to git yo' voice sweetened?"

"Sholy, sholy, Brer Rabbit. Let's we all hurry about it. I wants tuh serenade Miss Nancy from de piney woods tuh night."

"Well, den, open yo' mouf and poke out yo' tongue," says the rabbit.

No sooner did Mr. Dog poke out his tongue than Mr. Rabbit split it with a knife and ran for all he was worth to a hollow stump and hid hisself.

The dog has been mad at the rabbit ever since.

Anybody who don't believe it happened, just look at the dog's tongue and he can see for himself where the rabbit slit it right up the middle.

STEPPED ON A TIN, MAH STORY ENDS.

1926

Sweat

It was eleven o'clock of a Spring night in Florida. It was Sunday. Any other night, Delia Jones would have been in bed for two hours by this time. But she was a washwoman, and Monday morning meant a great deal to her. So she collected the soiled clothes on Saturday when she returned the clean things. Sunday night after church, she sorted them and put the white things to soak. It saved her almost a half day's start. A great hamper in the bedroom held the clothes that she brought home. It was so much neater than a number of bundles lying around.

She squatted in the kitchen floor beside the great pile of clothes, sorting them into small heaps according to color, and humming a song in a mournful key, but wondering through it all where Sykes, her husband, had gone with her horse and buckboard.

Just then something long, round, limp and black fell upon her shoulders and slithered to the floor beside her. A great terror took hold of her. It softened her knees and dried her mouth so that it was a full minute before she could cry out or move. Then she saw that it was the big bull whip her husband liked to carry when he drove.

She lifted her eyes to the door and saw him standing there bent over with laughter at her fright. She screamed at him.

"Sykes, what you throw dat whip on me like dat? You know it would skeer me—looks just like a snake, an' you knows how skeered Ah is of snakes."

"Course Ah knowed it! That's how come Ah done it." He slapped his leg with his hand and almost rolled on the ground in his mirth. "If you such a big fool dat you got to have a fit over a earth worm or a string, Ah don't keer how bad Ah skeer you."

"You aint got no business doing it. Gawd knows it's a sin. Some day Ah'm gointuh drop dead from some of yo' foolishness. 'Nother thing, where you been wid mah rig? Ah feeds dat pony. He aint fuh you to be drivin' wid no bull whip."

"You sho is one aggravatin' nigger woman!" he declared and stepped into the room. She resumed her work and did not answer him at once. "Ah done tole you time and again to keep them white folks' clothes outa dis house."

He picked up the whip and glared down at her. Delia went on with her work. She went out into the yard and returned with a galvanized tub and set it on the washbench. She saw that Sykes had kicked all of the clothes together again, and now stood in her way truculently, his whole manner hoping, *praying,* for an argument. But she walked calmly around him and commenced to re-sort the things.

"Next time, Ah'm gointer kick 'em outdoors," he threatened as he struck a match along the leg of his corduroy breeches.

Delia never looked up from her work, and her thin, stooped shoulders sagged further.

"Ah aint for no fuss t'night Sykes. Ah just come from taking sacrament at the church house."

He snorted scornfully. "Yeah, you just come from de church house on a Sunday night, but heah you is gone to work on them clothes. You ain't nothing but a hypocrite. One of them amen-corner Christians—sing, whoop, and shout; then come home and wash white folks clothes on the Sabbath."

He stepped roughly upon the whitest pile of things, kicking them helter-skelter as he crossed the room. His wife gave a little scream of dismay, and quickly gathered them together again.

"Sykes, you quit grindin' dirt into these clothes! How can Ah git through by Sat'day if Ah don't start on Sunday?"

"Ah don't keer if you never git through. Anyhow, Ah done promised Gawd and a couple of other men, Ah aint gointer have it in mah house. Don't gimme no lip neither, else Ah'll throw 'em out and put mah fist up side yo' head to boot."

Delia's habitual meekness seemed to slip from her shoulders like a blown scarf. She was on her feet; her poor little body, her bare knuckly hands bravely defying the strapping hulk before her.

"Looka heah, Sykes, you done gone too fur. Ah been married to you fur fifteen years, and Ah been takin' in washin' fur fifteen years. Sweat, sweat, sweat! Work and sweat, cry and sweat, pray and sweat!"

"What's that got to do with me?" he asked brutally.

"What's it got to do with you, Sykes? Mah tub of suds is filled yo' belly with vittles more times than yo' hands is filled it. Mah sweat is done paid for this house and Ah reckon Ah kin keep on sweatin' in it."

She seized the iron skillet from the stove and struck a defensive pose, which act surprised him greatly, coming from her. It cowed him and he did not strike her as he usually did.

"Naw you won't," she panted, "that ole snaggle-toothed black woman you runnin' with aint comin' heah to pile up on *mah* sweat and blood. You aint paid for nothin' on this place, and Ah'm gointer stay right heah till Ah'm toted out foot foremost."

"Well, you better quit gittin' me riled up, else they'll be totin' you out sooner than you expect. Ah'm so tired of you Ah don't know whut to do. Gawd! how Ah hates skinny wimmen!"

A little awed by this new Delia, he sidled out of the door and slammed the back gate after him. He did not say where he had gone, but she knew too well. She knew very well that he would not return until nearly daybreak also. Her work over, she went on to bed but not to sleep at once. Things had come to a pretty pass!

She lay awake, gazing upon the debris that cluttered their matrimonial trail. Not an image left standing along the way. Anything like flowers had long ago been drowned in the salty stream that had been pressed from her heart. Her tears, her sweat, her blood. She had brought love to the union and he had brought a longing after the flesh. Two months after the wedding, he had given her the first brutal beating. She had the memory of his numerous trips to Orlando with all of his wages when he had returned to her penniless, even before the first year had passed. She was young and soft then, but now she thought of her knotty, muscled limbs, her harsh knuckly hands, and drew herself up into an unhappy little ball in the middle of the big feather bed. Too late now to hope for love, even if it were not Bertha it would be someone else. This case differed from the others only in that she was bolder than the others. Too late for everything except her little home. She had built it for her old days, and planted one by one the trees and flowers there. It was lovely to her, lovely.

Somehow, before sleep came, she found herself saying aloud: "Oh well, whatever goes over the Devil's back, is got to come under his belly. Sometime or ruther, Sykes, like everybody else, is gointer reap his sowing." After that she was able to build a spiritual earthworks against her husband. His shells could no longer reach her. *Amen.* She went to sleep and slept until he announced his presence in bed by kicking her feet and rudely snatching the covers away.

"Gimme some kivah heah, an' git yo' damn foots over on yo' own side! Ah oughter mash you in yo' mouf fuh drawing dat skillet on me."

Delia went clear to the rail without answering him. A triumphant indifference to all that he was or did.

The week was as full of work for Delia as all other weeks, and Saturday found her behind her little pony, collecting and delivering clothes.

It was a hot, hot day near the end of July. The village men on Joe Clarke's porch even chewed cane listlessly. They did not hurl the cane-knots[1] as usual. They let them dribble over the edge of the porch. Even conversation had collapsed under the heat.

"Heah come Delia Jones," Jim Merchant said, as the shaggy pony came 'round the bend of the road toward them. The rusty buckboard was heaped with baskets of crisp, clean laundry.

"Yep," Joe Lindsay agreed. "Hot or col', rain or shine, jes ez reg'lar ez de weeks roll roun' Delia carries 'em an' fetches 'em on Sat'day."

"She better if she wanter eat," said Moss. "Syke Jones aint wuth de shot an' powder hit would tek tuh kill 'em. Not to *huh* he aint."

"He sho' aint," Walter Thomas chimed in. "It's too bad, too, cause she wuz a right pritty lil trick when he got huh. Ah'd uh mah'ied huh mahseff if he hadnter beat me to it."

Delia nodded briefly at the men as she drove past.

"Too much knockin' will ruin *any* 'oman. He done beat huh 'nough tuh kill three women, let 'lone change they looks," said Elijah Moseley. "How Syke kin stommuck dat big black greasy Mogul he's layin' roun' wid, gits me. Ah swear dat eight-rock[2] couldn't kiss a sardine can Ah done thowed out de back do' 'way las' yeah."

"Aw, she's fat, thass how come. He's allus been crazy 'bout fat women," put in Merchant. "He'd a' been tied up wid one long time ago if he could a' found one tuh have him. Did Ah tell yuh 'bout him come sidlin' roun' *mah*

1. The indigestible part of the sugarcane stalk.

2. The eight ball in pool, that is, Black.

wife—bringin' her a basket uh peecans outa his yard fuh a present? Yeah, mah wife! She tol' him tuh take 'em right straight back home, cause Delia works so hard ovah dat washtub she reckon everything on de place taste lak sweat an' soapsuds. Ah jus' wisht Ah'd a' caught 'im 'roun' dere! Ah'd a' made his hips ketch on fiah down dat shell road."

"Ah know he done it, too. Ah sees 'im grinnin' at every 'oman dat passes," Walter Thomas said. "But even so, he useter eat some mighty big hunks uh humble pie tuh git dat lil' 'oman he got. She wuz ez pritty ez a speckled pup! Dat wuz fifteen yeahs ago. He useter be so skeered uh losin' huh, she could make him do some parts of a husband's duty. Dey never wuz de same in de mind."

"There oughter be a law about him," said Lindsay. "He aint fit tuh carry guts tuh a bear."

Clarke spoke for the first time. "Taint no law on earth dat kin make a man be decent if it aint in 'im. There's plenty men dat takes a wife lak dey do a joint uh sugar-cane. It's round, juicy an' sweet when dey gits it. But dey squeeze an' grind, squeeze an' grind an' wring tell dey wring every drop uh pleasure dat's in 'em out. When dey's satisfied dat dey is wrung dry, dey treats 'em jes lak dey do a cane-chew. Dey thows 'em away. Dey knows whut dey is doin' while dey is at it, an' hates theirselves fuh it but they keeps on hangin' after huh tell she's empty. Den dey hates huh fuh bein' a cane-chew an' in de way."

"We oughter take Syke an' dat stray 'oman uh his'n down in Lake Howell swamp an' lay on de rawhide till they cain't say Lawd a' mussy. He allus wuz uh ovahbearin' niggah, but since dat white 'oman from up north done teached 'im how to run a automobile, he done got too biggety to live—an' we oughter kill 'im," Old Man Anderson advised.

A grunt of approval went around the porch. But the heat was melting their civic virtue and Elijah Moseley began to bait Joe Clarke.

"Come on, Joe, git a melon outa dere an' slice it up for yo' customers. We'se all sufferin' wid de heat. De bear's done got *me!*"

"Thass right, Joe, a watermelon is jes' whut Ah needs tuh cure de eppizudicks,"[3] Walter Thomas joined forces with Moseley. "Come on dere, Joe. We all is steady customers an' you aint set us up in a long time. Ah chooses dat long, bowlegged Floridy favorite."

"A god, an' be dough. You all gimme twenty cents and slice way," Clarke retorted. "Ah needs a col' slice m'self. Heah, everybody chip in. Ah'll lend y'll mah meat knife."

The money was quickly subscribed and the huge melon brought forth. At that moment, Sykes and Bertha arrived. A determined silence fell on the porch and the melon was put away again.

Merchant snapped down the blade of his jackknife and moved toward the store door.

"Come on in, Joe, an' gimme a slab uh sow belly an' uh pound uh coffee—almost fuhgot 'twas Sat'day. Got to git on home." Most of the men left also.

Just then Delia drove past on her way home, as Sykes was ordering magnificently for Bertha. It pleased him for Delia to see.

"Git whutsoever yo' heart desires, Honey. Wait a minute, Joe. Give huh two bottles uh strawberry soda-water, uh quart uh parched ground-peas, an' a block uh chewin' gum."

3. That is, epizootic; any fast-spreading disease.

With all this they left the store, with Sykes reminding Bertha that this was his town and she could have it if she wanted it.

The men returned soon after they left, and held their watermelon feast.

"Where did Syke Jones git da 'oman from nohow?" Lindsay asked.

"Ovah Apopka.[4] Guess dey musta been cleanin' out de town when she lef'. She don't look lak a thing but a hunk uh liver wid hair on it."

"Well, she sho' kin squall," Dave Carter contributed. "When she gits ready tuh laff, she jes' opens huh mouf an' latches it back tuh de las' notch. No ole grandpa alligator down in Lake Bell ain't got nothin' on huh."

Bertha had been in town three months now. Sykes was still paying her room rent at Della Lewis'—the only house in town that would have taken her in. Sykes took her frequently to Winter Park to "stomps."[5] He still assured her that he was the swellest man in the state.

"Sho' you kin have dat lil' ole house soon's Ah kin git dat 'oman outa dere. Everything b'longs tuh me an' you sho' kin have it. Ah sho' 'bominates uh skinny 'oman. Lawdy, you sho' is got one portly shape on you! You kin git *anything* you wants. Dis is *mah* town an' you sho' kin have it."

Delia's work-worn knees crawled over the earth in Gethsemane[6] and up the rocks of Calvary many, many times during these months. She avoided the villagers and meeting places in her efforts to be blind and deaf. But Bertha nullified this to a degree, by coming to Delia's house to call Sykes out to her at the gate.

Delia and Sykes fought all the time now with no peaceful interludes. They slept and ate in silence. Two or three times Delia had attempted a timid friendliness, but she was repulsed each time. It was plain that the breaches must remain agape.

The sun had burned July to August. The heat streamed down like a million hot arrows, smiting all things living upon the earth. Grass withered, leaves browned, snakes went blind in shedding and men and dogs went mad. Dog days!

Delia came home one day and found Sykes there before her. She wondered, but started to go on into the house without speaking, even though he was standing in the kitchen door and she must either stoop under his arm or ask him to move. He made no room for her. She noticed a soap box beside the steps, but paid no particular attention to it, knowing that he must have brought it there. As she was stooping to pass under his outstretched arm, he suddenly pushed her backward, laughingly.

"Look in de box dere Delia, Ah done brung yuh somethin'!"

She nearly fell upon the box in her stumbling, and when she saw what it held, she all but fainted outright.

"Syke! Syke, mah Gawd! You take dat rattlesnake 'way from heah! You *gottuh*. Oh, Jesus, have mussy!"

"Ah aint gut tuh do nuthin' uh de kin'—fact is Ah aint got tuh do nothin' but die. Taint no use uh you puttin' on airs makin' out lak you skeered uh dat snake—he's gointer stay right heah tell he die. He wouldn't bite me cause Ah knows how tuh handle 'im. Nohow he wouldn't risk breakin' out his fangs 'gin *yo'* skinny laigs."

4. A town in Florida some ten miles from Eatonville.
5. Raucous dance parties.
6. The garden outside Jerusalem that was the scene of Jesus's agony and arrest (Matthew 26:36–57).

"Naw, now Syke, don't keep dat thing 'roun' heah tuh skeer me tuh death. You knows Ah'm even feared uh earth worms. Thass de biggest snake Ah evah did see. Kill 'im Syke, please."

"Doan ast me tuh do nothin' fuh yuh. Goin' 'roun' tryin' tuh be so damn asterperious.[7] Naw, Ah aint gonna kill it. Ah think uh damn sight mo' uh him dan you! Dat's a nice snake an' anybody doan lak 'im kin jes' hit de grit."

The village soon heard that Sykes had the snake, and came to see and ask questions.

"How de hen-fire did you ketch dat six-foot rattler, Syke?" Thomas asked.

"He's full uh frogs so he caint hardly move, thass how Ah eased up on 'm. But Ah'm a snake charmer an' knows how tuh handle 'em. Shux, dat aint nothin'. Ah could ketch one eve'y day if Ah so wanted tuh."

"Whut he needs is a heavy hick'ry club leaned real heavy on his head. Dat's de bes' way tuh charm a rattlesnake."

"Naw, Walt, y'll jes' don't understand dese diamon' backs lak Ah do," said Sykes in a superior tone of voice.

The village agreed with Walter, but the snake stayed on. His box remained by the kitchen door with its screen wire covering. Two or three days later it had digested its meal of frogs and literally came to life. It rattled at every movement in the kitchen or the yard. One day as Delia came down the kitchen steps she saw his chalky-white fangs curved like scimitars hung in the wire meshes. This time she did not run away with averted eyes as usual. She stood for a long time in the doorway in a red fury that grew bloodier for every second that she regarded the creature that was her torment.

That night she broached the subject as soon as Sykes sat down to the table.

"Syke, Ah wants you tuh take dat snake 'way fum heah. You done starved me an' Ah put up widcher, you done beat me an Ah took dat, but you done kilt all mah insides bringin' dat varmint heah."

Sykes poured out a saucer full of coffee and drank it deliberately before he answered her.

"A whole lot Ah keer 'bout how you feels inside uh out. Dat snake aint goin' no damn wheah till Ah gits ready fuh 'im tuh go. So fur as beatin' is concerned, yuh aint took near all dat you gointer take ef yuh stay 'roun' *me*."

Delia pushed back her plate and got up from the table. "Ah hates you, Sykes," she said calmly. "Ah hates you tuh de same degree dat Ah useter love yuh. Ah done took an' took till mah belly is full up tuh mah neck. Dat's de reason Ah got mah letter fum de church an' moved mah membership tuh Woodbridge—so Ah don't haftuh take no sacrament wid yuh. Ah don't wantuh see yuh 'roun' me atall. Lay 'roun' wid dat 'oman all yuh wants tuh, but gwan 'way fum me an' mah house. Ah hates yuh lak uh suck-egg dog."[8]

Sykes almost let the huge wad of corn bread and collard greens he was chewing fall out of his mouth in amazement. He had a hard time whipping himself up to the proper fury to try to answer Delia.

"Well, Ah'm glad you does hate me. Ah'm sho' tiahed uh you hangin' ontuh me. Ah don't want yuh. Look at yuh stringey ole neck! Yo' rawbony laigs an' arms is enough tuh cut uh man tuh death. You looks jes' lak de devvul's doll-baby tuh *me*. You cain't hate me no worse dan Ah hates you. Ah been hatin' *you* fuh years."

7. That is, astorperious; haughty (possibly a fusion of *Astor*, the name of a wealthy family, and *imperious*, or arrogant).

8. A dog that steals chicken eggs.

"Yo' ole black hide don't look lak nothin' tuh me, but uh passle uh wrinkled up rubber, wid yo' big ole yeahs flappin' on each side lak uh paih uh buzzard wings. Don't think Ah'm gointuh be run 'way fum mah house neither. Ah'm goin' tuh de white folks about *you,* mah young man, de very nex' time you lay yo' han's on me. Mah cup is done run ovah."[9] Delia said this with no signs of fear and Sykes departed from the house, threatening her, but made not the slightest move to carry out any of them.

That night he did not return at all, and the next day being Sunday, Delia was glad she did not have to quarrel before she hitched up her pony and drove the four miles to Woodbridge.

She stayed to the night service—"love feast"—which was very warm and full of spirit. In the emotional winds her domestic trials were borne far and wide so that she sang as she drove homeward,

> "Jurden[1] water, black an' col'
> Chills de body, not de soul
> An' Ah wantah cross Jurden in uh calm time."

She came from the barn to the kitchen door and stopped.

"Whut's de mattah, ol' satan, you aint kickin' up yo' racket?" She addressed the snake's box. Complete silence. She went on into the house with a new hope in its birth struggles. Perhaps her threat to go to the white folks had frightened Sykes! Perhaps he was sorry! Fifteen years of misery and suppression had brought Delia to the place where she would hope *anything* that looked towards a way over or through her wall of inhibitions.

She felt in the match safe behind the stove at once for a match. There was only one there.

"Dat niggah wouldn't fetch nothin' heah tuh save his rotten neck, but he kin run thew whut Ah brings quick enough. Now he done toted off nigh on tuh haff uh box uh matches. He done had dat 'oman heah in mah house, too."

Nobody but a woman could tell how she knew this even before she struck the match. But she did and it put her into a new fury.

Presently she brought in the tubs to put the white things to soak. This time she decided she need not bring the hamper out of the bedroom; she would go in there and do the sorting. She picked up the pot-bellied lamp and went in. The room was small and the hamper stood hard by the foot of the white iron bed. She could sit and reach through the bedposts—resting as she worked.

"Ah wantah cross Jurden in uh calm time." She was singing again. The mood of the "love feast" had returned. She threw back the lid of the basket almost gaily. Then, moved by both horror and terror, she sprang back toward the door. *There lay the snake in the basket!* He moved sluggishly at first, but even as she turned round and round, jumped up and down in an insanity of fear, he began to stir vigorously. She saw him pouring his awful beauty from the basket upon the bed, then she seized the lamp and ran as fast as she could to the kitchen. The wind from the open door blew out the light and the darkness added to her terror. She sped to the darkness of the yard, slamming the door after her before she thought to set down the lamp. She did not feel safe even on the ground, so she climbed up in the hay barn.

9. "My cup runneth over," Psalm 23:5.
1. The river Jordan, mentioned in the Bible, signifies deliverance.

There for an hour or more she lay sprawled upon the hay a gibbering wreck.

Finally she grew quiet, and after that, coherent thought. With this, stalked through her a cold, bloody rage. Hours of this. A period of introspection, a space of retrospection, then a mixture of both. Out of this an awful calm.

"Well, Ah done de bes' Ah could. If things aint right, Gawd knows taint mah fault."

She went to sleep—a twitch sleep—and woke up to a faint gray sky. There was a loud hollow sound below. She peered out. Sykes was at the wood-pile, demolishing a wire-covered box.

He hurried to the kitchen door, but hung outside there some minutes before he entered, and stood some minutes more inside before he closed it after him.

The gray in the sky was spreading. Delia descended without fear now, and crouched beneath the low bedroom window. The drawn shade shut out the dawn, shut in the night. But the thin walls held back no sound.

"Dat ol' scratch[2] is woke up now!" She mused at the tremendous whirr inside, which every woodsman knows, is one of the sound illusions. The rattler is a ventriloquist. His whirr sounds to the right, to the left, straight ahead, behind, close under foot—everywhere but where it is. Woe to him who guesses wrong unless he is prepared to hold up his end of the argument! Sometimes he strikes without rattling at all.

Inside, Sykes heard nothing until he knocked a pot lid off the stove while trying to reach the match safe in the dark. He had emptied his pockets at Bertha's.

The snake seemed to wake up under the stove and Sykes made a quick leap into the bedroom. In spite of the gin he had had, his head was clearing now.

"Mah Gawd!" he chattered, "ef Ah could on'y strack uh light!"

The rattling ceased for a moment as he stood paralyzed. He waited. It seemed that the snake waited also.

"Oh, fuh de light! Ah thought he'd be too sick"—Sykes was muttering to himself when the whirr began again, closer, right underfoot this time. Long before this, Sykes' ability to think had been flattened down to primitive instinct and he leaped—onto the bed.

Outside Delia heard a cry that might have come from a maddened chimpanzee, a stricken gorilla. All the terror, all the horror, all the rage that man possibly could express, without a recognizable human sound.

A tremendous stir inside there, another series of animal screams, the intermittent whirr of the reptile. The shade torn violently down from the window, letting in the red dawn, a huge brown hand seizing the window stick, great dull blows upon the wooden floor punctuating the gibberish of sound long after the rattle of the snake had abruptly subsided. All this Delia could see and hear from her place beneath the window, and it made her ill. She crept over to the four-o'clocks and stretched herself on the cool earth to recover.

She lay there. "Delia, Delia!" She could hear Sykes calling in a most despairing tone as one who expected no answer. The sun crept on up, and he

2. A nickname of the devil; here refers to the serpent.

called. Delia could not move—her legs were gone flabby. She never moved, he called, and the sun kept rising.

"Mah Gawd!" She heard him moan, "Mah Gawd fum Heben!" She heard him stumbling about and got up from her flower-bed. The sun was growing warm. As she approached the door she heard him call out hopefully, "Delia, is dat you Ah heah?"

She saw him on his hands and knees as soon as she reached the door. He crept an inch or two toward her—all that he was able, and she saw his horribly swollen neck and his one open eye shining with hope. A surge of pity too strong to support bore her away from that eye that must, could not, fail to see the tubs. He would see the lamp. Orlando with its doctors was too far. She could scarcely reach the Chinaberry tree, where she waited in the growing heat while inside she knew the cold river was creeping up and up to extinguish that eye which must know by now that she knew.

1926

How It Feels to Be Colored Me

I am colored but I offer nothing in the way of extenuating circumstances except the fact that I am the only Negro in the United States whose grandfather on the mother's side was *not* an Indian chief.

I remember the very day that I became colored. Up to my thirteenth year I lived in the little Negro town of Eatonville, Florida. It is exclusively a colored town. The only white people I knew passed through the town going to or coming from Orlando. The native whites rode dusty horses, the Northern tourists chugged down the sandy village road in automobiles. The town knew the Southerners and never stopped cane chewing when they passed. But the Northerners were something else again. They were peered at cautiously from behind curtains by the timid. The more venturesome would come out on the porch to watch them go past and got just as much pleasure out of the tourists as the tourists got out of the village.

The front porch might seem a daring place for the rest of the town, but it was a gallery seat for me. My favorite place was atop the gate-post. Proscenium box[1] for a born first-nighter. Not only did I enjoy the show, but I didn't mind the actors knowing that I liked it. I usually spoke to them in passing. I'd wave at them and when they returned my salute, I would say something like this: "Howdy-do-well-I-thank-you-where-you-goin'?" Usually automobile or the horse paused at this, and after a queer exchange of compliments, I would probably "go a piece of the way" with them, as we say in farthest Florida. If one of my family happened to come to the front in time to see me, of course negotiations would be rudely broken off. But even so, it is clear that I was the first "welcome-to-our-state" Floridian, and I hope the Miami Chamber of Commerce will please take notice.

During this period, white people differed from colored to me only in that they rode through town and never lived there. They liked to hear me "speak pieces" and sing and wanted to see me dance the parse-me-la, and gave me generously of their small silver for doing these things, which seemed strange to me for I wanted to do them so much that I needed bribing to stop. Only

1. The box seats in a theater on either side of and nearest to the stage.

they didn't know it. The colored people gave no dimes. They deplored any joyful tendencies in me, but I was their Zora nevertheless. I belonged to them, to the nearby hotels, to the county—everybody's Zora.

But changes came in the family when I was thirteen, and I was sent to school in Jacksonville. I left Eatonville, the town of the oleanders, as Zora. When I disembarked from the river-boat at Jacksonville, she was no more. It seemed that I had suffered a sea change. I was not Zora of Orange County any more, I was now a little colored girl. I found it out in certain ways. In my heart as well as in the mirror, I became a fast[2] brown—warranted not to rub nor run.

But I am not tragically colored. There is no great sorrow dammed up in my soul, nor lurking behind my eyes. I do not mind at all. I do not belong to the sobbing school of Negrohood who hold that nature somehow has given them a lowdown dirty deal and whose feelings are all hurt about it. Even in the helter-skelter skirmish that is my life, I have seen that the world is to the strong regardless of a little pigmentation more or less. No, I do not weep at the world—I am too busy sharpening my oyster knife.[3]

Someone is always at my elbow reminding me that I am the granddaughter of slaves. It fails to register depression with me. Slavery is sixty years in the past. The operation was successful and the patient is doing well, thank you. The terrible struggle that made me an American out of a potential slave said "On the line!" The Reconstruction said "Get set!"; and the generation before said "Go!" I am off to a flying start and I must not halt in the stretch to look behind and weep. Slavery is the price I paid for civilization, and the choice was not with me. It is a bully adventure and worth all that I have paid through my ancestors for it. No one on earth ever had a greater chance for glory. The world to be won and nothing to be lost. It is thrilling to think—to know that for any act of mine, I shall get twice as much praise or twice as much blame. It is quite exciting to hold the center of the national stage, with the spectators not knowing whether to laugh or to weep.

The position of my white neighbor is much more difficult. No brown specter pulls up a chair beside me when I sit down to eat. No dark ghost thrusts its leg against mine in bed. The game of keeping what one has is never so exciting as the game of getting.

I do not always feel colored. Even now I often achieve the unconscious Zora of Eatonville before the Hegira.[4] I feel most colored when I am thrown against a sharp white background.

For instance at Barnard. "Beside the waters of the Hudson" I feel my race. Among the thousand white persons, I am a dark rock surged upon, and overswept, but through it all, I remain myself. When covered by the waters, I am; and the ebb but reveals me again.

Sometimes it is the other way around. A white person is set down in our midst, but the contrast is just as sharp for me. For instance, when I sit in the drafty basement that is The New World Cabaret with a white person, my color comes. We enter chatting about any little nothing that we have in common and are seated by the jazz waiters. In the abrupt way that jazz

2. Colorfast.
3. An allusion to Shakespeare's *The Merry Wives of Windsor* 2.2.3–4: "Why, then the world's mine oyster, / Which I with sword will open."
4. In Islam, Muhammad's emigration from Mecca to Medina in 622 C.E.; here, the journey to Jacksonville.

orchestras have, this one plunges into a number. It loses no time in circumlocutions, but gets right down to business. It constricts the thorax and splits the heart with its tempo and narcotic harmonies. This orchestra grows rambunctious, rears on its hind legs and attacks the tonal veil with primitive fury, rending it, clawing it until it breaks through to the jungle beyond. I follow those heathen—follow them exultingly. I dance wildly inside myself; I yell within, I whoop; I shake my assegai[5] above my head, I hurl it true to the mark *yeeeeooww!* I am in the jungle and living in the jungle way. My face is painted red and yellow and my body is painted blue. My pulse is throbbing like a war drum. I want to slaughter something—give pain, give death to what, I do not know. But the piece ends. The men of the orchestra wipe their lips and rest their fingers. I creep back slowly to the veneer we call civilization with the last tone and find the white friend sitting motionless in his seat, smoking calmly.

"Good music they have here," he remarks, drumming the table with his fingertips.

Music. The great blobs of purple and red emotion have not touched him. He has only heard what I felt. He is far away and I see him but dimly across the ocean and the continent that have fallen between us. He is so pale with his whiteness then and I am *so* colored.

At certain times I have no race, I am *me*. When I set my hat at a certain angle and saunter down Seventh Avenue, Harlem City, feeling as snooty as the lions in front of the Forty-Second Street Library,[6] for instance. So far as my feelings are concerned, Peggy Hopkins Joyce on the Boule Mich[7] with her gorgeous raiment, stately carriage, knees knocking together in a most aristocratic manner, has nothing on me. The cosmic Zora emerges. I belong to no race nor time. I am the eternal feminine with its string of beads.

I have no separate feeling about being an American citizen and colored. I am merely a fragment of the Great Soul that surges within the boundaries. My country, right or wrong.

Sometimes, I feel discriminated against, but it does not make me angry. It merely astonishes me. How *can* any deny themselves the pleasure of my company? It's beyond me.

But in the main, I feel like a brown bag of miscellany propped against a wall. Against a wall in company with other bags, white, red and yellow. Pour out the contents, and there is discovered a jumble of small things priceless and worthless. A first-water diamond,[8] an empty spool, bits of broken glass, lengths of string, a key to a door long since crumbled away, a rusty knife-blade, old shoes saved for a road that never was and never will be, a nail bent under the weight of things too heavy for any nail, a dried flower or two still a little fragrant. In your hand is the brown bag. On the ground before you is the jumble it held—so much like the jumble in the bags, could they be emptied, that all might be dumped in a single heap and the bags refilled without altering the content of any greatly. A bit of colored glass more or less would not matter. Perhaps that is how the Great Stuffer of Bags filled them in the first place—who knows?

1928

5. Spear.
6. The headquarters of the New York Public Library.
7. The elegant Boulevard St. Michel in Paris.
8. A diamond of the highest quality.

The Gilded Six-Bits

It was a Negro yard around a Negro house in a Negro settlement that looked to the payroll of the G and G Fertilizer works for its support.

But there was something happy about the place. The front yard was parted in the middle by a sidewalk from gate to door-step, a sidewalk edged on either side by quart bottles driven neck down into the ground on a slant. A mess of homey flowers planted without a plan but blooming cheerily from their helter-skelter places. The fence and house were whitewashed. The porch and steps scrubbed white.

The front door stood open to the sunshine so that the floor of the front room could finish drying after its weekly scouring. It was Saturday. Everything clean from the front gate to the privy house. Yard raked so that the strokes of the rake would make a pattern. Fresh newspaper cut in fancy edge on the kitchen shelves.

Missie May was bathing herself in the galvanized washtub in the bedroom. Her dark-brown skin glistened under the soapsuds that skittered down from her wash rag. Her stiff young breasts thrust forward aggressively like broad-based cones with the tips lacquered in black.

She heard men's voices in the distance and glanced at the dollar clock on the dresser.

"Humph! Ah'm way behind time t'day! Joe gointer be heah 'fore Ah git mah clothes on if Ah don't make haste."

She grabbed the clean meal sack at hand and dried herself hurriedly and began to dress. But before she could tie her slippers, there came the ring of singing metal on wood. Nine[1] times.

Missie May grinned with delight. She had not seen the big tall man come stealing in the gate and creep up the walk grinning happily at the joyful mischief he was about to commit. But she knew that it was her husband throwing silver dollars in the door for her to pick up and pile beside her plate at dinner. It was this way every Saturday afternoon. The nine dollars hurled into the open door, he scurried to a hiding place behind the cape jasmine bush and waited.

Missie May promptly appeared at the door in mock alarm.

"Who dat chunkin' money in mah do'way?" She demanded. No answer from the yard. She leaped off the porch and began to search the shrubbery. She peeped under the porch and hung over the gate to look up and down the road. While she did this, the man behind the jasmine darted to the chinaberry tree. She spied him and gave chase.

"Nobody ain't gointer be chuckin' money at me and Ah not do 'em nothin'," she shouted in mock anger. He ran around the house with Missie May at his heels. She overtook him at the kitchen door. He ran inside but could not close it after him before she crowded in and locked with him in a rough and tumble. For several minutes the two were a furious mass of male and female energy. Shouting, laughing, twisting, turning, tussling, tickling each other in the ribs; Missie May clutching onto Joe and Joe trying, but not too hard, to get away.

"Missie May, take yo' hand out mah pocket!" Joe shouted out between laughs.

"Ah ain't, Joe, not lessen you gwine gimme whateve' it is good you got in yo' pocket. Turn it go, Joe, do Ah'll tear yo' clothes."

1. A number significant in mysticism.

"Go on tear 'em. You de one dat pushes de needles round heah. Move yo' hand Missie May."

"Lemme git dat paper sack out yo' pocket. Ah bet its candy kisses."

"Tain't. Move yo' hand. Woman ain't go no business in a man's clothes nohow. Go way."

Missie May gouged way down and gave an upward jerk and triumphed.

"Unhhunh! Ah got it. It 'tis so candy kisses. Ah knowed you had somethin' for me in yo' clothes. Now Ah got to see whut's in every pocket you got."

Joe smiled indulgently and let his wife go through all of his pockets and take out the things that he had hidden there for her to find. She bore off the chewing gum, the cake of sweet soap, the pocket handkerchief as if she had wrested them from him, as if they had not been bought for the sake of this friendly battle.

"Whew! dat play-fight done got me all warmed up." Joe exclaimed. "Got me some water in de kittle?"

"Yo' water is on de fire and yo' clean things is cross de bed. Hurry up and wash yo'self and git changed so we kin eat. Ah'm hongry." As Missie said this, she bore the steaming kettle into the bedroom.

"You ain't hongry, sugar," Joe contradicted her. "Youse jes' a little empty. Ah'm de one whut's hongry. Ah could eat up camp meetin', back off 'ssociation, and drink Jurdan[2] dry. Have it on de table when Ah git out de tub."

"Don't you mess wid mah business, man. You git in yo' clothes. Ah'm a real wife, not no dress and breath.[3] Ah might not look lak one, but if you burn me, you won't git a thing but wife ashes."

Joe splashed in the bedroom and Missie May fanned around in the kitchen. A fresh red and white checked cloth on the table. Big pitcher of buttermilk beaded with pale drops of butter from the churn. Hot fried mullet, crackling bread, ham hock atop a mound of string beans and new potatoes, and perched on the window-sill a pone[4] of spicy potato pudding.

Very little talk during the meal but that little consisted of banter that pretended to deny affection but in reality flaunted it. Like when Missie May reached for a second helping of the tater pone. Joe snatched it out of her reach.

After Missie May had made two or three unsuccessful grabs at the pan, she begged, "Aw, Joe gimme some mo' dat tater pone."

"Nope, sweetenin' is for us men-folks. Y'all pritty lil frail eels don't need nothin' lak dis. You too sweet already."

"Please, Joe."

"Naw, naw. Ah don't want you to git no sweeter than whut you is already. We goin' down de road a lil piece t'night so you go put on yo' Sunday-go-to-meetin' things."

Missie May looked at her husband to see if he was playing some prank. "Sho nuff, Joe?"

"Yeah. We goin' to de ice cream parlor."

"Where de ice cream parlor at, Joe?"

"A new man done come heah from Chicago and he done got a place and took and opened it up for a ice cream parlor, and bein' as it's real swell, Ah wants you to be one de first ladies to walk in dere and have some set down."

"Do Jesus, Ah ain't knowed nothin' 'bout it. Who de man done it?"

2. The Jordan River. "'ssociation": a religious gathering.

3. Imitation wife.

4. A type of baked or fried bread.

"Mister Otis D. Slemmons, of spots and places—Memphis, Chicago, Jacksonville, Philadelphia and so on."

"Dat heavy-set man wid his mouth full of gold teethes?"

"Yeah. Where did you see 'im at?"

"Ah went down to de sto' tuh git a box of lye and Ah seen 'im standin' on de corner talkin' to some of de mens, and Ah come on back and went to scrubbin' de floor, and he passed and tipped his hat whilst Ah was scourin' de steps. Ah thought Ah never seen *him* befo'."

Joe smiled pleasantly. "Yeah, he's up to date. He got de finest clothes Ah ever seen on a colored man's back."

"Aw, he don't look no better in his clothes than you do in yourn. He got a puzzlegut on 'im and he so chuckle-headed, he got a pone behind his neck."

Joe looked down at his own abdomen and said wistfully, "Wisht Ah had a build on me lak he got. He ain't puzzle-gutted, honey. He jes' got a corperation. Dat make 'm look lak a rich white man. All rich mens is got some belly on 'em."

"Ah seen de pitchers of Henry Ford and he's a spare-built man and Rockefeller[5] look lak he ain't got but one gut. But Ford and Rockefeller and dis Slemmons and all de rest kin be as many-gutted as dey please, Ah'm satisfied wid you jes' lak you is, baby. God took pattern after a pine tree and built you noble. Youse a pritty man, and if Ah knowed any way to make you mo' pritty still Ah'd take and do it."

Joe reached over gently and toyed with Missie May's ear. "You jes' say dat cause you love me, but Ah know Ah can't hold no light to Otis D. Slemmons. Ah ain't never been nowhere and Ah ain't got nothin' but you."

Missie May got on his lap and kissed him and he kissed back in kind. Then he went on. "All de womens is crazy 'bout 'im everywhere he go."

"How you know dat, Joe?"

"He tole us so hisself."

"Dat don't make it so. His mouf is cut cross-ways, ain't it? Well, he kin lie jes' lak anybody else."

"Good Lawd, Missie! You womens sho is hard to sense into things. He's got a five-dollar gold piece for a stick-pin and he got a ten-dollar gold piece on his watch chain and his mouf is jes' crammed full of gold teethes. Sho wisht it wuz mine. And whut make it so cool, he got money 'cumulated. And womens give it all to 'im."

"Ah don't see whut de womens see on 'im. Ah wouldn't give 'im a wink if de sheriff wuz after 'im."

"Well, he tole us how de white womens in Chicago give 'im all dat gold money. So he don't 'low nobody to touch it at all. Not even put dey finger on it. Dey tole 'im not to. You kin make 'miration at it, but don't tetch it."

"Whyn't he stay up dere where dey so crazy 'bout 'im?"

"Ah reckon dey done made 'im vast-rich and he wants to travel some. He say dey wouldn't leave 'im hit a lick of work. He got mo' lady people crazy 'bout him than he kin shake a stick at."

"Joe, Ah hates to see you so dumb. Dat stray nigger jes' tell y'all anything and y'all b'lieve it."

"Go 'head on now, honey and put on yo' clothes. He talkin' 'bout his pritty womens—Ah want 'im to see *mine*."

5. Henry Ford (1863–1947), U.S. automobile manufacturer. John D. Rockefeller (1839–1937), U.S. oil magnate.

Missie May went off to dress and Joe spent the time trying to make his stomach punch out like Slemmons' middle. He tried the rolling swagger of the stranger, but found that his tall bone-and-muscle stride fitted ill with it. He just had time to drop back into his seat before Missie May came in dressed to go.

On the way home that night Joe was exultant. "Didn't Ah say ole Otis was swell? Can't he talk Chicago talk? Wuzn't dat funny whut he said when great big fat ole Ida Armstrong come in? He asted me, 'Who is dat broad wid de forte shake?' Dat's a new word. Us always thought forty was a set of figgers but he showed us where it means a whole heap of things. Sometimes he don't say forty, he jes' say thirty-eight and two and dat mean de same thing. Know whut he tole me when Ah wuz payin' for our ice cream? He say, 'Ah have to hand it to you, Joe. Dat wife of yours is jes' thirty-eight and two. Yessuh, she's forte!' Ain't he killin'?"

"He'll do in case of a rush. But he sho is got uh heap uh gold on 'im. Dat's de first time Ah ever seed gold money. It lookted good on him sho nuff, but it'd look a whole heap better on you."

"Who, me? Missie May youse crazy! Where would a po' man lak me git gold money from?"

Missie May was silent for a minute, then she said, "Us might find some goin' long de road some time. Us could."

"Who would be losin' gold money round heah? We ain't even seen none dese white folks wearin' no gold money on dey watch chain. You must be figgerin' Mister Packard or Mister Cadillac[6] goin' pass through heah."

"You don't know whut been lost 'round heah. Maybe somebody way back in memorial times lost they gold money and went on off and it ain't never been found. And then if we wuz to find it, you could wear some 'thout havin' no gang of womens lak dat Slemmons say he got."

Joe laughed and hugged her. "Don't be so wishful 'bout me. Ah'm satisfied de way Ah is. So long as Ah be yo' husband, Ah don't keer 'bout nothin' else. Ah'd ruther all de other womens in de world to be dead than for you to have de toothache. Less we go to bed and git our night rest."

It was Saturday night once more before Joe could parade his wife in Slemmons' ice cream parlor again. He worked the night shift and Saturday was his only night off. Every other evening around six o'clock he left home, and dying dawn saw him hustling home around the lake where the challenging sun flung a flaming sword from east to west across the trembling water.

That was the best part of life—going home to Missie May. Their whitewashed house, the mock battle on Saturday, the dinner and ice cream parlor afterwards, church on Sunday nights when Missie outdressed any woman in town—all, everything was right.

One night around eleven the acid ran out at the G. and G. The foreman knocked off the crew and let the steam die down. As Joe rounded the lake on his way home, a lean moon rode the lake in a silver boat. If anybody had asked Joe about the moon on the lake, he would have said he hadn't paid it any attention. But he saw it with his feelings. It made him yearn painfully for Missie. Creation obsessed him. He thought about children. They had been married for more than a year now. They had money put away. They ought to be making little feet for shoes. A little boy child would be about right.

He saw a dim light in the bedroom and decided to come in through the kitchen door. He could wash the fertilizer dust off himself before present-

6. Two lines of expensive cars.

ing himself to Missie May. It would be nice for her not to know that he was there until he slipped into his place in bed and hugged her back. She always liked that.

He eased the kitchen door open slowly and silently, but when he went to set his dinner bucket on the table he bumped it into a pile of dishes, and something crashed to the floor. He heard his wife gasp in fright and hurried to reassure her.

"Iss me, honey. Don't get skeered."

There was a quick, large movement in the bedroom. A rustle, a thud, and a stealthy silence. The light went out.

What? Robbers? Murderers? Some varmint attacking his helpless wife, perhaps. He struck a match, threw himself on guard and stepped over the door-sill into the bedroom.

The great belt on the wheel of Time slipped and eternity stood still. By the match light he could see the man's legs fighting with his breeches in his frantic desire to get them on. He had both chance and time to kill the intruder in his helpless condition—half in and half out of his pants—but he was too weak to take action. The shapeless enemies of humanity that live in the hours of Time had waylaid Joe. He was assaulted in his weakness. Like Samson awakening after his haircut.[7] So he just opened his mouth and laughed.

The match went out and he struck another and lit the lamp. A howling wind raced across his heart, but underneath its fury he heard his wife sobbing and Slemmons pleading for his life. Offering to buy it with all that he had. "Please, suh, don't kill me. Sixty-two dollars at de sto'. Gold money."

Joe just stood. Slemmons looked at the window, but it was screened. Joe stood out like a rough-backed mountain between him and the door. Barring him from escape, from sunrise, from life.

He considered a surprise attack upon the big clown that stood there laughing like a chessy cat.[8] But before his fist could travel an inch, Joe's own rushed out to crush him like a battering ram. Then Joe stood over him.

"Git into yo' damn rags, Slemmons, and dat quick."

Slemmons scrambled to his feet and into his vest and coat. As he grabbed his hat, Joe's fury overrode his intentions and he grabbed at Slemmons with his left hand and struck at him with his right. The right landed. The left grazed the front of his vest. Slemmons was knocked a somersault into the kitchen and fled through the open door. Joe found himself alone with Missie May, with the golden watch charm clutched in his left fist. A short bit of broken chain dangled between his fingers.

Missie May was sobbing. Wails of weeping without words. Joe stood, and after awhile he found out that he had something in his hand. And then he stood and felt without thinking and without seeing with his natural eyes. Missie May kept on crying and Joe kept on feeling so much and not knowing what to do with all his feelings, he put Slemmons' watch charm in his pants pocket and took a good laugh and went to bed.

"Missie May, whut you cryin' for?"

"Cause Ah love you so hard and Ah know you don't love *me* no mo'."

Joe sank his face into the pillow for a spell then he said huskily, "You don't know de feelings of dat yet, Missie May."

7. See Judges 16:17, where Samson tells Delilah: "If I be shaven, then my strength will go from me, and I shall be like any other man."

8. An allusion to the grinning Cheshire cat in Lewis Carroll's *Alice's Adventures in Wonderland* (1865).

"Oh Joe, honey, he said he wuz gointer give me dat gold money and he jes' kept on after me—"

Joe was very still and silent for a long time. Then he said, "Well, don't cry no mo', Missie May. Ah got yo' gold piece for you."

The hours went past on their rusty ankles. Joe still and quiet on one bed-rail and Missie May wrung dry of sobs on the other. Finally the sun's tide crept upon the shore of night and drowned all its hours. Missie May with her face stiff and streaked towards the window saw the dawn come into her yard. It was day. Nothing more. Joe wouldn't be coming home as usual. No need to fling open the front door and sweep off the porch, making it nice for Joe. Never no more breakfast to cook; no more washing and starching of Joe's jumper-jackets and pants. No more nothing. So why get up?

With this strange man in her bed, she felt embarrassed to get up and dress. She decided to wait till he had dressed and gone. Then she would get up, dress quickly and be gone forever beyond reach of Joe's looks and laughs. But he never moved. Red light turned to yellow, then white.

From beyond the no-man's land between them came a voice. A strange voice that yesterday had been Joe's.

"Missie May, ain't you gonna fix me no breakfus'?"

She sprang out of bed. "Yeah, Joe. Ah didn't reckon you wuz hongry."

No need to die today. Joe needed her for a few more minutes anyhow.

Soon there was a roaring fire in the cook stove. Water bucket full and two chickens killed. Joe loved fried chicken and rice. She didn't deserve a thing and good Joe was letting her cook him some breakfast. She rushed hot biscuits to the table as Joe took his seat.

He ate with his eyes on his plate. No laughter, no banter.

"Missie May, you ain't eatin' yo' breakfus'."

"Ah don't choose none, Ah thank yuh."

His coffee cup was empty. She sprang to refill it. When she turned from the stove and bent to set the cup beside Joe's plate, she saw the yellow coin on the table between them.

She slumped into her seat and wept into her arms.

Presently Joe said calmly, "Missie May, you cry too much. Don't look back lak Lot's wife and turn to salt."[9]

The sun, the hero of every day, the impersonal old man that beams as brightly on death as on birth, came up every morning and raced across the blue dome and dipped into the sea of fire every evening. Water ran down hill and birds nested.

Missie knew why she didn't leave Joe. She couldn't. She loved him too much, but she could not understand why Joe didn't leave her. He was polite, even kind at times, but aloof.

There were no more Saturday romps. No ringing silver dollars to stack beside her plate. No pockets to rifle. In fact the yellow coin in his trousers was like a monster hiding in the cave of his pockets to destroy her.

She often wondered if he still had it, but nothing could have induced her to ask nor yet to explore his pockets to see for herself. Its shadow was in the house whether or no.

One night Joe came home around midnight and complained of pains in the back. He asked Missie to rub him down with liniment. It had been three

9. According to Genesis 19:26, Lot's wife was turned into a pillar of salt for looking back on the destroyed city of Sodom.

months since Missie had touched his body and it all seemed strange. But she rubbed him. Grateful for the chance. Before morning, youth triumphed and Missie exulted. But the next day, as she joyfully made up their bed, beneath her pillow she found the piece of money with the bit of chain attached.

Alone to herself, she looked at the thing with loathing, but look she must. She took it into her hands with trembling and saw first thing that it was no gold piece. It was a gilded half dollar. Then she knew why Slemmons had forbidden anyone to touch his gold. He trusted village eyes at a distance not to recognize his stick-pin as a gilded quarter, and his watch charm as a four-bit piece.

She was glad at first that Joe had left it there. Perhaps he was through with her punishment. They were man and wife again. Then another thought came clawing at her. He had come home to buy from her as if she were any woman in the long house. Fifty cents for her love. As if to say that he could pay as well as Slemmons. She slid the coin into his Sunday pants pocket and dressed herself and left his house.

Halfway between her house and the quarters[1] she met her husband's mother, and after a short talk she turned and went back home. Never would she admit defeat to that woman who prayed for it nightly. If she had not the substance of marriage she had the outside show. Joe must leave *her*. She let him see she didn't want his old gold four-bits too.

She saw no more of the coin for some time though she knew that Joe could not help finding it in his pocket. But his health kept poor, and he came home at least every ten days to be rubbed.

The sun swept around the horizon, trailing its robes of weeks and days. One morning as Joe came in from work, he found Missie May chopping wood. Without a word he took the ax and chopped a huge pile before he stopped.

"You ain't got no business choppin' wood, and you know it."

"How come? Ah been choppin' it for de last longest."

"Ah ain't blind. You makin' feet for shoes."

"Won't you be glad to have a lil baby chile, Joe?"

"You know dat 'thout astin' me."

"Iss gointer be a boy chile and de very spit of you."

"You reckon, Missie May?"

"Who else could it look lak?"

Joe said nothing, but he thrust his hand deep into his pocket and fingered something there.

It was almost six months later Missie May took to bed and Joe went and got his mother to come wait on the house.

Missie May delivered a fine boy. Her travail was over when Joe came in from work one morning. His mother and the old women were drinking great bowls of coffee around the fire in the kitchen.

The minute Joe came into the room his mother called him aside.

"How did Missie May make out?" he asked quickly.

"Who, dat gal? She strong as a ox. She gointer have plenty mo'. We done fixed her wid de sugar and lard to sweeten her for de nex' one."

Joe stood silent awhile.

"You ain't ast 'bout de baby, Joe. You oughter be mighty proud cause he sho is de spittin' image of yuh, son. Dat's yourn all right, if you never git

1. The dwellings in which the workers lived.

another one, dat un is yourn. And you know Ah'm mighty proud too, son, cause Ah never thought well of you marryin' Missie May cause her ma used tuh fan her foot round right smart and Ah been mighty skeered dat Missie May was gointer git misput on her road."

Joe said nothing. He fooled around the house till late in the day then just before he went to work, he went and stood at the foot of the bed and asked his wife how she felt. He did this every day during the week.

On Saturday he went to Orlando to make his market. It had been a long time since he had done that.

Meat and lard, meal and flour, soap and starch. Cans of corn and tomatoes. All the staples. He fooled around town for awhile and bought bananas and apples. Way after while he went around to the candy store.

"Hellow, Joe," the clerk greeted him. "Ain't seen you in a long time."

"Nope, Ah ain't been heah. Been round in spots and places."

"Want some of them molasses kisses you always buy?"

"Yessuh." He threw the gilded half dollar on the counter. "Will dat spend?"

"Whut is it, Joe? Well, I'll be doggone! A gold-plated four-bit piece. Where'd you git it, Joe?"

"Offen a stray nigger dat come through Eatonville. He had it on his watch chain for a charm—goin' round making out iss gold money. Ha ha! He had a quarter on his tie pin and it wuz all golded up too. Tryin' to fool people. Makin' out he so rich and everything. Ha! Ha! Tryin' to tole off folkses wives from home."

"How did you git it, Joe? Did he fool you, too?"

"Who, me? Naw suh! He ain't fooled me none. Know whut Ah done? He come round me wid his smart talk. Ah hauled off and knocked 'im down and took his old four-bits way from 'im. Gointer buy my wife some good ole lasses kisses wid it. Gimme fifty cents worth of dem candy kisses."

"Fifty cents buys a mighty lot of candy kisses, Joe. Why don't you split it up and take some chocolate bars, too. They eat good, too."

"Yessuh, dey do, but Ah wants all dat in kisses. Ah got a lil boy chile home now. Tain't a week old yet, but he kin suck a sugar tit and maybe eat one them kisses hisself."

Joe got his candy and left the store. The clerk turned to the next customer. "Wisht I could be like these darkies. Laughin' all the time. Nothin' worries 'em."

Back in Eatonville, Joe reached his own front door. There was the ring of singing metal on wood. Fifteen times. Missie May couldn't run to the door, but she crept there as quickly as she could.

"Joe Banks, Ah hear you chunkin' money in mah do'way. You wait till Ah got mah strength back and Ah'm gointer fix you for dat."

1933

Characteristics of Negro Expression

Drama

The Negro's universal mimicry is not so much a thing in itself as an evidence of something that permeates his entire self. And that thing is drama.

His very words are action words. His interpretation of the English language is in terms of pictures. One act described in terms of another. Hence the rich metaphor and simile.

The metaphor is of course very primitive. It is easier to illustrate than it is to explain because action came before speech. Let us make a parallel. Language is like money. In primitive communities actual goods, however bulky, are bartered for what one wants. This finally evolves into coin, the coin being not real wealth but a symbol of wealth. Still later even coin is abandoned for legal tender, and still later for checks in certain usages.

Every phase of Negro life is highly dramatized. No matter how joyful or how sad the case there is sufficient poise for drama. Everything is acted out. Unconsciously for the most part of course. There is an impromptu ceremony always ready for every hour of life. No little moment passes unadorned.

Now the people with highly developed languages have words for detached ideas. That is legal tender. "That-which-we-squat-on" has become "chair." "Groan-causer" has evolved into "spear" and so on. Some individuals even conceive of the equivalent of check words, like "ideation" and "pleonastic." Perhaps we might say that *Paradise Lost* and *Sartor Resartus*[1] are written in check words.

The primitive man exchanges descriptive words. His terms are all close fitting. Frequently the Negro, even with detached words in his vocabulary—not evolved in him but transplanted on his tongue by contact—must add action to it to make it do. So we have "chop-ax," "sitting-chair," "cook-pot" and the like because the speaker has in his mind the picture of the object in use. Action. Everything illustrated. So we can say the white man thinks in a written language and the Negro thinks in hieroglyphics.

A bit of Negro drama familiar to all is the frequent meeting of two opponents who threaten to do atrocious murder one upon the other.

Who has not observed a robust young Negro chap posing upon a street corner, possessed of nothing but his clothing, his strength and his youth? Does he bear himself like a pauper? No, Louis XIV could be no more insolent in his assurance. His eyes say plainly "Female, halt!" His posture exults "Ah, female, I am the eternal male, the giver of life. Behold in my hot flesh all the delights of this world. Salute me, I am strength." All this with a languid posture, there is no mistaking his meaning.

A Negro girl strolls past the corner lounger. Her whole body panging[2] and posing. A slight shoulder movement that calls attention to her bust, that is all of a dare. A hippy undulation below the waist that is a sheaf of promises tied with conscious power. She is acting out. "I'm a darned sweet woman and you know it."

These little plays by strolling players are acted out daily in a dozen streets in a thousand cities, and no one ever mistakes the meaning.

Will to Adorn

The will to adorn is the second most notable characteristic in Negro expression. Perhaps his idea of ornament does not attempt to meet conventional standards, but it satisfies the soul of its creator.

1. A combination of fiction, essay, and autobiography published by Thomas Carlyle (1795–1881) in 1833. *Paradise Lost,* the most famous epic poem in the English language, is by John Milton (1608–1674).
2. As in pangs of hunger.

In this respect the American Negro has done wonders to the English language. It has often been stated by etymologists that the Negro has introduced no African words to the language. This is true, but it is equally true that he has made over a great part of the tongue to his liking and has his revision accepted by the ruling class. No one listening to a Southern white man talk could deny this. Not only has he softened and toned down strongly consonanted words like "aren't" to "aint" and the like, he has made new force words out of old feeble elements. Examples of this are "ham-shanked," "battle-hammed," "double-teen," "bodaciously," "mufflejawed."

But the Negro's greatest contribution to the language is: (1) the use of metaphor and simile; (2) the use of the double descriptive; (3) the use of verbal nouns.

1. METAPHOR AND SIMILE

One at a time, like lawyers going to heaven.
You sho is propaganda.
Sobbing hearted.
I'll beat you till: (*a*) rope like okra, (*b*) slack like lime, (*c*) smell like onions.
Fatal for naked.
Kyting along.
That's a lynch.
That's a rope.
Cloakers—deceivers.
Regular as pig-tracks.
Mule blood—black molasses.
Syndicating—gossiping.
Flambeaux—cheap café (lighted by flambeaux).
To put yo'self on de ladder.

2. THE DOUBLE DESCRIPTIVE

High-tall.
Little-tee-ninchy (tiny).
Low-down.
Top-superior.
Sham-polish.
Lady-people.
Kill-dead.
Hot-boiling.
Chop-ax.
Sitting-chairs.
De watch wall.
Speedy-hurry.
More great and more better.

3. VERBAL NOUNS

She features somebody I know.
Funeralize.
Sense me into it.
Puts the shamery on him.
'Taint everybody you kin confidence.
I wouldn't friend with her.
Jooking—playing piano or guitar as it is done in Jook-houses (houses of ill-fame).
Uglying away.
I wouldn't scorn my name all up on you.
Bookooing (beaucoup) around—showing off.

NOUNS FROM VERBS

Won't stand a broke.
She won't take a listen.
He won't stand straightening.
That is such a compliment.
That's a lynch.

The stark, trimmed phrases of the Occident seem too bare for the voluptuous child of the sun, hence the adornment. It arises out of the same impulse as the wearing of jewelry and the making of sculpture—the urge to adorn.

On the walls of the homes of the average Negro one always finds a glut of gaudy calendars, wall pockets and advertising lithographs. The sophisticated white man or Negro would tolerate none of these, even if they bore a likeness to the Mona Lisa. No commercial art for decoration. Nor the calendar nor the advertisement spoils the picture for this lowly man. He sees the beauty in spite of the declaration of the Portland Cement Works or the butcher's announcement. I saw in Mobile a room in which there was an overstuffed mohair living-room suite, an imitation mahogany bed and chifferobe, a console victrola. The walls were gaily papered with Sunday supplements of the *Mobile Register.* There were seven calendars and three wall pockets. One of them was decorated with a lace doily. The mantel-shelf was covered with a scarf of deep home-made lace, looped up with a huge bow of pink crêpe paper. Over the door was a huge lithograph showing the Treaty of Versailles being signed with a Waterman fountain pen.

It was grotesque, yes. But it indicated the desire for beauty. And decorating a decoration, as in the case of the doily on the gaudy wall pocket, did not seem out of place to the hostess. The feeling back of such an act is that there can never be enough of beauty, let alone too much. Perhaps she is right. We each have our standards of art, and thus are we all interested parties and so unfit to pass judgment upon the art concepts of others.

Whatever the Negro does of his own volition he embellishes. His religious service is for the greater part excellent prose poetry. Both prayers and sermons are tooled and polished until they are true works of art. The supplication is forgotten in the frenzy of creation. The prayer of the white man is considered humorous in its bleakness. The beauty of the Old Testament does not exceed that of a Negro prayer.

Angularity

After adornment the next most striking manifestation of the Negro is Angularity. Everything that he touches becomes angular. In all African sculpture and doctrine of any sort we find the same thing.

Anyone watching Negro dancers will be struck by the same phenomenon. Every posture is another angle. Pleasing, yes. But an effect achieved by the very means which an European strives to avoid.

The pictures on the walls are hung at deep angles. Furniture is always set at an angle. I have instances of a piece of furniture in the *middle* of a wall being set with one end nearer the wall than the other to avoid the simple straight line.

Asymmetry

Asymmetry is a definite feature of Negro art. I have no samples of true Negro painting unless we count the African shields, but the sculpture and carvings are full of this beauty and lack of symmetry.

It is present in the literature, both prose and verse. I offer an example of this quality in verse from Langston Hughes:[3]

3. Poet (1902–1967). The poem is his "Evil Woman" (1927).

I aint gonna mistreat ma good gal any more,
I'm just gonna kill her next time she makes me sore.

I treats her kind but she don't do me right,
She fights and quarrels most ever' night.

I can't have no woman's got such low-down ways
Cause de blue gum woman aint de style now'days.

I brought her from the South and she's goin on back,
Else I'll use her head for a carpet track.

It is the lack of symmetry which makes Negro dancing so difficult for white dancers to learn. The abrupt and unexpected changes. The frequent change of key and time are evidences of this quality in music. (Note the St. Louis Blues.)

The dancing of the justly famous Bo-Jangles and Snake Hips are excellent examples.

The presence of rhythm and lack of symmetry are paradoxical, but there they are. Both are present to a marked degree. There is always rhythm, but it is the rhythm of segments. Each unit has a rhythm of its own, but when the whole is assembled it is lacking in symmetry. But easily workable to a Negro who is accustomed to the break in going from one part to another, so that he adjusts himself to the new tempo.

Dancing

Negro dancing is dynamic suggestion. No matter how violent it may appear to the beholder, every posture gives the impression that the dancer will do much more. For example, the performer flexes one knee sharply, assumes a ferocious face mask, thrusts the upper part of the body forward with clenched fists, elbows taut as in hard running or grasping a thrusting blade. That is all. But the spectator himself adds the picture of ferocious assault, hears the drums and finds himself keeping time with the music and tensing himself for the struggle. It is compelling insinuation. That is the very reason the spectator is held so rapt. He is participating in the performance himself—carrying out the suggestions of the performer.

The difference in the two arts is: the white dancer attempts to express fully; the Negro is restrained, but succeeds in gripping the beholder by forcing him to finish the action the performer suggests. Since no art ever can express all the variations conceivable, the Negro must be considered the greater artist, his dancing is realistic suggestion, and that is about all a great artist can do.

Negro Folklore

Negro folklore is not a thing of the past. It is still in the making. Its great variety shows the adaptability of the black man: nothing is too old or too new, domestic or foreign, high or low, for his use. God and the Devil are paired, and are treated no more reverently than Rockefeller and Ford.[4] Both

4. Henry Ford (1863–1947), U.S. automobile manufacturer. John D. Rockefeller (1839–1937), U.S. oil magnate.

of these men are prominent in folklore, Ford being particularly strong, and they talk and act like good-natured stevedores or mill-hands. Ole Massa is sometimes a smart man and often a fool. The automobile is ranged alongside of the oxcart. The angels and the apostles walk and talk like section hands.[5] And through it all walks Jack, the greatest culture hero of the South; Jack beats them all—even the Devil, who is often smarter than God.

Culture Heroes

The Devil is next after Jack as a culture hero. He can out-smart everyone but Jack. God is absolutely no match for him. He is good-natured and full of humor. The sort of person one may count on to help out in any difficulty.

Peter the Apostle is the third in importance. One need not look far for the explanation. The Negro is not a Christian really. The primitive gods are not deities of too subtle inner reflection; they are hard-working bodies who serve their devotees just as laboriously as the suppliant serves them. Gods of physical violence, stopping at nothing to serve their followers. Now of all the apostles Peter is the most active. When the other ten fell back trembling in the garden, Peter wielded the blade on the posse.[6] Peter first and foremost in all action. The gods of no peoples have been philosophic until the people themselves have approached that state.

The rabbit, the bear, the lion, the buzzard, the fox are culture heroes from the animal world. The rabbit is far in the lead of all the others and is blood brother to Jack. In short, the trickster-hero[7] of West Africa has been transplanted to America.

John Henry is a culture hero in song, but no more so than Stacker Lee, Smokey Joe or Bad Lazarus. There are many, many Negroes who have never heard of any of the song heroes, but none who do not know John (Jack) and the rabbit.

EXAMPLES OF FOLKLORE AND THE MODERN CULTURE HERO

Why de Porpoise's Tail is on Crosswise

Now, I want to tell you 'bout de porpoise. God had done made de world and everything. He set de moon and de stars in de sky. He got de fishes of de sea, and de fowls of de air completed.

He made de sun and hung it up. Then He made a nice gold track for it to run on. Then He said, "Now, Sun, I got everything made but Time. That's up to you. I want you to start out and go round de world on dis track just as fast as you kin make it. And de time it takes you to go and come, I'm going to call day and night." De Sun went zoonin' on cross de elements. Now, de porpoise was hanging round there and heard God what he told de Sun, so he decided he'd take dat trip round de world hisself. He looked up and saw de Sun kytin' along, so he lit out too, him and dat Sun!

So de porpoise beat de Sun round de world by one hour and three minutes. So God said, "Aw naw, this aint gointer do! I didn't mean for nothin' to be faster than de Sun!" So God run dat porpoise for three

5. Track layers for a railroad company.
6. John 18:10: "Then Simon Peter having a sword drew it, and smote the high priest's servant, and cut off his right ear."
7. The hero of many West African tales is frequently a trickster who prevails by using his wits, not physical force.

days before he run him down and caught him, and took his tail off and put it on crossways to slow him up. Still he's de fastest thing in de water.

And dat's why de porpoise got his tail on crossways.

Rockefeller and Ford

Once John D. Rockefeller and Henry Ford was woofing at each other. Rockefeller told Henry Ford he could build a solid gold road round the world. Henry Ford told him if he would he would look at it and see if he liked it, and if he did he would buy it and put one of his tin lizzies[8] on it.

Originality

It has been said so often that the Negro is lacking in originality that it has almost become a gospel. Outward signs seem to bear this out. But if one looks closely its falsity is immediately evident.

It is obvious that to get back to original sources is much too difficult for any group to claim very much as a certainty. What we really mean by originality is the modification of ideas. The most ardent admirer of the great Shakespeare cannot claim first source even for him. It is his treatment of the borrowed material.

So if we look at it squarely, the Negro is a very original being. While he lives and moves in the midst of a white civilization, everything that he touches is re-interpreted for his own use. He has modified the language, mode of food preparation, practice of medicine, and most certainly the religion of his new country, just as he adapted to suit himself the Sheik haircut made famous by Rudolph Valentino.

Everyone is familiar with the Negro's modification of the whites' musical instruments, so that his interpretation has been adopted by the white man himself and then re-interpreted. In so many words, Paul Whiteman is giving an imitation of a Negro orchestra making use of white-invented musical instruments in a Negro way. Thus has arisen a new art in the civilized world, and thus has our so-called civilization come. The exchange and re-exchange of ideas between groups.

Imitation

The Negro, the world over, is famous as a mimic. But this in no way damages his standing as an original. Mimicry is an art in itself. If it is not, then all art must fall by the same blow that strikes it down. When sculpture, painting, dancing, literature neither reflect nor suggest anything in nature or human experience we turn away with a dull wonder in our hearts at why the thing was done. Moreover, the contention that the Negro imitates from a feeling of inferiority is incorrect. He mimics for the love of it. The group of Negroes who slavishly imitate is small. The average Negro glories in his ways. The highly educated Negro the same. The self-despisement lies in a middle class who scorns to do or be anything Negro. "That's just like a Nigger" is the most terrible rebuke one can lay upon this kind. He wears drab clothing, sits through a boresome church service, pretends to have no interest in the

8. Small, cheap automobiles.

community, holds beauty contests, and otherwise apes all the mediocrities of the white brother. The truly cultured Negro scorns him, and the Negro "farthest down" is too busy "spreading his junk" in his own way to see or care. He likes his own things best. Even the group who are not Negroes but belong to the "sixth race," buy such records as "Shake dat thing" and "Tight lak dat." They really enjoy hearing a good bible-beater preach, but wild horses could drag no such admission from them. Their ready-made expression is: "We done got away from all that now." Some refuse to countenance Negro music on the grounds that it is niggerism, and for that reason should be done away with. Roland Hayes was thoroughly denounced for singing spirituals until he was accepted by white audiences. Langston Hughes is not considered a poet by this group because he writes of the man in the ditch, who is more numerous and real among us than any other.

But, this group aside, let us say that the art of mimicry is better developed in the Negro than in other racial groups. He does it as the mockingbird does it, for the love of it, and not because he wishes to be like the one imitated. I saw a group of small Negro boys imitating a cat defecating and the subsequent toilet of the cat. It was very realistic, and they enjoyed it as much as if they had been imitating a coronation ceremony. The dances are full of imitations of various animals. The buzzard lope, walking the dog, the pig's hind legs, holding the mule, elephant squat, pigeon's wing, falling off the log, seabord (imitation of an engine starting), and the like.

Absence of the Concept of Privacy

It is said that Negroes keep nothing secret, that they have no reserve. This ought not to seem strange when one considers that we are an outdoor people accustomed to communal life. Add this to all-permeating drama and you have the explanation.

There is no privacy in an African village. Loves, fights, possessions are, to misquote Woodrow Wilson, "Open disagreements openly arrived at."[9] The community is given the benefit of a good fight as well as a good wedding. An audience is a necessary part of any drama. We merely go with nature rather than against it.

Discord is more natural than accord. If we accept the doctrine of the survival of the fittest there are more fighting honors than there are honors for other achievements. Humanity places premiums on all things necessary to its well-being, and a valiant and good fighter is valuable in any community. So why hide the light under a bushel? Moreover, intimidation is a recognized part of warfare the world over, and threats certainly must be listed under that head. So that a great threatener must certainly be considered an aid to the fighting machine. So then if a man or woman is a facile hurler of threats, why should he or she not show their wares to the community? Hence the holding of all quarrels and fights in the open. One relieves one's pent-up anger and at the same time earns laurels in intimidation. Besides, one does the community a service. There is nothing so exhilarating as watching well-matched opponents go into action. The entire world likes action, for that matter. Hence prize-fighters become millionaires.

9. From President Wilson's January 8, 1918, "Address to Congress." The actual quotation is "Open covenants of peace, openly arrived at."

Likewise love-making is a biological necessity the world over and an art among Negroes. So that a man or woman who is proficient sees no reason why the fact should not be moot. He swaggers. She struts hippily about. Songs are built on the power to charm beneath the bed-clothes. Here again we have individuals striving to excel in what the community considers an art. Then if all of his world is seeking a great lover, why should he not speak right out loud?

It is all in a view-point. Love-making and fighting in all their branches are high arts, other things are arts among other groups where they brag about their proficiency just as brazenly as we do about these things that others consider matters for conversation behind closed doors. At any rate, the white man is despised by Negroes as a very poor fighter individually, and a very poor lover. One Negro, speaking of white men, said, "White folks is alright when dey gits in de bank and on de law bench, but dey sho' kin lie about wimmen folks."

I pressed him to explain. "Well you see, white mens makes out they marries wimmen to look at they eyes, and they know they gits em for just what us gits em for. 'Nother thing, white mens say they goes clear round de world and wins all de wimmen folks way from they men folks. Dat's a lie too. They don't win nothin, they buys em. Now de way I figgers it, if a woman don't want me enough to be wid me, 'thout I got to pay her, she kin rock right on, but these here white men don't know what do wid a woman when they gits her—dat's how come they gives they wimmen so much. They got to. Us wimmen works jus as hard as us does an come home an sleep wid us every night. They own wouldn't do it and its de mens fault. Dese white men done fooled theyself bout dese wimmen.

"Now me, I keeps me some wimmens all de time. Dat's whut dey wuz put here for—us mens to use. Dat's right now, Miss. Y'll wuz put here so us mens could have some pleasure. Course I don't run round like heap uh men folks. But if my ole lady go way from me and stay more'n two weeks, I got to git me somebody, aint I?"

The Jook

Jook is the word for a Negro pleasure house. It may mean a bawdy house. It may mean the house set apart on public works where the men and women dance, drink and gamble. Often it is a combination of all these.

In past generations the music was furnished by "boxes," another word for guitars. One guitar was enough for a dance; to have two was considered excellent. Where two were playing one man played the lead and the other seconded him. The first player was "picking" and the second was "framming," that is, playing chords while the lead carried the melody by dexterous finger work. Sometimes a third player was added, and he played a tom-tom effect on the low strings. Believe it or not, this is excellent dance music.

Pianos soon came to take the place of the boxes, and now player-pianos and victrolas are in all of the Jooks.

Musically speaking, the Jook is the most important place in America. For in its smelly, shoddy confines has been born the secular music known as blues, and on blues has been founded jazz. The singing and playing in the true Negro style is called "jooking."

The songs grow by incremental repetition as they travel from mouth to mouth and from Jook to Jook for years before they reach outside ears. Hence the great variety of subject-matter in each song.

The Negro dances circulated over the world were also conceived inside the Jooks. They too make the round of Jooks and public works before going into the outside world.

In this respect it is interesting to mention the Black Bottom. I have read several false accounts of its origin and name. One writer claimed that it got its name from the black sticky mud on the bottom of the Mississippi river. Other equally absurd statements gummed the press. Now the dance really originated in the Jook section of Nashville, Tennessee, around Fourth Avenue. This is a tough neighborhood known as Black Bottom—hence the name.

The Charleston is perhaps forty years old, and was danced up and down the Atlantic seaboard from North Carolina to Key West, Florida.

The Negro social dance is slow and sensuous. The idea in the Jook is to gain sensation, and not so much exercise. So that just enough foot movement is added to keep the dancers on the floor. A tremendous sex stimulation is gained from this. But who is trying to avoid it? The man, the woman, the time and the place have met. Rather, little intimate names are indulged in to heap fire on fire.

These too have spread to all the world.

The Negro theater, as built up by the Negro, is based on Jook situations, with women, gambling, fighting, drinking. Shows like "Dixie to Broadway" are only Negro in cast, and could just as well have come from pre-Soviet Russia.

Another interesting thing—Negro shows before being tampered with did not specialize in octoroon chorus girls. The girl who could hoist a Jook song from her belly and lam it against the front door of the theater was the lead, even if she were as black as the hinges of hell. The question was "Can she jook?" She must also have a good belly wobble, and her hips must, to quote a popular work song, "Shake like jelly all over and be so broad, Lawd, Lawd, and be so broad." So that the bleached chorus is the result of a white demand and not the Negro's.

The woman in the Jook may be nappy headed and black, but if she is a good lover she gets there just the same. A favorite Jook song of the past has this to say:

> *Singer:* It aint good looks dat takes you through dis world.
> *Audience:* What is it, good mama?
> Singer: Elgin movements[1] in your hips
> Twenty years guarantee.

And it always brought down the house too.

> Oh de white gal rides in a Cadillac,
> De yaller[2] gal rides de same,
> Black gal rides in a rusty Ford
> But she gits dere just de same.

The sort of woman her men idealize is the type that is put forth in the theater. The art-creating Negro prefers a not too thin woman who can shake like jelly all over as she dances and sings, and that is the type he put forth on the stage. She has been banished by the white producer and the Negro who takes his cue from the white.

1. Like an Elgin watch.

2. A light-skinned African American.

Of course a black woman is never the wife of the upper class Negro in the North. This state of affairs does not obtain in the South, however. I have noted numerous cases where the wife was considerably darker than the husband. People of some substance, too.

This scornful attitude towards black women receives mouth sanction by the mud-sills.[3]

Even on the works and in the Jooks the black man sings disparagingly of black women. They say that she is evil. That she sleeps with her fists doubled up and ready for action. All over they are making a little drama of waking up a yaller wife and a black one.

A man is lying beside his yaller wife and wakes her up. She says to him, "Darling, do you know what I was dreaming when you woke me up?" He says, "No honey, what was you dreaming?" She says, "I dreamt I had done cooked you a big, fine dinner and we was setting down to eat out de same plate and I was setting on yo' lap jus huggin you and kissin you and you was so sweet."

Wake up a black woman, and before you kin git any sense into her she be done up and lammed you over the head four or five times. When you git her quiet she'll say, "Nigger, know whut I was dreamin when you woke me up?"

You say, "No honey, what was you dreamin?" She says, "I dreamt you shook yo' rusty fist under my nose and I split yo' head open wid a ax."

But in spite of disparaging fictitious drama, in real life the black girl is drawing on his account at the commissary. Down in the Cypress Swamp[4] as he swings his ax he chants:

Dat ole black gal, she keep on grumblin,
New pair shoes, new pair shoes,
I'm goint to buy her shoes and stockings
Slippers too, slippers too.

Then adds aside: "Blacker de berry, sweeter de juice."

To be sure the black gal is still in power, men are still cutting and shooting their way to her pillow. To the queen of the Jook!

Speaking of the influence of the Jook, I noted that Mae West in "Sex" had much more flavor of the turpentine quarters[5] than she did of the white bawd. I know that the piece she played on the piano is a very old Jook composition. "Honey let yo' drawers hang low" had been played and sung in every Jook in the South for at least thirty-five years. It has always puzzled me why she thought it likely to be played in a Canadian bawdy house.

Speaking of the use of Negro material by white performers, it is astonishing that so many are trying it, and I have never seen one yet entirely realistic. They often have all the elements of the song, dance, or expression, but they are misplaced or distorted by the accent falling on the wrong element. Every one seems to think that the Negro is easily imitated when nothing is further from the truth. Without exception I wonder why the black-face comedians *are* black-face; it is a puzzle—good comedians, but darn poor niggers. Gershwin[6] and the other "Negro" rhapsodists come under this same axe. Just about as Negro as caviar or Ann Pennington's[7] athletic Black Bottom. When the Negroes who knew the Black Bottom in its cradle saw the

3. The lowest members of a given community.
4. In Florida.
5. Southern Black rural communities where turpentine was made.
6. George Gershwin (1898–1937), American composer of *Rhapsody in Blue*.
7. White dancer (1892–1971).

Broadway version they asked each other, "Is you learnt dat *new* Black Bottom yet?" Proof that it was not *their* dance.

And God only knows what the world has suffered from the white damsels who try to sing Blues.

The Negroes themselves have sinned also in this respect. In spite of the goings up and down on the earth, from the original Fisk Jubilee Singers[8] down to the present, there has been no genuine presentation of Negro songs to white audiences. The spirituals that have been sung around the world are Negroid to be sure, but so full of musicians' tricks that Negro congregations are highly entertained when they hear their old songs so changed. They never use the new style songs, and these are never heard unless perchance some daughter or son has been off to college and returns with one of the old songs with its face lifted, so to speak.

I am of the opinion that this trick style of delivery was originated by the Fisk Singers; Tuskegee and Hampton followed suit and have helped spread this misconception of Negro spirituals. This Glee Club style has gone on so long and become so fixed among concert singers that it is considered quite authentic. But I say again, that not one concert singer in the world is singing the songs as the Negro song-makers sing them.

If anyone wishes to prove the truth of this let him step into some unfashionable Negro church and hear for himself.

To those who want to institute the Negro theater, let me say it is already established. It is lacking in wealth, so it is not seen in the high places. A creature with a white head and Negro feet struts the Metropolitan boards. The real Negro theater is in the Jooks and the cabarets. Self-conscious individuals may turn away the eye and say, "Let us search elsewhere for our dramatic art." Let 'em search. They certainly won't find it. Butter Beans and Susie, Bo-Jangles[9] and Snake Hips are the only performers of the real Negro school it has ever been my pleasure to behold in New York.

Dialect

If we are to believe the majority of writers of Negro dialect and the burnt-cork artists, Negro speech is a weird thing, full of "ams" and "Ises." Fortunately we don't have to believe them. We may go directly to the Negro and let him speak for himself.

I know that I run the risk of being damned as an infidel for declaring that nowhere can be found the Negro who asks "am it?" nor yet his brother who announces "Ise uh gwinter." He exists only for a certain type of writers and performers.

Very few Negroes, educated or not, use a clear clipped "I." It verges more or less upon "Ah." I think the lip form is responsible for this to a great extent. By experiment the reader will find that a sharp "I" is very much easier with a thin taut lip than with a full soft lip. Like tightening violin strings.

If one listens closely one will note too that a word is slurred in one position in the sentence but clearly pronounced in another. This is particularly true of the pronouns. A pronoun as a subject is likely to be clearly enunciated, but slurred as an object. For example: "You better not let me ketch yuh."

8. A celebrated 19th-century group of young singers who toured to raise funds for the university.

9. Bill "Bojangles" Robinson (1876–1949) was a dance star of stage and screen. Jodie "Butterbeans" Edwards (1897–1967) and Susie Hawthorn were popular Black entertainers known for their husband-and-wife sketches.

There is a tendency in some localities to add the "h" to "it" and pronounce it "hit." Probably a vestige of old English. In some localities "if" is "ef."

In story telling "so" is universally the connective. It is used even as an introductory word, at the very beginning of a story. In religious expression "and" is used. The trend in stories is to state conclusions; in religion, to enumerate.

I am mentioning only the most general rules in dialect because there are so many quirks that belong only to certain localities that nothing less than a volume would be adequate.

Now He told me, He said: "You got the three witnesses. One is water, one is spirit, and one is blood. And these three correspond with the three in heben—Father, Son, and Holy Ghost."

Now I ast Him about this lyin in sin and He give me a handful of seeds and He tole me to sow 'em in a bed and He tole me: "I want you to watch them seeds." The seeds come up about in places and He said: "Those seeds that come up, they died in the heart of the earth and quickened and come up and brought forth fruit. But those seeds that didn't come up, they died in the heart of the earth and rottened.

"And a soul that dies and quickens through my spirit they will live forever, but those that dont never pray, they are lost forever."

(Rev. Jessie Jefferson.)[1]

1934

From Mules and Men

[NEGRO FOLKLORE]

I was glad when somebody told me, "You may go and collect Negro folklore."

In a way it would not be a new experience for me. When I pitched headforemost into the world I landed in the crib of negroism. From the earliest rocking of my cradle, I had known about the capers Brer Rabbit is apt to cut and what the Squinch Owl says from the house top. But it was fitting me like a tight chemise. I couldn't see it for wearing it. It was only when I was off in college, away from my native surroundings, that I could see myself like somebody else and stand off and look at my garment. Then I had to have the spy-glass of Anthropology to look through at that.

Dr. Boas[1] asked me where I wanted to work and I said, "Florida," and gave, as my big reason, that "Florida is a place that draws people—white people from all over the world, and Negroes from every Southern state surely and some from the North and West." So I knew that it was possible for me to get a cross section of the Negro South in the one state. And then I realized that I was new myself, so it looked sensible for me to choose familiar ground.

First place I aimed to stop to collect material was Eatonville, Florida.

And now, I'm going to tell you why I decided to go to my native village first. I didn't go back there so that the home folks could make admiration

1. A local minister observed by Hurston.

1. Franz Boas (1858–1952), pioneering American anthropologist; he was a professor at Columbia University when Hurston was a Barnard student (1925–28).

over me because I had been up North to college and come back with a diploma and a Chevrolet. I knew they were not going to pay either one of these items too much mind. I was just Lucy Hurston's daughter, Zora, and even if I had—to use one of our down-home expressions—had a Kaiser baby, and that's something that hasn't been done in this Country yet, I'd still be just Zora to the neighbors. If I had exalted myself to impress the town, somebody would have sent me word in a match-box that I had been up North there and had rubbed the hair off of my head against some college wall, and then come back there with a lot of form and fashion and outside show to the world. But they'd stand flat-footed and tell me that they didn't have me, neither my shampolish, to study 'bout. And that would have been that.

I hurried back to Eatonville because I knew that the town was full of material and that I could get it without hurt, harm or danger. As early as I could remember it was the habit of the men folks particularly to gather on the store porch of evenings and swap stories. Even the women folks would stop and break a breath with them at times. As a child when I was sent down to Joe Clarke's store, I'd drag out my leaving as long as possible in order to hear more.

Folk-lore is not as easy to collect as it sounds. The best source is where there are the least outside influences and these people, being usually underprivileged, are the shyest. They are most reluctant at times to reveal that which the soul lives by. And the Negro, in spite of his open-faced laughter, his seeming acquiescence, is particularly evasive. You see we are a polite people and we do not say to our questioner, "Get out of here!" We smile and tell him or her something that satisfies the white person because, knowing so little about us, he doesn't know what he is missing. The Indian resists curiosity by a stony silence. The Negro offers a featherbed resistance. That is, we let the probe enter, but it never comes out. It gets smothered under a lot of laughter and pleasantries.

The theory behind our tactics: "The white man is always trying to know into somebody else's business. All right, I'll set something outside the door of my mind for him to play with and handle. He can read my writing but he sho' can't read my mind. I'll put this play toy in his hand, and he will seize it and go away. Then I'll say my say and sing my song."

I knew that even *I* was going to have some hindrance among strangers. But here in Eatonville I knew everybody was going to help me. So below Palatka I began to feel eager to be there and I kicked the little Chevrolet right along.

I thought about the tales I had heard as a child. How even the Bible was made over to suit our vivid imagination. How the devil always out-smarted God and how that over-noble hero Jack or John—not *John Henry,* who occupies the same place in Negro folk-lore that Casey Jones does in white lore and if anything is more recent—outsmarted the devil. Brer Fox, Brer Deer, Brer 'Gator, Brer Dawg, Brer Rabbit, Ole Massa and his wife were walking the earth like natural men way back in the days when God himself was on the ground and men could talk with him. Way back there before God weighed up the dirt to make the mountains. When I was rounding Lily Lake I was remembering how God had made the world and the elements and people. He made souls for people, but he didn't give them out because he said:

> "Folks ain't ready for souls yet. De clay ain't dry. It's de strongest thing Ah ever made. Don't aim to waste none thru loose cracks. And then men got to grow strong enough to stand it. De way things is now,

if Ah give it out it would tear them shackly bodies to pieces. Bimeby, Ah give it out."

So folks went round thousands of years without no souls. All de time de soul-piece, it was setting 'round covered up wid God's loose raiment. Every now and then de wind would blow and hist up de cover and then de elements would be full of lightning and de winds would talk. So people told one 'nother that God was talking in de mountains.

De white man passed by it way off and he looked but he wouldn't go close enough to touch. De Indian and de Negro, they tipped by cautious too, and all of 'em seen de light of diamonds when de winds shook de cover, and de wind dat passed over it sung songs. De Jew come past and heard de song from de soul-piece then he kept on passin' and all of a sudden he grabbed up de soul-piece and hid it under his clothes, and run off down de road. It burnt him and tore him and throwed him down and lifted him up and toted him across de mountain and he tried to break loose but he couldn't do it. He kept on hollerin' for help but de rest of 'em run hid 'way from him. Way after while they come out of holes and corners and picked up little chips and pieces that fell back on de ground. So God mixed it up wid feelings and give it out to 'em. Way after while when He ketch dat Jew, He's goin' to 'vide things up more ekal'.

So I rounded Park Lake and came speeding down the straight stretch into Eatonville, the city of five lakes, three croquet courts, three hundred brown skins, three hundred good swimmers, plenty guavas, two schools, and no jailhouse.

Before I enter the township, I wish to make acknowledgments to Mrs. R. Osgood Mason[2] of New York City. She backed my falling in a hearty way, in a spiritual way, and in addition, financed the whole expedition in the manner of the Great Soul that she is. The world's most gallant woman.

As I crossed the Maitland-Eatonville township line I could see a group on the store porch. I was delighted. The town had not changed. Same love of talk and song. So I drove on down there before I stopped. Yes, there was George Thomas, Calvin Daniels, Jack and Charlie Jones, Gene Brazzle, B. Moseley and "Seaboard." Deep in a game of Florida-flip. All of those who were not actually playing were giving advice—"bet straightening" they call it.

"Hello, boys," I hailed them as I went into neutral.

They looked up from the game and for a moment it looked as if they had forgotten me. Then B. Moseley said, "Well, if it ain't Zora Hurston!" Then everybody crowded around the car to help greet me.

"You gointer stay awhile, Zora?"

"Yep. Several months."

"Where you gointer stay, Zora?"

"With Mett and Ellis, I reckon."

"Mett" was Mrs. Armetta Jones, an intimate friend of mine since childhood and Ellis was her husband. Their house stands under the huge camphor tree on the front street.

"Hello, heart-string," Mayor Hiram Lester yelled as he hurried up the street. "We heard all about you up North. You back home for good, I hope."

2. Charlotte Mason (1854–1946), also known as "Godmother," was Hurston's patron and confidante for several years, starting in 1927.

"Nope, Ah come to collect some old stories and tales and Ah know y'all know a plenty of 'em and that's why Ah headed straight for home."

"What you mean, Zora, them big old lies we tell when we're jus' sittin' around here on the store porch doin' nothin'?" asked B. Moseley.

"Yeah, those same ones about Ole Massa, and colored folks in heaven, and—oh, y'all know the kind I mean."

"Aw shucks," exclaimed George Thomas doubtfully. "Zora, don't you come here and tell de biggest lie first thing. Who you reckon want to read all them old-time tales about Brer Rabbit and Brer Bear?"

"Plenty of people, George. They are a lot more valuable than you might think. We want to set them down before it's too late."

"Too late for what?"

"Before everybody forgets all of 'em."

"No danger of that. That's all some people is good for—set 'round and lie and murder groceries."

"Ah know one right now," Calvin Daniels announced cheerfully. "It's a tale 'bout John and de frog."

"Wait till she gets out her car, Calvin. Let her get settled at 'Met's' and cook a pan of ginger bread then we'll all go down and tell lies and eat ginger bread. Dat's de way to do. She's tired now from all dat drivin'."

"All right, boys," I agreed. "But Ah'll be rested by night. Be lookin' for everybody."

So I unloaded the car and crowded it into Ellis' garage and got settled. Armetta made me lie down and rest while she cooked a big pan of ginger bread for the company we expected.

Calvin Daniels and James Moseley were the first to show up.

"Calvin, Ah sure am glad that you got here. Ah'm crazy to hear about John and dat frog," I said.

"That's why Ah come so early so Ah could tell it to you and go. Ah got to go over to Wood Bridge a little later on."

"Ah'm glad you remembered me first, Calvin."

"Ah always like to be good as my word, and Ah just heard about a toe-party over to Wood Bridge tonight and Ah decided to make it."

"A toe-party! What on earth is that?"

"Come go with me and James and you'll see!"

"But, everybody will be here lookin' for me. They'll think Ah'm crazy—tellin' them to come and then gettin' out and goin' to Wood Bridge myself. But Ah certainly would like to go to that toe-party."

"Aw, come on. They kin come back another night. You gointer like this party."

"Well, you tell me the story first, and by that time, Ah'll know what to do."

"Ah, come on, Zora," James urged. "Git de car out. Calvin kin tell you dat one while we're on de way. Come on, let's go to de toe-party."

"No, let 'im tell me this one first, then, if Ah go he can tell me some more on de way over."

James motioned to his friend. "Hurry up and tell it, Calvin, so we kin go before somebody else come."

"Aw, most of 'em ain't comin' nohow. They all 'bout goin' to Wood Bridge, too. Lemme tell you 'bout John and dis frog:

> It was night and Ole Massa sent John, his favorite slave, down to the spring to get him a cool drink of water. He called John to him.

"John!"

"What you want, Massa?"

"John, I'm thirsty. Ah wants a cool drink of water, and Ah wants you to go down to de spring and dip me up a nice cool pitcher of water."

John didn't like to be sent nowhere at night, but he always tried to do everything Ole Massa told him to do, so he said, "Yessuh, Massa, Ah'll go git you some!"

Ole Massa said: "Hurry up, John, Ah'm mighty thirsty."

John took de pitcher and went on down to de spring. There was a great big ole bull frog settin' right on de edge of de spring, and when John dipped up de water de noise skeered de frog and he hollered and jumped over in de spring.

John dropped de water pitcher and tore out for de big house, hollerin' "Massa! Massa! A big ole booger[3] done got after me!"

Ole Massa told him, "Why, John, there's no such thing as a booger."

"Oh, yes it is, Massa. He down at dat Spring."

"Don't tell me, John. Youse just excited. Furthermore, you go git me dat water Ah sent you after."

"No, indeed, Massa, you and nobody else can't send me back there so dat booger kin git me."

Ole Massa begin to figger dat John musta seen somethin' sho nuff because John never had disobeyed him before, so he ast: "John, you say you seen a booger. What did it look like?"

John tole him, "Massa, he had two great big eyes lak balls of fire, and when he was standin' up he was sittin' down and when he moved, he moved by jerks, and he had most no tail."

Long before Calvin had ended his story James had lost his air of impatience.

"Now, Ah'll tell one," he said. "That is, if you so desire."

"Sure, Ah want to hear you tell 'em till daybreak if you will," I said eagerly.

"But where's the ginger bread?" James stopped to ask.

"It's out in the kitchen," I said. "Ah'm waiting for de others to come."

"Aw, naw, give us ours now. Them others may not get here before forty o'clock and Ah'll be done et mine and be in Wood Bridge. Anyhow Ah want a corner piece and some of them others will beat me to it."

So I served them with ginger bread and buttermilk.

"You sure going to Wood Bridge with us after Ah git thru tellin' this one?" James asked.

"Yeah, if the others don't show up by then," I conceded.

So James told the story about the man who went to Heaven from Johnstown.[4]

You know, when it lightnings, de angels is peepin' in de lookin' glass; when it thunders, they's rollin' out de rain-barrels; and when it rains, somebody done dropped a barrel or two and bust it.

One time, you know, there was going to be big doin's in Glory and all de angels had brand new clothes to wear and so they was all peepin' in the lookin' glasses, and therefore it got to lightning all over de sky.

3. A bogey man [*Hurston's note*].

4. A town in Pennsylvania that was the site of the great flood of May 31, 1899, in which a dam broke and twenty-one hundred lives were lost.

God tole some of de angels to roll in all de full rain barrels and they was in such a hurry that it was thunderin' from the east to the west and the zigzag lightning went to join the mutterin' thunder and, next thing you know, some of them angels got careless and dropped a whole heap of them rain barrels, and didn't it rain!

In one place they call Johnstown they had a great flood. And so many folks got drownded that it jus' look like Judgment day.

So some of de folks that got drownded in that flood went one place and some went another. You know, everything that happen, they got to be a nigger in it—and so one of de brothers in black went up to Heben from de flood.

When he got to the gate, Ole Peter let 'im in and made 'im welcome. De colored man was named John, so John ast Peter, says, "Is it dry in dere?"

Ole Peter tole 'im, "Why, yes it's dry in here. How come you ast that?"

"Well, you know Ah jus' come out of one flood, and Ah don't want to run into no mo'. Ooh, man! You ain't *seen* no water. You just oughter seen dat flood we had at Johnstown."

Peter says, "Yeah, we know all about it. Jus' go wid Gabriel and let him give you some new clothes."

So John went on off wid Gabriel and come back all dressed up in brand new clothes and all de time he was changin' his clothes he was tellin' Ole Gabriel all about dat flood, jus' like he didn't know already.

So when he come back from changin' his clothes, they give him a brand new gold harp and handed him to a gold bench and made him welcome. They was so tired of hearing about dat flood they was glad to see him wid his harp 'cause they figgered he'd get to playin' and forget all about it. So Peter tole him, "Now you jus' make yo'self at home and play all de music you please."

John went and took a seat on de bench and commenced to tune up his harp. By dat time, two angels come walkin' by where John was settin' so he throwed down his harp and tackled 'em.

"Say," he hollered, "Y'all want to hear 'bout de big flood Ah was in down on earth? Lawd, Lawd! It sho rained, and talkin' 'bout water!"

Dem two angels hurried on off from 'im jus' as quick as they could. He started to tellin' another one and he took to flyin'. Gab'ull went over to 'im and tried to get 'im to take it easy, but John kept right on stoppin' every angel dat he could find to tell 'im about dat flood of water.

Way after while he went over to Ole Peter and said: "Thought you said everybody would be nice and polite?"

Peter said, "Yeah, Ah said it. Ain't everybody treatin' you right?"

John said, "Naw. Ah jus' walked up to a man as nice and friendly as Ah could and started to tell 'im 'bout all dat water Ah left back there in Johnstown and instead of him turnin' me a friendly answer he said, 'Shucks! You ain't seen no water!' and walked off and left me standin' by myself."

"Was he a *ole* man wid a crooked walkin' stick?" Peter ast John.

"Yeah."

"Did he have whiskers down to here?" Peter measured down to his waist.

"He sho did," John tol' 'im.

"Aw shucks," Peter tol' im. "Dat was Ole Nora.[5] You can't tell *him* nothin' 'bout no flood."

There was a lot of horn-honking outside and I went to the door. The crowd drew up under the mothering camphor tree in four old cars. Everybody in boisterous spirits.

"Come on, Zora! Le's go to Wood Bridge. Great toe-party goin' on. All kinds of 'freshments. We kin tell you some lies most any ole time. We never run outer lies and lovin'. Tell 'em tomorrow night. Come on if you comin'—le's go if you gwine."

So I loaded up my car with neighbors and we all went to Wood Bridge. It is a Negro community joining Maitland on the north as Eatonville does on the west, but no enterprising souls have ever organized it. They have no schoolhouse, no post office, no mayor. It is lacking in Eatonville's feeling of unity. In fact, a white woman lives there.

While we rolled along Florida No. 3, I asked Armetta where was the shindig going to be in Wood Bridge. "At Edna Pitts' house," she told me. "But she ain't givin' it by herself; it's for the lodge."

"Think it's gointer be lively?"

"Oh, yeah. Ah heard that a lot of folks from Altamonte and Longwood is comin'. Maybe from Winter Park too."

We were the tail end of the line and as we turned off the highway we could hear the boys in the first car doing what Ellis Jones called bookooing before they even hit the ground. Charlie Jones was woofing[6] louder than anybody else. "Don't y'all sell off dem pretty li'l pink toes befo' Ah git dere."

Peter Stagg: "Save me de best one!"

Soddy Sewell: "Hey, you mullet heads! Get out de way there and let a real man smoke them toes over."

Gene Brazzle: "Come to my pick, gimme a vaseline brown!"

Big Willie Sewell: "Gimme any kind so long as you gimme more'n one."

Babe Brown, riding a running-board, guitar in hand, said, "Ah want a toe, but if it ain't got a good looking face on to it; don't bring de mess up."

When we got there the party was young. The house was swept and garnished, the refreshments on display, several people sitting around; but the spot needed some social juices to mix the ingredients. In other words, they had the carcass of a party lying around up until the minute Eatonville burst in on it. Then it woke up.

"Y'all done sold off any toes yet?" George Brown wanted to know.

Willie Mae Clarke gave him a certain look and asked him, "What's dat got to do with you, George Brown?" And he shut up. Everybody knows that Willie Mae's got the business with George Brown.

"Nope. We ain't had enough crowd, but I reckon we kin start now," Edna said. Edna and a sort of committee went inside and hung up a sheet across one end of the room. Then she came outside and called all of the young women inside. She had to coax and drag some of the girls.

"Oh, Ah'm shame-face-ted!" some of them said.

"Nobody don't want to buy *mah* ole rusty toe." Others fished around for denials from the male side.

I went on in with the rest and was herded behind the curtain.

"Say, what *is* this toe-party business?" I asked one of the girls.

5. Noah [*Hurston's note*].

6. Aimless talking [*Hurston's note*]. "Bookooing": loud talking, bullying, woofing. From French *beaucoup* [*Hurston's note*].

"Good gracious, Zora! Ain't you ever been to a toe-party before?"

"Nope. They don't have 'em up North where Ah been and Ah just got back today."

"Well, they hides all de girls behind a curtain and you stick out yo' toe. Some places you take off yo' shoes and some places you keep 'em on, but most all de time you keep 'em on. When all de toes is in a line, sticking out from behind de sheet they let de men folks in and they looks over all de toes and buys de ones they want for a dime. Then they got to treat de lady dat owns dat toe to everything she want. Sometime they play it so's you keep de same partner for de whole thing and sometime they fix it so they put de girls back every hour or so and sell de toes agin."

Well, my toe went on the line with the rest and it was sold five times during the party. Everytime a toe was sold there was a great flurry before the curtain. Each man eager to see what he had got, and whether the other men would envy him or ridicule him. One or two fellows ungallantly ran out of the door rather than treat the girls whose toe they had bought sight unseen.

Babe Brown got off on his guitar and the dancing was hilarious. There was plenty of chicken perleau[7] and baked chicken and fried chicken and rabbit. Pig feet and chitterlings and hot peanuts and drinkables. Everybody was treating wildly.

"Come on, Zora, and have a treat on me!" Charlie Jones insisted. "You done et chicken-ham and chicken-bosom wid every shag-leg[8] in Orange County *but* me. Come on and spend some of *my* money."

"Thanks, Charlie, but Ah got five helpin's of chicken inside already. Ah either got to get another stomach or quit eatin'."

"Quit eatin' then and go to thinking. Quit thinkin' and start to drinkin'. What you want?"

"Coca-Cola right off de ice, Charlie, and put some salt in it. Ah got a slight headache."

"Aw now, my money don't buy no sweet slop. Choose some coon dick."

"What is coon dick?"

"Aw, Zora, jus' somethin' to make de drunk come. Made out uh grape fruit juice, corn meal mash, beef bones and a few mo' things. Come on le's git some together. It might make our love come down."

As soon as we started over into the next yard where coon dick was to be had, Charlie yelled to the barkeep, "Hey, Seymore! fix up another quart of dat low wine—here come de boom!"

It was handed to us in a quart fruit jar and we went outside to try it.

The raw likker known locally as coon dick was too much. The minute it touched my lips, the top of my head flew off. I spat it out and "choosed" some peanuts. Big Willie Sewell said, "Come on, heartstring, and have some gospel-bird[9] on me. My money spends too." His Honor Hiram Lester, the Mayor, heard him and said, "There's no mo' chicken left, Willie. Why don't you offer her something she can get?"

"Well there *was* some chicken there when Ah passed the table a little while ago."

"Oh, so you offerin' her some chicken *was*. She can't eat that. What she want is some chicken *is*."

7. That is, pilaf; a rice dish.
8. Fellow, slightly pejorative; akin to ne'er-do-well.
9. Chicken. Preachers are supposed to be fond of them [*Hurston's note*].

"Aw shut up, Hiram. Come on, Zora, le's go inside and make out we dancin'." We went on inside but it wasn't a party any more. Just some people herded together. The high spirits were simmering down and nobody had a dime left to cry so the toe-business suffered a slump. The heaped-up tables of refreshments had become shambles of chicken bones and empty platters anyway so that there was no longer any point in getting your toe sold, so when Columbus Montgomery said, "Le's go to Eatonville," Soddy Sewell jumped up and grabbed his hat and said, "I heard you buddy."

Eatonville began to move back home right then. Nearly everybody was packed in one of the five cars when the delegation from Altamonte arrived. Johnnie Barton and Georgia Burke. Everybody piled out again.

"Got yo' guitar wid you, Johnnie?"

"Man, you know Ah don't go nowhere unless Ah take my box wid me," said Johnnie in his starched blue shirt, collar pin with heart bangles hanging on each end and his cream pants with the black stripe. "And what make it so cool, Ah don't go nowhere unless I play it."

"And when you git to strowin' yo' mess and Georgy gits to singin' her alto, man it's hot as seven hells. Man, play dat 'Palm Beach'."

Babe Brown took the guitar and Johnnie Barton grabbed the piano stool. He sung. Georgia Burke and George Thomas singing about Polk County where the water taste like wine.

> My heart struck sorrow, tears come running down.

At about the thirty-seventh verse, something about:

> Ah'd ruther be in Tampa with the Whip-poor-will,
> Ruther be in Tampa with the Whip-poor-will,
> Than to be 'round here—
> Honey with a hundred dollar bill,

I staggered sleepily forth to the little Chevrolet for Eatonville. The car was overflowing with passengers but I was so dull from lack of sleep that I didn't know who they were. All I knew is they belonged in Eatonville.

Somebody was woofing in my car about love and I asked him about his buddy—I don't know why now. He said, "Ah ain't got no buddy. They kilt my buddy so they could raise me. Jus' so Ah be yo' man Ah don't want no damn buddy. Ah hope they kill every man dat ever cried, 'titty-mamma' but me. Lemme be yo' kid."

Some voice from somewhere else in the car commented, "You sho' Lawd is gointer have a lot of hindrance."

Then somehow I got home and to bed and Armetta had Georgia syrup and waffles for breakfast.

1935

From Their Eyes Were Watching God

Chapter 1

[THE RETURN]

Ships at a distance have every man's wish on board. For some they come in with the tide. For others they sail forever on the horizon, never out of sight, never landing until the Watcher turns his eyes away in resignation, his dreams mocked to death by Time. That is the life of men.

Now, women forget all those things they don't want to remember, and remember everything they don't want to forget. The dream is the truth. Then they act and do things accordingly.

So the beginning of this was a woman and she had come back from burying the dead. Not the dead of sick and ailing with friends at the pillow and the feet. She had come back from the sodden and the bloated; the sudden dead, their eyes flung wide open in judgment.

The people all saw her come because it was sundown. The sun was gone, but he had left his footprints in the sky. It was the time for sitting on porches beside the road. It was the time to hear things and talk. These sitters had been tongueless, earless, eyeless conveniences all day long. Mules and other brutes had occupied their skins. But now, the sun and the bossman were gone, so the skins felt powerful and human. They became lords of sounds and lesser things. They passed nations through their mouths. They sat in judgment.

Seeing the woman as she was made them remember the envy they had stored up from other times. So they chewed up the back parts of their minds and swallowed with relish. They made burning statements with questions, and killing tools out of laughs. It was mass cruelty. A mood come alive. Words walking without masters; walking altogether like harmony in a song.

"What she doin' coming back here in dem overhalls? Can't she find no dress to put on?—Where's dat blue satin dress she left here in?—Where all dat money her husband took and died and left her?—What dat ole forty year ole 'oman doin' wid her hair swingin' down her back lak some young gal?—Where she left dat young lad of a boy she went off here wid?—Thought she was going to marry?—Where he left *her*?—What he done wid all her money?—Betcha he off wid some gal so young she ain't even got no hairs—why she don't stay in her class?—"

When she got to where they were she turned her face on the bander log and spoke. They scrambled a noisy "good evenin'" and left their mouths setting open and their ears full of hope. Her speech was pleasant enough, but she kept walking straight on to her gate. The porch couldn't talk for looking.

The men noticed her firm buttocks like she had grape fruits in her hip pockets; the great rope of black hair swinging to her waist and unraveling in the wind like a plume; then her pugnacious breasts trying to bore holes in her shirt. They, the men, were saving with the mind what they lost with the eye. The women took the faded shirt and muddy overalls and laid them away for remembrance. It was a weapon against her strength and if it turned out of no significance, still it was a hope that she might fall to their level some day.

But nobody moved, nobody spoke, nobody even thought to swallow spit until after her gate slammed behind her.

Pearl Stone opened her mouth and laughed real hard because she didn't know what else to do. She fell all over Mrs. Sumpkins while she laughed. Mrs. Sumpkins snorted violently and sucked her teeth.

"Humph! Y'all let her worry yuh. You ain't like me. Ah ain't got her to study 'bout. If she ain't got manners enough to stop and let folks know how she been makin' out, let her g'wan!"

"She ain't even worth talkin' after," Lulu Moss drawled through her nose. "She sits high, but she looks low. Dat's what Ah say 'bout dese ole women runnin' after young boys."

Pheoby Watson hitched her rocking chair forward before she spoke. "Well, nobody don't know if it's anything to tell or not. Me, Ah'm her best friend, and *Ah* don't know."

"Maybe us don't know into things lak you do, but we all know how she went 'way from here and us sho seen her come back. 'Tain't no use in your tryin' to cloak no ole woman lak Janie Starks, Pheoby, friend or no friend."

"At dat she ain't so ole as some of y'all dat's talking."

"She's way past forty to my knowledge, Pheoby."

"No more'n forty at de outside."

"She's 'way too old for a boy like Tea Cake."

"Tea Cake ain't been no boy for some time. He's round thirty his ownself."

"Don't keer what it was, she could stop and say a few words with us. She act like we done done something to her," Pearl Stone complained. "She de one been doin' wrong."

"You mean, you mad 'cause she didn't stop and tell us all her business. Anyhow, what you ever know her to do so bad as y'all make out? The worst thing Ah ever knowed her to do was taking a few years offa her age and dat ain't never harmed nobody. Y'all makes me tired. De way you talkin' you'd think de folks in dis town didn't do nothin' in de bed 'cept praise de Lawd. You have to 'scuse me, 'cause Ah'm bound to go take her some supper." Pheoby stood up sharply.

"Don't mind us," Lulu smiled, "just go right ahead, us can mind yo' house for you till you git back. Mah supper is done. You bettah go see how she feel. You kin let de rest of us know."

"Lawd," Pearl agreed, "Ah done scorched-up dat lil meat and bread too long to talk about. Ah kin stay 'way from home long as Ah please. Mah husband ain't fussy."

"Oh, er, Pheoby, if youse ready to go, Ah could walk over dere wid you," Mrs. Sumpkins volunteered. "It's sort of duskin' down dark. De booger man might ketch yuh."

"Naw, Ah thank yuh. Nothin' couldn't ketch me dese few steps Ah'm goin'. Anyhow mah husband tell me say no first class booger would have me. If she got anything to tell yuh, you'll hear it."

Pheoby hurried on off with a covered bowl in her hands. She left the porch pelting her back with unasked questions. They hoped the answers were cruel and strange. When she arrived at the place, Pheoby Watson didn't go in by the front gate and down the palm walk to the front door. She walked around the fence corner and went in the intimate gate with her heaping plate of mulatto rice. Janie must be round that side.

She found her sitting on the steps of the back porch with the lamps all filled and the chimneys cleaned.

"Hello, Janie, how you comin'?"

"Aw, pretty good, Ah'm tryin' to soak some uh de tiredness and de dirt outa mah feet." She laughed a little.

"Ah see you is. Gal, you sho looks *good*. You looks like youse yo' own daughter." They both laughed. "Even wid dem overhalls on, you shows yo' womanhood."

"G'wan! G'wan! You must think Ah brought yuh somethin'. When Ah ain't brought home a thing but mahself."

"Dat's a gracious plenty. Yo' friends wouldn't want nothin' better."

"Ah takes dat flattery offa you, Pheoby, 'cause Ah know it's from de heart." Janie extended her hand. "Good Lawd, Pheoby! ain't you never goin' tuh gimme dat lil rations you brought me? Ah ain't had a thing on mah stomach today exceptin' mah hand." They both laughed easily. "Give it here and have a seat."

"Ah knowed you'd be hongry. No time to be huntin' stove wood after dark. Mah mulatto rice[1] ain't so good dis time. Not enough bacon grease, but Ah reckon it'll kill hongry."

"Ah'll tell you in a minute," Janie said, lifting the cover. "Gal, it's *too* good! you switches a mean fanny round in a kitchen."

"Aw, dat ain't much to eat, Janie. But Ah'm liable to have something sho nuff good tomorrow, 'cause you done come."

Janie ate heartily and said nothing. The varicolored cloud dust that the sun had stirred up in the sky was settling by slow degrees.

"Here, Pheoby, take yo' ole plate. Ah ain't got a bit of use for a empty dish. Dat grub sho come in handy."

Pheoby laughed at her friend's rough joke. "Youse just as crazy as you ever was."

"Hand me dat wash-rag on dat chair by you, honey. Lemme scrub mah feet." She took the cloth and rubbed vigorously. Laughter came to her from the big road.

"Well, Ah see Mouth-Almighty is still sittin' in de same place. And Ah reckon they got *me* up in they mouth now."

"Yes indeed. You know if you pass some people and don't speak tuh suit 'em dey got tuh go way back in yo' life and see whut you ever done. They know mo' 'bout yuh than you do yo' self. An envious heart makes a treacherous ear. They done 'heard' 'bout you just what they hope done happened."

"If God don't think no mo' 'bout 'em then Ah do, they's a lost ball in de high grass."

"Ah hears what they say 'cause they just will collect round mah porch 'cause it's on de big road. Mah husband git so sick of 'em sometime he makes 'em all git for home."

"Sam is right too. They just wearin' out yo' sittin' chairs."

"Yeah, Sam say most of 'em goes to church so they'll be sure to rise in Judgment. Dat's de day dat every secret is s'posed to be made known. They wants to be there and hear it *all*."

"Sam is *too* crazy! You can't stop laughin' when youse round him."

"Uuh hunh. He says he aims to be there hisself so he can find out who stole his corn-cob pipe."

"Pheoby, dat Sam of your'n just won't quit! Crazy thing!"

"Most of dese zigaboos is so het up over yo' business till they liable to hurry theyself to Judgment to find out about you if they don't soon know. You better make haste and tell 'em 'bout you and Tea Cake gittin' married, and if he taken all yo' money and went off wid some young gal, and where at he is now and where at is all yo' clothes dat you got to come back here in overhalls."

"Ah don't mean to bother wid tellin' 'em nothin', Pheoby. 'Tain't worth de trouble. You can tell 'em what Ah say if you wants to. Dat's just de same as me 'cause mah tongue is in mah friend's mouf."

"If you so desire Ah'll tell 'em what you tell me to tell 'em."

"To start off wid, people like dem wastes up too much time puttin' they mouf on things they don't know nothin' about. Now they got to look into me

1. Rice and peas.

loving Tea Cake and see whether it was done right or not! They don't know if life is a mess of corn-meal dumplings, and if love is a bed-quilt!"

"So long as they get a name to gnaw on they don't care whose it is, and what about, 'specially if they can make it sound like evil."

"If they wants to see and know, why they don't come kiss and be kissed? Ah could then sit down and tell 'em things. Ah been a delegate to de big 'ssociation of life. Yessuh! De Grand Lodge, de big convention of livin' is just where Ah been dis year and a half y'all ain't seen me."

They sat there in the fresh young darkness close together. Pheoby eager to feel and do through Janie, but hating to show her zest for fear it might be thought mere curiosity. Janie full of that oldest human longing—self revelation. Pheoby held her tongue for a long time, but she couldn't help moving her feet. So Janie spoke.

"They don't need to worry about me and my overhalls long as Ah still got nine hundred dollars in de bank. Tea Cake got me into wearing 'em—following behind him. Tea Cake ain't wasted up no money of mine, and he ain't left me for no young gal, neither. He give me every consolation in de world. He'd tell 'em so too, if he was here. If he wasn't gone."

Pheoby dilated all over with eagerness, "Tea Cake gone?"

"Yeah, Pheoby, Tea Cake is gone. And dat's de only reason you see me back here—cause Ah ain't got nothing to make me happy no more where Ah was at. Down in the Everglades there, down on the muck."

"It's hard for me to understand what you mean, de way you tell it. And then again Ah'm hard of understandin' at times."

"Naw, 'tain't nothin' lak you might think. So 'tain't no use in me telling you somethin' unless Ah give you de understandin' to go 'long wid it. Unless you see de fur, a mink skin ain't no different from a coon hide. Looka heah, Pheoby, is Sam waitin' on you for his supper?"

"It's all ready and waitin'. If he ain't got sense enough to eat it, dat's his hard luck."

"Well then, we can set right where we is and talk. Ah got the house all opened up to let dis breeze get a little catchin'.

"Pheoby, we been kissin'-friends for twenty years, so Ah depend on you for a good thought. And Ah'm talking to you from dat standpoint."

Time makes everything old so the kissing, young darkness became a monstropolous old thing while Janie talked.

Chapter 2

[PEAR TREE]

Janie saw her life like a great tree in leaf with the things suffered, things enjoyed, things done and undone. Dawn and doom was in the branches.

"Ah know exactly what Ah got to tell yuh, but it's hard to know where to start at.

"Ah ain't never seen mah papa. And Ah didn't know 'im if Ah did. Mah mama neither. She was gone from round dere long before Ah wuz big enough tuh know. Mah grandma raised me. Mah grandma and de white folks she worked wid. She had a house out in de back-yard and dat's where Ah wuz born. They was quality white folks up dere in West Florida. Named Washburn. She had four gran'chillun on de place and all of us played together and dat's how come Ah never called mah Grandma nothin' but Nanny, 'cause dat's what everybody on de place called her. Nanny used to ketch us in our devilment and lick every youngun on de place and Mis' Washburn did de same. Ah reckon dey never hit us ah lick amiss 'cause dem three boys and us two girls wuz pretty aggravatin', Ah speck.

"Ah was wid dem white chillun so much till Ah didn't know Ah wuzn't white till Ah was round six years old. Wouldn't have found it out then, but a man come long takin' pictures and without askin' anybody, Shelby, dat was de oldest boy, he told him to take us. Round a week later de man brought de picture for Mis' Washburn to see and pay him which she did, then give us all a good lickin'.

"So when we looked at de picture and everybody got pointed out there wasn't nobody left except a real dark little girl with long hair standing by Eleanor. Dat's where Ah wuz s'posed to be, but Ah couldn't recognize dat dark chile as me. So Ah ast, 'where is me? Ah don't see me.'

"Everybody laughed, even Mr. Washburn. Miss Nellie, de Mama of de chillun who come back home after her husband dead, she pointed to de dark one and said, 'Dat's you, Alphabet, don't you know yo' ownself?'

"Dey all useter call me Alphabet 'cause so many people had done named me different names. Ah looked at de picture a long time and seen it was mah dress and mah hair so Ah said:

"'Aw, aw! Ah'm colored!'

"Den dey all laughed real hard. But before Ah seen de picture Ah thought Ah wuz just like de rest.

"Us lived dere havin' fun till de chillun at school got to teasin' me 'bout livin' in de white folks' back-yard. Dere wuz uh knotty head gal name Mayrella dat useter git mad every time she look at me. Mis' Washburn useter dress me up in all de clothes her gran'chillun didn't need no mo' which still wuz better'n whut de rest uh de colored chillun had. And then she useter put hair ribbon on mah head fuh me tuh wear. Dat useter rile Mayrella uh lot. So she would pick at me all de time and put some others up tuh do de same. They'd push me 'way from de ring plays and make out they couldn't play wid nobody dat lived on premises. Den they'd tell me not to be takin' on over mah looks 'cause they mama told 'em 'bout de hound dawgs huntin' mah papa all night long. 'Bout Mr. Washburn and de sheriff puttin' de bloodhounds on de trail tuh ketch mah papa for whut he done tuh mah mama. Dey didn't tell about how he wuz seen tryin' tuh git in touch wid mah mama later on so he could marry her. Naw, dey didn't talk dat part of it atall. Dey made it sound real bad so as tuh crumple mah feathers. None of 'em didn't even remember whut his name wuz, but dey all knowed de bloodhound part by heart. Nanny didn't love tuh see me wid mah head hung down, so she figgered it would be mo' better fuh me if us had uh house. She got de land and everything and then Mis' Washburn helped out uh whole heap wid things."

Pheoby's hungry listening helped Janie to tell her story. So she went on thinking back to her young years and explaining them to her friend in soft, easy phrases while all around the house, the night time put on flesh and blackness.

She thought awhile and decided that her conscious life had commenced at Nanny's gate. On a late afternoon Nanny had called her to come inside the house because she had spied Janie letting Johnny Taylor kiss her over the gatepost.

It was a spring afternoon in West Florida. Janie had spent most of the day under a blossoming pear tree in the back-yard. She had been spending every minute that she could steal from her chores under that tree for the last three days. That was to say, ever since the first tiny bloom had opened. It had called her to come and gaze on a mystery. From barren brown stems to glistening leaf-buds; from the leaf-buds to snowy virginity of bloom. It stirred her tremendously. How? Why? It was like a flute song forgotten in another existence and remembered again. What? How? Why? This singing she heard that had nothing to do with her ears. The rose of the world was breathing out smell. It followed her through all her waking moments and caressed her in her sleep. It connected itself with other vaguely felt matters that had struck her outside observation and buried themselves in her flesh. Now they emerged and quested about her consciousness.

She was stretched on her back beneath the pear tree soaking in the alto chant of the visiting bees, the gold of the sun and the panting breath of the breeze when the inaudible voice of it all came to her. She saw a dustbearing bee sink into the sanctum of a bloom; the thousand sister-calyxes arch to meet the love embrace and the ecstatic shiver of the tree from root to tiniest branch creaming in every blossom and frothing with delight. So this was a marriage! She had been summoned to behold a revelation. Then Janie felt a pain remorseless sweet that left her limp and languid.

After a while she got up from where she was and went over the little garden field entire. She was seeking confirmation of the voice and vision, and everywhere she found and acknowledged answers. A personal answer for all other creations except herself. She felt an answer seeking her, but where? When? How? She found herself at the kitchen door and stumbled inside. In the air of the room were flies tumbling and singing, marrying and giving in marriage. When she reached the narrow hallway she was reminded that her grandmother was home with a sick headache. She was lying across the bed asleep so Janie tipped on out of the front door. Oh to be a pear tree—*any* tree in bloom! With kissing bees singing of the beginning of the world! She was sixteen. She had glossy leaves and bursting buds and she wanted to struggle with life but it seemed to elude her. Where were the singing bees for her? Nothing on the place nor in her grandma's house answered her. She searched as much of the world as she could from the top of the front steps and then went on down to the front gate and leaned over to gaze up and down the road. Looking, waiting, breathing short with impatience. Waiting for the world to be made.

Through pollinated air she saw a glorious being coming up the road. In her former blindness she had known him as shiftless Johnny Taylor, tall and lean. That was before the golden dust of pollen had beglamored his rags and her eyes.

In the last stages of Nanny's sleep, she dreamed of voices. Voices far-off but persistent, and gradually coming nearer. Janie's voice. Janie talking in whispery snatches with a male voice she couldn't quite place. That brought her wide awake. She bolted upright and peered out of the window and saw Johnny Taylor lacerating her Janie with a kiss.

"Janie!"

The old woman's voice was so lacking in command and reproof, so full of crumbling dissolution,—that Janie half believed that Nanny had not seen her. So she extended herself outside of her dream and went inside of the house. That was the end of her childhood.

Nanny's head and face looked like the standing roots of some old tree that had been torn away by storm. Foundation of ancient power that no longer mattered. The cooling palma christi leaves that Janie had bound about her grandma's head with a white rag had wilted down and become part and parcel of the woman. Her eyes didn't bore and pierce. They diffused and melted Janie, the room and the world into one comprehension.

"Janie, youse uh 'oman, now, so—"

"Naw, Nanny, naw Ah ain't no real 'oman yet."

The thought was too new and heavy for Janie. She fought it away.

Nanny closed her eyes and nodded a slow, weary affirmation many times before she gave it voice.

"Yeah, Janie, youse got yo' womanhood on yuh. So Ah mout ez well tell yuh what Ah been savin' up for uh spell. Ah wants to see you married right away."

"Me, married? Naw, Nanny, no ma'am! Whut Ah know 'bout uh husband?"

"Whut Ah seen just now is plenty for me, honey, Ah don't want no trashy nigger, no breath-and-britches, lak Johnny Taylor usin' yo' body to wipe his foots on."

Nanny's words made Janie's kiss across the gatepost seem like a manure pile after a rain.

"Look at me, Janie. Don't set dere wid yo' head hung down. Look at yo' ole grandma!" Her voice began snagging on the prongs of her feelings. "Ah don't want to be talkin' to you lak dis. Fact is Ah done been on mah knees to mah Maker many's de time askin' *please*—for Him not to make de burden too heavy for me to bear."

"Nanny, Ah just—Ah didn't mean nothin' bad."

"Dat's what makes me skeered. You don't mean no harm. You don't even know where harm is at. Ah'm ole now. Ah can't be always guidin' yo' feet from harm and danger. Ah wants to see you married right away."

"Who Ah'm goin' tuh marry off-hand lak dat? Ah don't know nobody."

"De Lawd will provide. He know Ah done bore de burden in de heat uh de day. Somebody done spoke to me 'bout you long time ago. Ah ain't said nothin' 'cause dat wasn't de way Ah placed you. Ah wanted yuh to school out and pick from a higher bush and a sweeter berry. But dat ain't yo' idea, Ah see."

"Nanny, who—who dat been askin' you for me?"

"Brother Logan Killicks. He's a good man, too."

"Naw, Nanny, no ma'am! Is dat whut he been hangin' round here for? He look like some ole skullhead in de grave yard."

The older woman sat bolt upright and put her feet to the floor, and thrust back the leaves from her face.

"So you don't want to marry off decent like, do yuh? You just wants to hug and kiss and feel around with first one man and then another, huh? You wants to make me suck de same sorrow yo' mama did, eh? Mah ole head ain't gray enough. Mah back ain't bowed enough to suit yuh!"

The vision of Logan Killicks was desecrating the pear tree, but Janie didn't know how to tell Nanny that. She merely hunched over and pouted at the floor.

"Janie."

"Yes, ma'am."

"You answer me when Ah speak. Don't you set dere poutin' wid me after all Ah done went through for you!"

She slapped the girl's face violently, and forced her head back so that their eyes met in struggle. With her hand uplifted for the second blow she saw the huge tear that welled up from Janie's heart and stood in each eye. She saw the terrible agony and the lips tightened down to hold back the cry and desisted. Instead she brushed back the heavy hair from Janie's face and stood there suffering and loving and weeping internally for both of them.

"Come to yo' Grandma, honey. Set in her lap lak yo' use tuh. Yo' Nanny wouldn't harm a hair uh yo' head. She don't want nobody else to do it neither if she kin help it. Honey, de white man is de ruler of everything as fur as Ah been able tuh find out. Maybe it's some place way off in de ocean where de black man is in power, but we don't know nothin' but what we see. So de white man throw down de load and tell de nigger man tuh pick it up. He pick it up because he have to, but he don't tote it. He hand it to his womenfolks. De nigger woman is de mule uh de world so fur as Ah can see. Ah been prayin' fuh it tuh be different wid you. Lawd, Lawd, Lawd!"

For a long time she sat rocking with the girl held tightly to her sunken breast. Janie's long legs dangled over one arm of the chair and the long braids of her hair swung low on the other side. Nanny half sung, half sobbed a running chant-prayer over the head of the weeping girl.

"Lawd have mercy! It was a long time on de way but Ah reckon it had to come. Oh Jesus! Do, Jesus! Ah done de best Ah could."

Finally, they both grew calm.

"Janie, how long you been 'lowin' Johnny Taylor to kiss you?"

"Only dis one time, Nanny. Ah don't love him at all. Whut made me do it is—oh, Ah don't know."

"Thank yuh, Massa Jesus."

"Ah ain't gointuh do it no mo', Nanny. Please don't make me marry Mr. Killicks."

"'Tain't Logan Killicks Ah wants you to have, baby, it's protection. Ah ain't gittin' ole, honey. Ah'm *done* ole. One mornin' soon, now, de angel wid de sword is gointuh stop by here. De day and de hour is hid from me, but it won't be long. Ah ast de Lawd when you was uh infant in mah arms to let me stay here till you got grown. He done spared me to see de day. Mah daily prayer now is tuh let dese golden moments rolls on a few days longer till Ah see you safe in life."

"Lemme wait, Nanny, please, jus' a lil bit mo'."

"Don't think Ah don't feel wid you, Janie, 'cause Ah do. Ah couldn't love yuh no more if Ah had uh felt yo' birth pains mahself. Fact uh de matter, Ah loves yuh a whole heap more'n Ah do yo' mama, de one Ah did birth. But you got to take in consideration you ain't no everyday chile like most of 'em. You ain't got no papa, you might jus' as well say no mama, for de good she do yuh. You ain't got nobody but me. And mah head is ole and tilted towards de grave. Neither can you stand alone by yo'self. De thought uh you bein' kicked around from pillar tuh post is uh hurtin' thing. Every tear you drop squeezes a cup uh blood outa mah heart. Ah got tuh try and do for you befo' mah head is cold."

A sobbing sigh burst out of Janie. The old woman answered her with little soothing pats of the hand.

"You know, honey, us colored folks is branches without roots and that makes things come round in queer ways. You in particular. Ah was born back due in slavery so it wasn't for me to fulfill my dreams of whut a woman oughta be and to do. Dat's one of de hold-backs of slavery. But nothing can't stop you from wishin'. You can't beat nobody down so low till you can rob 'em of they will. Ah didn't want to be used for a work-ox and a brood-sow and Ah didn't want mah daughter used dat way neither. It sho wasn't mah will for things to happen lak they did. Ah even hated de way you was born. But, all de same Ah said thank God, Ah got another chance. Ah wanted to preach a great sermon about colored women sittin' on high, but they wasn't no pulpit for me. Freedom found me wid a baby daughter in mah arms, so Ah said Ah'd take a broom and a cook-pot and throw up a highway through de wilderness for her. She would expound what Ah felt. But somehow she got lost offa de highway and next thing Ah knowed here you was in de world."

* * *

1937

What White Publishers Won't Print

I have been amazed by the Anglo-Saxon's[1] lack of curiosity about the internal lives and emotions of the Negroes, and for that matter, any non-Anglo-Saxon peoples within our borders, above the class of unskilled labor.

This lack of interest is much more important than it seems at first glance. It is even more important at this time than it was in the past. The internal affairs of the nation have bearings on the international stress and strain, and this gap in the national literature now has tremendous weight in world affairs. National coherence and solidarity is implicit in a thorough understanding of the various groups within a nation, and this lack of knowledge about the internal emotions and behavior of the minorities cannot fail to bar out understanding. Man, like all the other animals, fears and is repelled by that which he does not understand, and mere difference is apt to connote something malign.

The fact that there is no demand for incisive and full-dress stories around Negroes above the servant class is indicative of something of vast importance to this nation. This blank is NOT filled by the fiction built around upper-class Negroes exploiting the race problem. Rather, it tends to point it up. A college-bred Negro still is not a person like other folks, but an interesting problem, more or less. It calls to mind a story of slavery time. In this story, a master with more intellectual curiosity than usual, set out to see how much he could teach a particularly bright slave of his. When he had gotten him up to higher mathematics and to be a fluent reader of Latin, he called in a neighbor to show off his brilliant slave, and to argue that Negroes had brains just like the slave-owners had, and given the same opportunities, would turn out the same.

1. By "Anglo-Saxon" Hurston means, broadly speaking, white people. See also her use of "Nordics" later in the essay.

The visiting master of slaves looked and listened, tried to trap the literate slave in Algebra and Latin, and "failing to do so in both, fumed to his neighbor and said:

"Yes, he certainly knows his higher mathematics, and he can read Latin better than many white men I know, but I cannot bring myself to believe that he understands a thing that he is doing. It is all an aping of our culture. All on the outside. You are crazy if you think that it has changed him inside in the least. Turn him loose, and he will revert at once to the jungle. He is still a savage, and no amount of translating Virgil and Ovid is going to change him. In fact, all you have done is to turn a useful savage into a dangerous beast."

That was in slavery time, yes, and we have come a long, long way since then, but the troubling thing is that there are still too many who refuse to believe in the ingestion and digestion of western culture as yet. Hence the lack of literature about the higher emotions and love life of upper-class Negroes and the minorities in general.

Publishers and producers are cool to the idea. Now, do not leap to the conclusion that editors and producers constitute a special class of unbelievers. That is far from true. Publishing houses and theatrical promoters are in business to make money. They will sponsor anything that they believe will sell. They shy away from romantic stories about Negroes and Jews because they feel that they know the public indifference to such works, unless the story or play involves racial tension. It can then be offered as a study in Sociology, with the romantic side subdued. They know the skepticism in general about the complicated emotions in the minorities. The average American just cannot conceive of it, and would be apt to reject the notion, and publishers and producers take the stand that they are not in business to educate, but to make money. Sympathetic as they might be, they cannot afford to be crusaders

In proof of this, you can note various publishers and producers edging forward a little, and ready to go even further when the trial balloons show that the public is ready for it. This public lack of interest is the nut of the matter.

The question naturally arises as to the why of this indifference, not to say skepticism, to the internal life of educated minorities.

The answer lies in what we may call THE AMERICAN MUSEUM OF UNNATURAL HISTORY. This is an intangible built on token belief. It is assumed that all non-Anglo-Saxons are uncomplicated stereotypes. Everybody knows all about them. They are lay figures mounted in the museum where all may take them in at a glance. They are made of bent wires without insides at all. So how could anybody write a book about the non-existent?

The American Indian is a contraption of copper wires, eternal war-bonnet, with no equipment for laughter, expressionless face and that says "How" when spoken to. His only activity is treachery leading to massacres. Who is so dumb not to know all about Indians, even if they have never seen one, nor talked with anyone who ever knew one?

The American Negro exhibit is a group of two. Both of these mechanical toys are built so that their feet eternally shuffle, and their eyes pop and roll. Shuffling feet and those popping, rolling eyes denote the Negro, and no characterization is genuine without this monotony. One is seated on a stump picking away on his banjo and singing and laughing. The other is a most amoral character before a share-cropper's shack mumbling about injustice. Doing this makes him out to be a Negro "intellectual." It is as simple as all that.

The whole museum is dedicated to the convenient "typical." In there is the "typical" Oriental, Jew, Yankee, Western, Southerner, Latin, and even out-of-favor Nordics like the German, the Englishman "I say old chappie," and the gesticulating Frenchman. The least observant American can know them all at a glance. However, the public willingly accepts the untypical in Nordics, but feels cheated if the untypical is portrayed in others. The author of *Scarlet Sister Mary*[2] complained to me that her neighbors objected to her book on the grounds that she had the characters thinking, "and everybody know that Nigras don't think."

But for the national welfare, it is urgent to realize that minorities do think, and think about something other than the race problem. That they are very human and internally, according to natural endowment, are just like everybody else. So long as this is not conceived, there must remain that feeling of insurmountable difference, and difference to the average man means something bad. If people were made right, they would be just like him. The trouble with the purely problem arguments is that they leave too much unknown. Argue all you will or may about injustice, but as long as the majority cannot conceive of a Negro or a Jew feeling and reacting inside just as they do, the majority will keep right on believing that people who do not look like them cannot possibly feel as they do, and conform to the established pattern. It is well known that there must be a body of waived matter, let us say, things accepted and taken for granted by all in a community before there can be that commonality of feeling. The usual phrase is having things in Common. Until this is thoroughly established in respect to Negroes in America, as well as to other minorities, it will remain impossible for the majority to conceive of a Negro experiencing a deep and abiding love and not just the passion of sex. That a great mass of Negroes can be stirred by the pageants of Spring and Fall; the extravaganza of summer, and the majesty of winter. That they can and do experience discovery of the numerous subtle faces as a foundation for a great and selfless love, and the diverse nuances that go to destroy that love as with others. As it is now, this capacity, this evidence of high and complicated emotions, is ruled out. Hence the lack of interest in a romance uncomplicated by the race struggle has so little appeal.

This insistence on defeat in a story where upper-class Negroes are portrayed perhaps says something from the subconscious of the majority. Involved in western culture, the hero or the heroine, or both, must appear frustrated and go down to defeat, somehow. Our literature reeks with it. Is it the same as saying, "You can translate Virgil, and fumble with the differential calculus, but can you really comprehend it? Can you cope with our subtleties?"

That brings us to the folklore of "reversion to type." This curious doctrine has such wide acceptance that it is tragic. One has only to examine

2. Title of a 1928 novel by white American author Julia Peterkin (1880–1961). The story is set in the Low Country of South Carolina among the Gullah people, an African American ethnic group whose culture, perhaps due to their relative geographic isolation, has to this day preserved significant strains of their African heritage.

the huge literature on it to be convinced. No matter how high we may seem to climb, put us under strain and we revert to type, that is, to the bush. Under a superficial layer of western culture, the jungle drums throb in our veins.

This ridiculous notion makes it possible for that majority who accept it to conceive of even a man like the suave and scholarly Dr. Charles S. Johnson[3] to hide a black cat's bone on his person, and indulge in a midnight voodoo ceremony, complete with leopard skin and drums if threatened with the loss of the presidency of Fisk University, or the love of his wife. "Under the skin . . . better to deal with them in business, etc., but otherwise keep them at a safe distance and under control. I tell you, Carl Van Vechten,[4] think as you like, but they are just not like us."

The extent and extravagance of this notion reaches the ultimate in nonsense in the widespread belief that the Chinese have bizarre genitals, because of that eye-fold that makes their eyes seem to slant. In spite of the fact that no biology has ever mentioned any such difference in reproductive organs makes no matter. Millions of people believe it. "Did you know that a Chinese has . . ." Consequently, their quiet contemplative manner is interpreted as a sign of slyness and a treacherous inclination.

But the opening wedge for better understanding has been thrust into the crack. Though many Negroes denounced Carl Van Vechten's *Nigger Heaven* because of the title, and without ever reading it, the book, written in the deepest sincerity, revealed Negroes of wealth and culture to the white public. It created curiosity even when it aroused skepticism. It made folks want to know. Worth Tuttle Hedden's *The Other Room*[5] has definitely widened the opening. Neither of these well-written works takes a romance of upper-class Negro life as the central theme, but the atmosphere and the background is there. These works should be followed up by some incisive and intimate stories from the inside.

The realistic story around a Negro insurance official, dentist, general practitioner, undertaker and the like would be most revealing. Thinly disguised fiction around the well-known Negro names is not the answer, either. The "exceptional" as well as the Ol' Man Rivers has been exploited all out of context already. Everybody is already resigned to the "exceptional" Negro, and willing to be entertained by the "quaint." To grasp the penetration of western civilization in a minority, it is necessary to know how the average behaves and lives. Books that deal with people like in Sinclair Lewis' *Main Street* is the necessary métier.[6] For various reasons, the average, struggling, non-morbid Negro is the best-kept secret in America. His revelation to the public is the thing needed to do away with that feeling of difference which inspires fear, and which ever expresses itself in dislike.

It is inevitable that this knowledge will destroy many illusions and romantic traditions which America probably likes to have around. But then, we have no record of anybody sinking into a lingering death on finding out that

3. Johnson (1893–1956), an American sociologist and the first Black president of Fisk, was a powerful champion of racial equality whom some saw as too conservative because he opted to work for change collaboratively with whites.
4. White American writer and photographer (1880–1964) and a prominent patron of the Harlem Renaissance. His controversial novel *Nigger Heaven* (1946) was intended to show how Black people actually lived in Harlem.
5. A 1949 novel by Hedden (1896–1985), a white American. *The Other Room*, which sold widely, deals with the relationship between a white woman and a Black man at a college in New Orleans.
6. Occupation, activity, strength.

there was no Santa Claus. The old world will take it in its stride. The realization that Negroes are no better nor no worse, and at times just as bonny as everybody else, will hardly kill off the population of the nation.

Outside of racial attitudes, there is still another reason why this literature should exist. Literature and other arts are supposed to hold up the mirror to nature. With only the fractional "exceptional" and the "quaint" portrayed, a true picture of Negro life in America cannot be. A great principle of national art has been violated.

These are the things that publishers and producers, as the accredited representatives of the American people, have not as yet taken into consideration sufficiently. Let there be light!

1950

NELLA LARSEN
1893–1964

Of all the fiction published during the Harlem Renaissance, Nella Larsen's *Passing* (1929) is arguably the most sophisticated attempt to question the very idea of race: the notion that there are identifiable differences among groups of human beings (even if, as Irene Redfield puts it in the book, they are "not definite or tangible"). Whereas George Schuyler's irreverent science fiction satire *Black No More* (1931) is unrelenting in its sending-up of the American hysteria around race in the period, Larsen's novel is notable for its psychological depth, its investigation of the moral complexity of "passing" (that is, the phenomenon of light-skinned Blacks who choose to pass for white), and its focus on the implications of racial identity for women in particular.

Larsen's childhood is so shrouded in mystery that a contemporary who attempted to sketch her biography labeled her "Madame X." Larsen's father, a Black West Indian, is reported to have died two years after her birth; her mother, a Dane, married "a man of her own race and nationality" shortly thereafter, and thus Larsen (like Helga Crane, the protagonist of Larsen's first novel, *Quicksand*) grew up as the only Black member of a white family. Larsen attended Fisk University (1909–10); audited classes at the University of Copenhagen (1910–12); and then began studying at the Lincoln School for Nurses in New York, where she completed the nursing program in 1915. She immediately went to Alabama to serve as the head nurse at the John A. Andrew Hospital and Nurse Training School at Tuskegee Institute. She did not care for the South, however. Returning to New York a year later, she worked as assistant superintendent of nurses at Lincoln Hospital from 1916 to 1918 and then for the New York Department of Health.

In 1921, when Larsen left nursing to work in the New York Public Library, she was put in charge of the children's room at the 135th Street branch in Harlem. She had already begun to publish essays, reviews, and short fiction in magazines such as *The Brownies Book* and *The Messenger* and soon became a regular at Harlem Renaissance events, meeting many of the major literary figures of the era. In October 1925, she took a leave of absence from her job, apparently for health reasons, and resigned from the library in January 1926. During her convalescence, she wrote *Quicksand*. A powerful dissection of the impact of racial attitudes and middle-class expectations on the life of its young light-skinned protagonist, *Quicksand* was an instant critical success when it appeared in 1928. W. E. B. Du Bois hailed it as "the best piece of fiction that Negro America has produced since the heyday of Chesnutt." By the fall of the same year Larsen had completed a draft of *Passing* (which like *Quicksand* was published by Knopf), a novel centering on the relationship between two light-skinned Black women, Clare Kendry and Irene Redfield, and specifically on Irene's attempt to make sense of Clare's choice to pass for white.

Why Larsen produced no other novels in the remaining thirty-five years of her life is a matter of much speculation among scholars, who often cite two possible contributing factors. The first is the public charge of plagiarism brought in connection with her 1930 short story "Sanctuary," which bore a striking resemblance to the story "Mrs. Adis" by Sheila Kaye-Smith, a contemporary writer. Larsen defended herself in an open letter to the magazine that had published the story, but seems never to have recovered from the accusation. Another factor might have been the collapse around 1931 of her marriage to Dr. Elmer S. Imes, a physicist. When Imes headed south to take a position at Fisk, she spent a year traveling in Europe on a Guggenheim fellowship in preparation for a novel that never materialized. After they were divorced in 1933, Larsen was awarded alimony that enabled her to live without working until 1941; but this freedom produced no new novels. Imes's death in 1941 forced her to return to nursing.

During the last three decades of her life, Larsen became relatively reclusive. Circulating a rumor that she had left the United States for South America, she refused to correspond with most of her friends. In 1964, about five years before an upsurge of interest in women writers resulted in a reprinting of *Quicksand* and established Larsen as one of the central artists of the Harlem Renaissance, she was found dead in her New York apartment.

Passing

for
Carl Van Vechten
and
Fania Marinoff[1]

One three centuries removed
From the scenes his fathers loved,
Spicy grove, cinnamon tree,
What is Africa to me?
—Countée Cullen[2]

Part One: Encounter

One

It was the last letter in Irene Redfield's little pile of morning mail. After her other ordinary and clearly directed letters the long envelope of thin Italian paper with its almost illegible scrawl seemed out of place and alien. And

1. Writer and photographer Carl Van Vechten (1886–1964) and his wife, actress Fania Marinoff (1887–1972).

2. From "Heritage" by Countee Cullen (1903–1946).

there was, too, something mysterious and slightly furtive about it. A thin sly thing which bore no return address to betray the sender. Not that she hadn't immediately known who its sender was. Some two years ago she had one very like it in outward appearance. Furtive but yet in some peculiar, determined way a little flaunting. Purple ink. Foreign paper of extraordinary size.

It had been, Irene noted, postmarked in New York the day before. Her brows came together in a tiny frown. The frown, however, was more from perplexity than from annoyance; though there was in her thoughts an element of both. She was wholly unable to comprehend such an attitude towards danger as she was sure the letter's contents would reveal; and she disliked the idea of opening and reading it.

This, she reflected, was of a piece with all that she knew of Clare Kendry. Stepping always on the edge of danger. Always aware, but not drawing back or turning aside. Certainly not because of any alarms or feeling of outrage on the part of others.

And for a swift moment Irene Redfield seemed to see a pale small girl sitting on a ragged blue sofa, sewing pieces of bright red cloth together, while her drunken father, a tall, powerfully built man, raged threateningly up and down the shabby room, bellowing curses and making spasmodic lunges at her which were not the less frightening because they were, for the most part, ineffectual. Sometimes he did manage to reach her. But only the fact that the child had edged herself and her poor sewing over to the farthermost corner of the sofa suggested that she was in any way perturbed by this menace to herself and her work.

Clare had known well enough that it was unsafe to take a portion of the dollar that was her weekly wage for the doing of many errands for the dressmaker who lived on the top floor of the building of which Bob Kendry was janitor. But that knowledge had not deterred her. She wanted to go to her Sunday school's picnic, and she had made up her mind to wear a new dress. So, in spite of certain unpleasantness and possible danger, she had taken the money to buy the material for that pathetic little red frock.

There had been, even in those days, nothing sacrificial in Clare Kendry's idea of life, no allegiance beyond her own immediate desire. She was selfish, and cold, and hard. And yet she had, too, a strange capacity of transforming warmth and passion, verging sometimes almost on theatrical heroics.

Irene, who was a year or more older than Clare, remembered the day that Bob Kendry had been brought home dead, killed in a silly saloon-fight. Clare, who was at that time a scant fifteen years old, had just stood there with her lips pressed together, her thin arms folded across her narrow chest, staring down at the familiar pasty-white face of her parent with a sort of disdain in her slanting black eyes. For a very long time she had stood like that, silent and staring. Then, quite suddenly, she had given way to a torrent of weeping, swaying her thin body, tearing at her bright hair, and stamping her small feet. The outburst had ceased as suddenly as it had begun. She glanced quickly about the bare room, taking everyone in, even the two policemen, in a sharp look of flashing scorn. And, in the next instant, she had turned and vanished through the door.

Seen across the long stretch of years, the thing had more the appearance of an outpouring of pent-up fury than of an overflow of grief for her dead father; though she had been, Irene admitted, fond enough of him in her own rather catlike way.

Catlike. Certainly that was the word which best described Clare Kendry, if any single world could describe her. Sometimes she was hard and apparently without feeling at all; sometimes she was affectionate and rashly impulsive. And there was about her an amazing soft malice, hidden well away until provoked. Then she was capable of scratching, and very effectively too. Or, driven to anger, she would fight with a ferocity and impetuousness that disregarded or forgot any danger; superior strength, numbers, or other unfavourable circumstances. How savagely she had clawed those boys the day they had hooted her parent and sung a derisive rhyme, of their own composing, which pointed out certain eccentricities in his careening gait! And how deliberately she had—

Irene brought her thoughts back to the present, to the letter from Clare Kendry that she still held unopened in her hand. With a little feeling of apprehension, she very slowly cut the envelope, drew out the folded sheets, spread them, and began to read.

It was, she saw at once, what she had expected since learning from the postmark that Clare was in the city. An extravagantly phrased wish to see her again. Well, she needn't and wouldn't, Irene told herself, accede to that. Nor would she assist Clare to realize her foolish desire to return for a moment to that life which long ago, and of her own choice, she had left behind her.

She ran through the letter, puzzling out, as best she could, the carelessly formed worlds or making instinctive guesses at them.

". . . For I am lonely, so lonely . . . cannot help longing to be with you again, as I have never longed for anything before; and I have wanted many things in my life. . . . You can't know how in this pale life of mine I am all the time seeing the bright pictures of that other that I once thought I was glad to be free of. . . . It's like an ache, a pain that never ceases. . . ." Sheets upon thin sheets of it. And ending finally with, "and its your fault, 'Rene dear. At least partly. For I wouldn't now, perhaps, have this terrible, this wild desire if I hadn't seen you that time in Chicago. . . ."

Brilliant red patches flamed in Irene Redfield's warm olive cheeks.

"That time in Chicago." The words stood out from among the many paragraphs of other words, bringing with them a clear, sharp remembrance, in which even now, after two years, humiliation, resentment, and rage were mingled.

Two

This is what Irene Redfield remembered.

Chicago. August. A brilliant day, hot, with a brutal staring sun pouring down rays that were like molten rain. A day on which the very outlines of the buildings shuddered as if in protest at the heat. Quivering lines sprang up from baked pavements and wriggled along the shining car-tracks. The automobiles parked at the kerbs were a dancing blaze, and the glass of the shop-windows threw out a blinding radiance. Sharp particles of dust rose from the burning sidewalks, stinging the seared or dripping skins of wilting pedestrians. What small breeze there was seemed like the breath of a flame fanned by slow bellows.

It was on that day of all others that Irene set out to shop for the things which she had promised to take home from Chicago to her two small sons, Brian junior and Theodore. Characteristically, she had put it off until only a few crowded days remained of her long visit. And only this sweltering one was free of engagements till the evening.

Without too much trouble she had got the mechanical aeroplane for Junior. But the drawing-book, for which Ted had so gravely and insistently given her precise directions, had sent her in and out of five shops without success.

It was while she was on her way to a sixth place that right before her smarting eyes a man toppled over and became an inert crumpled heap on the scorching cement. About the lifeless figure a little crowd gathered. Was the man dead, or only faint? someone asked her. But Irene didn't know and didn't try to discover. She edged her way out of the increasing crowd, feeling disagreeably damp and sticky and soiled from contact with so many sweating bodies.

For a moment she stood fanning herself and dabbing at her moist face with an inadequate scrap of handkerchief. Suddenly she was aware that the whole street had a wobbly look, and realized that she was about to faint. With a quick perception of the need for immediate safety, she lifted a wavering hand in the direction of a cab parked directly in front of her. The perspiring driver jumped out and guided her to his car. He helped, almost lifted her in. She sank down on the hot leather seat.

For a minute her thoughts were nebulous. They cleared.

"I guess," she told her Samaritan, "it's tea I need. On a roof somewhere."

"The Drayton, ma'am?" he suggested. "They do say as how it's always a breeze up there."

"Thank you. I think the Drayton'll do nicely," she told him.

There was that little grating sound of the clutch being slipped in as the man put the car in gear and slid deftly out into the boiling traffic. Reviving under the warm breeze stirred up by the moving cab, Irene made some small attempts to repair the damage that the heat and crowds had done to her appearance.

All too soon the rattling vehicle shot towards the sidewalk and stood still. The driver sprang out and opened the door before the hotel's decorated attendant could reach it. She got out, and thanking him smilingly as well as in a more substantial manner for his kind helpfulness and understanding, went in through the Drayton's wide doors.

Stepping out of the elevator that had brought her to the roof, she was led to a table just in front of a long window whose gently moving curtains suggested a cool breeze. It was, she thought, like being wafted upward on a magic carpet to another world, pleasant, quiet, and strangely remote from the sizzling one that she had left below.

The tea, when it came, was all that she had desired and expected. In fact, so much was it what she had desired and expected that after the first deep cooling drink she was able to forget it, only now and then sipping, a little absently, from the tall green glass, while she surveyed the room about her or looked out over some lower buildings at the bright unstirred blue of the lake reaching away to an undetected horizon.

She had been gazing down for some time at the specks of cars and people creeping about in streets, and thinking how silly they looked, when on taking up her glass she was surprised to find it empty at last. She asked for more tea and while she waited, began to recall the happenings of the day and to wonder what she was to do about Ted and his book. Why was it that almost invariably he wanted something that was difficult or impossible to get? Like his father. For ever wanting something that he couldn't have.

Presently there were voices, a man's booming one and a woman's slightly husky. A waiter passed her, followed by a sweetly scented woman in a fluttering dress of green chiffon whose mingled pattern of narcissuses, jonquils, and hyacinths was a reminder of pleasantly chill spring days. Behind her there was a man, very red in the face, who was mopping his neck and forehead with a big crumpled handkerchief.

"Oh dear!" Irene groaned, rasped by annoyance, for after a little discussion and commotion they had stopped at the very next table. She had been alone there at the window and it had been so satisfyingly quiet. Now, of course, they would chatter.

But no. Only the woman sat down. The man remained standing, abstractedly pinching the knot of his bright blue tie. Across the small space that separated the two tables his voice carried clearly.

"See you later, then," he declared, looking down at the woman. There was pleasure in his tones and a smile on his face.

His companion's lips parted in some answer, but her words were blurred by the little intervening distance and the medley of noises floating up from the streets below. They didn't reach Irene. But she noted the peculiar caressing smile that accompanied them.

The man said: "Well, I suppose I'd better," and smiled again, and said good-bye, and left.

An attractive-looking woman, was Irene's opinion, with those dark, almost black, eyes and that wide mouth like a scarlet flower against the ivory of her skin. Nice clothes too, just right for the weather, thin and cool without being mussy, as summer things were so apt to be.

A waiter was taking her order. Irene saw her smile up at him as she murmured something—thanks, maybe. It was an odd sort of smile. Irene couldn't quite define it, but she was sure that she would have classed it, coming from another woman, as being just a shade too provocative for a waiter. About this one, however, there was something that made her hesitate to name it that. A certain impression of assurance, perhaps.

The waiter came back with the order. Irene watched her spread out her napkin, saw the silver spoon in the white hand slit the dull gold of the melon. Then, conscious that she had been staring, she looked quickly away.

Her mind returned to her own affairs. She had settled, definitely, the problem of the proper one of two frocks for the bridge party that night, in rooms whose atmosphere would be so thick and hot that every breath would be like breathing soup. The dress decided, her thoughts had gone back to the snag of Ted's book, her unseeing eyes far away on the lake, when by some sixth sense she was acutely aware that someone was watching her.

Very slowly she looked around, and into the dark eyes of the woman in the green frock at the next table. But she evidently failed to realize that such intense interest as she was showing might be embarrassing, and continued to stare. Her demeanour was that of one who with utmost singleness of mind and purpose was determined to impress firmly and accurately each detail of Irene's features upon her memory for all time, nor showed the slightest trace of disconcertment at having been detected in her steady scrutiny.

Instead, it was Irene who was put out. Feeling her colour heighten under the continued inspection, she slid her eyes down. What, she wondered, could be the reason for such persistent attention? Had she, in her haste in the taxi, put her hat on backwards? Guardedly she felt at it. No. Perhaps there was a streak of powder somewhere on her face. She made a quick pass over it with her handkerchief. Something wrong with her dress? She shot a glance over it. Perfectly all right. *What* was it?

Again she looked up, and for a moment her brown eyes politely returned the stare of the other's black ones, which never for an instant fell or wavered. Irene made a little mental shrug. Oh well, let her look! She tried to treat the woman and her watching with indifference, but she couldn't. All her efforts to ignore her, it, were futile. She stole another glance. Still looking. What strange languorous eyes she had!

And gradually there rose in Irene a small inner disturbance, odious and hatefully familiar. She laughed softly, but her eyes flashed.

Did that woman, could that woman, somehow know that here before her very eyes on the roof of the Drayton sat a Negro?

Absurd! Impossible! White people were so stupid about such things for all that they usually asserted that they were able to tell; and by the most ridiculous means, finger-nails, palms of hands, shapes of ears, teeth, and other equally silly rot. They always took her for an Italian, a Spaniard, a Mexican, or a gipsy. Never, when she was alone, had they even remotely seemed to suspect that she was a Negro. No, the woman sitting there staring at her couldn't possibly know.

Nevertheless, Irene felt, in turn, anger, scorn, and fear slide over her. It wasn't that she was ashamed of being a Negro, or even of having it declared. It was the idea of being ejected from any place, even in the polite and tactful way in which the Drayton would probably do it, that disturbed her.

But she looked, boldly this time, back into the eyes still frankly intent upon her. They did not seem to her hostile or resentful. Rather, Irene had the feeling that they were ready to smile if she would. Nonsense, of course. The feeling passed, and she turned away with the firm intention of keeping her gaze on the lake, the roofs of the buildings across the way, the sky, anywhere but on that annoying woman. Almost immediately, however, her eyes were back again. In the midst of her fog of uneasiness she had been seized by a desire to outstare the rude observer. Suppose the woman did know or suspect her race. She couldn't prove it.

Suddenly her small fright increased. Her neighbour had risen and was coming towards her. What was going to happen now?

"Pardon me," the woman said pleasantly, "but I think I know you." Her slightly husky voice held a dubious note.

Looking up at her, Irene's suspicious and fears vanished. There was no mistaking the friendliness of that smile or resisting its charm. Instantly she surrendered to it and smiled too, as she said: "I'm afraid you're mistaken."

"Why, of course, I know you!" the other exclaimed. "Don't tell me you're not Irene Westover. Or do they still call you 'Rene?"

In the brief second before her answer, Irene tried vainly to recall where and when this woman could have known her. There, in Chicago. And before her marriage. That much was plain. High school? College? Y. W. C. A. committees? High school, most likely. What white girls had she known well enough to have been familiarly addressed as 'Rene by them? The woman before her didn't fit her memory of any of them. Who was she?

"Yes, I'm Irene Westover. And though nobody calls me 'Rene any more, it's good to hear the name again. And you—" She hesitated, ashamed that she could not remember, and hoping that the sentence would be finished for her.

"Don't you know me? Not really, 'Rene?"

"I'm sorry, but just at the minute, I can't seem to place you."

Irene studied the lovely creature standing beside her for some clue to her identity. Who could she be? Where and when had they met? And through her perplexity there came the thought that the trick which her memory had played her was for some reason more gratifying than disappointing to her old acquaintance, that she didn't mind not being recognized.

And, too, Irene felt that she was just about to remember her. For about the woman was some quality, an intangible something, too vague to define, too remote to seize, but which was, to Irene Redfield, very familiar. And that voice. Surely she'd heard those husky tones somewhere before. Perhaps before time, contact, or something had been at them, making them into a voice remotely suggesting England. Ah! Could it have been in Europe that they had met? 'Rene. No.

"Perhaps," Irene began, "you—"

The woman laughed, a lovely laugh, a small sequence of notes that was like a trill and also like the ringing of a delicate bell fashioned of a precious metal, a tinkling.

Irene drew a quick sharp breath. "Clare!" she exclaimed, "not really Clare Kendry?"

So great was her astonishment that she had started to rise.

"No, no, don't get up," Clare Kendry commanded, and sat down herself. "You've simply got to stay and talk. We'll have something more. Tea? Fancy meeting you here! It's simply too, too lucky!"

"It's awfully surprising," Irene told her, and seeing the change in Clare's smile, knew that she had revealed a corner of her own thoughts. But she only said: "I'd never in this world have known you if you hadn't laughed. You are changed, you know. And yet, in a way, you're just the same."

"Perhaps," Clare replied. "Oh, just a second."

She gave her attention to the waiter at her side. "M-mm, let's see. Two teas. And bring some cigarettes. Y-es, they'll be all right. Thanks." Again that odd upward smile. Now, Irene was sure that it was too provocative for a waiter.

While Clare had been giving the order, Irene made a rapid mental calculation. It must be, she figured, all of twelve years since she, or anybody that she knew, had laid eyes on Clare Kendry.

After her father's death she'd gone to live with some relatives, aunts or cousins two or three times removed, over on the west side: relatives that nobody had known the Kendry's possessed until they had turned up at the funeral and taken Clare away with them.

For about a year or more afterwards she would appear occasionally among her old friends and acquaintances on the south side for short little visits that were, they understood, always stolen from the endless domestic tasks in her new home. With each succeeding one she was taller, shabbier, and more belligerently sensitive. And each time the look on her face was more resentful and brooding. "I'm worried about Clare, she seems so unhappy," Irene remembered her mother saying. The visits dwindled, becoming shorter, fewer, and further apart until at last they ceased.

Irene's father, who had been fond of Bob Kendry, made a special trip over to the west side about two months after the last time Clare had been to see them and returned with the bare information that he had seen the relatives and that Clare had disappeared. What else he had confided to her mother, in the privacy of their own room, Irene didn't know.

But she had had something more than a vague suspicion of its nature. For there had been rumours. Rumours that were, to girls of eighteen and nineteen years, interesting and exciting.

There was the one about Clare Kendry's having been seen at the dinner hour in a fashionable hotel in company with another woman and two men, all of them white. And *dressed!* And there was another which told of her driving in Lincoln Park with a man, unmistakably white, and evidently rich. Packard limousine, chauffeur in livery, and all that. There had been others whose context Irene could no longer recollect, but all pointing in the same glamorous direction.

And she could remember quite vividly how, when they used to repeat and discuss these tantalizing stories about Clare, the girls would always look knowingly at one another and then, with little excited giggles, drag away their eager shining eyes and say with lurking undertones of regret or disbelief some such thing as: "Oh, well, maybe she's got a job or something," or "After all, it mayn't have been Clare," or "You can't believe all you hear."

And always some girl, more matter-of-fact or more frankly malicious than the rest, would declare: "Of course it was Clare! Ruth said it was and so did Frank, and they certainly know her when they see her as well as we do." And someone else would say: "Yes, you can bet it was Clare all right." And then they would all join in asserting that there could be no mistake about its having been Clare, and that such circumstances could mean only one thing. Working indeed! People didn't take their servants to the Shelby for dinner. Certainly not all dressed up like that. There would follow insincere regrets, and somebody would say: "Poor girl, I suppose it's true enough, but what can you expect. Look at her father. And her mother, they say, would have run away if she hadn't died. Besides, Clare always had a—a—having way with her."

Precisely that! The words came to Irene as she sat there on the Drayton roof, facing Clare Kendry. "A having way." Well, Irene acknowledged, judging from her appearance and manner, Clare seemed certainly to have succeeded in having a few of the things that she wanted.

It was, Irene repeated, after the interval of the waiter, a great surprise and a very pleasant one to see Clare again after all those years, twelve at least.

"Why, Clare, you're the last person in the world I'd have expected to run into. I guess that's why I didn't know you."

Clare answered gravely: "Yes. It is twelve years. But I'm not surprised to see you, 'Rene. That is, not so very. In fact, ever since I've been here, I've more or less hoped that I should, or someone. Preferably you, though. Still, I imagine that's because I've thought of you often and often, while you—I'll wager you've never given me a thought."

It was true, of course. After the first speculations and indictments, Clare had gone completely from Irene's thoughts. And from the thoughts of others too—if their conversation was any indication of their thoughts.

Besides, Clare had never been exactly one of the group, just as she'd never been merely the janitor's daughter, but the daughter of Mr. Bob Kendry, who, it was true, was a janitor, but who also, it seemed, had been in college with some of their fathers. Just how or why he happened to be a janitor, and a very inefficient one at that, they none of them quite knew. One of Irene's brothers, who had put the question to their father, had been told: "That's something that doesn't concern you," and given him the advice to be careful not to end in the same manner as "poor Bob."

No, Irene hadn't thought of Clare Kendry. Her own life had been too crowded. So, she supposed, had the lives of other people. She defended her—their—forgetfulness. "You know how it is. Everybody's so busy. People leave, drop out, maybe for a little while there's talk about them, or questions; then, gradually they're forgotten."

"Yes, that's natural," Clare agreed. And what, she inquired, had they said of her for that little while at the beginning before they'd forgotten her altogether?

Irene looked away. She felt the telltale colour rising in her cheeks. "You can't," she evaded, "expect me to remember trifles like that over twelve years of marriages, births, deaths, and the war."

There followed that trill of notes that was Clare Kendry's laugh, small and clear and the very essence of mockery.

"Oh, 'Rene!" she cried, "of course you remember! But I won't make you tell me, because I know just as well as if I'd been there and heard every unkind word. Oh, I know, I know. Frank Danton saw me in the Shelby one night. Don't tell me he didn't broadcast that, and with embroidery. Others may have seen me at other times. I don't know. But once I met Margaret Hammer in Marshall Field's.[3] I'd have spoken, was on the very point of doing it, but she cut me dead. My dear 'Rene, I assure you that from the way she looked through me, even I was uncertain whether I was actually there in the flesh or not. I remember it clearly, too clearly. It was that very thing which, in a way, finally decided me not to go out and see you one last time before I went away to stay. Somehow, good as all of you, the whole family, had always been to the poor forlorn child that was me, I felt I shouldn't be able to bear that. I mean if any of you, your mother or the boys or—Oh, well, I just felt I'd rather not know it if you did. And so I stayed away. Silly, I suppose. Sometimes I've been sorry I didn't go."

Irene wondered if it was tears that made Clare's eyes so luminous.

"And now 'Rene, I want to hear all about you and everybody and everything. You're married, I s'pose?"

Irene nodded.

"Yes," Clare said knowingly, "you would be. Tell me about it."

And so for an hour or more they had sat there smoking and drinking tea and filling in the gap of twelve years with talk. That is, Irene did. She told Clare about her marriage and removal to New York, about her husband, and about her two sons, who were having their first experience of being separated from their parents at a summer camp, about her mother's death, about the marriages of her two brothers. She told of the marriages, births, and deaths in other families that Clare had known, opening up, for her, new vistas on the lives of old friends and acquaintances.

Clare drank it all in, these things which for so long she had wanted to know and hadn't been able to learn. She sat motionless, her bright lips slightly parted, her whole face lit by the radiance of her happy eyes. Now and then she put a question, but for the most part she was silent.

Somewhere outside, a clock struck. Brought back to the present, Irene looked down at her watch and exclaimed: "Oh, I must go, Clare!"

A moment passed during which she was the prey of uneasiness. It had suddenly occurred to her that she hadn't asked Clare anything about her own life and that she had a very definite unwillingness to do so. And she was quite well aware of the reason for that reluctance. But, she asked herself, wouldn't it, all things considered, be the kindest thing not to ask? If

3. A chic Chicago department store.

things with Clare were as she—as they all—had suspected, wouldn't it be more tactful to seem to forget to inquire how she had spent those twelve years?

If? It was that "if" which bothered her. It might be, it might just be, in spite of all gossip and even appearances to the contrary, that there was nothing, had been nothing, that couldn't be simply and innocently explained. Appearances, she knew now, had a way sometimes of not fitting facts, and if Clare hadn't—Well, if they had all been wrong, then certainly she ought to express some interest in what had happened to her. It would seem queer and rude if she didn't. But how was she to know? There was, she at last decided, no way; so she merely said again. "I must go, Clare."

"Please, not so soon, 'Rene," Clare begged, not moving.

Irene thought: "She's really almost too good-looking. It's hardly any wonder that she—"

"And now, 'Rene dear, that I've found you, I mean to see lots and lots of you. We're here for a month at least. Jack, that's my husband, is here on business. Poor dear! in this heat. Isn't it beastly? Come to dinner with us tonight, won't you?" And she gave Irene a curious little sidelong glance and a sly, ironical smile peeped out on her full red lips, as if she had been in the secret of the other's thoughts and was mocking her.

Irene was conscious of a sharp intake of breath, but whether it was relief or chagrin that she felt, she herself could not have told. She said hastily: "I'm afraid I can't, Clare. I'm filled up. Dinner and bridge. I'm so sorry."

"Come tomorrow instead, to tea," Clare insisted. "Then you'll see Margery—she's just ten—and Jack too, maybe, if he hasn't got an appointment or something."

From Irene came an uneasy little laugh. She had an engagement for tomorrow also and she was afraid that Clare would not believe it. Suddenly, now, that possibility disturbed her. Therefore it was with a half-vexed feeling at the sense of undeserved guilt that had come upon her that she explained that it wouldn't be possible because she wouldn't be free for tea, or for luncheon or dinner either. "And the next day's Friday when I'll be going away for the week-end, Idlewild,[4] you know. It's quite the thing now." And then she had an inspiration.

"Clare!" she exclaimed, "why don't you come up with me? Our place is probably full up—Jim's wife has a way of collecting mobs of the most impossible people—but we can always manage to find room for one more. And you'll see absolutely everybody."

In the very moment of giving the invitation she regretted it. What a foolish, what an idiotic impulse to have given way to! She groaned inwardly as she thought of the endless explanations in which it would involve her, of the curiosity, and the talk, and the lifted eyebrows. It wasn't she assured herself, that she was a snob, that she cared greatly for the petty restrictions and distinctions with which what called itself Negro society chose to hedge itself about; but that she had a natural and deeply rooted aversion to the kind of front-page notoriety that Clare Kendry's presence in Idlewild, as her guest, would expose her to. And here she was, perversely and against all reason, inviting her.

4. A summer resort founded in 1912 in Michigan, catering to middle- and upper-class African Americans.

But Clare shook her head. "Really, I'd love to, 'Rene," she said, a little, mournfully. "There's nothing I'd like better. But I couldn't. I mustn't, you see. It wouldn't do at all. I'm sure you understand. I'm simply crazy to go, but I can't." The dark eyes glistened and there was a suspicion of a quaver in the husky voice. "And believe me, 'Rene, I do thank you for asking me. Don't think I've entirely forgotten just what it would mean for you if I went. That is, if you still care about such things."

All indication of tears had gone from her eyes and voice, and Irene Redfield, searching her face, had an offended feeling that behind what was now only an ivory mask lurked a scornful amusement. She looked away, at the wall far beyond Clare. Well, she deserved it, for, as she acknowledged to herself, she *was* relieved. And for the very reason at which Clare had hinted. The fact that Clare had guessed her perturbation did not, however, in any degree lessen that relief. She was annoyed at having been detected in what might seem to be an insincerity; but that was all.

The waiter came with Clare's change. Irene reminded herself that she ought immediately to go. But she didn't move.

The truth was, she was curious. There were things that she wanted to ask Clare Kendry. She wished to find out about this hazardous business of "passing," this breaking away from all that was familiar and friendly to take one's chance in another environment, not entirely strange, perhaps, but certainly not entirely friendly. What, for example, one did about background, how one accounted for oneself. And how one felt when one came into contact with other Negroes. But she couldn't. She was unable to think of a single question that in its context or its phrasing was not too frankly curious, if not actually impertinent.

As if aware of her desire and her hesitation, Clare remarked, thoughtfully: "You know, 'Rene, I've often wondered why more coloured girls, girls like you and Margaret Hammer and Esther Dawson and—oh, lots of others—never 'passed' over. It's such a frightfully easy thing to do. If one's the type, all that's needed is a little nerve."

"What about background? Family, I mean. Surely you can't just drop down on people from nowhere and expect them to receive you with open arms, can you?"

"Almost," Clare asserted. "You'd be surprised, 'Rene, how much easier that is with white people than with us. Maybe because there are so many more of them, or maybe because they are secure and so don't have to bother. I've never quite decided."

Irene was inclined to be incredulous. "You mean that you didn't have to explain where you came from? It seems impossible."

Clare cast a glance of repressed amusement across the table at her. "As a matter of fact, I didn't. Though I suppose under any other circumstances I might have had to provide some plausible tale to account for myself. I've a good imagination, so I'm sure I could have done it quite creditably, and credibly. But it wasn't necessary. There were my aunts, you see, respectable and authentic enough for anything or anybody."

"I see. They were 'passing' too."

"No. They weren't. They were white."

"Oh!" And in the next instant it came back to Irene that she had heard this mentioned before; by her father, or, more likely, her mother. They were Bob Kendry's aunts. He had been a son of their brother's, on the left hand. A wild oat.

"They were nice old ladies," Clare explained, "very religious and as poor as church mice. That adored brother of theirs, my grandfather, got through every penny they had after he'd finished his own little bit."

Clare paused in her narrative to light another cigarette. Her smile, her expression, Irene noticed, was faintly resentful.

"Being good Christians," she continued, "when dad came to his tipsy end, they did their duty and gave me a home of sorts. I was, it was true, expected to earn my keep by doing all the housework and most of the washing. But do you realize, 'Rene, that if it hadn't been for them, I shouldn't have had a home in the world?"

Irene's nod and little murmur were comprehensive, understanding.

Clare made a small mischievous grimace and proceeded. "Besides, to their notion, hard labour was good for me. I had Negro blood and they belonged to the generation that had written and read long articles headed: 'Will the Blacks Work?' Too, they weren't quite sure that the good God hadn't intended the sons and daughters of Ham to sweat because he had poked fun at old man Noah once when he had taken a drop too much. I remember the aunts telling me that that old drunkard had cursed Ham and his sons for all time."[5]

Irene laughed. But Clare remained quite serious.

"It was more than a joke, I assure you, 'Rene. It was a hard life for a girl of sixteen. Still, I had a roof over my head, and food, and clothes—such as they were. And there were the Scriptures, and talks on morals and thrift and industry and the loving-kindness of the good Lord."

"Have you ever stopped, to think, Clare," Irene demanded, "how much unhappiness and downright cruelty are laid to the loving-kindness of the Lord? And always by His most ardent followers, it seems."

"Have I?" Clare exclaimed. "It, they, made me what I am today. For, of course, I was determined to get away, to be a person and not a charity or a problem, or even a daughter of the indiscreet Ham. Then, too, I wanted things. I knew I wasn't bad-looking and that I could 'pass.' You can't know, 'Rene, how, when I used to go over to the south side, I used almost to hate all of you. You had all the things I wanted and never had had. It made me all the more determined to get them, and others. Do you, can you understand what I felt?"

She looked up with a pointed and appealing effect, and, evidently finding the sympathetic expression on Irene's face sufficient answer, went on. "The aunts were queer. For all their Bibles and praying and ranting about honesty, they didn't want anyone to know that their darling brother had seduced—ruined, they called it—a Negro girl. They could excuse the ruin, but they couldn't forgive the tar-brush. They forbade me to mention Negroes to the neighbours, or even to mention the south side. You may be sure that I didn't. I'll bet they were good and sorry afterwards."

She laughed and the ringing bells in her laugh had a hard metallic sound.

"When the chance to get away came, that omission was of great value to me. When Jack, a schoolboy acquaintance of some people in the neighbourhood, turned up from South America with untold gold, there was no one to tell him that I was coloured, and many to tell him about the severity and the religiousness of Aunt Grace and Aunt Edna. You can guess the rest.

5. A reference to Genesis 9:20–27, where Noah's son Ham is cursed as a punishment for witnessing his father's nakedness and drunkenness; the story was used as a justification for slavery.

After he came, I stopped slipping off to the south side and slipped off to meet him instead. I couldn't manage both. In the end I had no great difficulty in convincing him that it was useless to talk marriage to the aunts. So on the day that I was eighteen, we went off and were married. So that's that. Nothing could have been easier."

"Yes, I do see that for you it was easy enough. By the way! I wonder why they didn't tell father that you were married. He went over to find out about you when you stopped coming over to see us. I'm sure they didn't tell him. Not that you were married."

Clare Kendry's eyes were bright with tears that didn't fall. "Oh, how lovely! To have cared enough about me to do that. The dear sweet man! Well, they couldn't tell him because they didn't know it. I took care of that, for I couldn't be sure that those consciences of theirs wouldn't begin to work on them afterwards and make them let the cat out of the bag. The old things probably thought I was living in sin, wherever I was. And it would be about what they expected."

An amused smile lit the lovely face for the smallest fraction of a second. After a little silence she said soberly: "But I'm sorry if they told your father so. That was something I hadn't counted on."

"I'm not sure that they did," Irene told her. "He didn't say so, anyway."

"He wouldn't, 'Rene dear. Not your father."

"Thanks. I'm sure he wouldn't."

"But you've never answered my question. Tell me, honestly, haven't you ever thought of 'passing'?"

Irene answered promptly: "No. Why should I?" And so disdainful was her voice and manner that Clare's face flashed and her eyes glinted. Irene hastened to add: "You see, Clare, I've everything I want. Except, perhaps, a little more money."

At that Clare laughed, her spark of anger vanished as quickly as it had appeared. "Of course," she declared, "that's what everybody wants, just a little more money, even the people who have it. And I must say I don't blame them. Money's awfully nice to have. In fact, all things considered, I think, 'Rene, that it's even worth the price."

Irene could only shrug her shoulders. Her reason partly agreed, her instinct wholly rebelled. And she could not say why. And though conscious that if she didn't hurry away, she was going to be late to dinner, she still lingered. It was as if the woman sitting on the other side of the table, a girl that she had known, who had done this rather dangerous and, to Irene Redfield, abhorrent thing successfully and had announced herself well satisfied, had for her a fascination, strange and compelling.

Clare Kendry was still leaning back in the tall chair, her sloping shoulders against the carved top. She sat with an air of indifferent assurance, as if arranged for, desired. About her clung that dim suggestion of polite insolence with which a few women are born and which some acquire with the coming of riches or importance.

Clare, it gave Irene a little prick of satisfaction to recall, hadn't got that by passing herself off as white. She herself had always had it.

Just as she'd always had that pale gold hair, which, unsheared still, was drawn loosely back from a broad brow, partly hidden by the small close hat. Her lips, painted a brilliant geranium-red, were sweet and sensitive and a little obstinate. A tempting mouth. The face across the forehead and cheeks was a trifle too wide, but the ivory skin had a peculiar soft lustre. And the eyes were magnificent! dark, sometimes absolutely black, always luminous, and set in long, black lashes. Arresting eyes, slow and mesmeric, and with, for all their warmth, something withdrawn and secret about them.

Ah! Surely! They were Negro eyes! mysterious and concealing. And set in that ivory face under that bright hair, there was about them something exotic.

Yes, Clare Kendry's loveliness was absolute, beyond challenge, thanks to those eyes which her grandmother and later her mother and father had given her.

Into those eyes there came a smile and over Irene the sense of being petted and caressed. She smiled back.

"Maybe," Clare suggested, "you can come Monday, if you're back. Or, if you're not, then Tuesday."

With a small regretful sigh, Irene informed Clare that she was afraid she wouldn't be back by Monday and that she was sure she had dozens of things for Tuesday, and that she was leaving Wednesday. It might be, however, that she could get out of something Tuesday.

"Oh, do try. Do put somebody else off. The others can see you any time, while I—Why, I may never see you again! Think of that, 'Rene! You'll have to come. You'll simply have to! I'll never forgive you if you don't."

At that moment it seemed a dreadful thing to think of never seeing Clare Kendry again. Standing there under the appeal, the caress, of her eyes, Irene had the desire, the hope, that this parting wouldn't be the last.

"I'll try, Clare," she promised gently. "I'll call you—or will you call me?"

"I think, perhaps, I'd better call you. Your father's in the book, I know, and the address is the same. Sixty-four eighteen. Some memory, what? Now remember, I'm going to expect you. You've got to be able to come."

Again that peculiar mellowing smile.

"I'll do my best, Clare."

Irene gathered up her gloves and bag. They stood up. She put out her hand. Clare took and held it.

"It has been nice seeing you again, Clare. How pleased and glad father'll be to hear about you!"

"Until Tuesday, then," Clare Kendry replied. "I'll spend every minute of the time from now on looking forward to seeing you again. Good-bye, 'Rene dear. My love to your father, and this kiss for him."

The sun had gone from overhead, but the streets were still like fiery furnaces. The languid breeze was still hot. And the scurrying people looked even more wilted than before Irene had fled from their contact.

Crossing the avenue in the heat, far from the coolness of the Drayton's roof, away from the seduction of Clare Kendry's smile, she was aware of a sense of irritation with herself because she had been pleased and a little flattered at the other's obvious gladness at their meeting.

With her perspiring progress homeward this irritation grew, and she began to wonder just what had possessed her to make her promise to find time, in the crowded days that remained of her visit, to spend another afternoon with a woman whose life had so definitely and deliberately diverged from hers; and whom, as had been pointed out, she might never see again.

Why in the world had she made such a promise?

As she went up the steps to her father's house, thinking with what interest and amazement he would listen to her story of the afternoon's encounter, it came to her that Clare had omitted to mention her marriage name.

She had referred to her husband as Jack. That was all. Had that, Irene asked herself, been intentional?

Clare had only to pick up the telephone to communicate with her, or to drop her a card, or to jump into a taxi. But she couldn't reach Clare in any way. Nor could anyone else to whom she might speak of their meeting.

"As if I should!"

Her key turned in the lock. She went in. Her father, it seemed, hadn't come in yet.

Irene decided that she wouldn't, after all, say anything to him about Clare Kendry. She had, she told herself, no inclination to speak of a person who held so low an opinion of her loyalty, or her discretion. And certainly she had no desire or intention of making the slightest effort about Tuesday. Nor any other day for that matter.

She was through with Clare Kendry.

Three

On Tuesday morning a dome of grey sky rose over the parched city, but the stifling air was not relieved by the silvery mist that seemed to hold a promise of rain, which did not fall.

To Irene Redfield this soft foreboding fog was another reason for doing nothing about seeing Clare Kendry that afternoon.

But she did see her.

The telephone. For hours it had rung like something possessed. Since nine o'clock she had been hearing its insistent jangle. Awhile she was resolute, saying firmly each time: "Not in, Liza, take the message." And each time the servant returned with the information: "It's the same lady, ma'am: she says she'll call again."

But at noon, her nerves frayed and her conscience smiting her at the reproachful look on Liza's ebony face as she withdrew for another denial, Irene weakened.

"Oh, never mind. I'll answer this time, Liza."

"It's her again."

"Hello. . . . Yes."

"It's Clare, 'Rene. . . . Where *have* you been? . . . Can you be here around four? . . . What? . . . But, 'Rene, you promised! Just for a little while. . . . You can if you want to. . . . I am *so* disappointed. I had counted so on seeing you. . . . Please be nice and come. Only for a minute. I'm sure you can manage it if you try. . . . I won't beg you to stay. . . . Yes. . . . I'm going to expect you . . . It's the Morgan. . . . Oh, yes! The name's Bellew, Mrs. John Bellew. . . . About four, then. . . . I'll be so happy to see you! . . . Goodbye."

"Damn!"

Irene hung up the receiver with an emphatic bang, her thoughts immediately filled with self-reproach. She'd done it again. Allowed Clare Kendry to persuade her into promising to do something for which she had neither time nor any special desire. What was it about Clare's voice that was so appealing, so very seductive?

Clare met her in the hall with a kiss. She said: "You're good to come, 'Rene. But, then, you always were nice to me." And under her potent smile a part of Irene's annoyance with herself fled. She was even a little glad that she had come.

Clare led the way, stepping lightly, towards a room whose door was standing partly open, saying: "There's a surprise. It's a real party. See."

Entering, Irene found herself in a sitting-room, large and high, at whose windows hung startling blue draperies which triumphantly dragged attention from the gloomy chocolate-coloured furniture. And Clare was wearing a thin floating dress of the same shade of blue, which suited her and the rather difficult room to perfection.

For a minute Irene thought the room was empty; but turning her head, she discovered, sunk deep in the cushions of a huge sofa, a woman staring up at her with such intense concentration that her eyelids were drawn as though the strain of that upward glance had paralysed them. At first Irene took her to be a stranger, but in the next instant she said in an unsympathetic, almost harsh voice: "And how are you, Gertrude?"

The woman nodded and forced a smile to her pouting lips. "I'm all right," she replied. "And you're just the same, Irene. Not changed a bit."

"Thank you." Irene responded, as she chose a seat. She was thinking: "Great goodness! Two of them."

For Gertrude too had married a white man, though it couldn't be truthfully said that she was "passing." Her husband—what was his name?—had been in school with her and had been quite well aware, as had his family and most of his friends, that she was a Negro. It hadn't, Irene knew, seemed to matter to him then. Did it now, she wondered? Had Fred—Fred Martin, that was it—had he ever regretted his marriage because of Gertrude's race? Had Gertrude?

Turning to Gertrude, Irene asked: "And Fred, how is he? It's unmentionable years since I've seen him."

"Oh, he's all right," Gertrude answered briefly.

For a full minute no one spoke. Finally out of the oppressive little silence Clare's voice came pleasantly, conversationally: "We'll have tea right away. I know that you can't stay long, 'Rene. And I'm so sorry you won't see Margery. We went up the lake over the week-end to see some of Jack's people, just out of Milwaukee. Margery wanted to stay with the children. It seemed a shame not to let her, especially since it's so hot in town. But I'm expecting Jack any second."

Irene said briefly: "That's nice."

Gertrude remained silent. She was, it was plain, a little ill at ease. And her presence there annoyed Irene, roused in her a defensive and resentful feeling for which she had at the moment no explanation. But it did seem to her odd that the woman that Clare was now should have invited the woman that Gertrude was. Still, of course, Clare couldn't have known. Twelve years since they had met.

Later, when she examined her feeling of annoyance, Irene admitted, a shade reluctantly, that it arose from a feeling of being outnumbered, a sense of aloneness, in her adherence to her own class and kind; not merely in the great thing of marriage, but in the whole pattern of her life as well.

Clare spoke again, this time at length. Her talk was of the change that Chicago presented to her after her long absence in European cities. Yes, she said in reply to some question from Gertrude, she'd been back to America a time or two, but only as far as New York and Philadelphia, and once she had spent a few days in Washington. John Bellew, who, it appeared, was some sort of international banking agent, hadn't particularly wanted her to come with him on this trip, but as soon as she had learned that it would probably take him as far as Chicago, she made up her mind to come anyway.

"I simply had to. And after I once got here, I was determined to see someone I knew and find out what had happened to everybody. I didn't quite see how I was going to manage it, but I meant to. Somehow. I'd just about decided to take a chance and go out to your house, 'Rene, or call up and arrange a meeting, when I ran into you. What luck!"

Irene agreed that it was luck. "It's the first time I've been home for five years, and now I'm about to leave. A week later and I'd have been gone. And how in the world did you find Gertrude?"

"In the book. I remembered about Fred. His father still has the meat market."

"Oh, yes," said Irene, who had only remembered it as Clare had spoken, "on Cottage Grove near—"

Gertrude broke in. "No. It's moved. We're on Maryland Avenue—used to be Jackson—now. Near Sixty-third Street. And the market's Fred's. His name's the same as his father's."

Gertrude, Irene thought, looked as if her husband might be a butcher. There was left of her youthful prettiness, which had been so much admired in their high-school days, no trace. She had grown broad, fat almost, and though there were no lines on her large white face, its very smoothness was somehow prematurely ageing. Her black hair was clipt, and by some unfortunate means all the live curliness had gone from it. Her over-trimmed Georgette *crêpe* dress was too short and showed an appalling amount of leg, stout legs in sleazy stockings of a vivid rose-beige shade. Her plump hands were newly and not too competently manicured—for the occasion, probably. And she wasn't smoking.

Clare said—and Irene fancied that her husky voice held a slight edge—"Before you came, Irene, Gertrude was telling me about her two boys. Twins. Think of it! Isn't it too marvellous for words?"

Irene felt a warmness creeping into her cheeks. Uncanny, the way Clare could divine what one was thinking. She was a little put out, but her manner was entirely easy as she said: "That is nice. I've two boys myself, Gertrude. Not twins, though. It seems that Clare's rather behind, doesn't it?"

Gertrude, however, wasn't sure that Clare hadn't the best of it. "She's got a girl. I wanted a girl. So did Fred."

"Isn't that a bit unusual?" Irene asked. "Most men want sons. Egotism, I suppose."

"Well, Fred didn't."

The tea-things had been placed on a low table at Clare's side. She gave them her attention now, pouring the rich amber fluid from the tall glass pitcher into stately slim glasses, which she handed to her guests, and then offered them lemon or cream and tiny sandwiches or cakes.

After taking up her own glass she informed them: "No, I have no boys and I don't think I'll ever have any. I'm afraid. I nearly died of terror the whole nine months before Margery was born for fear that she might be dark. Thank goodness, she turned out all right. But I'll never risk it again. Never! The strain is simply too—too hellish."

Gertrude Martin nodded in complete comprehension.

This time it was Irene who said nothing.

"You don't have to tell me!" Gertrude said fervently. "I know what it is all right. Maybe you don't think I wasn't scared to death too. Fred said I was silly, and so did his mother. But, of course, they thought it was just a notion I'd gotten into my head and they blamed it on my condition. They don't know like we do, how it might go way back, and turn out dark no matter what colour the father and mother are."

Perspiration stood out on her forehead. Her narrow eyes rolled first in Clare's, then in Irene's direction. As she talked she waved her heavy hands about.

"No," she went on, "no more for me either. Not even a girl. It's awful the way it skips generations and then pops out. Why, he actually said he didn't care what colour it turned out, if I would only stop worrying about it. But, of course, nobody wants a dark child."

Her voice was earnest and she took for granted that her audience was in entire agreement with her.

Irene, whose head had gone up with a quick little jerk, now said in a voice of whose even tones she was proud: "One of my boys is dark."

Gertrude jumped as if she had been shot at. Her eyes goggled. Her mouth flew open. She tried to speak, but could not immediately get the words out. Finally she managed to stammer: "Oh! And your husband, is he—is he—er—dark, too?"

Irene, who was struggling with a flood of feelings, resentment, anger, and contempt, was, however, still able to answer as coolly as if she had not that sense of not belonging to and of despising the company in which she found herself drinking iced tea from tall amber glasses on that hot August afternoon. Her husband, she informed them quietly, couldn't exactly "pass."

At that reply Clare turned on Irene her seductive caressing smile and remarked a little scoffingly: "I do think that coloured people—we—are too silly about some things. After all, the thing's not important to Irene or hundreds of others. Not awfully, even to you, Gertrude. It's only deserters like me who have to be afraid of freaks of the nature. As my inestimable dad used to say, 'Everything must be paid for.' Now, please one of you tell me what ever happened to Claude Jones. You know, the tall, lanky specimen who used to wear that comical little moustache that the girls used to laugh at so. Like a thin streak of soot. The moustache, I mean."

At that Gertrude shrieked with laughter. "Claude Jones!" and launched into the story of how he was no longer a Negro or a Christian but had become a Jew.

"A Jew!" Clare exclaimed.

"Yes, a Jew. A black Jew, he calls himself. He won't eat ham and goes to the synagogue on Saturday. He's got a beard now as well as a moustache. You'd die laughing if you saw him. He's really too funny for words. Fred says he's crazy and I guess he is. Oh, he's a scream all right, a regular scream!" And she shrieked again.

Clare's laugh tinkled out. "It certainly sounds funny enough. Still, it's his own business. If he gets along better by turning—"

At that, Irene, who was still hugging her unhappy don't-care feeling of rightness, broke in, saying bitingly: "It evidently doesn't occur to either you or Gertrude that he might possibly be sincere in changing his religion. Surely everyone doesn't do everything for gain."

Clare Kendry had no need to search for the full meaning of that utterance. She reddened slightly and retorted seriously: "Yes, I admit that might be possible—his being sincere, I mean. It just didn't happen to occur to me, that's all. I'm surprised," and the seriousness changed to mockery, "that you should have expected it to. Or did you really?"

"You don't, I'm sure, imagine that that is a question that I can answer," Irene told her. "Not here and now."

Gertrude's face expressed complete bewilderment. However, seeing that little smiles had come out on the faces of the two other women and not recognizing them for the smiles of mutual reservations which they were, she smiled too.

Clare began to talk, steering carefully away from anything that might lead towards race or other thorny subjects. It was the most brilliant exhibition of conversational weight-lifting that Irene had ever seen. Her words swept over them in charming well-modulated streams. Her laughs tinkled and pealed. Her little stories sparkled.

Irene contributed a bare "Yes" or "No" here and there. Gertrude, a "You don't say!" less frequently.

For a while the illusion of general conversation was nearly perfect. Irene felt her resentment changing gradually to a silent, somewhat grudging admiration.

Clare talked on, her voice, her gestures, colouring all she said of wartime in France, of after-the-wartime in Germany, of the excitement at the time of the general strike in England,[6] of dressmaker's openings in Paris, of the new gaiety of Budapest.

But it couldn't last, this verbal feat. Gertrude shifted in her seat and fell to fidgeting with her fingers. Irene, bored at last by all this repetition of the selfsame things that she had read all too often in papers, magazines, and books, set down her glass and collected her bag and handkerchief. She was smoothing out the tan fingers of her gloves preparatory to putting them on when she heard the sound of the outer door being opened and saw Clare spring up with an expression of relief saying: "How lovely! Here's Jack at exactly the right minute. You can't go now, 'Rene dear."

John Bellew came into the room. The first thing that Irene noticed about him was that he was not the man that she had seen with Clare Kendry on the Drayton roof. This man, Clare's husband, was a tallish person, broadly made. His age she guessed to be somewhere between thirty-five and forty. His hair was dark brown and waving, and he had a soft mouth, somewhat womanish, set in an unhealthy-looking dough-coloured face. His steel-grey opaque eyes were very much alive, moving ceaselessly between thick bluish lids. But there was, Irene decided, nothing unusual about him, unless it was an impression of latent physical power.

"Hello, Nig," was his greeting to Clare.

Gertrude who had started slightly, settled back and looked covertly towards Irene, who had caught her lip between her teeth and sat gazing at husband and wife. It was hard to believe that even Clare Kendry would permit this ridiculing of her race by an outsider, though he chanced to be her husband. So he knew, then, that Clare was a Negro? From her talk the other day Irene had understood that he didn't. But how rude, how positively insulting, for him to address her in that way in the presence of guests!

In Clare's eyes, as she presented her husband, was a queer gleam, a jeer, it might be. Irene couldn't define it.

6. In May 1926 there was a one-week general strike by workers in the British railway, transport, steel, and coal-mining unions.

The mechanical professions that attend an introduction over, she inquired: "Did you hear what Jack called me?"

"Yes," Gertrude answered, laughing with a dutiful eagerness.

Irene didn't speak. Her gaze remained level on Clare's smiling face.

The black eyes fluttered down. "Tell them, dear, why you call me that."

The man chuckled, crinkling up his eyes, not, Irene was compelled to acknowledge, unpleasantly. He explained: "Well, you see, it's like this. When we were first married, she was as white as—as—well as white as a lily. But I declare she's gettin' darker and darker. I tell her if she don't look out, she'll wake up one of these days and find she's turned into a nigger."

He roared with laughter. Clare's ringing bell-like laugh joined his. Gertrude after another uneasy shift in her seat added her shrill one. Irene, who had been sitting with lips tightly compressed, cried out: "That's good!" and gave way to gales of laughter. She laughed and laughed and laughed. Tears ran down her cheeks. Her sides ached. Her throat hurt. She laughed on and on and on, long after the others had subsided. Until, catching sight of Clare's face, the need for a more quiet enjoyment of this priceless joke, and for caution, struck her. At once she stopped.

Clare handed her husband his tea and laid her hand on his arm with an affectionate little gesture. Speaking with confidence as well as with amusement, she said: "My goodness, Jack! What difference would it make if, after all these years, you were to find out that I was one or two per cent coloured?"

Bellew put out his hand in a repudiating fling, definite and final. "Oh, no, Nig," he declared, "nothing like that with me. I know you're no nigger, so it's all right. You can get as black as you please as far as I'm concerned, since I know you're no nigger. I draw the line at that. No niggers in my family. Never have been and never will be."

Irene's lips trembled almost uncontrollably, but she made a desperate effort to fight back her disastrous desire to laugh again, and succeeded. Carefully selecting a cigarette from the lacquered box on the tea-table before her, she turned an oblique look on Clare and encountered her peculiar eyes fixed on her with an expression so dark and deep and unfathomable that she had for a short moment the sensation of gazing into the eyes of some creature utterly strange and apart. A faint sense of danger brushed her, like the breath of a cold fog. Absurd, her reason told her, as she accepted Bellew's proffered light for her cigarette. Another glance at Clare showed her smiling. So, as one always ready to oblige, was Gertrude.

An on-looker, Irene reflected, would have thought it a most congenial tea-party, all smiles and jokes and hilarious laughter. She said humorously: "So you dislike Negroes, Mr. Bellew?" But her amusement was at her thought, rather than her words.

John Bellew gave a short denying laugh. "You got me wrong there, Mrs. Redfield. Nothing like that at all. I don't dislike them, I hate them. And so does Nig, for all she's trying to turn into one. She wouldn't have a nigger maid around her for love nor money. Not that I'd want her to. They give me the creeps. The black scrimy devils."

This wasn't funny. Had Bellew, Irene inquired, ever known any Negroes? The defensive tone of her voice brought another start from the uncomfortable Gertrude, and, for all her appearance of serenity, a quick apprehensive look from Clare.

Bellew answered: "Thank the Lord, no! And never expect to! But I know people who've known them, better than they know their black selves. And I read in the papers about them. Always robbing and killing people. And," he added darkly, "worse."

From Gertrude's direction came a queer little suppressed sound, a snort or a giggle. Irene couldn't tell which. There was a brief silence, during which she feared that her self-control was about to prove too frail a bridge to support her mounting anger and indignation. She had a leaping desire to shout at the man beside her: "And you're sitting here surrounded by three black devils, drinking tea."

The impulse passed, obliterated by her consciousness of the danger in which such rashness would involve Clare, who remarked with a gentle reprovingness: "Jack dear, I'm sure 'Rene doesn't care to hear all about your pet aversions. Nor Gertrude either. Maybe they read the papers too, you know." She smiled on him, and her smile seemed to transform him, to soften and mellow him, as the rays of the sun does a fruit.

"All right, Nig, old girl. I'm sorry," he apologized. Reaching over, he playfully touched his wife's pale hands, then turned back to Irene. "Didn't mean to bore you, Mrs. Redfield. Hope you'll excuse me," he said sheepishly. "Clare tells me you're living in New York. Great city, New York. The city of the future."

In Irene, rage had not retreated, but was held by some dam of caution and allegiance to Clare. So, in the best casual voice she could muster, she agreed with Bellew. Though, she reminded him, it was exactly what Chicagoans were apt to say of their city. And all the while she was speaking, she was thinking how amazing it was that her voice did not tremble, that outwardly she was calm. Only her hands shook slightly. She drew them inward from their rest in her lap and pressed the tips of her fingers together to still them.

Husband's a doctor, I understand. Manhattan, or one of the other boroughs?"

Manhattan, Irene informed him, and explained the need for Brian to be within easy reach of certain hospitals and clinics.

"Interesting life, a doctor's."

"Ye-es. Hard, though. And, in a way, monotonous. Nerve-racking, too."

"Hard on the wife's nerves at least, eh? So many lady patients." He laughed, enjoying, with a boyish heartiness, the hoary joke.

Irene managed a momentary smile, but her voice was sober as she said: "Brian doesn't care for ladies, especially sick ones. I sometimes wish he did. It's South America that attracts him."

"Coming place, South America, if they ever get the niggers out of it. It's run over—"

"Really, Jack!" Clare's voice was on the edge of temper.

"Honestly, Nig, I forgot." To the others he said: "You see how hen-pecked I am." And to Gertrude: "You're still in Chicago, Mrs.—er—Mrs. Martin?"

He was, it was plain, doing his best to be agreeable to these old friends of Clare's. Irene had to concede that under other conditions she might have liked him. A fairly good-looking man of amiable disposition, evidently, and in easy circumstances. Plain and with no nonsense about him.

Gertrude replied that Chicago was good enough for her. She'd never been out of it and didn't think she ever should. Her husband's business was there.

"Of course, of course. Can't jump up and leave a business."

There followed a smooth surface of talk about Chicago, New York, their differences and their recent spectacular changes.

It was, Irene thought, unbelievable and astonishing that four people could sit so unruffled, so ostensibly friendly, while they were in reality seething with anger, mortification, shame. But no, on second thought she was forced to amend her opinion. John Bellew, most certainly, was as undisturbed within as without. So, perhaps, was Gertrude Martin. At least she hadn't the mortification and shame that Clare Kendry must be feeling, or, in such full measure, the rage and rebellion that she, Irene, was repressing.

"More tea, 'Rene," Clare offered.

"Thanks, no. And I must be going. I'm leaving tomorrow, you know, and I've still got packing to do."

She stood up. So did Gertrude, and Clare, and John Bellew.

"How do you like the Drayton, Mrs. Redfield?" the latter asked.

"The Drayton? Oh, very much. Very much indeed," Irene answered, her scornful eyes on Clare's unrevealing face.

"Nice place, all right. Stayed there a time or two myself," the man informed her.

"Yes, it is nice," Irene agreed. "Almost as good as our best New York places." She had withdrawn her look from Clare and was searching in her bag for some non-existent something. Her understanding was rapidly increasing, as was her pity and her contempt. Clare was so daring, so lovely, and so "having."

They gave their hands to Clare with appropriate murmurs. "So good to have seen you." . . . "I do hope I'll see you again soon."

"Good-bye," Clare returned. "It was good of you to come, 'Rene dear. And you too, Gertrude."

"Good-bye, Mr. Bellew." . . . "So glad to have met you." It was Gertrude who had said that. Irene couldn't, she absolutely couldn't bring herself to utter the polite fiction or anything approaching it.

He accompanied them out into the hall, summoned the elevator.

"Good-bye," they said again, stepping in.

Plunging downward they were silent.

They made their way through the lobby without speaking.

But as soon as they had reached the street Gertrude, in the manner of one unable to keep bottled up for another minute that which for the last hour she had had to retain, burst out: "My God! What an awful chance! She must be plumb crazy."

"Yes, it certainly seems risky," Irene admitted.

"Risky! I should say it was. Risky! My God! What a word! And the mess she's liable to get herself into!"

"Still, I imagine she's pretty safe. They don't live here, you know. And there's a child. That's a certain security."

"It's an awful chance, just the same," Gertrude insisted. "I'd never in the world have married Fred without him knowing. You can't tell what will turn up."

"Yes, I do agree that it's safer to tell. But then Bellew wouldn't have married her. And, after all, that's what she wanted."

Gertrude shook her head. "I wouldn't be in her shoes for all the money she's getting out of it, when he finds out. Not with him feeling the way he does. Gee! Wasn't it awful? For a minute I was so mad I could have slapped him."

It had been, Irene acknowledged, a distinctly trying experience, as well as a very unpleasant one. "I was more than a little angry myself."

"And imagine her not telling us about him feeling that way! Anything might have happened. We might have said something."

That, Irene pointed out, was exactly like Clare Kendry. Taking a chance, and not at all considering anyone else's feelings.

Gertrude said: "Maybe she thought we'd think it a good joke. And I guess you did. The way you laughed. My land! I was scared to death he might catch on."

"Well, it was rather a joke," Irene told her, "on him and us and maybe on her."

"All the same, it's an awful chance. I'd hate to be her."

"She seems satisfied enough. She's got what she wanted, and the other day she told me it was worth it."

But about that Gertrude was sceptical. "She'll find out different," was her verdict. "She'll find out different all right."

Rain had begun to fall, a few scattered large drops.

The end-of-the-day crowds were scurrying in the direction of street-cars and elevated roads.

Irene said: "You're going south? I'm sorry. I've got an errand. If you don't mind, I'll just say good-bye here. It has been nice seeing you, Gertrude. Say hello to Fred for me, and to your mother if she remembers me. Good-bye."

She had wanted to be free of the other woman, to be alone; for she was still sore and angry.

What right, she kept demanding of herself, had Clare Kendry to expose her, or even Gertrude Martin, to such humiliation, such downright insult?

And all the while, on the rushing ride out to her father's house, Irene Redfield was trying to understand the look on Clare's face as she had said good-bye. Partly mocking, it had seemed, and partly menacing. And something else for which she could find no name. For an instant a recrudescence of that sensation of fear which she had had while looking into Clare's eyes that afternoon touched her. A slight shiver ran over her.

"It's nothing," she told herself. "Just somebody walking over my grave, as the children say." She tried a tiny laugh and was annoyed to find that it was close to tears.

What a state she had allowed that horrible Bellew to get her into!

And late that night, even, long after the last guest had gone and the old house was quiet, she stood at her window frowning out into the dark rain and puzzling again over that look on Clare's incredibly beautiful face. She couldn't, however, come to any conclusion about its meaning, try as she might. It was unfathomable, utterly beyond any experience or comprehension of hers.

She turned away from the window, at last, with a still deeper frown. Why, after all, worry about Clare Kendry? She was well able to take care of herself, had always been able. And there were, for Irene, other things, more personal and more important to worry about.

Besides, her reason told her, she had only herself to blame for her disagreeable afternoon and its attendant fears and questions. She ought never to have gone.

Four

The next morning, the day of her departure for New York, had brought a letter, which, at first glance, she had instinctively known came from Clare

Kendry, though she couldn't remember ever having had a letter from her before. Ripping it open and looking at the signature, she saw that she had been right in her guess. She wouldn't, she told herself, read it. She hadn't the time. And, besides, she had no wish to be reminded of the afternoon before. As it was, she felt none too fresh for her journey; she had had a wretched night. And all because of Clare's innate lack of consideration for the feelings of others.

But she did read it. After father and friends had waved goodbye, and she was being hurled eastward, she became possessed of an uncontrollable curiosity to see what Clare had said about yesterday. For what, she asked, as she took it out of her bag and opened it, could she, what could anyone, say about a thing like that?

Clare Kendry had said:

> 'Rene dear:
>
> However am I to thank you for your visit? I know you are feeling that under the circumstances I ought not to have asked you to come, or, rather, insisted. But if you could know how glad, how excitingly happy, I was to meet you and how I ached to see more of you (to see everybody and couldn't), you would understand my wanting to see you again, and maybe forgive me a little.
>
> My love to you always and always and to your dear father, and all my poor thanks.
>
> Clare.

And there was a postscript which said:

> It may be, 'Rene dear, it may just be, that, after all, your way may be the wiser and infinitely happier one. I'm not sure just now. At least not so sure as I have been.
>
> C.

But the letter hadn't conciliated Irene. Her indignation was not lessened by Clare's flattering reference to her wiseness. As if, she thought wrathfully, anything could take away the humiliation, or any part of it, of what she had gone through yesterday afternoon for Clare Kendry.

With an unusual methodicalness she tore the offending letter into tiny ragged squares that fluttered down and made a small heap in her black *crêpe de Chine* lap. The destruction completed, she gathered them up, rose, and moved to the train's end. Standing there, she dropped them over the railing and watched them scatter, on tracks, on cinders, on forlorn grass, in rills of dirty water.

And that, she told herself, was that. The chances were one in a million that she would ever again lay eyes on Clare Kendry. If, however, that millionth chance should turn up, she had only to turn away her eyes, to refuse her recognition.

She dropped Clare out of her mind and turned her thoughts to her own affairs. To home, to the boys, to Brian. Brian, who in the morning would be waiting for her in the great clamorous station. She hoped that he had been comfortable and not too lonely without her and the boys. Not so lonely that that old, queer, unhappy restlessness had begun again within him; that craving for some place strange and different, which at the beginning of her marriage she had had to make such strenuous efforts to repress, and which yet faintly alarmed her, though it now sprang up at gradually lessening intervals.

Part Two: Re-encounter

One

Such were Irene Redfield's memories as she sat there in her room, a flood of October sunlight streaming in upon her, holding that second letter of Clare Kendry's.

Laying it aside, she regarded with an astonishment that had in it a mild degree of amusement the violence of the feelings which it stirred in her.

It wasn't the great measure of anger that surprised and slightly amused her. That, she was certain, was justified and reasonable, as was the fact that it could hold, still strong and unabated, across the stretch of two years' time entirely removed from any sight or sound of John Bellew, or of Clare. That even at this remote date the memory of the man's words and manner had power to set her hands to trembling and to send the blood pounding against her temples did not seem to her extraordinary. But that she should retain that dim sense of fear, of panic, was surprising, silly.

That Clare should have written, should, even all things considered, have expressed a desire to see her again, did not so much amaze her. To count as nothing the annoyances, the bitterness, or the suffering of others, that was Clare.

Well—Irene's shoulders went up—one thing was sure: that she needn't, and didn't intend to, lay herself open to any repetition of a humiliation as galling and outrageous as that which, for Clare Kendry's sake, she had borne "that time in Chicago." Once was enough.

If, at the time of choosing, Clare hadn't precisely reckoned the cost, she had, nevertheless, no right to expect others to help make up the reckoning. The trouble with Clare was not only that she wanted to have her cake and eat it too, but that she wanted to nibble at the cakes of other folk as well.

Irene Redfield found it hard to sympathize with this new tenderness, this avowed yearning of Clare's for "my own people."

The letter which she just put out of her hand was, to her taste, a bit too lavish in its wordiness, a shade too unreserved in the manner of its expression. It roused again that old suspicion that Clare was acting, not consciously, perhaps—that is, not too consciously—but, none the less, acting. Nor was Irene inclined to excuse what she termed Clare's downright selfishness.

And mingled with her disbelief and resentment was another feeling, a question. Why hadn't she spoken that day? Why, in the face of Bellew's ignorant hate and aversion, had she concealed her own origin? Why had she allowed him to make his assertions and express his misconceptions undisputed? Why, simply because of Clare Kendry, who had exposed her to such torment, had she failed to take up the defence of the race to which she belonged?

Irene asked these questions, felt them. They were, however, merely rhetorical, as she herself was well aware. She knew their answers, every one, and it was the same for them all. The sardony[7] of it! She couldn't betray Clare, couldn't even run the risk of appearing to defend a people that were being maligned, for fear that that defence might in some infinitesimal degree lead the way to final discovery of her secret. She had to Clare Kendry a duty. She was

7. Apparently an original coinage by Larsen, from the adjective "sardonic."

bound to her by those very ties of race, which, for all her repudiation of them, Clare had been unable to completely sever.

And it wasn't, as Irene knew, that Clare cared at all about the race or what was to become of it. She didn't. Or that she had for any of its members great, or even real, affection, though she professed undying gratitude for the small kindnesses which the Westover family had shown her when she was a child. Irene doubted the genuineness of it, seeing herself only as a means to an end where Clare was concerned. Nor could it be said that she had even the slight artistic or sociological interest in the race that some members of other races displayed. She hadn't. No, Clare Kendry cared nothing for the race. She only belonged to it.

"Not another damned thing!" Irene declared aloud as she drew a fragile stocking over a pale beige-coloured foot.

"Aha! Swearing again, are you, madam? Caught you in the act that time."

Brian Redfield had come into the room in that noiseless way which, in spite of the years of their life together, still had the power to disconcert her. He stood looking down on her with that amused smile of his, which was just the faintest bit supercilious and yet was somehow very becoming to him.

Hastily Irene pulled on the other stocking and slipped her feet into the slippers beside her chair.

"And what brought on this particular outburst of profanity? That is, if an indulgent but perturbed husband may inquire. The mother of sons too! The times, alas, the times!"

"I've had this letter," Irene told him. "And I'm sure that anybody'll admit it's enough to make a saint swear. The nerve of her!"

She passed the letter to him, and in the act made a little mental frown. For, with a nicety of perception, she saw that she was doing it instead of answering his question with words, so that he might be occupied while she hurried through her dressing. For she was late again, and Brian, she well knew, detested that. Why, oh why, couldn't she ever manage to be on time? Brian had been up for ages, had made some calls for all she knew, besides having taken the boys downtown to school. And she wasn't dressed yet; had only begun. Damn Clare! This morning it was her fault.

Brian sat down and bent his head over the letter, puckering his brows slightly in his effort to make out Clare's scrawl.

Irene, who had risen and was standing before the mirror, ran a comb through her black hair, then tossed her head with a light characteristic gesture, in order to disarrange a little the set locks. She touched a powder-puff to her warm olive skin, and then put on her frock with a motion so hasty that it was with some difficulty properly adjusted. At last she was ready, though she didn't immediately say so, but stood, instead, looking with a sort of curious detachment at her husband across the room.

Brian, she was thinking, was extremely good-looking. Not, of course, pretty or effeminate; the slight irregularity of his nose saved him from the prettiness, and the rather marked heaviness of his chin saved him from the effeminacy. But he was, in a pleasant masculine way, rather handsome. And yet, wouldn't he, perhaps, have been merely ordinarily good-looking but for the richness, the beauty of his skin, which was of an exquisitely fine texture and deep copper colour.

He looked up and said: "Clare? That must be the girl you told me about meeting the last time you were out home. The one you went to tea with?"

Irene's answer to that was an inclination of the head.

"I'm ready," she said.

They were going downstairs, Brian deftly, unnecessarily, piloting her round the two short curved steps, just before the centre landing.

"You're not," he asked, "going to see her?"

His words, however, were in reality not a question, but, as Irene was aware, an admonition.

Her front teeth just touched. She spoke through them, and her tones held a thin sarcasm. "Brian, darling, I'm really not such an idiot that I don't realize that if a man calls me a nigger, it's his fault the first time, but mine if he has the opportunity to do it again."

They went into the dining-room. He drew back her chair and she sat down behind the fat-bellied German coffee-pot, which sent out its morning fragrance, mingled with the smell of crisp toast and savoury bacon, in the distance. With his long, nervous fingers he picked up the morning paper from his own chair and sat down.

Zulena, a small mahogany-coloured creature, brought in the grapefruit.

They took up their spoons.

Out of the silence Brian spoke. Blandly. "My dear, you misunderstand me entirely. I simply meant that I hope you're not going to let her pester you. She will, you know, if you give her half a chance and she's anything at all like your description of her. Anyway, they always do. Besides," he corrected, "the man, her husband, didn't call you a nigger. There's a difference, you know."

"No, certainly he didn't. Not actually. He couldn't, not very well, since he didn't know. But he would have. It amounts to the same thing. And I'm sure it was just as unpleasant."

"U-mm, I don't know. But it seems to me," he pointed out, "that you, my dear, had all the advantage. You knew what his opinion of you was, while he—Well, 'twas ever thus. We know, always have. They don't. Not quite. It has, you will admit, its humorous side, and, sometimes, its conveniences."

She poured the coffee.

"I can't see it. I'm going to write Clare. Today, if I can find a minute. It's a thing we might as well settle definitely, and immediately. Curious, isn't it, that knowing, as she does, his unqualified attitude, she still—"

Brian interrupted: "It's always that way. Never known it to fail. Remember Albert Hammond, how he used to be for ever haunting Seventh Avenue, and Lenox Avenue, and the dancing-places, until some 'shine' took a shot at him for casting an eye towards his 'sheba?'[8] They always come back. I've seen it happen time and time again."

"But why?" Irene wanted to know. "Why?"

"If I knew that, I'd know what race is."

"But wouldn't you think that having got the thing, or things, they were after, and at such risk, they'd be satisfied? Or afraid?"

"Yes," Brian agreed, "you certainly would think so. But, the fact remains, they aren't. Not satisfied, I mean. I think they're scared enough most of the time, when they give way to the urge and slip back. Not scared enough to stop them, though. Why, the good God only knows."

Irene leaned forward, speaking, she was aware, with a vehemence absolutely unnecessary, but which she could not control.

8. "'shine' . . . 'sheba'": derogatory slang terms for a Black man and woman, respectively.

"Well, Clare can just count me out. I've no intention of being the link between her and her poorer darker brethren. After that scene in Chicago too! To calmly expect me—" She stopped short, suddenly too wrathful for words.

"Quite right. The only sensible thing to do. Let her miss you. It's an unhealthy business, the whole affair. Always is."

Irene nodded. "More coffee," she offered.

"Thanks, no." He took up his paper again, spreading it open with a little rattling noise.

Zulena came in bringing more toast. Brian took a slice and bit into it with that audible crunching sound that Irene disliked so intensely and turned back to his paper.

She said: "It's funny about 'passing.' We disapprove of it and at the same time condone it. It excites our contempt and yet we rather admire it. We shy away from it with an odd kind of revulsion, but we protect it."

"Instinct of the race to survive and expand."

"Rot! Everything can't be explained by some general biological phrase."

"Absolutely everything can. Look at the so-called whites, who've left bastards all over the known earth. Same thing in them. Instinct of the race to survive and expand."

With that Irene didn't at all agree, but many arguments in the past had taught her the futility of attempting to combat Brian on ground where he was more nearly at home than she. Ignoring his unqualified assertion, she slid away from the subject entirely.

"I wonder," she asked, "if you'll have time to run me down to the printing-office. It's on a Hundred and Sixteenth Street. I've got to see about some handbills and some more tickets for the dance."

"Yes, of course. How's it going? Everything all set?"

"Ye-es. I guess so. The boxes are all sold and nearly all the first batch of tickets. And we expect to take in almost as much again at the door. Then, there's all that cake to sell. It's a terrible lot of work, though."

"I'll bet it is. Uplifting the brother's no easy job. I'm as busy as a cat with fleas, myself." And over his face there came a shadow. "Lord! how I hate sick people, and their stupid, meddling families, and smelly, dirty rooms, and climbing filthy steps in dark hallways."

"Surely," Irene began, fighting back the fear and irritation that she felt, "surely—"

Her husband silenced her, saying sharply: "Let's not talk about it, please." And immediately, in his usual, slightly mocking tone he asked: "Are you ready to go now? I haven't a great deal of time to wait."

He got up. She followed him out into the hall without replying. He picked up his soft brown hat from the small table and stood a moment whirling it round on his long tea-coloured fingers.

Irene, watching him, was thinking: "It isn't fair, it isn't fair." After all these years to still blame her like this. Hadn't his success proved that she'd been right in insisting that he stick to his profession right there in New York? Couldn't he see, even now, that it *had* been best? Not for her, oh no, not for her—she had never really considered herself—but for him and the boys. Was she never to be free of it, that fear which crouched, always, deep down within her, stealing away the sense of security, the feeling of permanence, from the life which she had so admirably arranged for them all, and desired so ardently to have remain as it was? That strange, and to her fantastic, notion of Brian's of going off to Brazil which, though unmentioned, yet lived within him; how it frightened her, and—yes, angered her!

"Well?" he asked lightly.

"I'll just get my things. One minute," she promised and turned upstairs.

Her voice had been even and her step was firm, but in her there was no slackening of the agitation, of the alarms, which Brian's expression of discontent had raised. He had never spoken of his desire since that long-ago time of storm and strain, of hateful and nearly disastrous quarrelling, when she had so firmly opposed him, so sensibly pointed out its utter impossibility and its probable consequences to her and the boys, and had even hinted at a dissolution of their marriage in the event of his persistence in his idea. No, there had been, in all the years that they had lived together since then, no other talk of it, no more than there had been any other quarrelling or any other threats. But because, so she insisted, the bond of flesh and spirit between them was so strong, she knew, had always known, that his dissatisfaction had continued, as had his dislike and disgust for his profession and his country.

A feeling of uneasiness stole upon her at the inconceivable suspicion that she might have been wrong in her estimate of her husband's character. But she squirmed away from it. Impossible! She couldn't have been wrong. Everything proved that she had been right. More than right, if such a thing could be. And all, she assured herself, because she understood him so well, because she had, actually, a special talent for understanding him. It was, as she saw it, the one thing that had been the basis of the success which she had made of a marriage that had threatened to fail. She knew him as well as he knew himself, or better.

Then why worry? The thing, this discontent which had exploded into words, would surely die, flicker out, at last. True, she had in the past often been tempted to believe that it had died, only to become conscious, in some instinctive, subtle way, that she had been merely deceiving herself for a while and that it still lived. But it *would* die. Of that she was certain. She had only to direct and guide her man, to keep him going in the right direction.

She put on her coat and adjusted her hat.

Yes, it would die, as long ago she had made up her mind that it should. But in the meantime, while it was still living and still had the power to flare up and alarm her, it would have to be banked, smothered, and something offered in its stead. She would have to make some plan, some decision, at once. She frowned, for it annoyed her intensely. For, though temporary, it would be important and perhaps disturbing. Irene didn't like changes, particularly changes that affected the smooth routine of her household. Well, it couldn't be helped. Something would have to be done. And immediately.

She took up her purse and drawing on her gloves, ran down the steps and out through the door which Brian held open for her and stepped into the waiting car.

"You know," she said, settling herself into the seat beside him, "I'm awfully glad to get this minute alone with you. It does seem that we're always so busy—I do hate that—but what can we do? I've had something on my mind for ever so long, something that needs talking over and really serious consideration."

The car's engine rumbled as it moved out from the kerb and into the scant traffic of the street under Brian's expert guidance.

She studied his profile.

They turned into Seventh Avenue. Then he said: "Well, let's have it. No time like the present for the settling of weighty matters."

"It's about Junior. I wonder if he isn't going too fast in school? We do forget that he's not eleven yet. Surely it can't be good for him to—well, if he is, I mean. Going too fast, you know. Of course, you know more about these things than I do. You're better able to judge. That is, if you've noticed or thought about it at all."

"I do wish, Irene, you wouldn't be for ever fretting about those kids. They're all right. Perfectly all right. Good, strong, healthy boys, especially Junior. Most especially Junior."

"We-ll, I s'pose you're right. You're expected to know about things like that, and I'm sure you wouldn't make a mistake about your own boy." (Now, why had she said that?) "But that isn't all. I'm terribly afraid he's picked up some queer ideas about things—some things—from the older boys, you know."

Her manner was consciously light. Apparently she was intent on the maze of traffic, but she was still watching Brian's face closely. On it was a peculiar expression. Was it, could it possibly be, a mixture of scorn and distaste?

"Queer ideas?" he repeated. "D'you mean ideas about sex, Irene?"

"Ye-es. Not quite nice ones. Dreadful jokes, and things like that."

"Oh, I see," he threw at her. For a while there was silence between them. After a moment he demanded bluntly: "Well, what of it? If sex isn't a joke, what is it? And what is a joke?"

"As you please, Brian. He's your son, you know." Her voice was clear, level, disapproving.

"Exactly! And you're trying to make a molly-coddle out of him. Well, just let me tell you, I won't have it. And you needn't think I'm going to let you change him to some nice kindergarten kind of a school because he's getting a little necessary education. I won't! He'll stay right where he is. The sooner and the more he learns about sex, the better for him. And most certainly if he learns that it's a grand joke, the greatest in the world. It'll keep him from lots of disappointments later on."

Irene didn't answer.

They reached the printing-shop. She got out, emphatically slamming the car's door behind her. There was a piercing agony of misery in her heart. She hadn't intended to behave like this, but her extreme resentment at his attitude, the sense of having been wilfully misunderstood and reproved, drove her to fury.

Inside the shop, she stilled the trembling of her lips and drove back her rising anger. Her business transacted, she came back to the car in a chastened mood. But against the armour of Brian's stubborn silence she heard herself saying in a calm, metallic voice: "I don't believe I'll go back just now. I've remembered that I've got to do something about getting something decent to wear. I haven't a rag that's fit to be seen. I'll take the bus downtown."

Brian merely doffed his hat in that maddening polite way which so successfully curbed and yet revealed his temper.

"Good-bye," she said bitingly. "Thanks for the lift," and turned towards the avenue.

What, she wondered contritely, was she to do next? She was vexed with herself for having chosen, as it had turned out, so clumsy an opening for what she had intended to suggest: some European school for Junior next year, and Brian to take him over. If she had been able to present her plan, and he had accepted it, as she was sure that he would have done, with other more favourable opening methods, he would have had that to look forward to as a break in the easy monotony that seemed, for some reason she was wholly unable to grasp, so hateful to him.

She was even more vexed at her own explosion of anger. What could have got into her to give way to it in such a moment?

Gradually her mood passed. She drew back from the failure of her first attempt at substitution, not so much discouraged as disappointed and ashamed. It might be, she reflected, that, in addition to her ill-timed loss of temper, she had been too hasty in her eagerness to distract him, had rushed too closely on the heels of his outburst, and had thus aroused his suspicions and his obstinacy. She had but to wait. Another more appropriate time would come, tomorrow, next week, next month. It wasn't now, as it had been once, that she was afraid that he would throw everything aside and rush off to that remote place of his heart's desire. He wouldn't, she knew. He was fond of her, loved her, in his slightly undemonstrative way.

And there were the boys.

It was only that she wanted him to be happy, resenting, however, his inability to be so with things as they were, and never acknowledging that though she did want him to be happy, it was only in her own way and by some plan of hers for him that she truly desired him to be so. Nor did she admit that all other plans, all other ways, she regarded as menaces, more or less indirect, to that security of place and substance which she insisted upon for her sons and in a lesser degree for herself.

Two

Five days had gone by since Clare Kendry's appealing letter. Irene Redfield had not replied to it. Nor had she had any other word from Clare.

She had not carried out her first intention of writing at once because on going back to the letter for Clare's address, she had come upon something which, in the rigour of her determination to maintain unbroken between them the wall that Clare herself had raised, she had forgotten, or not fully noted. It was the fact that Clare had requested her to direct her answer to the post office's general delivery.

That had angered Irene, and increased her disdain and contempt for the other.

Tearing the letter across, she had flung it into the scrap-basket. It wasn't so much Clare's carefulness and her desire for secrecy in their relations—Irene understood the need for that—as that Clare should have doubted her discretion, implied that she might not be cautious in the wording of her reply and the choice of a posting-box. Having always had complete confidence in her own good judgment and tact, Irene couldn't bear to have anyone seem to question them. Certainly not Clare Kendry.

In another, calmer moment she decided that it was, after all, better to answer nothing, to explain nothing, to refuse nothing; to dispose of the matter simply by not writing at all. Clare, of whom it couldn't be said that she was stupid, would not mistake the implication of that silence. She might—and Irene was sure that she would—choose to ignore it and write again, but that didn't matter. The whole thing would be very easy. The basket for all letters, silence for their answers.

Most likely she and Clare would never meet again. Well, she, for one, could endure that. Since childhood their lives had never really touched.

Actually they were strangers. Strangers in their ways and means of living. Strangers in their desires and ambitions. Strangers even in their racial consciousness. Between them the barrier was just as high, just as broad, and just as firm as if in Clare did not run that strain of black blood. In truth, it was higher, broader, and firmer; because for her there were perils, not known, or imagined, by those others who had no such secrets to alarm or endanger them.

The day was getting on toward evening. It was past the middle of October. There had been a week of cold rain, drenching the rotting leaves which had fallen from the poor trees that lined the street on which the Redfields' house was located, and sending a damp air of penetrating chill into the house, with a hint of cold days to come. In Irene's room a low fire was burning. Outside, only a dull grey light was left of the day. Inside, lamps had already been lighted.

From the floor above there was the sound of young voices. Sometimes Junior's serious and positive; again, Ted's deceptively gracious one. Often there was laughter, or the noise of commotion, tussling, or toys being slammed down.

Junior, tall for his age, was almost incredibly like his father in feature and colouring; but his temperament was hers, practical and determined, rather than Brian's. Ted, speculative and withdrawn, was, apparently, less positive in his ideas and desires. About him there was a deceiving air of candour that was, Irene knew, like his father's show of reasonable acquiescence. If, for the time being, and with a charming appearance of artlessness, he submitted to the force of superior strength, or some other immovable condition or circumstance, it was because of his intense dislike of scenes and unpleasant argument. Brian over again.

Gradually Irene's thought slipped away from Junior and Ted, to become wholly absorbed in their father.

The old fear, with strength increased, the fear for the future, had again laid its hand on her. And, try as she might, she could not shake it off. It was as if she had admitted to herself that against that easy surface of her husband's concordance with her wishes, which had, since the war had given him back to her physically unimpaired, covered an increasing inclination to tear himself and his possessions loose from their proper setting, she was helpless.

The chagrin which she had felt at her first failure to subvert this latest manifestation of his discontent had receded, leaving in its wake an uneasy depression. Were all her efforts, all her labours, to make up to him that one loss, all her silent striving to prove to him that her way had been best, all her ministrations to him, all her outward sinking of self, to count for nothing in some unperceived sudden moment? And if so, what, then, would be the consequences to the boys? To her? To Brian himself? Endless searching had brought no answer to these questions. There was only an intense weariness from their shuttle-like procession in her brain.

The noise and commotion from above grew increasingly louder. Irene was about to go to the stairway and request the boys to be quieter in their play when she heard the doorbell ringing.

Now, who was that likely to be? She listened to Zulena's heels, faintly tapping on their way to the door, then to the shifting sound of her feet on the steps, then to her light knock on the bedroom door.

"Yes. Come in," Irene told her.

Zulena stood in the doorway. She said: "Someone to see you, Mrs. Redfield." Her tone was discreetly regretful, as if to convey that she was reluctant to disturb her mistress at that hour, and for a stranger. "A Mrs. Bellew."

Clare!

"Oh dear! Tell her, Zulena," Irene began, "that I can't—No. I'll see her. Please bring her up here."

She heard Zulena pass down the hall, down the stairs, then stood up, smoothing out the tumbled green and ivory draperies of her dress with light stroking pats. At the mirror she dusted a little powder on her nose and brushed out her hair.

She meant to tell Clare Kendry at once, and definitely, that it was of no use, her coming, that she couldn't be responsible, that she'd talked it over with Brian, who had agreed with her that it was wiser, for Clare's own sake, to refrain—

But that was as far as she got in her rehearsal. For Clare had come softly into the room without knocking, and before Irene could greet her, had dropped a kiss on her dark curls.

Looking at the woman before her, Irene Redfield had a sudden inexplicable onrush of affectionate feeling. Reaching out, she grasped Clare's two hands in her own and cried with something like awe in her voice: "Dear God! But aren't you lovely, Clare!"

Clare tossed that aside. Like the furs and small blue hat which she threw on the bed before seating herself slantwise in Irene's favourite chair, with one foot curled under her.

"Didn't you mean to answer my letter, 'Rene?" she asked gravely.

Irene looked away. She had that uncomfortable feeling that one has when one has not been wholly kind or wholly true.

Clare went on: "Every day I went to that nasty little post-office place. I'm sure they were all beginning to think that I'd been carrying on an illicit love-affair and that the man had thrown me over. Every morning the same answer: 'Nothing for you.' I got into an awful fright, thinking that something might have happened to your letter, or to mine. And half the nights I would lie awake looking out at the watery stars—hopeless things, the stars—worrying and wondering. But at last it soaked in, that you hadn't written and didn't intend to. And then—well, as soon as ever I'd seen Jack off for Florida, I came straight here. And now, 'Rene, please tell me quite frankly why you didn't answer my letter."

"Because, you see—" Irene broke off and kept Clare waiting while she lit a cigarette, blew out the match, and dropped it into a tray. She was trying to collect her arguments, for some sixth sense warned her that it was going to be harder than she thought to convince Clare Kendry of the folly of Harlem for her. Finally she proceeded: "I can't help thinking that you ought not to come up here, ought not to run the risk of knowing Negroes."

"You mean you don't want me, 'Rene?"

Irene hadn't supposed that anyone could look so hurt. She said, quite gently, "No, Clare, it's not that. But even you must see that it's terribly foolish, and not just the right thing."

The tinkle of Clare's laugh rang out, while she passed her hands over the bright sweep of her hair. "Oh, 'Rene!" she cried, "you're priceless! And you haven't changed a bit. The right thing!" Leaning forward, she looked curiously into Irene's disapproving brown eyes. "You don't, you really can't mean exactly that! Nobody could. It's simply unbelievable."

Irene was on her feet before she realized that she had risen. "What I really mean," she retorted, "is that it's dangerous and that you ought not to run such silly risks. No one ought to. You least of all."

Her voice was brittle. For into her mind had come a thought, strange and irrelevant, a suspicion, that had surprised and shocked her and driven her to her feet. It was that in spite of her determined selfishness the woman before her was yet capable of heights and depths of feeling that she, Irene Redfield, had never known. Indeed, never cared to know. The thought, the suspicion, was gone as quickly as it had come.

Clare said: "Oh, me!"

Irene touched her arm caressingly, as if in contrition for that flashing thought. "Yes, Clare, you. It's not safe. Not safe at all."

"Safe!"

It seemed to Irene that Clare had snapped her teeth down on the word and then flung it from her. And for another flying second she had that suspicion of Clare's ability for a quality of feeling that was to her strange, and even repugnant. She was aware, too, of a dim premonition of some impending disaster. It was as if Clare Kendry had said to her, for whom safety, security, were all-important: "Safe! Damn being safe!" and meant it.

With a gesture of impatience she sat down. In a voice of cool formality, she said: "Brian and I have talked the whole thing over carefully and decided that it isn't wise. He says it's always a dangerous business, this coming back. He's seen more than one come to grief because of it. And, Clare, considering everything—Mr. Bellew's attitude and all that—don't you think you ought to be as careful as you can?"

Clare's deep voice broke the small silence that had followed Irene's speech. She said, speaking almost plaintively: "I ought to have known. It's Jack. I don't blame you for being angry, though I must say you behaved beautifully that day. But I did think you'd understand, 'Rene. It was that, partly, that has made me want to see other people. It just swooped down and changed everything. If it hadn't been for that, I'd have gone on to the end, never seeing any of you. But that did something to me, and I've been so lonely since! You can't know. Not close to a single soul. Never anyone to really talk to."

Irene pressed out her cigarette. While doing so, she saw again the vision of Clare Kendry staring disdainfully down at the face of her father, and thought that it would be like that that she would look at her husband if he lay dead before her.

Her own resentment was swept aside and her voice held an accent of pity as she exclaimed: "Why, Clare! I didn't know. Forgive me. I feel like seven beasts.[9] It was stupid of me not to realize."

"No. Not at all. You couldn't. Nobody, none of you, could," Clare moaned. The black eyes filled with tears that ran down her cheeks and spilled into her lap, ruining the priceless velvet of her dress. Her long hands were a little uplifted and clasped tightly together. Her effort to speak moderately was obvious, but not successful. "How could you know? How could you? You're free. You're happy. And," with faint derision, "safe."

Irene passed over that touch of derision, for the poignant rebellion of the other's words had brought the tears to her own eyes, though she didn't allow

9. Biblical reference to the beast with seven heads, described first in Revelation 13:1–10.

them to fall. The truth was that she knew weeping did not become her. Few women, she imagined, wept as attractively as Clare. "I'm beginning to believe," she murmured, "that no one is ever completely happy, or free, or safe."

"Well, then, what does it matter? One risk more or less, if we're not safe anyway, if even you're not, it can't make all the difference in the world. It can't to me. Besides, I'm used to risks. And this isn't such a big one as you're trying to make it."

"Oh, but it is. And it can make all the difference in the world. There's your little girl, Clare. Think of the consequences to her."

Clare's face took on a startled look, as though she were totally unprepared for this new weapon with which Irene had assailed her. Seconds passed, during which she sat with stricken eyes and compressed lips. "I think," she said at last, "that being a mother is the cruellest thing in the world." Her clasped hands swayed forward and back again, and her scarlet mouth trembled irrepressibly.

"Yes," Irene softly agreed. For a moment she was unable to say more, so accurately had Clare put into words that which, not so definitely defined, was so often in her own heart of late. At the same time she was conscious that here, to her hand, was a reason which could not be lightly brushed aside. "Yes," she repeated, "and the most responsible, Clare. We mothers are all responsible for the security and happiness of our children. Think what it would mean to your Margery if Mr. Bellew should find out. You'd probably lose her. And even if you didn't, nothing that concerned her would ever be the same again. He'd never forget that she had Negro blood. And if she should learn—Well, I believe that after twelve it is too late to learn a thing like that. She'd never forgive you. You may be used to risks, but this is one you mustn't take, Clare. It's a selfish whim, an unnecessary and—

"Yes, Zulena, what is it?" she inquired, a trifle tartly, of the servant who had silently materialized in the doorway.

"The telephone's for you, Mrs. Redfield. It's Mr. Wentworth."

"All right. Thank you. I'll take it here." And, with a muttered apology to Clare, she took up the instrument.

"Hello. . . . Yes, Hugh. . . . Oh, quite. . . . And you? . . . I'm sorry, every single thing's gone. . . . Oh, too bad. . . . Ye-es, I s'pose you could. Not very pleasant, though. . . . Yes, of course, in a pinch everything goes. . . . Wait! I've got it! I'll change mine with whoever's next to you, and you can have that. . . . No. . . . I mean it. . . . I'll be so busy I shan't know whether I'm sitting or standing. . . . As long as Brian has a place to drop down now and then. . . . Not a single soul. . . . No, don't. . . . That's nice. . . . My love to Bianca. . . . I'll see to it right away and call you back. . . . Good-bye."

She hung up and turned back to Clare, a little frown on her softly chiselled features. "It's the N. W. L. dance," she explained, "the Negro Welfare League,[1] you know. I'm on the ticket committee, or, rather, I *am* the committee. Thank heaven it comes off tomorrow night and doesn't happen again for a year. I'm about crazy, and now I've got to persuade somebody to change boxes with me."

"That wasn't," Clare asked, "Hugh Wentworth? Not *the* Hugh Wentworth?"

1. A fictional organization, the name of which is reminiscent of both the National Association for the Advancement of Colored People and the National Urban League.

Irene inclined her head. On her face was a tiny triumphant smile. "Yes, *the* Hugh Wentworth. D'you know him?"

"No. How should I? But I do know about him. And I've read a book or two of his."

"Awfully good, aren't they?"

"U-umm, I s'pose so. Sort of contemptuous, I thought. As if he more or less despised everything and everybody."

"I shouldn't be a bit surprised if he did. Still, he's about earned the right to. Lived on the edges of nowhere in at least three continents. Been through every danger in all kinds of savage places. It's no wonder he thinks the rest of us are a lazy self-pampering lot. Hugh's a dear, though, generous as one of the twelve disciples; give you the shirt off his back. Bianca—that's his wife—is nice too."

"And he's coming up here to your dance?"

Irene asked why not.

"It seems rather curious, a man like that, going to a Negro dance."

This, Irene told her, was the year 1927 in the city of New York, and hundreds of white people of Hugh Wentworth's type came to affairs in Harlem, more all the time. So many that Brian had said: "Pretty soon the coloured people won't be allowed in at all, or will have to sit in Jim Crowed sections."[2]

"What do they come for?"

"Same reason you're here, to see Negroes."

"But why?"

"Various motives," Irene explained. "A few purely and frankly to enjoy themselves. Others to get material to turn into shekels.[3] More, to gaze on these great and near great while they gaze on the Negroes."

Clare clapped her hand. "'Rene, suppose I come too! It sounds terribly interesting and amusing. And I don't see why I shouldn't."

Irene, who was regarding her through narrowed eyelids, had the same thought that she had had two years ago on the roof of the Drayton, that Clare Kendry was just a shade too good-looking. Her tone was on the edge of irony as she said: "You mean because so many other white people go?"

A pale rose-colour came into Clare's ivory cheeks. She lifted a hand in protest. "Don't be silly! Certainly not! I mean that in a crowd of that kind I shouldn't be noticed."

On the contrary, was Irene's opinion. It might be even doubly dangerous. Some friend or acquaintance of John Bellew or herself might see and recognize her.

At that, Clare laughed for a long time, little musical trills following one another in sequence after sequence. It was as if the thought of any friend of John Bellew's going to a Negro dance was to her the most amusing thing in the world.

"I don't think," she said, when she had done laughing, "we need worry about that."

Irene, however, wasn't so sure. But all her efforts to dissuade Clare were useless. To her, "You never can tell whom you're likely to meet there," Clare's rejoinder was: "I'll take my chance on getting by."

"Besides, you won't know a soul and I shall be too busy to look after you. You'll be bored stiff."

2. Segregated sections.

3. Slang for coins; cash (from Hebrew).

"I won't, I won't. If nobody asks me to dance, not even Dr. Redfield, I'll just sit and gaze on the great and the near great, too. Do, 'Rene, be polite and invite me."

Irene turned away from the caress of Clare's smile, saying promptly and positively: "I will not."

"I mean to go anyway," Clare retorted, and her voice was no less positive than Irene's.

"Oh, no. You couldn't possibly go there alone. It's a public thing. All sorts of people go, anybody who can pay a dollar, even ladies of easy virtue looking for trade. If you were to go there alone, you might be mistaken for one of them, and that wouldn't be too pleasant."

Clare laughed again. "Thanks. I never have been. It might be amusing. I'm warning you, 'Rene, that if you're not going to be nice and take me, I'll still be among those present. I suppose, my dollar's as good as anyone's."

"Oh, the dollar! Don't be a fool, Clare. I don't care where you go, or what you do. All I'm concerned with is the unpleasantness and possible danger which your going might incur, because of your situation. To put it frankly, I shouldn't like to be mixed up in any row of the kind." She had risen again as she spoke and was standing at the window lifting and spreading the small yellow chrysanthemums in the grey stone jar on the sill. Her hands shook slightly, for she was in a near rage of impatience and exasperation.

Clare's face looked strange, as if she wanted to cry again. One of her satin-covered feet swung restlessly back and forth. She said vehemently, violently almost: "Damn Jack! He keeps me out of everything. Everything I want. I could kill him! I expect I shall, some day."

"I wouldn't," Irene advised her, "you see, there's still capital punishment, in this state at least. And really, Clare, after everything's said, I can't see that you've a right to put all the blame on him. You've got to admit that there's his side to the thing. You didn't tell him you were coloured, so he's got no way of knowing about this hankering of yours after Negroes, or that it galls you to fury to hear them called niggers and black devils. As far as I can see, you'll just have to endure some things and give up others. As we've said before, everything must be paid for. Do, please, be reasonable."

But Clare, it was plain, had shut away reason as well as caution. She shook her head. "I can't, I can't," she said. "I would if I could, but I can't. You don't know, you can't realize how I want to see Negroes, to be with them again, to talk with them, to hear them laugh."

And in the look she gave Irene, there was something groping, and hopeless, and yet so absolutely determined that it was like an image of the futile searching and the firm resolution in Irene's own soul, and increased the feeling of doubt and compunction that had been growing within her about Clare Kendry.

She gave in.

"Oh, come if you want to. I s'pose you're right. Once can't do such a terrible lot of harm."

Pushing aside Clare's extravagant thanks, for immediately she was sorry that she had consented, she said briskly: "Should you like to come up and see my boys?"

"I'd love to."

They went up, Irene thinking that Brian would consider that she'd behaved like a spineless fool. And he would be right. She certainly had.

Clare was smiling. She stood in the doorway of the boys' playroom, her shadowy eyes looking down on Junior and Ted, who had sprung apart from their tusselling. Junior's face had a funny little look of resentment. Ted's was blank.

Clare said: "Please don't be cross. Of course, I know I've gone and spoiled everything. But maybe, if I promise not to get too much in the way, you'll let me come in, just the same."

"Sure, come in if you want to," Ted told her. "We can't stop you, you know." He smiled and made her a little bow and then turned away to a shelf that held his favourite books. Taking one down, he settled himself in a chair and began to read.

Junior said nothing, did nothing, merely stood there waiting.

"Get up, Ted! That's rude. This is Theodore, Mrs. Bellew. Please excuse his bad manners. He does know better. And this is Brian junior. Mrs. Bellew is an old friend of mother's. We used to play together when we were little girls."

Clare had gone and Brian had telephoned that he'd been detained and would have his dinner downtown. Irene was a little glad for that. She was going out later herself, and that meant she wouldn't, probably, see Brian until morning and so could put off for a few more hours speaking of Clare and the N. W. L. dance.

She was angry with herself and with Clare. But more with herself, for having permitted Clare to tease her into doing something that Brian had, all but expressly, asked her not to do. She didn't want him ruffled, not just then, not while he was possessed of that unreasonable restless feeling.

She was annoyed, too, because she was aware that she had consented to something which, if it went beyond the dance, would involve her in numerous petty inconveniences and evasions. And not only at home with Brian, but outside with friends and acquaintances. The disagreeable possibilities in connection with Clare Kendry's coming among them loomed before her in endless irritating array.

Clare, it seemed, still retained her ability to secure the thing that she wanted in the face of any opposition, and in utter disregard of the convenience and desire of others. About her there was some quality, hard and persistent, with the strength and endurance of rock, that would not be beaten or ignored. She couldn't, Irene thought, have had an entirely serene life. Not with that dark secret for ever crouching in the background of her consciousness. And yet she hadn't the air of a woman whose life had been touched by uncertainty or suffering. Pain, fear, and grief were things that left their mark on people. Even love, that exquisite torturing emotion, left its subtle traces on the countenance.

But Clare—she had remained almost what she had always been, an attractive, somewhat lonely child—selfish, wilful, and disturbing.

Three

The things which Irene Redfield remembered afterward about the Negro Welfare League dance seemed, to her, unimportant and unrelated.

She remembered the not quite derisive smile with which Brian had cloaked his vexation when she informed him—oh, so apologetically—that she had promised to take Clare, and related the conversation of her visit.

She remembered her own little choked exclamation of admiration, when, on coming downstairs a few minutes later than she had intended, she had rushed into the living-room where Brian was waiting and had found Clare there too. Clare, exquisite, golden, fragrant, flaunting, in a stately gown of shining black taffeta, whose long, full skirt lay in graceful folds about her slim golden feet; her glistening hair drawn smoothly back into a small twist at the nape of her neck; her eyes sparkling like dark jewels. Irene, with her new rose-coloured chiffon frock ending at the knees, and her cropped curls, felt dowdy and commonplace. She regretted that she hadn't counselled Clare to wear something ordinary and inconspicuous. What on earth would Brian think of deliberate courting of attention? But if Clare Kendry's appearance had in it anything that was, to Brian Redfield, annoying or displeasing, the fact was not discernible to his wife as, with an uneasy feeling of guilt, she stood there looking into his face while Clare explained that she and he had made their own introductions, accompanying her words with a little deferential smile for Brian, and receiving in return one of his amused, slightly mocking smiles.

She remembered Clare's saying, as they sped northward: "You know, I feel exactly as I used to on the Sunday we went to the Christmas-tree celebration. I knew there was to be a surprise for me and couldn't quite guess what it was to be. I am *so* excited. You can't possibly imagine! It's marvellous to be really on the way! I can hardly believe it!"

At her words and tone a chilly wave of scorn had crept through Irene. All those superlatives! She said, taking care to speak indifferently: "Well, maybe in some ways you will be surprised, more, probably, than you anticipate."

Brian, at the wheel, had thrown back: "And then again, she won't be so very surprised after all, for it'll no doubt be about what she expects. Like the Christmas-tree."

She remembered rushing around here and there, consulting with this person and that one, and now and then snatching a part of a dance with some man whose dancing she particularly liked.

She remembered catching glimpses of Clare in the whirling crowd, dancing, sometimes with a white man, more often with a Negro, frequently with Brian. Irene was glad that he was being nice to Clare, and glad that Clare was having the opportunity to discover that some coloured men were superior to some white men.

She remembered a conversation she had with Hugh Wentworth in a free half-hour when she had dropped into a chair in an emptied box and let her gaze wander over the bright crowd below.

Young men, old men, white men, black men; youthful women, older women, pink women, golden women; fat men, thin men, tall men, short men; stout women, slim women, stately women, small women moved by. An old nursery rhyme popped into her head. She turned to Wentworth, who had just taken a seat beside her, and recited it:

"Rich man, poor man,
Beggar man, thief,
Doctor, lawyer,
Indian chief."

"Yes," Wentworth said, "that's it. Everybody seems to be here and a few more. But what I'm trying to find out is the name, status, and race of the blonde beauty out of the fairy-tale. She's dancing with Ralph Hazelton at the moment. Nice study in contrasts, that."

It was. Clare fair and golden, like a sunlit day. Hazleton dark, with gleaming eyes, like a moonlit night.

"She's a girl I used to know a long time ago in Chicago. And she wanted especially to meet you."

"'S awfully good of her, I'm sure. And now, alas! the usual thing's happened. All these others, these—er—'gentlemen of colour' have driven a mere Nordic from her mind."

"Stuff!"

"'S a fact, and what happens to all the ladies of my superior race who're lured up here. Look at Bianca. Have I laid eyes on her tonight except in spots, here and there, being twirled about by some Ethiopian? I have not."

"But, Hugh, you've got to admit that the average coloured man is a better dancer than the average white man—that is, if the celebrities and 'butter and egg' men[4] who find their way up here are fair specimens of white Terpsichorean art."[5]

"Not having tripped the light fantastic with any of the males, I'm not in a position to argue the point. But I don't think it's merely that. 'S something else, some other attraction. They're always raving about the good looks of some Negro, preferably an unusually dark one. Take Hazelton there, for example. Dozens of women have declared him to be fascinatingly handsome. How about you, Irene? Do you think he's—er—ravishingly beautiful?"

"I do not! And I don't think the others do either. Not honestly, I mean. I think that what they feel is—well, a kind of emotional excitement. You know, the sort of thing you feel in the presence of something strange, and even, perhaps, a bit repugnant to you; something so different that it's really at the opposite end of the pole from all your accustomed notions of beauty."

"Damned if I don't think you're halfway right!"

"I'm sure I am. Completely. (Except, of course, when it's just patronizing kindness on their part.) And I know coloured girls who've experienced the same thing—the other way round, naturally."

"And the men? You don't subscribe to the general opinion about their reason for coming up here. Purely predatory. Or, do you?"

"N-no. More curious, I should say."

Wentworth, whose eyes were a clouded amber colour, had given her a long, searching look that was really a stare. He said: "All this is awfully interestin', Irene. We've got to have a long talk about it some time soon. There's your friend from Chicago, first time up here and all that. A case in point."

Irene's smile had only just lifted the corners of her painted lips. A match blazed in Wentworth's broad hands as he lighted her cigarette and his own, and flickered out before he asked: "Or isn't she?"

Her smile changed to a laugh. "Oh, Hugh! You're so clever. You usually know everything. Even how to tell the sheep from the goats. What do you think? Is she?"

He blew a long contemplative wreath of smoke. "Damned if I know! I'll be as sure as anything that I've learned the trick. And then in the next minute I'll find I couldn't pick some of 'em if my life depended on it."

"Well, don't let that worry you. Nobody can. Not by looking."

4. Slang for a big spender; also a 1926 jazz song ("Big Butter and Egg Man") written by Percy Venable and recorded by Louis Armstrong.

5. That is, the dancing ability of whites.

"Not by looking, eh? Meaning?"

"I'm afraid I can't explain. Not clearly. There are ways. But they're not definite or tangible."

"Feeling of kinship, or something like that?"

"Good heavens, no! Nobody has that, except for their in-laws."

"Right again! But go on about the sheep and the goats."

"Well, take my own experience with Dorothy Thompkins. I'd met her four or five times, in groups and crowds of people, before I knew she wasn't a Negro. One day I went to an awful tea, terribly dicty.[6] Dorothy was there. We got talking. In less than five minutes, I knew she was 'fay.'[7] Not from anything she did or said or anything in her appearance. Just—just something. A thing that couldn't be registered."

"Yes, I understand what you mean. Yet lots of people 'pass' all the time."

"Not on our side, Hugh. It's easy for a Negro to 'pass' for white. But I don't think it would be so simple for a white person to 'pass' for coloured."

"Never thought of that."

"No, you wouldn't. Why should you?"

He regarded her critically through mists of smoke. "Slippin' me,[8] Irene?"

She said soberly: "Not you, Hugh. I'm too fond of you. And you're too sincere."

And she remembered that towards the end of the dance Brian had come to her and said: "I'll drop you first and then run Clare down." And that he had been doubtful of her discretion when she had explained to him that he wouldn't have to bother because she had asked Bianca Wentworth to take her down with them. Did she, he had asked, think it had been wise to tell them about Clare?

"I told them nothing," she said sharply, for she was unbearably tired, "except that she was at the Walsingham. It's on their way. And, really, I haven't thought anything about the wisdom of it, but now that I do, I'd say it's much better for them to take her than you."

"As you please. She's your friend, you know," he had answered, with a disclaiming shrug of his shoulders.

Except for these few unconnected things the dance faded to a blurred memory, its outlines mingling with those of other dances of its kind that she had attended in the past and would attend in the future.

Four

But undistinctive as the dance had seemed, it was, nevertheless, important. For it marked the beginning of a new factor in Irene Redfield's life, something that left its trace on all the future years of her existence. It was the beginning of a new friendship with Clare Kendry.

She came to them frequently after that. Always with a touching gladness that welled up and overflowed on all the Redfield household. Yet Irene could never be sure whether her comings were a joy or a vexation.

Certainly she was no trouble. She had not to be entertained, or even noticed—if anyone could ever avoid noticing Clare. If Irene happened to be out or occupied, Clare could very happily amuse herself with Ted and Junior, who had conceived for her an admiration that verged on adoration, especially

6. Snobbish.
7. Derivative of "ofay," disparaging African American slang for a white person.
8. That is, trying to trick or fool me.

Ted. Or, lacking the boys, she would descend to the kitchen and, with—to Irene—an exasperating childlike lack of perception, spend her visit in talk and merriment with Zulena and Sadie.

Irene, while secretly resenting these visits to the playroom and kitchen, for some obscure reason which she shied away from putting into words, never requested that Clare make an end of them, or hinted that she wouldn't have spoiled her own Margery so outrageously, nor been so friendly with white servants.

Brian looked on these things with the same tolerant amusement that marked his entire attitude toward Clare. Never since his faintly derisive surprise at Irene's information that she was to go with them the night of the dance, had he shown any disapproval of Clare's presence. On the other hand, it couldn't be said that her presence seemed to please him. It didn't annoy or disturb him, so far as Irene could judge. That was all.

Didn't he, she once asked him, think Clare was extraordinarily beautiful?

"No," he had answered. "That is, not particularly."

"Brian, you're fooling!"

"No, honestly. Maybe I'm fussy. I s'pose she'd be an unusually good-looking white woman. I like my ladies darker. Beside an A-number-one sheba, she simply hasn't got 'em."

Clare went, sometimes with Irene and Brian, to parties and dances, and on a few occasions when Irene hadn't been able or inclined to go out, she had gone alone with Brian to some bridge party or benefit dance.

Once in a while she came formally to dine with them. She wasn't, however, in spite of her poise and air of worldliness, the ideal dinner-party guest. Beyond the aesthetic pleasure one got from watching her, she contributed little, sitting for the most part silent, an odd dreaming look in her hypnotic eyes. Though she could for some purpose of her own—the desire to be included in some party being made up to go cabareting, or an invitation to a dance or a tea—talk fluently and entertainingly.

She was generally liked. She was so friendly and responsive, and so ready to press the sweet food of flattery on all. Nor did she object to appearing a bit pathetic and ill-used, so that people could feel sorry for her. And, no matter how often she came among them, she still remained someone apart, a little mysterious and strange, someone to wonder about and to admire and to pity.

Her visits were undecided and uncertain, being, as they were, dependent on the presence or absence of John Bellew in the city. But she did, once in a while, manage to steal uptown for an afternoon even when he was not away. As time went on without any apparent danger of discovery, even Irene ceased to be perturbed about the possibility of Clare's husband's stumbling on her racial identity.

The daughter, Margery, had been left in Switzerland in school, for Clare and Bellew would be going back in the early spring. In March, Clare thought. "And how I do hate to think of it!" she would say, always with a suggestion of leashed rebellion; "but I can't see how I'm going to get out of it. Jack won't hear of my staying behind. If I could have just a couple of months more in New York, alone I mean, I'd be the happiest thing in the world."

"I imagine you'll be happy enough, once you get away," Irene told her one day when she was bewailing her approaching departure. "Remember, there's Margery. Think how glad you'll be to see her after all this time."

"Children aren't everything," was Clare Kendry's answer to that. "There are other things in the world, though I admit some people don't seem to suspect it." And she laughed, more, it seemed, at some secret joke of her own than at her words.

Irene replied: "You know you don't mean that, Clare. You're only trying to tease me. I know very well that I take being a mother rather seriously. I *am* wrapped up in my boys and the running of my house. I can't help it. And, really, I don't think it's anything to laugh at." And though she was aware of the slight primness in her words and attitude, she had neither power nor wish to efface it.

Clare, suddenly very sober and sweet, said: "You're right. It's no laughing matter. It's shameful of me to tease you, 'Rene. You are so good." And she reached out and gave Irene's hand an affectionate little squeeze. "Don't think," she added, "whatever happens, that I'll ever forget how good you've been to me."

"Nonsense!"

"Oh, but you have, you have. It's just that I haven't any proper morals or sense of duty, as you have, that makes me act as I do."

"Now you are talking nonsense."

"But it's true, 'Rene. Can't you realize that I'm not like you a bit? Why, to get the things I want badly enough, I'd do anything, hurt anybody, throw anything away. Really, 'Rene, I'm not safe." Her voice as well as the look on her face had a beseeching earnestness that made Irene vaguely uncomfortable.

She said: "I don't believe it. In the first place what you're saying is so utterly, so wickedly wrong. And as for your giving up things—" She stopped, at a loss for an acceptable term to express her opinion of Clare's "having" nature.

But Clare Kendry had begun to cry, audibly, with no effort at restraint, and for no reason that Irene could discover.

Part Three: Finale

One

The year was getting on towards its end. October, November had gone. December had come and brought with it a little snow and then a freeze and after that a thaw and some soft pleasant days that had in them a feeling of spring.

It wasn't, this mild weather, a bit Christmasy, Irene Redfield was thinking, as she turned out of Seventh Avenue into her own street. She didn't like it to be warm and springy when it should have been cold and crisp, or grey and cloudy as if snow was about to fall. The weather, like people, ought to enter into the spirit of the season. Here the holidays were almost upon them, and the streets through which she had come were streaked with rills of muddy water and the sun shone so warmly that children had taken off their hats and scarfs. It was all as soft, as like April, as possible. The kind of weather for Easter. Certainly not for Christmas.

Though, she admitted, reluctantly, she herself didn't feel the proper Christmas spirit this year, either. But that couldn't be helped, it seemed, any more than the weather. She was weary and depressed. And for all her trying, she couldn't be free off that dull, indefinite misery which with increasing tenaciousness had laid hold of her. The morning's aimless wandering through the teeming Harlem streets, long after she had ordered the flowers which had been her excuse for setting out, was but another effort to tear herself loose from it.

She went up the cream stone steps, into the house, and down to the kitchen. There were to be people in to tea. But that, she found, after a few words with Sadie and Zulena, need give her no concern. She was thankful. She didn't want to be bothered. She went upstairs and took off her things and got into bed.

She thought: "Bother those people coming to tea!"

She thought: "If I could only be sure that at bottom it's just Brazil."

She thought: "Whatever it is, if I only knew what it was, I could manage it."

Brian again. Unhappy, restless, withdrawn. And she, who had prided herself on knowing his moods, their causes and their remedies, had found it first unthinkable, and then intolerable, that this, so like and yet so unlike those other spasmodic restlessnesses of his, should be to her incomprehensible and elusive.

He was restless and he was not restless. He was discontented, yet there were times when she felt he was possessed of some intense secret satisfaction, like a cat who had stolen the cream. He was irritable with the boys, especially Junior, for Ted, who seemed to have an uncanny knowledge of his father's periods of off moods, kept out of his way when possible. They got on his nerves, drove him to violent outbursts of temper, very different from his usual gently sarcastic remarks that constituted his idea of discipline for them. On the other hand, with her he was more than customarily considerate and abstemious. And it had been weeks since she had felt the keen edge of his irony.

He was like a man marking time, waiting. But what was he waiting for? It was extraordinary that, after all these years of accurate perception, she now lacked the talent to discover what that appearance of waiting meant. It was the knowledge that, for all her watching, all her patient study, the reason for his humour still eluded her which filled her with foreboding dread. That guarded reserve of his seemed to her unjust, inconsiderate, and alarming. It was as if he had stepped out beyond her reach into some section, strange and walled, where she could not get at him.

She closed her eyes, thinking what a blessing it would be if she could get a little sleep before the boys came in from school. She couldn't, of course, though she was so tired, having had, of late, so many sleepless nights. Nights filled with questionings and premonitions.

But she did sleep—several hours.

She wakened to find Brian standing at her bedside looking down at her, an unfathomable expression in his eyes.

She said: "I must have dropped off to sleep," and watched a slender ghost of his old amused smile pass over his face.

"It's getting on to four," he told her, meaning, she knew, that she was going to be late again.

She fought back the quick answer that rose to her lips and said instead: "I'm getting right up. It was good of you to think to call me." She sat up.

He bowed. "Always the attentive husband, you see."

"Yes indeed. Thank goodness, everything's ready."

"Except you. Oh, and Clare's downstairs."

"Clare! What a nuisance! I didn't ask her. Purposely."

"I see. Might a mere man ask why? Or is the reason so subtly feminine that it wouldn't be understood by him?"

A little of his smile had come back. Irene, who was beginning to shake off some of her depression under his familiar banter, said, almost gaily: "Not at all. It just happens that this party happens to be for Hugh, and that Hugh happens not to care a great deal for Clare; therefore I, who happen to be giving the party, didn't happen to ask her. Nothing could be simpler. Could it?"

"Nothing. It's so simple that I can easily see beyond your simple explanation and surmise that Clare, probably, just never happened to pay Hugh the admiring attention that he happens to consider no more than his just due. Simplest thing in the world."

Irene exclaimed in amazement: "Why, I thought you liked Hugh! You don't, you can't, believe anything so idiotic!"

"Well, Hugh does think he's God, you know."

"That," Irene declared, getting out of bed, "is absolutely not true. He thinks ever so much better of himself than that, as you, who know and have read him, ought to be able to guess. If you remember what a low opinion he has of God, you won't make such a silly mistake."

She went into the closet for her things and, coming back, hung her frock over the back of a chair and placed her shoes on the floor beside it. Then she sat down before her dressing-table.

Brian didn't speak. He continued to stand beside the bed, seeming to look at nothing in particular. Certainly not at her. True, his gaze was on her, but in it there was some quality that made her feel that at that moment she was no more to him than a pane of glass through which he stared. At what? She didn't know, couldn't guess. And this made her uncomfortable. Piqued her.

She said: "It just happens that Hugh prefers intelligent women."

Plainly he was startled. "D'you mean that you think Clare is stupid?" he asked, regarding her with lifted eyebrows, which emphasized the disbelief of his voice.

She wiped the cold cream from her face, before she said: "No, I don't. She isn't stupid. She's intelligent enough in a purely feminine way. Eighteenth-century France would have been a marvellous setting for her, or the old South if she hadn't made the mistake of being born a Negro."

"I see. Intelligent enough to wear a tight bodice and keep bowing swains whispering compliments and retrieving dropped fans. Rather a pretty picture. I take it, though, as slightly feline in its implication."

"Well, then, all I can say is that you take it wrongly. Nobody admires Clare more than I do, for the kind of intelligence she has, as well as for her decorative qualities. But she's not—She isn't—She hasn't—Oh, I can't explain it. Take Bianca, for example, or, to keep to the race, Felise Freeland. Looks *and* brains. Real brains that can hold their own with anybody. Clare has got brains of a sort, the kind that are useful too. Acquisitive, you know. But she'd bore a man like Hugh to suicide. Still, I never thought that even Clare would come to a private party to which she hadn't been asked. But, it's like her."

For a minute there was silence. She completed the bright red arch of her full lips. Brian moved towards the door. His hand was on the knob. He said: "I'm sorry, Irene. It's my fault entirely. She seemed so hurt at being left out that I told her I was sure you'd forgotten and to just come along."

Irene cried out: "But, Brian, I—" and stopped, amazed at the fierce anger that had blazed up in her.

Brian's head came round with a jerk. His brows lifted in an odd surprise.

Her voice, she realized, *had* gone queer. But she had an instinctive feeling that it hadn't been the whole cause of his attitude. And that little straightening motion of the shoulders. Hadn't it been like that of a man drawing himself up to receive a blow? Her fright was like a scarlet spear of terror leaping at her heart.

Clare Kendry! So that was it! Impossible. It couldn't be.

In the mirror before her she saw that he was still regarding her with that air of slight amazement. She dropped her eyes to the jars and bottles on the table and began to fumble among them with hands whose fingers shook slightly.

"Of course," she said carefully, "I'm glad you did. And in spite of my recent remarks, Clare does add to any party. She's so easy on the eyes."

When she looked again, the surprise had gone from his face and the expectancy from his bearing.

"Yes," he agreed. "Well, I guess I'll run along. One of us ought to be down, I s'pose."

"You're right. One of us ought to." She was surprised that it was in her normal tones she spoke, caught as she was by the heart since that dull indefinite fear had grown suddenly into sharp panic. "I'll be down before you know it," she promised.

"All right." But he still lingered. "You're quite certain. You don't mind my asking her? Not awfully, I mean? I see now that I ought to have spoken to you. Trust women to have their reasons for everything."

She made a little pretence at looking at him, managed a tiny smile, and turned away. Clare! How sickening!

"Yes, don't they?" she said, striving to keep her voice casual. Within her she felt a hardness from feeling, not absent, but repressed. And that hardness was rising, swelling. Why didn't he go? Why didn't he?

He had opened the door at last. "You won't be long?" he asked, admonished.

She shook her head, unable to speak, for there was a choking in her throat, and the confusion in her mind was like the beating of wings. Behind her she heard the gentle impact of the door as it closed behind him, and knew that he had gone. Down to Clare.

For a long minute she sat in strained stiffness. The face in the mirror vanished from her sight, blotted out by this thing which had so suddenly flashed across her groping mind. Impossible for her to put it immediately into words or give it outline, for, prompted by some impulse of self-protection, she recoiled from exact expression.

She closed her unseeing eyes and clenched her fists. She tried not to cry. But her lips tightened and no effort could check the hot tears of rage and shame that sprang into her eyes and flowed down her cheeks; so she laid her face in her arms and wept silently.

When she was sure that she had done crying, she wiped away the warm remaining tears and got up. After bathing her swollen face in cold, refreshing water and carefully applying a stinging splash of toilet water, she went back to the mirror and regarded herself gravely. Satisfied that there lingered no betraying evidence of weeping, she dusted a little powder on her dark-white face and again examined it carefully, and with a kind of ridiculing contempt.

"I do think," she confided to it, "that you've been something—oh, very much—of a damned fool."

Downstairs the ritual of tea gave her some busy moments, and that, she decided, was a blessing. She wanted no empty spaces of time in which her mind would immediately return to that horror which she had not yet gathered sufficient courage to face. Pouring tea properly and nicely was an occupation that required a kind of well-balanced attention.

In the room beyond, a clock chimed. A single sound. Fifteen minutes past five o'clock. That was all! And yet in the short space of half an hour all of life had changed, lost its colour, its vividness, its whole meaning. No, she reflected, it wasn't that that had happened. Life about her, apparently, went on exactly as before.

"Oh, Mrs. Runyon. . . . So nice to see you. . . . Two? . . . Really? . . . How exciting! . . . Yes, I think Tuesday's all right. . . ."

Yes, life went on precisely as before. It was only she that had changed. Knowing, stumbling on this thing, had changed her. It was as if in a house long dim, a match had been struck, showing ghastly shapes where had been only blurred shadows.

Chatter, chatter, chatter. Someone asked her a question. She glanced up with what she felt was a rigid smile.

"Yes . . . Brian picked it up last winter in Haiti. Terribly weird, isn't it? . . . It *is* rather marvellous in its own hideous way. . . . Practically nothing, I believe. A few cents. . . ."

Hideous. A great weariness came over her. Even the small exertion of pouring golden tea into thin old cups seemed almost too much for her. She went on pouring. Made repetitions of her smile. Answered questions. Manufactured conversation. She thought: "I feel like the oldest person in the world with the longest stretch of life before me."

"Josephine Baker? . . . No. I've never seen her. . . . Well, she might have been in *Shuffle Along* when I saw it, but if she was, I don't remember her. . . . Oh, but you're wrong! . . . I do think Ethel Waters is awfully good. . . ."[9]

There were the familiar little tinkling sounds of spoons striking against frail cups, the soft running sounds of inconsequential talk, punctuated now and then with laughter. In irregular small groups, disintegrating, coalescing, striking just the right note of disharmony, disorder in the big room, which Irene had furnished with a sparingness that was almost chaste, moved the guests with that slight familiarity that makes a party a success. On the floor and the walls the sinking sun threw long, fantastic shadows.

So like many other tea-parties she had had. So unlike any of those others. But she mustn't think yet. Time enough for that after. All the time in the world. She had a second's flashing knowledge of what those words might portend. Time with Brian. Time without him. It was gone, leaving in its place an almost uncontrollable impulse to laugh, to scream, to hurl things about. She wanted, suddenly, to shock people, to hurt them, to make them notice her, to be aware of her suffering.

"Hello, Dave. . . . Felise. . . . Really your clothes are the despair of half the women in Harlem. . . . How do you do it? . . . Lovely, is it Worth or Lanvin? . . . Oh, a mere Babani.[1] . . ."

9. Waters (1896–1977), a celebrated blues singer and film actress. Baker (1906–1975), singer and dancer who became famous when she moved to France in 1925 to perform in shows such as *La Revue Nègre*. Before leaving New York, Baker was a chorus girl in the successful Black musical *Shuffle Along* (1921) by Aubrey Lyles and Flournoy Miller, with music by Noble Sissle and Eubie Blake.

1. Prominent fashion designers in Paris in the early 20th century.

"Merely that," Felise Freeland acknowledged. "Come out of it, Irene, whatever it is. You look like the second grave-digger."[2]

"Thanks, for the hint, Felise. I'm not feeling quite up to par. The weather, I guess."

"Buy yourself an expensive new frock, child. It always helps. Any time this child gets the blues, it means money out of Dave's pocket. How're those boys of yours?"

The boys! For once she'd forgotten them.

They were, she told Felise, very well. Felise mumbled something about that being awfully nice, and said she'd have to fly, because for a wonder she saw Mrs. Bellew sitting by herself, "and I've been trying to get her alone all afternoon. I want her for a party. Isn't she stunning today?"

Clare was. Irene couldn't remember ever having seen her look better. She was wearing a superlatively simple cinnamon-brown frock which brought out all her vivid beauty, and a little golden bowl of a hat. Around her neck hung a string of amber beads that would easily have made six or eight like one Irene owned. Yes, she was stunning.

The ripple of talk flowed on. The fire roared. The shadows stretched longer.

Across the room was Hugh. He wasn't, Irene hoped, being too bored. He seemed as he always did, a bit aloof, a little amused, and somewhat weary. And as usual he was hovering before the bookshelves. But he was not, she noticed, looking at the book he had taken down. Instead, his dull amber eyes were held by something across the room. They were a little scornful. Well, Hugh had never cared for Clare Kendry. For a minute Irene hesitated, then turned her head, though she knew what it was that held Hugh's gaze. Clare, who had suddenly clouded all her days. Brian, the father of Ted and Junior.

Clare's ivory face was what it always was, beautiful and caressing. Or maybe today a little masked. Unrevealing. Unaltered and undisturbed by any emotion within or without. Brian's seemed to Irene to be pitiably bare. Or was it too as it always was? That half-effaced seeking look, did he always have that? Queer, that now she didn't know, couldn't recall. Then she saw him smile, and the smile made his face all eager and shining. Impelled by some inner urge of loyalty to herself, she glanced away. But only for a moment. And when she turned towards them again, she thought that the look on his face was the most melancholy and yet the most scoffing that she had ever seen upon it.

In the next quarter of an hour she promised herself to Bianca Wentworth in Sixty-second Street, Jane Tenant at Seventh Avenue and a Hundred and Fiftieth Street, and the Dashields in Brooklyn for dinner all on the same evening and at almost the same hour.

Oh well, what did it matter? She had no thoughts at all now, and all she felt was a great fatigue. Before her tired eyes Clare Kendry was talking to Dave Freeland. Scraps of their conversation, in Clare's husky voice, floated over to her: ". . . always admired you . . . so much about you long ago . . . everybody says so . . . no one but you. . . ." And more of the same. The man hung rapt on her words, though he was the husband of Felise Freeland, and the author of novels that revealed a man of perception and a devastating irony. And he fell for such pish-posh! And all because Clare had a trick of sliding down

2. A reference to the character in act 5, scene 1 of Shakespeare's *Hamlet,* who is stumped by the first grave-digger's riddle.

ivory lids over astonishing black eyes and then lifting them suddenly and turning on a caressing smile. Men like Dave Freeland fell for it. And Brian.

Her mental and physical languor receded. Brian. What did it mean? How would it affect her and the boys? The boys! She had a surge of relief. It ebbed, vanished. A feeling of absolute unimportance followed. Actually, she didn't count. She was, to him, only the mother of his sons. That was all. Alone she was nothing. Worse. An obstacle.

Rage boiled up in her.

There was a slight crash. On the floor at her feet lay the shattered cup. Dark stains dotted the bright rug. Spread. The chatter stopped. Went on. Before her, Zulena gathered up the white fragments.

As from a distance Hugh Wentworth's clipt voice came to her, though he was, she was aware, somehow miraculously at her side. "Sorry," he apologized. "Must have pushed you. Clumsy of me. Don't tell me it's priceless and irreplaceable."

It hurt. Dear God! How the thing hurt! But she couldn't think of that now. Not with Hugh sitting there mumbling apologies and lies. The significance of his words, the power of his discernment, stirred in her a sense of caution. Her pride revolted. Damn Hugh! Something would have to be done about him. Now. She couldn't, it seemed, help his knowing. It was too late for that. But she could and would keep him from knowing that she knew. She could, she would bear it. She'd have to. There were the boys. Her whole body went taut. In that second she saw that she could bear anything, but only if no one knew that she had anything to bear. It hurt. It frightened her, but she could bear it.

She turned to Hugh. Shook her head. Raised innocent dark eyes to his concerned pale ones. "Oh, no," she protested, "you didn't push me. Cross your heart, hope to die, and I'll tell you how it happened."

"Done!"

"Did you notice that cup? Well, you're lucky. It was the ugliest thing that your ancestors, the charming Confederates ever owned. I've forgotten how many thousands of years ago it was that Brian's great-great-grand-uncle owned it. But it has, or had, a good old hoary history. It was brought North by way of the subway. Oh, all right! Be English if you want to and call it the underground. What I'm coming to is the fact that I've never figured out a way of getting rid of it until about five minutes ago. I had an inspiration. I had only to break it, and I was rid of it for ever. So simple! And I'd never thought of it before."

Hugh nodded and his frosty smile spread over his features. Had she convinced him?

"Still," she went on with a little laugh that didn't, she was sure, sound the least bit forced, "I'm perfectly willing for you to take the blame and admit that you pushed me at the wrong moment. What are friends for, if not to help bear our sins? Brian will certainly be told that it was your fault.

"More tea, Clare? . . . I haven't had a minute with you. . . . Yes, it is a nice party. . . . You'll stay to dinner, I hope. . . . Oh, too bad! . . . I'll be alone with the boys. . . . They'll be sorry. Brian's got a medical meeting, or something. . . . Nice frock you're wearing. . . . Thanks. . . . Well, good-bye; see you soon, I hope."

The clock chimed. One. Two. Three. Four. Five. Six. Was it, could it be, only a little over an hour since she had come down to tea? One little hour.

"Must you go? . . . Good-bye. . . . Thank you so much. . . . So nice to see you. . . . Yes, Wednesday. . . . My love to Madge. . . . Sorry, but I'm filled up for Tuesday. . . . Oh, really? . . . Yes. . . . Good-bye. . . . Good-bye. . . ."

It hurt. It hurt like hell. But it didn't matter, if no one knew. If everything could go on as before. If the boys were safe.

It did hurt.

But it didn't matter.

Two

But it did matter. It mattered more than anything had ever mattered before.

What bitterness! That the one fear, the one uncertainty, that she had felt, Brian's ache to go somewhere else, should have dwindled to a childish triviality! And with it the quality of the courage and resolution with which she had met it. From the visions and dangers which she now perceived she shrank away. For them she had no remedy or courage. Desperately she tried to shut out the knowledge from which had risen this turmoil, which she had no power to moderate or still, within her. And half succeeded.

For, she reasoned, what was there, what had there been, to show that she was even half correct in her tormenting notion? Nothing. She had seen nothing, heard nothing. She had no facts or proofs. She was only making herself unutterably wretched by an unfounded suspicion. It had been a case of looking for trouble and finding it in good measure. Merely that.

With this self-assurance that she had no real knowledge, she redoubled her efforts to drive out of her mind the distressing thought of faiths broken and trusts betrayed which every mental vision of Clare, of Brian, brought with them. She could not, she would not, go again through the tearing agony that lay just behind her.

She must, she told herself, be fair. In all their married life she had had no slightest cause to suspect her husband of any infidelity, of any serious flirtation even. If—and she doubted it—he had had his hours of outside erratic conduct, they were unknown to her. Why begin now to assume them? And on nothing more concrete than an idea that had leapt into her mind because he had told her that he had invited a friend, a friend of hers, to a party in his own house. And at a time when she had been, it was likely, more asleep than awake. How could she without anything done or said, or left undone or unsaid, so easily believe him guilty? How be so ready to renounce all confidence in the worth of their life together?

And if, perchance, there were some small something—well, what could it mean? Nothing. There were the boys. There was John Bellew. The thought of these three gave her some slight relief. But she did not look the future in the face. She wanted to feel nothing, to think nothing; simply to believe that it was all silly invention on her part. Yet she could not. Not quite.

Christmas, with its unreality, its hectic rush, its false gaiety, came and went. Irene was thankful for the confused unrest of the season. Its irksomeness, its crowds, its inane and insincere repetitions of genialities, pushed between her and the contemplation of her growing unhappiness.

She was thankful, too, for the continued absence of Clare, who, John Bellew having returned from a long stay in Canada, had withdrawn to that other life of hers, remote and inaccessible. But beating against the walled prison of Irene's thoughts was the shunned fancy that, though absent, Clare Kendry was still present, that she was close.

Brian, too, had withdrawn. The house contained his outward self and his belongings. He came and went with his usual noiseless irregularity. He sat across from her at table. He slept in his room next to hers at night. But he was remote and inaccessible. No use pretending that he was happy, that things were the same as they had always been. He wasn't and they weren't. However, she assured herself, it needn't necessarily be because of anything that involved Clare. It was, it must be, another manifestation of the old longing.

But she did wish it were spring, March, so that Clare would be sailing, out of her life and Brian's. Though she had come almost to believe that there was nothing but generous friendship between those two, she was very tired of Clare Kendry. She wanted to be free of her, and of her furtive comings and goings. If something would only happen, something that would make John Bellew decide on an earlier departure, or that would remove Clare. Anything. She didn't care what. Not even if it were that Clare's Margery were ill, or dying. Not even if Bellew should discover—

She drew a quick, sharp breath. And for a long time sat staring down at the hands in her lap. Strange, she had not before realized how easily she could put Clare out of her life! She had only to tell John Bellew that his wife—No. Not that! But if he should somehow learn of these Harlem visits—Why should she hesitate? Why spare Clare?

But she shrank away from the idea of telling that man, Clare Kendry's white husband, anything that would lead him to suspect that his wife was a Negro. Nor could she write it, or telephone it, or tell it to someone else who would tell him.

She was caught between two allegiances, different, yet the same. Herself. Her race. Race! The thing that bound and suffocated her. Whatever steps she took, or if she took none at all, something would be crushed. A person or the race. Clare, herself, or the race. Or, it might be, all three. Nothing, she imagined, was ever more completely sardonic.

Sitting alone in the quiet living-room in the pleasant firelight, Irene Redfield wished, for the first time in her life, that she had not been born a Negro. For the first time she suffered and rebelled because she was unable to disregard the burden of race. It was, she cried silently, enough to suffer as a woman, an individual, on one's own account, without having to suffer for the race as well. It was a brutality, and undeserved. Surely, no other people so cursed as Ham's dark children.

Nevertheless, her weakness, her shrinking, her own inability to compass the thing, did not prevent her from wishing fervently that, in some way with which she had no concern, John Bellew would discover, not that his wife had a touch of the tar-brush—Irene didn't want that—but that she was spending all the time that he was out of the city in black Harlem. Only that. It would be enough to rid her forever of Clare Kendry.

Three

As if in answer to her wish, the very next day Irene came face to face with Bellew.

She had gone downtown with Felise Freeland to shop. The day was an exceptionally cold one, with a strong wind that had whipped a dusky red into Felise's smooth golden cheeks and driven moisture into Irene's soft brown eyes.

Clinging to each other, with heads bent against the wind, they turned out of the Avenue[3] into Fifty-seventh Street. A sudden bluster flung them around the corner with unexpected quickness and they collided with a man.

"Pardon," Irene begged laughingly, and looked up into the face of Clare Kendry's husband.

"Mrs. Redfield!"

His hat came off. He held out his hand, smiling genially.

But the smile faded at once. Surprise, incredulity, and—was it understanding?—passed over his features.

He had, Irene knew, become conscious of Felise, golden, with curly black Negro hair, whose arm was still linked in her own. She was sure, now, of the understanding in his face, as he looked at her again and then back at Felise. And displeasure.

He didn't, however, withdraw his outstretched hand. Not at once.

But Irene didn't take it. Instinctively, in the first glance of recognition, her face had become a mask. Now she turned on him a totally uncomprehending look, a bit questioning. Seeing that he still stood with hand outstretched, she gave him the cool appraising stare which she reserved for mashers,[4] and drew Felise on.

Felise drawled: "Aha! Been 'passing,' have you? Well, I've queered that."[5]

"Yes, I'm afraid you have."

"Why, Irene Redfield! You sound as if you cared terribly. I'm sorry."

"I do, but not for the reason you think. I don't believe I've ever gone native[6] in my life except for the sake of convenience, restaurants, theatre tickets, and things like that. Never socially I mean, except once. You've just passed the only person that I've ever met disguised as a white woman."

"Awfully sorry. Be sure your sin will find you out and all that. Tell me about it."

"I'd like to. It would amuse you. But I can't."

Felise's laughter was as languidly nonchalant as her cool voice. "Can it be possible that the honest Irene has—Oh, do look at that coat! There. The red one. Isn't it a dream?"

Irene was thinking: "I had my chance and didn't take it. I had only to speak and to introduce him to Felise with the casual remark that he was Clare's husband. Only that. Fool. Fool." That instinctive loyalty to a race. Why couldn't she get free of it? Why should it include Clare? Clare, who'd shown little enough consideration for her, and hers. What she felt was not so much resentment as a dull despair because she could not change herself in this respect, could not separate individuals from the race, herself from Clare Kendry.

"Let's go home, Felise. I'm so tired I could drop."

"Why, we haven't done half the things we planned."

"I know, but it's too cold to be running all over town. But you stay down if you want to."

"I think I'll do that, if you don't mind."

3. Fifth Avenue, an exclusive shopping district in Manhattan.
4. Aggressively flirtatious men.
5. That is, ruined or undermined it.
6. An ironic inversion of the British imperial phrase for the adoption of the customs and habits of an indigenous population.

And now another problem confronted Irene. She must tell Clare of this meeting. Warn her. But how? She hadn't seen her for days. Writing and telephoning were equally unsafe. And even if it was possible to get in touch with her, what good would it do? If Bellew hadn't concluded that he'd made a mistake, if he was certain of her identity—and he was nobody's fool—telling Clare wouldn't avert the results of the encounter. Besides, it was too late. Whatever was in store for Clare Kendry had already overtaken her.

Irene was conscious of a feeling of relieved thankfulness at the thought that she was probably rid of Clare, and without having lifted a finger or uttered one word.

But she did mean to tell Brian about meeting John Bellew.

But that, it seemed, was impossible. Strange. Something held her back. Each time she was on the verge of saying: "I ran into Clare's husband on the street downtown today. I'm sure he recognized me, and Felise was with me," she failed to speak. It sounded too much like the warning she wanted it to be. Not even in the presence of the boys at dinner could she make the bare statement.

The evening dragged. At last she said good-night and went upstairs, the words unsaid.

She thought: "Why didn't I tell him? Why didn't I? If trouble comes from this, I'll never forgive myself. I'll tell him when he comes up."

She took up a book, but she could not read, so oppressed was she by a nameless foreboding.

What if Bellew should divorce Clare? Could he? There was the Rhinelander case.[7] But in France, in Paris, such things were very easy. If he divorced her—If Clare were free—But of all the things that could happen, that was the one she did not want. She must get her mind away from that possibility. She must.

Then came a thought which she tried to drive away. If Clare should die! Then—Oh, it was vile! To think, yes, to wish that! She felt faint and sick. But the thought stayed with her. She could not get rid of it.

She heard the outer door open. Close. Brian had gone out. She turned her face into her pillow to cry. But no tears came.

She lay there awake, thinking of things past. Of her courtship and marriage and Junior's birth. Of the time they had bought the house in which they had lived so long and so happily. Of the time Ted had passed his pneumonia crisis and they knew he would live. And of other sweet painful memories that would never come again.

Above everything else she had wanted, had striven, to keep undisturbed the pleasant routine of her life. And now Clare Kendry had come into it, and with her the menace of impermanence.

"Dear God," she prayed, "make March come quickly."

By and by she slept.

Four

The next morning brought with it a snowstorm that lasted throughout the day.

After a breakfast, which had been eaten almost in silence and which she was relieved to have done with, Irene Redfield lingered for a little while in

7. A sensational 1925 court case in which the socialite Leonard "Kip" Rhinelander sought a divorce from his wife, Alice, on the basis that she had misled him into believing she was white.

the downstairs hall, looking out at the soft flakes fluttering down. She was watching them immediately fill some ugly irregular gaps left by the feet of hurrying pedestrians when Zulena came to her, saying: "The telephone, Mrs. Redfield. It's Mrs. Bellew."

"Take the message, Zulena, please."

Though she continued to stare out of the window, Irene saw nothing now, stabbed as she was by fear—and hope. Had anything happened between Clare and Bellew? And if so, what? And was she to be freed at last from the aching anxiety of the past weeks? Or was there to be more, and worse? She had a wrestling moment, in which it seemed that she must rush after Zulena and hear for herself what it was that Clare had to say. But she waited.

Zulena, when she came back, said: "She says, ma'am, that she'll be able to go to Mrs. Freeland's tonight. She'll be here some time between eight and nine."

"Thank you, Zulena."

The day dragged on to its end.

At dinner Brian spoke bitterly of a lynching that he had been reading about in the evening paper.

"Dad, why is it that they only lynch coloured people?" Ted asked.

"Because they hate 'em, son."

"Brian!" Irene's voice was a plea and a rebuke.

Ted said: "Oh! And why do they hate 'em?"

"Because they are afraid of them."

"But what makes them afraid of 'em?"

"Because—"

"Brian!"

"It seems, son, that is a subject we can't go into at the moment without distressing the ladies of our family," he told the boy with mock seriousness, "but we'll take it up some time when we're alone together."

Ted nodded in his engaging grave way. "I see. Maybe we can talk about it tomorrow on the way to school."

"That'll be fine."

"Brian!"

"Mother," Junior remarked, "that's the third time you've said 'Brian' like that."

"But not the last, Junior, never you fear," his father told him.

After the boys had gone up to their own floor, Irene said suavely: "I do wish, Brian, that you wouldn't talk about lynching before Ted and Junior. It was really inexcusable for you to bring up a thing like that at dinner. There'll be time enough for them to learn about such horrible things when they're older."

"You're absolutely wrong! If, as you're so determined, they've got to live in this damned country, they'd better find out what sort of thing they're up against as soon as possible. The earlier they learn it, the better prepared they'll be."

"I don't agree. I want their childhood to be happy and as free from the knowledge of such things as it possibly can be."

"Very laudable," was Brian's sarcastic answer. "Very laudable indeed, all things considered. But can it?"

"Certainly it can. If you'll only do your part."

"Stuff! You know as well as I do, Irene, that it can't. What was the use of our trying to keep them from learning the word 'nigger' and its connotation?

They found out, didn't they? And how? Because somebody called Junior a dirty nigger."

"Just the same you're not to talk to them about the race problem. I won't have it."

They glared at each other.

"I tell you, Irene, they've got to know these things, and it might as well be now as later."

"They do not!" she insisted, forcing back the tears of anger that were threatening to fall.

Brian growled: "I can't understand how anybody as intelligent as you like to think you are can show evidences of such stupidity." He looked at her in a puzzled harassed way.

"Stupid!" she cried. "Is it stupid to want my children to be happy?" Her lips were quivering.

"At the expense of proper preparation for life and their future happiness, yes. And I'd feel I hadn't done my duty by them if I didn't give them some inkling of what's before them. It's the least I can do. I wanted to get them out of this hellish place years ago. You wouldn't let me. I gave up the idea, because you objected. Don't expect me to give up everything."

Under the lash of his words she was silent. Before any answer came to her, he had turned and gone from the room.

Sitting there alone in the forsaken dining-room, unconsciously pressing the hands lying in her lap, tightly together, she was seized by a convulsion of shivering. For, to her, there had been something ominous in the scene that she had just had with her husband. Over and over in her mind his last words: "Don't expect me to give up everything," repeated themselves. What had they meant? What could they mean? Clare Kendry?

Surely, she was going mad with fear and suspicion. She must not work herself up. She must not! Where were all the self control, the common sense, that she was so proud of? Now, if ever, was the time for it.

Clare would soon be there. She must hurry or she would be late again, and those two would wait for her downstairs together as they had done so often since that first time, which now seemed so long ago. Had it been really only last October? Why, she felt years, not months, older.

Drearily she rose from her chair and went upstairs to see about the business of dressing to go out when she would far rather have remained at home. During the process she wondered, for the hundredth time, why she hadn't told Brian about herself and Felise running into Bellew the day before, and for the hundredth time she turned away from acknowledging to herself the real season for keeping back the information.

When Clare arrived, radiant in a shining red gown, Irene had not finished dressing. But her smile scarcely hesitated as she greeted her, saying: "I always seem to keep C.P. time,[8] don't I? We hardly expected you to be able to come. Felise will be pleased. How nice you look."

Clare kissed a bare shoulder, seeming not to notice a slight shrinking.

"I hadn't an idea in the world, myself, that I'd be able to make it; but Jack had to run down to Philadelphia unexpectedly. So here I am."

Irene looked up, a flood of speech on her lips. "Philadelphia. That's not very far, is it? Clare, I—?"

8. "Colored People's time," that is, late.

She stopped, one of her hands clutching the side of her stool, the other lying clenched on the dressing-table. Why didn't she go on and tell Clare about meeting Bellew? Why couldn't she?

But Clare didn't notice the unfinished sentence. She laughed and said lightly: "It's far enough for me. Anywhere, away from me, is far enough. I'm not particular."

Irene passed a hand over her eyes to shut out the accusing face in the glass before her. With one corner of her mind she wondered how long she had looked like that, drawn and haggard and—yes, frightened. Or was it only imagination?

"Clare," she asked, "have you ever seriously thought what it would mean if he should find you out?"

"Yes."

"Oh! You have! And what you'd do in that case?"

"Yes." And having said it, Clare Kendry smiled quickly, a smile that came and went like a flash, leaving untouched the gravity of her face.

That smile and the quiet resolution of that one word, "yes," filled Irene with a primitive paralysing dread. Her hands were numb, her feet like ice, her heart like a stone weight. Even her tongue was like a heavy dying thing. There were long spaces between the words as she asked: "And what should you do?"

Clare, who was sunk in a deep chair, her eyes far away, seemed wrapped in some pleasant impenetrable reflection. To Irene, sitting expectantly upright, it was an interminable time before she dragged herself back to the present to say calmly: "I'd do what I want to do more than anything else right now. I'd come up here to live. Harlem, I mean. Then I'd be able to do as I please, when I please."

Irene leaned forward, cold and tense. "And what about Margery?" Her voice was a strained whisper.

"Margery?" Clare repeated, letting her eyes flutter over Irene's concerned face. "Just this, 'Rene. If it wasn't for her, I'd do it anyway. She's all that holds me back. But if Jack finds out, if our marriage is broken, that lets me out. Doesn't it?"

Her gentle resigned tone, her air of innocent candour, appeared, to her listener, spurious. A conviction that the words were intended as a warning took possession of Irene. She remembered that Clare Kendry had always seemed to know what other people were thinking. Her compressed lips grew firm and obdurate. Well, she wouldn't know this time.

She said: "Do go downstairs and talk to Brian. He's got a mad on."

Though she had determined that Clare should not get at her thoughts and fears, the words had sprung, unthought of, to her lips. It was as if they had come from some outer layer of callousness that had no relation to her tortured heart. And they had been, she realized, precisely the right words for her purpose.

For as Clare got up and went out, she saw that that arrangement was as good as her first plan of keeping her waiting up there while she dressed—or better. She would only have hindered and rasped her. And what matter if those two spent one hour, more or less, alone together, one or many, now that everything had happened between them?

Ah! The first time that she had allowed herself to admit to herself that everything had happened, had not forced herself to believe, to hope, that nothing irrevocable had been consummated! Well, it had happened. She knew it, and knew that she knew it.

She was surprised that, having thought the thought, conceded the fact, she was no more hurt, cared no more, than during her previous frenzied endeavours to escape it. And this absence of acute, unbearable pain seemed to her unjust, as if she had been denied some exquisite solace of suffering which the full acknowledgment should have given her.

Was it, perhaps, that she had endured all that a woman could endure of tormenting humiliation and fear? Or was it that she lacked the capacity for the acme of suffering? "No, no!" she denied fiercely. "I'm human like everybody else. It's just that I'm so tired, so worn out, I can't feel any more." But she did not really believe that.

Security. Was it just a word? If not, then was it only by the sacrifice of other things, happiness, love, or some wild ecstasy that she had never known, that it could be obtained? And did too much striving, too much faith in safety and permanence, unfit one for these other things?

Irene didn't know, couldn't decide, though for a long time she sat questioning and trying to understand. Yet all the while, in spite of her searchings and feeling of frustration, she was aware that, to her, security was the most important and desired thing in life. Not for any of the others, or for all of them, would she exchange it. She wanted only to be tranquil. Only, unmolested, to be allowed to direct for their own best good the lives of her sons and her husband.

Now that she had relieved herself of what was almost like a guilty knowledge, admitted that which by some sixth sense she had long known, she could again reach out for plans. Could think again of ways to keep Brian by her side, and in New York. For she would not go to Brazil. She belonged in this land of rising towers. She was an American. She grew from this soil, and she would not be uprooted. Not even because of Clare Kendry, or a hundred Clare Kendrys.

Brian, too, belonged here. His duty was to her and to his boys.

Strange, that she couldn't now be sure that she had ever truly known love. Not even for Brian. He was her husband and the father of her sons. But was he anything more? Had she ever wanted or tried for more? In that hour she thought not.

Nevertheless, she meant to keep him. Her freshly painted lips narrowed to a thin straight line. True, she had left off trying to believe that he and Clare loved and yet did not love, but she still intended to hold fast to the outer shell of her marriage, to keep her life fixed, certain. Brought to the edge of distasteful reality, her fastidious nature did not recoil. Better, far better, to share him than to lose him completely. Oh, she could close her eyes, if need be. She could bear it. She could bear anything. And there was March ahead. March and the departure of Clare.

Horribly clear, she could now see the reason for her instinct to withhold—omit, rather—her news of the encounter with Bellew. If Clare was freed, anything might happen.

She paused in her dressing, seeing with perfect clearness that dark truth which she had from that first October afternoon felt about Clare Kendry and of which Clare herself had once warned her—that she got the things she wanted because she met the great condition of conquest, sacrifice. If she wanted Brian, Clare wouldn't revolt from the lack of money or place. It was as she had said, only Margery kept her from throwing all that away. And if things were taken out of her hands—Even if she was only alarmed, only suspected that such a thing was about to occur, anything might happen. Anything.

No! At all costs, Clare was not to know of that meeting with Bellew. Nor was Brian. It would only weaken her own power to keep him.

They would never know from her that he was on his way to suspecting the truth about his wife. And she would do anything, risk anything, to prevent him from finding out that truth. How fortunate that she had obeyed her instinct and omitted to recognize Bellew!

"Ever go up to the sixth floor, Clare?" Brian asked as he stopped the car and got out to open the door for them.

"Why, of course! We're on the seventeenth."

"I mean, did you ever go up by nigger-power?"

"That's good!" Clare laughed. "Ask 'Rene. My father was a janitor, you know, in the good old days before every ramshackle flat had its elevator. But you can't mean we've got to walk up? Not here!"

"Yes, here. And Felise lives at the very top," Irene told her.

"What on earth for?"

"I believe she claims it discourages the casual visitor."

"And she's probably right. Hard on herself, though."

Brian said "Yes, a bit. But she says she'd rather be dead than bored."

"Oh, a garden! And how lovely with that undisturbed snow!"

"Yes, isn't it? But keep to the walk with those foolish thin shoes. You too, Irene."

Irene walked beside them on the cleared cement path that split the whiteness of the courtyard garden. She felt a something in the air, something that had been between those two and would be again. It was like a live thing pressing against her. In a quick furtive glance she saw Clare clinging to Brian's other arm. She was looking at him with that provocative upward glance of hers, and his eyes were fastened on her face with what seemed to Irene an expression of wistful eagerness.

"It's this entrance, I believe," she informed them in quite her ordinary voice.

"Mind," Brian told Clare, "you don't fall by the wayside before the fourth floor. They absolutely refuse to carry anyone up more than the last two flights."

"Don't be silly!" Irene snapped.

The party began gaily.

Dave Freeland was at his best, brilliant, crystal clear, and sparkling. Felise, too, was amusing, and not so sarcastic as usual, because she liked the dozen or so guests that dotted the long, untidy living-room. Brian was witty, though, Irene noted, his remarks were somewhat more barbed than was customary even with him. And there was Ralph Hazelton, throwing nonsensical shining things into the pool of talk, which the others, even Clare, picked up and flung back with fresh adornment.

Only Irene wasn't merry. She sat almost silent, smiling now and then, that she might appear amused.

"What's the matter, Irene?" someone asked. "Taken a vow never to laugh, or something? You're as sober as a judge."

"No. It's simply that the rest of you are so clever that I'm speechless, absolutely stunned."

"No wonder," Dave Freeland remarked, "that you're on the verge of tears. You haven't a drink. What'll you take?"

"Thanks. If I must take something, make it a glass of ginger ale and three drops of Scotch. The Scotch first, please. Then the ice, then the ginger ale."

"Heavens! Don't attempt to mix that yourself, Dave darling. Have the butler in," Felise mocked.

"Yes, do. And the footman." Irene laughed a little, then said: "It seems dreadfully warm in here. Mind if I open this window?" With that she pushed open one of the long casement-windows of which the Freelands were so proud.

It had stopped snowing some two or three hours back. The moon was just rising, and far behind the tall buildings a few stars were creeping out. Irene finished her cigarette and threw it out, watching the tiny spark drop slowly down to the white ground below.

Someone in the room had turned on the phonograph. Or was it the radio? She didn't know which she disliked more. And nobody was listening to its blare. The talking, the laughter never for a minute ceased. Why must they have more noise?

Dave came with her drink. "You ought not," he told her, "to stand there like that. You'll take cold. Come along and talk to me, or listen to me gabble." Taking her arm, he led her across the room. They had just found seats when the door-bell rang and Felise called over to him to go and answer it.

In the next moment Irene heard his voice in the hall, carelessly polite: "Your wife? Sorry. I'm afraid you're wrong. Perhaps next—"

Then the roar of John Bellew's voice above all the other noises of the room: "I'm *not* wrong! I've been to the Redfields and I know she's with them. You'd better stand out of my way and save yourself trouble in the end."

"What is it, Dave?" Felise ran out to the door.

And so did Brian. Irene heard him saying: "I'm Redfield. What the devil's the matter with you?"

But Bellew didn't heed him. He pushed past them all into the room and strode towards Clare. They all looked at her as she got up from her chair, backing a little from his approach.

"So you're a nigger, a damned dirty nigger!" His voice was a snarl and a moan, an expression of rage and of pain.

Everything was in confusion. The men had sprung forward. Felise had leapt between them and Bellew. She said quickly: "Careful. You're the only white man here." And the silver chill of her voice, as well as her words, was a warning.

Clare stood at the window, as composed as if everyone were not staring at her in curiosity and wonder, as if the whole structure of her life were not lying in fragments before her. She seemed unaware of any danger or uncaring. There was even a faint smile on her full, red lips, and in her shining eyes.

It was that smile that maddened Irene. She ran across the room, her terror tinged with ferocity, and laid a hand on Clare's bare arm. One thought possessed her. She couldn't have Clare Kendry cast aside by Bellew. She couldn't have her free.

Before them stood John Bellew, speechless now in his hurt and anger. Beyond them the little huddle of other people, and Brian stepping out from among them.

What happened next, Irene Redfield never afterwards allowed herself to remember. Never clearly.

One moment Clare had been there, a vital glowing thing, like a flame of red and gold. The next she was gone.

There was a gasp of horror, and above it a sound not quite human, like a beast in agony. "Nig! My God! Nig!"

A frenzied rush of feet down long flights of stairs. The slamming of distant doors. Voices.

Irene stayed behind. She sat down and remained quite still, staring at a ridiculous Japanese print on the wall across the room.

Gone! The soft white face, the bright hair, the disturbing scarlet mouth, the dreaming eyes, the caressing smile, the whole torturing loveliness that had been Clare Kendry. That beauty that had torn at Irene's placid life. Gone! The mocking daring, the gallantry of her pose, the ringing bells of her laughter.

Irene wasn't sorry. She was amazed, incredulous almost.

What would the others think? That Clare had fallen? That she had deliberately leaned backward? Certainly one or the other. Not—

But she mustn't, she warned herself, think of that. She was too tired, and too shocked. And, indeed, both were true. She was utterly weary, and she was violently staggered. But her thoughts reeled on. If only she could be as free of mental as she was of bodily vigour; could only put from her memory the vision of her hand on Clare's arm!

"It was an accident, a terrible accident," she muttered fiercely. "It *was*."

People were coming up the stairs. Through the still open door their steps and talk sounded nearer, nearer.

Quickly she stood up and went noiselessly into the bedroom and closed the door softly behind her.

Her thoughts raced. Ought she to have stayed? Should she go back out there to them? But there would be questions. She hadn't thought of them, of afterwards, of this. She had thought of nothing in that sudden moment of action.

It was cold. Icy chills ran up her spine and over her bare neck, and shoulders.

In the room outside there were voices. Dave Freeland's and others that she did not recognize.

Should she put on her coat? Felise had rushed down without any wrap. So had all the others. So had Brian. Brian! He mustn't take cold. She took up his coat and left her own. At the door she paused for a moment, listening fearfully. She heard nothing. No voices. No footsteps. Very slowly she opened the door. The room was empty. She went out.

In the hall below she heard dimly the sound of feet going down the steps, of a door being opened and closed, and of voices far away.

Down, down, down, she went, Brian's great coat clutched in her shivering arms and trailing a little on each step behind her.

What was she to say to them when at last she had finished going down those endless stairs? She should have rushed out when they did. What reason could she give for her dallying behind? Even she didn't know why she had done that. And what else would she be asked? There had been her hand reaching out towards Clare. What about that?

In the midst of her wonderings and questionings came a thought so terrifying, so horrible, that she had had to grasp hold of the banister to save herself from pitching downwards. A cold perspiration drenched her shaking body. Her breath came short in sharp and painful gasps.

What if Clare was not dead?

She felt nauseated, as much at the idea of the glorious body mutilated as from fear.

How she managed to make the rest of the journey without fainting she never knew. But at last she was down. Just at the bottom she came on the others, surrounded by a little circle of strangers. They were all speaking in whispers, or in the awed, discreetly lowered tones adapted to the presence of disaster. In the first instant she wanted to turn and rush back up the way she had come. Then a calm desperation came over her. She braced herself, physically and mentally.

"Here's Irene now," Dave Freeland announced, and told her that, having only just missed her, they had concluded that she had fainted or something like that, and were on the way to find out about her. Felise, she saw, was holding on to his arm, all the insolent nonchalance gone out of her, and the golden brown of her handsome face changed to a queer mauve colour.

Irene made no indication that she had heard Freeland, but went straight to Brian. His face looked aged and altered, and his lips were purple and trembling. She had a great longing to comfort him, to charm away his suffering and horror. But she was helpless, having so completely lost control of his mind and heart.

She stammered: "Is she—is she—?"

It was Felise who answered. "Instantly, we think."

Irene struggled against the sob of thankfulness that rose in her throat. Choked down, it turned to a whimper, like a hurt child's. Someone laid a hand on her shoulder in a soothing gesture. Brian wrapped his coat about her. She began to cry rackingly, her entire body heaving with convulsive sobs. He made a slight perfunctory attempt to comfort her.

"There, there, Irene. You mustn't. You'll make yourself sick. She's—" His voice broke suddenly.

As from a long distance she heard Ralph Hazelton's voice saying: "I was looking right at her. She just tumbled over and was gone before you could say 'Jack Robinson.' Fainted, I guess. Lord! It was quick. Quickest thing I ever saw in all my life."

"It's impossible, I tell you! Absolutely impossible!"

It was Brian who spoke in that frenzied hoarse voice, which Irene had never heard before. Her knees quaked under her.

Dave Freeland said: "Just a minute, Brian. Irene was there beside her. Let's hear what she has to say."

She had a moment of stark craven fear. "Oh God," she thought, prayed, "help me."

A strange man, official and authoritative, addressed her. "You're sure she fell? Her husband didn't give her a shove or anything like that, as Dr. Redfield seems to think?"

For the first time she was aware that Bellew was not in the little group shivering in the small hallway. What did that mean? As she began to work it out in her numbed mind, she was shaken with another hideous trembling. Not that! Oh, not that!

"No, no!" she protested. "I'm quite certain that he didn't. I was there, too. As close as he was. She just fell, before anybody could stop her. I—"

Her quaking knees gave way under her. She moaned and sank down, moaned again. Through the great heaviness that submerged and drowned her she was dimly conscious of strong arms lifting her up. Then everything was dark.

Centuries after, she heard the strange man saying: "Death by misadventure, I'm inclined to believe. Let's go up and have another look at that window."

1929

JEAN TOOMER

1894–1967

Although he never attained the lofty goals he set for himself, Jean Toomer was conspicuously a seeker, a man who viewed life as a search for the attainment of spiritual balance; Toomer apparently was interested in issues of race only insofar as they contributed to his achievement of inner peace. Claimed with equal passion by the race-conscious and the modernist camps for his groundbreaking work *Cane* (1923), Toomer spent his later years wondering why the reading public failed to see that "*Cane* was a song of an end," a song that had helped Toomer to put the racial disquiet within himself to rest. With that turmoil behind him, it was only natural for a man of his spiritual temperament to remark, "Why people have expected me to write a second and a third and a fourth book like *Cane* is one of the queer misunderstandings of my life."

Toomer was born in Washington, D.C., in late 1894, to Nathan and Nina Pinchback Toomer. When Nathan, a farmer from Georgia, deserted his wife less than a year later, she moved with her son into the home of her parents, where Toomer spent most of his childhood. P. B. S. Pinchback, Toomer's remarkable maternal grandfather, had built a political career in Reconstruction Louisiana on his claim that he was Black—although Jean Toomer himself would later assert that there was no proof in the matter. After the radical Republicans lost power and local whites regained control of the South, Pinchback could no longer reasonably expect to survive as a politician, and eventually settled in a white neighborhood in Washington, embittered by his fall from prominence.

In 1906, having remarried, Toomer's mother took him to live with her new husband in New Rochelle, New York. Toomer remained there until his mother's death in 1909, when he returned to Washington, D.C., to live with his grandparents, who were resettling from the middle-class white neighborhood where he had spent his boyhood to a Black part of town. Attending the M Street High School, Toomer adapted quickly to his new environment. Toomer, who once described himself as descended from a mixture of "Scotch, Welsh, German, English, French, Dutch, Spanish, and some dark blood," apparently had the issue of race brought home to him personally for the first time in his life at this point. His reaction to the matter was to hold the United States responsible for living up to its image as a melting pot; rather than viewing himself as Black or white, he stayed the issue of race by referring to himself as an American.

After graduating from high school, he devoted four years to higher education, but spent them at five different institutions (including the University of Wisconsin, the

American College of Physical Training in Chicago, and the City College of New York) between 1914 and late 1917. He never remained anywhere long enough to take a degree, and he financed his education by taking all sorts of jobs: he sold cars, taught physical education, and worked in a shipyard.

His decision to become a writer came in 1919. With literary contacts such as Waldo Frank, Hart Crane, Edward Arlington Robinson, and Van Wyck Brooks impressed by his promise, he was not long in making a small reputation for himself. However, the turning point in his career came with a stay in Sparta, Georgia, in 1921, where he served as acting superintendent of a school for Blacks. Out of the four months Toomer spent amid the rural Blacks of Georgia grew *Cane,* which catapulted its author in 1923 into a position of prominence among the younger writers in the African American world.

Although *Cane* contains several poems and brief sketches that had already appeared in magazines, the overwhelming impression left by the book on its appearance was one of freshness and modernity. *Cane* comprises three sections. In the first part, Toomer depicts in lyrical language the Black folk of rural Georgia; in the second, he turns his attention to urban Blacks, particularly those in Chicago and Washington, D.C.; and in the third section, a long, loosely autobiographical, dramatic piece titled "Kabnis," he attempts to synthesize the preceding sections by depicting an urban Black in a rural setting. Waldo Frank, who had first encouraged Toomer to collect his magazine pieces in book form, seemed to speak for the majority of critics in his highly laudatory introduction to the book. *Cane* was an unprecedented success, important enough not only to serve as the foundation of Toomer's career but also to sustain his reputation through a succession of failures.

Toomer had written other racially charged pieces before 1923. Of these, his best known was *Balo,* a one-act play included in the anthology *Plays of Negro Life* by Alain Locke and Montgomery Gregory. (Another play, *Natalie Mann,* and the short story "Withered Skins of Berries," though of interest to scholars, are probably as unfamiliar to the reading public as the philosophical and theological writings which followed from his pen.) After 1923, however, Toomer lost all interest in the issue of race. Indeed, he complained that Alain Locke had "tricked and misused" him by incorporating part of his work in his *The New Negro* in 1925.

With *Cane* and the racial tensions that had engendered it ostensibly behind him, Toomer began his long association with George I. Gurdjieff, an Armenian spiritualist who incorporated mysticism, yoga, Freudian psychoanalysis, and elements of dance into a system sometimes known as Unitism. Toomer, who had never shown a particular interest in religion, spent the summer of 1924 (and several later summers) at Gurdjieff's Institute for the Harmonious Development of Man in France; his goal in visiting the institute was apparently the attainment of "objective consciousness," a recognition of the self as a component in a larger whole. The themes of Unitism quickly began to dominate Toomer's writing. Working in the 1920s as a proselyte for Unitism in Harlem, Toomer temporarily attracted such people as Wallace Thurman, Aaron Douglas, and Nella Larsen as pupils. In all likelihood, however, they were drawn to Toomer less for bringing them Gurdjieff's message than for having written one of the most powerful texts of the Harlem Renaissance.

In 1932, Toomer married one of his white students, a writer named Margery Latimer, who died a year later during childbirth. He then married Marjorie Content, another white woman, in 1934. After they settled in Pennsylvania, Toomer formally broke with Gurdjieff and began to gain interest in the Society of Friends, though he did not become a Quaker until 1940.

In 1936, he wrote a long poem called *Blue Meridian* about the fusion of black-, white-, and red-skinned people into a new entity, the blue man. *Blue Meridian,* which appeared in *The New Caravan,* was the last major publication of Toomer's career. His studies *An Interpretation of Friends Worship* (1947) and *The Flavor of Man* (1949) appeared after his conversion to Quakerism. Much of the unpublished material that Toomer produced before turning his back on fiction and poetry in the mid-1940s has been collected in Darwin Turner's *The Wayward and the Seeking*

(1980). Turner's objective was to cull the most interesting pieces from a body of work that Nellie Y. McKay not unjustly called "largely didactic, tedious, and dull."

Even though Toomer insisted years before his death in 1967 that he was "of no particular race," his loss was deeply felt by the African American community. In the words of Arna Bontemps, Harlem had gone "quietly mad" when *Cane* appeared. If Toomer was indeed a one-book author, he was a one-book author of the first order. Many of the other luminaries of the Harlem Renaissance were more prolific, but few were more powerful as artists. Toomer once reflected: "Perhaps our lot on this earth is to seek and to search. Now and again we find just enough to enable us to carry on. I now doubt that any of us will completely find and be found in this life."

Cane[1]

Karintha

Her skin is like dusk on the eastern horizon,
O cant you see it, O cant you see it,
Her skin is like dusk on the eastern horizon
. . . When the sun goes down.

Men had always wanted her, this Karintha, even as a child, Karintha carrying beauty, perfect as dusk when the sun goes down. Old men rode her hobby-horse upon their knees. Young men danced with her at frolics when they should have been dancing with their grown-up girls. God grant us youth, secretly prayed the old men. The young fellows counted the time to pass before she would be old enough to mate with them. This interest of the male, who wishes to ripen a growing thing too soon, could mean no good to her.

Karintha, at twelve, was a wild flash that told the other folks just what it was to live. At sunset, when there was no wind, and the pine-smoke from over by the sawmill hugged the earth, and you couldnt see more than a few feet in front, her sudden darting past you was a bit of vivid color, like a black bird that flashes in light. With the other children one could hear, some distance off, their feet flopping in the two-inch dust. Karintha's running was a whir. It had the sound of the red dust that sometimes makes a spiral in the road. At dusk, during the hush just after the sawmill had closed down, and before any of the women had started their supper-getting-ready songs, her voice, high-pitched, shrill, would put one's ears to itching. But no one ever thought to make her stop because of it. She stoned the cows, and beat her dog, and fought the other children . . . Even the preacher, who caught her at mischief, told himself that she was as innocently lovely as a November cotton flower. Already, rumors were out about her. Homes in Georgia are most often built on the two-room plan. In one, you cook and eat, in the other you

1. *Cane* comprises three general sections. The first two, "Karintha" and "Seventh Street," are preceded by a single arc; two arcs precede the third section, "Kabnis." "Karintha" is set in the rural South, with an emphasis on stories of individual women. "Seventh Street" takes place, for the most part, in urban settings, such as Washington, D.C., and Chicago. "Kabnis" is a drama set in a single locality in the South.

sleep, and there love goes on. Karintha had seen or heard, perhaps she had felt her parents loving. One could but imitate one's parents, for to follow them was the way of God. She played "home" with a small boy who was not afraid to do her bidding. That started the whole thing. Old men could no longer ride her hobby-horse upon their knees. But young men counted faster.

Her skin is like dusk,
O cant you see it,
Her skin is like dusk,
When the sun goes down.

Karintha is a woman. She who carries beauty, perfect as dusk when the sun goes down. She has been married many times. Old men remind her that a few years back they rode her hobby-horse upon their knees. Karintha smiles, and indulges them when she is in the mood for it. She has contempt for them. Karintha is a woman. Young men run stills[2] to make her money. Young men go to the big cities and run on the road.[3] Young men go away to college. They all want to bring her money. These are the young men who thought that all they had to do was to count time. But Karintha is a woman, and she has had a child. A child fell out of her womb onto a bed of pine-needles in the forest. Pine-needles are smooth and sweet. They are elastic to the feet of rabbits. . . . A sawmill was nearby. Its pyramidal sawdust pile smouldered. It is a year before one completely burns. Meanwhile, the smoke curls up and hangs in odd wraiths about the trees, curls up, and spreads itself out over the valley. . . . Weeks after Karintha returned home the smoke was so heavy you tasted it in water. Some one made a song:

Smoke is on the hills. Rise up.
Smoke is on the hills, O rise
And take my soul to Jesus.

Karintha is a woman. Men do not know that the soul of her was a growing thing ripened too soon. They will bring their money; they will die not having found it out. . . . Karintha at twenty, carrying beauty, perfect as dusk when the sun goes down. Karintha . . .

Her skin is like dusk on the eastern horizon,
O cant you see it, O cant you see it,
Her skin is like dusk on the eastern horizon
. . . When the sun goes down.

Goes down . . .

Reapers

Black reapers with the sound of steel on stones
Are sharpening scythes. I see them place the hones
In their hip-pockets as a thing that's done,
And start their silent swinging, one by one.
Black horses drive a mower through the weeds,
And there, a field rat, startled, squealing bleeds.
His belly close to ground. I see the blade,
Blood-stained, continue cutting weeds and shade.

2. Make liquor illegally. 3. Work for the railroad companies.

November Cotton Flower

Boll-weevil's[1] coming, and the winter's cold,
Made cotton-stalks look rusty, seasons old,
And cotton, scarce as any southern snow,
Was vanishing; the branch, so pinched and slow,
Failed in its function as the autumn rake;
Drouth fighting soil had caused the soil to take
All water from the streams; dead birds were found
In wells a hundred feet below the ground—
Such was the season when the flower bloomed.
Old folks were startled, and it soon assumed
Significance. Superstition saw
Something it had never seen before:
Brown eyes that loved without a trace of fear,
Beauty so sudden for that time of year.

Becky

Becky was the white woman who had two Negro sons. She's dead; they've gone away. The pines whisper to Jesus. The Bible flaps its leaves with an aimless rustle on her mound.

Becky had one Negro son. Who gave it to her? Damn buck nigger, said the white folks' mouths. She wouldnt tell. Common, God-forsaken, insane white shameless wench, said the white folks' mouths. Her eyes were sunken, her neck stringy, her breasts fallen, till then. Taking their words, they filled her, like a bubble rising—then she broke. Mouth setting in a twist that held her eyes, harsh, vacant, staring . . . Who gave it to her? Low-down nigger with no self-respect, said the black folks' mouths. She wouldnt tell. Poor Catholic poor-white crazy woman, said the black folks' mouths. White folks and black folks built her cabin, fed her and her growing baby, prayed secretly to God who'd put His cross upon her and cast her out.

When the first was born, the white folks said they'd have no more to do with her. And black folks, they too joined hands to cast her out . . . The pines whispered to Jesus . . . The railroad boss said not to say he said it, but she could live, if she wanted to, on the narrow strip of land between the railroad and the road. John Stone, who owned the lumber and the bricks, would have shot the man who told he gave the stuff to Lonnie Deacon, who stole out there at night and built the cabin. A single room held down to earth . . . O fly away to Jesus . . . by a leaning chimney . . .

Six trains each day rumbled past and shook the ground under her cabin. Fords, and horse- and mule-drawn buggies went back and forth along the road. No one ever saw her. Trainmen, and passengers who'd heard about her, threw out papers and food. Threw out little crumpled slips of paper scribbled with prayers, as they passed her eye-shaped piece of sandy ground. Ground islandized between the road and railroad track. Pushed up where a blue-sheen God[1] with listless eyes could look at it. Folks from the town took turns,

1. A beetle notorious for destroying crops.

1. Perhaps the locomotive.

unknown, of course, to each other, in bringing corn and meat and sweet potatoes. Even sometimes snuff . . . O thank y Jesus . . . Old David Georgia, grinding cane and boiling syrup, never went her way without some sugar sap. No one ever saw her. The boy grew up and ran around. When he was five years old as folks reckoned it, Hugh Jourdon saw him carrying a baby. "Becky has another son," was what the whole town knew. But nothing was said, for the part of man that says things to the likes of that had told itself that if there was a Becky, that Becky now was dead.

The two boys grew. Sullen and cunning . . . O pines, whisper to Jesus; tell Him to come and press sweet Jesus-lips against their lips and eyes . . . It seemed as though with those two big fellows there, there could be no room for Becky. The part that prayed wondered if perhaps she'd really died, and they had buried her. No one dared ask. They'd beat and cut a man who meant nothing at all in mentioning that they lived along the road. White or colored? No one knew, and least of all themselves. They drifted around from job to job. We, who had cast out their mother because of them, could we take them in? They answered black and white folks by shooting up two men and leaving town. "Godam the white folks; godam the niggers," they shouted as they left town. Becky? Smoke curled up from her chimney; she must be there. Trains passing shook the ground. The ground shook the leaning chimney. Nobody noticed it. A creepy feeling came over all who saw that thin wraith of smoke and felt the trembling of the ground. Folks began to take her food again. They quit it soon because they had a fear. Becky if dead might be a hant,[2] and if alive—it took some nerve even to mention it . . . O pines, whisper to Jesus . . .

It was Sunday. Our congregation had been visiting at Pulverton, and were coming home. There was no wind. The autumn sun, the bell from Ebenezer Church, listless and heavy. Even the pines were stale, sticky, like the smell of food that makes you sick. Before we turned the bend of the road that would show us the Becky cabin, the horses stopped stock-still, pushed back their ears, and nervously whinnied. We urged, then whipped them on. Quarter of a mile away thin smoke curled up from the leaning chimney . . . O pines, whisper to Jesus . . . Goose-flesh came on my skin though there still was neither chill nor wind. Eyes left their sockets for the cabin. Ears burned and throbbed. Uncanny eclipse! fear closed my mind. We were just about to pass . . . Pines shout to Jesus! . . the ground trembled as a ghost train rumbled by. The chimney fell into the cabin. Its thud was like a hollow report, ages having passed since it went off. Barlo and I were pulled out of our seats. Dragged to the door that had swung open. Through the dust we saw the bricks in a mound upon the floor. Becky, if she was there, lay under them. I thought I heard a groan. Barlo, mumbling something, threw his Bible on the pile. (No one has ever touched it.) Somehow we got away. My buggy was still on the road. The last thing that I remember was whipping old Dan like fury; I remember nothing after that—that is, until I reached town and folks crowded round to get the true word of it.

Becky was the white woman who had two Negro sons. She's dead; they've gone away. The pines whisper to Jesus. The Bible flaps its leaves with an aimless rustle on her mound.

2. A ghost.

Face

Hair—
silver-gray,
like streams of stars,
Brows—
recurved canoes
quivered by the ripples blown by pain,
Her eyes—
mist of tears
condensing on the flesh below
And her channeled muscles
are cluster grapes of sorrow
purple in the evening sun
nearly ripe for worms.

Cotton Song

Come, brother, come. Lets lift it;
Come now, hewit! roll away!
Shackles fall upon the Judgment Day
But lets not wait for it.

God's body's got a soul,
Bodies like to roll the soul,
Cant blame God if we dont roll,
Come, brother, roll, roll!

Cotton bales are the fleecy way
Weary sinner's bare feet trod,
Softly, softly to the throne of God,
"We aint agwine t wait until th Judgment Day!

Nassur; nassur,
Hump.
Eoho, eoho, roll away!
We aint agwine t wait until th Judgment Day!"

God's body's got a soul,
Bodies like to roll the soul,
Cant blame God if we dont roll,
Come, brother, roll, roll!

Carma[1]

Wind is in the cane. Come along.
Cane leaves swaying, rusty with talk,

1. Or karma, the Hindu concept of the force of destiny or faith.

Scratching choruses above the guinea's squawk,
Wind is in the cane. Come along.

Carma, in overalls, and strong as any man, stands behind the old brown mule, driving the wagon home. It bumps, and groans, and shakes as it crosses the railroad track. She, riding it easy. I leave the men around the stove to follow her with my eyes down the red dust road. Nigger woman driving a Georgia chariot down an old dust road. Dixie Pike is what they call it. Maybe she feels my gaze, perhaps she expects it. Anyway, she turns. The sun, which has been slanting over her shoulder, shoots primitive rockets into her mangrove-gloomed, yellow flower face. Hi! Yip! God has left the Moses-people[2] for the nigger. "Gedap." Using reins to slap the mule, she disappears in a cloudy rumble at some indefinite point along the road.

(The sun is hammered to a band of gold. Pine-needles, like mazda, are brilliantly aglow. No rain has come to take the rustle from the falling sweet-gum leaves. Over in the forest, across the swamp, a sawmill blows its closing whistle. Smoke curls up. Marvelous web spun by the spider sawdust pile. Curls up and spreads itself pine-high above the branch, a single silver band along the eastern valley. A black boy . . . you are the most sleepiest man I ever seed, Sleeping Beauty . . . cradled on a gray mule, guided by the hollow sound of cowbells, heads for them through a rusty cotton field. From down the railroad track, the chug-chug of a gas engine announces that the repair gang is coming home. A girl in the yard of a whitewashed shack not much larger than the stack of worn ties piled before it, sings. Her voice is loud. Echoes, like rain, sweep the valley. Dusk takes the polish from the rails. Lights twinkle in scattered houses. From far away, a sad strong song. Pungent and composite, the smell of farmyards is the fragrance of the woman. She does not sing; her body is a song. She is in the forest, dancing. Torches flare . . . juju men, greegree,[3] witch-doctors . . . torches go out . . . The Dixie Pike has grown from a goat path in Africa.

Night.

Foxie, the bitch, slicks back her ears and barks at the rising moon.)

Wind is in the corn. Come along.
Corn leaves swaying, rusty with talk,
Scratching choruses above the guinea's squawk,
Wind is in the corn. Come along.

Carma's tale is the crudest melodrama. Her husband's in the gang.[4] And its her fault he got there. Working with a contractor, he was away most of the time. She had others. No one blames her for that. He returned one day and hung around the town where he picked up week-old boasts and rumors . . . Bane accused her. She denied. He couldnt see that she was becoming hysterical. He would have liked to take his fists and beat her. Who was strong as a man. Stronger. Words, like corkscrews, wormed to her strength. It fizzled out. Grabbing a gun, she rushed from the house and plunged across the road into a canebrake . . There, in quarter heaven shone the crescent moon . . . Bane was afraid to follow till he heard the gun go off. Then he wasted half an hour gathering the neighbor men. They met in

2. Ancient Hebrews.
3. A charm, associated with Africa. "Juju men": conjurers.
4. That is, a chain gang.

the road where lamp-light showed tracks dissolving in the loose earth about the cane. The search began. Moths flickered the lamps. They put them out. Really, because she still might be live enough to shoot. Time and space have no meaning in a canefield. No more than the interminable stalks . . . Some one stumbled over her. A cry went up. From the road, one would have thought that they were cornering a rabbit or a skunk . . . It is difficult carrying dead weight through cane. They placed her on the sofa. A curious, nosey somebody looked for the wound. This fussing with her clothes aroused her. Her eyes were weak and pitiable for so strong a woman. Slowly, then like a flash, Bane came to know that the shot she fired, with averted head, was aimed to whistle like a dying hornet through the cane. Twice deceived, and one deception proved the other. His head went off. Slashed one of the men who'd helped, the man who'd stumbled over her. Now he's in the gang. Who was her husband. Should she not take others, this Carma, strong as a man, whose tale as I have told it is the crudest melodrama?

Wind is in the cane. Come along.
Cane leaves swaying, rusty with talk,
Scratching choruses above the guinea's squawk,
Wind is in the cane. Come along.

Song of the Son

Pour O pour that parting soul in song,
O pour it in the sawdust glow of night,
Into the velvet pine-smoke air to-night,
And let the valley carry it along.
And let the valley carry it along.

O land and soil, red soil and sweet-gum tree,
So scant of grass, so profligate of pines,
Now just before an epoch's sun declines
Thy son, in time, I have returned to thee,
Thy son, I have in time returned to thee.

In time, for though the sun is setting on
A song-lit race of slaves, it has not set;
Though late, O soil, it is not too late yet
To catch thy plaintive soul, leaving, soon gone,
Leaving, to catch thy plaintive soul soon gone.

O Negro slaves, dark purple ripened plums,
Squeezed, and bursting in the pine-wood air,
Passing, before they stripped the old tree bare
One plum was saved for me, one seed becomes

An everlasting song, a singing tree,
Caroling softly souls of slavery,
What they were, and what they are to me,
Caroling softly souls of slavery.

Georgia Dusk

The sky, lazily disdaining to pursue
The setting sun, too indolent to hold
A lengthened tournament for flashing gold,
Passively darkens for night's barbecue,

A feast of moon and men and barking hounds,
An orgy for some genius of the South
With blood-hot eyes and cane-lipped scented mouth,
Surprised in making folk-songs from soul sounds.

The sawmill blows its whistle, buzz-saws stop,
And silence breaks the bud of knoll and hill,
Soft settling pollen where plowed lands fulfill
Their early promise of a bumper crop.

Smoke from the pyramidal sawdust pile
Curls up, blue ghosts of trees, tarrying low
Where only chips and stumps are left to show
The solid proof of former domicile.

Meanwhile, the men, with vestiges of pomp,
Race memories of king and caravan,
High-priests, an ostrich, and a juju-man,[1]
Go singing through the footpaths of the swamp.

Their voices rise . . . the pine trees are guitars,
Strumming, pine-needles fall like sheets of rain . . .
Their voices rise . . . the chorus of the cane
Is caroling a vesper to the stars . . .

O singers, resinous and soft your songs
Above the sacred whisper of the pines,
Give virgin lips to cornfield concubines,
Bring dreams of Christ to dusky cane-lipped throngs.

Fern

Face flowed into her eyes. Flowed in soft cream foam and plaintive ripples, in such a way that wherever your glance may momentarily have rested, it immediately thereafter wavered in the direction of her eyes. The soft suggestion of down slightly darkened, like the shadow of a bird's wing might, the creamy brown color of her upper lip. Why, after noticing it, you sought her eyes, I cannot tell you. Her nose was aquiline, Semitic. If you have heard a Jewish cantor sing, if he has touched you and made your own sorrow seem trivial when compared with his, you will know my feeling when I follow the curves of her profile, like mobile rivers, to their common delta. They were strange

1. A conjurer.

eyes. In this, that they sought nothing—that is, nothing that was obvious and tangible and that one could see, and they gave the impression that nothing was to be denied. When a woman seeks, you will have observed, her eyes deny. Fern's eyes desired nothing that you could give her; there was no reason why they should withhold. Men saw her eyes and fooled themselves. Fern's eyes said to them that she was easy. When she was young, a few men took her, but got no joy from it. And then, once done, they felt bound to her (quite unlike their hit and run with other girls), felt as though it would take them a lifetime to fulfill an obligation which they could find no name for. They became attached to her, and hungered after finding the barest trace of what she might desire. As she grew up, new men who came to town felt as almost everyone did who ever saw her: that they would not be denied. Men were everlastingly bringing her their bodies. Something inside of her got tired of them, I guess, for I am certain that for the life of her she could not tell why or how she began to turn them off. A man in fever is no trifling thing to send away. They began to leave her, baffled and ashamed, yet vowing to themselves that some day they would do some fine thing for her: send her candy every week and not let her know whom it came from, watch out for her wedding-day and give her a magnificent something with no name on it, buy a house and deed it to her, rescue her from some unworthy fellow who had tricked her into marrying him. As you know, men are apt to idolize or fear that which they cannot understand, especially if it be a woman. She did not deny them, yet the fact was that they were denied. A sort of superstition crept into their consciousness of her being somehow above them. Being above them meant that she was not to be approached by anyone. She became a virgin. Now a virgin in a small southern town is by no means the usual thing, if you will believe me. That the sexes were made to mate is the practice of the South. Particularly, black folks were made to mate. And it is black folks whom I have been talking about thus far. What white men thought of Fern I can arrive at only by analogy. They let her alone.

Anyone, of course, could see her, could see her eyes. If you walked up the Dixie Pike most any time of day, you'd be most like to see her resting listless-like on the railing of her porch, back propped against a post, head tilted a little forward because there was a nail in the porch post just where her head came which for some reason or other she never took the trouble to pull out. Her eyes, if it were sunset, rested idly where the sun, molten and glorious, was pouring down between the fringe of pines. Or maybe they gazed at the gray cabin on the knoll from which an evening folk-song was coming. Perhaps they followed a cow that had been turned loose to roam and feed on cotton-stalks and corn leaves. Like as not they'd settle on some vague spot above the horizon, though hardly a trace of wistfulness would come to them. If it were dusk, then they'd wait for the search-light of the evening train which you could see miles up the track before it flared across the Dixie Pike, close to her home. Wherever they looked, you'd follow them and then waver back. Like her face, the whole countryside seemed to flow into her eyes. Flowed into them with the soft listless cadence of Georgia's South. A young Negro, once, was looking at her, spellbound, from the road. A white man passing in a buggy had to flick him with his whip if he was to get by without running him over. I first saw her on her porch. I was passing with a fellow whose crusty numbness (I was from the North and suspected of being prejudiced and stuck-up) was melting as he found me warm. I asked him who she was. "That's Fern," was all that I could get from him. Some folks already thought that I was given to nosing around; I let it go at that, so far as questions were concerned. But at first sight of her I felt as if I heard a Jewish cantor sing. As if his singing rose above the unheard chorus of a folk-song. And I felt bound to her. I too had my dreams: something I would do for her. I have knocked about from town to town too much not to know the futility of mere change of place. Besides, picture if you can, this cream-colored solitary girl sitting at a tenement window looking down on the indifferent throngs of Harlem. Better that she listen to folk-songs at dusk in Georgia, you would say, and so would I. Or, suppose she came up North and married. Even a doctor or a lawyer, say, one who would be sure to get along—that is, make money. You and I know, who have had experience in such things, that love is not a thing like prejudice which can be bettered by changes of town. Could men in Washington, Chicago, or New York, more than the men of Georgia, bring her something left vacant by the bestowal of their bodies? You and I who know men in these cities will have to say, they could not. See her out and out a prostitute along State Street in Chicago. See her move into a southern town where white men are more aggressive. See her become a white man's concubine . . . Something I must do for her. There was myself. What could I do for her? Talk, of course. Push back the fringe of pines upon new horizons. To what purpose? and what for? Her? Myself? Men in her case seem to lose their selfishness. I lost mine before I touched her. I ask you, friend (it makes no difference if you sit in the Pullman[1] or the Jim Crow as the train crosses her road), what thoughts would come to you—that is, after you'd finished with the thoughts that leap into men's minds at the sight of a pretty woman who will not deny them; what thoughts would come to you, had you seen her in a quick flash, keen and intuitively, as she sat there on her porch when your train thundered by? Would you have got off at the next station and come back for her to take her where? Would you have completely forgotten her as soon as you reached Macon, Atlanta, Augusta, Pasadena, Madison, Chicago, Boston, or New Orleans? Would you tell your wife or sweetheart about a girl you saw? Your thoughts can help me, and I would like to know. Something I would do for her . . .

One evening I walked up the Pike on purpose, and stopped to say hello. Some of her family were about, but they moved away to make room for me. Damn if I knew how to begin. Would you? Mr. and Miss So-and-So, people, the weather, the crops, the new preacher, the frolic, the church benefit, rabbit and possum hunting, the new soft drink they had at old Pap's store, the schedule of the trains, what kind of town Macon was, Negro's migration north, bollweevils,[2] syrup, the Bible—to all these things she gave a yassur or nassur, without further comment. I began to wonder if perhaps my own emotional sensibility had played one of its tricks on me. "Lets take a walk," I at last ventured. The suggestion, coming after so long an isolation, was novel enough, I guess, to surprise. But it wasnt that. Something told me that men before me had said just that as a prelude to the offering of their bodies. I tried to tell her with my eyes. I think she understood. The thing

1. Sleeping car on the railroad; Blacks were generally barred from these in the South.

2. Beetles.

from her that made my throat catch, vanished. Its passing left her visible in a way I'd thought, but never seen. We walked down the Pike with people on all the porches gaping at us. "Doesnt it make you mad?" She meant the row of petty gossiping people. She meant the world. Through a canebrake that was ripe for cutting, the branch was reached. Under a sweet-gum tree, and where reddish leaves had dammed the creek a little, we sat down. Dusk, suggesting the almost imperceptible procession of giant trees, settled with a purple haze about the cane. I felt strange, as I always do in Georgia, particularly at dusk. I felt that things unseen to men were tangibly immediate. It would not have surprised me had I had vision. People have them in Georgia more often than you would suppose. A black woman once saw the mother of Christ and drew her in charcoal on the courthouse wall . . . When one is on the soil of one's ancestors, most anything can come to one . . . From force of habit, I suppose, I held Fern in my arms—that is, without at first noticing it. Then my mind came back to her. Her eyes, unusually weird and open, held me. Held God. He flowed in as I've seen the countryside flow in. Seen men. I must have done something—what, I dont know, in the confusion of my emotion. She sprang up. Rushed some distance from me. Fell to her knees, and began swaying, swaying. Her body was tortured with something it could not let out. Like boiling sap it flooded arms and fingers till she shook them as if they burned her. It found her throat, and spattered inarticulately in plaintive, convulsive sounds, mingled with calls to Christ Jesus. And then she sang, brokenly. A Jewish cantor singing with a broken voice. A child's voice, uncertain, or an old man's. Dusk hid her; I could hear only her song. It seemed to me as though she were pounding her head in anguish upon the ground. I rushed to her. She fainted in my arms.

There was talk about her fainting with me in the canefield. And I got one or two ugly looks from town men who'd set themselves up to protect her. In fact, there was talk of making me leave town. But they never did. They kept a watch-out for me, though. Shortly after, I came back North. From the train window I saw her as I crossed her road. Saw her on her porch, head tilted a little forward where the nail was, eyes vaguely focused on the sunset. Saw her face flow into them, the countryside and something that I call God, flowing into them . . . Nothing ever really happened. Nothing ever came to Fern, not even I. Something I would do for her. Some fine unnamed thing . . . And, friend, you? She is still living, I have reason to know. Her name, against the chance that you might happen down that way, is Fernie May Rosen.

Nullo

A spray of pine-needles,
Dipped in western horizon gold,
Fell onto a path.
Dry moulds of cow-hoofs.
In the forest.
Rabbits knew not of their falling,
Nor did the forest catch aflame.

Evening Song

Full moon rising on the waters of my heart,
Lakes and moon and fires,
Cloine tires,
Holding her lips apart.

Promises of slumber leaving shore to charm the moon,
Miracle made vesper-keeps,
Cloine sleeps,
And I'll be sleeping soon.

Cloine, curled like the sleepy waters where the moon-waves start,
Radiant, resplendently she gleams,
Cloine dreams,
Lips pressed against my heart.

Esther

1

NINE[1]

Esther's hair falls in soft curls about her high-cheek-boned chalk-white face. Esther's hair would be beautiful if there were more gloss to it. And if her face were not prematurely serious, one would call it pretty. Her cheeks are too flat and dead for a girl of nine. Esther looks like a little white child, starched, frilled, as she walks slowly from her home towards her father's grocery store. She is about to turn in Broad from Maple Street. White and black men loafing on the corner hold no interest for her. Then a strange thing happens. A clean-muscled, magnificent, black-skinned Negro, whom she had heard her father mention as King Barlo, suddenly drops to his knees on a spot called the Spittoon. White men, unaware of him, continue squirting tobacco juice in his direction. The saffron fluid splashes on his face. His smooth black face begins to glisten and to shine. Soon, people notice him, and gather round. His eyes are rapturous upon the heavens. Lips and nostrils quiver. Barlo is in a religious trance. Town folks know it. They are not startled. They are not afraid. They gather round. Some beg boxes from the grocery stores. From old McGregor's notion shop. A coffin-case is pressed into use. Folks line the curb-stones. Business men close shop. And Banker Warply parks his car close by. Silently, all await the prophet's voice. The sheriff, a great florid fellow whose leggings never meet around his bulging calves, swears in three deputies. "Wall, y cant never tell what a nigger like King Barlo might be up t." Soda bottles, five fingers full of shine,[2] are passed to those who want them. A couple of stray dogs start a fight. Old Goodlow's cow comes flopping up the street. Barlo, still as an Indian fakir,[3] has not moved. The town bell strikes six. The sun slips in behind a heavy mass of

1. Esther's age in this section.
2. That is, moonshine, or illegal whisky.
3. Magician.

horizon cloud. The crowd is hushed and expectant. Barlo's under jaw relaxes, and his lips begin to move.

"Jesus has been awhisperin strange words deep down, O way down deep, deep in my ears."

Hums of awe and of excitement.

"He called me to His side an said, 'Git down on your knees beside me, son, Ise gwine t whisper in your ears.'"

An old sister cries, "Ah, Lord."

"'Ise agwine t whisper in your ears,' he said, an I replied, 'Thy will be done on earth as it is in heaven.'"

"Ah, Lord. Amen. Amen."

"An Lord Jesus whispered strange good words deep down, O way down deep, deep in my ears. An He said, 'Tell em till you feel your throat on fire.' I saw a vision. I saw a man arise, an he was big an black an powerful—"

Some one yells, "Preach it, preacher, preach it!"

"—but his head was caught up in the clouds. An while he was agazin at th heavens, heart filled up with th Lord, some little white-ant biddies came an tied his feet to chains. They led him t th coast, they led him t th sea, they led him across th ocean an they didnt set him free. The old coast didnt miss him, an th new coast wasnt free, he left the old-coast brothers, t give birth t you an me. O Lord, great God Almighty, t give birth t you an me."

Barlo pauses. Old gray mothers are in tears. Fragments of melodies are being hummed. White folks are touched and curiously awed. Off to themselves, white and black preachers confer as to how best to rid themselves of the vagrant, usurping fellow. Barlo looks as though he is struggling to continue. People are hushed. One can hear weevils[4] work. Dusk is falling rapidly, and the customary store lights fail to throw their feeble glow across the gray dust and flagging of the Georgia town. Barlo rises to his full height. He is immense. To the people he assumes the outlines of his visioned African. In a mighty voice he bellows:

"Brothers an sisters, turn your faces t th sweet face of the Lord, an fill your hearts with glory. Open your eyes an see th dawnin of th mornin light. Open your ears—"

Years afterwards Esther was told that at that very moment a great, heavy, rumbling voice actually was heard. That hosts of angels and of demons paraded up and down the streets all night. That King Barlo rode out of town astride a pitch-black bull that had a glowing gold ring in its nose. And that old Limp Underwood, who hated niggers, woke up next morning to find that he held a black man in his arms. This much is certain: an inspired Negress, of wide reputation for being sanctified, drew a portrait of a black madonna on the courthouse wall. And King Barlo left town. He left his image indelibly upon the mind of Esther. He became the starting point of the only living patterns that her mind was to know.

2

SIXTEEN

Esther begins to dream. The low evening sun sets the windows of McGregor's notion shop aflame. Esther makes believe that they really are aflame. The

4. Boll weevils; beetles notorious for destroying crops.

town fire department rushes madly down the road. It ruthlessly shoves black and white idlers to one side. It whoops. It clangs. It rescues from the second-story window a dimpled infant which she claims for her own. How had she come by it? She thinks of it immaculately. It is a sin to think of it immaculately. She must dream no more. She must repent her sin. Another dream comes. There is no fire department. There are no heroic men. The fire starts. The loafers on the corner form a circle, chew their tobacco faster, and squirt juice just as fast as they can chew. Gallons on top of gallons they squirt upon the flames. The air reeks with the stench of scorched tobacco juice. Women, fat chunky Negro women, lean scrawny white women, pull their skirts up above their heads and display the most ludicrous underclothes. The women scoot in all directions from the danger zone. She alone is left to take the baby in her arms. But what a baby! Black, singed, woolly, tobacco-juice baby—ugly as sin. Once held to her breast, miraculous thing: its breath is sweet and its lips can nibble. She loves it frantically. Her joy in it changes the town folks' jeers to harmless jealousy, and she is left alone.

TWENTY-TWO

Esther's schooling is over. She works behind the counter of her father's grocery store. "To keep the money in the family," so he said. She is learning to make distinctions between the business and the social worlds. "Good business comes from remembering that the white folks dont divide the niggers, Esther. Be just as black as any man who has a silver dollar." Esther listlessly forgets that she is near white, and that her father is the richest colored man in town. Black folk who drift in to buy lard and snuff and flour of her, call her a sweet-natured, accommodating girl. She learns their names. She forgets them. She thinks about men. "I dont appeal to them. I wonder why." She recalls an affair she had with a little fair boy while still in school. It had ended in her shame when he as much as told her that for sweetness he preferred a lollipop. She remembers the salesman from the North who wanted to take her to the movies that first night he was in town. She refused, of course. And he never came back, having found out who she was. She thinks of Barlo. Barlo's image gives her a slightly stale thrill. She spices it by telling herself his glories. Black. Magnetically so. Best cotton picker in the county, in the state, in the whole world for that matter. Best man with his fists, best man with dice, with a razor. Promoter of church benefits. Of colored fairs. Vagrant preacher. Lover of all the women for miles and miles around. Esther decides that she loves him. And with a vague sense of life slipping by, she resolves that she will tell him so, whatever people say, the next time he comes to town. After the making of this resolution which becomes a sort of wedding cake for her to tuck beneath her pillow and go to sleep upon, she sees nothing of Barlo for five years. Her hair thins. It looks like the dull silk on puny corn ears. Her face pales until it is the color of the gray dust that dances with dead cotton leaves.

3

ESTHER IS TWENTY-SEVEN

Esther sells lard and snuff and flour to vague black faces that drift in her store to ask for them. Her eyes hardly see the people to whom she gives change. Her body is lean and beaten. She rests listlessly against the counter, too weary to sit down. From the street some one shouts, "King Barlo has come back to town." He passes her window, driving a large new car. Cut-out open.[5] He veers to the curb, and steps out. Barlo has made money on cotton during the war.[6] He is as rich as anyone. Esther suddenly is animate. She goes to her door. She sees him at a distance, the center of a group of credulous men. She hears the deep-bass rumble of his talk. The sun swings low. McGregor's windows are aflame again. Pale flame. A sharply dressed white girl passes by. For a moment Esther wishes that she might be like her. Not white; she has no need for being that. But sharp, sporty, with get-up about her. Barlo is connected with that wish. She mustnt wish. Wishes only make you restless. Emptiness is a thing that grows by being moved. "I'll not think. Not wish. Just set my mind against it." Then the thought comes to her that those purposeless, easy-going men will possess him, if she doesnt. Purpose is not dead in her, now that she comes to think of it. That loose women will have their arms around him at Nat Bowle's place tonight. As if her veins are full of fired sun-bleached southern shanties, a swift heat sweeps them. Dead dreams, and a forgotten resolution are carried upward by the flames. Pale flames. "They shant have him. Oh, they shall not. Not if it kills me they shant have him." Jerky, aflutter, she closes the store and starts home. Folks lazing on store windowsills wonder what on earth can be the matter with Jim Crane's gal, as she passes them. "Come to remember, she always was a little off, a little crazy, I reckon." Esther seeks her own room, and locks the door. Her mind is a pink meshbag filled with baby toes.

Using the noise of the town clock striking twelve to cover the creaks of her departure, Esther slips into the quiet road. The town, her parents, most everyone is sound asleep. This fact is a stable thing that comforts her. After sundown a chill wind came up from the west. It is still blowing, but to her it is a steady, settled thing like the cold. She wants her mind to be like that. Solid, contained, and blank as a sheet of darkened ice. She will not permit herself to notice the peculiar phosphorescent glitter of the sweet-gum leaves. Their movement would excite her. Exciting too, the recession of the dull familiar homes she knows so well. She doesnt know them at all. She closes her eyes, and holds them tightly. Wont do. Her being aware that they are closed recalls her purpose. She does not want to think of it. She opens them. She turns now into the deserted business street. The corrugated iron canopies and mule- and horse-gnawed hitching posts bring her a strange composure. Ghosts of the commonplaces of her daily life take stride with her and become her companions. And the echoes of her heels upon the flagging are rhythmically monotonous and soothing. Crossing the street at the corner of McGregor's notion shop, she thinks that the windows are a dull flame. Only a fancy. She walks faster. Then runs. A turn into a side street brings her abruptly to Nat Bowle's place. The house is squat and dark. It is always dark. Barlo is within. Quietly she opens the outside door and steps in. She passes through a small room. Pauses before a flight of stairs down which people's voices, muffled, come. The air is heavy with fresh tobacco smoke. It makes her sick. She wants to turn back. She goes up the steps. As if she were mounting to some great height, her head spins. She is violently dizzy. Blackness

5. A car without a steel top.

6. World War I (1914–18).

rushes to her eyes. And then she finds that she is in a large room. Barlo is before her.

"Well, I'm sholy damned—skuse me, but what, what brought you here, lil milk-white gal?"

"You." Her voice sounds like a frightened child's that calls homeward from some point miles away.

"Me?"

"Yes, you Barlo."

"This aint th place fer y. This aint th place fer y."

"I know. I know. But I've come for you."

"For me for what?"

She manages to look deep and straight into his eyes. He is slow at understanding. Guffaws and giggles break out from all around the room. A coarse woman's voice remarks, "So thats how the dictie niggers[7] does it." Laughs. "Mus give em credit fo their gall."

Esther doesnt hear. Barlo does. His faculties are jogged. She sees a smile, ugly and repulsive to her, working upward through thick licker fumes. Barlo seems hideous. The thought comes suddenly, that conception with a drunken man must be a mighty sin. She draws away, frozen. Like a somnambulist she wheels around and walks stiffly to the stairs. Down them. Jeers and hoots pelter bluntly upon her back. She steps out. There is no air, no street, and the town has completely disappeared.

Conversion

African Guardian of Souls,
Drunk with rum,
Feasting on a strange cassava,[1]
Yielding to new words and a weak palabra[2]
Of a white-faced sardonic god—
Grins, cries
Amen,
Shouts hosanna.

Portrait in Georgia

Hair—braided chestnut,
    coiled like a lyncher's rope,
Eyes—fagots,[1]
Lips—old scars, or the first red blisters,
Breath—the last sweet scent of cane,
And her slim body, white as the ash
    of black flesh after flame.

7. Educated Blacks.
1. An edible, tuberous tropical root, served cooked or used as a starch or flour.
2. Word or talk (Spanish).
1. A bundle of sticks or branches bound together, usually to be used in a fire.

Blood-Burning Moon[1]

1

Up from the skeleton stone walls, up from the rotting floor boards and the solid hand-hewn beams of oak of the pre-war cotton factory, dusk came. Up from the dusk the full moon came. Glowing like a fired pine-knot, it illumined the great door and soft showered the Negro shanties aligned along the single street of factory town. The full moon in the great door was an omen. Negro women improvised songs against its spell.

Louisa sang as she came over the crest of the hill from the white folks' kitchen. Her skin was the color of oak leaves on young trees in fall. Her breasts, firm and up-pointed like ripe acorns. And her singing had the low murmur of winds in fig trees. Bob Stone, younger son of the people she worked for, loved her. By the way the world reckons things, he had won her. By measure of that warm glow which came into her mind at thought of him, he had won her. Tom Burwell, whom the whole town called Big Boy, also loved her. But working in the fields all day, and far away from her, gave him no chance to show it. Though often enough of evenings he had tried to. Somehow, he never got along. Strong as he was with hands upon the ax or plow, he found it difficult to hold her. Or so he thought. But the fact was that he held her to factory town more firmly than he thought for. His black balanced, and pulled against, the white of Stone, when she thought of them. And her mind was vaguely upon them as she came over the crest of the hill, coming from the white folks' kitchen. As she sang softly at the evil face of the full moon.

A strange stir was in her. Indolently, she tried to fix upon Bob or Tom as the cause of it. To meet Bob in the canebrake, as she was going to do an hour or so later, was nothing new. And Tom's proposal which she felt on its way to her could be indefinitely put off. Separately, there was no unusual significance to either one. But for some reason, they jumbled when her eyes gazed vacantly at the rising moon. And from the jumble came the stir that was strangely within her. Her lips trembled. The slow rhythm of her song grew agitant and restless. Rusty black and tan spotted hounds, lying in the dark corners of porches or prowling around back yards, put their noses in the air and caught its tremor. They began plaintively to yelp and howl. Chickens woke up and cackled. Intermittently, all over the countryside dogs barked and roosters crowed as if heralding a weird dawn or some ungodly awakening. The women sang lustily. Their songs were cotton-wads to stop their ears. Louisa came down into factory town and sank wearily upon the step before her home. The moon was rising towards a thick cloud-bank which soon would hide it.

Red nigger moon. Sinner!
Blood-burning moon. Sinner!
Come out that fact'ry door.

2

Up from the deep dusk of a cleared spot on the edge of the forest a mellow glow arose and spread fan-wise into the low-hanging heavens. And all around the air was heavy with the scent of boiling cane. A large pile of

1. A reddish moon is said to portend a night of violence.

cane-stalks lay like ribboned shadows upon the ground. A mule, harnessed to a pole, trudged lazily round and round the pivot of the grinder. Beneath a swaying oil lamp, a Negro alternately whipped out at the mule, and fed cane-stalks to the grinder. A fat boy waddled pails of fresh ground juice between the grinder and the boiling stove. Steam came from the copper boiling pan. The scent of cane came from the copper pan and drenched the forest and the hill that sloped to factory town, beneath its fragrance. It drenched the men in circle seated around the stove. Some of them chewed at the white pulp of stalks, but there was no need for them to, if all they wanted was to taste the cane. One tasted it in factory town. And from factory town one could see the soft haze thrown by the glowing stove upon the low-hanging heavens.

Old David Georgia stirred the thickening syrup with a long ladle, and ever so often drew it off. Old David Georgia tended his stove and told tales about the white folks, about moonshining and cotton picking, and about sweet nigger gals, to the men who sat there about his stove to listen to him. Tom Burwell chewed cane-stalk and laughed with the others till some one mentioned Louisa. Till some one said something about Louisa and Bob Stone, about the silk stockings she must have gotten from him. Blood ran up Tom's neck hotter than the glow that flooded from the stove. He sprang up. Glared at the men and said, "She's my gal." Will Manning laughed. Tom strode over to him. Yanked him up and knocked him to the ground. Several of Manning's friends got up to fight for him. Tom whipped out a long knife and would have cut them to shreds if they hadnt ducked into the woods. Tom had had enough. He nodded to Old David Georgia and swung down the path to factory town. Just then, the dogs started barking and the roosters began to crow. Tom felt funny. Away from the fight, away from the stove, chill got to him. He shivered. He shuddered when he saw the full moon rising towards the cloud-bank. He who didnt give a godam for the fears of old women. He forced his mind to fasten on Louisa. Bob Stone. Better not be. He turned into the street and saw Louisa sitting before her home. He went towards her, ambling, touched the brim of a marvelously shaped, spotted, felt hat, said he wanted to say something to her, and then found that he didnt know what he had to say, or if he did, that he couldnt say it. He shoved his big fists in his overalls, grinned, and started to move off.

"Youall want me, Tom?"

"Thats what us wants, sho, Louisa."

"Well, here I am—"

"An here I is, but that aint ahelpin none, all th same."

"You wanted to say something? . . ."

"I did that, sho. But words is like th spots on dice: no matter how y fumbles em, there's times when they jes wont come. I dunno why. Seems like th love I feels fo yo done stole m tongue. I got it now. Whee! Louisa, honey, I oughtnt tell y, I feel I oughtnt cause yo is young an goes t church an I has had other gals, but Louisa I sho do love y. Lil gal, Ise watched y from them first days when youall sat right here befo yo door befo th well an sang sometimes in a way that like t broke m heart. Ise carried y with me into th fields, day after day, an after that, an I sho can plow when yo is there, an I can pick cotton. Yassur! Come near beatin Barlo yesterday. I sho did. Yassur! An next year if ole Stone'll trust me, I'll have a farm. My own. My bales will buy yo what y gets from white folks now. Silk stockings an purple dresses—course I dont believe what some folks been whisperin as t how y gets them things now.

White folks always did do for niggers what they likes. An they jes cant help alikin yo, Louisa. Bob Stone likes y. Course he does. But not th way folks is awhisperin. Does he, hon?"

"I dont know what you mean, Tom."

"Course y dont. Ise already cut two niggers. Had t hon, t tell em so. Niggers always tryin t make somethin out a nothin. An then besides, white folks aint up t them tricks so much nowadays. Godam better not be. Leastawise not with yo. Cause I wouldnt stand f it. Nassur."

"What would you do, Tom?"

"Cut him jes like I cut a nigger."

"No, Tom—"

"I said I would an there aint no mo to it. But that aint th talk f now. Sing, honey Louisa, an while I'm listenin t y I'll be makin love."

Tom took her hand in his. Against the tough thickness of his own, hers felt soft and small. His huge body slipped down to the step beside her. The full moon sank upward into the deep purple of the cloud-bank. An old woman brought a lighted lamp and hung it on the common well whose bulky shadow squatted in the middle of the road, opposite Tom and Louisa. The old woman lifted the well-lid, took hold the chain, and began drawing up the heavy bucket. As she did so, she sang. Figures shifted, restlesslike, between lamp and window in the front rooms of the shanties. Shadows of the figures fought each other on the gray dust of the road. Figures raised the windows and joined the old woman in song. Louisa and Tom, the whole street, singing:

Red nigger moon. Sinner!
Blood-burning moon. Sinner!
Come out that fact'ry door.

3

Bob Stone sauntered from his veranda out into the gloom of fir trees and magnolias. The clear white of his skin paled, and the flush of his cheeks turned purple. As if to balance this outer change, his mind became consciously a white man's. He passed the house with its huge open hearth which, in the days of slavery, was the plantation cookery. He saw Louisa bent over that hearth. He went in as a master should and took her. Direct, honest, bold. None of this sneaking that he had to go through now. The contrast was repulsive to him. His family had lost ground. Hell no, his family still owned the niggers, practically. Damned if they did, or he wouldnt have to duck around so. What would they think if they knew? His mother? His sister? He shouldnt mention them, shouldnt think of them in this connection. There in the dusk he blushed at doing so. Fellows about town were all right, but how about his friends up North? He could see them incredible, repulsed. They didnt know. The thought first made him laugh. Then, with their eyes still upon him, he began to feel embarrassed. He felt the need of explaining things to them. Explain hell. They wouldnt understand, and moreover, who ever heard of a Southerner getting on his knees to any Yankee, or anyone. No sir. He was going to see Louisa tonight, and love her. She was lovely—in her way. Nigger way. What way was that? Damned if he knew. Must know. He'd known her long enough to know. Was there something about niggers that you couldnt know? Listening to them at church didnt tell you anything. Looking at them didnt tell you anything. Talking to them didnt tell you anything—unless it was gossip, unless they wanted to talk. Of course, about farming, and licker, and craps—but those werent nigger. Nigger was something more. How much more? Something to be afraid of, more? Hell no. Who ever heard of being afraid of a nigger? Tom Burwell. Cartwell had told him that Tom went with Louisa after she reached home. No sir. No nigger had ever been with his girl. He'd like to see one try. Some position for him to be in. Him, Bob Stone, of the old Stone family, in a scrap with a nigger over a nigger girl. In the good old days . . . Ha! Those were the days. His family had lost ground. Not so much, though. Enough for him to have to cut through old Lemon's canefield by way of the woods, that he might meet her. She was worth it. Beautiful nigger gal. Why nigger? Why not, just gal? No, it was because she was nigger that he went to her. Sweet . . . The scent of boiling cane came to him. Then he saw the rich glow of the stove. He heard the voices of the men circled around it. He was about to skirt the clearing when he heard his own name mentioned. He stopped. Quivering. Leaning against a tree, he listened.

"Bad nigger. Yassur, he sho is one bad nigger when he gets started."

"Tom Burwell's been on th gang three times fo cuttin men."

"What y think he's agwine t do t Bob Stone?"

"Dunno yet. He aint found out. When he does—Baby!"

"Aint no tellin."

"Young Stone aint no quitter an I ken tell y that. Blood of th old uns in his veins."

"Thats right. He'll scrap, sho."

"Be gettin too hot f niggers round this away."

"Shut up, nigger. Y dont know what y talkin bout."

Bob Stone's ears burned as though he had been holding them over the stove. Sizzling heat welled up within him. His feet felt as if they rested on red-hot coals. They stung him to quick movement. He circled the fringe of the glowing. Not a twig cracked beneath his feet. He reached the path that led to factory town. Plunged furiously down it. Halfway along, a blindness within him veered him aside. He crashed into the bordering canebrake. Cane leaves cut his face and lips. He tasted blood. He threw himself down and dug his fingers in the ground. The earth was cool. Cane-roots took the fever from his hands. After a long while, or so it seemed to him, the thought came to him that it must be time to see Louisa. He got to his feet and walked calmly to their meeting place. No Louisa. Tom Burwell had her. Veins in his forehead bulged and distended. Saliva moistened the dried blood on his lips. He bit down on his lips. He tasted blood. Not his own blood; Tom Burwell's blood. Bob drove through the cane and out again upon the road. A hound swung down the path before him towards factory town. Bob couldnt see it. The dog loped aside to let him pass. Bob's blind rushing made him stumble over it. He fell with a thud that dazed him. The hound yelped. Answering yelps came from all over the countryside. Chickens cackled. Roosters crowed, heralding the bloodshot eyes of southern awakening. Singers in the town were silenced. They shut their windows down. Palpitant between the rooster crows, a chill hush settled upon the huddled forms of Tom and Louisa. A figure rushed from the shadow and stood before them. Tom popped to his feet.

"Whats y want?"

"I'm Bob Stone."

"Yassur—an I'm Tom Burwell. Whats y want?"

Bob lunged at him. Tom side-stepped, caught him by the shoulder, and flung him to the ground. Straddled him.

"Let me up."

"Yassur—but watch yo doins,[2] Bob Stone."

A few dark figures, drawn by the sound of scuffle, stood about them. Bob sprang to his feet.

"Fight like a man, Tom Burwell, an I'll lick y."

Again he lunged. Tom side-stepped and flung him to the ground. Straddled him.

"Get off me, you godam nigger you."

"Yo sho has started somethin now. Get up."

Tom yanked him up and began hammering at him. Each blow sounded as if it smashed into a precious, irreplaceable soft something. Beneath them, Bob staggered back. He reached in his pocket and whipped out a knife.

"Thats my game, sho."

Blue flash, a steel blade slashed across Bob Stone's throat. He had a sweetish sick feeling. Blood began to flow. Then he felt a sharp twitch of pain. He let his knife drop. He slapped one hand against his neck. He pressed the other on top of his head as if to hold it down. He groaned. He turned, and staggered towards the crest of the hill in the direction of white town. Negroes who had seen the fight slunk into their homes and blew the lamps out. Louisa, dazed, hysterical, refused to go indoors. She slipped, crumbled, her body loosely propped against the woodwork of the well. Tom Burwell leaned against it. He seemed rooted there.

Bob reached Broad Street. White men rushed up to him. He collapsed in their arms.

"Tom Burwell. . . ."

White men like ants upon a forage rushed about. Except for the taut hum of their moving, all was silent. Shotguns, revolvers, rope, kerosene, torches. Two high-powered cars with glaring searchlights. They came together. The taut hum rose to a low roar. Then nothing could be heard but the flop of their feet in the thick dust of the road. The moving body of their silence preceded them over the crest of the hill into factory town. It flattened the Negroes beneath it. It rolled to the wall of the factory, where it stopped. Tom knew that they were coming. He couldnt move. And then he saw the searchlights of the two cars glaring down on him. A quick shock went through him. He stiffened. He started to run. A yell went up from the mob. Tom wheeled about and faced them. They poured down on him. They swarmed. A large man with dead-white face and flabby cheeks came to him and almost jabbed a gun-barrel through his guts.

"Hands behind y, nigger."

Tom's wrists were bound. The big man shoved him to the well. Burn him over it, and when the woodwork caved in, his body would drop to the bottom. Two deaths for a godam nigger. Louisa was driven back. The mob pushed in. Its pressure, its momentum was too great. Drag him to the factory. Wood and stakes already there. Tom moved in the direction indicated. But they had to drag him. They reached the great door. Too many to get in there. The mob divided and flowed around the walls to either side. The big man shoved him through the door. The mob pressed in from the sides. Taut humming. No words. A stake was sunk into the ground. Rotting floor boards piled around it. Kerosene poured on the rotting floor boards. Tom bound to the stake. His breast was bare. Nails' scratches let little lines of blood trickle down and mat

2. Actions.

into the hair. His face, his eyes were set and stony. Except for irregular breathing, one would have thought him already dead. Torches were flung onto the pile. A great flare muffled in black smoke shot upward. The mob yelled. The mob was silent. Now Tom could be seen within the flames. Only his head, erect, lean, like a blackened stone. Stench of burning flesh soaked the air. Tom's eyes popped. His head settled downward. The mob yelled. Its yell echoed against the skeleton stone walls and sounded like a hundred yells. Like a hundred mobs yelling. Its yell thudded against the thick front wall and fell back. Ghost of a yell slipped through the flames and out the great door of the factory. It fluttered like a dying thing down the single street of factory town. Louisa, upon the step before her home, did not hear it, but her eyes opened slowly. They saw the full moon glowing in the great door. The full moon, an evil thing, an omen, soft showering the homes of folks she knew. Where were they, these people? She'd sing, and perhaps they'd come out and join her. Perhaps Tom Burwell would come. At any rate, the full moon in the great door was an omen which she must sing to:

Red nigger moon. Sinner!
Blood-burning moon. Sinner!
Come out that fact'ry door.

Seventh Street[1]

Money burns the pocket, pocket hurts,
Bootleggers in silken shirts,
Ballooned, zooming Cadillacs,
Whizzing, whizzing down the street-car tracks.

Seventh Street is a bastard of Prohibition and the War.[2] A crude-boned, soft-skinned wedge of nigger life breathing its loafer air, jazz songs and love, thrusting unconscious rhythms, black reddish blood into the white and whitewashed wood of Washington. Stale soggy wood of Washington. Wedges rust in soggy wood . . . Split it! In two! Again! Shred it! . . . the sun. Wedges are brilliant in the sun; ribbons of wet wood dry and blow away. Black reddish blood. Pouring for crude-boned soft-skinned life, who set you flowing? Blood suckers of the War would spin in a frenzy of dizziness if they drank your blood. Prohibition would put a stop to it. Who set you flowing? White and whitewash disappear in blood. Who set you flowing? Flowing down the smooth asphalt of Seventh Street, in shanties, brick office buildings, theaters, drug stores, restaurants, and cabarets? Eddying on the corners? Swirling like a blood-red smoke up where the buzzards fly in heaven? God would not dare to suck black red blood. A Nigger God! He would duck his head in shame and call for the Judgment Day. Who set you flowing?

Money burns the pocket, pocket hurts,
Bootleggers in silken shirts,
Ballooned, zooming Cadillacs,
Whizzing, whizzing down the street-car tracks.

1. The stories and sketches in this section are set in Washington, D.C., except for "Bona and Paul," which is set in Chicago.
2. World War I.

Rhobert

Rhobert wears a house, like a monstrous diver's helmet, on his head. His legs are banty-bowed and shaky because as a child he had rickets. He is way down. Rods of the house like antennae of a dead thing, stuffed, prop up in the air. He is way down. He is sinking. His house is a dead thing that weights him down. He is sinking as a diver would sink in mud should the water be drawn off. Life is a murky, wiggling, microscopic water that compresses him. Compresses his helmet and would crush it the minute that he pulled his head out. He has to keep it in. Life is water that is being drawn off.

Brother, life is water that is being drawn off.
Brother, life is water that is being drawn off.

The dead house is stuffed. The stuffing is alive. It is sinful to draw one's head out of live stuffing in a dead house. The propped-up antennæ would cave in and the stuffing be strewn . . shredded life-pulp . . in the water. It is sinful to have one's own head crushed. Rhobert is an upright man whose legs are banty-bowed and shaky because as a child he had rickets. The earth is round. Heaven is a sphere that surrounds it. Sink where you will. God is a Red Cross man with a dredge and a respiration-pump who's waiting for you at the opposite periphery. God built the house. He blew His breath into its stuffing. It is good to die obeying Him who can do these things.

A futile something like the dead house wraps the live stuffing of the question: how long before the water will be drawn off? Rhobert does not care. Like most men who wear monstrous helmets, the pressure it exerts is enough to convince him of its practical infinity. And he cares not two straws as to whether or not he will ever see his wife and children again. Many a time he's seen them drown in his dreams and has kicked about joyously in the mud for days after. One thing about him goes straight to the heart. He has an Adam's-apple which strains sometimes as if he were painfully gulping great globules of air . . air floating shredded life-pulp. It is a sad thing to see a banty-bowed, shaky, ricket-legged man straining the raw insides of his throat against smooth air. Holding furtive thoughts about the glory of pulp-heads strewn in water. . He is way down. Down. Mud, coming to his banty knees, almost hides them. Soon people will be looking at him and calling him a strong man. No doubt he is for one who has had rickets. Lets give it to him. Lets call him great when the water shall have been all drawn off. Lets build a monument and set it in the ooze where he goes down. A monument of hewn oak, carved in nigger-heads. Lets open our throats, brother, and sing "Deep River"[1] when he goes down.

Brother, Rhobert is sinking.
Lets open our throats, brother,
Lets sing Deep River when he goes down.

Avey

For a long while she was nothing more to me than one of those skirted beings whom boys at a certain age disdain to play with. Just how I came to

1. African American spiritual.

love her, timidly, and with secret blushes, I do not know. But that I did was brought home to me one night, the first night that Ned wore his long pants. Us fellers were seated on the curb before an apartment house where she had gone in. The young trees had not outgrown their boxes then. V Street[1] was lined with them. When our legs grew cramped and stiff from the cold of the stone, we'd stand around a box and whittle it. I like to think now that there was a hidden purpose in the way we hacked them with our knives. I like to feel that something deep in me responded to the trees, the young trees that whinnied like colts impatient to be let free . . . On the particular night I have in mind, we were waiting for the top-floor light to go out. We wanted to see Avey leave the flat. This night she stayed longer than usual and gave us a chance to complete the plans of how we were going to stone and beat that feller on the top floor out of town. Ned especially had it in for him. He was about to throw a brick up at the window when at last the room went dark. Some minutes passed. Then Avey, as unconcerned as if she had been paying an old-maid aunt a visit, came out. I dont remember what she had on, and all that sort of thing. But I do know that I turned hot as bare pavements in the summertime at Ned's boast: "Hell, bet I could get her too if you little niggers weren't always spying and crabbing everything." I didnt say a word to him. It wasnt my way then. I just stood there like the others, and something like a fuse burned up inside of me. She never noticed us, but swung along lazy and easy as anything. We sauntered to the corner and watched her till her door banged to. Ned repeated what he'd said. I didnt seem to care. Sitting around old Mush-Head's bread box, the discussion began. "Hang if I can see how she gets away with it," Doc started. Ned knew, of course. There was nothing he didnt know when it came to women. He dilated on the emotional needs of girls. Said they werent much different from men in that respect. And concluded with the solemn avowal: "It does em good." None of us liked Ned much. We all talked dirt; but it was the way he said it. And then too, a couple of the fellers had sisters and had caught Ned playing with them. But there was no disputing the superiority of his smutty wisdom. Bubs Sanborn, whose mother was friendly with Avey's, had overheard the old ladies talking. "Avey's mother's ont her," he said. We thought that only natural and began to guess at what would happen. Some one said she'd marry that feller on the top floor. Ned called that a lie because Avey was going to marry nobody but him. We had our doubts about that, but we did agree that she'd soon leave school and marry some one. The gang broke up, and I went home, picturing myself as married.

Nothing I did seemed able to change Avey's indifference to me. I played basket-ball, and when I'd make a long clean shot she'd clap with the others, louder than they, I thought. I'd meet her on the street, and there'd be no difference in the way she said hello. She never took the trouble to call me by my name. On the days for drill,[2] I'd let my voice down a tone and call for a complicated maneuver when I saw her coming. She'd smile appreciation, but it was an impersonal smile, never for me. It was on a summer excursion down to Riverview that she first seemed to take me into account. The day had been spent riding merry-go-rounds, scenic-railways, and shoot-the-chutes. We had been in swimming and we had danced. I was a

1. A street in a densely populated African American neighborhood in Washington, D.C.

2. Marching as part of the military training in high school.

crack swimmer then. She didnt know how. I held her up and showed her how to kick her legs and draw her arms. Of course she didnt learn in one day, but she thanked me for bothering with her. I was also somewhat of a dancer. And I had already noticed that love can start on a dance floor. We danced. But though I held her tightly in my arms, she was way away. That college feller who lived on the top floor was somewhere making money for the next year. I imagined that she was thinking, wishing for him. Ned was along. He treated her until his money gave out. She went with another feller. Ned got sore. One by one the boys' money gave out. She left them. And they got sore. Every one of them but me got sore. This is the reason, I guess, why I had her to myself on the top deck of the *Jane Mosely* that night as we puffed up the Potomac, coming home. The moon was brilliant. The air was sweet like clover. And every now and then, a salt tang, a stale drift of sea-weed. It was not my mind's fault if it went romancing. I should have taken her in my arms the minute we were stowed in that old lifeboat. I dallied, dreaming. She took me in hers. And I could feel by the touch of it that it wasnt a man-to-woman love. It made me restless. I felt chagrined. I didnt know what it was, but I did know that I couldnt handle it. She ran her fingers through my hair and kissed my forehead. I itched to break through her tenderness to passion. I wanted her to take me in her arms as I knew she had that college feller. I wanted her to love me passionately as she did him. I gave her one burning kiss. Then she laid me in her lap as if I were a child. Helpless. I got sore when she started to hum a lullaby. She wouldnt let me go. I talked. I knew damned well that I could beat her at that. Her eyes were soft and misty, the curves of her lips were wistful, and her smile seemed indulgent of the irrelevance of my remarks. I gave up at last and let her love me, silently, in her own way. The moon was brilliant. The air was sweet like clover, and every now and then, a salt tang, a stale drift of seaweed . . .

The next time I came close to her was the following summer at Harpers Ferry. We were sitting on a flat projecting rock they give the name of Lover's Leap. Some one is supposed to have jumped off it. The river is about six hundred feet beneath. A railroad track runs up the valley and curves out of sight where part of the mountain rock had to be blasted away to make room for it. The engines of this valley have a whistle, the echoes of which sound like iterated gasps and sobs. I always think of them as crude music from the soul of Avey. We sat there holding hands. Our palms were soft and warm against each other. Our fingers were not tight. She would not let them be. She would not let me twist them. I wanted to talk. To explain what I meant to her. Avey was as silent as those great trees whose tops we looked down upon. She has always been like that. At least, to me. I had the notion that if I really wanted to, I could do with her just what I pleased. Like one can strip a tree. I did kiss her. I even let my hands cup her breasts. When I was through, she'd seek my hand and hold it till my pulse cooled down. Evening after evening we sat there. I tried to get her to talk about that college feller. She never would. There was no set time to go home. None of my family had come down. And as for hers, she didnt give a hang about them. The general gossips could hardly say more than they had. The boarding-house porch was always deserted when we returned. No one saw us enter, so the time was set conveniently for scandal. This worried me a little, for I thought it might keep Avey from getting an appointment in the schools. She didnt care. She had finished normal school.[3] They could give her a job if they wanted to. As time went on, her indifference to things began to pique me; I was ambitious. I left the Ferry earlier than she did. I was going off to college. The more I thought of it, the more I resented, yes, hell, thats what it was, her downright laziness. Sloppy indolence. There was no excuse for a healthy girl taking life so easy. Hell! she was no better than a cow. I was certain that she was a cow when I felt an udder in a Wisconsin stock-judging class. Among those energetic Swedes, or whatever they are, I decided to forget her. For two years I thought I did. When I'd come home for the summer she'd be away. And before she returned, I'd be gone. We never wrote; she was too damned lazy for that. But what a bluff I put up about forgetting her. The girls up that way, at least the ones I knew, havent got the stuff: they dont know how to love. Giving themselves completely was tame beside just the holding of Avey's hand. One day I received a note from her. The writing, I decided, was slovenly. She wrote on a torn bit of note-book paper. The envelope had a faint perfume that I remembered. A single line told me she had lost her school and was going away. I comforted myself with the reflection that shame held no pain for one so indolent as she. Nevertheless, I left Wisconsin that year for good. Washington had seemingly forgotten her. I hunted Ned. Between curses, I caught his opinion of her. She was no better than a whore. I saw her mother on the street. The same old pinch-beck, jerky-gaited creature that I'd always known.

Perhaps five years passed. The business of hunting a job or something or other had bruised my vanity so that I could recognize it. I felt old. Avey and my real relation to her, I thought I came to know. I wanted to see her. I had been told that she was in New York. As I had no money, I hiked and bummed my way there. I got work in a ship-yard and walked the streets at night, hoping to meet her. Failing in this, I saved enough to pay my fare back home. One evening in early June, just at the time when dusk is most lovely on the eastern horizon, I saw Avey, indolent as ever, leaning on the arm of a man, strolling under the recently lit arc-lights of U Street.[4] She had almost passed before she recognized me. She showed no surprise. The puff over her eyes had grown heavier. The eyes themselves were still sleepy-large, and beautiful. I had almost concluded—indifferent. "You look older," was what she said. I wanted to convince her that I was, so I asked her to walk with me. The man whom she was with, and whom she never took the trouble to introduce, at a nod from her, hailed a taxi, and drove away. That gave me a notion of what she had been used to. Her dress was of some fine, costly stuff. I suggested the park, and then added that the grass might stain her skirt. Let it get stained, she said, for where it came from there are others.

I have a spot in Soldier's Home[5] to which I always go when I want the simple beauty of another's soul. Robins spring about the lawn all day. They leave their footprints in the grass. I imagine that the grass at night smells sweet and fresh because of them. The ground is high. Washington lies below. Its light spreads like a blush against the darkened sky. Against the soft dusk sky of Washington. And when the wind is from the South, soil of my homeland

3. A teacher-training institution. Although a normal school was not considered the equivalent of a four-year college, during the 1920s completion of a normal-school degree program qualified one to teach in elementary or secondary schools.
4. Another street in a densely populated African American neighborhood in Washington, D.C.
5. A park.

falls like a fertile shower upon the lean streets of the city. Upon my hill in Soldier's Home, I know the policeman who watches the place of nights. When I go there alone, I talk to him. I tell him I come there to find the truth that people bury in their hearts. I tell him that I do not come there with a girl to do the thing he's paid to watch out for. I look deep in his eyes when I say these things, and he believes me. He comes over to see who it is on the grass. I say hello to him. He greets me in the same way and goes off searching for other black splotches upon the lawn. Avey and I went there. A band in one of the buildings a fair distance off was playing a march. I wished they would stop. Their playing was like a tin spoon in one's mouth. I wanted the Howard Glee Club to sing "Deep River,"[6] from the road. To sing "Deep River, Deep River," from the road . . . Other than the first comments, Avey had been silent. I started to hum a folk-tune. She slipped her hand in mine. Pillowed her head as best she could upon my arm. Kissed the hand that she was holding and listened, or so I thought, to what I had to say. I traced my development from the early days up to the present time, the phase in which I could understand her. I described her own nature and temperament. Told how they needed a larger life for their expression. How incapable Washington was of understanding that need. How it could not meet it. I pointed out that in lieu of proper channels, her emotions had overflowed into paths that dissipated them. I talked, beautifully I thought, about an art that would be born, an art that would open the way for women the likes of her. I asked her to hope, and build up an inner life against the coming of that day. I recited some of my own things to her. I sang, with a strange quiver in my voice, a promise-song. And then I began to wonder why her hand had not once returned a single pressure. My old-time feeling about her laziness came back. I spoke sharply. My policeman friend passed by. I said hello to him. As he went away, I began to visualize certain possibilities. An immediate and urgent passion swept over me. Then I looked at Avey. Her heavy eyes were closed. Her breathing was as faint and regular as a child's in slumber. My passion died. I was afraid to move lest I disturb her. Hours and hours, I guess it was, she lay there. My body grew numb. I shivered. I coughed. I wanted to get up and whittle at the boxes of young trees. I withdrew my hand. I raised her head to waken her. She did not stir. I got up and walked around. I found my policeman friend and talked to him. We both came up, and bent over her. He said it would be all right for her to stay there just so long as she got away before the workmen came at dawn. A blanket was borrowed from a neighbor house. I sat beside her through the night. I saw the dawn steal over Washington. The Capitol dome looked like a gray ghost ship drifting in from sea. Avey's face was pale, and her eyes were heavy. She did not have the gray crimson-splashed beauty of the dawn. I hated to wake her. Orphan-woman . . .

Beehive

Within this black hive to-night
There swarm a million bees;
Bees passing in and out the moon,
Bees escaping out the moon,

6. Black American spiritual. Howard University is in Washington, D.C.

Bees returning through the moon,
Silver bees intently buzzing,
Silver honey dripping from the swarm of bees
Earth is a waxen cell of the world comb,
And I, a drone,
Lying on my back,
Lipping honey,
Getting drunk with silver honey,
Wish that I might fly out past the moon
And curl forever in some far-off farmyard flower.

Storm Ending

Thunder blossoms gorgeously above our heads,
Great, hollow, bell-like flowers,
Rumbling in the wind,
Stretching clappers to strike our ears . . .
Full-lipped flowers
Bitten by the sun
Bleeding rain
Dripping rain like golden honey—
And the sweet earth flying from the thunder.

Theater

Life of nigger alleys, of pool rooms and restaurants and near-beer saloons soaks into the walls of Howard Theater[1] and sets them throbbing jazz songs. Black-skinned, they dance and shout above the tick and trill of white-walled buildings. At night, they open doors to people who come in to stamp their feet and shout. At night, road-shows volley songs into the mass-heart of black people. Songs soak the walls and seep out to the nigger life of alleys and near-beer saloons, of the Poodle Dog and Black Bear cabarets. Afternoons, the house is dark, and the walls are sleeping singers until rehearsal begins. Or until John comes within them. Then they start throbbing to a subtle syncopation. And the space-dark air grows softly luminous.

John is the manager's brother. He is seated at the center of the theater, just before rehearsal. Light streaks down upon him from a window high above. One half his face is orange in it. One half his face is in shadow. The soft glow of the house rushes to, and compacts about, the shaft of light. John's mind coincides with the shaft of light. Thoughts rush to, and compact about it. Life of the house and of the slowly awakening stage swirls to the body of John, and thrills it. John's body is separate from the thoughts that pack his mind.

Stage-lights, soft, as if they shine through clear pink fingers. Beneath them, hid by the shadow of a set, Dorris. Other chorus girls drift in. John feels them in the mass. And as if his own body were the mass-heart of a

1. In an African American section of Washington, D.C. The audiences and performers were Black. "Near-beer saloons": establishments that sell low-proof beer.

black audience listening to them singing, he wants to stamp his feet and shout. His mind, contained above desires of his body, singles the girls out, and tries to trace origins and plot destinies.

A pianist slips into the pit and improvises jazz. The walls awake. Arms of the girls, and their limbs, which . . jazz, jazz . . by lifting up their tight street skirts they set free, jab the air and clog the floor in rhythm to the music. (Lift your skirts, Baby, and talk t papa!) Crude, individualized, and yet . . monotonous . . .

John: Soon the director will herd you, my full-lipped, distant beauties, and tame you, and blunt your sharp thrusts in loosely suggestive movements, appropriate to Broadway. (O dance!) Soon the audience will paint your dusk faces white, and call you beautiful.[2] (O dance!) Soon I . . . (O dance!) I'd like . . .

Girls laugh and shout. Sing discordant snatches of other jazz songs. Whirl with loose passion into the arms of passing show-men.

John: Too thick. Too easy. Too monotonous. Her whom I'd love I'd leave before she knew that I was with her. Her? Which? (O dance!) I'd like to . . .

Girls dance and sing. Men clap. The walls sing and press inward. They press the men and girls, they press John towards a center of physical ecstasy. Go to it, Baby! Fan yourself, and feed your papa! Put . . nobody lied . . and take . . when they said I cried over you. No lie! The glitter and color of stacked scenes, the gilt and brass and crimson of the house, converge towards a center of physical ecstasy. John's feet and torso and his blood press in. He wills thought to rid his mind of passion.

"All right, girls. Alaska. Miss Reynolds, please."

The director wants to get the rehearsal through with.

The girls line up. John sees the front row: dancing ponies. The rest are in shadow. The leading lady fits loosely in the front. Lack-life, monotonous. "One, two, three—" Music starts. The song is somewhere where it will not strain the leading lady's throat. The dance is somewhere where it will not strain the girls. Above the staleness, one dancer throws herself into it. Dorris. John sees her. Her hair, crisp-curled, is bobbed. Bushy, black hair bobbing about her lemon-colored face. Her lips are curiously full, and very red. Her limbs in silk purple stockings are lovely. John feels them. Desires her. Holds off.

John: Stage-door johnny; chorus-girl. No, that would be all right. Dictie,[3] educated, stuck-up; show-girl. Yep. Her suspicion would be stronger than her passion. It wouldn't work. Keep her loveliness. Let her go.

Dorris sees John and knows that he is looking at her. Her own glowing is too rich a thing to let her feel the slimness of his diluted passion.

"Who's that?" she asks her dancing partner.

"Th manager's brother. Dictie. Nothin doin, hon."

Dorris tosses her head and dances for him until she feels she has him. Then, withdrawing disdainfully, she flirts with the director.

Dorris: Nothin doin? How come? Aint I as good as him? Couldnt I have got an education if I'd wanted one? Dont I know respectable folks, lots of

2. During the 1920s, producers and directors of all-Black musical shows often preferred African American females who were light-skinned. The white audience would think of such women as white and thus beautiful.

3. Educated, middle-class African American (slang); connotes being stuck-up or snobbish. "Stage-door johnny": a man who dates actresses, singers, and dancers (slang).

em, in Philadelphia and New York and Chicago? Aint I had men as good as him? Better. Doctors an lawyers. Whats a manager's brother, anyhow?

Two steps back, and two steps front.

"Say, Mame, where do you get that stuff?"

"Whatshmean, Dorris?"

"If you two girls cant listen to what I'm telling you, I know where I can get some who can. Now listen."

Mame: Go to hell, you black bastard.

Dorris: Whats eatin at him, anyway?

"Now follow me in this, you girls. Its three counts to the right, three counts to the left, and then you shimmy[4]—"

John: —and then you shimmy. I'll bet she can. Some good cabaret, with rooms upstairs. And what in hell do you think you'd get from it? Youre going wrong. Here's right: get her to herself—(Christ, but how she'd bore you after the first five minutes)—not if you get her right she wouldnt. Touch her, I mean. To herself—in some room perhaps. Some cheap, dingy bedroom. Hell no. Cant be done. But the point is, brother John, it can be done. Get her to herself somewhere, anywhere. Go down in yourself—and she'd be calling you all sorts of asses while you were in the process of going down. Hold em, bud. Cant be done. Let her go. (Dance and I'll love you!) And keep her loveliness.

"All right now, Chicken Chaser.[5] Dorris and girls. Where's Dorris? I told you to stay on the stage, didnt I? Well? Now thats enough. All right. All right there, Professor?[6] All right. One, two, three—"

Dorris swings to the front. The line of girls, four deep, blurs within the shadow of suspended scenes. Dorris wants to dance. The director feels that and steps to one side. He smiles, and picks her for a leading lady, one of these days. Odd ends of stage-men emerge from the wings, and stare and clap. A crap game in the alley suddenly ends. Black faces crowd the rear stage doors. The girls, catching joy from Dorris, whip up within the footlights' glow. They forget set steps; they find their own. The director forgets to bawl them out. Dorris dances.

John: Her head bobs to Broadway. Dance from yourself. Dance! O just a little more.

Dorris' eyes burn across the space of seats to him.

Dorris: I bet he can love. Hell, he cant love. He's too skinny. His lips are too skinny. He wouldnt love me anyway, only for that. But I'd get a pair of silk stockings out of it. Red silk. I got purple. Cut it, kid. You cant win him to respect you that away. He wouldnt anyway. Maybe he would. Maybe he'd love. I've heard em say that men who look like him (what does he look like?) will marry if they love. O will you love me? And give me kids, and a home, and everything? (I'd like to make your nest, and honest, hon, I wouldnt run out on you.) You will if I make you. Just watch me.

Dorris dances. She forgets her tricks.[7] She dances.

Glorious songs are the muscles of her limbs.

And her singing is of canebrake loves and mangrove feastings.

The walls press in, singing. Flesh of a throbbing body, they press close to John and Dorris. They close them in. John's heart beats tensely against her dancing body. Walls press his mind within his heart. And then, the shaft of

4. A popular dance movement that emphasized an erotic vibration of the torso.
5. Another dance.
6. A nickname for a band leader or pianist.
7. Her practiced or stylized dance routine.

light goes out the window high above him. John's mind sweeps up to follow it. Mind pulls him upward into dream. Dorris dances . . . John dreams:

> Dorris is dressed in a loose black gown splashed with lemon ribbons. Her feet taper long and slim from trim ankles. She waits for him just inside the stage door. John, collar and tie colorful and flaring, walks towards the stage door. There are no trees in the alley. But his feet feel as though they step on autumn leaves whose rustle has been pressed out of them by the passing of a million satin slippers. The air is sweet with roasting chestnuts, sweet with bonfires of old leaves. John's melancholy is a deep thing that seals all senses but his eyes, and makes him whole.
>
> Dorris knows that he is coming. Just at the right moment she steps from the door, as if there were no door. Her face is tinted like the autumn alley. Of old flowers, or of a southern canefield, her perfume. "Glorious Dorris." So his eyes speak. And their sadness is too deep for sweet untruth. She barely touches his arm. They glide off with footfalls softened on the leaves, the old leaves powdered by a million satin slippers.
>
> They are in a room. John knows nothing of it. Only, that the flesh and blood of Dorris are its walls. Singing walls. Lights, soft, as if they shine through clear pink fingers. Soft lights, and warm.
>
> John reaches for a manuscript of his, and reads. Dorris, who has no eyes, has eyes to understand him. He comes to a dancing scene. The scene is Dorris. She dances. Dorris dances. Glorious Dorris. Dorris whirls, whirls, dances . . .

Dorris dances.

The pianist crashes a bumper chord. The whole stage claps. Dorris, flushed, looks quick at John. His whole face is in shadow. She seeks for her dance in it. She finds it a dead thing in the shadow which is his dream. She rushes from the stage. Falls down the steps into her dressing-room. Pulls her hair. Her eyes, over a floor of tears, stare at the whitewashed ceiling. (Smell of dry paste, and paint, and soiled clothing.) Her pal comes in. Dorris flings herself into the old safe arms, and cries bitterly.

"I told you nothin doin," is what Mame says to comfort her.

Her Lips Are Copper Wire

whisper of yellow globes
gleaming on lamp-posts that sway
like bootleg licker[1] drinkers in the fog

and let your breath be moist against me
like bright beads on yellow globes

telephone the power-house
that the main wires are insulate

(her words play softly up and down
dewy corridors of billboards)

1. Liquor illegally distilled, especially during Prohibition, the period from 1919 to 1933 when U.S. law prohibited the manufacture, transportation, and sale of alcoholic beverages.

then with your tongue remove the tape
and press your lips to mine
till they are incandescent

Calling Jesus

Her soul is like a little thrust-tailed dog that follows her, whimpering. She is large enough, I know, to find a warm spot for it. But each night when she comes home and closes the big outside storm door, the little dog is left in the vestibule, filled with chills till morning. Some one . . . eoho[1] Jesus . . . soft as a cotton boll brushed against the milk-pod cheek of Christ, will steal in and cover it that it need not shiver, and carry it to her where she sleeps upon clean hay cut in her dreams.

When you meet her in the daytime on the streets, the little dog keeps coming. Nothing happens at first, and then, when she has forgotten the streets and alleys, and the large house where she goes to bed of nights, a soft thing like fur begins to rub your limbs, and you hear a low, scared voice, lonely, calling, and you know that a cool something nozzles moisture in your palms. Sensitive things like nostrils, quiver. Her breath comes sweet as honeysuckle whose pistils bear the life of coming song. And her eyes carry to where builders find no need for vestibules, for swinging on iron hinges, storm doors.

Her soul is like a little thrust-tailed dog, that follows her, whimpering. I've seen it tagging on behind her, up streets where chestnut trees flowered, where dusty asphalt had been freshly sprinkled with clean water. Up alleys where niggers sat on low door-steps before tumbled shanties and sang and loved. At night, when she comes home, the little dog is left in the vestibule, nosing the crack beneath the big storm door, filled with chills till morning. Some one . . . eoho Jesus . . . soft as the bare feet of Christ moving across bales of southern cotton, will steal in and cover it that it need not shiver, and carry it to her where she sleeps: cradled in dream-fluted cane.

Box Seat[1]

1

Houses are shy girls whose eyes shine reticently upon the dusk body of the street. Upon the gleaming limbs and asphalt torso of a dreaming nigger. Shake your curled wool-blossoms, nigger. Open your liver lips to the lean, white spring. Stir the root-life of a withered people. Call them from their houses, and teach them to dream.

Dark swaying forms of Negroes are street songs that woo virginal houses.

Dan Moore walks southward on Thirteenth Street. The low limbs of budding chestnut trees recede above his head. Chestnut buds and blossoms are

1. Call.

1. Expensive theater seat usually elevated along a side wall. Box seats are considered the best seats in the theater.

wool he walks upon. The eyes of houses faintly touch him as he passes them. Soft girl-eyes, they set him singing. Girl-eyes within him widen upward to promised faces. Floating away, they dally wistfully over the dusk body of the street. Come on, Dan Moore, come on. Dan sings. His voice is a little hoarse. It cracks. He strains to produce tones in keeping with the houses' loveliness. Cant be done. He whistles. His notes are shrill. They hurt him. Negroes open gates, and go indoors, perfectly. Dan thinks of the house he's going to. Of the girl. Lips, flesh-notes of a forgotten song, plead with him . . .

Dan turns into a side-street, opens an iron gate, bangs it to. Mounts the steps, and searches for the bell. Funny, he cant find it. He fumbles around. The thought comes to him that some one passing by might see him, and not understand. Might think that he is trying to sneak, to break in.

Dan:[2] Break in. Get an ax and smash in. Smash in their faces. I'll show em. Break into an engine-house, steal a thousand horsepower fire truck. Smash in with the truck. I'll show em. Grab an ax and brain em. Cut em up. Jack the Ripper.[3] Baboon from the zoo. And then the cops come. "No, I aint a baboon. I aint Jack the Ripper. I'm a poor man out of work. Take your hands off me, you bull-necked bears. Look into my eyes. I am Dan Moore. I was born in a canefield. The hands of Jesus touched me. I am come to a sick world to heal it. Only the other day, a dope fiend brushed against me—Dont laugh, you mighty, juicy, meat-hook men. Give me your fingers and I will peel them as if they were ripe bananas."

Some one might think he is trying to break in. He'd better knock. His knuckles are raw bone against the thick glass door. He waits. No one comes. Perhaps they havent heard him. He raps again. This time, harder. He waits. No one comes. Some one is surely in. He fancies that he sees their shadows on the glass. Shadows of gorillas. Perhaps they saw him coming and dont want to let him in. He knocks. The tension of his arms makes the glass rattle. Hurried steps come towards him. The door opens.

"Please, you might break the glass—the bell—oh, Mr. Moore! I thought it must be some stranger. How do you do? Come in, wont you? Muriel? Yes. I'll call her. Take your things off, wont you? And have a seat in the parlor. Muriel will be right down. Muriel! Oh Muriel! Mr. Moore to see you. She'll be right down. You'll pardon me, wont you? So glad to see you."

Her eyes are weak. They are bluish and watery from reading newspapers. The blue is steel. It gimlets[4] Dan while her mouth flaps amiably to him.

Dan: Nothing for you to see, old mussel-head. Dare I show you? If I did, delirium would furnish you headlines for a month. Now look here. Thats enough. Go long, woman. Say some nasty thing and I'll kill you. Huh. Better damned sight not. Ta-ta, Mrs. Pribby.

Mrs. Pribby retreats to the rear of the house. She takes up a newspaper. There is a sharp click as she fits into her chair and draws it to the table. The click is metallic like the sound of a bolt being shot into place. Dan's eyes sting. Sinking into a soft couch, he closes them. The house contracts about him. It is a sharp-edged, massed, metallic house. Bolted. About Mrs. Pribby. Bolted to the endless rows of metal houses. Mrs. Pribby's house. The rows of houses belong to other Mrs. Pribbys. No wonder he couldn't sing to them.

2. Throughout this story, a colon indicates that the thoughts, not the spoken words, of the character will follow.

3. The name given by newspapers to an unidentified individual in 19th-century London who killed and mutilated several prostitutes.

4. A gimlet is a small tool for piercing holes.

Dan: What's Muriel doing here? God, what a place for her. Whats she doing? Putting her stockings on? In the bathroom. Come out of there, Dan Moore. People must have their privacy. Peeping-toms. I'll never peep. I'll listen. I like to listen.

Dan goes to the wall and places his ear against it. A passing street car and something vibrant from the earth sends a rumble to him. That rumble comes from the earth's deep core. It is the mutter of powerful underground races. Dan has a picture of all the people rushing to put their ears against walls, to listen to it. The next world-savior is coming up that way. Coming up. A continent sinks down. The new-world Christ will need consummate skill to walk upon the waters where huge bubbles burst . . . Thuds of Muriel coming down. Dan turns to the piano and glances through a stack of jazz music sheets. Ji-ji-bo, JI-JI-BO! . .

"Hello, Dan, stranger, what brought you here?"

Muriel comes in, shakes hands, and then clicks into a high-armed seat under the orange glow of a floor-lamp. Her face is fleshy. It would tend to coarseness but for the fresh fragrant something which is the life of it. Her hair like an Indian's. But more curly and bushed and vagrant. Her nostrils flare. The flushed ginger of her cheeks is touched orange by the shower of color from the lamp.

"Well, you havent told me, you havent answered my question, stranger. What brought you here?"

Dan feels the pressure of the house, of the rear room, of the rows of houses, shift to Muriel. He is light. He loves her. He is doubly heavy.

"Dont know, Muriel—wanted to see you—wanted to talk to you—to see you and tell you that I know what you've been through—what pain the last few months must have been—"

"Lets dont mention that."

"But why not, Muriel? I—"

"Please."

"But Muriel, life is full of things like that. One grows strong and beautiful in facing them. What else is life?"

"I dont know, Dan. And I dont believe I care. Whats the use? Lets talk about something else. I hear there's a good show at the Lincoln this week."

"Yes, so Harry was telling me. Going?"

"Tonight."

Dan starts to rise.

"I didnt know. I dont want to keep you."

"Its all right. You dont have to go till Bernice comes. And she wont be here till eight. I'm all dressed. I'll let you know."

"Thanks."

Silence. The rustle of a newspaper being turned comes from the rear room.

Muriel: Shame about Dan. Something awfully good and fine about him. But he dont fit in. In where? Me? Dan, I could love you if I tried. I dont have to try. I do. O Dan, dont you know I do? Timid lover, brave talker that you are. Whats the good of all you know if you dont know that? I wont let myself. I? Mrs. Pribby who reads newspapers all night wont. What has she got to do with me? She *is* me, somehow. No she's not. Yes she is. She is the town, and the town wont let me love you, Dan. Dont you know? You could make it let me if you would. Why wont you? Youre selfish. I'm not strong enough to buck it. Youre too selfish to buck it, for me. I wish you'd go. You irritate me. Dan, please go.

"What are you doing now, Dan?"

"Same old thing, Muriel. Nothing, as the world would have it. Living, as I look at things. Living as much as I can without—"

"But you cant live without money, Dan. Why dont you get a good job and settle down?"

Dan: Same old line. Shoot it at me, sister. Hell of a note, this loving business. For ten minutes of it youve got to stand the torture of an intolerable heaviness and a hundred platitudes. Well, damit, shoot on.

"To what? my dear. Rustling newspapers?"

"You mustnt say that, Dan. It isnt right. Mrs. Pribby has been awfully good to me."

"Dare say she has. Whats that got to do with it?"

"Oh, Dan, youre so unconsiderate and selfish. All you think of is yourself."

"I think of you."

"Too much—I mean, you ought to work more and think less. Thats the best way to get along."

"Mussel-heads get along, Muriel. There is more to you than that—"

"Sometimes I think there is, Dan. But I dont know. I've tried. I've tried to do something with myself. Something real and beautiful, I mean. But whats the good of trying? I've tried to make people, every one I come in contact with, happy—"

Dan looks at her, directly. Her animalism, still unconquered by zoo-restrictions and keeper-taboos, stirs him. Passion tilts upward, bringing with it the elements of an old desire. Muriel's lips become the flesh-notes of a futile, plaintive longing. Dan's impulse to direct her is its fresh life.

"Happy, Muriel? No, not happy. Your aim is wrong. There is no such thing as happiness. Life bends joy and pain, beauty and ugliness, in such a way that no one may isolate them. No one should want to. Perfect joy, or perfect pain, with no contrasting element to define them, would mean a monotony of consciousness, would mean death. Not happy, Muriel. Say that you have tried to make them create. Say that you have used your own capacity for life to cradle them. To start them upward-flowing. Or if you cant say that you have, then say that you will. My talking to you will make you aware of your power to do so. Say that you will love, that you will give yourself in love—"

"To you, Dan?"

Dan's consciousness crudely swerves into his passions. They flare up in his eyes. They set up quivers in his abdomen. He is suddenly over-tense and nervous.

"Muriel—"

The newspaper rustles in the rear room.

"Muriel—"

Dan rises. His arms stretch towards her. His fingers and his palms, pink in the lamplight, are glowing irons. Muriel's chair is close and stiff about her. The house, the rows of houses locked about her chair. Dan's fingers and arms are fire to melt and bars to wrench and force and pry. Her arms hang loose. Her hands are hot and moist. Dan takes them. He slips to his knees before her.

"Dan, you mustnt."

"Muriel—"

"Dan, really you mustnt. No, Dan. No."

"Oh, come, Muriel. Must I—"

"Shhh. Dan, please get up. Please. Mrs. Pribby is right in the next room. She'll hear you. She may come in. Dont, Dan. She'll see you—"

"Well then, lets go out."

"I cant. Let go, Dan. Oh, wont you please let go."

Muriel tries to pull her hands away. Dan tightens his grip. He feels the strength of his fingers. His muscles are tight and strong. He stands up. Thrusts out his chest. Muriel shrinks from him. Dan becomes aware of his crude absurdity. His lips curl. His passion chills. He has an obstinate desire to possess her.

"Muriel, I love you. I want you, whatever the world of Pribby says. Damn your Pribby. Who is she to dictate my love? I've stood enough of her. Enough of you. Come here."

Muriel's mouth works in and out. Her eyes flash and waggle. She wrenches her hands loose and forces them against his breast to keep him off. Dan grabs her wrists. Wedges in between her arms. Her face is close to him. It is hot and blue and moist. Ugly.

"Come here now."

"Dont, Dan. Oh, dont. What are you killing?"

"Whats weak in both of us and a whole litter of Pribbys. For once in your life youre going to face whats real, by God—"

A sharp rap on the newspaper in the rear room cuts between them. The rap is like cool thick glass between them. Dan is hot on one side. Muriel, hot on the other. They straighten. Gaze fearfully at one another. Neither moves. A clock in the rear room, in the rear room, the rear room, strikes eight. Eight slow, cool sounds. Bernice. Muriel fastens on her image. She smooths her dress. She adjusts her skirt. She becomes prim and cool. Rising, she skirts Dan as if to keep the glass between them. Dan, gyrating nervously above the easy swing of his limbs, follows her to the parlor door. Muriel retreats before him till she reaches the landing of the steps that lead upstairs. She smiles at him. Dan sees his face in the hall mirror. He runs his fingers through his hair. Reaches for his hat and coat and puts them on. He moves towards Muriel. Muriel steps backward up one step. Dan's jaw shoots out. Muriel jerks her arm in warning of Mrs. Pribby. She gasps and turns and starts to run. Noise of a chair scraping as Mrs. Pribby rises from it, ratchets down the hall. Dan stops. He makes a wry face, wheels round, goes out, and slams the door.

2

People come in slowly . . . mutter, laughs, flutter, wishadwash,[5] "I've changed my work-clothes—" . . . and fill vacant seats of Lincoln Theater. Muriel, leading Bernice who is a cross between a washerwoman and a blue-blood lady, a washer-blue, a washer-lady, wanders down the right aisle to the lower front box. Muriel has on an orange dress. Its color would clash with the crimson box-draperies, its color would contradict the sweet rose smile her face is bathed in, should she take her coat off. She'll keep it on. Pale purple shadows rest on the planes of her cheeks. Deep purple comes from her thick-shocked hair. Orange of the dress goes well with these. Muriel presses her coat down from around her shoulders. Teachers are not supposed to have bobbed hair.[6] She'll keep her hat on. She takes the first chair, and

5. The sounds made by a theater audience during the time before the curtain rises.

6. A short hairstyle of the 1920s that was considered fashionable and daring for women.

indicates that Bernice is to take the one directly behind her. Seated thus, her eyes are level with, and near to, the face of an imaginary man upon the stage. To speak to Berny she must turn. When she does, the audience is square upon her.

People come in slowly . . . "—for my Sunday-go-to-meeting dress. O glory God! O shout Amen!" . . . and fill vacant seats of Lincoln Theater. Each one is a bolt that shoots into a slot, and is locked there. Suppose the Lord should ask, where was Moses when the light went out? Suppose Gabriel should blow his trumpet![7] The seats are slots. The seats are bolted houses. The mass grows denser. Its weight at first is impalpable upon the box. Then Muriel begins to feel it. She props her arm against the brass box-rail, to ward it off. Silly. These people are friends of hers: a parent of a child she teaches, an old school friend. She smiles at them. They return her courtesy, and she is free to chat with Berny. Berny's tongue, started, runs on, and on. O washer-blue! O washer-lady!

Muriel: Never see Dan again. He makes me feel queer. Starts things he doesnt finish. Upsets me. I am not upset. I am perfectly calm. I am going to enjoy the show. Good show. I've had some show! This damn tame thing. O Dan. Wont see Dan again. Not alone. Have Mrs. Pribby come in. She *was* in. Keep Dan out. If I love him, can I keep him out? Well then, I dont love him. Now he's out. Who is that coming in? Blind as a bat. Ding-bat. Looks like Dan. He mustnt see me. Silly. He cant reach me. He wont dare come in here. He'd put his head down like a goring bull and charge me. He'd trample them. He'd gore. He'd rape! Berny! He wont dare come in here.

"Berny, who was that who just came in? I havent my glasses."

"A friend of yours, a *good* friend so I hear. Mr. Daniel Moore, Lord."

"Oh. He's no friend of mine."

"No? I hear he is."

"Well, he isnt."

Dan is ushered down the aisle. He has to squeeze past the knees of seated people to reach his own seat. He treads on a man's corns. The man grumbles, and shoves him off. He shrivels close beside a portly Negress whose huge rolls of flesh meet about the bones of seat-arms. A soil-soaked fragrance comes from her. Through the cement floor her strong roots sink down. They spread under the asphalt streets. Dreaming, the streets roll over on their bellies, and suck their glossy health from them. Her strong roots sink down and spread under the river and disappear in blood-lines that waver south. Her roots shoot down. Dan's hands follow them. Roots throb. Dan's heart beats violently. He places his palms upon the earth to cool them. Earth throbs. Dan's heart beats violently. He sees all the people in the house rush to the walls to listen to the rumble. A new-world Christ is coming up. Dan comes up. He is startled. The eyes of the woman dont belong to her. They look at him unpleasantly. From either aisle, bolted masses press in. He doesnt fit. The mass grows agitant. For an instant, Dan's and Muriel's eyes meet. His weight there slides the weight on her. She braces an arm against the brass rail, and turns her head away.

Muriel: Damn fool; dear Dan, what did you want to follow me here for? Oh cant you ever do anything right? Must you always pain me, and make me hate you? I do hate you. I wish some one would come in with a horse-whip

7. The Christian concept that, at the end of the world, the angel Gabriel will blow a horn to announce Judgment Day.

and lash you out. I wish some one would drag you up a back alley and brain you with the whip-butt.

Muriel glances at her wrist-watch.

"Quarter of nine. Berny, what time have you?"

"Eight-forty. Time to begin. Oh, look Muriel, that woman with the plume; doesnt she look good! They say she's going with, oh, whats his name. You know. Too much powder.[8] I can see it from here. Here's the orchestra now. O fine! Jim Clem at the piano!"

The men fill the pit. Instruments run the scale and tune. The saxophone moans and throws a fit. Jim Clem, poised over the piano, is ready to begin. His head nods forward. Opening crash. The house snaps dark. The curtain recedes upward from the blush of the footlights. Jazz overture is over. The first act is on.

Dan: Old stuff. Muriel—bored. Must be. But she'll smile and she'll clap. Do what youre bid, you she-slave. Look at her. Sweet, tame woman in a brass box seat. Clap, smile, fawn, clap. Do what youre bid. Drag me in with you. Dirty me. Prop me in your brass box seat. I'm there, am I not? because of you. He-slave. Slave of a woman who is a slave. I'm a damned sight worse than you are. I sing your praises, Beauty! I exalt thee, O Muriel! A slave, thou art greater than all Freedom because I love thee.

Dan fidgets, and disturbs his neighbors. His neighbors glare at him. He glares back without seeing them. The man whose corns have been trod upon speaks to him.

"Keep quiet, cant you, mister. Other people have paid their money besides yourself to see the show."

The man's face is a blur about two sullen liquid things that are his eyes. The eyes dissolve in the surrounding vagueness. Dan suddenly feels that the man is an enemy whom he has long been looking for.

Dan bristles. Glares furiously at the man.

"All right. All right then. Look at the show. I'm not stopping you."

"Shhh," from some one in the rear.

Dan turns around.

"Its that man there who started everything. I didnt say a thing to him until he tried to start something. What have I got to do with whether he has paid his money or not? Thats the manager's business. Do I look like the manager?"

"Shhhh. Youre right. Shhhh."

"Dont tell me to shhh. Tell him. That man there. He started everything. If what he wanted was to start a fight, why didnt he say so?"

The man leans forward.

"Better be quiet, sonny. I aint said a thing about fight, yet."

"Its a good thing you havent."

"Shhhh."

Dan grips himself. Another act is on. Dwarfs, dressed like prizefighters, foreheads bulging like boxing gloves, are led upon the stage. They are going to fight for the heavyweight championship. Gruesome. Dan glances at Muriel. He imagines that she shudders. His mind curves back into himself, and picks up tail-ends of experiences. His eyes are open, mechanically. The dwarfs pound and bruise and bleed each other, on his eyeballs.

8. Face powder, to make the skin seem lighter.

Dan: Ah, but she was some baby! And not vulgar either. Funny how some women can do those things. Muriel dancing like that! Hell. She rolled and wabbled. Her buttocks rocked. She pulled up her dress and showed her pink drawers. Baby! And then she caught my eyes. Dont know what my eyes had in them. Yes I do. God, dont I though! Sometimes I think, Dan Moore, that your eyes could burn clean . . . burn clean . . . BURN CLEAN! . .

The gong rings. The dwarfs set to. They spar grotesquely, playfully, until one lands a stiff blow. This makes the other sore. He commences slugging. A real scrap is on. Time! The dwarfs go to their corners and are sponged and fanned off. Gloves bulge from their wrists. Their wrists are necks for the tight-faced gloves. The fellow to the right lets his eyes roam over the audience. He sights Muriel. He grins.

Dan: Those silly women arguing feminism. Here's what I should have said to them. "It should be clear to you women, that the proposition must be stated thus:

> Me, horizontally above her.
> Action: perfect strokes downward oblique.
> Hence, man dominates because of limitation.
> Or, so it shall be until women learn their stuff.

So framed, the proposition is a mental-filler, Dentist, I want gold teeth. It should become cherished of the technical intellect. I hereby offer it to posterity as one of the important machine-age designs. P.S. It should be noted, that because it *is* an achievement of this age, its growth and hence its causes, up to the point of maturity, antedate machinery. Ery . . ."

The gong rings. No fooling this time. The dwarfs set to. They clinch. The referee parts them. One swings a cruel upper-cut and knocks the other down. A huge head hits the floor. Pop! The house roars. The fighter, groggy, scrambles up. The referee whispers to the contenders not to fight so hard. They ignore him. They charge. Their heads jab like boxing-gloves. They kick and spit and bite. They pound each other furiously. Muriel pounds. The house pounds. Cut lips. Bloody noses. The referee asks for the gong. Time! The house roars. The dwarfs bow, are made to bow. The house wants more. The dwarfs are led from the stage.

Dan: Strange I never really noticed him before. Been sitting there for years. Born a slave. Slavery not so long ago. He'll die in his chair. Swing low, sweet chariot. Jesus will come and roll him down the river Jordan. Oh, come along, Moses, you'll get lost; stretch out your rod and come across. LET MY PEOPLE GO![9] Old man. Knows everyone who passes the corners. Saw the first horse-cars. The first Oldsmobile. And he was born in slavery. I did see his eyes. Never miss eyes. But they were bloodshot and watery. It hurt to look at them. It hurts to look in most people's eyes. He saw Grant and Lincoln. He saw Walt—old man, did you see Walt Whitman?[1] Did you see Walt Whitman! Strange force that drew me to him. And I went up to see. The woman thought I saw crazy. I told him to look into the heavens. He did, and smiled. I asked him if he knew what that rumbling is that comes up from the ground. Christ, what a stroke that was. And the jabbering idiots crowding around. And the crossing-cop leaving his job to come over and wheel him away . . .

9. "Swing Low, Sweet Chariot," "Roll, Jordan, Roll," and "Let My People Go" are African American spirituals.

1. A 19th-century American poet who celebrated democracy and brotherhood; he served as a nurse during the Civil War.

The house applauds. The house wants more. The dwarfs are led back. But no encore. Must give the house something. The attendant comes out and announces that Mr. Barry, the champion, will sing one of his own songs, "for your approval." Mr. Barry grins at Muriel as he wabbles from the wing. He holds a fresh white rose, and a small mirror. He wipes blood from his nose. He signals Jim Clem. The orchestra starts. A sentimental love song, Mr. Barry sings, first to one girl, and then another in the audience. He holds the mirror in such a way that it flashes in the face of each one he sings to. The light swings around.

Dan: I am going to reach up and grab the girders of this building and pull them down. The crash will be a signal. Hid by the smoke and dust Dan Moore will arise. In his right hand will be a dynamo. In his left, a god's face that will flash white light from ebony. I'll grab a girder and swing it like a walking-stick. Lightning will flash. I'll grab its black knob and swing it like a crippled cane. Lightning . . . Some one's flashing . . . some one's flashing . . . Who in hell is flashing that mirror? Take it off me, godam you.

Dan's eyes are half blinded. He moves his head. The light follows. He hears the audience laugh. He hears the orchestra. A man with a high-pitched, sentimental voice is singing. Dan sees the dwarf. Along the mirror flash the song comes. Dan ducks his head. The audience roars. The light swings around to Muriel. Dan looks. Muriel is too close. Mr. Barry covers his mirror. He sings to her. She shrinks away. Nausea. She clutches the brass box-rail. She moves to face away. The audience is square upon her. Its eyes smile. Its hands itch to clap. Muriel turns to the dwarf and forces a smile at him. With a showy blare of orchestration, the song comes to its close. Mr. Barry bows. He offers Muriel the rose, first having kissed it. Blood of his battered lips is a vivid stain upon its petals. Mr. Barry offers Muriel the rose. The house applauds. Muriel flinches back. The dwarf steps forward, diffident; threatening. Hate pops from his eyes and crackles like a brittle heat about the box. The thick hide of his face is drawn in tortured wrinkles. Above his eyes, the bulging, tight-skinned brow. Dan looks at it. It grows calm and massive. It grows profound. It is a thing of wisdom and tenderness, of suffering and beauty. Dan looks down. The eyes are calm and luminous. Words come from them . . . Arms of the audience reach out, grab Muriel, and hold her there. Claps are steel fingers that manacle her wrists and move them forward to acceptance. Berny leans forward and whispers:

"Its all right. Go on—take it."

Words form in the eyes of the dwarf:

Do not shrink. Do not be afraid of me.
Jesus
See how my eyes look at you.
the Son of God
I too was made in His image.
was once—
I give you the rose.

Muriel, tight in her revulsion, sees black, and daintily reaches for the offering. As her hand touches it, Dan springs up in his seat and shouts:

"JESUS WAS ONCE A LEPER!"

Dan steps down.

He is as cool as a green stem that has just shed its flower.

Rows of gaping faces strain towards him. They are distant, beneath him, impalpable. Squeezing out, Dan again treads upon the corn-foot man. The man shoves him.

"Watch where youre going, mister. Crazy or no, you aint going to walk over me. Watch where youre going there."

Dan turns, and serenely tweaks the fellow's nose. The man jumps up. Dan is jammed against a seat-back. A slight swift anger flicks him. His fist hooks the other's jaw.

"Now you have started something. Aint no man living can hit me and get away with it. Come on on the outside."

The house, tumultuously stirring, grabs its wraps and follows the men.

The man leads Dan up a black alley. The alley-air is thick and moist with smells of garbage and wet trash. In the morning, singing niggers will drive by and ring their gongs . . . Heavy with the scent of rancid flowers and with the scent of fight. The crowd, pressing forward, is a hollow roar. Eyes of houses, soft girl-eyes, glow reticently upon the hubbub and blink out. The man stops. Takes off his hat and coat. Dan, having forgotten him, keeps going on.

Prayer

My body is opaque to the soul.
Driven of the spirit, long have I sought to temper it unto the spirit's longing,
But my mind, too, is opaque to the soul.
A closed lid is my soul's flesh-eye.
O Spirits of whom my soul is but a little finger,
Direct it to the lid of its flesh-eye.
I am weak with much giving.
I am weak with the desire to give more.
(How strong a thing is the little finger!)
So weak that I have confused the body with the soul,
And the body with its little finger.
(How frail is the little finger.)
My voice could not carry to you did you dwell in stars,
O Spirits of whom my soul is but a little finger . .

Harvest Song

I am a reaper whose muscles set at sundown. All my oats are cradled.
But I am too chilled, and too fatigued to bind them. And I hunger.

I crack a grain between my teeth. I do not taste it.
I have been in the fields all day. My throat is dry. I hunger.

My eyes are caked with dust of oatfields at harvest-time.
I am a blind man who stares across the hills, seeking stack'd fields of other harvesters.

It would be good to see them . . crook'd, split, and iron-ring'd
handles of the scythes. It would be good to see them, dust-caked
and blind. I hunger.

(Dusk is a strange fear'd sheath their blades are dull'd in.)
My throat is dry. And should I call, a cracked grain like the oats . . .
eoho—

I fear to call. What should they hear me, and offer me their grain,
oats, or wheat, or corn? I have been in the fields all day. I fear
I could not taste it. I fear knowledge of my hunger.

My ears are caked with dust of oatfields at harvest-time.
I am a deaf man who strains to hear the calls of other harvesters
whose throats are also dry.

It would be good to hear their songs . . reapers of the sweet-stalk'd
cane, cutters of the corn . . even though their throats cracked
and the strangeness of their voices deafened me.

I hunger. My throat is dry. Now that the sun has set and I am
chilled, I fear to call. (Eoho, my brothers!)

I am a reaper. (Eoho!) All my oats are cradled. But I am too fatigued
to bind them. And I hunger. I crack a grain. It has no taste to
it. My throat is dry . . .

O my brothers, I beat my palms, still soft, against the stubble of my
harvesting. (You beat your soft palms, too.) My pain is sweet.
Sweeter than the oats or wheat or corn. It will not bring me
knowledge of my hunger.

Bona and Paul[1]

1

On the school gymnasium floor, young men and women are drilling. They are going to be teachers, and go out into the world . . thud, thud . . and give precision to the movements of sick people who all their lives have been drilling. One man is out of step. In step. The teacher glares at him. A girl in bloomers, seated on a mat in the corner because she has told the director that she is sick, sees that the footfalls of the men are rhythmical and syncopated. The dance of his blue-trousered limbs thrills her.

Bona:[2] He is a candle that dances in a grove swung with pale balloons.

Columns of the drillers thud towards her. He is in the front row. He is in no row at all. Bona can look close at him. His red-brown face—

Bona: He is a harvest moon. He is an autumn leaf. He is a nigger. Bona! But dont all the dorm girls say so? And dont you, when you are sane, say so?

1. This story, set in Chicago, is the only story in the section not located in Washington, D.C.
2. Throughout this story, a colon usually precedes the thoughts, not the spoken words, of the character involved.

Thats why I love—Oh, nonsense. You have never loved a man who didnt first love you. Besides—

Columns thud away from her. Come to a halt in line formation. Rigid. The period bell rings, and the teacher dismisses them.

A group collects around Paul. They are choosing sides for basket-ball. Girls against boys. Paul has his. He is limbering up beneath the basket. Bona runs to the girl captain and asks to be chosen. The girls fuss. The director comes to quiet them. He hears what Bona wants.

"But, Miss Hale, you were excused—"

"So I was, Mr. Boynton, but—"

"—you can play basket-ball, but you are too sick to drill."

"If you wish to put it that way."

She swings away from him to the girl captain.

"Helen, I want to play, and you must let me. This is the first time I've asked and I dont see why—"

"Thats just it, Bona. We have our team."

"Well, team or no team, I want to play and thats all there is to it."

She snatches the ball from Helen's hands, and charges down the floor.

Helen shrugs. One of the weaker girls says that she'll drop out. Helen accepts this. The team is formed. The whistle blows. The game starts. Bona, in center, is jumping against Paul. He plays with her. Out-jumps her, makes a quick pass, gets a quick return, and shoots a goal from the middle of the floor. Bona burns crimson. She fights, and tries to guard him. One of her team-mates advises her not to play so hard. Paul shoots his second goal.

Bona begins to feel a little dizzy and all in. She drives on. Almost hugs Paul to guard him. Near the basket, he attempts to shoot, and Bona lunges into his body and tries to beat his arms. His elbow, going up, gives her a sharp crack on the jaw. She whirls. He catches her. Her body stiffens. Then becomes strangely vibrant, and bursts to a swift life within her anger. He is about to give way before her hatred when a new passion flares at him and makes his stomach fall. Bona squeezes him. He suddenly feels stifled, and wonders why in hell the ring of silly gaping faces that's caked about him doesnt make way and give him air. He has a swift illusion that it is himself who has been struck. He looks at Bona. Whir. Whir. They seem to be human distortions spinning tensely in a fog. Spinning . . dizzy . . spinning . . . Bona jerks herself free, flushes a startling crimson, breaks through the bewildered teams, and rushes from the hall.

2

Paul is in his room of two windows.

Outside, the South-Side L[3] track cuts them in two.

Bona is one window. One window, Paul.

Hurtling Loop-jammed[4] L trains throw them in swift shadow.

Paul goes to his. Gray slanting roofs of houses are tinted lavender in the setting sun. Paul follows the sun, over the stock-yards where a fresh stench is just arising, across wheat lands that are still waving above their stubble, into the sun. Paul follows the sun to a pine-matted hillock in Georgia. He sees the slanting roofs of gray unpainted cabins tinted lavender. A Negress chants a

3. Elevated train.

4. Crowded with passengers coming from the Loop, a section of downtown Chicago that was once the center of the shopping district.

lullaby beneath the mate-eyes of a southern planter. Her breasts are ample for the suckling of a song. She weans it, and sends it, curiously weaving, among lush melodies of cane and corn. Paul follows the sun into himself in Chicago.

He is at Bona's window.

With his own glow he looks through a dark pane.

Paul's room-mate comes in.

"Say, Paul, I've got a date for you. Come on. Shake a leg, will you?"

His blond hair is combed slick. His vest is snug about him.

He is like the electric light which he snaps on.

"Whatdoysay, Paul? Get a wiggle on. Come on. We havent got much time by the time we eat and dress and everything."

His bustling concentrates on the brushing of his hair.

Art: What in hell's getting into Paul of late, anyway? Christ, but he's getting moony. Its his blood. Dark blood: moony. Doesnt get anywhere unless you boost it. You've got to keep it going—

"Say, Paul!"

—or it'll go to sleep on you. Dark blood; nigger? Thats what those jealous she-hens say. Not Bona though, or she . . from the South . . wouldnt want me to fix a date for him and her. Hell of a thing, that Paul's dark: youve got to always be answering questions.

"Say, Paul, for Christ's sake leave that window, cant you?"

"Whats it, Art?"

"Hell, I've told you about fifty times. Got a date for you. Come on."

"With who?"

Art: He didnt use to ask; now he does. Getting up in the air. Getting funny.

"Heres your hat. Want a smoke? Paul! Here. I've got a match. Now come on and I'll tell you all about it on the way to supper."

Paul: He's going to Life this time. No doubt of that. Quit your kidding. Some day, dear Art, I'm going to kick the living slats out of you, and you wont know what I've done it for. And your slats will bring forth Life . . beautiful woman . . .

Pure Food Restaurant.

"Bring me some soup with a lot of crackers, understand? And then a roast-beef dinner. Same for you, eh, Paul? Now as I was saying, you've got a swell chance with her. And she's game. Best proof: she dont give a damn what the dorm girls say about you and her in the gym, or about the funny looks that Boynton gives her, or about what they say about, well, hell, you know, Paul. And say, Paul, she's a sweetheart. Tall, not puffy and pretty, more serious and deep—the kind you like these days. And they say she's got a car. And say, she's on fire. But you know all about that. She got Helen to fix it up with me. The four of us—remember the last party? Crimson Gardens![5] Boy!"

Paul's eyes take on a light that Art can settle in.

3

Art has on his patent-leather pumps and fancy vest. A loose fall coat is swung across his arm. His face has been massaged, and over a close shave, powdered.

5. A nightclub.

It is a healthy pink the blue of evening tints a purple pallor. Art is happy and confident in the good looks that his mirror gave him. Bubbling over with a joy he must spend now if the night is to contain it all. His bubbles, too, are curiously tinted purple as Paul watches them. Paul, contrary to what he had thought he would be like, is cool like the dusk, and like the dusk, detached. His dark face is a floating shade in evening's shadow. He sees Art, curiously. Art is a purple fluid, carbon-charged, that effervesces beside him. He loves Art. But is it not queer, this pale purplc facsimile of a red-blooded Norwegian friend of his? Perhaps for some reason, white skins are not supposed to live at night. Surely, enough nights would transform them fantastically, or kill them. And their red passion? Night paled that too, and made it moony. Moony. Thats what Art thought of him. Bona didnt, even in the daytime. Bona, would she be pale? Impossible. Not that red glow. But the conviction did not set his emotion flowing.

"Come right in, wont you? The young ladies will be right down. Oh, Mr. Carlstrom, do play something for us while you are waiting. We just love to listen to your music. You play so well."

Houses, and dorm sitting-rooms are places where white faces seclude themselves at night. There is a reason . . .

Art sat on the piano and simply tore it down. Jazz. The picture of Our Poets hung perilously.

Paul: I've got to get the kid to play that stuff for me in the daytime. Might be different. More himself. More nigger. Different? There is. Curious, though.

The girls come in. Art stops playing, and almost immediately takes up a petty quarrel, where he had last left it, with Helen.

Bona, black-hair curled staccato, sharply contrasting with Helen's puffy yellow, holds Paul's hand. She squeezes it. Her own emotion supplements the return pressure. And then, for no tangible reason, her spirits drop. Without them, she is nervous, and slightly afraid. She resents this. Paul's eyes are critical. She resents Paul. She flares at him. She flares to poise and security.

"Shall we be on our way?"

"Yes, Bona, certainly."

The Boulevard is sleek in asphalt, and, with arc-lights and limousines, aglow. Dry leaves scamper behind the whir of cars. The scent of exploded gasoline that mingles with them is faintly sweet. Mellow stone mansions overshadow clapboard homes which now resemble Negro shanties in some southern alley. Bona and Paul, and Art and Helen, move along an island-like, far-stretching strip of leaf-soft ground. Above them, worlds of shadow-planes and solids, silently moving. As if on one of these, Paul looks down on Bona. No doubt of it: her face is pale. She is talking. Her words have no feel to them. One sees them. They are pink petals that fall upon velvet cloth. Bona is soft, and pale, and beautiful.

"Paul, tell me something about yourself—or would you rather wait?"

"I'll tell you anything you'd like to know."

"Not what I want to know, Paul; what you want to tell me."

"You have the beauty of a gem fathoms under sea."

"I feel that, but I dont want to be. I want to be near you. Perhaps I will be if I tell you something. Paul, I love you."

The sea casts up its jewel into his hands, and burns them furiously. To tuck her arm under his and hold her hand will ease the burn.

"What can I say to you, brave dear woman—I cant talk love. Love is a dry grain in my mouth unless it is wet with kisses."

"You would dare? right here on the Boulevard? before Arthur and Helen?"

"Before myself? I dare."

"Here then."

Bona, in the slim shadow of a tree trunk, pulls Paul to her. Suddenly she stiffens. Stops.

"But you have not said you love me."

"I cant—yet—Bona."

"Ach, you never will. Youre cold. Cold."

Bona: Colored; cold. Wrong somewhere.

She hurries and catches up with Art and Helen.

4

Crimson Gardens. Hurrah! So one feels. People . . . University of Chicago students, members of the stock exchange, a large Negro in crimson uniform who guards the door . . . had watched them enter. Had leaned towards each other over ash-smeared tablecloths and highballs and whispered: What is he, a Spaniard, an Indian, an Italian, a Mexican, a Hindu, or a Japanese? Art had at first fidgeted under their stares . . what are *you* looking at, you godam pack of owl-eyed hyenas? . . but soon settled into his fuss with Helen, and forgot them. A strange thing happened to Paul. Suddenly he knew that he was apart from the people around him. Apart from the pain which they had unconsciously caused. Suddenly he knew that people saw, not attractiveness in his dark skin, but difference. Their stares, giving him to himself, filled something long empty within him, and were like green blades sprouting in his consciousness. There was fullness, and strength and peace about it all. He saw himself, cloudy, but real. He saw the faces of the people at the tables round him. White lights, or as now, the pink lights of the Crimson Gardens gave a glow and immediacy to white faces. The pleasure of it, equal to that of love or dream, of seeing this. Art and Bona and Helen? He'd look. They were wonderfully flushed and beautiful. Not for himself; because they were. Distantly. Who were they, anyway? God, if he knew them. He'd come in with them. Of that he was sure. Come where? Into life? Yes. No. Into the Crimson Gardens. A part of life. A carbon bubble. Would it look purple if he went out into the night and looked at it? His sudden starting to rise almost upset the table.

"What in hell—pardon—whats the matter, Paul?"

"I forgot my cigarettes—"

"Youre smoking one."

"So I am. Pardon me."

The waiter straightens them out. Takes their order.

Art: What in hell's eating Paul? Moony aint the word for it. From bad to worse. And those godam people staring so. Paul's a queer fish. Doesnt seem to mind . . . He's my pal, let me tell you, you horn-rimmed owl-eyed hyena at that table, and a lot better than you whoever you are . . . Queer about him. I could stick up for him if he'd only come out, one way or the other, and tell a feller. Besides, a room-mate has a right to know. Thinks I wont understand. Said so. He's got a swell head when it comes to brains, all right. God, he's a good straight feller, though. Only, moony. Nut. Nuttish. Nuttery. Nutmeg . . . "What'd you say, Helen?"

"I was talking to Bona, thank you."

"Well, its nothing to get spiffy about."

"What? Oh, of course not. Please lets dont start some silly argument all over again."

"Well."

"Well."

"Now thats enough. Say, waiter, whats the matter with our order? Make it snappy, will you?"

Crimson Gardens. Hurrah! So one feels. The drinks come. Four high-balls. Art passes cigarettes. A girl dressed like a bareback rider in flaming pink, makes her way through tables to the dance floor. All lights are dimmed till they seem a lush afterglow of crimson. Spotlights the girl. She sings. "Liza, Little Liza Jane."

Paul is rosy before his window.

He moves, slightly, towards Bona.

With his own glow, he seeks to penetrate a dark pane.

Paul: From the South. What does that mean, precisely, except that you'll love or hate a nigger? Thats a lot. What does it mean except that in Chicago you'll have the courage to neither love or hate. A priori.[6] But it would seem that you have. Queer words, arent these, for a man who wears blue pants on a gym floor in the daytime. Well, never matter. You matter. I'd like to know you whom I look at. Know, not love. Not that knowing is a greater pleasure; but that I have just found the joy of it. You came just a month too late. Even this afternoon I dreamed. Tonight, along the Boulevard, you found me cold. Paul Johnson, cold! Thats a good one, eh, Art, you fine old stupid fellow, you! But I feel good! The color and the music and the song . . . A Negress chants a lullaby beneath the mate-eyes of a southern planter. O song! . . And those flushed faces. Eager brilliant eyes. Hard to imagine them as unawakened. Your own. Oh, they're awake all right. "And you know it too, dont you Bona?"

"What, Paul?"

"The truth of what I was thinking."

"I'd like to know I know—something of you."

"You will—before the evening's over. I promise it."

Crimson Gardens. Hurrah! So one feels. The bare-back rider balances agilely on the applause which is the tail of her song. Orchestral instruments warm up for jazz. The flute is a cat that ripples its fur against the deep-purring saxophone. The drum throws sticks. The cat jumps on the piano keyboard. Hi diddle, hi diddle, the cat and the fiddle. Crimson Gardens . . hurrah! . . jumps over the moon. Crimson Gardens! Helen . . O Eliza . . rabbit-eyes sparkling, plays up to, and tries to placate what she considers to be Paul's contempt. She always does that . . Little Liza Jane . . . Once home, she burns with the thought of what she's done. She says all manner of snidy things about him, and swears that she'll never go out again when he is along. She tries to get Art to break with him, saying, that if Paul, whom the whole dormitory calls a nigger, is more to him than she is, well, she's through. She does not break with Art. She goes out as often as she can with Art and Paul. She explains this to herself by a piece of information which a friend of hers had given her: men like him (Paul) can fascinate. One is not responsible for fascination. Not one girl had really loved Paul; he fascinated them. Bona didnt; only thought she did. Time would tell. And of course, *she* didn't. Liza . . . She plays up to, and tries to placate, Paul.

6. In advance of the fact (Latin). A priori conclusions are judgments based on preconceived theories rather than on actual study and analysis.

"Paul is so deep these days, and I'm so glad he's found some one to interest him."

"I dont believe I do."

The thought escapes from Bona just a moment before her anger at having said it.

Bona: You little puffy cat, I do. I do!

Dont I, Paul? Her eyes ask.

Her answer is a crash of jazz from the palm-hidden orchestra. Crimson Gardens is a body whose blood flows to a clot upon the dance floor. Art and Helen clot. Soon, Bona and Paul. Paul finds her a little stiff, and his mind, wandering to Helen (silly little kid who wants every highball spoon her hands touch, for a souvenir), supple, perfect little dancer, wishes for the next dance when he and Art will exchange.

Bona knows that she must win him to herself.

"Since when have men like you grown cold?"

"The first philosopher."

"I thought you were a poet—or a gym director."

"Hence, your failure to make love."

Bona's eyes flare. Water. Grow red about the rims. She would like to tear away from him and dash across the clotted floor.

"What do you mean?"

"Mental concepts rule you. If they were flush with mine—good. I dont believe they are."

"How do you know, Mr. Philosopher?"

"Mostly a priori."

"You talk well for a gym director."

"And you—"

"I hate you. Ou!"

She presses away. Paul, conscious of the convention in it, pulls her to him. Her body close. Her head still strains away. He nearly crushes her. She tries to pinch him. Then sees people staring, and lets her arms fall. Their eyes meet. Both, contemptuous. The dance takes blood from their minds and packs it, tingling, in the torsos of their swaying bodies. Passionate blood leaps back into their eyes. They are a dizzy blood clot on a gyrating floor. They know that the pink-faced people have no part in what they feel. Their instinct leads them away from Art and Helen, and towards the big uniformed black man who opens and closes the gilded exit door. The cloak-room girl is tolerant of their impatience over such trivial things as wraps. And slightly superior. As the black man swings the door for them, his eyes are knowing. Too many couples have passed out, flushed and fidgety, for him not to know. The chill air is a shock to Paul. A strange thing happens. He sees the Gardens purple, as if he were way off. And a spot is in the purple. The spot comes furiously towards him. Face of the black man. It leers. It smiles sweetly like a child's. Paul leaves Bona and darts back so quickly that he doesnt give the door-man a chance to open. He swings in. Stops. Before the huge bulk of the Negro.

"You're wrong."

"Yassur."

"Brother, you're wrong.

"I came back to tell you, to shake your hand, and tell you that you are wrong. That something beautiful is going to happen. That the Gardens are purple like a bed of roses would be at dusk. That I came into the Gardens, into life in the Gardens with one whom I did not know. That I danced with her, and did not know her. That I felt passion, contempt and passion for her whom I did not know. That I thought of her. That my thoughts were matches thrown into a dark window. And all the while the Gardens were purple like a bed of roses would be at dusk. I came back to tell you, brother, that white faces are petals of roses. That dark faces are petals of dusk. That I am going out and gather petals. That I am going out and know her whom I brought here with me to these Gardens which are purple like a bed of roses would be at dusk."

Paul and the black man shook hands.

When he reached the spot where they had been standing, Bona was gone.

Kabnis

1

Ralph Kabnis, propped in his bed, tries to read. To read himself to sleep. An oil lamp on a chair near his elbow burns unsteadily. The cabin room is spaced fantastically about it. Whitewashed hearth and chimney, black with sooty saw-teeth. Ceiling, patterned by the fringed globe of the lamp. The walls, unpainted, are seasoned a rosin yellow. And cracks between the boards are black. These cracks are the lips the night winds use for whispering. Night winds in Georgia are vagrant poets, whispering. Kabnis, against his will, lets his book slip down, and listens to them. The warm whiteness of his bed, the lamp-light, do not protect him from the weird chill of their song:

White-man's land.
Niggers, sing.
Burn, bear black children
Till poor rivers bring
Rest, and sweet glory
In Camp Ground.

Kabnis' thin hair is streaked on the pillow. His hand strokes the slim silk of his mustache. His thumb, pressed under his chin, seems to be trying to give squareness and projection to it. Brown eyes stare from a lemon face. Moisture gathers beneath his arm-pits. He slides down beneath the cover, seeking release.

Kabnis: Near me. Now. Whoever you are, my warm glowing sweetheart, do not think that the face that rests beside you is the real Kabnis. Ralph Kabnis is a dream. And dreams are faces with large eyes and weak chins and broad brows that get smashed by the fists of square faces. The body of the world is bull-necked. A dream is a soft face that fits uncertainly upon it. . . God, if I could develop that in words. Give what I know a bull-neck and a heaving body, all would go well with me, wouldnt it, sweetheart? If I could feel that I came to the South to face it. If I, the dream (not what is weak and afraid in me) could become the face of the South. How my lips would sing for it, my songs being the lips of its soul. Soul. Soul hell. There aint no such thing. What in hell was that?

A rat had run across the thin boards of the ceiling. Kabnis thrusts his head out from the covers. Through the cracks, a powdery faded red dust sprays down on him. Dust of slavefields, dried, scattered. . . No use to read. Christ, if he only could drink himself to sleep. Something as sure as fate was going to happen. He couldnt stand this thing much longer. A hen, perched on a shelf in the adjoining room begins to tread. Her nails scrape the soft wood. Her feathers ruffle.

"Get out of that, you egg-laying bitch."

Kabnis hurls a slipper against the wall. The hen flies from her perch and cackles as if a skunk were after her.

"Now cut out that racket or I'll wring your neck for you."

Answering cackles arise in the chicken yard.

"Why in Christ's hell cant you leave me alone? Damn it, I wish your cackle would choke you. Choke every mother's son of them in this God-forsaken hole. Go away. By God I'll wring your neck for you if you dont. Hell of a mess I've got in: even the poultry is hostile. Go way. Go way. By God, I'll . . ."

Kabnis jumps from his bed. His eyes are wild. He makes for the door. Bursts through it. The hen, driving blindly at the window-pane, screams. Then flies and flops around trying to elude him. Kabnis catches her.

"Got you now, you she-bitch."

With his fingers about her neck, he thrusts open the outside door and steps out into the serene loveliness of Georgian autumn moonlight. Some distance off, down in the valley, a band of pine-smoke, silvered gauze, drifts steadily. The half-moon is a white child that sleeps upon the tree-tops of the forest. White winds croon its sleep-song:

rock a-by baby . . .
Black mother sways, holding a white child on her bosom.
when the bough bends . . .
Her breath hums through pine-cones.
cradle will fall . . .
Teat moon-children at your breasts,
down will come baby . . .
Black mother.

Kabnis whirls the chicken by its neck, and throws the head away. Picks up the hopping body, warm, sticky, and hides it in a clump of bushes. He wipes blood from his hands onto the coarse scant grass.

Kabnis: Thats done. Old Chromo in the big house there will wonder whats become of her pet hen. Well, it'll teach her a lesson: not to make a hen-coop of my quarters. Quarters. Hell of a fine quarters, I've got. Five years ago; look at me now. Earth's child. The earth my mother. God is a profligate red-nosed man about town. Bastardy; me. A bastard son has got a right to curse his maker. God. . .

Kabnis is about to shake his fists heavenward. He looks up, and the night's beauty strikes him dumb. He falls to his knees. Sharp stones cut through his thin pajamas. The shock sends a shiver over him. He quivers. Tears mist his eyes. He writhes.

"God Almighty, dear God, dear Jesus, do not torture me with beauty. Take it away. Give me an ugly world. Ha, ugly. Stinking like unwashed niggers. Dear Jesus, do not chain me to myself and set these hills and valleys, heaving with folk-songs, so close to me that I cannot reach them. There is a radiant beauty in the night that touches and . . . tortures me. Ugh. Hell. Get up, you damn fool. Look around. Whats beautiful there? Hog pens and chicken yards. Dirty red mud. Stinking outhouse. Whats beauty anyway but ugliness if it hurts you? God, he doesnt exist, but nevertheless He is ugly.

Hence, what comes from Him is ugly. Lynchers and business men, and that cockroach Hanby, especially. How come that he gets to be principal of a school? Of the school I'm driven to teach in? God's handiwork, doubtless. God and Hanby, they belong together. Two godam moral-spouters. Oh, no, I wont let that emotion come up in me. Stay down. Stay down, I tell you. O Jesus, Thou art beautiful. . . Come, Ralph, pull yourself together. Curses and adoration dont come from what is sane. This loneliness, dumbness, awful, intangible oppression is enough to drive a man insane. Miles from nowhere. A speck on a Georgia hillside. Jesus, can you imagine it—an atom of dust in agony on a hillside? Thats a spectacle for you. Come, Ralph, old man, pull yourself together."

Kabnis has stiffened. He is conscious now of the night wind, and of how it chills him. He rises. He totters as a man would who for the first time uses artificial limbs. As a completely artificial man would. The large frame house, squatting on brick pillars, where the principal of the school, his wife, and the boarding girls sleep, seems a curious shadow of his mind. He tries, but cannot convince himself of its reality. His gaze drifts down into the vale, across the swamp, up over the solid dusk bank of pines, and rests, bewildered-like, on the court-house tower. It is dull silver in the moonlight. White child that sleeps upon the top of pines. Kabnis' mind clears. He sees himself yanked beneath that tower. He sees white minds, with indolent assumption, juggle justice and a nigger. . . Somewhere, far off in the straight line of his sight, is Augusta. Christ, how cut off from everything he is. And hours, hours north, why not say a lifetime north? Washington sleeps. Its still, peaceful streets, how desirable they are. Its people whom he had always half-way despised. New York? Impossible. It was a fiction. He had dreamed it. An impotent nostalgia grips him. It becomes intolerable. He forces himself to narrow to a cabin silhouetted on a knoll about a mile away. Peace. Negroes within it are content. They farm. They sing. They love. They sleep. Kabnis wonders if perhaps they can feel him. If perhaps he gives them bad dreams. Things are so immediate in Georgia.

Thinking that now he can go to sleep, he re-enters his room. He builds a fire in the open hearth. The room dances to the tongues of flames, and sings to the crackling and spurting of the logs. Wind comes up between the floor boards, through the black cracks of the walls.

Kabnis: Cant sleep. Light a cigarette. If that old bastard comes over here and smells smoke, I'm done for. Hell of a note, cant even smoke. The stillness of it: where they burn and hang men, you cant smoke. Cant take a swig of licker.[1] What do they think this is, anyway, some sort of temperance school? How did I ever land in such a hole? Ugh. One might just as well be in his grave. Still as a grave. Jesus, how still everything is. Does the world know how still it is? People make noise. They are afraid of silence. Of what lives, and God, of what dies in silence. There must be many dead things moving in silence. They come here to touch me. I swear I feel their fingers. . . Come, Ralph, pull yourself together. What in hell was that? Only the rustle of leaves, I guess. You know, Ralph, old man, it wouldnt surprise me at all to see a ghost. People dont think there are such things. They rationalize their fear, and call their cowardice science. Fine bunch, they are. Damit, that was a noise. And not the wind either. A chicken maybe. Hell, chickens dont wander around this time of night. What in hell is it?

1. Liquor.

A scraping sound, like a piece of wood dragging over the ground, is coming near.

"Ha, ha. The ghosts down this way havent got any chains to rattle, so they drag trees along with them. Thats a good one. But no joke, something is outside this house, as sure as hell. Whatever it is, it can get a good look at me and I cant see it. Jesus Christ!"

Kabnis pours water on the flames and blows his lamp out. He picks up a poker and stealthily approaches the outside door. Swings it open, and lurches into the night. A calf, carrying a yoke of wood, bolts away from him and scampers down the road.

"Well, I'm damned. This godam place is sure getting the best of me. Come, Ralph, old man, pull yourself together. Nights cant last forever. Thank God for that. Its Sunday already. First time in my life I've ever wanted Sunday to come. Hell of a day. And down here there's no such thing as ducking church. Well, I'll see Halsey and Layman, and get a good square meal. Thats something. And Halsey's a damn good feller. Cant talk to him, though. Who in Christ's world can I talk to? A hen. God. Myself. . . I'm going bats, no doubt of that. Come now, Ralph, go in and make yourself go to sleep. Come now . . in the door . . thats right. Put the poker down. There. All right. Slip under the sheets. Close your eyes. Think nothing . . a long time . . nothing, nothing. Dont even think nothing. Blank. Not even blank. Count. No, mustnt count. Nothing . . blank . . nothing . . blank . . space without stars in it. No, nothing . . nothing . .

Kabnis sleeps. The winds, like soft-voiced vagrant poets sing:

White-man's land.
Niggers, sing.
Burn, bear black children
Till poor rivers bring
Rest, and sweet glory
In Camp Ground.

2

The parlor of Fred Halsey's home. There is a seediness about it. It seems as though the fittings have given a frugal service to at least seven generations of middle-class shop-owners. An open grate burns cheerily in contrast to the gray cold changed autumn weather. An old-fashioned mantelpiece supports a family clock (not running), a figure or two in imitation bronze, and two small group pictures. Directly above it, in a heavy oak frame, the portrait of a bearded man. Black hair, thick and curly, intensifies the pallor of the high forehead. The eyes are daring. The nose, sharp and regular. The poise suggests a tendency to adventure checked by the necessities of absolute command. The portrait is that of an English gentleman who has retained much of his culture, in that money has enabled him to escape being drawn through a land-grubbing pioneer life. His nature and features, modified by marriage and circumstances, have been transmitted to his great-grandson, Fred. To the left of this picture, spaced on the wall, is a smaller portrait of the great-grandmother. That here there is a Negro strain, no one would doubt. But it is difficult to say in precisely what feature it lies. On close inspection, her mouth is seen to be wistfully twisted. The expression of her face seems to shift before one's gaze—now ugly, repulsive; now sad, and somehow beautiful in its pain. A tin wood-box rests on the floor below. To the right of the great-grandfather's portrait hangs a family group: the father, mother, two brothers, and one sister of Fred. It includes himself some thirty years ago when his face was an olive white, and his hair luxuriant and dark and wavy. The father is a rich brown. The mother, practically white. Of the children, the girl, quite young, is like Fred; the two brothers, darker. The walls of the room are plastered and painted green. An old upright piano is tucked into the corner near the window. The window looks out on a forlorn, box-like, whitewashed frame church. Negroes are gathering, on foot, driving questionable gray and brown mules, and in an occasional Ford, for afternoon service. Beyond, Georgia hills roll off into the distance, their dreary aspect heightened by the gray spots of unpainted one- and two-room shanties. Clumps of pine trees here and there are the dark points the whole landscape is approaching. The church bell tolls. Above its squat tower, a great spiral of buzzards reaches far into the heavens. An ironic comment upon the path that leads into the Christian land. . . Three rocking chairs are grouped around the grate. Sunday papers scattered on the floor indicate a recent usage. Halsey, a well-built, stocky fellow, hair cropped close, enters the room. His Sunday clothes smell of wood and glue, for it is his habit to potter around his wagon-shop even on the Lord's day. He is followed by Professor Layman, tall, heavy, loose-jointed Georgia Negro, by turns teacher and preacher, who has traveled in almost every nook and corner of the state and hence knows more than would be good for anyone other than a silent man. Kabnis, trying to force through a gathering heaviness, trails in behind them. They slip into chairs before the fire.

Layman: Sholy[2] fine, Mr. Halsey, sholy fine. This town's right good at feedin folks, better'n most towns in th state, even for preachers, but I ken say this beats um all. Yassur. Now aint that right, Professor[3] Kabnis?

Kabnis: Yes sir, this beats them all, all right—best I've had, and thats a fact, though my comparison doesnt carry far, y'know.

Layman: Hows that, Professor?

Kabnis: Well, this is my first time out—

Layman: For a fact. Aint seed you round so much. Whats th trouble? Dont like our folks down this away?

Halsey: Aint that, Layman. He aint like most northern niggers that way. Aint a thing stuck-up about him. He likes us, you an me, maybe all—its that red mud over yonder—gets stuck in it an cant get out. (Laughs.) An then he loves th fire so, warm as its been. Coldest Yankee I've ever seen. But I'm goin t get him out now in a jiffy, eh, Kabnis?

Kabnis: Sure, I should say so, sure. Dont think its because I dont like folks down this way. Just the opposite, in fact. Theres more hospitality and everything. Its diff—that is, theres lots of northern exaggeration about the South. Its not half the terror they picture it. Things are not half bad, as one could easily figure out for himself without ever crossing the Mason and Dixie[4] line: all these people wouldnt stay down here, especially the rich, the ones that could easily leave, if conditions were so mighty bad. And then too, sometime back, my family were southerners y'know. From Georgia, in fact—

Layman: Nothin t feel proud about, Professor. Neither your folks nor mine.

2. Surely.
3. The term "professor" was often used among Blacks as a term of respect for teachers, ministers, and musicians.
4. The Mason-Dixon Line is the border between British colonies surveyed between 1763 and 1767 by Charles Mason and Jeremiah Dixon; it came to symbolize the boundary between the northern and southern United States. "Dixie" is a slang term for the South.

Halsey (in a mock religious tone): Amen t that, brother Layman. Amen (turning to Kabnis, half playful, yet somehow dead in earnest). An Mr. Kabnis, kindly remember youre in th land of cotton—hell of a land. Th white folks get th boll; th niggers get th stalk. An dont you dare touch th boll, or even look at it. They'll swing y sho. (Laughs.)

Kabnis: But they wouldnt touch a gentleman—fellows, men like us three here—

Layman: Nigger's a nigger down this away, Professor. An only two dividins: good an bad. An even they aint permanent categories. They sometimes mixes um up when it comes t lynchin. I've seen um do it.

Halsey: Dont let th fear int y, though, Kabnis. This county's a good un. Aint been a stringin up I can remember. (Laughs.)

Layman: This is a good town an a good county. But theres some that makes up fer it.

Kabnis: Things are better now though since that stir about those peonage cases,[5] arent they?

Layman: Ever hear tell of a single shot killin moren one rabbit, Professor?

Kabnis: No, of course not, that is, but then—

Halsey: Now I know you werent born yesterday, sprung up so rapid like you aint heard of th brick thrown in th hornets' nest. (Laughs.)

Kabnis: Hardly, hardly, I know—

Halsey: Course y do. (To Layman) See, northern niggers aint as dumb as they make out t be.

Kabnis (overlooking the remark): Just stirs them up to sting.

Halsey: T perfection. An put just like a professor should put it.

Kabnis: Thats what actually did happen?

Layman: Well, if it aint sos only because th stingers already movin jes as fast as they ken go. An been goin ever since I ken remember, an then some mo. Though I dont usually make mention of it.

Halsey: Damn sight better not. Say, Layman, you come from where theyre always swarmin, dont y?

Layman: Yassur. I do that, sho. Dont want t mention it, but its a fact. I've seed th time when there werent no use t even stretch out flat upon th ground. Seen um shoot an cut a man t pieces who had died th night befo. Yassur. An they didnt stop when they found out he was dead—jes went on ahackin at him anyway.

Kabnis: What did you do? What did you say to them, Professor?

Layman: Thems th things you neither does a thing or talks about if y want t stay around this away, Professor.

Halsey: Listen t what he's tellin y, Kabnis. May come in handy some day.

Kabnis: Cant something be done? But of course not. This preacher-ridden race. Pray and shout. Theyre in the preacher's hands. Thats what it is. And the preacher's hands are in the white man's pockets.

Halsey: Present company always excepted.

Kabnis: The Professor knows I wasnt referring to him.

Layman: Preacher's a preacher anywheres you turn. No use exceptin.

Kabnis: Well, of course, if you look at it that way. I didnt mean—But cant something be done?

5. A reference to the practice in the U.S. South in which Blacks, especially prisoners, were indentured to work without pay for white landowners.

Layman: Sho. Yassur. An done first rate an well. Jes like Sam Raymon done it.

Kabnis: Hows that? What did he do?

Layman: Th white folks (reckon I oughtnt tell it) had jes knocked two others like you kill a cow—brained um with an ax, when they caught Sam Raymon by a stream. They was about t do fer him when he up an says, "White folks, I gotter die, I knows that. But wont y let me die in my own way?" Some was fer gettin after him, but th boss held um back an says, "Jes so longs th nigger dies—" An Sam fell down ont his knees an prayed, "O Lord, Ise comin to y," and he up an jumps int th stream.

Singing from the church becomes audible. Above it, rising and falling in a plaintive moan, a woman's voice swells to shouting. Kabnis hears it. His face gives way to an expression of mingled fear, contempt, and pity. Layman takes no notice of it. Halsey grins at Kabnis. He feels like having a little sport with him.

Halsey: Lets go t church, eh, Kabnis?

Kabnis (seeking control): All right—no sir, not by a damn sight. Once a days enough for me. Christ, but that stuff gets to me. Meaning no reflection on you, Professor.

Halsey: Course not. Say, Kabnis, noticed y this morning. What'd y get up for an go out?

Kabnis: Couldnt stand the shouting, and thats a fact. We dont have that sort of thing up North. We do, but, that is, some one should see to it that they are stopped or put out when they get so bad the preacher has to stop his sermon for them.

Halsey: Is that th way youall sit on sisters up North?

Kabnis: In the church I used to go to no one ever shouted—

Halsey: Lungs weak?

Kabnis: Hardly, that is—

Halsey: Yankees are right up t th minute in tellin folk how t turn a trick. They always were good at talkin.

Kabnis: Well, anyway, they should be stopped.

Layman: Thats right. Thats true. An its th worst ones in th community that comes int th church t shout. I've sort a made a study of it. You take a man what drinks, th biggest licker-head around will come int th church an yell th loudest. An th sister whats done wrong, an is always doin wrong, will sit down in th Amen corner[6] an swing her arms an shout her head off. Seems as if they cant control themselves out in th world; they cant control themselves in church. Now dont that sound logical, Professor?

Halsey: Reckon its as good as any. But I heard that queer cuss over yonder—y know him, dont y, Kabnis? Well, y ought t. He had a run-in with your boss th other day—same as you'll have if you dont walk th chalk-line. An th quicker th better. I hate that Hanby. Ornery bastard. I'll mash his mouth in one of these days. Well, as I was sayin, that feller, Lewis's name, I heard him sayin somethin about a stream whats dammed has got t cut loose somewheres. An that sounds good. I know th feelin myself. He strikes me as knowin a bucketful bout most things, that feller does. Seems like he doesnt want t talk, an does, sometimes, like Layman here. Damn queer feller, him.

6. A popular term for the section of the congregation in a Black church that is vocal in its support of the preacher and choir with exhortations and exclamations of "Amen!"

Layman: Cant make heads or tails of him, an I've seen lots o queer possums in my day. Everybody's wonderin about him. White folks too. He'll have t leave here soon, thats sho. Always askin questions. An I aint seed his lips move once. Pokin round an notin somethin. Noted what I said th other day, an that werent for notin down.

Kabnis: What was that?

Layman: Oh, a lynchin that took place bout a year ago. Th worst I know of round these parts.

Halsey: Bill Burnam?

Layman: Na. Mame Lamkins.

Halsey grunts, but says nothing.

The preacher's voice rolls from the church in an insistent chanting monotone. At regular intervals it rises to a crescendo note. The sister begins to shout. Her voice, high-pitched and hysterical, is almost perfectly attuned to the nervous key of Kabnis. Halsey notices his distress, and is amused by it. Layman's face is expressionless. Kabnis wants to hear the story of Mame Lamkins. He does not want to hear it. It can be no worse than the shouting.

Kabnis (his chair rocking faster): What about Mame Lamkins?

Halsey: Tell him, Layman.

The preacher momentarily stops. The choir, together with the entire congregation, sings an old spiritual. The music seems to quiet the shouter. Her heavy breathing has the sound of evening winds that blow through pinecones. Layman's voice is uniformly low and soothing. A canebrake, murmuring the tale to its neighbor-road would be more passionate.

Layman: White folks know that niggers talk, an they dont mind jes so long as nothing comes of it, so here goes. She was in th family-way, Mame Lamkins was. They killed her in th street, an some white man seein th risin in her stomach as she lay there soppy in her blood like any cow, took an ripped her belly open, an th kid fell out. It was living; but a nigger baby aint supposed t live. So he jabbed his knife in it an stuck it t a tree. An then they all went away.[7]

Kabnis: Christ no! What had she done?

Layman: Tried t hide her husband when they was after him.

A shriek pierces the room. The bronze pieces on the mantel hum. The sister cries frantically: "Jesus, Jesus, I've found Jesus. O Lord, glory t God, one mo sinner is acomin home." At the height of this, a stone, wrapped round with paper, crashes through the window. Kabnis springs to his feet, terror-stricken. Layman is worried. Halsey picks up the stone. Takes off the wrapper, smooths it out, and reads: "You northern nigger, its time fer y t leave. Git along now." Kabnis knows that the command is meant for him. Fear squeezes him. Caves him in. As a violent external pressure would. Fear flows inside him. It fills him up. He bloats. He saves himself from bursting by dashing wildly from the room. Halsey and Layman stare stupidly at each other. The stone, the crumpled paper are things, huge things that weight them. Their thoughts are vaguely concerned with the texture of the stone, with the color of the paper. Then they remember the words, and begin to shift them about in sentences. Layman even construes them grammatically. Suddenly the sense of them comes back to Halsey. He grips Layman by the arm and they both follow after Kabnis.

7. This description is based on the events of the 1918 lynching of Mary Turner in Valdosta, Georgia.

A false dusk has come early. The countryside is ashen, chill. Cabins and roads and canebrakes whisper. The church choir, dipping into a long silence, sings:

My Lord, what a mourning,
My Lord, what a mourning,
My Lord, what a mourning,
When the stars begin to fall.

Softly luminous over the hills and valleys, the faint spray of a scattered star. . .

3

A splotchy figure drives forward along the cane- and corn-stalk hemmed-in road. A scarecrow replica of Kabnis, awkwardly animate. Fantastically plastered with red Georgia mud. It skirts the big house whose windows shine like mellow lanterns in the dusk. Its shoulder jogs against a sweet-gum tree. The figure caroms off against the cabin door, and lunges in. It slams the door as if to prevent some one entering after it.

"God Almighty, theyre here. After me. On me. All along the road I saw their eyes flaring from the cane. Hounds. Shouts. What in God's name did I run here for? A mud-hole trap. I stumbled on a rope. O God, a rope. Their clammy hands were like the love of death playing up and down my spine. Trying to trip my legs. To trip my spine. Up and down my spine. My spine. . . My legs. . . Why in hell didnt they catch me?"

Kabnis wheels around, half defiant, half numbed with a more immediate fear.

"Wanted to trap me here. Get out o there. I see you."

He grabs a broom from beside the chimney and violently pokes it under the bed. The broom strikes a tin wash-tub. The noise bewilders. He recovers.

"Not there. In the closet."

He throws the broom aside and grips the poker. Starts towards the closet door, towards somewhere in the perfect blackness behind the chimney.

"I'll brain you."

He stops short. The barks of hounds, evidently in pursuit, reach him. A voice, liquid in distance, yells, "Hi! Hi!"

"O God, theyre after me. Holy Father, Mother of Christ—hell, this aint no time for prayer—"

Voices, just outside the door:

"Reckon he's here."

"Dont see no light though."

The door is flung open.

Kabnis: Get back or I'll kill you.

He braces himself, brandishing the poker.

Halsey (coming in): Aint as bad as all that. Put that thing down.

Layman: Its only us, Professor. Nobody else after y.

Kabnis: Halsey. Layman. Close that door. Dont light that light. For godsake get away from there.

Halsey: Nobody's after y, Kabnis, I'm tellin y. Put that thing down an get yourself together.

Kabnis: I tell you they are. I saw them. I heard the hounds.

Halsey: These aint th days of hounds an Uncle Tom's Cabin,[8] feller. White folks aint in fer all them theatrics these days. Theys more direct than that. If what they wanted was t get y, theyd have just marched right in an took y where y sat. Somebodys down by th branch chasin rabbits an atreein possums.

A shot is heard.

Halsey: Got him, I reckon. Saw Tom goin out with his gun. Tom's pretty lucky most times.

He goes to the bureau and lights the lamp. The circular fringe is patterned on the ceiling. The moving shadows of the men are huge against the bare wall boards. Halsey walks up to Kabnis, takes the poker from his grip, and without more ado pushes him into a chair before the dark hearth.

Halsey: Youre a mess. Here, Layman. Get some trash an start a fire.

Layman fumbles around, finds some newspapers and old bags, puts them in the hearth, arranges the wood, and kindles the fire. Halsey sets a black iron kettle where it soon will be boiling. Then takes from his hip-pocket a bottle of corn licker which he passes to Kabnis.

Halsey: Here. This'll straighten y out a bit.

Kabnis nervously draws the cork and gulps the licker down.

Kabnis: Ha. Good stuff. Thanks. Thank y, Halsey.

Halsey: Good stuff! Youre damn right. Hanby there dont think so. Wonder he doesnt come over t find out whos burnin his oil. Miserly bastard, him. Th boys what made this stuff—are y listenin t me, Kabnis? th boys what made this stuff have got th art down like I heard you say youd like t be with words. Eh? Have some, Layman?

Layman: Dont think I care for none, thank y jes th same, Mr. Halsey.

Halsey: Care hell. Course y care. Everybody cares around these parts. Preachers an school teachers an everybody. Here. Here, take it. Dont try that line on me.

Layman limbers up a little, but he cannot quite forget that he is on school ground.

Layman: Thats right. Thats true, sho. Shinin[9] is th only business what pays in these hard times.

He takes a nip, and passes the bottle to Kabnis. Kabnis is in the middle of a long swig when a rap sounds on the door. He almost spills the bottle, but manages to pass it to Halsey just as the door swings open and Hanby enters. He is a well-dressed, smooth, rich, black-skinned Negro who thinks there is no one quite so suave and polished as himself. To members of his own race, he affects the manners of a wealthy white planter. Or, when he is up North, he lets it be known that his ideas are those of the best New England tradition. To white men he bows, without ever completely humbling himself. Tradesmen in the town tolerate him because he spends his money with them. He delivers his words with a full consciousness of his moral superiority.

Hanby: Hum. Erer, Professor Kabnis, to come straight to the point: the progress of the Negro race is jeopardized whenever the personal habits and examples set by its guides and mentors fall below the acknowledged and hard-won standard of its average member. This institution, of which I am the humble president, was founded, and has been maintained at a cost of

8. A reference to the scene in which Eliza flees, pursued by bloodhounds, across the Ohio River to freedom in the novel *Uncle Tom's Cabin* (1852) by American author and abolitionist Harriet Beecher Stowe (1811–1896).

9. Moonshining, that is, making liquor illegally.

great labor and untold sacrifice. Its purpose is to teach our youth to live better, cleaner, more noble lives. To prove to the world that the Negro race can be just like any other race. It hopes to attain this aim partly by the salutary examples set by its instructors. I cannot hinder the progress of a race simply to indulge a single member. I have thought the matter out beforehand, I can assure you. Therefore, if I find your resignation on my desk by to-morrow morning, Mr. Kabnis, I shall not feel obliged to call in the sheriff. Otherwise. . ."

Kabnis: A fellow can take a drink in his own room if he wants to, in the privacy of his own room.

Hanby: His room, but not the institution's room, Mr. Kabnis.

Kabnis: This is my room while I'm in it.

Hanby: Mr. Clayborn (the sheriff) can inform you as to that.

Kabnis: Oh, well, what do I care—glad to get out of this mud-hole.

Hanby: I should think so from your looks.

Kabnis: You neednt get sarcastic about it.

Hanby: No, that is true. And I neednt wait for your resignation either, Mr. Kabnis.

Kabnis: Oh, you'll get that all right. Dont worry.

Hanby: And I should like to have the room thoroughly aired and cleaned and ready for your successor by to-morrow noon, Professor.

Kabnis (trying to rise): You can have your godam room right away. I dont want it.

Hanby: But I wont have your cursing.

Halsey pushes Kabnis back into his chair.

Halsey: Sit down, Kabnis, till I wash y.

Hanby (to Halsey): I would rather not have drinking men on the premises, Mr. Halsey. You will oblige me—

Halsey: I'll oblige you by stayin right on this spot, this spot, get me? till I get damned ready t leave.

He approaches Hanby. Hanby retreats, but manages to hold his dignity.

Halsey: Let me get you told right now, Mr. Samuel Hanby. Now listen t me. I aint no slick an span slave youve hired, an dont y think it for a minute. Youve bullied enough about this town. An besides, wheres that bill youve been owin me? Listen t me. If I dont get it paid in by tmorrer noon, Mr. Hanby (he mockingly assumes Hanby's tone and manner), I shall feel obliged t call th sheriff. An that sheriff'll be myself who'll catch y in th road an pull y out your buggy an rightly attend t y. You heard me. Now leave him alone. I'm takin him home with me. I got it fixed. Before you came in. He's goin t work with me. Shapin shafts and buildin wagons'll make a man of him what nobody, y get me? what nobody can take advantage of. Thats all . . .

Halsey burrs off into vague and incoherent comment.

Pause. Disagreeable.

Layman's eyes are glazed on the spurting fire.

Kabnis wants to rise and put both Halsey and Hanby in their places. He vaguely knows that he must do this, else the power of direction will completely slip from him to those outside. The conviction is just strong enough to torture him. To bring a feverish, quick-passing flare into his eyes. To mutter words soggy in hot saliva. To jerk his arms upward in futile protest. Halsey, noticing his gestures, thinks it is water that he desires. He brings a glass to him. Kabnis slings it to the floor. Heat of the conviction dies. His arms crumple. His upper lip, his mustache, quiver. Rap! rap, on the door. The sounds slap Kabnis. They bring a hectic color to his cheeks. Like huge cold finger tips they touch his skin and goose-flesh it. Hanby strikes a commanding pose. He moves toward Layman. Layman's face is innocently immobile.

Halsey: Whos there?

Voice: Lewis.

Halsey: Come in, Lewis. Come on in.

Lewis enters. He is the queer fellow who has been referred to. A tall wiry copper-colored man, thirty perhaps. His mouth and eyes suggest purpose guided by an adequate intelligence. He is what a stronger Kabnis might have been, and in an odd faint way resembles him. As he steps towards the others, he seems to be issuing sharply from a vivid dream. Lewis shakes hands with Halsey. Nods perfunctorily to Hanby, who has stiffened to meet him. Smiles rapidly at Layman, and settles with real interest on Kabnis.

Lewis: Kabnis passed me on the road. Had a piece of business of my own, and couldnt get here any sooner. Thought I might be able to help in some way or other.

Halsey: A good baths bout all he needs now. An somethin t put his mind t rest.

Lewis: I think I can give him that. That note was meant for me. Some Negroes have grown uncomfortable at my being here—

Kabnis: You mean, Mr. Lewis, some colored folks threw it? Christ Almighty!

Halsey: Thats what he means. An just as I told y. White folks more direct than that.

Kabnis: What are they after you for?

Lewis: Its a long story, Kabnis. Too long for now. And it might involve present company. (He laughs pleasantly and gestures vaguely in the direction of Hanby.) Tell you about it later on perhaps.

Kabnis: Youre not going?

Lewis: Not till my month's up.

Halsey: Hows that?

Lewis: I'm on a sort of contract with myself. (Is about to leave.) Well, glad its nothing serious—

Halsey: Come round t th shop sometime why dont y, Lewis? I've asked y enough. I'd like t have a talk with y. I aint as dumb as I look. Kabnis an me'll be in most any time. Not much work these days. Wish t hell there was. This burg[1] gets to me when there aint. (In answer to Lewis' question.) He's goin t work with me. Ya. Night air this side th branch aint good fer him. (Looks at Hanby. Laughs.)

Lewis: I see . . .

His eyes turn to Kabnis. In the instant of their shifting, a vision of the life they are to meet. Kabnis, a promise of a soil-soaked beauty; uprooted, thinning out. Suspended a few feet above the soil whose touch would resurrect him. Arm's length removed from him whose will to help. . . There is a swift intuitive interchange of consciousness. Kabnis has a sudden need to rush into the arms of this man. His eyes call, "Brother." And then a savage, cynical twist-about within him mocks his impulse and strengthens him to repulse Lewis. His lips curl cruelly. His eyes laugh. They are glittering needles, stitching. With a throbbing ache they draw Lewis to. Lewis brusquely wheels on Hanby.

1. Town.

Lewis: I'd like to see you, sir, a moment, if you dont mind.

Hanby's tight collar and vest effectively preserve him.

Hanby: Yes, erer, Mr. Lewis. Right away.

Lewis: See you later, Halsey.

Halsey: So long—thanks—sho hope so, Lewis.

As he opens the door and Hanby passes out, a woman, miles down the valley, begins to sing. Her song is a spark that travels swiftly to the near-by cabins. Like purple tallow flames, songs jet up. They spread a ruddy haze over the heavens. The haze swings low. Now the whole countryside is a soft chorus. Lord. O Lord. . . Lewis closes the door behind him. A flame jets out. . .

The kettle is boiling. Halsey notices it. He pulls the wash-tub from beneath the bed. He arranges for the bath before the fire.

Halsey: Told y them theatrics didnt fit a white man. Th niggers, just like I told y. An after him. Aint surprisin though. He aint bowed t none of them. Nassur. T nairy a one of them nairy an inch nairy a time. An only mixed when he was good an ready—

Kabnis: That song, Halsey, do you hear it?

Halsey: Thats a man. Hear me, Kabnis? A man—

Kabnis: Jesus, do you hear it.

Halsey: Hear it? Hear what? Course I hear it. Listen t what I'm tellin y. A man, get me? They'll get him yet if he dont watch out.

Kabnis is jolted into his fear.

Kabnis: Get him? What do you mean? How? Not lynch him?

Halsey: Na. Take a shotgun an shoot his eyes clear out. Well, anyway, it wasnt fer you, just like I told y. You'll stay over at th house an work with me, eh, boy? Good t get away from his nobs, eh? Damn big stiff though, him. An youre not th first an I can tell y. (Laughs.)

He bustles and fusses about Kabnis as if he were a child. Kabnis submits, wearily. He has no will to resist him.

Layman (his voice is like a deep hollow echo): Thats right. Thats true, sho. Everybody's been expectin that th bust up was comin. Surprised um all y held on as long as y did. Teachin in th South aint th thing fer y. Nassur. You ought t be way back up North where sometimes I wish I was. But I've hung on down this away so long—

Halsey: An there'll never be no leavin time fer y.

4

A month has passed.

Halsey's work-shop. It is an old building just off the main street of Sempter. The walls to within a few feet of the ground are of an age-worn cement mixture. On the outside they are considerably crumbled and peppered with what looks like musket-shot. Inside, the plaster has fallen away in great chunks, leaving the laths, grayed and cobwebbed, exposed. A sort of loft above the shop proper serves as a break-water for the rain and sunshine which otherwise would have free entry to the main floor. The shop is filled with old wheels and parts of wheels, broken shafts, and wooden litter. A double door, midway the street wall. To the left of this, a work-bench that holds a vise and a variety of wood-work tools. A window with as many panes broken as whole, throws light on the bench. Opposite, in the rear wall, a second window looks out upon the back yard. In the left wall, a rickety smoke-blackened chimney, and hearth with fire blazing. Smooth-worn chairs grouped about the hearth suggest the village meeting-place. Several large wooden blocks, chipped and cut and sawed on their upper surfaces are in the middle of the floor. They are the supports used in almost any sort of wagon-work. Their idleness means that Halsey has no worth-while job on foot. To the right of the central door is a junk heap, and directly behind this, stairs that lead down into the cellar. The cellar is known as "The Hole." Besides being the home of a very old man, it is used by Halsey on those occasions when he spices up the life of the small town.

Halsey, wonderfully himself in his work overalls, stands in the doorway and gazes up the street, expectantly. Then his eyes grow listless. He slouches against the smooth-rubbed frame. He lights a cigarette. Shifts his position. Braces an arm against the door. Kabnis passes the window and stoops to get in under Halsey's arm. He is awkward and ludicrous, like a schoolboy in his big brother's new overalls. He skirts the large blocks on the floor, and drops into a chair before the fire. Halsey saunters towards him.

Kabnis: Time f lunch.

Halsey: Ya.

He stands by the hearth, rocking backward and forward. He stretches his hands out to the fire. He washes them in the warm glow of the flames. They never get cold, but he warms them.

Kabnis: Saw Lewis up th street. Said he'd be down.

Halsey's eyes brighten. He looks at Kabnis. Turns away. Says nothing. Kabnis fidgets. Twists his thin blue cloth-covered limbs. Pulls closer to the fire till the neat stings his shins. Pushes back. Pokes the burned logs. Puts on several fresh ones. Fidgets. The town bell strikes twelve.

Kabnis: Fix it up f tnight?

Halsey: Leave it t me.

Kabnis: Get Lewis in?

Halsey: Tryin t.

The air is heavy with the smell of pine and resin. Green logs spurt and sizzle. Sap trickles from an old pine-knot into the flames. Layman enters. He carries a lunch-pail. Kabnis, for the moment, thinks that he is a day laborer.

Layman: Evenin, gen'lemun.

Both: Whats say, Layman.

Layman squares a chair to the fire and droops into it. Several town fellows, silent unfathomable men for the most part, saunter in. Overalls. Thick tan shoes. Felt hats marvelously shaped and twisted. One asks Halsey for a cigarette. He gets it. The blacksmith, a tremendous black man, comes in from the forge. Not even a nod from him. He picks up an axle and goes out. Lewis enters. The town men look curiously at him. Suspicion and an open liking contest for possession of their faces. They are uncomfortable. One by one they drift into the street.

Layman: Heard y was leavin, Mr. Lewis.

Kabnis: Months up, eh? Hell of a month I've got.

Halsey: Sorry y goin, Lewis. Just gettin acquainted like.

Lewis: Sorry myself, Halsey, in a way—

Layman: Gettin t like our town, Mr. Lewis?

Lewis: I'm afraid its on a different basis, Professor.

Halsey: An I've yet t hear about that basis. Been waitin long enough, God knows. Seems t me like youd take pity on a feller if nothin more.

Kabnis: Somethin that old black cockroach over yonder doesnt like, whatever it is.

Layman: Thats right. Thats right, sho.

Halsey: A feller dropped in here tother day an said he knew what you was about. Said you had queer opinions. Well, I could have told him you was a queer one, myself. But not th way he was driftin. Didnt mean anything by it, but just let drop he thought you was a little wrong up here—crazy, y'know. (Laughs.)

Kabnis: Y mean old Blodson? Hell, he's bats himself.

Lewis: I remember him. We had a talk. But what he found queer, I think, was not my opinions, but my lack of them. In half an hour he had settled everything: boll weevils, God, the World War. Weevils and wars are the pests that God sends against the sinful. People are too weak to correct themselves: the Redeemer is coming back. Get ready, ye sinners, for the advent of Our Lord. Interesting, eh, Kabnis? but not exactly what we want.

Halsey: Y could have come t me. I've sho been after y enough. Most every time I've seen y.

Kabnis (sarcastically): Hows it y never came t us professors?

Lewis: I did—to one.

Kabnis: Y mean t say y got somethin from that celluloid-collar-eraser-cleaned old codger over in th mud hole?

Halsey: Rough on th old boy, aint he? (Laughs.)

Lewis: Something, yes. Layman here could have given me quite a deal, but the incentive to his keeping quiet is so much greater than anything I could have offered him to open up, that I crossed him off my mind. And you—

Kabnis: What about me?

Halsey: Tell him, Lewis, for godsake tell him. I've told him. But its somethin else be wants so bad I've heard him downstairs mumblin with th old man.

Lewis: The old man?

Kabnis: What about me? Come on now, you know so much.

Halsey: Tell him, Lewis. Tell it t him.

Lewis: Life has already told him more than he is capable of knowing. It has given him in excess of what he can receive. I have been offered. Stuff in his stomach curdled, and he vomited me.

Kabnis' face twitches. His body writhes.

Kabnis: You know a lot, you do. How about Halsey?

Lewis: Yes. . . . Halsey? Fits here. Belongs here. An artist in your way, arent you, Halsey?

Halsey: Reckon I am, Lewis. Give me th work and fair pay an I aint askin nothin better. Went over-seas an saw France; an I come back. Been up North; an I come back. Went t school; but there aint no books whats got th feel t them of them there tools. Nassur. An I'm atellin y.

A shriveled, bony white man passes the window and enters the shop. He carries a broken hatchet-handle and the severed head. He speaks with a flat, drawn voice to Halsey, who comes forward to meet him.

Mr. Ramsay: Can y fix this fer me, Halsey?

Halsey (looking it over): Reckon so, Mr. Ramsay. Here, Kabnis. A little practice fer y.

Halsey directs Kabnis, showing him how to place the handle in the vise, and cut it down. The knife hangs. Kabnis thinks that it must be dull. He jerks it hard. The tool goes deep and shaves too much off. Mr. Ramsay smiles brokenly at him.

Mr. Ramsay (to Halsey): Still breakin in the new hand, eh, Halsey? Seems like a likely enough faller once he gets th hang of it.

He gives a tight laugh at his own good humor. Kabnis burns red. The back of his neck stings him beneath his collar. He feels stifled. Through Ramsay, the whole white South weighs down upon him. The pressure is terrific. He sweats under the arms. Chill beads run down his body. His brows concentrate upon the handle as though his own life was staked upon the perfect shaving of it. He begins to out and out botch the job. Halsey smiles.

Halsey: He'll make a good un some of these days, Mr. Ramsay.

Mr. Ramsay: Y ought t know. Yer daddy was a good un before y. Runs in th family, seems like t me.

Halsey: Thats right, Mr. Ramsay.

Kabnis is hopeless. Halsey takes the handle from him. With a few deft strokes he shaves it. Fits it. Gives it to Ramsay.

Mr. Ramsay: How much on this?

Halsey: No charge, Mr. Ramsay.

Mr. Ramsay (going out): All right, Halsey. Come down an take it out in trade. Shoe-strings or something.

Halsey: Yassur, Mr. Ramsay.

Halsey rejoins Lewis and Layman. Kabnis, hangdog-fashion, follows him.

Halsey: They like y if y work fer them.

Layman: Thats right, Mr. Halsey. Thats right, sho.

The group is about to resume its talk when Hanby enters. He is all energy, bustle, and business. He goes direct to Kabnis.

Hanby: An axle is out in the buggy which I would like to have shaped into a crow-bar. You will see that it is fixed for me.

Without waiting for an answer, and knowing that Kabnis will follow, he passes out. Kabnis, scowling, silent, trudges after him.

Hanby (from the outside): Have that ready for me by three o'clock, young man. I shall call for it.

Kabnis (under his breath as he comes in): Th hell you say, you old black swamp-gut.

He slings the axle on the floor.

Halsey: Wheeee!

Layman, lunch finished long ago, rises, heavily. He shakes hands with Lewis.

Layman: Might not see y again befo y leave, Mr. Lewis. I enjoys t hear y talk. Y might have been a preacher. Maybe a bishop some day. Sho do hope t see y back this away again sometime, Mr. Lewis.

Lewis: Thanks, Professor. Hope I'll see you.

Layman waves a long arm loosely to the others, and leaves. Kabnis goes to the door. His eyes, sullen, gaze up the street.

Kabnis: Carrie K.'s comin with th lunch. Bout time.

She passes the window. Her red girl's-cap, catching the sun, flashes vividly. With a stiff, awkward little movement she crosses the doorsill and gives Kabnis one of the two baskets which she is carrying. There is a slight stoop to her shoulders. The curves of her body blend with this to a soft rounded charm. Her gestures are stiffly variant. Black bangs curl over the forehead of her oval-olive face. Her expression is dazed, but on provocation it can melt into a wistful smile. Adolescent. She is easily the sister of Fred Halsey.

Carrie K.: Mother says excuse her, brother Fred an Ralph, fer bein late.

Kabnis: Everythings all right an O.K., Carrie Kate. O.K. an all right.

The two men settle on their lunch. Carrie, with hardly a glance in the direction of the hearth, as is her habit, is about to take the second basket down to the old man, when Lewis rises. In doing so he draws her unwitting attention. Their meeting is a swift sun-burst. Lewis impulsively moves towards her. His mind flashes images of her life in the southern town. He sees the nascent woman, her flesh already stiffening to cartilage, drying to bone. Her spirit-bloom, even now touched sullen, bitter. Her rich beauty fading. . . He wants to—He stretches forth his hands to hers. He takes them. They feel like warm cheeks against his palms. The sun-burst from her eyes floods up and haloes him. Christ-eyes, his eyes look to her. Fearlessly she loves into them. And then something happens. Her face blanches. Awkwardly she draws away. The sin-bogies of respectable southern colored folks clamor at her: "Look out! Be a *good* girl. A *good* girl. Look out!" She gropes for her basket that has fallen to the floor. Finds it, and marches with a rigid gravity to her task of feeding the old man. Like the glowing white ash of burned paper, Lewis' eyelids, wavering, settle down. He stirs in the direction of the rear window. From the back yard, mules tethered to odd trees and posts blink dumbly at him. They too seem burdened with an impotent pain. Kabnis and Halsey are still busy with their lunch. They havent noticed him. After a while he turns to them.

Lewis: Your sister, Halsey, whats to become of her? What are you going to do for her?

Halsey: Who? What? What am I goin t do? . .

Lewis: What I mean is, what does she do down there?

Halsey: Oh. Feeds th old man. Had lunch, Lewis?

Lewis: Thanks, yes. You have never felt her, have you, Halsey? Well, no, I guess not. I dont suppose you can. Nor can she. . . Old man? Halsey, some one lives down there? I've never heard of him. Tell me—

Kabnis takes time from his meal to answer with some emphasis:

Kabnis: Theres lots of things you aint heard of.

Lewis: Dare say. I'd like to see him.

Kabnis: You'll get all th chance you want tnight.

Halsey: Fixin a little somethin up fer tnight, Lewis. Th three of us an some girls. Come round bout ten-thirty.

Lewis: Glad to. But what under the sun does he do down there?

Halsey: Ask Kabnis. He blows off t him every chance he gets.

Kabnis gives a grunting laugh. His mouth twists. Carrie returns from the cellar. Avoiding Lewis, she speaks to her brother.

Carrie K.: Brother Fred, father hasnt eaten now goin on th second week, but mumbles an talks funny, or tries t talk when I put his hands ont th food. He frightens me, an I dunno what t do. An oh, I came near fergettin, brother, but Mr. Marmon—he was eatin lunch when I saw him—told me t tell y that th lumber wagon busted down an he wanted y t fix it fer him. Said he reckoned he could get it t y after he ate.

Halsey chucks a half-eaten sandwich in the fire. Gets up. Arranges his blocks. Goes to the door and looks anxiously up the street. The wind whirls a small spiral in the gray dust road.

Halsey: Why didnt y tell me sooner, little sister?

Carrie K.: I fergot t, an just remembered it now, brother.

Her soft rolled words are fresh pain to Lewis. He wants to take her North with him. What for? He wonders what Kabnis could do for her. What she could do for him. Mother him. Carrie gathers the lunch things, silently, and in her pinched manner, curtsies, and departs. Kabnis lights his after-lunch cigarette. Lewis, who has sensed a change, becomes aware that he is not included in it. He starts to ask again about the old man. Decides not to. Rises to go.

Lewis: Think I'll run along, Halsey.

Halsey: Sure. Glad t see y any time.

Kabnis: Dont forget tnight.

Lewis: Dont worry. I wont. So long.

Kabnis: So long. We'll be expectin y.

Lewis passes Halsey at the door. Halsey's cheeks form a vacant smile. His eyes are wide awake, watching for the wagon to turn from Broad Street into his road.

Halsey: So long.

His words reach Lewis halfway to the corner.

5

Night, soft belly of a pregnant Negress, throbs evenly against the torso of the South. Night throbs a womb-song to the South. Cane- and cotton-fields, pine forests, cypress swamps, sawmills, and factories are fecund at her touch. Night's womb-song sets them singing. Night winds are the breathing of the unborn child whose calm throbbing in the belly of a Negress sets them somnolently singing. Hear their song.

White-man's land.
Niggers, sing.
Burn, bear black children
Till poor rivers bring
Rest, and sweet, glory
In Camp Ground.

Sempter's streets are vacant and still. White paint on the wealthier houses has the chill blue glitter of distant stars. Negro cabins are a purple blur. Broad Street is deserted. Winds stir beneath the corrugated iron canopies and dangle odd bits of rope tied to horse- and mule-gnawed hitching-posts. One store window has a light in it. Chesterfield cigarette and Chero-Cola cardboard advertisements are stacked in it. From a side door two men come out. Pause, for a last word and then say good night. Soon they melt in shadows thicker than they. Way off down the street four figures sway beneath iron awnings which form a sort of corridor that imperfectly echoes and jumbles what they say. A fifth form joins them. They turn into the road that leads to Halsey's workshop. The old building is phosphorescent above deep shade. The figures pass through the double door. Night winds whisper in the eaves. Sing weirdly in the ceiling cracks. Stir curls of shavings on the floor. Halsey lights a candle. A good-sized lumber wagon, wheels off, rests upon the blocks. Kabnis makes a face at it. An unearthly hush is upon the place. No one seems to want to talk. To move, lest the scraping of their feet . .

Halsey: Come on down this way, folks.

He leads the way. Stella follows. And close after her, Cora, Lewis, and Kabnis. They descend into the Hole. It seems huge, limitless in the candle light. The walls are of stone, wonderfully fitted. They have no openings save a small iron-barred window toward the top of each. They are dry and warm.

The ground slopes away to the rear of the building and thus leaves the south wall exposed to the sun. The blacksmith's shop is plumb against the right wall. The floor is clay. Shavings have at odd times been matted into it. In the right-hand corner, under the stairs, two good-sized pine mattresses, resting on cardboard, are on either side of a wooden table. On this are several half-burned candles and an oil lamp. Behind the table, an irregular piece of mirror hangs on the wall. A loose something that looks to be a gaudy ball costume dangles from a near-by hook. To the front, a second table holds a lamp and several whiskey glasses. Six rickety chairs are near this table. Two old wagon wheels rest on the floor. To the left, sitting in a high-backed chair which stands upon a low platform, the old man. He is like a bust in black walnut. Gray-bearded. Gray-haired. Prophetic. Immobile. Lewis' eyes are sunk in him. The others, unconcerned, are about to pass on to the front table when Lewis grips Halsey and so turns him that the candle flame shines obliquely on the old man's features.

Lewis: And he rules over—

Kabnis: Th smoke an fire of th forge.

Lewis: Black Vulcan?[2] I wouldnt say so. That forehead. Great woolly beard. Those eyes. A mute John the Baptist of a new religion—or a tongue-tied shadow of an old.

Kabnis: His tongue is tied all right, an I can vouch f that.

Lewis: Has he never talked to you?

Halsey: Kabnis wont give him a chance.

He laughs. The girls laugh. Kabnis winces.

Lewis: What do you call him?

Halsey: Father.

Lewis: Good. Father what?

Kabnis: Father of hell.

Halsey: Father's th only name we have fer him. Come on. Lets sit down an get t th pleasure of the evenin.

Lewis: Father John it is from now on . . .

Slave boy whom some Christian mistress taught to read the Bible. Black man who saw Jesus in the ricefields, and began preaching to his people. Moses- and Christ-words used for songs. Dead blind father of a muted folk who feel their way upward to a life that crushes or absorbs them. (Speak, Father!) Suppose your eyes could see, old man. (The years hold hands. O Sing!) Suppose your lips. . .

Halsey, does he never talk?

Halsey: Na. But sometimes. Only seldom. Mumbles. Sis says he talks—

Kabnis: I've heard him talk.

Halsey: First I've ever heard of it. You dont give him a chance. Sis says she's made out several words, mostly one—an like as not cause it was "sin."

Cora laughs in a loose sort of way. She is a tall, thin, mulatto woman. Her eyes are deep-set behind a pointed nose. Her hair is coarse and bushy. Seeing that Stella also is restless, she takes her arm and the two women move towards the table. They slip into chairs. Halsey follows and lights the lamp. He lays out a pack of cards. Stella sorts them as if telling fortunes. She is a beautifully proportioned, large-eyed, brown-skin girl. Except for the twisted line of her mouth when she smiles or laughs, there is about her no suggestion of the life she's been through. Kabnis, with great mock-solemnity, goes

2. The blacksmith god in Roman mythology.

to the corner, takes down the robe, and dons it. He is a curious spectacle, acting a part, yet very real. He joins the others at the table. They are used to him. Lewis is surprised. He laughs. Kabnis shrinks and then glares at him with a furtive hatred. Halsey, bringing out a bottle of corn licker, pours drinks.

Halsey: Come on, Lewis. Come on, you fellers. Heres lookin at y.

Then, as if suddenly recalling something, he jerks away from the table and starts towards the steps.

Kabnis: Where y goin, Halsey?

Halsey: Where? Where y think? That oak beam in th wagon—

Kabnis: Come ere. Come ere. Sit down. What in hell's wrong with you fellers? You with your wagon. Lewis with his Father John. This aint th time fer foolin with wagons. Daytime's bad enough f that. Ere, sit down. Ere, Lewis, you too sit down. Have a drink. Thats right. Drink corn licker, love th girls, an listen t th old man mumblin sin.

There seems to be no good-time spirit to the party. Something in the air is too tense and deep for that. Lewis, seated now so that his eyes rest upon the old man, merges with his source and lets the pain and beauty of the South meet him there. White faces, pain-pollen, settle downward through a cane-sweet mist and touch the ovaries of yellow flowers. Cotton-bolls bloom, droop. Black roots twist in a parched red soil beneath a blazing sky. Magnolias, fragrant, a trifle futile, lovely, far off. . . His eyelids close. A force begins to heave and rise. . . Stella is serious, reminiscent.

Stella: Usall is brought up t hate sin worse than death—

Kabnis: An then before you have y eyes half open, youre made t love it if y want t live.

Stella: Us never—

Kabnis: Oh, I know your story: that old prim bastard over yonder, an then old Calvert's office—

Stella: It wasnt them—

Kabnis: I know. They put y out of church, an then I guess th preacher came around an asked f some. But thats your body. Now me—

Halsey (passing him the bottle): All right, kid, we believe y. Here, take another. Wheres Clover, Stel?

Stella: You know how Jim is when he's just out th swamp. Done up in shine[3] an wouldnt let her come. Said he'd bust her head open if she went out.

Kabnis: Dont see why he doesnt stay over with Laura, where he belongs.

Stella: Ask him, an I reckon he'll tell y. More than you want.

Halsey: Th nigger hates th sight of a black woman worse than death. Sorry t mix y up this way, Lewis. But y see how tis.

Lewis' skin is tight and glowing over the fine bones of his face. His lips tremble. His nostrils quiver. The others notice this and smile knowingly at each other. Drinks and smokes are passed around. They pay no neverminds to him. A real party is being worked up. Then Lewis opens his eyes and looks at them. Their smiles disperse in hot-cold tremors. Kabnis chokes his laugh. It sputters, gurgles. His eyes flicker and turn away. He tries to pass the thing off by taking a long drink which he makes considerable fuss over. He is drawn back to Lewis. Seeing Lewis' gaze still upon him, he scowls.

Kabnis: Whatsha lookin at me for? Y want t know who I am? Well, I'm Ralph Kabnis—lot of good its goin t do y. Well? Whatsha keep lookin for?

3. Drunk, intoxicated.

I'm Ralph Kabnis. Aint that enough f y? Want th whole family history? Its none of your godam business, anyway. Keep off me. Do y hear? Keep off me. Look at Cora. Aint she pretty enough t look at? Look at Halsey, or Stella. Clover ought t be here an you could look at her. An love her. Thats what you need. I know—

Lewis: Ralph Kabnis gets satisfied that way?

Kabnis: Satisfied? Say, quit your kiddin. Here, look at that old man there. See him? He's satisfied. Do I look like him? When I'm dead I dont expect t be satisfied. Is that enough f y, with your godam nosin, or do you want more? Well, y wont get it, understand?

Lewis: The old man as symbol, flesh, and spirit of the past, what do you think he would say if he could see you? You look at him, Kabnis.

Kabnis: Just like any done-up preacher is what he looks t me. Jam some false teeth in his mouth and crank him, an youd have God Almighty spit in torrents all around th floor. Oh, hell, an he reminds me of that black cockroach over yonder. An besides, he aint my past. My ancestors were Southern blue-bloods—

Lewis: And black.

Kabnis: Aint much difference between blue an black.

Lewis: Enough to draw a denial from you. Cant hold them, can you? Master; slave. Soil; and the overarching heavens. Dusk; dawn. They fight and bastardize you. The sun tint of your cheeks, flame of the great season's multi-colored leaves, tarnished, burned. Split, shredded: easily burned. No use . . .

His gaze shifts to Stella. Stella's face draws back, her breasts come towards him.

Stella: I aint got nothin f y, mister. Taint no use t look at me.

Halsey: Youre a queer feller, Lewis, I swear y are. Told y so, didnt I, girls? Just take him easy though, an he'll be ridin just th same as any Georgia mule, eh, Lewis? (Laughs.)

Stella: I'm goin t tell y somethin, mister. It aint t you, t th Mister Lewis what noses about. Its t somethin different, I dunno what. That old man there—maybe its him—is like m father used t look. He used t sing. An when he could sing no mo, they'd allus come f him an carry him t church an there he'd sit, befo th pulpit, aswayin an aleadin every song. A white man took m mother an it broke th old man's heart. He died; an then I didnt care what become of me, an I dont now. I dont care now. Dont get it in y head I'm some sentimental Susie askin for yo sop.[4] Nassur. But theres somethin t yo th others aint got. Boars an kids an fools—thats all I've known. Boars when their fever's up. When their fever's up they come t me. Halsey asks me over when he's off th job. Kabnis—it ud be a sin t play with him. He takes it out in talk.

Halsey knows that he has trifled with her. At odd things he has been inwardly penitent before her tasking him. But now he wants to hurt her. He turns to Lewis.

Halsey: Lewis, I got a little licker in me, an thats true. True's what I said. True. But th stuff just seems t wake me up an make my mind a man of me. Listen. You know a lot, queer as hell as y are, an I want t ask y some questions. Theyre too high fer them, Stella an Cora an Kabnis, so we'll just excuse em. A chat between ourselves. (Turns to the others.) You-all cant listen in on

4. Bread soaked in gravy or sauce; metaphorically, a gift or gesture of charity.

this. Twont interest y. So just leave th table t this gen'lemun an myself. Go long now.

Kabnis gets up, pompous in his robe, grotesquely so, and makes as if to go through a grand march with Stella. She shoves him off, roughly, and in a mood swings her body to the steps. Kabnis grabs Cora and parades around, passing the old man, to whom he bows in mock-curtsy. He sweeps by the table, snatches the licker bottle, and then he and Cora sprawl on the mattresses. She meets his weak approaches after the manner she thinks Stella would use.

Halsey contemptuously watches them until he is sure that they are settled.

Halsey: This aint th sort o thing f me, Lewis, when I got work upstairs. Nassur. You an me has got things t do. Wastin time on common low-down women—say, Lewis, look at her now—Stella—aint she a picture? Common wench—na she aint, Lewis. You know she aint. I'm only tryin t fool y. I used t love that girl. Yassur. An sometimes when th moon is thick an I hear dogs up th valley barkin an some old woman fetches out her song, an th winds seem like th Lord made them fer t fetch an carry th smell o pine an cane, an there aint no big job on foot, I sometimes get t thinkin that I still do. But I want t talk t y, Lewis, queer as y are. Y know, Lewis, I went t school once. Ya. In Augusta. But it wasnt a regular school. Na. It was a pussy Sunday-school masqueradin under a regular name. Some goody-goody teachers from th North had come down t teach th niggers. If you was nearly white, they liked y. If you was black, they didnt. But it wasnt that—I was all right, y see. I couldnt stand em messin an pawin over m business like I was a child. So I cussed em out an left. Kabnis there ought t have cussed out th old duck over yonder an left. He'd a been a better man tday. But as I was sayin, I couldnt stand their ways. So I left an came here an worked with my father. An been here ever since. He died. I set in f myself. An its always been; give me a good job an sure pay an I aint far from being satisfied, so far as satisfaction goes. Prejudice is everywheres about this country. An a nigger aint in much standin anywheres. But when it comes t pottin round an doin nothin, with nothin bigger'n an ax-handle t hold a feller down, like it was a while back befo I got this job—that beam ought t be—but tmorrow mornin early's time enough f that. As I was sayin, I gets t thinkin. Play dumb naturally t white folks. I gets t thinkin. I used to subscribe t th *Literary Digest*[5] an that helped along a bit. But there werent nothing I could sink m teeth int. Theres lots I want t ask y, Lewis. Been askin y t come around. Couldnt get y. Cant get in much tnight. (He glances at the others. His mind fastens on Kabnis.) Say, tell me this, whats on your mind t say on that feller there? Kabnis' name. One queer bird ought t know another, seems like t me.

Licker has released conflicts in Kabnis and set them flowing. He pricks his ears, intuitively feels that the talk is about him, leaves Cora, and approaches the table. His eyes are watery, heavy with passion. He stoops. He is a ridiculous pathetic figure in his showy robe.

Kabnis: Talkin bout me. I know. I'm th topic of conversation everywhere theres talk about this town. Girls an fellers. White folks as well. An if its me youre talkin bout, guess I got a right t listen in. Whats sayin? Whats sayin bout his royal guts, the Duke? Whats sayin, eh?

Halsey (to Lewis): Well take it up another time.

5. A weekly general-interest magazine published in New York from 1890 to 1938.

Kabnis: No nother time bout it. Now. I'm here now an talkin's just begun. I was born an bred in a family of orators, thats what I was.

Halsey: Preachers.

Kabnis: Na. Preachers hell. I didnt say wind-busters. Y misapprehended me. Y understand what that means, dont y? All right then, y misapprehended me. I didnt say preachers. I said orators. O R A T O R S. Born one an I'll die one. You understand me, Lewis. (He turns to Halsey and begins shaking his finger in his face.) An as f you, youre all right f choppin things from blocks of wood. I was good at that th day I ducked th cradle. An since then, I've been shapin words after a design that branded here. Know whats here? M soul. Ever heard o that? Th hell y have. Been shapin words t fit m soul. Never told y that before, did I? Thought I couldnt talk. I'll tell y. I've been shapin words; ah, but sometimes theyre beautiful an golden an have a taste that makes them fine t roll over with y tongue. Your tongue aint fit f nothin but t roll an lick hog-meat.

Stella and Cora come up to the table.

Halsey: Give him a shove there, will y, Stel?

Stella jams Kabnis in a chair. Kabnis springs up.

Kabnis: Cant keep a good man down. Those words I was tellin y about, they wont fit int th mold thats branded on m soul. Rhyme, y see? Poet, too. Bad rhyme. Bad poet. Somethin else youve learned tnight. Lewis dont know it all, an I'm atellin y. Ugh. Th form thats burned int my soul is some twisted awful thing that crept in from a dream, a godam nightmare, an wont stay still unless I feed it. An it lives on words. Not beautiful words. God Almighty no. Misshapen, split-gut, tortured, twisted words. Layman was feedin it back there that day you thought I ran out fearin things. White folks feed it cause their looks are words. Niggers, black niggers feed it cause theyre evil an their looks are words. Yallar niggers feed it. This whole damn bloated purple country feeds it cause its goin down t hell in a holy avalanche of words. I want t feed th soul—I know what that is; th preachers dont—but I've got t feed it. I wish t God some lynchin white man ud stick his knife through it an pin it to a tree. An pin it to a tree. You hear me? Thats a wish f y, you little snot-nosed pups who've been makin fun of me, an fakin that I'm weak. Me, Ralph Kabnis weak. Ha.

Halsey: Thats right, old man. There, there. Here, so much exertion merits a fittin reward. Help him t be seated, Cora.

Halsey gives him a swig of shine. Cora glides up, seats him, and then plumps herself down on his lap, squeezing his head into her breasts. Kabnis mutters. Tries to break loose. Curses. Cora almost stifles him. He goes limp and gives up. Cora toys with him. Ruffles his hair. Braids it. Parts it in the middle. Stella smiles contemptuously. And then a sudden anger sweeps her. She would like to lash Cora from the place. She'd like to take Kabnis to some distant pine grove and nurse and mother him. Her eyes flash. A quick tensioning throws her breasts and neck into a poised strain. She starts towards them. Halsey grabs her arm and pulls her to him. She struggles. Halsey pins her arms and kisses her. She settles, spurting like a pine-knot afire.

Lewis finds himself completely cut out. The glowing within him subsides. It is followed by a dead chill. Kabnis, Carrie, Stella, Halsey, Cora, the old man, the cellar, and the work-shop, the southern town descend upon him. Their pain is too intense. He cannot stand it. He bolts from the table. Leaps up the stairs. Planges through the work-shop and out into the night.

6

The cellar swims in a pale phosphorescence. The table, the chairs, the figure of the old man are amœba-like shadows which move about and float in it. In the corner under the steps, close to the floor, a solid blackness. A sound comes from it. A forcible yawn. Part of the blackness detaches itself so that it may be seen against the grayness of the wall. It moves forward and then seems to be clothing itself in odd dangling bits of shadow. The voice of Halsey, vibrant and deepened, calls.

Halsey: Kabnis. Cora. Stella.

He gets no response. He wants to get them up, to get on the job. He is intolerant of their sleepiness.

Halsey: Kabnis! Stella! Cora!

Gutturals, jerky and impeded, tell that he is shaking them.

Halsey: Come now, up with you.

Kabnis (sleepily and still more or less intoxicated): Whats th big idea? What in hell—

Halsey: Work. But never you mind about that. Up with you.

Cora: Oooooo! Look here, mister, I aint used t bein thrown int th street befo day.

Stella: Any bunk whats worked is worth in wages moren this. But come on. Taint no use t arger.

Kabnis: I'll arger. Its preposterous—

The girls interrupt him with none too pleasant laughs.

Kabnis: Thats what I said. Know what it means, dont y? All right, then. I said its preposterous t root an artist out o bed at this ungodly hour, when there aint no use t it. You can start your damned old work. Nobody's stoppin y. But what we got t get up for? Fraid somebody'll see th girls leavin? Some sport, you are. I hand it t y.

Halsey: Up you get, all th same.

Kabnis: Oh, th hell you say.

Halsey: Well, son, seeing that I'm th kindhearted father, I'll give y chance t open your eyes. But up y get when I come down.

He mounts the steps to the work-shop and starts a fire in the hearth. In the yard he finds some chunks of coal which he brings in and throws on the fire. He puts a kettle on to boil. The wagon draws him. He lifts an oak-beam, fingers it, and becomes abstracted. Then comes to himself and places the beam upon the work-bench. He looks over some newly cut wooden spokes. He goes to the fire and pokes it. The coals are red-hot. With a pair of long prongs he picks them up and places them in a thick iron bucket. This he carries downstairs. Outside, darkness has given way to the impalpable grayness of dawn. This early morning light, seeping through the four barred cellar windows, is the color of the stony walls. It seems to be an emanation from them. Halsey's coals throw out a rich warm glow. He sets them on the floor, a safe distance from the beds.

Halsey: No foolin now. Come. Up with you.

Other than a soft rustling, there is no sound as the girls slip into their clothes. Kabnis still lies in bed.

Stella (to Halsey): Reckon y could spare us a light?

Halsey strikes a match, lights a cigarette, and then bends over and touches flame to the two candles on the table between the beds. Kabnis asks for a cigarette. Halsey hands him his and takes a fresh one for himself. The girls, before the mirror, are doing up their hair. It is bushy hair that has gone through some straightening process. Character, however, has not all been ironed out. As they kneel there, heavy-eyed and dusky, and throwing grotesque moving shadows on the wall, they are two princesses in Africa going through the early-morning ablutions of their pagan prayers. Finished, they come forward to stretch their hands and warm them over the glowing coals. Red dusk of a Georgia sunset, their heavy, coal-lit faces . . . Kabnis suddenly recalls something.

Kabnis: Th old man talked last night.

Stella: And so did you.

Halsey: In your dreams.

Kabnis: I tell y, he did. I know what I'm talkin about. I'll tell y what he said. Wait now, lemme see.

Halsey: Look out, brother, th old man'll be getting int you by way o dreams. Come, Stel, ready? Cora? Coffee an eggs f both of you.

Halsey goes upstairs.

Stella: Gettin generous, aint he?

She blows the candles out. Says nothing to Kabnis. Then she and Cora follow after Halsey. Kabnis, left to himself, tries to rise. He has slept in his robe. His robe trips him. Finally, he manages to stand up. He starts across the floor. Half-way to the old man, he falls and lies quite still. Perhaps an hour passes. Light of a new sun is about to filter through the windows. Kabnis slowly rises to support upon his elbows. He looks hard, and internally gathers himself together. The side face of Father John is in the direct line of his eyes. He scowls at him. No one is around. Words gush from Kabnis.

Kabnis: You sit there like a black hound spiked to an ivory pedestal. An all night long I heard you murmurin that devilish word. They thought I didnt hear y, but I did. Mumblin, feedin that ornery thing thats livin on my insides. Father John. Father of Satan, more likely. What does it mean t you? Youre dead already. Death. What does it mean t you? To you who died way back there in th 'sixties. What are y throwin it in my throat for? Whats it goin t get y? A good smashin in th mouth, thats what. My fist'll sink int y black mush face clear t y guts—if y got any. Dont believe y have. Never seen signs of none. Death. Death. Sin an Death. All night long y mumbled death. (He forgets the old man as his mind begins to play with the word and its associations.) Death . . . these clammy floors . . . just like th place they used t stow away th worn-out, no-count niggers in th days of slavery . . . that was long ago; not so long ago . . . no windows (he rises higher on his elbows to verify this assertion. He looks around, and, seeing no one but the old man calls.) Halsey! Halsey! Gone an left me. Just like a nigger. I thought he was a nigger all th time. Now I know it. Ditch y when it comes right down t it. Damn him anyway. Godam him. (He looks and re-sees the old man.) Eh, you? T hell with you too. What do I care whether you can see or hear? You know what hell is cause youve been there. Its a feelin an its ragin in my soul in a way that'll pop out of me an run you through, an scorch y, an burn an rip your soul. Your soul. Ha. Nigger soul. A gin soul that gets drunk on a preacher's words. An screams. An shouts. God Almighty, how I hate that shoutin. Where's th beauty in that? Gives a buzzard a windpipe an I'll bet a dollar t a dime th buzzard ud beat y to it. Aint surprisin th white folks hate y so. When you had eyes, did you ever see th beauty of th world? Tell me that. Th hell y did. Now dont tell me. I know y didnt. You couldnt have. Oh, I'm drunk an just as good as dead, but no eyes that have seen beauty ever lose their sight. You aint got no sight. If you had, drunk as I am,

I hope Christ will kill me if I couldnt see it. Your eyes are dull and watery, like fish eyes. Fish eyes are dead eyes. Youre an old man, a dead fish man, an black at that. Theyve put y here t die, damn fool y are not t know it. Do y know how many feet youre under ground? I'll tell y. Twenty. An do y think you'll ever see th light of day again, even if you wasnt blind? Do y think youre out of slavery? Huh? Youre where they used t throw th worked-out, no-count slaves. On a damp clammy floor of a dark scum-hole. An they called that an infirmary. Th sons-a . . . . Why I can already see you toppled off that stool an stretched out on th floor beside me—not beside me, damn you, by yourself, with th flies buzzin an lickin God knows what they'd find on a dirty, black, foul-breathed mouth like yours . . .

Some one is coming down the stairs. Carrie, bringing food for the old man. She is lovely in her fresh energy of the morning, in the calm untested confidence and nascent maternity which rise from the purpose of her present mission. She walks to within a few paces of Kabnis.

Carrie K.: Brother says come up now, brother Ralph.

Kabnis: Brother doesnt know what he's talkin bout.

Carrie K.: Yes he does, Ralph. He needs you on th wagon.

Kabnis: He wants me on th wagon, eh? Does he think some wooden thing can lift me up? Ask him that.

Carrie K.: He told me t help y.

Kabnis: An how would you help me, child, dear sweet little sister?

She moves forward as if to aid him.

Carrie K.: I'm not a child, as I've more than once told you, brother Ralph, an as I'll show you now.

Kabnis: Wait, Carrie. No, thats right. Youre not a child. But twont do t lift me bodily. You dont understand. But its th soul of me that needs th risin.

Carrie K.: Youre a bad brother an just wont listen t me when I'm tellin y t go t church.

Kabnis doesnt hear her. He breaks down and talks to himself.

Kabnis: Great God Almighty, a soul like mine cant pin itself onto a wagon wheel an satisfy itself in spinnin round. Iron prongs an hickory sticks, an God knows what all . . . all right for Halsey . . . use him. Me? I get my life down in this scum-hole. Th old man an me—

Carrie K.: Has he been talkin?

Kabnis: Huh? Who? Him? No. Dont need to. I talk. An when I really talk, it pays th best of them t listen. Th old man is a good listener. He's deaf; but he's a good listener. An I can talk t him. Tell him anything.

Carrie K.: He's deaf an blind, but I reckon he hears, an sees too, from th things I've heard.

Kabnis: No. Cant. Cant I tell you. How's he do it?

Carrie K.: Dunno, except I've heard that th souls of old folks have a way of seein things.

Kabnis: An I've heard them call that superstition.

The old man begins to shake his head slowly. Carrie and Kabnis watch him, anxiously. He mumbles. With a grave motion his head nods up and down. And then, on one of the down-swings—

Father John (remarkably clear and with great conviction): Sin.

He repeats this word several times, always on the downward nodding. Surprised, indignant, Kabnis forgets that Carrie is with him.

Kabnis: Sin! Shut up. What do you know about sin, you old black bastard. Shut up, an stop that swayin an noddin your head.

Father John: Sin.

Kabnis tries to get up.

Kabnis: Didnt I tell y t shut up?

Carrie steps forward to help him. Kabnis is violently shocked at her touch. He springs back.

Kabnis: Carrie! What . . how . . Baby, you shouldnt be down here. Ralph says things. Doesnt mean to. But Carrie, he doesnt know what he's talkin about. Couldnt know. It was only a preacher's sin they knew in those old days, an that wasnt sin at all. Mind me, th only sin is whats done against th soul. Th whole world is a conspiracy t sin, especially in America, an against me. I'm th victim of their sin. I'm what sin is. Does he look like me? Have you ever heard him say th things youve heard me say? He couldnt if he had th Holy Ghost t help him. Dont look shocked, little sweetheart, you hurt me.

Father John: Sin.

Kabnis: Aw, shut up, old man.

Carrie K.: Leave him be. He wants t say somethin. (She turns to the old man.) What is it, Father?

Kabnis: Whatsha talkin t that old deaf man for? Come away from him.

Carrie K.: What is it, Father?

The old man's lips begin to work. Words are formed incoherently. Finally, he manages to articulate—

Father John: Th sin whats fixed . . . (Hesitates.)

Carrie K. (restraining a comment from Kabnis): Go on, Father.

Father John: . . . upon th white folks—

Kabnis: Suppose youre talkin about that bastard race thats roamin round th country. It looks like sin, if thats what y mean. Give us somethin new an up t date.

Father John:—f tellin Jesus—lies. O th sin th white folks 'mitted when they made th Bible lie.

Boom. Boom. BOOM! Thuds on the floor above. The old man sinks back into his stony silence. Carrie is wet-eyed. Kabnis, contemptuous.

Kabnis: So thats your sin. All these years t tell us that th white folks made th Bible lie. Well, I'll be damned. Lewis ought t have been here. You old black fakir—

Carrie K.: Brother Ralph, is that your best Amen?

She turns him to her and takes his hot cheeks in her firm cool hands. Her palms draw the fever out. With its passing, Kabnis crumples. He sinks to his knees before her, ashamed, exhausted. His eyes squeeze tight. Carrie presses his face tenderly against her. The suffocation of her fresh starched dress feels good to him. Carrie is about to lift her hands in prayer, when Halsey, at the head of the stairs, calls down.

Halsey: Well, well. Whats up? Aint you ever comin? Come on. Whats up down there? Take you all mornin t sleep off a pint? Youre weakenin, man, youre weakenin. Th axle an th beam's all ready waitin f y. Come on.

Kabnis rises and is going doggedly towards the steps. Carrie notices his robe. She catches up to him, points to it, and helps him take it off. He hangs it, with an exaggerated ceremony, on its nail in the corner. He looks down on the tousled beds. His lips curl bitterly. Turning, he stumbles over the bucket of dead coals. He savagely jerks it from the floor. And then, seeing Carrie's eyes upon him, he swings the pail carelessly and with eyes downcast and swollen, trudges upstairs to the work-shop. Carrie's gaze follows him till he is gone. Then she goes to the old man and slips to her knees before him. Her lips murmur, "Jesus, come."

Light streaks through the iron-barred cellar window. Within its soft circle, the figures of Carrie and Father John.

Outside, the sun arises from its cradle in the tree-tops of the forest. Shadows of pines are dreams the sun shakes from its eyes. The sun arises. Gold-glowing child, it steps into the sky and sends a birth-song slanting down gray dust streets and sleepy windows of the southern town.

1923

GEORGE SAMUEL SCHUYLER
1895–1977

Despite the historical value of George Schuyler's autobiography, *Black and Conservative* (1966), to scholars interested in the New York of Schuyler's youth, and the value of his novel *Slaves Today* (1931) to those concerned with twentieth-century slavery in Liberia, Schuyler's literary reputation probably rests on two texts: the novel *Black No More; Being an Account of the Strange and Wonderful Workings of Science in the Land of the Free* (1931) and an essay, "The Negro-Art Hokum" (1926). *Black No More* was the first book-length satire on race by a Black American, preceding Wallace Thurman's better-known *Infants of the Spring* by a year. The story of Dr. Crookman, a Black man who has devised a scientific process for the blanching of dark skins and hair-straightening (in other words, a way to make Blacks indistinguishable from whites), the tale is a trenchant commentary on race relations in America but cuts as mercilessly against Blacks as it does against whites. "The Negro-Art Hokum" is important primarily for having provoked Langston Hughes's famous rejoinder, "The Negro Artist and the Racial Mountain" (both articles appeared in the *Nation* in June 1926); but it remains a lively and persuasive defense of the assimilationist position among African Americans, a position that has become unfashionable but continues to appeal to many Blacks.

Schuyler's assimilationism appears to have been based on immense self-confidence. Throughout his life, he maintained that it was impossible for him to feel inferior to whites both because of his ancestors' participation in the Revolutionary War (one of his great-grandfathers served on the American side) and because his family had been free legally as far back as anyone had traced its genealogy. Born in Providence, Rhode Island, he moved with his family to Syracuse, New York, when he was three. He attended public school there until 1912, when he dropped out to join the army. Seven years later, he left the service as a first lieutenant. He spent a few years working at odd jobs in Syracuse and New York City before a short-lived flirtation with socialism brought him into contact with A. Philip Randolph, who, in 1923, hired him to work for the *Messenger.* Schuyler remained with Randolph as assistant editor until just after his marriage to a white woman, Josephine Cogdell, in 1928. Though he lived in New York, Schuyler worked much of his life for the *Pittsburgh Courier,* a popular Black weekly newspaper for which he had begun to write columns in 1924. He stayed with the *Courier* in various capacities until 1966, by which time his controversial views, including the characterization of Martin Luther King Jr. as a "sable Typhoid Mary," had made him unpopular with *Courier* readers. While working for the *Courier,* however, he became almost as well known to the white world of journalism as he was to the Black and, at one time, formed a close friendship with H. L. Mencken, on whose famously iconoclastic approach to journalism Schuyler clearly modeled his own work.

In the early 1950s, Schuyler joined the McCarthy camp; an intense animosity toward communism remained one of the defining characteristics of his writing for the rest of his life. Later, in 1967, he began working for William Loeb's ultraconservative *Union Leader,* published in New Hampshire. That year, his only child, Phillipa Duke Schuyler, a concert pianist and classical composer, was killed while on assignment in Vietnam for Loeb's publication. His wife died two years later.

Schuyler spent the remaining eight years of his life working as passionately as ever to propagate his own conservative beliefs. At his death, he was regarded by many Blacks as something of a traitor to his race. Nevertheless, his reputation is secure as one of the most independent and vigorous writers in the history of African American literature.

The Negro-Art Hokum[1]

Negro art "made in America" is as non-existent as the widely advertised profundity of Cal Coolidge, the "seven years of progress" of Mayor Hylan,[2] or the reported sophistication of New Yorkers. Negro art there has been, is, and will be among the numerous black nations of Africa; but to suggest the possibility of any such development among the ten million colored people in this republic is self-evident foolishness. Eager apostles from Greenwich Village, Harlem, and environs proclaimed a great renaissance of Negro art just around the corner waiting to be ushered on the scene by those whose hobby is taking races, nations, peoples, and movements under their wing. New art forms expressing the "peculiar" psychology of the Negro were about to flood the market. In short, the art of Homo Africanus was about to electrify the waiting world. Skeptics patiently waited. They still wait.

True, from dark-skinned sources have come those slave songs based on Protestant hymns and Biblical texts known as the spirituals, work songs and secular songs of sorrow and tough luck known as the blues, that outgrowth of rag-time known as jazz (in the development of which whites have assisted), and the Charleston, an eccentric dance invented by the gamins[3] around the public market-place in Charleston, S.C. No one can or does deny this. But these are contributions of a caste in a certain section of the country. They are foreign to Northern Negroes, West Indian Negroes, and African Negroes. They are no more expressive or characteristic of the Negro race than the music and dancing of the Appalachian highlanders or the Dalmation[4] peasantry are expressive or characteristic of the Caucasian race. If one wishes to speak of the musical contributions of the peasantry of the South, very well. Any group under similar circumstances would have produced something similar. It is merely a coincidence that this peasant class happens to be of a darker hue than the other inhabitants of the land. One recalls the

1. For a reply to this article, see Langston Hughes's "The Negro Artist and the Racial Mountain."
2. John F. Hylan (1868–1936), mayor of New York City (1917–25). Calvin Coolidge (1872–1933), thirtieth U.S. president (1923–29), was known for the brevity of his speeches.
3. Street urchins.
4. Dalmatia is a region of Croatia.

remarkable likeness of the minor strains of the Russian mujiks[5] to those of the Southern Negro.

As for the literature, painting, and sculpture of Aframericans—such as there is—it is identical in kind with the literature, painting, and sculpture of white Americans: that is, it shows more or less evidence of European influence. In the field of drama little of any merit has been written by and about Negroes that could not have been written by whites. The dean of the Aframerican literati is W. E. B. Du Bois, a product of Harvard and German universities; the foremost Aframerican sculptor is Meta Warwick Fuller, a graduate of leading American art schools and former student of Rodin, while the most noted Aframerican painter, Henry Ossawa Tanner,[6] is dean of American painters in Paris and has been decorated by the French Government. Now the work of these artists is no more "expressive of the Negro soul"—as the gushers put it—than are the scribblings of Octavus Cohen or Hugh Wiley.[7]

This, of course, is easily understood if one stops to realize that the Aframerican is merely a lampblacked Anglo-Saxon. If the European immigrant after two or three generations of exposure to our schools, politics, advertising, moral crusades, and restaurants becomes indistinguishable from the mass of Americans of the older stock (despite the influence of the foreign-language press), how much truer must it be of the sons of Ham[8] who have been subjected to what the uplifters call Americanism for the last three hundred years. Aside from his color, which ranges from very dark brown to pink, your American Negro is just plain American. Negroes and whites from the same localities in this country talk, think, and act about the same. Because a few writers with a paucity of themes have seized upon imbecilities of the Negro rustics and clowns and palmed them off as authentic and characteristic Aframerican behavior, the common notion that the black American is so "different" from his white neighbor has gained wide currency. The mere mention of the word "Negro" conjures up in the average white American's mind a composite stereotype of Bert Williams, Aunt Jemima, Uncle Tom, Jack Johnson, Florian Slappey,[9] and the various monstrosities scrawled by the cartoonists. Your average Aframerican no more resembles this stereotype than the average American resembles a composite of Andy Gump, Jim Jeffries, and a cartoon by Rube Goldberg.[1]

Again, the Africamerican is subject to the same economic and social forces that mold the actions and thoughts of the white Americans. He is not living in a different world as some whites and a few Negroes would have us believe. When the jangling of his Connecticut alarm clock gets him out of his Grand Rapids bed to a breakfast similar to that eaten by his white brother across the street; when he toils at the same or similar work in mills, mines, factories, and commerce alongside the descendants of Spartacus, Robin Hood, and

5. Peasants.
6. Tanner (1859–1937). Du Bois (1868–1963), editor of *Crisis* magazine. Fuller (1877–1963) attracted the attention of French sculptor Auguste Rodin (1840–1917) in her second year in Paris.
7. Cohen (1891–1959) and Wiley (1884–1969) were white writers who capitalized on existing stereotypes of Blacks in their work.
8. According to one reading of the Bible (see, for example, Genesis 9:22–25 and 10.1), Blacks were descendants of Ham.
9. One of Octavus Cohen's fictional creations. Williams (ca. 1875–1922), a popular Black entertainer who performed before Black and white audiences wearing blackface makeup over his fairly light skin. Johnson (1878–1946), the first Black heavyweight boxing champion of the world.
1. Goldberg (1883–1970), known for his cartoons of complicated inventions designed to do simple things. Gump was a cartoon character created by Robert Sidney Smith and others. Jeffries (1875–1953), white champion boxer who at the end of his career lost to Jack Johnson.

Eric the Red;[2] when he wears similar clothing and speaks the same language with the same degree of perfection; when he reads the same Bible and belongs to the Baptist, Methodist, Episcopal, or Catholic church; when his fraternal affiliations also include the Elks, Masons, and Knights of Pythias; when he gets the same or similar schooling, lives in the same kind of houses, owns the same makes of cars (or rides in them), and nightly sees the same Hollywood version of life on the screen; when he smokes the same brands of tobacco, and avidly peruses the same puerile periodicals; in short, when he responds to the same political, social, moral, and economic stimuli in precisely the same manner as his white neighbor, it is sheer nonsense to talk about "racial differences" as between the American black man and the American white man. Glance over a Negro newspaper (it is printed in good Americanese) and you will find the usual quota of crime news, scandal, personals, and uplift to be found in the average white newspaper—which, by the way, is more widely read by the Negroes than is the Negro press. In order to satisfy the cravings of an inferiority complex engendered by the colorphobia of the mob, the readers of the Negro newspapers are given a slight dash of racialistic seasoning. In the homes of the black and white Americans of the same cultural and economic level one finds similar furniture, literature, and conversation. How, then, can the black American be expected to produce art and literature dissimilar to that of the white American?

Consider Coleridge-Taylor, Edward Wilmot Blyden, and Claude McKay, the Englishmen; Pushkin, the Russian; Bridgewater, the Pole; Antar, the Arabian; Latino, the Spaniard; Dumas, *père* and *fils*, the Frenchmen; and Paul Laurence Dunbar, Charles W. Chesnutt, and James Weldon Johnson,[3] the Americans. All Negroes; yet their work shows the impress of nationality rather than race. They all reveal the psychology and culture of their environment—their color is incidental. Why should Negro artists of America vary from the national artistic norm when Negro artists in other countries have not done so? If we can foresee what kind of white citizens will inhabit this neck of the woods in the next generation by studying the sort of education and environment the children are exposed to now, it should not be difficult to reason that the adults of today are what they are because of the education and environment they were exposed to a generation ago. And that education and environment were about the same for blacks and whites. One contemplates the popularity of the Negro-art hokum and murmurs, "How come?"

This nonsense is probably the last stand of the old myth palmed off by Negrophobists for all these many years, and recently rehashed by the sainted Harding,[4] that there are "fundamental, eternal, and inescapable differences" between white and black Americans. That there are Negroes who will lend this myth a helping hand need occasion no surprise. It has been

2. Norse mariner (ca. 950). Spartacus (d. 71 B.C.E.), Thracian leader of a slave rebellion.

3. Prominent writer and civil rights leader (1871–1938). Samuel Coleridge Taylor (1875–1912), composer. Blyden (1882–1912), educator and journalist. McKay (1891–1948), Jamaican-born poet whose *Harlem Shadows* appeared in 1922. Alexander Pushkin (1799–1837), author of verse novels, including *Eugene Onegin*. George Augustus Polgreen Bridgewater (1799–1860), concert violinist. Antar-bin Shedad (ca. 500), Egyptian poet. Juan Latino "el negro" (1516–1597), African-born poet and professor. Alexandre Dumas père (1802–1870), author of *The Three Musketeers*. Alexandre Dumas fils (1824–1895), author of *The Lady of the Camellias*. Dunbar (1872–1906), the foremost African American poet at the turn of the century. Chesnutt (1858–1932), author of *The Conjure Woman*.

4. Warren G. Harding (1865–1963), twenty-ninth U.S. president (1921–23).

broadcast all over the world by the vociferous scions[5] of slaveholders, "scientists" like Madison Grant and Lothrop Stoddard,[6] and the patriots who flood the treasury of the Ku Klux Klan; and is believed, even today, by the majority of free, white citizens. On this baseless premise, so flattering to the white mob, that the blackamoor is inferior and fundamentally different, is erected the postulate that he must needs be peculiar; and when he attempts to portray life through the medium of art, it must of necessity be a peculiar art. While such reasoning may seem conclusive to the majority of Americans, it must be rejected with a loud guffaw by intelligent people.

1926

From Black No More

Being an Account of the Strange and Wonderful Workings of Science in the Land of the Free, A.D. 1933–1940

Chapter 1

Max Disher stood outside the Honky Tonk Club puffing a panatela and watching the crowds of white and black folk entering the cabaret. Max was tall, dapper and smooth coffee-brown. His negroid features had a slightly satanic cast and there was an insolent nonchalance about his carriage. He wore his hat rakishly and faultless evening clothes underneath his raccoon coat. He was young, he wasn't broke, but he was damnably blue. It was New Year's Eve, 1933, but there was no spirit of gaiety and gladness in his heart. How could he share the hilarity of the crowd when he had no girl? He and Minnie, his high "yallah" flapper, had quarreled that day and everything was over between them.

"Women are mighty funny," he mused to himself, "especially yallah women. You could give them the moon and they wouldn't appreciate it." That was probably the trouble; he'd given Minnie too much. It didn't pay to spend too much on them. As soon as he'd bought her a new outfit and paid the rent on a three-room apartment, she'd grown uppity. Stuck on her color, that's what was the matter with her! He took the cigar out of his mouth and spat disgustedly.

A short, plump, cherubic black fellow, resplendent in a narrow-brimmed brown fedora, camel's hair coat and spats, strolled up and clapped him on the shoulder: "Hello, Max!" greeted the newcomer, extending a hand in a fawn-colored glove, "What's on your mind?"

"Everything, Bunny," answered the debonair Max. "That damn yallah gal o' mine's got all up-stage and quit."

"Say not so!" exclaimed the short black fellow. "Why I thought you and her were all forty."

"Were, is right, kid. And after spending my dough, too! It sure makes me hot. Here I go and buy two covers at the Honky Tonk for tonight, thinkin' surely she'd come and she starts a row and quits!"

5. Descendants.
6. Author of several white-supremacist texts (1883–1950). Grant (1865–1937), pro-white author, co-founder of the New York Zoological Society, opponent of easy immigration to the United States.

"Shucks!" exploded Bunny, "I wouldn't let that worry me none. I'd take another skirt. I wouldn't let no dame queer my New Year's."

"So would I, Wise Guy, but all the dames I know are dated up. So here I am all dressed up and no place to go."

"You got two reservations, ain't you? Well, let's you and me go in," Bunny suggested. "We may be able to break in on some party."

Max visibly brightened. "That's a good idea," he said. "You never can tell, we might run in on something good."

Swinging their canes, the two joined the throng at the entrance of the Honky Tonk Club and descended to its smoky depths. They wended their way through the maze of tables in the wake of a dancing waiter and sat down close to the dance floor. After ordering ginger ale and plenty of ice, they reared back and looked over the crowd.

Max Disher and Bunny Brown had been pals ever since the war when they soldiered together in the old 15th regiment in France. Max was one of the Aframerican Fire Insurance Company's crack agents, Bunny was a teller in the Douglass Bank and both bore the reputation of gay blades[1] in black Harlem. The two had in common a weakness rather prevalent among Aframerican bucks: they preferred yellow women. Both swore there were three things essential to the happiness of a colored gentleman: yellow money, yellow women and yellow taxis. They had little difficulty in getting the first and none at all in getting the third but the yellow women they found flighty and fickle. It was so hard to hold them. They were so sought after that one almost required a million dollars to keep them out of the clutches of one's rivals.

"No more yallah gals for me!" Max announced with finality, sipping his drink. "I'll grab a black gal first."

"Say not so!" exclaimed Bunny, strengthening his drink from his huge silver flask. "You aint thinkin' o' dealin' in coal, are you?"

"Well," argued his partner, "it might change my luck. You can trust a black gal; she'll stick to you."

"How do you know? You ain't never had one. Ever' gal I ever seen you with looked like an ofay."

"Humph!" grunted Max. "My next one may be an ofay, too! They're less trouble and don't ask you to give 'em the moon."

"I'm right with you, pardner," Bunny agreed, "but I gotta have one with class. None o' these Woolworth dames for me! Get you in a peek o' trouble . . . Fact is, Big Boy, ain't none o' these women no good. They all get old on the job."

They drank in silence and eyed the motley crowd around them. There were blacks, browns, yellows, and whites chatting, flirting, drinking; rubbing shoulders in the democracy of night life. A fog of tobacco smoke wreathed their heads and the din from the industrious jazz band made all but the loudest shrieks inaudible. In and out among the tables danced the waiters, trays balanced aloft, while the patrons, arrayed in colored paper caps, beat time with the orchestra, threw streamers or grew maudlin on each other's shoulders.

"Looky here! Lawdy Lawd!" exclaimed Bunny, pointing to the doorway. A party of white people had entered. They were all in evening dress and in their midst was a tall, slim, titian-haired[2] girl who had seemingly stepped from heaven or the front cover of a magazine.

1. Dashing young men.
2. With reddish or gold hair, after the women in many paintings by the Italian artist Titian (ca. 1488–1576).

"My, my, my!" said Max, sitting up alertly.

The party consisted of two men and four women. They were escorted to a table next to the one occupied by the two colored dandies. Max and Bunny eyed them covertly. The tall girl was certainly a dream.

"Now that's my speed," whispered Bunny.

"Be yourself," said Max. "You couldn't touch her with a forty-foot pole."

"Oh, I don't know, Big Boy," Bunny beamed self-confidently, "You never can tell! You never can tell!"

"Well, I can tell," remarked Disher, "'cause she's a cracker."

"How you know that?"

"Man, I can tell a cracker a block away. I wasn't born and raised in Atlanta, Georgia, for nothin', you know. Just listen to her voice."

Bunny listened. "I believe she is," he agreed.

They kept eyeing the party to the exclusion of everything else. Max was especially fascinated. The girl was the prettiest creature he'd ever seen and he felt irresistibly drawn to her. Unconsciously he adjusted his necktie and passed his well-manicured hand over his rigidly straightened hair.

Suddenly one of the white men rose and came over to their table. They watched him suspiciously. Was he going to start something? Had he noticed that they were staring at the girl? They both stiffened at his approach.

"Say," he greeted them, leaning over the table, "do you boys know where we can get some decent liquor around here?[3] We've run out of stuff and the waiter says he can't get any for us."

"You can get some pretty good stuff right down the street," Max informed him, somewhat relieved.

"They won't sell none to him," said Bunny. "They might think he was a Prohibition officer."

"Could one of you fellows get me some?" asked the man.

"Sure," said Max, heartily. What luck! Here was the very chance he'd been waiting for. These people might invite them over to their table. The man handed him a ten dollar bill and Max went out bareheaded to get the liquor. In ten minutes he was back. He handed the man the quart and the change. The man gave back the change and thanked him. There was no invitation to join the party. Max returned to his table and eyed the group wistfully.

"Did he invite you in?" asked Bunny.

"I'm back here, ain't I?" answered Max, somewhat resentfully.

The floor show came on. A black-faced comedian, a corpulent shouter of mammy songs[4] with a gin-roughened voice, three chocolate soft-shoe dancers and an octette of wriggling, practically nude, mulatto chorines.

Then midnight and pandemonium as the New Year swept in. When the din had subsided, the lights went low and the orchestra moaned the weary blues. The floor filled with couples. The two men and two of the women at the next table rose to dance. The beautiful girl and another were left behind.

"I'm going over and ask her to dance," Max suddenly announced to the surprised Bunny.

3. Although Prohibition (1919–33) outlawed the manufacture, transportation, and sale of alcohol in the United States, some restaurants and nightclubs still illegally provided liquor to customers or helped them find places to buy it.

4. Songs associated with the vaudeville tradition of blackface performance, often drawing on stereotypical portrayals of African American life and culture.

"Say not so!" exclaimed that worthy. "You're fixin' to get in dutch,[5] Big Boy."

"Well, I'm gonna take a chance, anyhow," Max persisted, rising.

This fair beauty had hypnotized him. He felt that he would give anything for just one dance with her. Once around the floor with her slim waist in his arm would be like an eternity in heaven. Yes, one could afford to risk repulse for that.

"Don't do it, Max!" pleaded Bunny. "Them fellows are liable to start somethin'."

But Max was not to be restrained. There was no holding him back when he wanted to do a thing, especially where a comely damsel was concerned.

He sauntered over to the table in his most sheikish manner and stood looking down at the shimmering strawberry blonde. She was indeed ravishing and her exotic perfume titilated his nostrils despite the clouds of cigarette smoke.

"Would you care to dance?" he asked, after a moment's hesitation.

She looked up at him haughtily with cool green eyes, somewhat astonished at his insolence and yet perhaps secretly intrigued but her reply lacked nothing in definiteness.

"No," she said icily, "I never dance with niggers!" Then turning to her friend, she remarked: "Can you beat the nerve of these darkies?" She made a little disdainful grimace with her mouth, shrugged daintily and dismissed the unpleasant incident.

Crushed and angry, Max returned to his place without a word. Bunny laughed aloud in high glee.

"You said she was a cracker," he gurgled, "an' now I guess you know it."

"Aw, go to hell," Max grumbled.

Just then Billy Fletcher, the headwaiter, passed by. Max stopped him. "Ever see that dame in here before?" he asked.

"Been in here most every night since before Christmas," Billy replied.

"Do you know who she is?"

"Well, I heard she was some rich broad from Atlanta up here for the holidays. Why?"

"Oh, nothin'; I was just wondering."

From Atlanta! His home town. No wonder she had turned him down. Up here trying to get a thrill in the Black Belt but a thrill from observation instead of contact. Gee, but white folks were funny. They didn't want black folks' game and yet they were always frequenting Negro resorts.

At three o'clock Max and Bunny paid their check and ascended to the street. Bunny wanted to go to the breakfast dance at the Dahomey Casino but Max was in no mood for it.

"I'm going home," he announced laconically, hailing a taxi. "Good night!"

As the cab whirled up Seventh Avenue, he settled back and thought of the girl from Atlanta. He couldn't get her out of his mind and didn't want to. At his rooming house, he paid the driver, unlocked the door, ascended to his room and undressed, mechanically. His mind was a kaleidoscope: Atlanta, sea-green eyes, slender figure, titian hair, frigid manner. "I never dance with niggers." Then he fell asleep about five o'clock and promptly dreamed of her. Dreamed of dancing with her, dining with her, motoring with her, sitting beside her on a golden throne while millions of manacled

5. To get in trouble.

white slaves prostrated themselves before him. Then there was a nightmare of grim, gray men with shotguns, baying hounds, a heap of gasoline-soaked faggots[6] and a screeching, fanatical mob.

He awoke covered with perspiration. His telephone was ringing and the late morning sunshine was streaming into his room. He leaped from bed and lifted the receiver.

"Say," shouted Bunny, "did you see this morning's *Times?*"

"Hell no," growled Max, "I just woke up. Why, what's in it?"

"Well, do you remember Dr. Junius Crookman, that colored fellow that went to Germany to study about three years ago? He's just come back and the *Times* claims he's announced a sure way to turn darkies white. Thought you might be interested after the way you fell for that ofay broad last night. They say Crookman's going to open a sanitarium in Harlem right away. There's your chance, Big Boy, and it's your only chance." Bunny chuckled.

"Oh, ring off," growled Max. "That's a lot of hooey."

But he was impressed and a little excited. Suppose there was something to it? He dressed hurriedly, after a cold shower, and went out to the newsstand. He bought a *Times* and scanned its columns. Yes, there it was:

NEGRO ANNOUNCES REMARKABLE
DISCOVERY
Can Change Black to White in Three Days.

Max went into Jimmy Johnson's restaurant and greedily read the account while awaiting his breakfast. Yes, it must be true. To think of old Crookman being able to do that! Only a few years ago he'd been just a hungry medical student around Harlem. Max put down the paper and stared vacantly out of the window. Gee, Crookman would be a millionaire in no time. He'd even be a multimillionaire. It looked as though science was to succeed where the Civil War had failed. But how could it be possible? He looked at his hands and felt at the back of his head where the straightening lotion had failed to conquer some of the knots. He toyed with his ham and eggs as he envisioned the possibilities of the discovery.

Then a sudden resolution seized him. He looked at the newspaper account again. Yes, Crookman was staying at the Phyllis Wheatley Hotel. Why not go and see what there was to this? Why not be the first Negro to try it out? Sure, it was taking a chance, but think of getting white in three days! No more jim crow. No more insults. As a white man he could go anywhere, be anything he wanted to be, do most anything he wanted to do, be a free man at last . . . and probably be able to meet the girl from Atlanta. What a vision!

He rose hurriedly, paid for his breakfast, rushed out of the door, almost ran into an aged white man carrying a sign advertising a Negro fraternity dance, and strode, almost ran, to the Phyllis Wheatley Hotel.

He tore up the steps two at a time and into the sitting room. It was crowded with white reporters from the daily newspapers and black reporters from the Negro weeklies. In their midst he recognized Dr. Junius Crookman, tall, wiry, ebony black, with a studious and polished manner. Flanking him on either side was Henry ("Hank") Johnson, the "Numbers" banker, and Charlie ("Chuck") Foster, the realtor, looking very grave, important and possessive in the midst of all the hullabaloo.

6. Bundles of brush or twigs.

"Yes," Dr. Crookman was telling the reporters while they eagerly took down his statements, "during my first year at college I noticed a black girl on the street one day who had several irregular white patches on her face and hands. That intrigued me. I began to study up on skin diseases and found out that the girl was evidently suffering from a nervous disease known as vitiligo.[7] It is a very rare disease. Both Negroes and Caucasians occasionally have it, but it is naturally more conspicuous on blacks than whites. It absolutely removes skin pigment and sometimes it turns a Negro completely white but only after a period of thirty or forty years. It occurred to me that if one could discover some means of artificially inducing and stimulating this nervous disease at will, one might possibly solve the American race problem. My sociology teacher had once said that there were but three ways for the Negro to solve his problem in America," he gestured with his long slender fingers, "'To either get out, get white or get along.' Since he wouldn't and couldn't get out and was getting along only differently, it seemed to me that the only thing for him was to get white." For a moment his teeth gleamed beneath his smartly waxed mustache, then he sobered and went on:

"I began to give a great deal of study to the problem during my spare time. Unfortunately there was very little information on the subject in this country. I decided to go to Germany but I didn't have the money. Just when I despaired of getting the funds to carry out my experiments and studies abroad, Mr. Johnson and Mr. Foster," he indicated the two men with a graceful wave of his hand, "came to my rescue. I naturally attribute a great deal of my success to them."

"But how is it done?" asked a reporter.

"Well," smiled Crookman, "I naturally cannot divulge the secret any more than to say that it is accomplished by electrical nutrition and glandular control. Certain gland secretions are greatly stimulated while others are considerably diminished. It is a powerful and dangerous treatment but harmless when properly done."

"How about the hair and features?" asked a Negro reporter.

"They are also changed in the process," answered the biologist. "In three days the Negro becomes to all appearances a Caucasian."

"But is the transformation transferred to the off-spring?" persisted the Negro newspaperman.

"As yet," replied Crookman, "I have discovered no way to accomplish anything so revolutionary but I am able to transform a black infant to a white one in twenty-four hours."

"Have you tried it on any Negroes yet?" queried a skeptical white journalist.

"Why of course I have," said the Doctor, slightly nettled. "I would not have made my announcement if I had not done so. Come here, Sandol," he called, turning to a pale white youth standing on the outskirts of the crowd, who was the most Nordic looking person in the room. "This man is a Senegalese, a former aviator in the French Army. He is living proof that what I claim is true."

Dr. Crookman then displayed a photograph of a very black man, somewhat resembling Sandol but with bushy Negro hair, flat nose and full lips. "This," he announced proudly, "is Sandol as he looked before taking my treatment. What I have done to him I can do to any Negro. He is in good physical and mental condition as you all can see."

7. A skin condition in which sections of the skin progressively lose pigmentation and thus color.

The assemblage was properly awed. After taking a few more notes and a number of photographs of Dr. Crookman, his associates and of Sandol, the newspapermen retired. Only the dapper Max Disher remained.

"Hello, Doc!" he said, coming forward and extending his hand. "Don't you remember me? I'm Max Disher."

"Why certainly I remember you, Max," replied the biologist rising cordially. "Been a long time since we've seen each other but you're looking as sharp as ever. How's things?"

The two men shook hands.

"Oh, pretty good. Say, Doc, how's chances to get you to try that thing on me? You must be looking for volunteers."

"Yes, I am, but not just yet. I've got to get my equipment set up first. I think now I'll be ready for business in a couple of weeks."

Henry Johnson, the beefy, sleek-jowled, mulatto "Numbers" banker, chuckled and nudged Dr. Crookman. "Old Max ain't losin' no time, Doc. When that niggah gits white Ah bet he'll make up fo' los' time with these ofay girls."

Charlie Foster, small, slender, grave, amber-colored, and laconic, finally spoke up: "Seems all right, Junius, but there'll be hell to pay when you whiten up a lot o' these darkies and them mulatto babies start appearing here and there. Watcha gonna do then?"

"Oh, quit singin' th' blues, Chuck," boomed Johnson. "Don't cross bridges 'til yuh come tuh 'em. Doc'll fix that okeh. Besides, we'll have mo' money'n Henry Ford by that time."

"There'll be no difficulties whatever," assured Crookman rather impatiently.

"Let's hope not."

Next day the newspapers carried a long account of the interview with Dr. Junius Crookman interspersed with photographs of him, his backers and of the Senegalese who had been turned white. It was the talk of the town and was soon the talk of the country. Long editorials were written about the discovery, learned societies besieged the Negro biologist with offers of lecture engagements, magazines begged him for articles, but he turned down all offers and refused to explain his treatment. This attitude was decried as unbecoming a scientist and it was insinuated and even openly stated that nothing more could be expected from a Negro.

But Crookman ignored the clamor of the public, and with the financial help of his associates planned the great and lucrative experiment of turning Negroes into Caucasians.

The impatient Max Disher saw him as often as possible and kept track of developments. He yearned to be the first treated and didn't want to be caught napping. Two objects were uppermost in his mind: To get white and to Atlanta. The statuesque and haughty blonde was ever in his thoughts. He was head over heels in love with her and realized there was no hope for him to ever win her as long as he was brown. Each day he would walk past the tall building that was to be the Crookman Sanitarium, watching the workmen and delivery trucks; wondering how much longer he would have to wait before entering upon the great adventure.

At last the sanitarium was ready for business. Huge advertisements appeared in the local Negro weeklies. Black Harlem was on its toes. Curious throngs of Negroes and whites stood in front of the austere six-story building gazing up at its windows.

Inside, Crookman, Johnson and Foster stood nervously about while hustling attendants got everything in readiness. Outside they could hear the murmur of the crowd.

"That means money, Chuck," boomed Johnson, rubbing his beefsteak hands together.

"Yeh," replied the realtor, "but there's one more thing I wanna get straight: How about that darky dialect? You can't change that."

"It isn't necessary, my dear Foster," explained the physician, patiently. "There is no such thing as Negro dialect, except in literature and drama. It is a well-known fact among informed persons that a Negro from a given section speaks the same dialect as his white neighbors. In the South you can't tell over the telephone whether you are talking to a white man or a Negro. The same is true in New York when a Northern Negro speaks into the receiver. I have noticed the same thing in the hills of West Virginia and Tennessee. The educated Haitian speaks the purest French and the Jamaican Negro sounds exactly like an Englishman. There are no racial or color dialects; only sectional dialects."

"Guess you're right," agreed Foster, grudgingly.

"I know I'm right. Moreover, even if my treatment did not change the so-called Negro lips, even that would prove to be no obstacle."

"How come, Doc," asked Johnson.

"Well, there are plenty of Caucasians who have lips quite as thick and noses quite as broad as any of us. As a matter of fact there has been considerable exaggeration about the contrast between Caucasian and Negro features. The cartoonists and minstrel men have been responsible for it very largely. Some Negroes like the Somalis, Filanis, Egyptians, Hausas and Abyssinians[8] have very thin lips and nostrils. So also have the Malagasys of Madagascar. Only in certain small sections of Africa do the Negroes possess extremely pendulous lips and very broad nostrils. On the other hand, many so-called Caucasians, particularly the Latins, Jews and South Irish, and frequently the most Nordic of peoples like the Swedes, show almost Negroid lips and noses. Black up some white folks and they could deceive a resident of Benin. Then when you consider that less than twenty per cent of our Negroes are without Caucasian ancestry and that close to thirty per cent have American Indian ancestry, it is readily seen that there cannot be the wide difference in Caucasian and Afro-American facial characteristics that most people imagine."

"Doc, you sho' knows yo' onions," said Johnson, admiringly. "Doan pay no 'tenshun to that ole Doubtin' Thomas. He'd holler starvation in a pie shop."

There was a commotion outside and an angry voice was heard above the hum of low conversation. Then Max Disher burst in the door with a guard hanging onto his coat tail.

"Let loose o' me, Boy," he quarreled. "I got an engagement here. Doc, tell this man something, will you?"

Crookman nodded to the guard to release the insurance man. "Well, I see you're right on time, Max."

"I told you I'd be Johnny-on-the-spot,[9] didn't I?" said Disher, inspecting his clothes to see if they had been wrinkled.

8. English term for Ethiopians. "Filanis": Fulanis, the Fula people, one of the largest groups in West and Central Africa.

9. Slang phrase for a person who is precisely on time.

"Well, if you're all ready, go into the receiving room there, sign the register and get into one of those bathrobes. You're first on the list."

The three partners looked at each other and grinned as Max disappeared into a small room at the end of the corridor. Dr. Crookman went into his office to don his white trousers, shoes and smock; Johnson and Foster entered the business office to supervise the clerical staff, while white-coated figures darted back and forth through the corridors. Outside, the murmuring of the vast throng grew more audible.

Johnson showed all of his many gold teeth in a wide grin as he glanced out the window and saw the queue of Negroes already extending around the corner. "Man, man, man!" he chuckled to Foster, "at fifty dollars a th'ow this thing's gonna have th' numbah business beat all hollow."

"Hope so," said Foster, gravely.

Max Disher, arrayed only in a hospital bathrobe and a pair of slippers, was escorted to the elevator by two white-coated attendants. They got off on the sixth floor and walked to the end of the corridor. Max was trembling with excitement and anxiety. Suppose something should go wrong? Suppose Doc should make a mistake? He thought of the Elks' excursion every summer to Bear Mountain,[1] the high yellow Minnie and her colorful apartment, the pleasant evenings at the Dahomey Casino doing the latest dances with the brown belles of Harlem, the prancing choruses at the Lafayette Theater, the hours he had whiled away at Boogie's and the Honky Tonk Club, and he hesitated. Then he envisioned his future as a white man, probably as the husband of the tall blonde from Atlanta, and with firm resolve, he entered the door of the mysterious chamber.

He quailed as he saw the formidable apparatus of sparkling nickel. It resembled a cross between a dentist's chair and an electric chair. Wires and straps, bars and levers protruded from it and a great nickel headpiece, like the helmet of a knight, hung over it. The room had only a skylight and no sound entered it from the outside. Around the walls were cases of instruments and shelves of bottles filled with strangely colored fluids. He gasped with fright and would have made for the door but the two husky attendants held him firmly, stripped off his robe and bound him in the chair. There was no retreat. It was either the beginning or the end.

Chapter 2

Slowly, haltingly, Max Disher dragged his way down the hall to the elevator, supported on either side by an attendant. He felt terribly weak, emptied and nauseated; his skin twitched and was dry and feverish; his insides felt very hot and sore. As the trio walked slowly along the corridor, a blue-green light would ever and anon blaze through one of the doorways as a patient was taken in. There was a low hum and throb of machinery and an acid odor filled the air. Uniformed nurses and attendants hurried back and forth at their tasks. Everything was quiet, swift, efficient, sinister.

He felt so thankful that he had survived the ordeal of that horrible machine so akin to the electric chair. A shudder passed over him at the memory of the hours he had passed in its grip, fed at intervals with revolting concoctions.

1. A state park on the Hudson River in New York. The Benevolent and Protective Order of Elks is a U.S. fraternal order and social club founded in 1868.

But when they reached the elevator and he saw himself in the mirror, he was startled, overjoyed. White at last! Gone was the smooth brown complexion. Gone were the slightly full lips and Ethiopian nose. Gone was the nappy hair that he had straightened so meticulously ever since the kink-no-more lotions first wrenched Aframericans from the tyranny and torture of the comb. There would be no more expenditures for skin whiteners; no more discrimination; no more obstacles in his path. He was free! The world was his oyster and he had the open sesame of a pork-colored skin!

The reflection in the mirror gave him new life and strength. He now stood erect, without support and grinned at the two tall, black attendants. "Well, Boys," he crowed, "I'm all set now. That machine of Doc's worked like a charm. Soon's I get a feed under my belt I'll be okeh."

Six hours later, bathed, fed, clean-shaven, spry, blonde and jubilant, he emerged from the out-patient ward and tripped gaily down the corridor to the main entrance. He was through with coons,[2] he resolved, from now on. He glanced in a superior manner at the long line of black and brown folk on one side of the corridor, patiently awaiting treatment. He saw many persons whom he knew but none of them recognized him. It thrilled him to feel that he was now indistinguishable from nine-tenths of the people of the United States; one of the great majority. Ah, it was good not to be a Negro any longer!

As he sought to open the front door, the strong arm of a guard restrained him. "Wait a minute," the man said, "and we'll help you get through the mob."

A moment or two later Max found himself the center of a flying wedge of five or six husky special policemen, cleaving through a milling crowd of colored folk. From the top step of the sanitarium he had noticed the crowd spread over the sidewalk, into the street and around the corners. Fifty traffic policemen strained and sweated to keep prospective patients in line and out from under the wheels of taxicabs and trucks.

Finally he reached the curb, exhausted from the jostling and squeezing, only to be set upon by a mob of newspaper photographers and reporters. As the first person to take the treatment, he was naturally the center of attraction for about fifteen of these journalistic gnats. They asked a thousand questions seemingly all at once. What was his name? How did he feel? What was he going to do? Would he marry a white woman? Did he intend to continue living in Harlem?

Max would say nothing. In the first place, he thought to himself, if they're so anxious to know all this stuff, they ought to be willing to pay for it. He needed money if he was going to be able to thoroughly enjoy being white; why not get some by selling his story? The reporters, male and female, begged him almost with tears in their eyes for a statement but he was adamant.

While they were wrangling, an empty taxicab drove up. Pushing the inquisitive reporters to one side, Max leaped into it and yelled "Central Park!" It was the only place he could think of at the moment. He wanted to have time to compose his mind, to plan the future in this great world of whiteness. As the cab lurched forward, he turned and was astonished to find another occupant, a pretty girl.

"Don't be scared," she smiled. "I knew you would want to get away from that mob so I went around the corner and got a cab for you. Come along with me and I'll get everything fixed up for you. I'm a reporter from *The Scimitar.*

2. A derogatory term for Blacks.

We'll give you a lot of money for your story." She talked rapidly. Max's first impulse had been to jump out of the cab, even at the risk of having to face again the mob of reporters and photographers he had sought to escape, but he changed his mind when he heard mention of money.

"How much?" he asked, eyeing her. She was very comely and he noted that her ankles were well turned.

"Oh, probably a thousand dollars," she replied.

"Well, that sounds good." A thousand dollars! What a time he could have with that! Broadway for him as soon as he got paid off.

As they sped down Seventh Avenue, the newsboys were yelling the latest editions. "Ex—try! Ex—try! Blacks turning white! Blacks turning white! . . . Read all about the gr-r-reat dis—covery! Paper, Mister! Paper! . . . Read all about Dr. Crookman."

He settled back while they drove through the park and glanced frequently at the girl by his side. She looked mighty good; wonder could he talk business with her? Might go to dinner and a cabaret. That would be the best way to start.

"What did you say your name was?" he began.

"I didn't say," she stalled.

"Well, you have a name, haven't you?" he persisted.

"Suppose I have?"

"You're not scared to tell it, are you?"

"Why do you want to know my name?"

"Well, there's nothing wrong about wanting to know a pretty girl's name, is there?"

"Well, my name's Smith, Sybil Smith. Now are you satisfied?"

"Not yet. I want to know something more. How would you like to go to dinner with me tonight?"

"I don't know and I won't know until I've had the experience." She smiled coquettishly. Going out with him, she figured, would make the basis of a rattling good story for tomorrow's paper. "Negro's first night as a Caucasian!" Fine!

"Say, you're a regular fellow," he said, beaming upon her. "I'll get a great kick out of going to dinner with you because you'll be the only one in the place that'll know I'm a Negro."

Down at the office of *The Scimitar*, it didn't take Max long to come to an agreement, tell his story to a stenographer and get a sheaf of crisp, new bills. As he left the building a couple of hours later with Miss Smith on his arm, the newsboys were already crying the extra edition carrying the first installment of his strange tale. A huge photograph of him occupied the entire front page of the tabloid. Lucky for him that he'd given his name as William Small, he thought.

He was annoyed and a little angered. What did they want to put his picture all over the front of the paper for? Now everybody would know who he was. He had undergone the tortures of Doc Crookman's devilish machine in order to escape the conspicuousness of a dark skin and now he was being made conspicuous because he had once had a dark skin! Could one never escape the plagued race problem?

"Don't worry about that," comforted Miss Smith. "Nobody'll recognize you. There are thousands of white people, yes millions, that look like you do." She took his arm and snuggled up closer. She wanted to make him feel at home. It wasn't often a poor, struggling newspaper woman got a chap with a big bankroll to take her out for the evening. Moreover, the description she would write of the experience might win her a promotion.

They walked down Broadway in the blaze of white lights to a dinner-dance place. To Max it was like being in heaven. He had strolled through the Times Square district before but never with such a feeling of absolute freedom and sureness. No one now looked at him curiously because he was with a white girl, as they had when he came down there with Minnie, his former octoroon lady friend. Gee, it was great!

They dined and they danced. Then they went to a cabaret, where, amid smoke, noise and body smells, they drank what was purported to be whiskey and watched a semi-nude chorus do its stuff. Despite his happiness Max found it pretty dull. There was something lacking in these ofay places of amusement or else there was something present that one didn't find in the black-and-tan resorts in Harlem. The joy and abandon here was obviously forced. Patrons went to extremes to show each other they were having a wonderful time. It was all so strained and quite unlike anything to which he had been accustomed. The Negroes, it seemed to him, were much gayer, enjoyed themselves more deeply and yet they were more restrained, actually more refined. Even their dancing was different. They followed the rhythm accurately, effortlessly and with easy grace; these lumbering couples, out of step half the time and working as strenuously as stevedores[3] emptying the bowels of a freighter, were noisy, awkward, inelegant. At their best they were gymnastic where the Negroes were sensuous. He felt a momentary pang of mingled disgust, disillusionment and nostalgia. But it was only momentary. He looked across at the comely Sybil and then around at the other white women, many of whom were very pretty and expensively gowned, and the sight temporarily drove from his mind the thoughts that had been occupying him.

They parted at three o'clock, after she had given him her telephone number. She pecked him lightly on the cheek in payment, doubtless, for a pleasant evening's entertainment. Somewhat disappointed because she had failed to show any interest in his expressed curiosity about the interior of her apartment, he directed the chauffeur to drive him to Harlem. After all, he argued to himself in defense of his action, he had to get his things.

As the cab turned out of Central Park at 110th Street he felt, curiously enough, a feeling of peace. There were all the old familiar sights: the all-night speakeasies, the frankfurter stands, the loiterers, the late pedestrians, the chop suey joints, the careening taxicabs, the bawdy laughter.

He couldn't resist the temptation to get out at 133rd Street and go down to Boogie's place, the hangout of his gang. He tapped, an eye peered through a hole, appraised him critically, then disappeared and the hole was closed. There was silence.

Max frowned. What was the matter with old Bob? Why didn't he open that door? The cold January breeze swept down into the little court where he stood and made him shiver. He knocked a little louder, more insistently. The eye appeared again.

"Who's 'at?" growled the doorkeeper.

"It's me, Max Disher," replied the ex-Negro.

"Go 'way f'm here, white man. Dis heah place is closed."

3. Dock workers who load and unload cargo ships.

"Is Bunny Brown in there?" asked Max in desperation.

"Yeh, he's heah. Does yuh know him? Well, Ah'll call 'im out heah and see if he knows you."

Max waited in the cold for about two or three minutes and then the door suddenly opened and Bunny Brown, a little unsteady, came out. He peered at Max in the light from the electric bulb over the door.

"Hello Bunny," Max greeted him. "Don't know me, do you? It's me, Max Disher. You recognize my voice, don't you?"

Bunny looked again, rubbed his eyes and shook his head. Yes, the voice was Max Disher's, but this man was white. Still, when he smiled his eyes revealed the same sardonic twinkle—so characteristic of his friend.

"Max," he blurted out, "is that you, sure enough? Well, for cryin' out loud! Damned 'f you ain't been up there to Crookman's and got fixed up. Well, hush my mouth! Bob, open that door. This is old Max Disher. Done gone up there to Crookman's and got all white on my hands. He's just too tight, with his blond hair, 'n everything."

Bob opened the door, the two friends entered, sat down at one of the small round tables in the narrow, smoke-filled cellar and were soon surrounded with cronies. They gazed raptly at his colorless skin, commented on the veins showing blue through the epidermis, stroked his ash-blond hair and listened with mouths open to his remarkable story.

"Watcha gonna do now, Max?" asked Boogie, the rangy, black, bullet-headed proprietor.

"I know just what that joker's gonna do," said Bunny. "He's goin' back to Atlanta. Am I right, Big Boy?"

"You ain't wrong," Max agreed. "I'm goin' right on down there, brother, and make up for lost time."

"Whadayah mean?" asked Boogie.

"Boy, it would take me until tomorrow night to tell you and then you wouldn't understand."

The two friends strolled up the avenue. Both were rather mum. They had been inseparable pals since the stirring days in France. Now they were about to be parted. It wasn't as if Max was going across the ocean to some foreign country; there would be a wider gulf separating them: the great sea of color. They both thought about it.

"I'll be pretty lonesome without you, Bunny."

"It ain't you, Big Boy."

"Well, why don't you go ahead and get white and then we could stay together. I'll give you the money."

"Say not so! Where'd you get so much jack all of a sudden?" asked Bunny.

"Sold my story to *The Scimitar* for a grand."

"Paid in full?"

"Wasn't paid in part!"

"All right, then, I'll take you up, Heavy Sugar." Bunny held out his plump hand and Max handed him a hundred-dollar bill.

They were near the Crookman Sanitarium. Although it was five o'clock on a Sunday morning, the building was brightly lighted from cellar to roof and the hum of electric motors could be heard, low and powerful. A large electric sign hung from the roof to the second floor. It represented a huge arrow outlined in green with the words BLACK-NO-MORE running its full length vertically. A black face was depicted at the lower end of the arrow while at the top shone a white face to which the arrow was pointed. First would appear the outline of the arrow; then, BLACK-NO-MORE would flash on and off. Following that the black face would appear at the bottom and beginning at the lower end the long arrow with its lettering would appear progressively until its tip was reached, when the white face at the top would blazon forth. After that the sign would flash off and on and the process would be repeated.

In front of the sanitarium milled a half-frozen crowd of close to four thousand Negroes. A riot squad armed with rifles, machine guns and tear gas bombs maintained some semblance of order. A steel cable stretched from lamp post to lamp post the entire length of the block kept the struggling mass of humanity on the sidewalk and out of the path of the traffic. It seemed as if all Harlem were there. As the two friends reached the outskirts of the mob, an ambulance from the Harlem Hospital drove up and carried away two women who had been trampled upon.

Lined up from the door to the curb was a gang of tough special guards dredged out of the slums. Grim Irish from Hell's Kitchen, rough Negroes from around 133rd Street and 5th Avenue (New York's "Beale Street")[4] and tough Italians from the lower West Side. They managed with difficulty to keep an aisle cleared for incoming and outgoing patients. Near the curb were stationed the reporters and photographers.

The noise rose and fell. First there would be a low hum of voices. Steadily it would rise and rise in increasing volume as the speakers became more animated and reach its climax in a great animal-like roar as the big front door would open and a whitened Negro would emerge. Then the mass would surge forward to peer at and question the ersatz Nordic. Sometimes the ex-Ethiopian would quail before the mob and jump back into the building. Then the hardboiled guards would form a flying squad and hustle him to a waiting taxicab. Other erstwhile Aframericans issuing from the building would grin broadly, shake hands with friends and relatives and start to graphically describe their experience while the Negroes around them enviously admired their clear white skins.

In between these appearances the hot dog and peanut vendors did a brisk trade, along with the numerous pickpockets of the district. One slender, anemic, ratty-looking mulatto Negro was almost beaten to death by a gigantic black laundress whose purse he had snatched. A Negro selling hot roasted sweet potatoes did a land-office business while the neighboring saloons, that had increased so rapidly in number since the enactment of the Volstead Law[5] that many of their Italian proprietors paid substantial income taxes, sold scores or gallons of incredibly atrocious hootch.

"Well, bye, bye, Max," said Bunny, extending his hand. "I'm goin' in an' try my luck."

"So long, Bunny. See you in Atlanta. Write me general delivery."

"Why, ain't you gonna wait for me, Max?"

"Naw! I'm fed up on this town."

"Oh, you ain't kiddin' me, Big Boy. I know you want to look up that broad you saw in the Honky Tonk New Year's Eve," Bunny beamed.

4. A reference to the street in downtown Memphis, Tennessee, that is famous for its blues and jazz clubs.

5. The National Prohibition Act, passed by Congress in 1919 to enforce the ban on alcohol prescribed by the Eighteenth Amendment to the U.S. Constitution, was also known as the "Volstead Act" after Andrew Volstead (1860–1947), the Minnesota politician who was chairman of the House Judiciary Committee at the time.

Max grinned and blushed slightly. They shook hands and parted. Bunny ran up the aisle from the curb, opened the sanitarium door and without turning around, disappeared within.

For a minute or so, Max stood irresolutely in the midst of the gibbering crowd of people. Unaccountably he felt at home here among these black folk. Their jests, scraps of conversation and lusty laughter all seemed like heavenly music. Momentarily he felt a disposition to stay among them, to share again their troubles which they seemed always to bear with a lightness that was yet not indifference. But then, he suddenly realized with just a tiny trace of remorse that the past was forever gone. He must seek other pastures, other pursuits, other playmates, other loves. He was white now. Even if he wished to stay among his folk, they would be either jealous or suspicious of him, as they were of most octoroons and nearly all whites. There was no other alternative than to seek his future among the Caucasians with whom he now rightfully belonged.

And after all, he thought, it was a glorious new adventure. His eyes twinkled and his pulse quickened as he thought of it. Now he could go anywhere, associate with anybody, be anything he wanted to be. He suddenly thought of the comely miss he had seen in the Honky Tonk on New Year's Eve and the greatly enlarged field from which he could select his loves. Yes, indeed there were advantages in being white. He brightened and viewed the tightly-packed black folk around Inn with a superior air. Then, thinking again of his clothes at Mrs. Blandish's, the money in his pocket and the prospect for the first time of riding into Atlanta in a Pullman car and not as a Pullman porter, he turned and pushed his way through the throng.

He strolled up West 139th Street to his rooming place, stepping lightly and sniffing the early morning air. How good it was to be free, white and to possess a bankroll! He fumbled in his pocket for his little mirror and looked at himself again and again from several angles. He stroked his pale blond hair and secretly congratulated himself that he would no longer need to straighten it nor be afraid to wet it. He gazed raptly at his smooth, white hands with the blue veins showing through. What a miracle Dr. Crookman had wrought!

As he entered the hallway, the mountainous form of his landlady loomed up. She jumped back as she saw his face.

"What you doing in here?" she almost shouted. "Where'd you get a key to this house?"

"It's me, Max Disher," he assured her with a grin at her astonishment. "Don't know me, do you?"

She gazed incredulously into his face. "Is that you sure enough, Max? How in the devil did you get so white?"

He explained and showed her a copy of *The Scimitar* containing his story. She switched on the hall light and read it. Contrasting emotions played over her face, for Mrs. Blandish was known in the business world as Mme. Sisseretta Blandish, the beauty specialist, who owned the swellest hair-straightening parlor in Harlem. Business, she thought to herself, was bad enough, what with all of the competition, without this Dr. Crookman coming along and killing it altogether.

"Well," she sighed, "I suppose you're going down town to live, now. I always said niggers didn't really have any race pride."

Uneasy, Max made no reply. The fat, brown woman turned with a disdainful sniff and disappeared into a room at the end of the hall. He ran lightly upstairs to pack his things.

An hour later, as the taxicab bearing him and his luggage bowled through Central Park, he was in high spirits. He would go down to the Pennsylvania Station and get a Pullman straight into Atlanta. He would stop there at the best hotel. He wouldn't hunt up any of his folks. No, that would be too dangerous. He would just play around, enjoy life and laugh at the white folks up his sleeve. God! What an adventure! What a treat it would be to mingle with white people in places where as a youth he had never dared to enter. At last he felt like an American citizen. He flecked the ash of his panatela out of the open window of the cab and sank back in the seat feeling at peace with the world.

1931

RUDOLPH FISHER

1897–1934

A skilled physician, brilliant writer, and musical arranger, as well as a witty and informed conversationalist, Rudolph Fisher was by many accounts probably the most intellectually gifted member of the Harlem Renaissance. The son of Glendora Fisher and the Reverend John Wesley Fisher, he was born in Washington, D.C., but grew up in Providence, Rhode Island, where he graduated from Classical High School in 1915 with honors. Other honors came readily throughout the rest of his brief life. Attending Brown University as a prize scholar, he won an important award in German as a freshman, first prize in a prestigious speaking contest as a sophomore, and yet another major university award as a junior. Later, he wryly referred to Brown as "a most generous institution" that gave him "a great many prizes and scholarships, the degree of A.B. and A.M. in 1919 and 1920, and all of the keys—Phi Beta Kappa, Delta Sigma Rho and Sigma Xi. There was undoubtedly an oversupply that year."

The year 1924 was particularly eventful for Fisher: he took his M.D. (with highest honors) from Howard University Medical School, where he studied roentgenology (the diagnostic and therapeutic uses of x-rays); began his internship at Freedmen's Hospital in Washington, D.C.; and married Jane Ryder. In New York, he became a fellow of the National Research Council at Columbia University's College of Physicians and Surgeons. He specialized in roentgenology at Columbia for two years before opening a private practice in Harlem in 1927.

Despite the demands of his medical work, Fisher found time to write. In 1925, he published his first short story, "The City of Refuge," in the *Atlantic Monthly*, which brought him instant fame among the Harlem literary set because of its vividly dramatic depiction of Harlem street life as seen through the consciousness of a southern migrant. In the next two years, he published his short fiction in several other respected journals, including *McClure's*, *Survey Graphic*, *Redbook*, and *Story Magazine*. His essay "The Caucasian Storms Harlem" (1927) was the liveliest piece yet published on Harlem as a living cultural force. Fisher also published two novels: *The Walls of Jericho* (1928) and *The Conjure Man Dies: A Mystery Tale of Dark Harlem* (1932). The first was apparently written on a bet that Fisher could not create a unified narrative out of all the diverse elements of Harlem society. The second, *The Conjure Man Dies*, in which a doctor, John Archer, uses his medical expertise to help unravel a murder mystery, was hailed as the first Black detective novel; he was the forerunner of Chester Himes and Ishmael Reed. This work was first produced in dramatic form at the Lafayette Theatre in 1936, more than a year after Fisher's untimely death from intestinal cancer, perhaps brought on by the machines he used in his medical practice.

Many critics have noted Fisher's consistent return to a handful of themes, including the conflicts between generations of African Americans and the values of settled Harlemites as opposed to those of Black migrants fresh from the South or the Caribbean. This consistency may be seen in other ways. Certain characters in *Jericho* reappear in *Conjure Man,* and some characters in *Conjure Man* make it into later pieces of short fiction. Generally speaking, however, Fisher's treatment of such material improves with each return; one can only speculate about what he might have accomplished as a writer if he had not died so young.

The City of Refuge

I

Confronted suddenly by daylight, King Solomon Gillis stood dazed and blinking. The railroad station, the long, white-walled corridor, the impassible slot-machine, the terrifying subway train—he felt as if he had been caught up in the jaws of a steam-shovel, jammed together with other helpless lumps of dirt, swept blindly along for a time, and at last abruptly dumped.

There had been strange and terrible sounds: "New York! Penn Terminal[1]—all change!" "Pohter, hyer, pohter, suh?" Shuffle of a thousand soles, clatter of a thousand heels, innumerable echoes. Cracking rifleshots—no, snapping turnstiles. "Put a nickel in!" "Harlem? Sure. This side—next train." Distant thunder, nearing. The screeching onslaught of the fiery hosts of hell, headlong, breath-taking. Car doors rattling, sliding, banging open. "Say, wha' d'ye think this is, a baggage car?" Heat, oppression, suffocation—eternity—"Hundred'n turdy-fif[2] next!" More turnstiles. Jonah emerging from the whale.

Clean air, blue sky, bright sunlight.

Gillis set down his tan-cardboard extension-case and wiped his black, shining brow. Then slowly, spreadingly, he grinned at what he saw: Negroes at every turn; up and down Lenox Avenue, up and down One Hundred and Thirty-Fifth Street; big, lanky Negroes, short, squat Negroes; black ones, brown ones, yellow ones; men standing idle on the curb, women, bundle-laden, trudging reluctantly homeward, children rattle-trapping about the sidewalks; here and there a white face drifting along, but Negroes predominantly, overwhelmingly everywhere. There was assuredly no doubt of his whereabouts. This was Negro Harlem.

Back in North Carolina Gillis had shot a white man and, with the aid of prayer and an automobile, probably escaped a lynching. Carefully avoiding the railroads, he had reached Washington in safety. For his car a Southwest bootlegger had given him a hundred dollars and directions to Harlem; and so he had come to Harlem.

Ever since a traveling preacher had first told him of the place, King Solomon Gillis had longed to come to Harlem. The Uggams were always talking about it; one of their boys had gone to France in the draft and, returning,

1. A major train station in Manhattan.

2. Or 135th Street, in central Harlem.

had never got any nearer home than Harlem. And there were occasional "colored" newspapers from New York: newspapers that mentioned Negroes without comment, but always spoke of a white person as "So-and-so, white." That was the point. In Harlem, black was white. You had rights that could not be denied you; you had privileges, protected by law. And you had money. Everybody in Harlem had money. It was a land of plenty. Why, had not Mouse Uggam sent back as much as fifty dollars at a time to his people in Waxhaw?[3]

The shooting, therefore, simply catalyzed whatever sluggish mental reaction had been already directing King Solomon's fortunes toward Harlem. The land of plenty was more than that now: it was also the city of refuge.[4]

Casting about for direction, the tall newcomer's glance caught inevitably on the most conspicuous thing in sight, a magnificent figure in blue that stood in the middle of the crossing and blew a whistle and waved great white-gloved hands. The Southern Negro's eyes opened wide; his mouth opened wider. If the inside of New York had mystified him, the outside[5] was amazing him. For there stood a handsome, brass-buttoned giant directing the heaviest traffic Gillis had ever seen; halting unnumbered tons of automobiles and trucks and wagons and pushcarts and street-cars; holding them at bay with one hand while he swept similar tons peremptorily on with the other; ruling the wide crossing with supreme self-assurance; and he, too, was a Negro!

Yet most of the vehicles that leaped or crouched at his bidding carried white passengers. One of these overdrove bounds a few feet and Gillis heard the officer's shrill whistle and gruff reproof, saw the driver's face turn red and his car draw back like a threatened pup. It was beyond belief—impossible. Black might be white, but it couldn't be that white!

"Done died an' woke up in Heaven," thought King Solomon, watching, fascinated; and after a while, as if the wonder of it were too great to believe simply by seeing, "Cullud policemans!" he said, half aloud; then repeated over and over, with greater and greater conviction, "Even got cullud policemans—even got cullud—"

"Where y'want to go, big boy?"

Gillis turned. A little, sharp-faced yellow man was addressing him. "Saw you was a stranger. Thought maybe I could help y'out."

King Solomon located and gratefully extended a slip of paper. "Wha' dis hyeh at, please, suh?"

The other studied it a moment, pushing back his hat and scratching his head. The hat was a tall-crowned, unindented brown felt; the head was brown patent-leather, its glistening brush-back flawless save for a suspicious crimpiness near the clean-grazed edges.

"See that second corner? Turn to the left when you get there. Number forty-five's about halfway the block."

"Thank y', suh."

"You from—Massachusetts?"

"No, suh, Nawth Ca'lina."

"Is 'at so? You look like a Northerner. Be with us long?"

"Till I die," grinned the flattered King Solomon.

3. A town in south-central North Carolina.

4. See Numbers 35:11, where God instructs Moses: "Appoint you cities to be cities of refuge for you; that the slayer may flee thither, which killeth any person at unawares." Later in the story, Gillis claims that the homicide was accidental.

5. That is, that part of New York which is aboveground. Gillis has spent his time to this point in subway stations, and the like.

"Stoppin' there?"

"Reckon I is. Man in Washin'ton 'lowed I'd find lodgin' at dis address."

"Good enough. If y' don't, maybe I can fix y' up. Harlem's pretty crowded. This is me." He proffered a card.

"Thank y', suh," said Gillis, and put the card in his pocket.

The little yellow man watched him plod flat-footedly on down the street, long awkward legs never quite straightened, shouldered extension-case bending him sidewise, wonder upon wonder halting or turning him about. Presently, as he proceeded, a pair of bright-green stockings caught and held his attention. Tony, the storekeeper, was crossing the sidewalk with a bushel basket of apples. There was a collision; the apples rolled; Tony exploded; King Solomon apologized. The little yellow man laughed shortly, took out a notebook, and put down the address he had seen on King Solomon's slip of paper.

"Guess you're the shine[6] I been waitin' for," he surmised.

As Gillis, approaching his destination, stopped to rest, a haunting notion grew into an insistent idea. "Dat li'l yaller nigger was a sho' 'nuff gen'man to show me de road. Seem lak I knowed him befo'—" he pondered. That receding brow, that sharp-ridged, spreading nose, that tight upper lip over the two big front teeth, that chinless jaw—He fumbled hurriedly for the card he had not looked at and eagerly made out the name.

"Mouse Uggam, sho' 'nuff! Well, dog-gone!"

II

Uggam sought out Tom Edwards, once a Pullman porter, now prosperous proprietor of a cabaret, and told him:—

"Chief, I got him: a baby jess in from the land o' cotton and so dumb he thinks ante bellum's an old woman."

"Where d'you find him?"

"Where you find all the jay birds[7] when they first hit Harlem—at the subway entrance. This one come up the stairs, batted his eyes once or twice, an' froze to the spot—with his mouth open. Sure sign he's from 'way down behind the sun an' ripe f' the pluckin'."

Edwards grinned a gold-studded, fat-jowled grin. "Gave him the usual line, I suppose?"

"Didn't miss. An' he fell like a ton o' bricks. 'Course I've got him spotted, but damn 'f I know jess how to switch 'em on to him."

"Get him a job around a store somewhere. Make out you're befriendin' him. Get his confidence."

"Sounds good. Ought to be easy. He's from my state. Maybe I know him or some of his people."

"Make out you do, anyhow. Then tell him some fairy tales that'll switch your trade to him. The cops'll follow the trade. We could even let Froggy flop into some dumb white cop's hands and 'confess' where he got it. See?"

"Chief, you got a head, no lie."

"Don't lose no time. And remember, hereafter, it's better to sacrifice a little than to get squealed on. Never refuse a customer. Give him a little credit. Humor him along till you can get rid of him safe. You don't know

6. A Black person (derogatory term used by whites). 7. Simpletons.

what that guy that died may have said; you don't know who's on to you now. And if they get you—I don't know you."

"They won't get me," said Uggam.

King Solomon Gillis sat meditating in a room half the size of his hencoop back home, with a single window opening into an airshaft.

An airshaft: cabbage and chitterlings cooking; liver and onions sizzling, sputtering; three player-pianos out-plunking each other; a man and woman calling each other vile things; a sick, neglected baby wailing; a phonograph broadcasting blues; dishes clacking; a girl crying heartbrokenly; waste noises, waste odors of a score of families, seeing issue through a common channel; pollution from bottom to top—a sewer of sounds and smells.

Contemplating this, King Solomon grinned and breathed, "Doggone!" A little later, still gazing into the sewer, he grinned again. "Green stockin's," he said; "loud green!" The sewer gradually grew darker. A window lighted up opposite, revealing a woman in camisole and petticoat, arranging her hair. King Solomon, staring vacantly, shook his head and grinned yet again. "Even got culled policemans!" he mumbled softly.

III

Uggam leaned out of the room's one window and spat maliciously into the dinginess of the airshaft. "Damn glad you got him," he commented, as Gillis finished his story. "They's a thousand shines in Harlem would change places with you in a minute jess f' the honor of killin' a cracker."

"But, I didn't go to do it. 'Twas a accident."

"That's the only part to keep secret."

"Know whut dey done? Dey killed five o' Mose Joplin's hawses 'fo he lef'. Put groun' glass in de feed-trough. Sam Cheevers come up on three of 'em one night pizenin' his well. Bleesom beat Crinshaw out o' sixty acres o' lan' an' a year's crops. Dass jess how 't is. Soon's a nigger make a li'l sump'n he better git to leavin'. An' 'fo long ev'ybody's goin' be lef'!"

"Hope to hell they don't all come here."

The doorbell of the apartment rang. A crescendo of footfalls in the hallway culminated in a sharp rap on Gillis's door. Gillis jumped. Nobody but a policeman would rap like that. Maybe the landlady had been listening and had called in the law. It came again, loud, quick, angry. King Solomon prayed that the policeman would be a Negro.

Uggam stepped over and opened the door. King Solomon's apprehensive eyes saw framed therein, instead of a gigantic officer, calling for him, a little blot of a creature, quite black against even the darkness of the hallway, except for a dirty, wide-striped silk shirt, collarless, with the sleeves rolled up.

"Ah hahve bill fo' Mr. Gillis." A high, strongly accented Jamaican voice, with its characteristic singsong intonation, interrupted King Solomon's sigh of relief.

"Bill? Bill fo' me? What kin' o' bill?"

"Wan bushel appels. T'ree seventy-fife."

"Apples? I ain' bought no apples." He took the paper and read aloud, laboriously, "Antonio Gabrielli to K. S. Gillis, Doctor—"

"Mr. Gabrielli say, you not pays him, he send policemon."

"What I had to do wid 'is apples?"

"You bumps into him yesterday, no? Scatter appels everywhere—on de sidewalk, in de gutter. Kids pick up an' run away. Others all spoil. So you pays."

Gillis appealed to Uggam. "How 'bout it, Mouse?"

"He's a damn liar. Tony picked up most of 'em; I seen him. Lemme look at that bill—Tony never wrote this thing. This baby's jess playin' you for a sucker."

"Ain' had no apples, ain' payin' fo' none," announced King Solomon, thus prompted. "Didn't have to come to Harlem to git cheated. Plenty o' dat right wha' I come fum."

But the West Indian warmly insisted. "You cahn't do daht, mon. Whaht you t'ink, 'ey? Dis mon loose 'is appels an' 'is money too?"

"What diff'ence it make to you, nigger?"

"Who you call nigger, mon? Ah hahve you understahn' "—

"Oh, well, white folks, den. What all you got t' do wid dis hyeh, anyhow?"

"Mr. Gabrielli send me to collect bill!"

"How I know dat?"

"Do Ah not bring bill? You t'ink Ah steal t'ree dollar, 'ey?"

"Three dollars an' sebenty-fi'cent," corrected Gillis. " 'Nuther thing: wha' you ever see me befo'? How you know dis is me?"

"Ah see you, sure. Ah help Mr. Gabrielli in de store. When you knocks down de baskette appels, Ah see. Ah follow you. Ah know you comes in dis house."

"Oh, you does? An' how come you know my name an' flat an' room so good? How come dat?"

"Ah fin' out. Sometime Ah brings up here vegetables from de store."

"Humph! Mus' be workin' on shares."

"You pays, 'ey? You pays me or de policemon?"

"Wait a minute," broke in Uggam, who had been thoughtfully contemplating the bill. "Now listen, big shorty. You haul hips on back to Tony. We got your menu all right"—he waved the bill—"but we don't eat your kind o' cookin', see?"

The West Indian flared. "Whaht it is to you, 'ey? You can not mind your own business? Ah hahve not spik to you!"

"No, brother. But this is my friend, an' I'll be john-browned[8] if there's a monkey-chaser in Harlem can gyp him if I know it, see? Bes' thing f' you to do is catch air, toot sweet."[9]

Sensing frustration, the little islander demanded the bill back. Uggam figured he could use the bill himself, maybe. The West Indian hotly persisted; he even menaced. Uggam pocketed the paper and invited him to take it. Wisely enough, the caller preferred to catch air.

When he had gone, King Solomon sought words of thanks.

"Bottle it," said Uggam. "The point is this: I figger you got a job."

"Job? No I ain't! Wh' at?"

"When you show Tony this bill, he'll hit the roof and fire that monk."

"Wha ef he do?"

"Then you up 'n ask f' the job. He'll be too grateful to refuse. I know Tony some, an' I'll be there to put in a good word. See?"

King Solomon considered this. "Sho' needs a job, but ain' after stealin' none."

"Stealin'? 'T wouldn't be stealin'. Stealin' 's what that damn monkey-chaser tried to do from you. This would be doin' Tony a favor an' gettin' y'self out o' the barrel. What's the hold-back?"

8. After John Brown (1800–1859), leader of the raid on Harpers Ferry, who was executed.

9. Americanization of *tout de suite*, French for "immediately."

"What make you keep callin' him monkey-chaser?"

"West Indian. That's another thing. Any time y' can knife a monk, do it. They's too damn many of 'em here. They're an achin' pain."

"Jess de way white folks feels 'bout niggers."

"Damn that. How 'bout it? Y' want the job?"

"Hm—well—I'd ruther be a policeman."

"Policeman?" Uggam gasped.

"M—hm. Dass all I wants to be, a policeman, so I kin police all de white folks right plumb in jail!"

Uggam said seriously, "Well, y' might work up to that. But it takes time. An' y've got to eat while y're waitin'." He paused to let this penetrate. "Now, how 'bout this job at Tony's in the meantime? I should think y'd jump at it."

King Solomon was persuaded.

"Hm—well—reckon I does," he said slowly.

"Now y're tootin'!" Uggam's two big front teeth popped out in a grin of genuine pleasure. "Come on. Let's go."

IV

Spitting blood and crying with rage, the West Indian scrambled to his feet. For a moment he stood in front of the store gesticulating furiously and jabbering shrill threats and unintelligible curses. Then abruptly he stopped and took himself off.

King Solomon Gillis, mildly puzzled, watched him from Tony's doorway. "I jess give him a li'l shove," he said to himself, "an he roll' clean 'cross de sidewalk." And a little later, disgustedly, "Monkey-chaser!" he grunted, and went back to his sweeping.

"Well, big boy, how y' comin' on?"

Gillis dropped his broom. "Hay-o, Mouse. Wha' you been las' two-three days?"

"Oh, around. Gettin' on all right here? Had any trouble?"

"Deed I ain't—'ceptin' jess now I had to throw 'at li'l jigger out."

"Who? The monk?"

"M—hm. He sho' Lawd doan like me in his job. Look like he think I stole it from him, stiddy[1] him tryin' to steal from me. Had to push him down sho' 'nuff 'fo I could git rid of 'im. Den he run off talkin' Wes' Indi'man an' shakin' his fis' at me."

"Ferget it." Uggam glanced about. "Where's Tony?"

"Boss man? He be back direckly."

"Listen—like to make two or three bucks a day extra?"

"Huh?"

"Two or three dollars a day more'n what you're gettin' already?"

"Ain' I near 'nuff in jail now?"

"Listen," King Solomon listened. Uggam hadn't been in France for nothing. Fact was, in France he'd learned about some valuable French medicine. He'd brought some back with him,—little white pills,—and while in Harlem had found a certain druggist who knew what they were and could supply all he could use. Now there were any number of people who would buy and pay well for as much of this French medicine as Uggam could get. It was good

1. Instead of.

for what ailed them, and they didn't know how to get it except through him. But he had no store in which to set up an agency and hence no single place where his customers could go to get what they wanted. If he had, he could sell three or four times as much as he did.

King Solomon was in a position to help him now, same as he had helped King Solomon. He would leave a dozen packages of the medicine—just small envelopes that could all be carried in a coat pocket—with King Solomon every day. Then he could simply send his customers to King Solomon at Tony's store. They'd make some trifling purchase, slip him a certain coupon which Uggam had given them, and King Solomon would wrap the little envelope of medicine with their purchase. Mustn't let Tony catch on, because he might object, and then the whole scheme would go gaflooey. Of course it wouldn't really be hurting Tony any. Wouldn't it increase the number of his customers?

Finally, at the end of each day, Uggam would meet King Solomon some place and give him a quarter for each coupon he held. There'd be at least ten or twelve a day—two and a half or three dollars plumb extra! Eighteen or twenty dollars a week!

"Dog-gone!" breathed Gillis.

"Does Tony ever leave you heer alone?"

"M—hm. Jess started dis mawnin'. Doan nobody much come round 'tween ten an' twelve, so he done took to doin' his buyin' right 'long 'bout dat time. Nobody hyeh but me fo' 'n hour or so."

"Good. I'll try to get my folks to come 'round here mostly while Tony's out, see?"

"I doan miss."

"Sure y' get the idea, now?" Uggam carefully explained it all again. By the time he had finished, King Solomon was wallowing in gratitude.

"Mouse, you sho' is been a friend to me. Why, 'f't had n' been fo' you—"

"Bottle it," said Uggam. "I'll be round to your room to-night with enough stuff for to-morrer, see? Be sure'n be there."

"Won't be nowha' else."

"An' remember, this is all jess between you 'n me."

"Nobody else but," vowed King Solomon.

Uggam grinned to himself as he went on his way. "Dumb Oscar![2] Wonder how much can we make before the cops nab him? French medicine—Hmph!"

V

Tony Gabrielli, an oblate Neapolitan of enormous equator, wabbled heavily out of his store and settled himself over a soap box.

Usually Tony enjoyed sitting out front thus in the evening, when his helper had gone home and his trade was slackest. He liked to watch the little Gabriellis playing over the sidewalk with the little Levys and Johnsons; the trios and quartettes of brightly dressed, dark-skinned girls merrily out for a stroll; the slovenly gaited, darker men, who eyed them up and down and commented to each other with an unsuppressed "Hot damn!" or "Oh, no, now!"

2. Any stupid person (slang).

But to-night Tony was troubled. Something was different since the arrival of King Solomon Gillis. The new man had seemed to prove himself honest and trustworthy, it was true. Tony had tested him, as he always tested a new man, by apparently leaving him alone in charge for two or three mornings. Tony's store was a modification of the front rooms of his flat and was in direct communication with it by way of a glass-windowed door in the rear. Tony always managed to get back into his flat via the side-street entrance and watch the new man through this unobtrusive glass-windowed door. If anything excited his suspicion, like unwarranted interest in the cash register, he walked unexpectedly out of this door to surprise the offender in the act. Thereafter he would have no more such trouble. But he had not succeeded in seeing King Solomon steal even an apple.

What he had observed, however, was that the number of customers that came into the store during the morning's slack hour had pronouncedly increased in the last few days. Before, there had been three or four. Now there were twelve or fifteen. The mysterious thing about it was that their purchases totaled little more than those of the original three or four.

Yesterday and to-day Tony had elected to be in the store at the time when, on the other days, he had been out. But Gillis had not been overcharging or short-changing; for when Tony waited on the customers himself—strange faces all—he found that they bought something like a yeast cake or a five-cent loaf of bread. It was puzzling. Why should strangers leave their own neighborhoods and repeatedly come to him for a yeast cake or a loaf of bread? They were not new neighbors. New neighbors would have bought more variously and extensively and at different times of day. Living near by, they would have come in, the men often in shirtsleeves and slippers, the women in kimonos, with boudoir caps covering their lumpy heads. They would have sent in strange children for things like yeast cakes and loaves of bread. And why did not some of them come in at night when the new helper was off duty?

As for accosting Gillis on suspicion, Tony was too wise for that.

Patronage had a queer way of shifting itself in Harlem. You lost your temper and let slip a single "*nègre*."[3] A week later you sold your business.

Spread over his soap box, with his pudgy hands clasped on his preposterous paunch, Tony sat and wondered. Two men came up, conspicuous for no other reason than that they were white. They displayed extreme nervousness, looking about as if afraid of being seen; and when one of them spoke to Tony it was in a husky, toneless, blowing voice, like the sound of a dirty phonograph record.

"Are you Antonio Gabrielli?"

"Yes, sure." Strange behavior for such lusty-looking fellows. He who had spoken unsmilingly winked first one eye then the other, and indicated by a gesture of his head that they should enter the store. His companion looked cautiously up and down the Avenue, while Tony, wondering what ailed them, rolled to his feet and puffingly led the way.

Inside, the spokesman snuffled, gave his shoulders a queer little hunch, and asked, "Can you fix us up, buddy?" The other glanced restlessly about the place as if he were constantly hearing unaccountable noises.

Tony thought he understood clearly now. "Booze, 'ey?" he smiled. "Sorry—I no got."

3. Nigger.

"Booze? Hell, no!" The voice dwindled to a throaty whisper. "Dope. Coke, milk, dice—anything. Name your price. Got to have it."

"Dope?" Tony was entirely at a loss. "What's a dis, dope?"

"Aw, lay off, brother. We're in on this. Here." He handed Tony a piece of paper. "Froggy gave us a coupon. Come on. You can't go wrong."

"I no got," insisted the perplexed Tony; nor could he be budged on that point.

Quite suddenly the manner of both men changed. "All right," said the first angrily, in a voice as robust as his body. "All right, you're clever, You no got. Well, you will get. You'll get twenty years!"

"Twenty year? Whadda you talk?"

"Wait a minute, Mac," said the second caller. "Maybe the wop's[4] on the level. Look here, Tony, we're officers, see? Policemen." He produced a badge. "A couple of weeks ago a guy was brought in dying for the want of a shot, see? Dope—he needed some dope—like this—in his arm. See? Well, we tried to make him tell us where he'd been getting it, but he was too weak. He croaked next day. Evidently he hadn't had money enough to buy any more.

"Well, this morning a little nigger that goes by the name of Froggy was brought into the precinct pretty well doped up. When he finally came to, he swore he got the stuff here at your store. Of course, we've just been trying to trick you into giving yourself away, but you don't bite. Now what's your game? Know anything about this?"

Tony understood. "I dunno," he said slowly; and then his own problem, whose contemplation his callers had interrupted, occurred to him. "Sure!" he exclaimed. "Wait. Maybeso I know somet'ing."

"All right. Spill it."

"I got a new man, work-a for me." And he told them what he had noted since King Solomon Gillis came.

"Sounds interesting. Where is this guy?"

"Here in da store—all day."

"Be here to-morrow?"

"Sure. All day."

"All right. We'll drop in to-morrow and give him the eye. Maybe he's our man."

"Sure. Come ten o'clock. I show you," promised Tony.

VI

Even the oldest and rattiest cabarets in Harlem have sense of shame enough to hide themselves under the ground—for instance, Edwards's.[5] To get into Edwards's you casually enter a dimly lighted corner saloon, apparently—only apparently—a subdued memory of brighter days. What was once the family entrance is now a side entrance for ladies. Supporting yourself against close walls, you crouchingly descend a narrow, twisted staircase until, with a final turn, you find yourself in a glaring, long, low basement. In a moment your eyes become accustomed to the haze of tobacco smoke. You see men and women seated at wire-legged, white-topped tables, which are covered with half-empty bottles and glasses; you trace the slow-jazz accompaniment you heard as you came down the stairs to a pianist, a cornetist, and a drummer

4. Derogatory term for an Italian.
5. Based on Edmond's Cellar, a cabaret made famous by singer Ethel Waters (1896–1977).

on a little platform at the far end of the room. There is a cleared space from the foot of the stairs, where you are standing, to the platform where this orchestra is mounted, and in it a tall brown girl is swaying from side to side and rhythmically proclaiming that she has the world in a jug and the stopper in her hand.[6] Behind a counter at your left sits a fat, bald, tea-colored Negro, and you wonder if this is Edwards—Edwards, who stands in with the police, with the political bosses, with the importers of wines and worse. A white-vested waiter hustles you to a seat and takes your order. The song's tempo changes to a quicker; the drum and the cornet rip out a fanfare, almost drowning the piano; the girl catches up her dress and begins to dance. . . .

Gillis's wondering eyes had been roaming about. They stopped.

"Look, Mouse!" he whispered. "Look a-yonder!"

"Look at what?"

"Dog-gone if it ain' de self-same gal!"

"Wha' d' ye mean, self-same girl?"

"Over yonder, wi' de green stockin's. Dass de gal made me knock over dem apples fust day I come to town. 'Member? Been wishin' I could see her ev'y sence."

"What for?" Uggam wondered.

King Solomon grew confidential. "Ain but two things in dis world, Mouse, I really wants. One is to be a policeman. Been wantin' dat ev'y sence I seen dat cullud traffic-cop dat day. Other is to git myse'f a gal lak dat one over yonder!"

"You'll do it," laughed Uggam, "if you live long enough."

"Who dat wid her?"

"How'n hell do I know?"

"He cullud?"

"Don't look like it. Why? What of it?"

"Hm—nuthin—"

"How many coupons y' got to-night?"

"Ten." King Solomon handed them over.

"Y'ought to've slipt 'em to me under the table, but it's all right now, long as we got this table to ourselves. Here's y' medicine for to-morrer."

"Wha'?"

"Reach under the table."

Gillis secured and pocketed the medicine.

"An' here's two-fifty for a good day's work." Uggam passed the money over. Perhaps he grew careless; certainly the passing this time was above the table, in plain sight.

"Thanks, Mouse."

Two white men had been watching Gillis and Uggam from a table near by. In the tumult of merriment that rewarded the entertainer's most recent and daring effort, one of these men, with a word to the other, came over and took the vacant chair beside Gillis.

"Is your name Gillis?"

"Tain' nuthin' else."

Uggam's eyes narrowed.

The white man showed King Solomon a police officer's badge.

"You're wanted for dope-peddling. Will you come along without trouble?"

6. From a popular blues song of the 1920s.

"Fo' what?"

"Violation of the narcotic law—dope-selling."

"Who—me?"

"Come on, now, lay off that stuff. I saw what happened just now myself." He addressed Uggam. "Do you know this fellow?"

"Nope. Never saw him before tonight."

"Didn't I just see him sell you something?"

"Guess you did. We happened to be sittin' here at the same table and got to talkin'. After a while I says I can't seem to sleep nights, so he offers me sump'n he says'll make me sleep, all right. I don't know what it is, but he says he uses it himself an' I offers to pay him what it cost him. That's how I come to take it. Guess he's got more in his pocket there now."

The detective reached deftly into the coat pocket of the dumbfounded King Solomon and withdrew a packet of envelopes. He tore off a corner of one, emptied a half-dozen tiny white tablets into his palm, and sneered triumphantly. "You'll make a good witness," he told Uggam.

The entertainer was issuing an ultimatum to all sweet mammas who dared to monkey around her loving man. Her audience was absorbed and delighted, with the exception of one couple—the girl with the green stockings and her escort. They sat directly in the line of vision of King Solomon's wide eyes, which, in the calamity that had descended upon him, for the moment saw nothing.

"Are you coming without trouble?"

Mouse Uggam, his friend. Harlem. Land of plenty. City of refuge—city of refuge. If you live long enough—

Consciousness of what was happening between the pair across the room suddenly broke through Gillis's daze like flame through smoke. The man was trying to kiss the girl and she was resisting. Gillis jumped up. The detective, taking the act for an attempt at escape, jumped with him and was quick enough to intercept him. The second officer came at once to his fellow's aid, blowing his whistle several times as he came.

People overturned chairs getting out of the way, but nobody ran for the door. It was an old crowd. A fight was a treat; and the tall Negro could fight.

"Judas Priest!"

"Did you see that?"

"Damn!"

White—both white. Five of Mose Joplin's horses. Poisoning a well. A year's crops. Green stockings—white—white—

"That's the time, papa!"

"Do it, big boy!"

"Good night!"

Uggam watched tensely, with one eye on the door. The second cop had blown for help—

Downing one of the detectives a third time and turning to grapple again with the other, Gillis found himself face to face with a uniformed black policeman.

He stopped as if stunned. For a moment he simply stared. Into his mind swept his own words like a forgotten song, suddenly recalled:—

"Cullud policemans!"

The officer stood ready, awaiting his rush.

"Even—got—cullud—policemans—"

Very slowly King Solomon's arms relaxed; very slowly he stood erect; and the grin that came over his features had something exultant about it.

1925

ERIC WALROND
1898–1966

Published by Boni and Liveright in 1926, *Tropic Death*, the debut collection of short stories by Eric Walrond, was one of the most dazzling accomplishments of the Harlem Renaissance as well as one of the first great works of Caribbean literature in English. Even if the movement saw the emergence of a number of talented writers of short fiction (Jean Toomer and Zora Neale Hurston foremost among them), Walrond's work was absolutely unique in style and mood, with a riveting gothic sensibility that lurched between lush impressionism and raw naturalism. The Jamaican Claude McKay was the other most important writer of Caribbean origin in the period, but McKay spent most of the period in Europe, and his first two novels were set in the United States and the south of France. It was Walrond's writing more than any other that foregrounded the Caribbean contours of the movement, both by drawing attention to the pivotal presence in Harlem of migrants from the islands and by exposing Harlem readers to vivid depictions of Black life elsewhere, especially in the Panama Canal Zone.

Born in Georgetown, British Guiana (now Guyana), to a Guyanese father and a Barbadian mother, Walrond was raised largely by his mother after his father migrated to Panama to find work. After a fire devastated Georgetown in 1905, Walrond's mother moved the family to Barbados. In 1911 they joined Walrond's father in Panama, which was then a country still in its infancy (having only declared independence from Colombia in 1903), literally riven from ocean to ocean by the U.S.-led project to dig what would in 1914 become the Panama Canal. Walrond's family was part of an enormous labor pool that gravitated to the Zone from various points in the Caribbean basin, and as a child he experienced first-hand the tumult of uprooted populations and poor migrant communities that settled in the volatile slums of Colón, at the eastern edge of the canal. Forced to seek employment after high school, Walrond worked as a reporter for the Panama *Star and Herald*, where, as he later recounted, he was assigned to write articles on a dizzying variety of topics: "brawls, murders, political scandals, voodoo rituals, labor confabs, campaigns, concerts, dramatic affairs, shipping intelligence, etc."

Walrond came to New York via Ellis Island in 1918, at the height of a period that saw a large influx of Caribbean migrants to Harlem. There he encountered what he later described as a "wide cleavage" between native-born African Americans and recent Caribbean immigrants, with mistrust and prejudice on both sides. As he explained in a 1927 article, the Caribbean migrant in New York often finds himself "bewildered—that is, if he is not 'clear' enough to pass as a Greek or Spaniard or Italian—at being shoved down certain blocks and alleys 'among his own people.' He is angry and amazed at the futility of seeking out certain types of employment for which he may be specially adapted." Despite his own experience and gifts as a writer, Walrond initially had trouble finding work as a journalist and took a variety of other jobs (as a secretary, elevator operator, switchboard operator, janitor, and dishwasher). He finally found a position in 1920 with the *Weekly Review*, a small newspaper run by Marcus Garvey. The following year he won first prize in the literary contest sponsored by the *Negro World*, Garvey's flagship periodical, and soon parlayed the prize into a position, working as an editorial assistant on the paper from December 1921 to April 1923. He wrote a range of material (editorials, reviews, and sketches) for the *Negro World*, but by late spring 1922 he was growing disillusioned with Garvey, whom he would characterize in print the following year as a "megalomaniac" and a "mental Lilliputian" prone to "preposterous mistakes" of strategy and organization. Even in 1922 he began to publish with an intriguing range of white-owned periodicals (the *Dearborn Independent, Current History*, the *International Interpreter*, the *New Republic*), and his first short stories appeared in fall 1923 in *Opportunity* and in H. L. Mencken's magazine *Smart Set*. He continued his studies at City College and Columbia University, but did not earn a degree. By the middle of the decade his genial personality and obvious talent made him a popular figure on the Harlem literary scene, and Alain Locke included his short story "The Palm Porch" in *The New Negro*. From 1925 to 1927 he worked as business manager for *Opportunity*.

Walrond's move away from the *Negro World* was in part a matter of artistic maturation, as he came to realize that he could not tolerate literature that was simply a vehicle of propaganda. Interestingly, the earliest hint of this position appeared in his December 1921 *Negro World* article "Art and Propaganda," which focuses on René Maran's *Batouala*. Walrond argued that in order to "create a lasting work of art," the American Negro needed to "first purge himself of the feelings and sufferings and emotions of an outraged being, and think and write along colorless sectionless lines." The "most potent form of literary expression," according to Walrond, was realism, "the form that brought Maran the Goncourt award." When the Black writer turns to realism, he added, "it is not going to be in any half-hearted, wishy washy manner, but straight from the shoulder, slashing, murdering, disemboweling!" It is no accident that Walrond became one of the masters of folk regionalism in Black fiction, able to capture the speech patterns and idioms of characters from numerous Caribbean islands; he believed that "it is important to reproduce accurately the nuances of Negro speech, for the impetus to present the Negro as he is and not as others fancy him to be was the seed from which the renaissance sprang."

The success of *Tropic Death* prompted Boni and Liveright to issue a second printing and to give Walrond a contract for *The Big Ditch*, a book he planned to write about the building of the Panama Canal. Walrond won a Harmon Award in Literature and Guggenheim Award to support his "travel and study in the West Indies for the purpose of obtaining material for a series of novels and short stories depicting native life there," and he left New York in the fall of 1928 to spend the next year and a half in Panama and traveling around the Caribbean. Except for a short visit to see his family in 1931, he never returned to the United States. He settled in France (where he shared an apartment at one point with Countee Cullen) and in 1932 moved to Wiltshire, England, where he lived the rest of his life in such obscurity that many of his Harlem friends assumed he had died. In two invaluable collections, *"Winds Can Wake Up the Dead": An Eric Walrond Reader* (1998) and *In Search of Asylum: The Later Writings of Eric Walrond* (2011), scholars Louis J. Parascandola and Carl A. Wade have shown that, in fact, Walrond wrote throughout his life, contributing articles to Marcus Garvey's London-based *Black Man* in the 1930s and to Adam Clayton Powell, Jr.'s *People's Voice* in the 1940s. For reasons that remain mysterious, Walrond was admitted to Roundway Hospital, a psychiatric institution in Wiltshire, as a voluntary patient in 1952. Even during the five years he spent there he published portions of his never-finished work on the Panama Canal in the *Roundway Review*.

Walrond produced an impressive body of sketches and essays; among other things, his writings provide the most sustained reflection on the Caribbean immigrant experience in Harlem of the 1920s. But *Tropic Death* remains his towering achievement due to its unity of tone and singular style. The ten stories in the book are set in various locales around the Caribbean: four in Barbados, one in British Guiana, one aboard a ship traveling from Honduras to Jamaica, three in the Canal Zone of Panama, and one (the loosely autobiographical title story) following a family migrating from Barbados to Panama. As the seemingly oxymoronic title implies, the tropics are portrayed not as a region of luxuriance and exotic abundance, but instead as a place of death, as the tales provide a gruesome compendium of lurid demise (by dagger, by the bite of a vampire bat, by shark attack, by smoke asphyxiation, by leprosy, by the gun of an American Marine). Throughout, Walrond's language is inimitable, spondaic, at once overripe and oblique, as when a lecherous British client of the whorehouse in "The Palm Porch" is described as "red-faced, red-eyed, red-haired. Yellow-teethed, dribbled-lipped, swobble-mouthed, bat-eared." The story "Drought" concludes with the stream-of-consciousness of a man horrified to learn that his young daughter has died of starvation: "It came to Coggins in swirls. Autopsy. Noise comes in swirls. Pounding, pounding—dry Indian corn pounding. Ginger. Ginger being pounded in a mortar with a bright, new pestle. Pound, pound. And. Sawing. Butcher shop. Cow foot is sawed that way. Stew—or tough hard steak. Then the drilling—drilling—drilling to a stone cutter's ears! Ox grizzle. Drilling into ox grizzle. . . ." Relentless and raw, *Tropic Death* documents the squalor and treachery, draped in an ambience of murky superstition, pointless suffering, and petty disputes, among volatile populations of African descent as they intermixed in the region.

The Wharf Rats

I

Among the motley crew recruited to dig the Panama Canal were artisans from the four ends of the earth. Down in the Cut[1] drifted hordes of Italians, Greeks, Chinese, Negroes—a hardy, sun-defying set of white, black and yellow men. But the bulk of the actual brawn for the work was supplied by the dusky peons of those coral isles in the Caribbean ruled by Britain, France and Holland.

At the Atlantic end of the Canal the blacks were herded in boxcar huts buried in the jungles of "Silver City";[2] in the murky tenements perilously poised on the narrow banks of Faulke's River, in the low, smelting cabins of Coco Té. The "Silver Quarters" harbored the inky ones, their wives and pickaninnies.

As it grew dark, the hewers at the Ditch, exhausted, half-asleep, naked but for wormy singlets, would hum queer creole tunes, play on guitar or piccolo, and jig to the rhythm of the *coombia*.[3] It was a *brujerial* chant, for *obeah*,[4] a heritage of the French colonial, honeycombed the life of the Negro laboring camps. Over smoking pots, on black, death-black nights legends of the bloodiest were recited till they became the essence of a sort of Negro Koran. One refuted them at the price of one's breath. And to question the verity of the *obeah*, to dismiss or reject it as the ungodly rite of some lurid, crack-brained Islander was to be an accursed pale-face, dog of a white. And the *obeah* man, in a fury of rage, would throw a machete at the heretic's head or—worse—burn on his doorstep at night a pyre of Maubé bark or green Ganja weed.

1. In other words, the open excavation of the canal.
2. A colloquial name for the city of Colón, Panama, at the eastern side of the Panama Canal.
3. Also known as *cumbia*, a form of music with West African and indigenous influences that developed in Colombia and became popular throughout Latin America.
4. A term used in the Caribbean to refer to religious practices and folk magic derived from West African traditions, especially Igbo traditions in Nigeria. "*Brujerial*": linked to popular sorcery or witchcraft (Spanish).

On the banks of a river beyond Cristobal, Coco Té sheltered a colony of Negroes enslaved to the *obeah*. Near a roundhouse, daubed with smoke and coal ash, a river serenely flowed away and into the guava region, at the eastern tip of Monkey Hill. Across the bay from it was a sand bank—a rising out of the sea—where ships stopt for coal.

In the first of the six chinky cabins making up the family quarters of Coco Té lived a stout, pot-bellied St. Lucian, black as the coal hills he mended, by the name of Jean Baptiste. Like a host of the native St. Lucian emigrants, Jean Baptiste forgot where the French in him ended and the English began. His speech was the petulant *patois* of the unlettered French black. Still, whenever he lapsed into His Majesty's English, it was with a thick Barbadian bias.

A coal passer at the Dry Dock, Jean Baptiste was a man of intense piety. After work, by the glow of a red, setting sun, he would discard his crusted overalls, get in starched *crocus bag*,[5] aping the Yankee foreman on the other side of the track in the "Gold Quarters," and loll on his coffee-vined porch. There, dozing in a bamboo rocker, Celestin, his second wife, a becomingly stout brown beauty from Martinique, chanted gospel hymns to him.

Three sturdy sons Jean Baptiste's first wife had borne him—Philip, the eldest, a good-looking black fellow; Ernest, shifty, cunning; and Sandel, aged eight. Another boy, said to be wayward and something of a ne'er-do-well, was sometimes spoken of. But Baptiste, a proud, disdainful man, never once referred to him in the presence of his children. No vagabond son of his could eat from his table or sit at his feet unless he went to "meeting." In brief, Jean Baptiste was a religious man. It was a thrust at the omnipresent *obeah*. He went to "meeting." He made the boys go, too. All hands went, not to the Catholic Church, where Celestin secretly worshiped, but to the English Plymouth Brethren[6] in the Spanish city of Colon.

Stalking about like a ghost in Jean Baptiste's household was a girl, a black ominous Trinidad girl. Had Jean Baptiste been a man given to curiosity about the nature of women, he would have viewed skeptically Maffi's adoption by Celestin. But Jean Baptiste was a man of lofty unconcern, and so Maffi remained there, shadowy, obdurate.

And Maffi was such a hardworking *patois* girl. From the break of day she'd be at the sink, brightening the tinware. It was she who did the chores which Madame congenitally shirked. And towards sundown, when the labor trains had emptied, it was she who scoured the beach for cockles for Jean Baptiste's epicurean palate.

And as night fell, Maffi, a long, black figure, would disappear in the dark to dream on top of a canoe hauled up on the mooning beach. An eternity Maffi'd sprawl there, gazing at the frosting of the stars and the glitter of the black sea.

A cabin away lived a family of Tortola[7] mulattoes by the name of Boyce. The father was also a man who piously went to "meeting"—gaunt and hollow-cheeked. The eldest boy, Esau, had been a journeyman tailor for ten years; the girl next him, Ora, was plump, dark, freckled; others came—a string of ulcered girls[8] until finally a pretty, opaque one, Maura.

5. A canvas bag or gunny sack.
6. A conservative Evangelical Christian movement that originated in Dublin, Ireland, in the 1820s.
7. The largest and most populous of the British Virgin Islands.
8. Most likely scarred by leprosy.

Of the Bantu tribe Maura would have been a person to turn and stare at. Crossing the line into Cristobal or Colon—a city of rarefied gayety—she was often mistaken for a native *señorita* or an urbanized Cholo[9] Indian girl. Her skin was the reddish yellow of old gold and in her eyes there lurked the glint of mother-of-pearl. Her hair, long as a jungle elf's was jettish, untethered. And her teeth were whiter than the full-blooded black Philip's.

Maura was brought up, like the children of Jean Baptiste, in the Plymouth Brethren. But the Plymouth Brethren was a harsh faith to bring hemmed-in peasant children up in, and Maura, besides, was of a gentle romantic nature. Going to the Yankee commissary at the bottom of Eleventh and Front Streets, she usually wore a leghorn hat.[1] With flowers bedecking it, she'd look in it older, much older than she really was. Which was an impression quite flattering to her. For Maura, unknown to Philip, was in love—in love with San Tie, a Chinese half-breed, son of a wealthy canteen proprietor in Colon. But San Tie liked to go fishing and deer hunting up the Monkey Hill lagoon, and the object of his occasional visits to Coco Té was the eldest son of Jean Baptiste. And thus it was through Philip that Maura kept in touch with the young Chinese Maroon.

One afternoon Maura, at her wit's end, flew to the shed roof to Jean Baptiste's kitchen.

"Maffi," she cried, the words smoky on her lips, "Maffi, when Philip come in to-night tell 'im I want fo' see 'im particular, yes?"

"*Sacre gache!*[2] All de time Philip, Philip!" growled the Trinidad girl, as Maura, in heartaching preoccupation, sped towards the lawn. "Why she no le' 'im alone, yes?" And with a spatter she flecked the hunk of lard on Jean Baptiste's stewing okras.

As the others filed up front after dinner that evening Maffi said to Philip, pointing to the cabin across the way, "She—she want fo' see yo'."

Instantly Philip's eyes widened. Ah, he had good news for Maura! San Tie, after an absence of six days, was coming to Coco Té Saturday to hunt on the lagoon. And he'd relish the joy that'd flood Maura's face as she glimpsed the idol of her heart, the hero of her dreams! And Philip, a true son of Jean Baptiste, loved to see others happy, ecstatic.

But Maffi's curious rumination checked him. "All de time, Maura, Maura, me can't understand it, yes. But no mind, me go stop it, *oui*, me go stop it, so help me—"

He crept up to her, gently holding her by the shoulders.

"Le' me go, *sacre!*" She shook off his hands bitterly. "Le' me go—yo' go to yo' Maura." And she fled the room, locking the door behind her.

Philip sighed. He was a generous, good-natured sort. But it was silly to try to enlighten Maffi. It wasn't any use. He could as well have spoken to the tattered torsos the lazy waves puffed up on the shores of Coco Té.

II

"Philip, come on, a ship is in—let's go." Ernest, the wharf rat, seized him by the arm.

"Come," he said, "let's go before it's too late. I want to get some money, yes."

9. A derogatory term for persons of mixed Spanish and Amerindian parentage (Spanish).
1. A hat made from the dried and bleached straw of an Italian variety of wheat.
2. A French oath.

Dashing out of the house the two boys made for the wharf. It was dusk. Already the Hindus in the bachelor quarters were mixing their *rotie*[3] and the Negroes in their singlets were smoking and cooling off. Night was rapidly approaching. Sunset, an iridescent bit of molten gold, was enriching the stream with its last faint radiance.

The boys stole across the lawn and made their way to the pier.

"Careful," cried Philip, as Ernest slid between a prong of oyster-crusted piles to a raft below, "careful, these shells cut wussah'n a knife."

On the raft the boys untied a rowboat they kept stowed away under the dock, got into it and pushed off. The liner still had two hours to dock. Tourists crowded its decks. Veering away from the barnacled piles the boys eased out into the churning ocean.

It was dusk. Night would soon be upon them. Philip took the oars while Ernest stripped down to loin cloth.

"Come, Philip, let me paddle—" Ernest took the oars. Afar on the dusky sea a whistle echoed. It was the pilot's signal to the captain of port. The ship would soon dock.

The passengers on deck glimpsed the boys. It piqued their curiosity to see two black boys in a boat amid stream.

"All right, mistah," cried Ernest, "a penny, mistah."

He sprang at the guilder as it twisted and turned through a streak of silver dust to the bottom of the sea. Only the tips of his crimson toes—a sherbet-like foam—and up he came with the coin between his teeth.

Deep sea gamin,[4] Philip off yonder, his mouth noisy with coppers, gargled, "This way, sah, as far as yo' like, mistah."

An old red-bearded Scot, in spats and mufti, presumably a lover of the exotic in sport, held aloft a sovereign.[5] A sovereign! Already red, and sore by virtue of the leaps and plunges in the briny swirl, Philip's eyes bulged at its yellow gleam.

"Ovah yah, sah—"

Off in a whirlpool the man tossed it. And like a garfish Philip took after it, a falling arrow in the stream. His body, once in the water, tore ahead. For a spell the crowd on the ship held its breath. "Where is he?" "Where is the nigger swimmer gone to?" Even Ernest, driven to the boat by the race for such an ornate prize, cold, shivering, his teeth chattering—even he watched with trembling and anxiety. But Ernest's concern was of a deeper kind. For there, where Philip had leaped, was Deathpool—a spawning place for sharks, for baracoudas!

But Philip rose—a brief gurgling sputter—a ripple on the sea—and the Negro's crinkled head was above the water.

"Hey!" shouted Ernest, "there, Philip! Down!"

And down Philip plunged. One—two—minutes. God, how long they seemed! And Ernest anxiously waited. But the bubble on the water boiled, kept on boiling—a sign that life still lasted! It comforted Ernest.

Suddenly Philip, panting, spitting, pawing, dashed through the water like a streak of lightning.

"Shark!" cried a voice aboard ship, "Shark! There he is, a great big one! Run, boy! Run for your life!"

3. Or *roti*, from the Sanskrit for "bread"; a South Asian unleavened bread made from stoneground wholemeal flour.

4. A young child; urchin (French).

5. A British gold coin with a value of one pound sterling.

From the edge of the boat Philip saw the monster as twice, thrice it circled the boat. Several times the shark made a dash for it endeavoring to strike it with its murderous tail.

The boys quickly made off. But the shark still followed the boat. It was a pale green monster. In the glittering dusk it seemed black to Philip. Fattened on the swill of the abattoir[6] nearby and the beef tossed from the decks of countless ships in port it had become used to the taste of flesh and the smell of blood.

"Yo' know, Ernest," said Philip, as he made the boat fast to a raft, "one time I thought he wuz rubbin' 'gainst me belly. He wuz such a big able one. But it wuz wuth it, Ernie, it wuz wuth it—"

In his palm there was a flicker of gold. Ernest emptied his loin cloth and together they counted the money, dressed, and trudged back to the cabin.

On the lawn Philip met Maura. Ernest tipped his cap, left his brother, and went into the house. As he entered Maffi, pretending to be scouring a pan, was flushed and mute as a statue. And Ernest, starved, went in the dining room and for a long time stayed there. Unable to bear it any longer, Maffi sang out, "Ernest, whey Philip dey?"

"Outside—some whey—ah talk to Maura—"

"Yo' sure yo' no lie, Ernest?" she asked, suspended.

"Yes, up cose, I jes' lef' 'im 'tandin' out dey—why?"

"Nutton—"

He suspected nothing. He went on eating while Maffi tiptoed to the shed roof. Yes, confound it, there he was, near the stand-pipe,[7] talking to Maura!

"Go stop *ee, oui*," she hissed impishly. "Go 'top ee, yes."

III

Low, shadowy, the sky painted Maura's face bronze. The sea, noisy, enraged, sent a blob of wind about her black, wavy hair. And with her back to the sea, her hair blew loosely about her face.

"D'ye think, d'ye think he really likes me, Philip?"

"I'm positive he do, Maura," vowed the youth.

And an ageing faith shone in Maura's eyes. No longer was she a silly, insipid girl. Something holy, reverent had touched her. And in so doing it could not fail to leave an impress of beauty. It was worshipful. And it mellowed, ripened her.

Weeks she had waited for word of San Tie. And the springs of Maura's life took on a noble ecstasy. Late at night, after the others had retired, she'd sit up in bed, dreaming. Sometimes they were dreams of envy. For Maura began to look with eyes of comparison upon the happiness of the Italian wife of the boss riveter at the Dry Dock—the lady on the other side of the railroad tracks in the "Gold Quarters" for whom she sewed—who got a fresh baby every year and who danced in a world of silks and satins. Yes, Maura had dreams, love dreams of San Tie, the flashy half-breed, son of a Chinese beer seller and a Jamaica Maroon, who had swept her off her feet by a playful wink of the eye.

"Tell me, Philip, does he work? or does he play the lottery—what does he do, tell me!"

6. Slaughterhouse.
7. A freestanding pipe fitted with a tap, installed along a road as a water source for an area without a running supply to buildings.

"I dunno," Philip replied with mock lassitude, "I dunno myself—"

"But it doesn't matter, Philip. I don't want to be nosy, see? I'm simply curious about everything that concerns him, see?"

Ah, but Philip wished to cherish Maura, to shield her, be kind to her. And so he lied to her. He did not tell her he had first met San Tie behind the counter of his father's saloon in the Colon tenderloin, for he would have had to tell, besides, why he, Philip, had gone there. And that would have led him, a youth of meager guile, to Celestin Baptiste's mulish regard for anisette which he procured her. He dared not tell her, well-meaning fellow that he was, what San Tie, a fiery comet in the night life of the district, had said to him the day before. "She sick in de head, yes," he had said. "Ah, me no dat saht o' man—don't she no bettah, egh, Philip?" But Philip desired to be kindly, and hid it from Maura.

"What is it to-day?" she cogitated, aloud, "Tuesday. You say he's comin' fo' hunt Saturday, Philip? Wednesday—four more days. I can wait. I can wait. I'd wait a million years fo' 'im, Philip."

But Saturday came and Maura, very properly, was shy as a duck. Other girls, like Hilda Long, a Jamaica brunette, the flower of a bawdy cabin up by the abattoir, would have been less genteel. Hilda would have caught San Tie by the lapels of his coat and in no time would have got him told.

But Maura was lowly, trepid, shy. To her he was a dream—a luxury to be distantly enjoyed. He was not to be touched. And she'd wait till he decided to come to her. And there was no fear, either, of his failing to come. Philip had seen to that. Had not he been the intermediary between them? And all Maura needed now was to sit back, and wait till San Tie came to her.

And besides, who knows, brooded Maura, San Tie might be a bashful fellow.

But when, after an exciting hunt, the Chinese mulatto returned from the lagoon, nodded stiffly to her, said good-by to Philip and kept on to the scarlet city, Maura was frantic.

"Maffi," she said, "tell Philip to come here quick—"

It was the same as touching a match to the *patois* girl's dynamite. "Yo' mek me sick," she said. "Go call he yo'self, yo' ole hag, yo' ole fire hag[8] yo.'" But Maura, flighty in despair, had gone on past the lawn.

"Ah go stop *ee, oui*," she muttered diabolically, "Ah go stop it, yes. This very night."

Soon as she got through lathering the dishes she tidied up and came out on the front porch.

It was a humid dusk, and the glowering sky sent a species of fly—bloody as a tick—buzzing about Jean Baptiste's porch. There he sat, rotund, and sleepy-eyed, rocking and languidly brushing the darting imps away.

"Wha' yo' gwine, Maffi?" asked Celestin Baptiste, fearing to wake the old man.

"Ovah to de Jahn Chinaman shop, mum," answered Maffi unheeding.

"Fi' what?"

"Fi' buy some wash blue, mum."

And she kept on down the road past the Hindu kiosk to the Negro mess house.

8. In folklore, an old woman who sheds her skin at night and becomes a ball of fire.

IV

"Oh, Philip," cried Maura, "I am so unhappy. Didn't he ask about me at all? Didn't he say he'd like to visit me—didn't he giv' yo' any message fo' me, Philip?"

The boy toyed with a blade of grass. His eyes were downcast. Sighing heavily he at last spoke. "No, Maura, he didn't ask about you."

"What, he didn't ask about me? Philip? I don't believe it! Oh, my God!"

She clung to Philip, mutely; her face, her breath coming warm and fast.

"I wish to God I'd never seen either of you," cried Philip.

"Ah, but wasn't he your friend, Philip? Didn't yo' tell me that?" And the boy bowed his head sadly.

"Answer me!" she screamed, shaking him. "Weren't you his friend?"

"Yes, Maura—"

"But you lied to me Philip, you lied to me! You took messages from me—you brought back—lies!" Two *pearls*, large as pigeon's eggs, shone in Maura's burnished face.

"To think," she cried in a hollow sepulchral voice, "that I dreamed about a ghost, a man who didn't exist. Oh, God, why should I suffer like this? Why was I ever born? What did I do, what did my people do, to deserve such misery as this?"

She rose, leaving Philip with his head buried in his hands. She went into the night, tearing her hair, scratching her face, raving.

"Oh, how happy I was! I was a happy girl! I was so young and I had such merry dreams! And I wanted so little! I was carefree—"

Down to the shore of the sea she staggered, the wind behind her, the night obscuring her.

"Maura!" cried Philip, running after her. "Maura! come back!"

Great sheaves of clouds buried the moon, and the wind bearing up from the sea bowed the cypress and palm lining the beach.

"Maura—Maura—"

He bumped into some one, a girl, black, part of the dense pattern of the tropical night.

"Maffi," cried Philip, "have you seen Maura down yondah?"

The girl quietly stared at him. Had Philip lost his mind?

"Talk, no!" he cried, exasperated.

And his quick tones sharpened Maffi's vocal anger. Thrusting him aside, she thundered, "Think I'm she keeper! Go'n look fo' she yo'self. I is not she keeper! Le' me pass, move!"

Towards the end of the track he found Maura, heartrendingly weeping.

"Oh, don't cry, Maura! Never mind, Maura!"

He helped her to her feet, took her to the stand-pipe on the lawn, bathed her temples and sat soothingly, uninterruptingly, beside her.

V

At daybreak the next morning Ernest rose and woke Philip.

He yawned, put on the loin cloth, seized a "cracked licker" skillet[9] and stole cautiously out of the house. Of late Jean Baptiste had put his foot down on his sons' copper-diving proclivities. And he kept at the head of his

9. A frying pan used in processing cane.

bed a greased cat-o-nine-tails which he would use on Philip himself if the occasion warranted.

"Come on, Philip, let's go—"

Yawning and scratching Philip followed. The grass on the lawn was bright and icy with the dew. On the railroad tracks the six o'clock labor trains were coupling. A rosy mist flooded the dawn. Out in the stream the tug *Exotic* snorted in a heavy fog.

On the wharf Philip led the way to the rafters below.

"Look out fo' that *crapeau*,[1] Ernest, don't step on him, he'll spit on you."

The frog splashed into the water. Prickle-backed crabs and oysters and myriad other shells spawned on the rotting piles. The boys paddled the boat. Out in the dawn ahead of them the tug puffed a path through the foggy mist. The water was chilly. Mist glistened on top of it. Far out, beyond the buoys, Philip encountered a placid, untroubled sea. The liner, a German tourist boat, was loaded to the bridge. The water was as still as a lake of ice.

"All right, Ernest, let's hurry—"

Philip drew in the oars. The *Kron Prinz Wilhelm* came near. Huddled in thick European coats, the passengers viewed from their lofty estate the spectacle of two naked Negro boys peeping up at them from a wiggly *bateau*.[2]

"Penny, mistah, penny, mistah!"

Somebody dropped a quarter. Ernest, like a shot, flew after it. Half a foot down he caught it as it twisted and turned in the gleaming sea. Vivified by the icy dip, Ernest was a raving wolf and the folk aboard dealt a lavish hand.

"Ovah, yah, mistah," cried Philip, "ovah, yah."

For a Dutch guilder Philip gave an exhibition of "cork." Under something of a ledge on the side of the boat he had stuck a piece of cork. Now, after his and Ernest's mouths were full of coins, he could afford to be extravagant and treat the Europeans to a game of West Indian "cork."

Roughly ramming the cork down in the water, Philip, after the fifteenth ram or so, let it go, and flew back, upwards, having thus "lost" it. It was Ernest's turn now, as a sort of end-man, to scramble forward to the spot where Philip had dug it down and "find" it; the first one to do so, having the prerogative, which he jealously guarded, of raining on the other a series of thundering leg blows. As boys in the West Indies Philip and Ernest had played it. Of a Sunday the Negro fishermen on the Barbadoes coast made a pagan rite of it. Many a Bluetown dandy got his spine cracked in a game of "cork."

With a passive interest the passengers viewed the proceedings. In a game of "cork," the cork after a succession of "rammings" is likely to drift many feet away whence it was first "lost." One had to be an expert, quick, alert, to spy and promptly seize it as it popped up on the rolling waves. Once Ernest got it and endeavored to make much of the possession. But Philip, besides being two feet taller than he, was slippery as an eel, and Ernest, despite all the artful ingenuity at his command, was able to do no more than ineffectively beat the water about him. Again and again he tried, but to no purpose.

Becoming reckless, he let the cork drift too far away from him and Philip seized it.

He twirled it in the air like a crap shooter, and dug deep down in the water with it, "lost" it, then leaped back, briskly waiting for it to rise.

1. A poisonous toad; derived from the French *crapaud* (Creole).

2. Skiff; flat-bottomed boat (French).

About them the water, due to the ramming and beating, grew restive. Billows sprang up; soaring, swelling waves sent the skiff nearer the shore. Anxiously Philip and Ernest watched for the cork to make its ascent.

It was all a bit vague to the whites on the deck, and an amused chuckle floated down to the boys.

And still the cork failed to come up.

"I'll go after it," said Philip at last, "I'll go and fetch it." And, from the edge of the boat he leaped, his body long and resplendent in the rising tropic sun.

It was a suction sea, and down in it Philip plunged. And it was lazy, too, and willful—the water. Ebony-black, it tugged and mocked. Old brass staves—junk dumped there by the retiring French—thick, yawping mud, barrel hoops, tons of obsolete brass, a wealth of slimy steel faced him. Did a "rammed" cork ever go that deep?

And the water, stirring, rising, drew a haze over Philip's eyes. Had a cuttlefish, an octopus, a nest of eels been routed? It seemed so to Philip, blindly diving, pawing. And the sea, the tide—touching the roots of Deathpool—tugged and tugged. His gathering hands stuck in mud. Iron staves bruised his shins. It was black down there. Impenetrable.

Suddenly, like a flash of lightning, a vision blew across Philip's brow. It was a soaring shark's belly. Drunk on the nectar of the deep, it soared above Philip—rolling, tumbling, rolling. It had followed the boy's scent with the accuracy of a diver's rope.

Scrambling to the surface, Philip struck out for the boat. But the sea, the depths of it wrested out of an æon's slumber, had sent it a mile from his diving point. And now, as his strength ebbed, a shark was at his heels.

"Shark! Shark!" was the cry that went up from the ship.

Hewing a lane through the hostile sea Philip forgot the cunning of the doddering beast and swam noisier than he needed to. Faster grew his strokes. His line was a straight, dead one. Fancy strokes and dives—giraffe leaps . . . he summoned into play. He shot out recklessly. One time he suddenly paused—and floated for a stretch. Another time he swam on his back, gazing at the chalky sky. He dived for whole lengths.

But the shark, a bloaty, stone-colored mankiller, took a shorter cut. Circumnavigating the swimmer it bore down upon him with the speed of a hurricane. Within adequate reach it turned, showed its gleaming belly, seizing its prey.

A fiendish gargle—the gnashing of bones—as the sea once more closed its jaws on Philip.

Someone aboard ship screamed. Women fainted. There was talk of a gun. Ernest, an oar upraised, capsized the boat as he tried to inflict a blow on the coursing, chop-licking maneater.

And again the fish turned. It scraped the waters with its deadly fins.

At Coco Té at the fledging of the dawn, Maffi, polishing the tinware, hummed an *obeah* melody

> Trinidad is a damn fine place
> But *obeah* down dey. . . .

Peace had come to her at last.

1926

PAUL ROBESON
1898–1976

One of the most remarkable American personalities of the mid-twentieth century, Paul Robeson was renowned for his accomplishments across a range of fields: he was a star athlete and riveting orator as well as a brilliant stage actor and singer, graced with a powerful physique and a rich bass-baritone voice. He was among the most beloved of performers, but even as his fame crested around the world Robeson came to be feared and reviled in the United States due to his outspoken politics, and was largely forgotten or dismissed by the time he died. Nevertheless his impact in his time was almost unparalleled; as the actor Ossie Davis put it in the 1970s, Robeson was "a man and a half, and we have no category, even now, to hold the size of him."

Robeson's mother perished in a household fire when he was six, and he and his siblings were raised in New Jersey by their father, an ordained minister who had been born into slavery. One of the few Blacks to attend Somerville High School, Robeson showed early signs of his immense talents, and as a senior placed first in a statewide competitive exam for a scholarship to Rutgers College. Despite facing prejudice in college, Robeson excelled in his studies, and was twice named an all-American in football. After graduation in 1919, he briefly played professional football while attending law school at New York University and then Columbia University, where he met and married Eslanda Goode, a chemist who became head histological chemist in the pathology department at New York Presbyterian Hospital. In June 1920, with her encouragement, he made his acting debut in the title role in a revival of Ridgely Torrence's *Simon the Cyrenian* at the Harlem YMCA. Even before he graduated from law school in 1923, Robeson began to find success as an actor, starring in a production of Mary Hoyt Wiborg's *Taboo* that traveled to England. Discouraged by the racism he encountered working as an estate lawyer, Robeson decided to concentrate on his theatrical career, and later in 1923 he gained attention for his lead performances in two plays by Eugene O'Neill: *All God's Chillun Got Wings* (which was controversial due to its depiction of an interracial relationship) and a revival of *The Emperor Jones*, in the title role that had been originally performed in 1920 by the legendary Charles Gilpin. Robeson also made his film debut in Oscar Micheaux's silent "race film" *Body and Soul* (1924).

In the spring of 1925, Robeson began rehearsing classic spirituals like "Go Down, Moses," "Joshua Fit de Battle of Jericho," and "Steal Away" with the pianist Lawrence Brown. Carl Van Vechten helped arrange a public performance for the duo in April at the Greenwich Village theater of the Provincetown Players, and Harlem figures including James Weldon Johnson and Walter White joined a capacity audience to see a performance that one reviewer described as "the embodiment of the aspirations of the New Negro." Although he was not the only singer who performed concerts of spirituals (others included Roland Hayes, Jules Bledsoe, and Taylor Gordon), Robeson was widely praised for the emotional depth and unpretentious delivery of his performances. The Victor Company offered Robeson and Brown an exclusive recording contract, and soon thereafter Robeson became a major star of musicals on both sides of the Atlantic: the 1928 London production of *Show Boat* by Jerome Kern and Oscar Hammerstein II was hugely successful due in no small part to Robeson's rendition of "Ol' Man River."

By the end of the decade the Robesons had settled in England, where they remained until the eve of World War II. By the mid-1930s, Robeson was an international movie star, having appeared in American productions such as *The Emperor Jones* (1933) as well as a series of British films such as *Sanders of the River* (1935), *King Solomon's Mines* (1937), and *The Proud Valley* (1940). Robeson underwent a political awakening during this period, traveling in 1934 to the Soviet Union (at the invitation of director Sergei Eisenstein), where he was impressed by what he considered to be a lack of racial prejudice. In London he took on the title part in *Toussaint Louverture* (1936), a play about the Haitian Revolution by the Trinidadian writer and activist C. L. R. James, who was startled by the "great gentleness" as well as the "great command" of Robeson's physical presence: "the moment he came onto the stage," James commented later, "the whole damn thing changed."

Robeson became deeply involved in efforts to support the anti-fascist struggle in the Spanish Civil War, declaring that "the artist must take sides. He must elect to fight for freedom or slavery. I have made my choice. I had no alternative." The following year, he co-founded and served as chairman of the Council on African Affairs, which strove to develop solidarity between African Americans and colonized peoples in Africa and Asia. To Robeson such political links were only logical, for he believed that "the Negro—and I mean American Negroes as well as West Indians and Africans—has a direct and first-hand understanding, which most other people lack, of what imperialist exploitation and oppression is. With him, it is no far-off theoretical problem. In his daily life he experiences the same system of job discrimination, segregation and denial of democratic rights whereby the imperialist overlords keep hundreds of millions of people in colonial subjection throughout the world."

Robeson's popularity peaked during World War II, especially after CBS Radio broadcast his stirring performance of John LaTouche and Earl Robinson's patriotic song "Ballad for Americans" in the fall of 1939. Four years later, Robeson played the title role in *Othello*, the first time an African American had played the lead with a white supporting cast on Broadway, in what became the longest-running Shakespeare production ever. But in the tense atmosphere of the Cold War, Robeson's unflinching criticism of racism and segregation in the United States and his vocal praise of the Soviet Union made him an increasingly controversial figure. In 1947 the city council of Peoria, Illinois, voted not to allow Robeson to use any public gathering place for an upcoming concert because of his "un-American" beliefs, and he was subsequently banned at other locations around the country. In 1949, after it was inaccurately reported that Robeson said in a speech that it was "unthinkable" that African Americans would ever go to war against the Soviet Union, violent protests forced the cancellation of an outdoor concert in Peekskill, New York. In 1950 the U.S. government refused to give Robeson a passport to travel, and over the next eight years he was a pariah in his own country, denied access to the stage as well as to radio, television, and recording studios. Although he embarked on a world comeback tour in 1958 as soon as he was allowed to travel, he never achieved the same success, and persistent health concerns forced him to spend much of the rest of his life after 1963 in seclusion at home in New York and Philadelphia.

In the period of the Harlem Renaissance, Robeson was primarily known as an actor and a singer, but struck a prominent figure in the Harlem social scene and also published essays in periodicals such as the *Messenger* and *Opportunity*. However, his most important writings are his essays from the mid-1930s in England when, convinced that others had neglected the depth and complexity of African culture, he set himself a serious program of study. Originally intending to pursue a Ph.D. in philology, Robeson enrolled at the School of Oriental Languages in London, where he took courses in African languages including Swahili, Zulu, Mende, Ashanti, Ewe, and Hausa. Aside from the moving essay "I Want to Be African," where he makes a case that peoples of African descent around the world share a common "sense of rhythm," his major statement emerging from these studies is the 1934 *Spectator* article "The Culture of the Negro," in which Robeson wrote that the spirituals "are to negro culture what the works of the great poets are to English culture: they are the soul of the race made manifest." A number of years before the *Négritude* poet Léopold Sédar Senghor began to make similar arguments, Robeson contended that "the white man has made a fetish of intellect and worships the God of thought; the negro feels rather than thinks, experiences emotions directly rather than interprets them by roundabout and devious abstractions, and apprehends the outside world by means of intuitive perception instead of through a carefully built up system of logical analysis." For the rest of his life, Robeson remained determined to acknowledge what he considered to be the African cultural inheritance that underlay his artistry.

I Want to Be African

I am a Negro. The origin of the Negro is African. It would therefore seem an easy matter for me to assume African nationality.

Instead it is an extremely complicated matter, fraught with the gravest importance to me and some millions of coloured folk.

Africa is a Dark Continent not merely because its people are dark-skinned or by reason of its extreme impenetrability, but because its history is lost. We have an amazingly vivid reconstruction of the culture of ancient Egypt, but the roots of almost the whole remainder of Africa are buried in antiquity.

They are, however, rediscoverable; and they will in time be rediscovered.

I am confirmed in this faith by recent researches linking the *culture* of the Negro with that of many peoples of the East.

Let us consider for a moment the problem of my people—the African Negroes in the Occident, and particularly in America.

We are now fourteen millions strong—though perhaps "strong" is not the apt word; for nearly two and a half centuries we were in chains, and although to-day we are technically free and officially labelled "American Citizen," we are at a great economic disadvantage, most trades and many professions being practically barred to us and social barriers inexorably raised.

Consequently the American Negro in general suffers from an acute inferiority complex; it has been drummed into him that the white man is the Salt of the Earth and the Lord of Creation, and as a perfectly natural result his ambition is to become as nearly like a white man as possible.

He is that tragic creature, a man without a nationality. He claims to be American, to be British, to be French—but you cannot assume a nationality as you would a new suit of clothes.

In the country of his adoption, or the country that ruthlessly adopted his forebears, he is an alien; but (herein lies his tragedy) he believes himself to have broken away from his true origins; he has, he argues, nothing whatever in common with the inhabitant of Africa to-day—and that is where I believe he is wrong.

It may be asked "Why disturb him if he is happy in his present state?"

There are two sufficient answers to that; one that he is *not* happy, except in so far as his natural gaiety of disposition overcomes his circumstances—and the fact that a sick man laughs is surely no reason for not attempting to cure his sickness; and the other is that there is a world-necessity above and beyond his immediate needs.

This world-necessity is for an understanding between the nations and peoples which will lead ultimately to the "family of nations" ideal.

To this world-community every nation will contribute whatever it has of culture; and unless the African Negro (including his far-flung collaterals) bestirs himself and comes to a realization of his potentialities and obligations there will be no culture for him to contribute.

At present the younger generation of Negroes in America looks towards Africa and asks "What is there *there* to interest me? What of value has Africa to offer that the Western world cannot give me?"

At first glance the question seems unanswerable. He sees only the savagery, devil-worship, witchdoctors, voo-doo, ignorance, squalor, and darkness taught in American schools.

Where these exist, he is looking at the broken remnants of what was in its day a mighty thing; something which perhaps has not been destroyed, but only driven underground, leaving ugly scars upon the earth's surface to mark the place of its ultimate reappearance.

We know that in China there was a great and mighty culture—mighty in the sense not of pomp but of potency. An exiled Chinese to-day, at University in Manchester or Birmingham, might look towards China and ask the self-same question—"What has that chaos of conflicting misgovernments and household gods and superstitions to offer me?"—but we know enough of history to be aware that great cultures do not completely die, but are soil for future growths.

That portion of China that is only Buddhist is negligible, the publicized part, the unscratched surface; below are the vast depths of spirituality of which Taoism[1] in its present-day form is the broken relic.

Somewhere, sometime—perhaps at the Renaissance, but I think much earlier—a great part of Religion went astray. A blind groping after Rationality resulted in an incalculable loss in pure Spirituality. Mankind placed a sudden dependence on that part of his mind that was brain, intellect, to the discountenance of that part that was sheer evolved instinct and intuition; we grasped at the shadow and lost the substance . . . and now we are not even altogether clear what the substance was.

Now the pendulum is swinging back. Preaching in London not long ago, Father Bede Frost[2] is reported to have said:

> The epoch that began at the end of the sixteenth century is now ending. You can see the tiles fall from the roof, the walls beginning to crack. . . .
>
> During that epoch men's minds have been influenced by three dogmas:
>
> The perfectability of man in himself,
> The inevitability of progress towards a golden age,
> The infallibility of physical science.

Mankind is gradually feeling its way back to a more fundamental, more primitive, but perhaps truer religion; and religion, the orientation of man to God or forces greater than himself, must be the basis of all culture.

This religion, this basic culture, has its roots in the Far East, *and in Africa*.

What links the American Negro to this culture? It would take a psycho-anthropologist to give it a name; but its nature is obvious to any earnest inquirer.

1. Ancient Chinese religious tradition that emphasizes harmony with the energy or "way" (*tao* or *dao*) of the universe.

2. English writer, missionary, and Anglican priest (1875–1961).

Its manifestation occurs in his forms of religion and of art. It has recently been demonstrated beyond a possibility of doubt that the dances, the songs, and the worship perpetuated by the Negro in America are identical with those of his cousins hundreds of years removed in the depths of Africa, whom he has never seen, of whose very existence he is only dimly aware.

His peculiar sense of rhythm alone would stamp him indelibly as African; and a slight variation of this same rhythm-consciousness is to be found among the Tartars and Chinese, to whom he is much more nearly akin than he is to the Arab, for example.

Not long ago I learned to speak Russian, since, the Russians being so closely allied through the Tartars to the Chinese, I expected to find myself more in sympathy with that language than with English, French, or German. I was not disappointed; I found that there were Negro concepts which I could express much more readily in Russian than in other languages.

I would rather sing Russian folk-songs than German grand opera—not because it is necessarily better music, but because it is more *instinctive* and less *reasoned* music. It is in my blood.

The pressing need of the American Negro is an ability to set his own standards. At school, at university, at law school, it didn't matter to me whether white students passed me or I passed them. What mattered was, if I got 85 marks, *why didn't I get* 100? If I got 99, *why didn't I get* 100? "To thine own self be true" is a sentiment sneered at to-day as merely Victorian—but upon its observance may well depend the future of nations and peoples.

It is of course useful and even necessary from an economic and social standpoint for the Negro to *understand* Western ideas and culture, for he will gain nothing by further isolating himself; and I would emphasize that his mere physical return to his place of origin is not the essential condition of his regeneration. In illustration of this take the parallel case of the Jews.

They, like a vast proportion of Negroes, are a race without a nation; but, far from Palestine, they are indissolubly bound by their ancient religious practices—*which they recognize as such.* I emphasize this in contradistinction to the religious practices of the American Negro, which, from the snake-worship practised in the deep South to the Christianity of the revival meeting, are patently survivals of the earliest African religions; *and he does not recognize them as such.*

Their acknowledgment of their common origin, species, interest, and attitudes binds Jew to Jew; a similar acknowledgment will bind Negro and Negro.

I realize that this will never be accomplished by viewing from afar the dark rites of the witch-doctor—a phenomenon as far divorced from fundamental reality as are the petty bickerings over altar decorations and details of vestment from the intention of Christ.

It may be accomplished, or at least furthered, by patient inquiry. To this end I am learning Swahili, Tivi,[3] and other African dialects—which come easily to me *because their rhythm is the same as that employed by the American Negro in speaking English;* and when the time is ripe I propose to investigate, on the spot, the possibilities of such a regeneration as I have outlined.

3. A language of the Niger-Congo family, spoken in northern Nigeria.

Meanwhile in my music, my plays, my films I want to carry always this central idea: to be African.

Multitudes of men have died for less worthy ideals; it is even more eminently worth living for.

1934

The Culture of the Negro

Critics have often reproached me for not becoming an opera star and never attempting to give recitals of German and Italian songs as every accomplished singer is supposed to do. I am not an artist in the sense in which they want me to be an artist and of which they could approve. I have no desire to interpret the vocal genius of half a dozen cultures which are really alien to me. I have a far more important task to perform.

When I first suggested singing negro spirituals for English audiences a few years ago, I was laughed at. How could these utterly simple, indeed, almost savage songs interest the most sophisticated audience in the world? I was asked. And yet I have found response amongst this very audience to the simple, direct emotional appeal of negro spirituals. These songs are to negro culture what the works of the great poets are to English culture: they are the soul of the race made manifest. No matter in what part of the world you may find him the negro has retained his direct emotional response to outside stimuli; he is constantly aware of an external power which guides his destiny. The white man has made a fetish of intellect and worships the God of thought; the negro feels rather than thinks, experiences emotions directly rather than interprets them by roundabout and devious abstractions, and apprehends the outside world by means of intuitive perception instead of through a carefully built up system of logical analysis. No wonder that the negro is an intensely religious creature and that his artistic and cultural capacities find expression in the glorification of some deity in song. It does not matter who the deity is. The American and West Indian negro worships the Christian God in his own particular way and makes him the object of his supreme artistic manifestation which is embodied in the negro spiritual. But, what of the African negro? What is the object of his strong religious sense, and how does his artistic spirit manifest itself? These are the questions I have set myself to answer.

As a first step I went to the London School of Oriental Languages and, quite haphazardly, began by studying the East Coast languages, Swahili and the Bantu group which forms a sort of Lingua Franca[1] of the East Coast of Africa. I found in these languages a pure negro foundation, dating from an ancient culture, but intermingled with many Arabic and Hamitic[2] impurities. From them I passed on to the West Coast Negro languages and immediately found a kinship of rhythm and intonation with the negro-English dialect which I had heard spoken around me as a child. It was to

1. Language used between people with differing primary languages.

2. "Hamites" was the name formerly used for some North African peoples.

me like a homecoming, and I felt that I had penetrated to the core of African culture when I began to study the legendary traditions, folksong and folklore of the West African negro. I hope to be able to interpret this original and unpolluted negro folksong to the Western world, and I am convinced that there lies a wealth of uncharted musical material in that source which I hope, one day, will evoke the response in English and American audiences which my negro spirituals have done; but for me this is only one aspect of my discovery.

Culturally speaking, the African negro, as well as his American and West Indian brothers, stands at the parting of the ways. The day is past when they were regarded as something less than human and little more than mere savages by the white man. Racial tolerance and political equality of status have taken the place of oppression and slavery for the greater part of the negro race. But the sufferings he has undergone have left an indelible mark on the negro's soul, and at the present stage he suffers from an inferiority complex which finds its compensation in a desire to imitate the white man and his ways; but I am convinced that in this direction there is neither fulfilment nor peace for the negro. He is too radically different from the white man in his mental and emotional structure ever to be more than a spurious and uneasy imitation of him, if he persists in following this direction. His soul contains riches which can come to fruition only if he retains intact the full spate of his emotional awareness and uses unswervingly the artistic endowments which nature has given him.

It is astonishing and, to me, fascinating to find a flexibility and subtlety in a language like Swahili sufficient to convey the teachings of Confucius, for example, and it is my ambition to make an effort to guide the negro race by means of its own peculiar qualities to a higher degree of perfection along the line of its natural development. Though it is a commonplace to anthropologists, these qualities and attainments of negro languages are entirely unknown to the general public of the Western world and, astonishingly enough, even to the negroes themselves. I have met negroes in the United States who believed that the African negro communicated his thoughts solely by means of gestures, that, in fact, he was practically incapable of speech and merely used sign language!

It is my first concern to dispel this regrettable and abysmal ignorance of the value of its own heritage in the negro race itself. As a first step in this direction I intend to make a comparative study of the main language groups: Indo-European, Asiatic and African, choosing two or three principal languages out of each group, and indicate their comparative richness at a comparable stage of development. It may take me five years to complete this work, but I am convinced that the results will be adequate to form a concrete foundation for a movement to inspire confidence in the negro in the value of his own past and future.

1934

MARITA BONNER
1899–1971

Among the best educated of the writers and artists of the Harlem Renaissance, Marita Odette Bonner (sometimes identified as Marieta Bonner) was also one of the more versatile and talented.

Bonner never lived in Harlem, and seldom visited New York, but certainly left her mark on the literary movement. She was born in Brookline, Massachusetts, near Boston. After excelling as a student in Brookline High School, she entered Radcliffe College in nearby Cambridge in 1918. There she studied English and comparative literature (she would eventually become fluent in German) and made a name for herself as a singer. Admitted to an acclaimed and highly competitive writing seminar, she also laid, while at Radcliffe, the foundations for her literary career.

After receiving a bachelor's degree in 1922, Bonner taught for two years at the Bluefield Colored Institute in Bluefield, Virginia. Then, responding to the growing excitement among young African Americans about literature and culture, her writing began to mature with her move to Washington, D.C., in 1924 to teach at a high school. An important mentor was the poet Georgia Douglas Johnson, who welcomed Bonner to the celebrated weekly salon at her S Street home that at one time included Langston Hughes, Jean Toomer, Alain Locke, Willis Richardson, and most of the African American writers living in the district.

So multitalented was Bonner that she was able to win, in the 1920s, important prizes in the field of the essay, the short story, drama, and music. Her keen awareness of herself as a woman and an African American in an age of profound social change led to her remarkable landmark essay "On Being Young—a Woman—and Colored," which appeared in December 1925 in the *Crisis.* Her dramatic writing, which included plays such as *The Pot Maker* (1927), *The Purple Flower* (1928), and *Exit: An Illusion* (1929), also brought her widespread recognition among Black Americans as an important figure in the theater movement that included W. E. B. Du Bois and the Krigwa group in New York and Willis Richardson and other playwrights in Washington, D.C. In the 1920s, she also published several stories that further enhanced her reputation.

With her marriage in 1930 to an accountant, William Occomy, Bonner left Washington and settled in Chicago, where she lived for the rest of her life. In the following years she concentrated on the demands of her family, including three children, but also wrote fiction, principally short stories, that responded to the realities of Chicago life, especially among Black Americans living there. Around 1941, she more or less stopped writing, although to the end of her life she cherished literature and saw herself as a writer. In 1941, she resumed teaching, first at the Phillips High School in Chicago, and then, between 1950 and 1963, at the Doolittle School (also in Chicago), which served children who had not previously received educational advantages. In 1971 she died following a fire at her Chicago home.

In almost everything she wrote, Bonner showed a keen interest in exploring the distance between the private, inner self of an individual and the suppositions about that individual generated by prejudices about race, class, and gender. She brought a special insight to her depictions of Black feminine consciousness but never sought to limit herself to this subject. Her best stories, such as "Drab Rambles" (1927), "Tin Can" (1934), and "A Sealed Pod" (1936), are often presented as filtered through a complex, subjective consciousness; at their best, they fascinate the reader with their poetical and highly sensitive depictions of human character.

On Being Young—a Woman—and Colored

You start out after you have gone from kindergarten to sheepskin covered with sundry Latin phrases.

At least you know what you want life to give you. A career as fixed and as calmly brilliant as the North Star. The one real thing that money buys. Time. Time to do things. A house that can be as delectably out of order and as easily put in order as the doll-house of "playing-house" days. And of course, a husband you can look up to without looking down on yourself.

Somehow you feel like a kitten in a sunny catnip field that sees sleek, plump brown field mice and yellow baby chicks sitting coyly, side by side, under each leaf. A desire to dash three or four ways seizes you.

That's Youth.

But you know that things learned need testing—acid testing—to see if they are really after all, an interwoven part of you. All your life you have heard of the debt you owe "Your People" because you have managed to have the things they have not largely had.

So you find a spot where there are hordes of them—of course below the Line—to be your catnip field while you close your eyes to mice and chickens alike.

If you have never lived among your own, you feel prodigal. Some warm untouched current flows through them—through you—and drags you out into the deep waters of a new sea of human foibles and mannerisms; of a peculiar psychology and prejudices. And one day you find yourself entangled—enmeshed—pinioned in the seaweed of a Black Ghetto.

Not a Ghetto, placid like the Strasse[1] that flows, outwardly unperturbed and calm in a stream of religious belief, but a peculiar group. Cut off, flung together, shoved aside in a bundle because of color and with no more in common.

Unless color is, after all, the real bond.

Milling around like live fish in a basket. Those at the bottom crushed into a sort of stupid apathy by the weight of those on top. Those on top leaping, leaping; leaping to scale the sides; to get out.

There are two "colored" movies, innumerable parties—and cards. Cards played so intensely that it fascinates and repulses at once.

Movies.

Movies worthy and worthless—but not even a low-caste spoken stage.

Parties, plentiful. Music and dancing and much that is wit and color and gaiety. But they are like the richest chocolate; stuffed costly chocolates that make the taste go stale if you have too many of them. That make plain whole bread taste like ashes.

There are all the earmarks of a group within a group. Cut off all around from ingress from or egress to other groups. A sameness of type. The smug self-satisfaction of an inner measurement; a measurement by standards known within a limited group and not those of an unlimited, seeing, world. . . . Like the blind, blind mice. Mice whose eyes have been blinded.

Strange longing seizes hold of you. You wish yourself back where you can lay your dollar down and sit in a dollar seat to hear voices, strings, reeds that have lifted the World out, up, beyond things that have bodies and walls.

1. Street (German).

Where you can marvel at new marbles and bronzes and flat colors that will make men forget that things exist in a flesh more often than in spirit. Where you can sink your body in a cushioned seat and sink your soul at the same time into a section of life set before you on the boards for a few hours.

You hear that up at New York this is to be seen; that, to be heard.

You decide the next train will take you there.

You decide the next second that that train will not take you, nor the next—nor the next for some time to come.

For you know that—being a woman—you cannot twice a month or twice a year, for that matter, break away to see or hear anything in a city that is supposed to see and hear too much.

That's being a woman. A woman of any color.

You decide that something is wrong with a world that stifles and chokes; that cuts off and stunts; hedging in, pressing down on eyes, ears and throat. Somehow all wrong.

You wonder how it happens there that—say five hundred miles from the Bay State[2]—Anglo Saxon intelligence is so warped and stunted.

How judgment and discernment are bred out of the race. And what has become of discrimination? Discrimination of the right sort. Discrimination that the best minds have told you weighs shadows and nuances and spiritual differences before it catalogues. The kind they have taught you all of your life was best: that looks clearly past generalization and past appearance to dissect, to dig down to the real heart of matters. That casts aside rapid summary conclusions, drawn from primary inference, as Daniel did the spiced meats.[3]

Why can't they then perceive that there is a difference in the glance from a pair of eyes that look, mildly docile, at "white ladies" and those that, impersonally and perceptively—aware of distinctions—see only women who happen to be white?

Why do they see a colored woman only as a gross collection of desires, all uncontrolled, reaching out for their Apollos and the Quasimodos[4] with avid indiscrimination?

Why unless you talk in staccato squawks—brittle as seashells—unless you "champ" gum—unless you cover two yards square when you laugh—unless your taste runs to violent colors—impossible perfumes and more impossible clothes—are you a feminine Caliban craving to pass for Ariel?[5]

An empty imitation of an empty invitation. A mime; a sham; a copy-cat. A hollow re-echo. A froth, a foam. A fleck of the ashes of superficiality?

Everything you touch or taste now is like the flesh of an unripe persimmon.

. . . Do you need to be told what that is being . . . ?

Old ideas, old fundamentals seem worm-eaten, out-grown, worthless, bitter; fit for the scrap-heap of Wisdom.

What you had thought tangible and practical has turned out to be a collection of "blue-flower" theories.

If they have not discovered how to use their accumulation of facts, they are useless to you in Their world.

Every part of you becomes bitter.

2. Massachusetts.
3. See Daniel 1:8–16, where he refused to "defile himself with the portion of the king's meat."
4. Quasimodo is the central character in Victor Hugo's novel *The Hunchback of Notre Dame* (1831).
5. Savage and ugly trying to pass as noble and beautiful. Caliban and Ariel are characters in Shakespeare's *The Tempest*.

But—"In Heaven's name, do not grow bitter. Be bigger than they are"—exhort white friends who have never had to draw breath in a Jim-Crow train. Who have never had petty putrid insult dragged over them—drawing blood—like pebbled sand on your body where the skin is tenderest. On your body where the skin is thinnest and tenderest.

You long to explode and hurt everything white; friendly; unfriendly. But you know that you cannot live with a chip on your shoulder even if you can manage a smile around your eyes—without getting steely and brittle and losing the softness that makes you a woman.

For chips make you bend your body to balance them. And once you bend, you lose your poise, your balance, and the chip gets into you. The real you. You get hard.

. . . And many things in you can ossify . . .

And you know, being a woman, you have to go about it gently and quietly, to find out and to discover just what is wrong. Just what can be done.

You see clearly that they have acquired things.

Money; money. Money to build with, money to destroy. Money to swim in. Money to drown in. Money.

An ascendancy of wisdom. An incalculable hoard of wisdom in all fields, in all things collected from all quarters of humanity.

A stupendous mass of things.

Things.

So, too, the Greeks . . . Things.

And the Romans. . . .

And you wonder and wonder why they have not discovered how to handle deftly and skillfully, Wisdom, stored up for them—like the honey for the Gods on Olympus—since time unknown.

You wonder and you wonder until you wander out into Infinity, where—if it is to be found anywhere—Truth really exists.

The Greeks had possessions, culture. They were lost because they did not understand.

The Romans owned more than anyone else. Trampled under the heel of Vandals and Civilization, because they would not understand.

Greeks. Did not understand.

Romans. Would not understand.

"They." Will not understand.

So you find they have shut Wisdom up and have forgotten to find the key that will let her out. They have trapped, trammeled, lashed her to themselves with thews and thongs and theories. They have ransacked sea and earth and air to bring every treasure to her. But she sulks and will not work for a world with a whitish hue because it has snubbed her twin sister, Understanding.

You see clearly—off there is Infinity—Understanding. Standing alone, waiting for someone to really want her.

But she is so far out there is no way to snatch at her and really drag her in.

So—being a woman—you can wait.

You must sit quietly without a chip. Not sodden—and weighted as if your feet were cast in the iron of your soul. Not wasting strength in enervating gestures as if two hundred years of bonds and whips had really tricked you into nervous uncertainty.

But quiet; quiet. Like Buddha—who brown like I am—sat entirely at ease, entirely sure of himself; motionless and knowing, a thousand years before the white man knew there was so very much difference between feet and hands.

Motionless on the outside. But on the inside?

Silent.

Still . . . "Perhaps Buddha is a woman."

So you too. Still; quiet; with a smile, ever so slight, at the eyes so that Life will flow into and not by you. And you can gather, as it passes, the essences, the overtones, the tints, the shadows; draw understanding to yourself.

And then you can, when Time is ripe, swoop to your feet—at your full height—at a single gesture.

Ready to go where?

Why . . . Wherever God motions.

1925

STERLING A. BROWN
1901–1989

James Weldon Johnson seems to have spoken for the majority of modern African American critics when he declared that the use of dialect in literature was fundamentally limited to the expression of humor and pathos. While admitting the exception of Paul Laurence Dunbar, who for Johnson was the first poet to use dialect "as a medium for the true interpretation of Negro character and psychology," Johnson nonetheless argued in the influential preface to his 1922 *Book of American Negro Poetry* that dialect, given its long-standing association with minstrelsy and its stock of racist stereotypes, was unable to capture the full richness of modern Black life in the United States. But when Johnson revised and expanded his anthology in 1931, his additions included two young writers who had, he recognized, broken the "mold of convention" of dialect poetry, demonstrating its potential as a literary instrument: Langston Hughes and Sterling A. Brown. The next year Johnson wrote the preface to Brown's first book, *Southern Road* (1932), praising the way Brown "infused his poetry with genuine characteristic flavor by adopting as his medium the common, racy, living speech of the Negro in certain phrases of *real* life." On the basis of that single collection of verse, Brown established himself as a major voice in the renaissance, equaled only by Hughes and Zora Neale Hurston in his use of Black vernacular speech and culture as a literary resource.

Brown was born in Washington, D.C., with advantages and options that were available to few Blacks at the turn of the century. His father, Sterling Nelson Brown, who had counted Frederick Douglass and Paul Laurence Dunbar among his friends, had been enslaved and then worked his way through Fisk University and Oberlin College Seminary before becoming a professor of religion at Howard University as well as the pastor of Lincoln Temple Congregational Church. The young Brown attended Dunbar High School, where he encountered such teachers as Angelina Grimké and Jessie Redmon Fauset. He graduated from Williams College in 1922, then went on to earn a master's degree in English from Harvard the following year. Nevertheless, he maintained throughout his life that his best teachers were the poor Black folk of the South, particularly in the Lynchburg, Virginia, area, where he taught English at the Virginia Seminary and College for three years. In Lynchburg, and then while teaching at Lincoln University in Missouri and Fisk in Tennessee, Brown immersed himself in Black Southern life, above all the culture of everyday folk as he encountered it in bars, "jook joints," and barbershops. At the same time he began to establish a reputation in the renaissance, publishing his first essay in *Opportunity* in 1925; his poems began to appear regularly there and in the *Crisis*, as well as in prominent collections such as V. F. Calverton's *Anthology of Negro American Literature* (1927) and Countee Cullen's *Caroling Dusk* (1927).

In 1929, Brown joined the faculty at Howard University. Three years later, when *Southern Road* appeared, he found himself popular with almost all the critics—except for his fellow English professors, who tended to look down on his passion for jazz and the blues. Though he was unable to find a publisher for his second collection of verse, *No Hiding Place*, Brown remained productive, turning his attention to criticism and to prose sketches. Throughout the 1930s, he wrote a column for *Opportunity* called "The Literary Scene: Chronicle and Comment," and, while still underappreciated by critics, his articles and essays make the most sustained case that Black folk forms such as the blues and spirituals should be recognized as literary accomplishments. As early as 1930, in essays such as "The Blues as Folk Poetry," Brown noted the stunning range and nuance of vernacular forms, contending that "at their most genuine they are accurate, imaginative transcripts of folk experience, with flashes of excellent poetry." He published two groundbreaking books of criticism, *The Negro in American Fiction* (1937) and *Negro Poetry and Drama* (1937).

But his most important contributions may have been editorial: from 1936 to 1940 he served as the national editor of Negro Affairs for the Federal Writers' Project, supervising the production of guidebooks and histories for individual states across the United States. His influence in this role has not been adequately assessed by historians. To take one small example, in 1936 he wrote admirably concise guidelines for the transcription of Black speech (in the oral histories of formerly enslaved people conducted by Project employees in numerous states), observing that "exact phonetic transcription" goes too far when it results in "pages sprinkled with misspellings, commas and apostrophes," and counseling pragmatism: "Truth to idiom is more important, I believe, than truth to pronunciation." When he left the Federal Writers' Project, Brown turned his energies to one of the most important compilations in African American history, *The Negro Caravan* (1941, edited with Arthur P. Davis and Ulysses Lee), the first anthology to make the case that vernacular sources such as spirituals, blues, hollers, work songs, ballads, and folk tales must be seen as part of the Black literary tradition, in an approach that set the tone for every major anthology since.

Although a key figure in the period, Brown was consistently skeptical of the term "Harlem Renaissance," preferring to describe the upsurge of creativity as the "New Negro Renaissance." When asked to participate in a 1955 conference on "The New Negro Thirty Years Afterwards," he offered an eloquent explanation of his hesitation: "the New Negro is not to me a group of writers centered in Harlem during the second half of the twenties. Most of the writers were not Harlemites; much of the best writing was not about Harlem, which was the show-window, the cashier's till, but no more Negro America than New York is America. The New Negro movement had temporal roots in the past and spatial roots elsewhere in America, and the term has validity, it seems to me, only when considered to be a continuing tradition."

Although he remained at Howard until 1969, Brown taught for three semesters at Vassar College, where in 1945 he was offered a full-time position. That such a prestigious institution should invite an African American to join its faculty was rare enough to be national news at the time. However, Brown's devotion to Howard, where he was extremely popular with students, was such that he declined this offer. In 1971, Howard awarded him an honorary doctorate. In 1975, Brown at last published his second collection of verse, *The Last Ride of Wild Bill and Eleven Narratives; Southern Road* was also reprinted. Five years later, the poet Michael S. Harper brought out *The Collected Poems of Sterling A. Brown,* which included much of the material from the rejected volume *No Hiding Place,* and in 2007, the scholars John Edgar Tidwell and Mark A. Sanders compiled *A Negro Looks at the South*, an unfinished but voluminous book project Brown had undertaken in the early 1940s, with dozens of subtle and evocative sketches of Black life across the South. When Brown died in 1989, it was amid a revival of critical interest in his work that seems likely to endure.

Odyssey of Big Boy

Lemme be wid Casey Jones,[1]
  Lemme be wid Stagolee,[2]
Lemme be wid such like men
  When Death takes hol' on me,
    When Death takes hol' on me. . . .

Done skinned[3] as a boy in Kentucky hills,
  Druv steel dere as a man,
Done stripped tobacco in Virginia fiel's
  Alongst de River Dan,[4]
    Alongst de River Dan;

Done mined de coal in West Virginia,
  Liked dat job jes' fine,
Till a load o' slate curved roun' my head,
  Won't work in no mo' mine,
    Won't work in no mo' mine;

Done shocked de corn in Marylan',
  In Georgia done cut cane,
Done planted rice in South Caline,
  But won't do dat again,
    Do dat no mo' again.

Been roustabout in Memphis,
  Dockhand in Baltimore,
Done smashed up freight on Norfolk wharves,
  A fust class stevedore,
    A fust class stevedore. . . .

Done slung hash yonder in de North
  On de ole Fall River Line,
Done busted suds[5] in li'l New York,
  Which ain't no work o' mine—
    Lawd, ain't no work o' mine.

1. U.S. train engineer and folk hero (1864–1900).
2. Also known as Stacker Lee (or Stackerlee), a prominent figure in African American folklore.
3. Hunted animals for their pelts.
4. A river in south-central Virginia.
5. That is, worked as a dishwasher or launderer. "Fall River Line": a boat line from Fall River, Massachusetts, to New York.

Done worked and loafed on such like jobs,
Seen what dey is to see,
Done had my time wid a pint° on my hip *of liquor*
An' a sweet gal on my knee,
Sweet mommer on my knee:

Had stovepipe blond in Macon,
Yaller gal in Marylan',
In Richmond had a choklit brown,
Called me huh monkey man—
Huh big fool monkey man.

Had two fair browns in Arkansaw
And three in Tennessee,
Had Creole gal in New Orleans,
Sho Gawd did two time me—
Lawd two time, fo' time me—

But best gal what I evah had
Done put it over dem,
A gal in Southwest Washington
At Four'n half and M[6]—
Four'n half and M. . . .

Done took my livin' as it came,
Done grabbed my joy, done risked my life;
Train done caught me on de trestle,° *bridge*
Man done caught me wid his wife,
His doggone purty wife. . . .

I done had my women,
I done had my fun;
Cain't do much complainin'
When my jag° is done, *spree*
Lawd, Lawd, my jag is done.

An' all dat Big Boy axes
When time comes fo' to go,
Lemme be wid John Henry,° steel drivin' man, *Black folk hero*
Lemme be wid old Jazzbo,
Lemme be wid ole Jazzbo. . . .

1927

6. On M Street, between Fourth and Fifth streets.

When de Saints Go Ma'ching Home

(To Big Boy Davis,[1] Friend.
In Memories of Days Before He Was
Chased Out of Town for Vagrancy.)

I

He'd play, after the bawdy songs and blues,
After the weary plaints
Of "Trouble, Trouble deep down in muh soul,"
Always one song in which he'd lose the rôle
Of entertainer to the boys. He'd say,
"My mother's favorite." And we knew
That what was coming was his chant of saints,
"When de saints go ma'chin' home. . . ."
And that would end his concert for the day.

Carefully as an old maid over needlework,
Oh, as some black deacon, over his Bible, lovingly,
He'd tune up specially for this. There'd be
No chatter now, no patting of the feet.
After a few slow chords, knelling and sweet—
Oh when de saints go ma'chin' home,
Oh when de sayaints goa ma'chin' home. . . .
He would forget
The quieted bunch, his dimming cigarette
Stuck into a splintered edge of the guitar;
Sorrow deep hidden in his voice, a far
And soft light in his strange brown eyes;
Alone with his masterchords, his memories. . . .
    Lawd I wanna be one in nummer
    When de saints go ma'chin' home.
Deep the bass would rumble while the treble scattered high,
For all the world like heavy feet a-trompin' toward the sky,
With shrill-voiced women getting 'happy'
All to celestial tunes.
The chap's few speeches helped me understand
The reason why he gazed so fixedly
Upon the burnished strings.
For he would see
A gorgeous procession to 'de Beulah Land,'[2]—
Of saints—his friends—*"a-climbin' fo' deir wings."*
Oh when de saints go ma'chin' home. . . .
Lawd I wanna be one o' dat nummer
When de saints goa m'achin' home. . . .

1. Calvin "Big Boy" Davis, a traveling performer Brown met in Lynchburg, Virginia, while teaching at the Virginia Theological Seminary.

2. A biblical name for the Promised Land; from Isaiah 62:4.

II

There'd be—so ran his dream:
"Ole Deacon Zachary
With de asthmy° in his chest, *asthma*
A-puffin' an' a-wheezin'
Up de golden stair;
Wid de badges of his lodges
Strung acrost his heavin' breast
An' de hoggrease jes' shinin'
In his coal black hair. . . .

"An' ole Sis Joe
In huh big straw hat,
An' huh wrapper flappin',
Flappin' in de heavenly win',
An' huh thin-soled easy walkers
Goin' pitty pitty pat,—
Lawd she'd have to ease her corns
When she got in!"

Oh when de saints go ma'chin' home.
"Ole Elder Peter Johnson
Wid his corncob jes' a-puffin',
An' de smoke a-rollin'
Lak stormclouds out behin';
Crossin' de cloud mountains
Widout slowin' up fo' nuffin,
Steamin' up de grade
Lak Wes' bound No. 9.

"An' de little brown-skinned chillen
Wid deir skinny legs a-dancin',
Jes' a-kickin' up ridic'lous
To de heavenly band;
Lookin' at de Great Drum Major
On a white hoss jes' a-prancin',
Wid a gold and silver drumstick
A-waggin' in his han'."
Oh when de sun refuse to shine
Oh when de mo-on goes down
In Blood
"Ole Maumee Annie
Wid huh washin' done,
An' huh las' piece o' laundry
In de renchin' tub,
A wavin' sof' pink han's
To de much obligin' sun,
An' her feet a-moverin' now
To a swif' rub-a-dub;

"An' old Grampa Eli
Wid his wrinkled old haid,

A-puzzlin' over summut
He ain' understood,
Intendin' to ask Peter
Pervidin' he ain't skyaid,
'Jes' what mought be de meanin'
Of de moon in blood?'[3] . . ."
When de saints go ma'chin' home. . . .

III

"Whuffolks,"° he dreams, *"will have to stay outside* — *white folks*
Being so onery."° But what is he to do — *ornery*
With that red brakeman who once let him ride
An empty going home? Or with that kind-faced man
Who paid his songs with board and drink and bed?
Or with the Yankee Cap'n who left a leg
At Vicksburg? *Mought be a place, he said,*
Mought be another mansion fo' white saints,
A smaller one than his'n . . . not so gran'.
As fo' the rest . . . oh let 'em howl and beg.
Hell would be good enough—if big enough—
Widout no shade trees, lawd, widout no rain.
Whuffolks sho' to bring nigger out behin',
Excep'—"when de saints go ma'chin' home."

IV

Sportin' Legs would not be there—nor lucky Sam,
Nor Smitty, nor Hambone, nor Hardrock Gene,
An' not too many guzzlin', cuttin' shines,
Nor bootleggers to keep his pockets clean.
An' Sophie wid de sof' smile on her face,
Her foolin' voice, her strappin' body, brown
Lak coffee doused wid milk—she had been good
To him, wid lovin', money and wid food.—
But saints and heaven didn't seem to fit
Jes' right wid Sophy's Beauty—nary bit—
She mought stir trouble, somehow, in dat peaceful place
Mought be some dressed-up dudes in dat fair town.

V

Ise got a dear ole mudder,
She is in hebben I know—
He sees:
        Mammy,

3. An allusion to the biblical prescription in Acts 2:20 that "The sun shall be turned into darkness, and the moon into blood, before that great and notable day of the Lord come."

Li'l mammy—wrinkled face,
Her brown eyes, quick to tears—to joy—
With such happy pride in her
Guitar-plunkin' boy.
Oh kain't I be one in nummer?

Mammy
With deep religion defeating the grief
Life piled so closely about her,
Ise so glad trouble doan last alway,
And her dogged belief
That some fine day
She'd go a-ma'chin'
When de saints go ma'chin' home.

He sees her ma'chin' home, ma'chin' along,
Her perky joy shining in her furrowed face,
Her weak and quavering voice singing her song—
The best chair set apart for her worn out body
In that restful place. . . .
I pray to de Lawd I'll meet her
When de saints go ma'chin' home.

VI

He'd shuffle off from us, always, at that,—
His face a brown study beneath his torn brimmed hat,
His broad shoulders slouching, his old box strung
Around his neck;—he'd go where we
Never could follow him—to Sophie probably,
Or to his dances in old Tinbridge flat.

1927

Long Gone

I laks yo' kin' of lovin',
Ain't never caught you wrong,
But it jes' ain' nachal
Fo' to stay here long;

It jes' ain' nachal
Fo' a railroad man,
With a itch fo' travelin'
He cain't understan'. . . .

I looks at de rails,
An' I looks at de ties,
An' I hears an ole freight
Puffin' up de rise,

An' at nights on my pallet,
When all is still,
I listens fo' de empties[1]
Bumpin' up de hill;

When I oughta be quiet,
I is got a itch
Fo' to hear de whistle blow
Fo' de crossin' or de switch,[2]

An' I knows de time's a-nearin'
When I got to ride,
Though it's homelike and happy
At yo' side.

You is done all you could do
To make me stay;
'Tain't no fault of yours I'se leavin'—
I'se jes dataway.

I is got to see some people
I ain't never seen,
Gotta highball thu some country
Whah I never been.

I don't know which way I'm travelin'—
Far or near,
All I knows fo' certain is
I cain't stay here.

Ain't no call at all, sweet woman,
Fo' to carry on—
Jes' my name and jes' my habit
To be Long Gone. . . .

1931

Southern Road

Swing dat hammer—hunh[1]—
Steady, bo';
Swing dat hammer—hunh—
Steady, bo';
Ain't no rush, bebby,
Long ways to go.

1. The empty, and therefore rattling, train cars.
2. A device for diverting trains from one track to another.

1. The groan of the chain-gang worker as his hammer strikes.

Burner tore his—hunh—
Black heart away;[2]
Burner tore his—hunh—
Black heart away;
Got me life,[3] bebby,
An' a day.

Gal's on Fifth Street[4]—hunh—
Son done gone;
Gal's on Fifth Street—hunh—
Son done gone;
Wife's in de ward,[5] bebby,
Babe's not bo'n.

My ole man died—hunh—
Cussin' me;
My ole man died—hunh—
Cussin' me;
Ole lady rocks, bebby,
Huh misery.

Doubleshackled—hunh—
Guard behin';
Doubleshackled—hunh—
Guard behin';
Ball an' chain, bebby,
On my min'.

White man tells me—hunh—
Damn yo' soul;
White man tells me—hunh—
Damn yo' soul;
Got no need, bebby,
To be tole.

Chain gang nevah—hunh—
Let me go;
Chain gang nevah—hunh—
Let me go;
Po' los' boy, bebby,
Evahmo'. . . .

1931

2. That is, he shot a man in the heart. "Burner": gun.
3. That is, he was sentenced to life imprisonment.
4. His daughter is now a prostitute.
5. In the hospital.

Strong Men

The strong men keep coming on.
SANDBURG.[1]

They dragged you from homeland,
They chained you in coffles,[2]
They huddled you spoon-fashion in filthy hatches,
They sold you to give a few gentlemen ease.

They broke you in like oxen,
They scourged you,
They branded you,
They made your women breeders,
They swelled your numbers with bastards. . . .
They taught you the religion they disgraced.

You sang:
Keep a-inchin' along
Lak a po' inch worm. . . .

You sang:
Bye and bye
I'm gonna lay down dis heaby load. . . .

You sang:
Walk togedder, chillen,
Dontcha git weary. . . .
The strong men keep a-comin' on
The strong men git stronger.

They point with pride to the roads you built for them,
They ride in comfort over the rails you laid for them.
They put hammers in your hands
And said—Drive so much before sundown.

You sang:
Ain't no hammah
In dis lan',
Strikes lak mine, bebby,
Strikes lak mine.

They cooped you in their kitchens,
They penned you in their factories,
They gave you the jobs that they were too good for,
They tried to guarantee happiness to themselves
By shunting° dirt and misery to you. *shifting*

You sang:
Me an' muh baby gonna shine, shine

1. Carl Sandburg (1878–1967), American poet.

2. A group of enslaved people chained together.

Me an' muh baby gonna shine.
The strong men keep a-comin' on
The strong men git stronger. . . .

They bought off some of your leaders
You stumbled, as blind men will . . .
They coaxed you, unwontedly° soft-voiced. . . . *unusually*
You followed a way.
Then laughed as usual.

They heard the laugh and wondered;
Uncomfortable;
Unadmitting a deeper terror. . . .
The strong men keep a-comin' on
Gittin' stronger. . . .

What, from the slums
Where they have hemmed you,
What, from the tiny huts
They could not keep from you—
What reaches them
Making them ill at ease, fearful?
Today they shout prohibition at you
"Thou shalt not this"
"Thou shalt not that"
"Reserved for whites only"
You laugh.

One thing they cannot prohibit—
The strong men . . . coming on
The strong men gittin' stronger.
Strong men. . . .
Stronger. . . .

1931

Ma Rainey[1]

I

When Ma Rainey
Comes to town,
Folks from anyplace
Miles aroun',
From Cape Girardeau,
Poplar Bluff,[2]
Flocks in to hear
Ma do her stuff;

1. Celebrated blues singer (1886–1939).
2. The seat of Butler County, in southeastern Missouri. Cape Girardeau is a city (and county) in southeastern Missouri.

Comes flivverin'[3] in,
Or ridin' mules,
Or packed in trains,
Picknickin' fools. . . .
That's what it's like,
Fo' miles on down,
To New Orleans delta
An' Mobile° town, *Alabama seaport*
When Ma hits
Anywheres aroun'.

II

Dey comes to hear Ma Rainey from de little river settlements,
From blackbottom° cornrows and from lumber camps; *fertile land*
Dey stumble in de hall, jes a-laughin' an' a-cacklin',
Cheerin' lak roarin' water, lak wind in river swamps.

An' some jokers keeps deir laughs a-goin' in de crowded aisles,
An' some folks sits dere waitin' wid deir aches an' miseries,
Till Ma comes out before dem, a-smilin' gold-toofed smiles
An' Long Boy ripples minors on de black an' yellow keys.[4]

III

O Ma Rainey,
Sing yo' song;
Now you's back
Whah you belong,
Git way inside us,
Keep us strong. . . .
O Ma Rainey,
Li'l an' low;
Sing us 'bout de hard luck
Roun' our do';
Sing us 'bout de lonesome road
We mus' go. . . .

IV

I talked to a fellow, an' the fellow say,
"She jes' catch hold of us, somekindaway.
She sang Backwater Blues one day:

'It rained fo' days an' de skies was dark as night,
Trouble taken place in de lowlands at night.

'Thundered an' lightened an' the storm begin to roll
Thousan's of people ain't got no place to go.

3. Riding in a flivver, or a small, cheap automobile.

4. Plays songs on the piano in minor key signatures.

'Den I went an' stood upon some high ol' lonesome hill,
An' looked down on the place where I used to live.'

An' den de folks, dey natchally bowed dey heads an' cried,
Bowed dey heavy heads, shet dey moufs up tight an' cried,
An' Ma lef' de stage, an' followed some de folks outside."

Dere wasn't much more de fellow say:
She jes' gits hold of us dataway.

1932

Cabaret

(1927, Black & Tan Chicago)[1]

Rich, flashy, puffy-faced,
Hebrew and Anglo-Saxon,
The overlords sprawl here with their glittering darlings.
The smoke curls thick, in the dimmed light
Surreptitiously, deaf-mute waiters
Flatter the grandees,[2]
Going easily over the rich carpets,
Wary lest they kick over the bottles[3]
Under the tables.

The jazzband unleashes its frenzy.

Now, now,
To it, Roger; that's a nice doggie,
Show your tricks to the gentlemen.

The trombone belches, and the saxophone
Wails curdlingly, the cymbals clash,
The drummer twitches in an epileptic fit

Muddy water
Round my feet
Muddy water

The chorus sways in.
The 'Creole Beauties from New Orleans'
(By way of Atlanta, Louisville, Washington, Yonkers,
With stop-overs they've used nearly all their lives)
Their creamy skin flushing rose warm,
O, le bal des belles quarterounes![4]
Their shapely bodies naked save
For tattered pink silk bodices, short velvet tights,

1. A reference to Duke Ellington's popular recording "Black and Tan Fantasy" (1927).
2. Patrons with money.
3. Liquor bottles, during Prohibition.
4. Oh, the ball of the beautiful quadroons (French). A quadroon is a person of one-quarter African ancestry.

And shining silver-buckled boots;
Red bandannas on their sleek and close-clipped hair;
To bring to mind (aided by the bottles under the tables)
Life upon the river—

Muddy water, river sweet

(Lafitte the pirate, instead,
And his doughty[5] diggers of gold)
There's peace and happiness there
I declare

(In Arkansas,
Poor half-naked fools,[6] *tagged with identification numbers,*
Worn out upon the levees,
Are carted back to the serfdom
They had never left before
And may never leave again)

Bee—dap—ee—DOOP, dee—ba—dee—BOOP

The girls wiggle and twist

Oh you too,
Proud high-stepping beauties,
Show your paces to the gentlemen.
A prime filly, seh.
What am I offered, gentlemen, gentlemen. . . .

I've been away a year today
To wander and roam
I don't care if it's muddy there

(Now that the floods recede,
What is there left the miserable folk?
Oh time in abundance to count their losses,
There is so little else to count.)

Still it's my home, sweet home

From the lovely throats
Moans and deep cries for home:
Nashville, Toledo, Spout Springs, Boston,
Creoles from Germantown;—
The bodies twist and rock;
The glasses are filled up again. . . .

(In Mississippi
The black folk huddle, mute, uncomprehending,
Wondering 'how come the good Lord
Could treat them this a way')

5. Courageous and dependable. "Lafitte": Jean Lafitte (ca. 1780–ca. 1825), French pirate.
6. Black prisoners in work gangs.

shelter
Down in the Delta[7]

Along the Yazoo[8]
The buzzards fly over, over, low,
Glutted, but with their scrawny necks stretching,
Peering still.)

I've got my toes turned Dixie ways
Round that Delta let me laze

The band goes mad, the drummer throws his sticks
At the moon, a *papier-mâché* moon,
The chorus leaps into weird posturings,
The firm-fleshed arms plucking at grapes to stain
Their coralled mouths; seductive bodies weaving
Bending, writhing, turning

My heart cries out for
MUDDY WATER

(Down in the valleys
The stench of the drying mud
Is a bitter reminder of death.)

Dee da dee D A A A A H

1932

Break of Day

Big Jess fired on the Alabama Central,
Man in full, babe, man in full.
Been throwing on coal for Mister Murphy
From times way back, baby, times way back.

Big Jess had a pleasing woman, name of Mamie,
Sweet-hipted Mama, sweet-hipted Mame;
Had a boy growing up for to be a fireman,[1]
Just like his pa, baby, like his pa.

Out by the roundhouse Jess had his cabin,
Longside the tracks, babe, long the tracks,
Jess pulled the whistle when they high-balled[2] past it
"I'm on my way, baby, on my way."

Crackers[3] craved the job what Jess was holding,
Times right tough, babe, times right tough;

7. At the mouth of the Mississippi River.
8. A river running through western Mississippi.
1. A stoker, whose job it is to tend the fire in a steam locomotive.
2. Went at full speed; from the name of the railway signal indicating that the path ahead is clear.
3. A dismissive term for whites, used among African Americans.

Warned Jess to quit his job for a white man,
Jess he laughed, baby, he jes' laughed.

He picked up his lunch-box, kissed his sweet woman,
Sweet-hipted Mama, sweet-hipted Mame;
His son walked with him to the white-washed palings,
"Be seeing you soon, son, see you soon."

Mister Murphy let Big Jess talk on the whistle
"So long sugar baby, so long babe";
Train due back in the early morning
Breakfast time, baby, breakfast time.

Mob stopped the train crossing Black Bear Mountain
Shot rang out, babe, shot rang out.
They left Big Jess on the Black Bear Mountain,
Break of day, baby, break of day.

Sweet Mame sits rocking, waiting for the whistle
Long past due, babe, long past due.
The grits are cold, and the coffee's boiled over,
But Jess done gone, baby he done gone.

1938

Sam Smiley

I

The whites had taught him how to rip
   A Nordic belly with a thrust
Of bayonet,[1] had taught him how
   To transmute Nordic flesh to dust.

And a surprising fact had made
   Belated impress on his mind:
That shrapnel bursts and poison gas
   Were inexplicably color blind.

He picked up, from the difficult
   But striking lessons of the war,
Some truths that he could not forget,
   Though inconceivable before.

And through the lengthy vigils, stuck
   In never-drying stinking mud,
He was held up by dreams of one
   Chockfull of laughter, hot of blood.

1. That is, to attack German soldiers in World War I.

II

On the return Sam Smiley cheered
  The dirty steerage[2] with his dance,
Hot-stepping boy! Soon he would see
  The girl who beat all girls in France.

He stopped buckdancing[3] when he reached
  The shanties at his journey's end;
He found his sweetheart in the jail,
  And took white lightning[4] for his friend.

One night the woman whose full voice
  Had chortled so, was put away
Into a narrow gaping hole,[5]
  Sam sat beside till break of day.

He had been told what man it was
  Whose child the girl had had to kill,
Who best knew why her laugh was dumb,
  Who best knew why her blood was still.

And he remembered France, and how
  A human life was dunghill cheap,
And so he sent a rich white man
  His woman's company to keep.

III

The mob was in fine fettle, yet
  The dogs were stupid-nosed,[6] and day
Was far spent when the men drew round
  The scrawny woods where Smiley lay.

The oaken leaves drowsed prettily,
  The moon shone down benignly there;
And big Sam Smiley, King Buckdancer,
  Buckdanced on the midnight air.

1932 1975

2. The part of a ship designated for passengers with the cheapest tickets.
3. Dancing happily.
4. Cheap whiskey.
5. A grave.
6. Slow to pick up Sam's scent. "Fettle": condition.

GWENDOLYN B. BENNETT
1902–1981

Poet, artist, and journalist of the Harlem Renaissance, Gwendolyn B. Bennett was born in Giddings, Texas, in 1902—"unofficially" because that state denied official birth certificates to Blacks well into the twentieth century. Her parents soon took her to Nevada, where they worked as teachers on an American Indian reservation until 1906 or 1907. They then moved to Washington, D.C., so that Bennett's father could study law. When the marriage failed, Gwendolyn's mother gained custody of her. However, her father kidnapped his eight-year-old daughter and dragged her into a nomadic life of hiding (mainly in Pennsylvania) that lasted until her junior year in high school, when they finally settled in Brooklyn.

An excellent student, Bennett became the first Black member of the literary and dramatic societies in her high school, wrote the main graduation speech and lyrics to her graduation song, composed poetry, and took part in art competitions. After graduation, she studied fine arts at Columbia University and the Pratt Institute, where she earned a bachelor's degree in 1924. Having already established herself as a promising member of Harlem's literary and artistic set, she left New York for Washington, D.C., to teach art at Howard University. The next year, she won a $1,000 scholarship from the Delta Sigma Theta sorority that enabled her to study art in Paris for a year. Returning to New York in the summer of 1926, she found the Harlem Renaissance in full swing and immediately secured a prominent place in its ranks, especially with her poetry ("Heritage" had been published in 1923) and her illustrations for such magazines as *Opportunity*, the *Crisis*, and the short-lived *Fire!!* She also started a column called *The Ebony Flute*, which she described as a forum for "literary and social chit-chat," in Charles S. Johnson's *Opportunity*. This column aimed to satisfy anyone curious about the whereabouts, the recent accomplishments, or the plans of personalities such as the artist Aaron Douglas and the singer-actor Paul Robeson. Bennett kept her lively column going even after her return to Howard as an instructor. Indeed, the column lasted until May

A drawing by Gwendolyn Bennett on the cover of *Opportunity*.

1928, when Bennett accompanied her husband, Alfred Jackson, to Florida, where he wanted to establish a private medical practice.

Bennett soon found the rigid segregation of the South intolerable and convinced her husband to return to New York. Unfortunately, by this time the deepening Depression had virtually wiped out the Harlem Renaissance. The death of her husband forced Bennett further away from the life of art. Though she managed to publish a few new poems and essays, making a living began to consume most of her creative energy. She spent several years in government-sponsored positions before postwar anti-Communist hysteria claimed her—unfairly—as one of its victims. For a time she worked at the Consumers Union in Mount Vernon, New York, with the poet Helene Johnson; remarried, she spent the remainder of her life as an antiques dealer in Kutztown, Pennsylvania.

Some students of the Harlem Renaissance view Bennett as a figure whose literary reputation rests solely on her having been in the right place (Harlem) at the right time (the 1920s); but her poetry tells a different story—that of an active and artistic intelligence and consciousness. Keenly aware as an artist of the grace and loveliness of people of African descent, especially women and girls, Bennett wrote lyrics that expressed her admiration in interesting ways. She was among the more judiciously race conscious of the Harlem writers, but her poetry quietly celebrated the physical and emotional qualities not always appreciated by Blacks themselves in a time of intense segregation.

Heritage

I want to see the slim palm-trees,
Pulling at the clouds
With little pointed fingers. . . .

I want to see lithe Negro girls,
Etched dark against the sky
While sunset lingers.

I want to hear the silent sands,
Singing to the moon
Before the Sphinx-still face. . . .

I want to hear the chanting
Around a heathen fire
Of a strange black race.

I want to breathe the Lotus flow'r,
Sighing to the stars
With tendrils drinking at the Nile. . . .

I want to feel the surging
Of my sad people's soul
Hidden by a minstrel-smile.

1923

To a Dark Girl

I love you for your brownness
And the rounded darkness of your breast.
I love you for the breaking sadness in your voice
And shadows where your wayward eye-lids rest.

Something of old forgotten queens
Lurks in the lithe abandon of your walk,
And something of the shackled slave
Sobs in the rhythm of your talk.

Oh, little brown girl, born for sorrow's mate,
Keep all you have of queenliness,
Forgetting that you once were slave,
And let your full lips laugh at Fate!

1927

WALLACE THURMAN
1902–1934

Of himself and his many roles in the Harlem Renaissance, the versatile and mercurial Wallace Thurman wrote in 1929: "Three years in Harlem have seen me become a New Negro (for no reason at all and without my consent), a poet (having had 2 poems published by generous editors), an editor (with a penchant for financially unsound publications), an exotic (see articles on Negro life and literature in *The Bookman, New Republic, Independent, World Tomorrow,* etc.), an actor (I was a denizen of Cat Fish Row in *Porgy*), a husband (having been married all of six months), a novelist (viz: *The Blacker the Berry.* Macaulay's, Feb. 1, 1929: $2.50), a playwright (being co-author of *Black Belt*). Now—what more could one do?"

Born and reared in Salt Lake City, Thurman attended the University of Utah before transferring to the University of Southern California in 1922. He supported himself in Los Angeles by working for the postal service (with another Harlem Renaissance figure, Arna Bontemps) and writing a column called "Inklings" for a local Black newspaper. He was apparently thinking of becoming a doctor when news of the Harlem Renaissance reached him. Hoping to spark a West Coast version of the movement, he founded the *Outlet,* a magazine that failed after half a year. Thurman moved to Harlem in 1925. He worked at first as both reporter and editor at *The Looking Glass,* then served as managing editor at *The Messenger.* In 1926, he improbably became circulation manager for *The World Tomorrow,* a religious magazine run by whites and aimed mainly at whites. That same year saw the first and only number of the ill-fated magazine *Fire!!,* the brainchild of Thurman, Langston Hughes, Bruce Nugent, Zora Neale Hurston, and others, who all agreed that Thurman should be its editor. In 1928, Thurman started his own magazine, *Harlem: A Forum of Negro Life,* but it also failed after its first issue. In the meantime, he was hired at Macaulay's Publishing Company as the only Black reader in any of the major publishing houses of New York.

In 1929, his first play, *Harlem: A Melodrama of Negro Life in Harlem,* written in collaboration with the white dramatist William Jourdan Rapp, reached Broadway. Also that year his first novel, *The Blacker the Berry,* became both a critical and a popular success. In part, the book examines the prejudices of the African American community against its darker-skinned members, an issue about which the dark-skinned Thurman was sensitive. For sustained insight into Harlem life in the 1920s, however, Thurman's most important achievement is probably *Infants of the Spring* (1932), a roman à clef that mercilessly satirizes the Harlem Renaissance as a movement. His third and final novel, an exposé of hospital abuses called *The Interne* (1932), written in collaboration with the white author Abraham L. Furman, does not touch on racial issues and was generally disregarded by the Harlem community.

Thurman worked at Macaulay's until he was recruited by a filmmaker to write screenplays. Hired (reportedly) at an outrageously high salary, he moved back to California, where he wrote two scripts before a number of factors, including declining health and excessive drinking, led him to return to New York in 1934. There, he collapsed at a reunion party with his friends and was immediately hospitalized; he died a few months later of tuberculosis.

Langston Hughes captured some of the conflicts of Thurman's psychology when he wrote in 1940 that Thurman "wanted to be a *very* great writer, like Gorki or Thomas Mann, and he felt that he was merely a journalistic writer." Thurman compared his work with that of Proust, Melville, Tolstoy, and others and "found his own pages vastly wanting. So he contented himself by writing a great deal for money, laughing bitterly at his fabulously concocted 'true stories,' . . . drinking more and more gin, and then threatening to jump out of windows at people's parties and kill himself."

The chapter of *Infants of the Spring* included here offers, albeit in a veiled and satirical way, one of the most illuminating contemporary views of the Harlem Renaissance. Here, thinly disguised, are most of the major personalities of the movement, including Langston Hughes, Zora Neale Hurston, Alain Locke, Countee Cullen, and Rudolph Fisher, who assemble in the apartment of the principal character, Raymond (who most resembles Thurman himself), to discuss the renaissance.

From Infants of the Spring

Chapter XXI

[HARLEM SALON]

After Stephen's unexpected visit and their long conversation together, Raymond[1] seemed to have developed a new store of energy. For three days and nights, he had secluded himself in his room, and devoted all his time to the continuance of his novel. For three years it had remained a project. Now he was making rapid progress. The ease with which he could work once he set himself to it amazed him, and at the same time he was suspicious of this unexpected facility. Nevertheless, his novel was progressing, and he intended to let nothing check him.

In line with this resolution, he insisted that Paul[2] and Eustace hold their nightly gin parties without his presence, and they were also abjured to steer all company clear of his studio.

Stephen had gone upstate on a tutoring job, Lucille had not been in evidence since the donation party, and Raymond had made no attempt to get in touch with her. There was no one else in whom he had any interest. Aline

1. Based on Thurman himself.
2. Probably based on Richard Bruce Nugent (1906–1987), a painter, writer, and professional actor.

and Janet he had dismissed from his mind, although Eustace and Paul had spent an entire dinner hour telling him of their latest adventures. Both had now left Aline's mother's house and were being supported by some white man, whom Aline had met at a downtown motion picture theater. They had an apartment in which they entertained groups of young colored boys on the nights their white protector was not in evidence.

Having withdrawn from every activity connected with Niggeratti Manor, Raymond had also forgotten that Dr. Parkes[3] had promised to communicate with him, concerning some mysterious idea, and he was taken by surprise when Eustace came into the room one morning, bearing a letter from Dr. Parkes.

"Well, I'm plucked," Raymond exclaimed.

"What's the matter?" Eustace queried.

"Will you listen to this?" He read the letter aloud.

"My dear Raymond:

I will be in New York on Thursday night. I want you to do me a favor. It seems to me that with the ever increasing number of younger Negro artists and intellectuals gathering in Harlem, some effort should be made to establish what well might become a distinguished salon. All of you engaged in creative work, should, I believe, welcome the chance to meet together once every fortnight, for the purpose of exchanging ideas and expressing and criticizing individual theories. This might prove to be both stimulating and profitable. And it might also bring into active being a concerted movement which would establish the younger Negro talent once and for all as a vital artistic force. With this in mind, I would appreciate your inviting as many of your colleagues as possible to your studio on Thursday evening. I will be there to preside. I hope you are intrigued by the idea and willing to cooperate. Please wire me your answer. Collect, of course.

Very sincerely yours,

DR. A. L. PARKES."

"Are you any more good?" Raymond asked as he finished reading.

"Sounds like a great idea," Eustace replied enthusiastically.

"It *is* great. Too great to miss," Raymond acquiesced mischievously. "Come on, let's get busy on the telephone."

Thursday night came and so did the young hopefuls. The first to arrive was Sweetie May Carr.[4] Sweetie May was a short story writer, more noted for her ribald wit and personal effervescence than for any actual literary work. She was a great favorite among those whites who went in for Negro prodigies. Mainly because she lived up to their conception of what a typical Negro should be. It seldom occurred to any of her patrons that she did this with tongue in cheek. Given a paleface audience, Sweetie May would launch forth into a saga of the little all-colored Mississippi town where she claimed to have been born. Her repertoire of tales was earthy, vulgar and funny. Her darkies always smiled through their tears, sang spirituals on

3. Based on Alain Locke (1886–1954), champion of the Harlem Renaissance and editor of *The New Negro* (1925). "Niggeratti Manor": Iolanthe Sydney's rooming house in Harlem, where Thurman and other figures of the renaissance stayed at one time or another; Thurman and Zora Neale Hurston coined the term.

4. Based loosely on Zora Neale Hurston (1891–1960), author of *Mules and Men* and *Their Eyes Were Watching God.*

the slightest provocation, and performed buck dances when they should have been working. Sweetie May was a master of southern dialect, and an able raconteur, but she was too indifferent to literary creation to transfer to paper that which she told so well. The intricacies of writing bored her, and her written work was for the most part turgid and unpolished. But Sweetie May knew her white folks.

"It's like this," she had told Raymond. "I have to eat. I also wish to finish my education. Being a Negro writer these days is a racket and I'm going to make the most of it while it lasts. Sure I cut the fool. But I enjoy it, too. I don't know a tinker's damn about art. I care less about it. My ultimate ambition, as you know, is to become a gynecologist. And the only way I can live easily until I have the requisite training is to pose as a writer of potential ability. *Voila!* I get my tuition paid at Columbia. I rent an apartment and have all the furniture contributed by kind hearted o'fays.[5] I receive bundles of groceries from various sources several times a week . . . all accomplished by dropping a discreet hint during an evening's festivities. I find queer places for whites to go in Harlem . . . out of the way primitive churches, sidestreet speakeasies. They fall for it. About twice a year I manage to sell a story. It is acclaimed. I am a genius in the making. Thank God for this Negro literary renaissance! Long may it flourish!"

Sweetie May was accompanied by two young girls, recently emigrated from Boston. They were the latest to be hailed as incipient immortals. Their names were Doris Westmore and Hazel Jamison.[6] Doris wrote short stories. Hazel wrote poetry. Both had become known through a literary contest fostered by one of the leading Negro magazines.[7] Raymond liked them more than he did most of the younger recruits to the movement. For one thing, they were characterized by a freshness and naïveté which he and his cronies had lost. And, surprisingly enough for Negro prodigies, they actually gave promise of possessing literary talent. He was most pleased to see them. He was also amused by their interest and excitement. A salon! A literary gathering! It was one of the civilized institutions they had dreamed of finding in New York, one of the things they had longed and hoped for.

As time passed, others came in. Tony Crews,[8] smiling and self-effacing, a mischievous boy, grateful for the chance to slip away from the backwoods college he attended. Raymond had never been able to analyze this young poet. His work was interesting and unusual. It was also spotty. Spasmodically he gave promise of developing into a first rate poet. Already he had published two volumes, prematurely, Raymond thought. Both had been excessively praised by whites and universally damned by Negroes. Considering the nature of his work this was to be expected. The only unknown quantity was the poet himself. Would he or would he not fulfill the promise exemplified in some of his work? Raymond had no way of knowing and even an intimate friendship with Tony himself had failed to enlighten him. For Tony was the most close-mouthed and cagey individual Raymond had ever known when it came to personal matters. He fended off every attempt to probe into his inner self and did this with such an unconscious and naive air that the prober soon came to one of two conclusions: Either Tony had no depth whatsoever, or else he was too deep for plumbing by ordinary mortals.

5. Whites, a disparaging term.

6. Based on the poet Helene Johnson (1907–1995). Westmore is based on Johnson's cousin Dorothy West (1907–1998), author of *The Living Is Easy* (1948).

7. *Crisis* and *Opportunity* both sponsored literary contests in the 1920s.

8. Based on Langston Hughes (1902–1967); his two volumes of poetry in the 1920s were *The Weary Blues* (1926) and *Fine Clothes to the Jew* (1927).

DeWitt Clinton,[9] the Negro poet laureate, was there, too, accompanied, as usual, by his *fideles Achates,* David Holloway.[1] David had been acclaimed the most handsome Negro in Harlem by a certain group of whites. He was in great demand by artists who wished to paint him. He had become a much touted romantic figure. In reality he was a fairly intelligent school teacher, quite circumspect in his habits, a rather timid beau, who imagined himself to be bored with life.

Dr. Parkes finally arrived, accompanied by Carl Denny, the artist, and Carl's wife, Annette. Next to arrive was Cedric Williams,[2] a West Indian, whose first book, a collection of short stories with a Caribbean background, in Raymond's opinion, marked him as one of the three Negroes writing who actually had something to say, and also some concrete idea of style. Cedric was followed by Austin Brown, a portrait painter whom Raymond personally despised, a Dr. Manfred Trout,[3] who practiced medicine and also wrote exceptionally good short stories, Glenn Madison, who was a Communist, and a long, lean professorial person, Allen Fenderson, who taught school and had ambitions to become a crusader modeled after W. E. B. Du Bois.

The roster was now complete. There was an hour of small talk and drinking of mild cocktails in order to induce ease and allow the various guests to become acquainted and voluble. Finally, Dr. Parkes ensconced himself in Raymond's favorite chair, where he could get a good view of all in the room, and clucked for order.

Raymond observed the professor closely. Paul's description never seemed more apt. He was a mother hen clucking at her chicks. Small, dapper, with sensitive features, graying hair, a dominating head, and restless hands and feet, he smiled benevolently at his brood. Then, in his best continental manner, which he had acquired during four years at European Universities, he began to speak.

"You are," he perorated, "the outstanding personalities in a new generation. On you depends the future of your race. You are not, as were your predecessors, concerned with donning armor, and clashing swords with the enemy in the public square. You are finding both an escape and a weapon in beauty, which beauty when created by you will cause the American white man to reestimate the Negro's value to his civilization, cause him to realize that the American black man is too valuable, too potential of utilitarian accomplishment, to be kept down-trodden and segregated.

"Because of your concerted storming up Parnassus,[4] new vistas will be spread open to the entire race. The Negro in the south will no more know peonage, Jim Crowism, or loss of the ballot, and the Negro everywhere in America will know complete freedom and equality.

"But," and here his voice took on a more serious tone, "to accomplish this, your pursuit of beauty must be vital and lasting. I am somewhat fearful of the decadent strain which seems to have filtered into most of your work. Oh, yes, I know you are children of the age and all that, but you must not, like your paleface contemporaries, wallow in the mire of post-Victorian

9. Based on Countee Cullen (1903–1946), whose first collection of poetry, *Color,* appeared in 1925.
1. Based on Harold Jackman (1900–1960), whose portrait (by Winold Reiss) had appeared in the "New Negro" issue of *Survey Graphic. "Fideles Achates"*: faithful Achates (Latin). Jackman was probably Cullen's closest friend and is, therefore, compared to Achates, Aeneas's most faithful companion in the *Aeneid,* a Roman epic poem by Virgil.
2. Based on Eric Walrond (1898–1966), author of *Tropic Death* (1926). The Dennys are based on Aaron (1898–1979) and Alta Douglas (ca. 1899–1958).
3. Based on Rudolph Fisher (1897–1934), whose "City of Refuge" appeared in the *Atlantic Monthly* (1925).
4. A mountain in central Greece, traditionally associated with the muses and artistic production.

license. You have too much at stake. You must have ideals. You should become . . . well, let me suggest your going back to your racial roots, and cultivating a healthy paganism based on African traditions.

"For the moment that is all I wish to say. I now want you all to give expression to your own ideas. Perhaps we can reach a happy mean for guidance."

He cleared his throat and leaned contentedly back in his chair. No one said a word. Raymond was full of contradictions, which threatened to ooze forth despite his efforts to remain silent. But he knew that once the ooze began there would be no stopping the flood, and he was anxious to hear what some of the others might have to say.

However, a glance at the rest of the people in the room assured him that most of them had not the slightest understanding of what had been said, nor any ideas on the subject, whatsoever. Once more Dr. Parkes clucked for discussion. No one ventured a word. Raymond could see that Cedric, like himself, was full of argument, and also like him, did not wish to appear contentious at such an early stage in the discussion. Tony winked at Raymond when he caught his eye, but the expression on his face was as inscrutable as ever. Sweetie May giggled behind her handkerchief. Paul amused himself by sketching the various people in the room. The rest were blank.

"Come, come, now," Dr. Parkes urged somewhat impatiently, "I'm not to do all the talking. What have you to say, DeWitt?"

All eyes sought out the so-called Negro poet laureate. For a moment he stirred uncomfortably in his chair, then in a high pitched, nasal voice proceeded to speak.

"I think, Dr. Parkes, that you have said all there is to say. I agree with you. The young Negro artist must go back to his pagan heritage for inspiration and to the old masters for form."

Raymond could not suppress a snort. For DeWitt's few words had given him a vivid mental picture of that poet's creative hours—eyes on a page of Keats, fingers on typewriter, mind frantically conjuring African scenes. And there would of course be a Bible nearby.

Paul had ceased being intent on his drawing long enough to hear "pagan heritage," and when DeWitt finished he inquired inelegantly:

"What old black pagan heritage?"

DeWitt gasped, surprised and incredulous.

"Why, from your ancestors."

"Which ones?" Paul pursued dumbly.

"Your African ones, of course." DeWitt's voice was full of disdain.

"What about the rest?"

"What rest?" He was irritated now.

"My German, English and Indian ancestors," Paul answered willingly. "How can I go back to African ancestors when their blood is so diluted and their country and times so far away? I have no conscious affinity for them at all."

Dr. Parkes intervened: "I think you've missed the point, Paul."

"And I," Raymond was surprised at the suddenness with which he joined in the argument, "think he has hit the nail right on the head. Is there really any reason why *all* Negro artists should consciously and deliberately dig into African soil for inspiration and material unless they actually wish to do so?"

"I don't mean that. I mean you should develop your inherited spirit."

DeWitt beamed. The doctor had expressed his own hazy theory. Raymond was about to speak again, when Paul once more took the bit between his own teeth.

"I ain't got no African spirit."

Sweetie May giggled openly at this, as did Carl Denny's wife, Annette. The rest looked appropriately sober, save for Tony, whose eyes continued to telegraph mischievously to Raymond. Dr. Parkes tried to squelch Paul with a frown. He should have known better.

"I'm not an African," the culprit continued. "I'm an American and a perfect product of the melting pot."

"That's nothing to brag about." Cedric spoke for the first time.

"And I think you're all on the wrong track." All eyes were turned toward this new speaker, Allen Fenderson. "Dr. Du Bois has shown us the way. We must be militant fighters. We must not hide away in ivory towers and prate of beauty. We must fashion cudgels and bludgeons rather than sensitive plants. We must excoriate the white man, and make him grant us justice. We must fight for complete social and political and economic equality."

"What we ought to do," Glenn Madison growled intensely, "is to join hands with the workers of the world and overthrow the present capitalistic régime. We are of the proletariat and must fight our battles allied with them, rather than singly and selfishly."

"All of us?" Raymond inquired quietly.

"All of us who have a trace of manhood and are more interested in the rights of human beings than in gin parties and neurotic capitalists."

"I hope you're squelched," Paul stage whispered to Raymond.

"And how!" Raymond laughed. Several joined in. Dr. Parkes spoke quickly to Fenderson, ignoring the remarks of the Communist.

"But, Fenderson . . . this is a new generation and must make use of new weapons. Some of us will continue to fight in the old way, but there are other things to be considered, too. Remember, a beautiful sonnet can be as effectual, nay even more effectual, than a rigorous hymn of hate."

"The man who would understand and be moved by a hymn of hate would not bother to read your sonnet and, even if he did, he would not know what it was all about."

"I don't agree. Your progress must be a boring in from the top, not a battle from the bottom. Convert the higher beings and the lower orders will automatically follow."

"Spoken like a true capitalistic minion," Glenn Madison muttered angrily.

Fenderson prepared to continue his argument, but he was forestalled by Cedric.

"What does it matter," he inquired diffidently, "what any of you do so long as you remain true to yourselves? There is no necessity for this movement becoming standardized. There is ample room for everyone to follow his own individual track. Dr. Parkes wants us all to go back to Africa and resurrect our pagan heritage, become atavistic. In this he is supported by Mr. Clinton. Fenderson here wants us all to be propagandists and yell at the top of our lungs at every conceivable injustice. Madison wants us all to take a cue from Leninism and fight the capitalistic bogey. Well . . . why not let each young hopeful choose his own path? Only in that way will anything at all be achieved."

"Which is just what I say," Raymond smiled gratefully at Cedric. "One cannot make movements nor can one plot their course. When the work of a given number of individuals during a given period is looked at in retrospect, then one can identify a movement and evaluate its distinguishing characteristics. Individuality is what we should strive for. Let each seek his own salvation. To me, a wholesale flight back to Africa or a wholesale allegiance to Communism or a wholesale adherence to an antiquated and for the most part ridiculous propagandistic program are all equally futile and unintelligent."

Dr. Parkes gasped and sought for an answer. Cedric forestalled him.

"To talk of an African heritage among American Negroes *is* unintelligent. It is only in the West Indies that you can find direct descendents from African ancestors. Your primitive instincts among all but the extreme proletariat have been ironed out. You're standardized Americans."

"Oh, no," Carl Denny interrupted suddenly. "You're wrong. It's in our blood. It's . . ." he fumbled for a word, "fixed. Why . . ." he stammered again, "remember Cullen's poem, *Heritage*:

"'So I lie who find no peace
Night or day, no slight release
From the unremittant beat
Made by cruel padded feet
Walking through my body's street.
Up and down they go, and back,
Treading out a jungle track.'[5]

"We're all like that. Negroes are the only people in America not standardized. The feel of the African jungle is in their blood. Its rhythms surge through their bodies. Look how Negroes laugh and dance and sing, all spontaneous and individual."

"Exactly," Dr. Parkes and DeWitt nodded assent.

"I have yet to see an intelligent or middle class American Negro laugh and sing and dance spontaneously. That's an illusion, a pretty sentimental fiction. Moreover your songs and dances are not individual. Your spirituals are mediocre folk songs, ignorantly culled from Methodist hymn books. There are white men who can sing them just as well as Negroes, if not better, should they happen to be untrained vocalists like Robeson, rather than highly trained technicians like Hayes.[6] And as for dancing spontaneously and feeling the rhythms of the jungle . . . humph!"

Sweetie May jumped into the breach.

"I can do the Charleston better than any white person."

"I particularly stressed . . . intelligent people. The lower orders of any race have more vim and vitality than the illuminated tenth."

Sweetie May leaped to her feet.

"Why, you West Indian . . ."

"Sweetie, Sweetie," Dr. Parkes was shocked by her polysyllabic expletive.

Pandemonium reigned. The master of ceremonies could not cope with the situation. Cedric called Sweetie an illiterate southern hussy. She called him all types of profane West Indian monkey chasers. DeWitt and David were shocked and showed it. The literary doctor, the Communist and Fenderson moved uneasily around the room. Annette and Paul giggled. The two child prodigies from Boston looked on wide-eyed, utterly bewildered and dismayed. Raymond leaned back in his chair, puffing on a cigarette, detached and amused. Austin, the portrait painter, audibly repeated over and over to himself: "Just like niggers . . . just like niggers." Carl Denny interposed himself between Cedric and Sweetie May. Dr. Parkes clucked for civilized behavior, which came only when Cedric stalked angrily out of the room.

5. Lines 64–70.
6. Roland Hayes (1887–1977) studied music in Europe for two years. Paul Robeson (1898–1976) appeared in a number of musicals on and off Broadway.

After the alien had been routed and peace restored, Raymond passed a soothing cocktail. Meanwhile Austin and Carl had begun arguing about painting. Carl did not possess a facile tongue. He always had difficulty formulating in words the multitude of ideas which seethed in his mind. Austin, to quote Raymond, was an illiterate cad. Having examined one of Carl's pictures on Raymond's wall, he had disparaged it. Raymond listened attentively to their argument. He despised Austin mainly because he spent most of his time imploring noted white people to give him a break by posing for a portrait. Having the gift of making himself pitiable, and having a glib tongue when it came to expatiating on the trials and tribulations of being a Negro, he found many sitters, all of whom thought they were encouraging a handicapped Negro genius. After one glimpse at the completed portrait, they invariably changed their minds.

"I tell you," he shouted, "your pictures are distorted and grotesque. Art is art, I say. And art holds a mirror up to nature. No mirror would reflect a man composed of angles.[7] God did not make man that way. Look at Sargent's[8] portraits. He was an artist."

"But he wasn't," Carl expostulated. "We . . . we of this age . . . we must look at Matisse, Gauguin, Picasso and Renoir[9] for guidance. They get the feel of the age. . . . They . . ."

"Are all crazy and so are you," Austin countered before Carl could proceed.

Paul rushed to Carl's rescue. He quoted Wilde in rebuttal: Nature imitates art,[1] then went on to blaspheme Sargent. Carl, having found some words to express a new idea fermenting in his brain, forgot the argument at hand, went off on a tangent and began telling the dazed Dr. Parkes about the Negroid quality in his drawings. DeWitt yawned and consulted his watch. Raymond mused that he probably resented having missed the prayer meeting which he attended every Thursday night. In another corner of the room the Communist and Fenderson had locked horns over the ultimate solution of the Negro problem. In loud voices each contended for his own particular solution. Karl Marx and Lenin[2] were pitted against Du Bois and his disciples. The writing doctor, bored to death, slipped quietly from the room without announcing his departure or even saying good night. Being more intelligent than most of the others, he had wisely kept silent. Tony and Sweetie May had taken adjoining chairs, and were soon engaged in comparing their versions of original verses to the St. James Infirmary,[3] which Tony contended was soon to become as epical as the St. Louis Blues. Annette and Howard began gossiping about various outside personalities. The child prodigies looked from one to the other, silent, perplexed, uncomfortable, not knowing what to do or say. Dr. Parkes visibly recoiled from Carl's incoherent expository barrage, and wilted in his chair, willing but unable to effect a courteous exit. Raymond sauntered around the room, dispensing cocktails, chuckling to himself.

Such was the first and last salon.

1932

7. A reference to Cubism, an important movement in the visual arts at the time.
8. John Singer Sargent (1856–1925), American painter.
9. Auguste Renoir (1841–1919), Henri Matisse (1869–1954), Paul Gauguin (1848–1903), and Pablo Picasso (1881–1973), all innovative painters.
1. A satiric slogan of the Art for Art's Sake movement, with which Oscar Wilde (1856–1900) was associated.
2. Pseudonym of Vladimir Ilyich Ulyanov (1870–1924), Russian revolutionary leader and Soviet premier from 1918 to 1924. Marx (1818–1883), author of *The Communist Manifesto* with Friedrich Engels.
3. A blues number popularized by Black entertainer Gladys Bentley.

LANGSTON HUGHES
1902–1967

Langston Hughes enjoys a special relationship to the Harlem Renaissance for two main reasons. He helped define the spirit of the age, from a literary point of view, through his brilliant poetry and other writings, in a career that continued to flourish when most of the other writers of the movement had fallen silent. He also produced, in a section of his autobiography *The Big Sea* (1940), the finest first-person account of the renaissance, a treasure trove of impressions and memories on which virtually all scholars and students of the cultural movement have depended in their own writings.

Hughes was among the first of the writers and artists drawn to Harlem by its promise as a center of African American cultural activity. Born in Joplin, Missouri, Hughes grew up in Lawrence, Kansas, and Lincoln, Illinois, before going to high school in Cleveland, Ohio, and spending a year in Mexico, near Mexico City. Hughes was descended from a distinguished family. His maternal grandmother's first husband died at Harpers Ferry fighting in John Brown's band; her second husband, Langston's maternal grandfather, was prominent in Kansas politics during Reconstruction, before racism drove him from the field; and his brother, John Mercer Langston, was one of the most famous Black Americans of the nineteenth century, a congressman from Virginia and the founding dean of the law school of Howard University. However, Hughes's mother, Carrie Langston Hughes, and his father, James N. Hughes, separated not long after his birth. His father emigrated to Mexico, where he was successful in business. Langston grew up lonely and near poverty.

In September 1921, aided by his father, he arrived in New York ostensibly to attend Columbia University but really, he later claimed, to see Harlem. The previous June, he had published one of his greatest poems, "The Negro Speaks of Rivers," in the *Crisis,* where his talent was immediately spotted by its literary editor, Jessie Fauset. Hughes lasted only one year at Columbia, where he did well but never felt comfortable. He took a succession of jobs, including stints as a delivery boy, vegetable farmer, and mess boy on a ship anchored in the Hudson River. In 1923, he sailed to Africa as a member of the crew of a merchant steamer; the following year he traveled the same way to Europe, where he jumped ship and spent several months in Paris working in the kitchen of a nightclub. Through all these jobs and experiences, Hughes continued to work on his poetry, which he published mainly in the *Crisis.* By 1924, his poetry showed the powerful influence of the blues and jazz. In fact, his poem "The Weary Blues" helped launch his career when it won first prize in the poetry section of the 1925 literary contest organized by *Opportunity* magazine. Aided by Carl Van Vechten, a friend of his for life, Hughes won a book contract from Knopf and published *The Weary Blues,* his first collection of verse, in 1926.

Although Hughes's earliest influences as a mature poet came from Walt Whitman and Carl Sandburg ("my guiding star"), Claude McKay stood for him in the early 1920s as the embodiment of the cosmopolitan and yet racially confident and committed Black poet Hughes hoped to be. Hughes was also indebted to older figures such as Du Bois and James Weldon Johnson, both of whom admired his work and helped him. Images and sentiments such as those in "Poem" ("The night is beautiful, / So the faces of my people") and "Dream Variations" ("Night coming tenderly / Black like me") endeared his work to a wide range of African Americans.

His major step, encouraged in part by Sandburg's example (in publishing poems about jazz) but anchored by his own near-worship of Black music as the major form of art within the race, was his adaptation of traditional poetic forms first to jazz, then to the blues, in which Hughes sometimes used dialect but in a way radically different from that of earlier writers. In these steps Hughes was well served by his early experimentation with a loose form of rhyme that frequently gave way to an inventively rhythmic free verse ("Me an' ma baby's / Got two mo' ways, / Two mo' ways to do de buck!"). His landmark poem "The Weary Blues" was the first by any poet to make use of the basic blues form.

Even more radical experimentation with the blues form led to his next collection, *Fine Clothes to the Jew* (1927). Among his most distinctive books, *Fine Clothes* was also his least successful in terms of sales and, in the Black press (though not the white), critical reception. Several reviewers in Black newspapers and magazines were distressed by Hughes's fearless and, to them, tasteless evocation of elements of lower-class Black culture, including its sometimes raw eroticism, never before treated in serious poetry. The book was "about 100 pages of trash [reeking] of the gutter and sewer," wrote one man; another found the poems "insanitary, insipid and repulsing." These reviewers probably gave *Fine Clothes to the Jew* a harsher reception than that accorded any other book of American poetry, with the exception of Whitman's *Leaves of Grass.*

In response to his critics, Hughes was adamant about his determination to write about such people and to experiment with blues and jazz. The year before, 1926, he had published in the *Nation* an essay in defense of the freedom of the Black writer, "The Negro Artist and the Racial Mountain." "We younger Negro artists who create now intend to express our individual dark-skinned selves without fear or shame," he had declared. "We know we are beautiful. And ugly too." This essay quickly became a manifesto for many of the younger writers who wished to assert their right to explore and exploit allegedly degraded aspects of Black life.

Also in 1926, Hughes returned to school, this time at the historically Black (although the faculty was almost entirely white) Lincoln University in Pennsylvania, from which he graduated in 1929. In 1927, his life took an extraordinary turn when he met Charlotte Osgood Mason, a wealthy white patron of the arts then in her seventies, who had been led to Hughes by Alain Locke. During the next three years, Mason, who believed passionately in parapsychology, intuition, and folk culture, dominated Hughes's life with gifts of money and powerful advice about virtually every aspect of his life and art. She was directly involved in supervising the writing of his 1930 novel *Not without Laughter,* in which Hughes drew on his boyhood in Kansas to depict the life of a Black child, Sandy, growing up in a representative midwestern African American home.

In 1930, in a dispute that involved Zora Neale Hurston, who was also being supported by Mason, the relationship between Hughes and his patron came to an explosive end. Hurt and baffled by Mason's rejection, in 1931 Hughes used money from a prize to spend several weeks recovering in Haiti. When he returned to the United States, he made a sharp turn toward the political left, although social and political consciousness, and an interest in socialism, had always been a feature of his verse. He published verse and essays in *New Masses,* a journal controlled by the Communist Party, and later that year began a tour of the South and the West designed to take poetry to the people, with Hughes reading his poems in churches and schools. In 1932, he boarded a ship in New York and sailed for the Soviet Union with a group of young African Americans invited to take part in a film about American race relations. For Hughes, the renaissance was long over, replaced by a sense of the need for political struggle and for an art that reflected this radical approach.

Unlike most of the writers of the renaissance, Hughes's career survived the end of the movement; there was never a year, or even a month or a week, when he did not produce art in keeping with his sense of himself as a thoroughly professional writer. In 1934, he published his first collection of short stories, the often acerbic and even embittered *The Ways of White Folks.* However, in the 1930s Hughes's main concern was probably the theater. His drama of miscegenation and the South, *Mulatto* (1935), was the longest running play by an African American on Broadway until Lorraine Hansberry's *A Raisin in the Sun* in the 1960s. Some of his plays were comedies, others were dramas of domestic African American life or were radical in their politics, as with *Don't You Want to Be Free?* which Hughes's Harlem Suitcase Theater staged in 1938.

With the start of World War II, Hughes returned to the political center. His first autobiography, *The Big Sea,* with its memorable portrait of the renaissance, appeared in 1940. In poetry, he returned to some of his old themes and forms, including the blues, as in the collection *Shakespeare in Harlem* (1942). In 1943, in his weekly column for the Chicago *Defender,* he introduced one of his enduring fictional triumphs, the character Jesse B. Semple, or Simple, a Harlem everyman whose comic manner hardly obscured some of the serious themes raised by Hughes in relating Simple's exploits. In 1947, as lyricist for the Broadway musical *Street Scene,* with music by Kurt Weill, Hughes earned enough money to purchase a house in his beloved Harlem, where he lived for the rest of his life.

His output became prodigious. In addition to books of verse, including the bebop-shaped *Montage of a Dream Deferred* (1951), a suite (gathering many of Hughes's best-known short poems, such as "Ballad of the Landlord," "Dream Boogie," "Harlem," "Motto," and "Theme for English B") about a changing Harlem, fertile with humanity but in decline, he published another volume of autobiography, two more volumes of short stories, a second novel, about a dozen books for children, five books drawn from the Simple columns (which ran for twenty years), several plays and musicals (including pioneering examples of the gospel musical), a history of the NAACP, various libretti for operas and cantatas, and landmark anthologies of African American writing (notably *Poetry of the Negro,* 1949) and of African literature.

By the end of his life Hughes was almost everywhere recognized, because of his versatility and skill, as the most representative writer in the history of African American literature and also as probably the most original of all Black American poets. He cherished and even encouraged the often-bestowed title of "Poet Laureate of the Negro Race," which captures the importance he placed on writing literature both about and for African Americans as well as the sense that he had accomplished the central goal of his life.

The Negro Speaks of Rivers

I've known rivers:
I've known rivers ancient as the world and older than the
  flow of human blood in human veins.

My soul has grown deep like the rivers.

I bathed in the Euphrates when dawns were young.
I built my hut near the Congo and it lulled me to sleep.
I looked upon the Nile and raised the pyramids above it.
I heard the singing of the Mississippi when Abe Lincoln
  went down to New Orleans,[1] and I've seen its muddy
  bosom turn all golden in the sunset.

1. Lincoln's determination to end slavery was said to have started when, as a young man, he visited New Orleans for the first time.

I've known rivers:
Ancient, dusky rivers.

My soul has grown deep like the rivers.

1921

Mother to Son

Well, son, I'll tell you:
Life for me ain't been no crystal stair.
It's had tacks in it,
And splinters,
And boards torn up,
And places with no carpet on the floor—
Bare.
But all the time
I'se been a-climbin' on,
And reachin' landin's,
And turnin' corners,
And sometimes goin' in the dark
Where there ain't been no light.
So boy, don't you turn back.
Don't you set down on the steps
'Cause you finds it's kinder hard.
Don't you fall now—
For I'se still goin', honey,
I'se still climbin',
And life for me ain't been no crystal stair.

1922

Danse Africaine

The low beating of the tom-toms,
The slow beating of the tom-toms,
  Low . . . slow
  Slow . . . low—
  Stirs your blood.
    Dance!
A night-veiled girl
  Whirls softly into a
  Circle of light.
  Whirls softly . . . slowly,
Like a wisp of smoke around the fire—
  And the tom-toms beat,
  And the tom-toms beat,
And the low beating of the tom-toms
  Stirs your blood.

1922, 1926

Jazzonia

O, silver tree!
Oh, shining rivers of the soul!

In a Harlem cabaret
Six long-headed jazzers play.
A dancing girl whose eyes are bold
Lifts high a dress of silken gold.

Oh, singing tree!
Oh, shining rivers of the soul!

Were Eve's eyes
In the first garden
Just a bit too bold?
Was Cleopatra gorgeous
In a gown of gold?

Oh, shining tree!
Oh, silver rivers of the soul!

In a whirling cabaret
Six long-headed jazzers play.

1923

Dream Variations

To fling my arms wide
In some place of the sun,
To whirl and to dance
Till the white day is done.
Then rest at cool evening
Beneath a tall tree
While night comes on gently,
  Dark like me—
That is my dream!

To fling my arms wide
In the face of the sun,
Dance! Whirl! Whirl!
Till the quick day is done.
Rest at pale evening . . .
A tall, slim tree . . .
Night coming tenderly
  Black like me.

1924, 1926

The Weary Blues

Droning a drowsy syncopated tune,
Rocking back and forth to a mellow croon,
  I heard a Negro play.
Down on Lenox Avenue[1] the other night
By the pale dull pallor of an old gas light
  He did a lazy sway. . . .
  He did a lazy sway. . . .
To the tune o' those Weary Blues.
With his ebony hands on each ivory key
He made that poor piano moan with melody.
  O Blues!
Swaying to and fro on his rickety stool
He played that sad raggy tune like a musical fool.
  Sweet Blues!
Coming from a black man's soul.
  O Blues!
In a deep song voice with a melancholy tone
I heard that Negro sing, that old piano moan—
  "Ain't got nobody in all this world,
  Ain't got nobody but ma self.
  I's gwine to quit ma frownin'
  And put ma troubles on the shelf."
Thump, thump, thump, went his foot on the floor.
He played a few chords then he sang some more—
  "I got the Weary Blues
  And I can't be satisfied.
  Got the Weary Blues
  And can't be satisfied—
  I ain't happy no mo'
  And I wish that I had died."
And far into the night he crooned that tune.
The stars went out and so did the moon.
The singer stopped playing and went to bed
While the Weary Blues echoed through his head.
He slept like a rock or a man that's dead.

1923 1925

I, Too

I, too, sing America.
I am the darker brother.
They send me to eat in the kitchen
When company comes,
But I laugh,

1. Major Harlem thoroughfare, now Malcolm X Boulevard.

And eat well,
And grow strong.

Tomorrow,
I'll be at the table
When company comes.
Nobody'll dare
Say to me,
"Eat in the kitchen,"
Then.

Besides,
They'll see how beautiful I am
And be ashamed—

I, too, am America.

1925, 1959

Jazz Band in a Parisian Cabaret

Play that thing,
Jazz band!
Play it for the lords and ladies,
For the dukes and counts,
For the whores and gigolos,
For the American millionaires,
And the school teachers
Out for a spree.
Play it,
Jazz band!
You know that tune
That laughs and cries at the same time.
You know it.

May I?
Mais oui.[1]
Mein Gott![2]
Parece una rumba.[3]
Play it, jazz band!
You've got seven languages to speak in
And then some,
Even if you do come from Georgia.
Can I go home wid yuh, sweetie?
Sure.

1925

1. But yes (French).
2. My God! (German).
3. Seems like a rumba (Spanish). "Rumba": an Afro-Cuban dance.

Johannesburg Mines

In the Johannesburg mines
There are 240,000
Native Africans working.
What kind of poem
Would you
Make out of that?
240,000 natives
Working in the
Johannesburg mines.

1925

Homesick Blues

De railroad bridge's
A sad song in de air.
De railroad bridge's
A sad song in de air.
Ever time de trains pass
I wants to go somewhere.

I went down to de station.
Ma heart was in ma mouth.
Went down to de station.
Heart was in ma mouth.
Lookin for a box car
To roll me to de South.

Homesick blues, Lawd,
'S a terrible thing to have.
Homesick blues is
A terrible thing to have.
To keep from cryin'
I opens ma mouth an' laughs.

1926

Mulatto

I am your son, white man!

Georgia dusk
And the turpentine[1] woods.
One of the pillars of the temple fell.

1. Oil and resin mixture from pine trees.

You are my son!
Like hell!

The moon over the turpentine woods.
The Southern night
Full of stars,
Great big yellow stars.
What's a body but a toy?
Juicy bodies
Of nigger wenches
Blue black
Against black fences.
O, you little bastard boy,
What's a body but a toy?
The scent of pine wood stings the soft night air.
What's the body of your mother?
Silver moonlight everywhere.
What's the body of your mother?
Sharp pine scent in the evening air.
A nigger night,
A nigger joy,
A little yellow
Bastard boy.

Naw, you ain't my brother.
Niggers ain't my brother.
Not ever.
Niggers ain't my brother.

The Southern night is full of stars,
Great big yellow stars.
O, sweet as earth,
Dusk dark bodies
Give sweet birth
To little yellow bastard boys.

Git on back there in the night,
You ain't white.

The bright stars scatter everywhere.
Pine wood scent in the evening air.
A nigger night,
A nigger joy.

I am your son, white man!

A little yellow
Bastard boy.

1927

Red Silk Stockings

Put on yo' red silk stockings,
Black gal.
Go out an' let de white boys
Look at yo' legs.

Ain't nothin' to do for you, nohow,
Round this town,—
You's too pretty.
Put on yo' red silk stockings, gal,
An' tomorrow's chile'll
Be a high yaller.

Go out an' let de white boys
Look at yo' legs.

1927

Song for a Dark Girl

Way Down South in Dixie
(Break the heart of me)
They hung my black young lover
To a cross roads tree.

Way Down South in Dixie
(Bruised body high in air)
I asked the white Lord Jesus
What was the use of prayer.

Way Down South in Dixie
(Break the heart of me)
Love is a naked shadow
On a gnarled and naked tree.

1927

Gal's Cry for a Dying Lover

Heard de owl a hootin',
Knowed somebody's 'bout to die.
Heard de owl a hootin',
Knowed somebody's 'bout to die.
Put ma head un'neath de kiver,
Started in to moan an' cry.

Hound dawg's barkin'
Means he's gonna leave this world.
Hound dawg's barkin'

Means he's gonna leave this world.
O, Lawd have mercy
On a po' black girl.

Black an' ugly
But he sho do treat me kind.
I'm black an' ugly
But he sho do treat me kind.
High-in-heaben Jesus,
Please don't take this man o' mine.

1927

Dear Lovely Death

Dear lovely Death
That taketh all things under wing—
Never to kill—
Only to change
Into some other thing
This suffering flesh,
To make it either more or less,
But not again the same—
Dear lovely Death,
Change is thy other name.

1928

Afro-American Fragment

So long,
So far away
Is Africa.
Not even memories alive
Save those that history books create,
Save those that songs
Beat back into the blood—
Beat out of blood with words sad-sung
In strange un-Negro tongue—
So long,
So far away
Is Africa.

Subdued and time-lost
Are the drums—and yet
Through some vast mist of race
There comes this song
I do not understand
This song of atavistic[1] land,

1. Of primitive ancestry.

Of bitter yearnings lost
Without a place—
So long,
So far away
Is Africa's
Dark face.

1930

Negro Servant

All day subdued, polite,
Kind, thoughtful to the faces that are white.
O, tribal dance!
O, drums!
O, veldt° at night! *African grassland*
Forgotten watch-fires on a hill somewhere!
O, songs that do not care!
At six o'clock, or seven, or eight,
You're through.
You've worked all day.
Dark Harlem waits for you.
The bus, the sub°— *the subway*
Pay-nights a taxi
Through the park.
O, drums of life in Harlem after dark!
O, dreams!
O, songs!
O, saxophones at night!
O, sweet relief from faces that are white!

1930

Christ in Alabama

Christ is a nigger,
Beaten and black:
Oh, bare your back!

Mary is His mother:
Mammy of the South,
Silence your mouth.

God is His father:
White Master above
Grant Him your love.

Most holy bastard
Of the bleeding mouth,
Nigger Christ

On the cross
Of the South.

1931

Cubes

In the days of the broken cubes of Picasso
And in the days of the broken songs of the young men
A little too drunk to sing
And the young women
A little too unsure of love to love—
I met on the boulevards of Paris.
An African from Senegal.

God
Knows why the French
Amuse themselves bringing to Paris
Negroes from Senegal.

It's the old game of the boss and the bossed,
    boss and the bossed,
        amused
          and
        amusing,
    worked and working,
Behind the cubes of black and white,
          black and white,
    black and white

But since it is the old game,
For fun
They give him the three old prostitutes of France—
Liberty, Equality, Fraternity[1]—
And all three of 'em sick
In spite of the tax to the government
And the legal houses
And the doctors
And the *Marseillaise*.[2]

Of course, the young African from Senegal
Carries back from Paris
A little more disease
To spread among the black girls in the palm huts.
He brings them as a gift
    disease—
From light to darkness
        disease—
From the boss to the bossed
            disease—

1. National motto of France, with origins in the French Revolution (1789–99).

2. The French national anthem.

From the game of black and white
disease
From the city of the broken cubes of Picasso
d
i
s
e
a
s
e

1934

Ballad of the Landlord

Landlord, landlord,
My roof has sprung a leak.
Don't you 'member I told you about it
Way last week?

Landlord, landlord,
These steps is broken down.
When you come up yourself
It's a wonder you don't fall down.

Ten Bucks you say I owe you?
Ten Bucks you say is due?
Well, that's Ten Bucks more'n I'll pay you
Till you fix this house up new.

What? You gonna get eviction orders?
You gonna cut off my heat?
You gonna take my furniture and
Throw it in the street?

Um-huh! You talking high and mighty.
Talk on—till you get through.
You ain't gonna be able to say a word
If I land my fist on you.

Police! Police!
Come and get this man!
He's trying to ruin the government
And overturn the land!

Copper's whistle!
Patrol bell!
Arrest.

Precinct Station.
Iron cell.
Headlines in press:

MAN THREATENS LANDLORD

TENANT HELD NO BAIL

JUDGE GIVES NEGRO 90 DAYS IN COUNTY JAIL

1940, 1955

Madam and the Rent Man

The rent man knocked.
He said, Howdy-do?
I said, What
Can I do for you?
He said, You know
Your rent is due.

I said, Listen,
Before I'd pay
I'd go to Hades
And rot away!

The sink is broke,
The water don't run,
And you ain't done a thing
You promised to've done.

Back window's cracked,
Kitchen floor squeaks,
There's rats in the cellar,
And the attic leaks.

He said, Madam,
It's not up to me.
I'm just the agent,
Don't you see?

I said, Naturally,
You pass the buck.
If it's money you want
You're out of luck.

He said, Madam,
I ain't pleased!
I said, Neither am I.

So we agrees!

1943

Trumpet Player

The Negro
With the trumpet at his lips
Has dark moons of weariness
Beneath his eyes
Where the smoldering memory
Of slave ships
Blazed to the crack of whips
About his thighs.

The Negro
With the trumpet at his lips
Has a head of vibrant hair
Tamed down,
Patent-leathered[1] now
Until it gleams
Like jet—
Were jet a crown.

The music
From the trumpet at his lips
Is honey
Mixed with liquid fire.
The rhythm
From the trumpet at his lips
Is ecstasy
Distilled from old desire—

Desire
That is longing for the moon
Where the moonlight's but a spotlight
In his eyes,
Desire
That is longing for the sea
Where the sea's a bar-glass
Sucker size.

The Negro
With the trumpet at his lips
Whose jacket
Has a *fine* one-button roll,
Does not know
Upon what riff[2] the music slips
Its hypodermic needle
To his soul—

But softly
As the tune comes from his throat
Trouble
Mellows to a golden note.

1947

1. Shiny leather; sometimes synthetic material.
2. Improvised passage.

Song for Billie Holiday[1]

What can purge my heart
Of the song
And the sadness?
What can purge my heart
But the song
Of the sadness?
What can purge my heart
Of the sadness
Of the song?

Do not speak of sorrow
With dust in her hair,
Or bits of dust in eyes
A chance wind blows there.
The sorrow that I speak of
Is dusted with despair.

Voice of muted trumpet;
Cold brass in warm air.
Bitter television blurred
By sound that shimmers—
Where?

1949

Dream Boogie

Good morning, daddy!
Ain't you heard
The boogie-woogie[1] rumble
Of a dream deferred?

Listen closely:
You'll hear their feet
Beating out and beating out a—

You think
It's a happy beat?

Listen to it closely:
Ain't you heard
something underneath
like a—

What did I say?

Sure,
I'm happy!

1. Blues and jazz singer (1915–1959).

1. A style of dancing and music.

Take it away!

Hey, pop!
Re-bop!
Mop!

Y-e-a-h!

1951, 1959

Harlem

What happens to a dream deferred?

Does it dry up
like a raisin in the sun?
Or fester like a sore—
And then run?
Does it stink like rotten meat?
Or crust and sugar over—
like a syrupy sweet?

Maybe it just sags
like a heavy load.

Or does it explode?

1951, 1959

Motto

I play it cool
And dig all jive.
That's the reason
I stay alive.

My motto,
As I live and learn,
is:
Dig And Be Dug
In Return.

1951, 1967

Theme for English B

The instructor said,

Go home and write
a page tonight.

And let that page come out of you—
Then, it will be true.

I wonder if it's that simple?
I am twenty-two, colored, born in Winston-Salem.
I went to school there, then Durham,[1] then here
to this college[2] on the hill above Harlem.
I am the only colored student in my class.
The steps from the hill lead down into Harlem,
through a park, then I cross St. Nicholas,
Eighth Avenue, Seventh, and I come to the Y,
the Harlem Branch Y, where I take the elevator
up to my room, sit down, and write this page:

It's not easy to know what is true for you or me
at twenty-two, my age. But I guess I'm what
I feel and see and hear, Harlem, I hear you:
hear you, hear me—we two—you, me, talk on this page.
(I hear New York, too.) Me—who?
Well, I like to eat, sleep, drink, and be in love.
I like to work, read, learn, and understand life.
I like a pipe for a Christmas present,
or records—Bessie, bop, or Bach.[3]
I guess being colored doesn't make me *not* like
the same things other folks like who are other races.
So will my page be colored that I write?
Being me, it will not be white.
But it will be
a part of you, instructor.
You are white—
yet a part of me, as I am a part of you.
That's American.
Sometimes perhaps you don't want to be a part of me.
Nor do I often want to be a part of you.
But we are, that's true!
As I learn from you,
I guess you learn from me—
although you're older—and white—
and somewhat more free.

This is my page for English B.

1949

The Negro Artist and the Racial Mountain[1]

One of the most promising of the young Negro poets said to me once, "I want to be a poet—not a Negro poet," meaning, I believe, "I want to write

1. Winston-Salem and Durham are cities in North Carolina.
2. City College of New York.
3. Johann Sebastian Bach (1685–1750), German composer and musician. Bessie Smith (1894–1937), blues singer. "Bop": jazz music of the 1940s, characterized by discord and dissonance.

1. This essay originally appeared in *The Nation* in response to George S. Schuyler's essay "The Negro-Art Hokum," which was printed in *The Nation* the previous week.

like a white poet"; meaning subconsciously, "I would like to be a white poet"; meaning behind that, "I would like to be white." And I was sorry the young man said that, for no great poet has ever been afraid of being himself. And I doubted then that, with his desire to run away spiritually from his race, this boy would ever be a great poet. But this is the mountain standing in the way of any true Negro art in America—this urge within the race toward whiteness, the desire to pour racial individuality into the mold of American standardization, and to be as little Negro and as much American as possible.

But let us look at the immediate background of this young poet. His family is of what I suppose one would call the Negro middle class: people who are by no means rich yet never uncomfortable nor hungry—smug, contented, respectable folk, members of the Baptist church. The father goes to work every morning. He is a chief steward at a large white club. The mother sometimes does fancy sewing or supervises parties for the rich families of the town. The children go to a mixed school. In the home they read white papers and magazines. And the mother often says "Don't be like niggers" when the children are bad. A frequent phrase from the father is, "Look how well a white man does things." And so the word white comes to be unconsciously a symbol of all virtues. It holds for the children beauty, morality, and money. The whisper of "I want to be white" runs silently through their minds. This young poet's home is, I believe, a fairly typical home of the colored middle class. One sees immediately how difficult it would be for an artist born in such a home to interest himself in interpreting the beauty of his own people. He is never taught to see that beauty. He is taught rather not to see it, or if he does, to be ashamed of it when it is not according to Caucasian patterns.

For racial culture the home of a self-styled "high-class" Negro has nothing better to offer. Instead there will perhaps be more aping of things white than in a less cultured or less wealthy home. The father is perhaps a doctor, lawyer, landowner, or politician. The mother may be a social worker, or a teacher, or she may do nothing and have a maid. Father is often dark but he has usually married the lightest woman he could find. The family attend a fashionable church where few really colored faces are to be found. And they themselves draw a color line. In the North they go to white theaters and white movies. And in the South they have at least two cars and a house "like white folks." Nordic manners, Nordic faces, Nordic hair, Nordic art (if any), and an Episcopal heaven. A very high mountain indeed for the would-be racial artist to climb in order to discover himself and his people.

But then there are the low-down folks, the so-called common element, and they are the majority—may the Lord be praised! The people who have their hip of gin on Saturday nights and are not too important to themselves or the community, or too well fed, or too learned to watch the lazy world go round. They live on Seventh Street in Washington or State Street in Chicago and they do not particularly care whether they are like white folks or anybody else. Their joy runs, bang! into ecstasy. Their religion soars to a shout. Work maybe a little today, rest a little tomorrow. Play awhile. Sing awhile. O, let's dance! These common people are not afraid of spirituals, as for a long time their more intellectual brethren were, and jazz is their child. They furnish a wealth of colorful, distinctive material for any artist because they still hold their own individuality in the face of American standardizations. And perhaps these common people will give to the world its truly great Negro artist, the one who is not afraid to be himself. Whereas the better-class Negro would tell the artist what to do, the people at least let him alone when he does appear. And they are not ashamed of him—if they know he exists at all. And they accept what beauty is their own without question.

Certainly there is, for the American Negro artist who can escape the restrictions the more advanced among his own group would put upon him, a great field of unused material ready for his art. Without going outside his race, and even among the better classes with their "white" culture and conscious American manners, but still Negro enough to be different, there is sufficient matter to furnish a black artist with a lifetime of creative work. And when he chooses to touch on the relations between Negroes and whites in this country with their innumerable overtones and undertones surely, and especially for literature and the drama, there is an inexhaustible supply of themes at hand. To these the Negro artist can give his racial individuality, his heritage of rhythm and warmth, and his incongruous humor that so often, as in the Blues, becomes ironic laughter mixed with tears. But let us look again at the mountain.

A prominent Negro clubwoman in Philadelphia paid eleven dollars to hear Raquel Meller sing Andalusian[2] popular songs. But she told me a few weeks before she would not think of going to hear "that woman," Clara Smith,[3] a great black artist, sing Negro folksongs. And many an upper-class Negro church, even now, would not dream of employing a spiritual in its services. The drab melodies in white folks' hymnbooks are much to be preferred. "We want to worship the Lord correctly and quietly. We don't believe in 'shouting.' Let's be dull like the Nordics," they say, in effect.

The road for the serious black artist, then, who would produce a racial art is most certainly rocky and the mountain is high. Until recently he received almost no encouragement for his work from either white or colored people. The fine novels of Chesnutt[4] go out of print with neither race noticing their passing. The quaint charm and humor of Dunbar's[5] dialect verse brought to him, in his day, largely the same kind of encouragement one would give a sideshow freak (A colored man writing poetry! How odd!) or a clown (How amusing!).

The present vogue in things Negro, although it may do as much harm as good for the budding colored artist, has at least done this: it has brought him forcibly to the attention of his own people among whom for so long, unless the other race had noticed him beforehand, he was a prophet with little honor. I understand that Charles Gilpin[6] acted for years in Negro theaters without any special acclaim from his own, but when Broadway gave him eight curtain calls, Negroes, too, began to beat a tin pan in his honor. I know a young colored writer, a manual worker by day, who had been writing well for the colored magazines for some years, but it was not until he recently broke into the white publications and his first book was accepted by a prominent New York publisher that the "best" Negroes in his city took the trouble to discover that he lived there. Then almost immediately they decided to give a grand dinner for him. But the society ladies were careful to whisper to his mother that perhaps she'd better not come. They were not sure she would have an evening gown.[7]

2. From a region of Spain.
3. Major blues singer (1885–1935).
4. Charles Chesnutt (1858–1932), author of three novels, *The House behind the Cedars* (1900), *The Marrow of Tradition* (1901), and *The Colonel's Dream* (1905); a biography of Frederick Douglass; and two short story collections, *The Conjure Woman* (1899) and *The Wife of His Youth and Other Stories of the Color Line* (1899).
5. Paul Laurence Dunbar (1872–1906), poet and author of the novel *Sport of the Gods* (1907).
6. American actor (1878–1930).
7. This incident, which happened to Hughes himself in 1925, is related in his autobiography *The Big Sea* (1940).

The Negro artist works against an undertow of sharp criticism and misunderstanding from his own group and unintentional bribes from the whites. "Oh, be respectable, write about nice people, show how good we are," say the Negroes. "Be stereotyped, don't go too far, don't shatter our illusions about you, don't amuse us too seriously. We will pay you," say the whites. Both would have told Jean Toomer not to write *Cane*.[8] The colored people did not praise it. The white people did not buy it. Most of the colored people who did read *Cane* hate it. They are afraid of it. Although the critics gave it good reviews the public remained indifferent. Yet (excepting the work of Du Bois[9]), *Cane* contains the finest prose written by a Negro in America. And like the singing of Robeson,[1] it is truly racial.

But in spite of the Nordicized Negro intelligentsia and the desires of some white editors we have an honest American Negro literature already with us. Now I await the rise of the Negro theater. Our folk music, having achieved world-wide fame, offers itself to the genius of the great individual American composer who is to come. And within the next decade I expect to see the work of a growing school of colored artists who paint and model the beauty of dark faces and create with new technique the expressions of their own soul-world. And the Negro dancers who will dance like flame and the singers who will continue to carry our songs to all who listen—they will be with us in even greater numbers tomorrow.

Most of my own poems are racial in theme and treatment, derived from the life I know. In many of them I try to grasp and hold some of the meanings and rhythms of jazz. I am as sincere as I know how to be in these poems and yet after every reading I answer questions like these from my own people: Do you think Negroes should always write about Negroes? I wish you wouldn't read some of your poems to white folks. How do you find anything interesting in a place like a cabaret? Why do you write about black people? You aren't black. What makes you do so many jazz poems?

But jazz to me is one of the inherent expressions of Negro life in America; the eternal tom-tom beating in the Negro soul—the tom-tom of revolt against weariness in a white world, a world of subway trains, and work, work, work; the tom-tom of joy and laughter, and pain swallowed in a smile. Yet the Philadelphia clubwoman is ashamed to say that her race created it and she does not like me to write about it. The old subconscious "white is best" runs through her mind. Years of study under white teachers, a lifetime of white books, pictures, and papers, and white manners, morals, and Puritan standards made her dislike the spirituals. And now she turns up her nose at jazz and all its manifestations—likewise almost everything else distinctly racial. She doesn't care for the Winold Reiss[2] portraits of Negroes because they are "too Negro." She does not want a true picture of herself from anybody. She wants the artist to flatter her, to make the white world believe that all Negroes are as smug and as near white in soul as she wants to be. But, to my mind, it is the duty of the younger Negro artist, if he accepts any duties at all from outsiders, to change through the force of his art that old whispering "I want to be white," hidden in the aspirations of his people, to "Why should I want to be white? I am a Negro—and beautiful!"

8. A collection (1923) of stories, poetry, and drama about the rural South and the urban North.

9. W. E. B. Du Bois (1868–1963) helped found the NAACP and edited its journal, *Crisis*, from 1910 to 1934; he is best known for *The Souls of Black Folk* (1903).

1. Paul Robeson (1898–1976), actor and singer.

2. Portrait painter (1886–1953).

So I am ashamed for the black poet who says, "I want to be a poet, not a Negro poet," as though his own racial world were not as interesting as any other world. I am ashamed, too, for the colored artist who runs from the painting of Negro faces to the painting of sunsets after the manner of the academicians because he fears the strange un-whiteness of his own features. An artist must be free to choose what he does, certainly, but he must also never be afraid to do what he might choose.

Let the blare of Negro jazz bands and the bellowing voice of Bessie Smith[3] singing Blues penetrate the closed ears of the colored nearintellectuals until they listen and perhaps understand. Let Paul Robeson singing "Water Boy," and Rudolph Fisher writing about the streets of Harlem, and Jean Toomer holding the heart of Georgia in his hands, and Aaron Douglas[4] drawing strange black fantasies cause the smug Negro middle class to turn from their white, respectable, ordinary books and papers to catch a glimmer of their own beauty. We younger Negro artists who create now intend to express our individual dark-skinned selves without fear or shame. If white people are pleased we are glad. If they are not, it doesn't matter. We know we are beautiful. And ugly too. The tom-tom cries and the tom-tom laughs. If colored people are pleased we are glad. If they are not, their displeasure doesn't matter either. We build our temples for tomorrow, strong as we know how, and we stand on top of the mountain, free within ourselves.

1926

3. Blues singer (1894–1937).
4. Artist and educator (1899–1979). Fisher (1897–1934), author of two novels, *The Walls of Jericho* (1928) and *The Conjure Man Dies* (1932).

NICOLÁS GUILLÉN
1902–1989

In April 1929 the aspiring poet Nicolás Guillén published an article titled "El Camino de Harlem" ("The Path of Harlem") in the conservative Havana newspaper *Diario de la Marina.* Noting the persistence of racial prejudice in Cuba, he observed that "unknowingly, we are separated in many arenas where we should be united," and argued that Cubans needed to transcend their differences in the interest of national unity. Otherwise, he warned, there might come a day when every town would have its "barrio negro" (Black neighborhood), "as in the land of our Northern neighbors." This was something to be avoided at all costs, Guillén counseled; it was "the path of Harlem."

But within a year, Guillén met a poet visiting Havana who gave him a more concrete image of the "Negro capital" to the North. The following March, he published another article in the newspaper based on his "Conversation with Langston Hughes," who Guillén noted "looks exactly like a Cuban 'little mulatto.'" He described Hughes as "one of the minds most sincerely interested in the things of the black race" who "more than any other poet in his language has managed to incorporate into North American literature the purest manifestations of popular music in the U.S., so deeply influenced by blacks." Hughes told him that going to West Africa in 1923 (as a crew member on a freighter) and seeing the suffering of Blacks under colonial rule had made him understand that he had to be "their friend, their voice, their support: their poet."

Within a month of Hughes's visit, Guillén published in the same newspaper a group of eight poems under the title *Motivos de son* ("*Son* Motifs") that have come to be recognized as one of the major events in the history of Cuban poetry. In the previous decade there had emerged an "Afro-Hispanic movement" among writers including the Puerto Rican Luís Palés Matos and the Cubans José Zacarías Tallet and Ramón Guiro; but whereas their verses luxuriated in exotic portraits of Black life, Guillén's poems were stark and authentic: encapsulations of the everyday lives of Black Cubans, in their own voices, taking up issues (skin color prejudice, poverty, erotic desire) that until then had never been considered proper material for poetic inspiration. Guillén had read some of Hughes's poems, like the emblematic "I, Too," in the Spanish translations of the white journalist Fernández de Castro. It is difficult to gauge the degree to which Guillén's revolutionary new work was influenced by reading these translations or by meeting Hughes. There is no question, however, that Guillén discovered in the Black Cuban popular music of the *son* a resource for his poetry in a manner strikingly parallel to the way Hughes had come to base his writing on the blues and jazz. As Guillén put it in another article, "without either the *son* being equal to the blues, or Cuba and the U.S. South being similar places, the *son*, in my view, is an appropriate form in which to write vernacular poems, perhaps because it is also, in fact, our most representative music."

Born in Camagüey a mere seven weeks after Cuba achieved independence, Guillén planned to study law but found himself inexorably drawn to literature. At the end of the 1920s he met the poet and journalist Gustavo Urrutia, who invited Guillén to contribute to "Ideales de una raza" ("Ideals of a Race"), a supplement on Black Cuban culture published in the *Diario de la Marina*. He published *Motivos de son* as a limited-edition pamphlet in the fall of 1930 and included its eight poems in his first full-length book, *Sóngoro cosongo*, a year later. The book's prologue was a remarkable manifesto in which Guillén first made the case that a properly Cuban poetry would have to be informed by Black culture. "These are mulatto verses," Guillén proclaimed. They "share the same elements that enter into the ethnic composition of Cuba," where "the Negro . . . contributes vital essences to our cocktail." Even if the races appeared to be distant, they were hooked together by "submarine" links, Guillén concluded, "like those underwater bridges which secretly join two continents. Therefore the spirit of Cuba is mixed-race [*mestizo*]."

Hughes was excited by Guillén's experiments, and as early as 1930 he began publishing translations of the poems in *Motivos de son* and *Sóngoro cosongo* in American periodicals, especially *Opportunity*. Eventually he collaborated with the Howard University professor Ben Frederic Carruthers to publish *Cuba Libre* (1948), a collection of translations of poems from *Motivos de son, Sóngoro cosongo*, and *Cantos para soldados y sones para turistas* ("Songs for Soldiers and *Sones* for Tourists") (1937). Their translations are a fascinating case study in the similarities and divergences between African American and Afro-Cuban vernacular culture. The English versions of some poems such as "Chévere" (translated as "Blade") are ingenious in concocting African American equivalents to the Cuban context, though at other times (as when a section of "West Indies, Ltd." identified as a *son* is simply retitled "Blues" for the English version) the parallels seem forced. *Cuba Libre* included a translation of "Little Ode," which appeared in *Sóngoro cosongo* but was actually written in 1929 before Guillén's encounter with Hughes. The poem was also published under the title "Pequeña oda a un Negro Boxeador Cubano" ("Little Ode to a Black Cuban Boxer") and is dedicated to Eligio Sardinias y Montalbo, the legendary Cuban fighter known as "Kid Chocolate" who moved to New York in 1928 and was World Junior Lightweight Champion in the early 1930s.

In the 1930s the purview and ambition of Guillén's poetry broadened: while his early work emphasized Black popular life on the island, the focus expanded in *West Indies, Ltd.* (1934), which criticized the domination of outside forces (especially

U.S. corporations) across the Caribbean region. At the end of the decade Guillén participated in international writers' movements, including the Congress of the League of Revolutionary Writers and Artists (1937) in Mexico and the Second International Congress of Writers for the Defense of Culture (1938) in Spain, where he again spent time with Hughes, and these travels are reflected in books such as *España: Poema en cuatro angustias y una esperanza* ("Spain: Poem in Four Anxieties and a Hope") (1937). Guillén also joined the Cuban Communist Party and edited left-wing periodicals. After a period in exile in France due to his political activities, he came back to Havana in January 1959 a few weeks after the Cuban Revolution; his first public reading upon his return took place at the invitation of Che Guevara at an event for the soldiers of the victorious rebel army. In 1961 he was proclaimed Cuba's National Poet and named president of UNEAC (the Union of Cuban Writers and Artists), a position he would hold until the end of his life.

Among Guillén's great later works are book-length suites such as the allegorical bestiary *El Gran Zoo* ("The Great Zoo"; 1967) and the sardonic historical montage *El diario que a diario* ("The Daily Daily"; 1972), which have both appeared in English translation. Among the compilations of selected poems by Guillén available in English, *Man-Making Words* (1972), translated by Robert Máquez and David Arthur McMurray, contains all six of the magnificent *Elegias* ("Elegies"; 1958) that are the major product of Guillén's mid-century exile, including poems dedicated to Emmett Till and the Haitian writer Jacques Roumain as well as the "family elegy" titled "El apellido" ("My Last Name"), a profound meditation on diasporic identity.

Little Ode[1]

Gloves ready poised
at the ends of your squirrel-like body,
Oh, the punch of your smile!
Up North it's fierce and cold, boxer,
but Broadway
pulses like the blood in your veins,
and stamps enthusiastically around those rings
where you leap like a modern monkey of elastic
needing neither ropes nor the pillows of the clinch;
Broadway
spreads wide its melon-like mouth
in surprise at your sport-model car,
your hair sleek black rubber,
your shoes of patent leather.

This same Broadway
extends its beast-like lips
in a great wet bridge
to lick greedily
at the blood of our cane fields.
Certainly you don't keep in touch with things
that happen here,
nor with the current events up there,
because training is hard
and muscles are traitorous

1. Also published under the title "*Pequeña oda a un Negro Boxeador Cubano*" ("Little Ode to a Black Cuban Boxer"), this poem was dedicated to Eligio Sardinias y Montalbo, also known as "Kid Chocolate" (1910–1988), the great Cuban boxer who moved to New York in 1928 and was World Junior Lightweight Champion from 1931 to 1933.

and you must be "strong like a bull"—
as you've learned to say—
so that your blows will hurt more.
Your English,
even worse
than your bad Spanish,
is still enough for you
to understand in the ring
those guys who spit at you
their dirty slang
while you
mow them down,
jab by jab.

I really don't think you need much
because, as you're certainly aware,
you've made your place—
which is what interests you,
and us, as well.
The best thing, after all,
is to get a punching bag,
lose weight in the sun,
jumping,
sweating,
swimming,
from rope to shadow boxing,
from the showers to the table,
to come out glowing, fine strong,
like a newly made cane,
hard and aggressive
as a blackjack.

Now that the white world
toasts its body in our sun
and looks for *rumbas*[2] in Havana,
shine in your blackness, kid,
while the crowd applauds.
Envied by the whites,
speak for the blacks indeed!

1948

My Last Name

A family elegy

I

Ever since school
and even before . . . Since the dawn, when I was
barely a patch of sleep and wailing,
since then

2. Popular Cuban music and dance with strong roots in West African traditions.

I have been told my name. A password
that I might speak with stars.
Your name is, you shall be called . . .
And then they handed me
this you see here written on my card,
this I put at the foot of all poems:
thirteen letters
that I carry on my shoulders through the street,
that are with me always, no matter where I go.
Are you sure it is my name?
Have you got all my particulars?
Do you already know my navigable blood,
my geography full of dark mountains,
of deep and bitter valleys
that are not on the maps?
Perhaps you have visited my chasms,
my subterranean galleries
with great moist rocks,
islands jutting out of black puddles,
where I feel the pure rush
of ancient waters
falling from my proud heart
with a sound that's fresh and deep
to a place of flaming trees,
acrobatic monkeys,
legislative parrots and snakes?
Does all my skin (I should have said),
Does all my skin come from that Spanish marble?
My frightening voice too,
the harsh cry in my throat?
Are all my bones from there?
My roots and the roots
of my roots and also
these dark branches swayed by dreams
and these flowers blooming on my forehead
and this sap embittering my bark?
Are you certain?
Is there nothing more than this that you have written,
than this which you have stamped
with the seal of anger?
(Oh, I should have asked!)

Well then, I ask you now:
Don't you see these drums in my eyes?
Don't you see these drums, tightened and
beaten with two dried-up tears?
Don't I have, perhaps,
a nocturnal grandfather
with a great black scar
(darker still than his skin)
a great scar made by a whip?
Have I not, then,
a grandfather who's Mandingo, Dahoman, Congolese?
What is his name? Oh, yes, give me his name!

Andrés? Francisco? Amable?
How do you say Andrés in Congolese?
How have you always said
Francisco in Dahoman?
In Mandingo, how do you say Amable?
No? Were they, then, other names?
The last name then!
Do you know my other last name, the one that comes
to me from that enormous land, the captured,
bloody last name, that came across the sea
in chains, which came in chains across the sea.

Ah, you can't remember it!
You have dissolved it in immemorial ink.
You stole it from a poor, defenseless Black.
You hid it, thinking that I would
lower my eyes in shame.
Thank you!
I am grateful to you!
Noble people, thanks!
Merci!
Merci bien!
Merci beaucoup!
But no . . . Can you believe it? No.
I am clean.
My voice sparkles like newly polished metal.
Look at my shield: it has a baobab,
it has a rhinoceros and a spear.
I am also the grandson,
great grandson,
great great grandson of a slave.
(Let the master be ashamed.)
Am I Yelofe?
Nicolás Yelofe, perhaps?
Or Nicolás Bakongo?
Maybe Gullén Banguila?
Or Kumbá?
Perhaps Guillén Kumbá?
Or Kongué?
Could I be Guillén Kongué?
Oh, who knows!
What a riddle in the waters!

II

I feel immense night fall
on profound beasts,
on innocent castigated souls;
but also on ready voices,
which steal suns from the sky,
the brightest suns,
to decorate combatant blood.
From some flaming land pierced through
by the great equatorial arrow,

I know there will come distant cousins,
my ancestral anguish cast upon the winds;
I know there will come portions of my veins,
my ancestral blood,
with calloused feet bending frightened grasses;
I know there will come men whose lives are green,
my ancestral jungle,
with their pain open like a cross and their breasts red with flames.
Having never met, we will know each other by the hunger,
by the tuberculosis and the syphilis,
by the sweat bought in a black market,
by the fragments of chain
still clinging to the skin;
Having never met we will know each other
by the dream-full eyes
and even by the rock-hard insults
the quadrumanes[1] of ink and paper
spit at us each day.
What can it matter, then.
(What does it matter now!)
ah, my little name
of thirteen letters?
Or the Mandingo, Bantu,
Yoruba, Dahoman name
of the sad grandfather drowned
in notary's ink.
Good friends, what does it matter?
Oh, yes, good friends
come look at my name!
My name without end,
made up of endless names;
My name, foreign,
free and mine, foreign and yours,
foreign and free as the air.

1958

1. Archaic term for non-human primates.

COUNTEE CULLEN
1903–1946

In their adherence to a traditional poetic format, on the one hand, and their troubled perception of the issue of race, on the other, the lines "Yet do I marvel at this curious thing: / To make a poet black, and bid him sing!" may rightly serve as the signature couplet for the brilliant poet Countee Cullen, who produced some of the most haunting lyrics of the Harlem Renaissance. An African American determined to succeed in the white-dominated field of literature, Cullen was probably the figure from the Harlem Renaissance who most closely corresponded to Alain Locke's idea of the New Negro. Because he wanted to succeed as a poet not by innovation but by adhering to the traditional standards and practices of English verse, Cullen shied away from being labeled a racial writer; yet he won his greatest poetic renown for his most race-conscious lyrics. His determined resistance to the theme that proved most fruitful for him is clear in one of his most frequently quoted remarks: "I find that I am actuated by a strong sense of race consciousness. This grows upon me, I find, as I grow older, and although I struggle against it, it colors my writing, I fear, in spite of everything I can do." Ambivalent though he may have been toward this theme in his own writing, many people were impressed by his power as an artist. In the mid-1920s, none of the younger Harlem poets, not even Langston Hughes, seemed more promising to Harlem readers than Countee Cullen.

Cullen's origins were long shrouded in mystery. However, it now seems clear that shortly after his birth in 1903 to Elizabeth Lucas in Louisville, Kentucky, Cullen was left in the care of Elizabeth Porter, who may have been his paternal grandmother. Cullen remained at Porter's New York residence until her death in 1918, at which time he was taken into the home of Reverend Frederick Cullen, pastor of the prominent Salem Methodist Episcopal church in Harlem, and his wife, Carolyn. With strong ties to the NAACP and the National Urban League, the Cullens were deeply interested in race matters. Their adopted son, grateful for their kindness but more romantic than they were, later described life with the religious couple as a constant posing of the problem of "reconciling a Christian upbringing with a pagan inclination." Cullen excelled as a student and as a poet at the predominantly white De Witt Clinton High School, from which he graduated in 1922, and then at New York University. While there, he won prizes in the Witter Bynner Poetry Contest (open to all American undergraduate college students) in 1923, 1924, and 1925. In 1925 he graduated Phi Beta Kappa and then began working on his master's degree at Harvard. Also that year, his first volume of poetry, *Color,* was published. His "Threnody for a Brown Girl" won him the John Reed Memorial Prize from *Poetry* magazine and his "Two Moods of Love" the Spingarn Award from the *Crisis.* He also took prizes in contests sponsored by *Palms* and *Opportunity.* The eminent literary critic Irving Babbit hailed Cullen's "Ballad of the Brown Girl" as the finest poem of its type ever written by an American.

In 1927, after returning to New York to work for Charles S. Johnson as assistant editor at *Opportunity,* Cullen published two more books of poetry, *Copper Sun* and *The Ballad of the Brown Girl: An Old Ballad Retold.* These books reflected his commitment to conservative forms. At Harvard he had studied poetry composition under Robert Hillyer, who required his pupils to master the Spenserian stanza, rime royal, terza rima, and other conventional poetic forms. Like Claude McKay, Cullen felt most at ease when working within a fairly rigid structure; he had little use for dialect verse or for blues and jazz as influences on poetry.

Throughout the 1920s he earned several honors. Cullen received the Harmon Foundation Literary Award in 1927, when he published his invaluable anthology of African American poetry, *Caroling Dusk.* His influence grew with the appearance of his column, "The Dark Tower," in *Opportunity* magazine. In 1928, Cullen received a Guggenheim fellowship. That year, he married Nina Yolande Du Bois, daughter of W. E. B. Du Bois, in perhaps the single most spectacular event of the Harlem Renaissance. More than one thousand guests and a host of onlookers witnessed this wedding at Reverend Cullen's Harlem church. The marriage, however, was a failure. Cullen left for Europe without Yolande only two months after the ceremony and formalized the divorce from Paris in 1930.

By that time, his career as a writer also was in decline. *The Black Christ and Other Poems* appeared in 1929, but left his admirers wondering about the future of a poet who had once seemed the brightest talent of the Harlem Renaissance. Cullen's only novel, *One Way to Heaven* (1932), was also a disappointment. One of its two plots concerns the relationship between Mattie Johnson, who works as a maid in Harlem, and a one-armed Texas con man, Sam Lucas, who supports himself by moving from town to town and faking his conversion to Christianity. The other plot focuses on Constancia Brandon, Mattie's wealthy Black employer, who hosts literary gatherings of pretentious people who rarely read anything. The two plots seem fundamentally unrelated; according to the acerbic Rudolph Fisher, Cullen was guilty of "exhibiting a lovely pastel and cartoon on the same frame." Cullen went on to collaborate with Harry Hamilton in adapting the novel to the stage, but it was never produced professionally.

In 1934, Cullen began teaching French and English at the Frederick Douglass Junior High School in New York. A year later, he brought out *The Medea and Some Poems,* based on his translation of Euripides; but it did little to revive his career as a writer. Later came two collections of children's stories, *The Lost Zoo* (1940) and *My Lives and How I Lost Them* (1942). Cullen's last major artistic endeavor was a collaboration with Arna Bontemps that resulted in the dramatization of Bontemps's novel *God Sends Sunday* as *St. Louis Woman.* Unfortunately for Cullen, several members of the Black cultural elite objected to its emphasis on life among the African American lower class. Cullen considered this criticism unjust and was deeply hurt by it. He died suddenly, only two and a half months before *St. Louis Woman* was produced in New York. After his death came *On These I Stand: An Anthology of the Best Poems of Countee Cullen,* a collection Cullen himself had arranged.

One of Cullen's main admirers, James Weldon Johnson, noted: "Cullen himself has declared that, in the sense of wishing for consideration or allowances on account of race or of recognizing for himself any limitation to 'racial' themes and forms, he has no desire or intention of being a Negro poet. In this he is not only within his right; he is right. Yet, strangely, it is because Cullen revolts against these 'racial' limitations—technical and spiritual—that the best of his poetry is motivated by race." The truth seems to be that Cullen was as gifted as any writer of the Harlem Renaissance and that in his vacillations and insecurities he mirrored enduring truths about the psychological state of many African Americans. Some of his poems are unforgettable, so capable was Cullen of setting down in precise language the subtle feelings that made him one of the most intriguing writers in African American literature.

Yet Do I Marvel

I doubt not God is good, well-meaning, kind,
And did He stoop to quibble could tell why
The little buried mole continues blind,
Why flesh that mirrors Him must some day die,
Make plain the reason tortured Tantalus[1]
Is baited by the fickle fruit, declare
If merely brute caprice dooms Sisyphus[2]
To struggle up a never-ending stair.
Inscrutable His ways are, and immune
To catechism[3] by a mind too strewn
With petty cares to slightly understand

1. In Greek myth, he was punished after death by being placed by a pool of water that retreated whenever he stooped to drink and under trees whose branches lurched upward whenever he reached for their fruit.
2. He spent eternity struggling to roll uphill a boulder that forever rolled back down.
3. Knowledge gained from questions and answers.

What awful brain compels His awful hand.
Yet do I marvel at this curious thing:
To make a poet black, and bid him sing!

1925

Incident

(For Eric Walrond)[1]

Once riding in old Baltimore,
Heart-filled, head-filled with glee,
I saw a Baltimorean
Keep looking straight at me.

Now I was eight and very small,
And he was no whit bigger,
And so I smiled, but he poked out
His tongue, and called me, "Nigger."

I saw the whole of Baltimore
From May until December;
Of all the things that happened there
That's all that I remember.

1925

The Shroud of Color

(For Llewellyn Ransom)

"Lord, being dark," I said, "I cannot bear
The further touch of earth, the scented air;
Lord, being dark, forewilled to that despair
My color shrouds me in, I am as dirt
Beneath my brother's heel; there is a hurt
In all the simple joys which to a child
Are sweet; they are contaminate, defiled
By truths of wrongs the childish vision fails
To see; too great a cost this birth entails.
I strangle in this yoke drawn tighter than
The worth of bearing it, just to be man.
I am not brave enough to pay the price
In full; I lack the strength to sacrifice.
I who have burned my hands upon a star,
And climbed high hills at dawn to view the far
Illimitable wonderments of earth,

1. Author of *Tropic Death* (1926).

For whom all cups have dripped the wine of mirth,
For whom the sea has strained her honeyed throat
Till all the world was sea, and I a boat
Unmoored, on what strange quest I willed to float;
Who wore a many-colored coat[1] of dreams,
Thy gift, O Lord—I whom sun-dabbled streams
Have washed, whose bare brown thighs have held the sun
Incarcerate until his course was run,[2]
I who considered man a high-perfected
Glass where loveliness could lie reflected,
Now that I sway athwart Truth's deep abyss,
Denuding man for what he was and is,
Shall breath and being so inveigle me
That I can damn my dreams to hell, and be
Content, each new-born day, anew to see
The steaming crimson vintage of my youth
Incarnadine° the altar-slab of Truth? *stain red*

Or hast Thou, Lord, somewhere I cannot see,
A lamb imprisoned in a bush for me?[3]
Not so? Then let me render one by one
Thy gifts, while still they shine; some little sun
Yet gilds these thighs; my coat, albeit worn,
Still hold its colors fast; albeit torn,
My heart will laugh a little yet, if I
May win of Thee this grace, Lord: on this high
And sacrificial hill 'twixt earth and sky,
To dream still pure all that I loved, and die.
There is no other way to keep secure
My wild chimeras,[4] grave-locked against the lure
Of Truth, the small hard teeth of worms, yet less
Envenomed than the mouth of Truth, will bless
Them into dust and happy nothingness.
Lord, Thou art God; and I, Lord, what am I
But dust? With dust my place. Lord, let me die."

Across the earth's warm, palpitating crust
I flung my body in embrace; I thrust
My mouth into the grass and sucked the dew,
Then gave it back in tears my anguish drew;
So hard I pressed against the ground, I felt
The smallest sandgrain like a knife, and smelt
The next year's flowering; all this to speed
My body's dissolution, fain to feed
The worms. And so I groaned, and spent my strength
Until, all passion spent, I lay full length
And quivered like a flayed and bleeding thing.

1. An allusion to Joseph's coat of many colors (Genesis 37:3).
2. Bathed in the sun from morning to night.
3. Just as Abraham was about to sacrifice his son, Isaac, God stopped him and told him to slaughter instead a ram caught in the bushes nearby (Genesis 22:12–13).
4. Imaginings; traditionally, a mythical creature having a lion's head, a goat's body, and a serpent's tail.

So lay till lifted on a great black wing
That had no mate nor flesh-apparent trunk
To hamper it; with me all time had sunk
Into oblivion; when I awoke
The wing hung poised above two cliffs that broke
The bowels of the earth in twain, and cleft
The seas apart. Below, above, to left,
To right, I saw what no man saw before:
Earth, hell, and heaven; sinew, vein, and core.
All things that swim or walk or creep or fly,
All things that live and hunger, faint and die,
Were made majestic then and magnified
By sight so clearly purged and deified.
The smallest bug that crawls was taller than
A tree, the mustard seed loomed like a man.
The earth that writhes eternally with pain
Of birth, and woe of taking back her slain,
Laid bare her teeming bosom to my sight,
And all was struggle, gasping breath, and fight.
A blind worm here dug tunnels to the light,
And there a seed, racked with heroic pain,
Thrust eager tentacles to sun and rain;
It climbed; it died; the old love conquered me
To weep the blossom it would never be.
But here a bud won light; it burst and flowered
Into a rose whose beauty challenged, "Coward!"
There was no thing alive save only I
That held life in contempt and longed to die.
And still I writhed and moaned, "The curse, the curse,
Than animated death, can death be worse?"

"Dark child of sorrow, mine no less, what art
Of mine can make thee see and play thy part?
The key to all strange things is in thy heart."[5]

What voice was this that coursed like liquid fire
Along my flesh, and turned my hair to wire?

I raised my burning eyes, beheld a field
All multitudinous with carnal yield,
A grim ensanguined° mead whereon I saw *bloodied*
Evolve the ancient fundamental law[6]
Of tooth and talon, fist and nail and claw.
There with the force of living, hostile hills
Whose clash the hemmed-in vale with clamor fills,
With greater din contended fierce majestic wills
Of beast with beast, of man with man, in strife
For love of what my heart despised, for life
That unto me at dawn was now a prayer
For night, at night a bloody heart-wrung tear

5. At this point, the speaker is cast along the lines of a biblical prophet, such as Ezekiel, and experiences divine visions.
6. That is, of evolution or survival of the fittest.

For day again; for *this,* these groans
From tangled flesh and interlocked bones.
And no thing died that did not give
A testimony that it longed to live.
Man, strange composite blend of brute and god,
Pushed on, nor backward glanced where last he trod:
He seemed to mount a misty ladder flung
Pendant from a cloud, yet never gained a rung
But at his feet another tugged and clung.
My heart was still a pool of bitterness,
Would yield nought else, nought else confess.
I spoke (although no form was there
To see, I knew an ear was there to hear),
"Well, let them fight; they *can* whose flesh is fair."

Crisp lightning flashed; a wave of thunder shook
My wing; a pause, and then a speaking, "Look."

I scarce dared trust my ears or eyes for awe
Of what they heard, and dread of what they saw;
For, privileged beyond degree, this flesh
Beheld God and His heaven in the mesh
Of Lucifer's revolt,[7] saw Lucifer
Glow like the sun, and like a dulcimer
I heard his sin-sweet voice break on the yell
Of God's great warriors: Gabriel,
Saint Clair and Michael, Israfel and Raphael.
And strange it was to see God with His back
Against a wall, to see Christ hew and hack
Till Lucifer, pressed by the mighty pair,
And losing inch by inch, clawed at the air
With fevered wings; then, lost beyond repair,
He tricked a mass of stars[8] into his hair;
He filled his hands with stars, crying as he fell,
"A star's a star although it burns in hell."
So God was left to His divinity,
Omnipotent at that most costly fee.

There was a lesson here, but still the clod
In me was sycophant unto the rod,
And cried, "Why mock me thus? Am I a god?"

"One trial more: this failing, then I give
You leave to die; no further need to live."

Now suddenly a strange wild music smote
A chord long impotent in me; a note
Of jungles, primitive and subtle, throbbed
Against my echoing breast, and tom-toms sobbed
In every pulse-beat of my frame. The din

7. In Christianity, Lucifer (the name of the morning star as well as of Satan) led a revolt against God just before the world was created.

8. The fallen third of the host of heaven that Satan is reported to have enlisted on his side of the battle.

A hollow log bound with a python's skin
Can make wrought every nerve to ecstasy,
And I was wind and sky again, and sea,
And all sweet things that flourish, being free.

Till all at once the music changed its key.

And now it was of bitterness and death,
The cry the lash extorts, the broken breath
Of liberty enchained; and yet there ran
Through all a harmony of faith in man,
A knowledge all would end as it began.
All sights and sounds and aspects of my race
Accompanied this melody, kept pace
With it; with music all their hopes and hates
Were charged, not to be downed by all the fates.
And somehow it was borne upon my brain
How being dark, and living through the pain
Of it, is courage more than angels have. I knew
What storms and tumults lashed the tree that grew
This body that I was, this cringing I
That feared to contemplate a changing sky,
This that I grovelled, whining, "Let me die,"
While others struggled in Life's abattoir.° *slaughterhouse*
The cries of all dark people near or far
Were billowed over me, a mighty surge
Of suffering in which my puny grief must merge
And lose itself; I had no further claim to urge
For death; in shame I raised my dust-grimed head,
And though my lips moved not, God knew I said,
"Lord, not for what I saw in flesh or bone
Of fairer men; not raised on faith alone;
Lord, I will live persuaded by mine own.
I cannot play the recreant° to these; *traitor*
My spirit has come home, that sailed the doubtful seas."
With the whiz of a sword that severs space,
The wing dropped down at a dizzy pace,
And flung me on my hill flat on my face;
Flat on my face I lay defying pain,
Glad of the blood in my smallest vein,
And in my hands I clutched a loyal dream,
Still spitting fire, bright twist and coil and gleam,
And chiseled like a hound's white tooth.
"Oh, I will match you yet," I cried, "to truth."

Right glad I was to stoop to what I once had spurned,
Glad even unto tears; I laughed aloud; I turned
Upon my back, and though the tears for joy would run,
My sight was clear; I looked and saw the rising sun.

1925

Heritage

(For Harold Jackman)[1]

What is Africa to me:
Copper sun or scarlet sea,
Jungle star or jungle track,
Strong bronzed men, or regal black
Women from whose loins I sprang
When the birds of Eden sang?
One three centuries removed
From the scenes his fathers loved,
Spicy grove, cinnamon tree,[2]
What is Africa to me?

So I lie, who all day long
Want no sound except the song
Sung by wild barbaric birds
Goading massive jungle herds,
Juggernauts of flesh that pass
Trampling tall defiant grass
Where young forest lovers lie,
Plighting troth beneath the sky.

So I lie, who always hear,
Though I cram against my ear
Both my thumbs, and keep them there,
Great drums throbbing through the air.
So I lie, whose fount of pride,
Dear distress, and joy allied,
Is my somber flesh and skin,
With the dark blood dammed within
Like great pulsing tides of wine
That, I fear, must burst the fine
Channels of the chafing net
Where they surge and foam and fret.

Africa? A book one thumbs
Listlessly, till slumber comes.
Unremembered are her bats
Circling through the night, her cats
Crouching in the river reeds,
Stalking gentle flesh that feeds
By the river brink; no more
Does the bugle-throated roar
Cry that monarch[3] claws have leapt
From the scabbards where they slept.
Silver snakes that once a year
Doff the lovely coats you wear,
Seek no covert in your fear

1. A Harlem schoolteacher (1900–1960), probably Cullen's closest friend.
2. Despite this line, the cinnamon tree is not native to Africa.
3. Lion, king of the jungle.

Lest a mortal eye should see;
What's your nakedness to me?
Here no leprous flowers rear
Fierce corollas[4] in the air;
Here no bodies sleek and wet,
Dripping mingled rain and sweat,
Tread the savage measures of
Jungle boys and girls in love.
What is last year's snow to me,
Last year's anything? The tree
Budding yearly must forget
How its past arose or set—
Bough and blossom, flower, fruit,
Even what shy bird with mute
Wonder at her travail there,
Meekly labored in its hair.
One three centuries removed
From the scenes his fathers loved,
Spicy grove, cinnamon tree,
What is Africa to me?

So I lie, who find no peace
Night or day, no slight release
From the unremittant beat
Made by cruel padded feet
Walking through my body's street.
Up and down they go, and back,
Treading out a jungle track.
So I lie, who never quite
Safely sleep from rain at night—
I can never rest at all
When the rain begins to fall;
Like a soul gone mad with pain
I must match its weird refrain;
Ever must I twist and squirm,
Writhing like a baited worm,
While its primal measures drip
Through my body, crying, "Strip!
Doff this new exuberance.
Come and dance the Lover's Dance!"
In an old remembered way
Rain works on me night and day.

Quaint, outlandish heathen gods
Black men fashion out of rods,
Clay, and brittle bits of stone,
In a likeness like their own,
My conversion came high-priced;
I belong to Jesus Christ,
Preacher of humility;
Heathen gods are naught to me.

4. The petals collectively.

Father, Son, and Holy Ghost,
So I make an idle boast;
Jesus of the twice-turned cheek,
Lamb of God, although I speak
With my mouth thus, in my heart
Do I play a double part.
Ever at Thy glowing altar
Must my heart grow sick and falter,
Wishing He I served were black,
Thinking then it would not lack
Precedent of pain to guide it,
Let who would or might deride it;
Surely then this flesh would know
Yours had borne a kindred woe.
Lord, I fashion dark gods, too,
Daring even to give You
Dark despairing features where,
Crowned with dark rebellious hair,
Patience wavers just so much as
Mortal grief compels, while touches
Quick and hot, of anger, rise
To smitten cheek and weary eyes.
Lord, forgive me if my need
Sometimes shapes a human creed.

All day long and all night through,
One thing only must I do:
Quench my pride and cool my blood,
Lest I perish in the flood.
Lest a hidden ember set
Timber that I thought was wet
Burning like the dryest flax,
Melting like the merest wax,
Lest the grave restore its dead.
Not yet has my heart or head
In the least way realized
They and I are civilized.

1925

To John Keats,[1] Poet, at Spring Time

(For Carl Van Vechten)[2]

I cannot hold my peace, John Keats;
There never was a spring like this;
It is an echo, that repeats
My last year's song and next year's bliss.
I know, in spite of all men say
Of Beauty, you have felt her most.

1. English Romantic poet (1795–1821).

2. Writer and photographer (1880–1964).

Yea, even in your grave her way
Is laid. Poor, troubled, lyric ghost,
Spring never was so fair and dear
As Beauty makes her seem this year.

I cannot hold my peace, John Keats,
I am as helpless in the toil
Of Spring as any lamb that bleats
To feel the solid earth recoil
Beneath his puny legs. Spring beats
Her tocsin[3] call to those who love her,
And lo! the dogwood petals cover
Her breast with drifts of snow, and sleek
White gulls fly screaming to her, and hover
About her shoulders, and kiss her cheek,
While white and purple lilacs muster
A strength that bears them to a cluster
Of color and odor; for her sake
All things that slept are now awake.

And you and I, shall we lie still,
John Keats, while Beauty summons us?
Somehow I feel your sensitive will
Is pulsing up some tremulous
Sap road of a maple tree, whose leaves
Grow music as they grow, since your
Wild voice is in them, a harp that grieves
For life that opens death's dark door.
Though dust, your fingers still can push
The Vision Splendid to a birth,
Though now they work as grass in the hush
Of the night on the broad sweet page of the earth.

"John Keats is dead," they say, but I
Who hear your full insistent cry
In bud and blossom, leaf and tree,
Know John Keats still writes poetry.
And while my head is earthward bowed
To read new life sprung from your shroud,
Folks seeing me must think it strange
That merely spring should so derange
My mind. They do not know that you,
John Keats, keep revel with me, too.

1925

3. An alarm sounded on a bell.

From the Dark Tower

(To Charles S. Johnson)[1]

We shall not always plant while others reap
The golden increment of bursting fruit,
Not always countenance, abject and mute,
That lesser men should hold their brothers cheap;
Not everlastingly while others sleep
Shall we beguile their limbs with mellow flute,[2]
Not always bend to some more subtle brute;
We were not made eternally to weep.

The night whose sable breast relieves the stark,
White stars is no less lovely being dark,
And there are buds that cannot bloom at all
In light, but crumple, piteous, and fall;
So in the dark we hide the heart that bleeds,
And wait, and tend our agonizing seeds.

1927

1. Founder and editor of *Opportunity* magazine (1893–1956).

2. Relax them with music.

RICHARD BRUCE NUGENT
1906–1987

Richard Bruce Nugent made his way to Harlem from Washington, D.C., where one evening in the summer of 1925 he met Langston Hughes at Georgia Douglas Johnson's salon. Dazzled by Hughes (who was only a few years older but had traveled to Africa and Europe and was already a published poet), Nugent accompanied him to New York to attend the *Crisis* awards dinner. Within the year Nugent had met most of the Harlem literary world, seen his poem "Shadow" printed in the October issue of *Opportunity*, contributed the sketch "Sahdji" to Alain Locke's *The New Negro*, and moved into an apartment on West 136th Street with Wallace Thurman. By the following March, when one of his drawings was featured on the cover of *Opportunity*, Nugent was ensconced in the irreverent coterie of younger writers (including Thurman, Hughes, Gwendolyn Bennett, and Zora Neale Hurston) who that fall would edit and publish their own journal, *Fire!!*

Nugent grew up in modest comfort in Washington until the age of thirteen, when his father died of tuberculosis and his mother moved the family to New York. While his precocious younger brother Gary Lambert (known as Pete) made a name for himself as a tap dancer, eventually leaving home to tour, Nugent took a series of menial if diverting jobs: when he worked as a delivery boy for Youmans Hats on Fifth Avenue, his customers included the actor Buster Keaton; later, as a bellhop at the women-only

Drawings for Mulattoes, Number 2, by Nugent, an illustration for the 1927 anthology *Ebony and Topaz.*

Martha Washington Hotel, he fell in love with a Panamanian kitchen employee named Juan José Viana, who he later said was the model for "Beauty" in the story "Smoke, Lilies and Jade." Nugent also took art classes at the New York Evening School of Industrial Arts and the Traphagen School of Fashion. In late 1924, he told his mother that as an artist, he had decided he would no longer work for a living; she promptly sent him back to Washington to live with his grandmother. But he found his way back to New York with Hughes only a few months thereafter.

In the fall of 1927, Nugent responded to an open call for actors for DuBose and Dorothy Heyward's play *Porgy* and was hired (along with fellow writers Thurman and Dorothy West) for a non-speaking role. The show was a hit, and Nugent stayed through its extended run on Broadway as well as the subsequent national tour and a trip to England in 1929.

Nugent continued sporadically to publish his writing and illustrations in journals and anthologies and collaborated with Locke in expanding his sketch "Sahdji" into a full-length "African Ballet" that (with music by the Black composer William Grant Still and choreography by Thelma Biracree) was performed in 1931 at the Eastman School of Music in Rochester, and then in 1932 at the University of Illinois in Chicago. In New York, Nugent even danced himself with some of the pioneers of African American dance in the period, including Hemsley Winfield and Asadata Dafora. In the late 1930s Nugent worked (as did Claude McKay, Waring Cuney, Roi Ottley, and Ralph Ellison, among others) for the Federal Writers' Project. Over the coming decades, as Nugent continued to refuse to take on a steady job (to support himself, he took occasional part-time positions, including in a hardware supply company in lower Manhattan), he wrote a good deal of fiction but only published one short stand-alone work, *Beyond Where the Stars Stood Still*, in a limited edition in 1945.

In the 1970s and 1980s, Nugent, as one of the few surviving members of the renaissance generation, became a sought-after interview subject for scholars writing about the period. Gregarious, eloquent, and still debonair, he provided invaluable information about the goings-on among the younger writers, especially the raucous gatherings at the home he shared with Thurman (which they ironically called "Niggerrati Manor") and about the genesis and premature demise of *Fire!!*, which lasted only one issue but was notorious for what Alain Locke described disapprovingly as "the strong sex radicalism of many of the contributions."

The most scandalous contribution to *Fire!!* was Nugent's loosely autobiographical story "Smoke, Lilies and Jade," with its languid evocations of the bohemian existence, its vaguely Orientalist suggestions of decadence ("oh the joy of being an artist and of blowing blue smoke through an ivory holder inlaid with red jade and green . . ."), and especially its overt homoeroticism. Although there is reason to believe that sexual experimentation was just as prevalent in Harlem as downtown in the 1920s—and in particular that a number of the most prominent male writers in the renaissance were attracted to, or had sexual relationships with, other men—Nugent was unique in his forthrightness about his sexual orientation. "I have never been in what they call 'the closet,'" he remarked many years later. "It has *never* occurred to me that it was anything to be ashamed of, and it never occurred to me that it was anybody's business but mine." His voluminous unpublished writings, selections from which were edited by Thomas H. Wirth in 2002, are remarkable not only for their documentation of Black gay life in the Harlem Renaissance, but also for their refreshing humor and unrepentant hedonism and eroticism. As Nugent wrote in one of his unpublished novels, *Geisha Man*: "Is it wrong to love bodies? Just bodies? To cover myself with the sight of bodies, like I clothe myself in magnolia scent? Bodies call. Often, a body passing in night mystery will pierce my vision with the poignancy of a gull's cry. Of course, a gull's cry leaves a void even as it fills. But why not play a wonderful song on bodies, like one plucks the strings of a zither?"

Smoke, Lilies and Jade

He wanted to do something . . . to write or draw . . . or something . . . but it was so comfortable just to lie there on the bed . . . his shoes off . . . and think . . . think of everything . . . short disconnected thoughts . . . to wonder . . . to remember . . . to think and smoke . . . why wasn't he worried that he had no money . . . he *had* had five cents . . . but he had been hungry . . . he *was* hungry and still . . . all he wanted to do was . . . lie there comfortably smoking . . . think . . . wishing he were writing . . . or drawing . . . or something . . . something about the things he felt and thought . . . but what did he think . . . he remembered how his mother had awakened him one night . . . ages ago . . . six years ago . . . Alex . . . he had always wondered at the strangeness of it . . . she had seemed so . . . so . . . so just the same . . . Alex . . . I think your father is dead . . . and it hadn't seemed so strange . . . yet . . . one's mother didn't say that . . . didn't wake one at midnight every night to say . . . feel him . . . put your hand on his head . . . then whisper with a catch in her voice . . . I'm afraid . . . ssh don't wake Lam . . . yet it hadn't seemed as it should have seemed . . . even when he had felt his father's cool wet forehead . . . it hadn't been tragic . . . the light had been turned very low . . . and flickered . . . yet it hadn't been tragic . . . or weird . . . not at all as one should feel when one's father died . . . even his reply of . . . yes he is dead . . . had been commonplace . . . hadn't been dramatic . . . there had been no tears . . . no sobs . . . not even a sorrow . . . and yet he must have realized that one's father couldn't smile . . . or sing anymore . . . after he had died . . . everyone remembered his father's voice . . . it had been a lush voice . . . a promise . . . then that dressing together . . . his mother and himself . . . in the bathroom . . . why was the bathroom always the warmest room in the winter . . . as they had put on their clothes . . . his mother had been telling him what he must do . . . and cried softly . . . and that had made him cry too but you mustn't cry Alex . . . remember you have to be a little man now . . . and that was all . . . didn't other wives and sons cry more for their dead than that . . . anyway people never cried for beautiful sunsets . . . or music . . . and those were the things that hurt . . . the things to sympathize with . . . then out into the snow and dark of the morning . . . first to the undertaker's . . . no first to Uncle Frank's . . . why did Aunt Lula have to act like that . . . to ask again and again . . . but when did he die . . . when did he die . . . I just can't believe it . . . poor Minerva . . . then out into the snow and dark again . . . how had his mother expected him to know where to find the night bell at the undertaker's . . . he was the most sensible of them all though . . . all he had said was . . . what . . . Harry Francis . . . too bad . . . tell mamma I'll be there first thing in the morning . . . then down the deserted streets again . . . to grandmother's . . . it was growing light now . . . it must be terrible to die in daylight . . . grandpa had been sweeping the snow off the yard . . . he had been glad of that because . . . well he could tell him better than grandma . . . grandpa . . . father's dead . . . and he hadn't acted strange either . . . books lied . . . he had just looked at Alex a moment then continued sweeping . . . all he said was . . . what time did he die . . . she'll want to know . . . then passing through the lonesome street toward home . . . Mrs. Mamie Grant was closing a window and spied him . . . hallow Alex . . . an' how's your father this mornin' . . . dead . . . get out . . . tch tch tch an' I was just around there with a cup a' custard yesterday . . . Alex puffed contentedly on his cigarette . . . he was hungry and comfortable . . . and he had an ivory holder inlaid with red jade and green . . . funny how the smoke seemed to climb up that ray of sunlight . . . went up the slant just like imagination . . . was imagination blue . . . or was it because he had spent his last five cents and couldn't worry . . . anyway it was nice to lie there and wonder . . . and remember . . . why was he so different from other people . . . the only things he remembered of his father's funeral were the crowded church and the ride in the hack . . . so many people there in the church . . . and ladies with tears in their eyes . . . and on their cheeks . . . and some men too . . . why did people cry . . . vanity that was all . . . yet they weren't exactly hypocrites . . . but why . . . it had made him furious . . . all these people crying . . . it wasn't *their* father . . . and he wasn't crying . . . couldn't cry for sorrow although he had loved his father more than . . . than . . . it had made him so angry that tears had come to his eyes . . . and he had been ashamed of his mother . . . crying into a handkerchief . . . so ashamed that tears had run down his cheeks and he had frowned . . . and someone . . . a woman . . . had said . . . look at that poor little dear . . . Alex is just like his father . . . and the tears had run fast . . . because he *wasn't* like his father . . . he couldn't sing . . . he didn't want to sing . . . he didn't want to sing . . . Alex blew a cloud of smoke . . . blue smoke . . . when they had taken his father from the vault three weeks later . . . he had grown beautiful . . . his nose had become perfect and clear . . . his hair had turned jet black and glossy and silky . . . and his skin was a transparent green . . . like the sea only not so deep . . . and where it was drawn over the cheek bones a pale beautiful red appeared . . . like a blush . . . why hadn't his father looked like that always . . . but no . . . to have sung would have broken the wondrous repose of his lips and maybe that was his beauty . . . maybe it was wrong to think thoughts like these . . . but they were nice and pleasant and comfortable . . . when one was smoking a cigarette through an ivory holder . . . inlaid with red jade and green . . . .

he wondered why he couldn't find work . . . a job . . . when he had first come to New York he had . . . and he had only been fourteen then . . . was it because he was nineteen now that he felt so idle . . . and contented . . . or because he was an artist . . . but was he an artist . . . was one an artist until one became known . . . of course he was an artist . . . and strangely enough so were all his friends . . . he should be ashamed that he didn't work . . . but . . . was it five years in New York . . . or the fact that he was an artist . . . when his mother said she couldn't understand him . . . why did he vaguely pity her instead of being ashamed . . . he should be . . . his mother and all his relatives said so . . . his brother was three years younger than he and yet he had already been away from home a year . . . on the stage . . . making thirty-five dollars a week . . . had three suits and many clothes and was going to help mother . . . while he . . . Alex . . . was content to lay and smoke and meet friends at night . . . to argue and read Wilde . . . Freud . . . Boccacio and Schnitzler . . . to attend Gurdjieff meetings and know things . . . Why did they scoff at him for knowing such people as Carl . . . Mencken . . . Toomer . . . Hughes . . . Cullen . . . Wood . . . Cabell[1] . . . oh the whole lot of them . . . was it because it seemed incongruous that he . . . who was so little known . . . should call by first names people they would like to know . . . were they jealous . . . no mothers aren't jealous of their sons . . . they are proud of them . . . why then . . . when these friends accepted and liked him . . . no matter how he dressed . . . why did mother ask . . . and you went looking like that . . . Langston was a fine fellow . . . he knew there was something in Alex . . . and so did Rene and Borgia . . . and Zora and Clement and Miguel[2] . . . and . . . and . . . and all of them . . . if he went to see mother she would ask . . . how do you feel Alex with nothing in your pockets . . . I don't see how you can be satisfied . . . Really you're a mystery to me . . . and who you take after . . . I'm sure I don't know . . . none of my brothers were lazy and shiftless . . . I can never remember the time when they weren't sending money home and when your father was your age he was supporting a family . . . where you get your nerve I don't know . . . just because you've tried to write one or two little poems and stories that no one understands . . . you seem to think the world owes you a living . . . you should see by now how much is thought of them . . . you can't sell anything . . . and you won't do anything to make money . . . wake up Alex . . . I don't know what will become of you . . . .

it was hard to believe in one's self after that . . . did Wilde's parents or Shelley's or Goya's[3] talk to them like that . . . but it was depressing to think in that vein . . . Alex stretched and yawned . . . Max had died . . . Margaret had died . . . so had Sonia . . . Cynthia . . . Juan-Jose and Harry . . . all people he had loved . . . loved one by one and together . . . and all had died . . . he never loved a person long before they died . . . in truth he was tragic . . . that was a lovely appellation . . . The Tragic Genius . . . think . . . to go through life known as The Tragic Genius . . . romantic . . . but it was more or less true . . . Alex turned over and blew another cloud of smoke . . . was all life like that . . . smoke . . . blue smoke from an ivory holder . . . he

1. James Branch Cabell (1879–1958), white American novelist. Oscar Wilde (1854–1900), Irish writer. Sigmund Freud (1856–1939), Austrian psychoanalyst. Giovanni Boccaccio (1313–1375), Italian poet. Arthur Schnitzler (1862–1931), Austrian playwright and novelist. George Ivanovich Gurdjieff (ca. 1866–1949), Russian spiritual teacher and educator. Carl Van Vechten (1880–1964), writer and photographer. H. L. Mencken (1880–1956), critic, satirist, and editor. Jean Toomer (1894–1967), Harlem Renaissance fiction writer and poet. Langston Hughes (1902–1967), Harlem Renaissance poet. Clement Wood (1888–1950), white American poet and fiction writer.

2. Miguel Cocarrubias (1904–1957), Mexican artist and illustrator who moved to New York in 1923. Rene Borgia was the pseudonym of Venezuelan poet, screenwriter, and journalist Napoleón Acevedo (1892–1961). Harlem Renaissance author and folklorist Zora Neale Hurston (1891–1960).

3. Percy Bysshe Shelley (1792–1822), British poet. Francisco de Goya (1746–1828), Spanish painter.

wished he were in New Bedford[4] . . . New Bedford . . . New Bedford was a nice place . . . snug little houses set complacently behind protecting lawns . . . half-open windows showing prim interiors from behind waving cool curtains . . . inviting . . . like precise courtesans winking from behind lace fans . . . and trees . . . many trees . . . casting lacy patterns of shade on the sun-dipped sidewalks . . . small stores . . . naively proud of their pseudo grandeur . . . banks . . . called institutions for saving . . . all naive . . . that was it . . . New Bedford was naive . . . after the sophistication of New York it would fan one like a refreshing breeze . . . and yet he had returned to New York . . . and sophistication . . . was he sophisticated . . . no because he was seldom bored . . . seldom bored by anything . . . and weren't the sophisticated continually suffering from ennui[5] . . . on the contrary . . . he was amused . . . amused by the artificiality of naiveté and sophistication alike . . . but maybe that in itself was the essence of sophistication or . . . was it cynicism . . . or were the two identical . . . he blew a cloud of smoke . . . it was growing dark now . . . and the smoke no longer had a ladder to climb . . . but soon the moon would rise and then he would clothe the silver moon in blue smoke garments . . . truly smoke was like imagination . . . .

Alex sat up . . . pulled on his shoes and went out . . . it was a beautiful night . . . and so large . . . the dusky blue hung like a curtain in an immense arched doorway . . . fastened with silver tacks . . . to wander in the night was wonderful . . . myriads of inquisitive lights . . . curiously prying into the dark . . . and fading unsatisfied . . . he passed a woman . . . she was not beautiful . . . and he was sad because she did not weep that she would never be beautiful . . . was it Wilde who had said . . . a cigarette is the most perfect pleasure because it leaves one unsatisfied . . . the breeze gave to him a perfume stolen from some wandering lady of the evening . . . it pleased him . . . why was it that men wouldn't use perfumes . . . they should . . . each and every one of them liked perfumes . . . the man who denied that was a liar . . . or a coward . . . but if ever he were to voice that thought . . . express it . . . he would be misunderstood . . . a fine feeling that . . . to be misunderstood . . . it made him feel tragic and great . . . but maybe it would be nicer to be understood . . . but no . . . no great artist is . . . then again neither were fools . . . they were strangely akin these two . . . Alex thought of a sketch he would make . . . a personality sketch of Fania[6] . . . straight classic features tinted proud purple . . . sensuous fine lips . . . gilded for truth . . . eyes . . . half opened and lids colored mysterious green . . . hair black and straight . . . drawn sternly mocking back from the false puritanical forehead . . . maybe he would make Edith[7] too . . . skin a blue . . . infinite like night . . . and eyes . . . slant and gray . . . very complacent like a cat's . . . Mona Lisa lips . . . red and seductive as . . . as pomegranate juice . . . in truth it was fine to be young and hungry and an artist . . . to blow blue smoke from an ivory holder . . . .

here was the cafeteria . . . it was almost as though it had journeyed to meet him . . . the night was so blue . . . how does blue feel . . . or red or gold or any other color . . . if colors could be heard he could paint most wondrous tunes . . . symphonious . . . think . . . the dulcet clear tone of a blue like night . . . of a red like pomegranate juice . . . like Edith's lips . . . of the

4. Fishing town in Massachusetts.
5. Boredom (French).
6. Fania Marinoff (1887–1971), actress.
7. Edith Wilson (1896–1981), African American singer, vaudeville performer, and musical theater star.

fairy tones to be heard in a sunset . . . like rubies shaken in a crystal cup . . . of the symphony of Fania . . . and silver . . . and gold . . . he had heard the sound of gold . . . but they weren't the sounds he wanted to catch . . . no . . . they must be liquid . . . not so staccato but flowing variations of the same caliber . . . there was no one in the cafe as yet . . . he sat and waited . . . that was a clever idea he had had about color music . . . but after all he was a monstrous clever fellow . . . Jurgen[8] had said that . . . funny how characters in books said the things one wanted to say . . . he would like to know Jurgen . . . how does one go about getting an introduction to a fiction character . . . go up to the brown cover of the book and knock gently . . . and say hello . . . then timidly . . . is Duke Jurgen there . . . or . . . no because if one entered the book in the beginning Jurgen would only be a pawnbroker . . . and one didn't enter a book in the center . . . but what foolishness . . . Alex lit a cigarette . . . but Cabell was a master to have written Jurgen . . . and an artist . . . and a poet . . . Alex blew a cloud of smoke . . . a few lines of one of Langston's poems came to describe Jurgen . . . . .

Somewhat like Ariel
Somewhat like Puck
Somewhat like a gutter boy
Who loves to play in muck.
Somewhat like Bacchus
Somewhat like Pan
And a way with women
Like a sailor man . . . .

Langston must have known Jurgen . . . suppose Jurgen had met Tonio Kroeger[9] . . . what a vagrant thought . . . Kroeger . . . Kroeger . . . Kroeger . . . why here was Rene . . . Alex had almost gone to sleep . . . Alex blew a cone of smoke as he took Rene's hand . . . it was nice to have friends like Rene . . . so comfortable . . . Rene was speaking . . . Borgia joined them . . . and de Diego Padro . . . their talk veered to . . . James Branch Cabell . . . beautiful . . . marvelous . . . Rene had an enchanting accent . . . said sank for thank and souse for south . . . but they couldn't know Cabell's greatness . . . Alex searched the smoke for expression . . . he . . . he . . . well he has created a fantasy mire . . . that's it . . . from clear rich imagery . . . life and silver sands . . . that's nice . . . and silver sands . . . imagine lilies growing in such a mire . . . when they close at night their gilded underside would protect . . . but that's not it at all . . . his thoughts just carried and mingled like . . . like odors . . . suggested but never definite . . . Rene was leaving . . . they all were leaving . . . Alex sauntered slowly back . . . the houses all looked sleepy . . . funny . . . made him feel like writing poetry . . . and about death too . . . an elevated[1] crashed by overhead scattering all his thoughts with its noise . . . making them spread . . . in circles . . . then larger circles . . . just like a splash in a calm pool . . . what had he been thinking . . . of . . . a poem about death . . . but he no longer felt that urge . . . just walk and think and wonder . . . think and remember and smoke . . . blow smoke that mixed with his thoughts and the night . . . he would like to live in a large white palace . . . to wear a long black cape . . . very full and lined with vermilion . . . to have many cushions and to lie

8. The main character in *Jurgen: A Comedy of Justice* (1919), fantasy novel by American writer James Branch Cabell (1879–1958).

9. The protagonist of the 1903 novella *Tonio Kröger* by German writer Thomas Mann (1875–1955).

1. An elevated subway train.

there among them . . . talking to his friends . . . lie there in a yellow silk shirt and black velvet trousers . . . like music-review artists talking and pouring strange liquors from curiously beautiful bottles . . . bottles with long slender necks . . . he climbed the noisy stair of the odorous tenement . . . smelled of fish . . . of stale fried fish and dirty milk bottles . . . he rather liked it . . . he liked the acrid smell of horse manure too . . . strong . . . thoughts . . . yes to lie back among strangely fashioned cushions and sip eastern wines and talk . . . Alex threw himself on the bed . . . removed his shoes . . . stretched and relaxed . . . yes and have music waft softly into the darkened and incensed room . . . he blew a cloud of smoke . . . oh the joy of being an artist and of blowing blue smoke through an ivory holder inlaid with red jade and green . . .

the street was so long and narrow . . . so long and narrow . . . and blue . . . in the distance it reached the stars . . . and if he walked long enough . . . far enough . . . he could reach the stars too . . . the narrow blue was so empty . . . quiet . . . Alex walked music . . . it was nice to walk in the blue after a party . . . Zora had shone again . . . her stories . . . she always shone . . . and Monty was glad . . . everyone was glad when Zora shone . . . he was glad he had gone to Monty's party . . . Monty had a nice place in the village . . . nice lights . . . and friends and wine . . . mother would be scandalized that he could think of going to a party . . . without a copper to his name . . . but then mother had never been to Monty's . . . and mother had never seen the street seem long and narrow and blue . . . Alex walked music . . . the click of his heels kept time with a tune in his mind . . . he glanced into a lighted cafe window . . . inside were people sipping coffee . . . men . . . why did they sit there in the loud light . . . didn't they know that outside the street . . . the narrow blue street met the stars . . . that if they walked long enough . . . far enough . . . Alex walked and the click of his heels sounded . . . and had an echo . . . sound being tossed back and forth . . . back and forth . . . someone was approaching . . . and their echoes mingled . . . and gave the sound of castanets . . . Alex liked the sound of the approaching man's footsteps . . . he walked music also . . . he knew the beauty of the narrow blue . . . Alex knew that by the way their echoes mingled . . . he wished he would speak . . . but strangers don't speak at four o'clock in the morning . . . at least if they did he couldn't imagine what would be said . . . maybe pardon me but are you walking toward the stars . . . yes, sir, and if you walk long enough . . . then may I walk with you . . . I want to reach the stars too . . . perdone me señor tiene usted fósforo[2] . . . Alex was glad he had been addressed in Spanish . . . to have been asked for a match in English . . . or to have been addressed in English at all . . . would have been blasphemy just then . . . Alex handed him a match . . . he glanced at his companion apprehensively in the match glow . . . he was afraid that his appearance would shatter the blue thoughts . . . and stars . . . ah . . . his face was a perfect compliment to his voice . . . and the echo of their steps mingled . . . they walked in silence . . . the castanets of their heels clicking accompaniment . . . the stranger inhaled deeply and with a nod of content and a smile . . . blew a cloud of smoke . . . Alex felt like singing . . . the stranger knew the magic of blue smoke also . . . they continued in silence . . . the castanets of their heels

2. "Excuse me, sir: do you have a match?" (Spanish).

clicking rhythmically . . . Alex turned in his doorway . . . up the stairs and the stranger waited for him to light the room . . . no need for words . . . they had always known each other . . . .

as they undressed by the blue dawn . . . Alex knew he had never seen a more perfect being . . . his body was all symmetry and music . . . and Alex called him Beauty . . . long they lay . . . blowing smoke and exchanging thoughts . . . and Alex swallowed with difficulty . . . he felt a glow of tremor . . . and they talked and . . . slept . . .

Alex wondered more and more why he liked Adrian so . . . he liked many people . . . Wallie . . . Zora . . . Clement . . . Gloria . . . Langston . . . John . . . Gwenny[3] . . . oh many people . . . and they were friends . . . but Beauty . . . it was different . . . once Alex had admired Beauty's strength . . . and Beauty's eyes had grown soft and he had said . . . I like you more than anyone Dulce[4] . . . Adrian always called him Dulce . . . and Alex had become confused . . . was it that he was so susceptible to beauty that Alex liked Adrian so much . . . but no . . . he knew other people who were beautiful . . . Fania and Gloria . . . Monty and Bunny . . . but he was never confused before them . . . while Beauty . . . Beauty could make him believe in Buddha . . . or imps . . . and no one else could do that . . . that is no one but Melva . . . but then he was in love with Melva . . . and that explained that . . . he would like Beauty to know Melva . . . they were both so perfect . . . such compliments . . . yes he would like Beauty to know Melva because he loved them both . . . there . . . he had thought it . . . actually dared to think it . . . but Beauty must never know . . . Beauty couldn't understand . . . indeed Alex couldn't understand . . . and it pained him . . . almost physically . . . and tired his mind . . . Beauty . . . Beauty was in the air . . . the smoke . . . Beauty . . . Melva . . . Beauty . . . Melva . . . Alex slept . . . and dreamed . . . . .

he was in a field . . . a field of blue smoke and black poppies and red calla lilies . . . he was searching . . . on his hands and knees . . . searching . . . among black poppies and red calla lilies . . . he was searching and pushed aside poppy stems . . . and saw two strong white legs . . . dancer's legs . . . the contours pleased him . . . his eyes wandered . . . on past the muscular hocks to the firm white thighs . . . the rounded buttocks . . . then the lithe narrow waist . . . strong torso and broad deep chest . . . the heavy shoulders . . . the graceful muscled neck . . . squared chin and quizzical lips . . . Grecian nose with its temperamental nostrils . . . the brown eyes looking at him . . . like . . . Monty looked at Zora . . . his hair curly and black and all tousled . . . and it was Beauty . . . and Beauty smiled and looked at him and smiled . . . said . . . I'll wait Alex . . . and Alex became confused and continued his search . . . on his hands and knees . . . pushing aside poppy stems and lily stems . . . a poppy . . . a black poppy . . . a lily . . . a red lily . . . and when he looked back he could no longer see Beauty . . . Alex continued his search . . . through poppies . . . lilies . . . poppies and red calla lilies . . . and suddenly he saw . . . two small feet olive-ivory . . . two well-turned legs curving gracefully from slender ankles . . . and the contours soothed him . . . he followed them . . . past the narrow rounded hips to the tiny waist . . . the fragile firm breasts . . . the graceful slender throat . . . the soft rounded chin . . . slightly parting lips and straight little nose with its slightly flaring nostrils . . . the black eyes with lights in them . . . looking at

3. Gwendolyn Bennett (1902–1981). "Wallie": Wallace Thurman (1902–1934). Both were Harlem Renaissance writers.

4. A term of endearment, literally "sweet" (Spanish).

him . . . the forehead and straight cut black hair . . . and it was Melva . . . and she looked at him and smiled and said . . . I'll wait Alex . . . and Alex became confused and kissed her . . . became confused and continued his search . . . on his hands and knees . . . pushed aside a poppy stem . . . a black-poppy stem . . . pushed aside a lily stem . . . a red-lily stem . . . a poppy . . . a poppy . . . a lily . . . and suddenly he stood erect . . . exultant . . . and in his hand he held . . . an ivory holder . . . inlaid with red jade . . . and green . . . .

and Alex awoke . . . Beauty's hair tickled his nose . . . Beauty was smiling in his sleep . . . half his face stained flush color by the sun . . . the other half in shadow . . . blue shadow . . . his eyelashes casting cobwebby blue shadows on his cheek . . . his lips were so beautiful . . . quizzical . . . Alex wondered why he always thought of that passage from Wilde's Salome . . . when he looked at Beauty's lips . . . I would kiss your lips[5] . . . he *would* like to kiss Beauty's lips . . . Alex flushed warm . . . with shame . . . or was it shame . . . he reached across Beauty for a cigarette . . . Beauty's cheek felt cool to his arm . . . his hair felt soft . . . Alex lay smoking . . . such a dream . . . red calla lilies . . . red calla lilies . . . and . . . what could it all mean . . . did dreams have meanings . . . Fania said . . . and black poppies . . . thousands . . . millions . . . Beauty stirred . . . Alex put out his cigarette . . . closed his eyes . . . he mustn't see Beauty yet . . . speak to him . . . his lips were too hot . . . dry . . . the palms of his hands too cool and moist . . . through his half-closed eyes he could see Beauty . . . propped . . . cheek in hand . . . on one elbow . . . looking at him . . . lips smiling quizzically . . . he wished Beauty wouldn't look so hard . . . Alex was finding it difficult to breathe . . . breathe normally . . . why *must* Beauty look so long . . . and smile *that* way . . . his face seemed nearer . . . it was . . . Alex could feel Beauty's hair on his forehead . . . breathe normally . . . breathe normally . . . could feel Beauty's breath on his nostrils and lips . . . and it was clean and faintly colored with tobacco . . . breathe normally Alex . . . Beauty's lips were nearer . . . Alex closed his eyes . . . how did one act . . . his pulse was hammering . . . from wrist to finger tip . . . wrist to finger tip . . . Beauty's lips touched his . . . his temples throbbed . . . throbbed . . . his pulse hammered from wrist to finger tip . . . Beauty's breath came short now . . . softly staccato . . . breathe normally Alex . . . you are asleep . . . Beauty's lips touched his . . . breathe normally . . . and pressed . . . pressed hard . . . cool . . . his body trembled . . . breathe normally Alex . . . Beauty's lips pressed cool . . . cool and hard . . . how much pressure does it take to waken one . . . Alex sighed . . . moved softly . . . how does one act . . . Beauty's hair barely touched him now . . . his breath was faint on . . . Alex's nostrils and lips . . . Alex stretched and opened his eyes . . . Beauty was looking at him . . . propped on one elbow . . . cheek in his palm . . . Beauty spoke . . . scratch my head please Dulce . . . Alex was breathing normally now . . . propped against the bed head . . . Beauty's head in his lap . . . Beauty spoke . . . I wonder why I like to look at some things Dulce . . . things like smoke and cats . . . and you . . . Alex's pulse no longer hammered from . . . wrist to finger tip . . . wrist to finger tip . . . the rose dusk had become blue night . . . and soon . . . soon they would go out into the blue . . . .

5. A line from Oscar Wilde's one-act play *Salomé* (1891), originally written in French.

the little church was crowded . . . warm . . . the rows of benches were brown and sticky . . . Harold was there . . . and Constance and Langston and Bruce and John . . . there was Mr. Robeson[6] . . . . how are you Paul . . . a young man was singing . . . Caver . . . Caver was a very self-assured young man . . . such a dream . . . poppies . . . black poppies . . . they were applauding . . . Constance and John were exchanging notes . . . the benches were sticky . . . a young lady was playing the piano . . . fair . . . and red calla lilies . . . who had ever heard of red calla lilies . . . they were applauding . . . a young man was playing the viola . . . what could it all mean . . . so many poppies . . . and Beauty looking at him like . . . like Monty looked at Zora . . . another young man was playing a violin . . . he was the first real artist to perform . . . he had a touch of soul . . . or was it only feeling . . . they were hard to differentiate on the violin . . . and Melva standing in the poppies and lilies . . . Mr. Phillips was singing . . . Mr. Phillips was billed as a basso . . . and he had kissed her . . . they were applauding . . . the first young man was singing again . . . Langston's spiritual . . . Fy-ah-fy-ah-Lawd . . . fy-ah's gonna burn ma soul . . . Beauty's hair was so black and curly . . . they were applauding . . . encore . . . Fy-ah Lawd had been a success . . . Langston bowed . . . Langston had written the words . . . Hall bowed . . . Hall had written the music[7] . . . the young man was singing it again . . . Beauty's lips had pressed hard . . . cool . . . cool . . . fy-ah Lawd . . . his breath had trembled . . . fy-ah's gonna burn ma soul . . . they were all leaving . . . first to the roof dance . . . fy-ah Lawd . . . there was Catherine . . . she was beautiful tonight . . . she always was at night . . . Beauty's lips . . . fy-ah Lawd . . . hello Dot . . . why don't you take a boat that sails . . . when are you leaving again . . . and there's Estelle . . . everyone was there . . . fy-ah Lawd . . . Beauty's body had pressed close . . . close . . . fy-ah's gonna burn my soul . . . let's leave . . . have to meet some people at the New World . . . then to Augusta's party . . . Harold[8] . . . John . . . Bruce . . . Connie . . . Langston . . . ready . . . down one hundred thirty-fifth street . . . fy-ah . . . meet these people and leave . . . fy-ah Lawd . . . now to Augusta's party . . . fy-ah's gonna burn ma soul . . . they were at Augusta's . . . Alex half lay . . . half sat on the floor . . . sipping a cocktail . . . such a dream . . . red calla lilies . . . Alex left . . . down the narrow streets . . . fy-ah . . . up the long noisy stairs . . . fy-ahs gonna bu'n ma soul . . . his head felt swollen . . . expanding . . . contracting . . . expanding . . . contracting . . . he had never been like this before . . . expanding . . . contracting . . . it was that . . . fy-ah . . . fy-ah Lawd . . . and the cocktails . . . and Beauty . . . he felt two cool strong hands on his shoulders . . . it was Beauty . . . lie down Dulce . . . Alex lay down . . . Beauty . . . Alex stopped . . . no no . . . don't say it . . . Beauty mustn't know . . . Beauty couldn't understand . . . are you going to lie down too Beauty . . . the light went out expanding . . . contracting . . . he felt the bed sink as Beauty lay beside him . . . his lips were dry . . . hot . . . the palms of his hands so moist and cool . . . Alex partly closed his eyes . . . from beneath his lashes he could see Beauty's face over his . . . nearer . . . nearer . . . Beauty's hair touched his forehead now . . . he could feel his breath on his nostrils and

6. Paul Robeson (1898–1976), African American actor, singer, and political activist.

7. The African American composer Francis Hall Johnson (1888–1970) wrote musical settings for a number of poems by Langston Hughes, including "Fire," a poem in Hughes's second collection, *Fine Clothes to the Jew* (1927).

8. Harold Jackman (1901–1961) high-school teacher, model, actor, and writer. Augusta Savage (1892–1962), Black sculptor associated with the Harlem Renaissance.

lips . . . Beauty's breath came short . . . breathe normally Beauty . . . breathe normally . . . Beauty's lips touched his . . . pressed hard . . . cool . . . opened slightly . . . Alex opened his eyes . . . into Beauty's . . . parted his lips . . . Dulce . . . Beauty's breath was hot and short . . . Alex ran his hand through Beauty's hair . . . Beauty's lips pressed hard against his teeth . . . Alex trembled . . . could feel Beauty's body . . . close against his . . . hot . . . tense . . . white . . . and soft . . . soft . . . soft . . . .

they were at Forno's . . . everyone came to Forno's once . . . maybe only once . . . but they came . . . see that big fat woman Beauty . . . Alex pointed to an overly stout and bejeweled lady making her way through the maze of chairs . . . that's Maria Guerrero[9] . . . Beauty looked to see a lady guiding almost the whole opera company to an immense table . . . really Dulce . . . for one who appreciates beauty you do use the most abominable English . . . Alex lit a cigarette . . . and that florid man with white hair . . . that's Carl . . . Beauty smiled . . . The Blind Bow-Boy . . . he asked . . . Alex wondered . . . everything seemed so . . . so just the same . . . here they were laughing and joking about people . . . there's Rene . . . Rene this is my friend Adrian . . . after that night . . . and he felt so unembarrassed . . . Rene and Adrian were talking . . . there was Lucrecia Bori[1] . . . she was bowing at their table . . . oh her cousin was with them . . . and Peggy Joyce[2] . . . everyone came to Forno's . . . Alex looked toward the door . . . there was Melva . . . Alex beckoned . . . Melva this is Adrian . . . Beauty held her hand . . . they talked . . . smoked . . . Alex loved Melva . . . in Forno's . . . everyone came there sooner or later . . . maybe only once . . . but . . . .

up . . . up . . . slow . . . jerk up . . . up . . . not fast . . . not glorious . . . but slow . . . up . . . up into the sun . . . slow . . . sure like fate . . . poise on the brim . . . the brim of life . . . two shining rails straight down . . . Melva's head was on his shoulder . . . his arm was around her . . . poised . . . the down . . . gasping . . . straight down . . . straight like sin . . . down . . . the curving shiny rail rushed up to meet them . . . hit the bottom then . . . shoot up . . . fast . . . glorious . . . up into the sun . . . Melva gasped . . . Alex's arm tightened . . . all goes up . . . then down . . . straight like hell . . . all breath squeezed out of them . . . Melva's head on his shoulder . . . up . . . up . . . Alex kissed her . . . down . . . they stepped out of the car . . . walking music . . . now over to the Ferris Wheel . . . out and up . . . Melva's hand was soft in his . . . out and up . . . over mortals . . . mortals drinking nectar . . . five cents a glass . . . her cheek was soft on his . . . up . . . up . . . till the world seemed small . . . tiny . . . the ocean seemed tiny and blue . . . up . . . up and out . . . over the sun . . . the tiny red sun . . . Alex kissed her . . . up . . . up . . . their tongues touched . . . up . . . seventh heaven . . . the sea had swallowed the sun . . . up and out . . . her breath was perfumed . . . Alex kissed her . . . drift down . . . soft . . . soft . . . the sun had left the sky flushed . . . drift down . . . soft down . . . back to earth . . . visit the mortals sipping nectar at five cents a glass . . . Melva's lips brushed his . . . then out among the mortals . . . and the sun had left a flush on Melva's cheeks . . . they walked hand in hand . . . and the moon came out . . . they walked in silence on the silver strip . . . and the sea sang for them . . .

9. María Guerrero Torija (1867–1928), Spanish theater actress and director.

1. Lucrezia Bori (1887–1960), Spanish opera singer.

2. Joyce (1893–1957), American actress and celebrity.

they walked toward the moon . . . we'll hang our hats on the crook of the moon Melva . . . softly on the silver strip . . . his hands molded her features and her cheeks were soft and warm to his touch . . . where is Adrian . . . Alex . . . Melva trod silver . . . Alex trod sand . . . Alex trod sand . . . the sea *sang* for her . . . Beauty . . . her hand felt cold in his . . . Beauty . . . the sea *dinned* . . . Beauty . . . he led the way to the train . . . and the train dinned . . . Beauty . . . dinned . . . dinned . . . her cheek *had* been soft . . . Beauty . . . Beauty . . . her breath *had* been perfumed . . . Beauty . . . Beauty . . . the sands *had* been silver . . . Beauty . . . Beauty . . . they left the train . . . Melva walked music . . . Melva said . . . don't make me blush again . . . and kissed him . . . Alex stood on the steps after she left him . . . and the night was black . . . down long streets to . . . Alex lit a cigarette . . . and his heels clicked . . . Beauty . . . Melva . . . Beauty . . . Melva . . . and the smoke made the night blue . . .

Melva had said . . . don't make me blush again . . . and kissed him . . . and the street had been blue . . . one *can* love two at the same time . . . Melva had kissed him . . . one *can* . . . and the street had been blue . . . one *can* . . . and the room was clouded with blue smoke . . . drifting vapors of smoke and thoughts . . . Beauty's hair was so black . . . and soft . . . blue smoke from an ivory holder . . . was that why he loved Beauty . . . one *can* . . . or because his body was beautiful . . . and white and warm . . . or because his eyes . . . one *can* love . . . .

. . . *To Be Continued* . . .

1926

HELENE JOHNSON
1907–1995

The youngest of the poets associated with the Harlem Renaissance, Helen Johnson (her pen name, Helene, was suggested to her by an aunt) was born in Boston, where she attended public schools and, for a time, Boston University. She came to New York in 1926 for *Opportunity* magazine's annual ceremony for the winners of its poetry contest, in which she had earned honorable mention, and stayed. When she moved into the only apartment building in mid-Manhattan that allowed Black tenants, another tenant was Zora Neale Hurston, and the two became friends. Johnson was also helped by her closeness to her cousin Dorothy West and later to Gwendolyn Bennett, both prominent figures in the Harlem Renaissance.

Johnson's early years in New York were her most productive. She published work in numerous magazines and anthologies, including *Opportunity, Vanity Fair, Fire!!*, and Cullen's *Caroling Dusk*. However, with her marriage (to William Warner Hubbell) and particularly after the birth of her daughter, Abigail, in 1940, Johnson wrote less. After she and her husband separated, Johnson returned to Massachusetts for some years before failing health brought her back to Manhattan, where she died. Of her own writings, she largely agreed with her critics in seeing the two dozen or so poems that she published in the late 1920s and early 1930s as her strongest work. Her poetry is marked by an often lovely lyricism in which a genteel sensuality and a usually muted expression of racial pride are blended.

Poem

Little brown boy,
Slim, dark, big-eyed,
Crooning love songs to your banjo
Down at the Lafayette[1]
Gee, boy, I love the way you hold your head,
High sort of and a bit to one side,
Like a prince, a jazz prince. And I love
Your eyes flashing, and your hands,
And your patent-leathered feet,

And your shoulders jerking the jig-wa.° *a dance*
And I love your teeth flashing,
And the way your hair shines in the spotlight
Like it was the real stuff.
Gee, brown boy, I loves you all over.
I'm glad I'm a jig.° I'm glad I can *a Black person*
Understand your dancin' and your
Singin', and feel all the happiness
And joy and don't-care in you.
Gee, boy, when you sing, I can close my ears
And hear tomtoms just as plain.
Listen to me, will you, what do I know
About tomtoms? But I like the word, sort of,
Don't you? It belongs to us.
Gee, boy, I love the way you hold your head,
And the way you sing and dance,
And everything.
Say, I think you're wonderful. You're
All right with me,
You are.

1927

Sonnet to a Negro in Harlem

You are disdainful and magnificent—
Your perfect body and your pompous gait,
Your dark eyes flashing solemnly with hate,
Small wonder that you are incompetent
To imitate those whom you so despise—
Your shoulders towering high above the throng,
Your head thrown back in rich, barbaric song,

1. The Lafayette Theatre on 132nd Street and Seventh Avenue in New York.

Palm trees and mangoes stretched before your eyes.
Let others toil and sweat for labor's sake
And wring from grasping hands their meed° of gold. *reward*
Why urge ahead your supercilious feet?
Scorn will efface each footprint that you make.
I love your laughter arrogant and bold.
You are too splendid for this city street.

1927

Invocation

Let me be buried in the rain
In a deep, dripping wood,
Under the warm wet breast of Earth
Where once a gnarled tree stood.
And paint a picture on my tomb
With dirt and a piece of bough
Of a girl and a boy beneath a round, ripe moon
Eating of love with an eager spoon
And vowing an eager vow.
And do not keep my plot mowed smooth
And clean as a spinster's bed,
But let the weed, the flower, the tree,
Riotous, rampant, wild and free,
Grow high above my head.

1931

Timeline

African American Literature in Context

1492–1775

1492 Pedro Alonzo Nino, traditionally considered the first of many New World explorers of African descent, sails with Christopher Columbus

1526 African slaves brought to what is now the United States by the Spanish

1619 Twenty Africans brought to Jamestown, Virginia, on Dutch ship and sold as indentured servants

1623 William Tucker, in Jamestown, is the first Black child born in the English North American colonies

1641 Massachusetts becomes the first colony to legally recognize slavery

1645 First American slave ships sail, from Boston; triangular trade route brings enslaved Africans to West Indies in exchange for sugar, tobacco, and wine, which are then sold for manufactured goods in Massachusetts

1646 John Wham and his wife are freed, becoming first recorded free Blacks in New England

1652 Rhode Island passes first North American law against slavery

1662 Virginia is the first colony to declare that mother's status determines whether a child is born free or into slavery

1663 Major conspiracy by Black and white indentured servants in Virginia is betrayed by servant

1688 Pennsylvania Quakers sign first official written protest against slavery in North America

1712 New York City slave revolt is quelled by militia • Pennsylvania becomes first colony to outlaw slave trade

1734 "Great Awakening" religious revival begins; Methodist and Baptist churches attract Blacks by offering "Christianity for all"

1739 South Carolina enslaved people launch Stono Rebellion, killing 30 whites

1740 In response to the Stono Rebellion, South Carolina outlaws teaching enslaved people to write

1746 Lucy Terry writes "**Bars Fight**," the first poem extant by an African American (not published until 1895)

1756–63 African Americans fight in French and Indian War

1757 Phillis Wheatley purchased in Boston

1758 First Black Baptist church in colonies is erected on plantation in Virginia

1760 Jupiter Hammon, "**An Evening Thought: Salvation by Christ with Penitential Cries**," printed as a broadside, the first poetry published by an African American

1773 Phillis Wheatley, ***Poems on Various Subjects, Religious and Moral***, published in London, first book published by an African American and second book published by an American woman • Enslaved people in Massachusetts petition legislature for freedom for first time

1774 Continental Congress prohibits importation of enslaved people after December 1, 1774

1775–83 American Revolutionary War; battles fought by African Americans include Bunker Hill, Lexington, Concord

1775 First antislavery society organized by Philadelphia Quakers • Royal governor of Virginia offers freedom to any enslaved man joining British army; 800 respond to form "Ethiopian Regiment" • Second Continental Congress resolves against importation of enslaved people. "**The Last & Dying Words of MARK**," the earliest extant slave narrative published in North America

1776–1818

1776 Declaration of Independence adopted without antislavery statement proposed by Thomas Jefferson

1777 Vermont is one of the first states to abolish slavery in state constitution • New York is the first state to extend vote to Black males, but limits voting in 1815 and 1821 with permit, property, and residency requirements

1780 Pennsylvania becomes the first state to allow interracial marriage • Free Blacks in Massachusetts protest "taxation without representation" and petition for exemption from taxes

1783 Massachusetts Supreme Court grants Black taxpayers suffrage

1786 Free Blacks join in Shay's Rebellion, protesting the Massachusetts government's lack of concern over harsh conditions of farmers

1787 Constitution ratified, classifying one enslaved person as three-fifths of one person for congressional apportionment, postponing prohibition of slave importation until 1808, and demanding return of fugitive enslaved people to masters • Congress passes Northwest Ordinance, banning slavery in Northwest Territories and all land north of Ohio River • Absalom Jones and Richard Allen organize Philadelphia Free African Society • Rhode Island free Blacks establish African Union Society to promote repatriation to Africa, a position opposed by Philadelphia Free African Society

1789 Olaudah Equiano, ***The Interesting Narrative of the Life of Olaudah Equiano, or Gustavus Vassa, the African***

1790 Pennsylvania abolitionists submit first antislavery petitions to U.S. Congress

1793 U.S. Congress passes first Fugitive Slave Law • Invention of cotton gin increases demand for slave labor in South

1794 U.S. Congress prohibits slave trade with foreign countries • French National Convention abolishes slavery in French territories (ban will be repealed by Napoleon in 1802) • Richard Allen founds first African Methodist Episcopal church (AME), in Philadelphia

1796 Lucy Terry Prince becomes first woman to argue before Supreme Court, successfully defending against a white man trying to steal her family's land • Joshua Johnson, first Black portrait painter to gain recognition in the United States, opens studio in Baltimore

1798 Georgia is last state to abolish slave trade • Venture Smith, ***A Narrative of the Life and Adventures of Venture, a Native of Africa***

1800 U.S. citizens are prohibited from exporting enslaved people • Pennsylvania free Blacks petition U.S. Congress to outlaw slavery • Gabriel Prosser and Jack Bowler organize 1,000 fellow slaves to seize Richmond, but plan is quelled by militia and leaders are executed along with many others

1802 Haitians force French government to end slavery in Haiti; François-Dominique Toussaint-Louverture is made governor

1803 Louisiana Purchase doubles size of the United States

1804 York, an enslaved man, serves as guide for Lewis and Clark expedition to Pacific • Ohio sets precedent with passage of first "Black Laws" restricting rights and movements of free Blacks in North

1807 United States outlaws importation of new slaves after January 1, 1808, but law is widely ignored • Britain abolishes the trade in enslaved people

1811 Slave revolt in Louisiana led by Charles Deslandres ends with over 100 enslaved people killed or executed by U.S. troops

1812 Enslaved and free Blacks fight in War of 1812

1815 Quaker Levi Coffin establishes Underground Railroad to help enslaved persons escape to Canada

1816–18 First Seminole War, involving runaway slaves and Native Americans fighting the U.S. federal government in Florida

1816 American Colonization Society formed in Washington, D.C., to promote African repatriation of freedpeople to ease U.S. race problems; the society is supported by leading white members of Congress

1817 Over 3,000 free Blacks in Philadelphia meet to oppose American Colonization Society

1818 President given power to use armed vessels in Africa to halt illegal trade in enslaved people • U.S. Congress allots $100,000 to transport illegally imported slaves back to Africa

1820–1851

1820 Missouri Compromise reached, allowing Maine into Union as free state, Missouri as slave state in 1821, and outlawing slavery in all new Northern Plains states • American Colonization Society sends expedition to begin establishment of Liberia, a Black republic in West Africa; first repatriation ship, *Mayflower of Liberia,* leaves from New York City with 86 Blacks

1821 African Grove Theatre, first all-Black U.S. acting troupe, begins performances in New York City

1822 Denmark Vesey organizes slave revolt to take over Charleston, South Carolina, but is betrayed by a servant • Liberia formally founded by African American colonizers

1823 Alexander L. Twilight graduates from Middlebury College, Vermont, becoming first African American college graduate

1826 First U.S. colony for free Blacks, Nashoba, established near Memphis, Tennessee

1828 **"Theresa, A Haytien Tale"** published in *Freedom's Journal.* This is quite possibly the first published work of African American fiction.

1829 David Walker, ***David Walker's Appeal*** • George Moses Horton, ***The Hope of Liberty*** • Three-day race riot breaks out in Cincinnati; more than 1,000 Blacks flee to Canada after whites attack them and burn their homes

1830 First National Negro Convention convenes in Philadelphia

1831 Maria W. Stewart, **"Religion and the Pure Principles of Morality"** • Nat Turner leads slave uprising in Southampton County, Virginia; at least 57 whites are killed; 3,000 soldiers and Virginia militiamen react by killing Blacks indiscriminately; Turner is captured and hanged

1832 Stewart, first American woman to engage in public political debates, begins speaking tour in Boston

1833 Oberlin College is founded as first coeducational U.S. college and is integrated from its inception

1834 Henry Blair, inventor of corn planter, is first recorded African American to receive patent • Antiabolitionist riots in Philadelphia and New York • British Parliament abolishes slavery in British Empire

1835–42 Second Seminole War

1836 U.S. House of Representatives passes first "gag rule," preventing any antislavery petition or bill from being introduced, read, or discussed

1837 Victor Séjour, **"The Mulatto"**

1838 Frederick Douglass escapes from slavery • Joshua Giddings of Ohio is first abolitionist elected to U.S. Congress

1839 Cinque leads successful slave revolt on Spanish ship *Amistad* • U.S. State Department rejects passport application by Philadelphia Black man on basis that African Americans are not citizens

1840 Pope Gregory XVI states opposition to slave trade and slavery

1841 Quintuple Treaty signed by England, France, Russia, Austria, and Prussia, allowing mutual search of vessels on high seas to halt slave trade • Frederick Douglass makes his first antislavery speech, in Nantucket, Massachusetts

1843 Henry Highland Garnet delivers **"An Address to the Slaves of the United States"** at National Negro Convention, Buffalo, New York • Vermont and Massachusetts defy 1793 Fugitive Slave Act

1845 Frederick Douglass, ***Narrative of the Life of Frederick Douglass, an American Slave, Written by Himself***

1847 William Wells Brown, ***Narrative of William W. Brown*** • Liberia declares independence and becomes first African republic

1848 Frederick Douglass speaks at first Women's Rights Convention in Seneca Falls, New York • Ohio reverses "Black Laws"

1849 Harriet Tubman escapes from slavery and begins work with Underground Railroad • Massachusetts Supreme Court upholds "separate but equal" ruling in first U.S. integration suit

1850 Clay Compromise strengthens 1793 Fugitive Slave Act, outlaws slave trade in Washington, D.C., admits California as free state, and admits Utah and New Mexico as either slave or free • Lucy Session becomes first recorded African American woman college graduate, receiving her degree from Oberlin College, in Ohio

1851 Sojourner Truth delivers **"Ar'n't I a Woman?"** at Women's Rights Conference in Akron, Ohio

1852–1889

1852 Harriet Beecher Stowe, *Uncle Tom's Cabin* • Martin R. Delany, ***The Condition, Elevation, Emigration, and Destiny of the Colored People of the United States*** • Mary Ann Shadd, ***A Plea for Emigration; or, Notes of Canada West***

1853 Brown, ***Clotel*** • J. M. Whitfield, ***America and Other Poems***

1854–64, 1885–89 Charlotte Forten Grimké writes **journals**

1854 Frances E. W. Harper, ***Poems on Miscellaneous Subjects*** • Kansas-Nebraska Act repeals Missouri Compromise of 1820 • Republican Party founded to oppose extension of slavery

1855 Douglass, ***My Bondage and My Freedom*** • "Bleeding Kansas" fighting begins as antislavery and proslavery settlers hold separate state conventions • John Mercer Langston is elected clerk of Brownhelm Township, Ohio, becoming first African American elected to political office

1857 Supreme Court declares African Americans are not citizens in *Dred Scott* decision

1859 Harriet Wilson, ***Our Nig***, first novel published in America by an African American • John Brown leads abolitionist raid in Harpers Ferry, West Virginia • Last U.S. slave ship lands in Alabama

1860 William Craft and Ellen Craft, ***Running a Thousand Miles for Freedom*** • South Carolina is first state to secede from Union

1861–65 American Civil War

1861 Harriet Jacobs, ***Incidents in the Life of a Slave Girl*** • Harper's **"The Two Offers"** is first short story published by an African American woman

1862 Congress bans slavery in District of Columbia and U.S. territories • President Lincoln issues Emancipation Proclamation, effective January 1, 1863, freeing enslaved people in rebel states • U.S. recognizes Liberia as free nation

1863 Slavery abolished in all Dutch colonies

1864 Fugitive Slave Laws repealed

1865 General Sherman orders up to 40 acres given to each Black family, but President Johnson later reverses policy • Slavery outlawed by 13th Amendment • Freedmen's Bureau established • "Black Codes" issued in former Confederate states, severely limiting rights of freed women and men • President Lincoln assassinated • Ku Klux Klan founded in Tennessee

1866 Congress passes first Civil Rights Act declaring freed Blacks U.S. citizens and nullifying Black codes • Edward G. Walker and Charles L. Mitchel are first Blacks elected to state legislature

1867 Congress passes First Reconstruction Act, granting suffrage to Black males in rebel states, among other rights

1868 Congress passes 14th Amendment, granting Blacks equal citizenship and civil rights • Elizabeth Keckly, ***Behind the Scenes; or, Thirty Years a Slave, and Four Years in the White House***

1869 National Women's Suffrage Association formed • Wyoming Territory is first to grant women suffrage in the United States

1870 Congress passes 15th Amendment, guaranteeing suffrage to all male U.S. citizens • Congress passes Enforcement Acts to control Ku Klax Klan and to federally guarantee civil and political rights • Rev. Hiram R. Revels of Mississippi is first Black U.S. senator • Joseph H. Rainey is seated as first Black U.S. representative; 5 other Black men are also elected to U.S. House of Representatives • Richard T. Greener is first African American graduate of Harvard College

1871 Congress passes second Ku Klux Klan Act to enforce 14th Amendment

1874 Women's Christian Temperance Union founded in Ohio

1875 Congress passes Civil Rights Act of 1875, giving equal treatment "to all citizens" in public places and access to jury duty

1877 Federal troops withdraw from South, officially ending Reconstruction

1879–80 Migration of African Americans from the South to Kansas ("Exodusters"), the first large-scale exodus following the Civil War

1881 Booker T. Washington founds Tuskegee Institute

1883 Supreme Court overturns Civil Rights Act of 1875

1884 Moses Fleetwood Walker plays baseball for Toledo Blue Stockings as one of first Black major leaguers

1889 Charles Chesnutt, **"Dave's Neckliss"**

1890–1927

1890 Oklahoma admitted as first state with women's suffrage • Mississippi limits Black suffrage through "understanding" test, setting precedent for other southern states

1892 Anna Julia Cooper, *A Voice from the South* • Harper, *Iola Leroy*

1893 Paul Laurence Dunbar, *Oak and Ivy*

1894 *The Woman's Era*, later to become the official organ of the National Association of Colored Women, begins publication

1895 Booker T. Washington delivers **"Atlanta Exposition Address"** • Alice Moore Dunbar Nelson, ***Violets and Other Tales*** • Ida B. Wells-Barnett, ***A Red Record*** • Victoria Earle Matthews, **"The Value of Race Literature"**

1896 Supreme Court approves segregation with "separate but equal" ruling in *Plessy v. Ferguson* • National League of Colored Women and National Federation of Afro-American Women merge to form National Association of Colored Women

1898 Spanish-American War

1899 Charles W. Chesnutt, ***The Conjure Woman, The Wife of His Youth and Other Stories of the Color Line***

1900 Washington, ***Up from Slavery*** • Pauline E. Hopkins, ***Contending Forces***.

1903 W. E. B. Du Bois, ***The Souls of Black Folk***

1904 *AME Church Review* calls for a "New Negro Renaissance"

1905 Niagara Movement, dedicated to "aggressive action" for equal rights, is founded by Du Bois and others

1906 Madame C. J. Walker opens hair-care business, becoming one of the first female American millionaires

1907 Alain Locke is first African American Rhodes Scholar

1908 Jack Johnson becomes first African American world heavyweight champion

1909 National Association for the Advancement of Colored People (NAACP) founded by Du Bois

1910–30 Migration of over 1 million southern Blacks to northern cities

1912 James Weldon Johnson, ***The Autobiography of an Ex-Colored Man*** • Claude McKay, *Songs of Jamaica* and *Constab Ballads*

1913 Fenton Johnson, ***A Little Dreaming***

1914–18 World War I

1916 Angelina Weld Grimke's *Rachel* is performed in Washington, D.C., the first full-length play written, performed, and produced by African Americans in the twentieth century • Marcus Garvey comes to the United States from Jamaica and begins "Back to Africa" movement • Margaret Sanger opens first birth control clinic in the United States

1917 United States enters World War I • Blacks march down Fifth Avenue in New York to protest racial inequalities • Claude McKay, **"The Harlem Dancer"** • Hubert Harrison, **"The East Louisville Horror"**

1918 Georgia Douglas Johnson, **"The Heart of a Woman"** • Garvey establishes the newspaper *Negro World*

1919–40 Harlem Renaissance

1919 Du Bois organizes first Pan-African Congress in Paris • 83 lynchings recorded during "Red Summer of Hate" • American Communist Party organized • Harrison, **"Two Negro Radicalisms"**

1920 Ratification of 19th Amendment, granting suffrage to women

1921 René Maran, ***Batouala***

1922 Johnson, ***The Book of American Negro Poetry*** • McKay, **"Harlem Shadows"** • Dyer Anti-Lynching bill passes U.S. House of Representatives but fails in Senate

1923–25 Garvey, ***The Philosophy and Opinions of Marcus Garvey***

1923 Jean Toomer, ***Cane*** • Oklahoma declares martial law to curb KKK

1925–27 Annual literary contests sponsored by *Crisis* and *Opportunity*

1925 Alain Locke, **"The New Negro"** and **"The Legacy of the Ancestral Arts"** • Countee Cullen, ***Color*** • 40,000 KKK members parade in Washington, D.C. • Josephine Baker becomes sensation in Paris through *La Revue Negre*

1926 Eric Walrond, ***Tropic Death*** • Langston Hughes, **"The Weary Blues"** • Richard Bruce Nugent, **"Smoke, Lilies, and Jade"** • Zora Neale Hurston,**"The Eatonville Anthology"**

1927 Charles S. Johnson's anthology *Ebony and Topaz* • Cullen's anthology *Caroling the Dusk* • *The Jazz Singer* is first "talkie" motion picture, with white actor Al Jolson as black-faced minstrel singer • Sterling Brown, **"When de Saints go Ma'ching Home"**

1928–1957

1928 McKay, ***Home to Harlem*** • Nella Larsen, ***Quicksand*** and ***Passing*** • Langston Hughes, **"Johannesburg Mines"**

1929 Jessie Fauset, ***Plum Bun*** • Claude McKay, *Banjo* • Stock Market Crash ushers in Great Depression

1930 W. D. Fard founds Nation of Islam

1931 Arna Bontemps, *God Sends Sunday* • "Scotsboro boys" unjustly convicted of raping two white women in Alabama, prompting nationwide protest • George Samuel Schuyler, ***Black No More***

1932 Sterling A. Brown, **"Southern Road"** • Thurman, ***Infants of the Spring***

1933 President Roosevelt pushes "New Deal" through Congress

1934 Nancy Cunard, *Negro, An Anthology* • Paul Robeson, **"I Want to Be African"** and **"The Culture of the Negro"** • Langston Hughes, **"Cubes"**

1935 Zora Neale Hurston, ***Mules and Men*** • National Council of Negro Women founded

1936 Jesse Owens wins four gold medals at "Nazi Olympics" in Berlin

1937 Hurston, ***Their Eyes Were Watching God*** • Joe Louis becomes boxing's world heavyweight champion

1938 Richard Wright, ***Uncle Tom's Children*** • Crystal Bird Fauset elected to Pennsylvania House of Representatives, becoming first African American woman state legislator • Sterling Brown, **"Break of Day"**

1939–45 World War II

1939 Marian Anderson sings at Lincoln Memorial after her concert at Constitution Hall was prevented by Daughters of American Revolution

1940 Wright, *Native Son* • Hughes, *The Big Sea* • Robert Hayden, ***Heart-Shape in the Dust***

1941 A. Philip Randolph of the Brotherhood of Sleeping Car Porters organizes march on Washington to protest segregation in the military and employment discrimination; President Roosevelt issues executive order forbidding racial and religious discrimination in government training programs and defense industries; Randolph calls off march • United States enters war after Japanese attack on Pearl Harbor

1942 Hurston, ***Dust Tracks on a Road*** • Margaret Walker, **"For My People"**

1943 First successful "sit-in" demonstration staged by Congress of Racial Equality (CORE) • Over 40 killed in race riots in Detroit and Harlem

1944 Melvin B. Tolson, ***Rendezvous with America*** • Chester Himes, **"Cotton Gonna Kill Me Yet"**

1945 Wright, ***Black Boy*** • Gwendolyn Brooks, ***A Street in Bronzeville***

1946 Ann Petry, *The Street*

1947 Tolson named Poet Laureate of Liberia

1948 Dorothy West, ***The Living Is Easy*** • President Truman approves desegregation of the military and creates Fair Employment Board

1950–53 Korean War

1950 Brooks wins Pulitzer Prize for *Annie Allen* (1949), the first African American to win Pulitzer in any category • Ralph J. Bunche is first African American to receive Nobel Peace Prize

1951 Hughes, *Montage of a Dream Deferred*

1952 Ralph Ellison, ***Invisible Man***

1953 Tolson, *Libretto for the Republic of Liberia* • Brooks, ***Maud Martha*** • James Baldwin, *Go Tell It on the Mountain* and **"Stranger in the Village"** • Wright, *The Outsider*

1954 In *Brown v. Board of Education*, Supreme Court declares segregated schools unconstitutional, overturning *Plessy v. Ferguson* (1896)

1955 Baldwin, ***Notes of a Native Son*** • Rosa Parks arrested for refusing to give seat on bus to white man, setting off bus boycott led by Martin Luther King Jr. • 14-year-old Emmett Till lynched in Mississippi • Supreme Court orders speedy integration of schools • Interstate Commerce Commission orders integration of buses, trains, and waiting rooms for interstate travel

1956 101 southern congressmen sign "Southern Manifesto" against school desegregation • Baldwin, ***Giovanni's Room***

1957 Congress approves Civil Rights Act of 1957 • Federal troops sent to Alabama to enforce school desegregation • Ghana is first African nation to gain independence from colonial rule

1959–1969

1959 Lorraine Hansberry's ***A Raisin in the Sun*** is first Broadway play by an African American woman • Paule Marshall, *Brown Girl, Brownstones*

1960 Sit-in staged by four Black students at Woolworth's lunch counter in North Carolina • Student Non-violent Coordinating Committee (SNCC) founded • Congress passes Civil Rights Act of 1960 • Gwendolyn Brooks, **"A Bronzeville Mother Loiters in Mississippi . . . "**

1961 Hughes, *The Best of Simple* • Hoyt Fuller revives *Negro Digest* • LeRoi Jones (Amiri Baraka), **"Preface to a Twenty Volume Suicide Note"** • Baraka, ***Dutchman*** • 13 "freedom riders" sponsored by CORE take bus trip across South to force integration of terminals

1962 Hayden, **"Ballad of Remembrance"** • Baldwin, *Another Country* • Riots break out after Supreme Court orders University of Mississippi to accept James Meredith as first Black student; 12,000 federal troops are employed to restore order and ensure Meredith's admission

1963 National support for civil rights roused after police attack Birmingham, Alabama, demonstration led by Martin Luther King Jr. • King writes **"Letter from Birmingham Jail"** • March on Washington attracts over 200,000 demonstrators; King delivers "I Have a Dream" speech • Ku Klux Klan bombing of the 16th Street Baptist Church in Birmingham kills four girls • President Kennedy assassinated

1964 Tolson, ***Harlem Gallery*** • Ellison, ***Shadow and Act*** • Baraka's ***Dutchman*** wins Obie Award • Malcolm X founds Organization of Afro-American Unity, officially splitting with Elijah Muhammad and the Black Muslims • 3 civil rights workers murdered in Mississippi by white segregationists, setting off Mississippi "Freedom Summer" • King wins Nobel Peace Prize • 24th Amendment ratified, outlawing poll tax used to limit Black suffrage • Congress passes Civil Rights Act of 1964 and Economic Opportunity Act • Sidney Poitier wins Academy Award for *Lilies of the Field* • Cassius Clay wins world heavyweight boxing championship, subsequently converts to Islam and changes name to Muhammad Ali • Adrienne Kennedy, ***Funnyhouse of a Negro*** • Baraka, **"A Poem for Willie Best,"** "Black Dada Nihilismus," ***The Slave*** • Mari Evans, **"Vive Noir!"**

1965–73 Vietnam War

1965 Malcolm X, ***The Autobiography of Malcolm X*** • A. B. Spellman, *The Beautiful Days* • King leads march from Selma to Montgomery, Alabama • Malcolm X assassinated in New York City • Watts riot • Black Arts Movement started by Baraka in Harlem • David Henderson, **"Keep on Pushing"** • Daniel Moynihan publishes *The Negro Family: The Case For National Action*, a controversial report that shapes policy in the late 1960s

1966 Black Panther Party founded • National Organization for Women founded • Senator Edward W. Brooke (R-MA) becomes first elected Black senator since Reconstruction • "Black Power" concept is adopted by CORE and SNCC

1967 Haki R. Madhubuti, ***Think Black*** • Jay Wright, *Death as History* • King announces opposition to Vietnam War • Detroit riot kills 43; major riots in Newark and Chicago • Thurgood Marshall becomes first Black U.S. Supreme Court justice • Supreme Court overturns law against interracial marriage • Calvin Hernton, **"Jitterbugging in the Streets"** • Baraka, ***Slave Ship***

1968 Etheridge Knight, ***Poems from Prison*** • Nikki Giovanni, ***Black Feeling*** • Eldridge Cleaver, ***Soul on Ice*** • Quincy Troupe's anthology ***Watts Poets: A Book of New Poetry and Essays*** • Carolyn Rodgers, ***Paper Soul*** • Earnest Gaines, ***Bloodline*** • Audre Lorde, ***The First Cities*** • June Jordan, ***Who Look at Me*** • Alice Walker, ***Once: Poems*** • King assassinated in Memphis • Senator Robert F. Kennedy assassinated in Los Angeles • Shirley Chisholm becomes first Black woman elected to U.S. Congress • Baraka and Larry Neal edit *Black Fire*, a major collection of Black Arts poetry, prose, and drama including Stewart's **"The Development of the Black Revolutionary Artist"** • Amus Mor, "Poem to the Hip Generation"

1969 Sonia Sanchez, **"homecoming"** • Jayne Cortez, ***Pisstained Stairs and the Monkey Man's Wares*** • Lucille Clifton, ***Good Times*** • Al Young, *Dancing: Poems* • Major antiwar demonstrations in Washington • Raymond Patterson, ***Twenty-Six Ways of Looking at a Blackman and Other Poems*** • Baraka, **"Ka 'Ba"** • Sonia Sanchez, ***Sister Son/ji; Homecoming*** • Haki Madhubuti, ***Don't Cry, Scream***

1970–1993

1970 Maya Angelou, ***I Know Why the Caged Bird Sings*** • Toni Morrison, *The Bluest Eye* • Michael S. Harper, **"Dear John, Dear Coltrane"** • Toni Cade Bambara edits *The Black Woman* • Baraka, **"It's Nation Time"** • Sanchez, ***We a BaddDDD People*** • Nikki Giovanni, ***Black Feeling, Black Talk/Black Judgment***

1971 Gaines, *Autobiography of Miss Jane Pittman* • Supreme Court approves busing as method of desegregation • Supreme Court rules closing of Mississippi swimming pools to avoid desegregation is constitutional

1972 Reed, ***Mumbo Jumbo*** • Congress passes Equal Rights Amendment, which goes to states for ratification • Chisholm is first Black woman to run for U.S. president • Toni Cade Bambara, ***Gorilla My Love***

1973 Morrison, ***Sula*** • Supreme Court prohibits state restrictions on abortions in *Roe v. Wade*

1974 Charles Johnson, *Oxherding Tale* • Albert Murray, ***Train Whistle Guitar***

1975 Ntozake Shange's ***for colored girls who have considered suicide/when the rainbow is enuf*** is second play by an African American woman to reach Broadway • Sherley Anne Williams, ***Peacock Poems*** • Gayl Jones, ***Corregidora***

1976 Alex Haley awarded special Pulitzer Prize for *Roots* • Kennedy, *A Movie Star Has to Star in Black and White* • Octavia Butler, *Patternmaster* • Audre Lorde, ***Coal***

1977 Toni Morrison, *Song of Solomon* • TV miniseries based on Alex Haley's *Roots* attracts more viewers than any television program in history • Michael S. Harper, ***Images of Kin: New and Selected Poems***

1978 James Alan McPherson wins Pulitzer Prize for *Elbow Room* • Supreme Court disallows quotas for college admissions but gives limited approval to affirmative action programs • Audre Lorde, ***The Black Unicorn***

1979 Walker edits *I Love Myself When I Am Laughing: A Zora Neale Hurston Reader*

1980 Liberian president William Tolbert ousted by Staff Sargeant Samuel K. Doe, ending over 130 years of Americo-Liberian rule over indigenous Africans • June Jordan, ***Passion: New Poems, 1977–1980***

1982 Marshall, ***Reena and Other Stories*** • Lorde, ***Zami: a new spelling of my name*** • Equal Rights Amendment fails after 10 years, 3 states short of ratification

1983 Alice Walker wins Pulitzer Prize for ***The Color Purple***

1984 John Wideman, ***Brothers and Keepers*** • August Wilson's *Ma Rainey's Black Bottom* opens on Broadway • Jesse Jackson is first serious Black contender for the U.S. presidency, winning 17 percent of popular vote in Democratic primary • Vanessa Williams crowned first Black Miss America • Christopher Gilbert, *Across the Mutual Landscape*

1985 Jamaica Kincaid, ***Annie John***

1986 Essex Hemphill, ***Conditions*** • Martin Luther King's birthday officially celebrated as federal holiday • Wole Soyinka of Nigeria is first person of African descent to win Nobel Prize for Literature

1987 Wilson wins Pulitzer Prize for Broadway play *Fences* • Dove wins Pulitzer Prize for ***Thomas and Beulah***

1988 Morrison wins Pulitzer Prize for *Beloved* • Naylor, ***Mama Day***

1989 500,000 march in Washington for prochoice rally • L. Douglas Wilder of Virginia is first elected Black governor • General Colin Powell becomes first Black Chief of Staff for U.S. Armed Forces • Supreme Court approves state limits on abortion

1990 Wilson wins Pulitzer Prize for *The* ***Piano Lesson*** • Johnson's *Middle Passage* wins National Book Award • Elizabeth Alexander, ***The Venus Hottentot***

1991 Clarence Thomas confirmed Supreme Court justice, despite Anita Hill's sexual harassment testimony

1992 Police acquitted of beating Rodney King, setting off riots in Los Angeles • Carol Moseley Braun of Illinois becomes first African American woman elected to the U.S. Senate • Supreme Court rules against state bans of "hate speech" • Derek Walcott is first West Indian to win Nobel Prize for Literature • Edward P. Jones, ***Lost in the City***

1993 Yusef Komunyakaa wins Pulitzer Prize for ***Neon Vernacular*** • Caryl Phillips, ***Crossing the River*** • Toni Morrison is first African American to win Nobel Prize for Literature • Maya Angelou reads "On the Pulse of Morning" at Clinton inauguration, becoming the first Black poet to participate in a U.S. presidential inauguration • Supreme Court disallows congressional districts drawn to increase Black representation

1994–2011

1994 Henry Louis Gates Jr., *Colored People* • Edwidge Danticat, ***Breath, Eyes, Memory*** • Rita Dove named U.S. Poet Laureate • David Levering Lewis wins Pulitzer Prize in Biography for *W. E. B. Du Bois: Biography of a Race*, 1868–1919 • O. J. Simpson accused of murdering ex-wife and her friend; ensuing trial grips nation

1995 Rita Dove, ***Mother Love*** • Harryette Mullen, ***Muse & Drudge*** • O. J. Simpson acquitted of murder charges • Million Man March in Washington organized by Nation of Islam minister Louis Farrakhan • Colin Powell considered as a presidential candidate of the Republican Party • Barack Obama, *Dreams from My Father* • Samuel Delaney, *Atlantis: Three Tales* • John Keene, ***Annotations***

1996 Wilson, *Seven Guitars*, on Broadway • Percival Everett, **"The Appropriation of Cultures"**

1997 California passes state ban on all forms of affirmative action (Proposition 209) • Randall Kennedy's *Race, Crime, and the Law* tracks discrimination in the criminal justice system

1998 Washington State abolishes all state affirmative action • Unexpurgated edition of Chester Himes's *Yesterday Will Make You Cry*

1999 Ralph Ellison's second novel, *Juneteenth*, published posthumously

2000 One month after contested presidential election results, the Supreme Court rules against recounts in Florida and effectively declares George W. Bush president with 271 electoral votes • Lucille Clifton, ***Blessing the Boats*** (wins National Book Award)

2001 President Bush appoints Colin Powell Secretary of State and Condoleezza Rice National Security Advisor • Halle Berry first African American woman to win Academy Award for Best Actress • Lewis wins second Pulitzer Prize in Biography for *W. E. B. Du Bois: The Fight for Equality and the American Century, 1919–1963* • On September 11, terrorists hijack four commercial jetliners; two crash into World Trade Center in New York, one into Pentagon, and one into a field in Pennsylvania • Kevin Young, *To Repel Ghosts*

2002 University of Michigan Law School's affirmative action policy ruled constitutional • Suzan-Lori Parks wins Pulitzer in Drama for ***Topdog/Underdog*** • Hannah Crafts, ***The Bondswoman's Narrative***, the first African American novel (written before 1861), is published

2003 Illinois governor George Ryan grants clemency to all 160 death-row inmates after his 2002 blue-ribbon Commission on Capital Punishment finds systemic failures • President Bush orders U.S. Justice Department to file briefs urging Supreme Court to rule as unconstitutional University of Michigan's affirmative action policies in undergraduate and law school admissions • Edward P. Jones, *The Known World* (wins Pulitzer Prize for fiction) • Kevin Young, ***Jelly Roll*** • *Forbes* reveals Oprah Winfrey as the first African American woman to become a billionaire

2004 Rita Dove, ***American Smooth*** • Barack Obama elected as U.S. senator from Illinois

2005 Condoleezza Rice named first female African American secretary of state under President George W. Bush • Hurricane Katrina hits the American southeast, crippling New Orleans, Louisiana, and the Gulf Coast of Mississippi and Alabama • August Wilson completes *Radio Golf*, the final play in his century cycle, only months before his death

2006 Edward P. Jones, *Aunt Hagar's Children*

2007 300 Tuskegee Airmen and their widows given Congressional Gold Medal for their service in World War II • Natasha Trethewey, *Native Guard* (wins the Pulitzer Prize for poetry) • Gregory Pardlo, ***Totem***

2008 Barack Obama elected as the first African American president of the United States • M. NourbeSe Philip, ***Zong!***

2009 Obama wins the Nobel Peace Prize • Eric Holder becomes the first African American to serve as United States Attorney General

2010 An earthquake measuring 7.0 on the Richter Scale shakes Haiti, killing over 100,000 • Trethewey, ***Beyond Katrina*** • Terrance Hayes, *Lighthead* (wins National Book Award for poetry)

2011 Tracy K. Smith, ***Life on Mars*** (wins Pulitzer Prize for poetry) • Kevin Young, ***Ardency*** • Following a 2003 invasion and years of occupation, American combat forces leave Iraq • Amidst widespread protests, Troy Anthony Davis is executed after being convicted of murdering a police officer in 1989

2012–2024

2012 Obama elected to second term as president • Trethewey named Poet Laureate of the United States

2013 George Zimmerman, tried for the murder of African American teenager Trayvon Martin, acquitted of second degree murder and manslaughter • Jesmyn Ward, ***Men We Reaped***

2014 Claudia Rankine, ***Citizen: An American Lyric*** • Teju Cole, **"Black Body: Rereading James Baldwin's 'Stranger in the Village'"** • Black Lives Matter movement gains prominence in response to police brutality, particularly the killings of several unarmed Black men by the police

2015 Supreme Court rules that the U.S. Constitution guarantees same-sex couples the right to marry in *Obergefell v. Hodges*

2016 *The Fire This Time*, anthology edited by Jesmyn Ward; it includes Rachel Kaadzi Ghansah's **"The Weight of James Arthur Baldwin"** • Donald Trump elected as the 45th president of the United States

2017 Ta-Nehisi Coates, ***We Were Eight Years in Power: An American Tragedy*** • #MeToo movement gains prominence, drawing increased societal attention to sexual abuse

2018 Kendrick Lamar wins Pulitzer Prize in Music for *DAMN*

2020–23 COVID-19 pandemic causes global societal disruption, illness, and death, including hundreds of thousands of deaths in the United States and millions worldwide

2020 The murder of George Floyd during his arrest by police office Derek Chauvin in Minneapolis, Minnesota, triggers worldwide protests against police brutality and racism that continue into the following year • Kamala Harris, on the ticket with Joe Biden, elected as the first Black and first female vice president of the United States

2022 Supreme Court rules that the U.S. Constitution does not confer a right to abortion in *Dobbs v. Jackson Women's Health Organization*, reversing the precedent of *Roe v. Wade*

2023 Supreme Court rules against race-conscious affirmative action in college admissions programs in *Students for Fair Admissions, Inc. (SFFA) v. President & Fellows of Harvard College* and *SFFA v. University of North Carolina*

2024 Kamala Harris becomes the first African American woman to seek election to the U.S. presidency on the ticket of a major party

Suggested General Readings

Additional bibliographies can be found at **digital.wwnorton.com/africanamericanlit4**.

Political, Social, and Cultural History

In the twentieth century African American history moved from a footnote shaped by its status as "the Negro Problem" to a rich and complex textual independence informed by both national and international perspectives. For a sense of the profound changes in the study of race in history, see August Meier and Elliott Rudwick's *Black History and the Historical Profession 1915–1980* (1986) and John Hope Franklin's *Race and History: Selected Essays 1938–1988* (1989). An excellent resource for students is *The Harvard Guide to African-American History* (2001), edited by Evelyn Brooks Higginbotham et al. Historical studies include John Hope Franklin's *From Slavery to Freedom: A History of Negro Americans* (1947); Herbert Aptheker's *To Be Free: Studies in American Negro History* (1948); *The Making of Black America: Essays in Negro Life and History* (1969), edited by August Meier and Elliott Rudwick; Philip Foner's *Essays in Afro-American History* (1978); Bettina Aptheker's *Woman's Legacy: Essays on Race, Sex, and Class in American History* (1982); *The Southern Enigma: Essays on Race, Class, and Folk Culture* (1983), edited by Walter J. Fraser Jr. and Winfred B. Moore Jr.; *History and Tradition in Afro-American Culture* (1984), edited by Günter H. Lenz; Paula Giddings's *When and Where I Enter: The Impact of Black Women on Race and Sex in America* (1984); *In Resistance: Studies in African, Caribbean, and Afro-American History* (1986), edited by Gary Y. Okihiro; Benjamin Quarles's *The Negro in the Making of America* (1987); and Ira Berlin's *Many Thousands Gone: The First Two Centuries of Slavery in America* (1998). Several reference works on history and culture are *The Afro-American Encyclopedia* (1974), edited by Martin Rywell and Charles H. Wesley; *The Encyclopedia of African-American Culture and History* (1993), edited by Jack Salzman, David Lionel Smith, and Cornel West; *The African American Century: How Black Americans Have Shaped Our Country* (2000), edited by Henry Louis Gates Jr. and Cornel West; and *African American Lives*, edited by Henry Louis Gates Jr. and Evelyn Brooks Higginbotham (2004). For Pan-African perspectives, see *Africa and the Afro-American Experience: Eight Essays* (1977), edited by Lorraine A. Williams; Gregory U. Rigsby's *Alexander Crummell: Pioneer in Nineteenth-Century Pan-African Thought* (1987); Paul Gilroy's *The Black Atlantic: Modernity and Double-Consciousness* (1993); and John Cullen Gruesser's *Black on Black: Twentieth-Century African American Writing about Africa* (2000). See also Isabel Wilkerson, *Caste: The Origins of Our Discontents* (2020); Henry Louis Gates Jr., *The Black Box: Writing the Race* (2024); and Sarah Lewis, *The Unseen Truth: When Race Changed Sight in America* (2024).

Colonial and Antebellum Years

Studies of African American history of the colonial and antebellum periods include Lorenzo Johnston Greene's *The Negro in Colonial New England* (1969); A. Leon Higginbotham's *In the Matter of Color: The Colonial Period* (1978); Daniel F. Littlefield's *Africans and Creeks: From the Colonial Period to the Civil War* (1979); *Slavery and Freedom in the Age of the American Revolution* (1983), edited by Ira Berlin and Ronald Hoffman; William Dillion Piersen's *Black Yankees: The Development of an Afro-American Subculture in Eighteenth-Century New England* (1988); Jean Fagin Yellin's *Women and Sisters: The Antislavery Feminists in American Culture* (1989); Peter Michael Voelz's *Slave and Soldier: The Military Impact of Blacks in the Colonial Americas* (1993); Joseph Douglas Deal's *Race and Class in Colonial Virginia: Indians, Englishmen, and Africans on the Eastern Shore during the Seventeenth Century* (1993); Donald R. Wright's *African Americans in the Colonial Era: From African Origins Through the American Revolution* (2000); Barbara A. Faggins's *Africans and Indians: An Afrocentric Analysis of Contacts between Africans and Indians in Colonial Virginia* (2001); *Another's Country: Archaeological and Historical Perspectives on Cultural*

Interactions in the Southern Colonies (2002), edited by J. W. Joseph and Martha Zierden; and John Ernest's *Liberation Historiography: African American Writers and the Challenge of History, 1794–1861* (2004) and *A Nation within a Nation: Organizing African-American Communities before the Civil War* (2011). See also *Witness for Freedom: African American Voices on Race, Slavery, and Emancipation* (1993), edited by C. Peter Ripley.

Nineteenth Century

Studies of slave culture include Herbert Aptheker's *American Negro Slave Revolts* (1963); Eugene D. Genovese's *Roll, Jordan, Roll: The World the Slaves Made* (1976); Albert J. Raboteau's *Slave Religion: The "Invisible Institution" in the Antebellum South* (1978); John Blassingame's *The Slave Community* (1979); Orlando Patterson's *Slavery and Social Death: A Comparative Study* (1982); Sterling Stuckey's *Slave Culture* (1987); Wilma King's *Stolen Childhood: Slave Youth in Nineteenth-Century America* (1995); and *Slave Cultures and the Cultures of Slavery* (1995), edited by Stephan Palmié. Nineteenth-century studies include *The Black Man in America Since Reconstruction* (1970), edited by David M. Reimers; Dorothy Sterling's *We Are Your Sisters: Black Women in the Nineteenth Century* (1984); R. J. M. Blackett's *Beating against the Barriers: Biographical Essays in Nineteenth-Century Afro-American History* (1986); Hazel Carby's *Reconstructing Womanhood* (1987); *The African American Family in the South, 1861–1900* (1994), edited by Donald G. Nieman; Martha Elizabeth Hodes's *White Women, Black Men: Illicit Sex in the Nineteenth-Century South* (1997); James Oliver and Lois E. Horton's *In Hope of Liberty: Culture, Community, and Protest among Northern Free Blacks, 1700–1860* (1997); Saidiya V. Hartman's *Scenes of Subjection: Terror, Slavery, and Self-Making in Nineteenth-Century America* (1997); Chungchan Gao's *African Americans in the Reconstruction Era* (1999); Katherine Clay Bassard's *Spiritual Interrogations: Culture, Gender, and Community in Early African American Women's Writing* (1999); Eddie S. Glaude's *Exodus! Religion, Race, and Nation in Early Nineteenth-Century Black America* (2000); John Stauffer's *The Black Hearts of Men: Radical Abolitionists and the Transformation of Race* (2002); Jerrold M. Packard's *American Nightmare: The History of Jim Crow* (2002); William L. Andrews, *Slavery and Class in the American South: A Generation of Slave Narrative Testimony, 1840–1865* (2019), and Henry Louis Gates Jr., *Stony the Road: Reconstruction, White Supremacy, and the Rise of Jim Crow* (2019).

Twentieth and Early Twenty-First Centuries

Crucial texts for political and social history include Gunnar Myrdal's *An American Dilemma: The Negro Problem and Modern Democracy* (1944); E. Franklin Frazier's *Black Bourgeoisie: The Rise of a New Middle-Class in the United States* (1962); Gilbert Osofsky's *Harlem: The Making of a Ghetto* (1963); William Van DeBurg's *New Day in Babylon: The Black Power Movement and American Culture, 1965–1975* (1992); Michael Omi and Howard Winant's *Racial Formation in the United States: From the 1960s to the 1990s* (1994); and Rayford Logan's *The Betrayal of the Negro: From Rutherford Hayes to Woodrow Wilson* (1997). The March 2000 issue of *Sage*, edited by Elijah Anderson and Tukufu Zuberi, revisits the philosophy of Du Bois in *The Study of African American Problems: W. E. B. Du Bois's Agenda, Then and Now*. See also *Negro Protest Thought in the Twentieth Century* (1971), edited by August Meier, Elliott Rudwick, and Francis L. Broderick; Kevin Kelly Gaines's *Uplifting the Race: Black Leadership, Politics, and Culture in the Twentieth Century* (1996); *The House That Race Built: Black Americans, U.S. Terrain* (1997), edited by Wahneema Lubiano; *African Americans and Jews in the Twentieth Century: Studies in Convergence and Conflict* (1998), edited by V. P. Franklin et al.; *Black American Intellectualism and Culture: A Social Study of African American Social and Political Thought* (1999), edited by James L. Conyer Jr.; Mary L. Dudziak's *Cold War Civil Rights: Race and the Image of American Democracy* (2000); and Anthony Dawahare's *Nationalism, Marxism, and African American Literature between the Wars: A New Pandora's Box* (2003). Studies of contemporary history include Andrew Billingsley's *Climbing Jacob's Ladder: The Enduring Legacy of African American Families* (1992) and *Against the Odds: Scholars Who Challenged Racism in the Twentieth Century* (2002), edited by Benjamin P. Bowser, Louis Kushnick, and Paul Grant. Other important studies include Bruce Michael Tyler's *From Harlem to Hollywood: The Struggle for Racial and Cultural Democracy, 1920–1943* (1992) and *Radical Revisions: Rereading 1930s Culture* (1996), edited by Bill Mullen and Sherry Lee Linkon. See also Beth Tompkins Bates's *Pullman Porters and the Rise of Protest Politics in Black America, 1925–1945* (2001) and Zhang Aimin's *The Origins of the African American Civil Rights Movement, 1865–1956* (2002). On the 1960s, see *In Black America, 1968: The Year of Awakening* (1969), edited by Patricia W. Romero; *Race, Politics, and Culture: Critical Essays on the Radicalism of the 1960's* (1986), edited by Adolph Reed Jr.; Jennifer B. Smith's *An International History of the Black Panther Party* (1999); and James C. Hall's *Mercy, Mercy Me: African American Culture and the American Sixties* (2001).

For women's history, see the collection of tapes and transcripts *Black Women Oral History Project Interviews* (1976–81) at Schlesinger Library, Radcliffe College; *Black*

Women in United States History (1990–95), edited by Darlene Clark Hine; *"We specialize in the wholly impossible": A Reader in Black Women's History* (1995), edited by Darlene Clark Hine, Wilma King, and Linda Reed; Darlene Clark Hine and Kathleen Thompson's *A Shining Thread of Hope: The History of Black Women in America* (1998); *A Companion to American Women's History* (2002), edited by Nancy A. Hewitt, 2002. See also *Unequal Sisters: A Multicultural Reader in U.S. Women's History* (2000), edited by Vicki L. Ruiz and Ellen Carol DuBois; Saidiya Hartman, *Wayward Lives, Beautiful Experiments: Intimate Histories of Riotous Black Girls, Troublesome Women, and Queer Radicals* (2019); Erica Edwards, *The Other Side of Terror: Black Women and the Culture of U.S. Empire* (2021); and Courtney Thorsson, *The Sisterhood: How a Network of Black Women Writers Changed American Culture* (2023).

Critical studies of the impact of migration on African Americans include Spencer R. Crew's *Field to Factory: Afro-American Migration, 1915–1940* (1987); E. Marvin Goodwin's *Black Migration in America from 1915 to 1960: An Uneasy Exodus* (1990); *Black Exodus: The Great Migration from the American South* (1991), edited by Alferdteen Harrison; and Isabel Wilkerson, *The Warmth of Other Suns: The Epic Story of America's Great Migration* (2010).

Historical studies that focus on the economic system of the United States are numerous. For a history of African American labor, see *The Black Worker: A Documentary History from Colonial Times to the Present* (1978), edited by Philip S. Foner and Ronald L. Lewis. Studies of work and economics include Jacqueline Jones's *The Dispossessed: America's Underclasses from the Civil War to the Present* (1992) and *American Work: Four Centuries of Black and White Labor* (1998); Julius Wilson's *When Work Disappears: The World of the New Urban Poor* (1997); Robert E. Weems's *Desegregating the Dollar: African American Consumerism in the Twentieth Century* (1998); Paul R. Mullins's *Race and Affluence: An Archaeology of African America and Consumer Culture* (1999); and Bruce Nelson's *Divided We Stand: American Workers and the Struggle for Black Equality* (2001).

On the role of law in African American history, see Mary Frances Berry's *Black Resistance/White Law: A History of Constitutional Racism in America* (1971); C. Vann Woodward's *The Strange Career of Jim Crow* (1974); Eric Foner's *Reconstruction: America's Unfinished Revolution, 1863–1877* (1988); *The Black Abolitionist Papers* (1985–92), edited by C. Peter Ripley et al.; *African Americans and the Living Constitution* (1995), edited by John Hope Franklin and Genna Rae McNeil; A. Leon Higginbotham's *Shades of Freedom: Racial Politics and Presumptions of the American Legal Process* (1996); *Plessy v. Ferguson: A Brief History with Documents* (1997), edited by Brook Thomas; Gail Williams O'Brien's *The Color of the Law: Race, Violence, and Justice in the Post-World War II South* (1999); and *Local Matters: Race, Crime, and Justice in the Nineteenth-Century South* (2001), edited by Christopher Waldrep and Donald G. Nieman. See also *Interracialism: Black-White Intermarriage in American History, Literature, and Law* (2000), edited by Werner Sollors, and Richard Rothstein, *The Color of Law: A Forgotten History of How Our Government Segregated America* (2017).

For studies of African American culture, see *African American Culture* (1996), edited by Sandra Adell, Thomas L. Morgan, and Patrick Roney; George E. Kent's *Blackness and the Adventure of Western Culture* (1972); *The Greatest Taboo: Homosexuality in Black Communities* (2001), edited by Deloy Constantine-Simms; *Sports Matters: Race, Recreation, and Culture* (2002), edited by John Bloom and Michael Nevin Willard; and Frances Smith Foster's *'Til Death or Distance Do Us Part: Love and Marriage in African America* (2010). For the role of periodicals in African American culture, see *The Negro and His Folklore in Nineteenth-Century Periodicals* (1977), edited by Bruce Jackson; *The Black Press in the Middle West, 1865–1985* (1996), edited by Henry Lewis Suggs; and *African-American Newspapers and Periodicals: A National Bibliography* (1998), edited by James P. Danky and Maureen E. Hady. See also Suggs's *P. B. Young, Newspaperman: Race, Politics, and Journalism in the New South, 1910–1962* (1988); Abby Arthur Johnson and Ronald Maberry Johnson's *Propaganda and Aesthetics: The Literary Politics of African-American Magazines in the Twentieth Century* (1991); and Eric Gardner's *Unexpected Places: Relocating Nineteenth-Century African American Literature* (2009).

For an assessment of the roles of religion in African American history, see Hans A. Baer and Merrill Singer's *African-American Religion in the Twentieth Century: Varieties of Protest and Accommodation* (1992); Evelyn Brooks Higginbotham's *Righteous Discontent: The Women's Movement in the Black Baptist Church, 1880–1920* (1993); *African-American Religion: Interpretive Essays in History and Culture* (1997), edited by Timothy E. Fulop and Albert J. Raboteau; and Henry Louis Gates Jr., *The Black Church: This Is Our Story, This Is Our Song* (2021). See also *Religion and American Culture: A Reader* (1995), edited by David G. Hackett.

An important study is *Chant of Saints: A Gathering of Afro-American Literature, Art, and Scholarship* (1979), edited by Michael S. Harper and Robert B. Stepto. Two classic studies of African American music are Maud Cuney-Hare's *Negro Musicians and Their Music* (1996) and Eileen Southern's *The Music of Black Americans* (1997). See also Brent Hayes Edwards, *Epistrophies: Jazz and the Literary Imagination* (2017); Daphne Brooks, *Liner Notes for the Revolution: The Intellectual Life of Black Feminist Sound* (2021); and Adam Bradley, *The Anthology of Rap* (2010) and *Book of Rhyme: Poetics of Hip-Hop* (rev. ed. 2017).

For African American art, see Albert Boime's *The Art of Exclusion: Representing Blacks in the Nineteenth Century* (1990); Gus C. McElroy's *Facing History: The Black Image in American Art, 1710–1940* (1990); Sharon F. Patton's *African-American Art* (1998); and Michael D. Harris's *Colored Pictures: Race & Visual Representation* (2003). Richard Powell produced several studies: the essays collected in *Harlem Renaissance: Art of Black America* (1987) and *Rhapsodies in Black: Art of the Harlem Renaissance* (1997). See also his *Black Art and Culture in the Twentieth Century* (1997). Studies of performance include *African Dance: An Artistic, Historical, and Philosophical Inquiry* (1996), edited by Kariamu Welsh Asante; John O. Perpener's *African-American Concert Dance: The Harlem Renaissance and Beyond* (2001); and Arthur Knight's *Disintegrating the Musical: Black Performance and American Musical Film* (2002).

Genre Studies

For studies of the vernacular tradition, see J. Mason Brewer's *American Negro Folklore* (1968); Lawrence Levine's *Black Culture and Black Consciousness: Afro-American Folk Thought from Slavery to Freedom* (1977); Mary F. Berry and John Blassingame's *Long Memory: The Black Experience in America* (1982); Dolan Hubbard's *The Sermon and the African American Literary Imagination* (1994); and Bertram D. Ashe's *From within the Frame: Storytelling in African-American Fiction* (2002).

Studies of African American poetry include Sterling A. Brown's *Outline for the Study of Poetry of American Negroes* (1931) and *Negro Poetry and Drama* (1937); J. Saunders Redding's *To Make a Poet Black* (1939); William H. Robinson's *Early Black American Poets* (1969); Jean Wagner's *Black Poets of the United States* (1973); Stephen Henderson's *Understanding the New Black Poetry: Black Speech and Black Music as Poetic References* (1973); *Black Sister: Poetry by Black American Women, 1746–1980* (1981), edited by Erlene Stetson; Mari Evans's *Black Women Writers, 1950–1980: A Critical Evaluation* (1984); D. H. Melham's *Heroism in the New Black Poetry: The Will and the Spirit* (1990); Fahamisha Patricia Brown's *Performing the Word: African-American Poetry as Vernacular Culture* (1999); *The Furious Flowering of African American Poetry* (1999), edited by Joanne V. Gabbin; *Reading Race in American Poetry: An Area of Act* (2000), edited by Aldon Lynn Nielsen; Lorenzo Thomas's *Extraordinary Measures: Afrocentric Modernism and Twentieth-Century American Poetry* (2000); Cheryl Clarke's *"After Mecca": Women Poets of the Black Arts Movement* (2005); and Lauri Ramey's *Slave Songs and the Birth of African American Poetry* (2008). Poetry has been collected in several anthologies and critical editions. Important studies include Joan R. Sherman's *Invisible Poets: Afro-Americans of the Nineteenth Century* (1989); *Collected Black Women's Poetry* (1988) in *The Schomburg Library of Nineteenth-Century Black Women Writers*; and *African-American Poetry of the Nineteenth Century: An Anthology* (1992). See also *The Garden Thrives: Twentieth-Century African-American Poetry* (1996), edited by Clarence Major.

For critical studies of drama and performance, see *The Theater of Black Americans: A Collection of Critical Essays* (1987), edited by Errol Hill; Leslie Catherine Sanders's *The Development of Black Theater in America: From Shadows to Selves* (1988); *Black Theatre and Performance: A Pan-African Bibliography* (1990), compiled by John Gray; Geneviève Fabre's *Drumbeats, Masks, and Metaphors: Contemporary Afro-American Theatre* (1993); Dana A. Williams's *Contemporary African American Female Playwrights: An Annotated Bibliography* (1998); *A Sourcebook of African-American Performance: Plays, People, Movements* (1999), edited by Annemarie Bean; Kimberly W. Benston's *Performing Blackness: Enactments of African-American Modernism* (2000); and *African-American Performance and Theater History: A Critical Reader* (2001), edited by Harry J. Elam Jr. On drama from specific periods, see Daphne A. Brooks's *Bodies in Dissent: Spectacular Performances of Race and Freedom, 1850–1910* (2006); David Krasner's *A Beautiful Pageant: African American Theatre, Drama, and Performance in the Harlem Renaissance, 1910–1927* (2002); David Savran's *Highbrow/Lowbrow: Theater, Jazz, and the Making of the New Middle Class* (2010); *Black Theatre: Ritual Performance in the African Diaspora* (2002), edited by Paul Carter Harrison; Mance Williams's *Black Theatre in the 1960s and 1970s: A Historical-Critical Analysis of the Movement* (1985); *Contemporary Black Men's Fiction and Drama* (2001), edited by Keith Clark; and Soyica Diggs Colbert's *The African American Theatrical Body: Reception, Performance, and the Stage* (2011).

For an understanding of the slave narrative and its place in the literary tradition, see *Great Slave Narratives* (1969), edited by Arna Bontemps; Robert B. Stepto's *From behind the Veil: A Study of Afro-American Narrative* (1979); Frances Smith Foster's *Witnessing Slavery: The Development of Ante-bellum Slave Narratives* (1994); *The Art of Slave Narrative: Original Essays in Criticism and Theory* (1982), edited by John Sekora and Darwin T. Turner;

The Slave's Narrative (1990), edited by Charles T. Davis and Henry Louis Gates Jr.; *The Classic Slave Narratives* (1987), edited by Henry Louis Gates Jr.; *Pioneers of the Black Atlantic: Five Slave Narratives from the Enlightenment, 1772–1815* (1998), edited by Henry Louis Gates Jr. and William L. Andrews; *The Civitas Anthology of African American Slave Narratives* (1999), edited by William L. Andrews and Henry Louis Gates Jr.; Ashraf H. A. Rushdy's *Neo-slave Narratives: Studies in the Social Logic of a Literary Form* (1999); *Black Imagination and the Middle Passage* (1999), edited by Maria Diedrich, Henry Louis Gates Jr., and Carl Pedersen; *The Cambridge Companion to the African American Slave Narrative* (2007), edited by Audrey Fisch; and *Slave Narratives after Slavery* (2011), edited by William L. Andrews.

On the development of the autobiographical tradition, see Stephen Butterfield's *Black Autobiography in America* (1974); William L. Andrews's *To Tell a Free Story: The First Century of Afro-American Autobiography, 1760–1865* (1986); *Sisters of the Spirit: Three Black Women's Autobiographies of the Nineteenth Century* (1986), edited by William L. Andrews; Mary Helen Washington's *Invented Lives* (1988); Joanne M. Braxton's *Black Women Writing Autobiography* (1989); *African American Autobiography: A Collection of Critical Essays* (1993), edited by William L. Andrews; and Frances Smith Foster's *Written by Herself: Literary Production of Early African American Women Writers* (1993).

On the narrative tradition, see also *Journeys in New Worlds: Early American Women's Narratives* (1990), edited by William L. Andrews et al.; Joycelyn Moody's *Sentimental Confessions: Spiritual Narratives of Nineteenth-Century African American Women* (2001); Yolanda Pierce's *Hell without Fires: Slavery, Christianity, and the Antebellum Spiritual Narrative* (2005); and P. Gabrielle Foreman's *Activist Sentiments: Reading Black Women in the Nineteenth Century* (2009).

Studies of the African American novel include Vernon Loggins's *The Negro Author* (1931); Nick Aaron Ford's *The Contemporary Negro Novel: A Study in Race Relations* (1936); Sterling A. Brown's *The Negro in American Fiction* (1937); Hugh Gloster's *Negro Voices in American Fiction* (1948); Robert Bone's *The Negro Novel in America* (1965); Noel Schraufnagel's *From Apology to Protest: The Black American Novel* (1973); Bernard W. Bell's *The Afro-American Novel and Its Tradition* (1987); Thomas H. Nigel's *From Folklore to Fiction: A Study of Folk Heroes and Rituals in the Black American Novel* (1988); John Callahan's *In the African-American Grain: The Pursuit of Voice in Twentieth-Century Black Fiction* (1990); Farah Jasmine Griffin's *"Who Set You Flowin'?" The African-American Migration Narrative* (1995); J. Lee Greene's *Blacks in Eden: The African American Novel's First Century* (1996); Claudia Tate's *Psychoanalysis and Black Novels: Desire and the Protocols of Race* (1998); Lawrence R. Rodgers's *Canaan Bound: The African-American Great Migration Novel* (1997); and J. Lee Greene, *The Diasporan Self: Unbreaking the Circle in Western Black Novels* (2008).

For the tradition in women's literature, see Barbara Christian's *Black Women Novelists* (1980); Hazel Carby's *Reconstructing Womanhood* (1987); Susan Willis's *Specifying: Black Women Writing the American Experience* (1987); Michael Awkward's *Inspiriting Influences: Tradition, Revision, and Afro-American Women's Novels* (1989); Karla F. C. Holloway's *Moorings and Metaphors: Figures of Culture and Gender in Black Women's Literature* (1992); *The Schomburg Library of Nineteenth-Century Black Women Writers* (1988–91), edited by Henry Louis Gates Jr. et al.; Madhu Dubey's *Black Women Novelists and the Nationalist Aesthetic* (1994); and Cheryl A. Wall's *Worrying the Line: Black Women Writers, Lineage, and Literary Tradition* (2005).

Studies in the short story are *The Black American Short Story in the 20th Century: A Collection of Critical Essays* (1977), edited by Peter Bruck; Robert Bone's *Down Home: Origins of the Afro-American Short Story* (1988); and *The African American Short Story, 1970 to 1990: A Collection of Critical Essays* (1993), edited by Wolfgang Karrer and Barbara Puschmann-Nalenz. For the essay, see Cheryl B. Butler's *The Art of the Black Essay: From Meditation to Transcendence* (2003). For the tradition in oratory, see *With Pen and Voice: A Critical Anthology of Nineteenth-Century African-American Women* (1995), edited by Shirley Wilson Logan.

Literary History

Guides to the literature include Blyden Jackson's *A History of Afro-American Literature* (1989); *The Oxford Companion to African American Literature* (1997), edited by William L. Andrews, Frances Smith Foster, and Trudier Harris, and their *Concise Oxford Companion to African American Literature* (2001); and Dickson D. Bruce's *The Origins of African American Literature, 1680–1865* (2001). For critical issues affecting literary history, see Houston A. Baker's *Long Black Song: Essays in Black American Literature and Culture* (1972); Charles T. Davis's *Black Is the Color of the Cosmos: Essays on Afro-American Literature and Culture, 1942–1981* (1982), edited by Henry Louis Gates Jr.; *Redefining American Literary History* (1990), edited by LaVonne Brown Ruoff and Jerry W. Ward Jr.; Dickson D. Bruce's *Black American Writing from the Nadir: The Evolution of a Literary Tradition, 1877–1915* (1989); *The Black Columbiad: Defining Moments in African American Literature and Culture* (1994), edited by Werner Sollors and

Maria Dietrich; and *Genius in Bondage: Literature of the Early Black Atlantic* (2001), edited by Vincent Carretta and Philip Gould. Excellent resources on authors and literary movements can be found in the volumes edited by Trudier Harris and Thadious M. Davis in The Dictionary of Literary Biography series: *Afro-American Writers before the Harlem Renaissance; Afro-American Writers from the Harlem Renaissance to 1940; Afro-American Writers after 1955: Dramatists and Prose Writers;* and *Afro-American Poets since 1955*. See also *Black American Poets between Worlds, 1940–1960* (1986), edited by R. Baxter Miller; Lorraine Elena Roses and Ruth Elizabeth Randolph's *Harlem Renaissance and Beyond: Literary Biographies of 100 Black Women Writers, 1900–1945* (1990); Michel Fabre's *From Harlem to Paris: Black American Writers in France, 1840–1980* (1991); Elizabeth McHenry's *Forgotten Readers: Recovering the Lost History of African-American Literary Societies* (2002); and John Ernest's *Chaotic Justice: Rethinking African American Literary History* (2009).

Literary Theory and Criticism

An excellent overview of theory can be found in *African American Literary Theory: A Reader* (2000), edited by Winston Napier. For individual texts, see *Black Literature and Literary Theory* (1984), edited by Henry Louis Gates Jr.; Houston A. Baker Jr.'s *Blues, Ideology, and Afro-American Literature: A Vernacular Theory* (1984); *"Race," Writing, and Difference* (1986), edited by Henry Louis Gates Jr.; Henry Louis Gates Jr.'s *Figures in Black: Words, Signs, and the "Racial" Self* (1987) and *The Signifying Monkey: A Theory of Afro-American Literary Criticism* (1988); *Changing Our Own Words: Essays on Criticism, Theory, and Writing by Black Women* (1989), edited by Cheryl A. Wall; Sandra Adell's *Double-Consciousness/Double Bind: Theoretical Issues in Twentieth-Century Black Literature* (1994); and Hortense Spillers's *Black, White, and in Color: Essays on American Literature and Culture* (2003). Important texts for feminist criticism and theory include Barbara Smith's *Toward a Black Feminist Criticism* (1977); *Conjuring: Black Women, Fiction, and Literary Tradition* (1985), edited by Marjorie Pryse and Hortense J. Spillers; *Black Feminist Criticism and Critical Theory* (1989), edited by Joe Weixlmann and Houston A. Baker; *Reading Black, Reading Feminist: A Critical Anthology* (1990), edited by Henry Louis Gates Jr.; Houston A. Baker's *Workings of the Spirit: The Poetics of Afro-American Women's Writing* (1991); *Theorizing Black Feminisms: The Visionary Pragmatism of Black Women* (1993), edited by Stanlie M. James and Abena P. A. Busia; Deborah E. McDowell's *"The Changing Same": Black Women's Literature, Criticism, and Theory* (1995); Joyce Ann Joyce's *Warriors, Conjurers and Priests: Defining African-Centered Literary Criticism* (1994); Barbara Christian's *Black Feminist Criticism: Perspectives on Black Women Writers* (1997); *Female Subjects in Black and White: Race, Psychoanalysis, Feminism* (1997), edited by Elizabeth Abel, Barbara Christian, and Helene Moglen; *African American Literary Criticism, 1773 to 2000* (1999), edited by Hazel Arnett Ervin; *The Black Feminist Reader* (2000), edited by Joy James and T. Denean Sharpley-Whiting; Gina Wisker's *Post-Colonial and African American Women's Writing: A Critical Introduction* (2000); and *Black Feminist Cultural Criticism* (2001), edited by Jacqueline Bobo.

Excellent collections of critical approaches to African American literature and culture include *Within the Circle: An Anthology of African American Literary Criticism from the Harlem Renaissance to the Present* (1994), edited by Angelyn Mitchell; *Literary Influence and African-American Writers: Collected Essays* (1996), edited by Tracy Mishkin; Ross Posnock's *Color & Culture: Black Writers and the Making of the Modern Intellectual* (1998); and Robert E. Washington's *The Ideologies of African American Literature from the Harlem Renaissance to the Black Nationalist Revolt: A Sociology of Literature Perspective* (2001). For critical studies of nineteenth-century literature, see *Slavery and the Literary Imagination* (1989), edited by Deborah E. McDowell and Arnold Rampersad; Houston A. Baker's *Long Black Song: Essays in Black American Literature and Culture* (1990); Claudia Tate's *Domestic Allegories of Political Desire: The Black Heroine's Text at the Turn of the Century* (1992); *The Culture of Sentiment: Race, Gender, and Sentimentality in Nineteenth-Century America* (1992), edited by Shirley Samuels; Eric J. Sundquist's *To Wake the Nations: Race in the Making of American Literature* (1993); John Ernest's *Resistance and Reformation in Nineteenth-Century African-American Literature* (1995); and Farah Jasmine Griffin, *Read Until You Understand: The Profound Wisdom of Black Life and Literature* (2021).

The Harlem Renaissance has generated tremendous scholarly interest. For a sense of the culture and politics of the period, see James Weldon Johnson's *Black Manhattan* (1930); Claude McKay's *Harlem: Negro Metropolis* (1940); *The Harlem Renaissance Remembered: Essays* (1984), edited by Arna Bontemps; David Levering Lewis's *When Harlem Was in Vogue* (1997); and George Hutchinson's *The Harlem Renaissance in Black and White* (1985). See as well Steven Watson's *Circles of the Twentieth Century: The Harlem Renaissance* (1995); Cary D. Winty's *Black Culture and the Harlem Renaissance* (1988); Carole Marks and Diana Edkins's *The Power of Pride: Stylemakers and Rulebreakers of the Harlem Renaissance* (1999); and *Remember Me to Harlem: The Letters of Langston Hughes and*

Carl Van Vechten, 1925–1964 (2001), edited by Emily Bernard. The anthology *The New Negro: Readings on Race, Representation, and African American Culture, 1892–1938* (2007), edited by Henry Louis Gates Jr. and Gene Andrew Jarrett, provides a history of the key metaphor of the period. Jonathan Gill's *Harlem: The Four Hundred Year History from Dutch Village to Capital of Black America* (2012) is an invaluable general history. For the central place Harlem holds in African American culture, see *Harlem on My Mind: Cultural Capital of Black America, 1900–1968* (1995), edited by Allon Schoener, and Sharifa Rhodes-Pitts's *Harlem Is Nowhere: A Journey to the Mecca of Black America* (2011).

Important critical issues in literature are examined in several works. For conjunctions of identities, see *Comparative American Identities: Race, Sex, and Nationality in the Modern Text*, (1991), edited by Hortense J. Spillers; *Subjects and Citizens: Nation, Race, and Gender from Oroonoko to Anita Hill* (1995), edited by Michael Moon and Cathy N. Davidson; Werner Sollors's *Neither Black nor White yet Both: Thematic Explorations of Interracial Literature* (1999); *Separate Spheres No More: Gender Convergence in American Literature, 1830–1930* (2000), edited by Monika M. Elbert; Mia Bay's *The White Image in the Black Mind* (2000); and *Race and the Archaeology of Identity* (2001), edited by Charles E. Orser Jr. Cultural history is examined in *Afro-American Literary Study in the 1990s* (1989), edited by Houston A. Baker Jr. and Patricia Redmond; *History and Memory in African-American Culture* (1994), edited by Geneviève Fabre and Robert O'Meally; and *The African Diaspora: African Origins and New World Identities* (1999), edited by Isidore Okpewho, Carole Boyce Davies, and Ali A. Mazrui. Critical studies of literary history include several works by Houston A. Baker Jr.: *The Journey Back: Issues in Black Literature and Criticism* (1980); *Afro-American Poetics: Revisions of Harlem and the Black Aesthetic* (1988); *Turning South Again: Re-Thinking Modernism/Re-Reading Booker T.* (2001); and *Critical Memory: Public Spheres, African American Writing, and Black Fathers and Sons in America* (2001). See also *Recovering the Black Female Body: Self-Representations by African American Women* (2001), edited by Michael Bennett and Vanessa D. Dickerson; and Trudier Harris-Lopez's *South of Tradition: Essays on African American Literature* (2002).

PERMISSIONS ACKNOWLEDGMENTS

TEXT

Roger Abrahams, "Shine and the *Titanic,*" from DEEP DOWN IN THE JUNGLE: BLACK AMERICAN FOLKLORE FROM THE STREETS OF PHILADELPHIA. Reprinted by permission of Taylor and Francis Group, LLC, a division of Informa plc.

Gwendolyn B. Bennett, "Heritage" and "To a Dark Girl" from *Opportunity* (March 1934). By Gwendolyn B. Bennett. Copyright © Manuscripts, Archives and Rare Books Division, Schomburg Center for Research in Black Culture, The New York Public Library.

John Bennett, "All God's Chillen Had Wings," from THE DOCTOR TO THE DEAD by John Bennett. Copyright 1943, 1946 by John Bennett. Reprinted by permission of the University of South Carolina Press.

Sterling A. Brown, "Break of Day," "Cabaret," "Long Gone," "Ma Rainey," "Odyssey of Big Boy," "Sam Smiley," "Southern Road," "Strong Men," and "When the Saints Go Ma'ching Home" from THE COLLECTED POEMS OF STERLING A. BROWN, selected by Michael S. Harper. Copyright © 1980 by Sterling A. Brown. Reprinted by permission of the John L. Dennis Revocable Trust.

Willie Dixon, "I'm Your Hoochie Coochie Man" words and music by Willie Dixon. Copyright © 1954. HOOCHIE COOCHIE MUSIC. Copyright renewed. All Rights Administered by BMG Rights Management (US) LLC. All Rights Reserved. Used by permission. Reprinted by permission of Hal Leonard LLC.

Angelina Weld Grimké, "A Winter Twilight," "The Black Finger," "When the Green Lies Over the Earth," and "Tenebris" from SELECTED WORKS OF ANGELINA WELD GRIMKÉ are reprinted by permission of Moorland-Spingarn Research Center, Howard University, Washington, D.C.

Charlotte Forten Grimké, "A Parting Hymn" and excerpts from "Journals" reprinted by permission of Moorland-Spingarn Research Center, Howard University, Washington, D.C.

Nicolas Guillen, "Little Ode," trans. by Langston Hughes from THE COLLECTED WORKS OF LANGSTON HUGHES, vol. 16. Copyright © 1948 by Ben Frederick Carruthers and Langston Hughes. Copyright renewed 1976 by George Houston Bass. Reprinted by permission of Harold Ober Associates Incorporated. "My Last Name" from MAN-MAKING WORDS: SELECTED POEMS OF NICOLAS GUILLEN. Copyright © 1972 by Robert Marquez and David Arthur McMurray. Reprinted by permission of the publisher, the University of Massachusetts Press.

Sam "Lightning" Hopkins, "It's a Sin to Be Rich" words and music by Sam "Lightning" Hopkins. Copyright © 1972 Prestige Music c/o Concord Music Publishing. Copyright renewed. All rights reserved. Used by permission. Reprinted by permission of Hal Leonard LLC.

Eddie "Son" House, "Death Letter Blues," words and music by Eddie "Son" House. Copyright 1965 Sondick Music. Copyright renewed. All rights administered by BMG Rights Management (US) LLC. All rights reserved. Reprinted by permission of Hal Leonard LLC.

Langston Hughes, "Theme for English B," "Dream Boogie," "Ballad of the Landlord," "Harlem (2)," "Cubes," "Motto," Trumpet Player," "Negro Servant," "Christ in Alabama," "Madam and the Rent Man," "Afro-American Fragment," "Song for Billie Holiday," from THE COLLECTED POEMS OF LANGSTON HUGHES, edited by Arnold Rampersad with David Roessel, associate editor, copyright © 1994 by the Estate of Langston Hughes. Used by permission of Alfred A. Knopf, an imprint of the Knopf Doubleday Publishing Group, a division of Random House LLC. All rights reserved.

Zora Neale Hurston, Excerpts from "Introduction," "Big Talk," "Member Youse a Nigge," "Why the Sister in Black Works Hardest," and "What the Rabbit Learned" from MULES AND MEN by Zora Neale Hurston. Copyright 1935 by Zora Neale Hurston; renewed © 1963 by John C. Hurston and Joel Hurston. Chapters 1 and 2 from THEIR EYES WERE WATCHING GOD. Copyright 1937 by Zora Neale Hurston; renewed © 1965 by John C. Hurston and Joel Hurston. Reprinted by permission of HarperCollins Publishers.

Nehemiah "Skip" James, "Hard Time Killing Floor Blues" written by Nehemiah "Skip" James. Copyright © 1931 by Nehemiah James. Reprinted by permission of Wynwood Music Co., Inc.

Helene Johnson, "Poem," "Sonnet to a Negro in Harlem," and "Invocation" from THIS WAITING FOR LOVE: HELENE JOHNSON, POET OF THE HARLEM RENAISSANCE. Copyright © 2000 by University of Massachusetts Press. Reprinted by permission of the publisher.

Robert Johnson, "Hellhound on My Trail," words by Robert Johnson. Copyright © 1990 by Lehsem Music LLC / Claude I. Johnson. Reprinted by permission of Music and Media International, Inc.

Julius Lester, "Brer Rabbit Tricks Brer Fox Again," from THE TALES OF UNCLE REMUS: THE ADVENTURES OF BRER RABBIT by Julius Lester, text copyright © 1987 by Julius Lester. Used by permission of Dial Books for Young Readers, an imprint of Penguin Young Readers Group, a division of Penguin Random House LLC. All rights reserved.
Alain Locke, From "Apropos of Africa" from THE WORKS OF ALAIN LOCKE, ed. by Charles Molesworth (2012). By permission of Oxford Publishing Limited.

John A. Lomax and Alan Lomax, "Rosie," collected, adapted, and arranged by John A. Lomax and Alan Lomax. Copyright © 1934 (Renewed) Global Jukebox Publishers, Marshall, TX. TRO-Ludlow Music, Inc., New York, NY, controls all publishing rights for the world outside the U.S.A. International copyright secured. Made in the U.S.A. All rights reserved including public performance for profit. Used by permission. Written and arranged by C. B. Cook and John Lomax. Reprinted by permission of Global Jukebox Publishing.

Minnie McCoy, "Chickasaw Train Blues," works and music by Minnie McCoy. Copyright © 1934 by UNIVERSAL MUSIC CORP. Copyright renewed. All rights reserved. Used by permission. Reprinted by permission of Hal Leonard LLC.

McIntosh County Shouters, "Kneebone Bend," "Watch the Star," and "Farewell, Last Goin'" reprinted by permission of the McIntosh County Shouters.

Paul Robeson, "I Want to Be African" from PAUL ROBESON SPEAKS (1978) is reprinted by permission of Paul Robeson, Jr. "The Culture of the Negro" from *The Spectator*, June 15, 1934. Copyright © 1934 The Spectator. Reprinted by permission of the publisher.

Jimmy Rushing, Count Basie, and Ed Durham, "Good Morning Blues," words and music by Count Basie, Jimmy Rushing, and Ed Durham. Copyright © 1938 (Renewed) WB MUSIC CORP. All rights reserved. Used by permission of Alfred Music Publishing.

George Samuel Schuyler, "The Negro-Art Hokum" by George Schuyler is reprinted with permission from the June 16, 1926, issue of *The Nation*. Copyright © 1926 The Nation Company.

Victor Séjour, "The Mulatto," translated by Philip Barnard, is reprinted by permission of the translator.

Anne Spencer, "Before the Feast of Shushan" and "The Wife-Woman" from TIME'S UNFADING GARDEN (Louisiana State University Press, 1977), edited by J. L. Greene. Reprinted by permission of J. L. Greene.

Phillis Wheatley, from THE POEMS OF PHILLIS WHEATLEY, ed. and with an introduction by Julian D. Mason, Jr. Copyright © 1966 by the University of North Carolina Press, renewed 1989. Used by permission of the publisher.

IMAGES

2: Corbis Historical/Getty Images; **8:** Music Division, The New York Public Library. "Eli Green's Cake-Walk," The New York Public Library Digital Collections. 1896. https://digitalcollections.nypl.org/items/510d47e3-fc4f-a3d9-e040-e00a18064a99; **10:** A Negro Camp Meeting in the South from *Harper's Weekly*, 10th August 1872 (engraving) (b&w photo), Eytinge Solomon (1833–1905) (after) / Private Collection / The Bridgeman Art Library; **26:** David Gahr/Getty Images; **38:** Library of Congress Prints & Photographs Division Lomax Collection LC-USZ62-23008; **56:** *Uncle Remus and His Friends; Old Plantation Stories, Songs, and Ballads, with Sketches of Negro Characters* by Joel Chandler Harris. Illustrated by A. B. Frost. 1892, Boston, New York, Houghton, Mifflin and Company/Internet Archive; **70:** Library of Congress; **75:** The Picture Art Collection/Alamy Stock Photo; **76:** incamerastock / Alamy Stock Photo; **77:** Library of Congress Rare Book and Special Collections Division Washington, D.C. 20540 USA, LC-USZC4-5321; **86:** Bettmann/Getty Images; **89:** Collection of Massachusetts Historical Society; **117:** akg-images / British Library; **142:** American Antiquarian Society; **143:** Library of Congress Rare Book and Special Collections Division, Washington, D.C. 20540 USA, LC-USZC4-5316; **193:** Internet Archive/frontispiece from *Twelve years a slave. Narrative of Solomon Northup, a citizen of New-York, kidnapped in Washington city in 1841, and rescued in 1853, from a cotton plantation near the Red River in Louisiana.* New York: C. M. Saxton, 25 Park Row. 1859; **229:** University of Rochester; **334:** Artokoloro / Penta Springs Limited / Alamy Stock Photo; **436:** Schomburg Center NYPL / Art Resource NY; **510:** Library of Congress; **512:** "The Negro in The War," *Frank Leslie's Illustrated*, January 1863, artist's impression, zoomable image, *House Divided: The Civil War Research Engine* at Dickinson College, https://hd.housedivided.dickinson.edu/node/41475. Scanned by Archives and Special Collections, Dickinson College; **515:** MARBL Emory University; **517** Library of Congress; **573:** (left and right) Cleveland Public Library Digital Collection; **707:** Kansas Historical Society; **724:** Library of Congress Prints and Photographs Division, Washington, D.C. 20540. LC-DIG-ppmsca-37818 (digital file from original item); **725:** Wikimedia Commons; **822:** Robert N. Dennis Collection of Stereoscopic Views, Miriam and Ira D. Wallach Division of Art Prints and Photographs, The New York Public Library, Astor, Lenox, and Tilden Foundations; **926:** Courtesy of the Ohio Historical Society; **954:** Bettmann / Getty Images; **956:** National Archives; **957:** *Protest Parade*, 1924. James VanDerZee. © Donna Mussenden VanDerZee; **960:** © 2024 Heirs of Aaron Douglas / Licensed by VAGA at Artists Rights Society (ARS), NY. W. W. Norton & Company, Inc., wishes to thank the Crisis Publishing Co., Inc., the publisher of the magazine of the National Association for the Advancement of Colored People, for the use of the image first published in the May 1928 issue of *Crisis Magazine*; **961:** *Chicago Defender* (May 3, 1924); **962:** Courtesy of The Frank Driggs Collection at Jazz at Lincoln Center; **971:** Bridgeman Images; **984:** © Morgan and Marvin Smith. Photographs and Prints Division, Schomburg Center for Research in Black Culture, The New York Public Library; **1011:** Municipal Cultural Center in Olkusz; **1012:** The Michael C. Rockefeller Memorial Collection, Bequest of Nelson A. Rockefeller, 1979. The Metropolitan Museum of Art; **1019:** NY Daily News via Getty Images; **1027:** W. W. Norton & Company, Inc., wishes to thank the Crisis Publishing Co., Inc., the publisher of the magazine of the National Association for the Advancement of Colored People, for the use of the image first published in the May 1922 issue of *Crisis Magazine*; **1047:** James Weldon Johnson Memorial Collection of Negro Arts and Letters at Yale. Used with permission from the Zora Neale Hurston Trust and Victoria Sanders & Associates LLC; **1319:** General Research & Reference Division, Schomburg Center for Research in Black Culture, The New York Public Library, Astor, Lenox and Tilden Foundations; **1371:** Yale Collection of American Literature, Beinecke Rare Book and Manuscript Library, Yale University.

Index